D0607363

THE OFFICIAL ENCYCLOPEDIA OF BRIDGE

THIRD EDITION, NEW, REVISED, AND EXPANDED

CONTRIBUTING EDITORS

THE OFFICIAL ENCYCLOPEDIA OF BRIDGE

THIRD EDITION, NEW, REVISED, AND EXPANDED

Authorized by the American Contract Bridge League

and Prepared with the Assistance of Its Staff

RICHARD L. FREY

Editor in Chief

ALAN F. TRUSCOTT

Executive Editor

AMALYA L. KEARSE

Editor, Third Edition

CROWN PUBLISHERS, INC. • NEW YORK

00044

EDITORIAL ADVISORY BOARD

Library of Congress Cataloging in Publication Data

American Contract Bridge League.
  The official encyclopedia of bridge.

  1. Contract bridge—Dictionaries. I. Frey,
Richard L. II. Truscott, Alan F. III. Kearse, Amalya.
IV. Title.
GV1282.3.A45 1976   795.4'15'03   76-17053
ISBN 0-517-52724-3

FOREWORD

Since my initial proposal, in 1964, that the American Contract Bridge League compile this work, *The Official Encyclopedia of Bridge* has become a living panorama of the game, combining past history with present kaleidoscopic change. Even while changing, its purpose remains: "To provide an official and authoritative answer to any question a reader might ask about the game of contract bridge and its leading players." To accomplish this has made necessary two major expansions and continuous exploration, not only of today but also of yesterday.

We have seen rapid and radical developments in bidding systems; explosion of new cheating scandals and employment of devices to prevent them; the creation of techniques for warning opponents about bids that have unusual meanings so that new ideas can flourish under conditions that give them a fair trial. All these "news" are presented, plus an occasional flashback into history. For example, there is the newly uncovered evidence that bridge was known and played before the earliest previous accreditation (to Russia) of its origin and its name. (See "History of Bridge.")

Hundreds of experts (some of whose contributions date back to the only other modern work of this kind, Ely Culbertson's 1935 *Encyclopedia of Bridge*) have aided in the preparation of the technical material that is the heart of this work. To mention only a few such major contributions, I cite Eric Crowhurst's "Suit Combinations"; Monroe Ingberman's exhaustive studies of the "Squeeze"; Albert Dormer's articles on "False-carding" and "Deceptive Play"; Marshall Miles on Match-Point Bidding, Defense, and Play; Edgar Kaplan's "International Match-Point Tactics"; "Play from Equals" analyzed by Jeff Rubens. The panel of contributing editors lists many others who have added their expertise—including, alas, a growing number of those who have made their final contributions to the game. To all of them, bridge in general and this work in particular owe deepest thanks.

However, a major share of credit for the worth of this Encyclopedia must go to:

—Executive Editor Alan Truscott, who came to the United States from his native Britain primarily to produce the 1964 edition and has since become a permanent resident and the Bridge Editor of *The New York Times.* Many of the unsigned technical entries, as well as much of the other content of this book, have been prepared by him.

—The late Albert H. Morehead, whose title of Chairman of the Editorial Advisory Board does not begin to cover the contributions he made. This book owes much to his encyclopedic knowledge of contract bridge and bridge history, to his long career as Truscott's predecessor at *The Times,* to the facility he gained as Editor in Chief of other reference works, and, most of all, to his great love of the game.

—Amalya L. Kearse, a bright new star of bridge both as player and author, who is largely responsible for the organization, revision, and expansion of this third edition.

—Thomas M. Smith, whose efforts in the preparation of the second edition have continued with his considerable contributions to this third edition.

Grateful recognition is also due to Edith Simon, ACBL Librarian, who, with the noteworthy assistance of Mae Dean Smith, performed the monumental task of updating League records for this edition; also to Rhoda Barrow Lederer, whose earlier work in producing a British edition is reflected in this one as well.

In a sense, however, major credit must go to the 200,000 members of the American Contract Bridge League, and to its Board of Directors, who gave the project official sponsorship and authorized the use of the League's records, without which this project could not have been undertaken.

—RICHARD L. FREY
Editor in Chief

HOW TO USE THIS ENCYCLOPEDIA

For easy reference, this book is divided into four main parts: I. General Information (technical—bidding and play; historical; procedural—tournament organization, laws, etc.; geographical; and terminological); II. Biographies; III. Tournament Results; IV. Bibliography.

I. General Information.

Technical. When more than one name is in use for a specific system, convention, etc., the major entry is under the term more commonly used in America, and this is also used in other articles. A cross-reference will be found for alternative names.

Appearance of a term or name in small capitals indicates that a separate entry is to be found either in Part I or in the biographical section.

The reader who wishes to study a particular field of bidding or play is advised to consult one of the following major headings. In each case, a number of cross-references permit investigation of the subject in depth: ARTIFICIAL BID; BIDDING; BIDDING SYSTEMS; COMPETITIVE BIDDING; COUP; DEFENSE; DEFENSIVE BIDDING; DOUBLES; DUMMY PLAY; ENTRY; FOUR NO TRUMP CONVENTIONS; LIMIT; MATHEMATICS OF BRIDGE; NO TRUMP BIDDING; ONE CLUB SYSTEMS; OPENING BID; OPENING LEADS; RESPONDER'S REBID; RESPONSE; SIGNALS; SLAM CONVENTIONS; SQUEEZE; TWO-BID; TWO CLUB SYSTEMS.

Historical. Every effort has been made to record the history of the American Contract Bridge League and other major national and international organizations. Information of importance—some of it newly discovered—will also be found under HISTORY OF BRIDGE, HISTORY OF PLAYING CARDS, and the entries of historic figures in the biographical section.

Procedural. The Laws of Rubber Bridge (1963) and of Duplicate Bridge (1975) are given in full. Various aspects of tournament organization are presented or cross-referenced in the article DUPLICATE BRIDGE, in the preparation of which the Editors are indebted to Terry Smith and to the late Arthur Marks for considerable help. ˙

Geographical. National bridge organizations throughout the world are listed, and histories and descriptions of them are provided. Concluding most such entries is a list of the leading bridge players of the country.

Terminological. An effort has been made to list and define all terms, both regular and colloquial, in common use throughout the English-speaking world.

II. Biographies. Under the heading "Leading Bridge Personalities" are listed more than twenty-five hundred American and foreign bridge notables. Occupations given are not necessarily current ones but indicate that the individual was at some time primarily engaged in that vocation. Where an individual is given credit for a contribution to bridge in the main body of the Encyclopedia, his last name appears in small capitals to indicate that a separate entry for this person is in the biographical section.

Noteworthy achievements by an increasing number of players who have appeared on the scene since the first (1964) edition of this Encyclopedia have imposed new and stricter criteria for including individual biographies. It has been necessary to de-list many players who have won fewer than three major regional events, or whose failure to win recent events suggests that they have become inactive; to drop the recording of second place finishes in events of less than major national ranking; to omit the complete detailing of regional titles from the biographies of those who have to their credit many such triumphs, or whose national and international achievements overshadow such victories. However, all such successes are to be found recorded in the history of the event itself, as detailed in Part III.

III. Tournament Results. Except for WORLD CHAMPIONSHIPS and USBA GRAND NATIONALS results (listed under these headings in Part I), all North American and most of the important international tournament results have been divided into three Appendixes: Appendix I—North American Championships: the three ACBL National tournaments, the Grand National team play-off, and the ACBL Continentwide and Intercollegiate Championships; Appendix II—ACBL Regional Championships; Appendix III—International Championships: European, Far East, and South American Zonal Championships.

IV. Bibliography. Significant books on all aspects of bridge and its evolution are here listed according to subject.

The American Contract Bridge League, 2200 Democrat Road, Memphis, Tenn. 38116, will endeavor to render library service to owners of this encyclopedia who send a request for information with a self-addressed stamped envelope.

GENERAL INFORMATION

A

ABA. AMERICAN BRIDGE ASSOCIATION.

ABL. AMERICAN BRIDGE LEAGUE.

ABPA. American Bridge Press Association.

ABTA. AMERICAN BRIDGE TEACHERS' ASSOCIATION.

ACBL. AMERICAN CONTRACT BRIDGE LEAGUE.

ACBL BULLETIN. See BULLETIN, THE CONTRACT BRIDGE.

ACBL CHARITY FOUNDATION. See CHARITY PROGRAM OF THE ACBL.

ACBL HANDBOOK. A handbook that sets forth under one cover the regulations and practices followed by the American Contract Bridge League in several important phases of its activities. Interested persons or groups may secure copies of the handbook or sections thereof from ACBL HEADQUARTERS.

ACBL HEADQUARTERS. 2200 Democrat Road, Memphis, Tennessee 38116.

ACBL PLAYER NUMBER . See PLAYER NUMBER.

AWL. AMERICAN WHIST LEAGUE.

A POSTERIORI PROBABILITIES. See PROBABILITIES, A POSTERIORI.

A PRIORI PROBABILITIES. See PROBABILITIES, A PRIORI.

ABOVE THE LINE. A phrase denoting all scores in rubber bridge entered above a horizontal line on the score sheet, including penalties and the premiums for honors, slams, rubbers, overtricks, and fulfilling a doubled or redoubled contract. See PREMIUM SCORE.

ABSOLUTE FORCE. A bid which makes it incumbent on partner to guarantee that another bid can be made by the player making the absolute force. Unless the bid is overcalled or doubled immediately, the partner is under conventional obligation to make some call other than a pass. See DEMAND BID, FORCING BID.

ABSY CONVENTION. A form of STAYMAN popular in France devised by Dr. Rafael Absy of Paris. A two club response promises at least 8 high-card points, unlike the standard version in which the responder may be very weak. All two-level rebids show minimum no trump hands, with two no trump guaranteeing both major suits. Maximum hands rebid at the three-level, with three clubs denying a major and three diamonds promising both majors. If opener has rebid three diamonds, rebids of four clubs and four diamonds by responder transfer to four hearts and four spades respectively.

ACCIDENTS. From time to time a player may suffer from some misfortune. He may miscount his points, missort his hand, mishear the bidding, or pull out a wrong card. In such circumstances he should be particularly careful not to react in any way when he discovers his error. A player who ostentatiously and angrily takes a card from one part of his hand and jabs it into a different location may be giving information to his partner, and be subject to penalty. See LAWS (Law 16). Such behavior by a declarer would be simply unwise, but not improper.

The error may sometimes be corrected legally, and in such a case the auction may puzzle the other three players. For example:

WEST	NORTH	EAST	SOUTH
1 ♠	Pass	Pass	1 NT
Pass	Pass	2 ◊	4 ♡

The most likely explanation of South's curious behavior is that he has a void diamond: after the two diamond bid, he inspected his diamond holding only to find that both his red suits were hearts.

ACCORDING TO HOYLE. A phrase indicating that a procedure is sanctioned both legally and ethically; in addition, that it has the backing of custom. The prestige of Edmond HOYLE was so great that the phrase "according to Hoyle" came to mean correct procedure in general.

ACE. The suit card with only a single pip. In most games, including all those of the bridge family, it is the highest ranking card; hence, a top performer in any field.

In England, the ace of spades was the card which indicated that the duty had been paid (see TAXES ON PLAYING CARDS) and its printing was controlled by the government. Ever since the wrapper carried the duty or tax notation, the card has remained ornate in England and the United States, where each manufacturer developed an individual design to serve as a trademark.

In other countries, other aces have served to carry the trademarks: clubs in France, hearts in Germany. See: ACE-SHOWING RESPONSES; HONOR TRICKS; OPENING LEADS; POINT-COUNT.

ACE FROM ACE-KING. The traditional lead of the king from an ace-king holding has been abandoned by many players in favor of the ace lead. Some players lead the ace against no trump contracts only, because an ace lead against no trump is unlikely to be attractive if the king is not held.

The argument in favor of leading the ace is that it avoids certain ambiguities which arise if the king is led:

(1) After the lead of the king against a suit contract, the opening leader's partner is unsure whether to high-low with a small doubleton combination. He would wish to do so if the lead is from ace-king, but not if it is from king-queen. The same would apply if the leader's partner holds a doubleton jack.

(2) After the lead of the king against any contract, the opening leader's partner is uncertain whether to signal with his second card holding the jack and two small cards. In this situation he would wish to signal if the lead was from king-queen but not if it was from ace-king. (It is assumed in all cases that dummy holds three worthless cards.)

Against this, the proponents of the king lead point out that the lead of an unsupported ace is not uncommon against a suit contract, and the leader's partner may wish to know whether the king is held.

Holding a doubleton ace-king this special procedure is reversed: the king is led followed by the ace.

Whatever convention is being used, the ace lead is tactically advisable against a slam contract: the king is too revealing when the opposing hands have a singleton opposite a combination headed by queen-jack.

For an alternative method of avoiding the ambiguity arising from the king lead, see RUSINOW LEAD.

ACE-GRABBER. A player who leads or takes his aces at his first opportunity, thereby automatically setting up tricks for the opponents or making the play easier for them.

ACE-HIGH. (1) A term dating from whist days indicating that the ace is the highest card in the suit or the cut. Obsolescent in bridge because the alternative procedures associated with other games have been generally forgotten. (2) Descriptive of a suit held by one player in which the ace is the top card.

ACE IDENTIFICATION. An extension of the Gerber convention devised by Norman Squire (England) to discover which ace a partnership is missing.

When responder has shown one or two aces in response to four clubs, four no trump asks for further information. If responder has one ace, he bids the suit of the ace. If he has two aces, he bids:

5 ♣	with aces of the same color
5 ♢	with aces of the same rank
5 ♡	with mixed aces

This may assist in deciding whether to bid a small slam, and possibly a grand slam if the four no trump bidder has a void. See also GERBER and ROMAN GERBER.

ACE LEAD. Against no trump, by a convention of long standing, this lead requires partner to play his highest card of the suit led. This may be helpful if the opening leader has A K J 10 x x, and his partner holds the queen, but these situations are not common. This is not applicable of course if a partnership uses ACE FROM ACE-KING as a standard lead.

ACE SHOWING. See CUE-BIDS TO SHOW CONTROLS.

ACE-SHOWING RESPONSES. Answers to forcing opening bids that are based on the theory that the opener with a powerful unbalanced hand is more interested in his partner's first-round controls than in his long suit or general strength.

This is sometimes employed over FORCING TWO-BIDS, but is also common in conjunction with conventional TWO CLUB STRONG ARTIFICIAL OPENINGS, especially in Europe (see P. ALBARRAN). A minimum response, other than a negative one, shows the ace of the suit bid. The responses to a conventional two club bid would be:

two diamonds	negative
two hearts or spades	ace-showing
two no trump	8 points at least, but aceless
three clubs or diamonds	ace-showing
three no trump	two aces

French experts vary this scheme in two ways. A two no trump response is permitted with two kings; and a hand holding two aces can make a more precise response:

three hearts	two mixed aces (♠ and ♢, or ♡ and ♣)
three spades	two aces of the same color
three no trump	two aces, both major, or both minor

The opening bidder can subsequently ask for kings by using the bid normally employed to ask for aces—four no trump or four clubs at choice.

A method suggested by C.S. HOBLIT, of Detroit, Michigan, for use over natural forcing two-bids, requires responder to show top trump honors, if any, along with his aces. The responses are:

single raise	one trump honor, no ace
double raise	two trump honors, no ace
new suit	ace in suit, no trump honor
jump in new suit	ace in suit, one trump honor
double jump in new suit	ace in suit, two trump honors
two no trump	no trump honors, no ace
three no trump	no trump honors, two aces

An alternative scheme is to respond according to the *step* principle, showing aces and kings simultaneously. See STEP RESPONSES. See also BLUE TEAM CLUB, CAB SYSTEM, DYNAMIC NO TRUMP, SCHENKEN SYSTEM (two diamond opening), SKINNER TWO BIDS, TAM II TWO CLUB OPENING.

ACE VALUES. A method of distributional valuation developed as part of the BARON SYSTEM.

When valuing a hand for a raise, the HONOR TRICK value of the hand is added to the following distributional values:

	with 3 trumps	with 4 trumps
void	2	3
singleton	1	2
doubleton	½	1

(But a second shortage counts at half-value unless five trumps are held).

The total is the level to which responder should raise playing LIMIT RAISES. For example:

♠ Q J 3 2   ♡ K Q 6   ◇ K 6 5 2   ♣ 9 6

In response to a one spade opening bid, this hand counts three ace values (two for honor tricks plus one for the club doubleton), and therefore justifies a raise to three spades.

If the opening bidder is planning to raise his partner's response, he subtracts two from his ace values and raises to the level of the answer: i.e., with four ace values he raises to the two-level, with five to the three-level, and so on. See DISTRIBUTIONAL COUNTS.

ACES OVER TWO-BIDS. See ACE-SHOWING RESPONSES.

ACES SCIENTIFIC SYSTEM. A detailed system formulated by the ACES TEAM with the aid of a computer for research and experimentation. Precise standards are set for all phases of bidding, including detailed methods for dealing with opponents' interference in constructive auctions. The main features of the system, as described by R. GOLDMAN, are:

(1) 15½ to 18 point no trump openings. Responses of two diamonds and two hearts are JACOBY TRANSFERS; two spades promises both minor suits and is a mild slam try; three clubs and three diamonds are weak; three hearts and three spades, both artificial, are mild slam tries in clubs and diamonds respectively.

Two clubs is non-forcing STAYMAN, following which responder may: rebid three clubs to seek a 4–4 minor suit fit; or rebid three diamonds (artificial) to show a long minor suit and slam interest; or rebid three of the other major suit to show four-card support for opener's major, an unidentified singleton and slam interest.

(2) Major suit openings promise at least five cards; a one no trump response is forcing for one round; two-level responses are virtually forcing to game. Jump raises are limit, and forcing raises may be made in one of six ways to show specific point ranges and hands with and without singletons. See UNBALANCED SWISS, VALUE SWISS.

Jump shifts into minor suits show solid suits with at least 6½ playing tricks; opener's rebids below three no trump show stoppers rather than suits.

(3) Minor suit openings promise at least three-card suits. Immediate jump raises are limit; jumps to three of the *other* minor suit are forcing raises. These jump shifts and delayed jump raises are forcing to

three no trump or four of a minor. Jump shift responses into major suits promise either a solid suit, or an excellent suit in a no trump type hand, or a strong suit with strong support for opener.

(4) TWO CLUB openings (strong and artificial) are usually forcing to game. Responses of two diamonds are neutral; other suits are natural with good values in the suit; and two and three no trump deny any aces and show balanced hands with no suit worse than J x x. Two-level openings other than clubs are WEAK TWO-BIDS.

(5) Slam conventions include modern Roman responses to BLACKWOOD, GERBER, and SUPER GERBER, plus a fifth step to show two aces and a useful void, and additional steps to show one ace and a useful void. Further slam tries may be made after the ace-asking response. Five no trump, even after Blackwood, asks about trump quality whenever a fit has been agreed.

ACES TEAM. A full-time professional bridge team, organized in 1968 by Dallas financier Ira CORN for the express purpose of returning the world team championship to the United States.

In an attempt to duplicate the unity and team spirit of Italy's famed BLUE TEAM, Corn selected six players from among America's leading young experts, paying each a salary, plus tournament expenses, to undertake a full-time career of studying and playing bridge. Selection, beginning with a Texas pair, James JACOBY and Robert WOLFF, was based on the player's ability to function harmoniously within the team framework and to adjust to the pressures of training and championship play. Three additional players, William EISENBERG, Robert GOLDMAN, and Michael LAWRENCE, accepted the offer in 1968; Robert HAMMAN, the sixth member, joined the team in 1969. Meanwhile, in 1968 retired Air Force Colonel Joseph MUSUMECI was added as trainer and coach. Since its operations were centered in Dallas, Texas, the team originally became known as the Dallas Aces, later shortened to the Aces; the name US Aces under which they were incorporated was not accepted by the ACBL.

Using a computer to analyze results and to generate specific sets of hands to provide practice in given areas of the game—slam hands, pre-emptive openings, etc.—the Aces spent 50 to 60 hours a week perfecting the three partnerships' bidding systems and discussing problems encountered at the table. Complete records of all hands played by the team were compiled for critical analysis. From the intensive study and analysis emerged three bidding systems or styles: the ORANGE CLUB, used by Wolff and Jacoby; the similar BLACK CLUB, used by Hamman and Eisenberg; and the ACES SCIENTIFIC SYSTEM, used by Goldman and Lawrence. Besides competing in National tournaments and Regional knockout team-of-four contests, the Aces also engaged many of America's top experts in practice matches in Dallas and staged a series of exhibition matches. See SHARIF BRIDGE CIRCUS.

In 1968, the Aces captured the Spring National Men's Teams, and that summer Eisenberg-Goldman and Jacoby-Wolff finished first and second respectively in the Life Master Pairs, which qualified both pairs for the INTERNATIONAL OPEN TEAM SELECTION trials. Eisenberg-Goldman subsequently earned a place on the 1969 North American International Team, as did Hamman, who was not then a member of the Aces. In 1969, the team achieved the first major goal set by Corn by winning the Spingold Knockout Teams and later routing the Vanderbilt champions by 141 IMPs in a play-off match that earned the Aces the right to represent North America in the 1970 Bermuda Bowl in Stockholm, Sweden. With the Blue Team retired, the Aces swept the 1970 World Championship and returned the Bermuda Bowl to North America for the first time since 1954. The Aces successfully defended their world title in 1971. See WORLD CHAMPIONSHIPS.

Thereafter the makeup of the Aces' team began to change. In 1971 Eisenberg left the team and was replaced by Paul SOLOWAY; in early 1973 Soloway was replaced by Mark BLUMENTHAL. In mid-1973 Lawrence and Jacoby left the team and were replaced by Eric MURRAY and Sammy KEHELA. Following the 1974 Bermuda Bowl, Goldman and Blumenthal left the team and were replaced by Don KRAUSS and Edwin KANTAR, who themselves were replaced shortly thereafter by Soloway, returning, and John SWANSON. In 1975 the Aces were Hamman and Wolff, Murray and Kehela, Soloway and Swanson. By June of 1972 the team had become a part-time effort, with the players being paid only their expenses rather than salaries.

Following their initial successes in 1968, the Aces continued to perform well in international and national competition. They were World Champions in 1970 and 1971; runners-up in World Championships in 1972, 1973, 1974 and 1975*, winners of the SPINGOLD TROPHY in 1969, runners-up in 1970; winners of the VANDERBILT CUP (1) in 1971, 1973, runners-up in 1970; co-winners of the REISINGER MEMORIAL TROPHY in 1970. In 1972 Hamman, Wolff, and Goldman were members of the team that won the World Olympiad Mixed Team Championship. In 1974 Hamman and Wolff won the World Open Pair Championship in Las Palmas.

ACOL DIRECT KING CONVENTION. A bid of four no trump to ask about kings by a player whose partner has already made a bid specifically showing the number of aces he holds. This convention can be used with such conventions as GAMBLING THREE NO TRUMP, when it has been agreed that this bid denies an outside ace, and STEP RESPONSES TO STRONG ARTIFICIAL TWO-BIDS.

ACOL FOUR NO TRUMP OPENING. A specialized bid asking for aces. The responses are:

5 ♣	no ace
5 ◇	ace of diamonds
5 ♡	ace of hearts
5 ♠	ace of spades
5 NT	2 aces
6 ♣	ace of clubs

ACOL SYSTEM. The system which is "standard" in British tournament play, and widely used in other parts of the world. The originators were a group of players which included M. HARRISON-GRAY, I. MAC LEOD, J. C. H. MARX, T. REESE, and S. J. SIMON, and it was called Acol because it was first played in 1934 in the small North London bridge club on the street of the same name. Many of the ideas were derived from the early writings of Ely CULBERTSON.

The chief features of the system are:

(1) The weak no trump not vulnerable and the strong no trump vulnerable. The original ranges were 13–15 and 16–18, but 12–14 has become standard for the weak range, and 15–17 is often preferred to 16–18. (The system is frequently used with a weak or strong no trump at all vulnerabilities (see also THREE-QUARTER NO TRUMP).)

(2) LIMIT RAISES and no trump responses. Raises and no trump responses are never forcing in their own right. After an opening bid of one spade, a response of two no trump or three spades is encouraging but not forcing, showing about 11 points or the distributional equivalent.

(3) Jump rebids are not forcing unless in a new suit.

(4) Opening suit bids tend to be slightly weaker than in American methods, especially if a six-card major suit is held.

(5) TWO-OVER-ONE RESPONSES are made more freely than in American methods: 8 points with a five-card suit, or 7 points with a six-card suit may be sufficient.

(6) Fourth-suit bids are used conventionally by most Acol experts. See FOURTH SUIT FORCING.

(7) Two clubs, artificial strong opening, forcing to two no trump.

(8) ACOL TWO-BID, forcing for one round.

(9) GAMBLING THREE NO TRUMP. A long strong minor suit with at least two other suits protected.

(10) Four no trump opening asks for specific aces. See ACOL FOUR NO TRUMP OPENING.

Other regular features of the system are listed separately: CULBERTSON FOUR-FIVE NO TRUMP or BLACKWOOD; STAYMAN; GRAND SLAM FORCE; TRIAL BID. Optional features of Acol listed separately include: ACOL DIRECT KING CONVENTION; BARON SLAM TRY; BENJAMIN; CROWHURST; FLINT THREE DIAMONDS; FLINT TWO DIAMONDS; GERBER; INTEREST-SHOWING BIDS; KOCK-WERNER REDOUBLES; RESPONSIVE DOUBLE; RO-MAN BLACKWOOD; ROMAN TWO DIAMOND; SHARPLES; SHORT-SUIT GAME TRIES; STRONG NO TRUMP AFTER PASSING; SWISS; TEXAS; UNUSUAL NO TRUMP; VOID-SHOWING BIDS; WEISSBERGER.

ACOL TWO-BID. A type of intermediate two-bid, strong and forcing for one round. A strong distributional hand is required with at least eight playing tricks:

(a)	(b)
♠ A K Q 8 7 5 4	♠ 8
♡ A J 4	♡ A Q J 10 5 4
◇ 9 6	◇ A K 9 8 5
♣ 2	♣ 9
Two spades	Two hearts

A suit of six or more cards is normal, but the bid can be used with two strong five-card suits.

The negative response is two no trump (although some use the next highest suit by special partnership agreement), after which a simple rebid or a bid of a lower-ranking suit at the three-level is non-forcing.

A suit take-out response approximates to a standard two-over-one take-out, but can be weaker at the level of two. A single raise is highly constructive, suggesting a slam, and virtually promising an ace. A double raise shows about 10 points but no ace. If responder has moderate strength but no marked distributional feature and no slam ambitions, he can make a negative response and then bid game. See BENJAMIN.

ACORNS. One of the suits in old-time PLAYING CARDS. See also PACK.

ADEQUATE TRUMP SUPPORT. See TRUMP SUPPORT.

ADJUSTED SCORE. An arbitrary score assigned by the tournament director. An adjusted score may be exactly an average score, if the director finds that neither side was at fault. A pair may be awarded a score below average if the director decides that it was guilty of a violation of law or procedure; or a pair may be awarded an above-average score if the director decides that their score was damaged by a violation of law or procedure by another pair. The North-South and East-West scores are not necessarily complementary. See LAWS OF DUPLICATE (Laws 12, 82, 84).

ADVANCE CUE-BID. A cue-bid of a first-round control (in rare cases, a second-round control) made before the cue-bidder's partner knows the agreed trump suit. The purpose of this cue-bid is to distinguish between a normal raise and a raise based on controls plus a good distributional fit that offers some hope for slam if partner has the right distribution or high-card structure.

For example, the bidding goes:

SOUTH	NORTH
1 ♠	2 ♡
3 ♠	4 ♣

North holds:

♠ J 6 5
♡ A Q 9 7 3
♢ 9 2
♣ A 10 4

If South holds a solid spade suit, the king of hearts and a diamond control, slam at spades will be a reasonable undertaking, but might not be reached unless North shows his slam interest by cue-bidding the ace of clubs before supporting spades. From South's seat, however, the four club bid is ambiguous. North could have a heart-club two-suiter or be making an advance cue-bid.

The cue-bid might also be used after a jump shift:

SOUTH	NORTH
1 ♠	1 NT
3 ♢	4 ♣

North holds:

♠ 7
♡ Q 10 6 4
♢ K 8 7 3 2
♣ A 5 2

North's hand has grown to slam proportions after South's jump shift, so he makes a slam try by cue-bidding the club ace *before* raising diamonds. Here also South is not yet certain whether North has a legitimate club suit, or is cue-bidding in support of diamonds, or possibly spades.

Variations of this cue-bid occur in many no trump sequences, but cannot be considered "true" advance cue-bids because the trump suit is set by implication. For example:

SOUTH	NORTH		SOUTH	NORTH		SOUTH	NORTH
1 NT	3 ♠		2 NT	3 ♡		1 ♣	1 ♠
4 ♢			4 ♣			2 NT	3 ♡
						4 ♢	

The logical interpretation of South's last bid in each of these auctions is that he has strong support for partner's last named suit, a maximum for his previous bid(s), a wealth of first- and second-round controls and, usually, a ruffing value and the ace of the cue-bid suit. Without these features, South would support North's suit or rebid three no trump, as North's bidding requested. See also RESPONSES TO ONE NO TRUMP AND TWO NO TRUMP.

ADVANCE SAVE. A sacrifice bid made before the opponents have reached their probable optimum contract. This may have two objects: first to leave the opposition in doubt about whether the sacrifice bidder expects to make his contract; second to make the opponents guess at a high level without giving them full opportunity to exchange information.

For example, East-West are vulnerable and the bidding goes:

WEST	NORTH	EAST	SOUTH
1 ♣	1 ♡	2 ♡	6 ♡

South holds:

♠ 5 3
♡ Q 7 5 3 2
♢ J 7 5 3 2
♣ 6

It is highly probable that East-West are headed for a slam in a black suit, so South aims to set his opponents a problem. South is prepared to concede a penalty of 900 or thereabouts, which may prove an accurate sacrifice and also may goad East-West into attempting an impossible contract. See also SACRIFICE.

ADVANCED SENIOR MASTER. The second highest in the ranking of players in the AMERICAN CONTRACT BRIDGE LEAGUE. See RANKING OF PLAYERS.

ADVERSARY. Either opponent of declarer, or, during the auction, a player on the other side. The laws of 1963 use "opponent" for the latter and "defender" for the former. Senior adversary was synonymous with declarer's left-hand opponent, and junior adversary with his right-hand opponent.

AFRICA. See the following areas and countries, listed separately as African Bridge Federations: CENTRAL AFRICA, EGYPTIAN BRIDGE ASSOCIATION, MOROCCO, SOUTH AFRICA.

AGGREGATE SCORE. See TOTAL POINT SCORING.

ALBERT MOREHEAD CHAPTER OF THE IBPA. The American section of the INTERNATIONAL BRIDGE PRESS ASSOCIATION, formed in 1967 and named in honor of Albert H. Morehead, former bridge editor of *The New York Times,* who was critically ill at that time. In 1975, the President of the chapter, and also President of the IBPA, was Richard L. Frey.

ALBERT TWO CLUBS. An artificial opening bid, used by the Venezuelan team in the 1966 and 1967 WORLD CHAMPIONSHIPS, that describes a powerful hand, generally forcing to game.

The responses are:

2 ◇: 7 or more points
2 ♡: 0–6 points
2 ♠: five-card or longer spade suit
2 NT: five-card or longer heart suit
3 ♣ or 3 ◇: natural
3 ♡: 0–2 points, balanced hand
3 ♠: six-card suit headed by three honors
3 NT: six-card heart suit headed by three honors
4 ♡ or 4 ♠: solid six- or seven-card suit

ALCATRAZ COUP. A coup in contract bridge is a term applied to any strategic play. A few situations can come up which are not covered by the rules. The Alcatraz Coup is one of these; as the name suggests, it is considered a form of robbery that almost warrants a prison term for the perpetrator. The following is an example:

DUMMY	A J 10
DECLARER	K x

Declarer, to make three tricks in the suit, calls the jack from dummy and, receiving a small card from right-hand opponent, fails to follow suit. Fourth hand either produces the queen or a small card. If a small card, declarer corrects his revoke by substituting the small card, leads to his king, and has the ace in dummy for the third trick. If fourth hand produces the queen, declarer "corrects his revoke" by producing the king, sweetly permitting his left-hand opponent to change his play, and finesses the located queen on the next lead.

The coup could be perpetrated unintentionally, and in the following example there is no unethical intent.

DUMMY	X X X
DECLARER	A Q 10 8

Dummy is on lead, and when right-hand opponent follows suit declarer unintentionally revokes by ruffing. As it happens, left-hand opponent overruffs, exposing the position. Declarer corrects his revoke and is able to take the marked "finesse" of the eight.

Whenever the coup occurs, whether or not it is intentional, the defenders are entitled to redress and should receive an adjusted score in accordance with LAWS OF DUPLICATE (Laws 12A, 47F). No director would permit a declarer to gain an advantage of this type, and any such swindle attempted deliberately should meet with a serious penalty on ethical charges.

ALERTING. A method of drawing opponents' attention to the fact that a particular bid has a conventional or unusual meaning. In 1971 the ACBL adopted a CONVENTION CARD that provided boxes for a partnership to check off its basic bidding agreements, thereby eliminating the need to list all partnership understandings. In addition, the ACBL has made it mandatory for a player to alert his opponents whenever his partner makes a bid that has a special partnership meaning and that is other than a "Class A" CONVENTION. The recommended procedure is that when such a bid occurs, the player announces to his right-hand opponent, "Alert." The opponent can request an explanation at that time or can reserve the right to inquire at the conclusion of the auction. See EXPLANATION OF CONVENTIONAL CALL OR PLAY. A player must use the alert procedure unless his opponents specifically request him not to do so before the auction begins. See CONVENTION. A player who gains information from his partner's alert should avoid taking advantage of it. However, if his partner has alerted in error or has given a wrong explanation, it is improper for him to correct the error immediately or to indicate in any manner that a mistake has been made; and he is under no legal or moral obligation to offer a correction later. If, as a result of alerting, whether or not an explanation is requested, a partnership either avoids a misunderstanding or becomes aware of a misunderstanding, an ADJUSTED SCORE may be awarded. See LAWS OF DUPLICATE (Laws 16, 40, and Proprieties II, IV).

Use of diagonal bidding SCREENS in national and (in 1975) in World Championship play made it necessary in many cases for the bidder himself to point silently to an "alert" sign for the benefit of his left-hand opponent; this procedure was then repeated by his partner for the benefit of the latter's left-hand opponent on his side of the screen. In a few instances the explanations of the two partners differed and it then became necessary for the director, or a tournament committee, to decide on the need to adjust a score or replay a deal. In the absence of screens, an informal method of alerting used in many international events is to tap on the table.

ALL-AMERICAN REGIONAL CHAMPION-SHIPS. A four-day event held annually in the Midwest, beginning in 1938. This tournament is usually staged in Cleveland or Akron (and in past years Toledo and Detroit) over Memorial Day. For past results, see Appendix II.

ALL INDIA BRIDGE FEDERATION. See BRIDGE FEDERATION OF INDIA.

ALL INDONESIA BRIDGE ASSOCIATION (GABUNGAN BRIDGE SELURUH INDONESIA). Founded in 1953, and by 1968 had a membership of approximately 6,000. The Association is a member of the Far East Bridge Federation, and participates in the Far East Championships and World Olympiads. Indonesia won the Far East Championships in 1962, 1964, 1972, 1973, and 1974. National tournaments include an annual Intercity Championship and biennial events for Open Pairs, Mixed Pairs, and Women's Teams (odd-numbered years) and Open Teams and Women's Pairs (even-numbered years). Players listed separately are Tan Hok San, Oei King Hian, H. Lasut, E. Manoppo, F. Manoppo, W. Moniaga, W. Wuwungan.

Officers, 1975:
President: Dr. Sunawar Sukowati.
Secretary: Abdul Majid, Jln. Cik Di Third
     Djakarta, Indonesia.

ALLEN OVER NO TRUMP. A convention suggested by Larry ALLEN of Summerville, South Carolina, for use in conjunction with JACOBY TRANSFER BIDS to initiate a search for a 4–4 minor suit fit. After responder has bid two clubs STAYMAN and opener has responded in a major suit, a rebid of the other major by responder asks opener to show another four-card suit if he has one. If opener has rebid two diamonds in response to Stayman, a three-club bid by responder is also a minor suit inquiry. Opener rebids three diamonds with 3–3–4–3 distribution, rebids three no trump with 3–3–3–4 distribution, and rebids three of his shorter major suit if he has four cards in each minor suit. See also BARON COROLLARY.

ALLEN OVER TWO CLUBS. A method devised by Ellen ALLEN of Summerville, South Carolina, to describe three-suited hands of game-forcing strength. A two-club strong artificial opening is used, with an automatic TWO DIAMOND ARTIFICIAL RESPONSE; a jump rebid by opener to three of a major suit or four of a minor suit shows 4–4–4–1 or 5–4–4–0 distribution, with shortness in the suit bid.

ALPHA ASKING BIDS. (1) Asking bids in the ROMAN SYSTEM concerned with controls in a side suit. See ROMAN ASKING BIDS. (2) Asking bids in the SUPER PRECISION system concerned with responder's support for the one club opener's suit. See SUPER PRECISION ASKING BIDS.

ALTERNATE THREAT SQUEEZE. See COMPOUND SQUEEZE.

ALTERNATIVE SQUEEZE (Either-Or Squeeze). A simple squeeze played as a double squeeze.

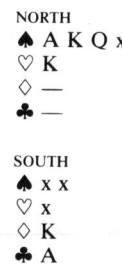

NORTH
♠ A K Q x
♡ K
◊ —
♣ —

SOUTH
♠ x x
♡ x
◊ K
♣ A

Suppose that West has the ace of hearts, and East has the ace of diamonds. Spades cannot be guarded by both opponents, so that North's small spade technically cannot be a DOUBLE MENACE because it is not possible for opponents to hold four spades each. However, when South leads the ace of clubs, whichever opponent is actually guarding spades must unguard that suit in order to keep his ace. If West keeps his ace of hearts, North discards the heart king; if West started with four or more spades the squeeze has worked on him. Alternatively, if West started with fewer than four spades, East is now squeezed.

                                        M. I.

AMBIGUOUS BIDS. See PARTNERSHIP MISUNDERSTANDINGS.

AMERICAN AUCTION BRIDGE LEAGUE. See AMERICAN BRIDGE LEAGUE.

AMERICAN BRIDGE ASSOCIATION. The national organization founded in 1932 to encourage duplicate bridge among black players. It continued to develop steadily, reaching a total membership of about 5,000 in 1975, including 1,500 Life Masters. It conducts two annual National tournaments, a Spring National, usually held in April since 1969, and a Summer National, usually held in August since 1934, with pair championships for Open, Mixed, Men's and Women's Pairs, an Individual, and team championships for Open, Mixed, Men's and Women's Teams. The earliest National championships were held in New York, but since that time have been held in many major cities all over the US. For past results of the ABA Open Teams and Open Pairs, see Appendix I.

In the early days of contract bridge, Negroes were excluded from most major tournaments. In 1932, a small group of black players in the Greater New York area decided to foster and promote duplicate bridge among themselves. To that end, they conceived the idea of establishing a national organization and made contact with similar groups in other parts of the country. The result was the foundation of the American Bridge Association by Dr. M. E. Du Bissette (President, 1932–35), Horace R. Miller (President, 1936), and L. C. Collins, with John W. Cromwell, Jr., of Washington, D.C.

In 1936 the ABA merged with the Eastern Bridge League, a group of New York City clubs headed by Morgan S. Jensen. There followed a period of steady expansion under the presidency of Dr. E. T. Belsaw (1936–49). Four geographical sections were formed, subsequently expanded to seven, which conducted sectional tournaments equivalent to ACBL Regional tournaments. A master-point system was established for rating players. The bi-monthly *ABA Bulletin*, edited by W. R. Tatem from 1944–53, became an outstanding publication, and its high standards were maintained under the succeeding editors, Clarence Farmer (1953–70) and Mrs. Bobbye Caldwell (1970–).

Official recognition of the growing acceptance of Negro participation in tournaments came in 1952, when the ACBL passed an amendment proposed by Gen. R. Gill by which each unit became the sole judge of membership qualifications in its territory.

Enactment of Federal legislation which forbade the exclusion of Negroes from hotels, etc., was speedily followed in 1964 by an ACBL regulation ensuring the right of any ACBL member to play in any National tournament no matter where held.

The last barrier to ACBL membership for Negroes was removed in 1967 when the ACBL included in its bylaws the proviso that "no person shall be denied membership because of race, color, or creed."

An outstanding achievement of the ABA administration under Victor R. Daly, Washington, D.C. (President, 1949–64), was the conduct of negotiations leading to the building of mutual rapport and respect between the ACBL and the ABA. Hundreds of ABA members joined the ACBL, and several became Life Masters. The first Negro Life Master of the ACBL was Marion Wildy of Aiea, Oahu, Hawaii, and the first ABA player to achieve Life Master ranking in the ACBL was Leo Benson of Chicago.

The close association of the ACBL and the ABA continued under the ABA presidency of Maurice Robinson, New York, N.Y. (President, 1964–69). At the suggestion of the ABA, representatives of the ABA and the Greater New York Bridge Association, a unit of the ACBL, met in two exhibition matches in New York in 1969 resulting in one win for each organization.

The leading master-point holders of the ABA in 1975 were Roscoe Rigmaiden of Philadelphia and Robert Price of Chicago. William Sides was the leading player on the West Coast. The leading ABA woman player was Joyce Williams of Chicago, who was also its fourth-ranking master-point holder.

ABA President (1976): Dr. Jacqueline Sheppard, 6125 Washington Ave., Philadelphia, Pa. 19143
Executive Secretary: Ken Cox, 1740 Mulford Ave., Apt. 15A, Bronx, N.Y.

AMERICAN BRIDGE LEAGUE. An organization founded in 1927 at Hanover, N.H. (see HISTORY OF BRIDGE). The original title was "American Auction Bridge League," but the word "Auction" was dropped in 1929. The League amalgamated with the UNITED STATES BRIDGE ASSOCIATION in 1937 to form the AMERICAN CONTRACT BRIDGE LEAGUE. ABL presidents are listed under PRESIDENTS, and ABL results are listed with ACBL results under Fall Nationals and Summer Nationals in Appendix I.

AMERICAN BRIDGE OLYMPICS. American winners of the WORLD PAR CONTESTS are listed under that title.

The Culbertson organization staged a national Olympic in 1932, distinct from the World event. The winners were: North-South, Dr. and Mrs. Monte F. Meyer; East-West, James M. Magner, Jr., and William C. Campbell.

AMERICAN BRIDGE TEACHERS' ASSOCIATION. A non-profit professional organization composed primarily of bridge teachers, but also includes tournament directors and bridge writers, dedicated to promoting higher standards of bridge teaching and playing.

The ABTA was founded in 1957 by a charter membership of 150. At the initial meeting, held in New York City, the fourteen members attending, including Deborah N. Glover, the organizing secretary and George S. COFFIN, the organizing treasurer, proposed that the goal of the organization be "to provide and protect the standards of bridge teaching and its practitioners, to establish a code of ethics and minimal fees insofar as is practical, and to make known in the public and professional interest any information in the bridge profession."

The Association is divided into ten regions, each headed by a Vice President, who, with the assistance of state chairmen, arrange frequent meetings where teachers learn new techniques and have an opportunity to examine the latest teaching equipment. In addition, there is an annual meeting, usually held in conjunction with the Summer Nationals of the ACBL, where several days are spent listening to outstanding bridge teachers and players. Most of the leading bridge personalities have addressed this convention at least once and many have appeared on several occasions.

Applicants for membership in the ABTA are required to pass an entrance exam. Once accepted, members are rated according to experience, training, and attendance at teachers' seminars, with the highest rating available being "Master Bridge Teacher."

The Association publishes a quarterly bulletin, which includes news of the organization's activities, articles on teaching techniques, and an exchange of ideas for promoting business. See BIBLIOGRAPHY, P.

Presidents of the ABTA have been: Jo Woods of Arkansas 1958–59, Margaret M. Wales of Texas 1960–61, Deborah N. Glover of Florida 1962, George S. Gooden of California 1963, Dorothy Jane Cook of Illinois 1964, Kenneth Turner of Ontario 1965, Nellie Harrington of West Virginia 1966, Helen Albano of New Jersey 1967, Thelma Smith of Texas 1968–69, Helen Cale of California 1969–70, Effie L. Long of Connecticut 1971–72, Edward L.

Gordy of Florida 1973–75, Eloene Griggs of Washington, D.C. 1975–.

Secretary, 1974–75: Dr. T. B. Lyons, 113 Hillson Avenue, Pittsburgh, Pa. 15227.

AMERICAN CONTRACT BRIDGE LEAGUE. The NATIONAL AUTHORITY and governing body for organized bridge activities and promotion on the North American continent; it is by far the largest bridge organization in the world. The ACBL, as it is usually referred to in this book, traces its history from the organization of the American Auction Bridge League in Hanover, N.H., at the 1927 congress (tournament) of the AMERICAN WHIST LEAGUE, by a group sparked by Ralph R. RICHARDS, Detroit, including E. J. TOBIN and Robert W. HALPIN, Chicago, Henry P. JAEGER and C. W. Aldrich, Cleveland. Tobin was named Executive Secretary. CONTRACT BRIDGE was introduced into the second congress held in Cleveland in 1928, during which year the infant organization acquired the services of William E. MC KENNEY, whose originality, drive, and organizational ability did much to establish the League. The increased popularity of contract bridge at the expense of the older game, auction bridge, led to the name change to AMERICAN BRIDGE LEAGUE in 1929. A merger of this group with the UNITED STATES BRIDGE ASSOCIATION was effected in 1937, with McKenney, first named Executive Secretary in 1929, remaining at the helm of the organization until 1947, shortly before his death in 1950.

In 1948–49 a major reorganization of the League was carried out by W. von ZEDTWITZ, as President and Chairman, aided by the Steering Committee of R. GILL, R. GRESHAM, L. HAZEN, B. LEBHAR, R. MC GROVER, and A. MOREHEAD and the By-Laws Committee headed by L. WEISS of Boston.

McKenney was succeeded by R. BALDWIN, who was appointed Business Manager of the League and remained so until his recall to active duty with the US Army in 1951, at which time A. LANDY was named acting Business Manager. In 1952, Landy was advanced to the position of Executive Secretary, remaining in that post until his death in 1967. Tom STODDARD, then Executive Administrator, served briefly as Executive Secretary pro tem until Easley BLACKWOOD was appointed to that post in 1968, retiring after three years, as he had planned, on March 1, 1971. R. GOLDBERG, Assistant Executive Secretary under both Landy and Blackwood, was named as Blackwood's successor.

The membership of the League grew spectacularly from the 270 who joined the American Auction Bridge League to more than 15,000 at its twentieth birthday in 1947; following merger in 1956 with the PACIFIC BRIDGE LEAGUE, which became the ACBL's Western Division, headed by Stoddard, growth accelerated to 170,000 in 1970 and approached 200,000 in 1975.

During these years, the League moved to New York from the Midwest in 1934; then to its own building in Greenwich, Connecticut, in 1967. This became sole national headquarters in 1968 when the western office was closed. In 1972 the League erected its own building in Memphis, Tennessee, opened in late November at 2200 Democrat Road, with adequate space for its then needs and provision for anticipated expansion.

In addition to the growth in membership, there has been a tremendous increase in the scope and influence of the League's activities. Beyond the authorization and supervision of bridge tournament activities from the level of National and Regional CHAMPIONSHIP TOURNAMENTS to the games run in some 5,000 affiliated duplicate bridge clubs, ACBL activities include: formulation and publication of the LAWS, both OF CONTRACT (Rubber) BRIDGE and OF DUPLICATE CONTRACT BRIDGE; conduct of charity games and other activities which raised nearly three million dollars through 1974 (see CHARITY PROGRAM); cooperation with other national bridge organizations, through membership in the WORLD BRIDGE FEDERATION for which it hosted two WORLD TEAM OLYMPIADS (1964, 1972) as well as seven WORLD CHAMPIONSHIPS for the BERMUDA BOWL, following the inception of that event in 1950 in Bermuda through its 25th anniversary in 1975.

Two major forces in the League's growth are the MASTER-POINT PLAN and the RANKING OF PLAYERS, both of which were important considerations in the League's consolidation with USBA and the Pacific Bridge League. In 1961, the huge task of issuing and recording members' master points was computerized, and in 1975, when this service had grown to require mailing some 38,000 notification cards per semi-monthly cycle, it was streamlined to a once-a-month operation. The League's BULLETIN, published monthly, is the most widely distributed and one of the most highly respected publications in its field. The League has also compiled and published records and selected hands of all world championships and team Olympiads since 1953. See BIBLIOGRAPHY, G.

In addition to units in the United States, the ACBL encompasses units in Bermuda, Canada, and Mexico as well. The major championship tournaments conducted by the ACBL thrice annually are North American Championships, and are recognized by the World Bridge Federation as Zonal Championships. See WORLD BRIDGE FEDERATION PLAYER RANKINGS.

Members of the ACBL BOARD OF DIRECTORS and BOARD OF GOVERNORS are chosen by the membership. See DISTRICT, UNIT. PRESIDENTS, CHAIRMEN, and HONORARY MEMBERS of the League are elected by the Board of Directors. Copies of the BY-LAWS and ACBL HANDBOOK are available to members on request from ACBL HEADQUARTERS.

AMERICAN CONTRACT BRIDGE LEAGUE CHAMPIONSHIPS. Tournaments held twice a year from 1937, and three times a year since 1958 in various North American cities (see FALL NATIONALS, SPRING NATIONALS, and SUMMER NATIONALS). These tournaments, now called North American Championships, have usually consisted of four or more NATIONAL CHAMPIONSHIPS, some minor national events, and SIDE GAMES held two or three times, but usually four times, during each twenty-four hours.

Between 1964 and 1968, the Friday evening preceding the start of the championships was allocated to the playing of the Continentwide Charity Game or Olympiad Fund Game. These events have been held on the second Friday of the tournament since 1969, when the National championships were rescheduled to open a day earlier. The playing of the Continentwide Charity Game at the 1968 Spring Nationals, acting as hub of the continental effort, set a record by attracting 1,526 pairs. The largest Continentwide game, 17,524 pairs, was held at 375 sites during the 1972 Spring Nationals. GOLD POINTS, 25 of which are a requirement for LIFE MASTER ranking for players who began accumulating master points as of January 1, 1969, may be won in open or master national events. RED POINTS, 30 of which are one of the requirements for the status of Life Master, may be won in all national events. REGIONAL POINTS, 50 of which may be used instead of the 30 national red points for Life Master designation, may be won in side games. (In the regular side games, half of the points are given in regional red points, and half in black. In the Charity Pairs, Olympiad Fund Pairs, and International Fund Pairs, all points won are regional red points, which are converted in the ratio of 30 national red points to 50 regional red points.) The bookings for the Nationals have grown to be the fifth largest convention in the hotel ratings. The selection of cities and hotels for such mammoth tournaments presents great problems; allocations are usually made five years in advance. With three North American Championships, 80 Regionals, and 772 Sectionals in 1975—an increase each year—the ACBL reservations for hotel space are believed to be the largest for any field of activity.

AMERICAN LEADS. Leads devised at whist to give partner a count when a solid suit was being led. The lead of the jack followed by the queen, for example, showed a solid seven-card suit. The inventors were "CAVENDISH" of London, and N. B. Trist of New Orleans. Although they have been long obsolete, American leads were a milestone in the development of defensive signals.

AMERICAN WHIST LEAGUE. Founded in Milwaukee in 1891 as a central organization to control and promulgate the laws of whist. Its sponsorship of tournaments between representatives of member clubs did much to stimulate the competitive aspects of games of the bridge family. Within the first few years of the life of this League its members worked out official laws, rules, a code of ethics, boards, methods of scoring, and movements of boards and players for all sorts of games up to teams of sixteen.

The tournaments of the American Whist League (called congresses) were contested for the Hamilton Trophy (Club Teams of Four), 1892–1934; the Minneapolis Trophy (Club Pairs), 1895–1934; the Brooklyn Trophy (Auxiliary Association members), 1896–1911; Associate Members Trophy (Mixed Pairs), 1901–34; Manhattan Trophy (Mixed or Women's Pairs), 1908–34; the Congress Trophies (Men's Pairs), 1908–34.

By the end of the thirties, the League existed in name only, although whist congresses, attended by a few lifelong devotees, continued into the fifties. The careers of many of the players prominent in whist continued into auction bridge and contract, including such names listed in this encyclopedia as R. F. FOSTER, R. HALPIN, N. KELLY, S. LENZ, W. LIGGETT, JR., A. MOUAT, C. PATTON, R. RICHARDS, P. H. SIMS, C. WALLACE, W. WHITEHEAD, M. WORK.

The AWL prolonged its life by adding an Auction Team event in 1924 and an Auction Pair event in 1930. A Contract Whist event in 1934 did not prove popular and was dropped, but the Contract Pair event began in 1930 and the Team event in 1932 continued through 1937, with the winners as listed below:

ALL-AMERICAN TEAMS OF FOUR

1932	P. H. Sims, W. S. Karn
	D. Burnstine, H. Schenken
1933	L. H. Watson, C. S. Lochridge
	W. Malowan, S. Fry, Jr.
1934	L. H. Watson, A. M. Barnes
	H. H. Boscowitz, S. Fry, Jr.
1935	H. S. Vanderbilt, O. Jacoby
	A. M. Barnes, B. J. Becker
1936	E. Hymes, Jr., M. D. Maier
	O. Jacoby, L. J. Haddad
1937	R. W. Halpin, H. Kempner
	M. S. Becker, Jr., M. N. Besser

ALL-AMERICAN OPEN PAIRS

1930	D. R. Sims, W. von Zedtwitz
1931	F. C. Thwaits, R. E. Smith
1932	W. J. Pray, J. E. Cain
1933	L. H. Watson, S. Fry, Jr.
1934	L. H. Watson, S. Fry, Jr.
1935	W. von Zedtwitz, B. J. Becker
1936	R. F. Rubel, Allyne Paris
1937	A. Glatt, A. Weiss

AMERICAN WHIST MOVEMENT. A schedule for conducting duplicate contests between teams of four originated for tournaments at whist, later adapted to auction bridge and contract. See TEAM-OF-FOUR MOVEMENTS.

ANALYSIS. The appraisal of a bidding or playing situation. It is generally used in reference to the play of the cards. A good analyst will recognize the possibilities inherent in a particular deal and act accordingly, so as to give his side the best mathematical or psychological chance in either dummy play or defense.

ANCHOR SUIT. See ASTRO.

ANGLO-AMERICAN MATCHES. Teams representing Great Britain (or England) and the United States (or North America) have met on many occasions.

There have been five official meetings in World Championship competition:

| 1950 | Bermuda | United States won |
| 1955 | New York | Great Britain won |

1960	Turin	Great Britain won*
1962	New York	North America won
1965	Buenos Aires	North America won†

(Details of teams and scores are given under WORLD CHAMPIONSHIP.)

The following semi-official or unofficial matches have been played:

(1) London, 1930. America (Mr. and Mrs. E. Culbertson, T. Lightner, and W. von Zedtwitz) beat England (Col. W. Buller, Mrs. G. Evers, C. Kehoe, and Dr. N. Wood-Hill) by 4,845 total points over 200 boards.

(2) London, 1933. For the SCHWAB CUP. America (Mr. and Mrs. E. Culbertson, T. Lightner, and M. Gottlieb) beat England (Lt. Col. H. M. Beasley, Sir G. Domville, P. V. Tabbush, G. Morris, G. Mathieson, and Lady D. Rhodes) by 11,110 total points over 300 boards.

(3) London, 1934. For the SCHWAB CUP. America (Mr. and Mrs. E. Culbertson, T. Lightner, and A. Morehead) beat England (R. Lederer, W. Rose, H. St. J. Ingram, and S. Hughes; with Col. G. G. J. Walshe [capt.] and A. Frost as alternates) by 3,600 total points over 300 boards.

(4) London, 1949. For the CROWNINSHIELD CUP. England beat America by 330 total points, the net result of two matches. England (M. Harrison-Gray [capt.], K. Konstam, T. Reese, and B. Schapiro) beat America (J. Crawford, G. Rapee, S. Stayman, and P. Leventritt) by 2,950 total points. The same American team beat England (E. Kempson [capt.], Mrs. R. Markus, K. Konstam, L. Dodds, E. Rayne, J. Pavlides, and G. Mathieson) by 2,620 total points. Both matches were of 96 boards.

(5) London, 1954. England (T. Reese, B. Schapiro, K. Konstam, A. Meredith, and E. Mayer) beat America (C. Bishop, M. Ellenby, D. Steen, L. Mathe, and D. Oakie; W. Rosen was absent) by 81 IMPs over 100 boards.

(6) Miami, 1955. America (W. von Zedtwitz, H. Harkavy, W. Root, A. Weiss, E. Burns, W.

---

*Great Britain (T. Reese, B. Schapiro, A. Rose, N. Gardener, R. Swimer, and J. Flint) beat the United States, Vanderbilt 1 (J. Crawford, S. Silodor, B. J. Becker, N. Kay, T. Stone, and G. Rapee) by 50 IMPs in the 40-board qualifying round and by 66 IMPs in the 60-board round-robin final. In the final, Great Britain beat the United States, Spingold 1 (O. Jacoby, I. Rubin, V. Mitchell, W. Grieve, M. Rubinow, and S. Stayman) by 40 IMPs; and beat the United States, Spingold 2 (C. Goren, H. Sobel, H. Schenken, H. Ogust, L. Mathe, and P. Allinger) by 4 IMPs, scoring 3–1 in victory points.

In the 1964 Team Olympiad in New York, the United States (S. Stayman, V. Mitchell, R. Jordan, A. Robinson, R. Hamman, and D. Krauss) beat Great Britain (T. Reese, B. Schapiro, K. Konstam, M. Harrison-Gray, J. Flint, and J. Tarlo) by 38 IMPs in the 18-board qualifying round-robin match.

In the 1972 Team Olympiad in Miami, the United States (R. Goldman, R. Hamman, J. Jacoby, M. Lawrence, P. Soloway, R. Wolff) beat Great Britain (J. Cansino, C. Dixon, J. Flint, A. Priday, C. Rodrigue, R. Sheehan) 20–0 victory points in the 20-board qualifying round-robin match.

†After T. Reese and B. Schapiro were accused of cheating, non-playing captain of the British team, R. Swimer, forfeited the match against North America, in which Britain was leading by 46 IMPs with twenty boards to be played. See BUENOS AIRES AFFAIR.

Seamon, H. Vanderbilt, C. Goren, and C. Whitebrook) beat Great Britain (T. Reese, K. Konstam, L. Dodds, A. Meredith, J. Pavlides) by 150 total points over 100 boards.

(7) London, 1956. England (T. Reese, B. Schapiro, K. Konstam, L. Dodds, and E. Mayer) beat America (S. Stayman, C. Goren, C. Solomon, M. Field, L. Hazen, and R. Kahn) by 79 IMPs over 100 boards.

See also Joshua CRANE.

ANTICIPATION. See PREPAREDNESS, PRINCIPLE OF.

ANTI-FRAGMENT BIDS. See SPLINTER BIDS.

APPEAL. An appeal may deal only with an illegal or improper act by a contestant or an action or decision of the director. The appeal must be joined by both members of a partnership or a majority of a team to receive consideration.

Should a player be dissatisfied with a ruling by a director as to a matter of fact that occurred at a table, the player, his partner agreeing, may ask for an appeal (sometimes termed a "protest") of the ruling. The director may act on the appeal himself, on his own initiative, or by consultation with others, overruling his own decision or that of one of his assistants. If he does not do so, and the appeal is pursued, he turns it over to the tournament committee for adjudication if it is a matter of fact. The director himself rules on any question of a decision on a point of law.

In hearing an appeal, the tournament committee should give primary consideration to the director's statements of facts occurring in his presence.

An appeal from a ruling of law by the director or of fact by a tournament committee may be appealed further to the National Authority. If practical, the National Authority will hear the case on the spot; if impractical, the director is required to forward the appeal with a written statement of the facts as found by the committee or the director, and an expression of his views on the legal aspects of the case, as well as such written statements as the appellants may desire to make. See COMMITTEE; DIRECTOR; LAWS OF DUPLICATE (Laws 88, 89); PROTEST.

APPENDIX TABLE. A method of expanding sections to accommodate extra tables without increasing the number of boards in play; particularly useful for adding late pairs or tables to HOWELL MOVEMENTS. The result of adding appendix tables to the seven-table Howell game has led to the THREE-QUARTER MOVEMENT for eight, nine, and up to twelve tables.

The use of appendix tables in MITCHELL MOVEMENT games is possible, although infrequently employed, except as adapted into certain GUIDE CARD movements for two-session events. One use that is popular is that of a NOVICE TABLE appendix to a regular game where inexperienced players may be accommodated without delaying the regular game. The application of the appendix table principle by former National Tournament Director Paul Marks has made the RAINBOW INDIVIDUAL MOVEMENT adaptable for numbers of tables one or even two greater than a prime number (such as 7, 11, 13, 17, etc.).

The technique of handling an appendix table is simple. In a Howell movement, a table (or tables) may be appended to any table where there are two moving pairs. The North-South pair at the base table is instructed to remain stationary as is the East-West pair at the appended table. Boards are constantly relayed from the base table to the appended table, and as moving pairs arrive at the base table to sit North-South, they are instructed to play at the appended table, then to resume their regular progression. In a Mitchell game, a table may be appended to any section that consists of a prime number of tables. Boards are placed on the base table and are relayed with the appended table. Throughout the game the boards move regularly to the next lower table within the prime section. The East-West pair at the base table remains stationary, as does the North-South pair at the appended table. All other pairs move each round, East-West moving to the next higher table and North-South skipping one table to the next higher table.

APPROACH-FORCING SYSTEM. A term applicable to most standard methods of bidding, including GOREN or STANDARD AMERICAN. The CULBERTSON SYSTEM was the earliest of these, and was the basis on which many other systems were built. The original objective of Culbertson was to emphasize the need for slow suit exploration, in preference to a precipitate excursion into no trump. See APPROACH PRINCIPLE.

APPROACH PRINCIPLE. The precept of Ely Culbertson favoring opening suit-bids and a slow exchange of information in preference to no trump opening bids and responses. He described it this way:

In view of the fact that in making an opening bid, the player is venturing into unknown territory, it is wise for him to proceed cautiously, to feel his way, and thus, protected by a network of approach suit-bids of one, act with care until he learns something about the distribution of honor strength held by both his partner and his adversaries.

The Approach Principle, as applied to contract, may be stated as follows: *Whenever a hand contains a biddable suit, even a shaded four-card minor, that suit and not notrump should usually first be bid.* The "notrump complex," which suggests that the opening bid on a hand should be notrump even when the hand contains a biddable suit, is a disease especially prevalent among advanced players. The logical place for notrump bidding is after information has been exchanged as to suit lengths and distribution. Notrump bids in the early stages crowd the bidding too much and eliminate many valuable suit-bids, while the bid of a suit always leaves the alternative of notrump without increasing the contract. The use of the Approach Principle does not decrease, but, as a matter of fact, increases the number of safe notrump contracts undertaken.

Culbertson's dislike of indiscriminate no trump bids stemmed from experience. Too many of his contemporaries carried over from auction the phobia created by the scoring table (where if the opponents held three honors in a suit they might outscore the declarer who made only two-odd or three-odd). Thus they tended to bid one no trump with almost any hand lacking a suit headed by three honors. Hampered by lack of a Stayman convention to discover a 4–4 fit after the no trump opening, far too often the wrong contract was reached.

In support of the approach idea, Culbertson quoted the following hands:

WEST (dealer)	EAST
♠ A Q x x	♠ J x x x
♡ A x	♡ x
♢ A J x	♢ K x x x
♣ A 10 x x	♣ K x x x

Culbertson's suggested bidding was:

WEST	EAST
1 ♠	2 ♠
3 NT	4 ♠
Pass	

A few years later, most good players—including Culbertsonites—would open with one club, and arrive at the same final contract. But in citing this example, he was shooting at the flaw of opening a no trump with more than the desirable strength, as well as the danger of missing the spade fit.

In the beginning, Culbertson recommended no trump openings on a range of three honor tricks not vulnerable to four-plus honor tricks vulnerable. His zeal for approach principles caused him to limit the bid to 4–3–3–3 distribution with an occasional exception for 4–4–3–2, including a strong doubleton—not less than Q x.

Thus, analysis of the 1937 prototype World Championship reveals that the Culbertson team did not use a single opening bid of one no trump. As methods of responding to one no trump were improved so as to discover suit fits after the no trump opening, Culbertson gradually relaxed his strictures against opening no trumps on hands of the "wrong" distribution in order to use the bid on more hands of the "right" high-card strength. Thus, by 1949, 4–4–3–2 and 5–3–3–2 distributions (but not five-card majors) were officially included in the no trump family—no longer as exceptions. But while the distributional range was spread, the high-card range was narrowed, standardized at three and one-half to four-plus honor tricks which were later interpreted—by Culbertson as well as by others—as 16–18 high-card points, with even 6–3–2–2 distributions admitted to the no trump family on hands of proper high-card strength and strong doubletons.

In spite of these changes, over a span of more than thirty years the Culbertson Approach Principle remained, with but little alteration, a basic principle of bidding. A few more hands containing biddable suits were opened with one no trump; the standards for biddable suits in the responder's hand were shaded down. But it remained standard practice to avoid indiscriminate no trump openings, and especially to avoid responses of one no trump to partner's suit bid if a response could be given at the one-level in another suit. The no trump response may result in a suit fit being missed, and may lead to the weak hand becoming the declarer at no trump. Many experts play that a response of one no trump to one diamond, for example, absolutely denies holding a four-card major suit. Others, however, would not choose to respond in a worthless four-card suit. See BIDDABLE SUITS.

ARABIA. See SAUDI ARABIA.

ARGENTINE BRIDGE ASSOCIATION. A member of the South American Bridge Confederation, with a membership that grew from 750 in 1969 to 2,300 in 1975; sponsor of the team that has won the South American Championships ten times. Until Venezuela triumphed in 1965, Argentina was the only country to represent South America in the World Championship, doing so on six occasions, beginning in 1958. National competitions include Open Teams, Open Pairs, and Masters Individual; also the Gabarret Cup, given for the most master points in a year. Players listed separately are: R. Argerich, L. Attaguile, A. Berisso, A. Blousson, D. Blum, J. Bosco, C. Cabanne, L. Casabal, H. Cramer, C. Dibar, A. Gabarret, A. Jaques, A. Klein, R. Lerena, Dr. M. Lerner, E. Marquardt, A. Olmedo, C. Ottolenghi, E. Rocchi, A. Santamarina, M. Santamarina, A. Saravia, Dr. L. Schenone, Mrs. M. de Schenone, Mrs. E. de Vergara.

Officers, 1975:
President: Dr. Luis M. de Santa Coloma.
Secretary: Dr. Luis Pérez Colman, Lavalle 1145,
  Buenos Aires, Argentina.

ARNO. See LITTLE ROMAN.

ARRANGEMENT OF CARDS. The act of sorting the cards in one's own hand or (by the declarer) in the dummy's hand, which includes the conventional placing of trumps to the declarer's left in the dummy's hand. Most players sort their cards into suits, red and black alternately, and place the cards in each suit according to rank. It is regarded as an offense against the proprieties of bridge for any player to draw inferences about another player's hand by noting the position of the cards. But some players split suits and avoid singletons at the end of the hand to protect themselves against players with better eyesight than ethics.

ARRANGEMENT OF TABLES. At a duplicate tournament, the arrangement of tables depends on the size and shape of the playing space and the expected number of tables which must be accommodated (see TABLE SPACING). A hairpin type of arrangement is more desirable than a straight line arrangement for sections in order to bring the last table into proximity with the first in each section.

Care must be taken that players do not inadvertently see hands in play at other tables. An arrangement of tables in a pattern like

$$1 \quad 2 \quad 3 \quad 4 \quad 5 \quad 6 \quad 7 \quad 8$$
$$15 \quad 14 \quad 13 \quad 12 \quad 11 \quad 10 \quad 9,$$

although convenient and conserving space because rows can be closer together, makes it very difficult for players not to see a hand of another player at a different table.

ARRANGEMENT OF TRICKS. In duplicate bridge, the act of turning a card face down on the edge of the table immediately in front of a player after four cards have been played to a trick, with the long axis of the card pointing to the players who won the trick; in rubber bridge, the act of collecting the cards played to a trick by a member of the side that won the trick and then turning them face down on the table so that the tricks are identifiable in proper sequence. See LAWS (Law 66); LAWS OF DUPLICATE (Law 65).

ARRANGING.
(1) A term having reference to the aligning of the cards of the dummy as that hand is being spread on the table just after the opening lead has been made. The declarer may arrange the cards to his own satisfaction when he states that he is doing so.
(2) A statement by a player before he has bid in the first round of bidding meaning that he has been lax in picking up his hand or looking at it, and is not in a position to act when it becomes his turn. A call of some sort should follow this remark with reasonable dispatch.
(3) The act of sorting one's own cards. See ARRANGEMENT OF CARDS.

ARROW. The symbol on the duplicate board which indicates the alignment required so that the North player receives the hand designated for him. Table cards have the compass points printed on the edges; the boards have the arrow symbol pointing to the North hand; the arrow point and the printed direction coinciding, each player's hand is directly in front of him in the board. See: ARROW SWITCH; SCRAMBLED MITCHELL MOVEMENT.

ARROW SWITCH. The right-angle turning of the table guide card between rounds of a Mitchell duplicate movement, to produce a SCRAMBLED MITCHELL MOVEMENT. The field is thus combined to one field instead of two for scoring purposes.
A single arrow switch does not provide balanced comparisons by any means, as adjoining North-South pairs play all but four boards in direct competition in a thirteen-table game, and all but two boards in a larger game. To secure balanced comparisons, an arrow switch should be made two to four times during the play, and the number of rounds in each position should be varied. Alex GRONER, in his *Duplicate Bridge Direction,* offers a table for the arrow switch. See SCRAMBLED MITCHELL.

ARTIFICIAL CALL. An arbitrary call which can be

correctly interpreted by partner only if agreement has been reached about its meaning in advance.

Certain artificial bids are now so standard that their apparent normal meaning would be considered as an "artificial" convention. For example: a take-out double; a two no trump "bust response" to an opening two-bid, etc.

At the extreme of artificiality are "cipher" bids which bear no relation to the suit named, or to any other suit. The commonest examples are the STAYMAN responses of two clubs and three clubs over one no trump and two no trump respectively, and the responses to Blackwood. Other examples are the conventional two club opening bid with a powerful hand, and the FLINT THREE DIAMOND convention.

Cipher bids are developed to the maximum by the French RELAY SYSTEM, in which one player can make a series of artificial bids to discover the details of his partner's hand.

Cipher bids are common also in the Italian systems, which abound with semi-artificial bids. Examples of the latter in the ROMAN SYSTEM are the opening one-bid which will frequently be a three-card suit; the opening bid of two in a major suit which announces a secondary suit of clubs; and a jump overcall of an opponent's opening which shows a particular two-suited hand.

Semi-artificial bids in use among standard bidders are TEXAS and other transfer bids, and the UNUSUAL NO TRUMP.

The multiplication of artificial bids of all kinds in the postwar years led to some objections. The American Contract Bridge League, the French Bridge Federation, and the English Bridge Union, among others, restrict the use of artificial systems and conventions, such as the Italian systems and others of similar complexity, in normal tournament play. It is considered that the users of such systems gain an unfair advantage against opponents unfamiliar with the methods employed. This is particularly true in pair tournaments and other events in which a small number of boards are played in each round.

Defensive bids take on a different meaning against artificial systems, and the meanings of doubles, no trump bids, and bids in the opponent's suit have to be carefully considered. A further point is that a defender can afford to pass over an artificial forcing bid holding a strong hand, knowing that he will get a further opportunity to bid.

At the international level the use of artificial systems often causes debate, but legislation against them is hardly possible: it would appear to discriminate against the successful European users of such methods.

A highly artificial British system, the LITTLE MAJOR, was invented as an attempt at *reductio ad absurdum,* pushing artificiality to the furthest possible limits. This does not count, however, as the strangest system ever played seriously by top-ranking players. That distinction belongs to the Italian MARMIC SYSTEM.

In the early thirties there was some doubt about the legality of certain artificial bids. In 1933 the Portland Club in London, one of the law-making bodies, ruled that the Culbertson Four-Five No Trump convention and others that could indicate the possession of specific cards were illegal. The decision was based on the idea that a bid that showed possession of a particular card amounted to the exposure of that card.

This ruling was quickly challenged in America, and the Whist Club gave an opposite verdict.

Many different articles are included in this book dealing with artificial bids. Those connected with SLAM BIDDING are listed under SLAM CONVENTIONS. Others include: ACE-SHOWING RESPONSES; ASPRO; ASTRO; ASTRO CUE-BIDS; BENJAMIN; BLUE TEAM TWO DIAMONDS; BROZEL; COMPETITIVE DOUBLE; DEFENSE TO STRONG ARTIFICIAL OPENINGS; DOUBLE FOR SACRIFICE; DRURY; DYNAMIC NO TRUMP; FLANNERY TWO DIAMONDS; FLINT; FOUR DIAMONDS; FOURTH SUIT, FORCING AND ARTIFICIAL; GLADIATOR; JACOBY TRANSFER BIDS; LANDY; LEBENSOHL; LIMIT JUMP RAISE TO SHOW SINGLETON; MEXICAN TWO DIAMONDS; MICHAELS CUE-BID; OKUNEFF; ROMAN TWO DIAMONDS; RUBIN TRANSFERS; SOUTH AFRICAN TEXAS; SWISS; TEXAS CONVENTION; TRANSFER BIDS; TRANSFER OPENING THREE-BIDS; TWO CLUBS; TWO-SUITER conventions; TWO-WAY GAME TRIES; TWO-WAY STAYMAN; UNBID MINOR SUIT FORCE.

ARTIFICIAL CLUB BIDS. See ONE CLUB SYSTEMS.

ARTIFICIAL RESPONSES AND REBIDS AFTER NATURAL NO TRUMP. See NO TRUMP BIDDING.

ARTIFICIAL TWO DIAMOND AND TWO CLUB OPENINGS. The bids and responses as advocated by S. Stayman are:

Two diamonds corresponds to the strong artificial two club bid usually used with weak two-bids. Two hearts is the negative response. The bidding may die below game only after the sequences:

$$2 \diamondsuit - 2 \heartsuit \quad \text{or} \quad 2 \diamondsuit - 2 \heartsuit$$
$$2 \text{ NT} \qquad\qquad\qquad 2 \spadesuit - 2 \text{ NT}$$
$$\qquad\qquad\qquad\qquad\qquad 3 \spadesuit$$

When two diamonds is thus used, two clubs shows a strong intermediate hand, usually based on one or both major suits. Responder almost always bids two diamonds, after which opener bids:

Two, three, or four of a major to show a single-suited hand with eight, nine, or ten tricks respectively.

Two no trump to show a 19–20-point hand.

Three clubs and three diamonds (conventional) to show major two-suiters worth eight tricks and nine tricks respectively.

Four of a minor (conventional) shows a major two-suiter worth ten tricks, with a void in the minor bid.

Other responses to two clubs are:

A minimum suit-bid to show a 3- or 4-point hand with a six-card major or a seven-card minor.

2 no trump to show a weak minor two-suiter.

3 no trump to show a strong minor two-suiter.

It follows that opening bids of one heart or one spade are limited, showing less than eight playing tricks and less than 19 points.

See also BENJAMIN, ROMEX.

ASBURY PARK. The scene of many of the most important national championships in the early years of contract bridge. The nine-day SUMMER NATIONALS of the ABL and later of the ACBL were held there from 1930 to 1941 inclusive, making it the focal point of the bridge tournament year. In the early forties the Asbury Park Convention Hall became too small to accommodate a national championship. From 1958 through 1969 it was the scene of the annual regional tournament of the New York–New Jersey Conference.

See CITY OF ASBURY PARK TROPHY.

ASIA. See the following listed separately as Asian bridge federations: CHINA, FAR EAST, HONG KONG, INDIA, INDONESIA, JAPAN, LEBANON, MALAYSIA, PAKISTAN, PHILIPPINES, SINGAPORE, THAILAND, TURKEY.

ASKING BIDS. A method by which one player can discover specific CONTROLS held by his partner when exploring a possible slam contract; they were devised by A. Morehead and developed by E. Culbertson.

The following are asking bids:

(1) After a suit has been raised, a bid of a new suit at level of four or higher.

SOUTH	NORTH	or	SOUTH	NORTH
1 ♠	3 ♠		1 ♣	1 ♠
4 ◇ ?			3 ♠	4 ◇ ?

(2) An unnecessary jump bid in a new suit at the level of three or higher. (Unnecessary means one level higher than needed for a normal forcing jump bid.)

SOUTH	NORTH	or	SOUTH	NORTH
1 ♣	3 ♠ ?		1 ♣	3 ♠ ?
4 ◇ ?				

Should there by any doubt as to the agreed suit, the suit bid immediately before the asking bid is treated as agreed.

Responses to Asking Bids. The examples cited below are based on the examples in (1) above: spades is the agreed suit, four diamonds, the asking bid.

(a) Lacking first-round control of any suit, or with two or more quick losers in the asking suit, sign off in the agreed suit at the lowest level (four spades).

(b) First- or second-round control in the asked suit and two aces in the hand; the minimum bid in no trump (four no trump).

(c) First- or second-round control in the asked suit and three aces in the hand; jump in no trump (five no trump). The responder may or may not have the ace of the asked suit.

(d) First- or second-round control in the asked suit, and one first-round control; bid the suit of the first-round control. Jump in the agreed suit if the ace is in that suit (four hearts, five clubs, five diamonds, or five spades).

(e) Void in the asked suit with two aces elsewhere in the hand; jump in either of the two suits neither agreed nor asked (five hearts or six clubs).

Controls:

First-round:	ace or void
Second-round:	king or singleton
Third-round:	queen or doubleton

But voids do not count as aces for purposes of a no trump response.

Further Asking Bids may be made in four different ways:

(1) In the same suit after a negative response. Partner shows second-round control but no ace by bidding a minimum number of no trump, shows third-round control by bidding any outside first-round control, signs off by minimum bid in the agreed suit.

(2) In a new suit after a negative response. Responses are the same as to the original asking bid.

(3) In the same suit after positive response (asks for third-round control). Negative answer, sign off in agreed suit; positive answer, bid a void or second-round control in another suit, or bid minimum number of no trump.

(4) In new suit after positive response (asks for second-round control). Negative, sign off in agreed trump suit; positive, bid an unrevealed second-round control or void, or a minimum number of no trump. A third asking bid in the same suit would ask for third-round control. See also AUSTRALIAN ASKING BIDS; FULWILER CONVENTION; PRECISION ASKING BIDS; ROMAN ASKING BIDS; SUPER PRECISION ASKING BIDS; and TRUMP ASKING BID. For other uses of such bids, see FRAGMENT BID; INTEREST-SHOWING BID; SPLINTER BID; and VOID-SHOWING BID.

ASOCIACIÓN DEL BRIDGE ARGENTINO. See ARGENTINE BRIDGE ASSOCIATION.

ASOCIACIÓN PARAGUAYA DE BRIDGE. See PARAGUAY BRIDGE ASSOCIATION.

ASOCIACIÓN PERUANA DE BRIDGE. See PERUVIAN BRIDGE ASSOCIATION.

ASOCIACIÓN URUGUAYA DE BRIDGE. See URUGUAY BRIDGE ASSOCIATION.

ASPRO. A method of defending against one no trump openings based on Astro, devised by Terence REESE. (The name is borrowed from a popular British brand of aspirin.)

The term "astronaut" is used to designate the overcaller, and the term "relay" to describe the responses in the neutral suit. Astro is varied in three respects:

(1) *Major two-suiters* are bid differently. The two club overcall is often used with a major two-suiter. With five spades and four or five hearts, the astronaut bids two clubs and follows with two spades over the two diamond relay.

With four spades and five hearts the treatment varies with the strength of the overcaller's hand. Normally he bids two clubs followed by two hearts, giving responder the opportunity to show spades.

With a stronger hand he bids two diamonds followed by two no trump.

(2) *Pronounced two-suiters* (6–5 or 6–6 distribution). Specific bids are laid down for each two-suited hand:

two no trump	black suits
three clubs	minor suits
three diamonds	red suits
three hearts	major suits

With the odd two-suiters (spades-diamonds or hearts-clubs), bid two of the minor suit and follow with a jump in a six-card suit.

(3) *A redouble* by the astronaut or the responder is an SOS. For alternative methods of defending against one no trump, see ASTRO, BROZEL, EXCLUSION BID, LANDY, and RIPSTRA.

ASSIGNMENT OF SEATS. At a duplicate tournament the seating assignments are made on the entry blank which is purchased by the contestants. In the second session of pair events, when there has been a qualifying session, this may be done by giving GUIDE CARDS to the players which show their seating assignment for all rounds. See SEED, SEEDING.

In a club game, the North-South seats are sometimes given to the better players in the interest of accurate scoring, but this unbalances the North-South and East-West fields. As most players prefer to sit North-South in MITCHELL MOVEMENT games, the most equitable procedure is a cut with a limited deck, using the size of the card to indicate the TABLE NUMBER, and the color of the card to indicate the direction at the table.

ASSIST. To raise a suit first bid by partner. See RAISE.

ASSOCIATION OF AMERICAN PLAYING CARD MANUFACTURERS TROPHY. Awarded to the winners of the two-session Comm. & Ind. Team Championship held at the Summer Nationals until 1965, donated by the Association of American Playing Card Manufacturers, an organization founded in 1939 to promote the playing of card games. Until it ceased to exist in 1964 it was managed by the J. Walter Thompson agency. Consultants on card games to the Association were: G. Mott-Smith, 1939–60; A. Ostrow, 1960–62; W. Root, 1962–64. In 1965 the trophy was replaced by the UNITED STATES PLAYING CARD TROPHY.

ASSUMPTIONS, IN PLAY. When a contract depends on the positions of two or three key cards, it often helps to make a definite assumption about one of them. If you can afford to have it wrong, assume that it is wrong; if you must have it right, assume that it is right and build up your picture of the opposing hands on that basis.

The following is a difficult example of "second-degree" assumption:

NORTH
♠ A K 10 6 3
♡ Q 5
◇ Q 4
♣ K Q 6 2

WEST
♡ K led

SOUTH
♠ Q J 9 4 2
♡ 7
◇ A J 6 3
♣ 8 7 4

West deals at game all and the bidding goes:

SOUTH	WEST	NORTH	EAST
—	1 ♡	Dbl.	2 ♡
3 ♠	Pass	4 ♠	Pass
Pass	Pass		

West leads the king of hearts and continues with the ace of hearts. South ruffs and draws trumps in two rounds. What should he play next? The contract will fail only if South loses two tricks in clubs and one in diamonds. Suppose that he leads a club, which looks obvious. If East holds the ace of clubs, then surely West will hold the king of diamonds, and South will be defeated. Playing a diamond first, on the other hand, South is completely safe. If West holds the king of diamonds, and puts it up, there will be two club discards on declarer's diamond ace-jack. But if East holds the king of diamonds, then assuredly West will hold the ace of clubs. It is a puzzling but instructive hand. This is the distribution against which South has to guard:

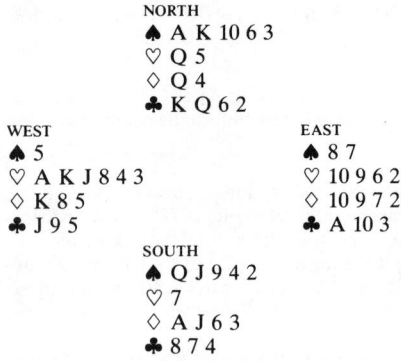

NORTH
♠ A K 10 6 3
♡ Q 5
◇ Q 4
♣ K Q 6 2

WEST
♠ 5
♡ A K J 8 4 3
◇ K 8 5
♣ J 9 5

EAST
♠ 8 7
♡ 10 9 6 2
◇ 10 9 7 2
♣ A 10 3

SOUTH
♠ Q J 9 4 2
♡ 7
◇ A J 6 3
♣ 8 7 4

T. R. Quoted from *The Expert Game*

ASSUMPTIONS, MATHEMATICAL. See MATHEMATICAL ASSUMPTIONS.

ASTERISK BIDS. Bidding conventions not in general use, though permitted.

The name derived from the format of the convention card adopted in 1960 by the American Contract Bridge League, on which these bids were marked by * with a footnote that the use of these bids must be called to opponents' attention. Later regulations require ALERTING to such bids.

ASTRO. Over one no trump, a specialized use of minor suit overcalls to show two-suited hands. The name of the convention is derived from the initial letters of the inventors' names: Allinger–STern–ROsler. After a strong or a weak no trump, in the direct or the reopening position:

2 ♣   shows *hearts* and a minor suit
2 ◇   shows *spades* and another suit

The Astro bidder promises at least nine cards in two suits; and his suits must have some solidity if he is vulnerable.

The Astro bidder's partner has a choice of these actions:

(1) Two of the anchor major (i.e., the particular major suit guaranteed by the overcaller): shows at least three cards in the suit and no game ambitions.

(2) Three of the anchor major: a game invitation with at least four-card support. The strength depends mainly on the vulnerability situation, and to a lesser extent on the strength of the no trump opening.

(3) Four of the anchor major: natural.

(4) Pass: a weak hand, and a long suit (probably of six cards) in the minor bid by partner.

(5) Two of the neutral suit (i.e., the next suit above the Astro bid): a negative action, denying the ability to make any other response. Indicates at least a doubleton in the neutral suit and usually fewer than three cards in the anchor suit.

(6) Two no trump: artificial and forcing. Shows some support for the anchor major, and suggests game prospects without guaranteeing a further bid.

(7) New suit take-out or jump (includng a jump in the neutral suit and a "raise" of the take-out bid): shows a six-card or longer suit.

The Astro bidder has a choice of rebids after a neutral response. He may pass with five cards in the neutral suit, or show five cards in the anchor suit by "rebidding" it. He may show his second suit at the level of three, indicating a probable six-card suit and more than minimum playing strength.

In most sequences, two no trump by either player is artificial and forcing. As responder's second bid, it is likely to be weak:

WEST		EAST	
♠ A 5 2		♠ Q 4 3	
♡ A J 10 5 4		♡ 6	
◇ 6		◇ Q 8 5 3 2	
♣ K 10 8 5		♣ Q 9 6 4	

SOUTH	WEST	NORTH	EAST
1 NT	2 ♣	Pass	2 ◇
Pass	2 ♡	Pass	2 NT
Pass	3 ♣	Pass	Pass
Pass			

Astro Variations. Some partnerships use a variation

of Astro similar to the BROZEL convention, called Pinpoint Astro, which is more explicit as to the two suits held.

2 ♣   shows hearts and clubs
2 ◇   shows hearts and diamonds
2 ♡   shows hearts and spades
2 ♠   shows spades and a minor suit

A modification adopted by many Roth-Stone players uses both two-level and three-level overcalls in order to show precisely which suits are held:

2 ♣   shows clubs and spades
2 ◇   shows diamonds and spades
3 ♣   shows clubs and hearts
3 ◇   shows diamonds and hearts
Double shows hearts and spades

Yet another variation, devised by M. GRANOVET-TER, uses a double to show spades and another suit. Two clubs shows clubs and hearts; two diamonds shows diamonds and hearts.

Defense. The opening bidder's partner has several choices if his side appears to have the balance of strength. He can double with a defensive hand, usually with a good holding in the anchor major and the suit he doubles; cue-bid the anchor major when his hand is unsuited to defense; or pass to await developments (remembering that there *might* not be any). A non-jump new-suit bid (including a "raise" in the Astro bidder's minor) would be unconstructive. Two no trump would be natural. For an alternative defense to Astro, see LEBENSOHL CONVENTION.

For alternative defensive conventions against no trump openings, see ASPRO, BROZEL, EXCLUSION BID, LANDY, and RIPSTRA.

ASTRO CUE-BIDS. Devised by the authors of the ASTRO convention, these are used to show certain two-suited hands.

An immediate cue-bid in the suit bid by the opener shows a long minor together with a shorter major suit. The bid shows clubs and hearts unless one of these suits has been bid, in which case the next-higher suit is assumed.

(a)	(b)
♠ 5 3	♠ 5
♡ A K J 6	♡ K 10 6 5 2
◇ 7	◇ Q 10 9 7 4 3
♣ A Q 10 8 5 2	♣ 6

With hand (a), the cue-bid would be used over one diamond or one spade. This is an inconvenient hand to bid with standard methods. Note that the problem is less acute if the minor suits are reversed. Over one spade, for example, a double would then be appropriate, followed by a diamond bid over a club response.

With hand (b), two clubs can be bid over one club at favorable vulnerability. As clubs have been bid, the cue-bid must show the red suits.

The Astro cue-bid is not well defined in terms of point-count. When vulnerable, the cue-bidder shows a hand equivalent to a sound overcall in the promised minor; when not vulnerable, it is equivalent to a weak jump overcall. The cue-bid should be avoided by a player holding low-card honors in short suits, because partner may misevaluate the defensive potential and take a defensive save.

The precise nature of the cue-bid allows responder to bid naturally and accurately in the next round. If the cue-bidder voluntarily bids his major suit, he promises a five-card suit.

ATTACK. To take the initiative in bidding or play at some risk. Used particularly with reference to the opening lead.

ATTACKING LEAD. A risky lead away from a high-card combination such as A Q, K J, or an unsupported high honor. This is common against a no trump contract, but less common against a suit contract when a PASSIVE LEAD is often called for. See OPENING LEADS.

The term "attacking lead" used to be applied to a lead from an honor sequence, but this meaning is obsolete.

Several situations deserve special mention:

(1) An attacking lead is desirable when the leader holds four or more trumps, or can deduce that his partner holds four or more trumps.

(2) An attacking lead is desirable when the opponents have reached a suit game tentatively after bidding three suits. For example:

WEST	EAST
1 ♣	1 ♠
2 ♠	3 ♣
3 ♡	3 ♠
4 ♠	Pass

The opening leader can expect his partner to have any missing high diamond honor, because both North and South have avoided no trump. It is probably desirable to take diamond tricks before declarer can get discards, and also to force the declarer, whose trump fit is likely to be four-three.

(3) An attacking lead has to be considered against a contract at a high level, either in a suit or no trump, if the bidding suggests that declarer will have a long suit in his hand or the dummy.

(4) An attacking lead should not be made against a seven contract. (However, in the 1958 European Championships, a Belgian declarer made seven no trump redoubled when the player on lead refused to lead from a king: the other defender held the ace of the same suit. See SWING HAND.)

ATTITUDE. The interest or disinterest of a defender in having a suit led or continued by his partner. The usual method of encouraging the lead or continuation of a suit is a HIGH LOW SIGNAL. See also ODD-EVEN DISCARDS and UPSIDE-DOWN SIGNALS.

AUCTION. The bidding by the four players for the contract. The dealer is the first bidder after the cards are dealt. He may pass or bid. The bidding proceeds clockwise around the table. Each player may pass, make a bid or raise a preceding bid, or double or redouble. The bidding ends when three players have passed in succession (or four players on the first round of bidding).

In the Midwest, "auction" is sometimes used as a synonym for "final contract": "Four spades was a fine auction."

AUCTION BRIDGE. The third step in the evolution of the general game of bridge. Its predecessors were WHIST and BRIDGE WHIST. The great innovation in auction bridge was the introduction of competitive bidding. It was first played in 1903 or 1904, but the precise circumstances are disputed. The first code of laws governing the play of auction was set forth in 1908, the product of a joint committee of the Bath Club and the Portland Club. The popularity of auction bridge increased enormously, and the activity in whist and bridge whist decreased proportionately. After the introduction of CONTRACT BRIDGE in 1926, auction bridge lost favor rapidly.

In auction bridge the aim was to keep the contract as low as possible because the declarer's side was credited with the number of tricks won, whether contracted for or not. For example, the declarer may have bid two spades and actually won six tricks over his book. He is credited with making a small slam. Penalties and premiums in auction are the same without regard to vulnerability. Honor scoring in auction bridge is different from contract bridge—so important, in fact, that it may distort the bidding, especially in duplicate auction.

Auction bridge scoring is as follows:

Scoring—Provided declarer has won at least the number of odd tricks named in his contract, declarer's side scores for each odd trick won:

	Undoubled	Doubled	Redoubled
With no trump	10	20	40
With spades trump	9	18	36
With hearts trump	8	16	32
With diamonds trump	7	14	28
With clubs trump	6	12	24

Game and Rubber. When a side scores, in one or more hands, 30 points or more for odd tricks, it has won a game and both sides start fresh on the next game. When a side has won two games it wins the rubber and adds to its score 250 points.

Doubles and Redoubles. If a doubled contract is fulfilled, declarer's side scores 50 points bonus plus 50 points for each odd trick in excess of his contract. If a redoubled contract is fulfilled, declarer's side scores 100 points bonus plus 100 points for each odd trick in excess of his contract. These bonuses are additional to the score for odd tricks, but do not count toward game.

Undertricks. For every trick by which declarer falls short of his contract, his opponents score 50 points; if the contract is doubled, 100 points; if it is redoubled, 200 points.

Honors. The side which holds the majority of the trump honors (A, K, Q, J, 10), or of the aces at no trump, scores:

For 3 honors (or aces) 30
For 4 aces in one hand at no trump 100
For 5 honors in one hand 100
For 4 trump honors in one hand 80
For 4 trump honors in one hand, 5th in partner's hand 90
For 4 aces in one hand at no trump 100
For 5 honors in one hand 100

Slams. A side which wins twelve of the thirteen tricks, regardless of the contract, scores 50 points for a small slam. A side which wins all thirteen tricks, regardless of the contract, scores 100 points for grand slam.

Points for overtricks, undertricks, honors, and slams do not count toward game. Only odd tricks count toward game, and only when declarer fulfills his contract.

Contract Bridge for Auction Players, by Ely Culbertson, gives the complete details of auction bidding contrasted, in parallel columns, with contract bidding. See also *Auction Bridge Complete* by Milton C. Work.

National championships at auction:

American Bridge League

MEN'S TEAM OF FOUR

1927 E. Culbertson, W. von Zedtwitz
     T. A. Lightner, R. R. Richards
1928 M. W. Kastriner, E. M. Baker
     S. L. Guggenheim, P. E. Leon
1929 G. Reith, Com. W. Liggett, Jr.
     P. H. Sims, Sir D. J. Wernher
1930 C. T. Robertson, M. Maschke
     V. F. Boland, J. H. Law
1931 } W. von Zedtwitz, P. H. Sims
1932 } O. Jacoby, D. Burnstine

MEN'S PAIR

1927 H. P. Jaeger, C. Apthorp
1928 S. L. Guggenheim, P. E. Leon
1929 E. Culbertson, P. H. Sims
1930 R. R. Richards, F. S. Eaton
1931 W. von Zedtwitz, P. H. Sims
1932 W. von Zedtwitz, P. H. Sims
1933 M. Maschke, G. W. Parratt

WOMEN'S TEAM OF FOUR

1927 Mrs. E. Culbertson, Mrs. A. O. Lynch
     Mrs. O. Gilman, Mrs. L. G. Russ
1928 Mrs. C. W. Nokes, Mrs. H. E. Parsons
     M. Beech, Mrs. H. D. Stahl
1929 Mrs. S. Lovell, Dr. E. Dafter
     Mrs. M. K. Alexander, Mrs. R. Fleischer
1930 Mrs. E. P. Sawhill, Mrs. C. T. Robertson
     Mrs. C. W. Nokes, Mrs. G. H. Schryver
1931 Mrs. H. White, Mrs. A. C. Hoffmeier
     Mrs. Carl T. Robertson, Mrs. A. Rosenfield
1932 E. Murdoch, Mrs. M. Stengel
     Mrs. H. L. Peterson, Mrs. J. S. Jones, Jr.

WOMEN'S PAIR

1927 Mrs. S. Lovell, Mrs. E. Evans
1928 Mrs. H. D. Stahl, M. Beech
1929 Mrs. P. H. Sims, Mrs. E. F. Clement
1930 Mrs. A. Rosenfield, Mrs. C. T. Robertson
1931 Mrs. J. S. Jones, Jr., Mrs. H. L. Peterson
1932 E. Murdoch, Mrs. M. Stengel

American Whist League

ALL-AMERICAN TEAM OF FOUR TROPHY

1924 S. S. Lenz, Com. W. Liggett, Jr.
     P. H. Sims, E. A. Wetzlar
1925 R. A. Amerman, H. C. Wallace
     H. E. Bidwell, C. F. Snow
1926 E. Culbertson, Mrs. E. Culbertson
     R. R. Richards, T. A. Lightner
1927 C. R. Apthorp, H. P. Jaeger
     M. Maschke, C. T. Robertson
1928 Mrs. A. R. Coffin, E. J. Tobin
     Mrs. C. T. Robertson, Mrs. G. C. Buschmann
1929 D. R. Sims, C. L. Downs
     T. A. Lightner, O. Jacoby
1930 E. C. Wolfe, M. W. Kastriner
     P. E. Leon, S. L. Guggenheim
1931 P. H. Sims, O. Jacoby
     W. S. Karn, D. Burnstine
1932 P. H. Sims, W. S. Karn
     W. von Zedtwitz, D. Burnstine
1933 D. Burnstine, O. Jacoby
     H. H. Boscowitz, E. A. Wetzlar
1934 Mrs. H. Scranton, G. Unger
     Mrs. A. Rosenfeld, Sir D. J. Wernher

AUGUST CONVENTION. See TWO-WAY STAYMAN.

AUSTRALIAN ASKING BIDS. A slight modification of the original Culbertson ASKING BIDS. Holding a singleton in the asked suit and two aces, a jump is made in the suit of the lower-ranking ace. In some cases the asking bid can be made below the four-level: two spades in response to one heart, for example, is used as an asking bid.

AUSTRALIAN BRIDGE. An independent bimonthly magazine, published from GPO 3805, Sydney, NSW, established in 1970 with Denis HOWARD as editor. He was succeeded in 1972 by Ron KLINGER, a contributing editor to this Encyclopedia.

AUSTRALIAN BRIDGE FEDERATION. Founded in 1934 as the Australian Bridge Council, with New South Wales, Victoria, and South Australia as original members. Later the Australian Capital Territory, Queensland, Tasmania, and Western Australia joined the Federation, and associate members are the Northern Territory and the Territory of Papua and New Guinea. From 2,000 members in 1970 the Federation had grown to approximately 11,000 members in 1974. Australia participates in the Far East Championships, winning the Open Teams in 1968 and 1970, the Women's Teams in 1973 and 1974, and the Far East Pairs in 1971 and 1972. The WBF Zone 7 Championship has been held since 1970 (except for 1972), Australia winning in 1970, 1971, and 1974. Australia competes in the World Olympiads and participated in the 1971 Bermuda Bowl, finishing third. It annually sponsors an Interstate Congress, consisting of Teams, Pairs, and Individual Championships, an annual Open Teams event, and Youth (under-30) Championships, and also sponsored a Par Point event for Pairs from 1956 to 1963. It awards the McCutcheon Trophy for most master points won in a year. Players listed separately are: F. Altman, D. Anderson, F. Beale, J. Borin, N. Borin, P. Brown, H. Cayley, R. Cummings, I. Dahler, R. Eaton, D. Evans, M. Freedman, W. Golding, E. Griffin, C. Grigg, A. Hancock, D. Hoffman, D.

Howard, F. Landy, P. Lavings, R. Klinger, W. Lipscomb, M. McMahon, A. Markovics, Z. Nagy, J. O'Sullivan, E. Poulsen, H-G. Rosendorff, J. Rothfield, T. Seres, R. Smilde, G. Stern, G. Tabak, V. Vahala, W. Wallace, A. Walsh.

Officers of the Federation, 1975:
President: James De Courcy O'Sullivan.
Secretary: Wilfred Wallace, Box 3805, GPO, Sydney, 2001, Australia.

AUSTRALIAN TRUMP-ASKING BID. A trump-asking bid initiated by either partner's use of the cheapest bid in no trump immediately after a major suit has been agreed. The inquiry, which could be made as low as the two level, focuses on the king and queen of trumps. Lacking both king and queen, the partner of the asking bidder signs off in the trump suit. The other responses are in steps, not counting the trump suit as a step:

1st step	queen
2nd step	king
3rd step	king and extra length
4th step	king and queen
5th step	king and queen and extra length

For alternative methods see TRUMP ASKING BID.

AUSTRIAN BRIDGE FEDERATION (ÖS-TERREICHISCHER BRIDGE VERBAND). Founded in 1928–29 by Dr. Paul Stern, inventor of the VIENNA (AUSTRIAN) SYSTEM, who became its first president, by 1975 it had 850 members. The Federation is a member of the European Bridge League and participates in European Championships, organizing the events in Vienna in 1934 and 1957. Austrian teams recorded a double victory in the 1937 World Championships, winning both the Open and Women's Team events. Austria won the World Open Pair Olympiad in 1970. In the European championships, Austria won the Open Team in 1932, 1933, and 1936, and the Women's Team in 1935 and 1936. Among the many events which the Federation sponsors each year are tournaments at Loiren and Salzburg and the International Bridge Week at Velden in the spring. Austrian players listed separately are: F. Babsch, K. von Bluhdorn, Dr. E. Frischauer, Dr. E. Gluttig, H. Hartwich, W. Herbert, H. Jellinek, P. Manhardt, Mrs. R. Markus, M. Reithoffer, W. von Scala, K. Schneider, Dr. P. Stern.

Officers, 1975:
President: Karl Rohan.
Secretary: Mrs. Inge Babsch, A-1100 Wien, Fernkorng, 44/II/14, Austria.

AUSTRIAN SYSTEM. See VIENNA SYSTEM.

AUTOBRIDGE. A commercial device by means of which lesson hands can be used for self-teaching bidding and play. A deal sheet is inserted in a special board so that only the player's own cards are shown. As the deal progresses, the player finds that his own bids and plays are automatically corrected, and that the bids and plays of the other players are automatically revealed. The board and deal sheets are accompanied by a booklet, in which the hands are set out and the bidding and play explained by experts.

Experts who have composed Autobridge hands include Ely and Josephine CULBERTSON, Albert MOREHEAD, Richard FREY, Charles GOREN, Alfred SHEINWOLD, and Alan TRUSCOTT.

AUTOMATIC ACES. A way of showing the number of aces held in certain situations.

After an opening bid of one no trump or two no trump receives a forcing response in a new suit at the level of three, if the opener has a fit with responder's suit and slam ambitions, he shows the number of aces he holds by a step method.

NORTH	SOUTH
2 NT	3 ♠
4 ◇	

This shows good spade support and three aces (four clubs would show two aces; four hearts, four aces). If the opening bid was a weak no trump, the first step response would show one ace. If the opening bidder has no slam ambitions he raises responder's suit or bids three no trump.

AUTOMATIC SQUEEZE. A simple squeeze which will operate against either opponent.

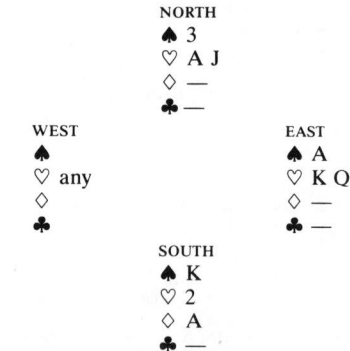

The lead of South's diamond ace squeezes East, and would also squeeze West if the defenders' hands were exchanged. Whatever West discards, the spade three is thrown from dummy.

This situation contrasts with a POSITIONAL SQUEEZE, when only the player who plays immediately after the squeeze card is under pressure, and the declarer's discard from the third hand varies with the defender's discard. See also SQUEEZE.

AUTOMATON CONTRACT BRIDGE PLAYER. An obsolete electric machine designed by William

Patzer to play a specific bridge hand against anyone who would put a coin into the machine to start the proceedings. The machine would make winning plays against various stratagems used by the declarer—i.e., the paying customer. See also ROBOT BRIDGE PLAYER.

In the days of whist there were several very popular machines which it was claimed were able to play whist. The first, invented by an American named Balcom and adapted for exhibition by Maelzel, was exhibited c. 1829–31. An automaton called "Psycho" was exhibited by John Maskelyne at the Egyptian Hall, Piccadilly, London for several decades beginning in 1875. The *New York Journal* exhibited an automaton whist player, named the "Yellow Kid," in New York in 1896.

AVERAGE EXPECTANCY. The term applied to the expected holding of the partner of the opening bidder; it may refer to one-third of the missing cards of a suit or one-third of the missing honor strength. The fraction will vary as the bidding progresses. It was much used in the Culbertson system in his arguments for pre-emptive bids.

AVERAGE HAND. A hand that contains ten high-card points. An ace, king, queen, and a jack, or one-fourth of all the high honors, is the average expectation of each player before the hands are seen. This basic assumption furnishes the player with a simple yardstick for measuring the relative high-card strength of a given hand, and may assist materially in estimating the game potential or penalty expectancy of any bid. Hence, two or three points added to an average hand is the valuation of a hand with a minimum opening bid.

AVERAGE SCORE. One-half the match points possible on a given hand or in a particular session of a match point pairs tournament.

In IMP pair games "average" on a given board is the arithmetical mean of all scores on that board, usually excluding the highest and the lowest. This constructed "average" is called a "datum." See INTERNATIONAL MATCH POINTS.

The average score is usually the basis on which adjusted scores are awarded when a particular hand cannot be properly played. When the hand cannot be played through no fault of one pair, the adjustment is usually 20% of the average score added to the average score. Deduction from the average score is made by the tournament director when one of the pairs is at fault. These are referred to as Average-plus or Average-minus.

AVOIDANCE. A plan of play designed to prevent a particular opponent from gaining the lead.

There are two main reasons for pursuing such a plan. First, it may be necessary to prevent a defender with established winners from gaining the lead, especially at no trump. Second, declarer may have a suit combination which is vulnerable to a lead from a particular side. Both aspects of avoidance arise if either of these suit combinations is held:

(a)	(b)
DUMMY	DUMMY
3 2	2
DECLARER	DECLARER
A J 4	K J 4 3

In each case South is playing three no trump and West leads the five to East's queen. If South wins the trick, East becomes the dangerous hand, but if South holds up twice, West becomes the opponent to be feared. South's play at the first trick must therefore be determined by an examination of the whole hand to discover which opponent is more likely to secure the lead. If a vital king or queen is missing in a side suit, it is usually obvious which opponent may gain the lead. If the missing card is an ace, there will often be an inference available from the bidding. In the examples above, West would be likely to have a side ace if he has volunteered a bid, and unlikely to have one if he has passed throughout.

The suit combination which most commonly indicates the need for an avoidance play is a guarded king or the equivalent: a guarded queen when one top honor has been played, or, as in the examples above, a guarded jack when two top honors have been played; a guarded ten would operate in the same way if three honors had been played.

But if declarer may have to lose the lead twice, the danger suit may be one in which he has one sure guard and a partial guard:

(a)	(b)	(c)
DUMMY	DUMMY	DUMMY
J 4 3 2	A 3 2	K 3 2
DECLARER	DECLARER	DECLARER
A 10	Q 4	Q 4

In each case the right-hand opponent is the danger hand. In (a) and (b) there is a certainty of two stoppers if the suit is led from the left. In (c), suppose that the left-hand opponent holds the ace. Declarer then has two tricks if the suit is led from his left, but only one trick if it is led from the right.

The danger hand may suddenly change. Suppose that in (a) the danger hand secures the lead and plays a low card. The ten loses to an honor, and the ace is knocked out. The left-hand opponent has suddenly become the danger hand: he may have one small card remaining, which he can lead to allow his partner to score two tricks.

Similarly, in (c), the right-hand opponent may gain the lead and play a low card. Declarer puts up the queen, which holds the trick. It is obvious that the left-hand opponent must not be permitted to gain the lead.

Avoidance play may require unusual handling of a suit which needs development:

(d)	(e)	(f)
DUMMY	DUMMY	DUMMY
K J 8	K 9 2	K 9
DECLARER	DECLARER	DECLARER
A 10 9 5 2	A J 4 3	A Q 4 3 2

The left-hand opponent is the danger hand. In (d) declarer runs the ten or nine: it would be quite wrong to play the ace first, because the queen may have three guards. In (e) a deep finesse of the nine is taken if South is trying for three tricks. The danger hand can secure the lead only if it has both the missing honors. In (f) the nine is "finessed" with the virtual certainty that it will lose. (If the danger hand held both honors, he would play one.) This ensures four tricks against any normal break, and keeps the danger hand from the lead unless it has J 10 x x.

Another type of avoidance play is possible in this situation:

```
                      NORTH
                      A K 3 2
WEST                                       EAST
Q 8 7                                      J 10 9
                      SOUTH
                      6 5 4
```

South needs three tricks in this suit, but must not permit East to gain the lead. Declarer leads twice from his hand, permitting West to win a trick with the queen if he plays it at any stage. If West is able to make a discard on the suit led from dummy back to declarer's hand, he can thwart South's plan by the spectacular discard of his queen.

Avoidance play can also be effected by LOSER-ON-LOSER technique, or by DUCKING.

B

BA. Bridge Association.

BL. Bridge League.

BABY BLACKWOOD. The use of a three no trump bid conventionally to discover the number of aces held by partner. The convention is usually applied after a forcing double raise in a major suit. For example:

SOUTH	NORTH
1 ♡	3 ♡ (forcing)
3 NT	

South's three no trump bid is a request for aces. North bids four clubs with no aces (or four aces), four diamonds with one ace, and so on. Similarly, an immediate jump to three no trump in response to a one heart or one spade opening may be used as Baby Blackwood.

An alternative proposal is to use two no trump to uncover the number of aces partner holds. Whenever either player bids two no trump, partner bids

three clubs with no aces, three diamonds with one ace, etc. Subsequent bids of three no trump, four no trump and five no trump can then be used to locate the number of kings, queens, and jacks, respectively held by partner. See BLACKWOOD.

BACK IN. To make the first bid for one's side, after passing on a previous round, in the face of opposing bidding. See BALANCING.

BACK SCORE. The summary sheet on which the results of each rubber are credited to the winners and debited against the losers, in rubber bridge or Chicago. Results are entered in hundreds of points, with 50 points ignored in England but counted as 100 in the United States. The back score is referred to by more colorful names in England, as "flogger" or "washing list," while many American clubs refer to it as a "ledger."

BACKWARD FINESSE. An unnatural finessing maneuver which may sometimes be made for special reasons.

```
                        (a)
                       NORTH
                       ♠ A 3 2
WEST                                       EAST
♠ Q 5 4                                    ♠ 10 8 7 6
                       SOUTH
                       ♠ K J 9

                        (b)
                       NORTH
                       ♠ K 3 2
WEST                                       EAST
♠ A J 4                                    ♠ 9 7 6 5
                       SOUTH
                       ♠ Q 10 8
```

In (a), the normal play is to finesse the jack, which is an even chance. As the cards lie, it is easy to see that the winning play is to lead the jack. If this is covered, South finesses the nine on the way back.

Similarly in (b), the normal play is to finesse the ten after leading to the king, but the lead of the ten is essential in the position given, with a finesse of the eight to follow. (The position of the ace is irrelevant.)

There are three possible reasons for selecting the backward finesse. First, there may be a good reason to believe that the natural finesse will fail, based on an inference from an opening bid, for example, or a failure to open the bidding.

Second, the backward finesse may be an AVOIDANCE play. Suppose that in each of the above cases the declarer has an extra small card in his own hand and in the dummy, and needs three tricks without allowing West to gain the lead. His best play is the jack in (a) and the ten in (b). It is doubtful whether this should be classified as a backward finesse, because South may well reject the finesse on the way back.

Third, the play may be selected when SHOOTING for a top in a pair event, or playing for a SWING in a team-of-four match.

In defense the backward finesse can be a natural play dictated by cards visible in dummy.

BACKWASH SQUEEZE. A unique type of TRUMP SQUEEZE in which both menaces are in the same hand and the player sitting behind the hand with the menaces holds both guards plus a losing trump, and is caught in the "backwash" of a squeeze by means of a ruff taken in the hand holding the menaces. Analyzed and described by Geza Ottlik in the February 1974 issue of *The Bridge World,* the backwash squeeze can have any of a number of other end game characteristics. Three such hands are used here by permission of *The Bridge World.*

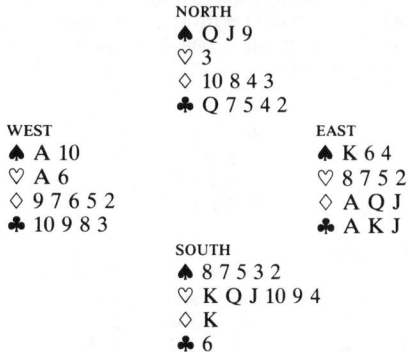

```
            NORTH
            ♠ Q J 9
            ♡ 3
            ◇ 10 8 4 3
            ♣ Q 7 5 4 2
WEST                    EAST
♠ A 10                  ♠ K 6 4
♡ A 6                   ♡ 8 7 5 2
◇ 9 7 6 5 2             ◇ A Q J
♣ 10 9 8 3             ♣ A K J
            SOUTH
            ♠ 8 7 5 3 2
            ♡ K Q J 10 9 4
            ◇ K
            ♣ 6
```

South has arrived in two spades doubled after a strong one club opening by East showing 17 or more points, and a CARD SHOWING DOUBLE by West promising 6–8 points. Clubs were led and continued, with South ruffing the second round. South tried to slip the nine of hearts through but West took his ace and shifted to the ace and another trump. When East won his king he cashed the diamond ace and continued with the queen. Declarer had lost five tricks and apparently had one more to lose—if he drew the last trump he could not return to the closed hand to run the hearts. Because of the blockage in the North-South spades, East's spade six prevented ordinary suit-establishment. However, South ruffed the diamond queen and cashed three top hearts, East being forced to follow suit, leaving this position:

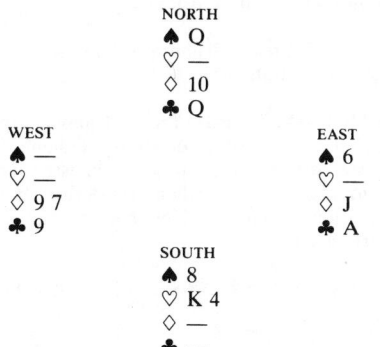

```
            NORTH
            ♠ Q
            ♡ —
            ◇ 10
            ♣ Q
WEST                    EAST
♠ —                     ♠ 6
♡ —                     ♡ —
◇ 9 7                   ◇ J
♣ 9                     ♣ A
            SOUTH
            ♠ 8
            ♡ K 4
            ◇ —
            ♣ —
```

South led a heart, ruffed it with dummy's queen of spades—and East was squeezed. If he underruffed, the South hand would be high. If he discarded a plain suit he would promote one of dummy's cards which would be led, forcing East to ruff and allowing South to overruff.

The backwash squeeze can be used to strip a defender of his exit cards preparatory to a throw-in play.

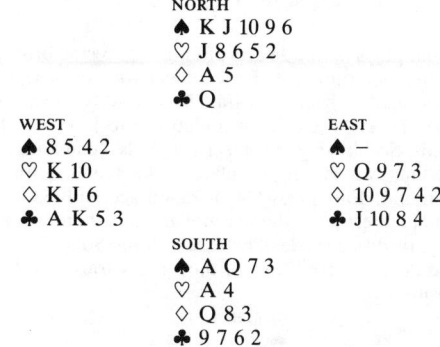

```
            NORTH
            ♠ K J 10 9 6
            ♡ J 8 6 5 2
            ◇ A 5
            ♣ Q
WEST                    EAST
♠ 8 5 4 2               ♠ —
♡ K 10                  ♡ Q 9 7 3
◇ K J 6                 ◇ 10 9 7 4 2
♣ A K 5 3              ♣ J 10 8 4
            SOUTH
            ♠ A Q 7 3
            ♡ A 4
            ◇ Q 8 3
            ♣ 9 7 6 2
```

South has arrived in four spades after a 13–15 no trump opening by West and an ASTRO two diamond bid by North, showing spades and another suit. West led the club king and forced dummy with a second club. Planning to set up dummy, declarer led ace and another heart. West won and forced dummy again in clubs. Declarer ruffed a heart high, then led a low spade to dummy and discovered the unfortunate spade division. Suddenly a simple hand had become complicated. North was on lead, with declarer needing five of the last six tricks:

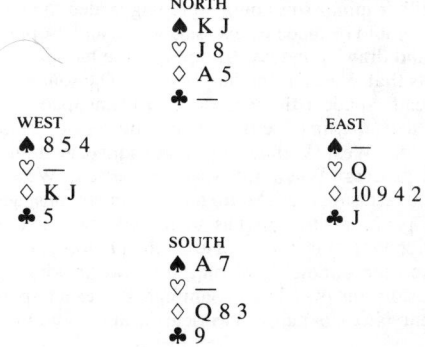

```
            NORTH
            ♠ K J
            ♡ J 8
            ◇ A 5
            ♣ —
WEST                    EAST
♠ 8 5 4                 ♠ —
♡ —                     ♡ Q
◇ K J                   ◇ 10 9 4 2
♣ 5                     ♣ J
            SOUTH
            ♠ A 7
            ♡ —
            ◇ Q 8 3
            ♣ 9
```

Declarer ruffed a heart with the spade ace—and the backwash caught West in its undertow. An underruff would let declarer draw trumps; and a diamond pitch would allow South to cash the ace of diamonds and then lead the jack of hearts, throwing a club. Thus, West had to part with his club—his only exit card. South cashed the king and jack of spades and led the last heart. West ruffed, but was end-played.

Occasionally the backwash squeeze can be used as a DISCOVERY play. The following example requires a VIENNA COUP for the execution of the squeeze.

NORTH
♠ A 10 8 5 4 2
♡ 10 7 3
◇ 9 2
♣ K J

SOUTH
♠ 6
♡ K Q J 8
◇ K Q 10 5
♣ A 10 9 3

South plays in four hearts after having rested briefly in three no trump until East doubled for a spade lead. West leads a heart and East plays low. South wins with the eight and leads a club to the jack, which holds. So far, so good. Declarer leads a diamond to the king, which wins, a club to the king, and another diamond. East plays the diamond ace and leads a trump. West plays the ace and another trump while East throws a spade. The lead is in the South hand, and declarer needs five of the last six tricks, in this position:

NORTH
♠ A 10 8 5 4 2
♡ —
◇ —
♣ —

WEST
♠ 3
♡ 9
◇ J 6
♣ Q 7

SOUTH
♠ 6
♡ K
◇ Q 10
♣ A 10

If either minor-suit honor were unguarded the contract could be made by guessing which and dropping it, and drawing the last trump. But the bidding suggests that West has the hand shown. The solution is to lead a spade to the ace, and ruff a losing spade with the master trump, setting up an unnecessary trump trick for West (Vienna Coup), but squeezing him in the process. When the spade is ruffed, West is backwash-squeezed. South may, of course, misguess the position—he still has to read West's holding correctly. But he is no worse off than before; he will have seen another card played before making the decision and will have confirmed the exact spade count. No other play will work in the above ending.

BAD CARD HOLDER. A player who seems consistently to hold less than his fair share of honor cards at rubber bridge. Although many losing players explain their losses by claiming to be bad card holders, lack of skill is a more likely explanation. Both mathematics and practical tests suggest that any given player and any given partnership will hold close to an average holding over a long period in terms of percentage.

BAD CARDS. (1) Consistently inferior cards in a session of rubber bridge. (2) Cards that are expected, on the basis of the bidding, to be of little or no value to partner. If partner shows an unbalanced distribution with one very long suit or two long suits, minor honors in the other suits are unlikely to be of value to him. Similarly, tenace holdings or single honors other than the ace deteriorate if the suit is bid by the left-hand opponent.

If partner has bid two suits, a holding of three small cards in the suit which is not going to be trumps represents a liability, and four small cards is almost as bad. See WORKING CARDS.

BAD HANDS. Hands with little honor strength.

S. J. Simon pointed out that underbidding with a bad hand is a common error of the average player. He gave this spectacular example of the need to bid with a weak hand:

EAST
♠ 4 3 2
♡ K 2
◇ 5 4 3 2
♣ 5 4 3 2

The bidding:

NORTH	EAST	SOUTH	WEST
1 ◇	Pass	2 ♣	2 ◇
3 ♣	Pass	3 ◇	4 ♣
4 ◇	Pass	5 ♣	5 ◇
Pass	5 ♠	Pass	6 ♠
Pass	?		

East has been forced to express a choice between the major suits, and has shown no strength whatever. He has the vital heart king, and West must be confident of making twelve tricks without that card. Therefore the heart king must be the thirteenth trick, and East should bid the grand slam.

If partner shows great strength, a player should always ask himself whether his hand is better than it might be in the light of his earlier bidding.

BAD POINTS. See BAD CARDS (2).

BAHAMAS CONTRACT BRIDGE CLUB. An ACBL unit organized in 1965; joined WBF in 1970. Participated in 1972 World Team Olympiad. Player listed separately: Fred C. Rubbra.

President, 1975: Fred C. Rubbra, P.O. Box N–1036, Nassau, N.P., Bahamas.

BAIRD TROPHY. Awarded for the National Open Individual Championship, donated by James C. Baird in memory of his wife in 1948; contested at the Fall Nationals until 1957, then transferred to the Spring Nationals, under which heading the past results are listed.

BALANCE OF POWER. A concept first put forth by

S. Garton CHURCHILL involving the calculation of the safety of entering the auction based on actions taken by the opponents. See BALANCING.

BALANCE OF STRENGTH. The concept of calculating which side holds the majority of the high-card points. If a player adds his own point-count to the minimum shown by his partner, and the total is more than twenty, he knows that his side has the balance of strength. Sometimes he can infer that his side is likely to have the balance of strength by relying on the normal expectation of strength in his partner's hand.

(a)		(b)		(c)	
NORTH	EAST	NORTH	EAST	EAST	SOUTH
1 ♠	Dbl.	1 ♠	1 NT	1 NT	
				(weak—12–14	
				points)	

In cases (a) and (b) South can be sure his side has the balance of strength if he has ten points or more, and can reasonably expect it if he has nine. In (a) he redoubles and in (b) he doubles, in each case suggesting that he is hoping for a good penalty.

In (c) South doubles with 15 points or more because his side will have the balance of strength if the missing points are shared equally between West and North.

If South fails to make a balance of strength bid in these cases, North will usually assume that he was not strong enough to do so. See BALANCING.

BALANCED COMPARISONS. A principle embodied in most types of duplicate movement. If two pairs in competition play a given number of boards in the same direction (North-South or East-West), the movement is perfectly balanced if the same result is achieved by comparing either pair with a third pair.

Any full MITCHELL MOVEMENT is automatically balanced, because the players do not change direction, and the stationary players, like the moving players, compare with each other throughout.

A SCRAMBLED MITCHELL apparently cannot be completely balanced. To determine a plan of arrow switches which is even close to a perfect balance is a complex mathematical problem, and a computer experiment in 1964 in a specific case failed to discover even a near-solution. However, some imperfection in this respect is not a serious fault.

The original HOWELL MOVEMENTS were not balanced, nor were the later schedules prepared by R. BALDWIN and W. MC KENNEY. The first completely balanced Howell schedules were prepared by Jacques ACH and Charles KENNEDY in 1935.

In modern tournaments in which two or more sections may be scored as a unit, the director may have to take special care to avoid infringing the principle of balanced comparisons.

BALANCED DISTRIBUTION (or pattern). A hand that appears suitable for no trump rather than trump contracts. Standard types are 4–4–3–2, 4–3–3–3, and 5–3–3–2; 5–4–2–2 and 6–3–2–2 are borderline cases.

See EXPECTED NUMBER OF CONTROLS IN BALANCED HANDS. The completely balanced 4–3–3–3 distribution can be described colloquially as flat, square, or round, an example of the strangeness of bridge geometry.

Balanced distribution can also refer to an even division of one suit around the table, but this is a rare usage.

BALANCING (or protection, which is the normal term in England). Reopening with a bid or double when the opposing bidding has stopped at a low level.

After a suit opening.

WEST	NORTH	EAST	SOUTH
1 ◇	Pass	Pass	?

East's hand is known to be extremely weak, so South can balance with a hand of medium strength on the assumption that his partner has unrevealed strength.

The normal range for a simple suit bid by South in this situation would be 8–13 points in high cards. The spade suit is particularly significant: possession of spades favors balancing action, and lack of spades counts against it.

In more general terms, a shortage in an unbid suit, especially a major, militates against balancing, and a shortage in the opponent's suit favors it.

♠ 3
♡ A Q 6 4
◇ K J 5 3
♣ Q 6 4 2

South has sufficient strength to bid one heart, but that would be dangerous. The opponents almost certainly have a spade fit, which they are likely to discover if given the opportunity. It is perhaps better policy to allow them to play one diamond, which may be a poor contract for them.

But if the opening bid had been one spade, balancing action (in this case a double) would be automatic. It is now probable that East-West are in their best denomination, that North-South have a fit somewhere, and that North has some strength. North will frequently pass a strong hand with length and strength in the opponent's suit, but South can discount that possibility if he himself has the opponent's suit.

If South jumps in a new suit, he shows a hand too good for a simple balancing bid, probably a six-card or strong five-card suit and about 12–16 points.

A balancing double closely resembles a take-out double by the second player: there is virtually no upper limit, but with only moderate strength it should usually indicate a shortage in the opponent's suit and at least three-card support for each unbid suit. A balancing double may be slightly weaker (a minimum of about 10 points with ideal distribution) than an immediate take-out double. See also BALANCING TWO CLUBS FOR TAKE-OUT. A balancing double is unattractive with a void in the opponent's suit and 5–4–4–0 distribution, because the second player will often pass for penalties. Marshall MILES suggests that the cue-bid in the opponent's suit should be used freely in this position: it would not guarantee a game or even a second bid, and second hand bids as he would in response to a take-out double.

A balancing bid of one no trump is a weakish action, but exactly how weak is a matter of opinion. Standard treatment suggests the equivalent of a weak no trump opening, with about 11–14 points. KAPLAN-SHEINWOLD indicates an 8–10 point range, because a stronger hand would double. Others advise a 12–16 point range, because hands of this strength may otherwise present problems: a double may not be convenient with three or four cards in the opponent's suit and a doubleton in an unbid suit.

After a suit opening and response.

The most important consideration is whether the opening side seems to have a fit. If the opening bid is raised to the two-level and the opener passes, balancing action is strongly indicated, especially if the opening bid was in a minor suit.

WEST	NORTH	EAST	SOUTH
1 ♣	Pass	2 ♣	Pass
Pass	?		

In this situation North should almost invariably balance. Holding:

      ♠ A J 5 3
      ♡ K J 4 2
      ◇ J 3
      ♣ 6 4 2

he doubles. If South bids two diamonds, North corrects to two hearts, leaving South the option of continuing with two spades.

When one side has a fit, their opponents are almost sure to have a fit also. If the opening bid was one diamond raised to two diamonds, balancing is usually called for. For this reason many players continue to three of the minor suit as a pre-emptive maneuver to forestall balancing action.

WEST	NORTH	EAST	SOUTH
1 ♣	Pass	2 ♣	Pass
3 ♣			

                or

WEST	NORTH	EAST	SOUTH
1 ◇	Pass	2 ◇	Pass
3 ◇			

See PRE-EMPTIVE RE-RAISE.

Balancing action is desirable in theory but more difficult in practice if a major suit has been opened and raised. The player who balances must be prepared for his side to land at the three-level, although a balancing bid of two spades over two hearts can occasionally be risked with a four-card suit.

When a suit is raised directly, it is almost certain that the opening side has a combined eight-card or better fit. The same applies if the responder's suit is raised. Balancing action is strongly indicated after:

WEST	NORTH	EAST	SOUTH
1 ♣	Pass	1 ♡	Pass
2 ♡	Pass	Pass	?

There are other situations in which the opening side seems likely to have an eight-card fit:

(a)		(b)		(c)	
WEST	EAST	WEST	EAST	WEST	EAST
1 ♡	1 NT	1 ♡	1 NT	1 ◇	1 ♡
2 ♡	Pass	2 ◇	2 ♡	1 NT	2 ◇
			or Pass		

In each case North and South are likely to have a spade fit and should usually try to contest the auction, either with a spade bid or a balancing double.

In (a), (b), and (c) both North and South are in a position to take balancing action. Although North (South in case [c]) is not in the pass-out position, he knows that East and West will probably drop the auction at the level of two.

If the opening side bids three or four suits, or drops the bidding at one no trump, balancing is less attractive. The hand will frequently be a misfit for both sides, and it will pay to defend rather than contest.

WEST	NORTH	EAST	SOUTH
1 ♡	Pass	1 NT	Pass
Pass	Dbl.		

WEST	NORTH	EAST	SOUTH
1 ♡	Pass	1 ♠	Pass
1 NT	Dbl.		

In these sequences, North is implying that he passed originally on a strong hand because he holds strength and length in the opener's heart suit. He is hoping for a penalty, although South might choose to bid if his hand is very weak and he has a long suit.

After a one no trump opening.

A one no trump bid passed by the opener's partner produces a situation in which balancing is often not expedient. The probabilities are that the opening side has no good fit, and therefore that the defending side also has no good fit. The best policy, therefore, generally is to remain silent. To bid a five-card suit in the pass-out position may produce a double from opener's partner and a singleton trump in the dummy. However, some risks may have to be taken at board-a-match or pair scoring; conventional machinery such as ASTRO or LANDY can prove helpful.

With an UNUSUAL NO TRUMP, **q.v.**

BALANCING TWO CLUBS FOR TAKE-OUT. A

convention used in the ROTH-STONE SYSTEM in which a BALANCING bid of two clubs is artificial and shows 6–9 points with support for the unbid suits. The balancing take-out double is reserved for hands worth 10 or more points.

BALDWIN MEMORIAL TROPHY. For the four-session Swiss Team event contested at the summer nationals, presented by the widow of Colonel Russell J. Baldwin in his memory. First awarded in 1970. Past winners are listed under Summer Nationals, Appendix I.

BALTIC CONGRESS. An international bridge festival held annually in Gdánsk, Poland, since 1961. The main event is for Intercity Teams, restricted to selected city teams which compete for the Baltic Bowl, but there are also events for Open Teams, Open Pairs, Mixed Pairs, and Individuals. The Baltic Bowl contest was first held in 1963, and in 1968 attracted teams from Norway, Sweden, Belgium, Italy, Czechoslovakia, Hungary, and Russia.

BAMBERGER POINT-COUNT. See ROBERTSON POINT-COUNT and VIENNA SYSTEM.

BANGKOK CLUB. A system developed principally by Somboon NANDHABIWAT of Thailand and used by the Thai pairs in the 1966, 1967, and 1969 WORLD CHAMPIONSHIPS. The chief features are:

One club opening is a one-round force, denies possession of any five-card suit other than clubs, and shows 12–20 points. Responder bids one diamond with 0–6 points or 7–8 points and no biddable suit, one heart or one spade with 7–10 points, two clubs or two diamonds with 8–10 points, or one no trump with 11 points or more, which is game-forcing. A jump response in a suit shows a six-card suit with 4–6 points, and a jump to two no trump is made with 9–10 points with no four-card major and no five-card minor.

After a semi-positive response of one heart or one spade, a new suit by opener on the two-level, other than clubs, is natural and forcing to game. Over a minor-suit response, a new suit asks for a control, with two no trump as the positive response. After a one no trump response, opener may show a suit naturally on the two-level, raise to two no trump with a minimum balanced hand, or show various strengths of strong balanced hands by specialized rebids on the three-level.

If an opponent overcalls the one club opening, responses are natural. If an opponent doubles, responses on the one-level are natural, equivalent to a positive response, jump responses are pre-emptive, and a redouble shows 11 points or more.

One diamond, one heart, or one spade openings guarantee a five-card suit with 11–17 points.

One no trump opening shows 18 points or more with a five-card suit, or 21 points and up with balanced distribution. Two clubs is the conventional negative response (0–6 points), over which opener may ask for a major by rebidding two diamonds.

With 7 points or more, responder may bid a five-card suit, or raise to two no trump to deny a five-card suit, over which opener may ask for a major by rebidding three clubs.

Two-bids are natural, game-forcing, with two no trump as the conventional negative response.

BANNING OF BRIDGE IN RUSSIA. See RUSSIA.

BAR, BARRED.

(1) A bid out of rotation during the auction, or an insufficient bid if corrected in certain permissible ways, or exposure of certain cards has, as a penalty, the requirement that the partner of the offender must pass whenever it is his turn to call or at his next opportunity to do so. Such an infraction will bar the partner.

(2) An ethical player, when his partner has hesitated and then passed at some point during the auction, will bar himself from taking any action on his cards that is in any way questionable; that is, he will lean over backwards to avoid taking advantage of his partner's hesitation.

(3) A player may be technically "barred" from further bidding, especially if he has limited his hand previously. See, e.g., PRE-EMPTIVE RE-RAISE, SIGN-OFF BID.

(4) A player may be prohibited by the methods he is using from making a certain bid. For example, pairs using psychic responses to WEAK TWO BIDS may agree that opener is barred from rebidding past three of his own suit.

BARBADOS BRIDGE LEAGUE. Founded in 1966. Competes annually with Trinidad and Tobago in Open and Women's teams. Competes regularly in CACBF events. National events include two Interclub series, a Knockout Interclub event, and a four-session Open Pairs.

President, 1970: E. L. Cozier, 3 Diocesan House, Bridgetown, Barbados.

BARCLAY MOVEMENT. A movement designed by Shepard BARCLAY in the late twenties so that competition between any two teams is completed in the same round of play. The necessity of relaying boards led to its early discontinuance as the size of the fields increased. Lawrence ROSLER, in 1963, designed a movement incorporating the good features of this movement for larger fields. See TEAM-OF-FOUR MOVEMENT.

BARCLAY TROPHY. Awarded for the National Masters Mixed Team Championship, donated by Shepard G. Barclay in 1929; replaced by the LEBHAR TROPHY in 1948. Formerly contested at the Summer Nationals, under which heading past results are listed.

BARCO SQUEEZE. A triple-double squeeze, exerting pressure on both opponents in three suits.

The most famous example was played by Edward T. Barco, and described by him in *The Bridge World* (Dec. 1935).

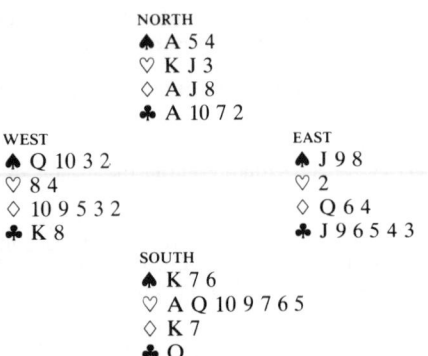

```
                    NORTH
                    ♠ A 5 4
                    ♡ K J 3
                    ◇ A J 8
                    ♣ A 10 7 2
WEST                                    EAST
♠ Q 10 3 2                              ♠ J 9 8
♡ 8 4                                   ♡ 2
◇ 10 9 5 3 2                            ◇ Q 6 4
♣ K 8                                   ♣ J 9 6 5 4 3
                    SOUTH
                    ♠ K 7 6
                    ♡ A Q 10 9 7 6 5
                    ◇ K 7
                    ♣ Q
```

West led a trump against South's contract of seven hearts, and declarer ran five trump tricks to reach this ending:

```
                    NORTH
                    ♠ A 5 4
                    ♡ —
                    ◇ A J 8
                    ♣ A 10
WEST                                    EAST
♠ Q 10 3 2                              ♠ J 9 8
♡ —                                     ♡ —
◇ 10 9 5                                ◇ Q 6 4
♣ K                                     ♣ J 9
                    SOUTH
                    ♠ K 7 6
                    ♡ 7 6
                    ◇ K 7
                    ♣ Q
```

South led a further heart, on which West and North discarded a spade. East was squeezed, and had to discard a spade also. The last trump squeezed West in three suits. However, if he had discarded a diamond, declarer would have had to make the double-dummy play of entering dummy and leading the diamond jack. See HEXAGON SQUEEZE.

BAROMETER. A device originated in Sweden in which all groups of boards are played simultaneously. Running scores are posted on the "Barometer" shortly after the conclusion of each round, thus heightening the interest for both players and spectators. Toward the end of an event, the known positions of the pairs in contention will influence the tactics they choose in attempting to win.

Barometer scoring was first used in world championship play in the WORLD PAIR OLYMPIAD in 1970. In the United States it was first used on the national level at the 1974 Spring National tournament in the final session of a secondary event.

BARON COROLLARY. An adjunct to TWO-WAY STAYMAN, of increasing popularity in Canada, that is designed to discover 4–4 minor suit fits. After re-

sponder has bid two diamonds (forcing to game), and opener has bid two no trump, denying a four-card major or a five-card minor, a three club rebid by responder asks opener's precise distribution. Opener rebids three diamonds with 3–3–4–3, three no trump with 3–3–3–4, or three of his longer major if he has two four-card minors. See also ALLEN OVER NO TRUMP.

BARON NO TRUMP OVERCALL. An equivalent to a weak take-out double. It is usually made with a singleton or void in the opponent's suit, and the most likely distribution is 4–4–4–1. The maximum strength is 13 points, and the minimum depends on vulnerability. It has achieved little popularity, because one no trump is valuable as a natural overcall. For an alternative method of making a weak take-out double, see MICHAELS CUE-BID.

BARON SLAM TRY. An invitation to a slam contract if partner holds good trumps.

A bid of the suit next below the agreed suit at the five or six level specifically asks partner whether he holds good trumps. So if spades are agreed, five hearts invites six spades, and six hearts invites seven spades.

What constitutes good trumps depends on the previous auction. Partner must ask himself how much worse his trump holding might be in the light of his previous calls.

BARON SYSTEM. An English system developed in the 1940s by Leo Baron, Adam Meredith, and others. Its exponents have had considerable success in British tournament play, and many of the ideas of the system have taken root in the general theory of the game. Examples of this are (1) the weak no trump opening bid combined with a one no trump constructive rebid; (2) bidding UP THE LINE with four-card suits; (3) relaxed requirements for BIDDABLE SUITS; (4) the five-card suit requirement for a response of two hearts to an opening of one spade; (5) the lead of ACE FROM ACE-KING.

Other distinctive features of the system are: (6) A bid of the third suit by the opener is forcing (e.g., one club—one heart—one spade; or one spade—two clubs—two diamonds). Some experts using standard methods follow this theory when the response was at the level of two. (7) An immediate raise requires at least four-card trump support. (8) Suit opening bids are highly prepared, with a four-card spade suit being opened ahead of a five-card heart suit regardless of quality. (9) Simple overcalls are strong and jump overcalls weak.

See also: ACE VALUES; BARON NO TRUMP OVERCALL; BARON SLAM TRY; TWO NO TRUMP OPENING; TWO NO TRUMP RESPONSE.

BARON TWO NO TRUMP RESPONSE. See TWO NO TRUMP RESPONSE.

BARRAGE. The French term for PRE-EMPTIVE BID. Sometimes used by English writers to describe a series of obstructive bids.

BARRICADE. An obsolete term for PRE-EMPTIVE BID or BARRAGE, coined by P. Hal Sims.

BARTON ONE CLUB. An English system popular in the thirties. The one club opening bid promised three and one-half quick tricks or more.

BATH COUP. A simple hold-up of the ace when the jack is also held:

(a)

	NORTH	
	4 3 2	
WEST		EAST
K Q 10 9 6		7 5
	SOUTH	
	A J 8	

(b)

	NORTH	
	A 3 2	
WEST		EAST
K Q 10 9 6		7 5
	SOUTH	
	J 8 4	

In each case the king is led and is allowed to win. If declarer holds two small cards, as in (b), he should generally play the higher one. This play may cause West to think that East has begun a high-low, and induce him to continue the suit to South's advantage.

The play dates from the days of whist, and is presumably named after the English watering place of Bath.

BATTLE, SARAH. A character invented by Charles Lamb to embody his idea of what a perfect whist player should be. In his *Essays of Elia* he wrote: "She loved a thorough-paced partner, a determined enemy. She took and gave no concessions. She never made a revoke nor even passed it over in her adversary without exacting the utmost forfeiture. She fought a good fight—cut and thrust. She sat bolt upright, and neither showed you her cards, nor desired to see yours. . . . I never in my life—and I knew Sarah Battle many of the best years of it—saw her take out her snuffbox when it was her turn to play, or snuff a candle in the midst of a game or ring for a servant until it was fairly over. She never introduced or connived at miscellaneous conversation during its progress. As she emphatically observed, 'cards were cards,' and if I ever saw mingled distaste in her fine last-century countenance, it was at the airs of a young gentleman of a literary turn, who had been with difficulty persuaded to take a hand, and who, in his excess of candor, declared that he thought there was no harm in unbending the mind now and then, after serious studies, in recreations of that kind! She could not bear to have her noble occupation, to which she wound up her faculties, considered in that light. It was her business, her duty, the thing she came into the world to do—and she did it. She unbent her mind afterwards over a book."

BECHGAARD SIGNALS. A method of discarding to show the length of a suit, devised by Kai Bechgaard, South Africa.

With five cards, a *delayed* signal is used: three, four, and then two, for example.

With six cards, a *continued* signal is used: four, three, and then two.

With seven cards, a *double* signal is used: three, two, five, and then four.

The following hand is an illustration:

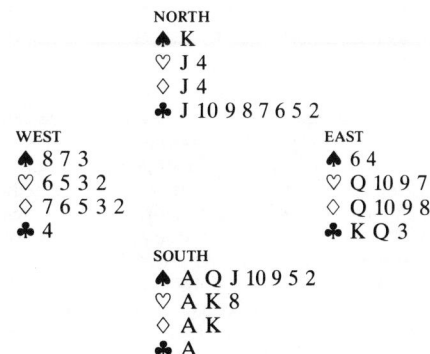

South plays in seven spades, and West leads a trump, the only lead to defeat the contract. South plays all his black suit winners, and East must decide which red suit to retain.

Using Bechgaard signals, West discards the three, five, and two of diamonds to show a five-card holding, and East knows that he must retain hearts.

For alternative methods of treating this type of situation, see LENGTH SIGNALS.

BELATED SUPPORT. Support for the opener's original suit on the second round after opener has rebid two no trump (as distinguished from PREFERENCE and JUMP PREFERENCE).

WEST	EAST
1 ♡	1 ♠
2 NT	3 ♡

A forcing sequence, which would show exactly three-card support if LIMIT RAISES are being used. If the opener then bids three spades, he also shows three-card support.

If the opener's suit is a minor, a small minority of players would regard the belated support as non-forcing.

BELGIAN ROYAL BRIDGE FEDERATION (FÉDÉRATION ROYALE BELGE DU BRIDGE, BELGISCHE BRIDGE FEDERATIE). Founded in 1932 by a group of thirteen clubs headed by the Cercle Privé du Royal Automobile Club of Brussels. The Federation annually sends teams to the European Championships, organizing the 1935 event in Brussels and the 1965 and 1973 tournaments in Ostend. Among the events it sponsors are the Belgian Team Championship, played by teams of clubs, and an

Open Pair event. The Federation had approximately 1,750 members in 1975. Belgian players listed separately are: J. van den Borre, L. Devroede, A. Finckelstein, C. de Hemricourt, L. Klenovicz, Mrs. E. Köver, A. Littman-Lemaitre, S. Lipschutz, L. Luyten, J. Mardulyn, C. Monk, Miss S. Moulia, Mrs. C. Myrans, E. Polak, S. Rubin, N. Savostin, R. Silberwasser.

Officers, 1968:
President: Charles Mathys.
Secretary: Jean Mardulyn, Fédération Belge du Bridge, 57, Avenue Louis Lepoutre, Brussels 6, Belgium 1060.

BELONG. An expression to indicate which side can legitimately expect to buy the contract. A player who says he knew that "the hand belonged to the opponents" indicates that he judged the opposition could make the highest positive score on the deal. In such circumstances, it may pay to take an ADVANCE SAVE or other pre-emptive action. Alternatively, a player who judges that he will be outgunned in high cards may prefer to remain silent on the theory that he will end up as a defender and does not wish to give information that may help the declarer.

An alternative meaning of the word in modern bridge jargon, especially in a POST-MORTEM, is to indicate the most desirable contract for a side: "We belong in five diamonds."

BELOW THE LINE. Points at rubber bridge entered below the horizontal line on the score sheet. These points are solely those made by bidding and making part-scores or games. All other points are scored above the line only. Points scored below the line count toward winning a game or rubber. At duplicate bridge or Chicago, the term may be used loosely to refer to trick-score. See SCORING.

BENJAMIN. Convention permitting an Acol player to use WEAK TWO-BIDS in the major suits; invented by Albert Benjamin (Scotland). Opening bids of two spades and two hearts are weak. An opening bid of two diamonds is equivalent to an Acol bid of two clubs, and almost guarantees game. The negative response is two hearts, and the sequence two diamonds—two hearts—two no trump, showing 23–24 points, can be passed.

An opening bid of two clubs shows a normal Acol one round forcing two-bid in an unspecified suit, and promises at least eight playing tricks. The negative response is two diamonds, and any positive response is forcing to game. With this method it is possible to see an Acol two-bid when clubs is the primary suit. See ACOL SYSTEM.

BENNETT MURDER. A historic tragedy which took place in Kansas City, Kan., in 1931. The victim was John S. Bennett, a prosperous perfume salesman, who met his death as a result of a game of contract in which he played with his wife against another married couple. His wife became so infuriated at her husband's play that she shot him following a bitter quarrel. She was tried for murder later the same year, and acquitted.

The following account of the episode appeared in the New York *Evening Journal:*

"As the game went on," Mrs. Hoffman said, "The Bennetts' criticism of each other grew more and more caustic. Finally a spade hand was bought by them in the following manner: Bennett bid a spade. My husband overcalled with two diamonds. Mrs. Bennett promptly boosted the original spade bid to four. I passed. Mrs. Bennett, as Dummy, laid down a rather good hand. But her husband was set. This seemed to infuriate his wife and she began goading him with remarks about 'bum Bridge players.' He came right back at her. I don't remember the exact words. This kept up for several minutes. We tried to stop the argument by demanding cards, but by this time the row had become so pronounced that Bennett, reaching across the table, grabbed Myrtle's arm and slapped her several times. We tried to intervene, but it was futile. While Mrs. Bennett repeated over and over in a strained sing-song tone, 'Nobody but a bum would hit a woman,' her husband jumped up and shouted, 'I'm going to spend the night at a hotel. And tomorrow I'm leaving town.' His wife said to us: 'I think you folks had better go.' Of course, we started to do so."

While the Hoffmans were putting on their things Mrs. Bennett dashed into the bedroom of her mother, Mrs. Alice B. Adkins, and snatched the family automatic from a dresser drawer. "John's going to St. Joseph," she explained to the older woman, "and wants to be armed." Bennett had gone to his "den," near the bathroom, to pack for the intended trip. Hoffman, adjusting his muffler, turned back and saw his friend alone for the moment. While Mrs. Hoffman waited in the doorway, her husband advanced toward Bennett, hoping to say a word or two that would dispel this angry depression. The two men were in conversation as Mrs. Bennett darted in, pistol in hand. Bennett saw her, ran to the bathroom, slammed the door just as two bullets pierced the wooden paneling. Hoffman, rigid with astonishment, remained in the den. His wife, hearing the shots, ran down the hall and began pounding on the door of the next apartment. It is thought Bennett died from two bullets fired as he neared the door leading to the street. He staggered to a chair—the Hoffmans agree—moaning, "She got me." Then he slumped, unconscious, to the floor. Mrs. Bennett was standing at the other side of the living room, the gun dangling loosely from her fingers. As Bennett fell, her daze broke. She ran toward him. Police found her bent over him, giving vent to wild sobs.

The alleged hand was as follows:

```
                    NORTH
                    ♠ A 10 6 3
                    ♡ 10 8 5
                    ◇ 4
                    ♣ A 9 8 4 2
WEST                                    EAST
♠ Q 7 2                                 ♠ 4
♡ A J 3                                 ♡ Q 9 4
◇ A Q 10 9 2                            ◇ K J 7 6 3
♣ J 6                                   ♣ Q 7 5 3
                    SOUTH (D)
                    ♠ K J 9 8 5
                    ♡ K 7 6 2
                    ◇ 8 5
                    ♣ K 10
```

The bidding:

SOUTH	WEST	NORTH	EAST
1 ♠	2 ◇	4 ♠	Pass
Pass	Pass		

Mr. Bennett opened the bidding without sufficient values for an opening bid, and suffered an unusually heavy penalty. However, four spades was not an impossible contract, and Ely Culbertson analyzed the deal as follows:

> We have heard of lives depending on the play of a card. It is not often that we find that figure of speech literally true. Here is a case in point. Mr. Bennett had overbid his hand. Of that there can be no doubt, but even with this, so kind were the gods of distribution that he might have saved his life had he played his cards a little better. Mr. Hoffman opened the diamond Ace, then shifted to the club suit when he saw the Dummy void of diamonds, and led the club Knave. This Mr. Bennett won with his King and started to pull the adverse trumps. Here again he flirted with death, as people so frequently do when they fail to have a plan either in the game of Bridge or the game of life. He still could make his contract and save his life. The proper play before drawing the trumps would have been to establish the club suit, after ruffing the last diamond in the closed hand, upon which to discard losers in his own hand. Suppose Mr. Bennett, when he took the club trick with his King, had led his last diamond and trumped it with one of Dummy's small trumps. He could then lead a trump and go up with the King. . . . Now he would lead the club ten, and, when Mr. Hoffman followed suit, his troubles would be over. He would play the Ace of clubs and lead the nine or eight. If Mrs. Hoffman put up the Queen, Mr. Bennett should trump and let Mr. Hoffman overtrump if he pleased. If Mr. Hoffman, after winning this trick, led a heart, the contract and a life would be saved. If he led a diamond the same would be true. A lead of the trump might still have permitted the fatal dénouement but at least Mr. Bennett would have had the satisfaction of knowing that he had played the cards dealt him by fate to the very best of his ability.

The episode was entertainingly described at length by Alexander Woollcott in *While Rome Burns.*

BERMUDA. An ACBL unit, hosted the first of the present World Championships series held in 1950, and gave its name to the World Championship Trophy. Leading players listed separately are N. M. Bach, T. Denninger, and W. F. E. Tucker.

Secretary, 1969–70: Mrs. Roy S. Mucklow, P.O. Box 1568, Hamilton, Bermuda.

BERMUDA BOWL. The annual World Team Championship; the trophy at stake therein.

The first postwar world contract bridge team championship was played in Bermuda in 1950 on the initiative of Norman M. Bach. The contest was a three-cornered match between teams representing the United States, Great Britain (the European champions), and Europe (a combined Sweden-Iceland team).

The next six Bermuda Bowl contests were two-team events between the United States and the winners of the European Championships.

In 1958, the contest became a three-cornered event with the inclusion of the South American Champions.

In 1960, 1964, 1968, and 1972, which were Team Olympiad years, there was no Bermuda Bowl competition. In 1974 the WBF voted to conduct the Bermuda Bowl in odd-numbered years only. To provide a transition, for 1976 both the Bermuda Bowl and the World Team Olympiad were scheduled for consecutive play in Monte Carlo.

In 1961, France was included, as holder of the Olympiad title. From 1962 onward, the current holders of the Bermuda Bowl title were made automatically eligible. From 1950 to 1963 inclusive, the Bermuda Bowl was organized under the auspices of the ACBL and the European Bridge League with the collaboration of the South Amercan Bridge Federation from 1958. Since 1963 the Bermuda Bowl has been conducted by the World Bridge Federation.

In 1965, the WBF voted to expand the championship to a five-team contest with the inclusion of the Far East Champions, who became eligible for Bermuda Bowl competition in 1966.

In 1971, and again in 1974, the championship became a six-team contest when Australia, and then New Zealand, exercised the right to represent the South Pacific Zone.

For a full listing of Bermuda Bowl results, see WORLD CHAMPIONSHIPS. See also EUROPEAN CHAMPIONSHIP RESULTS; INTERNATIONAL BRIDGE LEAGUE; SOUTH AMERICAN CHAMPIONSHIP RESULTS; and WORLD BRIDGE FEDERATION.

BERMUDA INCIDENT. In 1975, during the early qualifying stages of the WORLD CHAMPIONSHIPS, being played in Bermuda in celebration of the 25th anniversary of the Bermuda Bowl, Gianfranco

FACCHINI, a member of the Italian team, was accused of giving foot signals to his partner, Sergio ZUCCHELLI.

The first person to notice unusual foot movements was Bruce KEIDAN, an American news correspondent monitoring the match between Italy and France. Keidan reported his observation to the North American NPC, Alfred SHEINWOLD, and to Edgar KAPLAN, a member of the WBF Appeals Committee. Kaplan informed WBF President Julius ROSENBLUM. Rosenblum himself observed for a time, then he assigned special observers from the Appeals Committee, Johannes HAMMERICH of Venezuela and James O'SULLIVAN of Australia, to monitor the Italian pair.

According to Keidan, Hammerich, and O'Sullivan, Facchini reached out with his feet on several occasions during auctions and before opening leads, and apparently touched Zucchelli on the toes once or more; Zucchelli's feet remained completely immobile, and Facchini did not move his feet at other times. Rosenblum, Hammerich, and WBF Vice President ORTIZ-PATINO of Switzerland therefore decided to monitor Italy's next qualifying match, using European observers. Before this plan could be implemented, however, the WBF was informed that the North American team would refuse to play against Zucchelli and Facchini in this next scheduled match. This, plus the fact that rumors of the foot-movement accusation were already rampant, caused the WBF to inform all team captains of what had transpired, to postpone the Italy-North American match, and to convene a hearing immediately.

The WBF Appeals Committee heard testimony from observers Keidan, Hammerich, O'Sullivan, Rosenblum, and Tracy DENNINGER. Facchini did not deny moving his feet, but attributed his movements to nervous tension. Zucchelli testified that he was unaware of any foot actions by his partner. Oswald JACOBY, who had analyzed some of the hands, was called as a witness, but the Committee was unable to find specific correlation between the foot movements observed and the bidding or play of the hands—a factor usually considered essential to conclusive proof of cheating. The WBF therefore resolved that Facchini and Zucchelli ". . . be severely reprimanded for improper conduct with respect to the actions of Mr. Facchini moving his feet unnaturally and touching his partner's feet during the auction and before the opening lead." Coffee tables were thereafter placed beneath the card tables to block any possibility of further such movements.

Sheinwold promptly issued a statement: "The North American team endorses the verdict of guilty but deplores the failure of the World Bridge Federation to bar this pair from further international competition." The word "guilty" had not appeared in the original verdict, but a later statement from Rosenblum corrected this omission by declaring that the accused pair "had been found guilty only of improper foot movements." The first meeting between the Italian and North American teams, postponed from Sunday afternoon, was played that evening. Italian NPC SALVETTI kept the suspect pair

out of the lineup, saying that their nerves were frayed by the accusations. Two days later, the pair also sat out the second qualifying match against North America, although they had played in other matches in the interim.

On the morning of the first session of the finals between Italy and North America, when Sheinwold learned that Facchini and Zucchelli were listed in Italy's starting lineup, he announced that the North American team would not play against this pair unless instructed to do so by the ACBL. ACBL representatives in Bermuda unanimously ordered the team to play. Italy fared poorly with the accused pair in the lineup, and it was only after they had been benched at the request of Garozzo and Belladonna that her team staged an "impossible" rally to retain the world title.

An unfortunate consequence of the nature of the verdict was that it caused wide though scarcely justified criticism of the conduct of the American players, the ACBL officials, and the WBF. Pre-tournament publication of an article by Sheinwold about the Italian players—written before he had been named captain of the American team—had brought forth official protests and created an atmosphere in which the actions of Sheinwold were taken into greater account than the admonishment of the accused players at the hands of the WBF. At the next subsequent meeting of the ACBL Board of Directors (Honolulu, 1975), Sheinwold's name was removed from the list of possible future captains and, in protest, he resigned as chairman of the National Laws Commission. The fact remained that the partnership of the accused players was broken up and the WBF advised Italian bridge officials that it would not welcome the nomination of either player to any event it conducted in the immediately foreseeable future. See BUENOS AIRES AFFAIR; CAPTAIN; CHEATING; CHEATING ACCUSATIONS.

BERMUDA REGIONAL CHAMPIONSHIPS. First played in 1962. For past results, see Appendix II.

BETA ASKING BIDS.
(1) Asking bids in the ROMAN and SUPER PRECISION SYSTEMS concerned with responder's support for the suit bid by the one club opener. After the negative response of one diamond, opener initiates the inquiry by jumping in a major suit (or, in Roman, by simply rebidding a minor suit). The responses are as set out in ROMAN ASKING BIDS.
(2) Asking bids in the SUPER PRECISION system concerned with the quality of a side suit after responder has made a positive response in no trump are also sometimes called Beta Asking Bids, although the difference in schedule of responses has led them to be designated Delta Asking bids in the version of Super Precision used by Belladonna and Garozzo. See SUPER PRECISION ASKING BIDS.

BETS. Betting is illegal in tournament play sanctioned by the American Contract Bridge League, or any of its affiliated groups.

Occasionally rather sizable bets have been made

on the results of challenge bridge matches, notably the CULBERTSON-LENZ MATCH of 1931–32 and the CULBERTSON-SIMS MATCH of 1935.

Bets on the outcome of a rubber or match are based on the side winning the larger number of points rather than the rubber bonus or bonuses, and are thus distinguished from STAKES, which are based on the difference in points earned at so much per point.

BEYNON TROPHY. Donated by George Beynon in 1947 and formerly awarded for the Senior Masters Individual Championship. This event was part of the Life Masters Individual Championship and was played as an independent tournament. In 1958 it became part of the Fall Nationals until 1960, when it was withdrawn. Past results are listed under Fall Nationals. From 1965 to 1971, the trophy was returned to competition and awarded to the winners of a two-session event for non-qualifiers in the Flight B Masters Pairs at the Summer Nationals, under which past results are listed.

BIBLIOGRAPHY. See page 849.

BID. A call by which a player proposes a contract that his side will win at least as many odd tricks (one to seven) as his bid specifies, provided the hand is played at the denomination named. See LAWS (Law 38).

BID OF MORE THAN SEVEN. A call by a player contracting for more than seven-odd tricks, and one which is, therefore, inadmissible. See LAWS (Law 38).

BID OUT OF ROTATION. A call by a player, not in turn. See LAWS (Law 31).

BID-RITE TEAM. The team that won the Eastern Team-of-Four Championship in 1933. The members were Howard Schenken, David Bruce (Burnstine), Richard L. Frey, and Charles Lochridge. Named for the Bid-Rite Playing Card Co., the first manufacturer of four-color cards. Clubs were blue, and diamonds were orange.

BID WHIST. An outgrowth of whist somewhat similar to auction bridge in method of bidding but differing considerably in method of scoring. The bidding is opened by the player to the left of the dealer; highest bidder leads after he has named the trump suit. Seventeen points is the maximum score on a deal, each trick counting one and the four face cards of the trump suit counting one each to the player who takes them in a trick. Sometimes confused with BRIDGE WHIST, this game, now obsolete, was not a direct link in the chain between whist and contract. See HISTORY OF BRIDGE.

BIDDABLE SUITS. The minimum requirements for a bid in terms of the length and strength of the suit.

In the thirties, the CULBERTSON SYSTEM laid down Q J 3 2 as a minimum biddable suit, but permitted this to be shaded slightly in certain circumstances.

Modern writers tend to reject a generalized rule for biddable suits, recognizing that the requirements must depend on the circumstances in which the bid is made. Four main situations can be listed.

Opening bids. The higher the rank of the suit, the higher the suit requirements tend to be. One club is often used as a prepared bid with a three-card suit, usually with 4–3–3–3 pattern and a minimum or near-minimum opening bid. Most authorities require that the three-card suit be headed by a high honor, but in an extreme case this requirement might be waived:

♠ A J 10 5
♡ A K J
♢ 5 4 2
♣ 8 4 3

Many players using standard methods would bid one club and hope for the best.

If the red suits were reversed in this example, most experts would open one diamond, regarding the quality of the suit as of greater importance than the convenience of rebid provided by an opening of one club. But this is an exceptional case. A bid of one diamond usually shows at least a four-card suit, but no guarantee is made about the quality of the suit. Four small cards may be sufficient in certain circumstances.

Standards are generally higher for major-suit openings (not taking into account players who favor FIVE-CARD MAJORS). Few experts are prepared to open with one heart or one spade unless the suit is biddable in the original Culbertson sense. A few players distinguish between hearts and spades, opening four-card heart suits much more readily than four-card spade suits.

Responses to suit bids. A similar principle applies: the most economical bid may sometimes be made with a three-card suit, especially a minor suit, while the most space-consuming bid usually indicates a five-card or longer suit.

(a)	(b)	(c)
♠ K 7 5	♠ 9 7 5	♠ 9 7 5
♡ A 5 2	♡ A 5 4 2	♡ A K 4
♢ A 6 3	♢ K 6 3	♢ 6 4 3
♣ 9 6 4 3	♣ A 6 3	♣ 8 7 4 3

With hand (a), most experts would select a response of one diamond to an opening bid of one club. This is a waiting bid which can come to little harm, and there is no good alternative unless a two no trump response is being used as a limit bid.

Hand (b) presents a problem when responding to an opening bid of one spade. Two hearts is clearly ruled out because nearly all experts reserve this space-consuming response for hands containing a five-card or longer heart suit. The hand is not strong enough for two no trump (unless this is played as limit). So the general expert choice would be two clubs.

It is usually dangerous to bid a three-card major suit, but Pierre JAïs, of France, recommends one heart in response to one diamond with hand (c), or one spade in response to one heart if the major suits are reversed. This is an extreme treatment, but illustrates the general principle of striving to make the most economical bid.

Conversely, a response at the two-level in the suit ranking immediately below the opener's almost always shows a minimum of five cards, as with the response of two hearts to one spade.

The most controversial problem concerning biddable suits is whether a weak four-card major suit should be bid at the one-level in preference to one no trump. The authorities who favor five-card majors require a four-card suit of any strength to be shown at the level of one, but other leading writers are divided or noncommittal on this point.

Rebids. This is similarly controversial when the choice lies between showing a weak four-card major suit and rebidding one no trump. In 1959, a panel of American experts were asked whether they subscribed to the idea of "giving highest priority to finding a major-suit fit." There were 29 panelists who answered yes, without reservations; 38 panelists answered yes, with reservations; 17 replied that they would bid the four-card major suit only if it was worth showing. On this specific hand:

♠ 7 4 3 2
♡ 5 3
◇ A Q 7
♣ A Q J 7

the panelists were asked to choose between a rebid of one spade and a rebid of one no trump after opening one club and receiving a response of one heart. There were 49 votes for one spade, and 43 for one no trump.

In a survey conducted by *Bridge World* magazine in 1967, 90 leading experts were asked whether a one no trump rebid after an opening bid of one club and a response of one heart denied a four-card spade suit. Sixty-five percent replied yes, indicating that the modern tendency is toward bidding major suits regardless of their quality.

The problem is slightly different at the level of two, when the choice lies between rebidding a five-card suit and introducing a weak four-card suit. A bid in the four-card suit, if lower ranking, would probably be the preference of the majority, in most situations.

Overcalls. In most situations, the overcaller can apply the standards of a rebiddable suit (see OPENER'S REBID), but standards must vary widely in accordance with such factors as vulnerability, level of the auction, and pre-emptive effect. See OVERCALL.

BIDDER. A player who makes a BID. Occasionally the term is used to indicate a player who is prone to overbid, or one who will prefer taking on a doubtful contract rather than defending in competitive bidding situations. Also, any player during the auction period.

BIDDING. The period following the deal, and ending after the third successive pass of any bid. Aspects of this phase of the game are listed under the following group headings: ARTIFICIAL BIDS; BIDDING SYSTEMS; COMPETITIVE BIDDING; DOUBLES; NO TRUMP BIDDING; OPENING BID; SLAM CONVENTIONS; VALUATION. Other articles include: APPROACH PRINCIPLE; ARTIFICIAL BID; BAD CARDS; BALANCE OF STRENGTH; BELATED SUPPORT; BIDDABLE SUITS; BIDDING SPACE; BORDERLINE OPENING BIDS; CANAPÉ; CHANGE OF SUIT; CHOICE OF SUIT; DELAYED GAME RAISE; DOUBLE RAISE; DRURY; FAST ARRIVAL, PRINCIPLE OF; FIVE-CARD MAJORS; FORCING SEQUENCES; GUARD; IMP TACTICS; IMPOSSIBLE BID; INVERTED MINOR SUIT RAISES; INVITATIONAL BID; JUMP REBIDS BY RESPONDER; LIMIT BID; LIMIT JUMP RAISE; LIMIT JUMP RAISE TO SHOW SINGLETON; MATCH-POINT BIDDING; ONE NO TRUMP RESPONSE; ONE OVER ONE RESPONSE; OPENER'S REBID; PART-SCORE BIDDING; PASSED HAND; PRE-EMPTIVE BID; PRE-EMPTIVE RE-RAISE; PRE-EMPTIVE RESPONSE; PREFERENCE; PSYCHIC BIDDING; PSYCHIC CONTROLS; RESPONDER'S REBIDS; SHOOTING; SHORT CLUB; SHORT SUIT GAME TRIES; SIGN-OFF BID; SINGLE RAISE; SKINNER PSYCHIC CONTROLS; SLAM BIDDING; STRENGTH-SHOWING BIDS; STRONG NO TRUMP AFTER PASSING; SWISS CONVENTION; THREE-CARD SUITS, BIDS IN; THREE NO TRUMP RESPONSE; TRAP BID; TRIAL BID; TRIPLE RAISE; TRUMP SUIT; TRUMP SUPPORT; TWO NO TRUMP RESPONSE; TWO OVER ONE RESPONSE; TWO-WAY GAME TRIES; UP THE LINE; VALUE OF GAME; WAITING BID; WEAK JUMP RESPONSES; WEAK SUIT; WEAK TWO-BIDS; WEAKNESS RESPONSE; WORKING CARDS.

BIDDING BOXES. A device, used extensively in the Scandinavian countries, that permits silent bidding. To make a bid, the player takes the appropriate card from a box attached to the corner of the table on his right and places it in front of him on the table. All bidding cards remain on the table until the auction is concluded, thus avoiding the need for a review of the bidding, as well as the possibility of mishearing or misunderstanding a bid. The boxes were used successfully in the World Pair Olympiads in Sweden in 1970 and Las Palmas in 1974, and in the 1975 WORLD CHAMPIONSHIP in Bermuda. A poll of the players and captains of the teams in the Bermuda Bowl showed that the bidding boxes, combined with the bidding SCREENS that were used, were an unqualified success.

BIDDING CONTESTS. See INTERNATIONAL BRIDGE ACADEMY.

BIDDING SCREEN. See SCREEN.

BIDDING SPACE. The economy or otherwise of bids, in terms of bids which have been skipped. A response of one heart to one diamond, for example, uses no bidding space, but a response of two clubs would use up all the possible bidding space. The general theory is that the length of a suit tends to increase as the bidding space consumed in bidding it increases.

(1) In opening the bidding, one club is not infrequently a three-card suit, and the length expectancy increases up the line. One spade is usually a five-card suit, even for players who do not require five-card majors.

(2) Similarly in responding, a response using no bidding space, e.g., one club—one diamond, may occasionally be a three-card suit. A response using all the bidding space (e.g., one spade—two hearts) is nearly always a five-card suit.

(3) In rebidding by the opener, a rebid in the original suit is most likely to be a five-card suit if it consumes no space (one heart—two diamonds—two hearts), but almost sure to be a six-card suit if all the bidding space has been used (one heart—one spade—two hearts).

(4) Overcalls represent exceptions, for tactical reasons. One spade over an opposing bid of one club is slightly more likely to be a four-card suit than it would be over one heart. In the former case the overcaller may be taking a calculated risk in the hope of shutting the opponents out of a heart fit.

BIDDING SYSTEMS. Specific methods of bidding are discussed under the following headings: ACES SCIENTIFIC; ACOL; BARON; BIG DIAMOND; BISSELL; BLUE TEAM CLUB; BULLDOG; CAB; CANARY CLUB; CULBERTSON; EFOS; FOUR ACES; FRENCH CLUB; GOREN; KAPLAN-SHEINWOLD; LEVINREW; LITTLE MAJOR; LITTLE ROMAN; MARMIC; NEW SOUTH WALES; NOTTINGHAM CLUB; OFFICIAL; PRECISION CLUB; REITH'S ONE OVER ONE; RELAY; ROMAN; ROMEX; ROTH-STONE; SCHENKEN; SIMS; STANDARD AMERICAN; STAYMAN; TREFLE SQUEEZE; VANDERBILT CLUB; VIENNA; WALSH; WINSLOW.

BIDDING TO THE SCORE. See PART-SCORE BIDDING.

BIFF. Colloquial for trumping the led suit, particularly a winning card on an early lead.

BIG CLUB. See SCHENKEN SYSTEM.

BIG DIAMOND SYSTEM. A method introduced by G. Robert NAIL and Robert STUCKER, the cornerstone of which is a forcing one diamond opening, promising an unbalanced hand with at least 17 points. One heart is the negative response (0–9), and one no trump shows a positive response in hearts. After a negative response, minimum rebids by opener show 17–21 points; jump rebids ask responder to define his support and strength by steps, or to jump to game with good support and a void or singleton. Double jump rebids by opener are game-forcing, and responder shows his support by steps. Opener may then bid a new suit to ask for controls in that suit. After a positive response, opener jumps to show a self-sustaining suit, or rebids two no trump (18–20) or three no trump (21–23) with no fit for responder's suit and all unbid suits stopped. Other openings include:

(1) One club, forcing, showing a balanced hand not suitable for a one no trump opening (14–16) or a two no trump opening (20–21). A one diamond response is negative (0–10).

(2) Two clubs, non-forcing, showing 12–15 points with 4–4 or better in the minor suits. Over a two no trump response, opener rebids three of a minor suit if he has five cards in the suit, or three of a major with three cards in that suit.

(3) Two diamonds, showing 14–16 points and 4–4 or 5–4 in the major suits. Responses of three diamonds, three hearts, and three spades are invitational; two no trump is game-forcing and opener rebids three clubs or three diamonds with 4–4 in the majors and three cards in the minor suit bid, or rebids three hearts or three spades with five cards in the major bid.

BIG TOP. The highest match-point score on a board when two or more sections are scored together. Common big tops are 25 and 39. See SCORING ACROSS THE FIELD.

BIOGRAPHIES. See Section II.

BIRITCH, or Russian Whist. The historic four-page pamphlet, thought to be the earliest publication of the rules of bridge. Authorship has now been traced to John Collinson of London, in whose name copyright was entered July 14, 1886. The original copy in the British Museum was destroyed in the blitz, but a reproduction, made available through the courtesy of Cambridge University Library, is now in the ACBL library. The principal innovations from short whist are described as follows:

> . . . No card is turned up for trumps.
> The dealer, after the cards have been looked at, has the option of declaring the suit he elects for trumps, or of saying "Pass," in which latter case his partner *must* declare trumps.
> In either case, the one declaring may, instead of declaring trumps, say "BIRITCH," which means that the hands shall be played *without trumps.*
> . . . Either of the adversaries may say *"Contre,"* in which case the value of all tricks taken is *doubled,* the dealer or his partner may however thereupon say *"Sur contre,"* in which latter case the value of all tricks taken is *quadrupled,* and so on *ad infinitum.*
> . . . The person to the left of the dealer leads a card. Then the partner of the dealer exposes all his cards, on the table, which are played by the dealer as at *Dummy Whist.*

> GAMES AND RUBBERS

> A game is won by the first side which scores *in play* 30 points. The honours do not score towards the game.
> The *Rubber* consists . . . of two games out of three.

> SCORING

> The *odd tricks* count as follows:
> If "Biritch" is declared . . . . each 10 points
> If "Hearts" are made trumps . . . . " 8 "
> If "Diamonds" are made trumps . . . . " 6 "
> If "Clubs" are made trumps . . . . " 4 "
> If "Spades" are made trumps . . . . " 2 "

> If *all* the tricks are taken by one side they add 40 extra points. This is called "GRAND SLAMM."
> If *all* the tricks *but one* are taken by one side they add 20 extra points. This is called "PETIT SLAMM."
> The *winners* of each rubber add 40 points to their score. This is called "CONSOLATION."
> There are *four honours* if "BIRITCH" is declared, which are the *four aces.*

Equality in aces counts nothing.

3 aces .... 3 tricks
4 " .... 4 tricks
4 " in one hand .... 8 tricks

There are *five honours,* viz: Ace, King, Queen, Knave, and Ten, if *trumps* are declared.

Simple honours (3) .... 2 tricks
4 " .... 4 tricks
4 " in one hand .... 8 tricks
5 " in one hand .... 1 trick additional
to the score for four honours

If one hand has *no trumps* (trumps having been declared), his side, in case of it scoring honours, adds the value of simple honours to its honour score, or, in case of the other side scoring honours, the value of simple honours is deducted from the latter's honour score. This is called "CHICANE."

Despite existence of this pamphlet, derivation of the name *bridge* from *biritch* was long disputed on the ground that no such word existed in Russian. Recent research by R. TRUE found that earlier Russian dictionaries did include the term, defined as *herald, town crier, announcer,* making it a logical name for a game which introduced the new idea of announcing the declaration at which the hand was to be played. It is interesting to observe the designation of *biritch* for the declaration of no trump, a feature never part of whist. Use in the pamphlet of the French terms for double and redouble would tend to confirm that bridge was played earlier in France, or in those diplomatic circles where French was the prevailing language. (See HISTORY OF BRIDGE.)

BISSELL. An original method for showing distribution with the first bid, devised by Harold Bissell of New York and published in 1936. It attracted favorable attention from B. Jay Becker, Louis Watson, and Edward Hymes, and anticipated some modern European systems, such as ROMAN and RELAY.

Valuation. This was by a distributional point-count which ingeniously took into account the strength of combined honors as well as suit lengths. Honor cards were valued at 3, 2, and 1 point respectively if there were 0, 1, or 2 higher honors missing in the same suit. For example:

ace	3	king	2	ace	3
queen	2	queen	2	jack	1
ten	1	jack	2		4
	6		6		

To these were added distributional points: 1 for the fourth card in any suit; and 4 for the fifth and succeeding cards in any suit.

The grand total bore a direct relation to the playing-trick strength of a hand (three times the number of playing tricks) and was therefore an accurate measure of the power of the hand.

Opening bids. One club was artificial and forcing, and was normally based on a two-suited hand or occasionally a powerful distributional hand of any type. A one diamond response was a positive relay, asking for further information.

A one diamond opening was artificial and forcing, showing a three-suited hand or possibly a powerful balanced hand.

One heart or one spade showed a five-card suit and the equivalent of 12–16 points in normal point-count. One no trump represented about 13–17 points in normal point-count. Opening two-bids were strong but not forcing.

BLACK CLUB. A modified version of BLUE TEAM CLUB used by Bill EISENBERG and Bob HAMMAN in the 1971 World Championship.

The one club opening promises 17 or more points; all other openings are limited. The opening bid style is mildly CANAPÉ. The one no trump opening shows 16–17 HCP, or 13–15 points and a 3–3–3–4 or 3–3–2–5 distribution.

Other methods include FLANNERY TWO DIAMOND, weak 2's in the majors, GLADIATOR over two no trump openings, and cue-bids for slam exploration, with first- and second-round controls treated as equals and shown up-the-line.

BLACK POINTS. Master points won other than in regional or national championships. See GOLD POINTS; RANKING OF PLAYERS; RED POINTS; REGIONAL AND NATIONAL POINTS.

BLACK AND RED GERBER. A variation of the GERBER convention devised by Irving Cowan, Shedden, Ont., which uses four clubs as the ace-asking bid only when a red suit has been agreed on as trumps. When clubs or spades are to be trumps, the ace-asking bid is four diamonds. This modification retains a lower-level ace-asking bid than BLACKWOOD, while avoiding the ambiguity of using four clubs as Gerber, with clubs as the agreed suit.

BLACKPOOL MOVEMENT. A movement popular in England in which ten tables play twenty-four boards. Two boards are played in each round, and bye-stands are placed between tables 1 and 10, and between 5 and 6. Players and boards move as in a normal MITCHELL MOVEMENT for eleven rounds, so that in the eleventh round original opponents are again in opposition. For the twelfth round East-West pairs deduct their pair number from 11 and move to the indicated table.

BLACKWOOD. A convention in which a four no trump bid is used to discover the number of aces held by partner. It was invented by Easley Blackwood of Indianapolis in 1933, and has attained worldwide popularity.

The conventional responses to the four no trump bid are:

5 ♣	no ace or four aces
5 ◇	one ace
5 ♡	two aces
5 ♠	three aces

If the four no trump bidder continues by bidding five no trump he is asking for kings in a similar fashion. As this must be an attempt to reach a grand slam, the five no trump bid guarantees that the partnership holds all four aces.

Requirements. There are no specific requirements, but the four no trump bidder should feel safe at the level of five, and have an expectation of twelve playing tricks in the combined hands. He should expect to be able to make a successful decision on the basis of his partner's response, and should therefore usually be well provided with second- and third-round playing tricks in the combined hands. It is seldom wise to use the convention when holding a void suit or a worthless doubleton.

If the intention is to play in a minor-suit slam, discretion must be exercised if the four no trump bidder has fewer than two aces. Blackwood may be used with one ace if the intended trump suit is diamonds, but not if it is clubs.

In some circumstances it may be possible to play in five no trump. If the Blackwood bidder next bids an unbid suit at the five-level, he is requesting responder to bid five no trump.

Void suits. Void suits may not be counted as aces, but there are several methods in which voids can be indicated.

(1) Make the normal response, but at the level of six, to show the indicated number of aces and an unspecified void. Thus six clubs shows no ace and a void; six diamonds shows one ace and a void, etc.

(2) Bid six clubs to show one ace and a void; six diamonds to show two aces and a void. (Used by the GARDENER-ROSE partnership.)

(3) Bid five no trump to show two aces and a void; six of a suit ranking below the agreed trump suit to show a void in that suit and one ace; six of the agreed trump suit to show one ace and a higher-ranking void. (Introduced by the JORDAN-ROBINSON partnership.)

(4) Holding two aces, make the response that normally shows no aces; holding three aces, make the response that normally shows one ace. When the four no trump bidder signs off, the responder does not pass, but now bids the suit of his void. Responses at the six level show one ace and a void, as in (3) above. (Devised by Jeff RUBENS.)

(5) Using a three step set of normal responses to Blackwood in which five clubs shows 0 or 3 aces, five diamonds shows 1 or 4, and five hearts shows two aces, make a bid higher than five hearts to show a void. Five spades shows a spade void and one ace; other responses are as in (3) above. (Used in ROMEX.)

Interference bidding. See DEFENSE TO INTERFERENCE WITH BLACKWOOD.

Non-conventional. There are a number of situations in which four no trump should be treated as a natural bid. Experts sometimes disagree on specific situa-

tions, but there is general agreement on the following rule:

A four no trump bid is a natural bid whenever the partnership has not bid a suit genuinely. For example:

SOUTH	NORTH	SOUTH	NORTH	SOUTH	NORTH
1 NT	4 NT	2 ♣	2 ◇	1 NT	2 ♣
		2 NT	4 NT	2 ◇	4 NT
		(using an artificial two club bid)			

But there are other circumstances in which the four no trump bid should be treated as natural. Careful partnership agreement is needed. The following rule is generally valid: If, during the auction, one player bids three no trump and his partner bids four of a minor suit as a slam suggestion, a subsequent four no trump bid by either player should be a natural sign-off bid. For example:

SOUTH	NORTH		SOUTH	NORTH
1 ♠	2 ♡		1 ♠	2 ♣
3 NT	4 ◇		3 NT	4 ♣
4 NT			4 NT	

In these sequences the final bid rejects the slam invitation and expresses a desire to play in four no trump.

A more general rule is recommended by Terence Reese: Four no trump is natural when no suit has been agreed, either directly or by inference.

This covers a wide range. For example:

SOUTH	NORTH
1 ♠	2 ♡
3 NT	4 NT

Many players would regard this as conventional, but on Reese's rule it would be natural.

SOUTH	NORTH
1 ♡	2 NT
4 NT	

This type of four no trump bid is listed as conventional by Blackwood himself, but would be natural on Reese's rule. If South wishes to bid four no trump conventionally, he can make a forcing bid at the level of three and follow with four no trump on the next round.

By agreement, a raise from two no trump to four no trump at any stage can be regarded as natural: a conventional four no trump can always be postponed. But judgment may be required when three no trump is followed by four no trump.

SOUTH	NORTH
1 ♠	3 ♡
3 NT	4 NT

This is clearly conventional. North may be planning to play in either major suit, but has had no opportunity to fix a suit below game level.

Also, any sudden jump from a suit bid to four no trump is of necessity conventional.

See also: BABY BLACKWOOD; BOWERS; BYZANTINE BLACKWOOD; CULBERTSON FOUR-FIVE NO TRUMP; DECLARATIVE-INTERROGATIVE FOUR NO TRUMP; GERBER CONVENTION; NORMAN FOUR NO TRUMP; ROMAN BLACKWOOD; ROMAN GERBER; SAN FRANCISCO CONVENTION; SUPER BLACKWOOD; SUPER GERBER; and SUPPRESSING THE BID ACE.

BLACKWOOD THEORY OF DISTRIBUTION. A formula applied when missing four cards including the queen.

NORTH
♠ K J 10 7 4

SOUTH
♠ A 8 6 2

South lays down the ace and both defenders play low. On the second round West plays low, and South has to decide whether to finesse or play for the drop.

Mathematically it is extremely close. Easley Blackwood suggests a rule based on the LAW OF SYMMETRY: If the combined North-South holding in their shortest suit is:

(a) five cards, or four cards
divided two-two: play for the drop
(b) four cards divided three-
one or four-zero, or fewer
than four cards: finesse

This formula was tested on a large number of published hands, and produced excellent results. However, it can apply only when there are no indications from the bidding and play, which is rarely the case.

BLANK. A VOID. Used as an adjective, it indicates lack of a protecting small card for an honor, as a *blank* king. As a verb, it means to discard a protecting small card, as to *blank* a king.

Blank honors, whether singleton or doubleton, are slightly devalued in most POINT-COUNT methods.

BLANK HAND. A hand with seemingly no trick-taking potential (see YARBOROUGH).

BLANK SUIT. See VOID.

BLIND LEAD. The first lead on any hand, so called because the opening leader has not seen the dummy. Particularly is this term applied when the leader's partner has not bid, and the declarer's side has bid only one denomination.

Terence Reese, noted English bridge player, is quoted as saying, "Blind leads are for deaf players." See OPENING LEAD.

BLIND PLAYERS. Blindness is not an insurmountable obstacle to bridge. Bridge decks can be marked by Braille symbols on the corners, and each player calls the card he plays to each trick. A blind player may at any time ask that the remaining cards in the dummy be read to him.

J. P. DUNNE and Dr. A. DYE were among the first blind players to play in American Contract Bridge League National tournaments. Dr. Lois Zwart (now Wiley) of Chicago commenced playing a few years later, accompanied by her Seeing Eye dog. It was interesting that early Braille markings were not standardized, and often players could not read one another's Braille.

Dr. Dye, Dr. WILEY, and John L. Larsen of Minneapolis, Minnesota, have earned the LIFE MASTER rating. The American Contract Bridge League furnishes hundreds of decks for Brailling each year.

An organization devoted to teaching bridge to the blind is Bridge for the Blind, 248 Elwood Ave., Newark, N.J. 07106. This nonprofit corporation, founded and directed by Helen D. ALBANO, purchases and distributes Brailled lessons and cards, enrolls and trains teachers of the blind, certifies qualified teachers, and issues diplomas to students who have attended the required bridge courses and certificates to contributors to the organization. In 1974, there were 84 enrolled teachers in the United States, 5 in Canada, 1 in South Africa, and 5 in Iran. See also HANDICAPPED PLAYERS.

BLOCK. A situation in which entry problems within a particular suit make it difficult or impossible to cash winners or possible winners in that suit. This occurs when both members of a partnership (the declaring side or the defense) hold significant honor cards, and one of them has no accompanying small cards. For example:

NORTH	NORTH
K Q J 10	Q J 3 2
SOUTH	SOUTH
A	A K

In these cases the block is complete, and the honor cards in dummy cannot be utilized unless a side entry is available. Sometimes the block may be less embarrassing:

NORTH	NORTH
A J 4 3 2	A 4 3 2
SOUTH	SOUTH
K Q	K Q J

If there is no side entry to dummy, South must sacrifice an honor by overtaking the last honor in his own hand. He needs a 3–3 division of the defenders' cards to make more than three tricks.

The general rule for resolving blocked situations, or for avoiding unnecessary blocks, is that high cards must be played from the shorter hand as quickly as possible. See also UNBLOCKING and INTERNAL BLOCK.

BLOCKBUSTER. A bridge hand of seemingly tremendous trick-taking potential. Frequently, however, these hands have a weakness and give rise to very large sets when the partner's hand contains no protective features, and the trump suit divides unfavorably. See also MONSTER and ROCK-CRUSHER.

BLOCKED SQUEEZE. See Criss-cross Squeeze, under SIMPLE SQUEEZE. For other types of blocked squeeze, see ENTRY SQUEEZE and STEPPINGSTONE SQUEEZE.

BLOCKING. Playing so as to create a block in the opponent's suit. For example:

NORTH
♠ A 5 2

WEST   EAST
♠ K 10 8 6 3   ♠ Q 9

SOUTH
♠ J 7 4

West leads the spade six against three no trump. The normal play is to hold up the ace twice, but this is useless if West rather than East is likely to gain the lead. In that case South should put up dummy's ace, abandoning the chance that the lead is from king-queen. Whenever East holds a doubleton honor the spade suit is blocked for the defense.

Notice that if the defensive entry was held by East, he would need to unblock with the queen on the first trick.

Another position:

NORTH
♠ A 6 4

WEST   EAST
♠ Q 9 8 5 3   ♠ K J

SOUTH
♠ 10 7 2

In this position West leads the five and South puts up dummy's ace, hoping for East to hold two honors doubleton. When the defenders gain the lead, they can cash only one spade trick.

NORTH
♠ 8 6

WEST   EAST
♠ A 9 4 3 2   ♠ K J 10

SOUTH
♠ Q 7 5

When East wins the lead of the three with the king, and returns the jack, South should cover and so block the suit. He assumes that West's three is an honest fourth-best lead, in which case West cannot have six spades, and East cannot have a doubleton. If there were two small spot cards missing, suggesting a six-card suit with West, South should play low on the jack.

NORTH
♠ A 3

WEST   EAST
♠ K J 7 5 4   ♠ Q 8

SOUTH
♠ 10 9 6 2

On the lead of the five, South blocks the suit by putting up dummy's ace. This permits a triumph for the rare player who underleads K Q J x x (see OPENING LEADS).

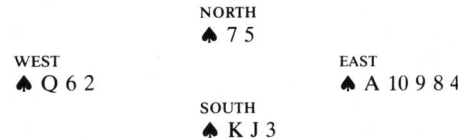

NORTH
♠ 7 5

WEST   EAST
♠ Q 6 2   ♠ A 10 9 8 4

SOUTH
♠ K J 3

West leads the two to East's ace, and the ten is returned. If South judges that West has led from an honor, he puts up the king and achieves a block.

See also UNBLOCKING.

BLUE PETER. A humorous term for a high-low signal invented in 1834 by Lord Henry Bentinck. This was probably the first defensive signal in any game of the whist family. The name is nautical in origin, referring to a signal hoisted in harbor to denote that a ship is ready to sail. Bentinck's signal was used in a side-suit to indicate to partner a desire to have trumps led. For uses of the high-low or echo in contract, see SIGNALS, SIGNALING.

BLUE RIBBON PAIR CHAMPIONSHIP, NATIONAL. An event contested annually for the CAVENDISH CLUB TROPHY at the Fall National Tournament, under which heading past results are listed. Entry is limited to (1) players who, within a specified period of time, have finished high in national championship events, or have finished first or second in regional-rated events, (2) the top 100 master-point holders, (3) members of current official teams representing the ACBL or any of its member countries in international competition, and (4) winners of Grand National District championships.

BLUE TEAM. The popular name of the Italian international bridge team which gained a remarkable series of successes beginning in 1956. The name is apparently derived from the 1956 Italian Trials, when the Blue Team defeated the Red Team.

Federico Rosa, the late Secretary of the Italian Bridge Federation, explained that the successes of the Blue Team were closely connected with the name of Carl' Alberto PERROUX, the Technical Commissioner of the Italian Bridge Federation. He undertook this duty in 1950, and scored his first success in the following year when the team which he had selected won the European Championship in Venice. But the subsequent World Championship encounter with the United States at Naples showed that the young Italian champions were lacking in experience and team discipline.

But this did not cause Perroux to lose heart. He wrote then that the Italians had wished to reach the moon too quickly. This was a promise and a threat. From that day, two groups of enthusiasts, under the paternal leadership of the Technical Commissioner, dedicated themselves to a profound and detailed study of the game. As a result the two schools—the Neapolitan and the Roman—gave birth not only to the most accurate bidding systems ever devised, including ARNO (LITTLE ROMAN), an offshoot of the ROMAN SYSTEM, but also to the great story of the Blue Team, made up of men such as Avarelli, Belladonna, Chiaradia, d'Alelio, Forquet, Garozzo, Pabis Ticci, and Siniscalco.

The Italians did not have to wait too long before avenging the 1951 defeat. From 1956 the Blue Team, captained by Perroux through 1966, Guido Barbone in 1967, and Angelo Tracanella in 1968–69, went from victory to victory, and finally reached the moon. They set an international record which will probably never be equalled: four consecutive European Championship wins, ten consecutive World Championship victories in the Bermuda Bowl, and three consecutive World Team Olympiad victories.

With the universe theirs, the Blue Team announced its retirement after winning the 1969 World Championship. After the ACES' victories in the 1970 and 1971 Bermuda Bowls, the Blue Team briefly returned to world competition for the 1972 World Team Olympiad. With Umberto Barsotti as their non-playing captain and using modifications of the PRECISION CLUB system, the Blue Team won the round robin and went on to defeat the Aces in the finals 203–138. Italy continued its domination of the Bermuda Bowl in 1973, 1974, and 1975 with Sandro Salvetti as NPC, but with only two or three members of the traditional Blue Team in the lineup.

BLUE TEAM CLUB. An increasingly popular offspring of the NEAPOLITAN system, developed principally by Benito GAROZZO. See BIBLIOGRAPHY C. The chief features of Blue Team Club are:

One club opening is forcing and normally shows 17 or more points (4–3–2–1 count). Occasionally distributional factors may dictate a one club bid with slightly less than 17, or a weaker opening with exactly 17.

Responses show controls by steps, counting an ace as 2 controls and a king as 1. One diamond shows 0–2 controls, less than 6 points; one heart shows 0–2 controls, 6 points or more; one spade shows 3 controls, and so on up to two diamonds, which shows 6 controls and two no trump showing 7. Jump responses of two of a major show a six-card suit headed by two honors but less than 6 points.

If one club is overcalled at the one-level, a pass is equivalent to the first step response and a double to the second. Other responses are control-showing, except that two hearts and two spades retain the same meaning as if there were no intervention. After a jump overcall the responses follow a similar pattern: pass is the weakest bid, double shows 6 or more points, suit responses are forcing for a round, a response in no trump shows 3 or 4 controls, and a cue-bid shows 5 or more controls.

One club is generally forcing to one no trump if the response is one diamond, or to two no trump if the response is one heart. The partnership is committed to game after any other control-showing response.

The opener can force to game by a jump rebid in a

suit. If he rebids one or two no trump, the responder can use STAYMAN. Responder usually makes his first rebid in his best suit, and subsequently shows significant features.

One diamond, one heart, and one spade openings are natural limited bids, showing 12–16 points and at least a four-card suit. Occasionally one diamond may be opened on a three-card suit. With two suits of equal length, opener bids the higher-ranking. With two suits of unequal length, the shorter suit is bid first unless the hand is a minimum and the long suit is higher-ranking.

Most responses are normal. Jump raises are limited. A two no trump jump response is invitational, showing 11–12 points and 4–3–3–3 distribution. Jump shifts show solid or near-solid suits and 13 points or more. Strong hands are bid according to the CANAPÉ principle. Responder's first suit may not be a real suit if his second is higher-ranking.

A response at the two-level is forcing for one round, or to two no trump. Opener must rebid a five-card suit if he has one. After a one heart or one spade opening, a second-round jump by responder to four clubs or four diamonds agrees opener's suit as trump and shows a control in the bid suit. See BLUE TEAM FOUR CLUB-FOUR DIAMOND CONVENTION.

If opener has a maximum opening, usually 14–16 points, he may make a jump rebid or reverse. Concentration of points in the bid suits favors the selection of a strong rebid.

One no trump opening shows a balanced hand, either 13–15 points with a club suit and exactly three cards in each major, or 16–17 points. Minor-suit responses are artificial. Two clubs normally shows 8–11 points and requests opener conventionally to rebid two spades with the strong no trump, or make some other two-level bid to describe the strength and club length of the 13–15 no trump. After a two-spade rebid, two no trump by responder asks for majors; minor-suit rebids are non-forcing. After any other rebid by opener, responder's rebids are mostly non-forcing, though encouraging in some cases.

A two diamond response shows a minimum of 12 points and is forcing to game. With a strong no trump, opener bids a four-card major or bids three clubs with no major, after which three diamonds by responder inquires about the minors. With a weak no trump, opener rebids two no trump, after which three clubs by responder requests opener to describe his strength and number of clubs in four steps.

Jump responses to the three-level show six-card suits headed by two of the top three honors with 6–7 points. Jump responses of four clubs and four diamonds are transfers to four hearts and four spades respectively.

Two club opening shows a good club suit of at least five cards and 12–16 points. If a second suit is held, opener will usually have a minimum of 15. A response of two diamonds is artificial and asks opener to bid a secondary suit. If he does not have one, he rebids either two no trump with stoppers in two of the outside suits, or three clubs with a stopper in only one outside suit. Three diamonds by responder then requests opener to pinpoint his stoppers. Other two-level responses are natural and non-forcing. Jump responses are forcing to game.

Two diamond opening shows a powerful three-suited hand (4–4–4–1) with 17–24 points. See BLUE TEAM TWO DIAMONDS.

Two heart and two spade openings are WEAK TWO-BIDS with a normal range of 8–11. Two no trump is the only forcing response.

Three club opening is a natural pre-empt and shows a minimum of seven playing tricks, including one outside the club suit.

GAMBLING THREE NO TRUMP.

Other opening bids are standard.

Blackwood is used on the first and second rounds of bidding, or in later rounds if a jump bid. Responses are ROMAN BLACKWOOD style, with five clubs showing one ace or four, and five diamonds showing none or three. In other situations four no trump is a natural slam invitation. Partner can cooperate by showing an additional feature. He may pass, but more often signs off in the agreed suit. See DECLARATIVE INTERROGATIVE FOUR NO TRUMP.

Defensive bidding is normal, but overcalls are made freely, especially at the one-level. Jump overcalls are intermediate. In response to take-out double, the cheapest bid may be a HERBERT NEGATIVE.

BLUE TEAM FOUR CLUB–FOUR DIAMOND CONVENTION. A delayed game raise used in the BLUE TEAM CLUB system to describe responder's minor suit controls. When opener bids and rebids a major suit or opens a major suit and rebids in no trump and responder has excellent support for opener's suit, he responds as follows:

(1) Two clubs followed by four clubs shows first- or second-round control of clubs and denies first- or second-round control of diamonds;

(2) Two diamonds followed by four diamonds shows first- or second-round control of diamonds and denies first- or second-round control of clubs;

(3) Two clubs followed by four diamonds shows either first-round control of both clubs and diamonds or second-round control of both suits;

(4) Two diamonds followed by four clubs shows first-round control of one minor and second-round control of the other.

See also NEAPOLITAN FOUR DIAMOND CONVENTION.

BLUE TEAM TWO DIAMONDS. A bid showing a hand worth 17–24 high-card points, with 4–4–4–1 distribution. An integral part of the BLUE TEAM CLUB system, this convention can also be used with standard methods. Responses fall into one of four categories:

(1) *Immediate sign-off:* with a very weak hand (about 0–5 points) and three or more spades, responder bids two spades. Opener will normally pass unless he has either a singleton spade or a maximum hand with four spades. With a singleton spade, opener rebids two no trump, allowing responder to select one of the other three suits.

(2) *Discouraging response with long broken suit:* with a hand worth 5–6 points containing a broken six-card suit, responder bids three of his suit. If that suit

is opener's singleton he will pass unless he has a maximum. If opener has four cards in responder's suit he may either bid game or try for slam by cue-bidding his singleton. After the cue-bid, responder bids in steps to show whether he has the ace or king of his suit, and whether or not he has any singleton.

(3) *Encouraging response with long good suit:* with a hand worth about 6 or 7 points containing a six-card suit headed by any three honors or two of the top three honors, responder bids two no trump. This bid asks opener to bid the suit *below* his singleton. At his next turn responder bids his suit (or bids three no trump if his suit is clubs and opener has shown a singleton club by rebidding three spades). If opener's singleton is in responder's long suit, opener may pass with a minimum, or may bid game in no trump or in responder's suit with a maximum. If opener has four cards in responder's suit the partnership is committed to game, and opener may try for slam by cue-bidding. Responder then cue-bids a singleton if he has one.

(4) *Relay response:* with a hand unsuitable for any of the above responses, responder bids two hearts, an artificial bid that asks opener for information. With a minor suit singleton and/or a maximum (21–24), opener bids the denomination below his singleton; rebids of two no trump and three clubs show minimum hands and rebids of three diamonds through three no trump show maximums. If opener has instead a minimum (17–20) and a major suit singleton, he rebids two spades; responder then rebids two no trump asking opener to bid three clubs with a singleton heart, three diamonds with a singleton spade and 17–18 HCP, or three hearts with a singleton spade and 19–20. Responder may then cue-bid opener's known singleton to ask about various features of opener's hand such as point count, controls, and queens.

BLUFF. A bid or play made with deceptive intent. See PSYCHIC BID and DECEPTIVE PLAY.

BLUFF FINESSE. See CHINESE FINESSE.

BOARD. (1) A duplicate board. (2) The table on which the cards are played. (3) The dummy's hand, so called because it lies on the table. See LAWS OF DUPLICATE (Law 2).

BOARD, DUPLICATE. An oblong or square board used in various forms of duplicate bridge, slotted with four sections, each deep enough to hold one quarter of a standard deck of playing cards.

The face, or top, of each board has listings appropriate to the board's use, as follows: numbered so that it can be quickly distinguished from companion boards of the same set, one slot marked to indicate the dealer, vulnerability conditions marked both in the slot itself (usually with red paint) and on the face of the board.

Sometimes the cards to be placed in the slots are shuffled by the players and dealt at the beginning of each contest, but for larger tournaments organizers usually obtain preshuffled or machine-prepared hands to be put into play instead of player-dealt hands.

As adapted for use in contract bridge, the boards are usually packed in sets of thirty-two or thirty-six in a carrying case designed for them. Dealer and vulnerability follow a standardized pattern, with North dealing the first board, East the second, South the third, and West the fourth with the same rotation repeated for every subsequent set of four. Vulnerability is arranged in a sixteen-board pattern as follows:

Board	1	2	3	4	5	6	7	8
Dealer	N	E	S	W	N	E	S	W
Vulnerability	No	N-S	E-W	Both	N-S	E-W	Both	No

Board	9	10	11	12	13	14	15	16
Dealer	N	E	S	W	N	E	S	W
Vulnerability	E-W	Both	No	N-S	Both	No	N-S	E-W

Thus every player deals in each of the four possible vulnerability situations. George Beynon notes that this pattern can be put into a magic square, in which N means N-S vulnerable; E, E-W; B means Both; and O for no vulnerability thus:

$$O\ N\ E\ B$$
$$N\ E\ B\ O$$
$$E\ B\ O\ N$$
$$B\ O\ N\ E$$

In England the boards in use have the deal 180° out of phase, South dealing on board #1.

The first duplicate boards (then called trays) were devised by Cassius M. Paine and J. L. Sebring in 1891. They were square boards, called Kalamazoo after the company that manufactured them. The first oblong boards were produced by W. MC KENNEY in 1928 using paper, and the first metal boards were manufactured in 1931 by F. D. COURTENAY.

Square and circular boards are also used, and paper, cardboard, wood, and plastic are alternative materials. Wallets made of plastic and foldable when not in use are popular in Europe and South America.

BOARD OF DIRECTORS OF THE ACBL.
The body that manages and controls the business and activities of the ACBL. The Board is composed of one director elected by each DISTRICT for a three-year term. The terms of the directors are staggered, with approximately one-third of the directors being elected each year. There are three regular meetings each year, usually just preceding a national tournament.

BOARD OF GOVERNORS OF THE ACBL.
A body that has the power to make recommendations to the BOARD OF DIRECTORS OF THE ACBL, and to receive reports from and to ratify certain actions taken by that Board. It is composed of five members from each DISTRICT, and, in addition, all past Presidents of the ACBL and all past Chairmen of the Board of Governors. Three regular meetings a year are held, usually during a national tournament.

BOARD-A-MATCH SCORING.
A method of scoring multiple team matches where each team plays against a variety of opponents, in which each board has exactly the value of 1 match-point. The highest match-point score among those in direct competition is the winner. Although this method used to be prevalent, it has been replaced in large part by INTERNATIONAL MATCH POINTS with SWISS MOVEMENT pairing.

The movement is so arranged that if the North-South pair of a given team plays a board against the East-West pair of an opposing team, the East-West pair of the given team plays the same board against the North-South pair of the same opposing team. If the total of a team's North-South and East-West scores on the same board is positive, that team receives 1 match-point. If it is negative, the team receives 0 match-points. If the total is exactly zero (that is, if both teams achieve the same score), both teams receive ½ match-point.

This method is virtually unknown in Europe, where it is sometimes termed "point-a-board." For movements employed see AMERICAN WHIST; NEW ENGLAND RELAY; PATTON; ROSLER. For other forms of team events see AGGREGATE; DOUBLE ELIMINATION; KNOCKOUT; HYBRID SCORING; QUOTIENT; ROUND ROBIN; SWISS.

BODY.
A term used to describe a hand with useful intermediate cards such as tens, nines, and eights. Some authorities advocate counting a ten as half a point, sometimes only for no trump purposes. The ten is of greatest value in combination with one or two higher honors, such as K 10 x, Q 10 x, or K Q 10. It has least value when isolated (10 x x) or in a solid suit (A K Q J 10). Similarly a nine may be valuable in combination (Q 10 9) but almost worthless in isolation.

Body may be a decisive factor in making a bidding decision:

♠ K 10 5 4
♡ A Q 9
♢ Q 10 9
♣ K J 8

This hand counts 15 points in high cards, but the intermediate cards make it a "good" 15, and most experts would treat it as a 16-point hand, and open with a standard 16–18 no trump.

Body is a factor to consider when making BORDERLINE OPENING BIDS. As the bidding proceeds, a player can often revalue his intermediate cards. A holding of 109x is certainly worthless if the bidding marks partner with a singleton or a void, and very probably worthless opposite a doubleton. But there is a good chance that the ten-nine will be valuable opposite a probable three-card suit: partner may have something like A J x, K J x, or Q 8 x.

BOLAND CLUB SYSTEM.
An early (1931) system devised by Vincent F. Boland of Shaker Heights, Ohio. The one club bid was *either* an artificial bid promising between three and five honor tricks *or* a

normal club bid. In the latter case the clubs were rebid on the second round. Other one-bids showed that the opening was about a minimum in honor strength. Two-bids were strong and forcing. The system was popular in the Cleveland area.

BOLAND CONVENTION. A method of slam exploration after a natural raise to four no trump, devised by M. M. Miller and C. Boland, Toronto. After the bidding:

WEST	EAST
1 NT	4 NT

West declines the invitation by passing if he has a minimum. With an average hand in terms of point count (i.e., 17 points using a standard 16–18 no trump) he bids five of his lowest ranking biddable suit. Responder acts accordingly, and may jump to the six-level in another suit without excluding other contracts. A five no trump rebid would deny a biddable suit.

With a maximum hand, the opener jumps to the six-level in his lowest ranking biddable suit in similar fashion.

The convention can be used in the same way after any natural jump from two no trump to four no trump.

BOLSTER. A PARTIAL STOPPER in a suit which is likely to be led by the opponents in no trump. A holding of J x x, for example, while valueless in itself, promotes a holding of Q x in partner's hand into a single stopper, or A 10 x into a double stopper.

BONNEY'S SQUEEZE. A triple squeeze against one opponent combined with a simple squeeze against the other. (Analyzed by Norman Bonney, Boston, Mass.)

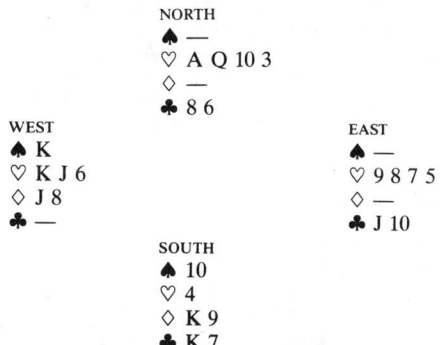

South leads the king of diamonds on which he throws a club from dummy. East is squeezed and must discard a heart. Now the lead of the club king squeezes West in three suits.

At the start South has all but *two* of the remaining tricks, but he manages to win all six by means of the squeeze.

M. I.

BONUS. A term used in all types of bridge to describe various premiums given under the scoring rules to sides or partnerships who accomplish specified aims, to wit: In rubber bridge, bonuses are awarded for the winning of the rubber by scoring two games before the opponents have scored two games. A bonus of 700 points is credited to the side winning a two-game rubber before the opponents have won even one game. If the opponents have won a game, the bonus becomes 500 points. A bonus of 50 points is paid any side scoring a successful doubled or redoubled contract. A bonus is scored above the scoring line for a side which, in the given hand, has held honors in trump, or all the aces in one hand at no trump. This bonus is either 100 or 150 points. (See HONORS.) Bonus scores are given to sides who successfully bid and make any slam contract. (See SLAM.) If a rubber of bridge has to be terminated before its regular conclusion, a bonus of 300 points is given to a side that is a game ahead, and a part-score earns a 50-point bonus. In CHICAGO bridge, bonuses can occur on each of the four hands, inasmuch as in this type of contest each deal is really almost a separate game of itself. A non-vulnerable side scoring a game in Chicago is credited with 300 points immediately, and a vulnerable side, 500. Slam bonuses are the same as in rubber bridge, and honors are likewise scored. A partial score achieved on the fourth or final deal, however, acquires an extra bonus in Chicago of 100 points. This bonus, however, is awarded only for partials actually acquired on the last deal—there is no premium for a partial remaining open at the conclusion of a four-deal chukker. In duplicate bridge, a bonus is awarded for the making of any partial score (a below-game score) on a given deal. The bonus is 50 points. The regular slam premiums apply in duplicate scoring as explained above, but there are no bonuses for honors, except in total-point scoring. In duplicate, the regular Chicago bonuses for games bid and made apply, e.g., 300 for making a non-vulnerable game and 500 for making a vulnerable game.

BOOK. The tricks won by a side which have no value in the score; a whist term with little significance at contract bridge. For the declarer, the first six tricks taken constitute his book; for the adversaries, the amount of the declarer's bid subtracted from seven, or the maximum number of tricks the adversaries may take without defeating declarer's contract. The origin of the term apparently lies in the old practice of forming the first six tricks into a "book" by placing them all in one stack.

BOOK GAME. Style of a player who is acquainted with the situations described in the books about bridge, and rigorously follows this pattern of bidding and play. It features theoretical knowledge, but implies lack of skill from practice and lack of versatility.

BOOK PLAYER. A player who plays a BOOK GAME. "The book player is a safe partner, but is not very dangerous as an adversary." (A. W. Drayton: *Art of Practical Whist*)

BOOKS. See BIBLIOGRAPHY.

BORDERLINE OPENING BIDS. When the decision seems to be close between opening the bidding with one of a suit and passing, a number of considerations may influence a good player.

Position at the table. The third player can open relatively freely, with a point or two less than he would normally require. This is partly because there is no necessity to rebid, and partly because the opening may inconvenience the fourth player, who is likely to have the best hand at the table. The fourth player may also open, especially at match-point scoring, with one point below the normal requirements in the hope of snatching a part-score; but in this situation the spade suit is crucial; if the fourth player is weak in spades he should usually refrain from opening a doubtful hand.

Vulnerability. This may sway a borderline decision, especially at match-points. With a 5–3–3–2 hand, for example, when the five-card suit is weak, there is a distinct possibility of playing a part-score down two to save an opposing part-score. The vulnerability would then make the difference between a good score and a bad one.

Location of honors. In general, a hand with honors in its long suits is well placed in attack, while a hand with honors in its short suits is more effective in defense. This factor is allowed for to some extent in most point-count systems, which devalue singleton kings, queens, and jacks, and doubleton queens and jacks.

Consider the following two hands:

(a)	(b)
♠ 9 4 3	♠ A J 4
♡ A J 7 5 3	♡ J 7 5 3 2
◇ A Q 5 4	◇ J 5 4 3
♣ 3	♣ A

The distribution and point-count are the same, but hand (a) has a sound opening bid, and hand (b) does not—although it could have an acceptable opening bid in some situations. The difference lies in the location of the honor cards.

Rebid prospects. The ease or difficulty of the rebid will often be a determining factor.

(a)	(b)	(c)
♠ A J 10 4	♠ A 8 7 5	♠ 8 6
♡ 6 4 3	♡ A 9 6 3 2	♡ A 7 6 3 2
◇ K J 6 2	◇ 7	◇ 5
♣ K 7	♣ K 8 4	♣ A Q 9 4 3

Hand (a) can give trouble on standard methods, because there would be no acceptable rebid if the bidding started one spade—two hearts or one diamond—two clubs. An opening bid is permissible

on bidding styles which allow a minimum hand to raise partner's response to the level of three (ACOL) or to rebid two no trump (several modern systems). But if the minor suits are transposed, one club can be bid without hesitation because there is no rebid problem.

Hand (b) is best passed because any opening bid can lead to problems. This hand combines two danger signals: a four-card suit ranking immediately above a five-card suit, and a weak five-card suit ranking immediately above a singleton. Either of these features should be counted against an opening bid. Change a small heart into a small spade, and an opening bid of one spade is in order, followed if necessary by two hearts.

Hand (c) will present a rebid problem if the bidding starts one heart—two diamonds or one club—one spade. An opening bid would be much more attractive if the heart suit were spades or diamonds, in which case there would be no rebid trouble.

Majors or minors. The possession of a major suit, and particularly spades, favors an opening bid. An opening bid in a major has some obstructive value, and the prospects of outbidding the opponents and of scoring a game are slightly improved.

BOSTON CHESS CLUB. The oldest club devoted to games in the United States, founded in 1857 in Boston, Massachusetts. In 1926, bridge-playing replaced chess as the chief activity of the club, and in modern times contract has been played almost exclusively.

BOTTOM. In tournament play, the lowest score on a particular hand in the group in direct competition. It is extended to indicate an excruciatingly bad result.

BOWERS VARIATION OF BLACKWOOD. A method of responding to BLACKWOOD credited to Stewart Bowers of New York. A response of five diamonds shows an ace of a suit bid by the partnership, and five hearts shows an unbid ace. Five spades shows two aces, and five no trump three aces.

BOX A CARD. To place a hand in a duplicate board with a card, usually not the top card, turned face up.

BRAZILIAN BRIDGE CONFEDERATION (CONFEDERAÇÃO BRASILEIRA DE BRIDGE). Founded in 1955, and formed of the bridge leagues of Guanabara, São Paulo, Bahia, Rio Grande do Sul, Pernambuco, Minas Gerais, and Rio de Janeiro. By 1969, it had a membership of approximately 3,500, competing in local championships and an annual National Championship for Open Teams and Open Pairs. Brazil participates in South American Championships and World events. The Confederation won the South American Championships in 1949, 1955, 1956, 1967, 1968, 1969, 1970, 1971, 1972, 1973, 1974, the Women's Team Championships in 1954, 1955, 1956, 1958, 1959, 1965, 1966, 1972, 1973, and represented the South American Confederation in the 1969, 1970, 1971, 1973, 1974, and 1975 World Championships. Players listed separately are: E. Amaral, P. P. Assumpcao, P. P. de Barros, E. Bastos, P. P. Branco, M. Branco, G. Chagas, G. Cintra, A. D'Ave, L. Decsi, N. Ferreira, S. Ferreira, C. Fonseca, T. Kenedi, Dr. S. Leite-Ribiero, C. C. Pereira de Sousa.

Officers, 1975:
President: Georges Vero.
Secretary: Ernesto D'Orsi, Praca de República, 177–1° andar., São Paulo—S.P., Brazil.

BREAK. The distribution of the outstanding cards in a suit in a manner favorable to the declarer. This may imply that a suit was divided evenly or nearly so, or that an adversely held honor was positioned so that it did not develop into a winning trick. The term "break" is also used to indicate the actual distribution of the cards outstanding in the suit; or with the adjective "bad" to indicate unfavorable distribution from the declarer's standpoint.

In most contexts, "split" may be used as a synonym for "break," both as a noun and a verb: "the suit *split* (or broke) badly (or well)." "There was a bad *split* (or break) in spades." For expectations as to how a suit will break, see MATHEMATICAL TABLES 4, 4A.

BREAKAGE. A rubber bridge term for rounding off the score to the nearest one hundred points. Should the value of an overtrick determine the breakage, some experts will go through a long rigmarole of adding up the score while playing the final hand to determine exactly how many tricks are needed for the additional points.

BREAKING TIES. The breaking of ties in duplicate contests, when it is a question of the winner, is done for the purpose of awarding of trophies when it is not feasible to award duplicates to the tying pairs or teams. Master-point awards in ACBL tournaments are awarded equally to each tying group, the amount being one half the sum of the awards for first and second places. The main occasion for breaking of ties during the course of the competition is to determine which of two or more pairs, tied for the last qualifying position or positions, is entered into the final session. In either case, for pair events, the method is similar. All boards played by all tying groups are considered, and 1 point awarded for an above-average score and ½ point awarded for an average score if the board or boards were not played in direct comparison. If the tying pairs are in direct comparison on any board, 1 point is awarded to the pair with the better match-point result on that board, ½ point if their match-point result is a tie. In team events, the result of the match between the two tying teams is used with BOARD-A-MATCH SCORING. In head-to-head team competition, such as knockout events, additional boards are played, usually about one-third of the number of boards in the original match. The method of breaking ties should be approved by the

SPONSORING ORGANIZATION or announced in the CONDITIONS OF CONTEST, before being used.

BRIDGE. A partnership game of cards derived from WHIST and played by four persons. The term can refer to three distinct games, which are listed under BRIDGE WHIST, AUCTION BRIDGE, and CONTRACT BRIDGE. All these games have been referred to simply as "bridge" during their periods of dominance, and the term "bridge whist" was not used when the game was in vogue (1894–1904). It was coined subsequently to distinguish the game from its successors.

The earliest printed mention of "bridge" appears to be in a pamphlet published in 1886 entitled "Biritch, or Russian Whist." Although there is no certainty that the game is Russian, the fact that it was christened "Russian Whist" gave weight to the idea that it originated in Russia. It does, as a matter of fact, bear a close resemblance to Vint, Preference, and similar games; and Vint certainly is of Russian origin. See BIRITCH; HISTORY OF BRIDGE; RUSSIA.

BRIDGE BATTLE OF THE CENTURY. See CULBERTSON-LENZ MATCH.

BRIDGE BUFF'S BULLETIN. A bulletin published quarterly since 1974 by Bill Sachen of Waukegan, Ill., in the interests of bridge book collectors. New and old books and periodicals are reviewed, master lists of all known bridge and whist books have been published, and subscribers can publicize lists of books they wish to purchase or sell. See BIBLIOGRAPHY, O.

BRIDGE COLUMNS. Ever since the game of auction bridge became popular, newspapers and periodicals have had columns in which bridge is featured. These columns are quite varied, frequently containing local bridge news including results of local duplicate contests, anecdotes, interesting results; other columns are of a didactic nature such as quizzes and problems; while others feature outstanding and unusual bridge hands with explanations of bidding and play and sidelines on the personalities involved. Some are distributed to newspapers through national syndicates, appearing in hundreds of papers; others are produced locally for one, two, or three papers. Most of them are prepared by either local players or nationally known players.

The popularity of bridge columns is attested to by the fact that very few papers have ever dropped one permanently, because every such attempt met with violent protest from the readers of the paper.

BRIDGE FEDERATION OF INDIA. Formed in 1958 by Ramniwas Ruia who was its President from founding until 1970. Member of WBF since 1959, Far East Federation since 1972. Principal National tournaments sponsored yearly include Team of Four (Ruia Gold Trophy), Open Pairs (Holkar Trophy), Open Teams (Singhania Trophy), Mixed Pairs (Lalbhai Trophy) and Inter-State Championship. Players listed separately are O. Campos, S. Ghosh,

J. Kohli, S. D. Panjabi, R. Roy, R. R. Ruia, S. Sethi, Dr. N. S. Tibrewala.

Officers, 1975:
President: K. K. Birla.
Secretary: M. C. Mitter, Ibcon Private, Ltd., Brady House, The Mall, Kanpurul, India.

BRIDGE GOLF. See GOLF.

BRIDGE HEADQUARTERS. Name given to an organization formed in the 1930s to exploit the OFFICIAL SYSTEM. It turned out to be abortive, perhaps because the only binding force among its individual members was an ambition to emulate the success of ELY CULBERTSON.

BRIDGE HISTORY. See HISTORY OF BRIDGE.

BRIDGE JOURNAL, THE. A bi-monthly magazine intended for the edification of and exchange of ideas by serious players, founded and first published in 1963 by Paul Heitner and Jeff Rubens and aimed at improving technical and mechanical aspects of the game, especially at tournament level. Some of the regular features of this publication were a Spotlight on Bidding match between experts, a problem forum on bidding and play, and a Systems Corner. When Rubens became Associate Editor of *The Bridge World* in 1967, the *Journal* ceased independent publication and merged with *The Bridge World*. See BIBLIOGRAPHY, O.

BRIDGE MAGAZINE. An English monthly with an international reputation published in Leeds. It was founded in 1926 by A. E. Manning-Foster, and is therefore the oldest bridge periodical (as at 1964). Publication was suspended, however, during the war years, and in number of issues *Bridge Magazine* is therefore exceeded by *The Bridge World*. Ewart Kempson became the editor when publication was resumed in 1946, and continued in that capacity after the merger with the *British Bridge World* in 1964. After his death in 1966 Eric C. Milnes assumed the post of editor. See BIBLIOGRAPHY, O.

BRIDGE MATHEMATICS. See MATHEMATICS OF BRIDGE.

BRIDGE-O-RAMA. A method of displaying bridge competition to a large audience. The technique was devised in Italy, and first used in the 1958 World Championship. The forerunner of this development was used in the thirties when an electric display board was used in exhibitions in department stores. The features of Bridge-O-Rama include a large display board on which the hands can be placed in frames, so that the representations of the actual cards are lighted, along with devices for indicating the winning card, tricks won by declarer or defender, the contract, and other information. In addition to the display board there is a "console," or bank of light switches, by which the lights of the display

board are controlled. Explanations and comments on the bidding and play are provided by an expert panel.

The largest audience for a Bridge-O-Rama showing was the crowd of 1,500 that attended the finals of the 1964 Olympiad in the Hotel Americana in New York City. The size of the crowd made necessary the simultaneous VU-GRAPH screening of the hands for spectators too far away to see the Bridge-O-Rama board.

Because setting up the deals for Bridge-O-Rama slowed up the play and required a large staff, exhibitions since the 1971 World Championship in Taiwan have been almost exclusively by means of Vu-Graph, enhanced in some cases by closed circuit television of the play in the open room.

BRIDGE OLYMPICS. See WORLD PAR CONTESTS.

BRIDGE IN PRISON CAMPS. The absorbing character of duplicate bridge to such an extent that one is unaware of the passage of time has made it an ideal activity for prisoners of war confined in military prison camps. A POW returning in 1973 from a Vietnamese prison camp described the materials improvised to run a duplicate game twice a week for three years: porcelain covered metal plates sometimes served as both the duplicate board and the traveling score sheet—the hands, each wrapped with a scrap of paper showing its compass position, were stacked atop an upside down plate for passing from one "table" (a folded blanket) to another; the eating side of the plate carried the traveling score diagram; when pencils were not available for scoring on the plates, toilet paper was used for score sheets, with scores entered by use of cotton-tipped bamboo sticks dipped in homemade ink.

BRIDGE IN PRISONS. In 1972, recognizing that bridge is such an absorbing and constructive activity that it might assist in the rehabilitation of the prisoners, the ACBL Board of Directors and the ACBL Charity Foundation instituted a policy of encouraging the playing of duplicate bridge in penal institutions.

The League and various member units have donated cards, boards, bridge books, and other instructional materials to prison duplicate clubs. In 1973 the ACBL Charity Foundation made a $5,000 contribution to the Foundation for the Advancement of Inmate Rehabilitation and Recreation. The American Bridge Teachers' Association has assisted the program by waiving its initiation fees and dues for prison inmates who qualify as bridge teachers and pass the ABTA examination. Local clubs have encouraged their players to participate in prison duplicate games. By early 1975 there were some two dozen duplicate clubs in penal institutions.

It is perhaps fitting that bridge be encouraged in prisons since the idea of playing with one hand exposed as the dummy may have originated in Newgate Prison, where whist was played in this manner as a three-handed game prior to 1820.

BRIDGE TOURNAMENT FOR CLUBS IN COPEN-HAGEN. The world's oldest yearly bridge event, played every year since 1927. Invitations are issued to all clubs in Copenhagen, of any sort, including clubs promoting relations between countries, clubs of doctors, engineers, women's liberation, etc. Each year the Tournament is played on the second Monday of each month from November through April. Since 1927 it has had only three chairmen: in 1975 he was bridge journalist and author Svend Novrup.

BRIDGE WEEK. A Regional championship held annually in Los Angeles since 1935, usually in May or June. From 1935 through 1947 the tournament was also called The All-Western. From 1948 through 1955 the name Bridge Week was also given to the annual San Francisco tournament, which is now called The All-Western. Bridge Week has always been the biggest Regional Championship, and the 1965 figure of 10,948 tables set a world attendance record for regionals. For past results, see Appendix II.

BRIDGE WHIST. The game which succeeded WHIST in popularity until AUCTION BRIDGE became the vogue early in the twentieth century. Chief differences between bridge whist and whist are the manner of selection of the trump suit, the introduction of play at no trump, the exposure of the dummy hand, and the innovation of the double and redouble calls, which could continue indefinitely. This re- and re-doubling feature introduced the element of gambling for very high stakes into the staid game of whist, which caused a storm of disapproval. The *Whist Reference Book,* published in 1898, called doubling "the most objectionable feature of the game." Instead of the trump suit being selected by the turn of the last card dealt, the dealer or his partner has the privilege of naming the trump suit or no trump. It was a requirement of the game that the leader ask, "Partner, may I lead?" to which his partner, if he did not plan to double, was required to respond, "Pray do." The play then proceeded as in auction or contract bridge. The scoring is different from whist, in which each trick counted only one point. In bridge whist, the four suits and no trump have varying values. Spades are the lowest of the suits in value, followed in ascending order by clubs, diamonds, hearts, and no trump. Honors, games, rubbers, and slams are also scored. The greatest exponent of the strategy and tactics of bridge whist was Joseph B. ELWELL, who wrote many books on the subject, chief among them, *Advanced Bridge,* published in 1904.

Contemporary players and writers referred to the game simply as "bridge." As the shorter term was also used later to refer to auction bridge and contract bridge, card historians invented the term "bridge whist" to identify the original form of bridge.

BRIDGE WORLD, THE. The oldest continuously published magazine dealing with contract bridge, founded and first published by Ely Culbertson in October, 1929. Published monthly, it was a comparative success from the start, and such events as the CULBERTSON-LENZ challenge MATCH of 1931–32 and the CULBERTSTON-SIMS MATCH later did much to further interest.

Culbertson, who held the post of editor in chief until September of 1943, founded it with the idea of making it a widely popular publication, and for a short time it was placed on newsstand sale, but this proved uneconomical. It soon became what it has remained: a magazine for better than average players, and a sounding board for new and improved theories (having been first to present such ideas as the Stayman convention; the Roth-Stone and Kaplan-Sheinwold systems; Lavinthal suit-preference signals; unusual no trump bids, and many other ideas). *The Bridge World*'s "Master Solvers' Club," featuring a panel of experts who vote for and explain why they chose what they consider the correct bid in a monthly series of problems, has been copied by almost every other bridge publication.

Publication was taken over from Culbertson in 1943 by A. H. Morehead, who edited it in association with R. L. Frey, Mrs. Culbertson, A. Moyse, Jr., and others until 1946, when it was taken over by Moyse, who ran it under the Culbertson aegis until the death of the Culbertsons, Dec. 1955–May 1956, when he became sole owner and editor. In Nov. 1963, the magazine was bought by the McCall Corporation, with Moyse retained as editor. When Moyse retired at the end of 1966, McCall's divested itself of the magazine. E. Kaplan and J. Rubens became sole owners, with Kaplan assuming the role of editor and Rubens associate editor. Much of the material that Rubens had been publishing in *Bridge Journal* appeared in *The Bridge World,* including a highly popular series of bidding matches between expert partnerships. The list of sometime editors and contributing editors includes, in addition to the Culbertsons, Morehead, Frey, and Moyse, many of the famous bridge writers: T. Lightner, S. Fry, Jr., G. Mott-Smith, O. Jacoby, C. Goren, B. J. Becker, A. M. Sobel, W. Malowan, W. J. Huske, A. Shein-wold, A. Truscott, W. von Zedtwitz, and others.

BRIDGE WORLD STANDARD. A "system" arrived at largely by consensus of experts and other subscribers through a series of polls conducted by *The Bridge World.* It provides the standard for the bidding problems posed to the Master Solvers Club, a monthly feature in the magazine, and is as well a useful frame of reference for casual partnerships. The principal elements are:

(1) *Opening bids:* strong no trumps (15 to a "bad" 18), with non-forcing STAYMAN, and pre-emptive jump responses to three of a minor suit; strong four-card major suits may be opened if a convenient rebid is available; WEAK TWO-BIDS; TWO CLUBS is strong and artificial, with natural positive responses;

(2) *Responses and rebids:* limit jump raises, with three no trump response and SWISS used as forcing raises; up-the-line responses with four-card major suits; a response of one no trump to one club shows

8–10 points; reverse rebids by opener forcing; jump rebids by responder not forcing except in opener's minor or in a new suit; responder's non-jump rebids of new suits over opener's one no trump rebid are not forcing; opener's bid of a new suit after a single raise is a natural game try;

(3) *Slam conventions:* Blackwood over suit bids; Gerber over no trump bids; grand slam force;

(4) *Competitive conventions and treatments:* negative doubles through three spades; responsive doubles after take-out doubles; non-forcing non-jump responses after an overcall over partner's one no trump opening; pre-emptive re-raises; two no trump response over opponent's double shows a limit raise of opener's suit, with other changes of suit and jump shifts non-forcing; pre-emptive jump overcalls; unusual two no trump overcall for the two lower unbid suits; Landy; take-out doubles of pre-empts through four hearts, with penalty doubles of higher pre-empts; jump responses to partner's one no trump overcall are invitational, with a cue-bid the only force.

BRIDGE WORLD TEAM. A name applied to several teams in the early thirties whose members were particularly associated with *The Bridge World.* The most famous of these teams comprised Ely and Josephine CULBERTSON, Waldemar von ZEDTWITZ, and Theodore LIGHTNER. Their successes included the VANDERBILT CUP of 1930, and the first of the ANGLO-AMERICAN MATCHES.

BRIDGERAMA. The European term for BRIDGE-O-RAMA.

BRIDGESAMBANDS ISLANDS. See ICELANDIC BRIDGE UNION.

BRIDGETTE. A bridge game for two players invented by Prince Djoli Kansil (the former Joel D. Gaines), with the assistance of Waldemar von Zedtwitz, and acclaimed by many experts as the best of all two-handed bridge games. It is played with a 55-card deck—the standard pack plus three extra cards called *colons.* The *colons* are used in the play to force the opponent to discontinue the suit he is leading. In an advanced version of Bridgette, "cue-bids" are used to elicit specific information about the opponent's distribution.

BRING IN. To establish a suit and make effective use of the established winners. The ability to bring in a suit may be affected by considerations of ENTRIES, TEMPO, CONTROLS, or DUCKING, or by the SUIT COMBINATION in the suit being established.

BRITISH BRIDGE. Direct methods of bidding advocated in the thirties by a group of English players headed by Walter BULLER and Ewart KEMPSON, as opposed to the approach-forcing methods popularized by Ely CULBERTSON.

BRITISH BRIDGE LEAGUE. Founded in 1931 by A. E. Manning-Foster, since 1938 it has been a federal body, with the English Bridge Union, the Northern Ireland Bridge Union, the Scottish Bridge Union, and the Welsh Bridge Union as its chief constituents. Among other bodies affiliated to the League are India, New Zealand, and South Africa.

The League selects British teams for European Championships and World events. Their successes include World Championship 1955, and European Championship 1948, 1949, 1950, 1954, 1961, 1963. The British Women's Team won the World Women's Team Olympiad in 1964 and the European Women's Championship on numerous occasions.

The League organizes the CAMROSE TROPHY for home international competition, the Gold Cup for Open Teams, the Portland Cup for Mixed Pairs, and the Lady Milne Cup for Women's Team of Four.

Names of British players are listed under ENGLISH BRIDGE UNION; NORTHERN IRELAND BRIDGE UNION; SCOTTISH BRIDGE UNION; WELSH BRIDGE UNION.

Officials, 1975:
President: R. F. Corwen.
Secretary: Mrs. H. D. Newton, 21, Sandringham Road, Wrexham, Clwyd LL11 2RF, Wales.

BRITISH BRIDGE WORLD. An English monthly publication founded in 1932 by Hubert Phillips. It was revived in 1956 as a successor to the *Contract Bridge Journal,* and continued until 1964 when it merged with *Bridge Magazine.* See BIBLIOGRAPHY, O.

BROZEL. Developed by Bernard Zeller of West Orange, N.J., as a defense against an opposing one no trump opening, and may be used either in the direct or balancing position.

A double shows a one-suited hand. If partner does not wish to defend, he bids two clubs and passes the doubler's next bid. All overcalls on the two-level show two suits as follows:

2 ♣ shows hearts and clubs
2 ♢ shows hearts and diamonds
2 ♡ shows hearts and spades
2 ♠ shows spades and a minor
2 NT shows clubs and diamonds

An overcall on the three-level shows a singleton or void in the bid suit and support for the other three suits.

After a weak response to a one no trump opening, a double again describes a one-suited hand. Without suitable defense, partner bids the next higher-ranking suit, then passes the doubler's next bid. All simple overcalls show the bid suit and the next higher-ranking unbid suit. Two no trump is a take-out for the three unbid suits, and a cue-bid is a stronger take-out, implying game possibilities.

For alternative defensive conventions against no trump openings, see ASPRO; ASTRO; EXCLUSION BID; LANDY, and RIPSTRA.

BUDAPESTI BRIDZS EGYESÜLET. See HUNGARIAN BRIDGE ASSOCIATION.

BUENOS AIRES AFFAIR. In 1965, the international bridge world was rocked by a widely publicized charge that Terence REESE and Boris SCHAPIRO, representing Great Britain in the WORLD CHAMPIONSHIPS at Buenos Aires, Argentina, had transmitted information about the heart suit by finger signals.

The accusers, B. Jay BECKER and Mrs. Dorothy HAYDEN, members of the North American team, and Alan TRUSCOTT, Bridge Editor for *The New York Times,* testified that the British pair were observed to be holding their cards in a varying manner, with a different number of fingers, either closed or spread, showing at the back of their hands from deal to deal. After comparing findings, it was suggested that Reese and Schapiro were signaling the number of hearts they held (two fingers for two or five hearts, depending on whether the fingers were closed or spread, three fingers for three or six hearts, and so forth). The evidence was presented to John GERBER, (npc, North American team), who, in turn, brought it to the attention of Ralph SWIMER (npc, British team), and Geoffrey BUTLER, Chairman of the British Bridge League and member of the World Bridge Federation Executive Committee and Chairman of its Appeals Committee. After an independent investigation, Butler called a meeting of the Appeals Committee to present his observations, to study the evidence further, and to inform Reese and Schapiro of the charges against them. Both denied the allegations. The matter was then brought to the attention of the WBF Executive Committee. On the last day of the World Championship, by a vote of 10–0 (Carl 'Alberto PERROUX abstaining, one absentee), the Executive Committee found Reese and Schapiro guilty of using illegal signals, and the evidence was turned over to the British Bridge League for final disposition. Swimer conceded the Great Britain–Argentine match, which Great Britain had won 380–184, and the Great Britain–North American match, in which Great Britain was leading 288–242 with twenty boards to play.

After receiving the WBF report, the British Bridge League set up an independent inquiry to study the charges, headed by Sir John Foster, Queens Counsel, and General Lord Bourne, assisted on the technical aspects of the case by Alan Hiron and Richard Anthony PRIDAY. The Foster report, released after more than ten months' consideration, found Reese and Schapiro "not guilty" of the cheating allegation. In the opinion of Sir John Foster, the technical evidence appeared to indicate that Reese and Schapiro had not profited in the bidding or play from a foreknowledge of the heart suit, and thus failed to substantiate the testimony of the prosecution's witnesses.

After learning of this verdict, which was released after the 1966 WBF meeting, WBF President Charles SOLOMON stated, "It is doubtful that the WBF can accept the decision of the London hearing. . . ." His position was that the WBF had rendered the verdict in Buenos Aires and had submitted its report to the British Bridge League to determine what punitive action would be taken.

At its annual meeting in 1967, the WBF Executive Committee reaffirmed its earlier guilty verdict and passed a resolution that the Chairman of the Credentials Committee refer applications of any player found guilty of irregular practices in WBF-sponsored tournaments to the Executive Council. The implication was that applications by Reese and Schapiro would not be accepted, and the implication became fact in 1968 when the Executive Council so answered a query from the British Bridge League concerning possible entry of Reese and Schapiro in the 1968 OLYMPIAD. As a result, the British Bridge League elected not to participate in the Olympiad.

In 1968, the Executive Council restored Reese and Schapiro to good standing on the ground that the three-year ban that had been in effect since 1965 constituted adequate punishment.

The repercussions of the episode during the years of controversy spanned the American and European continents. An article by Rixi MARKUS defending Reese that appeared in *The Bridge World* resulted in a libel suit by Swimer, and the reluctance of Reese and Swimer to play against each other created problems in the 1968 British Team Trials. The evidence for both sides was presented in books by two of the controversy's leading figures: Reese's *Story of an Accusation* and Truscott's *The Great Bridge Scandal.* See BIBLIOGRAPHY, P. See also BERMUDA INCIDENT; CHEATING ACCUSATIONS.

BULLDOG SYSTEM. Devised by William Hanna and Douglas Steen. The name is derived from the first names of the authors: Bill-Doug.

Features of the system include:

(1) A variable one no trump opening: 12–14 not vulnerable, 17–19 vulnerable.

(2) KIVI convention: one no trump—four diamonds asks for precise point-count; opener bids four hearts with minimum, four spades with average hand, and four no trump with maximum. Applies in similar situations when a jump to four diamonds follows a no trump bid.

(3) Artificial JUMP SHIFT to three clubs on powerful hands, permitting other jump shifts to be made preemptively.

(4) OKUNEFF convention. After a cue-bid used to invite three no trump if partner holds a stopper, the lowest possible bid in an unbid suit shows a partial stopper in the opponent's suit. If this is not possible below three no trump, a bid suit may be utilized.

(5) STAYMAN on the second round, after no trump rebids.

Other conventions listed separately include RESPONSIVE DOUBLES and RUSH ASKING BIDS.

BULLETIN, THE CONTRACT BRIDGE. A monthly magazine, official organ of the American Contract Bridge League, with by far the largest circulation of any bridge periodical, since it goes to all members of the League, totaling nearly 200,000 in 1975. Published originally as *The Bulletin of the American Bridge League* in 1934; the word "Contract" was added when the name of the League was changed in 1937. It became *The Contract Bridge Bulletin* of the ACBL in 1962.

Earliest issues, edited by Geoffrey Mott-Smith and William Huske, consisted of a four-page tabloid newspaper listing tournament results and facts concerning upcoming tournaments. In subsequent years it was edited by George Beynon and then Alfred Sheinwold.

In May 1958, editorship was assumed by Richard L. FREY, who instituted radical changes in format and content. In June of 1958 the directory of bridge clubs was included in *The Bulletin* for the first time. In June 1959, increasing circulation made possible a switch to offset printing. In 1960, the publication went from ten issues a year to a full twelve-issue monthly. Pages jumped from 408 in 1958 to 968 in 1969. Technical content increased steadily and a new Master Pointers section was begun in February 1964.

In 1970, Frey retired and his duties were assumed by three of his assistants. Steven BECKER was appointed Executive Editor, responsible for all functions of the Bulletin Department; Tannah HIRSCH became the Editor; and Thomas SMITH was named Business Manager.

Major changes in the top editorial positions occurred again in 1972, when the ACBL moved its headquarters to Memphis. In 1973 Henry FRANCIS became Executive Editor; Sue Emery was appointed Editor; Richard Oshlag became Business and Advertising Manager.

BULLETINS. Daily bulletins are issued at some International championships and by the ACBL at all National championships. These are available on subscription.

Many ACBL units issue unit bulletins giving local news and some technical material. Among these are *Post-Mortem, Florida Bridge News, New England Bridge Conference Bulletin, The ALACBU News,* and *The Forum.*

Regular bridge periodicals, some of which are entitled "bulletin," are listed in the periodical section of the BIBLIOGRAPHY.

BUMBLEDOG AND BUMBLEPUPPY. Humorous terms applied to bad players or the bad playing of whist. The terms were originally used to denote groups of players who were in ignorance of most of the rules and conventions of the game; they were occasionally employed in denigration of certain players of contract bridge as late as the early thirties.

BUMP MITCHELL. An adaptation of the MITCHELL MOVEMENT invented by Forrest Sharpe for the accommodation of an extra half table. The extra pair plays North-South, sitting out the first round, taking the highest North-South number. After the first round, this pair, keeping its number, plays North-South at table 1 for the remainder of the session. The North-South pair originally at table 1 sits out round 2 and bumps the North-South pair at table 2. They remain number one, but play at table 2 for the balance. Similarly, pair two bumps pair three after sitting out the third round; pair three bumps pair four after sitting out a round.

Whenever, without the half table, the boards are set out without the use of a BYE STAND, a "bump Mitchell" is practical, and probably the least undesirable alternative. If, without the extra pair, the requirements of the game demand a bye stand, the extra pair should be placed North-South at a table replacing the bye stand. The half table without a bump movement must be completed for as many rounds as there are tables in play to prevent a great amount of factoring at the end.

BURNER. A colloquialism used in bridge tournaments to refer to a photo-copying machine by means of which raw scores (i.e., not match-pointed) are made available to players a few minutes after the end of a session.

BUSINESS DOUBLE. See PENALTY DOUBLE.

BUSINESS PASS. See PENALTY PASS.

BUST. Bridge slang term for a seemingly valueless hand. See YARBOROUGH.

BUSY CARD AND IDLE CARD. These terms were originated by Ely CULBERTSON, and used in his *Red Book on Play* (see BIBLIOGRAPHY). His definitions are:

A busy card is one which will have a definite duty in the play of the hand, either as a trick winner or as a guard to a card which will or may eventually win a trick. The idle cards have no such function; they serve the holder only in that he may discard them and save his busy cards for a better purpose.

If a suit is distributed as shown in the diagram, then West's small card is idle, but both the king and queen are busy.

```
                    NORTH
                    A J 10
WEST                                      EAST
K Q x                                     x x x
                    SOUTH
                    x x x
```

The terms arise in connection with squeeze play, whose object is to force the discard of a busy card by an opponent.

BYE.

(1) In team-of-four competition, an advance to a later round without the necessity of winning or playing a match. This occurs at some point in the play in order to reduce the field to a multiple of two when the number of entries does not conform ideally to the elimination pattern.

(2) In pair contests, a BYE STAND is used as a temporary resting place for boards not in play during a particular round.

(3) In pair matches, when an uneven number of pairs compete, there is one table, a bye table, at which traveling pairs find no opponents, or where a stationary pair has no opponents come to them. This results in a bye round for the opponentless pairs (see FACTORING).

(4) A slang term, unsanctioned by law, for "I pass." Sometimes also "Bye me," or "I go bye." Such terms are to be avoided since, unless they are always used, they infringe the warning against different designations for the same call. See LAWS OF DUPLICATE, PROPRIETIES IIIA3.

BYE STAND. A stand (it may be a chair or small side table) where one or more sets of boards rest during rounds in which they are not in play. The bye stand is usually placed in such position that the boards will be conveniently available to the table where they will be in play next.

The most common use of a bye stand is described under MITCHELL MOVEMENT. A pamphlet (available on request from the ACBL office) instructs the tournament director what procedure to follow to correct the omission or misplacement of the bye stand in a Mitchell movement. The use of a bye stand in a Mitchell game is necessary only when it is desired to play all the boards. (See EIGHT TABLES; TWELVE TABLES.) If one or more sets of boards are not to be played, the SKIP MOVEMENT eliminates the need for the bye stand.

BYLAWS OF THE ACBL. The ACBL Bylaws govern principally such matters as the elections, meetings, and powers of the BOARD OF DIRECTORS, BOARD OF GOVERNORS, and officers. With respect to membership in the ACBL, the Bylaws provide as follows:

A. Any person of good moral character is eligible to membership in the American Contract Bridge League. No person shall be denied membership because of race, color, or creed. Upon application, favorably acted upon by a Unit with jurisdiction, such applicant shall become and remain a member unless:

(1) he has failed to pay his dues in accordance with regulations established by the American Contract Bridge League.

(2) he is suspended or expelled in accordance with paragraph "E" hereof.

B. Each Unit may determine the qualifications for membership, but such qualifications for membership shall not contravene any provision of these Bylaws or the Certificate of Incorporation.

C. A member may belong only to the Unit within whose jurisdiction he resides, unless there are District Regulations to the contrary.

D. Honorary members may be elected by the Board of Directors. They shall be exempt from the payment of dues and shall be honorary members for life.

E. A member of the League may be censured, suspended, expelled, or otherwise disciplined in accordance with regulations established by the American Contract Bridge League; provided, however, that such regulations shall conform to the rules of due process applicable to Membership Corporations.

BYZANTINE BLACKWOOD. A complex modern variation of the four no trump ace-asking convention, devised by J. C. H. MARX of Great Britain, in which the responses are given in the style of ROMAN BLACKWOOD and may be based on a "key suit" king instead of one of the aces normally shown. Key suits include the trump suit, any genuine side suit that has been bid and supported, and any suit bid by a player whose partner's first bid was in no trump. Byzantine is not used when there are more than two key suits. If there is only one key suit, a king of a "half-key" suit, i.e., a genuine suit that has been bid but not supported, may be shown.

When there is only one key suit the Byzantine responses to four no trump are:

five clubs	No ace, or three aces, or two aces plus the key suit king
five diamonds	One ace, or four aces, or three aces plus the key suit king
five hearts	Two aces, or the ace, king and queen of the key suit, or the ace-king of the key suit plus the king of the half-key suit
five spades	Two aces plus the king and queen of the key suit, or three aces plus the king of the half-key suit
five no trump	Three aces plus the king and queen of the key suit, or all the aces plus the king of the key suit

When there are two key suits, half-key kings are not shown and the higher Byzantine responses are expanded as follows:

five hearts	Two aces or the ace, king, and queen of a key suit, or one ace and both key suit kings
five spades	Two aces plus the king and queen of a key suit, or two aces and both key suit kings, or one ace plus the king of one key suit and the king and queen of the other key suit
five no trump	Three aces plus the king and queen of a key suit, or three aces and both key suit kings, or all the aces plus one key suit king, or two aces plus the king of one key suit and the king and queen of the other, or one ace and the kings and queens of both key suits

See also CULBERTSON FOUR-FIVE NO TRUMP, KEY CARD BLACKWOOD, ROMAN BLACKWOOD.

C

CACBF. CENTRAL AMERICAN AND CARIBBEAN BRIDGE FEDERATION.

CBA. Contract Bridge Association.

CBAI. Contract Bridge Association of Ireland.

CBL. Contract Bridge League.

CAB. A British system of bidding which incorporates some of the features of the STANDARD AMERICAN style:

(1) Strong no trump opening bids, with GLADIATOR responses. (But responses of two diamonds, hearts, and spades are constructive and non-forcing.)

(2) Jump raises and two no trump responses are forcing except in competition.

(3) Suit opening bids are unprepared. One spade is bid with:

> ♠ A K 10 6
> ♡ A 5 3
> ◇ 5 2
> ♣ Q 9 7 2

After a response at the level of two (10 points or more), the opener can rebid two no trump with a minimum hand.

(4) A conventional TWO CLUBS, with ACE-SHOWING RESPONSES. A subsequent four no trump bid asks for kings on the BLACKWOOD principle.

(5) CUE-BIDS TO SHOW CONTROLS are used extensively, and in some situations are compulsory.

(6) ACOL TWO-BIDS: a suit response at the two-level may consist of no more than a fair five-card suit.

(7) Opening three-bids in a minor suit invite three no trump: either the suit is solid, or it is nearly solid and there is an outside entry.

The initials CAB stand for two Clubs, Ace-showing, and Blackwood. The chief contributions to the development of the system were made by Leslie DODDS.

CADDY. An assistant at a bridge tournament. Duties of the caddy are to "dress" the tables (putting pick-up slips, pencils, and private scores on the tables), pick up the completed entry blanks, assemble the boards at the conclusion of play, and otherwise make himself useful. In pairs events or team events scored by BOARD-A-MATCH, the caddy picks up the score slips at the completion of each round and assists the scorer in checking doubtful slips. In a KNOCKOUT TOURNAMENT or a team game with a SWISS MOVEMENT there are no score slips to be picked up, and the caddy's chief duty during the session is to transport the boards played at one table of each match to the other table of that match.

Assignment of caddies to work various sessions of a duplicate tournament is the responsibility of the local tournament committee. Generally selection is made from interested high-school boys and girls.

CALCUTTA. A duplicate tournament with a feature making possible a fair-sized financial gain to any player or other participant. After the entries have been made, an auction is held at which players, spectators, and others bid for and "buy" the contesting pairs. The total of the moneys bid for the players is put into a POOL which is distributed to the purchasers of the winning entries. In addition, cash prizes or other worthwhile stimuli are provided so that the contestants themselves have a stake in the results. It is usually a proviso that a contestant may purchase from the buyer up to 50% interest in his own partnership at the original price.

Because of the gambling feature involved in the auctioning of the participants, the American Contract Bridge League does not sanction a Calcutta, and master points are not awarded. See GAMBLING AT BRIDGE.

CALIFORNIA CUE-BID. See WESTERN CUE-BIDS; CUE-BIDS IN OPPONENT'S SUIT.

CALIFORNIA SCORING. A method of computing the East-West pairs' match-point score by assigning them the same score as their North-South opponents, rather than the reciprocal. Using this method the East-West pair with the lowest score is then the winner. Alternatively, each East-West score may be subtracted from the maximum possible match-point total to produce the same score that would have been achieved using regular match-point scoring methods. California Scoring derived its name from its popularity primarily in California and other western clubs. See TRAVELING SCORE SLIP.

CALL. Any bid, double, redouble, or pass. See LAWS OF CONTRACT BRIDGE.

CALL AFTER THE AUCTION IS CLOSED. See LAWS (Law 39).

CALL IN ROTATION AFTER AN ILLEGAL CALL. See LAWS (Law 34).

CALL OUT OF TURN. See LAWS (Laws 28–35).

CALLING A CARD OR A SUIT. The privilege of compelling an opponent to lead or play a certain card or a certain suit, to play his highest or lowest, or to win or lose a trick. See LAWS (Laws 26, 27c, 30b, 31b, 32a, 36a, 37, 38, 39b, 50, 52, 56b, 57, 73). See LAWS OF DUPLICATE (Laws 46, 51).

CAMROSE TROPHY. Competed for annually by England, Scotland, Northern Ireland, Wales, and formerly Eire, under the auspices of the British Bridge League. Presented by Lord Camrose in 1936, and won on every occasion by England until Scotland succeeded in 1964.

CANADIAN-AMERICAN REGIONAL CHAMPIONSHIPS. A four-day event held annually during the spring. Beginning in 1951, the tournament has usually been staged in Montreal, Ottawa, Quebec, or upstate New York. It was the successor of a historic tournament which began in the thirties. For past results, see Appendix II.

CANADIAN BRIDGE FEDERATION. The official National Contract Bridge Organization, as recognized by the WORLD BRIDGE FEDERATION, for the 24 Canadian Units of the ACBL. Founded in 1967 for the purpose of promoting a national identity and union of Canadian bridge players, it designates Canada's representatives to WBF Olympiad events, publishes a magazine, *The Canadian Bridge Digest,* and promotes the ACBL Canadian Charitable Fund, whose trustees are executive members of the Federation. Canadian players are eligible to compete for places on the North American team for the BERMUDA BOWL. Eric Murray achieved this honor in 1962, 1966, 1967, and 1974; Sammy Kehela in 1966, 1967, and 1974. Players listed separately who have represented Canada include: Mrs. J. Begin, H. Bork, Mrs. M. Bowden, N. M. Burns, R. Cohen, B. Elliott, Mrs. C. Fisher, Dr. R. Forbes, S. Gold, B. Gowdy, J. Howell, S. Kehela, J. Klein, A. Lando, W. Lebovic, Mrs. L. Mark, E. Murray, D. Phillips, Mrs. J. Phillips, Mrs. F. Pielsticker, D. Richmond, Mrs. M. Roncarelli, Dr. G. Sereny, P. Sheardown, Mrs. H. Smith.

Officers, 1975:

President: Jack Murphy.

Executive Secretary: Alvin Baragar, Canadian Bridge Federation, 6608 — 84 Street, Edmonton, AB, Canada.

CANADIAN NATIONAL REGIONAL CHAMPIONSHIPS.

A six-day event held annually in Toronto since 1951. For past results, see Appendix II.

CANAPÉ.

A bidding method in which the long suit is usually bid on the second round. This was developed by Pierre ALBARRAN in France, where it has had a considerable following. By contrast, standard methods are described in France as *la longue d'abord* (long suit first). Canapé has influenced Italian bidding theory, and is incorporated in both the BLUE TEAM and ROMAN systems.

Albarran's definition of canapé is: "With a two-suited hand of more than minimum strength, the higher-ranking suit must be bid on the first round if it has four cards, and on the second round if it has more than four cards."

Four-card major suits are usually bid ahead of any minor suit; five-card major suits are bid on the first round if the hand is a minimum. Normal reverse sequences are inverted (*inversés*):

♠ A Q 10 x x
♡ K Q x x
◇ K x
♣ x x

Using canapé, the opening bid is one heart, and two spades is bid on the next round. A heart preference is highly improbable, so the canapé player can stay safely at the level of two.

Canapé is admittedly in difficulty with certain minimum hands, such as those with four spades and five clubs. One spade followed by three clubs would exaggerate the strength, and one club followed by one spade would imply a five-card spade suit.

A modified version called "canapé tendency" (*tendance canapé*) has been used successfully in international competition by Pierre JAÏS and Roger TRÉZEL. They bid minimum hands in normal fashion, but adopt the canapé principle for hands of maximum strength and some hands of intermediate strength.

CANARY CLUB.

An artificial bidding system developed in 1964 by John LOWENTHAL and Paul HEITNER. The name of the system is derived from its chief features—CANAPÉ, RELAY bids, and one CLUB forcing.

One club opening shows 17 points or more, or a strong distributional hand. Responses tend to follow the BLUE TEAM control-showing pattern with certain exceptions, and after the initial response the auction tends to develop naturally with a variety of asking bids available once the trump suit is agreed.

If an opponent overcalls, responder may double for penalties, bid a suit naturally (less than three controls), jump in a suit (pre-emptive), bid the cheapest no trump with three or more controls but less than three controls outside the opponent's suit, jump in no trump with less than three controls with a stopper in the opponent's suit, or cue-bid with three or more controls outside the opponent's suit.

One diamond, one heart, and one spade openings are natural according to the canapé principle, but do not guarantee any defensive strength. Major-suit raises or jump raises are limited bids. Two hearts over one spade is non-forcing, and jump shifts are pre-emptive with the exception of three hearts over one spade. The cheapest response is a relay and requests opener to rebid his longest suit. If it coincides with the relay suit, opener bids either one no trump or two of the suit depending on the strength of his opening bid. After a one diamond or one heart opening, a one no trump response shows at least five hearts or five spades, respectively, and is forcing. New suits by responder are also forcing and are made in five-card or longer suits. A jump response of two no trump is a specialized bid, agreeing opener's suit as trump and requesting opener to rebid his longest suit. New suits by responder are then asking bids and three no trump is an inquiry about trump quality.

One no trump opening shows a balanced hand with 12–16 points.

Two clubs opening is natural, at least a six-card club suit, no four-card major, with 11–16 points. Responses in the majors are natural and invitational. Two diamonds requests opener to show a three-card major, and two no trump requests opener to define the strength of his opening and to show a singleton with a maximum.

Two diamonds opening is equivalent to a ROMAN two club bid. A response of three no trump shows a solid suit, and jumps in a suit are specialized asking bids.

Two hearts and two spades openings are similar to the ROMAN system; clubs cannot be longer than the major. If responder jumps in a suit, it is an asking bid with the major the agreed trump suit.

CANNIBAL SQUEEZE. See SUICIDE SQUEEZE.

CAPTAIN.

Teams representing major bridge countries in international play normally have a non-playing captain (although Great Britain won three successive European Championships 1948–50 with M. HARRISON-GRAY as playing captain). The captain's chief function is to decide who shall play at each stage in the contest, taking into account such factors as the ability and stamina of the players at his command, the caliber of the opposition, the closed and open room, and BRIDGE-O-RAMA. In addition, the captain represents the team in discussions relating to the conditions of play, and in protests and appeals. He also acts as the team's spokesman on all social occasions.

The importance of the captain's role has been recognized in recent years, and it is usual for the ACBL to appoint an experienced player whose decisions will be respected and accepted by the players in his charge. At one time the president of the ACBL was automatically designated non-playing captain of its international team, but this practice was discontinued after 1961. With the inception of the play-off method of selection from the winners of the four major team championships, each team was required to select a non-playing captain from a panel of eligible captains selected by the ACBL BOARD OF DIRECTORS, and the captain of the winning team was virtually an automatic selection for the World Championship, although subject to Board confirmation. Usually the non-playing captaincy of a team is not a controversial role. In 1974, however, the ACBL appointment of Alfred SHEINWOLD as non-playing captain of the 1975 North American team caused considerable controversy. Sheinwold had published articles on the previous Bermuda Bowl contest in *Popular Bridge* in which he impugned the ethics of Italian bridge. Italian officials protested the naming of Sheinwold, and the European Bridge League wrote an unprecedented letter to the ACBL asking the latter to reconsider its appointment of Sheinwold. The ACBL refused, a decision it later had cause to regret. See BERMUDA INCIDENT.

Carlo Alberto PERROUX, of Italy, who made a considerable contribution to the remarkable series of victories compiled by the BLUE TEAM, earned a reputation as one of the most powerful and successful non-playing captains in the history of bridge.

CAPTAINCY. The control of the auction assumed by one partner in certain situations. For example, in BLACKWOOD auctions the four no trump bidder is the captain, and his partner simply follows instructions in making the agreed responses. But captaincy may shift from one partner to the other in a single auction. For example, if the Blackwood bidder continues with five no trump, indicating his side's possession of all the aces, in some circumstances the responder may take responsibility for a grand slam contract. In many auctions there is no captain, and both players simply use their judgment in arriving at what they hope will be the best contract.

CARD, DAMAGED OR MARKED. See DAMAGED CARD.

CARD COMMITTEE. In private clubs it is customary that a committee of two or more members is charged with the responsibility of order and decorum in the club's card room. Referred to this committee are disputes which arise in the play that cannot be settled by reference to the rules of the game in question. Also under the jurisdiction of this committee

come such questions as what games will be permitted, rules of procedure for forming tables, maximum stakes, and unpaid wagers. With respect to contract bridge tournaments, see COMMITTEE.

CARD FEE. See ENTRIES.

CARD PLAYED. See PLAYED CARD.

CARD READING. Drawing correct inferences about the nature of the opponent's holdings and distribution from information disclosed by the fall of the cards.

```
NORTH
♠ A 8
♡ K Q J 7 6
◇ J 8 7
♣ 6 5 3

SOUTH
♠ Q J 10 4 3 2
♡ A 5 3
◇ A K
♣ 10 7
```

South plays in four spades after East has opened the bidding with one club. West leads the two of clubs and East wins with the ace, and shifts to the nine of hearts. A seemingly secure contract is now in some jeopardy. East clearly has a singleton heart, and very likely three trumps including the king. Obviously his plan is to win the second trump lead and put partner in with a club honor for a heart ruff. Declarer can foil this defense by playing East for the queen of diamonds (not unlikely on the bidding). Winning the heart in dummy, he plays off the ace and king of diamonds before crossing to the ace of spades. The jack of diamonds is led from dummy, East covering and South discarding his last club, thus effectively severing communication between the defenders. The complete deal:

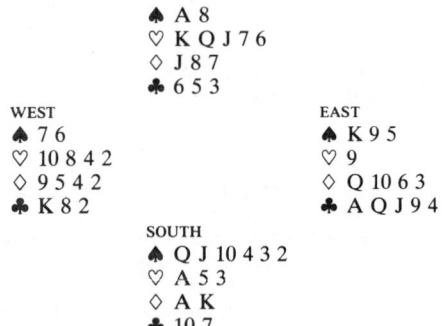

```
        NORTH
        ♠ A 8
        ♡ K Q J 7 6
        ◇ J 8 7
        ♣ 6 5 3
WEST                        EAST
♠ 7 6                       ♠ K 9 5
♡ 10 8 4 2                  ♡ 9
◇ 9 5 4 2                   ◇ Q 10 6 3
♣ K 8 2                     ♣ A Q J 9 4
        SOUTH
        ♠ Q J 10 4 3 2
        ♡ A 5 3
        ◇ A K
        ♣ 10 7
```

Combining accurate card-reading with counting often provides valuable clues for the defense. Careful examination of the evidence provided East with the opportunity to defeat the contract on this hand:

```
                    NORTH
                    ♠ 10 8 6 2
                    ♡ K 6 5
                    ◊ Q 5
                    ♣ A J 7 6
WEST                                    EAST
♠ J 7 4 3                               ♠ A Q 9 5
♡ Q 7 4 2                               ♡ J 10
◊ 9 6 3 2                               ◊ A 8 7
♣ 8                                     ♣ Q 5 4 3
                    SOUTH
                    ♠ K
                    ♡ A 9 8 3
                    ◊ K J 10 4
                    ♣ K 10 9 2
```

The bidding has been:

SOUTH	NORTH
1 ♣	1 ♠
1 NT	2 NT
3 NT	

West leads the deuce of hearts, and East's ten loses to declarer's ace. A club is led to dummy's ace, and the jack run, West discarding the two of diamonds. The queen of diamonds is taken by East, and he reviews the situation.

He knows that South has four club tricks, and at least two in hearts. What about the diamonds? West's diamond discard on the second club is revealing: he is unlikely to have parted with one from 10 x x x or J x x x. Could West have started with five diamonds? Not very likely, for in that case he might have led one. South can therefore be assumed to have three diamond tricks, enough for his contract, should he regain the lead. The only hope for the defense seems to lie in spades. If East's estimate of the situation is correct, then West had started with a 4–4–4–1 distribution, marking declarer with a singleton spade—very likely the king, considering his bidding.

Declarer's play of the club suit seems to bear this out; having a two-way finesse, he chose to take it into the hand that was less likely to shift to spades, if it lost. On this reasoning East lays down the ace of spades, dropping declarer's king, and continues with a small card to his partner's jack. A third round of spades permits East to score the queen and nine to defeat the contract. See also COUNTING THE HAND and INFERENCE.

For full discussions of card reading, see *Card Reading* by Eric JANNERSTEN, *The Art of Card Reading at Bridge* by Fred KARPIN, and *How To Read Your Opponent's Cards* by Mike LAWRENCE. (BIBLIOGRAPHY, D.)

　　　　　　　　　　　　　　　　　　S. K.

CARD SENSE. A special aptitude for playing card games, specifically (in this context) bridge.

Until psychological research and army selection procedures satisfactorily demonstrated the existence of special aptitudes, there was considerable controversy about whether card sense existed.

Although he changed his mind later, Culbertson was originally among the skeptics, commenting as follows: "One hears a good deal about that elusive something called 'card sense.' It is spoken of as though it were some mysterious, deeply inborn faculty which cannot be taught. Lack of 'card sense' is always said to be the great bugaboo blocking the prospective bridge player's path to improvement. As a matter of fact, 'card sense'—whatever those who use the term mean—is a certain facility at cards shown by some players and entirely lacking in others."

Among good bridge players, it is virtually impossible to distinguish between what is the result of card sense and what is the result of experience. Card sense is more easily distinguishable among beginners, when it appears to be a compound of various elements: intelligence, interest, and youth.

There is probably a high correlation between ability to learn the elements of bridge and mathematical aptitude, and a rather lower correlation with intelligence quotient.

See also INTUITION.

CARD-SHOWING DOUBLE. A double that does not promise any particular distribution but instead shows general high card strength. The amount of strength promised by a double that shows "cards" obviously varies according to the circumstances in which the double is made. For example, the DOUBLE OF TWO CLUB RESPONSE to a WEAK NO TRUMP would show strength equivalent to that of a double of a one no trump opening; the double of interference with a PRECISION CLUB opening bid, however, promises about 5–8 points.

CARDS. Used in a colloquial sense, usually in describing the meaning of certain doubles, to mean high card strength. See CARD-SHOWING DOUBLE.

CARDS, NEUTRAL AND POSITIVE. The only information disclosed by the play of a neutral card is the obvious point that the player has that particular card. The essence of this is that the player is not void of the suit, and even this knowledge will generally have little or no effect on problems of probability.

A card may be said to have positive value when: (1) the holder was deemed certain to have played it, or; (2) it indicates the position of one or more other specified cards, or suggests their probable location, or; (3) it indicates the distribution of all the outstanding cards of a suit.

```
                    NORTH
                    ♠ 5 4 3
                    ♡ A K 2
                    ◊ A J 8 6 5
                    ♣ K 3


                    SOUTH
                    ♠ A J 2
                    ♡ Q 8 4 3
                    ◊ K 10 7
                    ♣ A J 5
```

South plays in no trump, and West leads the spade king. South assumes that West holds the spade king, queen, and ten. If he also assumes that West was certain to make this lead, there will be odds of 13 to 10 that East has the diamond queen:

(a) If East follows with a low spade, these odds are only very slightly altered. East's card is neutral, and indicates only that West does not have seven spades. The elimination of all distributions where West holds seven spades removes more cases favorable to East's holding the diamond queen than unfavorable cases. The odds are a very little less than 13 to 10, and the difference may be disregarded.

(b) If East plays a heart at trick 1, there will be positive significance in the fact that he has played a non-spade, though the card itself is neutral. The odds are 13 to 6 that East holds the diamond queen. We know now that East is not void of hearts, but we cannot say that he was certain to play a heart whatever cards he holds.

(c) If East discards a club at trick 1, the odds are again 13 to 6 that he has the diamond queen.

CARDS OF A SUIT IN OPPONENT'S HAND. See SUIT, NUMBER OF CARDS IN.

CARIBBEAN CHAMPIONSHIPS. Organized in 1964 as an informal international championship for countries in the Caribbean area. The first Caribbean Championship was held in Curaçao, Netherlands Antilles, and the two subsequent tournaments were staged in Barranquilla, Colombia, and Caracas, Venezuela, respectively. Venezuela won the first two events and Colombia won the championship in 1968.

There were four participating nations in the 1968 event, Colombia, Ecuador, Netherlands Antilles, and Venezuela, but it is expected that teams from Jamaica, Panama, Puerto Rico, and other Caribbean countries will take part in future competitions. See CENTRAL AMERICAN AND CARIBBEAN BRIDGE FEDERATION.

CARRY-OVER SCORES. Under the regulations of the American Contract Bridge League, certain events in tournaments of sectional or higher rating are conducted in more than one session. These events may or may not involve elimination of some of the contestants from the main event (see CONSOLATION EVENT).

If no players are eliminated from the event, their match-point score is carried over from one session to the succeeding session, and the event decided upon the total score in all sessions. Regulations require that if a later session of a play-through multi-session event has a different top score on a board, provision is made for adjusting to the top score in the first session. See FACTORING.

When the original starting field is reduced for later sessions, regulations provide that scores in the early (qualifying) round or rounds be carried over into the final session on the basis of a formula.

$$\text{carry-over} = \frac{M \; Q^2 a \; B}{E \; S}$$

where M represents the number of match points in the qualifying round or rounds which a contestant scores, Q^2 is the square of the number of pairs in the final session, a is the average on a board in the finals, B the number of boards in the qualifying round or rounds, E the number of pairs entered in the event, and S is the sum of all qualifying scores of pairs eligible for the finals.

If there is one qualifying round and one final, the total spread from top to bottom score is reduced to twice the top score on a board in the finals; if there are two qualifying rounds and one final, the total is reduced to three and a half boards; and for two qualifying rounds and two final rounds, five boards. The formula may give a smaller spread.

CASH. To play a winning card and win the trick.

CASH IN. To take a series of tricks by playing winning cards one after another. The term is usually applied to a situation where a player realizes that he is on lead for what is probably going to be the last time during that particular hand, and while in control, he will now take his tricks. The term can be applied to a declarer as well as defenders.

CAVALIER. A fourth COAT CARD, which is still maintained in some playing cards as an alternative for the JACK. See PACK.

CAVENDISH CLUB (New York City). Founded in 1925 by W. C. Whitehead, in association with G. Scott, and E. Wetzlar, the Club was housed for the first eight years at the Mayfair House, and then moved to the Ambassador Hotel. From 1950–65 it was at the Ritz Tower Hotel. From 1965 to 1974 it occupied premises on Central Park South. In 1974 it moved to the Carlton House.

Since 1941 the Cavendish Club has been a non-profit membership corporation, managed by the Club secretary, B. Jay Becker 1941 to 1947, Rudolf Muhsam from 1947 to 1973 and subsequently Thomas M. Smith. The presidents have been G. Scott 1925–35, Frank Crowninshield 1935–47, Nate Spingold 1948–58, Samuel Stayman 1958–62, Howard Schenken 1963–64, Harold Ogust 1965–67, Leonard Hess 1968–70, Edward Loewenthal 1971–73, and Roy Titus elected in 1974. Members have included very many players of international reputation: B. J. Becker, J. R. Crawford, W. Eisenberg, P. Feldesman, M. Field, H. Fishbein, R. L. Frey, S. Fry, Jr., C. Goren, W. Grieve, E. Hymes, O. Jacoby, R. Kahn, E. Kaplan, N. Kay, Mrs. E. Kemp, B. Koytchou, P. Leventritt, T. Lightner, A. Meredith, A. H. Morehead, A. Moyse, Jr., H. Ogust, G. Rapee, A. Roth, I. Rubin, A. Sheinwold, H. Sobel Smith, C. Solomon, S. Stearns, T. Stone, A. Truscott, D. Truscott, H. S. Vanderbilt, W. von Zedtwitz. Honorary members include General Alfred Gruenther, the late Baron Robert de Nexon, and George S. Kaufman.

CAVENDISH TROPHY. Awarded for the National Open Pair Championship; donated by the Cavendish Club of New York in 1928; contested at the Fall

times a year is required to hold at least one one-session charity club championship annually, the proceeds of which must be contributed to the ACBL Charity Foundation or the Canadian Charitable Fund. This game receives 70% of sectional rating. An ACBL club that holds a weekly game is entitled to hold a second one-session charity club championship annually, which also receives 70% of sectional rating. It is hoped that the club will select the Foundation as the beneficiary of the second game also, but the club may instead contribute the proceeds to a local charity of its choice, provided that the selected charity is tax exempt according to the Internal Revenue Service. When a local charity is selected, the Charity Tournament Report form must include the name of the charity and the amount contributed. Regardless of the recipient, the proceeds contributed must amount to at least $1.00 per player per session. A club may substitute one or more sessions of club charity tournaments for one or more sessions of its club tournaments. However, such substitutions earn only club championship rating.

Similar regulations apply to the ACBL units. Each unit may conduct two charity events annually of one or two sessions; each event receives sectional rating. This is in addition to the two annual Continentwide Charity games, which are normally run by the unit and which also are sectionally rated. The amount contributed from a Unit Charity game must amount to at least $1.50 per player per session, while for the Continentwide events a minimum donation of $1.75 per player is required.

Advance applications for unit charity tournaments must be submitted to the office of the ACBL Tournament Coordinator prior to scheduling. The need to apply well in advance and on the appropriate form cannot be emphasized too strongly. The very minimum is sixty days in advance of the requested date, and even more time should be allowed if possible. It frequently happens that the requested date conflicts with some other activity in the vicinity and cannot be used for the charity game. Sufficient time is then necessary for selection of a new date. Clubs, however, do not have to make advance application for their charity tournaments.

A number of sectional and regional tournaments have added a charity game to the regular schedule of events. This practice is encouraged, provided the charity game is *added* to the regular events, and not *substituted* for one of them. In such a case, the charity game receives sectional rating, and is usually scheduled on the evening before the start of the tournament proper.

Experience has proved that attendance at a charity game can be greatly increased, even doubled or more, by advance planning and thorough promotion. This, of course, reacts to the advantage of the beneficiary; but it also has important benefits for the sponsoring organization.

A big problem for any bridge group is to make new contacts, to interest new people, and the charity game is the best opportunity to do it. A good charity campaign will make contacts with scores of potential new members, people who like bridge, but haven't yet taken up duplicate. Every duplicate player knows

the fascination of the game, and if a new person can be induced to play it even once, he is likely to become a regular player and a club member.

The Charity Program has very great advantages in attracting favorable attention to the ACBL, providing additional master points for its members, and enabling its local groups to expand their activities and membership. However, these benefits can be realized only if fully exploited at the local level. They accrue directly to the members, clubs, and units, but only to the extent that they take advantage of the opportunities. See CONTINENTWIDE GAMES.

The earliest charity games of the ABL and ACBL began in 1934 on the initiative of William MC KENNEY, and these efforts were continued in subsequent years, especially in New York City. The chief beneficiaries were various children's organizations, including the Children's Cancer Fund, Inc., and the WAR ORPHANS SCHOLARSHIP, INC.

From 1951 to 1964 one or two charities were nominated annually as the beneficiaries of the ACBL's national charity program:

1951–52	Damon Runyon Memorial Fund	$ 25,713.21
1952–53	American Heart Association	38,846.64
1953–54	March of Dimes	53,345.68
1954–55	American Cancer Society	60,469.48
1955–56	National Society for Crippled Children	76,431.71
1956–57	American Heart Association	85,831.76
1957–58	American Cancer Society	104,809.61
1958–59	Arthritis and Rheumatism Foundation	136,814.67
1959–60	Red Cross Disaster Fund	163,540.01
1960–61	National Association for Mental Health	173,395.82
1961–62	Family Service Association of American National Kidney Disease Foundation	157,632.76
1962–63	National Multiple Sclerosis Society, Institute of Logopedics	229,541.46
1963–64	American Cancer Society, United Cerebral Palsy Associations	221,493.00

The desire to aid less well-known but thoroughly worthwhile causes with smaller contributions, rather than to make one or two very large contributions to a national group each year, led the Board of Directors of the ACBL to establish its own Charity Foundation on July 1, 1964. From 1964 to 1975, the Foundation approved grants totaling more than $1.26 million to twenty-three organizations:

Albany Medical College	$ 10,000.00
Allergy Foundation of America	47,000.00
American Cancer Society	228,600.00
Arthritis Foundation	113,700.00
Child Welfare League of America	40,000.00
Family Service	7,500.00
Foundation for Advancement of Inmate Rehabilitation and Recreation	5,000.00
Homemaker Services	7,500.00
Howe Laboratory of Ophthalmology	56,000.00
Leader Dogs for the Blind	10,000.00
Muscular Dystrophy Association of America	25,000.00
Myasthenia Gravis Foundation	10,000.00
National Association for Mental Health	22,500.00
National Association for Retarded Children	30,000.00
National Cystic Fibrosis Foundation	122,000.00
National Foundation for Neuromuscular Diseases	43,000.00
National Jewish Hospital at Denver	6,800.00
National Kidney Foundation	24,000.00
National Multiple Sclerosis Society	80,000.00
National Society for Crippled Children and Adults	20,000.00
National Tuberculosis Association	73,000.00
Salk Institute for Biological Studies	65,000.00
United Cerebral Palsy Research Foundation	222,200.00

The League appointed as original trustees of the Foundation a group composed of: General Alfred M. Gruenther (President), Benjamin O. Johnson, John E. Simon, Jerry M. Lewis, and Sidney B. Fink. Presidents following Gruenther's retirement in 1965 have been Fink (1965–67), Johnson (1968–73), Joseph J. Stedem (1973–74), and Percy X. Bean (since 1975). The Treasurer is Lee Hazen. In 1975 the Trustees of the Foundation, who are responsible for disbursing the funds raised, were:

Percy X. Bean
Fred B. Ensminger
Joseph J. Stedem
Mrs. L. W. McConnell
Joseph Weintraub

Trustees Emeriti are:
Benjamin O. Johnson
Gen. Alfred Gruenther
Abner Parker
Julius Rosenblum
John E. Simon
Samuel Stayman

CHARLES GOREN FOUNDATION. See INTER-
COLLEGIATE BRIDGE TOURNAMENT.

CHEAPER MINOR. See DEFENSE TO OPENING THREE-
BID; SECOND NEGATIVE RESPONSE AFTER ARTIFICIAL
FORCING OPENING.

CHEAPEST BID. The most economical bid available at any particular point in the auction, such as
one diamond in response to one club. Many conventional bids and systems make use of this principle
of economy by attaching special meanings to club
bids at various levels, and occasionally to diamond
bids. The same principle of economy is followed in
making natural opening bids and responses. See
CHOICE OF SUIT and UP THE LINE.

CHEATING. Throughout history, card cheats have
always been held in contempt. It is so with bridge.

The LAWS OF CONTRACT BRIDGE are not designed to
prevent cheating or to provide redress. The lawgivers have presumably taken the view that it would
be wrong to accord cheats a status by providing legal
remedies against their activities. This also is the
policy of the ACBL; permanent exclusion from
membership would be the inevitable penalty for
premeditated cheating, but a case of momentary
weakness might be dealt with by temporary suspension. ("The penalty of cheating is exclusion from
society," wrote the great whist authority, Cavendish.)

Cheating at Rubber Bridge. At rubber bridge,
cheating is not a problem. Short of actually manipu-
lating or marking the cards, it is impracticable for a
lone player to cheat effectively. The fact that good
bridge is so exact an art militates against cheating, for
a player who made bids or plays which were against
the odds but which proved consistently successful
would soon excite suspicion. Cheating in clubs is
therefore rare.

Traditional forms of cardsharping are unreward-
ing in bridge because each deal is almost equally
important. A sharper can hardly make a killing by
awaiting a suitable opening as in such games as
poker, and if he just "happened" to pick up good
cards every time he dealt, his career would be short-
lived. The dealing of "seconds," therefore, the
classic technique of the cardsharping aristocracy, is
not an effective means of winning. (An accomplished
sharp, dealing from a marked pack, sees when a high
card is about to go to an opponent, and deals that
opponent the next card instead, keeping the high
card for himself or his partner.) For the same reason,
another time-honored device of sharps, ringing in a
cold deck, will not yield a reward commensurate with
the risk.

In general it is fair to say that such cheating as has
occurred in clubs is not the work of sharps but of a
few disorientated and amoral persons, who nevertheless should be mercilessly shunned.

Cheating at Duplicate. The fact that duplicate is a
game for fixed partnerships as opposed to the cut-in
style of rubber bridge makes dishonesty more
practicable. Fortunately, in duplicate there is a
powerful safeguard; success gained otherwise than
by fair combat is empty to a true bridge player, and
cheating presents no attraction to a normal person. It
is happily true that to most competitors their own
self-respect is at least as important as the kudos to be
gained from tournament successes.

There is reason to believe that the rare cases which
do occur are not the work of a partnership which has
an explicit agreement to cheat, but are rather the
result of the opportunism of an unscrupulous player
to which his partner turns a blind eye. In such a case,
the partner must be considered as morally blame-
worthy as the cheat himself.

Cheating at duplicate is by no means easy to
define. Although the Laws do not recognize cheats,
the section called "The Proprieties" defines two
main types of improper conduct: breaches of ethics
and breaches of etiquette. Breaches of ethics are
commonly thought of as unfair practices which fall
short of deliberate cheating, but it is possible for the
difference to be one of degree only. For example, a
pair who took note of inflections in bidding would be
considered unethical, while a pair who set out to
impart similar information by secret signals would be
considered cheats. Common sense is a surer guide
than legal definition. (See also ETHICS, ETIQUETTE,
and PROPRIETIES.)

Apart from the traditional forms of cardsharping
which have been briefly mentioned under RUBBER
BRIDGE—and which of course present no advantage
whatsoever at DUPLICATE—the following are some
examples of infringements which are peculiar to the
tournament world. By their aggravated nature they
can be classified as cheating and have been dealt with
as such by the ACBL.

Spying on upcoming boards. Disciplinary action
has been taken against players who have been observed to take note of the play at other tables. One
player who cheated too discreetly to be detected by
ordinary surveillance was found out when an

observant tournament director noticed that he seemed to score consistently better on even-numbered boards than on odd-numbered boards. Observation over a period of time proved that he made a practice of listening to conversations at adjoining tables when he had finished a set of boards, making notes on his private scorecard.

All players can help to apprehend such cheats by being careful to restrict their attention to their own table while waiting for the table change. So far as possible, players should avoid leaving the playing area during sessions, but where this is unavoidable they should always select a route which takes them as far away from the playing tables as possible. When this is done by all honest players, would-be cheats are more conspicuous.

Altering score sheets. The ACBL's policy of posting BURNER copies of the recap sheets (containing each player's total point score on each board as well as his match-point score) within a few minutes of the end of play has virtually killed this kind of cheating. The risk of detection when victimized opponents inspect the recap sheet is far too great.

Secret signals. Various forms of signaling, usually by the defenders, have been attempted. Generally the purpose is either to suggest an opening lead or to convey the hand pattern held—i.e., 4–5–3–1, etc. The result of such cheating, if attended by any degree of success, is inevitable. The suspicions of competent players are soon aroused, and in a short time the offenders are marked men. Even if they abandon their cheating methods in order to escape final detection, the game is never the same for them again; they have forfeited forever the friendship of decent players.

Many of the tournament procedures which have been devised by the ACBL are unobtrusive but effective safeguards against cheating. (For more obtrusive safeguards, see use of coffee tables in BERMUDA INCIDENT.) Thus, in the LAWS OF DUPLICATE, some of the examples cited as irregularities for which the tournament director may impose disciplinary penalties are anticheating safeguards. These are:

"86 B.3. Any discussion of the bidding, play, or result of a board, which may be overheard at another table.

"86 B.4. Any comparison of scores with another contestant during a session.

"86 B.5. Any touching or handling cards belonging to another player."

Experienced players realize that these and other procedures are for the benefit of all. (See BERMUDA INCIDENT, BUENOS AIRES AFFAIR, CHEATING ACCUSATIONS.)

H. G. and A. D.

CHEATING ACCUSATIONS. Accusations of CHEATING are rare in serious tournament bridge, and substantiated accusations are even rarer. It is gener-

ally recognized that an allegation that is not supported by solid evidence should not be made, and that "accusation by rumor" is highly improper.

At the international level there have been very few cases of charges being brought. Most of these were disposed of, without widespread publicity, by the national or international committees concerned. The notable exceptions occurred in the 1965 and 1975 World Championships. See BERMUDA INCIDENT; BUENOS AIRES AFFAIR.

Several suggestions have been made, aimed at preventing cheating and of forestalling accusations of cheating. Screens called FRANCO BOARDS were introduced in Italian events years ago, but did not find general acceptance. In 1974, the proposal of WBF President Julius Rosenblum to use bidding SCREENS in the 1975 Bermuda Bowl in order to eliminate accusations of cheating met with a sharp division of opinion, with many taking the position that such screens would be demeaning to the players and to bridge itself. Nevertheless, in 1975 bidding screens were used for the first time in World Championship play, and their use in combination with BIDDING BOXES virtually eliminated any problems relating to the inadvertent exchange of unauthorized information and the ethical problems resulting from hesitations. The response of the players to the screens and boxes was overwhelmingly positive. The irony of the 1975 Bermuda Bowl was, however, that while the screens designed to eliminate cheating accusations were being enthusiastically received, an Italian pair was accused of cheating by using foot signals under the table. See BERMUDA INCIDENT.

CHECKBACK STAYMAN. See STAYMAN ON SECOND ROUND.

CHESS PLAYERS. Nobody has ever reached the highest levels at both chess and bridge, perhaps because life is too short. But many have been expert at one game and near-expert at the other.

High-ranking bridge players who are also strong chess players include Oswald JACOBY, Alan TRUSCOTT, and Sol RUBINOW. Among chess players, two former world champions, Emanuel Lasker and José Raoul Capablanca, were contributing editors of *The Bridge World* in the early thirties.

However, G. le B. DESCHAPELLES excelled at whist and chess, and was acknowledged as the finest player of his day at both games.

CHICAGO (Four-Deal Bridge). A form of the game much played in clubs and well suited to home play. Its effect is to avoid long rubbers of uncertain duration; a member never need wait longer than the time (about twenty minutes) required to complete four deals. The game is called "Chicago" for the city in which it originated, and sometimes "club bridge."

Basic rules. The LAWS OF CONTRACT BRIDGE and rules for CLUB PROCEDURE are followed, except as modified by the following rules.

The rubber. A rubber consists of a series of four deals that have been bid and played. If a deal is passed out, the same player deals again, and the deal passed out does not count as one of the four deals.

A fifth deal is void if attention is drawn to it at any time before there has been a new cut for partners or the game has terminated; if the error is not discovered in time for correction, the score stands as recorded. A sixth or subsequent deal is unconditionally void, and no score for such a deal is ever permissible.

In case fewer than four deals are played, the score shall stand for the incomplete series unless attention is drawn to the error before there has been a new cut for partners, or the game has terminated.

When the players are pivoting, the fact that the players have taken their proper seats for the next rubber shall be considered a cut for partners.

Vulnerability. Vulnerability is not determined by previous scores but by the following schedule:

first deal: neither side vulnerable

second and   dealer's side vulnerable, the
third deals: other side not vulnerable

fourth deal: both sides vulnerable

Premiums. For making or completing a game (100 or more trick points), a side receives a premium of 300 points if on that deal it is not vulnerable, or 500 points if on that deal it is vulnerable. There is no additional premium for winning two or more games, each game premium being scored separately.

The score. As a reminder of vulnerability, two intersecting diagonal lines should be drawn near the top of the score pad, as follows:

The numeral "1" should be inserted in one of the four angles thus formed that faces the first dealer. After play of the first deal is completed, "2" is inserted in the next angle in clockwise rotation, facing the dealer of the second deal. The numerals "3" and "4" are subsequently inserted at the start of the third and fourth deals respectively, each in the angle facing the current dealer.

A correctly numbered diagram is conclusive as to vulnerability. There is no redress for a bid influenced by the scorer's failure to draw the diagram or for an error or omission in inserting a numeral or numerals in the diagram. Such error or omission should, upon discovery, be immediately corrected, and the deal or deals should be scored or rescored as though the diagram and the number or numbers thereon had been properly inserted.

Part-scores. A part-score or -scores made previously may be combined with a part-score made in the current deal to complete a game of 100 or more trick points. The game premium is determined by the vulnerability, on that deal, of the side that completes the game. When a side makes or completes a game, no previous part-score of either side may thereafter be counted toward game.

A side that makes a part-score in the fourth deal, if the part-score is not sufficient to complete a game, receives a premium of 100 points. This premium is scored whether or not the same side or the other side has an uncompleted part-score. There is no separate premium for making a part-score in any other circumstances.

Deal out of turn. When a player deals out of turn, and there is no right to a redeal, the player who should have dealt retains his right to call first, but such right is lost if it is not claimed before the actual dealer calls. If the actual dealer calls before attention is drawn to the deal out of turn, each player thereafter calls in rotation. Vulnerability and scoring values are determined by the position of the player who should have dealt, regardless of which player acutally dealt or called first. Neither the rotation of the deal nor the scoring is affected by a deal out of turn. The next dealer is the player who would have dealt next if the deal had been in turn.

Optional rules and customs. The following practices, not required, have proved acceptable in some clubs and games.

(1) Since the essence of the game is speed, if a deal is passed out, the pack that has been shuffled for the next deal should be used by the same dealer.

(2) The net score of a rubber should be translated into even hundreds (according to American custom) by crediting as 100 points any fraction thereof amounting to 50 or more points: e.g., 750 points count as 800; 740 points count as 700 points.

(3) No two players may play a second consecutive rubber as partners at the same table. If two players draw each other again, the player who has drawn the highest card should play with the player who has drawn the third-highest, against the other two players.

(4) Any player may announce, prior to the auction and before he has looked at his hand, which deal it is and who is vulnerable; or may for his own information inquire as to these facts when it is his turn to call. There is no redress if no announcement is made or if incorrect information is given.

(5) To avoid confusion as to how many deals have been played: Each deal should be scored, even if there is no net advantage to either side (for example, when one side is entitled to 100 points for undertrick penalties and the other side is entitled to 100 points for honors). In a result that completes a game, preminimums for overtricks, game, slam, or making a doubled contract should be combined with the trick score to produce one total, which is entered below the line; for example, if a side makes two spades doubled and vulnerable with an overtrick, 870 should be scored below the line, not 120 below the line and 50, 500, and 200 above the line.

(6) In some clubs, notably the Cavendish (N.Y.C.), the vulnerability on the second and third deals is reversed. The objective is to give the non-vulnerable side an opportunity to pre-empt as declarer.

CHICAGO TROPHY. Awarded for the National Open Team Championship (board-a-match scoring) until 1965 when it was replaced by the REISINGER MEMORIAL TROPHY; contested at the Fall Nationals (under which heading past results are listed). The Chicago Trophy was donated by the Auction Bridge Club of Chicago in 1929. (In 1928, the open team competition was for the Harold S. Vanderbilt Cup.)

CHICANE. A term from BRIDGE WHIST referring to a hand that is void of trumps. It was scored the same as three honors. In contract bridge, the term is obsolete in its original sense, though it is occasionally used to describe a void suit, as "chicane in hearts."

CHILDREN. Youth is no bar to contract bridge, and many children play as well as their parents. Among the outstandingly successful children are Mark Goldstein, Hopkins, Minn., who played creditably in the Charity Game of the Summer Nationals in 1962 at the age of seven, appearing later on a panel show in company with the nation's bridge greats; Dianne Barton, San Francisco, who had won over 10 master points at the age of eleven; and August Boehm, New York, who was the youngest player competing in the first National Teen-Year Pairs, winning the title at the age of thirteen. See YOUNGEST LIFE MASTER.

CHILEAN BRIDGE FEDERATION (FEDERACIÓN CHILENA DE BRIDGE). Founded in 1951, with a membership of 300 in 1969 in 17 affiliated clubs. Chile participates in all South American Championships, hosting the 1951, 1957, 1965, and 1972 events in Santiago, and occasionally in World Olympiads. National events held annually are for Men's and Women's Championships. The following Chilean players are listed separately: Walter Kohn, Jorge Ovalle, E. Palocz, Mrs. E. Palocz.

President, 1975: Mario Vilensky, Casilla 14911, Santiago, Chile.

CHINA. See NATIONAL CONTRACT BRIDGE LEAGUE OF THE REPUBLIC OF CHINA.

CHINESE FINESSE. An attempt to win a trick by leading an unsupported honor.

NORTH
♣ A 5

WEST   EAST
♣ K 8 6 2   ♣ J 10 7

SOUTH
♣ Q 9 4 3

If South needs to avoid a loser in this suit, he may dismiss the remote chance of dropping the singleton king, and try the effect of leading the queen from his hand. In the diagrammed situation West may well decide to duck, fearing that South has Q J 10, with or without the nine.

CHOICE, RESTRICTED. See RESTRICTED CHOICE.

CHOICE OF PACKS AND SEATS. The winner (or highest card) of the cut for first deal has the choice of which seat he will take and which of the two packs he wishes to deal. Presumably, unless the wrong player deals, at some subsequent point, the cards will continue to be dealt by this player and his partner, the other pack by their opponents.

CHOICE OF SUIT. In opening the bidding and responding, a long suit is normally bid ahead of a short one, but a few exceptions should be noted:

(1) A three-card minor suit, particularly clubs, is often bid ahead of a four-card major suit. Using FIVE-CARD MAJORS, the prepared minor-suit bid is made in all situations. In standard methods the major suit will usually be preferred if the suit is biddable and there will not be any rebid difficulty. In practice a four-card major is rarely bid with a 4–3–3–3 distribution: a minimum hand needs to keep the bidding at a low level; a hand of medium strength normally opens one no trump; and a maximum hand bids one club in order to make it easy for partner to respond.

(2) A strong four-card suit is often bid ahead of a five-card suit ranking immediately below it. This is necessary with a minimum or near-minimum hand; with hands of intermediate strength, a REVERSE from the long suit into the short suit becomes possible. There can be an acute problem if both suits are of poor quality:

♠ A x x x
♥ A x x x x
♦ A J x
♣ x

It would be risky to bid one spade followed by two hearts. The least evil is perhaps to bid one heart, and rebid two diamonds if responder bids two clubs.

(3) A five-card suit may be bid ahead of a six-card suit ranking immediately below it if the hand is a minimum:

♠ x
♥ A J x x x
♦ A Q x x x x
♣ x

One diamond followed by a heart bid would not be justified by the strength of the hand, and opposing bidding might shut out the heart suit. Most players will bid one heart, treating the hand as a five-five distribution.

(4) In response to one spade, a three-card club suit is sometimes bid in preference to a four-card heart suit.

(5) In response to an opening bid in a red suit, a major suit is sometimes bid at the one-level in preference to a five- or six-card minor suit at the two-level. This may be because the hand is not strong

enough to bid at the level of two, or to avoid concealing the major suit when the hand is not worth two constructive bids.

See also BIDDABLE SUITS; CANAPÉ; THREE-CARD SUITS, BIDS IN; WALSH.

With two or three suits of equal length, the choice is more complicated:

(6) With five-card suits (or six-card suits) the opener normally bids the higher-ranking unless he has both black suits. Some players bid one spade with two five-card black suits if the hand is strong enough to make a rebid at the level of three.

An exception can arise when a player holds a minimum hand and a void. With 5–0–5–3 or 3–5–0–5, some players bid the minor suit for reasons of preparedness.

With two or three four-card suits the opener's choice is usually the suit below the shortage, or most nearly below it. But if this rule produces a weak four-card major suit, most players would search for another bid. This may prove particularly difficult if the hand is a minimum and it includes a doubleton club:

```
-    ♠ J x x x    ♠ J x x x    ♠ A K x
     ♡ J x x x    ♡ A K x     ♡ J x x x
     ◇ A K x      ◇ J x x x    ◇ J x x x
     ♣ A 10       ♣ A 10       ♣ A 10
```

Many players would open these hands with one diamond, and would hope not to be faced by the problem of finding a rebid over a response of two clubs.

If the opener's hand is strong, there is rarely a rebid problem. In that case a minor suit is often bid in preference to a major, with the idea of keeping the bidding low and giving partner the maximum opportunity to respond with a weak hand.

If the opener holds both minor suits, he usually has a free choice, and may be guided by tactical or lead-inhibiting considerations; he will hardly ever wish to bid both suits. However, one diamond is clearly preferable holding a worthless trebleton heart:

```
♠ A J
♡ 10 x x
◇ K J x x
♣ K J x x
```

One club would leave the opener with an impossible rebid after an overcall of one heart and a response of one spade.

With three four-card suits, the "middle" suit may sometimes fare better than the suit below the shortage:

```
♠ K Q x x
♡ K Q x x
◇ A x x x
♣ x
```

Players who require responder to show a four-card major at the one-level if possible, often prefer to bid one heart rather than one spade. This avoids the awkward rebid decision which faces the opener if he opens one spade, and receives a response of one no trump or two clubs.

(8) With five-card suits, responder invariably prefers the higher-ranking for his response. For responder's choice with four-card suits, see UP THE LINE.

CHUKKER. A term for four deals of CHICAGO. It is also used in a long team match for a group of boards followed by comparison of scores. The term is borrowed from polo.

CHURCHILL STYLE. The methods of bidding advocated by S. Garton Churchill of New York. The main features are:

(1) A weak no trump opening. Churchill was among the first leading American theorists to advocate this bid and his followers were the exclusive advocates of it for many years. In this style, however, not all weak balanced hands are opened with one no trump. One heart would be bid with

```
♠ x x
♡ A Q x x
◇ A J x x
♣ Q 10 x
```

Hence, the one no trump rebid might be made with as little as 2½ HONOR TRICKS.

(2) A "utility" one no trump response with a wide variety of weak hands. One no trump would be the response to one heart with any of the following:

```
♠ Q x x          ♠ Q x x
♡ K x x          ♡ K x x x
◇ x x x          ◇ x x x x
♣ x x x x        ♣ x x

♠ Q x x x x      ♠ Q 10 x x x x
♡ K x            ♡ x x
◇ x x x          ◇ x
♣ x x x          ♣ 10 x x x
```

On the last example, responder would bid spades at his next opportunity. The corollary is that all other responses, including a single raise in the opener's suit, imply a forward-going response.

After the "utility" one no trump response, the opening bidder, unless his holding is inflexible, will normally rebid a suit lower in rank, although, with a reasonably good balanced hand, he is allowed to pass, and oftentimes does. This was the forerunner of the forcing ROTH-STONE one no trump response.

(3) Light opening bids with distributional patterns such as 5–4–3–1, 5–4–4–0, 4–4–4–1, 6–4–3–0, 5–5–3–0, 6–5–1–1, etc.

(4) Frequent bids in short suits; Churchill was well before his time in using such bids as all-purpose bids for exploring for games and slams, or steering the contract into a particular hand, etc.

(5) Constructive overcalls; forcing jump overcalls.

(6) Four-card openings in suits of any strength.

(7) "Picture Bidding": jump rebids and responses used essentially to describe solid or near-solid suits as well as slam aspirations.

(8) No strength-showing forcing opening bid.

(9) Sparing use of pre-emptive bids.

(10) BALANCE OF POWER bidding (see BALANCING).

CIPHER BID. See ARTIFICIAL BID.

CIRCUS. See SHARIF BRIDGE CIRCUS.

CITY OF ASBURY PARK TROPHY. Awarded for the Challenge Team-of-Four Championship, an event held from 1930 until 1937 at the Summer Nationals, under which the results are reported. The trophy was a statuette carved and cast by Dorothy Rice Sims, and donated by her and her husband.

The conditions of the event made it unique in that the runners-up could challenge the winners to play for the championship; on the few occasions when this happened, however, the winners retained the title. The championship was equivalent in status to the SPINGOLD event which took its place in 1938. Thereafter the trophy was turned over to the New York–New Jersey Conference, which awarded it annually from 1958 through 1969 to the winner of the most master points at their summer regional. When the conference regional was moved from Asbury Park that city, to which the trophy had originally been presented, requested its return.

CLAIM OR CONCESSION. The claim or concession of tricks by declarer or defender is probably the greatest source of calls for the director.

It is rarely advisable for the defending side to claim or concede tricks. There are times when, in the interest of speeding up the game, the declarer might wish to terminate play by claiming some or all of the balance of the tricks. There is one, and only one, proper way in which this can be done. Declarer faces his hand on the table, stating the exact order in which he proposes to play his cards. See LAWS OF DUPLICATE, Laws 68–71.

See also LAWS OF CONTRACT BRIDGE, Laws 70–74. The two sets of laws are somewhat different because of the absence of a director at most rubber bridge tables. Law 69 of the Duplicate Laws lists the prohibitions against the declarer if his claim is questioned.

Claims or concessions of tricks by a defender can be even more severely penalized, because such claim or concession by one defender may give information about his holding to his partner. This makes his partner's cards penalty cards subject to the call of the declarer.

```
              DUMMY
               x x
   CLAIMER
    K x                 A x
              DECLARER
               Q J
```

Claimer states, "My partner holds ace and small, and we win the balance." Declarer plays the queen;

if claimer covers, declarer may require claimer's partner to win with the ace; if claimer plays small, declarer may require claimer's partner to play small also.

The correct procedure for a defender wishing to expedite the play is to show his cards to the declarer. This should be done in the late stages of the play if declarer has a finesse-guessing position and the defender knows that any play fails.

CLARAC SLAM TRY. A feature of the PRO SYSTEM based principally on a four club bid to ask about aces and other controls. The name CLARAC is an acronym for CLub Asking, Respond Aces and Controls.

Responses to the four club bid vary according to whether or not the partner of the four club bidder has shown a good hand. By a limited hand, the responses to four clubs are: four diamonds with no aces and no king-queen combinations; four no trump with no aces but with reasonable king-queen values; four hearts, four spades, or five clubs with one ace plus first- or second-round control in the suit named; five diamonds, five hearts, five spades, or six clubs with two aces plus second-round control in the suit named; five no trump with three aces and no other control. By a good hand, the responses to four clubs show one ace more than they do by a limited hand.

Over any response but four diamonds, a suit bid by the four club bidder is an asking bid in that suit. Responses are: cheapest suit to deny first- or second-round control; cheapest no trump to show second-round control; raise to show two of the top three honors; any other suit to show the ace of the asked suit plus second-round control in the bid suit. More asking bids may follow.

CLASH SQUEEZE. A squeeze in three suits, distinguished by the presence of a special type of long menace called a "clash menace," analyzed and named by Chien-Hwa Wang (in *Bridge Magazine* articles 1956–57).

```
                    NORTH
                     A 2
   WEST                            EAST
    K                             J 10
                    SOUTH
                      Q
```

South's queen is a clash menace against West's king.

```
                    NORTH
                    A x x
   WEST                            EAST
    Q J                           9 x x
                    SOUTH
                    K 10
```

South's ten is a clash menace against West's queen and jack.

The following are the basic positions for a clash squeeze.

(1) Simple Squeeze

Positional

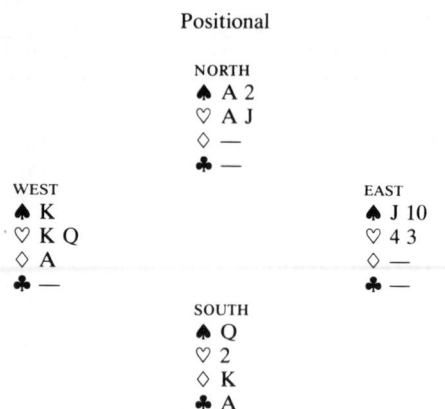

```
              NORTH
              ♠ A 2
              ♡ A J
              ◇ —
              ♣ —
WEST                        EAST
♠ K                         ♠ J 10
♡ K Q                       ♡ 4 3
◇ A                         ◇ —
♣ —                         ♣ —
              SOUTH
              ♠ Q
              ♡ 2
              ◇ K
              ♣ A
```

South leads the ace of clubs, which squeezes West in three suits (if West discards a spade, South cashes the queen and then crosses to the ace of hearts in order to take the ace of spades).

Delayed (secondary)

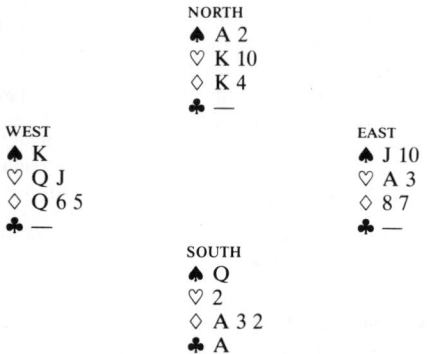

```
              NORTH
              ♠ A 2
              ♡ K 10
              ◇ K 4
              ♣ —
WEST                        EAST
♠ K                         ♠ J 10
♡ Q J                       ♡ A 3
◇ Q 6 5                     ◇ 8 7
♣ —                         ♣ —
              SOUTH
              ♠ Q
              ♡ 2
              ◇ A 3 2
              ♣ A
```

South leads the ace of clubs, which squeezes West in three suits. West must discard a heart, and North throws a spade. Now South can lead a heart, and establish a trick in that suit. See also VICE SQUEEZE.

(2) Double Squeeze (non-simultaneous and positional). A double clash squeeze consists of two parts: a clash squeeze against one opponent, then a simple squeeze against the other.

```
              NORTH
              ♠ A 2
              ♡ —
              ◇ K 4 3
              ♣ —
WEST                        EAST
♠ K                         ♠ J 10
♡ A                         ♡ K
◇ Q 6 5                     ◇ 8 7
♣ —                         ♣ —
              SOUTH
              ♠ Q
              ♡ Q
              ◇ A 2
              ♣ A
```

South leads the ace of clubs, and West is clash squeezed. He must discard a heart, after which South plays the king then ace of diamonds to squeeze East in the majors.

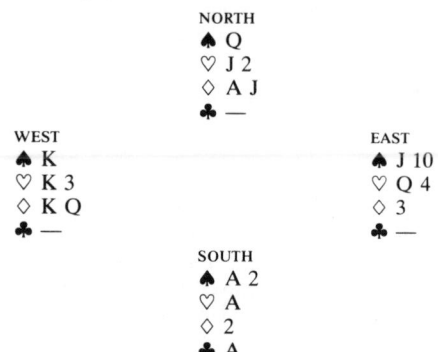

```
              NORTH
              ♠ Q
              ♡ J 2
              ◇ A J
              ♣ —
WEST                        EAST
♠ K                         ♠ J 10
♡ K 3                       ♡ Q 4
◇ K Q                       ◇ 3
♣ —                         ♣ —
              SOUTH
              ♠ A 2
              ♡ A
              ◇ 2
              ♣ A
```

The ace of clubs lead by South clash squeezes West, and forces him to discard a heart. South cashes the ace of hearts (VIENNA COUP), then crosses to the ace of diamonds, squeezing East in the majors.

(3) Double Squeeze (simultaneous)

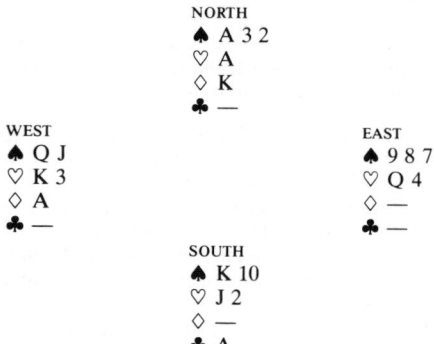

```
              NORTH
              ♠ A 3 2
              ♡ A
              ◇ K
              ♣ —
WEST                        EAST
♠ Q J                       ♠ 9 8 7
♡ K 3                       ♡ Q 4
◇ A                         ◇ —
♣ —                         ♣ —
              SOUTH
              ♠ K 10
              ♡ J 2
              ◇ —
              ♣ A
```

On the lead of the ace of clubs West must discard a heart, North throws a diamond, and East is squeezed in the majors.

This is a positional squeeze.

Secondary

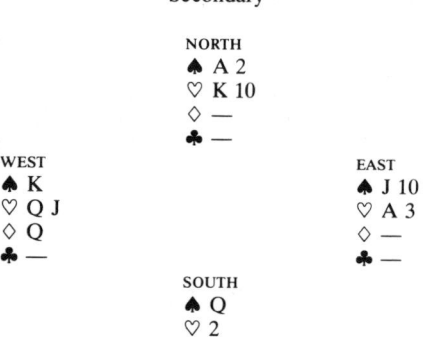

```
              NORTH
              ♠ A 2
              ♡ K 10
              ◇ —
              ♣ —
WEST                        EAST
♠ K                         ♠ J 10
♡ Q J                       ♡ A 3
◇ Q                         ◇ —
♣ —                         ♣ —
              SOUTH
              ♠ Q
              ♡ 2
              ◇ 3
              ♣ A
```

South leads the ace of clubs. If West discards a heart, North throws a spade, and East throws a heart. South leads a heart to establish a trick in that suit, with the ace of spades for an entry. If West throws a spade, North throws a heart as does East. South cashes the queen of spades and leads a heart to throw in East who must give the last trick to North's ace of spades.

(4) Trump Squeeze

Single

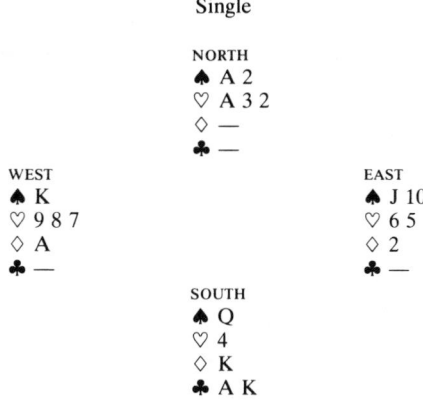

```
                    NORTH
                    ♠ A 2
                    ♡ A 3 2
                    ◇ —
                    ♣ —
WEST                                    EAST
♠ K                                     ♠ J 10
♡ 9 8 7                                 ♡ 6 5
◇ A                                     ◇ 2
♣ —                                     ♣ —
                    SOUTH
                    ♠ Q
                    ♡ 4
                    ◇ K
                    ♣ A K
```

With clubs as trumps, South leads the king of that suit. West can do no better than discard a heart, but now South can ruff out that suit, using the ace of spades as a re-entry. This squeeze is positional.

Double

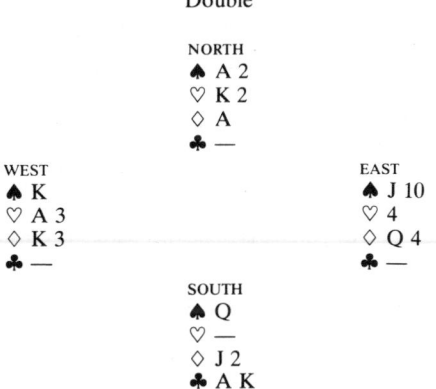

```
                    NORTH
                    ♠ A 2
                    ♡ K 2
                    ◇ A
                    ♣ —
WEST                                    EAST
♠ K                                     ♠ J 10
♡ A 3                                   ♡ 4
◇ K 3                                   ◇ Q 4
♣ —                                     ♣ —
                    SOUTH
                    ♠ Q
                    ♡ —
                    ◇ J 2
                    ♣ A K
```

Clubs are trumps. South leads the trump king, and West must throw a diamond. North and East discard hearts. South cashes the ace of diamonds, and ruffs a heart which squeezes East in spades and diamonds.

M. I.

CLEAR A SUIT. At no trump play, to clear a suit is to force out, by continued leads of the suit, adversely held high cards so that the remainder of the cards in that suit are winners. At suit play, the term is used also to indicate a line of play which cashes winners in one side-suit and trumps out the balance of the cards in that suit so as to eliminate all cards of the suit from both the declarer's and dummy's hand. Then if a trick is lost to the defense later, a further lead of this suit gives declarer the option of trumping in one hand while discarding a potential loser in the other. See also ELIMINATION and STRIP PLAY.

CLOSED HAND. The hand of the declarer, as distinct from the "open hand," which is now legally referred to as the "dummy." The terms date from auction bridge, the first of the predecessors of contract bridge to make declarer's partner's hand visible to all, and under the direction of the declarer. Because declarer's partner had no control of the play of the cards dealt him, he was referred to as the dummy, which term became so universally used as to become official.

CLOSED ROOM. In team-of-four matches, particularly in the knockout matches, the two pairs of a team play in different rooms or different areas of the same room. One of these rooms is designated the open room, one the closed room. Normally, spectators are permitted in the open room, and these spectators are free to come and go, without hindrance. However, if spectators are permitted in the closed room, they are restricted to one table, and are not permitted to leave until the match they are watching is terminated. As soon as one of the matches in the closed room has been terminated, the original open room becomes a closed room, to which no other spectators are permitted entrance, and to which no contestant or spectator may be readmitted after leaving until the last open room contest has terminated.

In important matches where arrangements are made for play-by-play relaying of information to a large group of spectators, the boards are originally played in a closed room with a starting time appreciably earlier than that for the replay. Thus information may be kept from the players in the replay but made available to spectators in the theatre, who can contrast the results of the first play with what is going on in the replay. Spectators thus are more fully informed of what has gone on than are any of the actual contestants.

In some major events such as the European Championship, the open room is always open, but players are not permitted to leave the closed room until the open half of their match is completed. See BRIDGE-O-RAMA.

CLOTHESLINE. An arrangement by which traveling score slips can be displayed for study by the players when the recapitulation sheet does not show information beyond the match-point score itself.

CLUB. (1) The symbol ♣, which appears on the thirteen cards of the lowest ranking of the four suits in a bridge deck, stems from the French (*trèfle*), but the name seems to be of Spanish or Italian origin as a translation of *basto* or *bastone*. (2) The club suit consists of the thirteen cards bearing this symbol. Since the club suit as trump is the least likely final declaration when a choice of trump suits is available, many systems make use of the naming of this suit to show conventional holdings. See CLUB CONVENTIONS.

CLUB BRIDGE. See CHICAGO.

CLUB CHARITY GAMES. See CHARITY PROGRAM OF THE ACBL.

CLUB CONVENTIONS. The low-ranking club suit is particularly well suited for conventional uses of various kinds. The VANDERBILT CLUB was the original "club convention" and has had many successors (see ONE CLUB SYSTEMS and TWO CLUB SYSTEMS). Conventional club bids at higher levels include TWO CLUB STRONG ARTIFICIAL OPENING, STAYMAN, and GERBER.

CLUB PROCEDURES. See HOUSE RULES. Each bridge club will find that there are situations in its operation that are not covered by the LAWS, or occasionally, points where the laws do not agree with the desire of the members of the club on such points as precedence in entering a table, complement of a table, personal dislikes of certain players, methods of settling games for stakes, and like problems. Procedures used in such cases should always be consistent and definitely formulated for future reference.

CLUB SYSTEMS. See ONE CLUB SYSTEMS, TWO CLUB SYSTEMS.

CLUB TRICK. A trick in the club suit.

CLUBS. Organizations or groups of bridge players who form units acting as centers of interest for players in a particular community. All over the world may be found clubs catering to the needs and wishes of people in all walks of life who have one common interest, contract bridge. They may prefer duplicate or rubber bridge, either for stakes or not, or they may be devotees of the recently developed CHICAGO form of bridge, which consists of rapid, usually action-packed deals, four in number, allowing all members easy access to a playing table without too long a wait. Clubs are today so diversified as to type of premises and rules of membership that a comprehensive description is impossible. It can be said, however, that large cities all over the world have at least one and often many more such clubs. Those who prefer to play for stakes can always be accommodated, providing they pass whatever standards are set up, and people who prefer duplicate can usually find an open game-club devoted to such purposes. In smaller towns throughout America, the emphasis has shifted to duplicate bridge, and a club for that purpose is almost always available to the players of the community. The ACBL issues annual directories of all clubs operating under its auspices. In 1975 the total was 4,993. A club can be located at an American Legion post or country club or in a YMCA or other civic-sponsored quarters. Games usually occur at regular periods, with specially scheduled Club championship events every calendar quarter. Fees are charged for each participation, and in some cases annual dues as well. In big cities such as New York, Philadelphia, or Chicago there is a huge play at duplicate clubs that are largely proprietary in nature—that is, run for the benefit of the owner or group of members controlling the club. But there has consistently been much play at rubber bridge and Chicago at clubs in large cities too. Many clubs of this type are also proprietary in nature, open for two sessions each day, and in some cases also have weekly duplicates which are open to all comers. There are also clubs restricted to operation on a membership basis. These are also usually to be found in large cities. Annual dues are charged and members also pay card fees whenever they play. Clubs of this type usually have boards of directors or governors. Various committees exist, too, for the purpose of controlling membership applications or tournament activities, etc. Typical clubs belonging to this category are the CAVENDISH and REGENCY in New York, CROCKFORD'S, PORTLAND, and HAMILTON in London. See also CROCKFORD'S CLUB (N.Y.) and WHIST CLUB.

COAT CARDS. The original term in English for the three cards of each suit which represent costumed human figures: the king, queen, and jack. In some countries, a fourth coat card, variously the valet or courtier, is included in the deck. The term has been superseded by a corruption, "court cards." See FACE CARDS.

COFFEE-HOUSE BRIDGE. Card playing in European coffee houses frequently featured conversational or other gambits designed to mislead opponents, and the term "coffee-house bridge" became a synonym for legal but unethical gambits. Such questions as "Did you bid a *spade?*" with a rising inflection to inform partner of a sound spade holding in one's own cards, or "What did you bid first over one diamond?" to right-hand opponent when one wants his partner to lead that suit against a no trump contract, are easily caught, and the player ostracized at rubber bridge or the offense adjudicated when a director is present. Action on a doubtful hand after a slow pass by partner is somewhat harder to classify, but the ethical player will pass all such doubtful hands after such a slow pass by partner.

Conversational gambits, even when made without any devious intent, have no place at the bridge table among serious, ethical players.

COFFEE-HOUSING. Indulging in unethical actions, with full intent to mislead opponents. See COFFEE-HOUSE BRIDGE.

COFFIN TROPHY. Awarded for the National Women's Team Championship, donated by Charles Emmet Coffin in 1933, contested at the Fall Nationals until 1963, when it was transferred to the Spring Nationals, under which heading past results are listed.

COLD. Bridge slang term describing an easily makable contract. In post-mortem heat, players tend to exaggerate the degrees of coldness.

COLLECTION AND ARRANGEMENT OF TRICKS. See LAWS OF CONTRACT BRIDGE (Law 66); LAWS OF DUPLICATE (Law 65).

COLLECTIONS OF PLAYING CARDS. These collections, public and private, are fairly numerous; quite a few museums have cards as part of their material on graphic arts.

The largest collection in the United States is in Cincinnati, Ohio, a gift of the United States Playing Card Company to the Museum of Art. In New York City, the Morgan Library has a few of the oldest and most valuable cards. Yale University has a collection of more than 3,000 packs, uncut sheets, and card printers' woodblocks acquired by the late Melbert and Mary Cary and willed to Yale University in 1967.

The French collection is in the Bibliothèque Nationale in Paris; London has two collections, one in the British Museum, the other in the Guildhall; others are in Vienna, Nuremberg, Dresden, Munich, and Budapest.

There are two associations of collectors of playing cards in the United States, some members collecting packs, while many collect only card backs.

COLLEGE BRIDGE. Colleges are fertile breeding grounds for bridge experts of the future. Most competition at college level has been on a national basis using computer-dealt hands which replaced par hands in 1969. (See INTERCOLLEGIATE BRIDGE TOURNAMENT.) The Eastern Collegiate Bridge League was formed in 1962, with two subdivisions. The New England Conference consists of Brandeis, Harvard, MIT, Massachusetts, Tufts, and Yale. The Mid-Atlantic Conference includes Columbia, Lafayette, Lehigh, Princeton, and Rutgers. Each college plays two 24-board matches (home and away) against each other within its own group, and the winners meet in a final to decide the "World Series of Eastern Intercollegiate Bridge."

COLLOQUIALISMS. Bridge has evolved or adopted its share of colloquialisms. For example, see the following: BIFF; BLOCKBUSTER; DEATH HOLDING; DUB; FIXED FRAME; GAME HOG; GOULASH; HOOK; HORSE AND HORSE; JUNK; KIBITZ; KICK IT; KILLED; LAY-DOWN; LOCK; MAMA-PAPA BRIDGE; MAYONNAISE; PALOOKA; PHANTOM SACRIFICE; PIANOLA; PUMP; PUNCH; QUACK; RAGS; RIDE; SHAKE; SOCK; STIFF; SUCKER'S DOUBLE; TANK; UNDER THE GUN; and UPPERCUT.

COLOMBIAN BRIDGE FEDERATION (FEDERACIÓN COLOMBIANA DE BRIDGE). Founded in 1963 by Jorge Ospina, Ivan Hoyos, Francisco Soto Pombo, Rodolfo Segovia, and Jorge Combariza, representing the various clubs of Bogotá, Medellín, Barranquilla, Cali, and Pereira; by 1969 there were approximately 500 members. The Federation participates in South American Championships and Caribbean Championships, and its international successes include South American Women's Teams 1968, 1970, second 1964, and the Caribbean Championship 1968. National Championships for Open Teams, Open Pairs, and Masters Pairs, and Regional tournaments are held annually. Colombian players listed separately are: J. Atuesta, A. Cahn-Speyer, Mrs. B. de Hoyos, A. Rivas, B. Rivas, Mrs. M. C. de Rivas, R. Savdie, Mrs. A. de Soto.

Officers, 1975–77:
President: Dr. Santiago Sondono White.
Secretary: Carlos Reyes Gomez, Carrera 13, No. 54–78 Of. 204, Bogotá, D.E., Colombia.

COLONIAL ACOL. A version of ACOL popular in Canada; its basic elements were used by all three Canadian pairs in the 1972 World Team Olympiad. Major features include four-card major suit openings (one club opening may be prepared). Jump raises are usually limit, with either SWISS, JACOBY TWO NO TRUMP, or SPLINTERS used to show a strong raise. One no trump opening is 16–18, although some shade it to 15–17, with TWO-WAY STAYMAN. Opening bids of two diamonds, two hearts, or two spades are ACOL TWO BIDS; some partnerships use FLANNERY TWO DIAMONDS.

COLOR. A term occasionally used to distinguish suit-play as opposed to no trump play. In the bidding, to "change the color" means to bid a new suit. The term is virtually synonymous with "suit."

COLORFUL CUE-BID. Devised by Mrs. D. TRUSCOTT of Riverdale, N.Y., this is an immediate overcall in the opponent's major suit to show two unbid suits of the same color. See also CUE-BIDS IN OPPONENT'S SUIT; MICHAELS CUE-BID.

COLUMNS. See BRIDGE COLUMNS.

COMBINATION TEAM SCORING. A method of scoring team-of-four events that permits comparison of pair scores as well as team scores. After award of team scores on a win-half-loss basis, the North-South scores are match-pointed on the basis of the number of times the board was played, and the East-West scores also match-pointed on the same basis.

In theory this combination team scoring permits a team to analyze its game as to which of the pairs contributed to the winning or losing of boards by securing a less-than-average result.

This is also the method by which team scores are computed on a board that has been fouled between the times that the two halves of the team play it; the fields resulting from the fouling are match-pointed separately, and the combination of the percentages of the possible match points totaled for the two team halves; such a total of less than 70 losing the board, exceeding 130 winning it, and between these percentages being awarded a half on the board.

COME-ON, COME-ON SIGNAL. A defensive maneuver by which one player indicates to his partner that he wishes a suit, led by his partner, to be continued. The usual come-on is a HIGH-LOW SIGNAL, called also an "echo," and in England, a PETER. An alternative is the UPSIDE-DOWN SIGNAL.

COMIC NO TRUMP OVERCALL. An overcall of one no trump to show a weak hand with a long suit. Partner bids two clubs to locate the long suit. See also GARDENER NO TRUMP OVERCALL.

COMM. & IND. Commercial and Industrial.

COMMAND BID. A term suggested by G. ROSEN-KRANZ to describe a bid which compels partner to make a specific response but which: a) Does not promise a holding of the commanded suit (compare TRANSFER BID); b) does not promise any particular strength (compare DEMAND BID); c) does not ask about the holding in any suit (compare ASKING BID). E.g., FLINT THREE DIAMONDS over two no trump; ROMEX two hearts, two spades, or two no trump over two diamonds.

COMMERCIAL AND INDUSTRIAL TEAMS. See UNITED STATES PLAYING CARD TROPHY.

COMMITTEE. In tournaments of the American Contract Bridge League of sectional or higher ranking, a committee from the sponsoring organization is charged with the responsibility of making necessary arrangements. This is known as the tournament committee. The work of this committee is divided into two parts, before and during the tournament. Among the pre-tournament duties are arrangements for location, dates, securing of sanctions, arrangements for services to the players, prizes, obtaining the services of a director, publicity, and financing.

During the course of a tournament, the director may be called on to make a ruling where he is unable to secure agreement on the facts under question. In such cases, and in cases where the director uses his discretionary powers, a player may, through the director, appeal to the tournament committee. Such an appeal is based on questions of fact, not of law. See Chapter XI, LAWS OF DUPLICATE CONTRACT BRIDGE.

Appeals to the national authority on matters of conduct, deportment, or ethics can be taken to the National Conduct, Deportment, and Ethics Committee, and on questions of law to the National Laws Commission.

Occasionally, the tournament committee delegates to a subcommittee (known as an appeals committee) its duties at a particular tournament. See NATIONAL APPEALS COMMITTEE.

COMMON MARKET CHAMPIONSHIPS. A biennial tournament held in Western Europe starting in 1967 for member countries of the European Common Market. The tournament consists of several team events in which each country may enter one team, and several pair events in which each country may be represented by a number of pairs.

COMMON-SENSE SYSTEM. See CRANE SYSTEM.

COMMUNICATION BETWEEN PARTNERS. The act of conveying information within a partnership. It is a breach of ethics when information is conveyed intentionally by a remark, gesture, or mannerism. See LAWS (Proprieties, I). Information can of course be conveyed legitimately by bids and defensive plays.

COMMUNICATION PLAY. A play intended to preserve or establish communication (transfer of the lead) between partnership hands to make it possible at the strategic time to lead from the right hand; or a play to destroy such means of communication between the opponents. Various plays of this nature are discussed in the following articles: DESCHAPELLES COUP; DUCKING; ENTRY; ENTRY-KILLING PLAY; HOLDUP; MERRIMAC COUP; SCISSORS COUP.

COMMUTER BRIDGE. A set-to at bridge on trains, popular in Boston, Chicago, New York, Philadelphia, and other cities. Players who regularly use the same train for commuting arrange to have the first player to enter the train reserve a double seat, and the other players use the same car, joining the game as soon as they board the train. In New York, the cards are dealt as the last player boards, and play is continued until the train reaches the Newark or One Hundred and Twenty-fifth Street station, after which no further hands are dealt.

Originally, running scores in the form of rubbers prevailed, continuing from day to day with settlement of the wagers made monthly, but in the sixties four-deal bridge (CHICAGO) gained ground.

COMPANY BRIDGE. See NATIONAL INDUSTRIAL RECREATION ASSOCIATION TOURNAMENT.

COMPARING SCORES. Discussion of results already achieved by contestants in a duplicate competition. Making such comparisons with other contestants playing the same board, in tournament play before the session's play has been completed, has long been held to be unethical. Since 1963 these comparisons have been declared illegal, and the director is authorized to assess penalties for them.

The private scores kept by many tournament players furnish material for long and involved discussions of what might have been, and are very useful for later study and as a reminder of holdings.

In club games where traveling score slips are used to facilitate the scoring of the game, knowledge of previous results on an individual board is legitimately available to the players after the board has been played. Courtesy requires that the player responsible for scoring the result make the slip available to the other players who are entitled to see it; discussion of previous results should be held in abeyance until after both (or all) the boards of the current round have been completed. Score comparison is not regarded with disfavor in Europe. Players may compare scores on boards already played by both partnerships unless specifically instructed to the contrary. See ESTIMATION.

COMPARISONS. At duplicate, comparisons are made between pairs (or players) who played a board in the same direction, and consequently under similar conditions of dealer, vulnerability, and holding. See BALANCED COMPARISONS.

COMPASS POINTS. In discussing bridge hands, columnists describe the four players by using the points of the compass to distinguish the players. Thus North and South compete against East and West. In tournament play, too, the table markers designate the seating of the players for the original deals by compass directions at designated tables. In the usual MITCHELL type of tournament competition, the North and South players remain in the same seats throughout, doing the scoring and passing the boards, while the East and West players move from table to table in a direction opposite that in which the boards are passed. In pair competition the boards are moved to the next lower numbered tables while the traveling players move to the next higher numbered table. In team play, boards and players both move in the same direction, boards to the next lower numbered table, and players to the table below that to which the boards are delivered.

COMPETITION. (1) Any duplicate bridge contest. See TOURNAMENT. (2) A bidding situation in which both sides are active. Some experts announce "limit raises in competition," meaning that a LIMIT RAISE would apply after an overcall.

COMPETITIVE BIDDING. Bidding sequences in which both partnerships enter the auction. Doubling situations are listed under DOUBLE. Other articles dealing with competitive bidding include: BALANCING; CUE-BIDS IN OPPONENT'S SUIT; DEFENSE TO DOUBLE OF ONE NO TRUMP; DEFENSE TO ONE NO TRUMP; DEFENSE TO OPENING FOUR-BID; DEFENSE TO OPENING THREE-BID; DEFENSE TO STRONG ARTIFICIAL OPENINGS; DEFENSE TO TWO-SUITED INTERFERENCE; DEFENSIVE BIDDING; DIRECTIONAL ASKING BID; DOUBLE JUMP OVERCALL; FORCING PASS; FREE BID; GARDENER NO TRUMP OVERCALL; JUMP OVERCALL; KOCK-WERNER REDOUBLE; LEAD-DIRECTING BID; LEBENSOHL; ONE NO TRUMP OVERCALL; OVERCALL; OVERCALL IN OPPONENT'S MAJOR SUIT; OVERCALL IN OPPONENT'S MINOR SUIT; PHANTOM SACRIFICE; POSITIONAL FACTOR; PRESSURE BID; PUSH; REDOUBLE; ROMAN JUMP OVERCALLS; RULE OF TOTAL TRICKS; S O S REDOUBLE; SAFETY LEVEL; SAVE; TWO NO TRUMP OVERCALL; UNUSUAL NO TRUMP; WEAK JUMP OVERCALL; WEAK NO TRUMP OVERCALL.

COMPETITIVE DOUBLE. A double in a competitive auction which invites partner to bid game but gives him the option of signing off in a part-score or passing for penalties. One increasingly popular example is the MAXIMAL OVERCALL DOUBLE. Competitive doubles can be useful in contested auctions where the enemy suit has been bid and raised at a low level:

SOUTH	WEST	NORTH	EAST
1 ♡	2 ♣	2 ♡	3 ♣
Pass	Pass	?	

North may hold

♠ A 7 4 3 ♡ J 6 2 ◇ A 10 9 4 ♣ 8 3

He is too strong to pass and his holding in clubs is too weak to make either a penalty double or a cooperative double, but his aces are useful for either offense or defense. Since South will usually not have sufficient values in the opponents' suit to double for penalties in such an auction, and since any unilateral action could easily be wrong, some experts prefer to use this double as competitive. It says: "Partner, I have a good hand with two-way values and don't know what to do; *you* decide."

Another typical competitive double occurs when the doubler's previous bidding shows that he cannot possibly be strong in the suit he is doubling.

SOUTH	WEST	NORTH	EAST
1 ◇	Pass	1 NT	2 ♠
Pass	Pass	?	

North cannot have as many as four good spades in view of his original one no trump response, and his location in front of the spade bidder is hardly ideal for defensive purposes. Thus a double is competitive, showing a hand such as:

♠ A 6 3 ♡ J 6 4 ◇ A 6 ♣ 10 9 7 4 3

Partner is asked to decide whether to play for the penalty, or bid on in no trump.

COMPLEMENTARY SCORES. When two contestants play against each other in a match-point contest, their combined match-point scores add up to the match-point top available on that board, and the two scores are complements of each other. For example, if top score is 12 points and the North-South pair earns 8 points, the opposing East-West pair earns 4 points. Similarly if one pair earns 2½ points, the opposing pair earns 9½ points.

COMPLETE THE CUT. See CUT (2).

COMPLETE TABLE. In rubber bridge, four or more players. In club bridge, club rules sometimes specify six players as constituting a complete table. When a table is complete, no other player may cut in until or unless one of the players withdraws.

The alternative procedure, common in England, is for players to cut into any table which has completed a rubber, provided only that three players may not cut in unless there is only one table in play. This arrangement produces a greater circulation of players.

COMPOUND SQUEEZE. A preparatory triple squeeze, followed by a double squeeze, analyzed exhaustively by Dr. Clyde LOVE. This ending requires two double menaces (guarded by both opponents) and a one-card menace. The one-card menace must be placed to the left of the opponent threatened. Declarer has all remaining tricks but one.

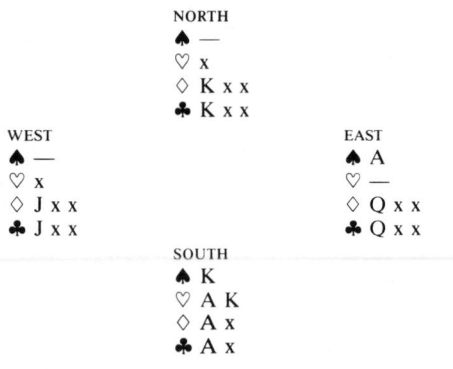

```
                  NORTH
                  ♠ —
                  ♡ x
                  ◊ K x x
                  ♣ K x x
WEST                              EAST
♠ —                              ♠ A
♡ x                              ♡ —
◊ J x x                          ◊ Q x x
♣ J x x                          ♣ Q x x
                  SOUTH
                  ♠ K
                  ♡ A K
                  ◊ A x
                  ♣ A x
```

South leads the ace of hearts, and East is squeezed in three suits. In order to avoid giving declarer a trick directly, East must unguard a minor suit. South cashes the king and ace of that suit, leaving West with the sole guard in that suit. Now the lead of South's remaining heart effects a double squeeze. Each of the double menaces must be accompanied by a winner in its suit to provide an entry.

The alternate threat squeeze is a hybrid form of compound squeeze with very special requirements.

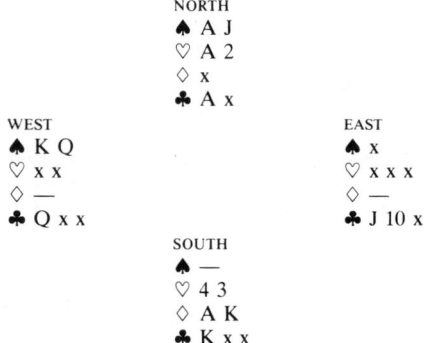

```
                  NORTH
                  ♠ A J
                  ♡ A 2
                  ◊ x
                  ♣ A x
WEST                              EAST
♠ K Q                            ♠ x
♡ x x                            ♡ x x x
◊ —                              ◊ —
♣ Q x x                          ♣ J 10 x
                  SOUTH
                  ♠ —
                  ♡ 4 3
                  ◊ A K
                  ♣ K x x
```

South leads the ace of diamonds, and West must discard one of his guards. Since a spade would give up a trick directly, West must throw a heart or a club. If he chooses a heart, the low heart is discarded by North on the king of diamonds continuation. Meanwhile, East has thrown a heart and a spade. Now a heart lead squeezes West (in spades and clubs), and the ace of spades which follows squeezes East (in hearts and clubs). If West chooses to discard a club on the ace of diamonds, declarer leads a club to the ace and cashes the ace of spades and returns to his hand with the king of clubs. Now the lead of the king of diamonds brings about a simultaneous double squeeze.

From this, the special requirements for this squeeze are: (1) a one-card menace accompanied by a winner and placed to the left of the threatened opponent; (2) a double menace (the alternate threat suit) accompanied by a winner and any two cards of that suit in the hand opposite.

In addition, the usual requirements for a compound squeeze must be present.

COMPOUND TRUMP SQUEEZE. A COMPOUND SQUEEZE in which at least one opponent is subject to a TRUMP SQUEEZE. The following ending was posed as a double dummy problem by William Whitfeld before 1900.

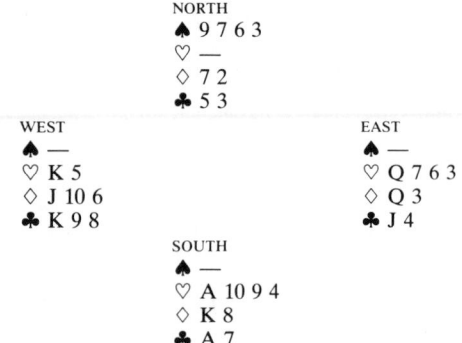

```
                  NORTH
                  ♠ 9 7 6 3
                  ♡ —
                  ◊ 7 2
                  ♣ 5 3
WEST                              EAST
♠ —                              ♠ —
♡ K 5                            ♡ Q 7 6 3
◊ J 10 6                         ◊ Q 3
♣ K 9 8                          ♣ J 4
                  SOUTH
                  ♠ —
                  ♡ A 10 9 4
                  ◊ K 8
                  ♣ A 7
```

South has the lead with spades as trumps and needs all the tricks.

South leads a low heart and trumps in dummy. A trump is led from dummy and East must discard a club or a diamond to avoid letting declarer establish an extra heart trick by ruffing. South discards whichever suit East discards, and leads that suit from dummy, winning in his hand. Declarer now cashes the ace of hearts, discarding a diamond from dummy, and leads a small heart, ruffing. When dummy's last trump is led, East obviously must keep his last heart and discard whichever minor suit he has retained. South discards his heart and West is squeezed in the minor suits.

R. T(rue)

COMPUTER-DEALT HANDS. An alternate expression for MACHINE-PREPARED HANDS, a modern method of presenting twinned hands for large tournament competition.

COMPUTERS (in their application to bridge organization). From 1961 to 1963 the ACBL used unit record equipment, and a staff of eight, to maintain master-point and membership records for 140,000 bridge players by a punched card method. This was superseded, in January 1964, by faster and more flexible magnetic tape equipment which is a form of computer with a "memory." This could be adapted for scoring a bridge tournament, and a nationwide tournament with an overall four-figure "top" became a possibility.

The first serious attempt to score a bridge tournament with computer assistance was in Ostend, Belgium, in the early fifties. The players used sensitized pencils to enter the scores on punched cards which were fed directly into a machine. Besides calculating the overall standings, the machine furnished each pair with a virtual reproduction of their personal score card, with the match points awarded on each board.

Other pioneering efforts were made in Denver in

1957, in the World Pair Olympiads in Cannes, France, 1962, Amsterdam, Holland, 1966, and Stockholm, Sweden, 1970, and in New York, N.Y., 1962. The many difficulties encountered were due partly to the difficulty of obtaining trained personnel and partly to the difficulty of dealing with fouled and protested boards. Many of these drawbacks were overcome in the 1970 Pair Olympiad when a new method, which had been used successfully in some of Europe's larger pair contests, was introduced. The boards were duplicated beforehand and each pair played the same boards simultaneously. After each round the scores were fed into the computer, and within minutes the match-point results for that round were posted.

The first application of computer scoring to an ACBL National Tournament was a highly organized large-scale effort. A Honeywell H-800 tallied the scores of each pair of players participating in the six-session Life Masters Pairs event held at the Biltmore Hotel in Los Angeles from July 28 to August 2, 1963.

Since the computer was located at a remote site, some five miles from where actual play was being conducted, a method of relaying all pertinent information concerning the play of the hands as quickly as possible had to be determined, as well as the return of the results to the participants themselves. This was accomplished in the following manner. Upon receipt of the individual tickets from the scoring staff of the ACBL, information was relayed by private telephone to a battery of key-punch operators who in turn punched this data onto standard 80-column tabulating cards in a pre-set format. The information punched on these cards was then read back via telephone against the original tickets for verification and checking purposes, to ensure a minimum of input error conditions for the computer. Once verified for accuracy, the score cards, each of which contained the result of a particular deal played by two pairs in a given section, were fed into the H-800 via a card reader at the rate of 650 cards per minute.

In addition to visual and verbal verification procedures, the computer program also checked all information which it received for any possible undetected errors, checking North-South and East-West pair numbers as a function of board and round numbers. Upon detection of such an error by the program, the erroneous score card would be re-punched and entered as a correction.

The computer program was equipped to handle such conditions as awarded scores due to fouled boards or penalties imposed, and to adjust the previous session's results if corrections were detected by the scorers or handed in by the players after completion of play. Cards containing the names of all pairs involved and their section, direction, and pair number assignments for a particular session were also entered for use on the printed output reports containing a breakdown of the results. Four types of reports, produced at the rate of 900 lines per minute, were generated by the H-800 following completion of the last round of play: an overall ranking of the top twenty pairs for the tournament to date; a list

of the scores of all individual pairs, section by section; a breakdown of the particular match-point awards for each raw score received on every board played; and a full recapitulation sheet for each section in the tournament.

Since the results were match-pointed dynamically as play progressed to a top score of 25, within minutes of transmission of the last score ticket, full results of the play of the session were available. All the above-mentioned reports were flashed back to the site of play via closed-circuit television monitors with the exception of the recapitulation sheet, which was returned to the hotel for posting.

CONCEDE. To yield one or more of the remaining tricks to the opponents. See LAWS (Laws 70, 73, 74); LAWS OF DUPLICATE (Laws 68, 70, 71).

CONCESSION. See CLAIM OR CONCESSION.

CONDITIONS OF CONTEST. A statement governing the competition in an event. In general there should be a preliminary statement as to the master-point requirements or other prerequisites for entry into the event, the number of sessions the event will run, the entry fee, how many qualifying sessions and how many final (or semi-final) sessions. In knockout team games there should also be a statement as to such matters as the number of boards to be played in each match; the seeding rights, i.e., the rights exercisable by the higher-ranked team with respect to the choice of seats and opponents; any restrictions on the right to have two pairs who played each other in the first half of the match play against each other in the second half; the method of resolution of the match in the event of a tie, and so forth. In SWISS MOVEMENT team games the conditions of contest must include statements as to the form of scoring used, including the scale of VICTORY POINTS, if any. In a pairs event a final statement, made up after the event is under way, includes the setup of the game, number to be qualified and method of qualification, whether at-large pairs will be qualified, and computation of the carryover, and the setup of the final (or semi-final) session(s).

CONDONING. An action immediately following an irregularity by the opposition which would have been a proper one if the preceding action had been proper.

At rubber bridge, an irregular bid can be condoned in this way unless the non-offending side has drawn attention to the irregularity. In duplicate such a bid can be condoned as a matter of law. In both forms of the game an irregular lead can be condoned in all circumstances. If a declarer leads from the wrong hand, a defender may follow in proper sequence, either on his own initiative or if his partner so requires. See LAWS 34, 53, 60; LAWS OF DUPLICATE (Laws 27, 53, 60).

CONDUCT. See ETHICS AND CONDUCT.

CONFEDERAÇAO BRASILEIRA DE BRIDGE. See BRAZILIAN BRIDGE FEDERATION.

CONFEDERACIÓN SUDAMERICANA DE BRIDGE. See SOUTH AMERICAN BRIDGE CONFEDERATION.

CONFERENCE. A voluntary association of neighboring ACBL units or districts organized to further the purposes of the ACBL and of its member units. The powers of a Conference are limited to those delegated to it by the member units. Among the reasons for organizing an ACBL Conference are the promotion of matters of mutual interest, such as tournament attendance, and the reduction of inter-unit and inter-district frictions.

CONGLOMERATE MAJOR RAISES. An extension of the SWISS CONVENTION designed to allow responder to make a forcing raise of a major suit opening while specifying whether it is based on a singleton somewhere in the hand, on great high-card strength, on very good trumps, or merely on general strength. Using the bids just beyond a jump raise (starting with three spades over one heart, or three no trump over one spade), responder bids as follows:

First step	shows a singleton (unidentified)
Second step	shows 17–18 HCP
Third step	shows four trumps headed by at least two of the top three honors, or more than four trumps headed by at least the ace or king
Fourth step	shows any hand worth a strong raise that does not meet the above criteria.

After responder has shown a singleton, opener can ask where it is by making the cheapest bid. Responder bids the suit of his singleton if he can do so without going past four of the trump suit; otherwise he bids four of the trump suit.

For alternative methods see SUPER SWISS, UNBALANCED SWISS RAISE, VALUE SWISS RAISES.

CONGRESS. Obsolete term for tournament, dating back to the days of whist.

CONOT TWO NO TRUMP. See ONE NO TRUMP OPENING (Responses).

CONSOLATION EVENT. In most SECTIONAL and higher rated TOURNAMENTS, the OPEN PAIR event and occasionally other events are held in two or more SESSIONS, one or more of which may be QUALIFYING SESSIONS. The players who do not qualify for the last session or sessions are eligible for competition in a secondary event played at the same time as the finals of the main event, which event is known as a CONSOLATION. In REGIONAL and NATIONAL TOURNAMENTS, where GOLD and RED POINTS are awarded for the main event, the consolation event awards are also partially in red points, and the balance in regular master points. See also SECONDARY EVENT.

CONSTRUCTIVE. A description applied to a bid that suggests game prospects but is not forcing. The partner will take further action more often than not. See ENCOURAGING (1).

SOUTH	WEST	NORTH	EAST
1 ♣	1 ♠	Pass	2 ◊

Some players treat East's bid of two diamonds as *constructive,* implying game ambitions; others regard it as *unconstructive,* expecting it to be passed unless West has a diamond fit.

CONSULTATION. This practice between partners regarding a penalty is forbidden under Law 11, LAWS OF DUPLICATE, and any such discussion cancels the right to penalize.

CONTESTANT. One or more players competing for a combined score. In an individual contest, each player enters as an individual, changing partners as the movement requires and receiving credit for his own score on each board he plays. In a pair contest, players enter as pairs, playing with the same partner throughout for a common score on all boards played. In a team contest, players enter as a team of four or more, changing partners among their own teammates as permitted by the tournament director, but competing for a common score.

CONTESTED AUCTION. See COMPETITIVE BIDDING.

CONTINENTWIDE GAMES. Four times annually, in conjunction with each national tournament and during the month of January, the ACBL conducts a game that is played at separate sites throughout the North American continent. All sections in each game are conducted virtually simultaneously, and the ACBL provides computer-dealt hands, one set for each section, so that all sections play identical hands. At the conclusion of the game the participants are provided with printed copies of the first thirty-six deals, accompanied by expert analyses. After comparing scores sent in from each game site, the ACBL determines a winner and runner-up on a best percentage score basis for each of its twenty-five districts and an overall winner and runner-up for the entire continent. For results, see Appendix I. The record winning score in a continentwide game is 82.95%, recorded in the March 1971 game. The low record for a winning score is 72.9% in the Fall 1966 game. The largest continentwide game, 17,524 pairs, was held during the 1972 Spring Nationals.

Continentwide games are conducted for the benefit of three special funds. The receipts of the games held at the Spring and Fall Nationals are donated to the ACBL Charity Foundation (see CHARITY PROGRAM OF THE ACBL). Proceeds from the Summer National continentwide game, for the Olympiad Fund, are distributed proportionally, according to the number of participants, to the four countries that comprise the ACBL (Bermuda, Canada, Mexico, and the United States) to assist in sending teams and pairs to World Olympiad contests. The monies raised by the January International Fund continentwide game are used to defray the expense of sending a North American team to the annual competition for the BERMUDA BOWL.

The first continentwide game was held at the Summer Nationals in 1962. At that time it was known as a nationwide game, but the name was changed to the present title prior to the Fall Nationals in 1964. All of the earliest games held at the nationals were for the benefit of charity, but in 1967, the Summer event became the Olympiad Fund continentwide game. The International Fund game was first held in 1966.

Each unit and affiliated club is invited to participate in the continentwide game by conducting a section of the event in its own playing quarters. The conditions under which a unit or club may participate are published by the ACBL shortly before each contest. All sections of the events are awarded master points on a sectional rating scale for each individual section.

Any unit or club may award prizes to the winners of its own game, if it so desires. See also OMNIUM.

CONTRACT. (1) The undertaking by declarer's side to win, at the denomination named, the number of odd tricks specified in the final bid, whether undoubled, doubled, or redoubled. (2) The game of contract bridge, loosely. See TRUMP SUIT.

CONTRACT BRIDGE. Fourth in the succession of partnership card games that began with WHIST and continued with BRIDGE WHIST and AUCTION BRIDGE. The essential point of difference from its predecessor is that no tricks won in the play are counted toward game except those which are contracted for in the bidding. A declarer contracting for and making 100 points in trick score has made a game and become vulnerable. Game contracts are: three no trump (first trick worth 40, and subsequent tricks 30 each); four of a major suit, hearts or spades, worth 30 each; five of a minor suit, diamonds or clubs, worth 20 each. The lowest bid in the auction is one club, followed by one of diamonds, hearts, spades, or no trump, and so on up to seven of any suit or no trump. It must be noted that a call of a higher number of tricks outranks a bid of a lower number, even though the lower number bid may be valued at a higher trick count. Contracts may be doubled, to increase premiums and penalties. There are bonuses for contracts of six and seven, called small and grand slams. See SCORING; MAJORITY CALLING.

Sides may be predetermined if two partnerships are pre-established. Otherwise the cards are CUT to establish partnerships and, in any case, to determine the first dealer. Partners face each other in seats arbitrarily named for compass points, North and South opposing East and West. The player at the dealer's left shuffles the cards and presents them to the dealer, who offers them to the player at his right for a cut. Normally, two decks of fifty-two cards are used, the dealer's partner shuffling the second deck and placing them after shuffling at his right, from where the next dealer offers the cards to the previous dealer for a cut. The dealer distributes the cards one at a time to each player in a clockwise manner beginning with the player on his left, and taking the last card himself, ending with each player having before him a hand of thirteen cards. The players study their hands, and the bidding period begins.

The dealer has the opportunity to open the bid-

ding, or he may pass. During the bidding, correct procedure requires that bids be made in a uniform manner, as, "pass," "one spade," "double," etc. Any variation from the standard formula is improper, as also are any gestures, remarks, mannerisms, or grimaces. See PROPRIETIES. The auction proceeds until three players have passed in succession following the last bid, double, or redouble. If all four players pass, the deal is abandoned and the next player deals. (In CHICAGO, the same dealer redeals.) At the end of the bidding, the declarer is determined as that player of the partnership who first named the denomination, suit, or no trump, of the final bid. This completes the bidding phase of the hand.

The player to the left of the declarer has the duty of making the OPENING LEAD. After he has led a card, declarer's partner places his hand face up on the table, and the play of his cards is at the management of the declarer. See ARRANGING.

The play consists of thirteen tricks, to each of which each player contributes one card in proper clockwise sequence. To each trick each player must play a card of the suit led, if able. If unable, he may play any card. Any trick containing a trump is won by the highest trump; any trick not containing a trump is won by the highest card of the suit led. The winner of each trick has the right and duty of leading to the next trick.

The declarer then attempts to make his contract, by taking as many tricks in excess of six as his final contract specified he would take. If he succeeds, he enters his trick points BELOW THE LINE and any extra tricks or bonuses he may have earned ABOVE THE LINE. When a partnership's total of trick points exceeds 100, that partnership is vulnerable, and a new GAME is started from a zero trick score on each side. The side first winning two games gets the bonus for winning the RUBBER. See SCORING.

If the declarer fails to make his contract, his opponents score points above the line for each UNDER-TRICK. These points are increased if the contract has been DOUBLED or REDOUBLED during the period of the auction.

The game grew out of its predecessor, Auction Bridge, via "contract auction" in the US and PLAFOND in France, in which the idea of trick score only for contracted tricks was introduced. It was not until 1925 however that Contract Bridge was devised and named by Harold VANDERBILT, who practiced and perfected the new scoring system while on an ocean trip from Los Angeles to Havana. Changes in the scoring since 1925 were fairly frequent in the early days, but minor in character.

Vanderbilt's contract bridge caught on very rapidly with many players of the game, but for several years there was no formal regulation of bridge, and in many clubs both auction and contract bridge were played. Rules adopted by the card committee of the WHIST CLUB (NYC) were probably the most widely used. Earlier laws produced by R. F. Foster and the Knickerbocker Whist Club were withdrawn in favor of the Whist Club version.

The first issue of *The Bridge World* magazine, edited by Ely CULBERTSON, in October 1929, advocated the promulgation of an international Code of Laws for Contract Bridge. Subsequently, committees representing the United States, England, and France were appointed, and the first International Code became effective November 1, 1932. See LAWS OF CONTRACT BRIDGE.

In September 1930, Ely Culbertson published his *Contract Bridge Blue Book,* which became a best seller, and appeared in annual revisions for four years (see BIBLIOGRAPHY). It was Culbertson, through his writings, his personality, his lectures, and his organization, who was most responsible for the wide vogue the game quickly attained. The international publicity resulting from the famous CULBERTSON-LENZ MATCH in 1931 and the ANGLO-AMERICAN MATCHES in 1930, 1933, and 1934 made the new game of Contract Bridge a household word. Although Culbertson's was the first widely accepted system of bidding in Contract Bridge, it became outmoded, and numerous other systems of bidding have come to the fore since his day. The GOREN methods, based on POINT-COUNT valuation, which became standard in the United States after 1950, are based firmly on the foundations laid by Culbertson.

CONTRACT BRIDGE ASSOCIATION OF IRELAND. Founded in Dublin in 1930, and controls the game in the twenty-six southern counties of Ireland. A group of individuals managed it until 1937, when numerical and geographical growth made it necessary to change to affiliated club membership, and the Association became a purely organizing body. In 1974 there were more than 300 clubs divided into ten regions, with a membership of over 12,000. Ireland hosted the 1967 European Championships in Dublin. For international participation, see IRISH BRIDGE UNION. Competitions include Open Teams and Pairs Championships, with twenty open Congresses held annually at different times of the year. Players listed separately are: Mrs. O. G. Giddings, J. Kelly, J. P. McHale, Mrs. I. McMenamin, E. McNeill, P. Pigot, G. F. Read, B. Seligman, Dr. M. Shrage.

Secretary, 1975: Col R. Dalton, 17 St. Johns Rd., Dublin 4, Ireland.

CONTRACT BRIDGE ASSOCIATION OF POLAND (POLSKI ZWIAZEK BRYDZA SPORTOWEGO). Founded in 1956 and known until 1962 as the Polish Bridge Union; by 1975 it had a membership of 6,200 in 547 clubs. The Association participates in European Championships, hosting the 1966 event in Warsaw and finishing second in 1970, annually sponsors the Baltic Bowl competition (see BALTIC CONGRESS), and took part in World Olympiads in 1962, 1964, 1966, 1970, 1972, and 1974. National Championships are held annually for Open Teams (a league event, divided into divisions, with automatic promotion and relegation of the winning and losing teams), Open Pairs, Mixed Teams, Mixed Pairs, and an Individual. Except for the Open Teams, national events are conducted on a multi-stage elimination method, also used to select Poland's international team. In 1968, more than 500 teams participated in

the Open Teams event, and 3,500 players contested for the Open Pairs title. The Association also awards master points and publishes a monthly magazine, *Brydz.* Polish players listed separately are: Dr. S. Achmatowicz, S. Bitner, Mrs. I. Czekańska, J. Czekański, J. Elżanowski, M. Frenkiel, L. Grosfeld, A. Jaworski, K. Jedrzejowski, M. Kasprzak, Mrs. E. Klukowska, J. Klukowski, Mrs. J. Krogulska, Z. Krogulski, C. Kuklewicz, L. Lebioda, S. Lowiński, A. Macieszczak, L. Michniewski, H. Niedźwiecki, J. Nowak, A. Olszewski, K. Pawlik, J. Poiec, F. Poprawa, A. Rożecki, A. Simon, Dr. J. Stachowicz, Z. Szurig, K. Wagrodzki, J. Wieczorkiewicz, A. Wilkosz, J. Wiśniewski, J. Wolosewicz.

Officers, 1975:
Chairman: F. Poprawa.
Secretary: Leonard Michniewski, Kniewskiego 9/4, Warsaw, Poland.

CONTRACT BRIDGE LAWS. For rubber bridge, see LAWS OF CONTRACT BRIDGE; for duplicate bridge, see LAWS OF DUPLICATE; for Chicago, see CHICAGO.

CONTRACT BRIDGE LEAGUE OF THAILAND. Founded in 1947 by Lt. William Howard Hunter, and in 1964 numbered 26 members. The League participates in World Team Olympiads and Far Eastern Championships, winning the event in 1961, 1963, 1965, and 1966. In 1966 Thailand became the first representative of the Far East Bridge Federation to participate in the Bermuda Bowl, and also represented the FEBF in the 1967 World Championships. Players listed separately are: Dr. T. Charusorn, B. Gimkiewicz, S. Nandhabiwat, K. W. Shen, Col. B. Soralampa, K. Suchartkul, Col. T. Sudasna, Dr. S. Unakul, M. Veeraburus.

Officers, 1975:
President: Air Marshal Suan Sukserm.
Secretary: Pitswong Guna Tilaka, Box 2588, Bangkok, Thailand.

CONTRACT GOLF. See GOLF.

CONTRACT WHIST. A cross between WHIST and CONTRACT BRIDGE. The four players bid in turn for the contract, but the play is that of whist, with all four hands concealed. The principles of the game were set forth in *Contract Whist,* by Hubert Phillips, published in 1932. It is played only occasionally, although considered by some to be a game requiring high skill.

CONTRACTING. A word which signifies the act of agreeing to take a certain number of tricks in a deal of bridge.

CONTRACTING SIDE. Declarer and his partner. The opponents are the defending side.

CONTROL MAINTENANCE. A strategy aimed at preventing a defender from gaining the mastery of a particular suit. In no trump hands, HOLD-UP PLAY is the key to control. In trump play, control usually refers to the struggle against a defender holding trump length. The following example is from Terence Reese's book *Reese on Play:*

A fairly well-known stratagem to avoid losing control of trumps is to refuse to ruff until dummy can cope with the suit which the opponents have led:

NORTH
♠ Q 10 8
♡ 9 8
◇ Q J 8 7
♣ K 9 8 7

WEST
♠ 7 6
♡ Q J 10 7 6
◇ A 9 4
♣ J 6 3

EAST
♠ 5 4 3 2
♡ K 5 4 3 2
◇ 10 5
♣ 10 2

SOUTH
♠ A K J 9
♡ A
◇ K 6 3 2
♣ A Q 5 4

The queen of hearts is led against four spades. If declarer draws three or four rounds of trumps, the 4–2 split is fatal for him. The right play is to draw two rounds of trumps and then clear diamonds. West wins with the ace and plays a second heart; South discards a club from hand and any further heart leads can be dealt with in dummy.

In the play of this hand declarer used two stratagems to protect himself from losing control; one was to clear the side suit before drawing trumps, and the other was to refuse to ruff the second heart.

CONTROL SWISS CONVENTION. See SWISS CONVENTION.

CONTROLLED PSYCHICS. See PSYCHIC CONTROLS.

CONTROLS. (1) Generally, holdings that prevent the opponents' winning one, two, or conceivably three immediate tricks in a specified suit.

First-round control: ace, or a void in a trump contract.
Second-round control: king, or a singleton in a trump contract.
Third-round control: queen, or a doubleton in a trump contract.
Controls may be discovered or revealed by means of ASKING BIDS or CUE-BIDS.
(2) Specifically, aces and kings. An ace is normally counted as two "controls," and a king as one. See BLUE TEAM CLUB.
See also EXPECTED NUMBER OF CONTROLS IN BALANCED HAND.

CONVENTION. A call that, by agreement, not inference, gives or requests information unrelated to the denomination named, as defined by the ACBL for its convention classification system. For example, if a bid of one club is understood to mean possession of general strength not necessarily in the club suit, or

perhaps not in the club suit at all, that is a convention, for ordinarily the bid of one club implies the bidder's willingness to play the hand at a club contract—that is, it implies the possession of general strength with either length or strength in the club suit. See ARTIFICIAL BID and LAWS OF DUPLICATE (Law 40). In addition, a play by a defender that conveys a meaning by agreement rather than by inference is a convention.

The ACBL lists bidding conventions that are acceptable in tournament play. Prior to 1969, these were listed in two general categories: Class I, those automatically allowed in all tournaments, and Class II, those dependent on the discretion of the tournament committee. With the increasing proliferation of conventions, the League adopted new regulations in 1969 and 1970. All conventions were placed in five general classes, A, B, C, D, and E, and, effective January 1, 1971, a new CONVENTION CARD and an alert procedure were introduced. Emphasis shifted from listing all partnership bidding agreements to listing only the most common understandings and ALERTING the opponents to special conventions and treatments. For this purpose, bids were classified as follows:

Convention: A call that, by agreement, not inference, gives or requests information unrelated to the denomination named.

TREATMENT: A call that indicates desire to play in the denomination named (or promises or requests values in that denomination) but that also, by agreement, gives or requests information on which further action can be based.

NATURAL CALL: A call that suggests itself as the final contract, without giving additional information on which further action could be based.

All natural calls and treatments were allowed in every class game; only conventions were subject to regulation. However, every player became responsible for alerting his opponents whenever his partner used an unusual treatment, or convention, not checked off on the convention card. In addition, a player must use the alert procedure unless his opponents specifically request him not to do so before the auction begins.

In 1975 the following bidding conventions were listed:

CLASS A

[Must be allowed in all local or higher-rated events except as noted above.]
Blackwood, and conventions to handle interference with Blackwood.
Gerber.
Grand Slam Force.
Stayman Club response to NT.
Lightner Double.
Take-out Double.
Unusual No Trump (by an unpassed hand must be at two-level or higher).
S O S Redouble.
Cue-bid for strong take-out.
2 club opening, forcing, strong, and artificial.
2 diamond negative response to forcing 2 club opening.
2 NT negative response to strong 2 opening bid.

CLASS B

[Must be allowed in championship events with sectional or higher rating.]
Negative Double.
4 NT slam conventions (Blackwood variations, San Francisco, etc.).
4 Club slam conventions (Gerber variations, etc.).
2 NT over opponent's take-out double as a conventional raise.
Stayman diamond response to NT.
Take-out bids over opponent's pre-empts.
Transfers (Jacoby & Texas).
Gambling 3 NT (maximum one side stopper).
Over opponent's 1 NT opening: 2 clubs for majors; 2 clubs for minors, 2 diamonds for majors; better minor for major suit take-out.
1 NT response to major forcing.
Defenses after opponents' conventional calls.
1 club forcing.
1 diamond artificial negative response to 1 club opening.
2 diamond artificial response to natural 2 club opening.
Second negative response after artificial forcing opening bid.

CLASS C

[Must be allowed in regional or higher-rated events.]
Asking bids (suit control and trump quality asking).
Flint (3 diamonds or 3 clubs).
Jump to 2 NT or 3 NT as forcing raise.
Jump and double-jump shift to show forcing raise.
Cue-bid for light take-out or two-suit take-out.
Responsive doubles.
Conventional responses and rebids after weak two-bids.
Conventional responses to natural strong two-bids.
Checkback or delayed Stayman.
Astro.
Brozel.
Calls which by agreement reveal a psych.
Drury.
Flannery 2 diamond opening.
Impossible negative.

CLASS D

[Must be allowed in national championship events.]
Strong ace asking other than 4 clubs or 4 NT.
Other artificial responses and rebids after natural NT.
2 diamond openings: Roman, Schenken, Precision, Stayman, Mexican.
Flannery 2 hearts.
Double of 3 NT for lead of specified suit.
Negative Slam Double.
Opening 2 NT or higher for minors.
1 NT overcall for take-out.
Balancing 2 clubs for take-out.
Competitive doubles.
Opening 4 clubs and 4 diamond transfers.
Artificial and step responses to artificial forcing opening bids.
Roman 2 suit jump overcalls.
2 club or 2 diamond opening (three suiter) at or near minimum opening.

CLASS E

[May be used only if approved in advance on Form 505 or approved by the Tournament Committee for extended team play.]
Herbert responses to take-out doubles and one-bids.
Strong artificial 1 diamond opening bid.
Dynamic 1 NT openings.
TAM II 2 diamonds.
Two suit non-forcing 2 club opening.

CLASS F

[May not be authorized for use in other than extended team play — matches of 16 boards or more.]
Big Diamond System, Pro System, Lea System, Roman System.

For descriptions and evaluations of these and other conventions see Kearse, *Bridge Conventions Complete,* BIBLIOGRAPHY, E.

CONVENTION CARD. In tournament bridge, the opponents are entitled to know the meaning of all bids made by a team. If any bid conveys a meaning to a partner that the opponents could not be expected to recognize, or that is not the standard meaning the bid would have, it is a "conventional bid." See CONVENTION and ARTIFICIAL BID. See also ALERTING. In order to facilitate such exchange of information, a card, on which generally used conventions and treatments may be checked off and which provides space to list other conventional bids, is provided. This convention card is often on the back of the card on which a partnership can keep a record of their scores on the boards played. See PRIVATE SCORE CARD.

CONVERSATION. Conversation is carried on at the bridge table in the LANGUAGE of the bidding and the play of the cards. Any other conversation during the bidding or play of the hand is either distracting (and therefore discourteous), revealing (and therefore improper and even illegal), or misleading. (See COFFEE-HOUSING, legal at poker but not at bridge.) Although bridge is a social game, any socializing or gossiping should be confined to the short period of the deal, or prior to the start of the game, or during a refreshment intermission.

COOPERATIVE DOUBLE. A double that leaves partner the option of passing for penalties or bidding further. (A special type is the OPTIONAL DOUBLE.) Originally used by Culbertson to describe a double of an opening three-bid, the term is now better reserved for some more complicated situations:

SOUTH	WEST	NORTH	EAST
1 ♡	1 ♠	2 ♡ or	2 ♠
		1 NT	
Pass	Pass	Dbl.	

As North's first bid showed limited strength, he is unlikely to have a hand on which he can be confident of defeating two spades. The double is a suggestion which leaves the final decision to South.

SOUTH	WEST	NORTH	EAST
1 ♣	Pass	Pass	Dbl.
1 ♠	2 ◇	Pass	Pass
Dbl.			

In the light of his previous bidding, South can hardly have any positive assurance of defeating two diamonds. He obviously has a maximum one-bid, perhaps 20 high-card points and 4–3–1–5 distribution. North has to consider whether he can contribute anything to the defense, and may decide to bid two spades, three clubs, two hearts, or pass.

This type of double can occur in many disguises, but the doubler has always limited his hand in such a way that he cannot be in a position to guarantee a penalty. See also COMPETITIVE DOUBLE; DOUBLE; MAXIMAL OVERCALL DOUBLE; OPTIONAL DOUBLE.

COPENHAGEN CONVENTION. A defensive bid designed by John TRELDE of Denmark to show a two-suited hand. After an opening bid, a jump to two no trump shows the two lowest unbid suits, three clubs the lowest and highest unbid suits, and three diamonds the two highest unbid suits.

CORRECT THE COUNT. See RECTIFYING THE COUNT.

CORRECT PACK. See PACK.

COUNT. A term used in three distinct senses, referring to: (1) the number of cards held in a suit, see COUNTING THE HAND, FOSTER ECHO, LENGTH SIGNALS, TRUMP ECHO; (2) the strength of a hand, see DISTRIBUTIONAL COUNTS, POINT-COUNT; (3) the number of tricks that must be lost for the operation of a squeeze; see RECTIFYING THE COUNT, SQUEEZE WITHOUT THE COUNT.

COUNT SQUEEZE. A squeeze that operates on a player who does not guard a crucial suit in such a way as to give declarer a count of the suit, allowing him to drop an honor off-side instead of taking a losing finesse.

```
                NORTH
              ♠ A Q
              ♡ K
              ◇ —
              ♣ —
 WEST                        EAST
 ♠ x x                       ♠ K
 ♡ A                         ♡ —
 ◇ —                         ◇ —
 ♣ —                         ♣ x x
                SOUTH
              ♠ x
              ♡ x
              ◇ —
              ♣ A
```

Suppose that West is known to have the ace of hearts. South leads the ace of clubs and West discards a spade. North can safely discard the king of hearts. South leads a spade, and West follows low. North's ace must be played for it is known that West's remaining card is the ace of hearts. If West had guarded spades, he would have been caught in a SHOW-UP SQUEEZE.

M. I.

COUNT, SQUEEZE WITHOUT THE. See SQUEEZE WITHOUT THE COUNT.

COUNTING CARDS. It is each player's responsibility to determine that the hand he is about to play contains exactly thirteen cards. This determination should be made before he looks at the face of any card. The LAWS (Law 7) OF DUPLICATE BRIDGE also require that the cards be recounted before being replaced in the board at completion of play.

COUNTING THE HAND. Deducing the distribution of the hidden hands from information gained during the bidding and early stages of play.

On many hands, the crucial play depends on the distribution of one particular suit. By observing or projecting the distributions of the other three suits, a player may be able to deduce how the key suit splits, *even if that suit has not yet been led.*

The procedure used is simple arithmetic, based on two facts: each suit has thirteen cards; each player started with thirteen cards in his hand.

The following is an elementary illustration of the basic technique of counting the hand: A decision which at first glance is a pure guess reduces to a certainty as a result of the play of the other suits.

WEST	EAST
♠ A Q 7	♠ K 5 3
♡ K Q 6	♡ A 4 2
◇ A K J 3	◇ Q 8 4 2
♣ A J 5	♣ K 10 3

West plays seven no trump, with the jack of spades led. He should delay his decision in clubs to the very end, by first cashing all his winners. South follows twice to each major, but discards clubs on the third round of each. He then follows to three rounds of diamonds, while North discards a heart on the third round. Now, by subtraction, North is known to have started with five cards in each major and two diamonds, hence only one club. So West cashes dummy's king of clubs, and (unless North drops the queen) finesse through South with certainty.

In the above example, counting the hand made declarer's final play a sure thing. More often, counting will indicate which play has the highest probability of success.

Suppose South had followed to four diamonds. Now it would be known that he started with five clubs, and North with two clubs. Then West should finesse through South as before, this time with odds of five to two that South has the missing queen. (When declarer finally takes the finesse, each defender has only one unknown card, but the odds determined from the count of the *initial* distribution are unchanged.) See PROBABILITIES, A POSTERIORI and A PRIORI.

In the illustration above, declarer's problem was simply which way to take a finesse. Sometimes counting the hand will help declarer decide between a squeeze and a finesse. Sometimes it will point up the necessity to handle a problem suit in a way radically different from what he would otherwise have attempted.

WEST	EAST
♠ A K Q	♠ 7 5 3
♡ A K Q	♡ 6 4 2
◇ A Q 8	◇ K 7 3
♣ K Q 7 3	♣ A 10 4 2

Again West plays seven no trump, with the jack of spades led. Apparently West must cash king and queen of clubs, hoping that North has two or more clubs or that the jack is singleton. But before playing clubs, West should cash his major-suit winners. On the third round of each, South discards diamonds. West then cashes the ace and queen of diamonds, and both opponents follow. Counting North's hand—five spades, five hearts, and two diamonds—shows that he has at most one club, which must be the eight, nine, or jack if West is to make the contract. So West abandons the normal play in clubs, and instead leads the three to dummy's ace. If North follows with the eight or nine, declarer leads a club from dummy and covers South's card, using the carefully preserved king of diamonds as a re-entry for a second finesse if South splits his holding.

The preceding examples were played at no trump, so declarer could count the hand by cashing his winners, and noting when the opponents showed out. In a suit contract, this type of play runs the risk of the opponents gaining a ruff. However, in a suit contract, declarer may be able to count the hand by using *his own* trumps for ruffing. For example, if dummy has A K x x in a side suit, and declarer has two small, declarer may be able to ruff the suit twice in his hand. He does not gain any tricks by doing this, as his long trumps were winners anyhow. In fact, in the process of ruffing he destroys any squeeze or throw-in threat in the suit. But he is sure to obtain the count of the suit, if that is the crucial factor in the play of the rest of the hand.

So far, we have considered only cases where declarer's information on the count was gained during the play. Inferences about suit lengths may also be drawn from the opponents' bidding (or failure to bid), from the opening lead, or from defenders' plays or signals (see DISCOVERY). These inferences are, of course, not as firm as when a player fails to follow suit.

Defensive Play. Counting the hand is as important for the defenders as for the declarer.

NORTH (Dummy)
♠ K J
♡ 10 5 3
◇ A 8 6 3
♣ A 8 7 2

EAST
♠ A Q 6
♡ J 9 7 6
◇ Q J 10
♣ J 9 5

South plays in five diamonds, no other suits having been bid. West leads the five of spades. East wins and leads a second high spade, which South ruffs. South cashes king and ace of diamonds; West follows once, then discards a spade. South now cashes the ace, king, and queen of hearts (West following three times), then leads a diamond. East wins and counts declarer's hand—one spade, three hearts, five diamonds, therefore four clubs. So East does not fall for declarer's trap, and return a club, jeopardizing West's doubleton king or queen. Instead he leads a major, yielding a useless sluff-ruff, and eventually sets the hand with a club trick.

In addition to absolute counts, as in the above example, and inferential counts from the bidding, the defenders have a counting aid not available to the declarer—the LENGTH SIGNAL. Most experts use such signals sparingly, to help partner in the play of one specific suit. The policy of some experts is to signal length in all suits, when they think partner will profit more than declarer from a complete count of the hand.

In general, when partner is unlikely to be misled, a defender should make it as difficult as possible for declarer to count the hand. For instance, if a suit has gone around three times, the defender should retain the thirteenth card as long as possible, to keep declarer in doubt as to its location. It is usually wrong for a defender's first discard to be a worthless card in a suit where he has five cards and dummy has four cards—an astute declarer may be able to use this inference in counting the hand.

For a full discussion of counting, see *All Fifty-Two Cards (How to Reconstruct the Concealed Hands at the Bridge Table)* by Marshall MILES (BIBLIOGRAPHY, D). See also CARD READING.

L. R.

COUP. A special maneuver by declarer in the play of the hand. More specifically, without further designation, it refers to an end play situation in which a defender's finessable trumps are trapped without a finesse. This may arise when there is no entry to take a finesse, or when there is no trump to lead for a finesse. Often the coup has to be prepared by shortening the trump length, reducing it to not more than the same length as the defender's. For example:

NORTH
♠ A Q 9 5 2
♡ K
◇ K J 6 4
♣ 8 4 2

WEST	EAST
♠ 10 6	♠ J 7 3
♡ 7	♡ Q 9 8 5 3
◇ A 10 9 7 5 3	◇ Q 8 2
♣ A Q J 3	♣ 9 7

SOUTH
♠ K 8 4
♡ A J 10 6 4 2
◇ —
♣ K 10 6 5

South plays in four hearts after West has shown minor suits by an unusual no trump overcall. The diamond ace is led and ruffed, and a heart is led to the king. South cashes the diamond king, ruffs a diamond, and plays three rounds of spades ending in dummy. A spade is ruffed, and a club is played. South must eventually make his two remaining trumps.

When the preparation of the coup makes it necessary to ruff a winner, the term GRAND COUP is used. Single, double, and triple grand coups refer to situations in which one, two, and three winners are ruffed respectively.

For the term coup applied in other special contexts, see ALCATRAZ; BATH COUP; COUP EN PASSANT; DESCHAPELLES COUP; MERRIMAC COUP; MORTON'S FORK COUP; PITT COUP; ROBERT COUP; SCISSORS COUP.

COUP EN BLANC. A term formerly used by some writers instead of DUCK.

COUP EN PASSANT. The lead of a plain suit card to promote a low trump behind a higher trump to a winning position. The term is taken from chess. See also ELOPEMENT.

In the following position, spades are trump. The lead is in the North hand.

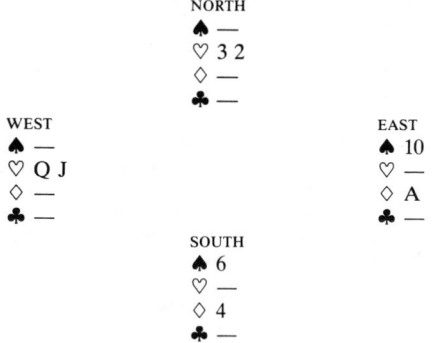

Declarer (South) holds no more winning cards. However, when a heart is led from the North hand, South makes a trick with the six of spades. If East discards, South ruffs the heart. If East ruffs with his master trump, the six of spades wins the final trick. In the above example, if East held 10 5 of spades, South would score the spade six "en passant" in a similar manner, overruffing if East ruffed low and discarding if East ruffed high.

COUP WITHOUT A NAME. See SCISSORS COUP.

COURT CARDS. The king, queen, and jack of each suit are represented by coated figures rather than pips, giving rise to the expression "coat card." This term was corrupted to "court card," and extended to include the ace, probably due to the association with the figures in a royal court.

COURTESY. Any bridge player should, at all times,

maintain a courteous attitude toward his partner and his opponents. See LAWS OF DUPLICATE, Proprieties, Section III. Also, see ETIQUETTE.

COURTESY BID. A response made on a very weak hand to allow for the possibility that the opener has great strength.

COURTESY OF THE TABLE. A feature of the laws of auction bridge, and the first laws of contract bridge. If dummy left the table, the defenders were required to take over dummy's duty of guarding declarer against the possibility of revoking. No penalty could be exacted against a declarer who revoked if the defenders had failed to ask the routine question, "Having no more?"

It was customary, although not legally necessary, for the dummy to ask for the "Courtesy of the Table" on leaving the table. This served to remind the defenders of their obligation in the matter.

This requirement was omitted from the first International edition of the LAWS, published in 1932.

COVERING HONORS. When an honor is led and the next player follows with a higher honor, he is said to have covered an honor with an honor. Second hand should usually cover an honor if he might establish a trick in that suit for himself or partner in the process.

If an honor is led from a sequence of touching honors, it is seldom proper to cover until the last of the sequentials is led. The following examples are typical:

(a)	NORTH	
	A x x	
WEST		EAST
K x x		10 x x
	SOUTH	
	Q J 9 x	

The queen is led. If West covers, then South can take a finesse against the ten. West must duck the first honor lead but cover at the second opportunity.

If West does cover, he can be expected to hold K, K x, or K 10.

(b)	NORTH	
	K x x	
WEST		EAST
Q x x		A 9 x x
	SOUTH	
	J 10 8	

South leads the jack and makes two tricks if West covers. If West ducks, East can win or duck, and South is held to one trick provided the defenders avoid leading the suit subsequently.

(c)	NORTH	
	A x x	
WEST		EAST
Q 9 x		K 8 x x
	SOUTH	
	J 10 x	

If West covers the jack he gives South two tricks.

The decision about whether to cover is generally more difficult when the honor is led by declarer. Generally, if dummy does not have the honor directly below declarer's card, it should be assumed that declarer has it, and the defender should wait and cover the next honor. If dummy has the honor below the card led by declarer, it is often proper to cover unless declarer is believed to have a TWO-WAY FINESSE. When in doubt, the best policy is usually to duck quickly. An exception to the rule about not covering a sequence occurs when the opposing suit can be blocked:

(d)

	NORTH	
	A K x x x	
WEST		EAST
Q 9 x		x x x
	SOUTH	
	J 10	

If dummy has no entry, West must cover the jack or ten to prevent declarer making five tricks.

(e)

	NORTH	
	Q J 10 9 x	
WEST		EAST
x x x		K x x x
	SOUTH	
	A	

If the queen is led and covered, the remainder of the suit is established in the North hand.

(f)

	NORTH	
	A x	
WEST		EAST
K x x		x x x
	SOUTH	
	Q J 10 x x	

If the queen is led West must not cover. He can ensure a trick in the suit because the ace must be played on the second round.

There are numerous exceptions to this rule, and a clever declarer can pose the defenders many problems, as in the following examples:

(g)

	NORTH	
	A x	
WEST		EAST
K x x		J 10 x x
	SOUTH	
	Q x x x	

If South needs to steal a trick in the suit, he can lead the queen and West may duck.

(h)

	NORTH	
	A x x	
WEST		EAST
K x		10 9 x
	SOUTH	
	Q J x x x	

If South leads the queen, West must cover with a doubleton king; otherwise South can continue with a small card, and drop the king.

(i)

	NORTH	
	Q J 10 8 x	
WEST		EAST
A x x x		K 9 x
	SOUTH	
	x	

At a trump contract, North leads the queen in a side suit. East must play the king. If he ducks, the king may be ruffed out eventually.

J. R.

CRACK. An expert player, partnership, or team. As a verb, there are three meanings: (1) to obtain bad results after a period of success; (2) to double; (3) to open a new suit during the play of the hand. The latter two meanings are bridge colloquialisms.

CRANE SYSTEM. An obsolete bidding system devised by Joshua CRANE, in which the full value of the hand was bid immediately in accordance with its point-count. A hand counting to 12–15 was bid at the one-level; a hand worth 16–19 was bid at the two-level, etc. This may have been the earliest published system to include a distributional point-count: both opener and responder counted 3 points for a singleton and 6 points for a void once the trump suit had been agreed. Also called, somewhat optimistically, the "common-sense system."

CRASHING HONORS. The deceptive play of a suit by declarer resulting in the defense wasting two high honors on one trick.

The most common situation in which the declarer can crash honors occurs when the declarer holds concealed length in his own hand. The lead of an honor from dummy may cause second hand to cover with an honor, crashing still a third honor in the other defender's hand. For example:

	NORTH	
	♠ J 8 5 3	
WEST		EAST
♠ A		♠ K 4
	SOUTH	
	♠ Q 10 9 7 6 2	

If the jack of spades is led from dummy (North), East may play the king in the hope that West holds 10 x, 10 9, or 10 x x of spades.

Declarer may also crash honors with a lead from his own hand toward the dummy. This play is most likely to work if dummy is apparently (or actually) short of entries, as the defenders may believe declarer did not have the option of taking a finesse. Thus:

	NORTH	
	♡ 9 8 7 6	
WEST		EAST
♡ K 4		♡ A
	SOUTH	
	♡ Q J 10 5 3 2	

With dummy (North) barren of entries, South leads the queen of hearts. If West believes declarer is trying to avoid a loser in the suit by leading the queen from ace, queen, jack, he may play the king.

More subtle examples of crashing honors can be found in holdings in which the declarer is missing several top cards. The choice of card to lead might not seem too important in this suit:

NORTH
◇ J 8 5 3

SOUTH
◇ 10 9 7 6 4

If possible, declarer (South) should start the diamond suit by leading the jack from dummy. East may play the ace from A Q 2, or may split honors from K Q 2.

Sometimes, it helps declarer's plan if the defenders know about his length in a suit. In the example below, South has indicated a six-card club suit.

NORTH
♣ J 8

WEST
♣ Q 5 3

EAST
♣ A K

SOUTH
♣ 10 9 7 6 4 2

South leads the two of clubs toward dummy's jack. As he would make the same play with A K 7 6 4 2 of clubs in his hand, West is faced with a guess. If West takes the wrong view, the defense will crash honors in clubs.

In a slightly different sense, declarer may sometimes crash a single honor by making it fall on a trick with low cards, so it will not interfere with the trick-taking potential of declarer's honor cards.

NORTH
♠ —

WEST
♠ A 5

EAST
♠ J 10 9

SOUTH
♠ K Q 8 7 6 4 3 2

South, who has opened with four spades, can afford to lose only one spade trick. His only chance is to lead the queen of spades from the closed hand. West may suspect that South has an even longer suit than he actually holds (or may make a mistake), and so play low. South can now crash the ace of spades with one of East's minor honors by leading a low spade, preserving his king for the third round of the suit.

J. R.

CRISSCROSS SQUEEZE. A blocked squeeze described under SIMPLE SQUEEZE.

CROCHET. See WINKLE SQUEEZE.

CROCKFORD'S CLUB, London, England, a famous proprietary club descending from a gambling club founded by William Crockford in 1827. In modern times it has been primarily a bridge club,

patronized by English players, including World Champions Terence Reese, Kenneth Konstam, and others. In Dec. 1961, Crockford's reverted to its gambling traditions by becoming the headquarters of *chemin-de-fer* in England.

CROCKFORD'S CLUB, New York (1932–38). Founded by Ely Culbertson, and named after the English club of the same name. The club was famous for its high-quality cuisine and for its luxurious appointments, as was its sister club in Chicago. Many famous American players of the thirties were members of Crockford's, including: Ely Culbertson, Josephine Culbertson, Richard Frey, Sam Fry, Jr., Michael Gottlieb, Oswald Jacoby, Theodore Lightner, Albert Morehead, Alphonse Moyse, Sidney Rusinow, Howard Schenken, Dorothy Sims, P. Hal Sims, Helen Sobel, Sherman Stearns, Harold Vanderbilt, and Waldemar von Zedtwitz. Many of the members were drawn from high society rather than from the tournament bridge world.

CROSSRUFF. A method of play whereby ruffing tricks are made in each of a partnership's hands, thus using the trumps separately.

When a crossruff is played, ruffing tricks are being taken in two side suits. It is usually a good idea to cash winners in the remaining suit at an early stage.

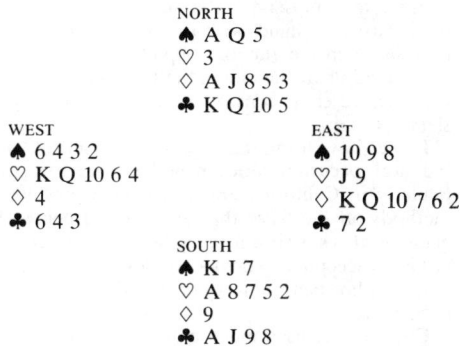

NORTH
♠ A Q 5
♡ 3
◇ A J 8 5 3
♣ K Q 10 5

WEST
♠ 6 4 3 2
♡ K Q 10 6 4
◇ 4
♣ 6 4 3

EAST
♠ 10 9 8
♡ J 9
◇ K Q 10 7 6 2
♣ 7 2

SOUTH
♠ K J 7
♡ A 8 7 5 2
◇ 9
♣ A J 9 8

After East opens three diamonds, West leads a trump against South's contract of six clubs. South can count only five top tricks outside of clubs and must therefore make all his remaining trumps separately. He must be careful to cash his three spade tricks immediately, else the defenders will discard spades when failing to follow to red suit tricks. If this happens, declarer will lose his good spades to opposing ruffs. If the spades cannot be cashed at once, there is no hope for the contract.

CROWHURST CONVENTION. A secondary Stayman inquiry after a one no trump rebid by opener, devised by Eric CROWHURST, of Reading, England, and widely used by British tournament players. Opener is assumed to have 12–16 HCP; the two club rebid by responder asks for further clarification. If opener has 15–16 he rebids two no trump (game forcing) regardless of his distribution; with 12–14 opener either (1) rebids a five-card major suit, (2) shows three-card support for responder's major suit,

(3) shows an unbid four-card major suit, or (4) bids two diamonds. See also STAYMAN ON SECOND ROUND.

CROWNINSHIELD TROPHY. Presented by Frank Crowninshield for British-American competition. Contested only once, in 1949, when an unofficial US team (J. Crawford, P. Leventritt, G. Rapee, S. Stayman) played matches against two British teams. The result was a win for Britain by 330 aggregate points. See ANGLO-AMERICAN MATCHES.

CUDGELS. The club suit.

CUE-BID. A forcing bid in a suit in which the bidder cannot wish to play. It is applied to (1) bids in the opponents' suit at any level; (2) bids to show controls at a high level after a suit has been agreed directly or by inference. These two types are discussed separately below.

CUE-BIDS IN OPPONENT'S SUIT. When a player bids a suit which has originally been called by his opponents, he is said to make a cue-bid. A cue-bid is not made in the expectation of actually playing in the relevant suit; it is made for exploratory or control-showing purposes.

In the early days of contract bridge, a cue-bid could be made in only two situations: The immediate overcall in the opponent's suit guaranteed a void (or at any rate, no losers) in the suit. This was later extended to strong hands with a singleton in the suit. At *later stages* in the auction, opposite a partner who had already bid, the cue-bid in the opponent's suit was used to show control of the suit, and suggest slam.

In the above form, the opportunity to make a cue-bid rarely occurred. Modern bidders, therefore, particularly in California and in England, developed methods on the basis that any cue-bid below the game level is simply a forcing bid. This concept has not been accepted by GOREN and some other conservative authorities, but has gained wide acceptance in expert circles.

Cue-bids are used much more extensively by experts than by others. In studying the meaning of various cue-bids, the subject is considered (1) from opener's viewpoint, (2) from responder's viewpoint, and (3) from defenders' viewpoint.

Cue-Bids by Opener. The level at which the cue-bid is made is a vital consideration. The meaning changes according to whether game has been reached.

Above the game level, there can be no doubt that the cue-bid is a slam try. The same is true in this sort of situation:

SOUTH	WEST	NORTH	EAST
1 ♠	2 ♡	3 ♠	Pass
4 ♡			

North-South are already committed to playing in at least a game in spades, so four hearts must be a slam try, showing control of the heart suit. First-round control of hearts (ace or void) is virtually guaranteed.

But when partnership is still searching for the *safest* game contract, the cue-bid by opener is much less precise. He may or may not have slam ambitions. He may or may not have a control in the cue-bid suit. Time will tell:

SOUTH	WEST	NORTH	EAST
1 ♣	1 ♡	1 ♠	Pass
2 ♡			

All North can tell at this stage is that South has an enormous hand, and wants to be in at least a game. North must make the most helpful bid he can think of, which is likely to be no trump if he has a heart stopper. If he has a double heart stopper and a *weak* hand he should jump to three no trump. This should serve as a warning to South that duplication is present.

South may have any of the following hands:

(a)
♠ A Q 7 4
♡ 6
◇ A 6 3
♣ A K J 5 4

South's hand offers good slam prospects, and it would be wrong to raise immediately to four spades. He plans to bid four spades on the next round, whatever rebid he gets from North. *A delayed raise to game always promises more than an immediate game bid.* See FAST ARRIVAL, PRINCIPLE OF.

(b)
♠ A 4
♡ 7 5
◇ A J 5
♣ A K Q J 5 4

Here the cue-bid is made, not as in slam try, but as a means of reaching the *best* game contract.

Although he has no spade fit and no heart control, South must insist on reaching game. He is too strong to bid three clubs, which could be passed. If North bids two no trump, South raises to three no trump. If North rebids two spades, South simply bids three clubs, and awaits developments.

(c)	(d)
♠ A J 6	♠ A 6 5
♡ 5	♡ 5 4
◇ A J 7	◇ K Q J 6
♣ A K Q 9 5 4	♣ A K Q J

On both these hands South will bid three spades if North bids two no trump in response to South's two heart cue-bid. In each case, the best contract may turn out to be four spades, which North will bid if he has a five-card suit or a strong four-card suit.

Notice that in no case does South have a void heart. With a void it will usually be better to make a *jump cue-bid.* This pinpoints a void specifically.

In some circumstances, a cue-bid is not even completely forcing to game. Consider the following:

SOUTH	WEST	NORTH	EAST
1 ♣	Pass	Pass	1 ♡
2 ♡			

or

SOUTH	WEST	NORTH	EAST
1 ♣	1 ♡	Pass	2 ♡
3 ♡			

South cannot be insisting on game here because he did not open with a forcing bid, and his partner's hand may be completely worthless. He may have either of these hands:

♠ A Q 5 4	♠ A K 3
♡ —	♡ —
◇ A K 7 2	◇ A J 8
♣ A Q J 8 6	♣ K Q J 8 7 3 2

This particular cue-bid, even without a jump, suggests a void in hearts. (With a singleton heart, a take-out double would be the normal action: South would then be less reluctant to hear his partner pass the double for penalties.)

The following example shows the advantage of playing the low-level cue-bid as a vague forcing bid, without any guarantee of control in the suit.

SOUTH	WEST	NORTH	EAST
1 ♣	2 ♠ (Weak)	3 ♡	Pass
3 ♠			

South holds:

♠ 7 5
♡ J 3
◇ Q 8 3
♣ A K Q 7 4 3

This use of the cue-bid to ask about stoppers is prevalent in the West and is called a Western cue-bid. It is the only way for South to steer the contract into three no trump if North has a spade guard. (If South had a spade stopper he could simply bid three no trump himself.) Unless the partnership has this understanding, South is forced to bid four clubs, or even four hearts, when the no trump game may easily be best (see DIRECTIONAL ASKING BID).

A cue-bid must always be considered within the framework of the bidding. If the cue-bidder and his partner have limited their hands by the earlier auction, the cue-bid may be made even in a part-score situation, when there is no intention of reaching game.

This is illustrated by the following example:

SOUTH	WEST	NORTH	EAST
1 ♣	1 ◇	Pass	1 NT
Pass	Pass	Dbl.	Pass
2 ◇			

South's hand was:

♠ Q J 10 6
♡ A 7 5 4
◇ 6
♣ K J 8 4

As he had passed over one no trump and then refused to stand the double, it was clear that South was weak. With North also limited by his original pass, the cue-bid was simply a useful maneuver to find a major-suit fit.

Cue-bids by Responder

SOUTH	WEST	NORTH	EAST
1 ♣	1 ♠	2 ♠	

Classically this would have shown a club fit with no losers in spades, and a desire to reach at least game. In the modern style, North could have any of the following hands:

(a)	(b)	(c)
♠ A 6	♠ 7 4 2	♠ K J
♡ A K J	♡ K J 7 3	♡ A J 7 4
◇ 9 6 5 3 2	◇ A 10 5	◇ A J 6
♣ J 4 2	♣ K Q 7	♣ 10 6 4 2

These examples are taken from Reese and Dormer's *Blueprint for Bidding* (English title: *The Acol System Today*).

All three hands would present problems without the use of the cue-bid. A bid of two hearts on (b) or (c) would suggest a five-card suit, and a bid of two diamonds on (a) is misleading with such a weak suit. In each case North raises to three no trump if South's rebid is two no trump, showing a spade stopper.

This usage in no way bars responder from making the cue-bid with its classical meaning. He follows with a club raise or a clear-cut slam move, and the situation becomes clear to opener.

When North has a spade void, he can show this unequivocally by a jump cue-bid of *three* spades. (Unusual jump bids which have no normal meaning can often be useful to show a specific void.)

The responder can cue-bid with great freedom on the second round of bidding:

SOUTH	WEST	NORTH	EAST
1 ♣	Pass	1 ◇	1 ♠
Pass	Pass	2 ♠	

North holds:

♠ Q 8
♡ A 10 5
◇ A J 8 7 4
♣ J 5 2

In this case South is limited by his failure to bid over one spade, which strongly suggests that his hand is minimum. North intends to pass if he gets a discouraging bid of three clubs or three diamonds from South. This is one case in which the bidding can die short of game after a cue-bid. If South has any game ambitions, he must make some more constructive bid.

Counter-cues and redoubles. If South has ♠ A x x or ♠ K x x, for example, he can make a counter-cue-bid of three spades, which steers three no trump into the North hand.

Having the contract played from the right side of the table is a consideration also on this deal:

Dlr.: S
Vul.: N-S

```
                    NORTH
                    ♠ Q 5
                    ♡ 6 2
                    ◇ K Q 3
                    ♣ A Q 8 7 6 4
WEST                                    EAST
♠ J 10 9 8 6 2                          ♠ K 7 4
♡ A K 10 3                              ♡ 9 8
◇ 7 4                                   ◇ J 9 8 5
♣ 5                                     ♣ J 10 9 2
                    SOUTH
                    ♠ A 3
                    ♡ Q J 7 5 4
                    ◇ A 10 6 2
                    ♣ K 3
```

SOUTH	WEST	NORTH	EAST
1 ♡	Pass	2 ♣	Pass
2 ◇	2 ♠	3 ♠	Dbl.
Redbl.	Pass	3 NT	Pass
Pass	Pass		

If the cue-bid were not available, North would be in trouble over two spades. Three clubs or three diamonds would be substantial underbids, likely to lead to a missed game.

East's double of three spades strongly suggests that he has a top spade honor, so North-South are able to play three no trump from the North position. When a cue-bid (in the opponent's suit or otherwise) is doubled, a redouble shows control of the suit; whether it is first- or second-round control is a matter for partnership agreement.

There are often opportunities for using the cue-bid after an original pass by the cue-bidder:

NORTH	EAST	SOUTH	WEST
Pass	Pass	1 ◇	1 ♠
2 ♠			

This shows a near opening bid, a balanced distribution, and insufficient spade strength to bid two no trump. For example:

```
      (a)                 (b)
♠ 7 4 3 2           ♠ A 6 4
♡ A Q 6             ♡ A K J
◇ Q 8 5             ◇ 10 9 8
♣ K 10 7            ♣ 10 9 7 3
```

Holding a fit with the opener's suit, the responder will rarely wish to look further than a raise of partner's suit. With the hands given, North would have an impossible bid to make. In each case he is hoping for three no trump, but with his partner to play it.

In the event of North wishing to make a cue-bid because he has a powerful diamond fit, he can still do so. But until North clarifies the situation on the next round, South must bid on the assumption that North's hand is balanced. Any simple bid by South on the second round, such as three clubs or three diamonds, may be passed. So if South wants to be in game he must make a counter-cue-bid of three spades or take some other strong action.

A Cue-bid in no trump. A cue-bid in no trump is both rare and rarely understood. Suppose the bidding goes:

SOUTH	WEST	NORTH	EAST
1 ◇	1 NT	2 NT	

What does North's bid mean? It cannot be a balanced hand trying for a no trump game, because any such hand would simply double one no trump and take a penalty.

Two no trump in this situation should be regarded as a cue-bid, simply forcing to game. It shows an unbalanced hand which does not wish to defend against no trump. A two-suiter is likely, such as:

```
          ♠ A Q 6 5 4 2
          ♡ A J 6 5 3
          ◇ 9
          ♣ 4
```

There should be game in one of the major suits, but a double will not work out well if, as is likely, West has a strong club suit.

Once the game level has been reached, the cue-bid becomes simply control-showing. Almost invariably it will show the ace or a void, but might occasionally be made with a second-round control. This can be ventured if the cue-bidder's trump holding is strong, as there is then no danger that partner will race for a grand slam missing a trick in the enemy suit.

Negative inferences. The failure to cue-bid can be very significant:

```
WEST                    EAST
♠ A Q 7 5 4 3           ♠ K J 8 5
♡ A K J 6 3             ♡ 7 2
◇ —                     ◇ A Q 10 8 3
♣ 9 4                   ♣ 10 6
```

WEST	NORTH	EAST	SOUTH
1 ♠	4 ♣	4 ♠	Pass
5 ♠	Pass	Pass	Pass

This asks only for control of clubs. If West had any other worries he would make a suitable cue-bid.

Similarly, a player who holds

```
          ♠ 5 2
          ♡ A Q 7 6 4 2
          ◇ —
          ♣ A K 8 7 3
```

can bid five hearts when his partner's one heart has been overcalled with one spade.

There are numerous possibilities for cue-bidding after partner's opening bid of one no trump. Frequently the cue-bid has to take the place of a STAYMAN inquiry which has been frustrated by the intervening bid.

♠ A K 7 3
♡ Q 6
♢ A 10 6 2
♣ K J 6

South holds this hand and the bidding goes:

SOUTH	WEST	NORTH	EAST
1 NT	2 ♡	3 ♡	Pass
3 ♠	Pass	3 NT	Pass
?			

North's bid of three hearts could have any of three meanings. He could be paving the way for a slam; he could be trying to find a 4–4 spade fit to play in four spades; or he could be worrying about the presence of a heart guard for three no trump.

The three no trump bid makes it clear that he has not got spades, nor is he seeking a slam. His only reason for not bidding three no trump directly was because he has no heart guard.

In these circumstances, West would enjoy three no trump, so South must bid four diamonds. He expects to play a game in spades, diamonds, or clubs.

Another curious cue-bid can arise after a one no trump opening bid:

SOUTH	WEST	NORTH	EAST
1 NT	Dbl.	2 NT	

This cannot be a natural bid, because a hand which is ready to suggest three no trump would prefer to redouble. The redouble is almost sure to produce a good score, probably from a penalty when the opponents play in some doubled contract at the two-level. So two no trump must be a forcing bid with a very unbalanced distribution—probably a two-suiter on which game seems feasible. Over West's double, a jump to three spades, for example, should be preemptive, not forcing, so two no trump is the only forcing bid at North's disposal.

Cue-bids by the Defenders. Cue-bids by the side which did *not* open the bidding are considered under two headings; cue-bids by second hand and cue-bids by fourth hand.
Cue-bids by second hand. The immediate overcall in the opponent's suit has been the subject of experiment in recent years. There are no fewer than five varieties:

(1) *Classical* (Culbertson-Goren). The equivalent of an opening forcing bid, guaranteeing a game. Goren insists that the cue-bid shows first-round control in the cue-bid suit, without explaining what to do if that feature is not present. Culbertson is less rigid, permitting the cue-bid with a singleton, and allowing for the possibility that the bidding may die short of game if the responding hand is very weak. Modern bidders contend that these interpretations weaken the value of the bid, since there is so rarely an opportunity to use it.

(2) *Modern* (Reese and Dormer). Here the cue-bid is used for most powerful hands with game prospects, when a take-out double is unsuitable because a penalty pass would be unwelcome. *Blueprint for*

Bidding gives these three examples of two diamonds after an opening one diamond:

(a)	(b)
♠ A K 10 8 4 3 2	♠ A Q 10 7 4
♡ K 4	♡ K J 8 7 5
♢ 7	♢ —
♣ A J 6	♣ A Q 5

(c)
♠ K Q 9 5 4
♡ A
♢ 9
♣ A K J 8 3 2

In (a), the spades are bid and rebid, and the bidding can die at three spades. If (b) gets a three club response, a repeat cue-bid of three diamonds is used to ask for a major suit. The bidding can stop at three hearts or three spades. If (c) gets a two heart response, which is likely, the rebid is three clubs, which can be passed.

(3) *Hypermodern* (the MICHAELS CUE-BID). Here there is a two-suited hand, usually less than opening bid strength. Over a minor suit it shows major suits; over a major suit it shows the unbid major and an unspecified minor. In the latter case the hand may be stronger. See also KANTAR CUE-BID.

It is generally true that two-suited hands are difficult to bid in defense, and this has given rise to various attempts, such as the unusual no trump, to show two suits with one bid. An alternative two-suiter cue-bid:

(4) *Artificial* (the ASTRO CUE-BID). This method is described by its inventors, Rosler, Stern, and Allinger. It shows a minor-major two-suiter—the lower unbid minor and the lower unbid major. The minor suit is always long, and the distribution is likely to be 6–5, 6–4, or 5–4. The strength will vary wildly. At favorable vulnerability, it might be a 5-point hand hoping for a sacrifice, while at unfavorable vulnerability the cue-bidder must have a sound hand able to play safely at the three-level. See also COLORFUL CUE-BID.

(5) *Natural.* There is a strong argument for playing an immediate overcall in an opponent's minor suit as a natural bid to show a suit, especially if the opponents do not open four-card major suits. In that case they will frequently bid a three-card minor suit, and the second player may want to bid the suit naturally.

Against opponents who open freely with weak four-card major suits, or even three-card major suits, the cue-bid may be used naturally at all times.

Of the five different methods listed above, the tendency in expert circles is to veer toward the second method, i.e., modern. Under this method, the second player may make a delayed cue-bid in a variety of circumstances. A common situation follows a take-out double:

SOUTH	WEST	NORTH	EAST
1 ♡	Dbl.	Pass	2 ♣
Pass	2 ♡		

Many years ago this bid was used as a natural bid to show a strong heart suit, and it was not forcing. This treatment has been abandoned, partly because such hands usually pass the opening heart bid, and partly because it is needed as a cue-bid with a variety of strong hands.

The precise meaning of the cue-bid is influenced by the type of *immediate* cue-bid being used. If this has the normal strong meaning, then the delayed cue-bid is certain to be less than a game-forcing hand. Using a specialized cue-bid—(3), (4), or (5) above—the delayed cue-bid has no upward limit. In either case the minimum should be a hand with about 20 points.

A cue-bid following partner's double is, of course, very different:

SOUTH	WEST	NORTH	EAST
1 ♠	Pass	Pass	Dbl.
Pass	2 ♠		

It would be unprofitable to reserve this cue-bid for a hand which can guarantee game, because West's original pass makes it unlikely that he has such a hand. The cue-bid here simply suggests a game, and West could have as little as:

> ♠ 8 7 4
> ♡ J 10 8 5
> ◊ A Q 10
> ♣ K 9 2

If East's next bid is three clubs or three diamonds, West can and should pass. Over three hearts, he can just afford to continue to game, because all his points are "working." If East has a good sound double, he will either bid a game directly or make a further cue-bid of three spades.

A pass followed by a bid in the opponent's suit may need a little study. Usually it is a natural bid, based on a strong suit which the opponent has stolen. For example:

SOUTH	WEST	NORTH	EAST
1 ♠	Pass	1 NT	Pass
Pass	2 ♠		

This indicates a good six-card spade suit. South and North may well have only four spades and one spade respectively, so West cannot allow himself to be talked out of playing in spades. He would be less inclined to bid two spades, perhaps, if the opening bid promised a five-card suit. See OVERCALL IN OPPONENT'S MAJOR SUIT.

The same would apply if the opening bid was in hearts, but the situation is different when the opening bid was in a minor suit:

SOUTH	WEST	NORTH	EAST
1 ◊	Pass	1 NT	Pass
Pass	2 ◊		

Now it is much less likely that West will want to bid two diamonds naturally, because North-South will almost always have six diamonds between them and usually more. It is more useful, therefore, to use the bid in the opponent's minor suit as a cue-bid for a major-suit take-out on this type of hand:

> ♠ K 8 5 3
> ♡ A 10 6 3
> ◊ 7 5 4
> ♣ K 2

West could not afford to make an original double with this hand, partly because his strength is insufficient, and partly because he is not prepared for a club response. It is highly probable after this auction that East-West have a 4–4 fit or better in one of the major suits, and the two diamond cue-bid is an effective way for East-West to balance themselves into a major suit.

If West makes a cue-bid of this type, and East is in any doubt about its significance, he can usually come to the right conclusion by considering his own holding in the cue-bid suit. If he has a misfit in the cue-bid suit, the bid is likely to be natural. If not, it is likely to be for a take-out.

To complete the picture as far as cue-bids by the second player are concerned, there is the rare no trump cue-bid. A bid of two no trump over an opening bid of one no trump is not simply an unusual no trump asking for minor suits. It shows a freak two-suited hand of any kind, and could be based on KQxxxx in both major suits.

Cue-bids by fourth hand. Here there is much more variety, and six common cases need consideration.

(1) *After two passes.* If South bids one diamond and East bids two diamonds in the pass-out position, the cue-bid should mean the same as if made by second hand. East bears in mind that West and North are limited by their original passes.

(2) *After a pass and a suit response*

SOUTH	WEST	NORTH	EAST
1 ◊	Pass	1 ♠	2 ♠

This is clearly forcing to game, but there is some difference of opinion about the meaning of a bid of two diamonds instead of two spades. The usual American interpretation is that this would also be a cue-bid, of a different order of strength. This is hardly necessary because a double is available as a request for a take-out, and one no trump can be given a similar meaning by agreement. The British treatment is different: if the opponents bid two suits, a bid in their original suit is natural. This applies more frequently when second hand has overcalled.

(3) *After an overcall and a pass*

SOUTH	WEST	NORTH	EAST
1 ◊	1 ♠	Pass	2 ◊

This is back to the earlier pattern: a strong hand which expects to go to game but does not know where to go. East might hold:

> ♠ K 3
> ♡ Q J 6 2
> ◊ 10 3
> ♣ A K 7 5 4

East expects to reach game, but this could be in any denomination except diamonds. West may show any additional feature: a second suit if he has one; a diamond guard by bidding no trump; or a good overcall including a six-card spade suit by jumping to *three* spades. If he can do no more than rebid two spades, East raises to three spades, which can be passed. If East-West are vulnerable, East might go to four spades over two spades. This depends on the partnership's overcalling standards.

Alternatively, East may hold a hand which is worth a raise to four spades, but offers some slam chances. If he bids two diamonds, and follows with four spades West may be able to continue.

Another treatment that has become increasingly popular among modern players is to use this cue-bid as responder's only strong bid, usually equivalent to a limit raise of the overcaller's suit.

For example, the bidding goes:

WEST	NORTH	EAST	SOUTH
1 ♡	1 ♠	Pass	2 ♡

South holds:

♠ K 9 5
♡ A 7 2
♢ K J 9 8 3
♣ 10 6

In standard methods, South would express the value of his hand by jump raising to three spades, but this may get his side too high. Employing the cue-bid as an invitational measure permits South to explore accurately for game without endangering the partial contract. If North rebids two spades, South passes, while if North shows additional values above a minimum overcall by jumping to three spades or introducing a new suit, South supports spades as cheaply as possible to describe the limited nature of his cue-bid. With a stronger hand, South would again cue-bid, but would take some further action over a minimum rebid by North. As a corollary, a double raise of an overcall is freed for use as a pre-emptive tactic. See also RESPONDING TO OVERCALLS.

(4) *After a double and a pass*
This is very common:

SOUTH	WEST	NORTH	EAST
1 ♢	Dbl.	Pass	2 ♢

East can hold any hand on which he expects to get to game, but does not know where. A typical hand would be:

♠ K 7 6 3
♡ K 7 6 3
♢ 9 3 2
♣ A K

Over two diamonds, West is almost sure to bid a major, which East raises to game. A raise to three spades would not be forcing, and would be appropriate if the club king were turned into the jack or a small card.

This last point involves an important principle. In general, a cue-bid is not completely forcing to game.

It loses its forcing quality when a limited position is reached. A raise is always limited, so the bidding can die below game. A minimum double and a minimum cue-bid may not have enough combined values for game. This allows East to make the cue-bid freely on hands which would otherwise present a problem.

(5) *After a double and a bid*

SOUTH	WEST	NORTH	EAST
1 ♢	Dbl.	1 ♡	2 ♡

This is similar to (2), in that the opponents have bid two suits. Two hearts is a normal cue-bid, with no interest in a heart contract. Holding four hearts or more, he would certainly double. But the only way to show diamonds at this point is to bid them, so two diamonds should simply mean a desire to play in that contract.

(6) *After a no trump overcall*

SOUTH	WEST	NORTH	EAST
1 ♢	1 NT	Pass	2 ♢

There are two schools of thought about this position. The normal interpretation is that it is a cue-bid, which can be used as a Stayman substitute.

Alternatively, two clubs can be retained as a Stayman bid, in which case two diamonds is a weak hand that wants to play in diamonds. This is not too unlikely because the no trump bidder has promised a good diamond holding.

Conclusion. Cue-bidding is an extremely broad subject. There are hundreds of situations in which low-level cue-bids can be used effectively, and most of them are impossible to classify because they occur on the second or third round of bidding. In these situations, cue-bids may provide an answer to bidding problems which would otherwise be insoluble. See also DOUBLE OF A CUE-BID and COLORFUL CUE-BID.

CUE-BIDS TO SHOW CONTROLS (see also CUE-BIDS IN OPPONENT'S SUIT). A bid in a suit in which the partnership cannot wish to play is usually a control-showing cue-bid if the partnership is already committed to a game contract. A slam invitation is implied:

(a)		(b)	
NORTH	SOUTH	NORTH	SOUTH
1 ♠	3 ♠	1 ♣	1 ♡
4 ♢		3 ♡	4 ♢

In each case the side is committed to game, and a suit has been firmly agreed. The final bid is a slam suggestion, and the cue-bidder's partner acts accordingly. If his hand is completely unsuitable for slam purposes, he signs off in the agreed trump suit at the lowest level. If he is willing to cooperate in a slam venture, he can bid a slam directly, or take some other strong action which will take the bidding past the game level. When in doubt, he can sometimes make a further cue-bid below the game level; in case (a), South can make a cue-bid of four hearts in his turn without taking the bidding past four spades.

The first cue-bid is assumed to show first-round control (usually the ace, but occasionally a void), although a hand which is known to be very weak might make a cue-bid with a king. Later cue-bids by either player may show second-round controls.

It is usual (and in some systems compulsory) to make the cheapest possible cue-bid. Therefore in case (a) above, North denies first-round club control, and in case (b), South denies first-round spade control.

An alternative recommended by Jeremy FLINT is to cue-bid first the higher ranking of two touching aces and the lower of two non-touching aces. (The trump suit is excluded in determining which suits are touching.) The intent is to create extra room for the partnership to show all its controls. A hand given in illustration by H. W. KELSEY in his book on Slam Bidding (see BIBLIOGRAPHY, C) is:

WEST	EAST
♠ A 7	♠ 3
♡ A 5 4	♡ K 8 6
◇ J 10 9 6 5 2	◇ A K Q 7
♣ K 4	♣ A Q 8 5 3

Using standard methods of bidding all controls as cheaply as possible, the auction would start:

WEST	EAST
1 ◇	3 ♣
3 ◇	4 ◇
4 ♡	5 ♣
5 ♠	?

East cannot be sure his partner has the club king and cannot find out without committing himself one way or another. Using the Flint style, however, the auction would be:

WEST	EAST
1 ◇	3 ♣
3 ◇	4 ◇
4 ♠	5 ♣
5 ♡	5 ♠
6 ♣	7 ◇

West's cue-bid of his aces in reverse order has created just one bit of extra space, but that one step is enough. The Flint method has its disadvantages, however, when the hand that initiates the cue-bidding has only one ace, for there will be second-round controls that the hand cannot show without promising first-round control.

A bluff cue-bid is made not infrequently to inhibit a lead:

NORTH	SOUTH
1 ♠	3 ♠
4 ♣	4 ♠
6 ♠	Pass

It is possible that North had a grand slam in mind, but abandoned that possibility when South made the discouraging return to four spades. But it is more likely, if North is a good player, that he was bent on six spades, and bid four clubs on the way to inhibit a

club lead. If East is also a good player he will see through the maneuver and lead a club, which opens the way for a double-cross genuine cue-bid.

Certain bids may at first sight appear to be cue-bids, but on inspection do not conform to the definition:

(a)		(b)	
NORTH	SOUTH	NORTH	SOUTH
1 ♡	2 ♣	1 ♡	2 ♣
3 ♣	3 ♠	4 ♣	4 ♡

In case (a), North-South are not committed to a game contract, because the bidding can die in four clubs. Three spades is not a cue-bid suggesting a slam, but a STRENGTH-SHOWING BID suggesting three no trump; the spade holding could be QJx.

In case (b), South's bid of four hearts is quite unconstructive. It simply suggests that four hearts may be a better contract than five clubs, and the heart support may be as little as a doubleton honor.

The above treatment should be regarded as standard unless a partnership agrees otherwise. For alternative treatments see: ASKING BID; INTEREST-SHOWING BID; and ROMAN ASKING BID. For related topics see also: DOUBLE OF A CUE-BID; OUT-OF-THE-BLUE CUE-BID; TRIAL BID; and VOID-SHOWING BID.

In the early years of contract, various authorities, including R. F. FOSTER, S. LENZ, G. REITH, and E. V. SHEPARD devised complex systems of cue-bidding. These were intended to offer alternatives to the Culbertson four-five no trump convention and other devices for locating aces, but they did not achieve any popularity.

CULBERTSON ASKING BID. See ASKING BID.

CULBERTSON FOUR-FIVE NO TRUMP. A slam convention showing aces and kings as well as asking for them. The four no trump bid promises either:

three aces, or
two aces and a king of a suit genuinely bid by the partnership.

The responses

Holding two aces, or one ace and all the kings of genuinely bid suits, bid: five no trump.
Holding no ace, bid: five of lowest genuinely bid suit.
Holding one ace, usually bid the ace suit (but if this is the lowest bid suit, a jump to six is necessary).

Notice that the sign-off is not in the agreed trump suit, but in the lowest suit which the partnership has genuinely bid. Responder can exercise some discretion when he holds one ace and no additional values. If his normal response would take the bidding above the five level in the agreed trump suit, he may invent some lower bid.

Holding two aces *and* a king, the responder is often interested in a grand slam. Provided his king is not in the agreed trump suit, he may bid the suit in which he holds a king. This may be temporarily misleading, but he can clarify the situation by making a constructive bid on the next round.

This convention was generally superseded by BLACKWOOD and other conventions, but retained popularity among some leading British players. See BYZANTINE BLACKWOOD.

CULBERTSON-LENZ MATCH. The "Bridge Battle of the Century," as it was called when it took place between December 1931 and January 1932, was a genuine milestone in the history of the development and promotion of bridge as it is known today. Combining as it did every feature designed to capture and hold the interest of the then bridge-mad multitudes, and starring the greatest celebrities then prominent in bridge, it was predestined to be an exciting and long-remembered event. These were the years when bridge was making its impact felt keenly in the United States for the first time. During the previous decade, many new styles of bidding and play had come to the forefront, and most prominent among these was the CULBERTSON SYSTEM. Conceived and popularized by a man who was a born molder of opinions and customs, and who was a superbly able practical psychologist as well, the Culbertson System took the nation by storm, and was indeed original in concept and, as practiced by its leading exponents, a successful and highly practical method of bidding in bridge. Naturally its success caused many rivalries and feuds among those players who were at the very top rungs of the bridge ability ladder. The principal leader of the various groups in opposition to the Culbertson methods was Sidney LENZ, a veteran of auction bridge. In his camp were other great luminaries of the game who also felt that their methods were superior to the Culbertson System. The name by which the Lenz forces' system was called was the OFFICIAL SYSTEM. A book on this system, which acknowledged its debt to Culbertson in that much of it was derived from his concepts, was later to be written by Milton WORK. The actual match was the result of a challenge made earlier in 1931 by Culbertson to the Lenz faction. There were many complications to be ironed out before agreement as to conditions could actually be achieved, but essentially the match was finally played on a pair-against-pair basis, with Culbertson wagering $5,000 against Lenz's $1,000 on the outcome, with the money going to charity no matter who won. In all, 150 rubbers were played, and during 88 of them Culbertson played with his wife, Josephine. His partners for the balance of the encounter were LIGHTNER, VON ZEDTWITZ, SCHENKEN, and GOTTLIEB. Lenz played the first 103 rubbers with Jacoby, who then resigned because of a difference of opinion on the play of a defensive situation. Lenz's partner for the remainder of the session was W. LIGGETT. The Culbertson team won by a margin of 8,980 points. Careful and accurate records of cards held for each deal were kept, and at the conclusion it was determined that each side had held fairly much the same number of high cards as the other. The first half of the match was held at New York's Chatham

Hotel, and the second part at the newly opened Waldorf-Astoria. The conditions of play and of protocol in general were governed by an agreement to which both Culbertson and Lenz were signatory, and the bridge laws under which the match was conducted were those published by the Whist Club of New York. Coverage by the press of the nation was stupendous. Stories about the match were on the front pages of newspapers all over America. Regular correspondents were dispatched to the scenes of play, and some of the great newspaper personalities of the time wrote articles for their papers and for syndicates. Complete statistics were collated, and records of every phase of the match carefully kept. However, the single most significant feature of the entire proceedings was the enormous impetus it gave bridge when the game's popularity was already great.

	CULBERTSON	LENZ
Points won	122,925	113,945
Rubbers won	77	73
Number of two-game rubbers	37	32
Size of average rubber won	934	866
Largest rubber won	2,580	2,825
Games	195	186
Small slams bid and made	9	8
Small slams defeated (not including sacrifices)	9	5
Grand slams defeated	0	1
Opening suit bids of one	366	289
Opening one no trump bids	43	45
Opening forcing bids	5	5
Small slams made but not bid (many owing to lucky breaks)	20	19
Games made but not bid (many owing to lucky breaks)	15	13
Successful contracts	273	273
Defeated contracts	142	162
Number of (exact) game contracts voluntarily bid and defeated	48	49
Number of penalties of 600 or more	7	14
Points lost in penalties of 600 or more	5,900	11,500
Aces	1,745	1,771
Kings	1,775	1,741
Honor tricks	3,649½	3,648
Points (4–3–2–1)	18,091	17,898
Value of average rubber	899	
Hands dealt	879	
Hands passed out	25	

CULBERTSON NATIONAL STUDIOS. An organization of bridge teachers which flourished in the thirties. Some 4,000 bridge teachers passed examinations in the CULBERTSON SYSTEM, and were granted certificates attesting their fitness to teach the Culbertson methods. A similar organization was developed later by Charles GOREN. See also AMERICAN BRIDGE TEACHERS' ASSOCIATION.

CULBERTSON-SIMS MATCH. A 150-rubber pair match held in March and April of 1935 with Ely and Josephine Culbertson on one side against P. Hal and Dorothy Sims. On the next-to-last day of the match, Culbertson played with A. Morehead and Sims with B. J. Becker, while the ladies took a holiday. The match was won by the Culbertsons by a margin of 16,130 points. In this match, which took place as a result of a challenge issued by Sims, accurate records were kept of the proceedings and of the cards and deals held by the participants. Publicity for the contest was not as widespread as in the Culbertson-

Lenz match three years earlier, but the nation's interest was aroused. Both sides took to the airwaves on weekly radio broadcasts to describe various features of the games and hands of particular merit were discussed. The match served to whet the public's already keen appetite for bridge and anything about it, as well as to reinforce the position of authority held by the Culbertson group.

CULBERTSON SYSTEM. The system of bidding developed by Ely Culbertson, revised periodically to incorporate new developments. For example, in 1930 Culbertson regarded a response in a new suit as non-forcing, which was a departure from his 1925 auction principles. He adhered to this in the 1933 *Blue Book,* which listed a one-over-one response as "99 44/100% forcing," but abandoned the idea in 1935 when it became clear that the mass of bridge players would not be converted.

Other non-forcing bids were featured in the early *Blue Books,* abandoned shortly afterward, and revived by others as "modern" innovations. Examples are: LIMIT RAISES; limit two no trump response; and WEAK NO TRUMP openings, non-vulnerable. All these became features of the ACOL style; and limit raises and weak no trumps regained some popularity among American tournament players in the sixties. The 1933 *Blue Book* also included the WEAK JUMP OVERCALL.

The Culbertson System, influenced both by the methods of the successful FOUR ACES and by pressure of public opinion, was crystallized in the 1936 *Gold Book.* The bidding set out in the *Gold Book,* with one notable exception, became standard practice in America for the next fifteen years, and was only slightly modified by the GOREN SYSTEM, which won the allegiance of the bridge-playing masses in the fifties. The chief features were:

(1) Valuation by HONOR TRICKS.

(2) Uniform standards for BIDDABLE SUITS, with QJxx a minimum four-card suit. This applied to the opening bidder, irrespective of whether the suit was a major or a minor. The responder could bid a shaded or conditional biddable suit.

(3) The APPROACH PRINCIPLE, emphasizing suit opening bids and responses in preference to no trump bids.

(4) The FORCING TWO-BID: any opening suit bid of two requiring the partnership to reach game. (Later modified, 1952–53, so that responder could pass after a sequence such as two spades—two no trump—three spades.)

(5) The forcing take-out (or JUMP SHIFT) showed 3½ honor tricks (or about 16 points). This requirement was raised by Goren and later authorities.

(6) STRONG NO TRUMP (4–4½ honor tricks) preferably limited to 4–3–3–3 distribution in accordance with the approach principle.

(7) Jump rebids by opener or responder (see OPENER'S REBIDS) not forcing unless in a new suit. (This principle was modified by later writers: see GOREN SYSTEM and STANDARD AMERICAN.)

(8) ASKING BIDS were introduced in 1936, and rein-troduced in 1953 with amplifications, but never gained substantial support.

In 1952–53 Culbertson also introduced his own DISTRIBUTIONAL COUNT.

CULBERTSON TROPHY. Any of a number of trophies donated by Mr. and Mrs. Ely Culbertson, all of them for minor events. In 1962 the name was given to the World Olympiad Pair Championship trophy, first contested at Cannes, France.

CULWOOD CONVENTION. (Thomas Bigelow): Responses to four no trump:

> no aces - five clubs
> one ace - five diamonds
> two aces - five hearts

In order to bid four no trump the bidder must have three aces or two aces and a king of a bid suit.

The response of five spades shows that the partnership holds all aces and the kings of all bid suits.

The response of five no trump shows that in addition to holding all the aces, the partnership holds two of the three top honors of the trump suit in the responding hand.

CUMBERLAND HAND. See DUKE OF CUMBERLAND'S HAND.

CUMULATIVE SCORE. In tournament bridge, when an event is scheduled for more than one session of play, and there is no elimination of players from the event, the winner of the event is decided by cumulative score; that is, the total of the scores made in each of the sessions. However, should there be a different "average score" for the two or more sessions (owing to playing a different number of boards, a no-show for the second session, or other reason), the later sessions' scores are factored by a multiplier that makes the sessions comparable to the first session, so that a particularly high score in any session would carry the same weight as in any other session.

In rubber bridge, where the partnerships change from rubber to rubber, a cumulative score of points won or lost in each rubber is kept so that each player's status of winnings or losses is shown at the termination of each rubber.

In progressive or party bridge, the cumulative score is the totality of points won at all tables at which the player played. Generally, only plus scores are considered, and losses are not deducted before being entered onto the cumulative score sheet.

In knock-out team-of-four matches, all points are scored both plus and minus for both pairs of both teams, and the team with a greater plus total than minus total is the winner. This is referred to as AGGREGATE SCORE and has been generally supplanted in head-to-head matches by international match points.

CUPS, SWORDS, MONEY, WANDS. Names of suits in Tarot. Tarot was a special deck of cards used in ancient Italy and elsewhere for various games and for fortunetelling.

CURIOSITIES. See FREAK HANDS.

CURSE OF SCOTLAND. A term applied to nine of diamonds, for which various explanations are given, none completely authoritative. *The Bridge Magazine* once listed six possible origins for the term as follows:

1. That in the once popular round game "Pope Joan," the nine of diamonds was called "the Pope," the antichrist of Scottish Reformers.

2. That the nine of diamonds was the chief card in the game "cornette," introduced into Scotland by the unhappy Queen Mary.

3. That "Butcher" Cumberland wrote the orders for the Battle of Culloden, 1746, on the back of the card. This is very doubtful.

4. That the order for the Massacre of Glencoe was signed on the back of this card.

5. That the dispositions for the fatal field of Flodden (1513) were drawn up on it by James IV of Scotland. Both these last have only the slightest authority.

6. That it is derived from the nine lozenges that formed the arms of the Earl of Stair, who was especially loathed for his connection with the Massacre of Glencoe and the union with England (1707).

CURT REISINGER TROPHY. See REISINGER MEMORIAL TROPHY; REISINGER TROPHY.

CURTAIN CARD. A record of a hand in a duplicate board. The curtain card is placed in the tray with the hand; the player is thus able to determine that the hand he has taken from the board is the one that was to have been there. Use of curtain cards is rare in the United States, but still found elsewhere. An advantage of curtain cards is that fouled boards are discovered immediately. See FOULED BOARD; HAND RECORD; MISSING CARD.

CUT. (1) At the commencement of rubber bridge play, a pack of cards is spread out, face downward, and each player draws one, turning it face up. Rank and suit of these cards determine the makeup of the first partnerships, and the original dealer. (2) At the conclusion of each hand, the cards are gathered together and reshuffled for the next deal. The new dealer presents the shuffled deck to the right-hand opponent, who cuts the pack by removing more than four but less than forty-eight cards from the top of the deck, and places the cards removed alongside the balance of the deck, nearer to the dealer. The dealer then completes the cut by placing the part of the pack which was originally on the bottom above the part originally on the top. (3) A colloquial term for the verbs "trump" or "ruff," used commonly in Scotland. (4) To terminate a movement before the scheduled completion. See CUTTING MOVEMENT DURING PLAY.

CUT IN. To assert the right to become a member of an incomplete table, or to become a member of a complete table at such time as it may become incomplete.

CUTTHROAT BRIDGE. A name applied to a traditional three-handed game (described under THREE-HANDED BRIDGE) and to a four-handed game with flexible partnerships.

In the four-handed version originated by S. B. Fishburne, Tulsa, Okla., and sometimes called "Reject" or "Let's Pick Partners," the opening bid must be natural and honest (at least 13 points in high cards, and at least four cards in the suit bid). The auction closes when a bid is followed by three passes; doubling and redoubling takes place later. No part-score contracts are played: the cards are thrown in, and the deal passes.

The player who makes the final bid is always declarer, and after the final pass he nominates one of the other three players as his partner. That player becomes the dummy, and moves into the seat opposite the declarer. Declarer's partner has the option of rejecting the partnership, in which case he scores with the defenders instead of with the declarer. Either defender may double and declarer (or dummy if he has not rejected) may redouble.

A separate score is kept for each player, using normal contract scoring as far as possible. The rubber bonus is only 500 if either defender has a game. Only plus scores are recorded, so no entry is made on the score of the one, two, or three players who are on the losing end of a deal. In the final scoring, each player has a reckoning with each other player.

Honors are scored only by the player holding them. A player becomes vulnerable in the usual way. A non-vulnerable player scores 300 if his vulnerable partner scores rubber points.

A weak point in this version of the game was the rejection of part-scores. Three no trump was seldom played, because a player with a weak hand could bid four clubs or four diamonds without risk; unless someone made a higher bid, the hands were thrown in.

This gave rise to another version which gained considerable popularity in New York clubs: After the (natural) opening bid, the next player must make a bid of four no trump or higher. Some games include a GOULASH feature.

CUTTING FOR DEAL, PARTNERS. At the beginning of each rubber, in order to establish partnerships and determine the original dealer, the four participating players each draw a card from an unfaced deck. The two players drawing the highest ranking cards play as partners, and the player with the higher of these two is the dealer on the first hand. An alternate method of determining deal and partners for second and subsequent rubbers is pivoting (see PIVOT BRIDGE).

At CHICAGO, a method combining both the CUT and the pivot is frequently used, the cut establishing partnerships and deal for the first round, the highest cut card determining the pivot player. After the first round, the pivot player remains stationary and plays with his original right-hand opponent for the second round, and then with his original left-hand opponent for the third round. The pivot player, who deals the first hand of each of the three rounds, is often termed the wheel. See LAWS (Law 3).

CUTTING MOVEMENT DURING PLAY. A method of terminating a game at a given time, without playing all of the boards scheduled under the movement in use. It is accomplished by omitting one or more of the rounds normally scheduled by the movement.

In general, any movement in which all boards in play at each round may be terminated at the end of any round, with no other defect than disturbance of balanced comparisons.

In a pair or individual movement involving either bye boards or relays, early termination also disrupts the scoring, for some boards will be played more often than others. This will result in a different top on certain boards, and a different possible score for some or all contestants. See TRUNCATED HOWELL MOVEMENT. See also NINE TABLES for an unusual cutting procedure in a MITCHELL game.

CUTTING OUT. It is frequently impractical to have exactly four players. When five players form a table, an order of omission from the table is established by drawing. The player with the lowest card sits out the first rubber, and other players sit out in their turn in the order thus established.

Alternatively, a fresh draw can be made after each rubber, with the lowest to sit out; only players who have not sat out participate in the draw. This is a matter of club procedure.

The draw for participation in the rubber is usually quite distinct from the draw, or cut, for partners. But see PIVOT BRIDGE.

CYCLIC MOVEMENT. A movement in which contestants follow each other in a regular sequence or series. When a move is called, each contestant moves to a position previously occupied by a given other contestant, whose name or number is known in advance. The HOWELL MOVEMENT for pairs is a typical cyclic movement. Many other movements for pairs, teams, or individuals use the cyclic feature in some form.

CZECHOSLOVAKIAN BRIDGE ASSOCIATION (CESKOSLOVENSKY BRIDZOVY SVAZ). Organized in 1961, the Association became a member of the European Bridge League in 1968 and a participant in European Championships. It hosted the first Junior European Championship in Prague in 1968. Czech teams have also competed in international matches between Poland and Hungary. National events include Open Teams and Open Pairs. Players listed separately are F. Joles, K. Stein.

Secretary, 1969: Dr. Karl Pražák, Czech Bridge Association, Veletržné 29, Prague, Czechoslovakia.

D

D.I. See DECLARATIVE-INTERROGATIVE FOUR NO TRUMP.

DEPO. See DEFENSE TO INTERFERENCE WITH BLACKWOOD.

DOPI. See DEFENSE TO INTERFERENCE WITH BLACKWOOD.

DAMAGED CARD. According to the LAWS, Law 7:

A pack containing a card so damaged or marked that it may be identified from its back must be replaced if attention is drawn to the imperfection before the first card of the current deal is dealt.

DANGER HAND. The declarer often strives to prevent one opponent, the "danger hand," from obtaining the lead. This may be because that player has established winners, or because he will be able to make a damaging lead through a vulnerable honor holding. See AVOIDANCE.

DANISH BRIDGE LEAGUE (DANMARKS BRIDGE FORBUND). Organized in 1939 as a consolidation of the "Dansk Bridge Union" and the "Dansk Bridge Liga," which had been functioning one east and one west of the Great Belt since 1933. As of 1974, there were approximately 190 clubs throughout Denmark, with a membership of 10,000. The League participated in the 1960, 1968, and 1972 World Team Olympiads, and annually sends teams to the European Championships; it sponsored the first post-war event in Copenhagen in 1948 at the urging of the late Herman Dedichen. The record of the Women's Teams in the European Championships is particularly noteworthy—they have won the title on six occasions, 1938, 1948, 1949, 1955, 1957, and 1958. The Danish Bridge League sponsors Open Team and Pairs Championships, the Danish Cup, adult education, and the magazine *Dansk Bridge*, and introduced a master-point program in 1970. Players listed separately are: J. Boeck, K.-Aa Boesgaard, S. Carstensen, Mrs. E. Dam, Mrs. O. Damm, H. Dedichen, Mrs. R. Fraenckel, J. Hulgaard, Mrs. L. Hulgaard, S. Moeller, Mrs. V. Petersen, P. Schaltz, Mrs. G. Skotte, K. Tarp, J. Trelde, A. Voigt, O. Werdelin, S. Werdelin, and G. Zabel.

Officers, 1975:
President: Bent Haestrup, Brunebjerg 24, 3400 Hilleroed.
Secretary: Mrs. Inge Wahlberg, Korsgade 62, Copenhagen N.

DATUM. A reference score from which the number of IMPs won or lost in an IMP pair game can be computed. See AVERAGE SCORE.

DEAD. Bridge jargon to describe a player in a hopeless situation. It usually refers to the play of the hand, as in, "North made a killing shift, and I was dead."

Also said of a hand, especially dummy, which has been robbed of (or never had) a re-entry.

DEAL. (1) To distribute the fifty-two cards at contract; (2) the privilege of thus distributing the cards; (3) the act of dealing; (4) the cards themselves when distributed. The dealer distributes the cards face down, one at a time in rotation into four separate hands of thirteen cards each, the first card to the player on his left and the last card to himself. If he deals two cards simultaneously or consecutively to the same player, or fails to deal a card to a player, he may rectify the error, provided he does so immediately and to the satisfaction of the other players.

The dealer must not allow the face of any card to be seen while he is dealing. Until the deal is completed, no player but the dealer may touch any card except to correct or prevent an irregularity. See LAWS (Laws 8, 9, 10), LAWS OF DUPLICATE BRIDGE (Law 6).

DEALER. The player who distributes the cards at a hand of bridge. At the start of a rubber of regular bridge or of Chicago, a cut is made for partners and for the deal privilege, the player who receives the highest card becoming "dealer." After the entire deck has been given out one by one in turn to each player starting at the left of the dealer, each fourth card going to the dealer himself, the dealer speaks first in the auction by either bidding or passing, subsequent calls proceeding normally clockwise from his position.

The term "dealer" is also a specialized slang word applying to a person who knows how to cheat at cards by arranging or "stacking" the pack in such fashion as to give himself and/or his partner by far the best of the cards continuously.

DEALING DEVICE. (1) a crank-operated machine which distributes the cards. (2) An electrically operated card table which accepts the used pack, shuffles it, and distributes the cards for the next deal. Neither has gained wide acceptance.

DEATH HOLDING. A holding in a suit which seems an a priori certainty to kill the partnership's chances of playing or defending successfully. The most common examples are (1) a holding of xx in the opponents' suit in a hand with slam possibilities; with a small doubleton in one hand it is likely that neither partner can adequately control the opponents' suit for slam play; (2) a defensive holding of Qx in front of a long suit headed by AK in the dummy's or declarer's hand; such a holding gives little hope of a trick on power, and no hope that declarer will misplay or misguess.

DECEPTION, MATHEMATICS OF. The rule of multiplication of probabilities (see PROBABILITY OF SUCCESSIVE EVENTS) is applicable when declarer has to decide whether a card is a DECEPTIVE PLAY. The probability that a suspected card is true is the probability that the player holds a distribution that leaves him no choice but to play it. The probability that it is false is the probability that he has a distribution from which the deceptive play would be attractive, multiplied by the probability that he would in fact decide to play the falsecard.

NORTH
A 8 3 2

SOUTH
K Q 10 4

After winning the opening lead, South plays the king. West follows low, and East plays the nine. The probability that this is a singleton is approximately 2.8%. However, East may hold J9xx, and the probability of this holding is about 8.4%. Consequently, if the probability that East would play the nine from J9xx is greater than 1/3, that distribution would be more likely than the singleton nine. Albert Dormer and Terence Reese have postulated that the play of the nine from J9xx is obligatory, in order to present South with a choice of plays on the second round. If South accepts this view, he must play the ace next time. (For simplicity, the assumption has been made that, if West held J765, he would play the low cards indiscriminately.)

The problem should be pursued a little further. Suppose that the only deception envisaged is the play of the nine from J9xx, that is to say that East holds either J9xx or the singleton nine when he plays the nine. With a side entry to dummy, South can now give himself a better chance. He enters dummy and leads low toward the queen-ten. If East shows out, South plays the queen, and has a marked finesse against West. To counteract this, East must not merely play the nine from J9xx, but also from 9xx and 9x. If he is deemed capable of this, there is little attraction for declarer in the play just described, since if East follows to a low card from dummy, declarer will have to guess whether to finesse the ten or play the queen. As 9xx and 9x each have a probability of about 10.2%, South would do better to play dummy's ace on the second round, unless he estimates only a very small probability of the nine being played from a doubleton or tripleton.

A detailed explanation of this case is as follows: It is assumed that East will always play the nine from J9xx. The possible plans for South are:

A. Low to the ace, so as to be able to finesse against East if West shows out.

B. Enter dummy with a side-suit, lead toward queen-ten, and finesse the ten if East follows.

C. Enter dummy with a side-suit, lead toward queen-ten, and play the queen if East follows:

The probabilities that the relevant distributions were dealt to East are: 9x or 9xx, 64%; J9xx, 27%; singleton 9, 9%. Let p = the probability that East will play the nine if he has 9x or 9xx. Then the chance of plan A succeeding is .64 times p + .27, and of plan B succeeding, .09 + .27. Therefore if p is less than 14%, plan A is preferable. That is, plan A should be preferred unless it is thought that West would not play the nine from 9x or 9xx at least seven times in fifty. The chance of plan C succeeding is .64 times p + .09, and plan C is thus clearly inferior to plan A. If entries permit, the two should be led from North's hand on the first round of that suit. It is now more difficult for East to play the nine from J 9 x x. West may hold the ten and the play of the nine could concede a trick unnecessarily.

A. T. and R. T.

DECEPTIVE BID. See LEAD-INHIBITING BID and PSYCHIC BIDDING.

DECEPTIVE LEAD. See OPENING LEAD.

DECEPTIVE OPENING LEADS. See FALSE-CARD-ING and OPENING LEAD.

DECEPTIVE PLAY. The term "deceptive play" could well be used of any play that aims to mislead an opponent. Discriminating writers, however, tend to restrict the use of the term to plays by the declarer. Deceptive play by the defenders is more suitably described as FALSE-CARDING, and is dealt with under that title.

Deceptive plays by the declarer are analyzed under these headings:

(1) Weakness-concealing plays.
(2) Strength-concealing plays.
(3) Honor-crashing plays.
(4) "Scrambling" plays that interfere with the defenders' signals.
(5) Miscellaneous deceptive plays.

Weakness-concealing plays. Bluff is the basis of most of these plays; the declarer deliberately does something which is not correct technique, in the hope that the deceptive effect of his play will outweigh its mathematical shortcoming.

```
              NORTH
              ♠ 8 6 3
              ♡ 9 2
              ◇ Q J 10 6 4
              ♣ K Q 7

              SOUTH
              ♠ A K 9 4
              ♡ A J
              ◇ K 9 8 3
              ♣ A 8 2
```

West leads a small heart against South's three no trump contract, and East puts up the queen. If perfect defense were to be assumed, South's best play would be to duck. After winning the next trick he would play diamonds, hoping that the defender with the diamond ace had no more hearts to play.

This plan has a slight but legitimate chance of success. In practice it is very much better to win the *first* trick, and drive out the diamond ace. If West has it, and the heart king as well, he may not find the right continuation. East's play of the heart queen on the opening lead has made it plain to West that declarer has the jack, but he does not know that it is

bare. West may conclude that his best chance of defeating the contract is to find East with a black ace, so that he can lead hearts through declarer's jack.

On other occasions the declarer tries to bluff his way through by opening up a weak suit himself.

```
              NORTH
              ♠ J 6 2
              ♡ A K 10
              ◇ 8 6 3
              ♣ A 10 9 7

              SOUTH
              ♠ Q 7 3
              ♡ Q 8 3
              ◇ A 10 2
              ♣ K Q 4 3
```

West leads the heart four against South's three no trump contract. Declarer's ninth trick can come only from spades, and then only if both ace and king are in one hand. Further, if declarer attacks spades himself, and is lucky enough to find the cards suitably placed, the defender will probably shift to diamonds.

Declarer's best plan is to take the opening lead in dummy, and lead diamonds himself, inserting the ten if East plays low and ducking if East puts up an honor. There is a reasonable chance that the defenders will attack spades.

Many weakness-concealing plays involve releasing a high card earlier than need be. Against a no trump contract, West leads the two of a suit in which dummy holds J x x and declarer Q x. If East plays the ace, it can do no harm for declarer to drop the queen. East will probably recognize that this is not a singleton, and he may assume that declarer's other card is the king. There are many variations of this theme.

Sometimes bluff is needed to extract tricks from an unpromising holding. A declarer who is reduced to the necessity of attempting to make two tricks with K x x in dummy and J x x in the closed hand does best to lead the king from the table. If the cards are distributed as follows:

```
                        NORTH
                        K x x
          WEST                        EAST
          A 10 x                      Q x x x
                        SOUTH
                        J x x
```

West may conclude that South is trying to establish a suit headed by the queen and jack in the closed hand. If West seeks to molest declarer's communications by holding up the ace, South has every chance of two tricks, for East is unlikely to put up the queen on the second round.

Strength-concealing plays. These are resorted to most frequently in no trump contracts. The usual occasion is when declarer wants the defenders to continue a suit which they have opened, rather than shift to a suit which he fears more.

NORTH
♠ K J 7 3
♡ 10 7 2
◇ Q J 10 5
♣ 8 7

SOUTH
♠ A Q 2
♡ J 8
◇ A 9 7 4 3
♣ A Q 6

West leads a small club against three no trump, and East plays the jack. Declarer can afford to win with the ace rather than the queen. He crosses to dummy with a spade and takes the diamond finesse, hoping that if it loses West will continue clubs rather than shift to hearts. The stratagem is a familiar one but can be effective.

Following is a play to conceal strength which can occur equally at a suit contract or at no trump:

NORTH
Q 5 2

SOUTH
A 10 9 8

South needs to develop a second trick in the suit, but entry difficulties make it necessary to lead from the closed hand. He has no indication of where the king is located.

Some players will lead the ten in the hope of putting pressure on West, but actually the eight is better, especially if West can be expected to realize that South has the ace. By leading the eight, declarer conceals the fact that he has a possible finesse against the jack. Hence, if West has the king, he is more likely to put it up, for from his viewpoint the declarer may have no option but to play dummy's queen. It is, therefore, sound psychology to lead the eight, and run it if West plays low.

Honor-crashing plays. Plays aimed at persuading the defenders to spend two honors—usually trumps—on one trick range from the simple to the subtle. Some examples are given under the title CRASHING HONORS, but there are others which have a more deceptive flavor.

NORTH
Q 7 x x

SOUTH
10 8 x x x

The usual way of playing this suit is by leading small toward the queen. Declarer loses only two tricks provided that the suit divides evenly, that West has the lone jack, or that West has A K x or A K J.

The fact that the defenders would expect declarer to play thus can make the lead of the queen from dummy effective. If the bidding rules out the possibility that East has a singleton, the queen lead cannot

cost and may tempt a cover from East if he has K J x or A J x.

Sometimes the best way of crashing the defenders' honors is to induce them to ruff with a small trump before the trump suit has been touched.

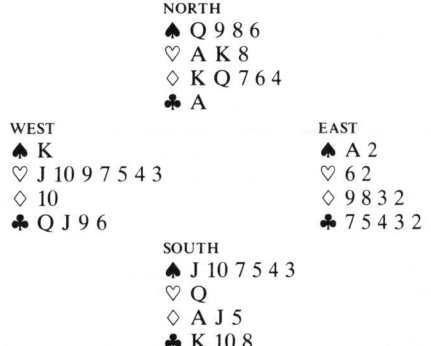

NORTH
♠ Q 9 8 6
♡ A K 8
◇ K Q 7 6 4
♣ A

WEST
♠ K
♡ J 10 9 7 5 4 3
◇ 10
♣ Q J 9 6

EAST
♠ A 2
♡ 6 2
◇ 9 8 3 2
♣ 7 5 4 3 2

SOUTH
♠ J 10 7 5 4 3
♡ Q
◇ A J 5
♣ K 10 8

In a pairs contest South plays four spades after West has made a pre-emptive bid in hearts. When West opens the heart jack, South's best deceptive play is to win in hand, cross to the club ace, and continue hearts, throwing a diamond from hand. If East ruffs in small on the third round, South overruffs and drops the enemy trumps together for a high matchpoint score.

"Scrambling" plays. When the declarer has pronounced views as to whether he wants the defenders to continue a suit or shift, he may be able to cut in on their signals. The general rule for declarer is to put out the same signals as he would if he were defending—a high card to encourage a continuation, a low card to discourage. The following is a basic position:

NORTH
9 7 4

WEST
A K J 3

EAST
10 8 5

SOUTH
Q 6 2

When West leads the king against a suit contract, South drops the six to make East's five look like the beginning of an echo.

If the declarer has more than two cards to signal with, it does not necessarily follow that he should play the highest.

NORTH
9 3 2

WEST
A K J

EAST
10 8 5

SOUTH
Q 7 6 4

When West leads the king and East plays the five, South should drop the six, not the seven. If he played the seven, West would realize that some deception was afoot, for it is a basic rule of defensive signaling that encouraging signals should be as high as is safely possible. East, therefore, would not start an echo with the five if he also held the six. So, if South dropped the seven in the above diagram, West would suspect that he held the six as well. Similarly:

```
                NORTH
                8 3
WEST                            EAST
Q J 10 5                        9 7
                SOUTH
                A K 6 4 2
```

South is playing a no trump contract, having concealed this suit in the bidding. West leads the queen, and South, needing to develop the suit, encourages in the hope that West will continue. In this diagram, both the four and the six are apt to be effective, but against players who themselves always false-card as high as possible the four is best; if West reasons that South would play the six to encourage, West will be all the more convinced that East's seven is the beginning of a signal.

It can be good policy for declarer to scramble the signals even when he has no immediate objective in mind.

```
                NORTH
                K Q 4
WEST                            EAST
J 9 5 2                         10 8 6
                SOUTH
                A 7 3
```

Suppose South wants to enter dummy to lead another suit. By leading the seven, rather than the three, he may confuse West's count of the hand. East's six may appear to West as the beginning of an echo; it may even suggest to him that East is holding up the ace.

There are some more advanced situations where the declarer has not only to play the right card—he has to know also which hand to lead from.

```
                NORTH
                K Q J 8 2
WEST                            EAST
9 6 5                           A 10 4
                SOUTH
                7 3
```

South is playing a no trump contract, and has no entries to dummy. He needs two tricks from the suit.

If South starts by playing the three toward dummy's king, West will play the five, and East will know that his partner has either three cards in the suit or a singleton. In neither case can it cost East to play his ace on the second round, so South will be thwarted in his endeavor.

Suppose instead that South leads the *seven* from hand; now, from East's angle his partner's five could be the beginning of an echo, showing a doubleton. In any case, East allows dummy to win the first trick, but the critical point comes on the second round: provided that the second lead comes from *dummy*,

East will have to make his decision without any sure guidance from partner.

On other occasions it can be better to make both leads from the closed hand:

```
                NORTH
                K Q J 2
WEST                            EAST
A 8 6                           10 9 4
                SOUTH
                7 5 3
```

This time South is playing a suit contract, and will be inconvenienced if the ace is held up until the third round. He leads the five from hand and dummy wins. Now he must re-enter the closed hand in another suit and lead the seven; West may place his partner with two or four cards, and in either event may release the ace. The principle followed is to make the defender with the stop card play *second* to the vital trick.

Also coming broadly under the heading of scrambling plays are those where the declarer has to follow suit with a particular card in order to make it more difficult for the defenders to gauge his holding.

```
                NORTH
                K J 6
WEST                            EAST
8 5                             A Q 10 7 4 2
                SOUTH
                9 3
```

South is playing a suit contract, and West leads the eight of this side suit, which East has bid. Dummy plays the jack, East the queen, and South drops the nine. If he plays the three instead, East knows that it is safe to continue with ace and another (unless the partnership is playing MUD leads). After the play of the nine, however, East has to take account of the possibility that declarer has a singleton.

In general, in such situations as above, the declarer follows suit with a card higher than the one led, but sometimes only a certain card will do.

```
                NORTH
                K 7 4 3
WEST                            EAST
2                               A Q 8 6 5
                SOUTH
                J 10 9
```

Again West leads a suit bid by his partner, and this time declarer wants to lose only one trick. (Discards are available elsewhere.) His best chance is to play low from dummy and drop the ten from hand. East may still read the situation correctly, but his task would be easier if declarer played either the jack or the nine; he would then be able to infer that partner would not have opened the two from either J 10 2 or 10 9 2.

Miscellaneous deceptive plays. One group of situations which does not fall readily under any other heading, and which has been little explored is the following:

	WEST	EAST
(a)	10 7 3 2	A K Q 6 4
(b)	J 6 5 4	A K 10 7 3
(c)	10 5 4 3	A K 8 6 2

In each case East is declarer, and these are his trump holdings. It costs nothing to lead the high card from West each time, intending, if North plays low, to overtake and play normally for the drop. Occasionally the deceptive precaution will pay dividends, as where North covers the ten with the jack from J 9 8 5 in example (a), enabling his cards to be picked up by subsequent finesses. Example (b) is similar, while in (c) East improves his chances not only when North has all four outstanding cards but also when he covers from J 9 7 or Q 9 7.

There are many similar positions, and the field is widened when account is taken of inferences from the bidding. For example:

	WEST	EAST
	10 4 3 2	A K 8 6

The ten lead costs only when North has the lone queen or jack. If the bidding precludes this possibility, the ten is liable to prove doubly effective, since North will be expecting declarer to play him for trump length. Further, North may not care to outbluff the declarer by playing low from a holding headed by queen and jack, since declarer may well run the ten in this situation.

The basis of another group of miscellaneous plays is that the lead should be made from dummy toward the closed hand:

NORTH

A Q x x

SOUTH

x x x

South has to develop this suit at no trump but does not need immediate tricks. Best play is to lead small from dummy on the first round. East may put up the king from a variety of holdings which would have ruined the declarer had he played any other way. Similarly:

NORTH

K x x x

SOUTH

Q x

At a suit contract, South leads from dummy on the first round, and the queen holds. Ordinary technique is to play low from both hands on the next round, and hope to ruff out the ace on the third. Entries permitting, however, it is better to re-enter dummy after the queen, and to lead again toward the closed hand. East may put up the ace, fearing that declarer started with both queen and jack.

A. D.

DECK. (1) The pack; a synonym used regularly in America but not in England. (2) A colloquial term for a big hand. "Holding the deck" refers to a hand with a disproportionate number of high cards, or to a session in which a player holds a number of such hands. See PACK.

DECLARATION. (1) Contract, e.g., a heart declaration. (2) A statement of intent as to further line of play made by the declarer at some point previous to the play of the last trick of any given hand. See also CALL.

DECLARATIVE-INTERROGATIVE (D. I.) FOUR NO TRUMP. The use of four no trump as a general slam investigation, rarely as BLACKWOOD; developed originally as part of the NEAPOLITAN system. Four no trump is Blackwood if it is a jump bid, or bid at the first opportunity after a sudden leap to game. Otherwise, it promises two aces if bid by an unlimited hand, or one ace by a limited hand, and requests partner to show an undisclosed feature (a first- or second-round control, or even a key queen) by bidding the suit containing the feature. The reply does not promise extra values unless it goes past five of the agreed trump suit. Responder may also answer by jumping to six of the agreed suit to deny interest in grand slam, or by bidding five no trump to announce a complete maximum and strong interest in grand slam. Over any normal five-level reply, a rebid of five no trump again asks for additional features in an effort to reach grand slam and promises one more ace than originally guaranteed.

In several systems such as KAPLAN-SHEINWOLD and BLUE TEAM CLUB, D. I. four no trump asks for features without promising a specific number of aces. In Blue Team when four no trump is bid in the course of a series of cue-bids it is a generalized slam try indicating that all suits are controlled, unless the player who bids four no trump bypasses a suit in which control has not been shown. Some expert partnerships have agreed that after a Blackwood four no trump and the ace-showing response, five no trump is always declarative-interrogative, asking for features rather than for the number of kings.

DECLARER. The player who first bid the denomination of the final bid. If the final bid is hearts, the player on the side making the final bid that first named hearts is the declarer. The declarer controls the play of his own hand and the dummy as a united force.

DECLARER'S CLAIM OR CONCESSION OF TRICKS. See CLAIM OR CONCESSION and LAWS (Law 70); LAWS OF DUPLICATE (Laws 68–71).

DEEP FINESSE. A finesse when three or more cards are missing higher in rank than the card finessed. This is often made in order to execute a DUCK or AVOIDANCE play, but can be a genuine play necessary to achieve the best result. Well-known situations are:

(a)	(b)	(c)
NORTH	NORTH	NORTH
Q 10 x	A J 9	A Q 9
SOUTH	SOUTH	SOUTH
x x x	x x x	x x x

With (a) the ten is finessed, although it might be right to put up the queen if West leads a low card: it would be unusual to lead from ace-jack or king-jack with Q 10 x visible in dummy.

With (b) and (c) the nine is finessed to give the maximum chance.

A rarer deep finesse can occur when a singleton is held opposite a five-card suit including J 108:

(d)	(e)	(f)
NORTH	NORTH	NORTH
A J 10 8 x	K J 10 8 x	Q J 10 8 x
SOUTH	SOUTH	SOUTH
x	x	x

In each case the best chance of developing three tricks is to finesse the eight on the first round.

See also FINESSE and SUIT COMBINATIONS.

DEFEAT THE CONTRACT. To prevent the declaring side from making as many tricks as required by the final contract.

DEFECTIVE TRICK. A trick that contains fewer or more than four legally played cards. See LAWS (Law 68); LAWS OF DUPLICATE (Law 67).

DEFENDER. An opponent of the declarer; one who attempts to prevent the declarer from making his contract. The secondary objective of preventing overtricks is of major importance at duplicate.

DEFENDER'S CLAIM OR CONCESSION OF TRICKS. See CLAIM OR CONCESSION and LAWS (Law 73); LAWS OF DUPLICATE (Laws 70, 71).

DEFENDING HAND. Either opponent of the declarer; occasionally used in the bidding to refer to an opponent of the player who opened the bidding.

DEFENSE, DEFENSIVE PLAY. The play by the opponents of the declarer. The primary object of defensive play is normally to defeat the contract, even at the expense of presenting declarer with overtricks if the chosen line of defense is unsuccessful. At duplicate, however, particularly at match-point play, holding declarer to a minimum number of tricks can be important, indeed. Articles dealing with defensive play that should be consulted are: COVERING HONORS; DESCHAPELLES COUP; DISCARDING; DISCOVERY; DUCK; ENTRY-KILLING PLAY; FALSE-CARDING; FORCING DECLARER TO RUFF; JETTISON; MATCH-POINT DEFENSE; MERRIMAC COUP; OVERRUFF; PLAY FROM EQUALS; RULE OF ELEVEN; SECOND HAND PLAY; SPOT CARDS; THIRD HAND PLAY; THROUGH STRENGTH; TRUMP PROMOTION;

UNDERRUFF; UP TO WEAKNESS; UPPERCUT. For all topics relating to OPENING LEADS, see that heading.

DEFENSE TO DOUBLE OF ONE NO TRUMP. In standard practice the double of a one no trump opening bid is for penalties. The usual means of escape is for opener's partner to bid a suit, and the traditional meaning of a redouble is to penalize the doubler. See DOUBLES OF NO TRUMP BIDS (Third hand problems). However, several alternatives are designed either to locate the partnership's best escape suit or to place the no trump opener as declarer, or both.

One suggested method is to use TRANSFER BIDS. Responder bids the suit next below his long suit. If responder's suit is clubs he redoubles to ask opener to bid clubs. If responder has no long suit but has seven or eight cards in the major suits, he can redouble, ostensibly transferring to clubs; but, after opener bids two clubs, responder bids two diamonds, asking opener to choose between hearts and spades.

In a simpler method, suggested by Martin COHN of Atlanta, Ga., suit bids by responder remain natural, and the redouble itself is used as a STAYMAN-type inquiry for the majors.

A third possibility is to use a response of two diamonds to ask opener to bid his better major suit, and to redouble to ask him to bid his better minor suit. In this method, responder's immediate run-out to two hearts or two spades would be natural, and his bid of two clubs would promise a long minor suit. If responder's suit is diamonds he runs to that suit over the double of two clubs that will presumably be forthcoming.

DEFENSE TO INTERFERENCE WITH BLACK-WOOD. The traditional method for dealing with opponents who overcall a four no trump BLACKWOOD bid has been to double whenever the size of the prospective penalty is attractive, and otherwise to pass with no aces and bid the cheapest suit with one ace, and so forth up the line. Modern conventions recognize that the penalty will rarely be sufficiently lucrative to warrant a double, and therefore give that call an artificial meaning related to the number of aces held by the Blackwood responder. The most common such conventions are:

(1) DEPO, which stands for Double Even, Pass Odd. A double shows zero, two, or four aces; a pass shows one or three.

(2) DOPI, which stands for Double Zero, Pass 1. A double shows no aces, pass shows 1, and two or more aces are shown by bidding up the line.

(3) PODI, which stands for Pass Zero, Double 1. The double and the pass have the reverse of the meanings they have using DOPI; other bids are the same.

DOPI is more widely used than PODI. A number of experts agree to use DOPI when the overcall is at the five-level, allowing room for bidding two or more aces up the line, and to use DEPO when the overcall is at the six-level and space is scarce.

DEFENSE TO ONE NO TRUMP. Specialized actions after an opposing opening bid of one no trump are discussed under other headings: ASPRO; ASTRO; BROZEL; DOUBLES OF NO TRUMP BIDS; EXCLUSION BID; LANDY; and RIPSTRA.

The general rule for the defenders is to pass when in doubt. An overcall is far more dangerous after a no trump opening than after a suit opening because the opening bidder has defined his hand precisely. The opener's partner is therefore in a position to judge the defensive prospects accurately.

This caution applies equally in the pass-out position. Although the fourth player has the advantage of knowing that the opposing strength has an upward limit of about 23 points, he should be discouraged by knowing that his side is unlikely to have a good suit fit. The opening bid and the pass by the opener's partner imply that those two hands are balanced. If the fourth player has a long suit, his partner is likely to be short in the same suit.

An overcall should therefore be assumed to be a six-card suit, although a non-vulnerable player might sometimes venture into the auction with a strong five-card suit. Even with a six-card suit and a good hand, it may be advisable to pass if the distribution is defensive (e.g., 6–3–2–2) rather than attacking (say, 6–4–2–1).

If the opening bid is a strong no trump, the opponents are unlikely to head for game and make it. But this is not so against a weak no trump, and responding to an overcall needs consideration. Some experts regard a bid of two no trump by the overcaller's partner as a forcing bid—a type of cue-bid in the opener's denomination. Suit take-outs of the overcall are then non-forcing.

DEFENSE TO OPENING FOUR-BID. Against an opponent's opening bid at the four-level it is standard to use the calls of double and four no trump in a variety of ways, depending on the suit of the opening bid.

Against an opening pre-empt of four clubs or four diamonds, a double is for take-out. Some partnerships use a bid of four no trump as a natural bid; some use it as BLACKWOOD.

Against a four heart opening, a double is for take-out and guarantees spade support. The prevailing agreement is that a four no trump bid is take-out for the minor suits.

Against a four spade opening a double is used for penalties. Hence a four no trump bid is for take-out.

DEFENSE TO OPENING THREE-BID. The following methods can be used as a defense against WEAK TWO-BIDS also:

(1) Standard. A double is primarily for take-out, but is sometimes described as "cooperative" or "optional" because the doubler's partner may sometimes decide to pass in the expectation of a penalty. A normal minimum for the double would be 16 points in high cards, or 13 points in the pass-out seat. The double implies support for the unbid major or

majors unless the doubler has considerable reserve strength.

Other bids would be natural, including three no trump, which would be a minimum of 18 points. Desirable features for this bid would be a double stopper in the opener's suit and a good minor suit.

(2) Fishbein. Devised by Harry Fishbein of New York. A double of a three-bid is for penalties, and the doubler's partner should rarely take any action. A bid in the cheapest available suit is a conventional bid to replace a take-out double. Three hearts over three diamonds, for example, would show a minimum of 16 points in high cards and a three-suited hand, or possibly a two-suited hand. The Fishbein take-out bid over three spades would be four clubs. The take-out bid is unconditionally forcing, because it might be based on a two-suited hand. The convention does not apply in the pass-out position.

(3) Cheaper (or lower) minor. The use of the cheaper available minor suit as a take-out bid: three diamonds over three clubs, and four clubs over other three-bids. As in the Fishbein convention, a double is for penalties, and the convention does not apply sitting under the three-bidder (although it can apply by partnership agreement). This convention is standard among English tournament players. A variation is known in America as the Smith convention, devised by Curtis SMITH, Houston. He recommends the use of four clubs as the take-out bid in all circumstances, even over three clubs.

(4) Optional double. A double that promises a balanced hand with both support for the unbid suits and some strength in the opener's suit. It invites the doubler's partner to pass for penalties.

(5) Weiss. The use of the cheaper minor for take-out as in (3) above, with the double used as an optional double as in (4).

(6) Three no trump for take-out. Rare in America, but combined with a double for penalties, this is standard procedure in England at rubber bridge. Partnerships must agree whether this applies in the pass-out position. A disadvantage is that three no trump is often needed as a natural bid.

(7) Reese. Three no trump for a take-out over major-suit three-bids only, with a double for penalties. Double for take-out over minor suits, and in fourth seat.

(8) Two-suiter take-outs. Overcalls of four in a minor suit after a major-suit three-bid can be used to show that suit and the unbid major. In combination with standard take-out doubles, this solves some difficult two-suiter problems. The single-suited minor-suit hand is often suitable for a three no trump overcall, or a jump to the five-level. The two-suiter bids can be applied in both second and fourth seats. (A minor two-suiter can be shown by a jump to an "unusual" four no trump.)

DEFENSE TO PRE-EMPTIVE BIDS. See DEFENSE TO OPENING FOUR-BID; DEFENSE TO OPENING THREE-BID and WEAK TWO-BIDS.

DEFENSE TO A SQUEEZE. The prerequisites for a true squeeze are: menace cards, properly located and oriented; sufficient entries to these menaces; and correct timing. Unless all these elements are present, the squeeze will not be effective unless the opponents misdefend. There are several principles which can assist the defenders to discard correctly.

(1) If one defender guards a two-card menace and two isolated menaces, then he should unguard the long menace when a choice must be made among the three suits.

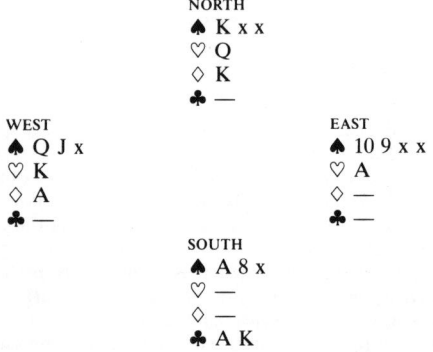

The lead of the club ace squeezes West in three suits. If he discards a diamond, then North's king becomes established. If he discards a heart, the ending leads to a twin-entry DOUBLE SQUEEZE. West must discard a spade, his guard to the long menace.

(2) When a defender guards two long menaces and one isolated menace, then he should unguard the long menace placed to his left.

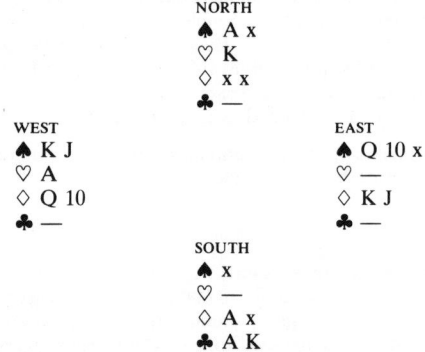

South leads the ace of clubs, which squeezes West in three suits. If he discards the ace of hearts, then North's king becomes established. If he discards a diamond, then South cashes the ace of that suit, which leads to a positional double squeeze. West must discard a spade, the guard to the long menace situated to his left.

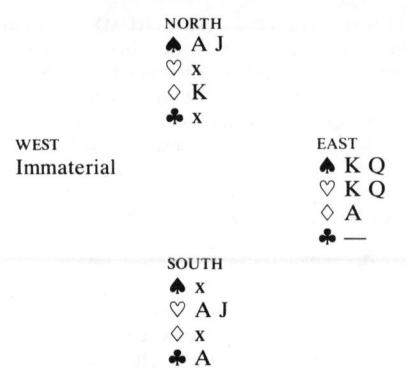

PROGRESSIVE SQUEEZE defense. In this example, South leads the ace of clubs, which squeezes East in three suits. Any discard costs a trick, so that East's objective must be to protect himself from a progressive squeeze, which would cost him two tricks. A heart is the only discard which will achieve this end.

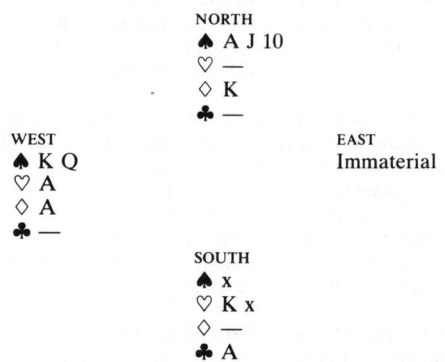

This resembles an automatic REPEATED SQUEEZE position, but it is faulty in that a one-card menace (the diamond king) is misplaced in the North hand. When South leads the ace of clubs, West must discard the ace of diamonds. Otherwise South can win all the remaining tricks.

(3) On rare occasions an underruff (see UNDER-RUFF) proves to be a defender's only safe play. The following hand from a par contest illustrates the point. (ROMANET).

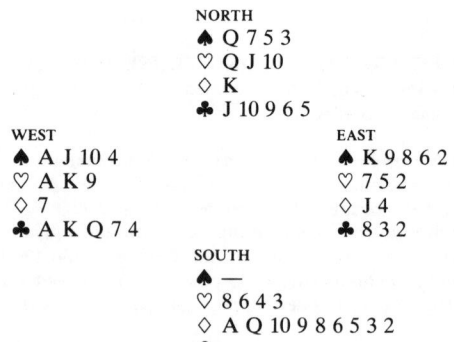

East is declarer in six spades. South leads the ace of diamonds, followed by the queen. West ruffs the second diamond with the ace, and North must under-ruff. Any other discard would enable declarer to establish a trick. When the trumps are run off, North cannot be squeezed since he discards after West, which hand contains all the menace cards.

Sometimes correct discarding will not save the defenders; an early attack against one of the basic elements of the squeeze may be the only means to break it up.

(a) Destruction of the menace. This can be effected in two ways: (1) by leading the suit at every opportunity, thus forcing declarer to play the menace card prematurely; and (2) by making it impossible to ISOLATE THE MENACE. This latter occurs usually at a trump contract. T. REESE provides this example to illustrate the attack on menace cards.

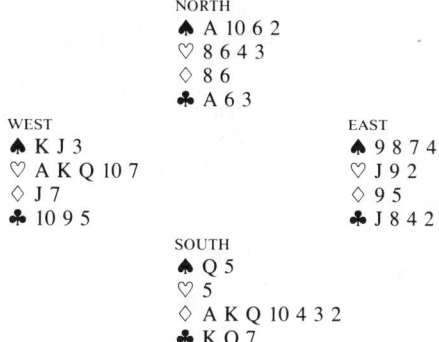

```
            NORTH
            ♠ A 10 6 2
            ♡ 8 6 4 3
            ◇ 8 6
            ♣ A 6 3
WEST                        EAST
♠ K J 3                     ♠ 9 8 7 4
♡ A K Q 10 7                ♡ J 9 2
◇ J 7                       ◇ 9 5
♣ 10 9 5                    ♣ J 8 4 2
            SOUTH
            ♠ Q 5
            ♡ 5
            ◇ A K Q 10 4 3 2
            ♣ K Q 7
```

South is declarer at six diamonds. West leads the king of hearts. If West continues with another heart, South ruffs, and after drawing trumps, enters dummy with the club ace to ruff a third heart, thus leaving West alone with the burden of guarding that suit as well as the spade suit. However, if West refrains from leading the second heart, then the heart menace cannot be isolated; East's jack cannot be ruffed out, West can discard all his hearts, relying on East to guard that suit.

(b) Attack on entries. This defense consists of playing the suit where declarer has a long menace. In this way a two-card menace may become an isolated menace, a twin-entry menace may be transformed into an ordinary two-card menace, etc.

```
            NORTH
            ♠ K x
            ♡ x
            ◇ K x
            ♣ —
WEST                        EAST
♠ x x                       ♠ Q J 10
♡ A K                       ♡ —
◇ x                         ◇ A x
♣ —                         ♣ —
            SOUTH
            ♠ A x x
            ♡ —
            ◇ —
            ♣ A K
```

Clubs are trumps, and West has the lead. If West leads a heart or a diamond, South can ruff and play his last trump, and East will be squeezed in diamonds and spades. The ending is a twin-entry simple squeeze. However, if West leads a spade, the twin-entry menace is reduced to a two-card menace of the usual sort and the squeeze must fail.

(c) Failure to rectify the count. Many times declarer must lose one or two tricks to the opponents in RECTIFYING THE COUNT for a squeeze. Defenders can withhold their cooperation in this maneuver, either by failure to cash established winners or by refusing to win a trick offered by the declarer. The example below, if permitted to succeed, is known as a SUICIDE SQUEEZE.

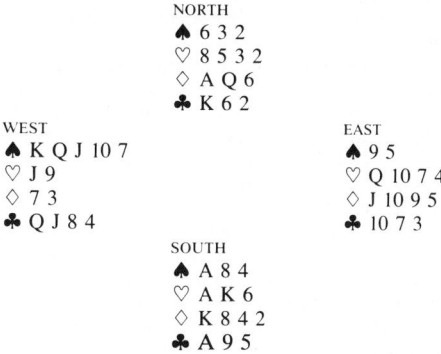

```
            NORTH
            ♠ 6 3 2
            ♡ 8 5 3 2
            ◇ A Q 6
            ♣ K 6 2
WEST                        EAST
♠ K Q J 10 7                ♠ 9 5
♡ J 9                       ♡ Q 10 7 4
◇ 7 3                       ◇ J 10 9 5
♣ Q J 8 4                   ♣ 10 7 3
            SOUTH
            ♠ A 8 4
            ♡ A K 6
            ◇ K 8 4 2
            ♣ A 9 5
```

South is declarer at three no trump, and West leads a spade. South wins the second round, and returns the suit. If West cooperates with declarer and cashes all his spades, then East can discard his clubs, but the second club lead won in dummy later squeezes him in the red suits. West cannot even cash the fourth spade without putting pressure on his partner. East can let go of two clubs on the third and fourth spades, but when declarer cashes his ace and king of clubs, East must either unguard the diamonds or discard a heart, whereupon declarer will be able to set up dummy's fourth heart for his ninth trick. West can cash only two spades, but then he must switch and declarer cannot make his contract.

B. Romanet gives the following hand:

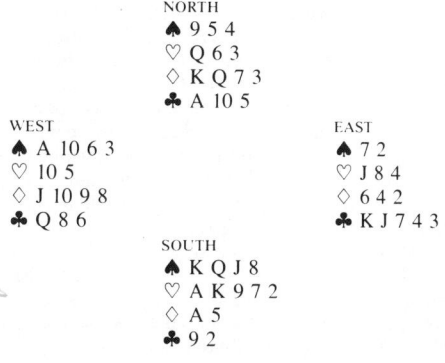

```
            NORTH
            ♠ 9 5 4
            ♡ Q 6 3
            ◇ K Q 7 3
            ♣ A 10 5
WEST                        EAST
♠ A 10 6 3                  ♠ 7 2
♡ 10 5                      ♡ J 8 4
◇ J 10 9 8                  ◇ 6 4 2
♣ Q 8 6                     ♣ K J 7 4 3
            SOUTH
            ♠ K Q J 8
            ♡ A K 9 7 2
            ◇ A 5
            ♣ 9 2
```

South is declarer at six hearts, and receives the lead of a diamond. After drawing trumps, he leads from North up to the king of spades. If West ducks two rounds of spades, the contract is unmakable. On the other hand, if he wins either of the first two rounds of spades, South can execute a spade-diamond squeeze against West.

M. I.

DEFENSE TO STRONG ARTIFICIAL OPENINGS. With the modern trend toward strong artificial opening bids, it becomes increasingly necessary for the defending side to have some conventional understanding about how to enter the auction, either to prepare for a possible sacrifice or to prevent the opponents from finding their best contract. Several methods are in current use, most of them based on the theory that the defending side will usually not find it profitable to enter the auction except with pre-emptive-type hands, containing either a long suit or two suits.

(1) The simplest defense, employed by the majority of tournament players, uses a double to show length in the major suits, and a one no trump overcall to show length in the minor suits. This treatment would apply directly over an artificial one club opening, or over an artificial one diamond response. Single suit bids are natural and show long suits; jump overcalls are pre-emptive. This method can be used over strong artificial two club and two diamond openings as well, but few pairs do so.

(2) Truscott defense. Devised by Alan TRUSCOTT, this method allows the defense to show all two-suited and one-suited hands. After a strong artificial opening, such as two clubs or SCHENKEN or BLUE TEAM one club, or the artificial negative diamond response, one-suited hands would be shown by a jump overcall. All simple overcalls would show a two-suiter, the bid suit and the next higher-ranking. The two non-touching suit combinations would be shown by a double (the doubled suit and the non-touching suit) or a no trump overcall (the other two suits). For example, after an artificial two club opening, a two diamond overcall shows diamonds and hearts, two spades shows spades and clubs, double shows clubs and hearts, and two no trump shows diamonds and spades. The only alteration after a negative two diamond response is that the double shows diamonds and spades and two no trump shows clubs and hearts.

A possible weakness with this convention occurs in the rare case where the defender holds a strong hand (either a balanced strong no trump or a strong one-suiter) and has no convenient way to enter the auction after a SCHENKEN or BLUE TEAM one club opening. A modification that would cover this eventuality is to use a double to show a strong hand, approximately equivalent to the minimum strength shown by the opening bid, and a no trump overcall to show the two non-touching suit combinations.

(3) Defense to PRECISION CLUB. A method developed by THE PRECISION TEAM to defend against PRECISION CLUB openings allows the defense to show either a pre-emptive one-suited or two-suited hand, or a strong hand. The double is used to show 16 or more points in a hand that may be balanced; it is roughly the equivalent of a standard double of a one

no trump opening. A one no trump overcall of one club shows length in the major suits; a two no trump overcall shows length in the minor suits. This defense could be used against other ONE CLUB SYSTEMS, but is most valuable against the Precision system because that system reduces the minimum high-card requirement for one club openings to 16 points. Hands in which the opener has only 16 points may well belong to the "defense," and the incidence of 16-point hands is more than 80% as high as the total incidence of 17- and 18-point hands.

(4) EXCLUSION BIDS.

DEFENSE TO TWO-SUITED INTERFERENCE. When an opponent makes a two-suited cue-bid such as a MICHAELS CUE-BID or a two-suited overcall such as the unusual TWO NO TRUMP OVERCALL or the ROMAN JUMP OVERCALL, the partner of the opening bidder has available several countermeasures to advance his side's cause: the double, the raise, the cue-bid, and the bid of the new suit not shown by the opponent's interference.

Standard practice: Responder doubles with a hand which would have been worth a redouble of a take-out double and which is interested primarily in defense. Responder makes a simple raise in opener's suit with a hand worth a traditional free single raise after an overcall. A cue-bid in either of the suits shown by the interference is a general force, with the more expensive cue-bid logically promising a stronger hand than the cheaper cue-bid.

"Unusual over Unusual": When the interference is in the form of an unusual two no trump overcall, some partnerships retain the standard meanings of the double and the raise, but assign a specific meaning to each cue-bid. Each cue-bid shows the strength of a limit raise or better, and each shows length in one of the suits not promised by the overcall. The lower cue-bid shows length in the lower suit, and the higher cue-bid shows length in the higher suit that was not shown by the overcall. For example:

NORTH	EAST	SOUTH
1 ♠	2 NT	3 ◊

South's three diamond bid shows a hand worth at least a limit raise in spades. Free bids are forcing to game.

For a convention dealing in part with two-suited interference over one no trump openings, see LEBENSOHL.

DEFENSIVE BIDDING. All the bidding by a side after the opponents have opened the auction. (However, the bidding by the opener's side can sometimes be "defensive.") Specific defensive actions are discussed under various other headings including: BALANCING; CUE-BIDS IN OPPONENT'S SUIT; DEFENSE TO OPENING THREE-BIDS; DEFENSE TO ONE NO TRUMP; DEFENSE TO STRONG ARTIFICIAL OPENINGS; DOUBLE; DOUBLE FOR SACRIFICE; JUMP OVERCALL; OVERCALLS; PENALTY DOUBLE; SACRIFICE; TAKE-OUT DOUBLE;

TWO-SUITER CONVENTIONS. Some specialized defensive methods are listed under various systems, such as ROTH-STONE and KAPLAN-SHEINWOLD.

Accurate defensive bidding requires considerable judgment and experience. In this department of the game, the expert has a much greater advantage over the average player than he has in normal constructive bidding. Some of the many factors which have to be taken into account are:

(1) *The risk involved.* Is there a real danger of being doubled and losing more than the opponents could score if left to their own devices? This may vary with the type of scoring, and with a psychological estimate of the opponents. Are they likely to be quick doublers?

(2) *The prospects* of achieving something by action. Possible goals are: (a) bidding and making a part-score, game, or slam; (b) saving effectively against a contract the opponents could make (see SAVE); (c) pushing the opponents to a level at which the defense may have a chance; (d) disrupting the opponents' bidding so that they reach the wrong contract. In general, the holding in the opponent's suit is a determining factor: a shortage favors action, and length and/or strength indicate passivity.

(3) *Vulnerability*, a paramount factor. Favorable vulnerability often generates aggressive action by the defenders, especially at duplicate. Both sides are very conscious of the fact that a three-trick defeat is a triumph for the defenders if it saves a vulnerable game, with the extra possibility that the opening side may permit itself to be pushed to a dangerous level. This situation becomes exaggerated at the slam level: a non-vulnerable pair can afford to go down seven tricks to save a vulnerable small slam, and eleven tricks to save a vulnerable grand slam.

(4) *Level of the auction.* If a bid has to be made at a higher level, it is obviously more dangerous, and it may also offer poorer prospects. A side that bids one spade over an opposing one diamond is more likely to buy the final contract than a player who bids two diamonds over one spade. For both these reasons a bid at a higher level indicates a better hand. Similarly a double of one club can be made more freely than a double of one spade, because the latter offers fewer prospects and is less safe.

(5) *Estimate of partner's hand.* Simple addition of the minimum point-counts shown by the opponents and the points held by a defender will often reveal that partner's hand is virtually worthless. If you hold 16 points and a balanced hand, and an opening bid of one spade on your left gets a response of two diamonds, partner's probable range is 0–3 points, and the lower end of that scale is the more likely. To bid in such a situation, which the Europeans call "in sandwich," is clearly dangerous. It would be less dangerous if the response was one no trump, and least dangerous if the opener's suit had been raised. If the opener's side has established a fit, the chance that the defending side has a good fit is increased.

(6) *Honor wastage.* Queens and jacks in suits bid by the opponents are not only worthless for attacking purposes but should be rated as a minus quantity; they increase the defensive prospects, and therefore the danger of a PHANTOM SAVE. Conversely, queens and jacks in a suit held by the defending side are probably worthless in defense. Queens and jacks in side-suits are likely to play a part in any contract.

(7) *Honor position.* Most honor holdings increase in value when the suit is bid by the right-hand opponent, and decrease in value when the suit is bid on the left. (The exceptions are solid sequences such as king-queen-jack, and an ace not backed by another honor.) Similarly, three small cards is a poor holding if the suit was bid on the right, but rather better if the suit was bid on the left; any honor holding which partner may have has lost or gained value as a result of the bidding.

(8) *Length of suit.* An immediate overcall of an opening suit bid is normally at least five cards. In most other situations, a suit bid by the defending side is likely to be based on six-card length; e.g., after a no trump opening, or after two suit bids by the opener's side.

(9) *Raise your partner.* The need to support partner freely increases as the auction becomes more competitive. For example, if both sides are vulnerable and the bidding goes:

SOUTH	WEST	NORTH	EAST
♡	1 ♠	4 ♡	?

If East has some honor strength, it might be right for him to bid four spades holding a singleton spade honor: the chance that West has a very substantial spade suit is greatly increased by the North-South bidding.

(10) *Preparation.* The defending side may have to prepare its bidding in the same way that the opener does. A minimum take-out double would be unprepared if the doubler has a doubleton in an unbid suit. Consider this hand after right-hand opponent has bid one heart:

       ♠ A Q 6 4 3
       ♡ 7
       ◊ 5
       ♣ A 10 9 8 6 3

At favorable vulnerability there are excellent chances of an effective save over an opposing four heart bid, so two clubs followed by a spade bid at the lowest available level on the next round is the indicated procedure. At unfavorable vulnerability, it is sufficient to overcall one spade. Unless partner can support spades there is no great future, and it would be too dangerous to make a second bid at a high level. At equal vulnerability the decision would be closer.

(11) *Fit in side-suit.* When a good fit has been established in one suit, the degree of fit in another suit may be an important consideration. In a competitive auction a player who has overcalled and found a fit should sometimes bid a second suit in order to help his partner judge the right action at a high level. If the overcaller's partner bids a side-suit after finding a fit, it is more likely to be for lead-directing purposes.

(12) *Holding in the opponent's suit.* Three small cards in the opponent's suit is usually a bad holding,

but it becomes better than a doubleton if the suit has been strongly bid and supported: partner can be expected to have a singleton or void.

(13) *Push*. The defenders frequently have to make "push" bids:

SOUTH	WEST	NORTH	EAST
1 ♠	2 ♣	2 ♠	3 ♣

East's club support may be only a doubleton honor. The bid is worthwhile if he thinks that each side can make about eight tricks. The risk is not great, and East gives his side the chance of a plus score if the opponents allow themselves to be pushed to three spades.

DEFENSIVE TRICK. A card or card combination that may be expected to win a trick if an opponent becomes the declarer.

In some situations a player with a solitary defensive trick may need to take positive action. If six hearts is reached voluntarily and the bidding has indicated that six spades is a possible SACRIFICE, a hand that is known to be very weak should usually double if it has one defensive trick. This should help partner to make the right decision (which may still be to bid six spades), and avoid a PHANTOM SACRIFICE. For artificial uses of doubles and passes to reveal whether or not the partnership has enough defensive tricks to defeat the slam, see DOUBLE FOR SACRIFICE.

DELAYED DUCK SQUEEZE. A particular form of SECONDARY SQUEEZE.

DELAYED GAME RAISE. A bidding sequence equivalent to a standard jump raise.

♠ K J 5 4
♡ A 5 3
◇ 8 2
♣ A Q 9 7

This hand is too strong to raise an opening one spade to four spades in any normal bidding style. Using LIMIT RAISES, a substitute for the forcing double raise is necessary, and two clubs followed by four spades is the usual device. This is not completely satisfactory if the opener's rebid is two spades because the nature of responder's hand is not clarified; but in that case the slam prospects are remote.

For alternative solutions to this problem, see SWISS convention, THREE NO TRUMP RESPONSE, and TWO NO TRUMP RESPONSE. These devices would be used on relatively balanced hands, in which case the delayed game raise can be reserved for markedly two-suited hands.

DELAYED RAISE. See BELATED SUPPORT; PREFERENCE.

DELAYED STAYMAN. See STAYMAN ON SECOND ROUND.

DELTA ASKING BIDS. See SUPER PRECISION ASKING BIDS.

DEMAND BID. A forcing bid. A term used occasionally to refer to a FORCING TWO-BID but otherwise obsolete.

DENIAL BID. A bid that indicates lack of support for partner's bid (an obsolescent term).

DENMARK. See DANISH BRIDGE LEAGUE.

DENOMINATION. The suit or no trump specified in a bid. See LAWS (Law 18).

DESCENDING ORDER. The order of the rank of the denominations: no trump, spades, hearts, diamonds, and clubs.

DESCHAPELLES COUP. The lead of an unsupported high honor in order to establish an entry to partner's hand. This sacrificial play was invented by Guillaume Deschapelles at whist.

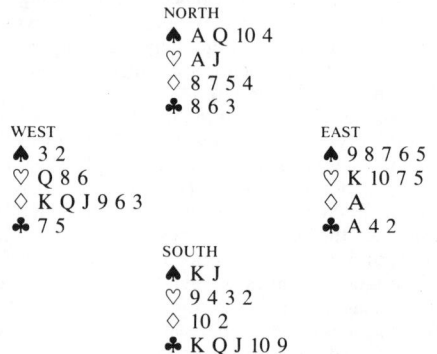

NORTH
♠ A Q 10 4
♡ A J
◇ 8 7 5 4
♣ 8 6 3

WEST
♠ 3 2
♡ Q 8 6
◇ K Q J 9 6 3
♣ 7 5

EAST
♠ 9 8 7 6 5
♡ K 10 7 5
◇ A
♣ A 4 2

SOUTH
♠ K J
♡ 9 4 3 2
◇ 10 2
♣ K Q J 10 9

The blocked diamond position makes it very difficult for the defense to defeat South's highly optimistic three no trump contract. East overtakes the diamond king lead with his ace, and must hope that his partner has a queen outside diamonds. If West has the club queen, the contract will be defeated automatically, so East assumes that his partner holds the heart queen. The return of the heart king is the key play. Whether or not South ducks, West's heart queen is established as an entry, and South can be held to five tricks. Any other play by East at the second trick permits South to make his contract. Note that the play of the heart king cannot give South his contract if West has the club queen: South's maximum would then be four spade tricks, three heart tricks, and one club trick.

For a similar defensive play aimed at destroying an entry instead of creating one, see MERRIMAC COUP.

DESPERATION LEAD OR PLAY. A lead or play made in defiance of the dictates of safety when defensive prospects seem poor. A tactic usually reserved for rubber bridge, not duplicate. For example, after this bidding:

NORTH	EAST	SOUTH	WEST
Pass	1 ♠	Pass	3 ♠
Pass	4 ♠	Pass	Pass
Pass			

South has to lead from:

> ♠ 8 7
> ♡ K 4
> ◇ J 8 5 4 2
> ♣ 9 7 4 3

The lead of the heart king is a desperation lead trying to promote a heart ruff in South's hand. North may hold heart ace, or heart queen and spade ace.

DEUCE. The two-spot, the lowest card, so named from the French *deux* coming from the Latin *duo*. The name is also applied to the two spots on a die, in gaming with dice, whence it is naïvely held that the imprecation, "What the deuce!" meaning distaste for an unexpected and unfortunate turn of events was derived.

In defensive play the deuce has definite meanings. When led against a no trump or suit contract, it usually indicates a suit of four cards, or perhaps three, headed by at least one honor. Some partnerships would lead the deuce from four small cards. When defender leads a deuce in a suit in which he is presumably short, it most likely indicates a singleton. When defender discards a deuce, he wishes to discourage the continuance of that particular suit or a subsequent switch to it.

DEUTSCHER BRIDGE-VERBAND. See GERMAN BRIDGE LEAGUE.

DEVIL'S BEDPOSTS. The four of clubs.

DEVIL'S COUP. Sometimes called the disappearing trump trick. The defenders' seemingly certain trump winner vanishes owing to a certain lie of the cards:

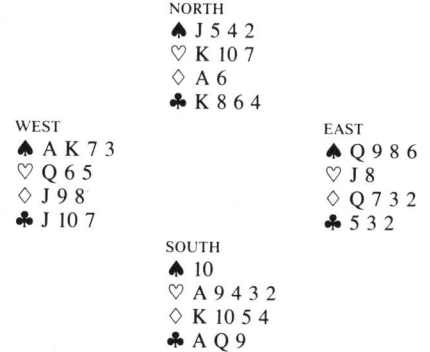

> NORTH
> ♠ J 5 4 2
> ♡ K 10 7
> ◇ A 6
> ♣ K 8 6 4

> WEST   EAST
> ♠ A K 7 3   ♠ Q 9 8 6
> ♡ Q 6 5   ♡ J 8
> ◇ J 9 8   ◇ Q 7 3 2
> ♣ J 10 7   ♣ 5 3 2

> SOUTH
> ♠ 10
> ♡ A 9 4 3 2
> ◇ K 10 5 4
> ♣ A Q 9

Declarer (South) reaches an optimistic six heart contract, apparently off a spade and a trump trick. However, West leads two rounds of spades. South ruffs the second, plays three rounds of clubs ending in dummy, and ruffs a spade. Ace, king, and a small diamond ruffed in dummy is followed by a ruff of dummy's last spade, arriving at the following end position:

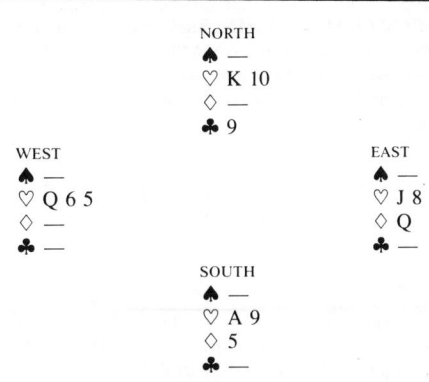

> NORTH
> ♠ —
> ♡ K 10
> ◇ —
> ♣ 9

> WEST   EAST
> ♠ —   ♠ —
> ♡ Q 6 5   ♡ J 8
> ◇ —   ◇ Q
> ♣ —   ♣ —

> SOUTH
> ♠ —
> ♡ A 9
> ◇ 5
> ♣ —

South leads his diamond and East-West are helpless to prevent him from taking the remainder of the tricks. If West trumps low, North overtrumps and makes the last two tricks with high trumps. If West ruffs with the queen, dummy overruffs with the king, and East's jack is finessed on the return.

For another type of disappearing trump trick, see SMOTHER PLAY.

DEVIL'S PICTURE BOOK, DEVIL'S TICKETS. Names given to playing cards by New England Puritans. From the time of their introduction in Europe, gambling at cards has been opposed: in 1387, John I, King of Castile, forbade dice and cards; in 1397, the Provost of Paris forbade playing at dice or cards on workdays; in 1404, the Synod of Langres forbade clergymen to play at dice or cards; in 1423, St. Bernardin preached against cards, and persuaded the people of Bologna to throw their cards into a fire; and in 1541, the Parliament of Paris forbade play at dice or cards in the homes of the town and suburbs.

The objections were usually against gambling or against workingmen wasting their time; but the Puritans, for example, held that the Second Commandment (graven images) was violated by face cards. Hence, some churches permitted games using decks without court cards.

The opposition to cards has dwindled steadily, and the term is used humorously today except in a few isolated communities.

DEVONSHIRE CLUB CUP. Awarded to winners of the RUBBER DUPLICATE tournament at the Devonshire Club, London, England.

DIAMOND. (1) The suit second lowest in rank, next above the club suit, represented by the symbol ◇; (2) the symbol. The suit originated in France in the sixteenth century; its name obviously comes from the diamond-shaped lozenge used for the pips.

DIAMOND TRICK. A trick in the diamond suit.

DINK. To shorten the trumps of either dummy or declarer by forcing him to ruff; a rarely used colloquialism.

DIRECT COMPETITION. Such competition exists between two contestants when they play hands which are identical with respect to cards, relative location, dealer, and vulnerability. See BALANCED COMPARISONS.

DIRECTION. The designation of North, South, East, West, or the hand held by these players.

DIRECTIONAL ASKING BID. A specialized use of a low-level CUE-BID IN OPPONENT'S SUIT to invite partner to bid no trump. Partner must bid no trump if he holds Qx, Jxx, or better in the opponent's suit. The directional asking bidder may have two objectives. First, he may wish to discover whether his side has a combined stopper in the opponent's suit when he himself holds Qx, Jxx, or a singleton king. Second, he may wish to steer the contract into his partner's hand. A player with Axx or Kxx should wish to be dummy if the right-hand opponent has bid the suit. The lead should come up to partner's possible Qx or Jxx.

However, the low-level cue-bid is regularly used on the West Coast and in England as a general-purpose forcing bid (or Western cue-bid). The cue-bidder will often have no stopper of any kind in the opponent's suit, and his partner bids no trump if, and only if, he has a full stopper in his own right. (In general, the Western cue-bid "asks" if opponents have bid only one suit, but shows a stopper if they have bid more than one.)

Each partnership must decide whether the low-level cue-bid shows a guard (East-Coast style), no guard (West-Coast style), or half a guard (directional asking bid). The last methods can be combined to some extent by regarding a repeat cue-bid below the game level as a directional asking bid:

SOUTH	WEST	NORTH	EAST
1 ♣	Pass	1 ◇	1 ♡
2 ♡	Pass	3 ♣	Pass
3 ♡			

South holds:

> ♠ A 4
> ♡ J 7 3
> ◇ 9
> ♣ A K Q 9 7 6 2

Three no trump can still be reached if North has as little as a singleton heart king or queen.

DIRECTOR. (1) Tournament director, the person designated to supervise a bridge tournament and to apply and interpret the LAWS OF DUPLICATE BRIDGE. These duties are outlined in Laws 77–87, and his responsibilities set forth. (2) Director of ACBL governing body at national or lower level. Throughout this encyclopedia, Director (capitalized) is used in sense (2). Tournament director is not capitalized.

DIRECTOR CLASSIFICATION. See TOURNAMENT DIRECTORS.

DIRECTOR'S INSTRUCTIONS. See INSTRUCTIONS, DIRECTOR'S.

DISAPPEARING TRUMP TRICK. See DEVIL'S COUP; SMOTHER PLAY.

DISCARD. (1) To play a card which is neither of the suit led, or of the trump suit, or (2) the card so played. Colloquialisms for discard include ditch, pitch, and shake. Defenders can and do convey information to each other by the specific nature of certain discards. See DEFENSE; DISCARDING; SIGNALING.

DISCARDING. Deciding what cards to keep in the late stages of the play is one of the basic arts of the game. Although there are no absolute rules, and each case must be considered on its merits, a number of general considerations are worth remembering.

(1) It is usually desirable to retain four cards in a useful side-suit held in the dummy:

> NORTH
> ♠ A K 8 2
>
> WEST
> ♠ 9 7 6 4

If South has a doubleton queen, West's anemic holding constitutes a vital stopper. In order to retain his spades, West should not hesitate, for example, to unguard a queen in another suit in which dummy is weak. In the unlikely event that declarer has AKJ, he is likely to finesse.

Notice that West's spade holding could be significant with the five instead of the nine: if South then held J93 or 1093 he would need a side entry to dummy to make four tricks.

The same consideration applies when the declarer is known to have or may have a four-card side-suit.

(2) Attention to the bidding will usually locate for the defender missing aces and kings, and sometimes queens and jacks. This is relatively easy when the declarer has made a no trump bid showing a specific point-count range, but may be possible in other situations. The defender should mentally reconstruct declarer's original hand, and decide whether his bidding would be consistent with or without a particular honor card. Suppose this is the position:

> NORTH
> ♣ K J 5
>
>   EAST
>   ♣ Q 8 6 3

When discarding, East must make up his mind who holds the ace. If South holds it, East must retain three clubs. If West has the ace, East should keep a doubleton.

If East held small cards only in the same situation, he should be careful to retain three cards if he believes that declarer holds the ace.

(3) A defender should usually discard established winners for which he has no conceivable entry. One exception arises in this common position:

NORTH
♣ A Q

WEST
♣ K 2

At the twelfth trick South is in a position to try for an overtrick by taking a finesse. If East has kept two clubs, the finesse can be taken safely. But if East has kept one club and a "useless" winner, South may not choose to jeopardize his contract.

(4) Signaling may help your partner to discard accurately, and attention to his signals should help you. Except in obvious cases, one need not worry about informing declarer. Declarers dislike being deceived and many do not place any reliance on the defenders' plays.

A valuable rule is to signal with the highest card that can be spared. It then follows that any high encouraging discard denies the next higher card, and promises the next lower.

NORTH
♣ 4 3 2

WEST
♣ A 8 5

If East has discarded the club king, declarer's clubs must be worthless, and West can lead the suit happily. If East has thrown the jack, West should lead the five, not the ace. East must have started with KJ109 or possibly J109x. But if East throws the queen, West must leave clubs alone. South's king can be trapped later.

The following illustrates the principle.

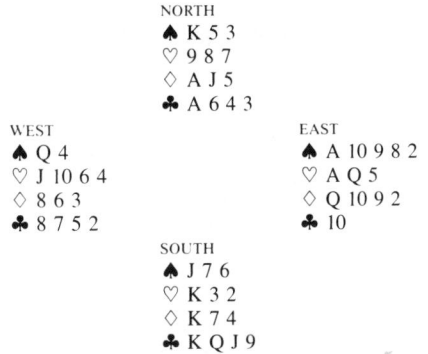

NORTH
♠ K 5 3
♡ 9 8 7
♢ A J 5
♣ A 6 4 3

WEST
♠ Q 4
♡ J 10 6 4
♢ 8 6 3
♣ 8 7 5 2

EAST
♠ A 10 9 8 2
♡ A Q 5
♢ Q 10 9 2
♣ 10

SOUTH
♠ J 7 6
♡ K 3 2
♢ K 7 4
♣ K Q J 9

South played in two no trump, and West led the heart four. East played the queen, a good third-hand play to prevent a hold-up by South, and South won. He finessed the diamond jack, losing to the queen, and the defense cashed three heart tricks. On the last heart East discarded the spade ten. West then knew enough *not* to lead spades. South was marked with the jack, and passive play left South a trick short. The lead of the spade queen by West would have given South his eighth trick.

(5) A player discarding from a worthless hand should do his best to help his partner, who may need information. If a defender has worthless holdings in two suits, he should normally be careful to discard from both suits as soon as possible. The discarding of two or three small cards from one suit only would raise a presumption that he had something to look after in the other suits.

If partner is likely to be interested in length rather than strength, one possible maneuver is to discard one suit completely. Alternatively, with a regular partner, it is possible to give LENGTH SIGNALS at each stage. With 97532, the sequence would be 2, 7, 3, 9, 5. The first discard is discouraging. Subsequently a low card means an odd number of cards *remaining*, and a high card means an even number.

(6) It will often be clear that, unless partner has certain cards, there is nothing to be done. Discards can then be made on the assumption that partner has those cards.

John Brown gives this example in his *Winning Defense*.

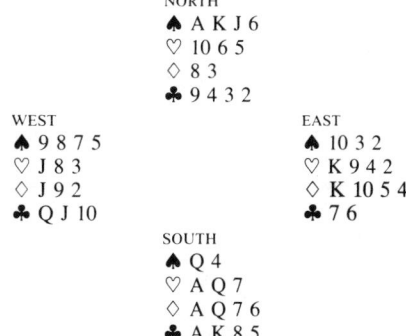

NORTH
♠ A K J 6
♡ 10 6 5
♢ 8 3
♣ 9 4 3 2

WEST
♠ 9 8 7 5
♡ J 8 3
♢ J 9 2
♣ Q J 10

EAST
♠ 10 3 2
♡ K 9 4 2
♢ K 10 5 4
♣ 7 6

SOUTH
♠ Q 4
♡ A Q 7
♢ A Q 7 6
♣ A K 8 5

South played in a wildly optimistic six no trump, and made it as a result of bad discarding. The club queen was led and won by the king, and South returned a low club. West won and shifted to a spade, taken by South's queen.

South crossed to the spade jack, finessed the heart queen, and cashed two club tricks and one more spade, leaving this position:

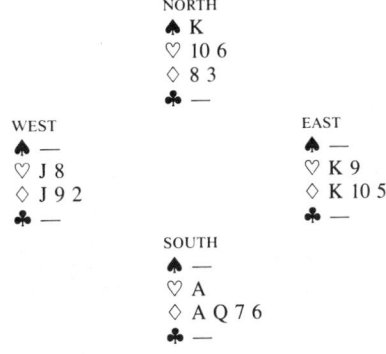

NORTH
♠ K
♡ 10 6
♢ 8 3
♣ —

WEST
♠ —
♡ J 8
♢ J 9 2
♣ —

EAST
♠ —
♡ K 9
♢ K 10 5
♣ —

SOUTH
♠ —
♡ A
♢ A Q 7 6
♣ —

On the last spade everyone discarded a diamond, and South finessed the diamond queen to make his contract. The fault lay primarily with East, for South's play had clearly marked him with at least three diamonds. Even if declarer held ace, queen, and jack of diamonds, he wouldn't be able to get back to dummy to repeat the diamond finesse and East's king would score a trick at the end. After East's error, however, West could still have saved the defense by realizing that his partner must be guarding hearts, and unless East also held a diamond honor, the contract was unbeatable. West would then discard a heart and all would have been well.

DISCIPLINARY CODE. The ACBL Disciplinary Code, approved in 1975, provides that every member charged should have a fair hearing. Disciplinary bodies in the ACBL are Units, Districts, the National Board of Directors, and Tournament Committees. The jurisdiction of these bodies, grounds for discipline, sanctions which may be imposed, appeal procedures, and procedural principles for the conduct of hearings are covered by the Code.

DISCIPLINE. The ability of both members of a partnership to follow an agreed system when partnership action is called for.

The ROTH-STONE SYSTEM was the first to stress partnership discipline as a requirement for use of the system, although all systems had implied its necessity without actually stressing it. Selection committees for teams in international competition have more and more stressed the importance of discipline under the heading of established partnerships.

DISCOURAGING BID. A bid indicating that game is unlikely but not impossible. Examples are: responder's raise of opener's suit from one to two, as a first response or as a rebid; responder's bid of one no trump as a first response or as a rebid; opener's minimum rebid of his suit after a one-round forcing response at the two-level; and in some styles a suit take-out in response to an overcall.

The bidder expects a combined point-count in the range of 18–22, or the distributional equivalent, and partner continues only if he has considerable additional strength in terms of high cards, distribution, or fit.

DISCOURAGING CARD. A card which denotes a lack of interest in a suit's being continued or led. Usually a low card, the six or lower, it may be played either when following suit or when discarding upon another suit. See also DISCARD and SIGNALS.

DISCOVERY. The process of maneuvering the play in order to learn vital information about the hidden hands.

Terence REESE gives this example in *The Expert Game:*

NORTH
♠ 10 8 4 2
♡ K 9 8 3
◇ A Q 4 3
♣ Q

WEST
♣ 9 led

SOUTH
♠ A Q J 9 7 5
♡ —
◇ 6 5 2
♣ A K 7 4

With neither vulnerable, South opens one spade in fourth seat. North raises to four spades, and South bids six spades.

South will look first to see if there is any reason for cashing the spade ace and play for some elimination position. The chances of this are obscure, so he may judge that the hand depends on one of two finesses and lead a spade for a finesse of the queen.

It is possible to improve on that play. At the second trick declarer should lead the heart king from dummy. If East covers with the ace, South ruffs and finesses the diamond queen. East wins with the king and leads the spade six. Now South has discovered for sure that East holds the heart ace and diamond king. Since West opened the club nine it is probable also that East holds jack-ten of clubs; if South wants to look further, he can place East with intermediate cards in both hearts and diamonds, for had West held a solid sequence in either suit he would presumably have led it.

In short, South has built up for East a hand on which, if it contained the king of spades as well, he might well have opened the bidding third hand. Having reached this point, South may decline the spade finesse and play for the drop of the singleton king.

A different type of discovery play can be aimed at determining a suit division.

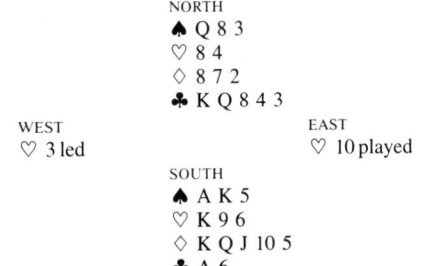

NORTH
♠ Q 8 3
♡ 8 4
◇ 8 7 2
♣ K Q 8 4 3

WEST
♡ 3 led

EAST
♡ 10 played

SOUTH
♠ A K 5
♡ K 9 6
◇ K Q J 10 5
♣ A 6

South opens two no trump and is raised to three no trump. He wins the first trick with the heart king, and has to choose between playing diamonds and clubs. The diamond play wins if the heart suit is split 4–4; the club play wins if the clubs split 3–3.

The even club split is slightly more likely mathematically, and the heart lead increases the chance that West has a five-card suit. But instead of plunging on clubs, South can give himself both chances if the defenders are good players. At the second trick he leads the club six to dummy's king, followed by a low club to the ace. West is likely to signal his club length (see LENGTH SIGNALS) by playing low from a three-card holding or high from two or four. If West's club plays indicate that the suit will not break, South abandons clubs, and tries diamonds. This preserves the chance of making the contract if the hearts are split evenly, and avoids a possible two-trick defeat.

Discovery plays by the defenders are very rare. The following example is from the 1961 British International Trials with Alan TRUSCOTT sitting West.

```
                    NORTH
                    ♠ 9 3
                    ♡ A 8 7 2
                    ◊ 7 6 4 2
                    ♣ K J 7
WEST                                EAST
♠ A Q 10 7                          ♠ 8 4
♡ K Q 9 4                           ♡ J 10 6 3
◊ Q J 3                             ◊ K 10
♣ A 2                               ♣ 10 8 6 5 3
                    SOUTH
                    ♠ K J 6 5 2
                    ♡ 5
                    ◊ A 9 8 5
                    ♣ Q 9 4
```

Both sides vulnerable; dealer East.

EAST	SOUTH	WEST	NORTH
Pass	Pass	1 ♡	Pass
2 ♡	2 ♠	Dbl.	2 NT
Pass	3 ◊	Dbl.	Pass
Pass	Pass		

West led the heart king, captured by dummy's ace. South led a spade to his jack, and West won with the queen. It was clearly necessary for the defenders to lead trumps, but the lead of the queen would have blocked the suit, and prevented the defenders from playing three rounds advantageously. West judged that his partner must have a high diamond honor or the club queen. To learn which, he led the club ace to get an ATTITUDE signal. When East dropped the club three it was clear that he did not hold the club queen, so West shifted to the diamond three. South was held to six tricks, losing 800.

DISCRETIONARY POWERS. See ADJUSTED SCORE and Laws 9–12 and 80–87 of the LAWS OF DUPLICATE.

DISQUALIFICATION. Law 87, LAWS OF DUPLICATE BRIDGE, provides that a director is specifically empowered to suspend a player for the balance of a session, or subject to the approval of the tournament committee or the sponsoring organization, to disqualify a player, pair, or team, for cause in order to maintain discipline or order.

DISTRIBUTION. The manner in which the cards of a suit are dispersed among the four hands of a deal, or the manner in which the number of cards in the four suits are distributed in one hand. Variations in distribution are the basis of various bidding systems in use. See BIDDING.

DISTRIBUTIONAL COUNTS. Distributional points added to high-card points are used to arrive at an overall hand valuation. There are various ways in which the standard 4–3–2–1 POINT-COUNT can be supplemented:

Goren count, devised by William Anderson of Toronto, and adopted and developed by Charles Goren.

void	counts 3 points
singleton	counts 2 points
doubleton	counts 1 point

This applies to the opener's hand, and these points are added to the high-card POINT-COUNT (subject to the usual corrections).

If the responding hand plans to raise the opener's suit, he applies a different count:

void	counts 5 points
singleton	counts 3 points
doubleton	counts 1 point

In addition, the responder makes certain corrections, deducting a point for each of the following; (a) a raise with 3 trumps; (b) a 4–3–3–3 distribution; (c) an insufficiently guarded high card. Also, a point is *added* for a king, queen, or jack in the trump suit provided this does not bring the total number of high-card points in the trump suit to over 4.

Karpin count, popularized by Fred Karpin of Silver Spring, Md., who was the first to achieve a large following with a distributional point-count method. Distributional points are assigned for length, one point for each card over four in any suit. Thus any five-card suit counts 1 point, any six-card suit 2 points, and so on.

Short suits are counted in raising partner according to the following schedule:

	with 4 or more trumps	with 3 trumps
void counts:	3	2
singleton counts:	2	1
doubleton counts:	1	0

These are in addition to points for length.

A simple version of the Karpin idea was published in 1947 by R. A. Miller of York, Pa. An even earlier pioneer of distributional point-count was Victor Porter of Boston, Mass. His method, published in 1938, allowed 4 points for each singleton and void, and 2 points for a doubleton in both hands.

Culbertson count, published by Ely Culbertson in 1952. For an opening suit bid, count each card over three in any suit as one point except that the fourth card does not count in the trump suit. When declarer's opening bid has been raised, he counts the fourth trump as a point, and adds 2 points when he holds six or more trumps. Responder also counts 2 points for holding six or more trumps when giving a raise and makes some minor correction: (a) 1 point is deducted for three-card trump support or 4–3–3–3 distribution; (b) 1 point is added for holding a void or two singletons.

Prior to Culbertson's adoption of point-count, he advocated a distributional count. Honor winners and long-suit winners were added, and the total of the combined hands represented the level to which the side could bid. A supporting hand counted ruffing values, but did not count length in side suits.

Roth count, devised by Alvin ROTH to quantify the POINT-COUNT adjustments in hand evaluation which experts make in light of the bidding. The Roth system retains the 4–3–2–1 WORK POINT-COUNT for honor cards and the basic 3–2–1 Goren count for shortness. It adds points for long suits: one point for any six-card major or for a good six-card minor; two points for any seven-card major or for a good seven-card minor.

Adjustments to shortness and length points are made in light of the degree of fit shown by one's partner's bidding. With 0–2 cards in partner's suit, no points are counted for shortness in a side suit; with 3 cards in partner's suit, the normal 3–2–1 scale of shortness count should be used; with 4 cards in partner's suit one extra point should be added for each singleton, plus one extra point if there are any doubletons. If one's own suit is raised by partner or if partner makes a no trump bid showing a balanced hand, one point is added for each card in the suit in excess of four.

Combination count, devised in England, uses lengths and shortages immediately. Karpin length points are supplemented by 2 for a void and 1 for a singleton. This is applied to both opener and responder in all situations with two provisos: (a) the opening bidder may not count more than 3 distributional points; (b) in responses and rebids no player may count more distributional points than he has cards in his partner's suit.

All distributional counts are an attempt to reach by formula the bid which an expert will make on the basis of experience. Their chief value is in giving guidance to inexperienced players; experts seldom make any conscious calculation of distributional points. See VALUATION.

DISTRIBUTIONAL POINT-COUNT. For the distributional value of certain short suit holdings translated into point-count, see DISTRIBUTIONAL COUNTS, DISTRIBUTIONAL VALUES.

DISTRIBUTIONAL VALUES. The trick-taking possibilities of a hand that depend on the distribution of the cards in the other three hands rather than on the rank of the cards in their respective suits; low-card

tricks in general, including long-suit tricks and ruffing tricks (short-suit tricks).

The classic example of the power of distribution *versus* points is the DUKE OF CUMBERLAND'S HAND. A slight variation, given below, has been immortalised by Ian Fleming in his "Moonraker."

The famous James Bond, sitting North and partnering "M," sets out to teach a lesson to the cheat "Drax."

Having pre-arranged the pack, Bond sees to it that the evil Drax gets the West hand and it will be clear that, no matter which of his three suits East chooses to lead, the final contract of seven clubs doubled and redoubled by Bond cannot be defeated. Playing for enormous stakes, this costs Drax something like £15,000—a salutary lesson indeed!

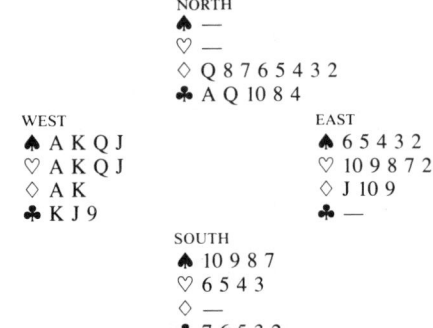

```
                 NORTH
                 ♠ —
                 ♡ —
                 ◇ Q 8 7 6 5 4 3 2
                 ♣ A Q 10 8 4
WEST                              EAST
♠ A K Q J                        ♠ 6 5 4 3 2
♡ A K Q J                        ♡ 10 9 8 7 2
◇ A K                            ◇ J 10 9
♣ K J 9                          ♣ —
                 SOUTH
                 ♠ 10 9 8 7
                 ♡ 6 5 4 3
                 ◇ —
                 ♣ 7 6 5 3 2
```

DISTRICT, DISTRICT ORGANIZATION. The territory of the ACBL is divided into 25 geographic Districts. Each District is represented on the ACBL BOARD OF DIRECTORS by one Director, and on the ACBL BOARD OF GOVERNORS by five Representatives. Areas included within each District are shown in Appendix II at the beginning of the recapitulation of the District Tournament results.

Each District is governed by a District Organization, whose functions include the organization of the REGIONAL TOURNAMENTS assigned to the District, the conduct of a District-wide contest to select a team to represent the District in the GRAND NATIONAL team playoffs, the coordination of the scheduling of SECTIONAL TOURNAMENTS within the District and with neighboring Districts, and the establishment of a DISTRICT JUDICIARY COMMITTEE.

DISTRICT CHAMPIONSHIP. See GRAND NATIONALS CHAMPIONSHIPS (2).

DISTRICT JUDICIARY COMMITTEE. A committee of the DISTRICT ORGANIZATION whose rights and responsibilities include hearing appeals from disciplinary action imposed on a member by a unit board of directors, and conducting disciplinary hearings *ab initio*, which may result in censure, suspension, or expulsion of a player.

DITCH. A colloquialism for DISCARD.

DOCTORS. The demands of the medical profession seldom permit its members to play bridge at the highest level. Dr. John FISHER, Dallas, Tex., and Dr. Richard KATZ, Los Angeles, Calif., are the only physicians who have reached the higher flights of the ACBL's master-point ranking. Dr. Louis MARK, Columbus, Ohio, was president of the ACBL, 1949, and held high ranking at his death in 1954. Several doctors represented the FRENCH BRIDGE FEDERATION during the postwar years, including Dr. Pierre JAÏS, Dr. Bertrand ROMANET, and Dr. Georges THERON.

DOOP. A device developed by Ronald ANDERSEN which permits "one table duplicate games," so that hands previously played in tournaments can be played in the home.

DOUBLE. A call that increases the scoring value of odd tricks or undertricks on an opponent's bid. See DOUBLES and LAWS (Law 19).

DOUBLE ACTION. In some bidding situations, a player will pass after some hesitation, squirming, gesture, or other mannerism that will alert his partner to the idea that he has some other possible action than a pass in mind. Such a hesitation on the part of one's partner should not deter a player from taking whatever action his own holdings might justify. However, it is unethical to re-open the bidding with a double to encourage partner to take whatever action he was considering. For a player who has so hesitated to take action after a double by his partner is highly questionable ethically.

DOUBLE AGAINST SLAM. See DOUBLE FOR SACRIFICE; LIGHTNER DOUBLE.

DOUBLE-BARRELED STAYMAN. A method of combining forcing and non-forcing Stayman. See TWO-WAY STAYMAN.

DOUBLE COUP. A trump coup in which two ruffs are necessary to achieve the required end position.

DOUBLE OF A CUE-BID. At a high level, a double of a suit bid in which there is no intention of playing can be used for lead-directing purposes, or perhaps to suggest a save. It is an indiscreet action if there is no positive purpose other than intimidation, because it gives the left-hand opponent the possibility of a pass or a redouble. There is no general agreement about the meaning of a redouble in this situation: in one style the redouble shows second-round control of the suit.

A double of a cue-bid at a low level would be lead-directing by a side which is on the defensive. But a double of a normally pre-emptive cue-bid such as a MICHAELS CUE-BID would, in standard practice, show a strong defensive hand. See DEFENSE TO TWO-SUITED INTERFERENCE.

DOUBLE DUMMY. (1) Play of a hand that could not be improved upon, as though declarer were looking at all the four hands as in DOUBLE DUMMY PROBLEMS.

It can also be used to refer to perfect play by the defenders.

Originally, Double Dummy was a two-handed form of whist in which each player had a dummy. Some players exposed all four hands, thus giving rise to the modern usage.

(2) Trademark of a two-hand contract game, introduced in 1975, in which each player has a dummy. Since each player already sees two hands, no dummy hand is put down on the table.

DOUBLE DUMMY PROBLEMS. Problems in the play of the hand in which the solver knows the holdings in all four hands. In attempting to discover the solution, the solver is usually required to make an unusual play such as losing a trick early in the play, discarding a high card, or unprotecting his own suit; the finish is usually a SQUEEZE or END PLAY. Since the solver must contend with perfect defense, the correct solution must include the best play by both sides, and any other plays that are just about as good; a second or third line of play is called a variation, and not a solution. A solution must include all variations. The following problem was devised by the late R. W. WILSON, Lower Burrell, Pa.

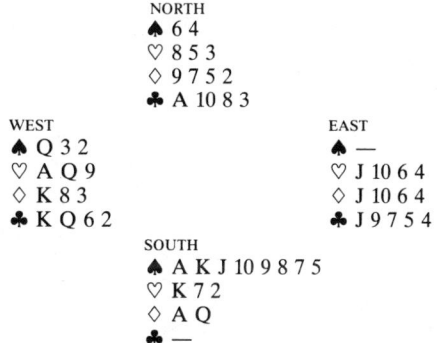

Opening lead, club king, South to make four spades. (Hint: West can avoid a red suit end play as long as he can lead a low club to East's J9.)

Solution

Tricks 1 and 2. North ducks two club leads; South discards a low heart, then ruffs the second club with a middle trump.

Trick 3. South leads a middle trump; West must win, else South wins all the trumps and two of the last four tricks.

Trick 4. North wins the trump return (any other return gives declarer a red trick, and the trump six provides entry to the club ace).

Tricks 5 and 6. South sheds a low heart on the ace of clubs, and ruffs the fourth club.

Tricks 7–10. South wins his trumps. West keeps the ace of hearts and king and eight of diamonds.

Trick 11. South leads king of hearts, and West is end-played for last two tricks.

Three of the most famous problems in bridge history are the VIENNA COUP (which is no longer regarded as a problem), the WHITFIELD SIX, and the VANIVA problem.

Plagiarism of double dummy end-game problems

is apparently simple. Suits and spot cards can be changed to produce a "new" form of an old problem. A method of defeating plagiarists was devised by R. F. FOSTER, based on the longest suit other than trumps in the problem (i.e., the suit in which most cards are used by the composer). The key code for the WHITFIELD SIX, for example, is 126/37. This indicates that South, the leader, has the first- second- and sixth-ranking cards of the longest suit, and that West has the third- and seventh-ranking cards of that suit.

R. W.

DOUBLE ELIMINATION. A method used in the VANDERBILT and SPINGOLD knockout team events in the annual ACBL spring and summer tournaments from the mid-1950s until 1966 and 1965 respectively, and occasionally in other knockout team events.

As is implied in the name, a knockout tournament is one in which a team that loses a head-on match is eliminated from further competition. In a double knockout, the usual procedure is modified to provide that no team is eliminated until it has lost two matches.

The first competition between teams thus results in a group of losers and a group of winners (usually termed winners' bracket and losers' bracket). Matches continue in the winners' bracket, with half the competing teams continuing in the winners' bracket in the next round, the balance joining the losers' bracket. Eventually there is one surviving team from the winners' bracket.

In the losers' bracket, head-on play continues between one-time losers. Winners of these matches continue play in the next round, with losers in this bracket being eliminated as they have then lost their second match. In each round of the losers' bracket, the winners of the previous round are joined for the next round by the losers in the preceding round from the winners' bracket. This can often lead to a possible rematch between two teams that have previously competed against each other, and the CONDITIONS OF CONTEST are usually designed to provide as few as possible of such rematches.

Special provisions must usually be made in the conditions for the last few matches, depending on whether the losers' bracket ends up in a round of two, three, four, or five.

DOUBLE FINESSE. A finesse against two outstanding honors. The classic situation is:

DUMMY
A Q 10

DECLARER
x x x

The only serious chance of making three tricks is to finesse the ten. A more difficult situation is:

DUMMY
A J 4 3 2

DECLARER
10 9 6 5

With this holding some players would play the ace, hoping for an honor to fall or for a 2–2 division. But the better percentage play is to take two finesses. See also DEEP FINESSE, FINESSE, and SUIT COMBINATIONS.

DOUBLE GRAND COUP. A play by which declarer twice ruffs winning cards in order to reduce the hand which is long in trumps to the same length as that of an opponent, in preparation for a COUP.

DOUBLE JUMP. A bid two levels higher than necessary. This may refer to a RAISE (one heart—four hearts), a RESPONSE (one heart—three spades or four clubs) or an OVERCALL (one heart, three spades or four clubs). The term is obsolescent, partly because it is frequently misunderstood or misused by inexperienced players who confuse a DOUBLE RAISE (one heart—three hearts) with a DOUBLE JUMP RAISE (one heart—four hearts).

DOUBLE JUMP OVERCALL. A pre-emptive jump after an opposing opening bid. As with all pre-emptive actions, the bidder must allow for the vulnerability and the level at which he has to bid. The bid normally requires a suit of at least seven cards, but some liberties may be taken at favorable vulnerability. Over one club, a jump to three spades may be tried with a hand as weak as:

♠ K Q J 10 3 2
♡ 3
♢ 10 9 7 5
♣ 8 4

This offers a definite possibility of shutting out the heart suit. In other situations the RULE OF TWO AND THREE should be applied. See PRE-EMPTIVE BID; PRE-EMPTIVE OVERCALL; and WEAK JUMP OVERCALL.

DOUBLE JUMP RAISE. A triple raise, such as one heart—four hearts; sometimes confused with a jump raise such as one heart—three hearts. See TRIPLE RAISE.

DOUBLE JUMP SHIFT REBID. See OPENER'S REBID.

DOUBLE JUMP TAKE-OUT. A pre-emptive response one level higher than a JUMP SHIFT, such as one heart—three spades, or one spade—four hearts. See PRE-EMPTIVE RESPONSES.

DOUBLE MENACE. In a double squeeze situation, the threat card in the suit guarded by both opponents.

DOUBLE MITCHELL. A form of duplicate tournament competition to permit comparison between a greater number of pairs than can be had in direct competition in a single section. The boards are carefully twinned (either at the table or beforehand) and a MITCHELL MOVEMENT used. In scoring the event, all North-South scores from both sections are entered on the same recapitulation sheet, and the match points are awarded across the pairs in both sections as one field. Similar treatment is accorded the East-West scores. Thus top score is increased from 12 to 25 on a board.

Double Mitchell is also used to describe a movement for two small sections which can be linked together to permit half of the boards to be played by the midway point. For example, suppose two parallel six-table sections in which the tables are numbered 1 through 6 and 11 through 16, sharing boards, 1 with 11, etc., on each round. Both sections move within themselves for three rounds using the normal Mitchell progression. The moving pairs then move to the adjoining section without progressing, i.e., from table 1 to 11, 2 to 12, etc. After a further three rounds of normal Mitchell progressions, all pairs have played all the boards then in play. New boards are then introduced in play and twinned. Players then take their positions for what would normally be the fourth round (add three or subtract three from their original pair number in the section they started in), and play three rounds in that section. After these three rounds, they make a move similar to that after the third round, and complete the last three rounds in the adjacent section. If all sections in a big tournament are thus subdivided, it becomes possible to commence the match-pointing in the middle of the play. In Europe, where all sections are matchpointed against the whole field, with top score occasionally in the hundreds, this is a distinct advantage.

DOUBLE NEGATIVE. A bid or rebid by responder after opener has opened with a strong two-bid or an artificial strong TWO CLUB bid, that denies a hand worth more than 0–3 points. Several such double negatives are in current use:

(1) TWO DIAMOND ARTIFICIAL RESPONSE TO FORCING TWO CLUB OPENING when using STEP RESPONSES (Kaplan modification), or a TWO HEART ARTIFICIAL RESPONSE as neutral.

(2) HERBERT NEGATIVE (touching suit) rebid after a negative response has previously been made to the forcing opening.

(3) Cheaper minor rebid after a negative response has previously been made to the forcing opening.

When the double negative is made by responder's rebid as in (2) and (3), it is sometimes called a SECOND NEGATIVE.

DOUBLE RAISE. A jump raise of opener's suit from one to three (one spade—three spades, or one diamond—three diamonds). The standard meaning is a hand with 13–15 points and at least four-card trump support, and the bid is forcing to game.

In accordance with an idea put forward by Marshall MILES, the responder may make the bid with a much stronger hand of similar distribution, with the intention of making a slam effort on the next round.

Many tournament players prefer to make the double raise encouraging but not forcing (see LIMIT JUMP RAISES). Some use the limit jump raise only when the suit is a minor, or only after an opponent has overcalled.

INVERTED MINOR SUIT RAISES are an alternative treatment. For substitutes for the standard forcing jump raise, see DELAYED GAME RAISE; SWISS CONVENTION; and THREE NO TRUMP RESPONSE.

DOUBLE RAISE IN MINOR, PRE-EMPTIVE. See INVERTED MINOR SUIT RAISES.

DOUBLE OUT OF ROTATION. See LAWS OF DUPLICATE, Law 32.

DOUBLE FOR SACRIFICE. A double of an opponent's voluntary slam bid after the doubler's side has bid and raised a suit pre-emptively, designed to help the defenders decide whether they have enough tricks to defeat the slam or should sacrifice. The double indicates how many tricks the doubler expects to take. There are two variations of the convention.

One method, called the Negative Slam Double, played by Ira RUBIN, requires the left-hand opponent of the slam bidder to double only if he has no defensive tricks. If his partner has fewer than two such tricks, he sacrifices. If the slam bidder's LHO has one or two tricks he passes and his partner doubles only if he has no tricks, allowing the slam to be played doubled if the pass was made with two tricks, or the sacrifice to be taken if the pass was made with one trick. For obvious reasons, R. L. FREY originally christened this convention the "Undouble."

An alternative method, called the Positive Slam Double, requires the slam bidder's LHO to double only if he has two defensive tricks. If instead he passes, his partner will sacrifice with no tricks, pass with two tricks, or double with one trick, allowing the slam to be played doubled if the pass was made with one trick, or the sacrifice to be taken if the pass was made with no tricks.

DOUBLE SHOWING ACES. See DEFENSE TO INTERFERENCE WITH BLACKWOOD.

DOUBLE IN SLAM-GOING AUCTION. See DEFENSE TO INTERFERENCE WITH BLACKWOOD; DOUBLE FOR SACRIFICE; DOUBLE OF A CUE-BID; LEAD DIRECTING DOUBLE; LIGHTNER DOUBLE.

DOUBLE SQUEEZE. A squeeze of both opponents. It involves three suits, which may be labeled A, B, and C; then one opponent is squeezed in suits A and B while the other is squeezed in suits B and C. Thus a double squeeze is a combination of two simple squeezes, one against each opponent. Every double squeeze requires a squeeze card, a double menace, and two isolated menaces, guarded by only one opponent. Declarer must have all but one of the remaining tricks. The following classifications are based on analysis by Bertrand ROMANET.

(1) Simultaneous. In a simultaneous double squeeze both opponents are squeezed on the same trick. There are three basic positions:

(a) Balanced

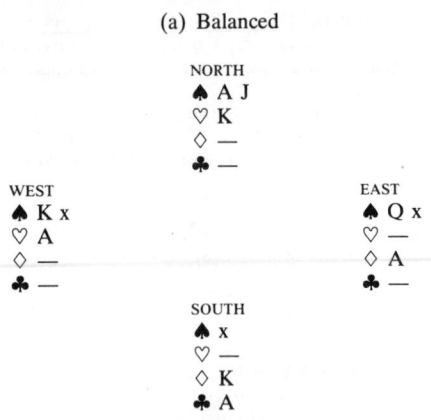

```
              NORTH
              ♠ A J
              ♡ K
              ◇ —
              ♣ —
WEST                        EAST
♠ K x                       ♠ Q x
♡ A                         ♡ —
◇ —                         ◇ A
♣ —                         ♣ —
              SOUTH
              ♠ x
              ♡ —
              ◇ K
              ♣ A
```

South leads the squeeze card, which is the ace of clubs. West is squeezed in the majors, and he must discard a spade. North throws a heart, and East is squeezed in spades and diamonds. This is a positional squeeze.

(b) Automatic

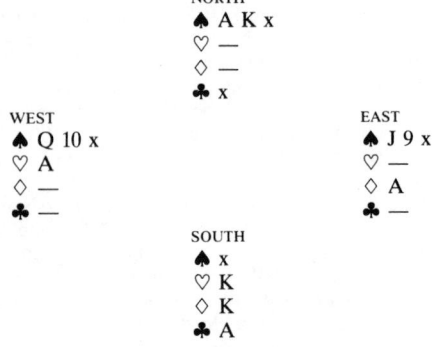

```
              NORTH
              ♠ A K x
              ♡ —
              ◇ —
              ♣ x
WEST                        EAST
♠ Q 10 x                    ♠ J 9 x
♡ A                         ♡ —
◇ —                         ◇ A
♣ —                         ♣ —
              SOUTH
              ♠ x
              ♡ K
              ◇ K
              ♣ A
```

South leads the ace of clubs, squeezing West in the majors. West must discard a spade, and now East is squeezed in spades and diamonds.

(c) Twin Entry

```
              NORTH
              ♠ K x
              ♡ K
              ◇ K
              ♣ —
WEST                        EAST
♠ Q 10 x                    ♠ J 9 x
♡ A                         ♡ —
◇ —                         ◇ A
♣ —                         ♣ —
              SOUTH
              ♠ A x x
              ♡ —
              ◇ —
              ♣ A
```

South leads the ace of clubs, West must throw a spade, North discards a heart, and East is squeezed in spades and diamonds. This is a positional squeeze.

(2) Non-Simultaneous. In a non-simultaneous double squeeze there are two separate squeeze cards. Declarer's last established trick in the fourth suit squeezes one opponent; a trick or more thereafter, the second squeeze card disposes of the other opponent. The second squeeze card lies opposite the first squeeze card, and it accompanies the isolated menace guarded by the opponent who was squeezed initially. There are four basic positions (Romanet):

(a) Inverted Left

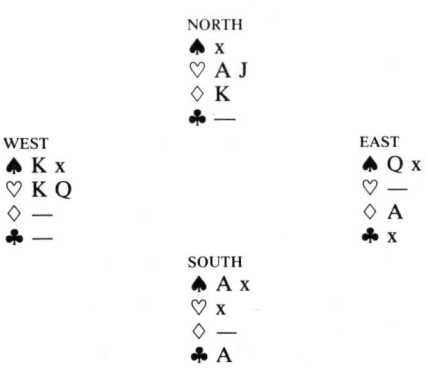

```
              NORTH
              ♠ x
              ♡ A J
              ◇ K
              ♣ —
WEST                        EAST
♠ K x                       ♠ Q x
♡ K Q                       ♡ —
◇ —                         ◇ A
♣ —                         ♣ x
              SOUTH
              ♠ A x
              ♡ x
              ◇ —
              ♣ A
```

South leads the ace of clubs, forcing West to discard a spade, and North throws a low heart. Now South leads a heart to the ace which squeezes East in spades and diamonds. This is a positional squeeze.

The term "inverted" refers to the fact that the double menace accompanies the squeeze card, which is unusual since the double menace ordinarily lies opposite the squeeze card. "Left" indicates that the isolated menace guarded on the left is accompanied by a winner.

(b) Inverted Right

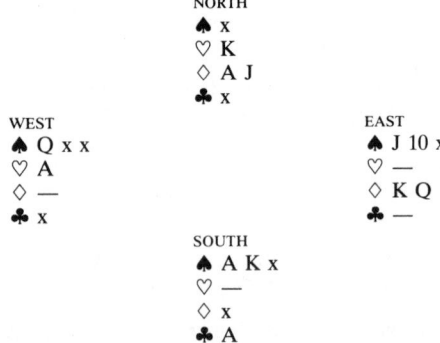

```
              NORTH
              ♠ x
              ♡ K
              ◇ A J
              ♣ x
WEST                        EAST
♠ Q x x                     ♠ J 10 x
♡ A                         ♡ —
◇ —                         ◇ K Q
♣ x                         ♣ —
              SOUTH
              ♠ A K x
              ♡ —
              ◇ x
              ♣ A
```

South leads the ace of clubs, forcing East to discard a spade. Now North wins the ace of diamonds, squeezing West in spades and hearts. This is an automatic squeeze.

For this squeeze an ordinary two-card menace against both opponents does not suffice; a recessed menace is required.

(c) Twin Entry Left

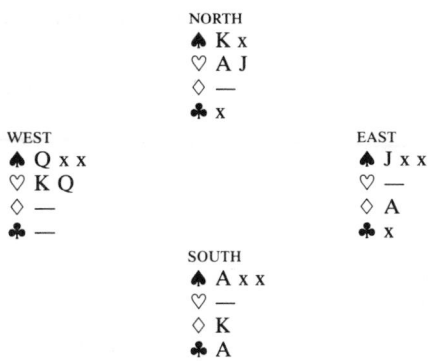

```
                    NORTH
                    ♠ K x
                    ♡ A J
                    ◇ —
                    ♣ x
WEST                                  EAST
♠ Q x x                               ♠ J x x
♡ K Q                                 ♡ —
◇ —                                   ◇ A
♣ —                                   ♣ x
                    SOUTH
                    ♠ A x x
                    ♡ —
                    ◇ K
                    ♣ A
```

South leads the ace of clubs, which forces West to discard a spade. Now a lead to the king of spades, followed by the ace of hearts squeezes East in spades and diamonds. This is a positional squeeze.

This ending combines elements of the balanced and twin-entry positions discussed above.

(d) Inverted Left Recessed

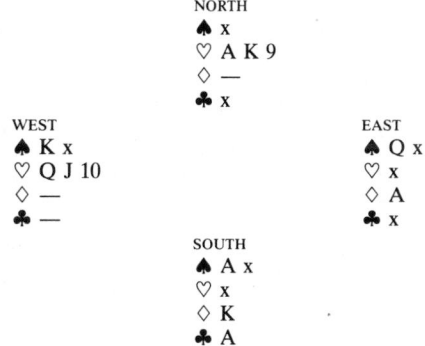

```
                    NORTH
                    ♠ x
                    ♡ A K 9
                    ◇ —
                    ♣ x
WEST                                  EAST
♠ K x                                 ♠ Q x
♡ Q J 10                              ♡ x
◇ —                                   ◇ A
♣ —                                   ♣ x
                    SOUTH
                    ♠ A x
                    ♡ x
                    ◇ K
                    ♣ A
```

South leads the ace of clubs, which forces West to discard a spade. Now North wins two top hearts, the last of which squeezes East in spades and diamonds. This is a positional squeeze.

The isolated menaces are arranged as in a balanced double squeeze, but the double menace is inverted. As compensation, North must have two winners, one of which is an entry. The last two positions illustrate the available endings.

See also BARCO SQUEEZE; BONNEY'S SQUEEZE; CLASH SQUEEZE; HEXAGON SQUEEZE; RECIPROCAL SQUEEZE.

M. I.

DOUBLE TENACE. A tenace in which the sequence is broken in two places, such as A Q 10 or K J 9.

DOUBLE TOP. In some individual tournaments it is not practical to maintain direct comparison within a group on all of the boards played. Thus every score will be duplicated to each of the two players who were partners on the board. In match-pointing the scores, thus, there are two identical entries for each score, and each award is entered twice, once to each of the players. Thus there are two top scores on each board; and a game so scored is referred to as scored with a double top.

The term is also used to refer to a scoring method more in use in other countries, whereby each match-point score is obtained by counting two points for each poorer score and one point for each equal score. This eliminates the half points in match-pointing. Thus with thirteen pairs in competition, top score would be 24 rather than 12, amounting to a "double top."

DOUBLE OF TWO CLUB RESPONSE TO NO TRUMP. The two club response to an opening bid of one no trump is usually used as the STAYMAN convention. When two clubs is bid in response to a strong no trump, a double by the LHO of the two club bidder is normally a lead directing bid showing concentrated strength in clubs, but not promising overall strength. See DOUBLES OF ARTIFICIAL BIDS FOR PENALTIES.

When the opening no trump bid is of the weak variety, however, the responder sometimes has a very weak hand with which he wishes to escape into a suit. See WEAK NO TRUMP. The escape is frequently initiated by a two club response. Consequently for most expert partnerships the double of the two club response to a weak opening no trump simply shows general strength. The double does not promise any particular distribution, but suggests that the doubler has a hand with which it would have been appropriate for him to double the no trump opening had he been sitting over the opener.

DOUBLER. A player who has doubled.

DOUBLES. The two main categories are PENALTY DOUBLES and TAKE-OUT DOUBLES, which are listed separately. Distinguishing between the two types is not always easy. The following is a sound general rule: *A double of a suit bid below the game level is for a take-out if partner has not bid.*

Conversely, a double is for penalties if:

(1) The bidding is at the game level or above; or
(2) The bid doubled is in no trump; or
(3) The doubler's partner has already bid.

But these generalities require some qualification in particular cases.

(1) Even at the game level, a double may have a take-out flavor. If the bidding goes one heart—pass—four hearts—double, the doubler is unlikely to be loaded with hearts. He indicates a hand with considerable high-card strength, and expects a take-out, although partner will often exercise his option of passing for penalties. If the suit were spades, the penalty aspect would be more dominant.

(2) A double of a response of one no trump is a special case (one heart—pass—one no trump—

double). This is primarily for take-out, although responder will often exercise his option to pass.

(3) Doubles on the second round have to be considered on their merits, and are sometimes ambiguous. The old theory was that a double of a suit rebid is for penalties when the same suit could have been doubled on the first round. This is true in cases like:

SOUTH	WEST	NORTH	EAST
1 ♠	Pass	2 ♣/1 NT	Pass
2 ♠	Dbl.		

West must have spade length and strength, and was lying in wait. The situation would not be so clear in a minor suit:

SOUTH	WEST	NORTH	EAST
1 ◇	Pass	1 NT	Pass
2 ◇	Dbl.		

West may have diamond strength, but equally, since both opponents are limited, he may be looking for a major suit. East's diamond length will usually enable him to interpret the double correctly.

If another take-out action is available, a double is clearly for penalties. The following sequences only look similar:

(a)

SOUTH	WEST	NORTH	EAST
1 ♣	Pass	1 ◇	Pass
2 ♣	Dbl.		

(b)

SOUTH	WEST	NORTH	EAST
1 ◇	Pass	2 ♣	Pass
2 ◇	Dbl.		

Sequence (a) is clearly for penalties: West would make a cue-bid of two diamonds holding the majors.* In sequence (b) the cue-bid is not available, so the double is ambiguous: it is likely to be for a take-out, but East must inspect his hand.

Experts disagree about the meaning of this sequence:

SOUTH	WEST	NORTH	EAST
1 ♡	Pass	1 NT	Pass
2 ♣	Dbl.		

The doubler can be expected to have some heart strength, but whether he has clubs is not clear.

A double is always for penalties if three suits have been bid: there are no longer two or more suits between which the responder can choose. However, if made at a low level, some expert partnerships nevertheless use such doubles as take-out, and some treat the double as a COOPERATIVE DOUBLE.

Doubles other than penalty doubles and take-out doubles may be used in a variety of situations to give information. In slam auctions, for example, doubles may be used offensively as a DEFENSE TO INTERFER-

ENCE WITH BLACKWOOD. Defensively, doubles may be used to exchange information as to when to sacrifice against a slam. See DOUBLES FOR SACRIFICE. See also CARD SHOWING DOUBLE, COMPETITIVE DOUBLE, DOUBLE OF TWO CLUB RESPONSE TO NO TRUMP, MAXIMAL OVERCALL DOUBLE.

Other doubling situations are discussed under: BALANCING; COOPERATIVE DOUBLE; DOUBLE OF CUE-BID; DOUBLES OF NO TRUMP BIDS; FREE DOUBLE; INHIBITORY DOUBLE; LEAD-DIRECTING DOUBLES; LIGHTNER DOUBLE; NEGATIVE DOUBLE; OPTIONAL DOUBLE; PENALTY PASS; RESCUE; RESPONSES OVER OPPONENT'S TAKE-OUT DOUBLE; RESPONSIVE DOUBLE; STRIPED-TAIL APE DOUBLE; SUCKER'S DOUBLE; as well as PENALTY DOUBLES and TAKE-OUT DOUBLES.

DOUBLES OF ARTIFICIAL BIDS FOR PENALTIES. At a high level the situation is clear-cut. A player who doubles a response to BLACKWOOD, or a GERBER four club bid, for example, is showing strength in the suit he has doubled in the hope of directing his partner to the right opening lead. There is a negative inference which is sometimes overlooked: the player who does *not* double a conventional bid on his right usually does not want that suit led.

At a low level, other considerations come into play. The double for business is the standard treatment when the hand seems sure to "belong" to the side that is doubled. This would apply if the bid doubled is: a conventional two clubs; a conventional response (negative or ace-showing) to a conventional two clubs; or a STAYMAN response to two no trump or a standard (strong) no trump. See also FISHER DOUBLE.

When the doubling side may well have the majority of the high-card strength, the double may be put to better use by partnership agreement—either to show general strength or in some more specialized way. Each situation needs examination in relation to the convention used by the opponent. See DOUBLE OF TWO CLUB RESPONSE TO NO TRUMP; JACOBY TRANSFER BIDS; ONE CLUB SYSTEMS; ROMAN SYSTEM; TEXAS, and WEAK NO TRUMP. For an alternative treatment of all such situations, see TWO-SUITER conventions.

DOUBLES OF NO TRUMP BIDS. In principle, such doubles are for penalties, and partner is not expected to take out the double unless he has a very poor defensive hand with a long suit. There is one important exception:

WEST	NORTH	EAST	SOUTH
1 ♡	Pass	1 NT	Dbl.

It is probably more useful to reserve South's double for a hand which would make a take-out double of one heart than for the rarer hand which would wish to punish one no trump, although North may often choose to pass for penalties.

A number of situations deserve separate comment:

---

* The same would apply to the sequence one diamond—pass—one no trump—pass—two clubs—double.

(1) *Doubles of strong no trump openings.* A very rare action, seldom justified unless a long strong suit is held together with side entries. Partner should hardly ever take out the double. A player with a balanced 17-point hand should usually pass a no trump opening, because the possible losses exceed the possible profits. The meaning of the double does not vary in fourth seat, and the opening leader tends to lead a short suit. For alternative treatments, see ASTRO, BROZEL.

(2) *Doubles of weak no trump openings.* A double by second hand should be at least as strong as the opening bid, and a good suit to lead is desirable but not essential. To pass a weak no trump with a balanced 15-point hand runs a serious risk of missing a game; to double with less leads to trouble when the opener's side has the balance of strength.

The double by fourth hand is a theoretical problem. Apparently the fact that opener's partner has passed should encourage the fourth player, but this is deceptive. Experienced players do not pass very weak hands when their partners have opened with one no trump; instead they scramble out into a suit at the level of two in an attempt to avert disaster. So when one no trump has been passed, the opener's side is more likely than not to hold the balance of strength, and the fourth player should be cautious about doubling. (But this sort of thinking might permit the third player to try a double cross by passing with a near-Yarborough.) Conversely, the fourth player should double a two-level suit take-out by third hand with any hand with which he would have doubled an opening weak no trump on his right. Many players extend this treatment to a double of a STAYMAN response to allow for the possibility that third hand is taking evasive action (see DOUBLE OF TWO CLUB RESPONSE TO NO TRUMP); this gives up the lead-directing double of a Stayman bid based on clubs.

The doubler's partner should take out only with a long suit and a very weak hand.

(3) *Double of a one no trump overcall.* By third player this is a simple indication that he has at least 8–9 points, and therefore expects his side to have the balance of strength. This principle applies to most no trump doubles: the double is made when the doubler thinks it more likely than not that his side has more than 20 high-card points. If the opener doubles one no trump, either by second or fourth hand, he shows a maximum one-bid, probably 19–21 in high cards.

(4) *Doubles of three no trump* are often lead-directing. See LEAD-DIRECTING DOUBLE.

(5) *Double of a no trump rebid.*

SOUTH	WEST	NORTH	EAST
1 ♣	Pass	1 ♡	Pass
1 NT	Dbl.		

or

SOUTH	WEST	NORTH	EAST
1 ♣	Pass	1 ♡	Pass
1 NT	Pass	Pass	Dbl.

In both sequences the double is intended for penalties. In the first case West has club strength, and in the second case East has heart strength.

Third hand problems. When an opening one no trump bid is doubled, the opening bidder's partner has four standard options.

(a) *Redouble.* A call indicating that the opener's side has the majority of the high-card strength, and that a penalty should be available if the doubling side escapes into a suit. A frequent action holding 9 points or opposite a weak (12–14) no trump. Opposite a standard (16–18) no trump, 5 points is theoretically sufficient, but slightly more is desirable in view of the likelihood that the doubler has a good suit to lead.

(b) *Two no trump.* A bid with no natural meaning, because a strong balanced hand would always redouble. It is therefore treated as a type of cue-bid, and is likely to be based on a strong two-suited hand.

(c) *Two clubs.* Not Stayman after a double. It is normally a natural bid with a long club suit, and should be assumed to be so by the opener. However, the bid is often made on a weak unbalanced hand with the intention of making an S O S redouble when doubled. This would be an appropriate action with a 4–4–1–4 distribution, for example.

(d) *Three of a suit.* An unlikely action opposite a standard no trump. Opposite a weak no trump it would be pre-emptive, with a six-card suit and no game ambitions.

For other options available to the partner of the opening no trump bidder, see DEFENSE TO DOUBLE OF ONE NO TRUMP.

DOUBLETON. An original holding of two cards in a suit. If an opening lead is made from a doubleton, the top card is customarily led first. For evaluation of a doubleton, see DISTRIBUTIONAL POINT-COUNT.

DOUBLY IMPROPER CALL. A call which is irregular in two respects, such as an insufficient bid out of rotation. See LAWS (Law 31).

DOWN. Defeated; said of a declarer who has failed to make a contract. The term is used in various ways, such as "We are down two" or "down 700," meaning the side has failed to make a contract by two tricks, or has incurred a penalty of 700 points.

DRAW FOR PARTNERS. See LAWS (Law 3).

DRAWING TRUMPS. The action of removing the trumps from the opponents' hands. When he first gains the lead, declarer should usually draw trumps, provided that in doing so he does not remove cards from his own hand or dummy which are necessary for some other purposes. There are various considerations which may persuade declarer to postpone drawing trumps.

Ruffs. Declarer may need to ruff some of his losers in the dummy. It may be necessary to give the lead to the opponents in the process of establishing and taking the ruffs, and they may lead trumps at every opportunity. Declarer must leave at least enough trumps in dummy to take care of his losers while allowing for such trump leads by the defense (see CROSSRUFF).

Entries. Often declarer can use dummy's trumps as entries. These entries may be required for finesses or development of a side suit in declarer's hand. If no other entries are available, these plays must be made while drawing trumps.

Sometimes declarer plans to establish dummy's suit. Once it has been established, the trump suit may provide the only entry to dummy. If this delayed entry would not be available after drawing trumps and taking ruffs in dummy, then either play must be postponed, and dummy's suit established first. Eventually the dummy may be entered by drawing the last trump, or by means of a ruff.

Stoppers. Dummy's trumps may serve as stoppers in a certain suit. However, it may not be expedient for declarer to ruff all his losers in that suit; instead he plans to establish discards, which may entail losing the lead to the opponents. Declarer seeks to leave one trump in dummy (to stop the opponents' suit) for each time he must lose the lead in this fashion.

Declarer may be able to use his trumps or dummy's trumps as stoppers. He may be unable to ruff in his hand lest he lose trump control. Therefore he must leave enough trumps in the dummy to cope with the opponents' suit while he proceeds with the development of the hand.

Timing. Declarer may put off drawing trumps because his plan for the hand as a whole requires him to deal first with other matters:

(1) Declarer may seek to establish a quick discard for a potential loser before the defenders can establish and cash their trick in that suit.

(2) Declarer has a side-suit which is not solid. Unless he has abundant trumps it is best to test the side-suit before all the trumps are drawn. This is important if the trump suit is broken.

(3) Declarer has a choice between the ruffing game and the long suit plan (particularly if the long suit is in dummy). By leading the long suit at once, declarer can vary his plan according to circumstances.

Weakness. If the trump length and strength is shared about equally between the two sides, declarer should usually avoid trump leads:

NORTH
J 5 4

SOUTH
K 9 7 2

In such situations South can hope to collect two or three trump tricks by leaving his holding intact for the end game.

With extreme weakness in trumps, declarer is on

the defensive. He may need to lead trumps to avoid opposing ruffs.

Master Trump. Declarer usually ceases to draw trumps when one defender has one or two master trumps. But a trump continuation may still be desirable to achieve a throw-in, or simply to get rid of the lead; and it may be necessary to drive out a master trump which would otherwise interrupt the run of dummy's established suit at a time when dummy has no remaining entry.

DRIVE OUT. To force the play of a high card, i.e., to lead or play a card sufficiently high in rank to force the play of an adverse commanding card to win the trick, or to continue until this result is achieved.

DROP. To capture an adverse potential winning card by the direct lead of a higher card or series of higher cards, as to drop an unguarded king by the play of an ace; also, the play which endeavors to capture an adverse card, as to "play for the drop," instead of finessing.

Whether to finesse or play for the drop is generally a case of determining the correct mathematical probabilities. However, this preference is considerably modified by information derived from the bidding and play, and it is the policy of good players to obtain as much information as possible, inferential as well as exact, before committing themselves. For example:

SOUTH	WEST	NORTH	EAST
	1 ♣	Pass	Pass
1 NT	Pass	3 NT	Pass
Pass	Pass		

If during the play, East shows up with an ace or king, it is highly unlikely that he will hold another high honor, since he passed his partner in one club. It would therefore be indicated for South to disregard the mathematical probabilities, and arbitrarily place all missing honors in the East hand.

DRURY. A convention that uses an artificial two club response by a PASSED HAND in response to a major suit opening.

	(a)		(b)
SOUTH	NORTH	SOUTH	NORTH
Pass	1 ♠	Pass	1 ♡
2 ♣	2 ◇	2 ♣	2 ◇

In both cases the two club bid asks the opener to clarify his strength, and the two diamond rebid is in principle negative, showing a sub-minimum opening.

In (a) South might hold:

♠ K 9 7 3		♠ 10 9 3
♡ K 6 4 2	or	♡ 6 5
◇ Q 7		◇ A J 7 4
♣ K J 8		♣ A 10 9 7

South continues with two spades, showing a stronger

hand than would have been indicated by an immediate raise to two spades.

The responder in no way guarantees a fit with opener's suit. He would bid two clubs in response to one spade with:

(c)	or	(d)
♠ J 5		♠ 3
♡ K J 10 7		♡ 9 3 2
◇ A J 7 5		◇ K J 9
♣ Q 7 3		♣ A J 10 9 6 5

With hand (c) responder avoids the routine two no trump response, partly because there may be a fit in hearts, and partly because two no trump may be too high opposite a light opening bid. He follows with two hearts, showing a four-card suit, if the rebid is two diamonds. Any other rebid would show a full opening bid.

With hand (d) the responder bids two clubs followed by three clubs. In this case the Drury player may end up one level higher than other players—usually the converse is true—but these hands are not common because a good six-card club suit will often justify an original one club or three club bid.

The two diamond rebid by the opener is not necessarily negative, and cannot be passed. He may hold a hand worth a full opening bid or more on which diamonds is his natural rebid. In that case he follows with a constructive bid of two no trump or a bid at the three-level, which makes the position clear to the responder.

The convention works similarly after an opening bid of one heart, but the frequency is much lower because responder will bid one spade if he can.

The inventor of the convention, the late Douglas DRURY, used a response of two no trump to show a balanced 11–12 points with a doubleton in partner's major and a trebleton in the unbid major. But his leading supporters never use the two no trump response, preferring to have the chance of playing at the level of two in a major suit.

If the two no trump response is ruled out for natural purposes, it can be used to show a balanced hand with a good major suit fit and about 11 points. The jump raise to the three-level would be unbalanced and semi-pre-emptive.

For an alternative device with a similar object, see SNAP.

DUB. At bridge, a dub is a player whose game is below the standards of the players with whom he competes.

DUCK. To play a small card, and surrender a trick which could be won, with the object of preserving an ENTRY. When the suit has been led by an opponent, the duck is mechanically identical to a HOLD-UP, in that a master card (or cards) is retained, but the objective is different. A player ducks in order to pursue his own aims, but holds up in order to thwart the opponents.

A *coup en blanc* is a ducking play for the purpose of winning a later trick.

Apart from a considerable number of situations listed under SAFETY PLAY, ducking plays may be listed under five main headings:

(1) *Suit combinations*

To make the maximum number of tricks in no trump with no side entry to dummy:

(a)	(b)
A K x x x	A Q x x x
DUMMY	DUMMY
x x or x x x	x x or x x x

In (a) the first trick is ducked and the declarer hopes for an even split to make four tricks; with three small, he may duck twice to make three tricks. The situation in (b) is similar, but declarer finesses on the second round; if declarer has three small cards, the first-round duck is slightly better than a finesse followed by a duck because right-hand opponent might hold a singleton king.

(c)	(d)
K Q 10 7 x x	K J 8 x x x x
DUMMY	DUMMY
x x	x x

These are harder, and declarer needs more optimism. In each case he must duck the first trick completely in the hope of finding the right-hand opponent with a singleton ace. If the required situation does exist, it would be brilliant play for the left-hand opponent to play his highest card in an attempt to deflect declarer from his purpose.

(2) *Trap combinations*

In no trump with no side entry in dummy:

(e)	(f)	(g)
A Q J x x x	A Q J x x	A Q 10 x x x
DUMMY	DUMMY	DUMMY
x x	x x x	x x x

In each case a small card is led, and left-hand opponent plays the king. A duck ensures the loss of only one trick, and is essential in (e): if left-hand opponent has brilliantly played the king from a doubleton or tripleton, he has gained a trick for his side.

In (f) and (g) declarer does slightly better to win the first trick, return to his hand, and plan to duck the second round if the king was singleton; but he requires a convenient entry, and there may be an AVOIDANCE consideration.

(h)	(i)
A K x x x	A Q x x x
DUMMY	DUMMY
J 10	J 10

If declarer's lead is covered, he must duck and hope for a three–three division. The only hope of five tricks is for left-hand opponent to fail to cover holding Q x x (or K x x). It is therefore better to lead the ten, following the principle of leading low from a sequence when you wish to avoid a cover.

(j)	(k)
A x x x x	A x x x x
DUMMY	DUMMY
Q J x	J 10 9

In both cases declarer leads a high card and must duck if left-hand opponent covers. In (k) the jack is the best lead: declarer plans to follow with the nine. If left-hand opponent is left with a doubleton honor, he may make the mistake of playing low, and declarer makes four tricks.

(3) *Double and triple*
Again in no trump with no side entry to dummy:

(l)	(m)
A x x x x	A 9 x x x
DUMMY	DUMMY
x x x	x x x x

With (l) two ducks and a three–two split are needed to make three tricks. (m) requires one duck if the suit splits two–two, giving four tricks; a three–one split requires two ducks, and gives three tricks; a four–zero split requires three ducks and gives two tricks. This is the only possible situation for a triple duck.

(4) *Control*
In a trump contract:

(n)	(o)	(p)
x x	A x	A x x
DUMMY	DUMMY	DUMMY
A x x	x x x	x x x

Declarer usually ducks with (n) unless there is a possibility of a seven–one division. This prepares for a ruff in dummy without the need for a side entry, and retains control of the suit if the opponents shift: this may be most important if they are able to draw dummy's trumps.

Declarer would not duck with (o) if a ruff is the only consideration, but it may be right to duck for control reasons. If the defenders can prevent a ruff, declarer is better placed with the ace still in dummy.

The duck with (p) could also be described as a hold-up. It interferes with the defensive communications, and may prevent the defense taking a second trick if the suit is divided five–two.

(5) *Defensive*
A defender in a trump contract often ducks to prepare for a ruff by his side or in order to prevent a ruff by declarer:

(q)		(r)	
WEST	EAST	WEST	EAST
x x	A x x x	x x	A x x

In (q) West leads a doubleton in a side suit in the hope of getting a ruff. East ducks if he can judge that the lead is more likely to be a doubleton than a singleton, and if he thinks that West is more likely to secure the lead.

The objective is reversed in (r), although the mechanics are the same. West leads a doubleton trump aiming to prevent a ruff in the dummy. Again

East ducks if he judges that West has a doubleton and the likely entry.

The suit combination plays described above for the declarer are also available for the defenders, almost always in no trump contracts. Some ducks that are simple for the declarer are very much harder for the defense:

(s)		(t)	
	DUMMY		DUMMY
	x x		J x x
WEST	EAST	WEST	EAST
K x x	A x x x x	K x x x x	A x x
	SOUTH		SOUTH
	Q J 10		Q x

In (s) West leads low and an entryless East must duck. In (t) the duck can be on the first or second round. The first-round duck may have the advantage of depriving dummy of an entry, because declarer can drop the queen under the ace. This would only lose if the lead was from Q x x x specifically. See also THIRD-HAND PLAY.

DUEL. A two-handed form of bridge invented by Norman B. Hasselriis, and described by him in *The Bridge World* magazine for February 1950.

DUFFER. A bridge player of inferior ability.

DUKE OF CUMBERLAND'S HAND. A phenomenal hand at whist. The Duke of Cumberland, son of George III, King of England, was an inveterate gambler for high stakes. One day, at the notorious gaming rooms in Bath, it is said that he was dealt the following hand:

♠ A K Q   ♡ A K Q J   ◇ A K   ♣ K J 9 7

The game being whist, the last card, a club, was turned to set the trump suit. The Duke, sitting at dealer's left, had the opening lead. In accordance with sound whist precepts, he opened the seven of clubs. Obviously it was to his interest to knock out all the opponents' trumps as quickly as possible to avoid the ruffing of any of his solid top cards.

The Duke's opponents proceeded to assert that he would not win a single trick, and to infuriate him into a bet.

The complete deal was:

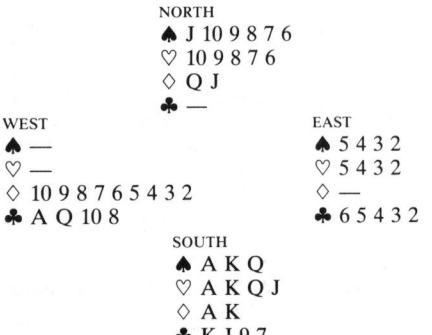

West won the club seven with the eight, and led a diamond which was trumped by his partner. East returned a club, the Duke's nine being taken by the ten, and a second diamond was trumped by East. East led his last trump into his partner's tenace over the Duke, and West won and led the final trump from his hand, felling the Duke's king. West's seven established diamonds won the last seven tricks.

This display of virtuosity by East-West cost the Duke the sum of £20,000 or nearly $100,000 (equal to $750,000 in modern terms).

Such is the story of the "Duke of Cumberland's Hand" as related by Professor Richard A. Proctor in *How to Play Whist* (1885). One wonders why the Duke, an experienced whist player, did not speculate on how his opponents could foretell the outcome. (Remember that no hand is exposed in whist.) A more plausible version of this legendary episode suggests that the South hand was given to the Duke, who knew that it was manufactured and ventured to bet in the face of that knowledge.

The victim may have been an earlier duke, "Butcher" Cumberland, son of George II, but the scant evidence favors the later duke.

DUMB BIDDER. A device to permit silent bidding. It consists of a small board placed in the center of the table on which the four suits, no trump, numbers from 1 to 7, double, redouble, and pass are inscribed. Each player makes his bid by tapping the appropriate sections with a pencil. This avoids any possible revealing inflections. This device is used particularly in Nottingham, England. For alternative methods SEE BIDDING BOXES, WRITTEN BIDDING.

DUMMY. (1) The declarer's partner after he has placed his cards face up on the table, which is done immediately after the opening lead is made by the opponent on the declarer's left; (2) the cards held by the declarer's partner, also called the dummy's hand. The name originated in dummy whist, in which there were only three players, the fourth hand being exposed as the "dummy," an imaginary and silent player (see HISTORY OF BRIDGE). The dummy in bridge takes no part in the play; he may not suggest by word or gesture any lead or play, but he may call attention to errors of play or violations of law. The dummy may ask his partner if he has any or none of the suit led, to prevent a revoke. If the dummy looks at his partner's hand or the hand of either adversary, he forfeits his right to protect his partner from revoking. See LAWS (Laws 42, 43).

DUMMY BRIDGE. A form of bridge for three. Player cutting low plays as dummy's partner for the entire game or rubber. Usually only single games are played before a new cut, the winner scoring a bonus of 50 points. Dealer or his partner names the trump suit. Dummy deals first and partner declares, having looked only at the dummy hand. When an opponent deals, however, he may pass to his partner the right to name trumps. Dealer's left-hand opponent is the only player who may double. The dummy is not exposed until after the opening lead. Otherwise, play is as in BRIDGE WHIST.

One theory of the origin of AUCTION BRIDGE attributes it to a game in which three British officers in a post in India remote from any fourth player evolved the idea of bidding for the dummy.

DUMMY PLAY. The management of the assets of the declarer and the dummy; synonymous with "declarer's play." The subject is dealt with under the following general headings: COUPS; END PLAY; MATHEMATICS OF BRIDGE; SQUEEZE. Also under the following particular titles: AVOIDANCE; BACKWARD FINESSE; BLACKWOOD THEORY OF DISTRIBUTION; BLOCKING; CARD READING; CONTROL; COUNTING THE HAND; CRASHING HONORS; CROSSRUFF; DECEPTIVE PLAY; DEEP FINESSE; DISCOVERY; DRAWING TRUMPS; DUCK; DUMMY REVERSAL; ENTRY; FINESSE; GAMBIT; HOLD UP; IMP TACTICS; JETTISON; LOSER ON LOSER; MATCH-POINT PLAY; NEGATIVE INFERENCE; OBLIGATORY FINESSE; OPTIONS; OVERTAKE; PERCENTAGE PLAY; PLAY FROM EQUALS; RUFF AND DISCARD; RUFF AND RUFF; RUFFING FINESSE; RULE OF ELEVEN; SAFETY PLAY; SHOOTING; SINGLETON KING; SMOTHER PLAY; SPOT CARDS; SUIT COMBINATIONS; THROW-IN; TRUMP PICK-UP; TRUMP SUIT MANAGEMENT; TWO-WAY FINESSE; UNBLOCKING; UNDERRUFF.

DUMMY REVERSAL. A procedure by which the dummy is made the master hand. Generally speaking, it is advantageous to ruff only in the hand that contains shorter trumps, but in a dummy reversal extra tricks may sometimes be developed by ruffing in the long hand and later using dummy's trumps to extract those of the opponents.

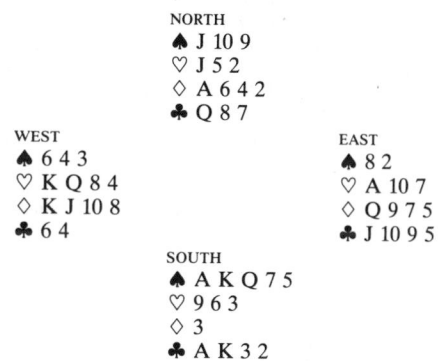

South plays in four spades, and the defense cash their three heart tricks before shifting to a diamond. Superficially it seems that declarer must bank on an even division in clubs or alternatively draw two rounds of trumps and then attempt to ruff the fourth club in dummy in case they divide unevenly. Both these lines are inferior to the dummy reversal which requires only a 3–2 break in trumps. Dummy wins the diamond, and a low diamond is ruffed with the ace of spades. Dummy is re-entered twice in spades—declarer conserving his small trumps for that purpose—to ruff the remaining diamonds with the king and queen, leaving this position:

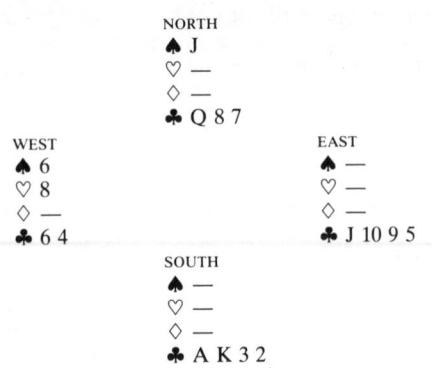

```
                 NORTH
                 ♠ J
                 ♡ —
                 ◇ —
                 ♣ Q 8 7
WEST                        EAST
♠ 6                         ♠ —
♡ 8                         ♡ —
◇ —                         ◇ —
♣ 6 4                       ♣ J 10 9 5
                 SOUTH
                 ♠ —
                 ♡ —
                 ◇ —
                 ♣ A K 3 2
```

Declarer now crosses to dummy's queen of clubs, and leads the jack of spades, extracting the last trump upon which he discards his losing club, and takes the last two tricks with the ace and king of clubs.

Sometimes the decision to "reverse," or establish the dummy in preference to his hand, is forced upon declarer by the character of his trump suit.

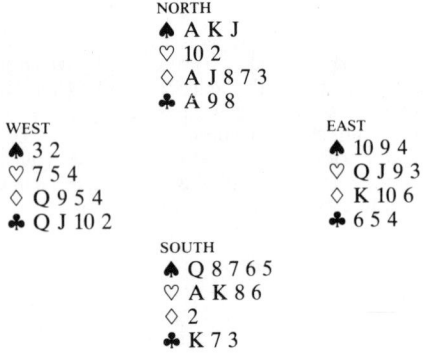

```
                 NORTH
                 ♠ A K J
                 ♡ 10 2
                 ◇ A J 8 7 3
                 ♣ A 9 8
WEST                        EAST
♠ 3 2                       ♠ 10 9 4
♡ 7 5 4                     ♡ Q J 9 3
◇ Q 9 5 4                   ◇ K 10 6
♣ Q J 10 2                  ♣ 6 5 4
                 SOUTH
                 ♠ Q 8 7 6 5
                 ♡ A K 8 6
                 ◇ 2
                 ♣ K 7 3
```

The contract is six spades, and West leads the queen of clubs. If declarer attempts to ruff his losing hearts in dummy he will promote a trump trick for East which together with the club loser would spell defeat. However, by ruffing three of dummy's diamonds in his hand—establishing the fifth diamond in the process—he can utilize dummy's trumps for drawing purposes, and loses only a club trick.

                                    S. K.

DUMMY WHIST. A variety of WHIST for three. The player who draws the lowest card plays with the dummy as his partner. The last card dealt is turned as trumps. Dummy is not exposed until after the opening lead is made. Each trick over book (six) counts as one point. Seven points are game.

DUMMY'S FORFEITURE OF RIGHTS. Invoked if the player whose hand is the dummy intentionally looks at his partner's or an opponent's hand. He then forfeits his privileges in protection of his partner against revokes or leading from the wrong hand. See LAWS (Laws 42, 43).

DUMMY'S HAND. It is the responsibility of all the players equally that dummy's hand shall be a proper one. No revoke can be claimed as a result of an improper play from the dummy. See DUMMY.

DUMMY'S RIGHTS AND LIMITATIONS. Dummy has certain absolute and limited rights as described in LAWS OF DUPLICATE (Laws 42, 43). In a rubber bridge game, particularly under social conditions in the home, the old rule of "courtesy of the table" required that the opponents inquire of the declarer whether a play to a trick constituted a revoke, and failure to so inquire waived the right to a penalty for such a revoke. Normally, however, such courtesy should be granted to the hostess or host who, as dummy, engages in cleaning ashtrays, replenishing drinks, and otherwise servicing the table.

DUPLICATE. A term applied to the playing of the same deal of cards by more than one table of players; successively applied to whist, auction bridge, and contract bridge. See DUPLICATE BRIDGE and HISTORY OF BRIDGE.

DUPLICATE, MATHEMATICS OF MATCH-POINT. See MATHEMATICS OF MATCH-POINT PLAY.

DUPLICATE BIDDING. The crucible of tournament play has led to many of the modern bidding tactics and systems used in rubber bridge. Several factors which are unimportant to rubber bridge, such as whether a part-score contract should be played in a minor suit or a less desirable major suit that could produce as many tricks, are discussed in MATCH-POINT BIDDING and IMP TACTICS. Slams, particularly grand slams, may be bid more frequently in duplicate. See SLAM BIDDING.

DUPLICATE BOARD. See BOARD, DUPLICATE.

DUPLICATE BRIDGE. The form of bridge in which the same hand is played more than once. Each competing unit (which may be an individual, pair, or team) has to try to perform better than one or more other units playing the identical deals in similar circumstances. The luck of the deal, so important in rubber bridge, is therefore eliminated, and bridge becomes a satisfactory test of skill. (But see CHANCE.)

The first application of the duplicate idea dates from whist. The pioneer in this field was John T. MITCHELL, who invented the first pair movement and whose book on duplicate whist was published in 1892. The long series of American Whist League Championships began in the same year. (See HISTORY OF BRIDGE.)

The duplicate principle was never applied to the original game of bridge (see BRIDGE WHIST) which flourished in the decade 1894–1904. It was generally believed that bridge, unlike whist, was not a suitable game for serious competition. This was perhaps partly because at this stage of its development bridge permitted unlimited redoubles, which emphasized the gambling element in the game and gave it a pokerlike character.

The first games of duplicate auction bridge were apparently held in 1914 under the auspices of the American Whist League, but another ten years elapsed before a national auction tournament was staged.

The application of duplicate to contract bridge was a rapid development, and the first national championship was held in 1928, when the game was less than three years old, under the auspices of the AMERICAN (auction) BRIDGE LEAGUE.

The most popular form of duplicate is the weekly club game. This usually consists of a 24- or 26-board pair event, lasting some 3½ hours. The number of tables varies widely, but is likely to be between eight and fifteen. The players pay a card fee that is usually between $2 and $3. Many clubs run several games a week, and a few clubs in large metropolitan areas run games each afternoon and evening throughout the year.

Players wishing to join a club can obtain free copies of a booklet entitled "Easy Guide to Duplicate" and of a Directory of Clubs by applying to ACBL HEADQUARTERS.

Duplicate bridge can be a satisfying home game for eight players. (See TWO TABLES.) It is also very popular as part of the recreation program of commercial and industrial organizations.

For the more complex organization of tournaments above the club level, see AMERICAN CONTRACT BRIDGE LEAGUE and CHAMPIONSHIP TOURNAMENTS.

The mechanics of play at duplicate are covered in LAWS OF DUPLICATE BRIDGE, Laws 2–8. In order to make replay of the hand possible, some modification of the mechanics of the deal, shuffle, and gathering of tricks from those of RUBBER BRIDGE or CHICAGO is necessary.

Essentially, the mechanics of duplicate require the following steps:

(1) Getting the right boards and correct opponents to the table. See MOVEMENTS.

(2) Withdrawal of the hand to be played from the board, counting the cards to ascertain the correctness of the hand.

(3) Determination of vulnerability and dealer on the board (see BOARD, DUPLICATE). The bidding then proceeds as in rubber bridge.

(4) The play to the trick. Instead of playing to the center of the table, each player faces his contribution or lead face up, in front of him, in turn. When the four cards have been played to the trick, each player turns his card face down, in a line, in front of him. The card is pointed toward his partner if they have won the trick, but placed with the length from right to left if the trick was won by the opposition.

(5) Determination of and agreement about the result. All four players should, as a result of the preceding paragraph, agree as to the number of tricks won by the declarer; if disagreement exists, the

cards should not be disturbed, but the result determined by the director, who should be summoned.

(6) Recounting the cards and replacing in the pockets of the duplicate board.

Articles dealing with various aspects of handling duplicate tournaments are: TWO, THREE, FOUR, etc., to FIFTEEN TABLES; movements: AMERICAN WHIST, BARCLAY, BLACKPOOL, BUMP MITCHELL, CYCLIC, HOWELL, INDIVIDUAL, MCKENNEY-BALDWIN, RAINBOW INDIVIDUAL, ROVER, SCRAMBLED MITCHELL, SHORT HOWELL, SWISS, TEAM-OF-FOUR, THREE-QUARTER HOWELL; ADJUSTED SCORE, APPENDIX TABLE, ARROW, ARROW SWITCH, ASSIGNMENT OF SEATS, BALANCED COMPARISONS, BREAKING TIES, BYE STAND, CALIFORNIA SCORING, CARRY-OVER SCORES, CONVENTION CARD, CUTTING MOVEMENT DURING PLAY, DUPLICATE SCORING, ENTRIES, FACTORING, FOULED BOARD, HALF TABLE, HAND RECORDS, HYBRID SCORING, INTERNATIONAL MATCHPOINTS, JUNIOR TABLE, MACHINE-PREPARED HANDS, MATCH-POINT, POSTING THE SCORE, PRIVATE SCORECARD, RECTIFICATION, ROUND ROBIN, SCORING CORRECTIONS, SEED/SEEDING, SLOW PLAY, STARTING TIME, SUBSTITUTE, SUSPENSION, TRAVELING SCORE, TOURNAMENT DIRECTOR.

DUPLICATE BRIDGE LAWS. See LAWS OF DUPLICATE.

DUPLICATE SCORING. The scoring of each deal is covered by the provisions of Laws 73 and 74 of LAWS OF DUPLICATE. A scoring table, listing all possible duplicate results, may be obtained from ACBL HEADQUARTERS free on request. After the score on any hand has been determined according to this table, a comparison of results becomes possible.

Most pair events and all individual events are scored on a match-point basis. After all the scores have been determined on a board, 1 match point is awarded to a team for every score that they have bettered, and ½ match point for every score that they have duplicated. Totaling of the match-point scores determines the winner for the session. When an event is held in two or more sessions without elimination, the total score is carried forward and the event winner determined by the largest total score.

Scores for a multi-session event where elimination is involved, however, do not carry over totals from the qualifying round. A maximum carry-over, ranging from the equivalent of five boards, depending on the number of qualifying rounds and the number of final rounds, is provided by league regulations. The maximum carry-over may not exceed this, but it may be less. For details of formula, see CARRY-OVER SCORES.

For team-of-four play, there are three methods of scoring in use: BOARD-A-MATCH; TOTAL POINTS; and INTERNATIONAL MATCH POINTS. (Other methods in use in Europe include COMBINATION TEAM SCORING and QUOTIENT scoring.)

In board-a-match, the most common type of team competition in the United States until the introduction of the enormously popular SWISS MOVEMENT in 1967, each board is scored as 1, ½, or 0 match points, depending on whether the total score on the two plays is greater than zero, zero, or less than zero. This system of scoring over-emphasizes the extra trick, the no trump versus suit play, the hair-trigger part-score doubles. An alternative, particularly in longer matches, is total-point scoring, which, however, has the defect of being able to determine the outcome of a match on two or so major SWING hands. The international match point method, which has gained considerable currency, is designed to eliminate the defects of both board-a-match and total-point scoring methods. In the present IMP scale (see Law 74), the small swings are rewarded with fewer points than larger swings, but the award to a large swing hand is still great in comparison.

IMP scoring may be used for pair events, where a pair's score on a board is determined by its reference to a mean score on the board (by averaging all except the upper and lower scores made) with an IMP award based on the difference. (See INTERNATIONAL MATCH POINTS; INTERNATIONAL OPEN TEAM SELECTION.)

DUPLICATE TECHNIQUE. See IMP TACTICS; MATCH-POINT BIDDING; MATCH-POINT PLAY.

DUPLICATE TOURNAMENT. See DUPLICATE BRIDGE and CHAMPIONSHIP TOURNAMENTS.

DUPLICATE TRAY. See BOARD, DUPLICATE.

DUPLICATE WHIST. The oldest form of duplicate competition, in which movements such as the MITCHELL and HOWELL were developed.

DUPLICATING BOARDS. See TWINNING.

DUPLICATION OF DISTRIBUTION. This occurs where the suit lengths in a partnership's hands are evenly matched. A distributional flaw that limits the trick-taking potential of a pair of hands, it manifests itself in the absence of a long suit that can be developed.

♠ A Q 10	♠ K J 9
♡ K Q J 9	♡ A 10 6 2
◇ A 10 3	◇ 9 7 6
♣ 6 4 2	♣ Q 7 3

The presence of a long card in either hand would permit the development of an additional trick, but with the above distribution, no game contract is likely to be fulfilled, though sufficient values are held.

DUPLICATION OF VALUES. A concentration of strength and control in the same suit between two partners. When too much of the combined strength of the partnership is concentrated at one point there are likely to be serious weaknesses elsewhere and an unsound contract is often reached.

WEST	EAST
♠ A K	♠ Q J
♡ K Q J 10 4	♡ A 9 7 5
◇ A 7 5	◇ K 6 4 3
♣ 4 3 2	♣ 8 6 5

The above hands contain sufficient values to warrant a game contract in hearts, which has to fail owing to the poor division of strength in the black suits.

Another form of duplication:

WEST	EAST
♠ 6	♠ A K Q 8 7
♡ A J 10 4 3	♡ K Q 7 6
◇ K Q 8 5	◇ 9
♣ 9 7 5	♣ 6 4 2

A contract of four hearts would be almost impossible to avoid, though declarer has four quick losers. Both hands contain, in effect, second-round control in spades and diamonds, leaving a glaring weakness in clubs. If West's king-queen of diamonds (5 points) were changed to the ace (4 points), the game would be a lay-down, for now East's singleton diamond would be pulling its weight.

Certain sequences have been devised to identify duplication of values at the slam level, for example, keeping out of six where there is a prospect of two immediate losers in a suit:

WEST	EAST
1 ♠	3 ♠
4 ◇	4 ♡
5 ♠	

Here the opener's last bid asks partner to bid a slam if he has as good as a second-round control in the unbid suit, clubs.

In a general way, duplication can be detected when a player has a void or singleton in a suit in which his partner has indicated some strength, for example:

WEST	NORTH	EAST
1 ♡	1 ♠	1 NT

West holds:

♠ —
♡ K Q 8 6 2
◇ A Q 9 3
♣ K J 7 4

and must tread warily, for his partner's values (in spades) seem to be misplaced for purposes of a suit contract.

DUTCH BRIDGE LEAGUE. See NETHERLANDS BRIDGE LEAGUE.

DYNAMIC NO TRUMP. A one no trump opening bid to show an unbalanced hand with 18–21 points. Developed by Dr. George ROSENKRANZ of Mexico City as a cornerstone of the ROMEX SYSTEM.

Responses are control-showing as in the BLUE TEAM style, counting an ace as two controls and a king as one. Two clubs shows no more than one control with 0–6 points; two diamonds shows less than two controls with 7 or more points; two hearts shows two controls; two spades shows three controls, etc.

Opener's rebids are natural except that after a two club response, two diamonds asks responder to bid a major. A no trump rebid describes a minor two-suiter.

With a balanced hand of less than 19 points, opener opens in a suit, then rebids either one no trump with 12–16 points or two no trump with 17–18 points.

E

EBL. European Bridge League.

EFOS. Economical Forcing System. See EFOS SYSTEM.

EAST. One of the four hands at the bridge table. East is the partner of West, and the left-hand opponent of North.

EASTERN SCIENTIFIC. A style of bidding in which the principal features are strong no trump openings with non-forcing Stayman and Jacoby Transfer bids, five-card major-suit openings with a forcing one no trump response and limit raises. Two-over-one responses are strong but not necessarily forcing to game. Other elements are weak two-bids, with a strong artificial two club opening forcing to two no trump or three of a major suit; also negative and responsive doubles.

EASTERN STATES REGIONAL CHAMPION-SHIPS. A ten-day tournament held annually in New York City, usually in May, since 1929. In its early years it was organized by the Knicker-bocker Whist Club under the title of Eastern Championships, and had the prestige of a National championship. The most important of the nine major events are the REISINGER TROPHY for Knockout Teams and the GOLDMAN TROPHY for Open Pairs. For past results, see Appendix II.

EASY ACES. In auction bridge, at no trump, no honors were scored when aces were divided two–two among the pairs.

Also, the name of a popular radio show in the thirties associated with Goodman Ace and his wife Jane. It was a comedy series which began with a bridge theme.

ECHO. See HIGH-LOW SIGNAL.

ECONOMY OF HONORS. A playing technique intended to preserve honor cards from capture by opposing honors or trumps. The opponents can sometimes be encouraged to give up their high cards in exchange for low ones.

K Q x x

J x x

South leads twice from his own hand in order to make three tricks when West holds A x. See ACE-GRABBER, which illustrates the opposite principle.

Michael J. Sullivan gives these examples of economy of honors.

(1)

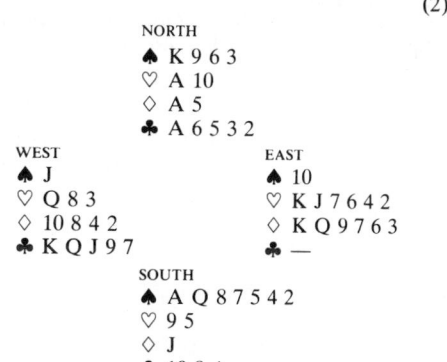

NORTH
♠ 10 6 3 2
♡ K 6
◇ K 9 6
♣ 8 6 4 3

WEST
♠ K J 9 4
♡ Q J 8 5
◇ J 8 5 2
♣ A

EAST
♠ Q 7
♡ 10 4 3 2
◇ Q 10 3
♣ J 10 9 7

SOUTH
♠ A 8 5
♡ A 9 7
◇ A 7 4
♣ K Q 5 2

South plays one no trump and receives the lead of the deuce of diamonds from West. Needing two club tricks and holding actual or potential stoppers in all other suits, South wins the diamond ace and, as insurance against the bare ace of clubs in the West hand, leads a low club. The ace drops and all is well, but even if it hadn't, the entries and tempos are available for two subsequent leads toward the ♣ K Q x.

(2)

NORTH
♠ K 9 6 3
♡ A 10
◇ A 5
♣ A 6 5 3 2

WEST
♠ J
♡ Q 8 3
◇ 10 8 4 2
♣ K Q J 9 7

EAST
♠ 10
♡ K J 7 6 4 2
◇ K Q 9 7 6 3
♣ —

SOUTH
♠ A Q 8 7 5 4 2
♡ 9 5
◇ J
♣ 10 8 4

West leads the king of clubs against South's contract of four spades. Unless the ace of clubs is ruffed, South has ten certain tricks. To guard against that lone possibility, declarer ducks the first round of clubs and subsequent club leads until West either shifts to another suit or permits South to ruff the fourth round of clubs. Eventually declarer gets to discard his losing heart on the carefully preserved ace of clubs.

ECUADOR BRIDGE ASSOCIATION (ASOCIACION DE BRIDGE DEL ECUADOR). The Association is a member of the South American Confederation and participates in South American Championships.

Officers, 1975:
President: Carlos Baquerizo Sotomayer.
Secretary: Jaime Vera, Asociación de Bridge del Ecuador, Casilla 521, Guayaquil, Ecuador.

EFOS SYSTEM. The "economical forcing system" used in international championships by leading Swedish players such as J. WOHLIN, N. LILLIEHÖÖK, and G. ANULF. A minimum suit response, such as one spade in reply to one heart, is treated artificially. The object is to give the opener every opportunity to make a natural descriptive rebid. A single raise of responder's artificial suit response is a strong bid indicating reversing values. For a similar idea, see RELAY SYSTEM.

EGYPTIAN BRIDGE ASSOCIATION (ASSOCIATION EGYPTIENNE DE BRIDGE). Founded in 1934; originally six clubs in Cairo and six clubs in Alexandria, as of 1964 had grown to fifteen clubs, with a membership of 1,500. The Association participates in the World Olympiads and formerly participated in European Championships. National events include Open Teams and Pairs and an Inter-Club tournament. The 1960 World Women's Team Olympiad was won by Egypt. Players listed separately are: Mrs. H. Camara, Mrs. A. Choucry, Mrs. S. Fathy, Mrs. L. Gordon, Mrs. J. Morcos, Mrs. S. Naguib, G. Nassif, O. Sharif, T. Trad, M. Zananiri.

Officers, 1975:
President: Hussain Motawi.
Secretary: Dr. Ahmed M. Ed-Morshidy, c/o Guezira Sporting Club, Zamalek, Cairo, Egypt.

EIGHT or EIGHT-SPOT. The seventh highest ranking card in each suit, having eight pips of the suit to which it belongs on the face. See: DISCARD; HIGH-LOW SIGNALS; OPENING LEAD; RULE OF ELEVEN.

EIGHT TABLES. At duplicate, eight tables provide for competition among thirty-two players as individuals, sixteen pairs, or eight teams of four.

Study of the chart below will show that this is a seven-table RAINBOW MOVEMENT, with the addition of stationary players numbered 29, 30, 31, and 32. All other players move. East moves to the next higher numbered table, South skips a table in the same direction, North skips two tables in the same direction; the boards move to the next lower numbered table, and West skips a table to the next lower numbered. However, the movement of each group is interrupted as a player goes to a seat occupied by a stationary player; the four players thus affected play instead, for that round only, at table 8, where the boards remain stationary. After playing at table 8, each player goes to the table determined by the seat from which he was displaced.

As a pair game, eight tables may be either MITCHELL or THREE-QUARTERS MOVEMENT. If the former, tables 1 and 2 relay boards, and a bye stand is placed between tables 5 and 6; the full eight rounds should be played to eliminate factoring. If three-quarters movement cards are used, thirteen rounds of two boards are played; if the SHORT HOWELL MOVEMENT is used, eleven rounds of two boards are provided.

As a team-of-four contest, the NEW ENGLAND RELAY MOVEMENT is suitable. Tables 1 and 5, 2 and 6, 3 and 7, and 4 and 8 have a continual relay of boards, with the second, fourth, sixth, and eighth sets in play the first round after traveling pairs move to the next

THIRTY-TWO PLAYER INDIVIDUAL MASTER SHEET
Based on Appendix Rainbow, devised by Paul N. MARKS

Sets	1	2	3	4	5	6	7	8
Round								
1 N/S E/W	T1 29–15 8–22	T2 2–16 30–23	T3 3–31 10–24	T4 4–18 11–32	T5 5–19 12–26	T6 6–20 13–27	T7 7–21 14–28	T8 1–17 9–25
2 N/S E/W	T7 4–19 13–23	T1 29–20 14–24	T2 6–21 30–25	T3 7–31 9–26	T4 1–16 10–32	T5 2–17 11–28	T6 3–18 12–22	T8 5–15 8–27
3 N/S E/W	T6 7–16 11–24	T7 1–17 12–25	T1 29–18 13–26	T2 3–19 30–27	T3 4–31 8–28	T4 5–21 9–32	T5 6–15 10–23	T8 2–20 14–22
4 N/S E/W	T5 3–20 9–25	T6 4–21 10–26	T7 5–15 11–27	T1 29–16 12–28	T2 7–17 30–22	T3 1–31 14–23	T4 2–19 8–32	T8 6–18 13–24
5 N/S E/W	T4 6–17 14–32	T5 7–18 8–27	T6 1–19 9–28	T7 2–20 10–22	T1 29–21 11–23	T2 4–15 30–24	T3 5–31 13–25	T8 3–16 12–26
6 N/S E/W	T3 2–31 12–27	T4 3–15 13–32	T5 4–16 14–22	T6 5–17 8–23	T7 6–18 9–24	T1 29–19 10–25	T2 1–20 30–26	T8 7–21 11–28
7 N/S E/W	T2 5–18 30–28	T3 6–31 11–22	T4 7–20 12–32	T5 1–21 13–24	T6 2–15 14–25	T7 3–16 8–26	T1 29–17 4–27	T8 4–19 10–23

higher numbered tables; thereafter, traveling pairs move to the next higher numbered tables, and North-South obtain boards from the relay tables and play them in ascending order.

There is also available an eight-table guide card movement, which is an adaptation of the standard team-of-four progression. The standard team-of-four progression, however, cannot be used without such adaptation for less than twelve teams, when the number of teams is even.

For seven and a half tables, use the eight-table Howell guide cards, making a stationary pair the phantom; in a Mitchell game, one of the North-South pairs at the relay table should be the phantom to avoid the necessity of relaying.

For eight and a half tables, see NINE TABLES. It is also possible to use a BUMP MITCHELL, which is particularly desirable if the extra half-table is a late arrival after the boards have been distributed.

EIRE. See CONTRACT BRIDGE ASSOCIATION OF IRELAND.

EITHER-OR SQUEEZE. See ALTERNATIVE SQUEEZE.

ELEVEN, RULE OF. See RULE OF ELEVEN.

ELEVEN TABLES. At duplicate, eleven tables afford excellent competition for either forty-four individuals, twenty-two pairs, or eleven teams-of-four.

As an individual tournament, eleven-table (eleven being a prime number) games are conducted under the RAINBOW MOVEMENT. Twenty-two boards are in play, for eleven rounds, and top is 10, average 110. It is also possible to extend the number of partnerships and boards to twenty-four or twenty-seven, by playing eight or nine rounds of three boards each. An interchange of partnerships by an exchange of seats between East and South, for two-board rounds, or by a counterclockwise movement by West in a three-board round, increases the number of partnerships, but usually slows down the speed with which the game can be conducted.

As a pair contest, twenty-two boards in eleven rounds complete either a MITCHELL or SCRAMBLED MITCHELL MOVEMENT. If more boards are desired, eight or nine rounds of three boards can be played. The THREE-QUARTERS HOWELL MOVEMENT provides for twenty-six boards in thirteen rounds with nine stationary pairs.

Standard team-of-four movement requires ten rounds. At thirty boards, it is too long, at twenty boards, too short for most sessions. Usually twenty-four boards are played, with the two middle rounds eliminated. After four rounds, traveling pairs return the boards just played to their home table and subtract three (or add eight) to their number to get their fifth-round assignment.

For ten and a half tables, see TEN TABLES. For eleven and a half tables, the phantom pair should be North-South at table 12, and a bye stand is inserted between tables 6 and 7. Since 1 and 12 would relay boards, the relay is eliminated in this manner. Traveling pairs leaving table 11 sit out the next

round. Using the three-quarters movement, the phantom pair should be one of the stationary assignments to keep top score on all boards the same. Moving pairs' scores must be factored up (by $1/12$) to make them comparable with those playing all the boards.

ELIMINATION. A type of end play in which (1) neutral suits are all played from both declarer's and dummy's hand, the last of such plays (2) saddling a defender with the lead, in order to force the defender to make a lead desired by the declarer. The play of the neutral cards is referred to as a STRIP PLAY, the saddling of a defender with the lead as a THROW-IN PLAY. See the latter for a discussion of various types and illustrations. See also PARTIAL ELIMINATION.

ELOPEMENT. A term coined by Géza OTTLIK in a series of *Bridge World* articles to describe coups by which a player scores a trick with a trump that would not ordinarily have sufficient rank to take a trick. The simplest type of elopement is a COUP EN PASSANT. In the following elopement spades are trump:

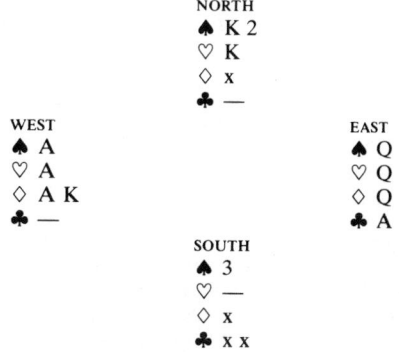

```
                    NORTH
                    ♠ K 2
                    ♡ K
                    ◇ x
                    ♣ —
WEST                                    EAST
♠ A                                     ♠ Q
♡ A                                     ♡ Q
◇ A K                                   ◇ Q
♣ —                                     ♣ A
                    SOUTH
                    ♠ 3
                    ♡ —
                    ◇ x
                    ♣ x x
```

South leads a club and, remarkably, takes three tricks. If West ruffs, a diamond is discarded from dummy. If West throws a diamond, the club is ruffed in dummy and a heart is ruffed in the South hand, and the lead of South's last club is a coup en passant. If West instead throws the heart ace, the club is ruffed and the king of hearts provides a discard for South's losing diamond while West ruffs with his master trump.

EN PASSANT. See COUP EN PASSANT.

ENCOURAGING. (1) A term applied to a bid which strongly urges partner to continue to game. The bid is usually one trick short of game (two no trump, three hearts, or three spades), and indicates that the combined hands are known to total 23–24 points (or the distributional equivalent), and that therefore game is in view. If partner has an unpromising hand with no values in reserve for his previous bidding, he may pass, but will usually continue to game.

The following bids are all encouraging in standard theory:

SOUTH	NORTH
1 ♣	1 ♡
2 NT	

SOUTH	NORTH
1 ♣	1 ♡
3 ♡	

SOUTH	WEST	NORTH	EAST
1 ♣	1 ♡	Pass	3 ♡

The last sequence, with a jump raise of an overcall, is treated as pre-emptive by some theorists.

In many other sequences, opinions are divided. For example, a jump bid by responder is always treated as forcing in STANDARD AMERICAN, especially as interpreted on the East Coast. But a jump by responder in no trump or in a suit already bid by the partnership is simply encouraging in the style of experts in other areas such as the West Coast, the Midwest, Texas, and England. See JUMP REBIDS BY RESPONDER.

"CONSTRUCTIVE" and "forward-going" are almost synonymous terms for encouraging.

(2) A term applied to a defensive signal by which a player urges his partner to continue playing the suit led. See COME-ON, HIGH-LOW SIGNAL, UPSIDE-DOWN SIGNALS.

END GAME FALSE-CARDING. See FALSE-CARDING.

END PLAY. A play taking place toward the end of the hand, usually at about the eleventh trick, though sometimes earlier. The preparation for an end play may begin as early as the first or second trick; its object is to win an additional trick. They are essentially of three types; the forced lead or throw-in play, the coup or trump-reducing play, and the squeeze play. Many variations of each type occur. Articles dealing with various end plays are listed under the general headings COUP and SQUEEZE, and under the particular headings RUFF AND DISCARD, RUFF AND RUFF, SMOTHER PLAY, THROW-IN, TRUMP PICK-UP, and UNDERRUFF.

ENGLISH BRIDGE UNION. Founded in 1938 as the successor to the Duplicate Bridge Control Board. It is a constituent member of the British Bridge League, and its players have achieved many international successes representing Great Britain. The EBU was host to the European Championship at Brighton in 1950 and 1975, and at Torquay in 1961. It had a membership of about 20,000 in 1974, and organizes many National events, of which the most important are the Life Masters Pairs, National Pairs, and Crockfords Cup. Players listed separately include: N. Bach, L. Baron, J. Brown, G. L. Butler, J. Cansino, B. Cohen, J. D. R. Collings, R. F. Corwen, E. Crowhurst, L. W. Dodds, A. Dormer, Mrs. J. Durran, Mrs. M. Edwards, Mrs. R. Evans, Mrs. A. G. Evers, F. Farrington, G. Fell, Mrs. A. L. Fleming, J. Flint, Dr. R. Forbes, G. C. H. Fox, H. Franklin, N. Gardener, C. Goldstein, Mrs. P. Gordon, Mrs. B. Harris, M. Harrison-Gray, N. Hart, Mrs. G. E. Higginson, Mrs. A. Hiron, H. St.

J. Ingram, E. Kempson, K. W. Konstam, J. Lazarus, E. Leader-Williams, R. Lederer, Dr. S. Lee, I. MacLeod, A. E. Manning-Foster, Mrs. R. Markus, J. C. H. Marx, G. F. Mathieson, E. Mayer, A. Meredith, E. Milnes, V. Mollo, Mrs. J. Moss, F. North, J. T. Pavlides, H. Phillips, R. Preston, R. A. Priday, Mrs. R. A. Priday, E. Rayne, T. Reese, Lady D. Rhodes, C. Rodrigue, A. Rose, W. Rose, B. Schapiro, Miss D. Shanahan, J. Sharples, R. Sharples, S. J. Simon, N. Squire, R. Swimer, H. P. F. Swinnerton-Dyer, J. Tarlo, L. Tarlo, R. L. Telfer, A. F. Truscott, G. G. Walshe, Mrs. M. Whittaker, Mrs. P. Williams.

Officials, 1975:
Chairman: J. G. Faulkner.
Secretary: Dr. E. Stuart Staveley, High Street, Thame, Oxon, England.

ENTRIES. Sold for events at a bridge tournament to provide a control of seating assignments. Each entry blank designates an individual's, pair's or team's original seating assignment as to table number (and direction if appropriate) and section.

Particular seating assignments are usually separated from others at multi-sectioned events for assignment to known expert players to distribute such players equitably throughout the field. See SEED, SEEDING, and ASSIGNMENT OF SEATS.

ENTRY. A means of securing the lead in a particular hand. Careful and effective use of entries is one of the basic arts of card play. In most situations it is sound strategy to maintain entries in both hands, which means preserving entries in the weaker hand where possible.

When both hands hold high cards, and there are more high cards than tricks, declarer should try to preserve a flexible entry situation:

NORTH
♠ A Q 10

SOUTH
♠ K J 9

Suppose the first spade trick is won with the ace. If South will need entries to dummy, he should drop his king; if he needs entries to his hand, he should drop the nine. The jack is definitely a bad play. Declarer should aim to have the sequence of cards alternate from hand to hand: dropping the jack would leave dummy's Q 10 in effective sequence.

Similarly when drawing trumps, declarer may leave himself with two low trumps in one hand and one in the other. He should try to arrange that the single trump ranks between the trumps in the opposite hand.

A 4–4 fit will often provide an entry with a spot card if the suit divides 3–2.

```
        NORTH
        ♠ A Q 10 3

        SOUTH
        ♠ K J 9 2
```

If dummy needs every possible entry, South should start by overtaking any high card as economically as possible. Later he repeats the process, and if the suit splits 3–2, he does so a third time, giving dummy a fourth-round entry with the three.

The same is true if the defenders have one, two, or three winners in the suit. If declarer has four small cards in each hand, he can arrange to win the fourth round in either hand, except in the rare case when the spot cards do not overlap at all.

Some special situations involving entries are dealt with under the following headings. DESCHAPELLES COUP; ENTRY-SHIFTING SQUEEZE; ENTRY SQUEEZE; GAMBIT; HOLD UP; MERRIMAC COUP; SCISSORS COUP; STEPPINGSTONE SQUEEZE; UNBLOCKING; UNBLOCKING SQUEEZE.

ENTRY-KILLING PLAY. A play made with the object of cutting the opponents' entry to a particular hand. Special varieties of this are discussed under MERRIMAC COUP (by the defense) and SCISSORS COUP (by declarer).

The following are typical maneuvers by second hand when dummy is entryless:

```
              NORTH
              ♠ A J 10 x x
WEST                              EAST
♠ Q x x                          ♠ K x x
              SOUTH
              ♠ x x
```

When South leads the suit, West must play the queen to hold South to one trick in the suit. If he plays low, East must allow the ten or jack to hold to prevent South making four tricks.

```
              NORTH
              ♠ A J 9 x
WEST                              EAST
♠ K 10 x                         ♠ Q 8 x x
              SOUTH
              ♠ x x
```

When South leads, West must again play high. If he plays low, South can make a second trick in the suit by finessing the nine.

Similarly, plays can be made by the declarer. If East were declarer in these two cases, he would play high from dummy on a lead from South if he could judge the situation accurately.

ENTRY-SHIFTING SQUEEZE. A squeeze described by Géza OTTLIK in which a shortage of normal entries is compensated for by the capability of winning the squeeze trick or a crucial later trick in either hand. A necessary ingredient is a balanced matrix in the squeeze suit, i.e., the suit must be divided equally between declarer's hand and dummy, with the two top cards split. The entry-shifting squeeze may be of either the trump or the no trump variety. Several hands from Ottlik's *Bridge World* articles are used here with permission.

West dealer, North-South vulnerable.

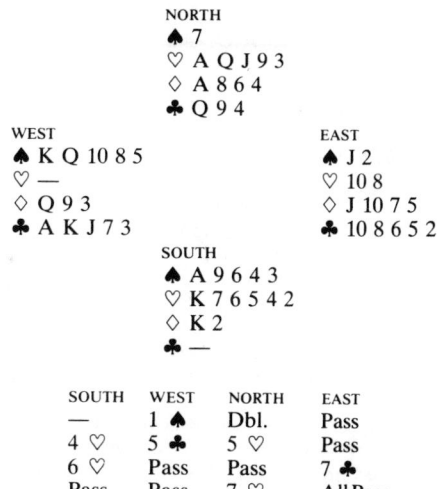

```
              NORTH
              ♠ 7
              ♡ A Q J 9 3
              ◇ A 8 6 4
              ♣ Q 9 4
WEST                              EAST
♠ K Q 10 8 5                     ♠ J 2
♡ —                              ♡ 10 8
◇ Q 9 3                          ◇ J 10 7 5
♣ A K J 7 3                      ♣ 10 8 6 5 2
              SOUTH
              ♠ A 9 6 4 3
              ♡ K 7 6 5 4 2
              ◇ K 2
              ♣ —
```

SOUTH	WEST	NORTH	EAST
—	1 ♠	Dbl.	Pass
4 ♡	5 ♣	5 ♡	Pass
6 ♡	Pass	Pass	7 ♣
Pass	Pass	7 ♡	All Pass

West would have liked to lead a heart to cut down on declarer's crossruffs, but having no hearts he settles on a spade lead as most likely to hurt declarer by prematurely removing a vital entry. South wins the spade lead and pulls one round of trumps hoping for a 1–1 division, which would allow him to crossruff for thirteen tricks. Discovering the 2–0 break, he abandons trumps temporarily. He cashes two rounds of diamonds and ruffs a diamond, ruffs a spade with the nine of hearts, followed by another diamond ruff and another spade ruff with the queen, leaving this position:

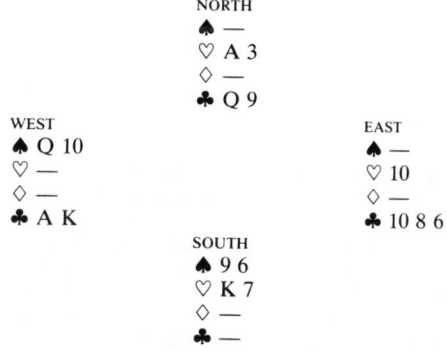

```
              NORTH
              ♠ —
              ♡ A 3
              ◇ —
              ♣ Q 9
WEST                              EAST
♠ Q 10                           ♠ —
♡ —                              ♡ 10
◇ —                              ◇ —
♣ A K                            ♣ 10 8 6
              SOUTH
              ♠ 9 6
              ♡ K 7
              ◇ —
              ♣ —
```

On the lead of the heart king, West is squeezed. If he throws a spade, the heart is ducked in dummy, allowing declarer to ruff out the remaining high spade. If West throws a club instead, the heart king is overtaken with dummy's ace, and a club ruff establishes a club trick.

The following hand illustrates alternative entry situations.

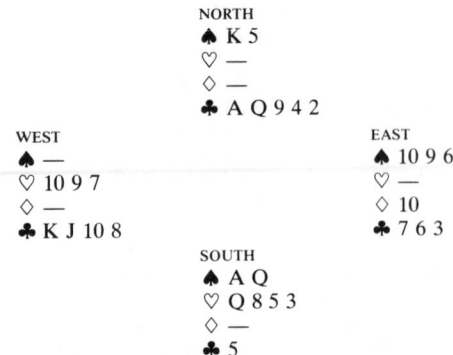

South plays in six no trump doubled by West; South had rested briefly in six hearts until West doubled that contract.

Alternative A: West leads the club jack. The queen is finessed successfully, but an entry has been eliminated prematurely. A spade is led to the ace, and the jack of diamonds is finessed and the ace cashed, felling the king. A third round of diamonds is cashed, West throwing his last spade, leaving this position:

NORTH
♠ K J
♡ 4
♢ 3
♣ A 9 4 2

WEST
♠ —
♡ J 10 9 7 6
♢ —
♣ K 10 8

EAST
♠ 10 9 6 4
♡ 2
♢ 10
♣ 7 6

SOUTH
♠ Q 8
♡ A K Q 8 5 3
♢ —
♣ —

On the lead of the eight of spades, West is squeezed. If he throws a heart, the spade is won with dummy's king, preserving South's queen as an entry to the hearts that are about to be set up. If West throws a club, the spade eight is won with dummy's jack, preserving the king as an entry to the clubs.

Alternative B: West's opening lead is the jack of hearts, which South must win immediately to prevent West from shifting to clubs and thus cutting communications in both long suits. South cashes another round of hearts, discarding a diamond, takes two rounds of diamonds, cashes the jack of spades,

and comes to hand with the third round of diamonds, leaving this position:

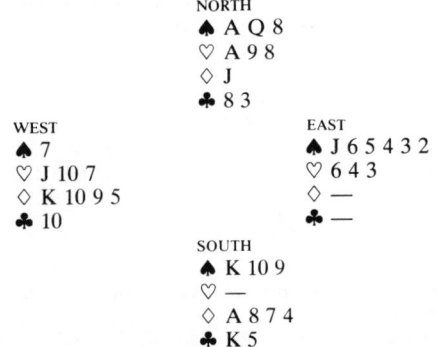

When the ace of spades is led, West is squeezed with the same effect as in *Alternative A*. If he discards a heart, the spade king will be unblocked from dummy to allow hearts to be established and cashed; if he throws a club, the spade five will be played, retaining the king for entry to the clubs.

Note that in *Alternative A* it was crucial for declarer to win the first spade trick with the ace in order to preserve the ability to win either or both of the last two spade tricks in dummy since dummy had a long suit in which declarer was void. In *Alternative B*, the reverse was true—declarer had a long suit in which dummy was void. Hence the ace and queen of spades had to be retained in South's hand to maximize the entries in that direction.

There appear to be two principal defenses to an entry-shifting squeeze. One is for a defender to play a card in the squeeze suit that deprives declarer of his flexibility on later tricks, for example:

NORTH
♠ A Q 8
♡ A 9 8
♢ J
♣ 8 3

WEST
♠ 7
♡ J 10 7
♢ K 10 9 5
♣ 10

EAST
♠ J 6 5 4 3 2
♡ 6 4 3
♢ —
♣ —

SOUTH
♠ K 10 9
♡ —
♢ A 8 7 4
♣ K 5

Playing in no trump, South needs all the tricks, but East is on lead and leads the *jack* of spades. This defense leaves South no way to produce the position he needs, i.e., the equivalent of A Q in dummy and K x in hand. Another defense is to delay winning a defense trick until such time as declarer can be forced to commit himself in the key suit before operating the squeeze. In the following position, spades are trump and South needs all but two of the remaining tricks.

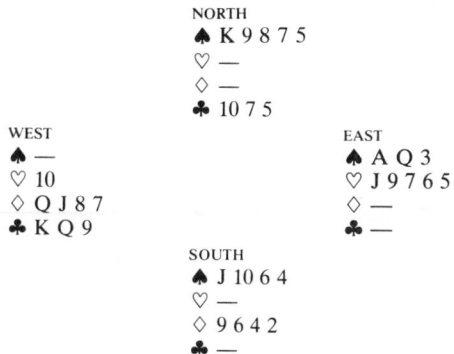

```
                    NORTH
                    ♠ K 9 8 7 5
                    ♡ —
                    ◇ —
                    ♣ 10 7 5
WEST                              EAST
♠ —                              ♠ A Q 3
♡ 10                             ♡ J 9 7 6 5
◇ Q J 8 7                        ◇ —
♣ K Q 9                          ♣ —
                    SOUTH
                    ♠ J 10 6 4
                    ♡ —
                    ◇ 9 6 4 2
                    ♣ —
```

South ruffs a diamond. If East overruffs and plays trumps to stop the crossruff, West can discard a heart on the ace of spades, but when East plays his last trump, West will be caught in an entry-shifting trump squeeze (assuming South plays the jack or ten on East's three). So East must refrain from overruffing until South has ruffed yet another diamond in dummy and two clubs in his hand, and has reached this position:

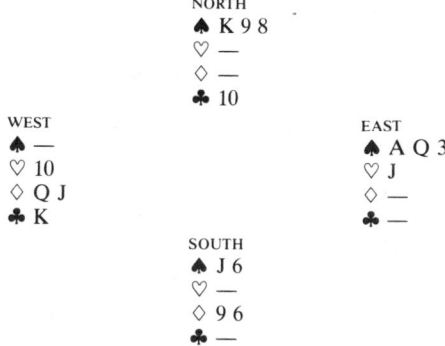

```
                    NORTH
                    ♠ K 9 8
                    ♡ —
                    ◇ —
                    ♣ 10
WEST                              EAST
♠ —                              ♠ A Q 3
♡ 10                             ♡ J
◇ Q J                            ◇ —
♣ K                              ♣ —
                    SOUTH
                    ♠ J 6
                    ♡ —
                    ◇ 9 6
                    ♣ —
```

Now when South ruffs a diamond in dummy, East overruffs and cashes his ace of spades. West can safely throw the heart ten, and the North and South hands are in effect squeezed in spades. Their trump plays must reveal which hand will win the twelfth trick, and West can discard appropriately on the eleventh trick, thus winning the last trick.

ENTRY SQUEEZE. A squeeze that is aimed at forcing a defender, or both defenders, to discard from a seemingly worthless holding so that declarer can create an extra entry to one hand or the other by overtaking a card of winning rank. Analyzed and described by Géza OTTLIK in the December 1967 issue of *Bridge World.* His article, entitled "The Quest," won the first INTERNATIONAL BRIDGE ACADEMY "Ar-

ticle of the Year" award in 1968, and three of the hands from this article have been used herein by permission of *Bridge World.*

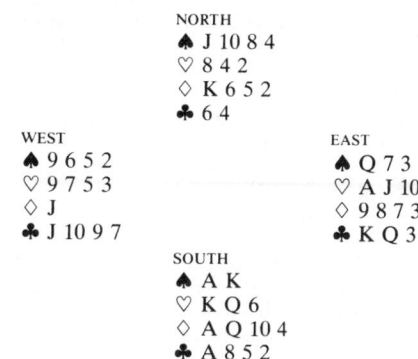

```
                    NORTH
                    ♠ J 10 8 4
                    ♡ 8 4 2
                    ◇ K 6 5 2
                    ♣ 6 4
WEST                              EAST
♠ 9 6 5 2                        ♠ Q 7 3
♡ 9 7 5 3                        ♡ A J 10
◇ J                              ◇ 9 8 7 3
♣ J 10 9 7                       ♣ K Q 3
                    SOUTH
                    ♠ A K
                    ♡ K Q 6
                    ◇ A Q 10 4
                    ♣ A 8 5 2
```

South declares three no trump after East has opened the bidding, and West leads the jack of clubs. East overtakes with the queen and continues with the king and a third club as declarer holds up the ace until the third round. The ace and queen of diamonds reveal the 4–1 division, but South can still get home if he concedes a club to West, which crushes East in three suits. Clearly East cannot let go of a spade, and if he discards a heart, one heart lead from dummy suffices to establish two tricks in that suit for declarer. So East is forced to discard one of his "useless" diamonds. Now declarer has two diamond entries to dummy by overtaking the ten with the king and can lead twice toward his heart honors. As Ottlik noted in his article: "Those silly little diamonds in East's hand have a function after all. Nondescript, irrelevant, or immaterial as they may be called, by their sheer existence they also serve. They stand and wait, in the way, blocking traffic, hindering enemy lines of communication. And having this value, however silent, taciturn and hidden, they are subject to the pressure of a squeeze."

Occasionally it may be necessary for declarer to unblock a spot card to create the position for an entry squeeze.

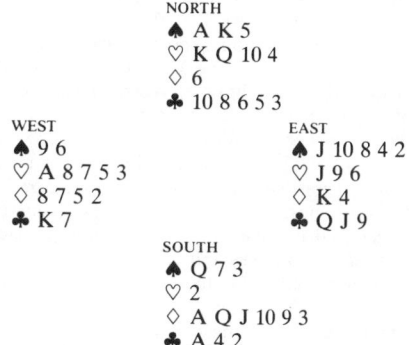

```
                    NORTH
                    ♠ A K 5
                    ♡ K Q 10 4
                    ◇ 6
                    ♣ 10 8 6 5 3
WEST                              EAST
♠ 9 6                            ♠ J 10 8 4 2
♡ A 8 7 5 3                      ♡ J 9 6
◇ 8 7 5 2                        ◇ K 4
♣ K 7                            ♣ Q J 9
                    SOUTH
                    ♠ Q 7 3
                    ♡ 2
                    ◇ A Q J 10 9 3
                    ♣ A 4 2
```

After an aggressive auction, in which West has over-called in hearts and has been raised by East, South lands in a near-hopeless contract of six diamonds. West's spade lead, however, gives declarer a chance, providing he wins the spade in dummy and carefully unblocks the seven from his hand. After a successful diamond finesse, South runs all his trumps but one, discarding four clubs from dummy, and on the fifth round East is squeezed. He cannot discard a heart; otherwise declarer plays a heart to the queen and returns the king, smothering East's jack. Nor can East let go of a club, which would allow South to lead a heart to the queen (West must duck), then concede a club. Thus, East is forced to come down to a single-ton spade. This merely postpones the inevitable though, for South leads a heart to the queen, ruffs a heart, and returns to dummy by overtaking the queen of spades with the ace. The king of hearts crashes the jack and ace and declarer's carefully preserved three of spades allows him entry to dummy's high heart.

The entry squeeze can also operate against both opponents in the form of a double squeeze.

NORTH
♠ A 6 4
♡ 10 6 5
◇ J 8 7 4
♣ 9 4 2

WEST
♠ J 10 8
♡ Q 7 4 2
◇ 10 6 5 2
♣ 7 6

EAST
♠ 9 7 5 2
♡ K 8 3
◇ Q 9 3
♣ 10 8 5

SOUTH
♠ K Q 3
♡ A J 9
◇ A K
♣ A K Q J 3

West leads the jack of spades against South's contract of six no trump. Rather than bank every-thing on finding East with both heart honors, or guessing which opponent might hold a doubleton honor, declarer wins the spade in hand and cashes five rounds of clubs, discarding a diamond and a heart from dummy. On the last club West is in some difficulty. If he holds fewer than three hearts, South can lead a heart from his hand to establish two tricks in that suit. Alternatively, if West comes down to fewer than three diamonds, declarer can cash the ace and king of diamonds, the king and ace of spades, then take the heart finesse; West, marooned with nothing but hearts, must then return a heart into declarer's tenace. So West is "squeezed" down to a singleton spade. East, in turn, is squeezed on the last club, for he must also hold three cards in each red suit and can hold no more than one spade. South has thus squeezed both opponents in a suit in which he started with three top winners and now makes his slam by overtaking the king of spades with the ace for a heart finesse. The six of spades provides entry to dummy for the second heart finesse.

A squeeze that is required because a blocked suit

prevents declarer from cashing one of his "sure" winners has also been called an entry squeeze, but these squeezes are more properly categorized under different headings. See UNBLOCKING SQUEEZE.

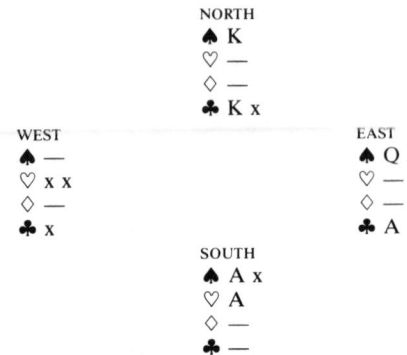

NORTH
♠ K
♡ —
◇ —
♣ K x

WEST
♠ —
♡ x x
◇ —
♣ x

EAST
♠ Q J
♡ —
◇ —
♣ A

SOUTH
♠ A x
♡ A
◇ —
♣ —

Also described as an overtaking squeeze. South leads the ace of hearts, discarding a club from dum-my, and East is squeezed in two suits. If he discards a spade, South can play the ace of spades, which estab-lishes his low spade. If East discards his ace of clubs, South leads a low spade to North's king, which enables him to cash the king of clubs.

The blocked menace contains two winners, with the length of the master card accompanying the squeeze card. The other hand contains a one-card menace against the same player who controls the blocked suit. Since the East and West cards could be interchanged and the squeeze would remain effec-tive, the squeeze is automatic.

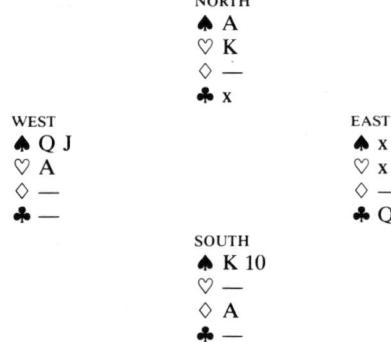

NORTH
♠ A
♡ K
◇ —
♣ x

WEST
♠ Q J
♡ A
◇ —
♣ —

EAST
♠ x
♡ x
◇ —
♣ Q

SOUTH
♠ K 10
♡ —
◇ A
♣ —

Also known as a jettison squeeze. South leads the ace of diamonds. If West discards the ace of hearts, South leads a spade to the ace and cashes the king of hearts. If West discards a spade, North discards (jet-tisons) the ace of spades and plays the king of that suit, establishing the ten.

These squeezes are sometimes called STEPPING-STONE SQUEEZES (Reese).

EQUALS. Cards that are in sequence, or cards that are in effect in sequence because all cards of inter-

vening rank have been played. See PLAY FROM
EQUALS.

EQUITY. The "equity rule" for adjusting scores.
See LAWS OF DUPLICATE (Law 12).

ERRORS IN SCORING. See LAWS OF DUPLICATE
(Law 75) and SCORING CORRECTIONS.

ESCAPE SUIT. A long suit held in reserve by a
player making a gambling or psychic bid. An overcall
of one no trump by a player with a weak hand and a
long broken suit is a well-worn tactic. It is not difficult to expose the maneuver by doubling and forcing
the overcaller to escape into his suit, but the tactic
has some positive value: a weak hand with a long suit
might otherwise be shut out of the auction unless
WEAK JUMP OVERCALLS are being used.

Psychic bids in a short suit with an escape suit in
reserve are seldom met with, because they tend to be
more dangerous to partner than to the opponents.
For a regular systemic use of a bid with an escape
suit, see GAMBLING THREE NO TRUMP.

ESTABLISH. To make a suit or an individual card
good by forcing out the opponent's guards or
winners. Thus one may establish K Q J 10 9 of a suit
for four tricks after conceding one to the ace.

ESTABLISHED CARD. A card that has been promoted to winning rank after all higher-ranking cards
in the other hands have been played.

ESTABLISHED ENTRY. An entry developed by
driving out a higher card.

ESTABLISHED REVOKE. A revoke which may not
be corrected. A revoke becomes established as soon
as the revoking player or his partner leads or plays to
the next trick, or, if the revoke is made in leading, as
soon as the revoking player's partner plays to the
trick on which the revoke is made; or by the act of
making a claim. A revoke made on the twelfth trick
never becomes established. See LAWS (Law 63).

ESTABLISHED SUIT. A long suit in which a player
holds all the remaining high cards, which at no trump
or after trumps have been drawn at a suit contract
will all be winners when the suit is led and run. The
object of no trump play is essentially to establish one
or more long suits, by drawing or forcing out
whatever high cards the opponents may hold in that
suit.

ESTIMATION. The attempt to judge the score that
one is likely to have earned in a duplicate game.
Generally a player estimates by comparing his result
on a hand with those likely to be obtained elsewhere.
As a result of this procedure, one can often alter
one's tactics toward the end of a session, playing a
somewhat chancier game if one is behind and needs
"tops" to win, or playing "down the middle" if one is
way ahead and can afford to coast. See SHOOTING.

In the normal American match-point pairs game,

which has a top of twelve, estimating can be quite
accurate. However, in large duplicates scored over a
wide field, when the top on a board is sometimes over
a hundred, estimation is less precise, and the best
one can do is to calculate in terms of percentage, or
to judge whether one's result will be:

bottom (O)
below average (A—)
average (A)
above average (A+)
top (T)

Alternatively, one can translate this formula into a
scale from 0 to 4, corresponding to the above; in this
case it is easy to remember that double the number of
boards already played represents an average score at
each stage of the game. Estimation can be very easy
when traveling score slips are in use; it becomes pro-
gressively more accurate as the contest continues,
reaching certainty on the last round. Traveling slips
are out of favor in the United States, however, for
tournaments above club level.

ETHICS AND CONDUCT. The term "ethics" is
commonly used in relation to the observance of fair
play. Breaches of ethics are generally thought of as
unfair practices which fall short of deliberate cheating.

The Laws deal with the whole question of proper
behavior at bridge under the general heading, "Proprieties." In popular thought, however, there is a
distinction between unethical conduct and bad
manners and this distinction is followed here. Thus
the provisions of the Proprieties which relate to good
behavior are dealt with under a separate entry, ETI-
QUETTE.

Of the five sections of the Proprieties in the LAWS
OF DUPLICATE BRIDGE, those dealing with ethics are
Nos. I (General Principles), II (Improper Informa-
tion), and IV (Partnership Agreements).

ETIQUETTE. Much of the popularity of contract
bridge is attributable to the high standards of etiquette which are observed by the players. No other
modern game leans so heavily on the expectation
that participants will conduct themselves in a highly
civilized manner.

In tournament bridge, violations of proper etiquette are to be expected from inexperienced
players, either through ignorance or inadvertence. A
well-mannered opponent who is the victim of such a
violation will, if he considers that comment is called
for, be at pains to make it clear that his comment is
intended to be helpful rather than admonitory.

At the other end of the scale is the noxious violation of the experienced player who complains
loudly—but unofficially—of a violation of ethics or
etiquette committed against him. "I wuz robbed!" is
never heard from a player of high standards of etiquette; he either makes an official protest or says
nothing.

The Laws of Contract Bridge deal with the whole
question of proper behavior under the heading,

"Proprieties." Matters of etiquette, as distinct from questions of ethics, are dealt with in Part III of the Proprieties.

Among the breaches of good manners frequently observed are the following: Discussion between two partners of a board just played when there is another board to play is unmannerly. Looking at an opponent's hand after it has been placed in the board without asking permission is unmannerly. Criticism of an opponent's bidding or any implication of bad faith on the part of the opponents without having previously called the director to the table is unmannerly. Appearing at a bridge tournament dressed carelessly or sloppily is an insult to the ladies and gentlemen against whom you will compete at the table.

Among the examples of good manners at the table are these items summed up by J. S. Weller, printed in the *Bridge Bulletin* of Johannesburg, South Africa.

(1) Good temper. Bring pleasure with you to this amusement. Take every event in good humor, and by no means incite ill humor.

(2) Silence. Never talk or twitch when someone is thinking—most rigidly enforced during the auction, when no questions are to be tolerated.

(3) Smooth action. Smooth flow of action without aggravating chitchat enhances the joy of the game, and gets hands finished faster. Have your bid ready before it is your turn.

(4) Advice. Don't give advice. Just think.

(5) Visitors. Visitors must remain still in one place until the hand is completed. They are bound by all proprieties even more strictly than the players. They are not even allowed to be careless, such as leaving a hand they feel is dull. They may never point out any infraction or impulsively correct a player.

(6) Sportsmanship. Feel that others are doing the best they can, considering the effect on them of your presence. No grown person, much less a bridge player, ever makes a condescending, belittling, or humiliating remark. Once in a while you will be gratified to observe an act deserving of a compliment. Give it.

(7) Winning. Winning makes a prize player feel very good indeed. It makes a child exult.

(8) Losing. Losing is accompanied by a grim, cheerful, determined, hopeful, anxious, patient demeanor. Never by a complaint or a grumble.

(9) Facts. When two cannot agree on what has occurred, the child is right. The bridge player will agree that he possibly could be. If a referee gives a decision, be gracious; don't talk back.

(10) Women. Women don't exist in a bridge game, nor do men; only bridge players. All are equally bound by etiquette. Courtesy exists, favors because of sex do not.

EUROPEAN BRIDGE LEAGUE. Founded in 1947 at Copenhagen, by delegates from the bridge federations of eight countries (Belgium, Denmark, Finland, France, Great Britain, the Netherlands, Norway, and Sweden). All were members of the Inter-

national Bridge League, which they voted to dissolve to form a new league, in a new setting, Denmark. A. J. E. Lucardie was elected President, and Herman Dedichen (at whose instigation the meeting was called) was named Honorary Secretary. Congresses of the league have always been combined with the European Championships. In 1948 the League was a member of the group of three, with the PORTLAND CLUB and ACBL, that issued the International Laws of Bridge. Membership of the EBL had grown by 1974 to a total of twenty-five countries, the original eight plus Austria, Czechoslovakia, Germany, Greece, Hungary, Iceland, Ireland, Israel, Italy, Lebanon, Monaco, Poland, Portugal, Spain, Switzerland, Turkey, and Yugoslavia.

The European Championship results, listed in Appendix III, include the prewar events held under the auspices of the International Bridge League. In 1937 the championship in Budapest was a World Championship as well as a European Championship, and the results are listed under WORLD CHAMPIONSHIP. Similarly, there were no European Championships in 1960, 1964, 1968, and 1972 because World Team Olympiads took place in those years. When the WBF decided to hold the BERMUDA BOWL competition in the odd-numbered years only, starting in 1977, the European Championships also became a biennial event, to be held shortly prior to each Bermuda Bowl.

Some of the many contributions of the European Bridge League and its constituent bodies to bridge on the international level include: European Match Points (later called INTERNATIONAL MATCH POINTS); procedure for recording in detail a large number of matches played simultaneously; the development of BRIDGE-O-RAMA; and the custom of using English as the international bridge language.

Considerable contributions to the development of international bridge in Europe have been made by: A. J. E. LUCARDIE (IBL President 1933–34 and 1938–39); Sir A. Noel MOBBS of England (EBL President 1948–50); Baron R. de NEXON (EBL President 1950–65); Count Carl BONDE (EBL President 1965–69); Marchese Silvio CARINI-MAZZACARA (EBL President 1969–73); Andre Littman-Lemaitre (1973–); Herman DEDICHEN (EBL Secretary 1947–58); Ernst HELDRING (EBL Secretary 1958–71); Wolf Achterberg (1971–). Because of their impressive contributions to the EBL, Baron R. de Nexon was elected President Emeritus upon his retirement in 1965, and Geoffrey Butler was elected President Emeritus in 1974.

Honorary Secretary, 1975: Wolf Achterberg.

EUROPEAN BRIDGE REVIEW. See BIBLIOGRAPHY, O.

EUROPEAN JUNIOR CHAMPIONSHIPS. A biennial event for players under the age of 27, first officially held in Delft, Holland, in 1972. Two previous events had been held in Prague in 1968 and Dublin in 1970, won by Sweden and Denmark, respectively.

Winners and runners-up in the official events have been:

SITE	WINNERS	RUNNERS-UP
1972—Delft	Poland	Israel
1974—Copenhagen	Sweden	Ireland

EVEN. A term applying to the equal distribution of the outstanding cards in a suit, as a 3–3 division of six outstanding cards.

EVENT. A contest of one or more sessions in duplicate bridge played to determine a winner.

EXCESS POINTS. When cumulative scoring was used in pair competition, the limit placed on the number of points that could be scored was, for the defenders, 600 if not vulnerable, 900 if vulnerable; for the declarer, 800 if not vulnerable, 1,000 if vulnerable. No limitation was placed if the contract was for a slam. Losers lost total points, winners were credited only with the maximum, and the balance carried to a special "excess points" column used only for breaking ties. In England, the 600 maximum for defenders was 700. Since match-point scoring has almost totally replaced total-point scoring, this provision was omitted from the Laws of 1943 and subsequently.

EXCLUSION. A Unit board of directors may vote to exclude a member of another Unit from its tournaments for cause. See also SUSPENSION.

EXCLUSION BID. A bid which shows a holding in every suit *except* the one named. This is a feature of the ROMAN SYSTEM. After an opening bid of two clubs or two diamonds, showing a three-suited hand, the opener rebids in his short suit if he receives the conventional positive response of two (see ROMAN TWO DIAMONDS). Similarly, the Roman System prescribes a bid in the shortest unbid suit in response to a take-out double; this has a transfer effect, and permits the stronger hand to become declarer. A take-out double is itself an exclusion call in a wide sense: it implies support for all suits except the one already bid.

Exclusion bids have been adopted by some partnerships as a defense against strong artificial opening bids. This device is useful for competing on three-suited hands in which no suit has been bid naturally. An extension of this convention devised by Andrew BERNSTEIN, which he calls the "Super Convention," is to use an overcall of an opponent's no trump opening as a two-way exclusion bid. The overcall thus shows either length in the suit bid, or shortness in the suit bid and support for all other suits. The partner of the overcaller is expected to treat the overcall as natural if he has fewer than three cards in the suit. Otherwise he is expected to take his choice of the other suits.

EXHAUST. To draw all cards of a suit from the hand of any player. A player becoming void of a suit

during the play is said to be exhausted of that suit, as distinguished from holding no cards of that suit originally.

EXHIBITION MATCHES. At certain major championship tournaments, advance arrangements are made for exhibition matches before a considerable audience. In such events, all contestants must agree, as a condition of entry, that they will, if required, participate in the exhibition matches at the announced time and place. The right of the governing body to impose this condition has been vigorously contested by some players, but without success. Since a considerable number of spectators are involved, the starting time must be rigidly observed, taking precedence over the convenience of the contestants. See BRIDGE-O-RAMA and VU-GRAPH.

EXIT. To "get out of one's hand," particularly when it is undesirable to lead from one's own hand, usually by making a lead which is not likely to jeopardize the value of any partnership holding.

EXIT CARD. A card by which one can exit from one's hand, offering an escape from an opponent's attempted throw-in or elimination play.

EXIT PLAY. A defensive unblocking maneuver executed in order to avoid a throw-in.

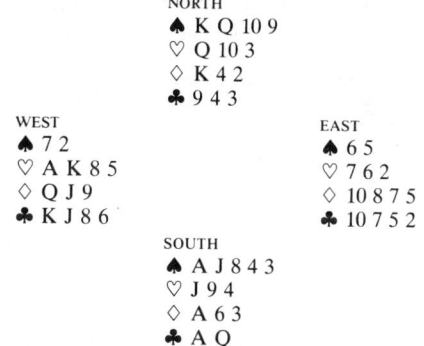

```
                    NORTH
                    ♠ K Q 10 9
                    ♡ Q 10 3
                    ◇ K 4 2
                    ♣ 9 4 3
    WEST                            EAST
    ♠ 7 2                           ♠ 6 5
    ♡ A K 8 5                       ♡ 7 6 2
    ◇ Q J 9                         ◇ 10 8 7 5
    ♣ K J 8 6                       ♣ 10 7 5 2
                    SOUTH
                    ♠ A J 8 4 3
                    ♡ J 9 4
                    ◇ A 6 3
                    ♣ A Q
```

South is in four spades after an opening bid on his left, and West leads three rounds of hearts. Declarer wins, draws trumps, and plays ace, king, and another diamond, hoping to throw West in for a favorable club lead. West, however, makes an exit play, disembarrassing himself of the queen and jack on the first two diamond leads, and retaining the nine, which his partner overtakes on the third round to play a club, defeating the contract.

S. K.

EXPECTANCY. What a player is entitled to expect in various circumstances governed by mathematical probabilities. (1) In the deal, a player's expectancy is one ace, one king, one queen, and one jack. (2) After looking at his hand and before any bidding has taken place, a player may expect his partner to hold one-third of the outstanding honor cards. (3) In some bidding situations, a player's expectation of partner's strength may be clear-cut. If a player with 17 points hears a bid of one no trump (16–18) bid on his right, the expectation of his partner's hand is 3 points. (4) In the play, expectancy depends on more complex mathematical calculations. (See MATHEMATICAL TABLES). The trick expectancy from the most promising line of play in many situations is given under SUIT COMBINATIONS. See also EXPECTATION.

EXPECTATION. The average result which would be achieved over a long trial period. In order to compute the expectation of a particular play, it is necessary to consider not only the frequency of gain or loss but the *amount* that is being risked. For example, let us compute the expectation of a pair that reaches a contract of four spades, not vulnerable, at rubber bridge. This contract, we will say, depends on winning one of two finesses (a 75% chance). Assuming the contract will either make or fail by one trick and that the pair will receive 300 points for making the game. The pair's expectation is:

(75%)	×	(+420)	+	(25%)	×	(−50)
chance		result		chance		result
of		of		of		of
success		success		failure		failure

This sum is 315 — 12.5 = 302.5. In making this computation we take into account that 75% of the time the pair will score +420 and 25% of the time the pair will score −50.

Let us contrast this expectation with that of a pair with the same cards that stops in three spades. The expectation of the latter is (assuming 50 points for a part score):

(75%)	×	(+170)	+	(25%)	×	(+140)
chance		result		chance		result
of an		with an		of just		when just
overtrick		overtrick		making		making

This sum is 127.5 + 35.0 = 162.5. Thus, the expectation of the pair bidding game is higher. This indicates that it is favorable to attempt the game under these conditions. By bidding the game, a pair will win an average of 302.5 points whereas by stopping short it will win an average of only 162.5. A similar calculation will indicate that it is not profitable (in the long run) to bid such a game which depends on two successful finesses (only a 25% chance).

In the play of the hand, the declarer may sometimes be unable to determine the correct play without resorting to (at least a rough) calculation of the expectation of different lines.

WEST	EAST
♠ A K 6 2	♠ 5 4
♡ A K 6 2	♡ 5 4
◇ A K 2	◇ 5 4
♣ 3 2	♣ A K Q 7 6 5 4

West plays six no trump against the opening lead of the queen of diamonds. East-West are vulnerable. How should West play?

A safety play for the contract is available. West needs only six club tricks for his contract. By ducking the first round of clubs (when North follows), he ensures his contract without an overtrick (+1440). By trying to run the clubs, he will make an overtrick (+1470) unless North holds all four clubs. If declarer fails to make the safety play and North has four clubs, he will be down three tricks (−300).

The expectation of the safety play is:

$$(100\%) \quad \times \quad +1440 \quad = \quad 1440$$

The expectation of trying to split the clubs is:

(5%)	×	(−300)	+	(90%)	×	(+1470)
chance				chance		
North has				clubs are		
four clubs				not 4–0		

$$+ \quad (5\%) \times (+1440)$$
chance
South has
four clubs
(West ducks
when North
shows out)

This expectation is only 1380. Therefore, the safety play is the superior play.

WEST	EAST
♠ Q 5 4 3	♠ J 2
♡ Q 5 4 3	♡ J 2
◇ A K 2	◇ 5 4
♣ 3 2	♣ A K Q 7 6 5 4

West plays in one no trump against an opening lead of the queen of diamonds. East-West are not vulnerable. Once again the safety play guarantees the contract (with an overtrick) for +120. If West fails to employ the safety play and North has all four clubs, he will be set two tricks for −100.

The expectation of the safety play is

$$(100\%) \quad \times \quad +120 \quad = \quad 120$$

while the expectation of trying to run the clubs without loss is

$$(5\%) \times (−100) \quad + \quad (90\%) \times (+150)$$
$$+ \quad (5\%) \times (+120) \quad = \quad 136$$

(assuming the defenders will discard correctly on the run of clubs).

In this case, the safety play is *not* the superior play. (This does not take into account the fact that if the clubs were four-zero there might have been some North-South bidding. Such a consideration makes the safety play even less desirable.)

J. R.

EXPECTED NUMBER OF CONTROLS IN BALANCED HANDS. A table of the number of controls statistically predictable in balanced hands of varying strength, analyzed and described by George ROSENKRANZ in the December 1974 issue of *Bridge World* and reprinted here with their permission. Knowledge of the average expectations of numbers of aces and kings for the strength point-count already shown is useful in determining whether or not to bid aggressively.

The table shows the approximate frequencies of specific numbers of controls (Ace=2, King=1) in all hands with 4–3–3–2, 4–4–3–2 or 5–3–3–2 distribution. Blanks indicate zero frequency; asterisks indicate usually less than one-half of 1 percent frequency.

EXPERT. A player of conceded skill. The caliber of the player accorded this title will vary with the circles in which he regularly plays; expertise cannot be measured by MASTER POINTS or in any other mechanical way, such as by having won one tournament or even by having played in international competition. (There was, for example, an anonymous lady recruited at the last moment in Budapest in 1937 to complete a US Women's team when it was a player short.)

The title of expert will probably be recognized as valid only when it has been awarded by a verdict of the expert's peers. It is, however, loosely used to characterize anyone who plays better than the usual level of the game in which the player plays.

EXPLANATION OF ANY CALL OR PLAY. Whenever a player makes a conventional call that is not a Class A CONVENTION, his partner should alert the opponents so that they may inquire as to its meaning. See ALERTING, PRIVATE CONVENTION. During the auction and before the final pass any player may, at his own turn to call, ask for a full explanation of any call made by an opponent. After the final pass and throughout the play, any player except dummy may, at his own turn to play, ask for an explanation of opposing calls or card play conventions. See FACE DOWN LEADS; LAWS OF DUPLICATE (Laws 20, 40).

A player who asks for an explanation of a bid should beware of giving information to his partner by his question. For example, a player who asks the meaning of a normal one club opening bid when he holds great club strength may be subject to penalty under Law 16. It is better to ask a question in general terms, rather than draw attention to one particular suit-bid, and so expose oneself to the suggestion that the question may be lead-directing.

When the auction is over, the ACBL recommends that the dummy should volunteer any explanation about his side's bidding which he may think necessary. Voluntary explanations during the auction are not advisable, because they may enlighten partner (or appear to enlighten him). If a player gains information as a result of his partner's explanation, he must carefully avoid taking advantage of it. However, it would be improper for him to offer an immediate correction of his partner's incorrect explanation of the partnership understanding, and he

EXPECTED NUMBER OF CONTROLS IN BALANCED HANDS

HCP	Relative Frequency	0	1	2	3	4	5	6	7	8	9	10	11	12
3	1216	67	33											
4	1891	40	39	21										
5	2505	23	48	29										
6	3129	12	41	47										
7	3795	5	30	46	19									
8	4192	2	19	44	28	7								
9	4377	*	10	35	44	11								
10	4379	*	5	24	44	27								
11	4179	*	2	14	40	33	11							
12	3755	*	1	8	30	42	17	2						
13	3242		*	3	20	39	34	4						
14	2687		*	1	11	33	38	17						
15	2115		*	*	5	24	42	23	6					
16	1596			*	2	14	36	37	10	1				
17	1155			*	1	8	27	39	24	1				
18	799			*	*	3	18	39	30	10				
19	526				*	1	10	32	40	15	2			
20	333				*	*	5	22	38	31	4			
21	201				*	*	2	13	35	35	15			
22	115					*	1	6	26	43	20	4		
23	62.9					*	*	3	17	38	35	7		
24	32.6					*	*	1	9	31	38	21		
25	16.0						*	*	4	21	43	26	6	
26	7.32							*	1	12	37	41	9	
27	3.21							*	*	6	28	41	25	
28	1.28								*	2	18	44	32	4
29	0.48								*	1	9	35	49	6

has no obligation to offer a correction at a later time. See LAWS OF DUPLICATE (Proprieties II, IV).

A tournament director may direct a player to leave the table while his partner gives an explanation; and it may be proper for him to depart voluntarily (at his partner's request or of his own volition) if a possibility of a misunderstanding exists.

EXPOSED CARD. For cards exposed during the bidding, see Law 23. Cards exposed during the play are covered by Laws 48, 49, and 73; LAWS OF DUPLICATE (Laws 48, 49, 70).

EXPOSED HAND. A hand placed in full view of all the players. This usually refers to dummy's hand, but it may also apply to the hand of declarer or a defender, which may become exposed by accident or in the process of making a claim. See LAWS 48, 49, 62, 64, 73; LAWS OF DUPLICATE (Laws 48, 49, 62, 64, 70).

EXTENDED GERBER. A method of pinpointing certain key cards in slam bidding, devised by Jerold A. Fink of Cincinnati, Ohio.

After a trump suit is established, a bid of four clubs requests partner to show controls (ace—2 controls, king—1 control). Four diamonds shows 0 or 1; four hearts shows 2; four spades shows 3; four no trump shows 4. With 5 or more controls, responder subtracts 5 and bids accordingly. After the conventional four diamond response, a four heart bid asks responder to clarify whether he holds 0 or 1 controls by bidding four spades with 0 controls (or 5 or 10), or four no trump with 1 control (or 6 or 11).

Other four-level bids by the asking bidder are sign-offs. The asking bidder may also sign off by bidding five clubs and passing partner's forced five diamond response, or by bidding five diamonds and passing partner's forced five heart response or correcting it to five spades. Other combinations of rebids on the five level are conventional, asking partner to show points (king—2 points, queen—1 point) in two specific suits by seven steps, ranging from 0 points for the first step to 6 points for the seventh step.

EXTENDED LANDY. The LANDY Convention is a two club take-out for the major suits over an opponent's no trump opening. An extension suggested by Martin COHN, of Atlanta, Ga., is to use a two club bid as a take-out for the majors over any call of one no trump by the opponents, whether it be a response, a rebid, or an overcall. In each of the examples below the two club bid requests partner to bid a major suit.

	NORTH	EAST	SOUTH	WEST
(a)	1 ♣	1 NT	2 ♣	
(b)	1 ♦	Dbl.	1 NT	2 ♣
(c)	1 ♠	1 NT	2 ♣	
(d)	1 ♡	Pass	1 ♠	Pass
	1 NT	2 ♣		

In example (c), the two club bidder would likely hold five hearts and three spades.

EXTRA TRICK. A trick scored in excess of the number of tricks required to fulfill a contract. Such tricks are scored above the line, and do not count toward game at their trick value. Extra tricks carry premium values if the contract has been doubled or redoubled. See OVERTRICK and SCORING.

F

FABER CUP. Awarded for the AWL National Auction Team Championship, donated by Eberhard Faber in 1927; contested as an Open Team event at the Summer Nationals until 1952, when it was withdrawn from competition and replaced by the MARCUS CUP.

FACE (of a card). The front of a playing card, containing the suit and rank of the card.

FACE CARDS. The cards which have a representation of a human figure, called originally coat cards, later court cards. Their design is virtually the same for all manufacturers in America and Britain, deriving from eighteenth century French patterns.

Earlier designs depended on the skill of the artists who carved the wood blocks, and gradually degenerated from representation of recognizable people and objects into meaningless figures. It has been said that Henry VIII was the model for all four kings; the oldest extant English cards have the same curling moustache and divided beard on the four kings, and legend has it that the queens were likenesses of Elizabeth of York, Henry VII's queen. The remainder of the design is clearly derived from cards made in Rouen, France; the faces differ, but the costumes, position of the hands, and weapons all show similarities.

The French packs developed along their own lines until 1813, when an official design was promulgated; the cards were all named, and even today the names appear on many packs:

	SPADES	HEARTS	DIAMONDS	CLUBS
KING	David	Charles	César	Alexandre
QUEEN	Pallas	Judith	Rachel	Argine
JACK	Hogier	Lahire	Hector	Lancelot

All represent real or mythical figures except Argine, an anagram of Regina.

In the Hungarian pack, eight of the face cards represent characters in Schiller's drama, *Wilhelm Tell*, laid in Switzerland:

SUITS	OBER	UNTER
Acorns	Wilhelm Tell	Rezsö Harras
Leaves	Ulrich Ruden	Walter Fürst
Bells	Vadász Stüssi	Itel Reding
Hearts	Herman Gezler	Pásztor Kuoni

But an oddity exists: the cards were never used in Switzerland.

The usual German packs do not have a queen, but have two jacks (or knaves), the Ober and the Unter. Some German packs, however, have four face cards, king-queen-jack-jack. The trappola pack (Spain and Italy) uses a mounted cavalier in place of the queen.

A. F.

FACE-DOWN LEADS. A procedure first introduced experimentally by the WBF in 1972 and adopted by the ACBL in 1975, requiring the opening leader to place his opening lead face down on the table, following which his partner may ask questions about the auction. This ensures that the partner of the leader will have the opportunity to ask questions about the auction before dummy is tabled, and that his questions will not influence the opening leader in his choice.

FACED CARD. A card exposed to all the players, which may be a card in the dummy, a penalty card, or a card exposed by a player making a claim or his opponent. No revoke penalty can be exacted for failure to play a faced card. See also PLAYED CARD.

FACT. A happening at a bridge table. When the facts are in dispute, or their interpretation is a matter of judgment, the matter may be referred to the tournament committee. This includes the significance or otherwise of hesitations. The committee may not overrule the director on a point of law, although an appeal may lie to the NATIONAL LAWS COMMISSION.

FACTORING. The process of adjusting match-point scores to the same base to make them comparable for ranking purposes. Percentage is a special type of factoring in which scores are adjusted to a basis of 1.000 or 100%.

When scores are to be compared for ranking within a group of contestants, it is necessary that the comparison be on the same base. For instance, in a 12½ table MITCHELL game, the usual procedure is to have a phantom pair 13 in the East-West field. Consequently all of the North-South players will have a bye round, and play 24 boards only, whereas the East-West players would play all 26 boards (in 13 rounds of play). Top on a board in such a case is 11, and the possible for East-West players is 286, but only 264 for the North-South players. To make the scores comparable, the North-South scores must be multiplied by the fraction 286/264 (13/12). To facilitate the computation, add 1/11 of the score obtained to the North-South scores.

There are several principles of factoring that should be observed. Scores should be factored up to the highest average rather than down to the lowest average, even if this means more scores are to be factored. There is a good reason for this: a winner must be .5 of a match point above the second-place finisher or the event is declared a tie. Factoring up will give a winner where factoring down may produce

a technical tie (less than ½ match-point difference) for first place.

In some half-table movements, certain boards are played more or less frequently than other boards, resulting in a higher top score on certain boards. In these cases, the possible score for each team should be computed and the percentage of this possible for each team found. To determine what percentage constitutes a clear win (equivalent to ½ match point), the percentage that constitutes ½ point should also be computed, and this used as a guide to determine technical ties; e.g., assume team A has 76.5 points out of a possible 132, and team B has 75 points out of a possible 129; team A's percentage is 57.95; team B's is 58.14, a difference of .19% which may or may not be a clear win. One-half point out of a possible 132 is .38%. The difference is less, and therefore the two teams are in a technical tie for first place. Team B would win the prize, but team A would share equally in any master-point award.

For one-session events in more than one section where there is a different top score in each section (an example would be one 14-table Mitchell section, top 12, average 156, and one 7-table three-quarters movement, top 6, average 78), the scores in the section with the lower top score would be factored up to those of the larger section (in this case, by simply doubling, 312/156 or 2 being the factor applied).

If the smaller section were an 11-table game with a three-quarters movement, 10 top, 130 average, the factor would be 312/260 or 6/5, one-fifth of their score being added to the scores in the smaller section.

In two-session events (without elimination) in which there are more or less contestants in the second session, and consequently the top score on a board is different, the second session is always adjusted to the possible score of the first session; in this case the factor to be used may be more or less than 1, and the factoring can be up or down.

For further information, the AMERICAN CONTRACT BRIDGE LEAGUE has a pamphlet entitled "Factoring" which explains the method in more detail.

FAILURE TO COMPLY WITH A LEAD OR PLAY PENALTY. The act of playing an INCORRECT CARD when a player is able to lead or play from an unfaced hand a card or suit required by law or specified by an opponent in accordance with an agreed penalty. See LAWS OF DUPLICATE, Law 52.

FALL, FALL OF THE CARDS. The play of a card or cards on a trick; the order in which they are played.

FALL NATIONAL CHAMPIONSHIPS. Often called the Winter Nationals, these contests were held annually from 1927 to 1936 under the auspices of the AMERICAN BRIDGE LEAGUE, and from 1937 on under the auspices of the AMERICAN CONTRACT BRIDGE LEAGUE. The Fall Nationals began as a four-day tournament and were enlarged to eight days four years later. Nine-day tournaments, held late in November, became standard in postwar years. In 1963, the addition of the International Fund Pairs lengthened the tournament to nine and one-half days and the Fall Nationals became a full ten-day tournament when the ACBL rescheduled the major events in 1969. The largest of these Nationals was the 1973 tournament in Las Vegas, when 13,464 tables participated.

In 1928 the major event of the ABL's "winter congress" was the Open Pairs played for the CAVENDISH TROPHY, presented by the Cavendish Club of New York City.

The CHICAGO TROPHY for Board-a-Match Teams-of-Four was put in play in 1929, and the HILLIARD TROPHY for Mixed Pairs, presented by Mrs. Olga Hilliard of New York, was introduced at the 1931 Fall Nationals. (For past results of Fall Nationals, see Appendix I.)

FALL NATIONALS

YEAR	SITE	TABLES	YEAR	SITE	TABLES
1927	Chicago		1954	Atlanta	(1,775)
1928	Cleveland		1955	Miami	(2,359)
1929	Chicago		1956	New Orleans	(2,777)
1930	Cleveland		1957	Los Angeles	(6,154)
1931	Philadelphia		1958	Detroit	(4,046)
1932	New York		1959	Coronado	(5,838)
1933	Cincinnati		1960	New York City	(6,391)
1934	New York		1961	Houston	(4,967)
1935	Chicago		1962	Phoenix	(6,468)
1936	Chicago		1963	Miami	(7,129)
1937	Washington		1964	Dallas	(8,686)
1938	Cleveland		1965	San Francisco	(11,198)
1939	Pittsburgh		1966	Pittsburgh	(8,896)
1940	Philadelphia		1967	New Orleans	(8,904)
1941	Richmond		1968	Coronado	(7,858)
1942	Syracuse		1969	Miami Beach	(9,069)
1943	New York		1970	Houston	(7,994)
1944	Atlantic City		1971	Phoenix	(7,080)
1945	Atlantic City		1972	Lancaster	(11,545)
1946	Hollywood, Fla.		1973	Las Vegas	(13,464)
1947	Atlantic City		1974	San Antonio	(8,419)
1948	Philadelphia		1975	New Orleans	(11,705)
1949	Philadelphia		1976	Pittsburgh	
1950	New Orleans		1977	Atlanta	
1951	Detroit		1978	Denver	
1952	Miami	(2,017)	1979	Cincinnati	
1953	Dallas	(1,798)	1980	Lancaster	

(Numbers in parentheses indicate total number of tables participating.)

FALSE-CARDING. A defender is said to false-card when he plays a card other than his lowest with the intention of deceiving the declarer. (Thus, a high card played as the beginning of an echo is not a false-card because there is no intention to deceive.)

The term "falsecard" derives from the fact that defenders normally play "true" cards in order to provide each other with information. The declarer, with no partner to worry about, is not obliged to play true cards, so for him there is no such thing as a false-card.

Deceptive play by the declarer may extend to the conduct of the whole hand, whereas in practical play the defenders are usually limited to the play of a single falsecard to one trick. It is, therefore, convenient to treat the subject of deceptive play by the defenders under the title "False-carding," dealing with declarer play under the title DECEPTIVE PLAY.

The defenders' advantage. Although the defenders are usually restricted to the choice of a single card, rather than a complete tactical plan, they have many more opportunities for skillful deception than the declarer, a fact which is not generally realized. Consider this situation:

(a)
NORTH
K 7 3

WEST   EAST
J 9 6 2   A Q 4

SOUTH
10 8 5

East is the declarer, and clearly there is no way for him to bring in the suit without loss. If dummy's jack is led, North covers and South's ten is promoted.

Now suppose instead that the declarer is South and that West is on lead. If West leads the jack, the declarer cannot be sure whether or not it is right to cover; he cannot see the defenders' cards. In the diagram, the king must be put on to make the ten a guard; but it may turn out that West has made a clever play from the queen-jack, the true position being:

(b)
NORTH
K 7 3

WEST   EAST
Q J 9 2   A 6 4

SOUTH
10 8 5

Now if the king is played on the first lead from West, East wins with the ace and returns the suit through South's ten; the defenders take all the tricks.

Suppose that in diagram (b) the declarer is East once more, and that he again leads an honor from dummy. If North covers, he allows declarer all the tricks, but North has no difficulty in playing low; seeing the queen-jack in dummy, he ducks the first lead, following the maxim that a defender should cover the last of touching honors—a complete answer to problems of this sort.

Clever false-carding aims at exploiting the defenders' advantage in situations of that kind. False-carding is analyzed under these headings: Playing a Known Card; Trump Suit False-Carding; Random Falsecards Which Cannot Deceive Partner; False Signals; Deceptive Opening Leads; False-Carding in the Middle or End Game.

Playing a known card. A well-established principle of defensive play is that in a critical position the defender should play a card which he is known to hold, if he can do so without sacrificing a trick. Example:

NORTH
A J 5

WEST   EAST
Q 10 3   8 6 2

SOUTH
K 9 7 4

South leads low, finesses dummy's jack, and continues with ace and another. When the ace is played, West can follow suit with two cards of equal value, the queen and ten. He should play the card he is known to hold, the queen, offering declarer the possibility of finessing the nine on the third round.

Such maneuvers are common in a keen game, even when the defender has no specific objective in mind.

NORTH
A K J 6

WEST   EAST
Q 5 4   10 8 3 2

SOUTH
9 7

South finesses dummy's jack. West should play the queen on the next round, for until he releases the queen, declarer knows that the suit cannot possibly be ruffed on his left. Similarly:

NORTH
A Q 7 5

WEST   EAST
K J 10 3   8 6 4 2

SOUTH
9

Playing a crossruff, South finesses dummy's queen and continues with ace and another, ruffing. Until West parts with the card he is known to hold, the king, declarer can safely ruff low.

More difficult to gauge is the early release of a high card whose position is not marked but soon will be. It may be necessary to have a grasp of the strategy of the entire hand before this sort of play is safe.

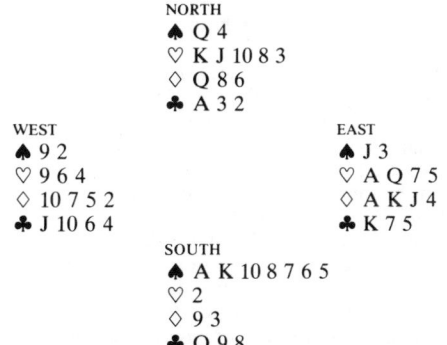

NORTH
♠ Q 4
♡ K J 10 8 3
◇ Q 8 6
♣ A 3 2

WEST   EAST
♠ 9 2   ♠ J 3
♡ 9 6 4   ♡ A Q 7 5
◇ 10 7 5 2   ◇ A K J 4
♣ J 10 6 4   ♣ K 7 5

SOUTH
♠ A K 10 8 7 6 5
♡ 2
◇ 9 3
♣ Q 9 8

South plays in four spades after East has opened the bidding. Diamonds are led and South ruffs the third round. Needing to establish two heart tricks, he finesses dummy's ten.

East wins with the ace, not the queen, and returns a trump. East judges that declarer will expect him to have the ace for his opening bid, so if he wins the first trick with the queen, declarer will take a ruffing finesse against the ace on the next round and make his contract. After East's deceptive play of the ace, however, declarer may try to bring down the queen

in West by ruffing the second round. If he tries that, shortage of entries prevents him establishing a second heart trick.

The following hand illustrates a different reason for releasing a high card whose location will soon be known to the declarer.

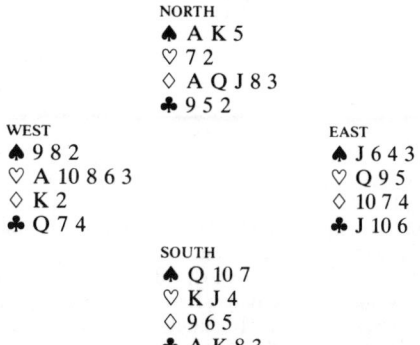

NORTH
♠ A K 5
♡ 7 2
◇ A Q J 8 3
♣ 9 5 2

WEST   EAST
♠ 9 8 2   ♠ J 6 4 3
♡ A 10 8 6 3   ♡ Q 9 5
◇ K 2   ◇ 10 7 4
♣ Q 7 4   ♣ J 10 6

SOUTH
♠ Q 10 7
♡ K J 4
◇ 9 6 5
♣ A K 8 3

In a pairs contest, West leads a small heart against three no trump, and the queen is topped by the king. South returns a diamond, and West, knowing that his king is lost, plays it immediately. Now South has a problem, even if he knows West as a guileful player. If he takes the trick, and it turns out that the king is singleton, he makes only nine tricks when he could have made ten by ducking, establishing the long card without letting East into the lead.

Trump suit false-carding. The suit combinations illustrated below can exist in any suit, whether trumps or not, but it is best to consider them as being trump. The fact that in every case the declarer has the majority of cards means that the suit usually will be trumps; also, the deceptive maneuvers require an exact appreciation of the layout of the suit, and in practical play this condition is seldom met unless the suit is trumps.

The essence of most of the following plays is that failure to false-card would leave the declarer no option but to adopt a winning line of play. The falsecard presents him with the possibility of following an alternative line, which will lose. This type of falsecard is still purposeful even if the declarer is unlikely to fall into the trap set for him. Had the falsecard not been played, there would have been no possibility of declarer's going wrong; after the falsecard there is such a possibility, however slight.

NORTH
A J 8 3

WEST   EAST
K 2   10 9 6

SOUTH
Q 7 5 4

South leads small and finesses dummy's jack. If East plays the six, declarer has no choice but to play the ace on the next round, making all the tricks. If East plays the nine or ten, declarer may enter the closed hand to lead the queen, which would be the winning play if East had ten-nine doubleton or a singleton.

There are some plays which appear dangerous at first sight but which in fact are obligatory if a high standard of play is to be assumed.

```
              NORTH
              A Q 6 2
WEST                         EAST
4                            K 10 8 3
              SOUTH
              J 9 7 5
```

When declarer leads small and finesses dummy's queen, only the eight from East offers hope of a second trick. If East wins with the king, the ace will be played on the next round, and a third-round finesse will pick up the suit. After the play of the eight, declarer may come to hand and lead the jack, which would be good play if East held 108 alone, but costs a trick in the actual diagram. Following is one of many variations of the theme.

```
              NORTH
              K Q 9 4
WEST                         EAST
10 8 6 3                     A
              SOUTH
              J 7 5 2
```

Unless West plays the eight when a low trump is led toward dummy's king, he has no chance of a second trick.

This next position also has variations:

```
              NORTH
              J 9 3
WEST                         EAST
8 5 4                        Q 10
              SOUTH
              A K 7 6 2
```

Whether South lays down the ace from hand or leads the three from dummy, East can probably read the position well enough to gauge that it is safe to drop the queen.

The following play is liable to score:

```
              NORTH
              Q 2
WEST                         EAST
J 10                         A 7 3
              SOUTH
              K 9 8 6 5 4
```

When South leads small to the queen, East ducks smoothly and the declarer probably continues by finessing the nine in his own hand. Had East taken the queen with the ace, South would have played to drop the jack on the next round, recognizing that there would be no purpose in finessing against A J 73 in East's hand. A similar position:

```
              NORTH
              7
WEST                         EAST
J 10 6                       A 5
              SOUTH
              K Q 9 8 4 3 2
```

Dummy's seven is led and the king wins. Unless West plays the ten or jack, declarer has no choice but to lead a low card to the next trick.

Many falsecards have a better chance of succeeding in a pairs contest, where declarers are willing to take measured risks for an extra trick.

```
              NORTH
              J 8 6 2
WEST                         EAST
Q 10 9 5                     3
              SOUTH
              A K 7 4
```

When South plays the ace, West drops the nine or ten. If declarer can afford to lose one trick, he does best to play small toward the jack, which preserves the position against any lie of the defenders' cards, but in a pairs contest he may decide instead to cross to dummy and lead the jack. This is equally safe against four cards in East's hand, and nets a big match-point score if West holds 109 alone.

Occasionally it is possible to forestall these defensive wiles.

```
              NORTH
              Q 8 4 2
WEST                         EAST
3                            J 9 6 5
              SOUTH
              A K 10 7
```

When declarer plays the ace from hand, the standard falsecard for East is the nine. If he fails to play the nine, declarer is bound to continue by leading toward the queen, discovering the finesse against the jack. After the play of the nine, declarer may continue with the king from hand, with the idea of finessing against West if he has J653.

Entries permitting, declarer in the above situation should make the first lead from dummy. Now it is dangerous for East to drop the nine, for partner could have the singleton ten.

There is another type of falsecard which, though not occurring in the trump suit, is associated with suit contracts. This is the play of a high card—perhaps setting up winners for declarer—to dissuade declarer from following a line of play which the defender knows must win. A bold player may sacrifice a high card in this way even though he may be unable to envisage the likely effect; it is sufficient for him that the declarer must be deflected from the course which he has apparently set. A classic hand of this kind was defended by the British player, Terence Reese, in his Oxford days.

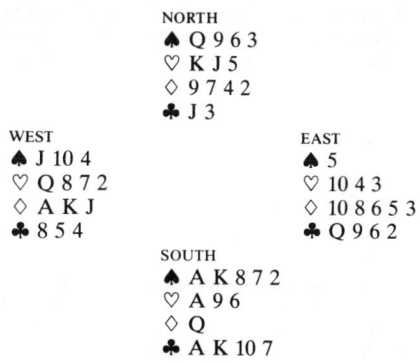

```
                    NORTH
                    ♠ Q 9 6 3
                    ♡ K J 5
                    ◇ 9 7 4 2
                    ♣ J 3
  WEST                                EAST
  ♠ J 10 4                            ♠ 5
  ♡ Q 8 7 2                           ♡ 10 4 3
  ◇ A K J                             ◇ 10 8 6 5 3
  ♣ 8 5 4                             ♣ Q 9 6 2
                    SOUTH
                    ♠ A K 8 7 2
                    ♡ A 9 6
                    ◇ Q
                    ♣ A K 10 7
```

West led diamonds against South's six spade contract. Having ruffed the second round, South played three rounds of clubs, ruffing in dummy. Since it was evident that the fourth club could be ruffed with impunity, Reese dropped the queen on the third round. The declarer continued with the spade queen and ace. When East showed out on the second trump, it appeared safe to lead the club ten, intending to discard a heart in dummy and subsequently ruff a heart. When the club ten was led, West made his trump jack to defeat a contract which would have been made routinely had not East false-carded.

Random falsecards which cannot deceive partner. The previous situations have been mainly those where an immediate purpose could be discerned, justifying the defender in breaching his duty to play true cards. There are, however, situations where it is permissible for a defender to false-card with the more general aim of harrying the declarer, and spoiling his count of the hand. The most common is where declarer has shown out of a suit; now, since both defenders know the exact distribution of the suit, they may false-card with no specific aim in mind.

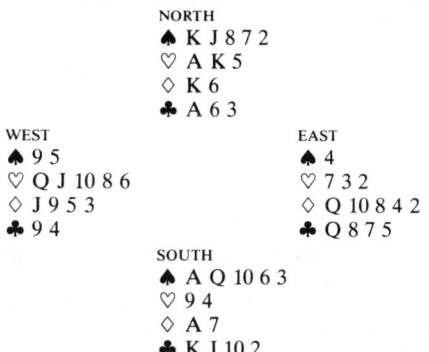

```
                    NORTH
                    ♠ K J 8 7 2
                    ♡ A K 5
                    ◇ K 6
                    ♣ A 6 3
  WEST                                EAST
  ♠ 9 5                               ♠ 4
  ♡ Q J 10 8 6                        ♡ 7 3 2
  ◇ J 9 5 3                           ◇ Q 10 8 4 2
  ♣ 9 4                               ♣ Q 8 7 5
                    SOUTH
                    ♠ A Q 10 6 3
                    ♡ 9 4
                    ◇ A 7
                    ♣ K J 10 2
```

West leads the heart queen against six spades. South's only problem is to locate the club queen for the overtrick and, though the hand does not lend itself to maneuver, declarer should endeavor to extract what information he can before putting himself to the club guess. After drawing trumps, he plays a

second and third round of hearts, ruffing. West must play his cards circumspectly; if he follows thoughtlessly with the six and eight, declarer will reflect that West probably had a five-card heart suit, since the lead of the queen is more attractive when both jack and ten are behind it. So slight a consideration as this would be enough to sway declarer's play of the clubs; South would play East for the club queen since, holding shorter hearts than West, he may hold longer clubs.

On the second and third round of hearts, West does best to play the six and ten. It may seem attractive to play the ten and jack, seeking to create the impression that East is the player with long hearts, but if declarer notices that East has played the seven on the third round although the six is still missing, he may begin to wonder.

If, in a situation like that, West really held the doubleton club queen, it is doubtful whether he would be well advised to play his hearts in such a way as to give declarer a true count of the suit, in the expectation that declarer would take the losing play in clubs. Such maneuvers fall into the category of pure bluff rather than tactics, and in a keen game the defenders usually do best to play accurately and let declarer guess.

Falsecards of that type are more effective if made before declarer actually shows out of the suit, since he is then more inclined to take them at face value.

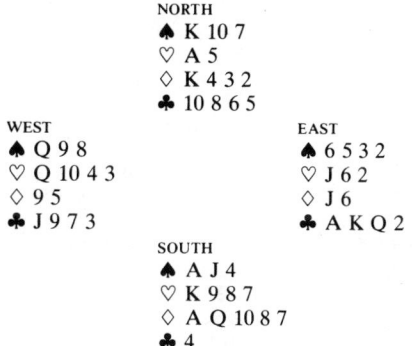

```
                    NORTH
                    ♠ K 10 7
                    ♡ A 5
                    ◇ K 4 3 2
                    ♣ 10 8 6 5
  WEST                                EAST
  ♠ Q 9 8                             ♠ 6 5 3 2
  ♡ Q 10 4 3                          ♡ J 6 2
  ◇ 9 5                               ◇ J 6
  ♣ J 9 7 3                           ♣ A K Q 2
                    SOUTH
                    ♠ A J 4
                    ♡ K 9 8 7
                    ◇ A Q 10 8 7
                    ♣ 4
```

South plays six diamonds after East has dealt and passed. When West leads the club three, East false-cards, winning with the king rather than the queen. (If the ace stands up on the next round, West will not be critical of the falsecard; if it doesn't, West knows all.) Declarer ruffs the ace, and has to guess the spade position to make his contract. Had East won the opening lead with the queen, South would have reflected (after finding the red jacks in East) that East might have opened the bidding had he held the spade queen and thirteen points in all.

False signals. The defenders labor under the disadvantage that most of their signals are sent "in clear" and so are liable to enemy interception. On a hand like the following, the declarer's task is easier if his opponents are known as conscientious signalers.

```
        NORTH
        ♠ 8 7
        ♡ K 8 7 5 4
        ◇ 8 6 2
        ♣ A 9 5


        SOUTH
        ♠ A K Q 10 6 5
        ♡ A 2
        ◇ A Q J
        ♣ K 7
```

South plays six spades in a pairs contest. Having won the club lead with the king and drawn trumps, South's problem is whether to try to ruff out the hearts for two discards or to finesse diamonds; shortage of entries means that he cannot try both. But, if the defenders echo to show two or four cards, declarer knows what to do after playing ace and another heart.

Best results are obtained by defenders who keep up with the game and at a given time are conscious whether a false signal could mislead partner. Very often it can be recognized that partner will not be misled. In such cases, defenders should vary their signals between true and false cards rather than try to outsmart the declarer.

False signals can be used to persuade the declarer to ruff unnecessarily, or to ruff high, in a critical trump situation.

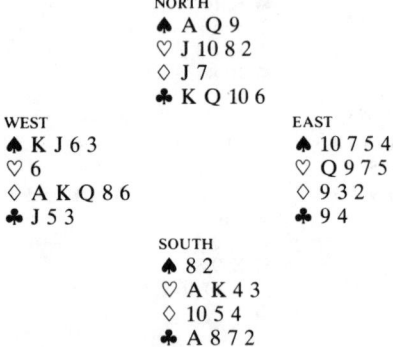

```
            NORTH
            ♠ A Q 9
            ♡ J 10 8 2
            ◇ J 7
            ♣ K Q 10 6
WEST                        EAST
♠ K J 6 3                   ♠ 10 7 5 4
♡ 6                         ♡ Q 9 7 5
◇ A K Q 8 6                 ◇ 9 3 2
♣ J 5 3                     ♣ 9 4
            SOUTH
            ♠ 8 2
            ♡ A K 4 3
            ◇ 10 5 4
            ♣ A 8 7 2
```

South plays four hearts after West has opened one diamond. On the king and ace of diamonds, East echoes with the nine and two. Since it is quite possible that East has a doubleton diamond, declarer may judge to ruff with the ten when West plays the third round. If he does so, he loses two trump tricks instead of one.

Deceptive opening leads. Defenders should seldom depart from the accepted conventional leads. To underlead an ace against a suit contract, or to lead an honor from the middle of a sequence, may score on a particular hand, but if it is done frequently, the loss in partnership accuracy will outweigh the gain thus made.

Because that is generally recognized as true, the occasional deceptive lead can be all the more effec-

tive. Some leads, such as the jack from queen-jack doubleton, are so well known as to lack any element of surprise. The following is also far from fresh:

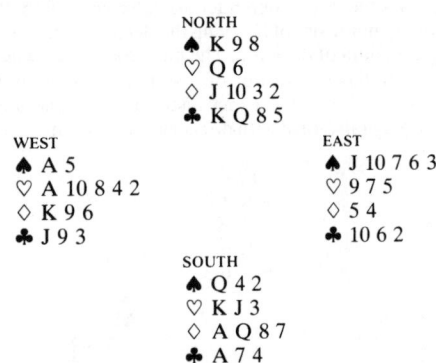

```
                    NORTH
                    J 6 4
WEST                                EAST
10 9 2                               Q 3
                    SOUTH
                    A K 8 7 5
```

Left to himself, the declarer loses no tricks in this trump suit when he plays to drop the doubleton queen. Some authorities have commended the opening lead of the nine, the theory being that declarer may put on the jack and play East for Q 10 3 2 or Q 10 x.

Declarer's protection against being duped too often is the knowledge that a good defender seldom leads a trump other than his lowest. To lead the nine from 9 2, for example, can never gain as compared with leading the two, and can cost in more than one way. Since most defenders are averse to leading a singleton trump, the declarer should look suspiciously at the lead of a nine or card of similar rank; particularly when, as in the above diagram, he himself holds the card of next lower rank, and knows that the card led cannot be the top of a sequence.

The deceptive lead of fifth-best instead of fourth-best against no trump is a more persuasive maneuver. It is liable to gain in many situations like the following:

```
            NORTH
            ♠ K 9 8
            ♡ Q 6
            ◇ J 10 3 2
            ♣ K Q 8 5
WEST                        EAST
♠ A 5                       ♠ J 10 7 6 3
♡ A 10 8 4 2                ♡ 9 7 5
◇ K 9 6                     ◇ 5 4
♣ J 9 3                     ♣ 10 6 2
            SOUTH
            ♠ Q 4 2
            ♡ K J 3
            ◇ A Q 8 7
            ♣ A 7 4
```

West's own wealth of high cards makes it unlikely that his partner can contribute to the defense, so he leads the heart two against three no trump. Dummy wins, the diamond jack runs to West's king, and a small heart comes back. Declarer cashes his diamonds, and both defenders discard spades. Now South has to decide whether to set up a spade or to seek his ninth trick in clubs. After cashing two rounds of clubs he is none the wiser and, taking the opening lead at its face value, he may think that hearts are 4–4 and that it is safe to play a spade.

No less effective is the lead of third-best in an attempt to create the impression that a five-card suit is held. This is the other side of the picture from the previous deal:

```
                  NORTH
                  ♠ Q 10 9
                  ♡ Q 6 2
                  ◇ A K 6
                  ♣ Q 9 7 5
WEST                              EAST
♠ A 7 3 2                        ♠ 8 5 4
♡ A 9                            ♡ 7 5 4 3
◇ J 10 5 3                       ◇ 7 4
♣ A 8 4                          ♣ J 6 3 2
                  SOUTH
                  ♠ K J 6
                  ♡ K J 10 8
                  ◇ Q 9 8 2
                  ♣ K 10
```

Again West knows that partner has little to fight with, so he leads the spade three against South's three no trump contract. After driving out the heart ace and receiving the return of the spade two, South has only eight tricks, and has to decide whether to play a club or test diamonds. If he knew that West had only four spades, he could safely play a club; after the deceptive lead, however, he may decide to try for the diamond break, in which case he establishes a setting trick for the defenders.

Other opportunities for a deceptive lead are sometimes missed. Suppose the declarer in a no trump contract opened the bidding with one no trump, and subsequently showed a spade suit in response to STAYMAN; since both defenders have a count of the spades, expecting declarer to have precisely four, there is no reason why the defender, if he decides to open up the suit, should give declarer free information by leading a conventional fourth-best; he can simply lead his lowest card.

False-carding in the middle or end game. At the opening lead, the defender is restricted in his deceptive maneuvers by the necessity of not misleading partner, and by a general lack of information. In the middle game, however, it is possible for both defenders to know the exact lie of the cards while declarer is still in doubt. When this is the case, defenders can deceive declarer without deceiving each other.

The position illustrated under the heading The Defenders' Advantage is a basic one to which there are many variations. Example:

```
                  NORTH
                  K 7 3
WEST                              EAST
A Q 8                            J 9 6 2
                  SOUTH
                  10 5 4
```

Judging in the middle game that three tricks are needed from this suit, West leads the queen. Declarer may duck twice, playing him for queen and jack.

```
                  NORTH
                  A J 9 4
WEST                              EAST
Q 10 5                           K 8 6
                  SOUTH
                  7 3 2
```

South leads low, intending to follow the percentages by finessing the nine the first time and the jack the second. By putting up the queen, West may persuade declarer that he has the king as well, and deflect him from his course. Similar positions arise when West is on lead:

```
                  NORTH
                  J 9 6
WEST                              EAST
K 10 5 2                         Q 8 3
                  SOUTH
                  A 7 4
```

If circumstances compel West to open this suit, the king is the card. Conversely, in a position such as the following, it may be best to lead small:

```
                  NORTH
                  J 9 7
WEST                              EAST
K Q 3                            10 6 5 2
                  SOUTH
                  A 8 4
```

There are a number of miscellaneous positions in the middle game where the play of a high card may alter declarer's whole plan of campaign:

```
                  NORTH
                  A Q 10 9
WEST                              EAST
7 4 3                            K J 8
                  SOUTH
                  6 5 2
```

When declarer finesses dummy's ten, East wins with the king instead of the jack. If declarer assumes that the jack is with West, and that he has three certain tricks by finessing the nine on the next round, he may fall into indiscretion.

In the end game there are occasions when a desperate lead offers the only hope of escaping from an elimination.

```
                  NORTH
                  A 9 7
WEST                              EAST
Q 8 2                            J 6 4 3
                  SOUTH
                  K 10 5
```

If South has staged an elimination which compels West to open this suit, the queen is best, offering declarer the possibility of winning in hand, and finessing against the jack. If West leads small instead, declarer can play only for split honors. Similarly:

```
                    NORTH
                    Q 9 5
WEST                                 EAST
J 8 4                                K 10 6 2
                    SOUTH
                    A 7 3
```

If West leads small, declarer may play low in dummy, and capture the ten with the ace; on the next round he probably finesses the nine. If West leads the jack on the first round, declarer may cover on the assumption that the nine sits behind the ten.

Suppose that in the above example the declarer is on lead, and plays small toward the table. Suppose also that East is marked with the king, and the declarer intends to insert dummy's nine, forcing East to lead away from the king or concede a ruff-sluff. On South's lead, West puts in the jack to make it appear that he has the ten as well, in which case declarer's play would be to duck in dummy.

For declarer's counterweapon, see DECEPTION, MATHEMATICS OF.

A. D.

FALSE PREFERENCE. A return to partner's original suit at the lowest level when holding greater length in the second suit. See PREFERENCE BIDS.

FAMILY (bridge-playing). Brothers B. Jay BECKER and Simon BECKER, with two sons each of Life Master quality (one of whom, Michael, has represented North America in Bermuda Bowl competition), can form perhaps the strongest family bridge team in the world. Other powerful family combinations include the JACOBYS; William SEAMON and his sisters Edith KEMP and Anne BURNSTEIN; the CROSSLEYS, a three-generation bridge-playing family whose youngest generation includes 1974 Vanderbilt winners David and Robert; Great Britain's GARDENERS; and Italy's Benito and Marisa BIANCHI, Anna VALENTI, the latter's sister-in-law and partner in many international titles, and Anna's husband (Marisa Bianchi's brother), Paolo Valenti, a former non-playing captain of the BLUE TEAM.

FAR EAST BRIDGE FEDERATION. Organized in 1957 and originally consisted of four participating members: Republic of China, Hong Kong, Japan, and the Philippines. Since then the Federation has expanded to include Indonesia, Republic of Korea, Malaysia, Okinawa Bridge Club, Pakistan, Saigon Sporting Club, Singapore, and Thailand. It annually sponsors a Far East championship, played for the possession of the Rebullida Trophy, and an International Pairs Championship, first held jointly with the 1959 Far East Championship. (For past results of the Far East Championships, see Appendix III.) In 1958, the delegates to the Federation's annual convention decided to adopt WRITTEN BIDDING as the official method in all future tournaments. The Far East Bridge Federation was admitted to participate in the World Team Championships in 1966 and was represented by the holders of the Far East Championship, Thailand. In 1969 and 1970 the Far East representatives, Republic of China, finished second in the World Championships.

Headquarters: P.O. Box 3362, Manila, Philippines.

FAST ARRIVAL, PRINCIPLE OF. The principle that the greater the speed with which a contract is reached, the weaker the hand that placed the contract and, conversely, that the more gradual the approach, the greater the suggestion that a higher contract may be appropriate. The most commonplace example is the obvious difference between North's bidding in examples (a) and (b):

(a)		(b)	
SOUTH	NORTH	SOUTH	NORTH
1 ♠	4 ♠	1 ♠	3 ♠ (forcing)

Similarly North's bidding in (c) below is more encouraging than it is in (d):

(c)		(d)	
SOUTH	NORTH	SOUTH	NORTH
1 NT	2 ♣	1 NT	2 ♣
2 ♠	3 ♦	2 ♠	4 ♠
3 NT	4 ♠		

FAST PASS. A lightning action which may improperly convey weakness. The prevention of a fast pass is one of the reasons for the SKIP-BID WARNING. See also RHYTHM.

FEATURE, FEATURE SHOWING. A feature is a particular holding of an ace or king (occasionally a queen) which may be of particular importance in a given hand. Showing of features in a hand through the bidding commences only when a suit is agreed on and a game is assured. Among the conventions that are in common use to determine features are ACE-SHOWING RESPONSES, ASKING BIDS, GERBER, BLACKWOOD, and other four no trump bids, the GRAND SLAM FORCE, CUE-BIDS, and various combinations or modifications thereof. See also WEAK TWO-BIDS.

FEDERAÇAO PORTUGESA DI BRIDGE. See PORTUGUESE BRIDGE FEDERATION.

FEDERACIÓN CHILENA DE BRIDGE. See CHILEAN BRIDGE FEDERATION.

FEDERACIÓN VENEZOLANA DE BRIDGE. See VENEZUELAN BRIDGE FEDERATION.

FÉDÉRATION BELGE DU BRIDGE. See BELGIAN BRIDGE FEDERATION.

FÉDÉRATION FRANÇAISE DE BRIDGE. See FRENCH BRIDGE FEDERATION.

FÉDÉRATION LIBANAISE DE BRIDGE. See LEBANESE BRIDGE FEDERATION.

FÉDÉRATION ROYAL MAROCAINE DE BRIDGE. See MOROCCO BRIDGE FEDERATION.

FEDERATION SUISSE DE BRIDGE. See SWISS BRIDGE FEDERATION.

FEDERAZIONE ITALIANA BRIDGE. See ITALIAN BRIDGE FEDERATION.

FELL FOR IT. See WENT FOR IT.

FICTION. See LITERATURE AND BRIDGE.

FIFTEEN TABLES. At duplicate, fifteen tables provide for competition among sixty players, thirty pairs, or fifteen teams.

As an Individual tournament, a group of sixty players is extremely awkward. A double Appendix onto a fifty-two-player RAINBOW is possible (though guide cards would have to be improvised) with the four stationary seats at tables 1 to 4 populating table 14 and those at tables 5 to 8 filling table 15, with stationary boards at tables 14 and 15. Bumped players resume their Rainbow progression as though they had not been bumped at subsequent rounds. Another possibility is to use a seven-table Rainbow and an eight-table Appendix Rainbow, and play the game in two sections. Top and average would be the same in both sections, and results would be moderately comparable.

As a pair game, the usual and simple solution is a MITCHELL, either straight or scrambled, depending on whether one or two winning pairs are desired. There are guide cards available for treating fourteen to twenty tables as appendix movements using only twenty-six boards. This is standard in many countries where direct comparison on all the boards in play is desired. It is also sometimes used as the last session of multi-session events, although twinned seven-, eight-, or nine-table sections give comparable results with proper seeding of the sections.

As a team game, twenty-eight boards are required to complete the movement. When twenty-four boards are desired, either the middle two, or the first and last rounds can be conveniently omitted.

Fifteen and a half tables at pair play should use a BUMP MITCHELL movement. Any other adaptation of Mitchell movements gives differing top scores on the boards that are out of play, and all pairs do not have the same possible or average score.

FIFTH HONOR. The ten-spot of the trump suit.

FINAL BID. The last bid in the auction, followed by three consecutive passes. There can be no further bidding. The final bid becomes the contract.

Note that it is bad practice for a player to lead instead of making the final pass, since unless he makes a FACE-DOWN LEAD, he will deprive his partner of the right to review the bidding or ask questions about it.

FINESSE. The attempt to gain power for lower-ranking cards by taking advantage of the favorable position of higher-ranking cards held by the opposition.

The most common uses of the finesse are:

(1) *To avoid losing a trick*

NORTH
♣ A Q

SOUTH
♣ 3 2

South cannot afford to lose a club trick. He therefore leads a club to North's queen, finessing against the king. If West has the king, the queen will win, and South will avoid a club loser.

NORTH
♠ Q 10 6 2

WEST
♠ J 9 3

EAST
♠ K 8 7 5

SOUTH
♠ A 4

West leads the three of spades, and South must avoid a spade loser. If South reads the position correctly, he will play the ten of spades from dummy, finessing against the jack. This enables South to avoid a spade loser.

(2) *To gain a trick with low-ranking cards*

NORTH
♡ A 3 2

SOUTH
♡ Q 6 5

Needing two heart tricks, South cashes North's ace and leads toward his queen. If East holds the king, the queen will score a trick for South.

NORTH
◇ Q 3 2

SOUTH
◇ 7 6 5

South needs one diamond trick. His best chance is to find West with both the ace and king. He therefore leads toward the queen in the North hand, in an attempt to finesse against the ace-king, thereby creating a trick for the queen.

(3) *To prepare for a second finesse in the same suit.* A finesse can often be used to create a second finesse. When this is done successfully, the second finesse usually results in the direct gain of a trick.

NORTH
♣ A J 10

SOUTH
♣ 4 3 2

Needing two club tricks, South leads low to dummy's ten. If this finesse loses to an honor in the East hand, declarer is in position to take two tricks via a second finesse if West has the remaining high honor.

NORTH
♠ A J 9

SOUTH
♠ 4 3 2

Needing two spade tricks, South leads low toward the North hand. When West follows low, he finesses the nine. If West started with K 10 or Q 10, this will drive a high honor from the East hand and a second finesse of the jack will result in two tricks for South.

(4) *To prepare for a pinning play in the same suit.* A finesse can also be preparatory to a different form of trick-gaining play in a suit. By taking an early finesse, it may be possible to reduce the length of the suit in one enemy hand.

NORTH
♡ Q 9 8 7

WEST   EAST
♡ J 5   ♡ K 10 6

SOUTH
♡ A 4 3 2

Needing three heart tricks, South leads low, and finesses dummy's seven. East wins with the ten, but declarer later enters the North hand, and pushes the queen through East, blotting out the entire defensive holding.

NORTH
◊ Q 10 8 3 2

WEST   EAST
◊ J 9 4   ◊ A K 7 6

SOUTH
◊ 5

With some other suit as trump, South must develop two diamond tricks. He leads low from his hand, finessing North's eight. Later, the queen is led from the North hand to ruff away East's remaining honor. The suit will now fall after the second ruff (see FALSE-CARDING).

(5) *As an avoidance play.* A finesse may prove useful for keeping a particular opponent off lead.

NORTH
♠ Q J 9
♡ A 10 9
◊ 10 7 5 4 2
♣ 3 2

WEST   EAST
♠ 3   ♠ A 6 5
♡ 5 4 3 2   ♡ 8 7 6
◊ Q 9 8   ◊ K J 6 3
♣ A Q 10 9 5   ♣ J 7 6

SOUTH
♠ K 10 8 7 4 2
♡ K Q J
◊ A
♣ K 8 4

Against South's four spade contract, West leads the spade three. East plays two round of spades.

South now leads a club from dummy. If East follows low, South should finesse the eight! This is an avoidance play, designed to keep East off lead and avoid the killing play of the third trump.

If East has the club ace, the next club lead will score the king, and produce the game-going trick. However, if West has the ace, East can be prevented from leading the third round of trump. South later enters dummy with a heart, and leads a club to his king. This loses to West's ace, but declarer cannot be prevented from ruffing his third club in dummy.

(6) *As a safety play.* A finesse is often part of a safety play.

NORTH
♠ K 9 2

SOUTH
♠ A J 5 4 3

South wishes to avoid losing two spade tricks. He cashes the ace and then leads toward dummy. If West follows with a small card, he finesses dummy's nine to guard against West having started with Q 10 x x (see SAFETY PLAY).

NORTH
♠ A 10 9 8

SOUTH
♠ K 7 6 5 4

South wishes to avoid losing two spade tricks. He leads from either hand, and finesses by playing low from the opposite hand. In this way, Q J x x in either hand can be picked up with only one loser.

(7) *To gain one or more entries*

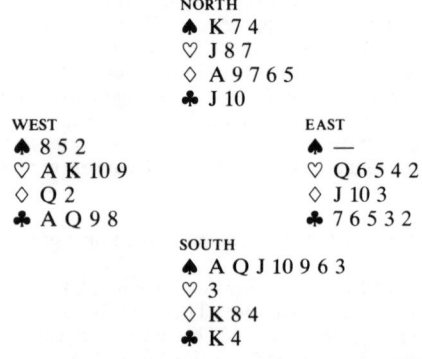

NORTH
♠ K 7 4
♡ J 8 7
◊ A 9 7 6 5
♣ J 10

WEST   EAST
♠ 8 5 2   ♠ —
♡ A K 10 9   ♡ Q 6 5 4 2
◊ Q 2   ◊ J 10 3
♣ A Q 9 8   ♣ 7 6 5 3 2

SOUTH
♠ A Q J 10 9 6 3
♡ 3
◊ K 8 4
♣ K 4

This hand demonstrates many techniques in the play of the cards. With best play on both sides, it hinges on repeated finesses to gain entries. South opens four spades in third position, and all pass. West leads the king of hearts which holds. West cannot continue with the ace of hearts, for declarer will discard a diamond from his hand, later establishing the diamond suit by ruffing (see LOSER-ON-LOSER), preventing a lead through the king of clubs. If West leads a lower heart, declarer will play the jack of hearts to force East's queen. He will later pass the eight of hearts to West while discarding a diamond and will thereby make his contract (see AVOIDANCE).

Nor can West shift to diamonds, for whereas declarer cannot establish diamonds without allowing East one lead if he must start the suit (see UNBLOCKING), if West leads a diamond, he can be forced to win a trick with the queen. Declarer can force this by leading low from his hand toward the dummy, but if West ducks, dummy must win and declarer must duck the next diamond. Now the diamonds cannot be unblocked before trump is drawn (see BLOCKING). However, if West shifts to the queen of diamonds, declarer will allow him to hold the trick. If West leads a low diamond, declarer will top East's honor with his king, and after drawing trump will allow West to hold the second diamond.

Since West cannot profitably lead clubs, his only chance is to shift to a trump. Because of the recurring finesse for entry position in the trump suit, it makes no difference which trump West plays.

Suppose West leads the deuce of spades. Declarer finesses dummy's four, which holds. The jack of hearts is played from dummy, East covers with the queen, and declarer ruffs with an honor. Now the king and ace of diamonds are cashed, West unblocking the queen of diamonds under the king to avoid being thrown in with that card. The eight of hearts is played. When East cannot cover, declarer's last diamong is discarded.

West wins and cannot lead a club or a heart, so he plays another trump. Declarer finesses the seven (or wins the king while unblocking from his hand if West plays the eight), underplaying with his six, ruffs a diamond to establish the suit, re-enters dummy with the remaining spade, and runs the diamonds.

On this deal, two finesses were taken against West's trump cards to obtain a third entry to dummy. Notice that if South must lead spades himself, he can enter dummy only twice against best defense by West. See also BACKWARD FINESSE; CHINESE FINESSE; DOUBLE FINESSE; SUIT COMBINATIONS.

FINESSING AGAINST PARTNER. See THIRD-HAND PLAY.

FINESSING PROBABILITIES. These and all finessing situations are listed under SUIT COMBINATIONS.

FINLANDS BRIDGEFORBUND. See FINNISH BRIDGE LEAGUE.

FINNISH BRIDGE LEAGUE (SUOMEN BRIDGE-LIITTO or FINLANDS BRIDGEFORBUND). Founded in 1936 by Helsingfors Bridge Club and Bridge Club Spades, the two clubs then in existence.

In 1975 there were approximately 1,300 active members in 50 clubs. Participants in European Championships since 1936, all Scandinavian Championships and the 1960, 1968, and 1972 World Olympiads. The European Championships were held in Helsinki in 1953 and the Scandinavian Championships in 1949 and 1957. Players listed separately are: J. Ehrnrooth, H. Forsblom, H. Guthwert, P. Immonen, M. Jalava, V. Jokinen, B. Laakso, K. Nortola, P. Nupponen, K. Nyman, L. Runeberg, U. Runeberg, R. Scholin, R. Skoroupo, K. Sorri, K. Walden.

Officers, 1974:
President: Lorenzo Runeberg.
Secretary: Siv Linden, 02260 Suomenoja, Livinsniemen Aukio 2, Finland.

FIRST HAND. The dealer, who is the first player to have the opportunity to bid or pass, has the "first hand." Should the first hand make a call other than a pass, he becomes the opening bidder. If the first hand passes, the opportunity to become the opening bidder passes to the opponent on his left.

FISHBEIN CONVENTION. See DEFENSE TO OPENING THREE-BID.

FISHBEIN TROPHY. Awarded to the player with the best overall individual performance record in the Summer Nationals, donated by Harry Fishbein of New York in 1952 in memory of his wife Sally. Winners are:

1952	J. Crawford	1964	P. E. Sheardown
1953	M. Ellenby	1965	A. Roth
1954	D. Carter	1966	A. Roth
1955	P. Hodge	1967	P. Feldesman
1956	T. Stone	1968	J. Jacoby
1957	J. Crawford	1969	R. Hamman
1958	H. Sobel	1970	D. Strasberg
1959	I. Rubin	1971	B. Rappaport
1960	B. Koytchou	1972	B. J. Becker
1961	M. Miles	1973	Dr. R. Katz
1962	I. Rubin	1974	R. Shepherd
1963	A. Roth	1975	G. Baze

FISHER DOUBLE. A lead directing double of a no trump contract asking for a minor-suit lead, developed by Dr. John FISHER of Dallas, Tex. After an opening bid of one or two no trump, if there have been no legitimate suit bids, a double of the final no trump contract asks for a club lead if Stayman has not been used and a diamond lead if it has.

FIT. A term referring to the effectiveness or ineffectiveness of two partnership hands in combination, commonly used to refer specifically to the TRUMP SUIT, under which heading various trump fits are discussed.

When the hand as a whole is considered, the fit may be distributional. With a sound trump fit, a shortage in each hand in different suits is likely to lead to an effective CROSSRUFF. (For an unsatisfactory fit, see DUPLICATION OF DISTRIBUTION.)

Fit can also be considered in terms of honor cards, which may or may not be effective in play (see GOOD CARDS).

FIVE or FIVE SPOT. The tenth ranking card in a suit, having five pips of the suit to which it belongs.

FIVE-ACE BLACKWOOD. See KEY-CARD BLACKWOOD.

FIVE-BID. Any bid at the five-level, to take eleven tricks if it becomes the final contract. As an opening bid, it indicates a hand of unusual power. As a bid made during the auction, it may be a slam invitation or part of a specialized slam convention. To play voluntarily five spades or five hearts and fail is one of the most ignominious results possible at the bridge table. Experts prefer to estimate slam possibilities below the game level.

See: ADVANCE SAVE; BLACKWOOD; FIVE OF A MAJOR OPENING; FIVE NO TRUMP OPENING; PRE-EMPTIVE BID; SUPER GERBER.

FIVE-CARD MAJORS. The concept according to which an opening bid of one spade or one heart guarantees at least a five-card suit. Many tournament players graft this rule onto standard bidding methods, although it is not usually applied after partner has passed. There are arguments for and against this procedure.

The knowledge that the opening bidder has a five-card suit often simplifies responder's problems, especially if there is competitive bidding. If the opening bid promises a five-card suit, a jump raise to three (either forcing or limit) can be made readily with three-card support, and a single raise can even be made with a doubleton. With this hand:

♠ K 2
♥ 8
♦ 10 8 6 4 3
♣ K 8 5 4 2

there is no sensible response to an opening bid of one spade. But two spades is attractive if the spade bidder has promised a five-card suit, and it may help to shut out an opposing heart contract.

There are two main arguments against the five-card rule. First, it forces the opening bidder to make frequent prepared, and slightly unnatural, bids in minor suits. Problems arise especially with two four-card majors and a club shortage (4–4–4–1 or 4–4–3–2 distributions) when the opening bid has to be one diamond, and a response of two clubs causes a difficulty. It is true that a major-suit fit can always be found if the opponents are silent; but a heart fit often remains undiscovered if there is an overcall of one spade.

Second, the extended use of the minor-suit opening gives more freedom to the opposition. A major-suit opening has distinct pre-emptive value, and may make it difficult for the opponents to enter the auction.

A possible compromise worth consideration is to bid four-card heart suits but not four-card spade suits. It is the one spade opening which commonly sets responder problems, and a spade fit, unlike a heart fit, seldom goes undiscovered after a minor-suit opening.

FIVE OF A MAJOR OPENING. Shows a hand missing both top honors in the trump suit, but with no outside losers. Partner is invited to raise accordingly with one or both of the missing key cards. Probably the rarest bid in bridge.

It could perhaps be used better as a pre-emptive bid with a freak hand, possibly a ten-card suit. With such a hand a four-level pre-emptive opening may not be high enough to keep the opposition out of the auction.

FIVE NO TRUMP OPENING. A very rare opening bid, showing a balanced hand which can guarantee eleven tricks. Responder is asked to raise the bidding one level for each ace, king, or queen which he holds.

FIVE-ODD. A term indicating five tricks over the book, or eleven tricks in all.

FIVE OR SEVEN. A phrase indicating the type of partnership holdings on which a successful play makes a grand slam, but if the play is not successful, the opponents can cash a second trick immediately, holding the result to five-odd. For a hand of this type, see MATCH-POINT BIDDING. In rubber bridge, probably the grand slam contract should be preferred, but there may be situations at duplicate where a six-odd contract is tactically better, even though this is neither the maximum nor the safest contract.

FIVE-SUIT BRIDGE. A game devised in 1937 by Dr. Marculin of Vienna, using a special 65-card deck. There were five suits of 13 cards, and each of the four players was dealt 16 cards. The remaining card was called the "widow," and placed face upwards on the table. After the dummy was exposed the declarer was entitled to exchange any card in his own hand or the dummy for the widow.

The fifth suit was green in color (except in England where it was blue), and was called "leaves" in Austria, "crowns" or "royals" in England, and "eagles" in America. Public interest was aroused when George VI bought some decks at an exhibition, and several books were written about the game, but it did not achieve lasting popularity.

FIVE TABLES. At duplicate, five tables provide competition for twenty players, ten pairs, or five teams.

As an individual, there are twenty rounds in four stanzas, with each set of boards going out of play at the end of each stanza. The master chart is as follows:

Rd.	N	S	E	W	Bd.	N	S	E	W	Bd.	N	S	E	W	Bd.	N	S	E	W	Bd.	N	S	E	W	Bd.
		Table 1						Table 2					Table 3					Table 4					Table 5		
1	20	1	10	12	1	19	5	9	11	2	18	4	8	15	3	17	3	7	14	4	16	2	6	13	5
2	20	2	7	15	2	19	1	6	14	3	18	5	10	13	4	17	4	9	12	5	16	3	8	11	1
3	13	9	20	3	3	12	8	19	2	4	11	7	18	1	5	15	6	17	5	1	14	10	16	4	2
4	4	20	11	6	4	3	19	15	10	5	2	18	14	9	1	1	17	13	8	2	5	16	12	7	3
5	8	14	5	20	5	7	13	4	19	1	6	12	3	18	2	10	11	2	17	3	9	15	1	16	4
6	20	6	15	2	6	18	10	14	1	7	17	9	13	5	8	16	8	12	4	9	19	7	11	3	10
7	20	7	12	5	7	18	6	11	4	8	17	10	15	3	9	16	9	14	2	10	19	8	13	1	6
8	3	14	20	8	8	2	13	18	7	9	1	12	17	6	10	5	11	16	10	6	4	15	19	9	7
9	9	20	1	11	9	8	18	5	15	10	7	17	4	14	6	6	16	3	13	7	10	19	2	12	8
10	13	4	10	20	10	12	3	9	18	6	11	2	8	17	7	15	1	7	16	8	14	5	6	19	9
11	20	11	5	7	11	17	15	4	6	12	16	14	3	10	13	19	13	2	9	14	18	12	1	8	15
12	20	12	2	10	12	17	11	1	9	13	16	15	5	8	14	19	14	4	7	15	18	13	3	6	11
13	8	4	20	13	13	7	3	17	12	14	6	2	16	11	15	10	1	19	15	11	9	5	18	14	12
14	14	20	6	1	14	13	17	5	15	11	12	16	9	4	11	11	19	8	3	12	15	18	7	2	13
15	3	9	15	20	15	2	8	14	17	11	1	7	13	16	12	5	6	12	19	13	4	10	11	18	14
16	20	16	19	17	16	5	1	4	2	17	6	7	10	8	18	11	12	15	13	19			Out		
17	20	17	18	19	17	4	5	3	1	18	10	6	9	7	19	15	11	14	12	20			of		
18	20	18	17	16	18	3	4	2	5	19	9	10	8	6	20	14	15	13	11	16			Play		
19	20	19	16	18	19	2	3	1	4	20	8	9	7	10	16	13	14	12	15	17					
20	18	17	19	16	20	1	2	5	3	16	7	8	6	9	17	12	13	11	14	18					

Since boards 16 to 20 are in play only four times, the total match-point scores on these boards should be multiplied by 4 and divided by 3 to make them comparable with the other boards. Nothing is lost should the game be terminated after the third, or even the second, stanza except that not all players will have partnered every other player. In this case, ten boards instead of five can be played in each stanza.

As a pair event, five rounds of five boards each as a MITCHELL game with a top of 4 and an average of 50 is sometimes used. The HOWELL MOVEMENT is available with nine rounds of three boards. For four and one-half tables, this is much preferable, with pair 10 as the phantom.

For team-of-four contests, see TEAM-OF-FOUR MOVEMENTS; the standard team-of-four progression (pairs skip a table down while boards move one table down) completes the game in four rounds, usually of six boards each. TOTAL POINT, BOARD-A-MATCH, or IMP scoring can be used.

FIXED. A colloquial term to designate a pair who have received a bad score through no fault of their own. Usually applied to a situation in which a player has made a technical error or suffered a legal misadventure, and gained a good result thereby. His innocent opponents, who suffered, but probably not in silence, can say that they have been "fixed."

FLAG-FLYING. An obsolete colloquialism for a bid made with full consciousness of its failure if allowed to stand, in the hope of avoiding a greater loss if the opponents are permitted to play the contract. The term was used to describe a bid made after the opponents had apparently reached their final contract, rather than one interjected during the auction. In this way it is distinguished from pre-emptive action (see PRE-EMPTIVE BID). "Sacrifice" and "save" are the modern terms.

FLANNERY TWO DIAMONDS. Developed by William FLANNERY of McKees Rocks, Pa., to show an 11-15 point hand with five hearts and four spades. Eleven-point hands must contain two and one-half defensive tricks.

Major-suit responses on the two-level are signoffs, though opener may raise with a maximum and a minor-suit void. Jump responses in the majors are invitational, and jumps to four clubs and four diamonds are transfers to four hearts and four spades respectively. If responder bids a minor on the three-level, opener bids three no trump with a fit (ace or king doubleton, or queen third). A two no trump response asks opener to clarify his strength and distribution. Opener rebids three hearts with 11-13 points or three spades with 14-15 points and two cards in each minor (or three no trump with 14-15 if his strength is concentrated in his minor suit doubletons), three clubs or three diamonds with three cards in the bid suit, or four clubs or four diamonds with four cards in the bid suit. See also FLANNERY TWO HEARTS.

FLANNERY TWO HEARTS. An opening bid of two hearts to show a hand worth 11-15 points with five hearts and four spades. Responses and rebids are the same as for the FLANNERY TWO DIAMOND convention, except that to sign off in hearts responder simply passes.

FLAT. (1) Hand: A hand without distributional values, particularly one with 4-3-3-3 distribution.

"Square" and "round" are also used to describe this type of hand.

(2) Board: A deal on which no variations in result are expected in the replays.

FLINT THREE CLUBS. A modification of the FLINT THREE DIAMOND convention designed to allow the partnership to rest in three diamonds after a two no trump opening bid, as well as in three of a major suit. The three club response to two no trump is a relay requiring opener to rebid three diamonds. Responder may pass if his suit is diamonds, or may bid a long major suit, which opener is expected to pass.

Using this variant, a response of three diamonds to the two no trump opening is used as a STAYMAN-type inquiry for major suits.

FLINT THREE DIAMONDS. Devised by Jeremy Flint, England, to permit a partnership to stop below game in a suit contract after an opening bid of two no trump. Although there is a FLINT THREE CLUB convention with the same goal, and a FLINT TWO DIAMOND convention for use with weak one no trump openings, the three diamond convention is the one that is commonly known simply as "Flint."

Over two no trump, a response of three diamonds, rarely needed as a natural bid, is artificial and demands a rebid of three hearts by the opener. If responder's suit is hearts he passes three hearts; otherwise he bids three spades, four clubs, or four diamonds, expecting opener to pass.

The opener may choose to continue to game if his hand is particularly suitable. For example:

(a)	(b)	(c)
♠ A K 5 4	♠ K 2	♠ A K 5 4
♡ K 2	♡ A K 4 3	♡ A K 4 3
◇ A K 4 3	◇ A K 5 4	◇ K 2
♣ A J 6	♣ A J 6	♣ A J 6

Opposite hand (a) the responder may have a very weak hand with a five-card spade suit. The bidding will then go:

OPENER	RESPONDER
2 NT	3 ◇
3 ♡	3 ♠
4 ♠	

As the opener has a good spade fit and good controls, there should be a play for game in spades.

With hand (b) the opener must prepare for the possibility that responder's suit is hearts, in which case game should be bid. He does this by bypassing the compulsory three hearts rebid:

OPENER	RESPONDER
2 NT	3 ◇
3 ♠	

This guarantees an excellent heart fit, and if responder has hearts, he bids four hearts. If his suit is spades, he passes three spades.

On hand (c) the opener has an excellent fit in both major suits, and wishes to be in game if responder holds either major. His rebid is three no trump, and the responder can pick a suit at the level of four.

Three diamonds can still be bid in a natural sense, if followed by a bid other than a minimum suit bid. Three diamonds followed by three no trump, for example, shows a genuine diamond suit and mild slam possibilities.

FLINT TWO DIAMONDS. A convention devised by Jeremy FLINT of England to invite game in no trump or a minor suit after a WEAK NO TRUMP opening. A two diamond response promises either a hand with a long solid minor suit or an unbalanced hand with at least four cards in each minor. With the former hand, responder rebids three clubs with a solid club suit or with a solid diamond suit and a club stopper; or he rebids three diamonds if he has a solid diamond suit and no club stopper. If responder has the unbalanced hand with both minors, he rebids his stronger major suit.

The two diamond response is forcing to three no trump or four of a minor suit. Opener is requested to bid a four card major suit if he has one; otherwise he bids two no trump. After responder clarifies his hand opener can either bid three no trump if he knows all suits are guarded, show an unbid stopper if he has one, sign off in four of a minor, or bid game in a minor.

FLITCH. See MR. AND MRS.

FLOGGER. See BACK SCORE.

FLOWER MOVEMENT. The Flower (or Endless Howell) movement is an adaptation of the HOWELL MOVEMENT so that the apparently haphazard movement of the players is replaced by an orderly progression by which one pair (North-South at table 1) is anchored, and remains stationary throughout. All other pairs progress, East-West moving toward the higher numbered table, until they reach the highest numbered table. After that round they merely switch directions at that table, and thereafter move to the next lower numbered table. As the players reach table 2, North-South, their next progression is to table 1, where they will sit East-West, then to table 2, East-West.

There must be one less set of boards in play than there are pairs.

Since this is a variation of the Howell movement, the arrangement of boards should be taken from the Howell cards. They must be redistributed properly by the director for each round. The regular progression of the players is attained by the sacrifice of a regular progression for the boards.

FLUKE. A fortuitous profit. An extreme case would be represented by a player dropping a card that appears disastrous but produces a brilliant result.

FORCE. (1) Noun: Any bid making it incumbent upon the bidder's partner to bid at least once more.

(2) Verb: To cause to ruff; to cause a player to use a high card.

FORCED BID. When a player makes a FORCING BID, his partner is required systemically to make some sort of response. The response may be a WEAKNESS RESPONSE, or a STRENGTH-SHOWING BID. It is possible that a PASS is a correct response (see PENALTY PASS) to a bid normally forcing.

FORCING BID. A bid which, because of system or convention, requires the partner to "keep the bidding open," by making some call other than a pass if there is no intervening call. Examples can be found under FORCING SEQUENCES and FORCING PASS.

Perhaps the most widely used forcing bids are the JUMP SHIFT by an unpassed hand and the ONE-OVER-ONE or TWO-OVER-ONE responses by an unpassed hand.

FORCING DECLARER TO RUFF. A method of defensive play, usually sound strategy when other forms of defense seem inadvisable or doubtful. When a defender, by the play of an established side-suit, forces declarer to use his valuable trumps, it sometimes causes the declarer to lose control of the play. Sometimes called "pumping declarer." In the following deal the insistent forcing of the declarer's strong trump hand enabled the defending partnership to defeat an otherwise sure game contract:

```
                NORTH
                ♠ 6 4 3 2
                ♡ K 10 8
                ◇ A Q J
                ♣ A J 10
WEST                              EAST
♠ K Q 10 9 5                     ♠ A 7
♡ A 5 4 3                        ♡ 7
◇ 10 3                           ◇ 7 6 5 4 2
♣ 7 2                           ♣ 9 6 5 4 3
                SOUTH
                ♠ J 8
                ♡ Q J 9 6 2
                ◇ K 9 8
                ♣ K Q 8
```

With West the dealer, the bidding went:

WEST	NORTH	EAST	SOUTH
1 ♠	Dbl.	Pass	3 ♡
Pass	4 ♡	Pass	Pass
Pass			

West's opening lead is the spade king, which East wins with the ace to unblock his partner's suit. East returns the spade seven, which West wins with the queen. West continues the suit, forcing South to ruff. South now leads a heart, which is won by West with the ace, and again West leads a spade, forcing South to ruff a second time. South leads a second round of hearts. At this point, it is obvious that South cannot make his contract, for West's greater length in

trumps gives him a trump winner. This was brought about by West's continued forcing, which battered down the declarer's trump fortress.

S. K.

FORCING LEADS. Plays by the opening leader aimed at weakening the declarer's trump suit. The lead is most effective when the leader has four trumps, and can visualize declarer's being forced to ruff prematurely and perhaps lose trump control.

Generally a forcing lead is made from a long suit, as in no trump, for should the attack succeed, the declarer may have to exhaust his attenuated trump suit in extracting the defender's trumps. Subsequently, if the defense regain the lead, they will be in a position to cash the established cards in their suit, for the hand will have been reduced to no trump.

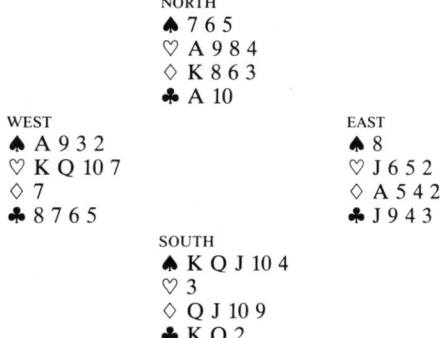

```
                NORTH
                ♠ 7 6 5
                ♡ A 9 8 4
                ◇ K 8 6 3
                ♣ A 10
WEST                              EAST
♠ A 9 3 2                        ♠ 8
♡ K Q 10 7                       ♡ J 6 5 2
◇ 7                              ◇ A 5 4 2
♣ 8 7 6 5                        ♣ J 9 4 3
                SOUTH
                ♠ K Q J 10 4
                ♡ 3
                ◇ Q J 10 9
                ♣ K Q 2
```

The contract is four spades by South. If the singleton diamond is led, the declarer has an easy ride, but holding four trumps, West should resist this temptation and attack in hearts. Declarer wins and forces out the ace of spades. West continues hearts, reducing South's trump length to his own. Declarer is now in a cleft stick: if he draws West's trumps and plays diamonds, East wins, and the defense secures two heart tricks. Alternatively, if he abandons trumps after discovering the bad break, West will score two of his small trumps.

Often the opening leader can diagnose the proper occasion for a forcing lead from the auction:

SOUTH	NORTH
1 ♠	2 ♣
2 ◇	2 NT
3 ♣	3 ♠
4 ♠	

West holds:

```
♠ 4
♡ K J 6
◇ 10 5 3 2
♣ Q 7 6 3 2
```

South's bidding has pinpointed a singleton or void heart; East almost certainly has at least four trumps. A forcing game should be initiated by leading the king of hearts (pinning a possible singleton queen in the South hand).

NORTH	SOUTH
2 ♠	2 NT
3 ♣	3 ♡
4 ♡	

West holds:

♠ 9 8
♡ Q J 10
◇ A J 8 2
♣ Q J 10 8

In this situation, the dummy can be visualized as having three trumps headed by the ace, king, and a singleton diamond. Accordingly, West should eschew the "normal" club lead in favor of the diamond ace, a forcing lead against dummy's trumps, in order to promote his trump holding.

See also ATTACKING LEADS.

S. K.

FORCING ONE NO TRUMP. Opening bids: see DYNAMIC NO TRUMP, LITTLE ROMAN CLUB SYSTEM. Overcalls: see COMIC NO TRUMP, GARDENER NO TRUMP OVERCALL, LEA SYSTEM, UNUSUAL ONE NO TRUMP OVERCALL. Responses: see ONE NO TRUMP RESPONSE TO MAJOR, FORCING.

FORCING PASS. A pass which forces partner to take further action, and informs him not to pass out the present contract. Such a pass may be made in the following situations:

(1) The opponents have taken an obvious sacrifice. A forcing pass denotes the desire to bid toward a higher contract if partner is willing.

(2) The opportunity for a sacrifice has arisen. A forcing pass denotes the desire to sacrifice, and asks partner to do so if he cannot double the opponents, and defeat their contract.

(3) A safety level has been established below which the contract cannot be sold. A forcing pass denotes inability to find a suitable call, or the desire to see if partner can double the enemy bid.

(4) After a slam-level sacrifice, a forcing pass sometimes denotes control of the enemy suit, and requests partner to bid a slam if he has the necessary outside values.

FORCING PRINCIPLE. In his early contract bridge books, Ely CULBERTSON described the basics of his system as the APPROACH and FORCING PRINCIPLES. This original statement of the principle has been expanded to include a great many FORCING SEQUENCES in modern bridge methods.

FORCING RAISE. See DOUBLE RAISE.

FORCING REBID. See OPENER'S REBIDS.

FORCING SEQUENCES. A series of bids by a partnership that require the bidding to continue. Some sequences cannot be passed by virtue of the strength shown by the last bid; certain others are considered to be forcing when the partnership has shown values for a game or slam while still bidding at a modest level. Again, some sequences commit the partnership to continue bidding until game is reached (or a worthwhile penalty extracted, should the opponents interfere); while others are merely forcing for one round.

Some common examples of forcing sequences follow, with the forcing bid underlined. (There is no unanimity of opinion as to the nature of many sequences. With the plethora of bidding systems and styles that abound, most sequences lend themselves to varying interpretations, not only from system to system, but from partnership to partnership.)

Sequences that are forcing for one round.

1. New suit by responder:

    a) 1 ♡　　1 ♠

    b) 1 ♡　　2 ♣

    c) 1 ♣　　1 ♠
       2 ♣　　2 ♡

    d) 1 ♣　　1 ♡
       1 NT　2 ♠

    (but not: 1 ♡—1 ♠—1 NT—2 ♡)

    e) 1 ♣　　1 ♡
       1 ♠　　2 ◇

    (see FOURTH SUIT FORCING)

2. Reverse bids by opener after a two-level response:

    a) 1 ♡　　2 ♣
       2 ♠

    b) 1 ♠　　2 ♡
       3 ♣

3. New suit by opener after the trump suit has been agreed:

    a) 1 ♠　　2 ♠
       3 ♣

Game-forcing sequences.

1. First-round jumps by responder:
    a) 1 ♠　　2 NT

    b) 1 ♠　　3 ♠
       and
       1 ♣　　3 ♣

    (see LIMIT RAISE)

    c) 1 ♡　　2 ♠

    (see WEAK JUMP RESPONSES)

2. Jump rebids by opener:

    a)   1 ♡   2 ♣
        3 ♡

       (but not: 1 ♡ —1 ♠ —3 ♡)

    b)   1 ♡   1 ♠
        3 ♣

3. Miscellaneous sequences:

    a)   1 ♡   1 ♠
        3 ♡   3 ♠

    b)   1 ♡   2 ◇
        2 NT   3 ♡

    c)   1 ♠   2 ♡
        3 ◇   3 NT
        4 ♣

4. JUMP REBIDS by responder:
This is a controversial topic, and is treated separately.

The above discussion has centered on forcing sequences that stem from opening bids of one of a suit. For other forcing sequences, see FORCING TWO-BID and ONE NO TRUMP OPENING.

                        S. K.

FORCING TAKE-OUT. See JUMP SHIFT.

FORCING TWO-BID. The traditional use of an opening two-bid in a suit to show a hand which can virtually guarantee game, or even slam. (Also referred to as Culbertson Two-Bid, Demand Bid, or Strong Two). It was a cornerstone of the CULBERTSON system, and remained standard practice in the US and many other parts of the world. In postwar years many experts abandoned the Forcing Two in favor of the WEAK TWO-BID, the ACOL TWO-BID, and other treatments. A variety of formulae have been put forward to determine whether a hand is worth a forcing two. Goren gives this schedule:

With a good five-card suit	25 high-card points.
With a good six-card suit	23 high-card points.
With a good seven-card suit	21 high-card points.

With a second good five-card suit, one point less is needed. If the game is to be in a minor suit, two points more are needed. Two more formulae were devised by Hy Lavinthal: (a) More honor tricks than possible losers. (This rule was incorporated into the Culbertson System.) (b) Rule of 24: add to the high-card point-count two points for every card over four in any suit; then subtract a point for any king or queen not in sequence with a next-ranking honor; bid two if the answer is 24 or more. However, the expert does not normally use such rules: he employs the forcing two-bid if he has reasonable game prospects opposite a worthless or nearly worthless hand. Another consideration is that a hand may be slightly too weak for a forcing two, but at the same time distinctly too strong for an opening bid of one in

a suit. In such circumstances, a slightly shaded two-bid may be a lesser evil than an overstrength one-bid.

However, the likelihood that a one-bid may be passed out is a further consideration. Highly distributional hands may safely be opened with a bid of only one, because if opener's partner passes it is most unlikely that both opponents will do so. Lacking controls of three suits therefore, the expert will tend to open with a one-bid and jump later to show distribution.

Culbertson later modified the "unconditionally" game-forcing character of the bid to permit partner to pass a bust hand if opener's call after a two no trump response was a simple rebid of his first suit, i.e.:

$$2 ♡ —2 NT—3 ♡$$

Responses. The conventional negative response is two no trump. Other responses are positive and natural, showing at least 7–8 points and seldom less than one quick trick (i.e., an ace, a king-queen, or two kings).

However, other responding treatments are used, including ACE-SHOWING RESPONSES and HERBERT NEGATIVE.

FORESIGHT. Looking ahead in the bidding or play. Examples of this are the prepared minor-suit opening bid to provide a convenient rebid over partner's or opponents' action, the early loss of a trick in order to set up a squeeze position, and a switch by defenders to a new suit in order to break up a possible later throw-in play. See BIDDING; END-PLAY; PREPAREDNESS, PRINCIPLE OF.

FORFEIT. To cancel a right or turn to call. See LAWS OF RUBBER BRIDGE (Law 15), LAWS OF DUPLICATE (Law 11).

FORK. See FOURCHETTE.

FORMOSA. See NATIONAL CONTRACT BRIDGE LEAGUE OF THE REPUBLIC OF CHINA.

FORTUNE. Chance may play an important role at the card table, but fortune can be significant in bridge events away from the table. There are three recorded instances of players achieving international honors as a result of fortuitous circumstances.

In 1937, the US Women's team at the World Championship at Budapest found itself one short. An American lady whose name has not been recorded was brought in to complete the team. She was a player with social bridge experience only who happened to be staying in Budapest at the time.

In 1961 at the Fall Nationals at Houston, Robert STUCKER, Houston, and Jack BLAIR, Tulsa, formed an impromptu partnership in order to complete a section in the Open Pairs and oblige the tournament director. They finished second in the event, and subsequently represented the United States in the

World Pair Championship in Cannes, 1962, in consequence of their success.

Mrs. Mary EDWARDS, of Esher, England, was brought in as a substitute in the 1959 British international women's trials to replace a player who had fallen ill. From an apparently hopeless position, trailing the rest of the field by a substantial margin, she qualified for the British team in partnership with Mrs. G. HIGGINSON, St. Annes-on-Sea, England. Subsequently they became European Champions when their team won in Palermo, Italy.

FORTUNETELLING. A pretense of predicting the future of an individual by giving "significance" to a pattern of playing cards spread before him. Standard packs can, of course, be used, but the TAROTS, with their individuality, provide a greater opportunity for imaginative divination for the edification and bewilderment of the gullible.

The first important book on divination by cards was written in the eighteenth century by Count de Gebelin, who explained a complex symbolism, more amusing than credible, supposedly derived from ancient Egypt. In the 1760s, a French hairdresser named Alliette (reversing his name to Etteilla for its Oriental sound) had new pictures put on each card, to which he assigned symbolism depending on the upright or inverted position of a card and those adjacent to it. Modern reproductions are available, and similarities to Tarot cards and de Gebelin's symbolism can be found.

Shortly afterward, Mademoiselle Lenormand designed a complete new pack for fortunetelling: a tiny playing card in the upper left, balanced by a single letter upper right. At the top a diagram of stars has some sort of "astrological" significance, and the cut and deal of the cards made by "astro-mytho-hermetic" methods. Packs of this type are made in several countries, mostly for children.

A. F.

FORUM, THE. The monthly bridge publication of the ACBL Western Conference, which appears in newspaper form; published privately by Tom STODDARD from 1925 to 1935, and subsequently on behalf of the PACIFIC BRIDGE LEAGUE.

FORWARD-GOING. See CONSTRUCTIVE.

FOSTER ECHO. A third-hand unblocking play against no trump, intended at the same time to show count. With a four-card holding, the first play is the second highest, followed by the third highest, reserving the lowest card for last. With a three-card holding, the first play is the second highest, then the highest.

FOULED BOARD. A board into which a card or cards or hands have been interchanged to incorrect pockets. Usually a fouled board occurs when the board is being discussed after the play, and various hands are interchanged across the table.

Fouling a board is perhaps the most heinous sin in bridge competition, because the scores prior to and after the fouling cannot be compared. When a board has been reported as fouled, the director must determine at what point in the competition the fouling occurred, and must match-point the results in some fair manner in the two fields thus created.

In pair play, one method is based on a formula devised by Col. Russell BALDWIN. To use this formula, the scores in the two fields are match-pointed as though the field were complete; i.e., with a 7-point top if the field has eight pairs. This is the X in the formula. A is the normal average (without any foul), N is the number of times the board was played in the group under consideration, and M is the award in match points to be given for the score.

$$M = \frac{A}{N} (2X + 1)$$

A board may be fouled by there being an incorrect number of cards in two of the pockets, such as 14 in one and 12 in another. In this case the director tries to locate which is the incorrect card in the long hand and checks with previous players to do this. Since the Laws of Duplicate Bridge require each player to verify that he holds the correct number of cards before looking at his hand and also before replacing the cards in the pocket, it is quite proper that penalties be assessed against the table where the fouling occurred. It is interesting to note that no pair has ever admitted responsibility for fouling a board—it has always been their opponents who must have done so; also, very rarely has a board been fouled in top competition after a moderately normal result.

Many tournament directors have announced automatic penalties against both pairs at the table where the fouling of the board occurred, usually of half the top score on a board for the session. To guard against the possibility of fouling a board, not more than one hand should be removed from the board at a time during discussions. This is particularly true when the opponents are not at the table.

In board-a-match team play, the correct manner of handling a fouled board is a matter of regulation, which has been changed from time to time. Under 1964 regulations of the ACBL, the scores, both North-South and East-West, are divided into two fields, before and after the fouling, each field is match-pointed independently, and the percentage of possible match points for each pair then is determined. For each team that played the board in different positions, the percentages are added and the board is won if the total is 130 or more, halved from 70 to 130, and lost with 70 or less. Results for teams that played the board in identical form are computed in the usual way, since the fouling occurred either before both halves of the teams had played it, or after both halves of the teams had played it.

FOUR or FOUR-SPOT. The eleventh ranking card of each suit, designated by four pips of the suit symbol on the face.

FOUR ACES POINT-COUNT. See FOUR ACES SYSTEM and POINT-COUNT.

FOUR ACES SYSTEM. Methods used by the FOUR ACES TEAM in winning many championships during the thirties. The main features of the system were:

(1) POINT COUNT of ace = 3; king = 2; queen = 1; jack = ½. This makes a total of 26 points in the pack, and 6½ represent an average hand; 9½ points represent a mandatory opening bid.

(2) *Limited one no trump* opening with a range of 11½–13 points. (Hands with less than seven honor cards are devalued by ½ point for each honor, and hands with more than seven honors similarly increased in value.) Establishment of this no trump range solved major rebidding headaches; in combination with point-count and rigidly prescribed responses, it precluded many of the no trump bidding faults that plagued inexpert players.

(3) *Minor-suit bids,* if need be in a three-card suit, as exploring maneuvers, either by the opener or the responder.

(4) WEAK JUMP OVERCALLS.

(5) PSYCHIC BIDS by third hand and occasionally first hand showing some high-card strength in the suit bid and little else.

(6) JUMP SHIFT to the level of two or three as a psychic control. The opener rebids two no trump with a psychic, and with any other rebid a slam is reached.

The Four Aces' book included a number of other original ideas, many of which have become standard practice.

FOUR ACES TEAM. The team that dominated tournament competition in the mid-thirties. The first appearance of this team was at the Summer Nationals in Asbury Park in 1933, when David (Burnstine) Bruce, Richard Frey, Oswald Jacoby, and Howard Schenken won the CITY OF ASBURY PARK TROPHY in the national teams event that was later to be superseded by the SPINGOLD. Burnstine and Jacoby had been original members of THE FOUR HORSEMEN. Burnstine, Schenken, and Frey (with Charles Lochridge) played as the BID-RITE TEAM earlier in 1933, when Jacoby and Michael T. Gottlieb were members of Culbertson teams. Gottlieb joined the team immediately afterward, and during 1934 the Four Aces' major wins included the VANDERBILT, the Spingold, the GRAND NATIONAL (the top team event of the United States Bridge Association), and the REISINGER. They successfully defended the Grand National in Feb. 1935, and also repeated in the Vanderbilt, with Sherman Stearns replacing Frey, who had resigned from the team when he became an executive in the Culbertson organization. Gottlieb retired in 1936 and was replaced by Merwin D. Maier. B. J. Becker and other experts played occasionally as members of the team, which did not play after Dec. 1941 but continued as an entity for purposes of book and newspaper publication until 1945.

The Four Aces played their own system, and wrote a book, *The Four Aces System of Contract Bridge* (see BIBLIOGRAPHY, C), which presented their original expert methods. Though the system was widely followed by tournament players, the book was not a commercial success.

FOUR-BID. A bid at the four-level, to take ten tricks if it becomes the final contract.

FOUR-CARD MAJORS. Opening bids of one spade or one heart holding a four-card suit. The old auction bridge idea of requiring a five-card suit for an opening bid has found a place in several modern systems such as ROTH-STONE and KAPLAN-SHEINWOLD. Nevertheless, an opening bid in a four-card major remains standard practice. Many authorities require a relatively strong four-card suit (see BIDDABLE SUITS).

FOUR-CARD SUIT BIDS. See BIDDABLE SUITS.

FOUR CLUB BLACKWOOD. See ACE IDENTIFICATION, BLACK AND RED GERBER, GERBER CONVENTION, EXTENDED GERBER, KEY CARD GERBER, ROMAN GERBER, and SUPER BLACKWOOD.

FOUR CLUB CONVENTIONS. See CLARAC SLAM TRY, FOUR CLUB BLACKWOOD, FOUR CLUB AND FOUR DIAMOND OPENING TRANSFERS, RUBIN TRANSFERS, SOUTH AFRICAN TEXAS, SWISS CONVENTION. See also SPLINTER BID, VOID-SHOWING BIDS.

An alternative usage, devised by Howard Robinson of New York City, is to use four clubs as a three-stage asking bid to determine singletons, aces, and trump honors.

When four clubs is a jump bid, or immediately follows a jump raise of another suit, partner is requested to bid a suit in which he holds a singleton or revert to the agreed trump suit with no singleton. The next ranking suit by the asking bidder then requests partner to show the number of aces he holds. If the asking bidder again bids the next ranking suit, responder shows his trump honors (ace, king, or queen) by three steps. The asking bidder signs off whenever he bypasses the asking denomination or reverts to the agreed trump suit.

FOUR CLUB AND FOUR DIAMOND OPENING TRANSFERS. An opening bid of four clubs promising a long heart suit or an opening of four diamonds promising a long spade suit. As most frequently used, opener promises a hand stronger than the normal direct opening of four of a major suit, although some pairs use the four-of-a-minor opening to show a weaker hand, or a hand with a solid major suit and nothing else.

Responder usually accepts the transfer by bidding four of opener's major. However, the bid of the next higher suit is available without getting the partnership beyond game, and can be used either as a re-transfer, making opener the declarer, or as an asking bid.

For an alternative treatment see RUBIN TRANSFERS.

FOUR-DEAL BRIDGE. See CHICAGO.

FOUR DIAMOND CONVENTIONS. See BLUE TEAM FOUR CLUB–FOUR DIAMOND CONVENTION; FOUR CLUB AND FOUR DIAMOND OPENING TRANSFERS; NEAPOLITAN FOUR DIAMOND CONVENTION; RUBIN TRANSFERS; SOUTH AFRICAN TEXAS; TEXAS CONVENTION.

FOUR DIAMOND OPENING TRANSFER. See FOUR CLUB AND FOUR DIAMOND OPENING TRANSFERS, RUBIN TRANSFERS.

FOUR-FIVE NO TRUMP CONVENTION. See CULBERTSON FOUR-FIVE NO TRUMP.

FOUR HORSEMEN. A champion team of the early thirties. It was formed by P. Hal Sims in 1931 to challenge the earlier success of the Culbertson team. The other "horsemen" were Willard S. Karn, David Burnstine (Bruce), and Oswald Jacoby. They won the two major team championships in 1932, the VANDERBILT and the ASBURY PARK, by large margins, and won the REISINGER convincingly in 1933. Sims's efforts to develop and promote his own system in opposition to Culbertson did not suit Jacoby and Bruce, who successively left the team (see FOUR ACES TEAM).

FOUR NO TRUMP CONVENTIONS. Since it is not frequent that a four no trump bid is QUANTITATIVE, and it is the lowest bid possible that is above the game level, it is a bid that is frequently used to initiate inquiries to lead either to a slam bid, or to stay below the slam level if the partnership hands cannot make a slam. Among the specialized uses of this bid are the following, dealt with in the following articles: ACOL FOUR NO TRUMP OPENING, BLACKWOOD, BOLAND CONVENTION, BOWERS VARIATION, BYZANTINE BLACKWOOD, CULBERTSON FOUR-FIVE NO TRUMP, CULWOOD, DECLARATIVE-INTERROGATIVE FOUR NO TRUMP, DEFENSE TO OPENING FOUR-BID, KEY-CARD BLACKWOOD, KING CONVENTION, NORMAN, ROMAN BLACKWOOD, SAN FRANCISCO, SUPPRESSING THE BID ACE.

For a discussion of the distinction between the quantitative and conventional uses of four no trump, see BLACKWOOD.

FOUR NO TRUMP OPENING. In standard methods, shows a balanced hand too strong to open three no trump. It should be a ten-trick hand with perhaps 28–30 points. This rare bid is in disuse in standard practice, because an opening two club bid followed by four no trump will serve equally well.

For alternative treatments, see ACOL FOUR NO TRUMP OPENING; FOUR NO TRUMP OPENING PRE-EMPT; RUBIN TRANSFERS.

FOUR NO TRUMP OPENING PRE-EMPT. Devised by T. REESE and J. FLINT as part of the LITTLE MAJOR SYSTEM and subsequently adopted by several American experts to distinguish between a strong and weak minor-suit game pre-empt.

An opening bid of four no trump shows a weak pre-empt of five clubs or five diamonds with less than five controls, counting an ace or void as two controls

and a king or singleton as one control. Consequently, an opening bid of five clubs or five diamonds would show a stronger pre-empt, five or more controls. For an alternative treatment see RUBIN TRANSFERS.

FOUR NO TRUMP OVERCALL. A bid of four no trump after an opposing opening bid is usually a form of the UNUSUAL NO TRUMP, calling for a minor suit. This could not apply after an opening bid of three clubs, three diamonds, or a weak two diamonds, in which case the bid would be BLACKWOOD. For treatment of four no trump overcall after an opening bid at the four-level see DEFENSE TO OPENING FOUR-BID.

FOUR-ODD. Four tricks over the book, or ten tricks in all.

FOUR OF A SUIT OPENING. A natural opening bid of four to show a long, strong suit with little side strength. A typical hand would contain a seven- or eight-card suit, but a six-card suit is possible.

♠ —
♡ K Q J 6 5 4
♢ K Q J 8 7
♣ 3 2

If this is the dealer's hand, four hearts has a lot to recommend it. An opening four in a minor would seldom be based on a solid suit, because of the possibility of three no trump. For alternative treatments, see FOUR CLUB AND FOUR DIAMOND OPENING TRANSFERS, LITTLE MAJOR, RUBIN TRANSFERS.

FOUR TABLES. At duplicate, four tables provide for competition among sixteen (or seventeen) players as individuals, eight pairs of players, or four teams of four.

As an individual tournament, it has the difficulty of being very short (fifteen or sixteen boards) or too long (thirty or thirty-two boards). Player assignments to seats and distribution of boards are shown under INDIVIDUAL MOVEMENT.

As a pair game, the HOWELL MOVEMENT, with seven rounds, is preferable to the MITCHELL MOVEMENT, with only four rounds. With seven pairs, the phantom should be pair 8. Either three or four boards may be played per round.

If the Mitchell movement is used, tables 1 and 2 should relay boards throughout, with a bye stand between tables 3 and 4. Boards move from 1 to 4 to bye stand, to 3, to 2 where they are shared with table 1. Traveling pairs move from 1 to 2 to 3 to 4 to 1 after each round. Three is top score on a board and average is one and one-half times the number of boards in play.

As a team-of-four event, three stanzas are required; in the first stanza, traveling pairs of teams 1 and 2 exchange places, as do the traveling pairs of 3 and 4; boards are relayed between tables 1 and 2 and between tables 3 and 4; in the second stanza, traveling pairs of teams 1 play at 3 and of team 3 at 1; similarly with teams 2 and 4; in the third stanza, teams 1 and 4 and teams 2 and 3 interchange traveling pairs, and relay the boards. Boards are reshuffled at the end of each stanza, and the six matches are scored individually. BOARD-A-MATCH, TOTAL POINT, or INTERNATIONAL MATCH-POINT SCORING can be used, and ties broken with summation from the three matches at board-a-match or total point or by quotient of points won divided by points lost at International Match Points.

FOUR-THREE-TWO-ONE COUNT. See POINT-COUNT.

FOURCHETTE. A tenace; an obsolete term for A Q, K J, or Q 10.

FOURTEEN TABLES. At duplicate, fourteen tables provide competition among fifty-six players, as individuals, twenty-eight pairs, or fourteen teams.

As an individual tournament, twinned RAINBOW sections of seven tables can be used with a thirteen-point top. This provides twenty-one boards with the same number of partnerships. Also possible is an Appendix Rainbow as described in EIGHT TABLES and TWELVE TABLES, where the "bumped" players will play boards 27 and 28 at table 14, with all other players moving and all players playing thirteen rounds, twenty-six boards, top 12, average 156. The Appendix Rainbow movement could be cut at eleven or twelve rounds if desired.

As a pair game, fourteen tables is becoming the basic unit for a section where there are many sections. When it is desired to pre-duplicate the hands from prepared hand records, the players who do the duplicating do not play the hand they duplicate; therefore it is necessary to have at least fourteen tables in each section in order to play the standard twenty-six boards.

As a one-session team game, there are two irregularities in the team-of-four movement; after the third round, traveling pairs skip an extra table toward lower numbers; after the ninth round, both the traveling pairs and the boards skip a table. This provides for meeting twelve of the thirteen teams with twenty-four boards played. If the thirteenth round is desired, boards are relayed between tables 1 and 8, 2 and 9, 3 and 10, etc., with the eleventh set of boards on table 1, boards being picked up from tables 8 through 14. Since the last round is completed within itself, it is desirable and feasible to distribute and shuffle boards anew for this round, scoring them to the right of the other boards on the summary sheet. In this way, all scores up to the last round can be totaled and checked while the last round is in play, and 0- to 2-point corrections added after the last round's play.

Fourteen and a half tables is extremely awkward when there is a phantom pair, and it is not recommended. The BUMP MITCHELL must be used, with one North-South pair not being bumped; consequently the bumping pair and the pairs that have been bumped must have their scores adjusted by adding one-twelfth.

FOURTH BEST. See FOURTH HIGHEST.

FOURTH HAND. The fourth player to have the opportunity to make a call, the player to the dealer's right.

FOURTH-HAND BIDS. For a discussion of minimum openings in fourth seat, see BORDERLINE OPENING BIDS.

The idea that the fourth player must have additional strength to open the bidding is now quite obsolete, and at duplicate a player may open slightly light in the hope of snatching a part-score.

Opening three-bids and weak two-bids in fourth position show maximum values, close to an opening bid, but rarely occur. Other opening bids are not affected by the positional factor. See also PASSED HAND.

FOURTH HIGHEST. Traditionally the fourth highest card of a long suit has been the lead when it is desired to develop long card tricks in a suit, or to give partner a count of the cards in the led suit at trump play. The application of the RULE OF ELEVEN when the led card is the fourth highest is a determining factor in third hand's play.

FOURTH SUIT FORCING AND ARTIFICIAL. If responder's rebid names a fourth suit, the bid is forcing in standard methods. Many players employ this as a waiting bid when no natural bid is available, and ACOL treats this as a convention: the opener assumes that responder is weak in the fourth suit, and must not bid no trump unless he guards the suit. The bid is often appropriate with two or three losers in the fourth suit:

NORTH	NORTH	NORTH
♠ 7 5 4	♠ A 3	♠ 8 4
♡ A 6 2	♡ 7 5 4	♡ K 6
◇ A K Q 4	◇ 9 7 2	◇ A K Q 6 4 2
♣ 8 4 3	♣ A K J 6 5	♣ 7 5 3

SOUTH	NORTH	SOUTH	NORTH	SOUTH	NORTH
1 ♣	1 ◇	1 ♠	2 ♣	1 ♠	2 ◇
1 ♡	1 ♠	2 ◇	2 ♡	2 ♡	3 ♣

The fourth suit is forcing for one round only, and promises a minimum of 10–11 points. Responder seldom wishes to bid the fourth suit in a natural sense, because he would then be able to bid no trump. See OUT-OF-THE-BLUE CUE-BID.

FRACTIONAL MASTER POINT CERTIFICATES. See RATING POINTS.

FRAGMENT. A term describing a suit of two or more cards that is not long enough to bid naturally; usually a three-card holding. The bid of a fragment is designed to imply shortness in an unbid suit. See FRAGMENT BID.

FRAGMENT BID. An unusual bid—usually a double jump—in a new suit on the second round of bidding, showing a fit with partner's suit and a shortage in the fourth suit (devised by M. INGBERMAN). The last bid in each of the following sequences is a fragment bid:

(a)		(b)		(c)	
NORTH	SOUTH	NORTH	SOUTH	NORTH	SOUTH
1 ♣	1 ♡	1 ♣	1 ♡	1 ♣	1 ♡
3 ♠		1 ♠	4 ◊	1 ♠	4 ♣

The fragment bidder usually has two or three cards in the fragment suit, and must have a singleton or void in the fourth suit—clubs in (b).

The fragment idea can be extended to this situation:

NORTH	SOUTH
1 ♡	2 ♣
2 ◊	3 ♠

Here the bid shows a fit with hearts and a diamond shortage. (The more orthodox treatment is to use this sequence to show a fit with diamonds, because South's hand has been improved by North's rebid.)

For alternative treatments of such sequences, see ASKING BID, SPLINTER BIDS, SWISS CONVENTION, and VOID-SHOWING BIDS.

Although fragment bids were originally devised as a use for the double jump shift, which was otherwise usually an IDLE BID, when a player has made a bid that denies a two-suited hand, a fragment bid may be made in a suit without jumping. The implication of the fragment bid is that the bidder has support for his partner's suit and a singleton in the remaining suit. See Soloway theory of JUMP SHIFTS.

FRAME. A colloquialism for a game. The term probably came from the appearance of the scoring pad used in rubber bridge: the vertical and horizontal lines, the edge of the single column pad, and the line drawn underneath the score when the game is completed "frame" the trick-score constituting the game.

FRANCE. See FRENCH BRIDGE FEDERATION.

FRANCHISED CLUBS. Groups of players desirous of holding periodic duplicate tournaments. These clubs are either cooperative organizations of players, groups within another organization such as a church, a YMCA, a commercial organization, or a proprietary club run by an individual, or small groups to which other players are invited. These clubs award Rating Point Certificates for their regularly scheduled games. For every twelve regularly scheduled games, or once each calendar quarter, a Club Tournament game may be held, for which the League office issues the first place award. All other points awards won at the Club Tournament are issued by the Club on Blue Ribbon Certificates. Two Charity Club Tournaments, one Olympiad Fund Club Tournament, and one Membership Tournament are also allocated to each Club annually under regulations of the League.

FRANCO-AMERICAN MATCHES. Teams representing France and the United States (or North America) have met on many occasions. There have been ten official meetings in World Championship competition.

1936	New York	1964	New York
	United States won		United States won*
1954	Monte Carlo	1967	Miami Beach
	United States won		North America won†
1956	Paris	1968	Deauville, France
	France won		United States won*
1960	Turin	1969	Rio de Janeiro
	France won*	.	North America won†
1961	Buenos Aires	1971	Taipei
	North America won		United States won†
1963	St.-Vincent, Italy	1972	Miami
	North America won		United States won*

(Details of teams and scores are given under WORLD CHAMPIONSHIPS).

The following semi-official or unofficial matches have been played:

(1) Paris 1930. US (Mr. and Mrs. E. Culbertson, T. Lightner, and W. von Zedtwitz) drew with France (P. Bellanger, P. Albarran, A. B. de Puchesse, R. de Nexon, G. Rousset, E. Tulumaris, and S. Venizelos). The match was played at PLAFOND, the forerunner of contract bridge, and, after a dispute, was abandoned as a draw shortly before the end when the scores were almost level.

(2) Paris, 1954. France beat US (C. Bishop, M. Ellenby, L. Mathe, D. Oakie, and D. Steen) by 17 IMP.

FRANCO BOARD. A screen invented by Italian international Mario FRANCO, and at one time used in

---

* In the 1960 World Team Olympiad, France (P. Jaïs, R. Trézel, P. Ghestem, R. Bacherich, C. Delmouly, and G. Bourchtoff) beat US Vanderbilt 2 (L. Harmon, S. Lazard, W. Hanna, M. Schleifer, D. Oakie, and I. Stakgold) by 25 IMPs in the 40-board qualifying round; beat the US Spingold 2 (C. Goren, H. Sobel, H. Schenken, H. Ogust, L. Mathe, and P. Allinger) by 7 IMPs in the qualifying, but lost to them by 8 in the 60-board final match; in the finals, beat US Vanderbilt 1 (J. Crawford, S. Silodor, B. J. Becker, N. Kay, T. Stone, and G. Rapee) by 36 IMPs and beat US Spingold 1 (O. Jacoby, I. Rubin, V. Mitchell, S. Stayman, W. Grieve, and M. Rubinow) by 29 IMPs.

In the 1964 World Team Olympiad, the US (S. Stayman, V. Mitchell, R. Jordan, A. Robinson, R. Hamman, and D. Krauss) beat France (G. Theron, G. Desrousseaux, H. Svarc, J.-M. Boulenger, R. Bacherich, and C. Deruy) by 14 IMPs, scoring 6–1 in victory points.

In the 1968 World Team Olympiad, the US (R. Jordan, A. Robinson, A. Roth, W. Root, E. Kaplan, and N. Kay) beat France (G. Bourchtoff, G. Desrousseaux, P. Steinberg, C. Delmouly, P. Sussel, and F. Versini) 14-6 victory points in the 20-board qualifying round robin match.

In the 1972 World Team Olympiad the US (R. Goldman, R. Hamman, J. Jacoby, M. Lawrence, P. Soloway, R. Wolff) beat France (G. Bourchtoff, P. Chemla, C. Delmouly, J.-P. Klotz, M. Lebel, D. Leclery) 14–6 in the 20-board qualifying round robin match.

† In 1967, NA defeated France 37-23 victory points in three, 32-board qualifying round robin matches.

In 1969, France defeated NA 37-19 victory points in three, 32-board qualifying round robin matches, but NA beat France in the 64-board playoff for third place by 35 IMPs.

In 1971 France defeated NA team 42–18 victory points in three, 32-board qualifying round robin matches, and defeated the United States (ACES) 31–29 victory points in the round robins; however, the Aces beat France in the 128-board finals.

major Italian events. It is placed diagonally across the table so that each player cannot see his partner and can see only one opponent. A trap in the center of the screen is raised before the start of the play so that all players can see the dummy. Combined with WRITTEN BIDDING, the board virtually removes any possibility of inadvertent exchange of illicit information, and greatly reduces the ethical problems resulting from hesitations. See BIDDING BOXES, BIDDING SCREEN.

FREAK. A single hand or a complete deal of abnormally unbalanced distribution. Usually a hand in which one player has more than seven cards in one suit, or more than eleven cards in two suits.

FREAK HANDS. In the field of bidding, there is no doubt that the expert has a tremendous advantage over the great majority of bridge players, for he has come across virtually every conceivable bidding situation, and has learned how to handle it. There is one type of bidding situation, however, that even the veriest of tyros handles as well (or as badly) as the expert. This is in the field of freak hands, hands that contain eight-, nine-, or ten-card suits, plus a void or two. (See DUKE OF CUMBERLAND'S HAND, MISSISSIPPI HEART HAND, and SWING HAND.) These hands defy scientific evaluation, and past experiences are of no help in appraising these anomalies. So the expert, like the average player, has to guess what he should bid; and when it comes to guessing, anybody is as good as anybody else.

Consider a few freak hands. The three deals which follow were all taken from National Championship events. The first one arose in the National Mixed Team-of-Four Championship of 1961.

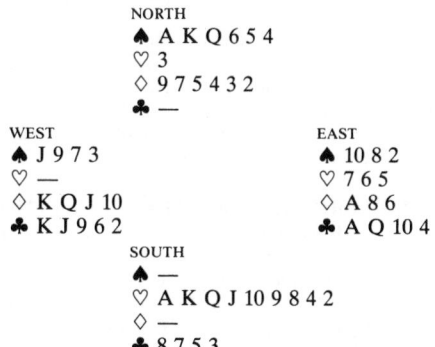

As is readily apparent, South can take thirteen tricks at hearts against any defense. When the board was played, East, as dealer, passed, and South either passed, bid one heart, bid four hearts, or bid six hearts. As to what the proper bid on the South hand was, there is no answer.

How freak hands can be wrecked on the rocks of distribution is evidenced in the following deal, which came up in the Mixed Team-of-Four Championship of 1949.

NORTH
♠ K Q J 5 4 3 2
♡ 3
◇ —
♣ A Q 10 7 4

WEST	EAST
♠ 9	♠ A 8 7
♡ 10 8 6 5	♡ K Q 9 4
◇ Q 10 8 4 2	◇ A K J
♣ 9 8 3	♣ K 5 2

SOUTH
♠ 10 6
♡ A J 7 2
◇ 9 7 6 5 3
♣ J 6

Neither side vulnerable. North dealer. The bidding at every table was identical.

NORTH	EAST	SOUTH	WEST
1 ♠	Dbl.	Pass	2 ◇
4 ♠	Dbl.	Pass	Pass
Pass			

Eleven tricks were made at every table, declarer's only losers being the ace of trumps and the king of clubs. Is there an authority, an expert, or an average player who would dare to say that East's business double of four spades was an improper bid?

We have all run into situations comparable to the one contained in this final deal, and there isn't a thing we can do about it in preparing ourselves to handle it in the future.

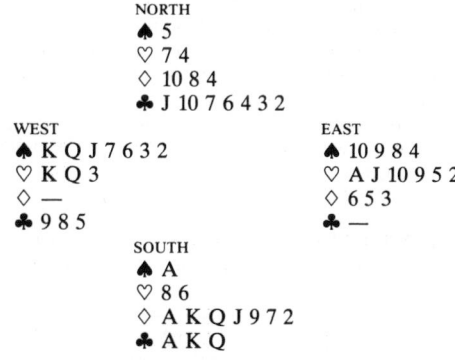

North-South vulnerable, South dealer, the bidding:

SOUTH	WEST	NORTH	EAST
2 ◇	2 ♠	Pass	4 ♠
5 ◇	5 ♠	6 ◇	6 ♠
Dbl.	Pass	Pass	Pass

It will be observed that West's only loser was the ace of trumps. Did South do something wrong when he doubled the slam contract?

F. K.

FREE BID. A bid made by a player whose partner's bid has been overcalled by right-hand opponent. In such circumstances partner will have another chance to bid, so it would seem unnecessary to bid with minimum values. Traditional theory therefore prescribed elevated standards for all "free" actions, equivalent to perhaps an additional king.

However, experts have tended to make free bids more freely, mainly because a pass with fair holdings is liable to put the opener's side at a disadvantage if there is further action by the opponents. Many players will respond with minimum values in the "free" position if they have an obvious bid to make.

There are three separate categories.

(1) One no trump (e.g., one club—one heart—one no trump). The traditional range is 10–12 or 9–12, but many players reduce this by partnership agreement, sometimes to as little as 7–10. In that case the minimum would apply only when holding a double stopper in the opponent's suit.

(2) Suit response (e.g., one club—one heart—one spade). A minimum of 9 points according to the textbooks, but partnership style may permit a lower limit. Some players would respond on 6 points if the suit is good. There is a strong tendency for the free response to show a five-card suit (especially playing NEGATIVE DOUBLES), or at least a strong four-card suit.

A free two-over-one response (e.g., one club—one heart—two diamonds) is usually held to show 11 points, or even 12; the standard should be slightly higher when the opener cannot rebid his suit at the level of two.

(3) Raises. In this category (e.g., one diamond—one spade—two diamonds), almost all experts have abandoned the idea that the raise shows greater strength than it would without the overcall. There is no disadvantage in raising exactly as if there had been no overcall, and a considerable tactical loss in adopting a waiting policy.

Free rebids by the opener follow similar principles. Any obviously suitable action should be taken, even with a minimum hand on which no desirable action is available.

FREE DOUBLE. A double of a contract which represents a game if undoubled. Usually confined to rubber bridge, when a part-score will convert an earlier part-score into game. If both sides have a part-score, judgment of a high level is required; all players may be straining their resources.

Doubles of game and slam contracts cannot properly be described as free. See PENALTY DOUBLE and SUCKER'S DOUBLE.

FREE FINESSE. A defensive lead which allows declarer to take a finesse without the risk of losing the trick, or a finesse which could not normally be taken at all:

(1) NORTH
     ♠ A J x

     SOUTH
     ♠ K x

(2) NORTH
     ♡ A Q x

     SOUTH
     ♡ Void

In (1), West's spade lead against South's heart contract presents declarer with the opportunity of finessing the jack without the risk of losing a trick to East's queen. In (2), with spades trumps, West leads a heart, giving South an opportunity to take a finesse he could not otherwise maneuver. Many experts consider this the only true example of the free finesse.

Like most gifts, however, it should be inspected with suspicion before acceptance. For example:

NORTH
♡ A Q x x x x

WEST   EAST
♡ 10 9 x x x   ♡ K J

SOUTH
♡ Void

West may lead a heart for the purpose of tempting South to finesse for a king which would otherwise fall on the first or second lead of the suit.

FREE RAISE. A single raise of opener's suit after an overcall. The classical theory that a free raise implies extra strength (8–10 points) has been generally abandoned; most experts maintain the normal range (6–9 points) irrespective of the overcall. However, the overcall may make it necessary to relax the requirements for trump support, especially if the overcall is in the suit ranking immediately below opener's:

(a)   (b)
♠ A x   ♠ x x
♡ x x   ♡ A x x x
♢ x x x x   ♢ Q x x x
♣ A J x x x   ♣ K x x

In (a), a raise to two spades would be appropriate when one spade has been overcalled by two hearts. In (b), one club should be raised to two clubs after an overcall of one spade. In each case the trump length is one card below standard. These examples assume that NEGATIVE DOUBLES are not being used.

FRENCH BRIDGE FEDERATION (FÉDÉRATION FRANÇAISE DE BRIDGE). Founded in 1935, and by 1974 had a membership of 15,000. French victories in international events include World Championship 1956, World Team Olympiad 1960, World Pair Olympiad 1962, European Championship 1953, 1955, 1962, 1966, 1970, 1974, European Women's Team Championship 1939, 1953, 1954, 1956, 1965, 1969. France hosted the World Championship in Monte Carlo in 1954, the World Pair Olympiad in Cannes 1962, the World Team Olympiad in Deauville 1968, and the European Championships in Paris 1949. National events held annually include Open Teams and Open Pairs. French players listed separately are: P. Albarran, A. Aron, R. Bacherich, Mrs. S. Baldon, P. Bellanger, J.-M. Boulenger, Mrs. A. Bourchtoff, G. Bourchtoff, J. Broutin, C. Delmouly, C. Deruy, G. Desrousseaux, P. Ghestem, Dr. F. Hervouët, P. Jaïs, B. Koytchou, M. Lebel, J. Le Dentu, Princess N. von Lichtenstein, C.

Mari, Mrs. C. Martin, Mrs. M. C. de Montaigu, R. de Nexon, Dr. J. Parienté, Mrs. E. Pouldjian, Dr. B. Romanet, J.-M. Roudinesco, P. Schemeil, R. Schlitz, J. Stetten, Dr. J.-L. Stoppa, Mrs. A. Sussel, H. Svarc, Mrs. S. de Temmermann, Dr. G. Theron, L. Tintner, R. Trézel.

Officers, 1974:
President: Michel Bongrand.
Secretary General: Francois Bonhoure, 53 Avenue Hoche, Paris 8ᵉ, France.

FRENCH CLUB. A simple one club forcing system in common use in France and other parts of the world. A standardized version, published by Pierre Ghestem in the *Revue Française de Bridge* (Dec. 1960), is the basis of the following summary.

One club is forcing and promises at least a doubleton club. There are two ranges:

(1) 13–17 points. Denies a five-card major suit or a four-card diamond suit (exception: five spades with four or five clubs and 13–15 points). It follows that one club will *tend* to be natural and include a club suit. Only when holding four cards in both majors can it become necessary to open one club with a doubleton.

With 13–15 points, a minimum rebid is made, with priority given to a major-suit bid. With 16–17 points over a response of, say, one heart, the opener jumps to two no trump, three clubs, or three hearts. (This does not deny holding four cards in the unbid major.)

(2) 18–23 points. Promises at least three clubs, and may have an outside five-card suit in which a jump will be made. If the response is one diamond, this range is shown by a rebid of two diamonds or anything higher.

After a positive response, two diamonds is forcing and semi-conventional: it may be made as a waiting bid with a three-card diamond suit.

Responses to one club:

(1) One diamond. Usually negative with less than 8 points, but may show a diamond suit and 10–11 points if followed by a non-forcing jump in diamonds or no trump. Other strong rebids by responder are forcing and show that the diamond bid was natural.

(2) One heart, one spade, or two clubs. Natural and forcing.

(3) One no trump. 8–10 points, no trump distribution, no four-card major.

(4) Two no trump. 11 points, natural.

(5) Two diamonds, two hearts, two spades. Semi-pre-emptive, four or five playing tricks.

(6) Three of a suit. A good suit and six playing tricks.

One diamond opening bid (13–18 points) is natural with at least a four-card suit, and denies a five-card major. A minimum rebid shows 13–15, and a jump rebid, 16–18. Responses are natural.

One spade or one heart opening bids are natural (12–17 points) and at least a five-card suit. A jump rebid, or a rebid of two no trump, is made with 16–17 points. Responses are natural with limit raises and limit jump responses of two no trump.

One no trump opening bid shows a balanced distribution and 18–20 points. A weak no trump non-vulnerable with a range of 12–15 is an optional variation.

Two club opening is conventional, showing 23 points or more. Other two-bids show 18–22 points, at least a five-card suit, and a club shortage.

FRENCH SCORING. In tournaments sanctioned by the French Bridge Federation, the value of the fourth odd trick in no trump contracts is reduced to 20 points. Thus ten or more tricks will be scored the same in either no trump or a major suit.

If it is assumed that a major game should be preferred to a no trump game, this scoring eliminates the edge given to the no trump contract when both will produce the same ten or more tricks.

FULFILLING CONTRACT. Taking as many tricks, in the play of the hand, as contracted for in addition to the book of six, i.e., eight tricks in a contract of two. A bonus of 50 points is awarded for a less-than-game contract in duplicate, 300 for a non-vulnerable game, and 500 for a vulnerable game.

FULWILER CONVENTION. A form of asking bid. After the trump suit has been established, any bid by either partner at the lowest range in another suit asks for control in that suit. Responses are in steps:

no control	1 step
singleton	2 steps
void	3 steps
king	4 steps
ace	5 steps
ace and king	6 steps

for example:

WEST	EAST
1 ♠	2 ♠
3 ♣	3 NT

(four steps, showing the king of clubs).

Subsequently, the opener can "ask" about trump honors. See ROMAN ASKING BIDS.

G

GABUNGAN BRIDGE SELURUH ASSOCIATION. See ALL INDONESIA BRIDGE ASSOCIATION.

GADGET. An artificial bidding device which can be grafted on to standard bidding methods but is not an integral part of any system. The term applies to nearly all the articles listed under ARTIFICIAL BIDS and SLAM CONVENTIONS.

GAMBIT. A deliberate sacrifice of a trick in order to gain additional tricks. The term is borrowed from chess.

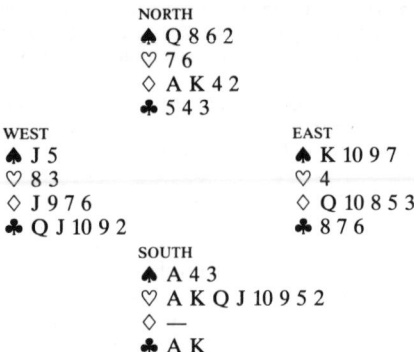

```
                   NORTH
                   ♠ Q 8 6 2
                   ♡ 7 6
                   ◇ A K 4 2
                   ♣ 5 4 3
WEST                                    EAST
♠ J 5                                   ♠ K 10 9 7
♡ 8 3                                   ♡ 4
◇ J 9 7 6                               ◇ Q 10 8 5 3
♣ Q J 10 9 2                            ♣ 8 7 6
                   SOUTH
                   ♠ A 4 3
                   ♡ A K Q J 10 9 5 2
                   ◇ —
                   ♣ A K
```

West leads the club queen against South's contract of six hearts. Declarer, at trick two, must play one of his two small trumps and concede an otherwise unnecessary trick to the eight. This forces a trump entry to the dummy, and permits South to discard his two spade losers on dummy's diamond winners. A spade lead would have defeated the contract.

GAMBLING AT BRIDGE. Playing for stakes is quite common in regular rubber bridge circles; in duplicate, however, it is officially frowned upon, and, in fact, absolutely prohibited in contests sponsored by the American Contract Bridge League. Bridge combines attractively the elements of both chance and skill. Chance, however, is considerably discounted, since in the long run cards will even out as to weight of holdings, and skill will always tell and be paramount. In clubs where bridge is played for stakes, the amount played for varies from a tenth of a cent a point on up to two or three cents or more per point. CHICAGO increases a given stake somewhat, since four-deal bridge is much faster, and one can win or lose more in less time. In duplicate pair contests or team-of-four events, betting has been done on the basis of match points or of number of boards by which a team wins or loses. However, gambling in duplicate events is not only against the regulations but also rare. See CALCUTTA, POOL.

GAMBLING THREE NO TRUMP. An opening bid based on a long, solid minor suit, a feature of the ACOL SYSTEM that has been adopted by many players using an artificial two club forcing opening bid.

```
   (a)                    (b)
♠ A 5                    ♠ 7
♡ K 2                    ♡ Q 8 3
◇ J 3                    ◇ A K Q 8 4 3 2
♣ A K Q J 7 4 3          ♣ J 3
```

The amount of outside strength required to make this bid varies with the individual partnership. In its original form, stoppers were needed in at least two side-suits, as in (a). The modern tendency is to make the bid (except in fourth position) with little or no outside strength, as in (b).

Responses:

(1) Four clubs shows extreme weakness and a desire to play at the four-level in opener's suit.

(2) Four diamonds is forcing. A good arrangement is for the opener to rebid his longer major suit. Any further bid by the responder is a slam invitation.

(3) Four spades and four hearts are natural, with a self-sufficient six-card suit or better.

(4) Four no trump is conventional, with responses downgraded because the opener has already shown an ace. A five diamond rebid would therefore show *two* aces.

(5) Five clubs shows a desire to play in five of opener's suit—possibly for pre-emptive reasons.

(6) Five diamonds is natural, implying that responder has a club honor and has therefore deduced that opener's suit is diamonds.

(7) Six clubs shows a desire to play a minor-suit slam.

Defenses:

The most effective method of bidding against a gambling three no trump opening bid is to use the RIPSTRA convention. Assuming adequate high-card strength, the bid of four of the better minor suit as a take-out for the majors gives the partnership the best chance of finding its best suit.

If three no trump has become the final contract, the best chance to defeat the contract is usually for the opening leader to cash a winner in order to take a look at dummy and to obtain information from his partner as to which hand controls which side suits.

GAME. The winning of 100 points below the line in bridge. Game can be attained by bidding and winning a succession of two or more part-scores, or can be bid in one contract after it is determined that the partnership has sufficient values in the combined hands. The first team to win two such games wins the rubber and the premium. In CHICAGO, a game may be bid and scored on each of four deals and it is theoretically possible for a side to win four games in one chukker.

GAME ALL. The situation when both sides are vulnerable. The term is rare in the United States but standard in England.

GAME BID. A bid for just enough odd tricks to complete the requirement for game in a particular suit or no trump. In duplicate bridge, this is a bid for three no trump, four of a major suit, or five of a minor suit. In rubber bridge, if a pair has a part-score, a game bid usually requires fewer tricks; a part-score of 40 points, for example, would make two no trump, two of a major, or three of a minor into game bids.

GAME CARDS. There are many games that are played with cards that are not the PACK of playing cards. Authors, Rook, and Old Maid are examples of games designed principally for children. Flash cards, such as those used in teaching word recognition and foreign languages in schools, are other types. Dominoes and Mah-Jongg can also be played with cards in place of the blocks and tiles.

Major manufacturers of card games are located in Salem and Springfield, Mass., but games are produced by a wide variety of individual manufacturers, and most are covered by patents.

GAME CONTRACT. An undertaking of a contract which, if successful, will earn enough points in TRICK-SCORE to make or complete the 100 required for a game. In no trump, three-odd, in hearts or spades, four-odd, in clubs or diamonds, five-odd tricks produce at least the 100 points necessary from a LOVE score. With a PART-SCORE, lower contracts become game contracts. Some rubber bridge players will DOUBLE a game contract more freely than below-game contracts, although such tactics are misconceived. See SUCKER'S DOUBLE.

GAME DEMAND BID. A bid which, once made, imposes an obligation upon the partnership to keep the bidding alive until game is reached or a satisfactory penalty inflicted upon the opponents. An obsolescent term. See FORCING TWO-BID.

GAME-FORCING BID. A bid which announces that the partnership should reach a game contract or higher, and thereby establishes a GAME-FORCING SITUATION.

GAME-FORCING SITUATIONS. A sequence of bidding which has committed both members of a partnership to reach a game contract. Many of these are listed under FORCING SEQUENCES.

GAME-GOING. A term applied to any hand or bidding situation which promises to develop a game for the partnership.

GAME HOG. A player who habitually distorts his own bidding in the expectation that all hands should be played at a game contract.

GAME IN. A colloquial expression meaning vulnerable.

GAME INVITATION. See COMPETITIVE DOUBLE; DRURY; INVITATIONAL BID; JUMP RAISE BY RESPONDER; LIMIT JUMP RAISE; LIMIT JUMP RAISE TO SHOW SINGLETON; MAXIMAL OVERCALL DOUBLE; SHORT-SUIT GAME TRIES; TWO-WAY GAME TRIES; WEAK-SUIT GAME TRY.

GAMMA TRUMP ASKING BIDS. Asking bids in the ROMAN and SUPER PRECISION systems concerned with the quality of responder's suit, which is inferentially agreed as trumps. The Roman responses are as follows:

1st step	— Queen or worse
2nd step	— King
3rd step	— Ace
4th step	— Two top honors
5th step	— Three top honors

For responses in the SUPER PRECISION system, which are identical to the trump-asking responses in standard PRECISION CLUB, see PRECISION ASKING BIDS.

GARBAGE. A colloquial term for a minimum type of holding whose majority values are in unsupported queens and jacks.

GARDENER NO TRUMP OVERCALL. A two-way bid, which may be either a natural no trump overcall with 16–18 points or a weak hand with a long suit. Partner usually bids two clubs to find out which type of overcall was made, and the overcaller rebids two no trump if he has the natural strong type. There is a technical reason for this procedure if strong jump overcalls are being used: a weak hand with a long suit has no convenient way to enter the auction. Devised by Nico Gardener, London.

GATHERING TRICKS. The taking in of tricks won by a side. The tricks taken by a side should be arranged in such a way that their number and sequence are apparent. See LAWS (Law 66).

GERBER CONVENTION. A four club bid to ask partner how many aces he holds. The responses are:

4 ◇	no ace
4 ♡	one ace
4 ♠	two aces
4 NT	three aces
5 ♣	four aces

By analogy to the BLACKWOOD convention, four diamonds can be used instead of five clubs to show the rare holding of four aces. The four club bidder uses the next available bid to ask for kings on the same principle, but cannot use the agreed trump suit for this purpose. For example, four spades asks for kings over a response of four hearts, unless spades is the agreed trump suit, in which case four no trump becomes the king-asking bid.

There may often be difficulty in distinguishing a conventional four club bid from a natural one. Some players restrict the use of the convention to situations in which no suit has been genuinely bid (e.g., after a one no trump or two no trump opening, or a conventional two club bid followed by two no trump or three no trump).

If four clubs is to be used more generally, there are three possible rules a partnership can adopt:

(1) Four clubs is conventional unless it is a direct club raise.

(2) Four clubs is conventional unless clubs have been genuinely bid by the partnership.

(3) Four clubs is conventional if it is a jump bid, or if a suit has been specifically agreed. This is perhaps the best of these rules.

A partnership also has to consider how responder should act holding a void, or when there is interference bidding.

Treatment of similar situations is discussed under Blackwood convention.

This convention, invented in 1938 by John GERBER of Houston, is sometimes referred to as Four Club Blackwood. See also ACE IDENTIFICATION; BLACK AND RED GERBER; CLARAC SLAM TRY; EXTENDED GERBER; KEY CARD GERBER; ROMAN GERBER; SUPER GERBER.

GERMAN BRIDGE LEAGUE (DEUTSCHER BRIDGE VERBAND). Founded in 1932, and by 1969 had approximately 6,000 members. The League participates in Olympiads and European Championships, hosting the 1963 event in Baden-Baden. The League also sponsors teams that compete in the Common Market Championships and the major European International Bridge Festivals. In the past, German teams contested for the Mitropa Cup, held annually in Austria, and have won the open division once and the women's event twice. The League awards master points and publishes a monthly magazine, *Deutsches Bridge Verbands-Blatt.* German players listed separately are: F. Chodziesner, E. von Dewitz, Mrs. E. Gotthelf, A. Littman-Lemaitre, L. Östör, K. Rachwalski, H. von Rotteck.

Officers, 1974:
Chairman: Dr. Heinz von Rotteck.
Secretary: Miss Elisabeth Kopf, 49 Herford, Kurfürstenstrasse 22, Germany.

GESTURE. A remark or mannerism that suggests a call, lead, play, or plan of play. See LAWS (Law 16).

GET A COUNT. To determine during the play the number of cards held in one or more suits by one of the hidden hands. See COUNTING THE HAND.

GHOULIES. See GOULASH.

GIVE COUNT. As a defender, to give a LENGTH SIGNAL to one's partner.

GLADIATOR. A method of responding to one no trump, devised in New Zealand, and used in slightly modified forms in the ROMAN and CAB systems.

A response of two clubs is a relay, requiring the opener to bid two diamonds. A minimum suit bid by responder then shows weakness, and the opener passes. Other rebids by the responder are limited.

A response of two diamonds is a STAYMAN-type inquiry for major suits, and is forcing to game. A response of two hearts or two spades is forcing, and higher suit responses are slam suggestions.

GO DOWN. Synonym for fail to make a contract.

GO UP. To play a high and possibly wining card when faced with a choice of playable cards.

GODDARD TROPHY. For the Men's and Women's Pair events; donated by the ACBL in 1937 and named after Ed Goddard, the organizing chairman of the series of Summer Nationals held at Asbury Park. Contested at the Summer Nationals, under which heading past results are listed.

GOING OUT. The act of making place, after each rubber, for any member who did not play the last rubber, in the event that there are more than four players at the table.

GOLD CUP. The Knock-out Team Championship of Great Britain, contested under the auspices of the BRITISH BRIDGE LEAGUE. (See also VON ZEDTWITZ GOLD CUP.)

GOLD POINT. Effective January 1, 1969, the ACBL added as a requirement for advancement to LIFE MASTER status the proviso that all players who had zero RED POINTS as of that date needed 25 gold points of the required 50 red points in order to achieve Life Master rank. These are master points awarded for overall placing or for winning a section top in regional or higher rated events that are not restricted by an upper master point limit. Gold points count toward the required red point total.

GOLDER CUP. A two-session contest for players eliminated from the Spingold competition, and other players of senior master or higher rank. Presented in memory of Benjamin Golder by his widow, subsequently Mrs. Charles Solomon. Results are under Summer Nationals.

GOLDMAN TROPHY. For the Open Pair Championship at the Eastern Regionals. Presented by Julian Goldman in 1929, and had the status of a National championship during the thirties.

GOLDWATER RULE. The satirical suggestion by Tournament Director Harry Goldwater that an opening lead out of turn should generally be accepted (see LAW 56 for declarer's other options). The rationale is that a player who does not know whose turn it is to lead probably doesn't know the right lead either.

GOLF. As many bridge-players also play golf, combined golf and bridge events are sometimes popular. An English plan conceived by D. Garfitt Clowes is to match-point the golf in the same way that a bridge event is scored (ten or more strokes on a hole counts as an automatic "bottom" or shared "bottom"). These scores are then divided by two, and the same pairs play a HOWELL or SCRAMBLED MITCHELL event to determine the winner on the combined scores.

GOOD. An adjective used to describe a hand which is better than the simple POINT-COUNT would suggest, as in "a good 18." This may be owing to distributional factors, to the presence of BODY, to the location of honors in long suits, or to a combination of these items.

GOOD CARDS. Cards which have been established during the play and which are winners that can be cashed.

In a wide sense, a player of a partnership holding good cards has more than a fair share of the honor strength.

But the term is sometimes used in a more precise technical meaning, referring to honor cards which have improved in value as a result of the auction. In a competitive auction, the improvement may arise because the significant honors are over the opponent who has bid the suit (see POSITIONAL FACTOR).

When one player shows an unbalanced hand, his partner can often judge that his cards are "good." This applies particularly when the bidding indicates a two-suiter. Suppose the bidding starts:

WEST	EAST
1 ♠	2 ♡
3 ◇	

If East is considering a slam in diamonds, he will know that any honors he may hold in spades and diamonds will be "good." Aces in the side-suits (hearts and clubs) will clearly be valuable, but minor honors in these suits are unlikely to pull their weight in a slam.

     ♠ 5
     ♡ A 7 4 3 2
     ◇ K 8 4 2
     ♣ A 6 3

With this hand, all the honor strength is working, and the spade shortage will help West ruff out the suit. East therefore has the values to bid six diamonds, although he may approach the slam gently. But if he held this hand:

     ♠ 6 2
     ♡ K Q 10 4 3
     ◇ J 8 5 2
     ♣ K Q

a simple bid of three no trump would be discreet. East has no "good" cards, and prospects of making six diamonds are poor unless West can bid further.

GOREN FOUNDATION. See INTERCOLLEGIATE BRIDGE TOURNAMENT.

GOREN POINT-COUNT. See POINT-COUNT and DISTRIBUTIONAL POINT-COUNT.

GOREN SYSTEM. The methods of bidding advocated by Charles H. Goren in many books since 1944. These have become synonymous with STANDARD AMERICAN, and correspond closely to the bidding structure set out in this encyclopedia unless otherwise stated. The following indicate some areas of doubt:

(1) The STAYMAN convention is part of "Standard" but is not an integral part of Goren. It is listed as an optional extra.

(2) In tournament play, WEAK TWO-BIDS are "Standard," as distinct from the FORCING TWO-BID advocated by Goren and used by most rubber bridge players.

(3) Jump bids by responder are forcing by implication in Goren's methods:

SOUTH	NORTH
1 ♣	1 ♡
1 ♠	2 NT

Culbertson and many modern authorities take an opposite view, rating this as encouraging but not forcing. The forcing interpretation is standard on the East Coast but practice varies elsewhere and is a matter of partnership agreement. See JUMP REBIDS BY RESPONDER.

GOREN TROPHY. Awarded for the National Men's Team Championship, donated by Charles H. Goren in 1946. Contested at the Fall Nationals until 1963, and then transferred to the Spring Nationals, under which heading the past results are listed.

GOULASH. A deal in which the cards are not shuffled, and are dealt five to each player for two circuits, and finally three to each player. The name is apparently derived from Hungarian goulash, a highly spiced mixture of meat and vegetables, and is intended to suggest a spicy and unusual mixture.

Players sometimes agree to play goulash when a hand has been passed out, particularly in private or commuter games. Goulashes are standard in CUT-THROAT BRIDGE and TOWIE.

A more extreme form, known as the "passing goulash," achieved some popularity in the twenties and thirties. Each partner was permitted to pass six cards to his partner after the conclusion of the deal, usually three cards followed by two cards followed by one card.

A goulash is sometimes referred to as "mayonnaise" or "hollandaise."

GRAND COUP. A play by which declarer deliberately shortens his trump holdings by ruffing a winner in order to achieve a finessing position over an adverse trump holding in an end position.

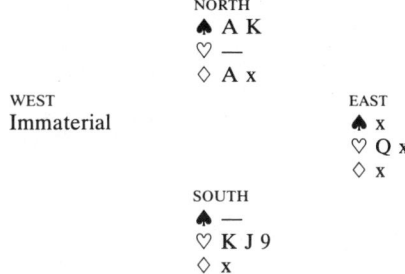

Declarer, in a heart contract, has discovered West to be void of hearts. With the lead in the dummy, declarer leads the ace of spades, and trumps it. He re-enters dummy with the ace of diamonds to lead any card at trick 12. East must ruff, and declarer overruffs.

GRAND MASTER. See WORLD BRIDGE FEDERATION PLAYER RANKINGS.

GRAND NATIONAL CHAMPIONSHIPS. (1) A series of annual championships first held in 1934 by the United States Bridge Association, and continued annually until 1937. For results, see USBA GRAND NATIONALS.

(2) A major ACBL Knockout team championship since 1973, for the Albert MOREHEAD TROPHY, patterned in many respects after the USBA's earlier event. The initial stages of the Grand Nationals are conducted over the course of several months in each of the individual ACBL DISTRICTS for members of Units within the District, to produce a district championship team. In 1973 a total of approximately 1,500 teams entered at the grass roots level. In 1974 more than 5,000 teams entered. In 1975, 6,135 teams entered.

The district champions compete within eight Grand National Zones for the Zonal Championship. The final playoffs of the Grand Nationals among the eight zonal champions are held at the Summer Nationals, under which heading the results are listed. The winning team is entitled to compete against the winners of the SPINGOLD TROPHY, REISINGER MEMORIAL TROPHY, and VANDERBILT CUP (1) for the right to represent North America or the United States in the next year's WORLD CHAMPIONSHIP. See INTERNATIONAL OPEN TEAM SELECTION.

GRAND OLD MAN OF BRIDGE. A term applied in the 1920s and early 1930s to Milton C. WORK and in later years to Sidney LENZ.

GRAND SLAM. The winning of all thirteen tricks by the declarer. The bonus for a grand slam, 1,000 points when not vulnerable and 1,500 when vulnerable, make a grand slam, bid and made, one of the best rewarded acccomplishments at rubber bridge, and one of the more effective methods of SHOOTING at duplicate. While the general tendency among rubber bridge players is to avoid bidding grand slams except in ironclad situations, the mathematics of the game suggest rather freer acceptance of the risks involved in view of the large rewards.

See SLAM BIDDING for an explanation of methods of exploration suitable to bidding grand slams, and the percentage or odds that justify such bids. For a brief period (1932–35) the grand slam bonuses were higher than they are now: 1,500 non-vulnerable, 2,250 vulnerable.

GRAND SLAM FORCE. A method of locating the top trump honors when a grand slam is in view. It was devised by E. CULBERTSON in 1936, was first described in a *Bridge World* article by Josephine CULBERTSON, and is often in consequence referred to in Europe as a "Josephine."

A bid of five no trump asks responder to bid a grand slam if he holds two of the top three trump honors. (This clearly does not apply if five no trump is a natural no trump raise, or if it is used as part of another slam convention.) A jump to five no trump fixes the last bid suit as trump unless another suit has been specifically agreed.

It is sometimes necessary to know whether responder has one of the top three honors. If the agreed trump suit is not clubs, one or more intermediate bids are available at the six-level for this purpose.

If diamonds are agreed, six diamonds should show one top honor. If a major suit has been agreed, several methods are in use, designed to permit a partnership to reach a grand slam missing Q x x in the trump suit.

One method is to divide the responses into four steps. The first step would show the weakest trump holding for the previous bidding (three or four small), the second step would show the queen, the third step the ace or king and the fourth step the ace or king with extra length. If hearts are agreed, the first and second steps are combined into one. If diamonds are the agreed suit, the first and second steps and the third and fourth steps are combined. For example,

NORTH
♠ K 5 3 2
♡ 6 5 4
◇ 8 5 3
♣ 10 7 2

SOUTH
♠ A 10 9 8 6 4
♡ A K
◇ A K Q 9 7
♣ —

SOUTH	NORTH
2 ♠	4 ♠
5 NT	6 ♡
7 ♠	

North's jump raise shows four spades, and his step response to the grand slam force shows the king. Since there is unlikely to be a trump loser, South bids the grand slam.

An alternate expert method, perhaps superior theoretically, is to sign off in the trump suit with the worst trump holding; other responses at the six-level are made inversely, the higher the bid the weaker the trump holding. In order to retain all four steps to show gradation of trump quality even when a suit other than spades has been agreed, some partnerships use jumps to five of the suit above the agreed trump suit, rather than to five no trump, as the grand slam force.

The grand slam force can also be used in conjunction with Blackwood. The ROMEX system uses a bid of five no trump as the grand slam force even after four no trump has been used as Blackwood. It is more common, however, for partnerships to use the MALOWAN SIX CLUB CONVENTION to ask about trump honors. After the conventional response to Blackwood a bid of six clubs is the grand slam force, providing clubs are not agreed.

In some systems, such as SCHENKEN, it is possible to agree on a trump suit and cue-bid first- and possibly second-round controls before four no trump is reached. R. P. Reed, Boulder, Colo., suggests that four no trump should then be used to pinpoint trump honors. Partner returns to the agreed trump suit with none of the top three honors, bids the lowest-ranking side suit with the king or queen, the next ranking side suit with the ace, the highest-ranking side suit with two of the top three honors, and five no trump with full control of the trump suit. See also BYZANTINE BLACKWOOD; TRUMP ASKING BIDS.

GREECE. See HELLENIC BRIDGE FEDERATION.

GREEN SUIT. The fifth suit in the American version of FIVE-SUIT BRIDGE, called Eagles. Prior to the introduction of five-suit bridge, the green suit was a non-existent fifth suit. See HIPPOGRIFFS.

GROUP SCORE. The score made by all the pairs in a group on a set of hands constituting a match. Competition between clubs and cities is sometimes based on a team of eight, twelve, or an even larger number of players. In such a game, each pair from one side meets each of the pairs on the competing side, all playing the same set of boards. The net score (plus and minus) of all pairs is included in the group score.

Also, in total point pair contests, the net score on a set of boards on which two particular pairs are in opposition.

GUAM CONTRACT BRIDGE LEAGUE. A unit of the ACBL which, because of its remoteness from the North American continent, plans to seek full membership in the FAR EAST BRIDGE FEDERATION. Participated Far East Championships 1974.

President, 1975: Raymond W. Volkwine, Box 3122, APO SF 96334, Guam.

GUARD (or Stopper). An honor holding in a particular suit which will or may prevent the opponents running the suit.

A guard may be:

(1) Positive: A, KQ, QJ10, J1098.
(2) Probable: KJx, K10x, QJx.
(3) Possible: Qxx, J9xx.
(4) Positional: Kx.
(5) Partial: K, Qx, Jxx, 10xxx.

GUARD SQUEEZE. A squeeze in three suits, in which an opponent holds guards in two suits, and his holding in a third suit prevents declarer from taking a winning finesse.

There are five basic endings, each of which resembles the basic double squeeze position. By contrast with the double squeeze, the guard squeeze takes place when the same opponent controls both isolated menaces, but as compensation the double menace contains finesse possibilities.

NORTH
♠ —
♡ K
◇ K
♣ A x

WEST
♠ —
♡ A
◇ A
♣ Q x

EAST
♠ x
♡ —
◇ —
♣ J x x

SOUTH
♠ A
♡ —
◇ —
♣ K 10 x

South leads the ace of spades, and West is squeezed in three suits. He must discard a club, but South leads a club to the ace (dropping the queen) and finesses the 10 on the way back.

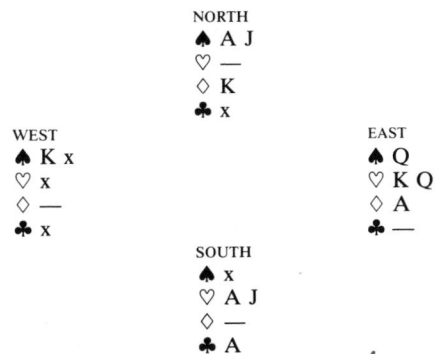

NORTH
♠ A J
♡ —
◇ K
♣ x

WEST
♠ K x
♡ x
◇ —
♣ x

EAST
♠ Q
♡ K Q
◇ A
♣ —

SOUTH
♠ x
♡ A J
◇ —
♣ A

South leads the ace of clubs, and East is squeezed in three suits. If he discards a spade, South can lead that suit, and finesse the jack.

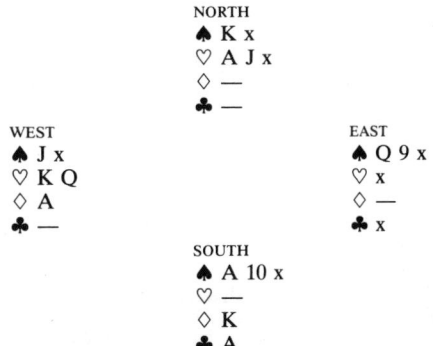

NORTH
♠ K x
♡ A J x
◇ —
♣ —

WEST
♠ J x
♡ K Q
◇ A
♣ —

EAST
♠ Q 9 x
♡ x
◇ —
♣ x

SOUTH
♠ A 10 x
♡ —
◇ K
♣ A

South leads the ace of clubs and West is squeezed in three suits. If he discards a spade, South leads a spade to the king (dropping the jack) and finesses the ten on the way back.

In each of the above positions the squeeze retains its effectiveness even if one of the isolated menaces is guarded by both opponents. This leads to a *double guard squeeze* whose constituents are a guard squeeze against one opponent and a simple squeeze against the other.

There are two other double guard squeeze positions:

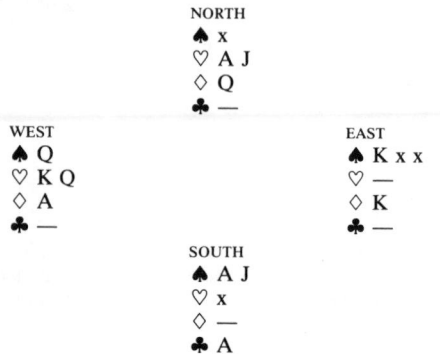

South leads the ace of clubs, and West is squeezed in three suits. He must discard a diamond. Now the ace of hearts squeezes East in spades and diamonds.

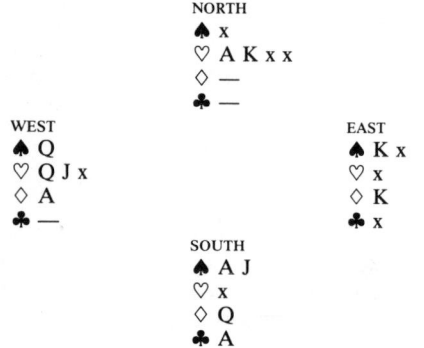

South leads the ace of clubs, and West is squeezed in three suits. He is forced to discard a diamond. South takes two top hearts, squeezing East in spades and diamonds.

See HEXAGON SQUEEZE; HEXAGON TRUMP SQUEEZE; TRUMP SQUEEZE.

M. I.

GUARDED HONOR or GUARDED SUIT. See GUARD.

GUIDE CARD. A card, usually printed, with pre-arranged instructions to each contestant, telling him which seat to occupy and which boards to play at each round. The guide card may also enable a contestant to check the positions and identities of his opponents.

Guide cards may be in the form of printed instruction cards remaining permanently at each table (suitable only for cyclic movements); or they may be in the form of separate cards to be hand-carried by each contestant (suitable for either cyclic or non-cyclic movements).

Guide cards are used for HOWELL MOVEMENT pair games, team games, and individual contests.

H

HALF TABLE. An extra pair at a duplicate game. To accommodate the extra pair, and still keep the game as a fair contest, requires a choice of methods by the director depending on the size of the game and the movement in use. For HOWELL MOVEMENTS, consider the half table as a full table with a PHANTOM PAIR. The phantom pair should be in the stationary position (or in one of the stationary positions in a THREE-QUARTER HOWELL). For MITCHELL MOVEMENTS, this same treatment is satisfactory provided the number of rounds to be played corresponds to the number of tables (including the half table) in play. (When this is an even number, the extra pair should sit East-West at one of the tables where the boards are relayed, thus avoiding the relay.) When the number of rounds to be played is less than the number of tables in play, either a BUMP MITCHELL or a one and one-half APPENDIX TABLE movement is proper. When the number of tables is over fourteen, the customary policy is to divide into two sections; however, the Bump Mitchell can be used, with scores factored up by adding 1/12 for those sitting out one round.

HALF TRICK. An original holding in a suit that will win a trick by virtue of being a high card about half the time. A queen held in company with an ace of the same suit, or a king with a guard, is a half trick on original valuation. The position of adverse bids as the bidding progresses may add to or detract from such a valuation.

HALL OF FAME. A plan for commemorating the achievements of outstanding bridge personalities, suggested by Lee HAZEN, New York, N.Y., and inaugurated in 1964 by *The Bridge World.* The first three members elected were Ely CULBERTSON, Charles GOREN, and Harold VANDERBILT; the next three were Oswald JACOBY, Sidney LENZ, and Milton WORK. The head of each member is cast in bronze, and put on permanent public display.

HAMILTON CLUB (London). One of the leading English card clubs, founded by Col. H. M. Beasley, 1939, in association with Carl Repelaer, who continued to manage the club after Beasley's death in 1949. The club was closed in the early 1970s; it had included among its members leading English players, such as L. Dodds, J. Pavlides, and R. Markus, who contributed to the development of the CAB SYSTEM. The club was regularly visited by American experts.

HAND. (1) A particular deal of fifty-two cards. (2) The cards held by one player. The term is also used to indicate the order in bidding rotation, as in "second hand" or "fourth hand."

HAND DISTRIBUTIONS. See HAND PATTERNS for general and specific distributions. See MATHEMATICAL TABLES for percentage frequency and hand distributions.

HAND HOG. A player who (often mistakenly) feels that he is the best qualified to manage the hands as declarer. The usual method of operation is to pass with minimum opening bids but to respond with jumps in no trump.

HAND PATTERNS. There are 39 possible hand patterns, ranging from the most balanced, 4–3–3–3, to the most unbalanced, 13–0–0–0. A player can hold specifically four spades, three hearts, three diamonds, and three clubs in 13C4 × 13C3 × 13C3 × 13C3 different ways, which computes to 16,726,-464,040 or 2.634% of the 635,013,559,600 hands he could hold (see number of possible hands). This, of course, is not the percentage probability that he will have a 4–3–3–3 hand, because the four card length need not be in spades, but could be in any of the four suits, so the chance of a 4–3–3–3 hand is 10.536%.

A rearrangement of the suits in a particular distributional pattern is termed a "permutation" in the pattern; 4–3–4–2 is a permutation of a 4–4–3–2 pattern. If we use the same letter of the alphabet to indicate the same length in a suit, there are three classes of hands:

A A A B, such as 4–3–3–3 or 4–4–4–1, etc.,
which has 4 permutations
A A B C, such as 4–4–3–2 or 5–5–2–1, etc.,
which has 12 permutations
A B C D, such as 5–4–3–1 or 7–3–2–1, etc.,
which has 24 permutations

Thus, the probability of five spades, four hearts, three diamonds, one club is .539%, but the probability of some 5–4–3–1 distribution is 24 times as great, or 12.931%. For all possible hand patterns, see MATHEMATICAL TABLES, Table 1.

A. T. and R. T.

HAND RECORDS. These records are a part of many important matches. At International matches, a recorder is usually present at every table, recording the bids made by the players, the cards as they are played, and the result of each hand. The board is then taken to another recorder, who makes a record of the actual cards in each of the four hands. A third recorder notes the bidding and play in the room where the replay of the board takes place. The three records are then combined to form the record of the hand.

When boards are twinned (see TWINNING boards) by computer-dealt hands, the players use machine-produced sheets (which can be made available in as many sets as required) that show the cards to be placed in each of the pockets. (Obviously, after putting the cards into the correct pockets, the players do not play that particular hand.) A set of these sheets is then kept as a hand record.

In some tournaments, particularly in Europe, the players make a record of each hand after they have played it on the first round. This card is then placed with the hand in the pocket, and can be used by succeeding players to check whether the cards they hold are the ones that were originally dealt into that hand. Such hand records are known as CURTAIN CARDS.

HANDBOOK, ACBL. See ACBL HANDBOOK.

HANDICAPPED PLAYERS. A number of bridge players have overcome serious physical handicaps to become high-ranking players. There are a number of BLIND PLAYERS who have earned LIFE MASTER status. The late Fred SNITE played from an iron lung. Life Master Mike WILSON, born without arms, uses his toes to sort and play his cards and to keep score.

Outstanding among the many players who participate from wheelchairs is Hermine BARON, who won the MCKENNEY TROPHY in 1964 and 1970, setting a master-point record in 1964. She represented the United States in international competition in 1968.

HANDICAPPING. A method of scoring in which each contestant is given a handicap (plus or minus) based on his previous performance. Handicaps may add to the social enjoyment of club or informal games, particularly among contestants of marked difference in skill. They are never used as the basis of master-point awards. Handicapping is frequently used to make the sale of weaker teams more productive in a CALCUTTA tournament.

An alternate method of handicapping is based on master-point status. For example, players can be debited with 1 percentage point for each step on the master-point ladder, ranging from 1 point for a Junior Master to 6 points for a Life Master. The points for the two players in a partnership are added together, and this percentage is deducted from their match-point score at the end of the session.

HANDLING CARDS. The handling of cards other than a player's own is improper. At duplicate, a player may ask to see his opponent's (or his partner's) card, and the player involved will turn it for him. There are some players who take a hand belonging to another player out of the board after play has been completed in order to discuss a matter of bidding or play. This practice is officially discouraged and is illegal if the opponents are not present. It is the cause of most fouled boards.

HANDS NOT PLAYED OUT. Hands can be concluded before the last trick for various reasons. Frequently declarer will table his hand and make a claim, even as early as after the opening lead. He should then make a statement of how he would play if he actually continued the physical motions of doing so, and if the line he intends to follow seems reasonable to the opposition and is not susceptible of any challenge by them, then the cards can be thrown in. See CLAIM OR CONCESSION BY DECLARER.

HEAD-TO-HEAD. A term used to describe any match in bridge of pre-arranged set opposition; that is, one team of four or more against another of the same number. Use of the term is restricted to two-team contests only.

HEART. The symbol ♡ for the second-ranking suit in bridge. Hearts are between spades and diamonds in value. The suit designation originated in France in the sixteenth century, and takes its name from the shape of the pips used in designating card rank.

HEART SUIT. The second ranking suit, with scarlet pips on each card in the shape of a heart. The suit ranks just below spades in bidding, and above diamonds.

HEART TRICK. A trick in the heart suit.

HEARTBREAKER. A term applied to a hand that fails in a big way to live up to one's original expectations of it. It can be a defensive hand where one has, for example, been dealt cards that enable one to double a certain final contract with the assurance of setting the opponents badly. If, because of the distributional situations or highly expert card play by declarer, the contract is made, then surely the "heartbreaker" term would follow. If, on the other hand, one is declarer at a contract that seems sure of success, and especially if the contract is a slam or a doubled or redoubled game bid, and is unable to make the hand or to avoid a large set in the process, then that hand is often called a "heartbreaker," too. Also applied to a session of duplicate which promises more than it achieves: in a head-to-head team match a pair may outplay their immediate opponents only to find their team score is negative.

HELLENIC BRIDGE FEDERATION. The national bridge organization of Greece, founded in 1965 by two clubs with approximately 320 members; in 1975 it had nine clubs as members, and three as affiliated organizations. The Federation participates in the European Championships, hosting the 1971 event in Athens, and participated in the 1968 World Team Olympiad. National events include Open Pair and Team Championships. Players listed separately are: N. Asmeniadis, G. Carlaftis, S. Delouca, E. Glykis, G. Gorgias, C. Kyriacos, S. Kyriakides, A. Kyriazis, E. Manoussakis, D. Papastavrou, G. Roussos, N. Spiliopoulos, R. Stucker, D. Yalirakis.

Officers, 1975:
President: E. C. Glykis.
Secretary: P. E. Economou, 6, Evripidou, Athens 122, Greece.

HELP SUIT GAME TRY. See WEAK SUIT GAME TRY.

HERBERT NEGATIVE. The idea that a negative response in a variety of situations can be made by making the cheapest possible suit response. It was advocated by Walter HERBERT when he was a member of the Austrian national team, and was applied in many ways in the VIENNA SYSTEM. Some of its many possible applications include: response to FORCING TWO-BID; response to TAKE-OUT DOUBLE; response to ACOL TWO-BID; as a SECOND NEGATIVE response to a strong forcing opening.

HERMAN TROPHY. Awarded to the player with the best overall individual performance record at the Fall Nationals, donated by Mrs. Sally Lipton (formerly Mrs. Lou Herman) of New York, in 1952, in memory of her husband. Winners:

1952	A. Roth	1965	M. Lawrence
1953	J. R. Crawford	1966	C. Coon
1954	P. Hodge	1967	S. Kehela
1955	M. Ellenby	1968	H. Bethe
1956	P. Hodge	1969	S. Stèin
1957	L. Mathe	1970	I. Rubin, *tied with*
1958	S. Stein		C. Burger
1959	M. Rubinow	1971	J. Grantham
1960	O. Jacoby	1972	S. Robinson
1961	P. Feldesman	1973	L. Cohen
1962	M. Miles	1974	F. Hamilton
1963	E. Murray	1975	W. Walvick
1964	H. Rockaway		

HESITATION. See HUDDLE.

HEXAGON SQUEEZE. A double guard squeeze in which each of the three menaces is protected by both opponents. (Analyzed and named by George COFFIN.)

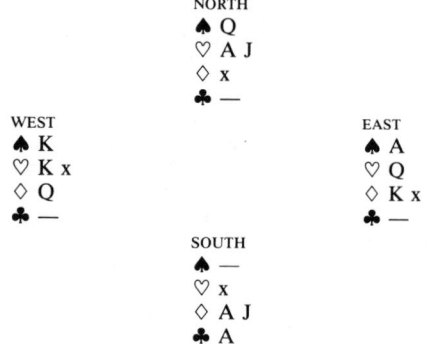

South leads the ace of clubs, and West must discard a spade. North discards a diamond, and East is squeezed in three suits. Once West discards his spade, East is caught in a standard guard squeeze. See also BARCO SQUEEZE.

M. I.

HEXAGON TRUMP SQUEEZE. A HEXAGON SQUEEZE in which both opponents are trump squeezed.

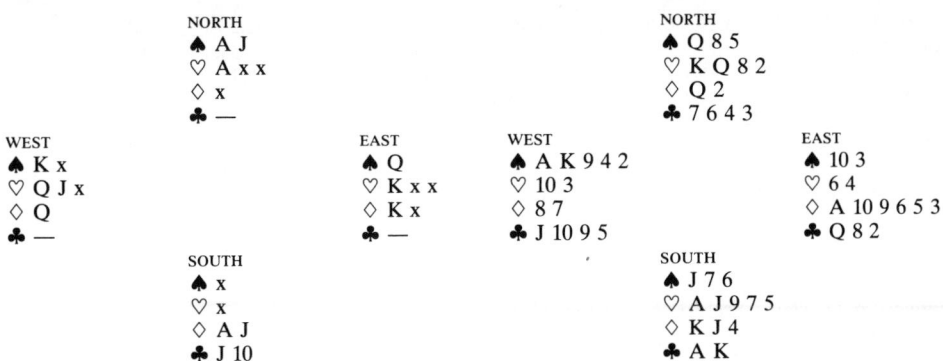

NORTH
♠ A J
♡ A x x
◇ x
♣ —

WEST   EAST
♠ K x   ♠ Q
♡ Q J x   ♡ K x x
◇ Q   ◇ K x
♣ —   ♣ —

SOUTH
♠ x
♡ x
◇ A J
♣ J 10

South is on lead needing all the tricks; clubs are trumps. South leads the jack of clubs. West must discard a heart, dummy can discard a diamond, and East is squeezed in three suits. If East discards a spade, West can be finessed. East obviously cannot discard a diamond, and if he lets go a heart, the ace of hearts and a heart ruff will establish an extra heart trick.

Alternatively, when West discards a heart on the jack of clubs, suppose North and East both discard spades. South leads to the ace of hearts and ruffs a heart. A spade to the ace then squeezes East in hearts and diamonds. In this variation the squeeze of East occurs three tricks later than the squeeze of West.

R. T(rue)

HIDDEN ENTRY. A low card, usually in the dummy hand, by which an entry may be made, usually established as such through the play of unnecessarily high cards by the declarer. Thus, if dummy has A Q 10 6 and declarer K J 9 5, the six may be set up as an entry by playing the king to the same trick as the ace, the jack to the same trick as the queen, and the nine to the same trick as the ten.

HIGH CARD. A ranking card; an honor card; a card that wins a trick by virtue of its being higher in pip value than the other three cards in the trick. A spot card which becomes the master card in the suit is said to be high.

HIGH-CARD TRICK. A term originally used to denote a trick won with an honor. The phrase had some currency in the OFFICIAL SYSTEM.

HIGH-LOW SIGNAL. Known also as echo or come-on, the high-low signal is probably the most important single weapon that the defenders possess in their arsenal of aggressive warfare. In its normal, recurring application, the high-low signal in a suit expresses the desire for a continuation of that suit, or an interest in that suit being played when partner obtains the lead. For example:

Against South's *four heart* contract, West opens the king of spades, dummy plays the five-spot, and East put up the *ten,* South dropping the six. West then continues with the spade ace, upon which East drops the three-spot. Observing that East has played high-low, urging the continuation of the spade suit, West plays a third round of spades, East trumping. The ace of diamonds is then cashed, for the setting trick.

Where the high-low signal is initiated by an unusually high card—such as the ten of spades in the above deal—it is of course rather simple for partner to recognize. But, on frequent occasions, one is not dealt an unusually high card as the top half of the doubleton and is forced to originate the signal with a low card. However, on the continuation of the suit, when a lower card is played, the high-low signal becomes unmistakable. Here is an illustration, taken from a tournament.

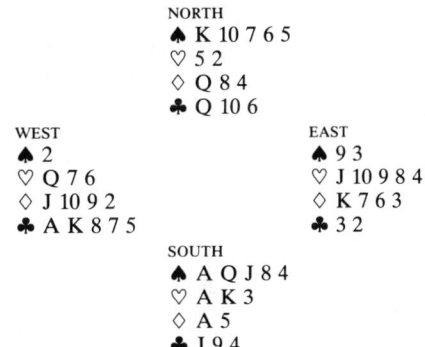

NORTH
♠ K 10 7 6 5
♡ 5 2
◇ Q 8 4
♣ Q 10 6

WEST   EAST
♠ 2   ♠ 9 3
♡ Q 7 6   ♡ J 10 9 8 4
◇ J 10 9 2   ◇ K 7 6 3
♣ A K 8 7 5   ♣ 3 2

SOUTH
♠ A Q J 8 4
♡ A K 3
◇ A 5
♣ J 9 4

Against South's *four spade* contract, West leads the king of clubs, East playing the three-spot. On this trick South drops the jack.

An unobservant West would probably now shift to the jack of diamonds, thereby allowing declarer to fulfill his contract. But our actual West defender observed that the *two* of clubs was missing. Either declarer still had that card, or third-hand had initiated a high-low signal with the three-spot. So West now led the club ace, upon which East played the missing two-spot. A third round of clubs was of course ruffed by East, and the four spade contract was ultimately defeated.

From East's point of view, it would have been nicer to have held, let us say, the 82 of clubs instead of the 32, so that a more violent signal could have been given with the eight-spot. But a high-low signal with the 32 nevertheless accomplished the purpose, thanks to West's observation. For alternative methods of signaling, see ODD-EVEN DISCARDS; UPSIDE-DOWN SIGNALS.

Unfortunately, as with all conventions, the high-low signal is often applied promiscuously, or misapplied, and is given merely because it is the "orthodox" thing to do. One sometimes forgets that the signal is given to get partner to continue the suit led *only* if it will attain an objective for the defenders. Here is an example of the misuse of the high-low signal.

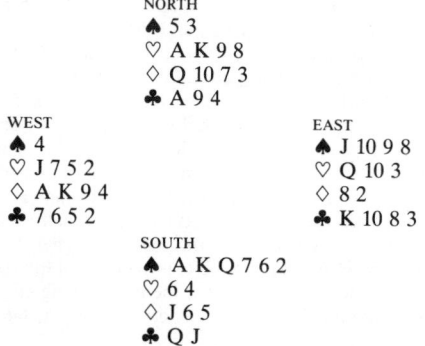

```
                NORTH
                ♠ 5 3
                ♡ A K 9 8
                ◇ Q 10 7 3
                ♣ A 9 4
WEST                              EAST
♠ 4                              ♠ J 10 9 8
♡ J 7 5 2                        ♡ Q 10 3
◇ A K 9 4                        ◇ 8 2
♣ 7 6 5 2                        ♣ K 10 8 3
                SOUTH
                ♠ A K Q 7 6 2
                ♡ 6 4
                ◇ J 6 5
                ♣ Q J
```

West opened the king of diamonds against South's *four spade* contract, and East mechanically played the eight-spot. West then continued with the ace, East dropping the deuce, after which a third diamond was led, East ruffing. From here in declarer had no problem. He drew trumps, and discarded his jack of clubs on dummy's high queen of diamonds.

On the opening lead of the diamond king, East should have played the discouraging deuce, not the eight. What did East have to gain by ruffing the third round of diamonds? Not a thing, since he possessed a natural trump trick which could never be taken away. Had he played the diamond deuce, West, at trick two, would unquestionably have shifted to a club. East would then have made his king of clubs, and declarer would have lost his contract.

There is a conventional situation in which a high-low signal is given not to denote an interest in the suit, but to indicate an *even number* of cards in that suit. This convention is discussed and illustrated in the section entitled LENGTH SIGNALS, but a passing illustration at this point would not be out of order.

It is a rather simple convention, and is most useful when a defensive holdup play must be employed. The setup to which it is applicable is the following:

When it is obvious that declarer is trying to establish a long suit in dummy (which has no outside entries), and that second hand's partner (or second hand himself) is going to have a problem as to when he should take his ace, second hand (or his partner)

gives a high-low signal when holding *two or four* cards of that suit; where second hand has *three* cards of that suit (say, 742), he plays his lowest card (the deuce) on the first lead, and then follows up by playing the next highest (the four). In this latter case, partner will know that the signaler has exactly three cards in that suit, since with two or four he would have given a high-low signal. Here is a practical application of this high-low convention:

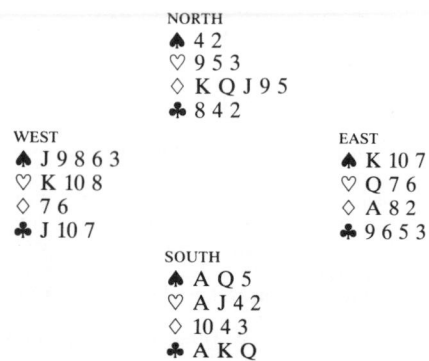

```
                NORTH
                ♠ 4 2
                ♡ 9 5 3
                ◇ K Q J 9 5
                ♣ 8 4 2
WEST                              EAST
♠ J 9 8 6 3                      ♠ K 10 7
♡ K 10 8                         ♡ Q 7 6
◇ 7 6                            ◇ A 8 2
♣ J 10 7                         ♣ 9 6 5 3
                SOUTH
                ♠ A Q 5
                ♡ A J 4 2
                ◇ 10 4 3
                ♣ A K Q
```

Against South's *three no trump* contract, West opened the six of spades, East's king falling to declarer's ace. South then led the ten of diamonds, West played the *seven-spot,* and North and East followed with low diamonds. Declarer then led the four of diamonds, West played the *six-spot,* and dummy's nine captured the trick when East properly declined to take his ace. Declarer now went down a trick, being unable to establish and cash dummy's diamonds.

West's high-low signal (7, 6) had told East that West had either two or four diamonds. That he had four became an impossibility when South led a second diamond, for if West had four diamonds then there were fourteen in the deck. Therefore East knew that West originally held precisely two diamonds, and that declarer still had a diamond left after the second diamond lead. See Lord Henry BENTINCK.

HIGH REVERSE. A non-jump bid in a third suit at the level of three. For example, one spade—two diamonds—three clubs. (This term is English usage, not current in the United States.) See OPENER'S REBID.

HIGHER BID. A bid higher in rank than the last previous bid; a sufficient bid. Usually a higher bid refers to a bid that is merely sufficient, i.e., does not use as much as a full level of bidding space. Where one or more levels of bidding space are used, it is termed a jump, skip, or pre-emptive bid.

HIGHEST SCORE. In American Contract Bridge League competition, several pairs have produced remarkable scores in major National events. S. Garton CHURCHILL and Cecil HEAD held the single-session record with a 77.4% game in the 1948 Life

Masters Pairs until 1963, when Erick MURRAY and Mrs. Agnes GORDON scored 77.9% (506½ match points on a 325 average) in the final session of the Fall Nat'l Mixed Pairs. This was subsequently beaten by Andrew BERNSTEIN and Gene NEIGER, who totaled 244 on a 156 average in the first session of the 1968 Spring Nat'l Open Pairs for 78.2%. For consistency in scoring, it is unlikely any pair can match the performance of Barry CRANE and Dr. John FISHER in the 1970 Spring Nat'l Open Pairs. Averaging 69.5% in the two qualifying rounds and 63.4% in the two final sessions, their winning total of 924 was the highest ever for a four-session pair championship.

In Regional competition, Paul Stern, Detroit–Bob Webber, Farmington, Mich., scored 257 (82.3%) in the Open Pairs at the 1973 Great Lakes Regional, only slightly below the 260 (83.3%)—highest on record for a 156 average game—scored by C. C. WEI–R. ANDERSEN in a single-session game at the 1974 NY Winter Regional.

HILLIARD TROPHY. Awarded for the National Mixed Pair Championship; donated by Mrs. Olga Hilliard in 1931. It was contested at the Fall Nationals until 1946, then transferred to the West Coast and played as part of Bridge Week until 1957, while retaining the status of a National Championship. Since 1958 it has been contested as a two-session event at the Spring Nationals, under which heading past results are listed.

HINDSIGHT. Most bridge players are able to find the perfect bid, the correct line of play, and the killing defense after the hand has been misbid, misplayed, or misdefended at the table. Players who regularly indulge in long discussions of this sort are known as RESULT PLAYERS or second-guessers.

HIPPOGRIFFS. Sometime humorous name of a mythical suit; chiefly used in a celebrated anecdote about a man who dreamed he held a perfect no trump hand with thirteen sure winners against a stranger (Satan), who was in the lead. The Devil then proceeded to run a thirteen-trick set against declarer by cashing all the cards of a weird greenish suit called hippogriffs.

HISTORY OF AMERICAN BRIDGE ASSOCIATION. See AMERICAN BRIDGE ASSOCIATION.

HISTORY OF BRIDGE. Bridge can trace its ancestry at least to the early sixteenth century in England (first reference 1529) and through succeeding centuries when prototype forms of whist were played under such names as triumph, trump, ruff, slamm, ruff and honours, whisk and swabbers, whisk, and whist. "Whisk" may have referred to the rapid action of sweeping up the cards after winning a trick, or "whist" to a call for silence. The game was popular under its modern name of whist by the middle of the seventeenth century, but it was not until 1742 that the first book devoted to whist appeared: Edmond

HOYLE's famous "Short Treatise" (see BIBLIOGRAPHY, A). This rapidly became a best-seller, and many pirated editions appeared immediately afterwards.

Whist maintained its popularity as a fashionable amusement, and in 1834 Lord Henry BENTINCK invented the HIGH-LOW SIGNAL. This was the forerunner of much research and writing by authorities on the game such as Clay, DESCHAPELLES, CAVENDISH, and many others.

The first game of duplicate whist was apparently played in London in 1857, under Cavendish's direction. It was intended to demonstrate the advantage accruing to skillful play, and a team of supposedly good players was deliberately pitted against supposedly poor opposition (there having been no previous criterion for judging them). The "good" players won easily. Cavendish observed that this procedure all but eliminated the luck of the deal, but his pioneering effort was not followed for nearly a quarter of a century.

The United States was slightly ahead of England in extending the duplicate method. A duplicate whist game was played privately in Chicago in 1880, and in a club in New Orleans in 1882. The first interclub match was played in Philadelphia, Pa., in 1883. The first duplicate match in the Old World was probably in Glasgow, Scotland, in 1888.

Duplicate offered the possibility of replacing private play by public contest. Major steps forward were the foundation of the AMERICAN WHIST LEAGUE in 1891; the invention of the Kalamazoo tray (first duplicate board) in the same year; and the first book on tournament organization, written in 1892 by J. T. Mitchell, who devised the first movement for pair play and decribed the method of match-pointing which has been used ever since.

Although the American Whist League was to flourish for some forty years, BRIDGE, the game which eventually led to its decline and fall, had come on the American scene early in the 1890s, at about the time it was also introduced in England. As chronicled by J. B. ELWELL and R. F. FOSTER, the game reached New York in 1893, thanks to Henry I. BARBEY, whose privately printed Laws of Bridge are dated 1892.

In London, the Portland Club began to play bridge in 1894 at the instance of Lord Brougham who had learned it in India from some army officers. (Some say that he learned it during a trip to Egypt.) But, according to a letter published in *Bridge Magazine* in 1932, Frank J. Nathan had played in the "first" English game in 1892 at St. George's Club, Hanover Square. It was introduced by a Colonel Studdy, who said it was of Levantine origin and that he had learned it in the trenches at Plevna during the Russo-Turkish war of 1877–78.

This earlier dating of the game and the probability that it was of Turkish or Russian origin is strongly supported by new evidence uncovered in 1974–75 by R. TRUE, who quotes from a 1904 issue of *Notes and Queries,* a letter from A. M. Keiley (nationality unknown): "I was in 1886 . . . a member of the Khedival Club in Cairo, and bridge was the principal card game played there at my entry and, as members told me, had long so been."

One of the names by which bridge was first known

on the Riviera was *Khedive,* presumably because players had met it in Cairo. Turkey held Egypt almost without interruption from the early sixteenth century until World War I and "Khedive" was the official title held by the Turkish viceroy.

A claim of even earlier existence of the game appears in the introduction to *Modern Bridge* by "Slam" published in London in 1901: "Bridge, known in Turkey as 'Britch,' . . . has been played in South-Eastern Europe . . . ever since the early sixties."

Although there are combinations of Turkish words pronounced somewhat similarly to "biritch," from the evidence thus far uncovered the origin of the name if not of the game seems clearly to be Russian. Both vint and another Russian game called "yeralash" include the no trump feature introduced by bridge, and, according to the rules in the 1886 pamphlet, "biritch" meant the declaration of no trump, with honor bonuses for the holding of three or four aces.

All this makes less plausible than ever the suggestion that the name of the game comes from the fact that the dealer "bridged" the bid when he passed his right of choice to his partner. It seems more likely that the term "I bridge it" when dealer did not wish to say "I make it ——" derived from the name of the game, rather than vice versa.

The pattern of the progress of the game, slow until it reached America and England, suggests that, unlike Whist, which began as a "below-stairs" game played by the serving class, bridge spread through diplomatic circles in such capitals as Constantinople and Cairo.

The origin of the word *bridge,* until recently characterized as "obscure," is often traced to an 1886 pamphlet in the British Museum entitled, "BIRITCH, or Russian Whist." But the clue that was earlier described as "slender"—on the ground that there was no such Russian word nor any game of that name played in Russia—has since gained considerable weight. The word *Biritch* is chronicled in Russian histories from the 10th through the 17th centuries; it meant, among other things, the town crier whose official duty it was to announce government edicts. It appears as "biritch" (accented on the second syllable) in dictionaries of Imperial days. In French, *annoncer* means to bid. Of course one of the major innovations of bridge was that the dealer or his partner had the right to announce or declare the trump suit, or to make it no trump.

An important change from whist was the exposure of one hand (dealer's partner) as the dummy, following the precedent of DUMMY WHIST, originated as a game for three players. According to one popular theory, this idea evolved from a game played first in India by three British officers so isolated they were unable to find a fourth. See THREE-HANDED BRIDGE; NEWGATE.

Another innovation was the introduction of the double and redouble. There was no limit to the number of redoubles, and this "gambling" feature of the new game, soon to be eliminated by the change to

Auction Bridge, was one of the strong arguments against bridge adduced by whist devotees.

The prototypical game of bridge, or bridge whist, had a short life. A great step forward was taken in 1904, when the auction principle was introduced, traditionally in India, possibly in England. Auction bridge grew steadily in popularity until 1927, though only toward the end of this period were auction bridge tournaments organized. For some reason it was believed that the duplicate principle, long popular among whist players, was not suitable for bridge.

The next major change may have been developed in France, where the game of PLAFOND was played in 1918 and perhaps earlier. A similar game, S.A.C.C., was described by Sir Hugh CLAYTON as having been "invented" in India in 1912, and similar games had been tried in the United States before 1915. In all such games each side had to bid to its "plafond" or ceiling: only tricks bid and made counted toward game. This variation rapidly became the standard French game, but did not succeed elsewhere in spite of occasional experiments.

Up to this point whist, bridge, auction, and plafond had simply grown, which is generally the way with card games. No individual can be given credit for inventing the dummy, the idea of bidding, the auction principle, or the ceiling principle of plafond. But in 1925 Harold S. VANDERBILT perfected a new form of the game, embodying the plafond principle but including the element of vulnerability and producing a scoring table that corrected the major faults in plafond. He succeeded so well that his game of "contract bridge" became the staple diet of card players everywhere. Afterward, he wrote:

Many years of experience playing games of the Whist family were, I think, a necessary prelude to acquiring the background and knowledge needed to evolve the game of Contract Bridge. Starting as a young boy about 70 years ago, I have played successively over the years Whist, Bridge, Auction Bridge, and Plafond.

. . . I compiled in the autumn of 1925 a scoring table for my new game. I called it Contract Bridge and incorporated in it, not only the best features of Auction and Plafond, but also a number of new and exciting feaures; premiums for slams bid and made, vulnerability, and the decimal system of scoring which by increasing both trick and game values and all premiums and penalties was destined to add enormously to the popularity of Contract Bridge.

An ideal opportunity to try out my new game presented itself while I was voyaging shortly after completing my scoring table with three Auction Bridge playing friends on board the steamship *Finland* from Los Angeles to Havana via the Panama Canal, a nine-day trip.

. . . At first, we were at a loss for a term, other than "game in," to describe the status of being subject to higher penalties because of having won a game. Fortunately for us, a young lady on board the *Finland* solved that problem by suggesting the word "vulnerable." . . .

We enjoyed playing my new game on board the *Finland* so much that, on my return to New York, I gave typed copies of my scoring table to several of my Auction Bridge playing friends. I made no other effort to popularize or publicize Contract Bridge. Thanks apparently to its excellence, it popularized itself and spread like wildfire.

No world-popular game in history—certainly none in the Whist family—can so accurately pinpoint its conception and the first time it was ever played. Recent research has established that the *Finland* reached Balboa on October 31, 1925, too late to proceed through the Canal or for passengers to go ashore. Francis Bacon III, in 1975 the sole surviving member of Vanderbilt's foursome, recalls that on that night the lady who suggested "vulnerable" was allowed to join their game of plafond and attempted to suggest some exotic and impractical changes based on a game she said she had played in China. This so irritated Vanderbilt that the next day, while the *Finland* passed through the Canal, he worked out the scoring table for contract which, except for no trump tricks then being valued at 35 points each, remained virtually unchanged half a century later. On that night, November 1, the game became Contract Bridge, scored under Vanderbilt's new rules.

Within two years, three codes of laws had been produced for the new game. Those of R. F. FOSTER and the Knickerbocker Whist Club (both 1927) were withdrawn in favor of the more authoritative code issued by the WHIST CLUB of New York. In 1928 the game was adopted in the major New York clubs, and late that year the first National Championship was held, with the VANDERBILT CUP as the prize.

In 1929 the American Auction Bridge League dropped the word "Auction" from its title and it became clear that contract had supplanted auction. The established auction authorities struggled to achieve expertise in the field of contract, but for the most part unsuccessfully. Leadership in the new game went to Ely CULBERTSON, who founded the first contract magazine in 1929 (*Bridge World*) and wrote his celebrated *Blue Book* in 1930. This revolutionary work set out the principles of approach-forcing bidding which became the nucleus of all modern standard systems.

Thanks to a thriving organization which exploited every phase of bridge activity and to his natural flair for publicity exhibited notably in the CULBERTSON-LENZ MATCH, Culbertson retained his leadership throughout the 1930s, untroubled by the tournament successes of the FOUR ACES.

Culbertson's interest and enthusiasm declined, and in the 1940s the leadership passed to Charles GOREN, who achieved great success by adapting Culbertson's methods to point-count valuation.

The growth of tournament bridge was hampered in the 1930s by the simultaneous activity of three separate organizing bodies, the AMERICAN BRIDGE LEAGUE, the AMERICAN WHIST LEAGUE, and the UNITED STATES BRIDGE ASSOCIATION. But from 1937 onward the AMERICAN CONTRACT BRIDGE LEAGUE had the field

to itself, and there followed a period of steady growth stimulated by the master-point plan.

1935 became the year of the first recognized World Championship, although several semi-official international matches had been played earlier. Later landmarks on the international scene were the first of the postwar World Championship series in 1950, the foundation of the WORLD BRIDGE FEDERATION in 1958, and the first team Olympiad in 1960.

The only major innovation in contract bridge during its first forty years of existence was the development of CHICAGO, the four-deal game which displaced traditional rubber bridge in many clubs during the early 1960s. But this, like contract bridge itself, was a change in scoring rather than in structure, and there have been few radical changes in the game nor do any seem likely in the immediate future.

HISTORY OF PLAYING CARDS. The earliest known cards were used in China, at least as long ago as 969 A.D. The pack was divided into four suits, fourteen cards in each, and was used for paper money as well as for games. This discredits the pleasant story that they were invented in 1120 A.D. to amuse the concubines of the Emperor Suen-ho. There is a tradition that a Venetian carried cards from China to his native city, the first place in Europe where they were known. This traveler may have been Niccolo Polo, who returned from China about 1269 with his brother Matteo, or it may have been Niccolo's son, the famed Marco, who accompanied his father and uncle on their second trip to that empire.

Some authorities favor India over China as the original source. A tenuous link has been suggested between early European cards and Ardhanari, the goddess of Hindu mythology. She was represented holding in her four hands a wand, a cup, a sword, and a ring (symbolizing money). Similar symbols appeared on some early European playing cards. One discredited theory suggests that cards were brought to Europe by the Gypsies, who may have belonged originally to an Indian race. They have been traced through Persia and Arabia into Egypt and then to Europe, and a body of over a hundred entered Paris in August 1427 (Pasquier: *Recherches Historiques*).

However, this date is too late to be significant. Cards were manufactured in many parts of Europe, notably in Nuremberg, Augsburg, and Ulm, in the fourteenth century, and perhaps even earlier. The Italian TAROT cards may have predated the German cards: they are mentioned in an Italian manuscript dated 1299. Johanna, Duchess of Brabant mentions cards in the Netherlands in 1379, and cards were known in Spain at least as early as 1371. The Moors or Saracens may have brought cards to Spain and Italy, but the attempt to show a resemblance between the Spanish word for cards (*naipes*) and the Arabic word (*nabi*, "a prophet"), is not well founded.

In 1392 in France, the monarch Charles VI ordered a hand-painted deck to be made by Jacquemin Gringonneur, and this historical fact gave rise to the

GROUP I

Cards designed
to avoid revoke.

New Index

Fassett's (England)

Nu fashion

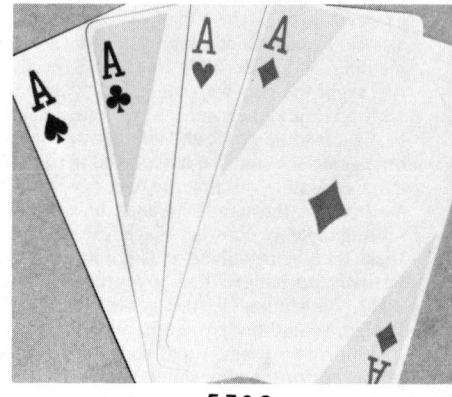

E-Z-2-C

GROUP II

Cards with artistic designs
replacing standard faces.

*All playing cards shown
from the collection
of Albert Field*

St. Hubert's (France)

De la Rue (England)

American Civil War

GROUP III

Cadine   *Hunt*

Two Queens—*Cadine:* On hand-made laid paper, printed from wood blocks and colored by stencil.

Jack and Ace—*Hunt:* The ace of spades indicating the tax paid per pack. These also are wood block. The aces were engraved by the government.

Samuel Hart & Co.: Indices were not used regularly on cards until about 1870. This pack is assumed to have been made about 1860.

Russell & Morgan: Made by the predecessor company of U. S. Playing Cards, this is one of the latest non-indexed cards.

GROUP IV

Round cards: have been intermittently made since 1874. The *concave* cards appeared in 1929. The *trapezoid* cards were produced in 1952, and the *barrel* cards are of modern English design. The *clipped* edges are French.

French: The basic design of the face cards was decided by Napoleon and has been followed ever since with artistic liberties being taken in recent times. The French name all their face cards. Note the double indices. (Most French who play bridge use copies of the cards common to the United States and England.)

German: German suits are leaves, bells, acorns, and hearts. The face cards are King, Ober, and Unter. Only in the last few years have indices been added.

Swiss: The Swiss use either the French pack or their own version of the German pack consisting of acorns, bells, flowers, and shields. The ten is on a flag.

Italian: There are at least ten different packs used in Italy. This is known as Venete and the suits are cups, swords, cudgels, and coins.

idea that cards originated in France. However, it seems clear that this order was for cards similar to others already in use. The royal treasurer, accounting for moneys paid out, mentions three packs of cards, painted "in gold and diverse colors, ornamented with many devices, for the diversion of our Lord, the King." Seventeen of these cards are on exhibition at the Bibliothèque Nationale (see COLLECTIONS OF PLAYING CARDS).

Cards probably reached England later than the other European countries. Chaucer, who died in 1400, never mentions cards, although he enumerates the amusements of the day: "They dance and they play at chess and tables." The reference to playing with four kings in the Wardrobe Rolls of Edward I in 1278 ("ad ludendum ad quattuor regis") almost certainly refers to some other game, perhaps a form of chess. The earliest clear-cut reference to playing cards in England dates from 1465, when manufacturers of playing cards petitioned Edward IV for protection against foreign imports, and were favored by an appropriate edict.

"There is a legend telling how the sailors with Columbus," writes C. P. Hargrave in *A History of Playing Cards,* "who were inveterate gamblers, threw their cards overboard in superstitious terror upon encountering storms in these vast and mysterious seas. Later, on dry land they regretted their rashness, and in the new country made other cards out of the leaves of the copys tree, which greatly interested the Indians." This seems to be more than a legend, for Garcilaso de la Vega (*Historia de la Florida,* Madrid, 1723) tells that the soldiers of Spain played with leather cards in the 1534 expedition. Cards were known to the early Mexicans as *amapatolli,* from *amatl* meaning paper and *patolli* meaning game.

The present pack of fifty-two cards, arranged in two black and two red suits, probably derived from the early Italian TAROT packs, in which there were four suits with ten SPOT CARDS and four COURT CARDS—KING, QUEEN, CAVALIER, and KNAVE. The queen was not included in early packs, and the chevalier still holds her position in some modern packs (see PACK). The knave has been variously represented by a VALET, and still carries this name, although modern usage changes it to the JACK. The chevalier, as apart from the queen, has been dropped from the fifty-two-card pack.

The Chinese playing cards differ considerably from the occidental; they are long and narrow, usually 2 to 2½ inches long and ½ to 1 inch wide, early cards longer and even narrower. In number of suits and cards, both the Chinese and Hindu decks differ markedly from ours. One Hindu deck includes 144 cards with eight suits of eighteen cards, another has 120 cards with ten suits of twelve cards; one Chinese deck has only thirty cards, three suits of nine cards and three extra cards of supreme value, but four suits were normal.

Long before bridge was heard of, playing cards were used in many forms of gambling and in fortune-telling, and acquired an unsavory reputation, being associated with all vices. The DEVIL'S PICTURE BOOK

and other names indicate the horror with which they were regarded by the virtuous and religious.

Playing cards, as a luxury, provided a source for much revenue in TAXES, first levied on them in England in 1615.

For information about the MANUFACTURE OF PLAYING CARDS at the present time, see that heading.

HIT. Slang used as two distinct transitive verbs: (1) To double. (2) To ruff.

HOLD. (1) To possess (a certain card or cards). (2) To win or guarantee the winning of a trick (by the play of a certain card). Thus, if partner plays the king when you hold the ace, and no ruff is impending, the king is said to hold the trick unless you decide to overtake it.

HOLD OFF. To refuse to play a winning card. See DUCK and HOLD UP.

HOLD UP. The "hold-up play" is the refusal to win a trick in order to maintain control of the suit which an opponent has led until such time as the control can be relinquished with comparative safety. Although there can be various reasons for the desire and necessity of maintaining control, one practical motive stands out above all others: to break the communication between the opponents' hands—that is, to eliminate from one of the opponents' hands the suit which has been led, so that if the devoided one obtains the lead subsequently, he will be unable to play back his partner's suit.

In this section, the hold-up play is discussed from the viewpoint of the declarer only. The play is also utilized by the defensive side, e.g., dummy, at a three no trump contract, possesses ♠52, ♡63, ◇632, ♣KQJ1092, and a defender, holding, for example, the A76 of clubs, holds up his ace long enough to prevent the establishment and cashing of dummy's club suit. See LENGTH SIGNALS.

The hold-up play is most frequently employed by declarer at no trump contracts, although there are many situations where it is also used to good advantage in suit contracts.

Let us examine a few illustrations of the hold-up play in action.

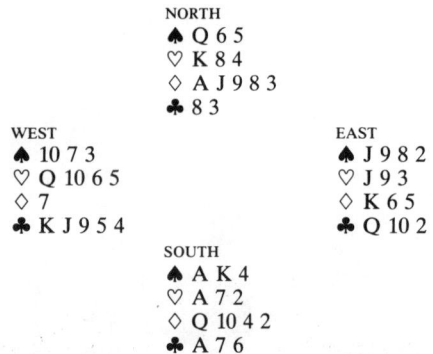

NORTH
♠ Q 6 5
♡ K 8 4
◇ A J 9 8 3
♣ 8 3

WEST
♠ 10 7 3
♡ Q 10 6 5
◇ 7
♣ K J 9 5 4

EAST
♠ J 9 8 2
♡ J 9 3
◇ K 6 5
♣ Q 10 2

SOUTH
♠ A K 4
♡ A 7 2
◇ Q 10 4 2
♣ A 7 6

Against South's three no trump contract, West opens

the five of clubs, East puts up the queen, and South employs the hold-up play, declining to take the ace. East continues with the ten of clubs, and once again South plays low, West overtaking with the jack. West then leads a third round of clubs, declarer winning with the ace. Clubs have now been eliminated from the East hand.

The diamond finesse is then tried, East taking the trick with the king. Whatever East returns, declarer will win and capture the remainder of the tricks.

It is apparent that if declarer had taken the first or second club trick, he would have been defeated. From this deal, it will be observed that the hold-up play is actually the counter-attack to the normal opening lead (against no trump contracts) of the fourth-best in the longest suit. The hold-up is based on the assumption that the leader usually has more cards in the suit led than does his partner; and each time declarer declines to win successive leads in that suit, the leader's partner, who started with few cards in that suit, must play another and another, until he finally has none left; and is "non-dangerous" when he later obtains the lead.

In a no trump contract, the hold-up play is designed to protect in all situations where the adversely led suit is divided in such a fashion that the opening leader has the greater number. When the suit that is led is divided evenly, say 4–4, the declarer requires no protection, since only three tricks will be lost in that suit (whether he captures the first, second, or third lead), plus one trick in the suit which he is going to establish (diamonds in the above deal). In this deal, had the eight adverse clubs been divided 4–4, any player would have fulfilled the three no trump contract. And if the diamond king were favorably located, again everybody would have made his contract whether he held up or not.

Thus, the hold-up play is what one might call comprehensive insurance; it takes care of everything: a bad division of the suit led, and a key card being adversely located.

Against a suit contract, especially when an opponent has overcalled, declarer sometimes has to guess whether or not to employ the hold-up play. For example:

NORTH
♠ 9 5 2
♡ A J 10 6
♢ 8
♣ K Q 7 5 3

SOUTH
♠ A 7 3
♡ Q 9 3
♢ A 4
♣ A J 10 6 4

The bidding:

SOUTH	WEST	NORTH	EAST
1 ♣	1 ♠	2 ♡	Pass
2 NT	Pass	4 ♣	Pass
4 ♡	Pass	5 ♣	Pass
Pass	Pass		

West, having overcalled in spades, opens the king of spades, and South has a rough problem. Shall he take the king, or shall he hold up? If West has the king of hearts, then no matter what declarer elects to do, he will come out all right, since he will in this case have no losers in hearts, diamonds, or clubs. But if East has the king of hearts, then the success of declarer's contract depends on his ability to diagnose whether East started with one or two spades.

If West has six spades, then if declarer wins the opening lead, draws trumps, and takes a heart finesse which loses to East, the latter will have no spade to play back. Declarer will now be able to discard one of his losing spades on dummy's fourth heart. Of course, if West has six spades, and declarer declines to win the opening lead, East will ruff the second spade—and East's king of hearts will ultimately become the setting trick.

But if West started with five spades (and East with two), then it becomes imperative for declarer to refuse to win the opening lead. If he doesn't, then when East wins the heart king, he will return his remaining spade, and West will make two spade tricks. If declarer does hold up, then when he wins the spade continuation at trick two, East will have no more spades. Declarer will now fulfill his contract.

As is obvious, it is a pure guess as to whether to win the first spade lead or "hold up" instead.

In duplicate bridge, the issue of whether to hold up or not can be a most difficult one to decide. Here is an example:

NORTH
♠ 9 7
♡ A 8 3
♢ K Q 10
♣ A J 10 9 5

SOUTH
♠ A 4 3
♡ K 6 5
♢ A J 8 3
♣ Q 8 7

With no adverse bidding, South arrives at a three no trump contract. West leads the six of spades, and East puts up the queen.

In rubber bridge, there would be no problem whatsoever. The ace would be held up until the third round, and this would just about guarantee the contract, regardless of the location of the club king.

But at match-points, the decision as to whether to hold up or not is not an easy one to make. If West has the club king, twelve tricks are there for the taking. If one plays safe, and holds up the spade ace for two rounds, then only eleven tricks will be made if the club finesse is successful. And if other North-South pairs choose to gamble on this deal for twelve tricks, the hold up will get a bad match-point score.

However, if the club king is held by East, then by taking the first or second club declarer might well go down at three no trump.

Probably the best course of action is to hold up on the first spade lead, and see what East plays back. This hold up cannot prove costly, since declarer can't ever make thirteen tricks. If East should return, let us say, the deuce of spades, then declarer should take it, for if the deuce is East's fourth best, then declarer will make nine tricks, since the eight adversely held spades will then be divided 4–4. And if the two of spades is East's remaining spade, then declarer will make either eleven or twelve tricks, depending on which opponent has the club king.

If, at trick two, East plays back, let us say, the ten of spades, probably declarer should hold up again. In this case, there is a real danger that West started with five spades, and East with three spades. And, in this latter situation, while holding up twice, declarer hopes that the club finesse loses, so that his technically correct rubber bridge play may receive its just deserts.

F. K.

HOLDING. (1) The cards one is dealt in a particular suit, as in the expression, "a club holding of king, queen, and two little." (2) A descriptive term used in reckoning one's entire hand, and often used in the question, "What would you bid holding five spades to the ace-queen, etc.?"

HOLLAND. See NETHERLANDS BRIDGE LEAGUE.

HOLLANDAISE. See GOULASH.

HOME TOWN RULING. An action by the director which accepts the credibility of players personally known to him as opposed to others from distant parts; the type of ruling sometimes given by club directors in favor of regular participants in the games as opposed to occasional drop-ins comes in this category and is even less defensible. Application of the published rules from the rule book for any and all players must in the long run provide the fairest competition and the most enjoyable game.

HONG KONG CONTRACT BRIDGE ASSOCIATION. Founded in 1951 by J. M. Remedios, E. M. Marchetti, and V. J. Zirinsky, with a nucleus of Hong Kong social clubs, by 1968 its membership was approximately 100. The Association was one of the original members of the Far East Bridge Federation and annually sends teams to compete in the Far East Championships. Hong Kong hosted the event in 1960, 1965, and 1973, and won the Far East Championships in 1959 and 1960. National events held annually are Open Teams, Masters Teams, Open Pairs, Masters Pairs, and Mixed Pairs. Hong Kong players listed separately are: Y. M. Chu, Y. T. Fong, H. Kuai, L. A. Ozorio, M. C. Siu, L. L. Sung, G. Tsiang, V. Zirinsky.

Officers, 1968:
Chairman: Leslie L. Sung
Vice-Chairman: V. J. Zirinsky, P.O. Box 1445, Hong Kong.

HONOR. One of the five top cards in a suit at bridge. An ace, king, queen, jack, or ten can properly be described as an honor.

HONOR CRASHING PLAYS. See CRASHING HONORS and DECEPTIVE PLAY.

HONOR LEAD. The lead of an honor, usually the top one of a sequence. The lead of an honor conventionally indicates possession of one or more lower touching honors, the exception being the lead of the king, which may be made from an ace-king or king-queen holding. The purpose of the honor lead is usually to establish the cards directly beneath it. In the middle game, the lead of an unsupported honor card is often correct.

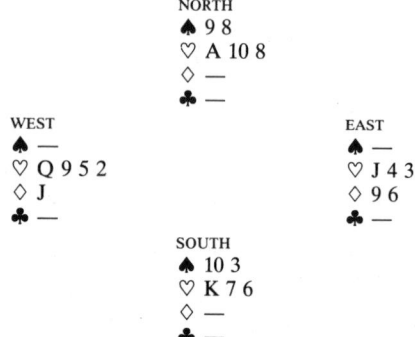

Spades are trump, and West is on lead and forced to open up the hearts. The queen is the proper play, for if he leads a low card, South simply plays the eight from dummy, forcing the jack from East. On the next round he has a simple finesse position with dummy's ace-ten over West's queen.

<pre>
        DUMMY (N)
        K 9 8
WEST
J 6 4 3
</pre>

West is on lead and has no further card of entry. Requiring three tricks fom this suit, he must lead the jack, hoping that his partner has ace, queen, ten.

See also INTERIOR SEQUENCE; JOURNALIST LEADS; OPENING LEAD; RUSINOW LEAD; ZERO OR TWO HIGHER LEADS.

HONOR SCORE. An extra bonus in rubber bridge and in CHICAGO scored above the line when claimed by a player (declarer, dummy, or defender) who held during the current deal any of certain honor card holdings in the trump suit as follows: For holding any four of the five top trump honors—100 points. For all five trump honors—150 points. For all the aces at no trump—150 points. Honors are not scored at duplicate except in total-point team-of-four play. See LAWS OF CONTRACT BRIDGE (Law 84), LAWS OF DUPLICATE (Law 73).

HONOR STRENGTH. The trick-taking value of a hand in honor tricks. This was of great importance as a basis for calculation of the power of a hand in the CULBERTSON SYSTEM.

HONOR TRICK. A unit of defensive valuation of honor cards and combinations. It is, of course, a combination which may also be expected to win a trick on the offensive. Valuations of combinations were made in accordance with the following table in the CULBERTSON SYSTEM:

2 HT	A K
1½ HT	A Q
1 HT	A, K Q, K J 10
½ HT	K x, Q J x
+ values	any queen (but not a singleton)
(about ¼ HT)	any jack combined with another honor (but no singleton or doubleton, and not A K Q J) any singleton or void (not more than one)

See DEFENSIVE TRICK and QUICK TRICK.

HONORARY MEMBERS. A title awarded by the American Bridge League and American Contract Bridge League. This title is awarded for long and meritorious service to the League.

ABL

1927	M. Work	1933	A. E. Manning-Foster
1928	W. Whitehead	1934	P. H. Sims
1929	Maurice Maschke	1935	N. S. Kelly
1930	E. Faber	1936	N. Spingold
1931	W. von Zedtwitz	1937	P. Steiner
1932	E. J. Tobin		

ACBL

1938	E. Culbertson	1956	G. Alderton, II
1939	H. Jaeger	1957	A. Landy
1940	Comdr. Corley	1958	L. Hazen
1941	H. Vanderbilt	1959	Dr. A. M. Dye
1942	Maj. Clarence Wyatt		C. Goren
1943	R. Baldwin	1960	T. Stoddard
1944	Gen. A. Gruenther	1961	C. Solomon
1945	Gen. R. Gill	1962	J. Simon
1946	A. Morehead	1963	B. Lebhar, Jr.
	M. O'Brien Bailey		M. Manchester
1947	B. Golder	1964	J. Glick
	Mrs. J. Baird	1965	S. B. Fink
1948	S. Barclay	1966	H. Fishbein
	A. Mouat	1967	O. Jacoby
	Mrs. A. Rutherford	1968	F. Westcott
1949	A. Sobel	1969	S. Stayman
1950	Dr. L. Mark	1970	J. Rosenblum
1951	J. Baird	1971	J. Stedem
1952	R. L. Miles, Jr.	1972	Mrs. S. Smith
1953	C. Reisinger	1973	Mrs. K. Buckman
1954	F. Snite, Jr.	1974	Mrs. L. Durham
1955	G. Beynon	1975	Mrs. P. Moody

HONORS. The five highest ranking cards in each suit; specifically, for the purpose of scoring honor premiums, the ace, king, queen, jack, and ten of the trump suit, or the four aces at no trump, are honors. See LAWS (Law 84), LAWS OF DUPLICATE (Law 73).

HOOK. Colloquialism for FINESSE.

HORSE AND HORSE. Slang term for both sides vulnerable.

HOSPITALITY. The general term for efforts by a host unit at a bridge tournament to make the players feel more comfortable and welcome. Among the forms that hospitality takes are souvenir programs and pencils; free orange juice (at Florida tournaments), coffee, or cokes; after-game refreshments; between-sessions buffets and even dinners; after-session dancing; morning tours to places of local interest; style shows and brunches; panel discussions; daily bulletins, etc.

HOUSE PLAYER. A player at a bridge club who is available for making up tables and for joining tables when a member wishes to leave. Generally house players receive some compensation for their services to the club, but arrangements vary from club to club regarding winnings or losings at play. Some clubs have a few regular players who make themselves available to help in forming tables in exchange for remission of fees for their play.

HOUSE RULES. Additions or amendments to the LAWS as required to meet conditions of play in a club or group. Proper subjects for house rules would be the posting of deposits to guarantee losses in rubber bridge games, clothing or dress rules, rules for cutting in to existent games, eligibility to play, pivoting regulations when time for play is limited, termination time of the game, etc.

HOWARD TROPHY. See PRESIDENT'S CUP.

HOWELL MOVEMENT. A method of producing one winner from a field at duplicate in which all pairs play each of the boards in play, with comparison in direct competition with other pairs on approximately half of the boards, and adverse comparison on the other boards. Because of the requirement that all pairs be met in head-on competition, the movement is not practical for many of the possible number of tables.

The four-table, five-table, six-table, and seven-table movements (requiring seven rounds of four boards, nine rounds of three boards, eleven rounds of two boards, and thirteen rounds of two boards, respectively) provide excellent competition. Starting assignments for these movements are given below, and positions and boards for each round subsequent can be got by the following rules: the highest numbered pair remains stationary throughout; each other pair replaces the pair with the next lower number for their next seat, with number 1 replacing the pair with the next to the highest number. Boards progress so that each table plays the boards in ascending order.

There are as many sets of boards in play during the session as there are rounds to be played. The extra sets are on a bye stand behind the highest numbered table. From here they are fed into the last table, and the boards at the bye stand are replenished from table 1. Note the special bye stand layout with four tables.

For eight to twelve tables, see THREE-QUARTER MOVEMENT. See also SHORT HOWELL.

Table 1		Table 2		Table 3		Table 4		Table 5		Table 6		Table 7	
Prs.	Bds.	Prs.	Bds.	Prs.	Bds.	Prs.	Bds.	Prs.	Bds.	Prs.	Bds.	Prs.	Bds.
8v1	1	3v6	4	2v7	6	5v4	7						
7v3	1	5v2	2	10v1	3	9v8	4	4v6	5				
12v1	1	6v7	4	11v4	6	3v9	8	2v5	9	10v8	11		
5v12	1	2v4	2	9v10	3	14v1	4	8v13	5	7v11	6	6v3	7

HUDDLE. A pause of longer than usual preceding an action in the bidding (usually) or the play of a hand. If the huddle is followed by a positive action, usually no harm is done to the opponents. However, the ethics of the game (all information is to be conveyed by the bids made, not the manner of making them) require that the partner of the huddler does not take cognizance of the information that the huddler "had a problem." See SLOW PASS.

One of the situations that used to cause difficulties was the problem that a player had after a pre-emptive bid on his right. Many hands seemed too good to pass, but did not offer a clear-cut alternative action. A huddle and following pass created an ethical problem for the partner. Should he take action on some sort of miscellaneous holding or not? Partner's huddle has reduced the danger that the right-hand opponent holds a powerful defensive hand. This frequently recurring problem was answered in the United States by the "skip-bid warning rule," which puts the player following the pre-empter under the obligation to take a huddle at all times when a skip-bid has been made so that his partner will have no ethical problem in connection with a valid huddle holding.

Players should strive for a rhythm in the tempo of bidding in order to obviate the necessity of huddling.

In the play, a hesitation by one defender will often reveal that he holds a key card. In that case his partner is not necessarily barred from making the indicated play, but should satisfy himself before doing so that he would have had sound technical reasons for playing in the same way without any hesitation.

A hesitation in the play when there is no possible reason to think (e.g., when playing a singleton, or when following suit with insignificant small cards) is an offense against the proprieties. In such cases the director may award an adjusted score under Law 12. However, the Laws in this matter are open to two interpretations. The statement that a player takes advantage of hesitations at his own risk is significant. See RHYTHM and SKIP-BID WARNING.

HUNGARIAN BRIDGE ASSOCIATION (BUDAPESTI BRIDZS EGYESULET). Revived in 1963 for organizing National Championships and international matches with Poland and Czechoslovakia, in 1975 there were approximately 600 members. In the prewar years Hungary was one of the dominant teams in the European Championships, winning the title in 1934 and 1938 and finishing second in 1935 and 1936. From 1939 to 1969 it did not participate in this tournament, but in 1968 the Association joined the European Bridge League and has participated since

that time. The Hungarian National Championships are held during the winter and there are regional championships during the summer. Players listed separately are: E. Alpár, R. Cohen, R. Darvas, L. Décsi, G. Ferenczy, Dr. G. Góth, I. Kaufman, A. Keleti, L. Klór, L. Kovács, F. von Leitner, L. Linczmayer, G. Ottlik, Dr. F. Proniewicz, Dr. T. Vég, Dr. L. Widder. P. Zankay.

Officers, 1975:
President: Gyorgy Antal.
General Secretary: Agoston Villanyi.
Foreign Relations Officer: Gabor Salgo, Hungarian News Agency MTI, H–1426 POB 3– Budapest, Hungary.

HYBRID SCORING. To combine the best features of IMP scoring and BOARD-A-MATCH scoring in team games where only short matches occur between two teams, a form of scoring has been developed by the ENGLISH BRIDGE UNION.

Three-board matches. A total of 10 points at stake in each match, divided as follows: 2 points for winning the board (ties on a board are awarded 1 each) for a total of 6 points. The additional 4 points to be awarded based on aggregate score, divided as follows:

$$0\text{–}240 \text{ divide } 2\text{–}2$$
$$250\text{–}490 \text{ divide } 3\text{–}1$$
$$500 \text{ and over, } 4\text{–}0$$

Four-board matches. A total of 13 points at stake in each match, divided as follows: 2 points for winning the board, for a total of 8 points. The additional 5 points based on aggregate score:

$$0\text{–}340 \text{ divide } 2\tfrac{1}{2}\text{–}2\tfrac{1}{2}$$
$$350\text{–}590 \text{ divide } 3 \ \text{–}2$$
$$600\text{–}990 \text{ divide } 4 \ \text{–}1$$
$$1{,}000 \text{ and over, } 5 \ \text{–}0$$

Five-board matches. A total of 16 points at stake, in each match, divided as follows: 10 points for boards won at 2 points per board, the additional 6 points based on aggregate score:

$$0\text{– } 440 \text{ divide } 3\text{–}3$$
$$450\text{– } 740 \text{ divide } 4\text{–}2$$
$$750\text{–}1{,}240 \text{ divide } 5\text{–}1$$
$$1{,}250 \text{ or over, } 6\text{–}0$$

A difference of 10 points on a board is considered to be a tie, as in IMP scoring, rather than a win, as in board-a-match scoring.

An alternate method of dividing the extra points based on aggregate score, when not all boards are played by all contesting teams, is as follows:

Add the net score on each of the boards to obtain

total aggregate score (this is without regard to whether the score is plus or minus).

Compute the net aggregate score as a percentage of the total aggregate score, and convert to VICTORY POINTS on the basis of:

0–5%	2	–2
over 5–10%	2½–1½	
over 10–15%	3	–1
over 15–25%	3½–	½
over 25%	4	–0

This scale was used in four-board matches in competition for the English Bridge Union's Pachabo Cup.

I

IBL. INTERNATIONAL BRIDGE LEAGUE.

IBM NUMBER. See PLAYER NUMBER.

IBPA. INTERNATIONAL BRIDGE PRESS ASSOCIATION.

ICELANDIC BRIDGE UNION (BRIDGE-SAM-BAND ISLANDS). Founded in 1948 by six of the leading bridge clubs in Iceland, and in 1974 there were approximately 1,200 members. The Union participates frequently in European Championships, finishing third in the 1950 event in Brighton, and also in the Scandinavian Championships, finishing third in 1966. In its first appearance in a World Team Olympiad 1968, Iceland finished tenth. Icelandic players listed separately are: J. Asbjornsson, P. Bergsson, H. Eliasson, S. Gudjohnsen, G. Gudmundsson, L. Karlsson, A. Palsson, T. Sigurdsson, K. Sigurhjartarson, H. Simonarson, S. Simonarson, E. Thorfinnsson.

Officers, 1975:
President: Hjalti Eliasson.
Secretary: Alfred G. Alfredsson, P.O. Box 256, Kopavogi, Iceland.

IDLE BIDS. Bids which have little or no natural function in a standard method of bidding, and which are therefore available for specialized use.

Bidding is a language with a limited vocabulary. If more bids can be added to a player's vocabulary without affecting other situations, efficiency tends to be increased. Theoreticians therefore search for idle bids, and try to assign useful meanings to them.

One example is a jump to two no trump when the opener's suit bid has been doubled. This is idle because a player with a strong balanced hand would automatically redouble. Many players therefore use this bid conventionally to show a useful hand, probably 10–11 in high cards, with at least four-card support for the opener's suit. The immediate jump raise over the double can then be reserved for preemptive use. See TWO NO TRUMP RESPONSE (OVER OPPONENT'S TAKE-OUT DOUBLE).

Another example is a response of five no trump to a one no trump opening. As four no trump is a natu-

ral invitation to six no trump, five no trump is not needed for that purpose. Some players therefore use it as an invitation to *seven* no trump, guaranteeing six. The same idea would apply to two no trump—five no trump. See also IMPOSSIBLE BID.

IDLE CARD. See BUSY CARD and IDLE CARD.

ILLEGAL CALL. A call out of rotation, insufficient, or otherwise improper, during the bidding period of a hand.

ILLOGICAL BID. See IMPOSSIBLE BID.

IMP. Abbreviation for INTERNATIONAL MATCH POINT. It is frequently used either as the three letters, or as the word "imp," in conversation.

IMP SCORING. See INTERNATIONAL MATCH POINTS.

IMP TACTICS. Bidding and play at IMPs is an intermediate stage between match points and rubber bridge. It is important to understand the mathematical factors that influence the bidding of games and slams.

The Odds. Bidding a close, non-vulnerable game can gain a swing of 250 points, 6 IMPs. If you go down, you may lose a swing of 190 points, 5 IMPs. So the odds are only 6 to 5 in your favor, without allowing for the badly splitting hand on which you get doubled in game. It is about even money.

Vulnerable games, though, gain 10 IMPs and lose only 6. Here the odds are much more favorable. So, bid any vulnerable game that seems faintly possible; but bid a non-vulnerable game only with solid expectation of making it.

For example, suppose you hold:

♠ K 8 4
♡ A 10 2
◇ K 7 3
♣ Q J 10 5

After two passes, you open one club. Partner jumps to two no trump. Push on to three no trump if vulnerable, but pass if you are not. Small slams are even-money bets at IMPs; you stand to gain or lose the same amount. However, tend to assume that any touch-and-go slam will not be bid at the other table. That's a fact of life. Thus, if you are comfortably ahead in the match, or playing a team you rate to beat easily, hold back; but if you are the underdog, play for the swing and bid. Actually, the best chance a weak team has to beat a stronger one is to bounce into slam whenever there seems to be a possibility of making.

Grand slams appear to have odds against them of only 15 to 11 non-vulnerable, or 17 to 13 vulnerable. These are not nearly so prohibitive as the 2 to 1 total-point odds—IMP scoring always reduces the big swing compared to the little one. But there is a hidden factor: at the other table, your opponents may not bid even a small slam. Then, going down in a grand slam vulnerable costs you 26 IMPs, the 13 you lose, plus the 13 you could have won; and making your grand slam gains only four IMPs extra. Perhaps you think it is next to impossible for the enemy to miss a small slam when you are thinking of a grand slam, but it has happened many, many times. So avoid grand slams unless you can count 13 tricks.

How does all this compare to match-point duplicate? There, it probably pays to bid any game with a 45% chance. (You never get a tremendous score for staying out of a close game even when it should go down, for the defense is too often poor; and, after all, you are trying to get a big score and win the tournament.) This means that a duplicate buff playing at IMP scoring should be less willing than usual to bid a non-vulnerable game, but more ready to bid a vulnerable game. Slam bidding is much the same at IMPs as at pairs, but you are a little readier to bid a doubtful small slam at pairs, since you are more likely to need points urgently. In pairs, as at IMPs, you steer clear of doubtful grand slams, for a small slam bid and made is usually a good score.

One- and Two-IMP Swngs. One major difference between IMPs and pair scoring is in the relative insignificance of tiny swings; overtricks, and the extra points for no trump or major suits. Play these North-South hands at three no trump against the lead of the diamond deuce:

NORTH
♠ 6 4
♡ 7 4
◊ A 8 3
♣ A K Q 7 5 2

SOUTH
♠ A K 10 5 2
♡ A J
◊ J 10 6 5
♣ 6 3

At match-point play, you should duck; this will probably allow you to make eleven tricks. Of course you will get a heart shift and will go down if clubs do not split, but you must try for the extra tricks. At IMP scoring, you rise with the diamond ace and concede a club, playing safe for your contract.

Now, suppose you ducked the diamond. Your heart stopper is knocked out; you test the clubs and they split 4–1. At match points you take a diamond finesse and cash out for down one; it may even be a good score, for everyone is in the same spot. At IMPs, if you neglected to play safe, you would play a spade to your ten, trying desperately to make your contract, because an extra undertrick does not bother you. Defense is very much simpler at IMPs than at match-point pairs, for your objective is always to defeat the contract, never to stop overtricks. For example:

NORTH
♠ A J 4 2
♡ 10 6 3
◊ 5
♣ K Q J 9 5

EAST
♠ 8 5
♡ A Q 2
◊ 10 8 6 3
♣ A 8 7 2

South opened one spade, North bid three spades, South four spades. You are East, and your partner leads the diamond king, won by declarer. Trumps are drawn and your club ace is knocked out. At match-points, you cash your heart ace, or, if hungry for a good score, you lead the heart deuce, hoping that declarer has K x x and will duck to ensure his contract.

At IMPs you have no choice; you lead the heart queen. Clearly, your best chance to defeat four spades (not to hold it to four, but to defeat it) is to find declarer with king-third or fourth in hearts and partner with jack-nine. Declarer is then likely to go wrong, playing you for queen-jack. Of course, most of the time you will lose your ace, declarer will hold king-jack or king doubleton, or king-nine; but then you never could have defeated the contract.

In bidding, also, you ignore tiny differentials at IMPs keeping your eye on the main chance, making your contract. Suppose you hold:

♠ Q 5
♡ Q 8 6 3
◊ 8 7
♣ A 10 7 4 2

Partner opens one club, you respond one heart, partner rebids one no trump. At match points, you might pass, hoping to make 120; at IMPs you bid two clubs. This must be safer, and you simply score 90 or 110 instead of 120 or 150.

Suppose you have the same hand when partner opens one spade. You bid one no trump; partner rebids two clubs. At match points it is surely right to give a false preference to two spades; at IMPs, it is surely better to raise clubs. Plus 110 and plus 140 are, in effect, the same at IMPs, and you look for the safest, not the largest, plus. Obviously, this applies even more forcibly to game and slam contracts. You are perfectly willing to play in a minor suit if it is safer; you never strain to play no trump or major suit contracts simply for the few extra points. Of course, whatever the scoring, it is hard to make five clubs and five diamonds, so these are not common contracts. However, they should be played at IMPs much more often than at match-point pairs. The answer is: never even consider swings of one or two IMPs. Ignore them in your thinking about dummy play, defense, or bidding. Of course, when your contract is secure (or when, on defense, you see that it is impossible to defeat the declarer), you can give yourself the pleasure of battling over the extra trick or tricks. But this is a frill. The business of IMP playing is making or setting contracts. The tiny swings almost always even out over a long match. And if your team goes out to win all the one-IMP and two-IMP swings, you are likely to lose the match.

Competing for Part-Scores. In many respects the fierce competition over part-score hands which characterizes match-point pairs should be carried over into IMPs. That is, you must do a lot of balancing; or, if you prefer, you must get into the auction early and very "lightly." One way or the other, you must not let the enemy buy a lot of contracts peacefully at the two-level. The difference between two hearts, making two, and three hearts down one, may be five IMPs, and a few swings like this can cost you a match.

Now, duplicate-oriented players usually do compete or balance at the two-level when playing IMPs. Where they tend to go wrong is in competing up at the three-level. Here there is a big difference between the two games. This is a common dilemma in pairs.

SOUTH	WEST	NORTH	EAST
1 ♠	Pass	2 ♠	Dbl.
Pass	3 ♡	Pass	Pass
?			

You, South, hold:

♠ A Q 8 6 4
♡ A 8 5
◇ K 10 4
♣ J 8

If the cards lie favorably for your side, you might well make three spades; you cannot get a good result defending. Likewise, if the lie is unfavorable, the opponents might make three hearts; then you might do better to go down at three spades. So at match points you should consider bidding.

At IMPs though, you should certainly pass. Whether you are plus 140 or plus 100 is a matter of one IMP; the same is true of minus 100 or minus 140. However, if both three hearts and three spades go down, not at all unlikely, the swing can be five IMPs. If your distribution were unbalanced, so that both contracts might make, then six IMPs might be gained by bidding. But with a flat hand you should expect that only one contract or the other can be made, according to whose finesses work. You cannot lose much by passing, only by bidding.

The key is to think about plus scores on part-score hands, not how big a plus or how small a minus. If both pairs can be plus on three-quarters of the small hands, the team can win almost any match.

Let us illustrate these two different competitive situations with hands from the 1962 World Championship.

NORTH
♠ 7 6 4
♡ K 4 3 2
◇ K 10 5
♣ 9 5 4

WEST
♠ Q 10 9 2
♡ Q 10 7 5
◇ 7 3
♣ A Q 2

EAST
♠ A K J 8 5
♡ 9 6
◇ J 8 4
♣ 8 6 3

SOUTH
♠ 3
♡ A J 8
◇ A Q 9 6 2
♣ K J 10 7

The bidding:

WEST	NORTH	EAST	SOUTH
Pass	Pass	Pass	1 ◇
Dbl.	1 ♡	1 ♠	2 ♡
Pass	Pass	Pass	

There are a number of points of interest in this auction, but consider East's final pass. This was poor rubber bridge thinking: "We are both passed hands; the opponents haven't bid game; let sleeping dogs lie." It cost six IMPs for two hearts made, and East-West made a spade partial at the other table.

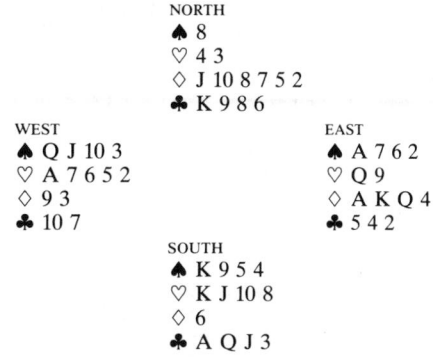

NORTH
♠ 8
♡ 4 3
◇ J 10 8 7 5 2
♣ K 9 8 6

WEST
♠ Q J 10 3
♡ A 7 6 5 2
◇ 9 3
♣ 10 7

EAST
♠ A 7 6 2
♡ Q 9
◇ A K Q 4
♣ 5 4 2

SOUTH
♠ K 9 5 4
♡ K J 10 8
◇ 6
♣ A Q J 3

The bidding:

SOUTH	WEST	NORTH	EAST
1 ♣	Pass	1 ◇	Pass
1 ♡	Pass	2 ♣	2 ♠
Dbl.	Pass	3 ♣	Pass
Pass	3 ♠	Pass	Pass
4 ♣	Pass	Pass	Pass

South's final bid looks like match-point thinking: "Partner has long clubs and short spades, so I should have a good play for four clubs; we can beat three spades but not for so good a score."

The moral is to fight your opponents up to the three-level, and then to play for any plus score.

Sacrifice Bidding. One area of difference between the match-point and the IMP approach is in sacrificing against game contracts. Sacrificing can be very rewarding at match points—it is a triumph to lose 300 rather than 420, or 500 rather than 620. At IMPs, though, for the swing of 120 points you earn three IMPs. And this is not a very good return on your investment, that is, for your gamble that the opponents could make their game. True, you are spared the worry of going for too much (losing 700 to save 620, for example); this costs only two IMPs. But if you take a PHANTOM SACRIFICE of 500 points against an unmakable game, you lose 12 IMPs. So the odds are not nearly as good as at duplicate.

The other side of this picture is that you are much more prone at IMPs than you are at duplicate to double an enemy sacrifice, rather than push on to five in a major. In a pair game you are reluctant to accept 500 points in exchange for a vulnerable game; it can almost be a zero. Playing IMPs though, you double a sacrifice bid unless you are a cinch for eleven tricks; the odds are greatly against bidding on.

Of course, this refers to the "match-point" type of sacrifice. In any game it pays to go for 100 or 300 against a vulnerable game. At any scoring it pays to bid on to five of a major on the chance you will make it when you feel that you may not beat the opponents by more than a trick. One should not say "never sacrifice" or "always double a sacrifice"; merely remember that the odds are quite different from those at match points, so your normal tendencies must be different also.

Actually, one type of sacrifice is popular among experienced IMP competitors; this is a premature sacrifice made in the hope of stampeding the opponents to the five-level. Thus, it aims at a 12 IMP, not a three IMP profit.

Suppose partner opens three hearts, not vulnerable against vulnerable, right-hand opponent doubles, and you hold:

♠ K 6
♡ A J 7 4
◇ Q 7 2
♣ 8 5 4 2

Jump to five hearts. You are likely to have to make this bid over four spades, so bid it immediately. Your left-hand opponent, under pressure, may bid five spades, down one.

Another time when a sacrifice aims at a large number of IMPs is when you save against a slam. Down six doubled, 1,100, can gain eight IMPs if your partners make 1,430. Here is an example:

West dealer:
East-West vulnerable:

```
                    NORTH
                    ♠ K 9 6 5 2
                    ♡ 5
                    ◇ Q 8 5 2
                    ♣ Q 8 4
     WEST                            EAST
     ♠ A 10 8 4                      ♠ Q J
     ♡ A Q J 9 7 2                   ♡ K 10 6 3
     ◇ A                             ◇ K
     ♣ 7 6                           ♣ A K J 9 5 3
                    SOUTH
                    ♠ 7 3
                    ♡ 8 4
                    ◇ J 10 9 7 6 4 3
                    ♣ 10 2
```

WEST	NORTH	EAST	SOUTH
1 ♡	2 ♡	Dbl.	7 ◇
Pass	Pass	Dbl.	Pass
Pass	Pass		

North's two heart bid was a MICHAELS CUE-BID, and South took desperate action fearing a grand slam. Actually, he was right in a way; East-West could make seven clubs, seven hearts or seven no trump, and seven diamonds doubled was down six for 1,100 on fine defense. This could gain 15 IMPs if a grand slam was bid at the other table, or 8 IMPs otherwise.

What happened? Only game was bid by the other East-West pair, so the sacrifice lost 12 IMPs.

This is the principal hazard in sacrificing against

vulnerable slams. It is hard to go for too much if your teammates bid the slam, but since they possibly won't, perhaps you should hope to defeat the contract rather than save against it, unless (1) your teammates are unusually aggressive slam bidders, or (2) there seems to be no chance at all of defeating the opposing slam.

Penalty Doubles. In almost all doubling situations at IMPs, the odds favor the coward, not the hero. Consider the position in which vulnerable opponents have crept up to four spades on a shaky auction. You can see that they are running into bad breaks and probably will go down, perhaps even two tricks. Then a double stands to gain 300 points for a two-trick set or lose 170 should the contract make; but the IMP odds are only 7 to 5. And if the opponent's contract is a silly one, your partners probably have stopped at a part-score; then a double stands to gain only an IMP or two, for you would have a handsome swing in your favor anyway.

This, actually, is quite similar to match-point thinking; why double the opponents if they have overbid, when you are getting most of the points anyway? And maybe they have not overbid; and perhaps your double will allow them to make a contract which otherwise would go down; this is particularly disastrous at IMPs.

An entirely different situation is the one in which you are debating whether to double an enemy overcall or to bid your own game contract. At match points the critical consideration is the vulnerability: can you score in penalties more than the value of your game? For example, suppose you hold:

♠ 7 2
♡ A Q 8
◇ K 9 8 3
♣ K 7 5 4

Partner opens one spade, right-hand opponent overcalls two diamonds. In a pair game you would certainly double if non-vulnerable against vulnerable: a two-trick set seems sure if partner stands the double. You would be reluctant to double at equal vulnerability, for fear that a two-trick set would not equal the score for the game which your side could probably make. At IMPs, in contrast, you should double at all but the most unfavorable vulnerability. If you lose 100 or 120 points (300 against 420, or 500 against 600), that is only three IMPs. But on the one deal in three when your cards will not produce game, you will win from 8 to 12 IMPs. So you will gain heavily in the long run, assuming that your own game contract is merely likely, not certain.

However, suppose you hold:

♠ Q J 6
♡ K 9 5
◇ K J 8 4
♣ A 10 3

With neither side vulnerable, partner opens one spade and right-hand opponent overcalls two diamonds. At match points you might double, hoping to collect 500 (when all you could make was 430 or 460). But at IMPs this swing is worth only 1 or 2 IMPs; and if you score 300 (against 430 or 460 at the other table) you lose four IMPs. So you will lose in the long run by doubling. Suppose this situation comes up three times in an evening. On each occasion you double the enemy when you have a laydown game yourself, and twice you beat them 500, once 300. At match points you would have two-thirds of the points, a winning percentage. At IMPs you would be minus.

The key question at IMPs, then, is whether or not your game is sure. With the first example, you can feel only that game is probable, so you are anxious to play for penalties. Holding the second example, you can hardly imagine a hand that partner can have which will not produce 10 or 11 tricks at no trump, so you are reluctant to double. In short, at IMPs, go for the surest, not the most sizable plus score.

One big difference between proper match-point and IMP approach is in doubling enemy part-scores on competitive auctions. If you have bid up to three hearts in a pair game and vulnerable opponents contest with three spades, you are likely to double any time you feel sure that your contract would make; you must try to get 200 instead of 100. Obviously, this is suicidal at IMPs. If you score 100 when 140 is made at the other table, you lose 1 IMP, and 200 would gain you only 2 IMPs. For this 3-IMP pickup, you are rising a loss of 12 IMPs when the doubled contract is made (and your teammates play it undoubled). At matchpoints, you would gain considerably by doubling such contracts even if one in three is made against you; at IMP scoring you would be a big loser.

Speculative lead-directing doubles (i.e., calling for a lead which does not ensure a set but merely increases your chances) are slightly better bets at IMPs than at total points. For example, suppose that you double a non-vulnerable three no trump contract to get a favorable lead. At match points you are gambling a top against a bottom, instead of settling for slightly below average; the odds are a little better than even money. To figure the odds at IMPs, assume that the game is bid and made at the other table. If you beat the contract, you gain 500, while if it makes, you lose 150; these total-points odds become 11 IMPs to 4. The chance of overtricks reduces this to about two to one in your favor. That is, you will break even if the lead you direct beats one game in three.

The odds become most attractive when it is a slam which you are doubling. Superficially, this does not seem to be so. If you double a non-vulnerable six spade contract you gain 1,080 (15 IMPs) when you beat it, while you lose 230 (6 IMPs) if you do not. But this assumes that the contract is the same at the other table, and this is an unwarranted assumption in the case of a close slam (as distinct from a touch-and-go game which probably will be bid). If only game is reached at the other table, your loss from doubling a makable slam is 1 IMP; and when your double was necessary to defeat the slam, your gain is 22 IMPs. (You gain 11 instead of losing 11.) At odds of 22 to 1, it is hard to go wrong.

General Tactics. There is another area of difference, though, caused not so much by the scoring as by the objectives of the two games. At match points, you are are trying to beat some huge (and ever increasing) number of competing pairs. At IMPs, you are trying to beat one team (at a time). And, in a pair contest, the huge field usually means that a great number of poor and inexperienced players are your direct or indirect opponents. But in an IMP team game you are not likely to meet any really bad opponents. What this means is that it is probably the winning style at match points to try to beat par, to try for unusually good results; in contrast, at IMP scoring, this is not the winning style (unless you are far behind or a decided underdog).

Par bridge, i.e., taking everything which is yours without trying to steal what belongs to the enemy, will win almost any IMP match. Of course, you and your teammates are bound to make a few errors, but if you play a steady game, and make fewer mistakes than your opponents, you will win. A 51% game is good enough. At match points, 51% is a disaster; even 60% games will not win tournaments. You must take more chances (and this means make more bad bids) to win a pair game. One illustration of this is in pre-emptive bidding.

    ♠ 6
    ♡ K Q 10 8 6 4
    ◇ A J 10 6 3
    ♣ 2

At match points one might open four hearts as dealer with neither side vulnerable. At IMPs better heart spots would be desirable, and there is a greater chance that the hand should be played in diamonds, so open one heart. At IMPs, there is less incentive to "steal."

Another illustration is in balancing in risky positions, i.e., when the opponents have not found a fit. Suppose that the auction goes as follows:

WEST	NORTH	EAST	SOUTH
1 NT*	Pass	Pass	?

With neither side vulnerable, you hold, sitting South:

    ♠ K 10 8 4 3
    ♡ 5
    ◇ A 10 6 5
    ♣ Q 7 4

At match points, bid two spades. If you pass, you are settling for a normal, under-average score; it would be better to try to beat par with an unsound overcall. At IMPs, you should pass, accepting the fact that it is "wrong" to overcall. The risk of a disastrous result is one you do not have to take when trying to beat one team instead of 200 pairs.

In the bridge world there are quite a few famous players whose great strength is their tactical bidding. (A "tactical" bid is a bad bid which gets a good re-

---

* 16–18.

sult.) These experts do very well at match points, winning far more than their share of tournaments, killing the weak fields. But they do poorly in team games.

So, save your bad bids for match points. When you play IMPs, try a cautious, cowardly style; leave the heroics to your opponents. Then, at the end of the match you can compliment them for some brilliant bid while they are congratulating you for winning. (Reprinted by permission from *The Bridge World*, Nov.-Dec. 1963.)

E. K(aplan)

IMPS FOR PAIR GAMES. Used for some pair events, particularly for team trial events. See INTERNATIONAL MATCH POINTS.

IMPERFECT PACK. A pack of playing cards which is incomplete or in which one or more cards are duplicated. See LAWS (Laws 11, 12), LAWS OF DUPLICATE (Laws 13, 14).

IMPOSSIBLE BID. Legally, an "inadmissible call" (see LAWS 36–39). A bid of eight is one example. A historic case was the double of "two cokes" ordered by the right-hand opponent. (It was suggested that this required a minimum holding of two Scotches.)

Technically, a bid which is inconsistent with previous bidding by the same player, and which therefore reveals that he is ignorant of bidding principles or has made a mistake.

For example, the bidding one no trump—three no trump—four no trump is impossible. If made by a good player, it would imply that the first bid was a mistake: probably there was an ace hidden when he counted his hand originally.

However, some impossible bids become possible on closer examination. A bid which is forcing but limited can often be employed in a sense which appears impossible. Marshall MILES suggested a response of two no trump to a suit bid with a balanced hand counting about 19 points. The idea was to follow with a natural four no trump bid, so describing accurately a hand which is difficult to define by normal methods. See also IDLE BIDS.

IMPOSSIBLE NEGATIVE. A method of responding over a PRECISION CLUB opening in order to show 4-4-4-1 distribution. Responder first makes the negative response of one diamond, then jumps in his short suit in order to show that he did not have a negative hand after all.

IMPROPER CALL. A bid or double during the auction when the caller is under obligation to pass.

IMPROPER REMARK. Any statement or question by a player during the play or bidding of a hand which refers to a possible holding or interpretation of an action of the current hand. The proprieties of the game state that any information must be exchanged between partners by proper calls at a steady rhythm, or by the order of play of cards when a choice of possible plays is present. See PROPRIETIES and COFFEE-HOUSE.

IMPROPRIETY. A violation or breach of ethical conduct; also the failure to observe proper etiquette. See ETHICS; ETIQUETTE; LAWS (Proprieties, I–III).

IN BACK OF. A term describing the relationship of a player to the opponent on his right; i.e., a player who plays after the player on his right is said to be "in back of" that player. An equivalent term is "over."

IN FRONT OF. The phrase used to describe the relationship between a player and his left-hand opponent; i.e., the player who plays before another player is said to be "in front of" that player. An equivalent term is "under."

IN THE RED. A seeming paradox in bridge terminology: in rubber bridge or CHICAGO it would mean being a loser, but in duplicate it describes a score good enough to earn master points, because rankings that qualify for points are indicated in red on the recap sheet.

INADMISSIBLE CALLS. See LAWS (Laws 36–39).

INADMISSIBLE DOUBLE OR REDOUBLE. See LAWS (Law 36).

INADVERTENT CALL. See LAWS (Law 24).

INADVERTENT INFRINGEMENT OF LAW. A violation of the proper procedure without deliberate attempt to do so. It is assumed that all infringements of laws are inadvertent, and the penalties prescribed for such infringements are designed to indemnify the non-offenders against potential loss as a result of such inadvertence.

INCOMPLETE HAND. An original holding of less than thirteen cards. Any missing card or cards are presumed to have been a part of the original hand, no matter where it or they may be found, unless attention is called to the imperfection. It is the responsibility of each player to count his cards at each deal. See LAWS (Law 11); LAWS OF DUPLICATE (Laws 13, 14).

INCOMPLETE PACK. A pack of cards from which one or more cards are missing. If a deal is made from an incomplete pack, the deal is void, if discovered within the legal time limits, and a new pack is substituted.

INCOMPLETE TABLE. (1) In club play, a table of four or five players in which there is room for a newcomer to cut in. Some clubs designate five players, some six, as a full complement of players. (2) In home play, two or three players in search of one or two. (3) In duplicate play, see HALF TABLE.

INCORRECT CARD. Any card played which is improper in that it may become a revoke, or is played out of turn. See LAWS OF DUPLICATE (Laws 52, 61–63.)

INDEMNIFY. To give redress to a side that has been injured by an infraction of the rules by the other side.

In duplicate bridge it is the duty of the tournament director to impose penalties for infractions. See LAWS OF DUPLICATE (Law 10). In rubber bridge a penalty may be imposed by agreement of the players, or by either member of the non-offending side (except dummy) so long as he does not consult his partner. See LAWS OF CONTRACT BRIDGE (Law 14).

INDIAN BRIDGE FEDERATION. See ALL INDIA BRIDGE FEDERATION.

INDICATOR. Gadget by which the final contract can be indicated on the table, to aid bridge players with memory lapses. However, players who forget the final contract during the play of the hand also forget to set the indicator. It has not proved popular. In BRIDGE-O-RAMA or VU-GRAPH exhibitions, however, the indicator of the final contract and the count of tricks won by declarer and defenders is very useful.

INDICES. Small identifying marks in the corners of playing cards, printed above the suit symbol.

The first use of indices is difficult to determine. Special packs of the seventeenth and eighteenth centuries (educational, heraldic, political, etc.) had so much of the card taken up with pictures and words that the identification consisted of a number or letter beside one pip in an upper corner. No one seems to have adapted this for use with regular playing cards for a long time. In the 1870s three American card makers tried different solutions to the problem. One put miniature cards in two corners (calling the style *Triplicate*); another used merely a letter or number and a small pip (called *Squeezers,* because they did not need to be fanned); the third put these in all four corners (*Quadruplicate*).

The use of double indices permits a hand to be fanned either right or left, and European cards today are usually so made; English and American players chose the single index at each end which is current today. In 1893 some packs were issued with a large corner pip, with a white index within it. Today some Swiss packs use no index pip, but put the index as a white numeral in the pip nearest the corner. Spanish and some Italian (trappola) packs have indices from 1 to 13, including both suit and court cards.

INDIVIDUAL MOVEMENT. A method of competition between bridge players, in which each contestant plays with many different partners. The movement most used is the RAINBOW MOVEMENT, in which the North players remain seated, South players progress to the next higher numbered table, East players skip a table to the higher numbered, West players skip a table to the lower numbered, and boards go to the lower numbered tables respectively.

This movement is effective only when the number of tables is prime: four rounds of six boards for a five-table competition, with the East player interchanging with South after the second board, and again with West after the fourth board of each round, all players resuming original directions after the round is completed; twenty-one boards in seven rounds of three boards each (players interchanging

after each board as before); eleven rounds of two boards each with eleven tables, South and East interchanging after the odd board has been played; and twelve or thirteen rounds of two boards each for thirteen tables with the interchange (as in eleven tables) for the even-numbered board.

For greater numbers of tables, it is frequently possible to break down into two sections with a prime number of tables in each: fourteen becomes two sevens; eighteeen becomes a seven and an eleven, etc. A perfect nine-table movement was used for many years in the Life Masters Individual. It requires five sessions of play.

For nine- and ten-table games, the least undesirable movement is the SHOMATE MOVEMENT, for which guide cards for each player are required. There is no regularity in this movement although it does provide for balanced comparisons of a sort.

Two tables with eight, nine, and ten players can be accommodated in an Individual tournament. The boards of each round are relayed between the two tables, with one less round than there are players. The game can be curtailed at any point, as all boards are completed after each round. In all cases, the players are assigned numbers, and replace the player with the next lower number at the end of each round. (In the eight-player movement, player number 8 is stationary, and number 1 replaces number 7.) Starting assignments are as follows:

	Table 1				Table 2			
	N	E	S	W	N	E	S	W
8 players	8	1	6	2	5	7	3	4
9 players	2	4	3	7	6	5	8	9
10 players	1	5	4	6	3	8	9	10

Three tables (twelve or thirteen players) can also compete. For twelve players the boards are also relayed among the three tables, making a minimum of three boards per round. Complete play thus requires thirty-three boards, but it may be curtailed after any set of boards has been finished. Original assignment at tables (in order, N, E, S, W) are: table 1: 12, 1, 5, 11; table 2: 4, 3, 10, 7; table 3: 2, 9, 6, 8. Player 12 is stationary, each player replacing the player with next lower number, 1 replacing 11 at the end of each round.

The thirteen-player movement runs thirteen rounds, two boards to a round. The tables play the boards in ascending order, the first set starting at table 1, sixth set at table 2 and twelfth set at table 3. Seating assignments are as follows: table 1: 1, 3, 5, 6; table 2: 7, 12, 13, 4; table 3: 2, 9, 8, 11. All players replace the next lower numbered player for the next round, player 1 replacing player 13.

Sixteen players play twelve rounds of two boards; tables 2 and 3 sharing boards throughout, additional boards feed in to table 4, and are out of play after three rounds. With seventeen players, the relay is unnecessary, thirteen rounds are played, the first three sets of boards on tables 1 to 3 and the sixth set on table 4, progressing to lower-numbered tables. In the original seating diagrams below, players with the four highest numbers remain stationary throughout, other players replace the player with the next lower number (1 following 12 in the sixteen-player game, and sitting out one round and replacing 13 in the 17-player game).

	Sixteen-player				Seventeen-player			
Table 1	16	1	6	10	17	8	1	3
Table 2	4	5	13	3	10	16	6	5
Table 3	8	15	12	9	9	13	15	12
Table 4	7	2	11	14	11	4	7	14

In the seventeen-player game, scores must be factored.

INDIVIDUAL TOURNAMENT. A bridge competition in which each contestant plays with many different partners, playing one or two hands with each. Obviously it is impractical to have partnership understandings with so many players in the limited time available for discussion, so that bidding systems are kept simple, and conventional bids held to a minimum. In order to eliminate a certain amount of the luck involved in indiscriminate partnerships, it is frequently desirable to break the field by master-point holdings into two or more flights. For movements used, see RAINBOW, APPENDIX (Rainbow) TABLE, and others discussed under the appropriate number of TABLES and INDIVIDUAL MOVEMENTS.

INDONESIA. See ALL INDONESIA BRIDGE ASSOCIATION.

INFERENCE. A conclusion drawn from a call or play made by partner or an opponent. Though the ability to gather and assimilate the most delicate clues is the hallmark of a fine player, the bidding and play of many hands abound with inferences that can be drawn by the average performer provided that he is alert and knows what to look for. Note that an inference implies uncertainty. An inference leaving no room for doubt would be a deduction.

A declarer's task is frequently lessened when the opponents have been in the auction; apart from yielding specific information about the enemy suit(s), interference bidding generally assists the declarer to "guess" better in the play of a critical suit. For example in playing a common combination such as:

NORTH
K J 10 9

SOUTH
A 8 7 6

declarer has to catch the queen, and with nothing to guide him, he must sometimes guess wrong. See TWO-WAY FINESSE. Suppose, however, that in the course of the auction West has made a pre-emptive bid marking himself with shortages elsewhere; the odds now clearly favor a finesse against his partner.

In taking advantage of the information provided by the bidding, a declarer frequently must resort to unusual plays:

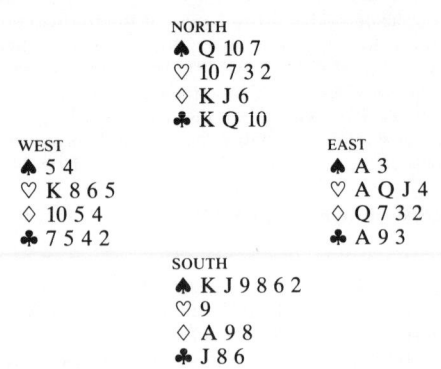

South is declarer in four spades after East has opened the bidding with one no trump. West leads a trump, and South, faced with three certain losers, has to avoid losing a diamond. The standard play of this combination is to finesse the jack, but in this instance declarer is fairly sure that East has the queen from his bid. His best chance is to take a backward finesse, leading the jack through East, and if covered, finessing against West for the ten on the second round.

Sometimes the defenders' side find themselves in the unhappy position of guiding declarer's play through not bidding:

NORTH
♠ K Q 4
♡ Q 6
◊ Q J 4 3
♣ A J 10 5

WEST
♠ 7 5
♡ A K 4 3
◊ K 7 6
♣ 8 7 4 2

EAST
♠ J 9 2
♡ J 9 7 5 2
◊ 10 9 8 5
♣ K

SOUTH
♠ A 10 8 6 3
♡ 10 8
◊ A 2
♣ Q 9 6 3

The bidding:

SOUTH	WEST	NORTH	EAST
	Pass	1 ♣	Pass
1 ♠	Pass	2 ♠	Pass
4 ♠	Pass	Pass	Pass

West cashes two hearts, and shifts to a trump, declarer drawing three rounds ending in dummy in order to take the diamond finesse. West wins and exits with a heart, South ruffing. The king of clubs is now marked with East, for in the play West has shown up with the ace, king of hearts, and king of diamonds, and if he also held the king of clubs he would have opened the bidding. Declarer's only chance is that the king is singleton. Accordingly, he plays a club to the ace, dropping East's lone king, winning both the contract and suspicious looks from the opposition.

Declarer has an even greater scope for making educated guesses based upon the play of the opponents' cards. This is particularly true when the defenders are forced to discard on a long suit, the order of their discards being most helpful to declarer. The accuracy of the inferences thus drawn varies with the skill of the opposition, for good players generally plan ahead in these situations, often leaving the declarer with little to go on. Nevertheless, it is the mark of a good player that he "guesses" the right play more often than not.

On rare occasions, the defenders are helpless to prevent declarer from gaining an inference.

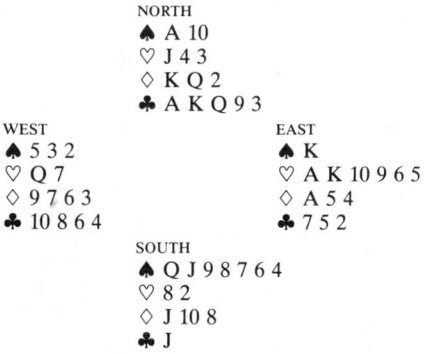

NORTH
♠ A 10
♡ J 4 3
◇ K Q 2
♣ A K Q 9 3

WEST
♠ 5 3 2
♡ Q 7
◇ 9 7 6 3
♣ 10 8 6 4

EAST
♠ K
♡ A K 10 9 6 5
◇ A 5 4
♣ 7 5 2

SOUTH
♠ Q J 9 8 7 6 4
♡ 8 2
◇ J 10 8
♣ J

The bidding:

SOUTH	WEST	NORTH	EAST
		1 ♣	1 ♡
3 ♠	Pass	4 ♠	Pass
Pass	Pass		

West leads the queen of hearts and continues the suit, East winning the king. After cashing the ace of diamonds, East is in a cleft stick: if he returns a third heart, South will ruff high and West's failure to over-ruff will mark the king of spades. On the other hand, if he does not continue hearts, South's suspicions will be aroused and he is bound to diagnose the position.

The defending side is sometimes better placed to make deductions, for they have the advantage of being able to gather clues from both declarer's and partner's actions.

In a general way, the defenders can make certain assumptions about the nature of declarer's holding by his approach. For example, at a suit contract, if he plays a side-suit before broaching trumps, he probably has a shaky trump suit. On the other hand, if trumps are drawn immediately, it is safe to infer that declarer intends to utilize a side-suit to dispose of his losers. At no trump, when declarer makes no attempt to establish a strong suit, it is reasonably certain that the suit is ready to run.

NORTH
♠ 8 7 6
♡ A 2
◇ K J 10 4 3
♣ Q 4 3

WEST
♠ K Q 10 9 4
♡ J 4 3
◇ 9 2
♣ A J 10

The bidding:

SOUTH	WEST	NORTH	EAST
1 NT	Pass	3 NT	Pass
Pass	Pass		

West leads the king of spades, which declarer wins with the ace. To the second trick, South leads a club; West plays the ace and then the queen of spades, dropping declarer's jack, and takes three further spade tricks to defeat the contract.

South held:

♠ A J
♡ K 9 7
◇ A Q 8 7
♣ K 9 5 2

West made two unusual plays: he rose with the ace of clubs in a position where it is customary to play low, and he continued spades at the risk of establishing the jack for declarer. The question is: how did he know? West reasoned that declarer could not have started with AJx of spades, for with that holding he would have surely refused the first spade, rendering the defense helpless. Either partner had the jack or, more likely, declarer had ace-jack alone. Further, declarer's failure to play on diamonds surely meant that the suit was solid, in which case, if declarer was permitted to steal a club, he would almost certainly have nine tricks: one spade, five diamonds, one club, and two hearts (he was likely to have the king of hearts for his bid).

Defenders are often misled into committing a blunder, basing their defense on the assumption that a declarer has adopted a reasonable line of play. Similarly, in deciding his play at a crucial point in a hand, a defender has to assume that his partner has played well. Terence Reese gives this example:

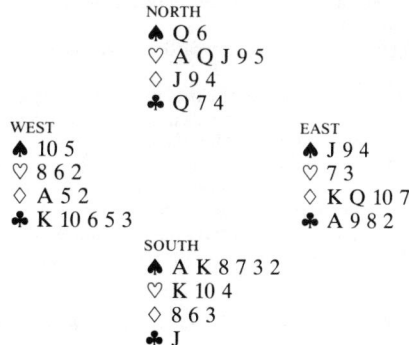

NORTH
♠ Q 6
♡ A Q J 9 5
◇ J 9 4
♣ Q 7 4

WEST
♠ 10 5
♡ 8 6 2
◇ A 5 2
♣ K 10 6 5 3

EAST
♠ J 9 4
♡ 7 3
◇ K Q 10 7
♣ A 9 8 2

SOUTH
♠ A K 8 7 3 2
♡ K 10 4
◇ 8 6 3
♣ J

South plays in four spades and West leads the club five to his partner's ace. East shifts to the king of diamonds and continues with the seven, declarer false-carding with the eight. West is now faced with the problem of "guessing" whether to attempt to cash the third diamond or the king of clubs. From his point of view, declarer might have well dropped the jack of clubs at trick one from Jx, and with apparently nothing to guide him he played the king of clubs, giving declarer the contract. West failed to draw the proper inference from his partner's play: if East had held five diamonds, leaving declarer with two, he would have realized that the defense could take only two diamond tricks and would have played the queen of diamonds to hold the lead before shifting back to clubs. See also CARD READING and COUNTING THE HAND.

S. K.

INFERENTIAL PROBLEM. A problem which requires the deduction of the lie of hidden cards through the use of information of a form not found in ordinary play.

Two examples of inferential problems follow. The first problem is of moderate difficulty, and provides a good introduction to inferential problems. The second problem is a harder nut to crack with only one clue given as to the makeup of the concealed hands.

Big Cassino and Little Cassino*

by Jeff Rubens

```
NORTH
♠ 3
♡ 9 6 4
◇ A 7 6
♣ K Q 9 5 4 2

SOUTH
♠ A Q 9 5 4
♡ 3 2
◇ K 9 5 3
♣ A 10
```

Contract: 6 ◇ by South
Clues:

(1) After the lead of any black card, South can make his contract by perfect play. However, after the lead of any red card, perfect defense can defeat the contract.

(2) (A "spot card" is any card from deuce through ten.)
The sum of East's spot cards in hearts subtracted from the sum of his spot cards in diamonds is exactly one third of the sum of all his black spot cards.

(3) Neither defender is void of hearts, and neither defender holds both big cassino (diamond ten) and little cassino (spade deuce).

What are the exact East-West hands and how does South fulfill his contract after a favorable lead?

Solution to "Big Cassino and Little Cassino"

As neither defender is void of hearts, South must discard all his hearts before losing the lead. Further, he cannot lose a trick to one of the three missing low trumps. If diamonds are 3–3, no discards can be taken. Therefore, diamonds must be 4–2 with West holding two blank honors. In this way, declarer can obtain two discards on the clubs in dummy. These discards must be taken after two trumps are drawn, therefore one ruff must establish the spade suit. This places East with ♠ K J 10 and four clubs. East's four clubs must include the jack as the lead of a black card must help declarer by providing an entry for a black suit finesse. Since the sum of East's black spot cards is divisible by three, East must hold ♣ J 8 6 3. Since West holds the spade deuce, East's diamond honor is the ten. Therefore, East holds two hearts with a spot total of 15 and the East-West hands are:

WEST	EAST
♠ 8 7 6 2	♠ K J 10
♡ A K Q J ? ?	♡ ? ?
◇ Q J	◇ 10 8 4 2
♣ 7	♣ J 8 6 3

After a black suit lead, declarer wins cheaply. He cashes the diamond king and diamond ace, takes the remaining black suit finesse, clears all the black suit tops in the South hand, ruffs a spade in dummy, and discards two hearts on good clubs. Clubs are now continued until East ruffs. If East ruffs low, South overruffs and leads good spades. If East ruffs high, South takes the balance easily. If East never ruffs, he is trump couped at trick 12.

East's two hearts must be 10 5, not 8 7, for if East held ♡ 8 7, the opening lead of ♡ 5 would not defeat the contract!

Inferential Problem*

by Terence Reese

```
NORTH
♠ 8 5 2
♡ J 6
◇ K 6 5 3 2
♣ 8 6 5

WEST
♠ K J 9 6
♡ K 7
◇ J 9 4
♣ Q 9 4 2
```

South played a contract of three no trump. West led the spade six, East won with the ace and returned the four. West won with the jack and played the king, on which East played the three, and all followed. West then cashed the thirteenth spade. The contract was just made.

---

footnotes

* Reprinted from *The Bridge Journal*, Jan.–Feb. 1964.

* Reprinted from *The Bridge World*, Feb. 1950.

"Nicely played," said West to declarer at the end of the hand. "There was nothing we could do, was there, partner?"

"Well, yes," said East. "If, at the fourth trick, you had played any card except the thirteenth spade we could have put them one down."

Assuming that East was right, what was South's hand?

Solution to "Inferential Problem"

The key lies in realizing that the last spade, in addition to making the timing right for a squeeze, gives South a chance to unblock in diamonds. The diamond holding is A Q 8 7, and the suit is blocked unless South can discard one of them. (The diamonds cannot be A Q 108 or A Q 107, for then a diamond lead by West would resolve the difficulty.)

Declarer has, at most, eight tricks on top. The ninth can come only from a squeeze in hearts and clubs. The hearts must be A Q alone—if A Q x, the lead of heart king would be fatal to the defense—and the clubs A K 73, for if they are as good as A K 10 x, the lead of club queen gives South three tricks in clubs, and enables him to end-play West. So the whole hand is:

♠ Q 10 7   ♡ A Q   ◇ A Q 8 7   ♣ A K 7 3

The play, when West leads the last spade, is to discard a heart from dummy and a diamond from declarer's hand. West exits with a diamond; declarer cashes the ace and king of clubs, and runs off the diamonds. The last diamond squeezes West in hearts and clubs.

J. R.

INFORMATION, UNAUTHORIZED. See UNAUTHORIZED INFORMATION.

INFORMATORY DOUBLE. An early name for the TAKE-OUT DOUBLE. More recently used by Robert EWEN in his book on doubles to encompass doubles designed to give the partner of the doubler a variety of options or information, such as the COMPETITIVE DOUBLE.

INFORMATORY PASS. See PENALTY PASS.

INHIBITORY DOUBLE. A psychic maneuver in a competitive auction aimed at intimidating the opponents. It usually takes the form of a double of a forcing bid after partner has made an overcall. For example:

SOUTH	WEST	NORTH	EAST
Pass	1 ♡	2 ♣	2 ♠
Dbl.			

East's two spade bid is clearly forcing, and if South held a good hand with spades he would be well advised to wait for better things. The doubler, in fact, usually has a bad hand with support for his partner's suit, to which the latter retreats at his turn.

Since it makes no impression on any but the very inexperienced players, it has an unethical flavor, and is seldom resorted to. It met with undeserved success on a hand from the 1955 World Championship.

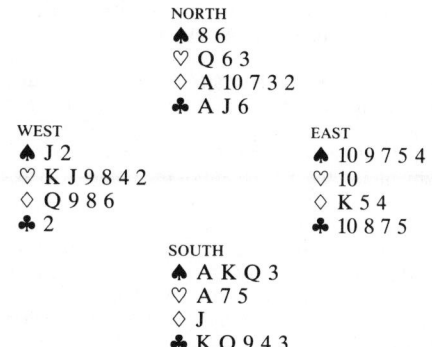

NORTH
♠ 8 6
♡ Q 6 3
◇ A 10 7 3 2
♣ A J 6

WEST
♠ J 2
♡ K J 9 8 4 2
◇ Q 9 8 6
♣ 2

EAST
♠ 10 9 7 5 4
♡ 10
◇ K 5 4
♣ 10 8 7 5

SOUTH
♠ A K Q 3
♡ A 7 5
◇ J
♣ K Q 9 4 3

In the closed room, the British pair (N-S) bid and made six clubs. In the open room, where Schapiro and Reese were East-West, for Great Britain this was the bidding:

SOUTH	WEST	NORTH	EAST
			Pass
1 ♣	1 ♠!	2 ◇	Dbl.
Pass	Pass!	3 ♣	Pass
3 NT	Pass	Pass	Pass

East's double was of the "impossible" variety, which West was expected to remove. Having made a psychic overcall, Reese was in no position to retreat to two spades, even though his partner's double indicated spade support, and he chose to pass rather than risk a complication by introducing his real suit.

INITIAL BID. The first bid of any deal. See OPENING BID.

INITIAL LEAD. The first lead of any deal. See OPENING LEAD.

INNER SEQUENCE. A sequence of which the top card is not the top card of the suit holding. See INTERMEDIATE SEQUENCE.

INSPECTION OF TRICKS. (1) The last trick may be inspected by any player, and each player required to identify his contribution to the trick, until the inspector has turned his own card face down on the table. (2) Until play ceases, QUITTED TRICKS may not be inspected except at the director's specific instruction. (3) After play ceases, the played and unplayed cards may be inspected to settle, e.g., a claim of a revoke or of the number of tricks won and lost; but no player should handle cards other than his own. See LAWS OF DUPLICATE, Law 66.

INSTINCT (or intuition). A term loosely applied to one's inherent feeling about the right play, or more seldom the right bid, to make during a deal of bridge.

Some players are said to be totally devoid of instinct or card sense (really sensitivity), and have to make calculations either rapid or involved for any play involving percentages. The concept of "instinct" as such has been challenged by many authorities, but those who possess it or claim to possess it maintain its definite existence. See TABLE PRESENCE.

INSTRUCTIONS (director's). The announcements by the director by which a movement in a session of duplicate bridge is completed. At the end of each round, the director instructs the players as to their movement and the movement of the boards in play. At determined times, this movement may vary for one or more rounds. The ARROW SWITCH, SKIP, and redistribution of boards are examples of such variations. Instructions are also given to the contestants for twinning of boards, methods of qualification, starting times for succeeding sessions, and other conditions of contest.

INSUFFICIENT BID. A bid which is lower in rank than a bid previously made in the same auction. For the penalties involved, see LAWS (Law 27).

INTERCITY MATCH. Many intercity matches have been played in various parts of North America. Notable among these were the series between New York and Philadelphia which the latter won regularly.

The first matches to have official status were those for the *Sports Illustrated* Trophy, subsequently for the Congress Playing Card Trophy when the United States Playing Card Company assumed chief sponsorship of the series in 1966 which it withdrew after the 1968 matches. These two-day events preceded the Summer Nationals from 1960 to 1973, and the city acting as host for the Nationals was the contender against the defending champions. The first contest was held in California in 1960. It was held twice that year, at the Summer Nationals and again·in the fall, and also in 1968 when New York hosted the Spring Nationals. Results are listed as follows:

YEAR	WINNER	LOSER
1960	Los Angeles	New York
1960	Los Angeles	New York
1961	Houston	Los Angeles
1962	Twin Cities	Houston
1963	Los Angeles	Twin Cities
1964	Los Angeles	Toronto
1965	Chicago	Los Angeles
1966	Chicago	Denver
1967	Montreal	Chicago
1968	Montreal	New York
1968	Minneapolis	Montreal
1969	Los Angeles	Minneapolis
1970	Boston	Los Angeles
1971	Boston	Chicago
1972	Boston	Denver
1973	Boston	Washington

INTERCOLLEGIATE BRIDGE TOURNAMENT. An annual event contested by universities and colleges throughout the United States and Canada, organized by Geoffrey Mott-Smith, 1940–60, William Root, 1961–65, Lawrence Rosler and Jeff Rubens, 1966–67 (who also assisted with the preparation of par hands from 1963–65), and subsequently by Roberta Applegate of Bradley University. The tournament is sponsored by the Association of College Unions—International, with the financial assistance of the Charles Goren Foundation and Celanese Corporation and technical assistance of the ACBL. When the Goren Foundation assumed financial sponsorship in 1969, the tournament became known as the Charles Goren Intercollegiate Bridge Tournament. In 1974 Celanese Corporation assumed full financial responsibility for the tournament. The ACBL grants master-point sanctions for all levels of the competition.

One of the unique features of the tournament for many years was the use of par hands. The earliest matches were conducted as a face-to-face contest for sixteen finalists, but in 1953, the procedure was changed to a mailing of par hands to each campus with the score cards rated in New York, N.Y. Under this plan, titles were awarded to the highest-scoring pair on the North-South hands and on the East-West hands. In 1965, the face-to-face final was restored and par hands were used in the qualifying round. Initially, the final was scored by match points, but international match-point scoring was adopted in 1967, and the conversion of IMPs to victory points was introduced in 1968. Par hands were eliminated in 1969, and the tournament became a three-stage contest, with an on-campus qualifying round and a regional semi-final in addition to the final.

From the restricted-to-Ivy-League beginnings of twelve colleges in 1940 and 1941, participation increased to 140 schools and 1,600 pairs in 1974. For a list of past Intercollegiate winners, see Appendix I.

INTEREST-SHOWING BIDS can be used as an alternative to CUE-BIDS when the opening and response have agreed on a major suit at the level of three or four. Having been often suggested and played in the United States without achieving popularity, they were developed in 1948 by some Cambridge University, England, players (E. M. L. and J. R. A. Beale, and H. P. F. Swinnerton-Dyer), and are an optional part of the ACOL SYSTEM.

If the bidding goes one spade—three spades; one spade—four spades; two spades—three spades; or two spades—four spades; or similarly in hearts, a change of suit which would normally be a cue-bid is made in a suit in which some support is needed. For example:

(a)	(b)
♠ A K 10 5 3	♠ K Q 9 5 4
♡ Q J 7 3	♡ A K J 6
◇ A	◇ Q 7 3
♣ K Q 7	♣ A

The opening bid of one spade is raised to three spades, an Acol limit raise showing about 11 points or the equivalent counting distribution.

On hand (a) the interest-showing bid would be four hearts, indicating that the opener needs some help in the form of heart honors or a heart shortage.

The interest-showing bid may well be made in a three-card suit. On hand (b) the opener rebids four diamonds to ask for support in that suit.

In each of these cases a normal cue-bid would

leave the responder in doubt about how to evaluate his hand for slam purposes.

For an alternative treatment, see ASKING BIDS.

INTERFERENCE BID. Any defensive overcall which is not attacking or strength-showing, but is designed to obstruct somewhat the path of the opponents, who have already opened the bidding. Sometimes interference is made with pre-emptive or jump-bid tactics. See NUISANCE BID and OVERCALLS.

INTERIM RESPONSE. See WAITING BID.

INTERIOR CARD. An intermediate card; formerly, the second card in sequence, as the jack in a holding of queen, jack, and others.

INTERIOR SEQUENCE. See INTERMEDIATE SEQUENCE.

INTERMEDIATE CARDS. See BODY and SPOT CARDS.

INTERMEDIATE JUMP OVERCALL. A jump overcall promising a good six-card suit and a hand approximately the strength of an opening bid. An ideal hand with which to make an intermediate jump overcall in hearts would be ♠xx ♡ A K J 9 x x ◇ A x ♣ J x x. For alternative uses of the jump overcall see JUMP OVERCALL, ROMAN JUMP OVERCALL, WEAK JUMP OVERCALL.

INTERMEDIATE SEQUENCE. A sequence within a suit such that the top card of the suit is not a part of the sequence, as the Q J 10 in a holding of A Q J 10, or the J 10 9 in a holding of A J 10 9. Some experts play that the lead of the jack against no trump denies a higher honor, and therefore lead the ten from A J 10 and K J 10. By extension, a lead of the ten can promise a higher honor by partnership agreement. The nine would then be led from a holding headed 10 9. See JOURNALIST LEADS; RUSINOW LEAD; ZERO OR TWO HIGHER LEADS.

INTERMEDIATE TWO-BID. An opening bid of two in a suit to show a strong hand somewhat short of game strength. In the original version, introduced about 1930, responder could pass the intermediate two-bid with a worthless hand, and some experts still play it in this fashion. Most, however, play it as a one-round force, with two no trump the required weakness response. See ACOL TWO-BID.

INTERNAL BLOCK. See UNBLOCKING.

INTERNATIONAL BRIDGE. There have been international tournaments and challenge matches since the earliest years of bridge. The first officially sponsored international tournament was held in Vienna in June 1930 under the auspices of the Austrian Bridge Union. The first international organization was the INTERNATIONAL BRIDGE LEAGUE, founded in 1932 by a small group of European countries, which conducted European championships until 1939. After World War II, the EUROPEAN BRIDGE LEAGUE was formed to replace the IBL.

Today there are a large number of regional international organizations or tournaments. See BALTIC CONGRESS; CENTRAL AMERICAN AND CARIBBEAN BRIDGE FEDERATION; COMMON MARKET CHAMPIONSHIPS; FAR EAST BRIDGE FEDERATION; NORDIC CHAMPIONSHIPS; SOUTH AMERICAN BRIDGE CONFEDERATION; SOUTHERN AFRICAN BRIDGE FEDERATION.

The first official world championship was held in New York in 1935 between France, reigning European champions, and a team representing the AMERICAN BRIDGE LEAGUE. The only other pre-war world championship was held in 1937 in Austria, hosted by the IBL. World championship play resumed in 1950 with the first of a series of contests for the BERMUDA BOWL. Since 1963 the Bermuda Bowl has been conducted by the WORLD BRIDGE FEDERATION, formed in 1958. The WBF also conducts quadrennial WORLD PAIR OLYMPIADS and WORLD TEAM OLYMPIADS.

INTERNATIONAL BRIDGE ACADEMY. Formed in 1965 at Ostend at the urging of J. Besse and P. Collet for the purpose of fostering the study of bridge as a science. The Academy holds biennial Congresses in conjunction with the World Team and Pair Olympiads and publishes journals in French and English after each Congress, which include a report on the meeting as well as articles on the scientific and technical aspects of bridge. Awarded its first literary prize in 1968 to Géza Ottlik of Hungary for his *Bridge World* article "The Quest." Since 1966 it has staged a world bidding contest for the Marcel Peeters Challenge Cup, which has attracted wider international participation each year since its inception. Sponsored by *Bridge World,* the United States joined the competition in 1969 and dominated the final standings by placing nine pairs among the ten overall leaders. Members of the Academy's Council of Directors in 1975 were: Alan Truscott, President; P. Collet, General Secretary, BP 111, 1040 Brussels, Belgium; C. Monk, Deputy General Secretary; G. Belladonna, J. Besse, H. Franklin, E. Kaplan, A. Traub, J. R. Vernes.

INTERNATIONAL BRIDGE LEAGUE. A forerunner of the WORLD BRIDGE FEDERATION, founded on June 10, 1932, at Scheveningen, Holland, by a small group of European countries. During the years 1932–39, the IBL organized annual championships, including a WORLD CHAMPIONSHIP in Budapest in 1937. The other tournaments ranked as EUROPEAN CHAMPIONSHIPS.

Presidents of the IBL were:

1932/3	A. E. Manning-Foster	Great Britain
1933/4	A. J. E. Lucardie	Holland
1934/5	R. D. van Gransberghe	Belgium
1935/6	Dr. E. Henriques	Sweden
1936/7	H. E. Tibor de Kallay	Hungary
1937/8	Johannes Brun	Norway

In 1936 and 1937 the IBL was subdivided into a European Division and an American Division. Albert MOREHEAD was President of the American Division.

**INTERNATIONAL BRIDGE PRESS ASSOCIA-
TION.** A worldwide organization of some four
hundred bridge writers, mostly professionals, whose
reports and articles appear in newspapers and other
periodicals in most countries where tournament
bridge is played. Authors of books, radio and TV
lecturers, etc., are also eligible for membership. At
the Oslo 1958 European Championships the bridge
journalists present formed the European Bridge
Press Association; at the first Olympiad played in
1960 in Turin, many non-European bridge writers
joined and the name was changed to International
Bridge Press Association (IBPA). The first president, G. Ramsey, died in office and was succeeded
by R. Halle (1960–64), J. Kelly (1964 until his death
in 1970), and R. Frey (1970–). E. Jannersten was
Executive Secretary-Treasurer from the foundation
of the organization and was for long its mainstay until
he resigned that post at the beginning of 1975, when
he was named Senior Vice-President for life. He was
editor of the IBPA's monthly bulletins until 1967,
when the then R. Barrow (later Lederer) assumed
the editorial duties, followed in turn by A. Dormer
who took over in 1973. Vice-presidents have included J. Vandenborre, L. Sapire, A. Jacques, H. Franklin, A. Morehead, A. Sheinwold, J. Le Dentu,
Henry Francis, and, in 1974, as Executive Vice-
President, H. Filarski. In addition, members of the
Executive Committee have included A. Trucott, C.
Cabanne, S. Moller, S. Carstensen, and A. Dormer,
who became Membership Secretary in 1975. E. von
Mutius, S. Carstensen, A. Moyse Jr., Gen. A. M.
Gruenther, and H. Schenken are among those to be
named as Honorary Member. The recruitment of
American members begun by Morehead was expanded by Frey until journalists of the Western
Hemisphere nearly equal the total of those elsewhere. The IBPA's functions have embraced negotiations with tournament organizers to improve
working conditions and accessibility of information
to the press; closer cooperation with national and
international bridge organizations; publication of
anthologies, such as Bridge Writers Choice (1964
and 1968); establishment and presentation of annual
awards for accomplishments in various fields of
bridge; the dissemination of news bulletins to
members and Associate Members, and the sponsorship of bridge promotions, such as the Bols Bridge
Tips Competition, offering substantial prizes to
invitees and journalists.

INTERNATIONAL CHAMPIONSHIPS. See WORLD
CHAMPIONSHIPS; Appendix III for European Championships, Far East Championships, South American Championships; Appendix I for North American
Championships.

INTERNATIONAL CODE. The Laws of Rubber
Bridge or of Duplicate Contract Bridge.

INTERNATIONAL FUND PAIRS. One-session pair
events held at the Spring and Fall National championships. These are in addition to the International
Fund CONTINENTWIDE GAME held in January. The proceeds are used to defray the expense of North American participation in Bermuda Bowl competition.

INTERNATIONAL MASTER. See WORLD BRIDGE
FEDERATION PLAYER RANKINGS.

INTERNATIONAL MATCH. A contest between
two (or more) countries. See ANGLO-AMERICAN
MATCHES; EUROPEAN CHAMPIONSHIP; FAR EAST CHAMPI-
ONSHIP; FRANCO-AMERICAN MATCHES; SOUTH AMERICAN
CHAMPIONSHIP; WORLD CHAMPIONSHIP.

INTERNATIONAL MATCH POINTS. A method of
scoring used frequently in team events, and occasionally in pair events.

The procedure appears to have been invented in
Vienna, and was first used at the international level
in the 1938 European Championship in Oslo. IMPs
were first used in a World Championship in 1951.

The original name was EMP, or European Match
Points. The original scale provided for a maximum
gain of 12 points, as follows:

Point Diff.	EMP	Point Diff.	EMP
10– 30	1	400– 490	7
40– 60	2	500– 590	8
70–100	3	600– 740	9
110–180	4	750–1490	10
190–290	5	1500–1990	11
300–390	6	2000 and up	12

A revised scale was adopted for the 1948 European
Championships in Copenhagen, with a maximum of
15 points. A further revision in 1961, devised by a
subcommittee of the World Bridge Federation,
brought the maximum to 25 points. This had the
effect of increasing the relative award to large gains,
and brought the scale slightly nearer to total-point
scoring.

1948 Scale		1961 Scale	
Point Diff.	IMPs	Point Diff.	IMPs
0– 10	0	0– 10	0
20– 60	1	20– 40	1
		50– 80	2
70– 130	2	90– 120	3
140– 210	3	130– 160	4
		170– 210	5
220– 340	4	220– 260	6
350– 490	5	270– 310	7
		320– 360	8
500– 740	6	370– 420	9
750– 990	7	430– 490	10
		500– 590	11
1000–1240	8	600– 690	12*
1250–1490	9	700– 790	13
		800– 890	14
1500–1990	10	900–1040	15
2000–2490	11	1050–1190	16
		1200–1340	17
2500–2990	12	1350–1490	18
3000–3490	13	1500–1740	19
		1750–1990	20
3500–3990	14	2000–2240	21
4000 and up	15	2250–2490	22
		2500–2990	23
		3000–3490	24
		3500 and up	25

* See LAWS OF DUPLICATE BRIDGE (Law 74) for the newer (1962)
scale, which differs from this point on.

The purpose of introducing international match points was to eliminate the inherent defects of other methods: total-point scoring accented one or two big swing boards; board-a-match reduced all boards to equal status. The general effect of the graduated scale of international match points is to flatten the value of high scores and to heighten the value of part-score contracts.

In team games, the international match points are awarded after the net score of the team (North-South and East-West) has been computed. The points are awarded to the team with a positive net score.

In pair events, each pair is compared with an "average" score, and the international match points awarded may be positive (for a score better than average) or negative (for a score below the average). The "average" score is the arithmetic mean of all scores, except that the best and worst scores are usually omitted in computing the comparison value. The purpose of this is to prevent one unusual result influencing scores at other tables. The best and worst scores, however, are used in computing the difference for that pair from the average. The net IMP scores on each "match" may be converted into victory points on a graduated scale.

This use of IMP scoring in pair events was originated by the British Bridge League under the Chairmanship of Geoffrey BUTLER, and is sometimes called the Butler method.

The most logical use of international match-point scoring in pair competition is in connection with qualifying events for pairs to compete in team events, as it adapts pair play to team scoring results. However, this method of scoring has been used successfully at the club level.

INTERNATIONAL OPEN TEAM SELECTION.

Many methods have been tried for selection of the North American team for Bermuda Bowl contests or of the United States team for World Olympiads. No method has proved satisfactory, but the following have been tried:

1950–60—Team Performance:

From 1950 to 1960, the ACBL selected the winners of the SPINGOLD, or the victors in a play-off between the Spingold and VANDERBILT winners. This had the advantage of producing a well-knit team, but it sacrificed the theoretical objective of fielding the "best" team: it is unlikely that the best six players, or the best three pairs, will form themselves into a voluntary team.

In 1960 the United States was entitled, by virtue of the size of the ACBL membership, to send four teams to the first World Team Olympiad. Two of the teams sent were the winners of the Vanderbilt and the Spingold. Each of the two other teams consisted of three pairs selected by a committee (the five most recent ACBL Presidents attending the 1959 Fall Nationals) from among the contestants remaining in the seventh or eighth round of the Vanderbilt and Spingold respectively. The four teams were:

Spingold Winners	*Vanderbilt Winners*
Oswald Jacoby	John Crawford
Ira Rubin	Sidney Silodor
Victor Mitchell	B. J. Becker
William Grieve	Norman Kay
Morton Rubinow	Tobias Stone
Samuel Stayman	George Rapee
Benjamin O. Johnson (npc)	Julius Rosenblum (npc)

Spingold 2	*Vanderbilt 2*
Charles H. Goren	Leonard Harmon
Helen Sobel	Sidney Lazard
Howard Schenken	William Hanna
Harold Ogust	Meyer Schleifer
Lewis L. Mathe	Donald Oakie
Paul Allinger	Ivar Stakgold
R. L. Miles Jr. (npc)	Harry Fishbein (npc)

1961—Direct Selection:

The ACBL International Team for 1961 consisted of three pairs selected by the ACBL Board of Directors from among the winners and runners-up in major national events. The direct selection method suffers from the disadvantage that it is virtually impossible to find selectors who are: technically competent; objective and unattached to particular players; not themselves candidates for the team. Italy solved this problem by appointing Carlo Alberto Perroux as "dictator" in charge of selection, but most countries would not accept this solution, even if a Perroux were available.

1962–69 Trials by Pairs:

In an effort to be fair and just, and to select pairs that are in effective current form, pairs trials were instituted in 1961 for the selection of the 1962 Team. From 1961 to 1966, the first three pairs in each trial were nominated as the international team for the following year, and the fourth-place pair became the alternate pair. Beginning with the 1967 trials, this automatic selection method was dropped and the non-playing captain was permitted to select any two of the top four pairs, and the third and alternate pair from among the remaining finalists. Julius Rosenblum exercised this option in 1967 when he named E. Kaplan and N. Kay, who had finished fourth in the trials, to the team and P. Feldesman and I. Rubin, the third-place pair, as alternates, the only time the top three pairs were not selected as the international team.

The scoring method used in the trials is that described under INTERNATIONAL MATCH POINTS.

1961 (Houston)	1 C. Coon, E. Murray
	2 G. R. Nail, M. Key
	3 L. Mathe, R. Von der Porten
	4 N. Kay, S. Silodor
1962 (Phoenix)	1 J. Jacoby, G. R. Nail
	2 R. Jordan, A. Robinson
	3 H. Schenken, P. Leventritt
	4 G. Michaud, D. Carter
1963 (Miami)	1 R. Hamman, D. Krauss
	2 S. Stayman, V. Mitchell
	3 R. Jordan, A. Robinson
	4 L. Mathe, E. O. Taylor
1964 (Dallas)	1 H. Schenken, P. Leventritt
	2 I. Erdos, K. Petterson
	3 B. J. Becker, D. Hayden
	4 R. Hamman, D. Krauss

1965 (San Francisco)	1 P. Feldesman, I. Rubin
	2 L. Mathe, R. Hamman
	3 E. Murray, S. Kehela
	4 B. J. Becker, D. Hayden
1966 (Pittsburgh)	1 E. Murray, S. Kehela
	2 E. Kaplan, N. Kay
	3 A. Roth, W. Root
	4 B. J. Becker, D. Hayden
1967 (Atlantic City)	1 R. Jordan, A. Robinson
	2 A. Roth, W. Root
	3 P. Feldesman, I. Rubin
	4 E. Kaplan, N. Kay
1968 (Atlantic City)	1 G. Rapee, S. Lazard
	2 W. Eisenberg, R. Goldman
	3 R. Hamman, E. Kantar
	4 I. Rubin, J. Westheimer

1970—Vanderbilt-Spingold Play-off:

The Pair-Team trials were discontinued in order to allow selection of an entire team rather than individual pairs to comprise a team. The 1970 International Team was selected by a direct 180-board play-off between the winners of the 1969 Vanderbilt and Spingold. However, this did not prove entirely satisfactory since it limited the number of teams that could challenge for international representation and reduced the prestige of the Fall National Championships, which previously had two events that qualified pairs for the trials.

1971–72—Placing-Points Play-offs:

Beginning with the 1969 Fall Nationals, the ACBL adopted a play-off among the teams with the best records over the course of a year. Teams placing high in the three major team championships (Reisinger, Vanderbilt, and Spingold) were awarded points according to the following scale:

Vanderbilt and Spingold		Reisinger	
1st	— 10 points	1st	— 6 points
2nd	— 4 points	2nd	— 4 points
3rd-4th	— 2 points	3rd	— 2 points

If a team accumulated 20 points it was to be automatically designated the International Team; otherwise teams with lesser numbers of points were to play off.

1973—Vanderbilt, Spingold, Reisinger, Grand Nationals Winners Play-off:

With the introduction of the GRAND NATIONAL CHAMPIONSHIPS (2) in 1972, the selection of the North American international team became a simple matter of a four-team play-off among the winners of the ACBL's four major team events: the Vanderbilt, Spingold, Reisinger, and Grand Nationals.

INTERNATIONAL PAIR EVENTS. See COMMON MARKET CHAMPIONSHIPS; LONDON SUNDAY TIMES PAIRS; PAN AMERICAN INVITATIONAL CHAMPIONSHIPS; WORLD PAIR OLYMPIAD.

INTERNATIONAL PALACE OF SPORTS. See KING OR QUEEN OF BRIDGE.

INTERNATIONAL TEAM PLAY-OFF MATCHES. See INTERNATIONAL OPEN TEAM SELECTION.

INTERNATIONAL TEAM TRIALS. See INTERNATIONAL OPEN TEAM SELECTION.

INTERNATIONAL WOMEN'S TEAM SELECTION. The United States has sent women's teams to each of the World Women's Team Olympiads, each selected by a different method. For the 1960 event, a committee consisting of the five most recent ACBL Presidents attending the 1959 Fall Nationals selected the team, by choosing three pairs of women who finished first or second in any national championship event during 1959.

For 1964, a trial by pairs was held, similar to the trials held during that period for the INTERNATIONAL OPEN TEAM SELECTION. For 1968 a round robin was held, for which four pairs qualified. Each pair played a 32-board match in partnership with each of the other pairs, and npc Margaret WAGAR was empowered to select any three of the four pairs.

For 1972, women's teams were to earn points in the major national team championships and play off to determine the US 1972 women's team. However, one team amassed so many points that it was designated without a play-off. The following were the US women's teams in the first four Olympiads:

1960	1964
Agnes Gordon	Agnes Gordon
Dorothy Hayden	Muriel Kaplan
Malvine Klausner	Alicia Kempner
Helen Portugal	Helen Portugal
Sylvia Schwartz	Stella Rebner
Jo Sharp	Jan Stone
C. J. Solomon (npc)	P. Hodge (npc)
1968	1972
Hermine Baron	Mary Jane Farell
Nancy Gruver	Emma Jean Hawes
Emma Jean Hawes	Marilyn Johnson
Dorothy Hayden	Jacqui Mitchell
Suzanne Sachs	Peggy Solomon
Rhoda Walsh	Dorothy Hayden Truscott
M. Wagar (npc)	M. Wagar (npc)

For 1976, women were permitted to earn "selection points," either as teams or as pairs, on all-women teams in the Vanderbilt, Spingold, Reisinger, and Spring National Women's Team events. The available points ranged from 1 point for being runner-up in the Spring Women's teams to 28 for winning the Vanderbilt or Spingold. To be selected intact, a team must have won more qualification points than any individual pair, except that if there were only one higher pair, a four-person team plus the high-ranking pair would form the six-member team. See also VENICE TROPHY.

INTERVENING BID. An overcall.

INTERWOVEN HOWELL. Two HOWELL games of equal size, so arranged that each plays (at each round) the boards which are not in play in the other.

Since a Howell game of X tables requires 2X — 1 sets of boards, X — 1 sets are out of play at a given time. By proper arrangement these boards may be used in a parallel or "interwoven" Howell game; except that there must be one pair of relay tables at which the same set of boards is in play simultaneously in both games.

INTUITION. See INSTINCT.

INVERTED MINOR SUIT RAISES. The combination of the following two procedures:

(1) *Single raise in minor strong:*

♠ K 6 4
♡ 5 3
♢ Q J 4
♣ K 10 5 4 2

With this hand, bid two clubs in response to one club. In KAPLAN-SHEINWOLD this is forcing, with a range of 9–20 points.

Also used in BARON, when it is simply constructive with a range of 7–10 points.

(2) *Double raise in minor pre-emptive:*
Used on hands on which the opponents may well hold the majority of the high-card strength, and are likely to have a major-suit fit:

♠ 6 5 3
♡ 8 2
♢ 9 3
♣ J 9 7 6 4 3

This would be sufficient for a non-vulnerable jump from one club to three clubs. If vulnerable, the bidder should have a singleton.

INVITATION. A bid which encourages the bidder's partner to continue to game or slam, but gives him the option of passing if he has no reserve values in terms of high-card strength or distribution.

In nearly all cases such bids are one level below the game or slam which is being suggested, so bids of two no trump or three of a major suit often come in this category.

INVITATIONAL BID. Bid indicating strong game prospects, which requests partner to continue if he has some reserve strength. The bidder announces that he can count about 23–24 points in the combined hands (including distribution).

A bid of two no trump is normally invitational:

WEST	EAST		WEST	EAST
1 NT	2 NT	or	1 ♡	2 ♣
			2 ♡	2 NT

but a jump by responder (response or rebid) is an exception, being forcing, in standard methods.

A jump rebid by the opener is invitational:

WEST	EAST
1 ♡	1 ♠
3 ♡	

and so is a single raise from two to three in the later stages of the auction:

WEST	EAST		WEST	EAST
1 ♠	2 ♣		1 ♠	2 ♣
2 ♠	3 ♠		2 ♡	3 ♡

For other sequences which are invitational in some styles but forcing in others, see JUMP REBIDS BY RESPONDER. See also conventions listed in GAME INVITATION.

IRELAND. See CONTRACT BRIDGE ASSOCIATION OF IRELAND; IRISH BRIDGE UNION; NORTH OF IRELAND BRIDGE UNION.

IRISH BRIDGE UNION. Founded in 1955, the Union consists of representatives from both the CONTRACT BRIDGE ASSOCIATION OF IRELAND and NORTH OF IRELAND BRIDGE UNION. It is responsible for selecting teams to represent the whole of Ireland in World Olympiads and European Championships (but not for Camrose Trophy matches), and for organizing All-Ireland events for Teams of Four and Pairs. Membership, comprising the total of both integral bodies, was about 13,500 in 1974.

Joint Honorary Secretaries, 1975:
Col. R. Dalton, 17 St. Johns Road, Dublin 4, Ireland. (CBAI)
John Grummitt. (NIBU)

IRON DUKE, NOT THROUGH THE. An expression indicating that the user holds a very strong hand. The remark is an improper one, and is usually made when the player splits cards of equal value to prevent a finesse.

IRREGULAR LEAD. A calculated departure from normal procedure occurring in the play of the first card to any trick by a defender.

IRREGULARITY. A deviation from correct procedures set forth in the LAWS and PROPRIETIES.

ISOLATING THE MENACE. A maneuver in squeeze-play technique.

A menace may be controlled by both opponents, in which case it is usually advantageous to have the full burden of guarding that suit imposed on one opponent. The term "isolating the menace" refers to declarer's efforts in that direction: he seeks to have the menace isolated so that it is protected by only one opponent.

	NORTH	
	A K x x	
WEST		EAST
Q J x x		10 x x
	SOUTH	
	x x	

If the diagram illustrates the distribution of a side suit at a trump contract, then North's menace can be isolated by playing off the ace and king followed by a ruff on the third round. At any contract a first-round duck would ensure that the menace was isolated.

ISRAEL BRIDGE FEDERATION. Revived in 1960, the Federation had over 1,000 members in 1974 in seven main branches: Tel Aviv, Haifa, Jerusalem, Netanya, Savyon, Beersheba, and Eilat. In 1963 Israel became a member of the European Bridge

League, and has participated in European Championships since 1965, hosting the 1974 event, and in Olympiads since 1964. Israel was runner-up in the 1975 European Championships, thereby winning the right to represent Europe in the 1976 Bermuda Bowl. The Federation sponsors an International Bridge Festival, held annually in Tel Aviv since 1966, and National Championships, which are held in the main branches throughout the year. The growth of popularity of bridge in Israel is attested to by the fact that in 1967 an official Hebrew bridge terminology was submitted to the Israeli Academy of Language for approval; since then, bridge columns in Israeli papers, formerly printed in English, German, or French, have appeared in Hebrew. The Federation also awards master points. Players listed separately are: D. Bardach, Dr. N. Bogair, Z. Duchovni, I. Elenberg, J. Frydrich, T. Hirsch, M. Hochzeit, M. Katz, R. Kunin, S. Lev, Y. Levit, P. Lukacs, Dr. N. Rand, P. Romik, Prof. L. Roseanu, A. Schwarz, E. Shaufel, M. Stampf.

Officers, 1975:
President: Reuben Kunen.
Secretary: David Bardach, 62 LaGuardia Street, P.O. Box 36376, Tel Aviv, Israel.

ITALIAN BRIDGE FEDERATION (FEDERAZIONE ITALIANA BRIDGE). Founded in 1936 in Milan by P. Baroni, F. Rosa, and E. Pontremoli. Reactivated after World War II, with Carl' Alberto Perroux as President, the Federation became an official body organizing regular National contests, which gave impetus to a national interest in the game. By 1974 there were about 12,500 members in 130 affiliated bodies and 160 clubs. About 50 tournaments are organized annually, including Open and Mixed Teams and the Knockout Teams for the Italian Cup, which attract an entry of 400 teams. The record of the Italian BLUE TEAM is an extraordinary one that is unlikely to be equalled. The first Italian team to compete in the European Championships in 1938 was the predecessor of the invincibles who became European Champions 1951, 1956, 1957, 1958, 1959, 1965, 1967, 1969, 1971, 1973, 1975, and sixteen times World Champions (Bermuda Bowl ten times from 1957–69, 1973–75, and World Olympiad winners 1964, 1968, 1972). Players listed separately are: W. Avarelli, P. Baroni, G. Belladonna, B. Bianchi, M. Bianchi, S. Brogi, S. Carini-Mazzacarra, E. Chiaradia, M. d'Alelio, S. DeFalco, G. Facchini, P. Forquet, A. Franco, M. Franco, G. Garabello, B. Garozzo, M. Giovine, R. Jabes, M. Ledeen, G. Messina, S. Osella, C. Pabis Ticci, G. Pelucchi, C. Perroux, V. Pittala, A. Ricci, A. Robaudo, C. Romanelli, F. Rosa, G. Siniscalco, A. Valenti, M. Venturini, S. Zucchelli.

Officers, 1974:
President: Prof. Luigi Firpo.
Secretary: Dino Mazza, Largo Augusto 3, 2022 Milan, Italy.

ITALIAN SYSTEMS. See BLUE TEAM CLUB; LEGHORN DIAMOND; LITTLE ROMAN CLUB; MARMIC SYSTEM; ROMAN SYSTEM; SUPER PRECISION.

J

JACK. The fourth ranking card in a suit. Also called knave. See COAT CARDS; COURT CARDS; VALET.

JACK, TEN, OR NINE SHOWING ZERO OR TWO HIGHER HONORS. See ZERO OR TWO HIGHER LEADS.

JACOBY INDIVIDUAL MOVEMENT. See RAINBOW INDIVIDUAL MOVEMENT.

JACOBY TRANSFER BIDS. Used in responding at the two-level to one no trump opening bids, or in responding at the three-level to two no trump openings. These transfers were introduced to the American bridge public by Oswald JACOBY in a *Bridge World* article in 1956, although they had been used in Sweden as early as 1953–54 as a result of a series of articles in *Bridge Tidningen* written by Olle WILLNER.

Two diamonds shows hearts and asks opener to bid two hearts.

Two hearts shows spades, and asks opener to bid two spades.

This convention greatly increases the chance that the strong hand will be the declarer in a suit contract. It also solves the problems created by many hands of intermediate strength:

(a)	(b)
♠ Q 10 8 7 6 4	♠ 8
♡ K 6 3	♡ A 10 9 5 4
◇ 4 3	◇ 10 5
♣ 7 5	♣ K Q 10 5 3

On hand (a) the response is two hearts, and the rebid of two spades is raised to three spades. This is a game invitation which the opener can pass if he wishes.

On hand (b) the response of two diamonds shows the heart suit, and responder continues with three clubs. This shows his two-suited hand, and leaves the next move to the opener. Three clubs is forcing, but might be made on a slightly weaker hand.

There are methods for extending transfers to the minor suits. One is to use a two spade response to transfer to three clubs and a three club response to transfer to three diamonds. Another is to use the two spade response as a minor two-suiter in a game-going hand with slam interest (see MINOR SUIT STAYMAN). A third alternative is to use the two spade response to show a game-going hand with one long minor suit and slam interest.

The defense against low-level artificial bids needs

consideration. With a balanced distribution the fourth hand can afford to wait for a round. He can bid an unusual no trump to indicate minor suits; double to show the suit doubled and the non-touching suit; cue-bid in responder's real suit to show the remaining possible two-suited combination (suits of the same color).

JACOBY TWO NO TRUMP. A method of increasing the accuracy of slam bidding, developed by Oswald JACOBY, and used in conjunction with limit major suit raises.

After a one heart or one spade opening, a jump to two no trump by an unpassed hand is a forcing raise of unlimited strength. As revised, opener's conventional rebids to clarify his strength and distribution are as follows: a new suit on the three-level shows a singleton or void in the bid suit, a new suit at the four-level shows 6–5–1–1 distribution (with a minimum one heart opening, opener should not show a spade suit); four of the agreed trump suit shows a minimum opening bid, no slam interest; three of the agreed trump suit shows 16 points or more, strong interest in slam; and three no trump describes a sound opening bid (14–15 points), but no distributional feature.

JAMAICA BRIDGE ASSOCIATION. An original member of CACBF founded in 1944, it had a total of 16 affiliated clubs in 1963, with a membership of 500. National events held annually are the Open Teams and Open Pairs. Jamaican players listed separately are: L. Alberga, O. Honiball, R. de Leon, Mrs. Ruby Lyons, F. Shalom.

Officers 1975:
President: Trevor Jones
Secretary: Calvin Wong, 47 West St., Kingston, Jamaica

JAPAN CONTRACT BRIDGE LEAGUE. Founded in Tokyo in 1953 with eleven members, and by 1974 the membership had grown to more than 2,000 in 55 affiliated clubs, with branches in Osaka, Nagoya, and Sapporo. Participates in the Far East Championships, hosting the 1958 and 1964 events, and in the World Par Championships; sent a team to the 1972 World Team Olympiad. National tournaments of importance include the Double Knockout Teams for the Prince Takamatsu Cup, Round Robin Teams for the Japan Times Cup, Teams-of-Four (modified board-a-match scoring) for the Fujiyama Cup, and Open Pairs for the Okazaki Club. Players listed separately are: T. Butcher, Mrs. P. Dudley, R. Fisher, U. Inoue, M. Kanazawa, K. Kawakami, S. Kimura, A. Kurokawa, E. Mizutani, J. Montalto, Y. Nakamura, K. Saburi, T. Sakurai, J. Wong, A. Yamada, F. Yamada.

Officers, 1974:
President: Toru Hagiwara.
Secretary: Tetsuji Hikawa, Room 202, Fudosan Kaikan, 5-ban Yotsuya 3-chome, Shinjuku-ku,

Tokyo 160, Japan, or CPO Box 1696, Tokyo 100–91, Japan.

JETTISON. The discard of a high-ranking honor, usually an ace or a king. The term was originated by G. Mott-Smith.

A typical example is the following:

```
                    NORTH
                    A 10 8 6 4 3
WEST                                    EAST
Q 2                                     J 9 5
                    SOUTH
                    K 7
```

In a no trump contract, South leads the king in a position in which East needs an entry. West must drop the queen, for otherwise South will allow the queen to hold on the next round.

The play may be necessary to effect an unblock, to create an entry, or to avert a ruff. The following jettison by a defender was necessary to avert a squeeze.

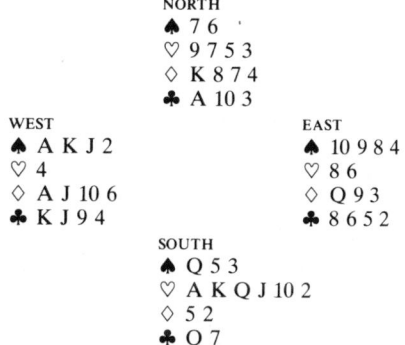

```
                    NORTH
                    ♠ 7 6
                    ♡ 9 7 5 3
                    ◇ K 8 7 4
                    ♣ A 10 3
WEST                                    EAST
♠ A K J 2                               ♠ 10 9 8 4
♡ 4                                     ♡ 8 6
◇ A J 10 6                              ◇ Q 9 3
♣ K J 9 4                               ♣ 8 6 5 2
                    SOUTH
                    ♠ Q 5 3
                    ♡ A K Q J 10 2
                    ◇ 5 2
                    ♣ Q 7
```

Against four hearts, West led the spade king, and shifted to a heart. South returned the spade queen, taken by the ace, and West played the spade jack. Dummy ruffed, and South ran all his trumps. West's only defense was to discard the diamond ace. See also ENTRY SQUEEZE.

JETTISON SQUEEZE. A form of ENTRY SQUEEZE.

JOKER. A fifty-third card in decks of cards, sometimes used as a substitute or "wild" card, but not used in bridge. See TAROT.

JOSEPHINE. The GRAND SLAM FORCE, associated in Europe with the name of Mrs. Josephine CULBERTSON, and therefore named after her. (Mrs. Culbertson was the first to write about the convention; it was devised by her husband, Ely Culbertson.)

JOURNALIST LEADS. A method of opening leads advocated by the *Bridge Journal* in 1964–65. The details are as follows:

Against no trump contracts:

A usually from A K J x (x x) or A K 10 x (x x). Third hand is requested to unblock a high honor if he can afford it, otherwise to give a length signal (high with an even number, low with an odd number of cards in the suit).

K from A K or K Q (assuming a high honor should be led).

Q from Q J (or K Q 10 9; third hand is requested to play the jack if he has it).

J from J 10. The jack denies a higher honor.

10 from A 10 9, K 10 9, Q 10 9, A J 10, K J 10. The ten guarantees a higher honor (queen, king, or ace).

9 from 10 9. The nine promises the ten and no higher honor.

Second highest or highest from lower spot cards to discourage suit continuation.

Usually lowest card from a long suit headed by one or two honors to encourage suit continuation.

The purpose of these leads is to make it easier for third hand to know whether to continue the attack on the suit led or to shift. The following hand shows what can happen when Journalist leads are not used.

IMP
Both sides vulnerable
North dealer

NORTH
♠ A J 10 6 3
♡ 5
◇ 7 4
♣ A K 10 7 2

EAST
♠ Q 9 5 2
♡ Q J 10 4
◇ A 6 3
♣ Q 5

NORTH	EAST	SOUTH	WEST
1 ♣	Pass	1 ♡	Pass
1 ♠	Pass	3 NT	Pass
Pass	Pass		

Using standard leads, West led the ten of diamonds to East's ace, South playing the deuce. Now if South started with a hand like: ♠ K x ♡ A K x x x ◇ Q J 2 ♣ x x x, East must continue diamonds. But if the ten was West's highest diamond, a heart shift is called for. East actually continued diamonds, and found South with: ♠ K x ♡ K x x x ◇ K Q J x ♣ J x x. Declarer won the diamond, cashed ace and king of clubs (because he could hardly afford to lose a finesse to East and get a heart through), and made ten tricks.

Using Journalist leads, West would have led the nine of diamonds, and East would have shifted to a heart, defeating the contract.

Against suit contracts Journalist Leads follow a different pattern. From two touching honors the second highest is led; from spot cards the highest card below the nine may be led to indicate a weak holding; otherwise, the third highest is led from an even number of cards or the lowest from an odd number of cards.

JUMP BID. A call of one more than is necessary to raise the previous bid, and made at any point after the auction has been opened. Bids of two or more than necessary are termed "double jumps," etc. SKIP BID is a more general term, embracing jumps to any level.

JUMP OVERCALL. A suit overcall at a level one higher than necessary:

SOUTH	WEST		SOUTH	WEST
1 ◇	2 ♠	or	1 ♠	3 ◇

In traditional methods this bid shows a strong six-card suit or a seven-card suit, and about 15–17 points in high cards. The jump in a minor suit is a strong invitation to three no trump, and the suit should be solid or nearly solid. With a still stronger hand the usual procedure is to double and bid the suit, perhaps with a jump, on the second round. For other uses of this jump, see INTERMEDIATE JUMP OVERCALL; ROMAN JUMP OVERCALL and WEAK JUMP OVERCALL.

One of the primary reasons for Ely Culbertson's initial introduction of the jump overcall as a strong bid was to take care of good two-suited hands, with which the player would not welcome a bid in a third suit or a penalty pass in response to a take-out double; many experts consider this to be of greater value than using the single-jump overcall as a weak preempt.

JUMP PREFERENCE. Returning to partner's original suit at a level one higher than necessary.

WEST	EAST
1 ♡	1 ♠ or 2 ♣ or 1 NT
2 ◇	3 ♡

In CULBERTSON and ACOL such bids are non-forcing. Many experts take an intermediate position, regarding them as forcing if the first response was at the two-level, and non-forcing otherwise. See also JUMP REBIDS BY RESPONDER.

If the opener gives jump preference, it is sometimes non-forcing:

WEST	EAST
1 ♣	1 ♡
2 ♣	2 ◇
3 ♡	

JUMP RAISE. See DOUBLE RAISE.

JUMP RAISE IN RESPONDER'S SUIT. See OPENER'S REBID.

JUMP REBID BY OPENER. See OPENER'S REBID.

JUMP REBIDS BY RESPONDER. Jump bids short of game by responder at his second turn.

This is an important area of bidding in which the practices of expert partnerships vary widely, and each partnership must make its own rules. In STANDARD AMERICAN (but not in CULBERTSON), it is generally understood—although rarely stated unequivocally—that all jump bids by responder are forcing to game. This treatment is followed by many East Coast experts.

The other extreme is represented by ACOL, in which all such bids (except the jump shift) are encouraging but not forcing. This style is followed by many experts in other parts of the United States,

balanced hand with more than 18 points. However, the last type is not easy to handle with a jump shift, and an alternative method is described under IMPOSSIBLE BIDS.

Many experts have less elevated standards for a jump shift, making the bid with about 17 points

JUMP REBIDS BY RESPONDER

Two No Trump	*Forcing Style*	*Non-forcing Style*
1 ♣ – 1 ♡ 1 ♠ – 2 NT	13–15, as an original 2 NT response. (An 11–12 point hand remains a problem.)	11–12. A 13–15 hand bids 3 NT, or makes a fourth-suit bid.
Jump Preference		
1 ♣ – 1 ♡ 1 ♠ – 3 ♣	13 or more.	11–12; perhaps only three-card support, but four or five is probable.
1 ♠ – 2 ♣ 2 ♡ – 3 ♠	13 or more. Probably three-card support, because of the failure to bid 3 ♠ originally.	11–12; three-card support if used in combination with limit raises.
1 ♡ – 1 ♠ 1 NT – 3 ♡	Shows game values, with the exact strength depending on the range of the 1 NT rebid.	Forcing—a special case. The strength depends on the strength of the 1 NT rebid.
1 ◇ – 1 ♠ 1 NT – 3 ◇	Ditto.	10–12, probably four-card support; weaker if the 1 NT rebid was constructive.
Jump Raise		
1 ♣ – 1 ♡ 1 ♠ – 3 ♠	13–15 and four-card support; equivalent to 1 ♠ – 3 ♠.	10–12 and four-card support; equivalent to a limit raise of 1 ♠ – 3 ♠. A stronger hand bids 4 ♠, or bids the fourth suit followed by 4 ♠ as a mild slam suggestion.
Jump Rebid		
1 ♣ – 1 ♡ 1 ♠ – 3 ♡	Game values and a six-card suit.	10–11 points and a six-card suit.
Jump Shift		
1 ♣ – 1 ♡ 1 ♠ – 3 ◇	Game values; usually a hand with a fit in opener's second suit, which has therefore improved to the point of slam prospects. But a two-suiter is possible.	As forcing style.

particularly California, Texas, and the Midwest. Many experts hold an intermediate position, treating some such bids as forcing and others as non-forcing.

The table above summarizes the two different styles.

JUMP SHIFT. A new suit response at a level one higher than necessary:

WEST	EAST		WEST	EAST
1 ♡	2 ♠	or	1 ♡	3 ♣

In standard methods this shows a hand of great strength which can almost guarantee a slam (19 points or more including distribution). The hand is usually one of four types: a good fit with opener's suit; a strong single-suiter; a strong two-suiter; or a

including distribution; in ACOL, 16 points or less with a good fit or a good suit. In this last case the response may be made in a three-card suit, either because the hand is balanced or because there is a fit with opener but no side suit.

A theory advanced by Paul SOLOWAY that is gaining adherence among experts is that jump shifts should be limited to three types of hands: (1) one-suiters, (2) semi-balanced hands, and (3) hands with a good fit for opener's suit. Responder clarifies his hand by his rebid. If he has a one-suited hand he rebids his suit. If he has a semi-balanced hand his next bid is in no trump. If he has a good fit for opener, he can make a FRAGMENT bid in a new suit to show a singleton in the fourth suit, or he can return to opener's suit to deny having a singleton. This method of showing a singleton and support for opener's suit is workable only if it is agreed that the jump shift cannot be made with a two-suited hand; under this agreement responder's bid of a new suit at his second turn cannot show a real suit.

Another method, proposed by R. P. Reed of Boulder, Colo., is to use a jump shift to show 19 or more points in support of opener's suit and the bid suit shows the lowest first-round control in responder's hand.

Perhaps the most unusual treatment of the jump shift is that used by W. PASSELL and D. STRASBERG. Their idea is that a jump shift shows a solid suit in the next high-ranking suit, opener's suit excepted. For example, after a one club opening, a jump to two spades shows a solid diamond suit. Opener normally accepts the transfer, which permits responder to cue-bid his other controls. If responder is unable to cue-bid, he supports the agreed suit, and a subsequent bid of four no trump by opener is not BLACKWOOD, but asks about the length of responder's suit.

Rebids by the opener after a jump shift are not standardized, but the opener should usually make the rebid he was planning after a non-jump response, only, of course, one level higher. There are two exceptions to this principle: a non-jump rebid of three no trump would not promise extra values, nor would a reverse.

This idea was originated by Ely Culbertson, who called it "jump take-out" or "forcing take-out."

For a pre-emptive use of this response, see WEAK JUMP SHIFT RESPONSES. See also PASSED HAND.

JUMP SHIFT REBID. See OPENER'S REBID.

JUMP TAKE-OUT. See JUMP SHIFT.

JUMP TO GAME IN MAJOR SUIT. See OPENER'S REBID for jump to game in responder's major suit or in opener's major suit. See also TRIPLE RAISE.

JUNIOR MASTER. A player who has achieved some minor success at duplicate bridge. See RANKING OF PLAYERS.

JUNK. A contemptuous term used to describe a hand or a holding felt to be particularly valueless by the person describing it. See BAD CARDS.

K

KANTAR CUE-BID. A specialized cue-bid after an opponent's overcall suggested by Edwin KANTAR. After, for example,

WEST	NORTH	EAST	SOUTH
1 ♠	2 ◇	3 ◇	

In this specialized usage, three diamonds shows a 5-4-4-0 or 4-4-4-1 hand with a shortage in the opponent's suit. The strength may be as little as 8-9 high-card points, but there is no upward limit.

For other uses of the cue-bid, see CUE-BID IN OPPONENT'S SUIT.

KANTAR THREE NO TRUMP. See THREE NO TRUMP OPENING.

KAPLAN-SHEINWOLD. A system devised by Edgar Kaplan and Alfred Sheinwold, based on the WEAK NO TRUMP and aimed at more precisely limiting the strength shown by all bids. The features of the system are:

(1) Weak no trump with 12–14 points. An 11-point hand may be opened with 2½–3 QUICK TRICKS, or a 15-point hand with less than two quick tricks. Responses of two diamonds, two hearts, two spades, three clubs, and three diamonds are weak sign-off bids. A bid of two clubs followed by a minor-suit rebid is strong and forcing. Other responses are standard, with non-forcing STAYMAN. A bid of two clubs followed by three hearts or three spades is forcing, and shows a more balanced pattern than an immediate jump. Whether doubled or not, responder runs from one no trump with less than 5 points, often into two clubs or two diamonds.

After an overcall, a double is negative and a new suit bid at the three-level is forcing.

(2) Minor-suit openings are sound (but any hand with three quick tricks must be opened). If balanced, 15–20 points and possibly a three-card suit; one no trump rebid shows 15–17 and two no trump rebid 18–20. A single raise of responder's major shows 15–17; a double raise 18–19; a triple raise 20–21 (in each case the requirements are reduced as distribution improves). A maximum unbalanced hand reverses or jump-shifts before raising.

Responder bids a major in response whenever possible. Opener's reverse is a one-round force, and two clubs following one diamond is treated as a reverse. A three no trump rebid shows a solid minor with outside stoppers.

For single and double raises, see INVERTED MINOR SUIT RAISES. Single raises are forcing and double raises are pre-emptive. A response of one no trump shows 5–8, and two no trump 12–15. A balanced 9–11 point hand may respond in the other minor.

If the opening is doubled, take-outs retain their meaning, but all raises are pre-emptive (redouble is the strong raise).

Opener may raise responder's major with three-card support in competiton.

(3) NEGATIVE DOUBLE.

(4) Jump shift by responder is pre-emptive in competition.

(5) FIVE-CARD MAJORS, which can be light: a 9-point hand with quick-trick and playing-trick strength is possible. Exceptionally, a strong four-card suit may be bid, with a balanced minimum with honors concentrated in two suits, or a touching lower-ranking weak five-card suit. ONE NO TRUMP RESPONSE FORCING, but opener passes with the rare balanced minimum hand.

LIMIT JUMP RAISES are used. The jump raise preceded by one no trump shows three-card support and a more balanced hand. A three no trump response is used instead of the standard (strong) jump raise. A two no trump response is standard. A minor-suit response is 12–13 minimum unless followed by a rebid in the minor, showing only a semi-solid suit headed by the ace; a delayed raise for opener or a two no trump rebid is game-forcing.

After one heart—one spade, opener rebids one no trump, two hearts, or two spades with a minimum. A bid of two clubs or two diamonds would be more constructive. After one spade—two hearts (minimum 10 and a five-card suit), minimum hands bid three hearts or two spades; maximum hands (18 or more) bid three clubs or three diamonds, which are the only forcing bids; other bids show 15–17, including two no trump which shows a singleton heart.

(6) Opening psychics are lead-directing, containing a legitimate suit with a high honor (2–6 points). A jump shift forces the opener to rebid in his suit or no trump, whichever is cheaper. Psychics are recommended only when non-vulnerable; at IMPS, only non-vulnerable versus vulnerable; at BOARD-A-MATCH, never.

(7) WEAK TWO-BIDS need one and one-half to two quick tricks and a semi-solid suit in first and second position. A single raise is pre-emptive, and other responses by an unpassed hand are forcing; two no trump asks the opener to bid a side honor.

(8) TWO CLUBS is the only forcing opening. After a two diamond negative response, the bidding can stop short of game if the opener rebids two no trump or bids and rebids one suit.

(9) THREE NO TRUMP opening shows a two no trump hand (20–22) with a long solid minor.

(10) CUE-BIDS are used, under game to suggest a slam, and over game to ask about an unbid suit. A subsequent four no trump bid is a natural slam invitation, as in BLUE TEAM CLUB.

(11) GERBER over no trump bids.

(12) BLACKWOOD in other situations.

(13) GRAND SLAM FORCE.

(14) ROMAN ASKING BIDS.

(15) TAKE-OUT DOUBLES emphasize distribution: there should be not less than three cards in each unbid suit. A cue-bid is the only forcing response.

(16) OVERCALLS have the same range as an opening bid. Responder should seldom pass if he would have responded to an opening bid.

(17) WEAK JUMP OVERCALLS, usually with a maximum of one and one-half tricks.

(18) ONE NO TRUMP OVERCALL shows 17–19. A two-level take-out is a sign-off, and a cue-bid is Stayman.

(19) Optional features of the system include: SHORT-SUIT GAME TRIES; FLINT; UNUSUAL NO TRUMP; LANDY; FRAGMENT BIDS; MICHAELS CUE-BID; ROMAN TWO DIAMONDS; WEAK JUMP SHIFT RESPONSES by passed hand; three clubs as "prelude to sign-off" over a jump rebid of two no trump; two diamonds as "forcing" Stayman; two no trump over opposing take-out double as semi-pre-emptive raise; three no trump after limit jump raise of major to ask for short suit.

E. K(aplan)

KEEPING SCORE. The process by which a record is kept of the activity during a rubber of bridge or of Chicago, and of the result on a board in duplicate. There can be more than one scorekeeper among a group of rubber bridge players, but in duplicate the score is usually kept by North.

KEEPING THE BIDDING OPEN. For the strength needed to make a response, see ONE OVER ONE RESPONSE. For opening action by the fourth player see BALANCING.

KELLY SOLID SUIT SIGNAL. Devised in the days of whist, by Nathan Kelly, Brookline, Mass. The play of second highest or highest card of a suit (originally led) to the second trick of the suit to show that the balance of the suit (five cards originally or longer at no trump play) is now established and will run.

	NORTH	
	8 4	
WEST		EAST
K 9 7 5 3		J 10 2
	SOUTH	
	A Q 6	

With the lead of the five of hearts, the jack forces declarer's queen. On a subsequent play, East obtains the lead, and leads the ten. If declarer plays the ace, the solid suit signal requires West to play the king. If declarer ducks, the second highest card (in this case, the nine) is played.

A variation for the original leader is the selection of which of touching honors shall be led against a no trump contract. From K Q J 4, the lead of the king followed by the queen shows a four-card suit; had the holding originally been K Q J 7 5, the lead of the jack would show five cards in the suit; had the original holding been K Q J 10 3 2, the ten would have been chosen as the second lead (the lower the second lead, the longer the suit).

KEM CARD TROPHY. For the Non-Masters Pair Championship, donated by the Kem Card Company in 1937; originally the National Amateur Pair Championship; contested at the Fall Nationals until 1966 and subsequently at the Spring Nationals, under which headings past results are listed.

KEM CARDS. The first successful plastic cards, manufactured in America since 1934. Each year several new designs are introduced, and lost or damaged cards can be replaced by the manufacturer. See PLASTIC CARDS.

KENYA BRIDGE ASSOCIATION. A group formed in 1963 with approximately 150 members.

Officers, 1975:
Chairman: N. Ajania.
Secretary: Mrs. J. H. Ayton, P.O. Box 49221, Nairobi, Kenya.

KEOHANE TROPHY. For the Open Individual Championship, contested at the Summer Nationals, donated by Mrs. Ethel Keohane in 1973 in memory of her husband, William H. Keohane. Past winners are listed under Summer Nationals.

KEY CARD BLACKWOOD. A form of BLACKWOOD in which the king of trumps is counted as a fifth ace. Responder bids five clubs with no aces or four aces, five diamonds with one ace or five aces, five hearts with two aces, and five spades with three aces. A subsequent bid of five no trump by the Blackwood bidder may be used in various ways. It may ask for kings in the normal manner, except that the king of trumps would not be shown. Or it may ask for an additional feature in the Blackwood responder's hand. See also BYZANTINE BLACKWOOD; CULBERTSON FOUR-FIVE NO TRUMP; KEY CARD GERBER; ROMAN KEY CARD BLACKWOOD.

KEY CARD GERBER. A modification of the GERBER CONVENTION in which trump honors may be counted as aces. When only the trump king is to be counted as an ace, responder bids four diamonds with no aces or four aces, four hearts with one ace or five aces, four spades with two aces, and four no trump with three aces. Some partnerships agree to count both the king and queen of trumps as aces. Using this agreement responder's four spade bid would show two or six aces. See BYZANTINE BLACKWOOD; ROMAN GERBER.

KHEDIVE. An early name for bridge as played on the French Riviera, which lends support to the belief that the game is of Turkish origin. (See HISTORY OF BRIDGE.)

KIBITZER. An onlooker at bridge or other games.

KIBITZER'S MAKE. A hand which seems to have sufficient controls, enough high-card winners, and sufficiently few losers to be successful in a contract, but which for reasons of entry problems, duplication of values, or lie of the cards is doomed. The term comes from the habit of some poorly trained kibitzers to indulge in analyses that careful scrutiny shows to be fallacious.

KIBITZING. The act of watching a game from the sidelines, sometimes including the making of comments about the bidding and play of the hand (if the game is bridge). Generally, the term "kibitzer" is used to refer to a person who spends most of his life at a session of bridge, wherever played, actually watching the play as opposed to participating in it. There are many arenas in which such kibitzing can take place, and the level of the behavior of the kibitzers will fluctuate accordingly. In serious play at top clubs in America and in Europe, the level of play is usually high and frequently, too, stakes are involved, so that there are unwritten, as well as written, rules concerning the deportment of any onlooker. See LAWS (Law 11, Proprieties, V). These onlookers know that it is extremely important for them not to give away any information about the nature of the hand or the holding that they are watching, and, too, they usually refrain from making comments about the bidding or play when the hand is ended. They often realize that they are permitted to observe the game only by sufferance of the players, and they guide themselves by the accepted norms of behavior in the particular surroundings. There are numerous stories and legends that have sprung up over the years about kibitzers and, although many of them are apocryphal, some are true, and others contain more than a germ of truth. Many of these tales are based on situations where the players are arguing vehemently about a bid or play, and it is decided that the matter be referred to the kibitzer for his opinion, with many varied and humorous endings. Then there are described systems of bidding in which an ace counts as so many points, a king one or two less, and a kibitzer still less, etc.

The word "kibitzer" itself derives from the German word for a green plover, a highly inquisitive bird. The role of the kibitzer grew somewhat in stature and in story as bridge itself expanded and progressed. In. H. T. Webster's regular series of bridge cartoons drawn for the New York *Herald Tribune,* the artist's attention was often turned to kibitzers, and the resulting drawings were among his most amusing. Some of the great humorists of the thirties and forties occasionally did pieces about kibitzers, and one of the wittiest was George S. Kaufman's "The Great Kibitzers' Strike." All of the comic and semi-serious articles written reflected the general mores and customs of the times regarding kibitzers and attitudes toward them. A classic story, and one of the few completely true ones, involved the players at a well-known New York club and their one kibitzer. The contract was five diamonds doubled, and with the opponents on lead to the tenth trick, declarer spread his hand, claiming the balance, just making contract. The opposition agreed, and the cards were just about to be thrown in, when the kibitzer pointed out a defensive lead which would have defeated the contract at that point. Bitter harangue and confusion then ensued and the matter was at length referred to the card committee. The final decision was that declarer should be credited with making five diamonds doubled, the defense with defeating the contract one trick, and the kibitzer ordered to pay the difference.

KICK IT. Colloquial term for "I double."

KILLED. (1) Captured, as in "The king was killed by the ace." (2) The fate of a player or pair playing well but scoring badly. At duplicate, the term implies that the opponents have played luckily and well on a group of boards. At rubber bridge it would refer to a session of poor cards and bad breaks. The term is always born of frustration and frequently of a desire to avoid admissions of poor play to one's teammates or oneself. (3) Denuded of whatever entries it may have had, as "The spade lead killed the dummy."

KING. The second highest ranking card in a suit in bridge. See COAT CARDS and COURT CARDS.

KING OR QUEEN OF BRIDGE. An honorary title bestowed each year by the International Palace of Sports, Inc., on the high school senior having the highest number of ACBL master points to his credit. As a part of the Kiwanis International Youth Career Awards Program, the International Palace of Sports, located in North Webster, Indiana, each year presents a plaque to the King or Queen of Bridge and awards a $1,000 scholarship to the alma mater of the winner, to be granted to a deserving student selected by the high school. The program is designed to inspire young people to better citizenship. Past holders of the title and their winning master point totals are:

1973	J. Merrill	470.41
1974	Jeff Meckstroth	479.91
1975	Bobby Levin	963.65

KING CONVENTION. A variation of the CULBERTSON FOUR-FIVE NO TRUMP convention in which responder with two aces and a king may sometimes bid the suit in which he holds the king.

KING LEAD. See JOURNALIST LEADS; OPENING LEADS; RUSINOW LEADS.

KISS OF DEATH. A penalty of 200 points on a partscore deal in a pair contest; usually down two vulnerable, or down one doubled vulnerable; down four not vulnerable rarely applies, because of the probability that the opponents can make a game. This minus 200 score is normally disastrous because it will rank lower than part-scores made in the opposite direction. The term can also be used by a defender, referring to the appearance from declarer's hand of a key card which kills all defensive hopes.

KIVI CONVENTION. See BULLDOG SYSTEM.

KNAVE. The jack, the fourth highest ranking card of a suit. This term is obsolete in American usage, and obsolescent elsewhere, although it had considerable currency in England and Continental Europe until the 1940s. One reason for the quick acceptance of the term "jack," instead of "knave," is that in reporting hands or in any abbreviated diagram or description of play the initial J can be used, whereas previously Kn had to be used, since a plain K would have been ambiguous. See COAT CARDS and COURT CARDS.

KNOCK. (1) An action, of doubtful propriety, consisting of hitting the table lightly instead of speaking the word "pass." While it is true that bridge laws technically condone passes executed in irregular style, provided the offender at least is consistent in passing that way all the time, the best practice and that most approved by top tournament directors remains the spoken word "pass." (2) An informal method of ALERTING.

KNOCK TOGETHER. See CRASHING HONORS.

KNOCKOUT TOURNAMENT. An event (usually for teams of four or more) in which one team plays against only one opposing team in a given session. The losers are eliminated. The winners remain in the contest, and meet new opponents at later sessions, until only one winning team remains.

In a double-knockout tournament, a team must lose twice before being eliminated. After its first loss, a team is transferred to the "loser's bracket," from which teams are eliminated after each round, and to which teams losing in the second or later rounds in the winner's bracket are added.

KOCK-WERNER REDOUBLE. A rescue device invented by the Swedish partnership of Rudolf KOCK and Einar WERNER. When partner's low-level overcall has been doubled, a redouble calls for a take-out. For example:

SOUTH	WEST	NORTH	EAST
1 ♣	1 ♡	Dbl.	Redbl.

East shows that he has a singleton or void in hearts, and requests a take-out into another suit. The possibility of playing in two clubs is not excluded: the best escape is often to a suit bid by the opposition.

Such redoubles are almost useless in a natural sense. If East is satisfied to play in one heart doubled, he simply passes.

(The treatment of the redouble needs special consideration if North-South are using NEGATIVE DOUBLES.)

See also S O S REDOUBLE.

L

LHO. Left-hand opponent, or the player on declarer's left.

LOL. An expression designating innocent-appearing bridge players who unexpectedly bid against you as though they were world champions. The letters originally designated "little old ladies," and were used as a term of some opprobrium, but the frequency with which little old ladies secured excellent results by simple common-sense action against pseudo-experts has caused the connotation to become more one of amusement and respect rather than of belittlement.

LANCIA TOURNAMENTS. In 1975 a team sponsored by Lancia Division of Fiat and consisting of W. AVARELLI, G. BELLADONNA, P. FORQUET, B. GAROZZO, O. SHARIF, and A. VIVALDI played four challenge matches in the United States against teams that had each earned the right to challenge the Lancia team by winning a qualifying Swiss tournament. The tour was organized by Goren International; the tournaments were sanctioned and conducted by the ACBL.

The prizes for any team that beat the Lancia team were five Lancia cars; if no team beat the Lancia team, the team with the best losing score would receive the five cars; the prizes for the team with the best score in losing to the Lancia team without winning any cars were steamship cruises.

The matches were played in New York, Los Angeles, Chicago, and Miami. The Lancia team was defeated in every match except Chicago. Thus every challenging team won prizes. Participants were: New York—M. GRANOVETTER, R. RUBIN, A. SONTAG, P. WEICHSEL; Los Angeles—L. COHEN, B. EISENBERG, E. KANTAR, Dr. R. KATZ; Chicago—L. BART, G. O'NEILL, W. ROSEN, M. ROSENBERG; Miami—R. BATES, S. DUBSON, J. MOHAN, Dr. G. ROSENKRANZ.

LANDY. A conventional overcall of two clubs after an opposing no trump opening as a request for a take-out with emphasis on the major suits, devised by the late Alvin Landy of New York. The overcaller promises at least four cards in each major suit, and is probably short in one or both minors. (A player with balanced distribution would normally double or pass.) The Landy bidder seldom has more than 15 high-card points.

Many players limit the convention to an immediate overcall of a weak no trump, but it can also be extended by agreement to the fourth position, and/or to strong no trump bids.

Responses to the Landy bid are not standardized, but the following scheme had the endorsement of the inventor of the convention:

(1) *Three clubs* is a forcing response unrelated to clubs, and asks the Landy bidder to describe his hand further. The responder may have equal length in the major suits. This is the *only* forcing response.

(2) *Three spades and three hearts* are game invitations, and might be based on a three-card suit.

(3) *Two no trump and three diamonds* are natural and encouraging but not forcing.

(4) *Two diamonds* shows a weak hand with diamond length.

(5) *Pass* shows a weak hand with club length.

Defense. A double of the Landy bid by the third player is often reserved for a good defensive hand which sees prospects of a good penalty (although one authority uses the double to show clubs). As a corollary, three clubs is natural and unconstructive with a long club suit.

Some of the other bids available to the opener's partner need careful consideration. Two spades and two hearts are unlikely to be needed as natural bids in the face of an announced major two-suiter, so a partnership can give these bids a specialized meaning.

A response of two no trump can be employed as "unusual," asking opener to bid a minor suit. A hand which would raise one no trump to two no trump without interference can double and bid two no trump on the next round.

(For alternative conventional defenses to one no

trump opening bids, see ASPRO; ASTRO; BROZEL; EXCLUSION BID; RIPSTRA.)

LANDY TROPHY. A trophy awarded in memory of Alvin LANDY to the winners of the Spring CONTINENT-WIDE charity game since 1969.

LANGUAGE. (1) Symbolic: The art of communication between partners; as, "the language of bidding" and "the language of signals." (2) Verbal: English is the official language of WBF tournaments and other international tournaments.

LATE PAIR. A pair desiring to enter an event after it has started. An ingenious director can usually add one or more pairs to a game during the first round (or even later) without disrupting play for those who have already started. See APPENDIX TABLE; HALF TABLE.

LATE PLAY. Play, after completion of a session, of one or more boards which would normally have been played during an earlier round.

A late play arises when the director observes that a given table has one or more boards to play in a given round when the rest have finished and are ready to move. The director may instruct the contestants not to start another board, but to return at the end of the contest to play the board then.

LAVINTHAL SIGNAL. See SUIT PREFERENCE.

LAW OF BALANCED DISTRIBUTION. A general principle relating to suit distributions, stated as follows by John A. TIERNEY, Annapolis: The more symmetrical of two specific holdings is the more probable. Two equally symmetric holdings are equally probable.

This does *not* mean that an even suit split is more likely than an uneven one, which is untrue with four cards (or a higher even number). It refers to specific layouts. If five cards are missing, the QJ432, all the following are equally probable: Q4; 32; Q43; 432. The following are less symmetric, and therefore less probable: Q; 2; QJ43; Q432.

LAW OF SYMMETRY. A theory of distribution suggested by Ely CULBERTSON. His idea was that imperfect shuffles tend to produce a suit pattern equivalent to a hand pattern in the same deal. A player with 5–4–3–1 distribution should expect the outstanding cards in his long suit to be divided 4–3–1 more frequently than the mathematical odds would suggest. There is no mathematical or empirical basis for this theory.

LAWS. See LAWS OF CONTRACT BRIDGE. In this encyclopedia "LAWS" refers to the Laws of both Contract and Duplicate unless separate reference is made to "LAWS OF DUPLICATE."

LAWS OF BRIDGE. In 1743, Edmond HOYLE published *A Short Treatise on the Game of Whist, Containing the Laws of the Game.* The laws as codified there became so universally accepted that they guided whist players for over one hundred years. The Arlington and Portland clubs revised the code in 1864, and the Portland Club remained as the recognized authority in the newer game of bridge, the laws of this newer game appearing under the pen name of Boaz in 1895. Other clubs adopted their own versions, until in 1902 a committee representing many card clubs promulgated an American code. This set of laws was not received with universal acclaim, and gradually the laws of the Whist Club (New York) became standardized.

Bridge, which had succeeded in surpassing whist, was itself superseded by auction bridge, and in 1909 the Portland and Bath clubs in England framed a Code of Laws of Auction Bridge; the Whist Club followed with its Laws of Auction Bridge in 1910. These were revised in 1911, 1912, 1915, 1917, and 1920, and in 1926 the most recent code was adopted. In the 1920s auction bridge began to be succeeded by the then new game of contract bridge, and in 1927 the Whist Club adopted a code based essentially on the 1926 Laws of Auction Bridge. This time the American clubs were ahead of their British counterparts, the Portland and other clubs adopting a code in 1929.

For several years thereafter, the Whist Club, the Portland Club, and the Commission Française du Bridge worked through their committees to make a code that would be international in scope, finally agreeing on one on October 19, 1932. This code was revised by equivalent groups in 1935, 1948, and 1963.

Meanwhile, the peculiar requirements of duplicate bridge, which was sweeping the country and much of the world, pointed up the necessity for a code to cover duplicate. The first such code was the result of a committee of the American Bridge League, adopted in November 1928. The 1932 revision of the *Laws of Contract Bridge* necessitated a 1933 revision of the duplicate laws. In America a further revision in 1943 of the laws of duplicate led to an international effort (1948–49 by the Portland Club, the European Bridge League, and the National Laws Commission for America) that revised the *Laws of Contract Bridge* and the *Laws of Duplicate Contract Bridge*. These laws remained in vogue throughout the world until the revision of both, under the same international groups, which became effective July 1, 1963.

The duplicate laws were further revised in 1975 under the auspices of the ACBL (with major contributions by Kaplan, Oakie, and Sheinwold) and the World Bridge Federation and thus became the first truly worldwide code. Representing the promulgating bodies were the following:

THE NATIONAL LAWS COMMISSION
of The American Contract Bridge League

Edgar Kaplan, *Chairman*

B. Jay Becker	Easley Blackwood
John Gerber	Richard Goldberg
Charles H. Goren	Oswald Jacoby
Thomas F. McCarthy	Donald Oakie
Carl B. Rubin	Edgar Theus

DRAFTING COMMITTEE
FOR DUPLICATE BRIDGE

Alfred Sheinwold, *Chairman*

John Gerber	Edgar Kaplan
Donald Oakie	Edgar Theus

THE LAWS COMMISSION OF THE
WORLD BRIDGE FEDERATION

Geoffrey L. Butler, *Chairman* (Great Britain)
Julius Rosenblum, *Ex-Officio* (USA)
Carlos Cabanne (Argentina)
Silvio Carini Mazzaccara (Italy)
Johannes Hammerich (Venezuela)
Edgar Kaplan (USA)
Andre LeMaitre (Belgium)
Dr. Ralph Mizroch (South Africa)
Donald Oakie (USA)
George Rosenkranz (Mexico)
Leslie Schneideman (New Zealand)
Alfred Sheinwold (USA)
Gunnar Zabel (Norway)
Victor Zirinsky (Hong Kong)

Representing the promulgating bodies on the international group in 1963 were the following:

THE NATIONAL LAWS COMMISSION
of the American Contract Bridge League

Harold S. Vanderbilt*† ⎱ *Chairmen*
Waldemar von Zedtwitz*† ⎰
Alvin Landy*†, Secretary

Russell J. Baldwin*†	Raymond J. McGrover
B. Jay Becker*	Albert H. Morehead*†
Charles H. Goren	Alfred Sheinwold*†
Lee Hazen	Alexander M. Sobel*
Thomas F. McCarthy	Charles J. Solomon*
Alfred M. Gruenther, Honorary Member	

CARD COMMITTEE
of the Portland Club

H. H. Renshaw, *Chairman*

E. H. Blain	Baron R. de Nexon
Sir Guy Domville, Bt.	G. L. Butler
K. Hurst-Brown	W. G. Purves
E. Rayne	Dr. J. S. Spickett

THE EUROPEAN BRIDGE LEAGUE

G. L. Butler, Delegate

LAWS OF CONTRACT BRIDGE

THE SCOPE OF THE LAWS
◆◆◆◆◆◆

The Laws are designed to define correct procedure and to provide an adequate remedy when-

---

* Drafting Committee for Duplicate Bridge
† Drafting Committee for Rubber Bridge

ever a player accidentally, carelessly or inadvertently disturbs the proper course of the game, or gains an unintentional but nevertheless unfair advantage. An offending player should be ready to pay a prescribed penalty graciously.

The Laws are not designed to prevent dishonorable practices and there are no penalties to cover intentional violations. In the absence of penalty, moral obligations are strongest. Ostracism is the ultimate remedy for intentional offenses.

The object of the Proprieties is twofold: to familiarize players with the customs and etiquette of the game, generally accepted over a long period of years; and to enlighten those who might otherwise fail to appreciate when or how they are improperly conveying information to their partners—often a far more reprehensible offense than a violation of a law.

When these principles are appreciated, arguments are avoided and the pleasure which the game offers is materially enhanced.

Part I

DEFINITIONS

◆◆◆◆◆◆

[For definitions of all terms except those set forth below, see definitions under LAWS OF DUPLICATE BRIDGE.*]

Defective Trick—A trick that contains fewer or more than four legally played cards.

Partial Designation—Incomplete specification by declarer of the rank or suit of a card to be played from dummy's hand (see Law 46).

Rubber—A unit in scoring denoting the winning of two games by a side.

Part II

PRELIMINARIES
TO THE RUBBER

◆◆◆◆◆◆

1. THE PLAYERS—THE PACK

Contract bridge is played by four players with a pack of 52 cards of identical back design and color, consisting of 13 cards in each of four suits. Two packs should be used, of which only one is in play at any time; and each pack should be clearly distinguishable from the other in back design or color.

2. RANK OF CARDS

The cards of each suit rank in descending order: Ace, King, Queen, Jack, 10, 9, 8, 7, 6, 5, 4, 3, 2.

3. THE DRAW

Before every rubber, each player draws a card from a pack shuffled and spread face down

---

* While certain definitions were reworded in the 1975 amendments to the duplicate laws, there were no substantive changes.

on the table. A card should not be exposed until all the players have drawn.

The two players who draw the highest cards play as partners against the two other players. When cards of the same rank are drawn, the rank of suits determines which is higher—spades (highest), hearts, diamonds, clubs.

The player with the highest card deals first and has the right to choose his seat and the pack with which he will deal. He may consult his partner but, having announced his decision, must abide by it. His partner sits opposite him. The opponents then occupy the two remaining seats as they wish and, having made their selection, must abide by it.

A player must draw again if he draws one of the four cards at either end of the pack, or a card adjoining one drawn by another player, or a card from the other pack; or if, in drawing, he exposes more than one card.

Part III

THE DEAL

◆◆◆◆◆◆

4. THE SHUFFLE

Before the cards are dealt they must be shuffled thoroughly, without exposure of the face of any card. The shuffle must be performed in full view of the players and to their satisfaction.

The pack to be used in each deal is prepared by the left-hand opponent of the player who will deal it. Preparation of the pack includes collecting the cards, shuffling them, and placing the shuffled pack face down at the left of the next dealer.

A pack properly prepared should not be disturbed until the dealer picks it up for his deal, at which time he is entitled to the final shuffle.

No player other than the dealer and the player designated to prepare the pack may shuffle.

5. THE CUT

The pack must always be cut immediately before it is dealt. The dealer presents the pack to his right-hand opponent, who lifts off a portion and places it on the table toward the dealer. Each portion must contain at least four cards. The dealer completes the cut by placing what was originally the bottom portion upon the other portion.

No player other than the dealer's right-hand opponent may cut the pack.

6. NEW CUT—NEW SHUFFLE

There must be a new cut if any player demands one before the first card is dealt. In this case the dealer's right-hand opponent cuts again.

There must be a new shuffle, followed by a cut:

(a) If any player demands one before the dealer has picked up the pack for his deal. In this case the player designated to prepare the pack shuffles again.

(b) If any player demands one after the dealer has picked up the pack but before the first card is dealt. In this case only the dealer shuffles.

(c) If a card is turned face up in shuffling. In this case the player who was shuffling shuffles again.

(d) If a card is turned face up in cutting. In this case only the dealer shuffles.

(e) If there is a redeal (see Law 10).

7. CHANGE OF PACK

The two packs are used alternately, unless there is a redeal.

A pack containing a card so damaged or marked that it may be identified from its back must be replaced if attention is drawn to the imperfection before the first card of the current deal is dealt.

A pack originally belonging to a side must be restored on demand of any player before the last card of the current deal has been dealt.

8. THE DEAL

The dealer distributes the cards face down, one at a time in rotation into four separate hands of thirteen cards each, the first card to the player on his left and the last card to himself. If he deals two cards simultaneously or consecutively to the same player, or fails to deal a card to a player, he may rectify the error, provided he does so immediately and to the satisfaction of the other players.

The dealer must not allow the face of any card to be seen while he is dealing. Until the deal is completed, no player other than the dealer may touch any card except to correct or prevent an irregularity.

9. ROTATION OF THE TURN TO DEAL

The turn to deal passes in rotation, unless there is a redeal. If a player deals out of turn, and attention is not drawn to the error before the last card has been dealt, the deal stands as though it had been in turn, the player who dealt the cards is the dealer, and the player who has missed his turn to deal has no redress; and the rotation continues as though the deal had been in turn, unless a redeal is required under Law 10.

10. REDEAL

When there is a redeal, the current deal is canceled; the same dealer deals again, unless he

was dealing out of turn; the same pack is used, unless it has been replaced as provided in Law 7; and the cards are shuffled and cut anew as provided in Laws 4 and 5.

There must be a redeal:

(a) If, before the last card has been dealt, it is discovered that

(i) a card has been turned face up in dealing or is face up in the pack or elsewhere;

(ii) the cards have not been dealt correctly;

(iii) a player is dealing out of turn or is dealing with a pack that was not shuffled or not cut, provided any player demands a redeal.

(b) If, before the first call has been made, it is discovered that a player has picked up another player's hand and has seen a card in it.

(c) If, before play has been completed, it is discovered that

(i) the pack did not conform in every respect to the requirements of Law 1, including any case in which a missing card cannot be found after due search;

(ii) one player has picked up too many cards, another too few;

(iii) two or more players on opposing sides have allowed any cards from their hands to be mixed together, following a claim that a redeal is in order.

11. MISSING CARD

When a player has too few cards and a redeal is not required by Law 10 (c), the deal stands as correct, and:

(a) If he has played more than one card to a previous trick, Law 68 applies;

(b) If a missing card is found elsewhere than in a previous trick, that card is deemed to have belonged continuously to the deficient hand and must be restored to that hand; it may become a penalty card, as provided in Law 23 or 49, and failure to have played it may constitute a revoke.

12. SURPLUS CARD

When a player has too many cards and a redeal is not required by Law 10 (c), the deal stands as correct, and:

(a) If the offender has omitted to play to a trick, Law 68 applies.

(b) If the offender has picked up a surplus card from a previous trick, or from dummy's hand, or from the other pack, or elsewhere, such surplus card must be restored to its proper place; and

(i) If the surplus card is in the offender's hand when it is discovered, there is no penalty.

(ii) If the surplus card has been led or played, the offender must substitute for it a card from his hand that he can legally play to the trick and if possible a card of the same suit as the surplus card, and the offense is subject to the rectification and penalty provisions of Laws 62 to 65.

Part IV

GENERAL LAWS
GOVERNING IRREGULARITIES
◆◆◆◆◆◆

13. PROCEDURE FOLLOWING AN IRREGULARITY

When an irregularity has been committed, any player—except dummy as restricted by Law 43—may draw attention to it and give or obtain information as to the law applicable to it. The fact that a player draws attention to an irregularity committed by his side does not affect the rights of the opponents.

After attention has been drawn to an irregularity, no player should call or play until all questions in regard to rectification and to the assessment of a penalty have been determined. Premature correction of an irregularity on the part of the offender may subject him to a further penalty (see Law 26).

14. ASSESSMENT OF A PENALTY

A penalty may not be imposed until the nature of the irregularity to be penalized has been determined and the applicable penalty has been clearly stated; but a penalty once paid, or any decision agreed and acted upon by the players, stands, even though at some later time it be adjudged incorrect.

With the exception of dummy, either member of the nonoffending side may impose a penalty, but without consulting his partner.

15. WAIVER OR FORFEITURE OF PENALTY

The right to penalize an offense is forfeited if a member of the nonoffending side
(a) waives the penalty;
(b) consults with his partner as to the imposition of a penalty before a penalty has been imposed;
(c) calls (Law 34) or plays (Law 60) after an irregularity committed by the opponent at his right.

Rectification or validation proceeds as provided in the law applicable to the specific irregularity.

16. UNAUTHORIZED INFORMATION

Any player except declarer may be subject to penalty if he conveys information to his partner other than by a legal call or play.

Information conveyed by an illegal call, play or exposure of a card is subject to the applicable law in Part V or VI.

If any player except declarer conveys information to his partner by means of a remark or an unmistakable gesture or mannerism that suggests a call,* lead, play, or plan of play; and if attention is drawn to the offense and the penalty is assessed forthwith, as provided in Laws 13 and 14:

(a) If the offense occurs before the auction closes, (penalty) either member of the nonoffending side may require both members of the offender's side to pass during the remainder of the auction; and if the offender becomes a defender, then when first it is the turn of the offender's partner to lead, including the opening lead, declarer may either
(i) require the offender's partner to lead a specified suit, or
(ii) prohibit the offender's partner from leading a specified suit; this prohibition continues for as long as the offender's partner retains the lead.

(b) If the offense occurs after the auction closes, (penalty) declarer or either defender, as the case may be, may prohibit the offender's partner from making:
(i) any lead based on the improper suggestion; this prohibition applies to any one lead, including the opening lead, and continues for as long as the offender's partner retains the lead; or
(ii) any play based on the improper suggestion; this prohibition may be applied to only one play.

The rights of the nonoffending side are not affected by an intervening call or play by the offending side. If the offender's partner has called after the offense, but before a member of the nonoffending side has subsequently called, his call may be canceled. If the offender's partner has led or played after the offense, and before a member of the nonoffending side has subsequently played, he may be required to withdraw his card and to substitute a card that does not conform to the improper suggestion, and a defender's card so withdrawn becomes a penalty card.

Part V

THE AUCTION
◆◆◆◆◆◆
Correct Procedure

17. DURATION OF THE AUCTION

The auction begins when the last card of a correct deal has been placed on the table. The

---

* After a deal has been completed, a player should not draw attention to the score, except to correct an error in recording. See Proprieties II (g).

dealer makes the first call, and thereafter each player calls in rotation. When three passes in rotation have followed any call, the auction is closed.

18. BIDS

Each bid must name a number of odd tricks, from one to seven, and a denomination. A bid supersedes the previous bid if it names either a greater number of odd tricks, or the same number of odd tricks in a higher denomination. A bid that fulfills these requirements is sufficient; one that does not is insufficient. The denominations rank in descending order: no-trump, spades, hearts, diamonds, clubs.

19. DOUBLES AND REDOUBLES

A player may double only the last preceding bid, and then only if it was made by an opponent and no call other than a pass has intervened.

A player may redouble only the last preceding double, and then only if it was made by an opponent and no call other than a pass has intervened.

A player should not, in doubling or redoubling, state the number of tricks or the denomination; but if he states either or both incorrectly, he is deemed to have doubled or redoubled the bid as it was made.

All doubles and redoubles are superseded by a subsequent legal bid. If there is no subsequent bid, scoring values are increased as provided in Law 84.

20. REVIEW OF THE AUCTION

A player who does not hear a call distinctly may forthwith require that it be repeated.

Before the auction closes, a player is entitled to have all previous calls restated when it is his turn to call, unless he is required by law to pass.

After the auction closes, declarer or either defender may require previous calls to be restated. A defender's right to such a review terminates when a member of his side has led or played to the first trick; declarer's right terminates when he has played to the first trick or dummy has spread any part of his hand.

A request to have calls restated should be responded to only by an opponent. Dummy or a player required by law to pass may review the auction at an opponent's request. Any player, including dummy or a player required by law to pass, may and should promptly correct an error in restatement.

21. CALL BASED ON MISINFORMATION

A player has no recourse if he has made a call on the basis of his own misunderstanding.

A player may, without penalty, change any call he may have made as a result of misinformation given him by an opponent, provided his partner has not subsequently called. If he elects to correct his call, his left-hand opponent may then, in turn and without penalty, change any subsequent call he may have made.

22. PROCEDURE AFTER THE AUCTION IS CLOSED

After the auction is closed:

(a) If no player has bid, the hands are abandoned and the turn to deal passes in rotation.

(b) If any player has bid, the final bid becomes the contract and play begins.

Irregularities

23. CARD EXPOSED OR LED DURING THE AUCTION

Whenever, during the auction, a player faces a card on the table or holds a card so that it is possible for his partner to see its face, every such card must be left face up on the table until the auction closes; and:

(a) If it is a single card below the rank of an honor and not prematurely led, there is no penalty, and when the auction closes the card may be picked up.

(b) If it is a single card of honor rank, or any card prematurely led, or if more than one card is so exposed, (penalty) the offender's partner must pass when next it is his turn to call; and if the offender subsequently becomes a defender, declarer may treat every such card as a penalty card (Law 50).

24. IMMEDIATE CORRECTION OF A CALL

A player may substitute his intended call for an inadvertent call, but only if he does so without pause. If legal, his last call stands without penalty; if illegal, it is subject to the applicable law.

25. CHANGE OF CALL

A call substituted for a call made previously at the same turn, when it is too late for correction as provided in Law 24, is canceled; and:

(a) If the first call was illegal, the offender is subject to the applicable law.

(b) If the first call was a legal one, the offender must either

    (i) allow his first call to stand and (penalty) his partner must pass when next it is his turn to call; or

    (ii) make any legal call and (penalty) his partner must pass whenever it is his turn to call.

The offender's partner may also be subject to a lead penalty as provided in Law 26.

26. UNAUTHORIZED INFORMATION GIVEN BY CHANGE OF CALL

When a player names a denomination not selected as his final call at that turn (as in changing a call* or in making or correcting an illegal call), then if he becomes a defender:

(a) If such denomination was a suit, (penalty) declarer may prohibit the offender's partner from leading that suit the first time the offender's partner has the lead, including the opening lead, and for as long as he retains the lead.

(b) If such denomination was no-trump, and if the offender's partner is to make the opening lead, (penalty) declarer may require the offender's partner to make the opening lead in a specified suit.

When a player has substituted another call for a double or redouble, the penalties provided in Law 27 (c) apply.

27. INSUFFICIENT BID

An insufficient bid made in rotation must be corrected, if either opponent draws attention to it, by substituting either a sufficient bid or a pass.† A double or redouble may not be substituted. If the call substituted is

(a) the lowest sufficient bid in the same denomination, the auction proceeds as though the irregularity had not occurred.

(b) any other sufficient bid, (penalty) the offender's partner must pass whenever it is his turn to call.

(c) a pass, (penalty) the offender's partner must pass whenever it is his turn to call; and if the offender's partner is to make the opening lead, declarer may either

(i) require the offender's partner to lead a specified suit, or

(ii) prohibit the offender's partner from leading a specified suit; this prohibition continues for as long as the offender's partner retains the lead.

If the offender attempts to substitute a double or redouble, it is canceled; he must pass and the offense is subject to the penalty provided in subsection (c) above.

If a player makes an insufficient bid out of rotation, Law 31 applies.

Call Out of Rotation

28. CALLS CONSIDERED TO BE IN ROTATION

A call is considered to be in rotation

(a) when it is made without waiting for the right-hand opponent to pass, if that opponent is required by law to pass.

(b) when it is made by the player whose turn it was to call, before a penalty has been

imposed for a call out of rotation by an opponent; it waives any penalty for the call out of rotation and the auction proceeds as though that opponent had not called at that turn.

29. PROCEDURE AFTER A CALL OUT OF ROTATION

A call out of rotation is canceled if either opponent draws attention to it. The auction reverts to the player whose turn it was to call. The offender may make any legal call in proper turn but may be subject to penalty under Law 30, 31 or 32.

30. PASS OUT OF ROTATION

When a player has passed out of rotation

(a) before any player has bid, or when it was the turn of the opponent on his right to call, (penalty) the offender must pass when next it is his turn to call.

(b) after any player has bid and when it was the turn of the offender's partner to call, (penalty) the offender must pass whenever it is his turn to call; the offender's partner may make a sufficient bid or may pass, but may not double or redouble at that turn; and if the offender's partner passes and subsequently is to make the opening lead, declarer may either

(i) require the offender's partner to lead a specified suit, or

(ii) prohibit the offender's partner from leading a specified suit; this prohibition continues for as long as the offender's partner retains the lead.

31. BID OUT OF ROTATION

When a player has bid out of rotation

. (a) before any player has called, (penalty) his partner must pass whenever it is his turn to call, and Law 26 may apply;

(b) after any player has called and when it was the turn of the offender's partner to call, (penalty) the offender's partner must pass whenever it is his turn to call; and if the offender's partner is to make the opening lead, declarer may either

(i) require the offender's partner to lead a specified suit, or

(ii) prohibit the offender's partner from leading a specified suit; this prohibition continues for as long as the offender's partner retains the lead.

(c) after any player has called and when it was the turn of the opponent on the offender's right* to call:

(i) If that opponent passes, the bid out of rotation, if sufficient, must be repeated and there is no penalty. If the bid out

---

* Except as permitted under Law 24.

† The offender is entitled to select his final call at that turn after the applicable penalties have been stated, and any call he has previously attempted to substitute is canceled, but Law 26 may apply.

*A call made after any player has called and when it is the turn of the opponent on the offender's left to call is treated as a change of calls and Law 25 applies.

of rotation was insufficient it must be corrected as provided in Law 27.

(ii) If that opponent makes a legal bid, double, or redouble,† the offender may in turn make any legal call and (penalty) the offender's partner must pass when next it is his turn to call, and Law 26 may apply.

32. DOUBLE OR REDOUBLE OUT OF ROTATION

When a player has doubled or redoubled out of rotation, and Law 36 or 37 does not apply:

(a) If it was the offender's partner's turn to call, (penalty) the offender's partner must pass whenever it is his turn to call; the offender may not thereafter, in turn, double or redouble the same bid he doubled or redoubled out of turn; and if the offender's partner is to make the opening lead, declarer may either

(i) require the offender's partner to lead a specified suit, or

(ii) prohibit the offender's partner from leading a specified suit; this prohibition continues for as long as the offender's partner retains the lead.

(b) If it was the turn of the opponent on the offender's right to call:

(i) If the opponent on the offender's right passes, the double or redouble out of rotation must be repeated and there is no penalty.

(ii) If the opponent on the offender's right bids, the offender may in turn make any legal call, and (penalty) the offender's partner must pass when next it is his turn to call, and Law 26 may apply.

33. SIMULTANEOUS CALLS

A call made simultaneously with one made by the player whose turn it was to call is deemed to be a subsequent call.

34. CALL IN ROTATION AFTER AN ILLEGAL CALL

A call by a member of the nonoffending side after an illegal call by the opponent on his right, and before a penalty has been imposed, forfeits the right to penalize that offense. The illegal call is treated as though it were legal, except that an inadmissible double or redouble or a bid of more than seven is treated as a pass; and Law 35 or 37 may apply.

35. RETENTION OF THE RIGHT TO CALL

A player may not be deprived of any turn to call by one or more passes following a pass out of rotation, when there has been no subsequent bid. All such passes are canceled, the bidding

† An illegal call by that opponent may be penalized in the usual way, after which this subsection (c) (ii) applies.

reverts to the player who has missed his turn, and the auction continues as though there had been no irregularity.

Inadmissible Calls

36. INADMISSIBLE DOUBLE OR REDOUBLE

Any double or redouble not permitted by Law 19 is canceled; and:

(a) If the offender has doubled or redoubled a bid that his side has already doubled or redoubled:

(i) The offender may substitute a legal bid, and (penalty) his partner must pass whenever it is his turn to call, and if the offender's partner is to make the opening lead, declarer may prohibit the lead of the suit illegally doubled or redoubled, for as long as the offender's partner retains the lead; or

(ii) The offender may substitute a pass, and (penalty) his partner must pass whenever it is his turn to call, either member of the nonoffending side may cancel all previous doubles or redoubles, and if the offender's partner is to make the opening lead, declarer may require the offender's partner to lead a specified suit, or prohibit the offender's partner from leading a specified suit; this prohibition continues for as long as the offender's partner retains the lead.

(b) If the offender has doubled a bid made by his side, redoubled an undoubled bid, or doubled or redoubled when there has been no bid, the offender in turn must make any legal call, and (penalty) his partner must pass when next it is his turn to call.

If the right of the nonoffending side to penalize is waived or forfeited, as provided in Law 15, the offender is deemed to have passed and the auction proceeds as though there had been no irregularity.

37. BID, DOUBLE OR REDOUBLE IN VIOLATION OF THE OBLIGATION TO PASS

A bid, double or redouble by a player who is required by law to pass is canceled, and (penalty) both members of the offending side must pass during the remainder of the auction, and if the offender's partner is to make the opening lead, declarer may either

(a) require the offender's partner to lead a specified suit, or

(b) prohibit the offender's partner from leading a specified suit; this prohibition continues for as long as the offender's partner retains the lead.

If the right of the nonoffending side to penalize is waived or forfeited, as provided in Law

15, the offender's bid, double or redouble, if otherwise legal, stands at that turn; but if the offender was required to pass for the remainder of the auction he must still pass at subsequent turns.

38. BID OF MORE THAN SEVEN

A bid of more than seven by any player is canceled, and (penalty) both members of the offending side must pass during the remainder of the auction, and if the offender's partner is to make the opening lead, declarer may either

(a) require the offender's partner to lead a specified suit, or

(b) prohibit the offender's partner from leading a specified suit; this prohibition continues for as long as the offender's partner retains the lead.

If the right of the nonoffending side to penalize is waived or forfeited, as provided in Law 15, the offender must substitute a pass; any call that may have been made subsequently is canceled; and the auction proceeds as though there had been no irregularity. No play or score at a contract of more than seven is ever permissible.

39. CALL AFTER THE AUCTION IS CLOSED

A call after the auction is closed is canceled, and:

(a) If it is a pass by a defender or any call by declarer or dummy, there is no penalty.

(b) If it is a bid, double or redouble by a defender, (penalty) declarer may either

(i) require the offender's partner, when first it is his turn to lead, to lead a specified suit; or

(ii) prohibit the offender's partner, when first it is his turn to lead, from leading a specified suit; this prohibition continues for as long as the offender's partner retains the lead.

Part VI

THE PLAY
◆◆◆◆◆◆◆
Correct Procedure

40. COMMENCEMENT OF PLAY

After the auction closes, the defender on declarer's left makes the opening lead. After the opening lead, dummy spreads his hand in front of him on the table, face up and grouped in suits with the trumps on his right. Declarer plays both his hand and that of dummy.

41. INFORMATION AS TO CONTRACT

After it is too late to have previous calls re-stated, as provided in Law 20, declarer or either defender is entitled to be informed what the contract is and whether, but not by whom, it was doubled or redoubled.

42. DUMMY'S RIGHTS AND LIMITATIONS

Dummy is entitled to give or obtain information as to fact or law; and provided he has not forfeited his rights (see Law 43) he may also:

(a) question players regarding revokes as provided in Law 61;

(b) draw attention to an irregularity, or try to prevent one.*

Except as provided in this law, dummy may not, on his own initiative, participate in the play, or make any comment on the bidding or play of the current deal, or draw attention to the score, and if he does so, Law 16 may apply. If dummy consults with declarer as to the imposition of a penalty, the right to penalize is forfeited as provided in Law 15.

43. FORFEITURE OF DUMMY'S RIGHTS

Dummy forfeits the rights provided in (a) and (b) of Law 42 if he exchanges hands with declarer, leaves his seat to watch declarer play, or, on his own initiative, looks at the face of a card in either defender's hand; and if, thereafter,

(a) He is the first to draw attention to a defender's irregularity, declarer may not enforce any penalty for the offense.

(b) He warns declarer not to lead from the wrong hand, (penalty) either defender may choose the hand from which declarer shall lead.

(c) He is the first to ask declarer if a play from declarer's hand constitutes a revoke or failure to comply with a penalty, declarer must substitute a correct card if his play was illegal, and the penalty provisions of Law 64 apply.

44. SEQUENCE AND PROCEDURE OF PLAY

The player who leads to a trick may play any card in his hand.† After the lead, each other player in turn plays a card, and the four cards so played constitute a trick.

In playing to a trick, each player must if possible follow suit. This obligation takes precedence over all other requirements of these Laws. If unable to follow suit, a player may play any card.*

A trick containing a trump is won by the player who has contributed to it the highest trump. A trick that does not contain a trump is won by the player who has contributed to it the highest card of the suit led. The player who has won the trick leads to the next trick.

---

* He may, for example, warn declarer against leading from the wrong hand.

† Unless he is subject to restriction after an irregularity committed by his side.

45. CARD PLAYED

Each player except dummy plays a card by detaching it from his hand and facing it near the middle of the table. Declarer plays a card from dummy's hand by moving the card toward the center of the table. If instructed by declarer to do so, dummy may play from his hand a card named or designated by declarer. In addition, a card must be played:

(a) If it is a defender's card held so that it is possible for his partner to see its face.

(b) If it is a card from declarer's hand that declarer holds face up in front of him and that is touching or near the table.

(c) If it is a card in dummy touched by declarer except for the purpose of arranging dummy's cards or of reaching a card above or below the card or cards touched.

(d) If the player who holds the card names or otherwise designates it as the card he proposes to play. A player may, without penalty, change an inadvertent designation if he does so without pause; but if an opponent has, in turn, played a card that was legal before the change of designation, that opponent may, without penalty, withdraw any card so played and substitute another.

(e) If it is a penalty card, subject to Law 50.

(f) If it is a card in dummy's hand that dummy has illegally suggested as a play, unless either defender forbids the play of such card, or an equal of it, or a card of the same suit, as provided in Law 16.

A card played may not be withdrawn except as provided in Law 47.

46. PARTIAL DESIGNATION OF A CARD TO BE PLAYED FROM DUMMY'S HAND

When declarer instructs dummy to play a card from dummy's hand, as permitted by Law 45, but names only a suit or only the rank of a card, or the equivalent, without fully specifying the card to be played, declarer must complete his partial designation. Dummy must not play a card before declarer has completed his partial designation, and if dummy prematurely plays a card, Law 16 applies on that trick only, unless a defender has subsequently played.

47. RETRACTION OF A CARD PLAYED

A card once played may be withdrawn only:

(a) to comply with a penalty, or to correct an illegal play;

(b) after a change of designation as permitted by Law 45 (d);

(c) after an opponent's change of play, to substitute a card for one played.

Penalty Card

48. EXPOSURE OF DECLARER'S CARDS

Declarer is not subject to penalty for ex-posing a card, and no card of declarer's or dummy's ever becomes a penalty card. Declarer is not required to play any card dropped accidentally.

When declarer faces his cards after an opening lead out of turn, Law 54 applies.* When declarer faces his cards at any other time, he is deemed to have made a claim or concession of tricks and Law 71 applies.

49. EXPOSURE OF A DEFENDER'S CARDS

Whenever a defender faces a card on the table, holds a card so that it is possible for his partner to see its face, or names a card as being in his hand, before he is entitled to do so in the normal course of play or application of the law, (penalty) each such card becomes a penalty card (Law 51).†

50. DISPOSITION OF A PENALTY CARD

A penalty card must be left face up on the table until it is played or is permitted to be picked up. When a penalty card is permitted to be picked up, it ceases to be a penalty card.

A penalty card must be played at the first legal opportunity, whether in leading, following suit, discarding, or trumping. If a defender has two or more penalty cards that can legally be played, declarer may designate which is to be played. The obligation to follow suit, or to comply with a lead or play penalty, takes precedence over the obligation to play a penalty card, but the penalty card must still be left face up on the table and played at the next legal opportunity.

When a defender has or first obtains the lead while his partner has a penalty card, declarer may require that defender to lead the suit of the penalty card, or may prohibit that defender from leading that suit for as long as he retains the lead. If declarer exercises this option, the penalty card may be picked up. If declarer does not exercise this option, the defender may lead any card; but the penalty card remains a penalty card. The defender may not lead until declarer has indicated his choice.

If a defender has two or more penalty cards in one suit, and declarer requires the defender's partner to lead that suit, the defender may pick up every penalty card in that suit and may make any legal play to the trick.

If a defender has penalty cards in more than one suit, declarer may prohibit the defender's partner from leading every such suit; but the defender may then pick up every penalty card

---

* Declarer should, as a matter of propriety, refrain from spreading his hand.

† Exposure of a card or cards by a defender who is making a claim or concession of tricks is subject to Law 73.

in every suit prohibited by declarer and may make any legal play to the trick.

51. PENALTY CARD ILLEGALLY PICKED UP

When a defender attempts illegally to restore a penalty card to his unfaced hand, such card must be replaced face up on the table on demand of declarer; but if in the meantime that defender has played another card and declarer has thereafter played from either his hand or dummy, the card illegally picked up ceases to be a penalty card and need not be replaced on the table.

52. FAILURE TO LEAD OR PLAY A PENALTY CARD

When a defender fails to lead or play a penalty card as required by Law 50, he may not, on his own initiative, withdraw any other card he may have played.

If a defender leads or plays another card when he could legally have led or played a penalty card,

(a) declarer may accept the defender's lead or play, and declarer must accept such lead or play if he has thereafter played from his or dummy's hand, but the unplayed penalty card remains a penalty card; or

(b) declarer may require the defender to substitute the penalty card for the card illegally led or played. Every card illegally led or played by the defender in the course of committing the irregularity becomes a penalty card.

Lead Out of Turn

53. LEAD OUT OF TURN ACCEPTED

Any lead out of turn may be treated as a correct lead. It becomes a correct lead if declarer or either defender, as the case may be, accepts it or plays a card before attention is drawn to the irregularity. A card so played by declarer from either hand may not be withdrawn unless its play constituted a revoke. Law 57 applies if such card is played by the defender at the right of the player from whose hand the lead out of turn was made.

54. OPENING LEAD OUT OF TURN

When a defender makes the opening lead out of turn:

(a) If declarer accepts the lead as provided in Law 53, dummy's hand is spread in accordance with Law 40 and the second card to the trick is played from declarer's hand; but if declarer first plays to the trick from dummy's hand, dummy's card may not be withdrawn except to correct a revoke.

(b) If declarer may have seen any of dummy's cards (except cards that dummy may

have exposed during the auction and that were subject to Law 23) he must accept the lead.

(c) If declarer begins to spread his hand as though he were dummy,* and in so doing exposes one or more cards, and if subsection (b) above does not apply, the lead must be accepted, declarer must spread his entire hand, and dummy becomes declarer.

When declarer requires the defender to retract his opening lead out of turn, Law 56 applies.

55. DECLARER'S LEAD OUT OF TURN

When declarer leads out of turn from his or dummy's hand and either defender requires him to retract such lead:

(a) If it was a defender's turn to lead, declarer restores the card led in error to his or dummy's hand without penalty.

(b) If declarer has led from the wrong hand when it was his turn to lead from his or dummy's hand, he withdraws the card led in error; he must lead from the correct hand, and, (penalty) if able to do so, a card of the same suit. Failure to observe this obligation in playing from his own hand may subject him to penalty under Law 65.

Either defender's drawing attention to declarer's lead out of turn is equivalent to requiring its retraction. Dummy's drawing attention to declarer's lead from the wrong hand does not affect the rights of the opponents.

56. DEFENDER'S LEAD OUT OF TURN

When declarer requires a defender to retract his lead out of turn:

(a) Declarer may treat the card illegally led as a penalty card and apply the provisions of Law 50; or

(b) Declarer may allow the card illegally led to be picked up; and if the offense occurred

(i) on the opening lead, or on a subsequent lead when it was the other defender's turn to lead, (penalty) declarer may require the offender's partner to lead the suit of the card led out of turn, or prohibit him from leading that suit for as long as he retains the lead.

(ii) when it was declarer's or dummy's turn to lead, declarer leads from the correct hand and (penalty) when first it is the turn of the offender's partner to lead, declarer may require him to lead the suit of the card led out of turn, or prohibit him from leading that suit for as long as he retains the lead.

---

* Declarer should, as a matter of propriety, refrain from spreading his hand.

Irregular Leads and Plays

57. PREMATURE LEAD OR PLAY BY A DEFENDER

When a defender leads to the next trick before his partner has played to the current trick, or plays out of turn before his partner has played, (penalty) declarer may require the offender's partner to play:

(a) his highest card of the suit led; or

(b) his lowest card of the suit led; or

(c) a card of another suit, specified by declarer.

Declarer must select one of these options, and if the offender's partner cannot comply with the penalty selected he may play any card, as provided in Law 59.

When, as a result of the application of the penalty, the offender's partner wins the current trick, he leads to the next trick; and any card led or played out of turn by the other defender becomes a penalty card (Law 50).

A defender is not subject to penalty for playing before his partner if declarer has played from both hands; but a singleton or one of two or more equal cards in dummy is not considered automatically played unless dummy has played the card or has illegally suggested that it be played—see Law 45 (f).

58. SIMULTANEOUS LEADS OR PLAYS

A lead or play made simultaneously with another player's legal lead or play is deemed to be subsequent to it.

If a defender leads or plays two or more cards simultaneously, and if only one such card is visible, he must play that card; if more than one card is exposed, he must designate the card he proposes to play and each other card exposed becomes a penalty card (Law 50).

If declarer leads or plays two or more cards simultaneously from either hand, he must designate the card he proposes to play and must restore any other card to the correct hand. A defender who has played to the only visible card played by declarer may, without penalty, withdraw the card played and substitute another.

If the error remains undiscovered until both sides have played to the next trick, Law 68 applies.

59. INABILITY TO LEAD OR PLAY AS REQUIRED

A player may play any correct card if he is unable to lead or play as required to comply with a penalty, either because he has no card of the required suit, or because he has only cards of a suit he is prohibited from leading, or because of his obligation to follow suit. The penalty is deemed to have been paid, except that the obligation to play a penalty card at the first legal opportunity continues.

60. PLAY AFTER AN ILLEGAL PLAY

A play by a member of the nonoffending side after the opponent on his right has led or played out of turn prematurely, and before a penalty has been imposed, forfeits the right to penalize that offense. The illegal play is treated as though it were legal, unless it constitutes a revoke. If the offending side had a previous obligation to play a penalty card or to comply with a lead or play penalty, the obligation remains at future turns (see Laws 52 and 65).

When a defender plays after declarer has been required to retract his lead out of turn from either hand, but before declarer has led from the correct hand, the defender's card becomes a penalty card (Law 50).

A play by a member of the offending side before a penalty has been imposed does not affect the rights of the opponents and may itself be subject to penalty.

The Revoke

61. FAILURE TO FOLLOW SUIT—
INQUIRIES CONCERNING A REVOKE

Failure to follow suit in accordance with Law 44 constitutes a revoke. Any player, including dummy,* may ask a player who has failed to follow suit whether he has a card of the suit led, and may demand that an opponent correct his revoke.

62. CORRECTION OF A REVOKE

A player must correct his revoke if he becomes aware of the occurrence of the revoke before it becomes established. To correct a revoke, the offender withdraws the card he played in revoking and follows suit with any card. A card so withdrawn becomes a penalty card (Law 50) if it was played from a defender's unfaced hand. The card may be replaced without penalty if it was played from declarer's or dummy's hand† or if it was a defender's faced card. Each member of the nonoffending side may, without penalty, withdraw any card he may have played after the revoke but before attention was drawn to it. Except as provided in the next paragraph, the partner of the offender may not withdraw his card unless it too constituted a revoke.††

A revoke on the twelfth trick never becomes established but must be corrected if discovered

---

* Subject to Law 43. A claim of revoke does not warrant inspection of quitted tricks except as permitted in Law 67.

† Subject to Law 43. A claim of revoke does not warrant inspection of quitted tricks except as permitted in Law 67.

†† In such case the card withdrawn becomes a penalty card if it was played from a defender's unfaced hand.

before it was the turn of the offender's partner to play to the twelfth trick, (penalty) declarer or either defender, as the case may be, may then require the offender's partner to play to that trick either of two cards he could legally have played.*

63. ESTABLISHMENT OF A REVOKE

A revoke in any of the first eleven tricks becomes established when the offender or his partner leads or plays to the following trick,† or names or otherwise designates a card to be so played, or makes a claim or concession of tricks orally or by facing his hand. The revoke may then no longer be corrected, and the trick on which the revoke occurred stands as played.

64. PROCEDURE AFTER ESTABLISHMENT OF A REVOKE

When a revoke has become established, (penalty) after play ceases, two tricks are transferred to the nonoffending side, if the side that has revoked has won two or more tricks after the revoke.†† Only one trick is transferred if the side that has revoked has won only one trick after the revoke. The trick on which the revoke occurred is counted as having been won after the revoke.§ There is no penalty for an established revoke:

(a) If the side that revoked did not win either the trick on which the revoke occurred or any subsequent trick.

(b) If the revoke was a subsequent revoke in the same suit by the same player.

(c) If the revoke was made in failing to play any card faced on the table or belonging to a hand faced on the table including a card from dummy's hand.

(d) If attention is first drawn to it after all players have abandoned their hands and permitted the cards to be mixed together.

65. FAILURE TO COMPLY WITH A LEAD OR PLAY PENALTY

When a player is able to lead or play from an unfaced hand a card or suit required by law or specified by an opponent in accordance with an agreed penalty, but instead plays an incorrect card:

(a) The offender must correct his error if he becomes aware of it before he or his partner plays another card. Any card played in rotation

by a member of the nonoffending side may, without penalty, be withdrawn if it was played after the error and before its correction. An incorrect card played from a defender's unfaced hand becomes a penalty card (Law 50).

(b) The offender may not withdraw any incorrect card he may have played if he or his partner has led or played to the following trick; and (penalty) the offense is subject to the penalty provisions of Law 64.

There is no penalty for failure to lead or play a faced card, including a penalty card* or a card from dummy's hand, but a member of the nonoffending side (except dummy) may demand rectification at any time before a member of his side has thereafter played a card.

Tricks

66. COLLECTION AND ARRANGEMENT OF TRICKS

The cards constituting each completed trick are collected by a member of the side that won the trick and are then turned face down on the table. Each trick should be identifiable as such, and all tricks taken by a side should be arranged in sequence in front of declarer or of one defender, as the case may be, in such manner that each side can determine the number of tricks it has won and the order in which they were taken.

67. INSPECTION OF TRICKS

Declarer or either defender may, until a member of his side has led or played to the following trick, inspect a trick and inquire what card each player has played to it. Thereafter, until play ceases, quitted tricks may be inspected only to account for a missing or surplus card. After play ceases, the tricks and unplayed cards may be inspected to settle a claim of a revoke, of honors, or of the number of tricks won or lost. If, after a claim has been made, a player on one side mixes the cards in such way that the facts can no longer be ascertained, the issue must be decided in favor of the other side.

68. DEFECTIVE TRICK

When a player has omitted to play to a trick, or has played too many cards to a trick, the error must be rectified if attention is drawn to the irregularity before a player on each side has played to the following trick. To rectify omission to play to a trick, the offender supplies a card he can legally play. To rectify the error of playing too many cards, the offender withdraws all but one card, leaving a card he can legally play. Each card so withdrawn becomes

---

* The text of this paragraph has been amended from previous printings for the purpose of clarification.

† Any such play, legal or illegal, establishes a revoke.

†† Failure to lead or play a card of suit specified by an opponent in accordance with an agreed penalty is not a revoke but may be subject to the same penalties (see Law 65).

§ For the scoring of tricks transferred see Law 80.

---

* A card played instead of the penalty card may be subject to penalty—see Law 52.

a penalty card (Law 50) if it was played from a defender's unfaced hand. After a card has been so withdrawn, each member of the non-offending side may, without penalty, withdraw any card he played after the irregularity but before attention was drawn to it.

When attention is drawn to a defective trick after a player on each side has played to the following trick, the defective trick stands as played and:

(a) A player with too few cards plays the remainder of his hand with fewer cards than the other players; he does not play to the final trick (or tricks); and if he wins a trick with his last card, the lead passes in rotation.

(b) A player with too many cards forthwith faces and adds a card to the defective trick, and if possible one he could legally have played to it. A card so contributed does not change the ownership of the trick.

69. TRICK APPROPRIATED IN ERROR

A trick appropriated by the wrong side must, upon demand, be restored to the side that has in fact won the trick by contributing the winning card to it. The scoring value of the trick must be credited to that side, subject to Law 81.

Claims and Concessions

70. DECLARER'S CLAIM OR CONCESSION OF TRICKS

Declarer makes a claim whenever he announces that he will win or lose one or more of the remaining tricks, or suggests that play may be curtailed, or faces his hand. Declarer should not make a claim if there is any doubt as to the number of tricks to be won or lost.

71. PROCEDURE FOLLOWING DECLARER'S CLAIM

When declarer has made a claim, play is temporarily suspended and declarer must place and leave his hand face up on the table and forthwith make a comprehensive statement as to his proposed plan of play, including the order in which he will play his remaining cards; and:

(1) Either defender may, at any time thereafter, demand that declarer clarify or amplify his statement in any particular.

(2) At any time after declarer's claim, either defender may face his hand for inspection by his partner, and declarer may not impose a penalty for any irregularity committed by a defender whose hand is so faced.

(3) Either defender may require that play continue as provided in Law 72.

Declarer's claim must be allowed if both defenders agree to it, or if either defender has allowed any of his remaining cards to be mixed with another player's cards.

72. CONTINUATION OF PLAY AFTER DECLARER'S CLAIM

Whenever either defender requires that play continue after declarer's claim, declarer must play on, leaving his hand face up on the table. Declarer may make no play inconsistent with any statement he may have made; and if he did not make an appropriate announcement at the time he made his claim, he may not exercise freedom of choice in making any play the success of which depends on finding either opponent with or without a particular unplayed card; and unless an opponent failed to follow to the suit of that card before the claim was made, declarer must play as directed by either defender. If declarer attempts to make a play prohibited under this law, either defender may accept the play or require declarer to withdraw the card so played and to substitute another that conforms to his obligations, provided neither defender has subsequently played. Any question not specifically dealt with should be resolved in favor of the defenders.*

73. DEFENDER'S CLAIM OR CONCESSION OF TRICKS

When a defender makes a claim or concession of tricks he may do so by showing any or all of his cards to declarer only, but this does not necessarily exempt the defender from penalty under Law 16. If in the course of making a claim or concession a defender faces his hand, names a card as being in his hand, or makes it possible for his partner to see one or more of his remaining cards, his cards do not become penalty cards but declarer may treat the remaining cards of the other defender as penalty cards.

74. CONCESSION WITHDRAWN

A concession may be withdrawn:

(a) If any player concedes a trick his side has, in fact, won; or if declarer concedes defeat of a contract he has already fulfilled; or if a defender concedes fulfillment of a contract his side has already defeated. If the score has been entered, it may be corrected, subject to Law 81.

(b) If a trick that has been conceded cannot be lost by any sequence of play of the remaining cards, however improbable, and if attention is drawn to that fact before the cards have been mixed together.

(c) If a defender concedes one or more tricks and his partner immediately objects, but Law 16 may apply.

---

* *Example:* Declarer may be required to draw, or not to draw, an outstanding trump that he may have overlooked and that is a possible winner.

Part VII

THE SCORE

✦✦✦✦✦✦

75. POINTS EARNED

The result of each deal played is recorded in points, which fall into two classes:

1. *Trick points.* Only declarer's side can earn trick points, and only by winning at least the number of odd tricks specified in the contract. Only the value of odd tricks named in the contract may be scored as trick points. (See Law 84.) Trick points mark the progression of the rubber toward its completion.

2. *Premium points.* Either side or both sides may earn premium points. Declarer's side earns premium points by winning one or more overtricks; by fulfilling a doubled or redoubled contract; by bidding and making a slam; by holding scorable honors in declarer's or dummy's hand; or by winning the final game of a rubber.* The defenders earn premium points by defeating the contract (undertrick penalty) or by holding scorable honors in either of their hands. (See Law 84.)

Each side's premium points are added to its trick points at the conclusion of the rubber.

76. PART SCORE—GAME

The basic units of trick scores are part score and game. A part score is recorded for declarer's side whenever declarer fulfills a contract for which the trick score is less than 100 points. Game is won by that side which is the first to have scored 100 or more trick points either in a single deal or by addition of two or more part scores made separately. No part score made in the course of one game is carried forward into the next game.

77. THE RUBBER

A rubber ends when a side has won two games. At the conclusion of the rubber, the winners of two games are credited in their premium score with 500 points if the other side has won one game, or with 700 points if the other side has not won a game. The trick and premium points scored by each side in the course of the rubber are than added. The side with the larger combined total wins the rubber, and the difference between the two totals represents the margin of victory computed in points.

78. METHOD OF SCORING

The score of each deal must be recorded and preferably a member of each side should keep score.

Scores are entered in two adjacent columns separated by a vertical line. Each scorer enters

---

* For incomplete rubber see Law 83.

points earned by his side in the left-hand column, and points earned by his opponents in the right-hand column.

Each side has a trick score and a premium score, separated by a horizontal line intersecting the vertical line. All trick points are entered, as they are earned, in descending order below the horizontal line; all premium points in ascending order above that line.

Whenever a game is won, another horizontal line is drawn under all trick scores recorded for either side, in order to mark completion of the game. Subsequent trick scores are entered below the line so drawn. Any line prematurely drawn must be erased, and a line incorrectly omitted must be drawn upon discovery of the error.

79. RESPONSIBILITY FOR THE SCORE

When play ceases, all four players are equally responsible for ascertaining that the number of tricks won by each side is correctly determined and that all scores are promptly and correctly entered.

80. TRANSFERRED TRICKS

A transferred trick is reckoned for all scoring purposes as though it had been won in play by the side to which it has been awarded.

81. CORRECTION OF THE SCORE

Any scoring error conceded by both sides may be corrected at any time before the score of the rubber is agreed upon; except that an error made by each scorer in recording a trick score, or failing to enter one, may not be corrected after the last card of the second succeeding correct deal has been dealt, unless the majority of the players consent. In case of disagreement among two or more scores kept, the recollection of the majority of the players as to the facts governs.

82. DEALS PLAYED WITH AN INCORRECT PACK

Scores recorded for deals played with an incorrect pack are not subject to change by reason of the discovery of the imperfection after the cards have been mixed together.

83. INCOMPLETE RUBBER

When, for any reason, a rubber is not finished, the score is computed as follows:

If only one game has been completed, the winners of that game are credited with 300 points; if only one side has a part score or scores in a game not completed, that side is credited with 50 points; the trick and premium points of each side are then added, and the side with the greater number of points wins the difference between the two totals.

84. SCORING TABLE

TRICK SCORE

Scored below the line by declarer's side, if the contract is fulfilled:

	IF TRUMPS ARE			
	♣	◊	♡	♠
For each trick over six, bid and made				
Undoubled	20	20	30	30
Doubled	40	40	60	60
Redoubled	80	80	120	120

	AT A NO-TRUMP CONTRACT		
	UNDOUBLED	DOUBLED	REDOUBLED
For the first trick over six, bid and made	40	80	160
For each additional trick over six, bid and made	30	60	120

The first side to score 100 points below the line, in one or more deals, wins a GAME. When a game is won, both sides start without trick score toward the next game. The first side to win two games wins the RUBBER.

PREMIUM SCORE

Scored above the line by declarer's side:

RUBBER, GAME, PART-SCORE, CONTRACT FULFILLED

For winning the RUBBER, if opponents have won no game	700
For winning the RUBBER, if opponents have won one game	500
UNFINISHED RUBBER—for having won one game	300
—for having the only part-score (or scores)	50
For making any DOUBLED or REDOUBLED CONTRACT	50

SLAMS

	NOT VULNERABLE	VULNERABLE
For making a SLAM		
Small Slam (12 tricks) bid and made	500	750
Grand Slam (all 13 tricks) bid and made	1000	1500

OVERTRICKS

	NOT VULNERABLE	VULNERABLE
For each OVERTRICK (tricks made in excess of the contract)		
Undoubled	Trick value	Trick value
Doubled	100	200
Redoubled	200	400

HONORS

Scored above the line by either side:

For holding four of the five trump HONORS (A, K, Q, J, 10) in one hand	100
For holding all five trump HONORS (A, K, Q, J, 10) in one hand	150
For holding all four ACES in one hand at a no-trump contract	150

UNDERTRICK PENALTIES

For tricks by which declarer fails to fulfill the contract; scored above the line by declarer's opponents if the contract is not fulfilled:

	NOT VULNERABLE		
	UNDOUBLED	DOUBLED	REDOUBLED
For the first undertrick	50	100	200
For each additional undertrick	50	200	400

	VULNERABLE		
	UNDOUBLED	DOUBLED	REDOUBLED
For the first undertrick	100	200	400
For each additional undertrick	100	300	600

PROPRIETIES

♦♦♦♦♦♦♦

I. GENERAL PRINCIPLES

Communication between partners during the auction and play periods should be effected only by means of the calls and plays themselves, not the manner in which they are made. Calls should be made in a uniform tone without special emphasis or inflection, and without undue haste or hesitation. Plays should be made without emphasis, gesture or mannerism, and so far as possible at a uniform rate.

Intentional infringement of a law is a serious breach of ethics, even if there is a prescribed penalty which one is prepared to pay. The offense may be the more serious when no penalty is prescribed.*

A player should carefully avoid taking any advantage which might accrue from an impropriety committed by his side. While one should not allow partner's hesitation, remark or mannerism to influence one's call, lead or play, it is not improper to draw inferences from an opponent's gratuitous hesitation, remark or mannerism, but such inferences are drawn at one's own risk.

There is no obligation to draw attention to an inadvertent infringement of law by one's own side; however, a player should not attempt to conceal such an infringement, as by committing a second revoke, concealing a card involved in a revoke, or mixing the cards prematurely.

It is proper to warn partner against infringing a law of the game, for example, against revoking, or against calling, leading or playing out of turn.

II. VIOLATIONS OF ETHICAL CONDUCT

The following acts should be carefully avoided and are considered breaches of ethics when committed intentionally.

a. A remark, question, gesture or mannerism which might convey information to partner or might mislead an opponent.

b. A call made with special emphasis, inflection, haste or undue hesitation.

c. A play made with emphasis, undue haste, or unreasonable delay, when the act might convey information to partner or might mislead an opponent.

---

* See the Scope of the Laws, page 215.

d. Any indication of approval or disapproval of partner's call, or of satisfaction with an opponent's call.

e. Indication of expectation or intention of winning or losing a trick before the trick has been completed.

f. Mixing the cards before the result of the deal has been agreed upon.

g. A comment or act during the auction or play period, calling attention to an incident thereof, the state of the score, or the number of tricks already taken or still required.

III. OBSERVANCE OF PROPER ETIQUETTE

A player should maintain at all times a courteous attitude toward his partner and opponents. He should carefully avoid any remark or action which might cause annoyance or embarrassment to another player or interfere with the enjoyment of the game.

Every player should follow uniformly correct procedure in calling and playing, since any departure from correct standards may interfere with the orderly progress of the game.

A player should refrain from:

a. The use of different designations for the same call.

b. Frequent review of the auction or play due to his own inattention.

c. Volunteering information that should be given only in response to a question.

d. Looking intently at any other player during the auction or play periods, or at another player's hand as for the purpose of observing the place from which he draws a card.

e. Making gratuitous comments during the play period as to the auction or the adequacy of the contract.

f. Exchanging hands with his partner, or letting his partner see his hand, whether or not a penalty may be incurred.

g. Detaching a card from his hand before it is his turn to lead or play.

h. Disorderly arrangement of completed tricks, which may make it difficult to determine the sequence of plays.

i. Making a claim or concession of tricks if there is any doubt as to the outcome of the deal.

IV. USE OF CONVENTIONS

It is improper to use, in calling or playing, any convention the meaning of which may not be understood by the opponents. Conventional calls or plays should be explained to the opponents before any player has looked at his cards. Advance notice may be given of the intention to use certain conventions of which full explanation may be deferred until the occasion arises. The explanation may be given only by the player whose partner made the conventional call or play. At any time this player must reply to an inquiry by an opponent as to the significance of a call or play that may be conventional, and should supply any information that may have been withheld.

Any sponsoring organization, club or tournament committee, or group of persons playing Contract Bridge, may restrict the use of conventions in games under its jurisdiction.

V. SPECTATORS

A spectator, or a member of a table who is not playing, should refrain from gratuitous remarks or mannerisms of any kind. He should not call attention to any irregularity or mistake, or speak on any question of fact or law except by request of a member of each side.

RULES FOR CLUB PROCEDURE

◆◆◆◆◆◆

The following rules, governing membership in new and existing tables, have proven satisfactory in club use over a long period of years.

A. DEFINITIONS

Member—An applicant who has acquired the right to play at a table either immediately or in his turn.

Complete Table—A table with six members.

Incomplete Table—A table with four or five members.

Cut In—Assert the right to become a member of an incomplete table, or to become a member of a complete table at such time as it may become incomplete.

B. TIME LIMIT ON RIGHT TO PLAY

An applicant may not play in a rubber unless he has become a member of a table before a card is duly drawn for the selection of players or partners.

C. NEWLY FORMED TABLES

Four to six applicants may form a table. If there are more than six applicants, the six highest-ranking ones become members. The four highest-ranking members play the first rubber. Those who have not played, ranked in their order of entry into the room, take precedence over those who have played; the latter rank equally, except that players leaving existing tables to join the new table rank lowest. Precedence between those of equal rank is determined by drawing cards, the player who draws the higher-ranking card having precedence.

D. CUTTING IN

An application establishes membership in a table either forthwith or (if the table is complete) as soon as a vacancy occurs, unless applications in excess of the number required to complete a table are made at the same time, in which case precedence between applicants is established by drawing cards, as provided in the preceding rule.

E. GOING OUT

After each rubber place must be made for any member who did not play the last rubber, by the member who has played the greatest number of consecutive rubbers at that table. Cards are drawn for precedence if necessary. A member who has left another existing table must draw cards, for his first rubber, with the member who would otherwise have played. A player who breaks up a game by leaving three players at a table may not compete against them for entry at another table until each of them has played at least one rubber.

F. MEMBERSHIP LIMITED TO ONE TABLE

No one may be a member of more than one table at the same time, unless a member consents, on request, to make a fourth at another table and announces his intention of returning to his former table as soon as his place at the new table can be filled. Failure to announce such intention results in loss of membership at his former table.

LAWS OF DUPLICATE BRIDGE. See LAWS OF DUPLICATE CONTRACT BRIDGE.

LAWS OF DUPLICATE CONTRACT BRIDGE. In 1975 the Laws of Duplicate Contract Bridge were revised under the auspices of the World Bridge Federation. This was the first revision since 1963. In many respects the changes in the new Laws are merely changes in language or terminology. In the American edition,* as set forth below, substantively new provisions are indicated by italics.

LAWS OF DUPLICATE CONTRACT BRIDGE

THE SCOPE OF THE LAWS

◆◆◆◆◆◆◆

The Laws are designed to define correct procedure and to provide an adequate remedy whenever a player accidentally, carelessly or in-

---

* Although considerably different in arrangement, the American version is substantively identical to the International edition.

advertently disturbs the proper course of the game, or gains an unintentional but nevertheless unfair advantage. An offending player should be ready to pay graciously any penalty or accept any adjusted score awarded by the Tournament Director.

The Laws are not designed to prevent dishonorable practices, but rather to redress damage inadvertently done.

THE OBJECT OF THE PROPRIETIES

◆◆◆◆◆◆◆

The object of the Proprieties is twofold: to familiarize players with the customs and etiquette of the game, generally accepted over a long period of years; and to enlighten those who might otherwise fail to appreciate when or how they are improperly conveying information to their partners—often a far more reprehensible offense than a violation of a law.

When these principles are appreciated, arguments are avoided and the pleasure that the game offers is materially enhanced.

CHAPTER I

DEFINITIONS

◆◆◆◆◆◆◆

Adjusted Score—An arbitrary score assigned by the Tournament Director (see Law 12).

Auction—1. The process of determining the contract by means of successive calls. 2. The aggregate of calls made. 3. The period during which calls are made.

Average—The arithmetic median between the greatest and least awarded scores available.

Bid—An undertaking to win at least a specified number of odd tricks in a specified denomination.

Board—A duplicate board as described in Law 2; or the four hands as originally dealt and placed in a duplicate board for play during that session.

Call—Any bid, double, redouble, or pass.

Contestant—In an individual event, a player; in a pair event, two players playing as partners throughout the event; in a team event, four or more players playing as teammates.

Contract—The undertaking by declarer's side to win, at the denomination named, the number of tricks specified in the final bid, whether undoubled, doubled, or redoubled.

Convention—A call that serves by partnership agreement to convey a meaning not necessarily related to the denomination named. 2. Defender's play that serves to convey a meaning by agreement rather than inference.

Deal—1. The distribution of the pack to form the hands of the four players. 2. The cards so distributed considered as a unit, including the auction and play thereof.

Declarer—The player who, for the side that

makes the final bid, first bid the denomination named in that bid. He becomes declarer when the auction is closed.

Defender—An opponent of declarer.

Denomination—The suit or no trump specified in a bid.

Director—A person designated to supervise a duplicate bridge contest and to apply these Laws.

Double—A call over an opponent's bid increasing the scoring value of fulfilled or defeated contracts (see Law 73).

Dummy—1. Declarer's partner. He becomes dummy when the auction is closed. 2. Declarer's partner's cards, once they are spread on the table after the opening lead.

Event—A contest of one or more sessions.

Follow Suit—Play a card of the suit that has been led.

Game—100 or more trick points scored on one deal.

Hand—The cards originally dealt to a player, or the remaining portion thereof.

Honor—Any Ace, King, Queen, Jack, or ten.

International Match Point [IMP]—A unit of scoring awarded according to a schedule established in Law 74 B.

Irregularity—A deviation from the correct procedures set forth in the Laws and Proprieties.

Lead—The first card played to a trick.

Match Point—A unit of scoring awarded to a contestant as a result of comparison with one or more other scores.

Odd Trick—Each trick won by declarer's side in excess of six.

Opening Lead—The card led to the first trick.

Opponent—A player of the other side; a member of the partnership to which one is opposed.

Overtrick—Each trick won by declarer's side in excess of the contract.

Pack—The 52 playing cards with which the game of Contract Bridge is played.

Partner—The player with whom one plays as a side against the other two players.

Part-Score—90 or fewer trick points scored on one deal.

Pass—A call specifying that a player does not, at that turn, elect to bid, double, or redouble.

Penalty—An obligation or restriction imposed upon a side for violation of these Laws.

Penalty Card—A card prematurely exposed by a defender.

Play—1. The contribution of a card from one's hand to a trick, including the first card, which is the lead. 2. The aggregate of plays made. 3. The period during which the cards are played.

Premium Points—Any points earned other than trick points (see Law 73).

Rectification—Adjustment made to permit the auction or play to proceed as normally as possible after an irregularity has occurred.

Redeal—A second or subsequent deal by the same player to replace his first deal.

Redouble—A call that increases the scoring value

of odd tricks or undertricks of a bid of one's own side that an opponent has doubled.

Revoke—The play of a card of another suit by a player who is able to follow suit or to comply with a lead penalty.

Rotation—The clockwise order in which the right to call or to play progresses.

Round—A part of a session played without progression of players.

Section—A group of contestants playing independently of any other group insofar as movement of boards and players is concerned.

Session—A period of play during which a specified number of boards is scheduled to be played.

Side—Two players who constitute a partnership against the other two players.

Slam—A contract to win twelve tricks, six odd tricks (called Small Slam), or to win all thirteen tricks, seven odd tricks (called Grand Slam); also the fulfillment of such a contract.

Specified Suit—Any suit that a player, in exacting a penalty, requires to be led or not to be led.

Suit—One of four groups of cards in the pack, each group comprising thirteen cards and having a characteristic symbol: spades (♠), hearts (♡), diamonds (♢), clubs (♣).

Team—Two pairs playing in different directions at different tables, but for a common score (applicable regulations may permit teams of more than four members).

Trick—The unit by which the outcome of the contract is determined, regularly consisting of four cards, one contributed by each player in rotation, beginning with the lead.

Trick Points—Points earned by declarer's side by fulfilling the contract (see Law 73).

Trump—Each card of the suit, if any, named in the contract.

Turn—The correct time when a player may call or play.

Undertrick—Each trick by which declarer's side falls short of fulfilling the contract (see Law 73).

Vulnerability—The condition of being exposed to greater undertrick penalties and entitled to greater premiums (see Law 73).

CHAPTER II

PRELIMINARIES
◆◆◆◆◆◆◆

1. THE PACK—RANK OF CARDS AND SUITS

Duplicate Contract Bridge is played with a pack of 52 cards, consisting of 13 cards in each of 4 suits. The suits rank downward in the order—Spades (♠), Hearts (♡), Diamonds (♢), Clubs (♣). The cards of each suit rank downward in the order—Ace, King, Queen, Jack, 10, 9, 8, 7, 6, 5, 4, 3, 2.

2. THE DUPLICATE BOARDS

A duplicate board containing a pack is provided for each deal to be played during a session. Each board is numbered and has four pockets to hold the four hands, designated North, East, South, and West. An arrow indicates the North hand. The dealer and vulnerability are designated as follows:

North Dealer	Boards	1	5	9	13
East Dealer	Boards	2	6	10	14
South Dealer	Boards	3	7	11	15
West Dealer	Boards	4	8	12	16
Neither Side Vulnerable	Boards	1	8	11	14
North-South Vulnerable	Boards	2	5	12	15
East-West Vulnerable	Boards	3	6	9	16
Both Sides Vulnerable	Boards	4	7	10	13

The same sequence is repeated for Boards 17–32, and for each subsequent group of 16 boards.

3. ARRANGEMENT OF TABLES

Four players play at each table, and tables are numbered in a sequence established by the Director. He designates one direction as North; other compass directions assume the normal relationship to North.

4. PARTNERSHIPS

The four players at each table constitute two partnerships or sides, North-South against East-West. In pair or team events the contestants enter as pairs or teams, and retain the same partnerships throughout a session (except in the case of substitutions authorized by the Director). In individual events each player enters separately, and partnerships change during a session.

5. ASSIGNMENT OF SEATS

A. Initial Position
The Director assigns an initial position to each contestant (individual, pair, or team) at the start of a session. Unless otherwise directed, the members of each pair or team may select seats, among those assigned to them, by mutual agreement. Having once selected a compass direction, a player may change it only upon instruction or permission of the Director.
B. Change of Direction or Table
Players change their initial compass direction or proceed to another table in accordance with the Director's instructions. The Director is responsible for clear announcement of instructions; each player is responsible for moving when and as directed, and for occupying the correct seat after each change.

CHAPTER III

PREPARATION AND PROGRESSION

6. THE SHUFFLE AND DEAL

A. The Shuffle
Before play starts, each pack is shuffled. *There must be a cut if either opponent so requests.*
B. The Deal
The cards must be dealt face down, one card at a time in rotation, into four hands of thirteen cards each; each hand is then placed face down in one of the four pockets of the board.
C. Representation of Both Pairs at Deal
A member of each side must be present during the shuffle and deal unless the Director instructs otherwise.
D. New Shuffle and Redeal
1. Cards Incorrectly Dealt or Card(s) Exposed
There must be a new shuffle and a redeal if it is ascertained before the last card is dealt that the cards have been incorrectly dealt, or that a player has seen the face of a card.
2. At Director's Instruction
There must be a new shuffle and a redeal when required by the Director for any reason he deems sufficient.
E. Director's Option of Shuffling and Dealing
1. By Players
The Director may instruct that the shuffle and deal be performed at each table immediately before play starts.
2. By Director
The Director may perform the shuffle and deal in advance, himself.
3. By Agents or Assistants
The Director may have his assistants, or other appointed agents, perform the shuffle and deal in advance.
4. Different Method of Dealing or Pre-dealing
The Director may require a different method of dealing or pre-dealing.
F. Duplication of Board
If required by the conditions of play, one or more exact copies of each original deal may be made under the Director's instructions.

7. CONTROL OF BOARDS AND CARDS

A. Placement of Board
When a board is to be played it is placed in the center of the table. The board remains in the center of the table until play is completed.
B. Removal of Cards from Board
After the four players are seated, each player takes a hand from the pocket corresponding to his compass position.
1. Counting Cards in Hand before Play
Each player must count his cards face down, before looking at the face of any card, to be sure he has exactly thirteen.

2. Control of Player's Hand

During play each player retains possession of his own cards, not permitting them to be mixed with those of any other player. No player should touch any cards other than his own (but declarer may play dummy's cards in accordance with Law 45) during or after play except by permission of the Director.

3. Counting Cards in Hand after Play

Each player should count his cards again after completion of play, just before returning them to the board.

C. *Returning Cards to Board*

Each player restores his original 13 cards to the pocket corresponding to his compass position. Thereafter no hand should be removed from the board unless a member of each side, or the Director, is present.

D. *Responsibility for Procedures*

The North player is responsible for the proper observance of these procedures, and for maintaining proper conditions of play at the table. However, if the East-West pair alone is stationary, the responsibility becomes East's.

8. SEQUENCE OF ROUNDS

A. *Movement of Boards*

1. Director's Instructions

At the start of each session, the Director instructs the players on the proper movement of board from table to table at each round.

2. Responsibility For Moving Boards

The North player at each table is responsible for moving the boards just completed at his table to the proper table for the following round, unless the Director instructs otherwise.

B. *End of Round*

In general, a round ends when the Director gives the signal for the start of the following round; but if any table has not completed play by that time, the round continues for that table until play has been completed and the score of the final board of the round has been agreed upon and entered on the proper scoring form.

C. *End of Last Round and End of Session*

The last round of a session, and the session itself, ends for each table when play of all boards scheduled at that table has been completed, and when all scores have been entered on the proper scoring forms.

CHAPTER IV

GENERAL LAWS
GOVERNING IRREGULARITIES
◆◆◆◆◆◆

9. PROCEDURE FOLLOWING AN IRREGULARITY

A. *Calling Attention to an Irregularity*

1. During the Auction Period

Any player may call attention to an irregularity during the auction, whether or not it is his turn to call.

2. During the Play Period

  (a) Declarer or Either Defender

    Any of the three active players may call attention to an irregularity that occurs during the play period.

  (b) Dummy (dummy's restricted rights are defined in Laws 42 and 43).

    (1) Dummy may not call attention to an irregularity during the play but may do so after play of the hand is concluded.

    (2) Dummy may attempt to prevent an irregularity from occurring (Law 42B2).

B. *After Attention is Called to an Irregularity*

1. Summoning the Director

  (a) When to Summon

    The Director must be summoned at once when attention is drawn to an irregularity.

  (b) Right to Summon

    Any player may summon the Director after attention has been drawn to an irregularity during the auction. Any player except dummy may summon the Director during the play.

  (c) Retention of Rights

    Summoning the Director does not cause a player to forfeit any rights to which he might otherwise be entitled.

  (d) Opponents' Rights

    The fact that a player draws attention to an irregularity committed by his side does not affect the rights of the opponents.

2. Further Bids or Plays

No player should call or play until the Director has explained all matters in regard to rectification and to the assessment of a penalty.

C. *Premature Correction of Irregularity*

Any premature correction of any irregularity by the offender may subject him to a further penalty (see Law 26).

10. ASSESSMENT OF A PENALTY

A. *Right to Assess Penalty*

The Director alone has the right to assess penalties when applicable. Players do not have the right to assess or waive penalties on their own initiative.

B. *Cancellation of Payment or Waiver of Penalty*

The Director may allow or cancel any payment or waiver of penalties made by the players without his instructions.

C. *Choice between Two or More Penalties*

1. Explanation of All Options

When these laws provide an option among penalties, the Director explains all the options available.

2. Declarer's Choice of Penalties

If the declarer has a choice of penalties he must make his selection without assistance from dummy.

11. FORFEITURE OF THE RIGHT TO PENALIZE

A. *Action by Non-Offending Side*

The right to penalize an irregularity may be

forfeited if either member of the non-offending side takes any action before summoning the Director.

B. Action by Player to Offender's Left

1. Call before Imposition of a Legal Penalty

The right to penalize an irregularity is definitely forfeited if the player to offender's left calls, after an irregularity by his right hand opponent, and before a legal penalty has been stated and imposed (Law 34).

2. Play before Imposition of a Legal Penalty

The right to penalize an irregularity in play is definitely forfeited if the player to the offender's left plays, after the irregularity by his right hand opponent, before a legal penalty has been stated and imposed (Law 60).

C. Consultation between Non-Offending Partners

1. Consultation Not Permitted

Consultation between partners regarding the imposition of a penalty is not permitted.

2. Consultation Has Taken Place.

When the Director considers that the non-offending partners have consulted regarding the imposition of a penalty, the partnership forfeits its right to penalize.

D. Irregularity Called by Spectator

1. Spectator Responsibility of Non-Offending Side

The right to penalize an irregularity may be forfeited if attention is first drawn to the irregularity by a spectator for whose presence at the table the non-offending side is responsible.

2. Spectator Responsibility of Offending Side

The right to correct an irregularity may be forfeited if attention is first drawn to the irregularity by a spectator for whose presence at the table the offending side is responsible.

E. Penalty after Forfeiture of the Right to Penalize

Even after the right to penalize has been forfeited under this law, the Director may assess a penalty under his exercise of discretionary powers.

12. DIRECTOR'S DISCRETIONARY POWERS

A. Right to Assign an Adjusted Score

The Director may assign an adjusted score (or scores), either on his own initiative, or on the application of any player, but only when these Laws empower him to do so (see Law 84), or:

1. Laws Provide No Indemnity

The Director may award an adjusted score when he judges that these Laws do not provide indemnity to the non-offending contestant *for the particular type of violation of law or propriety committed by an opponent.*

2. Normal Play of the Board is Impossible

The Director may assign an adjusted score if no rectification can be made that will permit normal play of the board.

3. Incorrect Penalty Has Been Paid

The Director may assign an adjusted score if an incorrect penalty has been paid.

B. No Adjustment for Undue Severity of Penalty

The Director may not assign an adjusted score on the ground that the penalty provided in these Laws is either unduly severe or advantageous to either side.

C. Assignment of Adjusted Score

1. How Assigned

An adjusted score is assigned by altering the total-point score on the board prior to match-pointing, or by the assignment of zero or more match points (see Law 84).

2. Point Assignment in Proportion to Irregularity

    (a) Point Award to Non-Offending Side

        The number of points assigned to the non-offending side should not exceed the number required to offset the irregularity.

    (b) Points Assigned to Offending Side

        The number of points assigned to the offending side to offset the irregularity may be reduced by penalty points.

3. Balance in Assigned Scores

The indemnity points awarded the non-offending side need not balance the penalty points assessed against the offending side.

13. INCORRECT NUMBER OF CARDS

A. No Player Has Seen Another Player's Card(s)

When the Director decides that one or more pockets of the board contained an incorrect number of cards, he should correct the discrepancy as follows and require that the board then be played and scored normally.

1. Hand Records

When hand records are available, the Director should distribute the cards in accordance with the records.

2. Consult Previous Players

If hand records are not available, the Director should correct the board by consulting with players who have previously played it.

3. Require a Redeal

If the board was incorrectly dealt, the Director should require a redeal (Law 6).

B. A Player Has Seen Another Player's Card(s)

When the Director determines that one or more pockets of the board contained an incorrect number of cards, and after restoration of the board to its original condition a player has seen one or more cards in another player's hand, if the Director deems:

1. The Information Gained is Inconsequential

That such information will not interfere with normal bidding or play, the Director should require that the board be played and scored normally.

2. The Information Will Interfere with Normal Play

That the information gained thereby is of sufficient importance to interfere with normal play, the Director should award an adjusted score and may penalize an offender.

14. MISSING CARD

A. Hand Found Deficient Before Play Commences

When three hands are correct and the fourth is

found to be deficient before the play period begins, the Director makes a search for the missing card, and:

1. Card Is Found

If the card is found, it is restored to the deficient hand.

2. Card Cannot Be Found

If the card cannot be found, the Director reconstructs the deal, as near to its original form as he can determine, by substituting another pack.

B. Hand Found Deficient During Play

When three hands are correct and the fourth is found to be deficient during play, the Director makes a search for the missing card, and:

1. Card is Found

    (a) If the card is found among the played cards, Law 67 applies.

    (b) If the card is found elsewhere, it is restored to the deficient hand, and penalties may apply (see 3., following).

2. Card Cannot Be Found

If the card cannot be found, the deal is reconstructed as nearly as can be determined in its original form by substituting another pack; and penalties may apply (see 3., following).

3. Possible Penalties

A card restored to a hand under the provisions of Section B of this Law is deemed to have belonged continuously to the deficient hand. It may become a penalty card (Law 50), and failure to have played it may constitute a revoke.

15. PLAY OF A WRONG BOARD

A. Players Have Not Previously Played Board

If players play a board not designated for them to play in the current round:

1. Designate a Late Play

The Director may require both pairs to play the correct board against each other later.

2. Score Board as Played

The Director should allow the score to stand if none of the four players have previously played the board.

B. One or More Players Have Previously Played Board

If any player plays a board he has previously played, with the correct opponents or otherwise, his second score on the board is cancelled both for his side and his opponents, and the Director should award an adjusted score to the contestants deprived of the opportunity to earn a valid score.

16. UNAUTHORIZED INFORMATION

A. Definition

1. Accidental Unauthorized Information

Any extraneous information a player receives about a board he is playing or has yet to play is accidental. This unauthorized information encompasses information received by looking at the

wrong hand; by overhearing calls, results or remarks; by seeing cards at another table, or by seeing a card belonging to another player at one's own table before the auction begins.

2. Illegal Unauthorized Information

Any information conveyed by a player, other than declarer, to his partner by means of a remark, *question, unmistakable hesitation, special emphasis, tone,* gesture, *movement,* mannerism, *or any other action* that *may* suggest a call, lead or plan of play, is illegal unauthorized information.

B. Report of Accidental Unauthorized Information

The Director shall be notified forthwith of the accidental receipt of any unauthorized information, preferably by the recipient.

1. Director's Action

    (a) Board Can Be Played Normally

        If the Director judges that the unauthorized information accidentally received is not of sufficient importance to interfere with normal bidding or play, he should require that the board be played and scored normally.

    (b) Board Cannot Be Played Normally

        If the Director judges that the board cannot be played normally:

        (1) Award Adjusted Score

            The Director may assign an adjusted score to the pairs involved or:

        (2) Substitute Player

            The Director may appoint a temporary substitute to replace the player who received unauthorized information.

C. Report of Alleged Illegal Information

1. Calling the Director

Any player *except dummy* may call the Director if it appears that illegal information has been conveyed by another player.

2. Director's Action

If attention is drawn to the offense and the Director is summoned forthwith, the Director *should require* that the auction or play continue, reserving his right to assign an adjusted score if he considers that the result *could have been* affected by the illegal information.

CHAPTER V

THE AUCTION

◆◆◆◆◆◆

PART I

Correct Procedure

Section One

Auction Period

17. DURATION OF THE AUCTION

A. Auction Period Starts

    The auction period begins for each player

when he looks at his hand after removing it from the board.

B. The First Call

The player designated by the board as dealer makes the first call.

C. Successive Calls

The player to dealer's left makes the second call, and thereafter each player calls in turn in a clockwise rotation.

D. End of Auction Period

The auction period ends when three passes in rotation have followed any call (but see Law 35).

18. BIDS

A. Proper Form

A bid must name a number of odd tricks, from one to seven, and a denomination. (Pass, double and redouble are calls but not bids.)

B. To Supersede a Bid

A bid supersedes a previous bid if it names either the same number of odd tricks in a higher-ranking denomination, or a greater number of odd tricks in any denomination.

C. Sufficient Bid

A bid that supersedes the immediately previous bid is a sufficient bid.

D. Insufficient Bid

A bid that fails to supersede the immediately previous bid is an insufficient bid.

E. Rank of the Denominations

The rank of the denominations in descending order is: no trump, spades, hearts, diamonds, clubs.

19. DOUBLES AND REDOUBLES

A. Doubles

1. Legal Double

A player must double only the last preceding bid. The bid must have been made by an opponent and no calls other than pass may have intervened.

2. Proper Form for Double

In doubling, a player should not state the number of odd tricks or the denomination. The only correct form is the single word "Double."

3. Double of Incorrectly Stated Bid

If a player, in doubling, incorrectly states the bid, or the number of odd tricks or the denomination, he is deemed to have doubled the bid as it was made. (*Law 16—Unauthorized Information—may apply.*)

B. Redoubles

1. Legal Redouble

A player may redouble only the last preceding double. The double must have been made by an opponent and no calls other than pass may have intervened.

2. Proper Form for a Redouble

In redoubling a player should not state the number of odd tricks or the denomination. The only correct form is the single word "Redouble."

3. Redouble of an Incorrectly Stated Bid

If a player, in redoubling, incorrectly states the doubled bid, or the number of odd tricks or the denomination, he is deemed to have redoubled the bid as it was made. (Law 16—Unauthorized Information—may apply.)

C. Double or Redouble Superseded

Any double or redouble is superseded by a subsequent legal bid.

D. Scoring a Doubled or Redoubled Contract

If a doubled or redoubled bid is not superseded by a subsequent legal bid, scoring values are increased as provided in Law 73.

20. REVIEW AND EXPLANATION OF CALLS

A. Call Not Clearly Heard

A player who does not hear a call distinctly may forthwith require that it be repeated.

B. Review of Auction during Auction Period

Before the auction closes, a player is entitled to have all* previous calls restated when it is his turn to call, unless he is required by law to pass.

C. Review after Close of Auction

1. Opening Lead Inquiry

After the final pass either defender has the right to ask if it is his opening lead (see Laws 47E and 41).

2. Review of Auction

Declarer or either defender may, *at his first turn to play,* require all* previous calls to be restated.

D. Who May Review the Auction

A request to have calls restated should be responded to only by an opponent.

E. Correction of Error in Review

Any player, including dummy or a player required by law to pass, may and should promptly correct an error in restatement.

F. Explanation of Conventional Meaning of Calls

1 During the Auction

During the auction and before the final pass, a full explanation of *any* call made by an opponent may be requested by any player, but only at that player's turn to call.

2. During the Play Period

After the final pass and *throughout the play period,* declarer or *either defender*** *may request such an explanation of opposing calls,* and declarer may request an explanation of the defenders' card play conventions, but only at his own turn to play (N.B.: Law 16 may apply).

21. CALL BASED ON MISINFORMATION

A. Call Based on Caller's Misunderstanding

A player has no recourse if he has made a call on the basis of his own misunderstanding.

---

* A player may not ask for a partial restatement of previous calls and should not halt the review before it has been completed.

** Sponsoring organizations are specifically authorized to establish different regulations applying to the defenders' questions before the first trick has been completed.

B. Call Based on Misinformation from an Opponent

1. Change of Call

A player may, without penalty, change a call he may have made as a result of misinformation given to him by an opponent (*failure to alert promptly to a conventional call or special understanding, where such alert is required by the sponsoring organization, is deemed misinformation*), provided that his partner has not subsequently called.

2. Change of Call by Opponent Following Correction

When a player elects to change a call because of misinformation (as in 1., preceding), his left hand opponent may then in turn change any subsequent call he may have made, without penalty (*unless his withdrawn call conveyed such substantial information as to damage the non-offending side, in which case the Director may assign an adjusted score*).

3. Too Late to Change Call

When it is too late to change a call, Law 40C may apply.

Section Two

Auction Is Closed

22. PROCEDURE AFTER THE AUCTION IS CLOSED

A. No Player Has Bid

After the auction is closed, if no player has bid, the hands are returned to the board without play. There *may not* be a redeal.

B. One or More Players Have Bid

If any player has bid, the final bid becomes the contract and play begins.

PART II

Irregularities in Procedure

Section One

Exposed Card, Auction Period

23. CARD EXPOSED OR LED DURING AUCTION

A. Director's Action

When the Director determines, during the auction, that a player has faced a card on the table, or held a card so that it is possible for his partner to see its face, he must require that every such card be left face up on the table until the auction closes; and (penalty) if the offender subsequently becomes a defender, declarer may treat *every* such card as a penalty card (Law 50). In addition:

1. Low Card Not Prematurely Led

If it is a single card below the rank of an honor and not prematurely led, there is no *further* penalty.

2. Single Card of Honor Rank, or Card Prematurely Led

If the card is a single card of honor rank, or is any card prematurely led, (penalty) offender's partner must pass when next it is his turn to call.

3. Two or More Cards are Exposed

If two or more cards are so exposed, (penalty)

offender's partner must pass when next it is his turn to call.

B. Enforced Pass May Damage Innocent Side

When the penalty for an irregularity, under this or any other Law, would compel the offender's partner to pass at his next turn, and when the Director deems that this enforced pass will *necessarily* damage the innocent side:

1. Direct That the Auction Continue

The Director may direct that the auction and play continue, reserving the right to assign an adjusted score if he considers that the result was affected by the illegal information, or:

2. Assign an Adjusted Score

The Director may forthwith assign an adjusted score.

Section Two

Changes of Calls

24. IMMEDIATE CORRECTION OF CALL

A. Correcting Inadvertent Call

A player may substitute his intended call for an inadvertent call but only if he does so, *or attempts to do so,* without pause *for thought.* If legal, his last call stands without penalty.

B. Correction to an Illegal Call

If the substituted call is an illegal call, it is subject to the applicable Law.

25. CHANGE OF CALL

A. Attempt to Change Illegal Call

A call substituted for an illegal call made previously at the same turn, when too late for correction as provided in Law 24, is cancelled. The offending side is subject to the applicable law for the illegal call, and may also be subject to Law 26.

B. Attempt to Change Legal Call

A call substituted for a legal call made previously at the same turn, when Law 24 does not apply, is cancelled. The legal call stands and (penalty):

1. Auction Period Penalty

The offender's partner must pass whenever it is his turn to call.

2. Lead Penalties

Offender's partner may be subject to the lead penalties of Law 26.

26. UNAUTHORIZED INFORMATION GIVEN BY CHANGE OF CALL

When a player illegally names a denomination not selected as his final call at that turn (as in changing a call except as permitted by Law 24, or in making or correcting a legal call), then if he becomes a defender:

A. Illegal Call Is a Suit Bid

If the illegal call is a suit bid:

1. Illegally Named Suit Is Not Conventional

When the illegally named suit is not conventionally related to another suit or suits, declarer may either (penalty):

(a) Require Lead of Illegally Named Suit

Require the offender's partner to lead the illegally named suit at his first turn to lead (includng the opening lead); or

(b) Prohibit Lead of Illegally Named Suit

Prohibit the offender's partner from leading the illegally named suit at his first turn to lead (including the opening lead) and for as long as the offender's partner retains the lead.

2. Illegally Named Suit Is Conventional

When the illegally named suit is conventionally related to another suit or suits, declarer may either (penalty):

(a) Require Lead of Conventionally Related Suit

Require the offender's partner to lead a card of a specified suit thus conventionally related at his first turn to lead (including the opening lead); or

(b) Prohibit Lead of Conventionally Related Suit

Prohibit the offender's partner from leading any card of any thus related suit at his first turn to lead (including the opening lead) and for as long as the offender's partner retains the lead.

B. *Illegal Call is No Trump Bid*

If the illegal call was a no trump bid,

1. No Trump Bid Is Not Conventional

When the illegal no trump bid is *not conventionally related to a suit or suits,* and if the offender's partner is to make the opening lead, (penalty) declarer may require the offender's partner to make the opening lead in a specified suit.

2. No Trump Bid Relates to Suit or Suits

When the illegal no trump bid conventionally relates to a suit or suits, Law 26A2 applies.

C. *Illegal Double or Redouble*

If another call has been substituted for an illegal double or redouble, the penalties provided in Law 27B3 apply.

Section Three

Insufficient Bid

27. INSUFFICIENT BID

A. *Insufficient Bid Accepted*

Any insufficient bid may be accepted (treated as legal) *at the option* of the opponent to offender's left. It is accepted if that player calls.

B. *Insufficient Bid Not Accepted*

If an insufficient bid made in rotation is not accepted, it must be corrected by the substitution of either a sufficient bid or a pass (the offender is entitled to select his final call at that turn after the applicable penalties have been stated, and any call he has previously attempted to substitute is cancelled, but Law 26 may apply).

1. Corrected by Lowest Sufficient Bid in Same Denomination

(a) No Penalty

If the insufficient bid is corrected by the lowest sufficient bid in the same denomi-

nation, the auction proceeds as though the irregularity had not occured (but see (b) following).

(b) Award of Adjusted Score

If the Director judges that the insufficient bid conveyed such substantial information as to damage the non-offending side, he may assign an adjusted score.

2. Corrected by Any Other Sufficient Bid

If the insufficient bid is corrected by any other sufficient bid, (penalty) the offender's partner must pass whenever it is his turn to call (and Law 26 may apply).

3. Corrected by a Pass

If the insufficient bid is corrected by a pass, (penalty) the offender's partner must pass whenever it is his turn to call; and if the offender's partner is to make the opening lead:

(a) Require Lead of Specified Suit

Declarer may require the offender's partner to lead a specified suit; or

(b) Prohibit Lead of a Specified Suit

Declarer may prohibit the offender's partner from leading a specified suit; this prohibition to continue for as long as offender's partner retains the lead.

4. Attempt to Correct by a Double or Redouble

If the offender attempts to substitute a double or redouble for his insufficient bid, the attempted call is cancelled; he must pass and the offense (penalty) is subject to the penalties provided in (3) preceding.

C. *Insufficient Bid Out of Rotation*

If a player makes an insufficient bid out of rotation, Law 31 applies.

Section Four

Call out of Rotation

28. CALLS CONSIDERED TO BE IN ROTATION

A. *Right Hand Opponent Required to Pass*

A call is considered to be in rotation when it is made by a player at his right hand opponent's turn to call, if that opponent is required by law to pass.

B. *Call by Correct Player Cancelling Call Out of Rotation*

A call is considered to be in rotation when made by a player whose turn it was to call, before a penalty has been assessed for a call out of rotation by an opponent; the call thus made waives any penalty for the call out of rotation and the auction proceeds as though the opponent had not called at that turn.

29. PROCEDURE AFTER A CALL OUT OF ROTATION

A. *Out of Rotation Call Cancelled*

A call out of rotation is cancelled (but see B following) and the auction reverts to the player whose turn it was to call. Offender may make any legal call in proper rotation, but may be subject to penalty under Laws 30, 31, or 32.

B. Forfeiture of Right to Penalize

Following a call out of rotation, the opponent next in rotation to the offender *may elect* to call, thereby forfeiting the right to penalize.

30. PASS OUT OF ROTATION

A. Before Any Player Has Bid

When a player has passed out of rotation before any player has bid, (penalty) the offender must pass when next it is his turn to call.

B. After Any Player Has Bid

1. At Offender's Right Hand Opponent's Turn to Call

After any player has bid, for a pass out of rotation made at the turn of offender's right hand opponent to call, (penalty) offender must pass when next it is his turn to call (*if the pass out of rotation relates by convention to a specific suit, or suits, thereby conveying information, Law 26 may apply*).

2. At Offender's Partner's Turn to Call
   (a) Action Required of Offender
      After any player has bid, for a pass out of rotation made at the offender's partner's turn to call, (penalty) the offender must pass whenever it is his turn to call (and Law 26 may apply).
   (b) Action Open to Offender's Partner
      Offender's partner may make any sufficient bid, or may pass, but may not double or redouble at that turn.
   (c) Offender's Partner Passes
      If offender's partner passes and subsequently is to make the opening lead:
      (1) Require Lead of a Specified Suit
         Declarer may require offender's partner to lead a specified suit; or
      (2) Prohibit Lead of a Specified Suit
         Declarer may prohibit offender's partner from leading a specified suit, such prohibition to continue for as long as he retains the lead.

3. At Offender's Left Hand Opponent's Turn to Call

After any player has bid, a pass out of rotation at offender's left hand opponent's turn to call is treated as a change of call and Law 25 applies.

31. BID OUT OF ROTATION

When a player has bid out of rotation (and the bid is cancelled, as the option to accept the bid has not been exercised—see Law 29):

A. Before Any Player Has Called

1. Offender's Right Hand Opponent's Turn to Call
   (a) Right Hand Opponent Passes
      When his right hand opponent passes, offender must repeat the bid out of rotation and there is no penalty.
   (b) Right Hand Opponent Bids
      If his right hand opponent bids, offender

may pass, double,* or make any legal call; if his call

(1) Repeats Denomination of Bid Out of Rotation
   Repeats the denomination of his bid out of rotation, (penalty) offender's partner must pass when *next* it is his turn to call (see Law 23B).

(2) Does Not Repeat Denomination of Bid Out Of Rotation
   Names a denomination other than that named in his call out of rotation, (penalty) offender's partner must pass whenever it is his turn to call (see Law 23B) and Law 26 must apply.

2. Offender's Partner's or Left Hand Opponent's Turn to Call

When a player has bid out of rotation, and it was the turn of either his partner or his left hand opponent to call, (penalty) offender's partner must pass whenever it is his turn to call (see Law 23B), and Law 26 may apply.

B. After Any Player Has Called

1. At Offender's Partner's Turn to Call

When a player has bid out of rotation, after any player has called, and when it was offender's partner's turn to call, (penalty) offender's partner must pass whenever it is his turn to call (see Law 23B), and Law 26 may apply; and if offender's partner is to make the opening lead:

   (a) Requiring the Lead of a Specified Suit
      Declarer may require offender's partner to lead a specified suit; or
   (b) Prohibiting the Lead of a Specified Suit
      Declarer may prohibit offender's partner from leading a specified suit, such prohibition to continue for as long as he retains the lead.

2. At Offender's Right Hand Opponent's Turn to Call
   (a) Right Hand Opponent Passes
      (1) Out of Rotation Bid Was Sufficient
         If the bid out of rotation was sufficient, and offender's right hand opponent now passes, offender must repeat his bid and there is no penalty.
      (2) Out of Rotation Bid Was Insufficient
         If the bid out of rotation was insufficient, and offender's right hand opponent now passes, offender's insufficient bid must be corrected as though it had been made in rotation, as provided in Law 27.
   (b) Right Hand Opponent Makes a Legal Bid, Double or Redouble†
      If offender's right hand opponent makes a legal bid, double or redouble, (penalty) *the penalty provisions of A1(b) preceding apply.*

---

* Law 23B may apply.

† An illegal call by that opponent may be penalized in the usual way, after which this subsection B2(b) applies.

3. At Offender's Left Hand Opponent's Turn to Call

Offender's bid out of rotation is treated as a change of call and Law 25 applies.

32. DOUBLE OR REDOUBLE OUT OF ROTATION

A. Inadmissible Double or Redouble Out of Rotation

An inadmissible double or redouble out of rotation is subject to Law 36.

B. Double or Redouble Out of Rotation, in Violation of Obligation to Pass

A double or redouble out of rotation when in violation of a legal obligation to pass, is subject to Law 37.

C. Doubles or Redoubles Out of Rotation Not Subject to Laws 36 or 37.

1. Made at Offender's Partner's Turn to Call

If a double or redouble out of rotation has been made when it was the offender's partner's turn to call, the offender's partner must pass whenever it is his turn to call (see Law 23B); the offender may not thereafter, in turn, double or redouble the same bid he doubled or redoubled out of turn; and if the offender's partner is to make the opening lead:

 (a) Requiring the Lead of a Specified Suit
    Declarer may require the offender's partner to lead a specified suit; or
 (b) Prohibiting the Lead of a Specified Suit
    Declarer may prohibit the offender's partner from leading a specified suit, such prohibition to continue for as long as the offender's partner retains the lead.

2. Made at Offender's Right Hand Opponent's Turn to Call

If a double or redouble out of rotation has been made at offender's right hand opponent's turn to call, then:

 (a) Offender's Right Hand Opponent Passes
    If offender's right hand opponent passes, offender must repeat his out of rotation double or redouble and there is no penalty.
 (b) Offender's Right Hand Opponent Bids
    If offender's right hand opponent bids, the offender may in turn make any legal call and the penalty provisions of 27B3 apply.

33. SIMULTANEOUS CALLS

A call made simultaneously with one made by the player whose turn it was to call, is deemed to be a subsequent call.

34. CALL IN ROTATION AFTER AN ILLEGAL CALL

A. Forfeiture of Penalty For Illegal Call

A call by a member of the non-offending side, after an illegal call by the opponent to his right, and before a penalty has been assessed, forfeits the right to penalize the offense.

B. Illegal Call Legalized

The illegal call is treated as though it were legal, *except that:*

1. Illegal Call Was a Bid of More Than Seven

A bid of more than seven is treated as a pass.

2. Illegal Call Was an Inadmissible Double or Redouble.

If the illegal call was an inadmissible double or redouble, *that call and all subsequent calls are cancelled; the auction reverts to the player whose turn it was to call and proceeds as though there had been no irregularity.* Law 35 or 37 may apply.

35. RETENTION OF RIGHT TO CALL

A. Player Retains Right to Call

A player may not be deprived of his right to call by one or more passes following a pass out of rotation, when there has been no subsequent bid.

B. Passes Cancelled

The Director should cancel all such passes, and the bidding reverts to the player who had missed his turn. The auction proceeds as though there had been no irregularity.

Section Five

Inadmissible Calls

36. INADMISSIBLE DOUBLE OR REDOUBLE

A. Definition

An inadmissible double or redouble is one not permitted by Law 19.

B. Inadmissible Double or Redouble Cancelled

Any inadmissible double or redouble is cancelled, and the offender must substitute a legal call; *Law 26 applies.*

C. Inadmissibly Doubled or Redoubled Bid Becomes Final Contract

If the bid that was inadmissibly doubled or redoubled becomes the final contract, either member of the non-offending side may specify that the contract be played undoubled.

D. Right to Penalize Inadmissible Double or Redouble is Forfeited

If the right of the non-offending side to penalize is forfeited, Law 34 applies.

37. BID, DOUBLE OR REDOUBLE IN VIOLATION OF OBLIGATION TO PASS

A. Bid, Double or Redouble Cancelled

If a player required by law to pass bids, doubles or redoubles, his call is cancelled, and:

1. Auction Penalty

Both members of the offending side must pass during the remainder of the auction.

2. Lead Penalties

If the offender's partner is to make the opening lead,

(a) Require Lead of Specified Suit
Declarer may require offender's partner to lead a specified suit; or
(b) Prohibit Lead of Specified Suit
Declarer may prohibit offender's partner from leading a specified suit, such prohibition to continue for as long as offender's partner retains the lead.

B. Right To Penalize Forfeited

If the right of the non-offending side to penalize is forfeited as provided in Law 11, the offender's bid, double or redouble, if otherwise legal, stands at that turn; but if the offender was required to pass for the remainder of the auction, he must still pass at subsequent turns.

38. BIDS OF MORE THAN SEVEN

No play or score at a contract of more than seven is ever permissible.

A. Bid of More Than Seven Cancelled

A bid of more than seven by any player is cancelled, and (penalty) both members of the offending side must pass during the remainder of the auction.

B. Lead Penalty

If a player bids more than seven, and his partner is to make the opening lead, declarer may either:

1. Require Lead of a Specified Suit
Require offender's partner to lead a specified suit; or

2. Prohibit Lead of Specified Suit
Prohibit offender's partner from leading a specified suit, such prohibition to continue for as long as offender's partner retains the lead.

C. Right to Penalize Forfeited

If the right to penalize is forfeited as provided in Law 11, the offender must substitute a pass; any call that may have been made subsequently is cancelled; and the auction proceeds as though there had been no irregularity.

39. CALL AFTER THE AUCTION IS CLOSED

A. Call after Auction Ends

A call made after the auction is closed is cancelled.

B. Pass by Defender

If a defender passes after the auction is closed there is no penalty.

C. Any Call by Declarer or Dummy

If declarer or dummy makes any call after the auction is closed there is no penalty.

D. Bid, Double or Redouble by a Defender

If a defender bids, doubles or redoubles after the auction is closed, declarer may either:

1. Require Lead of Specified Suit
Require offender's partner, when first it is his turn to lead, to lead a specified suit; or

2. Prohibit Lead of Specified Suit
Prohibit offender's partner, when first it is his turn to lead, from leading a specified suit, such

prohibition to continue for as long as the offender's partner retains the lead.

E. Right to Penalize Forfeited

If the right of the non-offending side to penalize is forfeited, as provided in Law 11, all calls made after the close of the auction are cancelled without penalty.

Section Six

Conventions and Agreements

40. PARTNERSHIP UNDERSTANDINGS

A. Right to Call

A player may make any call or play (including an intentionally misleading call—such as a 'psychic' bid—or a call or play that departs from commonly accepted, or previously announced, conventional practice), without prior announcement, provided that such call or play is not based on a partnership understanding.

B. Concealed Partnership Understandings Prohibited

A player may not make a call or play based on a partnership understanding, unless an opposing pair may reasonably be expected to understand its meaning, or unless his side discloses the use of such call or play in accordance with the regulations of the sponsoring organization.

Director's Option

If the Director decides that a side has been damaged through its opponents' failure to explain the meaning of a call or play, he may award an adjusted score.

D. Regulation of Conventions

The sponsoring organization may regulate the use of bidding or play conventions.

E. Convention Card

1. Right to Prescribe
The sponsoring organization may prescribe a convention card on which partners are to list their conventions, and may establish regulations for its use.

2. Referring to Opponents' Convention Card
During the auction *and play, any player except dummy may refer to his opponents' convention card at his own turn to* call or *play.*

CHAPTER VI

THE PLAY
◆◆◆◆◆◆
PART I

Procedure

Section One

Correct Procedure

41. COMMENCEMENT OF PLAY

A. The Opening Lead

After the auction closes, the defender on declarer's left makes the opening lead.

B. Spreading Dummy's Hand

After the opening lead has been made*, dummy spreads his hand in front of him on the table. The cards are face up, sorted in suits, with trumps to dummy's right.

C. Playing Dummy's Hand

Declarer plays both his hand and that of dummy.

D. Inquiry as to Final Contract

After it is too late to have previous calls restated, as provided in Law 20, declarer or either defender is entitled to be informed as to what the contract is and whether, but not by whom, it was doubled or redoubled.

42. DUMMY'S RIGHTS

A. Absolute Rights

1. Give or Obtain Information

Dummy is entitled to give or obtain information, *in the Director's presence,* as to fact or law.

2. Keep Track of Tricks

He may keep count of tricks won and lost by each side and may draw attention to the fact that another player's card, played to any preceding trick, has been pointed in the wrong direction.

3. Play as Declarer's Agent

He may play the cards of the dummy as declarer's agent and only as directed by him (see Law 16).

B. Qualified Rights

Dummy may exercise other rights subject to the limitations provided in Law 43.

1. Revoke Inquiries

Dummy may question players regarding revokes as provided in Law 61 (he may ask a player who has failed to follow suit to a trick whether he has a card of the suit led).

2. Attempt to Prevent Irregularity

He may try to prevent any irregularity (he may, for example, warn declarer against leading from the wrong hand).

3. Draw Attention to Irregularity

He may draw attention to any irregularity, *but only after play of the hand is concluded.*

43. DUMMY'S LIMITATIONS

A. Limitations on Dummy

1. General Limitations

(a) Calling the Director
Dummy should *not* call the Director *during play.*

(b) Calling Attention to Irregularity
Dummy may *not* call attention to an irregularity *during play* except to try to prevent an irregularity before it occurs (Law 42B2).

(c) Participate in or Comment on Play
Dummy may not participate in the play or make any comment on the bidding or play.

---

* The sponsoring organization may specify a delay (see footnote to Law 45).

2. Limitations Carrying Specific Penalty

(a) Exchanging Hands
Dummy *may not* exchange hands with declarer.

(b) Leave Seat to Watch Declarer
Dummy *may not* leave his seat to watch declarer's play of the hand.

(c) Look at Defender's Hand
Dummy *may not,* on his own initiative, look at the face of a card in either defender's hand.

B. Penalties for Violation

1. General Penalties

Dummy is liable to penalty under Law 86 for any violation of the limitations listed in A1 or A2 preceding.

2. Specific Penalties

If dummy, after violation of the limitations listed in A2 preceding:

(a) Draws Attention to Defender's Irregularity
Is the first to draw attention to a defender's irregularity, declarer may not enforce any penalty for the offense.

(b) Warns Declarer on Lead
Warns declarer not to lead from the wrong hand, (penalty) either defender may choose the hand from which declarer shall lead.

(c) Asks Declarer About Possible Irregularity
Is the first to ask declarer if a play from declarer's hand constitutes a revoke or failure to comply with a penalty, declarer must substitute a correct card if his play was illegal, and the penalty provisions of Law 64 apply.

44. SEQUENCE AND PROCEDURE OF PLAY

A. Lead to a Trick

The player who leads to a trick may play any card in his hand (unless he is subject to restriction after an irregularity committed by his side).

B. Subsequent Plays to a Trick

After the lead, each other player in turn plays a card, and the four cards so played constitute a trick. (For the method of playing cards and arranging tricks see Law 65.)

C. Requirement to Follow Suit

In playing to a trick, each player must follow suit if possible. This obligation takes precedence over all other requirements of these Laws.

D. Inability to Follow Suit

If unable to follow suit, a player may play any card (unless he is subject to restriction after an irregularity committed by his side).

E. Tricks Containing Trumps

A trick containing a trump is won by the player who has contributed to it the highest trump.

F. Tricks Not Containing Trumps

A trick that does not contain a trump is won by the player who has contributed to it the highest card of the suit led.

G. Lead to Tricks Subsequent to First Trick

The player who has won the trick leads to the next trick.

45. CARD PLAYED

A. Play of Card from a Hand

Each player except dummy plays a card by detaching it from his hand and facing* it on the table immediately before him.

B. Play of Card from Dummy

Declarer plays a card from dummy by naming the card, after which dummy picks up the card and faces it on the table, In playing from dummy's hand declarer may, if he prefers, pick up the desired card himself.

C. Compulsory Play of Card

1. Defender's Card

A defender's card held so that it is possible for his partner to see its face must be played to the current trick (if the defender has already made a legal play to the current trick, see Law 45E).

2. Declarer's Card

Declarer must play a card fom his hand held face up, touching or nearly touching the table, *or maintained in such a position as to indicate that it has been played.*

3. Dummy's Card

A card in the dummy must be played if it has been deliberately touched by declarer except for the purpose of arranging dummy's cards, or of reaching a card above or below the card or cards touched.

4. Named or Designated Card
   (a) Play of Named Card
   A card must be played if a player names or otherwise designates it as the card he proposes to play.
   (b) Correction of Inadvertent Designation
   A player may, without penalty, change an inadvertent designation if he does so without pause *for thought;* but if an opponent has, in turn, played a card that was legal before the change in designation, that opponent may withdraw without penalty the card so played and substitute another (see Law 47F).

5. Penalty Card

A penalty card must be played, subject to Law 50.

D. Card Misplayed by Dummy

If dummy places in. the played position a card that declarer did not name, the card must be withdrawn if attention is drawn to it before *each side* has played to the next trick, and a defender may withdraw (without penalty) a card played after the error but before attention was drawn to it (see Law 47F).

E. Fifth Card Played to Trick

1. By a Defender

A fifth card contributed to a trick by a defender

becomes a penalty card, subject to Law 50, unless the Director deems that it was led, in which case Laws 53 or 56 apply.

2. By Declarer

When declarer contributes a fifth card to a trick from his own hand or dummy, there is no penalty unless the Director deems that it was led, in which case Law 55 applies.

F. Dummy Indicates Card

After dummy's hand is faced, dummy may not touch or indicate any card (except for purpose of arrangement) without instruction from declarer. If he does so, the Director should be summoned forthwith. The Director should rule whether dummy's act did in fact constitute a suggestion to declarer, and if it did (penalty) he may forbid declarer to make any play predicated upon the suggestion.

G. Turning the Trick

No player should turn his card face down until all four players have played to the trick.

Section Two

Irregularities in Procedure

46. INCOMPLETE OR ERRONEOUS CALL OF CARD FROM DUMMY

A. Proper Form for Designating Dummy's Card

When calling a card to be played from dummy, declarer should clearly state both the suit and the rank of the desired card.

B. Incomplete or Erroneous Call

In case of an incomplete or erroneous call by declarer of the card to be played from dummy the following restrictions apply:

1. Incomplete Designation of Rank

If declarer, in playing from dummy, calls "high," or words of like import, he is deemed to have called the highest card of the suit indicated (*or if dummy is last to follow suit to the trick, the lowest winning card*); if he calls "low," or words of like import, he is deemed to have called the lowest.

2. Name of Suit but Not Rank

If declarer names a suit but not a rank, he is deemed to have called the lowest card of the suit indicated (*unless this was incontrovertibly not his intention*).

3. Name of Rank but Not Suit

If declarer names a rank but not a suit:
   (a) In Leading
   Declarer is deemed to have continued the suit in which dummy won the preceding trick, provided there is a card of the named rank in that suit.
   (b) All Other Cases
   In all other cases, declarer must play a card from dummy of the named rank if he can legally do so; but if there are two or more such cards that can be legally played, declarer must designate which is intended.

---

* *Sponsoring organizations may require an opening lead face down.*

4. Designated Card Not in Dummy

If declarer calls a card that is not in dummy, the call is void and declarer may designate any legal card.

5. No Suit or Rank Designated

If declarer indicates a play without naming either a suit or rank (as by saying, "play anything," or words of like import), either defender may designate the play from the dummy except when such play was incontrovertibly not declarer's intention.

47. RETRACTION OF CARD PLAYED

A. To Comply with Penalty

A card once played may be withdrawn to comply with a penalty (but see Law 49).

B. To Correct an Illegal Play

A played card may be withdrawn to correct an illegal play (but see Law 49).

C. To Change an Inadvertent Designation

A played card may be withdrawn without penalty after a change of designation as permitted by Law 45C4(b).

D. Following Opponent's Change of Play

After an opponent's change of play, a played card may be withdrawn without penalty to substitute another card for the one played.

E. Change of Play Based on Misinformation

1. Lead Out of Turn

A lead out of turn may be retracted without penalty if the leader was mistakenly informed by an opponent that it was his turn to lead.

2. Declarer's Retraction of Play

(a) Defender Has Not Subsequently Played

Declarer may retract a card played from his own hand or dummy after a mistaken explanation of a defender's conventional play and before a corrected explanation, but only if no card was subsequently played to that trick.

(b) One or More Subsequent Plays Made

When it is too late for declarer to correct a play, under (a) preceding, Law 40C applies.

F. Exposure of Retracted Card by Damaged Side

If a card retracted under sections D or E preceding gave substantial information to an opponent, the Director may award an adjusted score.

G. Illegal Retraction

Except as provided in A through E preceding, a card once played may not be withdrawn.

PART II

Penalty Card

48. EXPOSURE OF DECLARER'S CARDS

A. Declarer Exposes a Card

Declarer is not subject to penalty for exposing a card, and no card of declarer's or dummy's hand ever becomes a penalty card. Declarer is not required to play any card dropped accidentally.

B. Declarer Faces Cards

1. After Opening Lead Out of Turn

When declarer *inadvertently* faces his cards after an opening lead out of turn, Law 54 applies (*but it is a violation of propriety to spread his hand when he knows he is declarer*).

2. At Any Other Time

When declarer faces his cards at any time other than immediately after an opening lead out of turn, he *may be* deemed to have made a claim or concession of tricks, and Law 68 then applies.

49. EXPOSURE OF A DEFENDER'S CARDS

Whenever a defender faces a card on the table, holds a card so that it is possible for his partner to see its face, or names a card as being in his hand, before he is entitled to do so in the normal course of play or application of law, (penalty) each such card becomes a penalty card (Law 50); but see Law 70 (Defender's Claim or Concession of Tricks).

50. DISPOSITION OF PENALTY CARD

A. Definition of Penalty Card

A card prematurely exposed by a defender is a penalty card *unless the Director designates otherwise*.

B. Penalty Card Remains Exposed

A penalty card must be left face up on the table immediately before the player to whom it belongs, until it is played or until an alternate penalty has been selected.

C. Leader's Partner Has Penalty Card

1. Lead Must Be Held for Declarer's Option

When a defender has the lead while his partner has a penalty card, he may not lead until declarer has stated which of the options open to him he is selecting. If the defender leads prematurely, he is subject to penalty under Law 49.

2. Declarer's Options

(a) Require or Prohibit Lead of Penalty Card Suit

The declarer may require that defender to lead the suit of the penalty card, or may prohibit him from leading that suit for as long as he retains the lead. If declarer exercises this option, the penalty card may be picked up.

(b) Penalty Card to Remain Penalty Card

If declarer does not exercise the option provided in (a) preceding, the defender may lead any card, but the penalty card remains a penalty card.

(c) Two or More Penalty Cards

See Law 51.

D. Play of Penalty Card

A penalty card must be played at the first legal opportunity, whether in leading, following suit, discarding or trumping. If a defender has two or more penalty cards that can legally be played, declarer may designate which is to be played. The obligation to follow suit, or to comply with a lead or play penalty, takes precedence over the obligation to play a penalty card, but the penalty card must still be left face up on the table and played at the next legal opportunity.

51. TWO OR MORE PENALTY CARDS

A. Defender's Turn to Play
(See Law 50: If a defender has two or more penalty cards that can legally be played, declarer may designate which is to be played at that turn.)
B. Leader's Partner Has Two or More Penalty Cards
1. Penalty Cards in Same Suit
   (a) Declarer Requires Lead of That Suit
       When a defender has two or more penalty cards in one suit, and declarer requires the defender's partner to lead that suit, the defender may pick up every penalty card in that suit and may make any legal play to the trick.
   (b) Declarer Prohibits Lead of That Suit
       If the declarer prohibits the lead of that suit, the defender may pick up every penalty card in that suit and may make any legal play to the trick.
2. Penalty Cards in More Than One Suit
   (a) Declarer Requires Lead of a Specified Suit
       When a defender has penalty cards in more than one suit, declarer may require the defender's partner to lead any suit in which the defender has a penalty card (but B1(a) preceding then applies).
   (b) Declarer Prohibits Lead of Specified Suits
       When a defender has penalty cards in more than one suit, declarer may prohibit the defender's partner from leading every such suit; but the defender may then pick up every penalty card in every suit prohibited by declarer, and make any legal play to the trick.

52. FAILURE TO LEAD OR PLAY A PENALTY CARD

A. Defender Fails to Play Penalty Card
When a defender fails to lead or play a penalty card as required by Law 50, he may not, on his own initiative, withdraw any other card he may have played.
B. Defender Plays Another Card
1. Play of Card Accepted
   (a) Declarer May Accept Play
       If a defender has led or played another card when he could legally have led or played a penalty card, declarer may accept such lead or play.
   (b) Declarer Must Accept Play
       Declarer must accept such lead or play if he has thereafter played from his own hand or dummy.
   (c) Penalty Card Remains Penalty Card
       If the played card is accepted under either (a) or (b) preceding, the unplayed penalty card remains a penalty card.
2. Play of Card Rejected

Declarer may require the defender to substitute the penalty card for the card illegally played or led. Every card illegally led or played by the defender in the course of committing the irregularity becomes a penalty card.

PART III

Irregular Leads and Plays

Section One

Lead out of Turn

53. LEAD OUT OF TURN ACCEPTED

A. Lead Out of Turn Treated as Correct Lead
Any lead faced out of turn may be treated as a correct lead. It becomes a correct lead if declarer or either defender, as the case may be, accepts it (*by making a statement to that effect*), or if the player next in rotation plays* to the irregular lead. (If no acceptance statement or play is made the Director will require that the lead be made from the correct hand.)
B. Wrong Defender Plays Card to Declarer's Irregular Lead
If the defender at the right of the player from whose hand the lead out of turn was made plays* to the irregular lead, the lead stands and Law 57 applies.
C. Proper Lead Made Subsequent to Irregular Lead
If it was properly the turn to lead of an opponent of the player who led out of turn, that opponent may make his proper lead to the trick of the infraction without his card being deemed played to the irregular lead. When this occurs, the proper lead stands, and all cards played in error to this trick may be withdrawn without penalty (see Law 47F).

54. OPENING LEAD OUT OF TURN

A. Declarer Accepts Lead
When a defender faces the opening lead out of turn declarer may accept the irregular lead as provided in Law 53, and dummy is spread in accordance with Law 41.
1. Declarer Plays Second Card
The second card to the trick is played from declarer's hand.
2. Dummy Has Played Second Card
If declarer plays the second card to the trick from dummy, dummy's card may not be withdrawn except to correct a revoke.

B. Declarer Must Accept Lead
If declarer may have seen any of dummy's cards (except cards that dummy may have exposed during the auction and that were subject to Law 23), he must accept the lead.
C. Declarer Begins to Spread His Hand
If declarer inadvertently† begins to spread his

---

* But see C below.
† Declarer should, as a matter of propriety, refrain from spreading his hand when he knows that he is declarer.

hand as though he were dummy, and in so doing exposes one or more cards, and if subsection B preceding does not apply, the lead must be accepted, declarer must spread his entire hand and dummy becomes declarer.

D. Declarer Refuses Opening Lead

When declarer requires the defender to retract his opening lead out of turn, Law 56 applies.

55. DECLARER'S LEAD OUT OF TURN

A. Declarer's Lead Accepted

If declarer has led out of turn, either defender may accept the lead as provided in Law 53.

B. Declarer Required to Retract Lead

1. Defender's Turn to Lead

If declarer has led when it was a defender's turn to lead, and if either defender requires him to retract such lead, declarer restores the card led in error to the proper hand without penalty.

2. Lead in Declarer's Hand or Dummy's

If declarer has led from the wrong hand when it was his turn to lead from his hand or dummy's and if either defender requires him to retract the lead, he withdraws the card led in error. He must lead from the correct hand and, (penalty) if able to do so, a card of the same suit.

C. Failure to Comply with Penalty

Failure by declarer to comply with the lead penalty may subject him to penalty under Law 64.

56. DEFENDER'S LEAD OUT OF TURN

A. Declarer Accepts Lead

See Laws 53 and 54.

B. Declarer Requires Retraction of Lead

When declarer requires a defender to retract his lead out of turn, the card illegally led becomes a penalty card, and Law 50 applies.

Section Two

Other Irregular Leads and Plays

57. PREMATURE LEAD OR PLAY BY DEFENDER

A. Premature Lead or Play to Next Trick

When a defender leads to the next trick before his partner has played to the current trick, or plays out of turn before his partner has played, (penalty) the card so led or played becomes a penalty card, and declarer must select one of the following options. He may require the offender's partner:

1. Follow Suit with Highest Card

To play the highest card he holds of the suit led, or

2. Follow Suit with Lowest Card

To play the lowest card he holds of the suit led, or

3. Play Card of Another Suit

To play a legal card of another suit specified by declarer.

B. Offender's Partner Cannot Comply with Penalty

When offender's partner is unable to comply with the penalty selected by declarer, he may play any card, as provided in Law 59.

C. Declarer Has Played from Both Hands before Irregularity

A defender is not subject to penalty for playing before his partner if declarer has played from both hands; but a singleton, or one of two or more equal cards (cards of the same suit adjacent in rank) in dummy, is not considered automatically played unless dummy has played the card or has illegally suggested that it be played (see Law 45).

58. SIMULTANEOUS LEADS OR PLAYS

A. Play Made Simultaneously with Legal Play

A lead or play made simultaneously with another player's legal lead or play is deemed to be subsequent to it.

B. Defender Plays Two Cards Simultaneously

1. Only One Card Visible

If a defender leads or plays two or more cards simultaneously, and if only one such card is visible, he must play that card.

2. More Than One Card Exposed

If more than one card is exposed, he must designate the card he proposes to play, and each other card exposed becomes a penalty card (Law 50).

C. Declarer Plays Two or More Cards Simultaneously

1. Declarer Must Designate Correct Card

If declarer leads or plays two or more cards simultaneously from either hand, he must designate the card he proposes to play, and must restore any other card to the correct hand.

2. Declarer Withdraws Visible Card

If declarer withdraws a visible card and a defender has already played to that card, such defender may, without penalty, withdraw his card and substitute another (see Law 47F).

D. Error Not Discovered

If the error remains undiscovered until both sides have played to the next trick, Law 67 applies.

59. INABILITY TO LEAD OR PLAY AS REQUIRED

A player may play any correct card if he is unable to lead or play as required to comply with a penalty, whether because he holds no card of the required suit, or because he has only cards of a suit he is prohibited from leading, or because of his obligation to follow suit.

60. PLAY AFTER AN ILLEGAL PLAY

A. Play of Card after Irregularity

1. Forfeiture of Right to Penalize

A play by a member of the non-offending side after the opponent on his right has led or played out of turn or prematurely, and before a penalty has been assessed, forfeits the right to penalize that offense.

2. Irregularity Legalized

Once the right to penalize has been forfeited, the illegal play is treated as though it were legal (except as provided in Law 53) unless it constitutes a revoke.

3. Other Penalty Obligations Remain

If the offending side had a previous obligation to play a penalty card, or to comply with a lead or play penalty, the obligation remains at future turns (see Laws 52 and 64).

B. Defender Plays before Required Lead by Declarer

When a defender plays a card after declarer has been required to retract his lead out of turn from either hand, but before declarer has led from the correct hand, the defender's card becomes a penalty card (Law 50).

C. Play by Offending Side before Assessment of Penalty

A play by a member of the offending side before a penalty has been assessed does not affect the rights of the opponents and may itself be subject to penalty.

Section Three

The Revoke

61. FAILURE TO FOLLOW SUIT—INQUIRIES CONCERNING A REVOKE

A. Definition of Revoke

Failure to follow suit in accordance with Law 44, or failure to lead or play, when able, a card or suit required by law or specified by an opponent in accordance with an agreed penalty, constitutes a revoke (but see Law 59).

B. Right to Inquire about a Possible Revoke

Any player, including dummy (subject to Law 43), may ask a player who has failed to follow suit whether he has a card of the suit led (but a claim of revoke does not warrant inspection of quitted tricks, except at the Director's specific instruction—see Law 66).

62. CORRECTION OF A REVOKE

A. Revoke Must Be Corrected

A player must correct his revoke if he becomes aware of the irregularity before it becomes established.

B. Correcting a Revoke

To correct a revoke, the offender withdraws the card he played in revoking and follows suit with any card.

1. Defender's Card

A card so withdrawn becomes a penalty card (Law 50) if it was played from a defender's unfaced hand.

2. Declarer's or Dummy's Card, Defender's Faced Card

The card may be replaced without penalty if it

was played from declarer's or dummy's hand*, or if it was a defender's faced card.

C. Subsequent Cards Played to Trick

1. By Non-offending Side

Each member of the non-offending side may, without penalty, withdraw any card he may have played after the revoke but before attention was drawn to it (see Law 47F).

2. By Partner of Offender

Except as provided in subsection D following, the partner of the offender may not withdraw his card unless it too constituted a revoke (in which case, the card withdrawn becomes a penalty card if it was played from a defender's unfaced hand).

D. Revoke after Eleventh Trick

1. Must Be Corrected

After the eleventh trick, a revoke, even if established, must be corrected if discovered before all four hands have been returned to the board.

2. Offender's Partner Had Not Played to Trick Twelve

If the revoke occurred before it was the turn of the offender's partner to play to the twelfth trick, (penalty) declarer or either defender, as the case may be, may then require the offender's partner to play to that trick either of two cards he could legally have played.

63. ESTABLISHMENT OF A REVOKE

A. Revoke Becomes Established

A revoke becomes established:

1. Offending Side Leads or Plays to Next Trick

When the offender or his partner leads or plays to the following trick (any such play, legal or illegal, establishes the revoke).

2. A Member of Offending Side Indicates a Lead or Play

When the offender or his partner names or otherwise designates a card to be played to the following trick.

3. Member of Offending Side Makes a Claim or Concession

When a member of the offending side makes a claim or concession of tricks orally or by facing his hand (or in any other fashion).

B. Revoke May Not Be Corrected

Once a revoke is established, it may no longer be corrected (except as provided in Law 62D), and the trick on which the revoke occurred stands as played.

64. PROCEDURE AFTER ESTABLISHMENT OF A REVOKE

A. Penalty Assessed

1. Offending Side Has Won Revoke Trick

When a revoke is established, and the trick on which the revoke occurred was won by the offending side, (penalty) after play ceases, the trick on which the revoke occurred, plus one of any

---

* Subject to Law 43. A claim of revoke does not warrant inspection of quitted tricks except as permitted in Law 67.

subsequent tricks won by the offending side, are transferred to the non-offending side.

2. Offending Side Did Not Win Revoke Trick
When a revoke is established and the trick on which the revoke occurred was not won by the offending side (penalty) after play ceases, *one* of any subsequent tricks won by the offending side is transferred to the non-offending side.

B. *No Penalty Assessed*
1. Offending Side Fails to Win Revoke Trick or Subsequent Trick
The penalty for an established revoke does not apply if the offending side did not win either the revoke trick or any subsequent trick.
2. Second Revoke in Same Suit by Offender
The penalty does not apply to a subsequent revoke in the same suit by the same player.
3. Revoke by Failure to Play a Faced Card
The penalty does not apply if the revoke was made in failing to play any card faced on the table or belonging to a hand faced on the table, including a card from dummy's hand.
4. After Non-offending Side Calls to Next Deal
The penalty does not apply if attention was first drawn to the revoke after a member of the non-offending side has made a call on a subsequent deal.
5. After Round Has Ended
The penalty does not apply if attention was first drawn to the revoke after the round has ended.
6. Revoke after Eleventh Trick
The penalty does not apply to a revoke that was made after the eleventh trick.

C. *Director Responsible for Equity*
When, after any established revoke, including those not subject to penalty, the Director deems that the non-offending side is insufficiently compensated by this Law for the damage caused, he should assign an adjusted score.

PART IV

Tricks

65. ARRANGEMENT OF TRICKS

A. *Completed Trick*
When four cards have been played to a trick, each player turns his own card face down on the edge of the table before him.
B. *Keeping Track of the Ownership of Tricks*
1. Tricks Won
If the player's side has won the trick, the card is pointed lengthwise toward his partner.
2. Tricks Lost
If the opponents have won the trick, the card is pointed lengthwise toward the opponents.
C. *Orderliness Required*
Each player should arrange his own cards in an orderly overlapping row in the sequence played, in order to permit review of the play after its completion, if necessary to determine the number of tricks won by each side or the order in which the cards were played.

D. *Agreement on Results of Play*
A player should not disturb the order of his played cards until agreement has been reached on the number of tricks won.
E. *Noncompliance*
1. Rights Placed in Jeopardy
A player who fails to comply with the provisions of this Law may jeopardize his right to claim ownership of doubtful tricks or to claim a revoke.
2. Cards Incorrectly Pointed
Any player may request that a card incorrectly pointed be turned in the proper direction.

66. INSPECTION OF TRICKS

A. *Current Trick*
So long as his side has not led or played to the next trick, declarer or either defender may, *until he has turned his own card face down on the table*, require that all cards just played to the trick be faced for his inspection.
B. *Quitted Tricks*
Thereafter, until play ceases, quitted tricks may not be inspected (except at the Director's specific instruction, for example, to verify a claim of a revoke).
C. *After the Conclusion of Play*
After play ceases the played and unplayed cards may be inspected to settle a claim of a revoke, or of the number of tricks won or lost (or of honors in total point play); but no player should handle cards other than his own. If, after a claim has been made, a player mixes his cards in such a manner that the Director can no longer ascertain the facts, the issue must be decided in favor of the other side.

67. DEFECTIVE TRICK

A. *Irregularity Detected before Both Sides Have Played to Next Trick*
When a player has omitted to play to a trick, or has played too many cards to a trick, the error must be rectified if attention is drawn to the irregularity before a player on each side has played to the following trick.
1. Player Failed to Play Card
To rectify omission to play to a trick, the offender supplies a card he can legally play.
2. Player Contributed Too Many Cards
    (a) Offender Withdraws Surplus Card(s)
        To rectify the error of playing too many cards, the offender withdraws all but one card, leaving a card he can legally play. Each card so withdrawn becomes a penalty card (Law 50) if it was played from a defender's unfaced hand.
    (b) Change of Play by Non-offenders
        After a card has been so withdrawn, each member of the non-offending side may, without penalty, withdraw any card he played after the irregularity but before attention was drawn to it (see Law 47F).
B. *Irregularity Discovered after Both Sides Play*
When attention is drawn to a defective trick after

both sides play to the following trick, or when the Director later determines that there was a defective trick, from the fact that one player holds too few or too many cards and a corresponding improper number of played cards on the table before him, the defective trick stands as played and:

1. Player with Too Few Cards

A player with too few cards plays the remainder of his hand with fewer cards than the other players; he does not play to the final trick (or tricks), and if he wins a trick with his last card the lead passes in rotation.

2. Player with Too Many Cards

A player with too many cards *plays the remainder of his hand with more cards than the other players; all cards remaining unplayed after the final trick are added to that trick (but no card so contributed changes the ownership of that trick).*

3. Penalty on Offending Player

When it is no longer possibly to rectify a defective trick, failure to play a card to that trick, or the play of more than one card to that trick, is penalized as an established revoke. The Director should apply the penalty provisions and exemptions of Law 64. For this purpose the Director should attempt to determine the exact trick at which the irregularity took place, but should he be unable to do so with certainty, the defective trick is deemed to be the earliest one possible.

PART V

Claims and Concessions

68. DECLARER'S CLAIM OR CONCESSION OF TRICKS

A. Concession by Declarer

Declarer makes a concesssion when he announces that he will lose all the remaining tricks, or when he agrees to a defender's claim.

B. Claim by Declarer

Declarer makes a claim whenever he announces that he will win or lose one or more of the remaining tricks, or suggests that play be curtailed, or *intentionally* faces his hand.

C. Required Statement by Declarer

In making his claim declarer *is required* to state his proposed line of play.

D. Play Ceases

Play Ceases. When declarer has made a claim questioned by either defender the Director *must* be summoned immediately. *No action of any kind may be taken pending the Director's arrival (all play subsequent to a claim or concession must be voided by the Director). See Law 69.*

69. DIRECTOR'S RULING ON DECLARER'S CONTESTED CLAIM

A. General Objective

In ruling on a contested claim by declarer, the Director should adjudicate the result of the board as equitably as possible to both sides, but any doubtful points should be resolved in favor of the defenders. He should proceed as follows:

B. Investigatory Steps Director Should Follow

1. Require Declarer to Repeat Claim Statement

The Director should require declarer to repeat the statement he made at the time of his claim.

2. Require All Hands to be Faced

Next, the Director should require all players to put their remaining cards face up on the table.

3. Hear Defenders' Objections

The Director should then hear the defenders' objections to the claim.

C. There Is an Outstanding Trump

When a trump remains in one of the defenders' hands, the Director should award a trick or tricks to the defenders if:

1. Failed to Mention Trump

Declarer, in making his claim, made no statement about that trump, and

2. Was Probably Unaware of Trump

It is at all likely that declarer at the time of his claim was unaware that a trump remained in a defender's hand, and

3. Could Lose a Trick to the Trump

A trick could be lost to that trump by any normal play (including the careless or inferior but not the irrational).

D. Declarer Proposes a New Line of Play

The Director should not accept from declarer any proposed line of play inconsistent with his statement.

E. Declarer Failed to Make Appropriate Announcement

If declarer did not make an appropriate announcement at the time of his original claim, the Director should not accept from him any proposed line of play the success of which depends upon finding either opponent with or without a particular card, unless an opponent failed to follow to the suit of that card before the claim was made, *or would subsequently fail to follow to that suit on any conceivable line of play.*

70. DEFENDER'S CLAIM OR CONCESSION OF TRICKS

A. Defender's Claim

A defender makes a claim when he announces that he will win one or more of the remaining tricks, or when he shows any or all of his cards to declarer *for this purpose.*

1. Claim Pertains Only to Current Trick

If the claim pertains only to an uncompleted trick currently in progress, play proceeds normally; cards exposed or otherwise revealed by the defender in making his claim do not become penalty cards, but Law 16 may apply; and see Law 57.

2. Claim Pertains to Subsequent Tricks

  (a) Play Ceases

If the claim pertains to subsequent tricks, play must cease (any play subsequent to a claim or concession must be voided by the Director), and the defender is required to state his proposed line of defense.

  (b) Claim Questioned

When the claim is questioned by declarer, the Director must be summoned immediately and no action of any kind may be taken pend-

ing his arrival. The Director should adjudicate the result of the board as equitably as possible to both sides, but should award to the declarer any trick that the defenders could lose by normal (including the inferior or careless but not the irrational) play.

B. Defender's Concession

A defender makes a concession when he agrees to declarer's claim, or when he announces that he will lose one or more of the remaining tricks. (Concession cancelled, see Law 71.)

71. CONCESSION CANCELLED

A concession may be *cancelled by the Director:*

A. Illegal Concessions

1. Trick Side Has Won

*If any player concedes a trick his side has, in fact, won.

2. Contract Fulfilled

*If declarer concedes defeat of a contract he has already fulfilled.

3. Contract Defeated

*If a defender concedes the fulfillment of a contract his side has already defeated.

B. Concession of Trick That Cannot Be Lost

If a trick that has been conceded cannot be lost by any *probable* play of the remaining cards, and if the Director's attention is drawn to that fact before all four hands have been returned to the board.

C. Concession Disputed by Other Defender

If a defender concedes one or more tricks and his partner immediately objects, but Law 16 may apply.

CHAPTER VII

PROPRIETIES

◆◆◆◆◆◆

I. GENERAL PRINCIPLES

A. Observance of Laws

1. General Obligation on Contestants

Duplicate bridge tournaments should be played in strict accordance with the Laws.

2. Waiving of Penalties

In duplicate tournaments it is improper to waive a penalty for an opponent's infraction even if one feels that one has not been damaged.

3. Non-offender's Exercise of Legal Options

When these Laws provide the innocent side with an option after an irregularity committed by an opponent, it is proper to select that action most advantageous.

4. Offenders' Options

After the offending side has paid the prescribed penalty for an inadvertent infraction, it is proper for the offenders to make any call or play advantageous to their side, even though they thereby appear to profit through their own infraction.

---

* For a concession to be cancelled under this clause, the error must be reported to the Director within the correction period established under Law 75.

5. Responsibility for Enforcement of Laws

The responsibility for penalizing irregularities and redressing damage rests solely upon the Director and these Laws, not upon the players themselves.

B. Infraction of Law

1. Intentional

To infringe a law intentionally is a serious breach of propriety, even if there is a prescribed penalty that one is willing to pay. The offense may be the more serious when no penalty is prescribed.

2. Inadvertent Infraction

There is no obligation to draw attention to an inadvertent infraction of law committed by one's own side.

3. Concealing an Infraction

A player should not attempt to conceal an inadvertent infraction, as by committing a second revoke, concealing a card involved in a revoke, or mixing the cards prematurely.

II. IMPROPER INFORMATION

A. Proper Communication between Partners

1. How Effected

Communication between partners during the auction and play should be effected only by means of the calls and plays themselves.

2. Correct Form for Calls

Calls should be made in a uniform tone without special emphasis or inflection, and without undue haste or hesitation. (However, sponsoring organizations may require mandatory pauses, as on the first round of the auction, or following a skip bid.)

3. Correct Form for Plays

Plays should be made without emphasis, gesture, or mannerism, and so far as possible at a uniform rate.

B. Improper Communication between Partners

1. Gratuitous Information

It is improper for communication between partners to be effected through the manner in which calls or plays are made, through extraneous remarks or gestures, or through questions asked of the opponents or explanations given to them.

2. Prearranged Improper Communication

The gravest possible offense against propriety is for a partnership to exchange information through prearranged methods of communication other than those sanctioned by these Laws. The penalty imposed for infraction is normally expulsion from the sponsoring organization.

C. Player Receives Improper Information from Partner

When a player has available to him improper information from his partner's remark, question, explanation, gesture, mannerism, special emphasis, inflection, haste, or hesitation, he should carefully avoid taking any advantage that might accrue to his side.

D. Variations in Tempo

1. Inadvertent Variations

Inadvertently to vary the tempo or manner in which a call or play is made does not in itself constitute a violation of propriety, but inferences from such variation may properly be drawn only by an opponent, and at his own risk.

2. Intentional Variations

It is grossly improper to attempt to mislead an opponent by means of remark or gesture, through the haste or hesitancy of a call or play (such as a hesitation before the play of a singleton), or by the manner in which the call or play is made.

E. Deception

Any player may properly attempt to deceive an opponent through a call or play (so long as the deception is not protected by concealed partnership understanding). It is entirely proper to avoid giving information to the opponents by making all calls and plays in unvarying tempo and manner.

F. Violation of Proprieties

When a violation of the proprieties described in this part results in damage to an innocent opponent:

1. Player Acts on Improper Information

If the Director determines that a player chose from among logical alternative actions one that could reasonably have been suggested by his partner's tempo, manner or remark, he should award an adjusted score (see Law 16).

2. Player Injured by Deliberate Improper Deception

If the Director determines that an innocent opponent has drawn a false inference from deliberately and improperly deceptive information, he should award an adjusted score (see Law 12).

III. CONDUCT AND ETIQUETTE

A. Proper Attitude

1. Courtesy Toward Partner and Opponents

A player should maintain at all times a courteous attitude toward his partner and opponents.

2. Etiquette of Word and Action

A player should carefully avoid any remark or action that might cause annoyance or embarrassment to another player, or might interfere with the enjoyment of the game.

3. Conformity to Proper Procedure

Every player should follow uniform and correct procedure in calling and playing, since any departure from correct standards may disrupt the orderly progress of the game.

B. Etiquette

As a matter of courtesy a player should refrain from:

1. Lack of Attention

Paying insufficient attention to the game (as when a player obviously takes no interest in his hand, or frequently requests a review of the auction).

2. Making Gratuitous Comments

Making gratuitous comments during the play as to the auction or the adequacy of the contract.

3. Prematurely Detaching a Card

Detaching a card from his hand before it is his turn to lead or play.

4. Disorder in Played Cards

Arranging the cards he has played to previous tricks in a disordered manner, or mixing his cards before the result of the deal has been agreed upon.

5. Questionable Claims or Concessions

Making a claim or concession of tricks if there is any doubt as to the outcome of the deal.

6. Prolongation of Play

Prolonging play unnecessarily for the purpose of disconcerting the other players.

7. Disrespectful Summoning of the Director

Summoning the Director in a manner discourteous to him or to the other contestants.

C. Breaches of Propriety

It is a breach of propriety:

1. Variations in Calls

To use different designations for the same call.

2. Displaying Reaction to Calls or Plays

To indicate any approval or disapproval of a call or play.

3. Revealing Expectation of Trick Result

To indicate the expectation or intention of winning or losing a trick that has not been completed.

4. Pertinent Comment or Act during Auction or Play

To comment or act during the auction or play to call attention to a significant incident thereof, or to the state of the score, or to the number of tricks still required for success.

5. Volunteering Information

To volunteer information that should be given only in response to a question.

6. Staring at Other Players

To look intently at any other player during the auction or play, or at another player's hand as for the purpose of seeing his cards or observing the place from which he draws a card (but it is not improper to act on information acquired by inadvertently seeing an opponent's card).

7. Deliberate Variation of Tempo

To vary the normal tempo of bidding or play for the purpose of disconcerting the other players.

8. Unnecessary Departure from Table

To leave the table needlessly before the round is called.

IV. PARTNERSHIP AGREEMENTS

A. Concealed Partnership Agreements

It is improper to convey information to partner by means of a call or play based on special partnership agreement, whether explicit or implicit, unless such information is fully and freely available to the opponents (see Law 40).

B. Violations of Partnership Agreements

It is not improper for a player to violate an announced partnership agreement, so long as his partner is unaware of the violation (but habitual violations within a partnership may create implicit agreements, which must be disclosed). No player has the obligation to disclose to the opponents that he has violated an announced agreement; and if the opponents are subsequently damaged, as through drawing a false inference from such violation, they are not entitled to redress.

C. Answering Questions on Partnership Agreements

When explaining the significance of partner's call or play in reply to an opponent's inquiry (see Law 20), a player should disclose all special information conveyed to him through partnership agreement or partnership experience; but he need not disclose inferences drawn from his general bridge knowledge and experience.

D. Correcting Errors in Explanation

1. Explainer Notices Own Error

If a player subsequently realizes that his own explanation was erroneous or incomplete, he should immediately call the Director (who will apply Law 21 or Law 40C).

2. Error Noticed By Explainer's Partner

It is improper for a player whose partner has given a mistaken explanation to correct the error immediately, or to indicate in any manner that a mistake has been made (he must not take any advantage of the unauthorized information so obtained). He is under no legal or moral obligation at any later time to inform the opponents that the explanation was erroneous.*

V. SPECTATORS

A. Conduct During Bidding or Play

1. Personal Reaction

A spectator must not display any reaction to the bidding or play while a hand is in progress (as by shifting his attention from one player's hand to another's).

---

* Two examples may clarify responsibilities of the players (and the Director) after a misleading explanation has been given to the opponents. In both examples following, North has opened one no trump and South, who holds a weak hand with long diamonds, has bid two diamonds, intending to sign off; North explains, however, in answer to West's inquiry, that South's bid is strong and artificial, asking for major suits.

Example 1—Mistaken Explanation

The actual partnership agreement is that two diamonds is a natural sign-off; the mistake was in North's explanation. This explanation is an infraction of law, since East-West are entitled to an accurate description of the North-South agreement (when this infraction results in damage to East-West, the Director should award an adjusted score). If North subsequently becomes aware of his mistake, it is to his advantage immediately to notify the Director—this may serve to minimize the damage caused by his infraction. South must do nothing to correct the mistaken explanation during the auction period; if he becomes declarer or dummy, he may then volunteer a correction of the explanation.

Example 2—Mistaken Bid

The partnership agreement is as explained—two diamonds is strong and artificial; the mistake was in South's bid. Here there is no infraction of law, since East-West did receive an accurate description of the North-South agreement; they have no claim to an accurate description of the North-South hands. (Regardless of damage, the Director should allow the result to stand.) South must not correct North's explanation (or notify the Director) immediately, and he has no responsibility to do so subsequently.

In both examples, South, having heard North's explanation, knows that his own two diamond bid has been misinterpreted. This knowledge is "improper information" (see Proprieties, Part II), so South must be careful not to base subsequent actions on this information (if he does, the Director should award an adjusted score). For instance, if North rebids two no trump South has the improper information that this bid merely denies a four-card holding in either major suit; but South's responsibility is to act as though North had made a strong game try opposite a weak response, showing maximum values.

2. Mannerisms or Remarks

During the round, a spectator must refrain from mannerisms or remarks of any kind (*including conversation with a player*).

3. Consideration for Players

A spectator must not in any way disturb a player.

B. Spectator Participation

A spectator may not call attention to any irregularity or mistake, nor speak on any question of fact or law except by request of the Director.

CHAPTER VIII

THE SCORE
◆◆◆◆◆◆◆

72. DUPLICATE CONTRACT BRIDGE SCORING

A. Authorized Scoring

The Rubber Bridge scoring table applies to Duplicate Bridge with exceptions noted as follows:

B. Exceptions

1. Trick Points

Trick points scored on one board do not count toward making game on a board subsequently played.

2. Premium Points

Premium points are scored for making a part-score or game, not for winning a rubber.

3. Honors

Honors are not scored in match-point or international match-point play.

73. DUPLICATE BRIDGE SCORING TABLE

TRICK SCORE

Scored by declarer's side, if the contract is fulfilled:

		IF TRUMPS ARE		
	♣	◇	♡	♠
For each odd trick bid and made				
Undoubled	20	20	30	30
Doubled	40	40	60	60
Redoubled	80	80	120	120

	AT A NO TRUMP CONTRACT		
	Undoubled	*Doubled*	*Redoubled*
For the first odd trick bid and made	40	80	160
For each additional odd trick	30	60	120

A trick score of 100 points or more, made on one board, is GAME.
A trick score of less than 100 points is a PART-SCORE.

PREMIUM SCORE

Scored by declarer's side:

SLAMS

For making a SLAM	*Not vulnerable*	*Vulnerable*
Small Slam (12 tricks) bid and made	500	750
Grand Slam (all 13 tricks) bid and made	1,000	1,500

OVERTRICKS

For each OVERTRICK (tricks made in excess of the contract)	*Not vulnerable*	*Vulnerable*
Undoubled	Trick Value	Trick Value
Doubled	100	200
Redoubled	200	400

PREMIUMS FOR GAME, PART-SCORE, FULFILLING CONTRACT

For making GAME, vulnerable 500
For making GAME, not vulnerable 300
For making any PART-SCORE 50
For making any doubled or redoubled contract 50

HONORS

Scored by either side at total-point play, not at match-point play:
For holding four of the five trump HONORS
(A, K, Q, J, 10) in one hand 100
For holding all five trump HONORS
(A, K, Q, J, 10) in one hand 150
For holding all four ACES in one hand
at a no trump contract 150

UNDERTRICK PENALTIES

Scored by declarer's *opponents* if the contract is *not* fulfilled:

UNDERTRICKS
(tricks by which declarer falls
short of the contract)

	NOT VULNERABLE		
	Undoubled	Doubled	Redoubled
For first undertrick	50	100	200
For each additional undertrick	50	200	400

	VULNERABLE		
	Undoubled	Doubled	Redoubled
For first undertrick	100	200	400
For each additional undertrick	100	300	600

74. METHODS OF SCORING

A. Match-Point Scoring

In match-point scoring each contestant is awarded, for scores made by different contestants who have played the same board and whose scores are compared with his: two scoring units (match points or half match points) for each score inferior to his, one scoring unit for each score equal to his, and zero scoring units for each score superior to his.

B. International Match-Point Scoring

In international match-point scoring, on each board the total point difference (not including honors) between the two scores compared is converted into IMPs according to the following scale:

Difference in points	IMP	Difference in points	IMP
20– 40	1	750– 890	13
50– 80	2	900–1090	14
90–120	3	1100–1290	15
130–160	4	1300–1490	16
170–210	5	1500–1740	17
220–260	6	1750–1990	18
270–310	7	2000–2240	19
320–360	8	2250–2490	20
370–420	9	2500–2990	21
430–490	10	3000–3490	22
500–590	11	3500–3990	23
600–740	12	4000 and up	24

C. Total Point Scoring

In total point scoring, the net total point score (including honors) of all boards played is the score for each contestant.

D. Special Scoring Methods

Special scoring methods are permissible, if approved by the sponsoring organization. In advance of any contest the sponsoring organization should publish conditions of contest detailing conditions of entry, methods of scoring, determination of winners, breaking of ties, etc.

75. TRICKS WON

A. Agreement on Tricks Won

The number of tricks won should be agreed upon before all four hands have been returned to the board.

B. Disagreement on Tricks Won

If a subsequent disagreement arises, the Director must be called. No correction may be made unless the Director is called before the round has ended (see Laws 8 and 71).

C. Error in Score

1. Correction Period Specified

An error in computing or tabulating the agreed-upon score, whether made by a player or scorer, may be corrected until the expiration of the period specified for such corrections by the sponsoring organization.

2. Correction Period Not Specified

Unless otherwise specified by the sponsoring organization, the correction period expires 30 minutes after the official score has been completed and made available for inspection.

CHAPTER IX

TOURNAMENT SPONSORSHIP

◆◆◆◆◆◆

76. SPONSORING ORGANIZATION

A sponsoring organization conducting an event under these Laws has the following duties and powers:

A. Tournament Director

To appoint the tournament Director. If there is no tournament Director, the players should designate one of their own number to perform his functions.

B. Advance Arrangements

To make advance arrangements for the tournament, including playing quarters, accommodations, and equipment.

C. Session Times

To establish the date and time of each session.

D. Conditions of Entry

To establish the conditions of entry.

E. Supplementary Regulations

To publish or announce regulations supplementary to, but not in conflict with, these Laws.

CHAPTER X

TOURNAMENT DIRECTOR

◆◆◆◆◆◆

Section One

Responsibilities

77. DUTIES AND POWERS

A. Official Status

The director is the official representative of the sponsoring organization.

B. Restrictions and Responsibilities

1. Technical Management

The director is responsible for the technical management of the tournament.

2. Observance of Laws and Regulations

The director is bound by these Laws and by supplementary regulations announced by the sponsoring organization.

C. Director's Duties and Powers

The director's duties and powers normally include the following:

1. Assistants

To appoint assistants, as required to perform his duties.

2. Entries

To accept and list entries.

3. Conditions of Play

To establish suitable conditions of play, and to announce them to the contestants.

4. Discipline

To maintain discipline and to insure the orderly progress of the game.

5. Law

To administer and interpret these Laws.

6. Errors

To rectify any error or irregularity of which he becomes aware.

7. Penalties

To assess penalties when applicable.

8. Waiver of Penalties

To waive penalties, at his discretion, upon the request of the non-offending side.

9. Disputes

To adjust disputes, and to refer disputed matters to the appropriate committee when required.

10. Scores

To collect scores and tabulate results.

11. Reports

To report results to the sponsoring organization for official record.

D. Delegation of Duties

The Director may delegate any of the duties listed in C to assistants, but he is not thereby relieved of responsibility for their correct performance.

78. RECTIFICATION OF ERRORS OF PROCEDURE

A. Director's Duty

It is the duty of the Director to rectify errors of procedure and to maintain the progress of the game in a manner that is not contrary to these Laws.

B. Rectification of Error

To rectify an error in procedure the Director may:

1. Assignment of Adjusted Score

Assign an adjusted score as permitted by these Laws.

2. Specify Time of Play

Require or postpone the play of a board.

3. Reservation of Decision

Reserve his decision on any point of fact or law.

79. NOTIFICATION OF THE RIGHT TO APPEAL

If the Director believes that a review of his decision on a point of fact or exercise of his discretionary power might be in order (as when he assigns an adjusted score under Law 12), he should advise a contestant of his right to appeal.

Section Two

Rulings

80. RULINGS ON AGREED FACTS

When the Director is called to rule upon a point of law, procedure, or propriety, in which the facts are agreed upon, he should rule as follows:

A. No Penalty

If no penalty is prescribed by law, and there is no occasion for him to exercise his discretionary powers, he should direct the players to proceed with the auction or play.

B. Penalty Under Law

If a case is clearly covered by a law that specifies *a* penalty for the irregularity, he should assess that penalty and see that it is paid.

C. Player's Option

If a law gives a player a choice from among two or more penalties, the Director should explain the options and see that a penalty is selected and paid.

D. Director's Option

If the law gives the Director a choice between a specified penalty and the award of an adjusted score, he should attempt to restore equity, resolving any doubtful point in favor of the non-offending side.

E. Discretionary Penalty

If an irregularity has occurred for which no penalty is assessed by law, the Director may award an adjusted score.

81. RULINGS ON DISPUTED FACTS

When the Director is called upon to rule upon a point of law, procedure, or propriety, in which the facts are not agreed upon, he should proceed as follows:

A. Director's Assessment

If the Director is satisfied that he has ascertained the facts, he should rule accordingly.

B. Facts Not Determined

If the Director is unable to determine the facts to his satisfaction, he must make a ruling that will permit play to continue, and notify the players of their right to appeal.

Section Three

Correction of Irregularities

82. ADJUSTED SCORE IN TEAM PLAY

A. Normal Play Possible

When an irregularity occurs in team play, if these Laws provide a rectification that will permit normal play of the board, the Director should rule acordingly.

B. Normal Play Impossible

When no rectification will permit normal play of the board:

1. Time Available

If time permits, the Director should substitute a new board to be played at both tables:
(a) Equal Fault
  When neither team is at fault or if both teams have contributed to the error, or
(b) Board Not Played
  When the teammates of the players involved have not yet played the board.
2. No Time Available
When time will not permit the substitution of a new board, the Director should assign an adjusted score.
3. Board Played at Other Table
When the board has been played at the other table, the Director should assign an adjusted score, taking into consideration in his adjustment any unusually favorable result obtained by the non-offending team.

83. FOULED BOARD

A. Definition
  A board is considered to be 'fouled' if the Director determines that one or more cards were misplaced in the board, in such manner that contestants who should have had a direct score comparison did not play the board in identical form.
B. Scoring the Fouled Board
  In scoring a fouled board the Director determines as closely as possible which scores were made on the board in its correct form, and which in the changed form. He divides the score on that basis into two groups, and rates each group separately as provided in the regulations of the sponsoring organization.

Section Four

Penalties

84. AWARD OF INDEMNITY POINTS

In a pair or individual event, when a non-offending contestant is required to take an adjusted score through no fault or choice of his own, such contestant should be awarded a minimum of 60% of the match points available to him on that board, or the percentage of match points he earned on boards actually played during the session, if that percentage was greater than 60%.

85. PENALTIES IN INDIVIDUAL EVENTS

In individual events, the Director should enforce the penalty provisions of these Laws, and the provisions requiring the award of adjusted scores, equally against both members of the offending side, even though only one of them may be responsible for the irregularity. But the Director, in awarding adjusted scores, should not assess procedural penalty points against the offender's partner, if, in the Director's opinion, he is in no way responsible for the violation.

86. PROCEDURAL PENALTIES

A. Director's Authority
  The Director, in addition to enforcing the penalty provisions of these Laws, should also assess penalties for any offense that unduly delays or obstructs the

game, inconveniences other contestants, violates correct procedure, or requires the award of adjusted scores.
B. Offenses Subject to Penalty
  Offenses subject to penalty include but are not limited to:
1. Tardiness
Arrival of a contestant after the specified starting time.
2. Slow Play
Any unduly slow play by a contestant.
3. Loud Discussion
Any discussion of the bidding, play, or result of a board, which may be overheard at another table.
4. Comparing Scores
Any comparison of scores with another contestant during a session.
5. Touching Another's Cards
Any touching or handling of cards belonging to another player (Law 7).
6. Misplacing Cards in Board
Placing one or more cards in an incorrect pocket of the board.
7. Errors in Procedure
Any error in procedure (such as failure to count cards in one's hand, playing the wrong board, etc.) that requires an adjusted score for any contestant.
8. Failure to Comply
Any failure to comply promptly with tournament regulations, or with any instruction of the Director.
9. Improper Behavior
Any improper or discourteous behavior.

87. SUSPENSION AND DISQUALIFICATION OF PLAYERS

A. Director's Power to Suspend
  In performing his duty to maintain order and discipline, the Director is specifically empowered to suspend a player for the current session or any part thereof (the Director's decision under this clause is final).
B. Director's Right to Disqualify
  The Director is specifically empowered to disqualify a player, pair, or team for cause, subject to approval by the Tournament Committee or sponsoring organization.

CHAPTER XI

APPEALS

88. RIGHT TO APPEAL

A. Contestant's Right
  A contestant may appeal for a review of any ruling made by the Director or by one of his assistants.
B. Time of Appeal
  Any appeal of a Director's ruling must be made not later than thirty (30) minutes after the conclusion of the session during which the ruling was made.
C. How to Appeal
  All appeals must be made through the Director.
D. Concurrence of Appellants
  An appeal shall not be heard unless both members of a pair (except in an individual contest), or *the*

captain of a team, concurs in appealing. An absent member shall be deemed to concur.

89. PROCEDURES OF APPEAL

A. No Appeals Committee
The Chief Director should hear and rule upon all appeals if there is no Tournament or Appeals committee, or when a committee cannot meet without disturbing the orderly progress of the tournament.
B. Appeals Committee Available
If a committee is available:
1. Appeal Concerns Law
The Chief Director should hear and rule upon such part of the appeal as deals solely with the law. His ruling may be appealed to the committee.
2. All Other Appeals
The Chief Director must refer all other appeals to the committee for adjudication.
3. Adjudication of Appeals
In adjudicating appeals the committee may exercise all powers assigned by these Laws to the Director, except that the committee may not overrule the Director on a point of law or regulations, or on exercise of his disciplinary powers.
C. Appeal to National Authority
After the preceding remedies have been exhausted, further appeal may be taken to the national authority (on a point of law, in the ACBL the National Laws Commission, 2200 Democrat Road, Memphis, TN 38116).

For home play, see also PARTY CONTRACT BRIDGE; PIVOT BRIDGE; PROGRESSIVE BRIDGE; REPLAY DUPLICATE.

LAWYERS. The legal profession has made many contributions to the ranks of bridge experts. Lawyers who have represented North America in postwar years include Eric Murray, Toronto; Lee Hazen, New York City; and Marshall Miles, San Bernardino, Calif. Other leading personalities who have abandoned the practice of law include B. Jay Becker, New York City; Charles Goren, Miami Beach; Alvin Landy, New York City; and Charles Solomon, Philadelphia.
Three members of the Italian Blue Team come under this heading: Carlo Alberto Perroux, Walter Avarelli, and Massimo d'Alelio. Two English lawyers who have represented Great Britain on many occasions are the brothers Louis and Joel Tarlo.
At one time probably more top ranked players had been trained in the law than in any other single profession; more recently, the computer field appears to have taken over first place.

LAY DOWN. Verb: (1) to put the dummy's cards on the table; (2) to play a (high) card with the assurance of winning that particular trick.

LAY-DOWN. A colloquialism for a hand that can, virtually, be claimed for a successful contract as soon as the dummy is exposed. However, surprising things happen to lay-down hands with disconcerting frequency. PIANOLA is a synonym.

LEA SYSTEM. A one club system devised by Robert H. Lea, Denver, Colo. One club is bid with nearly all hands with 12 or more points. Responses are on a step system: 1 ◇, 0–5; 1 ♡, 6–8; 1 ♠, 9–11; etc. One no trump openings are weak. Other one openings show a six-card suit and 15 or 16 points including distribution.
No trump and minor suit overcalls show two-suited hands in all circumstances. No trump shows the two low-ranking unbid suits. Diamonds shows the two high-ranking unbid suits. Clubs shows the high-ranking suit and the low-ranking suit. If one no trump is overcalled, the opener is assumed to have clubs. Therefore two clubs over one no trump, for example, would show diamonds and spades.

LEAD. The first card played to a trick. See LAWS (Law 44).

LEAD-DIRECTING BID. A bid made primarily for the purpose of indicating a desired suit for partner to lead initially against an impending adverse contract. North holds, for example,

> ♠ 10 x x
> ♡ x x
> ◇ A K x x
> ♣ x x x x

and the bidding has proceeded:

NORTH	EAST	SOUTH	WEST
Pass	1 ♡	1 ♠	2 ♡

A bid of three diamonds by North in this position is a lead-directing bid. He has no intention of playing a diamond contract, and will retreat to three spades if doubled. He is merely maneuvering to secure a diamond opening lead if the final contract is in hearts.

LEAD-DIRECTING DOUBLE. The most frequent case is a double of a voluntarily bid contract at three no trump by the player not on lead. In current practice the double requests in order of priority: (a) the lead of the opening leader's suit; (b) the lead of the doubler's bid suit; (c) the lead of the first suit bid by dummy. However, it may not be right to lead dummy's suit if it has been rebid; and some authorities leave to judgment the situation in which both defenders have bid a suit. See also FISHER DOUBLE.
The lead-directing double may occur at the partscore level:

	(a)		
SOUTH	WEST	NORTH	EAST
Pass	Pass	1 ◇	Pass
2 NT	Pass	Pass	Dbl.

	(b)		
SOUTH	WEST	NORTH	EAST
1 ◇	Pass	1 NT	Pass
Pass	Dbl.		

In each case the double is suggesting the lead of a diamond.

A double of three no trump when neither side has bid a suit implies that the doubler has a solid suit which can be run immediately. The opening leader will tend to lead a short major suit in which he has no honor.

The double of a voluntarily bid suit game often has the same implications as a LIGHTNER DOUBLE of a slam contract:

SOUTH	WEST	NORTH	EAST
1 ♣	Pass	1 ♠	Pass
4 ♠	Dbl.		

West probably has a void club, and is gambling that he will be able to get two club ruffs, and defeat the contract.

A double of a conventional bid such as a response to BLACKWOOD has obvious lead-directing implications. There is also a negative inference: a player who does not double such a bid is likely to prefer another lead. See DOUBLES OF ARTIFICIAL BIDS FOR PENALTIES.

LEAD-INHIBITING BID. A tactical bid, in the nature of a semi-psychic call, which is designed to prevent the opponents from leading a specific suit. For example:

♠ K Q 6
♡ K J 7
◊ 8 5 2
♣ A Q 7 5

The normal opening bid should be one club followed by a rebid of one no trump. An opening bid of one diamond, made with the idea of discouraging a diamond lead against no trump, would be a lead-inhibiting bid.

Another common form of a lead-inhibiting bid:

♠ —
♡ K 7 6 5 2
◊ 9 5
♣ A K 8 5 3 2

After an opening bid of one heart by partner, one immediately thinks in terms of six or seven. A bid of three diamonds with this hand might stop the opponents from cashing the first two diamond tricks.

LEAD OUT OF TURN. An irregularity in play. See LAWS (Law 54 for opening lead out of turn. Law 55 for declarer's lead out of turn, and Law 56 for defender's lead out of turn).

LEAD OUT OF WRONG HAND (by declarer). A lead out of turn by declarer, leading either from his or dummy's hand incorrectly. See LAWS (Law 55).

LEAD THROUGH. To lead through a particular opponent is to initiate the lead in the hand to the right of that opponent, forcing that opponent to play to the trick before the leader's partner plays to it. See THROUGH STRENGTH; UP TO WEAKNESS.

LEAD THROUGH STRENGTH. See THROUGH STRENGTH.

LEAD UP TO. To lead with the object of enabling partner's hand to win a trick because of weakness in the hand on the leader's right. Occasionally, a strong hand may be led up to, when the object is not necessarily to win the trick. A lead is always "up to" the hand on the leader's right. See UP TO WEAKNESS.

LEAD UP TO WEAKNESS. See UP TO WEAKNESS.

LEADER. The person or player who first plays to any given trick, "as opening leader."

LEADING FROM HONORS. See ATTACKING LEAD, JOURNALIST LEADS, OPENING LEADS, THIRD HIGHEST LEAD.

LEAGUE. An organized association, which may be on a local, regional, national, or international scale. Members of the league may be individuals, clubs, teams, or other groupings. In this volume "the League" normally refers to the American Contract Bridge League. In England, "league" is commonly used as a synonym for ROUND ROBIN.

LEAP. A bid missing several levels, generally to game or slam, either in support of partner or in a new suit, inviting partner to pass at his next opportunity. Alternatively, a leap to a slam convention may be made.

LEAVE IN. See PENALTY DOUBLE.

LEAVES. One of the suits in early European PLAYING CARDS (a translation of German and Slavic words). See PACK.

LEBANESE BRIDGE FEDERATION (FÉDÉRATION LIBANAISE DE BRIDGE). Founded in 1949 by three Beirut bridge clubs, and in 1969 had approximately 400 members. The Federation usually sponsors teams to compete in the European Championships, and acted as host for the 1962 event in Beirut. The National Council of Tourism in Lebanon in conjunction with Middle East Airlines also sponsors an International Bridge Festival with cash prizes, held annually since 1963. Lebanese players listed separately are: F. Bustros, H. Dalati, H. Schoucair, A. Tosbath.

Officers, 1975:
President: Henri Schoucair.
Secretary: Charles Nasr, B. P. 375, Beirut, Lebanon.

LEBENSOHL CONVENTION. A convention designed by George BOEHM, of New York, to cope with an opponent's overcall over a one no trump opening. The mechanism varies depending on whether the overcall shows one suit or two, and whether it is made at the two-level or three-level.

Over a natural two-level overcall, a double is for

penalties, a two-level suit bid is non-forcing, a three-level suit bid is forcing, and a two no trump bid forces opener to rebid three clubs. Responder can pass opener's three club bid if he has a weak hand with long clubs, or can rebid; if he rebids a suit below the rank of the suit overcalled, it is a sign-off; if he rebids a suit above the rank of the suit overcalled, it is invitational to game.

Over a two-suited overcall such as LANDY, the double is penalty-oriented in at least one of the suits shown by the overcall. The two-level bid of a suit not shown by the overcall is not forcing, while the three-level bid of such a suit is forcing to game. Cue-bids are generally forcing to game. Only when the overcall shows two specific suits and responder cue-bids the cheaper may the partnership stop below game.

Over a three-level overcall, the double is a take-out for any suits not shown by the overcall. Suit bids at the three-level are forcing to game.

LEBHAR TROPHY. For the National Mixed Team Championship. Donated by Bertram Lebhar, Jr., in 1948, in memory of his wife Evelyn; a replacement for the BARCLAY TROPHY. Contested at the Summer Nationals, under which heading past results are listed.

LEBOVIC ASKING BID. A convention devised by Wolf LEBOVIC of Toronto, and publicized by Sammy KEHELA of Toronto; when two or three suits have been bid and a minor suit has been agreed as trumps, a double jump in an unbid suit asks about control in that suit. The last bid in each of the following auctions would be a Lebovic asking bid.

(a)		(b)	
SOUTH	NORTH	SOUTH	NORTH
1 ♣	1 ♡	1 ♠	2 ♢
1 ♠	3 ♣	3 ♢	4 ♡
4 ♢			

The responder to the asking bid answers as follows: with a singleton in the asked suit he bids six of the trump suit, with king doubleton or longer he bids four no trump, with the ace or a void he bids the asked suit, and with none of the above he makes the minimum bid in the trump suit.

LEDGER. See BACK SCORE.

LEFT-HAND PLAYER. The player on declarer's left. In assessing penalties, there has been a differentiation between left- and right-hand opponents as respects power or right to invoke penalties. Generally, however, the term is restricted to use in describing situations on play.

An alternative term is left-hand opponent, abbreviated to LHO.

LEG. A colloquial rubber bridge term to indicate a game already won. Partners who have a "leg" are vulnerable.

LEGAL. Applied to any call or play not in contravention of the mechanics of the game as set forth in the laws. A legal convention is one that is listed properly on the convention card that is either approved by the tournament committee or by the tournament director for use in that event. See LAWS, Sections I, II, and III, and PROPRIETIES.

LEGAL OPPORTUNITY. See LAWS (Law 50).

LEGHORN DIAMOND (LIVORNO) SYSTEM. Similar to the ROMAN SYSTEM, developed by Benito BIANCHI and Giuseppe MESSINA and used successfully in many EUROPEAN CHAMPIONSHIPS. The chief features are:

One club opening is forcing and may show any of four different types of hand: (1) 12–15 points, balanced distribution and no five-card major; (2) unbalanced with a long minor, 12–20 points, possibly with a side four-card major if the point range is 12 or 13; (3) unbalanced with a long major and no side four-card major or five-card minor, 16–20 points; or (4) a three-suiter with a singleton or void in a major, 12–13 points.

Two clubs (natural) and one diamond are both negative responses, showing less than 8 points. One heart and one spade responses are positive, 8 points or more, and one and two no trump deny a four-card major and are limited to 8–10 and 11–12 points respectively. Jump suit responses are natural and game forcing, except three clubs, which is forcing for only one round and suggests three no trump. A jump to two diamonds may be made on a four-card suit if responder intends to CANAPÉ into a major.

If one club is doubled, a pass is equivalent to the negative response and shows four-card support for clubs, although responder may have 8–11 points with three clubs in which case he will double, cue-bid, or bid no trump at his next turn; non-jump suit responses are limited to a maximum of 9 points; one no trump shows 10–11; and a redouble or a jump response shows 12 points or more. If one club is overcalled, a raise to two clubs shows a five-card suit and 5–7 points; a cue-bid is strong and asks for a stopper; one-level suit responses show 8–11; and two-level suit responses normally show 12 points or more.

The auction tends to develop naturally after the initial response. Minimum major-suit rebids by opener usually describe the weak balanced hand, but he may have the minimum major-minor two-suiter, or the three-suiter. With either of the unbalanced hands, opener makes a simple rebid in a minor with 12–17, jumps to the two-level in a major with 16–17, or jumps to the three-level in any suit with 18–20. After a positive response, a jump rebid by opener to two no trump shows exactly 15 points. After responding in a major, responder's second suit is his long suit.

One diamond opening is forcing and shows either a balanced hand with 19 points or more, or an unbalanced hand that is about a trick short of game, possibly a three-suiter with at least 20 points.

Suit responses show controls by steps (king=1 control; ace=2 controls). One heart shows no controls; one spade shows 1 control, and so on. With no controls but scattered queens and jacks, responder bids one no trump with 5–6 points or two no trump with 7 or more. If one diamond is doubled or overcalled, a pass is substituted for the first step and redouble or double for the second step.

A simple no trump rebid by opener describes a balanced hand with 19–21 points and a jump no trump rebid shows 22 points or more. If opener is unbalanced, he usually makes a minimum rebid in a suit, over which responder rebids conventionally by eight steps to show support. A new suit by opener is then a second asking bid, and the responses are on the same scale for that suit. After responder has made his support-showing step response to opener's second suit, a bid of the cheapest denomination by opener is a relay asking responder to choose between opener's suits.

One heart and one spade openings are natural but show two different types of hand: (1) less than 16 points with a five-card or longer major; or (2) a two-suiter, usually a four-card major and a five-card or longer side suit, with 14–19 points. To distinguish between the two types, opener normally rebids his major with the first type of hand, even if he has a side four-card suit, and bids his second suit (jumping with 17–19 points) with hand type two.

One no trump opening is standard (16–18) and denies a five-card major. A two club response is STAYMAN and other two-level responses are weak transfers to the next higher-ranking suit. The transfers to two hearts and two spades are presumed to be weak unless responder rebids. A rebid of two no trump by responder is BLACKWOOD. Two spades is ostensibly a transfer to three clubs, but may be preparatory to a sign-off in diamonds. Jump suit responses are strong and show interest in slam, and direct jumps to four diamonds and four hearts are transfers to four hearts and four spades respectively. A jump to four clubs shows 7 or more points with at least 5–5 distribution in the major suits. If opener has three or four aces and kings in the major suits his rebid is four diamonds, allowing responder to decide whether to sign off or to develop the auction with special asking bids. This structure of responding is also used after a one-diamond opening and a one no trump rebid.

Two club and two diamond openings show three-suited hands (4–4–4–1 or 5–4–4–0 distribution) with 12–16 and 17–19 points respectively. Responses and rebids are similar to the Roman System.

Two heart and two spade openings show two-suited hands, the bid major and a four- or five-card minor, with 9–12 points. Two no trump is the only forcing response and compels opener to bid his minor, after which a new suit by responder asks opener to define his hand pattern. Opener rebids his major with a six-card suit, rebids his minor with 5–5 distribution, bids a three-card fragment or bids three no trump with 5–4–2–2 distribution.

Two no trump opening shows at least five cards in each minor with 14–16 high-card points. Four clubs and four diamonds are the only strong responses and request opener to bid a six-card minor if he has one,

or (with 5–5 distribution) to bid four hearts with a minimum and four spades with a maximum.

Three-level suit openings are pre-emptive but are based on solid or semi-solid seven-card suits.

Three no trump opening is BLACKWOOD. During the auction three no trump is also Blackwood whenever it is an illogical bid, such as one club–three no trump, or one heart–one spade–three no trump.

Defensive bidding follows the general Italian style. Overcalls are made freely, and a take-out double shows opening bid strength but no particular distribution. In response to a double, the next suit may be a HERBERT NEGATIVE. With the perfect distribution for a take-out double (4–4–4–1 or 5–4–4–0), the overcaller cue-bids with 12–16 points, or jump cue-bids with more than 16, except over a one club opening; a two club overcall over one club is equivalent to a two club opening. If an opponent pre-empts at the three-level, a three no trump overcall shows two suits of the same rank and a double shows two suits of different rank. Jump overcalls are intermediate. See UNUSUAL NO TRUMP.

LENGTH. The number of cards held in a particular suit, usually referring to five or more; as opposed to STRENGTH, the high-card values held in a suit. See DISTRIBUTIONAL VALUES.

LENGTH OF SESSION. A session is generally thirteen rounds of two boards each, and experienced players should complete this in about three and a half hours. In no case may a tournament of the ACBL consist of less than twenty-two or more than thirty boards in pair competition. One board to a round may be used only in certain one-session team events or in individual contests; in some team events, particularly in head-on knockout competition, late rounds may be more than thirty boards. See ACBL HANDBOOK.

LENGTH SIGNALS. A method by which one defender can indicate to his partner the length held in a particular suit. The standard procedure is to play high-low with an even number of cards, and to play the lowest with an odd number of cards. (The reverse procedure, normal in Sweden, has some virtues. The higher card of a doubleton may be too high to be spared in standard methods.)

The normal application occurs when the declarer attacks a suit in which he is strong, but a signal can be made in a suit which is both led and dominated by the defenders. (See FOSTER ECHO.) In a high-level contract, the opening leader may need to know his partner's length in order to judge which tricks can be cashed quickly.

Accurate suit-length signals are the key to a golden treasury of defensive plays, seemingly brilliant, but in fact within the compass of everyone who is willing to count the cards. After a few tricks have been played, good defensive signalers may know nearly all about the unseen hands, and should be able to play just as accurately as declarer, if not more so.

NORTH
Dummy
♠ A J
♡ K 8 3
♢ A Q 9 8 6 2
♣ 8 2

WEST
♠ 4 2
♡ Q J 10
♢ J 10 7 3
♣ 9 6 5 3

NORTH	SOUTH
1 ◇	2 ♠
3 ◇	3 NT
6 NT	Pass

West leads the heart queen, and South wins with the ace. Dummy's spades win the next two tricks. South enters his hand with the club ace, and plays top spades. What does West discard?

If West is a tight defender, he will refuse to answer that question. He needs to know which cards *East* has played. So, let's start again. On the opening lead East drops the heart six. Remembering South's failure to bid hearts, this is easily read as a suit-length signal showing nine fourth. On dummy's spades, East echoes with the six and five—thereby telling West that South has a five-card suit. When declarer comes to hand with a club, East plays his lowest card, the four, indicating an odd number of cards. Remembering the bidding, this clearly places South with a four-card club suit. (With only two he would have rebid spades, supported diamonds, or bid hearts.)

Now West can figure declarer's hand as something like:

♠ K Q 9 7 3
♡ A 7 2
♢ 4
♣ A K J 7

When South runs his spade suit, the odds are heavily in favor of West's holding onto his four small clubs and letting the diamonds go—a play which would have been by no means obvious without East's suit-length signals.

Everyone agrees that when a defender *does* echo, he shows an even number of cards. And when he does not? Does that necessarily mean an odd number? Or has he decided not to echo for fear of giving information to the declarer? And why, if at all, is it permissible to try to mislead declarer by issuing a false signal?

It is possible for players to agree about every conceivable situation, but such an agreement is unethical if not explained to the opponents, and time-wasting if it is. Best is a commonsense approach which need not be announced at all.

When following a suit played by the declarer, always echo to show an even number of cards *unless it appears that this may help declarer;* then, don't echo at

all. But occasional false signals should be made in situations where it will not matter that partner is misled. See also TRUMP SIGNAL.

In this connection, there are two valid psychological points. First, it is not wise to try to outsmart the declarer continually by making false signals. The declarer usually comes out of a guessing game better than the defenders, and the reason is not hard to see. When the declarer has the lead, he has command of the play; he can come out of a huddle with a "rap-rap" which leaves the defenders no time for thought—and of course, a false signal has to be made smoothly and urbanely, if it is not to boomerang. So, false signals should be avoided unless the play has been thought out well in advance. But some false signals *must* be made: it is essential not to become typed as a player whose echoes are always dependable.

The second psychological point arises when a defender is afraid to signal for fear of tipping his hand to a declarer. If it seems a borderline case, it is better to signal. Declarers are desperately afraid of looking silly in a situation like this:

NORTH
K 9 5 3

WEST   EAST
10 8 6 2   J 7

SOUTH
A Q 4

South plays the ace and queen, and West, caught on the wrong foot, echoes with the six and two. Vain declarers, and those with critical partners, will not finesse dummy's nine on the third round. (Although the finesse is the percentage play; see RESTRICTED CHOICE.) They would rather be wrong five times in a situation like this than suffer the ignominy of letting East make a trick with J 10x. In a world of bluff and double-bluff, this human failing is something tangible to hold onto.

Usually the defenders have to cooperate if declarer is to be led astray. In a situation like the following, declarer is more likely to go wrong if both players false-card.

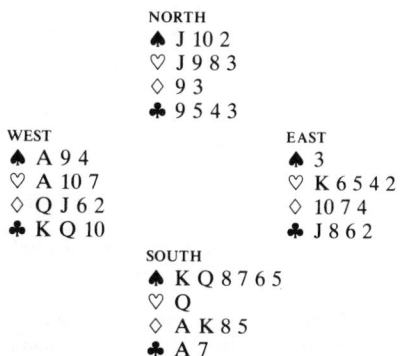

NORTH
♠ J 10 2
♡ J 9 8 3
♢ 9 3
♣ 9 5 4 3

WEST   EAST
♠ A 9 4   ♠ 3
♡ A 10 7   ♡ K 6 5 4 2
♢ Q J 6 2   ♢ 10 7 4
♣ K Q 10   ♣ J 8 6 2

SOUTH
♠ K Q 8 7 6 5
♡ Q
♢ A K 8 5
♣ A 7

West's one diamond opening is passed to South, who lands in four spades. West leads the club king and

South holds off in order to create a ruffing communication between dummy and the closed hand. South wins the second club and plays diamonds, intending to ruff the third round low and the fourth high. If East is awake, he will try to persuade declarer to ruff both diamonds high and rely on a 2–2 trump break. When South plays the ace and king of diamonds, East plays high-low with the ten and four. But West must keep up with the ball too, and withhold his normal suit-length signal; he should play the two followed by the six, supporting the theory that the diamonds are 5–2.

For a method by which declarer can plan to take advantage of length signals, see DISCOVERY.

A. D.

LENZ TROPHY. For the World Par-Point Championships of the WBF, donated in memory of Sidney Lenz by his long-time secretary, Mrs. Adele Hess. See WORLD PAR CONTESTS for results.

LESSON HANDS. Bridge teachers regularly offer prepared deals to their pupils, illustrating points in bidding and play covered by their lessons. The following hand is by Dorothy Jane Cook, of Vero Beach, Fla., a prominent teacher.

```
                    NORTH
                    ♠ K Q 8
                    ♡ A K 7 3
                    ◇ J 3
                    ♣ A Q J 7
WEST                                EAST
♠ J 10 9 6                          ♠ 7 4 3 2
♡ 9 8                               ♡ Q 10
◇ A Q 8 2                           ◇ 5 4
♣ 6 5 2                             ♣ 10 9 8 4 3
                    SOUTH
                    ♠ A 5
                    ♡ J 6 5 4 2
                    ◇ K 10 9 7 6
                    ♣ K
```

SOUTH	WEST	NORTH	EAST
Pass	Pass	1 ♣	Pass
1 ♡	Pass	4 ♡	Pass
4 NT	Pass	5 ♡	Pass
6 ♡	Pass	Pass	Pass

West leads the jack of spades.

The following comments are provided for the student:

South does not open the bidding because he lacks the two defensive tricks that are required for 13-point opening bids.

The opening lead is won with the spade ace, and South draws trumps. By discarding four diamonds from the South hand on the three clubs and the third spade in the dummy, South will avoid the loss of more than one diamond trick and make his slam by

taking three spade tricks, five heart tricks, and four club tricks.

LEVEL. The "odd-trick" count in excess of the book, that is, each trick over six. Thus an overcall of two clubs is a bid made at the two-level and a contract to make eight tricks. A four spade opening bid is said to be made at the four-level. See OVERCALLS.

LEVENTRITT TROPHY. For the Life Masters Pairs consolation event; donated by Peter A. Leventritt of New York in 1950. It was contested until 1972 at the Summer Nationals, under which heading past results are listed.

LEVINREW. A system devised by George Levinrew of Jerusalem, Israel, formerly of Brooklyn, N.Y. The chief features are:

(1) Weak two-bids with a range of 9–12 points. New suit responses are forcing. Two no trump and single raises are encouraging.

(2) Major-suit openings promise five cards. One spade, one heart, and one diamond show 15–23 points including distribution. One-level rebids normally show 15–17, two-level rebids 18–20, and three-level rebids 21–23, but a single raise counts as a one-level rebid, and so on.

(3) A response to a suit-bid may have as little as 4 high-card points, and can be artificial. A jump raise or a jump in a new suit is pre-emptive. One no trump response is weak, showing a lower-ranking suit of at least six cards.

(4) One club shows at least 12 points including distribution. A one-over-one response is not forcing.

(5) Weak no trump.

LIFE MASTER. The highest rank of player in the AMERICAN CONTRACT BRIDGE LEAGUE. (For qualification for this rank, see RANKING OF PLAYERS.) The category was created by the AMERICAN BRIDGE LEAGUE in 1936, and selection of the first Life Masters was based on national tournament successes, although a master-point program had been in effect since 1934. Initially, the rank was conferred on a group of ten players, ranked in order according to the number and importance of their national victories, and an eleventh player was made Life Master shortly thereafter. The first one hundred players to achieve the rank were:

1.	David Bruce	1936	12.	Charles	
2.	Oswald Jacoby	1936		Lochridge	1937
3.	Howard		13.	Charles H.	
	Schenken	1936		Goren	1938
4.	Waldemar		14.	A. Mitchell	
	von Zedtwitz	1936		Barnes	1938
5.	P. Hal Sims	1936	15.	Harry J.	
6.	B. Jay Becker	1936		Fishbein	1939
7.	Theodore A.		16.	Charles J.	
	Lightner	1936		Solomon	1939
8.	Richard L. Frey	1936	17.	Sally Young	1939
9.	Michael T.		18.	Fred D.	
	Gottlieb	1936		Kaplan	1939
10.	Sam Fry, Jr.	1936	19.	John R.	
11.	Merwin D.			Crawford	1939
	Maier		20.	Walter Jacobs	1939

21.	Morrie Elis	1939
22.	Phil Abramsohn	1940
23.	Edward Hymes, Jr.	1940
24.	Alvin Landy	1940
25.	Helen Sobel Smith	1941
26.	Sherman Stearns	1941
27.	Robert A. McPherran	1941
28.	Jeff Glick	1942
29.	Arthur Glatt	1942
30.	Dr. Richard Ecker, Jr.	1942
31.	Albert Weiss	1942
32.	Lee Hazen	1942
33.	Peggy Solomon	1942
34.	Alvin Roth	1942
35.	Sidney Silodor	1943
36.	Olive Peterson	1943
37.	Margaret Wagar	1943
38.	Peter Leventritt	1943
39.	Edson T. Wood	1944
40.	Ralph Kempner	1944
41.	Arthur S. Goldsmith	1944
42.	Simon Becker	1944
43.	Stanley O. Fenkel	1944
44.	George Rapee	1944
45.	Ruth Sherman	1944
46.	Robert Appleyard	1945
47.	Malcolm A. Lightman	1945
48.	Samuel Stayman	1945
49.	Edward N. Marcus	1945
50.	Charles A. Hall	1945
51.	Emily Folline	1946
52.	Joseph E. Cain	1946
53.	Harry Feinberg	1946
54.	Ambrose Casner	1946
55.	Samuel Katz	1946
56.	Jack Ehrlenbach	1946
57.	J. Van Brooks	1946
58.	Simon Rossant	1946
59.	Edward G. Ellenbogen	1946
60.	Sidney B. Fink	1946

61.	Bertram Lebhar, Jr.	1946
62.	Meyer Schleifer	1947
63.	Louis Newman	1947
64.	Elinor Murdoch	1947
65.	Paula Bacher	1947
66.	Florence Stratford	1947
67.	Jules Bank	1947
68.	William McGhee	1947
69.	Maynard Adams	1947
70.	Edith Kemp	1947
71.	David Carter	1947
72.	Jack Cushing	1947
73.	Dr. A. Steinberg	1947
74.	Jane Jaeger	1947
75.	Cecil Head	1947
76.	S. Garton Churchill	1947
77.	Edward S. Cohn	1947
78.	John Carlin	1947
79.	Lawrence Welch	1947
80.	Frank Weisbach	1947
81.	Charlton Wallace	1947
82.	Dr. Louis Mark	1947
83.	Edward Taylor	1947
84.	Dan Westerfield	1947
85.	Tobias Stone	1947
86.	Capt. Mark Hodges	1947
87.	Leo Roet	1947
88.	Sol Mogal	1947
89.	Herbert Gerst	1947
90.	Lewis Mathe	1947
91.	Ludwig Kabakjian	1947
92.	Gratian Goldstein	1947
93.	Allen P. Harvey	1947
94.	Lewis Jaeger	1947
95.	Mildred Cunningham	1947
96.	Elmer I. Schwartz	1947
97.	Mrs. W. L. Terry	1947
98.	Maurice Levin	1948
99.	Dave Warner	1948
100.	Ernest Rovere	1948

26.	Erik Paulsen	7,220
27.	Eric Murray	7,172
28.	Meyer Schleifer	7,121
29.	Malvine Klausner	7,084
30.	Don Oakie	7,059
31.	Charles Goren	7,045
32.	Robert Wolff	6,946
33.	Peter Pender	6,867
34.	Gunther Polak	6,836
35.	B. Jay Becker	6,791
36.	David Carter	6,675
37.	Charles Solomon	6,593
38.	Ethel Keohane	6,579
39.	Fred Hamilton	6,560
40.	Gerald Caravelli	6,539
41.	John Gerber	6,411
42.	Harold Guiver	6,397
43.	Margaret Wagar	6,384
44.	G. Robert Nail	6,296
45.	Vic Mitchell	6,152
46.	Marilyn Johnson	6,149
47.	Phil Leon	6,012
48.	John Crawford	5,989
49.	Jack Blair	5,893
50.	Kelsey Petterson	5,831
51.	Edward Rosen	5,774
52.	Gerald Bare	5,749
53.	Sidney Lazard	5,701
54.	Howard Schenken	5,652
55.	Paul Swanson	5,629
56.	Tobias Stone	5,621
57.	Murray Schnee	5,613
58.	Cliff Bishop	5,599
59.	Jack Ehrlenbach	5,559
60.	Edwin Kantar	5,553
61.	Carol Sanders	5,535
62.	Michael Moss	5,519

63.	Edith Kemp	5,510
64.	Robert Hamman	5,483
65.	Emma Jean Hawes	5,473
66.	Steve Robinson	5,465
67.	Nate Silverstein	5,389
68.	Mike McMahan	5,371
69.	Harry Steen	5,341
70.	Sam Stayman	5,298
71.	Rhoda Walsh	5,265
72.	Chester Davis	5,246
73.	Mike Cappelletti	5,210
74.	Jules Farell	5,204
75.	Richard Freeman	5,200
76.	Peggy Solomon	5,194
77.	Alex Tschekaloff	5,185
78.	William Rosen	5,159
79.	Robert Morris	5,159
80.	Chuck Burger	5,152
81.	Bud Creed	5,124
82.	George Rapee	5,084
83.	Marshall Miles	5,077
84.	J. David King	5,061
85.	Joan Remey	5,059
86.	Peter Leventritt	4,968
87.	Dorothy Truscott	4,967
88.	Lou Bluhm	4,888
89.	Milton Vernoff	4,873
90.	Sammy Kehela	4,856
91.	Holton Sexton	4,854
92.	Frank Weisbach	4,848
93.	Harry Fishbein	4,817
94.	Evan Bailey	4,816
95.	John Swanson	4,808
96.	Bruce Elliott	4,724
97.	Terry Michaels	4,717
98.	Nat Gerstman	4,693
99.	Jack Denny	4,687
100.	Jacqui Mitchell	4,660

LIFE MASTER INDIVIDUAL CHAMPIONSHIP, NATIONAL. See STEINER TROPHY.

LIFE MASTER MEN'S PAIR CHAMPIONSHIP, NATIONAL. See MOUSER TROPHY.

LIFE MASTER PAIR CHAMPIONSHIP, NATION-AL. See VON ZEDTWITZ TROPHY.

LIFE MASTER WOMEN'S PAIR CHAMPION-SHIP, NATIONAL. See SMITH TROPHY.

LIFT. A term meaning "raise."

LIGHTMAN TROPHY. For the charity event at the Spring Nationals, under which heading results are listed; presented in memory of M. A. Lightman of Memphis. First contested, under different circumstances, in 1958.

LIGHTNER DOUBLE. A lead-directing double of a slam contract. If competent opponents bid a slam voluntarily, it may be expected that they will fulfill their contract or fail by one trick. Thus a normal penalty double is unlikely to gain much. In 1929 Theodore Lightner of New York devised a more useful interpretation of this bid. A double by the hand not on lead is conventional. Partner is

As of June 30, 1975, 20,842 players had achieved that rank, and the top one hundred master-point holders were:

1.	Barry Crane	17,012
2.	Hermine Baron	14,285
3.	Mary Jane Farell	13,418
4.	James Jacoby	11,803
5.	Oswald Jacoby	11,534
6.	Dr. John Fisher	11,048
7.	Morris Portugal	10,870
8.	Al Roth	10,371
9.	Paul Soloway	9,681
10.	Alan Bell	9,591
11.	Norman Kay	9,529
12.	Edgar Kaplan	8,983
13.	Robert Sharp	8,354
14.	Helen Portugal	8,132
15.	Mark Blumenthal	8,113
16.	Peter Rank	8,024
17.	Richard Henderson	7,942
18.	Lew Mathe	7,926
19.	Hal Kandler	7,753
20.	Richard Walsh	7,560
21.	Mike Lawrence	7,518
22.	Mike Shuman	7,467
23.	Curtis Smith	7,458
24.	Gaylor Kasle	7,341
25.	Charles Coon	7,297

requested to choose an unusual lead which may result in the defeat of the slam. A conventional double of this sort excludes the lead of a trump, a suit bid by the defenders, or an unbid suit. The player who doubles expects to ruff the lead of a side suit mentioned by the opponents, or else to win two top tricks in that suit.

Some experts treat this double quite rigidly. They define the double to mean that partner must lead dummy's first-bid side suit. Other good players, including Lightner, interpret the bid more loosely. An unusual lead is requested and partner must deduce from the context which suit is required.

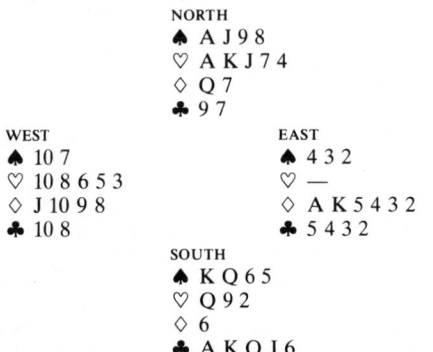

```
                 NORTH
                 ♠ A J 9 8
                 ♡ A K J 7 4
                 ◊ Q 7
                 ♣ 9 7
WEST                           EAST
♠ 10 7                         ♠ 4 3 2
♡ 10 8 6 5 3                   ♡ —
◊ J 10 9 8                     ◊ A K 5 4 3 2
♣ 10 8                         ♣ 5 4 3 2
                 SOUTH
                 ♠ K Q 6 5
                 ♡ Q 9 2
                 ◊ 6
                 ♣ A K Q J 6
```

South plays six spades, after opening one club and getting a response of one heart. East doubles, for an unusual lead. West leads a heart, East ruffs and cashes the diamond ace for the setting trick. Without the double West would have led a diamond which declarer would have covered from dummy. East would be forced to win the only trick the defense could take. See also LEAD-DIRECTING DOUBLES. For an alternative use of the double of a slam when the defenders have bid and raised a suit of their own, see DOUBLE FOR SACRIFICE.

LILIES. See ROYAL SPADES.

LIMIT. (1) The highest stake permitted in a bridge club. Most bridge clubs set a limit of one or two cents per point (in England, per hundred points, where a stake of a pound per hundred is about the US equivalent of three cents a point).

(2) A bid which shows a maximum as well as a minimum range of values in the bidder's hand. Various limit bids are discussed in the following articles: DELAYED GAME RAISE; DOUBLE RAISE; INVERTED MINOR SUIT RAISES; INVITATIONAL BID; LIMIT BID; LIMIT JUMP RAISE; NO TRUMP BIDDING; ONE NO TRUMP RESPONSE; SINGLE RAISE; STRONG NO TRUMP AFTER PASSING; THREE NO TRUMP RESPONSE; TRIPLE RAISE; and TWO NO TRUMP RESPONSE.

LIMIT BID. A bid with a limited point-count range, usually less than 4 points. Although a standard jump raise (one spade–three spades) is limited in the wide sense of the term, limit is normally applied only to non-forcing bids below the game level.

With some exceptions, a bid is limited and non-forcing if it is in no trump, if it is a raise, if it is a preference, or if it is a minimum rebid in a suit previously bid by the same player.

Opening no trump bids are invariably limited. Once we have decided that a certain bid is limited, the vital question arises: how wide can the limits be?

The answer involves a simple principle which hardly any players (or writers) are aware of, although they apply it.

The nearer the bidding is to game, the closer the limits must be. When the bidding reaches two no trump with the possibility of three no trump; or when the bidding reaches three spades, there is no longer any margin for exploration. So to give partner the chance of making an accurate decision, all such bids must have a range of only 2 points. Thus one heart–two no trump by a passed hand shows 11–12, and one heart–one no trump–two no trump shows 17–18; similarly one spade–three spades by a passed hand shows 10–11, or the equivalent, and one heart–one spade–three spades shows 17–18, or the equivalent. All these are typical *encouraging* bids, indicating that the partnership has a minimum of 23–24 points, and urging partner on to game if he has a little more than his promised minimum.

Conversely, any bid of one no trump, and any limited bid of two of a suit can afford a range of 3 or 4 points: there is still time for partner to make an encouraging bid below the game level. So one heart–one no trump or one heart–two hearts are each 6–9 (and may have to stretch a little further at that), and one heart–one spade–two spades is 13–16, or the distributional equivalent. In the same way, opening one no trump bids always have a range of 3 points (e.g., 16–18), but these could even be a point wider still without any disastrous loss of accuracy. (A 4-point range is not often used, because there is little compensating advantage for the modest loss of accuracy.) See OPENER'S REBID; RESPONDER'S REBID; and RESPONSE.

LIMIT JUMP RAISE. A feature of the ACOL and KAPLAN-SHEINWOLD systems, among others. A raise from one heart to three hearts, for example, is non-forcing but strongly encouraging. It shows a hand with about 11 high-card points or the distributional equivalent.

If the opening bidder has a minimum, he normally passes. If the nine-trick contract fails, it will often turn out that the opponents could have made a part-score or even a game.

Limit jump raises were a part of the original CULBERTSON SYSTEM (to 1934) and were revived for minor suits only in 1948. Some players use limit jump raises in competition only—that is, after a suit overcall by an opponent; and nearly all players ascribe to them a quite low limit, over an opponent's take-out double.

LIMIT JUMP RAISE TO SHOW A SINGLETON. A part of the WALSH SYSTEM, using an immediate jump raise of opener's major suit opening to show three or four trumps, 10–12 points, and a singleton somewhere in the hand. If opener is interested in locating responder's singleton, he makes the cheapest bid over the limit raise (See MATHE ASKING BID.)

This device can be used with other bidding styles if the partnership uses a forcing one no trump response to opening bids of one heart or one spade. The forcing no trump followed by a jump to three of opener's suit can be used to show a balanced limit raise.

LIMIT RAISE. A raise with closely defined limits of strength. Many such bids are limited in this way in standard methods, such as the single raise of opener's suit.

The chief application is the jump raise from one to three (see LIMIT JUMP RAISE). The bid would indicate at least four-card trump support with 10–11 points or the distributional equivalent.

The corollary is that a jump raise on the second round is invitational but non-forcing:

WEST	EAST	WEST	EAST
1 ♣	1 ♠	1 ♣	1 ♥
3 ♠		1 ♠	3 ♠

The second of these sequences is not clearly defined in standard methods. See JUMP REBIDS BY RESPONDER.

LIMIT RESPONSES. The combination of LIMIT RAISES with limit responses in no trump, so that responses of two no trump and three spades to an opening bid of one spade, for example, are both encouraging but not forcing.

LINE. The dividing horizontal marking on a score pad below which game and partial scores (trick scores) are written. See ABOVE THE LINE and BELOW THE LINE.

LITERATURE AND BRIDGE. Several full-length novels have focused on bridge. *Tickets to the Devil,* by Richard Powell, deals with the activities at a Spring National Championship, both at the tables and away from them. *Yarborough* by B. H. Friedman outlines the adolescence and young manhood of two precocious heroes. In one Agatha Christie mystery, *Cards on the Table,* the murder takes place during a bridge game and Hercule Poirot solves it by analyzing the score pad. A series of paperbacks by Don Von Elsner (*The Ace of Spies, The Jack of Hearts, The Jake of Diamonds, Kona Contract,* etc.) features a fictitious bridge pro, Jake Winkman, in a variety of adventures in tournament settings, in which the quality of the bridge hands is highly professional. Similarly, Frank THOMAS, a veteran actor of stage, movies, radio, and television, now a bridge teacher and editor of the ABTA *Quarterly,* has written two books about "Sherlock Holmes, Bridge Detective," which combine good storytelling with excellent bridge hands. In Sinclair Lewis's *Main Street* the local bridge club is a barometer of the protagonist's resistance and accommodation to the social life in Gopher Prairie, Minnesota. In Ian Fleming's *Moonraker,* James Bond rigged a variation of the DUKE OF

CUMBERLAND'S HAND in dealing with the villain of that book. (See DISTRIBUTIONAL VALUES.)

Among famous writers who have used a bridge theme for short story purposes are: Somerset Maugham ("The Three Fat Women of Antibes", "The Facts of Life"); Roald Dahl ("My Lady Love, My Dove"); Ring Lardner ("Contract"); and George S. Kaufman ("The Great Kibitzers' Strike of 1926"). See Cole, *Grand Slam,* BIBLIOGRAPHY B.

S. J. Simon, a European Champion and bridge writer, made some minor references to the game in the delightful series of novels he wrote with Caryl Brahms. C. S. Forester made his naval hero, Horatio Hornblower, a whist expert.

For Charles Lamb's view of whist players, see BATTLE, Sarah.

LITTLE MAJOR SYSTEM. An artificial system of bidding devised by Terence REESE and Jeremy FLINT, London, in the early sixties and now obsolete. In principle, an opening of one club denotes a heart suit and one diamond denotes a spade suit. Strong hands are opened with one heart, and minor suit hands with one spade.

(1) *One club* shows hearts, but might be only three hearts. One diamond is a negative response, but may be the first move with a big hand. Heart responses are natural and limited. Other minimum responses are positive with 8 points or more. A jump shift promises a good suit.

1 ♣	1 ◇
1 NT	

shows length in both majors. Other rebids by the opener are natural on the basis that he has already shown hearts.

(2) *One diamond* shows spades, but may be a strong balanced hand, in which case a suitable no trump rebid follows. One heart is a negative response, but may be the first move with a big hand.

1 ◇	1 ♥
1 NT	

shows 17–20

1 ◇	1 ♥
2 NT	

shows 23–24. Spade responses are natural and limited, and other responses are similar to one club responses.

(3) *One heart* is usually a strong hand, but may be used as a psychic with 2–6 points, in which case the opener passes the response. One heart is equivalent to any ACOL opening at the level of two (two clubs, two diamonds, etc., or two no trump). Responses are by steps: one spade negative; one no trump, one control; two clubs, one and one-half controls (i.e., ace and king or three kings); two diamonds, two or more controls.

(4) *One spade* is a minor suit hand, usually a diamond suit or both minors. Responses: One no trump

asks for suit. Two diamonds asks opener to bid a singleton major, a six-card minor, or two no trump; two no trump means playable in both minors.

(5) *One no trump* shows a balanced hand with 14–16. Two club response requires two diamonds rebid (GLADIATOR); two diamonds response is STAYMAN-type; two no trump response asks for four-card suits upwards; three clubs shows strength in one or both minors; three diamonds response is ROMAN BLACKWOOD; four clubs and four diamonds, SOUTH AFRICAN TEXAS.

(6) *Two clubs or two diamonds*, a natural minor-suit hand with useful values and natural responses.

(7) *Two hearts or two spades*, a major-minor two-suiter with useful values. Three club response shows desire to play in opener's minor. Two no trump response is forcing and opener bids the minor in which he is short.

(8) *Two no trump* shows a weak opening bid of three clubs or three diamonds. A response of four clubs is forcing.

(9) *Three clubs and three diamonds*, natural with a long, strong suit.

(10) *Three no trump* shows a solid minor suit.

(11) *Four clubs or four diamonds* bid transfers demands equivalent to four hearts and four spades respectively, but stronger.

RUSINOW leads are used (queen from king-queen, etc.). Some partnerships use ASPRO, and ASKING BIDS in some situations.

LITTLE ROMAN CLUB (ARNO) **SYSTEM.** Developed by Camillo PABIS TICCI and Massimo D'ALELIO, and first used successfully in the 1965 WORLD CHAMPIONSHIPS. The system is patterned closely on the principles of the ROMAN SYSTEM, especially the opening two-bids and structure of defensive overcalls. Its chief features are:

One club opening is forcing and shows either a balanced hand with 12–16 points, or a 17–20 point hand with a club suit or a two-suiter with at least four clubs. After a negative response of one diamond (less than 10 points), opener rebids on the one-level to show the balanced minimum opening. If responder makes a positive response of one heart or one spade, opener describes the minimum opening by raising with four-card support or rebidding one no trump with 12–14 points, or conventionally rebidding two clubs with 15–16 points. After a positive response in a minor, opener bids a suit on the two-level with 12–14 points or two no trump with 15–16 points. A response of one no trump is forcing to game, showing 12 points or more, over which opener bids a suit on the two-level with 12–13 points or raises to two no trump with 14–16 points. Jump responses are also forcing to game, and request opener to rebid conventionally by four steps to describe his strength and support for responder's suit.

With a strong distributional hand, opener bids his longest suit at a higher level than with a balanced hand.

One diamond, one heart, and one spade openings are forcing and natural according to the CANAPÉ principle with 12–20 points. The opening bid may be made in a

three-card suit with a minimum of 15 points or if opener's longest suit is clubs. The next higher suit by responder (one no trump over one spade) is the conventional negative, after which opener makes a simple rebid with 12–16 points or a jump rebid with a stronger hand. After a positive response, a normal rebid by opener is forcing for one round, and responder creates a game-force if his rebid is a reverse, a jump in a new suit, a raise of opener's second suit if it is a major, or a jump raise of opener's first suit. A one no trump response, if it is not a negative, shows a balanced hand with at least 12 points and is forcing to game.

If opener rebids in no trump after opening one diamond, he has a balanced hand with 17–20 points. Responder may then bid two clubs, forcing opener to rebid two diamonds and pass responder's next bid, or he may bid two diamonds to inquire about opener's major-suit holding and exact high-card strength.

One no trump opening is forcing and shows either a balanced hand with 21–24 points, or a powerful distributional hand that is forcing to game. Responder shows the number of aces he holds by steps, and opener rebids two no trump with the balanced hand, or canapés in a suit with the unbalanced hand. After a two no trump rebid, three clubs by responder is STAYMAN and three diamonds requests opener to rebid three hearts with a minimum and three spades with a maximum. This conventional treatment also applies to an auction of one diamond, one no trump, two no trump.

Two clubs, two diamonds, two hearts, and two spades openings are as in the ROMAN SYSTEM with certain variations in opener's rebids.

Two no trump opening shows a minimum of five cards in both minors with 12–16 points.

Jump overcall in the opponents' suit is equivalent to a strong take-out double.

Jump overcall of a one no trump opening describes a strong two-suiter, the bid suit and the next higher ranking suit. The non-touching combinations (spades and diamonds, or hearts and clubs) are shown by a two no trump overcall. Responder bids three clubs to allow the overcaller to define which combination he holds.

Take-out doubles may be made on either a balanced hand or a strong one-suited hand.

For other bidding treatments, see ROMAN SYSTEM.

LITTLE SLAM. See SMALL SLAM.

LIVORNO SYSTEM. See LEGHORN DIAMOND.

LOCAL TOURNAMENTS. See CHAMPIONSHIP TOURNAMENTS.

LOCK. A colloquial term, used principally in post mortems, to mean a 100% sure play or contract. For example, "Four spades was a lock." In certain ethical situations the term has a similar meaning: "After his partner's HUDDLE he had a lock to double."

LOCKED (IN OR OUT OF A HAND). To win a trick in a hand from which it is disadvantageous to make the lead to the next (or some later) trick is to be locked in. It usually refers to an end play against a defender (see THROW IN) or to a declarer who is forced to win a trick in the dummy hand, when he has high cards established in his own hand which he is unable to enter. Locked out refers to situations in which established cards in the dummy cannot be cashed because an entry is not available.

LONDON SUNDAY TIMES PAIRS. An invitational pair event sponsored by the London Sunday *Times*. The field is usually limited to 16–22 leading pairs from many countries. The winners:

1963	P. Jais, R. Trezel (France)
1964	T. Reese, B. Schapiro (England)
1965	No contest
1966	G. Theron, G. Desrousseaux (France)
1967	L. Tarlo, C. Rodrigue (England)
1968	C. Delmouly, L. Yallouze (France and Egypt)
1969	J. Besse, J. Collings (Switzerland and England)
1970	N. Gardener, R. A. Priday (England)
1971	C. Slavenburg, L. Tintner (Holland and France)
1972	L. Lebioda, A. Wilkosz (Poland)
1973	S. Altman, A. Sontag (U.S.A.)
1974	G. Facchini, S. Zucchelli (Italy)
1975	P. Weichsel, A. Sontag (U.S.A.)

LONG CARDS. Cards of a suit remaining in a player's hand after all other cards of that suit have been played.

LONG HAND. The hand of the partnership which has the greater length in the trump suit, or, in no trump play, the hand which has winners that are or may be established. See AVOIDANCE.

LONG SUIT. A suit in which four or more cards are held. Frequently it is used in connection with a hand of little strength but with great length in a particular suit. For bidding on such a hand, see PRE-EMPTIVE BID.

LONG TRUMP. Any card of the trump suit remaining after all other players' cards of the suit have been played.

LOSER. A card that must lose a trick to the adversaries if led, or if it must be played when the suit is led by an adversary. At no trump, all cards below the ace and not in sequence with it are possible losers, but may become winners if the play develops favorably. At a suit contract, the same may be said with the exception that losers may possibly be ruffed if the suit is short in one hand. A distinction must be made between possible losers and sure losers. The former may be discarded on a setup suit, or ruffed, or perhaps discarded on a setup card cashed by an adversary. If a loser cannot be disposed of, it must, of course, lose a trick to the opponents.

LOSER ON LOSER. The act of playing a card that must be lost on a losing trick in some other suit. This technique can be valuable in many situations, the most common of which are:

(1) *To allow a safe ruff to produce a trick:*

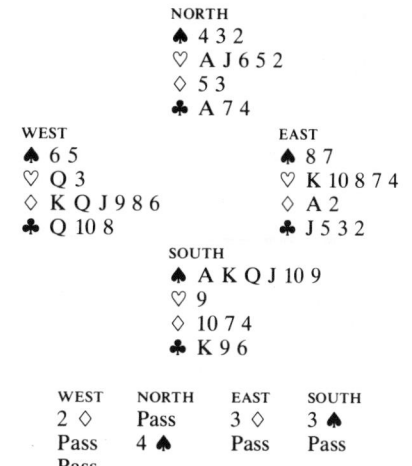

WEST	NORTH	EAST	SOUTH
2 ◇	Pass	3 ◇	3 ♠
Pass	4 ♠	Pass	Pass
Pass			

West leads the diamond king. East overtakes with the ace, and continues the suit. West wins and plays a third diamond. South realizes that East will be able to overruff dummy. He therefore plays a loser on a loser by discarding a club from dummy. Declarer can later ruff a club in dummy safely.

(2) *To allow a safe re-entry:*

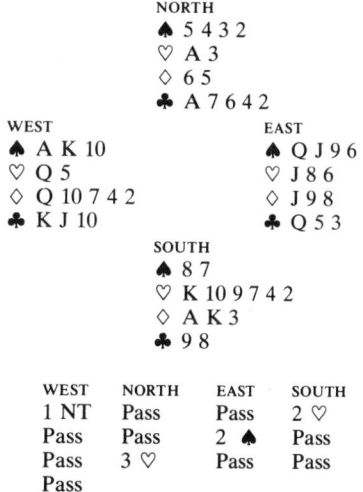

WEST	NORTH	EAST	SOUTH
1 NT	Pass	Pass	2 ♡
Pass	Pass	2 ♠	Pass
Pass	3 ♡	Pass	Pass
Pass			

West leads three rounds of spades, and declarer ruffs. Two rounds of diamonds are cashed and the third round is trumped in the North hand. After cashing the ace of hearts, declarer must now re-enter his hand to continue drawing trump. If he leads ace and another club, East will win and his spade continuation will create two trump tricks for the defense. Instead, declarer cashes dummy's ace of clubs and then leads a fourth round of spades, playing a loser on a loser by discarding his remaining club. The defense is now helpless. Declarer is fortunate in the distribution of the East-West minor suit cards but has nothing to lose by attempting this play.

(3) *To prevent a later overruff threat:*

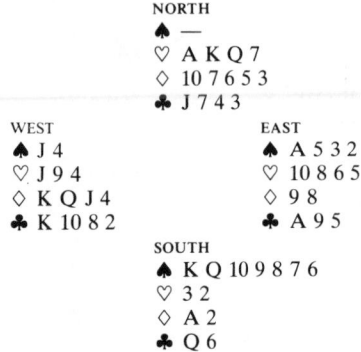

NORTH
♠ —
♡ A K Q 7
◇ 10 7 6 5 3
♣ J 7 4 3

WEST
♠ J 4
♡ J 9 4
◇ K Q J 4
♣ K 10 8 2

EAST
♠ A 5 3 2
♡ 10 8 6 5
◇ 9 8
♣ A 9 5

SOUTH
♠ K Q 10 9 8 7 6
♡ 3 2
◇ A 2
♣ Q 6

With East-West vulnerable, South opens four spades, and buys the contract. West leads the king of diamonds, which declarer wins. An immediate discard is necessary, so South takes three rounds of hearts, discarding his losing diamond. If South now fails to play the last heart, careful defense will obtain two club tricks and two trump tricks. East will lead his last heart at a later stage, promoting West's jack of trump (see TRUMP PROMOTION).

Instead, South uses the loser-on-loser technique. He leads dummy's remaining heart, discarding a club loser. East wins this trick, but the contract cannot be defeated.

(4) *To prevent a particular opponent from gaining the lead* (see AVOIDANCE):

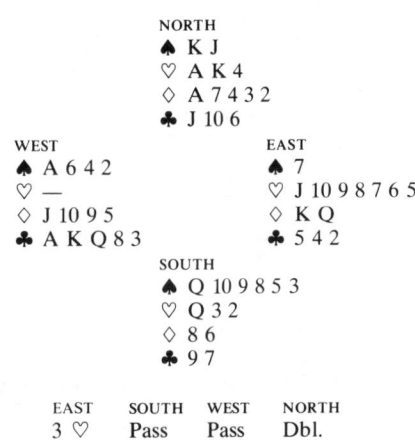

NORTH
♠ K J
♡ A K 4
◇ A 7 4 3 2
♣ J 10 6

WEST
♠ A 6 4 2
♡ —
◇ J 10 9 5
♣ A K Q 8 3

EAST
♠ 7
♡ J 10 9 8 7 6 5
◇ K Q
♣ 5 4 2

SOUTH
♠ Q 10 9 8 5 3
♡ Q 3 2
◇ 8 6
♣ 9 7

EAST	SOUTH	WEST	NORTH
3 ♡	Pass	Pass	Dbl.
Pass	3 ♠	Pass	Pass
Pass			

West leads the king of clubs and (erroneously) continues with the ace and queen. South observes that the bidding suggests West is void of hearts. He

therefore plays a loser on a loser by discarding a diamong on the third club. If South ruffs the third club, West will shift to diamonds after winning the second round of spades. South will then be unable to enter his hand without surrendering a heart ruff.

After South's discard on the third trick, his contract is safe.

(5) *To establish one or more tricks in the suit played:*

WEST
♠ A K J
♡ —
◇ A 3
♣ A K J 10 9 8 7 3

EAST
♠ 5 4 3
♡ K Q 4
◇ 10 7 6 5
♣ Q 6 2

Against West's contract of six clubs, North leads the king of diamonds. West wins and draws two trumps ending in the East hand. He should now lead the king of hearts from dummy, throwing a loser on a loser by discarding his diamond if East does not cover. If North wins the heart ace, the heart queen will provide a discard for the jack of spades. (Naturally, West has retained an entry to the East hand in clubs!) If South has the ace, either the king of hearts will win or the ace will be ruffed out. Declarer can now try the spade finesse for an overtrick.

(6) *To help establish a side suit* (see AVOIDANCE):

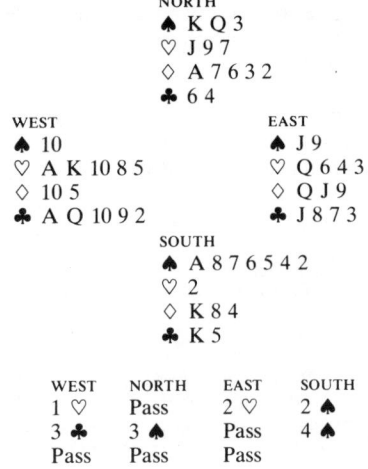

NORTH
♠ K Q 3
♡ J 9 7
◇ A 7 6 3 2
♣ 6 4

WEST
♠ 10
♡ A K 10 8 5
◇ 10 5
♣ A Q 10 9 2

EAST
♠ J 9
♡ Q 6 4 3
◇ Q J 9
♣ J 8 7 3

SOUTH
♠ A 8 7 6 5 4 2
♡ 2
◇ K 8 4
♣ K 5

WEST	NORTH	EAST	SOUTH
1 ♡	Pass	2 ♡	2 ♠
3 ♣	3 ♠	Pass	4 ♠
Pass	Pass	Pass	

West leads the king of hearts, and all follow. West, who has been reading this article, realizes that if he leads the ace of hearts, declarer will play a loser on a loser by discarding a dimond. This will allow the diamond suit to be established by ruffing, and prevent East from gaining the lead to annihilate the king of clubs.

West therefore shifts to a trump (a diamond has the same effect).

Declarer wins in dummy, playing the four from his own hand. Anxious to execute the loser-on-loser play, he leads the nine of hearts from dummy. East shakes off a yawn and rises with the queen to prevent the diamond discard. Declarer ruffs with the five, returns to dummy by leading the six of spades to the remaining honor in dummy. The jack of hearts is led from dummy. East cannot cover, and declarer sheds a low diamond. West wins and grudgingly cashes the ace of clubs to prevent an overtrick. Despite the best defense after the opening lead, declarer triumphs by continuing after his loser-on-loser play and careful unblocking in the spade suit (see UNBLOCKING).

(7) *To avoid a force:*

WEST	EAST
♠ A K Q J	♠ 10 8 5
♡ 3	♡ 9 8 7
◇ A 4 3	◇ 10 7 5
♣ A K J 9 5	♣ Q 10 8 2

Against West's four-spade contract (Don't ask me how he got there! It's a good contract, isn't it?), the defense begins with two rounds of hearts. To avoid weakening his trump holding, West should discard losing diamonds on the next two rounds of hearts. A fourth round of hearts can be ruffed in the East hand. If the trumps break 3–3 or 4–2, declarer romps home.

If declarer ruffs a heart too early, a 4–2 trump break may defeat him, the defense taking four hearts and one trump trick.

(8) *To execute an end play by creating a throw-in card:*

                   NORTH
                   ♠ K J 9 8 3
                   ♡ A 5
                   ◇ 3 2
                   ♣ 8 5 3 2

WEST	EAST
♠ A 4	♠ 2
♡ K Q 10 9	♡ J 8 7 4 3 2
◇ J 10 8 4	◇ 7 6 5
♣ A Q 7	♣ J 10 9

                   SOUTH
                   ♠ Q 10 7 6 5
                   ♡ 6
                   ◇ A K Q 9
                   ♣ K 6 4

Against South's four spade contract, West leads the king of hearts. Declarer wins with the ace, ruffs a heart, and leads a trump. West cautiously rises with the ace of spades, and exits with a spade. Declarer wins and tries to drop the jack, ten of diamonds. On the third diamond, a club is discarded from dummy. South then leads the fourth round of diamonds. When West covers, declarer makes use of loser-on-loser technique by discarding another club from dummy. West is in, and must give away a trick.

(9) *To execute an end play by forcing an opponent to remain on lead* (see RUFF AND DISCARD):

                   NORTH
                   ♠ A 3 2
                   ♡ A J
                   ◇ A 7 6
                   ♣ 10 9 6 4 3

WEST	EAST
♠ 4	♠ K Q J 9 8 7
♡ K Q 10 8 7 3 2	♡ 9 6
◇ J 10	◇ Q 9 5 3 2
♣ J 8 2	♣ —

                   SOUTH
                   ♠ 10 6 5
                   ♡ 5 4
                   ◇ K 8 4
                   ♣ A K Q 7 5

SOUTH	WEST	NORTH	EAST
1 ♣	2 ♡	3 ♡	4 ♠
Pass	Pass	5 ♣	Pass
Pass	Pass		

West leads the four of spades, which is won by North's ace. Declarer draws three rounds of trump and, placing West with seven hearts, cashes the two top diamonds and plays the ace and jack of hearts.

West is stuck on lead with all hearts remaining and must give up a ruff-and-discard. When he leads a heart, a diamond is thrown from dummy. South tosses a loser on a loser by discarding a spade from his own hand. West is forced to remain on lead. On the next heart, declarer ruffs in dummy and discards his last spade. He then crossruffs the balance of the tricks, having turned four losers into only two! West could counter brilliantly by permitting dummy's heart jack to win, after which declarer would have no recourse.

(10) *To rectify the count for a squeeze.* This use of the loser-on-loser technique has many variations. Some of the most esoteric play problems revolve around declarer's attempt to correct the count for a squeeze by losing a trick in the correct suit. The following hand illustrates the method in a fairly complex setting.

                   NORTH
                   ♠ A K 3
                   ♡ 8 4 3 2
                   ◇ Q 4 2
                   ♣ 6 5 3

WEST	EAST
♠ Q 10 7 2	♠ J 9 5
♡ 6	♡ 7
◇ A K 10 8 7 6 3	◇ J 9 5
♣ 7	♣ Q J 10 9 8 4

                   SOUTH
                   ♠ 8 6 4
                   ♡ A K Q J 10 9 5
                   ◇ —
                   ♣ A K 2

EAST	SOUTH	WEST	NORTH
3 ♣	4 ♡	5 ◇	5 ♡
Pass	6 ♡	Pass	Pass
Pass			

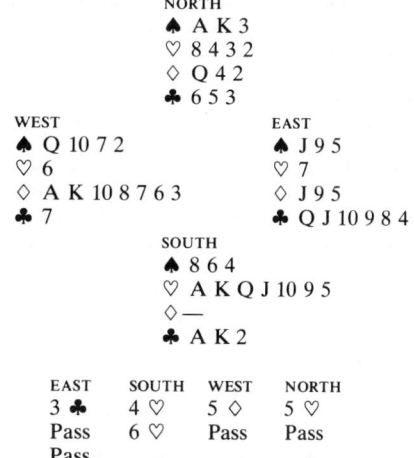

West leads the king of diamonds, and South surveys the situation. He realizes that if neither opponent is short of spades (a reasonable assumption on the bidding) an elimination will fail, and the only chance for the contract is a double squeeze. The queen of diamonds is a menace against West, and declarer's third club threatens East. But the count is wrong. Declarer must lose a trick before the squeeze will operate.

Where can this trick be lost? Certainly not in spades or clubs, for the loss of a trick in either of these suits will destroy the essential menace cards. Therefore, a trick must be lost in diamonds. Furthermore, this trick must be lost *at once*. If declarer attempts to give up a diamond trick later on, the defense will play a third diamond, quashing the diamond menace. Therefore, declarer must throw a loser on a loser on the first trick. He discards a spade.

West has no effective defense. His best play is a spade. Declarer wins and runs winners until this ending is reached.

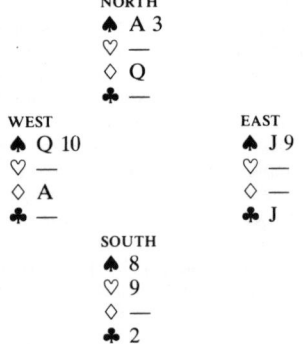

```
                    NORTH
                  ♠ A 3
                  ♡ —
                  ◇ Q
                  ♣ —
    WEST                      EAST
  ♠ Q 10                    ♠ J 9
  ♡ —                       ♡ —
  ◇ A                       ◇ —
  ♣ —                       ♣ J
                    SOUTH
                  ♠ 8
                  ♡ 9
                  ◇ —
                  ♣ 2
```

When South leads the nine of hearts, West must surrender a spade. Dummy discards the queen of diamonds, and East is squeezed in spades and clubs.

J. R.

LOSING-TRICK COUNT. A method of hand valuation. In 1934 the principle of assessing a hand in terms of "losers" was put forward by F. Dudley COURTENAY in his book, *The System the Experts Play*. The general idea was this: when a suit fit came to light, you added the number of worthless cards in your hand to the number of losers revealed by your partner's bidding; the total was subtracted from 18, and the answer would tell you how many odd tricks the combined hands were likely to take.

After years of semi-obscurity the LTC was revived by M. Harrison-Gray of London, and is now accepted as a reasonably accurate ready reckoner which pays due regard to the features that really matter.

This method of valuation is no longer treated with disdain by the expert. For instance, it is an integral part of the ROMAN SYSTEM, which has helped Italy to win seven world championships.

The Losing-Trick Count applies only to trump contracts. When a no trump contract is contemplated, the standard yardstick is the Milton Work Count.

Basic count of losers. With a void or singleton ace, count no loser in that suit; with any other singleton, or with A x or K x, count one loser; with any other doubleton, count two losers.

In each suit of three or more cards, including the trump suit, count one loser for each missing high honor (ace, king, or queen).

Do not count more than three losers in any one suit.

Count one loser only in a suit headed by A J 10.

Some distinction must obviously be made between A x x, K x x, and Q x x. The first is a better two-loser holding than K x x, and three losers must be counted in a queen-high suit unless: (a) it is the proposed trump suit; (b) the suit has been bid by the partner; (c) the queen is supported by the jack; (d) the queen is "balanced" by an ace in another suit.

The initial count. An opening bid of one is made with: (a) not more than seven losers; (b) adequate high-card values, including two defensive tricks; (c) a sound rebid.

A response in a new suit is made with: (a) at the one-level—not more than nine losers (sometimes ten with compensating values); (b) at the two-level—not more than eight losers (sometimes nine with compensating values).

The count on the second rounds. Neutral rebids by opener (e.g., one heart—one spade—two hearts, or one spade—two clubs—two diamonds, or one club—one spade—two spades) do not promise fewer than seven losers.

A jump rebid by the opener in his original suit (e.g., one club—one spade—three clubs) shows seven winners and (in most cases) only five losers.

A reverse rebid by the opener at two-level (e.g., one club—one spade—two hearts) shows five losers (sometimes six with a high point-count). A reverse at the three-level (e.g., one spade—two hearts—three clubs) shows not more than five losers.

A jump rebid by the responder in his original suit (e.g., one heart—one spade—two clubs—three spades) shows six losers.

A responder's reverse at the two-level (e.g., one diamond—two clubs—two diamonds—two hearts) shows six to seven losers. A reverse at the three-level (e.g., one heart—one spade—two hearts—three clubs) shows not more than six losers.

It soon becomes second nature to adjust the original count of losers in the light of the bidding. Trump control is an important factor, and a loser should be deducted whenever the quota of aces and other key features, such as a king or a singleton in the right spot, is better than it might be on the bidding. The LTC will put a non-expert player on the right track in a case like the following:

South dealer
East-West vulnerable

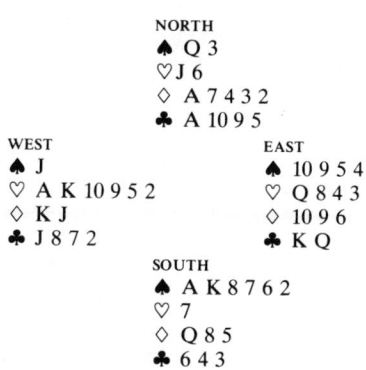

```
                    NORTH
                    ♠ Q 3
                    ♡ J 6
                    ◇ A 7 4 3 2
                    ♣ A 10 9 5
WEST                                    EAST
♠ J                                     ♠ 10 9 5 4
♡ A K 10 9 5 2                          ♡ Q 8 4 3
◇ K J                                   ◇ 10 9 6
♣ J 8 7 2                               ♣ K Q
                    SOUTH
                    ♠ A K 8 7 6 2
                    ♡ 7
                    ◇ Q 8 5
                    ♣ 6 4 3
```

The bidding:

SOUTH	WEST	NORTH	EAST
Pass	1 ♡	Pass	2 ♡
2 ♠	3 ♣	Pass	4 ♡
Pass	Pass	Dbl.	Pass
Pass	Pass		

West had six losers, and East was marked with nine; 15 from 18 suggested that even three hearts might fail through a dearth of top cards, but one of West's losers could be deducted for trump control, and a game try was in order. Three hearts would sound like mere contention, so he made a TRIAL BID in the spot where help was most needed. The onus was then on East, who saw two good reasons for jumping to game —his fourth trump and an ideal holding in the trial suit. The queen of spades was led and West could not go wrong, in view of South's initial pass, when he came to tackle diamonds.

Application of the LTC would have averted an inelegant result on the deal below:

South dealer
Both sides vulnerable

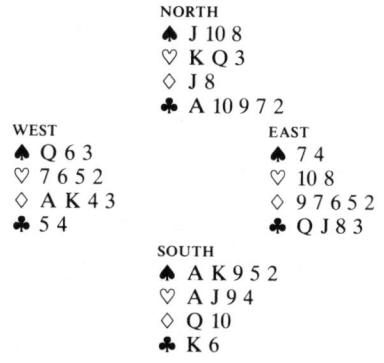

```
                    NORTH
                    ♠ J 10 8
                    ♡ K Q 3
                    ◇ J 8
                    ♣ A 10 9 7 2
WEST                                    EAST
♠ Q 6 3                                 ♠ 7 4
♡ 7 6 5 2                               ♡ 10 8
◇ A K 4 3                               ◇ 9 7 6 5 2
♣ 5 4                                   ♣ Q J 8 3
                    SOUTH
                    ♠ A K 9 5 2
                    ♡ A J 9 4
                    ◇ Q 10
                    ♣ K 6
```

The bidding:

SOUTH	WEST	NORTH	EAST
1 ♠	Pass	2 ♣	Pass
2 ♡	Pass	3 ♠	Pass
4 ♣	Pass	4 ♡	Pass
5 ♠	Pass	Pass	Pass

West could sit back and relax after cashing two diamonds. South made two common mistakes: his 17 points went to his head, and he read too much into a non-forcing preference bid. The LTC should serve as a halt sign. South has six losers, and his partner should have eight; if he deducts 14 from 18, he will see the futility of looking beyond four spades.

M. H.-G.

LOU HERMAN TROPHY. See HERMAN TROPHY.

LOVE. The state of the game, in rubber bridge, where there is as yet no score.

LOVE, TO PLAY FOR. To play rubber bridge without stakes.

LOVE ALL. A term, borrowed from tennis, used in some countries to describe that situation where neither side has made any score. Used in England at duplicate to indicate that neither side is vulnerable, but not used in the United States.

LOVE SCORE. Zero score; neither side vulnerable and no part-score.

LOW CARD. A card in a suit that is not an honor; any card from the deuce to the nine, usually represented by an x in card or hand descriptions.

LOW-LEVEL TEXAS. See JACOBY TRANSFER BIDS.

LOWER MINOR. See DEFENSE TO OPENING THREE-BID; SECOND NEGATIVE RESPONSE AFTER ARTIFICIAL FORCING OPENING.

LOWEST SCORE. The lowest score in major team-of-four play occurred in 1957, in the first Far East Team Championship at Manila. On the third set of eight boards in the match between Hong Kong and the Philippines, not one IMP was scored by either side. On each of the eight hands, both teams arrived at the same contract and made the same number of tricks. In a board-a-match team held at a Greater New York BA sectional tournament in 1975, one of the 74 teams entered scored only one-half board out of 26—a record that is unlikely to be broken, and if it is, it won't be by much. In pair play, the lowest recorded score is 13% (by opera star Lauritz Melchior).

LUCK. A basic reason for the success of duplicate bridge is that it incorporates the optimum degree of luck. Although this means that the best players do not invariably win, it adds greatly to the fascination of the game and to the interplay of psychological factors. Par contests, where the luck element is removed, are much less popular.

Individual contests contain by far the largest element of luck and are less highly regarded as a test of skill than other forms of duplicate. The hazardous nature of an individual contest derives partly from the constant change of partners. Good luck may take the form of being teamed with a strong and compatible partner on critical deals which require accurate bidding or play; it would be bad luck to be teamed with an incompatible partner on such deals, and a player would prefer to reserve such a partner for a set of flat boards. Similarly, being teamed against incompatible players on swingy deals could be good luck, and a player might pick up a high match-point score without taking an active part.

An illustration of the unpredictable nature of individual contests was afforded by the British Masters Individual in the days when this was an invitation event; a Master who had come bottom one year was reinvited the following year only after a divided vote, but he promptly won the Championship.

After individual contests, pair events contain the next highest proportion of luck. In a single-session event, a pair who are measurably stronger than the field will probably win less than half the time; but they will nearly always finish in the leading group. The greater the importance of a pair event, the greater the number of boards played, thus reducing the effect of luck. In the first World Pair Olympiad, held at Cannes, France, in 1962, the finalists each played a total of 286 boards. This is sufficient to minimize the role of luck, granted that the field is of reasonably level caliber.

Another facet of luck in pairs events is that toward the end of a contest an experienced pair who estimate that they have less than a winning score may adopt unusual tactics in an attempt to improve dramatically. Such tactics may take the form of bidding poor slams or games, or declining to bid good slams, in the hope that an improbable distribution of the cards will favor an unusual contract. Thus it is theoretically possible for a pair to have a comfortable lead with a few boards to go, to continue to bid and play perfectly, and yet be passed by a pair who have deliberately bid their way to faulty contracts or made imperfect plays. (See SHOOTING). The fact that this is so has given rise to the misconception that the structure of pairs scoring is necessarily faulty; an alternate view is that it adds to the excitement and affords more scope for judgment and opportunism.

It is in team-of-four games—particularly those where the scoring is by International Match Points—that luck is reduced to a minimum; consequently these events carry most prestige and are the accepted medium for international competition.

At the same time, the structure of team games is such that luck, when it does occur, is both more recognizable and more dramatic than in pairs contests. This adds greatly to the ways in which skill may be manifested. For example, a player who at a critical stage of a close match is faced with the decision whether to bid an even-money slam may bring into the reckoning such factors as the personal idiosyncrasies of his counterpart at the other table, the bidding systems being played there, whether the players there will be able to judge the score as accurately as he, and so on. Dramatic strokes of misfortune can also exert a profound psychological effect on the players and provide a stern test of character in the face of adversity.

Aside from close decisions, luck in team play may result in correct play being penalized by an unfortunate lie of the cards, while less sound play succeeds. In the first World Team Olympiad, held at Turin, Italy, in 1960, two teams landed in six spades on these cards:

WEST	EAST
♠ A Q J 9 8 6	♠ 4 2
♡ 9	♡ A K J 7 6 4 3
◇ A Q	◇ 5 4
♣ A K Q 8	♣ J 7

After a neutral lead, West's only problem was to avoid losing two trumps. B. Jay Becker for the US led a spade from the table and finessed the queen, which lost to the king. When he regained the lead Becker laid down the ace and found that North's king had been blank. He now had to lose a second trick to the guarded ten in South.

The Italian player initiated the suit by laying down the ace. When this dropped North's king, he entered dummy, finessed against the ten, and made seven-odd.

Laying down the ace may appear to be a safety play but it in fact gains in only one position—the actual one. Finessing the queen gains in three positions—where North has the blank three, five, or seven.

In team play an admitted but small mistake in technique can sometimes be penalized to an extent altogether out of proportion to the degree of error. Following were the cards in the crucial semi-final match between Britain and Italy in the second World Team Olympiad, held in New York City in 1964.

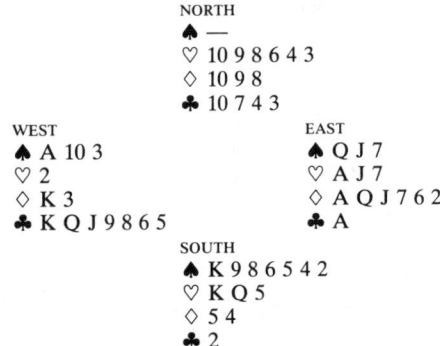

```
                         NORTH
                         ♠ —
                         ♡ 10 9 8 6 4 3
                         ◇ 10 9 8
                         ♣ 10 7 4 3
         WEST                              EAST
         ♠ A 10 3                          ♠ Q J 7
         ♡ 2                               ♡ A J 7
         ◇ K 3                             ◇ A Q J 7 6 2
         ♣ K Q J 9 8 6 5                   ♣ A
                         SOUTH
                         ♠ K 9 8 6 5 4 2
                         ♡ K Q 5
                         ◇ 5 4
                         ♣ 2
```

In the closed room the British bid to the best contract as follows:

WEST	EAST
Harrison-Gray	*Flint*
	2 NT
4 ♣	4 NT
7 NT	Pass

Seven no trump was a spread, and the British scored 2,220. When the deal was replayed on Bridge-O-Rama, the bidding was:

SOUTH	WEST	NORTH	EAST
Schapiro	*Avarelli*	*Reese*	*Belladonna*
		Pass	1 ◇
1 ♠	3 ♣	Pass	4 ◇
Pass	4 NT	Pass	5 NT
Pass	6 ◇	Pass	7 ◇
Pass	Pass	Pass	

This contract would be made unless North could ruff the opening lead or unless trumps were divided 5–0, the latter being only a 4% chance. Since seven diamonds bid and made gives a score of 2,140, normal expectation would be a swing of 2 international match points to the team which had bid seven no trump. In fact the British South opened a low spade against seven diamonds and his partner ruffed. The swing to Britain was thus 2,320, or 20 IMPs. Although the Italian bidding was imperfect, one might say that they suffered ill luck to the extent of perhaps 18 IMPs. See also FORTUNE.

LUNCH-TIME BRIDGE. Popular, especially in large corporations that have teams belonging to the various commercial bridge leagues. In lunchrooms where there is sufficient space, one may find occasional foursomes of a serious or semi-serious nature, and these develop into groups of decent ability from time to time. If a person is willing to take a good chunk of time away from his rest or eating period to play a card game, it stands to reason there must be keen interest. In larger luncheon groups, there are even lunchtime matches, consisting of six-board contests and lasting about forty minutes.

M

MACHINE-PREPARED HANDS. Used first in the Eastern States Regional Tournament in 1963, machine-prepared (computer-dealt is a synonymous phrase) hand records promise to be a solution for a practical, quick, inexpensive method of producing twinned hands in multi-section events. Martin Scheinberg and David Northrop devised the system by which such hand records could be produced; the machine simulates a shuffle producing a random

deal, sorts the resulting hands into suits, prints the hands, and assembles up to thirty-six hands into a set. Any number of complete sets can then be run off. All the NUMBER OF POSSIBLE HANDS may be generated at some time or other.

Fifty-two symbols are used, with each symbol having a translation into a particular card programmed into the memory unit of the machine. These symbols are then given a random distribution, simulating the perfect shuffling of a deck of cards, and then are distributed randomly into four groups of thirteen. Using the memory unit for symbol identification, the machine then puts each of the thirteen symbols representing spades, hearts, diamonds, and clubs respectively in order of ranking both of the suits and of the cards in the suit, and prints the result on a sheet in a style that resembles the duplicate board.

For a pairs event, it requires less than ten minutes for a member of the tournament staff to pass out the HAND RECORDS, and collect them after they have been used if the players have sorted the cards into suits. New cards in the boards, or arranging cards into suits prior to distribution speeds the process considerably.

With an even number of tables in a section, boards are moved normally before play. With an odd number of tables in a section, boards are passed in the normal direction, skipping an extra table.

At tournaments complaints are frequently heard about freakish distribution and unfortunate suit breaks, which are blamed on "those computer-dealt hands." (Such complaints are frequently heard even when machine-prepared hands have not been used.) The patterns of the 3,080 machine-prepared hands used in the round robin qualifying rounds of the 1972 World Team Olympiad were analyzed by *Bridge World* and the incidence of each hand pattern was found to have been very close to mathematical expectations. (See MATHEMATICAL TABLES, Table 1.) Suits were found to have broken evenly slightly more often than would be expected, and the most freakish deal of the tournament (a seven-card suit in one hand, a nine-card suit in another) was dealt *manually* after a protest had resulted in the computer-dealt hand being thrown out. Other analyses have indicated that manually dealt hands produce flat distributions somewhat more often than might be expected.

MACHLIN TROPHY. Donated by the Machlin family in memory of Sadie Machlin, long-time ACBL employee, and awarded to the winners of the Charity Game at the Fall Championships, under which heading past results are listed.

MAGAZINES. See BIBLIOGRAPHY, O.

MAGNETIC CARDS. Cards made from a very thin sheet of metal. Though not themselves magnetic, the cards are attracted to and held onto a magnetized board which is part of the set.

The principal advantage of these cards is that play can take place alongside outdoor pools, on breezy patios, or at the beach. Manufacture began in 1962, and prices are comparable to those of plastic cards and bridge tables.

MAJOR. A major suit, i.e., hearts or spades.

MAJOR SUIT. Either of the two highest-ranking suits, hearts and spades, so characterized because they outrank the third and fourth suits in the bidding and scoring.

MAJOR TENACE. An original holding of ace-queen (without the king) of a suit. After one or more rounds of a suit have played, the highest and third highest remaining cards of the suit in the hand of one player are called a major tenace (when the second highest remaining card is not held by the same player).

MAJORITY CALLING. The principle by which any bid outranks any other bid at a lower level, regardless of scoring value. The opposite principle, numerical calling, was standard in auction bridge, although abandoned in the United States in 1913. In this procedure four spades, for example, could follow a bid of five clubs because its scoring value was higher.

MAKE. Used in bridge in four different senses. As a verb, it may mean (1) to shuffle the deck; (2) to succeed in a contract; (3) to win a trick by the play of a card. As a noun, it means a successful contract, but usually a hypothetical one in the POST-MORTEM: "Five diamonds would have been a make."

MAKE UP. To shuffle the cards.

MAKE UP A TABLE. A player who, with at least three others, forms a table for play at rubber, or CHICAGO bridge, is said to make up a table.

MALAYSIAN CONTRACT BRIDGE ASSOCIATION. Founded in 1962 as the Malayan Contract Bridge Association; subsequently changed to its present title in 1964. By 1969 it had a membership of about 300. Its headquarters are in Kuala Lumpur, with branches in Selangor and Penang, and also in Singapore until that territory became a separate state in 1965. The Association participates in Far East Championships, hosting the 1968 event in Kuala Lumpur, and annually sponsors National Championships for the Tunku Abdul Rahman Trophy, Malaysia Cup, Jumabhoy Trophy, and various Interstate Team-of-Four contests. Players listed separately are: C. Brown, H. Chen, W. Fernando, Dr. T. Lim, K. Wong.

Officers, 1974:
President: Dr. Lim Eu Jin.
Secretary: Chin Tuck Meng, P.O. Box 137, Kuala Lumpur, W. Malaysia

MALOWAN SIX CLUB CONVENTION. A variation of the GRAND SLAM FORCE originated by Walter Malowan, New York City. After BLACKWOOD has been used, a five no trump bid is not available as a grand slam force because it would be a conventional bid asking for kings. Six clubs is therefore used as a substitute grand slam force unless clubs is the agreed trump suit.

The responses to six clubs must be influenced by the fact that the ace of trumps is already known. Marshall MILES suggests that the cheapest available bid should be used at the six-level to show the best possible trump holding, with increasingly strong bids showing increasingly worse holdings where available.

MALTAIS CONVENTION. See STAYMAN AFTER OVERCALL.

MAMA-PAPA BRIDGE. Slang for a bidding sequence employing little or no subtlety, few conventions, and careful adherence to a particular set of "rules."

MANNERISM. A peculiarity of action or behavior, which should be carefully avoided at the bridge table. Most unethical mannerisms are unconscious and not known by the player himself.

MANUFACTURE OF PLAYING CARDS. After the establishment of papermaking in America, several printers, including Benjamin Franklin, seem to have produced packs of cards as a sideline. The first man specifically listed as a maufacturer of playing cards was Jazaniah Ford of Milton, Mass., about 1800, followed by Thomas Crehore of Dorchester. Major companies in 1971, and their plant locations are:

United States Playing Card Company Cincinnati, Ohio	paper
Arrco Playing Card Company Chicago, Ill.	paper, plastic
Western P. & L. Company Racine, Wis.	paper
Stancraft Products St. Paul, Minn.	paper
Kem Playing Card Company Poughkeepsie and New York, N.Y.	plastic

The fundamental principle of manufacture has changed little over the century. The standard "poker" card measures $2\frac{1}{2} \times 3\frac{1}{2}$ inches, but bridge cards are a little narrower, $2\frac{1}{4} \times 3\frac{1}{2}$, to facilitate the holding of thirteen cards in a player's hand. The stock on which the cards are printed consists of two thin sheets of paper pasted together with a black paste. (A single sheet of heavier paper would not suffice; if a player had a lamp at his back, the light would show what he had in his hand, to the player across from him. The black paste makes the paper properly opaque.) Hence playing cards are sometimes called "pasteboards."

One or two full packs of cards are printed at a time on large sheets of pasteboard. The individual cards are then stamped out, one at a time, with a sharp die that works like a housewife's biscuit cutter, but one that cuts about 36,000 cards per hour. Simultaneously, and synchronized to the infinitesimal fraction of a second in which the die descends, the edges of the cards are pressed into a knife-edge, almost invisible to the naked eye, but enough to permit each card to slip between two other cards during a shuffle, and this retards the fraying of the edges.

Delicate operations like this require special machinery, designed for this specific purpose. Modern refinements on traditional processes have not been disclosed in patents, and rate among the world's most jealously guarded trade secrets.

The demand for playing cards is not likely to outrun supply, despite the paucity of manufacturers. It has been said that the largest playing-card plant (the U.S. Playing Card Company in Cincinnati) could, without effort, supply the wants of the card-playing world.

Modern cardplayers are accustomed to the "double-head" card, which can be read from either end, and to the INDICES in two corners, which permit one to recognize the card without seeing its entire face. Cards of this type did not become standard until the late 1870s. Until then a player had to look at a full face of the card, and hold it right-side up, to know what the card was.

Either superstition or habit prevents major changes in playing-card design. Unsuccessful attempts have been made to print the suits in four colors; to redesign the pips; to clothe the face cards in modern dress; and to introduce circular cards. Soviet Russia tried to replace the "anachronistic kings and queens" with revolutionary heroes, but so many packs were smuggled in that the conventional royalty cards were reinstated. (See also FIVE-SUIT BRIDGE.)

A more modest change reintroduced in 1964 and embodied in special decks used in the World Team Olympiad was to use a very pale blue-green tint instead of white for the background of the faces. This has been shown to reduce eyestrain. These cards with special backs have been used in World Championship competition in 1967, 1968, and 1969. For information on early cards and different packs, see HISTORY OF PLAYING CARDS; PACK; TAXES; TAROT.

MARCUS CUP. A board-a-match open team award, donated by friends in memory of Edward N. Marcus, of Boston, 1953. This event replaced the FABER CUP and is contested at the Summer Nationals, under which heading past results are listed.

MARK MEMORIAL TROPHY. A trophy donated in memory of Dr. Louis Mark. It is presented annually at the Spring Nationals, as part of the ACBL charity program, to the ACBL unit which has raised the largest amount of money in proportion to the size of its membership.

MARKED CARD. See DAMAGED CARD.

MARMIC SYSTEM. An Italian system, apparently obsolete, whose name is derived from the first names of the inventors (MARio Franco and MIChele Giovine). It is probably the most unusual system ever played in serious international competition by a major bridge country, and in some respects was a forerunner of the ROMAN SYSTEM. The chief feature was that a player was expected to pass in first or second position with balanced distribution and 16½–19 points. The same principle applied after an opponent's opening bid, and in each case the passer's partner was expected to balance with 5 points or more. This opened the possibility for trap passing by the opponents, and the system was amended to provide an opening one no trump bid, instead of the strong pass, at unfavorable vulnerability.

Other features of the system were:

(1) One club opening, with step responses by points. A very strong hand, or a normal opening with clubs, or an obligatory third- or fourth-hand opening with 5 points or more.

(2) One diamond opening, forcing with step responses. A natural hand with diamonds, or a very strong hand.

(3) One heart or one spade openings. Natural and limited (12–16).

(4) One no trump. 12–14 and balanced except at unfavorable vulnerability.

(5) Two clubs. A three-suiter with 13–16.

(6) Two diamonds. A three-suiter with 17 or more points.

(7) Weak two-bids in the major suits.

(8) Two no trump and three no trump opening bids pre-emptive with strong suits.

(9) Jump overcalls. Strong two-suiter in the unbid suits.

MARX TWO CLUBS. An alternate name, especially in England, for the STAYMAN convention. Originated by Jack Marx approximately at the same time as American counterpart devised by G. Rapee and S. Stayman.

MASTER. A player of some competence in the AMERICAN CONTRACT BRIDGE LEAGUE. See RANKING OF PLAYERS.

MASTER CARD. The highest unplayed card of a suit. It can also be thus characterized while actually being played.

MASTER HAND. The hand which controls the situation—more particularly, the one which controls the trump suit, leading out high trumps to prevent adverse ruffs, and retaining a trump or two to prevent the adverse run of a long side suit. It is usually the declarer's hand, but sometimes, when the declarer's trumps are more valuable as ruffers, the dummy is made the master hand. See DUMMY REVERSAL.

MASTER POINT. The unit which measures bridge achievement in tournament play.

The term first arose when eligibles for the ABL's 1934 von Zedtwitz Master Pairs (later Life Master Pairs) were chosen from a list of players credited with "master points" for winning tournaments run by the ABL and the AWL, as well as the Vanderbilt and Eastern Championships which at that time were independent events. In the following year, winners of many smaller tournaments that had applied for ABL sanction became eligible. To offset this rapid and somewhat haphazard inflation of "masters," in 1936 the League created the rank of LIFE MASTER, then awarded only to those who had won their points in national championships or the equivalent. These point awards were tiny. At the outset, 10 points was the qualifying minimum, and a scheme for deducting points each year made it necessary for Life Masters to continue successful competition in order to retain their status. Deductions were discontinued in 1944.

Meanwhile, the USBA announced its own master-point program and appears to have been the first to extend the idea to the club level. Effective Sept. 1, 1935, City Master Points were awarded for duplicate games in USBA-affiliated clubs. These were convertible at 10 for 1 into State Master Points, awarded for citywide tournaments, which were in turn convertible at 10 for 1 into National Master Points, awarded for State tournaments. A legal dispute over the ABL's claim of exclusive right to award "master points" was not resolved until 1937, when the USBA was merged into the ABL, becoming the ACBL. The ACBL introduced Rating Points (later called Fractional Master Points), worth $^1/_{100}$ of a master point, into club games effective Jan. 1, 1938. The result was a rapid acceleration in the growth of League membership, but it also led to the eventual need to distinguish among points won at local, regional, and national levels.

Reciprocal acknowledgment agreements have been reached between the ACBL and the ABA to enable their members to participate in Masters events in either organization.

Duplicate bridge was probably the first competitive recreational activity to develop a national system of rating for all its players. It was instituted in 1936, when a number of players were nominated as LIFE MASTERS.

For several years players were charged a fee for registering points. This was abandoned in favor of charging clubs and other organizations for the privilege of issuing certificates.

England adopted a master-point scheme in 1956, and was followed by many other countries. In most of these schemes the scales of awards are less generous, and the achievement of high rank is usually slower. Points won in foreign bridge leagues may be converted to ACBL Master Points under certain conditions. See GOLD POINTS; MASTER-POINT PLAN; RED POINTS; REGIONAL AND NATIONAL POINTS.

MASTER-POINT CERTIFICATE. See RATING POINTS.

MASTER-POINT PLAN. The method of awarding master points in bridge tournaments at club, sectional, regional, and national levels. Creation of the Master-Point Plan in 1936 must be credited to W. MC KENNEY and Ray EISENLORD, with many others contributing to later developments. The details of the method by which the plan operates at the club level are set out in the ACBL HANDBOOK.

Any club or group in the United States, Canada, Bermuda, or Mexico may apply for a franchise to issue master points at regularly scheduled duplicate games. The clubs are of three types: Open (to all

comers); Invitational (restricted to members of the group and invited guests); and Novice (restricted to players with not more than a stipulated number of master points).

The ACBL publishes an annual directory of clubs, which enables members to find bridge activity in any city they may visit.

Rating points must be awarded at every duplicate game conducted by a franchised club. Rating points are hundredths of a full point. The scale for invitational clubs is lightly lower; and novice clubs (or games) score at an even lower scale.

Once each calendar quarter a weekly club is entitled to a Club Tournament game with greatly increased rating point awards. Those clubs meeting less frequently are entitled to a Club Tournament for every 12 regular scheduled sessions.

At club tournament level and higher, events can be of various types: Open Pair; Mixed Pair; Men's Pair; Women's Pair; Individual; and team events of various kinds. The scale of awards increases steadily through the various levels— club, sectional, regional, and national. The highest award for any single event is given to the winners of the VANDERBILT and SPINGOLD championships, and to the winners of the Blue Ribbon Pairs Championship and Life Master Pair Championship. See also AMERICAN CONTRACT BRIDGE LEAGUE; DUPLICATE BRIDGE; DUPLICATE TOURNAMENT; FRANCHISED CLUBS; RANKING OF PLAYERS.

MASTER TOURNAMENT. An event or series of events at a bridge tournament where the requirements for entry into the competition include the holding of a high master-point rating. For most of the championship events in the Spring Nationals of the American Contract Bridge League, a rating of National Master is required; in the Summer Nationals, that of Senior Master. In the Open Pairs events, the top flight is frequently limited to Life Masters. See RANKING OF PLAYERS.

MASTERS MEN'S PAIRS. See MOUSER TROPHY.

MASTERS WOMEN'S PAIRS. See SMITH TROPHY.

MATCH. A session or event of head-to-head competition between two teams of four or more players.

The shortest matches in international competition were the 18-board qualifying round matches in the 1964 WORLD TEAM OLYMPIAD. The longest matches were played for the BERMUDA BOWL, from 1951 to 1957, when there were only two teams in competition, and 224 to 256 boards were played. Even longer matches have been played on semi-official occasions. See ANGLO-AMERICAN MATCHES.

MATCH PLAY. A team-of-four contest in which two teams are competing for an appreciable number of boards. Tactics at match play are described in IMP TACTICS and STATE OF MATCH.

MATCH POINT. A credit awarded to a contestant in pair or individual events for a score superior to that of another contestant in direct competition.

The number of match points available to a contestant is normally one less than the number of contestants in direct competition. For example, in a game of thirteen rounds there are thirteen North-South scores in direct competition and thirteen East-West scores in direct competition. The highest score in each group beats the other twelve scores in that group, and receives 12 match points, the greatest number available to it.

Other pairs receive 11, 10, 9 points, etc., according to the number of pairs beaten in direct competition. The lowest pair in each group beats no pair in direct competition and receives 0 match points.

When two or more pairs achieve identical scores, each pair receives ½ match point for each pair with which its score is tied (see Law 74, LAWS OF DUPLICATE).

When match-point scoring is used in team games, the score that is obtained by a team on a board is 1 match point if the score is plus, 0 if the score is minus, and ½ if the team score is neither plus nor minus. (Each board is thus scored as a match in itself, hence "board-a-match" scoring.) See also DOUBLE TOP; SCORING ACROSS THE FIELD.

MATCH-POINT BIDDING. If bridge were played double-dummy (if one could see all four hands whenever one had to make a decision), the bidding and play would be exactly the same at match-point duplicate as at rubber bridge. A minor exception is caused by the scoring of honors at rubber bridge. If one could see only partner's hand, the bidding would usually be the same. The objective on any one hand is the same for both forms of bridge: to score the maximum number of points or to allow the opponents to score a minimum number. Yet successful match-point tactics are quite different from successful rubber bridge tactics. For example, suppose the bidding, with both sides vulnerable, has gone as follows:

SOUTH	WEST	NORTH	EAST
1 ♡	Pass	2 ♡	Pass
Pass	?		

West holds:

♠ Q 9 8 x x
♡ x
◇ A x x x
♣ Q 10 x

The opponents' lack of enterprise marks East with at least 8 points, perhaps as many as 14. He may or may not fit West's hand. At either rubber or duplicate, West should bid two spades when East holds:

♠ K J x x
♡ x x x
◇ K J x
♣ K x x

West should pass when East holds:

♠ x
♡ K J 10 x
◇ J x x x
♣ K x x x

Since West does not know which type of hand his partner has, he must consider what he has to lose or gain by bidding. The best probable result from bidding is that East-West, instead of North-South, will make a part-score. This is equivalent to approximately a 250-point gain. A part-score is worth an additional 50 points at rubber bridge, the same as at duplicate. The worst likely result is a 500- or 800-point penalty. Which is more likely to occur? Surely the former.

A reopening two spade bid would probably work out as follows: Four times in ten the opponents would bid and make three hearts, in which case the reopening bid would have neither lost nor gained.

Four times in ten it would gain. Perhaps East-West would be plus 140 instead of plus 100, plus 110 instead of minus 110, minus 100 instead of minus 110, or plus 100 instead of minus 110 (because the opponents bid again).

The other two times the reopening bid would lose, perhaps quite heavily. The net loss from these two occasions would be greater than the gain from the other four.

In rubber bridge, it would not pay to reopen with a weak suit because, in the long run, a reopening bid would lose points. In duplicate, a reopening bid is advisable. This is true whether most of the other West players would bid or not, but it is easier to demonstrate if the potential reopener were a lone wolf. Passing would result in an average score, 6 match points out of 12. Whenever the reopening bid should gain, it would result in a top; whenever it should lose, it would result in a bottom. At rubber bridge, it is necessary to weigh the *amount* of gain against the *amount* of loss when considering any action. In duplicate, the main consideration is the *frequency* of gain or loss. The following hand illustrates a similar principle, except that the mystery is in regard to the opponents' holdings rather than partner's.

WEST	EAST
♠ A 10 x	♠ K Q x x
♡ 10 x	♡ x x
◇ A K J x	◇ Q 9 x x x x
♣ Q 10 9 x	♣ A

At rubber bridge, the bidding might well be as follows:

SOUTH	WEST	NORTH	EAST
Pass	1 ◇	Pass	1 ♠
Pass	2 ♠	Pass	4 ◇
Pass	5 ◇	Pass	Pass
Pass			

East has a good enough hand to be almost certain that five diamonds will be safe. Besides, a slam is still possible from his point of view. Consequently, he shows his excellent diamond support while still allowing West to return to spade with four-card spade support.

At duplicate, the bidding should start the same way, but East would probably bid four spades over the raise to two. A slam is unlikely, and with such a good four-card spade suit, East would not want to "risk" a final diamond contract. Perhaps the word "risk" seems unusual here, but at duplicate five diamonds is a much poorer gamble, hence a greater risk, than is four spades. At least 75% of the time, East-West will do better in spades than in diamonds; they cannot afford to "play safe" when the odds favor the more dangerous contract. This is true despite the fact that the gain in playing spades cannot exceed 20 to 50 points, while the loss, when the spades break badly, or the opening diamond lead is ruffed, can be several hundred points.

It has been stated that the same contract usually would be chosen at duplicate as at rubber bridge if one could see partner's hand. The following is an exception. Even the reason for the exception is that bridge is not a double-dummy game.

WEST	EAST
♠ A x	♠ x x
♡ A x x	♡ x x
◇ K Q J x x	◇ A x x
♣ 10 8 x	♣ A Q J 9 x x

The ideal contract at rubber bridge is seven clubs—despite the fact that the odds are slightly *against* making it! To simplify this discussion, assume that the diamonds are not 5–0, and the slam depends merely upon the club finesse. Normally two-to-one odds are needed to justify a grand slam bid, but these odds are based on the assumption that a small slam is safe. In this case, with a major suit lead, declarer will take either eleven or thirteen tricks, never twelve. By bidding seven, half the time declarer will score 1,440 or 2,140 points. At rubber bridge, a non-vulnerable game is worth approximately 300 points, even though no points are scored till the rubber is completed. When the club finesse fails, he will score minus 100 or minus 200. By bidding seven, he will average plus 670 not vulnerable or plus 970 vulnerable. This is better than he can score at any other contract.

Why is seven clubs not the ideal contract for duplicate also? The reason is that it will be very difficult, if not impossible, to get to *any* slam. The best contract is six clubs. Just bidding six, and making seven, will be good for a top board when no one else is in a slam. If the club finesse fails, down one may still be worth some points since the three no trump bidders may also be down one.

It is time to move on from theory to some practical applications.

SOUTH	WEST	NORTH	EAST
1 ♡	Pass	1 NT	Pass
2 ◇	Pass	?	

What should North bid with the following?

♠ Q 10 x
♡ 10 9 x
◇ J 10 x x
♣ Q J x

At rubber bridge, the answer is clear-cut. Pass, for two reasons. Two diamonds should be safer than two hearts, especially if South has only four hearts. Also, if North bids two hearts, South may bid again, while a pass will prevent him from doing so. Surely *two* diamonds will be safer than *three* hearts. Since game is out of the question, one should stop in the safest contract.

With	♠ x x x	or	♠ A x x
	♡ Q x x		♡ Q 10
	◇ K Q x x		◇ K x x
	♣ x x x		♣ x x x x x

a false preference for two hearts would be sound tactics at rubber bridge because game is still fairly likely.

At duplicate, a return to two hearts is advisable on all three hands. In the last two cases, the reason is the same as for rubber bridge: Game is still possible, and if opener has to pass, the hand may play as well (or within one trick as well) at hearts as at diamonds. In the first case, the reason is different. The hope is that opener will pass, and that he will pick up an extra 10 or 20 points in hearts. Quite frequently he will get too high or be defeated by a bad break, but the risk is justifiable because the odds are right.

SOUTH	WEST	NORTH	EAST
1 ♡	Pass	1 ♠	Pass
?			

What should South bid with:

♠ K x x
♡ A K x x x
◇ A 10 9 x
♣ x

At rubber bridge, the correct bid is surely two diamonds. Unless North can bid again, there will be no game. If he does bid again, the delayed spade support will describe this hand perfectly: a pretty good hand, three-card spade support, and a singleton club. This sequence has the best chance to indicate whether the two hands fit, whether they belong in game, and what the best game (or slam!) contract will be. For example, with:

♠ A x x x x
♡ 10 x
♢ K J x
♣ x x x

North would pass a raise to two spades, but would gladly bid four over the more descriptive sequence. Furthermore, responder would keep the bidding open by taking a false preference of two hearts over two diamonds with the hand just described—at rubber bridge.

At duplicate, South should raise to two spades immediately. North might have to pass either a two spade or a two diamond bid, and if so, two spades would surely be the better duplicate contract. The superior results at part-score contracts compensate for less efficient game and slam bidding since part-scores are just as important as games or slams at duplicate. When each hand is worth as much as another, one cannot afford to adopt a style of bidding which is bad for the part-score hands and good only for games and slams. Besides, there are hands such as the last example where responder would pass a two diamond rebid *at duplicate* (rather than risk an inferior part-score contract by giving a false preference) even though he would always bid again at rubber bridge. Competitive bidding is more competitive at duplicate. The first hand of this article illustrated a situation where it was advisable to reopen at duplicate and advisable to sell out at rubber bridge. It would be just as disastrous to let the opponents play two hearts when one could make two spades as it would be to take an 800-point set.

Dealer: North
Vulnerable: Both

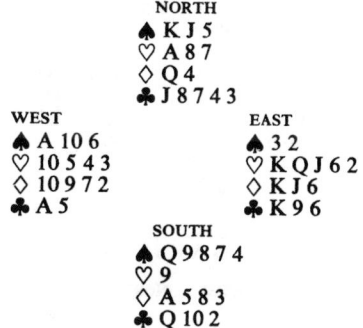

NORTH
♠ K J 5
♡ A 8 7
♢ Q 4
♣ J 8 7 4 3

WEST
♠ A 10 6
♡ 10 5 4 3
♢ 10 9 7 2
♣ A 5

EAST
♠ 3 2
♡ K Q J 6 2
♢ K J 6
♣ K 9 6

SOUTH
♠ Q 9 8 7 4
♡ 9
♢ A 5 8 3
♣ Q 10 2

SOUTH	WEST	NORTH	EAST
		Pass	1 ♡
Pass	2 ♡	Pass	Pass
2 ♠	3 ♡	3 ♠	Pass
Pass	Dbl.	Pass	Pass
Pass			

East-West must defend carefully to defeat three spades. As the cards lie, they can make four hearts. There are several interesting features about the bidding. The opening bid and raise were routine. So was the two spade bid—at duplicate. West properly bid three hearts since he had a maximum raise. The first questionable bid was North's raise to three spades. Usually, when the opponents are pushed one trick higher by a reopening bid, the percentage bid is to pass in all close situations. The reopener has already inferred from the opponents' bidding that his partner has high cards, and his partner has no business bidding again to show these same high cards. He should bid again only with good distribution or cards exceptionally well placed. The result from passing should be no worse than at other tables where someone failed to reopen, and it will be better when the opponents have been pushed beyond their depth. However, North's questionable bid would have gained him a top if West had not doubled. West knew that he would get a very poor score, perhaps 2 match points out of 12, if North-South should make exactly three spades. Consequently a double could not cost more than 2 match points. On the other hand, if North-South should make exactly eight tricks, it would be extremely costly not to double. West actually has a good defensive hand, and is tempted to double anyway; he would double with a poorer hand than he actually has. At rubber bridge a double which could convert a part-score into game would need about seven-to-one odds in its favor.

In duplicate, a double is sometimes the percentage bid even when the odds are *against* defeating the contract. Suppose, for example, that East-West were to bid four hearts over three spades. North-South are doomed to get a bottom anyway, since presumably other pairs will not bid game. So a double won't cost them a thing. If the hands were changed slightly so that four hearts could be defeated, a double would gain a few points, since plus 200 is better than North-South could do in spades. With nothing to lose and everything to gain, a double must be the right bid. If a double can lose only 2 points and may gain 9 or 10, it is a good gamble, even when one expects the contract to be made.

Another way it pays to be more competitive in duplicate is taking sacrifices. For example, suppose the bidding has gone as follows:

SOUTH	WEST	NORTH	EAST
1 ♡	Pass	3 ♣	Pass
3 ♢	Pass	3 ♡	Pass
4 NT	Pass	5 ♡	Pass
7 ♡	Pass	Pass	?

Only North-South are vulnerable, and East holds

♠ Q J 10 9
♡ x x
♢ x x x
♣ J 10 x x

At rubber bridge, he has no problem. It would be foolish to take a deliberate 2,100-point sacrifice to save a measly 110 points. The opponents are not infallible, and partner may win a trick with the queen of diamonds. At duplicate it is very tempting, and probably correct, to bid seven spades. North-South are unlikely to bid seven no trump with their unbalanced hands, and if they do, there is a good chance of setting them. The real problem is whether most North-South pairs will bid a grand slam. If not, minus 2,100 would be a bad result, and it is better to gamble on defeating seven hearts, just the same as at rubber bridge.

The more common dilemma is whether or not to take a sacrifice against a game contract. In rubber bridge, it is losing tactics to take a deliberate 500-point sacrifice against a vulnerable game when there is any reasonable hope of defeating it. In duplicate, the sacrifice is correct if the contract is a normal one and a favorite to make.

M. M.

MATCH-POINT DEFENSE. Defense at duplicate is often more difficult than at rubber bridge. In the latter, the objective is clear-cut: try to set the contract. It makes little difference when declarer makes an overtrick through an unsuccessful attempt to defeat him. At duplicate, the overtrick makes a great deal of difference.

of diamonds. At duplicate the right play is not clear-cut, but cashing the ace is probably correct. It loses in only two situations, and it gains (a trick) much more frequently—whenever declarer has the two red kings.

Suppose that West is on lead with:

♠ Q J 10 9
♡ A 7 8
♢ 9 5 3
♣ 7 5 2

After the following bidding:

SOUTH	WEST	NORTH	EAST
		1 ♣	Pass
2 ♢	Pass	2 NT	Pass
3 ♣	Pass	3 ♠	Pass
5 ♢	Pass	6 ♢	All Pass

North apparently has the king of hearts; South probably has two hearts. The best chance to set the contract is to lead a low heart, and hope that East has the queen and that either North or South has the jack. If that situation exists, declarer may misguess. The low heart lead is not correct at duplicate because it stands too good a chance of giving away an overtrick. The opponents may have both the king and queen of hearts, or they may be missing the queen *and* jack (in which case declarer would have to play dummy's king).

The defense against unusual contracts may be just as interesting as the play of unusual contracts.

Vulnerable: North-South

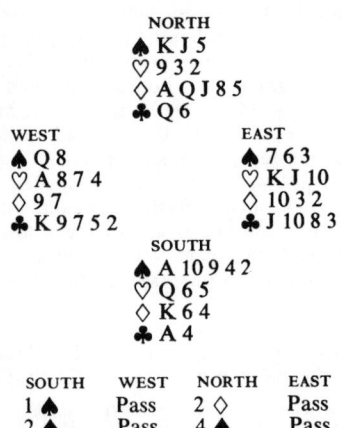

WEST leads a small club, won by dummy's queen. Declarer plays the king of spades, then takes a losing trump finesse to West's doubleton queen. What should West do? At rubber bridge, he should lead a low heart. This play will set the contract whenever it can be set—when East has king-queen-small or king-jack-ten of hearts; also when he has jack-ten-nine of hearts and the king

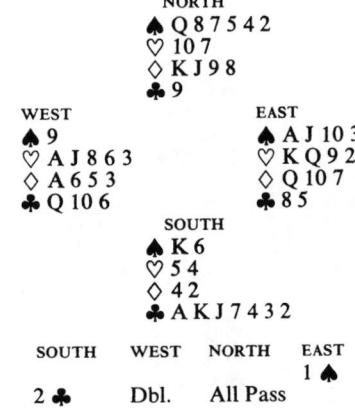

West's double is a gambling bid made only because of the favorable vulnerability. West leads his singleton spade, and ruffs the low spade return. At this point West can reconstruct the unseen hands almost card for card. Since East opened a four-card spade suit, he almost surely has four hearts. The queen of diamonds is necessary for the opening bid, and besides, East would have returned the jack or ten of spades as a suit preference signal if his diamonds were ten-high. West can see that four hearts is cold and easy to reach. Therefore he must gamble on a two-trick set. He does so by underleading the ace of diamonds. This play risks letting declarer make his contract, but the risk must be taken since plus 200 would be a poor result anyway. After stripping declarer's red cards, East will lead another spade to promote West's queen of trumps.

Suppose the hands were the same, but with neither side vulnerable, South overcalls four clubs. West doubles, of course, and the defense starts out the same way. This time West should not risk underleading the ace of diamonds. Plus 500 will be almost as good as plus 700, but plus 300 would be a bottom.

Another way in which the defense at duplicate varies from the defense at rubber bridge is that the defenders can take advantage of declarer's greed.

NORTH

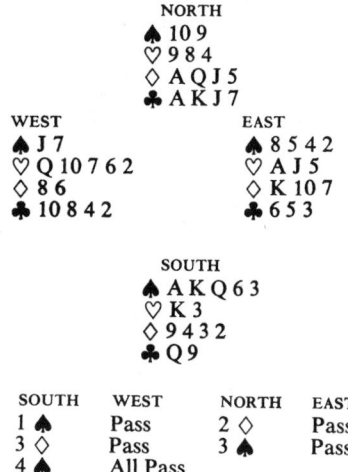

SOUTH

SOUTH	WEST	NORTH	EAST
1 ♠	Pass	2 ◇	Pass
3 ◇	Pass	3 ♠	Pass
4 ♠	All Pass		

The bidding is not recommended, but that is the way it went. West led the deuce of clubs, won by declarer's nine. He cashed three top spades and took the diamond finesse, which won. Dummy's clubs were now cashed for heart discards; East also discarded a heart on the last club. Declarer then ruffed a heart with his next-to-last trump in order to repeat the diamond finesse. This time the finesse lost. East cashed the good eight of spades, and the defenders took the remaining tricks. Down one!

Did East make the right play in refusing the first diamond finesse, or was he just lucky? By playing cautiously, declarer could have made an overtrick after East's duck. However East had a psychological factor working in his favor. Declarer risked his contract when he took the diamond finesse. If he wanted to play safe, he would have cashed his clubs first for heart discards. He did not play the hand this way because he was afraid of being stuck in the dummy, unable to take the diamond finesse. Since de-

clarer has risked his contract to take the diamond finesse, it would be inconsistent for him not to play to repeat the finesse, so as to make his apparently successful gamble pay off.

M. M.

MATCH-POINT DUPLICATE, MATHEMATICS OF. See MATHEMATICS OF MATCH-POINT PLAY.

MATCH-POINT PLAY. In duplicate play, the test for deciding between various alternatives is not how much (in total points) a given play could gain or lose, but how many match points it could gain or lose. (But see IMP TACTICS for a discussion of this specialized branch of duplicate play.) When the contract is a normal one, this means, "Does the play have better than a 50% chance of success?"

NORTH

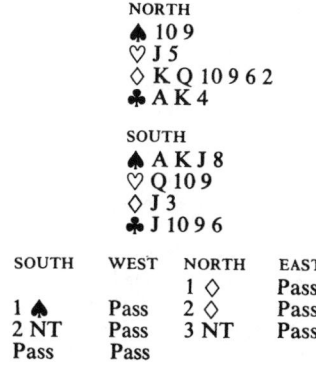

SOUTH

SOUTH	WEST	NORTH	EAST
		1 ◇	Pass
1 ♠	Pass	2 ◇	Pass
2 NT	Pass	3 NT	Pass
Pass	Pass		

The opening lead is the four of hearts to East's king. West ducks the seven of hearts return, playing the deuce. It is almost certain that three more heart tricks will be run by the opponents as soon as the lead is lost. Combined with the trick already lost and the ace of diamonds, that is one too many. At rubber bridge, the proper play would be to try for four spade tricks and four club tricks without touching the diamonds. Declarer's chances would not be good, but it would be worth a try with so much to gain, so little to lose. In duplicate, there is much more to lose. Down one should be almost an average board, while down two would surely be a cold bottom. The odds are greater than three to one that attacking the black suits will lose a trick rather than gain a trick, which means that playing to make the hand will result in three bottom boards for every top. When the odds are so unfavorable, it is better to play safe for eight tricks. The fact that the contract is for nine tricks is immaterial, since it is the contract everyone will reach.

Following is another example illustrating the same principle. In this case, however, declarer does not deliberately refuse to try to make his contract. He merely adopts a risky line of play which gives him a good opportunity for over-tricks.

```
              NORTH
              ♠ 7 5
              ♡ K 4
              ◇ A K 10 9 7 6
              ♣ A J 4

              SOUTH
              ♠ A 10 8
              ♡ A 10 7
              ◇ J 5
              ♣ 10 8 7 5 2
```

SOUTH	WEST	NORTH	EAST
		1 ◇	1 ♠
1 NT	Pass	3 NT	All Pass

A spade is led, and declarer holds up until the third trick, upon which West discards a heart. The correct rubber bridge play would be to attack the diamonds by cashing the ace and king. If West has the queen, it is unnecessary to finesse, since West has no spade to return, and only five diamonds tricks are needed. On the other hand, a losing finesse to East's singleton or doubleton queen would be disastrous. In duplicate, the better play is to take a first-round diamond finesse. This play will gain (a trick) approximately twice as often as it will lose (several tricks).

The finesse gains if West holds Q843, Q842, Q832, Q432, Q84, Q83, Q82, Q43, Q42, Q32 (ten distributions). The finesse loses if East holds Q, Q8, Q4, Q3, Q2 (five distributions). Each three-two division is slightly more likely than each four-one distribution.

Both the contracts shown were quite normal. It is proper to jeopardize one's normal contract when the odds are favorable. When a contract is exceptionally good, it is proper to play safe, just as at rubber bridge.

A hard-to-reach game or slam, or a doubled contract, would be an example of a good contract. When just making the contract will be worth 10 match points out of 12, only exceptionally good odds would justify jeopardizing the contract for an overtrick.

Some of the most interesting problems arise in the play of unusual contracts at duplicate.

Dealer: North
North-South Vulnerable:

```
              NORTH
              ♠ A 10 6 4 2
              ♡ 8 5
              ◇ Q 2
              ♣ Q 5 3 2

              SOUTH
              ♠ K J 9 5
              ♡ 4 2
              ◇ A K 10 9 3
              ♣ 6 4
```

SOUTH	WEST	NORTH	EAST
		Pass	1 ♡
1 ♠	4 ♡	4 ♠	Pass
Pass	Dbl.	Pass	Pass
Pass			

North's four spade bid was a bit odd, considering the vulnerability, and many South players would fail to overcall with a four-card suit. It is safe to say that four spades doubled will not be played at any other table, and down two will be a bottom, not even a tie for bottom. West leads the queen of hearts, followed by the jack. Next he plays the ace of clubs followed by the jack of clubs to East's king (dummy playing low). East returns the deuce of diamonds, and West does not cover the ten. The only problem is how to play the trump suit for no losers. If the spades are split 2–2 and the diamonds no worse than 4–2 the opponents cannot make four hearts; consequently minus 200 would be a bottom. Declarer must base his play on the assumption that four hearts can be made, and a singleton spade is more likely than a singleton diamond. It appears that West has five clubs to his partner's two, so if anyone has a singleton spade, it will be West. The proper play is to lead to the ace and finesse East for the queen. This works, since the four hands are as follows:

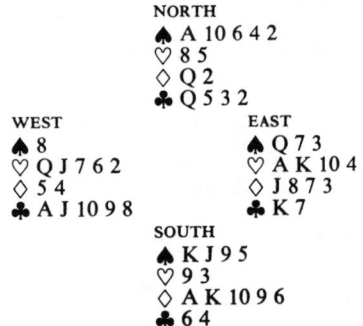

```
              NORTH
              ♠ A 10 6 4 2
              ♡ 8 5
              ◇ Q 2
              ♣ Q 5 3 2
WEST                         EAST
♠ 8                          ♠ Q 7 3
♡ Q J 7 6 2                  ♡ A K 10 4
◇ 5 4                        ◇ J 8 7 3
♣ A J 10 9 8                 ♣ K 7
              SOUTH
              ♠ K J 9 5
              ♡ 9 3
              ◇ A K 10 9 6
              ♣ 6 4
```

Suppose that the four hands and bidding were changed slightly. The only difference in the bidding is that the four-spade contract is not doubled.

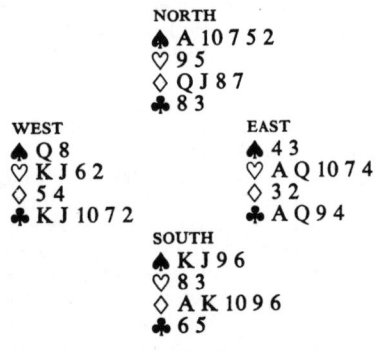

```
              NORTH
              ♠ A 10 7 5 2
              ♡ 9 5
              ◇ Q J 8 7
              ♣ 8 3
WEST                         EAST
♠ Q 8                        ♠ 4 3
♡ K J 6 2                    ♡ A Q 10 7 4
◇ 5 4                        ◇ 3 2
♣ K J 10 7 2                 ♣ A Q 9 4
              SOUTH
              ♠ K J 9 6
              ♡ 8 3
              ◇ A K 10 9 6
              ♣ 6 5
```

The defenders take the first four tricks in hearts and clubs, then exit with a diamond. Should declarer play the same as before? The fact that he is not doubled enables him to make an unusual type of safety play. He should bang down the ace and king of spades. If the queen does not fall, he doesn't care, because he knows that four hearts is cold, and minus 200 will be a good sacrifice. What he does not want to risk is a minus 200 when, as here, the opponents can only make three hearts. Minus 100 will beat all the minus 140 scores.

Dealer: South
East-West Vulnerable

NORTH
♠ 7 6 2
♡ K 7 6 2
◇ K 5 4 2
♣ 5 2

SOUTH
♠ K 3
♡ A Q 4 3
◇ Q J 3
♣ J 8 6 3

South opens with a weak no trump, and the other players pass. West leads the four of spades to East's ace. East returns the jack, and West plays the deuce. Before planning the play, declarer should evaluate his contract, and try to determine what other pairs in direct competition will be doing. If they buy the bid, most of them will be playing hearts. They will score 110 or 140, depending upon how the hand breaks. It is impossible to do as well at no trump as at hearts, no matter how badly the opponents defend, so the only hope to salvage the board is that the opponents can make something. Sure enough, North-South have a maximum of five defensive tricks against spades, and perhaps only three or four, depending upon the distribution. Since it is not possible to beat the pairs playing in hearts, the proper attitude is to forget about them and to concentrate on beating the pairs defending against spades. If North-South were vulnerable, it would be necessary to steal a diamond trick somehow—minus 200 would be no good at all. But not vulnerable, North-South can afford a two-trick set. Minus 100 should be just as good as minus 50. The proper play is not to try to steal anything, but just to hope that the hearts will break so that five tricks can be cashed. The whole hand is as follows:

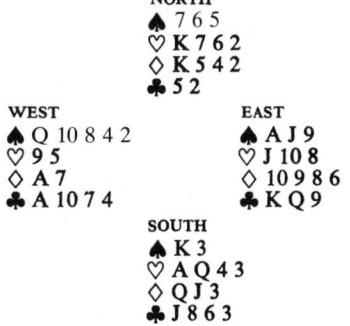

NORTH
♠ 7 6 5
♡ K 7 6 2
◇ K 5 4 2
♣ 5 2

WEST
♠ Q 10 8 4 2
♡ 9 5
◇ A 7
♣ A 10 7 4

EAST
♠ A J 9
♡ J 10 8
◇ 10 9 8 6
♣ K Q 9

SOUTH
♠ K 3
♡ A Q 4 3
◇ Q J 3
♣ J 8 6 3

At most tables, South opens with a suit bid, and West plays two or three spades after an overcall and a raise by his partner. Minus 100 is an excellent result for North-South, but minus 150 would be a bottom.

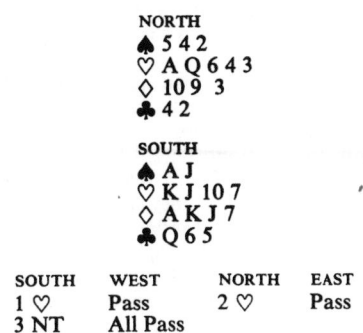

NORTH
♠ 5 4 2
♡ A Q 6 4 3
◇ 10 9 3
♣ 4 2

SOUTH
♠ A J
♡ K J 10 7
◇ A K J 7
♣ Q 6 5

SOUTH	WEST	NORTH	EAST
1 ♡	Pass	2 ♡	Pass
3 NT	All Pass		

West leads the king of spades. How should declarer play this contract? The first question is what will happen at the other tables. It seems quite likely that most of the field will be playing at four hearts. With the same spade lead, the declarers in four hearts will either make five by discarding a club on the fourth diamond, or be down one if the diamond finesse fails. What are the prospects in no trump? To make four or be down several if the diamond finesse fails. That is, down several if the finesse *is attempted* and fails. The only chance for a decent board is not to take the diamond finesse, and to hope that it does not work. If it does not work, down at three no trump will tie the field, which will be down one at four hearts. If the queen happens to be a doubleton, offside, refusing the finesse will result in an overtrick and a top.

NORTH
♠ K 6 5
♡ K 7
◇ 7 5 3 2
♣ 8 5 4 3

SOUTH
♠ A J 10 9 3
♡ A 8 4
◇ A Q
♣ A 10 6

The opening lead against three no trump is a small diamond, East playing the jack. At this point, nine tricks are cold, and an overtrick is made if declarer guesses the spades right. How many tricks will the four-spade bidders take? Presumably they will not get a diamond lead, and they will take nine or ten tricks, depending upon how they guess the spades. Nine or ten tricks can be taken at no trump, depending upon the spade guess. Nine tricks at no trump beat nine tricks at spades; ten tricks at no trump beat ten tricks at spades. If declarer can guess the spades the same way as the declarers playing four spades, he will automatically get a good result. The normal play in spades is to ruff the third round of hearts, then play the king of spades and finesse the jack on the next round. Playing at no trump, declarer should also finesse through East by playing the king and finessing the jack.

Suppose that East had played the king of diamonds at the first trick. Declarer would have the same nine or ten tricks at no trump as before, but with the diamond finesse working, the four spade bidders would take ten or eleven tricks, depending upon how they guess spades. The only chance for a good result at no trump would be to guess the spades right while the spade bidders guess wrong. Their normal play in spades would be the same whether the diamond finesse works or not. Since they will play East for the queen of spades, the no trump declarer should play West for the queen.

In the last example, the proper play depended upon what happened at the first trick. When the opening lead gave declarer a trick, he played one way. When it did not, he played another way. It happened that declarer was more concerned about beating declarers in another contract than beating declarers in his own contract. However, the opening lead also has an important influence upon the play of "normal" contracts.

NORTH
♠ J 10 5 2
♡ 6 3 2
◇ K Q 10 6
♣ A 3

SOUTH
♠ A Q 7 4 3
♡ A 7 4
◇ J 3 2
♣ Q 2

SOUTH	WEST	NORTH	EAST
1 ♠	Pass	2 ◇	Pass
2 ♠	Pass	3 ♠	Pass
4 ♠	Pass	Pass	Pass

West leads a club, a small card is played from dummy, and when East produces the jack, declarer wins with the queen. How should declarer play the spades? Normally he would take a finesse. However, the lead was very favorable. It gave declarer a trick he could never have won by himself. With a heart lead, declarer would have to be lucky to make four, and he would have no chance for more. Now he has a virtual cinch for contract and an overtrick. Rather than risk a losing spade finesse and a heart return before the diamonds are established, declarer should cash the ace of spades, and knock out the ace of diamonds. After the favorable lead, declarer should not jeopardize his advantage.

NORTH
♠ 8 3 2
♡ 7 6 3
◇ A J 10 5 4
♣ Q 6

SOUTH
♠ A 7 6
♡ A K
◇ Q 9 3
♣ A K J 10 5

SOUTH	WEST	NORTH	EAST
2 NT	Pass	3 NT	Pass
All Pass			

Surely every pair in the room will arrive, somehow, at three no trump. West goes into a long study, and finally leads the four of spades. Apparently West had no clear-cut lead, but he made a good guess. Without a spade lead, declarer would be cold for twelve or thirteen tricks, depending upon the diamond finesse. Should declarer hold up two rounds so as to shut out the thirteenth spade if the diamond finesse loses? He should not! If the diamond finesse is doomed to a poor result by West's fortunate lead. On the other hand, if South wins immediately and if the diamond finesse works, he will still take thirteen tricks. For that matter, the correct play at duplicate is probably to win the first trick even when West leads the king. Winning the first trick will always be worth a top or tie for top when the king of diamonds is on side. Therefore it is clearly the best play half the time. Even when the diamond finesse loses, declarer may tie with pairs who have held up, but not long enough. Holding up one round is best only when the finesse is off and East has a doubleton spade; holding up two rounds will lose to all other lines of play when the diamond finesse works, and it will be worth a top only when East has three spades with the king of diamonds.

M. M.

MATCH-POINT SCORING. In duplicate tournaments match-point scoring makes each board of equal importance with any other board, whether the hand involved is a part-score competitive bidding situation or a grand slam. Most pair tournaments are scored by match points. Most team contests and occasional important pair events are scored by IMPs, which make larger swings possible on big hands, and approach the tactics of rubber bridge. See DUPLICATE SCORING for the details of scoring procedures. For a fuller discussion of the effect of match-point scoring on bidding and play tactics, see MATCH-POINT BIDDING; MATCH-POINT PLAY; SHOOTING. See DUPLICATE BRIDGE for a full listing of the technical aspects of tournament organization. For the origins of the duplicate method, see HISTORY OF BRIDGE. See also LAWS OF DUPLICATE, Laws 72–76.

MATCH RECORDS. See HAND RECORD; BIBLIOGRAPHY, G.

MATHE ASKING BID. A method of locating a singleton in a hand that has responded with a limit jump major raise, devised by Lew MATHE of Los Angeles. Used principally by partnerships that use limit jump raises to promise a side singleton, the Mathe asking bid is opener's rebid of the cheapest denomination after responder's limit raise. If the suit that has been established is spades, responder simply bids four of the suit in which he has a singleton. If hearts is the agreed suit, responder rebids three no trump if he has a singleton spade, or bids his minor suit singleton.

Mathe Asking Bids may also be used where the limit raise has not guaranteed a singleton.

MATHEMATICAL ASSUMPTIONS. In all calculations of odds or probabilities, certain assumptions are made. The accuracy of an answer depends upon the validity of the assumptions. A condition that is taken for granted is that the pack has been sufficiently shuffled so that all possible deals are equally probable. Under the heading ODDS GOVERNING SPECIFIED CARDS, paragraph 7(b), is an example of another assumption that is specifically mentioned in the discussion.

Many controversies arise because the parties fail to mention the assumptions they make. By listing these clearly, the cause of dispute is often immediately apparent. An example is the following:

NORTH
5 4 3 2

SOUTH
A K 10 9 8

On the play of the ace, West plays the jack, and East the six. Dummy is entered and the three is led, East playing the seven. Should the king be played or the finesse taken? Only two cases have to be considered:

(a) Where West originally held
            QJ   52.17%   22C11
(b) Where West originally held
            J   47.83%   22C12
(the notation 22C11 can be read: the number of combinations of 22 things taken 11 at a time).

We can make any of the following assumptions:
(1) With queen-jack, West will always play the jack. In this case, playing for the drop is a 52% chance.
(2) With queen-jack, West will always play the queen. In this case, the finesse is a 100% chance (a sure thing).
(3) With queen-jack, West will play either honor indiscriminately. This means that in the 52.17% of the cases when he held the queen-jack, he will have played the queen 26% of the time, and the jack 26% of the time. When he has the singleton jack, he is bound to play it all 48% of the times. The odds are thus 24 to 13 in favor of the finesse.

Assumption (3) is based on a postulate to Bayes's Theorem, published over two hundred years ago, providing that in the absence of knowledge to the contrary, we assume that all prior probabilities are equal. It is the assumption a player should make in normal circumstances. See OPTIMUM STRATEGY; RESTRICTED CHOICE; SUIT COMBINATIONS.

A. T. and R. T

MATHEMATICAL TABLES. The tables below give a variety of information. When a percentage given is less than $1/10,000$ of 1%, the number of zeros before the first significant figure is indicated in parentheses. Thus 0.(6)3 should be read as .0000003.

TABLE 1

Probable Percentage Frequency of Distribution Patterns

This table may be used to determine percentages of various distribution patterns, both for hand patterns and suit patterns. Figures are expressed in percentage of hands. The percentage expectation of a particular pattern with the suits identified is given in the last column. For example, the chance that a given player has four spades, four hearts, three diamonds, and two clubs is 1.796%.

Pattern	Total	Specific
4–4–3–2	21.5512	1.796
4–3–3–3	10.5361	2.634
4–4–4–1	2.9932	0.748
5–3–3–2	15.5168	1.293
5–4–3–1	12.9307	0.539
5–4–2–2	10.5797	0.882
5–5–2–1	3.1739	0.264
5–4–4–0	1.2433	0.104
5–5–3–0	0.8952	0.075
6–3–2–2	5.6425	0.470
6–4–2–1	4.7021	0.196
6–3–3–1	3.4482	0.287
6–4–3–0	1.3262	0.055
6–5–1–1	0.7053	0.059
6–5–2–0	0.6511	0.027
6–6–1–0	0.0723	0.006
7–3–2–1	1.8808	0.078
7–2–2–2	0.5129	0.128
7–4–1–1	0.3918	0.033
7–4–2–0	0.3617	0.015
7–3–3–0	0.2652	0.022
7–5–1–0	0.1085	0.005
7–6–0–0	0.0056	0.0005
8–2–2–1	0.1924	0.016
8–3–1–1	0.1176	0.010
8–3–2–0	0.1085	0.005
8–4–1–0	0.0452	0.002
8–5–0–0	0.0031	0.0003
9–2–1–1	0.0178	0.001
9–3–1–0	0.0100	0.0004
9–2–2–0	0.0082	0.0007
9–4–0–0	0.0010	0.(4)8
10–2–1–0	0.0011	0.(4)4
10–1–1–1	0.0004	0.0001
10–3–0–0	0.00015	0.(4)1
11–1–1–0	0.(4)2	0.(5)2
11–2–0–0	0.(4)1	0.(5)1
12–1–0–0	0.(6)3	0.(7)3
13–0–0–0	0.(9)6	0.(9)2

TABLE 1A

Probable Frequency of High Card Content

This table gives the expectancies of having specific point counts, using the 4–3–2–1 count.

Point Count	%	Point Count	%
0	.3639	16	3.3109
1	.7884	17	2.3617
2	1.3561	18	1.6051
3	2.4624	19	1.0362
4	3.8454	20	.6435
5	5.1862	21	.3779
6	6.5541	22	.2100
7	8.0281	23	.1119
8	8.8922	24	.0559
9	9.3562	25	.0264
10	9.4051	26	.0117
11	8.9447	27	.0049
12	8.0269	28	.0019
13	6.9143	29	.0007
14	5.6933	30	.0002
15	4.4237	31–37	.0001

(a)	(b)	(c)	(a)	(b)	(c)
	6-6-1	1.414		5-2-1	12.727
	8-4-1	0.884		5-3-0	3.590
1	5-4-3	40.377		4-4-0	2.493
	6-4-2	14.683		6-1-1	1.414
	6-3-3	10.767		6-2-0	1.305
	5-5-2	9.911	6	3-2-2	33.939
	4-4-4	9.347		4-2-1	28.282
	7-3-2	5.873		3-3-1	20.740
	6-5-1	4.405		4-3-0	7.977
	7-4-1	2.447		5-1-1	4.242
	8-3-1	0.734		5-2-0	3.916
	8-2-2	0.601		6-1-0	0.870
2	4-4-3	26.170	7	3-2-1	53.333
	5-4-2	25.695		2-2-2	14.545
	5-3-3	18.843		4-1-1	11.111
	6-3-2	13.704		4-2-0	10.256
	6-4-1	5.710		3-3-0	7.521
	5-5-1	3.854		5-1-0	3.077
	7-3-1	2.284	8	2-2-1	41.211
	7-2-2	1.869		3-1-1	25.185
	6-5-0	0.791		3-2-0	23.247
3	4-3-3	27.598		4-1-0	9.686
	5-3-2	27.096		5-0-0	0.671
	4-4-2	18.817	9	2-1-1	48.080
	5-4-1	11.290		3-1-0	27.122
	6-3-1	6.021		2-2-0	22.191
	6-2-2	4.927		4-0-0	2.608
	7-2-1	1.642	10	2-1-0	66.572
	6-4-0	1.158		1-1-1	24.040
	5-5-0	0.782		3-0-0	9.388
4	4-3-2	45.160	11	1-1-0	68.421
	5-3-1	13.548		2-0-0	31.579
	5-2-2	11.085			

TABLE 2

Probability of Holding an Exact Number of Cards of a Specified Suit

This table gives the probability (a priori, before dealing) of holding an exact number of cards in a specified suit. The number of times the specified number of cards can be expected in any suit in the course of 100 deals is four times as great.

Number of Cards	%
0	1.279
1	8.006
2	20.587
3	28.633
4	23.861
5	12.469
6	4.156
7	0.882
8	0.117
9	0.009
10	0.0004
11	0.(5)9
12	0.(7)8
13	0.(9)16

TABLE 3

Probability of Distribution of Cards in Three Hidden Hands

This table gives probability of distribution of the remaining cards in a suit for a one-hand holding in column (a) among the other three hands, column (b) expressed as a percentage column (c). For brevity, probabilities of less than half of 1% are omitted.

(a)	(b)	(c)	(a)	(b)	(c)
0	6-4-3	25.921		3-3-3	11.039
	5-4-4	24.301		4-4-1	9.408
	5-5-3	17.497		6-2-1	4.927
	6-5-2	12.725		5-4-0	2.605
	7-4-2	7.069		6-3-0	1.390
	7-3-3	5.184	5	3-3-2	31.110
	8-3-2	2.121		4-3-1	25.925
	7-5-1	2.121		4-2-2	21.212

TABLE 4

Probability of Distribution of Cards in Two Hidden Hands

This table gives the probability of distribution of cards in two given hands. Column (a) shows number of cards in the two known hands; column (b) shows the number of outstanding cards in the two hidden hands; column (c) the ways in which these cards may be divided; column (d) shows the percentage of cases in which the distribution in column (c) occurs, followed by a bracketed figure showing the number of cases applicable. By dividing the percentage in column (d) by the bracketed figure, the probability that one opponent will hold particular specified cards of that remainder can be obtained.

(a)	(b)	(c)	(d)	
11	2	1–1	52	(2)
		2–0	48	(2)
10	3	2–1	78	(6)
		3–0	22	(2)
9	4	3–1	49.74	(8)
		2–2	40.70	(6)
		4–0	9.57	(2)
8	5	3–2	67.83	(20)
		4–1	28.26	(10)
		5–0	3.91	(2)
7	6	4–2	48.45	(30)
		3–3	35.53	(20)
		5–1	14.53	(12)
		6–0	1.49	(2)
6	7	4–3	62.17	(70)
		5–2	30.52	(42)
		6–1	6.78	(14)
		7–0	0.52	(2)
5	8	5–3	47.12	(112)
		4–4	32.72	(70)
		6–2	17.14	(56)
		7–1	2.86	(16)
		8–0	0.16	(2)
4	9	5–4	58.90	(252)

(a)	(b)	(c)	(d)
		6–3	31.41	(168)
		7–2	8.57	(72)
		8–1	1.07	(18)
		9–0	0.05	(2)
3	10	6–4	46.20	(420)
		5–5	31.18	(252)
		7–3	18.48	(240)
		8–2	3.78	(90)
		9–1	0.35	(20)
		10–0	0.01	(2)
2	11	6–5	57.17	(924)
		7–4	31.76	(660)
		8–3	9.53	(330)
		9–2	1.44	(110)
		10–1	0.10	(22)
		11–0	0.002	(2)
1	12	7–5	45.74	(1584)
		6–6	30.49	(924)
		8–4	19.06	(990)
		9–3	4.23	(440)
		10–2	0.46	(132)
		11–1	0.02	(24)
		12–0	0.0003	(2)
0	13	7–6	56.62	(3432)
		8–5	31.85	(2574)
		9–4	9.83	(1430)
		10–3	1.57	(572)
		11–2	0.12	(156)
		12–1	0.003	(26)
		13–0	0.(4)2	(2)

TABLE 4A

Probability of Distribution of Two
Residues between Two Hidden Hands

A residue is said to be favorably divided when it is divided as evenly as possible, e.g., 8 cards divided 4–4 or 7 cards divided 4–3. In this table, column (a) shows the number of cards outstanding in each of the two suits in the two hidden hands; column (b) shows the percentage of cases in which both residues will divide as evenly as possible; column (c) shows the percentage of cases in which at least one residue will divide favorably.

(a)	(b)	(c)
8–8	11.87%	53.57%
8–7	21.77	73.13
8–6	12.44	55.81
8–5	23.10	77.45
8–4	13.86	59.56
7–7	40.42	83.93
7–6	23.10	74.60
7–5	43.31	86.69
7–4	25.99	76.88
6–6	13.20	57.86
6–5	24.75	78.61
6–4	14.85	61.37
5–5	46.75	88.90
5–4	28.05	80.47
5–3	53.29	92.53

TABLE 5

Tables of Combinations (Values for nCr)

In making mathematical computation involving bridge (see MATHEMATICS OF BRIDGE), the formula nCr appears frequently. Since the formula involves factorial numbers, the computation is tedious (13 ! means 13 x 12 x 11 x 10 x 9 x 8 x 7 x 6 x 5 x 4 x 3 x 2 x 1). Values of nCr appear in the table below.

TOTAL NUMBER FROM WHICH
COMBINATIONS CAN BE TAKEN

r	2	3	4	5	6
2	1				
3	3	1			
4	6	4	1		
5	10	10	5	1	
6	15	20	15	6	1
7	21	35	35	21	7
8	28	56	70	56	28
9	36	84	126	126	84
10	45	120	210	252	210
11	55	165	330	462	462
12	66	220	495	792	924
13	78	286	715	1287	1716
14	91	364	1001	2002	3003
15	105	455	1365	3003	5005
16	120	560	1820	4368	8008
17	136	680	2380	6188	12376
18	153	816	3060	8568	18564
19	171	969	3876	11628	27132
20	190	1140	4845	15504	38760
21	210	1330	5985	20349	54264
22	231	1540	7315	26334	74613
23	253	1771	8855	33649	100947
24	276	2024	10626	42504	134596
25	300	2300	12650	53130	177100
26	325	2600	14950	65780	230230

	7	8	9	10
7	1			
8	8	1		
9	36	9	1	
10	120	45	10	1
11	330	165	55	11
12	792	495	220	66
13	1716	1287	715	286
14	3432	3003	2002	1001
15	6435	6435	5005	3003
16	11440	12870	11440	8008
17	19448	24310	24310	19448
18	31824	43758	48620	43758
19	50388	75582	92378	92378
20	77520	125970	167960	184756
21	116280	203490	293930	352716
22	170544	319770	497420	646646
23	245157	490314	817190	1144066
24	346104	735471	1307504	1961256
25	480700	1081575	2042975	3268760
26	657800	1562275	3124550	5311735

22C11 = 705432	25C11 = 4457400
23C11 = 1352078	25C12 = 5200300
23C12 = 1352078	25C13 = 5200300
24C11 = 2496144	26C11 = 7726160
24C12 = 2704156	26C12 = 9657700
24C13 = 2496144	26C13 = 10400600

TABLE 6

Sundry Odds

Various odds have been of interest to bridge players for many years. Below are a number of different possibilities, with odds computed.

Number of different hands a named player can receive
     52C13   635,013,559,600

Number of different hands a second named player can receive
     39C13   8,122,425,444

Number of different hands the third and fourth players can receive
     26C13   10,400,600

Number of possible deals
$52! \div 13!^4$
53,644,737,765,488,792,839,237,440,000

Number of possible auctions with North as dealer, assuming that East and West pass throughout
$2^{36} - 1 = 68,719,476,735$

Number of possible auctions with North as dealer, assuming that East and West do not pass throughout
$(4 \times 22^{35} - 1) \div 3 = 128,745,650,347,030,683,-$
120,231,926,111,609,371,363,122,697,557

Odds against each player having a complete suit
2,235,197,406,895,366,368,301,559,999 to 1

Odds against each player receiving identical hands except for difference of suit

♠ A K Q	♠ J 10 9	♠ 8 7 6	♠ 5 4 3 2
♡ J 10 9	♡ 8 7 6	♡ 5 4 3 2	♡ A K Q
◇ 8 7 6	◇ 5 4 3 2	◇ A K Q	◇ J 10 9
♣ 5 4 3 2	♣ A K Q	♣ J 10 9	♣ 8 7 6

Approx.: 55,976,427,337,829,109,025 to 1

Odds against receiving a hand
AKQ AKQ AKQ AKQJ
the J being in any of the four suits:
158,753,389,899 to 1

Odds against a YARBOROUGH
Approx. 1,827 to 1

Odds against both members of a partnership receiving Yarboroughs
546,000,000 to one

Odds against a hand with no card higher than 10
274 to 1

Odds against a hand with no card higher than jack
52 to 1

Odds against a hand with no card higher than queen
11 to 1

Odds against a hand with no aces
slightly more than 2 to 1

Odds against being dealt four aces
Approx. 378 to 1

Odds against being dealt four honors in one suit
Approx. 22 to 1

Odds against being dealt five honors in one suit
Approx. 500 to 1

Odds against being dealt at least one singleton
Slightly over 2 to 1

Odds against having at least one void
Approximately 19 to 1

Odds that two partners will be dealt 26 named cards between them, e.g., all the red cards.
495,918,532,948,103 to 1 against

Odds that no players will be dealt a singleton or void
Approximately 4 to 1 against

Odds that four specified cards will be cut by the four players
270,724 to 1 against

MATHEMATICAL VALUE OF GAME. See VALUE OF GAME.

MATHEMATICAL VALUE OF PART-SCORE. See PART-SCORE BIDDING.

MATHEMATICS OF BRIDGE. The mathematics of bridge runs the gamut from simply counting the number of cards in one's hand up to involved problems of probability theory. Some examples of the application of mathematics to bridge are:

(1) Bidding systems, methods, and conventions. Use may be made of the frequency with which various patterns occur (see MATHEMATICAL TABLES, Table 1).

A bidder will also find it valuable to know the ways in which the outstanding cards are likely to be divided among the three hidden hands. We may wish to determine the probability that a trick will not be lost in a suit in which we have a particular holding. It can be determined from Table 3 that with A K Q J x x there is a nearly 94% probability that no trick will be lost, but with AKQxxxx, the probability is only 84%.

(2) Sacrifice bidding.

(3) Choice among part-score, game, and slam. These are dependent on EXPECTATION, and of course, on correctly estimating the value of the players' hands.

(4) Percentage play. This is shown in MATHEMATICAL TABLES, Table 4.

(5) Safety play. This is governed by expectation. See SUIT COMBINATIONS.

(6) Countering false cards (see DECEPTION, MATHEMATICS OF; FALSECARDING).

To express and solve such mathematical problems are used the ordinary arithmetic symbols, and also the following two.

n! (read, n factorial), meaning that one multiplies all the numerals starting at 1, up to and including the number represented by n.

nCr (read, the number of combinations in which n things can be selected r at a time). Thus 52C13 is the number of different hands of 13 cards that can be dealt to a single player from a pack of 52 cards. The formula for finding this is:

$$\frac{n!}{(n-r)! \times r!} \quad \text{or} \quad \frac{52!}{39! \times 13!}$$

Applications of this formula are, among others,

(a) NUMBER OF POSSIBLE HANDS. DEALS
(b) The number of cards held in a suit
(c) Hand patterns
(d) ODDS GOVERNING SPECIFIED CARDS

The following headings also cover facets of mathematics of bridge: CARDS, NEUTRAL AND POSITIVE; DECEPTION, MATHEMATICS OF; EXPECTATION; HAND PATTERNS; MATHEMATICAL ASSUMPTIONS; BIBLIOGRAPHY, M; MATHEMATICS OF MATCH-POINT PLAY; NUMBER OF

POSSIBLE HANDS, DEALS; ODDS, IN BRIDGE; OPTIMUM STRATEGY; PERCENTAGE PLAY; PROBABILITIES, A POSTERIORI; PROBABILITIES, A PRIORI; PROBABILITY OF SUCCESSIVE EVENTS; SUIT, NUMBER OF CARDS IN; VALUE OF GAME.

A. T. and R. T.

MATHEMATICS OF DECEPTION. See DECEPTION, MATHEMATICS OF.

MATHEMATICS OF MATCH-POINT PLAY. The values of a game do not apply to duplicate at match points. A non-vulnerable game is always worth 300, a vulnerable game, 500, and a part-score 50 points, as opposed to the generally assumed values of 350, 500, or 700, and 100 points at rubber bridge.

This is particularly applicable to SAFETY PLAYS. In match-point duplicate, a safety play is used only if the distribution to be guarded against has a probability of more than 50%. Of course, if the contract is an excellent one that only a few other other competitors will arrive at, any safety play that will ensure it is used; similarly if the contract is a very bad one, the best chance to make a good score is that better contracts will be defeated by unusual distribution, so any possible safety play is used. For other considerations at match-point play, see MATCH-POINT BIDDING, MATCH-POINT PLAY, and MATCH-POINT DEFENSE.

MAX or MAXIMUM. The greatest number of tricks which can be made with any holding. However, "to play for the maximum" may be used technically to indicate the line of play which will produce the maximum average number of tricks in the long run. The term is used in this sense in the article on SUIT COMBINATIONS.

MAXIMAL OVERCALL DOUBLE. A type of COMPETITIVE DOUBLE used to invite game when the auction is too crowded for any other approach. The following situation is typical:

SOUTH	WEST	NORTH	EAST
1 ♠	2 ♡	2 ♠	3 ♡
?			

South may have a hand with which he wishes to sign off in three spades or a hand worth a game invitation. Either hand can be described if the maximal overcall double is used as a conventional bid inviting game and the three spade bid is reserved for use as a sign-off.

If the enemy competition is not in the "maximum" suit (the one just below South's), however, maximal overcall doubles are not needed if the partnership has agreed that opener's bid in the available side suit constitutes a general game try:

SOUTH	WEST	NORTH	EAST
1 ♠	2 ♢	2 ♠	3 ♢
?			

Here South can bid three hearts (conventional, forcing) to invite game in spades and bid three spades to sign off, so some advocates of maximal overcall doubles prefer to use this double for penalties. See also COMPETITIVE DOUBLES.

MAYONNAISE. Variant of GOULASH.

McCABE ADJUNCT. See WEAK TWO-BID.

McKENNEY. Standard term in Great Britain for the SUIT PREFERENCE signal, named for William McKenney of the American Contract Bridge League, who helped popularize it.

McKENNEY-BALDWIN MOVEMENT. One of a series of pair and individual movements planned by William E. McKenney and worked out by Russell J. Baldwin, then respectively secretary and tournament director of the American Bridge League.

The most widely used were two-session pair movements for 16 to 32 pairs, in which each contestant played against each of the others in the course of two sessions, with approximately balanced comparisons. One session consisted of an Appendix Scrambled Mitchell and the other of an interwoven Howell. Other movements were arranged for individual contests, and for pair contests of more than two sessions.

McKENNEY SIGNAL. See SUIT PREFERENCE.

McKENNEY TROPHY. The trophy presented to the ACBL member who has accumulated the most MASTER POINTS during the calendar year. It was donated by the USBA in recognition of W. E. McKenney. Winners are:

1937	C. H. Goren	1956	T. Stone
1938	M. Elis	1957	E. Kaplan
1939	M. D. Maier	1958	L. B. Harmon
1940	M. Elis	1959	O. Jacoby
1941	H. Sobel	1960	R. Jordan
1942	H. Sobel	1961	O. Jacoby
1943	C. H. Goren	1962	O. Jacoby
1944	H. Sobel	1963	O. Jacoby
1945	C. H. Goren	1964	H. Baron
1946	S. Silodor	1965	P. Rank
1947	C. H. Goren	1966	P. Pender
1948	C. H. Goren	1967	B. Crane
1949	C. H. Goren	1968	P. Soloway
1950	C. H. Goren	1969	P. Soloway
1951	C. H. Goren	1970	H. Baron
1952	B. Crane	1971	B. Crane
1953	W. Rosen	1972	Dr. J. Fisher
1954	D. Carter	1973	B. Crane
1955	N. Kay	1974	K. Shuman
		1975	B. Crane

MEAN SCORE. A score computed for a board at duplicate play, from which IMPs can be determined. See INTERNATIONAL MATCH POINTS (for pair games).

MECHANICS OF BRIDGE. Described in sections I, II, and III of the LAWS.

MEDIUM CARDS. The lower honor cards and the higher spot cards, those which provide BODY in long suit holdings or in support of a partner's bid suit.

MEMBER. (1) Of a table: one of the players constituting a table at rubber bridge, whether actively playing or awaiting re-entry to the table for the next rubber, or round of Chicago; (2) of a team: a player whose name was listed on the official entry blank whether actively playing or not (see RESERVE PLAYER); (3) of the ACBL: a person who has joined one of the geographical units chartered by the ACBL; see BYLAWS OF THE ACBL; (4) of a club: a player who is eligible to compete in duplicate play at clubs that are not open to all members of the ACBL.

MEMBERSHIP LIMIT. Table membership is limited to six players, unless exactly seven players are present (LAWS, "Rules for Club Procedure," Section F), and no player may be a member of two tables simultaneously. In order to make up tables with greater flexibility, many of the larger bridge clubs use HOUSE PLAYERS in order to be able to accommodate members as they arrive. For precedence in play at a table, see CUT IN.

MEMORY DUPLICATE. See REPLAY DUPLICATE.

MENACE. See THREAT CARD.

MEN'S PAIR CHAMPIONSHIP, NATIONAL. See WERNHER TROPHY.

MEN'S PAIRS. An event at duplicate competition between pairs of players, all of whom are men. Master-point awards are 20% lower than those for events of comparable size and duration open to all players. At most sectional tournaments, the men's pair event is held on Friday afternoon.

MEN'S TEAM CHAMPIONSHIP, NATIONAL. See GOREN TROPHY.

MENTAL PLAY. It is trite but true that hand valuation is "mental play." To estimate the trick-winning value of his hand, the player must foresee the conditions that will obtain when the cards are actually played. The better the player, the more accurate his valuation; for he can foresee only those plays which he can actually execute.

NORTH
♠ Q 10 2
♡ 10 8
♢ A Q J 6
♣ Q 10 8 2

WEST
♠ A
♡ A 6 5 3
♢ 9 7 5 3 2
♣ K J 6

EAST
♠ 8 7 5 3
♡ Q J 9 7 2
♢ —
♣ 9 5 4 3

SOUTH
♠ K J 9 6 4
♡ K 4
♢ K 10 8 4
♣ A 7

South dealt, both sides were vulnerable, and the bidding went:

SOUTH	WEST	NORTH	EAST
1 ♠	Pass	2 ♢	Pass
3 ♢	Pass	3 ♠	Pass
4 ♠	Dbl.	Pass	Pass
Pass			

South went for 1,100, and what valuation system could rate West's hand highly enough to predict even a one-trick defeat of the contract?

But because of North's diamond bid and South's diamond raise, West expected his partner to have at most a singleton in diamonds. West could therefore open a diamond; regain the lead on the first round of trumps; lead a second diamond for his partner to trump; and get in once again with the ace of hearts to give his partner a second ruff.

West's double was based upon mental play of a most elaborate sort, tantamount to a play-by-play forecast. But such a forecast is largely an unconscious and automatic one, for West did not repeat the series of plays to himself. He knew that a trump stopper and a quick entry outside, combined with a singleton in his partner's hand, add up to four tricks, and four tricks are enough to warrant doubling.

West opened the nine of diamonds, a suit-preference signal indicating that he preferred a heart to a club return. His hopes were more than realized when East was able to trump on the first round, not the second.

East read the suit-preference signal and led back the queen of hearts. South played low; there was not the remotest chance that East had the heart ace, and South did not wish to create two heart entries for West in case West had AJ. So the queen of hearts won the trick.

East continued with the heart jack, and West took his ace, then led the deuce of diamonds for East to trump.

The next lead by East was a club, and South had a problem because he could not see his opponents' hands and could not know that his play would make no difference. If East had started with only three spades, and if West had the club king (as indicated by his leading the diamond two, another suit-preference signal) South could save a trick by putting up his club ace and leading trumps. If East had the club king, South might save two tricks by playing his low club.

South decided to play his club ace and lead a spade. West took his spade ace, gave East a third diamond ruff, and won his king of clubs for the defenders' seventh trick.

The process of valuation by "mental play" permitted not only the diamond lead that gave the defenders a four-trick set but also West's double, which gained at least 700 points for the defenders.

MERRIMAC COUP. The deliberate sacrifice of a high card with the object of knocking out a vital entry in an opponent's hand, usually the dummy. Named after the *Merrimac,* an American coal-carrying ship sunk in 1898 in Santiago Harbor in an attempt to bottle up the Spanish fleet (often misspelled Merrimack, in confusion with the Civil War ironclad that fought the Monitor).

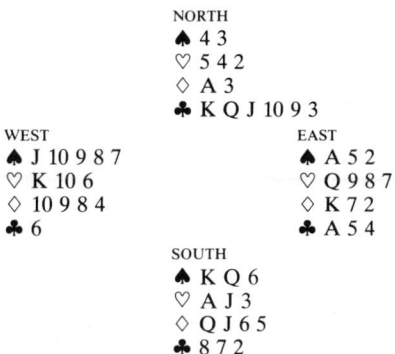

```
                    NORTH
                    ♠ 4 3
                    ♡ 5 4 2
                    ◇ A 3
                    ♣ K Q J 10 9 3
WEST                                    EAST
♠ J 10 9 8 7                            ♠ A 5 2
♡ K 10 6                                ♡ Q 9 8 7
◇ 10 9 8 4                              ◇ K 7 2
♣ 6                                     ♣ A 5 4
                    SOUTH
                    ♠ K Q 6
                    ♡ A J 3
                    ◇ Q J 6 5
                    ♣ 8 7 2
```

South is the declarer at a contract of three no trump. West leads the jack of spades which East wins with the ace. East at this point sees that the diamond ace is dummy's only entry after the club ace is knocked out, and East, realizing that this entry must be destroyed immediately, effectuates this by playing his diamond king to trick two. This defense holds declarer to eight tricks, and defeats the contract.

MEXICAN NATIONAL REGIONAL CHAMPIONSHIPS. A five-day tournament held in Mexico City, Mexico, beginning in 1955. This tournament became an annual event in 1964 when it acquired permanent Regional status. For past results, see Appendix II.

MEXICAN TWO DIAMONDS. A bid showing a balanced hand with 19–21 high-card points and 4–6 losers. A weak five-card major is permitted. Devised by Dr. G. Rosenkranz as a cornerstone of the ROMEX SYSTEM.

Negative responses (0–4 points) are: pass with diamond length; two hearts—transfer to two spades preparatory to a sign-off in clubs, hearts or spades (two hearts may also be a semi-positive with 5–6 points); two spades—transfer to two no trump.

Positive responses (7 points or more and game-forcing) include: Texas transfers; two spades—transfer to two no trump with 7–9 points, balanced distribution; two no trump—10 points or more, normally balanced; three of a suit—at least 10 points with a broken six-card suit. Responder's high-card requirements are reduced by 1 point for each five-card suit and by 2 points for a six-card major.

MEXICO. An independent member of the WORLD BRIDGE FEDERATION whose teams compete separately in the World Bridge Olympiad. Nationally and locally, however, Mexico's organized tournament bridge is conducted by two Units of the ACBL, and Mexican players are eligible to compete to represent North America on ACBL teams for the BERMUDA BOWL. The leading personality is Dr. G. Rosenkranz;

other players listed separately are F. D. Barroso, S. Dubson, C. Fua, R. C. Pike, Mrs. G. Rosenkranz.

MICHAELS CUE-BID. The use of an immediate cue-bid in the opponent's suit as a take-out double. Devised by the late M. MICHAELS of Miami Beach.

The bid is usually made with a two-suited rather than a three-suited hand:

```
♠ J 10 9 4 3          ♠ K Q 6 4
♡ A J 10 6 2          ♡ J 10 7 6 4
◇ 6                   ◇ A 4
♣ 8 7                 ♣ 8 7
```

If an opponent opens with a minor suit, the cue-bid is recommended with either of these hands unless the vulnerability is unfavorable. Over a minor suit the emphasis is on the major suits; there should be at least nine cards in the major suits and 6–11 points.

Over a major suit the cue-bid shows the unbid major suit and an unspecified minor suit:

```
♠ 7                   ♠ —
♡ Q J 10 9 5          ♡ 10 9 8 7 4
◇ 7 5                 ◇ A K J 6 2
♣ A J 10 6 2          ♣ Q 6 4
```

On each of these hands, two spades would be bid over one spade. If partner does not fit the unbid major, he can bid no trump as a request to the cue-bidder to show his minor suit.

The major-suit cue-bid is unlimited in point-count: the cue-bidder may have a strong hand, and plan to take further action.

Over either type of cue-bid, partner will usually bid the full value of his hand if there is a known fit; and in some circumstances he may put pressure on the opponents by making an advance sacrifice. He can also make use of a second cue-bid to ask for further definition of the cue-bidder's hand.

As with other devices which are partly obstructive, both the cue-bidder and his partner have to watch the vulnerability. At unfavorable vulnerability, freakish distribution is needed to make the cue-bid.

Defense. See DEFENSE TO TWO-SUITED INTERFERENCE.

MID-ATLANTIC CUP. For the charity event at the Summer National Championships. Presented by the Mid-Atlantic Bridge Conference in 1951.

MIDDLE CARD. The middle card of an original three-card holding. Generally referred to in connection with opening leads. See THREE SMALL CARDS, LEAD FROM.

MIDDLE GAME. The play, usually referring to the declarer's play, after the original lead or first few tricks won by the defenders, during which the plan of the play is developed, frequently leading to END PLAY positions or preparation for them. Aspects of the middle game are discussed in a number of articles listed under DEFENSE and DUMMY PLAY.

MIDDLE GAME FALSE-CARDING. See FALSE-CARDING.

MIDDLE SUIT. See DOUBLE MENACE.

MID-SOUTH SPRING REGIONAL CHAMPION-SHIPS. A five-day tournament held annually since 1941 in Western Tennessee or Alabama (and in past years Louisiana, Mississippi, and Arkansas). For past results, see Appendix II.

MILES CONVENTION. A convention devised by Marshall Miles of California, using a response of two no trump to a suit bid, followed by a natural rebid of four no trump to show a balanced hand with about 19 high-card points. Such a hand is difficult to describe using ordinary methods.

MILES RESPONSES TO TWO NO TRUMP OPEN-INGS. A method of responding to opening bids of two no trump devised by Mashall MILES of San Bernardino, Calif., to facilitate safe exploration for slams, games, or part-scores in any suit. The principal responses are as follows: Three clubs is STAYMAN; following a Stayman sequence, a four club rebid by responder is GERBER, and a four diamond rebid is a slam try that may be wholly artificial; JACOBY TRANSFER BIDS; jumps to the four-level are natural, showing a broken suit with slam interest; three no trump transfers to four clubs and promises a good suit, after which reponder may show a second suit if he has one; three spades transfers to three no trump, which responder may pass if he merely wanted to raise to game, or over which he may bid (1) four clubs to show a good diamond suit or a diamond-major two-suiter, (2) four of any other suit to show 4–4–4–1 distribution with shortness in the suit bid, or (3) four no trump to show 5–5 or longer in the minor suits.

MILES TROPHY. For the Masters Pair Championship (senior and advanced senior) at the Summer Nationals; donated by R. L. Miles, Jr., in 1950, for the Miles Masters Pairs, an event discontinued in 1954. Past winners are listed under Summer Nationals.

MILLER SLAM CONVENTION. On stronger hands there is an adjunct to the BOLAND CONVENTION advocated by M. M. Miller, Toronto, whereby one no trump—five clubs asks for precise point-count, five diamonds, five hearts, and five spades showing 16, 17, and 18 points respectively. It is forcing to a small slam, and a rebid by the five-club bidder of five no trump requires the opener to show his lowest four-card suit headed by a queen, or any five-card suit.

MINIMUM. A holding which justifies an original bid, response, or rebid with no high-card strength or distributional values in reserve. See BORDERLINE OPENING BIDS.

MINOR. A minor suit.

MINOR SUIT. Either of the two lower-ranking suits, diamonds or clubs.

MINOR SUIT STAYMAN. An artificial bid in response to an opening bid in no trump to explore for a minor suit game or slam or to determine whether or not no trump is playable. One such convention uses a two-diamond response to initiate the exploration. See TWO-WAY STAYMAN (2). An alternative is to use a two spade bid to ask about minor suits. If opener has four cards in one minor suit he bids that suit; if he has four cards in both minors he bids a major suit control; if he has no four card minor, he bids three no trump if he has no interest in a minor suit slam, or bids two no trump if he can tolerate further investigation. If responder rebids in a major suit he shows a singleton in that suit.

MINOR SUIT SWISS. A method devised by A. DORMER and T. REESE for use in conjunction with non-forcing minor suit jump raises, to show a strong hand in support of opener's minor suit without going past three no trump. In response to a one club opening, a jump to three hearts would show a very good club raise, and a jump to three diamonds would show a moderately good club raise. In response to a one diamond opening, a jump to three spades would show the very good raise and a jump to three hearts would show the moderately good raise. All these jumps are forcing either to three no trump or to four of opener's minor suit.

In determining which jump to make, principal emphasis is placed on the richness of responder's controls.

(a)	(b)
♠ x x	♠ A x
♡ K Q x	♡ x x x x
◇ K Q x x x	◇ K 10 x x x
♣ K x x	♣ A Q

Opposite a one diamond opening, responder would jump to three hearts with hand (a), and to three spades with hand (b). An alternative recommended by H. W. KELSEY is for responder not to attempt to distinguish between moderate and very good strength, but to choose among all three unbid suits and jump in the suit in which he holds the most secure stopper.

MINOR SUIT TEXAS. See SOUTH AFRICAN TEXAS.

MINOR TENACE. An original holding of king-jack (without the ace or queen) of a suit. After one or more rounds of a suit have been played, the second and fourth highest remaining cards of the suit in the hand of one player are also called a minor tenace. See TENACE.

MIRROR MITCHELL. See TEAM-OF-FOUR MOVEMENTS.

MISCOUNTING. A player who miscounts his points and later discovers the fact should beware of reacting in a revealing manner (see ACCIDENTS). When, as frequently happens, he has undervalued his hand slightly, he should beware of overbidding. Suppose a standard 16–18 point no trump is being used and the bidding proceeds:

WEST	EAST
1 NT	3 NT

If West now discovers that he holds 19 points, it would be foolish to make a further bid in the remote hope that a slam can be made. A bid of four no trump would suggest a holding of 3 or 4 more points than he had originally announced.

MISCUT. An illegal cut; a cut that leaves fewer than four cards in either portion of the deck.

MISDEAL. An imperfect deal, owing to an incorrect number of cards being dealt to any player, a card being exposed during the deal, etc. See LAWS (Laws 8–12); LAWS OF DUPLICATE (Laws 6, 13, 14).

MISFIT. A term used to describe a situation where two hands opposite each other in any given deal are unbalanced, each containing two long suits and extreme shortages or voids in its third and fourth suits, and further, where these lengths are met by shortages in the partner's hand and the short suits correspondingly met by lengths in the reverse hand. Where not even one four-four or better trump fit can be found in a set of twenty-six cards, the deal may be said to be a misfit as respects those two hands. An extreme example: North holds ♠ x ♡ x ◇ A Q x x x x ♣ A K x x x, while his partner was dealt ♠ A K x x x ♡ A Q J x x ◇ x ♣ x x. Even with 13 high-card points in one hand and 14 in the partner's, game is highly unlikely at any suit or no trump.

MISHEARING. For mishearing of a bid or called card there is no recourse. If a player is not sure what a previous bid was, he may and should ask for a review of the auction when it becomes his turn to bid. If left-hand opponent bids one spade, partner passes, and right-hand opponent bids four spades, a call of three diamonds is insufficient, even though the caller may have thought that right-hand opponent had bid two spades.

In the play, dummy should not put a card in the played position until he has ascertained that the card was specifically named by the declarer, and it is the declarer's duty to see that any card he has named is the one actually placed in the played position by the dummy. See ACCIDENTS.

MISNOMER. A bid or play improperly called. If a player bids one heart, for instance, when he meant to bid one spade, he may substitute his intended call if he does so without pause for thought; otherwise his call, if legal, stands, and if illegal, is subject to penalty. Should a player change a call after a pause, he is giving information to his partner to which his partner is not entitled, and a penalty under this provision should be enforced.

If a card is called by declarer from dummy in error, he may change the call if he does so without pause for thought, otherwise the called card, if a legal play, stands as the card played.

MISPLACED BYE STAND. A bye stand in a MITCHELL game with even number of tables placed at a position other than equidistant from the sharing tables. Adjustment can be made for a bye stand too near the head table or too far from it.

If the bye stand is too near, the game can proceed without change until the halfway mark; the next round is the correction round, and players should be warned of an unusual move. The first set of boards is placed on the bye stand, which is then placed in the proper spot. The highest set of boards does not move, but all other boards move down one table. East-West players make their normal move. The North-South players who have just finished playing the highest numbered boards, and the North-South players at the highest numbered table interchange for this round only (keeping their original table number after the correction round). During the correction round, and all subsequent rounds, the last two tables relay boards instead of the first and last tables. (During the correction round, the two interchanging North-South players play against the pairs they met on the first round, unavoidably.)

If the bye stand is too far, after the halfway mark, tables 1 and 3 relay boards instead of the relay between first and second tables. The final round can be omitted. For information on correcting errors in Mitchell games, see *Bridge Director's Manual,* by G. Beynon.

MISSING CARD. A card which is not in any of the four hands. If three of the four hands have a correct number of cards, and the fourth is deficient, and the fact is determined before play ends, a search for the card is conducted; if the card is located, it is deemed to have been in the hand which is deficient. In rubber bridge, if the card cannot be found, the hand is thrown out and a new deck of cards substituted. In duplicate, the director consults players who have played the hand, and a new deck is used to supply the board. When the missing card has either been found, or its denomination established, it is deemed to have been a member of the deficient hand, and may either be an exposed card or establish a discard on a previous trick as a revoke. See LAWS, (Law 11); LAWS OF DUPLICATE (Law 14).

MISSISSIPPI HEART HAND. A famous trick hand dating from the days of whist:

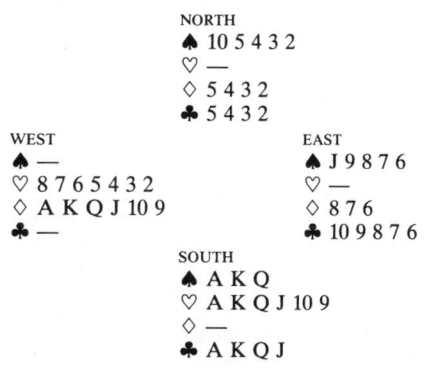

It will be seen that a diamond lead holds South to six tricks in a heart contract, and a game cannot be made in any denomination. South can make nine tricks in a spade contract, or ten tricks in a club contract.

An equivalent hand was given by Hoyle in 1747, and the modern version was given by Thomas Matthews in 1804. It was probably used by the card-sharps of the Mississippi River steamboats during the Civil War period, who hoped to persuade South to make a heavy bet on the odd trick with hearts as trumps. It grew in favor among the professional cheaters in the days of bridge whist. As doubling and redoubling could continue indefinitely, the odd trick in a low-stake game could become worth $10,000 (or as much as the client was considered good for) with the help of sufficient redoubles. Charles M. Schwab is reported to have paid off not less than $10,000 on this hand.

MISSORTING HAND. See ACCIDENTS.

MR. AND MRS. An event at a bridge tournament in which entries are limited to married couples, playing together. In England such a tournament has the name Flitch. When held, this event has been quite popular, particularly at tournaments held around St. Valentine's Day.

"MR. BRIDGE." A title conferred on Charles H. GOREN by the ACBL in 1969.

MITCHELL DIAMOND. A bidding system devised by Samuel M. STAYMAN and named for his frequent partner, V. MITCHELL. A one diamond opening is used for most strong hands worth 17–18 or more points. Other features are five-card major suit openings of limited strength, 16–17-point one no trump opening, a natural two diamond opening showing a five-card or longer diamond suit, and weak two bids in the major suits. The two club opening shows either a balanced hand worth 20–22 points or a hand worth an ACOL TWO-BID in a major suit. The two no trump opening shows a minor two-suiter. The one club opening is an all-purpose bid used for any hand of opening strength that does not fit any of the above bids.

MITCHELL-HOWELL MOVEMENT. A two-session pair movement, in which one session is played as a SCRAMBLED MITCHELL and the other as a twin or INTERWOVEN HOWELL.

Mitchell-Howell movements are available at the ACBL office for sixteen to thirty-eight pairs, and for forty-two pairs. Twinned twenties are used for forty pairs.

MITCHELL MOVEMENT. A method of play for duplicate whist originated by John T. Mitchell which has been continued through auction and contract. In the Mitchell movement, the North-South players remain stationary while the boards progress from table to next lower numbered table, and the East-West pairs move to next higher numbered tables at the completion of each round of play. The result of this type of movement is to divide each section in play into two fields which do not compete against each other but play separate contests. To produce one winner using this movement, see SCRAMBLED MITCHELL MOVEMENT.

In a Mitchell movement game, each pair takes as its number the table number at the table where they commence play for the first round, and boards are distributed, one set to each table for an odd number of tables. When there is an even number of tables in play, and it is desired to have as many rounds in play as there are tables in play, no boards are put on table 1, and a set of boards is left between tables after exactly half of the boards have been distributed. (For a twelve-table game, the extra set of boards is between tables 7 and 8; for an eight-table game, between 5 and 6; for a six-table game, between tables 4 and 5.) See BYE STAND. The balance of the boards are then distributed with the last set of boards on the highest numbered tables. Through the entire play, the boards at table 2 are relayed between tables 1 and 2, and at the end of each round, are passed to the highest numbered table. The boards at the table with the higher number above the bye stand are moved to the bye stand, and the lower numbered table gets its new boards from those previously at the bye stand.

If the game is not to play as many rounds as there are tables, and the game has an even number of tables, no bye stand is used. After half the rounds have been completed, the East-West players SKIP one table in their progression, with normal movement resumed after succeeding rounds have been played.

MIXED PAIR CHAMPIONSHIP, NATIONAL. See HILLIARD TROPHY; ROCKWELL TROPHY.

MIXED PAIRS. An event at duplicate competition between pairs, each of which has one man and one woman member. It is usually the most sociable of the events, and is held on Friday evening at most sectional tournaments.

MIXED TEAM CHAMPIONSHIP, NATIONAL. See BARCLAY TROPHY and LEBHAR TROPHY.

MIXED TEAM EVENTS. In tournaments in the United States, a mixed team is composed of four (occasionally five or six) players, who are obligated to compete at all times as two mixed pairs, one member of each partnership being of each sex. In the US formerly, and in some other countries still, a team is a mixed team if it has at least one member of opposite sex.

MIXING CARDS AFTER PLAY. Illegal if a claim has been made to inspect the cards for a revoke, or to ascertain honors or the number of tricks won or lost. See LAWS (Law 67).

MNEMONIC DUPLICATE. See REPLAY DUPLICATE.

MONACO SYSTEM. See RELAY SYSTEM.

MONSTER. A bridge hand of great trick-taking potential either because of a preponderance of high-card winners or because of concentrated strength in long suits and extreme shortness in weak suits. Also, a very big one-session score—a "big game."

MOREHEAD TROPHY. Donated by *The New York Times* in memory of its long-time bridge editor Albert H. Morehead. The trophy was originally awarded to the winners of a special knockout team event that followed the REISINGER team contest at the Fall Nationals in 1967, but was withdrawn when the event proved unpopular. The winners and runners-up were:

Winners	Runners-up
D. Rotman	G. Kendal
C. Peres	P. Munafo
S. Altman	F. Hoadley
M. Becker	N. Duvic
	P. Deal

Since 1973 the trophy has been awarded to the winners of the GRAND NATIONAL CHAMPIONSHIPS (2).

MOROCCO BRIDGE FEDERATION (FÉDÉRATION ROYALE MAROCAINE DE BRIDGE). Founded in Casablanca by M. Tazi Mohamed, in 1957, after independence was achieved by Morocco, succeeding the Moroccan unit of the Fédération Française de Bridge. In 1964 there were approximately 1,275 members, of whom more than half were in Casablanca. The Federation sponsors annual contests for teams and pairs.

MORTON'S FORK COUP. A maneuver by which declarer presents a defender with a choice of taking a trick cheaply or ducking to preserve an honor combination, only both decisions cost the defense a trick. If the defender wins the trick, he sets up another high card in the suit for declarer, while if he ducks, his winner disappears because declarer has a discard possibility. The name is derived from an episode in English history. Cardinal Morton, Chancellor under King Henry VII, habitually extracted money from wealthy London merchants for the royal treasury. His approach was that if the merchants lived ostentatiously, it was obvious that they had sufficient income to spare some for the king. Alternatively, if they lived frugally, they must be saving substantially and could therefore afford to contribute to the king's coffers. In either case, they were impaled on "Morton's Fork."

Dorothy Truscott gives this example of the coup:

```
                    NORTH
                    ♠ A Q 8 7
                    ♡ 5 4
                    ◊ Q 3 2
                    ♣ A 9 7 3
WEST                              EAST
♠ 2                               ♠ —
♡ K 10 9 8 3                      ♡ Q 7 6
◊ A J 8                           ◊ 10 9 6 5 4
♣ K Q 10 2                        ♣ J 8 6 5 4
                    SOUTH
                    ♠ K J 10 9 6 5 4 3
                    ♡ A J 2
                    ◊ K 7
                    ♣ —
```

South plays six spades after West has opened the bidding with one heart and receives the lead of the king of clubs. Since South cannot profitably discard on the ace of clubs, he ruffs the first round, draws the outstanding trump and leads a low diamond toward the queen. If West goes up with the ace, declarer subsequently discards two hearts on the queen of diamonds and ace of clubs, while if West withholds the ace of diamonds, declarer discards his losing diamond on the club ace and loses only one heart trick. Alternatively, had declarer judged that East held the diamond ace, he could have couped that defender by leading a low diamond toward his king.

MOTT-SMITH TROPHY. Awarded every year to the player with the best overall individual performance record in the Spring Nationals. Donated by friends in memory of Geoffrey Mott-Smith in 1961; made retroactive to 1958 in order to include all the winners.

WINNERS

1958	I. Stakgold	1967	L. Mathe
1959	L. Mathe	1968	N. Kay
1960	N. Kay	1969	Mrs. D. Sachs
1961	R. Jordan	1970	B. Crane
1962	R. Jordan	1971	B. Crane
1963	S. Silodor, N. Kay	1972	J. Blair, *tied with*
1964	L. Mathe		P. Swanson
1965	P. Feldesman	1973	R. Wolff
1966	P. Feldesman	1974	R. Andersen
		1975	R. Bates

MOUSER TROPHY. A trophy in memory of William H. MOUSER, presented by his friends in 1964. It is contested for the Fall National Life Master Men's Pairs.

MOVE. The change of seats in duplicate bridge after a round has been completed. The direction to move is one of the duties administered by the TOURNAMENT DIRECTOR.

MOVEMENT. A schedule of PROGRESSION for players, indicating the seat to be occupied and the boards to be played by each player at each round. The TOURNAMENT DIRECTOR announces the movement to be followed, which is usually arranged to provide each contestant with different opponents at each round.

Specific movements in common use are listed under the following headings: AMERICAN WHIST MOVEMENT; HOWELL MOVEMENT; MITCHELL; SCRAMBLED MITCHELL; SHORT HOWELL; THREE-QUARTER (Howell) MOVEMENT.

MOYSIAN FIT. A contract in which declarer's trump suit is divided 4–3, usually thus described when the selection is made deliberately. Named for A. MOYSE, Jr., whose ardent advocacy of this choice was part of his case in favor of opening four-card majors and raising with three trumps.

MUD. A lead convention in which the original lead from three small cards is the middle one, followed in play by the higher. The name comes from the letters of middle, up, down, the order in which the cards are played. See THREE SMALL CARDS, LEAD FROM.

MULTICOLORED TWO DIAMONDS. A conventional two diamond opening of British origin showing either a weak two-bid in one of the major suits or a three-suited hand worth 17–24 points. The responses assume that the opening was based on a weak two-bid, but allow for the slim possibility of the strong hand. The responses used by Dr. R. KATZ–L. COHEN are:

2 ♡	sign-off in opener's major, whatever it is
2 ♠	sign-off in spades, game invitation in hearts
3 ♣, 3 ◇	sign-off in the minor suit bid
3 ♡	sign-off in hearts, game invitation in spades
3 NT	Blackwood
4 ♣, 4 ◇	no-loser minor suits in support of opener's major, whatever it is
4 ♡	willingness to play game in opener's major, whatever it is
4 ♠	desire to play four spades even if opener's suit is hearts

A two no trump response asks opener for more information about his hand. Opener's rebids as follows:

3 ♣	weak two heart bid, maximum strength
3 ◇	weak two spade bid, maximum strength
3 ♡	weak two heart bid, minimum strength
3 ♠	weak two spade bid, minimum strength

Opener's rebids from three no trump through four hearts show the 17–24 point 4-4-4-1 hand, each bid showing a singleton in the next higher suit.

After a rebid showing the strong three-suited hand, responder's first bid of the known singleton asks opener to specify his point range in four steps, the first step showing 17–18, the second showing 19–20, the third showing 21–22, the fourth showing 23–24. Responder's second bid of opener's known singleton asks opener how many controls he has (king = 1, ace = 2). Opener replies in steps, starting with four controls if he has shown 17–20 points, or starting with six controls if he has shown 21–24 points. Responder's third bid of opener's known singleton asks opener how many queens he has.

MULTIPLICATING BOARDS. See TWINNING.

MURDER. See BENNETT "MURDER."

MURRAY CONVENTION. Devised by Eric MURRAY, Toronto, Canada. See TWO-WAY STAYMAN.

N

NCBO. National Contract Bridge Organization. A WBF term for an organization of any independent or self-governing country with at least 250 members.

The membership of the WORLD BRIDGE FEDERATION is comprised of approximately 60 NCBOs.

NIRA. See NATIONAL INDUSTRIAL RECREATION ASSOCIATION.

NPC. Non-playing captain. See CAPTAIN.

NAMYATS. Name sometimes applied to FOUR CLUB AND FOUR DIAMOND OPENING TRANSFERS. These transfers are used by Samuel STAYMAN and some other experts to show strong four heart and four spade openings. "Namyats" is Stayman spelled backwards.

NATIONAL AMATEUR PAIR CHAMPIONSHIP. See KEM CARD TROPHY.

NATIONAL AMATEUR TEAM-OF-FOUR CHAMPIONSHIP. See ROTHSCHILD TROPHY.

NATIONAL APPEALS COMMITTEE. The committee appointed at each national tournament by the ACBL Board of Directors to hear appeals from rulings of directors or complaints as to conduct or ethics. The power and jurisdiction of this committee end with the end of the national tournament for which its appointment is made. See also COMMITTEE.

NATIONAL AUTHORITY. The body which, in each country, has responsibility for sponsoring and promoting bridge in that country. For the names of such organizations, see entry under each country. Most national authorities are members of the WORLD BRIDGE FEDERATION. See NCBO. The national authority has jurisdiction over all competition in that country and APPEALS on matters of law and fact are taken to the group designated by the national authority to hear them. In the ACBL, the national authority on matters of law is the NATIONAL LAWS COMMISSION.

NATIONAL BLUE RIBBON PAIR CHAMPIONSHIP. See BLUE RIBBON PAIR CHAMPIONSHIP, NATIONAL; CAVENDISH TROPHY.

NATIONAL BRIDGE ASSOCIATION. See WORLD PAR CONTESTS.

NATIONAL CHAMPIONSHIP. A championship in a major event determined on a nationwide basis, usually at a NATIONAL TOURNAMENT. The ACBL holds three national tournaments each year; since Bermuda, Canada, and Mexico are member organizations of the ACBL, the major events at those tournaments are now called North American championships. See also GRAND NATIONAL CHAMPIONSHIPS. The major events are distributed as follows in 1975:

SPRING

MEN'S PAIRS for the Sir Derrick WERNHER TROPHY

WOMEN'S PAIRS for the Wilbur C. WHITEHEAD TROPHY

MEN'S TEAMS for the Charles H. GOREN TROPHY

WOMEN'S TEAMS for the Charles E. COFFIN TROPHY

OPEN TEAMS for the Harold S. VANDERBILT CUP

OPEN PAIRS for the Sidney SILODOR TROPHY

SUMMER

LIFE MASTERS PAIRS for the Waldemar von ZEDT-WITZ GOLD CUP

MASTER TEAMS for the Nate D. SPINGOLD TROPHY

MASTER MIXED TEAMS for the Evelyn LEBHAR MEMORIAL TROPHY

SENIOR and ADVANCED SENIOR MASTER PAIRS for the R. L. MILES TROPHY

GRAND NATIONAL CHAMPIONSHIP for the Albert H. MOREHEAD TROPHY

FALL

OPEN TEAMS for the REISINGER MEMORIAL TROPHY

MIXED PAIRS for the Helen ROCKWELL TROPHY

LIFE MASTER MEN'S PAIRS for the William H. MOUSER TROPHY

LIFE MASTER WOMEN'S PAIRS for the Helen Sobel SMITH TROPHY

BLUE RIBBON PAIRS for the CAVENDISH TROPHY

Winners of these events can be found under each tournament listing in Appendix I.

Other events are held at each of these tournaments that do not have National Championship status, but for which the competition is no less keen.

For National Championships outside North America, see under the appropriate country.

NATIONAL CONTRACT BRIDGE LEAGUE OF THE REPUBLIC OF CHINA. Founded in 1950 at Taipei, Taiwan (Formosa), and by 1968 had an approximate membership of 15,000. The League participates in World Olympiads and Far East Championships, hosting the latter events in Taipei in 1959, 1963, and 1969, and hosting the Bermuda Bowl in 1971. China won the Far East Championship in 1967, 1969, and 1971, and finished second in 1968. When Australia could not represent the Far East Bridge Federation in the 1969 World Championships, China was named as alternate, and succeeded in making the best showing of a Far East team by finishing second, a feat it repeated in 1970. The chief National Championship is for the Governor's Cup. Chinese players listed separately are: C. K. Cheng, C. Y. Dean, J. Y. Hsu, F. Huang, P. K. Huang, H. Lin, D. Mao, Dr. C. S. Shen, M. F. Tai, J. Wong.

Officers, 1975:
Chairman: S. F. Tung.
Executive Secretary: David Mao, P.O. Box 100, Taipei, Taiwan.

NATIONAL LAWS COMMISSION. A committee of the American Contract Bridge League charged with formulating and promulgating the official laws of Rubber and Duplicate Contract Bridge.

In the preparation of international codes, the Commission collaborates with various other bodies, which have included the WHIST CLUB of New York, the PORTLAND CLUB of London, and the EUROPEAN BRIDGE LEAGUE.

Former members of the Commission, now deceased, who have made substantial contributions to the development of the Laws include: Walter Beinecke, Edward Hymes, Jr., George Reith, William McKenney, Geoffrey Mott-Smith, and Harold Richard.

In 1975 the members of the Commission were: Donald Oakie, *Chairman;* B. Jay Becker, Easley Blackwood, John Gerber, Sam Gold, Richard Goldberg, Charles H. Goren, Oswald Jacoby, Edgar Kaplan, Amalya Kearse, Thomas F. McCarthy, Dr. George Rosenkranz, Carl B. Rubin, Edgar Theus. See LAWS OF BRIDGE.

NATIONAL LIFE MASTERS INDIVIDUAL CHAMPIONSHIP. See STEINER TROPHY.

NATIONAL LIFE MASTERS MEN'S PAIR CHAMPIONSHIP. See MOUSER TROPHY.

NATIONAL LIFE MASTERS PAIR CHAMPIONSHIP. See VON ZEDTWITZ GOLD CUP.

NATIONAL LIFE MASTERS WOMEN'S PAIR CHAMPIONSHIP. See SMITH TROPHY.

NATIONAL MARCUS CUP TEAM CHAMPIONSHIP. See MARCUS CUP.

NATIONAL MASTER. A ranking among the players in the AMERICAN CONTRACT BRIDGE LEAGUE. See RANKING OF PLAYERS.

NATIONAL MASTER MIXED PAIR CHAMPIONSHIP. See HILLIARD TROPHY; ROCKWELL TROPHY.

NATIONAL MASTER OPEN TEAM CHAMPIONSHIP. See SPINGOLD TROPHY.

NATIONAL MEN'S PAIR CHAMPIONSHIP. See WERNHER TROPHY.

NATIONAL MEN'S TEAM CHAMPIONSHIP. See GOREN TROPHY.

NATIONAL MIXED TEAM CHAMPIONSHIP. See BARCLAY TROPHY and LEBHAR TROPHY.

NATIONAL NON-MASTERS PAIR CHAMPIONSHIP. See KEM CARD TROPHY.

NATIONAL OPEN INDIVIDUAL CHAMPIONSHIP. See BAIRD TROPHY.

NATIONAL OPEN PAIR CHAMPIONSHIP. See CAVENDISH TROPHY; SILODOR TROPHY.

NATIONAL OPEN TEAM CHAMPIONSHIP. See VANDERBILT CUP; REISINGER MEMORIAL TROPHY.

NATIONAL POINTS. See REGIONAL AND NATIONAL POINTS.

NATIONAL SENIOR AND ADVANCED SENIOR MASTER PAIR CHAMPIONSHIP. See MILES TROPHY.

NATIONAL SENIOR MASTERS INDIVIDUAL CHAMPIONSHIP. See BEYNON TROPHY.

NATIONAL SUB-SENIOR MASTERS TEAM CHAMPIONSHIP. See ROTHSCHILD TROPHY.

NATIONAL TOURNAMENT. A tournament which determines the winners of various events on a nationwide basis. In the ACBL there are three such tournaments held yearly, each with a different schedule of major events. In 1975 these were renamed North American championships. See CHAMPIONSHIP TOURNAMENTS; NATIONAL CHAMPIONSHIP.

NATIONAL TRUMP. The establishing by a governing body of a particular suit as trump at whist.

NATIONAL WOMEN'S PAIR CHAMPIONSHIP. See WHITEHEAD TROPHY.

NATIONAL WOMEN'S TEAM CHAMPIONSHIP. See COFFIN TROPHY.

NATIONALIST CHINA. See NATIONAL CONTRACT BRIDGE LEAGUE OF THE REPUBLIC OF CHINA.

NATIONALS. A term for one of the NATIONAL TOURNAMENTS, now titled NORTH AMERICAN CHAMPIONSHIPS.

NATIONWIDE CHARITY GAME. See CONTINENTWIDE GAMES.

NATURAL CALLS. Calls which reflect the character of the hand and suggest a possible final contract. A natural call is contrasted with ARTIFICIAL CALL. However, some bids which have artificial meanings can be used as natural bids.

NATURAL FOUR NO TRUMP. See BLACKWOOD.

NEAPOLITAN. A system devised principally by Eugenio CHIARADIA, and played in many World Championship events by a group of Neapolitan players, which has included Pietro FORQUET, Guglielmo SINISCALCO, Massimo D'ALELIO and Benito GAROZZO. Since 1965 Garozzo, as the leading Neapolitan theorist, has gradually revised the system, renaming it the BLUE TEAM CLUB system. It is this version that has become increasingly popular in the United States and has been adopted as the official system of the SHARIF BRIDGE CIRCUS. See BLUE TEAM CLUB.

NEAPOLITAN FOUR DIAMOND CONVENTION. A form of delayed game raise used in the NEAPOLITAN SYSTEM. It is a jump bid which applies when a forcing jump in the intended trump suit is not available:

WEST	EAST		WEST	EAST		WEST	EAST
1 ♠	2 ♣		1 ♠	2 ♣		1 ♡	1 ♠
2 ♠	4 ◇		2 ♡	4 ◇		2 ♣	4 ◇
agrees spades			agrees hearts			agrees hearts	

See BLUE TEAM FOUR CLUB-FOUR DIAMOND CONVENTION.

NEAR-SOLID SUIT. See SEMI-SOLID SUIT.

NEDERLANDSE BRIDGE BOND. See NETHERLANDS BRIDGE LEAGUE.

NEGATIVE DOUBLE. The original name for a take-out double, in general use from 1915 to 1930, about which time the term "informatory" became current, later superseded by the more descriptive term "take-out" double. In 1957 Alvin Roth and Tobias Stone introduced a modern "negative double," in which what was formerly a penalty double of a suit overcall was used as a take-out bid. This feature of the ROTH-STONE SYSTEM was christened "Sputnik" because it was an important new device dating from the same period as that Russian space satellite.

NORTH	EAST	SOUTH
1 ◇	1 ♡	Dbl.
	or 1 ♠	
	or 2 ♣	

The double shows a hand on which any normal bid is unsatisfactory; it can be made at the one-level with as little as 7 points:

♠ K x x x
♡ x x
◇ K J x x x
♣ x x

Double if partner's one club opening is overcalled with one heart. See also CARD-SHOWING DOUBLE.

It may also be made on a hand worth an opening bid:

♠ A Q 9 x
♡ J x x x
◇ K
♣ A J x x

Double if partner's one diamond opening is overcalled with one heart; follow with a cue-bid if convenient. The double is preferred to a bid of one spade because a free bid is rarely made with a four-card suit.

The opening bidder responds to the double in accordance with his assessment of game prospects. A cue-bid would be the only absolute force. With strength in the opponent's suit, he can make a penalty pass.

The negative double treatment can be extended to the following situations:

(1) High-level overcalls, whether strong or pre-

emptive, up to and including four spades. The higher the overcall the more likely it is that the opener will decide to pass for penalties, so a shaded raise often should be given in preference to the double.

(2) A natural overcall at the two- or three-level in a minor suit after a no trump opening bid. The double would then show support for one or both major suits, but would not be forcing to game.

In KAPLAN-SHEINWOLD, negative doubles are used after non-jump overcalls only, and promise four cards in any unbid major. The strength is unlimited, and the opener rebids as though the indicated major had actually been bid. Free responses show no additional strength, but promise five-card suits when a negative double could have been made instead.

Defense. When the right-hand opponent has made a negative double, the situation is similar to a bid over an opposing take-out double. A redouble shows high-card strength, and may expose an opening psychic bid. A jump raise of the overcaller's suit would be pre-emptive.

NEGATIVE INFERENCE. Information deduced from a player's failure to take a specific action in the bidding or play. Though this type of inference is frequently available, it is often overlooked, the average player preferring to concentrate on more positive clues.

Here is a hand where the declarer was able to diagnose the location of a critical card based upon negative inferences gleaned from the bidding and play.

Dealer: South
North-South Vulnerable

```
                  NORTH
                  ♠ A 10 8 2
                  ♡ 8 4
                  ◇ A Q 10 4
                  ♣ J 6 4
WEST                              EAST
♠ K Q J 6 4                      ♠ 9 7 3
♡ A J 3                          ♡ K 10 6 5 2
◇ K 7 6 5                        ◇ 9 8 3
♣ K                              ♣ 9 3
                  SOUTH
                  ♠ 5
                  ♡ Q 9 7
                  ◇ J 2
                  ♣ A Q 10 8 7 5 2
```

The bidding:

SOUTH	WEST	NORTH	EAST
Pass	1 ♠	Pass	Pass
2 ♣	2 ◇	3 ♣	3 ♠
4 ♣	Pass	5 ♣	Pass
Pass	Pass		

West opened the king of spades, and the declarer, Arthur Robinson of Philadelphia, won with dummy's ace. With the ace, king of hearts to lose, de-

clarer had to pick up both minor-suit kings. The percentages favor a finesse in the club suit; nevertheless he led a club to his ace at trick two, dropping West's king. A successful diamond finesse gave him eleven tricks.

Robinson "guessed" the club position well. He reasoned that if West had held both top hearts he would surely have led one in order to inspect dummy and judge the best continuation. The absence of a heart lead therefore marked East with a high heart—if he held the club king in addition he would have responded on the first round. The only hope, therefore, was that West held a singleton king. See also INFERENCE.

S. K.

NEGATIVE RESPONSES. Artificial responses that show weakness. Examples are: a two no trump response to a FORCING TWO or an ACOL TWO; a one or two diamond response to an artificial one club or two club opening; or a two heart response to an artificial two diamond opening. See also DOUBLE NEGATIVE; HERBERT NEGATIVE; SECOND NEGATIVE RESPONSE AFTER ARTIFICIAL FORCING OPENING. For natural negative responses, see WEAKNESS RESPONSE.

NEGATIVE SLAM DOUBLE. See DOUBLE FOR SACRIFICE.

NET SCORE. The result of a rubber of bridge or of CHICAGO after the losing side's score is subtracted from the winning, or higher score. In rounding off to the nearest hundred, fifty points counts as an extra hundred in the United States, but is dropped in England.

The term is also used in team matches to designate the difference between the scores of two teams at the end of a session or a match; it can be expressed in total points or in INTERNATIONAL MATCH POINTS.

NETHERLANDS ANTILLES BRIDGE ASSOCIATION (BRIDGE BOND NEDERLANDSE ANTILLEN). Founded in 1963, and by 1969 had approximately 225 members. Participated in the World Team Olympiad 1964, 1968, 1972, World Pair Olympiad 1966, South American Championships 1963, as well as several international matches in South America. The Association consists of five affiliated clubs in two districts, Curaçao and Aruba. A system of master points was introduced in 1965, and National Championships have been held annually for Open Teams and Open Pairs since 1961. Netherlands Antilles player listed separately is Wouter Goetzee.

Officers, 1975:
President: H. G. A. Bongers, Blenchiweg 3, Curaçao.
Secretary: P. J. Van Gijn, Van Engelenweg, 20 Willemstad, Curaçao, Netherlands Antilles.

NETHERLANDS BRIDGE LEAGUE (NEDERLANDSE BRIDGE BOND). Founded in 1930 by the late A. J. E. Lucardie, and in 1975 had approximately 25,000 members. The League participates in World Olympiads, finishing fourth in 1968, and European Championships, hosting the 1932, 1939, and 1955 events. Holland finished second in the 1965 and 1966 European Championships and represented Europe in the 1966 Bermuda Bowl. Won 1966 World Open Pair Olympiad. National events are held annually. Many of the League's activities are designed to stimulate participation by young players and grass roots players. Dutch players listed separately are: H. Filarski, E. Goudsmit, F. Goudsmit, E. Heldring, K. Kaiser, R. Kaiser, J. C. Kokkes, J. T. M. Kreyns, N. D. Oudshoorn, C. Slavenburg.

President, 1975: Dr. G. Kramer.
Information: Nederlandse Bridge Bond, Emmapark 9, The Hague, Holland.

NEUTRAL CARDS. See CARDS, NEUTRAL AND POSITIVE.

NEUTRAL LEAD. See PASSIVE LEAD.

NEUTRAL SUIT. See ASTRO.

NEW DEAL. A fresh deal to take the place of a misdeal or to replace a deal void for any reason.

NEW ENGLAND REGIONAL CHAMPIONSHIPS. Originated in 1930 with the Boston Chess Club under the sanction of ABL first and then ACBL. In 1937, in some events, the Cavendish Club of Boston ran a second regional for the same New England area. In 1948 the New England Bridge Association took over both sets of regionals and from that time on each event was held only once a year, with the exception of the Men's and Women's Pairs in 1964 and either a Team or Pair event run concurrently with the Knockout Teams. The two-day Individual Championship, held annually since 1945, was developed by the late W. KEOHANE into the largest event of its kind. For past results, see Appendix II.

NEW ENGLAND RELAY. A movement for team-of-four contests originally used for competition at whist. When the number of competing teams was odd, the American Whist League movement was used, but this required the use of a phantom table when the number of competing teams was even. A movement first used in Boston eliminated this necessity by placing two parallel rows of tables, with the lower numbered tables in one row, and the higher numbered tables in the other. Boards are distributed with the first set at the first table, second set at a BYE STAND, third set at the second table, fourth set at a bye stand, etc., until all sets are distributed to half the tables and their bye stands. Traveling pairs move to the next lower table, and the boards are put on the bye stand toward the lower numbered table, and removed from the bye stand toward the higher numbered table at the conclusion of each round. During the play, each of the lower numbered tables relays the boards with the table in the adjacent row.

The movement is still in use at some tournaments, but has been largely supplanted by other movements. See TEAM-OF-FOUR MOVEMENT.

NEW SOUTH WALES SYSTEM. A variation of the VIENNA SYSTEM used by R. CUMMINGS and T. SERES of Australia. The principal features are five-card openings in diamonds, hearts, and spades, strong one no trump openings, weak two bids in the major suits. The two club opening, which is used sparingly, is game forcing; the two no trump opening shows a strong minor two-suiter, and the two diamond opening shows a balanced hand with at least 21 HCP. A forcing one club opening is used for all other hands, e.g., long club suit, or a balanced hand worth 12–14 or 19–20, or a hand of any strength with 4–4–4–1 distribution.

All responses in new suits are forcing, and jump shifts are used as modified CULBERTSON ASKING BIDS.

NEW ZEALAND BRIDGE ASSOCIATION. Founded in 1936, by 1975 it had a membership of approximately 14,500 in 87 clubs. Based on New Zealand's total population of 3,000,000, this Association is probably relatively the largest in the world. The Association participates in the Far East Championships and in competitions with Australia, and sent teams to the World Team Olympiad 1972, Bermuda Bowl 1974. National events include Open Teams and Pairs Championships, and an Inter-Provincial Teams of Four. Players listed separately are: S. Abrahams, Mrs. V. Bell, B. Bell, R. Brightling, J. Cordwell, M. Cornell, R. Evans, D. John Evitt, W. Haughie, A. Hollis, R. Hudson, J. Hutchison, R. Kerr, J. Kinsella, J. Knight, W. Linderman, F. Lu, J. Martin, Mrs. Z. Morris, L. Schneideman, R. Scott, Mrs. E. Taylor, Dr. J. Thomson, J. Wignall, G. Wilson.

Secretary, 1975: Mrs. Kitching, P.O. Box 12116, Wellington, New Zealand.

NEWGATE. A prison in England where, prior to 1820, whist was played as a three-handed game with one hand exposed as the dummy.

NEWLY FORMED TABLES. These can be created with four to six players ranking according to precedence, this generally being established by order of entry into the playing room. Players leaving an existing table to cut into the new table have lowest precedence. See RUBBER BRIDGE.

NINE or NINE-SPOT. That card ranking sixth highest in a suit, and being between the ten and eight in position.

NINE TABLES. At duplicate, nine tables provide for competition among thirty-six players as individuals, eighteen pairs, or nine teams-of-four.

As an individual tournament, nine tables present difficulties in entering to the recapitulation sheet, but provide good comparisons, using the SHOMATE MOVEMENT, for which guide cards are available. There are also guide cards available for a two-session game.

As a pair event, MITCHELL, THREE-QUARTER (Howell) MOVEMENT or SHORT HOWELL movements may be used. In the Mitchell game, either eight or nine rounds of three boards each can be played.

As a team-of-four event, nine tables provide an excellent movement for meeting against each of the other teams in an uninterrupted team-of-four progression, boards going to the next lower numbered tables, and players skipping a table toward the lower numbers.

For eight and a half tables at pair play, the phantom pair may be either North-South or East-West, but unless the entire nine rounds are played, there are different tops on the boards that are not out of play for a round, and numerous adjustments must be made. If this is impractical, and it is desired to play only eight rounds, a BUMP MITCHELL should be used, with the extra pair bumping North-South pair 1 after the first round. See BUMP MITCHELL, EIGHT TABLES. The nine-table Short Howell for twenty-two boards or Three-Quarter movement for twenty-six boards can be used, with the phantom pair being one of the stationary pairs.

For nine and a half tables, pair 10 East-West is the extra pair. Tables 1 and 9 should be close together and relay boards throughout. Use the straight Mitchell movement with a skip after the fourth round, traveling pairs sitting out after playing at table 9 and re-entering at table 1. All boards are played nine times in eight rounds, and have the same top. Two East-West players do not sit out, and those who do have their scores factored up by one-seventh. Nine and a half tables can also be handled using the Three-Quarter Howell movement, with one of the stationary pairs as a phantom. Factoring must be done for the players who are moving, and thus sit out one round, to compare with the players who are stationary and do not, but top on all boards is the same, 7. The same is true for the Short Howell, but only twenty boards are played by the players who sit out one round, and that is frequently too short a game. There is also available an East-West Bump Movement. Three East-West pairs have irregular movements. Guide cards are obtainable from the ACBL.

NO BID. A term meaning "I pass," common in England where there is some likelihood of confusion in the enunciation of *pass* and *hearts*. The term has been generally accepted by custom, but does not appear in the official laws and is subject to the warning (see LAWS OF DUPLICATE, Proprieties IIIA3) against use of different designations for the same call. Regulations for international play may specifically bar the term because it may be mistaken for another call, e.g., *double*.

NO CALL. An obsolete and inaccurate term occasionally used instead of PASS.

NO TRUMP. A denomination in which a player may bid at bridge. No trump is the ranking denomination during the auction, being just above spades in precedence. One is required to take only nine tricks

for game at no trump, since the first trick over book of six counts for 40 points and the subsequent tricks for 30 points each as in a major suit. As the name implies, contracts at no trump are played without a trump suit; the play therefore is entirely different from that of suit contracts, one of the chief differences being that declarer while planning his line of play attempts to count winners rather than losers. At no trump, a primary concern of the side contracting for game or partial is that there be stoppers in the suits bid or held by the opponents. More game contracts are played at no trump than at any other denomination.

NO TRUMP BIDDING. The standard point-count is particularly effective in its application to no trump bidding. A partnership aims to reach three no trump with 26 points in high cards in the combined hands, and is prepared to play in game with 25. Similarly, six no trump should be reached with 34 points, and 33 points will offer a fair play.

Different aspects of this subject are under: BOLAND CONVENTION; DYNAMIC NO TRUMP; EXPECTED NUMBER OF CONTROLS IN BALANCED HANDS; FIVE NO TRUMP OPENING; FOUR NO TRUMP OPENING; GERBER CONVENTION; GLADIATOR; JACOBY TRANSFER; ONE NO TRUMP OPENING; ONE NO TRUMP RESPONSE; OPENER'S REBIDS; RESPONDER'S REBIDS; SHARPLES; SIX NO TRUMP OPENING; SOUTH AFRICAN TEXAS; STAYMAN; TEXAS CONVENTION; THREE NO TRUMP OPENING; THREE NO TRUMP RESPONSE; THREE-QUARTER NO TRUMP; TWO NO TRUMP OPENING; TWO NO TRUMP RESPONSE; TWO-WAY STAYMAN; WEAK NO TRUMP; WEISSBERGER; WOODSON TWO-WAY NO TRUMP.

NO TRUMP DISTRIBUTION. A hand distribution suited to no trump play rather than a suit because of its balanced pattern. The three most common distributions are: 4-3-3-3, 4-4-3-2, 5-3-3-2. Occasionally 5-4-2-2 or 6-3-2-2 can be considered as no trump pattern.

NO TRUMP OPENING. See ONE NO TRUMP OPENING; TWO NO TRUMP OPENING; THREE NO TRUMP OPENING; FOUR NO TRUMP OPENING; FIVE NO TRUMP OPENING; SIX NO TRUMP OPENING.

NO TRUMP OVERCALL. See ONE NO TRUMP OVERCALL; TWO NO TRUMP OVERCALL; THREE NO TRUMP OVERCALL; FOUR NO TRUMP OVERCALL; UNUSUAL NO TRUMP.

NO TRUMP PLAY. Play and defense in no trump contracts are discussed in many of the headings listed under DEFENSE and DUMMY PLAY.

NO TRUMP RESPONSES TO SUIT OPENINGS. See ONE NO TRUMP RESPONSE; TWO NO TRUMP RESPONSE; TWO NO TRUMP RESPONSE OVER OPPONENT'S TAKE-OUT DOUBLE; THREE NO TRUMP RESPONSE.

NON-FORCING SEQUENCES. A sequence which permits either member of the partnership to drop the bidding. A sequence starting with a suit bid can be assumed to be non-forcing unless it is listed under FORCING SEQUENCES.

Before passing a non-forcing sequence, a player should satisfy himself that a game contract is unlikely to be a sound proposition. He should also be sure that he cannot convert safely to a superior part-score.

NON-MASTERS PAIRS CHAMPIONSHIP, NATIONAL. See KEM CARD TROPHY.

NON-PLAYING CAPTAIN. See CAPTAIN.

NON-VULNERABLE. The condition of a side that has not won a game in a rubber of bridge. In CHICAGO or four-deal bridge, each pair is non-vulnerable twice; that is to say, on the first deal and on either the second or third deal depending on local rules as respects dealer's vulnerability. In duplicate, deals or "boards" are marked according to vulnerability so that each tray clearly displays the vulnerability conditions, whether they be all non-vulnerable, or either side or neither side. When a pair is not vulnerable, it can bid with slightly more freedom than when vulnerable, because the schedule of penalties for undertricks is set up so as to levy more severe punishment on vulnerable pairs that incur penalties. Frequently, then, it will be found that a non-vulnerable pair will "take a save" rather than allow the opposition to make a game, the premium for which can be quite high, especially, if, conversely, the team scoring the game is vulnerable. See LOVE ALL.

NORDIC CHAMPIONSHIPS. Organized in 1946 by delegates from the bridge federations of the three Scandinavian nations (Denmark, Norway, Sweden) and Finland, meeting at Copenhagen, the Nordic Championships represented one of the first postwar efforts to revive international bridge competition in Europe. The initial tournament was staged later the same year in Oslo, and the Championships were held on an annual basis until 1949. Iceland joined the competition in 1949 and has been a regular participant ever since. After the European Championships were reactivated, the importance of a separate Nordic competition lessened, so the event became a biennial competition, except for a three-year lapse from 1959–62.

NORMAL EXPECTANCY. The holding in either high cards or distribution which a player might expect in partner's hand when he decides whether to open the bidding. This can be roughly approximated as one-third of the missing high cards or high-card points, and one-third of the remaining cards in the suit. Partner's responses and future actions modify this concept as the bidding progresses. See SUIT COMBINATIONS and TRUMP SUPPORT for further treatment.

NORMAN FOUR NO TRUMP. A slam convention in which kings and aces are shown with one bid. An ace is counted as 1 point and a king as ½ point, and responses are according to the following table:

Five clubs	less than 1½ points
Five diamonds	1½ points
Five hearts	2 points
Five spades	2½ points
Five no trump	3 points, etc.

The four no trump bidder can usually determine which aces and kings are held by responder.

This convention has been popular in England, where it is credited to Norman de Villiers Hart and Sir Norman Bennet, and was incorporated into the VIENNA SYSTEM. Several similar methods have been used in America, but only the SAN FRANCISCO convention achieved any substantial following.

Similar responding principles are used in the BLUE TEAM CLUB System and by some players after an artificial two-club opening.

NORSK BRIDGE FORBUND. See NORWEGIAN BRIDGE ASSOCIATION.

NORTH. A position in a bridge foursome or in a bridge diagram opposite South and to the left of West. In duplicate games the scoring is done by North. In newspaper columns North is usually the dummy.

NORTH AMERICAN CHAMPIONSHIPS. Name given in 1975 to the three AMERICAN CONTRACT BRIDGE LEAGUE CHAMPIONSHIP tournaments held each year for North America. (Formerly known as "NATIONALS.") Results are reported in Appendix I.

NORTH AMERICAN RUBBER BRIDGE CHAMPIONSHIPS. A form of nationwide bridge competition conducted in 1962 and 1963 by North American Van Lines of Fort Wayne, Ind., in connection with their sponsorship of the TV series "Championship Bridge with Charles Goren."

Entrants formed groups for home play. High scorers in each game center area qualified for a knockout rubber bridge competition, the two finalist pairs meeting next evening to play the same hands (pre-dealt centrally) as played in every city. The highest scoring pair east of the Mississippi met the highest scoring Western pair, face to face, in a final (played in 1962 in Chicago, Ill., in 1963 in New York City). Judges were Charles Goren, Alvin Landy, and Richard L. Frey.

	WINNERS	RUNNERS-UP
1962	Mrs. J. Garcia, G. Boone	J. Steele, S. Stone
1963	Mr. and Mrs. B. Howe	M. Phillips, I. Trivers

NORTH AMERICAN TEAM TRIALS. See INTERNATIONAL OPEN TEAM SELECTION.

NORTH OF IRELAND BRIDGE UNION. The controlling body of the six northern counties of Ireland, founded in 1932. By 1975 there were more than 30 clubs affiliated, with a total membership of about 1,500. The Union belongs to the British Bridge League, and competes annually with England, Scotland, and Wales for the CAMROSE TROPHY. For other international participation, see IRISH BRIDGE UNION. The NIBU hosted the European Championship at Dun Laoghaire in 1952. Players listed separately are: D. Cohen, D. Deery, H. M. Gabbey, E. Goldblatt, A. Lennon.

Secretary, 1975: John Grummitt.

NORWEGIAN BRIDGE ASSOCIATION (NORSK BRIDGE FORBUND). Founded in 1932, and in 1969 had a membership of about 13,000 with 561 clubs. The Association embraces 45 districts of sparsely populated countryside, which compete for the Norwegian Team and Pairs Championships. The 1974 Open Pairs Championship drew more than 9,000 players, and a National team event attracted 394 teams. Norway annually participates in the European Championships, finishing second in 1938 and 1969, and hosted the 1938, 1958, and 1969 events in Oslo; represented Europe 1970 World Championships. Norwegian players listed separately are: A. Amundsen, P. Breck, J. Brun, L. Christiansen, R. Halle, E. Hoie, T. Jensen, K. Koppang, B. Larsen, O. Larsen, R. Lien, H. Nordby, A. Olsen, P. Olsen, T. Pedersen, L. A. Strom.

Officers, 1974:
President, Baard Baardsen.
Secretary: Per Pettersen, Kirkevien 59, Oslo 3, Norway.

NOT VULNERABLE. See NON-VULNERABLE.

NOTTINGHAM CLUB. A system popular in the English Midlands. The chief features are:
   (1) One club opening bid with 16–21; negative response, one diamond with less than 8 points.
   (2) One diamond with 12–13 points and no four-card major suit. Minimum suit responses are non-forcing and show 0–11 points.
   (3) One heart and one spade, 12–15 with five-card suit.
   (4) One no trump, 13–15 points.
   (5) Two clubs, 12–15 with club length.
   (6) Two diamonds, forcing opening with 22 or more.
   (7) Two hearts or two spades, 12–15 with eight playing tricks.

NOVELS. See LITERATURE AND BRIDGE.

NOVICE GAMES. A method of promoting duplicate bridge among inexperienced players that has proved very helpful in stimulating interest and building up membership in duplicate clubs and the ACBL. At sectional and higher-rated tournaments, the novice game is often conducted as a special event, normally limited to players with fewer than 20 master points, with a pre-game talk on duplicate techniques, and occasionally as a separate section during regular play, where the pace of the game is usually slower and supervision of scoring and movements much closer than in games with more experienced players.

Usually 22 or 24 boards are scheduled in place of the normal 26, though this is not always practical. Wtih only one or two tables of inexperienced players NOVICE TABLES can be used.

The novice program received a boost in 1965 when the ACBL introduced analyzed sets of hands for novices—32 computer-dealt hands, 30 of which are analyzed—with sufficient printed analysis sheets for distribution to all participants. The analysis sheet permits the novice to compare his result with what could have or should have been done on the board, and is often used as a reference for an increasingly popular post-game show where four experts replay four, six, or eight of the novice deals on VU-GRAPH. Analyzed novice sets are available from ACBL HEADQUARTERS at a nominal charge of $5.50 per section.

When the ACBL revised its club regulations in 1969, novice games became a regular feature of many of the ACBL franchised clubs. Each club that holds a novice game at least once a month is awarded a "bonus factor," which allows the club to increase its master-point awards to the top finishers in its regular game.

NOVICE TABLE. An appendix table at a duplicate contest, usually a club game, where inexperienced players remain stationary, getting their boards from a table in the regular competition, relaying with the table to which it is appended. The players at the novice table keep their own scores, which can be entered on the recapitulation sheet on a separate line, match points being awarded in relation to the scores in the regular game. No harm is done if the novice table does not play all the boards, so the regular game is not appreciably slowed up. As players become more familiar with the techniques of duplicate, they join the regular game.

The pamphlet "Easy Guide to Duplicate Bridge," in which the use of novice tables and NOVICE GAMES is more fully described, is available from ACBL HEADQUARTERS.

NUISANCE BID. A bid made to hinder the opponents and dislocate the flow of their bidding. The following example is from the 1962 World's Championship Team Match, Great Britain vs. North America.

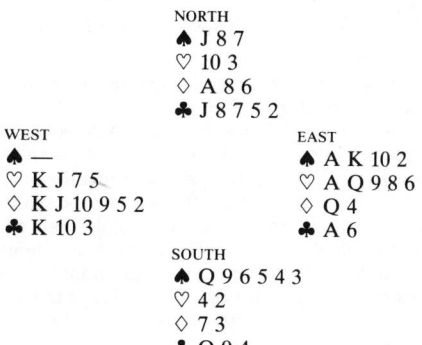

```
                        NORTH
                        ♠ J 8 7
                        ♡ 10 3
                        ◇ A 8 6
                        ♣ J 8 7 5 2
WEST                                        EAST
♠ —                                         ♠ A K 10 2
♡ K J 7 5                                   ♡ A Q 9 8 6
◇ K J 10 9 5 2                              ◇ Q 4
♣ K 10 3                                    ♣ A 6
                        SOUTH
                        ♠ Q 9 6 5 4 3
                        ♡ 4 2
                        ◇ 7 3
                        ♣ Q 9 4
```

The bidding proceeded as follows:

SOUTH	WEST	NORTH	EAST
	1 ◇	Pass	2 ♡
Pass	3 ♡	Pass	4 NT
5 ♠	Pass	Pass	5 NT
Pass	6 ◇	Pass	7 ♡
Pass	Pass	Dbl.	Pass
Pass	Pass		

G. Robert Nail, sitting South for North America, made a fine nuisance bid of five spades over the opposition ROMAN BLACKWOOD call. This interference bid caused the British players to overreach themselves. The contract was down one, and North America gained 19 IMPS.

NUMBER. Used as in "going for a number." "Number" as used here refers to the high numeral value of the set that a team sustains. If a team is set 500 or 700 or, when vulnerable, 800 or 1,100 or more, the team is said to have "gone for a number." A number usually represents a loss, because it exceeds the value of an opposing contract.

NUMBER OF POSSIBLE HANDS, DEALS.

(1) The number of hands any named player can have is

$$\frac{52\ !}{39!\ \times\ 13!}\ =\ 635{,}013{,}559{,}600$$

(2) The number of hands a second named player can have is:

$$\frac{39\ !}{26!\ \times\ 13!}\ =\ 8{,}122{,}425{,}444$$

(3) The number of ways the remaining twenty-six cards can be divided is

$$\frac{26\ !}{13!\ \times\ 13!}\ =\ 10{,}400{,}600$$

(4) The total number of possible deals is the three above numbers multiplied together, or

$$\frac{52\ !}{(13!)^4}\ =\ 53{,}644{,}737{,}765{,}488{,}792{,}839{,}237{,}440{,}000$$

These rather simple-appearing mathematical formulas for the first three are the number of combinations in which thirteen items can be combined from a supply of fifty-two, thirty-nine, and twenty-six respectively. The fourth figure is, as mentioned, the product of the other three. In each case the symbol ! (read "factorial") means that the number preceding it is multiplied successively by each smaller number down to 1. A rather elementary "program" enables an electronic calculator of sufficient scope to handle the fantastic arithmetic problem in a matter of minutes.

A. T. and R. T.

O

OBJECT OF THE GAME. The object of the game is to do the best one can with the cards one has been dealt on a particular deal, so that at the conclusion of the hand, one can feel the result well warranted by the efforts put into the planning and strategy of the hand. It is sometimes said that the *immediate* object when playing rubber bridge is to score game and rubber, so as to receive the scoring advantages thereto pertaining. Likewise, in CHICAGO, games should be bid, as there are substantial bonuses accruing as benefits. In duplicate, the object of the game is to score points on a particular deal or board, and various factors have to be weighed so as to determine the way to obtain the best score. Through the years, however, there has been one school of thought that has consistently maintained that the object of bidding in contract bridge should be to bid in such a way as to get the opponents into a contract they cannot make, and then double and set them. The points thus built up can attain significant proportions above the line. Of course this was largely a rubber bridge theory, and one that does not necessarily pertain to four-deal games or duplicate.

Objectives may be affected by considerations of partnership psychology. See RUBBER BRIDGE TACTICS.

OBLIGATION TO PASS. When a player bids out of turn, the Laws may require as a penalty that his partner must pass when next it is his turn to call, or for the duration of the auction. This is an "obligation to pass." If a player under such an obligation to pass makes a bid, double, or redouble, then both members of the offending side must pass for the entire auction. For the conditions which bring an obligation to pass, see LAWS (Laws 30, 31, 32, 36, 37, and 38). Lead penalties may also apply.

OBLIGATORY. A term characterizing a play which cannot lose but may win a trick, when the situation is such that not to make the play will gain nothing and will lose the opportunity of making a trick that might otherwise be sacrificed, as an obligatory duck, an obligatory finesse, etc.

OBLIGATORY FINESSE. The play of a small card on the second lead of a suit in the hope that the adversary yet to play holds only the commanding card of the suit. The object of the play is to limit the number of losers in the suit when only two of the five honors are held. It is usually made when the position of the master card is marked, and the adversaries originally held five cards of the suit. Thus, in the following situation:

NORTH
♠ Q 7 4 2
WEST   EAST
♠ A 5   ♠ J 10 9
SOUTH
♠ K 8 6 3

if South leads toward the North hand, and the ace is

not played by West, he puts up the queen and wins the first spade trick, and leads a low spade from North. When East plays one of his equals, South must play a small card in the hope that West originally held only one guard to the ace. This play can lose nothing, since if the cards are otherwise distributed at least two tricks must be lost in spades in any event. Hence, an "obligatory" finesse is a play which cannot lose but may gain a trick.

ODD-EVEN DISCARDS. Methods of signaling which assign different meanings to odd-numbered and even-numbered spot cards. When following to partner's opening lead in a suit, the ROMAN SYSTEM uses an odd-numbered card to encourage and an even-numbered card to discourage. The size of the card carries a suit preference message.

These signals are complicated in operation, because an odd card, or an even card, may not be available when required. They are also confusing for the opponents, and were therefore prohibited in ACBL tournament play.

ODD TRICK. A trick won by the declarer, in excess of the first six tricks. The term is a holdover from WHIST, in which the winning of the odd trick was paramount.

ODDS, IN BRIDGE. Odds describe a ratio between two probabilities, the probability that an event (such as a player holding a particular card) will occur to the probability that it will not occur. If such a probability is expressed as a decimal, the alternate probability is the difference between totality (1), and that decimal. MATHEMATICAL TABLES, Table 4, shows the probabilities of distribution of cards between two hidden hands. It shows, for instance, that the probability that three outstanding cards will divide 2–1 is 78%. Expressing this probability in terms of odds *on* a 2–1 division are 78–22 or 39–11. The odds *against* a 2–1 division is the opposite (converse) of these figures, or 11–39, (which is the odds *on* a 3–0 division). Odds represent what would be a fair bet.

Odds are often used to express the probability of two events that are mutually exclusive (cannot both happen at the same time, such as two winners in a prizefight). Thus in dealing with the division of four cards in a suit, Table 4 shows that the odds *against* a 2–2 division are 49.74 to 40.70 (approximately 5–4), provided that it is known that each opponent has at least one card of the suit. It should be noted that in this computation the possibility of a 4–0 split could be eliminated by one lead to test, and therefore odds could be expressed because there were left only two possible a priori divisions, 2–2 and 3–1.

A. T. and R. T.

ODDS GOVERNING SPECIFIED CARDS. (For explanation of the notations used in this article, see MATHEMATICS OF BRIDGE, and SUIT, NUMBER OF CARDS IN.)

(1) A player can have 1C1 × 51C12 hands in which he holds the ace of spades. He can have the ace and three other spades in 1C1 × 12C3 × 39C9 ways.

(2) If twenty-six cards are seen, of which n are spades, one of the other hands can have a singleton spade in (13-n)C1 × (26 = (13-n))C12 ways; that is, if six spades are seen, a singleton in an unseen hand can occur in 7C1 × 19C12 ways; he can have a named singleton, such as the queen of spades, in 1C1 × 19C12 ways.

(3) A player can have n specified cards in nCn × (52-n)C(13-n) ways. He can, for instance, have the ace of spades and the king-queen of hearts in 3C3 × 49C10 ways.

(4) If 26 cards are known, the formula in (3) above, becomes nCn × (26-n)C(13-n).

(5) If there are an equal number of unknown cards in two closed hands, there is a 50% chance that a named card will be in one of those hands.

(6) When the entire distribution of a suit is known: (a) the probability that a named card in the suit is in a particular hand is proportional to the number of cards held in the suit; and (b) the probability that a named card of another suit is in a particular hand is proportional to the number of cards other than those of the suit whose distribution is known.

As an example, if ten spades are held by East-West, and East is known to hold six, and West, therefore, four, the chance that a named spade is with East is 60% (6 to 4). The chance that East holds a named card in some other suit is 43.75% (7 to 9), since there are seven vacant places (non-spades) in East's hand as against nine such vacant places in West's.

(7) The vacant places method (see [6] above) can be used in only two cases: (a) where the entire distribution of one or more suits is known; then the odds governing any of the other cards are accurately shown by this method; (b) where the play of an opponent shows RESTRICTED CHOICE. An example would be: with no defense bidding and an opening lead of the heart queen from West. If we assume (see MATHEMATICAL ASSUMPTIONS) that this is from the queen-jack, and that West was certain to lead it, the odds on any other named card being with West are 11–13. (There are only 11 vacant places in the West hand, and 13 in East's.)

In the above case, the assumption was made that declarer's side held the ace and king of hearts. If only the ace of hearts is held, then it must be assumed that East holds it, and there are only 12 vacant places in the East hand and the odds become 11–12 instead of 11–13.

If East does not follow suit, the rule in (7)(a) applies because the exact distribution of hearts is known.

If East follows suit with an insignificant heart, the odds change only very slightly, because it is possible to exclude only those distributions in which East was void of hearts. This is so small that the vacant places method is still accurate. A fallacy to be avoided is to argue that since East followed with a nondescript heart, there are only 12 vacant places in his hand, and the odds are 11–12 that a missing card is with West. The fallacy ignores the difference between significant and insignificant cards, for which see CARDS, NEUTRAL AND POSITIVE.

A. T. and R. T.

OFFENDER. The player who commits an irregularity. The laws assume that an offender commits the irregularity without doing so deliberately, and the penalties are devised in order to rectify such an error as equitably as possible. For a player to commit an irregularity either with the intent of invoking a law to his advantage, or with the intent of gaining or giving information improperly is a violation of the proprieties of the game; it is unethical conduct, and is not to be considered by anyone under any conditions. In duplicate, Law 12 may be invoked.

OFFENSE. The attack; an offensive play or bid is an attacking move, as distinguished from a defensive play or bid. This is not to be confused with declarer or defender, since both of these must usually take offensive or defensive positions with certain suit holdings.

Also, a breach of law.

OFFICIAL LAWS. See LAWS OF CONTRACT BRIDGE and LAWS OF DUPLICATE.

OFFICIAL SCORE. In duplicate bridge, the account prepared by the director (or under his supervision) which sets forth each contestant's score for each board, and his score and rank for the session, and for the event. The basis for the official score is the set of traveling score cards on which all the results for each board are recorded, and sets of "pick-up slips," each showing a result on a board, team score slips, or other primary source. These primary sources are recorded on a "recapitulation sheet," from which match points and rankings are computed. It becomes the official score after the expiration of the "correction period." See LAWS (Law 77); PICK-UP SLIPS; RECAPITULATION SHEET; TRAVELING SCORE SLIP.

OFFICIAL SYSTEM. A system of contract bridge bidding devised and endorsed by a group of leading American authorities in 1931–32. They opposed themselves to Ely Culbertson, while acknowledging their debt to him in certain areas of theory. Prominent among the group were Milton C. Work, Sidney S. Lenz, Wilbur C. Whitehead, Winfield Liggett, Jr., and F. Dudley Courtenay. Other members of the Advisory Council were: Charles T. Adams, Shepard Barclay, Fred G. French, Henry P. Jaeger, Mrs. Madeleine Kerwin, Mrs. Guy Purdy, E. V. Shepard, Victor R. Smith, Charles S. Street, Edward C. Wolfe, and Walter F. Wyman.

Three of the principles which the Official System advocated in opposition to Culbertson have their place in the modern game: (1) the employment of the 4–3–2–1 count for no trump bidding; (2) the incorporation of an intermediate game invitation (non-forcing) suit bid of two; (3) the employment of an original opening forcing bid—the (artificial) TWO CLUB convention, designed not only for game but also for slam bidding. See BRIDGE HEADQUARTERS.

OGUST REBIDS. See WEAK TWO-BIDS.

OKUNEFF CONVENTION. See BULLDOG SYSTEM.

OLDEST PLAYER. Among the many players whose interest remained sharp at advanced ages were George BEYNON, actively playing and directing duplicate games, writing bridge columns, and conducting correspondence courses in club operation and direction after celebrating his centenary in 1964; Howard Foering, Sr., who celebrated his centenary on November 24, 1967, by attending a Continentwide Game; R. F. FOSTER, who played at the age of ninety; Tom Scott of Detroit, whose four sessions a week at the age of eighty-seven were publicized in the July 1955 *Bulletin;* Mrs. Alcinda M. Stebbins (1874–1975) of Tucson, Arizona, who celebrated her 100th birthday by playing bridge at the Tucson Bridge Club; Mrs. Willie Thalheimer, a regular player in her eighties (she was the mother of Louis Thalheimer, championship tennis player in the twenties and an excellent rubber bridge player); and Harold S. VANDERBILT, an expert rubber bridge player at the age of eighty.

OLYMPIAD. Worldwide competition at contract bridge, conducted by the WORLD BRIDGE FEDERATION. Team contests have been held in 1960, 1964, 1968, and 1972; pairs contests have been held in 1962, 1966, 1970, and 1972. The plans are to continue to hold the event every two years, alternating as a team and pair championship. For results of the events held to date, see WORLD CHAMPIONSHIPS.

OLYMPIAD FUND CONTINENTWIDE GAME. See CONTINENTWIDE GAMES.

OLYMPIC. A name first applied in bridge in the sense of a contest of skill at contract bridge in which anyone may participate. The first AMERICAN BRIDGE OLYMPIC and WORLD BRIDGE OLYMPIC were promoted, sponsored, and originated by Ely CULBERTSON in 1932. For results of this and other Olympics, see WORLD PAR CONTESTS. The term was modified to OLYMPIAD to describe WORLD CHAMPIONSHIP events conducted by the WORLD BRIDGE FEDERATION.

OLYMPIC PAR EVENTS. See WORLD PAR CONTESTS.

OMNIUM. A nationwide French tournament with many novel features, first played in 1963. The organizer was I. B. de Hérédia. Special decks with perforated edges were distributed to all playing centers, so that the players themselves could select the thirteen cards needed for each deal by inserting a metal pin in the appropriate hole. The deals were pre-played but not "prepared." Scoring was on a basis similar to a PAR CONTEST, with awards for good and bad results in bidding and play according to the decisions of an expert panel.

ONE-BID. A bid contracting to win one odd trick,

seven tricks in all. Articles appropriate to this heading are: BORDERLINE OPENING BIDS; CHOICE OF SUIT; ONE NO TRUMP OPENING; OPENING SUIT BID.

ONE CLUB ARTIFICIAL AND FORCING. Played in a variety of forms (see ONE CLUB SYSTEMS). The earliest in contract was H. Vanderbilt's "Club Convention," although R. F. Foster advocated a similar idea in auction.

ONE CLUB SYSTEMS. In the desire to conserve BIDDING SPACE, there are a number of systems which use an artificial bid of one club to originate investigations of the final contract. Such systems discussed in articles in this book are BANGKOK CLUB; BLUE TEAM CLUB; CANARY CLUB; FRENCH CLUB; LEA; LEGHORN DIAMOND; LEVINREW; LITTLE ROMAN; MARMIC; NOTTINGHAM; PRECISION; RELAY; ROMAN; ROTH CLUB SYSTEM; TRÉFLE SQUEEZE; VANDERBILT; VIENNA.

ONE DIAMOND NEGATIVE RESPONSE TO ONE CLUB. In most bidding systems that use an artificial opening of one club as a forcing bid, a one diamond response is used to deny certain values. In some systems the one diamond response denies certain point count; in others it denies a certain number of controls. For the parameters of the one diamond response in specific systems see ONE CLUB SYSTEMS.

ONE DIAMOND STRONG ARTIFICIAL OPENING. See BIG DIAMOND SYSTEM; LEGHORN DIAMOND; MITCHELL DIAMOND.

ONE NO TRUMP FORCING TAKE-OUT. See COMIC NO TRUMP OVERCALL; GARDENER NO TRUMP OVERCALL; LEA SYSTEM; UNUSUAL NO TRUMP.

ONE NO TRUMP OPENING. The development of no trump bidding is discussed under APPROACH PRINCIPLE. Limit bidding and the STAYMAN convention combine to make one no trump a cornerstone of modern bidding methods.

In considering an opening no trump bid, three aspects have to be reviewed.

(1) *Strength.* High-card points only are counted, but a five-card suit is worth a point, and the presence of tens can be taken into account. The standard range is 16–18, and alternatives are very rare at rubber bridge. In tournament play, on the other hand, many variations are met with. These include:

(a) 17–20. Used in the ROMAN SYSTEM.
(b) 15–18. A relaxation of the standard range, used by some who like to open one no trump as often as possible.
(c) 15–17. A reduction of the standard range. By including a 15-point hand the range for a one no trump rebid is reduced. The 18-point hand is then dealt with by a two no trump rebid (e.g., one club—one heart—two no trump).
(d) 14–16. Used in the LITTLE MAJOR SYSTEM.
(e) 13–15. Originally used non-vulnerable in the ACOL SYSTEM (now obsolete), and presently an integral feature of PRECISION.
(f) 12–14. The usual range for a WEAK NO TRUMP, used by many players using standard methods as well

as the followers of the KAPLAN-SHEINWOLD and BARON systems.

(g) 10–12. Used, at favorable vulnerability only, by Pierre Jaïs and Roger Trézel, France.
(h) Combinations. Two ranges, one weak and one strong, may be employed, depending on vulnerability and position at the table. The most common is 12–14 not vulnerable and 15–17 vulnerable, used in the Stayman System, the Acol System, and with a different valuation method, in the original CULBERTSON SYSTEM. Some favor a weak no trump at all vulnerabilities in fourth position, because a double is virtually impossible. See THREE-QUARTER NO TRUMP; WOODSON TWO-WAY NO TRUMP.

(2) *Distribution.* An orthodox no trump opening bid has one of the following distributions: 4–3–3–3; 4–4–3–2; or 5–3–3–2 with the five-card suit a minor. However, good players sometimes allow themselves the following exceptions:

(a) 5–3–3–2 with a five-card major-suit. May be tried either because tenace holdings make a no trump contract particularly attractive, or because a 16-point hand is held. The latter is likely to create a rebid problem after a one-level response or a single raise.
(b) 5–4–2–2. Two doubleton major-suit kings and a 16-point hand would be typical:

♠ K x
♡ K x
◇ K J x x
♣ A Q x x x

An opening bid in a minor suit would lead to a rebid problem after a major-suit response.

(c) 6–3–2–2. In this case also the doubletons are likely to be strong, and the strength of the hand is likely to be a minimum or sub-minimum; 15 points is likely using a 16-18 range.

(3) *Location of strength.* There is a tendency to prefer a no trump bid holding tenaces, making it likely that the opening lead will be an advantage to declarer. Conversely, a no trump bid is unattractive with points concentrated in two suits:

♠ x x x
♡ x x x
◇ A K J
♣ A K Q x

The concentration of honors in the minor suits would count against one no trump. On the other hand, a serious rebid problem will have to be faced after an opening of one club and a one-over-one suit response.

There is also a tendency, which some authorities make a rule, to avoid a one no trump bid holding a weak doubleton. The objection to this treatment is that it often creates a rebid problem:

♠ x x
♡ A J x
◇ A Q 10 x
♣ K Q x x

If the opening bid is one diamond (or one club) the rebid will be difficult after any one-level response (except one club—one no trump). For reasons of this kind many players open one no trump whenever the point-count and distribution are suitable, regardless of the location of the honor strength.

Responses to one no trump. The structure of responses is independent of the range of no trump opening being used. There is one tactical exception when a weak hand faces a WEAK NO TRUMP opening. See WEAK NO TRUMP. The point-counts for various responses are based on a 16–18 no trump. When a lower range is in use, the range for various responding bids must be scaled up accordingly.

(1) Two clubs. Almost invariably STAYMAN. One American expert who does not use Stayman is B. Jay Becker, who plays all suit responses to one no trump forcing. See also GLADIATOR, and SKINNER RESPONSES TO ONE NO TRUMP.

(2) Two diamonds. This can be used in various conventional ways. See JACOBY TRANSFER BIDS; TWO-WAY STAYMAN.

(3) Two diamonds (natural), two hearts, or two spades. An unconstructive bid showing at least a five-card suit and no interest in game. See WEAKNESS RESPONSE and JACOBY TRANSFER BID. Treatment of a hand with a long club suit is a matter of partnership agreement. Two clubs followed by three clubs is usual, but some bid three clubs directly and others pass.

(4) Two no trump. 8–9 points and relatively balanced; may have a long minor suit, in which case the point-count requirement is slightly lower. Unlikely to have a four-card major suit unless the distribution is 4–3–3–3. The BARON SYSTEM uses the two no trump response as a conventional forcing bid, asking the opener to bid his suits up the line.

Another alternative is to use the two no trump reponse as a relay, forcing opener to bid three clubs. Responder can pass three clubs with a weak hand and a long club suit, or bid three diamonds, an absolute sign-off, with a weak hand and a diamond suit. This method allows the partnership to use responder's immediate jump to three clubs or three diamonds as a slam try or a game try. If responder bids three hearts or three spades over opener's forced rebid of three clubs it can be used to show a three-suited hand with a singleton or void in the major suit bid.

A method deveoped by Robert Conot of Thousand Oaks, Calif., uses a two no trump response as a take-out for the minors. Responder may have a weak two-suiter, or he may be concerned about a no trump contract because of weakness in one of the majors, or he may be interested in a minor-suit slam. Opener bids his better minor, or bids three clubs if his minors are equal. If responder rebids in a major, he shows a singleton. Opener may then bid three no trump or try for a major suit game on a 4–3 fit. A raise of a minor suit opener has bid over the two no trump response, either direct or indirect, is a game try in that suit, while a rebid in the other minor is game-forcing and invitational to slam.

(5) Three clubs or three diamonds. Forcing to game, suggests a slam, and indicates at least a five-card suit. The opener should tend to bid a suit in which he has concentrated strength, and not necessarily length. This identifies duplication of values, and allows the partnership to rest in three no trump if the concentrated strength is opposite responder's singleton. These responses are weak in Kaplan-Sheinwold.

(6) Three hearts or three spades. Forcing to game, and indicates at least a five-card suit. The opener normally chooses between the suit game and no trump, bidding three no trump if he has only a doubleton in reponder's suit. A rebid in a new suit at the four-level is a slam try. It shows an excellent fit for responder's suit, the ace of the suit bid, a maximum no trump bid, and general suitability for a slam. See also AUTOMATIC ACES; EXPECTED NUMBER OF CONTROLS IN BALANCED HANDS.

Responder's bid may temporarily conceal slam ambitions. If it does, he may have more than a five-card suit. The bidding:

WEST	EAST
1 NT	3 ♡
3 NT	4 ♡

is a mild slam invitation, although rarely accepted. With a six-card suit and no slam interest, East would bid four hearts on the first round.

(7) Three no trump. If responder's hand is balanced, his range is likely to be 10–14. But often he holds a long minor suit and less high-card strength. A minor suit of A Q x x x x would justify a three no trump venture without any outside strength.

(8) Four clubs. Usually played as GERBER.

(9) Four diamonds. An IDLE BID unless TEXAS or SOUTH AFRICAN TEXAS is being used.

(10 Four hearts and four spades. A bid closing the auction. Usually a six-card suit with at least 7–8 points, but might be a strong five-card suit if there is an outside singleton or void. Four hearts might be TEXAS.

(11) Four no trump. A balanced hand, usually 4–3–3–3 distribution, with 15–16 points. A natural slam invitation, and the opener may show suits at the five-level in the hope of locating a 4–4 fit (see BOLAND CONVENTION).

(12) Five clubs or five diamonds. A freak hand with a long, broken minor suit, probably seven or eight cards in length, and little honor strength.

(13) Five no trump. An IDLE BID in standard methods. Used by some experts as an invitation to seven no trump, i.e., a hand slightly too strong to bid six no trump with 19–20. With a minimum, the opener must bid six no trump. Suits may be shown at the six level.

(14) Six no trump. A balanced hand, probably 4–3–3–3 with 17–18 points. Closes the auction.

ONE NO TRUMP OVERCALL. A direct overcall of one no trump shows a hand approximately equivalent to a one no trump opening bid in standard methods, and is therefore balanced with 16–18 points in high cards. Individual partnerships vary the range slightly, and may use 15–17, 15–18 or 16–19. Occasionally it may be expedient to overcall one no trump with a singleton:

♠ 5
♡ A Q 5
◇ A Q 7 3
♣ K J 6 4 2

If the right-hand opponent opens one heart or one diamond, one no trump is rather better than an overcall of two clubs or a TRAP PASS.

Responses by Overcaller's Partner. Partnerships should agree on one of the following methods:

(1) The cue-bid in the opener's suit is used as a STAYMAN-substitute. A response of two clubs is therefore natural and weak unless clubs was the opener's suit. This should be assumed to be standard unless another agreement is made.

(2) Overcaller's partner ignores the opening bid, responding exactly as he would have done to a no trump opening bid. In this case two clubs is always Stayman. The bid in the opponent's suit, other than clubs, is weak and natural. This is not unlikely if the opener's suit was diamonds.

(3) Combining methods (1) and (2) above, overcaller's partner bids two clubs as non-forcing Stayman, and makes a cue-bid in opener's suit, assuming it was not clubs, as forcing Stayman. This means that the overcaller's side will not be able to play in either two clubs or opener's suit, but it has the advantage of giving the overcaller's partner the tools to sign off, to invite, or to force to game.

(4) Overcaller's partner ignores the opening bid, responding as he would have done to one no trump except when the suit was clubs. In that case two diamonds is used as a Stayman substitute. This arrangement permits the overcaller's side to play in the opponent's minor suit, which will often be desirable.

Action by Opener's Partner. After a one no trump overcall, a new suit by the responder at the two-level is weak. He is likely to have a good five-card suit or a six-card suit, with less than 9 points in high cards. A jump to three-level in a new suit is a weak pre-emptive action with a six- or seven-card suit. With most strong hands (9 points or more) a double is appropriate. The only other strong action is a bid of two no trump (see CUE-BID IN OPPONENT'S SUIT) which suggests a freakish, unbalanced hand, probably a two-suiter, inadequate for defense.

For one no trump bids by opener's right-hand opponent, see BALANCING, UNUSUAL NO TRUMP; UNUSUAL ONE NO TRUMP OVERCALL.

ONE NO TRUMP REBID. A second call of one no trump by the opening bidder after a suit bid of one by responder. See OPENER'S REBID. For conventional actions by responder after the one no trump rebid see CROWHURST CONVENTION; STAYMAN ON SECOND ROUND; TWO CLUB REBID BY RESPONDER AS ONLY FORCE AFTER ONE NO TRUMP REBID; UNBID MINOR SUIT FORCE.

ONE NO TRUMP RESPONSE. A bid of one no

trump when partner has opened the bidding with a suit. The normal range for the bid is 6–9, but 10 is possible, particularly by a passed hand which does not wish to bid a four-card suit at the level of two.

One spade—one no trump is the commonest situation, and covers a wide range of hands. The responding hand may be quite unbalanced, but be unable to respond at the level of two:

♠ 3
♡ K 7 6 4 3
◇ K 10 8 7 2
♣ J 3

If the opener's rebid is two clubs, showing presumably 5–4 distribution, responder should bid two diamonds. This does not exclude a heart contract, because the opener will continue to two hearts with 5–3–1–4 distribution.

If the opener rebids a lower-ranking suit at the two-level, responder should very rarely go beyond two of the original suit. When he does so, the reason is usually a fine fit for opener's second suit:

(a)	(b)	(c)
♠ 5	♠ 5	♠ 5
♡ A 8 5 4 2	♡ A 7 4 3	♡ K 7 5 3
◇ K 7 4 3	◇ K 8 6 2	◇ 8 7 3 2
♣ 10 7 6	♣ J 8 5 3	♣ K Q 7 4

After

1 ♠   1 NT
2 ♡

hand (a) can jump to four hearts. The five-card trump support, combined with the singleton spade and two useful honors, is enormously powerful. With (b), three hearts is sufficient. Ten tricks may be out of reach if the opener has a minimum with a four-card heart suit. With hand (c) it would not be wrong to pass. If a try is to be made, some players would make it in clubs, showing a heart fit and some side strength in clubs. This helps the opener to make the right decision: with 5–4–3–1 distribution, for example, he will tend to sign off with a singleton club and bid game with a singleton diamond. This is a matter of partnership agreement; for many partnerships three clubs would simply show club length.

A two no trump rebid by responder is just conceivable in standard methods, but would be barred by some partnerships.

As the sequence

1 ♠   1 NT
2 ♡ (or ◇ or ♣)

has a very wide range (10–18 in high cards), some experts make a jump rebid of three hearts or three diamonds non-forcing. Three clubs then becomes an artificial game-force, unrelated to the club suit. The result is that the rebid at the level of two is more limited, and there is less temptation to try for game.

(The same principle would be applied to other jump shifts in a lower ranking suit, such as

| 1 ♡ | 1 NT |
| 3 ♣ | |

encouraging but non-forcing).

Other strong rebids available to the opener include:

(1) Two no trump. Showing about 17–18 points and probably a five card or even six-card spade suit; the failure to open one no trump is significant. If responder bids a new suit, it is long, weak and non-forcing

(2) A reverse:

| 1 ♡ | 1 NT |
| 2 ♠ | |

Also encouraging with about 17–18 points. Shows four spades and five (or six) hearts.

(3) A jump rebid:

| 1 ♠ | 1 NT |
| 3 ♠ | |

Encouraging but non-forcing, and roughly 16–17 points in high cards.

(4) Jump shift:

| 1 ♠ | 1 NT |
| 3 ♢ | |

Game-forcing, more than 18 points in high cards. Usually five spades and four or five diamonds, with a singleton or void in an unbid suit. (But see the alternative treatment above.)

(5) Three no trump. Usually a balanced distribution with 19–20 points, but might be somewhat less with a solid six- or seven-card spade suit.

(6) Jump rebid to game:

| 1 ♠ | 1 NT |
| 4 ♠ | |

An unbalanced hand with 8½ or more playing tricks, and at least a six-card suit.

The lower the rank of the opening bid, the lower the frequency of the one no trump response. This is because minimum responding hands have alternative possibilities without going to the level of two. Over one heart, one no trump denies a four-card spade suit (although some experts are prepared to conceal a very weak four-card spade suit).

Similarly, the one no trump response to a minor suit denies a four-card major suit in principle, and strongly suggests a balanced hand. Over one club, one no trump almost guarantees 4-3-3-3 distribution, and the four-card is normally a minor (see ONE NO TRUMP RESPONSE TO MINOR SUIT).

See also DRURY; ONE NO TRUMP RESPONSE TO MAJOR, FORCING; STRONG NO TRUMP AFTER PASSING.

ONE NO TRUMP RESPONSE TO MAJOR, FORCING. This response is used on a wide range of hands, including many which would qualify on standard systems for a single raise or a response at the two-level in a new suit. The main purpose is to narrow the range for a single raise. In ROTH-STONE a single raise is strong (10–12 points), and one no trump followed by a preference at the level of two is weak (6–9 points). KAPLAN-SHEINWOLD reverses this meaning which has some advantage in competitive auctions. The single raise, made immediately with a weak hand, has pre-emptive value. With a somewhat stronger hand, there is less reason to try to keep the opponents out of the auction.

As both systems guarantee five cards for a major-suit opening, it is assumed that the opener can take a further bid without strain. If he has a six-card suit, he rebids it. If not, he makes his rebid in his lowest-ranking three-card suit.

There are some inconvenient possibilities. If the opener's distribution is 4–5–2–2, the systems do not provide him with a rebid, and he may end up playing with six trumps in the combined hands. (This can also happen, for example, when the opener's distribution is 5–3–3–2 and responder has 1–3–3–6. The final contract may be two diamonds.) In this rare situation some players would break the rule and open one spade if the spade suit was a strong one.

ONE NO TRUMP RESPONSE TO MINOR SUIT. Most systems lay down 8–10 points as the requirement for a response of one no trump to an opening of one club; in GOREN, 9–11 are needed. This is because a weaker hand can usually always find some other bid; which may be a suit at the level of one, a raise to two clubs, or if need be a response of one diamond based on a three-card suit. Some players treat a response of one no trump to one diamond in the same way, but this creates problems when responder has a weak hand including a club suit.

A modern tendency is to relax these requirements and respond one no trump to one club with as little as 6 points. This has some pre-emptive value, because the fourth player cannot bid at the one-level; but it loses slightly in constructive efficiency.

In KAPLAN-SHEINWOLD the range is 5–8 points.

ONE-ODD. One trick more than six, the book. A bid of one-odd is a bid to win seven tricks.

ONE OVER ONE RESPONSE. A suit response at the level of one to an opening suit bid. For example, one club—one heart.

The minimum strength for this response is 6 points, but in some styles a response is permitted with 3 or 4 points and distributional features. The maximum is the level fixed for a JUMP SHIFT, i.e., about 17 points in standard methods and about 15 points in ACOL. For players using WEAK JUMP SHIFT responses, the one over one has no upper limit.

The longest suit is usually chosen for the response, and if two five-card suits are held, the higher-ranking is given preference. However, a four-card suit that can be bid at the one-level is often preferred to a five- or six-card suit which has to be bid at the two-level when the strength of the hand does not justify a two-over-one response.

For other aspects of this response, see CHOICE OF SUIT and UP THE LINE.

ONE-SPOT. A colloquial alternative for ACE.

ONE-SUIT SQUEEZE. A hybrid between a squeeze and a throw-in, described by Paul Lukacs. Most squeeze situations involve two or more suits.

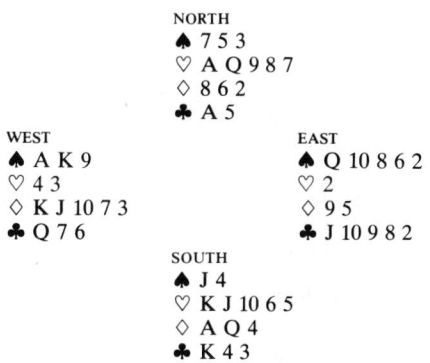

NORTH
♠ 7 5 3
♡ A Q 9 8 7
♢ 8 6 2
♣ A 5

WEST
♠ A K 9
♡ 4 3
♢ K J 10 7 3
♣ Q 7 6

EAST
♠ Q 10 8 6 2
♡ 2
♢ 9 5
♣ J 10 9 8 2

SOUTH
♠ J 4
♡ K J 10 6 5
♢ A Q 4
♣ K 4 3

The bidding:

SOUTH	WEST	NORTH	EAST
1 ♡	2 ♢	3 ♡	Pass
4 ♡	Pass	Pass	Pass

Spades are led three times and South ruffs. After ace, king, and a ruff in clubs and three rounds of trumps the position is:

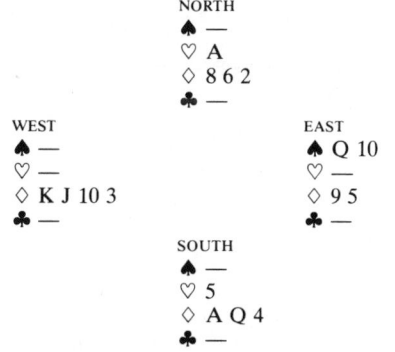

NORTH
♠ —
♡ A
♢ 8 6 2
♣ —

WEST
♠ —
♡ —
♢ K J 10 3
♣ —

EAST
♠ Q 10
♡ —
♢ 9 5
♣ —

SOUTH
♠ —
♡ 5
♢ A Q 4
♣ —

Ace of hearts is led. If West discards the three of diamonds, South merely ducks a diamond. If West discards the ten, South leads the six from dummy. If East ducks, so does South. If East puts up the nine, South covers, creating a tenace position. For a related situation, see RUFF AND RUFF.

ONE-SUITER. A hand with only one suit of more

than three cards. For opening the bidding with a one-suiter, see OPENING SUIT BID; PRE-EMPTIVE BID; WEAK TWO-BID.

ONE-TWO-THREE PRE-EMPTIVE. See PRE-EMPTIVE RE-RAISE.

OPEN. (1) To lead to the first trick in the play of the hand. (2) The bidding: to make the first bid in a given auction. (3) Teams, pairs: tournament contests in which any pair, whether mixed (man and woman) or not, or any team of whatever constituency may play. (4) Room: that room in a championship event in which spectators may be present in somewhat substantial numbers as opposed to a CLOSED ROOM that is limited as to both audience and egress. (5) Club: a game that allows all ACBL members to participate.

OPEN HAND. The dummy's hand, exposed on the table, as distinguished from the "CLOSED" HAND of the declarer.

OPEN INDIVIDUAL CHAMPIONSHIP, NATIONAL. See BAIRD TROPHY.

OPEN PAIR CHAMPIONSHIP, NATIONAL. See CAVENDISH TROPHY; SILODOR TROPHY.

OPEN PAIRS. An event of duplicate competition between pairs of players without regard to sex or master-point holding. Usually this is the most popular event at sectional tournaments, and is contested in two sessions on Saturday. When this is the main event of a tournament, it is necessary that the first session be a qualifying one, with about half of the field playing in the finals of the event. The eliminated players (and others, too) play in the consolation event that is run concurrently with the finals of the open pair. See CARRY-OVER SCORES, QUALIFYING.

OPEN TEAM CHAMPIONSHIP, NATIONAL. See VANDERBILT CUP; REISINGER MEMORIAL TROPHY.

OPENER'S REBID. The second bid by the opener who began with a suit-bid of one is frequently the crucial point in the auction. The following summary refers to standard methods (unless otherwise specified), and is limited to auctions in which responder made a non-jump bid in a new suit. Other rebids are dealt with separately under such headings as JUMP SHIFT; ONE NO TRUMP RESPONSE; TWO NO TRUMP RESPONSE; SINGLE RAISE and DOUBLE RAISE.

(1) *After a* ONE-OVER-ONE RESPONSE.

(a) *One no trump rebid.* 13–15 is the standard range using a 16–18 no trump opening, but 12 is possible. If the opening no trump is 15–17, the rebid is 12–14. For users of a weak no trump (12–14) the no trump rebid is a minimum of 15 (15–17 in KAPLAN-SHEINWOLD; 15–16 in ACOL).

The specific sequence one heart—one spade—one no trump can be given distinct treatment. In Kaplan-Sheinwold it shows 12–14, equivalent to a one no trump opening; and there is an argument for treating this sequence as strong when a strong no trump is being used.

(b) *Rebid in original suit.* These usually require a six-card suit, because the opener avoids rebidding a five-card suit if he can. A six-card suit is almost a certainty if the response was the most economical possible:

WEST	EAST	WEST	EAST
1 ♡	1 ♠	1 ♣	1 ♢
2 ♡		2 ♣	

In each case West had four other minimum rebids at his disposal, and chose to rebid his original suit. The opener is far more likely to rebid a five-card suit if the response used up bidding space:

WEST	EAST
1 ♣	1 ♠
2 ♣	

In these situations the opener may have an unbid four-card suit, or even a five-card suit, which he could not show without making a strength-showing reverse bid.

(c) *Rebid at the one-level.* For example, one club—one heart—one spade. This is a most unrevealing rebid, covering a very wide range of hands. The only information responder has is that the opener is unlikely to have as many as 19 high-card points, because he would then presumably have made a jump shift rebid. The black suit lengths remain shrouded in mystery. More often than not the club suit will be longer; five-four and six-four would be common distributions, and six-five possible. Even five-three and six-three are conceivable:

♠ A K 5	♠ A K 5
♡ 6 2	♡ 6 2
◇ 5 4	◇ 5 4 3
♣ A K Q 7 5 4	♣ A K Q 7 5

With both these hands many experts would open one club, and rebid one spade over one heart.

Equal black-suit lengths are common, four-four, five-five, or theoretically six-six. In exceptional cases the spades may be longer than the clubs:

♠ 7 5 4 3 2	♠ A Q 6 4
♡ 7 5	♡ 7 6 2
◇ A 3	◇ 9 8 2
♣ A K Q 4	♣ A K 6

Both these hands are awkward to bid, and in each case the lesser evil may be to bid one club and rebid one spade over one heart.

Similar considerations apply to the sequences one club—one diamond—one spade, and one club—one diamond—one heart, although in the latter case a five-five distribution is unlikely. One diamond—one heart—one spade is slightly more precise: a three-card diamond suit is improbable and so is five-five distribution.

(d) *Rebid in lower-ranking suit at the two-level.* Four sequences are possible, all consisting of a red-suit opening, a major-suit response, and a minor-suit rebid. For example:

WEST	EAST
1 ♡	1 ♠
2 ♣	

The most likely distribution for West is five-four, but five-five, six-four, and six-five are all possible. Four-five and four-four are possible in some styles, but should be avoided if possible because the responder may have to give preference to the original suit with a doubleton. When the rebid bypasses one no trump in this way, the responder can reasonably assume that the opener's original suit was a five-carder.

These sequences have a wide range in standard methods (10–18 in high cards), and are therefore difficult to handle. They are strong in Roth-Stone and Kaplan-Sheinwold, and in the latter system the sequence is virtually forcing if the opener bids both minor suits. The alternative is to try to avoid such rebids with as many as 17–18 points.

(e) *Reverse.* Four sequences are possible, all consisting of a minor-suit opening, a major-suit response, and a red-suit rebid. For example:

WEST	EAST
1 ♣	1 ♠
2 ♡	

The most likely distribution for West is five-four. His reverse bid promises more clubs than hearts, so obvious alternative distributions are six-four and six-five. A three-card heart suit is possible:

♠ Q 7 5	♠ Q 3
♡ A K 4	♡ A K 4
◇ 7 2	◇ 7 2
♣ A K J 8 3	♣ A Q J 9 5 3

These untypical reverses are often provoked by a weakness in the fourth suit. This factor may even cause the opener to break the rule that the first suit must be longer:

♠ Q 7 5
♡ A K 7 3
◇ 6 2
♣ A K Q 4

Even a five-five distribution is conceivable if a player with 3–5–0–5 distribution chooses to open one club.

The high-card strength for this reverse is normally 16–18, and it is highly encouraging but not forcing. Some systems treat the bid as forcing (Roth-Stone, Kaplan-Sheinwold, and Baron).

(f) *Single raise in responder's suit.* For example, one diamond—one spade—two spades. Usually 12–16 points, and an expectation of four-card trump support. Five-card trump support is theoretically possible if the sequence is one club—one spade—two spades. Three-card trump support is common, and is usually appropriate unless the hand is completely balanced or has a six-card suit to rebid.

Some authorities indicate that this single raise promises more than a minimum opening bid, but such treatment does not work well if the opener has a minimum hand: he may then be forced to break the rule or make a distorted rebid of some other kind.

(g) *Two no trump rebid.* The standard range is 19–20, i.e., a hand too strong to open a 16–18 one no trump. The responder continues to game unless he has made a sub-minimum response. The range is reduced to 18–19 for those using a 15–17 one no trump opening, and is 17–18 in Acol. A simple rebid in his own suit by the responder is ambiguous in standard methods. It would be a sign-off in Acol, but forcing in Kaplan-Sheinwold (which uses three clubs as preparatory to a sign-off). Other suit bids at the three-level are clearly forcing, including a bid in the opener's suit. See WOLFF CONVENTION.

(h) *Jump rebid in opener's suit.* For example one club —one heart—three clubs. This shows a good six-card suit or perhaps a seven-card suit and about 15–17 high-card points. The bid is encouraging, not forcing, and in a minor suggests three no trump. A new suit bid by responder at the three-level would show a no trump stopper and not necessarily length.

(i) *Jump raise in responder's suit.* For example, one diamond—one spade—three spades. Usually indicates 16–18 high-card points and four-card spade support. Three-card support is possible if the high-card strength is concentrated in the bid suits:

♠ A K 5
♡ 5 4 2
◇ A K J 6 3
♣ Q 5

Responder usually continues to game or slam, but may pass if his response was minimum or sub-minimum.

(j) *Jump shift rebid.* For example, one diamond— one spade—three clubs or three hearts. Shows an unbalanced hand and is forcing to game. The opener often has a fit for responder's suit which he plans to show later:

♠ A K 6 4
♡ 6
◇ A Q J 7 3
♣ A J 6

WEST	EAST
1 ◇	1 ♠
3 ♣	

intending to support spades later and so indicate heart shortage.

(k) *Three no trump rebid.* The standard range of 21–22 has been abandoned by virtually all experts, mainly as a result of the abandonment of the forcing two in favor of weak two-bids. The three no trump

rebid is therefore little used. It may be: (i) exactly 20 points and a balanced hand, if the opening no trump is 15–17 and a two no trump rebid is 18–19; (ii) 19–20 in Acol; (iii) a hand strong in minor-suit playing tricks:

♠ 5
♡ A 5 2
◇ A 9 3
♣ A K Q 10 6

The bidding is one club—one spade—three no trump.

(l) *Jump to game in responder's major suit.* For example, one diamond—one spade—four spades. This shows four-card support and sufficient values to justify game. The most common type of hand is relatively balanced with 19–20 points, because a powerful unbalanced hand is likely to prefer a jump shift rebid (see [j] above).

(m) *Jump to game in opener's major suit.* One heart—one spade—four hearts is the only possible sequence. Many powerful hands with a seven-card suit or even an eight-card suit would qualify. A six-card suit is possible:

♠ Q 5 4
♡ K Q J 10 7 3
◇ 6
♣ A K 3

In this case the opener's hand has been improved by the partial fit in spades. (The partial spade fit is automatically indicated in Acol, because other hands with sufficient playing strength would qualify for a two heart opening.)

(n) *Double jump rebid.* This can be a jump to four of opener's suit, or a double jump shift to the three-level or the four-level:

(a)		(b)		(c)	
WEST	EAST	WEST	EAST	WEST	EAST
1 ♣	1 ♡	1 ♣	1 ♡	1 ♣	1 ♡
4 ♣		3 ♠		4 ◇	

These sequences are virtually useless in a natural sense, although (b) could be used to show the rare 6–6 hand. Players using such bids normally do so as part of a slam convention. Auction (a) is normally used to show a hand worth a raise to game in hearts, but with a long and probably solid club suit. A typical hand would be

♠ x   ♡ K Q x x   ◇ A x   ♣ A K Q x x x

For other uses of these jump rebids see ASKING BID; FRAGMENT BID; SPLINTER BID; VOID-SHOWING BID.

(2) *After a* TWO OVER ONE RESPONSE.

(o) *Two no trump rebid.* For example, one heart— two clubs—two no trump. This is 15–18 in standard practice, and is never passed. It is theoretically forcing in Roth-Stone (13–16) and Kaplan-Sheinwold (15–17). It may be passed in Acol (15–17) because responder may have only 8 points.

(p) *Rebid in original suit.* For example, one spade—two diamonds—two spades. This shows a minimum opening bid with 10–14 or possibly 15 points in high cards. The suit will usually be a six-carder, but may be a good five-card suit if no alternative presents itself. The chance of a five-card suit is greatest if the response is in the suit ranking immediately below opener's: one spade—two hearts—two spades; one heart—two diamonds—two hearts; or one diamond—two clubs—two diamonds. On the other hand, the sequence one spade—two clubs—two spades nearly always represents a six-card suit: with only five spades the opener would usually be able to find an alternative rebid of three clubs, two no trump, two hearts or two diamonds.

If the opener's suit is a weak five-carder which will play badly opposite a possible singleton, many players would try to avoid rebidding it:

♠ J 6 4 3 2
♡ A 5
◇ A Q 5
♣ Q 4 2

If the response to one spade is two clubs, some experts would raise to three clubs. But this is ruled out by some authorities (see [r] below) in which case the choice lies between two diamonds, which is unlikely to come to harm, and rebidding the bad spades.

If the response to one spade is two hearts, two no trump and three hearts are both better rebids than two spades if the style used permits these rebids with a minimum hand.

(q) *Rebid in lower-ranking suit.* For example, one spade—two clubs—two diamonds. In standard practice this promises no additional strength and is not forcing: the opener may have 5–5 distribution and 11 high-card points. The opener should therefore try to avoid this minimum rebid with 16 points or more.

Some authorities treat the change of suit as forcing, in which case the bid has no upward limit of strength.

(r) *Single raise in responder's suit.* For example, one heart—two diamonds—three diamonds. There are two distinct schools of thought. Many textbooks class this bid as encouraging, with about 15–16 points in high cards; this makes it forcing in effect, and leaves unsolved the problem of minimum hands in which the natural action is to raise responder's suit. Other authorities therefore regard the single raise as a minimum rebid which does not promise extra strength and is in no way forcing.

(s) *Reverse at the two-level.* For example, one heart—two clubs—two spades. Forcing in standard methods, and virtually all non-standard ones. Some players would regard the bid as game-forcing. The first suit must be longer than the second, so that 5–4 is the expected distribution with the possibility of 6–4 or 6–5. Players who raise the two-level response with a minimum (see [r] above) may reverse into a three-card suit:

♠ A Q 5
♡ A Q 8 6 4
◇ 7 2
♣ K J 6

If the response to one heart is two clubs, two spades is best if three clubs would be a minimum. These sequences are strong (16 points or more) in all systems except Roth-Stone, in which the hand is likely to be a minimum and the distribution 4–4.

(t) *Second suit at the three-level (sometimes called "high reverse").* For example, one heart—two diamonds—three clubs. Forcing in all methods, and game-forcing in most. Players who do not regard this bid as game-forcing should agree on the circumstances in which the bidding can stop short of game. (Possible are: simple rebid by responder; simple preference by responder; simple rebid by responder followed by rebid of opener's first suit.) The distribution is usually 5–5 or 5–4; 5–5 is less likely if the suits are spades and clubs, because many players open one club with such hands. The opener's second suit will often be a three-carder:

♠ 5 2
♡ A Q 9 4 3
◇ A Q 8
♣ A Q 6

After one heart—two diamonds, three clubs would be the expert choice. If the clubs were K J 2, three clubs would still be chosen by those who do not regard three diamonds as encouraging (see [r] above).

(u) *Jump shift to the three-level.* For example, one spade—two clubs—three diamonds. Game-forcing, and may conceal a good fit for partner's clubs. Players who regard a two-diamond rebid as forcing usually reserve the jump shift for a marked two-suited hand—5–5 or better.

(v) *Jump rebid in opener's suit.* For example, one spade—two diamonds—three spades. Forcing in standard methods (but not in Acol) and shows a good six-card suit.

(w) *Jump to game in opener's suit.* For example, one spade—two diamonds—four spades. A strong six-card suit or better with values for game and no interest in a no trump contract. In Acol a moderate fit with responder's suit is implied because of the failure to open with a two-bid (compare [m]).

(x) *Jump raise in responder's suit.* Forcing in a minor suit, for example one spade—two diamonds—four diamonds and presumably four-card or five-card support (not forcing by definition in Acol, but some partnerships play it as forcing). One spade—two hearts—four hearts is a special case. It shows a hand slightly too good for three hearts (according to style) and may be three-card support because responder has promised a five-card suit.

(y) *Three no trump rebid.* For example, one spade—two diamonds—three no trump. Equivalent to a two no trump rebid over a one-level response, and therefore normally 19–20 points; but some experts would make this bid with 18 points or even 17.

(z) *Double jump shift.* For example, one spade—two clubs—four diamonds. As in [n] above.

OPENING BID. The first call in the auction other than a pass. The treatment of opening bids is discussed in the following separate articles: BIDDABLE

SUITS; BORDERLINE OPENING BIDS; CANAPÉ; CHOICE OF SUIT; FIVE-CARD MAJORS; FIVE OF A MAJOR OPENING; FIVE NO TRUMP OPENING; FORCING TWO; FOUR NO TRUMP OPENING; GAMBLING THREE NO TRUMP; ONE NO TRUMP OPENING; OPENING SUIT BID; PRE-EMPTIVE BID; SIX OF A SUIT OPENING; SIX NO TRUMP OPENING; THREE NO TRUMP OPENING; TWO CLUBS; TWO NO TRUMP OPENING; WEAK TWO-BID.

OPENING BIDDER. The player at a deal of contract who makes the first bid of an auction.

OPENING CALL. The original call made by the dealer to start the auction. See OPENING BID.

OPENING LEAD. After the bidding has been concluded, the play of the hand commences by the declarer's left-hand opponent making an original or opening lead. For selection of opening leads, see OPENING LEADS.

OPENING LEADS. Defense is regarded as the most difficult aspect of bridge. Since the opening lead is the only defensive play made while the dummy is concealed, it requires a kind of "detective" reasoning and considerable analysis of the meaning of every call in the auction, as well as agreed conventional leads and plays to the first trick. The opening lead is frequently the source of substantial profits and losses.

Choosing the Card. The card chosen for the opening lead should help pave the way for the defeat of the contract, insofar as this is possible, and should convey information to partner about the leader's holding in the suit. Some typical card choices, once the suit has been selected, are summarized in the accompanying table.

The "standard" approach has a substantial number of critics, and one important controversy concerns the lead from a sequence of honors. With holdings like A K Q, K Q J, or Q J 10, any of the honors can be led with equal trick-taking effect, so the main concern is to inform partner about the opening leader's holding. The customary practice is to lead the king from A K (unless it is doubleton, in which case the ace is led) and the top card from any other honor sequence. Similarly, the "standard" lead from holdings such as K 10 9 8 or Q 10 9 8 is the ten, the top of the *interior sequence*. However, standard leads create potentially costly confusion is certain instances. For example, the king is led from both A K 4 and K Q 4, so partner may have difficulty deciding whether to signal encouragement with J 8 2; and the ten is led from both K 10 9 8 and 10 9 8 2, so partner may have difficulty deciding whether to return the suit when he gains the lead. Therefore, conventional "non-standard" opening lead methods have become increasingly popular among experts, including ACE FROM ACE-KING; JOURNALIST LEADS; RUSINOW LEADS; and ZERO OR TWO HIGHER LEADS.

A second controversy has to do with the lead from three small cards against a suit contract. The top card is perhaps most common, but all three possibilities have been recommended. See THREE SMALL CARDS, LEAD FROM.

A third controversy concerns the standard fourth-best lead from a long suit. Against suit contracts, an increasing number of experts prefer to give count more accurately by leading the *third highest* card from an *even* number, and the *lowest* card from an *odd* number. Against no trump contracts, some use a low spot card lead to encourage the return of the suit and lead a high spot card to discourage a return; others object to this because the leader's partner can no longer use the RULE OF ELEVEN. These modifications are an integral part of JOURNALIST LEADS.

Choosing the Suit.

Clues from the bidding. Regardless of the carding method that is used, no table or convention can indicate the right *suit* to lead; judgment and deduction must be applied to each situation. In particular, the auction can provide the astute opening leader with valuable clues:

(1) If the opponents are strong in certain suits, the opening leader should look elsewhere for his selection.

(2) If the opponents are weak in a particular suit, the opening leader should attack it. See ATTACKING LEAD.

(3) If one opponent is likely to be void in a certain suit (as when he bids two suits several times and supports a third suit), the opening leader should not lead that ace if the enemy ends up in a suit contract.

(4) If dummy holds a long and strong side suit that will provide numerous discards (as when he has rebid it several times), the opening leader should be aggressive and try to take tricks in a hurry.

(5) If the opponents have staggered into their contract with little strength to spare, the opening leader should be cautious and avoid giving away the fulfilling trick.

(6) If the opponents have strength to spare, (at rubber bridge or IMPs) an aggressive lead has little to lose save an unimportant overtrick.

(7) If partner has indicated a good suit to attack by bidding it (see LEAD-DIRECTING BID), it is usually safe to lead it.

(8) If partner has denied length and strength in a suit by refusing to make a cheap one-level overcall when given the opportunity, the opening leader should not try to hit him in that suit.

(9) If partner has indicated general high-card strength by making a take-out double, it is relatively safe to lead away from an unsupported honor.

(10) If partner has denied general high-card strength by making a pre-emptive bid, it is not advisable to lead away from an unsupported honor.

(11) If partner has requested the lead of a specific suit by making a LEAD-DIRECTING DOUBLE or LIGHTNER DOUBLE, it is usually advisable to lead it.

Clues from the strength of the opening leader's hand. If the opponents bid game and the opening leader has 13 or 14 high-card points, he should visualize the near-Yarborough in partner's hand and reject any lead that requires substantial high-card help (such as the lead from an unsupported honor). When the opening leader's strength is mediocre, however, it is reasonable to expect some useful aid from partner.

The location of the opening leader's strength is

also important. If he holds finessable positions such as K 32 in front of suits bid by dummy, or a few small cards behind suits bid by declarer, the defenders are likely to be in trouble. Declarer's finesses rate to win, and the suits appear to be breaking well for the opponents. Holding length and weakness in dummy's long suit is also a bad sign, for declarer will probably be able to establish it with little difficulty. In such cases, an aggressive opening lead is often justified. But if the opening leader holds strength behind declarer's bid suits, and if he can see that important suits will be breaking badly for the enemy, a more conservative strategy is preferable.

Clues from the strength of the opening leader's suit. Other things being equal, it is frequently desirable to lead from stronger suits. Leading from Q 1043 is preferable to Q 432 because less help is needed from partner to build tricks (and avoid a disaster), while Q J 109 is superior to both holdings. However, as the preceding sections indicate, other things are often *not* equal; and many opening leaders go wrong by using the strength of one suit as their sole guide while ignoring valuable information available from other sources.

Leads against no trump contracts. Since declarer cannot ruff when he runs out of a suit, the defenders should usually try to establish length winners. Assuming that the bidding has not indicated the need for special action, the following guidelines apply:

(1) A five-card or longer holding in an unbid suit is usually an excellent choice, provided that the opening leader has at least one probable entry. For example, leading the three-spot from A Q 632 is ideal; even if declarer gets an undeserved trick with the king, three or four winners are likely to be established while the high cards are retained for use as entries.

(2) From a completely entryless hand, the opening leader should reject his own (weak) long suit and try to build length winners in partner's hand. An unbid *major* suit containing three cards or a strong doubleton is likely to be a good choice.

(3) From holdings such as J 109 x x, Q J 10 x x, K J 10 x x, or A J 10 x x in a suit bid by the enemy, the fourth-best card should be led. This avoids blocking the suit when partner has a useful doubleton, and is likely to tempt declarer into a fatal error in situations like this:

	NORTH	
	Q 2	
WEST		EAST
J 10 9 4 3		K 5
	SOUTH	
	A 8 7 6	

After the jack lead, South has two stoppers by covering. If the four is led instead, South inevitably plays dummy's queen.

(4) If no five-card or longer suit is held, a solid or nearly solid four-carder (such as Q J 109 or J 1093) is likely to build some winners without giving anything away.

(5) Leading from broken four-card suits is less desirable. Attacking from Q 1042 in an unbid suit is not unreasonable, since the lead has a good chance to pay off if partner has even one of the missing honors. However, a suit like A Q 32 should be avoided because the potential for length winners is too limited to justify giving declarer an undeserved trick.

(6) Against three no trump, leading an honor from A K 2 in an unbid suit can be very effective (especially at rubber bridge or IMPs). Partner may turn up with five to the queen, or with five small cards and a side entry. Even the lead of an honor from A Q 2 has at times paid similar dividends.

(7) If no attractive lead exists, a passive lead (as from three or four small cards) has the advantage of being relatively safe. Even the lead of a small doubleton may be correct (see SHORT-SUIT LEADS).

(8) In some instances, the opening leader may gain by disguising the length of his long suit. See FALSE-CARDING.

(9) After a two no trump opening bid, a passive lead is more frequently correct. Declarer's hand contains most of his side's strength, so he may have entry problems if left to his own devices.

(10) Against no trump partials, a passive lead is more frequently correct. The strength is more evenly divided between the two sides, so the defenders are less likely to have to collect tricks in a hurry.

(11) After a GAMBLING THREE NO TRUMP opening bid has been passed out, it is desirable to lead an ace. Declarer is trying to score nine fast tricks with the aid of a solid minor suit, so losing the lead even once may be fatal.

Leads against suit contracts. Here the defenders are less likely to gain by trying to build length winners, since declarer can simply ruff in when he runs out of a suit. Assuming that the bidding has not indicated the need for special action, the following guidelines apply:

(1) Leading from solid or nearly solid honor sequences, such as A K J 5, K Q J 73, Q J 102, or J 1095, is likely to be both constructive and safe. Leading from weaker honor holdings like K Q 73 or Q J 92 can also be effective, but may cost a trick when partner is weak in the suit.

(2) Leads from long suits are safer but less likely to establish several tricks, while leads from short side suits are riskier but more likely to establish several tricks. If the defenders must rush to collect their winners (as when dummy's bidding shows a long side suit that will provide numerous discards), it is better to lead from Q 75 in an unbid suit than from Q 8654. When safety considerations are more important, however, leading from length is preferable.

(3) When holding four or more trumps, it is particularly desirable to lead from a long suit. If declarer can be forced to ruff several times, his trumps may run out before the defenders' do and cause him to lose control of the hand. See FORCING LEADS.

(4) When no attractive lead exists, a passive lead (as from three or four small cards) has the advantage of being relatively safe.

(5) A trump lead is desirable in several situations: when the bidding indicates that declarer will try to ruff losers in dummy or crossruff; when the defenders hold substantial strength in all side suits, as when the opponents sacrifice against a contract

that the defenders expected to make on power; when a one-level contract is passed out; and when a passive lead is indicated and the opening leader holds a few small trumps. A trump lead is mandatory when a one-level take-out double is passed out. However, a trump lead should be avoided when the opening leader's holding is too precarious to lead from; when the bidding indicates that the defenders must take their tricks in a hurry; when the opening leader is very long is a suit declarer plans to ruff in dummy, indicating that partner will be able to overruff; when the opening leader has a singleton trump; and when the opening leader has four or more trumps, in which case the forcing game is preferable. See TRUMP LEADS.

(6) A side-suit singleton is likely to be effective when the opening leader has some extra low trumps to use for ruffing and a probable entry in trumps, so long as the leader's partner rates to have an entry or two. However, singleton leads should usually be avoided when the opening leader has no excess low trumps to ruff with (as when holding A Q or Q J 3); when he has four or more trumps, in which case the forcing game is preferable; or when the singleton is a king or queen.

(7) Side-suit doubletons are considerably less likely to produce ruffs than are singletons, and should be led for this purpose only when holding a quick entry *in trumps*. A small doubleton may be a satisfactory passive lead, however. In some infrequent cases, leading from K 2 or Q 2 may be justified because the opening leader is truly desperate (see DESPERATION LEAD OR PLAY).

(8) With an otherwise worthless hand, leading the king from K 7 4 3 in partner's bid suit can be effective.

If the king holds the trick, the opening leader may now be able to make a profitable attack through dummy in a different suit; while if the opening lead is the normal small card and declarer has a singleton, no further leads through dummy will be possible.

(9) Underleading the ace is normally avoided, but can be a winning choice. The defenders may need tricks in a hurry, and declarer may also be missing the queen and misguess; or it may be urgent to put partner on lead for an attack through declarer's hand or to obtain a ruff. See UNDERLEAD.

Leads against slam contracts. If the opponents reach a small slam and the opening leader holds K Q and an ace, it is obvious that the king should be led. However, fate usually does not conspire to deal all the defenders' high cards to the opening leader, so he often has to decide whether to lead away from an unsupported king or queen in an unbid suit. Fortunately, slam contracts often involve considerable amounts of bidding, which offer more clues to the opening leader. Normally, the following guidelines apply:

(1) Against a small slam, an attacking lead is preferable when dummy's bidding indicates a long, establishable suit. A passive lead is more appropriate if both declarer and dummy appear to have balanced hands, whether or not the contract is at no trump.

(2) Against suit small slams, an ace lead is desirable if it is in an unbid suit and the opening leader holds a probable second winner elsewhere, or if the bidding suggests that the opponents might be off two fast tricks. Otherwise the ace lead is more debatable, and should normally be avoided if it is in a suit bid by the enemy.

Opening Leads: Some Typical Card
Choices Once the Suit Has Been Selected

Suit Length	Holding in Suit	Lead vs. NT	Lead vs. Suits
Two Cards	Any non-trump doubleton	Top card	Top card
	Trumps: honor sequence or ace-any	—	Top card[1]
	Trumps: any other doubleton	—	Low card
Three Cards	9 8 7 or worse, not in trumps	Top card	Top card[2]
	Trumps: three small	—	2nd best[3]
	10 x x, J x x, Q x x, K x x	3rd best	3rd best
	Q 10 x, K 10 x, K J x	3rd best[4]	3rd best
	10 9 x, J 10 x, Q J x, K Q x	Top card	Top card
	Trumps: J 10 x	—	3rd best
	A x x, A 10 x	3rd best[5]	Ace
	A J x, A Q x	2nd best[6]	Ace
	A K x or better	King	King

[1] An old chestnut is to lead the jack from Q J or the nine from 10 9, hoping to induce declarer to misguess on the next round. However, this is unlikely to be necessary against a declarer familiar with RESTRICTED CHOICE.
[2] Middle and low are also popular. See THREE SMALL CARDS, LEAD FROM.
[3] Followed by the smallest, thus denying a doubleton.
[4] In some case, the jack from K J x is proper in order to unblock.
[5] The ace is preferable if partner does not figure to have a side entry.
[6] The ace is correct in some cases.

Four Cards	9 8 7 6 or worse	4th best[7]	4th best[7]
	10 x x x, J x x x, Q x x x, K x x x	4th best	4th best
	10 9 x x, J 10 x x, Q J x x	4th best	4th best[8]
	Q 10 x x, K 10 x x, K J x x	4th best	4th best
	Q 10 9 x, K 10 9 x, K J 10 x	2nd best	2nd best
	A 10 9 x, A J 10 x	2nd best	Ace
	10 9 7 x, J 10 8 x, Q J 9 x, K Q 10 x	Top card	Top card
	10 9 8 x, J 10 9 x, Q J 10 x, K Q J x	Top card	Top card
	A x x x, A 10 x x, A J x x, A Q x x	4th best	Ace
	K Q x x, K Q 9 x, A K x x, A K 10 x	4th best	King
	K Q 10 x, A K 10 9, A K J x, or better	King	King

Five Cards: The rules for four-card suits are frequently correct. Against *no trump* contracts, however, the degree of solidity of an honor sequence is particularly important. Compare the following situations:

10 9 7 x x, 10 9 8 x x, J 10 8 x x	4th best
10 9 7 6 x, 10 9 8 6 x, 10 9 8 7 x	Top card
J 10 8 7 x, J 10 9 7 x, J 10 9 8 x	Top card
Q J 9 x x, K Q 9 x x	4th best
J 10 9 x x, Q J 10 x x, K Q 10 x x, K Q J x x	Top card or 4th best[9]
Q J 9 8 x, K Q 10 9 x	2nd best[10]
Q J 10 8 x, Q J 10 9 x, K Q J 9 x, K Q J 10 x	Top card
Q 10 9 x x, K 10 9 x x, A 10 9 x x	4th best
Q 10 9 7 x, Q 10 9 8 x, K 10 9 7 x, K 10 9 8 x	2nd best
A 10 9 7 x, A 10 9 8 x	2nd best
K J 10 x x, A J 10 x x	2nd best or 4th best[10]
K J 10 8 x, K J 10 9 x, A J 10 8 x, A J 10 9 x	2nd best[11]
A K 10 9 x	King or ten[12]
A K J x x	King or 4th best[12]
A K J 10 x	Ace[13]

[7] The top card or second best may be led to deny an honor; see text.
[8] The queen from Q J x x is correct in some cases.
[9] Fourth best is preferable when the goal is to establish the whole suit, rather than play safe, and when an opponent is likely to have four cards in the suit.
[10] Partner is expected to play the immediately lower honor if he has it.
[11] King from K J 10 9 x x is correct in some cases.
[12] The king is preferable when a sure side entry is held.
[13] Partner is expected to play an honor if he has one, and to signal his count (high-low for even, low-high for odd) if he does not.

(3) Against suit small slams, singleton leads are often effective. However, they should be avoided if both opponents have bid the suit, in which case the lead may help them overcome a bad break; or if the opening leader has a sure winner (or a relatively strong hand), in which case the slam will be defeated anyway if partner can take a trick.

(4) Against suit small slams, a trump lead is dangerous; it may pick up partner's queen and save declarer a crucial guess. However, a trump lead may work well if the bidding plus the leader's holding indicates that partner has at most a singleton, the auction strongly suggests that declarer plans to do a great deal of ruffing in one or both hands, and the trump holding is safe to lead from.

(5) Against a grand slam, without an immediate

winner to cash, it is usually desirable to make a safe lead. Only one trick is needed to defeat the contract, so building winners is unnecessary. Trump leads are frequently desirable against suit grand slams, but should be avoided if partner may have the queen of trumps and a safe selection is available elsewhere.

Board-a-match and match-point considerations. At board-a-match scoring, the opening leader must be careful to avoid losing a board that his teammates at the other table have all but won. At match points, there are conflicting considerations. No trump contracts based on shaky stoppers are more common at this form of scoring, so the opening leader is more likely to gain by trying to run a long suit. Yet conceding even one undeserved trick can result in a bottom score, so care must be taken to avoid presenting declarer with a gift that his counterparts at other tables will not receive. Thus an unusual attempt to defeat a contract, correct at rubber bridge or IMPs, may be wrong at match points because it is too likely to concede the overtrick. (See MATCH-POINT DEFENSE.) Opening leads at match points are a source of considerable complexity (and headaches).

                                    R. E.

OPENING ONE NO TRUMP BID. See ONE NO TRUMP OPENING.

OPENING SUIT BID. An opening of one club, one diamond, one heart, or one spade has a normal range of 10–20 high-card points. It may sink below 10 in some freak cases—with 6–6 distribution, for example. It may rise above 20 with unbalanced hands, usually 4–4–4–1 or 5–4–3–1 patterns, unsuited to a two no trump opening and not quite strong enough for a forcing opening.

For special factors affecting the opening bid, see BIDDABLE SUITS; BORDERLINE OPENING BIDS; CHOICE OF SUIT.

OPPONENT. A member of the adverse team at bridge. An opponent can be a member of an opposing team of four, or five or six as well as merely a temporary adversary.

OPPONENT'S SUIT. A suit held or bid by one or both adversaries. In judging the bidding, a holding of three small cards in the opponent's suit is generally a danger signal. But if the opponent's suit is supported, a small tripleton may actually be better than a small doubleton because the chance of finding a singleton with partner is increased. For bids in the opponent's suit, see CUE-BIDS IN OPPONENT'S SUIT.

OPPOSITION. (1) The opponents on a hand, set of hands or rubber; (2) The contestants in DIRECT COMPETITION; (3) The balance of the field; (4) The other team in a head-on team event.

OPTIMUM STRATEGY. Plans of play adopted by declarer or defender in the light of different tactics which may be adopted by the opposing side.

The following is one example of the complications which can arise in considering alternative strategies:

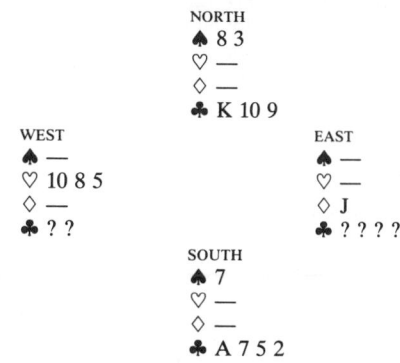

Spades are trumps. East is in.

Fruther conditions are that West is marked with three hearts and East with the diamond jack. Declarer knows, therefore, that the critical club suit is divided 2–4, but he doesn't know where the queen and jack of clubs are. Clubs are therefore designated with question marks on the diagram. Lest he give a ruff and discard, East must obviously lead a club, and, of course, declarer's aim is to make all the tricks.

The problem is to analyze the optimum strategy both from declarer's and (more important) defender's point of view.

The defender's clubs may break:

  (1) xx—QJxx .... 6 cases
  (2) Qx—Jxxx ....
      or
      Jx—Qxxx .... 8 cases
  (3) QJ—xxxx .... 1 case
               TOTAL   15 cases

Let us examine East's possible tactics.

(a) The "naïve" tactic. East is a weak player. He leads queen or jack in (1). He leads small in (2) and, perforce, in (3).

Against such an opponent it is clear that South will lose only in (3). He will win fourteen times out of fifteen.

(b) The "expert" tactic. East is a good player. He leads queen or jack whenever he has one (or both) of these cards.

Now declarer has to reverse his play. As (2) is more likely than (1), South should play for divided honors, i.e., cash the ace in hand and drop West's other honor next. So, South wins in (2) (eight cases) but loses in (1) (six cases).

Declarer, however, takes a little revenge in case (3) as Terence Reese points out in his *Expert Game.* For South can easily divine case (3) from the very fact that East had led a small card (having no alternative). So South wins also in case (3), hence, in nine cases out of fifteen.

To prevent this, East may lead sometimes small and sometimes high in case (2). Say 50% each. Which leads to:

(c) The shrewd tactic. East always leads an honor in (1), always small in (3), but in case (2) he leads half the time high and the rest small. Against this tactic,

South does better to revert to his behavior against tactic (a), playing East for both honors whenever he leads high, and only then.

South thus wins the six cases from (1) and four of the eight cases from (2), thus, on balance, ten cases out of fifteen.

This shrewd tactic is therefore no improvement, but we may now figure out the correct optimum strategy as follows:

(d) The optimum strategy. East leads, of course, always an honor in (1), but in case (2) he leads exactly, but "at random," a small card 12½% of the time, i.e., once out of eight times.

It is clear that declarer now has to play for split honors whenever East leads high (seven cases against six). But if East leads small, declarer may:

(i) play for split honors. He will win in $0 + (7 + 1) + 0 = 8$ cases (out of 15).

(ii) play for Q J with West. He will win in $0 + (7 + 0) + 1 = 8$ cases (out of 15).

Thus according to whether his strategy is naïve, expert, shrewd, or optimum, the defender wins a trick in fourteen, nine, ten, or eight cases out of fifteen. And declarer has no way to improve on those chances.

J. B.

(Reprinted by permission from *British Bridge World,* January 1960.)

OPTIONAL. A term applied to a bid, play, or point of law in which a player may have two or more choices; as distinguished from compulsory action, or procedure strictly regulated by law.

OPTIONAL DOUBLE. A COOPERATIVE DOUBLE showing a balanced hand with enough high cards to defeat the contract in all probability, and with support for any unbid suit. The partner of the doubler need not have a substantial trump holding in order to pass; he is expected to pass unless he has a good suit and unbalanced distribution. For example, the following hand would be appropriate for an optional double of a three heart opening pre-empt:

♠ A K 7
♡ A J 2
♢ 7 4 3
♣ A Q 6 5

See also DEFENSE TO OPENING THREE-BID; PENALTY DOUBLE; TAKE-OUT DOUBLE.

OPTIONS.

(1) Alternative actions available to a player in certain circumstances after an irregularity by the opposing side. An opening lead by the wrong defender is a case in which the declarer has four options. (See LAWS, Laws 54 and 56.)

(2) Alternative play possibilities available to a declarer. He should usually adopt a sequence of play which will "preserve options." A play which retains the possibility of trying for other possibilities is usually better than one which stands or falls on immediate success, even if the second is a better percentage chance.

George Coffin gives this example:

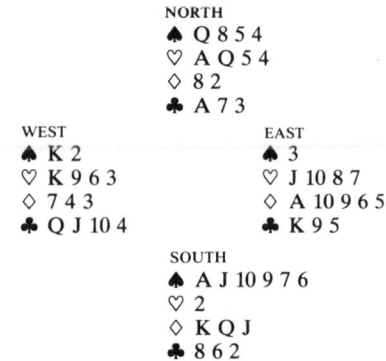

NORTH
♠ Q 8 5 4
♡ A Q 5 4
♢ 8 2
♣ A 7 3

WEST
♠ K 2
♡ K 9 6 3
♢ 7 4 3
♣ Q J 10 4

EAST
♠ 3
♡ J 10 8 7
♢ A 10 9 6 5
♣ K 9 5

SOUTH
♠ A J 10 9 7 6
♡ 2
♢ K Q J
♣ 8 6 2

West leads the four of clubs against four spades. South wins the club lead in dummy, leads the queen of spades, and rises with the ace if the king does not appear. This preserves the secondary option of the heart finesse, which works as the cards lie.

At match points this play would be doubtful, because it runs a serious risk of a disastrous two-trick defeat.

ORANGE CLUB. Strong club system used by J. JACOBY and R. WOLFF in the 1970, 1971, and 1972 World Championships.

The one club opening promises 17 or more points; responses show controls. Other opening bids are limited and natural according to the CANAPÉ principle. A one no trump opening shows a balanced hand with 13–15 points with a 4- or 5-card club suit, or 16–17 with any balanced distribution.

Other features include BLUE TEAM TWO DIAMONDS, FLANNERY TWO HEARTS, weak two bid in spades only; singleton- and void-showing forcing raises by a passed hand.

ORIGINAL BID. The first bid made in an auction. Reference is frequently made by a partner to one's "original bid" as having been in spades, or no trump, etc., as for example: "I returned you to spades, since that was your original bid."

ORIGINAL HOLDING. The cards one has in a given suit at the beginning of play, or at the beginning of the auction. Thus one might say, while describing the play of a hand, that one's original spade holding was five to the ace-jack-ten, and that at a certain point one was down to the ten and two little cards in the suit.

ORIGINAL LEAD. See OPENING LEAD.

ÖSTERREICHISCHER BRIDGE-VERBAND. See AUSTRIAN BRIDGE FEDERATION.

OUR HAND. A colloquial expression indicating that

a player thinks his side can make the highest positive score on a deal in which both sides take part in the auction. See BELONG.

OUT. A player who is a member of a table at rubber bridge, but not actively participating. The order in which players are out is established by cutting, the holder(s) of the lowest card or cards cut sitting out for the first rubber, other players going out in order.

OUT-OF-THE-BLUE CUE-BID. An unusual bid of a new suit which cannot be taken as a suit bid, indicating support for partner's last bid suit, strength in the cue-bid suit (often first-round control), and interest in reaching a high-level contract. The phrase was coined by Norman SQUIRE, England, in his *Theory of Bidding*.
For example:

NORTH	SOUTH
1 ♣	1 ♠
1NT	3 ♡
4 ◇	

North's four diamond bid cannot indicate a diamond suit. North is attempting to indicate good support for South's hearts, diamond control, and interest in a slam. North might hold (using strong no trumps): ♠ K x, ♡ A Q x x, ◇ A J, ♣ 109 x x x. See BLUE TEAM FOUR CLUB-FOUR DIAMOND CONVENTION.

OUT OF TURN. Not in rotation. For a bid out of rotation, see LAWS (Laws 30–32), for a lead out of turn, see Laws 54–56, for a play out of turn, see LAW 57.

OUT ON A LIMB. A phrase used to describe a player who has taken unusual or precipitate action during an auction, and is in great danger of being doubled at a contract that is both risky and untenable and susceptible of great loss as to points. During the play of a hand, one may be said to be out on a limb as respects a situation, for example, when one is "wide open" in a suit at no trump, although the opposition may not be aware of this, or when one is playing at a trump contract and not only does not have control of the trump suit but is extremely vulnerable to attack in that area.

OVER. A term used to indicate one's position at the table in respect to one's right-hand opponent. One may be correctly said to be over that opponent if one is West to his South, for example. This term may be used in bidding situations as well as in play. See RIGHT-HAND PLAYER.

OVERBID. A call offering to undertake a contract for a greater number of tricks than is justified by the bidder's holding. Matters of system are often involved; a call may be an overbid in one system but an underbid in another.
In competitive auctions, or auctions that are likely to become competitive, an apparent overbid may be an ADVANCE SAVE:

♠ 7
♡ Q J 9 8 7 6
◇ 5 3
♣ 10 8 5 2

With East-West vulnerable the bidding has gone:

SOUTH	WEST	NORTH	EAST
1 NT	Pass	4 ♡	All Pass
(12–14)			

North does not expect to make four hearts, but he does expect East-West to make four spades. But East may not be able to bid at the four-level.
The term overbid is sometimes erroneously used in referring to an OVERCALL. See SACRIFICE.

OVERBIDDER. A player who consistently bids higher than his high-card and distributional strength justify.
Playing with an overbidder, it is clearly necessary to be conservative, although this is no remedy holding extreme weakness. However, the overbidder must not be allowed to think that he is playing with an underbidder, or worse will follow. If the underbidder bids normally when he is due to be dummy he is little better off, because that is the situation in which the overbidder, vain of his dummy play, reaches for the moon. Ely Culbertson suggested a policy of overbidding with an overbidder in the hope of curing his excesses, but even if the overbidder were curable, life might be too short for a player trying to win.

OVERBOARD. The state of being (much) too high in a given auction. See SAFETY LEVEL.

OVERCALL IN OPPONENT'S MAJOR SUIT. Two hearts over one heart, or two spades over one spade, is most often used as a CUE-BID IN OPPONENT'S SUIT, in which case it can have any of a number of agreed-upon meanings.
The natural use of an overcall in an opponent's major suit is most beneficial when the opponents use a CANAPÉ style of bidding, in which a major suit opening may frequently be made on a suit of only three cards. It can sometimes be advantageous to treat a bid in a major suit as natural in response to a take-out double, even if that suit has been bid by responder over the double. If East-West are using RESPONSIVE DOUBLES, in the auction

SOUTH	WEST	NORTH	EAST
1 ◇	Dbl.	1 ♠	2 ♠

East's two spade bid should be natural, if only to expose what may be PSYCHIC BIDDING by North.

OVERCALL IN OPPONENT'S MINOR SUIT. Two clubs over one club, or two diamonds over one diamond, is often used naturally instead of as a cue-bid. Such treatment is most useful if the opponents are playing five-card majors, or any other method which requires frequent opening bids with prepared three-card minor suits. See also CUE-BIDS IN OPPONENT'S SUIT.

OVERCALLS. In a broad sense, the term overcall refers to any positive action by the player on the left of the opening bidder. In this article, only minimum bids in a suit will be considered. (For other actions, see INTERMEDIATE JUMP OVERCALL, JUMP OVERCALL, ONE NO TRUMP OVERCALL, PRE-EMPTIVE OVERCALL, TWO NO TRUMP OVERCALL, WEAK JUMP OVERCALL, etc.).

There are eight factors which may influence a player in making an overcall. In roughly descending order of importance, these are:

(1) *Length*. An overcall is nearly always based on a five- or six-card suit. A strong four-card suit may sometimes be sufficient if non-vulnerable at the level of one, but an obstruction factor (see [6] below) might be a consideration. A seven-card or longer suit will usually, but not always, qualify for action at a higher level. A vulnerable overcall at a two-level is more likely to be based on a six-card suit than a five-card suit.

(2) *Strength*. An average overcall is perhaps equivalent to a minimum suit bid, with perhaps 13 points in high cards. The maximum with a five-card suit is likely to be 15–16 points, i.e., a hand just short of the strength required to double and then bid the five-card suit. In favorable circumstances, not vulnerable at the level of one, a normal minimum is a hand with a king less than an opening bid. Even less is possible if the opponents are vulnerable, and the overcaller is visualizing a four-spade save against four hearts. In other circumstances, i.e., when vulnerable or when bidding at the level of two, the overcaller's partner should assume that the overcaller has an opening bid.

(3) *Vulnerability*. A non-vulnerable player can afford to make "unsound" overcalls. The opponents will be less eager to double for penalties, and when they do so, may find they have a poor bargain. This is particularly true at match points at the part-score level, when down two not vulnerable is a frequent source of profit against part-scores of 110 or more in the other direction.

(4) *Level*. One-level overcalls can obviously be made more freely than two-level overcalls. The latter are very much easier to double for penalties (see PENALTY DOUBLE).

(5) *Quality*. In borderline cases the texture of the suit can be important. QJ10987 is sure to be four playing tricks, but QJ5432 could turn out to be only one or two. Similarly, an overcall on a suit such as KQ10965 can have lead-directing advantages, if the opponents buy the contract and the overcaller's partner is on lead, whereas an overcall on a suit such as Q9752 is likely to result in embarrassment, or worse.

(6) *Obstruction*. An overcall which consumes the opponent's bidding space is always more attractive than one which does not. One spade over one club, two clubs over one diamond, two diamonds over one heart, and two hearts over one spade, all have a pre-emptive quality, leaving the opponents little room in which to maneuver. In each case a single raise is the only positive action open to the next opponent with a minimum responding hand.

(7) *Opponent's vulnerability*. At all forms of duplicate the overcaller must be sensitive to the opposing vulnerability. At favorable vulnerability he can show a profit by saving in four spades against four hearts and making seven tricks. At unfavorable vulnerability great discretion must be exercised. If a two club overcaller of one spade can be doubled and down two, he has met disaster with little prospect of gain. To overcall in such circumstances needs a solid six playing tricks, and even that may not be sufficient.

(8) *Opponent's methods*. Overcalls can be made slightly more freely against opponents using NEGATIVE DOUBLES. Overcalls of one spade over a minor suit should be made slightly more freely against opponents who do not open four-card major suits. There is then a greater chance that they can be prevented from finding a heart fit.

Responding to Overcalls

For action by the third player after an overcall, see FREE BID. Actions by the overcaller's partner come under four headings.

(1) *Raises*. The traditional treatment is for a raise to the two-level to be mildly encouraging, a raise to the three-level to be strongly encouraging (but not forcing), and for a raise to four to be natural and strong.

Suppose an opening bid of one club and a vulnerable overcall of one spade. If the responder has three-card support and 4–4–3–2 distribution, he would raise to two spades with 8–10, to three spades with 11–12, and to four spades with 13–15. Note that overcalls are regularly raised with three-card support, and might be raised with lesser holdings, especially if the third player bids. If the bidding went:

SOUTH	WEST	NORTH	EAST
1 ♡	1 ♠	4 ♡	4 ♠

with both sides vulnerable, it is conceivable that East, might hold a singleton spade honor and considerable honor strength in the minor suits.

If the overcall is not vulnerable at the level of one, partner must use more discretion in raising. The ranges given above should then be increased by about 2 points.

An alternative treatment put forward by Lawrence ROSLER and Roger STERN treats all raises of overcalls as pre-emptive, and uses a cue-bid in the opponent's suit as a constructive raise to the appropriate level. So when one club is overcalled with one spade, two clubs, three clubs and four clubs would be constructive raises to two, three, and four spades respectively.

A modification of the Rosler-Stern treatment, retaining all raises as pre-emptive, is to use the simple cue-bid as the start of any sequence to describe a hand worth at least a limit raise of the overcaller's suit. In this variation, the cue-bid is the only forcing response to the overcall; it allows the partner of the overcaller to clarify by his rebid whether he has a limit raise or a strong raise, or perhaps a strong hand with a good six-card suit of his own. His bid of a new suit after he has cue-bid is forcing for one round, although not to game.

(2) *No trump responses.* These are always constructive, but necessarily vary in strength with the vulnerability and level of the overcall.

After a one-level overcall the following ranges apply:

	NOT VULNERABLE	VULNERABLE
1 NT	9–12	9–10
2 NT	13–14	11–12
3 NT	15–16	13–16

The two no trump ranges are reduced slightly if the overcall was at the two-level.

(3) *Suit take-outs.* Non-forcing, except by special partnership agreement.

SOUTH	WEST	NORTH	EAST
1 ♣	1 ♡	Pass	1 ♠

East has a substantial spade suit, a strong five-carder at worst, and a heart misfit. He expects West to pass, although game might still be reached if there is a fit in spades. If East had bid his suit at the two-level—two diamonds—he would have a good six-card suit.

The meaning of a jump shift is a matter of partnership agreement. It may be forcing to game, forcing for one round, strongly encouraging, or pre-emptive, according to choice.

(4) *Cue-bid.* This is covered under CUE-BID IN OPPONENT'S SUIT. Note the special usage given to the cue-bid under *Raises* above.

OVERRUFF. To trump higher than the right-hand opponent after a plain-suit lead. An overruff is almost always good policy. The main exceptions occur when there is a possibility of achieving a trump promotion. A player who holds a certain trump trick together with a possibility of a second trick should usually refuse to overruff. This is an obvious position with spades as trumps:

```
                    NORTH
                    ♠ 4 3 2
WEST                             EAST
♠ A J                            ♠ 6 5
                    SOUTH
                    ♠ K Q 10 9 8 7
```

If East leads a suit of which South and West are both void, South may elect to ruff high. West then ensures two trump tricks by refusing to overruff.

The second trump trick may be an intermediate card apparently too low to be material. Suppose the following is the trump situation, and both defenders can lead a suit of which declarer and the other defender is void.

```
                    NORTH
                    ♠ 4 3 2
WEST                             EAST
♠ A 8 5                          ♠ 9 6
                    SOUTH
                    ♠ K Q J 10 7
```

East leads his long suit, and South must ruff high to prevent the eight making a trick. West refuses to overruff, but wins the first trump lead. In turn he leads his long suit, and East promotes a trick for the eight by an UPPERCUT with the nine.

OVERTAKE. To play a higher card than the one already played by partner for entry reasons. The objective may be suit establishment:

```
                    NORTH
                    ♣ A J 10 9 8 7
                    SOUTH
                    ♣ K
```

If five tricks are needed from this suit in a no trump contract, and there is only one entry in the North hand, the king must be overtaken by the ace. The same would apply if South held the queen singleton and North's suit was headed by the ace or king.

An alternative reason for overtaking would be an urgent need for an entry for finessing purposes.

```
WEST                             EAST
♠ A 6                            ♠ 7 3
♡ K                              ♡ A J 5 3
◇ A J 8 4                        ◇ 9 7 3 2
♣ A Q J 6 5 3                    ♣ 10 9 2
```

North leads a spade against West's three no trump contract. The only hope is to run the club suit, so West overtakes his heart king with the ace in order to take the club finesse. This sacrifices a heart trick, but makes the contract if the club finesse succeeds.

Another common reason for overtaking is dealt with under UNBLOCKING.

OVERTAKING SQUEEZE. A specialized form of triple squeeze in which the squeeze trick can be won in either hand (see OVER-UNDER SQUEEZE).

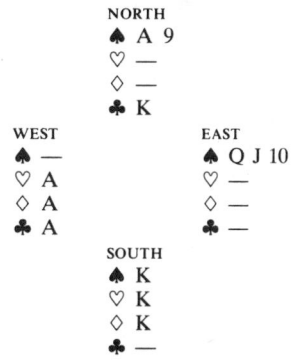

South leads the king of spades, and West is squeezed in three suits. If he discards a red ace, North plays low and South cashes the red king. If West discards the club ace, North overtakes and cashes the club king. South thus wins two tricks.

An analogous triple squeeze at a trump contract can give South all the tricks.

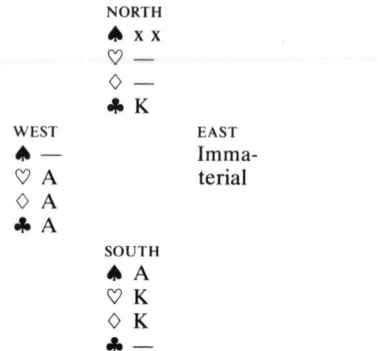

```
                    NORTH
                    ♠ x x
                    ♡ —
                    ♦ —
                    ♣ K
       WEST                    EAST
       ♠ —                     Imma-
       ♡ A                     terial
       ♦ A
       ♣ A
                    SOUTH
                    ♠ A
                    ♡ K
                    ♦ K
                    ♣ —
```

Spades are trump, and South leads the ace of that suit which squeezes West in three suits, enabling South to win the last three tricks.

M. I.

OVERTRICK. A trick taken by declarer in excess of the number of tricks required for contract. If a player is in four spades and takes twelve tricks, he is said to have made two overtricks. If a contract is doubled or redoubled, and an overtrick or overtricks are taken, the premium accruing to declarer's side can be substantial. Under certain conditions, redoubled overtricks can be worth more than the corresponding slam premium. At duplicate, the making of an overtrick can be all-important—it can actually win a board or even an entire tournament. This situation cannot occur in rubber bridge unless, again, the redoubled feature comes into consideration.

OVERTRUMP. See OVERRUFF.

OVER-UNDER SQUEEZE (sometimes called OVER-TAKING SQUEEZE). A trump squeeze, in which declarer depends on two ruffing menaces.

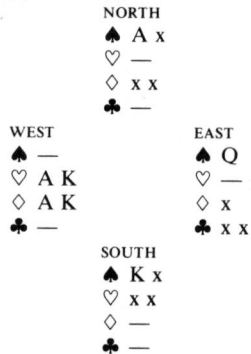

```
                    NORTH
                    ♠ A x
                    ♡ —
                    ♦ x x
                    ♣ —
       WEST                    EAST
       ♠ —                     ♠ Q
       ♡ A K                   ♡ —
       ♦ A K                   ♦ x
       ♣ —                     ♣ x x
                    SOUTH
                    ♠ K x
                    ♡ x x
                    ♦ —
                    ♣ —
```

With spades as trump, South cannot crossruff because East can overruff on a heart lead. South leads the king of spades, planning to overtake with the ace if West discards a diamond; in that case, South ruffs a diamond. North ruffs a heart, and cashes his established diamond. If West discards a heart on the king of spades, North follows low and a heart is ruffed by North, South re-enters his hand by ruffing a diamond, and cashes the established heart.

M. I.

P

PODI. See DEFENSE TO INTERFERENCE WITH BLACK-WOOD.

PRO. Pattern Relay Organized. See PRO SYSTEM.

PACIFIC BRIDGE LEAGUE. An organization founded by Tom STODDARD in 1933, and developed by him throughout the fifteen years of its existence. The League included the eleven far-western states, plus the territories of Hawaii and Alaska and the Canadian provinces of British Columbia and Alberta.

The League rapidly reached a four-figure membership, and promoted two major tournaments, in addition to many minor ones. The All-Western tournament was started in Los Angeles in 1935, and BRIDGE WEEK in 1936. The latter was held half in Los Angeles and half in San Francisco.

Collaboration between the ACBL and the Pacific BL began in 1940, when uniform master-point systems were agreed. A closer affiliation was planned in 1948, when the great services of Tom Stoddard to the Pacific BL were recognized. He was named President Emeritus of ACBL Western Division, with permanent status on the Executive Committee. The final merger was worked out by Tom Stoddard and Waldemar von Zedtwitz, and became effective Jan. 1, 1956.

PACIFIC NORTHWEST REGIONAL CHAMPIONSHIPS. A six-day tournament held annually since 1949 in Alaska, British Columbia, or Washington (and prior to 1967, in Oregon). Until 1958 this tournament was held over Washington's Birthday; then it was moved to early fall, and in 1968 it shifted to late April or early May. From 1963–67 the tournament was held twice annually, once in the spring and once in the fall. The spring event used various names including Polar-Canadian Regional, or Polar, Canadian, British Columbia Centennial, and Vancouver, but became known as the Pacific Northwest Regional in 1968 when the fall event was replaced by the Canadian and Puget Sound Regionals. For past results, see Appendix II.

PACIFIC SOUTHWEST REGIONAL CHAMPIONSHIPS. A six-day tournament held annually in Coronado, Calif. (in Anaheim, Calif. in 1968), beginning in 1946. For past results, see Appendix II.

PACK. A group of a specific number of cards of consistent composition, sold and used as a unit.

The makeup of a pack depends on the date and the country. In the Western world they are composed of four suits, with three FACE CARDS and up to thirteen SPOT CARDS, and have an extra card (JOKER) or cards. The tables below describe some of the many packs that have been in use. When ace is included with the face cards, it ranks high; when included with the spot cards, it ranks low, and is called the ONE-SPOT.

(1) Packs with one of each card:

No. of cards	Game or Country	Face Cards	Spot Cards	
62	500	A K Q J	*13 12 11 10 9 8 7 6 5 4 3 2	
60	Fantan	K Q J	12 11 10 9 8 7 6 5 4 3 2 1	
52	Bridge, Poker	A K Q J	10 9 8 7 6 5 4 3 2	
48	Alouette	K C J †	9 8 7 6 5 4 3 2 1	
48	Old German	K O U†	10 9 8 7 6 5 4 3 2	
40	Trappola	K C J †	7 6 5 4 3 2 1	
36	Schwerter (Ger.)	K O U†	10 9 8 7 6	2
36	Russian	K Q J	10 9 8 7 6	1
36	Sixettes	A K Q J	10 9 8 7 6	
32	Piquet	A K Q J	10 9 8 7	
32	German	K O U†	10 9 8 7	2
24	Schnaps	A K Q J	10 9	

(2) Packs with two of each suit:

64	Bezique	A K Q J	10 9 8 7
48	Pinochle	A K Q J	10 9
48	Gaigel	A K Q J	10 7

(3) With a group of extra cards not a part of the four suits (called in various countries, atouts or atutti):

97   Minchiate taroc (Florence) 41 atutti, and each suit has four face cards and ten spot cards.
78   Lombard tarot (Venice) 22 atutti, and each suit has four face cards and ten spot cards.
62   Tarocchino (Bologna) 22 atutti, and each suit has four face cards and six spot cards (10 9 8 7 6 1).
54   Tarok (German) 22 atutti, and each suit has four face cards and four spot cards, black suits 10 9 8 7 and red suits 4 3 2 1.
64   Sicilian 22 atutti, K Q C J 10 9 8 7 6 5 of four suits, and the ace and 4 of coins.

For the 22 atutti, see TAROT.

For bridge purposes, the pack is a set of fifty-two standard playing cards divided into four suits (spades, hearts, diamonds, and clubs) of thirteen cards each, ranking in descending order from the ace to the deuce. See LAWS (Law 1).

In the US the term "deck" is often preferred. See also HISTORY OF PLAYING CARDS; PLAYING CARDS.

A. F.

---

*Only two of the thirteen-spot cards are used.
† C = Cavalier, O = Ober, U = Unter.

PACKET. A portion of the deck held together, as in gathering tricks, or in dividing the cards for shuffling purposes.

PAIR. A twosome or partnership of two players. All games at bridge come down to the basic competitive situation of pair versus pair, bridge being a partnership, or pair, game.

PAKISTAN BRIDGE ASSOCIATION. Formed in 1973; participates in Far East Championships. Conducts national championship events. Players listed separately are: A. G. Cochinwala, A. S. Cochinwala, A. Jane, M. Tasneem.

Officers, 1975:
President: Amir Ali Fancy.
Secretary: M. Z. Farrukh, 60-D Block 6, Federal 'B' Area, Karachi, Pakistan.

PALOOKA. A run-of-the-mill bridge player, a nonexpert.

PANAMA BRIDGE ASSOCIATION. Founded in 1968; participates in CACBF, finishing second in Open Teams 1971, 1972, 1974; participated in 1974 Olympiad.

President, 1975: Alberto Calvo, Box 8103, Panama 7, Republic of Panama.

PAN-AMERICAN INVITATIONAL CHAMPIONSHIPS. An invitational pair championship first held in 1974 in Mexico, scored by IMPs. The winners:
1974   R. Hamman, R. Wolff, *tied with* P. Pender, G. Baze
1975   P. Pender, G. Baze

PAR, PAR SCORE. See PAR CONTEST.

PAR CONTEST. A tournament using prepared hands, each of which embodies a predetermined optimum ("par") result. The players' results are compared with par, rather than with each other.

In an ordinary duplicate tournament, how you fare depends to a large degree on how well or poorly your opponents play against you. In a par contest, your skill alone determines the result. You may not profit by an opponent's blunder if you have already erred.

World Championships on a par basis were held in 1961 and 1963 by the World Bridge Federation which prefers the term "par-point," perhaps because "par" can easily be confused with "pair." Until 1966 the Intercollegiate Bridge Tournament was the only par contest held annually in the United States. The National Industrial Recreational Association Tournament was conducted in 1963 and 1964 as a par contest but then adopted match-point scoring.

The following hand (from the 1963 National Industrial Recreation Association Par Tournament) illustrates the foundamental difference between a par contest and an ordinary duplicate.
Dealer: South
Both vulnerable

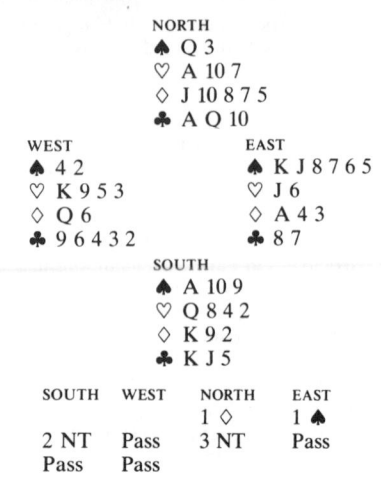

NORTH
♠ Q 3
♡ A 10 7
◇ J 10 8 7 5
♣ A Q 10

WEST
♠ 4 2
♡ K 9 5 3
◇ Q 6
♣ 9 6 4 3 2

EAST
♠ K J 8 7 6 5
♡ J 6
◇ A 4 3
♣ 8 7

SOUTH
♠ A 10 9
♡ Q 8 4 2
◇ K 9 2
♣ K J 5

SOUTH	WEST	NORTH	EAST
		1 ◇	1 ♠
2 NT	Pass	3 NT	Pass
Pass	Pass		

Opening lead: ♠ 4.

To earn par, East must not play an honor on the first trick, no matter what dummy plays. Then when West wins the queen of diamonds, he can play a spade, establishing East's suit while East still has the ace of diamonds for entry.

In a duplicate tournament, many defenders would defeat the contract after playing an honor on the first trick, because South would play incorrectly and win the trick. In a par contest, these defenders would not be awarded par.

In 1963, the World Bridge federation adopted an International Par Point Contract Bridge Code, drafted by M. J. Sullivan and R. E. Williams of Australia. This code deals primarily with irregularities and penalties. The basic decisions about the format of the contest are left to the organizers. Some of the factors to be considered below.

Par-point scoring may be used for individual, pair, or team contests, (but only pair games are common). For a pair game, the par-setters should strive to ensure that the North-South pairs and East-West pairs will meet problems of equal difficulty. Such judgments are necessarily subjective, however, and it is better to choose the North-South and East-West winners separately.

(1) *The Bidding.* The bidding problems should be arranged so as not unduly to favor or penalize any common system or convention. As a rule, par points are awarded on the basis of the final contract reached, not on the actual auction. Minor awards may be given to inferior contracts.

On some deals, players may be instructed (by a slip accompanying the board) to make specified preemptive bids, so that all pairs holding the other hands will be presented with uniform bidding problems. Furthermore, players are instructed to refrain from psychics or other unwarranted or misleading bids. Nevertheless, all the vagaries of competitive auctions cannot be anticipated. Some players will inevitably face more difficult opposition bidding than

others, and the par-setters may be called on to adjudicate. Despite this opportunity for redress, it is here that luck or the skill of one's opponents is most likely to affect one's score.

(2) *Before the Play.* So that all competitors face the same play or defense problems, it is usual to specify both the contract to be played and the opening lead. A traveling slip, accompanying the board for this purpose, is consulted after the bidding is over. The official contract need not be the same as the contract awarded maximum bidding par points, if a more interesting play problem is presented.

The par-setters may also provide a guidance auction, from which the players can derive information needed during the play. They are instructed to ignore the actual bidding at their table (but here again, some luck enters).

(3) *The Play.* At the discretion of the par-setters, the traveling slip may inform the players before the play begins whether the par is for the declarer or the defenders. This saves time by eliminating long huddles by the non-involved side, but adds another artificial aspect to the event.

In addition to the opening lead, the play to one or more tricks may be directed, and declarer or defenders may receive public or private instructions. The primary purpose is to obviate the awarding of "automatic pars," if the opponents should slip in advance of the anticipated problem. These instructions may also ensure the defeat of a misplaced contract or the fulfilment of a misdefended contract. This is of secondary importance, however, as the par would not be awarded in any case if the play at the table deviated from the prescribed line. Minor awards may be given for partially correct or slightly inferior lines of play or defense.

Note that an equitable two-way play par (that is, a separate par both for the declarer and the defenders on one deal) is almost impossible to arrange. For example, in the hand given above, South will not have a chance to make a par play (ducking the first trick) if East first makes *his* par play by ducking. Then that South would have to be awarded an unearned automatic par.

(4) *Movements.* Every player must play all the boards. No movement is necessary—a pair could well play the entire session against one pair of opponents, sharing the boards with the other tables. This arrangement also saves time, as the faster players need not wait for the slower ones to finish their boards each round. Nevertheless, for social and other reasons, some limited movement of the players is desirable.

It is recommended that a time limit for each group of boards be imposed. In important tournaments, the use of chess clocks should be considered.

L. R.

PAR HAND. A hand prepared for use in a PAR CONTEST. By extension, a randomly dealt hand suitable for inclusion in such a contest because a single technical aspect of play or defense is dominant.

PAR POINT BRIDGE. See PAR CONTEST.

PARAGUAY BRIDGE ASSOCIATION (ASOCIA-CIÓN PARAGUAYA de BRIDGE). The Association is a member of the South American Confederation and participates in South American Championships.

Officers, 1975:
President: Raúl Casabianca.
Secretary: Jose Burro, Asociación Paraguaya de Bridge, Alberdi 425, Asunción, Paraguay.

PART-SCORE. A partial; a trick-score of less than 100 points. In RUBBER BRIDGE, a part-score counts toward game, and enables a side, with the addition of further part-scores or a single part-score, should it be of sufficient point value, to make game. Sometimes it may happen that a side in possession of a part-score will have to bid up to game level in order to buy the contract, and, when the game is made, the entry on the scoring pad for that frame simply includes the total of both the game score and the previous part-score or scores. In cases where the adversaries score a game while one's side is in possession of a partial, that particular frame is then ended, and the only value of the part-score is as a part of the full score of one's side containing all the points above and below the line when added together at the conclusion of the rubber, or, as in CHICAGO, at the end of the fourth deal.

In DUPLICATE BRIDGE, any part-score, vulnerable or not, carries with it a premium or bonus of 50 points in addition to the trick-score itself. In rubber bridge, a partial is worth much more. An arbitrary figure of 100 points is usually applied to a part-score. More realistically, however, the true worth of a partial may be 200 points, depending upon the respective vulnerability and certain other factors. See PART-SCORE BIDDING.

PART-SCORE BIDDING. Bidding by a side which possesses a part-score is a subject which is scantily treated by textbooks, and produces considerable disagreement among experts. The following treatment is based on the opinion of a number of experts.

Forcing Bids. The most noticeable difference between part-score bidding and normal bidding results from the fact that many bids which would otherwise be forcing are no longer forcing when they complete the game. A new suit by responder, for example, is not forcing if it is sufficient for game. Similarly, a jump from one to three in a suit, or from one of a suit to two no trump may be passed. The jump shift remains forcing, however, regardless of the part-score.

Suit Bids. Because so many bids become non-forcing if they complete a partial, it is difficult for a partnership to conduct any lengthy bidding investigation. It is therefore of primary importance that whenever a partial exists, all suit bids should stress quality. Thus it would be poor policy to open a three-card minor with a partial. With 60 on score, holding ♠ A K J x, ♡ xxx, ◇ xxx, ♣ A J x, a player should open one spade, and pass partner's response (unless it is a jump shift). Similarly, responder should ignore a suit

of doubtful quality. With 70 on score, holding ♠ K x x, ♡ Q9x x, ◇ x x, ♣ A x x x, the response to one diamond should be one no trump, bypassing the poor heart holding. However, with ♠ K x x, ♡ x x, ◇ x x, ♣ Q J 109 x x, the response to one diamond should be two clubs; this response at the two-level does not promise as much high-card strength as at love score. Rather, it stresses the quality of the club suit. The opening bidder is expected to pass unless he has good reason to continue.

No Trump Bids. All no trump bids tend to have a slightly wider range when the bidder has a part-score. Using, normally, 16–18 point no trump bids, with 60 on the score, it would be correct tactics to open one no trump holding either

	(a)			(b)
♠	A J x	or	♠	A J x
♡	K J x		♡	K J x
◇	A Q x x		◇	Q x x x
♣	K J x		♣	K J x

Some experts allow themselves more latitude than others in the range of their opening no trump, but taking the average approach of the experts consulted, it can be stated that standard expert procedure is to widen the range for an opening one no trump by about a point in either direction when a part-score is held.

There are two reasons for this increase in the no trump range. First, there is always a tremendous tactical advantage in opening with one no trump. Partner is immediately in an excellent position either to place the contract or punish overzealous opponents. The opponents themselves are unable to compete at the one-level, and may find it too dangerous to begin their search for a fit at the two-level. To reopen in fourth seat after an opening no trump by opponents with a 60 partial is particularly dangerous, because opener's partner may pass with up to 13 high-card points, instead of being limited by his pass to 7 or less.

Tactical advantages exist for opening one no trump frequently at no score also, but in this case the problem of whether to reach game or settle for a partial is paramount; widening the range of the no trump would be against the interests of accuracy. With a substantial partial, the question of whether to reach game or not is already solved, and tactical considerations become more prominent. Naturally the prospect of missing a slam is a deterrent to increasing the upper limit unduly. With 60 on score, and a passed partner, it is surely good tactics to open one no trump with 19 points regardless of the normal range, as slam can hardly be missed.

The second, and less obvious, reason for increasing the range, and thus the frequency of the no trump opening, goes back to the stress on quality for opening suit-bids. If normal one no trump range is 15 to 17 points, and a partial of 40 is held, it would be proper to open one no trump holding ♠ K x x, ♡ A x x x, ◇ A x x x, ♣ K x. Ordinarily such a hand would be opened one heart or one diamond, depending on partnership attitude toward four-card majors. With the part-score, the suit-bid carries an added implication of quality. Partner will strain to raise the suit-bid, and the safer spot in no trump will be missed. If suit play is better, responder can choose the suit.

Other no trump bids are likewise affected by the partial. Most experts play 21–22 point opening two no trump bids. They increase this range, particularly the upper limit, when a partial exists. By far the most frequently used range (and, therefore, logically, the standard range) for an opening two no trump bid is 21–24 with a partial of 60 or more, and 20–24 with a lesser partial.

The opening strong three no trump bid becomes almost extinct in a part-score holding of 30 or more. It is better to open with two clubs, and rebid two no trump to a two diamond response. Any other response, and a slam can be investigated with impunity. Using strong two-bids, a two-bid in the best suit and a pass to the negative two no trump response are in order.

Of all the no trump bids, the simple response of one no trump is most affected by a part-score. Normally this bid shows 6–9 in STANDARD AMERICAN, but with a partial it tends to become 4–12. The lower limit is reduced because of the strain to keep the bidding open when game is so near; the upper limit is largely affected by distaste for bidding a weak suit.

The responses of two and three no trump remain close to their usual ranges. The 13–15 range for a two no trump response increases to 13–16 with a partial, and becomes non-forcing, of course. The three no trump range moves from 16–17 to 17–18. It is a common practice among average players to avoid both these responses on some theory that it is unnecessary to "get so high" with a partial. This is a fallacy. There should be no danger at this level opposite an opening bid. More important by far is the fact that these bids are extremely useful when the opening bidder has slam aspirations.

Raising Partner's Suit. As responder, when holding a fit with partner, it is imperative to show it immediately. The fact that one side has a fit increases the chances that the opponents have a fit and a profitable sacrifice. With a 90 part-score and an opening one spade bid by partner, holding ♠QJxx, ♡Kx, ♢Qxxx, ♣xxx, bid two spades immediately. If opener's hand is such that one spade is the partnership limit, fourth hand will take some action, and the necessary two spade bid on the next round will come after the opponents have found their fit. Immediate action may keep the opponents out altogether. With a part-score, it is standard to give a single raise with 6–12 points. The lower limit may be reduced as far as three points if the raise is necessary to complete the game. With 13–16 points it is still standard to give a jump raise from one to three in a suit. With a stronger hand, a jump shift is in order.

Stayman with a Partial. With a part-score of 60, the opening bid is one no trump, and the response is two clubs. In standard practice this is STAYMAN, but a substantial minority of experts regard two clubs as natural. Failing any partnership agreement, the opener

should assume the bid is conventional. This can at worst lead to a contract of three clubs instead of two clubs, while a pass of a conventional two club bid could be a complete disaster.

Forcing Two-Bids. Bridge authorities agree that with a part-score a forcing two-bid may be made with less than the normal requirements—perhaps a full playing trick less. This makes sense. A slam can be missed if partner has a little something, and if the one-bid is kept open because of the partial, on very little, a forcing rebid may get the combined hands overboard. By opening with a strong two-bid, the strength of the hand is announced in one bid, and can be bid conservatively thereafter. The texts maintain that the strong two-bid is a one-round force. Although the experts consulted agree in theory with this, many confessed that if they held nothing, they might pass in practice.

Tactical Considerations. With a part-score, is it wise to open lighter or stronger than usual? What about when the opponents have a partial? Or when both sides are on score? This is an area of wide disagreement. No standard approach exists, but the various schools of thought are presented so the reader may form his own opinions.

One school holds that as long as fewer tricks are required to make a game, opening bids may be slightly weaker with a partial. A second school recommends using stronger opening bids with a partial. This group reasons: If the bidding is opened with a partial, the opponents are very apt to compete. Responder will fight for the part-score on the strength of the opening bid; if this bid is subminimum, responder may push too high, presenting the opponents with a very attractive double, or, even worse, he may decide to "punish" competing opponents, and double them into game. A third school suggests opening light with spades, but normally or slightly over without spades. Obviously the side with spades has an advantage in any bidding battle. Still a fourth school feels that the advantages and disadvantages of either stronger or lighter bids just about cancel each other out, maintaining that normal bids will work out best in the long run. About half of the experts consulted recommended normal openings with a partial.

There are also various theories as to the best procedure when the opponents have a partial. A slight majority of the experts suggest opening light, believing that the best defense is an early offense. It is dangerous to overcall or balance against opponents who have a partial as they may have strength in reserve: hence the value of getting in first with the opening bid. Light take-out doubles and overcalls are also favored for the same reason. Many recommend the pre-emptive opening of one spade or one no trump with a slightly lighter range than usual. Culbertson, in his *Contract Bridge Complete*, says "Shade your bids downward if the opponents have a part-score and upward if you have the part-score." Then there are those who like to have stronger openings when the opponents have a partial; they would rather pass out a hand than open a minimum when they are at such a disadvantage in the score. Jaïs, in

How to Win at Rubber Bridge, remarks: "Under no circumstance open under strength. Do not invite a battle in which you are outgunned." Lastly there are those who stand steadfast for the normal opening.

A futher point arising when the opponents have a partial is often overlooked. When in doubt whether to bid game or settle for a part-score, it is better to stretch a bit, and bid game. The reason is that the value of success is substantially increased by the fact that the opponent's partial is wiped out.

When both sides have a part-score, the experts are split into two roughly equal camps: those favoring lighter openings and those favoring normal openings. Reasons given are various combinations of those above.

The Value of a Partial. Experts have long been aware that a part-score at rubber bridge is worth far more than the 50 points awarded in the rules for a partial in an unfinished rubber. Because of the many imponderable factors involved, including the identity of one's opponents, mathematicians cannot agree on the correct way to calculate the value mathematically. However, Jean Besse, Switzerland, kept a record of over a thousand part-score situations ("Autour de l'Étoile," *British Bridge World,* p. 34, August 1959). He compared the scores when a partial had just been achieved and again when the partial had been completed. Allowing 300 for any first game, 400 for the second game, and 500 for any third game, his results were as follows:

Value (over and above the trick score) of a non-vulnerable partial of 40 or more	90
Value of a vulnerable partial (opponents not vulnerable) of 40 or more	110
Value of a partial of 40 or more at game all	220

The tremendous value of a partial at game all he attributes partly, of course, to the increased value of game, but mainly to the increased difficulty encountered by vulnerable opponents in trying to defend.

In many of the bridge clubs of this country today, four-deal bridge, CHICAGO, has taken the place of rubber bridge. A partial must be worth somewhat less in this form of bridge, due to the limited time in which to capitalize on it. Naturally, a partial on the fourth deal is worth exactly the 100 points awarded for it in the rules.

                                                  D. H. T.

PART-SCORE BONUS. In duplicate competition, 50 points are scored as a bonus for fulfilling a part-score contract. In CHICAGO, a bonus of 100 points is given for a part-score contract successful on the last hand. For the mathematical value of a part-score see PART-SCORE BIDDING.

PARTIAL DESIGNATION. Incomplete specification by declarer of the rank or suit of a card to be played from dummy's hand. See LAWS (Law 46).

PARTIAL ELIMINATION. A throw-in play de-

pending on ruff-and-discard possibilities in which the stripping process is incomplete.

In a perfect elimination the declarer eliminates all the suits which a defender may safely lead and saddles him with the choice of conceding a ruff and sluff or leading into a tenace. A partial elimination, on the other hand, is so called because the declarer only partially eliminates the suits which a defender may safely lead; now, whether the defender will have to lead to the declarer's advantage will depend on distributional hazards.

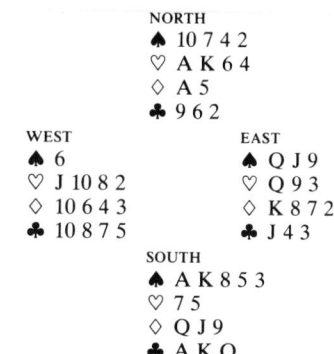

NORTH
♠ 10 7 4 2
♡ A K 6 4
◇ A 5
♣ 9 6 2

WEST
♠ 6
♡ J 10 8 2
◇ 10 6 4 3
♣ 10 8 7 5

EAST
♠ Q J 9
♡ Q 9 3
◇ K 8 7 2
♣ J 4 3

SOUTH
♠ A K 8 5 3
♡ 7 5
◇ Q J 9
♣ A K Q

Playing in six spades, South wins the heart lead and tests trumps. When West fails on the second round, South attempts an end play to avoid taking the diamond finesse. He plays the second top heart, ruffs the third round in his hand, and takes his three top clubs before throwing the lead to East's master trump. East fortunately has no hearts or clubs left and has to lead away from the diamond king.

South's maneuver is a *partial* elimination because he could only partially eliminate hearts. He did not have the entries to eliminate the hearts completely. This play had the added advantage that if East did have a club as an exit card he might have been unwilling to give declarer a ruff-sluff and led a diamond anyway. The ruff-sluff could not possibly help South because he had only one trump left and could not ruff both the club return and dummy's last heart.

In the above example the critical suit—hearts—was eliminated from two of the four hands. When the distribution is favorable, a partial elimination may succeed even though the critical suit be eliminated from only one hand:

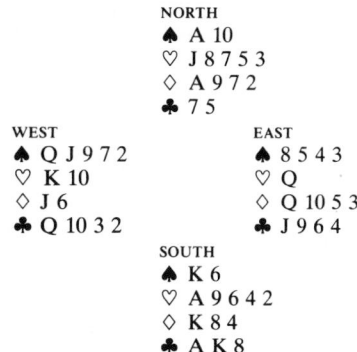

NORTH
♠ A 10
♡ J 8 7 5 3
◇ A 9 7 2
♣ 7 5

WEST
♠ Q J 9 7 2
♡ K 10
◇ J 6
♣ Q 10 3 2

EAST
♠ 8 5 4 3
♡ Q
◇ Q 10 5 3
♣ J 9 6 4

SOUTH
♠ K 6
♡ A 9 6 4 2
◇ K 8 4
♣ A K 8

With hearts as trumps, South can make twelve tricks by means of partial elimination. He wins the spade lead, plays off the trump ace, and eliminates the black suits. He cashes the ace and king of diamonds and exits with a trump. West wins, but he is the only player without a diamond in his hand. He has to return a black suit, and South ruffs on the table, at the same time sluffing a diamond from the closed hand.

A partial elimination can also operate when one of the defenders still has a trump in his hand:

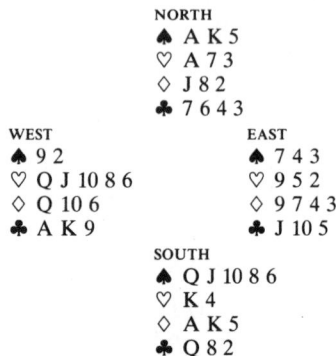

NORTH
♠ A K 5
♡ A 7 3
◇ J 8 2
♣ 7 6 4 3

WEST
♠ 9 2
♡ Q J 10 8 6
◇ Q 10 6
♣ A K 9

EAST
♠ 7 4 3
♡ 9 5 2
◇ 9 7 4 3
♣ J 10 5

SOUTH
♠ Q J 10 8 6
♡ K 4
◇ A K 5
♣ Q 8 2

West opens the bidding with one heart, and South reaches a contract of four spades instead of three no trump. After a heart lead, prospects are poor, but a partial elimination offers the best chance. However, it is essential to keep at least one trump in each hand to profit from a possible ruff and sluff; this means that South can afford to draw only two rounds of trumps, and must therefore rely on West's having no more than two trumps.

South wins the heart lead, plays off the ace and queen of trumps, and continues with a second and third round of hearts, ruffing. He then plays ace, king, and another diamond, throwing West into the lead. As expected, West has the outstanding high cards and has to offer a ruff and discard or concede a trick to the club queen.

PARTIAL SCORE. See PART-SCORES.

PARTNER. The player with whom one is paired in a game of bridge.

PARTNER'S SUIT. The suit bid or rebid by the player opposite one during an auction. It is usually advisable to support partner's suit when one can, as this builds firmness and reliability in a partnership. As respects defensive play situations, the leading of partner's suit raises many questions. Whether it should be led at all, and if so, which card of one's holding, etc., are all problems with which a good player constantly concerns himself.

PARTNERSHIP LANGUAGE. See SIGNALS and SYSTEMS.

PARTNERSHIP MISUNDERSTANDINGS. All partnerships have misunderstandings about the meaning of bids, although these should be infrequent in a well-established expert partnership. Some advance consideration can reduce the frequency of such errors.

Suth misunderstandings fall into four general categories:

(1) The strength of a bid. For example, the traditional strength of a two no trump opening is 22–24 points, but a majority of experts prefer 21–22 points as the range for this bid, and open with an artificial two club bid when they hold stronger hands.

(2) The nature of a bid: sign-off, discouraging, encouraging, or forcing (for one round or to game). A good example is a jump in a new suit over an opposing take-out double (see RESPONSES OVER OPPONENT'S TAKE-OUT DOUBLE). According to the partnership understanding, this bid can be pre-emptive, encouraging, forcing for one round, or forcing to game.

(3) Artificial or natural quality of a bid. Confusion can occur when a partnership has not specifically agreed whether a particular artificial device is being employed, such as LANDY over opposing no trump bids, especially with an unfamiliar partnership. Both players may normally use a convention, and be aware that the partner normally uses it, but still be in doubt about whether it is in use because it has not been discussed.

A more common source of difficulty is doubt about whether a convention is applicable to a particular situation. It is sometimes difficult to diagnose, for example, whether four no trump is natural or conventional; or whether a bid in the opponent's suit is a cue-bid or an attempt to play in that suit.

(4) The nature of a double. There may be doubt about whether a double is for penalties or for take-out. A failure to agree on the use of RESPONSIVE or NEGATIVE DOUBLES would be an example of this problem. There are also situations, usually after the first round of bidding, in which the intentions of the doubler are not clear.

The nature of a pass may also be crucial, especially if a FORCING PASS is a possibility.

No partnership can avoid misunderstandings altogether, but the following suggestions may help to reduce the incidence of disaster.

First, a regular partnership should have a detailed understanding.

Second, a player should avoid making an ambiguous bid when an unambiguous alternative is equally satisfactory.

Third, when an ambiguous bid is made, a partnership should apply some automatic rule. A reasonable rule is to take the weaker interpretation in each case, that is: the lower point range; non-forcing against forcing; natural as against conventional; and take-out rather than penalty double. The opposite rule is also playable, and so are a variety of hybrid rules. In any case, it is advisable to have some rule. This often avoids impending trouble, provided both players are aware of the possibility of trouble.

PARTNERSHIP PSYCHOLOGY. The art of keeping partner happy is worth more in terms of results than much advanced technical knowledge; but it is an art which many players, including some at the highest level, never learn.

At rubber bridge the player who encourages his partner instead of shouting at him, praising the occasional good plays instead of pointing out the obvious and frequent bad ones, earns large dividends. His partners then like to play with him, and play above themselves. On the other hand, a player who is subjected to a barrage of criticism is likely to play below his best not only for the remainder of the rubber but on subsequent occasions.

In tournament play, self-made partnerships ought in theory to be more compatible, but this is not always the case, and the same principles are applicable. Long-lived tournament partnerships usually consist of players who enjoy each other's company, and have a genuine respect for each other. Egotists whose main concern is to prove how brilliantly they themselves play and how foolishly their partners perform may have temporary successes, but they have to find new partners regularly.

PARTNERSHIP RUBBER BRIDGE. A style of rubber bridge popular in England whereby two players play as partners throughout a session. Players agree in advance to play as partners, as they would in a duplicate event, and there is no game for unpaired individuals. This tends to raise the standard of the game by excluding those who, through inferior ability or character deficiency, find it difficult to get a partner.

PARTNERSHIP UNDERSTANDING. An agreement between partners which enables them to draw information or inferences from the bidding and play. It is not to be confused with PRIVATE CONVENTION, which is illegal and unethical. It is the duty of all partnerships to make sure that any understanding they may have on the meanings of bids or plays of which the opponents could not reasonably be expected to have knowledge be clearly and concisely stated on their CONVENTION CARD in tournament play, and announced to the opponents in rubber bridge. See ALERTING, EXPLANATION OF CONVENTIONAL CALL OR PLAY.

PARTNERSHIPS. Either or both of the two sets of the players at a table, North-South and East-West. Players who play together frequently are considered an established partnership; players who pair up for a particular event, having played together either seldom or never, have a more casual partnership. Most of the bidding and play conventions were established as successful tactics by established partnerships; it is noteworthy that the use of these bids was carefully explained to opponents by their developers, and they were quite well known even before their publication.

PARTY BRIDGE. Private games consisting of at least two tables. The Chicago or four-deal method is customary. It is usual to give prizes to the players with the best scores, and the player with the worst score may receive a booby prize. The manner of mixing partnerships is manifold; some hostesses use commercial tallies which give seating assignments to players, by which players enjoy four hands with all the other players or, alternately, all the other players of opposite sex. Another form, where excellence of bridge is to be rewarded, provides that, after each round, the winning pairs move to the lower numbered table, except at the head table, where the losing pair goes to the highest numbered table.

Other possibilities are outlined under PARTY CONTRACT BRIDGE, LAWS OF, and PROGRESSIVE BRIDGE, LAWS OF.

PARTY CONTRACT BRIDGE, LAWS OF

DUPLICATE FOR HOME PLAY, AND COMPETITION
NOT IN DUPLICATE

The forms of Duplicate play described in the Laws are readily adapted to home play. Special games suitable to a small number of tables, or emphasizing the social above the competitive element, are described in the following pages.

For a single table, the available games are REPLAY DUPLICATE and PIVOT BRIDGE (non-Duplicate). For two or three tables there are INDIVIDUAL GAMES, and MITCHELL or HOWELL PAIR GAMES, and TEAM-OF-FOUR MATCHES. For a larger number of tables, where it is desired to emphasize the social element, the popular game is PROGRESSIVE BRIDGE.

In general, the Laws of Duplicate Contract Bridge apply to all forms of Duplicate and multiple-table play—from the simplest Replay contest to the most elaborate championship tournament.

Even in simple home games, such as Replay Duplicate, it is advisable to appoint one participant as Supervisor and to invest him with all the authority of a Tournament Director. Experience has shown that without a guiding hand even a social game is likely to be delayed or deadlocked by trivial irregularities.

REPLAY DUPLICATE

Replay Duplicate is a contest between two pairs. It is played in two sessions, called the Original Play and the Replay.

The players take places, one being designated North. The trays (boards) are shuffled, and are played with the arrows pointing North. Any number of trays is feasible.

A separate scoreslip is kept for each tray. At the close of the session the trays and scoreslips are laid aside where they will be undisturbed.

At some later time, the same four players take the same relative positions about the table. The trays are replayed with the arrows pointing East. Again a separate scoreslip is kept for each board.

The scoring may be by match-points or total points. If the former method is used, each deal is treated as a separate match. The pair having the better net score on a deal is credited with 1 point. The final scores are the totals of these match points.

If total point scoring is employed, the two slips for each deal are compared, and the pair having the greater plus or lesser minus is credited with the difference. The next scores for all deals, so determined, are totaled, and the pair having the larger total wins the difference.

Replay Duplicate is popular as a home game among foursomes that meet weekly for social bridge. It can easily be played in a continuous series of sessions. Half of the time in each session is devoted to the original play of new trays, and half to the replay of old trays.

The game tends to become a test of memory rather than of bridge skill. To check this tendency the following measures are recommended:

1. Do not play the trays in consecutive order. Choose the tray to be played next at random from the stack.

2. Avoid comment of any sort about the deal after its original play.

3. Allow at least a week to elapse between the original play and the replay.

It is sometims desired to make the game a test of skill in play alone. The bidding during the original play is then recorded, and for the replay this bidding is read to fix the contract and declarer.

INDIVIDUAL CONTESTS

In an individual game, each player plays once with every other as partner, and twice against every other as opponent.

The initial seating of the players in games for two or three tables is shown below:

TWO TABLES
N

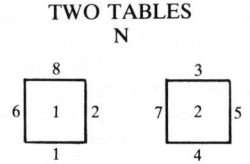

THREE TABLES

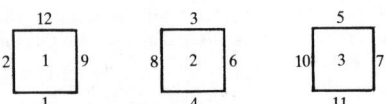

The game may be conducted without guide cards, thus:

1. Allow the players to take places at random. Reserve the North position at Table 1 for the Supervisor; this player is "anchor," retaining his seat throughout the game.

2. From this schedule inform each player of his number, and tell him who is the player of next-lower number.

3. Announce that after each round, all players but the anchor will progress, each player taking the seat vacated by the player of next-lower number. (Player 1 follows Player 7 or 11, respectively.)

A new set of trays is played in each round. The set is played at all tables, the trays being circulated at convenience. The eight-player game requires seven rounds, with a total of 14, 21, or 28 boards. The twelve-player game requires eleven rounds, and the only feasible number of boards is 33.

The scoring of individual contests is explained in the Laws of Duplicate Contract Bridge.

PROGRESSIVE RUBBER BRIDGE

Progressive Rubber Bridge is a variation of the usual progressive game. It has proved increasingly popular, and may in time supplant the usual form. It follows the methods of progression and change of partners described in the preceding laws, but the scoring is somewhat different.

Under this arrangement it is preferable to play 8 deals to a round, or to fix the length of a round by a definite time limit—say 30 minutes. If the length of a round is determined by a time limit, any deal which has been started before time is up may be completed, but no new hand may be dealt.

Rubber Bridge scoring is used. As many rubbers as possible are completed during the timed allotted. A rubber completed in two games carries a bonus of 700 points. A three-game rubber carries a bonus of 500 points. If a side has won one game toward a rubber and the other side has not won a game, 300 points are allowed for the single game won. If one side only has a part-score (a trick-score totaling less than 100) in an unfinished game of an unfinished rubber, that side adds 50 points to its score.

Vulnerability is determined by the state of the score and not according to Section 9 of the Progressive Code. A side is vulnerable when it has won a game and remains vulnerable until the conclusion of that rubber. However, vulnerability lapses at the conclusion of a round and a new rubber is started at the beginning of each new round.

At the end of a round each player enters on his tally only his net gain or loss—not his total score. At the end of the session these net gains and losses are totaled and the player's final score, plus or minus as the case may be, is entered at the bottom of his tally. (See Law 12 of PROGRESSIVE BRIDGE, LAWS OF.)

PASS. A call by which a player indicates that, at that turn, he does not choose to contract for a number of odd tricks at any denomination, nor does he choose, at that turn, to double a contract of the opponents or redouble a contract by his side that opponents have already doubled.

The proprieties require that only one term be used in passing. NO BID is an acceptable alternative (standard in England), but all calls must be made with uniform usage. See CALL, BID, PENALTY PASS, NO BID.

PASS OUT or THROW IN. A deal in which all four players pass on the first round of bidding. The score is zero. In duplicate, the hand is scored and returned to the board; in rubber bridge, the deal passes to the next player, but in CHICAGO a redeal by the same dealer is required. The term "pass out" is also applied to the action of the player who, after two passes, declines to reopen the bidding at a comparatively low level. He is said to be in the "pass-out seat" or the "pass-out position."

PASS OUT OF TURN. This can occur under two different circumstances: when it is the turn of the opponent on the right, or when partner's turn to call precedes the offender's turn to call. In the first case, no damage has been done, and the penalty is that the offender must echo his pass when next it is his turn to bid; in the latter case, damage has been done to the opponents, and the penalty is correspondingly more severe. See LAWS (Law 30, a, b). See also OBLIGATION TO PASS.

PASSED HAND. When partner has opened the bidding in third or fourth seat, the problems of the responder may be rather special. There are two complicating factors: (1) a change of suit is no longer forcing, so responder must be prepared for a "sudden death" pass of his response; (2) partner may have opened a sub-minimum hand, to direct a lead or to try for a small plus score, and will then be annoyed if responder gets up too high.

Since any response one makes may be passed, one must be very wary of responding in anemic suits. In general, the higher the response the greater is the chance that it will be dropped. This means that the responder can answer one diamond to one club with a weakish suit (four to the jack), since someone at the table will bail responder out. But if one responds one heart or, more particularly, one spade, one should have a respectable four-card suit (at least four to the queen-ten). And if the response is at the two-level, one must be prepared to play opposite a doubleton—partner is now even money to pass. So responder would want to have a six-card suit or at least a husky five-carder.

Suppose that one had passed this hand:

♠ K Q 2
♥ J 6 4 3
♦ A 9 6 3 2
♣ 7

If partner opens one club, respond one diamond. If, instead, he opens one diamond, respond three diamonds (not one heart, as one might if it were forcing). If partner opens one heart, one cannot temporize by answering two diamonds, so three hearts seems best. And if partner opens one spade, one must still avoid the two-diamond response, for one belongs in spades, not diamonds—responder may choose between two and three spades, and the jump raise is probably better in the long run.

Suppose that one had passed this hand:

♠ K 6
♥ Q 10 4 2
♦ K 10
♣ K 9 6 3 2

Again, one must be careful about bidding suits. Should partner open with one diamond, a one-heart response is preferable to two clubs. True, the hand is strong enough for a two-level response and for two bids; but (1) partner may pass before the second bid, and (2) partner is more likely to find a rebid if he can do so at the one-level, and (3) if partner does pass, one would rather be in the higher scoring major suit. What would be the response with this hand if partner opened one spade? Not two clubs, and certainly not two hearts. The best bet is two no trump; and this jump response could easily be right over one diamond or one club as well.

In contrast, if responder passed a hand that does contain a strong suit, he can give himself a little more freedom in bidding at the two-level. For example, holding:

♠ Q 7 5 2
♥ 7 4
♦ 2
♣ K Q 10 8 6 3

one would respond two clubs to a one-diamond opening if it was a passed hand, while one spade would be correct if it was not. What makes the difference? Once the responder passed, there is a fighting chance to play in two clubs when the responder bids it; and if partner rebids two diamonds, one can carry on with two spades without creating a forcing situation. What is more, it is dangerous to respond one spade—if partner passes there is no reason to believe that this is either the safest or most productive contract.

Since the requirements for a two-over-one suit take-out are shaded down, there is a worry about missing game when holding the normal solid values for this response. Consider these hands:

♠ 8 3   ♠ 7 4
♥ K Q 10 8 7 4 2 ♥ 6 2
♦ A 10 5   ♦ 8 5
♣ 5   ♣ A K Q 10 9 6 5

If, for some reason that appealed at the time, either hand has been passed, jump shift over partner's opening. Two hearts or two clubs in response to one spade is no longer nearly enough; one must jump to three. This puts partner on notice that there are game ambitions even opposite the bare minimum opening bid with which partner would pass a simple response. (Some experts, especially in England, use the jump shift by a passed hand as a one-round force with support for opener's suit.)

Jump bids should be made sparingly opposite a passed hand, because partner can have spare values for his opening. The last two examples are safe enough at the three-level, for there are seven winners, and partner should have the decency to provide two. But passed hand jump raises and jumps to two no trump entail considerable risk of a minus score. Consider these hands:

♠ K 8 6 2   ♠ A Q J 9   ♠ K 7 2   ♠ A Q 10 8 4
♡ J 10 4   ♡ 7 5 3   ♡ A Q J 3   ♡ K 10 6 2
◇ A Q 7 5   ◇ 10 2   ◇ Q 7 6 2   ◇ 9 8
♣ 7 3   ♣ K 10 8 2   ♣ 8 6   ♣ A 5

WEST	EAST
Pass	1 ♠
2 ♣	2 ♡
4 ♡	Pass

WEST	EAST
Pass	1 ♠
3 ♠	Pass

No one made a bad bid—East's third-hand opening is irreproachable, and West has the values for a passed-hand jump raise—but the final contract is dangerously high. Unless two finesses succeed, it will go down for a poor score. How do East-West get to two spades? It is no solution for West to temporize with two diamonds, as he might had partner opened in first seat, for he will be left in this unappetizing contract. Some players might bid only two spades with the West hand, fearing a light opening, but this risks missing game opposite a sound minimum, for the range of the single raise becomes impossibly broad (unless these players bid in delicately graded intonations; then they will get into a different kind of trouble).

Here is a similar problem:

♠ J 8 7 3   ♠ 9 6 2
♡ Q 10 4   ♡ A K J 2
◇ K J   ◇ Q 10 9 4
♣ A 9 4 2   ♣ J 6

WEST	EAST
Pass	1 ♡
2 NT	Pass

This contract is not likely to be a success. What went wrong? Surely, West could not bid only one no trump or two hearts; three hearts is a possible response, but it is almost certainly down one. A response of one spade would be passed, and declarer can develop ulcers playing in a trump suit like that. Perhaps light third- and fourth-hand openings are undesirable.

Not really. One will show a big match-point profit in the long run by opening these hands. When partner has a normal minimum count, one will earn a small plus or at least impede the opponents or direct a good lead. The examples above are unlucky, but there is an answer for them too.

A suggestion is to adopt the DRURY CONVENTION. When the bidding is opened in third or fourth seat with one of a major, the response of two clubs, by the passed hand, is artificial. It asks opener if he has a normal bid, or if he opened light. If opener has shaded his values, he answers two diamonds; if he has a reasonable hand, he makes his natural rebid.

In the examples above, West would respond two clubs, Drury. East would rebid two diamonds, and West would sign off safely at two of opener's major. Let us see an auction where opener has his full bid:

Here, the advantage of Drury is in making it easy to find the heart fit; without it, West would likely jump to three spades. However, the principal use of this convention is in staying at the two-level in case East's hand is:

♠ A J 9 8 4
♡ 6 2
◇ 9 8 4
♣ A J 5

The bidding then would be:

WEST	EAST
Pass	1 ♠
2 ♣	2 ◇
2 ♠	Pass

E. K(aplan)

PASSIVE DEFENSE. A defense which aims principally to avoid establishing tricks for declarer, rather than principally to establish tricks for the defense. A defender's continuation of a suit already led either by declarer or the defense, rather than attacking a new suit, is a common type of passive defense.

PASSIVE LEAD. An opening lead which is unlikely to hurt the defending side, but is not expected to have a positive value. A lead from three or four small cards is a typical passive lead, but in certain circumstances a trump lead may be passive, or a lead in an opposing suit which is likely to be solid. See ATTACKING LEAD; OPENING LEAD.

PASTEBOARDS. A name given to playing cards because a coating of black paste between two paper layers gave the stock on which the cards were printed an opacity that made it impossible to see through them. See MANUFACTURE OF PLAYING CARDS.

PATTERN RELAY ORGANIZED SYSTEM. See PRO SYSTEM.

PEETERS, MARCEL CHALLENGE CUP. See INTERNATIONAL BRIDGE ACADEMY.

PENAL INSTITUTIONS. See BRIDGE IN PRISONS.

PENALTY. (1) an obligation or restriction imposed upon a side for violation of the Laws of Bridge. In the language of the lawgivers, penalties are designed ". . . to provide an adequate remedy whenever a player accidentally, carelessly or inadvertently disturbs the proper course of the game. An offending player should be ready to pay graciously any penalty or adjusted score awarded by a Tournament Director."

(2) An amount scored above the line by the declarer's opponents when the declarer fails to make a contract. The penalty provisions of the score table are gauged so as to make competitive bidding a fine art.

Many of the great stories in the anecdotage of the game are concerned with penalties. The biggest penalty in a championship tournament was reported from the Men's Pairs Championship at the 1964 Summer Nationals held at Toronto, Canada.

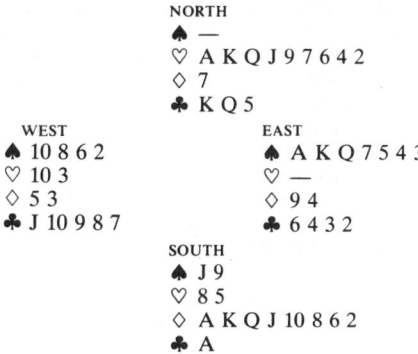

```
                    NORTH
                    ♠ —
                    ♡ A K Q J 9 7 6 4 2
                    ◇ 7
                    ♣ K Q 5
    WEST                            EAST
    ♠ 10 8 6 2                      ♠ A K Q 7 5 4 3
    ♡ 10 3                          ♡ —
    ◇ 5 3                           ◇ 9 4
    ♣ J 10 9 8 7                    ♣ 6 4 3 2
                    SOUTH
                    ♠ J 9
                    ♡ 8 5
                    ◇ A K Q J 10 8 6 2
                    ♣ A
```

With both sides vulnerable, the par contract is a seven-spade sacrifice by East-West, which costs 1,400 as compared with 2,220 for the grand slam which North-South can make in hearts. (Seven diamonds by South is defeated if West leads a heart.) At most tables the final contract was in fact seven spades doubled, but at a number of other tables the North-South pairs refused to be outbid and overcalled seven no trump, which was of course doubled and was usually redoubled. The auction at one such table was:

NORTH	EAST	SOUTH	WEST
2 ♡	2 ♠	3 ◇	Pass
4 NT	5 ♠	6 ♣	Pass
7 ♡	7 ♠	7 NT	Pass
Pass	Dbl.	Redbl.	Pass
Pass	Pass		

Spades were led, and West did not fail to unblock with the eight and ten. East Thus took the first seven tricks for a penalty of 4,000. At another table the bidding was:

NORTH	EAST	SOUTH	WEST
2 ♣	3 ♠	4 NT	Pass
6 ♡	Pass	7 NT	Pass
Pass	Dbl.	Redbl.	Pass
Pass	Pass		

West, doubtless attributing some unusual lead-

directing significance to his partner's double, led a club and the contract was made for a score of 2,930. The spread betwen top and bottom score was thus 6,930.

At a third table the penalty in favor of East-West became a penalty, in a different sense, in favor of North-South. North became the declarer in seven no trump redoubled, and East was just considering which of his high spades to lead when West led a club out of turn. North had to nominate a penalty, and after a few moments' deliberation he accepted the club lead and scored 2,930. If he had played South to have the spade ace instead of the club ace he would have lost 4,000.

Another remarkable penalty, which would have been even bigger but for the accident of vulnerability, occurred in a pair game at a London club, in December 1960. Robert Sharples playing with G. C. H. Fox held the East-West cards, vulnerable, against non-vulnerable opponents.

```
                    NORTH
                    ♠ J 9 3
                    ♡ Q 10 8
                    ◇ A K 10 6
                    ♣ K 10 3
    WEST                            EAST
    ♠ A 5                           ♠ Q 10 8 6 4 2
    ♡ A K 6 5                       ♡ 7 4 3
    ◇ J 4                           ◇ 5
    ♣ 9 7 6 4 2                     ♣ A Q J
                    SOUTH
                    ♠ K 7
                    ♡ J 9 2
                    ◇ Q 9 8 7 3 2
                    ♣ 8 5
```

WEST	NORTH	EAST	SOUTH
Pass	1 ◇	1 ♠	2 NT*
3 ♠	3 NT	Pass	Pass
Dbl.	Redbl.	Pass	Pass
Pass			

Sharples, on lead, produced the ace of hearts, and switched to the four of clubs, won by Fox with the jack. The heart return was won by the ace, and the nine of clubs lead suggested a spade return after Fox cashed his club jack and ace. Hoping for a one trick set, South played the king of spades, losing to the ace, and the marked spade return (after cashing the two long clubs by West) produced thirteen tricks for the defenders, for a penalty of 3,400 points.

PENALTY CARD. A card that has been prematurely exposed by a defender, and must be left face up on the table until legally played or permitted to be picked up. If it is a LEAD OUT OF TURN, the declarer has several options, some of which permit the penalty card to be picked up; if it remains a penalty card on a lead out of turn, or is prematurely exposed in any

---

* A rather injudicious "tactical bid."

other condition, it must be played at the first legal opportunity that the player may have to play it. See LAWS, Laws 23, 49–53, 55, 57, 58, and 62; LAWS OF DUPLICATE (Laws 23, 49–52, 54, 56–58, 62).

PENALTY DOUBLE. The distinction between penalty doubles and take-out doubles is discussed under DOUBLES. Normal penalty doubles can be considered in three categories:

(1) *Positive doubles.* Suppose an opening bid is overcalled and doubled, and the opener's hand seems unsuited to defense. Should he stand the double or take it out?

If the opening bid was of a sort which describes the hand within narrow limits, stand the double. If the opening bid is three spades with this hand:

> ♠ K J 8 7 6 4 3 2
> ♡ 3
> ◇ 2
> ♣ J 5 4

pass a double by partner of an overcall of four hearts. He does not expect the opener to have defensive strength.

Having opened with a three-bid, a four-bid, a weak two-bid, or any no trump bid, pass partner's double of an overcall. These are all bids which describe a hand within narrow limits.

Opponents seldom argue with a forcing two-bid, but when they do, retaliation must be swift and sure and there must be no partnership misunderstanding. The responder should beware of doubling on hands which contain a feature outside the enemy suit.

> ♠ A J 6 5   ♡ Q 8 7 4   ◇ 5 4 3   ♣ 7 2

After a two club opening by partner, do not double an overcall of two spades. Too often the hand will belong in a heart contract. In any event, the hand must be useful in attack, and game must be there. Experience shows that the double is best reserved for hands like

> ♠ Q 10 7 6 5   ♡ 8 7 4   ◇ 5 4 3   ♣ 7 2

If this is the partnership understanding, opener will pass the double with ♠ 4 ♡ A K J 5 ◇ A K J ♣ K Q J 8 3.

If the double is made on both hands above, the opener has a very tough decision. He will never know, with the last hand, whether he is surrendering game or slam for poor recompense.

Having opened with a two-bid, opener should accept partner's double of an intervening call *unless holding game in hand with fewer than five defensive tricks.*

(2) *Low-level doubles.* Partner deals and opens one spade, overcalled with two clubs. With equal vulnerability, consider

(a)		(b)
♠ 6 5	and	♠ Q J 8 4
♡ A 10 8 5		♡ 3 2
◇ K 10 4 3		◇ 8 7 4
♣ A K 6		♣ K Q 7 2

Here (a) holds no surprise for the overcaller, who knew that he was missing the ace-king of clubs. If the overcaller holds a seven-card suit and an outside trick, the double would score only 300, a poor substitute for the game.

The best doubles are made with unexpected trump tricks. J 10 6 5 with compensating outside values is a better double than A K 6, since the overcaller may not be expecting to lose any trump tricks.

There is a further reason for not doubling on hand (b). Although it contains a jolt for the enemy in clubs, the spade holding is too long. Experience shows that it is not winning bridge to double with length in partner's suit; the opponents will be short, and opener's high cards may not take tricks.

True, at match-point duplicate, particularly with vulnerable opponents, a double can be the winning bid even with three or four cards in opener's suit. Certainly it should be possible to secure as good results as would have been obtained if the opponents had not overcalled, and, of utmost significance in a keen game, is the partnership understanding that the doubler is short in the opener's suit. See IMP TACTICS, MATCH-POINT BIDDING.

Another critical situation: Vulnerable against not vulnerable opponents, partner opens one heart, overcalled by two diamonds.

> ♠ K 2   ♡ 7 6   ◇ A 10 5 4   ♣ K J 9 7 3

With different vulnerability, the double might be winning action. But with unfavorable vulnerability, a four-trick set is needed to outweigh the game. Probably two no trump is the most suitable call.

Supposing opener's bid was one spade instead of one heart, the two no trump bid is not as attractive. The absence of a heart stopper makes the double a more desirable action. When contemplating a tight double, consideration should be given to alternative actions. If they are happy alternatives, they should be preferred.

When the opponents overcall at the one-level, there are more alternatives to a double than when they bid at the two-level, so a double at the one-level should be based on better trumps. With ♠ A 10 8 4 ♡ 3 2 ◇ K J 8 2 ♣ J 5 4, if partner opens one club, bid one spade over a diamond overcall. If partner opens one heart, and the overcall is two diamonds, double; the bid of two spades is not a happy alternative.

Summarizing the above: Never double with four or more cards in partner's suit, be slow to double with three; save the hair-trigger doubles for occasions when short in opener's suit, singleton or doubleton. Do not double low-level overcalls unless trump tricks are of the "unexpected" variety. If there is an action that could have been taken without the overcall, prefer it.

Against experienced opponents, close doubles are profitable only when it is understood that partner is free to pull the double if his hand is unsuitable. Thus a double is not a death sentence from which there is no appeal. Rather, it is the duty of the doubler's partner to review the sentence. To stand pat on an unsuitable hand does not show confidence in partner; it shows rather a dereliction of duty.

A low-level double is simply a proposition, like many other calls in bridge. Partners expect each other to exercise judgment. The opener should not automatically pass.

Vulnerable, against not vulnerable opponents, opener bids one spade on ♠ A K 62 ♡ A Q 10 ◇ A 987 ♣ 52. Left-hand opponent overcalls two clubs, partner doubles. On no account should the double be pulled. *Partner knew opponents were not vulnerable when he doubled*, and his decision must be respected. If partner thinks two clubs can be beaten opposite a minimum opening, this hand should make a holiday in opener's heart. The penalty must be greater than the value of three no trump. But the double should be pulled with opener's holding ♠ J 9874 ♡ A K 1073 ◇ A 6 ♣ 2. Partner, doubling two clubs, *does not know about that heart suit*. The risk of partner having length in the unbid suit is too great.

The best low-level doubles, by far, are made when the partnership hands do not fit well. A further reason for pulling the double on the last hand is the fact that partner will probably intend to open your bid suit, and an opening from king small in spades could be horrible.

In deciding whether to pull a low-level double or not, quick tricks are as important as trumps. Doubler is entitled to expect a normal quota of defensive tricks implied by a sound opening bid.

♠ A K 7653　♡ Q 42　◇ A 9　♣ 64

Having opened one spade, most experts would stand for a double of a two club overcall; the doubler is expected to be short of spades, and that suit should produce two tricks; the ace of diamonds is the third, and there might even be a diamond ruff. If the hand were more unbalanced, the double should be pulled unless the clubs were better. Any hand that contains a void in the doubled suit is unsuited to standing a low-level double. Doubler does not *need* trump tricks from the opener, but there are many situations in play where even a single trump lead up to the doubler will be very worthwhile.

The above can be summarized: Stand a low-level double with three quick defensive tricks; pull it with fewer unless there is compensation in trump strength; pull the double nearly always with an unbid five-card suit. In a close decision, decide whether a lead of your bid suit will be welcome or not.

(3) Game doubles. Doubles of game contracts in a competitive auction are usually aimed at taking the maximum penalty from opponents who have taken a SAVE. However, the double may also act as a warning to partner not to proceed further. If a pass would be a FORCING PASS, then a double indicates a disinclination to go further. For this reason a player who anticipates disaster if his side bids further may double when his prospects of beating the opposing contract are no better than moderate.

Doubling a game contract which has been reached voluntarily without interference is very seldom good policy (unless the doubler suspects an advance save, for example, after three spades—four spades).

Doubling a game on the basis of high cards only is a costly exercise. For the double to be worthwhile,

both opponents must have limited their hands in such a way that it is clear that neither has any strength in reserve. For example:

WEST	EAST
1 ♣	1 ♡
2 ♡	2 NT
3 NT	

In this auction it is clear that both players are straining to reach game, and either opponent may double if the honor strength, especially in clubs and hearts, seems well placed for the defense.

If the contract is a suit, a double becomes attractive if the declaring side has run into a bad trump split. It is sometimes possible to double with a void because the other defender is marked by the bidding with five trumps. But it is still necessary for both opponents to be limited, so that all possibility of a redoubled overtrick is excluded.

DOUBLES OF NO TRUMP BIDS are listed separately. See also COOPERATIVE DOUBLE, DOUBLE FOR SACRIFICE, LEAD-DIRECTING DOUBLE, LIGHTNER DOUBLE, OPTIONAL DOUBLE.

A. D.

PENALTY EXCESS. See EXCESS POINTS.

PENALTY LIMITS. In social or progressive bridge, in order to prevent one hand from assuming overwhelming importance, it is customary to limit the plus score in premium points for doubled and redoubled undertrick penalties. Generally, 1,000 points is the limit. In TOTAL POINT SCORING for pair events, a method that is obsolescent if not obsolete, a similar though somewhat smaller limit was set. See EXCESS POINTS.

PENALTY PASS. A pass by a player after a TAKEOUT DOUBLE from his partner and a pass by right-hand opponent. For example:

SOUTH	WEST	NORTH	EAST
1 ◇	Dbl.	Pass	Pass

East's pass indicates considerable length and strength in diamonds; five cards headed by three honors would normally be the minimum diamond holding. Even holding five strong diamonds, a pass would be unwise with a two-suited hand, because the declarer would be likely to score ruffs. After such a pass, West has an obligation to lead a trump, because East will wish to draw South's trumps.

After a minor-suit opening, a penalty pass may come into consideration with nothing but trump length at unfavorable vulnerability. If the contract succeeds, even with an overtrick, the resulting score may be less than the opener's side could have scored in other ways.

A penalty pass becomes more attractive if the doubler was in a balancing position. Q J x x of trumps may be a sufficient trump holding.

PERCENTAGE. A quotient obtained by dividing

the actual match-point score of a contestant by the possible score of that contestant, which is then expressed as a percentage (of the possible score). Winning percentages tend to be higher (70 to 75%) in team games than in pair games (60 to 64%).

PERCENTAGE PLAY. A play influenced by mathematical factors when more than one reasonable line of play is available. See PROBABILITIES A POSTERIORI, SUIT COMBINATIONS, and MATHEMATICAL TABLES (Tables 4, 4A).

The following examples show how the above references can be used in bridge play.

(1) Neither the auction nor the play to the first trick has shown any marked UNBALANCED DISTRIBUTION in defenders' hands. Dummy has A K Q J 4 3 2, and declarer is void in the suit. There is about 36% probability that the suit will be divided 3–3.

(2)

NORTH
A K Q 10
SOUTH
4 3 2

The correct line of play, based solely on PROBABILITIES A PRIORI, is to play the ace, king, and queen unless East shows a singleton or void. From percentage play, probabilities are:

3–3 division	probability	35.53%
Jx (J9, J8, J7, J6, J5) in hand		16.15%
J singleton in hand		2.42%
J98765 with West		.74%
Jxxxx with West		6.05%
		60.89%

The alternative plan of taking a finesse on the third round unless the jack has been played, has the following probability.

J in West's hand	50.00%
Jx with East	8.07%
J singleton with East	1.21%

To make four tricks in the suit, the odds are slightly less than 61 to 59 on refusing the finesse.

(3)

NORTH
A Q 10 7 3 2
SOUTH
9 8 5

Declarer disregards the safety play in favor of trying for the maximum number of tricks. He plans to finesse the queen and make six tricks if West holds both honors doubleton or if East holds the singleton jack. He may also have to decide on his action if West plays low and the finesse loses. Reference to Table 4 shows that the distribution

64 opposite K J has a probability of 6.8%
J64 opposite K has a probability of 6.2%

The odds are therefore 34 to 31 on playing the ace on the second round after the finesse has lost, as against taking a second finesse.

Percentage play often requires calculations which, though not too difficult, require more involved operations. This may be valuable in subsequent analysis but not practical at the table. In the following, two lines of play present themselves.

NORTH
♠ —
♡ Q 3 2
♢ A K Q 10 4 3 2
♣ 7 5 4
SOUTH
♠ K Q J 6 3 2
♡ A K J 6 5 4
♢ —
♣ 3

South plays in six hearts. West leads the queen of clubs, then a second club on which East plays the king. South ruffs. As West presumably has the Q–J of clubs and East the A–K the play of this suit has not altered the ratio of the a priori odds, but in our more detailed calculations we must assume that East and West each originally held at least three clubs.

South's best line of play depends upon the probability of the divisions of the two red suits. To determine this accurately it is necessary to calculate the appropriate combinations as explained in SUIT, NUMBER OF CARDS IN. For a satisfactory approximate answer apply the rule of multiplying PROBABILITY OF SUCCESSIVE EVENTS. (This is an approximation because the distribution of the two suits is interdependent, not independent. We note the discrepancy when we give the result of our detailed calculations later.)

To the third trick South leads the ace of hearts, East and West both following. At the fourth trick South can
(a) lead the king of hearts;
(b) lead a low heart to dummy's queen;
(c) lead the jack of hearts.

In each case we must consider the position if (i) West follows to the second round of hearts, and (ii) West does not follow.

(a) (heart king) will win whenever

hearts are 2–2		40%
diamonds are 3–3	36%	
doubleton jack of diamonds	16%	
Total		52%

The probability that both will occur (hearts 2–2 and diamonds come home) is 40% of 52%, which equals 20.8%. If hearts actually divide 2–2 South leads the king of spades, and if this is covered his troubles are over. Assuming that West will cover half the time he holds the ace this gives another 4.8% (50% of 50% of 19.2%), bringing our total to 25.6%.

If West has three hearts (25%) South leads to dummy's queen of hearts and makes his contract with the above division of diamonds (52%). This gives another 13%. Similarly, we have a further 13% if East has three hearts and there is the above diamond division.

Our grand approximate total for (a) is thus 51.6%.

(b) (low heart) will win whenever

hearts are 2–2	40%
diamonds 4–2	48%
3–3	36%
singleton jack of diamonds	2%
any other diamond division provided West has the ace of spades	7%
Total	93%

Or

West has 3 hearts	25%
3 or 4 diamonds and the ace of spades	30%*
East has 3 hearts	25%
diamonds are 3–3	36%
doubleton jack of diamonds	16%
East has five small diamonds and two low spades, or jack four times diamonds and three low spades	2%
Total	54%

Our grand total for (b) is thus 40% of 93% + 25% or 84%, or 58.2%.

(c) (heart jack) is obviously inferior to (b). If West follows to the second round of hearts and we overtake the jack of hearts we lose if West has 3 hearts and 3 diamonds even if he also has the ace of spades. South has to return to his own hand twice—once to take the ruffing finesse in spades and once to draw West's last trump. One entry has to be the ruff of a fourth diamond, and West will overruff. If the jack of hearts is not overtaken the lead is not in dummy for the diamond suit to be led.

A more detailed calculation which takes account of the interdependence of the suit distributions gives us 48.99% for (a) and 52.62% for (b). We note that there is less difference between these two numbers than between our approximate calculations. This is due to the fact that (b) contains a larger number of unbalanced hands, the type of hand on which approximate calculations give misleadingly high figures.

PERCENTAGES. Since chance plays considerable part in the distribution of cards at a bridge table, it is understandable that expert players are interested in

the mathematical percentages applicable to different situations. Among the articles dealing with percentage are: MATHEMATICS OF BRIDGE, PERCENTAGE PLAY, SLAM BIDDING, SUIT COMBINATIONS, VALUE OF GAME, and PART-SCORE. MATHEMATICAL TABLES also deals with various percentage situations. Bridge writers frequently use a variation of percentage, ODDS IN BRIDGE, in discussing situations yielding to mathematical treatment.

PERFECT HAND. See MATHEMATICAL TABLES, Table 6, for the odds against receiving a perfect hand, one unable to lose a trick.

PERIODICALS. See BIBLIOGRAPHY.

PERMANENT TRUMP. At WHIST, a variation in which club card committees or other governing bodies declared a suit to be trump for all games under their jurisdiction. The rules of WHIST provided that the trump suit would be the suit of the last card dealt by the dealer to himself.

PERUVIAN BRIDGE ASSOCIATION (ASOCIACIÓN PERUANA DE BRIDGE). Founded in 1957, and in 1969 had approximately 170 members. Peru's representatives to the South American Championships are decided by annual tournaments, for both men's and women's events. The Association sent teams to the World Team Olympiad in 1972, hosted the 1956, 1961, 1967, and 1974 South American Championships in Lima, and won the Women's Team Championships in 1963 and 1969. Peruvian players listed separately are Alejandro Castro and Domingo Focacci.

Officers, 1975:
President: Dr. Enrique Elias.
Secretary: Dr. Jaime Garcia-Ribeyro, Avenida Orrantia 474, San Isidro, Lima, Peru.

PETER. A term used in Great Britain, but rarely elsewhere, to describe a high-low made in discarding, such as high-low in any given suit. Originally, in whist, the use of the term was restricted to a high-low in the trump suit only. See HIGH-LOW SIGNALS and BLUE PETER.

PHANTOM PAIR. In a pair contest with an odd number of pairs, the pair which would (if present) complete the last table. The contestant scheduled to play against the phantom pair has a bye round.

PHANTOM SACRIFICE (or phantom save). A sacrifice bid against a contract which would have been defeated. This is sometimes caused by a player with defensive values encouraging his partner to save. For example (neither side is vulnerable):

SOUTH	WEST	NORTH	EAST
1 ♣	1 ♠	2 ♡	?

East holds:

---

* We have omitted figures for 5 or 6 diamonds, which are negligible in an approximate calculation. The figure for 3 and 4 diamonds is too high, for we have assumed that it is a 50% chance that West has the ace of spades. But this is not so, for if West has 3 hearts, 4 diamonds and at least 3 clubs he cannot hold more than 3 of the 7 missing spades, so the probability that he holds the ace of spades is at most 43%.

♠ 4 3 2
♡ K J 9 3
◊ Q J 10 5 4
♣ 7

If East bids two spades, a natural action, West may be provoked into bidding four spades if the opponents reach four hearts, a contract East expects to defeat. It is therefore good tactics for East to pass, reserving the possibility of bidding three spades if North-South stop at the three-level.

PHENOMENAL HANDS. See FREAK HANDS.

PHILIPPINE CONTRACT BRIDGE LEAGUE. Organized in 1954, by 1975 its membership was over 500. The League participates in the Far East Championships, hosting the 1957, 1962, 1967, and 1974 events in Manila, and World Olympiads. Philippine teams won the Far East Championship in 1957 and 1958 and the Women's Team Championship in 1967 and 1968. National events are held annually for Knockout Teams, Open Teams, Mixed Teams, and Masters Pairs. Players listed separately are: M. Barredo, J. A. Cacho, Mrs. M. C. Cacho, S. Chua, M. R. Ciocon, G. J. Figueiredo, Mrs. L. Jalbuena, M. Ortegas, Jr., Mrs. L. de Padua, J. Reyes, M. Reyes, V. Reyes, L. da Silva, E. S. Teehankee, S. Tuason, K. T. Yang, R. Yap, A. Zamora.

Secretary, 1975: Tomas Quiogue, Sr., 356 Solana Street, Intramuros, P. O. Box 3362, Manila, Philippines.

PIANOLA. A hand at bridge which presents no problems to declarer, so easily playable that it almost plays itself. The name derives from the old player piano or "pianola" into which one placed a roll of music with specially punctured holes corresponding to notes of the keyboard. The roll would rotate and the keys would be depressed automatically, and the piano would "play" itself.

PICK UP. To capture or drop an outstanding high card.

PICK-UP BOY (GIRL). See CADDY.

PICK-UP SLIP. A form devised for the recording of the result on the play of one board on one round. Information contained on the slip includes identifying numbers of the pairs, the board number, which pair was the declarer, the final contract and by whom, whether doubled, redoubled, or undoubled, the result, trick-score, extra tricks, game or doubled bonuses, part-score bonus, slam bonus, or under-trick score. Usually the North (or South) player has the responsibility of making out the score, the East-West pair having responsibility for checking the entries and verifying the slip. After each round, the pick-up slips are collected and results of the round entered on the recapitulation sheet by the director or a designated scorer.

PIN. The lead of a high card when the right-hand opponent has an unguarded card slightly lower in rank. The play can be made either by declarer or by a defender.

NORTH
A 9 8 7 6
SOUTH
Q 10 5

If South must have five tricks from this suit, his only chance, a faint one, is to lead the queen and hope the singleton jack is on his right.

The defenders can sometimes falsecard in an attempt to avert an impending pin:

NORTH
♡ Q 10 3 2
WEST   EAST
♡ J 5 4   ♡ A K 8 7 6
SOUTH
♡ 9

South plays in a spade contract after East has bid hearts and West has raised them. If East plays in routine fashion by winning with the king and shifting to another suit, South can establish a heart trick in the dummy by ruffing a low heart and later leading the queen, or vice versa. But if East wins the first trick with the ace and returns a low heart, South is likely to conclude that West started with K x x.

The following position is similar:

NORTH
♡ J 9 6 3
WEST   EAST
♡ 10 7 2   ♡ K Q 8 5 4
SOUTH
♡ A

Again, East has bid hearts, West has raised, and South plays eventually in a spade contract. When West leads the two, dummy plays the three, and East plays the four, knowing that this will force the singleton ace.

If East gains the lead later and wishes to force South to ruff, he should usually lead a low card. South is almost certain to ruff. If East leads an honor instead, South has the possibility later of leading dummy's jack to pin the ten, and in any event the defense cannot force South again without establishing a trick in the dummy.

PINK POINTS. An obsolete term for REGIONAL POINTS. It was used to distinguish points won at a Regional tournament from those won at a National tournament (red points).

PINPOINT ASTRO. See ASTRO.

PIP. A small design indicating the suit to which a particular card belongs. The SPADE suit is indicated by a spearhead, the HEART suit by a heart, the

DIAMOND suit by a diamond-shaped tile, the CLUB suit by a clover leaf. The spot cards have as many pips as the rank of the card indicates, from one to ten in the standard deck, in addition to two INDICES, the lower half of which is a pip.

In German cards, the pips of LEAVES and ACORNS usually have stems, and are often attached as if on a branch. In the trappola PACK, the pips often vary in size and design, and the SWORDS and CUDGELS are usually interlaced. See SUIT and INDICES.

PITCH. A colloquial term for DISCARD.

PITCH COUNT. An old name for the 4-3-2-1 Point Count.

PITT COUP. A play by which the declarer places himself in a position to lead through his left-hand adversary in a suit in which the dummy holds a major tenace over the left-hand adversary's minor tenace. It frequently involves the unblocking of a trump suit in dummy, and also may include a deliberate higher-than-necessary ruff with an honor in the closed hand so as to be able to lead low through West.

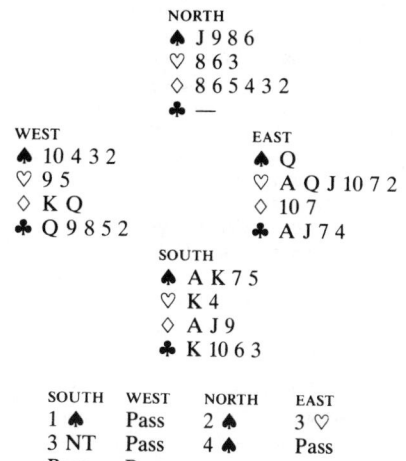

```
                    NORTH
                    ♠ J 9 8 6
                    ♡ 8 6 3
                    ◇ 8 6 5 4 3 2
                    ♣ —
WEST                              EAST
♠ 10 4 3 2                       ♠ Q
♡ 9 5                            ♡ A Q J 10 7 2
◇ K Q                            ◇ 10 7
♣ Q 9 8 5 2                      ♣ A J 7 4
                    SOUTH
                    ♠ A K 7 5
                    ♡ K 4
                    ◇ A J 9
                    ♣ K 10 6 3
```

SOUTH	WEST	NORTH	EAST
1 ♠	Pass	2 ♠	3 ♡
3 NT	Pass	4 ♠	Pass
Pass	Pass		

West opened the heart nine, won by East who returned the suit. South won with the king. The spade ace was led, on which declarer called for the eight from dummy (maintaining a two-way finesse situation against the ten). East's queen marked West with four spades to the ten. Declarer led ace and another diamond, hoping for and getting the 2–2 split in the suit. West won the second diamond, and returned a club, dummy discarding and East winning the ace. East returned the high heart, which declarer ruffed with the king. The lead of the spade seven permitted South to take a finesse, playing dummy's six; a further spade lead through West enabled declarer to unblock the high diamond from his hand on the fourth spade lead, and win the balance of the tricks in dummy.

The name is arbitrary, resulting from the use of

"Pitt," "Chatham," etc., in whist literature to designate particular players.

PIVOT BRIDGE, LAWS OF. (A form of social bridge played at home games where, instead of advancing from table to table as in party or progressive bridge, the players change or pivot among themselves at each individual table.)

Pivot bridge is played by four (or five and sometimes six) players at a table. This form may be used for a single table or for large gatherings in which it is desirable to have each table play as a separate unit without progression by the players.

The game is so arranged that each player plays with each other player at his table both as partner and opponent. There are two methods of play: first, four deals may be played to a round, one deal by each player, and the players change partners at the end of each four deals; second, rubbers may be played, and the players change partners at the end of each rubber.

If four deals to a round are played, the scoring is exactly the same as in Progressive Bridge; if rubbers are played, the scoring is exactly the same as in Rubber Bridge. The laws given below explain only the method of rotation in changing partners, not scoring, vulnerability, etc., which are covered elsewhere.

DRAW FOR PARTNERS

1. The players draw cards for partners and deal, and for a choice of seats and pack. The player who draws highest is the first pivot, and he deals first and has the choice of seats and packs. The player who draws second highest is the pivot's first partner; the player who draws third highest sits at the pivot's left during the first round; the player who draws fourth sits at the pivot's right; and if a fifth player is present, he does not participate in the first round or rubber.

CHANGING PARTNERS (FOR FOUR PLAYERS)

2. During the first three rounds or rubbers, the players change positions as indicated in the following diagram:

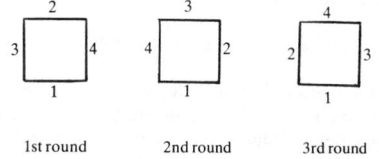

1st round   2nd round   3rd round

After the third round or rubber, the players again cut for position and partners.

CHANGING PARTNERS (FOR FIVE PLAYERS)

3. If five players desire to play at the same table, they may be accommodated in this manner:

For the first round or rubber, the players take the positions indicated by their draw for position under

Law No. 1. For rounds one to five, they take the positions indicated in the following diagram:

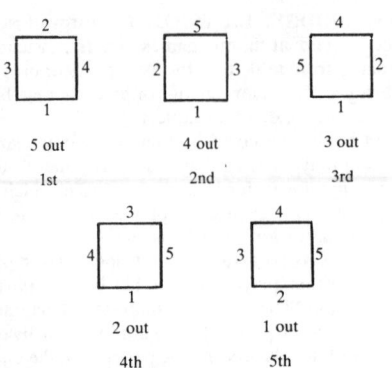

5 out   4 out   3 out

1st   2nd   3rd

2 out   1 out

4th   5th

At the end of each five rounds, the players again draw for positions and partners.

COMMENT

This arrangement permits each player to play with each other player once as partner and twice as opponent, and each player sits out one round in turn.

SIX PLAYER PIVOT

4. With six players at the same table, a complete pivot enabling each player to play once as partner and twice against each combination of opponents other than the player who is cut out at the same time, may be arranged by following this sequence of partnerships:

3–4	1–5	1–3	3–5	1–6	1–4	3–6	1–2
v	v	v	v	v	v	v	v
5–6	2–6	2–4	4–6	2–5	2–3	4–5	5–6

The player numbers correspond to the order in which they are cut out, with 1–2, 3–4 and 5–6 out simultaneously. If more than eight rounds are to be played, the pivot is resumed at round 3, or a new order may be determined by cutting so as to have different players out at the same time.

DETERMINATION OF THE WINNER

5. At the completion of each round or rubber, the player enters on his tally both his own score and that of his opponents. Each player totals his own and his opponents' scores separately and records the difference, plus or minus as the case may be, at the bottom of his tally. The player having the highest plus score is the winner and the others rank in descending order according to their scores.

PLACE THE CARDS, PLACING CARDS. See ASSUMPTIONS, IN PLAY; CARD READING.

PLACING THE LEAD. See AVOIDANCE.

PLAFOND. A French card game which was the immediate predecessor of contract. Harold Vanderbilt, the originator of contract bridge, used *plafond* (which means "ceiling") as the basis for his approach to the new game.

Pierre BELLANGER (*The Bridge World*, Sept. 1931) dates the origin of Plafond to 1918. where it was introduced at the Cercle Littéraire of Paris shortly after the Armistice. Only those tricks bid for and made were scored below the line and counted toward game. Tricks made above the bid scored 50 points above the line for each additional trick. Except for increasing the slam bonuses to 100 for a small slam and 200 for a grand slam, awarded whether the slam was bid or not, the trick scores and penalties were much as in Auction. However, a bonus of 50 points was scored for making any contract successfully; the first game for either side received a bonus of 100; winning the rubber was worth an additional 400. Bellanger also claims authorship of the words, "Contract Bridge," an appendix to his 1914 edition of *"Legislation du Bridge aux Enchéres"* mentioning *"Bridge avec Contrat."* But contract, as it was introduced in 1914 at the Automobile Club de France, was only an embryonic form of Plafond.

George F. HERVEY, bridge correspondent of *The Field*, cites a letter to that publication, dated February 8, 1941, in which Sir Hugh CLAYTON records that the contract principle was invented by four players in Poona (India) in 1912. The game was developed out of auction and named S.A.C.C., an acronym of the four men who invented it. On July 15, 1914, the rules of this game were published by Sir Hugh in *The Times of India*, and there is evidence that the game was played in various parts of India from that date until some years after promulgation of the first official code of laws to govern contract bridge (December 1929).

Milton C. WORK reported that similar games had been tried in the United States before 1914 but failed to become popular. Obviously, none of these games included the vulnerability feature and the scoring table devised by VANDERBILT, but it would appear that the "ceiling" principle of Plafond may have come to France from India or at least have originated there at an earlier date than reported by Bellanger.

There was a Franco-American Plafond Match in 1933 which ended about even, and which employed many of the newly established contract bridge methods, but most players essaying both games tended to prefer the more precise and demanding contract.

PLAIN SUIT. A suit other than the trump suit.

PLAN OF PLAY, PLANNING THE PLAY. The mental process by which declarer decides on how to use the assets of the combined hands to fulfill the contract, and, secondly, to develop overtricks or to minimize penalties. Among the things to be considered is the management of the trump suit, development of long cards in side suits, maintenance of communication between the two hands, if and how to finesse, development of end plays, safety plays against adverse distributions, and others. Declarer should mentally review these and other problems before playing to the first trick, even though such play may be automatic. Original plans should frequently be changed as more information about adverse holdings is developed, but the declarer should not require time to consider each play, and thus delay the tempo of the game. See NO TRUMP PLAY and TRUMP PLAY.

PLASTIC CARDS. Cards made of acetate cellulose or a vinyl or polyvinyl compound.

Since the wearing qualities of paper are limited, inventors searched for years for a substitute that would be more enduring. Success depended on two inventions, a method of making the thin material opaque so that no card could be identified from the back, and a formula for making ink that would adhere firmly to the plastic surface.

In 1932, Siegfried Klausner registered in Austria and other European countries a patent for making non-inflammable opaque plastic sheets and for making playing cards from them by coating the printed surfaces with a lacquer derived from the basic plastic. After manufacturing the cards under the trade name Mirakel, he sold domestic rights to Piatnik, the S. E. Europe monopoly, which took the cards off the market; but he retained US rights and in 1934 founded the Kem Company with E. Culbertson and others. The resulting KEM CARDS outwear paper cards, are resistant to soiling, and are easily cleaned.

Plastic cards are made by three companies in the United States, and by several in Japan and Europe. In spite of their proven superiority in many ways, they represent only about 2½% of the number of packs sold yearly. See MANUFACTURE OF PLAYING CARDS.

PLASTIC VALUATION. One of the phrases popularized in the writings of Ely CULBERTSON to describe the mental processes of the bidder as he receives more information regarding the makeup of his partner's hand. REVALUATION, PROMOTION OF TRUMP HONORS, and DISTRIBUTIONAL COUNTS were all covered in the one phrase.

PLAY (of the hand). See NO TRUMP PLAY and TRUMP PLAY.

PLAY AFTER AN ILLEGAL PLAY. Such action forfeits (waives) any penalty incurred by the illegal play, unless the illegal play constitutes a revoke. This is in accordance with the principle that the non-offending side may "condone" an offense. Such a play may be made only by the player to the left of the hand making the illegal play, and such right is not affected by partner calling attention to the illegality of the play. See LAWS (Law 60).

PLAY FROM EQUALS. When holding cards of

equal rank in a suit, it is often very important which card is chosen to be played to a particular trick. A defender's card may provide partner with important information, or it may deceive the declarer. A declarer's card may confuse the defense, or at least avoid giving away information unnecessarily.

Defensive play from equals. On the opening lead, there is a standard table which usually requires that the higher of two equal honors be led. The only exception to this is that the king is usually led from ace, king, and others (see OPENING LEADS). However, when the honor combination is bare (no small cards) the lower honor is sometimes led to inform partner of the situation. For example, the normal lead from A K x against a suit contract is the king. From A K alone, the usual lead is the ace. When this is followed by the king, the partner of the leader will know that the opening leader has exhausted the suit led (otherwise, the normal lead of the king would have been made).

This reversing order of plays can also be used later in the defense. Consider, for example, the deal below:

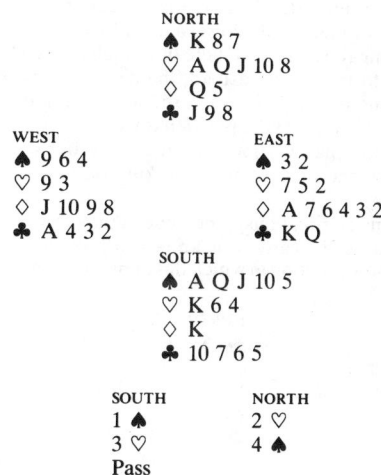

```
                    NORTH
                    ♠ K 8 7
                    ♡ A Q J 10 8
                    ◇ Q 5
                    ♣ J 9 8
   WEST                              EAST
   ♠ 9 6 4                           ♠ 3 2
   ♡ 9 3                             ♡ 7 5 2
   ◇ J 10 9 8                        ◇ A 7 6 4 3 2
   ♣ A 4 3 2                         ♣ K Q
                    SOUTH
                    ♠ A Q J 10 5
                    ♡ K 6 4
                    ◇ K
                    ♣ 10 7 6 5

   SOUTH            NORTH
   1 ♠              2 ♡
   3 ♡              4 ♠
   Pass
```

Against South's four spade contract, West leads the diamond jack.

East wins the ace of diamonds and sees at once that the defense must look to clubs for the setting tricks. East should shift to the queen of clubs, not the king. After the queen of clubs wins and East continues with the king of clubs, West should overtake to give East a club ruff. If East had started with three clubs to the king-queen, he would have made the normal shift to the club king. In this case, the deliberate play of the "wrong" honor from equals indicates no other cards in the suit led.

Sometimes, the lower honor is led from equal cards for the purpose of deceiving the declarer. In the deal below, the defense again needs three club tricks to defeat South's four spade contract.

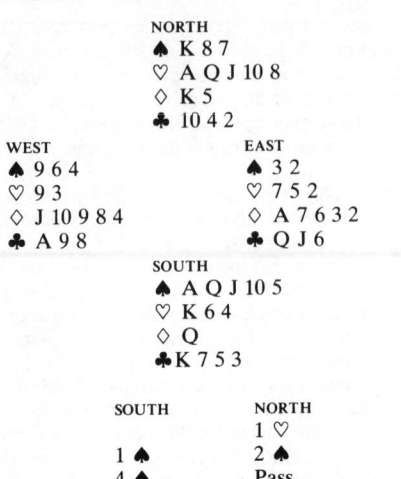

```
              NORTH
              ♠ K 8 7
              ♡ A Q J 10 8
              ◇ K 5
              ♣ 10 4 2
WEST                        EAST
♠ 9 6 4                     ♠ 3 2
♡ 9 3                       ♡ 7 5 2
◇ J 10 9 8 4                ◇ A 7 6 3 2
♣ A 9 8                     ♣ Q J 6
              SOUTH
              ♠ A Q J 10 5
              ♡ K 6 4
              ◇ Q
              ♣ K 7 5 3
```

SOUTH	NORTH
	1 ♡
1 ♠	2 ♠
4 ♠	Pass

West leads the jack of diamonds which East wins with the ace. East can see that the best chance to defeat the contract is to take three fast tricks in clubs. His best play is probably the club jack. An unwary declarer may decide that this places the ace and queen of clubs with West, and will cover the king, allowing the defense to take three club tricks. If East shifts to the queen instead, the declarer may place him with queen-jack and, if so, he will duck the first round of clubs. If the position is well known to both sides, this play will not succeed, for declarer's correct play on the first round is the king (see RESTRICTED CHOICE).

In many situations, a defender's play from equals should be the card he is known to hold. The most common situation in which this opportunity arises is:

```
              NORTH
              ♠ A J 2
WEST                        EAST
♠ Q 10 4                    ♠ 8 7 6
              SOUTH
              ♠ K 9 5 3
```

The declarer, South, leads the three of spades, and finesses dummy's jack. When the ace of spades is cashed, West should drop the queen. This card ranks equally with the ten, but the cards are not equivalent, as West is *known to hold the queen*. If West drops the ten under the ace, South must make four tricks in the suit. If West drops the queen on the second round, South is faced with a guess.

In some situations, the correct play from equals depends on the assumption of a possible distribution of the cards.

```
              NORTH
              ♡ A J 3
WEST                        EAST
♡ K Q 4 2                   immaterial
              SOUTH
              ♡ 7 led
```

When the declarer leads the seven of hearts, if West decides to split his honors, he should play the queen and not the king. It is possible that declarer is missing the ten, and can be put to a difficult guess on the second round of hearts. For example, the suit might be distributed:

```
              NORTH
              ♡ A J 3
WEST                        EAST
♡ K Q 4 2                   ♡ 10 6 5
              SOUTH
              ♡ 9 8 7
```

After the queen loses to the ace, declarer will later lead the suit from his own hand once again. If West ducks, declarer must reckon with the possibility that he made a "standard" falsecard with an original holding of Q 1042. Notice that the initial play of the king would not create this effect, as West could hardly afford to play the king from K 1042, lest declarer hold the queen in the concealed hand.

In other situations, the defense can play from imaginary equal cards:

```
              NORTH
              ♣ A K 10 9 7 6
WEST                        EAST
♣ J 8                       ♣ Q 2
              SOUTH
              ♣ 5 4 3
```

The declarer leads the five of clubs and West plays the jack. If the declarer suspects that West has split equals, he may later lose a trick to East's queen.

```
              NORTH
              ◇ A Q 9 4
WEST                        EAST
◇ 10 6 5                    ◇ J 8 7
              SOUTH
              ◇ K 3 2
```

The declarer cashes the diamond king, and leads the three. By playing the ten of diamonds with a naïve air, West may manufacture a surprise trick for the defense.

In choosing a deceptive card to play from equals, the best policy is to make the holding you are representing a believable one. In the following position, spades are trump and West chooses his opening lead in that suit:

```
              NORTH
              ♠ 4 3 2
WEST                        EAST
♠ 6                         ♠ Q J 7
              SOUTH
              ♠ A K 10 9 8 5
```

On the first trick, East should play the queen. South is more likely to believe that West led from J6 than that he led from Q6. If East plays the jack on the first trick, South will probably take a finesse against the queen.

An opening lead from equal cards is often made in consideration of what dummy is likely to hold in the suit led. On lead against a suit contract with A K 6 4 of a suit that dummy has bid strongly, the best lead is probably the ace. If the dummy's suit is headed by Q J without the ten, and the declarer holds a singleton, he may later take a ruffing finesse against third hand's imaginary king instead of choosing a different (possibly successful) line of play.

Another occasion for a deceptive lead from equal cards is when it is desirable to misrepresent the potential entry position. Let us suppose that West is on lead against the auction:

SOUTH	NORTH
1 NT	3 NT

West holds ♠ Q J 10 8 6 2. The best lead is the deceptive ten of spades. East's first play will look like a high signal, and declarer may believe that West has hit East's suit. If this plan succeeds, South will probably take losing finesses into the West hand.

Third hand's standard play from equal honors is the lowest of touching cards. Declarer may sometimes be deceived by a change of strategy.

NORTH
♠ 4 3

WEST
♠ 10 8 6 2

EAST
♠ K Q 7 5

SOUTH
♠ A J 9

Against South's no trump contract, West leads the deuce of spades. If East believes he will obtain the lead first for the defense, he might well play the king as a deceptive move.

When East later leads the five, South may decide his best chance is to hope that East has the ten.

When the declarer must guess which suit to attack, the defense can often mislead him with the play of an apparently unnecessarily high card from "equals."

NORTH
♠ A J 9 8 3

WEST
♠ 4 2

EAST
♠ K Q 10 5

SOUTH
♠ 7 6

Declarer plays a spade to dummy's nine. If East wins with the ten (equal with the king and queen on this trick), the declarer may look elsewhere for his tricks. If East wins with a high honor, however, declarer may continue the suit at his next opportunity, thus losing time (and possibly tricks).

The defense often uses a play from equals as a suit preference signal. This frequently occurs when a defender is establishing a suit against a no trump contract, and has a choice of equal cards to use to knock out the declarer's last stopper. The use of a high card shows a possible entry in a high-ranking suit, and the use of a low card shows a possible entry in a low-ranking suit. Another common play from equals involves the play of a high honor from equals to show strength in a high-ranking suit and a low honor from equals to show strength in a low-ranking suit. See SUIT PREFERENCE SIGNAL.

Declarer's play with equals. The selection of declarer's play with equal cards is designed to misguide the defense as much as possible. The selection of which equal to play depends upon declarer's specific objective.

NORTH
◇ 2

SOUTH
◇ K Q J 10 9

At a suit contract, declarer (South) must avoid a loser in diamonds (a side suit). If dummy holds a few trump cards, his best chance is to lead the nine of diamonds from his hand. If West holds the ace, he may duck on the assumption that East can win the trick cheaply.

Thus, declarer plays a low equal when he hopes the defense will not use their honor cards. If, in a similar situation, the declarer hopes to remove the ace quickly, he should play the king (or queen) on the first round.

At a no trump contract, the declarer is usually interested in concealing strength or feigning strength so that the defenders will not know whether or not they have hit a weak spot in declarer's armor.

NORTH
♣ 4 3

SOUTH
♣ K Q 10

Against South's no trump contract, West leads the club five on which East plays the jack. South should win with the king. By so doing, he may deceive West into believing that East holds the queen of clubs.

NORTH
♣ 4 3

SOUTH
♣ A K Q

Declarer has a weak spot elsewhere, and hopes the defense will continue clubs. When West leads the five of clubs and East plays the jack, declarer should play the king.

Once again this play may lead West to believe that East holds the queen of clubs. If declarer wins with the ace, West will know he has *something* else in clubs unless the unlikely situation of East holding K Q J exists. Thus, West may suspect some trickiness. (On the other hand, against an experienced West, the play of the ace may be a good double cross.)

If the declarer is afraid of a continuation of the suit led, he should put on a mock display of power.

NORTH
♠ 4 3

WEST
♠ A K 8 5 2

EAST
♠ 9 7 6

SOUTH
♠ Q J 10

On West's lead of the spade five, East plays the nine. South might well gobble this up with the ten, making sure West knows that he holds the queen and jack as well. If South wins a higher honor, West may tend to place East with more length because of the chance that the declarer lacks the ten of spades.

When the declarer has a very powerful holding in the suit led, he can often paint a very misleading picture.

NORTH
♡ Q 6 5

WEST
♡ 9 7 3 2

EAST
♡ 10 8

SOUTH
♡ A K J 4

Against South's three no trump contract, West leads the heart deuce. Dummy plays low and East plays the ten. To encourage the defense to continue the suit, South's best play is probably the king. In addition to concealing the jack, this play suggests that East may have started with A J 10. The play of the ace may present the same type of picture, but if holding the ace, declarer might have played dummy's queen on the first trick to gain a tempo by raking in a fast winner.

In general, declarer's best idea is to keep the defense in the dark as much as possible about his holding. However, he sometimes plays with a specific objective in mind.

NORTH
♠ 8 6 5

WEST
♠ A 2

EAST
♠ 7 3

SOUTH
♠ K Q J 10 9 4

Spades are trumps. In drawing trumps, many declarers think it is amusing to lead the eight from dummy and let it ride. This is a good way to let the dummy know the hand is not violently overbid, but it also gives away a lot of information. West may feel that declarer has taken a successful finesse, and he may adopt an active defense in a desperate attempt to defeat the contract. If this is to declarer's benefit, then this method of playing the trump suit is correct. However, if the declarer fears an active defense, he should play a low spade to his king or queen. West may now hope his partner held J 10 x of spades and that declarer must lose another trick in trump. He may therefore play safe, assuming that if he does not give away a trick with an aggressive lead, the contract will probably be defeated.

(As with all of these deceptive plays which leave possibilities open, how well declarer knows his opponents is an important factor.)

The purpose of declarer's play from equals is often to locate the defensive honors in a suit.

NORTH
♣ 4 3 2

SOUTH
♣ K Q 10

The declarer is anxious to discover the location of the ace of clubs. After he leads the suit from the dummy, his best play against inexperienced players is the king. Against more wary opposition, the queen may be more effective. In the first case, West may fear that the declarer holds the king as his only honor in the suit. However, a more experienced player may decide that the declarer is unlikely to start such a weak suit during the early play.

Declarer is anxious to have West take the ace if he holds it so that he will be able to take informed action on the second round of the suit.

In general, when declarer leads a suit, the play of his highest equal card will conceal his holding in the suit. For example, declarer might lead low to the queen with any of the following holdings:

NORTH	◇ 4 3 2	◇ 4 3 2	◇ 4 3 2
SOUTH	◇ A Q J	◇ Q J 10 6	◇ Q 6

◇ A Q J   ◇ Q J 10 6   ◇ Q 6

In the last example, of course, the declarer is trying to stop the defense from leading this suit when it gets the lead later in the play.

In a suit contract, the declarer can often conceal a potential ruff from the defense by playing carefully from equal cards.

NORTH
♡ Q J 10 4 3

WEST
♡ 9 8 7 6 5

EAST
♡ 2

SOUTH
♡ A K

West leads the nine of hearts against a spade contract. By playing low from dummy and winning with the ace, South may lead West to believe that East holds the king of hearts. An alternate form of this deception is to play the queen from the dummy before winning with the ace. This makes it look as if South gave East the opportunity to make a stupid play.

Declarer can often conceal the possibility of taking a deep finesse by leading low from equals.

NORTH
♠ Q 5

SOUTH
♠ A 10 9 8

By leading the eight of spades toward dummy's queen, declarer may induce West to pop in with his king, if he holds it. If the ten or nine is led, West may duck smoothly, being more likely to realize the possibility of a finesse against the jack.

NORTH
♡ Q 3 2

SOUTH
♡ A 9 8 7 6

Declarer has a choice of plays in this situation. By leading the six of hearts toward the dummy, he may conceal from West the possibility of an immediate double finesse on the first round. If West ducks smoothly, declarer should probably let the six ride and make a good guess on the next round. In this way, he may avoid two losers when West holds J x or 10 x in hearts (see SUIT COMBINATIONS).

The following situations are similar:

	NORTH			NORTH	
	◇ J 5 4			◇ J 5 4	
WEST		EAST	WEST		EAST
◇ Q 3 2		◇ K 10	◇ K 3		◇ Q 10 2
	SOUTH			SOUTH	
	◇ A 9 8 7 6			◇ A 9 8 7 6	

The declarer intends to lead toward dummy, and play West for 10 x (unless he receives information through action at the table). By leading the six, he can conceal the possibility of a finesse against the ten, and may find West jumping in with his king or queen (much to his subsequent embarrassment).

The following deal illustrates a deceptive play by declarer from a holding of "equals," countered by a brilliant defensive suit preference signal by an unusual play from equals.

```
                 NORTH
                 ♠ K 7 5 3 2
                 ♡ 3 2
                 ◇ J 6 4
                 ♣ Q 6 5
WEST                              EAST
♠ A 6 4                          ♠ Q 9 8
♡ 8                              ♡ 7 4
◇ Q 10 7 5 3 2                   ◇ A K 9 8
♣ J 9 7                          ♣ 10 8 3 2
                 SOUTH
                 ♠ J 10
                 ♡ A K Q J 10 9 6 5
                 ◇ —
                 ♣ A K 4
```

SOUTH	NORTH
2 ♡	2 NT
3 ♡	3 ♠
6 ♡	Pass

West leads a diamond which declarer ruffs. South realizes that he will have to guess the spade situation eventually. At trick two, therefore, South leads a spade. He chooses the ten so that West will not know that he has a possible finesse against the queen. West is likely to take his ace of spades (if he holds it) at once for fear that declarer has a singleton spade.

However, on the ten of spades lead, West calmly plays low. South, now faced with a guess, reasons that West might well have played the ace of spades if

he held it. Declarer therefore passes the ten of spades and the contract is defeated.

How did West know to make this ducking play? On the first trick, East deliberately played the ace of diamonds from his equal honor holding. This indicated a holding in spades. Clearly, this was the queen and not the queen-jack, so West knew that he could give the declarer a chance to misguess spades. East did not know that declarer held two spades, but as he held no possible defensive trick he felt that West would take the spade ace if he held a possible trick of his own. Declarer could not realize that a signal had taken place, for he did not know which defender held the king of diamonds.

The result was a deceptive play from equals countered by an informative play from equals.

J. R.

PLAY OUT. To continue the play of a hand, trick by trick, to its conclusion, usually at the request of a member of the side opposing declarer.

PLAY OUT OF TURN. A play is considered to be in turn if it is made after the player to the right has led or played, or if it is a lead by a player who has won the preceding trick. Any other order constitutes a play out of turn, and is covered by the rule for a premature lead or play by a defender, or lead or play from the wrong hand by declarer. See LAWS (Laws 54, 55, 56, and 57).

PLAYED CARD. Each player except dummy plays a card by detaching it from his hand, and facing it on the edge of the table immediately before him. Declarer plays a card from dummy's hand by naming the card he proposes to play; after which dummy picks up the card, and places it face up on his edge of the table. (In playing from dummy's hand, declarer may, if he prefers, pick up the desired card, and place it in such position as to indicate that it has been played.)

In addition, a card must be played if it is a defender's card held so that it is possible for his partner to see its face; or if it is a card from declarer's hand that declarer holds face up in front of him, and that is touching or near the table. Declarer must play a card in dummy that he touches for purposes other than arranging or in reaching for the card immediately above or below the card touched. Any player also plays a card by naming or otherwise designating it as the card he proposes to play. Also any penalty card must be played if it can be played legally (without revoking). See LAWS (Law 45).

PLAYER. A participant at a table of bridge, one of an active foursome engaged at bridge; one member of either pair playing against each other.

PLAYER NUMBER. A seven-digit number assigned by the ACBL to a member. The last digit is a self-checking device by which the key-punch machine throws out incorrect numbers. The method by which the checking digit is computed is interesting. Multiply the first six digits by 7, 6, 5, 4, 3, and 2 respectively; then add these products. Divide the total of the products by 11, and note the remainder. This remainder is then subtracted from the divisor, 11, and the resulting difference is the check digit. (If the net result of this work is a remainder of 1, then the number is not used.)

When a player achieves Life Master status, this is indicated by a change in his player number by the substitution of a letter for the first digit, alphabetically from J for 1 to R for 9.

PLAYER OF THE YEAR. The player who, during a given year, earns the greatest number of master points. This award may be made on a national basis (see MCKENNEY TROPHY), or on a unit basis for points won in unit sectional (or regional) tournaments, or even on a club basis for points won in the individual club's games. In many units, a separate award or recognition is given to the player who begins the year in a limited category (such as sub-National Master) who earns the most points in his category.

PLAYING CARDS. The cards, usually pasteboard, used in playing various games. (See also MAGNETIC CARDS, PLASTIC CARDS.) The standard bridge pack (or deck) consists of fifty-two cards, arranged in four suits of thirteen cards each. Among the principal games played in the US are bridge, canasta, casino, chemin-de-fer, cribbage, gin and other rummy games, hearts, piquet, twenty-one (also called blackjack and pontoon), and many varieties of solitaire and patience. Pinochle is played with a special deck, which can be formed from two decks of standard cards. (See PACK for non-standard packs and their makeup, and TAROT for a very special pack.) Each suit is divided into three COURT CARDS and ten SPOT CARDS. Of the latter, the ACE, or one-spot, ranks highest in bridge (but not necessarily so in other games). Below the ace in rank are the court cards—king, queen, and jack (which has replaced the older term, knave, almost completely)—followed by the spot cards—ten, nine, eight, seven, six, five, four, three (or trey), and two (or deuce). The suits are identified by the symbols ♠ for spades, ♡ for hearts, ♢ for diamonds, and ♣ for clubs, and rank in that order in bridge games. Today's cards have corner INDICES showing a letter or numeral above a PIP of the suit to which the card belongs, but this is a modern device. Cards lacked such an index as late as 1870.

For other articles in this book referring to playing cards, see COLLECTIONS OF PLAYING CARDS; DEVIL'S PICTURE BOOK; FACE CARDS; FORTUNETELLING; HISTORY OF PLAYING CARDS; MANUFACTURE OF PLAYING CARDS; SUIT; TAXES ON PLAYING CARDS; TEN OR TEN-SPOT and other-spot cards; TRANSFORMATION CARDS; and USES OF CARDS.

PLAYING KNOWN CARD. See FALSE-CARDING.

PLAYING TO THE SCORE. A variation in normal play of the cards which is motivated by the scores of the pairs involved in rubber bridge. The net score of each rubber is computed at the end of the rubber, but is carried to the summary sheet in amounts to the nearest hundred. If a certain line of play will produce a trick-score of 150 points if successful, but only 90 points if unsuccessful, while there is a different line of play that will guarantee 120 points, the declarer should mentally add the scores of each pair and obtain the net score before he determines which line of play to use. If the net score is 220 points, only a score of 150 points on the last deal would make the net score equal some 150 or more and be scored to the higher hundred. If the net score had been 240 points at that time, the need to get the added hundred would only have been 120 points, and the sure line of play should be adopted.

PLAYING TRICKS. Tricks that a hand may be expected to produce if the holder buys the contract; attacking tricks or winners, as distinguished from defensive tricks or winners when the holder must play against an adverse contract. In estimating the playing-trick strength of a hand, the holder assumes that his long suit (or suits) will break evenly among the other three hands, unless the auction has indicated otherwise, and adds the number of tricks his long suit (or suits) is likely to yield to his quick-trick total of the other suits. For example, the following hand

♠ K 5   ♡ A Q J 8 6 2   ♢ A Q 7   ♣ 9 3

contains about seven playing tricks—five in hearts, one-half quick trick in spades, one and one-half quick tricks in diamonds.

When the long suit is not solid or semi-solid, estimation of playing tricks becomes more difficult because a second factor must be considered—the position of the missing honor cards. Thus, this suit

♡ K J 8 6 5 3

is worth approximately three and one-half playing tricks. With normal distribution, the declarer might make four tricks if he can lead the suit from dummy or find the missing honors well placed, but could be limited to three tricks.

Assessment of playing tricks is particularly important when considering a pre-emptive bid or an overcall. See RULE OF TWO AND THREE.

PLAYS TO CONCEAL STRENGTH. See DECEPTIVE PLAY.

PLAYS TO CONCEAL WEAKNESS. See DECEPTIVE PLAY.

PLUS VALUE. An added feature of a hand or suit that should be weighed when one is planning a bid or series of bids. There are bidding developments which require evaluation of a hand on a fairly precise basis. Therefore, during a subsequent phase of the auction, if one has been somewhat rigid in describing his holding and does possess plus values such as jack-ten-nine combinations in suits otherwise protected or strengthened, or a guarded queen, etc., that may be felt to be of help to partner, one is sometimes more liberal in making a final placement of contract than without the aforementioned values.

The term was regularly used in counting HONOR TRICKS, but has little meaning when valuation is by points.

POCKET. One of four rectangular areas in a duplicate board which hold the four hands, designated North, South, East, and West. See LAWS OF DUPLICATE (Law 2).

POINT-COUNT. An almost universally used method of valuation. Many point-counts have become obsolete (see FOUR ACES, REITH, and ROBERTSON). In general use is the high-card valuation introduced by Bryant McCampbell in 1915 and publicized by Milton WORK after whom it was named:

Ace	4
King	3
Queen	2
Jack	1

This gives a total of 40 points in the pack, and makes an average hand worth 10 points.

The Work count is slightly less accurate mathematically than the Four Aces count, for example, but its simplicity favored its acceptance. It was regularly used by English experts in the thirties, but did not find favor with American experts until it was adopted and publicized by Fred Karpin and Charles Goren in the late forties. They supplemented the basic high-card count with valuation for distribution (see DISTRIBUTIONAL COUNTS).

All authorities recognize that the 4–3–2–1 count has some weaknesses, and recommend certain corrections:

(1) Aces are undervalued, so the presence or absence of aces materially affects the strength of a hand. Two methods are: add ½ point for each ace; or deduct a point for an aceless hand, and add a point for holding four aces.

(2) Tens are valuable cards, and are sometimes counted as ½ point or a plus value. One expedient is to consider aces and tens as a group, and to count an extra point if the hand contains three or more such cards.

(3) Unguarded or insufficiently guarded honor cards may not be worth their full point value. An extreme case is a singleton king, which some authorities count as 1 point instead of 3, and a singleton queen, which is sometimes counted as worthless. It is more normal to deduct one point from the value of a singleton king, queen, or jack. However, even the singleton ace is not quite as good as it looks, because it has little chance of capturing an opposing honor card, and is inflexible in the play.

Stayman goes to the extreme of recommending the deduction of a point for each of the following holdings:

K Q;   K J;   Q J;   Q x;   J x;   Q x x;   J x x.

It is true that these holdings have a reduced value if the partner has useless small cards in the suit. But if your side is destined to play the hand, there is a good chance that partner will hold a card which will combine effectively with the short honor holding.

(4) Honor combinations are slightly stronger than the same cards would be in different suits. For example, Q J x is more effective than Q x x in one suit and J x x in another suit. But so much depends on what partner can provide that it is better to make no adjustment in this respect unless there is reason to think that partner's hand will be worthless or nearly worthless; or unless the honor is in a suit bid by partner. For other methods of valuation, see BISSELL SYSTEM; HONOR TRICKS; and LOSING-TRICK COUNT.

POINTED. A term originally coined to describe the combination of the spade and diamond suits (for example a "pointed two-suiter"), since both suits have pips that are pointed at the top. The converse is "rounded," to indicate hearts and clubs.

POINTING CARDS. When four cards have been played to a trick in duplicate, each player turns his own card face down on the edge of the table immediately before him. If his side won the trick, the card is pointed lengthwise toward his partner; if the opponents won the trick, the card is pointed lengthwise toward his opponents. Each player should arrange his own cards in an orderly overlapping row in the sequence played.

At the completion of the play, each player has an accurate count of tricks won and lost; should there be a disagreement, the tricks can be inspected in turn, and the disagreement reconciled. Should any alteration of this order of play of the cards occur, the Director must assume the possibility that the player whose cards are disarranged is in error. This order of play should never be disturbed until the Director has been summoned in event of disagreement.

POINTS. (1) The score earned by a pair as a result of the play of a hand, including TRICK POINTS, PREMIUM SCORES, and BONUS. (2) A unit by which a hand is evaluated. See POINT-COUNT. (3) The holding of master points that have been credited to a player in the ACBL.

POKER BRIDGE. An epithet attached to a style of bidding that relies heavily on stabbing boldly with bids calculated to produce SWINGS on every hand. Players who can legitimately be accused of using "poker" tactics in bridge are those who constantly overbid or take long chances, and in general try to inculcate many more gambling features into bridge than rightfully belong there.

POLAND. See CONTRACT BRIDGE ASSOCIATION OF POLAND.

POLITICIANS. Many persons occupying high political or military offices have been known also as bridge players. Outstanding among these on a social level was the late President Dwight D. EISENHOWER, who made an appearance at the 1961 Summer Nationals in Washington. He was then accompanied by his wartime colleague General Alfred GRUENTHER, whose prewar reputation as the leading American tournament Director was somewhat eclipsed by his wartime services, and his subsequent appointments as supreme allied commander in NATO and president of the American Red Cross. Former Secretary of Agriculture Clinton P. Anderson was a prominent tournament player in the thirties.

Former Greek Premier VENIZELOS was a member of the French national team during the thirties, and was European Champion in 1935. In England, Winston CHURCHILL was playing bridge when the news of Germany's declaration of war on Russia interrupted his game. Ian MACLEOD had been a top tournament player and was one of the most influential cabinet ministers as Chancellor of the Exchequer at the time of his death in 1970. In Argentina, Ricardo ARGERICH was a player of international class until he retired to concentrate upon his diplomatic duties.

POLSKI ZWIAZEK BRYDZA SPORTOWEGO.
See CONTRACT BRIDGE ASSOCIATION OF POLAND.

POPULAR BRIDGE.
The only magazine dealing with contract bridge with newsstand distribution; founded and published bi-monthly by Gordon Behn and James Miller of Behn-Miller Publishers, Inc., Encino, Calif., who also publish two numismatic periodicals, *Coinage* and *Coin Mart,* and a non-fiction magazine on western history, *Westerner.* Publication began with the July-August issue in 1967 and the first issues contained mainly reprints from bridge books. As the magazine developed a character of its own, it attracted many of the leading bridge writers and increased its circulation to a point where it has become the second largest of all bridge periodicals. From inception, it has been directed primarily to appealing to the average player with attractive artwork and articles ranging from humor and mystery to some of the technical aspects of the game. Its contributors include A. Dormer, R. Frey, M. Hardy, T. Hirsch, E. Kantar, V. Mollo, A. Sheinwold, D. von Elsner, and others.

PORTLAND CLUB of London.
The principal bridge club of British gentry, nobility, and (at times) royalty; world-famous as promulgator of the laws used in many countries. Founded before 1815 as the Stratford Club, and reorganized 1825, according to tradition, in order to be rid of one objectionable member. Bridge, introduced in 1894 by Lord Brougham, was given a code of laws in 1895, and with subsequent revisions at intervals, gave the Portland Club its reputation as a law-making body (see LAWS). Famous members of the Club in its whist days included James Clay, William Pole, William Dalton, and Henry Jones (Cavendish). Geoffrey L. Butler, Chairman of the British Bridge League, has acted as the link between the Portland Club and international bodies such as the EUROPEAN BRIDGE LEAGUE and the WORLD BRIDGE FEDERATION.

PORTLAND RULES.
The laws of whist according to the English code, named after the Portland Club, which officially issued them.

In the early days of contract bridge and the later days of auction bridge, the use of bidding calls with conventional meaning (such as the Informatory Double of auction or the Vanderbilt Club Bid of contract) were decried by the card committee of the Portland Club, a staid, conservative, British stronghold, and barred in games held in their clubrooms. These rules were called Portland Rules at that time.

PORTUGUESE BRIDGE FEDERATION (FEDE-RAÇAO PORTUGUESA DI BRIDGE).
Founded in 1961 by Conde de Mangualde, and in 1975 had a membership of approximately 500 in three clubs, two in Lisbon and one in Oporto. The Federation is a member of the European Bridge League and participates in European Championships, hosting the 1970 event in Estoril. The main National competitions consist of two Team-of-Four and two Open Pairs events, one each of Portugal and one each of Lisbon. Players listed separately are: M. Antunes, F. Cabral, F. Calheiros, J. Cordeiro, J. Cruz, C. Debonnaire, J. Debonnaire, M. Melo, R. Pinto, J. Santos, R. Santos, C. Teixeira.

Officers, 1975:
President: Dr. Francisco de Sousa Tavares.
Secretary: Jose Pessanha Barbosa, Rua Dr. Silva Teles 13, Lisbon 1, Portugal.

POSITION.
The place at a table occupied by a player. The various positions are called by the compass points, i.e., North, South, East, and West. Also, the term "position" can correctly be used to describe one's place in the order of bidding during a given auction. "Second" position means that position directly to the left of the dealer. "Fourth" position is the seat to the dealer's right.

POSITIONAL FACTOR.
The value of honor cards during the bidding may improve or decline in accordance with the opposing bidding. A king becomes an almost sure trick when the suit is bid by the right-hand opponent, but is likely to be worthless if the suit is bid on the left, except as a no trump stopper if the holder of the king is declarer. See RIGHT SIDE.

Sidney Silodor gave the following example:

NORTH	EAST	SOUTH	WEST
1 ♡	Pass	2 ♡	3 ◇
3 ♡	Pass		

South holds:

♠ A J 7 3
♡ 10 6 3 2
◇ K 4 2
♣ 10 9

Although South has a relatively strong raise to two hearts, he should pass, because the diamond king has been devalued by the bid on the left. The decision to pass would be even clearer if the minor suits were interchanged and West bid three clubs. In that case North's failure to make the trial bid of three diamonds would imply a lack of interest in game.

POSITIONAL SQUEEZE. A squeeze which is effective against one opponent but not the other. This occurs when the hand opposite the squeeze card has nothing but busy cards; if that hand follows to the squeeze card before the opponent who is menaced, there can be no squeeze.

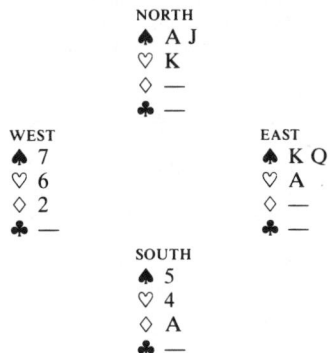

```
                NORTH
              ♠ A J
              ♡ K
              ◇ —
              ♣ —
WEST                        EAST
♠ 7                         ♠ K Q
♡ 6                         ♡ A
◇ 2                         ◇ —
♣ —                         ♣ —
                SOUTH
              ♠ 5
              ♡ 4
              ◇ A
              ♣ —
```

When the ace of diamonds is led, the North hand is squeezed before East must play, so that the latter is in no difficulty; however, if the East and West hands were reversed, the squeeze would be effective. Positional squeezes are characterized by the fact that the one-card menaces lie to the left of the opponent threatened. See also AUTOMATIC SQUEEZE and SIMPLE SQUEEZE.

M. I.

POSITIVE CARDS. See CARDS, NEUTRAL AND POSITIVE.

POSITIVE RESPONSE. A natural constructive response in a forcing situation which provides for an artificial negative response. See FORCING TWO-BID, TWO CLUB STRONG ARTIFICIAL OPENING.

POSITIVE SLAM DOUBLE. See DOUBLE FOR SACRIFICE.

POST-MORTEM. A term applied to discussion of bridge hands after the conclusion of the play or any time thereafter. Some players aver that they object to constant post-mortems, but it can sometimes be pointed out with a degree of correctness that what they object to is being reminded of their own mistakes. Generally speaking, post-mortems can be of significant value when engaged in by experts, as points of great interest are sometimes highlighted by this type of discussion, and unusual features of a hand brought into better perspective.

In tournament play, long post-mortems should be indulged in only if time permits at the end of a round.

POSTING THE SCORE. Among the duties of the tournament director (and his staff) is the posting of the score as rapidly and conspicuously as possible, for the inspection of the players. See CORRECTIONS TO THE SCORE, LAWS OF DUPLICATE BRIDGE (Law 77).

In club games, when traveling score slips are used, match points are awarded on the traveling score slips, and these are posted. Sometimes the match points are posted to a RECAPITULATION SHEET, where they are added and ranked. At no time is the score official until a PROTEST PERIOD has expired.

POWERHOUSE. A descriptive term signifying a really huge (in point value) hand at bridge. A powerhouse could also, but considerably less frequently, be a strong distributional hand with outside aces or ace combinations, or possibly void features. An alternative term is "rock crusher."

PRECEDENCE IN ENTERING A TABLE. In bridge clubs, precedence is given to that member who first appears in the playing room. The lowest priority belongs to a member leaving an existing table to join the new one. See HOUSE RULES.

PRECISION ASKING BIDS. The PRECISION CLUB system, in its most standard version, allows the one club opener to use asking bids for three purposes: (1) to find out about the length and quality of the trump suit, (2) to find out about responder's control of a particular suit, (3) to find out whether responder can fill in opener's SEMI-SOLID SUIT and what other aces he has.

Trump Asking. The most commonly used is the trump asking bid, which is initiated by the one club opener's single raise of responder's positive suit response. The responses are as follows:

1st step	No top honor
2nd step	Five cards with one top honor
3rd step	Five cards with two top honors
4th step	Six cards with one top honor
5th step	Six cards with two top honors
6th step	Three top honors

These asking bids and responses are used also in the SUPER PRECISION system, which designates them Gamma Trump Asking Bids. For other trump asking devices see TRUMP ASKING BIDS.

Control Asking. After a trump asking bid has been made and responded to, a bid in a new suit by opener asks about responder's controls in a side suit. The controls shown may be either high card or distributional. The responses are:

1st step	No control
2nd step	Third-round control
3rd step	Second-round control
4th step	First-round control
5th step	First- and second-round control

Ace asking. The third type of asking bid asks whether responder has one of the top three honors in a particular suit. It is initiated by a jump shift rebid by the one club opener after a positive response. The responses give information about another suit as well as about the asked suit. The responses are:

Cheapest no trump	No top honor, no aces
Single raise	Top honor in asked suit, no other aces
New suit	Ace of bid suit, no top honor in asked suit
Jump in new suit	Top honor in asked suit, ace in suit jumped in
Jump in no trump	No top honor in asked suit, but two side aces
Jump raise	Top honor in asked suit with two side aces

See also ASKING BIDS; ROMAN ASKING BIDS; ROMEX TRUMP ASKING BIDS; SUPER PRECISION ASKING BIDS.

PRECISION CLUB. A system developed principally by C. C. WEI and used successfully by the Chinese team in the 1967, 1968, and 1969 FAR EAST CHAMPIONSHIPS. The system attracted international attention during the 1969 WORLD CHAMPIONSHIP when Patrick HUANG, M. F. TAI, C. S. SHEN, and Frank HUANG, all using the Precision Club, spearheaded China's drive into the finals of the tournament. This was the closest a non-European, non-North American team had come to capturing the world team title. The Chinese team reached the finals again in 1970.

In the United States a number of top-level teams were sponsored by Wei to use and popularize the Precision System. One such team won three major ACBL knockout team events within a nineteen-month period. See PRECISION TEAM.

By 1972, when the Italian BLUE TEAM emerged from retirement to enter the World Team Olympiad, all three of its pairs were using versions of the Precision system. The version currently used by Belladonna and Garozzo is called SUPER PRECISION.

The chief features of the standard Precision System are as follows:

One club opening is forcing and artificial, and normally shows a minimum of 16 points. Suit responses, other than one diamond, which is the conventional negative, are positive, 8 points or more, guarantee at least a five-card suit and, in principle, are forcing to game. With a positive response and 4-4-4-1 distribution, there are two basic methods of responding. The partnership may agree to use the IMPOSSIBLE NEGATIVE: responder bids one diamond, then jumps in his singleton, or in no trump if his singleton is in opener's suit. Alternatively an UNUSUAL POSITIVE may be used: responder immediately jumps to two hearts, two spades, three clubs, or three diamonds over one club to show a singleton in the suit he jumps in, and four cards in every other suit. As a variation of the UNUSUAL POSITIVE, the jump can be made in the suit below the singleton, so that opener can economically cue-bid the singleton

to obtain additional information. Balanced hands are shown by responding either one no trump (8–10), two no trump (11–13, or 16 on up), or three no trump (14–15). After a negative response and a normal rebid, responder will usually bid again with 4–7 points.

If one club is overcalled, responder passes with less than 5 points, bids a five-card or longer suit, or makes a CARD-SHOWING DOUBLE with 5–8 points, jumps in no trump with the opponents' suit well stopped and 9–11 points, cue-bids with a hand too strong for a negative double, or bids the cheapest no trump with an unbalanced, game-forcing hand. If one club is doubled, normal responses are used, except that with a weak hand responder passes with clubs, bids one diamond without clubs, or redoubles with both major suits.

After a one diamond negative response, opener rebids one no trump with 16–18 points, two no trump with 19–21, or three no trump with 25–27. A non-jump rebid in a suit is non-forcing; a jump rebid is forcing to game unless opener rebids his suit at the three-level.

After a positive response, the auction develops naturally with one exception. A direct raise of responder's suit is an inquiry about the length of responder's suit and the number of top honors he holds, and subsequent suit bids by opener are asking bids. See PRECISION ASKING BIDS. See also SUPER PRECISION ASKING BIDS.

STAYMAN is used after all no trump responses and rebids.

One diamond, one heart, and one spade openings are natural, limited to a maximum of 15 points, and guarantee at least a four-card diamond suit or a five-card major.

One no trump response to a major-suit opening is forcing; three no trump is a strong balanced raise; double jumps are splinter bids, showing four-card support for opener's major and a singleton or void in the bid suit. Raises are limited and non-forcing, except after one diamond, two diamonds is forcing and three diamonds is pre-emptive. A jump response of two no trump shows 16 points or more.

One no trump opening is weak, 13–15 points. Two clubs and two diamonds are non-forcing and forcing STAYMAN, respectively.

Two clubs is a natural opening, showing a five-card or longer club suit and an unbalanced hand. Two diamonds is a conventional response: with a minimum, opener bids a four-card major; with a maximum, opener jumps in a four-card major, raises to three diamonds, or jumps to three no trump with a solid or semi-solid club suit. A rebid of two no trump shows a minimum hand with a six-card suit and two side suits stopped; responder may ask where the stoppers are by bidding three diamonds; the responses are three hearts to show hearts and diamonds, three spades to show spades and diamonds, and three no trump to show both major suits. A rebid of three clubs by opener over the two diamond response shows a six-card club suit with one side suit stopped; over a three diamond inquiry opener bids hearts or spades if that is where his stopper is, or bids three no trump if he has diamonds stopped.

Two diamonds is a specialized opening, describing a three-suited hand (4–4–1–4 or 4–4–0–5) with shortage in diamonds and 11–15 points. Three diamonds response requests opener to specify his exact distribution and point range of his opening bid. Other responses are limited and non-forcing.

Two hearts and two spades openings are weak two-bids.

Two no trump opening is standard (22–24 points).

Three no trump opening is gambling, showing a long, solid minor with little side strength.

Four clubs and four diamonds openings are four heart and four spade openings, respectively, showing a long, solid suit, with a side ace or king.

See SUPER PRECISION.

PRECISION TEAM. A highly successful team of young experts from the New York City area sponsored by C. C. WEI to use his PRECISION CLUB system between 1970 and 1973. While there have been a number of teams using the Precision system and coached by Wei, the designation "The Precision Team" came to mean the team whose nucleus was Steven ALTMAN, Thomas SMITH, Joel STUART, and Peter WEICHSEL, and which won three of the four major ACBL knockout team championships held between August 1970 and March 1972.

With David STRASBERG as a fifth member in 1970, the Precision Team defeated the World Champion ACES to win the Spingold. With Eugene NEIGER replacing Strasberg as the fifth member in 1971, the team successfully defended its Spingold title, becoming only the fifth team to do so since the event began in 1934. Adding Alan SONTAG as a sixth member, the team won the Vanderbilt in 1972.

In January 1973 four members of the Precision Team entered the LONDON SUNDAY TIMES pair event. Altman-Sontag and Smith-Weichsel finished first and second, respectively, in the select 22-pair field, marking the first time a United States pair had ever finished higher than fourth.

After failing to defend its titles successfully in the 1972 Spingold and 1973 Vanderbilt, the team was disbanded in mid-1973. In the meantime many international stars adopted Precision, including members of the Italian BLUE TEAM, the South American champions from Brazil, and a group of British stars headed by Terence REESE.

PRE-DEALING. A method of (1) producing twinned boards for play in more than two sections (when TWINNING is usually done), or (2) recording before a match so that duplicates of the hand records can be furnished to spectators or to those who prepare slides or frames for exhibition. The necessity for keeping the hand records secret until it is time for them to be used, and for checking the hands sorted into the boards for accurate reproduction must be borne in mind.

Perhaps the first use of pre-dealing of hands so that spectators could know the holdings of all four players occurred in Johannesburg, South Africa, in Dec.

1962 for an exhibition match between South African players and a visiting championship team from England.

For many years in the National Championships of the ACBL, hands for the final sessions of major events were pre-dealt by trusted employees, frequently by George Goff (Cleveland), who made up hand-record cards of each of the hundreds of deals required. These hand-record cards were then used for sorting hands and placing cards in the boards by caddies under the supervision of the head caddy; the completed sets were then checked in the scoring room by the tournament staff.

More recently (1963) a program was devised so that a simulated shuffling, dealing, and recording of hand records could be rapidly and inexpensively done by electronic machines. With this method available, the use of the same hands in all sections of an event and in CONTINENTWIDE or world wide games became entirely practical and economical. See COMPUTERS and MACHINE-PREPARED HANDS.

PRE-EMPTIVE BID or SHUT-OUT BID. An opening bid of three or more with a hand containing a long suit and limited high-card strength. The bid is usually defensive in purpose. The pre-emptive bidder hopes that opponents with strong hands will find it difficult to bid accurately when the auction has started at a high level.

The following considerations may influence the pre-emptive bidder.

(1) *Length of suit.* An opening three-bid is usually a seven-card suit or a strong six-card suit. An opening four-bid is usually an eight-card suit or a strong seven-card suit. An opening five-bid in a minor is usually a nine-card suit or a strong eight-card suit.

(2) *Vulnerability.* The traditional rule was to take the playing trick strength of the hand and add three tricks when not vulnerable or two tricks when vulnerable. This is an oversimplification, and most experts make pre-emptive bids more freely than this "two and three" rule would permit.

In the most favorable circumstances, third-hand not vulnerable against vulnerable opponents, some experts would venture three spades with a hand as weak as:

♠ K J 10 8 6 4
♡ 4
◇ 3 2
♣ 7 6 5 3

When vulnerable against non-vulnerable, on the other hand, the pre-emptive bidder should be within two tricks of his bid in his own hand, and even then may lose 500 to save 420.

(3) *Position at the table.* The third player is best placed to pre-empt, because he knows that he cannot pre-empt his partner, and the fourth player is almost sure to have the best hand at the table. Pre-emptive bids by the dealer are also attractive. They run the risk of finding partner with a strong hand, and therefore setting him problems, but there are two oppo-

nents who may have strength, and the odds are that the hand "belongs" to them.

Pre-emptive bids by the second player are less attractive, and should be slightly stronger than pre-empts by the dealer. Pre-empts by the fourth player are very rare, and should indicate a solid or near-solid suit if bid at the three-level.

(4) *Strength of suit,* and outside strength. The pre-emptive bidder prefers to have his honor strength concentrated in the suit bid. This automatically increases his playing strength, decreases the danger of suffering a substantial penalty, and decreases the chance of successful defense against an opposing contract. A doubleton queen in a side-suit is unlikely to play a part in attack, but may be an important factor in defense.

Some players make it a practice not to pre-empt when holding a four-card major side-suit but this rule is at best doubtful.

(5) *Bidding methods*. Opening three-bids tend to be weaker, and rarer, when using WEAK TWO-BIDS, which are a form of pre-emptive bid. The weak two is used with many hands which other players would open with three. The opponents' defensive methods also have to be taken into account. Opening four-bids tend to be weaker when the partnership is using artificial pre-emptive bids, which tend to be well defined in strength and suit texture. See FOUR CLUB AND FOUR DIAMOND OPENING TRANSFERS; FOUR NO TRUMP OPENING PRE-EMPT; RUBIN TRANSFERS; THREE NO TRUMP OPENING. See also TRANSFER OPENING THREE-BIDS. More discretion must be exercised in opening three-bids against players who double for penalties than against players who double for take-out. See DEFENSE TO OPENING THREE-BID.

Responses. Responses to opening three-bids are often of a tactical character, intended to reinforce the pre-emptive effect of the opening bid. If the dealer opens three spades, for example, and the third player holds three-card spade support or better, he should rarely pass unless he has sufficient defensive honor strength to defend against four hearts. If the third player has a hand so weak that he fears an adverse slam, he may take more positive action by bidding five spades, or six spades, or venturing some psychic maneuver. This would have the character of an ADVANCE SAVE.

The following points relate to normal constructive responses to pre-emptive bids.

(1) *Raise to game in a major suit* (e.g., three spades—four spades). Responder must take into account the vulnerability and other factors which influenced the opening bid. If vulnerable, he needs three sound playing tricks in the form of trump honors, aces, kings, and more ruffing values. Queens and jacks in side-suits must be discounted. If not vulnerable, he needs at least four playing tricks—more if circumstances favored a light pre-empt. But this raise is often made on a much weaker hand for the tactical reasons mentioned above.

(2) *Three no trump*. A bid which the opener should almost invariably pass. In response to a minor suit, it shows stoppers in at least two of the unbid suits, and probably a fitting honor in the opener's suit. In response to a major suit, it shows a hand capable of

making nine tricks without using the opener's suit. Responder is likely to have a solid minor suit, and might be void in opener's suit.

(3) *Three of a higher-ranking suit* (three clubs —three hearts). Forcing to game, showing that the pre-empt has found responder with a strong hand. The responder's suit should be a good five-card suit or better, and the opener should raise with any slight excuse. The opener should bid three spades if he has a spade stopper for no trump purposes; a rebid of three no trump in this situation would show a *diamond* stopper.

(4) *Four of a lower-ranking suit* (e.g., three spades —four clubs; but *not* three spades—four hearts, which would be natural). A slam try, inviting the opener to cooperate. Spades are provisionally, but not definitively, agreed on as the trump suit. (The same applies to five of a lower-ranking suit after an opening four-bid.) These bids can be used as ASKING BIDS.

(5) *Five of opener's suit* (e.g., three spades—five spades, or four spades—five spades). A natural slam invitation, implying that responder is not worried about two losers in any side suit. The quality of his trumps may decide opener's course of actions.

PRE-EMPTIVE JUMP OVERCALL. See WEAK JUMP OVERCALL.

PRE-EMPTIVE OVERCALL. A defensive overcall, usually a double or triple jump in a suit, aimed at obstructing the bidding by the opener's side. After an opening bid of one diamond, a jump to three hearts, three spades, or four clubs would be pre-emptive. Standards would be slightly higher than for opening pre-emptive bids at the same level, because the chance of seriously inconveniencing the opponents is reduced. A vulnerable jump to three spades suggests a hand with 7–8 playing tricks.

A jump to the game level is ambiguous. The over-caller is likely to have a pre-emptive hand, but may make the same bid with a strong hand, prepared to abandon hopes of slam in view of the opposing opening. See also DOUBLE JUMP OVERCALL and WEAK JUMP OVERCALL.

PRE-EMPTIVE RE-RAISE. A three-level rebid by opener in his own suit which has been raised by responder, in order to make it more difficult for the opponents to bid rather than to try for game. Responder is expected to pass this rebid.

In order to try for game, partnerships using pre-emptive re-raises must bid no trump or bid a new suit either naturally or as a SHORT SUIT GAME TRY, a TWO-WAY GAME TRY, or a WEAK SUIT GAME TRY. See also TRIAL BID.

PRE-EMPTIVE RESPONSE. A new suit response to a suit opening at a higher level than would be required for a jump shift:

SOUTH	NORTH
1 ♡	3 ♠ or 4 ♣ or 4 ◊ or 4 ♠

North normally holds a seven-card suit or eight-card suit, but the exact playing strength varies with circumstances. He must take the vulnerability into account, and also the likelihood of the opponents entering the auction. The suit will normally be a broken one; with a solid or near-solid suit a simple response followed by a jump is more appropriate.

As these responses are rarely used, they can be given conventional meanings. See ASKING BID, SPLINTER BIDS, SWISS, and VOID-SHOWING BID.

For other pre-emptive responses, see INVERTED MINOR SUIT RAISES and WEAK JUMP RESPONSES.

PREFERENCE. When a player bids two suits, and his partner returns to the original suit at the lowest possible level, he is giving simple preference. This is in no way strength-showing, and will usually be passed. Preference at an unnecessarily high level is termed jump preference, and is considered under RESPONDER'S REBID.

Simple preference can occur in five common situations:

(1) *After three bids at the one-level* (e.g., one club –one heart–one spade). With a minimum responding hand (5–7 points) and three cards in clubs and spades, it is usually best to pass. If the opener has to play a 4–3 spade fit instead of a 5–3 club fit at a higher level, it is no great hardship. A preference to two clubs would be appropriate with 8–9 points if diamond weakness rules out one no trump, and responder wishes to give the opener another chance in case he has 17–18 points.

If responder gives preference with three clubs, as he usually would with two spades and three clubs, he need not be afraid of a 3–3 fit. The opener will return to diamonds if he has opened with a prepared club.

The most difficult situation arises when the responder has not more than a doubleton in each of the opener's suits. A preference to two clubs should never be given with a doubleton, so the choice lies between a pass, leaving the opener to play in a 4–2 fit with the prospect of a club ruff, or one no trump if the partnership method permits this to be weak.

(2) *When opener bypasses one no trump* (e.g., one heart–one spade–two diamonds). Automatic preference to two hearts is called for if the responder has equal red-suit length (3–3 or 2–2). There is a strong probability that the opener has a five-card heart suit (see OPENER'S REBID). Some authorities suggest a timid pass when the response is a minimum instead of giving preference, but this is born of fear that the opener may continue bidding without justification. With 8–10 points, two hearts and three diamonds, false preference to two hearts may be appropriate in case the opener has a maximum rebid.

(3) *After a two-over-one response* (e.g., one spade –two clubs–two hearts). Preference to two spades is likely to be based on a doubleton, because with three-card support a raise might have been made on the first round. False preference with two spades and three hearts is not unlikely, especially if the partnership treats the two heart bid as forcing.

(4) *After a one no trump response* (e.g., one spade –one no trump–two hearts). The responder gives automatic preference, expecting the opener to hold five spades and four or five hearts. In the rare event

that the opener has chosen this sequence with four spades and five hearts, the wrong contract is reached.

If the opener's two suits are a major and a minor, false preference with two of the original suit and three of the second suit may be appropriate, especially at match points. This applies particularly after the sequence one spade–one no trump–two clubs, when the opener is virtually certain to have five spades and four clubs.

(5) *After a one no trump rebid* (e.g., one heart–one spade–one no trump–two clubs). A delicate situation, because the responder may hold a hand with four spades and five or six clubs which was not strong enough for an original response at the two-level. The opener should usually refrain from giving preference, even if he holds three spades. (Alternatively, a partnership may agree that with only four spades, responder should pass one no trump, in which contract the minor suit may prove useful.)

PREMATURE LEAD OR PLAY. A lead or play made before the proper time, or before the player's turn to do so. This may occur before the auction has closed, or after. There is no penalty for a premature lead or play by a declarer. See LAWS (Law 23 for card led during the auction, or Laws 54, 57).

PREMATURE SAVE. See ADVANCE SAVE.

PREMIUM. A score made above the line. See BONUS.

PREMIUM SCORE. The score ABOVE THE LINE, consisting of extra tricks, making doubled contracts, rubber bonus, slam awards, honors, and premiums for defeating opposition contracts.

PREPARED CLUB. See SHORT CLUB.

PREPARED HANDS. See MACHINE-PREPARED HANDS; PAR CONTESTS; PRE-DEALT HANDS; TWINNING.

PREPAREDNESS, PRINCIPLE OF. The idea, originally called "anticipation," of looking forward to the next round of bidding when selecting a bid. It applies regularly to the opening bidder, but may also apply to the responder or to the opponents of the player who opened the bidding. Specific cases are considered under CHOICE OF SUIT.

PRESIDENTS. American Bridge League, American Contract Bridge League, and United States Bridge Association:

ABL		ACBL	
1927	Ralph R. Richards	1937	Gordon M. Gibbs
1928	Henry P. Jaeger	1938	Nate B. Spingold
1929	Robert W. Halpin	1939	James H. Lemon
1930	Clayton W. Aldrich	1940	Elmer J. Babin
1931	Capt. Fred G. French	1941	Robert J. Gill
1932	Waldemar von Zedtwitz	1942	Morgan Howard
1933	Sir Derrick J. Wernher	1943	Albert H. Morehead
1934	Ray H. Eisenlord	1944	Richmond H. Skinner
1935	Louis J. Haddad	1945	George A. Alderton, II
1936	H. Huber Boscowitz	1946	Benjamin M. Golder

1947	Raymond J. McGrover	1964	Leo Seewald
1948	Waldemar von Zedtwitz	1965	Robin MacNab
1949	Dr. Louis Mark	1966	Eilif Andersen
1950	R. L. Miles, Jr.	1967	John W. Norwood
1951	Julius L. Rosenblum	1968	Joseph J. Stedem
1952	Joseph Cohan	1969	Edgar G. Theus
1953	Benjamin O. Johnson	1970	William A. Baldwin
1954	Peter A. Leventritt	1971	Carl Rubin
1955	Jefferson Glick	1972	Percy X. Bean
1956	Rufus L. Miles, Jr.	1973	Jerome R. Silverman
1957	James L. Ripstra	1974	Mrs. L. W. McConnell
1958	Charles J. Solomon	1975	Lewis L. Mathe
1959	Winslow Randall	1976	Donald Oakie
1960	Frank T. Westcott		
1961	James P. Ferguson	**USBA**	
1962	Max Manchester	1932–34	Milton C. Work
1963	Jerry Lewis	1935–37	Ely Culbertson

PRESIDENT'S CUP. Awarded to Non-Masters Pairs; presented by Morgan Howard in 1942. Restricted to players below the rank of senior masters. Results are listed under Summer Nationals.

PRESSURE BID. An overbid made necessary by opposing action. Suppose this bidding:

WEST	NORTH	EAST	SOUTH
1 ♡	3 ♣	?	

North's three clubs is a weak jump overcall, and East holds three-card heart support and 8 points in high cards. Although he could not have bid three hearts in the ordinary way, even using LIMIT JUMP RAISES, he should bid three hearts at this point under the pressure of the opposing bid. A pass would leave West to consider the possibility that East has a worthless hand. Three hearts is therefore less of an overbid than a pass would be an underbid.

In such circumstances three hearts shows the upper range of a raise to two hearts without interference. The opener allows for the pressure, and passes unless he would have considered a game after a single raise.

As a corollary, the responder must overbid similarly with a slightly stronger hand. If he would have made a limit jump raise to three hearts in normal circumstances, he must jump to four hearts over the bid of three clubs.

PRIMARY HONORS. Top honors, i.e., aces and kings. The king of a suit may instead be considered a SECONDARY HONOR when it is unaccompanied by the ace and when it is in a suit in which partner is known to be short. Primary honors usually carry more weight in suit contracts than in no trump.

PRIMARY TRICKS. A term first used by P. Hal Sims to describe high cards which will win tricks no matter who eventually plays the hand.

PRISONERS OF WAR. See BRIDGE IN PRISON CAMPS.

PRISONS, PRISONERS. See BRIDGE IN PRISONS.

PRIVATE CONVENTION. A partnership understanding which is not made known to the opponents. The use of such a convention is a violation of the laws and the Proprieties: "It is improper to convey infor-

mation to partner by means of a call or play based on special partnership agreement, whether explicit or implicit, unless such information is fully and freely available to the opponents (see Law 40)." LAWS OF DUPLICATE (Proprieties IV). This requirement is not easy to fulfill in tournament play. Many partnerships have elaborate understandings about the precise natural meaning to be allocated to certain bids and sequences. It is difficult to draw a hard-and-fast line to separate "convention" from "style."

ACBL standards require that the opponents automatically be alerted to any conventional bid embodying an understanding that is not classified as a Class A CONVENTION. See ALERTING. Other explanations should not be volunteered until the end of the auction. See also EXPLANATION OF CONVENTIONAL CALL OR PLAY.

PRIVATE SCORE CARD. A form designed to be carried by a player in a duplicate tournament in which results of the boards played can be noted, for later discussion or comparison with the official scores. Usually the private score card is on the reverse side of the CONVENTION CARD, although special forms have been devised for IMP team competition.

PRIZES. It is a strict rule of the ACBL that no cash prizes may be awarded at Sectional or higher tournaments, but most tournaments do provide individual prizes for the winners (and sometimes for the runners-up) in each event. These usually take the form of engraved trophies, important for their symbolic rather than their monetary value.

Many established tournaments have permanent floating trophies for each event upon which each year's winner's name is engraved, and held by the winner until the following year. The ACBL headquarters has on display all of the trophies from the NORTH AMERICAN CHAMPIONSHIPS and charity events.

The ACBL has a prize plan by which players may pyramid their awards into more elaborate prizes. Information may be obtained from ACBL HEADQUARTERS.

PRO SYSTEM. A system employed by a number of West Coast pairs, that uses many relay sequences in order to allow the stronger hand to control the auction and inquire about his partner's strength and pattern.

The principal features of PRO (Pattern Relay Organized) are: intermediate (14–16 HCP) no trump opening; forcing one club opening promising either a club suit or a balanced hand with 17–20 points; nonforcing two-over-one responses and jump shifts; four-card major suit openings, with a one no trump response that is virtually game forcing; reverses based on distribution rather than on high-card strength. The principal slam gadget is the CLARAC SLAM TRY.

PROBABILITIES A POSTERIORI. See PERCENTAGE PLAY; PROBABILITY OF SUCCESSIVE EVENTS.

(1)

NORTH
A Q 10 7 3 2

SOUTH
9 8 5

When dummy's queen is finessed and loses to East's king, there are two events. The first is that East has the king-jack, or alternatively, that he has the singleton king. The second is that in both cases, he would play the king. The second is regarded as certain; resultant probabilities are 6.8% and 6.2%. Assumed is that West has the same choice in both cases, to play either the six or the four. On a second lead, with West following with the other of the small cards, percentage play (slightly) favors the play of the ace.

(2)

NORTH
A J 10 7 3 2

SOUTH
9 8 5

The finesse of the nine loses to East's king. The a priori probabilities of relevant distributions are:

6 4 opposite K Q	6.8%
Q 6 4 opposite K	6.2%

In the first case there is no certainty that East will win with the king: he can equally well play the queen. If he is a good player the chances are about equal that he will play either honor, as any other method will be likely to help declarer. While the probability of the first event (that East holds king-queen) is 6.8%, the probability that he will play the king is 50%. Applying the rule for successive events, the probability that East will hold the king-queen, and play the king is 6.8% × 50% or 3.4%. The odds in favor of taking a second finesse are therefore 30 to 17.

(3)

NORTH
A K Q J 4 3 2

SOUTH
void

Assume that on the ace and king, East plays the seven and eight, and West the five and six. The only possible distributions are:

WEST	EAST	A Priori Probability
5 6 9	7 8 10	1.78%
5 6 10	7 8 9	1.78%
5 6 9 10	7 8	1.61%
5 6	7 8 9 10	1.61%

All the outstanding cards are insignificant (see CARDS, NEUTRAL AND POSITIVE) in that they cannot take a trick. It can be assumed that defenders play insignificant cards at random, avoiding giving declarer information unnecessarily. There are three ways in which each defender can select two cards from both the first two cases. Thus the play of the four cards in question from these cases is 3.56% × ¹/₉ = .39%. There are only six ways in which the particu-

lar played cards could occur from the last two cases in the table, so the probability of the selected play is 3.56% × ¹/₆ = .54%. The a priori probability of a 4–2 against a 3–3 division is exactly the same as the ratio between these a posteriori probabilities, .54 to .39.

(4) But it is not always apparent to a player that his cards are insignificant.

NORTH
4 3 2

WEST		EAST
J 10 9		Q 8 7

SOUTH
A K 6 5

West will appreciate that his cards are of equal value, but East will not know that his are. When West plays the nine on South's ace, East is unlikely to play the queen. The probabilities of the possible distributions can be calculated only on an assessment of how defenders are likely to play from each. Before South attacks the suit (at an early stage, and after a neutral lead) the odds are about 49 to 36 on a 4–2 division as against a 3–3. Declarer's interpretation of the play of the first two rounds may cause him to change his original plan. See MATHEMATICAL ASSUMPTIONS.

A. T. and R. T.

PROBABILITIES A PRIORI. Basic probabilities of a given distribution of cards is expressed as a fraction where the numerator is the total number of favorable cases, and the denominator the total number of (equally likely) possible cases. MATHEMATICS OF BRIDGE explains how these can be computed. Thus before the cards are seen (a priori), the probability a particular player will hold a 4–3–3–3 hand pattern is $\frac{66,905,856,160}{635,013,559,600}$. See HAND PATTERNS and NUMBER OF POSSIBLE HANDS.

In bridge, probability is most commonly shown as a percentage (100 times the above fraction). Play based on a priori probabilities is therefore known as PERCENTAGE PLAY.

Probability of any distribution varies at different stages of the game. Before one has seen any cards, there is a probability (see TABLES, MATHEMATICAL, Table 1) of 10.58% that one will hold a 5–4–2–2 hand pattern. There is the same probability that a particular suit will be distributed 5–4–2–2 to the four players. After a player looks at his hand and sees a suit of five cards, the probability that this suit is distributed 5–4–2–2 among the four players is 21.21% (Table 3). Thus 5–4–2–2 is now less than twice as likely as 5–5–2–1 whereas it was more than three times as probable before any cards were seen. (A priori has become a posteriori). The difference is because it is now known that one player does have five of the suit, and concern is only with the distribution of the remaining eight cards.

Subsequently, if partner's hand is seen to contain a doubleton of the five-card suit, the probability of a 5–4–2–2 distribution of the suit rises to 48.45% (Table 4), and 5–4–2–2 is now more probable than 5–3–3–2 although the latter was more probable in the earlier stages. Concern is now with the distribution of the remaining cards of the suit in only the other two hands.

It is apparent that a priori probabilities take no account of INFERENCES in bidding or play. Use should be made of the former only where more accurate probabilities cannot be drawn from such inferences.

When the opening lead has been made, strict a priori probabilities no longer apply; but if the lead gives no material information, they are altered only very slightly or not at all. See CARDS, NEUTRAL AND POSITIVE.

A. T. and R. T.

PROBABILITIES OF DISTRIBUTION. See MATHE-MATICAL TABLES, Tables 1, 3, 4, and 4A.

PROBABILITY OF SUCCESSIVE EVENTS. The probability that two events will occur is the product of the probability of each, the latter event's probability being calculated on the assumption that the former has taken place. See DECEPTION and PROBA-BILITIES A POSTERIORI and, for an unscientific, but practical application, the last example under PER-CENTAGE PLAY.

PROBABLE TRICK. A playing trick that can be reasonably counted upon when attempting to forecast the play during the bidding. K x of a suit bid voluntarily on the right is an example.

PROBLEMS. Usually of three types, SINGLE DUMMY PROBLEMS, DOUBLE DUMMY PROBLEMS, and INFEREN-TIAL PROBLEMS, which are listed in separate articles.

PROFESSIONAL PLAYERS. Bridge profession-alism takes several forms. Many bridge experts teach bridge to pupils of all levels of expertise, and some give lessons by playing with a pupil in a tournament. Some experts are also retained to play tournaments in partnership or on teams with lesser players, although here the teaching element is frequently lacking. Often such retainers add bonuses for success.

In addition, bridge has had its share of wealthy patrons who have sponsored expert bridge teams. In 1968, Dallas financier Ira CORN organized the ACES, the world's first full-time professional bridge team. The SHARIF BRIDGE CIRCUS was a part-time profes-sional team. In the 1970s, shipping magnate C. C. WEI sponsored several teams to popularize his PRE-CISION SYSTEM. See PRECISION TEAM. Some commer-cial concerns have sponsored teams in order to pro-mote their products. One of the earliest of these was Bid-Rite Playing Card Co. See BID-RITE TEAM. One of the most recent commercial sponsors was the Lancia Division of Fiat. See LANCIA TOURNAMENTS.

There are also those who make their living, in whole or in part, by playing bridge for high stakes, usually rubber bridge in CLUBS, but occasionally in Calcuttas or tournaments in which substantial money prizes are at stake.

Despite the variety of ways to earn money playing bridge, until the mid-1970s there was no formalized distinction between "professional" and "amateur" players in the sense that these terms apply in golf and

tennis. In 1975, however, the ACBL adopted regu-lations requiring registration by players who are paid substantial sums to play in tournaments. At the same time the ACBL planned to restrict certain of its events to non-registered players. There is a technical distinction in this classification. Although bridge may be the full-time profession of writers, editors, and lecturers, they are not considered professional players.

PROGRESSION. (1) The movement of players in duplicate; (2) the movement of the boards in duplicate; (3) the movement of players in PROGRES-SIVE BRIDGE. See PROGRESSIVE BRIDGE, LAWS OF (Laws 5 and 6).

PROGRESSIVE BRIDGE, LAWS OF. (A form of competition at CONTRACT BRIDGE played in the home or among social groups.)

ARRANGEMENT OF TABLES

1. The game is played by two or more tables of four players each. The tables are numbered consecu-tively from Table No. 1 to the highest number.

COMMENT

It is customary to provide each table with two decks of cards having different backs. The tables should be numbered conspicuously for the conveni-ence of the players, and each one should be provided with one or more pencils and a score pad showing contract scoring.

TALLY CARDS

2. Prior to the beginning of play, the game direc-tor or committee prepares individual tally cards, one for each player. Each tally card bears a table number and designates a position (North, South, East, or West) at the table.

The tally cards may be drawn at random by the players or assigned by the game director, as he prefers. When play is called, each player takes the position assigned by his tally card.

COMMENT

At mixed parties it is customary to arrange the tallies and seat assignments so that a gentleman will always have a lady as a partner and vice versa. This is accomplished by having tallies of two different colors, one for the ladies and the other for the gentle-men.

A ROUND

3. A round consists of four deals, one by each player. When all tables have completed play, the game director gives a signal and the players move to their positions for the next round according to the type of progression used.

COMMENT

Each round should take about 20 minutes and the average session of play is from 6 to 7 rounds.

A DEAL PASSED OUT

4. Only four hands are dealt at each table, one by each player. If a deal is passed out (that is, if all four players pass at their first opportunity to declare), the deal passes to the left and both sides score zero for that deal.

METHOD OF PROGRESSION

5. At the conclusion of each round, the winning pair at Table No. 1 remains and the losing pair moves to the last table. At all tables except Table No. 1, the losers remain and the winners move up one table toward Table No. 1.

COMMENT

The above is the standard method of progression, but this may be waived or altered to suit the wishes of the game director or the players. Special tallies may be arranged or obtained, assigning positions for each round in such a way as to give each player as wide a variety of partners as possible. Another method is to have the ladies progress one way and the gentlemen the other way.

SELECTION OF PARTNERS

6. At mixed parties, it is customary but not essential for a gentleman to play with a lady partner and vice versa. If the standard method of progression is used, the visiting lady at each table becomes the partner of the gentleman who remains.

If the players are all of the same sex, the four players at each table draw cards to determine partners at the start of each round. The two new arrivals at each table draw first, and the one drawing higher has choice of seats and is the first dealer; the one drawing lower sits at the left of the first dealer. The two players who remain at the table from the preceding round then draw, the higher becoming the partner of the dealer. Thus all players change partners after each round.

COMMENT

Since the chief function of progressive bridge is social, it is preferable to change partners at each round. However, if for some reason a pair contest is desired, the same partnerships may be retained throughout by simply progressing as described in Law No. 5 without changing partners at the next table. Another method is to have the original N-S pairs remain in the same positions throughout the game, and to have the E-W pairs progress one table at a time until they reach Table No. 1, and then go to the last table. In this case, the progression is followed automatically, regardless of which pair wins at each table.

DRAW FOR DEAL

7. Unless the dealer is already determined under Law No. 6, the four players at a table draw for first deal. The player who draws highest is the first dealer and may select either deck.

PROGRESSIVE BRIDGE SCORING

COMMENT

With the exceptions specifically mentioned below, the scoring for Progressive Bridge is exactly the same as for Duplicate Bridge and will be found explained in detail in Chapter VIII of the Duplicate Code. The most important points to remember about the scoring are:

Each deal is scored and recorded separately, and no trick points are carried over from one deal to the next.

Game is 100 points for tricks bid and made in one deal. The game premium is 300 points, if not vulnerable, and 500 points, if vulnerable, and it is allowed only when game is bid and made in one deal.

A premium of 50 points is scored for making any contract less than game. This premium is in addition to the value of the tricks made. Premiums for a small and grand slam are allowed only if bid for.

SCORING LIMITS

8. A side may not score more than 1,000 points in a single deal, except in the case of a slam contract fulfilled.

COMMENT

It is not correct to prohibit doubles or redoubles. The limitation of penalties avoids the necessity of this restriction.

VULNERABILITY

9. The first deal of each round shall be played and scored as if neither side were vulnerable.

The second and third deals of each round shall be played and scored as if the dealer's side were vulnerable and the other side not vulnerable.

The fourth deal of each round shall be played and scored as if both sides were vulnerable.

COMMENT

This is the most desirable method of determining vulnerability in Progressive Bridge, but if preferred all deals may be played as though both sides were vulnerable. In any event, the method should be announced before play starts.

THE SCORE

10. One of the four players at each table is appointed to record the score. He enters the result of each deal on the score pad separately and, at the end of the round, totals all the points made by each side.

He enters on the individual tally of each player the points made by that player's side and also the points made by the opponents.

COMMENT

Correctly designed tallies provide spaces to record both "My Score" and "Opponents' Score." It is important that both be entered on the tally, for otherwise the record would be meaningless.

COMPUTATION OF TOTAL SCORES

11. At the conclusion of the game, each player totals his score. He also totals the scores of his opponents, as recorded on his tally, and subtracts his opponents' total from his own. The difference, plus or minus as the case may be, is recorded in the space provided at the bottom of his tally.

COMMENT

Let us suppose that a player scores 2,460 points, and the opponents score 1,520 points against him. This makes his net score +940 for the entire session. On the other hand, if a player scores only 1,650 points, and the opponents score 1,940 points against him, then his net score for the session is −290 points. Do not make the mistake of recording only plus scores, for that method gives false results, and is likely to induce improper doubling and redoubling.

DETERMINATION OF THE WINNER

12. The player with the largest plus score is the winner. Other players with plus scores rank in descending order followed by the players with minus scores, the one with the largest minus being last.

COMMENT

The method of awarding prizes is left to the discretion of the game director. At mixed parties it is usual to award one or more prizes to the ladies and gentlemen, respectively, who have the best scores.

PROGRESSIVE SQUEEZE (or Repeated Squeeze or Repeating Triple Squeeze). A sequence of two squeezes which results in a gain of two tricks. In rare instances three tricks may be gained (see (9)). It is initiated by a triple squeeze which is followed by a simple squeeze, both against the same player. As in an ordinary triple squeeze, all but *two* of the remaining tricks must be in hand before pressure can be exerted. There are several types, of which (1) and (2) are most common.

(1) The requirements for a Type 1 progressive squeeze are:

(a) A one-card threat placed to the left of the opponent threatened.

(b) Two two-card menaces, one in each hand, for example:

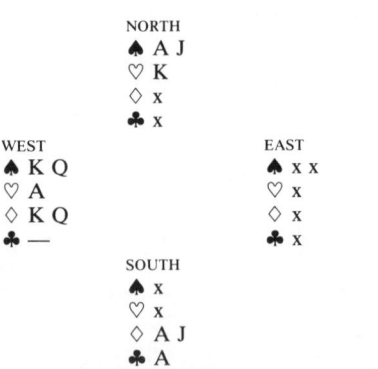

South leads the ace of clubs, and West is squeezed in three suits. If West discards a spade, South cashes two tricks in that suit which leads to an automatic squeeze against West in hearts and diamonds for the gain of a further trick. If West discards a diamond, South takes two diamonds, which results in a positional squeeze in the majors. Finally, if West discards a heart, South crosses to the ace of spades in order to play the king of hearts, which results in an automatic squeeze against West in spades and diamonds.

(2) The requirements for a Type 2 progressive squeeze are:

(a) A one-card threat placed to the right of the opponent threatened.

(b) The hand with the one-card threat has an entry in each of the other threat suits.

(c) The hand opposite the one-card threat contains the squeeze card, the remaining threat cards and entries in two of the three threat suits.

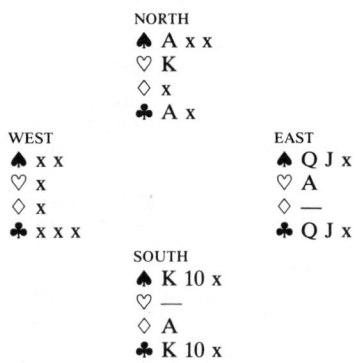

South leads the ace of diamonds, and East is squeezed in three suits. Any discard costs a trick, and leads to a simple squeeze for the loss of another trick by East.

(3) A third form of progressive squeeze may arise, with these requirements:

(a) An extended two-card menace (also called a double threat).

(b) Two one-card menaces opposite the extended threat.

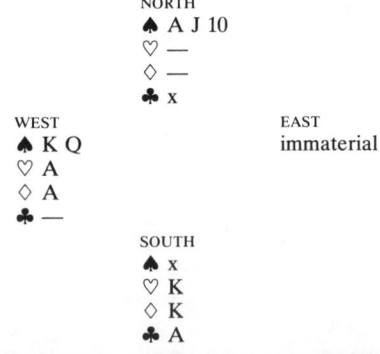

South leads the ace of clubs, and West is squeezed in three suits. If West discards a spade, it is at the cost of two tricks; if West discards a heart or a diamond, South continues with the king of that suit, effecting an automatic squeeze against West.

This squeeze is equally effective if the East and West cards are interchanged, so it is an automatic squeeze.

(4) (Described by Chien-Hwa Wang)

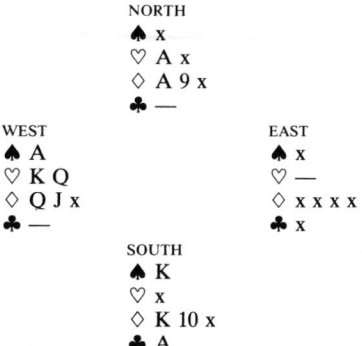

```
                NORTH
                ♠ x
                ♡ A x
                ◊ A 9 x
                ♣ —
  WEST                      EAST
  ♠ A                       ♠ x
  ♡ K Q                     ♡ —
  ◊ Q J x                   ◊ x x x x
  ♣ —                       ♣ x
                SOUTH
                ♠ K
                ♡ x
                ◊ K 10 x
                ♣ A
```

South leads the ace of clubs, and West is squeezed in three suits. If West discards a spade, then South leads the king of that suit, squeezing West in hearts and diamonds; a heart discard permits North to win his hearts, thereby squeezing West in spades and diamonds; if West discards a diamond, South cashes three diamonds, ending in his hand. The last of these squeezes West in the majors.

This is an automatic squeeze, since North's spade is an idle card. The requirements for this squeeze are as follows:

(a) A one-card menace placed to the right of the opponent threatened.

(b) A two-card menace in the hand opposite the one-card threat.

(c) A twin entry menace, with a menace card accompanying each winner.

The squeeze card lies in the same hand as the one-card menace.

(5)

```
                NORTH
                ♠ K 2
                ♡ K
                ◊ K
                ♣ x
  WEST                      EAST
  ♠ 7 x x                   ♠ Q J x
  ♡ x                       ♡ A
  ◊ x                       ◊ A
  ♣ —                       ♣ —
                SOUTH
                ♠ A 8 x x
                ♡ —
                ◊ —
                ♣ A
```

The lead of the ace of clubs squeezes East in three suits, and South eventually wins all the remaining tricks. (Variation of [2])

(6)

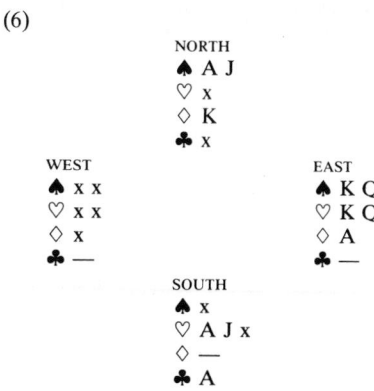

```
                NORTH
                ♠ A J
                ♡ x
                ◊ K
                ♣ x
  WEST                      EAST
  ♠ x x                     ♠ K Q
  ♡ x x                     ♡ K Q
  ◊ x                       ◊ A
  ♣ —                       ♣ —
                SOUTH
                ♠ x
                ♡ A J x
                ◊ —
                ♣ A
```

South leads the ace of clubs, and East is squeezed in three suits. The squeeze gains two tricks for South. (Variation of [2])

(7)

```
                NORTH
                ♠ J x x
                ♡ A
                ◊ A J
                ♣ —
  WEST                      EAST
  ♠ K Q                     ♠ x x
  ♡ K Q                     ♡ x x
  ◊ K Q                     ◊ x x
  ♣ —                       ♣ —
                SOUTH
                ♠ A
                ♡ J x
                ◊ x x
                ♣ A
```

South leads the ace of clubs, and West is squeezed in three suits. A spade discard gives North two spade tricks; a heart discard enables South to take the heart ace, spade ace, and jack of hearts, squeezing West in spades and diamonds; a diamond discard leads to a crisscross squeeze.

(8)

```
                NORTH
                ♠ K 8 x
                ♡ A J
                ◊ —
                ♣ x
  WEST                      EAST
  ♠ x x                     ♠ Q J 10
  ♡ x x                     ♡ K Q
  ◊ x                       ◊ A
  ♣ x                       ♣ —
                SOUTH
                ♠ A 9 x
                ♡ x
                ◊ K
                ♣ A
```

South leads the ace of clubs, and East is squeezed in three suits. If East discards a diamond, South takes two top spades ending in his hand, and plays the king of diamonds, squeezing East in the majors; a heart discard permits North to win two hearts which squeezes East in spades and diamonds; a spade discard enables South to win three spades ending in his hand, which squeezes East in the red suits.

(9) (Described by Clyde LOVE)

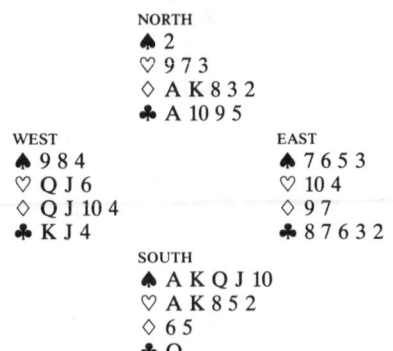

```
                  NORTH
                  ♠ 2
                  ♡ 9 7 3
                  ◊ A K 8 3 2
                  ♣ A 10 9 5
WEST                                  EAST
♠ 9 8 4                               ♠ 7 6 5 3
♡ Q J 6                               ♡ 10 4
◊ Q J 10 4                            ◊ 9 7
♣ K J 4                               ♣ 8 7 6 3 2
                  SOUTH
                  ♠ A K Q J 10
                  ♡ A K 8 5 2
                  ◊ 6 5
                  ♣ Q
```

South plays in seven spades doubled by West. West makes his normal lead of the queen of diamonds. South starts life with only ten top tricks, but after he has won the diamond lead and cashed three spades this is the position:

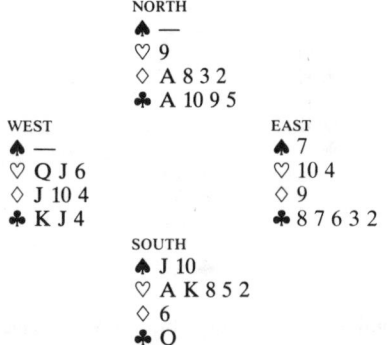

```
                  NORTH
                  ♠ —
                  ♡ 9
                  ◊ A 8 3 2
                  ♣ A 10 9 5
WEST                                  EAST
♠ —                                   ♠ 7
♡ Q J 6                               ♡ 10 4
◊ J 10 4                              ◊ 9
♣ K J 4                               ♣ 8 7 6 3 2
                  SOUTH
                  ♠ J 10
                  ♡ A K 8 5 2
                  ◊ 6
                  ♣ Q
```

When the fourth spade is led West cannot throw a heart or he will set up three tricks immediately. If West discards a diamond, a low club is discarded from dummy. Declarer then leads a diamond to the ace and ruffs a diamond to establish two tricks, and the cashing of these two new winners squeezes West in clubs and hearts to promote a third trick. The result would be the same if West had discarded a club rather than a diamond.

See also CLASH SQUEEZE; GUARD SQUEEZE; TRIPLE SQUEEZE.

M. I.

PROMOTION OF TRUMP HONORS. Revaluation after a trump fit has been found, with trump honors advanced in point value. Players of ability assign a higher value to an honor in a suit bid by partner than to a similar honor in a side suit. For instance, if partner bids hearts and the heart queen is held, it is almost surely of value, whereas the value of a queen in an unexplored side suit is problematical. Therefore an added value should be assigned when holding an honor in partner's suit.

Partner opens with one spade. Holding:

```
♠ K 7 6 5
♡ A 4 3
◊ 8 7 4 2
♣ 5 3
```

one raises to two spades. If partner bids again, one can happily bid four spades. However, holding:

```
♠ 8 7 6 4
♡ A 4 3
◊ K 7 5 4
♣ 5 3
```

again one would raise to two spades. If partner bids three clubs or three spades, a correction to three spades or a pass of that bid would be acceptable. See also GOOD CARDS.

For promotion in the play, see TRUMP PROMOTION.

PROPRIETIES. Three different kinds of improper conduct can be perceived: breaches of eithics, breaches of good manners, and cheating. Premeditated cheating is unforgivable; it is not dealt with by the Laws at all, for such a highly civilized game as bridge depends upon the assumption that players will not cheat.

Breaches of ETHICS and breaches of ETIQUETTE, however, are dealt with by the Laws. The proper code of behavior is set out in the Laws under the title, Proprieties. In the tournament world breaches of the Proprieties are punishable by the award of an adjusted score and by disciplinary penalties. In rubber bridge there is no way of adjusting the score except by agreement of the players or as provided in Law 16 (see LAWS).

PROTECT. (1) To guard with a small card, as an honor; (2) to make a bid in order that partner may have another opportunity to bid, thus "protecting" him if he has greater strength than his first call has implied (this usage is obsolescent); (3) in England, to balance; see BALANCING.

PROTECTED SUIT. See GUARD.

PROTECTION. An English term for BALANCING.

PROTEST PERIOD. The time in which corrections to the score can be filed, whether the error is made by the scorer or by a player at the table. The former are corrected when reported; the latter require the approval of a member of the opposing pair. When time permits, the protest period is usually about twenty-four hours, and its expiration is clearly indicated on the RECAPITULATION SHEET. When no time is specified, at least thirty minutes after the posting should be allowed.

PROTESTS. See APPEAL; COMMITTEE.

PROVEN FINESSE. A finesse whose success is guaranteed. For example:

NORTH
A Q J 7

SOUTH
10 9 5 3

The ten is led and wins, while right-hand opponent discards. Subsequent finesses in the suit are "proven" or "established."

PSEUDO ELIMINATION PLAY. See THROW-IN PLAYS.

PSEUDO SQUEEZE. A pseudo squeeze is a play intended to induce a wrong discard by a defender who mistakenly believes that he has been squeezed.

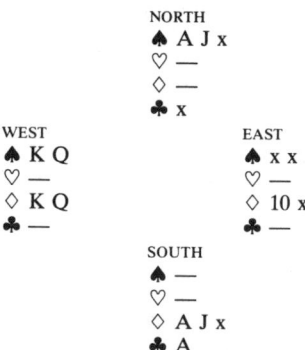

NORTH
♠ A J x
♡ —
♢ —
♣ x

WEST
♠ K Q
♡ —
♢ K Q
♣ —

EAST
♠ x x
♡ —
♢ 10 x
♣ —

SOUTH
♠ —
♡ —
♢ A J x
♣ A

Suppose that West is not aware that South has no spades. South leads the ace of clubs, and West may discard a diamond hoping that East can protect that suit.

M. I.

PSYCHIC BID. Any bid made primarily with the purpose of interfering with the opponent's bidding or play rather than with the idea of aiding the bidding and play of one's own side. See LAWS OF DUPLICATE BRIDGE (Law 40).

PSYCHIC BIDDING. A term coined in 1931 by Dorothy Rice SIMS, generally meaning bluffing calls to create the false illusion of strength or length in a particular suit, or to conceal a weakness. From about 1931–34 a wave of blind enthusiasm for psychic bidding swept the country's bridge tables, making it appear that a malignancy was threatening to deform the game that was still in its infancy. Most of these early psychics were hit-or-miss affairs, the bidder never knowing until it was all over whether his ploy had been brilliant or catastrophic

During this period Ely Culbertson, a keen strategist and psychologist who was not above making an occasional psychic himself,* was categorically opposed to psychic bidding for the masses. His reasoning was simply that the techniques of the CUL-

BERTSON SYSTEM were designed to create partnership harmony and confidence; any psychic bidding, unquestionably a unilateral and individualistic action, tended to destroy the precision his system was trying to create. He stated as follows:

"A psychic bid calculated to assure the opponents that the sure tricks and solid suits staring them in the face are not tricks at all—are simply mirages—has not a very good chance of succeeding. Even the weakest players trust their own eyesight. . . .

"The only rational reason for psychic bids of all descriptions is to lead the opponents to think that their kings and queens are apt to be trapped by superior honors, or that their suits will not break."†

Fortunately the early passion for psychics quickly subsided. Some two decades later, around 1952, psychic openings re-emerged in a more disciplined form as parts of the ROTH-STONE, STAYMAN, KAPLAN-SHEINWOLD, and BULLDOG systems. In the opinions of many experts, however, although the psychic opening had a tendency to force the opponents out of their familiar bidding patterns and into strange and uncomfortable situations, it was never terribly effective against sophisticated opponents, who would act positively when they had good cards in spite of the psychic. By 1964, the Roth-Stone system had eliminated the opening psychic because the complications it created outweighed the benefits it produced.

By and large the most effective psychic bids have been those that misdescribe the bidder's length in a particular suit. Sometimes these psychics promise extreme shortness in the suit (see (2) below); sometimes they promise considerable length in the suit, and when they find gaps in the opponents' defensive bidding conventions (see (1), (3), and (4) below), the results can be extremely profitable. The least successful type of psychic bid tends to be one which attempts a bluff as to wholesale strength (see (1), (5), and (6) below).

(1) The following deal was played in a team-of-four match in 1933. In the North seat was the late Edward Hymes, Jr.

NORTH
♠ J 10
♡ Q J 8
♢ K J 10 9 6 2
♣ 7 5

WEST
♠ A Q 9 5 4
♡ K 9
♢ 8 7 3
♣ Q 8 4

EAST
♠ K 6 3
♡ A 10 5 4 2
♢ 4
♣ A K 10 6

SOUTH
♠ 8 7 2
♡ 7 6 3
♢ A Q 5
♣ J 9 3 2

Neither side vulnerable. South dealer.

---

* In the CULBERTSON-LENZ MATCH of 1931–32, Mr. Culbertson bid *one* spade on ♠ 9 7 6 3 2, ♡ 7 6 4, ♢ Q 6, ♣ 8 6 3.

† *The New Gold Book of Bidding and Play,* by Ely Culbertson. The John Winston Company, Philadelphia, 1949.

SOUTH	WEST	NORTH	EAST
Pass	Pass	1 ♠	Dbl.
Pass	Pass	2 ♠	Dbl.
Pass	Pass	3 ♢	3 ♡
Pass	Pass	Pass	

As can be observed, East-West can make a game in hearts, or a slam in spades. Of course West is more to blame, but that is not the issue. The opponents were either duped by Mr. Hymes's bids, or they couldn't cope with the perplexing situation which was created.

When the board was replayed, North also made a psychic opening bid, but it didn't bother the East-West players:

SOUTH	WEST	NORTH	EAST
Pass	Pass	1 ♢	Dbl.
Pass	2 ♠	Pass	3 ♡
Pass	3 ♠	Pass	4 ♣
Pass	4 ♡	Pass	6 ♠
Pass	Pass	Pass	

(2) This is an example of a LEAD-INHIBITING psychic. The South player in this deal, which arose in 1934, was Richard Frey.

Both sides vulnerable. South dealer.

NORTH
♠ 9 6
♡ K Q 10 6 2
♢ 8 4
♣ K Q 3 2

WEST
♠ J 7 5
♡ 5 3
♢ A Q 9 5 2
♣ J 9 8

EAST
♠ 10 4 2
♡ 9 8
♢ K J 10 6
♣ 7 6 5 4

SOUTH
♠ A K Q 8 3
♡ A J 7 4
♢ 7 3
♣ A 10

SOUTH	WEST	NORTH	EAST
1 ♠	Pass	2 ♡	Pass
3 ♢	Pass	3 ♡	Pass
5 ♡	Pass	6 ♡	Pass
Pass	Pass		

East opened a club, and thirteen tricks were made. Of course, had West doubled three diamonds the story would have had a different ending.

(3) A psychic that has long been almost so standard a part of the repertoire that it is thought hardly worth using any more is the one spade butt-in over an opponent's take-out double of partner's one heart opening. Yet it was used to good effect in the finals of

the 1966 World Championships between Italy and North America.

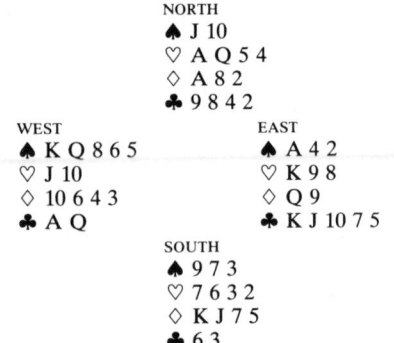

NORTH
♠ J 10
♡ A Q 5 4
♢ A 8 2
♣ 9 8 4 2

WEST
♠ K Q 8 6 5
♡ J 10
♢ 10 6 4 3
♣ A Q

EAST
♠ A 4 2
♡ K 9 8
♢ Q 9
♣ K J 10 7 5

SOUTH
♠ 9 7 3
♡ 7 6 3 2
♢ K J 7 5
♣ 6 3

Neither side vulnerable. North dealer.

NORTH	EAST	SOUTH	WEST
Mathe	*Belladonna*	*Hamman*	*Avarelli*
1 ♡	Dbl.	1 ♠	1 NT
Pass	2 ♣	Pass	2 ♢
Pass	2 NT	Pass	Pass
Pass			

Hamman's psychic spade response found a flaw in the Roman system: A double by Avarelli would have shown spade shortness rather than length. Still, the Italians could have recovered by bidding game in no trump. It was just as well that they did not, however, since after Mathe's opening spade jack was won by dummy's ace, Avarelli led a spade and covered Hamman's 7 with the 8, playing Hamman for a real suit, and lost a trick to Mathe's 10. Mathe wasted no time in shifting to a diamond to collect five tricks in all. In the replay West made eleven tricks in four spades.

(4) One of the most spectacularly successful psychics of recent years was an opening pre-emptive psychic by Martin COHN of Atlanta against Peter Leventritt and Howard Schenken in the 1970 Spring National Tournament. Holding a weak hand and a shortage of hearts, Cohn opened the bidding with three hearts and caught LHO Leventritt with a seven-card heart suit headed by the ace, king, and queen. Leventritt could not double for penalties since the partnership was using take-out doubles. He finally passed, but, understandably, found it difficult to do so in tempo, and three hearts, undoubled, became the final contract. Cohn, whose safety valve if doubled was a long club suit, was happy to concede the modest penalty, rather than the large score to which his opponents were entitled. He undoubtedly would not have attempted such a psychic had his opponents been using the FISHBEIN convention.

(5) This deal was a *cause célèbre* for many years after it arose in the National Team Championships of 1951.

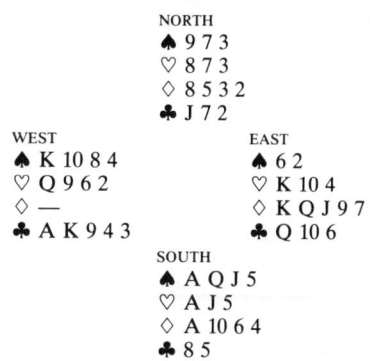

```
              NORTH
              ♠ 9 7 3
              ♡ 8 7 3
              ◊ 8 5 3 2
              ♣ J 7 2
WEST                        EAST
♠ K 10 8 4                  ♠ 6 2
♡ Q 9 6 2                   ♡ K 10 4
◊ —                         ◊ K Q J 9 7
♣ A K 9 4 3                 ♣ Q 10 6
              SOUTH
              ♠ A Q J 5
              ♡ A J 5
              ◊ A 10 6 4
              ♣ 8 5
```

North-South vulnerable. North dealer.

NORTH	EAST	SOUTH	WEST
1 ◊ (!)	Pass	1 ♠	Pass
Pass	Dbl.	2 ◊	2 ♠
Pass	Pass	3 ◊ (!)	Pass
Pass	Dbl.	Pass	Pass
Pass			

Of course South knew that North was psyching when he failed to provide his guaranteed rebid over one spade, but South felt that North had a diamond suit of some respectability, and he didn't want to sell out. It cost North-South 1,100 points.

(6) This final deal, which arose in the Masters Team-of-Four Championships of 1953, also became a *cause célèbre,* and probably more words were written about it than any other deal of that decade.

```
              NORTH
              ♠ A Q 9 8 6 5
              ♡ K 5
              ◊ 5 4
              ♣ K 7 3
WEST                        EAST
♠ 10 7 2                    ♠ 4 3
♡ —                         ♡ A J 9 7 6 4 2
◊ J 10 9 8 6 3              ◊ Q
♣ J 8 5 4                   ♣ 9 6 2
              SOUTH
              ♠ K J
              ♡ Q 10 8 3
              ◊ A K 7 2
              ♣ A Q 10
```

North-South vulnerable. West dealer.

WEST	NORTH	EAST	SOUTH
1 NT (!!)	2 ♠	4 ♡	Dbl.
Pass	Pass	Pass	

This went down six tricks, for a loss of 1,100 points. Probably very little would have been said about the deal if North-South had arrived at six no trump when the board was replayed, for that contract would have been fulfilled, for a score of 1,440 points, and the psy-

chic would have "paid off." But unfortunately, at the other table North-South arrived at a six spade contract, which was defeated with the heart opening and heart continuation, which was ruffed.

PSYCHIC CONTROLS. Devices intended to avert a partnership disaster following a psychic bid.

Controls are usually related to the "disciplined psychic" used in KAPLAN-SHEINWOLD and the original ROTH-STONE. In such cases the opener has 3–6 points, mainly in the suit which he has bid.

Responses of two no trump and three no trump can be used to show powerful balanced hands. Two no trump shows a hand with 21–22 points, and therefore interested in game even if the opener is psychic. Three no trump shows a stronger hand that is sure of game even opposite a psychic.

The jump shift remains forcing, and the opener must take care with his rebid. If he has made a psychic opening, he must rebid his suit or rebid in no trump, whichever is the more economical. Conversely, he must avoid these rebids holding a geniune opening. See also SKINNER PSYCHIC CONTROL.

Psychic controls are disallowed in some countries, notably in England, on the theory that the psychic bidder must be prepared to take his chances along with the opponents.

Open to much greater ethical doubt are psychic controls of other actions, such as responses. These are not sanctioned by any leading authority.

PSYCHIC LEAD. See OPENING LEAD.

PSYCHIC PLAY. See DECEPTIVE PLAY.

PSYCHOLOGY. See DECEPTIVE PLAY; FALSE-CARDING; PARTNERSHIP PSYCHOLOGY.

PULLING TRUMP. See DRAWING TRUMPS.

PUMP. A colloquialism for FORCE (2). FORCING DECLARER TO RUFF is frequently referred to as pumping the declarer.

PUNCH. Verb: to cause a player (usually dummy or declarer) to use a trump for ruffing; to shorten; noun: the act of shortening in trumps. See FORCING LEADS.

PUSH. (1) A raise of partner's suit, usually at the part-score level, aimed at pushing the opponents to a level at which they may be defeated. For example:

WEST	NORTH	EAST	SOUTH
1 ♠	2 ♡	2 ♠	

Neither side is vulnerable and South holds:

```
              ♠ 6 5 3
              ♡ K 9
              ◊ A 8 4 2
              ♣ Q 7 3 2
```

It seems likely to South that both sides will make about eight tricks, so he bids three hearts. North is marked with, at worst, a good five-card suit. If East-West continue to three spades, in which they will have more heart losers than they expect, they may be defeated, and South will have turned a minus score into a plus. The chance of being doubled in three hearts is slight, and North will be wary of continuing to game.

(2) A board in a team match, in which the result is the same in both rooms (also STAND-OFF).

(3) A rubber in which the net score is zero after ROUNDING OFF.

PUZZLES. In bridge, puzzles are referred to as PROBLEMS, and are usually of three types, DOUBLE DUMMY PROBLEMS, SINGLE DUMMY PROBLEMS, and INFERENTIAL PROBLEMS. Examples of each type appear in this book. Crossword puzzles and acrostics using bridge definitions or texts have been published as bridge magazine features.

Q

QUACK. A term to indicate either the queen or the jack in situations where it is of no consequence which of the two cards is held or played. See RESTRICTED CHOICE.

QUALIFYING. Finishing high enough in a QUALIFYING SESSION to continue competing in the final session(s) of the event. See CONDITIONS OF CONTEST.

QUALIFYING SESSION. In an event of two or more sessions, one or more of them may be designated as qualifying sessions, to select contestants eligible for continued play in the remaining sessions.

QUALITY. See STRENGTH. Ely CULBERTSON stressed "quality" and "quantity" in discussing hand valuation. More modern usage concerns control cards, suit strength or the presence of intermediate cards, etc. See also WORKING CARDS.

QUANTITATIVE. A bid is quantitative if it is natural, limited, and non-forcing. Quantitative is usually used to refer to a four no trump bid. For situations in which a four no trump bid is quantitative, see BLACKWOOD.

QUANTITATIVE FOUR NO TRUMP. A term covering a number of situations where four no trump is a natural bid. See BLACKWOOD.

QUANTITY. See LENGTH.

QUEEN. The third highest card in a suit, and the card most usually finessed for. The expression "dropping the queen" is frequently heard, and refers to situations where a declarer prefers to attempt to capture a queen by playing out higher honors.

QUEEN OF BRIDGE. See KING OR QUEEN OF BRIDGE.

QUEEN OVER JACK. The theory, or speculation, that the queen lies over the jack slightly more often than not. Credited to Clagett BOWIE, Baltimore, Md.

The assumption is based on the possibility that the queen may have captured the jack in the previous deal with the same deck, and that the cards may not have been separated in the shuffle. However, the manner in which the trick is gathered is an important, and uncertain, influence. The theory has meaning only at rubber bridge, if it has any value at all. See TWO-WAY FINESSE.

QUEEN FROM KING-QUEEN. See RUSINOW LEAD.

QUEEN LEAD. Traditionally, the lead of the queen from a long suit promises the jack and usually the ten or nine as well. See OPENING LEADS. In alternative methods the lead of the queen promises the king (see RUSINOW LEADS), or the ace and king. The JOURNALIST system of leads against no trump promises either the traditional holding headed by Q J 10, or a holding of K Q 10 9, and asks the partner of the opening leader to play the jack if he has it, enabling the opening leader to continue without fear of a BATH COUP by declarer.

QUESTIONS. For when to ask questions, see ALERTING; EXPLANATION OF CONVENTIONAL CALL OR PLAY; FACE DOWN LEADS.

QUICK TRICK. A high card holding that in usual circumstances will win a trick by virtue of the rank of the cards in either offensive or defensive play. Of course, in some distributional holdings, or FREAK HANDS, such defensive values evaporate. The accepted table of quick tricks is:

2 quick tricks	A K of same suit
1½	A Q of same suit
1	A or K Q of same suit
½	K x

QUITTED TRICK. A trick is quitted, in rubber bridge, when the four cards played to it have been gathered together and turned face down in a packet in front of the side which contributed the winning card. Any player has the right to inspect a quitted trick until either he or his partner has led or played to a subsequent trick.

In duplicate, a trick is quitted when all four players have played to it, and turned their cards face down. A quitted trick may not be inspected except at the director's specific instruction. If a player wishes to inspect the cards just played to a trick he may do so, assuming neither he nor his partner has led or played to the next trick, only if he has left his own card face up on the table. See LAWS OF DUPLICATE (Law 66).

QUOTIENT. A device used to determine the winner in team competition if a ROUND ROBIN ends in a tie, either in won and lost matches, or in VICTORY POINTS won and lost.

The number of IMPs won by a team is divided by

the number lost to determine the quotient. Italy has won two European Championships by quotient, over France in 1956 and over Great Britain in 1958. In the latter case Italy won 892 IMPs and lost 570, giving a quotient of 1.565. Great Britain won 769 IMPs and lost 550, giving them the inferior quotient of 1.4.

R

RHO. Right-hand opponent, or the player on declarer's right.

RONF. An abbreviation for "raise only non-force," used by pairs playing WEAK TWO-BIDS, to indicate that a response of two no trump or in a new suit is forcing for one round on the weak two-bidder.

RABBI'S RULE. "When the king is singleton, play the ace." A whimsical rule attributed to Milton Shattner, a New York attorney nicknamed "the Rabbi" because of his authoritative pronouncement of this and other convictions governing his play.

RACK. (1) A device used by handicapped players for holding a hand of cards. (2) A device to hold traveling score slips for inspection by the players after the game has been scored (see CLOTHESLINE). (3) Colloq., (verb) to ruin opponents by holding exceptionally good cards; (noun) a player who holds such cards; also called a "card-rack."

RAGS. A holding of only a few high cards, likely to be insignificant in the bidding or play of a hand.

RAINBOW INDIVIDUAL MOVEMENT. A movement for tournaments between players competing as individuals, in which contestants are divided into groups corresponding to their original starting directions, with separate instructions for progressing to each group. The guide cards are often printed in different colors to make the groups more easily distinguished, and hence the name for the movement. This movement was devised by Oswald Jacoby and Shepard Barclay.

In a typical set of guide cards (ACBL fifty-two-player Individual) the North players receive blue cards, and sit at the same table throughout. The East players receive yellow guide cards, moving two tables toward the higher number. South players receive white guide cards, and move to the next higher numbered table. West players receive pink guide cards, and skip a table toward lower numbers, while the boards go to the next lower numbered table. For identification purposes, players take a number: North, the table number; West, the table number plus 13; South, the table number plus 26; and East, the table number plus 39.

The movement in its simple form (as above) will work only when the number of tables is a prime number: 5, 7, 11, 13, 17, 19, or even 23. Paul MARKS, of Chicago, has devised a variation of this movement for prime number plus one tables (see EIGHT TABLES, TWELVE TABLES, FOURTEEN TABLES), which is based on the Rainbow.

With any prime number of tables, the movement can be carried out in any manner as long as it is remembered that there are five different movements for the four groups of players and the boards. As long as the groups and the boards have different progressions, and continue for succeeding rounds as they moved for the second, no difficulty is encountered. The number of rounds is equal to the number of tables, but can be cut short.

If it is desired to increase the number of partnerships, the South and West players interchange after the first boards in a two-board round, or the West player travels around the table counter-clockwise for three boards to a round; in all cases, the North player remaining stationary.

In no case does balanced comparison result. To secure fairly balanced comparisons, the game must be in more than one session, having one less round than there are players entered.

RAISE. Noun: an increase of the contract in the denomination named by partner; verb: to make a bid increasing the contract in the denomination named by partner. See SINGLE RAISE; DOUBLE RAISE; TRIPLE RAISE.

RAISE IN RESPONDER'S SUIT. See OPENER'S REBID.

RAISER. The player who bids for a greater number of tricks in a suit first bid by his partner.

RANDOM FALSECARDS. See FALSE-CARDING.

RANK. (1) The priority of suits in bidding and cutting. Starting at the bottom, the suits rank in alphabetical order: clubs, diamonds, hearts, spades, with no trump at the top of the list. (2) The trick-taking power of each card within a suit. The ace, king, queen, jack have priority in that order. The lower cards rank numerically.

RANKING BRIDGE PLAYER. See LIFE MASTER, the highest of the categories into which the ACBL ranks players. The ranking of players by means of MASTER POINTS won cannot be construed as definitive as between any two players, because of the difference in time during which points were earned, frequency of competition, ability to attend major regional and national CHAMPIONSHIP TOURNAMENTS. In any given year, among active participants, the MCKENNEY TROPHY winner must be considered the ranking player of that year in the ACBL.

RANKING OF PLAYERS. A part of the MASTER-POINT PLAN of the AMERICAN CONTRACT BRIDGE LEAGUE. The national offices of the league maintain a record for each player of points won in sanctioned tournaments. Rankings are based on the following table:

Sub-Master	A player who has less than 1 full master point recorded by the league.
Junior Master	A player who has 1 but less than 20 points credited.
Master	A player who has 20 but less than 50 points credited.
National Master	A player who has 50 but less than 100 points credited.
Senior Master	A player with 100 or more points credited.
Advanced Senior Master	A player with 200 or more points credited, including a minimum of 20 RED/GOLD POINTS.
Life Master	A player with 300 or more points credited, including a minimum of 50 RED POINTS. For players beginning to accumulate master points as of January 1, 1969, 25 of these 50 points must be RED/GOLD POINTS. Players with red points already to their credit prior to that date are not subject to this gold point requirement.

For the names of the top-ranking life masters, see LIFE MASTER. A life master, having fulfilled the above conditions, is also eligible to be elected as a life member of the American Contract Bridge League.

Comparable master-point plans are in effect in many other bridge-playing countries, although rankings and requirements differ from country to country. See MASTER-POINT PLAN. In addition, the World Bridge Federation has adopted its own master-point plan for the ranking of players of international calibre. See WORLD BRIDGE FEDERATION RANKINGS.

RATING POINT CERTIFICATE. See RATING POINTS.

RATING POINTS. Fractional master points awarded in ACBL club duplicate games or championships. Rating points are issued on certificates by the manager of the club in which they are won. Each rating point equals .01 master point, and certificates may be forwarded to the ACBL in blocks of 100 or more rating points within three years of their issuance for crediting to the member's master-point total.

REBIDDABLE SUITS. See OPENER'S REBID.

REBIDS IN ORIGINAL SUIT. See OPENER'S REBID.

RECAPITULATION SHEET (RECAP). A large printed form to which pickup slips are posted at bridge tournaments, and on which match points are assigned to scores, and totals computed. Recapitulation sheets are available in two forms, one for HOWELL MOVEMENT games or team-of-four play, and the other for MITCHELL MOVEMENT games. All sheets have a head on which space is provided for names of players and their SEATING ASSIGNMENTS and PLAYER NUMBERS, their overall RANKING, total score (for two or more session events or when FACTORING is involved), CARRY-OVER SCORE for two or more session events, and POINTS this session. These headings or copies thereof are the official records from which MASTER POINTS are awarded by the NATIONAL AUTHORITY, and serve as permanent records. To the right of this heading are boxes in which the individual scores on boards 1–36 (subsequent sheets can be appended for more boards) are entered and MATCH POINTS assigned. See also BURNER.

RECIPROCAL SQUEEZE. A variant of the double squeeze. The squeeze card is not an established card in the fourth suit; rather each opponent is squeezed in turn by a winner in the suit guarded by his partner. These are the basic positions:

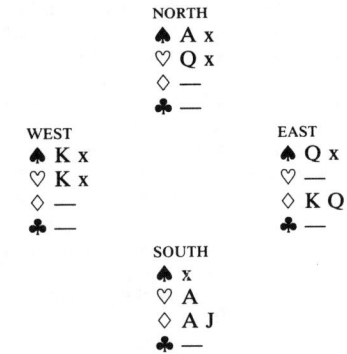

South leads the ace of hearts, which forces East to discard a spade. Now the lead of the ace of diamonds squeezes West in the majors.

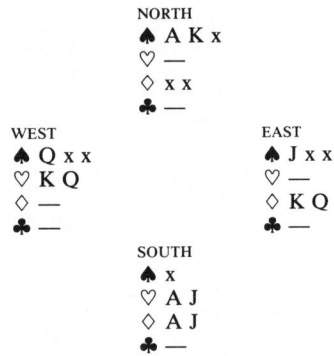

South leads the ace of hearts, which forces East to discard a spade. Now the lead of the diamond ace squeezes West in the majors.

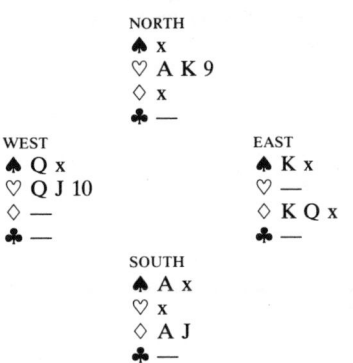

```
                NORTH
                ♠ x
                ♡ A K 9
                ◇ x
                ♣ —
WEST                        EAST
♠ Q x                       ♠ K x
♡ Q J 10                    ♡ —
◇ —                         ◇ K Q x
♣ —                         ♣ —
                SOUTH
                ♠ A x
                ♡ x
                ◇ A J
                ♣ —
```

South leads the ace of diamonds, which forces West to unguard spades. Now South leads hearts, and the second winner of that suit squeezes East in spades and diamonds.

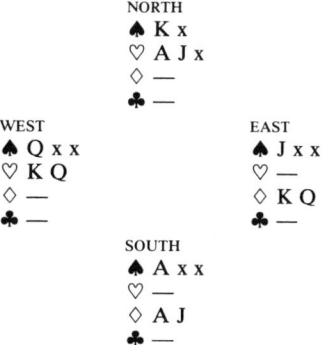

```
                NORTH
                ♠ K x
                ♡ A J x
                ◇ —
                ♣ —
WEST                        EAST
♠ Q x x                     ♠ J x x
♡ K Q                       ♡ —
◇ —                         ◇ K Q
♣ —                         ♣ —
                SOUTH
                ♠ A x x
                ♡ —
                ◇ A J
                ♣ —
```

South cashes the ace of diamonds, which forces West to unguard spades. A spade is led to the king followed by the ace of hearts, which squeezes East in spades and diamonds.

A double squeeze may be played as a reciprocal squeeze by running off all declarer's winners in the fourth suit (which is not guarded by either opponent). This has a dual advantage: it allows more room for defensive error, and it enables declarer to obtain additional information regarding the outstanding cards.

M. I.

RECORDING OF MASTER POINTS. The results of each MASTER POINT event are reported by the tournament director to the ACBL, and points are automatically recorded to the credit of the winners of club games, and to those players placing in local, sectional, or higher ranked tournaments provided a player number is given. A post-card announcement is sent to each member whenever new points are recorded for him, stating the amount of the new credit and his total to date in both total points and RED/GOLD POINTS.

Originally all recording was done manually, and the post-card acknowledgments were written out in longhand, and mailed to the players. In 1960 it be-

came evident that manual posting would not suffice to maintain individual records for many thousands of members, and a mechanical system of recording was installed.

Fractional master points are issued in the form of unrecorded certificates, to be retained by the player until he has accumulated fractions amounting to 1 full point or more. He may then send them to the ACBL office where each 100 fractional points will be recorded as 1 full master point.

The ACBL was first to develop a master-point plan, but similar plans are now in use by numerous other national bridge governing bodies.

RECORDING OF MATCHES. See BRIDGE-O-RAMA; HAND RECORD; VU-GRAPH.

RECTIFICATION. An adjustment made to permit the auction or play to proceed as normally as possible after an irregularity has occurred.

In the bidding stage, irregularities (other than violations of ethical procedure) are covered by specific penalties, as are most of the possible irregularities in the play. However, in the case of a failure to follow suit which is later corrected, it is possible that the offender inadvertently gains information that he is not entitled to under normal play; in this case, rectification is called for.

Occasionally the bidding will have started at a table when it is discovered that the traveling pair has come to the wrong table, and should not be playing the board against that opponent. In this case the director may seat the proper pair at the table and have the bidding repeated. If no additional information is gained, the board is permitted to stand; if the bidding progresses differently, then an adjusted score must usually be given. See ALCATRAZ COUP and LAWS OF DUPLICATE BRIDGE (Laws 12 and 16).

RECTIFYING THE COUNT. The process of losing a trick or tricks in order to reach a certain number of remaining losers, thus enabling a desired ending to be reached. The most common use of the play is to reduce the number of losers to one, enabling a simple squeeze to be executed.

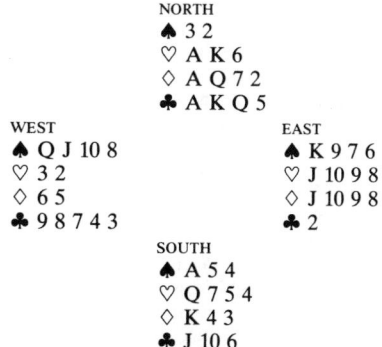

```
                NORTH
                ♠ 3 2
                ♡ A K 6
                ◇ A Q 7 2
                ♣ A K Q 5
WEST                        EAST
♠ Q J 10 8                  ♠ K 9 7 6
♡ 3 2                       ♡ J 10 9 8
◇ 6 5                       ◇ J 10 9 8
♣ 9 8 7 4 3                 ♣ 2
                SOUTH
                ♠ A 5 4
                ♡ Q 7 5 4
                ◇ K 4 3
                ♣ J 10 6
```

West leads the spade queen against South's six no trump contract. South has eleven winners. The contract will succeed if either hearts or diamonds are favorably divided. Another chance is a squeeze against an opponent holding guards in both red suits. This squeeze will operate only if South has but one loser remaining. If South wins the first trick, he can no longer make his contract. Instead, he should rectify the count by allowing West to hold the first spade. South wins any continuation, and runs his black winners, squeezing East between the red suits. For another example, see LOSER-ON-LOSER.

RED AND BLACK GERBER. See BLACK AND RED GERBER.

RED POINT. Master points won in regional and national CHAMPIONSHIP TOURNAMENTS are required for the advancement of players to ADVANCED SENIOR MASTER and LIFE MASTER status in the ACBL. To distinguish points won at these larger and more important events, the ACBL uses the term "red points." Fifty "colored" (red/gold) points are one of the requirements for promotion to Life Master status. See also GOLD POINT; RANKING OF PLAYERS; REGIONAL AND NATIONAL POINTS.

REDEAL. A second or subsequent deal by the same dealer to replace his first deal. See LAWS OF CONTRACT BRIDGE, Part III Section 10. Hands are never redealt at duplicate except in special cases on the director's instructions.

REDOUBLE. A call that increases the scoring value of odd tricks or undertricks at a bid that an opponent has doubled. It has the effect of multiplying a doubled penalty or premium by two.

When the standard of play is high, redoubled contracts are rare. Ill-judged doubles of game or slam contracts may lead to redoubles. At rubber bridge and IMP play, the mathematics of the scoring table favor redoubles at high levels.

In a high-level competitive auction, an expert may occasionally redouble when he expects his contract to fail by one trick. He is prepared to sacrifice 100 or 200 points in the hope of driving the opponents into continuing in their own suit and conceding a penalty.

A special situation arises when an artificial bid is doubled and redoubled. At a high level, when a CUE-BID has been doubled or a response to BLACKWOOD for example, the redouble is generally regarded as control-showing. Whether the control shown is first-round or second-round is a matter of partnership agreement. At a low level the situation is different:

SOUTH	WEST	NORTH	EAST
1 NT	Pass	2 ♣	Dbl.
Redbl.			

The redouble shows a desire to play in clubs: the opening bidder probably has a five-card club suit.

For other redoubling situations see DOUBLES OF NO TRUMP BIDS; KOCK-WERNER REDOUBLE; RESPONSES OVER OPPONENT'S TAKE-OUT DOUBLE; SOS REDOUBLE.

REDOUBLE OUT OF ROTATION. An improper bid when it is partner's or right-hand opponent's turn to call. If it is partner's turn to call, he must pass, and continue for the balance of the auction to pass when it is his turn to call. If the partner of the offender has the opening lead, declarer may require or forbid him to lead a specified suit. Also the offender is not permitted to redouble the same bid which he redoubled out of turn.

If it is the turn of the right-hand opponent to bid, the redouble must be repeated if this opponent passes; if the opponent bids, the offender may make any legal call, but his partner must pass at his next opportunity. See LAWS (Law 32).

RE-ENTRY. A card by which a player who has had the lead (including the opening lead) can regain it.

REFUSE. (1) Deliberate failure to win a trick because of reasons of strategy. (2) Used in the sense of refusing to finesse, i.e., not taking what was previously a winning finesse in order to ensure the contract. (3) An obsolete term formerly used in WHIST and AUCTION BRIDGE, the laws of which define it as "to fail to follow suit," as distinguished from RENOUNCE. See DISCARD. See DANGER HAND; DUCK; HOLD UP.

REGENCY WHIST CLUB (New York City). Formerly Regency Club, founded in 1936 and merged with the WHIST CLUB of New York in 1964. It has remained at 15 East 67th Street since it began its very successful career, with many of the outstanding bridge personalities among its members. These have included: the founder, Mrs. T. Charles Farrelly, a noted New York bridge teacher; B. Jay Becker, John Crawford, Sam Fry, Jr., Charles Goren, M. T. Gottlieb, Edward Hymes, Jr., Oswald Jacoby, Boris Koytchou, Peter Leventritt, T. A. Lightner, Charles Lochridge, Albert Morehead, Florence Osborn, Curt Reisinger, Howard Schenken, Alfred Sheinwold, Sherman Stearns, Alan Truscott, Harold S. Vanderbilt, Waldemar von Zedtwitz. Honorary members include Wingate Bixby, General Alfred Gruenther, Walter Malowan, and Harold S. Vanderbilt.

President, 1975: T. Suffern Tailer.
Secretary: Sam Fry, Jr.

REGIONAL AND NATIONAL POINTS. Regional points are master points won in championship events at regional tournaments under the earlier MASTER-POINT PLAN of the ACBL. This took cognizance of the larger fields and wider geographical distribution of players at its major tournaments by giving special recognition to winners of points in these tournaments (referred to as "red points," "regional reds," or "pink points"), keeping a record of these points separate from those won in lesser tournaments.

National points were a special award for success in National Championships (now NORTH AMERICAN CHAMPIONSHIPS). Each three National points were the equivalent of five Regional points.

Under the new program all red points are of the

same value and the old ratio for conversion of Regional to National point values is eliminated.

REGIONAL TOURNAMENT. Generally, see CHAMPIONSHIP TOURNAMENTS. For results of particular regional tournaments, see Appendix II.

REGISTERED PLAYER. See PROFESSIONAL PLAYERS.

REID CONVENTION. See RESPONSIVE DOUBLE.

REISINGER MEMORIAL TROPHY. Donated by the Greater New York BA in 1965 in memory of Curt H. Reisinger and awarded to the winners of the Fall Open Teams Championships under which heading past results are listed. Replaced the historic Chicago Trophy. The winners of the Reisinger are entitled to compete against the winners of the GRAND NATIONAL CHAMPIONSHIPS (2), SPINGOLD TROPHY, and VANDERBILT CUP (1) for the right to represent North America or the United States in the next year's WORLD CHAMPIONSHIPS. See INTERNATIONAL OPEN TEAM SELECTION.

REISINGER TROPHY. Donated by Curt H. Reisinger in 1930, for the Knockout Team-of-Four contest in the Eastern States Championships, under which heading past results are listed.

REITH ONE OVER ONE. A system of bidding described by George REITH in a series of five books published 1930–33. Approach bidding was used, and four-card suits were bid freely. Responses and bids were kept to minimum levels, and third-hand openings were somewhat shaded. The essence of the system, a forerunner of methods considered as "Standard" by postwar writers, was the principle of emphasizing distribution in early bidding rounds as opposed to showing strength. The one-over-one response made it incumbent upon opening bidder to bid at least once more. Defensive tactics featured wide usage of take-out doubles and the REITH POINT COUNT was employed in hand evaluation.

REITH POINT COUNT. An appraisal by George REITH of the relative values of high cards, primarily for no trump bidding. The values assigned were ace = 6, king = 4, queen = 3, jack = 2, ten = 1. See REITH ONE OVER ONE.

RELAY. (1) A minimum bid unrelated to the bidder's hand, aimed simply at keeping the bidding open so that the bidder's partner can describe his hand. An example is the LEBENSOHL rebid of three clubs, which is a forced bid. For the full development of this principle, see RELAY SYSTEM. (2) The practice of sharing boards at duplicate bridge, usually necessitated by a six-, eight-, or twelve-table MITCHELL MOVEMENT in which twenty-four boards are to be played. (3) In England, the equivalent of a BYE STAND.

RELAY STAND. See BYE STAND.

RELAY SYSTEM. A system devised by Pierre GHESTEM (France) and used by him in many world championship events in partnership with René BACHERICH. In 1963 it became the Monaco System, played by Pierre GHESTEM with Claude DELMOULY.

The one club opening is forcing but may be made with normal opening strength and either five or more clubs (shown by rebidding clubs), or no five card major suit (shown by rebidding a major). The chief features which distinguish this system from other one club systems are:

(1) Strength of the one no trump opening (13–15 not vulnerable; 18–20 vulnerable).

(2) Opening bids of two spades, two hearts, and two diamonds show 18–22 points and fewer than three cards in clubs. (With three clubs or more, open one club, and jump in the genuine suit on the next round.)

(3) The relay response of one diamond to a one club opening: a negative relay which can also be made with a strong hand.

(4) The rebid of two diamonds by the opener after the negative relay of one diamond: shows 18 points and upward, forcing for one round, asks responder to describe his hand.

The system aims to ensure that the contract is played from the right side of the table.

After one club, the responder must not use relays unless he has 11 points or more, i.e., when a game contract is in sight. Even with sufficient strength, he is not obliged to embark on relays. With a hand containing tenaces and guarded honors, he makes a natural response in hearts, spades, or no trump, showing a desire to be declarer.

When he does not desire to be declarer, the responder uses relays of one diamond, two diamonds, and if required, three diamonds and three hearts. (The latter two bids are TEXAS for the major suits.)

First Relay of One Diamond

The opener rebids in a major if he can. With both majors he rebids one heart, and follows with two spades over the second relay of two diamonds. With no major he rebids one no trump or two clubs.

If the responder still has problems, he can ask for further information.

Second Relay of Two Diamonds (forcing to game).

(1) If the rebid was one heart, opener shows a four-card spade suit or bids two no trump.

(2) If the rebid was one spade (denying hearts) opener rebids two hearts with a three-card suit; or three clubs with a good black two-suiter; otherwise two no trump.

(3) If the rebid was one no trump or two clubs, the opener now shows a three-card major, bidding two no trump with both majors. Three clubs would show a seven-card suit with no three-card major, and three diamonds would show 2–2–3–6.

Third Relay at Three-Level

Three diamonds may be used:

(1) To ask for a three-card spade suit when opener

has rebid one heart and two no trump. Opener now bids three spades or three no trump.

(2) To require a three heart bid when opener has shown three cards in both majors by a rebid of two no trump.

(3) To require a three no trump bid in other cases. Three hearts may be used:

(4) To require a three spade bid when the opener has shown three cards in both majors by a rebid of two no trump.

In all the above cases the opener's strength must be 12–17 points. With 18–23 points he makes a rebid higher than two clubs, or opens with a two-bid.

The following table summarizes the relays and rebids shown above:

1 ♣ opener has	over 1 ◊ relay he rebids	over 2nd relay of 2 ◊ he rebids	over 3rd relay of 3 ◊ he rebids	over 3rd relay of 3 ♡ he rebids
1. 4 ♡ & 4 ♠	1 ♡	2 ♠	3 NT	
2. 4 ♡ & 3 ♠	1 ♡	2 NT	3 ♠	
3. 4 ♡ & 2 ♠	1 ♡	2 NT	3 NT	
4. 3 ♡ & 3 ♠	2 ♣ or 1 NT	2 NT	3 ♡	3 ♠
5. 3 ♡ & 2 ♠	2 ♣ or 1 NT	2 ♡	3 NT	
6. 2 ♡ & 3 ♠	2 ♣ or 1 NT	2 ♠	3 NT	
7. 3 ♡ & 4 ♠	1 ♠	2 ♡	3 NT	
8. 2 ♡ & 4 ♠	1 ♠	2 NT	3 NT	
9. 2–2–3–6	2 ♣	3 ◊	—	3 NT
10. 7 ♣ and no 3-card major	2 ♣	3 ♣	3 NT	

Responses to One Club

(Note that the one club bid almost invariably contains at least three clubs. The only exception is a 4–4–3–2 hand.)

One Diamond may be: (a) Negative with less than eight points, in which case the responder passes or makes a weak rebid at his second turn. Or (b) Natural with 10–11 points and a diamond suit if followed by a jump in diamonds or no trump, which would be limit. Or (c) Conventional positive with at least 11 points if followed by the two diamond relay already described.

One heart, one spade, or two clubs are natural and forcing (they indicate a desire to be declarer). Two diamond rebid by opener is a relay.

One no trump and two no trump are natural limit bids.

Two diamonds, two hearts, and two spades are semi-pre-emptive transfer bids with four or five playing tricks.

Three of a suit shows a good suit and six playing tricks.

One Diamond Opening Bid

Shows at least four diamonds with 12–18 points, and denies a five-card major. A jump rebid may be made with a maximum over a positive response. A one heart response is a relay, and the opener's one no trump rebid shows the no trump range *not* in use

(i.e., 18–21 not vulnerable, and 12–15 vulnerable). Other responses are natural, but not forcing above two clubs.

One Heart and One Spade Opening Bids

Show at least a five-card suit and 10–17 points. One spade and one no trump are respectively relays. (This is the *only* situation in which one no trump can be a relay.) Two club response is natural and forcing. Two no trump response shows a three-suiter with a void in the opener's suit. Other responses are natural and non-forcing.

The sequences one heart—one spade—one no trump and one spade—one no trump—two clubs can show five different types of hand, and the opener clarifies his holding after the second relay.

In general, responses at the two-level to opening suit bids of one are transfer bids.

One No Trump Opening Bids

Shows 13–15 points not vulnerable or 18–20 points vulnerable. Two clubs is a relay response, and a two no trump rebid shows five clubs. Two no trump is a second relay by responder. Most suit responses are transfer bids.

Two Clubs Opening

Is forcing to game with specialized responses and rebids.

Responses: (1) Two diamonds is negative. (2) Two hearts shows one ace or four kings. (3) Two spades shows two aces or three kings. (4) Two no trump shows three aces or two kings. (5) Bids at the three level are natural but negative. A relay by the opener asks the responder to clarify his honor holding; and a super relay (one step higher) is also an asking bid. A jump rebid by the opener is limited.

Two Diamonds, Two Hearts and Two Spades Opening Bids

Show 18–22 points and fewer than three cards in clubs. A response at the three-level is a transfer bid. Opener shows a maximum by rebidding three clubs over a relay. The opener's suit has at least five cards.

Slam Conventions

Three clubs, four clubs, four no trump, and five no trump are used as a form of Blackwood, in which aces, kings, and queens are identified. Answers are by scales: one or four—one step; none or three—two steps; two of same rank—three steps; two of unlike color and rank—four steps; two of same color—five steps.

The three club conventional bid may be preceded by one relay after a major suit opening or two relays after a minor suit opening. Defensive bidding includes a number of two-suiter conventions.

Defensive Play

Lead ace from ace, king, and others. Lead a low card holding an odd number of cards, and a high card with an even number of cards. Suit preference signals; a low card asks for a suit just beneath the one which is played; a high card asks for a suit just above the one which is played.

RELAY TABLE. (1) One of the tables at which the players are sharing boards for that round with an adjacent table. (2) See BYE STAND.

REMAINDERS. The remaining cards of a four-card or longer suit, outstanding in the other three hands at the table. Two- and three-card remainders are called balanced remainders. One-card and four-card remainders, however, are called unbalanced remainders.

REMOVE. To bid on when partner has doubled for penalties.

RENEGE. A popular colloquial synonym for REVOKE. However, the term does not appear in the Laws of Bridge and is borrowed from such games as pinochle.

RENOUNCE. A term from AUCTION BRIDGE, meaning to fail to follow suit when able to do so; also (noun), the play involving such failure. The term was dropped from the 1935 LAWS OF CONTRACT BRIDGE, but was earlier used to designate a REVOKE that had not yet become established. See REFUSE.

REOPEN THE BIDDING. See BALANCING.

REPEATED SQUEEZE. See TRIPLE SQUEEZE.

REPEATING TRIPLE SQUEEZE. See PROGRESSIVE SQUEEZE.

REPLAY DUPLICATE. A form of duplicate in which just two pairs play against each other, playing the same boards but first in one position (i.e., North-South and then the other, East-West). Although this form of duplicate attained some currency in the twenties, it quickly became obsolete simply because a board could so easily be remembered by the players. Even the process of playing the boards one way one week and the other the next was of no avail against pairs who had even the merest semblance of competent memories.

REPUBLIC OF CHINA. See NATIONAL CONTRACT BRIDGE LEAGUE OF THE REPUBLIC OF CHINA.

RE-RAISE. A colloquialism for opener's rebid of three of his suit after responder has raised to two:

| 1 ♠ | 2 ♠ |
| 3 ♠ | |

RESCUE. To bid another suit, or conceivably no trump, when partner has been doubled for penalties.

The most common rescuing situation arises when an overcall has been doubled. There are three points for the overcaller's partner to consider:

(1) His length in the doubled suit. The more cards he holds, the less desirable a rescue becomes—it is rarely right with a doubleton, and virtually never right with more than two cards.

(2) The level of the potential rescue. Rescuing is more likely to be effective at the one-level, and may sometimes be attempted when holding a singleton or void in the doubled suit but no suit of more than five cards. See KOCK-WERNER REDOUBLE; SOS REDOUBLE. There is less case for rescuing if it must be done at a higher level.

(3) The quality of the rescuer's suit compared with the likely quality of the doubled suit. There must be a reasonable expectation that the rescuer's suit is more substantial than the doubled suit. In most circumstances a strong six-card suit or a seven-card suit is necessary.

Another common rescue situation occurs when a one no trump opening has been doubled. Here it is seldom right for responder to SIT if he has no high-card strength or if he has a long suit. See DEFENSE TO DOUBLE OF ONE NO TRUMP.

RESCUE BID. A bid, based on a long suit, made with less than normal values because of a misfit with partner's bid suit after it has been doubled.

RESERVE PLAYER. In an event for teams of four or more members, any team member not currently playing. A reserve player is eligible to replace an active member during the current or later sessions, but only under conditions announced by the director or published in advance. In major tournaments reserve players are usually barred from watching their teammates, or watching at an adjoining table.

RESOCK, REWIND. To redouble (obsolescent slang).

RESPOND. To answer in the language of bidding. To pass, however, is not to respond.

RESPONDER'S REBID. Many bids on the second round by the responding hand are covered under separate headings: DELAYED GAME RAISE; DOUBLE RAISE; FOURTH SUIT FORCING; JUMP REBIDS BY RESPONDER; ONE NO TRUMP RESPONSE; PREFERENCE; REVERSE; SINGLE RAISE; STAYMAN ON SECOND ROUND; THREE NO TRUMP RESPONSE; TRIAL BID; TRIPLE RAISE; TWO CLUB REBID BY RESPONDER AS ONLY FORCE AFTER ONE NO TRUMP REBID; TWO NO TRUMP RESPONSE; UNBID MINOR SUIT FORCE.

Other situations which can arise are discussed below.

(1) *After three suits at the one-level*
(a)

| 1 ♣ | 1 ♡ |
| 1 ♠ | 1 NT |

An ill-defined sequence in standard methods, but usually regarded as encouraging (8–10). This leaves unsolved problems at both ends of the range.

(a)	(b)
♠ 5	♠ J 7
♡ K 8 7 6 4	♡ A J 6 3 2
◇ Q J 7 4 2	◇ K J 5
♣ 9 3	♣ J 8 4

With hand (a) a pass is unthinkable; one spade is probably a 4–1 fit, and could even be a 3–1 fit. One no trump is the only conceivable action, but is a considerable overbid if one no trump is viewed as constructive. A plausible solution is to regard the one no trump rebid as having the same strength as an original one no trump response to one spade 6–9 or possibly 10.

Hand (b) offers an easy two no trump rebid if that is non-forcing (see Jump Rebids by Responder); but in standard methods, with two no trump forcing, responder must choose between an overbid of two no trump, an underbid of one no trump, or a "manufactured" two diamonds.

(b)

1 ♣	1 ♡
1 ♠	2 ♠

Usually indicates four-card trump support and 7–10 in high cards. But occasionally the raise must be given with three-card support, even without a ruffing value:

♠ K 7 2
♡ A K 4 2
♦ 7 3 2
♣ 10 8 6

After

1 ♣	1 ♡
1 ♠	

there is no sensible alternative to two spades.

Other sequences are listed under FOURTH SUIT FORCING; PREFERENCE; JUMP REBIDS BY RESPONDER.

(2) *After three suits ending at the two-level*

(c)

1 ♦	1 ♠
2 ♣	2 ♠

Normally a six-card suit and mildly encouraging; but if three spades is regarded as non-forcing, then two spades is discouraging.

(d)

1 ♦	1 ♠
2 ♣	2 NT

10–12 points in high cards, with at least a single stopper in the unbid suit. Similarly

1 ♠	2 ♣
2 ♡	2 NT

(e)

1 ♦	1 ♠
2 ♣	3 ♣

Also encouraging but not forcing, 10–12 points in high cards, and four-card, or conceivably five-card, club support.

Similarly

1 ♠	2 ♣
2 ♡	3 ♡

Other sequences are listed under Fourth Suit Forcing, Preference, and Jump Rebids by Responder.

(3) *After a one no trump rebid*

(f)

1 ♦	1 ♡
1 NT	2 ♡

A six-card heart suit, presumably, and highly discouraging. Opener almost invariably passes.

(g)

1 ♦	1 ♡
1 NT	2 ♦

Discouraging, but game might still be possible if opener is able to give delayed preference for hearts.

(h)

1 ♦	1 ♡
1 NT	2 ♣

Non-forcing and neutral. The opener should not rebid two no trump, but may give preference to two hearts or raise to three clubs, either of which might lead to a game. Responder is likely to have five hearts and four or five clubs. With only four clubs he should not retreat from one no trump automatically: with 3–5–1–4 distribution it may be best to leave one no trump, especially in a pair contest. This change of suit is forcing in Roth-Stone.

(i)

1 ♦	1 ♡
1 NT	2 NT

Non-forcing and encouraging. The strength depends on the range of the 1 NT rebid, but responder indicates that the combined hands have a minimum of 23–24 points.

(j)

1 ♦	1 ♡
1 NT	2 ♠

See REVERSE.

(k)

1 ♦	1 ♡
1 NT	3 ♣

A jump shift, forcing to game. An unbalanced distribution, and very likely a weakness in the unbid suit, spades.

(l)

1 ♦	1 ♡
1 NT	3 ♦

Forcing in standard methods, but non-forcing in ACOL and in some expert partnerships.

(m)

1 ♦	1 ♡
1 NT	3 ♡

Forcing in "standard," but the non-forcing treatment is popular and more logical. A game-going hand with a six-card heart suit can jump to four hearts.

(4) *After a minimum rebid in the original suit*

(n)

1 ♦	1 ♠
2 ♦	2 ♠

Encouraging with a six-card suit. With a hand without prospects, responder can pass two diamonds.

(o)

1 ◇	1 ♠
2 ◇	2 ♡ or 3 ♣

Forcing, probably with 5–5 or 5–4 distribution. But it may be necessary to make the rebid in a three-card suit:

♠ A Q 5 4 3   ♠ A Q 5 4 3
♡ A Q 4   ♡ 8 4
◇ J 6 2   ◇ J 6 2
♣ 8 4   ♣ A Q 4

(p)

1 ◇	1 ♠
2 ◇	2 NT

Encouraging but non-forcing. 10–12 points and presumably guards in both unbid suits.

(q)

1 ◇	1 ♠
2 ◇	3 ◇

Encouraging but not forcing. Probably 10–12 points and weak in the unbid suits.

(5) *After a single raise of responder's suit*

(r)

1 ◇	1 ♠
2 ♠	2 NT

Encouraging and non-forcing. Presumably stoppers in the unbid suits, 10–12 points, a four-card spade suit.

(s)

1 ◇	1 ♠
2 ♠	3 ◇

Encouraging and non-forcing. 10–12 points. Probably a four-card spade suit with four or five diamonds.

(t)

1 ◇	1 ♠
2 ♠	3 ♣

Forcing, and perhaps only a three-card club suit. Responder may be aiming for three no trump, or trying to find whether the opener has some reserve strength for a spade game.

(u)

1 ◇	1 ♠
2 ♠	3 ♠

Encouraging but not forcing. Probably a six-card spade suit with no special features in the unbid suits.

RESPONDING HAND. The hand, or player, facing opening bidder; the partner of the initial bidder.

RESPONSE. Usually bid by a player whose partner has opened the bidding, but may be used to describe a response to a take-out double, cue bid, conventional bid, etc. For responding to an opening bid of one,

see CHOICE OF SUIT; DOUBLE RAISE; JUMP SHIFT; ONE NO TRUMP RESPONSE; ONE OVER ONE RESPONSE; PRE-EMPTIVE RESPONSE; SINGLE RAISE; THREE NO TRUMP RESPONSE; TRIPLE RAISE; TWO NO TRUMP RESPONSE; TWO OVER ONE RESPONSE; UP THE LINE.

RESPONSES OVER OPPONENT'S TAKE-OUT DOUBLE. The usual treatment is:

(1) A *suit response* is non-forcing and unconstructive, but promises at least a five-card suit. At the two-level (e.g., one heart—double—two clubs) a six-card suit is probable.

(2) *One no trump* is mildly constructive, with about 7–9 points.

(3) A *single raise* is pre-emptive, and slightly weaker than it would be without the double.

(4) A *double raise* is pre-emptive, showing a distributional hand which would normally make a single raise.

(5) A *triple raise* is also pre-emptive, with extra playing-trick strength.

(6) A *redouble,* showing almost any strong hand with a minimum point-count of about 10. Usually the redoubler will have a defensive hand, and the opening bidder will not take a further bid at his next turn unless he has a distributional hand unsuited to defense.

With a four-card or better fit in the opener's suit, a redouble is unattractive because it makes it simple for the opponents to find a fit for a possible save. A direct raise to game in a major may be preferable, and there is a conventional possibility:

(7) *Two no trump* and *three no trump* have no natural meaning, because a good hand with balanced distribution would redouble. Some players, following the ACOL SYSTEM, use two no trump to denote a hand which would have made a LIMIT JUMP RAISE to three of opener's suit if there had been no double. By a logical extension, three no trump can be used to show a strong raise to game when the opening bid was a major suit. For alternative treatments, see TWO NO TRUMP RESPONSE (Over Opponent's Take-Out Double).

(8) *Jump suit responses* (e.g., one diamond—double—two spades). This bid shows at least a six-card suit, but the strength is a matter of partnership agreement. There are four schools of thought: (1) forcing to game; (2) forcing for one round; (3) not forcing and a hand of intermediate strength (about 9 points in high cards); (4) pre-emptive, say Q J x x x x and no other asset.

(9) A *pass* usually shows a weak hand unsuitable for any positive action. But a pass followed by a bid on the following round can be used to show a hand with fair defensive strength. For example:

♠ A 5 3
♡ Q 6 4
◇ K 6 3 2
♣ 7 4 3

If partner's one spade opening is doubled, a possible tactic is to pass and bid two spades on the next round. This must show a stronger hand than an immediate bid of two spades.

Some players treat a suit response over a double as

forcing, and a small minority bid exactly as they would have done without the double.

RESPONSIVE DOUBLE

RESPONSIVE DOUBLE (originated by Dr. F. Fielding-Reid, Dania, Fla.). The use of a double for take-out when there has been an immediate raise to the two- or three-level over partner's TAKE-OUT DOUBLE. For example:

WEST	NORTH	EAST	SOUTH
1 ◊	Dbl.	2 ◊	?

South holds:

♠ J 6 5 2
♡ Q 10 9 5
◊ 3
♣ Q 7 6 3

It would be cowardly to pass, and South is not nearly strong enough to make a CUE-BID of three diamonds. He does not want to guess which suit to bid, so he makes a responsive double. In this situation, it is very seldom that South will wish to make a PENALTY DOUBLE.

The double would also be used if East had raised to three diamonds instead of two diamonds.

The doubler may have a balanced hand if his high-card strength is somewhat improved:

♠ 4 3 2
♡ A Q 9
◊ Q 8 5 2
♣ J 8 6

This would be ideal for a responsive double if an opening spade bid were doubled and raised to two spades; and would be the most convenient action if the opposition had bid clubs, diamonds, or hearts.

The minimum strength required for a responsive double varies slightly with the level of the auction. With a balanced hand, a double of two clubs might be made with 6 points; a double of three spades would need at least 9 points.

The convention normally applies to any bid at the two- or three-level, but a few players use a double of three hearts or three spades for penalties.

An extension of the responsive idea can be used in the following situation:

NORTH	EAST	SOUTH	WEST
1 ♡	2 ♣	2 ♡	Dbl.

A penalty double of a free raise is very seldom required, so by partnership agreement West's double can show length in spades and diamonds.

RESTRICTED CHOICE

RESTRICTED CHOICE. The play of a card which may have been selected as a choice of equal plays increases the chance that the player started with a holding in which his choice was restricted.

The Rule of Restricted Choice is a rule of card play which can enable the declarer to take the correct action in situations which used to be thought of as guesswork.

The underlying principles were first discussed by Alan Truscott in the *Contract Bridge Journal*. Later, these principles were unified by Terence Reese in his book, *Master Play*.

THE BASIC PRINCIPLE

Following is the sort of card combination which can call the Rule of Restricted Choice into operation:

Example 1:

NORTH (dummy)
♠ Q J 9

SOUTH (declarer)
♠ 4 3 2

South has to develop a trick in this suit. He leads low to dummy's queen and East wins with the king. Upon regaining the lead, South again leads toward the North hand. Should South play the jack or nine from dummy? Is one play superior or is South faced with a guess?

If either East or West now holds both the ace and ten, South's play is immaterial. The jack will score if West holds the ace and East holds the ten. The nine is winning play if West holds the ten and East holds the ace. Thus the following summary of the situation can be constructed:

	West originally held:	East originally held:
Jack gains when	A	K 10
Nine gains when	10	A K

It is important to notice that this summary is sufficient, for when it comes time for South to make the final decision, he already knows that East held the king. Thus, South can exclude from the reckoning all distributions in which East does not hold the king.

The two possible distributions of the East-West honors given above are equally likely to occur, but the two plays are not of equal merit. To the statement, "the two crucial defensive holdings are equally likely," should be added, "provided there is no information regarding the distribution of honor cards in the suit."

In fact, there is such information. There is a direct inference to be drawn from the fact that East won the first trick with the *king*. Consider the first possible honor holding given above. If this is the actual distribution of East-West honor cards, East was forced to play his king of spades on the first round; his choice was restricted. This is not true in the second case, where East had the option of winning the first trick with the *ace* instead of the king. His choice was *not* restricted.

It can be presumed that if East started with A K, he would play the ace some percentage of the time. When East actually plays the king on the first round, the probability that he started with the ace and king is diminished because with both honors *he might have played the other one.*

For the sake of argument, assume that East would play his equal honors with equal frequency, winning with the king 50% of the time and winning with the ace 50% of the time. It can be demonstrated that this is, in fact, East's best strategy.

Under this assumption, imagine that declarer is playing the Example 1 combination 200 times. On 100 of these deals, East starts with ♠ K 10. On the other 100 deals, East starts with ♠ A K. Since, on the second 100 deals, East wins with the king only 50 times, certain things become clear.

East wins the king from an honor holding of K 10 on 100 occasions. But East wins the king from an honor holding of A K on only 50 occasions. On the other 50 deals on which East holds A K, he wins with the ace!

From this one may conclude that the jack is the superior play on the second round of spades. In fact, it is exactly twice as good a play as the nine. The position is exactly the same if East wins the first trick with the ace and not the king.

The above conclusions may be checked by examining all the possible honor distributions. If either defender holds *all three* honors, declarer will succeed or fail regardless of his plays, so these combinations can be omitted. This leaves the following possibilities, all equally probable before the suit is played for the first time:

	West holds	East holds
(a)	A K	10
(b)	A 10	K
(c)	K 10	A
(d)	A	K 10
(e)	K	A 10
(f)	10	A K

Each of the above situations is equally probable. Assume that each case occurs 100 times, 600 deals in all. Since East will (it is assumed) play equal honors with equal frequency, he wins a high honor on the first round on the following occasions:

		East wins with ♠ A	East wins with ♠ K
(a)		0	0
(b)		0	100
(c)		100	0
(d)		0	100
(e)		100	0
(f)		50	50
	TOTAL	250	250

Thus, East will win with a specified honor 250 times. Of these 250 times, declarer triumphs automatically in cases (b) or (c), a total of 100. Of the remaining 150, the jack is winning play 100 times in case (d) or (e) but the nine is right only 50 times in case (f).

Thus declarer's play of a card combination such as Example 1, far from being a blind guess, is subject to very definite analysis.

The logic behind the rule is simple and irrefutable. If the player in question had a choice of plays, he might have elected the other option. Therefore, there is a presumption that he did not have the option. Thus, in Example 1, when East wins with the king of spades, the chances favor the play of the jack

on the second round. The jack play caters to the situation in which East started with ♠ K 10, where he had no choice of plays on the first round, rather than the situation in which East had a choice of plays from A K.

Other Card Combinations. The rule of Restricted Choice can be applied to many more combinations:

Example 2:

> NORTH (dummy)
> J 9 4
>
> SOUTH (declarer)
> Q 3 2

South needs one trick, and is forced to attack the suit himself. He leads low to the queen, and West wins with a high honor. Later, South leads again toward the North hand. If West follows low, what should South do?

Applying the Rule of Restricted Choice, South should reason that if West held both high honors, he might have chosen the other one to capture the queen. But if West started with the high honor and the ten, his choice was restricted. The percentage play is the nine.

Example 3:

> NORTH (dummy)
> K 10 9
>
> SOUTH (declarer)
> 4 3 2

South leads toward the North hand and finesses the nine, losing to a middle honor. On the next lead, South should finesse the ten.

A Mistake to Avoid. Care must be taken to avoid mistaken applications of the rule of Restricted Choice.

Example 4:

> NORTH (dummy)
> K J 9
>
> SOUTH (declarer)
> 4 3 2

South requires one trick here. He leads up to the North hand, and decides to play the jack. East wins with the queen. Declarer has gained no information whatsoever as to the distribution of the outstanding honors. On the next lead declarer is faced with a guess. *There was no choice of plays involved for East,* who would win the jack with the queen whenever he held that card. The Rule of Restricted Choice does not apply.

Example 5:

> NORTH (dummy)
> ♠ A Q 10 7 6 5
>
> SOUTH (declarer)
> ♠ 4 3 2

South hopes to take six tricks here, and leads a spade

to North's queen, which East wins with the king. Later, South wants to pick up the remainder of the suit. Once again, there is no application of the Rule of Restricted Choice. The percentage play (barring side distributional inferences) is the ace.

Lower Odds. In the above examples of the Rule of Restricted Choice, declarer was faced with a choice of plays, one of which was exactly twice as good as the other. Restricted Choice situations do not always give such good odds as that.

There is a large class of card combinations in which declarer's correct play under the Rule of Restricted Choice gives him less than two-to-one odds.

Example 6:

NORTH (dummy)
K 10 9 8 7 6

SOUTH (declarer)
A 3 2

South leads the ace from his hand, West follows with the four and East drops the QUACK.* South leads toward the dummy, and West follows with the five. Assuming (as always) no important inferences to be drawn from the play of other suits, how should South play?

To answer that question, one starts by reflecting that the following distribution of East-West cards

(a)   WEST   EAST
           5 4   Q J

is *slightly* more probable (before the suit is played) than the following distribution:

(b)   WEST   EAST
           Q 5 4   J

Also, the chance of East holding Q J is *slightly* more probable than the following distribution:

(c)   WEST   EAST
           J 5 4   Q

But East is *less* likely to have Q J doubleton than he is to have a singleton *quack*. In other words, (b) and (c) together are greater than (a).

Thus, the correct play on the second round is to finesse. The odds favoring this play as opposed to the drop are slightly less than two to one.

Example 7:

NORTH (dummy)
A J 10 9 8 7

SOUTH (declarer)
4 3 2

South wishes to take five tricks. The best play is to take two finesses. This fails to bring in the suit (if such was possible) only when East holds K Q. It is easily

---

* We have already shown that from declarer's point of view it makes no difference whether East plays the queen or jack. Thus, terminology such as "quack" can be used to simplify both the discussion and the thinking.

---

seen that all other plays are inferior.

A common argument given about this combination is the following: It is best to take two finesses because it gains against more distributions than any other play. Once you have finessed the first time, you must follow through and finesse the second time.

This is an unfortunate way to get the right answer. According to the first part of this argument, if you finesse the jack and it loses to the king or queen, when you lead up to the dummy the second time, you have two possible combinations of cards:

	West holds	East holds
Case 1	6 5	K Q
Case 2 (a)	K 6 5	Q
(b)	Q 6 5	K

After the first trick, either Case 2 (a) or Case 2 (b) disappears, so only two relevant combinations remain, and the first is (initially) more probable. Therefore, the argument indicates playing for the drop on the second round.

The correct argument for the second finesse is that if East started with a singleton honor, his choice was restricted on the first round. Thus, the odds on the second finesse are *almost* two to one.

Another Mistake to Avoid. Some combinations are superficially similar to those in the last section, but do not admit exact application of the Rule of Restricted Choice.

Example 8:

NORTH (dummy)
A 2

SOUTH (declarer)
K Q 9 8 7 6

Declarer leads the six to the ace in dummy, and West plays the ten or jack. According to the principles developed in the previous section, although an original West holding of doubleton J 10 is more likely than the holding of a particular singleton honor, it is now more likely that West had a singleton honor than two honors doubleton.

That is true so far as it goes, but declarer should *not* finesse on the second round. West may well have J 10 3!

Example 9:

NORTH (dummy)
A 2

SOUTH (declarer)
K 9 8 7 6

South needs three tricks before the defense makes two. He leads the six to the ace, and West plays the jack. If West has the singleton jack, South must finesse coming back. Declarer must avoid a mistaken application of the Rule of Restricted Choice. It is true that singleton jack is more likely than either queen-jack or jack-ten doubleton. But the king is the right play if West has *either* of the two doubleton honor combinations, and these two together exceed the probability of a singleton jack.

Higher Odds. There are still other types of suit combinations that admit application of the Rule of Restricted Choice. Sometimes the declarer can obtain even higher odds than two-to-one in favor of the correct play. The odds mount appreciably in the following three examples:

Example 10:

NORTH (dummy)
A K Q 10

SOUTH (declarer)
4 3 2

Declarer plays off the ace and king, and the jack fails to drop. He later leads toward the tenace in the North hand. If West follows with a small card, the percentage play is the queen. Assuming no relevant information about the side suits, East is a slight favorite to hold the jack.

Example 11:

NORTH (dummy)
A K Q 9

SOUTH (declarer)
4 3 2

Dummy's holding is slightly weaker than in the previous example. Declarer cashes the ace and king. West follows with two small cards, but East drops an honor. Best play is to enter the South hand and finesse. If West follows to the third round with a small card, it is slightly less than two to one that he holds the missing honor.

Example 12:

NORTH (dummy)
A K Q 8

SOUTH (declarer)
4 3 2

Dummy's holding has been further debilitated—but the Rule of Restricted Choice is even more rewarding. When the ace and king are cashed, East drops two of the missing honors. Declarer's best play is to enter the South hand and finesse the eight.

The odds in favor of this play can be computed as follows. If East held J 109 originally, there were six ways in which he could have played two honors to the first two tricks. Only one of these ways was chosen; therefore the weight of this combination is only one-sixth its original chance. But if East held two blank honors originally, he still had two ways to play them and chose one of them. Therefore this combination carries only half its original weight. J 109 is slightly more likely than any particular doubleton (before any cards are played), but the finesse still has odds of almost three to one in its favor.

Following is an example of such a situation from actual play in a pair tournament:

Example 13:

NORTH (dummy)
2

SOUTH (declarer)
Q J 8 7 6 5 4

Declarer entered the North hand, and led the singleton deuce. East followed with the nine. South contributed the jack, and West won with the king. South later regained the lead, and was forced to lead a trump from his own hand. Should he play the queen or the eight?

If the suit originally split 4–1, the card played at this stage is of no significance. Thus a 3–2 division can be assumed. If the doubleton was in the East hand, the nine could have come from A 9 or 109, holdings which initially were equally likely. But if East had 109, he would presumably have played the ten half the time. Furthermore, if East held 109, West must have started with A K 3 and *he* might have won with the ace instead of the king. The Rule of Restricted Choice can be applied against *both* opponents in the same suit! Furthermore, the nine could have come from 1093.

Since the play of a small card on the second round caters to both applications of the Rule of Restricted Choice *and* guards against the false-card, it is clearly the superior play.

The odds in favor of this play as opposed to the play of the queen can be computed as follows: Disregarding the false-card, the odds in favor of the play of a small card are four to one. If East held A 9, the play of both opponents was restricted. There was only one way in which they could have played their cards. If East held 109, however, each opponent had a choice of two plays, giving them four different ways in which their cards could have been played.

Now consider the case in which East may have false-carded from 1093. This is another specific distribution of cards divided three and two, so it was originally equally likely as all the others. However, the weight of this combination must be decreased since the double application of the Rule of Restricted Choice still applies. Thus, the correct odds are five to one.

Applications. An application of the Rule of Restricted Choice would have saved the United States team several IMPs on this deal from the 1958 World Championship match against Italy.

Example 14:

NORTH
♠ K 4 2
♡ 8 3
◊ K 9 3 2
♣ A K 8 7

SOUTH
♠ A 5
♡ Q 10 9
◊ A Q J 7 6 5
♣ 10 4

SOUTH	NORTH
1 ◊	2 ♣
2 ◊	2 ♠
2 NT	3 NT
Pass	

West led the five of hearts which East won with the king. A low heart was returned and South was faced with a guess. After consideration, he played the queen. This proved to be the wrong move as West had led from ace-third.

The consensus of expert opinion was that South's play was correct. The *Bridge World* commentator wrote:

". . . I think South's play is correct. If the hearts are 4–4, South's play makes relatively little difference; only if the lead was from three is it crucial. And a lead from three to the jack seems a little more attractive than from three to an ace."

This point—and psychological considerations—are important factors in deciding which card to play. But such factors have a lot of ground to make up. On the auction, a heart lead might be expected from *any* holding of three to an honor. And according to the Rule of Restricted Choice, the ten is a two-to-one percentage favorite, for if East had started with five hearts to the ace-king, he might have played the ace on the first round. With five hearts to the king-jack, his choice was restricted to the play of the king. Another way of looking at it is that the combination of ace-third and king-third in West's hand are together twice as likely as jack-third. Here is another situation in which the Rule of Restricted Choice should be applied when the defenders attack a suit:

Example 15:

NORTH
♠ A K J 3
♡ Q
◇ 10 8 4
♣ A K J 10 5

SOUTH
♠ Q 10 9 8 6
♡ J 10 5
◇ K 3 2
♣ Q 9

At rubber bridge South is declarer at four spades with no East-West bidding.

West leads a small heart which East wins with the ace. It is apparent that the contract will be made unless the defense take three fast diamond tricks. East shifts to the quack of diamonds.

South knows that East is a good enough player to have shifted to the quack of diamonds from any of these holdings:

(1) ace, quack and small card(s)
(2) queen, jack and small card(s)
(3) quack and small card(s)

Even with restricted choice considerations put aside (which makes (2) less probable), playing low caters only to case (2) so South goes up with the king.

Naturally, West takes the ace of diamonds and continues with a small diamond. Now the nine becomes important. The only relevant holdings now are:

(4) East started with queen-jack and small card(s) but not the nine. (If East led from Q J 9, the game is over.)
(5) East started with quack-nine and possibly small card(s).

Queen-jack and quack-nine seem to be equally

likely possibilities but, as usual, the Rule of Restricted Choice tells us that with (4) East might have selected the other honor to lead. And so the correct play is the ten.

Similar considerations can arise when the declarer attacks a suit.

Example 16:

NORTH
♠ Q 10 9 7 6
♡ 4 2
◇ 5 3
♣ K 6 5 4

SOUTH
♠ A K J 8
♡ A K 3
◇ K 4 2
♣ 10 9 7

South plays in four spades at rubber bridge. West leads the diamond queen, East takes the ace, and returns the suit. South wins, ruffs his last diamond in dummy (East discarding a heart), plays a trump to the ace, and three rounds of hearts. West discards a diamond on the third round of hearts, which is ruffed in dummy. Now a spade to the king extracts both remaining trumps. Since both defenders have shown with two spades and 6–2 in the red suits, it is clear that both have three clubs, and the position is:

Example 17:

NORTH
♠ 10
♡ —
◇ —
♣ K 6 5 4

SOUTH
♠ J 8
♡ —
◇ —
♣ 10 9 7

South needs one club trick (or a ruff and sluff) to make his contract. He leads the nine (it can be verified that this is a superior play to the seven), and West plays the queen.

This play would be made from any of the holdings of ♣ A Q x, ♣ Q J x, or ♣ Q x x. Even with Restricted Choice set aside, the king is the best play. But East wins and returns a low club.

South must rely on the Rule of Restricted Choice and play the ten.

A little-known safety play shows that the Rule of Restricted Choice can be applied to spot cards as well as honors.

Example 18:

NORTH (dummy)
J 7 6 5

SOUTH (declarer)
A Q 9 8

South has adequate entries to both hands, and needs three tricks in this suit. The correct play is to lead low from the North hand, and finesse the queen. If this loses to the king, South next plays the ace. It is easily verified that this play will fail to produce three tricks only when West holds the blank king.

Suppose it be asked: why, after West wins the king, should declarer play West for the remaining cards rather than East?

Suppose East played the three on the first round of the suit. If East started with 10432, he had a choice of three low spots to play on the first round. He might equally well have played any of the low cards, therefore this holding can be counted only with a weight of one-third. On the other hand, if East started with the singleton three, his choice was restricted.

To check this computation, notice that if declarer goes after the suit with the intention of playing the ace on the second round, he loses only when West starts with singleton king (one distribution) but if he intends to play to the jack on the second round, he loses when East starts with the singleton four, three, or deuce (three distributions). As has been seen, the correct odds can always be discovered by returning to the original possibilities before any cards have been played (see Example 1).

The Rule of Restricted Choice may even be applied to the opening lead.

Example 19:

```
              NORTH
              ♠ A 4 3 2
              ♡ A K 4 3 2
              ◇ J 10
              ♣ J 2

              SOUTH
              ♠ K Q J 10 9 8
              ♡ 6 5
              ◇ K Q
              ♣ A Q 10
```

NORTH	SOUTH
1 ♡	4 NT
5 ♡	6 ♠
Pass	

West leads the seven of diamonds, and East wins with the ace. East shifts to a low club. Should South finesse?

There are two plays open to declarer. First, he can duck the club lead, hoping that East has the king. Second, he can rise with the ace, draw trump, and try to ruff out the heart suit. This play depends on a 3–3 heart split.

The chance of an even split in hearts is about 36%. The club finesse appears to offer a 50% chance, and therefore seems the better play. However, South must consider West's choice of opening leads. If East holds the king of clubs, West started with a collection of small cards in each minor suit. If this was the case, he would have led a club about half the time. Since

West did *not* lead a club, there is some presumption that his club-diamond holdings were not equivalent. If we assume West would lead a club half the time with equal minor suit holdings, the club finesse is only a 33% chance, and should therefore be rejected in favor of the attempt to split the hearts 3–3.

J. R.

RESULT PLAYER. A partner (or kibitzer) who helpfully suggests a line of play that would have been successful after his partner has failed with a line of play that he decided on. "Second guesser" is another term in use.

RETAIN THE LEAD. To continue to lead the first card to a trick, by virtue of having won the previous trick.

REVALUATION. The reassessment of a hand in the light of the bidding. Certain features of a hand may improve or deteriorate in value in the light of the bidding around the table. See DISTRIBUTIONAL COUNTS.

If partner shows a strong two-suited hand, minor suit honors are of greater significance in those suits, but are probably useless in the other suits. A shortage in partner's side suit, together with a few trumps, is more valuable than a shortage in another suit which is likely to be duplicated.

Kings and queens in a suit bid by an opponent improve if the bid was on the right, and deteriorate if the bid was on the left (see POSITIONAL FACTOR).

A holding of three small cards in a suit bid by an opponent at a low level is a liability, but improves if the opponents raise the suit strongly to a high level. It is then reasonable to assume that partner has not more than a singleton. In such circumstances a doubleton is less attractive, because there is an increased chance that there will be two losers.

REVERSE. An unforced rebid at the level of two or more, in a higher-ranking suit than that bid originally; a type of strength-showing bid. The original definition, used by Culbertson, was simpler: any rebid in a suit higher-ranking than the original one. This, however, permitted a one-level rebid to be described as a reverse, and as the term was in practice restricted to strength-showing sequences, the definition was modified accordingly.

The English definition of a reverse by the opener is slightly wider in scope: a bid of a third suit in an uncontested auction which prevents responder returning to the original suit at the level of two. This allows for the situation described in England as a HIGH REVERSE.

The following are standard reversing sequences:

WEST	EAST	WEST	EAST
1 ♣	1 ♠	1 ♡	2 ◇
2 ♡		2 ♠	

However, the opener's rebid in the following sequences is not a reverse:

WEST	NORTH	EAST	SOUTH
1 ♣	1 ♠	2 ◇	Pass
2 ♡			

WEST	NORTH	EAST	SOUTH
1 ◇	2 ♣	2 ♡	Pass
2 ♠			

The opposing overcall has in each case forced the bidding to a higher level, and it should be assumed that the opener's original intention was to rebid at the level of one.

All reverses, by opener or responder, show game possibilities, and the combined strength is rarely less than 23 points. Reverses by the responder are forcing in all standard systems; reverses by the opener are not forcing in STANDARD AMERICAN and ACOL, but are forcing in ROTH-STONE and KAPLAN-SHEINWOLD.

All reverses imply that the first-bid suit consists of at least five cards and that the second suit is shorter. It may sometimes be necessary to make a rebid in a three-card suit.

If all four suits are bid, it is doubtful whether the term "reverse" should be applied, and the inference that the reverser's original suit is at least five cards in length is less strong. For a conventional treatment see FOURTH SUIT FORCING AND ARTIFICIAL.

REVERSE DISCARDS. See UPSIDE-DOWN SIGNALS.

REVERSE FLANNERY. An opening bid of two hearts to show a minimum opening hand with four hearts and five spades. This convention is used almost solely by pairs that use CANAPÉ styles of bidding, e.g., BLUE TEAM CLUB, in which this distribution is difficult to show. Since such pairs usually use a two diamond opening for some other purpose, the reverse FLANNERY bid is usually two hearts.

REVERSE SEQUENCE LEAD. See RUSINOW LEAD.

REVERSE SWISS. The use of unusual jump shift rebids by opener to make a game raise of responder's suit, promising a wealth of high cards rather than just suitable distribution. For alternative uses of such jumps see FRAGMENT BIDS and SPLINTER BIDS.

REVERSING DUMMY. See DUMMY REVERSAL.

REVIEWING THE BIDDING. A player who does not hear a call distinctly may forthwith require that it be repeated. Any player may, when it is his turn to call, require that all previous calls be restated unless he is required by law to pass. In rubber bridge, after the auction is closed, any player may require such a review before his side has faced any cards. In duplicate, after the auction is closed, the declarer or either defender may require such a review at his own first turn to play. See LAWS (Law 20); LAWS OF DUPLICATE (Law 20). See also FACE DOWN LEADS; EXPLANATION OF CONVENTIONAL CALL OR PLAY.

REVOKE. The play of a card of another suit by a player who is able to follow suit, or comply with a lead penalty. Any player, including dummy if he has not forfeited his rights, may ask whether a play constitutes a revoke, and demand its correction.

If a revoke by a defender is corrected, the card played in error constitutes a penalty card.

A revoke becomes established after either member of the offending side leads or plays to the next trick, or if the revoking side makes a claim or concession. In rubber bridge there is a two-trick penalty if the revoking side won two or more tricks after the revoke trick, or a one-trick penalty if the revoking side won only one trick after the revoke trick. The trick on which the revoke occurred is counted as having been won after the revoke. In duplicate, if the revoking side won the revoke trick, that trick plus one of any tricks won thereafter by the revoking side are transferred from the revoking side; if the revoking side lost the revoke trick but won one or more tricks thereafter, the penalty is the transfer of one trick.

No player is ethically required to call attention to his own revoke, but a player should not commit a second revoke to conceal the first offense. See LAWS (Laws 61–64).

REVOLVING DISCARDS. A method of discarding which assigns a suit preference meaning to the first discard on any hand. There are two possible procedures which are similar in effect but vary slightly in execution.

(1) A low card calls for the suit below the suit in which the signal is given, and a high card for the suit above. The suits are considered in a circle with spades below clubs. Thus a low club discard on a heart lead would call for a spade, and a high club would call for a diamond. This version was developed in England, primarily for no trump defense, and is credited to J. Attwood.

(2) A low card calls for the lower-ranking of the other two suits, and a high card for the higher-ranking. This is advocated by Hy Lavinthal, the inventor of suit preference signaling, who gives this example:

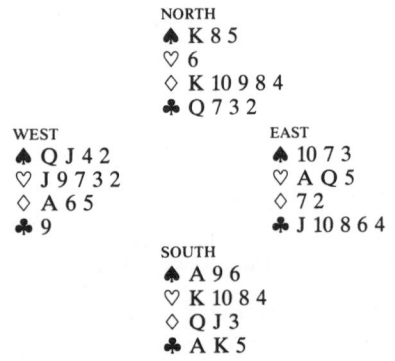

```
              NORTH
              ♠ K 8 5
              ♡ 6
              ◇ K 10 9 8 4
              ♣ Q 7 3 2
WEST                        EAST
♠ Q J 4 2                   ♠ 10 7 3
♡ J 9 7 3 2                 ♡ A Q 5
◇ A 6 5                     ◇ 7 2
♣ 9                         ♣ J 10 8 6 4
              SOUTH
              ♠ A 9 6
              ♡ K 10 8 4
              ◇ Q J 3
              ♣ A K 5
```

South plays in three no trump after opening one no trump. West leads the three of hearts, and East correctly plays the queen. (After the play of the ace there would be no way to defeat the contract.) South wins the heart queen with the king, and leads diamonds. West holds up the ace until the third round in order to get a signal from East. Normal signals would not help, because East cannot spare a heart, and a black-suit discard would be unenlightening. Using the Lavinthal discard signal the four of clubs asks for a heart, and the ten of spades would carry the same message. Using the revolving method given in (1), the three of spades or the jack of clubs would be appropriate.

REX BRIDGE. A Swedish variation on contract in which any player may introduce a Rex call at any time, ranking between spades and hearts. It is a no trump contract except that the ace of each suit ranks below the deuce, and the king is the high card in each suit, other cards maintaining their rank with respect to the king.

RHODESIA BRIDGE UNION. Formed in 1967 to replace the Central African Bridge Union when political matters broke communications between Zambia and Rhodesia. In 1975 the Union had approximately 1,100 members throughout Rhodesia, Malawi, and Mozambique. National events include Open Teams and Pairs, and Masters Pairs.

Officers, 1975:
Chairman: D. H. Salomon.
Secretary: Mrs. M. Freeman, P.O. Box 3204, Bulawayo, Rhodesia.

RHYTHM. Bidding and play at a uniform or nearly so speed. The stress here is on uniformity, and not on speed. An expert player attempts to foresee the possible problems that may evolve during the bidding of a hand before choosing his first action, so that he may avoid the agony of a later HUDDLE. Since a good player knows that a huddle followed by a pass, or even a double, places the onus on his partner not to be influenced by the fact that he had a problem, he will try to solve his future problems before they occur rather than later.

In the play of the hand, the shrewd declarer will sometimes attempt to cause opponents to be careless in the defense by playing with unusual rapidity, as though the hand was practically a PIANOLA. When confronted by a rapid tempo on declarer's part, a thoughtful defender will deliberately slow his own tempo so that he will have the opportunity to analyze declarer's play to see whether or not he has a problem.

In the play of the hand, too, the necessity for defenders to establish a rhythmic tempo to their play is important. In attempting to locate a particular card, such as an adversely held ace or queen, declarer is frequently put on the right track by applying the old adage "he who hesitates, has it." While a declarer takes advantage of a hesitation at his own risk (see PROPRIETIES), the opponent who hesitates before making a play with intent to deceive the declarer is being downright unethical.

RIDE. (1) To take a finesse with, fail to cover; for example, "dummy's jack was led and declarer let it ride." (2) A large penalty, derived from underworld argot in which a victim is "taken for a ride" by his would-be murderers.

RIFFLE. A light shuffle of the deck; a flexing of the deck with the cards bent, and held between the fingers so that a rapid motion ensues as the pack is straightened out.

RIGHT-HAND PLAYER. The player who, in rotation, acts before the referencing player. There are distinctions in the rules between irregular acts committed by the right-hand or left-hand player. The term is generally used, however, to refer to the player on declarer's right, after play commences. See RHO for a similar term.

RIGHT SIDE. The hand of the declaring partnership which can more successfully cope with the opening lead against the chosen contract. For example, assuming all other suits are adequately stopped, the hand holding A Q x opposite partner's x x x is the "right side" from which to play the hand. Sometimes there is no right or wrong side.

The "rightness" of one side and "wrongness" of the other may relate to factors other than the safety of the declarer's holding in the suit led; for example, the inability of one defender to lead the suit profitably (e.g., from K x x x when the declaring side has the ace and queen), or the inability of one defender to diagnose the most effective lead whereas from his partner's hand the right lead would be obvious.

Sometimes it is impossible to know on the basis of the two hands of the declaring partnership which side is the right side. For example, when East and West have the following heart holdings

WEST	EAST
♡ Q x	♡ A x

and a heart is led against three no trump, declarer does not know even upon seeing dummy whether or not the hand is being played from the right side. In this case the "right" side is the side that requires the hand with the heart king to be on lead.

RIGHTS, PLAYER'S. A player does not forfeit his rights if a director is called when an irregularity occurs. Neither does an opponent of the violator lose any rights if the violator or his partner is the first to call attention to the irregularity.

RIPSTRA. Over one no trump, the use of an overcall in a minor to show a three-suited hand, devised by J. G. Ripstra, Wichita, Kan. The bid guarantees a shortage in the unbid minor:

(a)	(b)
♠ A Q 4 3	♠ A Q 8 4 3
♡ K J 6 2	♡ K J 6 2
◇ K 10 6 3	◇ 6
♣ 8	♣ Q 6 3

On (a) bid two diamonds; on (b) bid two clubs. The strength qualifications for the bid naturally vary according to vulnerability. It can be made freely at favorable vulnerability, and should rarely be made at unfavorable vulnerability.

Some players use the convention with greater emphasis on the major suits, employing it with, for example, a 5–5–2–1 distribution.

A disadvantage of the convention is that it has a relatively low frequency. It is more suited to match-point events than to rubber bridge or IMP scoring. It is, however, useful in defense against a GAMBLING THREE NO TRUMP OPENING.

See also ASPRO; ASTRO; BROZEL; EXCLUSION BID; LANDY.

ROBERT COUP. The unnecessary expenditure of a trump in order to preserve a plain suit card to lead later in the play. (Analyzed and named by Robert DARVAS of Hungary.)

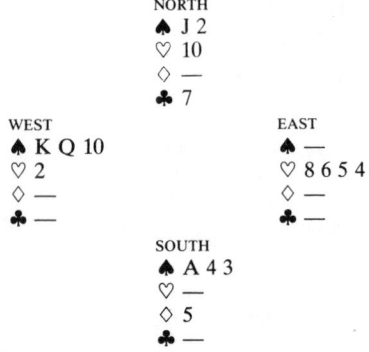

```
            NORTH
            ♠ J 2
            ♡ 10
            ◇ —
            ♣ 7
WEST                      EAST
♠ K Q 10                  ♠ —
♡ 2                       ♡ 8 6 5 4
◇ —                       ◇ —
♣ —                       ♣ —
            SOUTH
            ♠ A 4 3
            ♡ —
            ◇ 5
            ♣ —
```

Spades are trump and East leads the four of hearts. If South discards his diamond, his only other trick will be the ace of spades. But if South ruffs and *leads* the five of diamonds, West will be limited to one trump trick.

The coup may be executed early in the play as in this example given by Jeff RUBENS.

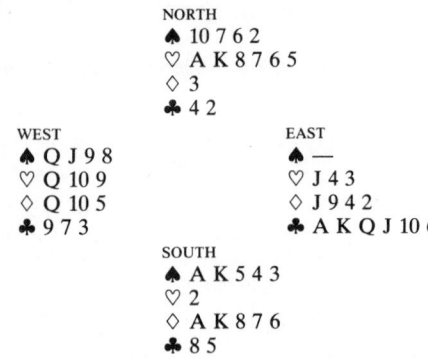

```
            NORTH
            ♠ 10 7 6 2
            ♡ A K 8 7 6 5
            ◇ 3
            ♣ 4 2
WEST                      EAST
♠ Q J 9 8                 ♠ —
♡ Q 10 9                  ♡ J 4 3
◇ Q 10 5                  ◇ J 9 4 2
♣ 9 7 3                   ♣ A K Q J 10 6
            SOUTH
            ♠ A K 5 4 3
            ♡ 2
            ◇ A K 8 7 6
            ♣ 8 5
```

Against South's four spade contract, West leads the nine of clubs. East overtakes with the ten, cashes the ace and, unwisely, continues with a third round of clubs. South ruffs in the closed hand and plays the king of spades; when the trump situation is revealed, declarer is obliged to play West for completely balanced distribution. The ace and king of diamonds and a diamond ruff, followed by the ace and king of hearts and a heart ruff, leads to this end position:

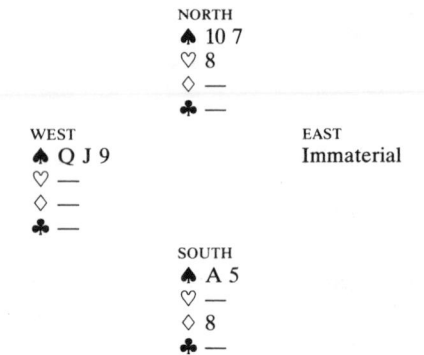

```
            NORTH
            ♠ 10 7
            ♡ 8
            ◇ —
            ♣ —
WEST                      EAST
♠ Q J 9                   Immaterial
♡ —
◇ —
♣ —
            SOUTH
            ♠ A 5
            ♡ —
            ◇ 8
            ♣ —
```

South produces his last diamond and West has no reply. The essential feature of the play was for South to reduce his trump holding by accepting the ruff and sluff in the long hand. The fifth spade could not be of use against any distribution but might get in the way if trumps broke badly. See also UNDERRUFF.

ROBERTSON POINT-COUNT. A point count published by Edmund Robertson in 1904.

> Ace counts 7 points
> King counts 5 points
> Queen counts 3 points
> Jack counts 2 points
> Ten counts 1 point.

A slight variation of this is the Bamberger point count used by the VIENNA SYSTEM, in which the jack counts one point and the ten is not counted.

With a total of 64 points in the pack, if both hands are balanced, 39 points should produce a game in no trump or a major suit; and 52 points should produce a small slam.

ROBOT BRIDGE PLAYER. A Bendix G-15 computer was built in the shape of a bridge robot, into which Prof. R. F. Jackson (University of Delaware) programmed bridge skills. It was displayed at a Western Regional in 1958, in a hand requiring a VIENNA COUP to make a grand slam. Opponents' plays were typed into Sputternik, as the robot was called, by the operator, and Sputternik typed out his and the dummy's plays. See AUTOMATON CONTRACT BRIDGE PLAYER.

ROCK-CRUSHER HANDS. Hands of really enormous proportions, laden with points. A forcing two opening bid would usually qualify as a rock-crusher.

ROCKWELL TROPHY. For the National Mixed Pair Championship, donated by Mrs. Helen Rockwell in 1946; it replaced the HILLIARD TROPHY contested as a four-session event at the Fall

Nationals, under which heading past results are listed.

ROMAN ASKING BIDS. A feature of the ROMAN SYSTEM which, in part, is also included in the 1969 version of the KAPLAN-SHEINWOLD SYSTEM. Both systems limit the use of the asking bids to jump bids that would otherwise be meaningless; so if an opening bid of one spade is raised to three spades, four clubs would be a cue-bid and five clubs would be an asking bid. The Roman responses are:

1st step	No control
2nd step	Singleton
3rd step	King
4th step	Ace
5th step	Void
6th step	Ace-king, or ace-queen (rare)

If responder cannot be short in the asked suit, the second and fifth steps are dropped. An older and better known version of Roman asking bids which is a feature of the Kaplan-Sheinwold system, restricts the responses to four steps. First step shows no control; second step shows king or singleton; third step shows ace or void; fourth step shows ace-king (rarely ace-queen) or perhaps singleton ace. These are called ALPHA ASKING BIDS.

Roman asking bids are also used in certain specialized sequences, the most common of which occur after a one club opening bid and a jump in a new suit by opener. Responder bids according to his holding in opener's suit as follows:

1st step	Two or three low cards
2nd step	Singleton or void
3rd step	Ace, king, or queen singleton or doubleton
4th step	Ace, king or queen third
5th step	Four low cards
6th step	Ace, king, or queen fourth
7th step	Two of the top three honors
8th step	Two of the top three honors fourth
9th step	Three top honors

These are called BETA ASKING BIDS. See also ASKING BIDS; FULWILER CONVENTION; PRECISION ASKING BIDS; ROMEX TRUMP ASKING BIDS; SUPER PRECISION ASKING BIDS; SPLINTER BIDS; VOID-SHOWING BIDS.

ROMAN BLACKWOOD. A four no trump convention which can help to determine which ace is missing if the partnership holds three. The responses are:

Five clubs	no ace or three aces
Five diamonds	one ace or four aces
Five hearts	two aces of the same color or rank
Five spades	two aces of unlike color and rank

A variation adopted by some BLUE TEAM CLUB users is to reverse the meanings of the traditional Roman responses of five clubs and five diamonds; the five club response is used to show one or four aces in order to facilitate further non-Blackwood exploration of slam on the hands where slam is a more likely proposition.

A subsequent five no trump bid asks for kings in the same way.

The four no trump bidder can easily determine from the previous auction the meaning of a five club or five diamond response. Five spades is also unambiguous, but five heart response does not pinpoint the aces precisely. If, for example, a player with the club ace receives the response of five hearts, he knows that his partner holds the heart ace and another ace.

A British variation is designed to avoid this ambiguity:

Five hearts	two aces of the same color
Five spades	two aces of the same rank
Five no trump	two aces of unlike color and rank

This may, however, rule out the possibility of asking for kings. The general advantage of the convention is that it may be effective when the four no trump bidder has a void. If his partner has two aces, it is usually possible to tell whether the void is facing an ace.

When making a decision to go to the six-level, it is usually sufficient to know the number of aces possessed by the partnership. But for grand slam purposes, the identity of a missing king may be vital. For this reason some partnerships abandon the precise identification of the two aces held, and use the five heart response to show two aces with no extra values, and the five spade response to show two aces in a hand with extra values. Alternatively, there can be advantages in using these Roman responses in combination with other conventions. See ACE-SHOWING RESPONSES; BYZANTINE BLACKWOOD; ROMAN GERBER; ROMAN KEY CARD BLACKWOOD.

ROMAN GERBER. A modified version of the GERBER four club slam convention. A response of four diamonds shows three aces or none; four hearts shows four aces or one; four spades shows two aces. If the four club bidder continues with the cheapest bid, he asks for kings and subsequently queens in the same way. The next-cheapest bid asks for clarification of the previous response. With one or three of the specified honor cards, responder bids the control he has or does not have. With two honors to be identified, he makes the minimum bid if they are of the same color; the second possible bid if they are unmatched in color and rank; and the third possible bid if both are majors or minors. See ACE IDENTIFICATION.

ROMAN JUMP OVERCALL. The use of a jump overcall to show a two-suited hand, specifically the suit bid and the next-higher-ranking suit excluding opener's suit. For example, if the opening bid is one diamond, an overcall of

two hearts	shows hearts and spades
two spades	shows spades and clubs
three clubs	shows clubs and hearts

The strength shown is about the minimum for an opening bid or slightly more. Very strong two-suiters are shown by a conventional overcall of two no trump.

ROMAN KEY CARD BLACKWOOD. A form of BLACKWOOD in which the king of trumps is counted as a fifth ace, and the responses are of the ROMAN BLACKWOOD space-saving variety:

Five clubs	0 or 3 aces
Five diamonds	1 or 4 aces
Five hearts	2 or 5 aces

The five spade response can be reserved to show two aces with extra values.

ROMAN LEADS. See RUSINOW LEADS and FOURTH HIGHEST.

ROMAN SYSTEM. Developed by Walter AVARELLI and Giorgio BELLADONNA, and used successfully in many WORLD CHAMPIONSHIPS. The chief features are:

One club opening is forcing, and may show four distinct types of hands. It usually shows 12–16 points with 4–3–3–3 or 4–4–3–2 distribution. After a negative response of one diamond (usually less than 9 points), the opener bids a major if he can, or one no trump. After a positive response in a suit (minimum of 8–11 points), the opener shows a minimum by a single raise, a rebid of one no trump, or a bid of a new suit on the same level.

Other positive responses are: one no trump, 12–16 points; two no trump, more than 16 points, over which opener rebids conventionally to show his exact point-count.

One club may also be bid with (1) 21–22 points and balanced distribution, in which case the rebid will be a jump in no trump; or (2) an unbalanced game-going hand, in which case the opener will jump rebid in a suit and responder rebids conventionally by six steps to show his holding in opener's suit; or (3) a two-suited hand with at least a four-card club suit and five cards in another suit and 17–20 points, in which case the opener will rebid in clubs.

If an opponent overcalls a one club opening, an immediate cue-bid by responder shows 12–16 points without a stopper and suggests a no trump contract.

One diamond, one heart, and one spade openings are natural (usually at least a four-card suit) and forcing, and guarantee at least one suit of more than four cards. With two suits, the shorter suit is opened (CANAPÉ principle), unless the shorter suit is clubs. With 5–3–3–2 distribution the opening suit is occasionally in the lower-ranking three-card suit other than clubs. A five-card suit may be opened and rebid with a minimum.

With fewer than 9 points, responder makes a single raise or makes the cheapest possible response, both of which are negative. Rebids are natural except for one no trump, which shows a minimum opening with five cards in the negatively bid suit. Other suit responses are positive, showing 9 points or more. No trump responses are as over one club (except one spade—one no trump, which is negative).

One no trump opening shows a balanced hand with 17–20 points. Responses of two clubs and two diamonds are GLADIATOR. Responses of two of a major or three of a minor are forcing to game, and opener rebids by steps to show support and opening-bid strength; the first two steps show minimum openings with poor and good support respectively; the third and fourth steps show maximum openings with poor and good support respectively. Other responses are natural and limited.

Two club and two diamond openings show three-suited hands (4–4–4–1 or 5–4–4–0 distributions) with 12–16 and 17–20 points respectively. A response of two no trump is positive and asks the opener to show his short suit. Minimum suit responses are negative and may sometimes have to be made in a three-card

suit. If the suit response strikes opener's shortage, he makes the cheapest possible suit rebid. See also ROMAN TWO DIAMONDS.

Two heart and two spade openings show at least a five-card suit, together with four or five clubs. A two no trump response asks opener to clarify his distribution by bidding a three-card suit with 5–4–3–1 distribution, three clubs with 5–4–2–2, three no trump with 5–5–2–1, four of a minor with 5–5–3–0, or rebidding a six-card suit.

Two no trump opening shows a balanced hand with 23–24 points. Responses are as over one no trump.

Asking bids are used after a suit has been agreed, usually a jump in a new suit at the level of four or higher. If responder can be short in the asked suit, the responses are by six steps: the first step shows no control, second step shows a singleton, third step shows the king, fourth step shows the ace, fifth step shows a void, and the sixth step shows the ace-king, or occasionally the ace-queen. If responder cannot be short in the asked suit, the second and fifth steps are deleted. Different asking bids are also used in certain special situations. See ROMAN ASKING BIDS.

Overcalls are limited to a maximum of 12 points, and are normally made only on a good suit.

Take-out doubles show 12–16 points. If third hand passes, responder bids his shortest suit if he can do so at the level of one or two. See EXCLUSION BID. Otherwise normal responses are given. If third hand bids, a double is for take-out.

One no trump overcall is equivalent to a one no trump opening bid, although the distribution might be slightly unbalanced. Responses are as over a one no trump opening.

Jump overcall shows a two-suiter, the bid suit and the next higher-ranking, excluding the opener's suit. The distribution is usually 5–5 or 5–6 with a five- to six-loser hand.

Two no trump jump overcall shows a strong two-suiter, excluding the opener's suit. Responder bids the lower unbid minor and the overcaller bids an unbid suit, holding the bid suit and partner's conventionally named suit, or three no trump with both unbid suits.

Overcalls in the opponent's suit are natural. A jump cue-bid shows a very strong three-suiter with a singleton or void in the opponents' suit and a four-loser hand. See also ROMAN BLACKWOOD.

ROMAN TWO DIAMONDS. A bid showing a strong hand with 5–4–4–0 or 4–4–4–1 distribution. This feature of the ROMAN system can be used with standard methods. The original range of 17–20 is sometimes increased by one or two points. A two no trump response is positive, and asks the opener to bid his short suit. Other responses are natural and negative, but may be in an economical three-card suit. If the response is in opener's shortage he makes the minimum possible rebid.

An alternative method of responding, proposed by Marshall Miles, is to respond two hearts on all weak hands. Other responses are natural and forcing to game. In all cases the opener bids his shortage on the second round, except that a no trump rebid shows a shortage in the suit bid by responder, whether naturally or artificially.

A version of the Roman Two Diamonds is also a part of BLUE TEAM CLUB. See BLUE TEAM TWO DIAMONDS.

ROMEX SYSTEM. A two club system with special bids to show hands of intermediate strength devised by Dr. George ROSENKRANZ of Mexico City. The distinguishing feature of the system is the use of the MEXICAN TWO-DIAMOND opening (showing a balanced hand with 19–20 HCP) and the DYNAMIC NO TRUMP opening (showing a balanced hand with 21–22 HCP or an unbalanced hand within one or two points of the requirements for a two club opening).

Two clubs (artificial, for very strong hands) and one-bids are normal, except that one-bids are limited by the failure to open two diamonds or one no trump. The lack of a natural no trump opening is balanced by the special one-bid limitation: opener, with a balanced hand, can make a minimum rebid in no trump with 13–16 HCP or jump with 17–18 HCP. An EASTERN SCIENTIFIC structure is used after major-suit openings.

Special methods include: No trump cue-bids to show the ace and king of the trump suit; special asking-bids, in preference to cue-bidding, after a strength- or weakness-showing opening; the "Romex raise" to show extra values through an otherwise impossible four no trump bid; step responses to many strong bids and asking-bids; emphasis on slam-bidding devices. See ROMEX TRUMP ASKING BIDS.

J. R.

ROMEX TRUMP ASKING BIDS. A series of asking bids designed to learn the strength of responder's holding in a particular suit, that suit being assumed to be trumps unless and until opener makes an asking bid in another suit. The asking bid, used after a game-forcing two club opening in the ROMEX System, is initiated by a jump shift rebid by opener. The responses are in steps:

1st step	void or singleton
2nd step	doubleton
3rd step	three cards
4th step	four or more cards
5th step	singleton ace, king, or queen

If responder shows any holding other than a singleton, opener can ask about responder's honor cards in the suit by making the cheapest no trump bid. The responses are

1st step	none of top three honors
2nd step	one of top three honors
3rd step	two of top three honors
4th step	all three top honors

If opener bids a new suit, he in effect changes the trump suit and the asking process begins anew. See also ASKING BIDS; PRECISION ASKING BIDS; ROMAN ASKING BIDS; SUPER PRECISION ASKING BIDS.

ROMEX TWO DIAMOND OPENING. See MEXICAN TWO DIAMONDS.

ROSLER MOVEMENT. See TEAM-OF-FOUR MOVEMENT.

ROTATION. The order in which actions take place at the bridge table. In the bidding stage, the dealer has the first action, followed in turn by the player on his left, his partner, and the right-hand opponent. In the play of the cards, the player to declarer's left has the initial lead. The duty of making the initial lead to each subsequent trick falls on the player whose card was the winning card played to the preceding trick. Any deviation from this clockwise rotation in bidding or play constitutes an irregularity; in tournaments, the director should be summoned when such an irregularity occurs.

ROTH CLUB SYSTEM. A ONE CLUB SYSTEM devised by Alvin ROTH and based on many facets of the ROTH-STONE SYSTEM, including strong no trump opening and five card majors. The one club opening promises at least 19 points if the hand is balanced, or at least 17 if unbalanced. A two club opening promises a genuine club suit and a five card spade suit. The one diamond opening is a catchall bid used for other hands, includng hands with long club suit.

ROTH POINT-COUNT. See DISTRIBUTIONAL COUNTS.

ROTH-STONE ASTRO. See ASTRO.

ROTH-STONE SYSTEM. Developed by Alvin ROTH and Tobias STONE. Many of their ideas have been adopted by tournament players using standard methods. Since the publication of the 1958 book on the system, Roth has modified the system considerably, describing his new ideas in a second book published in 1968. Among the features of the revised system are:

(1) Sound opening bids in first and second position. The minimum requirement is 14 points, including at least 10 high-card points, which is about 1 point more than in standard methods.

(2) Five-card majors in first and second position.

(3) ONE NO TRUMP RESPONSE TO A MAJOR, FORCING by an unpassed hand after a major-suit opening.

(4) A single raise in a major suit is constructive. It shows 10–12 points and is never passed by a first- or second-seat opener. With a void or singleton in a side suit and 10–12 points, responder, if he is an unpassed hand, jump raises to show shortness in the other major (e.g., one heart—three hearts shows a singleton or void in spades), or jumps to four clubs or four diamonds with shortness in the bid suit. A strong major raise is shown by a conventional jump to three clubs, which guarantees a minimum of four trumps and 13 points. Opener usually rebids conventionally to show whether or not he has a singleton, or, if not, the number of high trump honors he holds, but he may jump in a new suit as an asking bid.

(5) Two-over-one response (e.g., two clubs in re-

sponse to one spade) normally shows at least 11 points. It is forcing for one round and guarantees that responder will bid again.

(6) Opening bids of one club and one diamond may be prepared with a three-card suit. After a major-suit response, opener jumps to four of his minor with a strong six-card suit and weak four-card support for responder's major, jumps to four of the major with strong four-card support and a weak minor suit, jumps to four of the other minor (or to four hearts after a one spade response) with a singleton in the bid suit and a strong raise, or jumps to three of the other major with a strong, balanced hand and four-card support.

(7) Jump shift responses are weak, except by a passed hand in a non-competitive auction.

(8) Over one of a suit, a jump to two no trump by an unpassed hand is unlimited, at least 13 points, and a jump to three no trump is BABY BLACKWOOD.

(9) After a third- or fourth-seat major-suit opening, responder jumps to three no trump to show a strong, distributional raise, jumps to four clubs to show a distributional raise with slightly fewer high cards, or jumps to four diamonds to show a strong raise with no singleton or void.

(10) One no trump opening is standard (16–18). Responses of two clubs and two diamonds are forcing and slam-try STAYMAN respectively. Two no trump forces opener to bid a minor; if responder then rebids a major, it shows a singleton. Jump responses to the three-level are weak, but mildly invitational in the major suits. TWO-WAY STAYMAN is also used over two no trump (21–23), except that three clubs shows slam interest.

(11) TEXAS.

(12) GERBER over no trump openings.

(13) Two club opening is forcing to game. Two hearts is the conventional negative response and two diamonds is an artificial positive response, showing the equivalent of an ace and a king. Responses of two and three no trump show balanced hands with 8–9 and 10–12 scattered points respectively.

(14) WEAK TWO-BIDS with two no trump the only forcing response by an unpassed hand. Two no trump and a raise of opener's major are invitational by a passed hand.

(15) Three no trump opening shows a strong preempt in one of the four suits. If responder bids four clubs, he warns opener not to bid game in a minor.

(16) NEGATIVE DOUBLES.

(17) RESPONSIVE DOUBLES only after an overcall (e.g., one club—one spade—two clubs, double is responsive).

(18) WEAK JUMP OVERCALLS.

(19) UNUSUAL NO TRUMP.

(20) Bids in the opponent's suit are sometimes natural. After one club—pass—one spade, an overcall of two clubs or two spades would be natural.

(21) A take-out double may be light, 10 high-card points with 4-4-4-1 or 4-4-5-0 distribution. An immediate cue-bid of opponent's suit is equivalent to a strong take-out double, 18 points or more.

(22) When an opponent overcalls one no trump, two clubs is a weak take-out and double is a strong take-out, 8 points or more, but may be passed.

(23) When an opponent opens one no trump, two clubs and two diamonds show the bid minor and spades, three clubs and three diamonds show the bid minor and hearts, and double shows the major suits unless the no trump opening is weak, in which case it shows at least 15 high-card points.

(24) After one heart or one spade—pass—one no trump, two club and two diamond overcalls show the bid minor and the unbid major.

(25) After one club or one diamond—pass—one no trump, two club and two diamond overcalls show the unbid minor with spades or hearts respectively, and double shows the major suits.

(26) In a competitive auction where a sacrifice may be considered, a double of a slam contract at equal or favorable vulnerability shows no defensive tricks.

(27) A balancing bid of two clubs is equivalent to a light take-out double.

ROTHSCHILD TROPHY. For the Sub-Senior Masters Team Championship; donated by Mrs. Meyer D. Rothschild in 1938 for the National Amateur Team-of-Four Championship; contested at the Summer Nationals, under which heading past results are listed.

ROUND. A part of a session of bridge at a tournament, usually one-thirteenth, during which the players and the boards remain at a table. When two boards are played during a round, its duration should be about fifteen minutes.

In rubber bridge, a round refers to the three or four rubbers (or double rubbers) during which each of the players plays with each of the other players as partners.

ROUND HAND. A colloquialism for a hand with BALANCED DISTRIBUTION, particularly 4-3-3-3. Flat and square are also used to describe such a hand.

ROUND ROBIN. A form of competition in which each of the contesting groups (usually teams, though occasionally pairs) plays against each of the other groups entered in head-on competition. "League" is used as an equivalent term in England.

Round-robin team contests are increasing in popularity in individual playing areas, frequently requiring months to complete. KNOCKOUT TOURNAMENTS frequently end up in a round robin of surviving teams. The 1964 OLYMPIAD consisted of a round robin among the fifteen competing women's teams, and as a preliminary to the finals among the twenty-nine open teams.

When a round robin fails to establish a winner, some other device must be used, such as QUOTIENT.

ROUNDED. A term used to describe the combination of hearts and clubs, these suits having pips rounded at the tops. The converse is POINTED to indicate spades and diamonds.

ROUNDING OFF. At rubber bridge, it is customary to record the results of a rubber to the nearest 100 points. In America, 50 points are counted as an extra hundred, but in Europe it is customary to ignore them. For maintaining a running record of the results of a rubber game, a BACK SCORE sheet is used, showing each player as plus or minus some number of hundreds of points, and this provides the basis of settling the game. Some players use a banker who distributes poker chips at the beginning of a game, and rubbers are settled at the end of each by passing the chips from losers to winners, and they are redeemed by the banker at the end of the session.

ROVER MOVEMENT. An alternative method of handling an extra pair in duplicate tournaments to the PHANTOM PAIR or BUMP MITCHELL movements. The extra pair is given a North-South number, one greater than the number of tables in play. The pair enters the game by taking the place, for one round only, of any North-South pair, after sitting out the first round. After the round, the displaced pair resumes its original position, and the rover pair moves toward the lower numbered table (in the same direction as the boards) but skips a table for each move. If the number of tables in the game (not counting the rover) is even, the rover skips an extra table at the same time that the East-West traveling pairs skip one table. In an eight-table game plus a rover, the rover would play at tables 8, 6, 4, 2, then skip an extra table to 7, 5, and 3. The rover and all displaced pairs must have their scores factored up to be comparable to those pairs which did not miss a set of boards.

ROYAL SPADES (popularly LILIES). The spade suit when scored at 9 points per trick, in an early phase of bridge whist.

RUBBER. A unit of measurement of games at home or club bridge, hence the expression, "rubber bridge." A rubber must consist of at least two games, but not more than three. The first side to win two games wins the rubber, and a premium is earned on the basis of whether the opponents have won any game. If they have not, the winning side's premium is larger (700 as against 500). If a rubber is stopped before either side has actually won two games, it is called an "unfinished rubber," and there is a somewhat smaller bonus (300) to the side having won one game. If no game has been won by either side but a partial does exist, there is a small premium (50) to the side having the partial.

RUBBER BRIDGE. The original and always the most popular form of contract. However, DUPLICATE and CHICAGO bridge have increased in popularity. Rubber bridge was of course the basis for the development of the game that has occurred in the past thirty-five years, attracting much of the original in-terest of players all over the world. Rubber bridge is played for points, which sometimes may represent a monetary value per point. Tactics at this type of bridge differ from those used at tournament or dupli-cate. The premium for winning a rubber of two games where the opponents have not won a game is high, and even in a three-game rubber, that is, one where both sides have scored a game, the premium is substantial. In rubber bridge, therefore, consider-able effort is expended toward winning games, and risks in the bidding are taken to secure that end. (But see VALUE OF GAME.) Penalties can be inflicted by the opponents if too little regard for safety has been ob-served by a side. These penalties become more severe when the incurring side has won a game, that is, when they become vulnerable. The competitive features of rubber bridge are sometimes overlooked by players who manifest their principal bridge en-deavors in the tournament field. Many club players deplore the tendency toward Chicago and long for the days when rubber was the only game played. In fact, there are large clubs in the East and elsewhere where rubber bridge has disappeared entirely in favor of Chicago, rubber being a somewhat slower type of action, and Chicago being fast-paced. See PARTNERSHIP RUBBER BRIDGE.

RUBBER BRIDGE TACTICS. Should one be willing to go two down at equal vulnerability to save game?

At duplicate this is a matter of simple arithmetic. Each time the sacrifice will show a profit, for other things being equal, one concedes 300 or 500 against a game that is worth 400 or 600. At rubber bridge other things are rarely equal, and simple arithmetic is a poor guide. The issue is determined by the personal equation. With a good partner and mediocre oppo-nents, there is always the risk of phantom sacrifice, of going down to prevent them from going down.

Opponents may have a certain game, one that would be made "in the other room." But there is no other room, and mediocre opponents miss a good many certain games.

Conversely, when partner is the weakest player at the table, the cheapest sacrifice may prove expen-sive, for what attraction can there be in prolonging a rubber when you start every hand at a disadvantage?

Broadly speaking, there is little future in sacri-ficing at rubber bridge. The profit margin is too narrow, and it is generally best to leave this dubious pastime to the other side.

When the best slams are not so good. How about slams? At duplicate, the odds are clearly in favor of bidding a slam which depends on one of two finesses. At rubber bridge, the decision never rests with ab-stract figures, but always with concrete personalities.

Who will be declarer, you or partner? If it is partner and he goes down playing it his way, it will be poor consolation to know that he would have made it had he played it differently. It will be more painful still if on the next hand he concedes a needless penalty and then, through bad defense, allows oppo-nents to bring home an impossible slam.

Of course, when a good partner is in control, and opponents may be expected to slip in defense, you can bid slams with less than an even money chance. Faces alter cases, and it's the people, not the mathematical probabilities, that make the true odds.

Double the player, not the contract. If an overbidder calls four spades, double him if there seems any reason for doing so. But if the four spade call was made by an underbidder, pass. When in doubt, you double the man rather than the contract.

The statistically minded can look at it from another angle. The overbidder's record shows that he often goes down. He is a bad risk actuarially, and in doubling him the odds are favorable.

Not so the underbidder, who seldom gives away penalties. The best tactics against him are to open light, to intervene boldly, and to make a general show of strength. You may put him off, but you are not likely to score much above the line. The underbidder's main contribution to your welfare will come from the games and slams he makes but dares not bid.

Confusion—for confusion's sake. Psychic bids can be most rewarding, yet here again everything depends on the uncertain quality of partner and opponents. Each player must be studied separately and treated strictly on his demerits.

In principle it pays to create confusion for confusion's sake, so long as you remain in control. With little defense against opponent's major, but support for partner's minor, you can bid no trump. With support for partner's major you can bid a non-existent minor. If you are doubled, you have a ready-made escape, and meanwhile you may throw the other side off balance. Sometimes you will steal a hand that does not belong to you. Sometimes you will mislead an opponent in the play of the hand. But you will draw your biggest dividends on all those occasions, the vast majority, when you bid honestly and are unjustly suspected of bluffing. For it is not psyching but the reputation of psyching which creates confusion in the adversary's mind.

Much the same is true of inhibitory bids. If you have decided to bid six spades over partner's three spades, let us say, you may derive a twofold advantage from a spurious cue-bid. Holding a worthless doubleton in clubs, call four clubs on the way round. It may discourage a club lead, which you do not want. Better still, it may induce the lead you do want next time, when you make your cue-bid, deliberately, on A K J or A Q or K x. Of course, you must be careful to throw the bait to the *same* opponent. First sow suspicion, then exploit it. For it is the essence of rubber bridge to play the players, as well as the cards.

Every hand forms part of a pattern. In theory every hand must be treated in isolation, but in practice this is not true at all. At roulette red and black have equal chances every time the wheel spins regardless of how many reds or blacks have come up before. That is because the wheel is a purely mechanical device.

As soon as the human element is introduced, this no longer applies. Every move is influenced by those

that have preceded it, and neither emotion nor superstition can be left out of account.

If you have been doubled into game, you may take certain risks in part-score situations for the next half-hour or so—provided that you are up against the same opponents. They will surely hang back, fearful of suffering the same ignominy twice in quick succession.

The partner problem. Handling a weak partner is, perhaps, the most difficult art at rubber bridge. Of course, you want to prevent partner playing the hand, and of course you don't want him to know that you are trying to prevent him. Fortunately, weak players are singularly unobservant and with a little luck you will get away with it again and again.

On a balanced hand, intending to rebid no trumps, there is a good case for opening a weak minor in preference to a strong major. That way you are likely to get the no trump bid in first. At the same time, you may discourage an unwelcome lead. Even a one diamond opening on J x x may have something to commend it. It is a prepared bid—prepared to steer the contract into your own hand.

In defense, a little cynicism is seldom out of place. Opponents are in three no trump. What do you lead from K 7 6 in a suit bid by partner? The six? Are you sure that he deserves the compliment? Perhaps he was brought up to believe that it is sinful not to lead the highest of partner's suit. Humor him. Never hesitate to do the wrong thing with the right partner.

There are times when you can take advantage of partner's shortcomings, reversing on the sketchiest of values or false-carding wantonly. Opponents may be misled with impunity when partner is not good enough to be deceived.

When not to concentrate. The key to success at bridge at every level lies in concentration. But whereas at duplicate, and more especially in pairs events, concentration can never be relaxed, since every hand can be a top or bottom, at rubber bridge the good tactician takes an occasional breather, just as champions do at boxing or at tennis. If declarer can fulfill his contract of two diamonds he need not try too hard to make three or four. In terms of money the result will probably be the same, so why waste the effort? An extra ounce of mental energy may be all-important on the next hand or on the one after when the contract is a difficult game or slam.

The winning player has his lapses, but he usually knows when he can afford to have them, and is quick to concentrate and to give of his best when the need arises. That is why when he nods the cards so often forgive him. See also PARTNERSHIP PSYCHOLOGY.

V. M.

RUBBER DUPLICATE. A form of duplicate bridge using rubber bridge scoring. The boards are pre-duplicated by the director in preparation for a straight team-of-four match, and each deal is played simultaneously at the two tables. Play continues exactly as at rubber bridge, ignoring, of course, the vulnerability shown by the boards, until a rubber is scored at either table. The other table is then instructed to add up its score as an unfinished rubber, counting the normal 300 for a game and 50 for a part-score. The table at which a rubber was completed is entitled to know whether a rubber was scored in the other room also, but *not* by which side it was scored.

The final score is calculated by adding the precise results of all rubbers (i.e., not rounded off to the nearest 100) including the unfinished rubber, if any, when play ends. It is usual to play the match in two equal halves, with a change of opponents at half-time.

The director must move constantly between the two playing tables to observe the possibilities that a rubber will be completed. Table 1, for example, must not be permitted to start Board 8 if there is a chance that Table 2 will complete a rubber on Board 7.

Two matches can be conducted simultaneously using the same boards. In a sixteen-board half-match, Match A would start with Board 1 while Match B started with Board 9. This introduces the possibility of a fouled board, and the director should have an extra pre-duplicated board available to meet this situation.

Rubber duplicate is rarely played except in England, where the Devonshire Club Cup, a knock-out contest between leading London social clubs, is conducted on these lines. It has been won many times by the Royal Automobile Club.

RUBIN TRANSFERS. Devised by Ira RUBIN of Paramus, N.J., as a method of preventing the opponents from finding a cheap sacrifice against a game or slam, and used in the 1966 WORLD CHAMPIONSHIP.

Four clubs opening describes a hand containing either a long, semi-solid major suit with 3½ to 4 honor tricks, or a long minor suit with 2½ to 3 honor tricks and no voids. Responder will usually bid four diamonds to allow opener to show his suit. Major-suit responses are slam tries, and minor-suit responses show a solid suit missing the king, queen, or jack, which opener may raise to slam with three first-round controls.

Four diamonds opening shows a strong major suit with 2½ to 3 honor tricks. Four hearts is the normal response, while four spades shows active interest in a heart slam, but only mild interest in a spade slam. Responses in the minors are cue-bids, agreeing either major as trump, and four no trump is BLACKWOOD.

Four no trump opening shows a strong minor-suit hand with one or more voids. Responder bids five spades or five no trump with three or four aces respectively.

Game openings in any of the four suits are weak pre-empts, denying much high-card strength. Alternatively, a hand with greater high-card or playing strength can be shown by an opening bid of one followed by a jump to game.

See FOUR CLUB AND FOUR DIAMOND OPENING TRANSFERS.

RUFF. To trump a lead of a plain suit, other than the trump suit, winning the trick if no higher trump is played.

RUFF AND DISCARD (or Ruff and Sluff). When a defender leads a suit of which both declarer and dummy are void, the declarer gets a ruff and sluff; he can discard a loser from one hand and ruff in the other.

This may be declarer's only way of making a contract when too many losers are present. To compel a defender to give a ruff and sluff, he must be placed in the lead after all his safe exit cards have been removed.

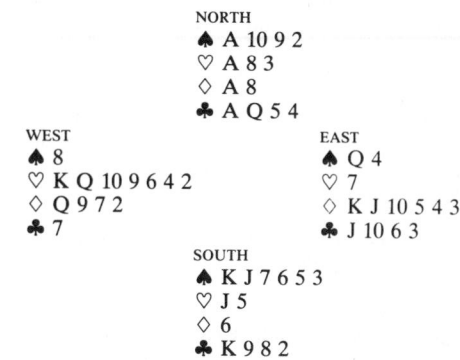

West opens three hearts, North doubles, South jumps to four spades, and North raises to six. Owing to the unfortunate club break, declarer apparently has a club loser as well as a heart. The two suits are guarded by different opponents, so no squeeze operates, and the only way to make the contract is by compelling a defender to concede a ruff and discard.

The heart lead is won, trumps are drawn and clubs are tested. Finding that he has a club loser, declarer continues by ruffing out diamonds and playing off the remaining clubs, throwing East into the lead. As expected after West's opening three-bid, East has no more hearts, and has to return a diamond. South throws the heart jack fom his own hand, and ruffs in dummy.

A defensive weapon

It can be winning defense to present declarer with a ruff and sluff even when the defender has safe exit cards in other suits. The usual occasion is when declarer is short of trumps, and has to lose the lead before he can develop a side suit.

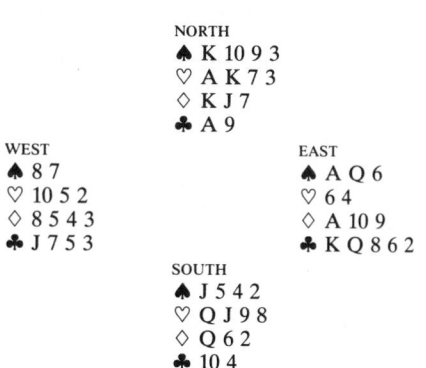

East's one club opening is passed to North, who doubles. South responds two hearts, and passes his partner's raise to three. West has no clue to the killing spade lead, and plays a club, which is won in dummy. After three rounds of trumps, South leads a spade to dummy's ten, and the queen wins, West starting an echo.

East may cash a club, and exit passively with ace and another spade, expecting to beat the hand if West has the diamond queen, for then the declarer would eventually lose two diamonds. If East follows that reasoning, the contract is made because South has the diamond queen.

By forcing declarer with repeated club leads, East succeeds no matter who has the diamond queen and despite giving South a ruff and sluff. After the spade queen, East plays a second and third round of clubs. It does not matter in which hand declarer ruffs, for when East comes in with the spade ace he plays another club, taking declarer's last trump. South has only eight tricks. East has three, and must make the diamond ace and the long club.

The lesser evil

In the above example the defender had no choice but to concede a ruff and sluff. Sometimes he has an option, albeit an unattractive one, such as leading into a tenace. If the situation does not lend itself to complete analysis, the defender should prefer to give a ruff and sluff rather than concede a trick in a side suit. This is particularly so when both declarer and dummy have four cards in the same side suit.

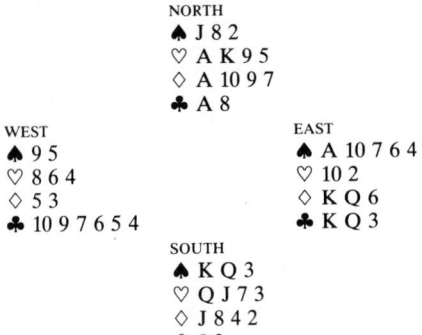

```
              NORTH
              ♠ J 8 2
              ♡ A K 9 5
              ◇ A 10 9 7
              ♣ A 8
WEST                        EAST
♠ 9 5                       ♠ A 10 7 6 4
♡ 8 6 4                     ♡ 10 2
◇ 5 3                       ◇ K Q 6
♣ 10 9 7 6 5 4             ♣ K Q 3
              SOUTH
              ♠ K Q 3
              ♡ Q J 7 3
              ◇ J 8 4 2
              ♣ J 2
```

East's one spade opening is passed to North, who doubles. South lands in four hearts, and the defense starts with two rounds of spades. Fearing a ruff, declarer pulls three rounds of trumps before touching the minor suits. South places East with all the missing high cards, and takes out the third round of spades before putting East on play with ace and another club. East counts declarer for four diamonds in his own hand as well as in dummy, so he gives him a ruff and sluff instead of leading a diamond. South still has to lose two diamonds, and is defeated, but had East returned a diamond the contract would have been made.

On the relatively few occasions when it is better to lead into a tenace than to concede a ruff and sluff, the usual reason is that a ruff and a sluff would enable declarer to establish a long card in a side suit. This suit will usually be distributed 4–3 between dummy and the declarer.

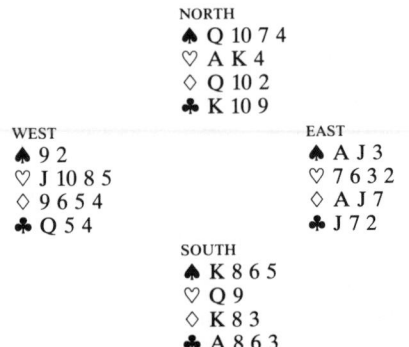

```
              NORTH
              ♠ Q 10 7 4
              ♡ A K 4
              ◇ Q 10 2
              ♣ K 10 9
WEST                        EAST
♠ 9 2                       ♠ A J 3
♡ J 10 8 5                  ♡ 7 6 3 2
◇ 9 6 5 4                   ◇ A J 7
♣ Q 5 4                     ♣ J 7 2
              SOUTH
              ♠ K 8 6 5
              ♡ Q 9
              ◇ K 8 3
              ♣ A 8 6 3
```

South opens one club and after a forcing two no trump response lands in four spades. West leads the heart jack, and South seeks to improve his chances by taking three rounds of hearts before leading a trump to the king and a trump back to dummy. East scores two trump tricks, but then has a choice of rotten apples. South had bid clubs, and if East plays the suit, declarer brings it in without loss, and makes his contract, for he has already discarded a diamond on the third round of hearts, and now loses only to the diamond ace. East's choice, therefore, lies between conceding a ruff and discard or playing a diamond.

Declarer had only eight ready tricks, so East willingly gives him a ninth by playing ace and another diamond. South still has to lose a club, and is defeated.

If East concedes a ruff and discard instead, South ruffs in hand, and sluffs a club from dummy. The third round of clubs is ruffed on the board, a diamond lead to South's king provides a ninth trick, and the long club is the tenth.

RUFF AND RUFF. A rare end-game situation described by Jean BESSE, Switzerland, in which the declarer is offered a ruff and discard, and the only winning play is to ruff in *both* declaring hands.

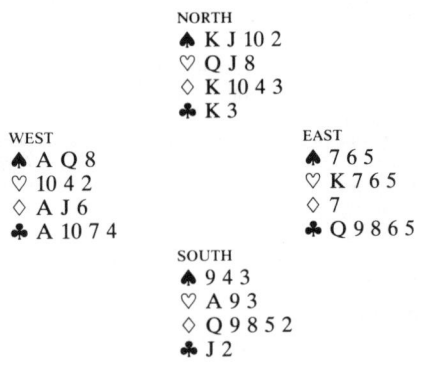

```
              NORTH
              ♠ K J 10 2
              ♡ Q J 8
              ◇ K 10 4 3
              ♣ K 3
WEST                        EAST
♠ A Q 8                     ♠ 7 6 5
♡ 10 4 2                    ♡ K 7 6 5
◇ A J 6                     ◇ 7
♣ A 10 7 4                  ♣ Q 9 8 6 5
              SOUTH
              ♠ 9 4 3
              ♡ A 9 3
              ◇ Q 9 8 5 2
              ♣ J 2
```

South plays in three diamonds after West has opened the bidding with one club, and the opening lead is the two of hearts. The eight of hearts forces the king, and the ace wins. A diamond is led to dummy's king, West naturally ducking, and dummy's two winning hearts are cashed.

A trump is continued, and West takes two trump tricks. He shifts to a low club, and South guesses right, putting up dummy's king. He returns a club, and West wins with the ace in this position:

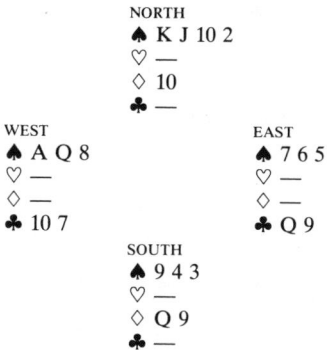

```
                NORTH
                ♠ K J 10 2
                ♡ —
                ◊ 10
                ♣ —
 WEST                           EAST
 ♠ A Q 8                        ♠ 7 6 5
 ♡ —                            ♡ —
 ◊ —                            ◊ —
 ♣ 10 7                         ♣ Q 9
                SOUTH
                ♠ 9 4 3
                ♡ —
                ◊ Q 9
                ♣ —
```

West returns a club, the best defense, and the only winning play for South is to ruff in dummy and over-ruff with his queen. He continues with the spade nine. If dummy discards any spade on the club lead, West can defend the position.

For a related situation, see ONE-SUIT SQUEEZE.

RUFF AND SLUFF. See RUFF AND DISCARD.

RUFFING FINESSE. A play by which a finesse is successful if the missing honor lies behind the finesse holding. With a singleton opposite a holding of ace, queen, jack, a simple finesse may be taken by leading the singleton and playing the jack, thus providing immediate discard on the ace if this is needed. The other possibility, granting no problem of entry, is to play for the king to be behind the high card holding. In this case the ace is played at the first trick, and the queen led. If the queen is covered, the trick can be ruffed; if no covered a sluff is taken. The bidding may give some clue to the missing king's location. When the declarer has no information to guide him, he should choose the ruffing finesse in preference to the simple finesse for the reason that the ruffing finesse will lose one less trick when it fails.

If the ten is missing, the ruffing finesse becomes less attractive:

```
                NORTH
                A Q J 3 2

                SOUTH
                4
```

The play of the ace followed by the queen cannot produce more than three tricks in all, with the help of two ruffs. Entries permitting, it is slightly better to ruff a low card on the second round and lead the queen later.

The all-out play of finessing the queen on the first round offers the chance of four tricks, with the help of one ruff, if the left-hand opponent began with Kxx.

Similarly, with a singleton opposite AKJ10x, a first-round finesse must be taken if it is essential to make five tricks in the suit.

This is another situation:

```
                NORTH
                K J 10 9 2

                SOUTH
                3
```

If the jack is finessed and loses to the queen, a later ruffing finesse is right both by percentages and psychology (West might have put up the ace if he had held that card). So if East began with AQxx and was sure about South's singleton, it would be a shrewd move for him to win the first trick with the ace.

RUFFING SQUEEZE. See TRUMP SQUEEZE.

RUFFING TRICK. A trick won by ruffing; usually a ruffing trick is a trick won by a trump which would otherwise be of little or no value. See COUP EN PASSANT; ELOPEMENT. Exceptions are the CROSSRUFF, where both hands contribute to the ruffing values, and the DUMMY REVERSAL, where the normal method of play is reversed and the hand containing the long trumps is used for ruffing. In hand evaluation under the POINT-COUNT system the responding hand, after finding a trump fit with partner, may add substantially for shortness in a side suit. See DISTRIBUTIONAL COUNTS.

RULE OF ELEVEN. A mathematical calculation applicable when the original lead is construed as a FOURTH-HIGHEST one. It is sometimes possible to obtain an exact reading of the distribution in all four hands.

The discovery of the rule is generally credited to R. F. Foster, and was published by him in his *Whist Manual.* First put in writing in a letter from Foster to a friend in 1890, it is said to have been discovered independently by E. M. F. Benecke of Oxford at about the same time.

The rule states: "Subtract the pips on the card led from eleven; the result gives the number of higher cards than the one led in the other three hands." Counting such cards in his own hand and in the dummy, both the leader's partner and the declarer can determine the number of such cards in the concealed hand of the other.

The application of the rule is easier than stating it. For example:

```
                DUMMY
                K 5 2
 7 led                    A 10 9 3
```

If the lead of the seven-spot is a fourth-best lead, third hand subtracts 7 from 11 and knows that four cards higher than the seven-spot are held in his, dummy's, and declarer's hands. He has three and dummy one, therefore declarer has no card higher than the seven, which can be permitted to ride.

Frequently only the declarer gains from the application of this rule.

DUMMY

A Q 9 5 4

6 led   3 played

10 7 2

Since declarer sees in his own hand and the dummy five cards higher than the six-spot, he can bring in the entire suit by successively finessing against the king, jack, and eight-spot.

The rule of eleven often spots a singleton lead. For example:

DUMMY

A 10 8 7 4

5 led   K 9 3 2

DECLARER

Q J 6

If five is subtracted from eleven, the third hand knows that this is the number of cards higher than the five-spot held by himself, dummy, and declarer. He sees six of them so declarer holds none if his partner's lead is a fourth best. Declarer ducks, the king is played, and declarer plays a seventh card higher than five. Third hand sees all cards lower than the five; therefore the lead is not from a doubleton, and can be presumed to be a singleton.

The rule is based on an honest lead of fourth best in a suit. There is a modern tendency to be less revealing on the opening lead, with the lead of a small card indicating a suit whose return is desired and a middle card to indicate a suit to be abandoned. Care must therefore be taken not to apply the rule rigorously when the lead is not certainly a fourth best.

RULE OF FIFTEEN. (1) A rule of thumb as to whether or not the bidding should be opened in fourth seat, after three passes: the rule states that fourth hand should open the bidding if the number of high-card points and the number of spades totals fifteen or more. The theory behind the rule is that if the high cards are likely very evenly divided between the two partnerships, fourth hand should open only with a spade suit that will facilitate his side's competing in the auction.

(2) A generalization of the RULE OF ELEVEN which allows third hand to determine what numerical "rule" to apply in conjunction with various types of spot-card leads other than fourth highest. The type of lead employed and the rule to be applied always total fifteen. For example, the rule of *eleven* is applicable to *fourth* best leads; the RULE OF TWELVE is used with *third* best leads; a rule of *ten* would be applicable to *fifth* best leads. See RULE OF ELEVEN.

RULE OF N-MINUS-ONE. A rule for squeezes published in the *Red Book on Play* by Ely CULBERTSON. This is his definition:

Count the number of busy cards in plain suits held by one adversary. This number is represented by the symbol N. N-minus-1 equals the number of uninterrupted winners the declarer needs for a squeeze.

This rule is applied at a time when the opponent to be squeezed has been stripped of all idle cards. At that point declarer must be capable of taking all but one of the remaining tricks. See RECTIFYING THE COUNT.

There are exceptions to this rule: see SQUEEZE WITHOUT THE COUNT; SECONDARY SQUEEZE; TRIPLE SQUEEZE.

RULE OF TOTAL TRICKS. A theory described by Jean-Rene Vernes, of Paris, in *The Bridge World*, designed to assist in competitive bidding situations. The rule is that in each deal, if each side played in its own trump suit, the total number of tricks theoretically available to both sides is approximately equal to the total number of trumps held by both sides, each in its respective suit. The rule of thumb suggested by this theory is that it is usually relatively safe to bid for as many tricks as your side has trumps. Factors that increase the safety of further competition include the existence of a double fit and the possession of all the honors in the trump suit.

RULE OF TWELVE. A mathematical calculation applicable when the original lead is construed as a THIRD HIGHEST one. The rule states, "Subtract the pips on the card led from twelve; the result gives the number of higher cards than the one led in the other three hands." The application of the rule is similar to the application of the RULE OF ELEVEN. For example:

DUMMY

K 10 7

6 led   A J 8 2

If the lead of the six-spot is a third-best lead, third hand subtracts 6 from 12 and knows that six cards higher than the six-spot are held in his hand, dummy's and declarer's hand. He has three and dummy has three, so if the lead was third highest, he will be able to win cheaply by topping whatever card is played from dummy. See RULE OF FIFTEEN (2).

RULE OF TWO AND THREE. A guide to pre-emptive opening bids and overcalls. The player taking pre-emptive action cannot afford to be set more than 500 unless he is saving against a slam. He can therefore risk being defeated by two tricks doubled vulnerable or three tricks doubled not vulnerable.

A simple way of considering this matter is to assume that a vulnerable partner can make two tricks, and a non-vulnerable partner three tricks. Therefore, a player who opens four spades should have an eight playing trick hand if he is vulnerable, and a seven playing trick hand if he is not vulnerable.

These traditional requirements are often modified by position at the table, methods of scoring, and other circumstances and have no mathematical validity, though sound psychologically. See PRE-EMPTIVE BID.

RULE OF X-PLUS-ONE. A formula conceived by Ely CULBERTSON as an aid to planning the play at no trump. If it is desired to establish long cards in a suit, estimate the number of losing tricks in the suit before it can be established (X) and add one to this number. This is the number of stoppers in opponents' long suit needed to be able to cash the long cards.

RULING. An adjudication by the director after an irregularity has occurred at a bridge tournament; in rubber bridge, an application of an applicable law by agreement among the players.

RULINGS OUT OF THE BOOK. In all tournament play, whether at the club level or at the level of International competition, the director should carry a rule book (LAWS OF DUPLICATE BRIDGE) to the table where an irregularity occurs, and quote the rule that applies directly from the book. The familiarity of the director with the provisions of the laws is not in question, but the player is far more apt to accept a ruling against him graciously if the rule is read to him directly. Particularly does this practice avoid the dubious one of a club director giving HOME TOWN RULINGS to his steady customers.

RUN. (1) Bidding: to take partner out in a different suit (or no trump) if he is doubled. (2) Play or run (a suit): to cash all the winning cards of an established or solid suit by playing them one after the other.

RUN OUT OF TRUMPS. To exhaust of trumps, usually by forcing the player to ruff. See CONTROL MAINTENANCE.

RUSH ASKING BID. A method of asking bids devised by Courtland RUSH, St. Joseph, Mo., and incorporated into the BULLDOG SYSTEM. It differs from other asking bid procedures in that it inquires about controls *outside* the asked suit.

The responder counts controls outside the asked suit on the NORMAN principle (each ace, 1 point; each king, ½ point) and responds on the following scale:

Cheapest available bid	0 or ½ or 2½
Next available bid	1 or 3
Third available bid	1½ or 3½
Fourth available bid	2 or 4

This scale is reduced by ½ point if responder is known to be very weak or if opener is known to be enormously strong.

Further bids are asking bids unless in the agreed trump suit or a jump. There are three types of repeat asking bids:

(1) In the original asked suit. A bid in the agreed trump suit is negative. A raise in the asked suit shows first-round control of it. A minimum no trump bid shows second-round control of the asked suit and no outside third-round control. A response in an outside suit shows a third-round control, together with second-round control of the asked suit.

(2) In a new suit. Return to agreed trump suit to deny third-round control in asked suit. Raise to show void or singleton. No trump response shows

third-round control. Side-suit response shows third-round control in asked suit and bid suit. Naming the original asked suit shows third-round control of second asked suit and first- or second-round control of first asked suit.

(3) In no trump. BLACKWOOD-type bid, asking for queens.

RUSINOW LEADS. The principle of leading the second-ranking of touching honors, devised by Sydney Rusinow and used by him, Philip Abramsohn, and Simon Rossant in the thirties. These leads were unaccountably barred in ACBL tournaments until 1964.

Ever since whist was *the* game, the standard lead from either ace-king or king-queen has been the king. This ambiguity often gives third hand an unsolvable problem. Here is only one example of many:

```
                    NORTH
                   ♠ 6 5 2
    WEST                        EAST
    ♠ K                         ♠ J 10 4
                    SOUTH
                    ♠ ?
```

Against a suit contract by South, West leads the king of spades. If he has king-queen, East wants to play the jack to encourage him to continue. But if he has ace-king, East wants to play low to get him to shift. (If East plays the jack, West may try to give East a ruff, and even if he shifts a trick will be lost if South has ♠ Q 9 x.)

Some players favor the lead of the ace from ace-king. Unfortunately this practice substitutes one problem for another. Often an ace should be led against a suit contract *without* the king. But if this lead convention is used, a guessing situation is created—so much so that one is reluctant to lead an unsupported ace even when it might be right to do so.

A sound solution was proposed thirty years ago by Sydney Rusinow—the lead of the second highest from touching honors (king from ace-king, queen from king-queen, etc.). Though endorsed by Ely Culbertson, these leads soon fell out of favor in America. They were adopted by many Europeans, however, notably the users of the ROMAN CLUB and later the LITTLE MAJOR. The details are:

A denies the king (except with ace-king doubleton —see below).

K from AK. Third hand should signal with the queen or a doubleton.

Q from KQ. Third hand should signal with the ace or jack, but not with a doubleton if dummy has three or four small. (Declarer may duck, and partner may continue into his AJ.)

J from QJ; 10 from J10; 9 from 109. Note that this blends nicely into MUD leads of second highest from three spot cards.

With more than two honors in sequence, the second highest is still led (Q from KQJ, etc.), followed by a lower one in most cases. The Romans lead second highest from an interior sequence also (10 from KJ10, 9 from K109 or Q109). This deserves more study; in any case, the problem is not too important, for the K J 10 is not usually a desirable combination to lead from, and the fourth highest is perhaps a better choice from the other two holdings.

Rusinow leads are used *only* on the first trick against a suit contract in a suit which partner has not bid. Later in the hand, or in partner's suit, the highest card should be led from touching honors.

If the touching honors to be led are doubleton, the top card should be led. Then when you play the second honor, partner will know you have no more of the suit. On the following hand, this special feature of the Rusinow leads was crucial. Match points. E-W vulnerable. North dealer.

NORTH
♠ 9 5 2
♡ K J 5
◇ A K J 9 4
♣ Q 3

WEST
♠ K Q
♡ A 4
◇ 10 5 2
♣ K 8 7 6 4 2

EAST
♠ A 8 6 4
♡ 8 6
◇ 8 7 3
♣ J 10 9 5

SOUTH
♠ J 10 7 3
♡ Q 10 9 7 3 2
◇ Q 6
♣ A

NORTH	EAST	SOUTH	WEST
1 ◇	Pass	1 ♡	Pass
2 ♡	Pass	4 ♡	Pass
Pass	Pass		

Playing Rusinow leads, West opens the king of spades, which East instantly identifies as a doubleton (if it is a singleton, South has a hidden five-card suit). He plays the eight, then overtakes the queen, and returns a spade for West to ruff, setting the contract.

Playing standard leads, East has to guess. He cannot be sure that West would have led low to the second trick holding ♠ K Q x, for West might have been afraid East would shift to a club. Nor would it have helped West to have opened the queen, for East would surely have overtaken and tried for a club trick.

Against No Trump Contracts. If Rusinow leads work so well against suit contracts, should they be used against no trump also? Many think not, because the purpose of a lead against no trump is entirely different. Against a suit, third hand has to know what specific honors the leader has, so the ace-king ambiguity must be resolved. Against no trump, third hand has to know whether partner has led his side's best suit—that is, whether he has honors in the suit led, not which specific ones they are. See JOURNALIST LEADS.

L. R.

RUSSIA. Bridge is little played in Russia, where chess is the dominant game, but the Russian whist variant Vint may have been a forerunner of bridge. Some of the leading chess players, notably Paul

Keres, play bridge as a recreation. Some tournament bridge is played in Estonia, especially at the University of Tartu. In the late 1960's Russia became more active in tournament competition and participated in several tournaments in iron curtain countries.

In 1973 the Associated Press reported from Moscow that the "bourgeois game of contract bridge" had been banned from play in clubs because the "passion for bridge" had been found to be "socially harmful" by the State Sports Committee. Bridge is, however, allowed to be played in private by consenting adults.

S

SAC. Colloquialism for SACRIFICE, as in "We took the sac."

S.A.C.C. A forerunner of PLAFOND, named for its originators and reported by Sir Hugh CLAYTON (probably one of them) in *The Times of India*, July 15, 1914, placing it five or six years earlier than BELLANGER's dating of the advent of Plafond in Paris. It does not appear to have caught on outside India.

A side received credit toward game only for tricks for which they had bid. Bonuses for slams were of an order that made it worth running the risk of being set: 1,000 for grand slam, 500 for small slam, 250 for five odd. (This idea of a demi-slam bonus, at times suggested for contract bridge, has always been rejected as overrewarding a timid approach to slam bidding.) Tricks not bid for received no score. In addition to scoring game for tricks bid for to a value of 30 points, a game was credited to the side that, since completion of a previous game, scored a total of 500 by honors, penalties, and points for slam. The avowed purpose of this rule was to discourage "flag-flying" and allow earlier completion of a rubber. From this distance in time, however, it would seem that the rule exaggerated one of the flaws in the auction scoring base used in S.A.C.C. and in Plafond—the penalties were already severe in ratio to a 250-point rubber bonus.

SNAP. Abbreviation for STRONG NO TRUMP AFTER PASSING. Frequently the initials are used as a word.

SACRIFICE (or SAVE). Sacrifice bidding over opponents' game contracts can be much more profitable at duplicate scoring than at rubber bridge. One will never see a successful "money" player chortling with triumph after going down 500 to stop a vulnerable game—one has saved very few points, if any, and would rather have had whatever small chance there was of setting the opponents' contract.

However, losing 500 instead of 620 at duplicate can yield a high match-point score.

Remember, though, that one will earn a fat score with one's sacrifice only when most of the field is bidding game with his opponents' cards. Suppose that one holds this hand; non-vulnerable against vulnerable:

♠ J 8 5
♡ 8 6 2
◇ J 7
♣ K 10 7 6 4

EAST	SOUTH	WEST	NORTH
1 ♡	Pass	2 ♡	2 ♠
3 ♡	Pass	Pass	3 ♠
Pass	Pass	4 ♡	Pass
Pass	?		

Certainly, the opponents will make their game more often than not—one has too good a fit with partner and too little defense to expect a set. Certainly, one will go down 500 or less at four spades. Should one sacrifice? The auction makes it clear that most of the twelve other pairs who hold the opponents' cards will not be in game. Say that this deal is played in a part-score eight times, in four hearts twice, in four spades doubled twice. Then, if four hearts makes, one will score 1 point for letting it play, or 3 points for saving; if four hearts goes down, one scores 11 points for letting it play or 1 point for saving. So one stands to gain 2 or lose 10—and the odds are nowhere near 5 to 1 that the game will make.

In contrast, suppose that one holds the same hand on this auction:

EAST	SOUTH	WEST	NORTH
1 ♡	Pass	3 ♡	3 ♠
4 ♡	?		

Now, the whole field is likely to be in game. Say that six pairs are allowed to play four hearts, while the other six double four spades. Either for passing or for bidding four spades one will score 9 points if he is right, 3 points if he is wrong—it is an even-money bet. At these odds, the price is right for a sacrifice, since four hearts will make perhaps three-quarters of the time. Remember that the determining factor in match-point play is not "how much?" but "how often?" Thus, the most important factor in sacrifice bidding at duplicate is the spirit of the enemy bidding: be reluctant to sacrifice when the opponents stagger into game even if one thinks they are likely to make; be alert to sacrifice against confident auctions when it appears that everyone else will be in game too.

Next in importance is the vulnerability. To be set more than the value of the enemy game is irritating at any scoring, but it is a major disaster at match points. Thus, one never really "sacrifices" when the vulnerability is unfavorable (vulnerable against not vulnerable). If one outbids the opponents, it must be with some notion that the contract might make; that if it goes down, it will be down only one. On equal vulnerability (both vulnerable or non-vulnerable),

one can loosen up, outbidding the opponents even when certainly going down. Here, there should be some hope of going down only one; otherwise, there is too much danger of down three for a zero. One cannot be really frisky with one's sacrifice bidding unless the vulnerability is favorable (not vulnerable against vulnerable) so that one can afford down three. For instance, suppose one holds:

♠ 2
♡ A Q J 8 4
◇ 8 5 2
♣ K Q 9 4

Open one heart; left-hand opponent doubles; partner raises to two hearts; and right-hand opponent jumps to four spades. It sounds as though the opponents have bid a normal game—should a sacrifice be considered? Obviously, pass if the vulnerability is unfavorable; there is no chance to win ten or eleven tricks. Equally obviously, bid five hearts if it is favorable; the opponents are more likely than not to make their game, and have little prospect of scoring 700. What about equal vulnerability?

The single most probable result is that the opponents can make their game while the defenders will be down only two. But it is advisable to pass. The combination of two less likely chances—(a) that one might beat four spades, plus (b) that one might go down three—outweighs the single most likely one. The opponents are merely favorites to make game; they might go down. And the defenders are merely a favorite to win nine tricks; after a single raise, a try for game would not be made, and this means there is no assurance of making even three hearts.

A hidden advantage of sacrifice bidding is the chance that the opponents will be pushed one higher and will go down. This accentuates the vulnerability differences. On unfavorable vulnerability, the opponents are longing to double the defenders; on equal vulnerability, they are willing to double; but on favorable vulnerability, they are reluctant to double and may well be pushed overboard. When the vulnerability is favorable, the odds favoring sacrifice bidding are simply magnificent. One should consider sacrificing against a confidently bid game whenever he and partner have a suit fit plus a little distribution. It is estimated that between one-third and one-half the time there is a paying non-vulnerable sacrifice available against a vulnerable suit game.

This means charge into the auction very boldly when the vulnerability is favorable. Loosen up the take-out doubles, and forget about all the strict requirements for overcalls. Any time there is exciting distribution, get in and bid. Do not worry about point-count. The weaker the hand, the more likely that the opponents have a vulnerable game. It is safe to bid, since the opponents hate to double low contracts which they will need to beat 700.

♠ 6 3
♡ 4
◇ K 10 7 3
♣ Q 8 7 4 3 2

does not meet the textbook requirements set for an overcall. However, there may be a good sacrifice if a club fit can be found.

When partner has overcalled on this vulnerability, raise him whenever a fit is held. His assumption should always be that a sacrifice is needed, not a game. But be wary of raising when one has a good deal of defensive strength. For example:

♠ Q 10 4
♡ Q J 8 6
♢ 8 5
♣ K Q 10 2

Left-hand opponent opens one club, partner overcalls one spade, right-hand opponent bids two hearts. Defender should pass. On unfavorable vulnerability, raise to two spades—if partner bids four spades, he expects to make it, and he will. However, on favorable vulnerability he will bid four spades as a sacrifice, and probably the enemy does not have game. See also ADVANCE SAVE and PHANTOM SACRIFICE.

SAFETY LEVEL. The maximum bid a partnership is willing to reach, presumably without undue risk, in order to investigate a higher contract or compete against enemy bids.

At times, one partner may wish to suggest a slam. If his hand is not strong enough to guarantee a contract above the level of game, he must make a slam try below game. The game level is then his safety level. If his hand is strong enough to guarantee the safety of an above-game contract (such as four no trump or five of a major suit), he may, if he wishes, make a slam try above game. In this case, the safety level is four no trump, five spades, or whatever.

When the bidding becomes competitive, the previous bids of a partnership often indicate they hold the strength to reach a certain level. This is their safety level, and the contract should not be sold (undoubled) to the opponents below this level. See RULE OF TOTAL TRICKS.

For example: South opens with a strong two-bid, forcing to game. If East-West enter the auction, North-South have a safety level at game, implicit in South's bid. North-South will not allow East-West to buy the contract below game unless they feel a satisfactory penalty will be obtained. See also FORCING BID; FORCING SEQUENCES; SLAM BIDDING.

SAFETY PLAY. The safety play appropriate to any particular SUIT COMBINATION is classified under that heading. The following discussion deals with applications of the safe-play idea.

In a broad sense, a "safety play" would be a play in which declarer is attempting to reduce to a minimum the risk of losing his contract. If safety play is defined in this manner, every hand would naturally be reduced to finding the safety play, and applying it.

However, as the term is actually used in bridge, it refers specifically to *the play of a suit,* as contrasted to the play of the entire hand. A safety play is the play of a suit in such a manner as to protect against an

abnormal or bad break in that suit, thereby either eliminating or minimizing the danger of losing the contract. Fundamentally, most types of safety plays are used almost exclusively in rubber bridge, although there are many standard safety plays which are applicable equally to both rubber bridge and duplicate bridge. Since in most safety-play situations, declarer sacrifices a possible overtrick to attain his objective, such a play is generally losing tactics at match-point duplicate play, where the overtrick can be worth as much as a game itself. See MATCH-POINT PLAY.

Let us examine a few illustrations of the safety play.

NORTH
♠ 7 5 4
♡ Q 9 6 4
♢ A 8 4
♣ A K 3

SOUTH
♠ A K 3
♡ A J 10 3 2
♢ K 2
♣ 6 5 2

Playing rubber bridge, South arrives at a four heart contract. West opens the jack of clubs, dummy's king is put up—and East drops the queen of clubs.

In rubber bridge, declarer has no problem as to how to proceed. He has ten sure tricks. So, with the safety of the contract being the sole consideration, a low trump is led,* taken with the ace, and a low trump is led back. West wins with the king, and the declarer is home safely. But if the trump finesse had been tried, declarer would not have enjoyed the future of the hand:

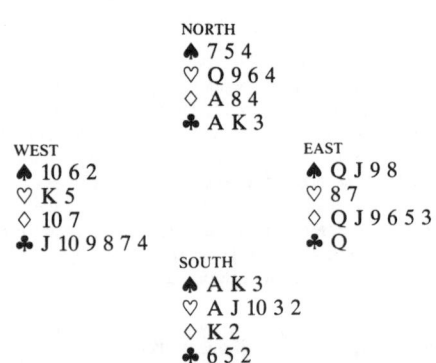

NORTH
♠ 7 5 4
♡ Q 9 6 4
♢ A 8 4
♣ A K 3

WEST
♠ 10 6 2
♡ K 5
♢ 10 7
♣ J 10 9 8 7 4

EAST
♠ Q J 9 8
♡ 8 7
♢ Q J 9 6 5 3
♣ Q

SOUTH
♠ A K 3
♡ A J 10 3 2
♢ K 2
♣ 6 5 2

As is evident, if declarer had taken the trump finesse, it would have lost, and West would have returned a club for East to trump. Declarer would then have gone down a trick.

In duplicate bridge, the proper play of the hand is

---
* Technically and psychologically, the queen of trumps should be led to entice East into covering if he possesses the king. But when East follows with a low trump, declarer will take his own queen with the ace, and then another trump is led to get rid of trumps as quickly as possible.

not as simple, for your objective cannot be defined specifically. Should you play safe, or should you try for the overtrick by taking the heart finesse? Obviously, East's queen of clubs is singleton, and the trump finesse, if it loses, will result in declarer's defeat. But can declarer, in a duplicate game, afford a safety play in the trump suit, and give up a fifty-fifty chance for an overtrick (if the trump finesse is successful)? If the trump finesse is taken successfully, declarer will get a top or a tie-for-top on the board. If it loses, he gets a bottom or tie-for-bottom on the board. Another factor which must be considered by declarer at match-point play is that at the other tables West might not open a club, in which case the declarers at those tables will all take the trump finesse, since they will have no reason to fear that East will trump a club.

Thus, in duplicate bridge, one can play for a top or a bottom by taking the trump finesse for the king. In rubber bridge, the finesse is not even considered, for the safety of the contract is the sole concern.

Here is another safety-play deal. The game is rubber bridge. South is declarer, playing a six spade contract.

```
                NORTH
                ♠ A 9 8 2
                ♡ A 6 5
                ◇ 8 3
                ♣ K Q 7 4

                SOUTH
                ♠ K 10 7 6 4
                ♡ K Q 8 2
                ◇ A K
                ♣ A 2
```

West opens the queen of diamonds, declarer winning with the king. It is apparent that if the four outstanding trumps are divided either 2–2 or 3–1, there is no problem, since in these cases South cannot possibly lose more than one spade trick. But if they are divided 4–0, then danger exists.

Proper safety-play technique, to avoid the loss of more than one spade trick, is to lead a low spade at trick two, and when West follows with a low spade, to insert the *eight-spot* from dummy. Either the eight will win, or it will be captured by East's jack (or queen). If East's jack wins, then there will remain but two outstanding spades, and declarer's ace and king will pick them up on the two succeeding rounds of trumps.

But to take this safety play in duplicate bridge would be losing tactics, for if the four outstanding trumps were divided 2–2, declarer would be throwing away an overtrick. And surely the four outstanding trumps are more likely to be divided 2–2 than 4–0.

In rubber bridge, the safety play is insurance against a bad break that would defeat declarer's slam contract. The cost of the insurance is the payment of a possible overtrick, worth 30 points. In duplicate bridge, the overtrick could be worth its weight in gold, and might well mean the difference between winning and losing a tournament, and the rubber bridge safety play becomes a duplicate bridge "unsafety" play.

The following deal depicts the infrequent situation in which a safety play should (probably) be taken in a duplicate game. It comes about when one has good reason to think that he is in a game or slam contract that will probably be reached by few (if any) other pairs; and one can thus afford to take a safety play to assure the contract.

```
                NORTH
                ♠ 7 5 2
                ♡ 8 4 3
                ◇ J
                ♣ A K Q 7 4 3

                SOUTH
                ♠ A 8 4 3
                ♡ J 10 9 2
                ◇ A K 5
                ♣ 5 2
```

Neither side vulnerable. West dealer.

WEST	NORTH	EAST	SOUTH
1 ◇	2 ♣	Pass	2 NT
Pass	3 NT	Pass	Pass
Pass			

West opened the four of diamonds, and dummy's jack won the trick. Declarer realized that his contract was guaranteed if he made just five club tricks. He therefore could afford to give away the first round of clubs as a safety play to guard against a 4–1 break in that suit. Certainly it appeared that bidding and making three no trump would be an excellent match-point result: the combined hands had only 22 high-card points, there had been an opening bid to overcome to reach game, and the opening lead had given declarer a present of a trick. Had hearts been attacked initially, there would have been no present of a trick, and declarer would have had no choice but to hope that the five outstanding clubs were divided 3–2.

At trick two, declarer led a low club out of dummy, and was rewarded nicely when the deal had ended, and the score was posted. This was the entire deal:

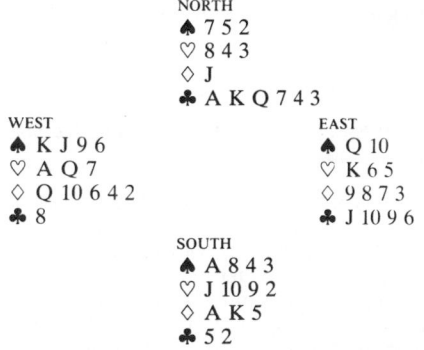

```
                NORTH
                ♠ 7 5 2
                ♡ 8 4 3
                ◇ J
                ♣ A K Q 7 4 3
WEST                                    EAST
♠ K J 9 6                               ♠ Q 10
♡ A Q 7                                 ♡ K 6 5
◇ Q 10 6 4 2                            ◇ 9 8 7 3
♣ 8                                     ♣ J 10 9 6
                SOUTH
                ♠ A 8 4 3
                ♡ J 10 9 2
                ◇ A K 5
                ♣ 5 2
```

See also EXPECTATION.

F. K.

SAN FRANCISCO CONVENTION. A four no

trump convention, sometimes called the Warren convention, with responses showing aces and kings in one bid. Aces are counted as three points and kings as one point, and the responses are:

Five clubs	less than 3 points
Five diamonds	3 points
Five hearts	4 points
Five spades	5 points
Five no trump	6 points, etc.

By inspecting his own hand, the four no trump bidder can almost always judge what his partner's response represents in aces and kings. A response of five hearts must show an ace and a king, or four kings.

The convention results in some disadvantage if the responder's hand is strong. If he has three aces, the response of six hearts may take his side too high.

SANCTION. The permission given by the ACBL to a Club, Unit, or District to hold a duplicate event within ACBL territory. In general a specific sanction to hold a tournament must be obtained from the League in advance of the date scheduled for the tournament. The League sends the sponsoring organization a form suitable for use in reporting the results of the tournament, and this report is used by the ACBL to record MASTER POINTS won by the contestants.

SANDWICH. A term used in Europe to describe an overcall or bid made in fourth position after both opponents have bid. For example:

SOUTH	WEST	NORTH	EAST
1 ◇	Pass	1 ♠	2 ♣

The term emphasizes the danger of bidding in such circumstances.

SANS ATOUT. No trump. The term is French.

SAUDI ARABIAN BRIDGE LEAGUE. Founded in 1968, joined WBF in 1970. National events held annually are Open Pairs, Teams of Four, Mixed Pairs.

President, 1975: Maxine Moats, P.O.B. 167, Jeddah, Saudi Arabia.

SAVE. See SACRIFICE.

SCANDINAVIAN CHAMPIONSHIPS. See NORDIC CHAMPIONSHIPS.

SCHENKEN SYSTEM. An artificial one club system devised by Howard SCHENKEN, New York City, and played by him in World Championship competition in partnership with Peter Leventritt.

The main features of the system are:

(1) One club opening. Forcing, and used on almost all strong hands. It shows a minimum of 17 high-card points or the distributional equivalent. There are three types: balanced no trump type with 19–22; slightly unbalanced hand with 17 or more; strong distribution with 14 or more.

One diamond is the conventional negative response, 0–6 points. Two clubs is also artificial, showing a semi-positive response of 7–8 points, including at least one king or ace, and promises a rebid. Other responses are positive, natural, and forcing to game. After an overcall up to three diamonds, a double is "positive," for take-out, and shows at least 9 points.

After a one diamond negative response, showing less than 9 points: a non-jump suit rebid may be passed; a jump suit rebid is forcing for one round; a one no trump rebid shows 19–20; a two no trump rebid shows 21–22.

STAYMAN is used after a one no trump response or rebid.

(2) One-bids in other suits are limited, with a maximum of 16 points. Responder normally passes with less than 8 points.

All raises and no trump responses are limited and non-forcing. A jump to game in a major may be based on high-card strength or distribution, because the limited opening has excluded slam chances. Three clubs response to a major is equivalent to a strong raise (16–17 points including distribution) and requests opener to bid a singleton.

(3) One no trump opening is standard (16–18). Two clubs response is non-forcing STAYMAN. Two diamonds shows an unbalanced responding hand (with a singleton or void), no four-card major, is game forcing and requests opener to show major suit stoppers.

(4) Two clubs is a natural opening with at least a good five-card club suit. A response of two diamonds asks opener to show a four-card major.

(5) Two diamonds. An artificial forcing opening bid used to locate specific honors. A two heart response denies an ace; other minimum responses are ace-showing, except that two no trump shows the heart ace. With two aces, responder jumps in the higher ranking ace with touching aces, three no trump with non-touching aces, or four clubs with the black aces. The opener follows with minimum rebids to locate kings and queens in the same way.

A two no trump rebid over two hearts shows 23–25, and may be passed. A three no trump rebid shows 26–27.

(6) Two spades and two hearts are weak two-bids, 8–12 points and a suit of reasonable strength. Two no trump is the only forcing response.

(7) Two no trump. Shows a minimum of five cards in each minor suit with 10–12 high-card points not vulnerable, 13–16 high-card points vulnerable.

(8) Three no trump opening is based on a solid minor suit with 8½–9 playing tricks and no side suit worse than Q x.

(9) Three clubs. A solid six- or seven-card suit, 10–15 points.

(10) Pre-emptive jump overcalls depending on the vulnerability.

SCHROEDER SQUEEZE. A triple trump squeeze without the count in a three-card position. This unique ending was executed in play by Dirk Schroeder of Wiesbaden, Germany.

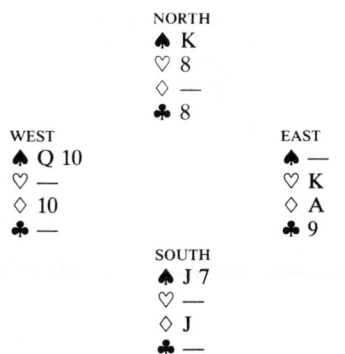

```
                  NORTH
                  ♠ K
                  ♡ 8
                  ◇ —
                  ♣ 8
WEST                        EAST
♠ Q 10                      ♠ —
♡ —                         ♡ K
◇ 10                        ◇ A
♣ —                         ♣ 9
                  SOUTH
                  ♠ J 7
                  ♡ —
                  ◇ J
                  ♣ —
```

With spades trump, and the lead in North, on the lead of the spade king East was squeezed. If he threw the winning heart or club South would have a winner to lead from dummy at the twelfth trick. If he threw the diamond ace, South would ruff something and score his diamond jack at the finish.

The complete deal was:

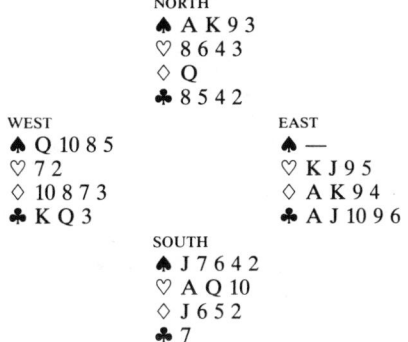

```
                  NORTH
                  ♠ A K 9 3
                  ♡ 8 6 4 3
                  ◇ Q
                  ♣ 8 5 4 2
WEST                        EAST
♠ Q 10 8 5                  ♠ —
♡ 7 2                       ♡ K J 9 5
◇ 10 8 7 3                  ◇ A K 9 4
♣ K Q 3                     ♣ A J 10 9 6
                  SOUTH
                  ♠ J 7 6 4 2
                  ♡ A Q 10
                  ◇ J 6 5 2
                  ♣ 7
```

In three spades doubled the defense led two rounds of clubs. South ruffed, entered dummy with a high spade, finessed the heart ten, and surrendered a diamond. After a third round of clubs was ruffed in the closed hand South ruffed a diamond, finessed the heart queen, and led the heart ace. West ruffed and led a diamond and then ruffed in dummy to produce the ending shown.

SCHWAB CUP. For the World Pairs Olympiad Championship, first contested in Cannes in 1962. Originally presented by Charles M. Schwab in 1933 for contest between the United States and England (see ANGLO-AMERICAN MATCHES). The trophy was redonated to the World Bridge Federation by the heirs of Ely Culbertson.

"SCIENTISTS" – "TRADITIONALISTS" MATCH. A 180-deal match, held in New York City in mid-January of 1965, sponsored by *The Bridge World* in an attempt to determine the value of highly technical and artificial bidding systems that had come to the fore in the sixties. The "Scientist" partnerships—Al Roth–Tobias Stone, Victor Mitchell–Sam Stayman, Robert Jordan–Arthur Robinson with

non-playing captains Julius Rosenblum and Edgar Kaplan—were allowed to use any artificial convention. Their "Traditionalist" adversaries—B. Jay Becker–Dorothy Hayden, Lew Mathe–Meyer Schleifer, Eric Murray–Sammy Kehela with non-playing captains Charles Solomon and Bill Root were restricted to standard bidding methods.

In a match that generated considerable public interest, the "Scientists" won by 53 IMPs, 367–314, but the result was generally considered inconclusive since the "Traditionalists" had led at one point by 108 IMPs. The swings were so huge that neither side was willing to concede the superiority of the other's bidding methods.

SCISSORS COUP. A play aimed at cutting the opponents' communications, usually in order to prevent a ruff (sometimes called less descriptively "the coup without a name").

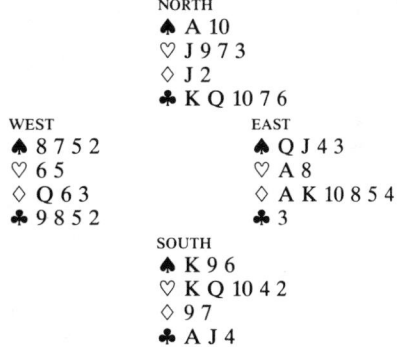

```
                  NORTH
                  ♠ A 10
                  ♡ J 9 7 3
                  ◇ J 2
                  ♣ K Q 10 7 6
WEST                        EAST
♠ 8 7 5 2                   ♠ Q J 4 3
♡ 6 5                       ♡ A 8
◇ Q 6 3                     ◇ A K 10 8 5 4
♣ 9 8 5 2                   ♣ 3
                  SOUTH
                  ♠ K 9 6
                  ♡ K Q 10 4 2
                  ◇ 9 7
                  ♣ A J 4
```

South plays in four hearts after East has opened the bidding with one diamond. South feels happy when it appears that there are only three losers, but feels much less happy when East wins the opening diamond lead with the king, and shifts to the club three. It is obvious that this is a singleton, and that West has a diamond entry to give his partner a ruff.

South must try to cut the diamond communication, so he cashes the ace and king of spades and leads the spade nine. Dummy's diamond is discarded, allowing East to win, and the defense can make only one more trick. South's play succeeds whenever East has both missing spade honors, or if East has a trebleton queen and fails to unblock.

SCORE. (1) Noun: the number of game or premium points earned as a result of the bidding and play of a hand, rubber, or session of bridge. (2) Verb: to record the score.

There is slight difference, due to the nature of the games, between the scoring at rubber bridge, Chicago, and tournament bridge. The latter, too, has different scoring procedures and values, depending on the type of event. See BOARD-A-MATCH SCORING; CUMULATIVE SCORE; INTERNATIONAL MATCH POINTS; LAWS (Laws 75 to 84); LAWS OF DUPLICATE (Laws 73, 74); MATCH POINT; MATCH-POINT SCORING.

SCORE CARD. See PICK-UP SLIP; SCORE PAD; RE-

CAPITULATION SHEET. A personal (or private) score card used in tournaments is called a CONVENTION CARD; when used in PARTY or PROGRESSIVE BRIDGE, it is called a TALLY.

SCORE PAD. A printed tablet of sheets of paper used to keep a record of the numerative functions of a game of rubber or Chicago bridge. Score pads come in various shapes and sizes, and some are imprinted with the name of the club at which they are used, but they are all ruled with printed lines, leaving spaces for entering game and partial score results and extra premiums such as undertrick penalties and slam and rubber bonuses and honors. Commercially printed pads for use in home games usually carry a back page with listings of the proper score for almost every situation that can occur in bridge. Chicago pads are printed on the top with inversely slanted lines, two in number and on the bias, for entering the number of each deal in the appropriate space thus obtaining.

SCORE SHEET. In club games, the summary sheet on which the MATCH POINTS won by a pair are entered for ease in totaling; in larger tournaments, the RECAPITULATION SHEET, to which the scores are posted from the PICK-UP SLIPS.

SCORER, OFFICIAL. See TOURNAMENT DIRECTOR.

SCORING. At duplicate, scoring is a fairly complicated operation. At club games, a slip for recording the results on each of the boards in play usually accompanies the board, folded so that it fits into a pocket, and previous results are not immediately apparent until the board has been played. See TRAVELING SCORE SLIP. After the board has been played, all four players are entitled to know the results of previous plays of that board.

In duplicate tournaments, individual PICK-UP SLIPS are provided at each table for recording the results on each board, for each round, individually. Spaces are provided for entry of contestant's number, board number, final contract, declarer, trick-score, extra trick-score, game, part-score, and doubled premium points, slam bonuses, and undertrick penalty points. If the points are won by North-South, they are entered on the left side of the slip; if won by East-West, on the right. Space is provided for the initials of one of the traveling pairs as a verification of the entries made, while it is the responsibility of the stationary pair to make out the original entries.

These slips are then collected by the director (or by the caddies under his supervision) and brought to the scorer who enters them on a RECAPITULATION SHEET. This sheet provides the information basic to awarding MATCH POINTS, the total of which is the session or overall total, from which winners and placers are determined.

SCORING CORRECTIONS. These are provided for in the regulations covering tournament bridge. Generally, the recapitulation sheet has a space in which the end of the correction period is noted, after which time the score becomes official.

Corrections are made by the scoring staff whenever the score slip is clearly in error—i.e., shows incorrect vulnerability, incorrect addition, etc., or when the slip has been incorrectly transcribed. When the correction involves a question of the results themselves—whether a contract was defeated one or two tricks, or whether extra tricks were scored—it may not be made after the end of the round in which the hand was played. See LAWS OF DUPLICATE, Law 75.

At rubber bridge, the rules set a time limit beyond which a correction may not be claimed—in most cases, after the score of the rubber has been determined and agreed upon.

SCORING ACROSS THE FIELD. A method of scoring a multi-section MATCH-POINT event designed to prevent inequitable score comparisons when the results in one section are at extreme variance with the results in other sections. The score on each board is match-pointed not just against other contestants in the same section but against the contestants in all sections playing in the same direction.

SCORING FORMS. Printed forms on which results of a duplicate board, a session, or an event are entered. Usually the North player enters the score on a TRAVELING SCORE SLIP or a PICK-UP SLIP. If the latter is used, the scorer enters the result on a RECAPITULATION SHEET. Match points are awarded either on the recapitulation sheet if pick-up slips are used, or on the traveling score slips. In team events of head-on competition, each pair keeps a running score of the results on the boards they play, and verification of these slips at each table makes it possible for each team to determine its own score, either in total point or IMP scoring.

SCORING TABLE. The current scoring table is set out in LAWS (Law 84) and LAWS OF DUPLICATE (Law 73). See also FRENCH SCORING and SCORING VARIANTS.

Today's scoring table includes few deviations from the original developed by Vanderbilt in 1925, having survived considerable tinkering, especially in the 1932 code. The 1927 Laws provided that each trick in a no trump contract was worth 35 points; that the premium for making a doubled contract was increased from 50 to 100 if vulnerable (if redoubled, the premiums were 100 and 200); and the penalties for undertricks increased as the tricks won fell farther short of contract, as follows:

PENALTIES

Undertricks (Scored in Adversaries' honor score):
	Points
If Undoubled (When Declarer is Not Vulnerable)	
per trick	50
If Undoubled (When Declarer is Vulnerable)	
for first trick	100
for subsequent tricks	200
If Doubled (When Declarer is Not Vulnerable)	
first two tricks, per trick	100
for third and fourth tricks, per trick	200
for subsequent tricks, per trick	400

If Doubled (When Declarer is Vulnerable)

for the first trick 200

for subsequent tricks, per trick 400

Redoubling doubles the doubled premiums and penalties.

Partly on the theory that the higher scores were largely responsible for the enormous popularity of contract bridge, the 1932 Laws sharply increased slam bonuses and also increased penalties, with nonvulnerable undertricks as well as vulnerable undertricks punished on a rising scale:

	PREMIUMS					
Not Vulnerable				Vulnerable		
Little Slam	500	500	500	750	750	750
Grand Slam	1500	1500	1500	2250	2250	2250

PENALTIES

Undertricks	Not Vulnerable		Vulnerable			
	Not	Re-	Not	Re-		
	Dbld	Dbld	Dbld	Dbld	Dbld	Dbld
First	50	100	200	100	200	400
Inc. ea. add. by	—	50	100	50	100	200
Thus:						
2nd is worth	50	150	300	150	300	600
3rd is worth	50	200	400	200	400	800

Furthermore, the value of tricks made in no trump contracts alternated: first, third, fifth, and seventh trick were worth 30 each; the second, fourth, and sixth, 40 each. Also, the premium for making a doubled contract was dropped.

The distortions imposed by this inflated scoring were corrected within three years—the shortest period ever for the issuance of a new laws code. In the forty years following issuance of the 1935 code, the only change in scoring was the restoration in the 1943 laws of a bonus for making a doubled contract, 50 points whether or not vulnerable.

SCORING VARIANTS. Several kinds of scoring variants have been introduced to make tournament bridge or rubber bridge a better competition. Among the more important are: (1) FRENCH SCORING, to make four of a major and four no trump of equal value. (2) PENALTY LIMITS in TOTAL POINT SCORING and PROGRESSIVE BRIDGE to limit the SWING on one hand. (3) Different TOPS in final competition of multi-session events or all sessions of important tournaments. (4) IMPS FOR PAIR GAMES, to make conditions comparable to INTERNATIONAL MATCH POINTS. (5) HYBRID SCORING to combine advantages of BOARD-A-MATCH and aggregate scores in team events.

SCOTTISH BRIDGE UNION. Consists of 249 clubs located in six regional districts, Western, Eastern, Northern, Southern, Central, and Ayrshire, with a membership in 1974 of approximately 10,500. The Union is affiliated with the British Bridge League, and annually competes for the Camrose Trophy, winning the event six times since 1964, two of those being jointly with England. The SBU also operates an independent master-point program; its awards are on an identical scale as the awards of the English

Bridge Union. Scottish players listed separately are: H. Barnett, S. Barnett, A. Benjamin, W. Coyle, T. Culbertson, Dr. R. Forbes, V. Goldberg, H. W. Kelsey, S. Leckie, J. MacLaren, Dr. J. Mathieson, B. Shenkin, V. Silverstone.

Secretary, 1975: Morag Malcolm, Shawboost, Johnstone, Scotland.

SCRAMBLED MITCHELL MOVEMENT. A modification of the MITCHELL MOVEMENT, used when it is desired to produce one winning pair. Each pair plays approximately one-half the boards North-South and the rest East-West. This is accomplished by switching the arrows designating North so that they point to the original East simultaneously at the end of certain rounds. The original East-West pairs, having adopted a moving pattern, continue to move, and the original North-South pairs remain at their tables, even though the arrows have been switched and they are playing the East-West hands.

Howell or Three-quarter movements are technically preferred. Balanced comparison is never achieved in the Scrambled Mitchell movement. Col. Russell Baldwin suggests that balanced comparisons can be approached by three ARROW SWITCHES so spaced that the rounds are divided into four unequal groups. George Beynon and Frank Farrington give the following table for various sized sections to approach balanced comparisons.

Tables	Arrow North	Arrow East
6	Rounds 1,2,5	3,4,6
7	Rounds 1,2,5	3,4,6,7
8	Rounds 1,2,5,6	3,4,7,8
9	Rounds 1,2,3,5,7	4,6,8,9
10	Rounds 1,2,3,6,8	4,5,7,9,10
11	Rounds 1,2,3,5,6,8	4,7,9,10,11
12	Rounds 1,2,3,6,7,9	4,5,8,10,11,12
13	Rounds 1,2,4,5,10,12,13	3,6,7,8,9,11
14	Rounds 1,2,4,5,10,12,13	3,6,7,8,9,11
15	Rounds 1,2,3,4,7,8,9,12	5,6,10,11,13

These were improved by Lawrence Rosler in 1964, as a result of prolonged mathematical calculations. The following tables give as close to a perfect balance of comparisons as can be obtained.

Tables	Arrow North	Arrow East
6	Rounds 1,2	3,4,5
7	Rounds 1,2,3,4,5	6,7
8	Rounds 1,4	2,3,5,6,7
9	Rounds 1,2,4,8,9	3,5,6,7
10	Rounds 1,4,5,7,8,9	2,3,6
11	Rounds 1,2,4,10	3,5,6,7,8,9.11
12	Rounds 1,2,4,6,7,8	3,5,9,10,11
13	Rounds 1,2,3,5,6,9	4,7,8,10,11,12,13
14	Rounds 1,3,9,13	2,4,5,6,7,8,10,11,12

SCRAMBLING PLAYS, SCRAMBLING SIGNALS. See DECEPTIVE PLAY.

SCREEN. An opaque barrier placed diagonally across the bridge table so that no player can see his partner. Perforce each player can see only one opponent. One type of screen consists of a curtain attached to runners along a wooden frame, the top of which is some 3–4 feet above the table. After the bidding is concluded, the screen is opened laterally by pulling on its drawstrings. A more elaborate type of screen is opened and closed vertically by turning a handle. For the play of the hand this screen may be raised just enough for dummy's cards to be visible, without allowing the defenders to see each other. For post mortems the screen may be raised completely. See also FRANCO BOARD.

Curtain-type screens were first used in World Championship play in the 1975 BERMUDA BOWL. Prior to 1975 there was such sharp division of opinion as to the desirability of screens that they were little used. Advocates felt that screens would help forestall charges of cheating. See CHEATING ACCUSATIONS. Those opposed felt that the use of screens would create the public impression that there was in fact cheating to be prevented; in addition they felt that screens would be a distracting and dehumanizing element. The screens used in the 1975 Bermuda Bowl, however, met with considerable approbation. A poll of the players and their captains conducted by WBF official J. HAMMERICH revealed that the great majority found that the use of screens, together with BIDDING BOXES, improved the general conditions of contest and made concentration easier, or at least no more difficult.

SEAT. The position which a contestant takes at a table; usually designated by one of the four principal points of the compass, North, South, East, or West. The first two and the last two are partners, and each pair is the opponent of the other pair.

SEATING ASSIGNMENTS. At duplicate tournaments, the ENTRIES sold to the players carry a section designator, a table number, and a direction. These are the seating assignments. For subsequent sessions of the same event, players either take their original seating assignments and await DIRECTOR'S INSTRUCTIONS, or pick up a new entry blank or GUIDE CARD for the subsequent session.

SECOND GAME. The second game of a rubber. Two games are required to win a rubber, and at the conclusion of a rubber a side may have won one, two, or no games during that rubber, but the winning of any second game immediately ends the rubber at that point.

SECOND GUESSER. See RESULT PLAYER.

SECOND HAND PLAY. The old whist rule of "second hand low" is sound enough as a rule of thumb, but there are many possible exceptions. The following are the most important and crucial situations.

(1) In a suit contract, declarer leads low toward a suit headed by K Q or K J. The left-hand defender has the ace, and he knows that the lead may be a singleton. Unless there is clear-cut reason for grabbing tricks quickly, the defender should usually duck without hesitation. If he fails to make his ace, it may not matter—declarer would presumably have been able to secure a discard. But if he puts up the ace, declarer is likely to benefit. If dummy has K Q two tricks are established, and if dummy has K J declarer avoids a guess.

The prompt duck is usually best in the reverse situation, when a singleton is led from dummy. The reasons are similar.

(2) In a suit contract declarer leads toward his hand in a suit in which dummy holds several small cards. There is a possibility that declarer has a singleton king. In this case the ace should be played if the defender has the queen or jack, because declarer cannot then make a losing guess.

(3) A second hand high play with a king or queen may be aimed at preventing a suit establishment.

NORTH
♣ A J 10 3 2

WEST   EAST
♣ K 5 4   ♣ Q 7 6
SOUTH
♣ 9 8

Dummy has no side entry. When South leads a club, West must play high (and would do the same with the queen instead of the king). South cannot make more than one club trick. If West wrongly played low, East would have to hold up his queen to prevent South's making four tricks in the suit.

Other reasons for playing second hand high include: an urgent need to establish partner's suit before his entry is removed; the need to avoid a throw-in; and the need to prevent declarer's ducking a trick to the other defender in an elimination position.

For other considerations involving second hand play see COVERING HONORS and PLAY FROM EQUALS.

SECOND NEGATIVE RESPONSE AFTER ARTIFICIAL FORCING OPENING. A rebid by a responder who has made a negative response to his partner's strong artificial opening bid, such as two diamonds in response to two clubs, that shows a hand worth about 0–3 points. Some partnerships use HERBERT NEGATIVE, the cheapest possible suit rebid by responder, as the second negative; others use the cheaper minor suit rebid. See also DOUBLE NEGATIVE; TWO DIAMOND ARTIFICIAL RESPONSE TO FORCING TWO CLUB OPENING.

SECONDARY EVENT. An event at a national tournament held concurrently with a championship event. Such events, which are open to players eliminated from the major events and to new players, are usually two sessions long and carry regional rating. See CHAMPIONSHIP TOURNAMENTS, SIDE GAME.

SECONDARY HONORS. The lower honors, i.e., queens and jacks. The king of a suit may also be considered a secondary honor when it is not accompanied by the ace. Secondary honors generally carry their weight better in no trump than in suit contracts, especially when they are not located in partner's long suits. See PRIMARY HONORS.

SECONDARY SQUEEZE. A squeeze in which the squeeze card is followed by the loss of one or more tricks to the opponents.

(1) *Squeeze Establishment* (also called delayed duck squeeze by Dr. Love and squeeze suit-out by Coffin). A squeeze establishment has these characteristics: one opponent possesses a guard to a long menace and a winner in a suit which declarer seeks to establish. The preliminary squeeze forces him to discard an additional winner or a card which may be led to his partner's winner.

The endings are based on simple squeeze positions except that declarer has two losers with no convenient way to RECTIFY THE COUNT. Thus, in effect, the rectification of the count takes place after the lead of the squeeze card. Some typical positions:

(a) Positional

NORTH
♠ A J
♡ Q J
◇ —
♣ —

WEST
♠ K Q
♡ A K
◇ —
♣ —

EAST
Imma-
terial

SOUTH
♠ x x
♡ x
◇ —
♣ A

(b) Twin Entry

NORTH
♠ K x
♡ Q J 10
◇ —
♣ —

WEST
Imma-
terial

EAST
♠ Q J 10
♡ A K
◇ —
♣ —

SOUTH
♠ A 9 x
♡ x
◇ —
♣ A

(c) Automatic

NORTH
♠ A 9 x
♡ x
◇ x
♣ —

WEST
Imma-
terial

EAST
♠ Q J 10
♡ A K
◇ —
♣ —

SOUTH
♠ K x
♡ Q J
◇ —
♣ A

(d) Automatic

NORTH
♠ A J
♡ x x
◇ —
♣ x

WEST
Imma-
terial

EAST
♠ K Q
♡ K Q J
◇ —
♣ —

SOUTH
♠ x
♡ A 10 x
◇ —
♣ A

(e) Crisscross

NORTH
♠ A
♡ 10 x x
◇ —
♣ x

WEST
Imma-
terial

EAST
♠ K Q
♡ K Q J
◇ —
♣ —

SOUTH
♠ J x
♡ A x
◇ —
♣ A

In all the above cases, South leads the ace of clubs. Defender must discard a heart in order to protect his spade guard. South can then lead a heart in order to establish a trick for himself in that suit.

In (a) through (e) above, a defender was forced to discard a second winner in the suit which declarer sought to establish. In a minor variation (sometimes called a squeeze elimination [ROMANET]), the opponent is squeezed out of a side winner or a card which may be led to partner's winner.

NORTH
♠ A J
♡ K x
◇ —
♣ —

WEST
♠ K Q
♡ A
◇ A
♣ —

EAST
♠ x
♡ x
◇ x x
♣ —

SOUTH
♠ x
♡ x
◇ x
♣ A

South leads his ace of clubs, and West is squeezed in three suits. He must discard the diamond winner, and North discards a spade. Now South can concede a heart and establish North's king. Had the diamond winner been with East and a small diamond in the West hand, West would have been forced to part with his exit card to his partner's winner.

(2) *Squeeze Throw-In* (also known as squeeze strip). An opponent guards a two-card menace which is in the form of a tenace combination, and he also holds a winner which corresponds to a low card in that suit held by declarer. Declarer intends to lead the low card, throwing the opponent into the lead, to force a play into the tenace.

If the opponent has been stripped of exit cards in all other suits, he still may have too many winners in the throw-in suit. In that case, the preliminary squeeze reduces the number of surplus winners which the defender can hold in the throw-in suit.

A. Declarer has a major tenace, and the throw-in is followed by two tricks for declarer. Declarer may have two or more losers.

(f)
NORTH
Imma-
terial

WEST
♠ K x
♡ —
◇ A K
♣ —

EAST
Imma-
terial

SOUTH
♠ A Q
♡ —
◇ x
♣ A

Squeeze card with tenace.

(g)
NORTH
♠ Q x
♡ —
◇ x
♣ x

WEST
♠ K x
♡ —
◇ A K
♣ —

EAST
Imma-
terial

SOUTH
♠ A x
♡ —
◇ x
♣ A

Split tenace.

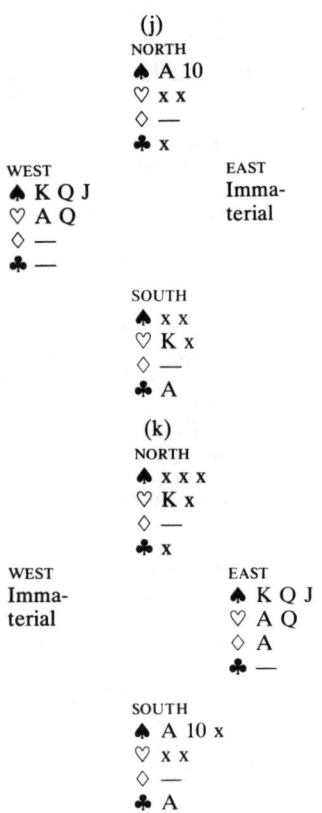

(h)
NORTH
♠ A Q
♡ —
◇ x
♣ x

WEST
Imma-
terial

EAST
♠ K x
♡ —
◇ A K
♣ —

SOUTH
♠ x x
♡ —
◇ Q
♣ A

Squeeze card opposite tenace.

In (f) through (h), the ace of clubs is led, forcing the defender to part with a diamond winner. Now South leads the diamond, and the defender is thrown in to lead away from his spade king. Note that the tenace may be with or opposite the squeeze card, or split between declarer and dummy.

B. Opponent has the major tenace, and the throw-in is followed by one trick for the declarer. Declarer has three losers.

(j)
NORTH
♠ A 10
♡ x x
◇ —
♣ x

WEST
♠ K Q J
♡ A Q
◇ —
♣ —

EAST
Imma-
terial

SOUTH
♠ x x
♡ K x
◇ —
♣ A

(k)
NORTH
♠ x x x
♡ K x
◇ —
♣ x

WEST
Imma-
terial

EAST
♠ K Q J
♡ A Q
◇ A
♣ —

SOUTH
♠ A 10 x
♡ x x
◇ —
♣ A

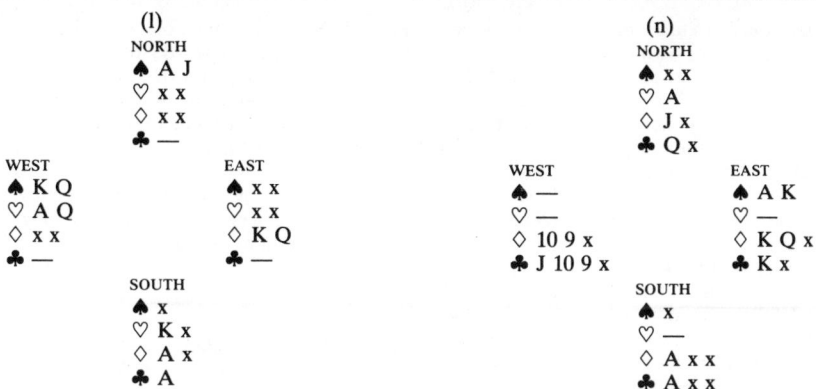

(l)

NORTH
♠ A J
♡ x x
◇ x x
♣ —

WEST
♠ K Q
♡ A Q
◇ x x
♣ —

EAST
♠ x x
♡ x x
◇ K Q
♣ —

SOUTH
♠ x
♡ K x
◇ A x
♣ A

(n)

NORTH
♠ x x
♡ A
◇ J x
♣ Q x

WEST
♠ —
♡ —
◇ 10 9 x
♣ J 10 9 x

EAST
♠ A K
♡ —
◇ K Q x
♣ K x

SOUTH
♠ x
♡ —
◇ A x x
♣ A x x

South leads the ace of clubs, which forces the defender to discard a surplus winner—jack of spades in (j), ace of diamonds in (k), or a potential exit card, the diamond, in (l). Now South takes his spade tricks, and exits in spades, so that he ends up by taking a trick with his king of hearts.

When declarer has a major tenace, so that the defenders cannot afford to lead away from his stopper (Dr. Love calls this a vulnerable stopper), then the end play is effective when declarer has two losers, as shown in A. The preliminary squeeze may force the defender to discard a surplus winner (as indicated) or an exit card. In this situation

South has four losers, and the squeeze must fail since East has a potential exit card in diamonds. North leads the ace of hearts, and East throws a spade. Now East wins the next spade, and plays a high diamond to the ace. He wins the next diamond, but he can now play a low diamond to West's ten, so that the end play is ineffective.

The squeeze establishment also has a three-suit variant which will gain a trick if declarer has three or more losers. Again, precisely three losers are required only if the defenders can kill one of the menace cards.

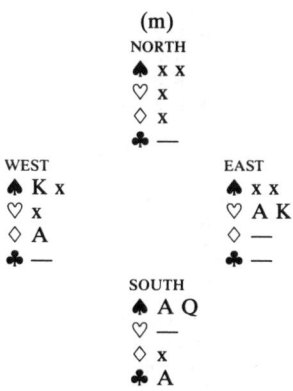

(m)

NORTH
♠ x x
♡ x
◇ x
♣ —

WEST
♠ K x
♡ x
◇ A
♣ —

EAST
♠ x x
♡ A K
◇ —
♣ —

SOUTH
♠ A Q
♡ —
◇ x
♣ A

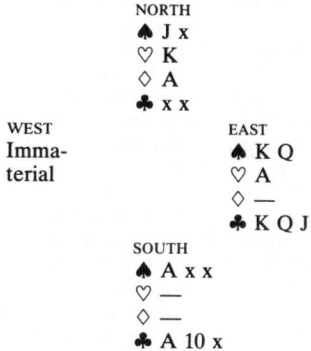

NORTH
♠ J x
♡ K
◇ A
♣ x x

WEST
Imma-
terial

EAST
♠ K Q
♡ A
◇ —
♣ K Q J

SOUTH
♠ A x x
♡ —
◇ —
♣ A 10 x

South leads the ace of clubs, and West is forced to discard his exit card in hearts. Now he can be thrown in with a diamond, and forced to lead a spade into declarer's tenace.

C. Three-suit variants: in the case where one opponent has guards in three suits, which include at least one vulnerable stopper (i.e., declarer has a major tenace in one of the suits), the squeeze works when declarer has three or more losers. Precisely three losers are required only if the defender has a potential exit card in one of the suits.

South has three tricks on top. The ace of diamonds is led and East is squeezed in three suits. He must discard a potential club trick. North leads a club, and declarer ducks, in order to establish his ten, which furnishes him with a fourth trick.

In certain squeeze-establishment plays, declarer may duck two or even three times in order to establish a trick for himself; understandably such positions arise rarely in play.

In another rare variant, the secondary squeeze involving three suits may result in the gain of two tricks to declarer: with three losers in hand, a squeeze-establishment play concedes one trick to the opponents, and adds one trick to declarer's stock. As a result, the count has been rectified, and declarer may be able to continue with a simple squeeze for the gain of another trick.

For related squeeze situations, see STEPPINGSTONE SQUEEZE; VICE SQUEEZE; WINKLE SQUEEZE.

M. I.

SECTION. A group of contestants who constitute a self-contained unit in the competition in one event for one session of a tournament. With up to seventeen tables, one section is usually used, with either a HOWELL (to seven tables), THREE-QUARTER (eight to eleven tables), SCRAMBLED MITCHELL (twelve or thirteen tables), SCRAMBLED MITCHELL or ACBL GUIDE CARD movement (fourteen to twenty-one tables). With twenty-one to thirty-six tables, two sections; thirty-seven to fifty-one tables, three sections; fifty-two to sixty-four tables, four sections; sixty-five to seventy-seven tables, five sections. Above seventy-eight tables, the layout of the room and the requirements of the scoring staff determine whether sections are built up in size or increased in number.

SECTIONAL, SECTIONAL TOURNAMENT. See CHAMPIONSHIP TOURNAMENTS.

SEED, SEEDING. The assignment of certain tables to particularly strong contestants when entries are sold to assure that there will be no preponderance of strong pairs in direct competition within any one section. It is desirable to seed weak pairs also to prevent an imbalance of weakness in a particular section. In pair events, tables 1 and 7 are usually reserved for seeded players; at national tournaments, tables 1, 6, and 11 or 2, 7, and 12 are reserved. In team competitions, adjacent pairs of tables such as 1 and 2, 9 and 10, 17 and 18, etc., are used for spotting the strongest teams through the field. In individual tournaments, an effort is made to assure that the North players, at least, are able to keep score. Tradition assigns the North-South seat at table 1 in section A to a defending pair, team 1 to a defending team.

In team-of-four knockout competition, at many important tournaments in the United States, seeding is based on the total master-point holding of the four starting players. This can accomplish a complete listing of all teams entered, and the usual bracketing by which the top two teams are placed in different halves of the bracketing is used, with the top team meeting the lowest ranked team, next highest meeting the next lowest, etc. When time does not permit complete seeding of the field, the top-ranked half of the field draw their opponents from the balance (unseeded half) by lot for the first-round pairings. As to the rights that may be given to the higher seeded team in a given knockout match, see CONDITIONS OF CONTEST.

ACBL National knockout events (Vanderbilt and Spingold) utilize various formulae for seeding which include not only master-point holdings but recent performances by the players.

SELECTION OF INTERNATIONAL TEAMS. See INTERNATIONAL OPEN TEAM SELECTION; INTERNATIONAL WOMEN'S TEAM SELECTION.

SEMI-FINAL. The round of four or six in a knockout team tournament. When the original draw is based on two, four, eight, or sixteen brackets, successive reduction of the field narrows it to four teams. In the semi-final round, the winners advance to the finals to determine the first and second place overall. When the original draw gives six or twelve brackets, successive reduction gives a semi-final round of six, the winners of the semi-final matches playing a round robin to determine the first three places, with the losers in the semi-final sharing the fourth to sixth position.

SEMI-PSYCHIC. A departure from normal bidding methods which is not a complete bluff but is still intended to deceive the opponents. The term usually refers to an opening bid well below minimum values, but LEAD-INHIBITING BIDS belong in the same category. Here is an illustration of a lead-directing semi-psychic from the National Open Team-of-Four Championships of 1952.

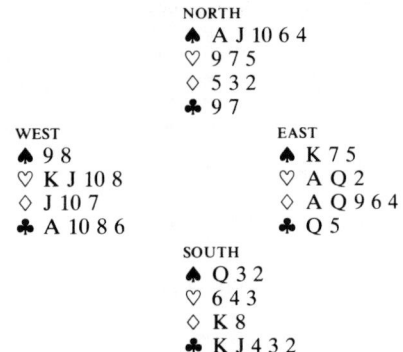

```
                    NORTH
                    ♠ A J 10 6 4
                    ♡ 9 7 5
                    ◇ 5 3 2
                    ♣ 9 7
WEST                               EAST
♠ 9 8                              ♠ K 7 5
♡ K J 10 8                         ♡ A Q 2
◇ J 10 7                           ◇ A Q 9 6 4
♣ A 10 8 6                         ♣ Q 5
                    SOUTH
                    ♠ Q 3 2
                    ♡ 6 4 3
                    ◇ K 8
                    ♣ K J 4 3 2
```

East-West vulnerable. North dealer.

NORTH	EAST	SOUTH	WEST
1 ♠	1 NT	Pass	2 NT
Pass	3 NT	Pass	Pass
Pass			

With the otherwise abnormal spade lead by South, the three no trump contract was defeated. With any other lead, it would have been fulfilled.

SEMI-SET GAME. A rubber bridge session involving five or more players in which one pair (sometimes two pairs), such as a husband and wife, play as partners except when one of them is cut out.

SEMI-SOLID SUIT. A suit of at least six cards which appears to contain only one loser; a suit that is one high card short of being a SOLID SUIT, for example, A K J 10 x x, A Q J x x x, A K x x x x, K Q J x x x x.

SENIOR AND ADVANCED SENIOR MASTER PAIR CHAMPIONSHIP, NATIONAL. See MILES TROPHY.

SENIOR MASTER. A high-ranking player in the AMERICAN CONTRACT BRIDGE LEAGUE. See RANKING OF PLAYERS.

SENIOR MASTERS INDIVIDUAL CHAMPION-SHIP, NATIONAL. See BEYNON TROPHY.

SEQUENCE. Two or more cards in consecutive order of rank, as A K Q (three-card sequence) or Q J 10 9 (four-card sequence). See PLAY FROM EQUALS.

SEQUENCE DISCARDS. The discard of an honor normally shows an honor sequence, of which the discard is the highest. Therefore the discard of a queen denies the king, and guarantees the jack and usually the ten.

The same principle applies in following suit when a top honor has already been played. This follows the more general principle of discarding the highest card which can be spared in transmitting a signal.

SEQUENCE OF ROUNDS. In a session of bridge the sequence of rounds is broken up for a few necessary irregularities. After about half the rounds have been played, the traveling pairs in a section with an even number of tables and no bye stand must skip a table. In team-of-four events, there is often an irregularity at the halfway point where traveling pairs make an irregular progression as do the boards they have just played. See PROGRESSION.

SEQUENCE RE-ENTRY. A type of suit preference signal. After leading a king against no trump from a combination headed by K Q J, the defender can follow with the queen or the jack at choice, in order to suggest a re-entry in a high- or low-ranking suit. See SUIT PREFERENCE SIGNAL.

SERES SQUEEZE. A rare triple squeeze in a three-card ending discovered by Tim Seres of Sydney, Australia in 1965. Playing in six clubs, he arrived at the following ending with the lead in dummy:

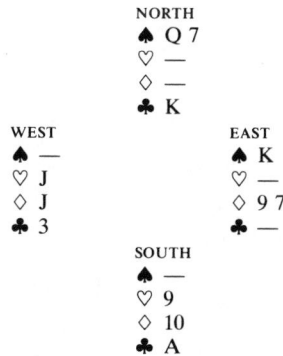

The spade seven was ruffed, establishing the queen, and West was triple squeezed. An unusual feature is that one of the three cards he is trying to retain is a trump loser. See BACKWASH SQUEEZE.

The complete deal was:

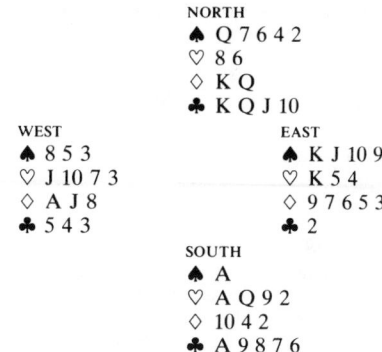

A club was led, and South won in dummy and finessed the heart queen. He cashed the spade ace and led a diamond. West put up the diamond ace and led a second trump. South won in dummy, ruffed a spade, and entered dummy with a diamond lead for another spade ruff. The heart ace and a heart ruff left the three-card ending shown above.

SERIES GAMES. Formerly duplicate sessions in a club which counted as a unit for points or prizes. As of January 1969, the ACBL no longer sanctioned series games for point awards.

SESSION. A period of play during which each contestant is scheduled to play a designated series of boards against one or more opponents. A session may consist of one or more rounds.

SET. Noun: the failure or defeat of a contract. Verb: to defeat a contract by at least one trick.

SET GAME. A pre-arranged match between two partnerships, with each pair almost always remaining the same for the duration of the contest. There have been set games where one of the players has been spelled for a while by some other player who had been waiting in reserve for such an instance, but generally set games involve only four people, and last for several rubbers as previously agreed upon.

The CULBERTSON-LENZ MATCH was the most publicized set game in history. However, there was wide interest in the more recent match between the SHARIF BRIDGE CIRCUS (Omar Sharif, Giorgio Belladonna, Benito Garozzo, and Claude Delmouly) and English experts Jonathan Cansino and Jeremy Flint (with Claude Rodrigue spelling Flint for part of the match), which was held in London in 1970. The stakes were enormous—£1 ($2.40) a point. Over the course of 80 rubbers, of which Sharif had agreed to play a minimum of 52, the Circus won by 5,470 points.

SET UP. To establish one or more cards in the hand of the player himself, his partner, or an opponent.

SET UP SUIT. See ESTABLISHED SUIT.

SEVEN or SEVEN-SPOT. The eighth-ranking card in a suit, located between the eight and the six.

SEVEN-ODD. Seven tricks over book, or thirteen tricks in all.

SEVEN TABLES. At duplicate, seven tables provide for competition among twenty-eight players as individuals, fourteen pairs, or seven teams-of-four. This is an ideal number of tables, and provides, therefore, a basic pattern for all numbers of tables up to thirteen for pair contests, and is an excellent base for larger individual tournaments.

Since 7 is a prime number, the RAINBOW MOVEMENT is suitable for an individual contest. Three boards to a round, with the West players moving counterclockwise around the table at the end of each board of the round, provides each player with twenty-one different partners. Six is top and 63 is average.

Thirteen rounds of two boards each makes the HOWELL MOVEMENT an ideal competition for pair events, each pair meeting every other pair, with almost perfectly balanced comparisons throughout the field and at least twelve and no more than fourteen direct comparisons between pairs. The MITCHELL MOVEMENT can also be used when two fields are desirable, six rounds of four boards, or seven rounds of three or four boards being the usual contest. (Seven rounds of four boards is a little long, seven rounds of three boards is a little short for most players.)

With six and a half tables as a pair contest, the phantom pair can, for convenience, be the stationary pair for a Howell game. If a Mitchell movement is used, any pair may be the phantom, but the entire seven rounds must be played to avoid factoring.

With seven and a half tables, the extra half table can be accommodated by a BUMP MITCHELL, using the seven table setup, or by a phantom pair in an EIGHT TABLE movement.

As a team contest, the regular team-of-four progression, boards going to the next lower and traveling pairs skipping a table to lower numbers, provides six uninterrupted rounds for twenty-four boards, without any irregularities in the progression.

SEXTET BRIDGE. A seldom played bridge game for six players, playing as two partnerships of three each. Two new suits were introduced, called rackets and wheels. The 50% increase in the number of suits and players in the game results in a total number of legal auctions with all players participating ($(6 \times 66^{49} -1)/5 = 1.7251787 \times 10^{89}$) that exceeds by a substantial margin the probable total number of atoms in the universe (about 10^{64} as estimated by physicist Sir James Jeans).

R. T(rue)

SHADE, SHADED. A bid made on slightly less than technical minimum requirements. For example:

♠ K Q 10 x x
♡ A J 10 x
◇ x x
♣ x x

is a shaded one spade opening bid. A shaded raise, a direct raise of partner's bid suit, may be made when strict requirements would dictate a pass. Often this may lessen the danger of missing a game or serve as a semi-pre-emptive nuisance bid.

The requirements for biddable suits may be lessened somewhat and therefore "shaded" in certain bidding situations, such as opening in third position with one spade, holding:

♠ K x x x
♡ A Q x
◇ Q x x
♣ x x x

Bidder in this situation is prepared to pass any response partner may make and may very well make a partial. If the opposition has the bulk of the cards, the one spade opening may serve as an obstacle in arriving at the proper contract.

SHAKE. A colloquialism meaning DISCARD.

SHARIF BRIDGE CIRCUS. A touring professional team of world class players, organized and headed by movie star Omar Sharif, to play a series of exhibition matches against leading European and North American teams.

The Circus made its debut late in 1967, when Sharif, Giorgio Belladonna, Claude Delmouly, Benito Garozzo, and Leon Yallouze, all playing the BLUE TEAM CLUB, defeated the Dutch international team in matches sponsored by newspapers and played in three Netherlands cities before enthusiastic audiences, who viewed the competition on BRIDGE-O-RAMA. Using this format—a match against a highly rated team with the play-by-play displayed to the audience accompanied by expert commentary—the Circus made an extended tour in 1968. It defeated teams in Italy and London, lost its first matches to Holland and Belgium in The Hague, and made a swing through six North American cities—Montreal, Toronto, Los Angeles, Dallas, New Orleans, and New York—winning the majority of the matches. (Several of the American matches were three-cornered contests involving the Circus, the local team, and the ACES.)

A second tour in 1970 received a spectacular send-off when Jeremy Flint and Jonathan Cansino challenged Sharif and company to a 100-rubber pair game in London (later reduced by time pressure to 80 rubbers). The stakes were an unprecedented British pound ($2.40) per point, plus an additional bonus of £1,000 on the net result of each four rubbers. The match attracted wide newspaper and magazine coverage in the United States as well as in Europe. Sharif won by a margin of 5,470 points and collected over $18,000 but this was a comparatively small sum against the expenses of staging the match and taping the highlights for a series of television shows planned for later syndication.

This was immediately followed by a tour of seven North American cities, Chicago, Winnipeg, Los Angeles, St. Paul, Dallas, Detroit, and Philadelphia. In addition to matches against powerful teams of local stars, the tour included a marathon 840-deal match against the Aces, who accompanied the Circus throughout the tour. The Circus defeated the all-star teams in Chicago, Winnipeg, and St. Paul, but lost all its other matches, bowing to the Aces by 101 IMPs (1,793–1,692) after the lead had seesawed excitingly from city to city. Pietro Forquet joined the Sharif team in Dallas but could not reverse the effect of the exhausting schedule, which included numerous personal appearances by Sharif.

Despite commercial sponsorship of more than $50,000 in 1970, neither of the American tours proved a financial success, although both resulted in wide publicity for bridge.

SHARK. An expert player, but more particularly one who specializes in playing for money, and is adept at this type of competition.

SHARPLES CONVENTION. Devised by James and Robert SHARPLES of England—a "natural" extension of the STAYMAN convention.

A responder who sees slam possibilities frequently faces a problem if he uses Stayman, and does not find an immediate fit. If the responder has 4–4–3–2 or 4–4–4–1 distribution, he may wish to explore the possibility of a 4–4 fit in a minor suit.

Opposite a 16- to 18-point no trump, responder holds:

♠ K J 7 5
♡ 4
♢ A Q 5 2
♣ A 10 5 3

The Sharples idea is to bid four of a minor suit on the second round, showing specifically a four-card suit and sufficient strength to play in at least four no trump:

OPENER	RESPONDER
1 NT	2 ♣
2 ♡	4 ♣

The opener rebids his hand naturally. If he has four-card club support, he raises to five clubs or six clubs in accordance with his estimation of slam prospects. If four-card club support is lacking, opener can make a natural suit bid of four diamonds or four spades (although in some styles a four-card spade suit may have been excluded by the two heart rebid). Four no trump and five no trump would be natural bids announcing that the opener's distribution was 4–3–3–3.

All no trump bids at any stage should be regarded as natural.

Suppose responder holds:

♠ J 3
♡ K J 7 5
♢ A Q 5 2
♣ A 5 3

The bidding goes:

OPENER	RESPONDER
1 NT	2 ♣
2 ♠	4 ♢

By jumping to four diamonds, responder denies a four-card club suit, and keeps open the possibility of playing a slam in a red suit.

SHIFT (or switch). To change suit from one originally led on defense; alternately, a change of suit by declarer in the development of his play. Shift can also be used to describe a bid in a new suit by either the opening bidder, his partner, or an overcaller or his partner, as JUMP SHIFT, ONE-OVER-ONE, etc.

SHOMATE MOVEMENT. For INDIVIDUAL TOURNAMENTS of EIGHT, NINE, or TEN TABLES. These movements are non-cyclic and must be conducted with GUIDE CARDS, and, while very difficult to post rapidly, provide excellent comparison among all the players entered in the competition.

SHOOTING. The art of playing deliberately for an abnormal result.

Occasionally near the end of a tournament, a couple of tops are needed in order to have any chance of winning. Two or three average results would be just as fatal to one's chances as bottoms. Under these circumstances, playing for abnormal results is justified. Playing for top or bottom is called shooting.

Many players, quite wrongly, think of shooting as equivalent to overbidding. In fact, good shooting will consist of underbidding as often as overbidding. The aim should be to arrive at a contract which is wrong but only slightly wrong.

To bid a game or a slam which has a 30–40% chance of success is an intelligent "shot"; but it is equally sensible to stop short of game or slam which is a 60–70% chance. In each case the shooter is hoping for the less likely result.

But the best chance to shoot intelligently is in the play of the hand.

NORTH
♠ x x
♡ x x x
◊ x x
♣ A 8 x x x x

SOUTH
♠ A Q x
♡ A K x x
◊ A Q x
♣ K 9 x

West leads a spade against South's three no trump contract. Declarer wins East's king with the ace, and attacks clubs. Normally he would play the king, and then duck a round. This is the percentage play because the odds are slightly against a 2–2 club break. Obviously if declarer plays the king, then leads the nine to dummy's ace, his contract will be placed in jeopardy. For one who wishes to shoot, this is a wonderful opportunity. By playing the ace on the second round (unless West shows out), he can be almost certain of a top (or bottom).

NORTH
♠ K 10
♡ x
◊ Q J x x
♣ A x x x x x .

SOUTH
♠ A J 9 x x x
♡ A x x x
◊ —
♣ K Q x

This hand is more complicated. West leads the king of hearts against the four spade contract. At rubber bridge, declarer would plan to ruff two hearts. This would be a safety play to guard against four trumps to the queen in one hand. At duplicate, there is a better play—to finesse the ten of spades at trick two. If the ten loses to the queen, the king will still provide a stopper against the running of the heart suit. Provided trumps are 3–2, this play will yield either twelve or thirteen tricks.

Suppose that one were shooting. How should one play? In weak competition this is not a good hand for shooting. The recommended play is greatly superior to any other line of play at duplicate, and if the rest of the field does not see it, one could "shoot" with very favorable odds by adopting it. In strong competition where most declarers could be expected to finesse the ten of spades, one could shoot by adopting the "rubber bridge play," but my preference would be to lead to the king, and finesse on the way back. This play would get a top whenever East had the queen, not more than three long. Of course when the finesse lost, it would result in a very cold bottom.

M. M.

SHORT CLUB. The short "prepared" or "convenient" club is an original opening bid made on a three-card club suit. It was first advocated by the FOUR ACES as a means of providing a comfortable rebid. In principle it requires a minimum of Qxx (to support a lead), and failing this, opener may choose instead to open with one diamond. It is most often used by the disciples of systems that require five cards for a major suit opening. For example:

♠ A 6 5 4
♡ A Q 3 2
◊ A 8
♣ 9 7 6

When playing FIVE-CARD MAJORS the hand is opened with one club. When the hand contains two clubs and three diamonds, an opening diamond bid is usually preferred. It is essential in these systems for responder to mention his four-card major holding, if at all feasible, in order to find the all-important major-suit "fit." All players, even those who initiate weak major-suit bids, will at times resort to the Short Club.
Consider:

♠ 8 7 6 2
♡ 9 6 4
◊ A K 5
♣ A K 7

This hand is not strong enough for an opening one no trump (if no trump is the correct contract, it will almost surely play better from your partner's hand), and the objection to one spade is that the player would have no sound rebid over a response in a new suit at the two-level. A "prepared" bid of one club will make his rebidding problem easier.

Responder should respond and rebid on the assumption that the one-club bid is genuine.

Some specialized bidding systems use an artificial club opening as an introduction to a very strong hand (see BLUE TEAM CLUB, SCHENKEN SYSTEM, VANDERBILT CLUB), but it is to be understood that the short club, per se, is not a system but an opening bid to facilitate future rebids, and may be passed by partner. When otherwise used it is more properly announced as ONE CLUB ARTIFICIAL AND FORCING, and in such cases it does not promise any particular length or strength in the club suit itself. See also CHOICE OF SUIT.

SHORT HAND. A term used to describe the hand of the partnership that contains the fewer cards in the trump suit, such as in the reference, "declarer (or the defenders) took the ruff in the short hand." Occasionally, the term may be applied to a hand that is short in a non-trump suit and therefore expects to ruff. During the auction, players frequently visualize possible shortness in partner's or one of the opponent's hand in a suit and draw certain inferences from this, and final contracts are often determined by just such estimations of shortness in a plain suit.

SHORT HOWELL MOVEMENTS. Methods of conducting a one-winner duplicate tournament when the object is to complete the game in just under three hours; provision is made for eleven rounds of two boards each. The six-table game is the regular HOWELL game, with APPENDIX TABLES being added for the seven-, eight-, nine-, and ten-table game.

To get BALANCED COMPARISONS, the stationary pairs other than the one with the highest number alternate between North-South and East-West positions, making the switch to and fro at various times. Guide cards are available giving complete information; the following table gives starting assignments, with numbers 12 and higher stationary. Boards are played in order at each table, starting with the set indicated in the table below. Pairs, in moving, replace the pair with the next lower number, number 1 replacing pair 11.

	6 tables		7 tables		8 tables		9 tables		10 tables	
#1	12v1	1	14v1	1	16v1	1	18v1	1	18v1	1
#2	11v6	3	4v6	2	4v15	2	5v17	2	5v17	2
#3	9v5	7	9v10	3	11v13	3	11v16	3	11v16	3
#4	3v2	8	7v3	4	14v10	4	2v10	4	10v19	4
#5	8v10	9	12v2	5	9v8	5	15v9	5	20v2	5
#6	7v4	11	11v13	6	5v7	6	7v8	6	15v9	6
#7			5v8	7	3v12	7	14v6	7	7v8	7
#8					2v6	8	4v13	8	14v6	8
#9							3v12	9	4v13	9
#10									3v12	10

SHORT SUIT. In an original hand of thirteen cards, a suit containing three cards or less. See SINGLETON, DOUBLETON.

SHORT-SUIT GAME TRIES. These were developed as part of the KAPLAN-SHEINWOLD SYSTEM, but can be used effectively with any standard system.

When the opening major-suit bid has been raised to two, the opener tries for game by bidding his shortest suit.
For example:

♠ A K 6 5 3
♡ A 5 2
◇ 8
♣ K J 7 4

The bidding goes:

OPENER	RESPONDER
1 ♠	2 ♠
3 ◇	

This asks responder to go to four spades if his values are mainly outside diamonds. If responder rebids three hearts, that would also be a short-suit try, expressing doubt about game prospects.

This method gives a partnership a chance of judging whether strength is duplicated. A disadvantage is that it may help the opponents to find a cheap save. One defender may double the short-suit try, and encourage his partner to take the save. It may also provide a clue to the most effective lead and subsequent defense.

It is best to restrict these bids to the situations when a major has been raised and there has been no interference.

The specific sequence one heart—two hearts—two spades may need special consideration. The two spade rebid may be needed as a natural rebid, especially if the opening bidder has not guaranteed a five-card heart suit.

For alternative methods see TWO-WAY GAME TRIES, WEAK SUIT GAME TRY.

SHORT-SUIT LEADS. An opening lead of a singleton or a doubleton is often indicated when the leader examines his hand in the light of the bidding.

Against either no trump or a trump contract, a short-suit lead is normal when partner has bid the suit. (Partner's bid suit is less automatic as a lead with greater length; against a trump contract it may be necessary to aim quickly for tricks elsewhere.)

The short-suit lead is also indicated when there is a bidding inference that this is partner's suit, and that he will have the entries to make use of it. Terence REESE gives this example:

SOUTH
♠ Q 5 3
♡ J 8 6 2
◇ 7 4
♣ Q 7 6 3

After the bidding:

WEST	EAST
1 ♣	1 ♠
2 ♣	2 NT
3 NT	

South should lead a diamond. The hand is too weak to hope to do much with hearts, so a diamond is led in the hope of hitting partner's strength. If South held the spade ace instead of the three, a heart lead would be indicated.

A short-suit lead may be made for passive reasons, usually because other leads seem unattractive. This is most likely to be desirable if the bidding suggests that the declaring side has no long suit, and that therefore there is no urgent need to attack.

In a suit contract a short-suit lead is most desirable if the trump holding suggests that there are real prospects of obtaining a ruff. (Ax, Axx, or Kxx would be ideal.) Conversely a short-suit lead, particularly of a singleton, may be a mistake when there is no ruffing prospect, because it may help declarer to play a suit which would have presented problems. A singleton trump is usually a bad lead (but see TRUMP LEADS).

Against no trump, a short-suit lead is indicated when the opening leader is very weak, and no entries are available to make use of a long weak suit. The leader should try to hit his partner's suit, although this may turn out to declarer's advantage. (For this reason the long weak suit may prove best as a passive lead.) A short-suit lead is required when the leader's partner has doubled no trump, and no suit has been bid:

SOUTH	WEST	NORTH	EAST
1 NT	Pass	3 NT	Dbl.
Pass	Pass	Pass	

SHORTEN. To force; to shorten in trumps by forcing to ruff. See FORCING LEADS.

SHOW OUT. To fail to follow suit for the first time during the play of that suit.

SHOW UP SQUEEZE. A squeeze of a player who guards a suit in which his holding could successfully be finessed, obviating the squeeze. It derives its name from the fact that after the squeeze card has been played the defender will have blanked his finessable card, so that it will show up when the suit is led toward the tenace. See also COUNT SQUEEZE.

SHOWING PREFERENCE. See PREFERENCE.

SHUFFLE. Noun: the mixing together of the pack of cards prior to the next, or first deal. Several thorough mixings, or shuffles, are required as it is important that the deck be mixed completely from deal to deal. Verb: to mix the cards. This is generally a two-handed operation, with each hand holding roughly half the deck between the thumb and fore and middle fingers. The halves are then blended together with a riffle effect.

SHUT-OUT BID. See PRE-EMPTIVE BID.

SIDE. A team of two in a rubber game or a Chicago game. The term can also describe a pairing in a duplicate contest, or, in team-of-four play, the entire team of whatever number.

SIDE GAME. A one-session event at a CHAMPION-SHIP TOURNAMENT, run concurrently with a championship event, and, at national tournaments, concurrently with SECONDARY EVENTS as well. Players who do not wish to compete in multisession events find single session competition in these games.

The greatest number of tables in play at National Championship tournaments compete in the side events. An extraordinary development in the early 1960s has been the size of the fields competing in special side games held in the morning at these tournaments, in addition to the afternoon and evening sessions.

SIDE SUIT. In bidding, a suit of at least four cards held by a player whose first bid is in another suit.

In play, a suit of at least four cards other than trumps held by declarer in his own hand or dummy.

SIGN-OFF BID. A bid which is intended to close the auction at the part-score level. It is usually a bid in a long suit when facing an announced no trump hand:

WEST	EAST		WEST	EAST
1 ♠	1 NT		1 ♣	1 ♠
2 ♠			1 NT	2 ♠

In each case the two spade bid announces spade length, probably six cards, and a complete lack of interest in game. In very rare circumstances, perhaps less than once in a hundred deals, partner may continue because he holds three-card spade support, a maximum hand, and honor strength in top cards.

Similar sequences ending at the three-level are regarded as sign-offs in some styles, notably ACOL:

WEST	EAST
1 ◇	1 ♠
2 NT	3 ♠

In KAPLAN-SHEINWOLD, East would sign off by bidding three clubs followed by three spades.

Some other bids, such as simple PREFERENCE bids, are similar in character because they expect partner to pass.

SIGNALS, SIGNALING. The language of defensive play, by which defenders can legitimately exchange information about the makeup of their hands. Various methods of signaling are discussed under the following titles: BECHGAARD SIGNALS; BLUE PETER; DISCARDING; HIGH-LOW; KELLY SOLID-SUIT SIGNALS; LENGTH SIGNALS; ODD-EVEN DISCARDS; REVOLVING DISCARDS; SUIT PREFERENCE SIGNAL; TRUMP SIGNAL; UPSIDE-DOWN SIGNALS.

SILENCE. Observed during the play of important matches, by consent of all, especially by the kibitzers. In the playing rooms of the top-level clubs, any noise or disturbance of the games is severely frowned upon, and should a disturbance occur, the officer of the day or other official will usually make the necessary remonstrance.

SILODOR TROPHY. For the Spring National Open Pair Championship. Presented in 1963 in memory of Sidney Silodor and made retroactive to include winners of the event since it started in 1958. Past results are listed under Spring Nationals.

SIMPLE. (as applied to an overcall or response). Non-jump; merely sufficient to overcall or respond.

SIMPLE FINESSE. A finesse for a single card held by the adversaries.

SIMPLE HONORS. A term in use in auction bridge to denote three honors in the trump suit, for which 30 points were scored.

SIMPLE OVERCALL. A minimum overcall.

SIMPLE SQUEEZE. A squeeze which acts against one opponent in two suits. The minimum requirements are: (1) a two-card menace and a one-card menace, both guarded by the same opponent; (2) all the remaining tricks but one.

The card which forces the defender to discard a busy card is called the squeeze card. The squeeze card must be a winner played from the hand opposite the two-card menace, so that the two menaces and the squeeze card cannot all be in the same hand. The two-card menace contains a master card, which provides an entry to one of the menaces.

The following are the basic endings for a simple squeeze:

(1) Positional (or one-way) squeeze:

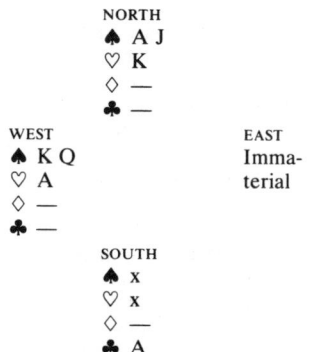

South plays the ace of clubs, and West is squeezed. When West discards one suit, North discards the other, and so takes the remaining tricks.

In this example, spades are the two-card menace and hearts the one-card menace. The squeeze card is the ace of clubs. Declarer has on top two of the remaining three tricks.

In this position both West and North have been reduced to busy cards, but West must discard first so that declarer can choose his discard accordingly, resulting in the gain of a trick. If, in this position, the East and West cards are interchanged, then the squeeze is inoperative.

(2) Split two-card menace:

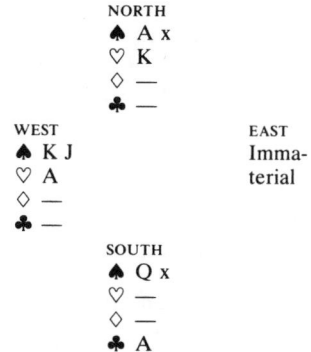

In this variation, the two-card menace is split between North and South. The North hand contains the master card (the ace of spades in this example), but the South hand contains the menace (here the queen of spades). The (split) two-card menace is still said to be opposite the squeeze card (here the ace of clubs) provided that a master card of that menace is properly situated, as here.

(3) AUTOMATIC SQUEEZE:

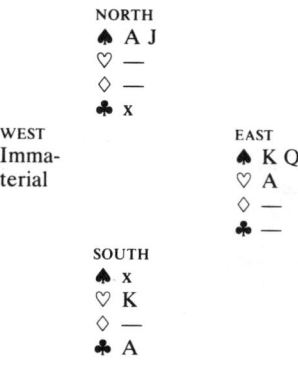

(a) As usual, the two-card menace is opposite the squeeze card, but now the one-card menace accompanies the squeeze card. This means that the North hand has an idle card (see BUSY CARD AND IDLE CARD) which can be played on the ace of clubs; that is, North's discard does not depend on the opponent's play. As a result, the squeeze is automatic in that it operates against either opponent if the same opponent guards both menace cards.

(b) Twin-entry menace:

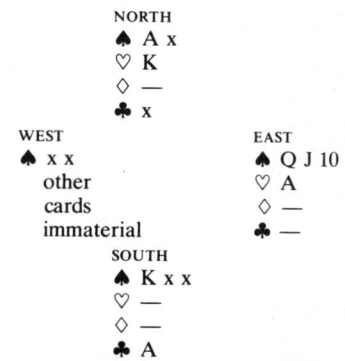

When South plays the ace of clubs, East is squeezed. The position is automatic; even though the one-card menace is opposite the squeeze card, there is compensation in the form of an extra winner in the long menace, which is now called a twin-entry two-card menace.

(c) Criss-cross squeeze:

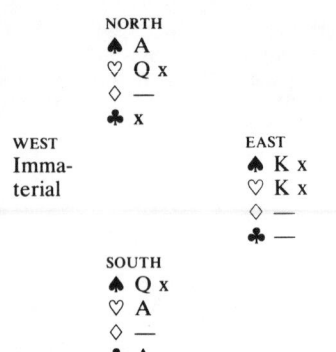

NORTH
♠ A
♡ Q x
◇ —
♣ x

WEST
Imma-
terial

EAST
♠ K x
♡ K x
◇ —
♣ —

SOUTH
♠ Q x
♡ A
◇ —
♣ A

South leads the ace of clubs, which forces East to unguard one of his major suit kings. If East discards a spade, declarer takes the ace of that suit, dropping East's king, returns to hand with the ace of hearts to cash the spade queen. If East can foresee the impending squeeze, he may be able to make a deceptive play, blanking one of his kings early, thereby presenting South with a guess as to what the end position is.

M. I.

SIMPLIFIED CLUB SYSTEM. Originated by Larry WEISS and played by him successfully in national competition. It combines some of the features of the BLUE TEAM CLUB and the ROMAN SYSTEM:

(1) One club shows 16 points or more, and responses show controls. A two-club rebid shows a stronger hand with game values, and the responses again show controls. A two-diamond rebid shows a strong three-suiter.

(2) One diamond, one heart, and one spade guarantee a two-suited hand, at least five-four, and the shorter suit is bid first unless it is clubs. One no trump is an artificial positive response showing at least 10 points. The suit immediately above the opener's is an artificial negative, but the responder is not required to use it if he has some fit with the opener.

(3) One no trump is 12–15 points.

(4) Two clubs is 11–16 and three-suited.

(5) Other two-bids show single-suited hands with 11–16 points. Club hands are shown by two no trump (14–17) or three clubs (11–14).

SIMPLIFIED PRECISION. A version of the PRECISION CLUB system that differs from Standard Precision essentially in that (1) it uses no asking bids, (2) its two diamond opening shows diamond length rather than diamond shortness, and (3) its four-level minor-suit openings are natural pre-empts. Compare also SUPER PRECISION.

SIMS-CULBERTSON MATCH. See CULBERTSON-SIMS MATCH.

SIMS SYSTEM. A system of contract bidding originated circa 1930–32 by P. Hal SIMS. The system stressed strong first- and second-hand opening bids (with corresponding "protection" by third or fourth hand); strong four-card biddable suits, with the opening bid made in the lower ranking. All opening bids of three or two in a suit were forcing, both showing hands strong in honor value, but the three-bid showing length as well. Weak defensive bids were not made when vulnerable. The system also employed forcing overcalls and informatory doubles.

SIMULTANEOUS CALLS, LEADS, OR PLAYS. Covered in appropriate sections of LAWS and LAWS OF DUPLICATE. The treatment is that, if one of the simultaneous acts is in legal rotation, that act stands; the other act, which is perforce out of rotation, is treated as a call, lead, or play out of rotation and the penalty applicable to such act is invoked.

SINGAPORE CONTRACT BRIDGE ASSOCIATION. Founded in 1965, when Singapore left the Malaysian Federation, the Association is a member of the Far East Bridge Federation and participates in Far East Championships, hosting the event in 1972. Honorary secretary, 1975: V. G. Kamath, c/o Singapore Contract Bridge Association, P.O. Box 47, Newton Post Office, Singapore 11.

SINGLE COUP. A coup in which declarer shortens his hand once in trumps by ruffing a card from dummy, in order to reduce his trump holding to the same number held by his right-hand opponent. See COUP.

SINGLE DUMMY PROBLEMS. A solver is given the two hands of a partnership holding, approximating the conditions facing a declarer at the bridge table. Among the foremost inventors of these problems is Paul LUKACS of Israel, who presents these.

(a)
NORTH
♠ 6 3 2
♡ Q J 4
◇ A Q 6 5 4
♣ 6 2

SOUTH
♠ A K 8
♡ 8
◇ K 8 2
♣ A K Q J 10 9

South plays six clubs against the lead of the heart five. East takes the first trick with the heart ace, and returns a low heart. Assuming that West holds the heart king, South can claim the contract. Why?

(b)

NORTH
♠ K 8 5
♡ 8 4 3 2
◊ 6
♣ A 10 9 8 7

SOUTH
♠ A Q 7
♡ K Q J
◊ K 10 9 8 4
♣ K 2

Against South's three no trump contract, West leads the four of clubs. East's jack is taken by South's king. Next comes a successful club finesse, East following suit. What is the right continuation?

Solutions. (a) South trumps the heart return; then plays all his trumps (discarding one diamond and two spades from the dummy). Diamond ace and king are cashed in that order. If both opponents follow, there is no problem. If West holds the diamond guard and the heart king, he is squeezed in the two red suits on the second spade lead. If East holds the diamond guard, after the third lead of diamonds, West has the heart king and East the diamond guard. Neither, then, has three spades, and declarer can claim the last three tricks in that suit.

(b) The solution hinges on the continuation of the club suit; should declarer play the ace and then the nine, he has an impossible discard to make on the second play; discarding either a second diamond or a heart gives the opponents a chance to establish that suit, while a spade discard costs a trick in the suit. Therefore, the potential club loser must be lost immediately, by leading the nine at trick three, before leading the ace.

SINGLE GRAND COUP. A GRAND COUP in which the declarer shortens his hand once in trumps, to reduce his holding to the same number as held by his right-hand opponent, by ruffing one winner from the dummy.

SINGLE RAISE. A raise of opener's one-level suit opening to the two-level. The normal range of the bid is 6–9 high-card points; but 10 is possible, and less than 6 is common when there is distributional compensation.

The higher the rank of the opener's suit, the less length is required by responder to raise. One spade tends to be a five-card suit, and can be raised freely with three-card support (and the five-card major-suit bidders might raise conceivably with a doubleton). One heart is often raised to two with three-card support, but a raise to two diamonds almost invariably indicates four cards or more. This is a possible exception:

♠ 4 3
♡ 5 2
◊ A 5 2
♣ Q 9 7 4 3 2

In reply to one club, even four-card support may not be sufficient. With a 3–3–3–4 hand, one diamond might be preferred to two clubs. (See BIDDABLE SUITS.)

For some special treatments of single raises see SINGLE RAISE IN MAJOR, CONSTRUCTIVE; INVERTED MINOR SUIT RAISES.

Rebids by the opener below the game level are almost always game invitations. (See SHORT-SUIT GAME TRIES; TRIAL BIDS; TWO-WAY GAME TRIES; WEAK SUIT GAME TRY. But see PRE-EMPTIVE RE-RAISE. Many partnerships make an exception if the opener raises again; this can conveniently be regarded as a pre-emptive measure, especially if the suit is a minor.

A rebid of two no trump (one heart—two hearts—two no trump) shows 17–18 points, and is not forcing. If responder then bids a lower-ranking suit, he is showing a long suit and general weakness, and expects to be passed.

SINGLE RAISE IN MAJOR, CONSTRUCTIVE. In ROTH-STONE, a raise from one spade to two spades or one heart to two hearts that shows 10–12 points and is very rarely passed.

♠ K 5 4
♡ A 9 6 3
◊ Q J 6
♣ 8 4 3

See ONE NO TRUMP RESPONSE TO MAJOR, FORCING.

SINGLE RAISE IN RESPONDER'S SUIT. See OPENER'S REBID.

SINGLETON. An original holding of exactly one card in a suit (see WORTHLESS SINGLETON/DOUBLETON). For valuation in a suit contract see DISTRIBUTIONAL VALUES.

SINGLETON KING. To drop a singleton king instead of taking a losing finesse is always satisfying. In the following deal, reported by Herman Filarski, the declarer dropped two singleton kings on the first two tricks:

WEST
♠ A
♡ J 10 9 7
◊ A Q J 5 4 2
♣ Q 5

EAST
♠ K J 8 3
♡ A Q 8 6 4
◊ 10 8 7
♣ A

East played in six hearts, against the opening lead of the diamond nine. He judged that South would be unlikely to underlead the diamond king, because there was no certainty that the diamond ace would be in dummy. The diamond ace was played, felling the singleton king in the North hand.

Declarer now realized that a losing trump finesse would expose him to a diamond ruff by North. In an effort to avert this possibility, he led to the heart ace —and dropped the singleton king. He made all the tricks by sound reasoning, but the opponents thought they were being cheated.

A singleton king can sometimes be dropped in this situation:

WEST   EAST
♣ J 10 9 8 5   ♣ A Q 2

West is the declarer and the club suit has not been bid. If he leads the jack and North plays low, there is an argument for putting up dummy's ace. North will almost always cover when he holds the king.

The popular notions are that singleton kings are more common than one might expect; that one singleton king suggests another; and that singleton kings of clubs are often to be found. These have no logical or mathematical justification, and can be classed as superstition.

SINGLETON-SHOWING BID. See SPLINTER BID.

SINGLETON SWISS. See SPLINTER BID.

SIT, SIT FOR. To pass one's partner's PENALTY DOUBLE or TAKE-OUT DOUBLE.

SITTING. Gerund: a session of bridge. Participle: descriptive term referring to one's position at the table, i.e., North, West, etc.; also used in a sentence to describe possession of a hand or a holding, in which case the exact holdings are always given. See SESSION, SEAT.

SIX or SIX-SPOT. The ninth highest card in a suit.

SIX NO TRUMP OPENING. A very rare opening bid showing a balanced hand with twelve sure tricks. Responder should raise if he holds an ace or a king. (To raise with a queen is doubtful.)

SIX OF A SUIT OPENING. The theoretical meaning of this bid is a twelve-trick hand which is missing only the ace or king of trumps. Such a hand has such low frequency that the bid is idle. It is perhaps more sensible to reserve it for a freak hand, possibly a complete two-suiter, which is likely to offer some play for twelve tricks. This has the required pre-emptive value, and does not encourage the opponents to save, as they would if the opener had guaranteed twelve tricks.

SIX-ODD. Six tricks over book, or twelve tricks in all.

SIX TABLES. At duplicate, six tables provide for competition among twenty-four players as individuals, twelve pairs, or six teams.

As an individual movement, the base is the twelve-player game, with two three-table sections playing the same boards, thus putting each board into play six times. By starting one of the sections at the second round while the others start at the third round, the necessity for twinning or relaying of boards is eliminated. Five is top, 55 is average. In addition, there is available a twenty-five player movement, which can be used for a one-session game using thirty boards, or a two-session game using only twenty-five boards.

As a pair contest, either the MITCHELL or HOWELL MOVEMENT can be used. If a Mitchell is used, tables 1 and 2 share boards by relay throughout, with a bye stand between tables 4 and 5, traveling pairs moving to higher numbered, and boards to lower numbered tables. The full six rounds must be played, usually four boards to the round. Top is 5, average is 72. If Howell movement is used, the full eleven-round, twenty-two-board movement is desirable for an early finish. For a longer game, the nine-round, three-boards-to-a-round, THREE-QUARTER MOVEMENT is excellent.

For five and a half tables, Mitchell, the phantom pair should be one of the North-South pairs at a relay table, eliminating the necessity for a relay; if a Howell movement is used, a stationary pair should be chosen for the phantom so that sit-outs always occur at the same table.

For a team game, tables 1 and 4, 2 and 5, and 3 and 6 should be close, as boards must be relayed between them each round. Boards 6–10 are on table 1, 16–20 on table 2, and 26–30 on table 3. North-South play boards in ascending order, getting them from bye stands, and traveling pairs move to the next lower numbered tables for the first and each subsequent round. See NEW ENGLAND RELAY movement.

For six and one half tables as a pair game, see SEVEN TABLES.

SKINNER PSYCHIC CONTROL (developed by Col. R. H. SKINNER, Wilmington, Del.). Use of certain forcing bids to guard against the possibility that the opener has made a disciplined (3- to 6-point) psychic bid. See PSYCHIC CONTROLS. The one no trump response to a major suit opening (nominally forcing) shows 6–13 points. It may be made with a hand which would normally make a direct pre-emptive raise to game; then, if the opener rebids, and so denies a psychic, responder jumps to game. A first-round raise of the major to game shows a powerful hand strong enough to make opposite a psychic. Similarly, a forcing single raise in a minor may be made with a strong hand. Responses of two no trump and three no trump show respectively 19–21 points, and more than 21 points.

SKINNER RESPONSES TO A ONE NO TRUMP OPENING (devised by Col. R. H. SKINNER, Wilmington, Del.). After a one no trump opening bid, two clubs requests opener to show a four-card major or rebid two no trump with a maximum, or to bid two diamonds with a minimum. If opener rebids two diamonds, responder will usually show a major, and opener either raises with four-card support, bids two spades over two hearts, or rebids two no trump with no major. A jump to three hearts or three spades after an initial response of two clubs shows a four-card suit and is game-forcing. To make a minor-suit slam try, responder jumps to three diamonds (natural), bids two clubs followed by three clubs (natural), or bids two clubs followed by three diamonds (both minors).

SKINNER TWO-BIDS (devised by Col. R. H. SKINNER, Wilmington, Del.). A method of responding to a strong two-bid that allows opener to pinpoint certain key cards in responder's hand. Two clubs opening is artificial and forcing to two no trump or three of a major. Two diamonds, two hearts, and two spades openings are natural, game-forcing, and request responder to bid a suit in which he holds an ace, bid two no trump with no ace, or to jump in the suit of the lowest-ranking ace with more than one ace. If opener's rebid is the cheapest call possible, responder shows his kings by bidding the suit, or suits containing the kings in the cheapest order. With no kings, or further kings to show, responder bids no trump. If opener again makes the cheapest possible call, responder shows his queens in the same manner. Whenever opener's rebid is not the cheapest call, he announces that his two-bid was based on high-card strength and that he is looking for general strength and distribution in responder's hand.

SKIP, SKIP MOVEMENT. An irregularity in the progression of the traveling pairs (or the boards) in a MITCHELL MOVEMENT pair game with an even number of tables, where it is not desired that all contestants play every board in play.

SKIP BID. In a wide sense, any bid at a level higher than is required by the previous auction. In practice, a skip bid is used to refer to weak pre-emptive actions, whether as an opening bid, an overcall, or a response. (See PRE-EMPTIVE BID, WEAK JUMP OVERCALL, and PRE-EMPTIVE RESPONSE.) To avoid the ethical problems that may arise after pre-emptive action, the SKIP-BID WARNING is usually used in the United States.

SKIP-BID WARNING. The interjection of a high-level pre-emptive bid by any bidder, by its very nature, poses a problem to the opposition. Whatever the bidder's mental processes up to that point might have been, the pre-emptive action by his right-hand opponent may well present him with a choice of actions. Should he pass immediately, his partner might well construe it as a sign of weakness, and be discouraged from taking aggressive action; should he double immediately partner might construe it for penalty rather than take-out; should he fidget and stew and then pass, partner could hardly help but be aware that some action has occurred to him, and encourage him to take such action by a reopening double. None of these actions would be particularly unethical by the player affected, but action based on them by his partner would be highly questionable. This very touchy ethical question ("What would I have done if my partner had acted entirely without nuance?") poses a definite dilemma to the ethical player, thus, giving an added and undeserved reward to the pre-empting side.

S. Fry, Jr., in 1938 proposed a compulsory pause after a skip bid, which the ACBL adopted in 1957 when it promulgated a regulation stating that "it was the duty of the player whose turn it became to pause for a duration of about ten seconds before taking any action whatsoever." It is recommended that the pre-emptive bidder alert the opposition to the fact that his bid is about to invoke this regulation by announcing, "I am about to make a skip-bid." In other jurisdictions, different practices have been adopted. In international matches, where there is a referee at the table, and a high level bid is made, he calls "stop" to halt all action until he gives a further word to proceed after a satisfactory interval. Another innovation which minimizes this problem, as well as many other ethical problems, is the FRANCO BOARD, or SCREEN, isolating each player from the sight of his partner.

SLAM. The winning of twelve tricks (SMALL SLAM, previously called little slam) or all thirteen tricks (GRAND SLAM). An original object in the earliest forms of whist (some of which were called "Slamm"), these results were rewarded by bonuses in bridge-whist and auction bridge regardless of the declaration, so much so that in auction bridge a side that bid seven and won twelve tricks still received the 50-point premium for small slam although the contract was down one. In contract bridge, however, slam bonuses are paid only when the slam is both bid and made.

SLAM BIDDING. The methods by which slam contracts are investigated. Accuracy in this department of the game is vital for the winning player, since successful slams are rewarded with large bonuses, and those that fail are severely penalized (the undertrick penalty *plus* the value of a game contract). Ironically, the history of championship matches is studded with failures in the slam zone.

The two vital ingredients of a successful slam contract are power and controls. Before launching into a slam a partnership must not only determine that it has the general values to take twelve or thirteen tricks in its best denomination; it must also be reasonably certain that the defense is unable to defeat the contract at the very start. To that end, a large part of modern slam bidding machinery is geared to the investigation of trump-suit solidity and first- and second-round controls. See SLAM CONVENTIONS.

The creation of a game-forcing situation in the early rounds of the bidding often provides the spark for slam investigation. See FAST ARRIVAL, PRINCIPLE OF. In addition, a variety of conventions have been devised to give slam-related information simultaneously with the announcement of a trump fit. See CONGLOMERATE MAJOR RAISES; JACOBY TWO NO TRUMP; SPLINTER BID; SUPER SWISS; UNBALANCED SWISS RAISE; VALUE SWISS RAISES.

After a satisfactory trump fit has been established, either player may activate the search if he suspects the possibility of a slam. There are various ways in which the slam may be approached.

Cue-Bidding of a control, usually an ace, invites partner to cooperate if his hand is suitable.

WEST	EAST
♠ A K J 10 4	♠ 8
♡ K J 9 8	♡ A Q 10 7 3 2
◇ 6 2	◇ Q 5 4
♣ K 9	♣ A J 3

The bidding:

WEST	EAST
1 ♠	2 ♡
4 ♡	5 ♣
5 ♡	—

In bidding five clubs, East shows the ace of that suit, and asks West how he feels about slam. Having nothing to spare for his bid, West signs off by returning to the agreed trump suit.

Frequently this slam try can be made below the game level:

WEST	EAST
♠ A K J 9 8	♠ Q 10 4 3
♡ 10 6	♡ K Q 9 7
◇ A 10 4	◇ K Q 2
♣ K J 9	♣ Q 2

The bidding:

WEST	EAST
1 ♠	3 ♠
4 ◇	4 ♠

Over East's forcing raise, West shows slam interest by bidding four diamonds, a convenient try which does not commit the partnership beyond game. Lacking primary controls, East declines.

WEST	EAST
♠ A J 8	♠ K Q 10 6 3
♡ K 10 7 6	♡ A 3
◇ A Q 10 7	◇ 8 3 2
♣ K 9	♣ A 8 6

The bidding:

WEST	EAST
1 NT	3 ♠
4 ◇	4 ♡
4 ♠	5 ♣
6 ♠	

The bid of four diamonds by West is not by way of suggesting an alternative trump suit; spades are agreed on by inference for, lacking spade support, West would simply bid three no trump. The four diamond bid is a slam try, showing in addition to the diamonds, a maximum no trump with good spade support. With two primary controls, East accepts the invitation by showing the ace of hearts. West has nothing further to say, but when his partner makes a further overture, he bids the slam.

After first-round controls have been cue-bid, subsequent cue-bids in the same suit indicate second-round control.

WEST	EAST
♠ A 10 3	♠ K J 9
♡ A K 9 8 2	♡ Q J 10 6 5
◇ A 4 3	◇ 8
♣ K 7	♣ A Q 8 6

The bidding:

WEST	EAST
1 ♡	3 ♡
3 ♠	4 ♣
4 ◇	4 ♠
5 ♣	5 ◇
7 ♡	

The hands lend themselves to a smooth sequence where first- and second-round controls are shown in turn, until West, having heard enough, bids the grand slam. See CUE-BIDS TO SHOW CONTROLS.

A Voluntary Bid Beyond the Game Level in an uninterrupted sequence is a specialized form of slam try usually inquiring about control of a specific suit.

WEST	EAST
♠ A K J 10 8 7	♠ Q 9
♡ Q 4	♡ 7 6
◇ A 10 7	◇ K Q 9 8 4
♣ K 6	♣ A Q 10 7

The bidding:

WEST	EAST
1 ♠	2 ◇
3 ♠	4 ♣
4 ◇	4 ♠
5 ♠	Pass

Since East did not raise the spades directly, his four club bid is interpreted by West as a mild slam try. With the minor suits under control, West's five spade bid requests his partner to bid the slam if he has as good as second-round control in the unbid suit, hearts, so that East, though holding quite a useful hand, is compelled to pass.

If the opponents have been in the bidding, a bid at the five-level in the agreed trump suit asks partner to bid a slam if he controls the enemy suit, unless one member of the partnership has already cue-bid that suit.

(a)

SOUTH	WEST	NORTH	EAST
1 ♡	2 ♠	3 ♡	Pass
5 ♡			

(b)

SOUTH	WEST	NORTH	EAST
1 ♡	1 ♠	3 ♡	Pass
3 ♠	Pass	4 ♡	Pass
5 ♡			

In (a) South has a powerful hand, but one which probably contains losing spades:

♠ 10 9
♡ A Q 10 9 7
◇ A K J 3 2
♣ A

In (b) South has shown control of spades, but he has poor trumps:

♠ —
♡ J x x x x x
◇ A K Q x x
♣ A K

This does not apply to sequences where opponents' bidding forces the auction to the five-level.

SOUTH	WEST	NORTH	EAST
1 ♡	1 ♠	3 ♡	4 ♠
5 ♡			

South has no slam pretensions; he merely feels that doubling four spades will not produce a satisfactory penalty, and prefers his chances of making eleven tricks in hearts.

Positional Slams. Occasionally a slam can be made from one side of the table, but may fail if played from the other. Thus a player with a vulnerable tenace holding should endeavor to become declarer to protect his tenuous assets from a possibly damaging opening lead.

NORTH
♠ A K Q 9 7 6 5 2
♡ 8 5
◇ K
♣ J 2

WEST	EAST
♠ J 4 3	♠ 10
♡ J 6 2	♡ K 7 4 3
◇ J 8 4	◇ 9 7 3 2
♣ A Q 10 7	♣ 8 6 5 4

SOUTH
♠ 8
♡ A Q 10 9
◇ A Q 10 6 5
♣ K 9 3

This hand is from the 1962 World Championship match between Great Britain and North America. In one room the American North played in four spades, making eleven tricks after a club lead.
The British bidding was:

SOUTH (Priday)	NORTH (Truscott)
1 ◇	2 ♠
3 ♡	4 ♠
4 NT	5 ◇
6 NT	

North's four spade bid, after his jump shift, showed a solid suit. Ascertaining through BLACKWOOD that the ace of clubs was missing, South bid the slam in no trump to protect his king of clubs from a possible fatal lead through.

WEST	EAST
♠ A J 10 8	♠ K Q 7 3 2
♡ K	♡ A 10 8 3
◇ A Q 10	◇ J 8 7
♣ K Q J 10 2	♣ 6

The bidding:

WEST	EAST
1 ♣	1 ♠
4 ♠	5 ♡
6 NT	

West accepts his partner's slam try, but corrects to no trump, realizing that, in six spades, a diamond lead might break the contract. See RIGHT SIDE.

Asking about Controls. Since controls are a necessary feature of successful slams, several conventions have been devised to determine the number of aces and kings held by a partnership. The most widely used is the BLACKWOOD convention:

WEST	EAST
♠ A	♠ K 8
♡ K 10 8 7	♡ A Q 9 6 3 2
◇ A 5	◇ K Q 10
♣ A Q 9 8 7 6	♣ 10 3

The bidding:

WEST	EAST
1 ♣	1 ♡
4 ♡	4 NT
5 ♠	5 NT
6 ◇	6 ♡
Pass	

The four no trump and five no trump bids are conventional, and West responds by showing his aces and kings (five spades = three aces; six diamonds = one king). Though East has a very powerful hand in light of his partner's strong bidding, he cannot venture beyond six, for he knows that one critical king is missing.

Blackwood, valuable in determining the *total number* of aces and kings held by a partnership, should not be used by a player interested in identifying a *specific control*.
West holds:

♠ A K Q 10 8 7 6
♡ 10
◇ 3 2
♣ A Q 3

and the bidding proceeds:

WEST	EAST
1 ♠	2 ♣
3 ♠	4 ♠

At this point West would like to be in a slam if his partner holds the ace of diamonds, but if East has only one ace and it is the ace of hearts there is a strong likelihood that the defense can take the first two diamond tricks before West gets in. Since a five diamond response to a Blackwood four no trump will leave him none the wiser, he is better off bidding five clubs, inviting his partner to cue-bid his ace if he has one. Alternatively, ASKING BIDS have been devised to allow inquiry into the amount and nature of control of a particular suit.

Trump Suit Quality. In investigating the prospects of a grand slam contract, the solidity of the trump suit is a critical factor. When a trump suit has been agreed upon, a five no trump bid can be used conventionally as the GRAND SLAM FORCE, requiring the responder to bid seven if he holds two of the top three trump honors.
West holds:

♠ Q J 8 7
♡ A K Q J 9
◇ —
♣ A K Q 2

and the bidding proceeds:

WEST	EAST
2 ♡	2 ♠

At this point West's sole concern is the spade suit and a bid of five no trump, agreeing spades by inference, will permit East to bid seven holding the ace and king, otherwise settling for a small slam.

Blasting. The success of slam contracts often turns on the opening lead. A more adventurous approach to slam bidding is therefore resorted to either when a player despairs of locating a key card in his partner's hand, or when he feels that the opponents are more likely to profit from a scientific investigation.

South holds:

♠ K 7 4 3
♡ A K J 10 6 2
◇ —
♣ 6 5 4

and the bidding proceeds:

NORTH	SOUTH
1 ♠	2 ♡
2 ♠	6 ♠

Six spades must have an excellent chance of coming home without a club lead and, rather than tip off the opponents, North prefers to blast. In the same vein, a player may take pains to bid a non-existent suit en route to a slam, to ward off a possibly lethal lead.

South holds:

♠ Q J 7 6 2
♡ —
◇ A K 10 8 3 2
♣ 3 2

In response to an opening spade bid by his partner, he may well bid six directly. However, against ingenuous opponents, it may pay to bid a psychic two clubs first in an effort to induce a favorable lead.

The bidding of slams in no trump usually involves a less arduous procedure, especially in sequences that stem from opening bids in no trump. The point-count formula, quite accurate in the evaluation of balanced hands, has reduced these to simple arithmetic: by adding his points to those shown by his partner's bid, the responder is usually in a position to place the final contract.
South holds:

♠ Q J 8
♡ A J
◇ K Q 3
♣ K J 8 4 2

In response to his partner's one no trump opening showing a minimum of 16 points, South can leap straight to six counting at least 33 points in the combined hands. With an in-between hand, the responder requires his partner's cooperation:

OPENER	RESPONDER
♠ K J 2	♠ Q 9 8 3
♡ A Q	♡ K J 4
◇ A K 8 7 6	◇ Q 10 9
♣ A Q 4	♣ J 10 6

The bidding:

OPENER	RESPONDER
2 NT	4 NT
6 NT	

In bypassing the game level, responder shows an interest in slam, and asks his partner to continue with a maximum holding. See EXPECTED NUMBER OF CONTROLS IN BALANCED HANDS.

Since in no trump sequences the four no trump bid has a quantitative meaning, the Blackwood convention is inoperative. A bid of four clubs, the GERBER convention, is used instead, to check on aces and kings.

Slams in Duplicate. In general, players tend to be conservative in the bidding of slams at match-point duplicate. This is conditioned by the form of scoring, where a minus score produces a poor result, and in missing a slam a cautious pair is likely to have lots of company. Having decided to scale the heights, players usually prefer the higher scoring denominations even though a slightly superior contract is available in a minor suit.
South holds:

♠ A
♡ K Q 4
◇ 9 3
♣ K Q J 10 9 5 4

The bidding:

NORTH	SOUTH
1 ♠	3 ♣
3 ◇	4 NT
5 ♡	6 NT

Though six clubs should be safe, South's final call is reasonable at match points. Specialized slam bidding conventions are listed under SLAM CONVENTIONS.

The percentages required to bid a small or grand slam have been calculated as below:

SMALL SLAM	Rubber Bridge					Chicago	IMP	Team
	N.V. N.V.	V. vs. N.V.	V. vs. N.V.	Both	N.V.	Vul.	N.V.	Vul.
	Game = 300	Game = 350	Game = 400	Game = 350				
Major	50	52	46	44	50	50	50	50	50
Minor	47	50	44	42	48	47	48	48	48
NT	50	53	47	45	50	50	50	50	50
GRAND SLAM								
Major	67	68	66	65	67	67	67	56	57
Minor	66	67	65	64	66	66	66	56	55
NT	68	69	66	65	67	68	67	56	57

The assumption is made that eleven tricks are a certainty for computing small slam percentages, and that twelve tricks are certain for the computation of grand slam percentages. Since these are by no means valid assumptions, the necessary percentages for bidding the slams are somewhat less than those shown, particularly for minor suit small slams.

At match-point play, a 50% chance of success justifies bidding a small slam, and a 67% chance justifies bidding the grand slam. Expert players will frequently take into account intangible factors such as the quality of the competition.

See VALUE OF GAME for the reasoning behind the inclusion of a value of 350 for the first game.

S. K.

SLAM CONVENTIONS. Specialized methods adopted for slam exploration include the following conventions which are listed separately: ACE IDENTIFICATION; ACE-SHOWING RESPONSES; ACOL DIRECT KING CONVENTION; ACOL FOUR NO TRUMP OPENING; ASKING BIDS; AUSTRALIAN ASKING BIDS; AUTOMATIC ACES; BABY BLACKWOOD; BARON COROLLARY; BARON SLAM TRY; BLACK AND RED GERBER; BLACKWOOD; BOLAND CONVENTION; BOWERS VARIATION; BYZANTINE BLACKWOOD; CLARAC SLAM TRY; CONGLOMERATE MAJOR RAISES; CONTROLS; CUE-BIDS TO SHOW CONTROLS; CULBERTSON FOUR-FIVE NO TRUMP; CULWOOD CONVENTION; DECLARATIVE-INTERROGATIVE FOUR NO TRUMP; DEFENSE TO INTERFERENCE WITH BLACKWOOD; FOUR CLUB BLACKWOOD; FRAGMENT BID; GERBER; GRAND SLAM FORCE; INTEREST-SHOWING BIDS; KEY-CARD BLACKWOOD; KEY-CARD GERBER; KING CONVENTION; LEBOVIC ASKING BID; MALOWAN SIX CLUB CONVENTION; MATHE ASKING BID; MINOR SUIT STAYMAN; NORMAN FOUR NO TRUMP; OUT-OF-THE-BLUE CUE-BID; ROMAN ASKING BIDS; ROMAN BLACKWOOD; ROMAN GERBER; ROMAN KEY CARD BLACKWOOD; RUSH ASKING BID; SAN FRANCISCO CONVENTION; SHARPLES CONVENTION; SPLINTER BID; SUPER BLACKWOOD; SUPER GERBER; SUPER SWISS; SUPPRESSING THE BID ACE; TRUMP ASKING BID; TWO-WAY STAYMAN; VOID-SHOWING BIDS. See also topics such as EXPECTED NUMBER OF CONTROLS IN BALANCED HANDS; FAST ARRIVAL, PRINCIPLE OF; RIGHT SIDE; SAFETY LEVEL.

SLAM DOUBLE CONVENTIONS. See DOUBLE FOR SACRIFICE; LIGHTNER DOUBLE.

SLAM LEADS. Opening leads against slam contracts frequently involve some special considerations. The general principle is to make passive leads against grand slams and active leads against small slams, but there are many exceptions to this.

An attacking lead against a small slam is often necessary when the bidding indicates a long, establishable suit in the dummy. It may then be necessary for the defense to lead from a king or a queen, in the hope of establishing a trick in the suit led before dummy's suit can be established for discards.

But if declarer and dummy both seem likely to have balanced hands, whether or not the contract is no trump, a passive lead is indicated. A deceptive lead is often appropriate, such as a third-best, a fifth-best, or the lower of touching honors. Misinforming the leader's partner is usually less important than misleading the declarer. Assessing the safety of a lead depends on the bidding as well as the suit holding. A low trump is safe from three small if the declaring side can be credited with at least nine trumps; but it would be unsafe against a likely eight-card trump fit, because partner may have Qx.

The lead of an ace is right more often than some authorities indicate. Apart from the obvious advantage at match-point play of preventing an overtrick, the ace lead is desirable if the opposing bidding has been crowded or rushed in such a way that two top losers are not unlikely. See also LIGHTNER DOUBLE.

SLIVER BID. An extension of the SPLINTER BID principle, devised by G. ROSENKRANZ for use with weaker responding hands. With four- or preferably, five-card trump support for a major suit opening and fewer than 10 HCP, the standard response would be a jump to game. When such a hand includes a singleton or void and a minimum of three controls including at least one king (2 controls—A or void; 1 control —K or singleton) possession of a "sliver" is indicated by a response of three no trump. Opener's rebids: Sign off in the major with more than five losers and a hand poor in HCP and controls. With at least six high-card controls, or five controls and a singleton, 15 or more HCP and fewer than six losers, opener explores slam possibilities by bidding the suit where responder's singleton or void will represent duplication and be of least value.

Responder's rebids: Sign off by bidding game in agreed suit if singleton or void is opposite partner's "exclusion" rebid. With shortage elsewhere, rebid by steps: 1st step: Singleton in lower unbid side suit. 2nd step: Singleton in higher suit. 3rd step: Void in lower unbid suit. 4th step: Void in higher unbid suit.

In counting steps, game bid in the agreed trump suit —the sign-off—is omitted.

SLOW PASS. A pass at a slow tempo which reveals that the passer was considering an alternative action. This may be quite harmless: if the passer takes the final decision for his side and becomes the declarer or the dummy, no ethical problem can arise.

In other circumstances the slow pass is liable to convey improper information to the partner, who must do his best not to be influenced by that information.

Four particular cases are worth distinguishing:

(1) A player who considers making an opening bid and then passes has implied that he holds close to an opening bid. In such circumstances, after he has hesitated, the player should prefer a subminimum opening to a subethical pass.

(2) A slow pass may reveal ambitions at a higher level. If a player passes slowly when his partner raises one spade to two spades, he has indicated faint game possibilities. Admittedly this information will not be significant unless an opponent indiscreetly balances.

(3) The slow pass is most revealing in competitive auctions. Some of the problems are solved by the SKIP-BID WARNING, but such situations often lead to protests. It is often difficult not to be influenced subconsciously. Some associations, notably the Greater New York BA, on the initiative of Edgar Kaplan, believe that adjustments should be made in such cases in the same way as offenses against the normal rules of the game. The slow-passing side is penalized in the same way that they would be for, say, a revoke, and there is no suggestion of unethical conduct. In order to provide standards and to avoid *ad hoc* judgments, some tournament protest committees apply a so-called 80% rule. If the Committee finds that there was in fact a slow pass, it will ordinarily rescind the action taken by the partner of the slow passer if it believes such an action would normally be taken less than 80% of the time.

(4) A slow pass which ends the auction may be revealing when the passer's partner will be on lead. There may be an indication that a lead-directing double was contemplated.

In one special case a slow pass is quite harmless. A forcing pass at a high level by the side which is on the offensive does not convey information, because partner does not know whether the alternative contemplated was a bid or a double.

See also HUDDLE.

SLOW PLAY. As opposed to careful or thoughtful play, slow play is discourteous not only to the opponents of the moment, but to all the other competitors in an event as well. In rubber bridge, it decreases the number of hands that can be played in a session; in duplicate tournaments, a consistently slow pair can delay the entire game by many minutes.

Contributing to slow play as defined here are some or all of these violations of the proprieties of duplicate play: (1) delay in coming to the table after the round has been called; (2) discussion of boards previously played; (3) failure to pass boards promptly, or pass one board if the other has not been completed; (4) inattention during the bidding necessitating frequent reviews of the auction; (5) postmortems of the first hand, particularly those involving the player whose duty it is to score the board just played; (6) failure to accept a ruling from the director pleasantly and promptly in the event of an infraction; (7) blaming previous opponents for present tardiness instead of concentrating on finishing the present hand; (8) waiting for a miracle to change opponent's aces to deuces so that a bad contract will not receive its deserved result. The LAWS OF DUPLICATE specifically provide that as a matter of courtesy a player should avoid "Prolonging play unnecessarily for the purpose of disconcerting the other players." (Proprieties III.)

In national and international championships a team which repeatedly exceeds the time limit allowed for play is subject to penalties. The penalty may take the form of a match-point or victory-point "fine," or may be as extreme as exclusion of a team from an event. The slowest performers on record are Pierre GHESTEM and René BACHERICH, France, who once took 40 minutes (including 3 minutes consumed by the opposition) to bid and play one deal, including 15 minutes for the play of one card. To allocate responsibility for slow play between two teams is always difficult. The use of a chess clock presents a possible remedy on important occasions.

SLUFF. To discard a worthless card; to dispose of a loser by throwing it off on the lead of a suit not held by the "sluffer." The word derives from "slough" —to cast off.

SMALL CARD. A card in a suit lower than the six, although the six itself on occasion might be considered a small card.

SMALL SLAM. The bidding and making of six-odd, or twelve tricks in all, for which the premium, scored above the line in rubber bridge, but in regular fashion in Chicago or duplicate, is 500 points when not vulnerable and 750 points when vulnerable. See SLAM BIDDING for a mathematical treatment of percentage expectation of success for the bid. See also MATHEMATICAL VALUE OF GAME.

SMITH CONVENTION. (1) A club take-out as a DEFENSE TO OPENING THREE-BID, devised by Curtis SMITH, (2) a four no trump slam convention devised by William S. Smith and Gertrude Smith of Waterbury, Conn., in 1935 and which was popular for many years. Identical in principle with the NORMAN FOUR NO TRUMP, but different in one detail. A response of five spades showed specifically one ace and three kings, while five no trump was used to show two aces and one king. (3) Also applied to the cheating device said to have been used at rubber bridge: holding a YARBOROUGH, one player announces that he has fourteen cards, and his partner, also with a poor hand, announces twelve, and rapidly mixes the two hands together. If partner has a good hand, he suggests a recount.

SMITH TROPHY. Awarded to the winners of the Life Master Women's pairs contested at the Fall Nationals, under which heading past results are listed. Donated by Charles H. Goren in 1969 in memory of his long-time partner Helen Sobel SMITH.

SMOLEN TRANSFER BID. An adjunct to STAYMAN and JACOBY TRANSFER BIDS for game-going hands, devised by Mike SMOLEN of Los Angeles, to allow the no trump opener to become the declarer in responder's long suit after responder has used Stayman with 5–4 or 6–4 in the major suits. Using Smolen Transfers, after the auction has started

NORTH	SOUTH
1 ♡	2 ♣
2 ◊	

South jumps to three of his four-card major suit, showing that he has more than four cards in the other major. If opener has three cards in the unbid major, he bids game in that major. If opener has only a doubleton he bids three no trump and, if responder has six cards in the unbid major, he continues by bidding four of the suit just below his unbid major, as a transfer bid.

SMOTHER PLAY. A rare end position that permits capture of a defender's virtually certain trump winner.

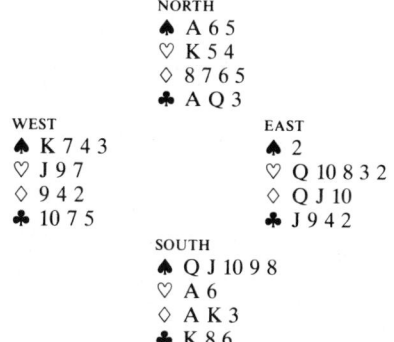

```
                    NORTH
                    ♠ A 6 5
                    ♡ K 5 4
                    ◊ 8 7 6 5
                    ♣ A Q 3
   WEST                         EAST
   ♠ K 7 4 3                    ♠ 2
   ♡ J 9 7                      ♡ Q 10 8 3 2
   ◊ 9 4 2                      ◊ Q J 10
   ♣ 10 7 5                     ♣ J 9 4 2
                    SOUTH
                    ♠ Q J 10 9 8
                    ♡ A 6
                    ◊ A K 3
                    ♣ K 8 6
```

South plays six spades. The contract appears doomed, for declarer must lose a diamond trick and West's trump king is sufficiently protected to elude capture by normal finessing. However, the opening lead of a diamond is won, and the ten and nine of spades are finessed, West declining to cover. South continues with three rounds of clubs, the ace, king, and a heart ruff in his own hand. The ace of diamonds is taken, leaving the following ending:

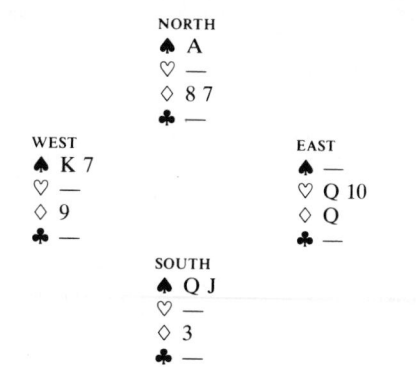

```
                    NORTH
                    ♠ A
                    ♡ —
                    ◊ 8 7
                    ♣ —
   WEST                         EAST
   ♠ K 7                        ♠ —
   ♡ —                          ♡ Q 10
   ◊ 9                          ◊ Q
   ♣ —                          ♣ —
                    SOUTH
                    ♠ Q J
                    ♡ —
                    ◊ 3
                    ♣ —
```

East is thrown in with a diamond and has nothing but hearts to return. South ruffs with the queen, and West is helpless. Also known as the "disappearing trump trick." See also DEVIL'S COUP.

SOCIAL BRIDGE. Played in a home for moderate or no stakes, bridge can still be highly skillful and competitive. For larger gatherings, see PARTY BRIDGE and PROGRESSIVE BRIDGE. In expert circles, social bridge increasingly is taking the form of team-of-four competition.

SOCK, SOCK IT. Slang for "I double." Used at the table, it is difficult to determine whether it is more impolite than unethical or vice versa.

SOLID SUIT. A holding which is expected as a trump or at no trump to win as many tricks as there are cards in the suit. Theoretically it should contain as many high cards as there are outstanding cards in the suit: A K Q x x x x x might lose a trick if all four cards are in the same hand. CULBERTSON gave as his definition of reasonable expectancy of the solidity of a suit the rule of thumb that a suit was solid if half the outstanding cards were in one hand, the entire suit could still be picked up by successive leads.

An alternate definition, similar in effect, is "a suit which can be expected to lose no tricks with a singleton in dummy, and may lose no tricks opposite a void." By this standard, A K Q x x x x and A K Q 10 x x qualify, but A K Q x x x does not.

SOLOMON TROPHY. A WBF trophy in honor of Charles J. SOLOMON awarded to the nation with the best overall victory-point record in the WORLD PAIR OLYMPIAD. Winners and runners-up are:

	WINNERS	RUNNERS-UP
1966	United States	Great Britain
1970	United States	Italy
1974	United States	Italy

SOLOWAY JUMP SHIFT. See JUMP SHIFT.

SORTING THE HAND. The act of arranging the cards of a hand into suits, and by order within suits after the cards have been dealt. Many fine players, after arranging their hand, then remove a couple of cards from a long suit and put them apart from the rest of the cards in the suit as a protection against an inadvertent glance of an opponent. Among the habits that experienced players develop are the placing of a singleton in the middle, rather than at an end of the hand, and the avoidance of rearranging a hand when a suit has been exhausted therefrom. It is a violation of the proprieties to note from what part of a hand an opponent or partner draws a card in order to get a clue as to his holding or distribution.

SOS REDOUBLE. A redouble calling on partner to select another denomination. It applies whenever there is no possibility of the redouble being applied in a natural sense.

SOUTH	WEST	NORTH	EAST
1 ♣	Dbl.	Pass	Pass
Redbl.			

South may have opened on a short club suit. His redouble requests North to bid his best suit outside of clubs as a rescue. However, in a major suit such a redouble would be strength-showing, not an S O S.

A double of an opening weak no trump bid often prompts an S O S redouble. For example:

SOUTH	WEST	NORTH	EAST
1 NT	Dbl.	2 ♣	Dbl.
Pass	Pass	Redbl.	

This sequence implies that North is planning to play in some other suit, and does not hold clubs. South should bid his lowest-ranking four-card suit, and if his only suit is clubs he should bid his lowest-ranking three-card suit.

If South retreats into two diamonds and an opponent doubles, North might redouble again to ask South to select a major suit. Similar situations arise when the opening no trump bid is doubled and redoubled. It is the doubling side which is then on the run, perhaps using S O S redoubles in an attempt to find the best part-score fit at the level of two.

In rare circumstances a player may redouble his partner's bid as an S O S instead of his own bid.

SOUTH	WEST	NORTH	EAST
1 ♣	Pass	Pass	Dbl.
Pass	Pass	Redbl.	

If North could not respond to one club he cannot wish to redouble naturally. The redouble therefore shows extreme shortage in clubs and begs South to pick another denomination.

For a specialized S O S redouble, see KOCK-WERNER REDOUBLE.

SOUND BIDDING. A bidding system stressing elevated standards for some opening bids and overcalls. ROTH-STONE opening bids in first or second position are examples of sound bids. A sound bidder refers to one whose bids, rebids, and responses are fully justified by his holding, and who, when choices of bids are available, will choose the more conservative action.

SOUTH. One of the compass points used in describing the players at the table. South is partnered by North, and is OVER the East hand but UNDER the West hand. In bridge writing for general reading, South is, conventionally, the declarer, and this usage is followed in this book. However, in reporting International Matches, the actual positions at the table are used.

SOUTH AFRICAN TEXAS. A special method of transfer bids at the level of four. After an opening bid of one no trump or two no trump, a jump to four clubs requires the opener to bid four hearts, and four diamonds asks for four spades.

This was the original form of David Carter's TEXAS convention, and was developed independently in South Africa. It was quickly abandoned in the US in favor of red-suit transfer bids which permit the use of four clubs as GERBER. The South African version has the psychological advantage that the responses do not sound natural, and the opener is protected from a lapse of memory.

SOUTH AMERICAN BRIDGE CONFEDERATION (CONFEDERACION SUDAMERICANA DE BRIDGE). Founded in 1948, and consists of the Bridge Associations of ten South American countries: Argentina, Bolivia, Brazil, Chile, Colombia, Ecuador, Paraguay, Peru, Uruguay, and Venezuela. The South American Confederation runs an annual team championship for its member countries, with the winning country gaining the right to represent South America in the World Championships. (For past results of the South American Championships, see Appendix III.)

Secretary General, 1975: Carlos Cabanne, Florida 1065, Buenos Aires, Argentina.

SOUTHERN AFRICAN BRIDGE FEDERATION. Formed in 1954, as the South African Bridge Federation, consisting at that time of the Transvaal Contract Bridge League, which represented the European Clubs, and the Transvaal Contract Bridge Board of Control, which represented the non-European Clubs. In 1963, the Central African Bridge Association was incorporated into the Federation, and the name was changed to the present title. With a total membership in 1974 of approximately 4,000, the Federation participates in the Olympiads, finishing second in the 1968 and 1972 World Women's Team Olympiad, and 1974 World Women's Pair Olympiad, and annually sponsors National Open Team and Open Pairs championships. The following South African players are listed separately: H. Butkow, Dr. A. A. Gordon, G. Goslar, Mrs. G. Goslar, Mrs. R. Jacobson, Mrs. P. Mansell, Dr. R. Mizroch, L. Sapire, M. Sapire, A. Shnieder, A. A. Traub, C. M. Vorajee.

Officers, 1975:
President: M. S. Nana
Secretary: David Goldfain, P.O. Box 3700, Johannesburg, South Africa.

SPADE TRICK. A trick in the spade suit.

SPADES. The highest ranking of the four suits at bridge. The thirteen cards of the suit are indicated with a black symbol, ♠; the ace of the suit usually carries a special design trade-marked by the manufacturer, on its face.

SPANISH BRIDGE FEDERATION (FEDERACIÓN ESPAÑOLA DE BRIDGE). Founded in 1941, by 1974 had 1,500 affiliated clubs in 13 associations throughout Spain. The Federation is a member of the European Bridge League and regularly sends teams to compete in both Open and Women's series; it also participates in World Olympiads, hosting the 1974 World Pair Olympiad. Tournaments are held on both the regional and national level. Players listed separately are: M. Calbeto, J. Diaz Agero, G. Gomez-Diaz, J. Gomez-Diaz, A. La Zerna, L. Matthews, E. de Meneses, M. Merino, R. Munoz, C. Paternina, R. Soler.

Secretary, 1974: Antonio Cabot, Traversera de las Corts 63, Barcelona 14, Spain.

SPECIFIED CARDS, ODDS GOVERNING. See ODDS GOVERNING SPECIFIED CARDS.

SPECIFIED SUIT. A suit of which the lead may be required or forbidden because of an irregularity earlier in the auction or play.

SPECTATOR. A person who watches a bridge tournament without actually taking part. This is differentiated from a KIBITZER, whose presence is limited to a particular table. The conduct of spectators is governed by the LAWS (Proprieties V). Misconduct by a kibitzer may result in a penalty against the side responsible for the kibitzer's presence. See LAWS OF DUPLICATE (Law 11).

Some of the larger championship events and all of the international and intercity matches draw large numbers of interested viewers for whom provision is usually made. Such provision is sometimes in the form of small raised grandstands surrounding the table to accommodate more spectators than can be taken care of in chairs, and range up to the BRIDGE-O-RAMA or VU-GRAPH facilities which enable hundreds of viewers to watch the play of all four hands simultaneously with the play itself. Of course the greatest number of spectators of a bridge match are the viewers of televised matches. See TELEVISION.

SPIDER MOVEMENT. A 26-board movement for 16–22 tables, devised by John "Spider" Harris. The movement consists of two subsections in which the boards (twinned) circulate independently, while the moving pairs progress to the highest numbered table in one subsection and then move to the other subsection. Boards are moved each round to the next lower numbered table until they reach the lowest numbered table in that subsection; then they go to a bye-stand to await re-entry at the highest numbered table in the subsection. The initial distribution of the boards is such that in one subsection the stationary pairs will play the boards in ascending order, while in the other subsection the stationary pairs will play boards in descending order. Charts for various numbers of tables are available from ACBL HEADQUARTERS.

SPINGOLD TROPHY. For the ACBL Masters Team Championships, donated by Nathan Spingold in 1934 for what was then called the World Championship Masters Team of Four and played originally as a separate knockout event. In 1938 this event became a part of the Summer Nationals (under which results are listed), superseding the CITY OF ASBURY PARK TROPHY event. In the 1950s and 1970s the Spingold helped to select a number of US international teams; it ranks with the Vanderbilt as the most highly prized trophy in the ACBL calendar. The winners of the Spingold are entitled to compete against the winners of the GRAND NATIONAL CHAMPIONSHIPS (2), REISINGER MEMORIAL TROPHY and VANDERBILT CUP (1) for the right to represent North America or the United States in the next year's WORLD CHAMPIONSHIP. See INTERNATIONAL OPEN TEAM SELECTION.

SPLINTER BID. A variation of the FRAGMENT BID idea, in which an unusual jump guarantees a fit for partner's last named suit, shows a singleton or void in the suit in which the jump is made, and suggests a slam. Alternatively known as an anti-fragment or singleton-showing bid, and often confused with the fragment bid. In general, any jump during the auction when a non-jump or lower-level jump would be forcing (assuming asking bids are not being used) may be considered a splinter bid. On this basis, the device can be used in a wide variety of situations. For example, the last bid in the following auctions would be a splinter:

	SOUTH		NORTH	
(1)	SOUTH		NORTH	
	1 ♠		4 ♣	
(2)	SOUTH		NORTH	
	1 ♡		3 ♠	
(3)	SOUTH		NORTH	
	1 ♣		1 ♠	
	4 ◇			
(4)	SOUTH		NORTH	
	1 ♠		2 ◇	
	4 ♣			
(5)	SOUTH		NORTH	
	1 ♠		2 ◇	
	2 ♡		4 ♣	
(6)	SOUTH	WEST	NORTH	EAST
	1 ♣	1 ♡	3 ♡	
(7)	SOUTH	WEST	NORTH	EAST
	1 ♡	1 ♠	2 ♣	3 ♡

There are two cases that require partnership agreement:

	SOUTH	NORTH
(8)	SOUTH	NORTH
	1 ♠	4 ♡

Most of those players who use splinter bids consider North's four heart bid a splinter, but the standard interpretation is also possible.

(9)

SOUTH	NORTH
1 ♠	2 ♣
3 ♡ or 4 ♡	

One of South's bids, but not both, should be a splinter.

For alternative treatments, see ASKING BIDS, CONGLOMERATE MAJOR RAISES, SWISS CONVENTION, VALUE SWISS RAISES, VOID-SHOWING BIDS.

SPLIT. See BREAK.

SPLIT EQUALS. See PLAY FROM EQUALS.

SPONSORING ORGANIZATION. The group which sponsors bridge tournaments conducted under the LAWS OF DUPLICATE (Law 76). Generally, this is a club or clubs for tournaments of local rating; a unit of the American Contract Bridge League for sectionally rated tournaments; a conference of units or a very large unit for regionally rated tournaments; and the American Contract Bridge League itself for national tournaments. See COMMITTEE.

SPONSORS. See PROFESSIONAL PLAYERS.

SPOT CARD LEADS. See JOURNALIST LEADS; OPENING LEADS; THREE SMALL CARDS, LEAD FROM.

SPOT CARDS. Cards ranking below the jack, from the ten down to the two.

Of the thirteen tricks which are won on each deal, approximately eight are won with aces, king, queens, and jacks; the remaining five tricks are won with the lower cards—the tens, nines, eights, sevens, etc. Generally speaking, a fraction more than five tricks is won by the lower cards in trump contracts, since the low trumps win tricks which are not available in no trump contracts.

Through the years, all the emphasis on winning tricks has been on aces, kings, queens, and jacks (HONOR TRICKS, POINT-COUNT) and quite naturally so, since these cards are the leaders in the area of winning tricks. However, as can be observed from the above, the lower cards are not merely pawns in the trick-taking field.

Here are two examples of the power of the spot cards. The South declarer in the first deal was Richard L. Frey.

```
              NORTH
              ♠ 10 9 2
              ♡ K 10 7 5
              ◇ A Q
              ♣ A 10 5 2
 WEST                        EAST
 ♠ 8 7                       ♠ Q J 5 3
 ♡ J 6 4                     ♡ 9
 ◇ J 7 6 2                   ◇ K 10 9 4 3
 ♣ Q 9 6 4                   ♣ J 7 3
              SOUTH
              ♠ A K 6 4
              ♡ A Q 8 3 2
              ◇ 8 5
              ♣ K 8
```

Against the sound six heart contract, West opened the eight of spades, dummy's nine was put up, East covered with the jack, and declarer's king captured the trick. Three rounds of trumps were then drawn, ending up in dummy. The ten of spades was then led, East played the queen, and declarer took the trick with his ace. On this trick West followed with the seven of spades.

It was now clear to declarer that East had the five and three of spades remaining, for surely if West had either of these cards he would not have dropped the seven-spot, which was the highest-ranking spade left.

Dummy was then re-entered via the club ace, and the deuce of spades was led. When East followed with the three-spot, declarer's four-spot was played, successfully finessing against East's five-spot.

The six of spades was now played, and on it dummy's queen of diamonds was discarded. All in all, thirteen tricks were taken, declarer ruffing out his losing diamond.

The following deal arose in the National Men's Pairs Championships of 1949. Keep your eye on West's singleton six of spades, because it is going to be promoted into a winning trick!

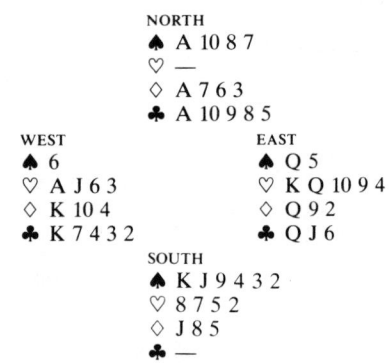

```
              NORTH
              ♠ A 10 8 7
              ♡ —
              ◇ A 7 6 3
              ♣ A 10 9 8 5
 WEST                        EAST
 ♠ 6                         ♠ Q 5
 ♡ A J 6 3                   ♡ K Q 10 9 4
 ◇ K 10 4                    ◇ Q 9 2
 ♣ K 7 4 3 2                 ♣ Q J 6
              SOUTH
              ♠ K J 9 4 3 2
              ♡ 8 7 5 2
              ◇ J 8 5
              ♣ —
```

The records do not indicate how South arrived at a five spade contract, but he did.

West opened the three of clubs, dummy's ace winning, with South discarding a diamond. A club was then ruffed, after which a heart was ruffed in dummy. Now another club was ruffed in the closed hand, and another heart ruffed on the board. A fourth club was then led, and East ruffed with his queen, South overruffing with the king. A third heart was ruffed in dummy, and the ace of diamonds was cashed next. On this trick, West unblocked with the king of diamonds.

Now came the fifth club, East ruffing with the five-spot, and South overruffing with the nine. Declarer's remaining heart was then ruffed with the board's last trump, the ace. A diamond was now led, and East climbed up with his queen. East then returned his fifth heart, the king, and declarer, with the J4 of trumps left, was fixed, for there was no way of preventing West from making his singleton six of spades. The two uppercuts by East really kayoed declarer (who did make eleven tricks, for a very poor score, since virtually every other North-South pair made twelve tricks).

The above deal demonstrates how important the spot cards can be in bridge: of the thirteen tricks played, seven were won by cards which ranked below the jack.

F. K.

SPREAD. (1) Verb: to spread the hand, either as a claim or as a concession of the remaining tricks. See CLAIM OR CONCESSION for the proper method of making such a claim. (2) Noun: the difference between the minimum and maximum values shown by a particular bid; in STANDARD AMERICAN, the range of values for an opening bid of one no trump is 16 to 18 high-card points, a spread of three, while an opening bid of one in a suit may have a high-card point-count spread of 11 to 24, or 14 points. Prior to 1971, the ACBL limited the spread of no trump openings to 4 points; of weak two-bid openings to 6 to 12 high-card points.

SPRING NATIONAL CHAMPIONSHIPS. An annual national tournament of the American Contract Bridge League first convening in 1958. The most important event is the VANDERBILT CUP contest. In 1968 the tournament attracted a total of 13,535 tables, a record for the series. For past results, see Appendix I.

Year	Site	Tables
1958	Atlantic City, N.J.	3,076
1959	Seattle, Wash.	4,124
1960	Jackson, Miss.	3,485
1961	Denver, Colo.	4,910
1962	Lexington, Ky.	4,703
1963	St. Louis, Mo.	6,556
1964	Portland, Ore.	6,950
1965	Cleveland, Ohio	8,128
1966	Louisville, Ky.	7,929
1967	Seattle, Wash.	7,098
1968	New York, N.Y.	13,535
1969	Cleveland, Ohio	8,958
1970	Portland, Ore.	7,025
1971	Atlanta, Ga.	9,706
1972	Cincinnati, Ohio	9,495
1973	St. Louis, Mo.	8,418
1974	Vancouver, B.C.	8,329
1975	Honolulu, Haw.	10,234
1976	Kansas City, Mo.	8,790
1977	Los Angeles, Calif.	
1978	Houston, Tex.	
1979	Norfolk, Va.	
1980	Fresno, Calif.	

SPUTNIK. See NEGATIVE DOUBLE.

SQUARE HAND. Bridge geometry is peculiar; square hand, flat hand, and round hand all describe BALANCED DISTRIBUTION.

SQUEEZE. A play which forces an opponent to discard a winner or a potential winner, or a card that protects a winner. A threat card (or menace card) is any card that will take a trick provided an opponent can be forced to unguard that suit. Every squeeze requires at least two THREATS, at least one of which must be accompanied by a winner in that suit. Such a threat is called a two-card threat. The hand opposite the two-card threats must contain a card in at least one such suit, which can be used as a means of reaching the two-card threat. A position must be achieved in which the opponent to be squeezed holds no idle cards (see RECTIFYING THE COUNT), but only winners or guards to winners. At this point the squeeze card is led: it is any card which forces the opponent in question to discard, thereby relinquishing one of his vital cards. Usually the squeeze card must be played from the hand opposite the two-card threat at the stage where the player can win all but one of the remaining tricks. If both menaces are in the same hand, only the opponent who is to the left of the squeeze card is affected. These are called positional (or one-way) squeezes. In an automatic squeeze, either opponent can be subjected to pressure. This occurs when the squeeze card is accompanied by a menace card, so that the hand opposite has one card which is immaterial, and furnishes an automatic discard.

The term "squeeze" was coined by Sidney LENZ well after the operation of a squeeze had been recognized and analyzed. Originally a squeeze was simply called a coup. In the heyday of American whist it was known as "putting the opponent to the discard." Circa 1910 ELWELL called squeeze play "forcing discards," and this term was in general use until Lenz in the middle twenties, inspired by a squeeze play in a professional baseball game, introduced his new term.

For various types of squeeze and aspects of squeeze play see ALTERNATIVE SQUEEZE; AUTOMATIC SQUEEZE; BACKWASH SQUEEZE; BARCO SQUEEZE; BONNEY'S SQUEEZE; BUSY CARD AND IDLE CARD; CLASH SQUEEZE; COMPOUND SQUEEZE; COMPOUND TRUMP SQUEEZE; COUNT SQUEEZE; CRISSCROSS SQUEEZE; DEFENSE TO A SQUEEZE; DOUBLE SQUEEZE; ENTRY SQUEEZE; ENTRY-SHIFTING SQUEEZE; GUARD SQUEEZE; HEXAGON SQUEEZE; HEXAGON TRUMP SQUEEZE; ISOLATING THE MENACE; JETTISON SQUEEZE; MENACE; ONE-SUIT SQUEEZE; OVERTAKING SQUEEZE; OVER-UNDER SQUEEZE; POSITIONAL SQUEEZE; PROGRESSIVE SQUEEZE; PSEUDO SQUEEZE; RECIPROCAL SQUEEZE; RECTIFYING THE COUNT; RULE OF N-MINUS-ONE; SCHROEDER SQUEEZE; SECONDARY SQUEEZE; SERES SQUEEZE; SHOW UP SQUEEZE; SIMPLE SQUEEZE; SQUEEZE FINESSE; SQUEEZE WITHOUT THE COUNT; SQUEEZED POSITION; STEPPINGSTONE; SUBMARINE SQUEEZE; SUICIDE SQUEEZE; THREAT CARD; TRANSFER SQUEEZE; TRANSFERRING THE MENACE; TRIPLE SQUEEZE; TRUMP SQUEEZE; UNBLOCKING SQUEEZE; VICE; VIENNA COUP; WINKLE.

SQUEEZE FINESSE. Closely related to the GUARD SQUEEZE. In each case, declarer threatens to take a successful finesse. In a guard squeeze, the opponents are not equally threatened, whereas the squeeze finesse is characterized by the presence of a symmetric menace which must be guarded with an equal number of cards by both opponents.

(1) Four-card squeeze finesse menaces:

Triple tenaces

NORTH			NORTH	
K 9			K 2	
WEST	EAST		WEST	EAST
Q 8	10 5	or	Q 8	10 5
SOUTH			SOUTH	
J 2			J 9	

These positions may lead to a squeeze or throw-in of either opponent.

Quadruple tenaces

NORTH			NORTH	
K 8			K 2	
WEST	EAST		WEST	EAST
Q 7	10 9	or	Q 7	10 9
SOUTH			SOUTH	
J 2			J 8	

In these positions, only West can be thrown in successfully.

(2) Six-card squeeze finesse menaces:

Triple tenaces

NORTH			NORTH	
K 9 x			K 3 2	
WEST	EAST		WEST	EAST
Q 8 x	10 5 x	or	Q 8 x	10 5 x
SOUTH			SOUTH	
A J 2			A J 9	

Either opponent may be thrown in.

Quadruple tenaces

NORTH			NORTH	
K 8 x			K 3 2	
WEST	EAST		WEST	EAST
Q 7 x	10 9 x	or	Q 7 x	10 9 x
SOUTH			SOUTH	
A J 2			A J 8	

Only West can be thrown in.

(3) Squeeze-Finesse positions (at no trump):

(a)

	NORTH	
	♠ K 8	
	♡ K	
	◇ —	
	♣ x	
WEST		EAST
♠ Q 7 3		♠ 10 9
♡ —		♡ A
◇ x		◇ A
♣ —		♣ —
	SOUTH	
	♠ J 2	
	♡ —	
	◇ Q	
	♣ A	

South has two of the remaining tricks. The ace of clubs is led and East is squeezed in three suits. He must discard a spade, and now South leads the jack of spades to smother the ten. If West's small diamond is exchanged for the king, this merely opens up the possibility of a squeeze throw-in against West.

(b)

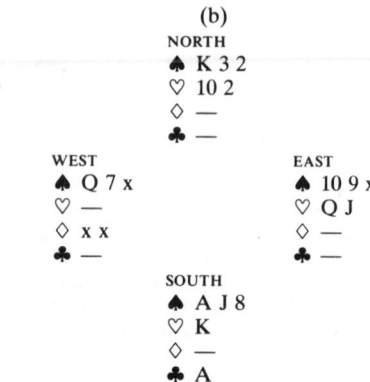

South has four of the remaining five tricks. The ace of clubs squeezes East in two suits. He must discard a spade, but declarer can now pick up three tricks in spades by leading the jack through West.

The squeeze fails if the eight and two of spades are interchanged.

(c)

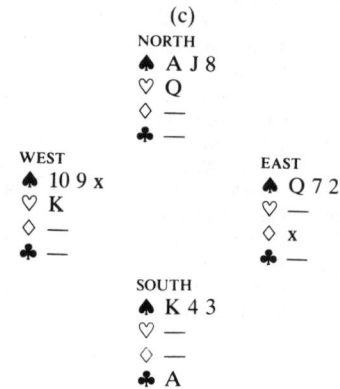

The ace of clubs squeezes West in two suits. West discards a spade, and declarer leads the ace of spades, and then runs the jack through East to pick up the suit.

The eight and two of spades may be interchanged without affecting the squeeze. East's small diamond may be exchanged for the ace of hearts, but the squeeze still works.

(4) Squeeze Finesse at Trumps (also called simply TRUMP SQUEEZE).

Simple

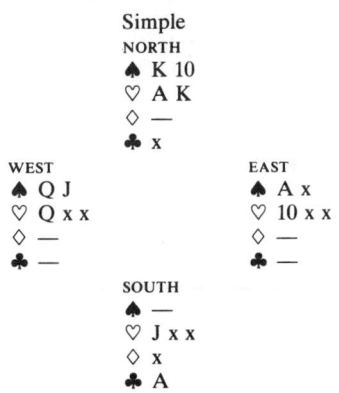

NORTH
♠ K 10
♡ A K
♢ —
♣ x

WEST
♠ Q J
♡ Q x x
♢ —
♣ —

EAST
♠ A x
♡ 10 x x
♢ —
♣ —

SOUTH
♠ —
♡ J x x
♢ x
♣ A

Diamonds are trumps. The ace of clubs is led and West is squeezed. If he discards a heart, declarer cashes the two top hearts, re-enters his hand by ruffing a spade to cash the jack of hearts. If West discards a spade, the king of spades can be led to ruff out the ace, and smother the queen, establishing North's ten.

Double

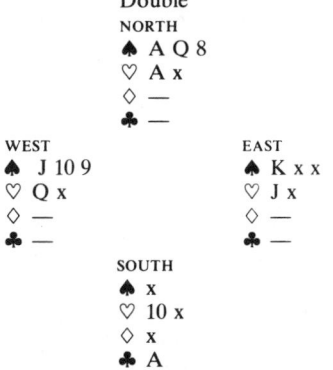

NORTH
♠ A Q 8
♡ A x
♢ —
♣ —

WEST
♠ J 10 9
♡ Q x
♢ —
♣ —

EAST
♠ K x x
♡ J x
♢ —
♣ —

SOUTH
♠ x
♡ 10 x
♢ x
♣ A

Diamonds are trumps. The ace of clubs is led and West is squeezed. If he discards a spade, the ace and queen of that suit are led, ruffing out the king and smothering West's honors. If West discards a heart, then North throws a heart and East is caught in a standard trump squeeze.

M. I.

SQUEEZE MNEMONICS. An acronym or other set of initials used as a reminder of the ingredients necessary for the operation of a squeeze. Among the more well-known mnemonics are:
   (1) Clyde Love's BLUE:
      B=Busy (one defender Busy in two suits)
      L=Loser (one Loser remaining)
      U=Upper (at least one threat in Upper hand)
      E=Entry (to the threat card)
   (2) George Coffin's EFG (to Enter Freedom, force the Guards):
      E=Entry (to the threat card)
      F=Forcing card
      G=Guards (in one defender's hand)
   (3) John Brown's STEM:
      S=Share-out or Substance
      T=Timing (count has been rectified)

E=Entries (to the threat card)
M=Menaces

R. T(rue)

SQUEEZE SUIT-OUT. A particular form of SECONDARY SQUEEZE.

SQUEEZE WITHOUT THE COUNT. An unusual variation of the squeeze. In order for a squeeze to be effective, declarer ordinarily must have all but one of the remaining tricks (see RULE OF N-MINUS-1). However, this is not invariably the case. In certain squeeze positions declarer gives up a trick after the squeeze. This is called a "squeeze without the count" (see SECONDARY SQUEEZE).

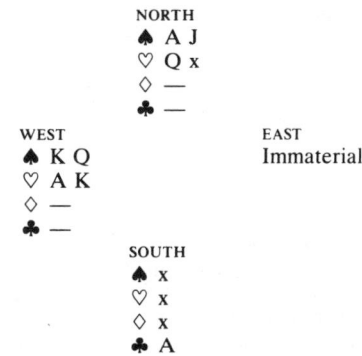

NORTH
♠ A J
♡ Q x
♢ —
♣ —

WEST
♠ K Q
♡ A K
♢ —
♣ —

EAST
Immaterial

SOUTH
♠ x
♡ x
♢ x
♣ A

South leads the ace of clubs which squeezes West, despite the fact that South has only two of the last four tricks. West must discard a heart; now South leads a heart to establish the queen.

SQUEEZED POSITION (PLAYING TO). In the development of the understanding of squeezes, Sidney Lenz invented the idea of a squeeze card, and this concept has dominated the analysis of squeeze play ever since. Indeed, some writers have even given special names, for example "reciprocal squeeze," where the actual squeeze card could not be identified.

(1)

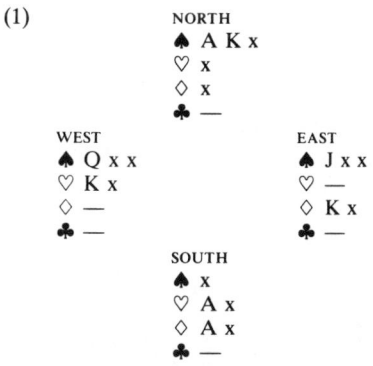

NORTH
♠ A K x
♡ x
♢ x
♣ —

WEST
♠ Q x x
♡ K x
♢ —
♣ —

EAST
♠ J x x
♡ —
♢ K x
♣ —

SOUTH
♠ x
♡ A x
♢ A x
♣ —

In this double automatic position, for instance, there is no separate and identifiable squeeze card. The two red aces are led, and each opponent is squeezed by the ace of his partner's suit.

As more and more squeeze positions have been

identified, the burden of remembering them for use in play has become impossible except for the most expert, and in trying to simplify the rules for the less expert players it has been found that, by abandoning the concept of a squeeze card, the number of end positions can be reduced, and, in particular, the more complex ones can be forgotten. This has probably always been the practice in expert circles, and was almost implied by Culbertson in his "Red Book."

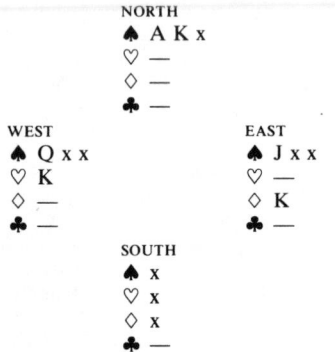

For example, in No. 1 above, if South cashes his red aces, he has achieved the "squeezed position." South is on lead, but both East and West have yet to play. This one position is all automatic double squeezes, and squeeze cards, reciprocal squeezes, simultaneous and interrupted automatic double squeezes, can all be forgotten.

The following are simple automatic squeezes:

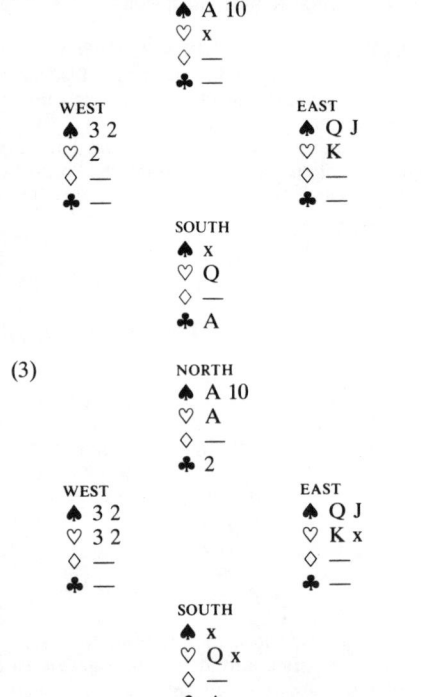

(4)
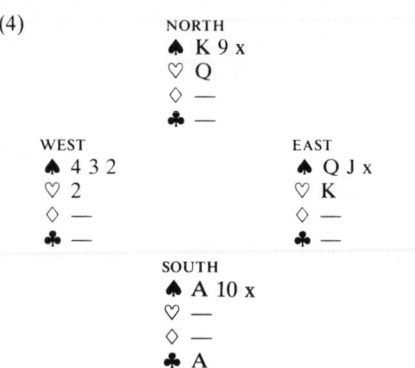

These three endings, Nos. 2, 3, and 4, can all be represented by one squeezed position, No. 5, with South on lead. North and South have both played, but the opponent with the high cards, either East or West, must now play and is squeezed. In No. 2 the ♣ A squeezes either East or West, the ♡ x being thrown from North. In No. 3 we first Vienna-Coup with the ♡ A, and then the ♣ A squeezes whichever opponent holds the high cards.

In No. 4 we have to imagine North as South in No. 5.

(5)
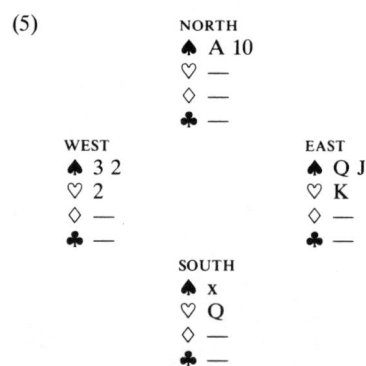

Examples could be given for all varieties of squeezes but this would be tedious, so let the following suffice:

(6)
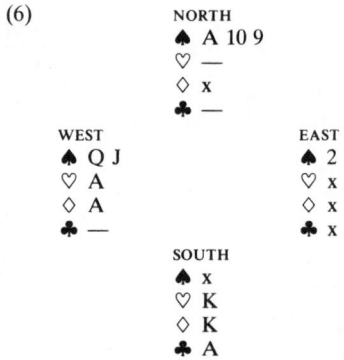

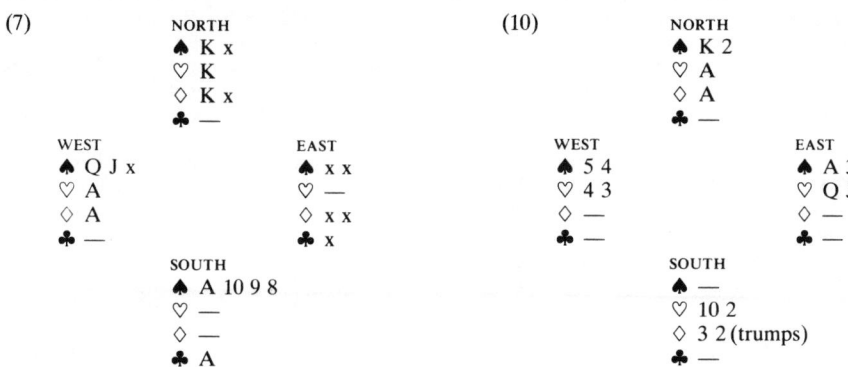

(7)

```
                NORTH
                ♠ K x
                ♡ K
                ◇ K x
                ♣ —
WEST                        EAST
♠ Q J x                     ♠ x x
♡ A                         ♡ —
◇ A                         ◇ x x
♣ —                         ♣ x
                SOUTH
                ♠ A 10 9 8
                ♡ —
                ◇ —
                ♣ A
```

(10)

```
                NORTH
                ♠ K 2
                ♡ A
                ◇ A
                ♣ —
WEST                        EAST
♠ 5 4                       ♠ A 3
♡ 4 3                       ♡ Q J
◇ —                         ◇ —
♣ —                         ♣ —
                SOUTH
                ♠ —
                ♡ 10 2
                ◇ 3 2 (trumps)
                ♣ —
```

Examples Nos. 6 and 7 are two triple squeeze positions, both automatic, in which the lead of the ♣ A squeezes opponent into promoting one of declarer's kings, then squeezing him a second time when that king is played, when the other ace or the guard to declarer's long suit must be given up. Example No. 8 is either of these reduced to the squeezed position, with South on lead. No. 7 has to be turned upside down to get to No. 8, but as the position is automatic, this is of no consequence.

Trump squeezes are always automatic. In No. 9 the lead of the ♣ 2, or in No. 10 the lead of a trump, squeezes the opponent (in this case East) who holds the high cards. If he throws a spade the ♠ 2 is led and trumped, North is re-entered and the ♠ K is cashed. If he throws a heart the ♡ A is cashed, a spade is ruffed, and the last heart made.

(8)

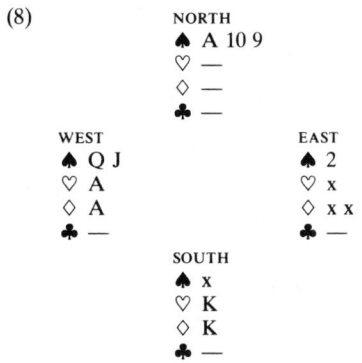

```
                NORTH
                ♠ A 10 9
                ♡ —
                ◇ —
                ♣ —
WEST                        EAST
♠ Q J                       ♠ 2
♡ A                         ♡ x
◇ A                         ◇ x x
♣ —                         ♣ —
                SOUTH
                ♠ x
                ♡ K
                ◇ K
                ♣ —
```

(11)

```
                NORTH
                ♠ K 2
                ♡ A K 2
                ◇ —
                ♣ —
WEST                        EAST
♠ 5 4                       ♠ A 3
♡ 4 3                       ♡ Q 8 5
◇ —                         ◇ —
♣ 3                         ♣ —
                SOUTH
                ♠ —
                ♡ 10 4 3
                ◇ 2 (trump)
                ♣ A
```

In No. 11 the ♣ A is led and North's ♡ 2 discarded. If East throws a spade North is entered with a heart, the ♠ 2 is ruffed, and North re-entered to make the ♠ K. If East throws a heart, North's ♡ A K are cashed and a spade ruff puts South in again to make the ♡ 10.

Finally, the simple trump squeeze. Although the three examples, Nos. 9, 10, and 11, all appear to be different, once one plays down to the squeezed position they all become the same.

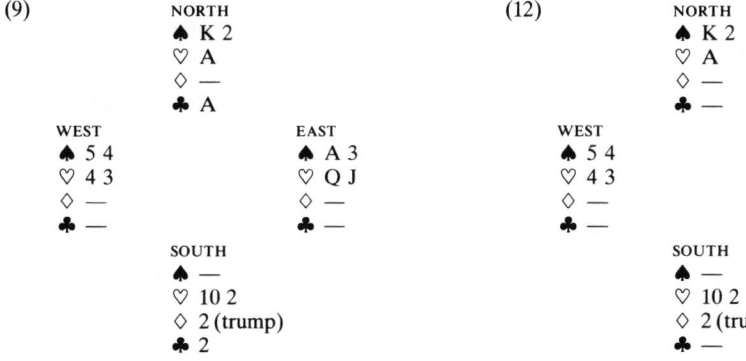

(9)

```
                NORTH
                ♠ K 2
                ♡ A
                ◇ —
                ♣ A
WEST                        EAST
♠ 5 4                       ♠ A 3
♡ 4 3                       ♡ Q J
◇ —                         ◇ —
♣ —                         ♣ —
                SOUTH
                ♠ —
                ♡ 10 2
                ◇ 2 (trump)
                ♣ 2
```

(12)

```
                NORTH
                ♠ K 2
                ♡ A
                ◇ —
                ♣ —
WEST                        EAST
♠ 5 4                       ♠ A 3
♡ 4 3                       ♡ Q J
◇ —                         ◇ —
♣ —                         ♣ —
                SOUTH
                ♠ —
                ♡ 10 2
                ◇ 2 (trump)
                ♣ —
```

Each of the above three cases reduces to the squeezed position, No. 12, with East to discard and then North to lead. This is a much simpler position to remember—in fact it is all simple trump squeezes, and is one position instead of three.

STACK, STACKED. The cards are said to be stacked against one when a single opponent holds all or nearly all of the cards in a crucial suit. To stack a deck is to arrange cards in an undealt deck in order to put predetermined holdings into one or more hands. See CHEATING.

STAKES. Rubber bridge is frequently played for stakes. Although it is a social game, the addition of stakes does provide an incentive to careful and accurate bidding and play.

In major bridge clubs, where membership and card fees are not inconsiderable, stakes range from ½ cent to 3 cents per point; in home and social games, stakes are usually much more modest, from 1/40 to 1/10 of a cent. Since in an evening of play, eight to ten rubbers are completed, with the scores of each rubber 500 to 700 points on the average, a penny a point might bring a fortunate player as much as 75 dollars in one session (or cause a comparable loss to a very unfortunate player). Stakes should never be so high that the possible loss in a sitting could financially hurt the loser, certainly no more than he would be prepared to pay for an evening's entertainment in another form. Rubbers are scored, almost universally, by rounding off to the nearest hundred points, with a score difference of 50 points counted as 100 in America but ignored in Europe. Another difference in usage is that stakes are quoted by the hundred points in England; thus a pound a hundred in England is approximately a 2-cent game in America. See SHARIF BRIDGE CIRCUS.

STAND, STAND FOR. To pass one's partner's PENALTY DOUBLE or TAKE-OUT DOUBLE.

STAND-OFF. A colloquialism for either a rubber with no net score (after ROUNDING OFF); a hand in which HONOR SCORE balances UNDERTRICK PENALTIES: or a deal in a team game (BOARD-A-MATCH, IMP, or TOTAL POINTS) in which neither team gains over the other.

STAND UP. In defensive play, a high card that wins a trick. A suit is said to stand up until it is trumped by the declarer. On the offense or on the defense, too, a high card is said to stand up if it wins the trick, even though a higher card may be outstanding in the suit. The queen stands up in an ace-queen combination, if led toward and the king is in front of it.

STANDARD AMERICAN. A nebulous term applied to the methods of bidding most commonly used in the United States. It approximates closely the methods advocated by Charles GOREN.

Among serious tournament players the WEAK TWO- BID is standard, while rubber bridge players continue to use the FORCING TWO.

Another debatable issue is the idea that jump bids by responder are always forcing. This is implicit in Goren's methods, but has limited acceptance in expert methods.

In parts of the United States, especially California, expert methods include limit bids, sign-off bids, and non-forcing jumps to a much greater extent than in the East, South, and Midwest.

STARTING TIME. Events at bridge tournaments are announced in the advertising material, and it is a measure of a director's and tournament committee's efficiency to have the games start promptly as scheduled. At or near the end of each session, the director clearly announces the starting time for the next session, and if it is a continuation of an event, may assess penalties for tardiness.

After the scheduled starting time, late players may be added to the event if the director can do so without restarting it or unduly delaying the game; such late entries are accepted by the director at his discretion, and no player has an automatic right to be so accepted.

STATE OF MATCH. In knockout team events intermediate scores are usually agreed at one or more stages during the match. In the late stages of a match a team in arrears may reach for optimistic games or slams in the hope of making up for lost ground (see SHOOTING). The side that is leading may decide to shoot also, in the hope of cancelling possible swings.

On the last board of a match a player may allow his decision to be determined by his estimate of the results on the preceding boards.

STAYMAN AFTER OVERCALL. When there is an overcall after a one no trump orening, all minimum minor-suit bids can be used to explore for major-suit contracts. After a two club overcall, two diamonds asks for a major. Three clubs over a two diamond overcall is similar, and the bidding can stop at four of a minor suit. After a major suit overcall, responder bids his longer minor to show length in the unbid major. This plan was devised by R. Maltais, Kenogami, Que.

STAYMAN CONVENTION. The response of two clubs to one no trump asking opener to bid a four-card major suit.

This device, which quickly became standard practice throughout the world, was played in a proto-type form in auction bridge, and in contract in the early thirties by Ewart KEMPSON in England and by a group of Boston players. Its modern form was devised independently by George RAPEE and S. M. STAYMAN, New York City, and by J. C. H. MARX, London, England; it was then published, developed, and popularized by Stayman, who has been responsible for several later developments.

The original convention provided for opener to rebid two diamonds with a minimum hand and two no trump with a maximum. S. J. SIMON, England, suggested the simplification which became generally adopted: opener automatically rebids two diamonds if he does not have a major suit.

The use of higher-level rebids by the opener (such as three clubs to show both major suits) is frowned on by the leading authorities: such bids tend to give excessive information to the opponents, and prevent responder's using Stayman with a weak unbalanced hand.

The authorities are divided on the right rebid for the opener holding both majors. It makes little difference and partnership agreement is not essential. Whether two spades or two hearts is preferred, the opener can bid the other major if responder rebids two no trump or three no trump.

Responder has a wide range of possible rebids, many of which are subject to varying interpretations.

(1) *Two of a major suit.* This can be treated in three ways.
(a) Forcing (usually described as *forcing Stayman*). The bidding must continue at least as far as two no trump. This permits a slow approach to the game, and slam level with strong hands; but most experts reject this treatment because strong hands can be bid satisfactorily by bidding the suit at the three-level on the first or second round.
(b) Encouraging (usually described as *non-forcing Stayman*). This is the standard procedure. Responder indicates game possibilities, together with a five-card suit, or possibly a six-card suit.
(c) Weak. This shows an unbalanced hand and no game interest. The suit bid is likely to be four cards only. If the opener has only a doubleton in the suit, he must make a further bid: over two hearts he bids two spades with a three-card suit, because responder presumably has spades; over two spades he bids three clubs if he has a club suit, and otherwise two no trump. (See article by Alan Truscott in *British Bridge World,* Feb./March 1959.)
(2) *Two no trump.* This is encouraging, showing the same strength as an immediate raise to two no trump. If the opener showed a major, responder now implies that he holds the other major. If the opener rebids two diamonds, responder simply indicates that he has one or both majors.
(3) *Three of a minor suit.* The standard treatment is for three clubs to be weak, with a six-card or seven-card club suit with no game interest. Three diamonds remains ambiguous, and can be treated as forcing or encouraging. (But see WEISSBERGER convention.) However, many experts use immediate jumps to three clubs and three diamonds as pre-emptive (as in ROTH-STONE and KAPLAN-SHEINWOLD) in which case the delayed bid of three clubs or three diamonds is clearly forcing to game; responder is exploring the possibility of a minor-suit game or slam.
(4) *Three of an unbid major suit* (always a jump unless opener bid spades). Forcing and shows a five-card suit. The distinction between this sequence and an immediate jump in the major suit is not clear: some players reserve the immediate jump for hands with slam ambitions; Kaplan-Sheinwold uses the delayed bid to show a strong five-card suit and a relatively balanced hand, leaving the opener to decide between a no trump and suit game. In ACOL, the delayed bid is an invitation to game, and is not forcing.

(5) *Raise to three of a major.* A natural invitation to game, showing four-card support for the major suit.
(6) *Three no trump.* A natural bid, implying that responder holds an unbid major (or possibly two unbid majors). The opener may continue in the unbid major if he has both. (However, in some partnerships the opener is barred from continuing. The ethics of this procedure are doubtful since it is designed simply to allow responder to use Stayman to confuse the issue for the opponents.)
(7) *Four of a minor suit.* When opener shows a major, four clubs can be Gerber by partnership agreement. In Acol, four clubs and four diamonds are used to show a suit of specifically four cards and a hand with slam ambitions (SHARPLES convention). All subsequent bids by both players are natural.
(8) *Four no trump.* An ambiguous bid, but most players who use Gerber would treat it as quantitative. A 4-3-3-3 hand would make an immediate raise to four no trump. (And a 4-4-3-2 hand could use the Sharples convention above.)

Other rebids by the responder are natural.

The above sequences apply to one no trump opening bids of any range. However, the employment of a weak no trump strengthens the argument for using non-forcing Stayman. See also GLADIATOR; ONE NO TRUMP OPENING; TWO-WAY STAYMAN.

STAYMAN ON SECOND ROUND. This is standard in one situation:

SOUTH	NORTH
2 ♣ (artificial)	2 ◇
2 NT	3 ♣

As no suit has been naturally bid, the responder can bid as he would opposite a two no trump opening, with the knowledge that the opener is slightly stronger.

By partnership agreement this can be extended to other no trump rebids:

SOUTH	NORTH
1 ♣	1 ♡
1 NT	2 ♣ (asking for a spade suit)

This checkback procedure permits the opener to conceal a four-card major suit on the second round if he wishes, but deprives the responder of some natural rebids. If the rebid is two no trump, three clubs is not available for players who use it as preparation for a sign-off at the three level (see WOLFF CONVENTION). See CROWHURST CONVENTION, TWO CLUB REBID BY RESPONDER AS ONLY FORCE AFTER ONE NO TRUMP REBID, UNBID MINOR SUIT FORCE.

STAYMAN SYSTEM. Specialized methods of bidding advocated by Sam STAYMAN, formerly played by him in international competition in partnership with Victor MITCHELL. The chief features are:
(1) Minor-suit opening bids often prepared, and

may be preparatory to major-suit CANAPÉ. Inverted raises in uncontested auction. Three no trump response, modified ROMAN BLACKWOOD. Weak jump shifts in competition or by unpassed hand. One no trump rebid, 16–18 points after a fourth-seat opening, otherwise 12–14. After one no trump response, two clubs is conventional and forcing, minor-suit jumps to the three-level are natural and not forcing, three hearts and three spades are canapé, not forcing.

(2) Major-suit opening bids, limited by failure to open two clubs, show less than eight playing tricks and less than 19 points; promise five cards in first or second position. One no trump response by unpassed hand is forcing. Two no trump response is a forcing raise. Three no trump response, modified Roman Blackwood. Limit raises. Jump shifts strong in uncontested auction, except 1 ♥ –2 ♠.

(3) One no trump opening bid, 15–18 points, 12–15 in fourth seat. Two club response, see STAYMAN CONVENTION. Two diamond response, either a transfer to hearts or a game invitational minor-suit hand. Two hearts transfers to two spades. Two spades shows a game forcing minor-suit hand. Two no trump, natural raise. TEXAS transfers at the four-level. Responses after a weak no trump opening are unchanged except two spades is natural and two no trump shows 5–5 or longer in two suits, excluding spades.

(4) Two clubs opening is artificial and forcing, major-suit oriented hand with at least eight playing tricks, or a 21-point balanced hand with all suits stopped.

(5) Two diamonds opening is artificial, usually forcing to game. Two heart response denies two kings or an ace and a king. Two no trump rebid shows a balanced hand, 23–24 points.

(6) Two no trump opening is pre-emptive with a long minor not vulnerable, except fourth seat; a good minor two-suiter vulnerable or in fourth seat.

(7) Gambling three no trump. In fourth seat, or in third seat with both sides vulnerable, shows eight or nine playing tricks with stopper in two outside suits. Otherwise it shows a solid seven- or eight-card minor with no outside stoppers.

(8) Four club or four diamond openings are transfers, equivalent to four heart or four spade openings respectively with possible slam interest.

(9) Four no trump opening, pre-emptive with a long minor, no slam interest.

STAYMAN TWO DIAMONDS. See ARTIFICIAL TWO DIAMOND AND TWO CLUB OPENINGS.

STEINER TROPHY. For the National Individual Masters Championship, donated by Albert and Philip Steiner in 1934. This event was played as an independent tournament. In 1958 it became part of the Fall Nationals until 1960, when it was withdrawn. Past results are listed under Fall Nationals.

STEP RESPONSES TO STRONG ARTIFICIAL TWO-BIDS. Responses to a TWO CLUB STRONG ARTIFICIAL OPENING that show, by steps, how many controls responder holds, counting a king as one

control and an ace as two. As described in THE BRIDGE JOURNAL, a two diamond response shows 0–1 control, a two heart response shows 2 controls, a two spade response shows an ace and a king (3 controls), a two no trump response shows three kings (3 controls), a three club response shows 4 controls and so on. The theory underlying using the two no trump response to show three kings is that if the hand is to be played in no trump it will more likely be played from the RIGHT SIDE. This method of responding is similar to that used in BLUE TEAM CLUB. See also NORMAN FOUR NO TRUMP.

A modification proposed by Edgar KAPLAN requires responder to bid two diamonds with 0–6 points and two hearts shows more than 6 points; both bids, however, show fewer than two controls. Most other responses are amended accordingly: a two spade response shows two controls, two no trump still shows three kings, three clubs shows one ace and one king, three diamonds shows four controls, and so forth. See ACE-SHOWING RESPONSES.

STEPPINGSTONE SQUEEZE. A secondary squeeze in which the opponents must choose between a throw-in and a suit establishment play, each of which enables declarer to gain a trick. (Analyzed and named by Terence REESE.)

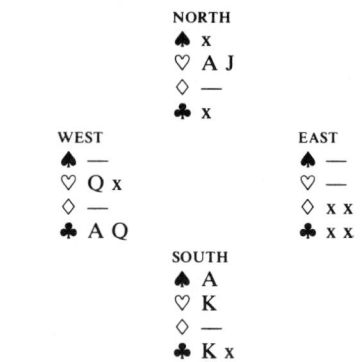

```
                    NORTH
                    ♠ x
                    ♥ A J
                    ◇ —
                    ♣ x
      WEST                          EAST
      ♠ —                           ♠ —
      ♥ Q x                         ♥ —
      ◇ —                           ◇ x x
      ♣ A Q                         ♣ x x
                    SOUTH
                    ♠ A
                    ♥ K
                    ◇ —
                    ♣ K x
```

South leads the ace of spades, and West is squeezed in two suits. In order to retain his guard in hearts, he must throw a club. If West discards the club queen, South takes the king of hearts, and exits with a club, forcing West to lead a heart to North's ace; if West discards the ace of clubs, South's king is established.

The blocked suit must include two winners, one in each hand, but the higher must be in dummy. South must have a one-card menace against the same player who protects the blocked suit. In the diagram position, if the East and West cards were reversed, the squeeze would still be effective. See also ENTRY SQUEEZE and WINKLE SQUEEZE.

M. I.

STERN SYSTEM. See VIENNA SYSTEM.

STIFF. (1) Adjective or noun: Colloquialism for SINGLETON, frequently used in reference to a major honor (ace, king, or queen) without guards. (2) Verb: Colloquially, to blank; to discard the guards.

STOP BID. A bid which fixes the final contract, and commands partner to pass. Responses of four spades or three no trump to an opening no trump bid are examples. SIGN-OFF BIDS are virtually stop bids, but in some cases the partner may have a reason to violate and continue with the auction. See PRE-EMPTIVE RE-RAISE.

STOPPER. A card which may reasonably be expected to or actually does stop the run of a suit. To be counted in the auction as a stopper, a high card, except an ace, must usually be accompanied by lower cards so that it will not have to be played on a higher one if the holder of the higher card decides to play for the drop. The number of low cards, or guards, needed is in inverse proportion to the rank of the honor. Thus, the king must ordinarily be accompanied by at least one guard, and the queen by at least two unless the bidding indicates that a higher ranking card is held by partner. Stoppers are particularly important at no trump contracts. See GUARD; NO TRUMP BIDDING.

STOPPING BELOW GAME. The decision to "stop on a dime" in two no trump or three of a major may be influenced by a variety of factors: vulnerability, method of scoring, and psychological reasons.

It is usually considered advisable to reach for optimistic vulnerable games at rubber bridge and international match-point scoring, but this theory is not borne out by the mathematics (see VALUE OF GAME). In match-point scoring, theory suggests that a game should be bid with a 50% chance, but in practice experts tend to be slightly conservative unless the opposition is weak. In such circumstances three no trump, down one, is likely to be a worse score than two no trump, made with an overtrick. It is desirable to make sure of a plus score.

The abilities of partner and opponents enter into the calculation at rubber bridge. Playing with a weak partner against good opponents, it may pay to strain to make a vulnerable game, which will lead to a change of partnership, but the converse is true when the first game is in prospect.

Contracts one below the game level are less frequent using STANDARD AMERICAN methods, in which many more bids are forcing than they are in a system in which more bids are limited and non-forcing.

STRAIN. A term encompassing all four suits plus no trump. See DENOMINATION.

STRENGTH. The top card holding in a suit, either as stoppers in no trump, for drawing adversely held trumps, for trick-taking potential, or to set up LONG CARDS as winners.

STRENGTH-CONCEALING PLAYS. See DECEPTIVE PLAY.

STRENGTH-SHOWING BIDS. In some special situations a suit bid can be used to show strength rather than length or control. This applies particularly when exploring for a three no trump contract as an alternative to an obvious minor-suit possibility.

The following are typical cases. The suit bid might conceivably be as weak as QJx, but would usually contain at least 4 points.

(a)

WEST	EAST
1 ◇	2 ♣
3 ♣	3 ♡

(b)

WEST	EAST
1 NT	3 ◇
3 ♡	

West can bid a strong three-card suit because East is unlikely to be interested in a major suit. This may reveal duplication if East is short in hearts, and permit a final contract of three no trump.

(c)

WEST	EAST
1 ◇	3 ◇
3 ♡	

(d)

WEST	EAST
3 ♣	3 ◇
3 ♡	

In each case the suit is unlikely to be raised. If it is, the choice lies between playing in a 3–4 fit or retreating into the minor suit.

STRIP PLAY. A method of play by which a chosen opponent is stripped of his cards in a certain suit with the purpose of later throwing the lead to that player, and thus compelling him to lead a suit desired by declarer. The term is also used for a method of play, termed elimination, by which declarer exhausts the cards in a suit or suits in both his and the dummy's hands so that a later lead by a defender will permit him to trump in one hand and sluff a loser from the other. Often combined with end play as in "strip and end play." See END PLAY; SQUEEZE; THROW IN.

STRIPED-TAIL APE DOUBLE. An inhibitory double of an opposing game contract made by a player who feels sure that his opponents can make a slam. The doubled contract with overtricks scores less than the score for bidding and making the slam. So named by John LOWENTHAL, Hackensack, N.J., and Samuel SCAFFIDI, Mingo Junction, Ohio, in a *Bridge Journal* article because the doubler flees like a striped-tail ape in the face of a redouble. The same tactics can be applied at the small slam level if a grand slam can be made.

STRONG ACE ASKING BIDS OTHER THAN FOUR CLUBS OR FOUR NO TRUMP. See SUPER GERBER.

STRONG JUMP OVERCALL. See JUMP OVERCALL.

STRONG MINOR RAISES. See INVERTED MINOR SUIT RAISES.

STRONG NO TRUMP. An opening bid of one no trump that meets the following requirements: the hand must have a point-count of 16, 17, or 18; must be of balanced distribution, 4–3–3–3, 4–4–3–2, or 5–3–3–2 with the proviso that the doubleton be headed by at least the queen; at least three suits must be protected and the fourth suit at least x x x. See ONE NO TRUMP OPENING.

Some players shade the requirements to 15 points, and some feel that 18 points is too strong for the bid. Many experts treat the other requirements flexibly. They may open one no trump with a weak doubleton because they foresee rebid problems after a suit opening; and they may occasionally open one no trump with a six-card minor and 6–3–2–2 distribution.

Even stronger one no trump opening bids are advocated in some systems, notably ROMAN, SIMS, and VANDERBILT. For strong no trump openings that are forcing for one round, see DYNAMIC NO TRUMP, LITTLE ROMAN CLUB SYSTEM, ROMEX SYSTEM.

STRONG NO TRUMP AFTER PASSING (abbreviated to SNAP). A response of one no trump by a passed hand as a strong bid, showing 9–12 points. An idea introduced by Jeremy FLINT and Tony PRIDAY.

This permits the bidding to stay in a comfortable low-level contract when the opener has a minimum or sub-minimum hand. The no trump bidder promises a relatively balanced hand, and denies holding a five-card major suit which could have been bid at the level of one. The idea often gives an advantage in a part-score deal, and is therefore of most value in a match-point event.

SNAP creates problems for some responding hands with 6–8 points. A 6-point hand may sometimes be passed, and an 8-point hand may respond at the level of two. The problems of the responder are most acute if the opening bid is one spade, for which reason some partnerships insist that a third- or fourth-hand spade opening bid should contain at least five cards, permitting a raise with a doubleton. A 7-point hand with 3–2–4–4 distribution presents a special problem, and a SNAP player might respond one spade.

Using SNAP, a two no trump response becomes an idle bid, and is used to show a relatively balanced limit jump raise in opener's suit.

For a device with similar objectives, see DRURY.

STRONG SUIT. A suit of four or more cards containing a minimum of six points.

STRONG TWO-BID. See FORCING TWO-BID.

SUBMARINE SQUEEZE. The concession of a trick by declarer in order to correct the count for a squeeze. If declarer gives up the trick on a lead by the opponents, he is said to be RECTIFYING THE COUNT; however, if the trick is conceded at a time when declarer holds the lead, some writers call this move a "submarine squeeze."

SUB-SENIOR MASTERS TEAM CHAMPIONSHIP, NATIONAL. See ROTHSCHILD TROPHY.

SUBSTITUTE. (1) Call. When a player makes an illegal call, he may be required to substitute a legal call, with appropriate penalties against his partner, under provisions of LAWS (Laws 25–27, 30–33, 36–38).

(2) Player. A player who, in rubber bridge, replaces a member of the table who is called away or must leave during or before the finish of a rubber. Such a substitute must be acceptable to all members playing at the table; and he would be assumed to have no financial responsibility unless agreed otherwise.

(3) Player. In duplicate play, a player who is permitted by the director to replace a player who is unable to finish a session or play in a second or later session. Such substitution is at the discretion of the director, guided by the league regulations contained in the ACBL HANDBOOK in the United States, or other regulatory bodies for tournament competition.

(4) Board. In team play, a board is introduced by the director at a table when an irregularity has occurred that makes a normal result impossible. Such a board is withdrawn after play, but reinstated when the teammates of the pairs who played it are scheduled to play that board. If the substitute board is needed on the replay (after the teammates have recorded a result), an offending side causing the substitution may be playing for at best a halved board.

SUCCESSIVE EVENTS, PROBABILITY OF. See PROBABILITY OF SUCCESSIVE EVENTS.

SUCKER'S DOUBLE. A double of a freely bid game or slam contract by a player who is relying solely on defensive high-card strength. Against good opponents such doubles rarely show more than a small profit. They can, however, show a disastrous loss, especially when the double helps declarer to make his contract. The probability is that the declaring side has distributional strength to compensate for the relative lack of high-card strength.

Such doubles are unwise mathematically as well as technically. A player who doubles four spades, not vulnerable, stands to gain 50 from a one-trick set, and to lose 170 if the contract is just made; and if the contract can be made, there is a possibility of a redouble. In slam contracts the odds are weighted even more heavily against the doubler, and the double is reserved for lead-directing purposes when the doubler's partner is on lead (see LIGHTNER DOUBLE).

These doubles are slightly more attractive at match-point scoring, when the small profit may be significant. But the doubler should consider that he will probably score well in any case if he scores a plus. See also PENALTY DOUBLE.

SUFFICIENT BID. A bid of the same number of a higher ranking denomination or of a greater number in a lower ranking suit or the same denomination. If the enforcement of a penalty permits a player to substitute a sufficient bid for an incorrect call, a double of an opponent's bid may not be substituted; even though such double is a legal call. See INSUFFICIENT BID.

SUICIDE SQUEEZE. A squeeze inflicted by a defender on his partner. (But as this name is hardly accurate, it is called by some the Cannibal Squeeze.) Inaccurate defense may lead to this position, but there are times when the opponents have no recourse.

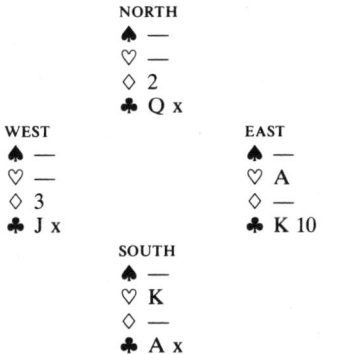

```
                    NORTH
                    ♠ —
                    ♡ —
                    ◇ 2
                    ♣ Q x
   WEST                        EAST
   ♠ —                         ♠ —
   ♡ —                         ♡ A
   ◇ 3                         ◇ —
   ♣ J x                       ♣ K 10
                    SOUTH
                    ♠ —
                    ♡ K
                    ◇ —
                    ♣ A x
```

West, on lead, produces a suicide squeeze on his partner if he cashes the high diamond. If East discards the ace of hearts, South discards the low club, winning two tricks. If East discards the ten of clubs, South discards the king of hearts. Proper defense calls for a club lead. If North were on lead, the small diamond lead would produce the simple squeeze against East.

This is essentially a simple squeeze position, with North on lead, but the squeeze card is a loser. Thus declarer must have all but two of the remaining tricks. In addition, the player who wins the squeeze card must have no other winner which he can cash. When these additional requirements are met, any simple squeeze ending may lead to a suicide squeeze, as can other squeeze positions.

M. I.

SUIT. The group to which each card in a pack belongs. Modern packs have four suits. Until the sixteenth century, there was no agreement as to number; Hindu cards had ten, and packs of five to eleven suits were used in one country or another. In the 1930s there was a brief flurry of interest in a fifth suit, but it faded.

Three different sets of symbols have been developed which are in use today:

International (British, American, French); spades, hearts, diamonds, and clubs.

Trappola (Italy, Spain, Latin countries); cups, coins, swords, and cudgels.

German (Germany, Austria, Bohemia, Poland, Hungary); hearts, leaves, bells, and acorns, with the Swiss modification of blossoms and shields for the latter two.

In 1862 an American chauvinist issued a patriotic deck of Union Playing Cards with suits of stars, flags, shields, and eagles. Card players were not chauvinistic.

Our club design is the clover-leaf of the French but the name is from the trappola deck; the diamond design is also French, but the name is an English descriptive term; the heart design is from the German pack; the spade design is the French pikehead, but the name is from the trappola deck.

The attribution of the suit names to the four orders of society—hearts for the church, spades for the military, clubs for the peasantry, and diamonds (tiles) for the merchants—was made long after the development of the suit names and symbols. See PLAYING CARDS.

A. F.

SUIT, NUMBER OF CARDS IN. For notations used, see MATHEMATICS OF BRIDGE.

(1) A player can have x cards of a given suit in $13Cx \times 39C(13-x)$ ways. The percentage probability is found by multiplying this by 100 and dividing by 52C13. A player can have exactly five spades, then, in $13C5 \times 39C8 = 79,181,063,676$ ways. The percentage is

$$\frac{7,918,106,367,600}{636,013,559,600} = 12.469\%$$

(2) A player can have x cards of one suit and y cards of another suit in $13Cx \times 13Cy \times 26C(13-x-y)$ ways. He can have five spades and four hearts, then, in $13C5 \times 13C4 \times 26C4 = 13,575,064,750$ ways. The percentage is 2.166%.

(3) If 26 cards are known (such as after the dummy is exposed), of which y are the cards of the suit in question, a player can have x cards in that suit in $(13-y)Cx \times (26-13+y)C(13-x)$ ways. If four spades are seen (y), he can have 5 spades in $9C5 \times 17C8$ ways. This computes to 3,063,060 ways, or a percentage of 29.451%.

SUIT COMBINATIONS. The correct treatment of particular suit combinations by declarer is a highly complex subject. The classified analysis on the following pages is the first attempt in bridge literature at a comprehensive coverage.

To find any particular combination, first count the number of high-card points held by the defense in the crucial suit. Find the appropriate section, which is subdivided according to the number of cards held by the declaring side.

The play of each combination is considered in two ways. First from the angle of safety plays, the number of tricks required is given together with the appropriate play and the percentage prospects. Second, where no particular number of tricks is required, but declarer simply wants to do as well as possible, the indicated maximum play (abbreviated to MAX) is given, with the expectation of tricks if this line is followed.

Whenever the symbol "x" is used, it should be assumed to be a completely insignificant spot card. In many cases the replacement of an x by an 8 or a 7 would affect the play or the percentages.

Dummy is always assumed to have the greater length. When the same holding occurs "the other way up," with the length in declarer's hand, the analysis and percentages are identical (except in very rare cases when psychological considerations apply).

Dummy Declarer	Tricks Required		% Chance of Success	Tricks per Deal

I. THE DEFENSE HAS NO POINTS

(a) Declarer Has Six Cards

1.	A K Q J 9 x	5	Cash top honors in the hope of dropping the ten	72	

(b) Declarer Has Seven Cards

2.	A K Q J 9 x x	6 5	Cash top honors Finesse the nine, in case East is void	86 99	
3.	A K Q J 9 x x	5	Cash top honors in the hope of dropping the ten	87	
4.	A K Q 9 x J x	5	Cash top honors in the hope of dropping the ten	87	
5.	A K Q J 8 x x	5	Cash top honors* (*But against defenders who would not false-card from 10 9x or 10 9xx, cash the jack and finesse the eight if the nine or ten appears from East)	84 85	
6.	A K Q 8 x J x	5	See (5) above	84	

(c) Declarer Has Eight Cards

7.	A K Q 8 x J x x	5	Cash the jack first in case East is void	98	

II. THE DEFENSE HAS ONE POINT

(a) Declarer Has Five Cards

8.	A K Q 10 x	4	Finesse the ten	50	

(b) Declarer Has Six Cards

9.	A K Q 10 9 x	5	Play off the top honors. This is fractionally better than the immediate finesse	36	
10.	A K Q 10 x x	5 4 Max	Finesse the ten Finesse the ten Finesse the ten	31 81	4.12
11.	A K Q 10 x x	4	Cash the queen, and then finesse the ten	50	
12.	A K Q 9 x x	4	Finesse the nine; hope that West has both the jack and ten	24	
13.	A K 10 x Q x	4	Cash the queen, and then finesse the ten	50	
14.	A K 9 x Q x	4	Play off the queen, king, and ace, hoping that the jack and ten fall in three rounds* (*But against defenders who would not false-card from J10x, cash the queen and finesse the nine if East drops an honor)	10 11	

(c) Declarer Has Seven Cards

15.	A K Q 10 9 x x	6	Cash the top honors	54	

Dummy Declarer	Tricks Required		% Chance of Success	Tricks per Deal

II. THE DEFENSE HAS ONE POINT (cont'd)

16.	A K Q 10 x x x	6 5 4 Max	Cash the top honors Finesse the ten Finesse the ten, in case East is void Cash the top honors	52 91 99	 5.37
17.	A K Q 10 9 x x	5	Play off the top honors	54	
18.	A K Q 10 x x x	5 4 Max	Play off the top honors Cash the ace, and finesse the ten Play off the top honors	52 93	 4.39
19.	A K Q 9 x x x	5 4 Max	Play off the top honors, hoping that the jack and ten drop in three rounds Lead small to the nine, in case East has a void or small singleton Play off the top honors* (*But against defenders who would not false- card from J10x, cash the ace and finesse the nine if East drops an honor)	 39 90 	 4.23 4.24
20.	A K 10 9 x Q x	5	Play off the top honors	54	
21.	A K 10 x x Q x	5 4 Max	Play off the top honors Cash the queen and finesse the ten Play off the top honors	52 93	 4.39
22.	A K 9 x x Q 10	5 4 Max	Cash the queen, king, and ace Cash the queen, and run the ten Cash the queen, and run the ten	54 100	 4.44
23.	A K x x x Q 10	5 4 Max	Finesse the ten Finesse the ten Finesse the ten	42 92	 4.34
24.	A K 9 x x Q x	5 4 Max	Play off the top honors Cash the queen, and finesse the nine if an honor drops from East Play off the top honors* (*But against defenders who would not false- card from J10x, cash the queen, and finesse the nine if an honor drops from East)	39 86 	 4.23 4.24
25.	A K Q 10 x x x	4	Cash the king and queen; if both follow, play the ace. This is 2% better than a third-round finesse	 61	
26.	A K Q 9 x x x	4	Cash the queen and king; if an honor drops from East, finesse the nine next. This is 6% better than cashing the three top honors regardless	 48	
27.	A K 10 x Q x x	4	See (25) above	61	
28.	A K 9 x Q x x	4	See (26) above	48	
29.	A K x x Q 10 x	4	Cash the ace, queen, and king. This is 4% better than a second-round finesse	 55	
30.	A 10 x x K Q x	4	See (25) above	61	
31.	A 9 x x K Q x	4	See (26) above	48	
32.	A x x x K Q 10	4	Cash the king, queen, and ace. This is 4% better than a second-round finesse	 55	

(d) **Declarer Has Eight Cards**

33.	A K Q 10 x x x x	7 6 Max	Play off the top honors Finesse the ten, in case East is void Play off the top honors	73 98	 6.70

Dummy Declarer	Tricks Required		% Chance of Success	Tricks per Deal

II. THE DEFENSE HAS ONE POINT (cont'd)

34.	A K Q 9 x x x x	6	Play off the top honors* (*But against defenders who would not false- card from J10x, cash the ace and finesse the nine if an honor appears from East)	68 70
		5	Lead small to the nine, in case East is void	98
35.	A K Q 8 x x 10 x	6	Play off the top honors	73
		5	Lead small to the ten	100
		Max	Play off the top honors	5.70
36.	K Q 9 x x x A x	6	Play off the top honors* (*But against defenders who would not false- card from J10x, cash the ace and finesse the nine if an honor appears from East)	68 70
37.	A K 9 x x Q 8 x	5	Cash the ace and queen (or the queen and ace), hoping for a 3–2 break or a singleton honor with East* (*But against defenders who would not false- card with J10x, cash the ace, and finesse the eight if West drops an honor)	 73 76
		4	Lead small to the eight or nine	100
38.	A K 10 x Q 9 x x	4	Cash the ace. If the eight falls, play the next top honor from the hand on the left of the eight. Otherwise guess which honor to play next (*Assuming that the eight is not a false-card from J8xx)	 92*
39.	A K 9 x Q 8 x x	4	Cash the ace. If an honor appears, cash the next top honor from the hand on the left of the J or 10	 79
40.	A K 9 x Q x x x	4	Cash the queen, in case West has J10xxx	75

(e) Declarer Has Nine Cards

41.	A K Q 8 x x x 9 x	7	Lead the nine, and play the ace whatever hap- pens. This saves a trick if West covers with J10xxx	 90+
42.	A K Q 7 x x 8 x x	6	Lead the eight, and play the ace whatever hap- pens. This saves a trick if West is lulled into covering with J109x	 90+
43.	A K 10 x x x Q 9 x	6	Lead the ace first in case either opponent is void	100
44.	A K 9 x x x Q x x	6	Play the queen first, in case East is void	95
45.	A K Q 7 x 8 x x x	5	Lead the eight, and play the ace whatever hap- pens. This saves a trick if West is lulled into covering with J109x	 90+
46.	A K 10 x x Q 9 x x	5	Cash the ace first, in case either opponent is void	100
47.	A K 9 x x Q x x x	5	Cash the queen first, in case East is void	95

III. THE DEFENSE HAS TWO POINTS

(a) Declarer Has Five Cards

48.	A K J 10 x	4	Finesse the jack. This line is 6% better than try- ing to drop the queen	11

(b) Declarer Has Six Cards

Dummy Declarer	Tricks Required		% Chance of Success	Tricks per Deal

III. THE DEFENSE HAS TWO POINTS (cont'd)

49. A K J 10 9 x	5	Finesse the jack	18	
50. A K J 9 8 x	5	Lead small to the jack or nine, playing West for Q10x or Q10	5	
	4	Lead small to the jack	58	
	Max	Lead small to the jack		3.63
51. A K J 9 x x	4	Finesse the nine; if this loses to the ten, finesse the jack	24	
	3	Finesse the jack and then the nine, *or* finesse the nine and then the jack	76	
52. A K 9 8 J x	4	Run the jack; if it is covered, finesse the nine next. West must have Q10, Q10x or Qxxxxx	6	
	3	Lead the jack; if it loses, finesse the nine next	76	
53. A K 9 x J x	3	Lead small to the jack. If this loses, finesse the nine	74	
54. A J 9 8 K x	4	Cash the king and, unless an honor appears from East, finesse the jack	6	
	3	Cash the king and, unless an honor appears from East, finesse the jack or nine*	69	
	Max	Cash the king and, unless an honor appears from East, finesse the jack or nine* (*This line is only fractionally better than running the nine, which will be superior if West is likely to have fewer cards in the suit than East)		2.75
55. A J x x K 9	3	Finesse the nine; if this loses to the ten, cash the king and ace	68	
56. A K 9 J x x	3	Lead small to the nine, hoping that West has both the queen and ten	24	
57. A K x J 9 8	3	*Either* run the nine *or* run the jack. Guess whether West has the bare queen or East the bare ten* (*But against defenders who can be relied upon to cover the nine with the ten, lead the nine, and play the ace and king if it is not covered; if the nine is covered, run the jack next)	24 29	

(c) Declarer Has Seven Cards

58. A K J 10 9 x x	6	Finesse the jack. This line is 8% better than try- ing to drop the queen	27	
59. A K J 9 8 7 x	6	Finesse the jack	19	
	5	Finesse the jack. This line is 2% better than cashing the ace and king, and 1% better than finessing the nine	71	
60. A K J 10 9 x x	5	Finesse the jack. Do not cash the ace first: Qxxx with West is more likely than Q with East	43	
61. A K J 9 x x x	5	Finesse the jack, alternatively cashing the ace first	19	
	4	Finesse the nine; if this loses to the ten, cash the ace and king	73	
	3	Finesse the nine, and then the jack *or* finesse the jack and then the nine, *or* cash the ace, and then finesse the jack or nine	94	
	Max	Finesse the nine; if this loses to the ten, cash the ace and king		3.85
62. A K 9 8 x J x	5	Run the jack *or* lead small to the nine	9	
	4	Cash the ace and then run the jack	73	
	Max	Run the jack. If it is covered, finesse the nine; if it loses, cash the ace; if it holds, cash the ace		3.79

Dummy Declarer	Tricks Required		% Chance of Success	Tricks per Deal

III. THE DEFENSE HAS TWO POINTS (cont'd)

Dummy Declarer	Tricks Required		% Chance of Success	Tricks per Deal
63. A K 9 x x J x	5	Run the jack *or* lead small to the nine. West must hold Q10x	7	
	4	Lead small to the jack; if it loses, cash the ace and king	68	
	3	Lead small to the jack; if it loses, finesse the nine	99	
	MAX	Lead small to the jack; if it loses, cash the ace and king		3.62
64. A J x x x K 9	5	Cash the king, and then finesse the jack	18	
	4	Lead small to the nine	68	
	3	Cash the king, and then finesse the jack	94	
	MAX	Cash the king, and then finesse the jack		3.74
64A. K J 9 x x A x	5	Cash the ace and then finesse the jack. (If East plays the ten, play for the queen to drop unless East is capable of a falsecard from 10 x x.)	20.99	
	4	Cash the ace and then finesse the jack or the nine. If East plays the queen, finesse the nine	69.04	
	MAX	Cash the ace and then finesse the jack.		3.84
65. A K J 10 x x x	4	Cash the ace, and finesse the ten	51	
66. A K J 9 x x x	4	Cash the ace, and finesse the jack	29	
	3	Cash the ace. Then lead toward dummy, and play the king if the ten fails to appear. Then lead up to the jack	85	
	MAX	Cash the ace, and finesse the jack		3.07
67. A K J x x x x	4	Cash the ace, and finesse the jack	18	
	3	Play off the ace and king, and then lead up to the jack	77	
	MAX	Cash the ace, and finesse the jack		2.87
68. A K 10 x J x x	4	Cash the ace, and then lead small to the ten. Don't lead the jack for the finesse; West may have Qx	28	
69. A K 9 8 J x x	4	Run the jack; if this is covered, finesse the nine	25	
	3	Play the ace, and if no honor appears, run the nine; if it loses, run the jack through next* (*Assuming East would not duck with Qxx, this line only loses when West has 10x. If East is a very good defender, play the king if the nine loses to the ten)	94	
			84	
	MAX	Run the jack; if this is covered, finesse the nine; if the jack loses, cash the ace and king		3.01
70. A K 9 x J x x	4	Lead small to the nine, hoping that West has Q10 or Q10x	9	
	3 } MAX }	Cash the ace and, unless the ten appears, lead small to the jack; if the jack loses, cash the king	84	2.88
71. A K x x J 10 9	4	Finesse the jack	50	
	3	Finesse the jack *or* play the ace, and then finesse the jack	100	
72. A K x x J 9 8	4	Run the nine and then the jack *or* run the jack and then the nine, hoping that West has Q10x or either Q or Qxxxx	8	
	3	Play the ace, and lead small to the jack	78	
	MAX	Run the nine; if it loses to the ten, run the jack next		2.85

Dummy Declarer	Tricks Required		% Chance of Success	Tricks per Deal

III. THE DEFENSE HAS TWO POINTS (cont'd)

	Dummy Declarer	Tricks Required		% Chance of Success	Tricks per Deal
73.	A K x x J 9 x	4	Play the ace, hoping that West has the singleton queen	1	
		3 } Max }	Play the ace and then lead small to the jack or nine	78	2.79
74.	A K x x J x x	3 } Max }	Play the ace and lead to the jack	69	2.69
75.	A J 9 8 K x x	4	Cash the king, and finesse the jack	29	
		3	Cash the king, and lead toward dummy, playing the ace unless the ten appears	85	
		Max	Cash the king, and finesse the jack		3.07
76.	A J 9 x K x x	4	Cash the king, and finesse the jack	29	
		3	Cash the king and ace; then lead to the jack	85	
		Max	Cash the king, and finesse the jack. If it loses, cash the ace		3.07
77.	A J x x K 9 x	4	Cash the king, and finesse the jack	19	
		3	Cash the king and ace; then lead to the jack	85	
		Max	Cash the king, and finesse the jack		2.98
78.	A J x x K x x	4	Cash the king, and finesse the jack	18	
		3	Cash the king and ace; then lead to the jack	77	
		Max	Cash the king, and finesse the jack		2.87
79.	K 9 x x A J x	4	Finesse the jack; then play the ace and king* (*Against defenders who would not falsecard from Q10x, finesse the nine if East drops the queen under the ace)	21 27	
		3	Lead small from dummy, and play the ace unless the ten appears. Then, unless West drops the ten, lead small to the jack	84	
		Max	Finesse the jack; then play the ace and king		3.03
80.	J 10 x x A K x	4	Cash the ace, and then run the jack. This line is only 1% better than cashing the two top honors	20	
81.	J 9 8 x A K x	4	Cash the ace and king, unless the queen drops from West* (*But if West is good enough to falsecard from Q10, we have to play the king, even if the queen falls under the ace)	12 11	
		3	Cash the ace and king; then lead to the jack	85	
82.	J x x x A K 9	4	Lead small to the nine, hoping that East has Q10 or Q10x	9	
		3 } Max }	Cash the ace and king; then lead to the jack	85	2.90

(d) Declarer Has Eight Cards

	Dummy Declarer	Tricks Required		% Chance of Success	Tricks per Deal
83.	A K J 10 9 x x x	7	Finesse the jack. This line is 4% better than playing off the ace and king	37	
84.	A K J 9 8 7 x x	7	Finesse the jack	34	
		6	Finesse the nine *or,* more profitably, finesse the jack	85	
85.	A K J 10 x x x x	6	Finesse the jack. Don't cash the ace first: Qxxx with West is more likely than Q with East	48	
		5	Finesse the jack	98	
		Max	Finesse the jack		5.46

	Dummy Declarer	Tricks Required		% Chance of Success	Tricks per Deal

III. THE DEFENSE HAS TWO POINTS (cont'd)

	Dummy Declarer	Tricks Required		% Chance of Success	Tricks per Deal
86.	A K J 9 x x x x	6	Finesse the jack, alternatively cashing the ace first*	37	
			(*Against defenders who would not falsecard from 10x, cash the ace, and play the king if the ten falls from East)	40	
		5 ⎰ Max ⎱	Cash the ace, and finesse the jack	88	5.22
87.	A K J x x x x x	6	Finesse the jack, alternatively cashing the ace first	34	
		5 ⎰ Max ⎱	Cash the ace, and then finesse the jack	85	5.17
88.	A K 9 8 7 x J x	6	Run the jack. If it is covered, guess whether to finesse for or drop the ten next	16	
		5 ⎰ Max ⎱	Run the jack. If it loses, cash the ace and king; if it is covered, guess as above	87	5.03
89.	A K 9 8 x x J x	6	Run the jack. If it is covered, guess whether to finesse or cash the ace next	16	
		5	Lead small to the jack, and then cash the ace and king (which will be best if West is likely to be short in the suit) *or*		
			Run the jack, cashing the ace and king if it loses, and guessing if it is covered (which will be best if East is likely to be short in the suit)	85	
		Max	Run the jack, guessing what to do next if it is covered		5.01
90.	A K 9 x x x J x	6	Run the jack. If it is covered, finesse the nine *or* cash the ace	14	
		5	Lead small to the jack; then cash the ace and king	85	
		4	Lead small to the jack	100	
		Max	Lead the jack, if it is covered, finesse the nine next		4.94
91.	A J 8 x x x K 9	6	Play the king. If the queen drops from East, run the nine; otherwise finesse the jack	37	
		5	Cash the king, and then lead the nine, and finesse the jack	88	
		4	Lead small to the nine	100	
92.	A J x x x x K 9	6	Cash the king, and finesse the jack	34	
		5	Cash the king, and lead the nine, intending to finesse the jack	88	
		4	Lead small to the nine	100	
		Max	Cash the king, and finesse the jack		5.20
93.	A K 9 8 x J x x	5	Play the ace. Then play the king unless the queen has appeared from East	30	
		4	Play the ace, and unless an honor appears, lead low to the jack	96	
		Max	Lead the jack. If it is covered, finesse the nine; if it loses, cash the ace		4.14
94.	A K 9 x x J x x	5	Play the ace and king (unless the queen drops from East)	30	
		4	Play the ace, and if the ten fails to appear, lead small to the jack	96	
		Max	Play the ace and king		4.09

Dummy Declarer	Tricks Required		% Chance of Success	Tricks per Deal

III. THE DEFENSE HAS TWO POINTS (cont'd)

95. A K 7 6 x J 9 8	5	Lead the nine to the ace. (This makes it harder for West to falsecard with queen from Q10, as it would help a declarer with J9.) If the queen falls, finesse accordingly; if not, cash the king		
		Assuming no falsecard:	33	
	4	Play the ace, and if no honor appears, lead low to the jack	98	
	Max	Cash the ace and king* (* If West would not falsecard from Q10)		4.11 4.14
96. A K x x x J 10 9	5	Finesse the jack. Don't cash the ace first: Qxxx with West is more likely than queen with East	48	
	4	Finesse the jack	100	
97. A K x x x J 9 8	5	Cash the ace and king* (*But against defenders who would not falsecard with Q10, finesse the nine if West drops the queen on the first round)	27 30	
	4	Play the ace, and lead small to the jack	88	
	3	Run the jack or lead small to the jack	100	
	Max	Cash the ace, and unless West is void, lead small to the king* (*If West would not falsecard with Q10)		4.01 4.04
98. A K x x x J 9 x	5	Play the ace and king* (*But against defenders who would not falsecard with Q10, finesse the nine if West drops the queen on the first round)	27 30	
	4	Play the ace, and lead small to the jack	88	
	Max	Play the ace and king		3.99
99. A J 9 x x K x x	5 } Max }	Cash the king, and finesse the jack* (*But against defenders who would not falsecard, it is fractionally better to play the ace if East drops the ten on the first round)	40	4.27
100. A J x x x K 9 x	5	Lead low to the jack* (*Against defenders who would not falsecard from Q10, finesse the nine next if the queen appears from West)	34 37	
	4	Play the ace, and unless an honor appears from West, lead low to the nine	96	
	3	Play either top honor	100	
	Max	Play the king, and finesse the jack		4.22
101. A 9 x x x K J x	5	Finesse the jack. Don't cash the ace first, for East may have the singleton queen	37	
	4	Play the king, and unless the ten appears, lead low to the jack	96	
	3	Finesse the jack, and cash the king or play the king and lead small to the jack	100	
	Max	Finesse the jack		4.30
102. J 9 8 x x A K x	5	Play the ace, and unless the queen appears from West, king* (*But if West would falsecard from Q10, cash the king next whatever happens)	33 30	
	4	Play the ace and king	88	
103. A K J 10 x x x x	4	Play the ace, and finessee the jack	53	
104. A K 9 x J x x x	4	Play the ace and king	30	
	3	Play the ace, and then lead small to the nine or jack	100	
	Max	Play the ace and king		3.21

Dummy Declarer	Tricks Required		% Chance of Success	Tricks per Deal

III. THE DEFENSE HAS TWO POINTS (cont'd)

105. A K 8 x J x x x	4 3 Max	Play the ace and king Play the ace; if the ten or nine appears from East, lead small to the jack Play the ace and king	27 92	 3.14
106. A K x x J 9 8 x	4 3 Max	Play the ace and king Play the ace, and unless the ten appears from East, run the nine Play the ace and king	33 100	 3.24
107. A J x x K 9 x x	4 3 Max	Finesse the jack Play the ace, and lead small to the nine Finesse the jack; if it loses, play the ace next	37 100	 3.34
108. A 10 8 x K J 9 x	4	Lead the jack to the ace *or* the ten to the king, and then take a second-round finesse. This gives the extra chance of a defender covering with Qx or Qxx	53+	

(e) Declarer Has Nine Cards

109. A K J x x x x x x	8 7 Max	Play the ace and king. This line is 8% better than a first-round finesse Finesse the jack, in case East is void Play the ace and king	53 95	 7.44
110. A K J x x x x x x	7	Play the ace and king. This line is 2% better than a second-round finesse	53	
111. A K 9 x x x x J x	7 6 Max	Play the ace and king Lead low to the jack Play the ace and king* (*But against defenders who would always cover the jack, and would not falsecard with Q10, lead the jack, and play the ace whatever happens, finessing the nine next if East plays the queen)	53 100	 6.44 6.48
112. A J x x x x x K 9	7 6 Max	Play the king and ace Lead small to the nine, in case West is void Play the king and ace	53 100	 6.48
113. A K J 10 x x x x x	6	Play the ace and king	58	
114. A K 9 x x x J x x	6 5	Play the ace and king Play the ace	53 100	
115. A K 8 x x x J x x	6 5 Max	Play the ace and king Lead small toward dummy, and cover whatever West plays Play the ace and king	53 100	 5.48
116. A K x x x x J 10 9	6	Lead the jack to the ace; then cash the king	53	
117. A K x x x x J 9 8	6 5 Max	Play the ace and king Lead small to the jack *or* (best) run the nine Play the ace and king	53 100	 5.48
118. A J x x x x K 9 x	6 5 Max	Play the ace and king Play the ace Play the ace and king	53 100	 5.53
119. A 9 x x x x K J x	6 5 Max	Play the ace and king Play the king Play the king and ace	53 100	 5.53

Dummy Declarer	Tricks Required		% Chance of Success	Tricks per Deal

III. THE DEFENSE HAS TWO POINTS (cont'd)

120. A K 8 x x J x x x	5	Play the ace and king* (*Against defenders who would always cover the jack, lead the jack, and play the ace whatever happens. If West covers and the ten or nine drops from East, finesse the eight next. This line will be better if East is likely to be short in the suit)	53 53	
	4 MAX	Lead small to the eight *or* small to the jack Play the ace and king	100	4.48
121. A K x x x J 10 9 x	5	Play the ace and king. This line is 2% better than a second-round finesse	58	
122. A J 9 x x K 10 8 x	5	Lead the jack to the king *or* lead the ten to the ace, and play for the drop on the second round. This gives the extra chance of a defender covering with Qxx	58	
123. A J x x x K 9 8 7	5 4	Play the king and ace, in case East is void Play the ace, in case West is void	58 100	
124. A J x x x K 9 x x	5 4	Cash the ace and king, preferably in that order Play the ace (best) *or* finesse the jack or nine	53 100	
125. A 9 x x x K J x x	5 4	Play the ace and king in either order Play the king (best), *or* finesse the jack	53 100	
126. A x x x x K J 9 8	5 4	Play the ace and king, in case West is void Play the king, in case East is void	58 100	
127. J 10 9 x x A K x x	5	Play the ace and king; this line is 2% better than a second-round finesse	58	
128. J x x x x A K 8 x	5 4 MAX	Play the ace and king Lead small to the eight, in case West is void Play the ace and king	53 100	4.48

(f) Declarer Has Ten Cards

129. A K 9 x x x x x J x	8	Lead the jack, and play the ace whatever happens. This line succeeds against all 2–1 breaks and when West is lulled into covering with Q10x	78+	
130. A K 9 x x x x J x x	7	See (129) above	78+	
131. A J x x x x x K x x	7	Lead the king, in case East is void	89	
132. A K 9 x x x J x x x	6	See (129) above	78+	
133. A J x x x x K x x x	6	See (131) above*	89	
133a. K x x x x x A J 9 8	6	*But if there is no side entry to dummy, play the ace, as the only way to avoid a suit block is to find a singleton queen	26	
134. A K 9 x x J x x x x	5	See (129) above	78+	
135. A J 9 x x K 10 x x x	5	Lead the ten to the ace, *or* lead the jack to the king. Guess who is most likely to be void	89	
136. A J x x x K x x x x	5	See (131) above	89	

	Dummy Declarer	Tricks Required		% Chance of Success	Tricks per Deal

IV. THE DEFENSE HAS THREE POINTS

A. THE KING

(a) Declarer Has Five Cards

| 137. | A Q J 9
x | 4
3
Max | The only hope is that West has K10 doubleton
Lead small to the nine
Lead small to the nine | 0.3
52 |

2.53 |

(b) Declarer Has Six Cards

138.	A Q J 9 8 x	5 4 Max	Finesse the queen. The only hope is that West has K10 doubleton Finesse the nine* Finesse the nine* (*The nine finesse is only 0.36% better than the queen finesse)	 1 41	 3.42
139.	A Q J 9 x x	4 3 ⎱ Max ⎰	Finesse the queen, hoping that West has K10 or K10x Finesse the queen. If it holds, finesse the jack; if it loses, cash the ace and jack* (*This assumes that East will duck the queen with Kx or Kxx. If not, it is better to finesse the nine if the queen loses)	 5 68 76	 2.73
140.	A Q 9 8 J x	4 3 ⎱ Max ⎰	Run the jack. If it is covered, finesse the nine next Run the jack. If it losses, finesse the nine; if it holds, finesse the queen* (*This assumes that West will cover the jack with Kxxxx or Kxxx, and that East will win with Kx or Kxx. If they would withhold the king in such circumstances, it is better to cash the ace and queen if the jack loses)	 5 76 68	 2.81
141.	A Q 9 x J x	3	Lead small to the jack and finesse the nine next whatever happens	56	
142.	A Q 8 x J 9	3	Lead the jack. If it holds, finesse the queen; if it loses, cash the ace; if it is covered, run the nine* (*The best defense is for East not to win with Kx or Kxx, and for West not to cover with Kxxxx or Kxxx)	 68	
143.	A Q x x J 9	3	Lead small to the nine, hoping that East has the singleton ten or king* (*Or that he will mistakenly play the king from Kx)	 50 54	
144.	A Q 9 J x x	3 Max	Lead small to the nine or (best) run the jack; if it is covered, finesse the nine Run the jack; if it is covered, finesse the nine next	 24	 2.24
145.	A Q x J 9 8	3 Max	Run the nine or (best) run the jack; if it is cov- ered, run the nine next Run the jack; if it is covered, run the nine next	 24	 2.24
146.	A x x Q J 9	3	Lead the queen. If it is covered, play the jack, if the queen holds, guess* (*But against defenders who might cover un- necessarily—let us assume half the time— finesse the nine if the queen is covered and lead the jack next if the queen holds)	 5 15	

Dummy Declarer	Tricks Required		% Chance of Success	Tricks per Deal

IV. THE DEFENSE HAS THREE POINTS (cont'd)

A. THE KING (cont'd)

(c) Declarer Has Seven Cards

	Dummy Declarer	Tricks Required		% Chance of Success	Tricks per Deal
147.	A Q J 9 8 7 x	6	Finesse the queen. The only hope is that West has K10 doubleton	2	
		5 } Max }	Finesse the queen; then cash the ace	62	4.63
148.	A Q J 9 x x x	6	Finesse the queen, hoping that West has K10 doubleton	2	
		5	Finesse the queen; then cash the ace	58	
		4	Finesse the nine; then cash the ace	92	
		3	Finesse the nine; then cash the ace	99	
		Max	Finesse the queen; then cash the ace		4.46
149.	A Q J 9 8 x x	5	Finesse the queen; if it loses, cash the ace and jack	19	
		4 } Max }	Finesse the queen; if it loses, cash the ace and jack	71	3.91
150.	A Q 9 8 x J x	5	Lead small to the nine *or* (best) run the jack, finessing the nine next if it is covered	9	
		4 } Max }	Run the jack. If it loses, cash the ace; if it is covered, finesse the nine; if it holds, finesse the queen	70	3.79
151.	A Q 9 x x J x	5	Lead small to the nine *or* (best) run the jack, finessing the nine next if it is covered	7	
		4	Lead small to the jack. If it holds, play the ace; if it loses, play the ace	58	
		3	Finesse the nine on the first or second round	93	
		Max	Run the jack. If it holds, finesse the nine; if it loses, cash the ace and queen; if it is covered, finesse the nine		3.54
152.	A Q x x x J 9	4	Lead small to the nine; if it loses, run the jack next*	49	
		3 } Max }	Lead small to the nine; if it loses, run the jack next*	93	3.42
			(*This line will also produce four tricks if East is tempted to play the king from Kx)	56	
153.	A Q x x x J x	4	Lead small to the jack, hoping that the suit divides 3–3 or that East has Kx	44	
		3	Play the ace, and lead small to the jack, in case West has the singleton king	86	
		Max	Lead small to the jack		3.29
154.	Q J 9 8 7 A x	5	Run the queen, cashing the jack next if it is covered	2	
		4	Play the ace, and lead to the queen	63	
		Max	Run the queen, cashing the jack next if it is covered*		3.63
			(*Playing the ace and leading to the queen makes only .004 tricks fewer, and will be the best line if West is more likely to be short in the suit)		
155.	Q J 9 x x A x	4	Play the ace, and lead to the queen	59	
		3	Play the ace, and lead to the nine	94	
		Max	Play the ace, and lead to queen		3.49
156.	Q J x x x A 9	4	Lead small to the nine	50	
		3	Lead small to the nine	93	
		Max	Lead small to the nine		3.43

Dummy Declarer	Tricks Required		% Chance of Success	Tricks per Deal

IV. THE DEFENSE HAS THREE POINTS (cont'd)
A. THE KING (cont'd)

157. A Q J x x x x	4 3 Max	Finesse the queen, hoping that West has Kxx Play the ace, and lead to the queen, in case East has the singleton king Finesse the queen	18 69	 2.86
158. A Q 10 x J x x	4	Lead small to the ten, and then small to the queen. Do not lead the jack in case West has K or Kx	27	
159. A Q 9 8 J x x	4 } Max } 3	Run the jack. If it is covered, finesse the nine; if it holds, lead to the nine; if it loses, cash the ace and queen Finesse the queen. If it holds, run the jack; if it loses, cash the jack and ace	25 79	3.03
160. A Q 9 x J x x	4 3 Max	Lead low to the nine, hoping that West has K10 or K10x Finesse the queen. If it loses, cash the jack and ace; if it holds, lead low to the nine Run the jack. If it is covered, finesse the nine; if it loses, cash the ace and queen	9 72	 2.78
161. A Q 8 7 J x x	4 3 } Max }	Run the jack, hoping that East has the singleton nine or ten Lead the jack. If it loses, cash the ace, and finesse the eight next if the nine or ten drops from East; if it holds, finesse the queen; if it is covered, finesse the eight and then the seven next* (*Assuming that West will not cover with Kxxx, K10xxx, or K9xxx)	2 59	 2.61
162. A Q 8 x J x x	3	Lead small to the queen. If it holds, lead the jack next unless the nine or ten has appeared from West; if it loses, cash the jack, and finesse the eight next if the ten or nine drops from East* (*This line is only slightly superior to the alternatives of leading small to the jack (56%) and running the jack (53%))	57	
163. A Q x x J 9 8	4 3 } Max }	Run the jack, and then the nine (best) or run the nine. Hope that West has K10x or either Kxxxx or K Lead the jack. If it loses, cash the ace; if it is covered, run the nine next	8 77	 2.85
164. A Q x x J 9 x	4 3 } Max }	Play the ace, hoping that West has the singleton king Play the ace, and lead small to the jack	1 64	 2.65
165. A 9 8 7 Q J x	4 3 Max	Lead the queen. If it holds or is covered, lead the jack next Lead small to the queen. If it holds, lead small to the jack; if it loses, cash the jack and ace Lead the queen. If it loses, cash the jack and ace; if it holds or is covered, lead the jack next	9 83	 2.88
166. A 9 x x Q J x	3 } Max }	Lead small to the queen. If it holds, lead small to the jack; if it loses, cash the jack and ace	83	2.83
167. Q J 9 x A x x	4 3 } Max }	Play the ace, hoping East has the singleton king Play the ace and then lead to the queen and jack	1 78	 2.79

Dummy Declarer	Tricks Required		% Chance of Success	Tricks per Deal

IV.   THE DEFENSE HAS THREE POINTS (cont'd)

A.   THE KING (cont'd)

168. Q J x x A x x	3	Play the ace, and lead low to the queen; then lead low to the jack	69	
169. J 9 8 7 A Q x	4	Run the nine. If it is covered, run the jack	10	
	3	Finesse the queen. If it holds, run the jack; if it loses, cash the ace and jack*	78	
		(*This line offers extra chances if West is tempted to win the queen with K10xxx)	83	
	Max	Run the jack. If it is covered, run the nine next		2.86
170. J 9 8 x A Q x	4	Finesse the queen. If it holds, run the nine, hoping that East has K10, Kx, or K	9	
	3	Finesse the queen. If it holds, lead the jack, if it loses, cash the ace and jack*	78	
		(*This line offers extra chances if West is tempted to win the queen with K10xxx)	83	
	Max	Finesse the queen. If it holds, run the nine; if it loses, cash the ace and jack		2.85
171. J 9 x x A Q x	4	Finesse the queen, and then cash the ace, hoping that East has K, Kx, or K10	9	
	3	Lead small to the ace, unless the ten appears from East; then lead to the queen and jack	69	
	Max	Finesse the queen, and then cash the ace		2.77
172. J x x x A Q 9	4	Lead small to the nine, hoping that East has K10 or K10x	9	
	3	Lead small to the queen. If it holds, finesse the nine; if it loses, cash the ace	71	
	Max	Lead small to the nine. If it loses, finesse the queen		2.77

(d)   Declarer Has Eight Cards

173. A Q J 9 x x x x	7	Finesse the queen, hoping that West has Kx or K10	14	
	6	Play the ace, and lead the queen	79	
	5	Finesse the nine, in case East is void	98	
	Max	Finesse the queen		5.86
174. A Q J 9 x x x x	6	Finesse the queen	34	
	5	Finesse the queen; if it loses, cash the ace	85	
175. A Q 9 8 x x J x	6	Finesse the queen, and run the jack if it holds or run the jack; if it loses, cash the ace; if it holds, finesse the queen; if it is covered, guess	14	
	5	As above	85	
176. A Q 9 x x x J x	6	Finesse the nine or finesse the queen or lead the jack and guess next time	14	
	5	Run the jack. If it is covered, finesse the nine next	82	
	4	Safeguard against East being void by leading the jack, leading to the jack or finessing the nine	98	
	Max	Run the jack. If it is covered, finesse the nine next		4.94
177. A Q x x x x J 9	5	Lead small to the jack	76	
	4	Lead small to the nine, in case West is void	98	
	Max	Lead small to the jack*		4.72
		(*But against defenders who would play the king from Kx as East, lead small to the nine and run the jack next)		4.73

Dummy Declarer	Tricks Required		% Chance of Success	Tricks per Deal

IV. THE DEFENSE HAS THREE POINTS (cont'd)

A. THE KING (cont'd)

	Dummy Declarer	Tricks Required		% Chance of Success	Tricks per Deal
178.	A Q x x x x J x	5 MAX	Play the ace. This succeeds if the suit divides 3–2 or there is a singleton king somewhere	73	4.70
179.	Q J 9 x x x A x	6	Lead the queen. If it is covered, finesse the nine, hoping East has Kx	10	
		5	Play the ace, and lead to queen	79	
		4	Play the ace; fails only if West is void	98	
		MAX	Lead the queen, finessing the nine next if it is covered		4.83
180.	A Q 10 x x J x x	5 MAX	Finesse the queen. Don't lead the jack in case West has the singleton king	37	4.33
181.	A Q 9 7 6 J 8 x	5	Run the jack. If it is covered, finesse the nine next	25	
		4	Run the jack *or* finesse the queen	90	
		MAX	Run the jack. If it is covered, finesse the nine next		4.14
182.	A Q 9 x x J 8 x	5	Finesse the queen. If it holds, guess whether to play the ace or the jack next*	16	
			(*If West would not falsecard with K10, finesse the eight if the king appears on the first round)	19	
		4	Finesse the queen *or* run the jack *or* play the ace and lead small to the jack	88	
		MAX	Finesse the queen, guessing what to do if it holds		4.04
183.	A Q 9 x x J x x	5	Finesse the queen *or* run the jack. Guess whether West has K10x, Kxx, or Kx	14	
		4	Finesse the queen, and lead to the nine if it holds *or* play the ace, and lead to the jack	88	
		3	Finesse the queen	98	
		MAX	Finesse the queen. If it loses, cash the jack; if it holds, lead to the nine		3.99
184.	A Q 8 x x J x x	5	Finesse the queen; if it holds, lead small to the eight*	14	
			(*If East would not falsecard from 109x, lead the jack if the nine or ten appears on the first round)	17	
		4	Lead small to the ace, unless the nine or ten appears from West; then lead low to the jack (best) *or* run the jack; if it is covered, lead low to the eight unless the nine or ten has dropped	79	
		3	Run the jack. If it is covered, lead low to the eight unless the nine or ten has dropped from East (best)	98	
		MAX	Finesse the queen. If it holds, lead small to the eight		3.86
185.	A Q x x x J 9 8	5	Lead the jack. If it holds, finesse the queen; if it is covered, guess whether to run the nine or play the ace next	16	
		4 MAX	Lead the jack. If it loses, cash the ace; if it holds, finesse the queen; if it is covered, run the nine	85	4.01
		3	Lead the jack (best) or lead small to the jack	100	
186.	A Q x x x J 9 x	5	Finesse the queen. If it holds, guess whether to lead the nine or the jack next*	14	
			(*If West would not falsecard from K10, finesse the nine if the king appears from West)	16	
		4	Play the ace, and lead small to the jack	79	
		3	Play the ace, or finesse the queen	98	
		MAX	Finesse the queen, and cash the ace next		3.88

Dummy Declarer	Tricks Required		% Chance of Success	Tricks per Deal

IV. THE DEFENSE HAS THREE POINTS (cont'd)

A. THE KING (cont'd)

187. A Q x x x J x x	5 4 Max	Finesse the queen, and then play the ace Play the ace, and lead toward the jack, in case East has the singleton king Finesse the queen	14 73	 3.80
188. A 9 x x x Q J x	5 4 3 Max	Lead the queen. If it holds, lead the jack, hoping that West has Kxx or K10 Lead small to the queen. If it holds, lead to the jack Lead small to the queen Run the queen. If it holds, lead the jack	14 93 100	 3.96
189. A x x x x Q J 9	5 4 3 Max	Lead the queen. If it is covered, play the jack next; if it holds, lead the jack next* (*This assumes that West will cover with Kx about once in four times—best defense) Lead small to the queen, and then small to the jack Lead the queen *or* lead small to the queen Lead the queen. If it is covered, play the jack; if it holds, lead the jack next* (*The best defense is now for West never to cover with Kx)	14 85 98	 3.85
190. Q J 9 x x A x x	5 4 Max	Lead the Queen. If it holds, lead the jack; if it is covered, finesse the nine* (*This assumes that East will cover with Kx half the time; if he always covers, this line will produce five tricks) Play the ace, and lead toward the queen Lead the queen. If it loses, play the ace; if it holds, play the ace; if it is covered, finesse the nine* (*But if West would not duck the queen with K10xx, lead the jack if the queen holds; and if East would always cover with Kx, lead the jack if the queen holds)	15 20 88	 3.93 3.98 4.03
191. J 9 8 x x A Q x	5 4 } Max }	Finesse the queen. If it holds, guess whether East has Kx or Kxx Finesse the queen. If it loses, cash the ace; if it holds, run the nine	16 93	 4.10
192. J x x x x A Q 9	5 4 } Max }	Finesse the queen *or* finesse the nine Finesse the queen. If it holds, lead small to the nine; if it loses, cash the ace	14 85	 3.96
193. A Q J x x x x x	4 3 Max	Finesse the queen Play the ace, and lead to the queen Finesse the queen	34 87	 3.18
194. A Q 10 x J x x x	4	Finesse the ten. Don't lead the jack in case West has the singleton king	37	
195. A Q 9 8 J x x x	4 3 Max	Lead the jack. If it is covered, finesse the nine; if it holds, lead small to the nine Lead small to the queen. If it loses, cash the ace; if it holds, lead to the nine Both the above lines produce	27 97	 3.16
196. A Q 9 x J x x x	4 3 } Max }	Finesse the queen *or* run the jack, guessing whether West has Kx or K10x Finesse the queen. If it loses, cash the jack; if it holds, finesse the nine	14 90	 3.03

Dummy Declarer	Tricks Required		% Chance of Success	Tricks per Deal
		IV. THE DEFENSE HAS THREE POINTS (cont'd)		
		A. THE KING (cont'd)		
197. A Q 8 x J x x x	4	Finesse the queen; if it holds, lead small to the eight*	14	
		(*If East would not falsecard from 109x, lead the jack next if the nine or ten drops)	17	
	3	Lead the jack. If it is covered, lead small to the eight unless the nine or ten has appeared from East	81	
	Max	Finesse the queen; if it holds, lead small to the eight		2.90
198. A Q x x J 9 8 x	4	Finesse the queen, hoping that West has K, Kxxx, K10, or Kx	19	
	3 } Max }	Finesse the queen. If it loses, play the ace; if it holds, run the nine	97	3.16
199. A Q x x J 9 x x	4	Finesse the queen. If it holds, guess whether to lead the jack or play the ace	16	
	3	Play the ace, and lead small to the queen	90	
	Max	Finesse the queen; then play the ace		3.03
200. A Q x x J x x x	4	Finesse the queen; then play the ace, hoping West has Kx	14	
	3	Play the ace, and lead small to either honor	73	
	Max	Finesse the queen; then play ace		2.84
201. A 9 8 x Q J x x	4	Lead the queen. If it is covered, cash the jack; if it holds, lead the jack. Hope that West has Kxx, K10, or Kxxx* (*It has been assumed that, if the queen is led, West will cover ⅓ of the time with Kx, and East will win ⅓ of the time with K10xx. This is the best defense)	16	
	3	Lead the queen (best). If it loses, cash the ace; if it holds, lead small to the nine *or* lead small to the queen. If it loses, cash the jack; if it holds, lead small to the nine	97	
	Max	Lead the queen. If it loses, cash the ace; if it is covered, run the nine; if it holds, lead small to the nine* (*It has been assumed that, if the queen is led West will cover ⅓ of the time with Kx, and East will win ⅓ of the time with K10xx. This is the best defense)		3.10
202. A x x x Q J x x	3	Play the ace, and lead to the queen. This fails only if East has a void or a small singleton	87	
203. Q J 9 x A x x x	4	Lead the queen. If it holds, lead the jack; if it is covered, finesse the nine next* (*This assumes that East will cover ½ the time with Kx; if he always covers, this line will produce four tricks)	15 20	
	3	Play the ace and lead to queen	90	
	Max	Lead the queen. If it holds, play the ace; if it is covered, finesse the nine* (*But if West would not duck the queen with K10xx, lead the jack next if the queen holds)		2.97 3.02
204. Q J x x A 9 x x	4	Lead the queen. If it holds, lead the jack; if it loses or is covered, cash the jack	14	
	3	Lead small to the queen. If it loses, cash the jack; if it holds, lead small to the nine	97	
	Max	Lead the queen, and play the jack next whatever happens		3.00

Dummy Declarer	Tricks Required		% Chance of Success	Tricks per Deal

IV. THE DEFENSE HAS THREE POINTS (cont'd)
A. THE KING (cont'd)

(e) Declarer Has Nine Cards

Dummy Declarer	Tricks Required		% Chance of Success	Tricks per Deal
205. A Q J 10 x x x x x	8	Finesse the queen; Kx with West is more likely than K with East	 27	
206. A Q 9 x x x x J x	7 6 Max	Finesse the queen Run the jack *or* lead small to the jack Finesse the queen	33 95	 6.23
207. Q J x x x x x A x	7 Max	Run the queen, hoping West has Kx Run the queen	20	 6.11
208. A Q 9 x x x J x x	6 ⎫ Max ⎬	Finesse the queen, hoping that West has Kxx, K10, Kx, or K	 33	 5.28
209. A Q 8 x x x J x x	6 5 Max	Finesse the queen Lead the jack, in case East is void Finesse the queen	27 95	 5.17
210. A Q 7 x x x J 9 8	6 5 Max	Finesse the queen Play the ace *or* finesse the queen Finesse the queen	33 100	 5.33
211. A Q x x x x J 9 8	6 5 Max	Finesse the queen, hoping that West has Kxx, K10, Kx, or K If West is more likely to be void, play the ace or finesse the queen; if East is more likely to be void, run the jack or lead small to the jack Finesse the queen	33 95	 5.28
212. A x x x x x Q J 9	6 5 Max	Run the queen Run the queen (best) *or* lead small to the queen Run the queen	27 95	 5.22
213. A x x x x x Q J x	6 5 Max	Run the queen Lead small to the queen, in case West is void Run the queen	20 95	 5.11
214. Q J 9 x x x A x x	6 ⎫ Max ⎬	Lead the queen. If it is covered, cash the Jack	27	5.22
215. Q J x x x x A x x	6 5 Max	Run the queen Play the ace, and lead to queen Run the queen	20 95	 5.11
216. J 9 8 x x x A Q x	6 5 Max	Finesse the queen Finesse the queen *or* play the ace Finesse the queen	33 100	 5.33
217. A Q J x x x x x x	5 Max	Finesse the queen Finesse the queen	45	 4.40
218. A Q 9 7 x J 8 x x	5 4	Finesse the queen. A singleton king with West is more likely than K10xx Finesse the queen, in case West is void	 33 100	
219. A Q 9 x x J x x x	5 Max	Finesse the queen Finesse the queen	33	 4.28
220. A Q 8 x x J x x x	5 4 Max	Finesse the queen Run the jack, in case East is void Run the jack. If it is covered, and the nine or ten drops from East, finesse the eight next	27 95	 4.21
221. A 9 8 x x Q J x x	5 4 Max	Run the queen. If it is covered, cash the jack Run the queen (best) *or* lead small to the queen Run the queen. If it is covered, cash the jack next	27 100	 4.27

Dummy Declarer	Tricks Required		% Chance of Success	Tricks per Deal

IV. THE DEFENSE HAS THREE POINTS (cont'd)
A. THE KING (cont'd)

222. A 9 x x x
    Q J x x
	5	Run the queen, hoping that West has Kxx, K10,
		    or Kx
			27	

	4	Lead small to the queen	100	
	Max	Run the queen		4.22
223. A x x x x Q J 9 x	5 ⎱ Max ⎰	Run the queen. If it is covered, cash the jack	27	4.22
224. A x x x x Q J x x	5	Run the queen, hoping that West has Kx	20	
	4	Play the ace, and lead to the queen	95	
	Max	Run the queen		4.11
225. Q J 9 x x A x x x	5 ⎱ Max ⎰	Run the queen. If it is covered, cash the jack	27	4.22
226. Q J x x x A x x x	5 4 Max	See (224) above	⎰20 ⎱95	 4.11

227. J 9 8 x x
    A Q x x
	5	Finesse the queen; then cash the ace. Unless
		    West plays the ten
			33	

	4	Finesse the queen (best) *or* cash the ace	100	
	Max	Finesse the queen; then cash the ace		4.33

(f) Declarer Has Ten Cards

228. A J 9 x x x x x Q x	8 ⎱ Max ⎰	Run the queen	50	7.50
229. A Q J x x x x x x x	7 ⎱ Max ⎰	Finesse the queen	50	6.50

230. A J 9 x x x x
    Q x x
	7 ⎱
	Max ⎰
		Run the queen. Don't finesse the jack in case
		    East is void
			50	6.50

231. Q J x x x x x A x x	7 ⎱ Max ⎰	Run the queen	39	6.39
232. A Q J x x x x x x x	6 ⎱ Max ⎰	Finesse the queen	50	5.50
233. A J 9 x x x Q x x x	6 ⎱ Max ⎰	See (230) above	50	5.50
234. Q J x x x x A x x x	6 ⎱ Max ⎰	Run the queen	39	5.39
235. A Q J x x x x x x x	5 ⎱ Max ⎰	Finesse the queen	50	4.50
236. A J 9 x x Q x x x x	5 ⎱ Max ⎰	See (230) above	50	4.50
237. A x x x x Q J x x x	5 ⎱ Max ⎰	Run the queen	39	4.39

(g) Declarer Has Eleven Cards

238. A Q J x x x
    x x x x x
	6	Play the ace. The singleton king with East is 2%
		    more likely than Kx with West
			52	

B. THE QUEEN-JACK
(a) Declarer Has Six Cards

239. A K 10 9 8
    x
	5	Play the ace and king, hoping that the queen-
		    jack are bare
			1	

	4	Lead small to the ten	45	
	Max	Lead small to the ten		3.46

Dummy Declarer	Tricks Required		% Chance of Success	Tricks per Deal

IV. THE DEFENSE HAS THREE POINTS (cont'd)
B. THE QUEEN-JACK (cont'd)

240.	A K 10 9 x x	4	Lead small to the ten, hoping that West has QJx or QJ	5
		3 } Max }	Finesse the ten; if this loses, finesse the nine next	76
				2.81
241.	A 9 x x K 10	3	Lead small to the ten; then cash the king and ace	55

(b) Declarer Has Seven Cards

242.	A K 10 9 x x x	5	Finesse the ten, hoping that West has QJx or QJ	9
		4	Finesse the ten; then finesse the nine	66
		3	Play the ace, and then finesse the ten *or* finesse the ten and then the nine	94
		Max	Finesse the ten; then finesse the nine	3.69
243.	A 10 x x x K 9	4	Lead small to the nine	61
		3	Lead small to the nine	92
243A.	A 10 9 x x K x	5	Play the king; then the ace	3
		4	Play the king, then the ace (unless East shows out)	61 3.54
		Max		
		3	Play the king, then finesse the nine or ten	93
244.	A K 10 9 x x x	4	Finesse the ten, hoping that West has both the queen and jack	24
		3	Finesse the ten; if it loses, cash the ace, and finesse the nine (best) *or* play the ace, and then finesse the ten and nine	78
		Max	Finesse the ten; if it loses, cash the ace, and finesse the nine	3.00
245.	A K 9 x 10 x x	4	Finesse the nine, hoping that West has QJx or QJ	9
		3	Play the ace. If no honor drops from East, lead small to the nine next	72
		Max	Finesse the nine	2.78
246.	A 10 9 x K 8 x	4	Play the king. If an honor drops from East, finesse the nine	4
		3 } Max }	Lead small to the eight. If it loses, run the ten next* (*This line fails only when West has QJ, QJx, or QJxx. In practical play, however, it might be better to lead small to the king, and then finesse the ten and nine: for East may split his honors with QJx, QJxx, etc.)	82 2.84
247.	A 10 x x K 9 x	4	Play the ace and king, hoping that the queen and jack are doubleton	3
		3 } Max }	Lead low to the nine; then cash the king and ace* (*This assumes that East would never split his honors from QJxx and longer; if this is not so, lead low to the king and then finesse the ten)	75 2.77
248.	A 10 x x K x x	3 } Max }	Play the king, and unless an honor appears from East, lead small to the ten* (*But if West might be tempted to split his honors, it might be better to play the king and ace and lead to the ten)	56 2.56

(c) Declarer Has Eight Cards

249.	A K 10 9 x x x x	6	Finesse the ten, hoping that West has QJ or QJx	14
		5	Play the ace. If an honor drops from East, play the king; otherwise finesse the ten	88
		Max	Finesse the ten. If it loses, play the ace and king	4.94

Dummy Declarer	Tricks Required		% Chance of Success	Tricks per Deal

IV. THE DEFENSE HAS THREE POINTS (cont'd)

B. THE QUEEN-JACK (cont'd)

	Dummy Declarer	Tricks Required		% Chance of Success	Tricks per Deal
250.	A 10 9 x x x K x	6	Play the ace and king, hoping that the queen-jack are doubleton	7	
		5 } Max }	Play the king, and unless an honor drops from East, lead small to the ten	88	4.92
251.	A 10 x x x x K 9	6	Play the king and ace, hoping that the queen-jack are doubleton	7	
		5	Lead small to the nine	82	
		4	Lead small to the nine	98	
		Max	Lead small to the nine		4.83
252.	A K 10 9 x x x x	5	Finesse the ten, hoping that West has QJxx, QJx, or QJ	22	
		4 } Max }	Finesse the ten. If it loses, cash the ace next	90	4.10
253.	A K 9 x x 10 x x	5	Run the ten, hoping that West has QJ or QJx* (*Or will cover with Qxx or Jxx)	14	
		4	Play the ace. Unless an honor appears, run the ten next	88	
		3	Play the ace	100	
		Max	Lead small to the nine		3.96
254.	A K 8 x x 10 x x	5	Play the ace and king, hoping that the queen-jack are doubleton	7	
		4	Play the ace, and lead small to the ten	82	
		3	Lead small to the ten	100	
		Max	Play the ace, and lead small to the ten		3.78
255.	A 10 9 x x K x x	5	Play the king. If an honor falls from East, finesse the ten	9	
		4	Play the king, and finesse the ten	88	
		3	Play the king, and finesse the ten	98	
		Max	Play the king, and finesse the ten		3.95
256.	A 10 x x x K 9 x	5	Play the king and ace, hoping that the queen-jack are doubleton	7	
		4	Lead low to the nine; then cash the king	90	
		3	Play the king, or lead small to the nine	100	
		Max	Play the king, and unless an honor appears, lead low to the ten		3.94
257.	A 10 x x x K 8 x	5	Play the king and ace, hoping that the queen-jack are doubleton	7	
		4	Play the king, and unless an honor drops from East, lead small to the ten (best), *or* lead small to the ten; if an honor appears from West, lead small to the eight next. The latter method might be better if West is more likely to be short in the suit	82	
		Max	Play the king, and unless an honor appears from East, lead small to the ten		3.87
258.	A 10 x x x K x x	5	Play the king and ace, hoping that the queen-jack are doubleton	7	
		4	Play the king, and unless an honor appears from East, lead small to the ten	82	
		3	Play the king, in case East is void	98	
		Max	Play the king, and unless an honor appears from East, lead small to the ten		3.87
259.	A K 10 9 x x x x	4	Finesse the ten	24	
		3 } Max }	Finesse the ten; if it loses, cash the ace	90	3.14
260.	A K 8 x 10 x x x	4	Play the ace and king, hoping that the queen-jack are bare	7	
		3	Play the ace. Then either lead small to the		

Dummy Declarer	Tricks Required		% Chance of Success	Tricks per Deal

IV. THE DEFENSE HAS THREE POINTS (cont'd)
B. THE QUEEN-JACK (cont'd)

		eight, *or* if an honor has appeared from West, small to the ten	82	
	Max	Play the ace. Unless an honor appears from West, lead small to the ten next		2.85
261.	A 10 9 8	4	Play the ace, and run the ten if an honor appears, *or* cash the king and finesse the ten if an honor appears	9
	K x x x			
		3 ⎫ Max ⎭	Run the ten. If an honor appears from East, finesse the eight next; if the ten loses, cash the king. Alternatively, if East is more likely to be short in the suit, finesse the ten first and cash the ace if it loses	94	3.00
262.	A 10 x x	4	Play the ace and king, hoping that the queen and jack will be doubleton	7	
	K 9 x x	3 ⎫ Max ⎭	Lead small to the ten, and then cash the ace, *or* lead small to the nine, and then cash the king; the latter line will be better if West is likely to be short in the suit	94	2.98
263.	A 10 x x	4	Play the ace and king, hoping that the queen-jack will be bare	7	
	K 8 x x	3	Lead small to the ten. If it loses, cash the ace; if West plays the jack or queen on the first round, lead small to the eight next	87	
		Max	Play the king, and unless an honor appears from East, lead small to the ten		2.91
264.	A 10 x x	4	Play the ace and king, hoping that the queen-jack will be bare	7	
	K x x x	3 ⎫ Max ⎭	Play the king, and unless an honor appears from East, lead small to the ten	84	2.91

(d) Declarer Has Nine Cards

265.	A K 10 9 x x	6 ⎫ Max ⎭	Play the ace. If an honor drops from East, finesse the ten	46	5.42
	x x x			
266.	A K 8 x x x	6	Play the ace and king	41	
	10 x x	5	Lead small to the eight, *or* run the ten, *or* lead small to the ten	95	
		Max	Lead the ten, and play the ace whatever happens; then play the king		5.36
267.	A 10 x x x x	6	Play the ace, and finesse the nine if an honor appears from West, *or* play the king, and finesse the ten if an honor appears from East	46	
	K 9 x	5	Lead small to the nine or ten	100	
		Max	Play the ace, and finesse the nine, *or* play the king and finesse the ten		5.42
268.	9 8 7 6 x x	6	Play the ace and king	41	
	A K 5	5	Lead small to the five	95	
		Max	Play the ace and king		5.31
269.	A K 10 9 x	5 ⎫ Max ⎭	Play the ace. If an honor drops from East, finesse the ten next; otherwise play the king	46	4.42
	x x x x			
270.	A K 9 x x	5 ⎫ Max ⎭	Play the ace. If an honor drops from East, finesse the nine	46	4.42
	10 x x x			
271.	A K 8 x x	5	Play the ace and king	41	
	10 x x x	4	Lead small to the eight, *or* run the ten, *or* lead small to the ten	95	
		Max	Lead the ten, and play the ace whatever happens; then play the king. This line saves a trick if West is tempted to cover with QJ9x.		4.31+

Dummy Declarer	Tricks Required		% Chance of Success	Tricks per Deal

IV. THE DEFENSE HAS THREE POINTS (cont'd)
B. THE QUEEN-JACK (cont'd)

272.	A 10 x x x	5	Play the ace (or king). If an honor falls, finesse the nine (or ten)	46	
	K 9 x x	4	Lead small to the nine or ten	100	
		Max	Play the ace (or king). If an honor falls, finesse the nine (or ten)		4.42

(e) Declarer Has Ten Cards

273.	A K x x x	5	Lead the ten, and play the ace whatever happens; this saves a trick when West is lulled into covering with QJx	78+	
	10 9 8 x x				
	etc.				

V. THE DEFENSE HAS FOUR POINTS
A. THE ACE

(a) Declarer Has Five Cards

274.	K Q J 9	3	Finesse the nine	50	
	x				

(b) Declarer Has Six Cards

275.	K Q J 9 8	4	Play the king, queen, and jack	36	
	x	Max	Play the king, queen, and jack		3.36
276.	K Q J 9 x	4	Finesse the nine	31	
	x	3	Finesse the nine	82	
		Max	Finesse the nine		3.13
277.	K Q J 9	3 }	Lead to the king; then finesse the nine	55	2.55
	x x	Max }			
278.	K Q 9 x	3	Lead to the jack, and run the eight next	51	
	J 8				
279.	K Q 9 x	3	Lead to the jack; then finesse the nine	51	
	J x				
280.	K Q x x	3	Finesse the nine	50	
	J 9				

(c) Declarer Has Seven Cards

281.	K Q J 9 x x	5	Lead to the king; then play the queen and jack	52	
	x	4	Finesse the nine	92	
		3	Finesse the nine, in case East is void	99	
		Max	Lead to the king; then play the queen and jack		4.38
282.	K Q J 9 8	4 }	Lead to the king; then lead to the queen	61	3.61
	x x	Max }			
283.	K Q J 9 x	4	Lead to the king; then lead to the queen	58	
	x x	3	Lead to the king; then finesse the nine	94	
		Max	Lead to the king; then lead to the queen		3.46
284.	K Q J x x	4	Lead to the king; then lead to the queen	44	
	9 x	3	Lead small to the nine, in case West has a void or small singleton	93	
		Max	Lead to the king; then lead to the queen		3.31
285.	K Q 9 x x	4	Lead to the jack; then play to the king and queen	54	
	J 8	3	Lead small to the eight, *or* (best) lead to the jack and then run the eight	100	
		Max	Lead to the jack; then play the king and queen		3.49
286.	K Q 9 x x	4	Lead to the jack, and then lead to the king	52	
	J x	3	Lead to the jack, and then finesse the nine	93	
		Max	Lead to the jack, and then lead to the king		3.40

Dummy Declarer	Tricks Required		% Chance of Success	Tricks per Deal

V. THE DEFENSE HAS FOUR POINTS (cont'd)

A. THE ACE (cont'd)

287.	K Q x x x J 9	4	Finesse the nine. This offers a 5% better chance than hoping for a 3–3 break	42
		3	Finesse the nine	93
		Max	Finesse the nine		3.25
288.	K Q J 9 x x x	3	Lead to the king, to the queen, and to the jack. This is fractionally better than the third-round finesse	78
289.	K Q 9 x J x x	3	Lead to the king, then to the jack, then to the queen. This is 2% better than the third-round finesse of the nine	62
290.	K Q x x J 9 x	3	Lead to the king; then lead to the jack	56
291.	K Q x x J x x	3	Lead to the king, and then to the queen. This is 8% better than leading to honors at random and hoping for a 3–3 break	45
292.	K 9 x x Q J x	3	Lead to the queen and then to the jack; play the king on the third round. This is 1% better than the third-round finesse of the nine	67
293.	K x x x Q J 9	3	Lead to the queen, and then to the jack	63

(d) Declarer Has Eight Cards

294.	K Q J 9 x x x x	6	Lead to the king; then play the queen and jack	76
		5	Finesse the nine, in case East is void	98
		Max	Lead to the king; then play the queen and jack		5.72
295.	K Q J x x x 9 x	5	Lead to the king; then play the queen and jack	76
		4	Lead small to the nine, in case West is void	98
		Max	Lead to the king, and then play the queen and jack		4.72
296.	K Q x x x x J 9	5	Lead to the jack, and then to the king	76
		4	Finesse the nine, in case West is void	98
		Max	Lead to the jack, and then to the king		4.72
297.	K Q 10 7 x J x x	4 ⎫ Max ⎬	Lead to the jack first; this fails only if West is void	98	3.98
298.	K Q 9 x x J 8 x	4	Lead to the king, and then to the jack	88
299.	K Q 9 x x J x x	4 ⎫ Max ⎬	Lead to the king, and then to the jack	88	3.86
300.	K Q 8 x x J x x	4	Play to a high honor, and play the jack on the first or second round	76
		3 ⎫ Max ⎬	Lead small to the jack. This fails only when West is void	98	3.74
301.	K Q x x x J 9 x	4 ⎫ Max ⎬	Lead to the king, and then to the jack, *or* lead to the jack and then to the king. The latter line is better if East is likely to be short in the suit	76	3.74
302.	K Q J 9 x x x x	3	Lead to the king first, in case West has the singleton ace	90
303.	K Q 9 x J 8 x x	3	Lead to the king, and then to the jack. This fails only when West has a small singleton	92
304.	K Q 9 x J x x x	3	Lead to the king, and then to the jack. This fails only when West has a void or a small singleton	90

Dummy Declarer	Tricks Required		% Chance of Success	Tricks per Deal

V. THE DEFENSE HAS FOUR POINTS (cont'd)
A. THE ACE (cont'd)

	Dummy Declarer	Tricks Required		% Chance of Success	Tricks per Deal
305.	K Q 8 x J x x x	3	Lead low to the jack first, in case East is void	78	
306.	K Q 7 x J 9 x x	3	Lead to the king and then to the queen* (*But if East would not falsecard from A108x, lead to the king, and if the eight drops from East, lead to the jack next; otherwise lead to the queen)	87 90	
307.	K Q x x J 9 x x	3	Lead to the king, and then to the queen	87	

(e) Declarer Has Nine Cards

308.	K Q 9 x x x J 8 x	5	Lead to the king	100	
309.	K Q 8 x x x J x x	5	Lead small to the jack. This fails only when West is void	95	
310.	K Q 9 x x J 8 x x	4	Lead small to the king	100	
311.	K Q 8 x x J x x x	4	Lead small to the jack, in case East is void	95	

B. THE KING-JACK

(a) Declarer Has Five Cards

312.	A Q 10 9 x	4	Finesse the queen, hoping that West has king-jack only	0.3	
		3 ⎱ Max ⎰	Finesse the ten. If it holds, play the ace and queen	13	2.14
313.	A Q 10 x x	3	Finesse the ten, hoping that West has both the king and jack	24	
		2	Finesse the queen and then the ten, *or* (best) finesse the ten and then the queen	76	
		Max	Finesse the ten; if it loses, finesse the queen		2.00
314.	A Q 9 x x	2	Finesse the nine, and then finesse the queen	63	
315.	A 10 9 Q x	3	Lead the queen, hoping that East has the singleton jack	0.2	
		2 ⎱ Max ⎰	Run the queen, finessing the ten next if it loses	76	1.76
316.	A 10 x Q x	2	Lead small to the queen. If it loses, finesse the ten	74	
317.	Q 10 9 A x	3	Play the ace, hoping that East has the singleton king	0.2	
		2 ⎱ Max ⎰	Play the ace, and guess whether to play the queen or ten next	53	1.53
318.	Q x x A 10	2	Finesse the ten	52	

(b) Declarer Has Six Cards

319.	A Q 10 9 8 x	5	Finesse the queen, hoping that West has the king-jack only	1	
		4	Finesse the ten. If it holds, play the ace and queen	23	
		Max	Finesse the ten; then play the ace and queen		3.24

	Dummy Declarer	Tricks Required		% Chance of Success	Tricks per Deal

V.   THE DEFENSE HAS FOUR POINTS (cont'd)
B.   THE KING-JACK (cont'd)

320.	A Q 10 9 x x	4 3 } Max }	Finesse the ten, hoping that West has KJ or KJx Finesse the ten; if it loses, finesse the nine	5 63	2.68
321.	A Q 10 8 x x	4 3 } Max } 2	Finesse the ten, hoping West has KJ9 only Finesse the eight, and guess whether to finesse the ten or queen next, *or* finesse the ten and guess whether to finesse the queen or eight next Finesse the eight, ten, or queen, and guess which finesse to take next	1 33 86	2.19
322.	A Q 9 8 x x	3 2 } Max }	Finesse the eight, and guess whether to finesse the nine or queen next Finesse the eight; if it loses, finesse the nine	 24 86	2.09
323.	A 10 9 x Q x	3 } Max }	Lead small to the queen, and finesse the nine next	 24	2.24
324.	Q 10 9 8 A x	3	Run the ten. Then play the ace and queen* (*But if East might be tempted to cover with Kxx, the best practical chance is to lead the queen first)	23 27	
325.	Q 9 x x A 10	3 } Max } 2	Finesse the ten, and then play the ace and queen Finesse the ten, *or* play the ace and run the ten	23 100	2.23
326.	Q x x x A 10	2 } Max }	Finesse the ten. If it loses to the jack, cash the ace, and if the king fails to appear, play small from the queen	 68	1.68
327.	A Q 10 x x x	3 2 Max	Finesse the ten Finesse the queen and then the ten, *or* (best) finesse the ten and then the queen Finesse the ten; if it loses, finesse the queen	24 76	 2.00
328.	A Q 9 x x x	2 } Max }	Finesse the nine, and then finesse the queen	63	1.63
329.	A Q x 10 x x	3 2 Max	Finesse the queen, hoping that West has king- jack only Play the ace, and lead low to the queen Lead toward the ace-queen, and play the ace unless the jack appears from West; then lead low to the queen	1 55 1.56	
330.	A Q x x x x	2 } Max }	Lead small from the ace-queen in case East has the singleton king; then finesse the queen* (*And if East panics into playing the king from Kx)	 50 54	1.50
331.	A 10 9 Q x x	3 2 } Max }	Lead the queen, hoping that East has the single- ton jack, *or* play the ace, hoping that West has the singleton king Lead small to the ten; if it loses to the jack, finesse the nine* (*But if East would play the king from Kx, run the ten first; if this loses to the jack, finesse the nine next)	 0.5 76 78	1.77
332.	A 10 x Q x x	2	Lead small to the queen; if it loses, finesse the ten next	74	
333.	A x x Q 10 9	3 2 } Max }	Lead the queen, hoping that East has the single- ton jack, *or* play the ace, hoping that West has the singleton king Run the ten; if it loses, run the queen* (*But if East would play the king from Kx, lead small to the ten; if this loses to the jack, run the queen next)	 0.5 76 78	1.77

Dummy Declarer	Tricks Required		% Chance of Success	Tricks per Deal

V. THE DEFENSE HAS FOUR POINTS (cont'd)
B. THE KING-JACK (cont'd)

(c) Declarer Has Seven Cards

334.	A Q 10 9 x x x	6	Finesse the queen, hoping that West has king-jack only	2
		5	Finesse the queen; then play the ace	40
		4	Lead toward the dummy, and play the ace unless the jack appears from West; then lead the queen	89
		Max	Finesse the queen; then play the ace		4.28
335.	A Q 10 9 x x x	5	Finesse the ten	9
		4	Finesse the ten; if it loses, finesse the nine next	59
		3	Finesse the queen, and lead to the ten if it holds, *or* (best) finesse the ten	93
		Max	Finesse the ten; if it loses, finesse the nine next		3.61
336.	A Q 9 8 x x x	4 } Max }	Finesse the nine, and finesse the queen next if it loses	33	3.09
		3	Finesse the nine, and finesse the eight next if it loses	82
337.	A Q x x x 10 x	4	Play the ace, and lead to the queen, *or* finesse the queen and then cash the ace, *or* (best) lead small to the ten, and then finesse the queen	18
		3	Lead small to the ten, and then finesse the queen* (*And there is the additional chance of East playing the king from Kx)	71 78
		2 } Max }	Lead small to the ten, and then finesse the queen. This fails only when West has the singleton jack	99	2.88
338.	A 10 9 x x Q x	4 } Max }	Run the queen, and finesse the ten next if it loses, *or* lead small to the ten and run the queen next	36	3.23
		3	Play the ace	89
		Max	Run the queen, and finesse the ten next if it loses, *or* lead small to the ten, and run the queen next		3.23
339.	Q x x x x A 10	4	Play the ace, and lead to the queen, *or* (best) finesse the ten	18
		3	Lead small to the ten	68
		2	Play the ace, and lead to the queen. This fails only when West has a void or a small singleton	94
		Max	Lead small to the ten		2.86
340.	A Q 10 9 x x x	4	Finesse the ten, hoping that West has both the king and jack	24
		3	Finesse the queen, and then the ten, *or* (best) finesse the ten and then the nine	76
		Max	Finesse the ten and then the nine		3.00
341.	A Q 10 8 x x x	4	Finesse the eight	11
		3	Finesse the queen; then finesse the ten	53
		2	Cash the ace, *or* (best) lead to the ten, and if it loses and the nine fails to appear on the second round, cash the ace next	91
		Max	Finesse the eight. If it loses, finesse the queen. If that loses, cash the ace		2.51
342.	A Q 10 x x x x	4	Finesse the ten, hoping that West has KJx	7
		3	Finesse the queen, and finesse the ten next	47
		2	Play the ace on the first or second round. The best line is to finesse the ten and cash the ace next if it loses	85
		Max	Finesse the ten, and finesse the queen next if it loses		2.36

Dummy Declarer	Tricks Required		% Chance of Success	Tricks per Deal

V. THE DEFENSE HAS FOUR POINTS (cont'd)

B. THE KING-JACK (cont'd)

343. A Q 9 8 / x x x

	3	Finesse the eight, and finesse the nine next if it loses	50	
	2	Finesse the eight. If it loses, (best) lead toward dummy and play the ace unless the jack or ten appears from West	91	
	MAX	Finesse the eight. If it loses, finesse the nine. If that loses, cash the ace		2.39

344. A Q 9 x / x x x

	3 / MAX	Finesse the nine, and finesse the queen next if it loses	32	2.08
	2	Play the ace, and lead to the nine, *or* (best) finesse the nine, and play the ace next	79	

345. A Q x x / 10 x x

	3	Play the ace, and unless the jack appears from East lead small to the queen* (*And if West would not falsecard from KJ, lead to the ten if the king appears from West on the first round)	21 / 22	
	2	Play the ace, and then lead low to the ten; then lead to the queen. This fails only when West has Jx	94	
	MAX	Finesse the queen; if it loses, lead small to the ten. If the queen holds, play the ace* (*And if West would not falsecard from KJ, lead to the ten i fthe king appears from West on the first round. But if East would play the king from Kx, the best practical play is to lead low to the ten; if this loses, finesse the queen)		2.05 / 2.06 / 2.10

346. A Q x x / x x x

	3	Play the ace, and lead to the queen, *or* finesse the queen	18	
	2	Lead low from dummy, then play the ace, and then lead to the queen	77	
	MAX	Play the ace, and lead to the queen		1.87

347. A 10 9 8 / Q x x

	4	Run the queen, hoping that East has the singleton jack	1	
	3 / MAX	Finesse the ten and then the nine, *or* (best) run the queen, and finesse the ten next if it loses	76	2.77

348. A 10 9 x / Q 8 x

	4	Run the queen, hoping that East has the singleton jack	1	
	3	Run the eight, and then run the queen, *or* (best) run the queen, and then finesse the ten	76	
	MAX	Run the queen, and finesse the ten next if it loses		2.77

349. A 10 9 x / Q x x

	3 / MAX	Lead small to the ten. If it loses to the jack, lead small to the nine. If the ten loses to the king, cash the queen, and finesse the nine	68	2.68

350. A 10 x x / Q 9 x

	3 / MAX	Lead small to the nine, and finesse the ten next if it loses to the jack. If East plays the king on the first round, finesse the nine next	52	2.52

351. A 10 x x / Q x x

	3	Lead small to the queen, and finesse the ten next if it loses. If East plays the king on the first round, cash the queen and ace	28	
	2 / MAX	Play the ace, and unless the jack appears from West, lead small to the queen	94	2.16

352. A x x x / Q 10 9

	3	Finesse the ten. If it loses to the king, finesse the nine. If the ten loses to the jack, run the queen next. If East plays the king on the first round, finesse the ten next* (*And if West omits to falsecard with KJx)	50 / 57	

353. Q 10 9 8 / A x x

	4	Play the ace, hoping that East has the singleton king	1	
	3 / MAX	Run the ten, and run the nine next if it loses	69	2.69

	Dummy Declarer	Tricks Required		% Chance of Success	Tricks per Deal

V. THE DEFENSE HAS FOUR POINTS (cont'd)

B. THE KING-JACK (cont'd)

	Dummy Declarer	Tricks Required		% Chance of Success	Tricks per Deal
354.	Q x x x A 10 9	3 } Max } 2	Finesse the ten, and finesse the nine next if it loses Finesse the ten and then the nine (best), *or* play the ace and run the ten	68 100	2.68
355.	Q x x x A 10 x	3 } Max } 2	Lead small to the queen, and finesse the ten next if it loses. If West plays the king on the first round, play the ace next Play the ace, and unless the jack appears from West, lead small to the ten. This fails only when West has Jx	26 94	2.12
356.	10 9 8 7 A Q x	4 3 Max	Run the ten, hoping that East has KJ or KJx Finesse the queen. If it loses, run the ten; if the queen holds, run the ten Run the ten, and finesse the queen next	9 62 	2.69
357.	10 9 x x A Q x	4 3 } Max }	Finesse the queen, hoping that East has king-jack only Finesse the queen. If it holds, play the ace; if the queen loses, run the ten next	2 47	2.48

(d) Declarer Has Eight Cards

	Dummy Declarer	Tricks Required		% Chance of Success	Tricks per Deal
358.	A Q 10 9 x x x x	7 6 } Max }	Finesse the queen, hoping that West has king-jack only Finesse the queen, in case East has the singleton jack	3 56	5.55
359.	A Q 10 9 x x x x	6 5 4 Max	Finesse the ten Finesse the queen, and then the ten, *or* (best) finesse the ten and then the queen Finesse the queen, *or* (best) finesse the ten Finesse the ten, and if it loses, finesse the nine	14 71 98	4.83
360.	A Q x x x x 10 x	5 4 3 Max	Play the ace, and then lead to the queen* (*But if East would play the king from Kx, lead to the ten, and then finesse the queen) Lead small to the ten, and then finesse the queen Lead small to the ten, in case either opponent is void Lead small to the ten, and then finesse the queen	37 44 93 100	4.27
361.	A 10 9 x x x Q x	5 } Max }	Run the queen. If it loses, finesse the jack next	60	4.53
362.	Q 9 x x x x A 10	5 Max	Play the ace, and then either run the ten or lead the ten to the queen Play the ace, and then either run the ten or lead the ten to the queen* (*The latter line is better against defenders who might cover the ten with Jxx)	59 	4.55
363.	Q x x x x x A 10	5 4 3 Max	Finesse the ten Play the ace, and lead to the queen Finesse the ten Finesse the ten	47 88 100	4.32
364.	A Q 10 9 x x x x	5 4 } Max }	Finesse the ten and then the nine Finesse the ten and then the nine	22 76	3.96
365.	A Q 10 8 x x x x	5 4 Max	Finesse the ten Finesse the queen; if it loses, finesse the ten Finesse the ten; if it loses, finesse the queen	16 66	3.70
366.	A Q 10 x x x x x	5 4 Max	Finesse the ten Finesse the queen; if it loses, finesse the ten Finesse the ten and then the queen	14 66	3.64

	Dummy Declarer	Tricks Required		% Chance of Success	Tricks per Deal

V. THE DEFENSE HAS FOUR POINTS (cont'd)
B. THE KING-JACK (cont'd)

	Dummy Declarer	Tricks Required		% Chance of Success	Tricks per Deal
367.	A Q 9 x x 10 x x	5 4 MAX	Lead small to the nine, *or* run the ten Finesse the queen, in case East has the singleton jack Finesse the nine and then the queen, *or* run the ten, and finesse the nine if it loses. The latter line will be better if East is likely to be short in the suit	14 71 	 3.80
368.	A Q 9 x x x x x	4 3 MAX	Finesse the nine and then the queen Finesse the nine. If it loses, finesse the queen (best), *or* play the ace Finesse the nine and then the queen	50 87	 3.35
369.	A Q x x x 10 x x	5 4 3 MAX	Finesse the queen, hoping that West has king-jack only Play the ace, and unless the king appears from West, lead small to the queen Play the ace, and lead small to the ten; this fails only if either opponent is void Lead to the ace, and unless West plays the king, lead small to the queen* (*If West plays the jack on the first round, finesse the queen immediately; good defenders, however, will play the king from king-jack only)	 3 50 96	 3.41
370.	A Q x x x x x x	4 3 } MAX }	Finesse the queen, *or* (best) play the ace, and lead small to the queen Play the ace, and lead small to the queen	34 85	 3.17
371.	A 10 9 x x Q x x	4 } MAX }	Finesse the ten and then the nine, *or* run the queen, and finesse the ten next if it loses. The latter line is better if East is likely to be short in the suit	71	3.69
372.	A 10 x x x Q x x	4 3 } MAX }	Play the ace, and lead small to the queen, *or* lead small to the queen, and if it loses, finesse the ten next Play the ace, and lead small to the queen. This fails only if either opponent is void	50 96	 3.46
373.	A 9 7 x x Q 10 8	5 4 } MAX }	Lead the queen, hoping that East has the singleton jack Lead the queen; if it loses, run the ten next* (*But if East would play the king from Kx, and West would not falsecard with KJ, lead low to the ten; if this loses to the jack, run the queen next)	3 76 83	 3.79 3.83
374.	A 9 x x x Q 10 8	5 4 3	Lead the queen, hoping that East has the singleton jack Lead the queen; if it loses, run the ten next* (*But if East would play the king from Kx and West would not falsecard with KJ, lead low to the ten; if this loses to the jack, run the queen) Lead the queen, *or* lead small to the ten, in case either opponent is void	3 74 83 100	 3.77 3.83
375.	A 9 x x x Q 10 x	4 } MAX } 3	Lead small to the ten; if it loses to the jack, run the queen next* (*And there is the extra chance that East will play the king from Kx) Lead small to the ten. This fails only if East is void	62 72 98	3.60

Dummy Declarer	Tricks Required		% Chance of Success	Tricks per Deal

V. THE DEFENSE HAS FOUR POINTS (cont'd)

B. THE KING-JACK (cont'd)

	Dummy Declarer	Tricks Required		% Chance of Success	Tricks per Deal
376.	A x x x x Q 10 9	4	Run the queen; if it loses, run the ten* (*But if West would not falsecard with KJ or KJx, lead small to the nine. If this loses to the jack, run the queen; if the nine loses to the king, finesse the ten. And if East would play the king from Kx:)	60 62 72	
		3	Lead small to the nine	98	
		Max	Lead small to the nine; if it loses to the jack, run the queen through next* (*And if West would not falsecard with KJ or KJx, finesse the ten if the nine loses to the king)		3.57 3.60
377.	A x x x x Q 10 x	4 } Max } 3	Play the ace, and then guess whether to lead to the queen or the ten Lead small to the ten. If it loses or holds, lead small to the queen next	50 90	3.36
378.	Q 10 9 x x A 8 x	5	Lead small to the ace, hoping that East has the singleton king	3	
		4 } Max }	Finesse the eight. If it loses to the jack, run the queen next; if the eight loses to the king, run the ten next* (*But if West would play the king from Kx, lead low to the ten; if this loses to the jack, finesse the eight next)	71 72	3.74
379.	Q 10 9 x x A x x	5	Play the ace, hoping that East has the singleton king	3	
		4 } Max }	Play the ace and lead small to the ten* (*But if West would play the king from Kx, lead small to the ten; if it loses to the jack, run the queen next)	67 72	3.68 3.70
380.	Q x x x x A 10 x	4	Play the ace, and unless the king appears from West, lead small to the queen	50	
		3	Play the ace, and lead small to the ten. This fails only if either opponent is void	96	
		Max	Lead small to the ten, and then cash the ace, or lead small to the queen, and finesse the ten next if it loses		3.41
381.	10 x x x x A Q x	5	Finesse the queen, hoping that East has king-jack only	3	
		4	Play the ace, and lead small to the queen, or finesse the queen, and then cash the ace	50	
		3	Play the ace, and lead small to the queen. This fails only if either opponent is void	96	
		Max	Finesse the queen, and then cash the ace		3.47
382.	A Q 10 9 x x x x	4	Finesse the ten	24	
		3	Either finesse the ten or finesse the queen; if it loses, finesse again	76	
		Max	Finesse the ten; if it loses, finesse the nine		3.00
383.	A Q 10 8 x x x x	4	Finesse the ten	16	
		3	Finesse the queen; if it loses, finesse the ten	68	
		Max	Finesse the ten; if it loses, finesse the queen		2.73
384.	A Q 9 x x x x x	3 } Max }	Finesse the nine, and then finesse the queen	52	2.38

Dummy Declarer	Tricks Required		% Chance of Success	Tricks per Deal

V. THE DEFENSE HAS FOUR POINTS (cont'd)

B. THE KING-JACK (cont'd)

385. A Q x x
10 x x x

	4	Finesse the queen, hoping that West has king-jack only	3	
	3	Finesse the queen, *or* play the ace, and lead small to the queen	50	
	2	Play the ace, and lead small to the queen	100	
	MAX	Lead small from the ten, and unless the jack appears, play the ace; then lead small to the queen		2.54

386. A Q x x
x x x x

	3	Finesse the queen, *or* play the ace, and lead small to the queen*	34	
		(*But if East would not falsecard from Jx, play the ace, and duck on the second round if the jack appears from East)	37	
	2 } MAX }	Play the ace, and lead small to the queen	87	2.21

387. A 10 9 8
Q x x x

	4	Lead the queen, hoping that East has the singleton jack, *or* play the ace, hoping that West has the singleton king	3	
	3 } MAX }	Finesse the ten; if it loses to the jack, finesse the nine*	78	2.81
		(*But if West would not falsecard with KJxx, and East would play the king from Kx, run the ten. If the ten loses to the jack, finesse the nine; if the king appears on the first round, play the ace next)	84	2.84

388. A 10 9 x
Q 8 x x

| | 4 | See 387 above | 3 | |
| | 3 | See 387 above | 78 | |

389. A 10 9 x
Q x x x

| | 3 | Finesse the ten, and then finesse the nine, *or* lead the queen, and finesse the ten next if it loses. The latter line is better if East is likely to be short in the suit | 73 | |

390. A 10 x x
Q 9 x x

| | 3 }
MAX } | Play the ace, and lead small to the nine* | 69 | 2.69 |
| | | (*But if East would play the king from Kx, lead small to the nine. If this loses to the jack, finesse the ten next; if East plays the king on the first round, play the ace next) | 71 | 2.71 |

391. A 10 x x
Q x x x

	3	Play the ace, and lead small to the queen (best), *or* lead small to the queen, and finesse the ten next if it loses, *or* lead small to the queen, and cash ace next if it loses	50	
	2	Play the ace, and either lead to the queen (best) or to the ten	100	
	MAX	Play the ace, and lead small to the queen		2.50

391A. Q x x x
A 10 8 7

	4	Lead the queen, hoping that East has the singleton jack	2.83 2.83	
	3 MAX	Lead the ace, followed by the seven or eight and guess whether to play the queen or duck in dummy. If East's first play is the nine, jack, or king, lead the ten on the second round intending to play low from dummy	61.62	2.62
	2	Play the ace	100	

Dummy Declarer	Tricks Required		% Chance of Success	Tricks per Deal

V. THE DEFENSE HAS FOUR POINTS (cont'd)

B. THE KING-JACK (cont'd)

	Dummy Declarer	Tricks Required		% Chance of Success	Tricks per Deal
392.	A x x x Q 10 9 x	4	Play the ace, hoping that West has the singleton king	3	
		3 ⎫ Max ⎭	Play the ace, and lead low to the ten* (*But if East would play the king from Kx, lead small to the ten. If it loses to the jack, run the queen next; if the king appears on the first round, play the ace next)	69 74	2.72 2.74
393.	A x x x Q 10 x x	3 ⎫ Max ⎭	Play the ace, and lead small to the ten	64	2.53
		2	Play the ace, and then lead low to the ten (best) or low to the queen	90	

(e) Declarer Has Nine Cards

	Dummy Declarer	Tricks Required		% Chance of Success	Tricks per Deal
394.	A Q 10 9 x x x x x	8 7 Max	Finesse the queen Finesse the queen (best), or finesse the ten Finesse the queen	20 72	 6.92
395.	A Q 10 x x x x x x	7 6 Max	Finesse the queen, hoping that West has Kxx, KJ, or Kx Play the ace, and lead small to the queen Finesse the queen; if it loses, cash the ace next	27 78	 5.94
396.	A Q x x x x x 10 x	7 6 5 Max	Finesse the queen Lead small from the ten, and play the ace unless the jack appears; then lead to the queen Lead small to the ten Finesse the queen	20 78 100	 5.87
397.	A 10 9 8 x x x Q x	7 6 ⎫ Max ⎭	Run the queen, hoping that East has the singleton jack Run the queen; if it loses, play the ace next	6 77	 5.83
398.	A 10 9 x x x x Q x	7 6 Max	Run the queen, hoping that East has the singleton jack Run the queen, and play the ace next if it loses, or lead small to the queen, and play the ace next if it loses. The latter line is better if West is more likely to be short in the suit Run the queen; if it loses, play the ace next	6 72	 5.78
399.	Q 10 9 x x x x A x	7 6 ⎫ Max ⎭	Play the ace, hoping that East has the singleton king Play the ace, and lead to the queen	6 78	 5.84
400.	Q x x x x x x A 10	6 ⎫ Max ⎭ 5	Play the ace, and lead to the queen Finesse the ten	78 100	5.73
401.	A Q 10 x x x x x x	6 5 Max	Finesse the queen Play the ace, and lead small to the queen Finesse the queen; if it loses, play the ace next	27 83	 4.98
402.	A Q x x x x	6 5 Max	Finesse the queen Play the ace, and lead small to the queen Finesse the queen	20 78	 4.92
403.	A Q x x x x x x x	6 5 Max	Finesse the queen Play the ace, and lead small to the queen Finesse the queen	20 72	 4.81
404.	A 10 9 x x x Q x x	6 5 ⎫ Max ⎭	Lead the queen, hoping that East has the singleton jack, or play the ace, hoping that West has the singleton king Play the ace, and lead small to the queen	6 78	 4.84

	Dummy Declarer	Tricks Required		% Chance of Success	Tricks per Deal

V. THE DEFENSE HAS FOUR POINTS (cont'd)
B. THE KING-JACK (cont'd)

	Dummy Declarer	Tricks Required		% Chance of Success	Tricks per Deal
405.	A 10 x x x x Q x x	5 ⎱ Max ⎰	Play the ace, and lead small to the queen	78	4.78
406.	A x x x x x Q 10 9	6	Lead the queen, hoping that East has the singleton jack, *or* play the ace, hoping that West has the singleton king	6	
		5	Play the ace and lead small to the queen* (*But if East would play the king from Kx, lead small to the ten; if it loses to the jack, run the queen next)	78 89	
		4	Run the ten, *or* lead small to the ten, *or* run the queen, and play the ace if it loses	100	
		Max	Play the ace, and lead small to the queen		4.79
407.	A x x x x x Q 10 x	6	Play the ace, hoping that West has the singleton king	6	
		5 ⎱ Max ⎰	Play the ace, and lead small to the queen	78	4.79
408.	Q 10 9 x x x A x x	6	Lead the queen, hoping that West has the singleton jack, *or* play the ace, hoping that East has the singleton king	6	
		5 ⎱ Max ⎰	Play the ace, and lead to the queen* (*But if West would play the king from Kx, lead small to the ten; if it loses to the jack, run the queen next)	83 89	4.89
409.	Q 8 x x x x A 10 9	6	Play the ace, hoping that East has the singleton King, *or* lead the queen, hoping that West has the singleton jack	6	
		5 ⎱ Max ⎰	Play the ace, and lead to the queen	83	4.89
410.	Q x x x x x A 10 x	5 ⎱ Max ⎰	Play the ace, and lead small to the queen	78	4.78
411.	10 x x x x x A Q x	6	Finesse the queen	20	
		5	Play the ace, and lead small to the queen	78	
		Max	Finesse the queen		4.92
412.	A Q 10 x x x x x x	5	Finesse the queen	27	
		4	Play the ace, and lead to the queen	83	
		Max	Finesse the queen; if it loses, play the ace next		3.98
413.	A Q x x x 10 x x x	5	Finesse the queen	20	
		4	Play the ace, and lead to the queen	78	
		Max	Finesse the queen		3.92
414.	A Q x x x x x x x	5	Finesse the queen	20	
		4	Play the ace, and lead to the queen	72	
		Max	Finesse the queen		3.81
415.	A 10 9 x x Q 8 x x	5	Lead the queen, hoping that East has the singleton jack, *or* play the ace, hoping that West has the singleton king	6	
		4 ⎱ Max ⎰	Play the ace, and lead small to the queen* (*But if East would play the king from Kx, lead small to the eight; if this loses to the jack, run the queen next)	83 94	3.89
416.	A 10 9 x x Q x x x	5	Lead the queen, hoping that East has the singleton jack, *or* play the ace, hoping that West has the singleton king	6	
		4 ⎱ Max ⎰	Play the ace and lead small to the queen* (*But if East would play the king from Kx, run the ten; if this loses to the jack, run the queen next)	78 84	3.84

	Dummy Declarer	Tricks Required		% Chance of Success	Tricks per Deal

	Dummy Declarer	Tricks Required		% Chance of Success	Tricks per Deal
417.	A 10 x x x Q 9 x x	5	Lead the queen, hoping that East has the single-ton jack, *or* play the ace, hoping that West has the singleton king	6	
		4 } Max }	Play the ace, and lead to the queen* (*But if East would play the king from Kx, lead small to the nine; if this loses to the jack, run the queen next)	83 89	3.89
418.	A 10 x x x Q x x x	4	Play the ace, and lead small to the queen	78	
419.	A x x x x Q 10 9 8	5	Lead the queen, hoping that East has the single-ton jack, *or* play the ace, hoping that West has the singleton king	6	
		4 } Max }	Play the ace, and lead to the queen* (*But if East would play the king from Kx, lead small to the ten, and run the queen next if it loses to the jack)	83 94	3.89
420.	A x x x x Q 10 9 x	5	Lead the queen, hoping that East has the single-ton jack, *or* play the ace, hoping that West has the singleton king	6	
		4 } Max }	Play the ace, and lead to the queen* (*But if East would play the king from Kx, lead small to the ten, and run the queen next if it loses to the jack)	83 89	3.89

(f) Declarer Has Ten Cards

	Dummy Declarer	Tricks Required		% Chance of Success	Tricks per Deal
421.	A Q 10 x x x x x x x etc.*	5 Max	Finesse the queen Finesse the queen	39	4.28
422.	A Q x x x 10 9 8 x x etc.*	5 } Max }	Lead the ten, and play the queen, giving an extra chance if West is tempted to cover with KJx	39	4.28
423.	A 10 9 x x Q x x x x etc.*	5 4 Max	Play the ace, hoping to drop the singleton king Lead small to the queen, *or* (best) lead small to the ten Play the ace	26 100	4.15

(g) Declarer Has Eleven Cards

	Dummy Declarer	Tricks Required		% Chance of Success	Tricks per Deal
424.	A Q 10 x x x x x x x x etc.*	6	Play the ace. This line is fractionally better than the queen finesse *N.B. Similar principles apply if declarer's ten or eleven cards are distributed differently between his hand and dummy	52	

VI. THE DEFENSE HAS FIVE POINTS

A. THE ACE-JACK

(a) Declarer Has Five Cards

	Dummy Declarer	Tricks Required		% Chance of Success	Tricks per Deal
425.	K Q 10 9 x	3	Finesse the ten	11	
426.	K Q 10 x x	2	Lead to the king, and whether it holds or loses, lead to the queen next* (*But this assumes that East will duck the king if he holds Ax(xxx), which is best defense. If he always wins with these holdings, lead to the king; if it holds, lead to the queen; if the king loses, finesse the ten next)	52 76	

	Dummy Declarer	Tricks Required		% Chance of Success	Tricks per Deal

VI. THE DEFENSE HAS FIVE POINTS (cont'd)

A. THE ACE-JACK (cont'd)

427.	K 10 x Q x	2	Lead to the queen, and then finesse the ten	50	
428.	K x x Q 10	2	Finesse the ten	50	

(b) Declarer Has Six Cards

429.	K Q 10 9 8 x	4	Finesse the ten, hoping that West has AJx, Jxx, AJ, Jx, or J	18	
430.	K Q 10 9 x x	4	Finesse the ten	14	
		3	Lead to the king; then play the queen. This line gains a trick when East has AJ, Jx, or J	72	
		Max	Finesse the ten		2.82
431.	K Q 10 9 x x	3	Finesse the ten	50	
432.	K Q 9 8 x x	3	Finesse the nine, hoping that West has AJ10, J10x, or J10	5	
		2 } Max }	Finesse the nine. If this loses to the jack or ten, finesse the eight next* (*But if East would not duck with Ax, Axx, A10xx, or AJxx, lead to the king; if it holds, lead to the queen; if the king loses, finesse the nine)	79 81	1.85
433.	K Q x x 10 x	2	Lead small to the ten. If the ten loses, play to the king; if the king holds, play small from the queen	56	
434.	K Q 10 x x x	2	Lead to the king and, whether it holds or loses, lead to the queen next* (*But if East would not duck the king if he holds the ace, lead to the king: if it loses, finesse the ten; if the king holds, lead to the queen)	55 76	
435.	K 10 x Q x x	2	Lead small to the queen, and then finesse the ten	51	

(c) Declarer Has Seven Cards

436.	K Q x x x x x	5	Duck one round, and then play the king (best), or lead the king	36	
		4	Duck one round; then either duck again or lead the king	86	
		Max	Duck one round, and then lead the king		4.20
437.	K Q 10 8 x x x	5	Finesse the ten. If the jack appears from West, duck the next round	21	
		4	Finesse the ten or the eight	68	
		3	Finesse the ten or the eight	94	
		2	Finesse the ten or the eight	99	
		Max	Finesse the ten		3.82
438.	K Q 10 9 x x x	4	Finesse the ten* (*But if East would not duck with Axx, lead to the king; if it holds, lead to the queen; if the king loses, finesse the ten)	42 43	
		3	Finesse the ten	93	
		Max	Finesse the ten		3.35

	Dummy Declarer	Tricks Required		% Chance of Success	Tricks per Deal

VI. THE DEFENSE HAS FIVE POINTS (cont'd)

A. THE ACE-JACK (cont'd)

	Dummy Declarer	Tricks Required		% Chance of Success	Tricks per Deal
439.	K Q 9 8 x x x	4	Lead to the king; if it holds, lead to the queen	21	
		3	Lead to the king, and whether it holds or loses, lead to the queen next* (*But if East would not duck with Ax, lead to the king; if it holds, lead to the queen; if the king loses, lead to the nine)	74 76	
		2	Lead to the king. If it loses, lead to the nine; if the king holds, lead to the queen or nine; *or* finesse the nine, and if it loses, finesse the eight	96	
		Max	Lead to the king, and whether it holds or loses, lead to the queen next* (*But if East would not duck with Ax, play to the nine if the king loses and to the queen if the king holds)		2.90 2.92
440.	K Q x x x 10 x	4	Lead small to the king; then lead to the queen	18	
		3	Lead small to the ten, and then lead to the king. This saves a trick when East has AJ only	61	
		2	Lead to the king and then to the queen, *or* lead small to the ten and then to the king. The latter line will be better if West is more likely to be short in the suit	93	
		Max	Lead to the king and then to the queen		2.71
441.	K Q 10 9 x x x	3	Lead to the king, and whether it holds or loses, finesse the ten next* (*This assumes that East will duck about half the time with Ax and Axx, which is the best defense. If he always wins with these holdings, play to the queen if the king holds, and finesse the ten if the king loses. Similarly, if East always ducks with Ax and Axx, play the queen if the king loses, and finesse the ten if the king holds)	51 54 52	
442.	K Q 9 8 x x x	3	Finesse the nine	24	
		2	Finesse the nine. If it loses, play to the king; if that loses, finesse the eight (best), *or* play to the king. If it loses, finesse the nine and, if necessary, the eight; if the king holds, play to the queen (best), or finesse the nine	89	
		Max	Finesse the nine. If it loses, lead to the king; if that loses, finesse the eight		2.13
443.	K 10 9 x Q x x	3	Lead small to the queen; then finesse the ten	53	
444.	K 10 x x Q 9 x	3 } Max }	Lead small to the queen; then finesse the ten. This is better than leading to the king first, for there is time to discover whether the insertion of the ace by East is from AJ doubleton or A singleton	31	2.31
445.	K x x x Q 10 9	3	Finesse the ten	50	
446.	K x x x Q 10 x	3 } Max }	Lead small to the ten and then small to the queen, hoping that East has AJ, AJx or Jxx	19	1.95
		2	Lead small to the queen and then small to the ten	77	
447.	10 9 8 7 K Q x	3	Lead to the king. If it holds, lead to the queen; if the king loses, cash the queen* (*This assumes that West will duck with Axx, which is the best defense. If he always wins with this holding, lead to the king: if it holds, lead to the queen; if the king loses, run the ten next)	36 45	

Dummy Declarer	Tricks Required		% Chance of Success	Tricks per Deal

VI. THE DEFENSE HAS FIVE POINTS (cont'd)
A. THE ACE-JACK (cont'd)

(d) Declarer Has Eight Cards

448.	K Q x x x x x x —	6 ⎫ MAX ⎭	Duck the first round, in case the ace is singleton; then play the king and queen	73	5.70
449.	K Q 10 x x x x x	6 5 4 MAX	Finesse the ten Finesse the ten Finesse the ten Finesse the ten	34 85 98 	 5.17
450.	K Q x x x x x x	6 ⎫ MAX ⎭ 5	Lead to the king, hoping that West has the double- ton ace Play small from both hands, in case the ace is sin- gleton; then play the king and queen	14 73	4.80
451.	K Q 10 x x x x x	5 ⎫ MAX ⎭ 4	Lead to the king. If it holds, lead to the queen; if the king loses, cash the queen next* (*But if East would not duck with Ax, finesse the ten if the king loses and lead to the queen if the king holds) Lead to the king. If it loses, finesse the ten; if the king holds, guess which honor to play next	47 54 88	4.30 4.40
452.	K Q x x x x 10 x	5 ⎫ MAX ⎭ 4 3	Lead to the king and then to the queen Lead to the king and then to the queen (best) or lead small to the ten Lead to the king or lead small to the ten. The latter line will be better if West is more likely to be short in the suit	34 85 98	4.17

(d) Declarer Has Eight Cards

453.	K Q 10 x x x x x	4 ⎫ MAX ⎭	Lead to the king, and whether it holds or loses, finesse the ten next* (*This assumes that East will duck about half the time with Ax. If he always ducks with this holding, finesse the ten if the king holds, and play the queen if the king loses. Similarly, if East always wins with Ax, finesse the ten if the king loses, and lead to the queen if the king holds)	55 59 57	3.43
454.	K 9 x x x Q 10 x	4 MAX	Lead small to the queen. If it holds, finesse the nine; if the queen loses, either play the king or finesse the nine Lead small to the queen, and then finesse the nine	46 	 3.42
455.	K x x x x Q 10 9	4 3 2 MAX	Finesse the ten Finesse the ten Finesse the ten (best), or lead to the queen Finesse the ten	48 98 100 	 3.46
456.	K x x x x Q 10 x	4 ⎫ MAX ⎭ 3	Lead small to the king, and then finesse the ten* (*The alternative is to lead small to the king or queen, playing the other top honor if it loses and ducking the next round if it holds, but this line is inferior against defenders who would not take the ace immediately) Lead small to the queen, and then lead small to the ten	37 88	3.20

Dummy Declarer	Tricks Required		% Chance of Success	Tricks per Deal

VI. THE DEFENSE HAS FIVE POINTS (cont'd)

A. THE ACE-JACK (cont'd)

457. K Q 10 x x x x x	3 Max	Lead to the king, and whether it holds or loses, finesse the ten next*	57	2.47
		(*This assumes that East will duck about half the time with Ax. If he always ducks with this holding, finesse the ten if the king holds, and play the queen if it loses.	61	
		Similarly, if East always wins with Ax, play to the queen if the king holds, and finesse the ten if the king loses)	59	
458. K 10 x x x Q x x x	3 Max	Lead to the queen, and then finesse the ten	40	2.27
	2	Play small from both hands; then lead to the queen	90	
459. K 9 8 7 Q x x x	3 Max	Lead to the queen, and then finesse the nine, hoping that East has 10, J, Ax, A10, AJ, or Axx; or lead to the king, and then run the nine. The latter line will be better if West is more likely to be short in the suit	23	2.12
	2	Finesse the nine. If this loses to the jack or ten, guess which honor to lead to next; if the jack or ten appears from West, run the eight, or run the nine. If this loses to the jack or ten, guess which honor to lead to next; if the jack or ten appears from East, finesse the eight	94	
460. K x x x Q 10 9 8	3	Lead to the queen, and then run the ten, or lead to the king, and then finesse the ten	56	
461. K x x x Q x x x	3 Max	Lead to either honor, and duck on the next round, hoping to find the right opponent with the doubleton ace	14	1.84
	2	Play low from both hands, in case the ace is singleton, and then lead to either honor	73	

(e) Declarer Has Nine Cards

462. K Q 8 x x x x 10 x	6 Max	Lead small to the king, and then small to the queen	72	5.67
	5	Lead small to the ten	100	
463. K Q 10 9 x x x x x etc.*	4	Lead small to the king; if it loses to the ace, lead to the queen next	77	
464. K 9 x x x Q 10 x x etc.*	4	Lead to the king, and play the queen next if it loses, or lead to the queen, and play the king next if it loses	59	
465. K 9 x x x Q x x x etc.*	4 Max 3	Lead small to the queen; if an honor appears from East, finesse the nine next Lead small to the queen, in case East is void	53 95	3.48
		*N.B. Similar principles apply, if declarer's nine cards are distributed differently between his hand and dummy		

(f) Declarer Has Ten Cards

466. K 8 x x x x Q 10 x x etc.*	5	Lead small to the king. This fails only if East is void	89	
		*N.B. Similar principles apply if declarer's ten cards are distributed differently between his hand and dummy		

Dummy Declarer	Tricks Required		% Chance of Success	Tricks per Deal

B. THE KING-QUEEN

(a) Declarer Has Five Cards

467.	A J 10 9 x	3	Finesse the jack; then play the ace	7	
468.	A J 10 x x	2	Finesse the jack; then finesse the ten	76	
469.	A J 9 x x	2	Finesse the nine; if it loses to an honor, finesse the jack next* (*If West inserts a high honor on the first round, still finesse the nine next, for West should falsecard with holdings like K10x, Q10x, etc. If he would not falsecard in this way, and would split high honors on the first round, finesse the jack next if the king or queen appears from West)	37 50	

(b) Declarer Has Six Cards

470.	A J 10 x x x —	4	Play the ace, and then lead small from the jack-ten, hoping that the king-queen are doubleton or tripleton	10	
		3 } Max }	Play the ace, and then lead small from the jack-ten, in case there is a doubleton honor	78	2.83
471.	A J 10 9 8 x	4	Finesse the jack, and then play the ace, hoping that West has xxxxx, KQx, KQ, Kx Qx, K, or Q	14	
472.	A J 10 9 x x	3	Finesse the jack, and then finesse the ten	50	
473.	A J 9 x x x	3	Finesse the jack, hoping that West has KQ10 only	1	
		2 } Max }	Finesse the nine. If it loses to the ten, play the ace and a small card; if the nine loses to a high honor, finesse the jack next* (*And if East omits to falsecard with KQ10)	41 42	1.42
474.	A J x x 10 x	2	Lead small to the ten; if it loses, play the ace, and lead small from the jack* (*But if East would play an honor from Qx, Kx, or Qxx, lead small to the ten, and finesse the jack next if it loses)	55 65	
475.	·A J 10 x x x	2	Finesse the jack, and then finesse the ten	76	
476.	A J 9 x x x	2	Finesse the nine, and then finesse the jack. If West inserts a high honor on the first round, still finesse the nine next; West should falsecard with K10x, etc.* (*But if West would split high honors and would not falsecard, finesse the jack next if West plays the king or queen on the first round)	38 50	
477.	A J 8 10 x x	2	Lead small to the eight. If this loses to a high honor, finesse the jack next* (*And if West is tempted to split his honors from KQ and others)	39 51	
478.	A J x 10 x x	2	Lead small to the jack; then play the ace* (*But if East might be tempted to play an honor from Kx, Qx, or Qxx, lead small to the ten, and then finesse the jack)	33 41	
479.	A x x J 10 9	2	Run the jack, and then run the ten	76	

Dummy Declarer	Tricks Required		% Chance of Success	Tricks per Deal

VI. THE DEFENSE HAS FIVE POINTS (cont'd)

B. THE KING-QUEEN (cont'd)

(c) Declarer Has Seven Cards

480. J 10 x x x x A	5	Play the ace, and then lead small from the jack-ten, hoping that the king-queen are doubleton	3	
	4	Play the ace, and then lead small from the jack-ten, in case there is a doubleton honor	65	
481. A J 10 9 x x x	5 }	Finesse the jack, and then cash the ace	23	4.08
	MAX } 4	Play the ace, and then lead the jack, in case East has a singleton honor	89	
482. A J 10 9 x x x	4 } MAX }	Finesse the jack, and then finesse the ten	53	3.45
	3	Finesse the jack	92	
483. A J 9 x x x x	4 } MAX }	Finesse the nine, and then finesse the jack	12	2.58
	3	Finesse the nine, and the jack	55	
	2	Finesse the nine, and the jack This fails only when West has a void or a singleton, or when East has a singleton ten	91	
484. A J 10 9 x x x	3	Finesse the jack, and then finesse the ten	76	
485 A J 10 x x x x	3 } MAX }	Finesse the jack, and then finesse the ten	45	2.28
	2	Play the ace, and lead small to the jack, *or* finesse the jack, and then play the ace	85	
486. A J 9 8 x x x	3	Finesse the eight, and then finesse the nine	37	
	2	Finesse the eight, the nine, and, if necessary, the jack (best), *or* finesse the jack, the eight, and then the nine	89	
	MAX	Finesse the eight, the nine, and, if necessary, the jack		2.26
487. A J 9 x x x x	3 } MAX }	Finesse the nine, and then finesse the jack, hoping that East has x, xx, xxx, Qxx, Kxx, or void	22	1.89
	2	Play the ace, and lead to the nine, *or* finesse the nine and the jack, *or* finesse the jack and the nine	68	
488. A J 8 x 10 x x	3	Lead small to the eight. If this loses to the king or queen, lead from the ten, and play the ace unless the nine appears from West*	26	
		(*And if West omits to falsecard with 9xxx	28	
		And if West is tempted to split his honors with KQx)	33	
	2	Play the ace, and unless an honor appears from West, lead small to the ten. This fails only when West has Kx or Qx	90	
	MAX	Lead small to the eight. If this loses to the king or queen, lead from the ten, and play the ace unless the nine appears from West. If the eight loses to the nine, lead small to the jack next*		2.15
		(*And if West omits to falsecard with 9xxx		2.16
		And if West splits his honors with KQx)		2.22
489. A J x x 10 x x	3	Lead small to the jack, hoping that West has KQ or KQx	9	
	2	Lead small to the ace, and unless an honor appears from West, lead small to the ten next. This fails only when West has Kx or Qx	87	

Dummy Declarer	Tricks Required		% Chance of Success	Tricks per Deal

VI. THE DEFENSE HAS FIVE POINTS (cont'd)

B. THE KING-QUEEN (cont'd)

	MAX	Lead small to the ace, and unless an honor appears from West, lead small to the ten*		1.90
		(*But if East would play an honor from Kx or Qx, lead small to the ten, and finesse the jack next if it loses to West)		1.93
490.	A 9 8 7 J x x	3	Run the nine. If this loses to the king or queen from West, run the jack next, hoping that East has 10 or 10x*	6
			(*But if East would not falsecard with 10x, run the nine; if the ten appears from East, play the ace next; if the king or queen appears from East or the nine loses to the king or queen from West, run the jack next.	8
			And if East would play a high honor from K10 or Q10, run the nine; if the king or queen appears from East, or the nine loses to the king or queen from West, run the jack next. This succeeds when East has 10, 10x, Q10, or K10)	9
	2 } MAX }	Run the jack. If it loses, finesse the nine next; if that loses, finesse the eight	89	1.90
491.	A x x x J 10 9	3 2	Run the jack and then the ten Run the jack and then the ten	28 100
492.	J x x x A 10 x	3 } MAX } 2	Lead small to the ten, and then play the ace, hoping that East has KQ or KQx Play the ace, and unless an honor appears from West, lead small to the ten	9 87	1.93

(d) Declarer Has Eight Cards

493.	A J 10 9 x x x x	6 } MAX }	Finesse the jack, and then play the ace	43	5.39
494.	A J 10 x x x 9 x	5 } MAX }	Lead small to the ten; then run the nine. Do not lead the nine for the first finesse: West may have a singleton honor	60	4.56
495.	A J 9 x x x x x	5	Finesse the nine, and then finesse the jack* (*If West would not falsecard with 10xx, play the ace if the nine loses to a high honor, and the ten fails to appear on the second round)	27 31
		4 } MAX }	Finesse the nine, and then finesse the jack	79	4.04
		3	Finesse the jack or the nine in case East is void	98
496.	A J x x x x 10 x	5	Lead small to the ten, and finesse the jack next, or run the ten and lead up to the jack next	24
		4 } MAX }	Lead small to the ten, and finesse the jack next	90	4.14
		3	Lead small to the ten	100
497.	A 9 8 x x x J x	5	Lead small to the jack, hoping that East has K10 or Q10	7
		4	Lead small to the jack and then to the nine, or play the ace, or run the jack, and finesse the nine next, or lead toward the ace, and play small unless an honor appears from West	85
		3	Lead small to the jack	100
	MAX	Lead small to the jack. If an honor wins from East, run the jack next; if East plays the ten on the first round, cash the ace next		3.92

Dummy Declarer	Tricks Required		% Chance of Success	Tricks per Deal

VI. THE DEFENSE HAS FIVE POINTS (cont'd)
B. THE KING-QUEEN (cont'd)

498.	A 9 x x x x J x	5	Lead small to the jack, hoping that East has K10 or Q10	7	
		4	Lead small to the jack; if the ten appears from East, finesse the nine next	73	
		MAX	Lead small to the jack. If an honor wins from East, run the jack next; if East plays the ten on the first round, finesse the nine		3.76
499.	A J 10 x x x x x	4 } MAX }	Finesse the jack, and then finesse the ten	63	3.50
		3	Finesse the jack, and then play the ace, or finesse the jack and then the ten (best)	90	
500.	A J 9 x x x x x	4 } MAX }	Finesse the nine, and then finesse the jack* (*If West would not falsecard from 10xx, play the ace if the nine loses to a high honor, and the ten fails to appear on the second round)	33 36	3.15
		3	Finesse the nine, and then finesse the jack	84	
501.	A J 8 7 x 10 x x	4 } MAX }	Run the ten. If it is covered, lead to the eight next; if the ten loses to East, finesse the jack next*	42	3.35
			(*But if West would not falsecard with K9 or Q9, and would not split his honors with KQ9, lead small to the eight. If this loses to the nine, lead to the ten next; if the eight loses to a high honor, finesse the seven next; and if the king or queen appears from West on the first round, run the eight next.	44	3.37
			And if West would split his honors with KQx or KQ9)	47	3.40
		3	Lead small to the jack. If it loses, lead small to the ten next. This fails only if West is void.	98	
502.	A J x x x 10 x x	4	Lead small to the jack, and then cash the ace	37	
		3	Play the ace, and lead small to the ten. This fails only to a 5–0 break	96	
		MAX	Lead small to the jack, and then cash the ace* (*But if East would play an honor from Kx or Qx, lead small to the ten, and then finesse the jack)		3.19 3.24
503.	A 9 8 7 x J x x	4	Run the nine. If it loses to the king or queen from West, run the jack; if the king or queen appears from East, either run the jack or cash the ace* (*This assumes that East will play an honor from K10 or Q10 about half the time, which is the best defense. If he would always play the high honor from these holdings, run the nine, and run the jack next if it loses to the king or queen on either side)	13 16	
		3	Run the nine. If this loses to the ten, run the jack next; if the nine loses to the king or queen on either side, lead small to the jack. This fails only when either opponent is void, or West has the singleton ten	93	
		MAX	Run the nine. If this loses to the ten, run the jack next; if the nine loses to the king or queen from West, run the jack next; if the king or queen appears from East on the first round, lead small to the jack next		2.97

Dummy Declarer	Tricks Required		% Chance of Success	Tricks per Deal

VI. THE DEFENSE HAS FIVE POINTS (cont'd)
B. THE KING-QUEEN (cont'd)

504. A x x x x	4	Run the jack and then the ten	54	
J 10 9	3	Run the jack and then the ten	96	
	2	Run the jack	100	
	MAX	Run the jack and then the ten		3.50
505. J 10 9 x x	4	Run the jack and then the ten	60	
A x x	3	Play the ace, *or* lead low to the jack. This fails only if West is void	98	
	MAX	Run the jack and then the ten		3.56
506. A J 10 9	3	Finesse the jack and then the ten	76	
x x x x				
507. A J 10 x	3 }	Finesse the jack and then the ten	65	2.54
x x x x	MAX }			
508. A J 9 x	3 }	Lead small to the nine; then finesse the jack* (*And if West would not falsecard with 10xx, play the ace if the nine loses to a high honor, and the ten fails to appear on the second round)	35	2.19
x x x x	MAX }			
			38	
	2	Play the ace, *or* take two finesses	84	
509. A J 8 x	3	Run the ten. If it loses to East, finesse the jack next; if the ten is covered, finesse the eight next		
10 x x x			44	
	2	Lead small to the jack, and finesse the eight next if it loses (best), *or* play the ace, and lead small to the ten	100	
	MAX	Finesse the jack; if it loses, finesse the eight next		2.37
510. A J x x	3 }	Finesse the jack; then cash the ace	37	2.32
10 x x x	MAX }			
	2	Play the ace, and lead small to either honor	100	
511. A 9 8 7	3	Run the nine. If it loses to the king or queen from West, run the jack; if East plays an honor on the first round, cash the ace next* (*But if East would play an honor from K10 or Q10, run the nine, and run the jack next if it loses to the king or queen on either side)	13	
J x x x			16	
	2	Run the nine. If this loses, lead small to the eight next. This fails only when West has the singleton ten	97	
	MAX	Play the ace, and then run the nine		2.05

(e) Declarer Has Nine Cards

512. A J 10 9 x x x x	7 }	Play the ace, *or* finesse the jack, and then play the ace	66	6.66
x	MAX }			
513. A J 10 9 x x x	6 }	Finesse the jack and then the ten	76	5.76
x x	MAX }			
514. A J 9 x x x x	6	Play the ace, and lead to the jack, *or* finesse the jack* (*But if West would not falsecard with K10x, Q10x, or 10x, lead toward dummy, and play the ace unless the ten appears from West. And if West splits his honors with KQx)	53	
x x			59	
			66	
	5	Finesse the jack or the nine, in case East is void	95	
	MAX	Finesse the jack* (*But if West would not falsecard with K10x, Q10x, or 10x, lead toward dummy, and play the ace if the ten fails to appear)		5.48
				5.50

Dummy Declarer	Tricks Required		% Chance of Success	Tricks per Deal

VI. THE DEFENSE HAS FIVE POINTS (cont'd)
B. THE KING-QUEEN (cont'd)

515. A 8 7 x x x x / J 10 — 6 } MAX / 5 — Run the jack, and then play the ace; this gains a trick when East has the singleton nine — 47 — 5.42 / Run the jack, in case East is void — 95

516. A J 10 x x x / x x x — 5 } MAX — Finesse the jack and then the ten — 76 — 4.71

517. A J 9 x x x / x x x — 5 } MAX — Finesse the nine. If this loses to the king or queen, finesse the jack next* — 57 — 4.53
(*But if West would not falsecard with K10x, Q10x, or 10x, lead toward dummy, and play the ace if the ten fails to appear. — 59 — 4.55
And if West splits his honors with KQx) — 66 — 4.61

518. A J x x x x / 10 x x — 5 } MAX — Lead small to the jack, *or* play the ace, and lead small to either honor — 66 — 4.66

519. A 9 x x x x / J x x — 5 — Play the ace, and lead small to the jack — 53
4 — Lead small to the jack — 100
MAX — Lead toward dummy, and play the nine if West follows small; otherwise play the ace, and lead small to the jack — — 3.48

520. A x x x x x / J 10 9 — 5 } MAX — Run the jack and then the ten — 71 — 4.71
4 — Run the jack — 100

521. A J 10 9 x / x x x x — 4 — Finesse the jack and then the ten — 76

522. A J 9 x x / x x x x — 4 } MAX — Finesse the nine; if this loses to the king or queen, finesse the jack next* — 57 — 3.53
(*But if West would not falsecard with K10x, Q10x, or 10x, lead toward dummy, and play the ace if the ten fails to appear from West. — 59 — 3.55
And if West splits his honors with KQx) — 66 — 3.61

523. A J x x x / 10 x x x — 4 } MAX — Finesse the jack, *or* play the ace, and lead small to either honor — 66 — 3.66

524. A 9 x x x / J x x x — 4 — Play the ace, and lead small to the jack — 53
3 — Lead small to the jack, *or* lead small to the nine — 100
MAX — Lead toward dummy, and play the nine if West follows small; otherwise play the ace, and lead to the jack — — 3.53

525. A x x x x / J 10 9 8 — 4 — Run the jack and then the ten — 76

(f) Declarer Has Ten Cards

526. A J 10 x x / x x x x x / etc.* — 4 } MAX — Lead to the jack, in case East is void — 89 — 3.89

*N.B. Similar principles apply if declarer's ten cards are distributed differently between his hand and dummy.

VII. THE DEFENSE HAS SIX POINTS
A. THE ACE-QUEEN

(a) Declarer Has Five Cards

527. K J 9 / x x — 2 } MAX / 1 — Finesse the nine and then the jack, *or* finesse the jack and then the nine — 24 — 1.02
Immaterial: take two finesses — 78

Dummy Declarer	Tricks Required		% Chance of Success	Tricks per Deal

VII. THE DEFENSE HAS SIX POINTS (cont'd)
A. THE ACE-QUEEN (cont'd)

(b) Declarer Has Six Cards

528.	K J 10 9 x x	3	Finesse the jack and then the ten	18	
529.	K J 9 8 x x	3	Finesse the eight, hoping that West has AQ10, Q10x, or Q10	5	
		2 } Max }	Finesse the eight; if this loses, finesse the nine next	63	1.68
530.	K x x x J 9	1	Lead small to the nine or jack; if this loses, lead to the king. Finessing the nine first will be better against East, who might be tempted to play an honor from AQ and others	75	
531.	K J 9 x x x	2	Finesse the jack or the nine	25	
		1	Immaterial: take two finesses	79	
		Max	Finesse the jack, and guess which to play next if the queen wins, or finesse the nine, and guess which to play next if the ten wins		1.04
532.	K J x x x x	2 } Max }	Lead to the jack, hoping that West has both the ace and queen	24	1.00
		1	Lead to the jack and then to the king (best), or lead to the king and then to the jack	76	
533.	K 9 8 J x x	2	Lead small to the king, hoping that West has AQ doubleton or the singleton queen	1	
		1 } Max }	Finesse the eight; if this loses to the ten, guess whether to play to the nine or king next* (*But if East would play a high honor from AQ and others, run the nine first; if this loses to the ten, lead to the king next)	80 88	0.81
534.	K x x J 9 x	2	Lead small to the king, hoping that West has the ace-queen doubleton or the queen singleton	1	
		1	Lead small to the king and then back to the jack or nine (best), or lead to the nine and then to the king, or lead to the jack and then to the king. The last two lines will be better if East is more likely to be short in the suit	76	
		Max	Lead small to the king and then back to the jack or nine		0.77
535.	K x x J x x	2	Lead small to the king, hoping that West has the ace-queen doubleton	1	
		1	Lead small to the king and then small to the jack (best), or lead small to the jack and then small to the king. The latter line will be better if East is more likely to be short in the suit* (*But if East would play an honor from AQ and others, lead small toward the jack, and duck whatever happens; then lead small to the king)	74 79	
		Max	Lead small to the king and then small to the jack		0.75

(c) Declarer Has Seven Cards

536.	K J 9 8 x x x	3	Finesse the eight, hoping that the queen and ten are both with West	24	
		2	Finesse the eight; if this loses to the ten, finesse the nine next (best), or finesse the jack, and then finesse the eight	76	
		Max	Finesse the eight and then the nine		2.00

Dummy Declarer	Tricks Required		% Chance of Success	Tricks per Deal

VII. THE DEFENSE HAS SIX POINTS (cont'd)

A. THE ACE-QUEEN (cont'd)

537.	K 10 8 x	3	Finesse the eight	20
	J x x	2	Finesse the ten. If it loses to the queen, lead small to the jack and then to the king; if the ten loses to the ace, finesse the eight next	79
		MAX	Finesse the eight. If this loses to the nine, finesse the ten next	1.95
538.	K 10 x x	3	Finesse the ten, hoping that West has AQ or AQx	9
	J x x	2	Lead small to the king; then lead small to the ten	69
		MAX	Finesse the ten. If this loses to the queen, lead small to the king next	1.76
539.	K 9 8 7	3	Run the jack, hoping that East has the singleton ten	1
	J x x	2	Run the jack, and then finesse the nine. If the ace appears from West on the first round, finesse the nine, and if necessary, the eight (best), *or* finesse the nine. If this loses to the queen, lead to the jack next; if the ace appears from West, finesse the nine next; if the nine loses to the ten, finesse the eight next*	76
			(*But if West would not falsecard with AQ10 or AQ10x, run the nine. If this loses to the ten, finesse the seven next; otherwise run the eight.	77
			And if East is tempted to play an honor from AQxxx)	78
		MAX	Run the jack. If it loses to the ace or queen from East, lead small to the nine next; if the ace appears from West on the first round, finesse the nine and, if necessary, the eight	1.77
540.	K x x x	2	Lead small to the jack, and then small to the ten. This fails only when West has AQ doubleton, AQ and at least two others, or the singleton or doubleton queen	75
	J 10 x			
541.	K x x x	2	Lead small to the nine. If the ten or queen appears from East, lead small from the king next; otherwise lead small to the king	47
	J 9 x	1 } MAX }	Lead small to the nine, then small to the jack, and then small to the king. This fails only when West has the Q10 doubleton	98 1.36
542.	K x x x	2 } MAX }	Lead to the jack, and then, unless the queen appears from East, lead to the king, *or* lead to the king and then to the jack. The latter line will be better if West is more likely to be short in the suit	26 1.12
	J x x	1	Lead small from both hands; then, unless the queen has appeared from West, lead to the jack; then lead to the king. This fails only when West has Qx	94

(d) Declarer Has Eight Cards

543.	K 10 8 x x	4	Run the jack. If this is covered, finesse the eight next	25
	J x x	3	Finesse the ten, and run the jack if it loses to the ace (best), *or* lead small to the king, and then small to the jack	90
		MAX	Finesse the ten; if this loses to the ace, run the jack	3.12

Dummy Declarer	Tricks Required		% Chance of Success	Tricks per Deal

VII. THE DEFENSE HAS SIX POINTS (cont'd)
A. THE ACE-QUEEN (cont'd)

544. K 9 8 x x J x x	4	Lead small to the king, hoping that West has the AQ only	3	
	3	Lead small to the eight. If it loses to the ten, finesse the nine next; if the ace appears from West on the first round, lead small to the jack	84	
	MAX	Finesse the eight. If it loses to the ten, finesse the nine next; if the ace appears from West on the first round, lead small to the king		2.82
545. K x x x x J 10 x	4	Lead small to the king, hoping that West has the AQ only	3	
	3 ⎱ MAX ⎰	Lead small to the jack, and then small to the ten	85	2.83
	2	Lead small to the jack. This fails only when East is void	98	
546. K x x x x J 9 x	4	Lead small to the king, hoping that West has AQ doubleton	3	
	3 ⎱ MAX ⎰	Lead small to the nine and then small to the king	63	2.58
	2	Lead small to the nine, and then small to the jack. This fails only if East is void	98	
547. K J 9 8 x x x x	3	Finesse the eight	27	
	2	Finesse the eight and then the jack (best), *or* finesse the jack and then the eight, *or* lead small to the king	83	
	MAX	Finesse the eight; if it loses to the ten, finesse the jack		2.10
548. K 10 8 x J x x x	3	Run the jack. If this is covered, finesse the eight next	27	
	2	Finesse the ten. If this loses to the queen, lead small to the jack; if the ten loses to the ace, run the jack (best), *or* lead small to the king, and then small to the jack	92	
	MAX	Finesse the ten. If this loses to the queen, lead small to the jack; if the ten loses to the ace, run the jack		2.16
549. K 9 8 7 J x x x	3	Lead small to the king, hoping that West has the ace-queen doubleton or the queen singleton	6	
	2 ⎱ MAX ⎰	Finesse the nine. If this loses to the queen, lead small to the jack; if the nine loses to the ten, finesse the eight	88	1.94
550. K x x x J 10 8 x	3 ⎱ MAX ⎰	Run the jack. If the ace appears from West, run the ten next; if the jack loses to the ace from East, guess whether to lead small or run the ten next; if the jack is covered, guess whether to lead to the ten or to the eight next*	14	
		(*This assumes that West will always play the ace from ace-queen doubleton and will cover with Qx about half the time, which is the best defense. If he always covers with Qx, lead to the eight if the jack is covered, lead the ten if the jack loses to the ace from East, and run the ten if the ace appears from West on the first round	17	2.01
		Similarly, if West never covers with Qx, lead small to the king if the jack loses to the ace from East, lead to the ten if the jack is covered, and run the ten if the ace appears from West on the first round)	17	2.01

Dummy Declarer	Tricks Required		% Chance of Success	Tricks per Deal

VII. THE DEFENSE HAS SIX POINTS (cont'd)

A. THE ACE-QUEEN (cont'd)

	2	Lead small to the jack, and then small to the king. This fails only when East has a void or a small singleton	92	
551. K x x x J 10 x x	3	Lead small to the king, hoping that West has AQ doubleton	3	
	2	Lead small to the king and then small to the jack, *or* lead small to the jack. The latter line will be better if East is more likely to be short in the suit	87	
	MAX	Lead small to the king, and then small to the jack		1.90
552. K x x x J 9 x x	3	Lead small to the king, hoping that West has AQ doubleton	3	
	2 } MAX }	Lead small to the king and then small to the nine	70	1.71
	1	Lead small to the nine (best), *or* lead toward the king, and duck if West fails to play an honor, *or* lead small to the jack	100	
553. K x x x J x x x	3	Lead small to the king, hoping that West has AQ doubleton	3	
	2	Lead toward the king, and duck if the queen fails to appear; then lead to the king (best), *or* lead to the king and then to the jack	50	
	1 } MAX }	Lead toward the king, and duck if the queen fails to appear; then lead to the king and finally to the jack	100	1.54

(e) Declarer Has Nine Cards

554. K J 9 x x x x x x*	4 MAX	Lead small to the jack Lead small to the jack	33	3.17
555. K J x x x x x x x*	4 MAX	Lead small to the jack Lead small to the jack	33	3.11
556. K 9 8 7 x J x x x*	4 3 MAX	Lead small to the king Lead small to the nine (best), *or* run the nine Lead small to the king	27 94	3.16
557. K x x x x J 10 9 8*	4	Run the jack	50	
558. K x x x x J 10 x x*	4 3 MAX	Lead small to the king Lead small to the king, in case West is void Lead small to the king	33 95	3.28
		*N.B. Similar principles apply if declarer's nine cards are distributed differently between his hand and dummy		

(f) Declarer Has Ten Cards

559. K J x x x x 10 x x x*	5	Finesse the jack	63	
560. K x x x x x J 10 9 x*	5	Run the jack	63	
		*N.B. Similar principles apply if declarer's ten cards are distributed differently between his hand and dummy		

Dummy Declarer	Tricks Required		% Chance of Success	Tricks per Deal

B. THE KING-QUEEN-JACK

(a) Declarer Has Five Cards

561.	A 10 9 8 x	2	Finesse the ten, and then play the ace	25	

(b) Declarer Has Six Cards

562.	A 10 9 8 x x	3 } Max } 2	Finesse the ten, and then play the ace	16	1.99
			Play the ace, and then lead low from the 1098; this gains a trick when East has a singleton or doubleton honor	87	
563.	A 10 9 8 x x	2	Finesse the ten and then the nine	77	

(c) Declarer Has Seven Cards

564.	A 10 9 8 x x x	4 } Max } 3 2	Finesse the ten, and then cash the ace	65	3.55
			Finesse the ten, and then play the ace (best), *or* play the ace	91	
			Finesse the ten, in case East is void	99	
565.	A 10 9 8 x x x	3 } Max } 2	Finesse the ten and then the nine; then play the ace	74	2.70
			Finesse the ten and then the nine (best), *or* play the ace	96	
566.	A 10 9 8 x x x	2	Finesse the eight, nine, and, if necessary, ten	89	
567.	A 10 9 x x x x	2	Finesse the ten and then the nine; then play the ace	68	
568.	A 10 x x 9 x x	2	Lead small to the nine. If this loses to West, finesse the ten next. If an honor appears from East on the first round, lead small to the nine again; if East shows out or plays another honor, finesse the ten next; otherwise play to the ace	51	

(d) Declarer Has Eight Cards

569.	A 10 9 8 x x x x	5 } Max } 4	Play the ace, in case East has a singleton honor	85	4.81
			Finesse the ten, in case East is void	98	
570.	A 10 9 8 x x x x	4 } Max } 3	Finesse the ten and then the nine	90	3.88
			Finesse the ten and then the nine	98	
571.	A 10 9 8 x x x x	3 } Max } 2	Finesse the ten and then the nine	92	2.90
			Finesse the ten and then the nine	98	
572.	A 10 x x x 9 x x	3 2 } Max }	Play the ace, and lead small to the nine	85	
			Lead small to the nine and then small to the ten	100	2.82
573.	A 8 7 x x 10 x x	3 } Max } 2	Run the ten, *or* lead small to the ten, in case East has the singleton nine	71	2.69
			Run the ten, *or* lead small to the ten, in case East is void	98	

Dummy Declarer	Tricks Required		% Chance of Success	Tricks per Deal

VII.   THE DEFENSE HAS SIX POINTS (cont'd)
B.   THE KING-QUEEN-JACK (cont'd)

574.	A 10 9 8 x x x x	2	Finesse the ten and then the nine; this fails only when West has a void or a small singleton	92

(e)   Declarer Has Nine Cards

575.	A 10 9 8 x x x x x	7 6 } MAX }	Play the ace, hoping for a 2–2 division Finesse the ten, and then play the ace	41 95	 6.36
576.	A 10 9 x x x x x x	6 5 } MAX }	Play the ace, hoping for a 2–2 division Finesse the ten, and then play the ace	41 95	 5.36
577.	A 10 x x x x 9 x x	5 4 MAX	Play the ace Lead small to the ten, *or* lead small to the nine Lead small to the ten or nine; then play the ace	41 95	 4.36
578.	A 10 x x x 9 x x x	4 3 MAX	Play the ace, hoping for a 2–2 division Lead small to the ten or nine Lead small to the ten or nine; then play the ace	41 95	 3.36

VIII.   THE DEFENSE HAS SEVEN POINTS
A.   THE ACE-KING

(a)   Declarer Has Five Cards

579.	Q J 9 8 x	2	Finesse the eight. If it loses to the ace or king on either side, lead the queen and jack next	11
580.	Q J 9 x x	1	Lead to the queen and then to the jack	78
581.	Q 9 x J x	1	Lead small to the jack. If it loses to West, finesse the nine next	62
582.	Q x x J 9	1	Finesse the nine	51

(b)   Declarer Has Six Cards

583.	Q J 9 8 x x	2	Finesse the nine	51
584.	Q x x x J 9	1	Finesse the nine. If it loses to the ten, play the jack and then low from the queen* (*This is only fractionally better than leading small to the jack and then ducking two rounds, and the latter line might be better if East is more likely to be short in the suit)	56
585.	Q J 9 x x x	1	Lead to the queen and then to the jack	79
586.	Q 9 x J x x	1	Lead small to the jack. If it loses to West, finesse the nine next	64
587.	Q x x J x x	1	Lead to either honor and then back to the other	49

(c)   Declarer Has Seven Cards

588.	Q J 9 x x x x	3 } MAX } 2 1	Lead to the queen and then to the jack Finesse the nine, and then lead to the queen Lead to the queen and then to the nine or jack (best), *or* finesse the nine, and then lead to the queen	38 80 96	2.12

Dummy Declarer	Tricks Required		% Chance of Success	Tricks per Deal

VIII. THE DEFENSE HAS SEVEN POINTS (cont'd)
A. THE ACE-KING (cont'd)

	Dummy Declarer	Tricks Required		% Chance of Success	Tricks per Deal
589.	Q J x x x 9 x	3 ⎱ Max ⎰	Lead to the queen and then to the jack	30	1.98
		2	Lead to the queen and then to the jack	73	
		1	Lead small to the nine. This fails only when West has the singleton ten	99	
590.	Q J 9 8 x x x	2 ⎱ Max ⎰	Lead small to the queen. If it loses, finesse the nine next	63	1.63
591.	Q J 9 x x x x	2 ⎱ Max ⎰	Lead small to the queen. If it loses, finesse the nine next	55	1.46
592.	Q J x x 9 x x	2 ⎱ Max ⎰	Lead to the queen and then to the jack	49	1.38
		1	Lead small to the queen. If it loses, lead small to the nine and then small to the jack. This fails only when West has the doubleton ten	95	
593.	Q J x x x x x	2 ⎱ Max ⎰	Lead to the queen and then to the jack	45	1.28
		1	Lead to the queen; if it loses, duck one round, and then lead to the jack (best), _or_ duck one round, and then lead to the queen and jack	85	
594.	Q 9 8 x J x x	2	Lead small to the jack. If it loses to West, finesse the nine next; if an honor appears from East on the first round, lead to the jack again	56	
595.	Q x x x J 9 x	2 ⎱ Max ⎰	Lead small to the nine. If it loses to a high honor from West, lead small to the queen; otherwise lead small to the jack	33	1.30
		1	Lead small to the nine and then small to the jack. This fails only if West has A10 or K10	97	
596.	Q x x x J x x	2	Lead small to the queen or jack, and then back to the other honor, hoping to find either opponent with AKx or the right opponent with AK doubleton	16	
		1	Lead toward the jack and duck; then lead to the jack and to the queen. This fails only when West has Kx or Ax	87	
		Max	Lead small to the jack. If it loses, duck the next round, and then lead to the queen		0.93

(d) Declarer Has Eight Cards

597.	Q J 10 6 x x 8 x	4 ⎱ Max ⎰	Lead to the queen and then to the jack	85	3.83
		3	Lead small to the eight, in case West is void	100	
598.	Q J 9 8 7 x x x	3	Lead small to the queen. If it loses, finesse the nine	75	
599.	Q J x x x x x x	3 ⎱ Max ⎰	Lead to the queen and then to the jack	63	2.50
600.	Q 10 9 6 x J x x	3 ⎱ Max ⎰	Lead the jack, in case East is void	98	2.98
601.	Q x x x x J 9 x	3	Lead small to the queen. If it loses to East, finesse the nine next; if an honor appears from West on the first round, lead to the queen again	48	
		2 ⎱ Max ⎰	Lead small to the nine and then small to the jack. This fails only if East is void	98	2.41
602.	Q J 9 8 x x x x	2	Lead small to the queen. If it loses, finesse the nine	77	

Dummy Declarer	Tricks Required		% Chance of Success	Tricks per Deal

VIII. THE DEFENSE HAS SEVEN POINTS (cont'd)
A. THE ACE-KING (cont'd)

603. Q 9 8 7
    J x x x — 2 — Lead small to the jack. If it loses to West, finesse the nine next — 66

604. Q 9 x x
    J x x x — 2 ⎱ Max ⎰ — Lead small to the jack. If it loses to West, finesse the nine next — 64 — 1.58
          1 — Finesse the nine (best), *or* lead small to the queen and then small to the jack, in case West has a bare honor — 100

605. Q x x x
    J x x x — 2 ⎱ Max ⎰ — Lead to the queen (or jack); if it loses, duck the next round — 37 — 1.32
          1 — Duck the first round, and then lead small to either honor — 100

(e) Declarer Has Nine Cards

606. Q J 7 x x x x
    9 x — 5 ⎱ Max ⎰ — Lead small to the queen and then to the jack — 84 — 4.79
          4 — Lead small to the nine, in case West is void — 100

607. Q x x x x x
    J 9 x — 4 — Finesse the nine. This only fails when West has AK10x, AK10, or 10 — 83

608. Q J 8 x x
    10 7 x x — 3 ⎱ Max ⎰ — Lead small to the queen, in case either opponent is void — 100 — 3.00

609. Q J x x x
    x x x x — 3 ⎱ Max ⎰ — Lead small to the queen and then small to the jack — 83 — 2.78

610. Q 9 x x x
    J x x x — 3 — Lead small to the jack and then small to the queen, *or* finesse the nine. The latter line will be better if West is more likely to be short in the suit — 83

B. THE ACE-QUEEN-JACK

(a) Declarer Has Five Cards

611. K 10 9
    x x — 1 — Finesse the ten and then the nine — 78

612. K 10 x
    x x — 1 — Finesse the ten and then lead to the king — 63

(b) Declarer Has Six Cards

613. K 10 9 8
    x x — 2 — Finesse the ten and then the nine — 50

614. K 10 9
    x x x — 1 — Finesse the ten and then the nine — 79

(c) Declarer Has Seven Cards

615. K 10 9 8
    x x x — 2 — Finesse the eight and then the nine — 76

616. K 10 9 x
    x x x — 2 ⎱ Max ⎰ — Finesse the nine and then the ten — 61 — 1.51

617. K 10 x x
    9 x x — 2 ⎱ Max ⎰ — Lead small to the ten and then small to the king — 37 — 1.25
          1 — Lead small to the king, and then, unless an honor appears from West, small to the nine (best), *or* lead to the ten and then to the nine — 90

Dummy Declarer	Tricks Required		% Chance of Success	Tricks per Deal

VIII. THE DEFENSE HAS SEVEN POINTS (cont'd)
B. THE ACE-QUEEN-JACK (cont'd)

618.	K 10 x x x x x	2 } Max } 1	Lead small to the ten and then small to the king Duck one round; then lead finesse the ten, and lead to the king	32 79	1.08
619.	K 9 8 7 x x x	2 1 } Max }	Lead to the nine and then to the king (best), *or* lead to the king, hoping that West has the ace and two other cards Finesse the seven and then the eight. This fails only if West has xx, x, or a void	 18 95	 1.11
620.	K x x x x x x	2 1 Max	Duck one round, and then lead to the king (best), *or* lead to the king, hoping that West has the ace and two other cards Duck two rounds, and then lead to the king Duck one round, and then lead to the king	 18 77	 0.87

(d) Declarer Has Eight Cards

621.	K 10 9 x x x x x	3 } Max } 2	Finesse the ten and then the nine Finesse the ten and nine (best), *or* lead to the king	75 92	2.66
622.	K 10 x x x 9 x x	3 } Max } 2	Finesse the ten, and then lead small to the king Finesse the ten. If it loses to the jack or queen, lead small to the nine next. This fails only if West is void	63 98	2.56
623.	K 10 9 8 x x x x	2	Finesse the eight and then the nine	83	
624.	K 10 x x x x x x	2 } Max }	Finesse the ten, and then lead to the king	52	1.38
625.	K x x x x x x x	2 1 Max	Lead small to the king, preferably ducking one round first Duck one round. Then either lead small to the king (best), *or* duck a second round Duck one round, and then lead small to the king	34 87 	 1.21

(e) Declarer Has Nine Cards

626.	K 10 9 x x x x x x	5 4 } Max }	Lead small to the king, hoping that West has the doubleton ace Finesse the ten. This gains a trick when East is void or has the singleton ace	20 89	3.98
627.	K 10 x x x x 9 x x	5 4 } Max }	Lead small to the king, hoping that West has the doubleton ace Finesse the ten, and then lead small to the king	20 89	4.03
628.	K 8 x x x x 10 x x	5 } Max } 4 3	Lead small to the king, hoping that West has the doubleton ace Lead toward the king, and play the king if the nine fails to appear from West* (*But West should falsecard from QJ9) Lead small to the ten	20 84 78 100	3.94
629.	K x x x x x x x x	5 } Max } 4	Lead small to the king, hoping that West has the doubleton ace Duck one round, and then lead small to the king	20 72	3.81

	Dummy Declarer	Tricks Required		% Chance of Success	Tricks per Deal

VIII. THE DEFENSE HAS SEVEN POINTS (cont'd)
B. THE ACE-QUEEN-JACK (cont'd)

	Dummy Declarer	Tricks Required		% Chance of Success	Tricks per Deal
630.	K 9 x x x x x x x	4 } Max } 3	Lead small to the king, hoping that West has the doubleton ace Duck one round, and then lead small to the king	20 72	2.81
631.	K 8 x x x 10 x x x	4 } Max } 3	Lead small to the king, hoping West has the doubleton ace Lead toward the king, and play the king if the nine fails to appear from West* (*But West should falsecard from QJ9)	20 84 78	2.98

IX. THE DEFENSE HAS EIGHT POINTS

(a) Declarer Has Five Cards

632.	Q 10 9 8 x	2	Finesse the ten, hoping that West has J, AJ, KJ, or Jx	2	
633.	Q 10 x x x	1	Finesse the ten, and then lead to the queen	37	

(b) Declarer Has Six Cards

634.	Q 10 9 8 x x	2	Finesse the ten and then the nine	18	
635.	Q 10 x x x x	2 1 } Max }	Lead to the queen, hoping that West has the AKJ only Lead to the ten and then to the queen	1 41	0.42
636.	Q 10 9 x x x	1	Finesse the ten and then the nine	51	
637.	Q 10 x x x x	1	Finesse the ten, and then lead to the queen	38	

(c) Declarer Has Seven Cards

638.	Q 10 x x x x x	3 } Max } 2 1	Lead to the ten and then to the queen Lead to the ten and queen Lead to the ten and queen	12 55 91	1.58
639.	Q 10 x x x x x	2 } Max } 1	Lead to the ten and then to the queen Lead to the ten and queen (best), or duck one round and then lead to the ten and queen, or lead to the queen and then to the ten	22 68	0.89
640.	Q 9 8 7 x x x	2 1 } Max }	Lead small to the queen Finesse the seven and then the eight	7 85	0.88
641.	Q x x x 10 9 x	2 1 } Max }	Lead small to the queen, hoping that West has AKx or AKJ Lead small to the ten and then small to the nine. This fails only when West has AJ or KJ	7 97	0.97
642.	Q x x x 10 x x	2 1 } Max }	Lead small to the queen, hoping that West has AKx or AKJ Lead small to the ten. If an honor appears from East, lead small to the ten again; if the ten loses to West on the first round, duck one round, and then lead to the queen	7 70	0.70

(d) Declarer Has Eight Cards

643.	Q 10 x x x x x x	3 } Max } 2	Finesse the ten, and then lead to the queen Finesse the ten, and then lead to the queen, in case East is void	33 84	2.15

Dummy Declarer	Tricks Required		% Chance of Success	Tricks per Deal

IX. THE DEFENSE HAS EIGHT POINTS (cont'd)

644.	Q x x x x 10 x x	3	Lead small to the queen. If the jack appears from West, cover with the queen, and duck the next round; if the ace or king appears on the first round, lead to the queen again	20	
		2 ⎱ Max ⎰	Lead toward the queen, and duck the trick. If an honor appears on the first round, lead small to the ten next; otherwise lead to the queen	90	1.95
		1	Lead small to the ten, in case West is void	100	
645.	Q x x x x x x x	3 ⎱ Max ⎰	Lead small to the queen	14	1.88
		2	Duck one round, and then, unless the ace or king appears from East, lead small to the queen	82	
646.	Q 10 x x x x x x	2 ⎱ Max ⎰	Finesse the ten, and then lead to the queen	35	1.19
647.	Q x x x 10 x x x	2 ⎱ Max ⎰	Lead small to the queen, and then, unless the jack appears from West, lead small to the ten	20	1.15
		1	Lead small to the queen and then small to the ten, *or* lead from the ten, and duck unless the jack appears from West; then, unless the ace or king appears from East, lead small to the queen. The latter line will be better if East is more likely to be short in the suit	94	
648.	Q x x x x x x x	2	Lead small to the queen	14	
		1	Duck one round, and then lead small to the queen	84	
		Max	Lead small to the queen		0.92

(e) Declarer Has Nine Cards

649.	Q 10 9 x x x x x x *	3	Finesse the ten	70	
		Max	Finesse the ten		2.66
650.	Q x x x x x x x x *	3 ⎱ Max ⎰	Lead small to the queen, *or* duck one round, and then lead small to the queen	53	2.48
			*N.B. Similar principles apply if declarer's nine cards are distributed differently between his hand and dummy.		

X. THE DEFENSE HAS NINE POINTS

(a) Declarer Has Seven Cards

651.	J 10 8 x x x x	1	Lead to the jack, and then either lead to the ten or finesse the eight	73	
652.	J 10 x x x x x	1	Lead to the jack and then to the ten	68	
653.	J x x x 10 x x	1	Lead small to the ten. If it loses to West, duck the next round, and then lead small to the jack	69	

(b) Declarer Has Eight Cards

654.	J x x x x 10 x x	2 ⎱ Max ⎰	Lead small to the ten. If it loses to West, lead small to the jack	88	1.88
		1	Lead small to the ten	100	
655.	J 10 x x x x x x	1	Lead small to the jack and then small to the ten	84	
656.	J x x x 10 x x x	1	Lead small to the jack (or ten). If it loses, lead small to the other honor	92	

E. C.

SUIT DISTRIBUTION. There are thirty-nine possible suit distributions. For the percentage play in handling any combination, see SUIT COMBINATIONS. For relative frequency of the occurrence of each pattern, see MATHEMATICAL TABLES, Table 1.

SUIT OPENING BID. See OPENING SUIT BID.

SUIT PATTERNS. For the thirty-nine suit patterns, ranging from a balanced 4-3-3-3 to an outlandish 13-0-0-0, and the percentage frequency of each, see MATHEMATICAL TABLES, Table 1.

SUIT PLACING. The process of marking during the bidding the suit lengths around the table. See CARD READING; COUNTING THE HAND.

SUIT PREFERENCE SIGNAL. A device in defensive play whereby a player may indicate a desire to have his partner lead one suit rather than another, when his partner has a choice. This method, devised by Hy LAVINTHAL of Trenton, N.J., in 1934, has had a greater effect on expert play than any other development of the twentieth century and ranks with the high-low signal and distributional echo of the nineteenth century. In various countries the suit preference signal is known by the names of bridge writers, especially W. E. MCKENNEY and B. J. BECKER, who adopted and publicized it but did not otherwise contribute to it.

The signal never applies to the suit led to the current trick, and seldom to the trump suit, so it is designed to guide partner's choice between the other two suits. The essence of the suit preference signal is this: When partner, having the lead, seems likely to switch suits, or when partner may have a choice of suits when next he obtains the lead, the play of a conspicuously high card calls for a lead in the higher-ranking suit in question, the play of a conspicuously low card calls for the lead of the lower-ranking suit.

Properly used, the suit preference signal does not interfere with conventional encouraging and discouraging plays and discards.

In the following example, the suit played is significant, so a suit preference does not apply, and the signal is a standard COME-ON.

NORTH
♠ A K Q J 10
♡ A K Q J 10
◇ 7
♣ 8 4

WEST
♠ 8 6 5
♡ 9 6 3 2
◇ A K 10 8 2
♣ 6

EAST
♠ 9 4 3
♡ 8 7
◇ Q J 6 5 4
♣ K 5 3

SOUTH
♠ 7 2
♡ 5 4
◇ 9 3
♣ A Q J 10 9 7 2

Against South's six club contract, West opens the king of diamonds. Glancing at the dummy, East may feel quite pessimistic, for at first glance, his king of trumps looks as if it will be trapped. But on further examination, East sees that if he can get his partner to continue diamonds, dummy will be reduced to one trump, and the king of clubs becomes untrappable. So on the lead of the diamond king, he plays the unnecessary high queen of diamonds, and when West continues the suit, forcing dummy to ruff, declarer can no longer take two finesses through the king of clubs.

The suit preference signal, at superficial glance, may appear to be related to East's come-on signal of the queen of diamonds in the above hand. Actually there is no relationship whatsoever.

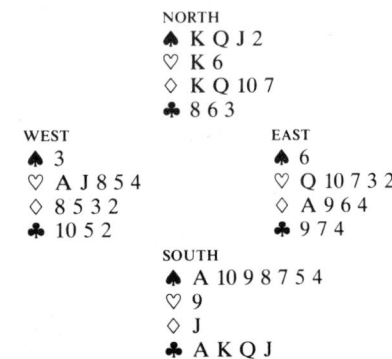

NORTH
♠ K Q J 2
♡ K 6
◇ K Q 10 7
♣ 8 6 3

WEST
♠ 3
♡ A J 8 5 4
◇ 8 5 3 2
♣ 10 5 2

EAST
♠ 6
♡ Q 10 7 3 2
◇ A 9 6 4
♣ 9 7 4

SOUTH
♠ A 10 9 8 7 5 4
♡ 9
◇ J
♣ A K Q J

How North-South arrived at a six spade contract, missing two aces, is irrelevant. Sufficient to say that it probably happens every day in every bridge club in the country. In a fair proportion of these situations, certainly, the defense slips, and declarer "steals" his unmakable contract.

Against the contract, West opened the ace of hearts, which won the trick. At a loss as to what to play next, West decided to shift to a club, and declarer waltzed home with his contract, discarding his diamond on the king of hearts. Had West shifted to a diamond at trick two, East would have cashed his ace. How could the defenders have gotten together to direct their defense? Answer: the suit preference signal.

The purpose of this signal is to eliminate the guesswork as to which of two suits partner should lead in situations like the one above. The reference to "two suits" may appear to be a typographical error, but actually it is not. Of the four suits, the trump suit is automatically eliminated, for when partner gives any signal whatsoever, it is never to direct the lead of the trump suit. Also, the suit being led, on which the suit-preference signal is being given, is excluded. That leaves the leader with a choice of two "obvious" suits. In the deal presented, after West cashed his ace of hearts, either a heart continuation or a trump lead were "impossible" plays. So it became a choice of clubs or diamonds.

On the lead of the ace of hearts, had East-West been employing this suit preference signal, East would have played the queen (or the ten) of hearts which, on examination of the dummy, should not have been construed as asking for a heart continuation. The queen of hearts would have said to West: "Play the higher ranking of the two obvious suits!"

Stating the suit preference signal as a principle, it comes to this: Whenever partner plays an unnecessarily high card which is obviously not a come-on-in-this-suit signal, it commands partner to lead the higher of the other two non-trump suits; whenever partner plays a very low card which is obviously not a no-interest-in-this-suit signal, that low card asks partner to shift to the lower of the two suits. If the partner of the leader has no interest in either of the two obvious suits, he will play some intermediate card in the suit being led.

When correctly applied, the play of either an unnecessarily high card or an obviously low card will be unmistakable. Partner will (almost) invariably make the right shift when he is properly directed.

It was mentioned that this convention is misapplied by a great many bridge players, the reason behind this is that offenders attempt to apply it indiscriminately.

```
                NORTH
                ♠ A K 6
                ♡ K 7 5
                ◇ J 8 7 3
                ♣ 9 4 2
   WEST
   ♠ 9 5 4 2
   ♡ Q 6 3
   ◇ Q 9 6 2
   ♣ A 6
```

Against South's four spade contract, West elects to open the ace of clubs, East plays the ten, and South, declarer, the three-spot. West, having discovered only recently the new toy called a suit preference signal, now demonstrates his recently acquired "knowledge" by banging down the queen of hearts, saying to himself, "My partner's ten of clubs was a command to me to lead the higher of the two obvious suits." Utter nonsense! East wanted clubs continued, and so he, in conventional fashion, played the unnecessarily high ten-spot. The suit preference signal is used only when it *must be obvious* that another suit is wanted.

The actual deal was:

```
                NORTH
                ♠ A K 6
                ♡ K 7 5
                ◇ J 8 7 3
                ♣ 9 4 2
   WEST                    EAST
   ♠ 9 5 4 2               ♠ 8
   ♡ Q 6 3                 ♡ 10 9 8 4 2
   ◇ Q 9 6 2               ◇ 10 4
   ♣ A 6                   ♣ K 10 8 7 5
                SOUTH
                ♠ Q J 10 7 3
                ♡ A J
                ◇ A K 5
                ♣ Q J 3
```

Probably the most frequent situation in which the suit preference signal is applied is when leading a suit which partner is obviously going to trump. It is necessary to direct him to play back a specific suit so that another ruff can be secured. The RANK of the card led when giving him the first ruff becomes the clear-cut signal; if an unnecessarily high card is led, partner is to return the higher of the two obvious suits (trumps and the suit being led are eliminated); if an obviously low card is led, he is to return the lower-ranking of the two suits.

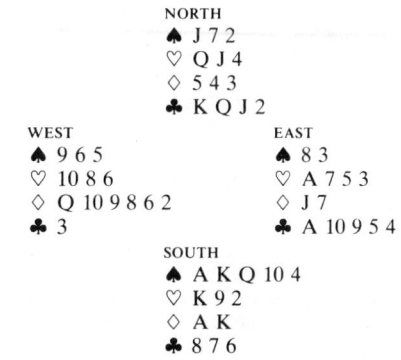

```
                NORTH
                ♠ J 7 2
                ♡ Q J 4
                ◇ 5 4 3
                ♣ K Q J 2
   WEST                    EAST
   ♠ 9 6 5                 ♠ 8 3
   ♡ 10 8 6                ♡ A 7 5 3
   ◇ Q 10 9 8 6 2          ◇ J 7
   ♣ 3                     ♣ A 10 9 5 4
                SOUTH
                ♠ A K Q 10 4
                ♡ K 9 2
                ◇ A K
                ♣ 8 7 6
```

Against South's four spade contract, West opens the three of clubs, dummy plays the jack, and East's ace captures the trick. It is, of course, perfectly apparent to East that the three-spot is a singleton, for it could not be fourth best, nor could it be the top of a worthless doubleton. So East is going to return a club for West to trump, and employing the suit preference signal, he returns the *ten*. When West trumps the trick, he recognizes the ten-spot as being unnecessarily high, and he now plays back a heart (as opposed to a diamond) which East wins, returning another club for West to trump for the setting trick. It is apparent that if West had not played back a heart, declarer would have captured any other return, drawn trumps, and fulfilled his contract.

Suppose this had been the situation:

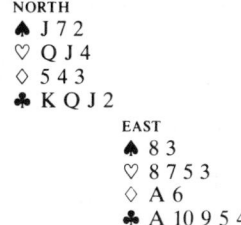

```
                NORTH
                ♠ J 7 2
                ♡ Q J 4
                ◇ 5 4 3
                ♣ K Q J 2
                           EAST
                           ♠ 8 3
                           ♡ 8 7 5 3
                           ◇ A 6
                           ♣ A 10 9 5 4
```

The three of clubs is led, and upon winning the opening lead, East would now lead back the four of clubs, an obviously low card, directing West to return the lower of the two non-trump suits (diamonds rather than hearts); and upon this return, East would now give his partner another ruff.

In expert circles, the suit preference convention has been extended to cover situations where the signal is given on the play of some side suit (any suit except the trump suit). The signal is made by high-low discards. Here is a hand which arose some years ago, George RAPEE and B. Jay BECKER sitting West and East respectively.

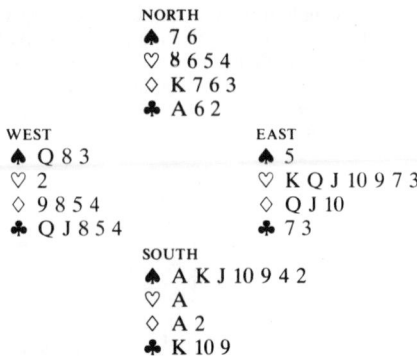

```
                    NORTH
                    ♠ 7 6
                    ♡ 8 6 5 4
                    ◇ K 7 6 3
                    ♣ A 6 2
    WEST                          EAST
    ♠ Q 8 3                       ♠ 5
    ♡ 2                           ♡ K Q J 10 9 7 3
    ◇ 9 8 5 4                     ◇ Q J 10
    ♣ Q J 8 5 4                   ♣ 7 3
                    SOUTH
                    ♠ A K J 10 9 4 2
                    ♡ A
                    ◇ A 2
                    ♣ K 10 9
```

After East opened with four hearts, North-South arrived at a six spade contract. West opened the two of hearts, which was quite obviously a singleton, dummy played the four, East the seven, and South won with the ace. The ace, king, and jack of trumps were then led, West winning the latter with the queen. On the last two spade plays, East discarded the king of hearts, then the three-spot.

It was apparent to West that East had gone out of his way to discard the king of hearts first, then the three-spot. Why did he not play normally? He was employing the suit preference signal, telling West that it was safe to play back the higher of the two remaining suits, diamonds as opposed to clubs. (West was known to have no more hearts, and probably no more spades.) Had an undirected West played back the queen of clubs, declarer would have fulfilled his contract.

This signal, as it was used by Becker and Rapee, is dangerous to employ unless it is handled with care. That is, if East had discarded the three of hearts at his first opportunity, and then a higher heart, it would have been wrong for West to suppose that East wanted the lower of the two suits, clubs instead of diamonds, led. The three-spot would have indicated merely that East had no positive interest in anything, and West would have been left to his own resources.

On the actual deal, the fact that East was employing the suit preference signal was obvious, because East had gone out of his way to play abnormally, by discarding the king first, whereas normally the three-spot would have been discarded first. It became apparent to West that East was not discarding the king because of an animosity toward nobility, but because he was trying to convey a HIGH-LOW message which the three-spot subsequently completed.

F. K.

SUIT SIGNALS. See LENGTH SIGNALS.

SUIT TAKE-OUT. See RESPONSE.

SUMMARY SHEET. See RECAPITULATION SHEET.

When the conditions of a bridge tournament event do not require the use of a recapitulation sheet (as for a knockout team event), the director will show the results during the event on some other type of sheet, such as a golf or tennis "draw" sheet with suitable modifications.

SUMMER NATIONALS. An annual tournament held since 1929, usually in July or early August. These championships, usually the largest of the three Nationals, were originally under the auspices of the ABL, and since 1938 have been controlled by the ACBL. In the thirties they were played at Asbury Park, N.J., and lasted eight days. In postwar years the program was gradually enlarged to nine days, and in 1969 it became a ten-day tournament.

In 1930 the knockout team event attracted an entry of 16 teams, and 22 pairs were entered for the Master Pairs for the von Zedtwitz Gold Cup. In the postwar years the tournaments expanded rapidly, partly as a result of the impetus given by the master-point scheme. A peak was reached in 1973 in Washington, D.C., with 16,043 tables, an all-time world record. The attendance record for the Spingold Knockout Teams was established in Los Angeles in 1969 (140 teams), and for the Life Masters Pairs in Boston in 1970 (360 pairs). For past results, see Appendix I.

The selection of cities and hotels for such mammoth tournaments presents great problems. Allocations are usually made five years in advance. See also NORTH AMERICAN CHAMPIONSHIPS, so designated beginning in 1975.

Year	Site	Tables
1929	Chicago, Ill.	
1930–41	Asbury Park, N.J.	
1942–47	New York, N.Y.	
1948–49	Chicago, Ill.	
1950	Columbus, Ohio	
1951	Washington, D.C.	
1952	Cincinnati, Ohio	3,093
1953	St. Louis, Mo.	3,054
1954	Washington, D.C.	4,496
1955	Chicago, Ill.	4,619
1956	New York, N.Y.	5,679
1957	Pittsburgh, Pa.	5,625
1958	Miami, Fla.	4,068
1959	Chicago, Ill.	6,939
1960	Los Angeles, Calif.	8,462
1961	Washington, D.C.	7,989
1962	Minneapolis, Minn.	5,820
1963	Los Angeles, Calif.	12,486
1964	Toronto, Ont.	11,150
1965	Chicago, Ill.	14,511
1966	Denver, Colo.	10,112
1967	Montreal, Que.	10,926
1968	Minneapolis, Minn.	9,857
1969	Los Angeles, Calif.	11,470
1970	Boston, Mass.	12,584
1971	Chicago, Ill.	13,566
1972	Denver, Colo.	11,449
1973	Washington, D.C.	16,043

1974	New York, N.Y.	15,310
1975	Miami Beach, Fla.	10,368
1976	Salt Lake City, Utah	
1977	Chicago, Ill.	
1978	Toronto, Ont.	
1979	Las Vegas, Nev.	
1980	Chicago, Ill.	
1981	Boston, Mass.	

SUOMEN BRIDGELIITTO. See FINNISH BRIDGE LEAGUE.

SUPER BLACKWOOD. A method of asking for aces when four no trump would be a natural bid.

Easley Blackwood lists three situations in which four no trump would be natural. (a) when the partnership has not bid a suit; (b) when no suit has been agreed, and the four no trump bidder has previously bid no trump; (c) when no suit has been agreed, and a no trump bid immediately preceded four no trump.

In each of these situations Blackwood suggests that a bid of four in the lowest-ranking unbid suit should ask for aces with step responses. A subsequent five no trump bid asks for kings in the same way.

The Super Blackwood bid will usually be four clubs, which lines it up with the GERBER convention.

SUPER CONVENTION. See EXCLUSION BID.

SUPER GERBER. An ace-asking convention devised by R. GOLDMAN for use when a minor suit fit has been established, or when the last bid was three no trump, so that a four no trump call would be natural. The Super Gerber bid is the lowest possible bid in an unbid suit or in a suit that cannot be deemed trumps; if all suits are unavailable or ambiguous, the Super Gerber bid is a jump to five clubs.

Over establishment of a minor suit fit, either expressly or by implication, the Super Gerber bid is a jump to four of the cheapest unbid suit:

(a)	(b)	(c)	(d)
1 ◇ 3 ◇	1 ♣ 3 ♣	1 ◇ 2 ◇	1 ◇ 1 ♡
3 ♡	4 ◇	4 ♣	3 ◇ 4 ♠

The last bid in each auction is Super Gerber. The use of Super Gerber in minor suit auctions is designed to allow four no trump to be used as a balanced general strength slam try, and to provide an ace-asking bid that does not risk getting the partnership beyond the game level with too few aces.

Responses as used by the ACES TEAM are in steps as follows:

1st step	0 or 3 aces
2nd step	1 or 4 aces
3rd step	2 aces
4th step	2 aces with extra value outside the trump suit
5th step	2 aces and a useful void
higher step	1 ace and a useful void

In showing one ace and a void, the void suit is bid if it ranks lower than the trump suit; the trump suit is bid if the void suit is higher ranking.

SUPER PRECISION. A version of the PRECISION CLUB system used by Georgio Belladonna and Benito Garozzo in which there are many specialized bids and asking sequences. It differs from standard Precision in the following essential respects:

No trump responses to one club are revised: one no trump is enlarged to encompass hands worth 8–13 points. A two no trump response shows 14 or more points, with no upper limit. A three no trump response shows a solid seven-card suit, with or without a side suit stopper. Opener's rebids over three no trump ask about high card controls, or identification of responder's suit.

Over interference with one club, controls are shown (ace=2, king=1). After a one-level overcall, a double shows 6 or more points with 0–2 controls, one no trump shows three controls and a stopper, two clubs shows three controls without a stopper, two diamonds shows four controls, two no trump shows five or more controls; bids of three clubs, three diamonds, and one, two, or three of a major are all natural, showing 0–2 controls.

Over a two-level overcall the double shows a balanced hand with as many as three controls; two no trump shows three or four controls with a stopper; a cue-bid shows five or more controls; suit bids are natural, showing unbalanced hands with 0–3 controls. Over a three-level overcall the responses are similar.

Two diamond opening may be 4–3–1–5 or 3–4–1–5 as well as 4–4–0–5 and 4–4–1–4. A two no trump response asks for clarification of distribution and strength. Three club and three diamond rebids show the hands with three spades and three hearts respectively; three heart and three spade rebids show 4–4–1–4 distribution, of minimum and maximum strength respectively; four club and four diamond rebids show 4–4–0–5 distribution, of minimum and maximum strength respectively; rebids of three no trump and four clubs show 4–4–0–5 distribution, minimum and maximum respectively.

Super Unusual Positive is used in responding to one club with 4–4–4–1 hands. An immediate jump to three clubs shows a singleton in a black suit, a jump to three diamonds shows a singleton in a red suit; both show minimum high card values. Opener's bid of the next suit asks where responder's singleton is; responder bids the first step with the minor suit singleton, or the second step with the major suit singleton. Immediate jump responses of three hearts, three spades, four clubs, and four diamonds over one club show maximum values and a singleton in the next higher suit.

Three-level minor suit openings are offensive rather than purely pre-emptive. Three clubs shows a seven-playing-trick hand with a semi-solid club suit and an outside entry. Three diamonds shows any solid seven-card suit with an outside entry (devised by Omar SHARIF). In response to three diamonds, three hearts is a sign-off to play in opener's suit; three spades is a general constructive bid. Over three spades opener bids three no trump if he has a minor suit, four clubs if his suit is hearts and he has a side void or singleton, four diamonds if his suit is spades and he has a side void or singleton; four hearts and four spades are natural and deny a side void or singleton. Responder may ask opener where his shortness lies.

Three no trump opening shows a pre-emptive minor suit opening similar to standard openings of four clubs or four diamonds. Responder retreats with a weak hand by bidding four clubs which opener passes if his suit is clubs, or corrects to four diamonds.

Asking bids of several kinds are used after a one club opening, each with its own series of responses. These include bids designated *Alpha*, in which opener asks about responder's support for opener's suit; *Beta*, in which opener asks about responder's length and strength in a particular suit; *Gamma*, which asks about trump honors; *Delta*, which asks about length and strength in a specific suit after a no trump bid or Stayman response. See SUPER PRECISION ASKING BIDS.

SUPER PRECISION ASKING BIDS.

Any of a number of types of asking bids in the SUPER PRECISION system as played by G. BELLADONNA and B. GAROZZO, used by the one club opener to ask a variety of questions, such as trump suit quality, high card or distributional controls, and responder's support for opener's suit.

Alpha Support Asking Bids. After a positive response in a suit, a new suit bid by opener asks about responder's support for opener's suit and his overall controls. Support is defined as Qxx or better. A hand with 0–2 controls is considered minimum, four or more controls is maximum, and three controls can be considered in either category. The responses are in five steps:

1st step	No support, minimum
2nd step	No support, maximum
3rd step	Support, minimum
4th step	Support, maximum
5th step	Four cards, maximum

Further definition of responder's support may follow.

Beta Suit Asking Bids. After a negative one diamond response to one club, a jump to two hearts or two spades by opener is a Roman-style asking bid inquiring about responder's strength and length in that suit. The responses are the first eight steps set out in ROMAN ASKING BIDS. See also Delta Suit Asking Bids below.

Gamma Trump Asking Bids. Initiated by the one club opener's single raise of responder's positive suit response, the responses show trump quality and length as set forth in PRECISION ASKING BIDS. Delayed trump asking bids are also available.

Delta Suit Asking Bids. After a positive response in no trump, a jump in a suit by opener is used to determine the number of cards and honors held by responder in that suit. The responses are:

1st step	no honors, doubleton or tripleton
2nd step	doubleton honor
3rd step	tripleton honor
4th step	four headed by an honor
5th step	two honors doubleton or tripleton
6th step	four headed by two honors

Control Asking Bids. After a suit fit has been established, a direct bid of four clubs is control asking. If cue-bidding has begun, four clubs is a cue-bid. There is one exception: if responder's first bid suit was clubs, then four diamonds is the control asking bid. Responses are in steps, with the first step showing none or one. See PRECISION ASKING BIDS. However, it may be agreed to vary the first step according to responder's previously shown strength.

Special Suit Asking Bids. After a Control Asking Bid, a new suit by opener asks responder to show his length and strength in the new suit as follows:

1st step	void or singleton
2nd step	doubleton
3rd step	tripleton
4th step	one of top three honors, any length
5th step	two of top three honors, any length
6th step	three top honors, any length

SUPER SWISS.

An expansion of the SWISS CONVENTION recommended by H. W. KELSEY that allows responder to make a forcing raise of opener's major suit while announcing immediately whether or not he has a singleton, and whether or not he has a void, and if he has neither, showing whether or not he has good controls. Responder bids one of four steps, the first step being the bid next above a single jump raise (three spades over one heart, three no trump over one spade):

1st step	void (unidentified)
2nd step	singleton (unidentified)
3rd step	two or three aces, denies a singleton or void
4th step	fewer than two aces, denies a singleton or void

After responder has shown a singleton or void, opener makes the cheapest bid to ask where responder's shortness lies; after the response, opener will usually be able to use BLACKWOOD to ask about aces.

For alternative methods see CONGLOMERATE MAJOR RAISES, UNBALANCED SWISS RAISE, VALUE SWISS RAISES.

SUPER UNUSUAL POSITIVE.

A set of artificial jump responses to a PRECISION CLUB opening to show 4-4-4-1 distribution and to specify minimum or maximum strength. See SUPER PRECISION.

SUPERSTITIONS.

Common as regards cards ever

since games were first played. In anything in which there is an element of luck or chance, superstition has a foothold. Some persons have the reputation of being good or bad cardholders. Substance is lent to such superstitions by the fact that a large number of instances is required to demonstrate the so-called law of averages. As with tossing coins, it may require one thousand tosses to arrive at a point where there exists even a rough parity in the number of head and tail tosses. It is similar with cards. If one collates records on a series of several hundred hands held, one will find that the honor trick holdings over the course will, to use point-count equivalents, average about ten points. There are numerous superstitions occurring at or applying to bridge games, such as shuffling the cards in a certain way, or positioning the deck after the cut, or using a certain pencil for scoring but for no other purpose, as does the Secretary of one of the most distinguished clubs, or getting up from one's seat and walking around one's chair or around the entire table "for luck" after a bad hand or bad run of cards. A common superstition involves choices of seats or decks of cards after the cut for partners. One expert who restricts himself generally to club play never allows a pencil to be thrust under the nap of the cover cloth, if the cloth is cut on a bias, allowing for open corners; another believes his luck will desert him if attention is drawn to it by calling him "lucky" or "the big winner," and so on, ad infinitum. See SINGLETON KING.

SUPPORT. Verb: to raise. Noun: (1) a raise; (2) whatever strength partner has in support of one's bid. See TRUMP SUPPORT.

SUPPRESSING THE BID ACE. Ace-asking conventions such as BLACKWOOD are occasionally used when the responding hand is already known to have a particular ace. The holder may have made a cue-bid, or shown a solid suit. In such cases partnership should agree whether the ace already identified should be shown when responding to the conventional bid. Similar questions arise when the partnership has used a VOID-SHOWING BID. It is preferable to agree that the ace of a suit in which partner is known to be void should not be shown. Lacking any agreement, however, the previous bidding should be disregarded and the number of aces shown in the normal way.

SURE TRICK. A trick that a player must win. For example: the ace of trumps, the guarded king of trumps when it is behind the ace, the ace of a suit you intend to lead against no trump.

The lead of an ace against a suit contract, even though it be from a short suit not mentioned in the bidding, is not necessarily a sure trick, as declarer or dummy may be void. See HONOR TRICK, QUICK TRICK.

The term is also used by George Coffin to describe single-dummy problems in which correct play will ensure the making of a specific number of tricks.

SURPLUS CARD. A card in excess of thirteen in a

bridge hand, before the play begins, or a card in excess of the number of tricks remaining to be played after play has commenced. See LAWS (Laws 11, 68), LAWS OF DUPLICATE (Laws 13, 67). See MISSING CARD.

SUSPENSION. See DISCIPLINARY CODE; EXCLUSION.

SVERIGES BRIDGEFORBUND. See SWEDISH BRIDGE LEAGUE.

SWEDISH BRIDGE LEAGUE (SVERIGES BRIDGEFORBUND). Founded in 1933, and in 1969 had approximately 25,000 members. The League participates in all European and Scandinavian Championships, and World Olympiads. Sweden won the World Women's Olympiad in 1968, the European Championships in 1939 and 1952, and the European Women's Championships in 1962 and 1967. Sweden hosted the European Championships in Stockholm in 1936 and 1956 and the Bermuda Bowl and World Pairs Olympiad in 1970. National events for Open Teams and Open Pairs attract 400 teams and 4,500 pairs, respectively. Swedish players listed separately are: G. Anulf, Mrs. B. Blom, Count C. Bonde, A. Brunzell, Mrs. K. Eriksson, S. Flodqvist, B. Hall, E. Jannersten, N. Jensen, R. Kock, N. Lilliehook, H. Lind, J. Lindqvist, Mrs. G. Linton, Mrs. E. Martensson, Mrs. M. Moore, M. Nilsand, L. Salsby, T. Sandgren, Mrs. R. Segander, Mrs. G. Silborn, P. Sundelin, E. Werner, Mrs. E. Werner, J. Wohlin, S. Zachrisson.

Officers, 1975:
President: Lars Erwail.
Secretary: Lars Salsby, Karlaplan 8, S-114 60 Stockholm, Sweden.

SWINDLE, SWINDLING. Legitimate methods of attempting to get better than deserved results are discussed under DECEPTIVE PLAY, FALSE-CARDING, LEAD-INHIBITING BID, and PSYCHIC BIDDING.

SWING. The difference between the actual score made on a deal and "what might have been" were the bidding, play, or defense different. Thus if poor dummy play by declarer results in down one on a vulnerable six spade contract, the swing is said to be 1,530 points.

The term is frequently used in team matches to name the actual gain or loss on a single hand. The term may be in total points or in IMPs. If North-South of a team make three spades for 140 points and their teammates defeat four spades by 50 points, the swing is 190 points or 5 IMPs. See SWING HAND.

SWING HAND. A term used to denote a hand on which successful or unsuccessful result by a partnership produces a very decisive change in overall results of a rubber or a match.

Consider this hand from a recent European championship:
North-South Vulnerable. South dealer.

```
                    NORTH
                    ♠ Q 5 3
                    ♡ A Q J
                    ◇ K
                    ♣ A Q J 9 4 3
    WEST                            EAST
    ♠ A 7 4                         ♠ K 10 9
    ♡ 10 8 5 2                      ♡ K 9 7 6 4 3
    ◇ 10 8 7 3                      ◇ 4
    ♣ 6 5                           ♣ 10 8 2
                    SOUTH
                    ♠ J 8 6 2
                    ♡ —
                    ◇ A Q J 9 6 5 2
                    ♣ K 7
```

NORTH	EAST	SOUTH	WEST
		1 ◇	Pass
3 ♣	3 ♡	4 ◇	4 ♡
4 NT	6 ♡	Pass	Pass
6 NT	Pass	7 ◇	Dbl.
7 NT	Dbl.	Pass	Pass
Redbl.	Pass	Pass	Pass

On the bidding above, East led a diamond, and North-South were plus 2,930 points. In the other room, North-South reached a contract of six clubs, down one, for a score of minus 100, a swing of over 3,000 points on a single hand.

SWISS BRIDGE FEDERATION (FÉDÉRATION SUISSE DE BRIDGE).

Founded in 1950 in Geneva, and by 1969 had a membership of approximately 1,000 in 33 affiliated clubs. The Federation annually sponsors teams in the European Championships, and hosted the tournament in Montreaux in 1954. It also participates in World Olympiads and finished fifth in 1964 and sixth in 1968. The Federation holds annual competitions for National Championships in Open Teams, Knockout Teams, Masters Pairs, Mixed Pairs, Open Pairs, a Par Contest, and limited Knockout Teams. The Swiss system of master point awards is unique in that master points cannot be carried forward from one year to the next. Players earn a permanent rank by winning a certain number of master points for several consecutive years, but this rank may be lost if a successful record is not maintained. Also, the master point value of a given tournament depends not only on the size and length of the tournament, but also on the number of participating National Series (highest ranking) players. In 1968, there were 14 players with the rank of National Series player. The following Swiss players are listed separately: M. Bardola, P. Béguin, P. Bernasconi, J. Besse, G. Catzeflis, T. Fenwick, L. Gordon, E. Jacobi, J. Ortiz, C. Reichenbach, T. Trad, T. VuMinh.

Officers, 1974:

President: Marc Hodler.

Secretary General: Wolfgang Achterberg, 54/56 Route de Vandoeuvres CH–1253 Vandoeuvres, Switzerland.

SWISS CONVENTION.

A response of four in a minor suit to an opening of one in a major suit shows a standard forcing raise to the three-level. This is a strength-showing substitute used by players employing limit jump raises. (Three no trump is sometimes used for the same purpose, for example in KAPLAN-SHEINWOLD.)

The usual high-card strength would be 13–15:

```
                    ♠ A Q x x
                    ♡ K J x x
                    ◇ A x x
                    ♣ x x
```

Over one heart or one spade, the response is four clubs or four diamonds to show a hand too strong in high cards to raise directly to game. It also suggests a relatively balanced hand, because responder would bid a side suit and raise to game on the second round with a two-suiter.

The distinction between four clubs and four diamonds is a matter of partnership agreement, but the trend is toward using four clubs as the more forward-going bid. When four clubs and four diamonds are the only forcing raises employed, one of the following treatments is usual:

(1) Trump quality: four clubs shows (and four diamonds denies) four trumps headed by at least two of the top three honors, or five or more trumps headed by at least the ace or king.

(2) Controls: four clubs shows (and four diamonds denies) three aces, or two aces and the king of trumps.

(3) Controls or Trumps: four clubs emphasizes good controls, and four diamonds emphasizes strong trumps.

Several methods have been developed which combine the jumps to four of a minor with other jump responses in order to allow for a finer distinction among types of strong raises. See CONGLOMERATE MAJOR RAISES, SUPER SWISS, UNBALANCED SWISS RAISE, VALUE SWISS RAISES.

For other conventional uses of four of a minor in response to one of a major, see ASKING BID, SPLINTER BID, and VOID-SHOWING BID.

SWISS MOVEMENT.

A partial round-robin movement similar to the method used for many years in major chess tournaments when insufficient time is available for a complete round robin.

The basic feature of a Swiss movement is that after the first round, winning teams or pairs are pitted against each other for the second round, and losers face each other as in a double elimination event, except that all teams continue to play throughout the event. For each succeeding round, new pairings are made on the basis of the records of the matched teams or pairs with the added proviso that no two teams or pairs may play a second match against each other. Scoring is usually by international match points, although BOARD-A-MATCH and HYBRID SCORING are feasible.

Team events: Although many attempts at adapting

the Swiss method to team contests have been made in the past, it was not until 1967 when John HAMILTON and Marc LOW developed the present method, which was first tried and proved successful at a Cincinnati Sectional, that Swiss team contests became popular. The idea caught on quickly throughout the ACBL and resulted in a spectacular increase in team attendance at sectional and regional tournaments, more than doubling the size of the previous board-a-match team events in many cases. The first National Swiss team was held at the 1970 Spring Nationals in Portland, Oregon.

The Hamilton-Low method consists of dividing the team event into a series of short, IMP-scored matches. The original field is seeded, with seeded teams competing against non-seeded teams for the first round. Pairings for each succeeding round are determined by the won-lost records of the teams. Since sufficient matches must be scheduled to produce a significant won-lost record, a minimum of two sessions of play is required. Usually more matches are scheduled than needed to reduce the field to one undefeated team, which may result in a tie. In that event, the tie is broken by either a play-off between the tied teams, by taking the result of the match between the tied teams if they played each other, or by comparing the results of all of the matches each of the tied teams played. An odd number of entries creates pairing difficulties and should be avoided.

An alternative method, used in Greater New York Bridge Association Swiss team events, is to convert IMP results into victory points. Pairings are then based on victory-point totals, not wins and losses, and the team with the most victory points is declared the winner. Another GNYBA innovation is to schedule a four-session Swiss movement on a weekend when no other events are held. This ensures a reasonable attendance and permits longer matches to be played.

Pair events: The ACBL introduced Swiss pair contests in 1970. As in the team event, the pairs play a series of short matches against each other, with each board IMPed against a computed average for the field. Pairings may be based on wins and losses or on victory points.

Some of the difficulties encountered are: (1) the boards must be duplicated for each round and (2) since pair events attract larger fields than team contests, it may be difficult to determine an overall winner in two sessions.

SWITCH. See SHIFT.

SWORDS. One of the suits in early PLAYING CARDS. Still used in the trappola deck (see SUIT).

SYMMETRY. See LAW OF SYMMETRY.

SYNDICATED ARTICLES. See BRIDGE COLUMNS.

SYSTEMS. See BIDDING SYSTEMS.

T

TABLE. Four players, two pairs, or one team, in duplicate play. For individual, pair, and team movements suitable to a particular number of tables, see TWO, THREE, FOUR, etc., to FIFTEEN TABLES.

The table most frequently used for bridge is a folding square table, about 30 inches on a side, and from 26½ to 27½ inches in height. The accouterments should include two score pads, two decks of bridge cards, two sharp pencils, ashtrays, coasters, and four chairs.

TABLE GUIDE CARD. A large card placed under the boards in the center of a table, containing instructions for the players. See GUIDE CARD.

TABLE MANNERS. Bridge is a social game, and good manners at the bridge table are as necessary for full enjoyment of the game as in any other form of sociability. See ETIQUETTE, PROPRIETIES.

TABLE NUMBERS. Rectangular, large cards in the center of the table, which give the number of the table in the section; sections are distinguished by the color of the table card, on a six-color repeating pattern; white for sections A, G, N, T, and Z; yellow for B, H, O, and U; green for C, J, P, and V; orange for D, K, Q, and W; blue for E, L, R, and X; pink for F, M, S, and Y.

TABLE PRESENCE. One of the features that make a good bridge player into an expert one is the undefinable something that is referred to as table presence. It is a combination of INSTINCT, if this quality actually exists; the drawing of correct inferences from any departure from RHYTHM by the opponents; the exercise of DISCIPLINE in bidding; and perhaps the most important, the ability to coax maximum performance from his partner, and the ability to make the opponents feel that they are facing a player of a higher order.

TABLE SPACING. The arrangement of tables in a hall for an event of a duplicate tournament. For comfortable play the ideal that is hoped for has spacing of nine feet between centers in rows spaced ten feet between centers apart. When the available space does not permit the ideal arrangement, reduction to eight feet between centers is practicable. The minimum spacing permitting any degree of comfort is a trifle over seven feet between centers in a row. When the rows cannot be spaced at least eight feet apart, staggering of tables in adjoining rows can be resorted to.

The setup of tables within the section should put the last table in the section near the first so that boards and players have a minimum of movement. This can be done with a hairpin arrangement, utilizing two rows of seven, eight, or nine tables in a row. When there are nine tables in a row, tables numbered 9 through 17 should be in one row, with number 16 adjacent to number 1, and number 18 in the row with numbers 1 to 8 next to number 1.

TABLES, MATHEMATICAL. See MATHEMATICAL TABLES.

TACTICS. Various maneuvers in the play of the hand, bidding nuances, and choices of action generally to adapt a player's usual rubber bridge games to the peculiarities inherent in tournament play owing to the methods of scoring, quality of the competition, and conditions of contests.

TAIWAN. See NATIONAL CONTRACT BRIDGE LEAGUE OF THE REPUBLIC OF CHINA.

TAKE-OUT. A bid at a denomination other than one previously named by partner, as distinguished from a raise. See JUMP SHIFT and RESPONSE.

TAKE-OUT DOUBLE. The use of a low-level double in certain circumstances as a request to partner to bid an unbid suit. This is a "natural" convention, because a penalty double of an opening suit bid of one can hardly exist: a player with great strength in the opponent's suit prefers to lie in wait (see TRAP PASS). The idea of doubling for a take-out appears to have been devised independently by Major Charles PATTON in New York and Bryant MC-CAMPBELL in St. Louis in 1912–13 and probably by others.

For the problems involved in distinguishing a take-out double from a penalty double, see DOUBLE.

By far the most common take-out double occurs when it immediately follows an opening bid of one in a suit. The doubler normally indicates a hand worth an opening bid with at least three-card support for all unbid suits. However, the respective vulnerability and the rank of the opener's suit may play a part in the decision.

♠ A Q x x
♡ x
◇ K x x
♣ J 10 x x x

At favorable vulnerability, a double of one heart can be ventured. If the doubler's partner can fit spades, a cheap save in four spades over four hearts is likely to materialize. There would be less reason to double if the opener's suit were a minor, or if the doubler held only three spades. A player who doubles a major-suit opening tends to hold four cards in the unbid major, and this may be a factor in deciding to double.

The high-card strength required for the double increases: (a) as the distribution becomes less suitable; (b) if the doubler is vulnerable; (c) if the opener's suit is spades, which will force a response at the two-level.

The following would be minimum vulnerable doubles of one spade:

♠ x	♠ x x	♠ x x x
♡ A Q x x	♡ A J x x	♡ A Q x
◇ K J x x	◇ K Q x x	◇ A J x x
♣ K x x x	♣ K J x	♣ K J x

A non-vulnerable double would be justified in each case if a jack were removed.

The distributional requirement, that at least three cards should be held in each unbid suit, should rarely be broken unless the doubler is very strong, with at least 17 high-card points:

♠ x x
♡ A Q x x x
◇ A Q x
♣ K Q x

Over one spade, one diamond, or one club, a double followed by a minimum bid in hearts is appropriate. The hand is clearly too strong for a simple overcall.

A take-out double is normally made with any strong hand unsuitable for other actions such as a one no trump overcall, a strong jump overcall, or a cue-bid. The maximum for a double is a hand just short of the requirements for an immediate cue-bid, unless the cue-bid is being used as a specialized bid (ASTRO, MICHAELS, etc.) in which case there is no upward limit. Very strong hands are often shown by doubling and following with a cue-bid: the idea that such bidding shows a desire to play in the opponent's suit is virtually obsolete.

Subsequent bidding

For action by the opener's partner, see RESPONSES OVER OPPONENT'S TAKE-OUT DOUBLE. The following summarizes possible actions by the doubler's partner if the bidding starts:

1 ◇   Dbl.   Pass   ?

(1) *Minimum suit response* (one heart or one spade or two clubs). A forced response which may have no high-card points. The normal maximum is 8 points, but see (3) below. Responder prefers a major suit to a minor, so two clubs is more likely to be five cards than four. One heart is not infrequently bid with a three-card suit because there is no alternative: if responder's only suit is diamonds he has to invent an economical bid. Even one spade might be a three-card suit, with 3–2–5–3 distribution for example.

The doubler passes these responses automatically if he has a minimum or near-minimum double. Further action shows that game is still possible in the face of responder's announced weakness. A raise of responder's suit or a bid in a new suit should show at least 17 points in high cards (or perhaps 16 if responder's jump shift would have been forcing). A minimum rebid in no trump is very constructive, suggesting a hand too strong to overcall one no trump (i.e., 19–20 points).

In one case responder may make an uneconomical response:

♠ A x x x
♡ K x x x
◇ x x x
♣ x x

One spade is a better response than one heart, as

responder can then continue readily to two hearts if, as is likely, the opponents contest with two clubs or two diamonds.

(2) *One no trump response*. Indicates a relatively balanced hand with moderate strength and a stopper in the opener's suit. The exact strength is a matter of style, and expert opinions vary. The conservative view is to reserve the bid for hands with 8–10 or perhaps 11 points. But this sets problems when responder has a hand such as:

♠ K J 10 x
♡ x x x
◇ Q x x
♣ x x x

Many authorities, such as Edgar KAPLAN, therefore recommend a range of 6–9.

(3) *Jump shift* (two hearts, two spades, or three clubs). There are two treatments. The majority of experts, and the majority of authorities, play this jump shift as encouraging but not forcing. The high-card strength is likely to be 9–11, but might be 8 with a five-card suit. The jump in a major suit is often a four-card suit; in a minor at least five cards are desirable.

However, some experts treat the jump as forcing. In this case the minimum strength should be 10–11. The disadvantage is that the range of the non-jump response becomes uncomfortably wide.

(4) *Cue-bid* (two diamonds). Shows any hand which can guarantee game but cannot be sure of the final resting place. The bid is totally unrelated to the opener's suit. Some players use the cue-bid slightly more freely:

♠ A Q x x
♡ K J x x
◇ J x x
♣ x x

Rather than make a non-forcing jump in one of the major suits, and perhaps pick the wrong suit, a possible treatment is to cue-bid two diamonds, intending to raise either major to the three-level. The doubler then passes with a minimum, because the responder would have bid game himself if he could.

(5) *Two no trump response*. Shows 11–12 points, and at least a single stopper in the opener's suit. The strength will depend slightly on the range adopted for the one no trump response, in (3) above. If that is 6–9 the two no trump bid may be made with 10; if one no trump is 8–11, two no trump is likely to be 12.

(6) *Three no trump response*. Usually a double stopper in the opener's suit and 13–16 points. Alternatively, responder may have a single stopper and a long minor suit which he expects to run with the help of doubler's expected fit. With more than 16 points, responder may suspect that the opener or the doubler has psyched, and proceed more slowly with a cue-bid.

(7) *Higher suit responses*. (3♡, 3♠, 4♣, 4♡, 4♠, 5♣). Natural limited bids based on a long suit

(usually six cards or longer). Responder expects to make his contract if doubler has a minimum.

(8) *Pass*. Great length and strength in diamonds (see PENALTY PASS).

After action by opener's partner
Action by third hand relieves the doubler's partner of his obligation to bid, but he should still make a "free" response if he has moderate values and can do so at a convenient level.

(9) *After a redouble*. A pass shows weakness. (The idea that responder should ignore the redouble, and therefore pass for penalties is virtually obsolete.) However, the responder is almost certain to have a hand with little strength, very probably less than 6 points. A suit bid should therefore not be construed as showing any strength: the chance that the doubler's side will wish to bid constructively toward game is negligible. Responder should usually show a four-card suit if he can do so at the level of one, and a five-card suit at the level of two. It is especially important for him to bid the cheapest suit, should he hold it and fear that partner may take out in a suit he cannot support.

(10) *After a change of suit by opener's partner*. If responder can bid a suit of his own at the one-level, he should usually do so with 5 points, and make the normal encouraging jump with 9. Slightly more is needed to bid at the two-level, but the free two-level response (1 ◇ –Dbl.–2 ♣ –2 ♠) should be made more freely than the jump shift when third hand has passed.

(11) *After a raise by opener's partner*. The opener's partner is trying to shut out the doubler's partner, who must often strain his resources in order to avoid being shut out. For a treatment of hands which do not offer an obvious bid, see RESPONSIVE DOUBLE.

Other take-out doubles
These can usually be identified by the general rule that a double of a suit bid at the level of one or two is for a take-out when partner has not bid. The most important cases are as follows:

(12) *The balancing double*. See BALANCING.

(13) *The double of two suits* (1 ♣ –Pass–1 ♡ –Dbl.). In standard practice this may show a relatively weak distributional two-suiter, or a strong relatively balanced hand. However, when both opponents are bidding and partner is silent, there are obvious dangers in entering the auction. ("Bidding in sandwich" is the European phrase.) Many tournament players therefore dispense with a natural one no trump overcall in this position (or two no trump if the bidding is at the two-level) and treat a no trump bid as UNUSUAL. This takes care of the distributional two-suited hands, and the double can be reserved for relatively balanced hands, strong in high cards.

(14) *The double of a one no trump response* (1 ♡ –Pass –1 NT–Dbl.). This is the only situation in which a double of a no trump bid is for take-out, but the take-out aspect is not very pronounced: partner will pass more often than he will pass any other take-out double. The double may have to be made with a strong balanced hand which would have overcalled one no trump if opportunity had offered.

(15) *The double of a raise* (1 ♡ –Pass–2 ♡ –Dbl.).
Vulnerability and the rank of opener's suit are
important considerations here. At favorable vulnerability a double of two hearts may be made lightly
with suitable distribution because a save in four
spades seems possible. A double of two spades
commits the doubler's side to the three-level, and
does not offer such good prospects of a save, so solid
values are needed by the doubler. The double of a
minor-suit raise emphasizes the major suits; and may
be made freely: the probability that the doubling side
has a fit is increased by the opening side's established
fit.

(16) *The double of a suit response to a one no trump
opening* (1NT–Pass–2 ♡ –Dbl.). Here again vulnerability and the rank of the suit are important factors.
If the suit is red, offering the possibility of play at the
two-level, a non-vulnerable player may double with
as little as 10 points and favorable distribution. He
can rely on strength in his partner's hand because the
opener's side has announced its intention of stopping
at the two-level, and is in effect balancing.

(17) *Doubles of weak two-bids and weak three-bids*
can be regarded as take-out. See DEFENSE TO OPENING
THREE-BIDS.

TALLIES. Prepared cards for the recording of
results at the end of each round (four deals) in PRO-
GRESSIVE or PARTY BRIDGE. These can be purchased at
most gift and stationery stores.

**TAM II TWO CLUB AND TWO DIAMOND
OPENINGS.** A system of strong artificial opening
bids for use with balanced hands of 22–29 high card
points or unbalanced game-going hands. The two
diamond opening shows a balanced hand with 22–25
points. Responses include transfers, STAYMAN-type
bids, and a two heart relay asking opener to specify
whether he has a minimum or maximum.

The two club opening may be made with a balanced hand with 26–29 points, which will be revealed
by a rebid in no trump. Or it may be made with an unbalanced hand, in which case opener will rebid in a
suit. A two no trump response is negative, denying as
much as one QUICK TRICK. A simple suit response
promises one or more quick tricks, shows an ace or
king in the suit bid, and denies the ace or king of any
lower ranking suit. A jump shift response shows at
least a six-card suit, headed by two of the top three
honors.

TANK. A colloquialism in the phrase "go into the
tank" meaning to fall into a protracted HUDDLE.

TAP. A colloquialism for shortening a hand in
trumps by forcing it to ruff. See FORCE (2).

TAP THE TABLE. (1) Give an informal ALERT. (2)
Make an informal PASS.

TARDINESS. Late arrival at rubber bridge games
curtails the length of time available for play, and is
inconsiderate of the host or hostess. At duplicate
tournaments far more people may be inconve-

nienced when the start of a second session may be
delayed some little time while the director seeks substitutes for non-shows. Purchase of an entry into an
event obligates the players to abide by the conditions
of play, including reporting on time for all following
sessions of the same event. See TIME LIMIT ON RIGHT
TO PLAY.

TAROT. The pack of twenty-two numbered cards
without suit signs that were part of the first pack
known to be used in Europe; or a pack containing
these twenty-two atouts (atutti, trumps) plus fifty-six
other cards divided into four suits, each with ten SPOT
CARDS and four COURT CARDS. Not all packs are alike,
but the basic cards were:

0   The fool (*Il Pazzo or Il Matto*), like a jester (most packs omit
    the numeral)
1   The juggler (*Bagatto*), wand or cup in hand, items of legerdemain
    on the table in front of him
2   The papess (*La Papessa*), double crowned, seated, book in hand
3   The empress (*L'Imperatrice*), singly crowned, scepter and shield
4   The emperor (*L'Imperator*), perhaps Charlemagne, scepter in
    hand
5   The pope (*Il Papa*), crowned, carrying staff, seated before two
    columns
6   Love (*Amore*), Cupid aiming a double arrow at two of three
    persons
7   The chariot (*La Carrozza*), shows one driver and two horses
8   Justice (*La Giustizia*), a woman, sword in one hand, scales in other
9   The hermit (*L'Eremita*), an old man, lantern in right hand
10 Wheel of fortune (*La Ruota della Fortuna*), a crowned figure with
    sword above a wheel with one figure going up and another down
11 Force (*La Forza*), either a man opening the jaws of a lion, or a
    woman breaking a pillar
12 The hanged man (*Il Penduto*), suspended upside-down by one
    foot
13 Untitled, picturing Death, a skeleton wielding a scythe over frag-
    ments of people
14 Temperance (*La Temperanza*), an angel pouring water from one
    jug into another
15 The devil (*Il Diavolo*), winged, with pitchfork and forked tail,
    threatening one or more figures
16 The tower (*La Torre*) being struck by lightning as two men fall
17 The star (*La Stella*), a nude woman pouring water from two jugs
    into a stream
18 The moon (*La Luna*), a profile face, riding over rooftops, with
    dogs baying below
19 The sun (*Il Sole*), full-face, shining on two boys in breechcloths
20 The angel (*L'Angelo*), blowing a trumpet over people rising from
    the grave
21 The world (*Il Mondo*), a female in a wreath; an angel, a winged
    beast, a cow, and a lion are in each corner

The first tarot cards appeared in Italy, probably in
the fourteenth century, and the original suits were
cups, coins, swords, and cudgels: the court cards,
king, queen, cavalier, and knave.

A. F.

TAXES ON PLAYING CARDS. The first tax on
playing cards in the United States was levied in 1862,
to raise money for the War Between the States,
varying from 1 to 15 cents (or 15% of the cost, whichever was greater), until 1866 when it became 6 cents
per pack. This tax was repealed in 1883, and not reinstated until the depression of Cleveland's second
administration, when a 2-cents-a-pack tax was
imposed under the Act of August 27, 1894. Since that
time it has been retained by the Federal Government
as a constant source of revenue. The levy remained
constant until the necessity of increased revenue following World War I caused an increase in 1920 to 8

The *tarot* pack consists of four suits, in this case Italian, plus 22 other cards numbered consecutively, each with its own name. Tarot packs are still produced in small quantities today.

From the collection of Albert Field

cents a pack, increased to 10 cents in 1925, and recently, 1961, to 13 cents. Revenues exceeded 5 million dollars in 1929, and over 8 million in 1962. This tax was lifted on July 1, 1965.

The first tax levied on playing cards, so far as the records show, was imposed in England in the reign of James I (1615). In the "Calendar of State Papers," Domestic Series, A.D. 1611–18, in the following minute: "1615, July 20. Westminister.—(19). Letters Patent granting to Sir Richard Coningsby, for rent of £200 per annum, the imposition of 5s. per gross on playing-cards, and the office of Inspector of all playing-cards imported in recompense of £1,800 due to him from the King, and of his patent for the sole export of Tin, granted by the late Queen. Warrant for the above granted July 19."

The proclamation of this patent is preserved in the library of the Society of Antiquaries; and following the proclamation is "The Copie of the Lord Treasourer's Letter," as under: "After my heartie commendations, whereby it had pleased his Majestie to direct a Privy Seal to me, touching the imposition of five shillings upon every grosse of Playing Cards that shall be Imported into this Kingdome or the Dominions thereof by vertue of his Majestie's Letters Patents granted to Sir Richard Coningsby knight under the Greate Seale of England. In regard whereof these are to wil and require you to take notice thereof and not to suffer any merchant to make any entry of Playing-Cards until the same impositions be payed according to the said Letters patents. Provided that the Patentees give caution for maintayning the Custome and Import accordng to a Medium thereof to be made as in such cases is used:

And so having signified his Majestie's pleasure to you in that behalfe I bid you heartily farewell.

"Your Loving Friend,
"Tho: Suffolke.

"From Northampton House the 29th of October, 1615"

This tax, it will be noted, was by warrant. It was in the reign of Queen Anne that playing cards were first subjected to tax under authority of Parliament. In 1710 an act was passed to obtain an annual sum of £186,670 as a fund or security for raising £2,602,200, "for carrying on the war, and for other her Majesty's Occasions." It was enacted that playing cards should pay a duty of sixpence a pack for a term of thirty-two years, commencing June 11, 1711.

It will thus be noted that the taxing of playing cards has had a close relationship to national and worldwide affairs, such as wars and panics. The plan to lay a tax on playing cards encountered much opposition. Several petitions against the tax were presented to Parliament, by card makers and importers of paper. For example: "Considerations in Relation to THE IMPOSITION ON CARDS, Humbly submitted to the Honorable House of Commons:—

Nine parts in ten of the cards now made are sold from 6s. to 24s., and even these six shillings in cards by this duty are subjected to pay £3 12s. tax per gross.

This with humble submission will destroy Nine Parts in Ten of this manufacture, for those Cards which are now bought for 3d. can't then be afforded under 10d. or a shilling, for every hand through which they pass will add again in consideration of the

Tax imposed and therefore the generality of the people will buy none at all.

If any of your Honors hope by this Tax to suppress expensive Card-playing, It is answered, That the Common sort who play for innocent diversion will by this tax be only hinder'd; for those sharp gamesters who play for money but do not use the Twentieth part of the Cards sold, will not by this Tax be discouraged; for those who play for many Pounds at a game will not be hindered by paying 12d. per pack: And the destruction of this manufacture will be attended with these ill consequences:—

First. Nothing (in comparison) will be (clear of all charges) raised by this duty imposed.

Secondly. All that depend upon this manufacture will be rendered incapable to maintain their numerous familes or pay their debts.

Thirdly. The English paper manufacture (which is the middle of the Cards) will be extremely prejudiced.

Fourthly. The importation of the Genoa White Paper (with which the Cards are covered) will be very much diminished; and in the consequence thereof.

Fifthly and lastly. Her Majesty will lose as much Paper duty as the clear duty on the Cards to be sold will amount unto.

And if it be intended to charge the Stock in hand, then the present Possessors will be thereby obliged to pay a Duty for Ten times more Cards than they will sell.

Wherefore it is humbly hoped, That your Honors will not lay a Duty, which it's humbly conceived will bring no profit to the Queen, but inevitably ruin many hundreds of her subjects."

In the reign of George II (1756) an additional tax of sixpence a pack was imposed on playing cards. In the reign of George III no less than seven Acts of Parliament were passed relating to cards and dice. All of this legislation tended to two ends: to impose additional taxes and to circumvent the evaders of the tax.

From and after July 5, 1765, makers of playing cards were required to send to the Stamp Office the paper on which the ace of spades was to be impressed. The Commissioners of Stamps were to print the ace of spades themselves, and had a special plate prepared for this purpose. The purpose of this provision, of course, was to make sure that all decks of playing cards sold paid revenue to the State. Again in 1789 and again in 1801 the tax was increased in sixpenny steps, till it reached the sum of half a crown a pack. In the year 1828 the half-a-crown tax was reduced to one shilling. The shilling duty, or tax, was to be denoted on the ace of spades, which came to be known as the "duty one shilling" ace, and also as "Old Frizzle," on account of the elaborate flourishes which adorned it, with which all cardplayers prior to 1864 were familiar.

The aces were supplied on credit to the card makers, the duty being exacted from time to time on their making up their packs for sale, when an officer had to attend to put on the wrappers, and to take an account of the numbers. Second-hand cards were permitted to be sold, except by licensed card makers, provided the words "second-hand cards" were legibly printed or written on the wrapper. Partly because of the heavy tax, the sale of second-hand cards became very extensive, and in June of 1862 the tax was fixed at threepence per pack. In the sixties the tax on playing cards was rescinded.

In some countries playing cards are a government monopoly. In France and Italy, for example, no imports are permitted even with duty and tax.

TEACHING IN BRIDGE. The first teacher of games in the bridge family was also one of the most successful. The ladies of good family to whom Edmund HOYLE taught whist were charged at the rate of one guinea an hour, equivalent to at least $50 an hour in modern terms. His celebrated "Short Treatise," published in 1743, which became a bestseller for over a century, was intended as a textbook for his students.

The first professional teacher of whist in America was Miss Kate Wheelock, who began teaching in Milwaukee in 1886. She achieved immediate success, and toured the continent lecturing in all the principal cities. The whistograph which she invented for use in her classes was the forerunner of the Vu-Graph used by the ACBL in modern times. She was the first woman to be made an associate member of the American Whist League, and Cavendish called her "The Whist Queen."

Whist teaching was a highly suitable occupation for ladies of some status and education who needed to supplement their incomes, and many others followed Miss Wheelock's example. The first prominent male teacher was Charles Stuart Street, of New York City, who began in 1890.

The most successful teacher of bridge whist, and of auction bridge up to the time of his death, was undoubtedly Joseph B. ELWELL. Among his most prominent successors was Josephine CULBERTSON. During the twenties Milton WORK and Wilbur WHITEHEAD organized conventions for teachers, and issued certificates to those who had completed courses. A similar procedure was followed later by Ely CULBERTSON, and later still by Charles GOREN, who was one of the highest-paid teachers of all time before he decided to concentrate on writing.

Many persons turned to bridge teaching as a temporary occupation during the depression years, and at its peak the membership of the Culbertson National Studios totaled some 6,000. The number of teachers dwindled markedly when prosperity returned, but increased again in the postwar years, particularly after Goren's point-count methods gained general currency.

In the sixties and seventies, the number of teachers has continuted to grow. Their ranks include many players of the highest quality, and for students with tournament ambitions the playing lesson has increased in popularity. See AMERICAN BRIDGE TEACHERS' ASSOCIATION, from which information about a wide range of teaching books and materials can be obtained. See also AUTOBRIDGE and LESSON HANDS.

TEAM. Four or more players competing as a unit in bridge tournaments. For one-session events, four players constitute a team; in two-session events, usually five players are permitted, with two of them playing only one session each. In multi-session events, a team of six players is usually permitted (REISINGER TROPHY, SPINGOLD TROPHY, VANDERBILT CUP events are examples). Frequently the six players consist of three established partnerships, although this is not compulsory.

In mixed team events, it is necessary not only that two of the players be of each sex, but that they play as mixed pairs, no two members of the same sex being permitted to play as partners.

TEAM-OF-EIGHT MATCH. A four-table team contest in which each team has eight active players.

TEAM-OF-FOUR EVENTS. Contests between teams of four, five, and occasionally six players are a standard part of duplicate tournaments at the sectional or higher level. These events are usually conducted according to the SWISS MOVEMENT with IMP scoring. (Board-a-match was the most popular form of scoring prior to the late 1960s.) Occasionally the field is divided into two flights, with master-point requirements of 50, 100, or higher for all team members in the higher flight. At regional tournaments, team contests limited to men, women, or mixed partnerships among the contestants are frequently held in addition to open team events.

Experienced duplicate bridge players generally consider that team-of-four competition is the most challenging and demanding. Most major international matches are at team-of-four competition. Specific conditions of contest vary from tournament to tournament as to type of scoring, number of members on a team (although only four play at any one time), and entry requirements. At sectional tournaments, the team-of-four competition is usually held on Sunday, frequently with limited pair events or individual events scheduled concurrently.

Other types of team-of-four contests have increased in popularity, but are not generally suitable for tournament play at sectional level: (1) KNOCKOUT; (2) DOUBLE ELIMINATION; (3) ROUND ROBIN. See also HYBRID SCORING, IMP SCORING, SWISS MOVEMENTS, TOTAL POINT SCORING.

TEAM-OF-FOUR MOVEMENTS. These are based, for small games, on the movement originated by the American Whist League in the nineteenth century. With an odd number of teams, the movement is completed in one round less than the number of competing teams, and each progression is the same, the boards moving toward the lower numbered tables, and the traveling pairs skipping a table to the next lower number. By omitting middle rounds, this is adaptable to large games by an irregularity in the movement at the midpoint. After half the boards are played, the traveling pairs return the boards just played to their home table, and get their new table assignment for the next round by adding 12 (if twenty-four boards constituted a session, 14 in a

twenty-eight-board session) to their original number, and going to the resultant sum for the next round. (If the sum is greater than the highest numbered table, subtract the number of tables in play from the sum, and progress to that table.)

With an even number of teams in competition, this movement does not provide competition between all teams, and this is compensated for by a phantom table so that one North-South and one East-West pair sit out each round.

To overcome this difficulty, Major C. L. PATTON devised a movement based on the HOWELL schedule, and a relay movement was produced later by Shepard BARCLAY. Both had advantages over the American Whist League movement for even-numbered teams. In the early 1950s, at the suggestion of Richard FREEMAN, the American Whist League movement was modified by two irregularities. After two (or three) fourteen-table rounds, traveling pairs skip an extra table, boards progressing normally; after all but two (or three) rounds, both the traveling pairs skip an extra table, and the boards skip a table. All but one match is completed by the end of the movement, and this last match can be played by relaying new boards as in a head-on match.

In 1963, Lawrence ROSLER devised a two-section team movement (very reminiscent of the Barclay movement of the 1930s). One of its salient features is that discussion of the last set or a glimpse of the next round's boards is not a defect of the movement. Sections of equal size are required. East-West pairs in the two sections interchange; after boards are twinned in the home section, a MITCHELL progression is used in both sections, except that in *one* of the sections, the East-West pairs remain stationary, and the North-South pairs move. This allows both pairs of a team to play a given board on the same round. However, it means that both partnerships of half the teams will be moving pairs, while both pairs of the remaining teams will be stationary.

A modification of the Rosler method called the Mirror Mitchell, which is used in most National Championship board-a-match events, allows each team to have one stationary pair. A regular Mitchell movement is used in one section. In the other sections the boards progress each round to the next lower numbered tables, while the pairs skip one table toward the lower numbered tables.

These movements apply to board-a-match and abbreviated IMP events. See SWISS MOVEMENTS.

TEAM OLYMPIAD. See WORLD TEAM OLYMPIAD.

TEAM-OF TWELVE (or more) MATCH. A team contest in which each team has twelve (or more) active players.

TEAM TRIALS. See INTERNATIONAL OPEN TEAM SELECTION.

TEAMMATES. A term applied to the other members of a team of four (five or six). During the play of an event, the term is usually used to refer to the other pair, rather than including one's partner in the term.

TELEVISION. The importance of bridge players as an audience with high rating has been clearly demonstrated by television. Perhaps the first regular television show featuring bridge was by Robert Lee Johnson in Los Angeles. In a later program in Miami, William Seamon presented challenging pairs who played rubber bridge against the previous week's winners. Much the same format was developed nationally by Charles Goren in his nationally distributed, sponsored program, "Championship Bridge." Another important TV show was headed by Easley Blackwood in Indianapolis, and the first bridge telecast on pay TV was devised by Alfred Sheinwold in Los Angeles in 1964. Many championship bridge events, including the 1957 and 1962 World Championships, have been televised locally, but the first to be shown on a national network were the finals of the Open Pairs event telecast from Los Angeles in the 1963 Summer Nationals.

Closed-circuit television has been an increasingly popular method of complementing and enhancing BRIDGE-O-RAMA or VU-GRAPH presentation of bridge contests. For the first time at a major event, the open room play of the 1967 World Championship final in Miami Beach was telecast to the Bridge-O-Rama audience. Closed-circuit television was also used extensively by the SHARIF BRIDGE CIRCUS to present its exhibition matches, and by the Swedish Bridge League for its coverage of the 1970 World Championship and World Olympiad Pairs in Stockholm.

TEMPO. (1) The element of timing in card play, with especial reference to the use of opportunities to make an attacking lead.

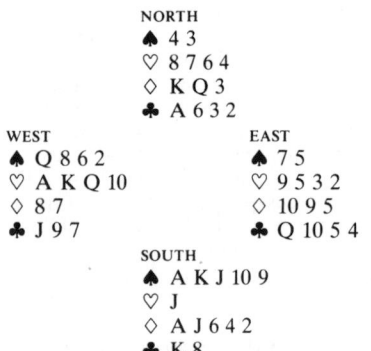

```
                    NORTH
                    ♠ 4 3
                    ♡ 8 7 6 4
                    ◇ K Q 3
                    ♣ A 6 3 2
WEST                                EAST
♠ Q 8 6 2                           ♠ 7 5
♡ A K Q 10                          ♡ 9 5 3 2
◇ 8 7                               ◇ 10 9 5
♣ J 9 7                             ♣ Q 10 5 4
                    SOUTH
                    ♠ A K J 10 9
                    ♡ J
                    ◇ A J 6 4 2
                    ♣ K 8
```

West leads two rounds of hearts against South's four spade contract. South should avoid losing a tempo by cashing the ace and king of spades immediately, and then starting his diamonds. The defenders can score the two remaining trumps but cannot damage the contract. If South loses a tempo by taking a spade finesse, the defense will continue hearts, reducing South's trumps to one fewer than West's. Should South allow this to happen, the defense will score a trick with a long heart, and defeat the contract.

(2) The speed with which a bid or a play is made. Experienced players attempt to adjust the speed of their own bidding and play so as always to use the same tempo, and thus not convey information to partner or to the opponents.

Players sometimes seek to force a rapid tempo of play, hoping to gain an advantage by encouraging an error by the opponents or by obtaining information from the opponents' pauses to think. The best defense against this somewhat unsporting tactic is to refuse to alter the tempo of one's own play, or even to slow the tempo down so as to protect one's partner. The term tempo, however, does not stretch to include deliberate hesitation when in fact a player has no problem.

TEMPORIZING BID. See WAITING BID.

TEN or TEN-SPOT. The fifth ranking card in each suit; at trump it is the lowest ranking honor card.

TEN TABLES. At duplicate, ten tables provide for competition among forty players as individuals, twenty pairs, or ten teams-of-four.

As an individual tournament, the SHOMATE MOVEMENT is at present the only feasible one-session movement available, but the entry of scores, matchpointing, and movement of players are difficult and conducive of hard-to-rectify errors. Try to get four more players, and use the forty-four-player RAINBOW.

As a pair game, it is usually not feasible to play thirty boards because of time limitation. Twenty-four or twenty-seven boards can be played as a MITCHELL MOVEMENT, eight or nine rounds with three boards to a round. After four or five rounds, there is an irregularity in the progression, the traveling pairs skipping a table to the higher numbers instead of going to the next higher numbered table. Boards move normally after all rounds to the next lower numbered tables.

With nine and a half tables, the eight-table game with one and one-half appendix is to be preferred to a Mitchell game with one phantom pair, as the latter method introduces different tops on boards that are played throughout. See NINE TABLES.

With ten and a half tables, the basic ten-table game should be used, and the extra pair given the number 11 and playing North-South, entering the game at table 1 after the first round. Original North-South pair 1 sits out the second round and re-enters (still with the number 1) at table 2 for the third round. See BUMP MITCHELL.

As a team game, the NEW ENGLAND RELAY movement can be used, and eight or nine rounds provide good competition for twenty-four or twenty-seven boards, meeting all teams or all teams except one.

The standard team-of-four progression can be used with two modifications. After the second round, the traveling pairs skip an extra table toward the lower number for their move, while the boards move normally; after the sixth round, both the traveling pairs and the boards skip an extra table toward the lower number. The game terminates after the eighth round, except that each team has not met one other team. If it is desired to complete the game, the traveling pairs move again, as usual skipping a table to the lower number. The omitted match is then set up, and the boards can be removed from tables 6 to 10, and the remaining boards relayed between tables 1 and 6, 2 and 7, 3 and 8, etc.

For an interesting variation for ten tables of pairs, so that all pairs play the same twenty-four boards, see BLACKPOOL MOVEMENT. This is also adaptable to nine and one-half tables.

TENACE. Two cards in the same suit of which one ranks two degrees lower than the other; the *major* tenace is A Q; the *minor* tenace is K J; more broadly, any holding of cards not in sequence in a suit.

TEXAS CONVENTION. A transfer bid, originated independently by David CARTER of St. Louis, Mo., and Olle WILLNER of Stockholm, Sweden. It is used after an opening one no trump or two no trump bid to make the strong hand declarer in a high suit contract. With a hand justifying a game contract, the responder jumps to four hearts holding a six-card or longer spade suit; the opener is required to bid four spades. Similarly, four diamonds requires the opener to bid four hearts.

The convention is usually limited to those sequences in which the responder has a major suit. But four clubs can be used in the same way to show diamonds, and four spades to show clubs.

A South African variation uses four clubs to ask for hearts, and four diamonds to ask for spades. This has a psychological advantage, alerting an absent-minded partner who might otherwise pass a four heart bid that asked for spades, but it has the disadvantage of ruling out the use of the GERBER convention.

As in the case of bidding against JACOBY TRANSFER BIDS, the fourth player can show a two-suited hand by previous partnership agreement. Four no trump would show minor suits; a double would show the suit doubled and the non-touching suit; and a cue-bid in responder's genuine suit would show two suits of the same color (COLORFUL CUE-BID).

THAILAND. See CONTRACT BRIDGE LEAGUE OF THAILAND.

THIN. An adjective used to describe (1) a hand without BODY; "a thin 15-count" indicates a hand with 15 high-card points but lacking intermediates; (2) a makeable game with fewer than 26 HCP between the two hands. Such a game is usually not a PIANOLA.

THIRD (similarly fourth, fifth, sixth, etc.). An adjective, that when used after naming a specific card, counts the number of cards held in the suit.

THIRD BEST. See THIRD HIGHEST LEAD.

THIRD HAND. In the bidding, the partner of the dealer; in the play, the partner of the leader to a trick. For considerations affecting the third hand in the bidding, after two passes, see BORDERLINE OPENING BIDS and PASSED HAND.

THIRD HAND BIDS. See BORDERLINE OPENING BIDS and PASSED HAND.

THIRD HAND PLAY. Correct play by the partner of the opening leader is often the key to successful defense. The old whist rule of "third hand high" is generally right when a small card is led and dummy has low cards.

If dummy has an honor which the third player can beat, he should play his second-highest card if that is a nine or better:

```
                    NORTH
                    Q 7 4
WEST                                    EAST
J 10 6 2                                K 9 3
                    SOUTH
                    A 8 5
```

West leads the two, dummy plays low, and East should play the nine. But if the nine and eight were interchanged, East should play high.

Sometimes the third player cannot afford to make any effort to win the trick:

```
                    NORTH
                    Q 10 2
WEST                                    EAST
J 9 7 3                                 K 6 4
                    SOUTH
                    A 8 5
```

If West leads the three, South plays low from dummy, East must play low. If he plays the king, South makes three easy tricks. After the duck, the third trick remains in contention.

The right play for the third player can depend on entry considerations:

```
                    NORTH
                    Q 7 2
WEST                                    EAST
J 9 5 3                                 K 8 4
                    SOUTH
                    A 10 6
```

If East has no card of entry he should play the eight-spot. (West can then continue the suit safely.) However, if East has the next entry he must play the king. (East can then continue the suit safely.)

The remainder of this article will deal with third hand play against no trump. Some of the suggested plays won't always work, but at least they are food for thought.

```
                    NORTH
                    X X
WEST                                    EAST
J x x x x                               A Q x
                    SOUTH
                    K 10 x
```

East should play the queen to the first trick to prevent South from making a hold-up play. The stronger East's hand the more important it is to play the queen. With no entry of any sort, the ace and then the queen is probably best. Partner can be misled by the play of the queen if he later regains the lead.

As declarer, you expect that a good defender will presumably play the ace and then queen only if he's entryless or if his original holding is AQJ. In the latter case South should win the second trick and block the suit.

A similar situation arises here:

```
                 NORTH
                  x x
WEST                          EAST
Q x x x x                     A J x
                 SOUTH
                 K 10 x
```

If East has a strong hand and a sure entry, it pays to play the jack rather than the ace and then the jack. Again the jack prevents declarer from holding up. If East is weak he should play the ace and then the jack. Partners who have led originally from K 10 x x x seldom appreciate the fine nuances of the jack to the first trick.

Similarly:

```
                 NORTH
                   x
WEST                          EAST
A 9 x x x                     K J x
                 SOUTH
                 Q 10 8 x
```

Here again the jack at trick one may be the only card to defeat the contract. If East's hand is entryless he should play the jack.

If East plays the king and then the jack, East-West can never realize their full potential in the suit. If East has a side entry he should still probably play the jack. Playing the king and then the jack might induce West to think that East has the ten. Indeed, with the K J 10 East would surely play that way.

Here's one where East should purposely fool his partner.

```
                 NORTH
                  x x
WEST                          EAST
A 9 x x x                     Q J 10
                 SOUTH
                  K x x
```

East must play the jack to the first trick rather than the ten. If the ten is played West may think that East has J 10 x, and wait for a lead through. However, when the jack drives out the king, West will know that either declarer has another stopper (K Q 10) and it won't cost to continue, or that partner has the queen and the rest of the tricks belong to the defense.

If you are fortunate or unfortunate enough to have a partner who leads short suits against no trump, you might remember these. Assume you are East and have not bid the suit:

```
                 NORTH
                  8 5 4
WEST                          EAST
3 2                           A K J 10 9
                 SOUTH
                 Q 7 6
```

West leads the three, and if East-West need five tricks, East should play the ace and then the jack. South will surely duck thinking that East has the doubleton. Also:

```
                 NORTH
                  7 6 5
WEST                          EAST
3 2                           A J 10 9 8
                 SOUTH
                 K Q 4
```

Assuming you have divined the situation, you should play the ten to the first trick, and if you regain the lead, try the jack. Again South will probably duck in the hope that the suit is blocked.

When the partner is known to have a four-card suit, and dummy has a doubleton nine, ten or jack, some unusual positions arise. For instance:

```
                 NORTH
                  10 5
WEST                          EAST
K 8 3 2                       A 9 4
                 SOUTH
                 Q J 7 6
```

Assuming dummy plays low, East saves a trick by playing the nine. One could interchange dummy's ten with either the jack or the queen, and the result is the same. It is good to remember this combination because if it comes up and you try the nine, the full position might be:

```
                 NORTH
                  10 5
WEST                          EAST
K Q 8 2                       A 9 4
                 SOUTH
                 J 7 6 3
```

In cases like this it pays to know when your play might have worked. Again in this position East should play his second best:

```
                 NORTH
                   9 2
WEST                          EAST
A 7 4 3                       J 8 5
                 SOUTH
                 K Q 10 6
```

Many tricks are given up by the defenders when third hand fails to play middle in these fairly common situations:

NORTH
10 2

WEST   EAST
K 8 6 4   Q 7 5

SOUTH
A J 9 3

Playing the seven if dummy plays low holds declarer to two tricks; playing the queen automatically gives declarer three. The position would be the same, of course, if North and South exchanged the nine and the ten.

Here are a few more:

NORTH
10 5

WEST   EAST
A 8 4 2   J 7 6

SOUTH
K Q 9 3

NORTH
8 5

WEST   EAST
K 9 4 3   Q 7 2

SOUTH
A J 10 6

In the first case, playing the six to trick one saves a trick, and in the second diagram, East is better off to play the seven. If East plays the seven, the defenders can at least garner two tricks with East needing the lead but once more. If East plays the queen, East will have to regain the lead two more times in order to get his rightful share.

Let's look at a few cases now where partner is likely to have a five-card suit.

NORTH
10 6 3

WEST   EAST
A 9 7 5 4   J 8 2

SOUTH
K Q

It should be fairly obvious that if East plays the jack to the first trick, declarer must make two tricks in the suit.

NORTH
10 5 2

WEST   EAST
Q 9 8 7 3   J 6 4

SOUTH
A K

It makes things much easier for West if he is the first to regain the lead if East plays low to the first trick. If East is the first to get the lead, it may not matter. However, if East plays low and finds the suit to be:

the result is disastrous.

Here is a fairly standard position:

NORTH
10 5 2

WEST   EAST
K Q 9 7 3   J 6 4

SOUTH
A 8

NORTH
10 2

WEST   EAST
A 9 7 4 3   Q 8 5

SOUTH
K J 6

Here East must play the eight or give North-South a trick that they do not deserve.

East also has the RULE OF ELEVEN to help him out. Consider the following layout:

NORTH
◇ 10 4 3

WEST   EAST
◇ A K 9 6 2   ◇ J 8 7

SOUTH
◇ Q 5

Using the rule of eleven, East knows that South has but one card above the six. As it can't be the nine (West would then have A K Q 6), the jack can't possibly be right. In fact, this is the actual hand:

NORTH
♠ x x x x
♡ A K x x
◇ 10 4 3
♣ x x

WEST   EAST
♠ x   ♠ Q J 10 9
♡ x x x   ♡ x x x
◇ A K 9 6 2   ◇ J 8 7
♣ K J x x   ♣ 10 x x

SOUTH
♠ A K x x
♡ Q J x
◇ Q 5
♣ A Q x x

South plays in 3NT and West leads the six of diamonds. Dummy plays low and if East casually plays the jack, there is no further defense.

South plays off his major suit winners ending up in his own hand and eventually exits with a diamond. West is forced to play into South's club tenace.

If East retains the jack, the hand cannot be made.

Any real bridge player would not dream of putting up the jack in the following situation:

```
              NORTH
              10 x x
   WEST                    EAST
   K Q 9 8                 J x x
              SOUTH
              A x x
```

If West leads the eight and dummy goes low the jack just can't be right.

When East has a doubleton picture and dummy the ten, East must ask himself who is more likely to get the next lead. If it is partner, it is usually right to duck if partner leads the seven:

```
              NORTH
              10 x x
   WEST                    EAST
   Q 9 8 7 x               J x
     or
   K 9 8 7 x
              SOUTH
              A K x
                or
              A Q x
```

Once again East does not look so good if West was leading from KQ97x.

Third hand must also consider the possibility of a suit block.

```
              NORTH
              x x
   WEST                    EAST
   A J 9 8                 Q 7 x x x
              SOUTH
              K 10
```

If East plays the queen in the diagram position, he blocks the suit.

Reprinted from an article by Edwin Kantar in the *American Bridge Digest*, August 1963.

THIRD HIGHEST LEAD. The lead of the highest card but two. This is standard when holding three cards headed by an honor. When the suit is longer, the third highest is led as a matter of system by some European players. It may also be used as a deceptive lead. A player who holds 10542 and a weak hand may choose to lead the four followed by the deuce. His purpose is to suggest a five-card suit, in the hope that declarer will make losing avoidance plays which are unnecessary, and which he would not have made if he had known that the opening leader's suit was a four-carder. For third hand play when third highest leads are used, see RULE OF TWELVE. See also THREE SMALL CARDS, LEAD FROM; JOURNALIST LEADS.

THIRD SUIT BID. A bid in a new suit by the opener after a ONE-OVER-ONE or TWO-OVER-ONE RESPONSE. Such bids are non-forcing in standard methods, but there are other treatments: (a) Forcing in KAPLAN-SHEINWOLD if opener bids both minor suits; (b) Forcing in ROTH-STONE after a two-over-one re-

sponse; strong after a one-over-one response and a rebid at the two-level; (c) Forcing in BARON in all situations. See OPENER'S REBID.

THIRTEEN TABLES. At duplicate, thirteen tables provide competition among fifty-two players as individuals, twenty-six pairs, or thirteen teams-of-four. In the development of bridge tournament movements, it was early recognized that thirteen rounds of two boards each, three and a half hours of play approximately, came close to being the ideal game. For this reason, thirteen tables is considered to be the ideal for section size because every player plays each of the boards in play.

Since thirteen is a prime number, the RAINBOW MOVEMENT is practical and is generally used for individual tournaments. This can be cut to eleven or twelve rounds for a shorter game without introducing any complications.

For a pair game, the simple MITCHELL MOVEMENT is used, either straight or scrambled. Playing twenty-six boards, top is 12 and average 156. For a two-session game, the SCRAMBLED MITCHELL is used for the first session and a MCKENNY-BALDWIN MOVEMENT for the second session in which North-South players of the first session meet each other head-on and the East-West original players do likewise.

As a team game, the regular team-of-four progression, boards to the next lower, players skipping a table to lower numbers, the entire game is played without interruption, every team meeting every other team.

For thirteen and a half tables, the ROVER MOVEMENT should be used. For twelve and a half tables, use the thirteen-table setup with any pair as the phantom.

THIRTEENER. The card remaining in a suit when all other cards in that suit have been played on the first three tricks of the suit.

THREAT CARD (or menace). A threat card is a potential winner. It will take a trick provided that the opponent's holding in that suit can be weakened sufficiently.

The term "menace" (or "threat card") may be used in one of the following specialized senses:

(1) Isolated menace: A menace consisting of one card, as the queen in the diagram.

```
              Q
         A         K
              x
```

(2) Two-card menace: A two-card holding, consisting of a winner in the suit accompanied by a menace, as in the diagram.

```
              A J
         K Q       x x
              x
```

(3) Split two-card menace: A two-card menace in

which the winner and the threat card are in opposite hands, as in this diagram:

```
        A x
     K J     x x
        Q x
```

(4) Double menace: A threat card against both opponents (the diagram for a one-card menace, above, shows a double menace).

(5) Extended two-card menace: A two-card menace accompanied by one or more cards in that suit with the property that if the two-card menace is established, then the whole suit will run, e.g.:

```
       A J 10
     K Q     x x x
        x x
```

In this diagram if West discards the queen (or king) he permits South to cash *two* additional tricks in the suit.

(6) Recessed menace: A menace card is accompanied by two (or more) winners in that suit, e.g.:

```
        A K 9
     Q J 10     x x x
         x
```

North's holding is a recessed menace against West.

(7) Twin entry menace: One hand contains a winner and one (or more) small card(s) while the opposite hand holds a winner, a menace, and one (or more) small card(s) in that suit, e.g.:

```
        K x
     Q J x
        A 10 x
```

This suit is a twin-entry menace against West.

THREE or THREE-SPOT. The second-lowest card in a given suit, ranking between the two and the four, sometimes also called "trey."

THREE-BID. See PRE-EMPTIVE BID.

THREE-CARD SUITS, BIDS IN. In many situations the most convenient bid available may be in a three-card suit. Some of the more common examples are:

(1) In opening the bidding. Most frequent is an opening bid of one club, to keep the bidding at a low level and avoid an opening in a poor four-card major suit. Less common is an opening of one diamond with a three-card suit, although this is standard practice with 4–4–3–2 distribution using five-card majors or with three small cards in clubs. Many play that a three-card suit must be no worse than Qxx. Semi-psychic opening bids of one spade with a three-card suit are sometimes made by European players, especially third-hand, non-vulnerable, with a sub-minimum opening. Opening bids in a three-card suit, of any rank, are often required in the ROMAN SYSTEM.

(2) In responding. A response in the lowest

possible suit is sometimes made with a three-card suit, especially if the suit is strong, because no good alternative presents itself:

(a)	(b)	(c)
♠ J x x	♠ A K x	♠ J x x x
♡ x x x	♡ x x	♡ Q x x
◇ A K x	◇ x x x x	◇ Q x x
♣ x x x x	♣ x x x x	♣ A Q x

(a) A response of one diamond to one club is slightly preferable to one no trump or two clubs.
(b) Some experts might choose to respond one spade to one heart, although the orthodox one no trump is, of course, not wrong.
(c) Two clubs would be the expert standard response to one spade. The hand is too strong for two spades, and not strong enough for two no trump or three spades.

(3) In rebidding. See OPENER'S REBID.

(4) In responding to a TAKE-OUT DOUBLE.

See also FOURTH SUIT FORCING AND ARTIFICIAL, FRAGMENT BID, INTEREST-SHOWING BID, TRIAL BID.

THREE CLUB RESPONSE AS MAJOR RAISE. A convention devised by Alvin ROTH to make a strong major suit raise while conserving space for exchange of information as to trump suit texture, singletons, and controls below the game level. Over the three club response, opener rebids three diamonds if he has any singleton; without a singleton he rebids three hearts, three spades or three no trump with two, one, or none of the top three trump honors, respectively. If opener has bid three diamonds, responder can show his own trump texture in the same way. Four-level bids show high card or distributional controls.

THREE CLUB RESPONSE TO ONE NO TRUMP. Used to ask for major suits. A STAYMAN prototype, completely obsolete.

THREE CLUBS STAYMAN. See TWO NO TRUMP OPENING.

THREE-HANDED BRIDGE. Many three-handed versions of bridge have been devised. Apart from TOWIE, described separately, two games deserve consideration.

In the traditional "cutthroat" game, the players bid for a hidden dummy. The bidding continues until a bid, doubled or redoubled, is followed by two passes. The player on declarer's left leads, and the dummy is spread between the two opponents. The scoring is normal, declarer scoring a 700 rubber bonus only if neither defender has a game. Plus scores only are recorded for each player, and settlement is made on the net difference in scores.

An alternative game with a pre-exposed dummy was devised by George S. COFFIN in 1932. It is sometimes called "triangle contract" or "trio bridge." The laws are as follows:

(1) The three players are designated as North, South, and East. North and South *bid* as well as play as partners against East and his exposed dummy.

There is no West player. Nor is there a second dummy, because North and South always play with closed hands, even if one or the other is declarer.

(2) To begin a game, the three players draw cards; the two players who draw the highest cards play as partners as North and South against East, who has the dummy for the entire rubber.

(3) For the first deal only, South shuffles either pack. Then East cuts and South deals while North shuffles the still pack. For the next hand, East cuts and North deals while South shuffles the still pack. Thereafter, North and South continue to deal alternately.

(4) East never deals or shuffles, but always cuts.

(5) Dummy is exposed before there is any bidding. Hence, if any dummy card is faced up during the deal, it is not treated as an exposed card. If a card is turned up in any other hand, there must, of course, be a new deal.

(6) South always calls first regardless of who dealt; North bids second. Dummy never bids, for East bids on the combined 26 East-West cards. If any player makes a bid, the auction continues indefinitely until two consecutive passes close it.

(7) As in four-handed bridge, the left-hand opponent (LHO) of declarer makes the opening lead. If South is declarer, dummy leads first; if North is declarer, East leads; or if East is declarer, South leads.

(8) If the revoke is established against East, he cannot be penalized for it unless South or North has called attention to East's failure to follow suit on the revoke trick. This special rule for three-handed bridge is called "the courtesy of the table," and it is due to the fact that East has no partner to say "having none?" This service is rendered by North and/or South.

(9) Regular contract bridge scoring is used. After the net amount of a finished rubber has been computed, East wins or loses *twice* the net amount because he collects dummy's gain or suffers dummy's loss.

(10) At the end of each rubber, North shifts into the vacant chair on his right and becomes redesignated as South and his former partner as East.

THREE NO TRUMP. The lowest, quantitatively, bid that produces a game from a zero score; nine tricks without benefit of a trump suit.

THREE NO TRUMP OPENING. Traditionally this shows a balanced hand with 25–27 points. But with such hands most experts bid two clubs followed by three no trump and therefore prefer to use the three no trump opening for some other purpose, such as:

(1) GAMBLING THREE NO TRUMP.

(2) Weak minor suit pre-empt, comparable to a standard four club or four diamond opening. This method is useful for those who use FOUR CLUB AND FOUR DIAMOND OPENING TRANSFERS to show strong major suit hands.

(3) Solid major suit pre-empt with no side suit aces and at most one side king. This use, suggested by Edwin KANTAR, is designed to ease responder's task

of judging his side's game or slam prospects. The recommended responses are as follows: four clubs asks opener to bid a side king if he has one; four diamonds transfers to opener's suit; four hearts or four spades indicates that responder wants to be declarer and has tried to guess opener's suit (if he misguesses, opener should correct); four no trump asks about queens; five no trump asks opener to bid a grand slam if he can play opposite a void.

THREE NO TRUMP OVERCALL. An overcall at the game level, usually made on a strong balanced hand or one of a pre-emptive nature.

NORTH	EAST
3 ♠	3 NT

In the above example East's hand might be:

♠ A J 9
♡ K 2
◇ A J 10 6 4
♣ K Q 2

It would be inadvisable for East to double three spades (OPTIONAL) since he has poor support for the "other major." Normally, the double of one major suit invites partner to bid the other if he can. East therefore "gambles" on three no trump. In these awkward situations it is generally a good idea arbitrarily to place 8 points in your partner's hand and proceed accordingly. An opponent's double or raise from partner will clarify the situation.

In many situations the three no trump overcall is gambling and semi-pre-emptive in nature. For example:

SOUTH	WEST
1 ♡	3 NT

or

NORTH	EAST	SOUTH	WEST
1 ♡	Pass	1 ♠	3 NT

In both examples West is trying to "steal" three no trump. His holding might be:

♠ 6
♡ K 5
◇ A K Q 7 6 3 2
♣ 8 7 6

If an opponent doubles, it usually is incumbent upon partner of overcaller to run out into four clubs if he has nothing of great value. A pass by partner would indicate a desire to play three no trump. Note that this bid is usually made when not vulnerable, and partner must exercise good judgment in determining his action, lest a catastrophe develop.

THREE NO TRUMP REBID. See OPENER'S REBID.

THREE NO TRUMP RESPONSE to an opening suit bid of one. There are a number of treatments which can be adopted:

(1) *Standard*. Shows 16–18 points and 4–3–3–3 distribution.

(2) *Limit*. Shows 13–15 points and 4–3–3–3 distribution (ACOL SYSTEM).

(3) *Conventional*. Used with limit raises to show a standard forcing jump raise of 13–15 points when the opening bid was in a major (invented by M. INGBERMAN). For alternative methods of solving this problem see DELAYED GAME RAISE and SWISS CONVENTION.

(4) *Distributional*. Shows a 13–15 point raise with a side suit singleton when the opening bid was in a major (ACES SCIENTIFIC SYSTEM).

(5) *Extra Strong or Distributional*. Shows one of a series of CONGLOMERATE MAJOR RAISES. In response to a one heart opening, three no trump would show 17–18 points. In response to a one spade opening, three no trump would be as in (4) above.

(6) *Ace-asking*. See BABY BLACKWOOD.

(7) *Psychic control*. Showing 23 points or more, and therefore a hand which offers a play for game opposite a psychic opening bid; this assumes a ROTH-STONE psychic with 3–6 points concentrated mainly in the bid suit. If the opening bidder has a normal opening he proceeds to a slam: the combined strength already suggests a grand slam.

THREE-ODD. Three tricks over book, or nine tricks in all.

THREE-QUARTER MOVEMENT. One of a series of pair movements arranged by Sam GOLD of Montreal, Que., for sixteen to twenty-four pairs inclusive. Each of the movements calls for twenty-six boards to be played against each of thirteen opposing pairs. The movement is usually controlled by printed guide cards placed in the center of each table, but may also be controlled by individual guide cards given to each pair.

The games are completed in one session, and all pairs are ranked as one field. The movements provide an approach to balanced comparisons, and are very desirable for clubs wishing to play exactly twenty-six boards, and to produce only one winning pair. The table below gives starting assignments for the first round. Pairs 1 through 13 move cyclically, replacing the lower numbered pair, with pair 1 replacing pair 13, while the boards are moved to the next lower numbered table, and from table 1 to the bye stand. Pairs 14 and higher remain stationary, but ARROW SWITCHES at these tables should be introduced to secure balanced comparisons among these pairs.

		16 Pairs	18 Pairs	20 Pairs
Table	1	16v1 1–2	18v1 1–2	20v1 1–2
	2	4v15 3–4	17v12 3–4	6v19 3–4
	3	11v13 5–6	8v5 5–6	18v8 5–6
	4	14v7 7–8	2v10 7–8	13v17 7–8
	5	10v9 9–10	13v9 9–10	3v7 9–10
	6	5v12 11–12	7v16 11–12	12v16 11–12
	7	3v8 13–14	15v6 13–14	15v2 13–14
	8	2v6 15–16	11v4 15–16	11v5 15–16
	9	Boards on	14v3 17–18	14v10 17–18
	10	bye stand	Boards on	9v4 19–20
	11	17–26	bye stand	Boards on
	12		19–26	bye stand
				21–26

		22 Pairs	24 Pairs
Table	1	7v8 1–2	7v8 1–2
	2	22v1 3–4	22v1 3–4
	3	21v3 5–6	21v3 5–6
	4	20v5 7–8	20v5 7–8
	5	2v19 9–10	2v19 9–10
	6	10v18 11–12	10v18 11–12
	7	12v17 13–14	12v17 13–14
	8	4v16 15–16	4v16 15–16
	9	15v11 17–18	15v11 17–18
	10	13v14 19–20	14v13 19–20
	11	6v9 21–22	6v23 21–22*
	12	Boards on	24v9 21–22*
		bye stand	*Constant
		23–26	relay;
			boards on
			bye stand
			23–26

THREE-QUARTER NO TRUMP. The use of a weak no trump in all situations except vulnerable against non-vulnerable. Players who combine this with a fourth-hand weak no trump at all vulnerabilities (safe because neither opponent can double and dummy must have some values) can be said to play 13/16ths.

THREE SMALL CARDS, LEAD FROM. There are three distinct schools of thought.

(1) *Top of nothing*. The traditional lead of the eight, for example, from 852, is advocated by most textbooks. This has the advantage of advising partner immediately that no high honor is held, but it has some disadvantages. It clarifies the suit distribution for the declarer also; it leads to ambiguity on the second round because partner cannot be sure whether the lead was from three cards or two; and it may waste a significant card, especially if the lead is an unsupported nine. Partners using this treatment must agree which card should be played on the second round of the suit. Most experts believe in following with the middle card, whether leading or following suit. This identifies a doubleton with certainty if the second card is the lowest possible. There is no technical objection to the alternative of following with the lowest card, in which case a doubleton is identified if the second card played is the highest possible.

Whether or not there is any partnership agreement, it is important to play quickly. Hesitation clearly shows the three-card holding, and is unethical.

(2) *Low Lead*. Some experts, mainly of the ROTH-STONE or JOURNALIST persuasion, lead the lowest of three small cards. (In pursuing this principle to the ultimate, Tobias Stone has been known to lead the 8 from 1098.) This avoids the disadvantages of the top of nothing lead, but leaves partner in doubt whether the lead is from an honor. (An obvious exception is the highest card is led in the suit that has been bid by partner and raised by the leader.)

(3) *Mud*. The lead of the middle card, usually to be followed by the top card. The term is derived from the initial letters of middle-up-down, and the lead is used by an increasing minority. It avoids most disadvantages, but may not be as clear to partner as the other methods. A few expert partnerships have no clear-cut agreement, but use the method which

seems best adapted to the particular situation. The top card is led if partner is likely to need to know about honors rather than length. The bottom card is led if length is the vital factor. And the middle card is chosen if it is desired to keep declarer in doubt.

In a no trump contract MUD can help the defense to decide which suit to establish:

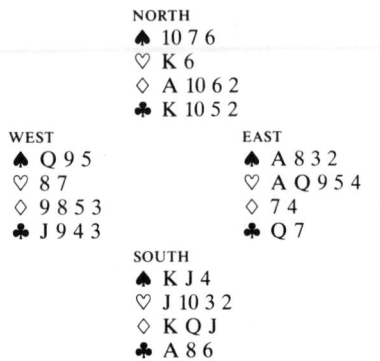

South opened one no trump, and North raised to three no trump. East willed his partner to lead a heart, and West obliged by laying down the eight-spot. East happily played out three rounds of hearts, and that was that. Declarer eventually came to a spade for his ninth trick.

Observe how easy it is to find the correct defense if East-West are playing mud. Since the eight is the highest low card West can hold, East knows immediately that there are only two hearts opposite, and that declarer started with J10xx. Therefore there can be no future in continuing hearts, so, after winning the first trick with the heart queen, East switches to a low spade, and collects three spades and two hearts before declarer can come to nine tricks.

THREE-SUITER. A hand with at least four cards in each of three suits, and therefore distributed 4-4-4-1 or 5-4-4-0. For opening the bidding with a three-suiter see BIDDABLE SUITS, BORDERLINE OPENING BIDS, and CHOICE OF SUIT. For specialized three-suiter conventions see BLUE TEAM TWO DIAMONDS, BROZEL, EXCLUSION BID, KANTAR CUE-BID, PRECISION CLUB (two diamond opening), ROMAN SYSTEM (two club opening), ROMAN TWO DIAMONDS. For systems of showing three-suiters in response to an artificial one club opening, see PRECISION CLUB (Impossible Negative; Unusual Positive), SUPER PRECISION (Super Unusual Positive). For a convention allowing the opening bidder to show a strong three-suiter, see ALLEN OVER TWO CLUBS.

THREE TABLES. At duplicate, three tables provide for competition among twelve (or thirteen) players as individuals, five or six pairs, or three teams-of-four.

As an individual tournament, eleven rounds are required for twelve players, twelve for thirteen players. Conduct of such a game is described under INDIVIDUAL MOVEMENT for twelve or thirteen players.

As a pair contest, the HOWELL MOVEMENT is far superior to the MITCHELL, as it provides that each pair of players will meet with each other pair as opponents. For the three-table Howell setup, see Howell Movement. If there are five pairs, pair 6 should be the phantom, and the other pairs sit out the round corresponding with their number.

A three-team round robin can be successfully conducted in two halves, using three sets of boards. Half of each team remains North-South in both halves. Setup of boards and players is as follows:

1st half Table	1 NS1 vs. EW2 first set of boards	
	2 NS2 vs. EW3 second set of boards	
	3 NS3 vs. EW1 third set of boards	
2nd half Table	1 NS1 vs. EW3 third set of boards	
	2 NS2 vs. EW1 first set of boards	
	3 NS3 vs. EW2 second set of boards	

Team 1 has met team 2 on the first set of boards and team 3 on the third set of boards, completing their two matches; and the match between teams 2 and 3 was completed on the second set of boards. Board-a-match scoring is possible, as is total point or International Match-Point scoring. If each team wins and loses one match, a winner can be determined by total boards won in both matches for BOARD-A-MATCH SCORING; total points in aggregate SCORING; or ratio of points won to points lost in IMP SCORING. See QUOTIENT.

For seven pairs (three and one-half tables) see FOUR TABLES.

THREE–TWO–ONE–ONE-HALF COUNTS. See FOUR ACES SYSTEM.

THROUGH STRENGTH. The old whist idea that one should lead "through strength" is one of the least valuable bridge rules of thumb. The implication is that the player on declarer's left should generally lead a suit in which dummy is strong.

In many situations it is much safer to lead a suit in which dummy is weak than a suit in which dummy is strong. The defender must consider carefully before leading away from an honor, just as he would in making an opening lead. To lead a suit with no card above the ten rarely costs a trick, although it may avoid a guess for the declarer.

Some situations need little discussion. If dummy has A K x, for example, a lead from a queen is dangerous, and other leads are safe or almost safe. The following examples deal with more difficult cases. In each case dummy is shown with three cards: the danger or lack of it is little affected if dummy has an extra small card.

(1) Dummy has A x x. A lead from a jack is relatively safe. A lead from the queen is more dangerous. A lead from the king worst of all.

(2) Dummy has A Q x or A J x. A lead from the king is again very dangerous. A lead from the jack (or queen) is less dangerous. From a holding headed by K J or K 10, the second honor should be led.

(3) Dummy has K Q x. A lead from the jack is dangerous. A lead from the ace is relatively safe.

(4) Dummy has K J x. A lead from the ace is safe. A lead from the queen is dangerous. However, this consideration may cause declarer to misguess if he holds a doubleton, and a lead is made from the queen.

(5) Dummy has K x x. All leads from single honors (except the ten) are bad. Worst is from the queen; least bad is from the ace.

(6) Dummy has Q x x. The lead from the king is now safest, and the lead from the ace is worst.

(7) Dummy has J x x. The lead from the ace is worst. It is better to lead from the queen than from the king.

(8) Dummy has x x x. In this case, the lower the honor to be led from, the safer the lead. Leading from the jack is almost completely safe, and leading from the queen costs only if declarer has A K J. The lead "through weakness" is usually safer than a lead "through strength."

For the converse situation, see UP TO WEAKNESS, under which heading a general principle covering the above situations is set out.

THROW AWAY. (1) To discard. (2) To defend or play so badly that a very poor score results.

THROW IN. (1) To make a THROW-IN PLAY. (2) To toss the cards into the center of the table, after four passes. Used in Great Britain as a synonym for PASS OUT.

THROW-IN PLAYS. The term "end play" originally referred to techniques applied during the last three or four tricks of a deal. Now an end play may be said to occur at any stage of the play provided that it involves a squeeze, a trump coup, or a throw-in. Loosely applied, end play is used incorrectly as a synonym for throw-in. In a throw-in play, an opponent gains the lead, but it costs him a trick (or more) to do so. There are three types of throw-in, according to the means whereby the opponent thrown in loses a trick.

(1) Tenace Throw-in (usually shortened to "throw-in"). An opponent is thrown in and forced to lead from a broken honor holding at the cost of a trick.

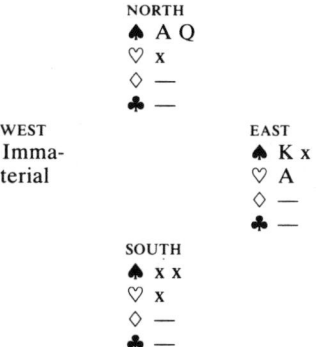

South has placed East with the king of spades. In order to avoid a losing finesse, a heart is led and East

is forced into the lead. He must lead into North's spade tenace.

(2) Trump Throw-in (also known as an "elimination play"). An opponent is thrown in and forced to concede a ruff and discard.

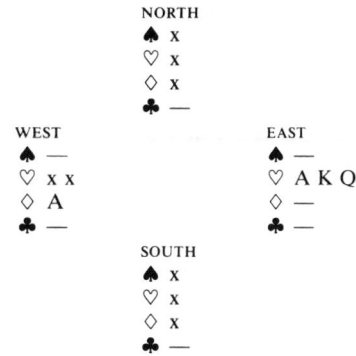

Spades are trumps, and South apparently has two unavoidable losers in hearts and diamonds. However, a heart is led, which forces East into the lead. He must continue a heart, permitting South to discard the losing diamond while ruffing the heart in the dummy.

The distinction between these two types of throw-in does not rest on the contract, trump or no trump, but on the mechanism involved. Both types may occur at a trump contract. At a trump contract, the opponent who is thrown in may be faced with a choice of plays, each of which costs a trick; thus the various categories of throw-in may overlap.

(3) Entry Throw-in. The opponent who gains the lead must play a suit in which declarer has established tricks to which there is no entry.

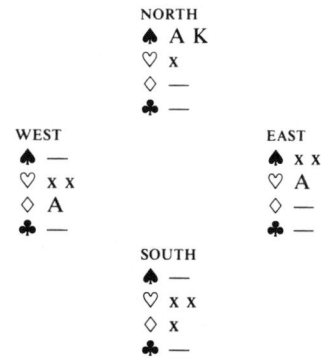

South has the lead in a no trump contract. North's two spade tricks are inaccessible. However, a heart lead saddles East with the necessity of leading a spade to the next trick, providing the entry to dummy's hand.

Proper execution of a throw-in play requires declarer to consider two questions: (a) the stripping, or elimination, process: this means that declarer must assure himself that, once thrown in, the defender has no safe lead; and (b) the throw-in card: at the judicious moment, declarer must be able to lose the lead to that opponent whose hand has been stripped of safe exit cards.

Declarer may strip an opponent's hand by plain suit leads, by ruffing, or by a preliminary squeeze (see SECONDARY SQUEEZE, SQUEEZE THROW-IN). Sometimes a perfect elimination is not possible, and declarer must hope for favorable distribution.

```
                NORTH
                ♠ Q x x x
                ♡ K x x
                ◇ A x x
                ♣ K x x
WEST                        EAST
♠ K J                       Imma-
♡ x x                       terial
◇ K J x x x
♣ Q J 10 x
                SOUTH
                ♠ A 10 x x x x
                ♡ A x x
                ◇ Q x
                ♣ A x
```

South has become declarer at a five spade contract reached by trying for a slam. A club was led by West, won by the ace. The ace of spades was cashed, followed by a club to the king and ruffing a third club (stripping both hands of clubs). Two top hearts were played, declarer hoping to strip West of exit cards in that suit, followed by a spade, throwing West into the lead. Since West in fact had no more hearts, his choice was between a club or diamond, either of which would forfeit a trick.

Certain suit combinations lend themselves to a throw-in. In the following combinations, the throw-in card is in the critical suit, which the defenders must return at the cost of a trick:

A Q 9   A J 10   K 10 x   Q J x   K 9 x   A 10 x
x x x   x x x   x x x   x x x   J x x   J 9 x

In each case, South leads low, and then simply covers the card played by West. Provided East has been stripped of all other exit cards, he will have to return this suit; in this way declarer can hold his losses in the suit to a minimum.

There are other combinations in which an extra trick is guaranteed, provided the opponents must open up the suit. The throw-in card must be in some other suit.

A 10 x   K x x   K 9 x   Q x x
J x x   x x x   Q 10 x   J x x

Finally, there are certain combinations in which declarer's prospects are improved if the opponents can be forced to lead the suit. Again, the throw-in card must be in some other suit:

A 10 x   A x   A x x
K 9 x   Q x   J 9 x

There are many suit combinations which can provide the means for a throw-in play. The most common is an eight-card holding. missing the king and queen, A x x opposite J x x x x. Declarer leads the ace, and then plays a small card in the suit after the elimination is complete. If either player holds K Q of that suit, he can be thrown in; even if he holds K x or Q x, he may neglect to unblock, or else it may cost him a trick to do so.

Many throw-in plays are named after the means employed to strip the hand or throw-in the opponents. One such would be a crossruff strip, and another a loser-on-loser elimination. The latter is a commonly available maneuver, although it is often missed in practice.

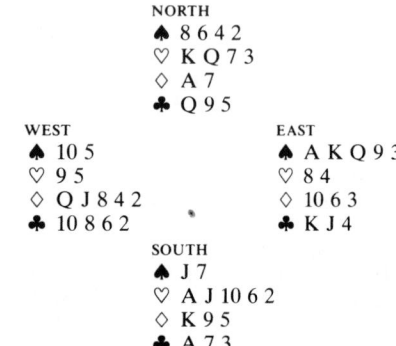

```
                NORTH
                ♠ 8 6 4 2
                ♡ K Q 7 3
                ◇ A 7
                ♣ Q 9 5
WEST                        EAST
♠ 10 5                      ♠ A K Q 9 3
♡ 9 5                       ♡ 8 4
◇ Q J 8 4 2                 ◇ 10 6 3
♣ 10 8 6 2                  ♣ K J 4
                SOUTH
                ♠ J 7
                ♡ A J 10 6 2
                ◇ K 9 5
                ♣ A 7 3
```

After East opened the bidding with one spade, South became the declarer at four hearts. Spades are led and declarer ruffs high on the third round. Placing East with the club king for his opening bid, South draws trumps in two rounds, plays the ace and king of diamonds, followed by a diamond ruff, ending in dummy. So dummy's last spade is led, on which South discards a losing club, throwing East into the lead. East must concede a ruff and sluff, or lead from his club tenace.

The throw-in usually follows the elimination, but this is not invariably the case.

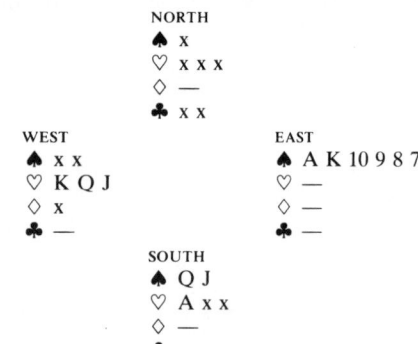

```
                NORTH
                ♠ x
                ♡ x x x
                ◇ —
                ♣ x x
WEST                        EAST
♠ x x                       ♠ A K 10 9 8 7
♡ K Q J                     ♡ —
◇ x                         ◇ —
♣ —                         ♣ —
                SOUTH
                ♠ Q J
                ♡ A x x
                ◇ —
                ♣ x
```

Clubs are trumps and South requires four of the remaining tricks, with only three in sight. A spade is led, won by East. On the spade continuation, North discards a heart. On the next spade, North discards another heart, while South ruffs. South can now lead the ace of hearts and win both of dummy's trumps for three more tricks.

In a double elimination, either opponent may win the throw-in card, but the declarer gains a trick in either case.

(4) Double Elimination.

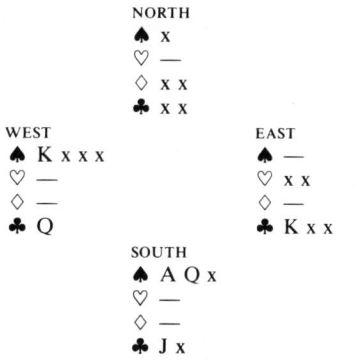

Diamonds are trumps, and South requires four of the remaining tricks. A club is led which may be won by either opponent. If West's queen holds, he must lead into South's spade tenace; if East overtakes with the king of clubs, South's jack is established.

There are certain rare positions in which the declarer can bring off a repeating elimination, in which the same defender can be thrown in several times to make a losing lead.

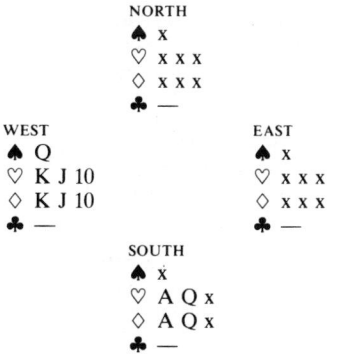

Spades are trump. South leads a spade and West is thrown in. Whatever card he returns, South wins two tricks in that suit and throws West in again with the third round of the suit. West must now give declarer two tricks in the second suit. South, starting with two tricks, ends up with four.

(5) Pseudo Elimination. A defender may believe that he has been thrown in and must concede a trick, although this may not be the case. Usually this occurs

when the defender fears to give declarer a ruff and sluff. This may not benefit declarer for either of two reasons: he may have concealed another card of that suit in his hand, or else the ruff and discard permits declarer to discard a card which was not a loser in any case.

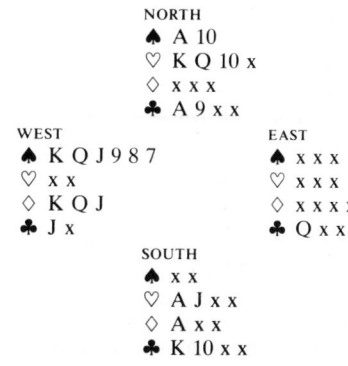

South is declarer at five hearts. A spade is led, won by the ace. Trumps are drawn, the ace of diamonds is taken, and the suit continued. West wins two diamonds and a spade. The only correct defense is a spade continuation, although South can discard a club in one hand while ruffiing the spade in the other. South still has a club loser. However, if West is reluctant to give the sluff and ruff, he will lead a club, permitting South to avoid a loser in that suit.

(6) Defense Against a Throw-in. Often the defenders can foresee an impending throw-in. They have several ways of escaping the end play.

(a) By retaining an Exit Card.

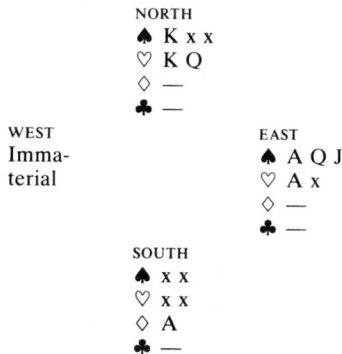

At no trump, South leads the ace of diamonds, throwing a spade from the North hand. East must discard a spade, not the small heart. If he discards the small heart, South can throw him in the lead with a heart, and East is forced to lead the spade. If he holds the small heart, he can exit with it after winning the ace of hearts, forcing the spade lead to come to him from North.

(b) By Unblocking.

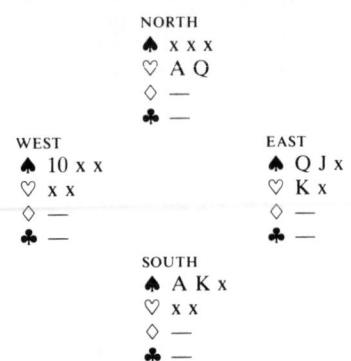

NORTH
♠ x x x
♡ A Q
♢ —
♣ —

WEST
♠ 10 x x
♡ x x
♢ —
♣ —

EAST
♠ Q J x
♡ K x
♢ —
♣ —

SOUTH
♠ A K x
♡ x x
♢ —
♣ —

South cashes the ace and king of spades, on which East must unblock by playing his honors, so that West can win the third round of spades with the ten, returning a heart, to ensure a trick for East's king.

(c) By Playing Second Hand High.

NORTH
A Q 8

WEST
10 x x

EAST
K J 9

SOUTH
x x x

South leads small, intending to insert the eight. East can win with the nine, but then must lead into North's tenace. When South plays small, West must rise with the ten to protect his partner from the end play.

(d) By Refusing to Assist in the Elimination.

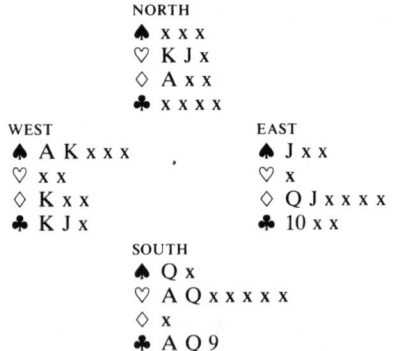

NORTH
♠ x x x
♡ K J x
♢ A x x
♣ x x x x

WEST
♠ A K x x x
♡ x x
♢ K x x
♣ K J x

EAST
♠ J x x
♡ x
♢ Q J x x x x
♣ 10 x x

SOUTH
♠ Q x
♡ A Q x x x x x
♢ x
♣ A Q 9

After West opened one spade, South became the declarer at four hearts. West took two top spades. West must switch to hearts or diamonds. South does not have enough entries to dummy to ruff out spades and diamonds to strip the West hand before leading a club. See also PARTIAL ELIMINATION.

M. I.

THROWING THE LEAD (into a desired defender's hand). See THROW-IN PLAYS.

TICKETS. A colloquialism used in various ways to refer to (1) pick-up slips, (2) private score cards, or (3) the right high cards for a particular action—"He had the tickets."

TIERCE. A term, obsolete in bridge, used to describe a sequence of three cards, one or more of which usually has honor rank.

TIES. The equality of scores in a session or event of bridge competition.

TIGHT. A colloquialism for SINGLETON, particularly in describing a singleton major honor. STIFF is also used.

TIME LIMIT ON RIGHT TO PLAY. This is usually at the discretion of the director. In some tournaments the sponsoring organization sets a deadline beyond which purchase of additional entries depends on the need to fill in sections. In second and later sessions of multi-session events, the director must seek substitutes for pairs who are late to report. If the qualified players do not appear within ten minutes of the scheduled time, their right to play is canceled, although usually they are permitted to enter subsidiary events if they have not gone into their second round. For other time limits, see SLOW PLAY.

TIME VALUATION. See TEMPO.

TIMING. An element in the play of a hand. The order in which trumps are pulled, losers are trumped, and side suits are developed are elements that enter into both declarer's and defenders' play. TEMPO is a synonym.

TOP. (1) On a board: the best score made in the play of a particular hand in a duplicate tournament; its value in match-point play is one less than the number of times the board was in competition. If one pair earns a top, their opponents must score zero points or a bottom. (2) Score: the best score for a session of play among the contestants in direct competition. (3) A card: to play a card higher in rank than the ones previously played by the second or third player to play to the trick.

TOP AND BOTTOM CUE-BID. An immediate overcall in the opponent's major suit to show the highest and lowest ranking unbid suits. See also MICHAELS CUE-BID.

TOP OF INTERIOR SEQUENCE. See INTERIOR SEQUENCE.

TOP OF NOTHING. See THREE SMALL CARDS, LEAD FROM.

TOP SCORE. The highest number of match points available to any contestant in direct competition. See MATCH POINT; SCORING ACROSS THE FIELD. Usually this is one less than the number of pairs in direct competition, although there are various other methods in use, as well as several methods of providing direct comparisons. In England, it is customary to make the top score double the above number (with thirteen pairs in direct competition, 24 is top) because this eliminates the need for half-points. Four pairs tied for top would score 10½ match points in the United States but 21 by the double top method. The top score is frequently 25 by scoring sections in pairs, bringing 26 pairs into direct competition (the selection of sections to be paired being arbitrary and based on the arrangement of the room, crossover, etc.). In Europe it is common to use much higher top scores, comparing across all sections in play, 77 points for top when six sections are duplicated, and even higher tops in some of the very large events.

TORINO BULL. The trophy for the World Women's Team Olympiad, presented by the City of Turin, Italy, on the occasion of the 1960 Olympiad. See WORLD CHAMPIONSHIPS for winners.

TOTAL POINT SCORING. Computation of scores based on points earned minus points lost, from the scoring table of contract bridge (see LAWS OF CONTRACT BRIDGE (Law 84), LAWS OF DUPLICATE (Law 73)); the scoring used at rubber bridge or Chicago.

As a form of scoring in pair tournaments, total point scoring was complicated by the imposition of PENALTY LIMITS and the resulting EXCESS POINTS. It has been almost wholly eliminated, generally in favor of MATCH-POINT SCORING, but occasionally, in important matches, by IMPS FOR PAIR GAMES or scoring by VICTORY POINTS.

As a form of scoring in team games, it is adaptable particularly for match play in head-on contests. IMP scoring has largely replaced total point scoring. The REISINGER TROPHY knockout teams in the EASTERN STATES REGIONAL was the last important knockout event to replace total point scoring with IMP scoring, doing so in 1965.

TOTAL SCORE. See TOTAL POINT SCORING.

TOTAL TRICKS, RULE OF. See RULE OF TOTAL TRICKS.

TOUCHING CARDS. (1) Cards that are in sequence in the same suit, as the ten and nine in a holding of king, ten, nine, six. See SEQUENCE and PLAY FROM EQUALS. (2) With fingers: in duplicate bridge, it is illegal for any player to touch any cards other than his own, unless he is arranging the dummy's cards and so declares. See LAWS OF CONTRACT BRIDGE (Law 7).

TOUCHING HONORS. A holding of two or more honors that are in sequence. In a holding of queen, jack, ten, and seven of a suit, the first three are touching honors.

TOUCHING SUITS. Suits that, within the order of ranking, are next to each other; spades and hearts, hearts and diamonds, and diamonds and clubs are touching suits. For some purposes, such as selecting the suit for an opening bid, clubs and spades are regarded as touching, with the clubs the "higher" suit.

TOURNAMENT. In the days of WHIST, gatherings of players for the purpose of competing at the game were termed "congresses." As auction bridge replaced whist, the term "congress" gave way to tournament, as the accent shifted from sociability to competition. Club games among local groups up to competition at national and international level are all so described.

The essentials of a tournament are the planning thereof by a SPONSORING ORGANIZATION, publicity and promotion, the programming of events, the competition itself, the SCORING and determination of winners, and the HOSPITALITY in connection therewith. Various aspects of tournament play and references to the results of important tournaments are treated in special articles in this book. See DUPLICATE BRIDGE and CHAMPIONSHIP TOURNAMENTS.

TOURNAMENT COMMITTEE. See COMMITTEE.

TOURNAMENT DIRECTOR. The official representative of the sponsoring organization, responsible for the technical management of the tournament, subject to the LAWS OF DUPLICATE and to supplementary regulations announced by the sponsor.*

Classification of Directors. Tournament directors are trained by the ACBL and ranked according to ability and experience, determining the kind of event each is qualified to direct. Exclusive of Local and Club directors authorized to conduct games at affiliated Duplicate CLUBS, in 1975 there were 223 such tournament directors of sectional rank or higher. In the following classifications, the figures in parentheses are the number qualified in that group as of 1975.

National directors (14). Full-time salaried employees of the ACBL, qualified to provide top-flight direction at International, National, and Regional Tournaments. When schedules permit, their services are also available as chief directors of Sectional tournaments, ensuring smooth conduct of these events as well as trained supervision of other directors on the staff.

Associate National directors (13): Although not usually full-time salaried ACBL employees, the members of this group are fully qualified to serve as chief directors at Regional and Sectional events.

Regional directors (86): Ranked at four levels, from R–1 through (highest) R–4 and certified as proficient in all aspects of tournament management. Qualified for assignment as director-in-charge for Sectional tournaments, as well as for staff service at Regional and National events.

Sectional directors (110): Certified by ACBL as fully qualified to assist a senior director at Sectional and higher-rated tournaments. Ranked S–1 through (highest) S–4.

Local directors: Recognized by the ACBL as qualified to assist higher-rated directors at Sectional tournaments in their home areas.

Trainee directors: Sponsoring Units may assign to their tournaments individuals as yet unrated directors/scorers for practice and training by the assigned

---

* Note: Throughout this book, "Director," when capitalized, refers to a member of the Board of Directors of a governing body, and not to a tournament director.

qualified director(s), who will give such trainees all possible assistance and instruction. Although they may be paid a small session fee, such trainees are not counted as members of the required professional staff. A trainee may work a maximum of eight sessions in that status. Thereafter, unless his work meets standards that would qualify him for rating as a local director, he may not be engaged as a professional assistant for further tournaments.

Scorer: If the director (or any assistant) has more than one score sheet to total at the end of a session, he is authorized to assign one competent scorer to match-point and total each extra sheet. This work is usually performed by one or more of the contestants after the game. No certification is required, but the director should select the best qualified individuals available.

Tournament directors listed by the ACBL in 1975 in its two top categories are:

NATIONAL TOURNAMENT DIRECTORS

Bill Adams	John Harris
Maury Braunstein	Jack Hudgins
Sid Davidson	Karl Johnson
Robert Dischner	Jerome Machlin
Michael Goldstein	Philip Merry
Harry Goldwater	John Wiser
John Hamilton	Phil Wood

ASSOCIATE NATIONAL TOURNAMENT DIRECTORS

George Cartwright	Nelson Rowe
Harry Clark	Paul Stehly
Esther DeRaad	Ken Stone
E. C. Donaghy	Stan Tench
Max Hardy	William Weyant
Michael Linah	Walter Wilson
Robert Roth	

TOWIE. A form of bridge devised for three players but intended to be played usually by four, five or more players, of whom only three play at one time but the others participate in the defenders' score against the declarer. The game originated in Paris in 1931, and was also much played in Rome in 1932; the originators were two Americans, J. Leonard Replogle and Paulding Fosdick, who were then living abroad. In 1935 Replogle with the assistance of W. Huske sought to make towie a popular game in the United States, with only moderate success, though it is still played. The principal books on the game were written by Huske and by Stuyvesant Wainwright, Jr.

The deal in towie conforms to that of certain earlier three-hand bridge games: After dealing four hands, the dealer turns up six cards of the dummy, after which the auction proceeds as in any three-handed game. Scoring is based on the 1932 INTERNATIONAL CODE, which differs from later codes in undertrick penalties and in the fact that no trump tricks count 35 each.

The three active players bid for the dummy. The high bidder becomes declarer. If he fulfills his contract, he collects from every other player, active or inactive; if he loses, he pays every such player. Ultimate settlement is made on the difference in scores. After each deal, one player is replaced by an inactive player, in order of precedence except that a player who is not vulnerable takes precedence over a vulnerable player.

If a game contract is not reached, the hands are thrown in, and a GOULASH follows. Scoring varies from 1963 contract bridge in the following respects: (1) a player scoring his first game gets a bonus of 500, and a rubber bonus of 1,000 goes to the first player to win two games. (2) In the trick-score, no trump counts 35 points per trick. (3) Undoubled overtricks are worth 50 each. (4) The bonus for making a doubled contract is 100 if vulnerable. (5) Penalties for doubled undertricks non-vulnerable total 100 for a one-trick defeat, 200 for a two-trick defeat, 400, 600, 1,000, 1,400, etc.; for undoubled undertricks vulnerable similarly total 100, 300, 500, etc.; for doubled undertricks vulnerable total 200, 600, 1,000, etc.

TRAIN BRIDGE. See COMMUTER BRIDGE.

TRANCE. A protracted break in the tempo of the play, in which a player attempts to solve a problem. Trances and huddles are frequent causes of ethical difficulties and disputes. See HUDDLE and SLOW PLAY.

TRANSFER BIDS. Bids aimed principally at making a strong hand declarer. It is often advantageous for the lead to come up to the stronger hand, and for it to remain concealed.

Transfer bids were first used in the United States by David CARTER (see TEXAS CONVENTION) and subsequently developed by Oswald JACOBY (see JACOBY TRANSFER BIDS). These bids were independently devised by Olle WILLNER of Stockholm, Sweden, who discussed the use of transfers in a series of articles in *Bridge Tidningen* in 1953–54.

The original form of transfer bid was the TEXAS convention, and SOUTH AFRICAN TEXAS is a revised form. See also French RELAY SYSTEM, SOUTH AFRICAN TEXAS.

Another purpose of transfer bids is to distinguish between weak and strong opening pre-empts, to enable responder to judge whether to try for slam. See FOUR CLUB AND FOUR DIAMOND OPENING TRANSFERS; FOUR NO TRUMP OPENING AS MINOR PRE-EMPT; RUBIN TRANSFERS.

TRANSFER OPENING PRE-EMPTS. See FOUR CLUB AND FOUR DIAMOND OPENING TRANSFERS; FOUR NO TRUMP OPENING PRE-EMPT; RUBIN TRANSFERS; TRANSFER OPENING THREE-BIDS.

TRANSFER OPENING THREE-BIDS. A development of the TEXAS principle. They have three technical advantages. First, the lead comes up to the hand which is likely to be strong in the side suits. Second, the defense is more difficult because little is known about the declarer's strength and distribution. Third, the opening bidder may be able to show a freak two-suited hand by bidding his second suit on the second round.

A technical disadvantage is that it is easier for the opponents to take action than it would be after a normal three-bid: a double and a cue-bid in the opener's genuine suit are available as take-out bids of varying strength. Also, a pre-emptive bid in clubs cannot be made at the level of three.

A practical disadvantage is that an absentminded partner may forget that the convention is being used. Also, it may gain an unfair advantage against opponents unfamiliar with the convention.

Used in the World Championship by Ghestem-Bacherich. Barred by the ACBL for tournament use.

TRANSFER SQUEEZE. A squeeze play which results from TRANSFERRING THE MENACE. The following hand was played by Alan Truscott in the 1958 European Championships:

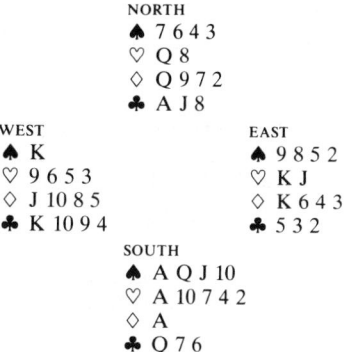

```
                  NORTH
                  ♠ 7 6 4 3
                  ♡ Q 8
                  ◇ Q 9 7 2
                  ♣ A J 8
   WEST                        EAST
   ♠ K                         ♠ 9 8 5 2
   ♡ 9 6 5 3                   ♡ K J
   ◇ J 10 8 5                  ◇ K 6 4 3
   ♣ K 10 9 4                  ♣ 5 3 2
                  SOUTH
                  ♠ A Q J 10
                  ♡ A 10 7 4 2
                  ◇ A
                  ♣ Q 7 6
```

West led the diamond jack against four spades, which was ducked around to the ace. A heart to the queen and king brought a spade return, and the finesse of the queen lost to the king. A heart was returned and won by South, who led a second round of trumps, revealing the bad split. A low heart was ruffed and overruffed, and East exited with his last trump. The jack of clubs was finessed, and the diamond queen was led to transfer the diamond menace. East covered, South ruffed, and two winning hearts squeezed West in the minor suits.

TRANSFERRED TRICK. A trick transferred to the non-offending side after a revoke has been established. See LAWS OF DUPLICATE (Law 64).

TRANSFERRING THE MENACE. The process whereby control of a suit is transferred from one opponent to the other.

```
                  NORTH
                  ♠ Q 10
                  ♡ A J
                  ◇ —
                  ♣ —
   WEST                        EAST
   ♠ J x                       ♠ K x x
   ♡ K Q                       ♡ x
   ◇ —                         ◇ —
   ♣ —                         ♣ —
                  SOUTH
                  ♠ A x
                  ♡ x
                  ◇ —
                  ♣ A
```

South has menaces in two suits, so that the material for a squeeze is present, but each opponent controls one menace, and neither can be squeezed. If the lead is in the North hand, the queen of spades is led forcing East to play the king which is taken by the ace. The spade menace is no longer the queen guarded by East's king but the ten guarded by West's jack, so that West has BUSY CARDS in two suits, and he is squeezed by the lead of the ace of clubs. But if the lead had been in the South hand, the lead of the club ace would have effected a GUARD SQUEEZE against West.

M. I.

TRANSFORMATION CARDS. These are specially designed packs whose faces include the various pips on the suit cards as part of an overall design.

During the last century, a number of artists tried their hands at creating pictures that would incorporate all of the pips, in their usual locations, into larger designs, generally of human or animal figures.

The first such cards seem to have been made by J. G. Cotta, in Tübingen, Germany, in 1805, with several different packs produced by him in the next few years. English transformation cards appeared first in Ackerman's *Repository* in 1818, and several other packs soon followed.

About 1850, sets of cards appeared in London, New York, Munich, Vienna, and Paris, partially duplicates in design, some cards being different while others appear in three or four of the packs. Because of the widespread copying, it is difficult to know which versions were original. Grimaud and Hart put their names on packs, and some artists' initials can be found, but precise dating appears impossible.

Issued in New York were the Eclipse Comic cards, designed by F. H. Lowerre in 1876. Tiffany & Company issued their Harlequin cards three years later; these same designs were used for the first series of Kinney Brothers Cigarette cards. A second Kinney series followed with all new designs. In 1895, the United States Playing Card Company published its own packs, called "Hustling Joe" and Vanity Fair."

A. F.

TRAP BID (or trap bidding). An inconsistent sequence of bids which traps partner by showing strength denied by an earlier bid.

For example:

SOUTH	NORTH
1 ♣	1 ♠
3 ♠	4 ♠
5 ♡	

South's raise to three spades was encouraging but non-forcing. North accepted the invitation to bid game, perhaps straining his values to do so, and is now faced by a slam invitation.

South's bidding cannot be correct. If he is strong enough to bid five hearts, he must have been too strong to make the invitational bid of three spades. His bidding means that his side must play below game or above game, but cannot stop in four spades. See also IMPOSSIBLE BID and PRESSURE BID.

TRAP PASS. A pass by a player holding a strong defensive hand, hoping that the opposition will bid themselves into difficulties. It is usually made by a player holding length and strength in the suit bid by the opener on his right:

     ♠ 6
     ♡ A Q 10 7 4
     ◇ K J 7
     ♣ A K 5 3

If the right-hand opponent opens the bidding with one heart, there is no good alternative to a pass. There is strong evidence that the hand is a misfit, and that it will pay to defend. If one heart is passed out, the result should be reasonable.

The same principle applies, only less forcefully, in a balancing position. A player with the above hand may consider passing if an opening bid of one heart is followed by two passes. This would certainly be sound tactics at match-point scoring against vulnerable opponents, as a score of 200 for the defense would beat all part-score results.

A trap pass becomes a doubtful proposition when holding 18 or 19 high-card points, and is usually unwise with 20 or more. The danger of passing up a game in favor of a small penalty becomes too great.

Passes with strong hands by the player on dealer's right after an opening suit bid and a suit response are similar in principle, although the motive is slightly different: the prospect of a penalty is reduced, but the danger of taking action is greater. With a hand of exceptional strength, the fourth player should not necessarily rely on the fact that responder's bid is technically forcing. It is not at all unlikely that the dealer has made a psychic bid, and if he passes, the other defender cannot be expected to balance with a very weak hand.

An unusual, and experimental, type of trap pass may sometimes be ventured by the partner of the opening bidder:

     ♠ 6
     ♡ K 8 5 3
     ◇ A J 4 2
     ♣ Q 10 5 4

If partner opens one spade and the next player passes, there is something to be said for a prompt pass if not vulnerable against vulnerable opponents. There is no certainty of a game, and if one spade is passed out the loss is unlikely to exceed 300. On the other hand, the fourth player may balance, in which case the penalty should not be less than 500 and might be 1,400. Such experiments should not be tried in match-pointed events (except when SHOOTING). See also MARMIC SYSTEM.

TRAP PLAY. See DECEPTIVE PLAY.

TRAVELING SCORE SLIP. The official score of each deal in a pair duplicate game may be recorded either of two ways: on a traveling score-slip or an individual pick-up card.

A majority of clubs and lesser championship events use the *traveling score-slip*. This slip travels with the board, folded and inserted in a pocket so that the scores for the tables which have played it earlier are not visible until the slip is opened after the board has been replayed. The score at the new table is then entered.

At the end of the session, when the board has been played at each table in the game, all the results will have been entered on the slip. The tournament director will then work out the match points as shown here:

OFFICIAL A.C.B.L. TRAVELING SCORE (Mitchell or Howell) NORTH PLAYER only keeps score							
ENTER PAIR NO. OF E-W PAIR Board No. 9							
N-S Pair	CON-TRACT	BY			NORTH-SOUTH Net Plus	Net Minus	E-W Pair	Match Points
1	4 S	N	5		450		6	5
2	4 S	N	4		420		1	2-
3	6 S	N	6		980		3	6
4	4 S	N	4		420		5	2-
5	6 S	N		1		50	7	0
6	4 S	N	4		420		2	2-
7	4 S	N	4		420		4	2-
8								
9								
10							1	3-
11							2	3-
							3	0
20							4	3-
21							5	3-
22							6	1
23							7	6
24							8	
25								

The completed traveling score slip gives you a full picture of how Match Points are awarded. First the North-South scores are figured. Each score is awarded 1 point for every poorer score; ½ point for every exactly equal score. It does not matter how much better one score is than another; the only thing that counts is how many pairs your score beats. Thus, the pair that bid and made six spades scored 530 points more than the next higher team, but got only one more Match Point. The pair that scored 450 for making five-odd got only 30 points more than each of the four pairs that bid and made exactly four, but that 30 points turns out to be worth 2½ Match Points more. The four pairs that got equal 420 scores were awarded 2½ Match Points; 1 for the one pair they beat; ½ for each of the three pairs they tied. The pair that was set at six spades got a zero.

The East-West pairs might be figured exactly the same way. But the simple way is to give East-West the reciprocal of the North-South score: that is, deduct the N-S score from the possible top score, 6, and give East-West the difference.

After several results have been entered, the contestants have an opportunity to compare their result with others previously recorded, and estimate an approximate final result. See CALIFORNIA SCORING, COMPARING SCORES, ESTIMATION.

TRAY. Whist term (still surviving) for the contraption to hold cards in duplicate competition. See BOARD, DUPLICATE.

TREASURERS of the American Bridge League and the American Contract Bridge League:

1927–28	C. W. Aldrich
1929	E. J. Tobin
1930–31	J. J. Lafferty
1932–34	R. Baldwin
1935	D. Burnstine
1936	G. M. Gibbs
1937	J. N. S. Brewster, Jr.
1938–40	G. M. Gibbs
1941–42	J. H. Block
1943–44	R. W. Gresham
1945–47	B. Lebhar, Jr.
1949–51	R. W. Gresham
1952–66	H. J. Fishbein
1966–69	S. Stayman
1969–70	P. X. Bean
1970–72	J. Silverman
1973–74	Walter O'Laughlin
1975–	Don Moeller

TREATMENT. A natural bid that indicates a desire to play in the denomination named (or promises or requests values in that denomination), but that also, by agreement, gives or requests additional information on which further action could be based. A treatment thus differs from a CONVENTION, which is a bid that gives or requests information unrelated to the denomination named. For example, a LIMIT JUMP RAISE is a treatment; but a LIMIT JUMP RAISE TO SHOW A SINGLETON in a side suit is a convention. INVERTED MINOR SUIT RAISES and PRE-EMPTIVE RE-RAISES are other examples of treatments.

TREFLE SQUEEZE SYSTEM. A one club system widely played in Belgium. One club shows *either* a hand with 17 points or more, regardless of distribution; *or* a normal opening bid (13–16 points) including at least five clubs. Responses are by point-count steps: one diamond, 0–5 points; one heart, 6–8 points; one spade, 9–11 points, etc. If there is an immediate overcall, a pass shows 0–5 points, the next higher suit 6–8, etc. The opener rebids clubs at the first opportunity to show the weak variety of club bid.

A two club opening is strong and artificial, also with step responses (two diamonds, 0–3; two hearts, 4–5, etc.). Other two bids show a strong suit and about 15 points. One no trump as an opening shows 15–16 points.

This system has more difficulty than most artificial systems in dealing with interference bids. See TWO-SUITER conventions.

TRELDE LEADS (developed by John Trelde of Holland). A method of leading from honor se-

quences to distinguish between a genuine sequence of three touching honors and a false sequence of only two touching honors. The principle is that from a genuine sequence the highest card is led and from a false sequence the second highest card is led. Partner should be able to determine which combination the lead is from by his and dummy's holding in the suit. Leads from ace-king doubleton, a suit headed by ace-king-queen, and internal sequences follow accepted practices.

TREY. The three or three-spot of each suit.

TRIAL BID. A game suggestion made by biddng a new suit after a major suit fit has been located:

SOUTH	NORTH
1 ♡	2 ♡
3 ♣	

North-South have provisionally agreed to play a heart contract, although a final contract of three no trump is not completely excluded. However, it is completely impossible that the right contract could be clubs, so the club bid can only be an exploring maneuver. If North has no interest in game, he signs off with three hearts. If he wants to accept the invitation, he bids four hearts or three no trump. As a rare alternative, he may bid an unbid suit in which he has strength, as a move toward three no trump.

The usual practice is for South to make his trial bid in a suit in which he needs support, so it will generally contain at least three cards and at least two losers. Possible holdings would be: xxx, Axx, K10xx, Jxxx, and many others.

The responder therefore takes his holding in the trial bid suit into account when making the decision whether to bid game. If his holding is neither maximum nor minimum in strength, he allows himself to be encouraged if he has honor strength or a shortage in the trial bid suit. Conversely, he should tend to reject the invitation if he has three or four small cards in the suit; a holding headed by the jack is only a slight improvement.

In one special case, the final contract may be in a suit other than the one originally agreed on:

SOUTH	NORTH
1 ♠	2 ♠
3 ♡	4 ♡

Four hearts may easily prove a superior contract to four spades. If South holds four hearts, and North holds four, five, or six, spades will be an inferior landing place if the spade fit is 5–3.

There are two other situations in which bids of similar types are made.

SOUTH	NORTH
1 ♣	1 ♠
2 ♠	3 ♡

North's bid invites four spades, and suggests some

length in hearts, in which he would welcome support.

SOUTH	NORTH
1 ♣	2 ♣
2 ♡	

This is not a trial bid, because no major suit has been agreed on. A heart fit is still possible, but it is very likely that the partnership will head for three no trump. South will tend to bid a suit in which he is strong, rather than a suit in which he is weak. His heart suit might be A Q x, but in no circumstances could it be x x x unless he was making a psychic effort to inhibit a lead.

Similarly:

SOUTH	NORTH
1 ♡	2 ♡
2 ♠	3 ♠

With three hearts and four spades in North, or with five hearts and four spades in South, the spade contract may be superior. However, restraint must be exercised. South's spade bid may be a three-card suit; hence a jump in spades by responder is unwise and unnecessary. See also INTEREST-SHOWING BID; PRE-EMPTIVE RE-RAISES; SHORT-SUIT GAME TRIES; SINGLE RAISE;TWO-WAY GAME TRIES; WEAK SUIT GAME TRY.

TRIALS. See INTERNATIONAL OPEN TEAM SELECTION.

TRICK. Consists of four cards played in rotation after an initial lead of one of the cards by the player whose turn it was to lead, or to play first to the trick. A trick of four cards can be won by virtue of the winning card being highest in rank (number) of the four played; or because the card led is "long," that is, a remaining card in one's hand of a suit not held by any other player; or by having a trump card played to it either by declarer or dummy, or either defender.

TRICK APPROPRIATED IN ERROR. A packet of the four cards played to a trick that has been gathered in by the pair of which neither contributed the winning card. Such a trick must be restored to the side that contributed the winning card if discovered before the second succeeding deal. See LAWS (Law 69).

TRICK POINTS. Points scored for fulfilled contracts toward the game. See BELOW THE LINE.

TRICK-SCORE. The value of the odd tricks of fulfilled contracts toward the winning of the game; in clubs or diamonds, 20 points each; in hearts or spades, 30 points each; at no trump, 40 points for the first and 30 for each subsequent trick. In French tournament play, the fourth trick at no trump has been reduced to 20 points so that four hearts, four spades, and four no trump each score 120 points. See FRENCH SCORING. Different trick scores operate in auction bridge and plafond.

TRINIDAD AND TOBAGO BRIDGE LEAGUE.

Competes annually with Barbados in an Open and Women's team event.

Information: Ken Hadley, 15 Springbank Ave., Cascade, Trinidad.

TRIPLE COUP. A series of plays by the declarer in which he trumps three cards from the dummy's hand in order to shorten his own trump suit to the number held by his right-hand opponent. The purpose is to lead a card from the dummy at the eleventh or twelfth trick which the right-hand opponent must trump (being void of all other suits), and thus permit declarer to win the last two tricks by virtue of his own trumps being over those of his opponent. If the cards deliberately trumped by the declarer are side suit winners in their own right, the coup is termed a grand coup. See COUP, TRIPLE GRAND COUP.

TRIPLE GRAND COUP. A grand coup in which the declarer shortens his hand three times in trumps, to reduce his holding to the same number as held by his right-hand opponent, by ruffing three winners from the dummy.

TRIPLE RAISE. A raise of partner's opening suit bid to the four-level. In a major suit the bid indicates that a fine distributional fit has been found, but that slam prospects are remote. A typical hand for responder would include an ace, a singleton, five trumps, and 7–10 points in high cards. None of these requirements is essential, but the hand should give promise of nine tricks opposite a minimum opening bid. The opener can assume that responder does not hold two aces, for he would then be likely to bid more slowly in case slam possibilities exist. See FAST ARRIVAL, PRINCIPLE OF.

In a minor suit the bid is rarer, and indicates an even more distributional hand. It is markedly pre-emptive in character, weaker in high cards than the major suit raise, and a typical distribution would be 6–5–2–0.

The raise of the major-suit opening to game can have a much wider range, up to perhaps 14 points in high cards, if the opening bid is limited as in the PRECISION, SCHENKEN, and BLUE TEAM CLUB systems. See also DOUBLE RAISE and DELAYED GAME RAISE.

TRIPLE SQUEEZE. A squeeze against one opponent in three suits. It is a combination of three simple squeezes against the same opponent, which justifies the term.

The term triple squeeze is often used to encompass squeezes which produce one trick and squeezes which produce two tricks. The latter is described under PROGRESSIVE SQUEEZE. See also BARCO SQUEEZE; CLASH SQUEEZE; COMPOUND SQUEEZE; GUARD SQUEEZE; HEXAGON SQUEEZE.

The minimum requirements for a triple squeeze are two one-card menaces and a two-card menace with an entry opposite the squeeze card.

These are the basic end positions:

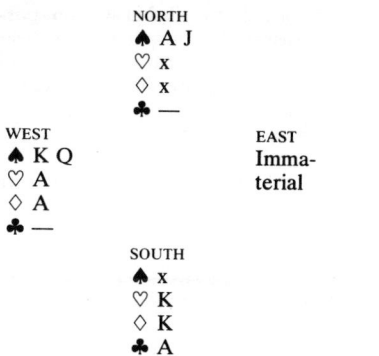

```
            NORTH
            ♠ A J
            ♡ x
            ◇ x
            ♣ —
WEST                    EAST
♠ K Q                  Imma-
♡ A                    terial
◇ A
♣ —
            SOUTH
            ♠ x
            ♡ K
            ◇ K
            ♣ A
```

South leads the ace of clubs, and West must surrender a spade, establishing a trick for South in that suit. (Any other discard permits South to win all four tricks.)

In this position the hand opposite the squeeze card has one menace. Since North has two idle cards, the position is automatic and either opponent may be squeezed.

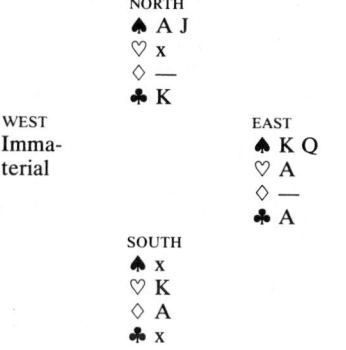

```
            NORTH
            ♠ A J
            ♡ x
            ◇ —
            ♣ K
WEST                    EAST
Imma-                  ♠ K Q
terial                 ♡ A
                       ◇ —
                       ♣ A
            SOUTH
            ♠ x
            ♡ K
            ◇ A
            ♣ x
```

South leads the ace of diamonds, and East is squeezed in three suits. He must part with a spade or a club to restrict declarer to three of the last four tricks.

In this position the hand opposite the squeeze card has two menaces. The ending shown is automatic and works equally well against either opponent.

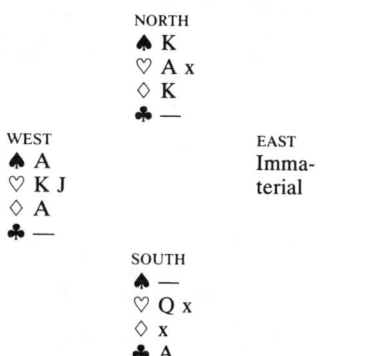

```
            NORTH
            ♠ K
            ♡ A x
            ◇ K
            ♣ —
WEST                    EAST
♠ A                    Imma-
♡ K J                  terial
◇ A
♣ —
            SOUTH
            ♠ —
            ♡ Q x
            ◇ x
            ♣ A
```

This is a variation of the above position, which is positional. If the East and West cards are transposed, the squeeze is ineffective. South leads the ace of clubs, and West is squeezed in three suits.

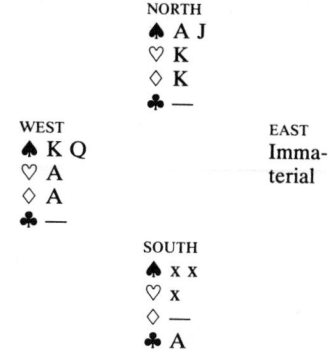

```
            NORTH
            ♠ A J
            ♡ K
            ◇ K
            ♣ —
WEST                    EAST
♠ K Q                  Imma-
♡ A                    terial
◇ A
♣ —
            SOUTH
            ♠ x x
            ♡ x
            ◇ —
            ♣ A
```

South leads the ace of clubs, and West is squeezed, permitting South to win two more tricks.

In all these squeezes South has all but *two* of the remaining tricks. This is a characteristic of triple squeezes.

In rare situations the triple squeeze may win two tricks immediately.

In this position there are three two-trick threats:

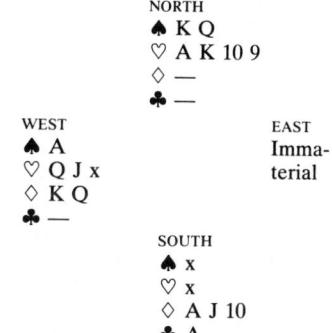

```
            NORTH
            ♠ K Q
            ♡ A K 10 9
            ◇ —
            ♣ —
WEST                    EAST
♠ A                    Imma-
♡ Q J x                terial
◇ K Q
♣ —
            SOUTH
            ♠ x
            ♡ x
            ◇ A J 10
            ♣ A
```

South has only four tricks on top, but the ace of clubs squeezes West in three suits, and any discard costs him two tricks.

Two two-trick threats (the great VIENNA COUP)

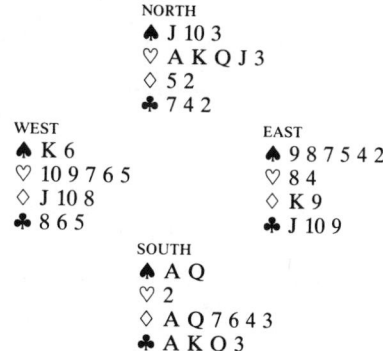

```
            NORTH
            ♠ J 10 3
            ♡ A K Q J 3
            ◇ 5 2
            ♣ 7 4 2
WEST                    EAST
♠ K 6                  ♠ 9 8 7 5 4 2
♡ 10 9 7 6 5           ♡ 8 4
◇ J 10 8               ◇ K 9
♣ 8 6 5                ♣ J 10 9
            SOUTH
            ♠ A Q
            ♡ 2
            ◇ A Q 7 6 4 3
            ♣ A K Q 3
```

Clubs are led and South must take all the tricks in a no trump contract.

South takes four club tricks, and West is squeezed in three suits. A discard of a spade or diamond costs two tricks, so West must throw a heart. South cashes the ace of spades, and then runs the hearts, squeezing West in spades and diamonds.

See also PROGRESSIVE SQUEEZE. For repeating triple squeezes, see BONNEY'S SQUEEZE; CLASH SQUEEZE; GUARD SQUEEZE; OVERTAKING SQUEEZE.

M. I.

TRIPLETON. A holding of three cards in a given suit in a particular hand. The term is usually used to describe an original, or dealt, combination; as, an ace-king tripleton in diamonds. For an opening lead from a small tripleton, see THREE SMALL CARDS, LEAD FROM.

TROPHIES. Those trophies competed for in International events are listed under the following headings: BERMUDA BOWL; CROWNINSHIELD TROPHY; CULBERTSON TROPHY; LENZ TROPHY; SCHWAB CUP; SOLOMON TROPHY; TORINO BULL; VANDERBILT CUP (2); VENICE TROPHY; WORLD BRIDGE FEDERATION TROPHY.

ACBL Trophies are listed separately: ASSOCIATION of AMERICAN PLAYING CARD MANUFACTURERS TROPHY; BAIRD TROPHY; BALDWIN MEMORIAL TROPHY; BARCLAY TROPHY; BEYNON TROPHY; CAVENDISH TROPHY; CHICAGO TROPHY; COFFIN TROPHY; FABER CUP; FISHBEIN TROPHY; GODDARD TROPHY; GOLDER CUP; GOREN TROPHY; HERMAN TROPHY; HILLIARD TROPHY; KEM CARD TROPHY; KEOHANE TROPHY; LANDY TROPHY; LEBHAR TROPHY; LEVENTRITT TROPHY; LIGHTMAN TROPHY; MACHLIN TROPHY; MC KENNEY TROPHY; MARCUS CUP; MID-ATLANTIC CUP; MILES TROPHY; MOREHEAD TROPHY; MOTT-SMITH TROPHY; MOUSER TROPHY; PRESIDENT'S CUP; REISINGER MEMORIAL TROPHY; ROCKWELL TROPHY; ROTHSCHILD TROPHY; SILODOR TROPHY; SMITH TROPHY; SPINGOLD TROPHY; STEINER TROPHY; VANDERBILT CUP (1); WERNHER TROPHY; WESTCOTT TROPHY; WHITEHEAD TROPHY; VON ZEDTWITZ GOLD CUP.

TRUMP. The suit named in the final bid, other than no trump. Such suit is the TRUMP SUIT, and a card of the trump suit, when played, is a winner over any card of a plain (not trump) suit; if two or more trumps are played on the same trick, the highest trump card played wins the trick.

TRUMP ASKING BID. A convention used to inquire about key cards in the trump suit. As used in conjunction with ASKING BIDS as developed by Ely CULBERTSON, a call of four no trump asked partner to describe his holding in the trump suit, as follows:

5 clubs	No ace, king, or queen
5 diamonds	One of three top honors
5 hearts	Two of three top honors
5 spades	All three top honors

If the four no trump bidder now bids five no trump, partner must show his trump length by a series of artificial responses. If the response to an asking bid is at the five level, five no trump can be used as a trump

asking bid for honor cards but it is not possible to follow up by asking for trump length. See also BARON SLAM TRY; BYZANTINE BLACKWOOD; GRAND SLAM FORCE; KEY CARD BLACKWOOD; KEY CARD GERBER; MALOWAN SIX CLUB CONVENTION; PRECISION ASKING BIDS; ROMEX TRUMP ASKING BIDS.

TRUMP CONTROL. See CONTROL MAINTENANCE and TRUMP SUIT MANAGEMENT.

TRUMP COUP. See COUP.

TRUMP ECHO. See TRUMP SIGNAL.

TRUMP KING. See conventions listed under TRUMP ASKING BID.

TRUMP LEADS. The opening lead of a trump is not a first-line lead, and it will turn out to be costly if the particular deal happens to be one where it was necessary for the defenders to cash tricks in a hurry, or not get them. Nevertheless, there are circumstances where an opening trump lead figures to be eminently proper. (Trump leads should *not* be made merely because one does not know what else to lead.)

Here are the major situations: (1) Where the bidding has indicated that dummy will be able to trump some of declarer's losing tricks; (2) Where the leader has reason to fear an aggressive lead in some other suit, lest it be beneficial to declarer; (3) Where there is a desire to mislead declarer as to the true state of affairs in the trump suit, as, for example, talking him out of taking finesse that he figures to take if left to his own resources.

The following hands illustrate some of the situations in which a trump opening should be made.

(1) Where the bidding has indicated that dummy will be able to trump some of declarer's losing tricks, a trump should be opened.

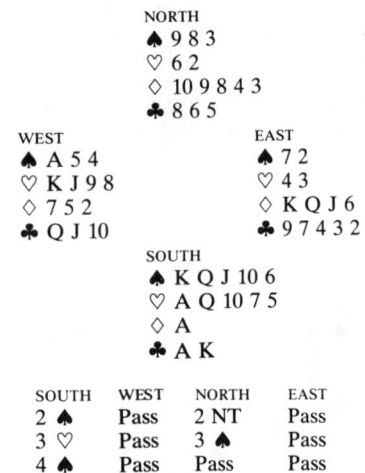

```
                NORTH
                ♠ 9 8 3
                ♡ 6 2
                ◇ 10 9 8 4 3
                ♣ 8 6 5
  WEST                        EAST
  ♠ A 5 4                     ♠ 7 2
  ♡ K J 9 8                   ♡ 4 3
  ◇ 7 5 2                     ◇ K Q J 6
  ♣ Q J 10                    ♣ 9 7 4 3 2
                SOUTH
                ♠ K Q J 10 6
                ♡ A Q 10 7 5
                ◇ A
                ♣ A K
```

SOUTH	WEST	NORTH	EAST
2 ♠	Pass	2 NT	Pass
3 ♡	Pass	3 ♠	Pass
4 ♠	Pass	Pass	Pass

What could be more "normal" than to open the queen of clubs? If made, this will be won by declarer and promptly he will bang down the ace and another heart. A belated shift by West to the ace and another trump permits South to trump one of his losing hearts with dummy's last trump; the closed hand entered with the ace of diamonds, picking up the last outstanding trump and conceding a further heart trick. Declarer makes four spades.

Based on the bidding, West should open the ace and follow with another trump. From South's bidding is it not apparent that he has a minimum of five spades and a minimum of five hearts? From North's bidding, is it not a fact that he prefers spades (however mildly) to hearts as the trump suit? From West's seat, should he not immediately make every effort to reduce dummy's ruffing power, to prevent dummy from ruffing hearts, especially since West has the KJ98 of hearts behind South's rebid suit?

With the ace of trumps lead, followed by another trump (and a third trump when West regains the lead in hearts), declarer will be defeated, losing three heart tricks and a trump trick.

(2) Where you have reason to be afraid to make an aggressive lead in some other suit, lest that lead be beneficial to declarer, lead a trump.

You, sitting West, hold: ♠843, ♡AJ76, ◇K74, ♣K63. The bidding proceeded:

SOUTH	WEST	NORTH	EAST
1 ♠	Pass	3 ♠	Pass
4 ♠	Pass	Pass	Pass

On the above bidding, it figures to be costly to lead either a heart, a diamond, or a club, since partner figures to have a virtual YARBOROUGH. The actual deal was:

NORTH
♠ K Q 9 6
♡ Q 4 2
◇ Q 5 2
♣ A 10 7

WEST
♠ 8 4 3
♡ A J 7 6
◇ K 7 4
♣ K 6 3

EAST
♠ 10
♡ 9 8 3
◇ 10 9 8 3
♣ Q 9 8 5 2

SOUTH
♠ A J 7 5 2
♡ K 10 5
◇ A J 6
♣ J 4

With the "safe" trump opening, declarer went down, losing two hearts, a diamond, and a club. Had either a heart, a diamond, or a club been opened, declarer would have fulfilled his contract; with the heart lead, declarer receives a present of a trick; with a low club lead, declarer would have played low from dummy, and would later have finessed West for the king of clubs; with the diamond lead, declarer would have won it with the jack (or queen), pulled trumps, then played the ace and another diamond, saddling West with the lead and forcing him to lead either a heart or a club. South *can* make four spades after the trump lead, but only by the double dummy expedient of pulling trumps and leading the heart king.

(3) Where you want to mislead declarer as to the true state of affairs in the trump suit; as, for example, talking him out of taking a finesse which he figures to take if left to his own resources, a trump lead may turn out to be the winning lead.

The deal which illustrates this point arose in the Men's Pair Championship of 1956. The West defender was Dr. Richard Greene.

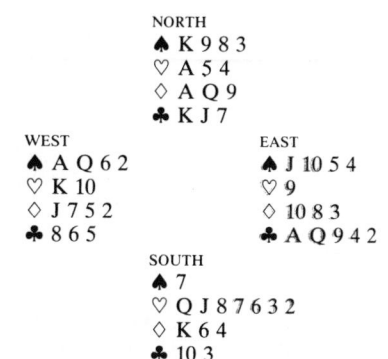

NORTH
♠ K 9 8 3
♡ A 5 4
◇ A Q 9
♣ K J 7

WEST
♠ A Q 6 2
♡ K 10
◇ J 7 5 2
♣ 8 6 5

EAST
♠ J 10 5 4
♡ 9
◇ 10 8 3
♣ A Q 9 4 2

SOUTH
♠ 7
♡ Q J 8 7 6 3 2
◇ K 6 4
♣ 10 3

North-South vulnerable, North deals. The bidding:

NORTH	EAST	SOUTH	WEST
1 NT	Pass	4 ♡	Pass
Pass	Pass		

West opened the ten of trumps on the reasoning:

(a) On the bidding, North figured to have the ace of hearts, and South figured to have a long heart suit.

(b) Even if South had something like an A Q J x x x and dummy the x x x of hearts, West would still make his king, since declarer couldn't possibly diagnose the situation. (Upon winning the opening lead with the jack, declarer would enter dummy, and lead a low heart, finessing East for the king.)

What would you, as declarer, have played to the first trick? Probably the same as our declarer did: he went up with the ace on the hope that West was leading from the doubleton 109 and, hence, East had the singleton king..

Had Dr. Greene not opened a trump, declarer, upon obtaining the lead, would probably have made the standard PERCENTAGE PLAY of leading the queen of trumps and finessing. As it was, he was "talked out" of finessing, and thus went down, losing two clubs, one spade, and, of course, the king of trumps.

The following specific situations suggest a trump lead, although circumstances may indicate another selection:

(1) The opponents have bid three suits and ended up in a fourth.

(2) Declarer, raised in his suit, has bid no trump, and been put back to his suit.

(3) The declaring side appears to have a good fit (5–4 or 4–4) in one suit and a misfit in the other suits. For example:

WEST	EAST
1 ♠	2 ◇
2 ♡	4 ♡

(4) The bidding indicates that dummy has exactly three trumps.

(5) A take-out double has been passed for penalties.

(6) An opening suit bid of one has been passed out, and the opening leader has a weak hand. Partner's failure to balance suggests long, strong trumps.

(7) Your side has been doubled for penalties, and one opponent has removed the double.

(8) Your side has opened the bidding with a no trump bid.

(9) Against a high-level sacrifice bid, when the declaring side appears to have little high-card strength.

Note also that a small trump is usually the desirable lead from holdings which would call for the highest in a plain suit: xxx; xx; or J 10x.

F. K.

TRUMP PETER. See TRUMP SIGNAL.

TRUMP PICK-UP. A play that reduces trump loss by plain suit leads. It usually involves the lead of a side suit through an opponent in order to pick up his seemingly inviolable trump holding.

```
                NORTH
                ♠ K Q
                ♡ 3
                ◇ K 4 3
                ♣ A K Q 10 7 3 2
WEST                            EAST
♠ 10 9 7 5 3 2                  ♠ J 6
♡ A 8 7 5                       ♡ K Q 10 2
◇ —                             ◇ J 9 7 6 2
♣ 8 6 4                         ♣ J 9
                SOUTH
                ♠ A 8 4
                ♡ J 9 6 4
                ◇ A Q 10 8 5
                ♣ 5
```

Against South's six diamond contract, West leads the ace of hearts and continues the suit in response to his partner's violent signal. Dummy ruffs and leads the king of diamonds, revealing the trump break. Declarer would have had no difficulty in finessing East out of his jack of trumps if dummy had not been forced to ruff; as it is, however, he has to utilize the club suit for that purpose. At trick three declarer leads a diamond to his eight and then starts the clubs. If East ruffs, declarer overruffs, draws trumps, and enters dummy with a spade to make the good clubs. If East refuses to ruff, South discards his spades and hearts until the following position is reached.

```
                DUMMY
                ♠ K Q
                ♡ —
                ◇ —
                ♣ 2
Imma-                           ♠ —
terial                          ♡ —
                                ◇ J 9 7
                                ♣ —
                ♠ —
                ♡ —
                ◇ A Q 10
                ♣ —
```

Dummy is on lead, and East is helpless to prevent declarer from taking the balance.

See COUP; DEVIL'S COUP; GRAND COUP; SMOTHER PLAY.

TRUMP PROMOTION. The creation of trump tricks through forcing the premature use of the trump cards of the opposition.

There are several ways in which trump tricks can be promoted: (1) forcing ruffs (see FORCING DECLARER TO RUFF) so as to make trump tricks by length; (2) COUP EN PASSANT so as to make trump tricks by position (see ELOPEMENT); (3) ruffing to force out honors (see UPPERCUT) so as to make trump tricks by force of cards; (4) threatening an overruff to force out honors so as to make trump tricks by force of cards.

In these examples, spades are trump, and East has led a plain suit of which both South and West are void. The best technique to promote trump tricks is to discard behind a player who has wasted a valuable card attempting to stop an overruff.

```
WEST
♠ A J
                        SOUTH
                        ♠ K Q 10 9 8 7 6 3
```

South must ruff with an honor to shut out West's jack. West discards and now has promoted a second trump trick. Notice that West must not overruff!

```
WEST
♠ K 10 2
                        SOUTH
                        ♠ A Q J 9 8 7 3
```

South must ruff with queen or jack to prevent West's ten from winning. West discards and now makes two trump tricks.

```
WEST
♠ J 3 2
                        SOUTH
                        ♠ A K Q 10 9 8 7
```

A trick is promoted for West's jack.

J. R.

TRUMP-REDUCING PLAY. A play designed to reduce the number of trumps in a hand, usually as a preparation for the trump pick-up. The principal trump-reducing plays are the simple and grand coup, the preliminary throw-in to force the lead of a ruffable suit, and the discard of a trump on a trick taken by a higher trump.

TRUMP SIGNAL. A play by defenders to indicate length of trump holding. The play of an intermediate card followed by a subsequent play of a lower card in the trump suit (HIGH-LOW SIGNAL) has the definite meaning that a third trump is held. The use of such a signal is important if the player has a potential RUFF-ING TRICK to indicate to partner that he still has the ability to trump a suit of which he is void. Note that the high-low trump signal to show a third card in the suit is the reverse of the meaning of an echo in a non-trump suit.

Some players use the trump signal whenever they hold three trumps. But as the defenders can count declarer's trumps from the bidding far more often than vice versa, it is better to confine its use to situations in which there is a real prospect of a ruff.

TRUMP SQUEEZE. A squeeze in which the ruffing power of the trump suit plays an essential part. Here is an example of the most common form of simple trump squeeze:

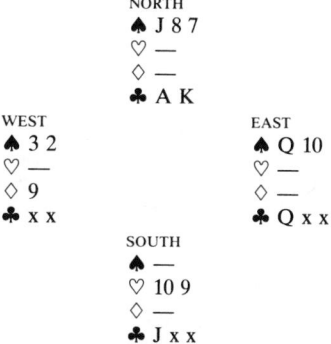

Hearts are trumps, and South leads a trump, discarding a spade from dummy. East is squeezed. If he discards a spade, dummy is entered with a club, and the spade queen is ruffed out. If East discards a club, then South cashes his winners in that suit, dropping the queen, and he returns to hand by ruffing a spade in order to cash the established jack of clubs. This squeeze is automatic, and it has a distinct resemblance to the CRISSCROSS SQUEEZE with a trump taking the place of an isolated master card in the other position.

These are the characteristic elements of the trump squeeze:

(1) *A split menace,* guarded on the right. But see BACKWASH SQUEEZE.

(2) A ruffing menace, also guarded on the right (a ruffing menace consists of two low cards in dummy, and a trick can be established by ruffing provided RHO weakens his guard in that suit).

(3) Dummy must have two entries, either in the split menace (as above) or by means of an additional entry in a third suit.

If both menaces are guarded on the left, the trump factor is not essential, and we have an ordinary simple squeeze against LHO.

It is worth noting that the squeeze takes place while declarer retains a trump; in most squeeze positions the last trump must be played before the pressure is felt.

There are two more simple trump squeeze positions:

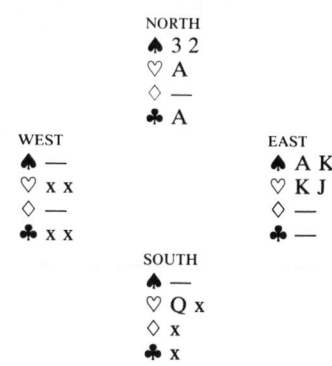

Diamonds are trumps. A club is led to the ace, and East is squeezed. A spade discard enables South to ruff out East's spade guard, and a heart discard permits North to cash the ace of that suit. The South hand is re-entered with a spade ruff, and the queen of hearts is cashed.

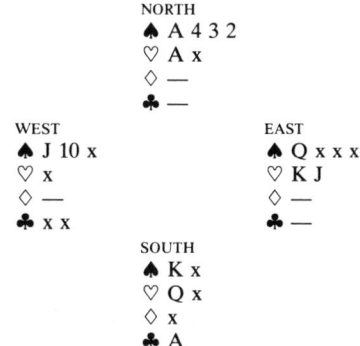

Diamonds are trumps. The ace of clubs is led and East is squeezed. A spade discard unguards his stopper, which can be ruffed out; a heart discard establishes the queen once the ace is cashed.

"Squeeze-Finesse at Trumps"
Simple

NORTH
♠ Q 9
♡ A K
◇ —
♣ x

WEST
♠ J 10
♡ Q x x
◇ —
♣ —

EAST
♠ A 6
♡ x x x
◇ —
♣ —

SOUTH
♠ —
♡ J x x
◇ x
♣ A

Diamonds are trumps. The ace of clubs squeezes West. If a heart is thrown, the ace and king of that suit are cashed, South re-enters his hand by ruffing a spade in order to cash the jack of hearts. If a spade is thrown, a heart is led to North, and the queen of spades is led to ruff out the ace and establish the nine.

Double

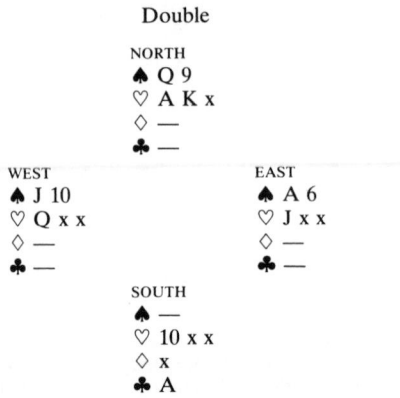

NORTH
♠ Q 9
♡ A K x
◇ —
♣ —

WEST
♠ J 10
♡ Q x x
◇ —
♣ —

EAST
♠ A 6
♡ J x x
◇ —
♣ —

SOUTH
♠ —
♡ 10 x x
◇ x
♣ A

Diamonds are trumps. South leads the ace of clubs, and West is squeezed. A spade discard enables South to ruff out East's stopper. If a heart is discarded, East is subjected to a simple trump squeeze.

Double

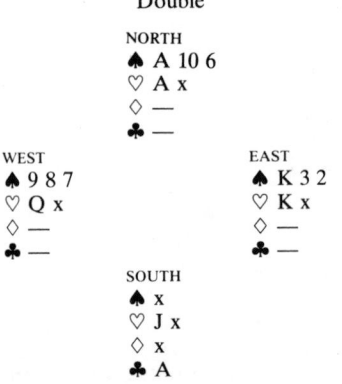

NORTH
♠ A 10 6
♡ A x
◇ —
♣ —

WEST
♠ 9 8 7
♡ Q x
◇ —
♣ —

EAST
♠ K 3 2
♡ K x
◇ —
♣ —

SOUTH
♠ x
♡ J x
◇ x
♣ A

Diamonds are trumps. South leads the ace of clubs, and West is squeezed. A spade discard enables South to establish a spade by leading to the ace, and returning the ten. A heart discard places East in a simple trump squeeze.

Trump Guard Squeeze

Simple

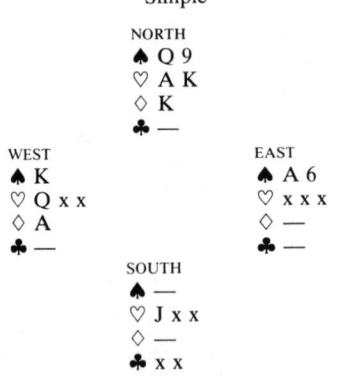

NORTH
♠ Q 9
♡ A K
◇ K
♣ —

WEST
♠ K
♡ Q x x
◇ A
♣ —

EAST
♠ A 6
♡ x x x
◇ —
♣ —

SOUTH
♠ —
♡ J x x
◇ —
♣ x x

Clubs are trumps. A trump is led, and West is squeezed in three suits. A diamond discard establishes the king; a heart discard permits South to play ace and king of that suit, establishing the jack, with a spade ruff as re-entry; a spade discard allows South to lead a heart to the king, and lead a spade, trump-finessing East's ace.

Double

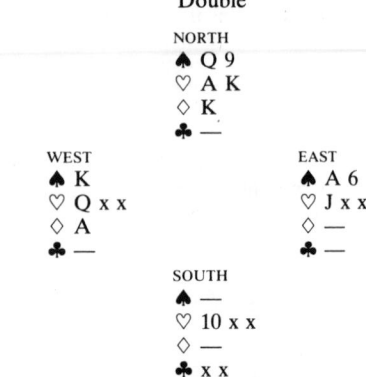

NORTH
♠ Q 9
♡ A K
◇ K
♣ —

WEST
♠ K
♡ Q x x
◇ A
♣ —

EAST
♠ A 6
♡ J x x
◇ —
♣ —

SOUTH
♠ —
♡ 10 x x
◇ —
♣ x x

Clubs are trumps. A trump is led, and West is squeezed in three suits. A diamond discard establishes the king; a heart discard places East in a simple trump squeeze; a spade lead permits South to ruff out East's ace.

M. I.

TRUMP SUIT. The principles governing the choice of a trump suit are well established. The following are basic rules, subject to certain exceptions.

(1) Eight cards or more between the partnership constitute a satisfactory trump suit.

(2) If the partnership can find an eight-card (or longer) fit in a major suit, the contract should usually be played in that suit.

(3) If the partnership has values for game (i.e., 25–26 points), the contract should be three no trump if no major-suit fit is available.

The following discussion centers on some of the exceptions.

When to play with less than eight trumps. Occasionally a trump suit in which the partnership has only seven cards may be the best bet, especially if the suit is strong (at least three of the top four honors) and one of the other suits appears to be weak. This type of hand is not uncommon:

♠ A Q 10 8 4   ♠ K 6
♡ 8 7   ♡ 9 3
◇ K 6 2   ◇ A Q J 10 7
♣ K Q 3   ♣ 10 8 6 4

These hands are on the borderline between part-score and game as far as values go. Clearly the only sound game contract is four spades, which needs a 3–3 break in spades, or the jack of spades falling doubleton. Notice the symptoms which point to this seven-card trump suit: a strong trump suit, and a marked weakness in another suit.

When the seven-card trump suit is split 4–3, a

strong trump suit and a weak side suit are still the signs to look for, but there is a further and most important complication. For the contract to be a good one, it is usually necessary for the hand which is shorter in the trump suit to be able to ruff the weak suit.

♠ A K J 5   ♠ Q 6 2
♡ 9 8 5   ♡ 3
◇ K 10 5   ◇ A Q J 9 2
♣ A 7 3   ♣ 10 8 6 4

Four spades is a lay-down, barring very bad breaks, and on a heart lead West can certainly make eleven tricks and perhaps twelve. Although the 5–3 fit in diamonds looks like a better bet than spades, five diamonds has no chance whatever. As the heart ruffs come in the long trump hand, ten tricks are the limit. The fact that the heart shortage is with the spade shortage is doubly advantageous; there is a positive profit, in that the heart ruffs score extra tricks, and a negative profit in that heart ruffs do not weaken control of the trump suit.

The converse position is much less attractive:

♠ A K J 5   ♠ Q 6 2
♡ 3   ♡ 9 8 5
◇ K 10 9 5 2   ◇ A Q J
♣ A 7 3   ♣ 10 8 6 4

If you play this hand in four spades, and ruff the second heart, you are uncomfortably placed. It looks as though a 4–2 spade break will be fatal, but the play is interesting. West should cash his king and jack of spades, leaving two trumps at large, and then play diamonds. A defender ruffs and plays another heart, and now West can please himself whether he ruffs and continues diamonds, or simply discards a club loser. Is there a simpler way of dealing with West's problems? He should, of course, quietly discard his two club losers on the second and third rounds of hearts, then a fourth heart can be ruffed in dummy.

So in this situation declarer has made ten tricks by skillful play, and can never make more; while in the previous case, with the heart and spade shortages in the same hand, he makes ten tricks without effort, and will often make more.

The moral is that a 4–3 fit in a strong suit will be satisfactory if the hand with three trumps has a shortage in the enemy suit. But if the hand with four trumps is going to be forced to ruff, the bidding should be more cautious: there will certainly be problems of control which may be difficult to solve.

Seven trumps divided 6–1 or 7–0, on the other hand, will usually prove adequate. But here also it is better for the suit to be fairly robust, and if a six-card suit has only one high honor, there may well be a better spot to play the hand.

To play with six trumps is nearly always a mistake. It is true that a strong 6–0 fit will play well, and occasionally a strong 5–1 fit may be the best spot; it is even possible to construct hands on which the only game to be made is in a strong 4–2 fit. But for practical purposes we can rule out any deliberate intention of playing in a trump suit in which the opposition have

the majority of cards. If, when dummy goes down, the combined hands prove to have only six trumps, then the bidding has probably failed.

When to reject an eight-card fit. There are three situations in which three no trump should be preferred to four of a major suit.

Type I:

♠ K J 7   ♠ A 4
♡ 9 7 6 3 2   ♡ K 8 4
◇ Q 10 7   ◇ K J 9
♣ A 3   ♣ K Q J 9 6

Although there is a ruff to be had in dummy, both hands are balanced and the heart suit is very feeble. If East opens one no trump (strong), West should simply raise to three no trump, and make no effort to play in hearts. If East has good hearts, the suit will pull its weight in no trumps. It is easy to see that three no trump is a virtual certainty, while four hearts needs a 3–2 heart break with the ace well placed.

Type II:

♠ A 4   ♠ 8 6
♡ A K Q J 8 3 ♡ 10 6 2
◇ A 5   ◇ J 7 4
♣ A 7 6   ♣ J 9 8 4 3

Here the possible trump suit, far from being weak, is absolutely solid. But there are nine sure tricks in no trump, and little chance of ten in hearts, because the East hand has no usable ruffing value. This is, of course, easy for West to spot, because he can count nine tricks in his own hand; but the position will be difficult and perhaps impossible to diagnose if some of West's strength is transferred to East. If West has eight tricks in his hand, he can sometimes take the gamble that East will produce the ninth, and that the opponents will not manage to cash five tricks.

To land this sort of contract the tricks have to be quick ones; aces in the side suits are essential, and the presence of minor honors will suggest that the suit contract is preferable. There is a paradoxical element in this: in a general way, the presence of aces normally suggests a suit contract, and the presence of minor honors suggests no trump.

Failure to recognize type III often does not show on the score sheet, so it usually stays unrecognized.

Type III:

♠ J 5 3 2   ♠ A Q
♡ K J 7 5   ♡ Q 6 3 2
◇ A Q   ◇ K J 7 5
♣ Q J 4   ♣ K 8 7

Suppose East opens one no trump (15–17). West should now reason along these lines: our combined count is about 30, so game is very easy, but there is no slam; even if there is a major-suit fit, the suit game may fail through a bad break, while three no trump is surely ironclad. So West raises to three no trump, which is impregnable, while four hearts would fail with a little bad luck, a 4–1 trump break, and the king of spades with South. These tactics may cost 20 or 50 points aggregate, but this is a good insurance except at match-point pairs.

In the slam zone there are other considerations which may cause us to reject a combined eight-card major suit holding. The most common symptom is a weak trump suit:

♠ A 8 6 3	♠ J 7 4 2
♡ A Q J 7	♡ K 3
◇ A K 6	◇ 4 2
♣ J 7	♣ A K Q 10 8

Twelve tricks are obviously a lay-down in clubs or no trump, but many players would arrive disastrously in six spades, which needs the 7% miracle of doubleton king-queen of spades. To avoid this type of trap often requires fine bidding judgment. This is another example in which the major suit has one loser only, but that denomination is still wrong:

♠ A 10 8 7 6 3	♠ K 5
♡ K Q 2	♡ 9 7 6
◇ A Q	◇ K 8 4
♣ J 6	♣ A K Q 10 8

Six spades again needs a miracle. Six no trump is a good contract, with slightly better than an even chance: as well as the ace of hearts with South, we can hope for a lucky spade position or a squeeze against North if he holds all the major-suit honors. But far and away the best contract is six clubs, in which the twelfth trick may come from hearts, or from ruffing out the spade suit. Again the strength of the trump suit proves more important than the length.

It may sometimes be advisable to reject an eight-card fit headed by the three trump top honors:

♠ A Q 7 5 4	♠ K 8 3
♡ K	♡ Q J 6 5
◇ A Q 9 3	◇ K
♣ K 9 4	♣ A Q 7 5 2

Six spades and six clubs are obviously both sound contracts, depending on a 3–2 trump break. But with a lot of general strength about, six no trump will often offer more chances. Here the no trump slam makes if either black suit breaks, or if a squeeze develops.

When to play in five of a minor. As it is much easier to make nine tricks than eleven, contracts of five in a minor suit are rare. It is nearly always possible to play in three no trump, or in a seven-card major-suit fit.

This is particularly true in match-point duplicate events, when a successful contract of five clubs or five diamonds usually scores badly: other pairs are likely to score slightly more by making ten tricks in no trump or a major.

To play in a minor-suit game with a 4–4 or 5–3 fit is very rare indeed. When it does happen, it is usually because *both* minor suits are held, and there is no seven-card fit in a major:

♠ x	♠ x x x x
♡ A x	♡ K x x
◇ A x x x	◇ K x x x
♣ A K x x x x	♣ x x

Five diamonds is the only possible game. It requires 3–2 breaks in both minor suits, representing a 46% chance.

This demonstrates two common symptoms of minor-suit games; a completely exposed suit, and obvious ruffing values (singleton or void) in each hand.

If a solid six-card minor suit is held opposite a balanced hand, three no trump is usually right. But in some cases it may be possible to diagnose a serious weakness, and play in the minor suit:

WEST	EAST
♠ x x x	♠ A K x
♡ x	♡ x x x
◇ A Q x x x x	◇ K x x x
♣ A K x	♣ Q J x

The bidding may start:

WEST	EAST
1 ◇	2 NT
3 ♣	3 ♠

after which the heart weakness is identified and the diamond game is reached. As is often the case when the choice lies between three no trump and a minor suit, the players bid suits in which they have strength but not necessarily length (see STRENGTH-SHOWING BIDS).

Interchanging East's rounded suits would produce a different contract:

WEST	EAST
♠ x x x	♠ A K x
♡ x	♡ Q J x
◇ A Q x x x x	◇ K x x x
♣ A K x	♣ x x x

In this case the first three bids would be the same, but East's second bid would be three no trump, showing stoppers in both major suits, and West would subside. Ten tricks in no trump are certain, and eleven are likely, while five diamonds needs a high heart lead or an end play to succeed.

TRUMP SUIT FALSE-CARDING. See FALSE-CARDING.

TRUMP SUIT MANAGEMENT. The manner in which declarer utilizes the trump suit in the play of the hand.

The proper technique in handling the trump suit varies, depending first upon the length and the division of the trump suit in the combined hands, i.e., declarer and dummy, and secondly the manner in which the outstanding trumps are distributed in the defenders' hands. Generally speaking, the minimum number of trumps required for a game contract is eight, and the most favorable distribution is four in the dummy and four in the declarer's hand, referred to as:

The 4–4 Fit: The main advantage of this division is that declarer can stand being forced to ruff twice in either hand, reserving the other for purposes of drawing trump. If one opponent holds four trumps, the situation will be much more satisfactory with a 4–4 than a 5–3 distribution; declarer must then take the precaution of looking to his side suits before tackling trumps:

```
                NORTH
              ♠ K J 10 4
              ♡ 8 7 6 3
              ◇ A K 2
              ♣ 4 3
WEST                        EAST
♠ 8                         ♠ 9 7 6 5
♡ A K 5                     ♡ Q J 9 2
◇ J 9 8 7                   ◇ 6 5 3
♣ 9 8 7 5 2                 ♣ A 10
                SOUTH
              ♠ A Q 3 2
              ♡ 10 4
              ◇ Q 10 4
              ♣ K Q J 6
```

Against four spades, West opens with the king of hearts. If the defense continues hearts, declarer ruffs the third round and knocks out the ace of clubs. East leads his last heart and South ruffs with the ace, draws trump, and takes the rest. On any other defense, declarer makes ten tricks by ruffing his losing club high in the dummy before drawing East's trumps.

The 4–4 distribution lends itself ideally to cross-ruffing; in this type of play the declarer must be careful to cash his side-suit winners before attempting to score his trumps separately.

```
                NORTH
              ♠ A 7 6 2
              ♡ A Q J 5
              ◇ —
              ♣ Q 10 6 3 2
WEST                        EAST
♠ J 9 5 3                   ♠ Q 4
♡ —                         ♡ 9 8 4 3 2
◇ 10 7 6                    ◇ A J 5 4
♣ A K J 8 5 4               ♣ 9 7
                SOUTH
              ♠ K 10 8
              ♡ K 10 7 6
              ◇ K Q 9 8 3 2
              ♣ —
```

The contract is four hearts, against which West leads the king of clubs. Declarer ruffs and is in a position to make ten tricks in spite of the vile distribution, provided he makes the ace and king of spades before he ruffs the third club. Failure to do so would give East an opportunity to discard a spade, and declarer would then be unable to enjoy both of his spade winners.

The 4–3 Fit: When the dummy holds only three trumps, facing four in declarer's hand, the play is unlikely to proceed favorably. These hands normally play better in no trump, especially at the higher

levels; exceptionally (e.g., when the opponents have an established suit), they are the only ones available. These contracts frequently call for delicate handling.

The problem of control is critical, and declarer must often establish his side-winners before embarking on drawing trumps.

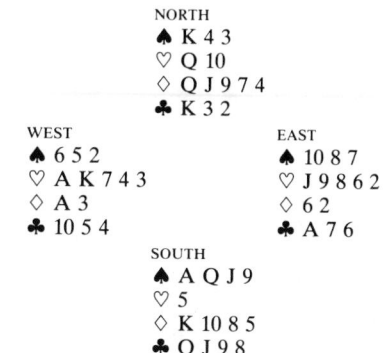

```
                NORTH
              ♠ K 4 3
              ♡ Q 10
              ◇ Q J 9 7 4
              ♣ K 3 2
WEST                        EAST
♠ 6 5 2                     ♠ 10 8 7
♡ A K 7 4 3                 ♡ J 9 8 6 2
◇ A 3                       ◇ 6 2
♣ 10 5 4                    ♣ A 7 6
                SOUTH
              ♠ A Q J 9
              ♡ 5
              ◇ K 10 8 5
              ♣ Q J 9 8
```

Four spades is the only possible game contract, and, as the cards lie, cannot be defeated. The defense does best to play hearts at every opportunity, and South ruffs the second round and plays diamonds. West plays a third round of hearts which is ruffed in dummy. Declarer now knocks out the ace of clubs and ruffs a further heart in dummy. Only now can he afford to draw trumps, and when they break he claims the balance with good diamonds and clubs.

Sometimes declarer can retain control of a shaky trump suit by refusing to ruff.

```
                NORTH
              ♠ K Q 10
              ♡ 4 3 2
              ◇ Q J 9 7
              ♣ A 10 4
WEST                        EAST
♠ 8 7 6 4                   ♠ 9 5
♡ A K Q 8 5                 ♡ J 9 7
◇ 10                        ◇ 8 6 5 2
♣ Q 6 5                     ♣ J 9 8 7
                SOUTH
              ♠ A J 3 2
              ♡ 10 6
              ◇ A K 4 3
              ♣ K 3 2
```

Against four spades, West leads three top hearts. If declarer ruffs and draws trump, West will be left with a long spade which he will use to interrupt the run of the diamonds, and cash his remaining heart winners. South can ensure the contract against all reasonable distributions by discarding his losing club on the third round of hearts. If the defense persists with a fourth round, he is able to ruff in dummy, preserving his own trump length, and is in a position to draw all West's trumps and take the rest of the tricks with minor-suit winners.

A less obvious example from the same family:

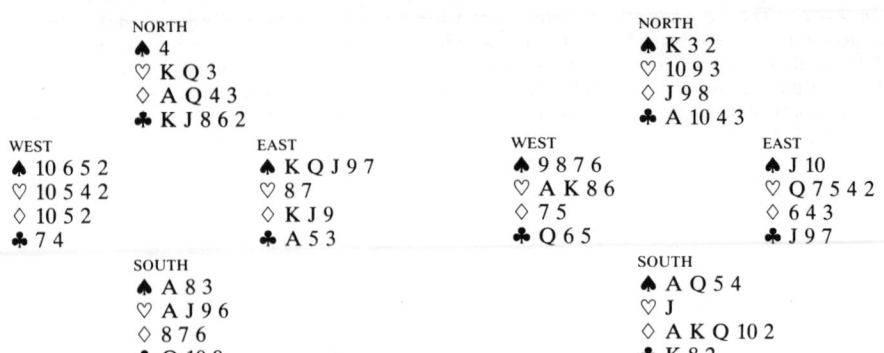

```
              NORTH                              NORTH
              ♠ 4                                ♠ K 3 2
              ♡ K Q 3                            ♡ 10 9 3
              ◇ A Q 4 3                          ◇ J 9 8
              ♣ K J 8 6 2                        ♣ A 10 4 3
WEST                     EAST          WEST                     EAST
♠ 10 6 5 2               ♠ K Q J 9 7   ♠ 9 8 7 6               ♠ J 10
♡ 10 5 4 2               ♡ 8 7         ♡ A K 8 6               ♡ Q 7 5 4 2
◇ 10 5 2                 ◇ K J 9       ◇ 7 5                   ◇ 6 4 3
♣ 7 4                    ♣ A 5 3       ♣ Q 6 5                 ♣ J 9 7
              SOUTH                              SOUTH
              ♠ A 8 3                            ♠ A Q 5 4
              ♡ A J 9 6                          ♡ J
              ◇ 8 7 6                            ◇ A K Q 10 2
              ♣ Q 10 9                           ♣ K 8 2
```

South plays in four hearts after East has bid spades, and West leads the two of spades, East playing the jack. Declarer's best play is to let East hold the trick, ruffing in dummy if spades are continued. Declarer is now in a position to draw trumps and give up a club trick while still maintaining control of the enemy suit. Attacking the trump suit by forcing declarer to ruff is by far the most effective form of defense against four–three trump contracts. Curiously enough, declarer can often turn this to his advantage and succeed in an otherwise impossible contract.

```
              NORTH
              ♠ Q 10 9
              ♡ 9 8 5 4
              ◇ J 5 2
              ♣ 7 5 3
WEST                     EAST
♠ 8 4 3                  ♠ 6 5 2
♡ A K J 10               ♡ Q 7 3
◇ 10 9 8                 ◇ K Q 7 6
♣ 10 6 2                 ♣ 9 8 4
              SOUTH
              ♠ A K J 7
              ♡ 6 2
              ◇ A 4 3
              ♣ A K Q J
```

Three no trump is safe as the cards lie but, unsure of the heart suit holding, North-South settled reasonably enough in four spades, West leading the king of hearts. If West shifts at trick two, South has four inescapable losers—two hearts and two diamonds—and must go one down. A heart continuation looks tempting however, and South ruffs the third round with the ace, leads the seven of spades to dummy's nine, and ruffs the fourth round of hearts with the king. He now overtakes the jack of spades to draw trump in dummy, discarding his losing diamond. Four club tricks plus the ace of diamonds (in addition to the five trump tricks) round out the contract.

It is sometimes possible for declarer to counter the forcing game, utilizing a strong side-suit for the purpose of weakening the defender's trump holding.

Against four spades, West leads two top hearts, declarer ruffing the second round. If South attempts to draw all the outstanding trumps, the hand collapses. In order to succeed, he must draw only two rounds of trumps with the ace and queen, and then start the diamonds. If West ruffs the third diamond to lead a heart, South ruffs with his last trump, crosses to dummy's ace of clubs, and draws West's last trump with the king, making eleven tricks. West does better by refusing to ruff, discarding his clubs instead. After finishing with the diamonds, South perforce leads a club. West ruffs and leads a third heart, and he cannot be prevented from scoring a further trump, but declarer still makes ten tricks. See also CONTROL MAINTENANCE; DRAWING TRUMPS; ELOPEMENT.

S. K.

TRUMP SUPPORT. A variable factor, depending on the nature of the bid which is being supported. (See BIDDABLE SUITS.) In general, a player will be very ready to give support if he knows that his side has eight cards in the suit; and may give a single raise when a combined seven-card holding is guaranteed and there are reasonable prospects of eight.

In most situations in constructive bidding, a suit bid promises four cards, and therefore four cards are needed for any kind of raise. But many special cases should be noted.

(1) *Five-card support* may be desirable if there is a fair chance that the suit being raised consists of three cards only. This applies particularly to minor-suit raises when the five-card major rule is being used and the incidence of prepared minors is therefore high. KAPLAN-SHEINWOLD, for example, insists on five-card support for a pre-emptive jump raise of a minor suit; and a single raise in a minor may be avoided with four-card support if there is any convenient alternative. In standard methods, there is a tendency to avoid raising one club with four-card support. With 3-3-3-4 distribution, an expert would often choose a response of one diamond in preference to a raise to two clubs.

(2) *Three-card support* may be given to any suit which is known or expected to be of at least five cards (e.g., a five-card major opening; a response of two hearts to one spade; or an overcall).

Three-card support is normally considered adequate for a single raise of a major suit bid by opener or responder at the first opportunity. Many players prefer the three-card holding to be headed by a high honor, but consider the following cases:

(a)	(b)
♠ 4 3 2	♠ 4 3 2
♡ 3 2	♡ 3 2
◇ 4 3 2	◇ A Q 2
♣ A Q 4 3 2	♣ A Q 4 3 2

In (a) an opening bid of one spade should be raised to two spades. Much more often than not the opener will hold more than four spades. The raise is a lesser evil than one no trump, because of the weakness in hearts. The responder does not wish to play no trump, nor to allow a heart bid by the opposition at the level of two.

Hand (b) opens the bidding with one club and gets a response of one spade. A raise to two spades is again a lesser evil than a rebid of one no trump, for similar reasons.

A jump raise or a raise of a secondary suit requires at least four-card support, but there are occasional exceptions on a least-evil basis:

(c)	(d)
♠ A Q 3	♠ K 6 4
♡ 10 8 5 4 2	♡ 4 2
◇ A 5 3 2	◇ A Q 6 4 3
♣ 2	♣ 5 4 2

Hand (c) has to respond to a fourth-hand opening bid of one spade and a jump to three spades is superior to a non-forcing bid of two hearts.

Hand (d) has responded one diamond to an opening bid of one club and the opener has rebid one spade. With the prospect of a ruffing value in hearts, responder is not unwilling to play in a four–three fit, and the mildly constructive raise to two spades is much better than a completely negative preference bid of two clubs.

(3) *Two-card support* may be given to any suit which is known or expected to be of at least six cards (e.g., any opening pre-emptive bid; a vulnerable overcall at the level of two; and almost any suit which has been bid twice [see REOPENER'S REBID]).

In an emergency, a doubleton may be sufficient to raise a suit which is known to be of at least five cards:

(e)	(f)
♠ 7 5	♠ K 7 6 5 3
♡ 2	♡ A 4
◇ A 8 6 5 3	◇ A Q 4 2
♣ J 7 6 5 2	♣ 8 6

Hand (e) should raise one spade to two spades playing five-card majors, partly for pre-emptive reasons and partly because there is no good alternative (unless a one no trump response is forcing). The alternative is a pass.

Hand (f) opens one spade, and the response is two hearts, showing at least a five-card suit. A raise to

three hearts is superior to a rebid of the anemic spade suit.

(4) *One-card support* is usually adequate only when the suit has been bid so strongly as to indicate that support is not needed. An exceptional case is suggested by Reese:

South holds:
♠ Q J 6 2
♡ 8 6 5 4
◇ A K 4 3
♣ Q

The bidding with neither vulnerable:

SOUTH	WEST	NORTH	EAST
1 ♡	2 ♣		2 ♡
?			

Reese's suggestion, endorsed by an expert panel, was to bid three clubs. With bidding all round the table North's overcall is likely to be a distributional one based on a good six-card suit; three clubs is likely to be the best contract for North-South; and East-West may be tempted to bid three hearts, which South can double effectively, and be surprised by the club situation. This is one case of a useful general rule: in competitive situations raises should be given more freely.

TRUMP SWISS CONVENTION. See SWISS CONVENTION.

TRUMP TRICK. A playing trick in the trump suit.

TRUNCATED HOWELL MOVEMENT. A shortening of the HOWELL MOVEMENT to terminate at the end of thirteen rounds, 26 boards. Since this did not give balanced comparison, it is no longer used but has been replaced by the THREE-QUARTER MOVEMENT.

TRUSCOTT DEFENSE. A system of two-suited take-outs that can be used over strong artificial openings of one club, two clubs, one diamond, or two diamonds. See DEFENSE TO STRONG ARTIFICIAL OPENINGS.

TRUSCOTT TWO DIAMONDS. See TWO-WAY STAYMAN.

TURKEY (TURKEY GAME, TURKEY SHOOT). A colloquial term used to describe events in a tournament other than major championships, such as secondary events, consolation events, and side games.

TURKISH BRIDGE FEDERATION (TÜRKIYE BRİÇ FEDERASYONU). Organized in the spring of 1965, its membership, which is governed by the Turkish Law of Associations, is limited to clubs, not individuals. As of 1974, there were nine member clubs with approximately 400 tournament players. The Federation became a member of the European Bridge League in 1968; it participated in its first European Championship in 1969, and sent representatives to the 1972 and 1974 World Olympiads. National events contested annually include Annual Pairs, Open Pairs, and Annual Teams of Four Championships. A master point program was introduced in the fall of 1968. Players listed separately are: N.

Akca, A. Benjenk, H. Dagli, M. Kortay, Y. Ozlem, K. Selcuk.

Officers, 1975:
President: Adnan Kocassian.
Secretary: Gunduz Pamuk, Harbiye Cumhuriyet Caddesi, Fransiz Gecidi Sokak No. 349, Istanbul, Turkey.

TURN. (1) Noun: the appropriate moment for a player to make a bid or play; (2) verb: to quit a card at duplicate or a trick at rubber bridge after all four players have played.

TWELVE, RULE OF. See RULE OF TWELVE.

TWELVE TABLES. At duplicate, twelve tables provide for competition among forty-eight players as individuals, twenty-four pairs, or twelve teams.

There are several movements available for a forty-eight player individual game, but for a one-session game, the appendix RAINBOW MOVEMENT devised by P. N. Marks provides the easiest movement and scoring. Four stationary player seats are assigned: 12, North at table 1; 24, East at table 2; 36, South at table 3; and 48, West at table 4. Players numbers 1 to 11 sit North at the corresponding tables; numbers 13 to 23 sit East at tables 1 to 11; numbers 25 to 35 sit South at tables 1 to 11; and numbers 37 to 47 sit West at tables 1 to 11. (However, four of these players, one from each group, find their new seats occupied by the stationary players, 45 to 48.) These players for the first round and their counterparts at every successive round play boards 23 and 24 at table 12. Otherwise, at the end of each round, North players skip a table to lower numbers, South players skip a table to higher numbers, East players go to the next higher numbered table, and West players skip two tables to higher numbers, boards going to next lower numbered tables. For purposes of progression and board numbers, table 12 is ignored, and is filled each round with players finding stationary players in the seats to which they are assigned. Each player thus plays twenty-two of the twenty-four boards in the eleven rounds. Ten is top and 110 average.

As a pair game, twenty-two boards can be played in eleven rounds, traveling players skipping a table after round number six. By inserting a bye stand between tables 7 and 8, and relaying boards between 1 and 2, twenty-four boards can be played. The game may be either straight or SCRAMBLED MITCHELL. THREE-QUARTER MOVEMENT HOWELL can be used for twenty-six boards; or eight or nine rounds of three boards played, utilizing the skip movement at the halfway point for a longer game.

As a team game, there are usually only two choices, two boards to a round, eleven rounds or three boards to a round, eight rounds missing three teams. The former is preferable as a competition. In this case, the standard team-of-four progression—boards to the next lower numbered table, traveling pairs skipping a table toward lower numbers—is used for two rounds, after which the traveling pairs skip an extra table. There is regular progression

thereafter for six more rounds. After the eighth round, both the traveling pairs and the boards skip a table. After ten rounds, the boards are removed from tables 7 to 12, and the boards are relayed between 1 and 7, 2 and 8, 3 and 9, etc., for the final round. East-West players add or subtract 6 from their team number for their seating assignment.

With twelve and a half tables as a pair game, see THIRTEEN TABLES. If it is desired to play less than twenty-six boards, however, a ROVER MITCHELL (straight or scrambled) must be used to avoid different top scores on the boards.

TWINNING. The process used for securing the play of the same boards in each of two (also used with some impropriety for three) sections. To twin the boards (either for social purposes or for scoring with a multiple top), the even boards are distributed to tables in one section, the odd boards to tables in the other section, where they are shuffled and played. While this is going on, a second board of the same number is put on the table to be twinned (reproduced card for card in each hand). The recommended procedure is to remove the cards from the board to be twinned, placing them face up in one or two stockpiles on the boards. Each player holds his own hand, and as a card in his hand appears at the top of a stockpile, he removes it and places it in front of him on the table. When the stockpiles are exhausted, each player checks his hand with the cards in front of him, replacing his original hand in the original board, and the duplicated hand in the second board. The twinned boards are then picked up by the director or an assistant and redistributed into the other section, where they are played without shuffling or dealing.

When boards are to be twinned over three sections, the first and third sections have boards distributed as above, shuffled, played, and duplicated. The second set of boards is twinned for use in the middle section (to which they are distributed) and a third board is given to the players for twinning to be used in the section that twinned the other boards of each set. Thus the middle section gets a later start than the others, but has both boards before the other sections have their second, and are able to complete the first round as soon as the other sections do.

Experienced directors find that duplicating across two sections requires about 15 minutes and across three, 20 minutes. In multisection events (more than three) other methods are available. See MACHINE-PREPARED HANDS and PRE-DEALING.

TWO or TWO-SPOT. The lowest-ranking card in any given suit. Sometimes referred to as the deuce, this card is just below the three in precedence.

TWO-BID. The bid of two in a suit as an opening bid is used in many different ways by various players. Specialized uses are referred to in the following articles: ACOL TWO-BID; ARTIFICIAL TWO DIAMOND AND TWO CLUB OPENINGS; BENJAMIN; BLUE TEAM TWO DIAMONDS; FLANNERY TWO DIAMONDS; FLANNERY TWO HEARTS; MEXICAN TWO DIAMONDS; ROMAN SYSTEM

(Two Club Opening); ROMAN TWO DIAMONDS; SKINNER TWO-BIDS; TAM II; TWO CLUB AND TWO DIAMOND OPENINGS; TWO CLUB STRONG ARTIFICIAL OPENING; WEAK TWO-BIDS.

TWO CLUB ARTIFICIAL BALANCING TAKE-OUT. See BALANCING TWO CLUBS FOR TAKE-OUT.

TWO CLUB CONVENTIONS. *Openings:* See TWO CLUB OPENING AS MULTI-SUITER; TWO CLUB SYSTEMS; TWO CLUBS STRONG ARTIFICIAL OPENING. *Responses:* See DRURY; GLADIATOR; STAYMAN CONVENTION; STAYMAN ON SECOND ROUND; TWO CLUB REBID BY RESPONDER AS ONLY FORCE AFTER ONE NO TRUMP REBID. *Take-outs:* See TWO-SUITER CONVENTIONS.

TWO CLUB OPENING AS MULTI-SUITER. The principal conventions that use a two club opening bid to show a two-suited or three-suited hand are features of the BID DIAMOND SYSTEM, ROMAN SYSTEM, and ROTH CLUB SYSTEM.

TWO CLUB REBID BY RESPONDER AS ONLY FORCE AFTER ONE NO TRUMP REBID. A convention devised by Edwin KANTAR to provide a full range of rebids by responder over a one no trump rebid by opener. Using two clubs as the only forcing rebid by responder, all other two-level suit bids are discouraging and jump bids at the three-level invite game. For example:

(a)		(b)	
1 ♣	1 ♡	1 ♣	1 ♡
1 NT	3 ♡	1 NT	3 ♦

The last bid in each of the above sequences is non-forcing but invitational. See also CROWHURST CONVENTION; STAYMAN ON SECOND ROUND; UNBID MINOR SUIT FORCE.

TWO CLUB RESPONSE TO NO TRUMP. See GLADIATOR; SKINNER RESPONSES TO A ONE NO TRUMP OPENING; STAYMAN CONVENTION.

TWO CLUB SYSTEMS. Many bidding systems use two clubs as the opening bid with strong hands, irrespective of the holding in the club suit. Information on such systems is included in the following articles: ACE-SHOWING RESPONSES; ACOL; ARTIFICIAL TWO DIAMOND AND TWO CLUB OPENINGS; BARON; BENJAMIN; BULLDOG; CAB; KAPLAN-SHEINWOLD; OFFICIAL; ROMEX; ROTH-STONE; STAYMAN; TAM II.

TWO CLUB STRONG ARTIFICIAL OPENING. An artificial opening bid on powerful hands which is the cornerstone of many systems. A response of two diamonds is usually negative. See TWO DIAMOND ARTIFICIAL RESPONSE TO FORCING TWO CLUB OPENING. See also SECOND NEGATIVE RESPONSE AFTER ARTIFICIAL FORCING OPENING. The first use of the bid of two clubs in this way is credited to David BURNSTINE at the Raymond Club, New York City, in 1929, but some experts used two clubs for all strong hands, and this concept gradually superseded the FORCING TWO-BID

in serious tournament play. It is usually used in combination with WEAK TWO-BIDS, but may be combined with INTERMEDIATE TWO-BIDS of various types.

Originally the two club bid was forcing to game. In modern practice many experts announce it as forcing to two no trump (after a two diamond response), to cover two common exceptions:

SOUTH	NORTH
2 ♣	2 ♦
2 ♡	2 NT
3 ♡	

North may pass. This widens the use of the two club opening to include a powerful one-suited hand where game may be missed if partner passes with 4–5 points, or slam may be missed because it becomes difficult for opener to show his strength clearly if he commences with a bid of one. The game-forcing nature of the opening two-bid was modified by CULBERTSON to exclude just such a situation after a two no trump response; opener made a minimum rebid of the same suit, viz.:

SOUTH	NORTH
2 ♡	2 NT
3 ♡	

Another exception tightens the gaps in the structure of no trump bids:

SOUTH	NORTH
2 ♣	2 ♦
2 NT	

North may pass. Under this method, instead of the book standard of 22–24 (or 21–23), a two no trump opener shows 21–22 (or 20–22) while two clubs followed by two no trump shows 23–24 (or 22–24).

If the opener's suit is a major, the two club bidder may be better off than the user of the forcing two:

SOUTH	NORTH
2 ♣	2 ♦
2 ♠	

The two club bidder has gained a round of bidding. North has given a negative response already, and can bid his hand naturally on the second round. Similarly playing forcing two:

SOUTH	NORTH
2 ♠	2 NT
3 ♠	

or

SOUTH	NORTH
2 ♡	2 NT
3 ♡	

Responder is unable to show lower ranking suit without going past three no trump, whereas with

SOUTH	NORTH
2 ♣	2 ♦
2 ♠	

responder can show any long suit without bypassing a no trump game. On the other hand, in one situation the forcing-two bidder may have the advantage if his suit is clubs:

SOUTH	NORTH
2 ♣	3 ◊

Using the two club bid, and with North holding a positive response in diamonds, the bidding is already at the level of three, and South has not bid clubs. If his opening is a minimum, he may not wish to bid four clubs and so go beyond three no trump.

The forcing-two player, however, can bid both suits naturally and remain at the two-level.

In rare situations, pre-emptive action by the opponents may also put the two club opener at a disadvantage in that he has not yet shown his suit (or one of two suits).

Standard for a positive response to two clubs varies, but most authorities insist on 1½ quick tricks (an ace and a king, or three kings). Others are satisfied with an ace, or a good suit headed by king and queen with some plus values; these treatments have the advantage that positive responses can be given more frequently. Two no trump can be regarded as an exception. Some players make this response with 8 points or more, irrespective of quick trick strength.

After a positive response, the opener will usually rebid as though the response had been negative. Therefore, two clubs—two hearts—two no trump, or two clubs—three clubs—three no trump, shows the balanced minimum hand with 23–24 points. Similarly, two clubs—two hearts—three no trump would show a balanced hand with 25–27 points.

In systems employing an artificial strength-showing bid of ONE CLUB, a bid of two clubs may be the equivalent of a standard one club opening, including a long club suit. See also ACE-SHOWING RESPONSES and FORCING TWO-BID.

TWO-DEMAND BID. See FORCING TWO-BID.

TWO DIAMOND ARTIFICIAL OPENING. As a strong forcing opening bid, see ARTIFICIAL TWO DIAMOND AND TWO CLUB OPENINGS, BENJAMIN convention, ROMEX SYSTEM, SCHENKEN SYSTEM, TAM II TWO CLUB AND TWO DIAMOND OPENINGS. As a two-suited or three-suited opening bid, see conventions listed in TWO DIAMOND OPENING AS MULTI-SUITER.

TWO DIAMOND ARTIFICIAL RESPONSE TO FORCING TWO CLUB OPENING. In response to a TWO CLUB STRONG ARTIFICIAL OPENING a two diamond response is usually negative, showing about 0–7 points. Alternatives are to use this response as:

(1) Automatic. The two diamond bid is non-descriptive, but gives opener room to describe his hand. See ALLEN OVER TWO CLUBS.

(2) Positive. Responder's two diamonds shows 8 or more points, but says nothing about his distribution. All other responses are negative, showing 0–7 points with length in the suit bid.

(3) Double Negative. Responder's bid shows

0–3 points. With this treatment it is possible to use a two heart response artificially either to show specifically 4–7 points (see STEP RESPONSES TO STRONG ARTIFICIAL TWO-BIDS), or as a neutral bid showing at least 4 high-card points and allowing opener to describe his hand.

(4) ACE-SHOWING RESPONSE.

TWO DIAMOND ARTIFICIAL RESPONSE TO ONE NO TRUMP OPENING. Conventions used in response to one no trump opening bids. An artificial convention designed to solve particular no trump bidding problems. In conjunction with the various conventions so used, a substitute sequence may be required to show a weak hand with a long diamond suit: an immediate three diamond bid; or two clubs followed by three diamonds; or two diamonds followed by three diamonds. See FLINT TWO DIAMONDS; GLADIATOR; JACOBY TRANSFER BID; TWO-WAY STAYMAN.

TWO DIAMOND OPENING AS MULTI-SUITER. There are several conventions that use a two diamond opening to show a two-suited or three-suited hand. The principal ones are BLUE TEAM TWO DIAMONDS, FLANNERY TWO DIAMONDS, ROMAN TWO DIAMONDS. In addition, a two diamond opening shows a three-suited hand in the PRECISION CLUB system and a hand with both major suits in the BIG DIAMOND SYSTEM.

TWO HEART ARTIFICIAL RESPONSE TO TWO CLUB OPENING. See STEP RESPONSES TO STRONG ARTIFICIAL TWO-BIDS; TWO DIAMOND ARTIFICIAL RESPONSE TO FORCING TWO CLUB OPENING.

TWO NO TRUMP OPENING. This shows a balanced hand with 21–22 points, and might be made with 20 points. This is the standard expert treatment. The traditional range of 22–24 continues to be used by most players who use FORCING TWO-BIDS. See also TWO NO TRUMP OPENING FOR MINORS.

Theoretically the distribution should be the same as for an opening no trump bid: 4–3–3–3, 4–4–3–2, or 5–3–3–2 with the five-card suit a minor. However, the two no trump opening often has to serve as a "least-evil" choice with hands too strong to open with one of a suit and not strong enough for a forcing opening. 5–3–3–2 with a major suit is frequently opened with two no trump, and occasional departures such as 6–3–2–2 or 5–4–2–2 are permissible.

Responses are as follows:

(1) *Three clubs.* Stayman, asking opener to bid a major suit. With no major he bids three diamonds, and if responder then bids a major, he shows a five-card suit. Holding both majors, either suit may be bid by partnership agreement, and agreement is not essential. If responder then bids three no trump, the opener bids his second major.

A rebid of four in a major suit, other than a raise, can be used to show a club/major two-suiter with mild slam ambitions.

A rebid of three no trump by the opener virtually does not exist in standard methods. It can be used by partnership agreement to show a hand with no interest in a major-suit contract, perhaps a doubleton in each.

A variation normal in England (due to the BARON SYSTEM) is for the opener to bid all his suits up the line. Three diamonds would show a diamond suit but would not deny a major. Three no trump would show that the opener's only suit was clubs. This method facilitates minor-suit slam bidding but is somewhat inefficient when responder is 5–4 or 4–5 in the major suits.

(2) *Three diamonds.* Used by many experts as the FLINT convention. In a natural sense the bid shows at least five diamonds, and is a slam suggestion.

(3) *Three hearts or three spades.* Forcing and shows a five-card suit. The suit may be longer [see (6) below]. The responder is asking the opener to choose between the major-suit game (with three-card support) or three no trump (with a doubleton in responder's suit). However, the responder may have slam interests, so the opener makes a cue-bid (2NT—3 ♡—4 ◊) if he has good support and a suitable hand for slam purposes. See also AUTOMATIC ACES; EXPECTED NUMBER OF CONTROLS IN BALANCED HANDS.

(4) *Three no trump.* A range of 4–10, although a thin 4-point hand may be passed. An occasional 3-point hand (Kxxxx) may be worth a raise.

(5) *Four clubs or four diamonds.* These bids are usually conventional (GERBER, TEXAS, or SOUTH AFRICAN TEXAS). In a natural sense they would show a strong suit, but are very rare.

(6) *Four hearts or four spades.* In standard methods this shows a six-card suit with mild slam ambitions. Holding a weaker hand with a six-card major, responder must bid his suit at the three-level and then rebid it. Many experts, especially in England, use the jump to game as a sign-off, in which case three of a major followed by four is a mild slam invitation.

(7) *Four no trump.* A natural invitation to six no trump, holding about 11 points. Responder's distribution is likely to be 4–3–3–3, but might be 4–4–3–2 or 5–3–3–2 if no major suit is held (see MILLER SLAM CONVENTION).

(8) *Five clubs or five diamonds.* A very unbalanced weak hand. A seven-card suit and a void would be typical. The opener is expected to pass, but might bid six with a fine fit and excellent controls.

(9) *Five hearts or five spades.* A strong invitation to bid six, based on a six-card suit.

(10) *Five no trump.* This has no natural meaning, but is used by some experts as an invitation to seven no trump. With no interest in a grand slam, the opener bids six no trump.

(11) *Six no trump.* A balanced hand, probably 4–3–3–3, with 12–14 points.

For an alternative system of responding, see MILES RESPONSES TO TWO NO TRUMP OPENINGS.

TWO NO TRUMP OPENING FOR MINORS. A

convention using a two no trump opening bid to show a hand worth 10–13 points not vulnerable or 14–16 points vulnerable, and at least five cards in each minor suit. Responses at the three- and four-level are not forcing.

TWO NO TRUMP OVERCALL. Can be used in six

different ways:

(1) *Natural.* To show a two no trump opening bid with about 22 points. This helps to define the range of a two no trump bid preceded by a take-out double, which would indicate 19–20. These two procedures can be interchanged by partnership agreement. STAYMAN would apply with partnerships that use it after a ONE NO TRUMP OVERCALL.

(2) *Unusual.* To show a minor two-suiter. The minimum strength would vary according to vulnerability. At favorable vulnerability, a 6–5 distribution with 6 points in the suits would usually be considered adequate. At unfavorable vulnerability both the hand and the suits should be distinctly stronger. The maximum strength would be a hand justifying an immediate CUE-BID in the opponent's suit.

Responder may have occasion to bid an unusual no trump in his turn:

```
            SOUTH
         ♠ 5 3 2
         ♡ A 6 4 3
         ◊ Q 7 2
         ♣ Q 6 3
```

With neither side vulnerable West deals and bids one spade. North bids two no trump (unusual) and East bids four spades. South expects a save in one of the minor suits, and bids four no trump to request North to pick a minor suit. If he has a six-five distribution it will be important to play in the six-card suit because spade leads will force declarer to ruff immediately.

In BLUE TEAM CLUB, two no trump applies over minor suits also and shows the lowest unbid suits: hearts and diamonds over one club, and hearts and clubs over one diamond. See DEFENSE TO TWO-SUITED INTERFERENCE.

(3) *Pre-emptive.* To indicate a long broken suit lower in rank than the opening bid, justifying a pre-emptive bid at the level of three. Partner is expected to bid three clubs if third hand passes, to permit his side to reach the appropriate suit; but third hand seldom passes. This is not needed playing WEAK JUMP OVERCALLS and has dubious value in any event.

(4) *Roman.* To show a strong two-suited hand, in which the suits are not specified. Responder bids the lowest unbid suit, and if the two no trump bidder shows a suit, he holds that suit and the suit in which responder made his artificial response. Three no trump would show the two unbid suits. (For weaker two-suited hands, see JUMP OVERCALL.)

(5) *Modern.* To show a strong hand with a near-solid minor suit, for example:

```
         ♠ A 2
         ♡ K 5
         ◊ J 4 2
         ♣ A Q J 9 6 2
```

Responder may raise to three no trump, or bid three clubs with no interest in game. In the latter case the overcaller passes or converts to three diamonds. In borderline cases, responder is guided by possession of a key card in his partner's minor. With a diamond honor he bids three clubs, and converts a three diamond rebid to three no trump. With a club honor he responds three diamonds, giving the overcaller the choice between three diamonds and three no trump.

(6) *Artificial.* When an immediate cue-bid in the opener's suit is given a specialized meaning (as in MICHAELS CUE-BID), two no trump can be used to show a hand of game-going strength, with three clubs as a conventional negative response.

TWO NO TRUMP REBID. See OPENER'S REBID.

TWO NO TRUMP RESPONSE (to Opening One No Trump Bid). Several treatments are in current usage: (1) as a balanced raise, showing 8–9 HCP (standard), (2) as a take-out for opener's better minor, (3) as a relay to three clubs, allowing responder principally to pass or to sign off in three diamonds, (4) as the Baron convention, initiating the bidding of four-card suits up the line in the hope of locating a four-four fit for play in slam. For elaboration of each method, see ONE NO TRUMP OPENING (Responses).

TWO NO TRUMP RESPONSE (to Opening Suit Bid of One). There are five treatments which can be adopted.

(1) *Standard.* 13–15 points and game forcing. The responder raises with any balanced distribution. If he rebids at the three-level in a suit, it will usually show an aversion to no trump: he is likely to have a singleton or void. The responder must then move cautiously:

♠ Q 3
♡ A 8 6 2
◇ A Q J
♣ J 8 5 3

The bidding:

NORTH	SOUTH
1 ♠	2 NT
3 ♣	3 ◇

The most useful bid South can make is a call at the three-level in a suit in which he holds considerable strength. If this corresponds to North's shortage, he will know that three no trump will be safe, and that there would be duplicated values in a high suit contract. But if North's shortage is in an unbid suit, he will know that a suit contract will be preferable to no trump. Responder should avoid raising opener's secondary minor suit, although he may do so at a later stage if circumstances warrant it.

A possible additional use for the two no trump response, suggested by Marshall MILES, is for balanced hands with about 19 points. Whatever the opener

rebids, the responder then suggests a slam, usually by rebidding four no trump. This makes it clear that responder cannot have the normal two no trump response.

(2) *Limit.* 11–12 points, encouraging but not forcing. The bidding can stop short of game in three ways: (a) an immediate pass by the opener, holding a minimum balanced hand; (b) after a rebid of his own suit by opener, showing a sub-minimum opening and, usually, a six-card suit (a typical ACOL sign-off bid); (c) after a bid of a new suit by the opener and a preference bid at the three level by responder. The responder must give jump preference to four hearts or four spades if his hand is particularly suitable for the suit game.

In choosing a rebid at the three-level, responder should consider the possibility of bidding a strong suit, as in (1) above. The Miles variation for balanced hands with about 19 points is not available since two no trump is not forcing.

If responder has passed originally, a response of two no trump is always a limit bid (unless DRURY or SNAP is being used).

(3) *Baron.* 16–18 points and game forcing. In this system the responses of two no trump and three no trump are inverted. After three no trump (12–14) it is usually easy for the opener to select a suitable game; and the two no trump response leaves more room for exploration on hands on which a slam is likely.

(4) *Psychic Control.* 21–22 points, and therefore offering prospects of game if the opening bidder has a systemic ROTH-STONE psychic.

In all the cases listed, with the possible exception of (4), the two no trump response normally has a 4-3-3-3 distribution, or 4-4-3-2 with the doubleton in the opener's suit.

(5) *Conventional.* Used with limit raises to show a standard forcing jump raise when the opening bid was in a major (invented by Oswald Jacoby). A rebid of four spades shows a minimum opening, and three no trump and three spades show hands of increasing strength. Rebids at three- and four-level in a new suit show singletons and voids respectively.

TWO NO TRUMP RESPONSE (Over Opponent's Take-out Double). An artificial response to an opening bid, which may be used in any of several ways, depending on whether the opening was in a suit or in no trump, and on the partnership's understanding: (1) as a limit raise over opener's suit bid, showing about 9 to 11 points with three or four trumps; (2) as a pre-emptive raise of opener's minor suit bid, normally promising five or six trumps and unbalanced distribution; this use allows responder to jump to three of opener's minor to show a limit raise, and permits opener to bid game in no trump from what is more likely to be the RIGHT SIDE; (3) when opener's bid was one no trump, as a relay to three clubs, see LEBENSOHL convention; (4) when opener's bid was one no trump, as a take-out bid implying that responder has a strong two-suiter, with which he cannot risk redoubling because the double may have been made on a long running suit.

TWO-ODD. Two tricks over book, or eight tricks in all.

TWO OVER ONE RESPONSE. A minimum response in a lower-ranking suit to an opening suit bid. For example, one heart—two clubs.

The minimum strength required for this response is 10 points in standard methods. Rather more is required in ROTH-STONE and KAPLAN-SHEINWOLD, when responder guarantees a second bid; rather less in ACOL, when 8 points may be sufficient.

The maximum strength is a hand just short of a JUMP SHIFT, i.e., about 17 points in standard methods or about 15 points in ACOL. For players using WEAK JUMP RESPONSES, the two over one has no upper limit.

The longest suit is usually chosen for the response, and if two five-card suits are held, the higher-ranking is given preference. If the sequence is specifically one spade—two hearts, the responder virtually guarantees a five-card suit, and the opener can raise confidently with three-card support or conceivably with a doubleton. Any response in the suit immediately lower in rank is likely to be at least five cards (one heart—two diamonds, or one diamond—two clubs).

For other aspects of this response, see CHOICE OF SUIT and UP THE LINE.

TWO-SUITER. A hand with one suit of more than four cards and another suit of more than three cards. The term used to be confined to hands with at least five cards in each of two suits. A 5–4 distribution was called a semi-two-suiter. For opening the bidding with a two-suiter, see BORDERLINE OPENING BIDS and CHOICE OF SUIT.

TWO-SUITER CONVENTIONS. Several defensive two-suiter conventions are listed under the following headings: ASTRO, ASTRO CUE-BIDS, BROZEL, COLORFUL CUE-BIDS, COPENHAGEN, DEFENSE TO STRONG ARTIFICIAL OPENINGS, LANDY, LEA SYSTEM, MICHAELS, ROMAN JUMP OVERCALLS, TOP AND BOTTOM CUE-BID, UNUSUAL NO TRUMP, UPPER SUITS CUE-BID. Offensive-type two-suited conventions include BIG DIAMOND SYSTEM (two club and two diamond openings); FLANNERY TWO DIAMONDS; FLANNERY TWO HEARTS; ROMAN SYSTEM (two heart and two spade openings).

TWO TABLES. At duplicate, two tables provide for competition among eight (or nine) players as individuals, four pairs of players, or two teams of four.

As an individual tournament among eight players, seven rounds are required so that each player will play with each other player as a partner. Conduct of this game is described under INDIVIDUAL MOVEMENTS for eight or nine players.

As a pair tournament, three rounds are required. In each round the boards are relayed between the two tables, and scores can be determined almost instantly by direct comparison. Pair 4 is North-South at table 1, facing pair 1 as East-West; at table 2, Pair 2 is North-South, and Pairs 3, East-West. The better score between the North-South pairs is awarded 1

point, the East-West players at the other table (having the better East-West score) also receiving a point.

New boards (or a reshuffling) are brought in for round 2, Pair 3 replacing 2, 2 replacing 1 and 1 replacing 3 for positions. This is repeated for the third round with a third set of boards. Eight boards to a round give about a three-hour game.

As a contest betwen two teams of four, the game may be divided into halves, if it is desired to have each pair of one team in head-on competition with both pairs of the other team. Otherwise it may be played straight through. In each half, one-quarter of the total number of boards to be played are shuffled at each table and played; the boards are then exchanged between tables. Scoring may be BOARD-A-MATCH, AGGREGATE (or total points), or scored by IMP. The latter is preferred by most top players.

For five pairs (two and one-half tables) see THREE TABLES.

TWO-WAY FINESSE. A recurring type of situation in which a FINESSE may be taken through either opponent. For example:

(a)	(b)
NORTH	NORTH
♠ A 10 3 2	♠ K 10 2
SOUTH	SOUTH
♠ K J 5 4	♠ A J 3

The question, of course, is whom to play for the queen of spades, East or West?

In many cases, in the absence of any clues revealed during the bidding or the play, it becomes a pure guess. Quite a few players, in these circumstances, will finesse West for the queen, on the theory of QUEEN OVER JACK. Of course, this method of taking a two-way finesse is rather on the unscientific side. In the absence of any external clues, a queen can frequently be located without resorting to guesswork. Here is such a case.

```
                    NORTH
                  ♠ K Q 3
                  ♡ K Q 7 5
                  ◊ K 10 9
                  ♣ Q J 4
  WEST                              EAST
♠ 8 4 2                          ♠ 9 7 6 5
♡ 6 4 3                          ♡ 10 8
◊ 7                              ◊ Q 8 6 5 3 2
♣ 10 9 8 6 5 2                   ♣ 7
                    SOUTH
                  ♠ A J 10
                  ♡ A J 9 2
                  ◊ A J 4
                  ♣ A K 3
```

South arrived at a seven no trump contract, against which West opened a club, dummy's jack winning. Declarer counted twelve tricks, and perceived that the thirteenth trick could be obtained only in the diamond suit. Whom to finesse for the diamond queen, East or West?

At trick two South cashed the king of clubs, East discarding a diamond. Three rounds of spades were then taken, everybody following suit. Next, three rounds of hearts were played and declarer paused to take inventory.

West was known to have started with six clubs, three spades, and three hearts. Hence he had, at most, one diamond. Dummy's king of diamonds was then played, and when West followed suit, all of his thirteen cards were accounted for. A diamond was now led off the board, and the jack of diamonds was finessed successfully, for declarer's thirteenth trick.

On occasion, when declarer is confronted with a two-way finesse, he can maneuver his play so that an opponent will lead that suit to him, thereby giving declarer a "free finesse." The deal which follows illustrates this point.

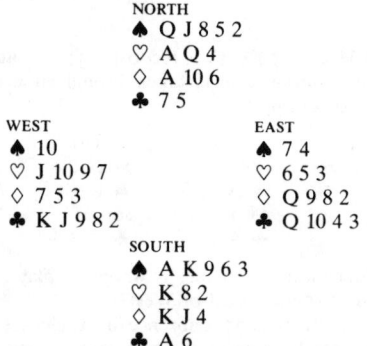

```
                    NORTH
                 ♠ Q J 8 5 2
                 ♡ A Q 4
                 ◇ A 10 6
                 ♣ 7 5
   WEST                           EAST
 ♠ 10                           ♠ 7 4
 ♡ J 10 9 7                     ♡ 6 5 3
 ◇ 7 5 3                        ◇ Q 9 8 2
 ♣ K J 9 8 2                    ♣ Q 10 4 3
                    SOUTH
                 ♠ A K 9 6 3
                 ♡ K 8 2
                 ◇ K J 4
                 ♣ A 6
```

South arrived at a six spade contract. West opened the jack of hearts, dummy's queen winning. The opponents' trumps were picked up in two rounds, after which the ace and king of hearts were cashed. Next came the ace of clubs, followed by another club, and this position was reached:

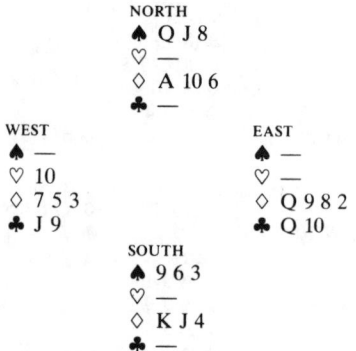

```
                    NORTH
                 ♠ Q J 8
                 ♡ —
                 ◇ A 10 6
                 ♣ —
   WEST                           EAST
 ♠ —                            ♠ —
 ♡ 10                           ♡ —
 ◇ 7 5 3                        ◇ Q 9 8 2
 ♣ J 9                          ♣ Q 10
                    SOUTH
                 ♠ 9 6 3
                 ♡ —
                 ◇ K J 4
                 ♣ —
```

It mattered not which opponent won the trick. If a heart or a club were returned, declarer would trump it in dummy, while simultaneously discarding the four of diamonds from his own hand. If the winner of the club lead led a diamond, declarer would surely make three diamond tricks.

In the actual play, West, who had won the club lead, led a diamond, East's queen falling to declarer's king via a free finesse.

The rules of thumb for taking two-way finesses fall under six headings. They all assume that other things are equal, which they very seldom are. In almost all cases, one defender will appear more likely to have missing honor cards, or to have greater length in the crucial suit.

(1) *Technical.* Play the left-hand opponent for the missing honor. Without the honor, he might have selected a passive opening lead in that suit. His selection of another opening lead is a slight indication that he may hold the missing queen.

(2) *Practical.* Declarer can often take advantage of the fact that the defenders are human.

```
                    DUMMY
                 ♡ A 10 8 4

                    DECLARER
                 ♡ K J 9 3
```

By leading the jack, South may induce West to cover with the queen (or think revealingly about covering). The cover would be necessary if South started with a doubleton jack (or with a tripleton jack, but in that case he would be unlikely to lead the jack). West has no temptation to cover if South has bid the suit, or if the nine is visible in dummy as well as the ten. If West plays low without thought, South plans to put up dummy's ace and finesse on the way back. Note that this would be risky technically if dummy did not hold the eight. East would be able to make a trick from an original holding of Q 8 7 x.

(3) *Unethical.* Think hard for two minutes (a long time) and lead rapidly from the wrong hand. The opponent who objects is likely to have the queen, because he is more interested in what declarer is doing. At the highest level of play, the converse would probably apply.

(4) *Counter-unethical.* Declarer holds the situation shown in (2) above, but fears that West, a stranger, may be in the habit of cheating by hesitating *without* the queen. Luckily South holds the following diamond suit:

```
                    DUMMY
                 ◇ A 3 2

                    DECLARER
                 ◇ K Q J
```

The jack is led, and South notes whether or not West hesitates. If West hesitates slightly, South will know what to do later if West hesitates or does not hesitate when the heart jack is led.

(5) *Superstitious.* The QUEEN-OVER-JACK rule is such a slight indication that it virtually ranks with the Belgian rule that the younger player always has the queen. If it has any value, then king-over-queen and ace-over-king must be very slightly superior rules, because more significant cards are involved.

Such rules normally have no applicability at tournament play, where the cards played to a trick are not gathered together. In England, however, it is habitual to sort the hand into suits at the end of each duplicate deal. If two adjacent honor cards were in the same hand on the previous deal and were not separated in the shuffle, the tendency will be for the jack to lie over the queen and the queen to lie over the king.

(6) *Dishonorable*. Holding the following trump suit at rubber bridge,

DUMMY

♠ K 9 4

DECLARER

♠ A J 10 8 3

declarer is said to have claimed 100 honors before tackling the trump suit. East dutifully recorded 100 to North-South on his score pad, and South finessed West for the spade queen. East produced the queen, announced "One down. No honors," and crossed them off his score pad.

(7) *Psychological*. P. Hal Sims claimed that the first defender to speak, light a cigarette, order a drink, or react in similar fashion could be expected to hold the queen. This would be an attempt to show nonchalant disinterest, but in fact betray nervousness.

Other two-way finesses.

(a)   (b)

DUMMY   DUMMY

♠ Q 10 5   ♠ J 9 5

DECLARER   DECLARER

♠ K 9 7   ♠ Q 8 4

(a) is a two-way finesse for the jack. (b) is a two-way finesse for the ten.

For other specific situations, see SUIT COMBINATIONS.

F. K.

TWO-WAY GAME TRIES (devised by Robert EWEN, New York, N.Y.). A method that combines both long-suit and short-suit game tries after a major-suit raise. If the auction starts one heart, two hearts, opener bids two no trump, three clubs, or three diamonds to make a short-suit try in spades, clubs, or diamonds respectively. A two spade rebid by opener forces responder to bid two no trump, after which opener bids three clubs, three diamonds, or three hearts to make a long-suit try in clubs, diamonds, or spades respectively. If the auction begins one spade, two spades, a new suit opener on the three-level is a short-suit try in the bid suit. A two no trump rebid by opener forces responder to bid three clubs, after which opener bids three diamonds, three hearts, or three spades to make a long-suit try in diamonds, hearts, or clubs respectively. Reraises of the major (one heart, two hearts, three hearts) are general-strength game tries. This method may be expanded to include raises of overcalls, or as a slam try after a forcing double raise.

TWO-WAY NO TRUMP. The use of two different point-count ranges for a one no trump opening bid. WOODSON TWO-WAY NO TRUMP is one form, as is the use of a WEAK NO TRUMP not vulnerable with a standard no trump vulnerable, and also the THREE-QUARTER NO TRUMP.

TWO-WAY STAYMAN. Any of a variety of conventions that use a two club response to a one no trump opening as STAYMAN and use a two diamond response to one no trump as a supplement to Stayman. The following describe the principal uses of the two diamond responses.

(1) *Double-barreled Stayman.* Two clubs is used for hands which cannot guarantee game, and two diamonds for hands which wish to force to game. After two clubs, the opener's rebids are normal, and the responder's rebids are all non-forcing. As responder's second-round jump to three spades, for example, would not be forcing, a two-level rebid can be regarded as weak. (See Stayman convention.) The meaning of two clubs followed by a jump to the four-level is a matter of partnership agreement.

Over two diamonds, the opener normally shows a major suit or rebids two no trump; but he can rebid at the three-level in a suit or in no trump if he wishes, showing a five-card suit, or a maximum 4–3–3–3 hand without a major. When there is a possibility of a minor-suit slam, a fit can be explored at the level of three because a forcing situation exists.

(2) *Stayman Two Diamonds.* A forcing to game response showing an unbalanced minor-suit hand: no four-card major suit, and a singleton or a void is a necessary requirement. The opener rebids in a suit to show concentrated strength (e.g., ace, king, jack—not necessarily a four-card suit) and two no trump to show scattered strength. If the concentrated strength proves to be opposite responder's shortage, he will know that three no trump is playable and that there is duplication of values for a suit contract. The subsequent bidding is also aimed at determining whether there is a serious no trump weakness.

(3) *Roth Two Diamonds.* A response that is forcing to game and invitational to slam. This convention allows slam exploration without getting past the game level.

Like Doubled-barreled Stayman, the two diamond response asks opener about his four-card majors; unlike Double-barreled Stayman, the two club response can be followed by rebids that are game-forcing as in simple STAYMAN. Opener's rebids show whether he has one or both four-card majors, or if he has none, whether he has a minimum or maximum no trump.

(4) *Murray Two Diamonds* asks the opener to bid his longer major suit, bidding a three-card suit if necessary. With equal length (4–4 or 3–3) in the majors the opener bids two hearts. One advantage of the convention is that it permits responder to bid weak unbalanced hands with 5–5 or 4–4 in the major suits. The responder does not promise any strength whatever, although he can have a strong hand. A rebid of two no trump by the responder asks the opener to bid four-card suits up the line.

The opener's rebid must be in a major suit unless he has two major-suit doubletons, in which case he bids a six-card minor suit or two no trump.

(5) *August Two Diamonds*, developed concurrently with Murray Two Diamonds and patterned on similar principles, is also a take-out for the majors with the added proviso that any suit rebid by responder is a sign-off. This permits responder to use the convention with a weak 4–5 major-minor two-suiter. If the opener rebids the wrong major, responder retreats to his minor. With a weak minor two-suiter, responder first bids two clubs (Stayman), then rebids three clubs.

(6) *Truscott Two Diamonds*, devised by Alan TRUSCOTT of New York and used widely in Israel. After the two diamond response, opener defines his distribution and responder uses relay bids, as follows: With 4–3–3–3 hands opener rebids two no trump and shows his suit after a three club relay. With 4–4–3–2 hands, opener bids three diamonds with both minors; with a major and a minor, he bids the suits in that order; with both majors he bids two hearts and then two no trump. In all cases after opener's two suits have been identified, the next relay by responder asks for a two-step clarification of opener's distribution; the first step shows that the doubleton ranks below the tripleton. With five hearts, spades, or clubs, opener bids the suit, and after a relay he rebids three hearts, three spades, or three no trump to show the lowest, middle, or highest ranking doubleton, respectively. If opener has a five-card diamond suit, he shows it and simultaneously identifies his doubleton by bidding three hearts, three spades, or three no trump directly over two diamonds. Responder can use a meaningless bid below the three no trump level to ask whether opener is minimum or maximum.

U

USBA. Abbreviation for UNITED STATES BRIDGE ASSOCIATION, one of the predecessor organizations from which AMERICAN CONTRACT BRIDGE LEAGUE emerged.

USBA GRAND NATIONALS. See UNITED STATES BRIDGE ASSOCIATION.

OPEN TEAM

YEAR	WINNERS	RUNNERS-UP
1934	H. Schenken,	W. Malowan
	M. T. Gottlieb, O. Jacoby	L. Langdon
	D. Burnstine, R. Frey	L. Bachner
		S. Rusinow
1935	H. Schenken, M. Gottlieb	W. Beinecke
	O. Jacoby, S. Stearns	J. Mattheys
	R. Frey	H. Jackson
		C. E. Van Vleck
1936	Mrs. J. Culbertson	E. Hymes, B. J. Becker
	W. von Zedtwitz	M. D. Maier
	S. Fry, M. Barnes	C. Lochridge
1937	D. Burnstine, O. Jacoby	E. Burns, L. Reiter
	M. D. Maier	S. Sanders
	H. Schenken	M. Schoenfield
	B. J. Becker	

MIXED TEAM

YEAR	WINNERS	RUNNERS-UP
1935	J. Sherman, R. Sherman	M. Kalman, R. Frey
	R. Kahn	Mrs. J. C. Planco
	Mrs. F. Greenebaum	J. A. Farrer
1936	Mrs. G. Harris	Mrs. R. Fuller
	J. Mattheys	M. Barnes, B. Collyer
	Mrs. J. C. Thaw, R. Balfe	W. von Zedtwitz

1937	H. Chanin	Mrs. S. A. Herzog
	Mrs. E. Clement	J. Shore
	C. Lochridge	Mrs. R. B. Fuller
	Mrs. N. Demarest	R. Appleyard

OPEN PAIR

YEAR	WINNERS	RUNNERS-UP
1934	H. Schenken	A. M. Barnes
	M. T. Gottlieb	E. Hymes, Jr.
1935	M. D. Maier, S. Stearns	M. Elis, F. Kaplan
1936	O. Jacoby, D. Burnstine	S. Stearns, J. Maier
1937	O. Jacoby, L. Bachner	W. von Zedtwitz
		M. D. Maier

MIXED PAIR

YEAR	WINNERS	RUNNERS-UP
1936	W. von Zedtwitz	M. Lovejoy
	B. Collyer	W. Liggett
1937	H. Chanin	Mrs. D. Tansill
	Mrs. E. Clement	R. Balfe

UNAUTHORIZED INFORMATION. Information which is given to a partner by means other than a legal call or play. Such information may be conveyed by questions, tone of voice, special emphasis, mannerisms, grimaces, remarks, squirms, or huddles. If such information is received, a player should be governed by Law 16 of either rubber or duplicate bridge. See ALERTING; EXPLANATION OF ANY CALL OR PLAY.

At times in duplicate games a player may inadvertently overhear a remark by a contestant about a particular board which he has not as yet played. Such a fact should be reported to the director who will act in a manner as fair as possible to the player so reporting. See LAWS (Law 16).

UNBALANCED DISTRIBUTION. Referring to either the distribution of the suits in a hand or the distribution of one suit among the four hands, unbalanced is opposed to BALANCED DISTRIBUTION. Among the requirements for unbalanced distribution is the combination of one or more long suits and one or more singletons or voids. A 5–4–2–2 distribution is on the borderline between balanced and unbalanced distribution.

UNBALANCED PATTERN. Hands which are eminently unsuited for no trump play or defensive properties. See MATHEMATICAL TABLES for frequency of occurrence. When a pattern is decidedly unbalanced, FREAK hands and results are to be suspected.

UNBALANCED SWISS RAISE. Part of the ACES SCIENTIFIC SYSTEM, used in combination with VALUE SWISS RAISES to provide a full range of game-forcing raises in response to a major suit opening. A jump response of three of the other major is used to show 10–12 points with a singleton somewhere in the hand; a jump to three no trump shows 13–15 points with a singleton.

Opener makes the cheapest bid to locate responder's singleton. Responder answers by bidding one of the next three steps; two of these steps will be natural suits and will show the singleton in the suit bid; the other step will be either three no trump or four of the trump suit, and will show a singleton in the remaining suit. See also CONGLOMERATE MAJOR RAISES, SUPER SWISS.

UNBEATABLE. See COLD.

UNBID MINOR SUIT FORCE. After opener has made a rebid of one no trump, it is sometimes useful for responder to have available a low-level forcing bid, either to inquire about opener's support for responder's suit, or to provide flexibility for responder's description of his own hand. Some pairs thus use a TWO CLUB REBID BY RESPONDER AS ONLY FORCE AFTER ONE NO TRUMP REBID; some use a two club rebid as STAYMAN ON SECOND ROUND. Both of these conventions can be amended slightly to allow responder to use the unbid minor suit as his forcing call; when the opening bid has been one club, this modification has the advantage of permitting responder to sign off in his partner's suit.

UNBID SUIT. Suit or suits which have not been bid by declarer or his partner during the auction. Frequently, without any attractive opening lead, a player will select a lead on the basis that a suit has been unbid. (This applies frequently to a major suit against a no trump contract.)

At some point in the auction, it may be desirable to make a bid in a previously unbid suit as a WAITING BID. See FOURTH SUIT FORCING AND ARTIFICIAL.

UNBLOCKING. Throwing a high card in play in order to gain some advantage for the hand opposite.

```
           NORTH
           A 10 6 2
WEST                   EAST
J 9 8 3                K 7 5
           SOUTH
           Q 4
```

Dummy has no side entry. West leads the three won by East's king. South unblocks with his queen, permitting a later finesse of the ten so that South makes two tricks. Similarly:

```
           NORTH
           A 9 5 3
WEST                   EAST
J 10 8 7               K 6 2
           SOUTH
           Q 4
```

Dummy has no side entry. West leads the jack, won by East's king. South unblocks the queen, and makes two tricks by a later finesse of the nine.

```
           NORTH
           Q 10 5 3
WEST                   EAST
K 8 7 2                6 4
           SOUTH
           A J 9
```

If South needs an entry to dummy later in spades, he must be careful to win the opening lead with the ace.

A blind spot for many players is the internal block:

```
NORTH            NORTH
A K Q 4 3        A 7 6 4 2
          or
SOUTH            SOUTH
10 8 7 6         K Q 9 8
```

If one defender holds J x x, five tricks cannot be run without a side entry to dummy. The perverse arrangement of the spot cards makes it impossible for South to win the fourth round of the suit with a low card in dummy. Declarer can sometimes maneuver to discard one of his spot cards on an opponent's suit.

The following examples of unblocking play are given by Roger Trézel in his monograph *Blocage et Déblocage* (See BIBLIOGRAPHY, D).

```
                 NORTH
                 ♠ A 3
                 ♡ A K
                 ◇ A 6 4
                 ♣ A K 7 4 3 2
WEST                              EAST
♠ Q 9 8 7                         ♠ 10 6 5 2
♡ 10 8 5                          ♡ 9 7 4 3
◇ K 10 7                          ◇ J 8 2
♣ Q 8 5                           ♣ J 10
                 SOUTH
                 ♠ K J 4
                 ♡ Q J 6 2
                 ◇ Q 9 5 3
                 ♣ 9 6
```

South plays in six no trump, and West sets an inadvertent trap for South by leading the spade seven. The right route to make twelve tricks is to win with the spade ace, cash two heart tricks, and develop clubs. As the cards lie, South can actually recover from the greedy error of winning the first trick in his hand. South cashes his winners in spades, hearts, and clubs and plays a third club, end-playing West.

The following is an unusual type of unblock in a suit in which declarer has no losers:

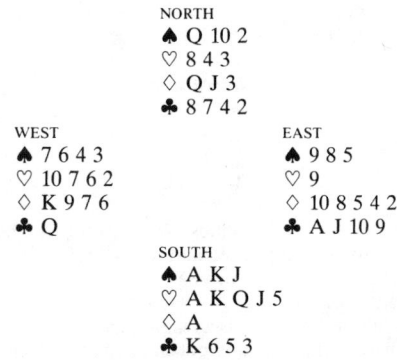

West leads the club queen against four hearts, won by East's ace. South covers the club jack return with the king, and West ruffs. West returns a trump, and South draws the remaining trumps.

The winning line is to cash the diamond ace, and

play two rounds of spades ending in dummy with the queen. The queen of diamonds is led, and South discards his remaining high spade—a winner-on-loser play. If West wins, and it does not help him to duck, he must return a spade or a diamond, and South's club losers are discarded on dummy's winners.

UNBLOCKING SQUEEZE.

A simple positional squeeze characterized by the fact that, although the last three tricks are "on top," lack of entries prevents declarer from cashing them.

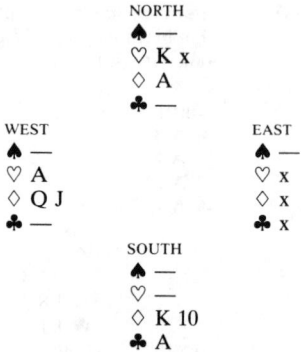

```
                    NORTH
                    ♠ —
                    ♡ K x
                    ◇ A
                    ♣ —
    WEST                        EAST
    ♠ —                         ♠ —
    ♡ A                         ♡ x
    ◇ Q J                       ◇ x
    ♣ —                         ♣ x
                    SOUTH
                    ♠ —
                    ♡ —
                    ◇ K 10
                    ♣ A
```

The club ace squeezes West. If he throws the heart ace dummy's two honors are established. If he throws a diamond dummy's diamond ace is unblocked, allowing South to cash the diamond king and ten.

The following deal, composed by G. A. Dickinson, is an attractive example which may be treated as a double dummy problem:

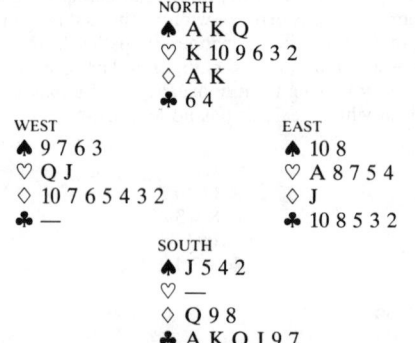

```
                    NORTH
                    ♠ A K Q
                    ♡ K 10 9 6 3 2
                    ◇ A K
                    ♣ 6 4
    WEST                        EAST
    ♠ 9 7 6 3                   ♠ 10 8
    ♡ Q J                       ♡ A 8 7 5 4
    ◇ 10 7 6 5 4 3 2            ◇ J
    ♣ —                         ♣ 10 8 5 3 2
                    SOUTH
                    ♠ J 5 4 2
                    ♡ —
                    ◇ Q 9 8
                    ♣ A K Q J 9 7
```

South plays in seven clubs, West leading the heart queen to the king, ace, and a low ruff by South. There are, in a way, thirteen tricks on top, but there are entry problems.

Solution: South leads a diamond to dummy's ace, and cashes the king and queen of spades. A club is then led and finessed and the clubs are then run. On the last trump West must discard the heart jack — which it is assumed that he won't do—or reduce his holding to either one spade or one diamond. North's

hand is unblocked by the discard of the ace of the suit bared by West, leaving South two tricks to cash in it. The second of these puts pressure on West again, the squeeze in hearts and the remaining suit being repeated. This may be termed a Repeating Jettison Squeeze. See also ENTRY SQUEEZE.

UNCONSTRUCTIVE. A bid which is distinctly discouraging, but does not bar partner from making a further move.

SOUTH	NORTH
1 ♣	1 ♠
1 NT	2 ♡

North announces that he dislikes no trump, that he has at least five spades and at least four hearts, and expects to play in two spades or two hearts. However, game is not completely excluded, and South may raise to three hearts, inviting game, if he has a maximum hand with four-card heart support.

UNDER. To the right of. Thus, South is under West, etc. A king or any other card may be said to be under another card if the positional factor applies as above.

UNDER THE GUN. A term borrowed from poker in which game the phrase refers to the hand betting immediately after the dealer. In bridge there are various meanings, both in bidding and play. The term can be used in bidding situations to cover the position where a hand or player can be said to be "under the gun" if he is bidding directly after a preemptive bidder and before a hand which has not yet been heard from. The term also can describe a position where a player has to meet a bid-or-double situation at the slam level. In play, it is used to describe the hand between dummy and declarer that has a high card or high cards that are finessable and are in a vulnerable position thereby.

UNDERBID. A bid lower than the value of the hand warrants. Although such bids are usually made because of inferior judgment, they may sometimes be made consciously and deliberately. One justification would be a tactical situation in which the opponents seem likely to save if the full value of the hand is bid. If the final contract is reached with, apparently, less assurance, the opponents may be deterred from saving. An underbid may also be made as an upside-down type of SHOOTING.

UNDERBIDDER. A player who regularly bids slightly less than the value of his hand warrants. He is rarer, and easier to play with, than the overbidder. His psychological motivation is usually a reluctance to be set in any contract. His tendencies manifest themselves in the later rounds of bidding, so that he will never push toward a borderline game. His partners therefore tend to overbid slightly in certain situations. After a two-over-one response, responder may choose to jump to three no trump at his second turn, holding 12 points, a hand on which he would normally be content to bid an invitational two no trump.

UNDERLEAD. The lead of a low card in a suit in which the master card or cards is held. This is routine in no trump contracts, but is unusual in trump contracts.

```
                    NORTH
                    K 7 2
WEST                                 EAST
A 10 8 3                             Q 9 6 5
                    SOUTH
                    J 4
```

If West gains the lead early in the play, and leads a low card, South should guess right. West would be unlikely to lead from the queen, and give South the chance of a trick he could not otherwise make. As the cards lie, one trick is all the defenders can make if they play passively.

But if West can find the lead of a low club originally, South is almost sure to go wrong and play low from dummy. Underleads of aces as the opening lead are distinctly daring, but may sometimes be risked if the bidding suggests strongly that dummy will have the king of the suit.

Another motive for an underlead is an urgent desire to get a particular lead from partner, perhaps for a ruff. The following celebrated example occurred in the 1958 World Championship.

```
                    NORTH
                    ♠ A K 8 4
                    ♡ A 7 6 3 2
                    ◊ 5
                    ♣ A J 8
WEST                                 EAST
♠ 10 6 5 3 2                         ♠ Q J 9
♡ 9                                  ♡ 10 5
◊ A J 10 8 7 4 3                     ◊ K Q 2
♣ —                                  ♣ K Q 6 5 4
                    SOUTH
                    ♠ 7
                    ♡ K Q J 8 4
                    ◊ 9 6
                    ♣ 10 9 7 3 2
```

Neither side was vulnerable. The bidding:

WEST	NORTH	EAST	SOUTH
			1 NT
		Pass	2 ♡
2 ♠	3 ♠	Pass	3 NT
5 ◊	5 ♡	Pass	Pass
Dbl.	Pass	Pass	Pass

Forquet, West for Italy, judged that his partner's most likely entry was the diamond king. He therefore led the diamond three, a suit preference signal. East duly won and returned the club king. West ruffed, and East had to make a club trick to defeat the contract.

In the other room the diamond ace was led against five hearts. The contract could not then be defeated. South was able to strip the hand and end-play East.

UNDERRUFF. To play a low trump when a trick has already been ruffed with a higher trump. It can be the right play whether the previous ruff was by an opponent or by partner. The undertrump, though unusual, is necessary in many situations.

(1) To avoid a trump surplus (simple trump coup). It is often a disadvantage to hold too many trumps. When reduced to only trump cards you may be forced to ruff a trick belonging to your partner, and then lead away from or into a tenace position.

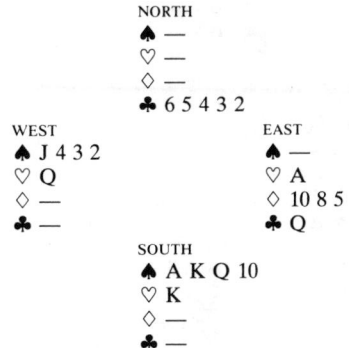

```
                    NORTH
                    ♠ —
                    ♡ —
                    ◊ —
                    ♣ 6 5 4 3 2
WEST                                 EAST
♠ J 4 3 2                            ♠ —
♡ Q                                  ♡ A
◊ —                                  ◊ 10 8 5
♣ —                                  ♣ Q
                    SOUTH
                    ♠ A K Q 10
                    ♡ K
                    ◊ —
                    ♣ —
```

South is declarer at a spade contract, and needs four tricks to make it. The lead is in North's hand. A club is led which East covers. South, knowing the trump position, realizes his only chance is to ruff high.

West must undertrump to avoid a trump end play. If West discards, South will lead his losing heart. West must ruff and lead into a spade tenace.

When West undertrumps, declarer is helpless. If he leads a heart, East will win and play a diamond through South's trump holding. (If South ruffs this high, West must undertrump perforce!)

In the following deal an underruff was necessary at the third trick, because East could not spare any cards in the side-suits.

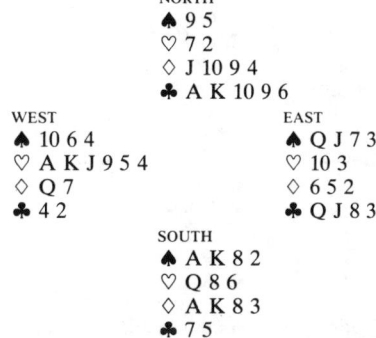

```
                    NORTH
                    ♠ 9 5
                    ♡ 7 2
                    ◊ J 10 9 4
                    ♣ A K 10 9 6
WEST                                 EAST
♠ 10 6 4                             ♠ Q J 7 3
♡ A K J 9 5 4                        ♡ 10 3
◊ Q 7                                ◊ 6 5 2
♣ 4 2                                ♣ Q J 8 3
                    SOUTH
                    ♠ A K 8 2
                    ♡ Q 8 6
                    ◊ A K 8 3
                    ♣ 7 5
```

South played in five diamonds, and West led two high hearts. East played high-low, perhaps wrongly, and when the diamond jack could not be overruffed at the third trick West was marked with the diamond queen. East had a discard problem which he solved by underruffing with the diamond deuce: any black-suit discard would have made the play easy for South.

The contract failed, although South could have

succeeded by very accurate play. Two high spades, a spade ruff, and four rounds of trumps would have squeezed East in the black suits.

(2) To create a trump end play immediately following COUP (EN PASSANT). By undertrumping at the right moment, it is sometimes possible to force an opponent to remain on lead against his wishes.

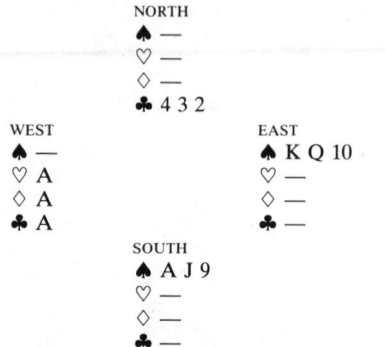

```
              NORTH
              ♠ —
              ♡ —
              ◇ —
              ♣ 4 3 2
   WEST                    EAST
   ♠ —                     ♠ K Q 10
   ♡ A                     ♡ —
   ◇ A                     ◇ —
   ♣ A                     ♣ —
              SOUTH
              ♠ A J 9
              ♡ —
              ◇ —
              ♣ —
```

Again North is on lead with South the declarer at a spade contract. South needs two more tricks for the contract. When a club is led from dummy, East must ruff high to prevent South from scoring the jack of spades.

South can now undertrump with the nine of spades, leaving East to lead into an established tenace. If South overruffs, he must concede two spade tricks to East.

(3) To be able to lead a plain suit card at a later time (ROBERT COUP). In certain positions, it is profitable to be able to lead a plain suit card rather than a trump.

```
              NORTH
              ♠ 10 2
              ♡ A Q
              ◇ 6
              ♣ —
   WEST                    EAST
   ♠ Q J 9                 ♠ A
   ♡ 4                     ♡ —
   ◇ 2                     ◇ Q J 10 5
   ♣ —                     ♣ —
              SOUTH
              ♠ K 8 6 4
              ♡ —
              ◇ —
              ♣ A
```

West leads against South's spade contract. South needs three tricks to produce the contract.

West leads the heart four which East ruffs with the ace of spades. This appears to give West two natural trump tricks, but South underruffs! East returns a diamond and South ruffs again. South now leads the ace of clubs. West must ruff with a high honor to prevent dummy's spade ten from winning this trick. Dummy discards and West must now lead away from his remaining spade honor.

If South does not preserve the club ace to lead toward dummy, he will be defeated. When a low

trump is led from the South hand, West wins with the jack *and dummy must follow suit*. West can now lead the queen of spades, smothering North's ten, and setting up the nine of spades for the setting trick.

(4) To avoid a premature squeeze (anti-positional squeeze). It is sometimes possible to avoid making a premature discard by undertrumping.

```
              NORTH
              ♠ Q J 10
              ♡ A 4 3 2
              ◇ A 4 3 2
              ♣ 9 2
   WEST                    EAST
   ♠ A 5                   ♠ 8 7 6
   ♡ Q J 10                ♡ 8 7 6 5
   ◇ Q J 10                ◇ 8 7 6 5
   ♣ A K Q J 10            ♣ 8 7
              SOUTH
              ♠ K 9 4 3 2
              ♡ K 9
              ◇ K 9
              ♣ 6 5 4 3
```

WEST	NORTH	EAST	SOUTH
2 NT	Pass	Pass	3 ♠
Pass	4 ♠	Pass	Pass
Pass			

East had a poor hand but he played the star role. West led the king of clubs and promptly shifted to ace and another trump. Dummy won and another club was won by West. West now shifted to the queen of hearts which declarer won with the king.

When declarer ruffed a club in dummy, East had to undertrump to defeat the contract. If he discarded from a red suit, South would have been able to establish a trick in that suit in dummy by ruffing, and the contract would have been made. After East underruffed, declarer was helpless.

J. R.

UNDERTRICK. Each trick by which declarer's side fails to fulfill its contract. For the penalties for each undertrick, see LAWS (Law 84), LAWS OF DUPLICATE (Law 73).

UNDERTRUMP. See UNDERRUFF.

UNDOUBLE. See DOUBLE FOR SACRIFICE.

UNFACED HAND. During the play, the hands of the declarer and both defenders. After the opening lead, the declarer's partner's hand is faced up on the table so that all players may see the cards (dummy's hand). Prior to the play, none of the hands is faced. A player in claiming or conceding tricks faces his hand in properly presenting his claim. See CLAIM OR CONCESSION; DEFENDING HAND; DUMMY.

UNFINISHED RUBBER. A rubber ended by agreement before either side has won two games. A side which has won one game is credited with a bonus of 300 points; a side which has a partial, if only one side, is credited with a bonus of 50 points.

UNINTENTIONAL. A violation of rules, ethics, or proprieties is assumed in bridge circles to be unintentional, not deliberate. It is the purpose of the LAWS to provide indemnities for the non-offending side to permit an accurate or fairly accurate result on the board or a hand. Any intentional violation is in contravention of the philosophy of the game, as a contest involving ladies and gentlemen. An assumption that a violation is intentional by an opponent is as much a violation of ethics as would be such an intentional violation itself.

UNIT-WIDE GAME. A game of Unit Championship rating held simultaneously at three or more locations in the Unit. Each Unit is entitled to hold one Unit-wide Championship a year for each full 200 members, up to a maximum of seven such championships. If more than one such game is held in a year, each game must be scheduled for a different day of the week. All master-point awards for unit-wide games are issued by the ACBL.

UNITED ARAB REPUBLIC BRIDGE FEDERATION. See EGYPTIAN BRIDGE ASSOCIATION.

UNITED STATES BRIDGE ASSOCIATION. One of the predecessor organizations which merged to form the AMERICAN CONTRACT BRIDGE LEAGUE. The purpose of this association was to organize a national tournament in which participation would be based on skill alone, and which would be a thorough enough test so that its winners could be clearly recognized as national champions.

The Grand National Plan which this organization evolved was a pyramiding series of qualifying tournaments starting with open local tournaments, city, state, and regional tournaments, and culminating in the GRAND NATIONAL (1).

In addition to the organization of tournaments truly national in scope, the United States Bridge Association was a charter member of the International Contract Bridge Union which was organized in 1934 under the joint sponsorship of the United States Bridge Association, the National Bridge Association of Great Britain, and the French Contract Bridge Association. Both the USBA and the ICBU owed much to Ely CULBERTSON, the first President of the international organization, and a member of the executive committee of the former (Milton C. Work, the Grand Old Man of Bridge, was President).

The American Bridge League (organized 1927) and the International Bridge League (headquarters at The Hague, Holland) existed concurrently, and some short-lived rivalry between the two organizations was eliminated in 1937 when the American Contract Bridge League resulted from the amalgamation of the two United States organizations.

Results of national tournaments prior to the merger are included under USBA GRAND NATIONALS.

UNITED STATES INTERNATIONAL REPRESENTATIVES. The names of players who have represented the US or North America in international team events may be found under ANGLO-AMERICAN MATCHES, FRANCO-AMERICAN MATCHES, INTERNATION-AL OPEN TEAM SELECTION, INTERNATIONAL WOMEN'S TEAM SELECTION, VENICE TROPHY, and WORLD CHAMPIONSHIPS.

UNITED STATES PLAYING CARD TROPHY. Donated by the United States Playing Card Company for the two-session Commercial & Industrial Team Championship held at the Summer Nationals, under which past results are listed. This event is open only to teams of four, five, or six players, all of whom are full-time or pensioned employees of the same commercial or industrial organization or government bureau. Replaced the ASSOCIATION OF AMERICAN PLAYING CARD MANUFACTURERS TROPHY in 1965.

UNITS OF THE ACBL. Totaling 324 in 1975, units of the ACBL have been formed at different times and under different conditions, and they differ widely among themselves in background, scope, and membership. Some limit their activity to a given town or city, others comprise two or more states.

The jurisdiction of a unit consists of a geographical area, bounded in its application and charter, and each unit has jurisdiction over its own members, while participating in the management of the League.

A new unit may be formed in any area where no unit exists, provided there are 100 or more members in the area to be organized. In the process of formation, a provisional charter may be granted with more than 50 members if a reasonable prospect of reaching the 100-member status exists.

The unit is expected to perform certain functions:

(1) Establish and maintain a membership of at least 100.

(2) Promote and stimulate interest in duplicate bridge among members and prospective members by providing an attractive program of bridge events.

(3) Expand and increase membership by interesting new players.

(4) Conduct or supervise tournament events at which master points and fractionals are awarded under League regulations.

(5) Establish and maintain contact with neighboring units, supporting each other's activities.

(6) Conduct annual election by popular vote for officers and/or Directors.

(7) Elect, in collaboration with other units in the district, a member of the National Board of Directors, a first and a second Alternate Director, and three representatives to the National Board of Governors.

(8) Adopt bylaws consistent with those of the ACBL, which must be approved.

(9) Assume fiscal responsibility for funds collected on behalf of the League, and membership dues from its members, submitting semi-annual financial reports to its officers; maintain accurate records.

UNLAWFUL. An action not in accordance with the mechanics of the game, as described in Parts I to III of LAWS.

UNLIMITED BID. A bid with wide limits in valuation. The bid with the widest limit of all is a STAYMAN response to a weak no trump, which could range from a worthless hand to a hand worth a forcing opening bid. Other unlimited bids are discussed under ONE OVER ONE, OPENING SUIT BID, and TAKE-OUT DOUBLE.

UNMAKABLE. A contract which cannot succeed if the defense does not cooperate with the declarer, i.e., does not do as well as can be done. Frequently an unmakable contract succeeds, however, because the defense is comparatively in the dark about the declarer's holding. Unmakable is the opposite of COLD (Unbeatable), and, like this term, is relative.

UNUSUAL JUMP. See ASKING BIDS; FRAGMENT BID; GRAND SLAM FORCE; LEBOVIC ASKING BID; ROMEX TRUMP ASKING BIDS; SPLINTER BID; SUPER GERBER; SUPER SWISS; VOID SHOWING BIDS.

UNUSUAL NO TRUMP. A method of showing two-suited hands in competitive situations. The convention, which normally indicates length in the minor suits, was devised by Alvin Roth, New York City, 1948 and developed by him with Tobias Stone.

An overall of two no trump after a major-suit opening is often used to show minor suits (see TWO NO TRUMP OVERCALL).

In many situations the unusual no trump is a balancing move:

(a)

SOUTH	WEST	NORTH	EAST
1 ♠	Pass	1 NT	Pass
2 ♠	Pass	Pass	2 NT

(b)

SOUTH	WEST	NORTH	EAST
1 ♠	Pass	2 ♠	Pass
Pass	2 NT		

In both cases the unusual no trump bidder wishes to contest the part-score, and invites his partner to pick a minor. Case (b) is slightly safer than (a), because the known fit for North-South in spades increases the chance that East-West have a fit.

The unusual no trump may be used when the auction is still very much alive:

(c)

SOUTH	WEST	NORTH	EAST
1 ♠	Pass	1 NT	Pass
2 ♠ or 2 ♡	2 NT		

(d)

SOUTH	WEST	NORTH	EAST
1 ♡	Pass	1 ♠	Pass
2 ♠	2 NT		

In (c) both North and South are limited and are unlikely to go beyond the level of two. West can rely on some strength from East, who should not entertain any hopes of game. In (d), North is not limited, but the North-South fit gives West some assurance of an East-West fit. If the vulnerability is favorable for

East-West, five clubs or five diamonds may prove a cheap save if North-South go to four spades.

An original pass may serve to identify the unusual no trump, as when the dealer overcalls one no trump after a fourth-hand major-suit opening bid. Many players apply the convention whenever the opponents have bid two suits:

(e)

SOUTH	WEST	NORTH	EAST
1 ♣	Pass	1 ♡	1 NT

(f)

SOUTH	WEST	NORTH	EAST
1 ♠	Pass	2 ♢	2 NT

It would seldom be right for East to make a no trump bid in a natural sense, because he would be laying himself open to a heavy penalty opposite a probably worthless dummy. With a strong defense hand he would prefer to stay out of the auction, and expect to defeat any game contract.

So in this case East's bid shows great length (at least 5–5) in the unbid suits. This is an extension of the convention (optional by partnership agreement) to situations not limited to minor suits.

The unusual no trump can be used when your side has already bid, and even when your side has opened the bidding:

(g)

SOUTH	WEST	NORTH	EAST
Pass	3 ♡	Dbl.	Pass
4 NT			

(h)

SOUTH	WEST	NORTH	EAST
1 ♣	4 ♠	4 NT	

In (g) South shows a good minor two-suiter, probably not far short of an opening bid. North may be able to jump to six clubs or six diamonds. In this case the unusual no trump is an attacking weapon.

When the bidding has been seriously crowded by an opponent's pre-emptive action, four no trump is usually a take-out bid rather than BLACKWOOD. In (h) Silodor suggested the four no trump bid on this hand:

♠ —
♡ K Q 6 5 3
♢ A J 9 8 3
♣ 9 7 2

The bid indicates a desire to play at the five-level, with a free choice left to partner.

The unusual no trump can operate when the user has already bid a minor suit:

(i)

SOUTH	WEST	NORTH	EAST
1 ♠	2 ♣	2 ♠	Pass
Pass	2 NT		

(j)

SOUTH	WEST	NORTH	EAST
1 ♣	1 ♡	Pass	4 ♡
4 NT			

In (i), West wishes to contest the part-score, and is likely to have five or six clubs and four diamonds. If his second suit was hearts he would double. In (j), South is likely to have five diamonds and six clubs: four no trump is his only way to indicate this distribution.

The unusual no trump is usually made by the side which did not open the bidding. In (h) and (j) above, its use by the opener's side is shown, and here are two further examples:

(k)

SOUTH	WEST	NORTH	EAST
1 ◇	1 ♠	Pass	4 ♠
4 NT			

(l)

SOUTH	WEST	NORTH	EAST
1 ♡	1 ♠	Pass	2 ♠
Pass	Pass	2 NT	

In (k), South's second suit must be hearts: with a minor two-suiter he would bid five clubs to offer an easy choice at the level of five. In (l) North cannot wish to play two no trump when he could not bid over one spade; clearly he has a weak minor two-suiter.

UNUSUAL NO TRUMP AND MINORS. See LEA SYSTEM.

UNUSUAL ONE NO TRUMP OVERCALL. An overcall of one no trump as a two-suited take-out rather than as the standard 16–18 point balanced hand. See also TWO NO TRUMP OVERCALL (2).

UNUSUAL POSITIVE. A set of artificial jump responses to a PRECISION CLUB opening to show 4–4–4–1 distribution.

UNUSUAL OVER UNUSUAL. See DEFENSE TO TWO-SUITED INTERFERENCE.

UP THE LINE. The practice of making the cheapest bid when responding or rebidding with two or three four-card suits, laid down as a principle by the BARON SYSTEM. The idea is employed in many bidding styles, with some reservations.

♠ K 8 4 3
♡ K 8 4 3
◇ A J
♣ K 10 5

A one heart response to an opening bid in either minor suit gives the opener the opportunity to rebid in spades. If he fails to do so, responder can assume that there is no spade fit, and bid three no trump.

This idea has validity but there are many circumstances in which expert players would depart from the principle.

(1) If there is a great disparity in the strength of the suits:

♠ A Q J 3
♡ 8 4 3 2
◇ A J
♣ Q 10 5

The chief arguments in favor of bidding one spade in response to a minor-suit opening are that a heart response might lead to a no trump contract with an unguarded heart suit, and that a high heart contract might result in a weak trump holding. The opposing view is that one heart may inhibit a heart lead in no trump, and that a one spade response may exclude a four-four fit in hearts.

(2) With two strong major suits:

♠ K Q J 3
♡ A Q 5 2
◇ 8 3
♣ 9 4 2

Some authorities recommend a response of one spade to an opening bid in a minor, with the intention of bidding hearts on the next round.

The choice of response is closely connected with the treatment of BIDDABLE SUITS. If the opener is not expected to rebid one spade with a bad four-card suit, the spade response is necessary to avoid missing a possible fit.

A disadvantage is that one spade followed by a heart bid tends to suggest a five-card spade suit. The "up the line" response of one heart, used by players who do not impose standards for biddable suits, leads to a problem if the opener rebids his suit. In that case an eccentric reverse bid of two spades may be tried.

(3) With one major suit and one minor suit:

(a)	(b)
♠ Q J 7 3	♠ 8 2
♡ 8 2	♡ Q J 7 3
◇ Q J 7 3	◇ Q J 7 3
♣ J 7 2	♣ J 7 2

In each of these cases there is a good argument for rejecting the one diamond response to one club in favor of the major suit. The danger of one diamond is that opposing intervention may shut out the major suit, which is a serious possibility in case (b). In case (a), one spade may work well by shutting out an opposing heart contract.

But if the responding hand is stronger, there is less likelihood of intervention, and therefore less reason to prefer the major-suit response.

If the response is at the two-level, the minor-suit response is preferable. The chance of interference is slight, and a response of two hearts to one spade is generally expected to show a five-card or longer suit.

UP TO. (1) Toward the hand that will play last to a particular trick, as in UP TO WEAKNESS. (2) Toward a vulnerable third-hand holding such as K x x or K Q x, as opposed to leading away from such a holding.

UP TO WEAKNESS. The old whist maxim recommending a lead "up to weakness" is valid but not very helpful. It is quite true that a lead by declarer's right-hand opponent up to a completely worthless holding in dummy will never give away a trick, although it may help the declarer if he is short of entries to dummy. But it is seldom that dummy is so obliging.

The following discussion will consider defender's problems in this situation on the assumption that the suit in question is distributed evenly around the table. If one player is known to be short or is likely to be short, the prospects are of course altered.

Crucial situations are classified in increasing order of dummy strength.

(1) Dummy has 9xx. Almost invariably a safe lead, but the defender should be careful to lead the ten from holdings headed by K10 or Q10.

(2) Dummy has 10xx. The defender must lead the jack from holdings headed by AJ or KJ. If leading from a single honor, the higher the honor the safer the lead. Axx is completely safe, while Jxx is the most dangerous.

(3) Dummy has Jxx. Again, the higher the honor the safer the lead. Axx is relatively safe, while Qxx is very dangerous.

(4) Dummy has Qxx. A lead from the jack is virtually safe. A lead from the ace or king is very dangerous.

(5) Dummy has Kxx. The lead from the ace is very dangerous. The lead from the jack or queen is almost completely safe.

(6) Dummy has Axx. All leads are relatively safe, with Jxx slightly the safest and Qxx the least safe.

The general principle applying in all the above cases is also applicable when leading through dummy. The defender should avoid breaking a suit in which an honor is poised over the honor ranking immediately below it. In other words, one should avoid leading from a jack up to a ten, a queen up to a jack, a king up to a queen, or an ace up to a king. Similarly, one should avoid leading from a jack through a queen, a queen through a king, or a king through an ace.

This applies also if dummy has two honors. It is obviously unwise to lead from a king up to A Q, or a queen up to A J or K J. See also THROUGH STRENGTH.

UPPER SUITS CUE-BID. An immediate overcall in the opponent's suit to show the two highest ranking unbid suits. See also MICHAELS CUE-BID.

UPPERCUT. A ruff, usually by a defender, aimed at promoting a trump trick for partner.

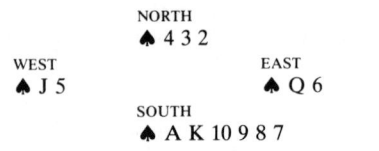

NORTH
♠ 4 3 2
WEST   EAST
♠ J 5   ♠ Q 6
SOUTH
♠ A K 10 9 8 7

In a spade contract, West leads a suit of which East and South are void. East ruffs with his spade queen, ensuring a trump trick for the defense. If South overruffs, the jack wins a trick.

A defender with a completely useless trump holding should usually ruff with his highest trump if he gets the opportunity. A ruff with a card as low as the six can possibly effect an uppercut and promote a trump trick for the defense.

UPSIDE-DOWN SIGNALS. The use of a low card in defense to encourage a continuation of a suit, or a shift to a suit, and a high card to discourage. The method is credited to Karl SCHNEIDER, Vienna, but seems to have been first published by E. K. O'Brien in a *Bridge World* article in 1937.

The chief theoretical advantage of this procedure is that a player may not be able to spare a high card from a strong holding:

NORTH
♠ 10 7 6 3
WEST   EAST
♠ J 5   ♠ K Q 9 2
SOUTH
♠ A 8 4

West leads the jack of spades against three no trump, because his own suit has been bid by declarer. East has to drop the deuce, because he cannot spare the nine. Using normal methods, it is now difficult for West to continue the suit when he gains the lead. But he continues happily using upside-down signals. Notice that if East had had a weak holding, such as Q842, he could have spared the eight as a discouraging card.

Other advantages claimed for this method are that it is harder for declarer to false-card effectively, and that a one-card discard signal during the defense may be clearer than with normal methods.

URUGUAY BRIDGE ASSOCIATION (ASOCIACIÓN URUGUAYA DE BRIDGE). Formed in 1948, the Association is a member of the South American Confederation and participates in South American Championships, hosting the event in 1950, 1953, 1958, 1964, and 1971. Uruguay won the Women's Team Championship in 1966, 1967, 1971, and 1974.

President, 1975: Juan Sagarra, Asociación Uruguaya de Bridge, Sarandi 584, Montevideo, Uruguay.

USES OF CARDS. Although playing cards are made for the playing of games, individual cards have been used for other purposes. Since the backs were (until about 120 years ago) blank and unmarked, paper was scarce and expensive, and playing cards used the very finest quality paper obtainable, cards were practical to use for purposes where standardization was an asset.

Both handwritten and printed visiting cards were made on card backs, as were tickets and identifying passes. Workmen dismantling the Bastille carried such passes to distinguish them from the crowds of curious visitors who interfered with their work.

In France and in Canada, cards were used in emergencies as money. Several libraries used them for their original index cards. At one time it was fashionable to write social invitations on them. Advertisements were printed and written on them.

Old cards and sheets of cards were used to stiffen the covers of books, and some of our knowledge of

early cards comes from discoveries of these fragments. And, of course, they are the building blocks
for constructing a house of cards.

A. F.

UTILITY. A British expression which summarizes
the straightforward bidding methods used there in
many rubber bridge clubs: strong no trump (16–18);
two clubs as the forcing opening; intermediate two
bids; and three no trump for take-out over opposing
three-bids.

UTILITY NO TRUMP RESPONSE. See CHURCHILL
STYLE.

V

VALET. One of the court cards in decks of cards
used centuries ago, decks that were ancestors of
present-day cards. The term survives in French,
meaning the equivalent of English jack or knave.

VALIDATION. In duplicate bridge, the certifying by
the director of the correctness of an auction or play;
the approval of the opponents to a correction of the
scoring of the results of a board of duplicate play; the
initialing of a pair score in team play by the
opponents of this pair on a set of boards.

VALUATION. Valuation of a hand is covered under
particular types of valuation in the following articles:
ACE VALUES; BISSELL SYSTEM; BODY; DISTRIBUTIONAL
COUNTS; DUPLICATION OF DISTRIBUTION; DUPLICATION
OF VALUES; GOOD CARDS; HONOR TRICK; LOSING TRICK
COUNT; PLUS VALUE; POINT COUNT; POSITIONAL FAC-
TOR; PROMOTION OF TRUMP HONORS; REVALUATION; and
ROBERTSON POINT-COUNT.

VALUE OF GAME. The calculation of the favorable
percentage necessary to justify bidding for game in
different situations is complicated by the uncertain
value of a PART-SCORE. The arbitrary figure of 50
assigned by the LAWS for the purposes of duplicate
bridge and unfinished rubbers is not realistic at rubber bridge. Assigning the more plausible figure of
150 when both sides are vulnerable, and 100 in other
situations, the following table can be constructed. It
is assumed that the choice lies between three spades
and four spades.

First game
  Profit from a successful game bid   200 (300 less 100)
  Loss from failing in game   240 (100 plus 90 plus 50)
  Odds required for bidding game:
  6 to 5 on, or 55%

Second game
  Profit from a successful game bid   300 (400 less 100)
  Loss from failing in game   290 (100 plus 90 plus 100)
  Odds required for bidding game:
  30 to 29 against or 49%

Game against vulnerable opponents
  Same as for first game

Deciding Game
  Profit from bidding game suc-
  cessfully   350 (500 less 150)
  Loss from failing in game   340 (150 plus 90 plus 100)
  Odds required for bidding game:
  35 to 34 against, or 49%

These figures may be regarded as slightly optimistic, in that no weight has been given to the situation
where opponents may double, increasing the loss by
50 or 100 points; or to those situations where neither
three nor four can be made, but four will be doubled
and defeated 300 or 500 to 500 or 800 points. Assuming correct bidding, it also must be assumed that the
doubled contract will be set far more often than it will
be made.

At any form of duplicate, the calculation is simpler. At match points, any game should be bid with a
50% chance, other things being equal. At IMPs,
games should be bid more freely: with a 37% chance
when vulnerable, or a 45% chance not vulnerable.

At CHICAGO, assuming a constant value of 100
points for a part-score, a non-vulnerable game
should be bid with a 55% chance or better, and a vulnerable game with a 43% chance or better.

D. H. T.

VALUE OF PART-SCORE. In duplicate, a bonus
of 50 points is awarded for successful less-than-game
contracts. In CHICAGO, a part-score remaining at the
end of four deals is not rewarded; except on the last
deal, a part-score earned is worth 100 points. These
values are not realistic in rubber bridge. See PART-
SCORE BIDDING.

VALUE SWISS RAISES. An expansion of the SWISS
CONVENTION used in the ACES SCIENTIFIC SYSTEM to
show a range of forcing balanced raises in response to
an opening bid of one heart or one spade. The ranges
shown are as follows:

12–13 HCP   one no trump, followed by four
             of opener's major
13–14 HCP   four diamonds
14–16 HCP   four clubs
16–18 HCP   two no trump followed by a
             strong return to opener's major

Each response denies a singleton or a good five-card
suit. UNBALANCED SWISS RAISES are used to show
raises based on distribution rather than on high-card
values. See also CONGLOMERATE MAJOR RAISES, SUPER
SWISS.

VANDERBILT CLUB SYSTEM. Harold S. Vanderbilt, who invented the game of Contract Bridge in
1925, was the first to advocate use of a one club opening bid as an artificial bid to show a strong hand, and
of a one diamond artificial negative response to show
a weak hand. He wrote three books, now long since
out of print, on his Club Convention prior to 1934;
and his Club Convention was very popular until his
books were no longer available.

After a lapse of about thirty years, interest in one

club systems revived. The BLUE TEAM CLUB, which helped to win many WORLD CHAMPIONSHIPS for Italy, uses an opening one club convention very like the Vanderbilt Club, and the SCHENKEN SYSTEM, used in two World Championships, is an even closer relation.

In 1964, Vanderbilt wrote a modernized version of his system entitled *The Club Convention Modernized*, which may be summarized as follows:

(1) *Opening Bids with Mediocre Suit Types of Hands*

Opening bids of one diamond, one heart, one spade, and two clubs have the same minimum high-card point requirement as opening bids of one in a suit in other systems, but the high-card point range is limited to about 6 points, or to one-half that of other systems, because with a good suit type of hand you open one club. Consequently, you give partner at the outset a better picture of your high card strength than when you open with one of a suit using other systems. This is the greatest of the many advantages of club systems.

To open two clubs, you should have not less than a five-card club suit including 5 points in high cards. When no other bid is available, open one diamond on a three-card 5 high-card point suit.

(2) *Opening Bids with Good Suit Types of Hands*

Open one club (a one-round force) whenever you hold a hand containing about 16 or more high-card points and five or more offensive tricks; except that, for expert use only, a two diamond (instead of one club) forcing to game, specific ace on the first round, and, if desired, king on the second round and queen on the third round asking bid is recommended when holding, say:

♠ A K J 8 7 4 3
♡ A Q 6
◇ —
♣ A K 5

in which case if responder holds:

♠ Q 9
♡ K 7 4
◇ 8 7 6 3
♣ Q 9 6 4

The partnership auction would go: two diamonds (specific aces?), two hearts (no ace), two spades (specific kings?), three hearts (king of hearts), three spades (specific queens?), five clubs (two queens of same color, but they must be black since opener holds the queen of hearts), seven spades, pass.

(3) *Responses to Any One Club Bid*

(a) Respond one diamond (the negative response and a one-round force) unless you hold at least: two aces; or three kings; or one ace, one king, and one queen; or two kings and two queens; or a six-card suit headed by the ace king; in any of which cases, force to game by responding with a natural bid other than one diamond.

(b) A two hearts, two spades, three clubs, or three diamonds response shows a solid five-card or longer suit.

(c) A three hearts, three spades, four clubs, or four diamonds response shows a six-card or longer suit requiring only the ace, king, or queen to make it solid, plus sufficient outside high-card strength to qualify for a positive response.

(d) A one no trump response shows a no trump type of distribution.

(e) A two no trump response shows a good hand with at least one high honor (ace, king, or queen) in every suit, and slam possibilities opposite a good one club opening.

(4) *Opening Bids with No Trump Types of Hands*

Open:

(a).One no trump with 16, 17, or 18 high-card points (the usual standard requirement).

(b) One club with 19 or 20 high-card points, followed by one no trump over a one diamond response.

(c) One club with 23 or 24 high-card points followed by two no trump over a one diamond response.

(d) Two no trump with 21 or 22 high-card points.

(e) One club with nine probable tricks and a stopper in every suit followed by three no trump over a one diamond response.

(f) Three no trump with about eight or nine probable tricks, most of them in minor suits. This bid is partly pre-emptive, and is best made third hand after two passes. For example, open three no trump, third hand holding:

♠ 7 5
♡ K 8
◇ A K Q 10
♣ A K Q J 10

(5) *Effect of an Overcall or a Double of a One Club Bid*

(a) A double of an overcall or a redouble of a double is the equivalent of a positive response. So is a one jump bid in no trump which is also the equivalent of responding two no trump to one club, after an intervening pass.

(b) A minimum no trump response is encouraging but not forcing, and shows a stopper in the suit of the overcall.

(c) A minimum suit response is encouraging but not forcing.

(d) A jump suit response is forcing for one round only. For example, holding:

♠ K Q 10 9 7 5
♡ 8 5
◇ Q 10 5
♣ 9 7

respond two spades after your partner's one club opening has been overcalled with one heart.

(6) *Other Opening Bids*

(a) Two hearts, two spades, and (except for expert use) two diamonds are defensive shut-out bids as in other systems that employ two clubs as the only forcing to game opening bid.

(b) Three clubs and three diamonds show solid seven- (exceptionally six-) card suits and invite three no trump.

(c) Three hearts and three spades show seven playing tricks but the suit need not be solid.

(7) Other Conventions
(a) STAYMAN: If the partnership bidding goes one club, one diamond, one no trump, two hearts or two spades; or one no trump, two hearts or two spades, opener must pass because of responder's failure to bid two clubs (Stayman) over one no trump before showing his major.
(b) The cheapest available of GERBER or BLACKWOOD. Since a one club opening does not rank as a bona fide club bid, it does not prevent the subsequent use of a Gerber four club jump bid to ask for aces.

H. V.

VANDERBILT CUP. (1) For the National Knockout Team Championship, donated by Harold S. Vanderbilt in 1928. The organizing body 1928–57 was the Vanderbilt Cup Committee. It was contested annually in New York until 1958 when it became part of the Spring Nationals, under which heading past results are listed. In the 1950s and 1970s the Vanderbilt helped to select a number of US international teams. Ranks with the Spingold as the most highly prized trophy in the ACBL calendar. The winners of the Vanderbilt are entitled to compete against the winners of the GRAND NATIONAL CHAMPIONSHIPS (2), REISINGER MEMORIAL TROPHY and SPINGOLD TROPHY for the right to represent North America or the United States in the next year's WORLD CHAMPIONSHIP. See INTERNATIONAL OPEN TEAM SELECTION. (2) For the World Olympiad Team Championship, presented by Harold S. Vanderbilt on the occasion of the first World Team Olympiad held in Turin, Italy, in 1960. See WORLD CHAMPIONSHIPS for winners. The two events are among the few (the Bermuda Bowl is another) for which the winners receive individual replicas of the trophy, a practice initiated by the donor from the first running of the events, and perpetuated by a $100,000 trust fund administered by the ACBL under the terms of Vanderbilt's will.

VANIVA PROBLEM. One of the most famous of all DOUBLE-DUMMY PROBLEMS; composed by Sidney Lenz in 1928 in a contest promoted by Vaniva Shaving Cream.

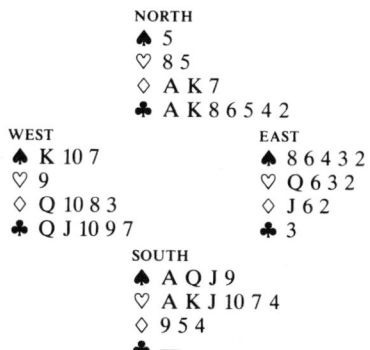

South to make seven hearts after the lead of the club queen. Solution: North wins the first trick, South discarding a diamond, North leads the other top club.

If East trumps, South overruffs, North ruffs out West's best spade, and one trump finesse captures East's queen.
If East sheds a spade, South ruffs, North ruffs out West's best spade, and South wins the trump finesse and his remaining spades. North wins a top diamond, and South ruffs a club. North wins another diamond and coups East's trumps.
If East sheds a diamond, South sheds a spade and finesses trumps. North wins a top diamond and South finesses trumps and runs all his trumps to triple squeeze West.

VENEZUELAN BRIDGE FEDERATION (FEDERACIÓN VENEZOLANA DE BRIDGE). Founded in 1955, by 1969 there were 320 members. The Federation participates in the South American Championships, hosting the 1963 and 1970 events and winning the Open Teams in 1963, 1965, and 1966, and represented the South American Confederation in the 1966 and 1967 World Championships. National events held annually are Open Teams and Open Pairs. Venezuelan players listed separately are: R. Benaim, D. A. Berah, M. Gonzales-Vale, J. Hammerich, E. Loynaz, M. Onorati, R. Rossignol, F. Vernon.

Officers, 1975:
President: Roberto Benaim.
Secretary: Lillian Morganti, Federación Venezolana de Bridge, Altamira Tennis Club, Tercera Avenida Altamira, Caracas, 106, Venezuela.

VENEZUELAN TRANSFERS. A systemized method of responding and rebidding to strong no trump openings, developed principally by Roberto BENAIM, and first used by the Venezuelan Team in the 1966 WORLD CHAMPIONSHIPS.
Responses to a one no trump opening are generally patterned after the JACOBY and TEXAS transfer principles. Two clubs is STAYMAN; two diamonds and two hearts are transfers to the next ranking suit; two spades is a minor-suit inquiry; three clubs and three diamonds are weak, showing at least a six-card suit headed by two of the top three honors; and four diamonds and four hearts are transfers to the majors. Special transfers are three hearts to four diamonds and three spades to four clubs.
After a Stayman response, opener rebids two no trump with both majors and a minimum no trump or three clubs with both majors and a maximum no trump. Opener accepts a two-level transfer, but with a maximum no trump he jumps in the transfer suit with four-card support, or rebids two no trump with two of the top three honors in the transfer suit. Over a two spade response, opener rebids two no trump with no minor suit, three clubs or three diamonds with at least four cards in the bid suit, three hearts with both minors and a better diamond suit, three spades with both minors and a better club suit, or three no trump with two of the top three honors in both minors.
If responder transfers on the two-level, then rebids two no trump, opener shows the strength of his no

trump opening and support for responder's suit by four steps. New suits by responder are then asking-bids or cue-bids. Three-level and four-level rebids by responder show different two-suiters.

A Stayman response is also used after a strong two no trump opening. Opener shows both majors by rebidding three no trump, over which responder transfers to hearts by bidding four clubs, and spades by bidding four diamonds. If opener denies a major, responder may inquire about the minors by rebidding four clubs. Opener rebids four diamonds with a diamond suit, four hearts with both minors and better diamonds, four spades with both minors and better clubs, or four no trump with a club suit. If responder transfers to a major on the three-level, opener bypasses the transfer and bids three no trump without support (responder may then transfer on the four-level), or, with two of the top three honors in the transfer suit, he again bypasses the transfer to show the number of aces he holds. The next ranking suit shows two. A four no trump rebid by responder is then BLACKWOOD for kings. Other rebids by responder show various types of two-suiters.

VENICE TROPHY. A trophy first awarded in 1974 to the winner of a challenge match between the European Bridge League Women's champions and a women's team representing the ACBL. In a 140-board match played in Venice concurrently with the 1974 Bermuda Bowl, the United States team defeated the world champion Italian women's team, which had theretofore been unbeaten in five years of women's competiton, by a score of 297–262.

UNITED STATES	ITALY
Mrs. B. Cohn	Mrs. M. Bianchi
Mrs. E. J. Hawes	Mrs. L. Canessa
Mrs. B. A. Kennedy	Mrs. R. Jabes
Mrs. M. Passell	Mrs. M. A. Robaudo
Mrs. C. Sanders	Mrs. A. Valenti
Mrs. D. Truscott	Mrs. M. Venturini
Mrs. R. McConnell (npc)	G. Pelucchi (npc)

In 1976 the trophy, donated by the City of Venice, was again played in Monte Carlo, where the United States team defeated the British, the Women's European Champions of 1975. It has since been accepted by the WBF as a continuing side event between an ACBL team and the current European Women's Champion or Olympiad Champion.

VERIFY (a score). In pair play, it is the duty of the North player to fill out the pick-up slip or traveling score card, and of the traveling pair or one of its members to verify (by initialing in a box provided on pick-up slips) the score as correct; in match play at teams-of-four, both pairs keep a record of their scores at each table, and each pair must verify the score slip of its opponents, from which the results of the match can be determined.

When recapitulation sheets are used for posting the results of play, a scorer noting an unusual score (such as 5 ♡ Dbld. for 650 points on a non-vulnerable board, or a set of four tricks undoubled with

both sides vulnerable) will indicate with a small check mark that the score has been verified as correct before he has posted it.

VICE SQUEEZE. A secondary squeeze that leads to a suit establishment play. (Analyzed and named by Terence REESE; the American spelling would be "vise.")

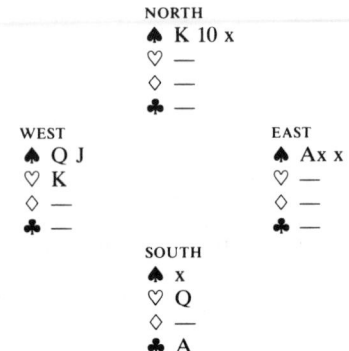

South leads the ace of clubs, and West is squeezed in two suits. If he discards the king of hearts, then South's queen will take a trick; if he discards a spade, South can establish a trick in that suit.

The position looks like an automatic squeeze against West which has been modified in a particular way: instead of a two-card menace we have a vice menace consisting of the second best card of the suit accompanied by a card which can be established if West weakens his second-round stopper.

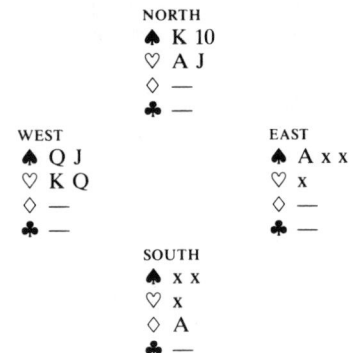

South leads the ace of diamonds, which forces West to unguard hearts or to discard his second-round trick in spades.

This position is a modification of the simple positional squeeze. The vice menace does not provide an entry, so that North's threat must be accompanied by a master card in the suit, which makes it a two-card threat.

In addition to the requirements stated above, East must have no trick to cash besides his stopper in the doubly guarded suit.

South loses a trick after the squeeze, so that he

needs all but two of the remaining tricks in the diagram positions.

M. I.

VICTORY POINTS. In a contest among a great number of teams with a limited number of sessions, each team plays a relatively small number of deals against each of the other teams, ranging from 32 in the round-robin of the WORLD CHAMPIONSHIPS to as few as two deals in some smaller events. Various methods have been devised to counteract the excessive rewards to a 10- or 20-point swing in BOARD-A-MATCH scoring, and to the slam contract made at one table and defeated at the other in IMP or TOTAL POINT SCORING.

The scoring method favored by many experts awards the IMP score on each board. The total IMP score on the boards of the match are then converted to victory points in accordance with a predetermined scale. This is the method most used in European Championships and in the round-robin portions of the Bermuda Bowl and World Team Olympiads.

The scale used in the 1964 World Bridge Olympiad was as follows:

Open Matches, 18 boards IMP Difference	Score	Women's Matches, 27 boards IMP Difference
0*– 3	4–3	0*– 5
4 – 9	5–2	6 –14
10 –17	6–1	15 –28
18 or more	7–0	29 or more

More commonly a 20-point scale is used, such as that used in the 20-board matches in the 1972 World Team Olympiad.

VIENNA COUP. An unblocking play made in preparation for a squeeze. Declarer plays off a master card which establishes a high card for an opponent. This clears the way for an automatic squeeze. Here is an example:

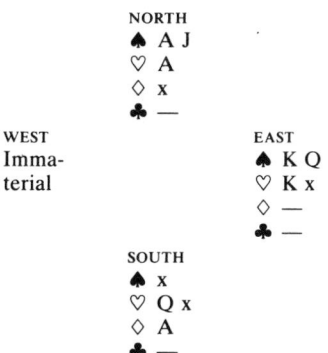

```
                 NORTH
                 ♠ A J
                 ♡ A
                 ◇ x
                 ♣ —
WEST                          EAST
Imma-                         ♠ K Q
terial                        ♡ K x
                              ◇ —
                              ♣ —
                 SOUTH
                 ♠ x
                 ♡ Q x
                 ◇ A
                 ♣ —
```

The menaces are correctly positioned for an automatic squeeze against East. Hearts should be a

one-card menace, and spades the two-card menace. Therefore the heart ace should be played before the squeeze card, which is the ace of diamonds.

If the ace of diamonds is played prematurely, as in the diagram position, then East can discard a heart with impunity, for declarer can establish the queen of hearts by crossing to the ace, but he cannot return to his hand to cash the queen.

M. I.

VIENNA SYSTEM. Based on an artificial one club bid for hands of normal strength, and an artificial one no trump bid for strong hands. Devised in 1935 by Dr. Paul Stern, this was the first highly conventional system to achieve international success. (See WORLD CHAMPIONSHIPS.) Also known as the Austrian System, it has been played in many countries. In postwar years its main adherents have been in Iceland and Australia.

The Bamberger point count (7–5–3–1) was originally used, but many Vienna players have preferred the standard 4–3–2–1 point-count which is employed in the following system summary. (References are to high-card points.)

(1) *One club* shows 11–17 points and no suit except clubs longer than four cards. One diamond is the negative, or HERBERT, response showing 0–7 points. With a six-card or longer suit, an alternative negative response is available: a negative jump to two of a major or three of a minor suit. Over one diamond the opener rebids at the one level, keeping the bidding as low as possible. (This treatment very closely resembles the ROMAN SYSTEM.)

Responses of one in a major or two in a minor are positive but limited, showing 8–11 points. The opener can pass or make a natural rebid: any jump rebid would be encouraging but not forcing.

The strongest response to one club is one no trump, showing 12 points or more. This almost always leads to game, but the responder can pass if the opener rebids two no trump at any stage.

(2) *One diamond, one heart, or one spade* shows a five-card suit with 11–17 points. Responses are standard except that two no trump is limit and non-forcing.

(3) *One no trump* shows 18 points at least, and is unlimited; any distribution is possible. With 0–7 points, the responder gives a negative response of two clubs or a negative jump to three diamonds, three hearts, or three spades.

With 12 points or more, responder bids a five-card suit; but the jump to three clubs is made only if the suit is very strong. With a broken five-card club suit, the response is sometimes two no trump, which denies a five-card diamond suit and also a total of five cards in the major suit. For other hands containing between five and eight cards in the major suits the response is two diamonds, which is therefore a two-way bid.

After a negative response of two clubs, a rebid of two diamonds asks for a major suit.

(4) *Two-bids* should be specialized asking bids, but most adherents of the system prefer standard methods.

(5) *Three-bids in a minor* are strong, with a powerful suit and an outside trick.

(6) *Other opening bids* are standard.

(7) *In defense* a take-out double is used as the approximate equivalent of a one club opening, and one no trump as the approximate equivalent of a one no trump opening. A Herbert negative is employed in response to a take-out double.

(8) *Slam conventions.* ASKING BIDS and the NORMAN convention are used.

VIOLATION. (1) The disregard of a law of propriety. It is assumed that any violation that occurs is either through carelessness or ignorance. A PENALTY for a violation is enforced in an attempt to INDEMNIFY the non-offending side, not to punish the offender. (2) A deliberate breach of a system agreement. Judgment may occasionally lead an expert player to pass a FORCING BID or to continue bidding after a SIGN-OFF BID, but such violations should be very rare if partnership confidence is to be maintained.

VIOLATION OF ETHICAL CONDUCT. An act of a player that deviates from the spirit or the form as described in PROPRIETIES; since there are no direct penalties for such violation, it is perhaps even more reprehensible than a deviation for which penalties are prescribed.

Most of the violations of ethical conduct are not deliberate on the part of the committer, but are due to ignorance of proper procedure or to inexperience. It is equally a violation of etiquette and manners to accuse opponents of lack of ethics indiscriminately as it is to be guilty of such a violation oneself. Inexperienced and beginning players should acquaint themselves with the proprieties and etiquette of the game, and should welcome any suggestions thereto when helpfully offered.

VIOLATION OF SYSTEM. A player is at any time entitled to violate his partnership agreement, and most players do so from time to time in minor ways. Major violations, such as passing a forcing bid, are very rare indeed among good players.

VISE SQUEEZE. See VICE SQUEEZE.

VOID. An original holding with no cards in a suit. CHICANE is a much older term, and BLANK a synonym in current use.

VOID-SHOWING BIDS. The use of a jump bid which has no natural meaning to show a void suit. The idea was revived by E. M. L. Beale, of Cambridge University, England, about 1948, following a prototype idea once adopted by Culbertson.

According to this idea, the last bid in each of the following sequences would show specifically a void in the suit bid, and, by inference, a good suit fit with partner.

	SOUTH	WEST	NORTH	EAST
(a)	1 ♡	Pass	4 ♣	
(b)	1 ♣	Pass	1 ♡	Pass
	3 ♠ or 4 ◇			
(c)	1 ◇	1 ♠	3 ♠	

The following are examples of opportunities for using the bid at later stages in the auction:

South dealer:

Both vulnerable:

```
                NORTH
                ♠ 10 6 2
                ♡ Q 8 7 5 4
                ◇ 4
                ♣ K 8 3 2
        WEST                    EAST
        ♠ A K J 9 5 3           ♠ 7
        ♡ J 2                   ♡ A 6 3
        ◇ A 10 9 6 5            ◇ K J 8 3 2
        ♣ —                     ♣ 10 6 5 4
                SOUTH
                ♠ Q 8 4
                ♡ K 10 9
                ◇ Q 7
                ♣ A Q J 9 7
```

This deal was reported in *The Bridge World,* August 1951, from the Masters Teams-of-Four final. Both teams reached five diamonds played by East after this bidding:

SOUTH	WEST	NORTH	EAST
1 ♣	2 ♠*	Pass	3 ◇
Pass	5 ◇	Pass	Pass
Pass			

If East-West had been using void-showing bids, West could have used one over three diamonds.

SOUTH	WEST	NORTH	EAST
1 ♣	2 ♠	Pass	3 ◇
Pass	5 ♣	Pass	5 ♡
Pass	7 ◇	Pass	Pass
Pass			

When East shows first-round control of hearts by his cue-bid, the grand slam becomes a good proposition. If East's diamonds turn out to be headed by queen-jack instead of the king, the opening bid by South suggests that the finesse will win. If East's diamonds had been still weaker, he would not have made the encouraging grand slam try of five hearts. As it was, he knew that all his high cards were working, and was able to visualize a crossruff.

Void-showing bids will sometimes make it possible

*Strong.

to apply the brakes when duplication of values is present:

South dealer:

East-West vulnerable:

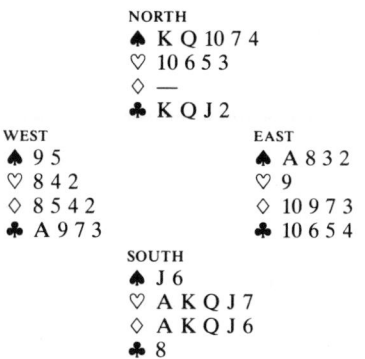

```
                    NORTH
                    ♠ K Q 10 7 4
                    ♡ 10 6 5 3
                    ◇ —
                    ♣ K Q J 2
   WEST                          EAST
   ♠ 9 5                         ♠ A 8 3 2
   ♡ 8 4 2                       ♡ 9
   ◇ 8 5 4 2                     ◇ 10 9 7 3
   ♣ A 9 7 3                     ♣ 10 6 5 4
                    SOUTH
                    ♠ J 6
                    ♡ A K Q J 7
                    ◇ A K Q J 6
                    ♣ 8
```

In the 1953 World Championship both the American and Swedish teams bid to six hearts missing two aces. This is a not uncommon disaster when one side holds everything else in the pack except two aces. Ace-showing conventions are of limited value when a void is present, although BLACK-WOOD has some void-showing possibilities. (See also SUPPRESSING THE BID ACE.)

Using a void-showing bid, the final contract would be five hearts:

(a) Using a strong two-bid

SOUTH	NORTH
2 ♡	4 ◇
4 ♡	5 ♡
Pass	

(b) Using a conventional two club bid

SOUTH	NORTH
2 ♣	2 ♠
3 ♡	5 ◇
5 ♡	Pass

For alternative treatments, see conventions listed under UNUSUAL JUMP.

VOLUNTARY BID. See FREE BID.

VON ZEDTWITZ GOLD CUP. For the Life Masters Pair Championship, donated by Waldemar von Zedtwitz of New York in 1930; the most highly regarded pair event in the ACBL calendar. It is contested at the Summer Nationals, under which heading past results are listed. Until Life Masters became numerous, the trophy was contested by master players who had qualified by winning a previous national championship. It was then a four-session event, and the field was limited to sixty-four pairs so that a complete movement could be played.

The trophy was originally presented on the basis that three wins by one player would secure him outright possession of the trophy, and this feat was achieved by Howard Schenken in 1934. The cup was subsequently put back into competition by the donor.

The cup was stolen in 1954 while in the possession of John Hubbell, who at that time held the Life Masters Pair title. The theft immediately followed a television appearance during which he had exhibited the trophy and given the address of his bridge club at which the cup was normally displayed. The trophy was not recovered and the present cup is an exact replica.

VU-GRAPH. A method of presenting an important match to an audience larger than can be accommodated around a bridge table. In the closed room, the board is dealt, bid, and played, with a recorder at the table noting the bidding, opening lead, and result obtained. The board and record are sent to a copier, who writes the hands, bidding, and play with wax pencil on a framed cellulose sheet, a form of hand record. The board is then sent to the open room where a microphone connected to the exhibition hall is used by a director in charge to relay the calls, leads, plays, and results to an operator in the exhibition hall. The frame is sent to the exhibition hall, where an operator, with a wax pencil, records the bids, plays, and results as announced from the open room on the frame which is put into an overhead projector, remaining visible to the audience in greatly enlarged form on a screen. Bidding is recorded in boxes on the printed frame, cards as played are crossed out from the hands, and results tabulated for further reference on the side of the screen.

Required for Vu-Graph presentation are a recorder in the closed room, a scribe, a director and commentator in the open room, and an operator at the projector who doubles as or is assisted by a commentator. Equipment needed is a dozen or so prepared frames, an overhead or rearview projector, a screen, and wax pencils. Frames are reusable, easily cleaned with carbon tetrachloride. For more elaborate setup, see BRIDGE-O-RAMA.

VULNERABILITY. The condition of being subject to greater undertrick penalties, and eligible to receive greater premiums as provided by the scoring table. In rubber bridge, vulnerability comes about by having won one game toward rubber. In duplicate bridge, vulnerability is arbitrarily assigned by board numbers.

Vulnerability in duplicate is on a sixteen-board cycle, repeating for each succeeding sixteen boards; boards 1, 8, 11 and 14 have no vulnerability; boards 2, 5, 12, and 15 have North-South vulnerable, East-West not vulnerable; boards 3, 6, 9, and 16 have East-West vulnerable, North-South not vulnerable; boards 4, 7, 10, and 13 have both sides vulnerable. This can be remembered fairly easily by the sixteen letters forming this arrangement:

```
O N E B
N E B O
E B O N
B O N E
```

where O stands for no vulnerability, N for North-South, E for East-West and B for both.

In CHICAGO, a four-hand variation of rubber bridge, the vulnerability also is arbitrarily assigned in similar fashion; no vulnerability on the first hand; dealer vulnerable on the second and third hands; and everyone vulnerable on the last hand. A variation in a few clubs that is technically perhaps a slight improvement assigns the vulnerability on the second and third hands to the opponents of the dealer.

The feature of vulnerability gives rise to many variations in the strategy of bidding and play; these variations probably are foremost among the reasons for the great interest which contract bridge has stimulated.

VULNERABLE. A term applied to a side which has won a game, and is thus exposed to greater undertrick penalties and entitled to greater premiums for slams and doubled overtricks. The term was suggested to Harold VANDERBILT by a fellow passenger on the cruise on which Vanderbilt devised the game of contract bridge.

W

WBF. See WORLD BRIDGE FEDERATION.

WBF MASTER POINTS. Points won in a tournament conducted by the WORLD BRIDGE FEDERATION or in WBF-approved ZONAL CHAMPIONSHIPS (1). See WORLD BRIDGE FEDERATION PLAYER RANKINGS.

WBF PLACING POINTS. Points, other than WBF MASTER POINTS, awarded by the WORLD BRIDGE FEDERATION to winners and very high finishers in WBF tournaments and Zonal team championships. A certain number of placing points are needed to achieve the WBF rankings of Grand Master and World Master. See WORLD BRIDGE FEDERATION PLAYER RANKINGS.

WAITING BID. A temporizing bid by a player who aims to extract information from partner rather than give information about his own holding. This is usually made in a minor suit, perhaps in a three-card suit.

A prepared opening bid of one club with a three-card suit is in a sense a waiting bid. For examples of waiting responses, see THREE-CARD SUITS, BIDS IN. The following is an example of a waiting rebid:

♠ A J 5
♡ A K 6
◇ Q 5 2
♣ K Q 7 3

After an opening bid of one club and a jump shift response of two diamonds, the best rebid is two no trump. The opener has no intention of stopping short of a small slam, and has thoughts of a grand slam, but his best move is to proceed cautiously, extracting more information from the responder before heading slamwards.

For another type of waiting bid, see the two no trump response described under IMPOSSIBLE BIDS.

WAIVE A PENALTY. In rubber bridge, either member of a partnership, without consulting the other member, may waive a penalty (condone an irregularity); if either member so elects, the right to enforce a penalty is forfeited. In duplicate, players do not have the right to waive penalties on their own initiative, and the director may allow or cancel any waiver of penalties made by the players without his instructions. However, the right to penalize an irregularity may be forfeited. See LAWS (Law 15), LAWS OF DUPLICATE (Laws 10, 11).

WALLET. British name for a form of DUPLICATE BOARD in which each pocket is formed in the fold of a wallet-shaped receptacle. The board can be folded into one-half size for ease in carrying. Plastic wallet boards are popular in Europe. They were used in the 1932 World Bridge Olympics.

WALSH SYSTEM. A style of bidding popular in the West, sometimes known as Western Roth-Stone or West Coast Scientific; its chief architect was Richard WALSH of Los Angeles. The principal features are strong one no trump openings with non-forcing STAYMAN and JACOBY TRANSFER BIDS, five-card major suit openings with a forcing one no trump response, and usually some form of SWISS major suit raises. Direct limit raises promise a side-suit singleton; jump shift responses are pre-emptive. Minor suit raises are INVERTED (see INVERTED MINOR SUIT RAISES), and a one diamond response to one club usually denies a four-card major suit.

Two-over-one responses are game forcing. Over a two club response to one diamond, opener has specialized responses: two hearts or two spades shows a four-card suit and no extra values; two no trump shows 4–4–3–2 distribution and no extra values, and two diamonds usually shows five or more diamonds, but may be forced with 3–3–4–3 distribution and poor clubs.

Other methods include MATHE ASKING BIDS, COMPETITIVE DOUBLES, rebid of new minor suit by responder forcing after opener's one no trump rebid, opening four club and four diamond bids to transfer to four hearts and four spades, respectively, negative and responsive doubles.

WAR ORPHANS SCHOLARSHIPS, INC. An educational foundation incorporated 1943 in New York State by officers and governors of ACBL; in the eight years of its existence it awarded about $800,000 in scholarship benefits to sons and daughters of members of the US armed services who in World War II suffered service-connected or battle-connected deaths. Tournament winners 1943–46 accepted printed certificates instead of prizes, the cost of trophies going to the scholarship fund, and special tournaments plus individual contributions and income from general solicitations made up the remainder of the fund. The board of WOS was composed of official representatives of the armed services of the US and officers of the ACBL. They were: Gen. Peter C. Harris, former Adjutant General, Chairman American Legion scholarship committee, Chairman; Gen. Frank T. Hines, Veterans Security Administrator, President; W. E. McKenney, Executive Secretary ACBL, Vice-President; A. H. Morehead, President ACBL, Secretary and Treasurer; Watson B. Miller, Federal Security Administrator, former Executive Secretary American Legion; Gen. James A. Ulio, Adjutant General USA; Adm. Randall Jacobs, Chief of Naval Personnel; Adm. Raymond Chalker, Commandant US Coast Guard; Gen. G. Peck, Commandant US Marine Corps.

WARNING PARTNER. A privilege of all players (including a dummy who has not intentionally looked at another hand) if the player feels that his partner is about to commit an irregularity. Examples: "It's not your lead, partner." "No hearts, partner?" "The lead is in the dummy, partner." It is not permitted during the auction to warn partner about a convention you or an opponent may be using, or to review the auction to apprise partner of a previous bid you think he may have misunderstood. See ALERTING.

WARREN. See SAN FRANCISCO.

WASHING-LIST. See BACK SCORE.

WEAK JUMP OVERCALL. The use of a jump overcall in a suit as pre-emptive. A FOUR ACES innovation of the thirties, credited to O. JACOBY, and embodied in ROTH-STONE and later systems.

Over a one diamond opening, two hearts, two spades, or three clubs would show the equivalent of a WEAK TWO-BID: 6–12 points, and a six-card or perhaps seven-card suit.

The weak jump overcall must always take the vulnerability situation into account. Not vulnerable against vulnerable, a weak jump to the level of two could be made on a good five-card suit and little else. A vulnerable jump to the three-level against non-vulnerable would almost always be too dangerous with a weak hand. For this reason, S. STAYMAN advises a strong jump overcall at unfavorable vulnerability.

The opening bidder's partner must bid aggressively with hands of medium strength when a weak jump overcall has been made. If he passes, the overcaller may achieve his objective and buy the contract cheaply. If a bid would have been made over a simple overcall, then a bid should still be made over a weak jump.

However, the increased level raises a problem. One solution is for minimum bids in a new suit to be non-forcing. In that case the only forcing bids would be a cue-bid in the opponent's suit, a jump in a new suit, and possibly, by agreement, two no trump.

The weak jump would not apply in the pass-out position, for there would be no object in pre-empting. In that situation a jump would be made with slightly less than the values needed for a strong jump. But if opponents bid two suits, the jump retains its pre-emptive character.

Some leading players, notably in Philadelphia, rely considerably on the negative inferences which can be available using the weak jump overcall. They treat simple overcalls as stronger than in standard methods, and respond to them as to an opening one-bid. See also DOUBLE JUMP OVERCALL.

WEAK JUMP SHIFT RESPONSES. The use of a jump response in a new suit as a pre-emptive bid. After an opening one club, a response of two spades would be made by a player whose only asset was ♠ KJ6542. This works for the sub-minimum responding hands with a six- or seven-card suit, but greatly increases the problem of bidding strong hands which would normally make a jump shift. The simple suit response becomes overloaded, because it may be made with a hand of any strength from 6 points upwards.

Like all pre-emptive bids, the weak jump shift response exerts pressure on an opponent with a good hand. The fourth player should bid as he would over an opening one-bid: double for a take-out, and bid two no trump on a hand which would open one no trump (16–18). See ROTH-STONE SYSTEM.

WEAK NO TRUMP. An opening one no trump with a minimum hand is an integral part of many systems. The usual range of the bid is 12–14 points, although the PRECISION SYSTEM uses a range of 13–15 points. The usual corollary is that a rebid of one no trump shows a hand too strong to open with one no trump (15–17 in KAPLAN-SHEINWOLD, 15–16 in the English systems).

Each of these systems has some special features in response, but with a suitable adjustment of range any normal principles of responding to a strong no trump can be followed.

A structure developed specifically for responding to a weak no trump opening by Mark Melchiori, Spring Arbor, Mich., relies extensively on transfer bids. With a weak hand responder may transfer to his longest suit by bidding the next lower-ranking suit, raise to two no trump as a take-out for the minors, or bid two clubs (STAYMAN) and over two diamonds by opener, rebid three diamonds as a take-out for the majors. With an invitational hand, responder will usually transfer and raise or rebid another suit; specialized invitations are a jump to three diamonds to invite game in hearts and a raise to two no trump followed by three no trump to invite a no trump game if opener has a fit for responder's minors and stoppers in the major suits. With a game-forcing hand, responder can transfer and jump in another suit, transfer to a minor and raise (slam invitational), or raise to two no trump and rebid a suit on the three-level (distributional game-force that could not be shown by other methods). See also FLINT TWO DIAMONDS.

Some special tactical situations arise when one no trump by the dealer has been passed and the responder is very weak. The fourth player is almost certain to have a strong hand, and there is a danger of conceding a heavy penalty, so third hand may have to take evasive action:

   ♠ 6 2
   ♡ 9 7 4 3
   ◇ J 10 7 3
   ♣ 9 5 3

Two diamonds is the best action because it will not be easy for the opponents to double for penalties. A pass is likely to lead to a contract of one no trump doubled, down three or four tricks. If the black suits were reversed, a conventional two club response would be possible with the intention of passing any rebid. But see DOUBLE OF TWO CLUB RESPONSE TO ONE NO TRUMP.

Responder has some unusual opportunities for psychic or semi-psychic bidding at favorable vulnerability with a long suit:

   ♠ 9 7 6 5 3 2
   ♡ 7
   ◇ 8 6 4 2
   ♣ 9 5

Not vulnerable against vulnerable opponents, a response of two spades would be unimaginative, for the opposition can surely make game in hearts and/or no trump. Four spades would be much better, and may not be easy for the opponents to double. Outrageous bids like two no trump, three no trump, or even two hearts may lead to a triumph. If one of these bids buys the contract undoubled and goes down a large number of tricks, there will still be a profit against a vulnerable game.

Competitive bidding is much more common and much more critical when the weak no trump is being used. The opponents frequently need some conventional defensive arrangement such as ASTRO, BROZEL, EXCLUSION BIDS, LANDY, or RIPSTRA. A double of a weak no trump should be for penalties, and partner should rarely remove the double: only a weak hand with a long suit would justify a take-out. The doubler should have a better hand than the no trump bidder, whether the double is made immediately or in the pass-out position.

When a weak no trump is doubled, opener's side will often need a conventional arrangement for escaping to their best suit contract. One method, proposed by Henry Shevitz, Detroit, Mich., is that a redouble by responder asks opener to bid his better minor, two diamonds is a request for his better major, and two clubs shows one minor, not necessarily clubs. If two clubs is doubled, responder corrects to diamonds if that is his suit.

The action by fourth hand after a two-level response needs consideration. A double of a STAYMAN two club response is usually taken to be an indication of a good club suit for lead-directing purposes. The modern tendency among some experts is to double two clubs or any suit take-out at the level of two with a hand which would have doubled if responder had passed one no trump.

For other details about no trump bidding, see JACOBY TRANSFER BIDS; ONE NO TRUMP OPENING; STAYMAN; TEXAS; etc.

WEAK NO TRUMP OVERCALL. The use of an overcall of one no trump is the equivalent of a weak no trump opening. This permits a defender to enter the auction on many hands which he would normally pass, but the value is doubtful because the overcaller will often be doubled for penalties with no escape. Sometimes confined to non-vulnerable situations.

The opener's partner follows the procedure for bidding over a normal strong no trump overcall. He usually doubles with 9 points or more, because his side is almost sure to have the balance of strength. With a weaker hand he can bid a five-card or longer suit at the two-level, which is unconstructive. And he can make a CUE-BID of two no trump with a strong unbalanced hand. See also BARON NO TRUMP OVERCALL.

WEAK SUIT. A suit which the opponents are likely to lead, and in which they can probably cash several tricks. Sometimes the term refers to an unstopped suit, but if a no trump contract is being considered it could also apply to a suit in which the opponents hold nine or more cards and in which only one stopper is held.

The weakness of a suit is relative to the auction. A small doubleton is often regarded as a weak suit for the purposes of a one no trump opening, although there are two schools of thought, and many players would not allow themselves to be deterred.

For the purposes of a no trump rebid, a small doubleton in an unbid suit is unthinkable, and a small tripleton is highly unattractive. The chance that the opponents will lead the suit is increased, and the chance that partner can guard it is decreased.

If a side has bid three suits, a no trump bid requires at least one positive stopper and preferably two in the fourth suit.

Sometimes anything less than a double stopper would certainly represent a weak suit:

SOUTH	WEST	NORTH	EAST
1 ◇	Dbl.	Pass	3 NT

As West is likely to have a diamond shortage, the jump to three no trump shows a double diamond stopper. Anything less would constitute a weak suit, unless perhaps East held a single stopper with a long strong club suit.

WEAK SUIT GAME TRY. A rebid by opener in his weakest suit to try for game after responder has raised the major suit opening bid to two. Sometimes called a "help suit game try." For example if opener holds:

♠ A K x x x   ♡ x x x   ◇ x   ♣ A Q J x

the bidding goes

OPENER	RESPONDER
1 ♠	2 ♠
3 ♡	

Opener's three heart bid asks responder to bid game in spades if he has either strength or shortness in hearts. Responder might hold any of the following hands:

(a)	(b)	(c)
♠ Q x x x	♠ Q x x x	♠ Q x x x
♡ J x x	♡ A x x x x	♡ x
◇ A x x x x	◇ J x x	◇ A J x x x
♣ x	♣ x	♣ x x x

With hand (a) responder would sign off in three spades since he has no help for opener's anemic hearts. With hand (b) or hand (c), however, responder would bid game in spades since his strength in (b) and his singleton in (c) can take care of the heart situation.

A disadvantage of weak suit game tries is that it usually reveals to the opponents the vulnerable spot of opener's hand, and therefore the defender's most advantageous point of attack.

WEAK TAKE-OUT. An English term for a natural unconstructive suit response to one no trump. See WEAKNESS RESPONSE.

WEAK TWO-BIDS. The use of suit openings of two other than clubs as a pre-emptive bid. A prototype of the weak two was used in auction bridge, and adopted in the VANDERBILT CLUB SYSTEM. Subsequently C. E. Van Vleck, New York, was responsible for an ultra-weak two-bid. Howard Schenken developed the modern weak two-bid along lines similar to Vanderbilt's. It was later incorporated into most modern American systems, and into the NEAPOLITAN and BLUE TEAM CLUB systems.

Most authorities require a six-card suit for a weak two-bid, with about 8–11 points in high cards mainly concentrated in the suit which is bid. But these requirements are commonly relaxed, especially in third seat, and many players simply announce a range of 6–12 high-card points. Vulnerability and position at the table may be a factor in deciding whether to make a weak two-bid.

Responses. There are a number of schools of thought, and the responses and rebids need precise partnership agreement.

(1) *Raise to four.* A two-way bid: perhaps a hand which expects to make game, or perhaps a preemptive action of the ADVANCE SAVE variety. The left-hand opponent may have a difficult decision with a strong hand.

(2) *Raise to three.* Originally a constructive invitation to opener to bid game, but many players use the raise pre-emptively. In the latter case the responder's trick-taking expectation for the combined hands may vary from nine tricks to as little as six tricks at favorable vulnerability.

(3) *Suit take-out.* Normally natural and forcing. Psychic responses are sometimes used, especially at the level of two.

An alternative treatment which has increased in popularity is to play suit take-outs as non-forcing and unconstructive, indicating that the responder has a misfit and expects a better result playing in his own long strong suit. Responder must bid two no trump whenever he wishes to make a forcing bid.

(4) *Two no trump.* Usually a one-round force. A rebid by opener in his own suit can be used to show a minimum; some players prefer to show a minimum by a three club rebid. Using either agreement, a rebid in another suit shows a high-card FEATURE and better than a minimum hand. If responder then gives a mere preference to opener's original suit on the second round, the defenders should find out whether the opener is encouraged or permitted to continue: if not, a psychic should be suspected. Similarly, it is important for both the opener's side and the defenders to know whether the opener is permitted to rebid above the level of three in his original suit. A raise of two no trump to three no trump, if permitted, should show a solid suit.

A system of rebidding to two no trump devised by Harold OGUST requires opener to describe the strength of his hand and the quality of his suit by a series of artificial bids. Ogust Rebids are as follows:

three clubs	minimum strength, poor suit
three diamonds	maximum strength, poor suit
three hearts	minimum strength, good suit
three spades	maximum strength, good suit

Some partnerships prefer to reverse the meanings of the three diamond and three heart rebids.

The McCabe Adjunct, described by J. I. McCabe, Columbia, S.C., in *The Bridge World,* Jan. 1955, is a method of playing at the three-level in a new suit. After the two no trump response, the opener is required to rebid three clubs, irrespective of his holding. The responder can now play in his long suit at the three-level, either by bidding it or by passing three clubs. Each partnership must decide the meaning of two no trump followed by a simple preference bid: this should be treated as constructive if an immediate raise would have been pre-emptive.

A two no trump response is occasionally used as a natural non-forcing invitation to three no trump; but it can very rarely be right to stop in two no trump after a weak two-bid.

Defense. Standard procedure is to bid as over a one-bid: double for take-out, and bid two no trump on a hand which would qualify for a strong no trump opening bid. But many other defensive arrangements are possible, including all the methods listed under DEFENSE TO OPENING THREE-BIDS.

To combat players addicted to psychic suit responses to a weak two-bid, some players use a double of the response for penalties. But if the suit response is natural and *non-forcing,* the double should be a normal take-out action. Weak two-bids are confined to the major suits by players who use a specialized two diamond convention such as BENJAMIN, BLUE TEAM, FLANNERY TWO DIAMONDS, or ROMAN.

WEAKNESS-CONCEALING PLAYS. See DECEPTIVE PLAY.

WEAKNESS RESPONSE. A natural response which indicates a strong desire to close the auction at that point.

The most common case is the response of two spades, two hearts, or two diamonds to an opening one no trump bid. Using standard methods, with the STAYMAN two club convention, responder shows at least a five-card suit and no desire to progress toward game.

In very rare circumstances the opener may make one further bid if he has a fine fit with responder, presumably four cards, and a maximum no trump opening consisting largely of top honors, usually including two of the three top honors in responder's suit. If opener raises to the three-level and the contract fails, it may prove that the raise has forestalled a successful balancing action by the opponents.

If the opener bids a new suit (one no trump—two hearts—three clubs), he implies a fit with responder's hearts plus a concentration of strength in clubs. This helps responder to evaluate game chances.

Another example of a weakness response:

SOUTH	WEST	NORTH	EAST
1 ♣	1 NT	2 ♡	

North's failure to double one no trump marks him with a weak hand (less than 8 or 9 points) and heart length. South will rarely be strong enough to attempt a game, and should rarely rescue. A suit bid or a simple raise over a take-out double is similar in principle.

Weakness responses, which are natural, are often confused with negative responses, which are conventional. Examples of these would be a negative two diamond response to a conventional two club bid, or a HERBERT NEGATIVE.

WEISS CONVENTION. See DEFENSE TO OPENING THREE BID.

WEISSBERGER CONVENTION. An extension of the STAYMAN convention to ask for three-card major suits, suggested by John PRESSBURGER and developed by Alan TRUSCOTT, New York, and Maurice Weissberger, London. It is intended for use with English-style Stayman in which a secondary jump to three hearts or three spades is invitational and not forcing, and is an optional feature of the ACOL system. Suppose the bidding proceeds:

OPENER	RESPONDER
1 NT	2 ♣
2 ◇	3 ◇

The bid of three diamonds has little or no natural meaning in Acol. The Weissberger idea is to use it to inquire for three-card major suits. This helps the responder to solve three types of bidding problems:

(1) A game-going hand with five spades and four hearts.

(2) A game-going hand with five spades and five hearts.

(3) A hand with five spades and five hearts on which game is doubtful.

As the responder is certain to have five spades, holding three spades the opener bids three spades with a minimum hand; four spades holding a maximum.

With only a doubleton spade, the opener bids three hearts holding a minimum hand and three no trump holding a maximum.

In all cases the responder has no problem in selecting the best final contract.

Notice that there are two other cases in which the convention is *not* needed:

(4) A game-going hand with four spades and five hearts. In this case the responder bids three hearts immediately over one no trump, and relies on the opener to show a four-card spade suit if he can.

(5) A hand with four in one major and five in the other on which game is doubtful. In this case the responder bids three of the five-card major suit over the opener's two diamond rebid. This sequence is strictly non-forcing in Acol.

WELSH BRIDGE UNION. Founded about 1934, and formed by three areas, North, West, and East, with a membership of 30 clubs and approximately 900 members in 1975. The Union competes nationally for five cups: Open Teams (Welsh Cup) and Women's Teams, both knockout events, International Pairs (restricted to Welsh International players), National Pairs, and a League event. Since 1961 the WBU has operated a master-point program with awards won by members of the English Bridge Union registrable with the EBU. Welsh players listed separately are: Dr. J. Butler, J. Carter, B. M. Clowes, Mrs. P. Fletcher, G. Fox, L. Murray, Dr. J. S. Spickett, Mrs. P. Spickett, P. Spurway, A. Stone, Maj. W. B. Tatlow.

Officers, 1975:
President: Mrs. Jessie Newton.
Secretary: Len Muller, 46 St. Isan Road, Heath, Cardiff CF 4 4LX, Wales.

WERNHER TROPHY. For the National Men's Pairs Championship, donated by Sir Derrick Wernher in 1934; contested at the Summer Nationals until 1962 and subsequently at the Spring Nationals, under which heading results are listed.

WEST. The player who sits at the left of South at a table of bridge. South is to his right and North to his left. He is the partner of East.

WEST COAST SCIENTIFIC. See WALSH SYSTEM.

WESTCOTT TROPHY. Awarded to the winner of

the Olympiad Fund Pairs at the Summer Nationals, donated in memory of Frank T. Westcott in 1974 by his widow.

WESTERN BRIDGE ASSOCIATION. A short lived Chicago-based membership organization which published *The Contract Bridge Magazine,* 1933–34, edited by E. M. LAGRON.

WESTERN CUE-BIDS. Generally, a cue-bid of a suit bid by an opponent to ask about stoppers for no trump play, rather than promising such stoppers. See CUE-BIDS IN OPPONENT'S SUIT; DIRECTIONAL ASKING BID.

WESTERN ROTH-STONE. See WALSH SYSTEM.

WETZLAR TROPHY. Awarded for distinguished services to bridge, this trophy was presented in memory of Edwin Wetzlar in 1935. The first winners were:

1935	H. H. Boscowitz	1938	Alfred Gruenther
1936	W. von Zedtwitz	1939	Nate B. Spingold
1937	Gordon Gibbs	1940	Harold S. Vanderbilt

After 1940 the Wetzlar was presented to ACBL HONORARY MEMBERS, under which heading the recipients are listed.

WHISK. An alternative name for whist. It was an English lower-class term, according to Dr. Samuel Johnson, used until about the end of the eighteenth century.

WHIST. A game of cards of English origin gradually evolved from several older games such as triumph, trump, ruff and honors, swabbers, and WHISK. Whist is played by four persons, two partners against two partners. A regular pack of 52 cards is dealt, 13 to each player. The last card dealt is turned face up on the table. Its suit becomes the trump suit. This card remains on the table until it is the dealer's turn to play to the first trick, when he may return it to his hand. The player at the left of the dealer makes the first lead, and the play proceeds as in bridge except that all four hands are concealed; there is no DUMMY. Six tricks taken make the BOOK. Each trick won over the book scores one point for the partners winning that trick. The range of possible scores for either set of partners is from one to seven. Any number of deals may be played. Scoring is by games. The English code of laws provides for rubber bonuses and honor bonuses. At the conclusion of play the side having the greatest number of points is the winner. The game of whist has, in general, been superseded in the United States by changing versions of the basic game—by bridge, AUCTION BRIDGE and CONTRACT BRIDGE. It is still played widely in Great Britain and the US. See also AMERICAN WHIST LEAGUE; BIBLIOGRAPHY; CONTRACT WHIST.

WHIST CLUB. A club of men interested in whist and later in all successive forms of bridge, founded in New York 1893, merged with the REGENCY CLUB of New York 1964. Because nearly all of its members were men of great wealth and prominence (including bridge prominence, such as H. Vanderbilt, J. Elwell,

M. Work, and E. Culbertson), unquestioned authority in the making of bridge laws for the US was accorded to the Whist Club for more than forty years. Two earlier codes of contract bridge laws were voluntarily withdrawn when in 1927 the Whist Club produced a code for contract bridge (formulated by a committee composed of H. Vanderbilt, H. C. Richard, Charles Cadley, Raymond Little, and William Talcott). Later the Whist Club's committees collaborated with the Portland Club of London and French Bridge Federation in producing the first and second international codes (1932, 1935), and Whist Club representatives have served continuously on the NATIONAL LAWS COMMISSION for the laws of 1943, 1948, 1949, and 1963.

WHITEHEAD TROPHY. For the National Women's Pair Championship, donated by Wilbur C. Whitehead in 1930; contested at the Summer Nationals until 1962 and subsequently at the Spring Nationals, under which heading results are listed.

WHITFIELD SIX. The father of all end-game problems, devised and published on January 31, 1885, by W. H. Whitfield, mathematical tutor at Cambridge, England, who was Cavendish's successor as Card Editor of the London *Field*. (Known as the "Whitfield Six" through a common mispronunciation of the inventor's name.)

Hearts are trumps. South must lead and make all the tricks.

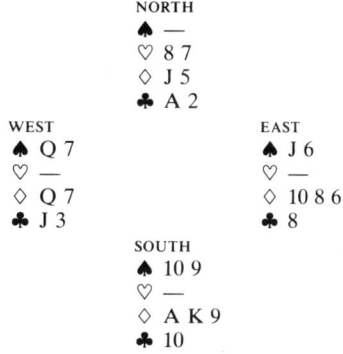

```
                NORTH
                ♠ —
                ♡ 8 7
                ◇ J 5
                ♣ A 2
    WEST                        EAST
    ♠ Q 7                       ♠ J 6
    ♡ —                         ♡ —
    ◇ Q 7                       ◇ 10 8 6
    ♣ J 3                       ♣ 8
                SOUTH
                ♠ 10 9
                ♡ —
                ◇ A K 9
                ♣ 10
```

Solution. South cashes the ace of diamonds, unblocking the jack from dummy to prepare for a possible finesse. A spade is ruffed and the last trump from dummy is cashed, on which South discards the club ten. The only temporary defense is for East to keep diamonds and the high spade, and for West to keep clubs and the diamond queen. The club ace from dummy then squeezes East. The Whitfield Six is a type of double guard squeeze.

WIDE OPEN. A phrase describing a suit in which declarer has no stopper or is extremely vulnerable to attack. For example, "Declarer was wide open in trumps."

WINKLE SQUEEZE. A secondary squeeze that

forces the opponents to choose between a throw-in or an unblock, each of which costs a trick. (Analyzed and named by Terence Reese.) Declarer has enough winners for all but one of the remaining tricks, but he cannot take all his tricks because of entry problems.

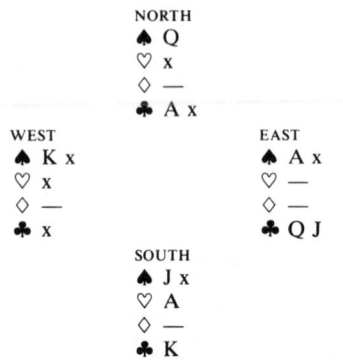

South leads the ace of hearts, and East is squeezed in two suits. In order to retain his club guard he must discard a spade. If East discards the ace of spades, South cashes the king of clubs, and exits with a spade, winning the jack of spades at the end; if East discards a small spade, the play proceeds the same way, but East wins the spade exit, and he must give North a club for the last trick.

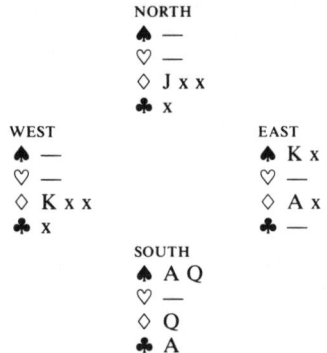

South leads the ace of clubs, and East is squeezed in two suits. A diamond must be discarded in order to protect the king of spades. If East discards a low diamond he will be thrown in to lead from his king of spades; if he discards the ace of diamonds, South takes the ace of spades, and then leads a diamond, eventually winning a trick with the jack. See also ENTRY SQUEEZE and STEPPINGSTONE SQUEEZE.

                                  M. I.

WINNER. (1) A card that may reasonably be expected to win a trick in dummy or declarer's hand. On defense, a card that will win a trick during the play of a given hand may be termed a winner as well. (2) The player, the pair, or team with the highest score in an event at a duplicate tournament. Winners and runners-up of duplicate games are eligible to compete in special WINNERS' GAMES.

WINNERS' GAMES. Sessions of club play at duplicate in which eligibility to compete was limited to players who had, within a prescribed period (usually one month) won one or placed second in two regularly scheduled sanctioned games, or won at least one full master point in a sectional or regional tournament within that time. This program is no longer in effect.

WINNING CARD. The card that takes the trick. In a no trump declaration this is always the highest card played in the suit that has been led; it may be a LONG CARD, led in a suit to which the other players cannot follow. In suit declarations, the above will apply, except that on a trick where more than one trump is played it is the highest trump that will win the trick.

WINSLOW SYSTEM. See WINSLOW, T. N. biography.

WITHDRAW A CARD. It is not permitted to withdraw a card previously played except to correct a revoke, or a card played by an opponent after such a card was withdrawn. Declarer may insist that a card he had called to be played from dummy be substituted for a card actually put into the playing position by the dummy. In this case, too, the opponent may without penalty withdraw his card and substitute a different proper card. See, however, ALCATRAZ COUP for a possible situation that calls for a redress under the general powers of the director.

WOLFF CONVENTION. Devised by R. WOLFF to allow responder to sign off at the three-level after opener has made a jump rebid of two no trump. Responder's rebid of three clubs asks opener to bid three of responder's suit if he has three-card support, and otherwise to bid three diamonds. Responder can then sign off by passing, by bidding four clubs, or by introducing a new suit of lower rank than his first suit; a rebid of three no trump by responder would be a mild slam try in clubs.

WOMEN'S INTERNATIONAL TEAM TRIALS. See INTERNATIONAL WOMEN'S TEAM SELECTION.

WOMEN'S PAIR CHAMPIONSHIP, NATIONAL. See WHITEHEAD TROPHY.

WOMEN'S PAIRS. An event at duplicate competition between pairs of women players. Awards are 25% lower than for events of comparable size and duration open to any players. At most sectional tournaments, the women's pairs event is held on Friday afternoon.

WOMEN'S TEAM CHAMPIONSHIP, NATIONAL. See COFFIN TROPHY.

WOODSON TWO-WAY NO TRUMP. This requires an opening no trump bid holding 10–12 points or 16–18 points and a hand with balanced distribution. It was devised in 1952 by William B. WOODSON, of Matthews N.C.

This two-way treatment sets problems for both sides, and its supporters believe that the defending side will frequently find its problems insoluble. The opener's partner can usually determine his partner's range without difficulty.

A response of two clubs to one no trump asks for clarification, and the rebids are:

Two diamonds or two hearts	10–12 points
Two spades or two no trump	16 points
Three clubs	17–18 points

Responder can use a bid of three diamonds on the second round to check for four-card major suits.

If one no trump is doubled, if one no trump bidder redoubles to show the weak no trump range of 10–12 and demand a rescue. (A reversal of this procedure would seem to have some advantages, with a redouble to show the strong range.)

Responder can sign off with two spades, two hearts, or two diamonds if he has no prospects of game opposite a strong no trump; and may head directly for game if he wishes to be in game opposite the weak variety.

Until the contrary is proved, the defenders should bid on the assumption that the no trump bid is weak. A double is in order with a full opening bid or better.

WORK POINT–COUNT. A 4–3–2–1 point-count based on the MC CAMPELL count of 1915, publicized and advocated by Milton WORK, circa 1923. See POINT-COUNT.

WORKING CARDS. High cards which, on the basis of the auction, rate to mesh well with partner's hand for suit play. For example, a SECONDARY HONOR or an unsupported king is usually discounted opposite a known singleton, whereas any of the top honors is likely to be "working" if it is in one of partner's suits. See also GOOD CARDS.

WORLD BIDDING CONTEST. See INTERNATIONAL BRIDGE ACADEMY.

WORLD BRIDGE FEDERATION. A successor of the INTERNATIONAL BRIDGE LEAGUE, was founded in Aug., 1958, at Oslo, Norway, by representatives of the American Contract Bridge League, the European Bridge League, and the Australian Bridge Council.

The WBF aims to provide a central organization to bind together the national controlling bridge organizations of the world. More specifically, its objects are:

(1) To promote, foster, and control the game of contract bridge.

(2) To apply the International Laws of contract bridge.

(3) To promote and conduct quadrennial WORLD CHAMPIONSHIP team tournaments on the basis of one team only for each country (the Olympiad).

(4) To conduct the BERMUDA BOWL contest, in every year in which there is no Team Olympiad.

(5) To promote and conduct quadrennial World Championship pair tournaments.

(6) To conduct World Championship par contests.

(7) To conduct such other contests as from time to time are agreed upon.

Member countries must have a minimum of 250 individual members, and belong to the zonal organization if one exists.

The zones of the WBF are: (1) Europe plus Israel and Lebanon, (2) North America, including Bermuda, (3) South America, (4) South Africa, (5) Open, (6) Far East, (7) South Pacific, (8) All countries not affiliated with any of the other zones, namely, Egypt, North African NCBOs, Iran, Saudi Arabia, islands in Central America and the Caribbean. In addition, the CENTRAL AMERICAN AND CARIBBEAN BRIDGE FEDERATION has been given provisional zonal recognition, reviewable in 1978.

The Federation's Board of Governors consists of one representative of each member country. It meets whenever and wherever a Team or Pair Olympiad is held.

The 1975 officers of the Federation were:

Julius L. Rosenblum, United States, President

Johannes Hammerich, Venezuela, 1st Vice-President

Jaime Ortiz Patino, Switzerland, 2nd Vice-President

André Littman-Lemaitre, Belgium, Secretary and Treasurer

Benjamin O. Johnson, United States, Assistant Secretary and Counsel

General Alfred M. Gruenther, United States, Honorary Chairman

EXECUTIVE COUNCIL

William A. Baldwin, United States
Geoffrey Butler, Great Britain
Carlos Cabanne, Argentina
Silvio Carini Mazzaccara, Italy
Richard Goldberg, United States
General Alfred M. Gruenther, United States*
Johannes Hammerich, Venezuela
Benjamin O. Johnson, United States*
André Littman-Lemaitre, Belgium
Robin MacNab, United States
Dr. Ralph Mizroch, South Africa
James O'Sullivan, Australia
Julius L. Rosenblum, United States
Leslie Schneiderman, New Zealand
Jerome Silverman, United States

Baron Robert de NEXON became the first President of the WBF in 1958 and was succeeded in 1964 by Charles SOLOMON, who had been the original Vice-President. In 1968, Count Carl BONDE was elected President. He held the post until the election of Julius ROSENBLUM in 1970. See also BERMUDA BOWL; INTERNATIONAL BRIDGE LEAGUE; WORLD PAR CONTESTS; WORLD CHAMPIONSHIPS.

WORLD   BRIDGE   FEDERATION   PLAYER RANKINGS. The ranking of players according to the world master-point plan of the World Bridge Federation. The three ranks, in descending order,

---

* Non-voting Member.

are Grand Master, World Master, and International Master.

The rank of Grand Master is achieved by accumulating 200 or more WBF MASTER POINTS (more than can be obtained by victory in any single WBF event) plus 10 WBF PLACING POINTS, and winning at least one major WBF event or four non-major events. The rank of World Master is achieved by accumulating 50 WBF points plus 5 WBF placing points, and winning at least one WBF championship or ZONAL CHAMPIONSHIP (1) or three NCBO championships. The rank of International Master may be achieved either by accumulating 10 WBF points, or by winning an NCBO championship and being nominated by an NCBO and being recognized by the appropriate WBF committee.

Each NCBO is allowed to nominate a certain number of players who have not won 10 WBF points to be International Masters. The number each NCBO may nominate is based principally on its membership population. In the United States the ACBL nominated as International Masters the top approximately 220 ACBL master-point holders who had won a national championship and who did not otherwise hold world ranking; the AMERICAN BRIDGE ASSOCIATION nominated several ABA players for such ranking.

Grand Masters, World Masters, and International Masters having 10 or more WBF points hold their ranks for life. International Masters with fewer than 10 WBF points hold their rank for four years and are then subject to review.

As of March 1975 the following players held the ranks of Grand Master and World Master:

GRAND MASTERS

1.	Belladonna, Giorgio	(Italy)	1,590
2.	Forquet, Pietro	(Italy)	1,450
3.	Garozzo, Benito	(Italy)	1,425
4.	d'Alelio, Massimo	(Italy)	1,260
5.	Avarelli, Walter	(Italy)	1,200
6.	Pabis Ticci, Camillo	(Italy)	910
7.	Hamman, Robert	(U.S.A.)	730
8.	Jacoby, Jim	(U.S.A.)	590
9.	Wolff, Robert	(U.S.A.)	570
10.	Goldman, Robert	(U.S.A.)	480
11.	Chiaradia, Eugenio	(Italy)	480
12.	Trézel, Roger	(France)	480
13.	Jaïs, Pierre	(France)	460
14.	Lawrence, Michael	(U.S.A.)	410
15.	Ghestem, Pierre	(France)	383
16.	Shapiro, Boris	(Gr. Br.)	353
17.	Bacherich, Rene	(France)	350
18.	Schenken, Howard	(U.S.A.)	330
19.	Reese, Terence	(Gr. Br.)	323
20.	Becker, B. Jay	(U.S.A.)	320
21.	Eisenberg, William	(U.S.A.)	300
22.	Stayman, Samuel	(U.S.A.)	295
23.	Rapee, George	(U.S.A.)	280
24.	Crawford, John	(U.S.A.)	255
25.	Markus, Mrs. Rixi	(Gr. Br.)	229
26.	Delmouly, Claude	(France)	228
27.	Siniscalco, Guglielmo	(Italy)	225
28.	Bianchi, Benito	(Italy)	213
29–30.	Kreyns, Hans	(Netherlands)	210
	Slavenburg, Cornelis	(Netherlands)	210
31.	Mathe, Lewis	(U.S.A.)	210
32.	Bourchtoff, Gerard	(France)	200

WORLD MASTERS — MEN

1.	Murray, Eric	(Can.)	363
2.	Kehela, Sammy	(Can.)	318

3–4.	Jordon, Robert	(U.S.A.)	275
	Robinson, Arthur G.	(U.S.A.)	275
5.	Kay, Norman	(U.S.A.)	255
6.	Roth, Alvin	(U.S.A.)	242
7.	Svarc, Henri	(France)	193
8.	Flint, Jeremy	(Gr. Br.)	190
9.	Boulenger, Jean-Michel	(France)	188
10.	Tai, M. F.	(China)	176
11.	Gardener, Nico	(Gr. Br.)	175
12.	Pittala, V.	(Italy)	170
13.	Huang, Patrick	(China)	169
14.	Leventritt, Peter	(U.S.A.)	160
15.	Roudinesco, J. M.	(France)	160
16.	Kaplan, Edgar	(U.S.A.)	155
17–18.	Babsch, Fritz	(Austria)	153
	Manhardt, P.	(Austria)	153
19.	Mayer, F.	(Italy)	150
20.	Root, William	(U.S.A.)	150
21.	Rose, Albert	(Gr. Br.)	148
22.	Goren, Charles H.	(U.S.A.)	140
23.	Mitchell, Victor	(U.S.A.)	140
24.	Soloway, Paul	(U.S.A.)	135
25.	Stoppa, Jean-Louis	(France)	135
26.	Stone, Tobias	(U.S.A.)	127
27.	Assumpcao, P. P.	(Brazil)	125
28.	Chagas, Gabriel	(Brazil)	123
29.	Cheng, Conrad	(China)	121
30–31.	Charney, G.	(Can.)	120
	Crissey, W.	(Can.)	120
32.	Rubin, Ira	(U.S.A.)	120
33.	Seres, Tim	(Australia)	113
34.	Tarlo, Joel	(Gr. Br.)	110
35.	Zanasi, I.	(Italy)	110
36.	Smilde, Roelof	(Australia)	108
37.	Fisher, Dr. John	(U.S.A.)	105
38.	Mondolfo, Renato	(Italy)	105
39–40.	Garabello, G.	(Italy)	100
	Krauss, Donald P.	(U.S.A.)	100
41.	Besse, Jean	(Switz.)	96
42.	Stetten, Jacques	(France)	95
43.	Tintner, Léon	(France)	95
44–45.	Cummings, Dick	(Australia)	95
	Howard, Denis	(Australia)	95
46.	Nail, G. R.	(U.S.A.)	90
47.	Cabanne, Carlos	(Argent.)	86.5
48.	Lin, Harry	(China)	86
49.	Hsiao, Elmer	(China)	85
50.	Desrousseaux, Gerard	(France)	83
51.	Rocchi, Egisto	(Argent.)	80
52.	Berisso, Alberto	(Argent.)	78.5
53.	Fonseca, Christiano	(Brazil)	78
54.	Shen, C. S.	(China)	78
55–57.	Bishop, Clifford	(U.S.A.)	75
	Ellenby, Milton Q.	(U.S.A.)	75
	Rosen, William A.	(U.S.A.)	75
58.	Chuang, Frank K.	(China)	73
59.	Cintra, Gabr.	(Brazil)	73
60.	Shen, K. W	(Thailand)	73
61.	Borin, Jim	(Australia)	73
62.	Feldesman, P.	(U.S.A.)	72
63–64.	Catzeflis, G.	(Switz.)	71
	Sucharitakul, K.	(Thailand)	71
65.	Lazard, Sidney	(U.S.A.)	70
66.	Hazen, Lee	(U.S.A.)	70
67.	Rodrigue, Claude	(Gr. Br.)	68
68.	Calvente, Ricardo	(Argent.)	66
69.	Branco, Marcelo C.	(Brazil)	65
70.	Ogust, Harold	(U.S.A.)	65
71.	Bernasconi, P.	(Switz.)	64
72.	Santamarina, A.	(Argent.)	63.5
73.	Franco, A.	(Italy)	60
74.	Branco, Pedro	(Brazil)	60
75–76.	Elliot, C. Bruce	(Can.)	60
	Sheardown, Percy E.	(Can.)	60
77.	Priday, R. A.	(Gr. Br.)	60
78.	Saulino, N.	(Italy)	60
79.	Attaguile, L.	(Argent.)	59.5
80.	Lerner, M.	(Argent.)	59
81.	Pariente, J.	(France)	55
82.	Wohlin, Jan	(Sweden)	55
83.	Ortiz-Patino, J.	(Switz.)	54
84.	Messina, Giuseppe	(Italy)	53
85–94.	Dodds, Leslie	(Gr. Br.)	50
	Kock, R.	(Sweden)	50

Lattes, Roger	(France)	50
Lightner, Theodore	(U.S.A.)	50
Lilliehöök, N. O.	(Sweden)	50
Oakie, Don	(U.S.A.)	50
Romanet, B.	(France)	50
Rosenblum, Julius L.	(U.S.A.)	50
Steen, Douglas	(U.S.A.)	50
Werner, Einar	(Sweden)	50

WORLD MASTERS — WOMEN

1.	Gordon, Mrs. Fritzi	(Gr. Br.)	194
2.	Truscott, Dorothy H.	(U.S.A.)	190
3.	Farell, Mary Jane	(U.S.A.)	135
4.	Priday, Jane	(Gr. Br.)	105
5.	Silborn, Mrs. Gunborg	(Sweden)	94
6.	Blom, Mrs. Britt	(Sweden)	91
7.	Jacobson, Rita	(S. Africa)	87
8.	Goslar, Gerda	(S. Africa)	85
9.	Johnson, Marilyn	(U.S.A.)	83
10.	Valenti, Anna	(Italy)	80
11.	Mansell, Petra	(S. Africa)	76
12.	Schnieder, Alma	(S. Africa)	76
13.	Gordon, Loula	(Switz.)	74
14.	Bianchi, Marisa	(Italy)	68
15.	Durran, Joan	(Gr. Br.)	65
16.	Shanahan, Dorothy	(Gr. Br.)	65
17.	Beron, Thelma	(S. Africa)	60
18.	Fleming, Dimmie	(Gr. Br.)	60
19.	Robaudo, Antionetta	(Italy)	60
20.	Jabes, Mrs. Rina	(Italy)	55
21.	Camara, Helen	(Egypt)	50
22.	Canessa, Luciana	(Italy)	50
23.	Chanfray, Annie	(France)	50
24.	Choucry, Aida	(Egypt)	50
25.	Eriksson, Karin	(Sweden)	50
26.	Fathy, Samika	(Egypt)	50
27.	Gruver, Nancy	(U.S.A.)	50
28.	Martenson, Eva	(Sweden)	50
29.	Morcos, Josephine	(Egypt)	50
30.	Morenas, Genevieve	(France)	50
31.	Moss, Mary	(Gr. Br.)	50
32.	Naguib, Suzanne	(Egypt)	50
33.	Portugal, Helen	(U.S.A.)	50
34.	Sachs, Suzanne	(U.S.A.)	50
35.	Segander, Rut	(Sweden)	50
36.	Serf, Mariane	(France)	50
37.	Venturini, Maria	(Italy)	50
38.	Werner, Britta	(Sweden)	50

WORLD BRIDGE FEDERATION POINTS. See WBF MASTER POINTS; WBF PLACING POINTS; WORLD BRIDGE FEDERATION PLAYER RANKINGS.

WORLD BRIDGE FEDERATION TROPHY. For the World Women's Olympiad Pair Championship. First contested in Cannes, France, in 1962. See WORLD CHAMPIONSHIPS for results.

WORLD BRIDGE OLYMPIC. See WORLD PAR CONTESTS.

WORLD CHAMPIONSHIPS. There have been four distinct categories of World Championship bridge.

I. Pre-World War II.

1935 (the first official meeting between the champions of Europe and the American Bridge League). New York, N.Y. United States defeated France by 2,810 points over 300 boards.

UNITED STATES	FRANCE
D. Burnstine	P. Albarran
M. Gottlieb	R. de Nexon
O. Jacoby	G. Rousset
H. Schenken	E. Tulumaris
	S. Venizelos

1937 (under the auspices of the International Bridge League). Budapest, Hungary. Austria defeated United States by 4,740 points.

OPEN WINNERS	OPEN RUNNERS-UP
Austria	United States
K. von Bluhdorn	E. Culbertson
E. Frischauer	Mrs. J. Culbertson
W. Herbert	Mrs. A. M. Sobel
H. Jellinek	C. C. Vogelhofer
U. von Meissl	
K. Schneider	
Dr. P. Stern (npc)	

WOMEN'S WINNERS	
Austria	
Mrs. M. Boschan	Mrs. L. Klauber
Mrs. G. Brunner	Mrs. R. Markus
Mrs. E. Ernst	Mrs. R. Riemer
Mrs. G. Joseffy	Mrs. G. Schlesinger

II. The Bermuda Bowl.

1950 (played in Bermuda). United States defeated Great Britain by 3,360 and Sweden-Iceland by 4,720; Sweden-Iceland defeated Great Britain by 1,940.

UNITED STATES	GREAT BRITAIN
J. R. Crawford	M. Harrison-Gray (c)
C. H. Goren	L. Dodds
G. Rapee	N. Gardener
H. Schenken	K. Konstam
S. Silodor	J. Tarlo
S. Stayman	L. Tarlo

SWEDEN-ICELAND	
E. Werner (c)	N. Lilliehöök
G. Gudmundson	E. Thorfinnson
R. Kock	J. Wohlin

1951 (played in Naples). United States defeated Italy by 116 IMPs.

UNITED STATES	ITALY
B. J. Becker	P. Baroni
J. R. Crawford	E. Chiaradia
G. Rapee	P. Forquet
H. Schenken	M. Franco
S. Stayman	A. Ricci
J. Rosenblum (npc)	G. Siniscalco
	C. A. Perroux (npc)

1953 (played in New York). United States defeated Sweden by 8,260 points.

UNITED STATES	SWEDEN
B. J. Becker	E. Werner (c)
J. R. Crawford	G. Anulf
T. A. Lightner	R. Kock
G. Rapee	R. Larsen
H. Schenken	N. Lilliehöök
S. Stayman	J. Wohlin
J. M. Cohan (npc)	

1954 (played in Monte Carlo). United States defeated France by 49 IMPs.

UNITED STATES	FRANCE
C. Bishop	J. Amouraben
M. Ellenby	R. Bacherich
L. Mathe	J. Besse (Switz.)
D. Oakie	P. Ghestem
W. A. Rosen	M. Kornblum
D. Steen	K. Schneider (Austria)
B. O. Johnson (npc)	

1955 (played in New York). England defeated the United States by 5,420 points.

ENGLAND	UNITED STATES
L. Dodds	C. Bishop
K. Konstam	M. Q. Ellenby
A. Meredith	L. Mathe
J. Pavlides	J. H. Moran
T. Reese	W. A. Rosen
B. Schapiro	A. Roth
R. Corwen (npc)	P. A. Leventritt (npc)

1956 (played in Paris). France defeated United States by a score of 342 IMPs to 288 IMPs.

FRANCE	UNITED STATES
R. Bacherich	M. Field
P. Ghestem	C. H. Goren
P. Jaïs	L. Hazen
R. Lattes	R. F. Kahn
B. Romanet	C. J. Solomon
R. Trézel	S. M. Stayman
R. de Nexon (npc)	J. Glick (npc)

1957 (played in New York). Italy defeated United States by a score of 10,150 points.

ITALY	UNITED STATES
W. Avarelli	C. H. Goren
G. Belladonna	B. Koytchou
E. Chiaradia	P. Leventritt
M. d'Alelio	H. Ogust
P. Forquet	W. Seamon
G. Siniscalco	Mrs. H. Sobel
C. A. Perroux (npc)	R. L. Miles, Jr. (npc)

1958 (played in Como, Italy). Italy defeated United States 211 to 174 IMPs and Argentina 239 to 167 IMPs. United States defeated Argentina 255 to 193 IMPs.

ITALY	UNITED STATES
W. Avarelli	B. J. Becker
G. Belladonna	J. R. Crawford
E. Chiaradia	G. Rapee
M. d'Alelio	A. Roth
P. Forquet	S. Silodor
G. Siniscalco	T. Stone
C. A. Perroux (npc)	J. G. Ripstra (npc)

ARGENTINA	
C. Cabanne	A. Blousson
A. Castro	R. Calvente
(co-captains)	M. Lerner

1959 (played in New York). Italy defeated United States 233 to 183 IMPs and Argentina 218 to 178 IMPs. United States defeated Argentina 252 to 209 IMPs.

ITALY	UNITED STATES
W. Avarelli	H. Fishbein
G. Belladonna	S. Fry, Jr.
E. Chiaradia	L. Harmon
M. d'Alelio	L. Hazen
P. Forquet	S. Lazard
G. Siniscalco	I. Stakgold
C. A. Perroux (npc)	C. J. Solomon (npc)

ARGENTINA	
A. Berisso	A. Jaques
R. Calvente	E. Rocchi
A. Castro	L. Santa Coloma (npc)
C. Dibar	

1961 (played in Buenos Aires). Italy defeated Argentina, 422 to 282; defeated France, 371 to 261, defeated North America, 382 to 262. North America defeated Argentina, 411 to 284; defeated France 262 to 236. France defeated Argentina, 339 to 287.

ITALY	NORTH AMERICA
W. Avarelli	J. Gerber
G. Belladonna	P. Hodge
E. Chiaradia	N. Kay
M. d'Alelio	P. Leventritt
P. Forquet	S. Silodor
B. Garozzo	H. Schenken
C. A. Perroux (npc)	F. Westcott (npc)

FRANCE	ARGENTINA
R. Bacherich	J. Bosco
C. Deruy	R. Calvente
P. Ghestem	A. Castro
J. Le Dentu	H. Cramer
R. Trézel	C. Dibar
R. de Nexon (npc)	E. Rocchi
	C. Cabanne (npc)

1962 (played in New York). Italy defeated Argentina 420 to 328; defeated Great Britain 365 to 286; defeated North America 331 to 305. North America defeated Argentina 400 to 242; defeated Great Britain 345 to 332. Great Britain defeated Argentina 318 to 311.

ITALY	NORTH AMERICA
W. Avarelli	C. Coon
G. Belladonna	M. Key
M. d'Alelio	L. Mathe
E. Chiaradia	E. Murray
P. Forquet	G. R. Nail
B. Garozzo	R. Von Der Porten
C. A. Perroux (npc)	J. Gerber (npc)

GREAT BRITAIN	ARGENTINA
N. Gardener	L. Attaguile
K. Konstam	A. Berisso
A. Priday	C. Cabanne
C. Rodrigue	R. Calvente
A. Rose	A. Jaques
A. Truscott	E. Rocchi
L. Tarlo (npc)	D. Blum (npc)

1963 (played in St. Vincent). Italy defeated United States 313 to 294; defeated France 421 to 236; defeated Argentina 372 to 282. United States defeated France 340 to 251; defeated Argentina 496 to 261. France defeated Argentina 453 to 319.

ITALY	NORTH AMERICA
G. Belladonna	P. Leventritt
E. Chiaradia	G. R. Nail
M. d'Alelio	J. Jacoby
P. Forquet	R. Jordan
B. Garozzo	A. Robinson
C. Pabis-Ticci	H. Schenken
C. A. Perroux (npc)	J. Gerber (npc)

FRANCE	ARGENTINA
R. Bacherich	L. Attaguile
G. Desrousseaux	R. Calvente
P. Ghestem	E. Rocchi
J. Stetten	M. Santamarina
G. Theron	A. Saravia
L. Tintner	L. Schenone
R. de Nexon (npc)	G. Malbran (npc)

1965 (played in Buenos Aires). Italy defeated United States 304–230; defeated Argentina 325–237; defeated Great Britain 354–233. United States defeated Argentina 359–250. Because of charges of irregular procedure against the partnership of Terence Reese and Boris Schapiro, non-playing captain Ralph Swimer of Great Britain forfeited the match with United States after leading 288–242 with twenty boards to play, and forfeited to Argentina after winning 380–184.

ITALY	UNITED STATES
W. Avarelli	B. J. Becker
G. Belladonna	I. Erdos
M. d'Alelio	Mrs. D. Hayden
P. Forquet	P. Leventritt
B. Garozzo	K. Petterson
C. Pabis Ticci	H. Schenken
S. Osella (npc)	J. Gerber (npc)
C. A. Perroux (co-captain)	

ARGENTINA	GREAT BRITAIN
L. Attaguile	J. Flint
A. Berisso	M. Harrison-Gray
C. Cabanne	K. Konstam
M. Lerner	T. Reese
E. Rocchi	A. Rose
A. Santamarina	B. Schapiro
E. Marquardt (npc)	R. Swimer (npc)

1966 (played in St. Vincent). Italy defeated North America 319–262; defeated Venezuela 362–203; defeated Netherlands 326–198; defeated Thailand 486–143. North America defeated Venezuela 398–260; defeated Netherlands 477–243; defeated Thailand 359–234. Venezuela defeated Netherlands 331–247; defeated Thailand 326–290. Netherlands defeated Thailand 293–230.

ITALY	NORTH AMERICA	BRAZIL
W. Avarelli	P. Feldesman	P. Assumpção
G. Belladonna	R. Hamman	M. Branco
M. d'Alelio	S. Kehela	G. Chagas
P. Forquet	L. Mathe	D. Coutinho
B. Garozzo	E. Murray	R. Mello
C. Pabis Ticci	I. Rubin	A. Porto D'Ave
C. A. Perroux (npc)	J. Rosenblum (npc)	P. Brum de Barros (ncp)

VENEZUELA	NETHERLANDS
R. Benaim	R. Blitzblum
D. Berah	P. Boender
M. Onorati	J. T. M. Kreyns
R. Rossignol	L. Oudshoorn
R. Straziota	R. De Leeuw
F. Vernon	C. Slavenburg
J. Alpert (npc)	G. Kramer (npc)

1970 (played in Stockholm). North America defeated Republic of China 64–14 victory points in the final; in the play-off for third place, Norway defeated Brazil 24–16 victory points. In the qualifying round robin, the scores were: North America 229, Republic of China 151, Brazil 136, Norway 118, Italy 105.

THAILAND
A. Boonsupa
E. Gaan
B. Gimkiewicz
H. Istenveli
S. Nandhabiwat
T. Raengkhan (captain)

NORTH AMERICA	REPUBLIC OF CHINA
W. Eisenberg	C. Cheng
R. Goldman	E. Hsiao
R. Hamman	P. Huang
J. Jacoby	H. Lin
M. Lawrence	M. Tai
R. Wolff	D. Mao (npc)
O. Jacoby (npc)	

1967 (played in Miami Beach). Italy defeated North America 338–227 in the final; in the playoff for third place, France defeated Thailand 182–133. In the qualifying round robin, the scores were: Italy 170, North America 161, France 132, Thailand 73, Venezuela 64.

NORWAY	BRAZIL
E. Höie	P. Assumpção
T. Jensen	P. de Barros
K. Koppang	E. Bastos
B. Larsen	O. de Faria
L. Ström	S. Ferreira
W. Varnås	G. Chagas
B. Baardsen (npc)	E. Amaral (npc)

ITALY	NORTH AMERICA
W. Avarelli	E. Kaplan
G. Belladonna	N. Kay
M. d'Alelio	S. Kehela
P. Forquet	E. Murray
B. Garozzo	W. Root
C. Pabis Ticci	A. Roth
G. Barbone (npc)	J. Rosenblum (npc)

ITALY
G. Barbarisi
E. Cesati
B. De Ritis
V. La Galla
A. Morini
R. Tersch
A. Tracanella (npc)

FRANCE	THAILAND
J. M. Boulenger	A. Boonsupa
J. Pariente	E. R. Gaan
J. M. Roudinesco	B. Gimkiewicz
J. Stetten	S. Nandhabiwat
H. Svarc	K. W. Shen
L. Tintner	C. Sitajitt
R. Huni (npc)	H. Lau (npc)

1971 (played in Taipei). The United States Aces defeated France 243–182 in the final; in the 64-board play-off for third place Australia defeated Republic of China 174–134; in the 32-board play-off for fifth place, Brazil defeated North America 79–63. In the qualifying round robin, the scores were: Aces 228, France 182, Australia 154, Republic of China 118, Brazil 103, North America 98.

VENEZUELA
R. Benaim
D. Berah
E. Loynaz
M. Romanelli
R. Rossignol
F. Vernon
R. Chapin (npc)

ACES	FRANCE
W. Eisenberg	J-M. Boulenger
R. Goldman	P. Jaïs
R. Hamman	J-M. Roudinesco
J. Jacoby	J-L. Stoppa
M. Lawrence	H. Svarc
R. Wolff	R. Trézel
O. Jacoby (npc)	R. Huni (npc)

1969 (played in Rio de Janeiro). Italy defeated Republic of China 429–182 in the final; in the playoff for third place, North America defeated France 150–115. In the qualifying round robin, the scores were: Italy 185, Republic of China 166, North America 141, France 126, Brazil 116.

AUSTRALIA	REPUBLIC OF CHINA
J. Borin	C. Cheng
N. Borin	S. Chua
R. Cummings	E. Hsaio
D. Howard	P. Huang
T. Seres	V. Reyes
R. Smilde	M. Tai
J. Rothfield (npc)	C. Wei (npc)

ITALY	REPUBLIC OF CHINA
W. Avarelli	F. Huang
G. Belladonna	P. Huang
M. d'Alelio	C. S. Shen
P. Forquet	K. W. Shen
B. Garozzo	K. Suchartkul
C. Pabis Ticci	M. Tai
R. Tracanella (npc)	C. C. Wei (npc)

BRAZIL	NORTH AMERICA
E. Amaral	E. Kaplan
P. P. Assumpção	N. Kay
G. Chagas	D. Krauss
G. Cintra	L. Mathe
A. D'Ave	J. Swanson
T. Kenedi	R. Walsh
A. Truscott (npc)	L. Hazen (npc)

NORTH AMERICA	FRANCE
W. Eisenberg	J. M. Boulenger
R. Goldman	G. Desrousseaux
R. Hamman	J. Stetten
E. Kantar	H. Svarc
S. Lazard	G. Theron
G. Rapee	L. Tintner
O. Jacoby (npc)	R. Huni (npc)

1973 (played in Guaruja). Italy defeated the United States Aces 330–205 in the final. In the qualifying round robin, the scores were: Aces 177, Italy 176, Brazil 148, North America 140, Indonesia 101.

ITALY	ACES
G. Belladonna	M. Blumenthal
B. Bianchi	R. Goldman
P. Forquet	R. Hamman
G. Garabello	J. Jacoby
B. Garozzo	M. Lawrence
V. Pittala	R. Wolff
S. Salvetti (npc)	I. Corn (npc)

BRAZIL	NORTH AMERICA
P. P. Assumpção	B. J. Becker
M. Branco	M. Becker
P. P. Branco	A. Bernstein
G. Chagas	J. Rubens
G. Cintra	P. Soloway
C. Fonseca	J. Swanson
A. D'Ave (npc)	R. Stern (npc)

INDONESIA
M. Aguw
J. Fransz
H. Lasut
E. Najoan
D. Sacul
F. Walujan
Ch. Bahasuan (npc)

1974 (played in Venice). Italy defeated North America 195–166 in the final. In the qualifying round robin, the scores were: Italy 149, North America 148, Brazil 111, Indonesia 82, France 71, New Zealand 17. In the semi-finals Italy defeated Indonesia 233–145; North America defeated Brazil 173–82.

ITALY	NORTH AMERICA
G. Belladonna	M. Blumenthal
B. Bianchi	R. Goldman
S. De Falco	R. Hamman
P. Forquet	S. Kehela
A. Franco	E. Murray
B. Garozzo	R. Wolff
S. Salvetto (npc)	I. Corn (npc)

BRAZIL	INDONESIA
P. P. Assumpção	M. Aguw
M. Branco	W. Karamoy
P. P. Branco	H. Lasut
G. Chagas	F. Manoppo
G. Cintra	M. Manoppo
C. Fonseca	W. Moniaga
S. Apoteker (npc)	D. Masengi (npc)

FRANCE	NEW ZEALAND
J-M. Boulenger	R. Brightling
M. Lebel	M. Cornell
C. Mari	R. Kerr
H. Svarc	P. Marston
C. Deruy (npc)	J. Wignall
	F. Lu (npc)

1975 (played in Bermuda). Italy defeated North America 215–189 in the final. In the qualifying round robin, the scores were: Italy 134, North America 116, France 105, Indonesia 90, Brazil 73. In the semi-finals Italy defeated Indonesia 280–134; North America defeated France 159–147.

ITALY	NORTH AMERICA
G. Belladonna	W. Eisenberg
G. Facchini	R. Hamman
A. Franco	E. Kantar
B. Garozzo	P. Soloway
V. Pittala	J. Swanson
S. Zucchelli	R. Wolff
S. Salvetti (npc)	A. Sheinwold (npc)

FRANCE	INDONESIA
J-M. Boulenger	I. Arwin
M. Lebel	H. Lasut
F. Leenhardt	F. Manoppo
C. Mari	M. Manoppo
H. Svarc	W. Moniaga
E. Vial	D. Sacul
R. Bacherich (npc)	O. Wullur (npc)

BRAZIL
M. Amaral
P. P. Assumpção
P. P. de Barros
G. Chagas
N. Ferreira
S. Ferreira
S. Apoteker (npc)

III. Team Olympiad, held quadrennially.

1960. Turin, Italy.

OPEN WINNERS	OPEN RUNNERS-UP
France (16 V.P.)	Great Britain (15 V.P.)
P. Jaïs	T. Reese
R. Trézel	B. Schapiro
G. Bourchtoff	A. Rose
C. Delmouly	N. Gardener
R. Bacherich	J. Flint
P. Ghestem	R. Swimer
R. de Nexon (npc)	L. Tarlo (npc)

WOMEN'S WINNERS
UAR
Mrs. H. Camara
Mrs. A. Choucry
Mrs. S. Fathy
Miss L. Gordon
Mrs. J. Morcos
Mrs. S. Naguib
S. de Polo (npc)

1964. New York, USA.

OPEN WINNERS	OPEN RUNNERS-UP
Italy	United States
W. Avarelli	R. Hamman
G. Belladonna	R. Jordan
M. d'Alelio	D. Krauss
P. Forquet	V. Mitchell
B. Garozzo	A. Robinson
C. Pabis Ticci	S. Stayman
S. Osella (npc)	F. Westcott (npc)

WOMEN'S WINNERS
Great Britain
Mrs. D. Fleming
Mrs. F. Gordon
Mrs. J. Juan
Mrs. R. Markus
Mrs. M. Moss
Miss D. Shanahan
H. Franklin (npc)

1968. Deauville, France.

OPEN WINNERS	OPEN RUNNERS-UP
Italy	United States
W. Avarelli	R. Jordan
G. Belladonna	E. Kaplan
M. d'Alelio	N. Kay
P. Forquet	A. Robinson
B. Garozzo	W. Root
C. Pabis Ticci	A. Roth
A. Tracanella (npc)	J. Rosenblum (npc)

WOMEN'S WINNERS
Sweden
Mrs. B. Blom
Mrs. K. Eriksson
Mrs. E. Martensson
Mrs. R. Segander
Mrs. G. Silborn
Mrs. B. Werner
Mrs. L. Saaby (npc)

1972. Miami, USA.

OPEN WINNERS	OPEN RUNNERS-UP
Italy	United States
W. Avarelli	R. Goldman
G. Belladonna	R. Hamman
M. d'Alelio	J. Jacoby
P. Forquet	M. Lawrence
B. Garozzo	P. Soloway
C. Pabis Ticci	R. Wolff
U. Barsotti (npc)	L. Hazen (npc)

WOMEN'S WINNERS	MIXED TEAMS*
Italy	United States
Mrs. M. Bianchi	Mrs. N. Alpaugh
Mrs. R. Jabes	R. Goldman
Mrs. A. Robaudo	J. Jacoby
Mrs. L. Romanelli	Mrs. H. Noland
Mrs. A. Valenti	Mrs. B. Wolff
Mrs. M. Venturini	R. Wolff
G. Pelucchi (npc)	

IV. Pair Olympiad, held quadrennially.

1962. Cannes, France.

OPEN PAIRS	WOMEN'S PAIRS
1st—P. Jais and R. Trézel	Mrs. R. Markus and
(France)	Mrs. F. Gordon (Great Britain)
2nd—T. Reese and	Mrs. F. Pariente and
B. Schapiro	Mrs. C. Serf
(Great Britain)	(France)

MIXED TEAMS*

1st—Mrs. R. Markus, Mrs. F. Gordon, B. Schapiro,
    N. Gardener (Great Britain)
2nd—Mrs. A. Westerfield, Mrs. Hoogenkamp,
    H. Filarski, A. Kornlijnslijper (Netherlands)

1966. Amsterdam, Netherlands.

OPEN PAIRS	WOMEN'S PAIRS
1st—C. Slavenburg and	Mrs. J. Durran and
J. T. M. Kreyns	Mrs. J. Juan
(Netherlands)	(Great Britain)
2nd—Dr. J. Fisher and	Mrs. D. Sachs and
J. Jacoby	Mrs. J. Gruver
(United States)	(United States)

MIXED PAIRS*

1st—Mrs. J. Farell and I. Erdos (United States)
2nd—Mrs. J. Durran and M. Weissberger (Great Britain)

1970. Stockholm, Sweden.

OPEN PAIRS	WOMEN'S PAIRS
1st—F. Babsch and	Mrs. J. Farell and
P. Manhardt	Miss M. Johnson
(Austria)	(United States)
2nd—B. Garozzo and	Mrs. R. Markus and
F. Mayer (Italy)	Mrs. F. Gordon (Great Britain)

MIXED PAIRS*

1st—Mrs. B. Brier and W. von Zedtwitz (United States)
2nd—Mrs. R. Markus and G. Catzeflis
    (Great Britain)   (Switzerland)

1974. Las Palmas, Spain.

OPEN PAIRS	WOMEN'S PAIRS
1st—R. Hamman and	Mrs. F. Gordon and
R. Wolff (United States)	Mrs. R. Markus (Great Britain)
2nd—L. Burgay and	G. Goslar and
A. Abate (Italy)	R. Jacobsen (South Africa)

MIXED PAIRS

1st—L. Gordon and T. Trad (Switzerland)
2nd—J. Mitchell and J. Cayne (United States)

---

* Non-World Championship event.

MIXED TEAMS

1st—J. Morse, P. Lipsitz, R. Lipsitz, S. Parker and
    S. Robinson (United States)
2nd—J. Cayne, M. Granovetter, J. Mitchell, V. Mitchell,
    J. Stayman (United States)

See also BERMUDA BOWL; INTERNATIONAL BRIDGE ACADEMY; INTERNATIONAL BRIDGE LEAGUE; WORLD BRIDGE FEDERATION; WORLD PAR CONTESTS.

WORLD MASTER. See WORLD BRIDGE FEDERATION PLAYER RANKINGS.

WORLD OLYMPICS. See WORLD PAR CONTESTS.

WORLD PAIR OLYMPIAD. A tournament conducted quadrennially by the World Bridge Federation, consisting principally of an open pair event, a women's pair event, and mixed team and mixed pair events. In the United States, pairs are selected to play in the open and women's pairs events on the basis of their performances in major ACBL national pairs championships. For results see WORLD CHAMPIONSHIPS (IV).

WORLD PAR CONTESTS. International events using prepared deals (see PAR CONTESTS). The idea of a series of par tournaments conducted throughout the world was conceived by Ely Culbertson and in 1932 the first World Bridge Olympic, using the par-hand format, was held. Culbertson founded the National Bridge Association, a non-profit corporation, in the same year, to conduct the tournaments. The bridge world's principal experts, regardless of their affiliation in the bridge politics of those times, constructed the prepared deals, and Culbertson's staff did the central management and scoring. Each contestant paid a fee of one dollar, of which half went to the game captain (who pre-arranged the hands and directed his game), and half was retained by the NBA. In 1932 and 1933, both American and World Olympics were conducted; from 1934 on, only the World Olympics. In 1934 self-dealing cards (marked on their backs to show which player should receive each card for the particular deal) and folding duplicate boards (later called bridge WALLETS) were supplied without extra charge by the NBA. The World Bridge Olympic reached its peak in 1934 with 70 countries and nearly 90,000 players entered, but even in that year the NBA lost money. In 1938 the ACBL took over the management, with W. Mc-Kenney in charge and G. Mott-Smith constructing the hands, but problems of foreign exchange as well as diminished interest caused the tournament to be abandoned after 1941.

The Olympic trophies were famous. For the American event, the two largest silver trophies of bridge history were provided. One of them is now the MC KENNEY TROPHY; the other was lost in circumstances that had a lasting effect on insurance law. A winner, entitled to one year's possession only, pawned the trophy. A court ruled that since it was his honest intention to redeem it within the year, he was not liable although he found himself later without funds to redeem it, nor was the pawnbroker responsible for having sold it when the time for redemption had passed. The insurance underwriter paid its value to the NBA. The two World trophies each contained $5,000 worth of pure platinum but Culbertson, who donated them, never relinquished personal title to them and sold them for their value in platinum when the tournament was discontinued. Individual prizes were given to all international and national winners and to state winners in the United States and provincial winners in Canada, both North-South and East-West, so the list of winners for each year was long indeed.

In 1951, the World Par Contest was revived by Australia and won by Dr. J. L. Thwaites and Dr. E. L. Field of Melbourne, Australia, in that year. It was held in 1961 and 1963 under the auspices of the World Bridge Federation. The WBF intended to hold this event biennially, but it has not been held since 1963. The organizers in 1961 and 1963 were M. J. Sullivan and R. E. Williams (Australia). Winners of these events, which had the status of World championships, were:

1932	N–S	Mr. and Mrs. B. E. Baldwin, East Orange, N.J.
	E–W	L. C. Frank, W. Mayer, Detroit, Mich.
1933	N–S	Mrs. J. H. Slager, F. Levy, Montgomery, Ala.
	E–W	Tied, L. D. Craine, J. F. Benedict, Sherburne, N.Y.
		O. Krefting, I. Nielson, Oslo, Norway
1934	N–S	Dr. E. Hilb, R. Darvas, Budapest, Hungary
	E–W	Mrs. G. Hill, Mrs. G. Whitaker, Winston-Salem, N.C.
1935	N–S	Dr. L. L. von Barkow, Mrs. C. von Kamensky, Dresden, Germany
	E–W	Mrs. P. Lotou, S. Zotos, Athens, Greece
1936	N–S	Tied, R. E. Horner, A. Harris, Ottawa, Canada S. Rivlin, Capt. W. H. Ricardo, Cardiff, Wales
	E–W	Dr. P. Stern, Dr. P. Kaltenegger, Vienna, Austria
1937	N–S	Dr. O. P. Hampton, Jr., W. L. Boeger, University City, Mo.
	E–W	W. Savery, Jr., J. E. Muckley, Seattle, Wash.
1938	N–S	T. Sandgren, B. Fant, Stockholm, Sweden
	E–W	I. H. Fisher, H. B. Karp, Baltimore, Md.
1940	N–S	J. M. Learmonth, E. Learmonth, Maracaibo, Venezuela
	E–W	Mrs. A. C. Bryant, Mrs. C. H. Drury, Ketchikan, Alaska
1941	N–S	R. P. Willson, G. Gooden, San Francisco, Calif.
	E–W	M. Foote, C. C. Miller, Jr., Phoenix, Ariz.
1961		T. Reese, C. Rodrigue, London, England
1963		G. Desrousseaux, B. Romanet, Paris, France

United States winners were:

1932	(International winners: see above.)	
1933	(International winners: see above.)	
1934	N–S	E. Powell, R. L. Powell, Freeport, Tex.
	E–W	(International winners: see above.)
1935	N–S	Mrs. H. L. Guthrie, G. A. Smith, Conneaut, Ohio
	E–W	Mrs. T. Ahrenbeck, Jr., M. O. McDonald, Houston, Tex.
1936	N–S	A. N. Cowperthwait, Tucson, Ariz., R. A. Cash, Phoenix, Ariz.
	E–W	G. Sherbaum, Memphis, Tenn., L. E. Shurlds, Shelby, Tenn.
1937	(International winners: see above.)	
1938	N–S	Mr. and Mrs. W. H. Gharrity, Chippewa Falls, Wis.
	E–W	(International winners: see above.)
1939	N–S	M. Miller, Dr. M. Shimberg, Leavenworth, Kan.
	E–W	A. Bugge, Mrs. C. C. Covington, Houston, Tex.
1940	N–S	G. R. Trimmer, D. Keating, Glasgow, Mont.
	E–W	Mrs. G. Morris, S. J. Lowery, Philadelphia, Pa.
1941	(International winners: see above.)	
1961	L. Rosler, Murray Hill, N.J., R. Stern, New York, N.Y.	
1963	L. Rosler, Murray Hill, N.J., R. Stern, New York, N.Y.	

WORLD TEAM OLYMPIAD. A WBF tournament conducted quadrennially starting in 1960, consisting of an open team event and a women's team event. In 1960 NCBOs having a very large number of members were allowed to enter more than one team. On this basis Sweden entered two teams and the United States entered four in the open event. Since 1960 each NCBO has been allowed to enter only one team in each event of the Olympiad. For results see WORLD CHAMPIONSHIPS (III); for method of team selection in the United States see INTERNATIONAL OPEN TEAM SELECTION, INTERNATIONAL WOMEN'S TEAM SELECTION.

WORTHLESS SINGLETON/DOUBLETON. A holding of one or two cards below honor rank in a suit; usually at no trump play such a holding is a detriment to success. In the trump suit, either holding is less than adequate for trump support until the suit has been rebid twice.

WRITTEN BIDDING. A variation in the bidding technique, so that each bidder writes his bid on a sheet (designed to facilitate the placing of each bid in a proper box) which is passed to him as it becomes his turn to bid. The theory is that any extra time a player might take in a huddle can be construed as a review of previous bidding, as shown on the sheet, and no information can be conveyed to the partner by mannerism, gesture, or inflection, and the need for a review of the bidding at any time is removed. The pad passed around is frequently referred to as the DUMB BIDDER. It has also been used in International Matches, because it lends itself to symbolic notation, understood even with a severe language barrier. See BIDDING BOXES. FRANCO BOARD.

WRONG BOARD. Occasionally the play of a wrong board is commenced before it is discovered that it is a wrong board. If this occurs, the director should be summoned and he will act under LAWS OF DUPLICATE, Law 15.

WRONG SIDE. The hand of the declaring partnership which is less well equipped to cope with the opening lead. See RIGHT SIDE.

X

X. (1) A symbol used in lower case in bridge literature to signify an insignificant small card in any suit, a card lower than a ten. Thus, K x x, means the king and two low cards in that suit. (2) A capital X indicates a double, and is used in recording bidding by hand in important matches. Similarly, XX means "redouble."

X PLUS ONE, RULE OF. See RULE OF X PLUS ONE.

Y

YARBOROUGH. Any hand at bridge containing no card higher than a nine, named after an English lord who customarily would wager 1,000 pounds to one against the chance of such a hand being held by a player. The odds against holding a Yarborough are 1,827 to one. In post-mortem discussions the term "Yarborough" has gained currency to describe bad hands which do not meet the strict requirements.

YOUNGEST LIFE MASTER. In 1975 this title belonged to Michael Freed of Beverly Hills, Calif., who became a Life Master just twenty days after his 15th birthday. Freed's accomplishment is all the more remarkable in light of his status as an honor student in school and an outstanding member of his high school wrestling team. In 1976 he was supplanted by Regina Barnes, the first to crack the 15 year age barrier. The following players were the youngest Life Masters at the time they achieved that status:

1952	Richard Freeman	19 yrs.
1961	Diane Barton Paine	18 yrs., 12 days
1963	Terry Crabbs	18 yrs.
1966	Kyle Larsen	15 yrs., 11 mos.
1968	Joseph Livezey	15 yrs., 5 mos.
1973	Bobby Levin	15 yrs., 4 mos.
1975	Michael Freed	15 yrs., 20 days
1976	Regina Barnes	14 yrs., 11 mos.

See also KING OR QUEEN OF BRIDGE.

YUGOSLAVIA BRIDGE FEDERATION (BRIDGE SAVEZ JUGOSLAVIJE). Reactivated in 1967 in Belgrade, with approximately 400 members, located principally in Belgrade, Zagreb, and Ljubljana. Prior to World War II, the League was an active member of the European Bridge League, tying for second place in the 1935 European Championships in Brussels, and finishing second in 1939 at The Hague. During the years when there was no official organization, Yugoslav players continued to enter international tournaments—World Pairs Olympiad 1962, European Championships, and International Bridge Festivals in Austria, Italy, and Yugoslavia—and national events were held for Open Teams and Open Pairs. The Federation is a member of the European Bridge League and has applied for membership in the WBF. Players listed separately are R. Antic, A. Bauer, M. Brkljacic, D. Perasic, Dr. L. Singer, A. Zepic.

Officers, 1975:
President: Dr. Lav Singer.
Foreign Correspondent: Fred Kulenovic, Kuhaceva 13, 41000 Zagreb, Yugoslavia.

Z

ZERO. The lowest score possible on a duplicate board, hence loosely, a very bad score. It also refers to a lost board in a team-of-four contest. Note that a score on a board of zero points (all four hands pass) may be any match-point score from none to top.

ZERO OR TWO HIGHER LEADS. An opening lead convention designed to eliminate the ambiguity of standard honor leads. The lead of the ten or nine promises either zero or two higher honors in the suit, while the lead of the jack denies any higher honors. Leads of the ace, king, and queen retain their standard meanings. These leads may be used against any contract or only against no trump, and may also be used throughout the deal. Proponents claim that the opening leader's partner usually has no trouble deducing the true situation, and that it keeps declarer in the dark better than do JOURNALIST LEADS or RUSINOW LEADS.

ZONAL CHAMPIONSHIP. (1) A championship held by and for one of the zones recognized by the WORLD BRIDGE FEDERATION. See WBF MASTER POINTS. (2) A championship in one of the eight geographical areas into which the ACBL is divided for the GRAND NATIONALS.

A

ABBOTT, E. Farrington, Jr., of Auburn, Me., shoe company president, born 1909; won several New England regional titles between 1947 and 1953.

ABRAHAMS, Stanley, of Aukland, New Zealand, born 1940 in Glasgow, Scotland; represented New Zealand World Championship 1974; World Team Olympiad 1972; Far East Championship 1973; won many major New Zealand tournaments, including Nat'l Teams 1972.

ABRAMS, Elsie, of Pompano Beach, Fla., registered nurse and bridge club director; won Fall Nat'l Mixed Pairs 1960; second Fall Nat'l Women's Team 1963; several regional wins including New England Knockout Teams 1960.

ACH, Jacques L., Sr., of London, England, formerly of Dayton, Ohio, born 1903, lawyer and accountant; tournament director; co-inventor of the Ach-Kennedy schedules (1935) which were the first HOWELL MOVEMENTS with perfectly BALANCED COMPARISONS.

ACHMATOWICZ, Dr. Selim, of Warsaw, Poland, university chemistry lecturer, born 1933; npc Poland's International Team 1961–64; won Baltic Bowl 1964, Hungarian Open Pairs 1959, Balaton Bowl 1963. National victories include Open Teams 1962, 1963, 1964, 1968; second 1961.

ACKER, Bill, of Freer, Tex., insurance agent, born 1926; won Fall Nat'l secondary Life Masters Men's Pairs 1970; several regional events.

ACKERMAN, Earl, of New York, N.Y., coffee importer, born 1896. Won Pacific Southwest Masters Pairs 1946, New England Spring Open Pairs 1951. President Pacific B.L. 1942–45 and served on many ACBL Committees.

ACKERMAN, Mrs. Earl, of New York, N.Y., born 1906; won several regional events including New England Open Teams 1951, 1953.

ACKERMAN, Gerald W., of Ridgewood, N.J., accountant, born 1925; won Marcus Cup 1954, second 1956.

ADAMS, Charles True, of Chicago, Ill. One of the first widely read authors of contract bridge books. His *Modern Contract Bridge* was published in 1930.

ADAMS, Dee (Mrs. Harrison), of Memphis, Tenn., real estate broker; winner of several Southern Conference regional events since 1961, including 1971 Memphis Regional Swiss Teams.

ADAMS, Earle G., of Vancouver, B.C., born 1901; won Northwest Open Teams 1958, Men's Pairs 1958. Former President Vancouver Unit ACBL.

ADAMS, Maynard D., of Northbrook, Ill., company president, born 1912; won Fall Nat'l Men's Teams 1946, Faber Cup 1948; won five Open Teams All-American, Central States, Midwest, and Western States Regionals between 1943 and 1956.

ADAMS, Mrs. Peggy (died 1974), of New York, N.Y., ACBL staff worker; won Fall Nat'l Women's Teams 1955; second 1952; several Eastern regional events including Eastern Women's Pairs 1951 and 1957.

ADAMS, Robert T., of Lafayette, Calif., chemist, born 1923; won Fall Nat'l Mixed Pairs 1957, secondary Mixed Pairs 1968, several regional wins including All-Western Knockout Teams 1967.

ADAMS, W. E., of Hamden, Conn., civil engineer, born 1917; won Nat'l Senior Masters Individual 1953, Fall Nat'l secondary Swiss Teams 1972; several regional wins including New England Open Teams 1961, 1968. Former ACBL Director, former President Connecticut BA.

ADAMS, W. Harrison, of Memphis, Tenn., lawyer, born 1926; several Southern Conference wins since 1958, including Masters Pairs, Men's Pairs, and 1971 Memphis Regional Swiss Teams.

ADKINS, Miles C., of Coulee City, Wash., wheat farmer, born 1928; winner of several regional events including Oregon Trail Masters Pairs 1968, Knockout Teams 1969.

ADLER, Betty (Mrs. Julian, formerly Mrs. Robert Goldberg), of Baltimore, Md., born 1927; won Summer Nat'l Women's Pairs 1959; second Summer Nat'l Mixed Team 1958, 1970, 1974; winner of many Mid-Atlantic regional events since 1961, including Keystone Swiss Teams 1971, 1972, 1973, 1974.

ADLER, Julian, of Baltimore, Md., clothing manufacturer, born 1917; second Summer Nat'l Non-Masters Pairs 1961; second Summer Nat'l Mixed

Team 1970, 1974; winner of several mid-Atlantic regional events since 1961, including Keystone Swiss Team 1971, 1972, 1973, 1974.

ADLER, Patricia. See SHEINWOLD, PATRICIA.

AGAY, Milton M., of Beverly Hills, Calif., furniture wholesaler, born 1901 (deceased); won several western regional events including Bridge Week Open Teams 1957, Masters Pairs 1960, Navajo Trail Knockout Teams 1970.

AGRAN, Nat, of Sarasota, Fla., attorney, born 1908; won Nat'l Senior Masters Individual 1948; Eastern States Mixed Pairs 1951, Mid-Atlantic Fall Open Teams 1955.

AGRAN, Violet (Mrs. Nat) (1923–1973), of Philadelphia, Pa., bridge teacher, won several eastern and southern regional events between 1951 and 1959.

AGRUSS, Billie (Mrs. Bernard), of Coronado, Calif., bridge teacher, born 1913; won several regional events between 1946 and 1955.

AKIN, Peg (Mrs. R. K.), of Springfield, Mo., bridge teacher; winner of several regional titles between 1940 and 1968.

ALBANO, Helen D., of Newark, N.J., bridge Bridge Teachers' Association; President and founder of "Bridge for the Blind," a non-profit organization for teaching bridge to the blind throughout the United States, Canada, South Africa, and Iran; author of *Analysis and Practical Application of the Goren Method,* which she had brailled for use as an instructional guide to bridge.

ALBARRAN, Pierre, of Paris, bridge authority, born of French parentage in the West Indies. The leading figure in French bridge until his death in 1960. European Champion 1935, represented France on many occasions including the World Championship against the FOUR ACES in 1936, and European Championship 1950. Won many national championships particularly in the period 1932–39. His chief contributions to theory were a distributional count, ACE-SHOWING RESPONSES to the two club forcing opening bid, and the development of CANAPÉ, or bidding a short suit before a long one. This principle has been followed by many leading French players, such as Jaïs and Trézel, and has influenced the ROMAN and NEAPOLITAN systems which have won many World Championships for Italy. He was also twice a member of the French Davis Cup team during the years when France was a tennis power. Many writings include *Canapé,* and *Encyclopédie du Bridge Moderne;* co-author with Baron de Nexon of *Notre Méthode de Bridge,* and with J. le Dentu *Le Memento du Bridge, Souvenirs et Secrets, Le Championnat du Monde de Bridge, Cent Donnes Extraordinaires.* See BIBLIOGRAPHY, E, G.

ALBERGA, Lionel, of Kingston, Jamaica, salesman, born 1904; fifteen wins in the National Open Team, including five in a row, 1949–53; twelve wins in National Interclub Championships, and other successes.

ALBERSHEIM, Alberta (Mrs. Walter J.), of Waban, Mass.; second Fall Nat'l Women's Pairs 1958; winner of several regional titles including Eastern States Mixed Pairs 1954, Mixed Teams 1967, New England Master Pairs 1972.

ALCORN, Margaret. See GAER, Margaret.

ALDERTON, George A., II, of Detroit, Mich., lawyer, born 1904; won Midwest Open Pairs 1949. Former President, Vice-President, and Honorary Member of ACBL; former President Midwest Conference and Michigan BA.

d'ALELIO, Massimo (Mimmo), of Naples, Italy, residing in Rome, lawyer and advertising man, born 1916; one of the world's great players; World Champion 1957, 1958, 1959, 1961, 1962, 1963, 1964, 1965, 1966, 1967, 1968, 1969, 1972; European Champion 1956, 1957, 1958, second 1955, 1962, 1963; National successes include Open Team 1953, 1956, 1957, 1959, 1963, 1964. See BLUE TEAM.

ALFANDRE, Ellen (Mrs. Larry), of Scarsdale, N.Y.; won Summer Nat'l Mixed Teams 1973; regional wins include Eastern States Mixed Teams 1969.

ALLEN, Ellen, of Summerville, S.C.; winner of many Mid-Atlantic regional events, including Summer Open Pairs 1967, Spring Open Pairs 1969, Women's Pairs 1972.

ALLEN, Larry C., of Summerville, S.C., general contractor; winner of several Mid-Atlantic regional events, including Summer Open Pairs 1967, Spring Open Pairs 1969, Swiss Teams 1971.

ALLEN, Zenobia (Mrs. Clarence, formerly Mrs. Robert Hall), of Detroit, Mich., bridge teacher (deceased), A top ranking woman player in the American Bridge Association from 1955. Winner of over 30 national championships, including the Mixed Pair ten times.

ALLINGER, Paul, of Alameda, Calif., accountant, born 1929; one of the leading players on the West Coast; represented US World Team Olympiad 1960; in Nationals won Fall Men's Pairs 1956, Spingold 1958, Chicago 1962, Fall Nat'l Men's Team 1962; second Fall Nat'l Men's Team 1956, Open Pair 1957, Men's Pairs 1961; regional wins include All-Western Open Team 1960, 1962, Masters Pairs 1965, Bridge Week Masters Teams 1955, Knockout Teams 1960, Open Teams 1961, 1962, Open Pairs 1956, 1960, and many more. Co-inventor of ASTRO.

ALLISON, Karen R., of Toronto, Ont., computer programming consultant; represented US in World Olympiad Women's Pairs 1970–74; won Fall Nat'l Women's Teams 1968, Spring Nat'l Women's Teams 1969; second Life Master Women's Pairs 1969; winner of several regional titles including Canadian-American Knockout Teams 1972.

ALOUF, Yehoshoua, of Ramat Gan, Israel, retired physical education supervisor, born in Russia 1900; publisher of Israeli magazine *Bridge;* originator and compiler of Hebrew glossary of bridge terminology.

ALPAR, Emeric (1905–1956), of Budapest, Hungary, stockbroker, from 1939 until his death a resident of London; European Champion 1934 representing Hungary, second 1935, 1936; won Masters Pairs (Great Britain) 1946.

ALPAUGH, Nancy. See ZOLLER, Nancy.

ALTAY, Andrew J., of Toronto, Ont., program analyst, born Budapest; winner of several Canadian regional events including Canadian Nat'l Knockout Teams 1973.

ALTMAN, Fred, of Melbourne, Australia; represented Australia World Team Olympiad 1968; npc Australian Team World Team Olympiad 1972.

ALTMAN, Ms. Marion, of Roslyn, N.Y., librarian; regional wins include Eastern States Women's Pairs 1970, New York Winter Women's Pairs 1974.

ALTMAN, Steven, of New York, N.Y., financial analyst, born 1943; one of the leading American players; won Spingold 1970, 1971, Vanderbilt 1972, Morehead Cup 1967, LONDON SUNDAY TIMES 1973; second Reisinger 1967, Spingold 1968; winner of several regional events since 1967, including Eastern States Open Pairs 1967, Long Island Knockout Teams 1971, 1972. One of the youngest to play in the finals of the Spingold. Coach US Team World Championship 1973. An original member of the PRECISION TEAM.

AMANN, Ross F., of Riverdale, Ill., physicist, born 1943; winner of several regional events including Central States Knockout Teams 1970.

AMANULLAH II (1892–1960), Emir of Afghanistan 1919–29; abdicated partly because of his obsession with auction bridge. This pastime displeased his Mohammedan subjects, especially because, with orthodox Mohammedans, it is a sacrilege to depict the human form on cards, or in any other way.

AMARAL, Eros, of São Paulo, Brazil, insurance agent and bridge writer, born 1915; represented Brazil World Olympiad 1964; won South American Open Team 1955, 1962, Brazilian Championship

1955, 1961, 1962; second South American Championship 1954, Brazilian Championship 1953, 1954, 1955. Writings include *The Limit System,* and a newspaper column.

AMER, J. Brian, of Whittier, Calif., attorney, born 1941; won several regional events including Pacific Southwest Knockout Teams 1970.

AMSBURY, Joe, of London, England, born 1929; writer and editor of *Popular Bridge Monthly;* won Gold Cup 1970, many other tournaments.

AMUNDSEN, Ambjörg, of Oslo, Norway, journalist, born 1910; npc Norwegian Women's Team European Championship since 1949; member of Executive Committee of Norwegian Bridge Association since 1947, and of the Tournament Committee since 1953. Author of daily bridge column, and contributor to several bridge publications.

ANDERSEN, Eilif B., of Los Angeles, Calif., born 1907; ACBL President 1966, Director 1956–58, 1961–67; Chairman Finance, Building Fund, Headquarters Site, and other ACBL committees; sponsored ACBL acceptance of district organization. Founder and first President of Ass'n of Los Angeles County Bridge Units 1960–62; President Western Conference 1967; founder and sometime editor of *Southern Californian Bridge News.* Won several regional events between 1953 and 1968.

ANDERSEN, Ronald E., of Wheaton, Ill., stockbroker; one of the most successful American players of the early 1970s; won Fall Nat'l Life Master Men's Pairs 1970, Summer Nat'l Mixed Teams 1971; Spring Nat'l Men's Teams 1974; Marcus 1965; second Vanderbilt 1974; Spring Nat'l Open Pairs 1974; winner of many regional events including Central States Knockout Teams 1972, 1973, New England Knockout Teams 1974. Won Mott-Smith Trophy 1974 with a record 260 points. Developer of DOOP; author of *Where & How High;* co-author of *Matchpoint Precision.*

ANDERSEN, Susan (Mrs. Ronald), of Wheaton, Ill., computer programmer; won Summer Nat'l Mixed Teams 1971, Spring Nat'l Women's Teams 1972; first Spring Nat'l Women's Swiss Teams 1973; Keystone Open Pairs 1973.

ANDERSON, A. Norman, of San Francisco, Calif., bridge teacher, born in Birkenhead, England; won Summer Nat'l secondary Swiss Teams 1972; winner dozens of regional events including Knockout Teams in All-Western 1970, Desert Empire 1970, Golden State 1971, Pacific Southwest 1971, Rocky Mountain 1971, Klondike 1972, Puget Sound 1973.

ANDERSON, Clinton P. (1895–1975), of Albuquerque, N.M., Senator and Cabinet member. Prominent in Southwest bridge in the thirties. Won USBA Open Teams, Southwest region, 1933.

ANDERSON, John, of California City, Calif.; won Summer Nat'l Mixed Teams 1971; winner of numerous regional events including Canadian Knockout Teams, Open Pairs, Master Pairs, Swiss Teams 1971, and Open Pairs Little Bridge Week 1973.

ANDERSON, Madeline L. (1901–1973), of Seattle, Wash., bridge writer, teacher, and club-owner; won Hawaiian Open Teams 1953, Hawaiian Masters Pairs 1953. Founder and former secretary of Wisconsin-Michigan BA and Midwest Bridge Conference, former secretary of ACBL, former Vice-President of ABTA, co-founder of Canadian-US Bridge Matches. Member ACBL Goodwill Committee.

ANDERSON, Virgil V., Jr., of Springfield, Mo., lawyer and manufacturer, born 1924; National Vice-President ACBL 1962–63; President Missouri Valley Conference 1962–63; President Southwest Missouri Unit 101 from 1955. Editor *Crossruff.*

ANDERSON, William, of Toronto, Ont., actuary; author of the most widely used DISTRIBUTIONAL POINT-COUNT.

ANDRES, Jim, of Vancouver, B.C.; winner of several regional events including British Columbia Open Pairs 1973, Oregon Trail and Peach Festival Swiss Teams 1974.

ANNIS, Marjorie (Mrs. Donald), of Omaha, Neb., died 1973; ACBL Director; long time Life Master and certified club director; member of Board of Nebraska Unit from its inception, Vice-President for eight years, President. Member National Goodwill Committee.

ANSAY, Nadine. See LIECHTENSTEIN, PRINCESS NADINE VON.

ANSIN, Mrs. Herbert, of Brookline, Mass.; one of the leading New England Women players in the forties; won Fall Nat'l Mixed Pairs 1947, many New England regional events between 1943 and 1946, including Knockout Teams 1944 (twice), 1945.

ANTUNES, Manuel Costa, of Lisbon, Portugal, civil engineer, born 1930; represented Portugal European Championships 1966, 1974; national wins include Open Teams six times, Open Pairs twice.

ANULF, Gunnar, of Lidingo, Sweden, government employee, born 1923; represented Sweden World Championship 1953, European Championships 1966, 1967; European Champion 1952, Scandinavian Champion 1955, 1957, 1963; National titles include

Open Team 1949, 1954, 1963, Open Pairs 1952, 1954.

APFEL, Dr. Kalman, of West Palm Beach, Fla., physician, born 1907; won Spingold 1956, Vanderbilt 1954, Summer Nat'l Golder Pairs 1952, Non-Masters Pairs 1942, Sub-Senior Masters Team 1946; winner of several regional events including Eastern States Knockout Teams 1966, New York Winter Swiss Teams 1974.

APPLETON, John P., Jr. (Jack), of Boston, Mass., insurance claims supervisor, born 1934; winner of several regional events, including New England Master Swiss Teams 1971, 1972.

APPLEYARD, Robert, of New York, N.Y., bridge teacher and club director, born 1909; won Chicago 1947, Vanderbilt 1948, Life Masters Pairs 1939, 1945; second Fall Nat'l Men's Team 1950, Life Masters Pairs 1936, Life Masters Individual 1950, 1956; regional successes include Central States Men's Pairs 1949, Florida Men's Team 1959, 1960, Mid-South Spring Masters Pairs 1945; second Mid-Atlantic Spring Open Team 1961.

ARGERICH, Ricardo Maria, of Buenos Aires, Argentina, diplomat, born 1923; South American Champion 1948, 1953; won Argentine Open Team 1949, Open Pairs 1952. Since 1955 retired from tournament play.

ARGERSINGER, Amelia (Mrs. Edward), of Ann Arbor, Michigan, born 1915; winner of several regional events including Motor City Women's Pairs 1968, Champagne Women's Pairs 1971, and Great Lakes Mixed Pairs 1971.

ARNDT, Ann, of Hermoga Branch, Calif., winner of several regional events including Golden State Open Pairs 1969 and Navajo Trail Women's Pairs 1970.

ARNOLD, Carrie (Mrs. I. G.), of Fort Lauderdale, Fla., born 1896; second Life Master Women's Pairs 1963, Fall Nat'l Women's Teams 1963; winner of several regional events including Southeastern Women's Teams 1962, 1963, 1964, 1967.

ARNOLD, Russell, of Miami, Fla.; won Spingold 1963, Grand Nat'l Teams 1973, second Vanderbilt 1960; won Florida Knockout Teams 1969, Mid-Atlantic Knockout Teams 1974.

ARNOTT, George W., of Kuala Lumpur, Malaya, agricultural chemist, born 1929; represented Malaya Far East Championship 1961, captain 1962; Club champion 1961, 1962. Secretary Malayan Contract Bridge Association.

ARON, Adrien, of Paris, writer, born 1902, European Champion 1935; represented France at Plafond against Ely Culbertson's US team 1933; French Open Team Champion 1932–39 inclusive. Author of many articles. See BIBLIOGRAPHY, G.

ARONSON, Sidney, of Arlington, Va., formerly of Brookline, Mass., lawyer, born 1911; won Fall Nat'l Open Teams 1949; winner of many regional events, including New England Masters Pairs 1942; Master Teams 1950; Mid-Atlantic Knockout Teams 1971, 1972.

ARST, Frieda (Mrs. B. H.), of Chicago, Ill., bridge teacher; won Spring Nat'l Women's Teams 1966, Life Master Women's Pairs 1973, Golder Pairs 1967; Fall Nat'l secondary Women's Pairs 1973, Spring Nat'l secondary Women's Swiss Teams 1972, tied 1973; second Spring Nat'l Women's Teams 1972; winner of many regional events including Central States Women's Pairs 1957, 1961, 1962, 1965, 1967.

ASCHEIM, Burton L., Jr., of Pittsburgh, Pa., born 1946; won Midwest Spring Open Pairs, 1967, Nat'l Sub-Senior Masters Teams 1965.

ASBER, A. Joseph, of Bethlehem, Pa., draftsman; regional wins include Eastern States Open Pairs 1971.

ASBJØRNSSON, Jon, of Reykjavik, Iceland, teacher; won Iceland National Open Teams 1970, 1971, 1972, Open Pairs 1970.

ASHLEY, David, of Las Vegas, Nev., dealer, born 1941; winner of many regional events including Rocky Mountain Knockout Teams 1971, Bridge Week Board-a-Match Teams 1972, All-Western Master Teams 1973.

ASKEW, Mrs. Mabs, of Downey, Calif.; won Golden State Masters Pairs 1965. President Association of Los Angeles County Bridge Units, which publishes *The Bridge News* monthly.

ASSUMPÇÃO, P. P., of São Paulo, Brazil, director of import-export company, born 1935; one of the leading players of South America; represented Brazil World Championship 1969, 1970, 1971, 1973, 1974, 1975, World Team Olympiad 1968, 1972; South American Champion 1967, 1968, 1969, 1970, 1971, 1972, 1973, 1974; winner of many Brazilian championships.

ATCHLEY, John C., of Los Angeles, Calif., attorney, born 1917; won Bridge Week Masters Pairs 1957, Life Masters Individual 1960, Mixed Team 1961.

ATTAGUILE, Luis, of Buenos Aires, Argentina, clerk, born 1926; represented Argentina World

Championships 1962, 1963, 1965, World Team Olympiad 1964; South American Champion 1961, 1962, 1964; won Argentine Open Teams 1959, 1961, 1962, 1964, 1968, 1970, 1973, 1974, Masters Pairs 1961, Open Pairs 1961.

ATUESTA, Jorge, of Bogotá, Colombia, engineer, born 1926; represented Colombia South American Championships 1964, 1966, 1968; National titles include Open Teams 1965, 1966, 1967, Master Pairs 1967.

AUGUST, William J., of Springfield, Mass., bridge teacher, born 1926; won Long Island Master Pairs 1969, Southeastern Open Teams 1970. Author of August Two-Diamond Convention. See TWO-WAY STAYMAN. President New England BC.

AVARELLI, Walter, of Rome, lawyer, born 1912; one of the world's great players; World Champion 1957, 1958, 1959, 1961, 1962, 1964, 1965, 1966, 1967, 1968, 1969, 1972; represented Italy World Olympiad 1960; European Champion 1956, 1957, 1958, 1959; won Italian Cup 1954, Italian Open Team 1954, 1959, 1960, 1963. Co-inventor of the ROMAN SYSTEM. See BLUE TEAM and BIBLIOGRAPHY, C.

D'AVE, Adelstano P., of Brazil, insurance broker, born 1928; South American Champion 1967, 1968, 1971, npc South American champion 1972, 1973, 1974; represented Brazil World Olympiad 1964, 1968, World Championships 1969, 1971, npc 1973, 1974; national wins include Open Teams 1967, 1968, 1969, 1970, 1972, 1974, Open Pairs 1960, 1970, 1974.

AWAD, George L., of Forest Hills, N.Y., engineer, born Cairo, Egypt 1923; represented Egypt World Team Olympiad 1964; winner of several regional events in US including Eastern States Knockout Teams 1972.

AWAD, Marie (Mrs. George), of Forest Hills, N.Y., tax consultant, born Cairo, Egypt; represented Egypt World Team Olympiad 1964; winner of several regional events in US including Eastern States Knockout Teams 1972.

AYRES, Richard, of Topeka, Kan., engineer, born 1914; winner of several regional events including District 15 Knockout Teams, Open Teams, Open Pairs 1968.

B

BABIN, Elmer J., of Cleveland, Ohio, attorney, born 1902; won American Whist League Open Pairs

1930; won Western States Open Team 1934, Open Pairs 1939. ACBL President 1940.

BABSCH, Fritz, of Vienna, Austria, civil engineer, born 1933; won World Olympiad Open Pairs 1970; represented Austria World Team Olympiad 1968; third European Championships 1969; various European international successes.

BACH, Norman M. (1903–1971), of Paget East, Bermuda, accountant; won Gold Cup (Great Britain) 1938; playing captain of Great Britain European Championships Team 1938, 1939. Initiated and organized the first postwar World Championships held in Bermuda 1950. See BERMUDA BOWL.

BACHER, Paula. See LEVIN, Paula.

BACHERICH, René, of Lille, France, merchant, born 1906; World Champion 1956, World Team Olympiad Champion 1960, represented France World Team Olympiad 1964, World Championships 1954, 1961, 1963; European Champion 1953, 1955, 1962, second 1956, 1961; national wins include Open Teams 1962, and other successes. See RELAY SYSTEM.

BACHNER, Lester R. (1897–1976), of New York, N.Y., attorney; won Grand National Open Pairs 1937, Vanderbilt 1942, Nat'l Mixed Team 1934.

BACKMAN, Joseph G., of Worcester, Mass., lawyer, born 1901; won USBA New England Team-of-Four 1936. First President Central Massachusetts Bridge Association.

BACON, Francis III, retired New York stockbroker; in 1975, as the only surviving member of the first game of contract bridge played aboard the S.S. *Finland,* Nov. 1, 1925, he contributed much new information regarding the background of the origin of the game and helped to pinpoint its date.

BAER, Henry, of Dallas, Tex., attorney, born Germany 1930; winner of several regional events including International City Open Pairs 1974.

BAILEY, Evan, of La Jolla, Calif., physicist, born 1929; won Golden State Open Pairs 1963, Bridge Week Masters Pairs 1968, All Western Masters Pairs 1967.

BAILEY, Maureen (formerly O'Brien) (1899–1963), bridge editor of the San Francisco *Chronicle* for about twenty-five years. Co-author, with Ivy Oeschger, of three books. Made an honorary member of ACBL in 1946. See BIBLIOGRAPHY, E.

BAIRD, Carol, of Seattle, Wash., travel agent; winner of several regional events including Puget Sound Open Pairs 1973, Yakima Valley Swiss Teams.

BAIRD, James C., of Baird, Miss. (1878–1963); won Mid-South Spring Master Individual 1951. He had played in forty of the fifty states, and in his honor, the town of Old Johnsonville had changed its name to Baird; President of the Mississippi Unit twice, he was also Honorary Member ACBL 1951. The Baird Trophy for National Open Individual was given by him, as a memorial for his wife who had died in 1947.

BAIRD, Mrs. James C., of Baird, Miss., died 1947. She was ACBL Honorary Member that year.

BAKER, H. Dean, Jr. (deceased), formerly of Rumford, R.I., executive, born 1902; won New England Knockout Teams 1949, 1953, Masters Teams 1951, Mixed Teams 1955, Men's Pairs 1959. Former Director ACBL, President New England BA.

BAKER, Royal (1904–1967), of Attleboro, Mass., lawyer; won New England Open Teams 1954, 1958, 1962, Knockout Teams 1949, 1956, 1963, Masters Pairs 1950.

BALAILA, Jack, of Haifa, Israel, travel agent, born 1923 in Beirut; represented Israel World Team Olympiad 1964, European Championship 1966; played with Lebanese team before moving to Israel 1954; member of Israeli Team for the following years; National successes include Open Pairs 1962.

BALANOW, Richard, of Houston, Tex., management financial consultant, born 1932; won Leventritt Pairs 1965, Mid-American–Canadian Open Pairs 1961, Central States Mixed Pairs 1963.

BALDON, Mrs. Suzanne, of Paris, born 1920; represented France World Women's Team Olympiad 1964; European Women's Champion 1953, 1954; represented France European Women's Championship 1957, 1967; national wins include Women's Team several times.

BALDWIN, Col. Russell J. (1898–1969), of Norwalk, Conn., formerly of Cleveland, Ohio, army officer and expert on tournament procedure. One of the leading American bridge personalities, he was active as an organizer from the earliest days of contract bridge, and became a Director of the American Bridge League and its Treasurer shortly after its foundation in 1927.

A member of the National Laws Commission (originally Committee) since its foundation in 1933, Baldwin was primarily responsible for the first Duplicate Code issued in 1935 and played a considerable part in formulating subsequent codes.

He was the author of the McKenny-Baldwin schedules for HOWELL MOVEMENTS, and constructed other movements. His many contributions to tournament procedure included the official ACBL method of dealing with fouled boards.

Baldwin was active as a tournament director 1927–41, and after war service became ACBL Business Manager, 1946–51. He was recalled to military service at the outbreak of the Korean War, and returned to the ACBL in charge of tournament scheduling 1958–63.

He was ACBL Honorary Member in 1943. His writings included many magazine contributions. Contributing Editor, *Bridge Encyclopedia*.

BALDWIN, William A., of Albuquerque, N.M., born 1906; general contractor; second Fall Nat'l Charity Game 1966. ACBL President 1970, Director since 1965. Chairman Board of Directors' Executive, Finance, Agenda Expediting, and many other committees. ACBL representative to WBF 1975–78.

BALFE, Raymond A. (1895–1969), of New York, N.Y.; a leading figure in auction bridge and in the early days of contract bridge; won All-American Open Pairs 1926 (auction) playing with W. VON ZEDTWITZ; USBA Grand National Mixed Team 1936 (contract).

BALLARD, Jude H. (Mrs. Neil), of Mercer Island, Wash., born 1931; second Spring Nat'l Women's Teams 1967; winner of several regional events including Northwest Masters Pairs 1963, Oregon Trail 1971, Women's Masters and Women's Pairs and Swiss Teams Inland Empire 1971.

BALLENTINE, Lyle, of Charleston, S.C., general contractor, born 1949; winner of several regional events including Mid-Atlantic Spring Knockout Teams 1974.

BALLESTEROS, Mrs. Carmen Veloso, of Rizal, Philippines, born 1922; Far East Champion 1957; represented Philippines World pairs Olympiad 1962; Far East Championships 1960, 1963; national titles include Mixed Teams 1965, second 1966; Mixed Pairs 1956, 1957; Open Pairs 1965; Open Teams 1961; Women's Pairs 1957, 1958; Women's Individual 1956.

BANCROFT, Mrs. Eleanor F. (1885–1962), of Boston, Mass.; won New England Women's Pairs 1931, 1933, 1937. Prominent bridge authority in the New England area in the thirties; proprietor and hostess for the Boston Chess Club.

BANDONI, Franco, of Toronto, Ont.; winner of several Canadian regional events including Canadian Nat'l Knockout Teams 1971; Masters Pairs 1974.

BANGS, Fred T., of Seal Beach, Calif., journalist, born 1886; won Open Pairs Championship 1934. Author of *Basic Bidding in Contract Bridge*.

BANK, Julius C., of Chicago, Ill., CPA; won Summer Nat'l Men's Teams 1946; second Spingold

1948 and twice in Vanderbilt; won All-American Open Teams 1944, Central States Open Teams 1956.

BARBEY, Henry I., of New York (1832–1906), banker, company director, and yachtsman. A cosmopolitan who lived in Europe for many years, Barbey is credited by Elwell and Foster with introducing bridge to New York in 1893. He wrote the first code of laws for the new game, dated 1892.

BARBONE, Guido, of Italy, columnist and bridge writer, npc World Championship Italian team 1967. Author of *The Complete Book of Bridge* (1964), *Funny Bridge* (1968), *The Complete Book of Duplicate Bridge* (1972).

BARBOUR, Kenneth, of Wellesley, Mass., formerly of Liverpool, England, programmer, born 1938; represented Great Britain in European Championships 1963; won English Team Trials 1962, Gold Cup 1963; second Summer Nat'l Mixed Teams 1970. Contributor to *Bridge World, British Bridge World,* and *Bridge Journal.*

BARCLAY, Shepard (1889–1955), bridge writer, publisher, lecturer, club director, born in St. Louis. During his career in bridge, 1927–55, he was a resident of New York City. In 1927 he bought *Auction Bridge Magazine* from J. T. Smith, and sought to make it a mass magazine, featuring the editorship of M. WORK and W. WHITEHEAD, cartoons by such famous illustrators as his brother McClelland Barclay, John Held, Jr., Tony Sarg, Jefferson Machamer, and H. T. WEBSTER, and articles by famous writers including Ring Lardner, Edgar Guest, and Clarence Buddington Kelland. The magazine failed (1929), and its mailing list was used by E. CULBERTSON to start *The Bridge World.* Barclay conducted a bridge page, with doggerel pertaining to bridge as a regular feature, in the New York *Herald Tribune,* 1929–34, and during those years also ranked the ten best (or most successful) players of each year annually for *Collier's* magazine. He conducted bridge clubs and duplicate games. Barclay wrote many books on bridge (see BIBLIOGRAPHY, E), and from 1932 until his death he wrote a daily syndicated newspaper feature on bridge for King Features Syndicate. He was a member of the executive committees of the ABL and ACBL 1936–49, and honorary member ACBL 1948.

BARD, George, of Bronxville, N.Y., publisher; a pioneer in bridge supplies and accessories, and at one time associated in this capacity with Ely Culbertson. Author of several books, including a self-teacher.

BARDACH, David, of Tel Aviv, Israel, book-publishing executive, born in Poland 1916; represented Israel in World Pairs Olympiad 1966, European Championships 1967; several national successes. Treasurer Israel Bridge Federation; Chairman Tel Aviv branch of the IBF 1969–72; chairman Israel Bridge Congresses 1969–74.

BARDOLA, Marcel, of Zurich, Switzerland, mathematician, born 1925; represented Switzerland European Championship 1959 through 1963; Nat'l titles include Open Team five times, Open Pairs 1953, 1959, 1961, 1962. Former Secretary-General of Swiss Bridge Federation.

BARE, Dorothy, of Pacific Palisades, Calif., travel agent; won Summer Nat'l Mixed Teams 1970, Pacific Southwest Open Teams 1966, Disneyland Open Teams 1970.

BARE, Gerald W., of Pacific Palisades, Calif., civil engineer, born 1933; won Summer Nat'l Mixed Teams 1970, second Reisinger 1966; winner of several regional events including Bridge Week Knockout Teams 1973.

BARLOW, Edward J., of Sunnyvale, Calif., computer programmer, born 1933; second Fall Nat'l Men's Teams 1965, Spring Nat'l Men's Teams 1967; winner of several regional events including District 21 Grand Nationals 1974.

BARNES, A. Mitchell, of New York, N.Y., bridge lecturer, travel agent, born 1906; one of the leading East Coast players; won AWL All-American Teams 1934, 1935, Spingold 1941, Chicago 1946, Fall Nat'l Open Pairs 1937, Summer Nat'l Men's Pairs 1946, USBA Grand National Open Teams 1936; second Vanderbilt 1933, Spingold 1938, Chicago 1938, 1941, Summer Nat'l Mixed Team 1934, Fall Nat'l Men's Team 1946, USBA Grand National Open Pairs 1934, Mixed Teams 1936; regional wins include Eastern States Knockout Teams 1935, 1937. Director of bridge activities for United States Lines and other shipping lines.

BARNETT, Harry, of Glasgow, Scotland, secretary, born 1914; represented Scotland in nine international matches; member of the victorious Camrose Trophy team twice. National titles include Open Teams and Open Pairs twice.

BARNETT, Lewis B., of Blacksburg, Va., biochemist, born 1934. Won Holland's Nat'l Open Team 1962, 1963, Jewish Nat'l Fund 1963, Mid-Atlantic Open Teams 1973. Contributor to *Bridge,* Holland's monthly bridge magazine.

BARNETT, Sol, of Glasgow, Scotland, furniture manufacturer, born 1913; represented Scotland in nineteen international matches; member of the winning Camrose Trophy team twice. National titles include Open Teams and Open Pairs.

BARON, Arthur, of Los Angeles, Calif., journalist, born 1923; won Bridge Week Masters Pairs 1957, Knockout Team 1961, Masters Team 1956.

BARON, Hermine (Mrs. Arthur), of Los Angeles, Calif.; one of the leading American women players; represented United States World Women's Team Olympiad 1968; won Spring Nat'l Women's Teams 1964, 1968, Women's Pairs 1968, Fall Nat'l Life Master Women's Pairs 1963, Summer Nat'l Life Master Pairs 1966; Fall Nat'l secondary Open Teams 1968, Summer Nat'l secondary Mixed Pairs 1972, Marcus Swiss Teams 1972; second Spring Nat'l Mixed Pairs 1961, Women's Teams 1967, Women's Pairs 1967, Fall Nat'l Blue Ribbon Pairs 1971, Women's Teams 1974. Has won hundreds of regional events including Bridge Week Knockout Teams 1969, 1970, Intermountain Open Pairs 1969, 1970, Open Teams 1969, 1970; Northern Rocky Mountain Open Teams 1962, 1965, 1966, 1967. Winner of McKenney Trophy 1964, 1970; her winning total of 1,370 master points in the 1964 McKenney competition stood as the all-time record until P. Soloway amassed 1,434 points in 1969. See HANDICAPPED PLAYERS.

BARON, Leo, of Salisbury, Southern Rhodesia, lawyer. Inventor of the BARON SYSTEM, and made many important contributions to bidding theory. British wins included Gold Cup 1946 and 1951. Retired from bridge after emigration to Southern Rhodesia in 1952. Co-author of *The Baron System of Contract Bridge.* (See BIBLIOGRAPHY, C.)

BARONI, Paolo, of Milan, Italy, technical director in silk industry and bridge writer, born 1911; European Champion 1951, second 1952; won Italian Open Team 1937, 1938, Mixed Team 1947. Founder Italian Bridge League. Italian delegate to IBL. Writer of bridge articles for Italian bridge magazine.

BAROUK, Nicholas T. (1916–1974), of Worcester, Mass., writer, teacher, lecturer. Former member Board of Governors; for many years Charity Chairman for District 1. Organized the Central Mass. Bridge Association in 1956 and served as its President in 1957. He also founded many bridge clubs, including the Cavendish Club of Worcester, where he pioneered a "Nassau" method of scoring IMP matches—two victory points awarded for the first half, two for the second half, and two more for the total. This method allows an underdog team a reasonable chance of collecting a few victory points from the favorite.

BARREDO, Manuel, of Manila, Philippines, businessman, born 1901; won Far East zone of the second World Par Championships; National Open Pairs 1954, 1959. First President of the Philippine Contract Bridge League.

BARRETT, Annette, of Miami, Fla., winner of

several regional events including Mid-Atlantic Fall Knockout Teams 1973.

BARRETT, William K., of Albany, Ga., born 1909; won Chicago 1930, and so became one of the youngest players ever to win a major National championship; regional wins include Southeastern Open Team 1931.

BARROSO, Fernando Diez (1918–1965), of Mexico City, business executive; represented Mexico World Olympiad 1964. Jai-alai Champion in Olympics 1950.

BARROW, Jim, of Pensacola, Fla., winner of several regional events including Missouri Valley Swiss Teams 1972.

BARROW, Rhoda. See LEDERER, Rhoda.

BARRY, Edward Owen, of Tipperary, Ireland, bank manager, born 1908; represented Ireland European Championship 1950, 1952, 1963; National successes include Irish Open Pairs twice and Open Teams four times, CBA of Ireland Open Teams four times and Men's Pairs twice.

BART, Leslie C., of Bethesda, Md., computer systems designer, born 1947; won Fall Nat'l Life Master Men's Pairs 1972; winner of many regional events including Tri-State Open Pairs 1975.

BARTH, Julian, of Miami, Fla., born 1891; won Eastern Open Teams 1931, Mexican Open Teams 1960, Southeastern Open Teams 1961. He played in teams with Schenken and Burnstine in the early days of contract, and made several contributions to theory during the late twenties and early thirties.

BARTH, Mrs. Julian, of Miami, Fla., born 1901; won Southeastern Open Teams 1961, Women's Teams 1968, 1969, Open Pairs 1943.

BARTON-PAINE, Dianne, of Berkeley, Calif., ACBL tournament director and student, born 1943; became Life Master in 1961 at age of 18, the youngest at that time to achieve that status. Formerly team photographer for Golden State Warriors professional basketball team.

BARTOSIK, Matt, of Los Angeles, Calif., deceased; won several regional events between 1968 and 1970.

BASTOS, Eduardo, of Rio de Janeiro, Brazil, insurance company branch manager, born 1930; represented Brazil World Championship 1970; South American Champion 1969.

BATES, Roger, of Tucson, Ariz.; one of the leading American players, Mott-Smith Trophy winner 1975. Won Vanderbilt 1975, Fall Nat'l Blue Ribbon Pairs 1971, Spring Nat'l secondary Swiss Teams 1974, Fall Nat'l secondary Open Pairs 1974; second Fall Nat'l Blue Ribbon Pairs 1974; winner of dozens of regional events since 1971 including Land of Coronado Knockout Teams, Swiss Teams, Men's Pairs 1972.

BAUER, Charles, of Louisville, Ky., restaurant owner, born 1924; regional wins include Midwest Men's Pairs 1959, 1960, 1973.

BAUSCHER, Dr. Larry P., of New Haven, Conn., chemist, born 1939; won Summer Nat'l Special Pairs 1972, Canadian-American Masters Pairs 1973, Long Island Swiss Teams 1973.

BAZE, Grant, of Fremont, Calif.; one of the leading players of the West Coast; won Spingold 1975, Reisinger 1970, Pan-American Invitational Pairs 1974, 1975, second Reisinger 1971, Spring Nat'l Men's Teams 1972. Winner of many regional events since 1969.

BEALE, Felicity (Mrs. Julian), of Melbourne, Australia, born Yugoslavia; Far East Women's Champion 1973.

BEAN, Percy X., of Olympia, Wash., industrial supplies executive, born 1916; member ACBL Board of Directors since 1964; President 1972; Chairman of Board 1973; President, ACBL Charity Foundation since 1974. One of principal sponsors of the GRAND NATIONAL (2); editor and publisher of *Mad Mad World of Bridge,* a newsletter principally to members of District 19, strongly championing the role of ACBL affairs of players of less than expert class. Member IBPA.

BEARD, Fran (Mrs. Sam), of Dallas, Texas; won Summer Nat'l secondary Women's Pairs 1974; tied second Spring Nat'l Women's Teams 1973; winner of several regional events including Texas Fall Women's Pairs 1973.

BEARD, Sam, of Dallas, Texas; won Summer Nat'l secondary Men's Pairs 1972, District 15 Mixed Pairs 1969; tied first Missouri Valley Men's Pairs 1971.

BEASLEY, Henry Mountifort ("Pops"), of London (1875–1949), army officer and bridge writer, born in India; one of the leading personalities in British bridge. Captained the British team in the Schwab Cup 1933, and played in one of the ANGLO-AMERICAN MATCHES of 1930. Won Gold Cup 1932. Co-founder and chairman of two of London's most important card clubs, CROCKFORD'S and the HAMILTON. Bridge columnist, author of a number of books, and the originator of a One Club system called after him.

BECHELY, Joseph, of Los Angeles, Calif., mathematician, born 1928; winner of several regional events since 1953, including Bridge Week Knockout Teams 1953, 1955, 1974.

BECKER, B. Jay, of Flushing, N.Y., attorney, bridge columnist, and bridge teacher; born 1904 in Philadelphia where he trained as a lawyer and lived until 1937. One of the greatest players of all time, Becker was World Champion 1951 and 1953, and also represented the United States in the 1958, 1965, and 1973 World Championship and the 1960 World Team Olympiad. He had the rare distinction of winning a national championship in his first year of tournament play. His introduction to duplicate play was early in 1932 when he entered and won a special pair contest organized by Alfred GRUENTHER, using unpublished hands from the just-concluded CULBERTSON-LENZ MATCH. In the Summer Nationals of that year he placed second in two major events, and he recorded a win in the Fall Nationals. This was in the Chicago Trophy, an event he was to win on seven subsequent occasions, 1939, 1942, 1943, 1950, 1953, 1954, 1956. Becker has had equal success in the other major team championships, winning the Spingold seven times, 1936, 1938, 1944, 1947, 1952, 1957, and the Vanderbilt seven times, 1944, 1945, 1951, 1955, 1956, 1957, 1959. His 1972 Spingold victory helped him to win the Fishbein Trophy in 1972.

Becker had the best record of any player in the Masters Individual Championship, winning in 1937 and 1948, and placing second in 1934, 1941, 1949, and 1955. It is curious to note that he has never won a national mixed pair or mixed team event, although his chief successes in the early sixties were with Mrs. Dorothy HAYDEN. In a two-year period, 1962–64, they won three of the four National Pair championships restricted by master-point qualifications, the Fall Nat'l Open Pairs 1962, the Blue Ribbon Pairs 1963, and the Life Master Pairs 1964.

Becker's other National wins include AWL All-American Open Pairs and Open Teams 1935, Life Masters pairs 1935, Fall Nat'l Open Pairs 1946, Men's Pairs 1938. He was second in 27 national events, and his regional wins include Eastern States Knockout Teams 1935, 1942, 1971, District 5 Keystone Open Teams 1965, Mid-Atlantic Summer Men's Pairs 1966, Spring Open Teams 1968, Tri-State Open Teams 1968, 1970, New England Winter Open Teams 1968.

Considered to be perhaps the most conservative of leading experts, Becker adopted very few bidding conventions, declining to play even the almost universally used STAYMAN convention. He was, however, among the first to adopt and recommend SUIT-PREFERENCE SIGNALS.

Becker managed three New York clubs, the Cavendish 1942–47, the New York Bridge Whist 1948–50, and the Regency 1951–56. He was associated with the New York Card School 1952–57, and became the bridge columnist for King Features Syndicate in 1956. He became a member of the National Laws Commission in 1954. Contributor *The Bridge World;* member of the Editorial Advisory Board of *Bridge Encyclopedia.* See also BUENOS AIRES AFFAIR, FAMILY.

BECKER, James W., of New York, N.Y., bridge teacher, born 1937; winner of many regional events including Tri-State Swiss Teams 1970, Mexican Nat'l Men's Pairs, Mixed Pairs 1970; won Intercollegiate Par Championship 1959, 1960; Keystone Men's Pairs 1972.

BECKER, Michael M., of N.Y., born 1943; one of the leading American players; represented North America World Championship 1973; won Morehead Cup 1967, Spingold 1972, Spring Nat'l secondary Mixed Pairs 1974; second Reisinger 1967, Spingold 1968; regional wins include New England Winter Teams 1968, Spring Nat'l Men's Team 1968; Eastern States Knockout Teams 1971. One of the youngest to play in the finals of the Spingold. See FAMILY.

BECKER, R. Jay, of New York, N.Y., actuary, lawyer, born 1944; won Summer Nat'l secondary Swiss Teams 1971; winner of several regional events including Long Island Men's Pairs 1969, 1972.

BECKER, Simon, of Philadelphia, Pa., court stenographer, born 1899; won Chicago 1944, second Spingold 1944, Chicago 1946, Fall Nat'l Open Pairs 1949, 1960; won Eastern States Knockout Teams 1942, Open Pairs 1964, Keystone Open Teams 1955, Men's Pairs 1966, and had many other National and Regional successes. See FAMILY.

BECKER, Steven, of Greenwich, Conn., bridge teacher and writer, born 1937; won New England Winter Open Teams 1968. Regular contributor to ACBL *Bulletin* (Executive Editor 1970–72). See also FAMILY.

BECKMAN, Terrence L., of Eden Prairie, Minnesota, printer, born 1947; winner of several regional events including Iowa Swiss Teams 1974.

BEERS, Dale G., of Springfield, Pa., insurance underwriter, born in 1950; won Summer Nat'l Senior/Advanced Senior Master Pairs 1974.

BEERY, James, of Fort Lauderdale, Fla.; radio engineer, won Grand Nationals 1973; Southeastern Men's Teams 1974.

BEGIN, Mrs. Jackie, of Montreal, Que., born 1917; represented Canada World Women's Team Olympiad 1968, 1972, World Olympiad Women's Pairs 1970; won Fall Nat'l Women's Team 1952; winner of many regional events including Canadian Nat'l Open Team 1963, Canadian-American Open Teams 1956, 1957, 1965.

BEGLEY, Francis P., of Bronx, N.Y., stockbroker, born 1906; won Spingold 1956, Vanderbilt 1954, Summer Nat'l Non-Masters Pairs 1942; second Life Masters Pairs 1957; won Eastern States Open Pairs 1948; other successes.

BÉGUIN, Pierre, of Geneva, Switzerland, architect, born 1911; playing captain of Swiss Team European Championships 1951, 1952, 1953, 1954, 1955, 1956; National titles include Open Team 1951, 1953, 1956, 1957, 1958, Open Pairs 1954, 1955, 1956, Swiss Cup 1952, 1955, 1956. Founder of the Swiss Bridge Federation.

BEINECKE, Walter (1888–1961), of New York, N.Y., corporation executive. A leading figure in bridge administration, he was a Vice-President of the USBA and the Whist Club of New York. A member of the Laws Commission from its formation in 1933, he assisted in the preparation of all the codes issued from that time until his death. Tournament successes included second Vanderbilt 1936. ACBL Director 1942–43.

BELL, Alan C., Los Angeles, Calif., bridge teacher, born 1925; formerly one of the leading players of the Middle West; second McKenney 1958, won Marcus 1962, Fall Nat'l Int'l Fund Pairs 1974, secondary Open Pairs 1974; winner of numerous regional events including All-American Open Teams 1958, 1961; Pacific Southwest Knockout Teams 1970, 1971. Director Chicago CBA, 1955–63.

BELL, Bruce C., of Auckland, N.Z., industrialist and bridge writer, born 1910; Fourth World Par Olympiad 1963; represented New Zealand Far East Championships 1964, 1972, npc 1973, 1974; won New Zealand Pairs 1950, 1957, 1958, 1966; New Zealand Open Teams twenty-one times between 1947 and 1972. Many other successes. Past President New Zealand CBA. Writings include bridge articles for newspapers and magazines in New Zealand, United States, and United Kingdom. Lecturer on bridge on and off television.

BELL, Frank, of Ann Arbor, Mich., student, born 1950; won Summer Nat'l secondary Swiss Teams 1974, several regional events including Canadian Nat'l Knockout Teams 1974.

BELL, Hazel (Mrs. James D.), Sun City, Ariz., born 1892 (deceased). ACBL Director and member of Board of Western Conference from 1956. Secretary of Denver Unit 1952–58.

BELL, Mrs. Valerie, of Christchurch, N.Z.; represented New Zealand Far East Women's Champion-

ships 1971; won New Zealand Pairs 1962, Canterbury Pairs 1962, Open Teams 1963.

BELLADONNA, Giorgio, of Rome, Italy, public official, born 1923; one of the world's greatest players; World Champion 1957, 1958, 1959, 1961, 1962, 1963, 1964, 1965, 1966, 1967, 1968, 1969, 1972, 1973, 1974, 1975; European Champion 1956, 1957, 1958, 1959, 1965, 1967, second 1962; Italian Cup 1954, Italian Open Team 1954, 1959, 1960, 1963. Belladonna is the only player who participated in all sixteen Italian world victories. Originally paired with Walter AVARELLI, since 1973 he has played in World Championship competition with Benito GAROZZO, a partnership considered by many to be the best in the world; won ACBL Spring Nat'l Men's Pairs 1971. Co-inventor ROMAN SYSTEM. See BIBLIOGRAPHY, C.

BELLANGER, Pierre, of Paris, bridge writer, born 1877. Captain of the first French team to play an international match against an American team (1933; see FRANCO-AMERICAN MATCHES). He was ahead of his time as a theorist in card play, and his book on finesses, *Les Impasses au Bridge* (See BIBLIOGRAPHY, D) was a notable work. He formulated the doctrine, which only received general endorsement after many years of debate, that a priori probabilities are a reliable guide to the play after some cards have appeared. If declarer discovers, for example, that West started with five clubs and East with two clubs, the odds of 5–2 in favor of West's holding the missing club queen are not affected by the fact that West has discarded three clubs. Bellanger also analyzed correctly a number of situations which were not generally understood until the principle of RESTRICTED CHOICE was formulated twenty years later.

Bellanger was Secretary-General of the Commission Française de Bridge in the thirties, and took an active part in formulating the 1935 Laws. His other writings included *Les 102 Donnes d'un Grand Match* as well as numerous magazine articles.

BEMMEL SUYCK, J. R. C. van, of The Hague, Holland, lawyer, born 1899; second European Championship 1932, 1933, 1934, and represented Holland on six other occasions, 1935, 1936, 1937, 1938, 1949, and 1950. Non-playing captain Holland team 1961 and 1962. Won 12 Nat'l team championships, 1931 through 1939, 1949, 1950, and 1951.

BENAIM, Roberto, of Caracas, Venezuela, publicity executive, born 1924; represented Venezuela World Team Olympiad 1968, World Championships 1966, 1967, South American Championships seven times. Won South American Championships 1965, 1966, National Open Teams eleven times.

BENEDICT, J. Frederic, of Des Moines, Iowa, building manager, born 1910; won World Olympic 1933, USBA Open Team 1933; regional successes include Gopher Open Teams 1972. ACBL Director, President Central New York BA.

BENJAMIN, Albert L., of Glasgow, Scotland, electrical merchant, bridge writer, and club owner, born 1909; won Scottish Open Teams six times; represented Scotland seventeen times in Camrose Trophy matches, and member of winning Scottish team in 1964. Co-author of *Tournament Bridge for Everyone,* daily bridge columnist, and regular contributor to *Bridge Magazine.* See BIBLIOGRAPHY, F.

BENNET, James E., Jr., of Hartford, Conn., insurance company supervisor, born 1936; winner of several regional events including Eastern States Knockout Teams 1965, New England Knockout Teams 1974.

BENONYSSON, Eggert, of Reykjavik, Iceland, radio technician, born 1908; represented Iceland European Championships 1958, 1961; National titles include Open Team six times from 1951 to 1963, Open Pairs 1959, 1962.

BENSON, Leo O., of Chicago, Ill., bridge columnist and teacher, born 1907; won Gopher Open Pairs 1958. The first player to achieve Life Master status in both the ACBL and the ABA. ACBL Regional Tournament Director.

BENTINCK, Lord Henry (1774–1839), of England. A well-known whist player who originated the BLUE PETER, probably the first defensive signal in any card game of the whist family.

BERAH, David, of Caracas, Venezuela, industrialist and bridge writer, born 1921; represented Venezuela World Team Olympiad 1960, 1964, 1968, World Pairs Olympiad 1966, World Championships 1966, 1967, South American Championships ten times. South American Champion 1963, 1965, 1966; National titles include Open Teams eleven times, Mixed Teams, Open Pairs and Mixed Pairs. Contributor to *The Contract Bridge Bulletin, The Bridge World,* and many other periodicals.

BERG, Mrs. Jack, of Clearwater, Fla.; bridge teacher and director; regional wins include Florida Life Masters Pairs 1970, Midwest Women's Pairs 1961 and 1962.

BERGEN, Marty A., of Hudson, N.Y., teacher, born 1948; won Summer Nat'l Sub-senior Masters Teams 1967; winner of several regional events including Mid-Atlantic Fall Knockout Teams 1973.

BERGER, Fred C., of Natchez, Miss., lawyer; winner of several regional events including Mid-South Open Teams 1962, Masters Pairs 1969, Men's Pairs 1970.

BERGER, Mark A., of Great Neck, N.Y., sales representative and bridge teacher, born 1927; second Summer Nat'l Mixed Teams 1974; regional wins include Tri-State Men's Pairs 1968, 1970.

BERGLUND, Sven Erik, of Hägersten, Sweden, accountant, born 1936; represented Sweden World Olympiad 1964, European Championships 1965; numerous national successes.

BERGOVOY, Bernie, of Oakland, Calif., won Spring Nat'l Men's Teams 1970, Marcus 1972; All-Western Knockout Teams 1969, Golden Gate Masters Pairs 1973.

BERISSO, Alberto, of Buenos Aires, Argentina, Doctor of Economics, born 1922; represented Argentina World Championships 1959, 1962, 1965, World Team Olympiad 1972; South American Champion 1958, 1959, 1961, 1962; won Argentine Open Team 1953, 1956, 1958, 1960, 1961, 1963, 1967, Open Pairs 1958, 1962.

BERKSON, Irving A., of Skokie, Ill., company president; won Summer Nat'l Non-Masters Pairs 1959; several regional titles between 1956 and 1960.

BERLIN, Norman, of Norfolk, Va., real estate investor, born 1907; regional wins include Mid-Atlantic Men's Pairs 1957, Men's Teams 1956, Open Teams 1964, 1965, Masters Pairs 1971.

BERNARD, Mrs. Joan, of Sarasota, Fla.; won Marcus 1971; winner of several regional events including Mid-South Master's Pairs 1974.

BERNASCONI, Pietro, of Geneva, Switzerland, bridge teacher and club manager, born 1932; represented Switzerland World Team Olympiad 1960, 1964, World Pair Olympiad 1962; European Championships 1958, 1959, 1961, 1962, 1963, 1965, 1967; National successes include Open Team five times and Open Pairs twice.

BERNSTEIN, Andrew, of Knoxville, Tenn., formerly of New York, N.Y., clinical psychologist, born 1942; one of the leading American players; represented North America World Championship 1973; won Spingold 1972; winner of several regional events including Eastern States Knockout Teams 1971, Goldman Pairs 1969. Developed two-way EXCLUSION BID overcall convention.

BERNSTEIN, Moshe, of Chicago, Ill.; won Spring Nat'l secondary CSNC Open Pairs 1973, tied first secondary Swiss Teams 1973; won Mississippi Valley Swiss Teams 1974.

BERRY, Peggy Jean. See SUTHERLIN, PEGGY JEAN.

BESSE, Jean, of Rome, Italy, director electronic computer program and bridge writer, born 1914; one of the outstanding bridge players in Europe; represented Switzerland World Team Olympiad 1960, 1964, 1968, European Championship twelve times; represented Europe World Championship

1954. National successes include French Open Team and Swiss Open Teams. Originator Swiss ACOL. Contributing Editor *Bridge Encyclopedia.*

BETHE, Henry, of New York, N.Y., arbitrageur, born 1944; won Fall Nat'l Life Master Men's Pairs 1968, Herman 1968; many regional events including New England Masters Pairs 1969, Pike's Peak Knockout Teams 1972. Associate editor *Bridge Journal* 1964–65.

BETTS, Laurence, of Delta, B.C., club director; winner of several regional events including Klondike Masters Pairs.

BEYNON, George W(illiam), (1864–1965), of St. Petersburg, Fla., tournament direction authority, born in Portage La Prairie, Manitoba. One of the leading personalities in the world of bridge, Beynon studied at Wesley University, Winnipeg, and his first career was that of a professional hockey player in Hamilton, Ont. He made music his major occupation, studying at La Scala in Milan, and later directing orchestras in Europe and America. After becoming an American citizen in 1904, Beynon developed a successful plan for synchronizing music with silent films. He was the musical director of *Birth of a Nation* (1915) and other early successes, and retired to East Orange, N.J., in 1917.

Forced out of retirement by the 1929 crash, Beynon made a new career in bridge. After directing games in New Jersey and writing a Newark bridge column, he joined the Culbertson organization in 1935 as office manager and became Secretary-General of the USBA. He rapidly became an authority on MOVEMENTS, and continued to report tournaments.

After the USBA amalgamated with the ABL in 1937, Beynon served the ACBL as Field Tournament Director 1937–55 and as *Bulletin* Editor 1939–52. After his second retirement in 1955 he was made consultant on matters of tournament direction and named ACBL Honorary Member.

After moving from New York to St. Petersburg in 1955, Beynon founded a successful correspondence school for directors, and began writing a weekly bridge column for the St. Petersburg *Times.* When he celebrated his one-hundredth birthday in September, 1964, he was probably the oldest working newspaperman in America.

His writings include *Bridge Director's Manual,* the standard work on duplicate organization (see BIBLIOGRAPHY, F) and many magazine articles. Contributing Editor of *Bridge Encyclopedia.*

BHARGAVA, Divakar, of Allston, Mass., engineer, born Sadabad, India 1945; won Fall Nat'l secondary Open Pairs 1972, California Capitol Masters Pairs 1971, New England Men's Pairs 1974.

BHAVNANI, Krishin H., of Carlisle, Mass., engineer; won District 5 Open Pairs 1960, Masters Pairs

1963, New England Knockout Teams 1967. Co-inventor American Relay system.

BIANCHI, Benito, of Leghorn, Italy, furrier, born 1924; Grand Master, co-developer LEGHORN DIAMOND (LIVORNO) SYSTEM and one of Europe's outstanding players; won World Championship 1973, 1974; European Championship 1965, 1967, 1969, 1971 (played on five other teams representing Italy in this event); Italian Cup (four times); Italian Mixed Teams (twice); Italian Open Team 1961.

BIANCHI, Marisa (Mrs. Benito), of Leghorn, Italy, born 1928; one of the world's great women players; won World Women's Olympiad, 1972; represented Italy in seven European Women's Championships, winning four straight: 1970, 1971, 1973, 1974; won European Common Market Women's Teams 1971, 1973; Italian Mixed Team Championship (twice); British Women's Team Championship 1973.

BICKEL, Fred L. (1924–1966), of Astoria, N.Y., accountant; second Winter Nat'l Men's Teams 1951; won Keystone Men's Pairs 1952, 1953, New York–New Jersey Open Pairs 1954, Eastern States Open Pairs 1965.

BIDDLE, John R., of Columbus, Ohio, born 1928; won Spring Nat'l Open Pairs 1965, winner of several regional events including Great Lakes Open Teams 1962, Midwest Spring Life Master pairs 1972.

BIERBAUM, Milton (deceased), formerly of Richmond Heights, Mo., school superintendent, born 1906; won Mississippi Valley Men's Pairs 1954. Former member ACBL Board of Directors.

BIERBAUM, Mrs. Milton, of Manchester, Mo., born 1910; won Mississippi Valley Mixed Pairs 1954, Open Individual 1954. Executive Secretary and President St. Louis Unit.

BIERMAN, Harry, of Culver City, Calif., lawyer, born 1910; won Bridge Week Knockout Teams and Masters Pairs 1953, Mixed Pairs 1962.

BIERMAN, Mrs. Harry, of Culver City, Calif., born 1906; won Bridge Week Mixed Pairs 1962, All-Western Mixed Pairs 1957, Pacific Southwest Open Teams 1958.

BINSKY, Robert, of Montreal, Canada, sales manager, born 1939; won Canadian Nat'l Open Teams 1970, Canadian-American Men's Pairs 1967; member of the Montreal Intercity Team that defeated Chicago in 1967. Syndicated Canadian bridge columnist.

BISHOP, Clifford W., of Detroit, Mich., advertising executive, born 1922; one of the leading players of the Middle West; World Champion 1954; represented US World Championship, 1955; won Spingold 1953, 1954; second Summer Nat'l Men's Pairs 1951, Fall Nat'l Men's Team 1953; winner of many regional events including All-American Open Teams 1948, 1960, Southeastern Swiss Teams, Men's Teams, Men's Pairs 1974.

BITNER, Stanislaw, of Warsaw, Poland, economist and bridge writer, born 1922; represented Poland in many international matches, including European Championships 1962, 1963, 1966, 1967; won Yugoslav Open Pairs 1965, second Open Teams 1964. Polish Player of the Year 1962. National successes include first Open Teams 1957, second Open Pairs 1962 and Individual 1960. Contributor to *Brydz.*

BITTMAN, Jack, of Denver, Colo.; won Pike's Peak Knockout Teams 1972, tied first Swiss Teams 1974; Rocky Mountain Open Pairs 1974.

BIXBY, Wingate, of New York, N.Y., banker, born 1900; won Fall Nat'l Mixed Pairs 1936; second Vanderbilt 1939; led unofficial United States teams which won Pan-American Championships in 1948, 1955, and 1958; President Regency Club 1950–63, and of Crockford's Club of Chicago, 1938.

BLACKERBY, Kirk, of San Jose, Calif., professor of economics, born 1941; winner of many regional events including five Knockout Teams—Oregon Trail 1970, All-Western 1971, California Capitol 1972, Intermountain 1972, Central California 1973.

BLACKWOOD, Easley, of Indianapolis, Ind., ACBL Executive Secretary (1968–71), writer, former insurance manager, born 1903; one of the famous bridge personalities in the world; won Midwest Fall Men's Pairs 1944, Southern Conference Open Team 1962; second Midwest Spring Mixed Pairs 1951. Originator of the BLACKWOOD four no trump convention. Author of *Bridge Humanics, Blackwood on Bidding,* and other books, many magazine articles, and a syndicated newspaper column. See BIBLIOGRAPHY, C, E.

BLAIR, Jack, of Tulsa, Okla., oil executive, born 1933; one of the leading American players; represented United States World Pair Championship 1962; won Fall Nat'l Men's Pairs 1960, Spring Nat'l Men's Teams 1972, Summer Nat'l Life Master Pairs 1973, secondary Swiss Teams 1973; co-winner, with Paul Swanson, of MOTT-SMITH Trophy 1972; second Fall Nat'l Open Pairs 1961, 1964, Reisinger 1973, Vanderbilt 1972; winner of many regional events, including Missouri Valley Open Teams 1965, Knockout Teams 1971, Swiss Teams 1971. See FORTUNE.

BLANCHARD, Katherine A., of West Los Angeles, Calif., teacher, born 1889; second Fall Nat'l Life Master Women's Pairs 1968; regional wins include Rocky Mountain Knockout Teams 1969.

BLASBAND, Mrs. Alfred, of Philadelphia, Pa.; won Fall Nat'l Women's Teams 1963, second Mixed Pairs 1966; won Texas Open Pairs 1962, Keystone Mixed Pairs 1959.

BLOM, Mrs. Britt, of Norrköping, Sweden, born 1924; won World Women's Team Olympiad 1968, European Women's Championships 1967, Scandinavian Women's Championships 1964, 1966, and six National women's titles.

BLOOM, Mildred (Mrs. Harry), of Passaic, N.J., secretary, born 1917; won Nat'l Beynon Pairs 1964.

BLOOMFIELD, Ruth (Mrs. I. M.), of Chicago, Ill.; won Fall Nat'l Life Master Women's Pairs 1972; Bermuda Mixed Pairs 1974.

BLOUSSON, Alberto (1908–1967), of Buenos Aires, Argentina, lawyer; represented Argentina World Championship 1958; South American Champion 1948, 1957, 1958; won Argentine Open Team 1938, 1942, 1949, 1955, Open Pairs 1942, 1943, 1947. Top record holder in Masters Individual Championship.

BLUHDORN, Karl von, born in Vienna, died 1960; resident of Paris after 1938; member Austrian World Champion team 1937.

BLUHM, Louis E., of Atlanta, Ga., born 1940; one of the leading American players; won Reisinger 1972, Spingold 1974; second Spring Nat'l Men's Teams; won Mid-Atlantic Open Pairs 1965, plus numerous regional events including Mid-Atlantic Summer Knockout Teams 1971, 1972, Fall Knockout Teams 1972, 1974.

BLUM, Desiderio (1906–1966), of Buenos Aires, Argentina, businessman; npc of Argentine Team in 1962 World Championship; South American Champion 1959, 1962, 1964; won Argentine Open Teams 1958, Open Pairs 1950, 1958. President Argentine Bridge Association 1957–1959.

BLUMENTHAL, Mark E., of Mount Prospect, Ill.; one of the leading American players; bridge and backgammon teacher, born 1942; represented United States World Team Olympiad 1972, represented North America World Championship 1973; member of ACES team 1972–73; won Marcus 1968, Vanderbilt 1972; second Spring Nat'l Men's Pairs 1966; second McKenny 1971; winner of dozens of regional events including the following Knockout Teams: Eastern States 1965, District 11 1971, Fun City 1971, New England 1971, Indy 500 1973, Keystone 1974, Mid-Atlantic 1974.

BLUMENTHAL, Maxine (Mrs. Herman), of Bellevue, Wash., department store executive; winner of several regional events including All-Western Masters Pairs 1974.

BLUSTEIN, Mary (Mrs. Maurice), of Seattle, Wash., secretary, born 1928; winner of several regional events including Oregon Trail Knockout Teams 1972, Yakima Valley Women's Pairs 1974.

BOECK, Jens, of Copenhagen, Denmark, clerk, born 1916; former editor of Danish magazine *Dansk Bridge,* contributor to foreign bridge magazines; author of numerous books on bridge including *The Small Bridge Dictionary, Bid Modern, Play Modern Bridge.* Contributing Editor *Bridge Encyclopedia.*

BOEHM, George A. W., of New York, N.Y., writer and editor, born 1922; won Eastern Open Teams 1955. Vice-President Greater New York BA and editor of its publication, *Post-Mortem,* during 1963. Popularized LEBENSOHL convention.

BOENDER, Pieter, deceased; formerly of The Hague, Holland, city official and bridge columnist, born 1919; represented Netherlands World Team Olympiad 1964, and European Championships 1956, 1959, 1961, 1963, 1965; won National Team Championships 1950, 1959, 1960, 1961, 1964, Masters Pairs 1961. Co-author of *Zak-encyclopedie voor Bridgers.*

BOESGAARD, Knud-Aage, of Copenhagen, Denmark, accountant, born 1950; won European Jr. Open Teams 1970; Nordic Jr. Open Teams 1971, 1973. Represented Denmark in European Open Teams 1975. Won all three major Danish National titles (open teams open pairs and the cup) 1975.

BOGAERTS, Louis, of Antwerp, Belgium, business manager, born 1907; represented Belgium in European Championships 1954, 1955, 1957, World Pair Championship 1962; won Belgian Open Teams 1956, 1959. President Belgian BF 1960–66.

BOGAIR, Dr. Nahum, of Tel Aviv, Israel, pediatrician and lecturer, born in Palestine 1912; represented Israel European Championships 1965; won Tel Aviv Open Team 1964, second Israel Open Pairs 1965. President Israel Bridge Federation.

BOLAND, Corti, of Downsview, Ont., lawyer, born 1914; won Winter Nat'l Open Teams 1951, and various Canadian championships including Canadian Nat'l Open Teams 1955 and Canadian-American Open Teams 1959.

BOMBECK, F. Ayres (died 1969), of Kansas City, Mo; won Marcus 1948; second Spingold 1953, 1954, Marcus 1963, Fall Nat'l Open Pairs 1954, Masters Individual 1954, Spring Nat'l Men's Team 1962; won many regional championships.

BONDE, Count Carl, of Moerkoe, Sweden, landed estates owner, born 1897; npc Swedish Open Team and Women's Team on many occasions. President of Swedish Bridge League for many years until his resignation in 1965. President European Bridge League 1965–69; Vice-President from 1950–65. President World Bridge Federation 1968–1970.

BONNEY, C. Jack, of Armonk, N.Y., accountant and bridge teacher, born 1904; won Mid-Atlantic Fall Open Teams 1953. Former President Westchester Unit ACBL. Author of several bridge teaching handbooks.

BONNEY, Mrs. Mildred (formerly Mrs. M. Betzler), of Armonk, N.Y., bridge teacher, born 1917; second Spring Nat'l Women's pairs 1952; won Mid-Atlantic Fall Open Teams 1953, Eastern Women's Pairs 1959, New England Open Pairs 1973.

BONNEY, Norman F. (died 1945), of Boston, Mass.; won Eastern States Open Pairs 1931, 1939, Men's Pairs 1939. Credited with BONNEY'S SQUEEZE.

BONOMI, Robert F., of Memphis, Tenn., born 1918 in Gem, Idaho. Public Relations director of ACBL from Oct. 1973. Member, Public Relations Soc. of America; long experienced in P.R. and news organizations, including editor, Associated Press, 1947–48.

BONWIT, Helen, of New York, N.Y.; won Fall Nat'l Women's Pair 1934, second 1942; second Nat'l Mixed Teams 1936; won Eastern Mixed Teams 1937, 1938.

BOOKSTAVER, John D., of San Francisco, Calif., marketing manager, born 1942; winner of several regional events including New England Knockout Teams 1972.

BOONSUPA, Ananta, of Bangkok, Thailand, marketing manager, born 1934; represented Thailand World Championship 1966, 1967, World Team Olympiad 1968, Far East Championships 1962, 1965, 1966, 1969, 1970; Far East Champion 1965; won Thailand Master Individual 1960, Open Pairs 1961, Open Teams 1963, 1964, 1965, Mixed Pairs 1964.

BORAK, Bernard, of New York, N.Y., insurance salesman, born 1910; third Winter Nat'l Open Pairs and Teams 1949; won Eastern Open Pairs 1962, second 1952. Represented Czechoslovakia in prewar European championships.

BORIN, Jim, of Melbourne, Australia, bridge teacher and writer, born London 1935; represented Australia World Championship 1971, World Team Olympiad 1972; winner of Zone 7 Championships 1970, 1971, Australia Nat'l Individual 1974, Interstate Teams 1962, 1968, many other events.

BORIN, Norma, of Melbourne, Australia, bridge teacher and writer; represented Australia World

Championship 1971, World Team Olympiad 1972; won Zone 7 Championships 1970, 1971, Australian Interstate Teams 1968.

BORK, Harry, of Hamilton, Ont., business manager, born 1909; represented Canada World Team Olympiad 1960; second Fall Nat'l Senior Masters Individual 1951; won Canadian Nat'l Mixed Pairs 1960, Knockout Teams 1968.

BORRE, Joseph van den. See VAN DEN BORRE, JOSEPH.

BORSTIBER, Rudolf, of New York, N.Y.; won Vanderbilt 1957, Eastern States Men's Pairs 1965.

BOSCO, Jorge, of Buenos Aires, Argentina, lawyer, born 1920; represented Argentina World Championship 1961; won Argentine Open Team 1951, 1953, 1966.

BOSCOWITZ, H. Huber, of New York, N.Y., sales manager, born 1902; won AWL All-American Open Teams 1934, Summer Nat'l Mixed Teams 1932; second Vanderbilt 1935; awarded Wetzlar Trophy 1935. As ABL President in 1936, he was responsible for introducing the MASTER-POINT PLAN, which became the basis of the ACBL's subsequent prosperity.

BOULENGER, Jean-Michel, of Paris, France, born 1934; one of the leading French players; represented France World Olympiad 1964, World Championships 1967, 1969, European Championships 1963, 1965; European Champion 1966, 1970, runner-up 1967; winner of many French national championships.

BOURCHTOFF, Andrée (Mrs. Gérard), of Paris, born 1923; European Women's Champion 1953, 1954; represented France 1957, 1958; National wins include Women's Teams.

BOURCHTOFF, Gérard, of Paris, company director, born 1923; World Team Olympiad Champion 1960; second European Championship 1956, 1959, and also represented France 1952. National wins include Open Team six times, including the years 1960, 1962, 1964, Open Pairs 1959, and English Master Pairs 1960. President French Bridge Federation Tournament Committee.

BOWDEN, Mary (Mrs. A. W.), of Toronto, Ont.; qualified to represent Canada Women's Team World Olympiad 1964 but was prevented from playing; won Fall Nat'l Women's Team 1950, Summer Nat'l Women's Pairs 1963, Fall Nat'l Mixed Pairs 1956, second 1955; won Canadian Nat'l Mixed Pairs 1967.

BOWIE, Clagett, of Falls Church, Va., industrial mathematician, born 1907; winner of several region-al events including Keystone Conference Open Pairs 1955, Goldman Open Pairs 1970. Credited with queen-over-jack rubber bridge theory (see TWO-WAY FINESSE).

BOWMAN, John T., of Ottawa, Ontario, born 1947; winner of several regional events including Cambrian Shield Knockout Teams 1973.

BRACHMAN, Malcolm K., Dallas, Tex., insurance and oil executive, born 1926; second Spingold 1973; winner of many regional events including Central States Knockout Teams 1968, Bridge Week Knockout Teams 1969, 1970, Big D Knockout Teams 1974; Mexican Nationals Swiss Teams 1974.

BRACHMAN, Minda (Mrs. Malcolm K.), of Dallas, Tex., born 1931; won Summer Nat'l Masters Mixed Teams 1968; second Summer Nat'l Life Masters Pairs 1971; winner of many regional events including Central States Knockout Teams 1968, Bridge Week Knockout Teams 1969, 1970, 1974.

BRADLEY, Kenn, of Tulsa, Oklahoma, attorney, born 1933; winner of several regional events including Missouri Valley Masters Pairs 1973.

BRADY, Phil, of Philadelphia, Pa., computer programmer, born 1947; winner of several regional events including Tri-State Open Pairs 1970.

BRALL, Carlyn (Mrs. Ira), of New York, N.Y., editorial consultant, born 1911; won Winter Nat'l Women's Teams 1955 and 1958; won Keystone Mixed Pairs 1957, New York–New Jersey Women's Pairs 1959, Eastern States Mixed Teams 1955, 1968. Former editor of Greater New York BA's *Post-Mortem.*

BRALL, Ira (1895–1966), of New York, N.Y., printer; won Eastern States Mixed Teams 1955. Former President, Vice-President and Tournament Director for the Greater New York Bridge Association.

BRAMLEY, Bart, of Waltham, Mass., computer programmer, born 1948; won Spring Nat'l secondary Men's Swiss Teams 1973; Summer Nat'l secondary Open Pairs 1974, winner of several regional events including Tri-State Swiss Teams 1974.

BRANCO, Marcelo C., of Rio de Janeiro, Brazil, construction engineer and government official, born 1945; one of the leading South American players; represented Brazil World Championship 1969, 1973, 1974; South American Champion 1968, 1971, 1972, 1973; won Brazilian Open Teams 1967, 1968, 1969, 1973, 1974, Open Pairs 1972.

BRANCO, Pedro Paulo C. ("P. P."), of Rio de Janeiro, Brazil, insurance technician, born 1940; one of the leading South American players; represented Brazil World Championships 1973, 1974, World Team Olympiad 1972; South American Champion 1969, 1972, 1973; won Brazilian Open Teams 1967, 1972, 1973, Open Pairs 1969.

BRANNON, Robert M., of Charlotte, N.C., bridge writer, born in Georgia in 1882; author of many early books on contract including *The Incomparable Club Convention,* a book on the VANDERBILT SYSTEM, and *Foolproof Contract.* See BIBLIOGRAPHY, C, E.

BRASHLER, Ted, of Lockport, Ill.; tied first Spring Nat'l secondary Swiss Teams 1972; won Tri-Unit Knockout Teams 1971, Central States Swiss Teams 1973.

BRATCHER, Robert L., of Carlsbad, Calif., tournament director, born 1930; winner of several regional titles including Midwest Open Teams 1963, Mid-Atlantic Mixed Pairs 1963. Several ABA titles, including Nat'l Open Teams 1962.

BRAUNSTEIN, Maurice F., of Schenectady, N.Y., computer processing director, born 1914; regional wins include Canadian-American Open Team 1955, New England Open Team 1955. ACBL National Tournament Director since 1968. Originator of several duplicate movements, including stanza movement. Director at world championships since 1972.

BRAUNSTEIN, Marian (Mrs. Maurice), of Schenectady, N.Y., auditor, born 1917; won Summer Nat'l Non-Masters Teams 1956.

BRENNAN, Patrick J., Jr., of Chickasha, Okla., sales manager, born 1933; won Fall Nat'l Secondary Men's Pairs 1974; second Spingold 1972; winner of several regional events including Land Coronado Knockout Teams 1970.

BRENNER, James J., of Ft. Lauderdale, Fla., accountant; winner of several regional events including Florida Life Masters Pairs 1969.

BRICKLIN, Albert R., of Scottsdale, Ariz., automobile manufacturer, born 1913; won Fall Nat'l secondary Men's Swiss Teams 1972; winner of several regional events including Motor City Men's Pairs 1974.

BRIER, Barbara (Mrs. Jerry), of North Miami, Fla., bridge teacher, born 1923; one of the leading American women players; won World Olympiad Mixed Pairs 1970, Summer Nat'l Master Mixed Teams 1965, Marcus 1958, second Mixed Teams

1956, Fall Nat'l Open Pairs 1955, Mixed Pairs 1963, Spring Nat'l Women's Pairs 1971; winner of several regional events including Eastern States Knockout Teams 1973, 1974, Southeastern Open Teams 1958.

BRIGHT, Mary A., of Cambridge, Mass., editor and writer; winner of several regional events including Canadian-American Knockout Teams 1974. Editor, *New England Bridge Bulletin.*

BRIGHT, Mildred (Mrs. M., formerly Mrs. S. L. Cytron), of Highland, Ill., bridge teacher, born 1906; won Spring Nat'l Women's Team 1962; winner of several regional events between 1947 and 1965, including Central States Open Teams 1953, Mid-South Open Teams 1965.

BRIGHTLING, Richard J., Christchurch, New Zealand, bridge teacher, born 1949; represented New Zealand World Championship 1974, Far East Championship 1973; won New Zealand Open Teams 1972.

BROCH, José, of Argentina, leather goods manufacturer, born in Austria 1938; national wins include Open Teams 1959, 1962, Open Pairs 1966, 1971.

BRODY, Harvey D., of San Francisco, Calif., controller, born 1939; winner of several regional events including All-Western Open Pairs 1972, Life Master Board-a-Match Teams 1974.

BROGI, Giovan Battista, of Livorno, Italy, manager wholesale drug company, born 1920; won Belgian Open Team 1961; second European Championship 1962; represented Italy European Championship 1961; Italian Cup 1955, 1957, 1961, Italian Open Team 1961, with other national and local successes. Tournament director since 1961.

BROOKS, Dorsey W., of Warren, Mich., financial administrator, born 1926; won Summer Nat'l Leventritt Pairs 1970, second Mixed Teams 1971; winner of several regional events including All-American Open Teams 1968; Nat'l Intercollegiate Champion 1949.

BROOKS, Zerrene (Mrs. Dorsey), of Warren, Mich., bridge teacher and recreational consultant; second Summer Nat'l Mixed Teams 1971; won Motor City Swiss Teams 1970.

BROTMAN, Oscar, of Flushing, N.Y., controller, born 1904; won Spingold 1940; Eastern States Open Team 1946. As a partner of Alvin Roth, he contributed to the early development of the ROTH-STONE SYSTEM.

BROUTIN, Joseph, of Paris, grain broker, born 1887; European Champion 1935; winner of many national championships 1933–39 as a member of group which included Albarran, Aron, de Nexon, Tulumaris, and Venizelos.

BROWN, Claude R., of Malaysia, company director, born 1930; represented Malaysia Far East Championships 1966, 1968, 1970.

BROWN, Dudley B., of Grandview, Wash., army reserve technician, born 1935; winner of Spring Nat'l Early Risers Pairs 1974, several regional events including Inland Empire Swiss Teams 1973. President District 19.

BROWN, H. Sanborn, of Grosse Pointe Farms, Mich., architect, born 1906; second in De La Rue International Pair Championship, London, 1957; won Marcus 1949, Life Masters Pairs 1957, Midwest Spring Open Pairs 1956. President Michigan BA.

BROWN, John, of Grimsby, England, director of a Kenyan coffee plantation, born 1887. Author of *Winning Tricks* and the classic *Winning Defence* and many magazine articles. See BIBLIOGRAPHY, C, D.

BROWN, Phyllis (Mrs. Hugh) of Brisbane, Australia, born 1926; Far East Women's Champion 1974; won Australian Women's Pairs 1973, Interstate Women's Teams 1973.

BRUCE, David (formerly Burnstine) (1900–1965), of Los Angeles, Calif. Leading player and tournament winner of the early 1930s; hence he became Life Master No. 1 when that category was inaugurated in 1936. He headed a group of players that made the Contract Bridge Club in New York the center of the most expert game of the times; he introduced the artificial two club opening bid to show a strong hand (including A K, A K, A) with other two bids not game-forcing—a method which became the most widely used among leading experts of the day, and later developed into the cornerstone of ACOL. He played as the partner of Oswald JACOBY and later of Howard SCHENKEN as a member of the first of the outstanding contract teams, the FOUR HORSEMEN, captained by P. Hal SIMS, and was author of the first book on that team's system (*Four Horsemen's One Over One*, 1932). In 1933, with Schenken, Jacoby, and R. L. FREY, joined shortly afterward by M. T. GOTTLIEB, he organized the FOUR ACES, the team that took the leadership in the field and held it, with several amendments in personnel, for the next decade. (Co-author with his teammates of *Four Aces System of Contract Bridge*, 1935. See BIBLIOGRAPHY, C.) In a brief interlude between the Four Horsemen and the Four Aces, Burnstine helped to organize and played as a member of the BID-RITE TEAM.

An all-around star, Burnstine's teammates were inclined to rate him as the best bidder in the game. Brashly self-confident, Burnstine frequently locked horns with Culbertson in duels of strategy and

repartee, and rarely came out second best. His impressive tournament record included a victory in the first official World Championship in 1935 and wins in the following National championships: AWL All-American Open Teams 1932; USBA Open Teams 1934, 1937, Open Pairs 1936; ABL Asbury Challenge Teams 1931, 1933, 1937; Spingold 1934, 1936, 1938; Vanderbilt 1931, 1934, 1935, 1937, 1938; Mixed Teams 1931, 1933; Master Pairs 1931, 1933, 1936; Men's Pairs 1934; Masters Individual 1933; Reisinger 1931–34.

BRUN, Johannes, of Oslo, Norway, army officer and bridge writer, born 1891; won most distinguished player award of the International Bridge League 1934; third European Championship 1932, 1933; second Open Pairs 1933. Co-founder European Bridge League 1932, director 1932–47; President International Bridge League 1938; Honorary Member European Bridge League 1947. Bridge editor *Aftenposten*, and contributor to several bridge publications.

BUCHMEIER, Horst, of Vienna, Austria, public relations manager. Represented Austria World Team Olympiad 1972, World Pair Olympiad 1970, 1974. Tournament successes include many Austrian titles.

BUCKMAN, Kate, of Toronto, Ont., bridge teacher, club owner. Honorary Member ACBL 1973. Introduced duplicate to Vancouver in 1951. Operates a duplicate and rubber bridge club in Toronto which teaches 300 to 350 students each year.

BUDIN, Barnett, of Philadelphia, Pa., printer, died 1964; ACBL Director 1963–64; Past President of Keystone Conference and Philadelphia Unit; co-author of *Bridge Players Digest of Conventions* (see BIBLIOGRAPHY, C).

BUFILL, Rafael, of Barcelona, Spain, engineer, born 1926; represented Spain World Team Olympiad 1964, European Championship 1967, npc European Women's Team Championship 1965; member of National Spanish Team, with national successes in Open Teams and Pair events.

BULLER, Lt. Col. Walter, of London (1887–1938); author, and a leading personality in British bridge in the thirties. Won first English National Pairs 1932; organized the first ANGLO-AMERICAN MATCH, 1930, and captained the English team. The leading protagonist of "British Bridge" or direct methods of bidding without conventional forcing bids. Bridge columnist and author of a number of books, including *Reflections of a Bridge Player*, and *From Auction to Contract*. See BIBLIOGRAPHY, E.

BURGER, C. F. (Chuck), of Oak Park, Mich., attorney, born 1936; one of the leading American players; represented US World Pair Olympiad 1970; won Blue Ribbon 1970, Life Masters Men's Pairs 1969, Spring Nat'l Masters Men's Teams 1969, second Summer Nat'l Masters Pairs 1969, 1973. Co-winner, with Ira Rubin, of Lou HERMAN TROPHY 1970. Winner of many regional titles, including Eastern States Open Pairs 1968, Southeastern Knockout Teams 1969, Central States Knockout Teams 1971.

BURKA, Paul J., of Austin, Texas, attorney; won Fall National secondary Open Pairs 1970; Texas Fall Masters Pairs, Men's Pairs 1973.

BURNHAM, Dr. Charles J., of Birmingham, Ala., ophthalmologist, born 1919; won Spring Nat'l Open Teams 1960; regional wins include Southern Conference Open Pairs, Men's Pairs 1962, Mid-South Open Teams 1974. Former President Alabama BA and Southern Conference.

BURNS, Edward, of Minneapolis, Minn., born 1906; represented US World Championship 1937; second Grand Nat'l Open Team 1936; won Fall Nat'l Men's Teams 1950, Masters Individual 1954; second Spingold 1953, 1954, Fall Nat'l Men's Pairs 1951.

BURNS, N. M., deceased; formerly of Toronto, Ont., salesman, born 1909; npc Canadian Team Olympiad 1960; won Canadian-American Mixed pairs 1958, Canadian National Mixed Pairs 1955, 1958. President Ontario Unit 1961–62.

BURNSTEIN, Anne (Mrs. Robert), of Las Vegas, Nev., one of the leading women players on the West Coast; won Life Masters Women's Pairs 1963, Fall Nat'l Women's Pairs 1951, 1962, Summer Nat'l Mixed Team 1952, 1953, Mixed Pairs 1946, 1952; second Life Masters Women's Pairs 1962, Fall Nat'l Women's Team 1955; regional wins include Desert Empire Open Team 1963, Southeastern Women's Team 1953, 1955, 1956, Women's Pairs 1951, and others. Sister of Mrs. Edith KEMP and William SEAMON.

BURNSTINE, David. See BRUCE, DAVID.

BURSTEIN, Frank, of Springfield, N.J., real estate investment business, born 1933; won Tri-State Regional Open Teams 1967, Keystone Conference Open Teams 1968 (tied); Fall Nat'l Men's Swiss Teams 1975; tied second, Summer Nat'l Swiss Teams 1975.

BUSSEY, Thomas E., of Vancouver, Wash., personnel director, born 1918; won Spring Nat'l Men's Teams 1967, Northern Rocky Mountain Open Pairs 1962. Former President Western Conference.

BUSTROS, Fady, of Beirut, Lebanon, newspaper manager and bridge columnist, born 1905; represented Lebanon World Team Olympiad 1960, 1964, European Championships 1954, 1956, 1957, 1961, 1962; national successes include Open Teams and Open Pairs, each six times.

BUTCHER, Harry C., of Santa Barbara, Calif., radio executive and naval captain, born 1901; acted as naval aide to General EISENHOWER 1942–45, and in that capacity made a fourth in several bridge games with the general.

BUTCHER, Thomas D., of Tokyo, Japan, English teacher, born 1932; represented Japan Far East Championships 1962, 1963, 1965, 1967; won Far East Open Pairs 1964; national wins include Knockout Teams, three times; Teams-of-Four, twice; Round Robin Teams; Open Pairs. Former Editor of the JCBL *Bulletin,* 1965–67; bridge columnist for the *Mainichi Daily News* since 1965.

BUTCHER, William, of Hartford, Conn., born 1918; won New England Knockout Teams 1960; Masters Teams 1967; winner of several regional events including Southeastern Open Teams 1974, Life Masters Pairs 1974.

BUTKOW, Hyman, of Johannesburg, South Africa, accountant, born 1927; represented South Africa World Team Olympiad 1968, 1972; won South African Open Pairs 1965, 1967, Open Teams 1971, 1972.

BUTLER, Geoffrey L., of London, England, journalist, born 1898; one of the leading personalities in the bridge world. Executive Member of World Bridge Federation and European Bridge League; Chairman British Bridge League, Vice-President English Bridge Union, and chairman of several of their committees; represented European Bridge League and Portland Club in preparation of 1963 Codes of Laws. Co-author of *Two Clubs System of Bidding.* Contributing editor to *Bridge Encyclopedia.* See BIBLIOGRAPHY, C; also BUENOS AIRES AFFAIR.

BUTLER, Dr. J., of Cardiff, Wales, physician, born 1921; won Welsh Open Teams three times, Master Pairs and Open Pairs twice. President Welsh Bridge Union 1963–64 and Vice-Chairman British BL.

C

CABANNE, Carlos, of Buenos Aires, Argentina, dentist, born 1917; a leading South American player; represented Argentina World Team Olympiad 1964, 1968, 1972, World Championship 1958, 1962, 1965, npc 1961; South American Champion 1948, 1950, 1953, 1954, 1957, 1959, 1961, 1962, 1964; won Argentine Open Teams 1945, 1946, 1949, 1961, 1963, 1965, 1967, 1971, Open Pairs 1948, 1953, 1956. President Argentine Bridge Association 1959–1963; Delegate World Bridge Federation 1961, 1962, 1964, South American Confederation 1949, 1950, 1951, 1956, 1957, 1959, 1961. Author of *Bridge Razonado para Principiantes,* 1968. Member Advisory Board *Bridge Encyclopedia.*

CABOT, Antonio, of Barcelona, Spain, industrialist, born 1933; represented Spain World Team Olympiad 1960, 1964, World Pairs Olympiad 1962, European Championships 1959, 1963.

CABRAL, Francisco Costa, of Lisbon, Portugal, technician, born 1943; represented Portuguese European Championships 1971; national wins include Open Teams twice.

CACHO, José Antonio, of Rizal, Philippines, born 1923; represented Philippines World Team Olympiad 1964, Far East Championships 1960; Director Philippine Contract Bridge League 1950–67.

CACHO, Maxine Carmelo (Mrs. José A.), of Rizal, Philippines, born 1922; won Far East Women's Championship 1967, Hong Kong–Manila Interport Tournament 1960. Secretary Philippines Contract Bridge League 1961–64.

CAHN-SPEYER, Aton, of Bogotá, Colombia, public accountant, born 1918 in Vienna, Austria; resident of Bogotá since 1938; represented Colombia South American Championships 1963, 1964, 1966, 1968, Caribbean Championships 1964, 1966; Caribbean Champion 1968; National successes include Open Teams 1962, 1964, 1965, 1966, 1967, Masters Pairs 1967, 1968, Open Pairs 1964.

CAIN, Joseph E. (1903–1963), of Indianapolis, Ind., company director; won Chicago 1935; All-American Open Team 1941, 1942, Central States Open Team 1943, Midwest Men's Pairs 1945, Western States Open Team 1944. He died in a plane crash in Florida on his way to the funeral of his regular bridge partner, Edson T. Wood, Jr.

CALBETO, Maria Rosa Ferrer de, of Barcelona, Spain; represented Spain European Championship 1974, many other international events.

CALDWELL, George A., of Providence, R.I., bridge teacher, club operator; won Canadian-Atlantic Open Pairs 1969, 1974, Knockout Teams 1971.

CALE, Helen, of Glendale, Calif., bridge teacher and writer, born 1912; won Nat'l Mixed Team 1949,

1950, second Fall Nat'l Mixed Pairs 1957; regional wins include Bridge Week Open Team 1948, Women's Pairs 1954, Master Women's Pairs 1971. President ACBL Western Division 1950; Chairman Los Angeles Unit, and other executive positions.

CALHEIROS, Francisco, of Lisbon, Portugal, economist, born 1929; former President Portuguese BF; represented Portugal European Championships 1967, 1971; national wins include Open Teams three times, Open Pairs twice.

CALLAHAM, Thomas M., of Covington, Va., pharmacist, born 1934; won several regional titles, including Mid-Atlantic Fall Masters Pairs 1970, Swiss Teams 1972, tied Spring Swiss Teams 1972.

CALVENTE, Ricardo, formerly of Buenos Aires, Argentina, industrialist, born 1918; represented Argentina World Championship 1958, 1959, 1961, 1962, 1963; South American Champion 1959, 1961; won Argentine Open Teams 1958, 1960, 1961, 1964, Open Pairs 1962, 1967.

CAMARA, Helen (Mrs. C. M., "Niny"), of Cairo, Egypt, born 1907 in Greece; World Women's Team Champion 1960; represented Egypt World Women's Team Olympiad 1964, Women's Team European Championship 1949, 1961, and Open Team 1956. National successes include Open Team 1937, 1946, 1950, 1953, 1959; Inter-Club Championships 1931, 1934, 1947; Mixed Teams 1959, 1960, 1961. Contributor to various bridge periodicals.

CAMPBELL, William C., of Harvard, Mass., born 1905; won American Bridge Olympic 1932, and played unofficial matches against English teams.

CANSINO, Jonathan, of London, England, stockbroker, born 1939; one of Europe's foremost players; represented Great Britain European Championships 1965, 1970, England in Camrose Trophy matches 1964, 1965; won Gold Cup 1965. National Pairs 1964, English Bridge Union Crockford's Cup 1964, 1966, 1968, 1972, Life Masters Pairs 1966, 1971.

CANTOR, Augusta, of New York, N.Y.; winner of several regional titles including Tri-State Masters Pairs 1972, Eastern States Masters Pairs 1963.

CAPPELLETTI, A. Michael, of Alexandria, Va., lawyer, born 1938; one of the leading players of the East Coast; won Summer Nat'l Mixed Teams 1967, Fall Nat'l secondary Open Teams 1970; second Blue Ribbon Pairs 1973, Fall Nat'l Mixed Pairs 1967; winner of many regional titles, including New England Knockout Teams 1965, Mid-Atlantic Open Teams 1967, 1970, Knockout Teams 1972.

CAPPELLETTI, Katherine H. (Mrs. A. Michael), of Alexandria, Va., born 1942; one of the leading women players of the East Coast; won Summer Nat'l Mixed Teams 1967, Fall Nat'l secondary Open Teams 1970; second Blue Ribbon Pairs 1973, Fall Nat'l Mixed Pairs 1967; won Keystone Open Teams 1966, Mid-Atlantic Open Teams 1967, 1970, Knockout Teams 1972.

CARAVELLI, Gerald A., of Des Plaines, Ill., financial analyst, born 1943; one of the leading players of the Middle West; won Fall Nat'l Mixed Pairs 1974, Summer Nat'l Mixed Teams 1975, Spring Nat'l secondary Open Teams 1974; second Summer Nat'l Senior & Advanced Senior Masters Pairs 1964, Spring Nat'l Men's Teams 1971; winner of numerous regional titles including Great Lakes Open Pairs 1968, 1971, Central States Knockout Teams 1969, 1972, 1973.

CARINI-MAZZACCARA, Marchese Silvio, of Florence, Italy, win industry executive, born 1907. Member of the Executive Committees of the European Bridge League, World Bridge Federation, Federazione Italiana Bridge. Contributor to *Bridge d'Italia*. Member of Editorial Advisory Board of the *Bridge Encyclopedia*.

CARLAFTIS, George M., of Greece, civil engineer, born 1937; one of the outstanding players of Greece; represented Greece European Championships 1967, 1969, 1970, 1971; won National Teams 1966 and 1968–74, National Open Pairs 1965, 1969, 1970; many other national successes.

CARLIN, John, of Chicago, Ill., died 1954; won Fall Nat'l Men's Team 1950; regional wins included Central States Open Team 1949, Midwest Spring Open Team 1951.

CARLSON, Mrs. E. N., of Webster Groves, Mo., bridge teacher, cruise conductor, club director; one of the early pioneers of bridge in the St. Louis area. Helped organize the St. Louis Unit in the thirties and the St. Louis Women's Bridge League, of which she has been President since 1939. Former President St. Louis Unit; former member ACBL Board of Directors, Good Will Committee, and Charity Committee.

CARMENA, Judy (Mrs. Thomas N.), of Las Vegas, Nev.; won Fall Nat'l Charity Pairs 1969, second Senior & Advanced Senior Masters Pairs 1969.

CARNEY, Mrs. Jean, of Chicago, Ill., bridge teacher; won Fall Nat'l secondary Swiss Teams 1970; winner of several regional titles, including Desert Empire Open Teams 1968, Women's Pairs 1972.

CARPENTER, Frederic, of Berkeley, Calif., writer, born 1903; won Northern Rocky Mountain Men's

Pairs 1956, Open Pairs 1958, All-Western Mixed Teams 1956; many other regional successes.

CARR, Mrs. A. N., of Birmingham, England, died 1959; European Women's Champion 1950; English successes included Women's Teams Championship.

CARROLL, Judith (Mrs. Gilbert), of Livingston, N.J., born 1941; regional wins include Mid-Atlantic Summer Women's Pairs 1964, Keystone Women's Teams 1974.

CARRUTHERS, John G., of Toronto, Ont., systems analyst; won Motor City Open Pairs 1972, Buffalo Centennial Open Pairs 1974; Canadian Nat'l Swiss Teams 1973.

CARSON, Mike, of Fort Lauderdale, Fla.; won Southeastern Men's Teams 1970, Life Masters Pairs 1971, 1972.

CARSTENSEN, Svend, of Copenhagen, Denmark, bridge writer and editor, born 1908. Pioneered electronic computer scoring system, and founded one of the biggest pair tournaments in the world. Bridge editor *Berlingske Tidende* 1946–69. Co-founder of IBPA.

CARTER, David C., of St. Louis, Mo., building and loan executive, born 1906; one of the leading bridge players of the Middle West; alternate for the 1963 North American World Championship Team; won Mc Kenney 1954, Life Masters Pairs 1954, Fall Nat'l Men's Team 1950, Men's Pairs 1957; second Spingold 1953, 1962, Marcus 1963, Fall Nat'l Open Pairs 1946, 1953, 1954; Men's Pairs 1960; numerous regional successes include All-American Open Pairs 1945, 1956, Men's Pairs 1954, Mississippi Valley Open Team 1955, 1963, Open Pairs 1952, 1953, Men's Pairs 1958, 1967, 1973, Mixed Pairs 1963, Masters Pairs 1967, Missouri Valley Open Team 1954, 1955, Open Pairs 1965, Men's Pairs 1959. President Missouri Valley Conference, Vice-President Midwest Conference. Originator of transfer bids in the form now known as SOUTH AFRICAN TEXAS (see also TEXAS). He also originated the double-barreled variety of TWO-WAY STAYMAN, in which two clubs is a one-round force, and two diamonds is forcing to game.

CARTER, Frances (Mrs. David C.), of St. Louis, Mo., born 1910; second Fall Nat'l Open Pairs 1946, Mixed Pairs 1957; regional successes include Mississippi Valley Women's Pairs 1954, 1960, Missouri Valley Open Teams 1954, 1955, Mid-South Spring Open Teams 1959.

CARTER, Jack, of Cardiff, Wales, local government official, born 1904; won six Welsh Open Team championships and three Mixed Team championships; represented Wales on many occasions; helped to found the Welsh Bridge Association (later Union) in 1933, and acted as its Honorary Secretary and Tournament Manager 1944–48.

CARTER, Kay, of Seminole, Fla., insurance executive, born 1921; started bridge at age of seven; second Summer Nat'l Women's Pairs 1962, Spring Nat'l Mixed Pairs 1965; regional wins include Keystone Mixed Pairs 1963.

CARTER, Richard M., of Port Charlotte, Fla., insurance executive, born 1909; winner of several regional titles including Midwest Open Teams 1954, 1964, 1971, Open Pairs 1954, 1964. Formerly member of ACBL Board of Directors and President of Midwest BC and Louisville BA, and many other executive positions.

CARTWRIGHT, George H. ("Duke"), of Toronto, Ont., teacher of commercial subjects, born 1906. ACBL Associate National Tournament Director.

CASABAL, León (1892–1965), of Buenos Aires, Argentina; pioneer of Argentine bridge; bridge columnist for *La Nación* in the early 1930s; participated in a radio match against Culbertson's team in 1936. Author of *Bridge de Hoy, 1930.*

CASEMENT, Robert, of Chicago, Ill., won Central States Life and Senior Masters Team 1961, Midwest Fall Open Team 1959; former editor of *The Kibitzer,* published by the Chicago Unit.

CASH, Ralph A., of Phoenix, Ariz., insurance agent, born 1904; one of the leading players of the Southwest; US winner World Olympic 1936; many regional successes including Desert Empire Open Team 1959, 1962, 1966, Knockout Teams 1967, Men's Pairs 1956, 1958, Spring Swiss Teams 1971. Many executive positions include former President of Western Division 1954, member of Nat'l Executive Committee and Western Conference Executive Committee, Chairman of Phoenix Unit, and General Chairman of Nat'l Fall Championships in Phoenix 1962.

CASNER, Ambrose (1903–1972), of New York, N.Y., greeting card manufacturer; won Fall Nat'l Open Pairs 1944; second Life Masters Pairs 1944, Summer Nat'l Men's Pairs 1944, Fall Nat'l Open Team 1945, Vanderbilt 1948, Spingold 1951, 1954; won Eastern States Open Pairs 1946, Reisinger 1951, Mixed Pairs 1945, Southeastern Men's Pairs 1956.

CASSON, Milton B., of Brookline, Mass., hotel supplier, born 1902; won New England Knockout Teams 1943, 1945, 1946 (twice), 1947, 1950, 1955, Mixed Teams 1945, Open Pairs 1932, 1942, 1950, Men's Pairs 1952, Mixed Pairs 1940, 1945.

CASTRO, Alejandro, of Lima, Peru, formerly of Argentina, merchant, born 1916; represented Argentina World Championship 1958, 1959, 1961; South American Champion 1948, 1953, 1954, 1957, 1958; many times winner in all Argentine events. Former Secretary of South American Bridge Federation, and member of World Bridge Federation Executive Committee.

CATON, Don J., of Pensacola, Fla., attorney, born 1941; first Spring Nat'l secondary Swiss Teams 1971; won Mid-South Open Pairs 1970, 1973, Men's Pairs 1970, 1971.

CATS, Martijn, of Amsterdam, Holland, shirtmaker, born 1915; represented Netherlands World Team Olympiad 1960, European Championship 1949, 1950, 1951, 1952, 1954, 1955, 1956, 1957, 1958, 1961, 1963, 1966, 1967; national successes include Open Pairs 1949, 1952, 1954, 1955, 1962, and Open Team 1947, 1950, 1951, 1952, 1953, 1954, 1955.

CATZEFLIS, Georges, of Lausanne, Switzerland, engineer, born 1931; represented Switzerland World Team Olympiad 1964, 1968, World Pairs Olympiad 1962, 1966, European Championships 1965; national titles include Masters Pairs 1963, 1964, 1965.

CAVENDISH, pseudonym of Henry Jones (1831–1899), a famous London whist authority. It was the name of the club to which he belonged, and the name he chose under which to publish his first book on whist in 1863. This book, *The Principles of Whist Stated and Explained, and Its Practice Illustrated on an Original System, by Means of Hands Played Completely Through,* became the most popular guide to the game of whist since Hoyle's *Short Treatise. Principles of Whist* went through many editions and revisions, incorporating Jones's latest and best theories. He was the author of a number of other books on whist, among them, *Whist Developments, American Leads, and the Plain-Suit Echo,* 1885, and *American Leads Simplified,* 1891. With N. B. Trist he developed the system of whist play named by him the "American Leads," which encountered rather violent opposition in some quarters, but nevertheless enjoyed great popularity in England, and even greater in America. Jones made a tour of America in 1893 during which he attended the third Annual Congress of the American Whist League, of which he was an honorary member. See BIBLIOGRAPHY, A.

CAYLEY, Henry Francis (Frank), of Sydney, Australia, author, historian, broadcaster, bridge writer and teacher, born 1910; npc Australia World Team Olympiad 1968; won Australian Par Championships, 1940, 1948, Australasian Par Point Championships 1953, 1958; fourth World Par Contest 1951. National victories include Open Teams 1964, 1965, 1967, Open Pairs 1959, 1967, Individual 1971. Conductor of bridge cruises to US and Europe. Former Chairman Australian Bridge Federation.

Former President New South Wales Bridge Association. Author of *Modern Contract Bridge, Contract Bridge—Bidding.*

CAYNE, James, of New York, N.Y., investment banker, born 1934; represented US World Pair Olympiad 1970; won Fall Nat'l Life Master Men's Pairs 1969, Spring Nat'l Men's Teams 1969, Summer Nat'l Masters Mixed Teams 1966; second Life Masters Pairs 1969, 1973; winner of many regional titles including Central States Life Masters Pairs 1963, Eastern States Open Pairs 1968, Metropolitan Knockout Teams 1974.

CEDERBORG, Warren J., of Hayward, Calif., teacher and writer, born 1945; winner of many regional titles since 1970, including Golden State Knockout Teams 1970, Men's Pairs 1971, Golden Gate Knockout Teams 1973.

CHAGAS, Gabriel P., of São Paulo, Brazil, commodity trading executive, born 1944; one of the leading South American players and personalities, generally considered to be South America's top player; winner of nine South American Championships 1967–75, many Brazilian Championships; represented Brazil in five World Championships, two World Team Olympiads and two World Pair Olympiads.

CHAIT, Gene, of Chicago, Ill., won Summer Nat'l President's Cup 1965, many regional titles including Gopher Open Teams, Open Pairs 1973, Masters Pairs 1974.

CHAMBERS, Neil, of Seattle, Wash., winner of many regional events including Inland Empire Knockout Teams 1970, Mid-Winter Holiday Knockout Teams 1971, British Columbia Knockout Teams 1972.

CHAN, Hin Cheung, of Malaysia, company director, born 1918; represented Malaysia Far East Championships 1963, 1965, 1966, 1968, 1970, 1972, 1973, 1974.

CHANG, Godfrey, of Honolulu, Haw., won Hawaii Men's Pairs 1969, Mixed Pairs 1972, Masters Pairs 1973.

CHANG, Morris, of Dallas, Texas, winner of several regional events including Big D Open Teams 1974, Masters Pairs 1972.

CHARUSORN, Dr. Thon, of Bangkok, Thailand, physician, born 1916; represented Thailand World Olympiad 1964.

CHATKIN, Robert T., deceased; formerly of Los Angeles, Calif., and of Brooklyn, N.Y., born 1891;

won Summer Nat'l Mixed Teams 1939, Eastern Open Pairs 1938; second Summer Nat'l Masters Individual 1944.

CHAZEN, Bernard (Bernie), of San Bruno, Calif., systems analyst, born 1942; won Spring Nat'l Men's Teams 1971, Fall Nat'l Mixed Pairs 1973, secondary Mixed Pairs 1974; winner of many regional titles, including Keystone Open Teams 1967, New England Master Men's Pairs 1968, Canadian National Open Teams 1969, Tri-State Open Teams 1971.

CHEATWOOD, F. D., of Oklahoma City, Okla., traffic manager, born 1913; won Rocky Mountain Masters Pairs 1952, Missouri Valley Open Pairs 1959, Texas Conference Mixed Pairs 1956, Masters Pairs 1954. One of the pioneers of bridge organization in Oklahoma. President Missouri Valley Regional; member Nat'l Goodwill Committee.

CHENG, Conrad K., of Hsinchu, Taiwan, trader, bridge writer, and teacher, born 1934; second World Championship 1970, represented China Far East Championship, 1961, 1962, 1965, 1966. Writings include *Modern Systems and Theory of Bidding* in Chinese.

CHERNOFF, Victor B., of Brentwood, Calif., actuary, born 1937; winner of several regional events, including Eastern States Open Pairs 1970, Keystone Open Pairs 1971, Mid-Atlantic Swiss Teams 1973.

CHIARADIA, Eugenio, of São Paulo, Brazil, professor of philosophy, born 1911; one of the world's great players; World Champion 1957, 1958, 1959, 1961, 1962, 1963; represented Italy World Team Olympiad 1960; European Champion 1951, 1956, 1957, 1958, 1959, second 1952, 1955, 1963; national successes include Italian Open Team 1951, 1956, 1957, 1959, 1963. Co-author of *Fiori Napolitano.* Coach to Brazilian national team.

CHILCOTE, Mary (Mrs. William), of Cleveland, Ohio, born 1926; won Fall Nat'l secondary Swiss Teams 1970, Spring Nat'l secondary Mixed Pairs 1973, second Fall Nat'l Mixed pairs 1970; winner of several regional titles including Las Vegas Knockout Teams 1971, Navajo Trail Open Teams 1973.

CHODZIESNER, Fritz, of Berlin, Germany, lawyer, born 1906; represented Germany in World Team Olympiad 1960, 1964, European Championships 1958, 1959, 1961, 1966, 1967, with many successes in Uruguay and Germany.

CHOUCRY, Mrs. Aida, of Cairo, Egypt, born 1922; World Women's Team Champion 1960; represented Egypt World Women's Team Olympiad 1964. National wins include Mixed Pairs 1959.

CHRISTIAN, Col. William, US Army, ret., of Metairie, La., born 1915; formerly one of the leading players of the East Coast; won Spingold 1946, Summer Nat'l Men's Pairs 1960; runner-up for McKenney 1948, Fall Nat'l Life Master Men's Pairs 1964; many regional successes including Bridge Week Knockout Teams 1974, New England Masters Teams 1965, Mid-South Spring Open Teams 1968, Missouri Valley Master's Pairs 1973.

CHRISTIANSEN, Leif, of Nordstradshogda, Norway, actuary and bridge columnist, born 1914; represented Norway European Championships 1938, 1939, 1948, 1951, 1952, 1955, 1956; Scandinavian Champion 1946, 1949; national successes include Open Teams 1938, 1942, 1947, 1949, 1951, 1952, Open Pairs 1946, 1956.

CHRISTOPHER, Jean (Mrs. Frank), of Forest Park, Ill.; won Fall Nat'l secondary Women's Pairs 1973, tied second Spring Nat'l Women's Teams 1973, tied first Central States Open Teams 1969.

CHU, Y. M., of Hong Kong, businessman, born 1922; Far East Champion 1959, second 1963, 1965, 1969; represented Hong Kong Far East Championships on other occasions; national wins include Master Teams 1960, 1963, 1968, Open Teams 1958, 1962, 1969, 1970, Master Pairs 1959, Open Individual 1958.

CHUA, Stephen, of Rizal, Philippines, businessman, born 1919; represented Philippines World Team Olympiad 1960, 1964; captain National team 1957, 1963; Far East Champion 1957, 1958; leading master point holder since 1955, and winner of many national titles.

CHURCHILL, S. Garton, of Great Neck, N.Y., attorney. One of the leading American bridge players and personalities. Won Life Master Pairs 1937 and 1948, setting two records on the second occasion in partnership with Cecil HEAD; they scored 65½% as an average of four sessions, and 77.4% in a single session. (The latter record was beaten in 1963, when Eric MURRAY and Mrs. Agnes GORDON recorded 78% in the final session of the Nat'l Mixed Pairs.) Won Chicago 1932, second 1933, 1939, 1941, 1942; second Summer Nat'l Mixed Teams 1937; Asbury Challenge Teams 1931. Many regional successes include Eastern States Knockout Teams 1937, 1938, 1939. Originator of the CHURCHILL SYSTEM. His many original theoretical ideas were set out in *Contract Bidding Tactics at Match-Point Play* (see BIBLIOGRAPHY, C).

CHURCHILL, Sir Winston (1874–1965). The great British war leader and historian played bridge in his younger days although it is doubtful whether he ever played contract. According to historian A. J. P. Taylor's biography of Lord Beaverbrook, "Aitken (Max Aitken, later Lord Beaverbrook) . . . went to Admiralty House with Smith (F. E. Smith, later

Lord Birkenhead). There they found Churchill with two Liberal friends. While waiting for news and for the Liberals to go away, four of them played bridge—seemingly a universal habit among politicians at this time. Aitken, as usual, was the odd man out. A dispatch box was brought in. It contained the news that Germany had declared war on Russia. Churchill . . . went off to mobilize the fleet. Aitken took over Churchill's partly played hand, finding himself 'in an extremely unfavorable tactical position.' Smith and Aitken remained at Admiralty House until it was almost morning, but Churchill did not return."

This was perhaps comparable to an episode in English history several centuries earlier, although Churchill did not follow the example of Sir Francis Drake in 1588: On hearing of the approach of the Spanish Armada, Drake, in no rush to interrupt his game, announced, "We can finish the rubber and beat the Spaniards too." However, the rubber that Drake was playing was not bridge but bowls. See POLITICIANS.

CINTRA, Gabino, of Rio de Janeiro, Brazil, exchange operations manager, born 1942. South American Champion 1970, 1972, 1973, Brazilian Champion 1970, 1972, 1973, 1974; represented Brazil World Championships 1971, 1973, 1974. Married to Lia B. CINTRA, the former Lia Penna, who in 1972 and 1973 won the South American Women's Championships while he won the open event.

CINTRA, Lia B. (Mrs. Gabino), of Rio de Janeiro, Brazil; South American Women's Champion 1971, 1972, 1973.

CIOCON, Manuel R., of Quezon City, Philippines, born 1922; represented Philippines Far East Championships 1963, 1965; member Interport Team to Taipei 1962.

CLARK, Douglas H., of Kingston, Ont., realtor, born 1930; winner of several regional events, including Canadian-American Knockout Teams 1973, Open Teams 1974.

CLARK, Ralph D., of Santa Monica, Calif., computer programmer, born 1938; won Fall Nat'l Comm. & Ind. Pairs 1959, Mid-Atlantic Summer Open Teams 1966, Pacific Southwest Masters Pairs 1968.

CLARKE, Gale (Mrs. Harry), of McLean, Va., bridge teacher; won Spring Nat'l Women's Pairs 1969, represented United States World Women's Pair Olympiad 1970.

CLARKE, Truesdale, of Rochester, N.Y., attorney, born 1905; won Canadian-American Open Pairs 1953, Open Team 1958, Men's Pairs 1953, Upper New York State Men's Pairs 1973.

CLARREN, David, of Minneapolis, Minn., bridge teacher; won Vanderbilt 1947; second Spingold 1949, 1953; winner of many regional events including Central States Open Team 1944, Gopher Open Team 1958, 1963, 1967, Knockout Teams 1967, 1971.

CLAY, James, of London (1805–73), the leading English whist authority between Hoyle and Cavendish. His chief work was *Treatise on the Game of Whist* (1864).

CLAYTON, Sir Hugh Byard, born in Queensland 1877, died in India 1947, one of the inventors of S.A.C.C., the initials of the four players living in India who developed this earlier prototype of Plafond about 1912. He served in the Intelligence Department, 1914–18, during the First World War; was Commissioner of Bombay 1919–28; knighted, 1938.

CLIFF, David L., of Basking Ridge, N.J., school teacher and principal, born 1932; winner of several regional events including New England Masters Teams 1956, Open Pairs 1960, Knockout Teams 1961.

CLINKINBEARD, Helen (Mrs. J. E.), of Knoxville, Tenn., born 1919; winner of several regional titles including Midwest Open Teams 1971, Mid-Atlantic Summer Open Pairs 1960, Masters Pairs 1960. Former President Tennessee Valley Unit 1962.

CLOWES, Barrington M., of Newport, Wales, textile technologist, born 1926; represented Wales Camrose Trophy matches ten times; National titles include International Masters Pairs twice, National Pairs, and Welsh Cup.

COFFIN, George S., of Waltham, Mass., author, publisher, and distributor of bridge books and supplies, born 1903. Won *The Bridge World* international problem-solving contest 1930. His principal bridge books include: *Endplays, Acol and the New Point Count, Bridge Play from A to Z,* and *Sure Tricks.* Author also of many volumes on games other than bridge (poker, pinochle, cribbage, etc.). Coffin's other important roles include: co-founder of ABTA and first editor of its quarterly magazine; development of THREE-HANDED BRIDGE; publisher of many bridge books, including Beynon's *Bridge Director's Manual,* as well as American publisher of British writers; creator of many items of bridge equipment; author of magazine and newspaper articles. Contributing Editor, *Bridge Encyclopedia.* See BIBLIOGRAPHY, C, D, E.

COHAN, Joseph (1908–1958), businessman of Wooster, Ohio, born in Canada; second Fall Nat'l Men's Team 1947, 1949; won All-American Men's

Pairs 1953, Mid-West Spring Mixed Pairs 1949, Mississippi Valley Open Team 1953. ACBL President 1952.

COHEN, Ben (1907–1971), of Hove, Sussex, England, author, publisher, and distributor of bridge books and stationery supplies. Pioneered duplicate bridge in the early thirties, and was one of the originators of the Acol system. Author of many books on Acol, bridge quizzes, etc.: co-editor of *The Bridge Players' Encyclopedia* (English edition of the *Official Encyclopedia of Bridge*); contributor to numerous bridge papers and journals, including the South African *Bridge Bulletin,* the Indian *Onlooker,* the Japanese *Bulletin.* Former editor of the *Bridge Magazine.* See BIBLIOGRAPHY, C, D, E, J.

COHEN, David, of Belfast, Ireland, born 1897; represented Ireland in European Championships 1956, and Northern Ireland in more than 70 Camrose Trophy matches, a record. Achieved a remarkable record in the 1969–70 season by winning eleven out of fifteen major Irish tournaments at age of seventy-two, perhaps the best performance ever by a veteran player. President Irish Bridge Union 1962–63; Chairman North of Ireland Bridge Union 1956.

COHEN, Harvey, of Los Angeles, Calif., lawyer, born 1935; Team trialist 1967; won Spring Nat'l Open Pairs 1967, Bridge Week Knockout Teams and Open Teams 1964.

COHEN, Israel, of Washington, D.C., merchant, born 1913; won Fall Nat'l Open Pairs 1952; second Chicago 1954, Summer Nat'l Mixed Team 1963, Open Individual 1956; regional wins include Eastern States Men's Pairs 1957, Keystone Conference Open Team 1959, Men's Pairs 1957, New York–New Jersey Open Team 1960.

COHEN, Jay, of Alexandria, Va., traffic engineer; winner of several regional events, including Mid-Atlantic Spring Masters Pairs 1967, Keystone Men's Teams 1971, 1972. Former President Washington B.L. 1964–65.

COHEN, Kenneth L., of Philadelphia, Pa., bridge teacher, born 1948; won Spring Nat'l secondary Masters Pairs 1972, second Fall Nat'l Mixed Pairs 1973; winner of several regional events, including Indy 500 Knockout Teams 1973, Bridge Week Men's Pairs 1974.

COHEN, Lawrence (Larry), of Los Angeles, Calif., pharmacist, born 1943; one of the most successful American players; in partnership with R. KATZ, won every major national team event once in a period of two years: Spingold 1973, Reisinger Team 1973, Grand Nat'l Teams 1974, Vanderbilt 1975; won Blue Ribbons 1968, Lou HERMAN TROPHY 1973; second Blue Ribbons 1969, Spring Nat'l Men's Teams 1971,

Vanderbilt 1973; won Spring Nat'l secondary Swiss Teams 1974. Numerous regional successes include Central States Knockout Teams 1965, 1972, 1973, Champagne Open Teams 1969, 1971, 1974. Intercollegiate Champion 1966, runner-up 1965. Coauthor of *Breakthrough in Bridge*.

COHEN, Louis J., of Southfield, Mich., sales manager, born 1910; second Fall Nat'l Mixed Pairs 1958; won several regionals including Midwest Men's Pairs 1956, All-American Open Teams 1968.

COHEN, Nathan, of Memphis, Tenn., ACBL division manager and assistant treasurer, born 1915; concerned with Bridge-O-Rama organization since 1959. Finance officer for all national tournaments, in charge of entry selling.

COHEN, Rafael, of Budapest, Hungary, retired merchant, born 1893; European Champion 1934, 1935, 1936; Hungarian Champion 1929–35, and 1960. Npc of Hungarian Team 1963–68.

COHEN, Ralph R., of Memphis, Tenn., Assistant Executive Secretary of the ACBL since 1971, born 1926; represented Canada World Team Olympiad 1964; regional wins include Canadian-American Open Teams 1952, 1954, and 1957, Men's Pairs 1957, New England Open Pairs 1965. Member Montreal's victorious Inter-City Team 1967, 1968.

COHEN, Robert, of Acton, Mass.; won Fleur-de-Lys Open Pairs 1974, Can-Am Knockout Teams 1974, Tri-State Masters Pairs 1974.

COHEN, Ruth (1915–1966), of Queens, N.Y., business executive, bridge teacher and director; charter member of American Bridge Teachers' Association (ABTA); author of many booklets, among them *How to Make Teaching a Paying Proposition, At-a-Glance Duplicate Scoring, How to Match Point.* See BIBLIOGRAPHY, D, E.

COHN, Bette L., of Atlanta, Ga.; won VENICE CUP 1974, Summer Nat'l Mixed Pairs 1966, Fall Nat'l Women's Teams 1967, Life Master Women's Pairs 1970; many regional successes including New England Master Pairs 1965, District 11 Knockout Teams 1969, Mid-Atlantic Open Teams 1970, Mid-South Women's Pairs 1974.

COHN, Edward F., of Philadelphia, Pa., insurance broker, died 1969; second Summer Nat'l Mixed Teams 1944; won Southeastern Open Teams 1953, 1954, and 1958, Mixed Pairs 1955.

COHN, Mrs. Janice, of Wheeling, Ill., bridge teacher; won Summer Nat'l Master Mixed Teams 1969, Midwest Fall Women's Pairs 1967, Gopher Open Teams 1973.

COHN, Martin J., of Atlanta, Ga., business executive, born 1923; second De La Rue International Pair Championship, London, 1957; won Life Master pairs 1957, Summer Nat'l Mixed Pairs 1966; second Fall Nat'l Men's Pairs 1961, Summer Nat'l Mixed Teams 1964, Spring Nat'l Men's Teams 1969. Winner of numerous regional titles including District 11 Knockout Teams 1969, Southern Conference Fall Open Teams 1962, Great Lakes Open Teams 1961, 1968, Thanksgiving Knockout Teams 1973, Texas Fall Knockout Teams 1964.

COHN, Steven, of Cincinnati, Ohio, computer operations supervisor, born 1942; won Fall Nat'l second flight Blue Ribbons 1970, District 5 Open Pairs 1969, District 11 Men's Pairs 1970, Open Teams 1974.

COKIN, Allan J., of Providence, R.I., bridge teacher and club owner, born 1942; won Summer Nat'l secondary Swiss Teams 1971, District 11 Open Teams 1971, tied Florida Men's Pairs 1973.

COLEMAN, Bernard, of Minneapolis, Minn.; won Champagne Men's Pairs 1969, Canadian Prairie Knockout Teams 1972, Buffalo Open Pairs 1972.

COLEMAN, C. N., of Corpus Christi, Tex., born 1896; won Mid-South Spring Men's Pairs 1949, Lone Star Men's Pairs 1962, South Texas Open Pairs 1971.

COLLIER, Gladys W., of New York, N.Y., mathematician; represented US World Olympiad Women's Pairs 1970; second Nat'l Life Master Women's Pairs 1969; won Keystone Mixed Pairs 1967, Southeastern Open Pairs 1968, Fun City Mixed Pairs 1971.

COLLINGS, John D. R., of London, England, sales executive, born 1933; one of Europe's leading players; represented Switzerland World Pair Olympiad 1970, European Championships 1970, Great Britain European Championships 1965, England Camrose Trophy matches 1961, 1964; won Gold Cup 1965, Daily Telegraph Cup 1959, 1965, English Bridge Union Crockford's Cup 1964, 1966, Life Masters Pairs 1966, London Sunday Times 1969. With Jack Nunes, won both Pairs and Team Championships at the 1965 international tournament at Juan-les-Pins, a record.

COLLYER, Barbara. See KACHMAR, BARBARA.

CONLIN, David A., Jr., of Phoenix, Ariz., real estate broker, born 1923; won Bridge Week Masters Pairs 1960, Desert Empire Open Teams 1959, Knockout Teams 1967.

COOK, Dean, of Oakland, Calif.; won many regionals including All-Western Open Teams 1957,

1963, Bridge Week Open Teams 1957, Crater Lake Open Teams 1970.

COOK, Mrs. Dorothy Jane, of Vero Beach, Fla., bridge teacher; won All-American Mixed Pairs 1945, Central States Mixed Pairs and Women's Teams 1947, Women's Pairs 1948, Life Masters Teams 1961. Former President, Executive Vice-President of ABTA. Author of *Learn to Play Better Bridge.*

COOK, Edward M., of Palos Verdes, Calif., investment manager, born 1901; won Summer Nat'l Men's Pairs 1935, 1937; regional wins include Bridge Week Men's Pairs 1958, Pacific Southwest Men's Pairs 1967.

COOLIK, Samuel, Jr., of Atlanta, Ga., stockbroker, born 1943; won Fall Nat'l secondary Men's Teams 1972; winner of many regional titles including Mid-South Men's Pairs 1971, 1972, Open Teams 1973.

COOMBS, Betty (Mrs. S. R.) (1901–1966), of Long Beach, Calif.; second Spring Nat'l Women's Pairs 1959; won Bridge Week Women's Pairs 1957, All Western Women's Pairs 1964, Rocky Mountain Open Teams 1958, Hawaiian Open Teams 1958, Women's Pairs 1957.

COOMBS, N. Dugan, Jr., of Hamilton, Ohio, consultant, born 1934; won Fall Nat'l secondary Special Pairs 1974; several regional wins including District 11 Men's Pairs 1963, Life Masters Pairs 1969.

COOMBS, William V., of Hamilton, Ohio, auditor, born 1943; winner of several regionals including Midwest Winter Swiss Teams 1974, Midwest Fall Master Pairs 1974.

COON, Charles, of Gloucester, Mass., bridge teacher, born 1931; one of the leading American players; represented North America 1962 World Championship; won 1961 Trials, Vanderbilt 1961, Summer Nat'l Mixed Teams 1962, Fall Nat'l Life Master Men's Pairs 1964, Blue Ribbon Pairs 1966; second Spring Nat'l Men's Teams 1968, winner of a great many regional titles including New England Knockout Teams 1957, 1958, 1961, 1964, Spring Open Teams 1956, 1959, 1960, 1961, 1963, Open Pairs 1955, 1962, Master Pairs 1974.

COOPER, Martin J., of Lincolnwood, Ill., pharmacist, born 1923; won Southeastern Mixed Pairs 1960, Open Pairs 1961, Midwest Mixed Pairs 1961.

COOPER, Roslyn (Mrs. Martin J.), of Lincolnwood, Ill., born 1926; won Southeastern Mixed Pairs 1960, Open Pairs 1961, Midwest Mixed Pairs 1961.

CORDOEIRO, José Antonio, of Lisbon, Portugal, born 1946; represented Portugal European Championships 1967, 1970, 1974; national wins include Open Pairs.

CORDWELL, John B., of Wellington, N.Z., insurance broker, born 1928; represented New Zealand World Team Olympiad 1972.

CORN, Ira G., Jr., of Dallas, Tex., corporation executive and director, born 1921; one of the leading bridge personalities in the Southwest area as organizer, financier, and captain of the Aces (the world's first professional bridge team), administrator for the Dallas Bridge Association, and successful tournament player. Won Spring Nat'l Mixed Pairs 1963, Men's Team 1968, Mid-South Summer Open Teams 1964, Golden Gate Knockout Teams 1968, Texas Fall Knockout and Open Teams 1968. Positions he has held in the Dallas Bridge Association include President 1968, Tournament Chairman 1966–67, and Director since 1965. ACBL Director since 1971. (See also ACES TEAM.)

CORNELL, Michael L., of Auckland, N.Z., accountant, born 1947; represented New Zealand World Championship 1974, World Team Olympiad 1972; won Nat'l Teams 1972, 1973.

CORNILLAUD, Mrs. Melvin, of Paducah, Ky., born 1904; won Spring Nat'l Women's Teams 1962.

CORWEN, Reginald F., of Leeds, England, clock importer; one of the leading European bridge personalities; npc Great Britain World Championship 1955 and many European Championships. Member European Bridge League Tournament committee; Chairman English Bridge Union since 1955.

COTT, Edward Van. See VAN COTT, EDWARD.

COURTENAY, F. Dudley, of South Dennis, Mass., manufacturer, bridge merchant and writer, born 1892. A major figure in the bridge battles of the early thirties, he founded BRIDGE HEADQUARTERS, and was a member of the group which produced the OFFICIAL SYSTEM in opposition to Ely Culbertson. Courtenay's chief contribution to theory was the development of the LOSING TRICK COUNT, an unusual and important method of hand valuation, which he described in his book *The System the Experts Play.* His other writings include *Standardized Code of Contract Bridge Bidding, The Losing Trick Count, The Standard Manual on Play,* and *Standardized Contract Bridge Complete.* See BIBLIOGRAPHY, C, D, and E.

Courtenay was the inventor and manufacturer of the first metal duplicate boards.

COWAN, Donald S., of Toronto, Ont., chartered accountant, born 1931; winner of several regional titles, including Canadian Nat'l Open Teams 1962, Knockout Teams 1971.

COX, David M., of San Antonio, Tex.; won Leventritt Pairs 1961, Summer Nat'l secondary Men's Pairs 1965.

COX, Karl C., of Medfield, Mass., accountant; won Eastern States Men's Pairs 1971, Canadian Nat'l Knockout Teams 1974, Open Teams 1974.

COX, Stephen P., of Indianapolis, Ind., student, born 1946; won Summer Nat'l secondary Swiss Teams 1973, Midwest Fall Knockout Teams 1973, tied Mid-Atlantic Spring Open Teams 1972.

COYLE, William, of Renfrew, Scotland, science and mathematics teacher, born 1937; represented Scotland in eleven international matches; member of the victorious Camrose Trophy team once. National titles include Open Teams twice. One of four Scottish players to compete in the *Sunday Times* International Pairs Championships and the British Trials.

CRAMER, Héctor (1901–1974), of Buenos Aires, Argentina; represented Argentina World Championship 1961; South American Champion 1954, 1957; won Argentine Open Teams 1935, 1938, 1940–43, 1949, 1952, 1954, 1964, Open Pairs 1935, 1942, 1943, 1955. Considered to be one of the world's great rubber bridge players.

CRANE, Barry, of Los Angeles, Calif., formerly of Detroit, Mich., television producer; one of the leading American players, and considered by many to be the top match-point player of all time; the world's top master-point holder; won McKenney 1952, 1967, 1971, 1973, second 1961, 1962, 1963, 1964; won Oeschger 1961, 1962, 1963, 1967, Nat'l Mixed Teams 1953, 1954, Spring Nat'l Open Pairs 1964, 1970, 1971, 1972, 1974; Men's Pairs 1966, Fall Nat'l Mixed pairs 1975; second Summer Nat'l Master Mixed Teams 1969, Fall Nat'l Mixed Pairs 1971, 1974, Spring Nat'l Men's Teams 1971; won Spring Nat'l secondary Open Pairs 1969, 1974, secondary Swiss Teams 1974. Won MOTT-SMITH TROPHY 1970, 1971. Winner of hundreds of regional championships including Bridge Week Knockout Teams 1967, Master Men's Pairs 1971, Open Pairs 1959, Champagne Open Teams 1971, 1974, Desert Empire Open Pairs 1958, 1964, 1965, Mississippi Valley Open Pairs 1960, 1962, 1967, 1971, 1974, Northwest Open Pairs 1960, 1961, 1966, 1968, and some four dozen other Open Pairs titles between 1970 and 1974. In October, 1968, Crane became the ACBL's leading master-point holder, replacing Oswald Jacoby who had held the top spot since 1962.

CRANE, Joshua (1869–1964), of Lantana, Fla., sportsman, bridge writer; an American long resident

in England who was prominent in polo, football, golf, and yacht racing as well as in bridge. In the mid-thirties he sponsored the visit of a New England team to London, where matches were played against leading English teams. His own system of bidding, the Crane System, was set out in *Common Sense in Contract Bidding.* See BIBLIOGRAPHY, C.

CRANE, Lois (Mrs. Walton E., formerly Mrs. E. Oke), of Granite Falls, Wash., bookkeeper, born 1922; winner of several regional titles including Northwest Open Team 1958, Masters Pairs 1960, Women's Pairs 1959.

CRAPKO, Boris D. ("Buddy"), of Richmond, B.C., land developer, born 1937; winner of many regional titles including Pacific Northwest Knockout Teams 1969, 1970, Masters Pairs 1966, Puget Sound Open Teams 1972.

CRAWFORD, Carol Stalkin (Mrs. John), of New York, N.Y.; second Spring Nat'l Women's Swiss Teams 1972, Summer Nat'l Mixed Teams 1974; won Spring Nat'l secondary Women's Teams 1972, tied 1973.

CRAWFORD, John R. (1915–1976), of New York, N.Y., bridge writer and teacher; one of the world's greatest players, his total of 37 ACBL titles won in ACBL Nationals up to 1964 exceeded any other player's record. By winning three consecutive World Championships 1950, 1951, and 1953, and by other performances abroad he established a solid international reputation. He also represented the United States in the World Championship contests of 1958 and 1960.

His ten wins in the Chicago Trophy, 1937, 1938, 1939, 1942, 1946, 1947, 1953, 1954, 1956, and 1961, set a record. The first of these wins, at the age of twenty-two, gave him his first national title at a younger age than any of the other great American players. Two years later he became Life Master No. 19, at that time much the youngest of a select band.

His other national wins include Spingold 1943, 1948, 1950, 1952, 1957; Vanderbilt 1941, 1946, 1950, 1951, 1955, 1956, 1957, 1959, 1960; Fall Nat'l Men's Teams 1961; Mixed Teams 1942, 1945, 1948, 1957; Life Masters Pairs 1943; Summer Nat'l Men's Pairs 1939; Fall Nat'l Mixed Pairs 1945, 1948, 1949, 1959; Masters Individual 1956. His 23 seconds in national events include five in the Life Masters Pairs.

In 1957 he achieved a unique grand slam of national team titles by holding simultaneously the Vanderbilt, Spingold, Chicago, Men's and Mixed Team Championships. He demonstrated his adaptability by achieving national successes with many different partners, and earned a reputation for competitive repartee, table presence, and psychological awareness.

An expert on many card games and forms of gambling, Crawford lectured extensively during his wartime army service in an attempt to help servicemen avoid being cheated. He helped to found the

New York Card School in 1950, and moved to New York City from Philadelphia in 1959.

Crawford's writings include *Crawford's Contract Bridge, How to Be a Consistent Winner in the Most Popular Card Games,* books on canasta and samba, and a column for *The Elks Magazine.* See BIBLIOGRAPHY, E.

CREED, Harold ("Bud"), of Dallas, Tex., engineer, born 1921; second Spring Nat'l Men's Pairs 1960; winner of many regional titles including All-American Open Teams 1952, Open Pairs 1957, 1958, Texas Open Teams 1970, International City Knockout Teams 1974.

CRISFORD, Mrs. Alison B., of Hove, England, born 1898; European Women's Champion 1950; represented Great Britain European Championship 1938; English successes include Women's Team Championship.

CRONEMILLER, Cmdr. Carl Frederick, Jr., of San Jose, Calif., retired naval officer, born 1922; represented South Vietnam Far East Championships 1962; won Japan Board-A-Match Teams 1959, Knockout Teams 1959, ACBL Spring Nat'l Individual 1967, Fall Nat'l secondary Swiss Teams 1970.

CROOKS, Bill, of Kansas City, Mo.; winner of several regional titles, including Missouri Valley Knockout Teams 1972, 1973.

CROSSLEY, Dr. C. F., Jr., of Las Vegas, Nev., physician, born 1924; winner of several regional titles, including All-Western Knockout Teams 1955, Desert Empire Open Teams 1962, 1963, Texas Mid-Winter Open Teams 1974. Present patriarch of bridge playing FAMILY which includes his wife Janet, sons David and Robert, and included his late father. Former President Western Conference 1959.

CROSSLEY, C. F., Sr. (1902–1968), of Palo Alto, Calif., contractor; won All-Western Open Teams 1955, Desert Empire Open Teams 1962.

CROSSLEY, David M., of Las Vegas, Nev., medical student and bridge teacher, born 1948; won Vanderbilt 1974; winner of several regional events including Golden Gate Knockout Teams 1974, Midwinter Holiday Knockout Teams 1974. See FAMILY.

CROSSLEY, Robert E., of San Rafael, Calif., bridge teacher, travel agent, student, born 1951; won Vanderbilt 1974; winner of several regional events including Golden Gate Knockout Teams 1974, Midwinter Holiday Knockout Teams 1974. See FAMILY.

CROUNSE, Eleanor (Mrs. George P.), of Paducah, Ky.; won Spring Nat'l Women's Teams 1962,

Summer Nat'l Mixed Pairs 1964; regional wins include District 11 Women's Pairs 1970.

CROWHURST, Eric, of Reading, England, accountant, born 1935; contributor to *British Bridge World,* ACBL *Bulletin,* and other periodicals. Contributor of the unique SUIT COMBINATIONS section to the *Bridge Encyclopedia.* Inventor of the CROWHURST CONVENTION, which is widely used by British tournament players.

CROWN, Ronald, of Palm Beach, Fla., formerly of London, England, bridge teacher, born 1927; represented England in Camrose Trophy matches 1961; won Tollemache Cup three times, Richard Lederer Cup twice. Regional successes include New England Winter Open Teams 1968, Eastern States Knockout Teams 1969. Contributor to *British Bridge World;* partner in the Card School of New York 1965–70.

CROWNINSHIELD, Frank (1872–1947), editor of *Vanity Fair* 1914–35 and subsequently associate editor of *Vogue* and Director of Condé Nast. A leading bridge personality who wrote *The Bridge Fiend* and other bridge books and articles under the name of Arthur Loring Bruce. President of the CAVENDISH CLUB, New York, 1935–47. Donor of the CROWNINSHIELD TROPHY.

CRUZ, Joao Nuño Moreira, of Lisbon, Portugal, lawyer, born 1936; represented Portugal European Championships 1965, 1966, 1967, 1970, 1971; national wins include Open Teams four times, Open Pairs three times.

CUDAHY, Mrs. R. E., of North Muskegon, Mich., born 1920; won Summer Nat'l Open Pairs 1962.

CULBERTSON, Ely (1891–1955), for many years principal authority on contract bridge, generally credited with making the game an internationally popular pastime, also author and lecturer on mass psychology and political science. He was born in Romania but was an American citizen from birth, by registration with the US consul, being the son of an American mining engineer who had been retained by the Russian government to develop the Caucasian oilfields and who had married a Russian woman. Culbertson belonged to a pioneer American family settled about Titusville, and Oil City, Pa., and later joined the Sons of the American Revolution to refute rumors that he had changed his name or falsified his ancestry. He attended *gymnasia* in Russia and matriculated at Yale (1908) and Cornell (1910), but in each case remained only a few months. Later (1913–14) he studied political science at l'École des Sciences Économiques et Politiques at the University of Paris (Sorbonne) and in 1915 at the University of Geneva in Switzerland, but he was largely self-educated, and the erudition for which he was admired can principally be attributed to a self-imposed and invariable regimen of reading for at least one hour a book designed to improve his knowledge before going to sleep each night. In this he was aided by an aptitude for languages. He conversed fluently in Russian, English, French, German, Czech, Spanish, and Italian, had a reading knowledge of Slavonic, Polish, Swedish, and Danish-Norwegian, and a classical knowledge of Latin and Greek.

In 1907 Culbertson participated as a student in one of the abortive Russian revolutions. He pursued his revolutionary ideas in labor disputes in the American Northwest and in Mexico and Spain (1911–12), serving as an agitator for the union and syndicalist sides.

[The foregoing biographical data, all of which is a matter of official record, is here given in detail because it has been disputed in various writings about Culbertson.]

After the Russian Revolution of 1917 wiped out his family's large fortune there, Culbertson lived for four years in Paris and other European cities by exploiting his skill as a card-player. In 1921 he returned to the US, almost penniless, and continued to derive his chief living from winnings in card games. In 1923, having acquired some reputation as a bridge player, he married Mrs. Josephine Murphy Dillon (see CULBERTSON, Josephine), one of the highly reputed bridge teachers in New York City. Together they became a successful pair as tournament players and bridge authorities.

Between 1926 and 1929, the then new game of contract bridge began to replace auction bridge, and Culbertson saw in this development an opportunity to overtake the firmly entrenched authorities on auction bridge. Culbertson planned a long-range campaign that included the construction of a dogmatic system; publication of a magazine to appeal to group leaders in bridge; authorship of a bridge textbook to serve as a "bible"; organization of professional bridge teachers; dramatization of himself and his wife as largely fictitious personalities; and expansion of the appeal of bridge by breaking down religious opposition to card playing.

The plan proved conspicuously successful. Culbertson founded his magazine, *The Bridge World*, in 1929, and through the same corporation published his earliest bridge books, all of which were best sellers; manufactured and sold bridge players' supplies including the introduction of Kem playing cards; maintained an organization of bridge teachers (Culbertson National Studios) which at its peak had 6,000 members; and conducted bridge competitions through the United States Bridge Association and the World Bridge Olympics and American Bridge Olympics. In its best year, 1937, The Bridge World, Inc., grossed more than $1,000,000 of which $220,000 were royalties payable to Culbertson before profits were calculated.

As a regular tournament competitor Culbertson had the best record in the earliest years of contract bridge. In 1930 he won the Vanderbilt and American Bridge League Knockout Team events, also the ABL Board-a-Match team event, and finished second in the masters' pairs. That year he led a team that played the first international match, in England, and defeated several teams there. In 1933 and 1934

his teams won the SCHWAB CUP. After 1934 Culbertson seldom played tournament bridge, but he was second in the ABL's 1935 match-point team contest and in the International Bridge League's first intercontinental tournament in 1937. Culbertson continued to play high-stake rubber bridge until about two years before his death.

The success of Culbertson's *Blue Book* in 1930 caused the established auction bridge authorities to join forces to combat its threatened domination of contract bridge. (See BRIDGE HEADQUARTERS and OFFICIAL SYSTEM.) Culbertson countered by challenging the leading player among his opposition, S. Lenz, to a test match, offering five-to-one odds. Culbertson's victory in this match, played in the winter of 1931–32, fortified his leading position (see CULBERTSON-LENZ MATCH). The great publicity accorded the match enriched Culbertson: he and his wife both acquired contracts for widely syndicated newspaper articles, he made a series of movie shorts for $360,000, and he received $10,000 a week for network radio broadcasts. In 1935 Culbertson tried to recapture the magic of his match against Lenz by playing a similar match against Mr. and Mrs. P. Hal Sims (see CULBERTSON-SIMS MATCH), but although the Culbertsons won this match also, there was no such publicity advantage as accrued from the Lenz match.

The publicity accorded Culbertson throughout his professional career can be attributed equally to his unquestioned abilities, his colorful personality, and his flamboyant way of life. Culbertson lived in the grand manner, with total disregard of expense whether at the moment he happened to be rich or penniless. Once he strolled into Sulka's, (then) on Fifth Avenue in New York, and bought $5,000 worth of shirts. He smoked a private blend of cigarettes that cost him $7 a day. When he decided to buy a Duesenberg automobile in 1934 he did not sell his Rolls Royce but gave it away. His home for years was an estate in Ridgefield, Conn., with a forty-five-room house, several miles of paved and lighted roads, greenhouses, cottages, lakes, and an enclosed swimming pool with orchids growing along its periphery. He always had caviar with his tea, and made special trips to Italy to buy his neckties. When he died in 1955, he owned five houses for his own use, four of them with swimming pools. But Culbertson rationalized these extravagances as publicity devices. He actually lived in one small room with a cot and a table, and he spent most of his time pacing the floor and thinking. In 1933, when a newspaper reporter asked him, "Mr. Culbertson, how did you get ahead of those other bridge authorities?" he answered, "I got up in the morning and went to work."

Culbertson's contributions to the science of contract bridge, both practical and theoretical, were basic and timeless. He devised the markings on duplicate boards for vulnerability and the bonuses for games and part-scores. He was the first authority to treat distribution as equal or superior to high cards in formulating the requirements for bids. Forcing bids, including the one-over-one, were original Culbertson concepts, as were four-card suit bids, limited no trump bids, the strong two-bid, and wholesale ace-showing including the four no trump slam try.

These were presented in the historic *Lesson Sheets on the Approach-Forcing System* (1927) and in numerous magazine articles written by Culbertson in the 1920s and early 1930s. Specific bridge principles attributable to Culbertson, separately described, include among others ASKING BIDS, the GRAND SLAM FORCE, JUMP BIDS, and the NEW-SUIT FORCING principle, which Culbertson first introduced and later repudiated.

In 1938, with war imminent in Europe, Culbertson lost interest in bridge, and thereafter devoted his time to seeking some grand achievement in political science. To effect world peace he proposed international control of decisive weapons and a quota for each major nation in tactical forces. After formation of the United Nations, to which Culbertson's ideas made a discernible contribution, he persisted in a campaign to give it adequate police power. At one time seventeen US Senators and forty-two US Congressmen subscribed to a proposed joint resolution of Congress advocating Culbertson's proposals. But in the course of these activities Culberton lost his position as the leading bridge authority; by 1950 or earlier, C. Goren had surpassed him in the sale of books and other bridge writings and in the adherence of bridge teachers and players. However, when a bridge "Hall of Fame" was inaugurated in 1964, nine years after his death, Culbertson was the first person elected.

Ely and Josephine Culbertson were divorced in 1938 and in 1947 Culbertson married Dorothy Renata Baehne, who was thirty-five years younger than he. There were two children by each of his marriages.

Culbertson suffered in late years from a lung congestion (emphysema), and died at his last home, in Brattleboro, Vt., of a common cold that proved fatal because of the lung condition.

BIBLIOGRAPHY. Minor works by Ely Culbertson, such as paperbound books and pamphlets, are literally too numerous to mention, and all or nearly all were written by members of Culbertson's staff, as also were most of the newspaper and magazine articles published under Culbertson's name from 1932 on. Earlier articles in bridge periodicals were written by Culbertson, as were the following of his major books, each of which was published in many editions: *Contract Bridge Blue Book,* 1930; *Culbertson's Self-Teacher,* 1933; *Red Book on Play,* 1934; *The Gold Book,* or, *Contract Bridge Complete,* 1936; and *Point-Count Bidding,* 1952.

Culbertson's autobiography, *The Strange Lives of One Man,* was published in 1940. His principal works on political science were *Total Peace,* 1943, and *Must We Fight Russia?* 1947.

See BIBLIOGRAPHY, C, D, E, G, K.

CULBERTSON, Josephine (Mrs. Ely) (1899–1956), bridge teacher and writer. She was born Josephine Murphy in Bayside, N.Y. (now part of New York City). In 1919 she married James Dillon, and was widowed by his suicide shortly thereafter. Her interest in bridge commenced when she became, ca.

1920, secretary to W. Whitehead. In 1923 she married E. Culbertson, and collaborated with him in the development and teaching of the Culbertson or approach-forcing systems of auction and contract bridge. During her teaching career, 1922–30, she was reputedly the highest-paid bridge teacher. Through the 1920s and into the 1930s, Mrs. Culbertson was known as "the modern miracle—the woman who can play on even terms with the best men." She was the first woman to achieve highest championship caliber, and as such was unique in her times, before the advent of Mrs. SOBEL and others. As a member of the Bridge World team, with W. von Zedtwitz as her partner and later M. Gottlieb and A. Morehead, Mrs. Culbertson won several national and international championships including the SCHWAB CUP 1933–34. Paired with her husband, she played many high-stake set games, won international matches in England and France, and achieved national fame in the CULBERTSON-LENZ MATCH, 1931–32, and CULBERTSON-SIMS MATCH, 1935. Mrs. Culbertson was co-founder of *Bridge World* magazine, 1929, and inaugurated its "Pro et Contra" department, which appeared under her name until her death. She was often on radio bridge shows, including two long series with her husband. She participated briefly in motion pictures made by her husband.

At all times, Mrs. Culbertson was an active editor of all books on the CULBERTSON SYSTEM. She was co-author of the historic *Lesson Sheets on the Approach-System* (1927) and made the first arrangement of material for *Culbertson's Summary* (1932), the largest-selling bridge book. However, her widely syndicated newspaper column, 1931–56, her *Bridge World* department, and the several books published under her name were largely prepared by the *Bridge World* technical staff; the best-known of these is *Contact Bridge for Beginners,* 1937.

Josephine and Ely Culbertson were divorced in an uncontested action brought by Mrs. Culbertson in Reno, Nev., in 1938, though they continued as business partners and co-editors. Mrs. Culbertson died in May, 1956, of a cerebral stroke shortly after her former husband's death.

Josephine Culbertson won ABL Open Challenge Team 1930; Vanderbilt 1930; second Life Master Pairs 1930; Open Pairs 1928 (both of these events played for the first time on these dates); Chicago 1935, Nat'l Women's Pairs 1930. See BIBLIOGRAPHY, E.

CUMMINGS, Michael, of Toronto, Ont., computer programming consultant, born 1944; winner of several regional events, including Great Lakes Open Teams 1970, Canadian-American Knockout Teams 1974.

CUMMINGS, Richard John, of Sydney, Australia, bridge teacher, born 1932; one of the leading Australian players; represented Australia World Championship 1971, World Team Olympiad 1960, 1964, 1968; national titles include Open Team 1959, 1962, 1963, 1974, Open Pairs 1957, Individual 1962, Par

1960, 1962, 1963. Delegate to Australian Bridge Federation, member of New South Wales Bridge Council. Contributor to overseas bridge magazines.

CUNNINGHAM, Mrs. Mildred, of Pompano Beach, Fla., bridge teacher, won Central States Mixed Pairs 1944, Masters Individual 1946, Women's Teams 1948, Open Pairs, Women's Pairs 1956, Mississippi Valley Women's Teams 1949, Southeastern Women's Teams 1967.

CURRENT, Dr. A. C., Jr., of Gastonia, N.C., dentist, born 1928; won Mid-Atlantic Spring Open Teams 1959, Men's Pairs 1967, Fall Open Teams 1961.

CUSHING, Jack, of New York, N.Y., textile importer, born 1902; won Marcus 1947, 1951; second Chicago 1939, Masters Individual 1947; among regional successes won Eastern States Knockout Teams 1948.

CZEKAŃSKA, Mrs. Irena, of Warsaw, Poland; represented Poland World Mixed Pairs Olympiad 1966, European Championships 1965; won Polish Mixed Teams 1964.

CZEKAŃSKI, Jerzy (1905–1967), of Warsaw, Poland; represented Poland World Mixed Pairs Olympiad 1966, European Championships 1957. National successes include Open Teams 1957, 1958, Mixed Teams 1964; second Individual 1958.

D

DA COSTA, Donald, of New Kingston, Jamaica, bridge club manager, born 1927; won Canadian Nat'l Open Teams 1961, Mixed Pairs 1965, Canadian-American Open Teams 1959, Mixed Pairs 1957.

DAHLER, Mrs. Ivy, of Toowoomba, Australia, born 1923; represented Australia World Women's Olympiad 1972.

DALATI, Henri, of Beirut, Lebanon; represented Lebanon World Team Olympiad 1960, 1964; European Championships 1954, 1956, 1957, 1961, 1962, 1963, with many national successes. Secretary of Lebanese Bridge Federation.

DALLAS, Richard N., of North Hollywood, Calif., chemical engineer, born 1916; won Fall Nat'l Open Pairs 1968, Mexican Nat'l Masters Pairs 1968, Orange County Open Teams 1972.

DALY, Victor, of Washington, D.C., Deputy Director United States Employment Service, born 1899. For many years the leading figure in the AMERICAN

BRIDGE ASSOCIATION, serving as its President from 1950 to 1964. Contributing Editor *Bridge Encyclopedia.*

DAM, Mrs. Else, of Copenhagen, Denmark, bridge teacher, born 1915; European Women's Champion 1948, 1949, second 1950, third 1952; won eleven Danish national titles.

DAMM, Mrs. Otti, of Copenhagen, Denmark, bridge teacher, born 1918; European Women's Champion 1949, 1955, 1957, 1958, second twice; other successes include Open Teams twice, and many Women's Team titles.

DANILENKO, Alex, of Philadelphia, Pa., photographer and accountant; won Spring Nat'l secondary Mixed Pairs 1969, 1970, Mid-Atlantic Open Teams 1951, 1952.

DARLING, Dean, of Washington, D.C., winner of several regional events, including Mid-Atlantic Summer Men's Pairs 1971, Fall Men's Pairs 1971, Master Pairs 1974.

DARVAS, Robert (1906–1957), of Budapest, Hungary; the best-known Hungarian bridge journalist; co-author of *Right Through the Pack* and *Spotlight on Cardplay;* contributor to the *European Bridge Review* and the *Bridge Magazine.* See BIBLIOGRAPHY, H.

DAUTELL, Eugene (Duke), of Los Angeles, Calif., insurance agent, bridge teacher, born 1921; won Fall Nat'l Men's Team 1951, Marcus 1952; Bridge Week Swiss Teams 1974, Midwest Open Teams 1957.

DAVIDSON, Isobel B. (Mrs. W. W.), of Edinburgh, Scotland; won many national and local tournaments including Scottish Open Teams and Scottish Women's Cup; represented Scotland twenty-one times in Camrose Trophy matches.

DAVIDSON, Sidney L., of San Francisco, Calif., National Tournament Director, born 1918; West Coast contributor to simplification of foul board calculations, carryover computations and use of MIRROR MITCHELL TEAM MOVEMENT.

DAVIS, Anita ("Pigeon"), of Beaumont, Tex., bridge columnist, born 1924; won Golder Pairs 1966, Fall Nat'l secondary Women's Teams 1972, tied 1968; winner of many regional titles including Texas Masters Pairs 1957, Women's Pairs 1958, 1968, Open Pairs 1961, Big D Mixed Pairs 1972. Bridge columnist for *Beaumont Enterprise* and *Beaumont Journal* since 1956.

DAVIS, Chester P., Jr., of Arlington, Mass., lawyer, born 1922; won Fall Nat'l secondary Masters Pairs

1973; winner of numerous regional championships including New England Knockout Teams 1963, 1969, 1973, Open Pairs 1966, Southeastern Men's Pairs 1967, Open Teams 1974, Life Masters Pairs 1974. Former President Eastern Massachusetts BA and member of ACBL Goodwill Committee.

DAVIS, Ltd. Col. Dougall M., of Oklahoma City, Okla., Air Force Officer, born 1921; represented Japan Far East Championships 1961; won four Japanese Team Championships 1961–63.

DAVIS, Edgar F., Jr., of Long Beach, Calif., systems analyst, born 1942; tied Fall Nat'l secondary Men's Teams 1971; winner of many regional titles, including Bridge Week Open Teams 1968, 1970, Mixed Pairs 1970, Pacific Southwest Knockout Teams 1970, Orange County Knockout Teams 1974.

DAVIS, Kerri. See SHUMAN, KERRI (MRS. MICHAEL).

DAVIS, Vickie (Mrs. Hugh D.), of Dallas Tex., home builder, born 1922; winner of several regional titles including Mississippi Valley Masters Pairs 1968, Texas Open Teams 1970, International City Knockout Teams 1974.

DAVIS, Wilfred M., of Atlanta, Ga., sales manager, born 1920; won Mid-Atlantic Fall Men's Pairs 1956 and 1958, Mixed Pairs 1961.

DAWKINS, George S., of Houston, Tex., professor of industrial engineering, born 1931; won Fall Nat'l Mixed Pairs 1970; winner of several regional championships including Mid-South Spring Masters Pairs 1963, Summer Open Teams 1967, Big D Knockout Teams 1970, Republic of Texas Knockout Teams 1970.

DAYBOCH, Ethel T., of St. Paul, Minn.; many regional wins including Gopher Masters Pairs 1958, Open Teams 1965, 1967, 1974, Knockout Teams 1968, 1969, Canadian Prairie Open Pairs 1967, 1968, Gopher Swiss Teams 1974.

DE. For names beginning with DE, see main element of name.

DEAN, Charles Y., of Taichung, Taiwan, aeronautical research worker and bridge writer, born 1918; represented China Far East Championship 1958, 1959; national wins include Open Team 1957, 1958, 1959, 1963 and Open Pairs 1960. Author *Dean's Diamond System.*

DEATON, Linda. See PERLMAN, LINDA.

DEBONNAIRE, Carlos Augusto, of Lisbon, Portugal, commercial director, born 1940; represented

Portugal European Championships 1965, 1966, 1970, 1974; national wins include Open Teams four times, Open Pairs once.

DEBONNAIRE, Jose Antonio, of Lisbon, Portugal, technician, born 1943; represented Portugal European Championships 1965, 1966, 1974; national wins include Open Teams three times, Open Pairs three times.

DECSI, Gabor, of Budapest, Hungary, technician, born 1912; won Hungarian Open Teams 1966; member of the victorious Hungarian team in matches with Germany 1964 and Brussels 1964.

DECSI, Leslie (Láslo), of São Paulo, Brazil, merchant and bridge writer, born in Budapest 1909; represented Brazil World Olympiad 1964; European Champion (representing Hungary) 1934; second 1935, 1936. Since 1947 has lived in Brazil. South American Champion 1955 representing Brazil. Co-author *The Limit System,* and a contributor to the *European Bridge Review.*

DEDICHEN, Herman, of Denmark, died 1958; honorary secretary of the European Bridge League from 1947 until his death. After World War II he invited the European countries to participate once again in the European Championships, and succeeded in reactivating these events in 1948. A member of the governing board of the Danmarks Bridge Forbund, he was considered one of the influential figures of the international scene.

DEERY, Desmond, of Belfast, Northern Ireland, solicitor and bridge columnist, born 1939; represented Ireland World Team Olympiad 1964, European Championship 1962, 1966, npc 1967; national wins include Open Team 1962, and Open Pairs 1959, 1961, 1963. Honorary Secretary of Northern Ireland Bridge Union and Irish Bridge Union. Leading Master Point holder in Ireland 1963–64.

DELMOULY, Claude, of Paris, bridge teacher and writer, born 1927; won World Team Olympiad 1960; represented France World Team Olympiad 1968, European Championships 1957, 1959, 1965; won Open Pairs 1959, Open Team 1960, 1962, English Master Pairs 1960, and many other successes. Author of *Tous les Secrets de Bridge* and co-author of the *Encyclopédie* with Pierre Albarran. Contributor to various bridge periodicals.

DELOUCA, Mrs. Sophie, of Greece, lawyer, born 1916; one of the leading Greek women players; represented Greece European Championship 1970, European Women's Championships 1966, 1969, 1971, 1973, 1974; won Nat'l Teams 1966, second 1970; won National Mixed Pairs 1967.

DENNARD, Dr. Robert W., of Ormond Beach, Fla., college administrator, born 1944; winner of several regional events including Southeastern Open Pairs 1971, Florida Open Teams 1974; second Intercollegiate Championships 1973.

DENNINGER, Tracy, Jr., of Bermuda, hotel manager, born 1924; represented Bermuda World Team Olympiad 1968, 1972; won Winter Nat'l Open Individual 1951, Bermuda Men's Pairs 1972.

DENNY, Jack, of N. Miami Beach, Fla., formerly of Akron, Ohio, bridge studio owner and teacher, born 1911; formerly one of the leading players of the Middle West; represented US World Pairs Olympiad 1962; won Fall Nat'l Men's Team 1951, secondary Open Pairs 1969, Marcus 1952; second Spring Nat'l Men's Pairs 1951, 1958; Open Pairs 1961; winner of many regional championships including Midwest Fall Open Teams 1960, 1966, All-American Open Teams 1967, Florida Knockout Teams 1970, Southeastern Men's Teams 1974.

DENNY, Jill (Mrs. Jack), of N. Miami Beach, Fla., formerly of Akron, Ohio, bridge teacher, born 1916; won Fall Nat'l secondary Open Pairs 1969; winner of several regional titles, including Midwest Fall Open Teams 1960, District 11 Open Teams 1962, All-American Open Teams 1967, 1969.

DERBY, Allan W., of Montreal, Que., cost accountant, born 1924; regional wins include Bermuda Masters Pairs 1972, Canadian-American Mixed Pairs 1956, Open Pairs 1960, Bermuda Open Pairs and Master Pairs 1972. Former President Montreal BL.

DERUY, Claude, of Vimy, Pas de Calais, France, bailiff; represented France World Pair Contest 1963; World Championship 1961, World Team Olympiad 1964; second European Championship 1961; national wins include Open Teams 1962.

DESCHAPELLES, Alexandre Louis Honoré Lebreton, sometimes referred to as **Guillaume le Breton** (1780–1847), a Frenchman of good family, was described by his contemporary, James Clay, English whist authority, as the finest whist player, "beyond any comparison, the world has ever seen." Deschapelles excelled at other games, among them billiards, Polish draughts, and chess. Fighting in one of the many wars of his time, he lost his right hand, but continued to play whist, and, more remarkably, billiards. He invented the coup which bears his name (see DESCHAPELLES COUP) and a number of other coups as well. He published only fragments of a projected extensive work on whist. See BIBLIOGRAPHY, A.

DESROUSSEAUX, Gérard, of Paris, bridge teacher and writer, born 1927; won World Par Contest 1963; represented France World Championship 1963,

1969, World Team Olympiad 1964, 1968, European Championship 1965, 1967; European Champion 1962; national wins include Open Team 1955, Open Pairs 1956, 1962, Mixed Team 1960, with other successes. Writings include articles for French periodicals.

DEUTER, Irving, of Detroit, Mich., bridge teacher and tournament director, born 1903; second Winter Nat'l Mixed Pairs 1945; won Mid-Atlantic Open Teams 1958, All-American Men's Pairs 1959; District 5 Men's Pairs 1964.

DEUTSCH, June, of Skokie, Ill.; won Spring Nat'l Women's Teams 1966, second 1972, won Fall Nat'l Life Masters Women's Pairs 1973, Spring Nat'l secondary Women's Teams 1972, tied 1973; winner of many regional titles, including Central States Women's Pairs 1961, 1962, 1965, 1967, Mixed Pairs 1967, 1970, Tri-Unit Women's Pairs 1970, 1973.

DEVROEDE, Léon, of Antwerp, Belgium (1901–1964); represented Belgium European Championships 1948, 1953; national wins included Open Pairs 1940, 1956.

DEWITT, Joan M., of Chicago, Ill., mathematics consultant, born 1938; won Motor City Open Teams 1972, Champagne Women's Pairs 1969, tied Iowa Women's Pairs 1974. Member of Chicago Intercity Team 1971.

DEWITZ, Egmont von, of Cologne, Germany, judge, born 1907; represented Germany World Team Olympiad 1960, 1964, and in almost every European Championship since 1938. National titles include Open Team fifteen times.

DIAZ, Eduardo, of Buenos Aires, Argentina, bank official, born 1933; national wins include Open Teams 1966, 1973, 1974.

DIBAR, Carlos F., (1911–1965), of Buenos Aires, Argentina, judge; represented Argentina World Championship 1959, 1961; South American Champion 1954, 1957; National wins include Open Team 1937, 1938, 1956, Open Pairs 1947, Master Pairs 1962. Secretary Argentine Bridge Commission 1936, 1938. Director Argentine Bridge Association 1962–63. Co-author Dibar system.

DI FELICE, Dom, of Hamilton Ont., math teacher, born 1949 in Gagliano, Italy. Won Canadian Nationals Master Pairs 1971, Mixed Pairs 1973, Canadian-American Open Pairs 1974.

DIONISI, Anthony H., of Tokyo, Japan, formerly of New York, N.Y., born 1934; won Reisinger 1970, second 1971, Spring Nat'l Men's Teams 1966; winner of several regional titles including Eastern States

Knockout Teams 1965, Open Pairs 1971, Mixed Pairs 1970, Keystone Open Teams 1965.

DISBROW, Bennett L., of Philadelphia, Pa., insurance broker, bridge teacher, and columnist; member board of directors Philadelphia Whist Assn. Co-author with Charles Solomon of *Slam Bidding and Point-Count* and *How to Bid and What to Lead*. See BIBLIOGRAPHY, C.

DISCHNER, Robert, of Santa Ana, Calif., US postal employee, born 1920; ACBL National Tournament Director.

DIVIS, Henry C. Jr., of Bethany, Okla., born 1947; won Big D Non-mixed Pairs 1974, Land of Coronado Knockout Teams 1974, Silver Anniversary Knockout Teams 1974.

DIXON, Christopher P., of London, England, bridge club proprietor, born 1944; second European Championship 1971, represented Great Britain World Team Olympiad 1972, England in Camrose Trophy matches 1972, 1973, 1974, 1975; won Gold Cup 1972, 1974. Regular contributor to *Bridge Magazine*.

DIXON, Maria L. (Mrs. Christopher P.), of London, England; represented Great Britain European Women's Championship 1974; won Whitelaw Cup 1974, Lady Milne Cup 1974.

DOANE, Alan H., of Halifax, N.S., realtor, born 1937; winner of several regional events including Canadian Atlantic Knockout Teams 1971, Swiss Teams 1973. Former President District 1.

DOCKMAN, Newton, of Minneapolis, Minn., born 1915; won Gopher Open Teams 1958 and 1960, Open Pairs 1959, Knockout Teams 1967, Mid-American–Canadian Open Teams 1961 and 1962. Inter-City Champion 1962.

DODDS, Leslie W(illiam), of London, England, import and export merchant, born 1903; World Champion 1955; European Champion 1948, 1949, 1950 and 1954; also represented Great Britain European Championship 1952, 1953, 1955; many national wins include Gold Cup 1938, 1949, 1956, 1960, Master Pairs 1955. One of the originators of the CAB SYSTEM, employed by a number of British experts.

DOERN, Helen J., of Portage, Ind., born 1920; won Central States Open Teams 1951, Life Masters Pairs 1953, Midwest Open Teams 1951.

DONAGHY, Ernest C., of Slippery Rock, Pa., statistician, born 1897; won Western States Open Team 1938. ACBL Associate National Tournament Director.

DONAGHY, George F., of Memphis, Tenn., service-division manager of the ACBL, born 1928; supervisor of supplies and playing arrangements at National tournaments; Regional Tournament Director before joining the ACBL staff.

DONALDSON, R. J., of Burnaby, B.C.; won Inland Empire Knockout Teams 1970, British Columbia Masters Pairs 1971, Klondike Open Teams 1974. From 1935 to 1974 won various events with 273 different partners.

DONNELL, Fitz, of Honolulu, Hawaii, born 1914; won Hawaiian Open Teams in four consecutive years, 1956–59, Hawaiian Men's Pairs 1961, 1968.

DONNELLY, John L., of Bellevue, Wash., industrial engineer, born 1905; won Northwest Open Team 1955, Northern Rocky Mountain Open Pairs 1958; Oregon Trail Men's Pairs 1966. Author of *Happiness Is a Squeeze*.

DORFMAN, Dr. George, of New Britain, Conn., gynecologist, born 1919; won New England Knockout Teams 1960.

DORMER, Albert G., of London, England, surveyor and bridge writer, born 1925; won Gold Cup 1958, 1963. Co-author of *The Acol System Today, The Bridge Player's Dictionary*, and *How to Play a Better Game of Bridge, Blueprint for Bidding,* and *Bridge for Tournament Players.* Editor of *British Bridge World,* 1962–64; contributing editor and former Associate Editor ACBL *Bulletin.* Editor WBF *News,* IBPA *Bulletin.* Contributing Editor *Bridge Encyclopedia.* See BIBLIOGRAPHY, C, F.

DORN, H. Charlie, of San Jose, Calif., bridge teacher, retired naval aviator; winner of many regional titles including All-Western Knockout Teams 1968, 1971, Open Teams 1968, Intermountain Knockout Teams 1972.

DOUGHTY, Richard E., of Baton Rouge, La., industrial sales manager, born 1943; won Spring Nat'l secondary Swiss Teams 1972, Summer Nat'l secondary Mixed Pairs 1973, Fall Nat'l secondary Mixed Pairs 1973, several regional events including Mid-South Open Teams 1969.

DOWNES, E. Hall, of Pittsburgh, Pa., bridge teacher and writer. Won Canadian-American Open Teams 1934. Writings included several self-teachers in the early thirties. A book by him on the Culbertson system provoked a law suit by Culbertson, who claimed that his name could not be used by other writers. Downes counterclaimed against Culbertson, who had warned booksellers not to sell Downes's books on pain of legal action. Downes won both suits, the courts holding that name of a system was public property. The case had permanent importance in legal history, both in respect of plagiarism and of unfair practices.

DREYFUS, Jack, of New York, N.Y., company president, born 1913; a leading bridge player reputed also to be the best American player of gin rummy.

DRUCKER, Ned, of Bronx, N.Y., salesman, born 1916; won Vanderbilt 1952 and 1954; second Life Masters Pairs 1951, Winter Nat'l Open Pairs 1943; won Eastern States Open Pairs 1945, Master Pairs 1968, New England Mixed Teams 1970.

DRURY, Douglas A. (1914–1967), of San Francisco, Calif., formerly of Toronto, Ont., bridge teacher; won Summer Nat'l Men's Pairs 1954, 1955, Mixed Teams 1956; second 1955; won Canadian Open Pairs 1957, Golden Gate Open Pairs 1962, Desert Empire Masters Pairs 1964, Bridge Week Knockout Teams 1965, Mixed Teams 1965, Northwest Men's Pairs 1964, All-Western Open Teams 1965, Oregon Trail Knockout Teams 1967. Former member ACBL Goodwill Committee. Originator of DRURY CONVENTION.

DRURY, Peggy (Mrs. Douglas), of Oakland, Calif.; won Navajo Knockout Teams 1969, Golden Gate Mixed Pairs 1971, Capital City Women's Pairs 1972.

DUCHOVNI, Zeev, of Tel Aviv, Israel, export manager, born 1912; represented Israel World Team Olympiad 1964, European Championship 1965, 1967; several national successes.

DUDLEY, Winifred (Mrs. Paul), of Honolulu, Hawaii, formerly of Yokohama, Japan, born 1915; won Prince Takamatsu Open Teams 1955, 1956, Princess Takamatsu Mixed Pairs 1958, with other successes.

DUFFY, Dr. Charles, of New Bern, N.C., physician, born 1905; won Mid-Atlantic Fall Open Team 1960; Winter Masters Pairs 1965, Southern Conference Masters Pairs 1964.

DUFOUR, R. W., Jr., of Edina, Minnesota, attorney, born 1940; winner of many regional titles including four events at the 1971 Canadian Nat'l Knockout Teams, Open Pairs, Masters Pairs, Open Teams (tied), Silver Anniversary Regional Master Pairs, 1974.

DUNN, James, of Inglewood, Calif., accountant, born 1913; won Nat'l Mixed Team 1946, All-Western Open Pairs 1956, Bridge Week Men's Pairs 1956,

1960, Open Pairs 1956, Mixed Teams 1961, Pacific Southwest Open Teams 1961, Men's Pairs 1961.

DUNN, Mrs. James, of Inglewood, Calif., won Nat'l Mixed Team 1946; second Fall Nat'l Women's Team 1959; won Bridge Week Women's Pairs 1945, 1946, 1958, 1959, Pacific Southwest Open Team 1961.

DUNNE, J. Patrick, of Miami, Fla. One of the best-known blind bridge players, and co-author of *Championship Bridge.* (See BIBLIOGRAPHY, K).

DUNPHY, Mrs. R. A. (formerly Mrs. R. E. Duncan), of St. Petersburg, Fla., born 1906; won Summer Nat'l Women's Pairs 1951, Western States Mixed Pairs 1944, Midwest Women's Pairs 1944.

DURHAM, Louise, of Durant, Miss., second Summer Nat'l Women's Pairs 1967; won Central States Women's Pairs 1951, Mid-South Open Teams 1957, Missouri Valley Women's Pairs 1954, and many other regional successes. Former ACBL Director and Secretary; Co-Chairman of Goodwill Committee and World Bridge Federation Friendship Committee; past president Mississippi Bridge Association. Honorary Member ACBL 1974.

DURRAN, Joan (Mrs. George), of Welwyn Garden City, England; one of the world's leading women players; won World Olympiad Women's Pairs 1966, European Women's Championships 1961, 1966; second World Olympiad Mixed Pairs 1966; represented Great Britain World Olympiad Women's Teams 1960, Women's Pairs 1970, European Women's Championships 1962, 1965, 1969; national successes include Hubert Phillips Bowl, Lady Milne Cup, and several victories in the Whitelaw Cup competition; runner-up in the Life Master Pairs in partnership with Mrs. J. PRIDAY, the highest placing ever by a women's pair.

DYE, Dr. Arthur M., of Charlotte, N.C., born 1896; won Mid-Atlantic Fall Mixed Pairs 1954. Former President of Mid-Atlantic BC; Honorary Member ACBL 1959.

E

EARL, Christopher W., of Portland, Ore., student, born 1951; winner of several regional events including Oregon Trail Open Teams 1972, Peach Festival Knockout Teams 1974.

EATON, Ruth (Mrs. F. N.), of Sydney, Australia, saleswoman; Far East Women's champion 1973, 1974; represented Australia World Women's Olympiad 1968; won National Women's Pairs 1969, 1972, ten Interstate Women's Team Championships between 1951 and 1972.

EBERSON, Mrs. Frederick, of St. Petersburg, Fla., won Winter Nat'l Women's Teams 1949; second Summer Nat'l Mixed Teams 1954, Spring Nat'l Women's Pairs 1960.

ECKER, Dr. Richard H., of New York, N.Y., dentist and lawyer; won Fall Nat'l Men's Pairs 1936, Masters Individual 1938; second Fall Nat'l Men's Pairs 1943. One of the founders of the Greater New York BA, active on its Board of Directors, chairman of the By-Laws, Ethics, and Goodwill committees.

ECKER, Wynne (Mrs. Richard H.), of New York, N.Y.; won Fall Nat'l Women's Teams 1954; second Summer Nat'l Women's Pairs 1956; won Eastern States Women's Pairs in 1955, 1958, New York–New Jersey Mixed Pairs 1967.

ECONOMIDY, Ann, of Manchester, Mo., won Spring National Women's Pairs 1973.

ECONOMIDY, Byron, of New Braunfels, Tex., second Grand Nat'l 1973, won Fall Nat'l secondary Life Masters Men's Pairs 1970, South Texas Mixed Pairs 1971.

EDWARDS, John M., of Rock Island, Ill., accountant, born 1940; won Spring Nat'l secondary Men's Pairs 1969, winner of several regional events including Canadian-American Open Pairs 1972.

EDWARDS, Mrs. Mary, of Esher, Surrey, England, born 1909; European Women's Champion 1959. See FORTUNE.

EHRLENBACH, Jack, of Los Angeles, Calif., bridge teacher, born 1894; one of the leading players of the West Coast; won Nat'l Mixed Teams 1949, 1950; regional successes include Bridge Week Open Teams 1939, 1940, 1945, 1946, 1948, Mixed Teams 1938, Mixed Pairs 1952, 1959, 1965, Open Pairs 1937, 1939, Men's Pairs 1947, Master Pairs 1959, All-Western Open Pairs 1937, Men's Pairs 1947, 1963, Desert Empire Open Pairs 1957, Northwest Fall Mixed Pairs 1958, Northwest Spring Open Team 1963, Men's Pairs 1960, Mixed Pairs 1963, Pacific Southwest Master Pairs 1961, Navajo Knockout Teams 1967. Became first Life Master on the West Coast 1946.

EISENBERG, William, of Los Angeles, Calif., bridge teacher, born 1937; one of the world's leading players; represented North America in World Championship 1969, 1975; World Champion 1970, 1971; won International Team Trials 1975, Spingold 1969, 1973, Summer Nat'l Open Teams 1961, Spring Nat'l Men's Teams 1968, Reisinger 1970, Vanderbilt 1971, Grand Nationals 1974, Life Master Pairs 1968; second Vanderbilt 1966, 1970, 1973, Spingold 1970, Team Trials 1968, Reisinger 1968, Spring Nat'l Men's Teams 1969; winner of many regional championships including Bridge Week Open Pairs 1968, Open Teams 1969, 1971, Knockout Teams 1972. Won World Backgammon Championship 1974. (See ACES TEAM.)

EISENHOWER, Dwight D. (1890–1969), as an officer in the United States Army from the time he was a captain, then as President of the United States and after retirement, never relinquished a keen interest in bridge. In Gibraltar on Nov. 7, 1942, the day of the landing at Casablanca which constituted the first Allied invasion after the fall of France, during the nerve-racking period when the landing had begun and the first news had not yet come back to his headquarters, he relaxed in a celebrated bridge game with Mark Clark, A. M. GRUENTHER, and H. BUTCHER. Similarly, he used bridge as a regular recreation while Supreme Allied Commander before the invasion in Normandy, while NATO chief in Paris, and while President in the White House; and after his retirement from the Presidency he was host at occasional games at his houses at Gettysburg, Pa., and Palm Springs, Calif. His skill has been characterized by O. JACOBY as "superior—capable of holding his own in the best club games below the most expert." When Gruenther phoned him from Chicago at 7 A.M. one day in 1960 to tell him to read *The New York Times* bridge column of that morning because it reported one of his hands, Eisenhower replied, "I've already read it."

EISENLORD, Ray H. (1884–1965), of Erie, Pa., accountant; won Pennsylvania State Open Team 1934. ABL President 1934, and one of the originators of the MASTER-POINT PLAN.

EKEBLAD, Russell A., of Pawtucket, R.I., company manager, born 1946; won Summer Nat'l Golder Pairs 1972, several regional events including Fun City Life Masters Pairs 1972.

ELENBERG, Itzhak, of Tel Aviv, Israel, merchant, born 1910; represented Israel World Team Olympiad 1964, European Championships 1965; won Israel Open Pairs 1965, Tel Aviv Open Team 1966, 1967, Open Pairs 1964, 1965. Chairman Israel Bridge Federation.

ELIASSON, Hjalti. of Kopavogi, Iceland, electrician, born 1929; represented Iceland World Team Olympiad 1960, and in European Championships 1963; national titles include Open Team 1962, Open Pairs 1963.

ELIS, ESTELLE (Mrs. Morrie, formerly Mrs. Drescher), of Oceanside, N.Y.; won Nat'l Mixed Team

1937; second 1945, won Fall Nat'l Women's Pairs 1940.

ELIS, Morrie, of Oceanside, N.Y., bridge teacher and lecturer; for many years one of the leading American players; winner of Mc Kenney 1938, 1940; won Vanderbilt 1949, Mixed Team 1937, Life Masters Pairs 1938, 1940, Life Masters Individual 1940, 1950; second Asbury Challenge Team 1937, Spingold 1937, 1938, Vanderbilt 1943, 1954, Fall Nat'l Open Pairs 1939, Life Masters Individual 1946, Fall Nat'l Men's Pairs 1934, 1937, 1938, 1939, 1940, 1947. Many regional wins include Eastern States Knockout Teams 1936.

ELLENBY, Milton Q., of Skokie, Ill., actuary, born 1923; one of the outstanding American players of the postwar period; World Champion 1954, also represented US in Bermuda Bowl 1955; won Spingold 1953, 1954, Life Masters Pairs 1953, Summer Nat'l Mixed Team 1957, Winter Nat'l Masters Pairs 1955, Spring Nat'l Men's Pairs 1951; second Summer Nat'l Men's Pairs 1954, Masters Team 1957; won Central States Life Masters Pairs 1956, Knockout Teams 1966, Mississippi Valley Open Teams 1951, Open Pairs 1954.

ELLIOTT, C. Bruce, of Weston, Ont., estimator, born 1922; one of the outstanding Canadian players; represented Canada World Olympiad 1960, 1968; won Spingold 1964, 1965; second Life Masters Pairs 1964; regional wins include Canadian-American Open Teams 1963, 1965, Open Pairs 1965, Canadian Nat'l Open Teams 1951, 1959, 1961, 1965, 1967, 1972, Open Pairs 1955, 1958, 1962, 1969, Men's Pairs 1960, Mixed Pairs 1952.

ELLIS, Mrs. Jean H., of Washington, D.C., congressional and governmental secretary, born 1897; one of the first woman Life Masters in the Capital District; finished second overall and first in the US in a Worldwide Tournament sponsored by the State Department in 1962. Former bridge lecturer, teacher, and director.

ELWELL, J(oseph) B(owne) (1873–1920), the principal American authority on the original game of bridge (bridge-whist) and on the early form of auction bridge. He was born February 23, 1873, in Cranford, N.J. Elwell is now remembered chiefly as the victim of one of the most celebrated murders of this century; it is said to have inspired the modern mystery novel. Elwell began his bridge career about 1900 as a bridge teacher, and quickly became a favorite of high society in New York City and Newport. He was a regular high-stake player at the Whist Club of New York and other clubs, and he and his regular partner, H. S. Vanderbilt, were considered the strongest American pair from about 1910 to 1920. Elwell amassed a considerable fortune, chiefly through speculation in Wall Street, and at the time of his death owned more than twenty race horses. His books, most of which went through several editions and sold in large quantities, included *Elwell on Bridge,* 1902; *Advanced Bridge,* 1904; *Practical Bridge,* 1906; *Bridge Axioms and Laws,* 1907; *Elwell on Auction Bridge,* 1910; *Elwell's New Auction Bridge,* 1920. His annotations of the hands played in a 1903 par-hand tournament (*Bridge Tournament Hands,* 1904) show great skill at analysis.

On the morning of June 11, 1920, Elwell's housekeeper found him fatally shot in the private house that he occupied alone on West 70th St., New York. He had been shot only about an hour earlier, and the motive was not robbery because none of the considerable amount of money and jewelry in the house was touched. Several women had keys to the house. Elwell was separated from his wife. The case received wide publicity, and has been the subject of several books and hundreds of articles. Officially the murder was never solved, though it is generally believed that the police knew the murderer but had insufficient evidence. Several novelists used the setting of the case for mystery novels in which they supplied their own solutions.

Mrs. J. B. Elwell remained active as a bridge teacher into the 1930s. See BIBLIOGRAPHY, A.

ELZANOWSKI, Jerzy, of Warsaw, Poland, managing director, born 1918; represented Poland European Championships 1962, 1966; npc Poland's International Team since 1967; won Beirut Festival Open Teams 1968. National successes include first Open Teams 1960, 1961, 1965, Individual 1960, Mixed Teams 1964, Open Pairs 1965; second Open Pairs 1959, Individual 1964.

EMERY, John (1926–1972), of Wichita Falls, Tex., tournament director, ACBL Associate National Tournament Director.

EMERY, Sue (Mrs. John), of Memphis, Tenn., bridge writer, teacher, and club owner, born 1920; won Texas Mixed Pairs 1963, Open Teams 1965. Associate Editor *Texas Bridge,* and regular member of ACBL press staff at National Championships since 1961. Editor ACBL *Bulletin* since 1972.

ENGEL, Michael, of New York, N.Y., stockbroker, born Berlin, Germany, 1935; second Chicago Trophy 1965; won New England Master Teams 1961, Open Teams 1964, Eastern States Men's Teams 1967.

ENSMINGER, Fred B., of Ann Arbor, Mich., born 1904; won Midwest Open Teams 1953, Mixed Pairs 1959, Mississippi Valley Men's Pairs 1965. Trustee ACBL Charity Foundation.

EPSTEIN, Mrs. Bert, of Beverly Hills, Calif., bridge teacher; won Spring Nat'l Women's Pairs 1959, Summer Nat'l secondary Women's Pairs 1969, Hawaiian Women's Pairs 1957, Golden State Women's Pairs 1965.

EPSTEIN, Isadore, of Tacoma, Wash., teacher, born 1908; won Northwest Spring Men's Pairs 1949, Open Team 1956, Masters Pairs 1957, Desert Empire Open Pairs 1952, Northern Rocky Mountain Open Team 1956, 1958; other regional successes.

EPSTEIN, James, of St. Louis, Mo., bridge instructor; won Senior Masters Individual 1951; many regional wins, including Midwest Spring Open Pairs 1962, Mississippi Valley Open Teams 1954, 1955, Open Pairs 1958, Men's Pairs 1959, 1960, 1966.

EPSTEIN, Mark, of South Orange, N.J.; won New York-New Jersey Mixed Pairs 1971, Fun City Men's Pairs 1972, Keystone Masters Pairs 1973.

EPSTEIN, Roberta (Mrs. Mark), of South Orange, N.J., senior systems designer, born 1936; won Nat'l Women's Teams 1960, 1961, second 1971, won Summer Nat'l secondary Women's Pairs 1971, Spring Nat'l secondary Women's Teams; winner of several regional events including Tri-State Women's Pairs 1973.

ERDENBAUM, Israel, of Israel, engraver, born 1920; represented Israel European Championship 1972, npc Israel Women's Team 1973; Israel's National Tournament Director; Tournament Director European Championship 1974, World Pair Olympiad 1974.

ERDOS, Ivan (1924–1967), of Los Angeles, Calif., travel agent, bridge teacher and writer; born in Budapest, resident of England 1939–1951; one of the leading American players; represented North America in World Championships 1965; won World Olympiad Mixed Pairs 1966, Fall Nat'l Men's Teams 1959; Spring Nat'l Men's Pairs 1962; second Team Trials 1964, Spingold 1953, 1957, Vanderbilt 1966, Spring Nat'l Mixed Pairs 1959, Open Pairs 1965. In regionals his wins include Bridge Week Masters Teams 1956, Open Teams 1953, Knockout Teams 1958, 1959, Rocky Mountain Open Teams 1954, Masters Pairs 1962, Desert Empire Masters Pairs 1959, 1966, Hawaiian Open Pairs, Mixed Pairs 1959, Missouri Valley Men's Pairs, 1955, Northern Rocky Mountain Mixed Pairs, Men's Pairs 1963, All-Western Open Pairs 1964, Golden Gate Open Teams 1965, District 5 Open Teams 1965, Pacific Southwest Open Teams 1965, Southeastern Men's Teams 1967; second All-Western Men's Pairs 1958, Bridge Week Men's Pairs 1958, Golden State Open Pairs 1963, Men's Pairs 1963. Bridge writings included contributions to *American Bridge Digest,* and editing of "Dupliquiz" for ACBL *Bulletin.* Author of *Bridge A La Carte.* Bridge editor *San Diego* magazine and several newspapers in Southern California.

ERICKSON, Nels, of San Diego, bridge teacher; won Leventritt Pairs 1969, many regional events including All-Western Knockout Teams 1972, Hawaii Men's Pairs 1973, Open Teams 1974.

ERIKSSON, Mrs. Karin, of Stockholm, Sweden, born 1914; won World Women's Team Olympiad 1968, Scandinavian Women's Championships 1957, 1966, 1968. National titles include Women's Pairs and Mixed Pairs.

EVANS, Donald Stewart, of Sydney, Australia, bridge teacher, born 1933; represented Australia World Team Olympiad 1964; National successes include Open Team (five times) and Individual Championship 1963.

EVANS, Hortense (Mrs. Eliot), of Evanston, Ill., born 1893; tied for first in Fall Nat'l Open Pairs 1929, won Fall Nat'l Mixed Pairs 1935, Nat'l Mixed Team 1936.

EVANS, Mrs. Ralph ("Penguin"), of Bournemouth, England, hotelier, born 1906; European Women's Team Champion 1950, 1951, 1952, second 1939; second Gold Cup 1950. Toured US 1953 as member of British Women's Team.

EVANS, Rex, of Auckland, New Zealand, public accountant and bridge writer, born 1918; represented New Zealand World Team Olympiad, De La Rue World Pair Championship 1957; won New Zealand Open Team twelve times, Open Pairs three times, winner in New Zealand section in Australasian Olympiads many times. President New Zealand Bridge Council, Auckland Bridge Council, Northern Council Bridge Club. Writings include magazine articles and newspaper columns.

EVERS, Mrs. Alice Gordon (1874–1950), of London; one of England's best women players in the thirties; represented England in first Anglo-American Match 1930; played in US Championships in 1934 by invitation.

EWEN, Ira, of Jamaica, N.Y., teacher; won New England Masters Teams 1963, Long Island Knockout Teams 1970; second Nat'l Senior & Advanced Senior Masters Pairs 1959. Bridge instructor for adult education classes.

EWEN, Robert B., of Miami, Fla., psychology professor and bridge author, born 1940; regional wins include Eastern States Knockout Teams 1972, Mid-Atlantic Knockout Teams 1973, Intercollegiate Champion 1958, 1963. Author of several books including *Opening Leads, Doubles for Takeout, Penalties and Profit,* and *Preemptive Bidding,* and *Bridge World* articles including the popular bridge word puzzles; former Associate Editor of *Bridge Journal;* creator of TWO-WAY GAME TRIES. Contributing editor *Bridge Encyclopedia,* and contributor to ACBL *Bulletin.* See BIBLIOGRAPHY, C, D.

F

FABER, Eberhard (1859–1946), New York City manufacturer; player of whist and bridge; member of the Knickerbocker Whist Club and president of American Whist League. Presented the Faber Challenge Trophy for the National Open Team Auction Bridge Championship. Honorary Member ABL 1930.

FACCHINI, Gianfranco, of Bologna, Italy, lawyer, born 1937; World Champion 1975; successes include Italy Cup 1970, 1974, London *Sunday Times* Pairs 1974, Monte Carlo Pairs 1974. Accused during 1975 Bermuda Bowl of illicit communications through foot signals. See BERMUDA INCIDENT.

FAIN, Ben (died 1976), of Houston, Tex., bridge club owner; won Spring Nat'l Men's Teams 1953, 1956, Life Master pairs 1955, Fall Nat'l Open Pairs 1956, Chicago 1955; second Chicago 1956, 1957; regional successes include Mid-South Mixed Pairs 1949, Texas Fall Open Teams 1962.

FAIRCHILD, Mrs. Shirley, of Dallas, Tex., born 1910; won Nat'l Women's Pairs 1952; second Nat'l Mixed Pairs 1951; won Mid-South Spring Open Team 1955, Mississippi Valley Mixed Pairs 1953.

FALENDER, Mrs. Arch, of Indianapolis, Ind., won Midwest Women's Pairs 1971, Spring Women's Pairs 1970, Indy 500 Women's Pairs 1973.

FALK, Charlotte F., of Atlanta, Ga.; won Fall Nat'l secondary Special Pairs 1974, tied secondary Swiss Teams 1972, tied Southeastern Women's Teams 1973.

FARELL, Jules, of Beverly Hills, Calif., bridge instructor; second Summer Nat'l Master Mixed Teams 1969; numerous regional wins including Pacific Southwest Masters Pairs 1956, Open Pairs 1965, Open Teams 1967, 1973, Golden Gate Open Teams 1967, Knockout Teams 1973.

FARELL, Mary Jane (Mrs. Jules, formerly Mrs. Arnold Kauder), of Beverly Hills, Calif., bridge teacher; one of the world's leading women players; won World Olympiad Mixed Pairs 1966, Women's Pairs 1970; represented US World Women's Team Olympiad 1972; won Spring Nat'l Women's Teams 1968, 1970, 1972, 1974, 1975, Nat'l Mixed Teams 1949, 1950, 1955, Fall Nat'l Women's Team 1957, 1964, secondary Swiss Teams 1973, Summer Nat'l Women's Pairs 1960, Spring Nat'l Mixed Pairs 1949, 1959; second Fall Nat'l Women's Pairs 1965, 1966, 1967, 1968, Spring Nat'l Women's Team 1967, 1973, Master Mixed Teams 1969; has won every event in the Western Regionals at least once, including Bridge Week Open Teams 1948, 1953, Knockout

Teams 1969, Mixed Teams 1950, 1960, 1969, Women's Pairs 1969, Open Pairs 1949, 1963, Pacific Southwest Masters Pairs 1956, Open Pairs 1956, 1965, Open Teams 1957, 1973, Women's Pairs 1973, and many more. In the summer of 1964 Mrs. Farell gained first placed among women in the master point rankings of the ACBL, displacing Mrs. Helen Sobel, and in 1970 advanced to third place in the all-time rankings, a place she still holds, behind B. Crane and H. Baron.

FARIA, Octavio G. de, of Brazil, company director, born 1920; South American Champion 1971, represented Brazil World Championship 1970; won Brazilian Open Teams 1969, 1973, 1974; many other successes.

FARQUHARSON, Donald Gordon, of Kingston, Jamaica, barrister and administrative manager, born 1906. Former Toronto player, he rose to the rank of Brigadier General in the Canadian Army during World War II. Won Chicago Trophy 1936; second Fall Nat'l Mixed Pairs 1956.

FARRER, J. Arnold (1872–1948), of Brookline, Mass., lawyer; won New England Knockout Teams 1930, 1935, 1938, 1940 (twice), Mixed Teams 1931, 1932.

FARRINGTON, Frank, of Bolton, Lancaster, England, textile consultant, born 1908; represented England Camrose match vs. Wales, England vs. France 1952, and London vs. Paris 1965. Won Gold Cup 1959, Crockford's Cup 1958, 1961. Author of *Duplicate Bridge Movements.* See BIBLIOGRAPHY, F.

FARRIS, Dr. Robert G. (1927–1970), of Austin, Tex., neurological surgeon; third Spingold 1960; won Texas Open Pairs 1960, Life Master Pairs 1966, Southern Spring Open Pairs 1966.

FASKOW, Donald R., of Pittsburgh, Pa., pension consultant, born 1934; second Chicago 1963, Life Masters Men's Pairs 1967, won Spring Nat'l secondary Open Pairs 1970; winner of many regional titles including Mid-Atlantic Fall Masters Pairs 1967, Open Teams 1970, Independence Day Open Teams 1969, 1970, Spring Men's Pairs 1972, Great Lakes Open Pairs 1973. Vice-President Pittsburgh Bridge Schools, Inc.

FATHY, Mrs. Samika, of Cairo, Egypt, born 1923; World Women's Team Champion 1960; represented Egypt World Women's Team Olympiad 1964; national wins include Mixed Team 1959, Inter-Club 1962.

FEIGUS, Jay T., of Brooklyn, N.Y., labor relations mediator, born 1892; won Vanderbilt 1948, Marcus 1951; second Spingold 1942; regional wins include Eastern States Knockout Teams 1947, 1949.

FEIN, Hal, of Eastchester, N.Y., music publisher, born 1913; credited with being creator of Rock & Roll music. Won Spring Nat'l secondary Men's Pairs 1971, secondary Men's Teams 1972; many regional successes including Eastern States Knockout Teams 1971, Tri-State Open Teams 1968, Men's Pairs 1971, 1975.

FEINBERG, Harry (1903–1966), of San Francisco, Calif., lawyer; won Chicago 1940, Vanderbilt 1947; second Fall Nat'l Mixed Pairs 1941; regional successes include All-American Open Pairs 1948, Mixed Pairs 1956, Bridge Week Knockout Team 1953, Mixed Pairs 1956, Pacific Southwest Open Team 1954.

FEINGOLD, Dr. Adolph, of Ottawa, Ont., professor of engineering; won Summer Nat'l secondary Open Pairs 1973, several regional titles including Cambrian Shield Knockout Teams 1973, Fleur-de-Lys Open Teams 1974.

FEJERVARY, John, of Palo Alto, Calif., president of chemical company, won All-Western Open Teams 1969, Knockout Teams 1971, Bridge Week Open Teams 1971, Palm Springs Knockout Teams 1973.

FELD, Marshall L., of Brookline, Mass., salesman; winner of several regional titles including New England Fall Men's Pairs 1972, Long Island Open Pairs 1970.

FELDESMAN, Philip, of New York, N.Y., diamond merchant, born 1919; one of the leading American players; represented US World Pair Olympiad 1962, Bermuda Bowl 1966; won International Team Trials 1965, third 1967; won Herman 1962, Mott-Smith 1965, 1966, Reisinger 1969, Vanderbilt 1965, 1966, Summer Nat'l Life Masters Pairs 1961, 1962, 1967, Mixed Teams 1973, Fall Nat'l Senior Masters Individual 1957, Open Pairs 1961, Spring Nat'l Men's Pairs 1961, 1962, Men's Teams 1962, 1963, 1966; second Spingold 1969, Vanderbilt 1969, Spring Nat'l Men's Teams 1965, Open Pairs 1967, Blue Ribbons 1967, Chicago 1965; regional successes include Eastern States Knockout Teams 1962, 1963, 1964, 1973, 1974, Masters Pairs 1961, Southeastern Men's Teams 1959, Open Pairs 1969, Knockout Teams 1969.

FELDHEIM, Harold, of Hamden, Conn., computer programmer, born 1936; regional wins include New England Knockout Teams 1968, New York–New Jersey Men's Pairs 1973; contributor to the ACBL *Bulletin.* Author *Weak Two-Bid in Bridge.*

FELDMAN, Mark D., of Brookline, Mass., won Spring Nat'l Men's Teams 1974, second Vanderbilt 1974; winner of many regional titles including New England Knockout Teams 1974, Open Pairs 1971, Fun City Knockout Teams 1972.

FELDSTEIN, Gretchen (Mrs. Harold), of Eau Gallie, Fla.; won Marcus 1950, Fall Nat'l Women's Teams 1953, Open Pairs 1965, Spring Nat'l Women's Pairs 1960, second 1953, Southeastern Women's Teams 1970.

FELDSTEIN, Harold, of Eau Gallie, Fla., computer systems analyst, born 1919; won Marcus 1950, Fall Nat'l Open Pairs 1965, second Men's Pairs 1948.

FELL, Geoffrey (1904–1971), of Steeton, Yorks., England, company managing director; represented England in many Camrose matches; npc Great Britain's Open Team and Women's Team European Championships, and England in several Camrose matches; won National Pairs 1950, EBU Mixed teams 1952. Member Yorkshire CBA committee since its inception; Honorary Tournament Secretary and member of the Council of the EBU.

FELS, Robert, of Avon, Conn., retailer, born 1902; New England Fall Open Teams 1948, 1949, Individual 1949, Masters Teams 1954; many regional successes in New England during years 1940 to 1950.

FENKEL, Stanley O., of Elkins Park, Pa., plastics manufacturer, born 1902; second Spingold 1944, Chicago 1946, Vanderbilt 1954. Secretary and Treasurer of the Cavendish Bridge Club of Philadelphia.

FENWICK, Thomas, of Geneva, Switzerland, director, born 1928; represented Switzerland World Team Olympiad, 1960, 1968, European Championships 1965; national titles include Masters Pairs 1963, 1964, 1965. Contributor to *Bridge World.*

FERENCZY, George, of Budapest, pianist, born 1902; European Champion 1938, second 1935; Hungarian Champion 1938.

FERER, Leland E., of Miami Beach, Fla., import manager and bridge writer, born 1927; won Winter Nat'l Mixed Team 1958; second Summer Nat'l Golder Pairs 1953, Mixed Teams 1967, Fall Nat'l Mixed Pairs 1972, Blue Ribbon Pairs 1966; won Central States Mixed Pairs 1951, Knockout Teams 1967, Florida Men's Teams 1961, Mixed Pairs 1967, Southeastern Open Teams 1966. Former Vice-President Florida Unit and editor of its *Bridge News.*

FERGUSON, James P., of Belle Vernon, Pa., candy manufacturer, born 1907. Former ACBL Director, President 1961; other executive positions have included President Keystone Conference, President Pittsburgh Unit, and organizer of District 5.

FERNANDO, William, of Malaysia, director of employer's organization, born 1917; represented Malaysia Far East Championships 1963, 1965, 1966, 1972, 1973, 1974.

FETZNER, Raymond J., Jr., of Laurel, Md., US government analyst and bridge teacher, born 1923; won Summer Nat'l Comm. & Ind. Team 1962; second Summer Nat'l Men's Pairs 1965. Director Washington BL.

FIELD, Albert, of Astoria, N.Y., teacher, playing card collector and historian; Contributing Editor, *Bridge Encyclopedia.*

FIELD, Myron (formerly Fuchs) (1912–1974), of New York, N.Y., stockbroker, one of the leading American players; represented North America World Championship 1956; won Spingold 1951, 1955, Chicago 1950, Vanderbilt 1941; second Spingold 1939, 1940, Chicago 1951, Vanderbilt 1950, 1953, Mixed Team 1951, Life Masters Pairs 1940, Life Masters Individual 1948, Reisinger 1939, 1940, Eastern States Open Pairs 1938; other regional successes.

FIGUEIREDO, Gustavo J., of Rizal, Philippines, pharmaceutical executive, born 1921; second Far East Championships 1967; represented Philippines World Team Olympiad 1968; won National Open Teams twice. Director Philippine Contract Bridge League.

FILARSKI, Herman, of Deil, Netherlands, wine merchant, bridge teacher, and journalist, born 1912; one of the leading European bridge personalities, resident of Amsterdam until 1963; represented Netherlands World Pair Olympiad 1962, second Mixed Team event; represented Netherlands frequently in European Championships and other events 1947 to 1962; many national successes including Open Pairs and Open Teams. Contributor to many bridge magazines and to fifteen Dutch periodicals. Author of several books and an editor of official magazine, *Nederlandse Bridge Bond.* Tournament Director World Team Olympiad 1960. Member IBPA Executive Committee.

FINCKELSTEIN, A., of Brussels, Belgium, bridge teacher and writer, born 1908; represented Belgium World Team Olympiad 1964; third in De La Rue International Pair Championship 1957; represented Belgium in many European Championships, and won many national titles. Technical director of Belgian magazine *Bridge.*

FINK, Sidney B. (1903–1967), of Cleveland, Ohio, lawyer; many regional wins including Western States Open Team 1934, Open Pairs 1934, 1939, Southeastern Open Team 1939, Midwest Open Pairs 1946,

Great Lakes Open Team 1960; Trustee ACBL Charity Foundation. ACBL Director 1959–62.

FISCHER, Gary, of Miami, Fla., computer programmer, won Florida Open Teams 1971, Southeastern Men's Teams 1971, tied Open Teams 1972.

FISCHER, Norman H., of Columbus, Ohio, research mathematician, born 1941; second Fall Nat'l Life Masters Men's Pairs 1969, tied second Spring Nat'l Men's Teams 1969, winner of several regional events including Mid-Atlantic Summer Masters Pairs 1971, District 11 Life Masters Pairs 1971, President, Central Ohio BA 1973–75.

FISHBEIN, Harry J. (1898–1976), of New York, N.Y.; president of Mayfair Bridge Club; one of the outstanding American bridge personalities and players; represented US World Championship 1959; npc US Team 1960 World Olympiad; won Vanderbilt 1936, 1943, 1947, 1949, 1958, Spring Nat'l Men's Teams 1965, Mixed Pairs 1967, Summer Nat'l Mixed Teams 1947, Life Masters Pairs 1939, 1940, Summer Nat'l Men's Pairs 1959, Fall Nat'l Mixed Pairs 1937, 1942, 1946, Masters Individual 1942, 1952, Marcus 1967; second Spingold 1937, 1943, 1945, 1958, Marcus 1963, Chicago 1942, 1957, 1959, Fall Nat'l Men's Teams 1953, 1960, Summer Nat'l Mixed Team 1945, Fall Nat'l Open Pairs 1934, 1937, 1940, 1941, 1942, Summer Nat'l Men's Pairs 1940, Masters Individual 1938, Spring Nat'l Open Pairs 1968. Treasurer ACBL 1952–66. Writings include *Fishbein Convention.* See BIBLIOGRAPHY, C.

FISHER, Cecille (Mrs. Alec), of Toronto, Ont.; represented Canada World Women's Team Olympiad 1964; won Canadian National Mixed Pairs 1959 and 1962.

FISHER, David C., of Columbia, S.C., business manager, born 1944; winner of several regional titles including Mid-South Open Pairs 1969, Mid-Atlantic Winter Knockout Teams 1972, 1973.

FISHER, Dr. John W., of Dallas, Tex., physician, born 1925; one of the leading American players; second World Olympiad Open Pairs 1966; won Mc Kenney 1972; won Vanderbilt 1965, Grand National 1975, Spring Nat'l Open Pairs 1970, 1971, 1972, 1974, Fall Nat'l Open Pairs 1958, Summer Nat'l Mixed Teams 1964; second Mixed Teams 1961, 1967, 1972, Spring Nat'l Men's Teams 1971, Fall Nat'l Men's Teams 1954, 1956, 1968; numerous regional successes include Texas Fall Open Team 1959, 1960, Open Pairs 1952, 1957, Men's Pairs 1953, 1957, Mixed Pairs 1960, Missouri Valley Open Teams 1970, 1973, 1974, Open Pairs 1974. President Dallas BA 1960–61. Invented the FISHER DOUBLE.

FISHER, Mrs. Margaret L., of Washington, D.C., publications editor and bridge columnist, born 1915;

won Sr. and Advanced Sr. Masters Pairs 1953; won Mid-Atlantic Fall Open Teams 1954 and 1960, Spring Open Pairs 1960. Former Secretary Mid-Atlantic BC.

FISHER, Richard C., of Tokyo, Japan, export manager, born 1921; won Northeastern Regional Open Teams 1943; since the war has won practically every major event in Japan; since 1947 active in forming duplicate tournaments and directing them; instrumental in having Japanese Master Players accepted by ACBL.

FLANNERY, William L., of McKees Rocks, Pa., born 1932; second Chicago 1963, Fall Nat'l Life Masters Men's Pairs 1967, Summer Nat'l Mixed Pairs 1968; winner of many regional titles including Upper New York State Open Teams 1963, 1965, Mid-Atlantic Fall Masters Pairs 1967, Winter Open Pairs 1968. Originator of FLANNERY TWO DIAMONDS convention.

FLASHER, Mrs. Mary, of Columbus, Ohio, retired bridge columnist and teacher, born 1901; won Midwest Spring Mixed Pairs 1949. Author of *You, Too, Can Play Bridge*.

FLEIG, Milton, of Laguna Hills, Calif., supervisor, born 1908; won Nat'l Comm. & Ind. Team 1959, Central States Men's Pairs 1955, Open Team 1956.

FLEISCHMAN, Richard K., Jr., of Hilo, Haw., professor, born 1941; winner of several regional championships including District 11 Knockout Teams 1969, Can-Am Knockout Teams 1972, Peach Festival Knockout Teams 1974.

FLEISCHMAN, Simon (Jimmy) (1896–1964) of New York, N.Y., export and import company president; European Champion 1932, 1933; represented Austria European Championships 1934, 1935.

FLEMING, Mrs. A. Leslie ("Dimmie"), of Tunbridge Wells, England, born 1911. One of the leading European women players. Won World Women's Team Olympiad 1964 and European Women's Champion 1951, 1952, 1959, 1963. Second European Open Championship 1953 (the only woman ever to represent Great Britain in the Open Series). Represented Great Britain on many other occasions, including World Women's Team Olympiad 1960, World Women's Pair Olympiad 1962, 1970, 1974, and tour of United States in 1953. National wins include Gold Cup 1950, British Women's Teams 1945, 1951, 1953, 1958, 1959, English Women's Teams 1947, 1951, 1953, 1958, 1959. Secretary of English Bridge Union 1956–75. Regular contributor to *Bridge Magazine*. Contributing Editor *Bridge Encyclopedia*.

FLETCHER, Mrs. Peggy, of Cardiff, Wales, born 1896; represented Great Britain World Women's

Pairs Olympiad 1962, and Wales in numerous Camrose Trophy and Lady Milne matches; national successes include Women's Teams 1945, 1953, 1955, 1960, 1964, 1965.

FLINT, Jeremy, of London, England, born 1928; one of the most successful players on both sides of the Atlantic; second World Team Olympiad 1960; European Champion 1963, second 1971; represented Great Britain World Pair Olympiad 1962, 1970, World Team Olympiad 1964, 1972, European Championship 1962, 1970, 1974; won Master Pairs 1963, 1964, Gold Cup 1964, Spring Foursomes 1971, 1972, 1973, Life Masters Pairs 1964, 1973; during his 1966 year's tour of the US, he won Mid-Atlantic Winter Open Teams, Men's Pairs, All-American Open Teams, Bridge Week Open Pairs, Northern Rocky Mountain Men's Pairs, Open Teams, New England Masters Pairs, Northwest Open Teams, Midwest Fall Open Teams, Open Pairs, District 4 Open Teams, Men's Pairs, Southern Spring Masters Pairs. Achieved the unique distinction of making Life Master of the ACBL within eleven weeks. Originator of the FLINT convention; other contributions to bidding theory include the LITTLE MAJOR. Author of *Tiger Bridge*. See BIBLIOGRAPHY, E.

FLINT, Honor (Mrs. Jeremy), of London, England; represented Great Britain World Women's Pairs Olympiad 1970, 1974, European Women's Championship 1970, 1971; national wins include English Women's Team 1970, 1972, Spring Foursomes 1971, 1972, 1973.

FLOREA, Harold R., of Winter Park, Fla., engineering manager, born 1914; won Fall National Masters Individual 1960, Florida Regional Mixed Pairs 1969. Introduced Swiss movement to bridge team play when director of 27-team Long Island Industrial Bridge League in 1962.

FLOURNOY, Carolyn C. (Mrs. Camp R.), of Shreveport, La., newspaper columnist; won Fall Nat'l Mixed Pairs 1970, several regional titles including South Texas Knockout Teams 1971, Open Teams 1971.

FLOYD, Jason H., of Gulfport, Miss., lawyer; won Mid-South Open Pairs 1942, Mixed Pairs 1942, Open Team 1962, Gulf Coast Mid-South Open Teams 1972.

FOCACCI, Domingo, of Lima, Peru, merchant, born 1904; npc South American Champion Women's Team 1963; represented Peru South American Championships 1962, 1963. President Peruvian Bridge Association.

FOERING, Howard (1910–73), of Bethlehem, Pa., electrical engineer; won Canadian–American Open

Team 1954, Open Pairs 1953. ACBL Associate National Tournament Director. ACBL communications specialist.

FOLLINE, Emily (Mrs. J. E.), of Columbia, S.C., born 1907; won Chicago 1949, Fall Nat'l Women's Team 1943, 1944, 1945, 1946, Nat'l Open Individual 1950; second Nat'l Women's Team 1942, Summer Nat'l Mixed Team 1946, 1947, Nat'l Open Individual 1947; won Mid-Atlantic Summer Open Teams 1964, Fall Open Teams and Mixed Pairs 1956.

FONG, Y. T., of Hong Kong, businessman; represented Hong Kong Far East Championship eight times; national wins include Open Teams, Master Teams, Open Pairs, Master Pairs.

FONSECA, Christiano G., of Brazil, operations manager, born 1940; South American Champion 1970, 1971, 1972, 1973, represented Brazil World Championship 1973, 1974, World Pair Olympiad 1974; national titles include Open Teams 1970, 1972, 1973, 1974.

FOOTE, Margery (Mrs. J. M.), of Phoenix, Ariz., born 1897; won World Par Contest 1941, Desert Empire Women's Pairs 1956, Pacific Southwest Open Teams 1951, Women's Pairs 1957.

FORBES, Dr. Robert Y., of Maidenhead, England, physician, born 1924; won Scottish National Pairs 1956, 1957, English Masters Individual 1959; represented Scotland seventeen times in Camrose Trophy matches; and other Scottish successes.

FORBES, Dr. Ronald, of Barrie, Ont., formerly of Jamaica, pathologist; represented Canada World Team Olympiad 1964; won Canadian-American Men's Pairs 1962, Canadian Nat'l Open Teams 1966.

FORBES, Sheila A., of Toronto, Ont., law clerk; winner of several regional titles including Canadian-American Knockout Teams 1972, Cambrian Shield Open Teams 1972.

FOREACRE, Joseph J. (1913–1969), of Kansas City, Mo., flight trainer operator; second Nat'l Open Individual 1945, Fall Nat'l Men's Team 1951; won Eastern States Mixed Pairs 1954.

FORQUET, Pietro, of Naples, Italy, banker, born 1925. One of the greatest players of all time, and considered by many to be the best player in the world. Won World Team Olympiad 1964, 1968, 1972 and World Championships 1957, 1958, 1959, 1961, 1962, 1963, 1965, 1966, 1967, 1969, 1973, 1974. Perhaps the greatest of the Italian players during the BLUE TEAM's remarkable string of ten consecutive World Championships from 1957–69, Forquet established a

reputation for calm, unruffled performances, apparently immune from the nervous tension which often afflicted his opponents. Using the NEAPOLITAN SYSTEM, he played equally well with three different partners, SINISCALCO, CHIARADIA, and GAROZZO. In 1972 he adopted the PRECISION SYSTEM which he used with GAROZZO in the Olympiad, and then in partnership with Benito BIANCHI in the 1973 and 1974 Bermuda Bowls. He won the European Title in 1951 when making his first appearance in the event at the age of twenty-six, and won the title again in 1956, 1957, 1958, 1959. Many Italian national successes include Open Teams 1951, 1956, 1957, 1959, 1963, 1967, 1968. See BLUE TEAM.

FORSTER, Dale E., of Eugene, Ore., realtor, born 1942; winner of several regional events including Rocky Mountain Open Pairs 1969, Mid-Winter Holiday Knockout Teams 1971.

FOSTER, Robert Frederick (1853–1945), of New York, N.Y., surveyor, and writer and lecturer on card games. Born in Scotland, his first profession, which he combined with prospecting for gold, took him to many parts of the world. After making and losing two fortunes, he established himself as the world's leading authority on card games of all kinds by writing *Foster's Complete Hoyle* (1897) (a copy was included in the time capsule at the 1939 New York World's Fair). Teaching and writing about whist was his chief occupation from 1888 onwards. His chief theoretical contribution was the discovery of the RULE OF ELEVEN, and he promoted many new ideas in his *Vanity Fair* magazine column, and his column in the New York *Sun*. His writings followed the successive developments of bridge, auction, and contract, and he wrote the first set of laws for the last-named game. He lectured on games in many countries throughout the world, and continued to teach and conduct duplicate games in New York up to the age of eighty-five. AWL Director. His books included *Whist Tactics* (1895), *Duplicate Whist and Whist Strategy* (1894), *Foster's Bridge* (1902), *Foster's Modern Bridge Tactics* (1925), *Foster on Auction and Contract* (1929), *Vanity Fair Bridge Problems* (1932), and many others. See BIBLIOGRAPHY, A, E, J.

FOX, Betty (Mrs. G. C.H., formerly Mrs. Trevor Harris), of London, England; won European Women's Championship 1966; represented Great Britain European Women's Championship 1965. In 1964, won English Bridge Union Women's Teams, County Teams of Four, British Women's Team of Four, Women's Individual, and London's Women's Pairs, a complete sweep of all the major women's events.

FOX, G. C. H., of London, bridge teacher and journalist, born 1914; author of *Sound Bidding at Contract* and *Duplicate Bridge, Its Procedures and Tactics,* bridge correspondent of the *Daily Telegraph,* and contributor to *British Bridge World* and *Bridge Magazine.* See BIBLIOGRAPHY, C, F.

FOX, George, of Cardiff, Wales, company director, born 1911; represented Wales in international events; national wins include Welsh Cup 1955, 1958, 1960; Open Pairs 1960, 1963.

FOX, Robert S., of Providence, R.I., cardboard products manufacturer, born 1919; winner of many regional championships including New England Knockout Team 1953, 1956, 1959, 1962, 1963, Open Team 1952, 1954, 1958, 1962.

FOX, Mrs. Siddy S., of Pittsburgh, Pa., programmer, born 1940; won Mid-Atlantic Women's Pairs 1969, Keystone Women's Pairs 1970, District 5 Women's Pairs 1970.

FRAENCKEL, Mrs. Rigmor, of Copenhagen, Denmark, bridge teacher, born 1909; third World Women's Team Olympiad 1960; represented Denmark World Women's Team Olympiad 1964; European Women's Champion 1948, 1949, 1955, 1957, 1958; Scandinavian Women's Team Champion four times; national titles include Open and Mixed Team.

FRANCIS, Henry G., of Memphis, Tenn. (formerly of Nahant, Mass.), editor, born 1926; won New England Open Pairs 1958, Canadian-Atlantic Knockout Teams 1968, 1969, 1970. Former Editor of the NEBL *Bulletin,* ACBL Associate National Tournament Director. Joined ACBL staff in 1972 as Associate Editor of *The Bulletin,* becoming its Executive Editor and Editor of World Championship Books in 1973; former News and Sports Editor, *Boston Herald Traveler;* President Professional Tournament Directors Assn. 1969–72.

FRANCO, Arturo, of Milan, Italy, insurance agent, born 1946; won World Championship 1974, 1975, European Champion 1973; won Italy Cup 1972, 1973, Mixed Teams 1967, 1970.

FRANCO, Mario, of Milan, Italy; European Champion 1951, runner-up 1952, 1955; represented Italy World Championships 1951; national successes include Italian Knockout Teams 1955, Open Teams 1955, and many others. Originator of the MARMIC SYSTEM.

FRANK, Aaron J., of Cleveland, Ohio, attorney, born 1909; second Spingold 1934, Chicago 1952, Fall Nat'l Open Pairs 1944, Men's Team 1954.

FRANKEL, Mrs. Jean, of New Orleans, La., bridge teacher, born 1926; second Summer Nat'l Mixed Teams 1961, Women's Pairs 1965, Spring Nat'l Women's Teams 1968; winner of many regional titles including Mid-South Summer Mixed Pairs 1962, 1966, 1970, Open Teams 1970, Mid-South Winter Knockout Teams 1973, Open Teams 1973.

FRANKLIN, Harold, of Leeds, England, tournament director and bridge writer, born 1915; represented Great Britain European Championship 1952, 1956; npc World Women's Team Olympiad Champions 1964, Women's Team European Championship 1965, 1967; won Gold Cup 1954, 1960, Master Pairs 1952, with other national championships. Member of Laws Commission of European Bridge League; Chief Tournament Director of English Bridge Union, and of several international tournaments, including World Pair Olympiad 1962 and European Championship 1961; member WBF Tournament Planning Committee; International Tournament Director of the World Bridge Federation since 1970. Bridge columnist of *Yorkshire Post,* and regular broadcaster. See BIBLIOGRAPHY, G.

FRASER, Douglas, of Montreal, Que.; tied second Summer Nat'l Mixed Teams 1974, tied Canadian Nat'l Open Teams 1973.

FREDD, Claudius G., of Atlanta, Ga., liquor distributor, born 1921. A top-ranking player of the American Bridge Association and Chairman of its Tournament Authority. Winner of more than 170 championships, more than any other ABA player.

FREEDMAN, Mrs. Minnie, of Perth, Western Australia, born 1907; represented Australia Women's Olympiad 1972, Far East Women's Championships 1971, 1972.

FREEDMAN, Richard N., of Waltham, Mass., computer programmer, born 1945; won New England Masters Pairs 1971, Eastern States Open Pairs 1972, Motor City Open Teams 1973.

FREEDMAN, Robert P., of Buffalo, N.Y., attorney, born 1926; represented US World Pair Olympiad 1970; won Summer Nat'l Mixed Teams 1956, Spring Nat'l secondary Open Pairs 1969; second Mixed Teams 1955, Life Master Pairs 1970; regional wins include Canadian Nat'l Open Teams 1957, Upper New York State Open Pairs 1957, 1972, Open Teams 1960, 1970, 1971, Master Pairs 1965. ACBL Director 1956–57.

FREEMAN, Louise K. (Mrs. Richard, formerly Mrs. W. C. Robinson), of Atlanta, Ga., born 1933; winner of many regional titles including Mid-Atlantic Fall Open Teams 1962, 1964, Spring Open Teams 1961, 1962, 1965, Summer Open Teams 1967.

FREEMAN, Richard, of Atlanta, Ga., manufacturing executive, born 1933; won Fall Nat'l Men's Team 1955, 1962, Summer Nat'l Mixed Teams 1961, Spring Nat'l Men's Teams 1966; second Spingold 1959, Fall Nat'l Men's Teams 1958, Open Teams 1965, Blue Ribbon Pairs 1970; winner of numerous regional titles including Mid-Atlantic Fall Open Teams 1951, 1956, 1962, 1964, Winter Open Teams 1958, 1965, Eastern States Knockout Teams 1960, 1961.

FREIER, Morris H., of St. Paul, Minn., transportation planner, born 1926; second Life Masters Pairs 1966, winner of many regional titles including Gopher Open Teams 1958, 1965, 1967, Men's Pairs 1964, Knockout Teams 1968.

FRENCH, Capt. Fred G., (1893–1958), army officer and bridge teacher and writer of Philadelphia, Pa.; ABL President 1931, member of Advisory Council of Bridge Headquarters which drafted and approved OFFICIAL SYSTEM.

FRENKIEL, Marian, of Warsaw, Poland, journalist for Polish Radio, born 1919; represented Poland World Mixed Pairs Olympiad 1966; won Baltic Bowl 1966, Polish Open Teams 1960, 1961, 1965, Open Pairs 1965, Mixed Pairs 1965; second Mixed Pairs 1964.

FREY, Mabel (Mrs. Richard L.), born 1905, a recorder at many international championships; set a record in 1935–36 by winning two consecutive Women's Pairs events at the Eastern Regionals in partnership with her mother, Mrs. G. Planco. Won New England Knockout Team 1936.

FREY, Richard L(incoln), writer, editor, and champion player, editor of the ACBL's *Contract Bridge Bulletin* 1958–70, and editor-in-chief of this *Bridge Encyclopedia,* born Feb. 12, 1905, in New York City. After his first major tournament victory, the Goldman Pairs in the Eastern Championships of 1930, and high position in the earliest masters' individual contests, as an original member of the BID-RITE TEAM (1931–32) and of the FOUR ACES (1933–35), he won most of the highest-ranked national championships. He had the best tournament record in 1934. He was No. 8 in the first group of players to be designated Life Masters when that designation was created. He temporarily dropped out of tournament play 1937–41, but resumed in 1942, and won both the Vanderbilt and Spingold events. For more than twenty years he had the highest percentage of national tournament victories out of events entered.

Other successes included Asbury Park Challenge Teams 1933, Vanderbilt, Spingold, Masters Pairs, and Grand National Teams all 1934, and Grand National Teams 1935. Second in seven other national championships and won five other regional championships.

In 1935 Frey resigned from the Four Aces to join the Culbertson organization as sales manager for Kem Playing Cards, an editor of *The Bridge World* magazine, technical consultant on the CULBERTSON SYSTEM and a player on Culbertson teams, often as Culbertson's partner. After the sale of Kem in 1937, Frey returned to the advertising business. He had begun a daily newspaper bridge column in 1937, took over writing the Four Aces column in 1944, and in 1954 merged the two in collaboration with Howard Schenken. In 1970, when he turned the column over to Schenken, his was the longest continuously published syndicated bridge feature in the US. His books

on canasta (1950–51) sold more than a million copies, and his *According to Hoyle* (1956), nearly two million. He is author of *How to Win at Contract Bridge in Ten Easy Lessons* (1958).

From the mid-forties until he joined the ACBL in 1958, Frey was a free-lance writer on diverse non-fiction subjects for some of the major magazines. Following his retirement from ACBL in 1970, he became chairman of the Goren Editorial Board, president of the International Bridge Press Association, and a consultant on various bridge projects.

Frey pioneered in bridge exhibitions and TV shows, initiated the Inter-City Challenge Matches (1960) and the North American Rubber Bridge Championship (1962); served as chief commentator at Bridge-O-Rama exhibitions of national and World Championships; edited twelve World Championship and World Olympiad Hand Books and the records of four International Team Trials. See BIBLIOGRAPHY, E, G.

FRIEDBERG, Joel M., of West Hempstead, N.Y., born 1954; won Summer Nat'l Senior and Advanced Senior Masters Pairs 1973.

FRIEDENBERG, Judi. See SOLODAR, JUDI.

FRIEDBERG, Robert, of Houston, Tex., attorney, born 1906; won Mexican Nat'l Open Teams 1962, Texas Conference Men's Pairs 1952; second Mexican Nat'l Masters Pairs 1960, Mid-South Spring Open Teams 1954.

FRIEDLANDER, Jerome M., of Little Falls, N.J., born 1906; won Eastern States Open Pairs 1945, Reisinger 1947, Canadian-American Open Team 1953, Canadian Nat'l Open Teams 1957, Upper New York Open Team 1960; second Canadian-American Open Team 1960, District 5 Open Team 1961. ACBL Regional Tournament Director.

FRISCHAUER, Dr. Edward (1895–1964), criminal lawyer and real-estate broker of Hollywood, Calif.; one of the greatest dummy-players of all time. He was born in Vienna and in World War I served in the Austro-Hungarian army; he emigrated to the United States in 1938, after Austria was annexed by Germany. World Champion 1937 as a member of the Austrian Team which played in Budapest; American successes included Nat'l Mixed Team 1953; second Spingold 1953; regional wins included Bridge Week Knockout Team 1952, Master Team 1951, Mixed Team 1953, Master Pairs 1944, Open Pairs 1944, Men's Pairs 1955, Mixed Pairs 1954, Pacific Southwest Open Team 1946, 1957, 1958, Open Pairs 1948, Men's Pairs 1950, Mixed Pairs 1950, All-Western Open Teams 1957; second All-Western Open Team 1958, Bridge Week Open Team 1959, Pacific Southwest Open Team 1950.

FRY, Sam, Jr., of New York, N.Y., secretary of REGENCY CLUB, New York, born 1909; one of the outstanding American bridge players and personalities; represented North America 1959 World Championship; won AWL Open Teams 1933, 1934, Open Pairs 1933, 1934; won USBA Open Teams 1936; won Asbury Challenge Teams 1933, Men's Pairs 1934, Spingold 1937, 1941, 1945, Vanderbilt 1958; second Vanderbilt 1933, 1935, 1942, Summer Nat'l Mixed Team 1957, Life Masters Pairs 1940, Fall Nat'l Open Pairs 1933, 1947. Won Reisinger 1935, other Eastern States titles from 1933, with many successes in other regional events. Numerous writings on bridge and other games include *How to Win at Bridge with Any Partner* and a modern edition of Watson's *Play of the Hand at Bridge*. Contributing editor of *The Bridge World* since 1932, and of the *Bridge Encyclopedia*. See BIBLIOGRAPHY, E.

FRYDRICH, Julian, of Tel Aviv, Israel, journalist, born in Poland 1937; European Champion 1975; represented Israel European Championships 1966, 1967, 1969, 1970, 1971, 1973, 1974, captain 1967; won Israel Open Pairs 1966, 1967, 1972, 1973, 1974, Tel Aviv Open Teams 1966. Editor Israeli publication *Bridge*. Sports Captain Israel Bridge Federation 1970–72.

FUA, Constant, of Cuernavaca, Mexico, business executive, bridge writer and director, born 1909; represented Mexico World Team Olympiad 1964; won Mexican Nat'l Knockout Team 1951–58 inclusive, Open Pairs 1962, Men's Pairs 1955, 1962, Mixed Pairs 1960; second Open Team 1960, Master Pairs 1960. Author of *Mexico Juega Bridge* and *Bridge International;* bridge correspondent of the Mexican *Excelsior*.

FUKUSHIMA, Everett A., of Honolulu, Haw.; won Fall Nat'l secondary Swiss Teams 1971, Desert Empire Men's Pairs 1972, Mount Shasta Open Teams 1974.

FULLER, H.E., of Portland, Ore.; won Spring Nat'l secondary Swiss Teams 1970, Oregon Trail Open Teams 1970, Knockout Teams 1971.

FULTON, Charles L., of Raleigh, N.C.; winner of several regional titles including Mid-Atlantic Spring Open Teams 1971, Summer Open Teams 1972.

FULWILER, C. H., of Albuquerque, N.M., investment and finance counselor, born 1886; wins and seconds in many regional events. ACBL Director, President Western Division ACBL 1940, Trustee Western Division ACBL. Inventor of FULWILER CONVENTION.

G

GABARRET, Adolfo (1890–1956) of Buenos Aires, Argentina, writer and journalist; pioneer of Argen-

tine bridge; long time participant in the Argentine Bridge Association and its tournament affairs; South American Champion 1954; won Argentine Open Teams 1940, 1941, 1943; participated in a radio match against Culbertson's team in 1936. Bridge columnist for both domestic and foreign magazines; author of several books and translations, including *Bridge Duplicado*, 1942; *Compendio de Bridge*, 1944; *El Carteo en Bridge Contrato*, 1948; *Codigo y Regalmento de Bridge y Organización de Torneos*, 1952.

GABBEY, Hugh Maurice, of Helen's Bay, Northern Ireland, banker, born 1907; represented Ireland European Championship 1958; national wins include Irish Open Team three times, Northern Ireland Open Pairs four times, and Mixed Pairs seven times.

GABRIEL, Charles, of Fort Worth, Tex., scientific analyst, born 1933; won Grand Nationals 1975; regional wins include North Texas Knockout Team 1961, Texas Conference Open Team 1961.

GABRILOVITCH, Andrew, of Stamford, Conn., physicist, born 1925; won Spingold 1961, second 1959; winner of many regional titles including Eastern States Knockout Teams 1961, Keystone Open Pairs 1958, Men's Pairs 1971, Men's Teams 1970, 1971, 1973, Knockout Teams 1974. President Washington BL 1962–63.

GAER, Gerald, of Phoenix, Ariz., insurance agent, born 1934; won Fall Nat'l secondary Men's Pairs 1971, Midwinter Knockout Teams 1970, California Capitol Knockout Teams 1970, 1971, Desert Empire Knockout Teams 1974.

GAER, Margaret E. (Mrs. Gerald, formerly Mrs. M. Alcorn), of Phoenix, Ariz., bridge teacher, born 1921; won Summer Nat'l Women's Pairs 1954, Fall Nat'l Women's Teams 1959, Mixed Pairs 1964, Life Master Women's Pairs 1964, Spring Nat'l Women's Pairs 1964; second Spring Nat'l Women's Pairs 1955. Regional victories include Missouri Valley Open Teams 1961, Desert Empire Open Teams 1974.

GAINES, Joel. See KANSIL, PRINCE DJOLI.

GALE, Bee. See SCHENKEN, BEE.

GALLAGHER, Jacqui. See MITCHELL, JACQUI.

GANZ, Elsa M. (Mrs. Frederick M.), of San Francisco, Calif., born 1904; winner of several regional championships including All-Western Masters Pairs 1959, Rogue River Valley Open Teams 1973, Pacific Southwest Open Teams 1973, Women's Pairs 1973.

GARDENER, Nico (formerly Goldinger), of London, England, bridge teacher, born 1908; one of the leading European players; represented Great Britain in World Team Olympiad 1960 (second), World Pair Olympiad 1962, and World Championship 1950 and 1962; won Mixed Team event World Pair Olympiad 1962; represented Great Britain in five European Championships, winning in 1950 and 1961, second in 1953; won Gold Cup 1946, 1951, 1954, 1958, 1967, 1968, and 1970, Master Pairs 1953; London *Sunday Times* 1970. Co-author of *Bridge for Beginners* and *Card Play Technique*. See BIBLIOGRAPHY, D, E; FAMILY. Inventor of GARDENER NO TRUMP OVERCALL CONVENTION.

GARDENER, Nicola, of London, England, bridge school director, born 1949; represented Great Britain European Women's Championships 1970, 1973, 1974, winning 1975; national successes include English Women's Teams 1971. See FAMILY.

GARDENER, Patricia (Mrs. Nico), of London, England; represented Great Britain European Women's Championships 1938, 1953, 1955, 1957; national successes include English Women's Teams 1970, 1972. See FAMILY.

GARDNER, James L., of Forsyth, Mont., warehouse manager; won Summer Nat'l Special Pairs 1974, District 5 Open Teams 1973, Midwest Open Teams 1973.

GARDNER, Robert R., of Chicago, Ill., accountant, born 1946; won Spring Nat'l secondary Swiss Teams 1973, several regional titles including Tri-Unit Men's Pairs 1970, Open Teams 1972, Mixed Pairs 1973.

GARFIELD, Evelyn (Mrs. Leonard), of Marblehead, Mass., accountant; winner of several regional titles including New England Knockout Teams 1960, Master Women's Pairs 1968, Open Teams 1971.

GARGRAVE, Jeffrey J., of W. Carrolton, Ohio, financial analyst, born 1949; won Summer Nat'l Special Pairs 1973, several regional titles including Great Lakes Open Teams 1973, Motor City Open Teams 1973, Masters Pairs 1973.

GARNER, Michael, of Chicago, Ill., option trader; winner of several regional titles including Keystone Men's Pairs 1970, Masters Pairs 1973, Puerto Rico Men's Pairs 1971, Open Pairs 1971, Open Teams 1971.

GAROZZO, Benito, of Rome, Italy, jewelry-store owner, born 1927; one of the world's greatest players; World Champion 1961, 1962, 1963, 1964, 1965, 1966, 1967, 1968, 1969, 1972, 1973, 1974, 1975; second World Pair Olympiad 1970. As of 1969, never on a losing team in international competition; formed one of the great partnerships of the world with Pietro FORQUET through 1972; since 1972 had

paired with Georgio BELLADONNA in what many consider to be the best partnership in the world. National wins include Italian Open Team 1958, 1963, 1967, 1968. See also BLUE TEAM.

GARVEY, Clarence Jr., of St. Louis, Mo., attorney and real estate broker, born 1917; won Mississippi Valley Masters Individual 1959. First Life Master in Hawaii. President Honolulu Unit 1951–53, Director St. Louis Unit 1957–59.

GATES, Georgiana C., of San Francisco, Calif., computer programmer, born 1945; winner of several regional titles including All-Western Women's Teams 1973, Mount Shasta Masters Pairs 1974.

GEERS, Donald C., of St. Louis, Mo., engineer, born 1924; won Spring Nat'l Individual 1963, Nat'l Comm. & Ind. Teams 1965, Pairs 1967.

GELEERD, William L., Jr., of Glenview, Ill., importer, born 1930; won Senior and Advanced Senior Master Pairs 1971.

GELMAN, Jerry, of Hollywood, Fla., sales director, born 1905; won Midwest Spring Mixed Pairs 1953, Rocky Mountain Open Team 1951, District 5 Men's Pairs 1958, Southeastern Open Pairs 1959.

GENUD, Maury, of Los Angeles, Calif., child psychologist and teacher, born 1940; Team Trialist 1967; won Spring Nat'l Open Pairs 1967, Mid-South Fall Open Teams 1967, Rocky Mountain Men's Pairs 1968, 1969, Knockout Teams 1969. ACBL analyst 1965 Team Trials report; contributor to *Bridge World;* columnist for *Los Angeles Bridge News.* President Westwood Unit.

GEOFFRION, C.A., of Montreal, Que., attorney, born 1916; won Canadian-American Men's Pairs 1951, Mixed pairs 1952, Open Teams 1952.

GERARD, Alice, of Orlando, Fla., accountant; won Summer Nat'l Marcus Teams 1971; winner of several regional titles including Florida Women's Teams 1961, Knockout Teams 1967, Florida Swiss Teams 1972.

GERBER, John, of Houston, Tex., manufacturer, born 1906; one of the leading American players and personalities; represented North America in World Championship 1961, npc North American Team World Championship 1962, 1963, 1965; won Summer Nat'l Mixed Teams 1964, Men's Pairs 1959, Chicago 1964, Fall Nat'l Men's Team 1953, 1965, 1968, Spring Nat'l Mixed Pairs 1956; second Spingold 1954, 1967, Chicago 1957, 1959, Summer Nat'l Open Teams 1963, Men's Pairs 1957, Mixed Teams 1967, Fall Nat'l Mixed Pairs 1953, 1968, Life Master Men's Pairs 1974; regional wins include Mid-South Spring Open Teams 1941, 1942, 1952, Open Pairs

1949, 1962, Men's Pairs 1966, Texas Spring Open Teams 1960, 1966, Texas Fall Mixed Pairs 1967, Knockout Teams 1969. Inventor of the GERBER (Four Club) Convention. Former ACBL Director. See BIBLIOGRAPHY, C; BUENOS AIRES AFFAIR.

GERDES, Franz Maurice, of Brooklyn, N.Y., pharmaceutical representative and bridge teacher, born 1932; first Life Master in Haiti; won Master Teams, Open Teams, Master Pairs, Open Pairs, and Individual in Haiti, all in 1959; won award as best player of the year 1959, 1961. Tournament director Haitian Bridge League 1962–63.

GERST, Herbert (1888–1963), of Norfolk, Va., laundry chain executive, served in the Navy in both World Wars; second Fall Nat'l Men's Teams 1949; won several Mid-Atlantic titles in Open Teams, Men's Pairs, and Mixed Pairs. ACBL Director.

GERSTMAN, Daniel M., of Buffalo, N.Y., insurance salesman, born 1948; won Summer Nat'l secondary Swiss Teams 1972, Fall Nat'l secondary Open Pairs 1972, Upper New York Men's Pairs 1972.

GERSTMAN, Nat, of Buffalo, N.Y. One of the leading players in his area, with close to 5,000 master points as of 1975, resulting from innumerable regional wins. These include New England Open Teams 1965, 1966; Swiss Teams 1969.

GHESTEM, Pierre, of Lille, France, merchant, born 1929; one of the leading players of the world; World Champion 1956; World Team Olympiad Champion 1960. Also represented France in World Championships 1954, 1961, 1963, European Championships 1965. European Champion 1953, 1955, 1962, second 1956, 1961. National wins include Open Teams 1962, 1964. Inventor of the complex RELAY SYSTEM (also called Monaco), with which he had many major successes in partnership with René BACHERICH.

GIDDINGS, Ruth (Mrs. O. G.), of Dublin, Ireland; represented Ireland World Women's Team Olympiad 1960, 1964; in many European Women's Championships, second 1954; National wins include four Irish Open Pairs and five CBA of Ireland Mixed Pairs.

GILL, Brigadier General Robert J., of Baltimore. Md., attorney; a leading personality in the American Contract Bridge League, Presdent 1941, Honorary Member 1945; Chairman of ACBL Committee on membership eligibility 1952.

GIMKIEWICZ, Benno, of Bangkok, Thailand, merchant, born 1922; represented Thailand World Team Olympiad 1964, World Pair Olympiad 1966, 1970, 1974; Far East Champion 1963, 1966; national successes include Masters Teams 1963, Open Team

1964, Masters Individual 1959, and Inter-Club Open Team 1963.

GINSBERG, Martin, of Atlantic Beach, N.Y., manufacturer, born 1935; won Marcus 1961, New York-New Jersey Open Pairs 1960, Men's Pairs 1961, Open Teams 1966, Bermuda Open Pairs 1968.

GIOVINE, Michele, of Milan, Italy, car agent and bridge writer, born 1922; Italian Cup Champion 1955, 1958, Italian Champion Open Team 1955; second European Championship 1952, 1955. Inventor of MARMIC system, and author of book in Italian on it.

GITTLEMAN, Mrs. Arthur, of Philadelphia, Pa., born 1905; won Eastern States Women's Pairs 1961, Southeastern Women's Team 1959, Keystone Women's Teams 1971.

GLATT, Arthur (1909–1975), of Lincolnwood, Ill., financial consultant, won Fall Nat'l Men's Pairs 1946, Men's Team 1946, Open Pairs 1951; second Spingold 1948, Chicago 1936, Mixed Pairs 1936, Life Masters Pairs 1949, 1952, Spring Men's Team 1962; numerous regional victories include All-American Open Team 1938, 1939, Open Pairs 1938, 1940, Midwest Open Team 1960. Technical advisor TV program "Championship Bridge."

GLENN, Richard M. C., of Richmond, Va., employment agent, born 1917; won Fall Nat'l International Fund Pairs 1973, winner of several regional titles including Mid-Atlantic Spring Men's Pairs 1956, 1971.

GLICK, Jefferson ("Jeff"), of Miami Beach, Fla., manufacturer's representative, born 1906. One of the leading American bridge personalities; npc United States team World Championship 1956; won Spingold 1949, Chicago 1949, Fall Nat'l Men's Teams 1947, 1948, 1954, 1958, Mixed Pairs 1941, Asbury Challenge Teams 1934; second Spingold 1934, 1952, Chicago 1952. Many regional successes include Southeastern Open Teams 1953, 1954, Men's Teams 1952, Men's Pairs 1952, Mixed Pairs 1944, Southern Conference Open Team 1956, Open Pairs 1953, 1957, Mixed Pairs 1936. Many executive positions include ACBL President 1955, Director since 1951; President Florida Unit 1947–59, Executive Manager since 1960. ACBL Honorary Member 1964.

GLICK, Maury J. (1891–1966), of Miami Beach, Fla., salesman; won Chicago 1940; second Fall Nat'l Mixed Pairs 1935; won Western States Open Team 1936.

GLICK, Vera (Mrs. Jefferson), of Miami Beach, Fla.; won Fall Nat'l Women's Team 1953, Mixed

Pairs 1941; winner of several regional titles including Southeastern Open Team 1953, 1954, Mixed Pairs 1944.

GLUTTIG, Dr. Erich, of Vienna, Austria, born 1929; second European Championship 1957, and represented Austria on five other occasions. National titles include Open Pair Championship four times.

GLYKIS, Evangelos, of Greece, industrialist, born 1920; represented Greece World Olympiad 1968; national successes include Team Trials 1968, Mixed Pairs 1968. Executive Secretary Hellenic BF since 1974.

GODFREY, Mrs. W. M., of Colorado Springs, Colo., bridge teacher; won Rocky Mountain Women's Pairs 1957, 1970, Desert Empire Master Pairs 1957, New England Fall Women's Pairs 1961.

GOETZEE, Wouter, of Curaçao, Netherlands Antilles, accountant, born 1921; national win: Open Team 1961. Former President Dutch BL Curaçao District. One of the pioneers of the Netherlands Antilles BA, of which he is an honorary member.

GOLD, Sam, of Montreal, Que., retailer and tournament director, born 1908; one of the leading Canadian players; represented Canada 1964 World Team Olympiad; semi-finalist Spingold 1947, 1949; won Canadian-American Open Teams 1952, 1954, 1966, 1967, Men's Pairs 1956, 1957. Inventor of THREE-QUARTER (Howell) MOVEMENT and other duplicate movements.

GOLDBERG, Freddie (Mrs. Richard), of Memphis, Tenn., earlier of Nashville, Tenn., and Stamford, Conn., former bridge teacher. Runner-up Spring National Individual 1965; winner Tri-State Women's Pairs 1968. Her active bridge career proved a valuable background for her role as wife of the ACBL Executive Secretary.

GOLDBERG, Herman H., of New York, N.Y., bridge club manager and tournament director, born 1897; second Spingold 1937, Vanderbilt 1948, Fall Nat'l Open Pairs 1934; won Eastern States Mixed Team 1949, Men's Pairs 1959, with many more regional successes.

GOLDBERG, Richard L., of Memphis, Tenn., formerly of Nashville; ACBL Executive Secretary and General Manager from 1971; civil engineer, born 1922. First official connection with ACBL was a Regional Tournament director, 1959, and National Director, 1961; brought to ACBL National Headquarters in New York to take over tournament scheduling, 1963–65; groomed for ACBL's top job

by serving as assistant to the Executive Secretary, 1965–71, when he succeeded Easley BLACKWOOD. The smooth transition of ACBL headquarters from Greenwich to Memphis was achieved under his aegis. Member of National Laws Commission; named representative to World Bridge Federation for Zone II, 1972. Member of the Editorial Board of this Encyclopedia.

GOLDBERG, Steve, of Miami, Fla.; won Reisinger 1972, Spingold 1974; tied second Spring Nat'l Men's Teams 1973; winner of many regional titles including Mid-Atlantic Spring Men's Pairs 1970, Summer Knockout Teams 1972, Masters Pairs 1972.

GOLDBERG, Victor, of Glasgow, Scotland, company director, born 1923; represented Great Britain World Pair Championship 1962; represented Scotland in the CAMROSE TROPHY on many occasions, including the Scottish victories in 1964, 1965. Scottish titles include Open Teams three times and Open Pairs once. One of the four Scottish players to compete in the *Sunday Times* International Pairs Championship and all British Trials.

GOLDBLATT, Eric, of Helen's Bay, Northern Ireland, wholesale merchant and bridge writer, born 1900; represented Ireland World Team Olympiad 1964; represented Northern Ireland on more than 80 occasions; national successes include Irish Open Pairs and every major NIBU title at least three times. Member of the selection committee Northern Ireland BU.

GOLDER, Col. Benjamin M. (1894–1946), of Philadelphia, Pa., congressman and attorney; ACBL President 1946, Honorary Member 1947.

GOLDING, Wendy M., of Perth, Western Australia, financier; represented Australia World Women's Team Olympiad 1972; Women's Pair Olympiad 1974.

GOLDMAN, Bernard, of Needham, Mass., engineer, born 1912; second Non-Masters Pairs 1942; won New England Knockout Teams 1955, Fall Men's Pairs 1952, Open Pairs 1945, Mixed Pairs 1944.

GOLDMAN, Robert, of Dallas, Tex., commercial real estate salesman, born 1938; one of the world's leading players; World Champion 1970, 1971; represented US World Championships 1969, 1970, 1971, 1973, 1974, World Team Olympiad 1972; won World Mixed Team Olympiad 1972; won Spingold 1969, Reisinger 1970, Vanderbilt 1971, 1973, Fall Nat'l Life Master Men's Pairs 1964, Men's Teams 1969, Life Master Pairs 1968, Spring Nat'l Men's Teams 1968; second Vanderbilt 1966, 1970, Spingold 1970, Fall Nat'l Men's Teams 1966, 1967, Blue Ribbon 1968, Reisinger 1968, Team Trials 1968, Spring Nat'l

Men's Teams 1969; regional successes include Golden Gate Knockout Teams 1968, Mexican National Open Teams 1968, Mid-South Summer Knockout Teams 1968, Texas Fall Knockout and Open Teams 1968. Originator of SUPER GERBER CONVENTION; author of *Aces Scientific*. (See ACES TEAM.)

GOLDRING, Frank (1935–1965), of Boston, Mass., credit manager; won Canadian-American Open Pairs 1961, New England Spring Open Team 1961, Open Pairs 1962.

GOLDSCHMIDT, David (1905–1955), of Hartford, Conn., machinery manufacturer; won New England Open Teams 1948, 1949, Men's Pairs 1948, 1952, Mixed Pairs 1952. Originator of the Goldschmidt no trump bidding features, which are still used in the Hartford area.

GOLDSCHMIDT, R., of Kitwe, Zambia, accountant, born 1925; one of the leading players in Central Africa; won Zambia Open Pairs 1959, 1962, 1963, Open Teams 1961, 1962, 1964, Southern Rhodesia Open Pairs 1963, 1964, Open Teams 1964, Central Africa Open Teams 1960, 1962; second in seven other major championships. Chairman Central Africa Bridge Association.

GOLDSMITH, Arthur S., of Cleveland, Ohio, attorney, born 1909; won Spingold 1949, Chicago 1949, Fall Nat'l Men's Team 1947, 1954, 1958, second Spingold 1946, 1952, Marcus 1951, Chicago 1952; won All-American Open Team 1953.

GOLDSTEIN, Abe, of Flushing, N.Y., bridge teacher and club director, born 1902; won Senior Masters Individual 1950, Eastern States Masters Pairs 1943, 1949, Reisinger 1949. Author of *Common-Sense Bridge for the Intermediate Player*. See BIBLIOGRAPHY, E.

GOLDSTEIN, Carol, of Johannesburg, South Africa, formerly of London, England, club proprietor, born 1928; represented Great Britain European Championships 1965, World Pairs Olympiad 1962; won English Bridge Union Mixed Pairs 1965, Crockford's Cup 1966, Mixed Teams 1966.

GOLDSTEIN, Gratian (Mrs. L. J.), of Coral Gables, Fla.; one of the leading women players of the Southeast; represented US World Olympiad Women's Pairs 1962, 1970; won Fall Nat'l Women's Teams 1948, 1953, Life Master Women's Pairs 1969, Summer Nat'l Women's Pairs 1947, 1948, Mixed Teams 1955, 1958; second Blue Ribbon Pairs 1966, Spring Nat'l Women's Teams 1971, Fall Nat'l Mixed Pairs 1972, Summer Nat'l Mixed Teams 1967; regional successes include Midwest Spring Open Pairs 1945, Florida Open Pairs 1961, Mixed Pairs 1967, Southeastern Open Teams 1966, Women's Teams 1970, Women's Pairs 1970.

GOLDSTEIN, Michael, of Silver Spring, Md., bridge teacher, born 1933; ACBL National Tournament Director. Contributor Washington BL *Bulletin*.

GOLDSTEIN, Stephen, of New York, N.Y.; won Spring Nat'l Men's Teams 1974, Spingold Consolation 1972; second Vanderbilt 1974, Reisinger 1974; winner of several regional titles including Fun City Knockout Teams 1972, New England Knockout Teams 1974.

GOLDWATER, Henry A. (Harry), of Yonkers, N.Y., tournament director, born 1901; won Eastern Regional Culbertson Trophy 1932, 1933, 1935, 1936. Advisor National Laws Commission since 1962. ACBL National Tournament Director since 1957. Contributing editor to *Bridge Encyclopedia*. Formulated the GOLDWATER RULE.

GOMEZ-DIAZ, Gala de Reschko, of Spain; represented Spain World Pair Olympiad 1962, 1966, World Women's Pair Olympiad 1970, 1974. European Championship 1966, European Women's Championship 1962, 1963, 1974. National successes include Open Teams, Women's Teams, Mixed Pairs.

GOMEZ-DIAZ, Juan Francisco, of Las Palmas, Spain, landowner, born 1916; represented Spain World Pair Olympiad 1962, 1966, European Championship 1966. National successes include Open Teams, Mixed Pairs.

GONZALEZ-VALE, Manuel, of Caracas, Venezuela, engineer, born 1923; represented Venezuela World Team Olympiad 1964, World Championships 1967; South American Champion 1963, 1966; won National Open Pairs.

GOODEN, George, of Carmel, Calif., writer, lecturer, tour conductor, born 1904; winner of World Olympic Par contest 1941; won Pacific Coast Open Pairs 1929, Pacific Coast Individual Champion 1932, All-Western Open Team 1936, 1937, 1938, Hawaiian Masters Pairs 1939, and other successes. ACBL Director 1959, President ABTA 1962–63. Has taught more than 250,000 pupils; other bridge activities include many radio and department-store lectures, and the preparation of many books and booklets for teaching purposes. These include *Contract Bridge Bidding and Play: Self-Teaching Lesson Course for Beginning Players* (1964), the first programed bridge instruction book for beginners. Co-author *Sherlock Holmes, Bridge Detective* (see BIBLIOGRAPHY, H).

GOODMAN, Aaron, of Montreal, Que., attorney, born 1904; won Summer Nat'l Men's Pairs 1942; won Canadian-American Open Teams 1952, 1954, 1966, 1967, Men's Pairs 1956.

GOODMAN, Alvin E., of South Pasadena, Calif., formerly Philadelphia, realtor (died 1975); won Summer Nat'l Golder Pairs 1959, several regional titles including Southeastern Men's Teams 1953, Keystone Conference Mixed Pairs 1954, Men's Pairs 1954.

GOPPERT, Clarence, of Prairie Village, Kan.; won Fall Nat'l secondary Swiss Teams 1974, winner of many regional championships including five Knock-out team titles and three Open team titles in 1973 and 1974.

GORDON, Dr. A. A., of Port Elizabeth, South Africa, physician, born 1916; national titles include Open Teams 1954, 1958, 1959, second 1955; Open Pairs 1963; won South African Congress Open Team 1961, 1963, second 1962.

GORDON, Agnes (Mrs. Ralph) (1906–1967), of Buffalo, N.Y.; one of the most successful American women players of all time; second World Women's Team Olympiad 1964; represented US World Women's Team Olympiad 1960, World Pairs Olympiad 1962; tied first Women's International Trials 1963; won Chicago 1948, Fall Nat'l Women's Teams 1948, 1950, 1964, 1965, Summer Nat'l Mixed Teams 1956, 1962, Women's Pairs 1961, Spring Nat'l Women's Teams 1967; second Fall Nat'l Women's Teams 1955, Summer Nat'l Mixed Teams 1951, 1955, Fall Nat'l Mixed Pairs 1956, 1963, Life Master Women's Pairs 1964, Summer Nat'l Women's Pairs 1959; regional wins include Canadian-American Open Teams 1953, 1958, Women's Pairs 1959, Mixed Pairs 1959, 1961, 1965, Canadian Nat'l Open Teams 1957, Women's Pairs 1966, Central States Women's Pairs 1966, All-American Mixed Pairs 1965, Great Lakes Open Teams 1965, New England Open Teams 1965, 1966, District 11 Women's Pairs 1967. Director ACBL 1963–66. In the final session of the 1963 Fall Nat'l Mixed Pairs, Mrs. Gordon and E. MURRAY recorded one of the highest single-session scores ever in a National Championship when they totaled 506½ match points on a 325 average.

GORDON, Dianna M., of Toronto, Ont., consultant, born 1944; won New England Open Teams 1973, Canadian Nat'l Knockout Teams 1973, Fleur-de-Lys Knockout Teams 1973.

GORDON, Fritzi (Mrs. Paul), of London, England, born 1916; one of the great women players of the world; World Women's Pairs Champion 1962; won World Olympiad Women's Teams 1964, Mixed Teams 1962, Women's Pairs 1974, second 1970; European Women's Champion 1950, 1951, 1952, 1959, 1961, 1963 and 1975, and represented Great Britain on eight other occasions; toured US 1953 as member of British Women's Team; won Gold Cup

1957 and 1961 and many other national championships. With Mrs. R. MARKUS forms the strongest women's partnership in world bridge.

GORDON, Loula, of Alexandria, Egypt, born 1918 of Greek parentage; World Women's Teams Champion 1960; Lebanon Pairs Champion 1954; several national championship wins in Open Teams and Open Pairs.

GORDON, Sam (1875–1968), of Portland, Ore., bridge columnist; writer, under the name of "The Kibitzer," of one of the longest-established bridge columns in the world, which appeared in Portland, Ore., and Seattle, Wash. Noted as a composer of bridge verse.

GOREN, Charles H(enry), born in Philadelphia March 4, 1901, and long resident also in New York City and Miami Beach, became the successor to Ely Culbertson as the world's foremost contract bridge authority; author, lecturer, teacher, TV personality, and star player, known to millions as "Mr. Bridge." Goren studied law at McGill University, LLB 1922 and Masters 1923; learned bridge there in a casual game with coeds; was admitted to the Pennsylvania Bar in 1923 and practiced law in Philadelphia for thirteen years, until publication of his first book, *Winning Bridge Made Easy,* 1936, when he turned "temporarily" to bridge as a business career, meantime retaining his membership in the bar. However, he never practiced again.

A late starter in the tournament world (1931), he won his first national events in 1933 (USBA and ABL Open Teams), worked for a while with Milton Work, and compared to names like Culbertson, Lenz, and Sims, was almost an unknown when the Chicago *Tribune* and New York *Daily News* chose to syndicate his daily newspaper articles as a replacement for Culbertson, who had moved to another syndicate. A fine writer and analyst, an excellent speaker, and an indefatigable worker, Goren soon knocked out Culbertson "on points." His remarkable string of tournament victories put him at the very top of the master point winners list—a place he held uninterruptedly from 1944 to 1962. And his introduction of point-count valuation, adding points for distribution to the high-card values of 4, 3, 2, 1 for ace, king, queen, jack, swept all other systems into the discard, and made his methods into what came to be called STANDARD AMERICAN. More important, because this valuation method proved much easier to learn, it helped make millions of new bridge players, giving the game a lift it had not enjoyed since the first boom of the early Culbertson years.

The name of Goren became synonymous with bridge to the millions; his importance as a world figure was recognized when he was front-covered by *Time* magazine. He made the first successful series of bridge shows on television, "Championship Bridge with Charles Goren," produced by Walter Schwimmer, continuing to run through 1964. In 1963, it was estimated that he had sold more than eight million books; in addition to his daily newspaper column (with a readership of over thirty-four million), he was writing a weekly column for *Sports Illustrated* and a monthly article for *McCall's Magazine,* not to mention regular contributions to *Bridge World* and to bridge magazines throughout the world, as well as sporadic appearances in more general publications. It was estimated that his annual income and his total earnings from bridge had far surpassed those of Culbertson.

He was made Honorary Member ACBL in 1959 and was one of the first three players elected to the Hall of Fame in 1963; has been a member of the National Laws Commission since 1956; is a contributing editor of *Bridge World* and a member of the Editorial Advisory Board of the *Bridge Encyclopedia,* and his writings on the game far outnumber those of anyone before him, with major works translated into a dozen different languages. His books include: *Better Bridge for Better Players,* 1942; *Standard Book of Bidding,* 1944; *Contract Bridge Made Easy: A Self-Teacher,* 1948; *Point Count Bidding in Contract Bridge,* 1949; *Goren Presents the Italian Bridge System,* 1958; *New Contract Bridge in a Nutshell,* 1959; *Sports Illustrated Book of Bridge,* 1961; *Goren's Winning Partnership Bridge,* 1961; *Charles Goren's Bridge Complete,* 1963; and *Goren on Play and Defense,* 1974.

A lifelong bachelor, Goren may genuinely be said to have been married to the game. In spite of his work as writer, lecturer, promoter, TV personality (unlike Culbertson, who grew bored with the game when he had become successful), Goren has always been devoted to tournament play. (He seldom plays rubber bridge, and never plays for high stakes; he considers his playing status amateur and once turned over to the Damon Runyon Cancer Fund the full amount of a $1,500 purse which he won in a charity tournament played in Las Vegas.) Before his retirement from active competition in 1966, he had captured virtually every major bridge trophy in US tournament play, including a record of eight McKenney "Player of the Year" trophies (1937, 1943, 1945, 1947, 1948, 1949, 1950, 1951). His tournament record includes: won Asbury Challenge Teams 1937, Spingold 1943, 1947, 1960, Chicago 1937, 1938, 1939, 1942, 1943, 1950, 1957, 1963, Vanderbilt 1944, 1945, Fall Nat'l Men's Team 1952, 1965, Mixed Team 1938, 1941, 1943, 1944, 1948, 1954, Life Masters Pairs 1942, 1958, Fall Nat'l Open Pairs 1940, Men's Pairs 1938, 1943, 1949, Mixed Pairs 1943, Life Masters Individual 1945, USBA and ABL Open Team 1933; second Spingold 1939, 1950, Chicago 1944, 1951, Vanderbilt 1934, 1936, 1949, 1950, 1953, 1955, 1959, 1962, Fall Nat'l Men's Team 1946, 1955, Mixed Team 1946, 1949, 1950, 1951, Life Masters Pairs 1953, Fall Nat'l Men's Pairs 1935, Mixed Pairs 1934; and a very large number of regional successes. Because of his many contributions to bridge, the ACBL Board of Directors, at its fall meeting in 1969, honored Goren by conferring on him the title "Mr. Bridge," and he was awarded the honorary degree of Doctor of Laws by McGill University in 1973. See BIBLIOGRAPHY, B, C, D, E, H, J.

GORFKLE, Kenneth, of Redmond, Wash., winner of many regional titles including All-Western Knockout Teams 1972, Masters Teams 1973, Golden Gate Knockout Teams 1971, Open Pairs 1974.

GORGIAS, George, of Greece, mechanical engineer, born 1935; one of the leading Greek players; represented Greece European Championship 1970; national wins include Open Teams 1968, 1971, 1972, 1973, 1974, Open Pairs 1967, 1969, 1971, 1974.

GOSLAR, Gerda, of Johannesburg, South Africa, bridge teacher, born in Germany; second Women's Team Olympiad 1968, 1972, Women's Pair Olympiad 1974; represented South Africa World Team Olympiad 1960, World Pairs Olympiad 1966, World Women's Pair Olympiad 1970; national titles include Individual 1957, Open Teams 1961, 1973, Open Pairs 1958, 1964. Co-founder of the first Women's Bridge Association in South Africa in 1961 and its Chairman until 1964.

GOSLAR, Gunter, of Johannesburg, South Africa, metal dealer, born 1915 in Hamburg, Germany; represented South Africa World Team Olympiad 1960, World Pair Olympiad 1962; national titles include Open Team 1961, 1973, Open Pairs 1958.

GOTH, Dr. Gabor, of Budapest, lawyer, born 1911; won Hungarian Open Teams 1961, 1962, 1964, 1965, 1967, Open Pairs 1962; member victorious Hungarian team against Czechoslovakia 1963, Germany 1964, Brussels 1964, and Austria 1965.

GOTTHELF, Mrs. Elisabeth, of Frankfurt, Germany, bridge teacher, born 1909; represented Germany World Women's Team Olympiad 1960, European Championships 1954, 1957, 1961, 1965, 1966. National wins include Open Teams (twice), Open Pairs (twice), Women's Pairs; won Mitropa Cup for Women's Teams (twice).

GOTTLIEB, Michael T., of Hillsborough, Calif., real estate broker, born 1902; one of the great players of all time. He was one of Ely Culbertson's partners in the Culbertson-Lenz match, and played on Culbertson's teams against France and England in 1933. Many successes 1934–36 as a member of the FOUR ACES included a win over France in the first official world championship in 1935. Retired in 1936 for business reasons. Won USBA Grand National Open Teams 1933, 1934, Grand National Pairs 1933, Asbury Challenge Teams 1934, Master Pairs 1931, Eastern Open Teams 1932, 1933, 1934, Spingold 1934, Vanderbilt 1929, 1934, 1935, Eastern Knockout Teams 1934; second Spingold 1932, Chicago 1932, Asbury Challenge Teams 1930. Co-author of *Four Aces System of Contract Bridge.* See BIBLIOGRAPHY, C.

GOUDSMIT, Dr. E. C. (1903–1967), of Amsterdam, Holland, lawyer; resident in US 1940–45;

second European Championships 1932, 1933, 1934, and represented Netherlands on many other occasions; many national wins include Open Teams 1933, 1935, 1936, 1938, 1939, 1951, 1952, 1953, 1954, 1955, 1956.

GOUDSMIT, Dr. F. W., of Amsterdam, Holland, lawyer and bridge columnist, born 1899; second European Championship 1932, 1933, 1934, and represented Netherlands on many other occasions; many national wins include Open Teams 1933, 1935, 1936, 1938, 1939, 1951, 1952, 1953, 1954, 1955, 1956. Author of several books on bidding and play. Translated several books from English into Dutch, including works by Ely Culbertson and S. J. Simon.

GOUGH, William L., of Oreland, Pa., bridge teacher, born 1951; winner of several regional titles including District 4 Open Pairs 1966, Keystone Open Teams 1970, 1974.

GOULANDRIS, Nicolas P., of Greece, shipping magnate; President of Hellenic BF.

GOULD, Edward A., Jr., of Manchester, N.H., sales representative, born 1928; President of District 25 and ACBL Director since 1973.

GOULD, Lawrence E., of Decatur, Ga., financial officer, born 1942; won Spingold 1974; Summer Nat'l secondary Swiss Teams 1973; tied second Spring Nat'l Men's Teams 1973, winner of many regional titles including Mid-Atlantic Fall Open Pairs 1970, 1973, Summer Knockout Teams 1971.

GOWDY, Bruce D., of Willowdale, Ont., chartered accountant and bridge club owner; one of the leading players of Canada; Life Master at the age of twenty after sixteen months of tournament bridge; represented Canada in World Olympiad 1960, 1972; won Spingold 1949, second 1964; won Canadian Nat'l Open Team five times consecutively 1949, 1950, 1951, 1952, 1953, Men's Pairs 1960, Mixed Pairs 1953. Former President Ontario Unit. The youngest player ever to win a major knockout event when he won the Spingold at the age of nineteen.

GRABEL, Ross, of Providence, R.I.; won Spring Nat'l secondary Non-Mixed Pairs 1972, New York Winter Open Pairs 1974, Upper New York State Knockout Teams 1974.

GRACE, Brian, of Wichita, Kans., lawyer, born 1942; won Nat'l Comm. & Ind. Pairs 1963, Flight B Men's pairs 1964, Missouri Valley Open Teams 1964, Masters Pairs 1973.

GRANOVETTER, Matthew, of New York, N.Y., bridge professional and music composer; won Spring

Nat'l Men's Teams 1975, tied Open Pairs 1972; second World Mixed Team Olympiad 1974; winner of many regional events including Long Island Men's Pairs 1971, Open Pairs 1974, Puerto Rico Men's Pairs 1972, Open Teams 1972, 1974.

GRANOVETTER, Zachary, of Jersey City, N.J.; won Puerto Rico Men's Pairs 1972, Open Teams 1974, tied Southeastern Open Teams 1972.

GRANTHAM, John M., of Amarillo, Tex., commodity broker, born 1944; won Blue Ribbon Pairs 1971, Summer Nat'l secondary Swiss Teams 1974; second Summer Nat'l secondary Mixed Pairs 1973; winner of numerous regional titles including Mount Shasta Open Teams 1972, Knockout Teams 1972, Land of Coronado Knockout Teams 1974, Open Teams 1974, Intermountain Men's Pairs 1974, Lou Herman Trophy Winner 1971.

GRANTHAM, Robin K(lar), of Houston, Tex., bridge professional; won Spring Nat'l Women's Pairs 1970; winner of several regional titles including Champagne Open Teams 1973, Land of Coronado Knockout Teams 1972, Open Teams 1972.

GRAVES, James Allan, of Vancouver, B.C., educator, born 1949; winner of many regional titles including All-Western Knockout Teams 1972, Masters Teams 1973, British Columbia Men's Pairs 1972, Open Pairs 1972.

GRAVES, S. Susan, of Indianapolis, Ind., nosologist, born 1942; won Spring Nat'l secondary Special Pairs 1972, 1973, Missouri Valley Open Pairs 1973.

GRAY, Maurice Harrison-. See HARRISON-GRAY, MAURICE.

GRAY, Mrs. Neva L., of Fort Lauderdale, Fla., born 1907; second Fall Nat'l Life Masters Women's Pairs 1963, Women's Teams 1963; winner of several regional titles including Southeastern Women's Pairs 1962, Women's Teams 1962, 1963, 1964, 1967.

GREEN, Farrell Bruce, of New Brighton, Minn., born 1937; winner of several regional titles including Gopher Open Teams 1959, 1961, 1974, Open Pairs 1960, 1962, 1967.

GREENBERG, Byron L., of Tulsa, Okla., restaurant owner, born 1927; won Fall Nat'l Open Pairs 1953, second Spingold 1972, Reisinger 1973; winner of many regional titles including Missouri Valley Knockout Teams 1971, 1974, Open Teams 1972, 1973. Past President Tulsa BA.

GREENBERG, Henry, of London, England, research scientist, born 1922; won ACBL Senior & Advanced Senior Masters Pairs 1968.

GREENBERG, Steve, of Oklahoma City, Okla., born 1932; won Nat'l Non-Masters Pairs 1953, Fall Nat'l secondary Mixed Pairs 1970; winner of many regional titles including Missouri Valley Knockout Teams 1971, 1974, Open Teams 1972.

GREENE, Dr. Richard, of New Orleans, La., dentist, born 1910; winner of many regional titles including Mid-South Open Teams 1944, 1948, 1960, 1963, Masters Pairs 1963, 1964. Former President Louisiana Association, former President Mid-South Conference.

GREENHUT, Carol A., of Redwood City, Calif., systems analyst, born 1945; won Fall Nat'l secondary Mixed Pairs 1974; second Spring Nat'l Women's Teams 1974; winner of several regional titles including District 22 Open Pairs, All-Western Women's Teams 1973, Masters Teams 1973.

GREGORY, Stephen C., of Alexandria, Va., law student, born 1947; won Mid-Atlantic Spring Open Pairs, Fall Knockout Teams 1972, 1973.

GRESHAM, Ralph, of New York, N.Y., died 1966; Treasurer of A.T.&T.; former Treasurer of ACBL and member of its Steering Committee during the crucial reorganization period 1948–49.

GRESHAM, William L. (died 1962), novelist and writer on history of playing cards. *Nightmare Alley,* Gresham's most famous novel, used the tarot pack as background material; in fact, in most of his books he used cards or card playing as a theme.

GRIEVE, William P., of New York, N.Y., mathematician, born 1929; one of the leading American players; represented US World Team Olympiad 1960; won Spingold 1959, second 1960, 1969; won Reisinger 1969, 1970, 1971, second 1972; won Summer Nat'l Mixed Teams 1960, Fall Nat'l Men's Pairs 1958, Spring Nat'l Men's Teams 1975. Regional successes include Eastern States Knockout Teams 1960, Mississippi Valley Open Team 1951, New England Knockout Team 1957, Open Team 1957, Mid-South Spring Open Team 1960.

GRIFFEY, Larry R., of Jacksonvile, Fla., statistics instructor, born 1944; winner of several regional titles including Southeastern Open Pairs 1971, Florida Open Teams 1974, Mixed Pairs 1974.

GRIFFIN, Edward F., of Sydney, Australia, solicitor, born 1947; Far East Pairs Champion 1972; represented Australia Far East Championships 1972, 1973, 1974; national successes include McCutcheon Trophy in 1973 for highest number of master points won.

GRIFFIN, Estee, of New York, N.Y., magazine editor, bridge writer; regional wins include Eastern States Mixed Teams 1961, Fun City Knockout Teams 1971, Long Island Knockout Teams 1968. Assistant Editor *Bridge World;* Associate Editor *Post Mortem;* former Promotion Director *The Bridge Journal.*

GRIFFIN, Thomas C., of New York, N.Y., social worker, born 1936; second Nat'l Senior & Advanced Senior Master Pairs 1959; regional wins include Fun City Knockout Teams 1971, New York–New Jersey Open Pairs 1967, Open Teams 1970, New England Open Teams (winter) 1968, Long Island Knockout Teams 1968. Former Associate Editor of *The Contract Bridge Bulletin* and *The Bridge Journal.*

GRIGG, Claire, of Perth, Western Australia; represented Australia World Women's Olympiad 1972.

GRIGGS, Eloene T., of Washington, D.C., bridge teacher; widow of Rear Admiral G.E. Griggs; officer of ABTA, president since 1975; member IBPA. Organizer of many service-connected women's clubs; member National Council of Women since 1959; listed in Who's Who of American Women since 1961.

GRONER, Alexander, of White Plains, N.Y., president of a corporate journalism company, former editorial writer for the *Cleveland Press,* correspondent for *Time, Life,* and *Fortune,* born 1914. Created Swiss Pairs and Multiple Teams tournament movements. Author of *Duplicate Bridge Direction.* See BIBLIOGRAPHY, F.

GROSFELD, Leon, of Warsaw, Poland, professor of history, born 1911; national titles include Open Teams 1958, 1959, 1960, 1961, Mixed Teams 1959, 1960, Mixed Pairs 1960.

GRUENTHER, General Alfred M., of Washington, D.C., born 1899; honorary President of the World Bridge Federation since its inception in 1958; considered the outstanding director of bridge tournaments in America in the thirties, acting as chief referee in the Culbertson-Lenz Match 1931–32; recognized as authority on duplicate contract bridge. Author of *Duplicate Bridge Simplified,* 1931, *Duplicate Bridge Guide,* and *Duplicate Contract Complete,* 1933; one of the authors of *Famous Hands of the Culbertson-Lenz Match,* 1932. Served 38 years in the US Army; his final military assignment Supreme Commander, Allied Powers, Europe, 1953–56. Retired Dec. 31, 1956, and from 1957 to 1964 served as president of the American Red Cross, serving with particular devotion and special interest in its youth program. Besides awards from other countries for International Red Cross league activities (nine Red Cross Societies), he has been decorated by fourteen governments other than the United States. Recipient of the DSM with two Oak Leaf clusters, and the

Legion of Merit from this country, he has honorary degrees from thirty-one American colleges and universities. Winner of Wetzlar Trophy 1938, 1944; Honorary Member ACBL 1944; Charter Member Nat'l Laws Commission, Honorary Member since 1948; on the Editorial Advisory Board of *Bridge Encyclopedia.* Chairman of ACBL Charity Foundation 1964–65. See BIBLIOGRAPHY, F, also EISENHOWER, DWIGHT D.

GRUVER, Nancy (Mrs. John A.), of Ellicott City, Md., born 1931; one of the leading American women players; second Women's Pairs Olympiad 1966; third Women's Team Olympiad 1968; won Spring Nat'l Women's Pairs 1965, Women's Teams 1966, 1973, second 1969; won Summer Nat'l Mixed Teams 1975, Fall Nat'l Life Master Women's Pairs 1967; regional titles include District 4 Women's Pairs 1965, Keystone Women's Pairs 1966, 1973, Women's Teams 1971, 1973. President Women's Bridge League of Maryland; Director Maryland BL.

GUDJOHNSEN, Stefan, of Reykjavik, Iceland, office manager and bridge columnist, born 1931; represented Iceland World Team Olympiad 1968, European Championships 1958, 1961, 1963, 1967, 1968, 1969, 1971, 1973; national titles include Open Team 1956, 1958, 1959, 1960, 1961, 1963, 1964, 1966, 1967, 1969, 1974, Open Pairs 1959. Radio broadcaster. President of Bridgefélag Reykjavikur.

GUDMUNDSSON, Gunnar, of Reykjavik, Iceland, banker, born 1920; represented Europe World Championship 1950; represented Iceland World Team Olympiad 1960, and European Championships 1950, 1951, 1956, 1961; national titles include Open Team 1953, 1954, 1957, 1962, 1965, 1973, Open Pairs 1955.

GUERIN, Donald H., of Los Angeles, Calif., real estate appraiser, born 1942; second Nat'l Senior & Advanced Senior Masters Pairs 1965; winner of several regional titles including District 11 Men's Pairs 1966, Orange County Knockout Teams 1972, Las Vegas Open Teams 1974.

GUIVER, Harold B., of Long Beach, Calif., owner of real estate investment company, born 1925; one of the leading players of the West Coast; won Chicago 1962, Spring Nat'l Men's Teams 1962, Fall Nat'l Men's Teams 1962, secondary Men's Teams 1972; second Chicago 1961, Vanderbilt 1961, 1963, Spring Nat'l Men's Teams 1974; third McKenney 1961. Many regional successes include All-Western Open Teams 1959, 1964, Masters Pairs 1971, Bridge Week Masters Pairs 1962, Knockout Teams 1967, Men's Pairs 1972.

GURVICH, Louis S., of New Orleans, La., president detective agency, born 1921; second Summer Nat'l Mixed Team 1961; regional successes include Mid-South Spring Open Pairs 1958, Open Teams

1962, 1965, 1967, 1973, Knockout Teams 1973, Mid-South Summer Men's Pairs 1962, Mixed Pairs 1962, 1965. ACBL Director since 1971; Chairman National Protests and Appeals Committee since 1970, many other committee positions; Chairman, Board of Governors 1967–71.

GURWITZ, Michael L., of San Francisco, Calif., computer programmer, born in Newark, N.J., 1947. Won Summer Nat'ls Spingold Consolation 1970; second Fall Nat'l Men's Pairs and Swiss Teams 1973. Also won many regionals including New England Knockout Teams 1972; New York–New Jersey Swiss Teams 1973, Bridge Week Knockout Teams 1974, Puget Sound Knockout Teams 1974.

GUTMAN, Josephine. See SHARP, JOSEPHINE.

GUTOWSKY, Ace, of Oklahoma City, Okla., aircraft sales representative, former professional football player, born 1909; won Fall Nat'l Men's Team 1951; regional successes include Texas Conference Open Team 1957, Masters Pairs 1954, Central States Open Pairs 1942, Mexican Nat'l Open Team 1955, Open Pairs 1955, Missouri Valley Open Pairs 1962, and many others. As a fullback with the Detroit Lions in 1935, won world football championship.

H

HABICHT, Val, of Wakefield, Mass.; winner of several regional championships including Tri-State Women's Pairs and Mixed Pairs 1971, New England Individual 1972.

HADDAD, Betty (Mrs. Said, formerly Miss Windley), painter, born 1924; represented US World Women's Pair Olympiad 1962; won Fall Nat'l Mixed Pairs 1954, Women's Pairs 1961, Keystone Mixed Pairs 1963, Open Teams 1956, 1961, Southeastern Open Teams 1965.

HADDAD, Said, of Arlington, Va., contractor, born 1916; won Fall Nat'l Mixed Pairs 1954, Nat'l Individual 1956, Eastern Men's Pairs 1960, Keystone Conference Open Teams 1951, 1956, Mixed Pairs 1963, Southeastern Open Pairs 1962, Open Teams 1965. Director and former Treasurer Washington BL.

HADDEN, Captain David, of Shreveport, La., environmental engineer; won Spring Nat'l Men's Pairs 1973.

HAGEDORN, Barry H., of Houston, Tex., business executive, born 1935; won Fall Nat'l secondary Open Pairs 1974; winner of many regional titles since

1968 including Republic of Texas Knockout Teams 1970, South Texas Knockout Teams 1971.

HAGEN, Fred, of Seattle, Wash., winner of several regional events including Pacific Northwest Knockout Teams 1969 and Men's Pairs Peach Festival 1974.

HALF, Ivan, of Pittsburgh, Pa., wholesale floor-covering merchant, born 1903; won Golder Pairs 1949. Former Vice-President ACBL.

HALL, Charles A. (1897–1958), of Cincinnati, Ohio; won Chicago 1933, Fall Nat'l Open Pairs 1933; second Life Masters Pairs 1935, Spingold 1934, 1951; won Midwest Spring Regional Open Team 1949, Open Pairs and Mixed Pairs 1957. He was for many years a member of the ACBL Board of Directors and was named "Mr. Bridge of Cincinnati" by a Cincinnati columnist.

HALL, James M., of Minneapolis, Minn., insurance salesman, born 1940; winner of several regional events since 1965 including Gopher Knockout Teams and Open Teams 1969, Iowa Swiss Teams and Men's Pairs 1974.

HALLE, Ranik, of Oslo, Norway, editor, born 1905; represented Norway European Championships ten times; second European Championships 1938; winner of twelve National Championships. President International Bridge Press Association 1960–64; honorary member and former president Norwegian Bridge Association; bridge columnist; member Editorial Advisory Board *Bridge Encyclopedia*.

HALLEE, Gerard F. (Jerry), of Los Angeles, Calif., partner computer corporation, born 1940; won Vanderbilt 1969, Senior & Advanced Senior Masters Pairs 1963; second Spring Nat'l Men's Pairs 1969. Regional wins include Rocky Mountain Masters Pairs 1964, Bridge Week Masters Men's Pairs 1967, Knockout Teams 1969, 1970, Golden State Open Pairs 1968.

HALLEN, Hans-Olof, of Morrum, Sweden, bridge consultant, born 1929; represented Sweden World Olympiad 1960, European Championships 1956; Swedish champion 1964; tournament director at World Championships 1970, 1974.

HALLER, Robert H., of Baker, Ore., retired rancher; winner of Fall Nat'l secondary Swiss Teams 1971; regional wins include Oregon Trail Masters Pairs 1970, Klondike Mixed Pairs 1972.

HALLER, Mrs. Robert H. ("Gert"), of Baker, Ore., retired rancher; winner of Fall Nat'l secondary Swiss Teams 1971, several regional championships including Oregon Trail Masters Pairs 1970, Klondike Mixed Pairs 1972.

HALLORAN, Julia, of Wooster, Ohio, writer, born 1928; winner of several regional championships including Midwest Women's Pairs 1957, Motor City Women's Pairs 1970, 1971.

HALPER, David, of New York, N.Y., attorney, born 1912; President Greater New York BA 1963, Chairman of the Board 1959–62, former Counsel. Chairman of ACBL committees 1962 and 1964 to study constitutional reforms.

HALPERIN, Richard, of Skokie, Ill., mortgage and real estate broker, born 1940; winner of several regional events including Great Lakes Open Pairs 1972, Men's Pairs 1963.

HALPERIN, Sue (Mrs. Richard), of Skokie, Ill., teacher of the blind, born 1938; winner of several regional events including Florida Knockout Teams 1970, Central States Women's Pairs 1974.

HALPIN, Robert W. (1896–1972), of Chicago, Ill., printing company president; one of the founders of the ABL, President in 1929; won Chicago 1929, Central States Open Pairs 1938, Open Team 1936, All-American Open Team 1944, Western States Open Pairs 1936; second Central States Open Pairs 1939, Open Team 1935, 1938, 1939, All-American Open Team 1944, Western States Open Pairs 1937.

HAMILTON, Frederick, of Los Angeles, Calif., bridge and backgammon professional; won International Team Trials 1975, Reisinger 1974, 1975, second Vanderbilt 1972, Grand National 1974, won Leventritt 1971, Fall Nat'l secondary Masters Pairs 1974; numerous regional championships since 1969 include Pheasant Knockout Teams 1970, Cambrian Shield Knockout Teams and Swiss Teams 1972, Canadian Nationals Knockout Teams 1974.

HAMILTON, John T., of Columbus, Ohio, National Tournament Director, born 1933; contributor to the SWISS TEAM MOVEMENT; Director Miami Valley Bridge Association 1960–66; Treasurer Central Ohio Bridge Association 1966–69; Vice-President Midwest Conference 1967–68; Treasurer, Professional Tournament Directors Association since 1970.

HAMILTON, Luther L., of Spring Hill, Ala., contractor, born 1907; won Summer Nat'l Non-Masters Pairs 1944, Southern Conference Individual 1956.

HAMMAN, Robert, of Dallas, Tex., insurance broker, born 1938; one of the world's great players; World Champion 1970, 1971; second World Championships 1973, 1974, 1975, World Team Olympiad 1964, 1972, won World Pair Olympiad 1974, Pan American Invitational Pairs 1974; represented North America World Championships 1966, 1969; won

International Team Trials 1963, second 1965, third 1968; won Vanderbilt 1964, 1966, 1971, 1973, Spingold 1969, Blue Ribbon Pairs 1964, Reisinger 1962, 1970, Grand Nationals 1975; Fishbein Trophy 1969, Comm. & Ind. Pairs 1959; second Vanderbilt 1970, Spingold 1970, Reisinger 1968, Spring Nat'l Men's Teams 1969; many regional successes. (See ACES TEAM.)

HAMMEL, Alma (Mrs. C. D.; formerly Mrs. Coleman), of San Francisco, Calif.; winner of several regional events including Bridge Week Knockout Teams 1971, All-Western Life Master Teams 1972.

HAMMERICH, Johannes J. J., of Caracas, Venezuela, lawyer and credit executive, born 1919; represented Venezuela World Team Olympiad 1960, World Pairs Olympiad 1966; npc Venezuela National Team 1957–62, Olympiad Team 1964; National wins include Open Teams three times, Open Pairs 1961, Mixed Teams 1963. Assistant Secretary World Bridge Federation 1964–67, Vice-President 1968–; Secretary General South American Confederation 1963–; co-founder Venezuelan Bridge Federation and its Vice-President from 1955.

HANCOCK, John W., of San Anselmo, Calif., mathematician, born 1923; won Spring Nat'l Mixed Team 1951, Mixed Pairs 1956; second Vanderbilt 1951; won Pacific Southwest Men's Pairs 1947, Open Pairs 1947, Palm Springs Knockout Teams 1967, Golden Gate Masters Pairs 1967, 1968, Open Pairs 1967, Open Teams 1968.

HANN, Gary, of New York, N.Y., kidney transplant technician; winner of several regional events including Great Lakes Swiss Teams 1971, Open Pairs 1974.

HANNA, William, of Englewood Cliffs, N.J., professor of political science and bridge writer; until he retired from active play in 1960, one of the leading players on the West Coast; represented US World Team Olympiad 1960; won Spingold 1958, Chicago 1960; regional successes include Mississippi Valley Open Team 1956, Rocky Mountain Open Pairs 1953, Men's Pairs 1953, 1954, Pacific Southwest Masters Pairs 1955, Open Team 1956. Co-author of BULLDOG SYSTEM. Bridge columnist and co-author of *Precision Power Bidding.* See BIBLIOGRAPHY, C.

HANSON, Keith, of Marion, Iowa, teacher; tied Summer Nat'l secondary Swiss Teams 1971; winner of several regional events including Gopher Masters Pairs 1972.

HARARI, Victor, of Argentina, wool materials representative, born in Egypt 1914; national wins include Open Teams 1939, Open Pairs 1970.

HARDIES, Bobb H. (1935–1975), of Cleveland Heights, Ohio, attorney; bridge editor, *Cleveland Press;* won Spring Nat'l secondary Open Teams 1969, many regional championships including All-American Open Pairs 1968, Swiss Teams 1973, District 5 Masters Pairs 1971, Swiss Teams 1972.

HARDING, Mrs. Frances (1900–1961), of Boston, Mass.; regional successes included Canadian-American Women's Pairs 1958, New England Knockout Teams 1932, Open Teams 1953, Mixed Teams 1951, 1957, Women's Pairs 1945, 1946, 1952, Mixed Pairs 1939 (twice), 1941, 1942, 1945, 1958.

HARDY, Max, of Camarillo, Calif., bridge teacher, writer, director, born 1932; regional successes include Copper State Knockout Teams 1974. ACBL Associate National Tournament Director. Author of *Five Card Majors, Western Style,* the only authoritative book on the WALSH SYSTEM (see BIBLIOGRAPHY, C).

HARKAVY, Harold (1915–1965), of Miami Beach, Fla., bridge club manager; one of the leading American players; won Spingold, 1956, 1963, Marcus 1946, Chicago 1952, Vanderbilt 1963, Summer Nat'l Mixed Team 1952, 1955, 1957, Summer Nat'l Men's Pairs 1953; second Spingold 1953, Chicago 1945, 1964, Summer Nat'l Mixed Team 1964, Men's Pairs 1962, Blue Ribbon Pairs 1963; regional successes include Eastern States Open Pairs 1946, Florida Men's Team 1962, Southeastern Open Team 1951, 1960, Men's Team 1957, 1958, Masters Pairs 1963.

HARKLEROAD, David, of Portland, Ore., car salesman, born 1910; won Northwest Open Team 1953, 1960, Fall Men's Pairs 1959.

HARMON, Leonard B., of New York, N.Y., insurance broker, born 1919; one of the most successful American players; represented North America World Championship 1959, US World Team Olympiad 1960; won McKenney 1958, Spingold 1962, Chicago and Vanderbilt 1958, Spring Nat'l Open Pairs 1958, Leventritt 1964; second Spingold 1958, Chicago 1959, Vanderbilt 1966, Summer Nat'l Mixed Teams 1959. Many regional successes include Eastern States Knockout Teams 1959, 1970, Masters Pairs 1958, Mixed Teams 1968, Keystone Open Teams 1962, Upper New York State Open Teams 1958. Treasurer of Greater New York BA 1959–64, President 1965.

HARPPORTE, Ronald de, of Minneapolis, Minn., sales executive, born 1938; winner of several regional titles including Gopher Master Teams 1968, 1969, 1971.

HARRIS, John, of Houston, Tex., ACBL National Tournament Director.

HARRIS, Marguerite (Mrs. R. F. S., "Tommy"), of New York, N.Y., former ACBL executive; won Fall Nat'l Women's Team 1954, second 1952; won Eastern States Mixed Team 1961, Women's Pairs 1951, 1957, New England Mixed Team 1947, New York-New Jersey Women's Pairs 1959. Former writer of ACBL *Bulletin* Club Corner.

HARRIS, Shirlee, of Houston, Texas, teacher, one of the leading women players of the Southwest, born 1934; represented US World Pair Championships 1962; won Spring Nat'l Mixed Pairs 1960, 1962; Central States Life and Senior Master Teams 1960, Rocky Mountain Mixed Pairs 1959, 1961, Midwest Fall Open Teams 1960, All-Western Women's Pairs 1965, Tri-Unit Mixed Pairs 1968.

HARRISON, Broma Lou, of Boulder, Colo., teacher, born 1932; winner of several regional events including Canadian Open Pairs 1969, Missouri Valley Swiss Teams 1974.

HARRISON, Payne, of Dallas, Tex., retired accountant and business executive; won Mid-South Spring Open Teams, Men's Pairs 1946, Rocky Mountain Open Pairs 1963, Texas Fall Regional Men's Pairs 1963, 1967, Open Pairs 1967, Mixed Pairs 1975, Texas Spring Regional Men's Pairs 1965, 1968, Knockout Teams 1969, Master Pairs 1969, Missouri Valley Knockout Teams 1967.

HARRISON-GRAY, Maurice ("Gray") (1900–1968), of London, England, bridge writer; one of the world's leading player-writers; European Champion 1948, 1949, 1950, and 1963 (acting as playing captain except in 1963); represented Great Britain in World Championship 1950, World Pair Olympiad 1962, World Team Olympiad 1964, and European Championship 1958; won Gold Cup 1937, 1947, 1949, 1962, 1966, 1967, 1968, and many other national championships. Bridge Editor of London *Evening Standard, Country Life,* and many other newspapers and periodicals. Author of *Country Life Book of Bridge;* co-author of *Winning Points at Match-Point Bridge.* A member of the group which developed the ACOL system in the thirties, and a leading exponent of the LOSING-TRICK COUNT. A contributing editor of the *Bridge Encyclopedia.* See BIBLIOGRAPHY, F.

HART, Norman de V., of London, bridge writer, born 1888; won English Inter-County Championship. Author of *Daily Telegraph Book of Contract Bridge, Bridge Player's Bedside Book.* Co-author of *Right Through the Pack, Vienna System of Contract Bridge, Quintessence of CAB.* See BIBLIOGRAPHY, C, H.

HARTLEY, Raphael (1900–1963), of Springfield, Mass., attorney; won New England Regional Open Pairs 1942, 1943, 1946, 1954.

HARTWICH, Hans, of Vienna, born 1923; second European Championship 1957, also represented

Austria 1950, 1956; national successes include Open Teams several times; playing captain Austrian Team World Team Olympiad 1960.

HARVEY, Allen P., Jr. (1917–1967), of Louisville, Ky.; won Life Masters Pairs 1947, second Spingold 1951, 1954, Fall Nat'l Men's Team 1955; won Mississippi Valley Open Pairs 1948, 1955, Men's Pairs 1955, Midwest Bridge Conference Open Pairs 1947, 1954, 1955, Open Team 1954.

HARVEY, Charles C., of Phoenix, Ariz., real estate broker, born 1906; won Spingold 1942; won New England Knockout Teams 1937, 1939, Mixed Teams 1935, 1938, Mixed Pairs 1935, Bridge Week Men's Pairs 1945, Masters Pairs 1960, and many others.

HARVEY, Harold H., of Minneapolis, Minn., born 1895; won Mid-American–Canadian Open Teams 1955, 1957, Men's Pairs 1955.

HATCH, Everett, of Fayetteville, N.Y., tax practitioner, born 1935; winner of several regional events including Upper New York State Open Pairs 1973.

HATHHORN, Thelma K. (Mrs. H. E.), of Belleaire, Fla., medical technician; second Fall Nat'l Women's Team 1951; won All-American Mixed Pairs 1953, Open Team 1952, Keystone Conference Women's Pairs 1953.

HATHORN, John B. (1925–64), of Houston, Tex., bridge writer and editor; a leading bridge personality of the Southwest; stricken by polio in 1954, but still achieved Life Master status in 1956. In 1959 he founded *Texas Bridge,* which he published and edited until his death; writings included many booklets on bidding and play, most in collaboration with G. Robert Nail. See BIBLIOGRAPHY, C, D.

HAUGHIE, William J., of Hamilton, N.Z., computer bureau manager, born 1942; represented New Zealand Far East Championships 1971; national wins include IMP Teams 1973, 1974.

HAWES, Emma Jean (Mrs. D. B.), of Fort Worth, Tex.; one of the leading American women players; third World Women's Team Olympiad 1968, 1972, World Women's Pairs 1974; won Venice Cup 1974; won Fall Nat'l Open Pairs 1958, Life Masters Women's Pairs 1966, Spring Nat'l Women's Teams 1967, 1970, 1972, 1974, 1975, Summer Nat'l Mixed Teams 1964; second Summer Nat'l Mixed Teams 1952, 1967, 1972, Spring Nat'l Women's Pairs 1968, Fall Nat'l Women's Teams 1967, Life Master Women's Pairs 1972; regional successes include a record Texas Open Team, Women's Pairs, Mixed Pairs, and a second in Masters Pairs in 1960; won Mid-South Spring Mixed Pairs 1949, 1965, Missouri

Valley Masters Pairs 1961, North Texas Knockout Team 1961, Open Teams 1963. Former President Forth Worth unit.

HAWKINS, Proctor, of Las Vegas, Nev., born 1937; winner of Fall Nat'l secondary Tournament of Champions 1973, many regional titles including Navajo Trail Knockout Teams 1973, Bridge Week Masters Pairs 1973, District 15 Masters Pairs 1974.

HAYASHI, James I., of San Jose, Calif., engineer, born 1943; won Summer Nat'l secondary Comm. & Ind. Teams 1969, several regional events including Central California Knockout Teams 1973.

HAYDEN, Dorothy. See TRUSCOTT, DOROTHY.

HAYDEN, Garey, of Lakewood, Col.; one of the most successful players of the Southwest; won Spring Nat'l Men's Teams 1973, Open Pairs 1975; secondary Open Pairs 1974, secondary Swiss Teams 1974, second Fall Nat'l Blue Ribbon 1972; winner of numerous regional championships since 1971, including more than a dozen Knockout Team events and ten Swiss Team events.

HAYNES, Nelle (Mrs. Lynn H.), of Knoxville, Tenn., born 1908; third Spring Nat'l Women's Pairs 1963; won Southern Conference Women's Pairs 1962. Member of National Goodwill Committee; President Tennessee Valley Unit.

HAYS, G. Gard, of Veradale, Wash., engineer, born 1933; won Fall Nat'l Men's Pairs 1961, Spring Nat'l Men's Pairs 1964, winner of many regional titles between 1963 and 1969 including Golden State Open Teams 1963, Oregon Trail Open Teams 1966, Pacific Northwest Knockout Teams 1969.

HAZEN, Lee, of New York, N.Y., attorney, born 1905; one of the leading American bridge players and personalities; represented US World Championship 1956, 1959; designated npc North American Team 1971 World Championships; won Spingold 1942, 1947, 1955, Marcus 1953, Chicago 1945, 1949, Vanderbilt 1939, 1942, 1949, 1958, Summer Nat'l Men's Pairs 1945, Masters Individual 1941; second Spingold 1945, 1958, Chicago 1941, 1942, Vanderbilt 1944, 1947, Life Masters Pairs 1946, Masters Individual 1940; regional successes include Reisinger. Honorary Member ACBL 1958. ACBL Director 1940, Vice-President 1945–47; ACBL attorney from 1942; and a driving force in the modernization of ACBL in the late forties. Member National Laws Commission since 1942. Founder and sometime Vice-President of Greater New York BA. Contributing Editor *Bridge Encyclopedia*.

HEAD, Cecil L., of New York, N.Y., attorney, born 1910; won Life Masters Pairs 1948; New England Knockout Team 1933, 1934, 1939, 1941 (twice), 1945, 1946 (twice), 1947, 1951, 1954; See S. G. CHURCHILL for records set by Head and Churchill when winning the Life Masters Pairs 1948.

HEALY, Raymond J. (1907–1966), of Newport Beach, Calif.; second AWL Nat'l Open Teams 1934; won All-American Open Teams 1954, Central States Open Teams 1956.

HEARD, Mrs. Helen ("Suzie"), of Altadena, Calif.; winner of several regional events including ALACBU Winter Open Pairs 1969, Intermountain Masters Pairs 1974.

HECKEL, Virginia, of Chicago, Ill.; won Spring Nat'l Women's Teams 1969, secondary Swiss Teams 1970, several regional titles including Central States Women's Pairs 1969, 1971.

HEINRICK, Sid J., of Franklin, Mich., chemical company president, born 1912; won All-American Open Teams 1943, Great Lakes Mixed Pairs 1965; member ACBL Finance Committee 1949, Goodwill Committee 1960–62.

HEITNER, Abigail (Mrs. Paul), of Hartsdale, N.Y., born 1946; winner of several regional titles including Canadian-Atlantic Knockout Teams 1970, 1973, Open Teams 1970, Transvaal Women's Teams 1974.

HEITNER, Paul L. (the "Whale"), of Hartsdale, N.Y., computer systems consultant, born 1939; won Life Masters Pairs 1970, second Spring Nat'l Men's Pairs 1972; winner of many regional events including Canadian-Atlantic Knockout Teams 1970, 1973, Open Teams 1969, 1970. A leading bridge theorist; co-developer with John LOWENTHAL of the CANARY CLUB system. Co-founder and Managing Editor of *Bridge Journal*.

HELDRING, Ernst (1904–1971), of Amsterdam, attorney, active in the European Bridge League, serving as a Director 1952–71, and as Secretary 1958–71. President Netherlands Bridge League 1949–59. Member of the Editorial Advisory Board *Bridge Encyclopedia*.

HELLER, Max, of St. Louis, Mo., public relations consultant, born 1916; won Midwest Fall Men's Pairs 1962, Mississippi Valley Men's Pairs 1961, 1967, 1970, Mixed Pairs 1960.

HEMANANI, J., of Bombay, business executive, born 1930; won National Master Pairs 1959, second 1960, 1961.

HEMMINGS, Robert S., of Chicago, Ill., insurance manager, born 1925; won Central States Open

Teams 1956, Life and Senior Masters Pairs 1967, Board-a-Match Teams 1971.

HEMRICOURT, Count Claude de, of Brussels, company director, born 1913; third World Mixed Teams 1962; represented Belgium in many European Championships; several times captain of Belgian Team; national titles include Open Teams 1948, 1949, 1951, 1952, 1955, 1956, 1959, Open Pairs 1949, Mixed Teams 1960, 1961, 1962. Member Belgian Bridge Commission. Vice-President European BL 1969–73.

HENDERSHOTT, Robert, of Seattle, Wash., fruit grower and tournament director, born 1925; won Northwest Men's Pairs 1958, 1962, Masters Pairs 1964, Oregon Trail Open Teams 1966, All-Western Men's Pairs 1963.

HENDERSON, Richard B., of Washington, D.C., formerly of Los Angeles, accountant, born 1933; winner of numerous regional titles since 1969 including Intermountain Open Teams 1970, Masters Pairs 1970, Open Pairs 1970, and more than a dozen Knockout Team events.

HENKE, Chuck, of Aurora, Colo., bridge lecturer and tournament director, born 1934; won Blue Ribbon 1965, Northwest Masters Pairs, Men's Pairs 1962, Inter-Mountain Open Teams 1965, Open Pairs 1966.

HENRY, Dr. Joseph L., of Newton Centre, Mass., professor of dentistry, dentist, born 1924; won Mid-Atlantic Summer Knockout Teams 1962. Top-ranking player of the ABA and has won over twenty ABA National Championship titles.

HERB, Jane, of Menlo Park, Calif.; second Nat'l Women's Team 1959; won Bridge Week Women's Pairs 1959, Mixed Team 1960.

HERBERT, Edmund J., of Phoenix, Ariz.; winner of several regional events including Desert Empire Masters Pairs 1973, Mixed Pairs 1973.

HERBERT, Walter (1902–1975), of San Diego, Calif., director and conductor San Diego Opera; member Austrian Team that won the first World Championship 1937; won Texas Conference Open Team 1962. Author of the HERBERT convention.

HERD, James D., of Los Angeles, Calif., teacher, born 1930; won Pacific Southwest Open Teams 1957, 1958; second Bridge Week Open Teams 1958, Open Pairs 1959. President Los Angeles BL 1957–58.

HÉRÉDIA, Irénée Bajos de, of Paris, tournament director; chief tournament director of the French

Bridge Federation, he directed many international tournaments including World Pair Championship, Cannes, 1962. Technical adviser to French Team European Championship 1965. Originator and organizer of OMNIUM.

HERLIHY, Rear Adm. Joseph L., of San Jose, Calif., Navy officer and bridge lecturer, born 1902; won Hawaiian Mixed Pairs 1955. Former President of three ACBL units.

HERMAN, Lou (1908–1950), of Houston, Tex., formerly of New York, N.Y., jeweler; won Mid-South Open Teams 1949. The Lou Herman Trophy was given in his memory by his widow, Mrs. Sally Lipton.

HERVEY, George F. (George John Frangopulo Hervey), free-lance British journalist, born 1897. Card correspondent of *The Field* (1940) and bridge correspondent of *The Western Morning News* (Plymouth 1953). Published six books on bridge, including *The Bridge Player's Bedside Book,* as well as other publications on card games.

HERVOUËT, Dr. François, of Paris, eye surgeon, born 1916; represented France World Championship as captain 1953; European Champion 1953; French Champion 1948, 1953.

HESS, Fred, of Naples, Fla., salesman, born 1907; won Upper New York State Open Pairs 1961, New England Men's Pairs 1957, Mixed Teams 1961.

HESS, Henrietta (Mrs. Arthur P.), of New York, N.Y.; won Summer Nat'l Sub-Senior Masters Teams 1943, Eastern States Women's Pairs 1948, Mixed Pairs 1953.

HETZER, Lloyd R., of N. Hollywood, Calif., controller, born 1946; won Fall Nat'l secondary Blue Ribbon 1970, District 10 Grand Nat'l Championships 1973, 1974, several regional events.

HEWITT, Richard G., of Scarsdale, N.Y., attorney, born 1927; regional successes include New England Open Teams 1974. President Westchester CBA, Director New York-New Jersey Conference.

HEWITT, Shirley (Mrs. R. G.), of Scarsdale, N.Y., born 1926; regional successes include Upper New York Women's Pairs 1961. Hostess 1968 Spring Nationals, 1974 Summer Nationals.

HIAN, Oei Kong, of Surabaya, Indonesia, merchant, born 1919; Far East Champion 1962, second 1961; national titles include Open Team 1960, 1962, and 1964, Open Pairs 1961.

HICKS, Adrian, of Vancouver, B.C., bridge teacher, born 1907; won Northwest Masters Pairs 1957, Men's Pairs 1958, 1960, Open Team 1956, Oregon Trail Men's Pairs 1958, Northern Rocky Mountain Open Teams 1958, 1960, 1963.

HIGASHIUCHI, K. A. (Jake), of Park Forest, Ill., chemist, born 1912; won Central States Mixed Pairs 1955, Life and Senior Masters Teams 1960, Knockout Teams 1963.

HIGGINSON, Mrs. G. E., of St. Annes-on-Sea, England, fashion house director; European Women's Champion 1959; national wins include Women's Teams 1961, 1962. See FORTUNE.

HILL, Kenneth P. (1890–1956), of Melrose, Mass., securities salesman; won New England Knockout Teams 1948, Master Teams 1949, Open Teams 1951, Mixed Teams 1946, 1948, 1949, 1950, Open Pairs 1946, Men's Pairs 1944.

HILLIARD, Olga, of New York, N.Y., born 1891; won Nat'l Mixed Team 1932, ABL Open Team 1932, Eastern Open Team 1932; second Nat'l Open Pairs 1931, ABL Mixed Pairs 1931, Women's Pairs 1931, Atlantic City Open Team 1931. Donor of ABL Trophy for Mixed Pairs.

HILTON, James R., of New York, N.Y., attorney, born 1946; won Spring Nat'l secondary Swiss Teams 1974, secondary Open Pairs 1974.

HIRON, Alan, of London, England, mathematician and bridge writer, born 1933; represented Great Britain European Championship 1967; npc Great Britain Women's Team European Championship 1969, 1974; won Gold Cup 1963, Crockfords 1964, 1966, Spring Foursomes 1966, 1974. Contributor to various magazines.

HIRON, Marjorie (Mrs. Alan, formerly Mrs. Van Rees), of London, England; European Women's Champion 1961; also represented Great Britain in European Women's Championships 1956, 1957, and 1958. Former Secretary of British Bridge League.

HIRSCH, Larry, of New York, N.Y. (died 1953); won Vanderbilt 1947, 1949, Chicago 1949, Eastern States Knockout Teams 1946, 1952; second Fall Nat'l Masters Individual 1953.

HIRSCH, Tannah, of Stamford, Conn., bridge writer, formerly of Johannesburg, South Africa, and Jerusalem, Israel, born 1933; won Congress Teams (South Africa) 1957, Natal Teams 1958, Jerusalem Pairs 1962, 1963, 1964, Mid-Atlantic Summer Men's Pairs 1968, Tri-State Swiss Teams 1970. Co-author of *Tournament Book of the 2nd World Olympiad Pairs.*

Editor ACBL *Bulletin* 1970, Editor European Championship *Daily Bulletin* 1965 and 1974. Contributor to *Bridge World, Nederlands Bridge, South African Bridge Bulletin, Popular Bridge.* See BIBLIOGRAPHY, G.

HIRSCHBERG, Ralph (1906–1962), of New York, N.Y., insurance broker. One of the leading American players, he set a record by winning the Reisinger Trophy six times, including four consecutive wins, 1946, 1952, 1956, 1957, 1958, 1959. Won Chicago 1958, Fall Nat'l Men's Team 1955, Open Pairs 1944; second Spingold 1960, Chicago 1945, Fall Nat'l Men's Team 1958, Men's Pair 1944, Life Master Pairs 1944. Regional wins included Eastern Master Pairs 1957, New York-New Jersey Mixed Pairs 1958, Keystone Conference Open Team 1954, 1957, 1960, Mixed Pairs 1957.

HIRSCHEY, Charles S., of Carthage, N.Y., industrialist, born 1912; won Canadian-American Open Teams 1958, Men's Pairs 1953, Open Pairs 1962.

HITCHENS, Robert M., of Seattle, Wash., sales manager, born 1937; winner of several regional events including Oregon Trail Open Pairs 1971.

HOADLEY, Frank M., of New Orleans,La., professor, born 1923; won Spring Nat'l Men's Pairs 1960; second Spingold 1959; regional successes include Keystone Open Team 1959, Mid-South Knockout Teams 1970, Men's Pairs 1973.

HOBLIT, Charles Sidney, of Detroit, Mich., former owner cab company, born 1901; regional successes include All-American Men's Pairs 1946, 1948, 1949, Midwest Spring Men's Pairs 1949. Devised a system of ACE-SHOWING RESPONSES to forcing two-bids. Former President Michigan Bridge Association.

HOCEVAR, Don, of Detroit, Mich., won Summer Nat'l secondary Marcus Teams 1970, Canadian Nat'l Knockout Teams 1971, Cambrian Shield Knockout Teams 1974.

HOCHFELD, Emanuel (1930–1972), of Chicago, Ill., stockbroker; one of the leading players of the Midwest; won Summer Nat'l Mixed Team 1961, Summer Nat'l Golder Pairs 1950, Fall Nat'l Open Pairs 1955, Men's Pairs 1951; second Spingold 1957, Vanderbilt 1951, Summer Nat'l Mixed Team 1953, Fall Nat'l Open Pairs 1959, Men's Team 1956; many regional wins including Central States Life and Senior Masters Teams 1957, 1961, Open Teams 1954, Life and Senior Masters Pairs 1956, Open Pairs 1960, 1961, 1963, Men's Pairs 1960, Knockout Teams 1968, 1970.

HOCHZEIT, Michael, of Israel, building contractor; European Champion 1975; third World Mixed Pairs

Olympiad 1970; represented Israel World Team Olympiad 1972, World Pair Olympiad 1974.

HODAPP, Thomas, of Cincinnati, Ohio, advertising executive, born 1942; won Spring Nat'l secondary Special Pairs 1972, 1973; winner of several regional championships including District 11 Life Masters Pairs 1972, Men's Pairs 1970, Mississippi Valley Open Pairs 1973.

HODGE, Paul, of Houston, Tex., attorney, born 1910; one of the leading bridge personalities of the Southwest; represented North America World Championship 1961, npc Women's Team World Olympiad 1964; winner of Fishbein 1955, Herman 1955, Marcus 1955, Chicago 1955, Fall Nat'l Men's Teams 1953, 1956, 1965, 1968, Open Pairs 1954, 1956, Mixed Pairs 1953, Summer Nat'l Life Masters Pairs 1955, second Marcus 1963, Chicago 1956, 1957, 1959, Vanderbilt 1959, Spingold 1967, Fall Nat'l Men's Teams 1960, Men's Pairs 1957, 1960. Regional successes include Mid-South Spring Open Teams 1941, 1942, Open Pairs 1949, Men's Pairs 1942, 1948, Texas Fall Open Teams 1954, 1963, Masters Pairs 1963, 1965, Open Pairs 1956, Texas Spring Open Teams 1966.

HOERSCH, Joel, of San Diego, Calif., newspaper composition programmer, born 1937; winner of several regional events including Bridge Week Open Pairs 1972.

HOFFER, Fred, of Montreal, Que., merchandiser, born 1937; second Spingold 1964; won Canadian Nat'l Open Pairs 1959, Open Teams 1960, Masters Pairs 1966, Canadian-American Open Pairs 1968.

HOFFMAN, David L., of Canberra, Australia, university lecturer, born 1945; represented Australia World Team Olympiad 1972, Far East Championships 1971.

HOFFMAN, H. D., of Hong Kong, textile manager, born 1922; second Far East Championship 1963; National successes include Master Team 1963, Open Team 1958, 1961, 1962, Open Pairs 1955. Vice-Chairman Hong Kong CBA 1957–62.

HOFFMAN, Michael, of Minneapolis, Minn., won Spring Nat'l Open Pairs 1973.

HÖIE, Erik, of Stavanger, Norway, tailor, born 1928; represented Norway World Championship 1970, European Championships 1959, 1961, 1965, 1969. Author of *Stavanger-grangen,* a work on one no trump opening bids and responses.

HOLDERNESS, William H. (1904–1965), of Greensboro, N.C., former member ACBL National Board of Directors 1958–61.

HOLLIS, Ailsa, of Auckland, New Zealand, bridge teacher, born 1910; represented New Zealand Far East Championships 1971; national wins include Australian Women's Team 1968, Women's Pairs 1968, New Zealand Teams 1971.

HOLT, Clarice K., of Fort Worth, Tex., oil executive, born 1911; won Summer Nat'l Women's Pairs 1962, Fall Nat'l Mixed Pairs 1962, second Fall Nat'l Women's Team 1964; won Mid-South Spring Open Pairs 1955, Women's Pairs 1955, Mid-South Summer Open Teams 1967, South Texas Knockout Teams 1971.

HONIBALL, Oscar, of Kingston, Jamaica, accountant, born 1905; won 26 National Championships, including Interclub nine times, five consecutively; Open Team six times and Open Pairs three times. Top Jamaica master point holder since 1950.

HOOD, Mrs. Pat L., of Austin, Tex., secretary, born 1936; won Fall Nat'l secondary Masters Pairs 1974, several regional events including Capital City Knockout Teams 1972.

HOOKER, Jim L., of Dallas, Tex., merchant, born 1937; won Grand Nationals 1975, Fall Nat'l secondary Swiss Teams 1973; winner of several regional titles including South Texas Swiss Teams 1973, Masters Pairs 1974.

HORN, James D. ("Stormy"), of El Paso, Tex., satellite meteorologist, born 1929; won Spring Nat'l secondary Men's Pairs 1973; winner of several regional championships including Rocky Mountain Men's Pairs 1970.

HORWITZ, Donald G., of Edina, Minn., salesman, born 1925; second US Zone World Par Olympiad 1963; won Summer Nat'l Leventritt Pairs 1962, several regional titles including Gopher Open Teams 1960, 1966, 1970, Men's Pairs 1960, Knockout Teams 1968, 1969. Contributing editor *Bridge Encyclopedia.*

HOWARD, Denis William, of Sydney, Australia, solicitor, born 1932; one of the leading Australian players; third World Championship 1971; represented Australia World Olympiad 1964, 1968; national titles include Open Teams 1958, 1959, 1961, 1962, 1963, 1964, 1965, 1967, Open Pairs 1957, 1961, 1962, 1964, 1965, 1971. New South Wales BA Councillor 1972–74, Australian BF Councillor 1960–74. Editor of *Australian Bridge.*

HOWARD, Mrs. Ward, of Newport News, Va., bridge teacher, born 1919; won Mid-Atlantic Fall Women's Pairs 1953 and 1955, Spring Mixed Pairs 1957.

HOWE, William A., of Atlanta, Ga., bridge club manager, born 1947; won Summer Nat'l secondary Marcus Teams 1971, tied Mid-Atlantic Winter Swiss Teams 1972.

HOWELL, Edwin C., professor of mathematics at Massachusetts Institute of Technology, born 1860; credited with the invention of the HOWELL MOVEMENT in 1897.

HOWELL, Jack, of Kemble, Ont., represented Canada World Team Olympiad 1964; won Canadian Nat'l Open Teams 1966.

HOYLE, Edmond (1679–1769), of London, barrister. The first authority on whist and other games, and the first professional teacher of whist. His famous work was perhaps the best seller of the eighteenth century, and had the longest title of any book ever written on cards: *A Short Treatise on the Game of Whist, Containing the Laws of the Game, and also Some Rules Whereby a Beginner May, with Due Attention to Them, Attain to the Playing It Well.* It was published in 1742, and quickly went through several editions as well as being pirated extensively.

Hoyle's technique was surprisingly modern. He introduced the idea of inferring the nature of unseen hands from the fall of the cards, and discussed matters of probability. He also included a Code of Ethics and Fair Play, which was embodied almost without change in the LAWS OF AUCTION BRIDGE nearly two centuries later.

He was the first person to establish a tradition of law and order in card games, whence the phrase, now used to describe correct procedure in anything, "according to Hoyle." The book of laws by Hoyle was reprinted verbatim through the years. The prominent London clubs eventually did make certain changes as to style and working from time to time, especially in the nineteenth century, but Hoyle's imprimatur remained on most editions. He achieved considerable fame during his lifetime, and his name has since become a household word. Any collection of rules of card, table, or board games is still termed a Hoyle. See BIBLIOGRAPHY, A.

HOYOS, Mrs. Beatriz de, of Bogotá, Colombia; represented Colombia South American Women's Championships 1963, 1964, 1965, 1966, 1967; national successes include second Open Teams 1967, third Masters Pairs 1967.

HSU, J. Y., of Taipei, Taiwan, textile merchant and bridge writer, born in Kiangsu, China 1916; Far East Open Pair Champion 1959, 1969; represented China in international events in 1960, 1962, 1966, 1967, 1972, 1973. Author of *Contract Bridge for Beginners* and *Conventions,* and translator of thirty bridge books into Chinese. Chief Editor of *Chinese Bridge Magazine.*

HUANG, Frank, of Silver Spring, Md., statistician, born 1940 in Shanghai; second 1969 World Championships as a member of the Chinese team; represented China World Team Olympiad 1964, Far East Championships 1958, 1959.

HUANG, Patrick K., of Taipei, Taiwan, born in Shanghai, China, 1943; one of the leading players of the Far East; second 1969, 1970 World Championships; represented China World Team Olympiad 1964; won Far East Open Pair Championships 1963, 1966, 1967, the only player to win the Pair event three times, Team Championships 1967, 1969, second 1959; represented China Far East Championships 1958, 1962, 1966; won Hong Kong–Taipei and Manila–Taipei Interport tournaments; numerous national and intercollegiate successes. The youngest player ever to represent his country in a major international championship when he participated in the Far East Championship in 1958 at the age of fifteen.

HUBBELL, John W., of Kansas City, Mo., bridge club owner, born 1903; won Life Masters Pairs 1954, Summer Nat'l Men's Pairs 1957; second Spingold 1953, 1954, 1962; regional wins include Mississippi Valley Open Team 1952, 1959, Open Pairs 1956, 1965.

HUDECEK, Carl J., of Toledo, Ohio, physicist, born 1934; won Fall Nat'l Life Masters Men's Pairs 1966, several regional events including Midwest Open Teams 1957, 1960, 1974. Former President Northwest Ohio BA, District 12 Organization, *Bridge World* contributor.

HUDGINS, John (Jack), of Norwood, Mass., National Tournament Director, born 1929; won Sub-Senior Masters Teams 1961. Regional wins include Mid-Atlantic Summer Knockout Teams 1962.

HUDSON, Robert R., of Dunedin, New Zealand, company director, born 1921; won New Zealand Open Teams 1966. Past President New Zealand CBA; Associate editor New Zealand Bridge Magazine.

HUGGARD, Richard T., of Ann Arbor, Mich., personnel manager, born 1936; winner of several regional championships including Cambrian Shield Knockout Teams 1974, Open Teams 1974.

HUGHES, Boyd R., of Columbia, S.C., died 1968; won Mid-Atlantic Fall Open Teams 1962, 1963; Mixed Pairs 1959; Former President Mid-Atlantic Conference and South Carolina Unit; author of booklet on club tournament direction.

HUGHES, Stanley (1889–1958), of London, England. Won Gold Cup 1936 and represented Britain Schwab Cup 1934.

HULGAARD, Dr. Johannes, of Aarhus, Denmark, orthopedic surgeon, born 1932; represented Denmark World Team Olympiad 1960, and European Championship 1956, 1957, 1965 1967, 1974, 1975; won Danish Open Teams 1956, 1957, 1960, 1961, 1963, 1964, 1965, 1966, 1973, 1974; Open Pairs 1969, 1970; Nordic Team Championships 1973. Co-author of *Modern Acol.*

HULGAARD, Mrs. Lida, of Aarhus, Denmark, lawyer, born 1939. Represented Denmark World Olympiad 1964; Open Teams 1974, 1975; European Ladies Teams 1963, 1967. Won Nordic Open Teams 1973. National titles include Open Team 1966, 1973, 1974; Open Pairs 1968, 1969.

HUME, Hampton (1924–1969), of Atlanta, Ga., publisher and mathematician; represented US World Pair Olympiad 1962; won Spring Nat'l Open Pairs 1961, second Summer Nat'l Mixed Team 1964; won Mid-Atlantic Fall Open Team 1962, Mid-Atlantic Spring Men's Teams 1957, Midwest Spring Men's Pairs 1965, Open Teams 1965, Missouri Valley Masters Pairs 1965, Southern Spring Open Teams 1965; second Mid-Atlantic Fall Mixed Pairs 1958, Mid-Atlantic Spring Open Team 1961, Men's Team 1957, Mid-South Mixed Pairs 1958. Former Publisher of *Modern Bridge.*

HUMER, Norman, of Waltham, Mass.; won Summer Nat'l Spingold Consolation Teams 1972, Spring Nat'l secondary Men's Swiss Teams; winner of several regional events including New England Knockout Teams 1969, 1973.

HUNT, August, of San Leandro, Calif.; won several regionals including Midwinter Knockout Teams 1970, California Capital Master Pairs and Swiss Teams 1972, Central California Swiss Teams 1973.

HUNT, Dr. E. J., of Terre Haute, Ind., surgeon, born 1895; won All-American Open Pairs 1941. Member of USBA Board of Governors.

HUNT, John J., of Bridgeport, Conn., attorney, born 1910; won New England Spring Individual 1961, 1965, Open Teams 1968. Past President of New England Conference and Connecticut BA.

HUSKE, William J. (1879–1945), born in Quebec; newspaper reporter and editor in the Midwest for thirty years; won USBA Open Team 1933; at one time bridge editor of the Cleveland *Plain Dealer,* he was editor of *The Bridge World* 1932–34, and associate editor 1943–45. He was the editor of the ACBL

Bulletin 1937–39, and wrote many articles on bridge and towie, the three-handed game he helped sponsor.

HUTCHINSON, Mary L. (Mrs. R. D.), of Corvallis, Ore., born 1916; won Hawaiian Open Team 1955, Northwest Masters Pairs 1959, 1962, Mixed Pairs 1959.

HUTCHINSON, R. D., of Corvallis, Ore., farmer, born 1905; won Hawaiian Men's Pairs 1955, Hawaiian Open Teams 1955, Rocky Mountain Men's Pairs 1960, Canadian Men's Pairs 1968.

HUTCHISON, Jean (Mrs. W. J.), of Petone, New Zealand, born 1899; represented New Zealand World Bridge Olympics 1934, Far East Women's Championships 1971, 1972, Australasian Par Point Championship 1962; New Zealand Open Team 1937, 1938, 1948, 1953, Open Pairs 1959.

HUTCHISON, Dr. W. J. (1898–1974), of Petone, New Zealand, physician; represented New Zealand Australasian Par Point Championship 1962; New Zealand Open Teams 1937, 1938, 1948, 1953, Open Pairs 1959. President New Zealand Contract BA.

HYERS, Earle W., of Berkeley, Ill.; won All-American Open Team 1954, Central States Men's Pairs 1955, Canadian-American Masters Pairs 1956.

HYMES, Edward, Jr. (1908–1962), of New York, N.Y., attorney; Life Master No. 14, and one of the leading American players until his retirement from tournament play; won Asbury Challenge Teams 1935, Spingold 1937, 1941, 1943, 1945, Vanderbilt 1940, Fall Nat'l Open Pairs 1935; second Spingold 1936, 1940, Asbury Challenge Teams 1933, USBA Open Teams 1936, Open Pairs 1934; regional wins included Eastern Mixed Pairs 1942, 1943; Honorary Member and lifetime director of CAVENDISH CLUB, New York.

I

IGNATZ, Rose (Mrs. Bennie), of Sacramento, Calif., pharmacist; won Fall Nat'l Mixed Team 1957. Chairman Sacramento BA.

IN DER MAUR, Gangolf, of Klagenfurt, Austria, born 1931; represented Austria World Team Olympiad 1968, several World Pair Olympiads and European Championships.

INGBERMAN, Monroe, of White Plains, N.Y., mathematician and bridge writer, born 1935; won Summer Nat'l secondary Men's Pairs 1969; winner of many regional titles including Central States

Knockout Teams 1962, 1966, Life and Senior Masters Pairs 1962, Men's Pairs 1963, Eastern States Knockout Teams 1970. Inventor of FRAGMENT BID, THREE NO TRUMP RESPONSE as forcing major raise. Contributor to various bridge periodicals; contributing editor *Bridge Encyclopedia*.

INGRAM, Henry St. John (1888–1974), of Farnborough, Kent, England, printer, bridge writer and editor; represented England in Schwab Cup 1936; captain of British team in some prewar championships; won Gold Cup 1936, and other national successes. Editor *Contract Bridge Journal* 1950–55; contributing editor for *Britannica* and *Chambers* encyclopaedias. Author of *How to Win at Bridge*. See BIBLIOGRAPHY, C, E.

INGVARSSON, Sveinn, of Reykjavik, Iceland, company director, born 1902; represented Iceland European Championship 1961, npc Icelandic Team 1962; national titles include many team and pair events.

IRWIN, Florence, of New York, N.Y., bridge teacher; author of the first book ever written on contract bridge: *Contract Bridge* (1927).

ISAACS, Bruce, of Phoenix, Ariz., retailer, born 1920; won Northwest Masters Pairs 1958, Desert Empire Open Team 1957, 1958, Men's Pairs 1958.

ISACKSON, Jeff, of Essexville, Mich.; won Summer Nat'l secondary Special Pairs 1974, tied secondary Swiss Teams 1973.

ISRAEL, Robert H., of Warren, Pa., physician, born 1900; won District 4 Men's Pairs 1960, Mixed Pairs 1958, Upper New York Open Pairs 1959, Men's Pairs 1960.

IVASKA, Paul, of Culver City, Calif., electrical engineer, born 1941; second World Bidding Contest 1973; won Fall Nat'l secondary Open Teams 1968, tied secondary Men's Swiss Teams 1971; winner of many regional titles including Bridge Week Knockout Teams 1973, Masters Pairs 1967, Men's Pairs 1971, Orange County Knockout Teams 1974.

J

JABON, Joseph A., of Seattle, Wash., salesman, born 1925 in New Orleans, where he was one of the so-called "Whiz Kids" team that included S. LAZARD, R. DREYFUS, H. DUVIC; won Nat'l Open Individual 1959, second Open Individual 1950, Fall Nat'l Open Pairs 1965; won Oregon Trail Open Teams 1963, 1966, 1968, Masters Pairs 1962, Northwest Masters Pairs 1961, Open Teams 1963, Open Pairs 1965.

JACKSON, Frank L., of San Francisco, Calif., bridge studio owner, teacher, columnist, born 1919; second Fall Nat'l Life Masters Individual 1959; won Bridge Week Open Pairs 1957, All-Western Open Pairs 1957, Open Team 1960, Masters Pairs 1961. Member of Western Conference Executive Committee, former ACBL Director.

JACOBI, Dr. Ernst, of Zurich, Switzerland, chemical engineer, born 1914; represented Switzerland in World Olympiad 1960 and in many European Championships; national successes include Open Team championships seven times, Open Pairs 1957, 1961, 1962, and Mixed Pairs 1963.

JACOBS, Jerome, of North Miami Beach, Fla.; won Central States Open Pairs 1951, Open Teams 1955, Midwest Open Teams 1952, 1957, Southeastern Men's Teams 1966, Knockout Teams 1967.

JACOBS, Walter L., of Miami, Beach, Fla., financier, born 1896; won Fall Nat'l Open Pairs 1936, 1939, All-American Open Teams 1938, Open Pairs 1939, Central States Open Teams 1938.

JACOBSON, Mrs. R., of Johannesburg, South Africa; second World Women's Team Olympiad 1968, 1972, World Olympiad Women's Pair 1974; represented South Africa World Women's Team Olympiad 1964, World Olympiad Women's Pairs 1962, 1966, 1970; national wins include Open Teams 1970, 1971, 1973, Open Pairs 1959.

JACOBUS, Marc S., of Allston, Mass., bridge teacher; won Fall Nat'l Life Master Men's Pairs 1972, second Reisinger 1974; won Long Island Open Teams 1974, Midwinter Holiday Open Teams 1974.

JACOBY, James O., of Richardson, Tex., born 1933; bridge teacher and backgammon teacher and writer, sharing a bridge column with his father, Oswald Jacoby, since 1965; one of the world's leading players; World Champion 1970, 1971, World Mixed Team Champion 1972, second World Championships 1973, World Team Olympiad 1972, World Olympiad Open Pairs 1966; represented North America World Championships 1963; won Spingold 1969, Marcus 1955, Chicago 1955, Vanderbilt 1965, 1967, 1971, Fall Nat'l Men's Pairs 1956, Spring Nat'l Men's Teams 1968, 1972, 1973, Summer Nat'l Masters Mixed Teams 1968, tied Reisinger 1970; second Spingold 1957, 1962, 1970, 1973, Vanderbilt 1970, Fall Nat'l Men's Teams 1954, 1968, Mixed Pairs 1963, Summer Nat'l Life Masters Pairs 1968, 1971, Spring Nat'l Men's Teams 1969. Winner of scores of regional events from Mid-South Spring Men's Pairs 1954, 1956, Open Teams 1954, through Big D Bridge Week Knockout Teams 1974. (See ACES TEAM.)

JACOBY, Mary Zita (Mrs. Oswald), of Dallas, Tex., born 1909; second Nat'l Mixed Team 1935; won Mid-

South Summer Open Team 1961, Texas Fall Open Teams 1960, Texas Spring Mixed Teams 1966; the only woman whose husband and son have won world titles; a former tennis champion.

JACOBY, Oswald, of Dallas, Tex., bridge columnist, actuary, one of the great players of all time. He first achieved international prominence as a bridge player as partner of Sidney Lenz in the CULBERTSON-LENZ MATCH, but he had already established himself as a champion at auction and contract. He next became a member of the famed FOUR HORSEMEN and FOUR ACES teams. His selection by Lenz over players of greater experience and with whom Lenz had practiced partnerships was early recognition of the brilliance and skill that were later to bring Jacoby to the top of the ACBL's list of all-time master-point winners.

Jacoby, born in Brooklyn, N.Y., in 1902, left Columbia University in his junior year to become an actuary, completing the examination of the Society of Actuaries in 1924 to become, at twenty-one, the youngest person ever to do so. After four years with Metropolitan Life, he went into business for himself, but his success was cut short by the 1929 market crash.

Jacoby's victory-studded career includes many oddities. He played in (and won) his first auction tournament in July, 1929—the National Team Championship of the American Whist League. But he had already won the first big contract pair tournament ever played, the Goldman Pairs event in the Eastern Championships held in February of that year. Later on he set a record by winning the Goldman three times in twenty years, the only occasions on which he entered. Afterward, he became a National Champion, winning two American Whist League pair and AWL team events.

After the Culbertson-Lenz match, Jacoby was for nearly two years secretary of the USBA, thus being associated with Culbertson. Late in 1933, however, he helped to form the original Four Aces team, which dominated the bridge world for the next several years. In this period, in addition to American Bridge League triumphs, he won two pair championships and four team championships of the United States Bridge Association. As of December 7, 1941, Jacoby held first place in the MASTER POINT ranking.

Jacoby had two months of army service in World War I, when he was fifteen. In 1941, he was playing in the national Open Pairs Championship in Richmond, Virginia, on December 7 when the Pearl Harbor attack was announced. He immediately left the tournament, and did not play again for four years, during most of which he was serving as a specialist in the Navy, from which he eventually was separated with rank of lieutenant commander. Returning to competition in 1945, he found Charles GOREN far ahead, and he had done very little about returning to the top when he again returned to duty in 1950 for service in the Korean action. This return to service cost him his place on the American team in the first Bermuda Bowl matches. However, he had represented the ABL in international competition as far

back as 1935 when the Four Aces team defeated the French, champions of Europe, in the first official World Championship encounter. (See WORLD CHAMPIONSHIPS.)

Returning from two years of Korean service, Jacoby found himself once again dropped out of the first ten. By 1958 he had managed to move back into sixth place, still far behind Goren, when he decided to make a determined effort to regain the number one position. By 1962, he had done so. Between 1959 and 1963, he won the MC KENNEY TROPHY four times in five years; the only player older than 50 to win the trophy, Jacoby won it at ages 57, 59, 60, and 61. In 1963, he became the first player to acquire more than 1,000 points in a single year. His winning total that year was 1,034. In 1967, he surpassed the 10,000-point mark, at which time he retired from active competition for the McKenney Trophy. Almost exactly one year later, he relinquished his position as top master-point holder to Barry Crane.

In 1950, Jacoby became the daily bridge columnist for the NEA syndicate, serving several hundred newspapers. He wrote books on poker, canasta, gin rummy, mathematical odds, etc. With all this bridge and games activity, Jacoby nevertheless continuously maintained a practice as a consulting actuary, served for six years as a member of the Board of Visitors of Harvard Observatory (for the last three, under the chairmanship of then Senator John F. Kennedy), became an expert on computers, and was frequently consulted on questions of tournament movements, elimination schedules, and scoring.

He won a National Championship with his son James (the Chicago in 1955); and scored many victories with his wife Mary Zita, hoping to add to his titles the missing one—most master points owned by any husband and wife, regardless of when acquired.

As player, writer, mathematician, and innovator, Jacoby's place among bridge immortals is assured. In 1965, he was elected to the Bridge Hall of Fame. As npc of the North American teams for 1969, 1970, and 1971, Jacoby captained the first North American World Champion teams in more than a decade.

His national wins include Spingold 1934, 1936, 1938, 1939, 1945, 1950, 1959; Vanderbilt 1931, 1934, 1935, 1937, 1938, 1946, 1965, Masters Mixed Teams 1968, Life Master Pairs 1936; Men's Team 1952, 1959; Open Pairs 1935, 1960, 1964; Men's Pairs 1934, 1939, 1949; Chicago 1955; Marcus 1955; Masters Individual 1935; USBA Grand National Open Teams 1934, 1935, 1937; Open Pairs 1936, 1937; very many seconds in national events, and wins in almost every regional tournament. In 1973 he won the World Championship of Backgammon.

Jacoby pioneered many bidding ideas, including the FORCING TWO, JACOBY TRANSFER BIDS, and WEAK JUMP OVERCALLS. More recently his innovations have included developments of GERBER and BLACKWOOD, and a specialized use of TWO NO TRUMP and THREE NO TRUMP RESPONSES. Among his writings are *The Four Aces System*, *What's New in Bridge*, *Win at Bridge with Oswald Jacoby*, *Win at Bridge With Jacoby Modern*, *The Backgammon Book* (with J. CRAWFORD), and many books on mathematics, gambling, poker, and other card games, including canasta, in which he had both of the two best-selling books. See BIBLIOGRAPHY, B, C, E, M.

JAEGER, Henry P., of Cleveland Heights, Ohio, manufacturer's representative, bridge writer and lecturer, born 1888; winner of many whist and auction trophies, won Ohio State Pairs 1930, and other wins in contract. ABL President 1928. Honorary Member ACBL 1939. A member of the group which promoted the OFFICIAL SYSTEM.

JAEGER, Jane (Mrs. Lewis M.), of Miami Beach, Fla., formerly of New York, born 1914; one of the leading East Coast women players; won Chicago 1947, Fall Nat'l Open Pairs 1945, Summer Nat'l Mixed Team 1951, Grand Nationals 1973; second Vanderbilt 1956; won Eastern States Knockout Teams 1945, Mixed Teams 1946, Mixed Pairs 1949, Women's Pairs 1966, Southeastern Women's Pairs 1966, Knockout Teams 1968.

JAEGER, Lewis M. (1901–1964), of Coral Gables, Fla., formerly of New York, manufacturer; was one of the leading East Coast players; won Chicago 1934, Fall Nat'l Open Pairs 1945; second Vanderbilt 1956, Nat'l Golder Pairs 1949; won Eastern States Knockout Teams 1945; Mixed Teams 1947, Mixed Pairs 1949.

JAÏS, Pierre, of Paris, physician, born 1913; one of the great players of the world. His partnership with Roger Trézel, one of the strongest in the world since 1950, demonstrated the efficiency of the *tendance canapé* (or modified canapé), and set a unique record by winning all three major world titles: World Championship 1956, World Team Olympiad 1960, World Pair Olympiad 1962. European Champion 1955, second 1954, 1956, 1959. Won London *Sunday Times* international pair contest 1963, and ten French national titles. Writings include *How to Win at Rubber Bridge, Apprenez à mieux jouer au bridge,* and many contributions to French periodicals. See BIBLIOGRAPHY, E.

JALAVA, Matti, of Helsinki, salesman, born 1926; represented Finland European Championships 1956, 1963, Scandinavian Championship 1962; national wins include Open Team 1949, 1958, 1960, 1962, 1963.

JALBUENE, Mrs. Lydia, of Manila, Philippines; represented Philippines World Team Olympiad 1964, Far East 1963, Women's World Pair Olympiad 1962, Mixed Team event 1962.

JANITSCHKE, Jan P., of Denver, Colo., bridge teacher, born 1947; winner of several regional events including Midwinter Holiday Knockout Team 1973, Missouri Valley Open Teams 1974.

JANITSCHKE, V. Craig, of Denver, Colo.; winner of several regional events including Midwinter Holiday Knockout Teams 1972, International City Masters Pairs 1974.

JANNERSTEN, Eric, of Stockholm, Sweden, editor and publisher, born 1912; one of the leading bridge personalities of Europe; represented Sweden on several occasions including European Championship 1951, and won many national titles. Editor of *Bridgetidningen* since 1939, bridge columnist since 1940. Publisher and editor of *European Bridge Review* 1949–51. Author of best-selling books on bridge, and publisher of about 40 bridge books. Headed a bridge school since 1938, with an estimated 150,000 pupils. Executive Secretary IBPA. Other activities include a radio program, "Bridge on the Air," directing World Team Olympiad 1960 and 1964, European Championship 1962, and other international tournaments, and acting as Bridge-O-Rama commentator.

JAQUES, Arturo, of Buenos Aires, Argentina, travel agent and bridge writer, born 1923; represented Argentina World Team Olympiad 1964, 1972, World Championships 1959, 1962; South American Champion 1958, 1959, 1961, second 1955, 1956; won Argentine Open Team 1950, 1954, 1958, 1960, 1961, 1963, 1965, 1967, 1969, 1971, Open Pairs 1951, 1959, 1960, 1964, 1965, 1974. Top Argentine Master-Point holder since 1960. Former Editor of *Bridge Argentino,* contributor to many bridge periodicals. Contributing editor *Bridge Encyclopedia.* Former Vice-President IBPA.

JAWORSKI, Antoni, of Warsaw, Poland, sanitation engineer, born 1930; represented Poland European Championships 1965, 1967; won Hungarian Balaton Bowl 1963, Belgian Open Pairs 1964, Baltic Bowl 1964, Polish Open Teams 1962, 1963, 1964, 1966; second Polish Open Teams 1965, Open Pairs 1964.

JAYE, Eli, of New York, N.Y., plumbing supplies manufacturer, born 1910; won Reisinger 1954, several regional titles including Keystone Conference Open Teams 1952, 1955; Eastern States Open Pairs 1964, Florida Men's Pairs 1970. Former president Greater New York BA.

JEANS, Christopher G., of Norristown, Pa., programmer, born 1944; second Fall Nat'l Life Masters Men's Pairs 1969; won several regional events including Keystone Knockout Teams 1973.

JEDRZEJOWSKI, Kyzysztof, of Warsaw, Poland, electronics engineer, born 1941; represented Poland European Championships 1967, European Junior Championships 1968; third World Par contest 1963; won Polish Open Teams 1966, 1968, Mixed Teams 1966; second Open Teams 1961, Mixed Pairs 1966.

JELLINEK, Hans, born in Vienna; deported by Germans from Norway 1940, died in concentration camp; World Champion 1937; European Champion 1936. His partnership with Karl SCHNEIDER was considered the strongest in Europe in the mid-thirties.

JENSEN, Nils E., of Stockholm, Sweden, president electric company, born 1920; represented Sweden World Mixed Teams Olympiad 1962 and Mixed Pairs Olympiad 1966; npc Sweden's European and Scandinavian Championships teams. President Swedish Bridge League since 1965.

JESNER, George David, of Canberra, Australia, formerly of Glasgow, Scotland, master draper, bridge teacher and writer, born 1925; member victorious Scottish Team, Camrose Trophy matches 1964; won Scottish Open Teams twice and Open Pairs.

JOHNSON, Benjamin O. (1906–76), of Spartanburg, S.C., attorney; npc US World Champion Team 1954; won Chicago 1949; second Marcus 1952; won Northwest Masters Pairs 1953, Mid-Atlantic Open Pairs 1953, Hawaiian Men's Pairs, Master Pairs and Mixed Pairs 1953, Texas Fall Men's Pairs 1966. ACBL President 1953. Chairman ACBL Charity Foundation. Counsel and member of Executive Committee WBF.

JOHNSON, Karl, of Moline, Ill., ACBL National Tournament Director, born 1924.

JOHNSON, Marilyn K., of Houston, Tex., librarian, born 1928; one of the world's leading women players; won World Olympiad Women's Pairs 1970, Fall Nat'l Mixed Pairs 1968, 1973; Spring Nat'l Women's Teams 1974, 1975; second Spring Nat'l Women's Pairs 1967, Mixed Pairs 1969, Women's Teams 1973, Summer Nat'l Masters Mixed Teams 1969; winner of many regional titles including All-Western Open Teams 1960, Knockout Teams 1967, Open Pairs 1970.

JOHNSON, Peter, of Chestnut Hill, Mass., bridge teacher, born 1912; second Fall Nat'l Mixed Pairs 1960; won New England Fall Knockout Teams 1943, Spring Open Teams 1953, 1955, Masters Pairs 1948, Mixed Teams 1957, Men's Pairs 1955, 1956.

JOHNSON, Robert L., of Los Angeles, Calif., bridge lecturer and broadcaster; a prominent pioneer in the teaching of bridge on radio and television.

JOHNSON, Mrs. Sallie, of Westport, Conn., bridge teacher, one of the leading American women players; represented United States World Olympiad Women's Pairs 1970; won Spring Nat'l Women's Teams 1955, 1958, 1960, 1961, 1968, second Women's Pairs 1969, Summer Nat'l Mixed Teams 1957, 1974, won Fall Nat'l secondary Women's

Teams 1968, 1969; regional wins include Eastern States Women's Pairs 1962, 1968, New England Fall Women's Pairs 1955, New York–New Jersey Open Teams 1963.

JOLMA, Lawrence, of Portland, Ore., business broker, born 1916; won Spring Nat'l Men's Teams 1967, Oregon Trail Knockout Teams 1974; ACBL Director since 1966.

JOLMA, Marge (Mrs. Lawrence), of Portland, Ore., born 1915; won Oregon Trail Knockout Teams 1974, Women's Pairs 1961, 1974.

JONES, Henry. See CAVENDISH.

JONES, Richard L., of Sacramento, Calif., real estate broker, born 1935; winner of several regional events including Oregon Trail Board-a-Match Teams 1967, Knockout Teams 1968, 1973.

JORDAN, Robert F., of Bala Cynwyd, Pa., born 1927; one of the outstanding American bridge players; second World Team Olympiad 1964, 1968; represented US World Pairs Olympiad 1962, and North America World Championships 1963; won International Team Trials 1967, second 1962, third 1963; won McKenney 1960, Mott-Smith 1961, 1962, Vanderbilt 1961, 1968, Reisinger 1966, 1967, Summer Nat'l Mixed Teams 1959, Spring Nat'l Open Pairs 1960, 1962; second Vanderbilt 1965, Chicago 1961, Spring Nat'l Mixed Pairs 1961, Fall Nat'l Men's Pairs 1956; regional successes include Eastern States 1956; regional successes include Eastern States Knockout Teams 1960, 1961, Mixed Teams 1958, Keystone Open Pairs 1958, Mid-Atlantic Summer Open Teams 1960, All-American Men's Pairs 1960, District 4 Open Pairs 1964, 1965, Open Teams 1965.

JOSEPH, William (1910–1968), of Wayne, N.J., construction director; won Life Masters Pairs 1952; second Fall Nat'l Men's Team 1949; won Canadian-American Mixed Pairs 1953, and many others. Many administrative positions include: ACBL Director, member By-Laws Commission; 1956 Nat'ls Planning Committee, President of New York–New Jersey Bridge Conference, North Jersey BA, Central New York BA, Secretary of Lehigh BA.

JOSFAY, George, of Budapest, Hungary, journalist and linguist, born 1938; managing editor of the Hungarian bridge magazine, *Bridzselet.*

JOTCHAM, Ray, of Don Mills, Ont., mathematics and computer science teacher, born 1941; second Spingold 1964; won several regional titles including Eastern States Open Pairs 1963, Canadian-American Open Teams 1964, 1967, 1969, Canadian-American Master Pairs 1974.

JOYCE, David J., of Chicago, Ill., commodity futures broker, born 1942; won Summer Nat'l Spingold Consolation, Fall Nat'l secondary Open Pairs, several regional titles including Bridge Week Masters Pairs 1970, 1974.

JOYCE, Randolph, of Raleigh, N.C., born 1947; winner of several regional events including Mid-Atlantic Open Teams 1968, 1971, 1972, 1973, 1974.

JUAN, Jane. See PRIDAY, Mrs. Anthony.

K

KABIAN, Ludwig J. (formerly Kabakjian), of Philadelphia, Pa., business consultant and bridge teacher, born 1909; won Chicago 1949, Nat'l Mixed Team 1947, Nat'l Open Individual 1947; second Nat'l Mixed Team 1948.

KACHMAR, Barbara (Mrs. John, formerly B. Collyer), of New York, N.Y., advertising copywriter and bridge writer, born 1911; one of the leading women players of the East Coast; won USBA Mixed Pairs 1936, Nat'l Women's Team 1960, 1961, Fall Nat'l Women's Pairs 1962; second Nat'l Mixed Team 1934, Nat'l Women's Team 1963; won Eastern States Mixed Team 1936. Writings include many entertaining contributions to *Bridge World, Modern Bridge,* and other periodicals.

KAHN, Richard, of New York, N.Y., motion picture sales executive, born 1911; one of the leading American players; represented North America World Championship 1956; won Chicago 1949, Vanderbilt 1953, Spingold 1955, Life Masters Pairs 1951, Fall Nat'l Mixed Pairs 1939, Summer Nat'l Mixed Team 1951, Grand Nat'l Mixed Team 1933; second Fall Nat'l Open Pairs 1951; won many regional titles including Eastern States Knockout Teams 1956, 1957, 1958, 1959, 1969, Open Pairs 1947, Masters Pairs 1960. Co-founder New York Card School 1950.

KAISER, Cornelis (Kees), of Utrecht, Holland, inspector of education, born 1926; represented Netherlands World Pair Olympiad 1962, World Team Olympiad 1964, and in European Championships 1954, 1957, 1958, 1966, 1967; National titles include Open Team 1949, 1958, 1962, Open Pairs 1954, 1955, 1963.

KAISER, Robert, of Maarn, Holland, civil engineer and bridge columnist, born 1927; represented Netherlands World Pair Olympiad 1962, European Championship 1954, 1957, 1958; National wins include Open Team 1949, 1958, 1962, Open Pairs 1954, 1958, 1959.

KAMINSKY, Amos, of New York, N.Y.; tied second Summer Nat'l Mixed Teams 1974; several regional wins including Rocky Mountain Knockout Teams 1973.

KANDLER, Harold, of Pico Rivera, Calif., bridge teacher, born 1927; second Fall Nationals and Masters Men's Pairs 1962; winner of many regional titles including All-Western Masters Pairs 1958, 1967, Pacific Southwest Open Teams 1967, Knockout Teams 1967, 1970, 1971.

KANSIL, Prince Djoli (formerly Joel D. Gaines), of Bali, Indonesia, born 1943 in New York; inventor of BRIDGETTE; co-founder of Eastern Collegiate Bridge League.

KANTAR, Edwin B., of Los Angeles, Calif., bridge teacher and writer, born 1932; one of the outstanding American player-writers; represented North America World Championships 1969, runner-up 1975; US World Olympiad Open Pairs 1970; third International Team Trials 1968; won Spingold 1961, 1962, 1974, Marcus 1960, Chicago 1962, 1965, Vanderbilt 1964, Grand Nationals 1974; second Vanderbilt 1961, 1968, 1973, Fall Nat'l Open Pairs 1962, Men's Pairs 1962, Reisinger 1968, Spring Nat'l Men's Pairs 1967; regional successes include Bridge Week Knockout Teams 1958, 1959, 1972, Open Teams 1961, 1962, Open Pairs 1958, All-Western Open Teams 1959. His frequent contributions to *Bridge World* and other periodicals include many "Test Your Play" features. Author of *A Comprehensive Bridge Manual for Beginners, Introduction to Declarer's Play, Introduction to Defender's Play, Bridge Conventions, Bridge Bidding Made Easy, Gamesman Bridge, Complete Defensive Play, Test Your Bridge Play.* Regular contributor to *Popular Bridge,* ACBL *Bulletin.* Former nationally ranked table tennis player. Contributing editor *Bridge Encyclopedia.* See BIBLIOGRAPHY, C, D, E.

KANTAR, Phyllis (former Mrs. Edwin), of Los Angeles, Calif., computer programmer; won Marcus Cup 1966; regional successes include Disneyland Open Pairs 1970. Editorial assistant *Popular Bridge.*

KANTOR, Dorothy, of Minneapolis, Minn., bridge club owner; winner of many regional championships including Pheasant Knockout Teams 1970, 1972, Canadian Prairie Knockout Teams 1972, Masters Pairs 1970, Gopher Master Pairs 1973. ACBL Director since 1974.

KANTOR, Dr. Simon W., of Ridgewood, N.J., research executive, born 1925; regional wins include New England Fall Mixed Team 1959, Long Island Men's Pairs 1972.

KAPLAN, Betty (Mrs. Edgar, formerly Mrs. Alfred Sheinwold), of New York, N.Y., former director of music school; won Summer Nat'l Mixed Teams 1963, Spring Nat'l Women's Teams 1965; second Summer Nat'l Mixed Team 1959, Spring Nat'l Women's Pairs 1962; regional successes include Eastern States Mixed Pairs 1962; Bermuda Open Teams 1972, 1974. Circulation Manager of *The Bridge World*.

KAPLAN, Edgar, of New York, N.Y., editor and publisher of *The Bridge World* since 1966, bridge teacher and writer, born 1925; one of the world's leading players; second World Olympiad 1968; represented North America World Championships 1967, 1971; Assistant Captain US team 1964, and many times coach to North American teams, which benefited from his detailed knowledge of European systems; second International Team Trials 1966; won McKenney 1957, Vanderbilt 1953, 1968, 1970, Spingold 1967, 1968, Chicago 1958, Marcus 1953, Spring Nat'l Men's Teams, Open Pairs 1966, Summer Nat'l Mixed Pairs 1967, Fall Nat'l Men's Teams 1955, 1966, Blue Ribbon Pairs 1974, Life Masters Men's Pairs 1973, Mixed Pairs 1965, Masters Mixed Teams 1963, Golder Pairs 1953, Masters Individual 1957, Reisinger 1966, 1967, 1971, second Reisinger 1969, Spingold 1965, 1971, Marcus 1949, Vanderbilt 1958, 1965, Fall Nat'l Men's Teams 1958, 1961, Life Masters Men's Pairs 1965, Summer Nat'l Masters Mixed Teams 1959, 1968, Spring Nat'l Men's Pairs 1970, Sub-Senior Masters Teams 1947, Golder Pairs 1950; regional successes include Eastern States Knockout Teams 1954, 1956, 1957, 1958, 1959, 1970, Open Teams 1957, Open Pairs 1951, Mixed Pairs 1962, Keystone Open Teams 1954, 1957, 1962. Writings include *How to Play Winning Bridge* (co-author), *The Complete Italian System of Winning Bridge, Winning Contract Bridge Complete, Competitive Bidding in Modern Bridge, Duplicate Bridge: How to Play, How to Win.* Co-inventor of the KAPLAN-SHEINWOLD system, and a partner in the Card School of New York, N.Y. Former ACBL Director. Contributing Editor *Bridge Encyclopedia.* See BIBLIOGRAPHY, C, E.

KAPLAN, Fred D. (1902–66), of New York, N.Y., attorney; won Vanderbilt 1936; second Spingold 1938; won Eastern States Knockout Teams 1936, Open Pairs 1939.

KAPLAN, Michael D., of Marina Del Ray, Calif., historical writer and researcher, born 1943; winner of several regional events including Desert Empire Knockout Teams 1974, Midwinter Holiday Knockout Teams 1972.

KAPLAN, Muriel, of New York, N.Y. (died 1970); second World Women's Team Olympiad 1964; won Women's International Team Trials 1963; second Nat'l Women's Team 1962; won Keystone Open Pairs 1959, New York-New Jersey Women's Pairs 1966.

KARLSSON, Larus, of Reykjavik, Iceland, accountant, born 1912; represented Iceland World

Team Olympiad 1960, in nine European Championships, and in Scandinavian Championships 1953, 1962; member winning Icelandic Team Iceland vs. Great Britain 1947; national titles include Open Teams 1949, 1953, 1954, 1957, 1962, Open Pairs 1956.

KARN, Willard S., of New York, N.Y. (1898–1950); executive and bridge writer, member of the FOUR HORSEMEN; winner of several American Whist League auction and contract events. Won ABL Open Team 1931, Vanderbilt 1931, 1932, Fall Nat'l Open Pairs 1931, 1932, and Masters Individual 1931; second Chicago 1931; regional wins included Reisinger 1931, Eastern Open Teams 1932. Writings include articles for *The Bridge World* and a book, *Karn's Bridge Service.* See BIBLIOGRAPHY, E.

KARP, Leonard, of Tenafly, N.J., bridge club owner and cruise director, born 1920; won Marcus 1954, second 1974.

KARPIN, Fred, of Silver Spring, Md., bridge teacher, lecturer, and writer, born 1913; one of the leading personalities of the East Coast; second Fall Nat'l Open Teams 1946. One of the originators of the POINT-COUNT method of distributional hand valuation. Author of: *Contract Bridge: the Play of the Cards, Psychological Strategy in Contract Bridge, How to Play (and Misplay) Slam Contracts,* and *Winning Play in Contract Bridge: Strategy at Trick One, The Finesse, The Art of Card Reading, Winning Play in Tournament and Duplicate Bridge: How the Experts Triumph;* co-author *The Complete Book of Duplicate Bridge.* Contributing Editor *Bridge Encyclopedia.* See BIBLIOGRAPHY, C, D, E.

KASDAY, Tony, of Scarborough, Me., businessman, born 1936; regional successes include Bridge Week Masters Pairs 1967, Canadian-Atlantic Knockout Teams 1974.

KASLE, Gaylor, of Tucson, Ariz., bridge professional, born 1941; won Spring Nat'l Men's Teams 1973, secondary Swiss Teams 1974, Fall Nat'l secondary Swiss Teams 1974, tied secondary Men's Teams 1969; winner of numerous regional titles including Southeastern Knockout teams 1973, Men's Teams 1970, 1971, Open Pairs 1972.

KASLE, Sharon (Mrs. Gaylor), of Tucson, Ariz., born 1937; won Spring Nat'l secondary Mixed Pairs 1971, several regional events including Texas Fall Mixed Pairs 1970.

KASPRZAK, Marek, of Warsaw, Poland, forestry engineer, born 1936; represented Poland European Championships 1965, 1967; won Hungarian Balaton Bowl 1963, Belgian Open Pairs 1964, Baltic Bowl 1964, Beirut Festival Open Teams 1968. National successes include Open Teams 1961, 1963, 1964, 1966.

KASS, Irving, of New York, N.Y., insurance agent, born 1915; won Vanderbilt 1952, Eastern States Knockout Teams 1950.

KASSAY, Michael B., of Huntington, N.Y., engineer, born 1926; member of Hungarian International Team 1955, and winner of five Hungarian National Championships; won Eastern States Mixed Teams 1962, New England Open Teams 1965, 1966.

KATZ, Emanuel, of Buffalo, N.Y., real estate insurance, born 1915; has won various Canadian national and regional events including Canadian Nat'l Open Teams 1957, and Canadian-American Open Teams 1953; won Upper New York State Open Pairs 1958, Mixed Pairs 1958, 1959, 1961, 1963, 1965.

KATZ, Harold, of Memphis, Tenn., ACBL *Bulletin* editorial assistant; won Mid-South Spring Open Teams 1971.

KATZ, Moshe, of Tel Aviv, Israel, sales manager, born 1920; represented Israel World Team Olympiad 1964, European Championships 1965, 1966, 1967; national successes include Tel Aviv Open Teams 1965, 1966.

KATZ, Dr. Richard Hart, of Los Angeles, Calif., physician, born 1942; one of the most successful American players; in partnership with L. COHEN, won every major national team event once in period of two years: Spingold 1973, Reisinger 1973, Grand Nationals 1974, Vanderbilt 1975; won Blue Ribbon Pairs 1968, FISHBEIN TROPHY 1973, Fall Nat'l Open Pairs 1967, Spring Nat'l secondary Swiss Teams 1974; second Vanderbilt 1973, Blue Ribbon Pairs 1969. Numerous regional successes. Intercollegiate Champion 1966, runner-up 1965. Co-author of *Breakthrough Bridge.*

KATZ, Samuel, of Miami Beach, Fla., stockbroker, deceased; one of the leading players of the Southeast; won Spingold 1940, Life Masters Pairs 1944, Fall Nat'l Men's Pairs 1948, Summer Nat'l Non-Masters Pairs 1933; second Spingold 1942, 1952, Chicago 1943, Vanderbilt 1946, 1947, Fall Nat'l Men's Pairs 1936, Men's Team 1952; regional wins include Florida Men's Teams 1959, Knockout Teams 1968, Southeastern Men's Pairs 1956, Men's Teams 1965, 1972, Midwestern Open Teams 1955.

KATZEN, David, of Johannesburg, South Africa, insurance broker, born 1929; won Southern Africa Open Pairs 1961; second Open Teams 1962; participated in a match against a touring British team 1962.

KAUDER, Arnold, of Los Angeles, Calif., electronics engineer, born 1908; won Nat'l Mixed Team 1949, 1950, 1955; regional wins include All-Western Master Pairs 1946, Bridge Week Open Team 1951,

Open Pairs 1949, Men's Pairs 1950, Mixed Pairs 1949, Pacific Southwest Open Pairs 1957, California Capital Open Pairs 1972.

KAUDER, James, of Los Angeles, Calif., attorney; regional successes include Eastern States Open Pairs 1966. Author, *The Bridge Philosopher;* contributor to *The Contract Bridge Bulletin* and *The Bridge World.*

KAUDER, Mary Jane. See FARELL, MARY JANE.

KAUFMAN, George S. (1889–1961), of New York, N.Y., dramatist; prominent rubber bridge player; honorary member of CAVENDISH CLUB, and member of CROCKFORD'S CLUB and REGENCY CLUB. Many humorous writings about bridge appeared in *The New Yorker* and other periodicals, and have often been reprinted. They included the "Kibitzers' Revolt," and the ingenious suggestion that clubs should post on the bulletin board the information that North-South (or East-West) are holding the good cards.

KAUFMAN, Istvan, of Budapest, Hungary, technician, born 1922; won Hungarian Open Teams 1961, 1962, 1964, 1965, 1967, Open Pairs 1959, 1960, Mixed Pairs 1961, 1962; member of victorious Hungarian team in matches with Czechoslovakia 1963, Germany 1964, Belgium 1964, and Austria 1965.

KAY, Judy (Mrs. Norman), of Narberth, Pa., born 1934; won Summer Nat'l secondary Mixed Pairs 1967; regional successes include Keystone Conference Women's Teams 1972.

KAY, Norman, of Narberth, Pa., investment executive, born 1927; one of the world's leading players. Represented US World Team Olympiad 1960, 1968, North America World Championships 1961, 1967, 1971; second International Team Trials 1966; won Mc Kenney 1955, Chicago 1961, Vanderbilt 1960, 1968, 1970, Fall Nat'l Men's Teams 1955, 1961, 1966, Men's Pairs 1962, Life Masters Men's Pairs, 1973, Blue Ribbon Pairs 1974, Spring Nat'l Open Pairs 1963, 1966, Men's Teams 1966, Men's Pairs 1958, Spingold 1967, 1968, Reisinger 1966, 1967, 1971, Life Masters Individual 1955; second Reisinger 1969, Spingold 1960, 1961, 1965, 1971, Chicago 1960, Vanderbilt 1958, 1965, 1970, Spring Nat'l Men's Teams 1963, Men's Pairs 1962, 1965, 1970, Summer Nat'l Men's Teams 1967, Fall Nat'l Men's Teams, Men's Pairs 1958. Many regional successes. Co-author of *The Complete Book of Duplicate Bridge.* See BIBLIOGRAPHY, F.

KAYE, Richard I., of Denver, Colo., business executive; won Spring Nat'l Men's Pairs 1970, several regional championships including Rocky Mountain Knockout Teams 1973, Men's Pairs 1974.

KEARSE, Amalya L., of New York, N.Y., attorney, writer; one of the leading American women players; won Spring Nat'l Women's Pairs 1971, Fall Nat'l Life

Master Women's Pairs 1972, secondary Open Pairs 1966, Spring Nat'l secondary Mixed Pairs 1974, secondary Women's Swiss Teams 1973; winner of seven ABA national championships in 1972 and 1973; several ACBL regional titles including Fun City Knockout Teams 1973, Keystone Open Pairs 1974. Author of *Bridge Conventions Complete;* cotranslator of *Championship Bridge* (Le Dentu, *Bridge A La Une*); member of Goren Editorial Board; Editor, third edition of this *Encyclopedia.* Chairman Greater New York BA Conduct and Ethics Committee since 1973. Listed in *Who's Who of American Women.* See BIBLIOGRAPHY, B, E.

KEENAN, Evva, of Chicago, Ill.; one of the leading bridge personalities of the Midwest; Secretary Chicago CBA 1947–63, Secretary Emeritus from 1963; ACBL Honorary Secretary 1950; member ACBL Goodwill and Membership Committee. Died 1970.

KEHELA, Sammy R., of Toronto, Ont., bridge teacher and writer, born 1934; one of the world's great players; represented Canada World Team Olympiad 1960, 1964, 1968, 1972, North America in World Championships 1966, 1967, 1974, coach North American team for World Championships 1962, 1963, 1965; won Team Trials 1966, 1973, third 1965; won Vanderbilt 1966, 1970, Spingold 1964, 1965, 1968, Blue Ribbon Pairs 1967, Fall Nat'l Life Masters Men's Pairs 1963, Open Pairs 1964, Spring Nat'l Men's Pairs 1963, Summer Nat'l Life Masters Pairs 1969; second Spingold 1963, Blue Ribbon Pairs 1969, Reisinger 1969, 1972, won Canadian Nat'l Open Teams 1959, 1961, 1965, 1967, Mixed Pairs 1959, 1962, Canadian-American Men's Pairs 1960, Canadian Prairie Masters Pairs 1967, Upper New York State Men's Pairs 1965, 1967, Open Pairs, 1963, Open Teams 1965. Former Editor Ontario *Kibitzer;* Contributing Editor *Bridge Encyclopedia.*

KEHOE, Robert A., of Natick, Mass., federal employee, born 1946; won Spring Nat'l secondary Swiss Teams 1974, several regional titles including Canadian-American Knockout Teams 1974.

KEIDAN, Bruce, of Philadelphia, Pa., bridge columnist; the first to notice unusual foot movements by one Italian pair during the 1975 Bermuda Bowl. See BERMUDA INCIDENT.

KEITH, Mrs. Seymour, of Coral Gables, Fla., born 1926; Southeastern Masters Pairs 1961, Women's Pairs 1960, 1963; second Summer Nat'l Women's Pairs 1961, Southeastern Women's Pairs 1961.

KELETI, Andor, of Budapest, hotel manager, born 1901; European Champion 1934, second 1935, 1936; Hungarian Champion 1933–35.

KELLEY, John J., of Germantown, Tenn., born Derby, Conn. Director of Administration of ACBL from 1968.

KELLY, Jack (1916–1970), of Sutton, Ireland, government accountant and bridge writer; represented Ireland World Team Olympiad 1960 and 1964, World Pair Olympiad 1962, European Championship 1954, 1959, 1965; national wins include every major event on the Irish calendar. Bridge editor of a newspaper, and contributor to *Bridge Magazine.* President IBPA 1964–70. Contributing Editor *Bridge Encyclopedia.*

KELLY, L. James, of Chicago, Ill., bridge teacher, born 1895; second Chicago 1929; won Mississippi Valley Open Teams 1949. Edited Chicago CBA *Kibitzer* 1950–56.

KELLY, Nathan (1876–1959), of Boston, Mass., lawyer and bridge teacher; a prominent player of whist, auction bridge, and contract bridge, and the inventor of KELLY SOLID SUIT SIGNALS; won many AWL national whist titles; regional successes at contract included New England Knockout Teams 1930, 1934, 1938, Men's Pairs 1944, Mixed Pairs 1943.

KELNER, Louis, of Forest Hills, N.Y., accountant, stockbroker, and ACBL Regional tournament director; won Spingold 1956, Summer Nat'l Golder Pairs 1952; second Life Master Pairs 1956; regional wins include Eastern States Individual 1952, Upper New York Men's Pairs 1957.

KELSEY, Hugh Walter, of Edinburgh, Scotland, novelist, bridge writer, and journalist, born 1926; represented Scotland in matches against Wales and Northern Ireland. National titles include Open Teams, Masters Pairs, and Masters Individual. Bridge columnist for P.A. Features Syndicate and *Edinburgh Evening News;* contributor to *Bridge Magazine* and other journals. Author of *Killing Defense at Bridge, Advanced Play at Bridge, Matchpoint Bridge,* and other books. See BIBLIOGRAPHY, D, E.

KEMP, Mrs. Edith (formerly Mrs. E. J. Seligman), of Miami Beach, Fla., bridge teacher; one of the great American women players of all time; won Vanderbilt and Spingold 1963, Chicago 1946, 1952, Spring Nat'l Women's Teams 1965, 1969, Fall Nat'l Women's Teams 1962, Mixed Teams 1942, Summer Nat'l Mixed Teams 1947, 1953, 1957, Open Pairs 1943, Women's Pairs 1941, 1942, 1943, 1946, Mixed Pairs 1968; second Spingold 1953, 1972, Fall Nat'l Open Teams 1964, von Zedtwitz 1962, Life Masters Women's Pairs 1973, 1974, Spring Nat'l Women's Teams 1971, Summer Nat'l Mixed Teams 1945, 1948, Women's Pairs 1957; won Eastern States Women's Pairs 1941, 1942, Mixed Pairs 1961, Southeastern Open Teams 1951, 1962, 1963, Women's Teams 1952, Open Pairs 1951, Women's Pairs 1955, 1958, 1960, Mixed Pairs 1951, 1957, Florida Life Master Pairs 1967, Open Pairs 1964. Sister of William SEAMON and Mrs. Anne BURNSTEIN.

KEMPNER, Alicia (Mrs. Ralph), of Los Angeles, Calif., bridge columnist; one of the leading women players on the West Coast; second Women's Team World Olympiad 1964; won Summer Nat'l Mixed Team 1946, 1960, Nat'l Mixed Team 1954, Fall Nat'l Women's Team 1962, Spring Nat'l Women's Teams 1969, secondary Swiss Teams 1970; second Fall Nat'l Mixed Pairs 1955, Spring Nat'l Women's Pairs 1965, Women's Teams 1969; regional successes include Bridge Week Masters Teams 1954, Open Pairs 1950, 1954, Mixed Pairs 1951, Women's Masters Pairs 1967, 1968, Southeastern Women's Teams 1965, Palm Springs Women's Pairs 1971.

KEMPNER, Ralph, of Los Angeles, Calif., stockbroker, formerly of Chicago; one of the leading players of the West Coast; won Fall Nat'l Open Pairs 1936, Spring Nat'l Mixed Pairs 1958; second Spingold 1948; regional successes include All-American Open Team 1939, Open Pairs 1939, All-Western Masters Team 1954, Men's Pairs 1952, Open Pairs 1950, Bridge Week Mixed Teams 1954, Masters Teams 1952, 1954, Men's Pairs 1965, Central States Open Teams 1938, Midwest Spring Men's Pairs 1954.

KEMPSON, Captain Ewart (1895–1966), of Gainford, England, army officer and bridge writer; one of the leading European bridge personalities; many tournament successes include English National Pair Championship; npc British Women's Team which won European title 1952 and toured the United States 1953; author of twenty-one books on bridge including *Kempson on Contract; How to Win at Contract Bridge; More Bridge Quizzes; First Book of Bridge Problems, Second Book of Bridge Problems* (with Paul Lukacs); *Tournament Bridge for Everyone;* co-author *Quintessence of CAB: The CAB System of Bridge; Bridge Quiz.* Editor and director of *Bridge Magazine* from 1949; in the thirties a leading protagonist of "British Bridge," or direct bidding without the use of forcing bids. Contributing editor *Bridge Encyclopedia.* See BIBLIOGRAPHY, C, E, F, G, H, J.

KENDRICK, Boots (Mrs. J. O.), of Anchorage, Alaska, born 1925; second Summer Nat'l Mixed Team 1961; regional wins include Mexican Nat'l Open Team 1960, Polar Mixed Pairs 1974.

KENEDI, Tibor, of São Paulo, Brazil, industrialist, born 1915; represented Brazil World Olympiad 1964, South American Championships four times; national successes include Open Team six times.

KENNEDY, Betty Ann (Mrs. J. E., formerly Mrs. J. F. Welch), of Shreveport, La., born 1931; one of the leading American women players; represented United States World Olympiad Women's Pairs 1974, won VENICE CUP 1974, Summer Nat'l Mixed Team 1960, second Fall Nat'l Life Masters Women's Pairs 1971; won Summer Nat'l secondary Women's Pairs 1972, 1973, many regional titles including Mid-South Knockout Teams 1972, Masters Pairs 1958, 1973, Open Pairs 1970, 1972.

KENNEDY, Charles T., of Cincinnati, Ohio, construction engineer; one of the leading Midwest tournament directors in the thirties, and co-inventor of the Ach-Kennedy schedules which provided the first HOWELL MOVEMENTS with perfectly balanced comparisons.

KENNEDY, George, of Kew Gardens, N.Y., bridge teacher and writer, born 1901; second Fall Nat'l Men's Pairs 1940; won Eastern States Mixed Team 1940. Originator of a bidding style which provides for control-showing bids in many situations. Author of *The Kennedy System of Bridge.* See BIBLIOGRAPHY, C.

KENNEDY, J. E., Jr., of Shreveport, La., industrialist, born 1920; won Spring Nat'l Men's Pairs 1973, several regional events including Mid-South Knockout Teams 1972, Masters Pairs 1971.

KEOHANE, Ethel (Mrs. William), of Wellesley Hills, Mass., secretary, born 1901; one of the most successful players in the New England area. Numerous regional successes include New England Mixed Pairs 1948, 1951, 1959, Open Teams 1951, 1967, 1968, 1974, Mixed Teams 1942, 1946, 1948, 1949, 1950, 1956, Knockout Teams 1949, Masters Teams 1949, Women's Pairs 1942, 1948, 1950, Open Pairs 1970, New England Fall–Swiss Teams 1974.

KEOHANE, William (1896–1972), of Wellesley Hills, Mass., consulting engineer, bridge teacher, and administrator; one of the leading New England bridge personalities; Chairman of the 1970 Summer Nationals in Boston and many times Chairman of the New England Individual Championship, the largest annual individual tournament in the world (in 1973, a record field of 768 players took part); also Chairman of many other New England Regional Championships. ACBL Board of Directors 1972.

KERR, Robert A., of Maywood, Calif., transportation analyst, born 1935; second Spring Nat'l Men's Pairs 1971, winner of several regional events including Bridge Week Open Pairs 1967.

KERR, Roy P., of Christchurch, New Zealand, professor of mathematics, born 1934; represented New Zealand World Championship 1974; national successes include Open Teams 1971, Open Pairs 1973.

KERWICK, Paul A., of Cranston, R.I., social administration adviser, born 1912; won New England Spring Open Pairs 1961. President of New England Bridge Conference 1961, Rhode Island Unit 1958.

KERWIN, Madeleine (1882–1965), of New York, N.Y., bridge writer and teacher. One of the pioneers of contract bridge, she introduced the game to a New York Club (the Cavendish) for the first time in 1926. She was also one of the originators of the FORCING TWO. Writings include the first book on the Sims System (*The One Over One for Everyone*, see BIBLIOGRAPHY, C), five other books, and many magazine contributions. Second President of ABL Associate Members 1931, and a member of the Advisory Council which codified the Official System in 1931. Honorary Member of the Cavendish Club, New York.

KEY, Mervin, of Houston, Tex., attorney, born 1929; one of the leading players of the Southwest; represented North America World Championships 1962, third International Team Trials 1961; won Fall Nat'l Open Teams 1964; second Chicago 1960, Fall Nat'l Men's Teams 1961, Life Masters Men's Pairs 1964; won North Texas Open Pairs 1959.

KHAUTIN, Richard L., of Woodside, N.Y., accountant, born 1940; won Fall Nat'l Blue Ribbon Pairs 1972; regional successes include Eastern States Men's Pairs 1972.

KIMURA, Seiji, of Tokyo, Japan, journalist and bridge writer; represented Japan Far East Championship 1961; won Open Teams, and many other national successes. Officer of Japan Contract BL; tournament chairman 1963. Author of bridge books in Japanese.

KINCAID, Arthur R., of Liberty, Mo., attorney, born 1911; second Spingold 1953; won Mississippi Valley Open Team 1952, Open Pairs 1951, Missouri Valley Open Team 1959, Open Pairs 1961, Men's Pairs 1961, 1965, District 15 Open Teams 1968, Open Pairs 1968. Former ACBL Director.

KING, Frank P., Jr., of Suitland, Md., Air Force sergeant, born 1933; winner of several regional events including Keystone Masters Pairs 1973, Open Pairs 1973, Mid-Atlantic Master Pairs 1974.

KING, J. David, of Miami Beach, Fla., bridge teacher, born 1923; winner of many regional events including Central States Life and Senior Masters Pairs 1960, Intermountain Open Teams 1970, Knockout Teams 1973.

KING, Jane (Mrs. Henry), of Springfield, Mo.; winner of several regional events including Land of Coronado Knockout Teams 1972, Open Teams 1972.

KING, Mary T. (Mrs. David), of Columbia, S.C., teacher, born 1943; winner of several regional events

including Mid-Atlantic Knockout Teams 1972, Women's Pairs 1973.

KINSELLA, Jocelyn (Mrs. A. E.), of Wellington, New Zealand, public relations consultant, born 1933; runner-up Far East Women's Teams 1971, represented New Zealand Far East Championships 1973; national successes include Pairs and Teams 1968, 1970.

KIRTLAND, Cmdr. S. W., of Miami, Fla., naval officer, born 1894; won Southeastern Open Team 1950, 1961, Open Pairs 1946, Men's Pairs 1971.

KIRTLAND, Mrs. S. W., of Miami, Fla., bridge teacher and club-owner, born 1905; won Southeastern Women's Team 1957, Open Team 1961, Florida Masters Pairs 1961. Manager Greater Miami CBL for several years.

KITZES, Dr. David, of Providence, R.I., cardiologist, born 1938; won New England Masters Teams 1962. Bridge theorist; helped formulate the principles of the American Design system, which was publicized in the *Bridge Journal*.

KIVEL, Joseph, of Bethesda, Md., science administrator, born 1934; winner of many regional events including Mid-Atlantic Open Teams 1970, 1973, Masters Pairs 1968, 1973.

KLAR, Carol (Mrs. Herman), of Houston, Tex., jewelry designer; won Spring Nat'l secondary Mixed Pairs 1967, Fall Nat'l secondary Women's Teams 1968, 1972; second Summer Nat'l Mixed Teams 1967, Fall Nat'l Mixed Pairs 1968. Regional successes include Texas Fall Mixed Pairs 1967, Mexican Nat'l Open Pairs 1968, Republic of Texas Open Pairs 1970.

KLAR, Robin. See GRANTHAM, ROBIN.

KLAS, Leo, of Prague, Czechoslovakia, technician, born 1921; represented Czechoslovakia European Championships 1966, 1967, against Poland 1961, 1962, and Hungary 1963; won Open Team events 1962, 1963, 1964.

KLAUSNER, Malvine (Mrs. Siegfried), of Beverly Hills, Calif., born 1902; one of the leading women players of the West Coast; represented US Women's Team World Olympiad 1960; won Summer Nat'l Mixed Teams 1953, second Fall Nat'l Mixed Pairs 1965; regional wins include Pacific Southwest Women's Pairs 1967, Bridge Week Masters Pairs 1951, 1959, Mixed Teams 1961, 1967, Open Team 1957, Women's Pairs 1956, Desert Empire Open Team 1957, 1958.

KLAUSNER, Siegfried (1898–1949), of Beverly Hills, Calif.; born in Vienna, and a leading Austrian player in the thirties; inventor of plastic cards (1932), those now manufactured in the United States under the name "Kem Cards."

KLEIN, Alejandro, of Buenos Aires, Argentina, plastics manufacturer, born 1913; won Argentine Open Teams 1959, 1962, Open Pairs 1954, 1971. Contributor to *Bridge Argentino.*

KLINGER, Ronald D., of Sydney, Australia, university lecturer, solicitor, bridge writer, born 1941; Far East Champion 1970; national successes include Interstate Teams 1968, 1969, Open Teams 1975. Editor *Australian Bridge;* founder Australian Bridge Institute.

KLÓR, Lásló (1905–1944), of Budapest, Hungary, bookkeeper; European Champion (representing Hungary) 1934, 1938, second 1935, 1936.

KLUEWER, Mrs. Ann, of Reseda, Calif., legal transcriber, born 1924; won Fall Nat'l secondary Open Pairs 1968, several regional events including Orange County Open Teams 1972.

KLUGMAN, Dr. David Julian, of Johannesburg, South Africa, physician, born 1938; represented South Africa World Team Olympiad 1964; won Southern Africa Open Teams 1965.

KLUKOWSKA, Mrs. Elzbieta (1936–1968), of Warsaw, Poland; represented Poland European Women's Championships 1965, 1966, 1967; won Hungarian Open Pairs 1963, Polish Mixed Teams 1965, 1966, Mixed Pairs 1966, Open Teams 1967; second Mixed Pairs 1965.

KLUKOWSKI, Julian, of Warsaw, Poland, mathematician, born 1939; represented Poland World Team Olympiad 1964, European Championships 1963, 1965, 1967; second World Par contest 1963; won Hungarian Balaton Bowl 1963, Baltic Bowl 1964. National successes include Open Teams 1962, 1963, 1964, 1966, 1967, Mixed Teams 1965, 1966, Mixed Pairs 1966; second Open Teams 1961, 1965, Mixed Pairs 1965.

KNIGHT, John W. J., of Aukland, New Zealand, company manager, born 1926; represented New Zealand World Team Olympiad 1972.

KOCK, Rudolf (Putte), of Stockholm, Sweden, radio and television executive, born 1901; represented Sweden World Championships 1950 and 1953; European Champion 1939, 1952, second 1948, 1949, 1950; national titles include Open Teams and Open Pairs many times. Writings include contributions to

Stockholmtidningen since 1938. Author of *Bridge i Toppklass.* Represented Sweden at football.

KOHLI, Jagdish, of Bombay, business executive, born 1920; represented India World Team Olympiad 1960; national successes include Open Teams 1960, 1961; second Master Pairs 1959.

KOHN, Walter Steiner, of Santiago, Chile, attorney and merchant, born 1908; represented Chile in South American Championships; won National Open Team, Individual 1958, 1961, National Mixed Pairs 1963, and many more successes. Many tournament wins in Czechoslovakian events prior to 1938, when he moved to Chile.

KOKISH, Eric O., of Montreal, Que., mining researcher, born 1947; represented Canada World Pair Olympiad 1974; won Vanderbilt 1974, second Spring Nat'l Men's Teams 1974; winner of numerous regional events including Canadian Nat'l Knockout Teams 1973, Open Teams 1970, New England Knockout Teams 1971, 1972.

KOKISH, Sharyn (formerly Linkovsky), of Montreal, Que., statistical clerk, born 1950; represented Canada World Women's Team Olympiad 1972; won Summer Nat'l secondary Golder Pairs 1971, several regional titles including Canadian Nat'l Knockout Teams 1973, Fleur-de-Lys Knockout Teams 1973.

KOKKES, Jacobus C. (Jaap), of Amsterdam, Holland, mathematics teacher, born 1923; second European Championships 1966; fourth World Team Olympiad 1968; represented Netherlands in World Pair Olympiad 1962, World Team Olympiad 1960, 1964, and European Championship 1957; national successes include Open Team 1962, Open Pairs 1963, 1964.

KOLKER, Larry, of Chesterfield, Mo., bridge club owner, born 1928; won Vanderbilt 1962, second Grand Nationals 1974; winner of several regional events including Mississippi Valley Open Teams 1962, Men's Pairs 1962, 1963, Missouri Valley Men's Pairs 1959.

KONSTAM, Kenneth W. (1906–1968), of London, England, journalist; long one of Europe's leading players; World Champion 1955, also represented Great Britain in World Championships 1950, 1962, 1965, Olympiad 1964, and in European Championships twelve times (a record), winning in 1948, 1949, 1950, 1954, 1961, 1963; won Gold Cup 1949, 1956, 1960, 1964, Master Pairs 1955 and other successes. Bridge editor of London *Sunday Times.* One of the leading exponents of the CAB system.

KOOPMAN, Richard C., of Dayton, Ohio, born 1942; winner of several regional events including All-

American Open Teams 1972 and Motor City Swiss Teams 1974.

KORNFELD, Warren, of New York, N.Y., data manager, born 1939; won Blue Ribbon Pairs 1972; several regional events including Eastern States Men's Pairs 1972.

KOSTAL, Irwin J. ("Irv"), of Sherman Oaks, Calif., computer programmer, born 1935; won Fall Nat'l secondary Open Pairs 1971; regional wins include Bridge Week Open Teams 1968.

KÓVACS, László, of Budapest, Hungary, technician, born 1910; won International Open Pair event, Budapest, 1937, Hungarian winner World Par Contest 1937; won Hungarian Open Team 1960, Open Pairs 1959, 1960; member winning Hungarian team against Poland 1963, Czechoslovakia 1963, Germany 1964, Brussels 1964, Austria 1965. Member World Bridge Federation Friendship Committee.

KÖVER, Helen (Mrs. Étienne), of Brussels, Belgium; third World Mixed Team event Cannes, 1962; represented Belgium in many European Women's Championships; finished second 1950, 1955, 1956, 1959; won Common Market Mixed Teams 1967, 1969, Women's Pairs 1969; national wins include Mixed Teams 1953, 1954, 1959, 1960, 1961, 1969, Mixed Pairs 1951, 1952, 1960, 1964, 1966, 1967.

KOYTCHOU, Boris, of New York, N.Y., bridge teacher and lecturer, born 1919, in France; one of the outstanding players in France, and later in US; represented France in European Championships 1948, 1949, 1950; represented North America World Championship 1957; won three French Nat'l Team Championships; won Spingold 1956, 1960, Chicago 1963; second Vanderbilt 1955, 1962, 1965; won Eastern States Knockout Teams 1954.

KOYTCHOU, Noreen (Mrs. Boris, formerly Mrs. Richard Walsh), of New York, N.Y.; won Bridge Week Open Teams 1963, Mixed Teams 1962, All-Western Masters Pairs 1963, Pacific Southwest Open Teams 1964.

KOZLOVE, Lawrence M., of Louisville, Ky., banker, born 1945; winner of many regional championships including All-American Open Pairs 1972, 1973, Men's Pairs 1974.

KRAMER, Albert, Jr. (1905–1968), of Sarasota, Fla.; won Bridge Week Open Team 1954, Mexican Nat'l Open Team 1953, Mixed Pairs 1953, Bridge Week Men's Pairs 1952.

KRANSBERG, Gladys (Mrs. Samuel), of North Miami Beach, Fla., born 1910; second Fall Nat'l

Mixed Pairs 1960; won New England Mixed Teams 1966, Women's Pairs 1968.

KRAUSS, Donald P., of Los Angeles, Calif., stockbroker, born 1937; one of the leading American players; second World Team Olympiad 1964; represented North America World Championships 1971; won International Team Trials 1963, International Play-off matches 1970, Vanderbilt 1964, Chicago 1962, Reisinger 1971, Spring Nat'l Men's Teams 1970; second Spingold 1971, Spring Nat'l Men's Teams 1972. Regional successes include Oregon Trail Open Teams 1961, Northern Rocky Mountain Masters Pairs 1961, All-Western Masters Pairs 1962, Pacific Southwest Mixed Pairs 1966, Bridge Week Knockout Teams 1966.

KREYNS, J. T. M. ("Hans"), of Rotterdam, Netherlands, painting contractor, born 1925; one of the world's great players; won World Olympiad Pairs 1966, second European Championships 1965, 1966, fourth 1968 World Team Olympiad; represented Holland World Championships 1966, World Pair Olympiad 1970, European Championships 1967; numerous national successes.

KROESEN, Willem Egbert (1872–1946), of The Hague, Holland, an official of the Dutch East Indies government, born in Batavia. Co-founder of the International Bridge League and its Honorary Secretary from 1936 until the IBL was ended by World War II. Secretary of the Dutch Bridge League.

KROGULSKA, Mrs. Jolanta, of Warsaw, Poland, mathematician, born 1940; represented Poland European Women's Championships 1965, 1966, 1967. National titles include Mixed Teams 1965, Open Teams 1967, 1968; second Mixed Pairs 1965.

KROGULSKI, Zbigniew, of Warsaw, Poland, building engineer, born 1935; won Baltic Bowl 1964, Polish Open Teams 1962, 1963, 1964, 1966, 1968, Mixed Teams 1965; second Open Teams 1961, 1965.

KRUSE, Ronald J., of San Pablo, Calif.; regional wins include Cambrian Shield Masters Pairs 1972.

KUAI, Henry, of Hong Kong, engineer; represented Hong Kong Far East Championships five times; national successes include Open Teams, Masters Teams, Open Pairs.

KUAI, S. Y., of Hong Kong, engineer, born 1912; Far East Champion 1959, 1960, second 1963, also represented Hong Kong Far East Championships 1962, with national successes in teams and pairs.

KUBISTA, Dr. Josef, of Prague, Czechoslovakia, pediatrician, born 1931; represented Czechoslovakia on many occasions, and won Baltic Cup international pair tournament 1963; national wins inlcude Open Teams 1961–62–63 and Open Pairs 1963.

KUKLEWICZ, Czeslaw, of Cracow, Poland, accountant, born 1926; represented Poland World Team Olympiad 1964, World Pairs Olympiad 1962, European Championships 1963, 1965; won Belgian Open Teams 1964; second Polish Open Teams 1967.

KUNKEL, John C., of Miami Beach, Fla., formerly of Pa., congressman; second Nat'l Mixed Teams 1938; won Southeastern Open Teams 1953, Men's Teams 1955, Men's Pairs 1954, Mixed Pairs 1959; Florida Men's Teams 1960, Master Pairs 1959, Men's Pairs 1959; Hawaiian Master Pairs 1963, Men's Pairs 1953.

KUNKEL, Mrs. John C., of Harrisburg, Pa.; won Southeastern Women's Pairs 1958, Women's Team 1954, second Open Team 1956; won New England Mixed Team 1952, Mid-Atlantic Fall Mixed Pairs 1955.

KUROKAWA, Akio, of Tokyo, Japan, bridge teacher and club operator, born 1937; represented Japan Far East Championships 1966, 1967; national titles include Knockout Teams three times, and Teams-of-Four, twice.

KUSHNER, Jack B. (1903–63), of Longmeadow, Mass., bridge teacher and writer; won Fall Nat'l Open Pairs 1950; won All-American Men's Pairs 1950; President New England Bridge Conference 1962. Co-inventor TNT system; author of *The Kushner System* and many booklets. See BIBLIOGRAPHY, C.

KYRIAKOS, Costas G., of Greece, bridge writer and automobile club director, born 1928; bridge columnist of Greek daily, *Apogevmatini,* and weekly *Epikaira.*

KYRIAKAIDES, Sosso (Mrs. John), of Greece, born 1915; outstanding woman player and official, represented Egypt World Women's Teams Championships 1937, placing third, many successes in Egypt 1936–61; national successes in Greece include Open Teams 1966, Mixed Pairs 1968, 1969. Co-founder of Hellenic BF, vice-president 1965–73.

KYRIAZIS, Agamemnon G., of Greece, tourist agent, born 1917; represented Greece European Championship 1970; national successes include Open Teams 1966, 1968, 1970, 1971, 1972, 1973, 1974, Open Pairs 1967, 1969, 1971, 1974, Mixed Pairs 1971.

L

LAAKSO, Bjarne, of Helsinki, Finland, salesman, born 1923; represented Finland in many European and Scandinavian Championships; national wins include Open Teams (eight times), and Open Pairs (twice). Director of Finnish Bridge League.

LABINS, Stephen H., of Hartford, Conn., manufacturer's representative, born 1933; many regional wins including New England Masters Teams 1966, Knockout Teams 1967, 1970, 1975, Men's Pairs 1967, 1971.

LACKMAN, HELEN (Mrs. Herman), of Cincinnati, Ohio, bridge teacher, born 1910; won Summer Nat'l Open Teams 1950; Midwest Spring Women's Pairs 1951.

LACOUR, Patricia, of Baton Rouge, La., won Summer Nat'l secondary Mixed Pairs 1973; Mid-South Women's Pairs 1973.

LACOUR, Ronald T., of Alexandria, La., bridge professional; winner of numerous regional championships including Intermountain Knockout Teams 1973, Open Pairs 1973, Klondike Knockout Teams 1974, Men's Pairs 1974.

LAFLEUR, Diane (formerly Mraz, née Wasserman), of La Jolla, Calif., born 1927; won Summer Nat'l secondary Swiss Teams 1972, several regional titles including Golden State Open Teams 1973, Inland Empire Knockout Teams 1973.

LAGRON, E. M., Chicago bridge teacher and lecturer, president, Western Bridge Assoc., 1933–34, and editor in chief of its *Contract Bridge Magazine;* author of *Defensive Bridge;* emceed the "Bridge Club of the Air," a twice-weekly Chicago radio show of the early thirties.

LAIR, Mark, of St. Louis, Mo., bridge professional, born 1947; second Blue Ribbon Pairs 1972, won Spring Nat'l secondary Masters Pairs 1971, Fall Nat'l secondary Swiss Teams 1974; winner of numerous regional titles including Missouri Valley Knockout Teams 1973, Gem State Knockout Teams 1974.

LAMB, Thomas, of Edinburgh, Scotland, civil servant, born 1922; represented Scotland Camrose Trophy matches five times; member of the victorious Scottish teams of 1964, 1965; other wins include Scottish Cup and 1959 Deauville Team-of-Four Championship.

LAMPREY, Charles V., of White Plains, N.Y., systems analyst, born 1938; one of the leading players of the East Coast; won Summer Nat'l secondary Golder Pairs 1971, secondary Men's Pairs 1971; winner of many regional titles including New England Master Teams 1966, 1970, 1973, Knockout Teams 1970, 1975.

LANDAU, Charles S., of Mt. Lebanon, Pa., purchasing and sales manager of electric supplies, born 1898; one of the most active bridge administrators in the Pittsburgh area. Chairman 1957 Summer National, 1966 Fall National; ACBL Director; former Treasurer, Vice-President, and President of the Pittsburgh Bridge Association.

LANDEN, Stephen, of Oak Park, Mich.; won Spring Nat'l secondary Non-mixed Pairs 1972, Summer Nat'l secondary Swiss Teams 1974, several regional titles including Canadian Nat'l Knockout Teams 1974.

LANDLEY, Wilson W., of Orlando, Fla., US Civil Service, born 1917; won Life Masters Pairs 1958, Fall Nat'l Men's Teams 1946.

LANDO, Albert M., of Toronto, Ont., accountant, born 1931; npc Canadian Team World Olympiad 1964, 1968; won Canadian-American Open Teams, Open Pairs 1962, Upper New York State Masters Pairs 1967.

LANDON, John T., Jr., of Rochester, N.Y., engineer, born 1944; won Nat'l Senior & Advanced Senior Masters Pairs 1968, Spring Nat'l secondary Men's Pairs 1969, Upper New York State Open Teams 1969, Mid-Atlantic Summer Open Pairs 1968.

LANDOW, William (Billy), of Cherry Hill, N.J., hospital supplies executive, born 1930; won District 4 Open Pairs 1963, Open Teams 1969, New York–New Jersey Open Pairs 1966, Open Teams 1967, Keystone Open Teams 1968, 1973.

LANDY, Alvin (1905–67), of Greenwich, Conn.; one of the outstanding bridge personalities of the world; Life Master #24; his record of four wins in the Fall Nat'l Men's Team (1947, 1948, 1954, 1958) has never been surpassed; won American BL Challenge Knockout Team 1936, second American Whist League Open Team 1934; won Spingold 1949, Marcus 1951, Chicago 1949, Nat'l Mixed Team 1939; second Spingold 1946, 1952, Marcus 1963, Life Masters Individual 1939; regional successes include Canadian Nat'l Men's Pairs 1963, District 5 Men's Pairs 1962, Western States Open Team 1936, Open Pairs 1938, All-American Open Pairs 1964. Secretary-Treasurer World Bridge Federation 1958–67; Executive Secretary ACBL 1951–67; Secretary National Laws Commission 1956–67; Honorary Member ACBL 1957. Inventor of the LANDY defense to no trump opening.

LANDY, Fay D. (Mrs. Thomas M.), of Brisbane, Australia, born 1925; represented Australia World Women's Team Olympiad 1972, Far East Women's Teams 1971.

LANGER, Edward, of Minneapolis, Minn., pharmacist, born 1907; won Mid-American–Canadian Open Teams 1955, 1957, 1961, and 1962, Gopher Masters Pairs 1959, 1966, Open Teams 1963, 1966, 1969, 1970, Open Pairs 1966.

LA NOUE, Jack, of New Orleans, La.; won Spring Nat'l secondary Open Teams 1972, Fall Nat'l secondary Open Pairs 1971, several regional titles including Mid-South Knockout Teams 1970, Masters Pairs 1969.

LAPIDES, Steven R., of Baltimore, Md., data processing engineer, born 1943; won Fall Nat'l Life Master Men's Pairs 1975; winner of several regional events including Mid-Atlantic Open Teams 1969, 1972.

LARSEN, Bjorn, of Bryn, Norway, inspector and bridge columnist, born 1921; third European Championship 1948; represented Norway British Bridge World Championship 1958, European Championships 1965, npc 1966; Scandinavian Champion three times; Norwegian Champion five times. Secretary Norwegian Bridge Federation 1954–62.

LARSEN, Kyle, of San Francisco, Calif., student, born 1950; won Spring Nat'l Men's Pairs 1968, Reisinger 1968, Nat'l Flight B Men's Pairs 1965, Teenyear Pairs 1965, second Vanderbilt 1971, Spring Nat'l Men's Teams 1970; many regional wins including All-Western Knockout Teams 1969, Bridge Week Knockout Teams 1971, Eastern States Knockout Teams 1973, 1974. The youngest player ever to win major National Pair and Team titles, both at age eighteen. Became a Life Master at age fifteen, the youngest player to do so at the time.

LARSON, Bernice E., of Greenfield, Wis.; nursing administrator, born 1911; won Fall Nat'l Life Masters Women's Pairs 1974, several regional events including Mississippi Valley Masters Pairs 1974.

LARSSON, Odd, of Oslo, Norway, born 1924; represented Norway European Bridge Championship several times; Norwegian Champion Open Team 1950, 1953, 1954, 1957, 1958, 1960, 1963, Open Pairs 1957, 1961.

LATTÈS, Robert, of Paris, mathematician; World Champion 1956; European Champion 1955; winner of many French national titles; contributor to *Bridge Magazine* and other periodicals.

LAVERY, Vivian. See WHALEN, VIVIAN.

LAVINGS, Paul W., of Sydney, Australia, bridge club owner, born 1946; WBF Zone 7 Champion 1974; won National Trials 1973, 1974, Open Teams 1975.

LAVINTHAL, Hy, of Trenton, N.J., retail store manager and bridge writer, born 1894; originated the SUIT PREFERENCE SIGNAL in 1933, and has been responsible for many innovations in bridge teaching. Former Associate Editor of *The Bridge World*. Writings include *Defense Tricks* and many contributions to periodicals. See BIBLIOGRAPHY, D.

LAWRENCE, Michael S., of Kelseyville, Calif., born 1940; one of the world's leading players; World Champion 1970, 1971, runner-up 1973, runner-up World Team Olympiad 1972; won Vanderbilt 1967, 1971, 1973, Spingold 1969, Reisinger 1965, 1970, International Play-off Match 1969, Spring Nat'l Men's Teams 1964, 1968, HERMAN TROPHY 1965; second Vanderbilt 1970, Spingold 1970, Fall Nat'l Blue Ribbon Pairs 1965, 1968, 1971, Spring Nat'l Men's Teams 1969; won Fall Nat'l secondary Men's Teams 1969, Summer Nat'l secondary Mixed Teams 1970, secondary Marcus Teams 1972, secondary Mixed Pairs 1972; numerous regional titles including more than a score of Knockout and Open Team events. Author of *How To Read Your Opponent's Cards.* (See ACES TEAM.)

LAY, James E., Jr., of Knoxville, Tenn., regional wins include District 11 Open Teams 1971.

LAZARD, Sidney H., of New Orleans, La., oil executive, born 1930; one of the most successful American players; represented North America in World Championships 1959, 1969, US in World Team Olympiad 1960; won International Team Trials 1968, Vanderbilt 1970, Spingold 1968, 1968, Chicago 1960, Summer Nat'l Mixed Teams 1963; second Spingold 1954, 1966, 1973, Spring Nat'l Men's Teams 1965, Men's Pairs 1967, Vanderbilt 1967, Reisinger 1968, 1969, Summer Nat'l Mixed Teams 1961, Fall Nat'l Mixed Pairs 1959, Men's Teams 1954, 1956, 1961; regional successes include All-American Men's Pairs, Bridge Week Open Pairs, Men's Pairs, Texas Summer Knockout Teams, Men's Pairs.

LAZARUS, Edmond P., of Baltimore, Md., army engineer project manager, born 1937; won Summer Nat'l Men's Pairs 1963, Spring Nat'l Men's Pairs 1968; regional successes include Upper New York State Masters Pairs 1964, Mid-Atlantic Summer Open Teams 1965, Spring Men's Pairs 1967, Independence Day Open Teams 1968, Eastern States Mixed Teams 1966, District 4 Open Teams 1968.

LAZARUS, Joseph, of Salford, Lancaster, England, company director, born 1909; represented Great Britain European Championship 1959, England

Camrose Trophy matches 1953, 1958, 1960; won Gold Cup 1959, National Pairs 1958, EBU Mixed Teams 1938, Crockford's Cup 1959; established a record with three consecutive wins in Northern Pairs 1956–58.

LAZARUS, Shirlee (Mrs. Julian), of Kenner, La., born 1932; winner of many regional championships including Mid-South Open Teams 1964, 1965, 1968, 1971, 1973.

LEARY, Pat, of Livermore, Calif.; won Spring Nat'l Women's Pairs 1974, Orange County Women's Pairs 1972.

LEAVITT, Arnold, of Lincolnwood, Ill., sales manager; second Fall Nat'l Open Pairs 1964; many regional successes include Midwest Open Teams 1961 and 1962, Central States Winter Knockout Teams 1962, Masters Pairs 1969, 1972, Tri-Unit Swiss Teams 1974.

LEAVITT, Carol ("Toddy," formerly Mrs. J. J. Ruther), of Chicago, Ill., bridge teacher, born 1936; second Spring Nat'l Women's Teams 1965; won Central States Life and Senior Masters Pairs 1960, All-American Women's Pairs 1961, Midwest Open Pairs 1963.

LEAVITT, Sandi (Mrs. Arnold), of Lincolnwood, Ill., born 1933; winner of many regional events including Central States Knockout Teams 1964, Open Teams 1971, Life and Senior Masters Pairs 1963, 1964, Tri-Unit Open Teams 1974.

LEBENSOLD, Kenneth W., of New York, N.Y., mathematics professor, born 1947; won Summer Nat'l Spingold Consolation 1972, tied Fall Nat'l secondary Men's Teams 1969, several regional titles including Fun City Knockout Teams 1972.

LEBHAR, Bertram, Jr. (1907–1972), of Atlantic, Fla., radio and television station owner. A noted sportscaster under the name "Bert Lee," and one of the leading American bridge personalities. Won Spingold 1940, Summer Nat'l Mixed Teams 1946; second Spingold, 1953, Life Masters Pairs 1945, Vanderbilt 1946, 1947, Chicago 1943, Nat'l Men's Pairs 1936. Many regional successes include Reisinger win 1951, second 1941, 1944. As Treasurer 1945–47 and a member of the Steering Committee, he made a major contribution to the modernization of the ACBL in the late forties, introducing the important principle of charging clubs for the issue of master points. Until that time players had paid a fee to register their points, at the rate of 50 cents per 100 fractional points. He was perhaps the first man to visualize the ACBL's vast potentiality for expansion, and his farsighted efforts were recognized when he was made ACBL Honorary Member in 1963. He was also one of the founders of the Greater New York BA, and its first President 1948.

LEBIODA, Lukasz, of Cracow, Poland, university chemist, born 1943; represented Poland World Pairs Olympiad 1966; won Juan-les-Pins Festival Individual 1965, second Open Teams 1966. Won Baltic Bowl 1965; second Polish Open Teams 1967, 1968.

LEBOVIC, Wolf, of Toronto, Ont., formerly of Budapest, builder; npc Canada Women's Team World Team Olympiad 1964; won Spring Nat'l Men's Pairs 1963, Individual 1965, Blue Ribbon 1967, Upper New York State Men's Pairs 1965.

LECKIE, Simon, of Glasgow, Scotland, accountant, born 1930; represented Great Britain World Pair Championship 1962; member of victorious Scottish Camrose Trophy Teams 1964, 1965. National titles include Open Teams twice. One of four Scottish players to compete in the *Sunday Times* International Pairs Championships and British Trials.

LEDERER, Richard, of London, England, bridge club owner and writer, born in Hungary 1895, died 1941; the first great figure in British bridge. Won Gold Cup 1933, 1934, and 1939; represented Britain in 1934 Schwab Cup match. With his great skill, charm, personality, and physical size, Lederer shared the spotlight with Ely Culbertson, then at the height of his fame. At the end of the thirties, Lederer's Club was the training ground for a group of players including Harrison-Gray, Konstam, Meredith, and Reese, subsequently dominant in the British tournament game. Lederer's writings included *Lederer Bids Two Clubs,* an exposition of his natural, aggressive two-club system. See BIBLIOGRAPHY, C.

LE DENTU, José, of Paris, lawyer, bridge journalist, and TV commentator, born 1917, in Madagascar; winner of five French team championship titles, retired from tournament play in 1957; played with Trézel in 1961 World Championship at Buenos Aires, and played virtually every board, probably a Bermuda Bowl record in this respect. Npc French Women's Team World Olympiad 1964. Author of *Bridge à la Une, 120 Donnes et Problèmes du Bridge;* co-author *Bridge pour tous, Memento du bridge, Le Championnat du monde, Cent donnes extraordinaires, Souvenirs et secrets, L'Aristocratie du Bridge,* and author of many newspaper columns and magazine articles. Competition editor of *Revue Française de Bridge.* Contributing editor *Bridge Encyclopedia.*

LEDERER, Rhoda (formerly Barrow), of England, bridge writer, columnist and teacher. Co-editor of *The Bridge Players' Encyclopedia* (British edition of the *Official Encyclopedia of Bridge*), and co-author of several bridge books. Editor IBPA *Bulletin* 1967–71. See BIBLIOGRAPHY, C, D, E.

LEE, Jerome, of Minneapolis, Minn., regional successes include Gopher Open Teams 1969, 1970.

LEE, Dr. Sidney, of London, England, physician, born 1912; npc winning British Women's Team European Championship 1951, and of Great Britain World Team Olympiad 1964; represented Great Britain European Championships 1965; won Gold Cup 1948, 1950, 1952, 1957; won English Open Teams three times.

LEE, Mrs. Sidney, of Dallas, Tex.; won Fall Nat'l Women's Pairs 1952, won Mexican Nat'l Open Teams, Mixed Pairs 1965.

LEESMENT, Otto, of Victoria, B.C., general contractor, born 1908 in Estonia; won Estonian Individual 1938, Spring Nat'l Mixed Pairs 1962, 1964, Polar Men's Pairs and Open Pairs 1963, Northwest Men's Pairs 1955, Canadian Prairie Open Teams 1965, Northern Rocky Mountain Men's Pairs 1967; second Northwest Open Team 1958, Mixed Pairs 1963, Intermountain Men's pairs 1970.

LEFEBVRE, Daniel H., of Los Angeles, Calif., purchasing agent, born 1920; won Northwest Open Teams, Open Pairs, and Men's Pairs 1963, Mixed Pairs 1960.

LE GROS, Travers J., of New York, N.Y., commercial executive, born 1901; second Nat'l Mixed Team 1937; won Eastern States Knockout Teams 1938.

LEIBENDERFER, Ralph J., of New York, N.Y., attorney, born 1882; one of the great players of auction bridge. Won Eastern Auction Open Teams 1927, 1928, and was a regular member of the famous Knickerbocker Whist Club team which included S. LENZ, W. LIGGETT, G. REITH, and P. H. SIMS. Associated with E. and J. CULBERTSON in the foundation of *The Bridge World* magazine, and acted as its counsel. Official referee for Culbertson in CULBERTSON-LENZ MATCH. Treasurer USBA 1935. Writings included articles for *The Bridge World* and *Vanity Fair,* and introductions to many books.

LEIBOWITZ, Seymour H., of Lebanon, Pa., clothing manufacturer, born 1918; won Summer Nat'l secondary Marcus Cup 1968, many regional titles including Keystone Open Teams 1971, 1973, 1974, Masters Pairs 1969, 1974.

LEITE-RIBEIRO, Dr. Samuel, of São Paulo, Brazil, physician, born 1902; South American Champion 1949, second 1950; won Brazilian Open Team 1950, 1962.

LEITNER, Francis von (1898–1958), of Budapest, Hungary, bookkeeper; European Champion representing Hungary 1934, second 1935, 1936.

LEMAITRE, A. Littman. See LITTMAN-LEMAITRE, A.

LEMON, James H., of Washington, D.C., stockbroker; won Eastern States Mixed Team 1939, other successes in ABL events. ACBL President 1939, and for many years a member of ABL and ACBL executive committees. Director Washington BL.

LENGYEL, George, of London, England, economist and importer, born in Hungary, 1911; represented Holland European Championship 1959; Dutch wins include Open Teams 1957, 1959. Contributor to *Bridge Magazine* and other periodicals.

LENNON, Aidan, of Belfast, Ireland, executive officer, born 1926; represented Ireland European Championships 1961; national successes include Northern Ireland Open Teams. Member Northern Ireland executive and selection committees.

LENZ, Sidney S(imon) (1873–1960), author and champion player at whist and all forms of bridge, expert in many games and sports. He was born near Chicago, July 12, 1873. Before he was twenty-seven a series of coups in the lumber business had made him prosperous, and when he was thirty he was rich. He promptly retired, and the rest of his life was devoted to competition, travel, reading, and writing. First he took up bowling, and one of his records, an average of 240 over twenty consecutive games (1909), stood up for nearly twenty years. In 1909 he became engrossed in whist, and in 1910 he won the AMERICAN WHIST LEAGUE's principal national team championship (Minneapolis Trophy). Altogether he won more than 600 whist and bridge competitions, ranging from club duplicate games to his 14 national championships. His Knickerbocker Whist Club auction bridge team (Lenz, W. Liggett, P. H. Sims, G. Reith and R. Leibenderfer) was considered the strongest in the country. He won the last tournament he played in, the Goldman Cup pairs at the Eastern Championships of 1932, then ranked as a national event.

Lenz had remarkable versatility in intellectual, coordinative, and athletic competitions. He played chess against José Capablanca and tennis against "Little Bill" Johnston with small odds. He was scratch at golf and "shot his age" at sixty-nine. At table tennis he was of championship caliber. Professional magicians considered him the best amateur magician in the US, and he was the first amateur ever elected honorary member of the American Society of Magicians. His special skill at dealing seconds impelled him to refuse to play card games for stakes. However, whist and bridge were his greatest loves, and he thought of himself primarily as a bridge player.

Lenz wrote several books on auction and contract bridge; and the first of them, *Lenz on Bridge* (1926), is ranked as a classic, partly in describing conditions of play as they actually exist in expert games, partly by using the vernacular and informal tone of experts in bridge-club conversations. Lenz also was able to write fiction that mass magazines would buy at top prices, and he wrote many short stories with bridge settings. As a part owner and associate editor of the former humorous magazine *Judge,* Lenz conducted double-dummy problem contests that served greatly to publicize bridge. He contributed articles on bridge to many other magazines including the bridge magazines, and occasionally wrote bridge columns for newspapers, including *The New York Times.* However, though at times it yielded substantial income, Lenz's writing was to him more a competitive than a professional matter.

In 1931 Lenz joined the advisory council of BRIDGE HEADQUARTERS, and contributed to the OFFICIAL SYSTEM. He represented this group in the CULBERTSON-LENZ MATCH, from which he acquired lasting fame despite his loss. In his later years Lenz appeared frequently at major tournaments as an honorary referee. He was unquestionably the most revered member of the bridge community.

At whist he won the American Whist League Open Pairs Championship 1910, 1918, 1919, 1920, representing the Knickerbocker Whist Club, and the Men's Pairs 1914, 1916, 1930, 1933, Open Teams 1929 and combination Open Teams and Pairs 1931; in auction in the American Whist League Championships he won Open Teams 1924, Open Pairs 1927, 1928, representing the Knickerbocker Whist Club; in contract he won the Eastern States Open Pairs 1932.

The technical contributions of Sidney Lenz to contract bridge are hard to define. His effort to introduce a new call, the "challenge," to replace the take-out double, was unsuccessful. His bidding system at contract bridge, the one-two-three, gave way to the artificial two-club bid with intermediate (strong) two-bids in other suits. The Lenz echo, a distribution-showing high-low from a four-card holding, remains standard among experts, but Lenz disclaimed credit for it, saying that it was standard among whist experts, and he merely taught auction players to use it. Nevertheless, by example in his masterful technique in both whist and bridge, Lenz may have contributed as much to the advancement of bridge science as any other person of this century. In 1965 he was elected to the Hall of Fame. See VANIVA PROBLEM and BIBLIOGRAPHY, A, E.

LEON, Philip H., of Grosse Pointe Farms, Mich., investments, born 1927; won Summer Nat'l secondary Marcus Teams 1970, secondary Swiss Teams 1974; many regional successes include Cambrian Shield Knockout Teams 1972, 1974, Indy 500 Knockout Teams 1973.

LEON, Rudolph de, of Kingston, Jamaica, owner and manager of bridge club, born 1915; represented Jamaica World Team Olympiad 1964.

LEONARD, Mrs. Verna (1906–66), of Sacramento, Calif., bookkeeper; won All-Western Mixed Pairs 1956, 1957, Women's Pairs 1937, Bridge Week Mixed Pairs 1956, Women's Pairs 1937, 1947. Former ACBL Director, former President Sacramento Unit.

LERENA, Raúl, of Buenos Aires, Argentina, bank official, born 1916; won Argentine Open Teams 1950, 1957; tournament director 1961, 1965 World Championships. Bridge writer and columnist; editor of *Bridge Argentino* since 1966.

LERNER, Dr. Marcelo Hector, of Buenos Aires, Argentina, physician and surgeon, born 1923; represented Argentina World Championship 1958, 1965, World Team Olympiad 1964, 1972; South American Champion 1957; won Argentine Open Teams 1955, 1963, 1965, 1967, 1969, Open Pairs 1964, 1965, 1969.

LESSER, Richard, of Glenmont, N.Y., educator, born 1924; won New England Knockout Team 1952, Masters Team 1958, Masters Pairs 1959, Upper New York State Open Team 1956; Intercollegiate Championship 1950.

LESSER, Thomas M., of North Hollywood, Calif., attorney, born 1943; tied Fall Nat'l secondary Men's Swiss Teams; regional wins include Bridge Week Swiss Teams 1970, Orange County Knockout Teams 1974.

LEVAN, Betty (Mrs. B. M.), of Los Angeles, Calif., born 1918; winner of several regional championships including Golden State Mixed Pairs 1963, 1964, 1965, Hawaii Open Pairs 1974, Mixed Pairs 1974.

LEVENTRITT, Peter A., of New York, N.Y., one of the outstanding American players, teachers and lecturers, born 1916; represented North America World Championships 1955 (npc), 1957, 1961, 1963, 1965; Coach South African Women's Team World Olympiad 1968; won Spingold 1956, 1960, Chicago 1941, 1949, Vanderbilt 1953, 1964, Life Masters Pairs 1944, 1951, Summer Nat'l Men's Teams 1949, 1950, 1959, Fall Nat'l Mixed Pairs 1950, Men's Teams 1966; second Chicago 1943, 1953, Vanderbilt 1947, 1948, 1955, 1959, 1962, 1967, Fall Nat'l Men's Teams 1955, Open Pairs 1948, 1951, Mixed Pairs 1944, 1949, Summer Nat'l Mixed Team 1947, Masters Individual 1952. Regional successes include events in Eastern States, Mid-South, New York–New Jersey, and others. President ACBL 1954, Assistant Treasurer 1945–46. Former President Greater New York BA. Co-founder and former president New York Card School. Pioneered the use of the SCHENKEN SYSTEM in partnership with its inventor.

LEVEY, Sydney, Jr., of Clovis, Calif., CPA, born 1927; regional wins include Bridge Week Open Teams 1960, 1961, Golden State Knockout Teams 1968. Member, Board of Governors; ACBL Board of Directors 1976.

LEVIN, Irving, of Minneapolis, Minn., salesman, born 1925; won Gopher Men's Pairs 1958, Open Teams 1959, 1961, Mid-American–Canadian Open

Pairs 1962; many other regional successes. Inter-City Champion 1962.

LEVIN, Maurice (1896–1963), of Short Hills, N.J., builder and philanthropist; won Nat'l Men's Teams 1949; Chairman ACBL Finance Committee 1949–50.

LEVIN, Muriel, of Chicago, Ill., born 1922; won Summer Nat'l Senior & Advanced Senior Masters Pairs 1965.

LEVIN, Paula (Mrs. Maurice, formerly Mrs. P. Bacher) of New York, N.Y., born 1908; one of the leading women players of the East Coast; won Chicago 1947, Spring Nat'l Women's Team 1951, Fall Nat'l Mixed Pairs 1946; second Spring Nat'l Women's Team 1946, Fall Nat'l Open Pairs 1952, Summer Nat'l Women's Pairs 1944, Fall Nat'l Mixed Pairs 1949. Many regional successes include Eastern States Mixed Teams 1943, 1947, Women's Pairs 1947, Southeastern Women's Pairs 1953, 1954, 1966, Mixed Pairs 1952, Women's Teams 1965, Knockout Teams 1968.

LEVIN, Robert, of North Miami, Fla., born 1957; achieved Life Master status in 1973 at the age of 15 years, four months, the youngest to do so at that time.

LEVIN, William K., of Brookline, Mass., attorney, bridge club director, born 1925; won New England Spring Open Team 1957, 1959, 1960, 1961, New England Fall Knockout Team 1961, Open Pairs 1960, with other regional successes.

LEVINSON, Delle (Mrs. Sidney A.), of Skokie, Ill., born 1920; won Nat'l Senior & Advanced Senior Masters Pairs 1965, Fall Nat'l Life Master Women's Pairs 1971.

LEVITT, Carolyn (Mrs. Jerry) (1922–1965), of Clayton, Mo., bridge teacher and club owner; won Vanderbilt 1962, Mississippi Valley Open Pairs 1957, Mixed Pairs 1956, Open Teams 1959.

LEVITT, Evelyn (Mrs. Harold), of Wilmington, Del., bridge teacher and director, born 1919; won Fall Nat'l Women's Teams 1968, second Mixed Pairs 1969; winner of several regional titles including Eastern States Mixed Pairs 1959, 1960, District 4 Grand Nat'l Championship 1973.

LEVITT, Jerry, of St. Louis, Mo., bridge teacher and club owner; won Vanderbilt 1962, second Grand Nat'l 1973; won Mississippi Valley Open Pairs 1953, 1961, Men's Pairs 1962, Mixed Pairs 1974, Missouri Valley Mixed Pairs 1968.

LEVITT, Paul, of Fort Worth, Tex., data processing consultant, born 1939; one of the leading players of the Southwest; won Fall Nat'l Mixed Pairs 1962, second Spingold, 1966, Vanderbilt 1967; winner of numerous regional titles including Mid-American–Canadian Masters Pairs 1959, 1960, Mid-South Spring Open Pairs 1963, Open Teams 1965, 1968, Summer Open Teams 1966, Open Pairs 1965, 1966, Texas Spring Knockout Teams 1968, Summer Knockout Teams 1967, Republic of Texas Open Teams 1973.

LEVY, Louis, of Fort Lee, N.J.; retired owner car-washing business, born 1921; second Life Masters Pairs 1958; won New York–New Jersey Men's Pairs 1968.

LEWIS, Lt. Col. Edwin R., of Metairie, La., born 1931; won seven Japanese Team Championships 1961–63; represented Japan in Far East Championships 1961; won Southern Spring Open Teams 1966, Mid-Atlantic Independence Day Masters Pairs 1968.

LEWIS, Harlow S., of Wynnewood, Pa., investment advisor, born 1932; won Reisinger 1970, Spring Nat'l Men's Pairs 1975, Fall Nat'l Life Masters Men's Pairs 1967, second Spingold 1974, Reisinger 1971, Men's Teams 1967; won Nat'l Intercollegiate Championship 1953; several regional championships including Eastern States Knockout Teams 1965, District 4 Open Teams 1966, Keystone Open Teams 1965. Member Goodwill Committee.

LEWIS, Jerry (1895–1965), of Dallas, Tex., sales executive; won Mid-South Spring Open Pairs 1956, Mixed Pairs 1962, North Texas Open Teams 1962. President ACBL 1963, Chairman of Board 1962, 1964; former Trustee ACBL Charity Foundation.

LEWIS, Nancy, of Warren, Ohio; won Summer Nat'l secondary Mixed Pairs 1970, Southeastern Women's Teams 1971, 1974.

LEWIS, Robert N., of McLean, Va., computer specialist, born 1937; third World Olympiad Mixed Teams 1974; winner of several regional titles including Mid-Atlantic Open Teams 1971.

LEWIS, Mrs. W. L., of Annapolis, Md.; winner of several regional events including Keystone Women's Pairs 1970.

LICHTENSTEIN, William Mason (1897–1970), of New York, N.Y., sales executive; won Vanderbilt 1948, second 1956; won Eastern States Knockout Teams 1945.

LIECHTENSTEIN, Princess Nadine von (formerly Nadine Ansay), of Paris, Frances; second World Women's Team Olympiad 1960; represented France in several European Women's Championships; won French Mixed Team and several times Women's Team. Organizer of annual international festivals at Deauville and Cannes.

LIGGETT, Cmdr. Winfield S., Jr. (1881–1937), executive officer of the U.S.S. *Montana* in World War I, retired from the Navy and became a bridge writer, teacher, and lecturer; one of the leading pre-war American bridge personalities; partnered Sidney Lenz during last part of the CULBERTSON-LENZ MATCH; won American Whist League Auction Open Team 1924, Auction Pairs 1927, 1932, Eastern Auction Open Team 1931, Pairs 1928, Auction and Contract Open Team 1930, Contract Pairs 1932, New England Auction Open Team 1930, ABL Men's Team 1929, Mixed Team 1930, Open Team 1931. Member of the Advisory Council on Official System. Author of *Contract Bridge Summary,* co-author of *Winning Leads at Contract Bridge.* See BIBLIOGRAPHY, E.

LIGHTMAN, Malcolm A. (1892–1958), of Memphis, Tenn; was associated with the motion picture industry. Won Life Masters Pairs 1945, Chicago 1947. See LIGHTMAN TROPHY.

LIGHTNER, Marie (Mrs. Theodore, formerly Mrs. M. Black), of New York, N.Y.; won Auction Mixed Pairs 1932, Nat'l Mixed Teams 1932, 1940; second Nat'l Women's Pairs 1933.

LIGHTNER, Theodore A., of New York, N.Y., stockbroker, born 1893; one of the great players of the world; a leading figure in bridge from the earliest days of contract, he partnered Ely Culbertson during a part of the CULBERTSON-LENZ MATCH. Lightner was a member of the Culbertson team which won victories over English teams in 1930, 1933, 1934 (see ANGLO-AMERICAN MATCHES). World Champion 1953, won Spingold 1937, 1939, 1945, Chicago 1947, Vanderbilt 1930, Life Masters Pairs 1932, 1935, Fall Nat'l Open Pairs 1928; second Spingold 1941, Chicago 1932, 1934, Vanderbilt 1937, 1938, 1939, 1941, 1945, Life Masters Pairs 1931, 1947, with many regional successes. A contributor to the development of the CULBERTSON SYSTEM, he was also the inventor of the LIGHTNER DOUBLE of slam contracts. His writings include *High Lights of the Culbertson System,* 1933, *Famous Hands of the Culbertson-Lenz Match* (co-author), 1932, and frequent contributions to *The Bridge World.*

LILIE, Harold J., of Woodmere, N.Y., insurance agent; winner of several regional titles including New York–New Jersey Open Teams 1973, Mixed Pairs 1972, 1973.

LILLIEHÖÖK, Nils Olof, of Lidingo, Sweden, lawyer, born 1915; represented Sweden World Championship 1950, 1953; European Champion

1952, second 1948, 1949, 1950; won six Scandinavian Championships and seven Swedish Championships. Co-inventor of EFOS SYSTEM. President of Stockholm Bridge League.

LIM, Dr. Teong Wah, of Malaysia, virologist, born 1932; represented Malaysia Far East Championship 1962, 1965, 1966, 1968, 1970, 1972, 1973.

LIN, HARRY S. C., of Taipei, Taiwan, bank employee, born 1939; second World Championship 1970; Far East Champion 1967, 1971; represented China Far East Championships 1965–68, 1970–74; national titles include Governor's Cup 1967.

LINDERMAN, Walter, of Auckland, New Zealand, manager importing company, born 1929; associate editor *New Zealand Bridge Magazine;* national wins include Scottish Nat'l Pairs 1958, Teams 1960, New Zealand Teams 1973, 1974.

LINDOP, David R., of Toronto, Ont., program analyst, born 1946; winner of several regional events including Canadian Nat'l Knockout Teams 1973, Canadian-American Masters Pairs 1972.

LINDSAY, Cameron A., of Vancouver, B. C., marketing analyst, born 1940; winner of several regional championships including Canadian-American Open Teams 1968, 1972.

LINHART, James, of Englewood Cliffs, N.J., bridge teacher, born 1936; Summer Nat'l Mixed Teams 1975, Marcus 1963, secondary Men's Pairs 1974; winner of several regional titles including Bridge Week Open Teams 1963, All Western Open Teams 1965, District 15 Knockout Teams 1969.

LIPIN, Max, of Birmingham, Mich., music and television distributor; won Southeastern Men's Teams, Open Teams 1962, District 5 Open Teams 1964.

LIPSCHUTZ, Salomon, of Antwerp, Belgium, diamond merchant, born 1905; won Belgian Individual 1952, Open Teams 1957, 1958, 1961, 1962.

LIPSCOMB, Winsom Mary, of Sydney, Australia; Far East Women's Champion 1973, 1974; represented Australia Women's Olympiad 1960, 1968; national titles include Interstate Women's Teams 1961, 1967, 1969, 1972, 1974, Nat'l Women's Pairs 1959, 1961.

LIPSITZ, Peggy (Mrs. Robert, formerly Mrs. Steve Parker), of Potomac, Md., bridge teacher, born 1941; won World Olympiad Mixed Teams 1974, Fall

Nat'l Mixed Pairs 1969, second Summer Nat'l Master Mixed Teams 1973; winner of several regional events including Mid-Atlantic Summer Masters Pairs 1970, Open Pairs 1970.

LIPSITZ, Robert H., of Potomac, Md., computer analyst, born 1942; won World Olympiad Mixed Teams 1974, second Summer Nat'l Master Mixed Teams 1973; winner of several regional events including New England Knockout Teams 1971, Keystone Open Teams 1971, Fun City Open Teams 1973.

LIPTON, Sally (Mrs. William, formerly Mrs. Lou Herman) (1913–1966), of New York, N.Y., ACBL office staff, tournament director; won Fall Nat'l Women's Team 1952; third Fall Nat'l Mixed Pairs 1952. Donor of (Lou) HERMAN TROPHY for best performance in Fall Nat'l Championships.

LIPTON, Dr. William V., of New York, N.Y., dentist, born 1901; one of the leading players of the East Coast; won Marcus 1953, Vanderbilt 1953, Fall Nat'l Men's Pairs 1942; second Marcus 1949, 1955, Chicago 1955; regional successes include Eastern States Knockout Teams 1947, 1949, 1955, Men's Pairs 1954, 1961, 1965, New England Master Pairs 1956. ACBL Vice-President, and director 1956–60; former President Greater New York BA, New York–New Jersey Conference. Introduced *Post-Mortem,* widely thought to have been the original author of its "Cynical Observer" column.

LISTON, John J. (1905–1952), of Cambridge, Mass., teacher; won New England Knockout Teams 1950, Mixed Teams 1936, 1937, Open Pairs 1936.

LITTMAN-LEMAITRE, André, of Antwerp, Belgium, business executive and bridge writer, born 1911; captain Belgian Team 1959–63, npc 1966, 1969–73; winner of German Open Teams 1956, 1968, 1961, 1962, 1965, Mixed Pairs 1968, Belgian Teams II 1966, Belgian Knockout Teams 1961, German Open Pairs 1955, 1956. Secretary World Bridge Federation since 1970, President European Bridge League since 1973. Member Tournament Committee European Bridge League since 1961, Chairman tournament division German Bridge Federation 1954–56, Director Belgian Federation since 1957, serving on various committees. Translated rules and established various tournament regulations for German Bridge Federation. Newspaper columnist and contributor to various bridge periodicals. IBPA "Bridge Man of the Year" award 1973. Contributing editor *Bridge Encyclopedia.*

LIVEZEY, Joseph, of Springfield, Pa., student, born in 1953; won several regional events including New England Mixed Teams 1968, Mid-Atlantic Master

Pairs 1974. In 1968, at the age of fifteen, he became the then youngest ACBL Life Master, breaking by six months the record formerly held by Kyle LARSEN.

LIVINGSTON, Mrs. Milton, of Paducah, Ky., born 1908; won Spring Nat'l Women's Teams 1962.

LOCHRIDGE, Charles (1905–1970), of New York, N.Y., president retailing company and bridge teacher; one of the great American players, noted for the brilliance of his dummy play; won Life Masters Pairs 1937, Vanderbilt 1937, 1939, Nat'l Mixed Teams 1931, Fall Nat'l Mixed Pairs 1932, Open Pairs 1934; second Vanderbilt 1937, 1944, Spingold 1938, 1940, Chicago 1941; won Reisinger 1933, 1938, 1941, 1944, Eastern States Open Pairs 1940; member of BID-RITE TEAM.

LOCKWOOD, Robert K., of Farmington, Mich., attorney, born 1922; won Japan Nat'l Mixed Pairs 1955, Open Pairs 1957; second Philippine Nat'l Individual 1958.

LOEWENTHAL, Edward, of New York, N.Y., stockbroker, born 1907; third World's Fair Open Pairs 1933; won Reisinger 1955, Eastern States Men's Pairs 1954, New York–New Jersey Open Pairs 1958, Southeastern Men's Teams 1959. Former President Greater New York BA.

LONG, Mrs. Effie, of Westport, Conn., bridge teacher and tournament director, born 1918; won Eastern States Mixed Team 1963. Director Connecticut Unit and New England Bridge Conference, President ABTA 1971–72.

LOOBY, James V., of Los Angeles, Calif., communications consultant, born 1947; winner of several regional events including Mid-Atlantic Knockout Teams 1973, 1974.

LOPATA, Monte, of St. Louis, Mo., accountant, born 1919; won Mississippi Valley Open Pairs and Men's Pairs 1961, 1970, Mid-South Open Pairs 1962, Midwest Men's Pairs 1962. Director St. Louis Unit ACBL; Chairman 1963 Spring Nat'l.

LORD, Roger E. III, of St. Louis, Mo., advertising executive, born 1941; second Grand Nat'l Championships 1973; won Fall Nat'l secondary Swiss Teams 1970, several regional titles including Missouri Valley Open Teams 1967, Open Pairs 1972.

LORTZ, Henry A., of Seattle, Wash., computer programmer, born 1950; winner of several regional events including Inland Empire Open Teams 1973, Masters Pairs 1973.

LOUVEAUX, Dr. J. T. C., of Elizabethville, Republic of Zaire, physician, born 1911; won Central Africa Open Teams 1962; Katanga Open Teams 1959, 1960; Zambia Open Teams 1956, 1957, 1959, 1960, 1963, 1965.

LOVE, Clyde E., of Ann Arbor, Mich., professor of mathematics, died 1960. A specialist on squeeze play whose writings included *Squeeze Play in Bridge, Bridge Squeezes Complete,* and many magazine articles. See BIBLIOGRAPHY, D.

LOW, Marc E., of Dayton, Ohio, mathematician, born 1935; won Marcus 1962, several regional championships including Missouri Valley Masters Pairs 1957, Central States Open Pairs 1962, Senior & Life Masters Teams 1964, All-American Open Teams 1968, Open Pairs 1971. Inventor of Swiss Team event which has substantially replaced board-a-match in sectional and regional tournaments.

LOWENTHAL, John, of Montvale, N.J., computer programmer, born 1938; won District 5 Masters Pairs 1962, Open Pairs 1964, New England Knockout Teams 1966, Open Teams 1968; co-inventor of the CANARY CLUB system.

LOWERY, Sylvester, of Philadelphia, Pa., builder and developer, born 1914; won US Zone World Bridge Olympics 1940; won Keystone Conference Mixed Pairs 1959, Texas Conference Open Pairs 1962. Former President Philadelphia Whist Assn.

LOWINSKI, Stefan (1908–1965), of Warsaw, Poland, teacher; one of the most popular personalities of Polish bridge, especially among the younger players; represented Poland World Pairs Olympiad 1962. Won Polish Open Teams 1957, 1958, 1960, 1961, Open Pairs 1965, Individual 1958. Because of his contributions to Polish bridge, one of Poland's bridge Congresses has been named in his honor.

LOYNAZ, Edgar, of Caracas, Venezuela, engineer, born 1908; represented Venezuela World Team Olympiad 1964, World Championships 1967, South American Championships five times; South American Champion 1963, 1966; won National Open Teams twice, Open Pairs three times.

LU, Frank P. S., of Christchurch, New Zealand, professor of industrial administration; represented New Zealand World Team Olympiad 1972, World Championships (npc) 1974; national wins include five national pairs championships, two team titles. President New Zealand CBA 1974–75.

LUDWIG, R. J., of Schenectady, N.Y., modern languages teacher, born 1918; second Nat'l Senior

Masters Individual 1954; won New England Masters Pairs 1954, Men's Pairs 1955, 1956.

LUKACS, Paul, of Tel Aviv, Israel, actuary, born 1915; represented Israel European Championships 1965; fourth World Par Championship 1961; won Tel Aviv Open Teams several times. Writings include articles for the Hungarian *Bridge Life,* and columns in the *European Bridge Review,* and *Bridge Magazine.* Contributor to *The Bridge World,* ACBL *Bulletin* and *Bridge Encyclopedia.* Co-author of *Spotlight on Cardplay, Second Book of Bridge Problems,* and *Bridge Hands for the Connoisseur.* See BIBLIOGRAPHY, H, J.

LUNDELL, Pär I., of Stockholm, Sweden, antique dealer, born 1926; represented Sweden European Championships 1958, 1961; Scandinavian Champion and national titles in Open Team and Open Pairs.

LUX, Thompson, of Kansas City, Mo., won several regional events in 1970, including District 15 Knockout Teams.

LUYTEN, Louis, of Antwerp, Belgium, born 1911; represented Belgium in European Championship, 1953; won Belgian Open Teams 1962, 1963.

LYONS, Mrs. Ruby, of Kingston, Jamaica, born 1901; Fall Nat'l Women's Team 1947; Jamaican national wins include Open Pairs, Open Teams, Inter-Club, and Master Individual. President Jamaica Bridge Association.

M

MacASLAN, David F., of Louisville, Ky., attorney; winner of several regional events including District 11 Knockout Teams 1974.

MacCRACKEN, Charles M., of Memphis, Tenn., ACBL Tournament Coordinator, born 1941; tied second, Spring Nat'l Men's Teams 1969; winner of many regional championships including Intermountain Knockout Teams 1968, 1969, Open Pairs 1971.

MacDUFF, R., of Coquitlam, B.C., winner of several regional events including Intermountain Knockout Teams 1971, Oregon Trail Open Pairs 1973.

MacHALE, J. P. (Joe), of Dublin, Ireland, university Secretary, born 1922; represented Ireland World Pair Olympiad 1962, World Team Olympiad 1972, European championships regularly since 1952; national wins include every major Irish title.

MACHLIN, Gertrude ("Trudy," Mrs. Jerome), of Silver Spring, Md., bridge teacher and director; won Fall Nat'l Mixed Pairs 1967.

MACHLIN, Jerome, of Silver Spring, Md., born 1913. ACBL National Tournament Director since 1957. Author of many articles in bridge publications.

MacLAREN, John M., of Edinburgh, Scotland, actuary, born 1926; won Scottish National Pairs 1956, 1957; represented Scotland twenty-six times in Camrose Trophy matches, and a member of winning teams in 1964, 1965; many other successes include Scottish Open Teams 1961. President Scottish Bridge Union 1967.

MacLEAN, Hugh C., of Wayzata, Minn., bridge teacher and writer, born 1938; represented US World Pair Olympiad 1974; won Fall Nat'l Life Master Men's Pairs 1970, Spring Nat'l Men's Teams 1974, second Open Pairs 1974; winner of numerous regional championships including Pheasant Knockout Teams 1970, 1972, Gopher Knockout Teams 1971, Masters Pairs 1973, Men's Pairs 1971.

MacLEOD, Ian (1913–70), of London, England, cabinet minister and journalist; won Gold Cup 1937; npc British team 1951. One of the originators of the ACOL SYSTEM. Author of *Bridge Is an Easy Game;* former Bridge Editor of the London *Sunday Times.* At the time of his death, he was Chancellor of the Exchequer, the second most powerful office in England's government. His former political positions included Minister of Health, Minister of Labour, Secretary of State for the Colonies, Leader of the House of Commons, and Chairman of the Conservative Party. See BIBLIOGRAPHY, E.

MacNAB, Robin B., of Bozeman, Mont., cattle rancher, born 1915; won Northern Rocky Mountain Masters Pairs 1957, Mid-Atlantic Fall Open Teams 1965. ACBL President 1965. ACBL Director since 1956 and former President Western Conference. Member World Bridge Federation Executive Council since 1956. Member US Olympic Track and Field Squad 1936.

MADDOCKS, Mrs. Judith, of Dearborn, Mich., teacher, born 1923; won Motor City Women's Pairs 1967, Mixed Pairs 1967. Editor of Michigan BA publication, *Table Talk,* since 1960.

MADDOX, Marilyn A. (Mrs. Myles), of Pleasant Ridge, Mich., born 1929; won Great Lakes Mixed Pairs 1967, 1968, tied Open Teams 1974.

MADDOX, Myles V., of Pleasant Ridge, Mich., high school teacher; winner of several regional titles including Great Lakes Mixed Pairs 1967, 1968, Open Teams 1971, tied 1974.

MAGEE, Lee T., of Kansas City, Mo., lawyer, born 1928; won several regional championships including Missouri Valley Knockout Teams 1973, Open Teams 1968, District 15 Open Teams 1968, Mid-American–Canadian Men's Pairs 1967.

MAHONEY, Mabel (Mrs. E. A.), of El Dorado, Ark.; winner of many regional championships including Canadian Knockout Teams 1970, Women's Pairs 1969, Klondike Knockout Teams 1972.

MAIER, Merwyn D. (1909–1942), of New York, N.Y., attorney, a member of the FOUR ACES 1937–42; one of the leading players of the pre-war period; won Spingold 1938, 1939, Vanderbilt 1937, 1938, Fall Nat'l Men's Pairs 1940, Life Master Pairs 1941, Masters Individual 1939; second Spingold 1936, 1941, Chicago 1934, Vanderbilt 1935, 1941, Individual 1936. Regional successes include Eastern States Open Pairs 1940.

MALOWAN, Walter (1882–1966), of New York, N.Y., exporter, born in Austria; one of the leading players of the period before World War II; won American Whist League Open Team 1933; second Vanderbilt 1930, 1931, Life Masters Pairs 1934; regional successes include Eastern States Mixed Team 1940, 1941, 1944, Mixed Pairs 1945, New England Knockout Teams 1936, Open Teams 1931, Open Pairs 1935, Atlantic City Open Team 1931, Open Pairs 1930, 1931, Mixed Team 1943. Member of Tournament Committee USBA; secretary of Crockford's Club, New York City; secretary and later honorary member Regency Club, New York City. Former contributing editor of *The Bridge World*. Author of many articles in bridge publications; collaborator with S. Lenz on newspaper articles. Originator of MALOWAN SIX CLUB CONVENTION.

MANCHESTER, Max (1914–1969), of Portland, Ore., director of state pension system; won Fall Nat'l Men's Pairs 1961; regional wins include Northwest Open Team 1955, Open Pairs 1950, Mixed Pairs 1961, Oregon Trail Knockout Teams 1968. President ACBL 1962, and Chairman of the Board 1960–61; former President of Western Conference and Chairman of the Board. Honorary Member ACBL 1963.

MANDEL, Larry A., of Los Angeles, Calif., insurance agent, born 1947; won 1974 US Int'l Team Trials; winner of several regional events including Desert Empire Open Teams 1974.

MANDELL, Jeffrey T., of Chicago, Ill., attorney; winner of several regional events including Central States Open Teams 1972, 1974.

MANDELL, Sidney, of Miami Beach, Fla., attorney and accountant, born 1906; won Vanderbilt 1952,

1954, several regional championships including Florida Men's Pairs 1972.

MANFIELD, Edward, of Arlington, Va., anti-trust economist, born 1943; won Keystone Open Teams 1967, Mid-Atlantic Independence Day Open Teams 1967, Mid-Atlantic Knockout Teams 1971.

MANGAN, Betty (Mrs. Michael), of San Antonio, Tex., bridge club operator; second Fall Nat'l Life Master Women's Pairs 1970; won South Texas Open Pairs 1968.

MANHARDT, Peter, of Vienna, Austria, director of Austrian road safety board, born 1936; won World Olympiad Open Pairs 1970; third European Championships 1969; various European national and international successes.

MANNING-FOSTER, Alfred Edye (1874–1939), of London; one of the leading pre-war bridge players; founder of *Bridge Magazine*, and its editor until 1939; foreign contributing editor of *The Bridge World;* bridge correspondent *The Times* (London) for many years. A leading figure in the European Bridge League, founder and first president of the British Bridge League 1934. ACBL Honorary Member 1933. Writings included *Auction Bridge for All, Contract Bridge for All,* and *Baby Contract Book*.

MANOS, Dr. John T., of East Norwich, N.Y., physician, born 1924; won several regional titles including Eastern Mixed Teams 1961, Bermuda Open Teams 1962, 1970, 1972.

MANOUSSAKIS, Emmanuel M., of Greece, civil engineer and industrialist, born 1926; national successes include Open Pairs 1966. Member Executive Council of Hellenic BF since 1971.

MANSELL, Mrs. Petra, of Durban, South Africa, bridge teacher, born 1923; runner-up World Women's Team Olympiad 1968, 1972; represented South Africa Women's Team Olympiad 1960, Open Team Olympiad 1964, World Pair Olympiad 1966; national titles include Open Teams 1965 and 1967 and Open Pairs 1960.

MANSFIELD, Warren, of Hartford, Conn., stockbroker and bridge writer, born 1893; won New England Fall Mixed Teams 1953, 1957, 1962, Mixed Pairs 1953, 1961, Open Teams 1961, Swiss Teams 1969. Former President Connecticut BA, Vice-President New England Bridge Conference.

MAO, David, of Taipei, Taiwan, president import-export corporation, born in Kiangsu, China, 1919; npc China World Championship 1970; represented China World Olympiad 1964, Far East Championships 1962, 1965, 1966, 1968; numerous national successes. Executive Secretary of the National Contract Bridge League of the Republic of China.

MARCUS, Edward N. (1895–1952), of Boston, Mass., clothing manufacturer; won Chicago 1949, second 1950, Spingold 1942, Nat'l Mixed Teams 1946; won New England Knockout Teams 1937, 1939, 1941 (twice), 1942, 1944 (twice), 1945, Open Pairs 1934, 1943, 1948, Masters Teams 1950, Mixed Pairs 1938, 1941, 1946, Mixed Teams 1938, 1943, Masters Pairs 1949, Men's Pairs 1935, 1938, 1941, 1943. Former ACBL Director, President New England BA.

MARGULIS, Sheldon, of Milwaukee, Wisc., rehabilitation counselor, born 1940; won Fall Nat'l Life Masters Pairs second flight 1969, District 5 Swiss Teams 1969, Great Lakes Open Pairs and Teams 1969, Motor City Teams 1969.

MARJANOVIĆ, Dragutin, of Zagreb, Yugoslavia, engineer, born 1907; represented Yugoslavia pre-World War II international competitions, including the European Championships; runner-up 1939 European Championships.

MARK, Dr. Louis (1893–1954), surgeon, of Columbus, Ohio. The first Life Master in Columbus. ACBL Honorary Member 1950, President 1949. See MARK TROPHY.

MARK, Louise (Mrs. Frederick), of Toronto, Ont., born Shanghai 1934; represented Canada Women's Team World Olympiad 1964; won Summer Nat'l Women's Pairs 1965. Director Ontario Unit.

MARKOVICS, Andrew M., of Sydney, Australia, bridge club proprietor, born 1947 in Hungary; WBF Zone 7 champion 1974; won Nat'l Trials 1974.

MARKS, Arthur (1908–1965), of New York, N.Y., mathematics teacher and tournament director; won Western States Open Pairs 1943. Contributing editor of *Bridge Encyclopedia.*

MARKS, Paul N. (1908–1968), of Maywood, Ill., accountant, mathematics and bridge teacher; ACBL National Tournament Director 1957 until his death. Devised APPENDIX movements for 7-, 11-, and 13-table RAINBOW INDIVIDUAL MOVEMENT. See EIGHT TABLES; TWELVE TABLES; FOURTEEN TABLES.

MARKUS, Mrs. Rika ("Rixi"), of London, England; born in Vienna; one of the greatest woman players of all time and one of the fastest analysts. First woman to become WBF Grandmaster. Winner of 12 international championships, more than any

other woman player. A key member of the Austrian Women's Team which, under the captaincy of Dr. Paul STERN, won the first two European Women's Championships, 1935 and 1936, and the World Women's Championship 1937. Became a British citizen after World War II, and formed a partnership with Mrs. F. GORDON, which established a serious claim to be regarded as the strongest pair in the world of feminine bridge by winning the World Women's Pairs Championship 1962, when they were also members of the winning Mixed Team, and the World Women's Team Olympiad 1964; they won the World Women's Pair Championship again in 1974, and finished second in 1970. Mrs. Markus represented Great Britain in many European Women's Championships, winning in 1951, 1952, 1959, 1961, 1963, 1966, 1975, and many Olympiad events, finishing second in the 1970 World Mixed Pairs; won Gold Cup 1961, Masters Pairs 1957; toured US 1953 as a member of the British Women's Team. Bridge Editor of the *Guardian* and the *Evening Standard* (London). Winner of IBPA Goren Award for bridge personality of the year 1974. Contributor to *The Bridge World, Bridge Magazine,* and other periodicals. Author of *Bid Boldly, Play Safe, Common Sense Bridge, Aces and Places* (see BIBLIOGRAPHY, H). See also BUENOS AIRES AFFAIR.

MARQUARDT, Eduardo, of Buenos Aires, Argentina, Attorney General, born 1910; npc Argentina World Team Olympiad 1964, World Championship 1965; represented Argentina South American Championship 1951; won Argentine Open Teams 1965.

MARSCH, John E., of Winnipeg, Man., businessman, born 1938; winner of several regional events including Calgary Knockout Teams 1973, Men's Pairs 1973.

MARSEE, Grant (1929–1967), of Livonia, Mich., bridge teacher; won Spring Nat'l Open Pairs 1962, second 1965; won Marcus 1965, Golder Pairs 1960, All-American Open Pairs 1955, Open Teams 1964, Men's Pairs 1964, Central States Masters Teams 1961, Great Lakes Open Teams 1961, Men's Pairs 1967, District 5 Men's Pairs 1964, Upper New York State Open Teams, Open Pairs 1965, Southeastern Men's Pairs 1966, Mississippi Valley Open Teams, Open Pairs 1967, Midwest Spring Open Teams 1967, Gopher Open Teams, Masters Pairs 1967.

MARSH, Edward, of Phoenix, Ariz., realtor, born 1927; won Canadian Nat'l Mixed Pairs 1949, Open Pairs 1951, and 1952, Canadian-American Men's Pairs 1949, Mixed Pairs 1951, Open Team 1949, 1952, 1954.

MARTENSSON, Mrs. Eva, of Stockholm, Sweden, born 1924; won World Women's Team Olympiad 1968, Scandinavian Women's Championships 1957, 1966, 1968.

MARTIN, Bruce, of El Paso, Tex.; winner of several regional events including Land of Coronado Masters Pairs 1974, Open Pairs 1972.

MARTIN, Mrs. Christianne, of Paris, born 1914; European Women's Team Champion 1939, 1954, 1956, represented France European Championships 1936, 1948, 1949, 1950, 1951, 1955, 1965, International Mixed Pairs twice; many national successes in Open and Mixed Teams. President of French National Tournament Committee.

MARTIN, John Frederick, of Auckland, N.Z., chemical engineer and bridge writer, born 1909; won World Bidding Contest 1953, New Zealand Open Team 1950, 1951, 1952, 1954, 1955, 1957, 1959, 1960, 1961, 1962, 1963, Open Pairs 1957, 1960, 1963. Delegate New Zealand Bridge Council. Vice-President Auckland Contract BC. Writings include articles in Auckland *Bridge Bulletin.*

MARTINEAU, Joel, of Vancouver, B.C.; winner of several regional events including Canadian Knockout Teams 1971, British Columbia Knockout Teams 1973.

MARTINO, Michael John, of Hamilton, Ont., lawyer, born 1936; won Spring Nat'l Men's Pairs 1969, several regional events including Canadian Nat'l Men's Pairs 1971.

MARTINS FERREIRA, Nelson, of São Paulo, Brazil, engineer, born 1921; represented Brazil World Team Olympiad 1960; won South American Championship 1956, 1974.

MARTINS FERREIRA, Synesio, of São Paulo, Brazil, businessman, born 1922; represented Brazil World Team Olympiad 1960, 1968, 1972, World Pair Olympiad 1970; won South American Championship 1966, 1969, 1974.

MARX, John C. H. ("Jack"), of London, England, economist and bridge columnist, born 1907; won European Championship 1950 and selected for British team in 1950 World Championship; won Gold Cup 1937, 1947, 1971. Regular contributor to *Contract Bridge Journal* 1946–48, and to *British Bridge World* 1950–56. One of the originators of the ACOL SYSTEM and an independent originator of the STAYMAN convention. Originator of the BYZANTINE convention. British Bridge League selector 1960–61.

MASON, David B., of Maplewood, N.J., accountant, born 1923; winner of many regional championships including Eastern States Knockout Teams 1972, Fun City Knockout Teams 1970, Long Island Knockout Teams 1969. President Greater New York BA 1964, and former Tournament Chairman.

MASON, Jane, of Maplewood, N.J., born 1933; winner of several regional titles including Fun City Knockout Teams 1970, Eastern States Knockout Teams 1972.

MASTRON, Victor, of Yorba Linda, Calif., physician, born 1920; winner of several regional events including Canadian Knockout Teams 1970, Golden Gate Knockout Teams 1971.

MATHE, Eugenie M. (Mrs. Lewis), of Los Angeles, Calif., born 1926; won Summer Nat'l Mixed Teams 1970, Fall Nat'l Mixed Pairs 1971, Bridge Week Mixed Team 1963, Mixed Pairs 1960, All-Western Open Teams 1966. Author of "LOL" column for *Southern California Bridge News* since 1966.

MATHE, Lewis L. ("Lew"), of Los Angeles, Calif., formerly of New York, N.Y., real estate investment consultant and bridge columnist, born 1915; one of the great bridge players of the world, noted for his adaptability and table presence. The leading exponent of the direct method of bidding favored on the West Coast. World Champion 1954, represented North America World Championships 1955, 1962, 1966, 1971, represented US World Olympiad 1960; won International Play-off Match 1970, Oeschger 1957, Mott-Smith 1959, 1964, 1967, Spingold 1954, Vanderbilt 1964, 1966, 1967, Chicago 1959, 1960, 1962, Reisinger 1971, Blue Ribbon 1964, Fall Nat'l Men's Teams 1957, 1962, Open Pairs 1957, Mixed Pairs 1971, Spring Nat'l Open Pairs 1959, Men's Teams 1970, Summer Nat'l Life Masters Pairs 1963, 1967, Mixed Teams 1970; second Team Trials 1965, Spingold 1953, 1971, 1974, Reisinger 1966, Blue Ribbon 1967, Summer Nat'l Mixed Teams 1953, Men's Pairs 1961, Spring Nat'l Open Pairs 1964, 1967, Men's Teams 1972, Mixed Pairs 1959; regional wins include Bridge Week Masters Teams 1956, Knockout Teams 1951, 1957, 1960, 1966, Open Teams 1949, 1950, 1959, Masters Pairs 1949, All-Western Open Teams 1961, 1962, 1966, Golden State Open Teams 1966. ACBL President 1975, Chairman of Board of Directors 1976. Three-time President Western Conference. ACBL Director 1958–61 and since 1970. Bridge Editor Los Angeles *Herald-Examiner.*

MATHEWS, Joseph M. (1912–1966), of Fort Worth, Tex., bridge writer and tournament director; writings included regular contributions to *Texas Bridge* and other periodicals. ACBL National Tournament Director from 1957 until his death.

MATHEWS, Luise. See EMBRY, MRS. ALLEN.

MATHIESON, Graham F. (1899–1972), of Caterham, Surrey, England, financial statistician; represented Great Britain in Schwab Cup match in 1933 and in European Championship 1937; won Gold Cup

1949, English Open Teams 1962. Chairman London County CBA.

MATHIS, James L., of Williamsville, N.Y., banking executive, born 1927; represented US World Pairs Olympiad 1970; won Spring Nat'l Open Pairs 1969; second Life Master Pairs 1970; regional successes include Upper New York State Open Teams 1964, 1970, 1971, Masters Pairs 1965.

MATSON, Elsie, of Ithaca, N.Y., bridge teacher, club director for over 35 years, died 1970. Helped found the Central New York Bridge Association in the 1930s, one of the first organized units, and the Upper New York State Regional in 1956. Executive Secretary CNYBA for 25 years and Upper New York Regional Conference for 12 years; ACBL Director 1958–60.

MATTHESS, Bob, of West Los Angeles, Calif.; won Spring Nat'l secondary Swiss Teams 1970, All-Western Knockout Teams 1973, tied Navajo Trail Open Pairs 1970.

MATTHEWS, Judge Ben G., of Shelbyville, Ky., born 1926; won several regional events including North Texas Masters Pairs 1962, Midwest Men's Pairs 1955, Open Teams 1971, Mississippi Valley Men's Pairs 1965. Member ACBL Goodwill Committee.

MATTHEYS, Jean (John) P. (1902–1967), of New York, N.Y., stockbroker; a prominent tournament player in the early days of contract; won Vanderbilt 1929, second 1931. Member USBA Tournament Committee.

MAUPIN, Evelyn, of Cocoa Beach, Fla., teacher; second Spring Nat'l Women's Team 1962; won Southeastern Women's Team 1961, Florida Women's Pairs 1974, Individual 1960.

MAURER, Marguerite (Mrs. Victor), of Skaneateles, N.Y., bridge club director, born 1921; won Canadian-American Women's Pairs 1960, Upper New York State Women's Pairs 1958, 1960. Member Board of Directors Onondaga County.

MAUSSER, Kathleen, of San Mateo, Calif., bridge teacher; won All-Western Women's Pairs 1954, 1961, Pacific Southwest Women's Pairs 1953.

MAY, Albert E., of Ft. Lauderdale, Fla., mathematician, born 1909; won Central States Open Teams 1964, 1968, Canadian-Atlantic Mixed Pairs 1973. Vice-President Midwest Bridge Conference.

MAY, Gideon, of North Hollywood, Calif., social worker, musician, born 1910; regional wins include

District 22 Masters Pairs 1973, Pacific Southwest Open Teams 1956.

MAY, Helene (Mrs. Albert), of Fort Lauderdale, Fla., born 1909; won Central States Open Teams

MAY, Helene (Mrs. Albert), of Fort Lauderdale, Fal., born 1909; won Central States Open Teams 1964, 1968, Canadian-Atlantic Mixed Pairs 1973.

MAY, Walter R., of Endicott, N.Y., university official, born 1930; second Golder Pairs 1959; won Upper New York Open Team 1956, New England Fall Open Team 1958, Masters Pairs 1959; District 3 Grand Nat'l Championship 1975.

MAYBIN, Laura, of Columbia, S.C., won Mid-Atlantic Women's Pairs 1972, 1974, tied Open Teams 1973.

MAYER, Edward, of London, England, lawyer, born 1901; represented Great Britain in Schwab Cup match 1933; won unofficial matches against American teams 1954 and 1956; won Gold Cup 1932, English Open Teams 1948. Council Member of British Bridge League; author of *Money Bridge;* bridge correspondent of London *Times* since 1953. See BIBLIOGRAPHY, E.

McALEAR, Allen L., of Bozeman, Mont., attorney, born 1928; won several regional events including Big Sky Knockout Teams 1971, Open Teams 1971, Calgary Master Pairs 1973.

McALLISTER, Donald, of Porthcawl, South Wales, chartered accountant, born 1909; represented Wales in pre-war international events, and for some years after; national successes include eight Open Team championships.

McBRIDE, Fred H., of Hollywood, Fla., shoe salesman, born 1917; winner of several regional titles including Mid-Atlantic Knockout Teams 1974, Open Pairs 1974.

McCABE, Joe I. (1906–1966), of Coral Gables, Fla., real estate broker; won Mid-Atlantic Fall Open Teams 1958. Devised McCabe Adjunct to WEAK TWO-BIDS.

McCAMPBELL, Bryant, of St. Louis, Mo., one of the most successful players of auction bridge and author of perhaps the first book (*Auction Tactics,* 1915) that described the strategy of the successful rubber-bridge player. He claimed invention of the TAKE-OUT DOUBLE and was one of the first bridge authors to publish it. He claimed also to be first to use the 4–3–2–1 POINT-COUNT. There is no reason to doubt that he arrived at both ideas independently, though perhaps not first.

McCAMPBELL, Leavelle, of New York, N.Y., Chairman of the Whist Club committee which produced the first generally accepted *Laws of Contract Bridge* in 1927; he assisted in many later revisions of the Laws.

McCLURKIN, Charles C., of Harrisburg, Pa., manufacturer, born 1913; ACBL Director 1969–71.

McCOMAS, Stanley, of Indianapolis, Ind., insurance bond manager, bridge writer, and teacher, born 1908; associated with Easley BLACKWOOD in his bridge writings; won Midwest Fall Open Team 1960, Mixed Pairs 1946.

McCONNELL, Ron E., of San Francisco, Calif., winner of several regional events including California Capitol Men's Pairs 1971, 1972.

McCONNELL, Ruth (Mrs. Lee W.), of Columbia City, Ind.; won several regionals including District 11 Mixed Pairs 1968, Mississippi Valley Women's Pairs 1970, npc US VENICE CUP team 1974. ACBL President 1974, first woman to hold that office. ACBL Director from 1965.

McCRACKIN, Nancy (Mrs. M. R.), of Albuquerque, N.Mex., born 1922; won Nat'l Individual 1953, several regional events including Desert Empire Open Teams 1965, Women's Pairs 1969, 1971.

McCRARY, Marilyn, of Lake City, Iowa; won Summer Nat'l Mixed Teams 1971.

McCRORY, Mary R., of San Diego, Calif.; won several regional events including Palm Springs Knockout Teams 1971.

McDANIEL, Garner (Mrs. Paul), of Houston, Tex., realtor; one of the most successful women players of the Southwest; won Spring Nat'l Women's Teams 1963, 1966, Women's Pairs 1967, second 1962; Spring Nat'l Women's Pairs 1963, 1966, Summer Nat'l Mixed Teams 1966; winner of several regional titles including Texas Knockout Teams 1970.

McDONALD, Al, of Ottawa, Ont., winner of several regional events including Fleur-de-Lys Knockout Teams 1974, Open Teams 1973.

McELWAIN, Constance (Mrs. John Alden), of Burlington, Mass., programmer, born 1931; won New England Fall Women's Pairs 1959, Mixed Teams 1963, Upper New York State Open Pairs 1962.

McGARRY, Dennis, of Cleveland, Ohio, born 1947; won Spring Nat'l secondary Men's Pairs 1972; winner of several regional events including Motor City Knockout Teams 1974.

McGERVEY, John D., of Cleveland Heights, Ohio, professor of physics, born 1931; regional wins include Keystone Open Teams 1955, 1959, District 5 Open Teams 1960.

McGHEE, William (1897–1966), of Lake Charles, La., automobile dealer; won Fall Nat'l Men's Teams 1946; Texas Men's Pairs 1954; was Vice-President ACBL, President of Midwest BA, Fort Worth Unit, and Texas Bridge Conference.

McGLYNN, Harry W., of Winnipeg, Man., born 1902; won Rocky Mountain Mixed Pairs 1962.

McGROVER, Raymond J. (1905–1974), of New York, N.Y., attorney; ACBL President 1947; in 1948 played a major role in the reorganization of the League. Member of the National Laws Commission since 1960 and assisted in formation of 1963 Laws. Chairman of ACBL subcommittee for laws of CHICAGO. President Long Island BL for seven years.

McKAIG, Mrs. W. H., of Rochester, N.Y., inventory clerk; won Upper New York State Women's Pairs 1960, 1966, Mixed Pairs 1956, second Open Pairs 1958; won Canadian-American Women's Pairs 1953, 1955, 1960. Past President Central New York BA, member Nat'l Goodwill Committee.

McKEE, Jay T., of Clinton, Miss., contractor, born 1948; second Spring Nat'l Men's Pairs 1971, won Fall Nat'l secondary Open Pairs 1971; winner of several regional titles including Golden Gate Knockout Teams 1971, Beef State Knockout Teams 1971.

McKENNEY, William E. (1891–1950), bridge columnist, pioneer in bridge administration, merchandising, and tournament direction. He was born in Cleveland, Ohio, but transferred his headquarters to New York City in 1934. He was a founder of the American Auction Bridge League, 1927; was made chairman of its committee on laws and then executive secretary in 1928; and continued as secretary of the succeeding ABL and ACBL until 1948. McKenney wrote a daily bridge column for NEA (Scripps-Howard newspapers) from 1929 until his death. He founded (1929) Bridge Supplies, Inc., which sold trophies, scoring supplies, and other bridge merchandise; in this connection he invented the oblong duplicate board, and collaborated in the MC KENNEY-BALDWIN MOVEMENTS. In 1936 he gave this corporation to the ABL. He founded the National Laws Commission in 1932 and was its chairman 1935–48; he founded also the ABL and ACBL charity activities, which he caused to endow the Children's Cancer Ward in Memorial Hospital, New York City, and War Orphans Scholarships.

McKenney's dedication to the ABL and later to the ACBL was complete: Often he contributed his privately earned income to their purposes, and nearly all his time was devoted to their interests. Unfortunately this led him to acquire a spirit of proprietary control, which became inconsistent with the interests of the League as its membership grew and its financial problems lessened, so that in 1948 he was deposed in pursuance of democratic control. McKenney's support through his newspaper column contributed greatly to the success of several bridge authors and authorities, and in the case of the SUIT-PREFERENCE SIGNAL it caused the convention to be called in European countries the McKenney convention instead of being attributed to its inventor, Hy LAVINTHAL. Though his contemporaries did not rank him highly as a player, McKenney became a Life Master and won the ABL Fall Nat'l Open Pairs 1929 and several lesser events.

McMAHAN, Mike, of Downey, Calif., manager office furniture store, born 1935; won Golder Pairs 1969, Fall Nat'l secondary Mixed Pairs 1971; second Reisinger 1966; won Desert Empire Open Teams 1959, All-Western Open Pairs 1963, Open Teams 1964, Pacific Southwest Masters Pairs 1963, Bridge Week Open Pairs 1965, Men's Masters Pairs 1968, Golden State Open Teams 1966.

McMAHAN, R. F., of Florence, S.C., electrical engineer, born 1930; won Mid-Atlantic Open Teams 1961, Knockout Teams 1973, Open Pairs 1973, Men's Pairs 1963. Bridge columnist for state paper; duplicate club owner.

McMAHON, Mary M., of Sydney, Australia, investor, Far East Open Champion 1970, Women's Champion 1973, 1974; represented Australia World Women's Olympiad 1960, 1968; national titles include Interstate Women's Teams 1951, 1954, 1962, 1963, 1964, 1965, 1969, 1970, 1972, Women's Pairs 1969, 1972, Women's Individual 1962, 1970.

McMENAMIN, Ina, of Dublin, Ireland, died 1974; captained Irish Open Team European Championship 1948; second European Women's Championship 1954; represented Ireland on many other occasions; won every national title, including Mixed Pairs six times. Co-author of *Modern Contract Bridge.*

McNUTT, Kathleen, of St. Petersburg, Fla., treasury clerk, born 1899; won Fall Nat'l Women's Team 1949, Mid-Atlantic Mixed Pairs 1958.

McPHERRAN, Robert A., of New York, N.Y., financial adviser and bridge teacher, born in Philadelphia 1915; one of the leading American players; won Spingold 1939, Marcus 1940, Vanderbilt 1940, 1941, Nat'l Mixed Teams 1936, Masters Individual 1946; second Vanderbilt 1939, Fall Nat'l Mixed Pairs 1940.

McWILLIAMS, William R., of North Hollywood, Calif., computer engineer, born 1928; won Bridge Week Masters Pairs 1958, Knockout Teams 1962, Mixed Teams 1966, Pacific Southwest Open pairs 1958, Rocky Mountain Open Pairs 1958, All-Western Knockout Teams 1973.

MELCHIOR, Edward F., of St. Louis, Mo., accountant, born 1909; won Mississippi Valley Open Teams 1957, 1960, Mixed Pairs 1967, Open Teams 1969, Central States Men's Pairs 1953.

MELO, Manuel Fontes Pereira de, of Estoril, Portugal, born 1921; represented Portugal European Championships 1966, 1967, 1974; national wins include Open Teams six times, Open Pairs five times.

MELTON, Dr. Robert A., of Wilmington, N.C., pediatrician, born 1930; won Mid-Atlantic Open Teams 1962, 1971, Mixed pairs 1966.

MENESIS, Enrique de, of Madrid, Spain, bridge writer and tournament organizer, born 1893; organizer of many international tournaments. Editor of Spanish bridge magazine; member of IBPA; bridge columnist for *Blanco y Negro.*

MERBLUM, Franklin P., of Hartford, Conn., student, born 1949; won Fall Nat'l secondary Swiss Teams 1972, New England Masters Teams 1968, Men's Pairs 1968.

MERCER, Mrs. Charles D., of Coronado, Calif.; won Upper New York Open Pairs 1956, Women's Pairs 1954, Canadian-American Women's Pairs 1955.

MEREDITH, Adam (1913–76), of New York, N.Y., formerly of London. One of the brilliant players of the world; noted for his skill in dummy play, especially in making "unmakable" contracts, and for unconventional bidding maneuvers. These usually consist of tactical bids in unbiddable suits such as opening bids of one spade with a three-card suit. Semi-retired from tournament play since moving from London to New York City in 1957. World Champion 1955; European Champion 1949 and 1954; also represented Great Britain in European Championship 1955, 1957, and 1959; British wins include Gold Cup 1948, 1950, 1952, 1953, 1956; Masters Pairs 1953. US regional wins include Eastern States Masters Pairs 1960 and others; co-author of *Baron System of Contract Bridge.* See BIBLIOGRAPHY, E.

MERINO, Maria L., of Madrid, Spain; represented Spain World Pair Olympiad 1966, 1970, 1974; several national successes.

MERIWETHER, Virginia (Mrs. Robert L.), of Des Moines, Iowa, born 1917; won Spring Nat'l secondary Women's Pairs 1973, Mid-American–Canadian Open Pairs 1958, District 15 Masters Pairs 1967.

MERRILL, Jay, of Rochester, N.Y., student, born 1955; second Reisinger 1974; winner of several regional events including Upper New York State Knockout Teams 1974, Men's Swiss Teams 1973, Men's Pairs 1974; KING OF BRIDGE Award 1973.

MERRIMAN, Mrs. William, of Camillus, N.Y.; winner of several regional events including Canadian-American Open Pairs 1953, Upper New York State Masters Pairs 1970, Women's Swiss Teams 1974.

MERRY, Philip H., of Tulsa, Okla., tournament director, born 1924; won Mid-South Spring Open Teams 1957. ACBL National Tournament Director since 1963. Contributing Editor *Bridge Encyclopedia.* Chairman of the Conduct Deportment and Ethics Committee of the Professional Tournament Directors Association.

MERSKY, Essie, of St. Paul, Minn., born 1919; winner of many regional events including Gopher Masters Teams 1968, Masters Pairs 1968, 1970.

MESSER, Alan W., of Upper Montclair, N.J., actuary, born 1934; won Fall Nat'l Men's Teams 1960, Eastern States Knockout Teams 1967, Long Island Knockout Teams 1968. Pioneered the Recorder system in the Greater New York BA.

MEYER, Florence (Mrs. B. W.,), of La Canada, Calif., born 1915; won several regional titles including Bridge Week Mixed Team 1960, 1963, Mixed Pairs 1958, Masters Pairs 1962, Women's Pairs 1971; tied Los Angeles Winter Women's Pairs 1974.

MEYER, "Babe" (Mrs. Frank H.), of Virginia Beach, Va.; second Fall Nat'l Mixed Pairs 1948; won Mid-Atlantic Spring Women's Pairs 1964.

MEYER, Mrs. Monte F. (1919–74), of New Orleans, La.; second Winter Nat'l Women's Teams 1950, Fall Nat'l Women's Teams 1967; won Southeastern Open Pairs 1946. Treasurer of Louisiana BA.

MICHAELS, Charles (1884–1962), of New York, N.Y.; was active in promoting bridge among the younger group; introduced contract as a course of study at Queens College while a teacher there, later taught in the Manhasset and Great Neck high schools, stimulating the juvenile interest in an unusual scientific manner. Founder of Barclay Bridge Supplies, Inc. See BIBLIOGRAPHY, E.

MICHAELS, Michael N. (1924–1966), of Miami Beach, Fla., bridge writer and lecturer; one of the leading players of the Southeast; won Marcus 1953; second Spingold 1959, Fall Nat'l Open Pairs 1960, Spring Nat'l Open Pairs 1962; won Missouri Valley Mixed Pairs 1959, Florida Open Pairs 1962, Southeastern Open Teams 1966. Inventor of MICHAELS CUE-BID, and long-time associate of Charles Goren in various journalistic enterprises.

MICHAELS, Mrs. Terry, of Washington, D.C., bridge teacher and tournament director, born 1927; one of the leading East Coast women players; won Nat'l Mixed Team 1955, Spring Nat'l Women's Teams 1963, 1965, 1973, Women's Pairs 1967; second Nat'l Mixed Teams 1963, Fall Nat'l Women's Teams 1961, 1962, 1963, 1969, Women's Pairs 1957, 1963; winner of many regional titles including Keystone Mixed Pairs 1959, Women's Pairs 1973, New York–New Jersey Open Teams 1960, Mid-Atlantic Spring Masters Pairs 1956, District 5 Women's Pairs 1966.

MICHAUD, Gerald L., of Wichita, Kan., attorney, born 1929; one of the leading players of the Middle West; International Team alternate 1963; won Summer Nat'l Life Masters Pairs 1974, Fall Nat'l Life Master Men's Pairs 1974; second Spingold 1962, Spring Nat'l Men's Teams 1962; winner of many regional championships including Rocky Mountain Open Teams 1953, Mid-American–Canadian Open Teams 1959, Open Pairs 1964, Missouri Valley Knockout Teams 1971, Open Teams 1973; Intercollegiate Champion 1951. President Kansas State BL 1960–61.

MICHELL, Jean, of Orinda, Calif., born 1925; winner of several regional events including Golden Gate Women's Pairs 1972.

MILES, Marshall, of San Bernardino, Calif., lawyer and bridge writer, born 1926; one of the leading American players; represented US World Pairs Olympiad 1962; won Fishbein 1961; won Spingold 1961, 1962, Marcus 1960, Chicago 1962, Life Masters Pairs 1961; second Vanderbilt 1961, Fall Nat'l Open Pairs 1962, Open Teams 1965, Men's Pairs 1962, Spring Nat'l Men's Pairs 1972; regional successes include Bridge Week Knockout Team 1958, 1959, 1972, 1974, Open Team 1957, 1961, Open Pairs 1953, 1958, Golden State Open Pairs 1966. Writings include *How to Win at Duplicate Bridge, All 52 Cards, Marshall Miles Teaches Logical Bridge,* and many articles for *The Bridge World, American Bridge Digest,* and the ACBL *Bulletin.* Contributing Editor *Bridge Encyclopedia.* See BIBLIOGRAPHY, F.

MILES, R. L., Jr. ("Skinny"), of Virginia Beach, Va., investment executive, born 1907; one of the leading American bridge personalities; npc North America World Championship team 1957 and US World Olympiad Team 1960; won Mid-Atlantic Fall Open Teams 1956, 1964, Spring Men's Teams 1956, Winter Open Teams 1965. President ACBL 1950, 1956, and member of many of its administrative committees for nearly two decades. Honorary member and former President of Mid-Atlantic Conference. See MILES TROPHY.

MILLER, Arthur M., of Beverly Hills, Calif., manufacturer and importer, born 1924; second Vanderbilt 1956, Chicago 1958; won Southern Conference Masters Pairs 1957, Southeastern Men's Pairs 1955.

MILLER, Bernard A., of Waltham, Mass., attorney, born 1940; won Summer Nat'l secondary Spingold Consolation 1972, Spring Nat'l secondary Men's Swiss Teams 1973; winner of several regional titles including New England Knockout Teams 1973, Men's Pairs 1970.

MILLER, Charles, of Houston, Tex., investment analyst, won Fall Nat'l Men's Teams 1964, Texas Spring Men's Pairs 1959, 1967, Mid-South Summer Mixed Pairs 1965, Southern Spring Men's Pairs 1965.

MILLER, Harvey H., Jr., of Chicago, Ill., real estate broker, born 1929; won several regional events including Midwest Fall Open Pairs 1964, Central States Knockout Teams 1974.

MILLER, Joseph P., of Denver, Colo.; winner of several regional events including Rocky Mountain Knockout Teams 1969.

MILLER, Martin E., of San Jose, Calif., rehabilitation counselor, born 1937; winner of several regional events including Central California Knockout Teams 1972, 1973.

MILLER, Mrs. Patricia, of St. Petersburg, Fla., bridge director, born 1910; won Florida Women's Pairs 1959; second Mid-Atlantic Spring Open Teams 1957. Founder of Northwest Ohio Unit.

MILLER, Portia (Mrs. William C.), of Pittsburgh, Pa.; won several regional events including Midwest Spring Open Team 1962, All-American Mixed Pairs 1963, 1973.

MILLER, Richard A., of York, Pa., stockbroker, bridge columnist of the *National Observer*, born 1911; one of the early exponents of the point-count method of evaluation; wrote *Point Count Bidding*, 1947, the first application of point-count to suit bid-

ding, and *It's a Bidder's Game*, 1955. Author of *Bridge Brilliance and Blunders*. Member National Board of Governors; former President Keystone Conference. See BIBLIOGRAPHY, C, H.

MILLERD, James A., of Dana Point, Calif., club manager, born 1927; won Leventritt Pairs 1955, Bridge Week Open Teams 1957, Mid-American–Canadian Open Pairs 1955.

MILLERD, John N., of Fountain Valley, Calif., actuary, born 1929; won Leventritt Trophy Summer Nat'l 1955, Bridge Week Open Teams 1957.

MILLION, Ruth (Mrs. C. E.), of Union City, Calif.; won Nat'l Mixed Team 1951, Mixed Pairs 1956; Hawaiian Master Pairs 1955.

MILLWARD, C. J., of Kitwe, Zambia, solicitor, born 1925; a leading player in Central Africa; won Zambia Open Pairs 1959, 1962, 1963, Open Teams 1961, 1962, 1964, Southern Rhodesia Open Pairs 1963, 1964, Open Teams 1964, Central Africa Open Teams 1960, 1962; second in seven other major championships. Vice-Chairman Central Africa Bridge Association.

MILNES, Eric Charles, of Bradford, Yorks, England, customs and excise officer, born 1912; won English Bridge Union Mixed Teams twice, Northern Pairs Championships twice. Editor of the *Bridge Magazine* since 1966. Co-author, *Improve Your Dummy Play*, and *Bridge Hands for the Connoisseur* (See BIBLIOGRAPHY, H).

MITCHELL, George, of Bellaire, Ohio, accountant, born 1928; won several regional events including All-American Open Pairs 1960, Great Lakes Open Teams 1962, District 5 Open Teams 1970.

MITCHELL, Jacqui (Mrs. Victor), of New York, N.Y., statistician, bridge teacher, born 1936; one of the outstanding American women players; second World Olympiad Mixed Teams 1974, World Olympiad Mixed Pairs 1974, represented United States World Women's Team Olympiad 1972; won Spring Nat'l Women's Teams 1965, 1970, 1974, 1975, Women's Pairs 1971, 1975, second Women's Teams 1973, Women's Pairs 1962, 1970, 1974; won Fall Nat'l secondary Swiss Teams 1973; winner of many regional championships including Eastern States Knockout Teams 1962, 1963, 1964, Mid-Atlantic Open Teams 1972. Won New York Player of the Year Award 1958 in her second year of tournament play.

MITCHELL, John T., of Chicago, Ill., known as the "Father of Duplicate Whist," and author of the first book on the subject, *Duplicate Whist* (1892). He invented many schedules for individual, pair, and team contests, notably the MITCHELL MOVEMENT. He helped to adapt the match-point scoring, used whist for the purposes of duplicate auction, and was a director of the American Whist League. See also HISTORY OF BRIDGE.

MITCHELL, Leslie, of Glasgow, Scotland, manufacturer's agent, born 1907; represented Scotland in the CAMROSE TROPHY on many occasions, including the unique Scottish victory in 1964. National titles include Open Teams seven times.

MITCHELL, Victor, of New York, N.Y., bridge teacher, born 1923; one of the outstanding American players; second World Olympiad Open Teams 1964, Mixed Teams 1974, represented US World Team Olympiad 1960; won Spingold 1956, 1959, Nat'l Men's Teams 1962, 1963, Nat'l Men's Pairs 1962, Summer Nat'l Life Masters Pairs 1965; second Chicago 1955, Vanderbilt 1969, Spingold 1969, Life Masters Pairs 1954, 1955, Nat'l Men's Pairs 1955, Spring Nat'l Men's Teams 1965, Fall Nat'l Life Master Men's Pairs 1965; many regional wins include Eastern States Knockout Teams 1955, 1962, 1963, 1964, Open Pairs 1958, Masters Pairs 1966, Southeastern Men's Teams 1973.

MITTELMAN, George, of Downsview, Ont.; winner of several regional events including Canadian Nat'l Knockout Teams 1973, Fleur-de-Lys Knockout Teams 1973.

MIZROCH, Dr. R., of Johannesburg, South Africa, dental surgeon, born 1923; npc South African Team World Olympiad 1964, Women's Olympiad Team 1968; member Executive Council World Bridge Federation. Bridge correspondent, Argus Group, South African newspapers.

MIZUTANI, Eizo, of Tokyo, Japan, author and director, born 1933; represented Japan Far East Championships 1962, 1965; won Knockout Teams five times, Round Robin Teams three times, Teams-of-Four twice. Executive Secretary of the Japan Contract Bridge League; co-author of *Contract Bridge Nyumon* and *Contract Bridge no Subete.*

MOELLER, Donald A., of Dayton, Ohio, banking executive and CPA, born 1926; ACBL Treasurer 1975; ACBL Director since 1973. First President of District 11.

MOFFATT, Mrs. James, of San Bernardino, Calif., born 1911; won Nat'l Mixed Team 1952; regional wins include Bridge Week Open Pairs 1953.

MOGAL, Sol, of New York, N.Y., importer; won Marcus 1951, Chicago 1949, Spingold 1946, 1949,

Fall Nat'l Men's Pairs 1947, Fall Nat'l Men's Teams 1947, 1948, 1954, second Spingold 1952; won Eastern States Knockout Teams 1952.

MOHAN, John A., of Beverly Hills, Calif., bridge professional, born 1939; one of the leading American players; won Vanderbilt 1975, Fall Nat'l Mixed Pairs 1972, Summer Nat'l secondary Swiss Teams 1972, secondary Men's Pairs 1972; winner of numerous regional championships including Missouri Valley Knockout Teams 1970, Pacific Southwest Knockout Teams 1972, Inland Empire Knockout Teams 1973.

MOHR, Mark D., of Roselle Park, N.J., teacher; won Nat'l Senior & Advanced Senior Masters Pairs 1961, Fun City Knockout Teams 1970, Tri-State Open Teams 1967, Keystone Open Teams 1968; member New York Intercity Team 1968. President, New Jersey Bridge League 1969–70; Editor *The Declarer* 1966–68.

MOELLER, Steffen Steen, of Copenhagen, Denmark, born 1939; represented Denmark World Team Olympiad 1968, 1972; European Championships 1966, 1969, 1970, 1971, 1974, 1975; captain, 1967; national titles include Danish Open Pairs 1974, Open Teams 1970, 1971, 1975. Bridge Editor *Berlingske Tidende* from 1970. Co-author *Systems and Conventions* and *Bid Modern, Play Modern Bridge.* Member executive committee IBPA.

MOLLO, VICTOR, of London, journalist, born 1909; national wins include Open Teams. Former bridge columnist of *London Evening Standard.* Books on bridge include *Streamlined Bridge: or Bidding Without Tears, Card Play Technique, Bridge for Beginners, Bridge Psychology, Bridge with a Master, Bridge: Modern Bidding, Success at Bridge, Bridge in the Menagerie, Bridge in the Fourth Dimension, The Bridge Immortals,* and *How Good Is Your Bridge?* See BIBLIOGRAPHY, C, D, E, L. Contributing Editor *Bridge Encyclopedia.*

MONK, Charles, of Brussels, Belgium, association manager and bridge columnist, born 1926; represented Belgium World Team Olympiad 1960, 1964, 1968, World Pair Olympiad 1962, 1968, European Championships 1961, 1965; national wins include Open Teams (three times), Mixed Teams, Open Pairs, Master Pairs, Mixed Pairs. Books include *Système Complet des Enchères Modernes* (see BIBLIOGRAPHY, C).

MONTAIGU, Mrs. Marie de, of Paris, born 1901; European Women's Team Champion 1939, 1953, 1954 (captain in 1953); European Women's Pair Champion 1935; represented France on other occasions, and won many national championships; retired from tournament bridge in 1956.

MONTGOMERY, Mrs. Gwen S., of Deerfield Beach, Fla., language teacher, born 1922; won Marcus 1954, Eastern States Mixed Teams 1960, Mixed Pairs 1958. Executive Secretary of New Jersey BA 1954–60, New York–New Jersey Bridge Conference 1956–59.

MORAN, Brian J., of Virginia Beach, Va., Associate National Tournament Director, born 1938; winner of several regional events including Mid-Atlantic Knockout Teams 1973, 1974. President Virginia State BA since 1972.

MORAN, John H., of Port Hueneme, Calif., bridge instructor and cruise director, born 1909; represented North America in World Championships 1955; won Spingold 1954, Blue Ribbon 1965, Marcus 1957; second Chicago 1958, Fall Nat'l Men's Team 1953, Fall Nat'l Mixed Pairs 1954; won Bridge Week Knockout Team 1956, Keystone Conference Open Teams 1954, Pacific Southwest Mixed Pairs 1949, Rocky Mountain Masters Pairs 1951, Open Pairs 1951, Men's Pairs 1962, Mixed Pairs 1956, Texas Open Teams, Open Pairs 1953, Northern Rocky Mountain Open Teams, Open Pairs 1965, Oregon Trail Knockout Teams 1967.

MORCOS, Mrs. Josephine, of Cairo, Egypt, born 1923; World Women's Team Champion 1960; represented Egypt World Women's Team Olympiad 1964; national wins include Mixed Pairs 1963.

MORDECAI, Daniel, of Denver, Colo., business consultant, born 1932; winner of many regional championships including Rocky Mountain Knockout Teams 1968, Open Teams 1961, 1969, Open Pairs 1974.

MOREHEAD, Albert H(odges) (1909–1966), of New York, N.Y., bridge author, writer and editor in general fields, born in Georgia. He was employed as a writer by E. Culbertson in 1932 and became technical editor of *The Bridge World* magazine in 1933, editor in 1934, and general manager of all Culbertson enterprises in 1934. He was publisher of *The Bridge World* 1943–46, and after 1947 the senior editor. He was chief editor of all Culbertson bridge books after 1933. He was an officer and director of the Bridge World, Inc., 1933–63; Kem Plastic Playing Cards, 1934–38; Crockford's Clubs of New York and Chicago, 1933–39; United States Bridge Association, 1933–38, and many others; after the merger of USBA and ABL in 1937, he became a Governor of ACBL, was President 1943, Chairman of the Board 1943–45, and Honorary Member 1946. From 1935 to the end of 1963 Morehead was bridge editor of the *New York Times*. His many books on games include six different "Hoyle" books. He was an original member of the National Laws Commission, and was in charge of production of the laws of 1943, 1948, 1949, and 1963. He was on the team that won the SCHWAB CUP in 1934, and he won or placed high in several national and regional tournaments before

retiring from tournament play at the end of 1935. Chief Editor *Encyclopedia of Bridge*, 1935, and Chairman, Editorial Advisory Board *Bridge Encyclopedia*. His bridge books include *Bridge the Expert Way, Contract Bridge Summary, Morehead on Bidding* (which won the International Bridge Press Association "Book of the Year" award in 1966), and many others. See BIBLIOGRAPHY, C, E.

MORENO, Mario, of Manila, Philippines, businessman, born 1910; Far East Open Pair Champion 1962, represented Philippines Far East Championships 1961, 1963, 1964; member Philippine Interport Team 1957–61; President Philippine Contract Bridge League 1964–65; Vice-President 1961–63.

MORRIS, Robert F., of Cincinnati, Ohio, advertising agency executive, born 1922; second Blue Ribbon 1969; regional wins include Midwest Spring Mixed Pairs 1956, All-American Open Teams 1968.

MORRIS, Zelda Melba, of Tokoroa, New Zealand, born 1915; represented New Zealand Far East Championships 1971, 1972, 1973, WBF Zone 7 Women's Teams six times.

MORSE, Dan, of Houston, Tex., pharmacist, born 1938; one of the leading players in the Southwest; won Fall Nat'l Mixed Pairs 1964, second Spingold 1967; won Spring Nat'l secondary Men's Pairs 1971, secondary Men's Swiss Teams 1972; winner of many regional titles including Southeastern Masters Pairs 1963, Open Teams 1969, 1970, Texas Masters Pairs 1965, Knockout Teams 1968, Men's Pairs 1967.

MORSE, Mrs. Jo, of Silver Spring, Md., born 1932; one of the leading women players of the East Coast; won World Olympiad Mixed Teams 1974; represented US World Women's Pair Olympiad 1974; won Spring Nat'l Women's Teams 1973, second Summer Nat'l Mixed Teams 1973; winner of many regional events including Mid-Atlantic Knockout Teams 1973, Keystone Masters Pairs 1970, 1971.

MOSHER, Robert, of Boston, Mass., mathematician, born 1937; won New England Masters Teams and Pairs 1962, Midwest Fall Open Teams 1965.

MOSS, Gail (Mrs. Michael), of New York, N.Y., bridge teacher; one of the leading American women players; second World Olympiad Mixed Teams 1972, represented US World Olympiad Women's Pairs 1974; won Fall Nat'l Women's Teams 1968, 1969, Summer Nat'l Masters Mixed Teams 1967, 1972, Spring Nat'l Women's Teams 1971, 1974, 1975, Women's Pairs 1975, second Women's Teams 1973, Women's Pairs 1970, 1972, 1974, Fall Nat'l Women's Teams 1967, won Spring Nat'l secondary Women's Teams 1973, Summer Nat'l secondary Mixed Teams 1970; winner of many regional championships including New England Masters Teams 1965, Mixed Teams 1966, Mixed Pairs 1971.

MOSS, Mary (Mrs. John), of London, born 1920; won World Women's Team Olympiad 1964, European Women's Championship 1963; also represented Great Britain World Women's Pair Olympiad 1962; national wins include Mixed Pairs.

MOSS, Michael, of New York, N.Y., stockbroker, born 1935; second World Olympiad Mixed Teams 1972, represented US World Pair Olympiad 1974; won Summer Nat'l Life Masters Pairs 1970, Master Mixed Teams 1967, 1972, secondary Mixed Teams 1970, secondary Mixed Pairs 1965; second Spring Nat'l Men's Pairs; winner of numerous regional championships including Eastern States Knockout Teams 1965, Southeastern Knockout Teams 1970, Men's Pairs 1965, 1972.

MOSS, Milton, of Tiburon, Calif., manufacturer's representative, born 1901; a prominent player, especially in the early years of contract; won Vanderbilt 1952, 1954; second Fall Nat'l Open Pairs 1943, Fall Nat'l Men's Team 1950; won Bridge Week Knockout Team 1962.

MOTT-SMITH, Geoffrey (1902–1960), of New York, N.Y., editor and cryptographer. Director and Hand-Setter of the Intercollegiate Par Contest from its inception. Director the US State Department World-Wide tournament. Games consultant for the American Playing Card Manufacturers Association. Collaborator in many Hoyles, and a frequent contributor to *The Bridge World*.

MOUAT, Andrew J., Wilmette, Ill., tournament director and whist teacher, born 1870. The leading personality in whist organization during the lifetime of the American Whist League. He was its chief tournament director for over forty years, serving as its president, secretary, and tournament committee chairman. Editor of *Whist Review* 1915–19; Honorary Member ACBL 1948.

MOULIA, Simone (1913–1970), of Brussels, Belgium, typewriter saleswoman; one of the leading European women players; represented Belgium World Women's Team Olympiad 1964; second European Women's Team 1950, 1955, 1956, 1959; represented Belgium on several other occasions; third Mixed Team event Cannes 1962; won fifteen national titles in open, mixed, and women's events.

MOUSER, Hal, of Woodmere, Ohio; winner of several regional events including Midwest Knockout Teams 1972.

MOUSER, William S. (1912–1963), speech therapist, and bridge columnist of Detroit, Mich., presumed dead when his private plane was lost over Lake Erie. Won All-American Open Team 1959. ACBL Director 1963, and served both as President and Treasurer of Michigan BA. See MOUSER TROPHY.

MOWRY, Oris, of Longview, Wash., school counselor; winner of several regional titles including Klondike Open Pairs 1972, Puget Sound Open Teams 1972.

MOYSE, Alphonse, Jr. (1898–1973), publisher and editor of *The Bridge World* from 1956 to 1966, bridge author and champion player. He was born in Summit, Miss., but spent most of his boyhood in Cincinnati, and then settled in New York City. When the crash of 1929 ended his career as a stockbroker, he adopted bridge as a profession. In 1934 he joined the organization of E. Culbertson, partly as an associate editor of *The Bridge World* but chiefly as writer of syndicated newspaper articles that were published under the names of Ely and Josephine Culbertson. From that time until 1956 he wrote two bridge columns each day, a total of more than 20,000, in addition to many magazine articles and editorial work on Culbertson books. Moyse was managing editor of *The Bridge World* 1939–43, and was publisher and chief editor 1946–56. On the death of Culberton in 1955 he bought the Bridge World, Inc., from the Culbertson estate, and was president and general manager of it until 1963 when he sold it to McCall Corp., remaining as publisher and editor of the magazine until his retirement in 1966. Perhaps Moyse's most admired writings are humorous articles about the bridge exploits of his wife, Jackie Moyse, whom he depicts as the typical member of ladies' luncheon-club bridge games. As an editor he made *The Bridge World* the most influential magazine in technical aspects of the game, being first to publish such historic suggestions as the Stayman convention, Roth-Stone and Kaplan-Sheinwold systems, Lavinthal suit-preference signals, Goren point-count, unusual no trump, and many others. Though a comparatively infrequent contestant in tournaments, he won Fall Nat'l Men's Teams 1949, Spring Nat'l Men's Team 1962; second Fall Nat'l Open Pairs 1938, Spring Nat'l Men's Pairs 1963; regional wins include Eastern States Open Pairs 1942. Original member Editorial Advisory Board *Bridge Encyclopedia*. See BIBLIOGRAPHY, G.

MUELLER, Jane (Mrs. A. H., formerly Mrs. Charles Hall), of Cincinnati, Ohio, clerical executive; represented US Women's Pairs World Olympiad 1962; won Spring Nat'l Women's Pairs 1960, Midwest Spring Open Teams 1948, 1949, Mixed Pairs 1957, Southwestern Women's Teams 1970, and others.

MUHSAM, Gertrude (Mrs. Rudolf), of New York, N.Y., assistant manager Cavendish Club of New York City, born 1909 in Austria; European Women's Team Champion 1935, 1936, 1937, captain 1935–37.

MUNAFO, Paul, of Huntsville, Ala., engineer, born 1939; winner of several regional events including Mid-South Masters Pairs 1966, 1969, Mid-South Men's Pairs 1973.

MUNN, Dorothy (Mrs. Charles), of San Francisco, Calif., born 1913; regional wins include Southeastern Mixed Pairs and Masters Pairs 1963, Bridge Week Mixed Teams 1965, Pacific Southwest Mixed Pairs 1966.

MURDOCH, Elinor, of Birmingham, Ala., bridge teacher, born 1901; won Nat'l Masters Individual 1934, second 1933; won Nat'l Mixed Teams 1933, Fall Nat'l Women's Pairs 1931, second 1930, Fall Nat'l Mixed Pairs 1931; won Nat'l Golder Pairs 1958, Southern Fall Women's Pairs 1964, Mexican Nat'l Masters Pairs 1965. Former president Alabama BA.

MURPHY, James A., of Chesapeake, Va., computer specialist; won Fall Nat'l secondary Masters Pairs 1972; winner of several regional events including Mid-Atlantic Knockout Teams (twice).

MURPHY, John Terence, of Calgary, Alta., locomotive engineer, born 1920; won Canadian Prairie Open Teams 1965. Vice-President Calgary Unit 1964–65. President Canadian BF since 1974.

MURRAY, David S., of Alexandria, Va., statistician, born 1921; second Summer Nat'l Mixed Team 1954; regional wins include Mid-Atlantic Fall Men's Pairs 1953, 1959.

MURRAY, Eric Rutherford, of Toronto, Ont., barrister and solicitor, born 1928; one of the world's outstanding bridge players and personalities; represented North America World Championships 1962, 1966, 1967, and Canada World Team Olympiad 1960, 1964, 1968, World Olympiad Open Pairs 1970; won International Team Trials 1966, third 1965; won Vanderbilt 1961, 1970, Spingold 1964, 1965, 1968, Marcus 1959, Fall Nat'l Life Masters Men's Pairs 1963, Men's Teams 1962, Mixed Pairs 1963, Summer Nat'l Life Masters Pairs 1969, Mixed Teams 1956, 1962, Men's Pairs 1954, 1955, Non-Masters Pairs 1949; second Blue Ribbon 1969, Reisinger 1969, 1972, Spring Nat'l Men's Pairs 1965, Marcus 1963, Chicago 1961, Summer Nat'l Mixed Teams 1954; regional successes include Canadian-American Open Pairs 1962, Men's Pairs 1960, Mixed Pairs 1959, 1961, Canadian Nat'l Open Teams 1959, 1961, 1965, 1967, Open Pairs 1957, 1958, 1962, Men's Pairs 1963, 1970. Organizing Chairman Summer Nat'ls 1964. Former President Eastern Canadian Bridge Conference and Ontario Unit ACBL, Director ACBL District 2. Devised MURRAY TWO-DIAMOND convention, co-author of DRURY convention. Contributing Editor *Bridge Encyclopedia*.

MURRAY, Laidlaw, of Swansea, Wales, born 1893; one of the founders of the Welsh Bridge Union. First Secretary of the Western Area; President of the WBU 1952; member of the Council since its inception. Represented Wales in many international competitions.

MURTINHO, Joao, of Rio de Janeiro, Brazil; chief organizer of 1969 Bermuda Bowl, first World Championship held in Brazil.

MUSUMECI, Lt. Col. Joseph, of Dallas, Tex., bridge teacher and writer, born 1921; won Texas Conference Open Teams 1955, 1961. Former President San Antonio BL; coach ACES TEAM.

MYERS, Mrs. Anne, of Winnipeg, Man., born 1912; won Mid-American–Canadian Masters Pairs and Women's Pairs 1962. Active in teaching bridge to disabled players.

MYRANS, Colette (Mrs. Samuel E.), of Deurle, Belgium, automobile parts saleswoman, born 1915; represented Belgium World Women's Team Olympiad 1964; second European Women's Championships 1955, 1956, 1959, and represented Belgium on several other occasions; national titles include Mixed Team 1955, 1956, 1961, second 1947, 1957, Women's Pairs 1954, 1955, 1960, 1963, Mixed Pairs 1958, second 1957.

N

NAGUIB, Mrs. Suzanne, of Cairo, Egypt, born 1921; World Women's Team Champion 1960; represented Egypt World Women's Team Olympiad 1964; national wins include Mixed Pairs 1953, Inter-Club 1963.

NAGY, Edward A., of San Francisco, Calif., salesman; winner of several regional events including California Capitol Knockout Teams 1971, Open Teams 1972.

NAGY, Zoltan, of Canberra, Australia, public servant; WBF Zone 7 Champion 1974; national successes include Interstate Teams 1970, 1974.

NAIL, Betty (Mrs. G. R., formerly Mrs. Betty Harding), of Houston, Tex., born 1923; won Spring Nat'l Women's Pairs 1958; third Fall Nat'l Women's Team 1958; Mississippi Valley Open Team 1958, Mixed Pairs 1962, Missouri Valley Women's Pairs 1957, South Texas Mixed Pairs 1974.

NAIL, G. Robert, of Houston, Tex., bridge teacher and writer, born 1925; one of the most successful American bridge players of the postwar period; represented North America World Championship 1962, 1963; won International Trials 1962, second 1961; won Fall Nat'l Men's Teams 1965, Vanderbilt 1967, Summer Nat'l Life Masters Pairs 1974, Fall Nat'l Life Master Men's Pairs 1974; second Chicago 1960, Spingold 1953, 1962, Fall Nat'l Men's Team 1961, Men's Pairs 1949, Spring Nat'l Men's Team 1964; regional wins include Mississippi Valley Open Team 1958, Mixed Pairs 1962, Missouri Valley Men's Pairs 1961, Masters Pairs 1968, 1971, Knockout Teams 1971, Open Pairs 1970, Mexican Nat'l Open Teams 1966, 1971. Originator of the BIG DIAMOND SYSTEM. Co-author of *Winning Duplicate, How to Play the Hand,* and *Revolution in Bridge.* (See BIBLIOGRAPHY, C, D.) See also NUISANCE BID.

NANDHABIWAT, Somboon, of Bangkok, Thailand, banker, born 1923; represented Thailand World Championships 1966, 1967, 1968, captain Thailand team World Olympiad 1964, Far East Champion 1961, 1963, 1966; national successes include all major events 1951–61. Honorary treasurer for the Bridge Association of Thailand 1951–61, 1967–74. Originator of the BANGKOK CLUB system.

NASSIF, Gabriel, of Cairo, Egypt, lawyer, born 1908; represented Egypt European Championships 1958; National Open Team Championships 1957, 1958, 1959, 1962, 1963.

NEDHAM, Shirley M., of Orinda, Calif., college instructor; winner of several regional events including Golden Gate Master Teams 1973.

NEEDHAM, Richard E., of Greenville, Pa., bridge writer and tournament organizer, died 1956. One of the most active tournament promoters for many years, active in western Pennslyvania, Ohio, West Virginia, and upstate New York. His most famous tournament was that at Conneaut Lake, Pa., which he managed from its foundation in 1927 until 1955. Writings included *Auction Bridge Sidelights,* 1927, and *Tournament Tactics at Contract Bridge,* 1934. ABL Director.

NEIGER, Eugene, of New York, N.Y., manufacturer; one of the leading East Coast players; won Spingold 1971, Vanderbilt 1972; winner of many regional championships including Long Island Knockout Teams 1972, California Capital Knockout Teams 1974. See PRECISION TEAM.

NEIL, G. Eloise (Mrs. Edmund), of Columbus, Ohio, bridge columnist and teacher, born 1892; won Spring Nat'l Women's Team 1950, second 1955; regional wins include All-American Open Teams

1943, Midwest Spring Women's Pairs 1965, District 11 Women's Pairs 1969. ACBL Secretary 1950, member of ACBL Goodwill Committee; former President Central Ohio BA.

NEILSON, Shirley (Mrs. Al), of Willowdale, Ont., travel agent and Associate National Tournament Director, born 1925; won All-American Mixed Pairs 1961, Canadian Nat'l Women's Pairs 1961; tied Upper New York State Women's Swiss Teams 1971.

NELSON, John A., of Omaha, Neb., electrical engineer, born 1926; won Nat'l Comm. & Ind. Teams 1959, Mid-American–Canadian Masters Pairs 1964.

NELSON, Morton, of New Orleans, La.; regional wins include District 15 Knockout Teams 1969.

NEUFELD, Richard, of Haifa, Israel, merchant, born 1910; represented Israel World Team Olympiad 1964; national successes include Open Team and Open Pairs. National captain 1960–63.

NEUMAN, Cyrus, of Miami, Fla., attorney, born 1921; won Spingold 1958, Nat'l Non-Masters Pairs 1951; second Spingold 1954; won Southeastern Open Pairs 1956, 1957, Men's Pairs 1961, Men's Team 1956, Open Team 1959.

NEVINS, Emilie (Mrs. Marshall), of Ft. Lauderdale, Fla.; won Summer Nat'l Senior and Advanced Senior Masters Pairs 1956, secondary Swiss Teams 1974; regional wins include Puerto Rico Masters Pairs 1973.

NEWBILL, Martha (Mrs. Charles M.), of Jacksonville Beach, Fla., bridge teacher, born 1908; won Mississippi Valley Women's Pairs 1952 and 1953, Mid-South Women's Pairs 1958, and many other tournament successes.

NEWMAN, Bert, of Detroit, Mich.; second Summer Nat'l Senior and Advanced Senior Master Pairs 1971; regional wins include Canadian Nat'l Knockout Teams 1974.

NEWMAN, Louis, of Los Angeles, Calif., liquor store proprietor; won Chicago 1940, second 1946; won Bridge Week Masters Pairs 1954.

NEWMAN, Lois (Mrs. Louis), of Los Angeles, Calif., born 1907; won Bridge Week Mixed Team 1962, Open Pairs 1961, Masters Pairs 1954, All-Western Women's Pairs 1966, Golden State Mixed Pairs 1967, 1968.

NEWTON, Jessie, of Wales; represented Wales in five Camrose Cup matches and numerous Lady Milne matches; national successes include two Open Team championships. Secretary British BL since 1966; President Welsh BU 1974–75.

NEXON, Baron Robert de (1892–1967), of Paris, France, perfume company president, racer and breeder of horses; one of the great figures in the world of international bridge; npc French Team World Olympiad 1960, 1964; European Champion 1935; and represented France World Championships 1935 against the FOUR ACES; npc European Championships 1953, 1955, 1962, runners-up 1954, 1956, 1959, 1961; winner of French Open Teams, Pairs, and many other events. President World Bridge Federation 1958–64, President Emeritus of World Bridge Federation 1964–67, and of European Bridge League 1965–67. President French Bridge Federation 1941–65, President European Bridge League 1950–65. Co-author with Pierre Albarran, in 1935, *Notre Méthode de bridge,* basis of the point-count system of today; also *Le Bridge pour tous, Le Memento de bridge* and *Souvenirs et secrets.*

NICKELL, Frank T. ("Nick"), of Raleigh, N.C., accountant; winner of many regional events including Mid-Atlantic Knockout Teams 1973, 1974, Open Teams 1968.

NICKLASSON, David, of San Diego, Calif., civil servant, born 1943; tied Summer Nat'l secondary Swiss Teams 1971, winner of several regional championships including Iowa Open Teams 1971, Open Pairs 1971.

NIEBERDING, Joseph H., of Chicago Heights, Ill., manufacturer's agent, born 1908; regional wins include Midwest Fall Masters Individual 1954, Mississippi Valley Men's Pairs 1968, Central States Men's Pairs 1974.

NIEDŹWIECKI, Henryk, of Warsaw, Poland, agricultural engineer, bridge writer, born 1899; represented Poland European Championships 1957; won Hungarian Balaton Bowl 1960, Czechoslovakian Open Teams 1965, Baltic Bowl 1967. National titles include Open Teams 1957, 1958, 1960, 1961, 1965, Open Pairs 1963, Individual 1963, 1966. Contributor to *Brydz.*

NIELSEN, Aksel J., of Copenhagen, Denmark, bridge writer, born 1900; national successes include Danish Teams and Pairs 1940. Author of several bridge books in Danish.

NIVER, Mabel (Mrs. F. J.), of Daytona Beach, Fla., bridge teacher and tournament director, born 1888; won Southeastern Open Teams 1957, Women's Teams 1962, Mixed Pairs 1953; former Director Florida Unit.

NOLAND, Helen ("Heitie," **Mrs. A. W.**), of Lake Charles, La., born 1920; won World Olympiad Mixed Teams 1972, second Spring Nat'l Women's Teams 1973; winner of several regional events including King Cotton Knockout Teams 1972, Lone Star Masters Pairs 1969, International City Women's Pairs 1974.

NORTH, Frederick L., of Hove, Sussex, England, bridge journalist; represented England in Camrose match vs. N. Ireland 1959, World Pairs Olympiad 1962, 1966. In 1957, swept the Torquay Congress by winning the Pre-Congress Pairs, Mixed Pairs, Master Pairs, Open Pairs, and Men's Teams. Co-author *Tiger Bridge.* See BIBLIOGRAPHY, E.

NORTON, Dorothea (Mrs. John F.), of Seattle, Wash., born 1925; won Northwest Open Teams 1964, 1965, Women's Pairs 1964, 1966.

NORWOOD, John W., Jr., of Greenville, S.C., insurance agent, born 1908; won Mid-Atlantic Summer Men's Pairs 1960, 1961, 1966, Open Teams 1961, Open Pairs 1964, Fall Masters Pairs 1962, Open Teams 1965. President ACBL 1967. ACBL Director 1961–67.

NOSZKA, Gloria (Mrs. Stanley), of Pittsburgh, Pa.; represented US World Women's Pair Olympiad 1970; won Spring Nat'l Women's Pairs 1969, secondary Mixed Pairs 1970; regional wins include Canadian Nat'l Open Teams 1971.

NOVAK, Mrs. Elmer, of Salem, Ill., born 1909; won Spring Nat'l Women's Teams 1962; regional successes include Champagne Open Pairs 1970. Member of National Goodwill and Membership Committees, Director St. Louis Unit.

NOVAK, Phyllis (Mrs. M. J.), of Seattle, Wash., geological assistant, born 1927; won Spring Nat'l Women's Pairs and Mixed Pairs 1958, Women's Teams 1962; winner of several regional events including Pacific Northwest Knockout Teams 1969, Northwest Open Teams 1964, 1965, Puget Sound Swiss Teams 1972.

NOWAK, Janusz, of Warsaw, Poland, born 1928; represented Poland European Championships 1966; won Polish Individual 1968; second Open Pairs 1967, Individual 1963.

NUGIT, Trudi, of Targana, Calif., born 1929; second Spring Nat'l Women's Teams 1974; regional successes include Mexican Nat'l Open Teams 1973.

NUPPONEN, Paavo, of Helsinki, bank accountant, born 1928; represented Finland in six European Championships and six Scandinavian; won five National Championships.

NUSINOFF, Alexander (1912–1966), of New York, N.Y., stockbroker; second Summer Nat'l Men's Pairs 1951; third Nat'l Senior Masters Individual 1952; won Canadian Nat'l Open Teams 1946.

O

OAKEY, Larry B., of Minneapolis, Min., auditor, born 1937; won Leventritt Pairs 1966; many regional successes include Calgary Knockout Teams 1973, Canadian Prairie Open Teams 1972, Open Pairs 1971, Men's Pairs 1970.

OAKIE, Donald A., of San Jose, Calif., bridge teacher, writer, professional player and consultant, born Donald Akira Aoki in Los Angeles, 1914; one of the leading American players and the first of Japanese descent to win the Bermuda Bowl; first ACBL member to become a Life Master with 300 red points. World Champion 1954; represented US World Olympiad 1960; Oeschger trophy winner 1959; won Spingold 1953, Chicago 1958; second Spring Nat'l Men's Pairs 1959. Numerous regional wins include Bridge Week Master Team 1952, Open Team 1937, 1938, 1958, 1959, Masters Pairs 1952, Open Pairs 1941, 1952, Knockout Teams 1965, Inland Empire Teams 1971, Desert Empire Knockout Teams 1972. Author and publisher of former *Monthly Bridge Letter* and a bridge correspondence course. ACBL President 1976; ACBL Director since 1967. Member Nat'l Laws Commission from 1967 and Chairman, 1975–; also member WBF Laws Commission; principal draftsman of revised American format of 1974 Laws of Duplicate; revised and rewrote *ACBL Handbook* 1973-4–5.

OAKLEY, RAY (1896–1973), of Sacramento, Calif., assistant city manager; ACBL National Tournament Director.

OAKS, Alan W., of Memphis, Tenn., Executive Secretary ACBL Charity Foundation, born 1938; won Oregon Trail Open Teams 1967, Pacific Northwest Open Pairs 1967.

ODDIE, T. H., of Little Rock, Ark., physicist; represented Australia World Olympiad 1960; various tournament successes in Australia 1933–60.

O'DOWD, John, of Hamilton, Ont., industrial engineer and bridge club owner; won Canadian National Open Team 1958, Knockout Teams 1968.

OGUST, Harold A., of New York, N.Y., plastics manufacturer and travel agent, born 1916; one of the most successful American bridge players; represented US World Championship 1957 and World Team Olympiad 1960; won Spingold 1956, 1960, Chicago 1957, 1963; second Spingold 1966, Chicago 1945, Vanderbilt 1955, 1959, 1962, Summer Nat'l Open Pairs 1943; won Western States Open Teams 1944.

Organizer of many Goren bridge cruises in his capacity as president of Travel-with-Goren and Goren International, Inc., which he founded. Originator of Ogust Rebids after WEAK TWO-BIDS.

OLIVIER, Réal, of Quebec, Que., railway mail clerk, born 1905; won Canadian-American Men's Pairs 1958, 1961. President Quebec, Que., Unit.

OLMEDO, Alejandro, of Buenos Aires, Argentina, solicitor, born 1902; South American Champion 1950, 1953, 1957; won Argentine Open Teams 1935, 1952, Open Pairs 1953, 1956.

O'LOUGHLIN, June (Mrs. Walter K.), of Towson, Md., secretary; won Mid-Atlantic Summer Women's Pairs 1962, Mixed Pairs 1968.

O'LOUGHLIN, Walter K., of Towson, Md., management consultant, born 1910; won Mid-Atlantic Summer Mixed Pairs 1968. President Maryland BA 1956, Director 1953, 1962; ACBL Director 1962–65, and since 1971. ACBL Treasurer 1973, 1974.

OLSEN, Arne, of Oslo, Norway, born 1939; represented Norway European Championships 1965, Scandinavian Championships 1964; Scandinavian Team champion 1965.

OLSEN, Jack, of Rollinsville, Colo., writer, born 1925; senior editor of *Sports Illustrated;* author of *The Mad World of Bridge;* co-author of *A New Approach to Bridge.* See BIBLIOGRAPHY, B.

OLSEN, Per, of Oslo, Norway, clerk, born 1941; represented Norway European Championships 1965, Scandinavian Championships 1964; won Norwegian Open Pairs 1965.

OLSZEWSKI, Andrzej, of Warsaw, Poland, born 1918; represented Poland European Championships 1962, 1966; won Polish Open Pairs 1963, Open Teams 1965.

O'MALIA, Bernard E. ("Barney"), of Hawthorne, Nev., industrialist; winner of several regional championships including Intermountain Knockout Teams 1969, Men's Pairs 1971, Pacific Southwest Knockout Teams 1969, Masters Pairs 1973.

ONORATI, Mario, of Caracas, Venezuela, business executive, born 1928; represented Venezuela World Team Olympiad 1960, 1964, 1968, World Championships 1966, 1967, South American Championships seven times; South American Champion 1963, 1965, 1966; national titles include Open Teams five times, Open Pairs, Mixed Teams.

OREFFICE, Paul F., of Coral Gables, Fla., chemical engineer, born 1927; won Spanish Open Pairs 1964, Southeastern Knockout Teams 1968, Florida Men's Pairs 1968.

O'REILLEY, Edward, of Kingston, Ont.; won Canadian-Atlantic Knockout Teams 1969, 1970, Open Teams 1970.

ORLETT, Paul V., of Kansas City, Mo., bridge club owner, born 1934; winner of several regional events including Missouri Valley Knockout Teams 1972, District 14 Masters Pairs 1969.

ORME, Maynard, of Seattle, Wash., real estate salesman, born 1905; won Northwest Open Team 1960, 1962, Open Pairs 1961, 1962, Mixed Pairs 1957, 1962.

ORTIZ, Jimmy (Ortiz-Patino, Jaime), of Geneva, Switzerland, company director, born 1928; represented Switzerland World Team Olympiad 1964, 1968, World Pair Olympiad 1962; fifth World Pair Olympiad 1961; represented Switzerland in European Championships 1955, 1956, 1959, 1961, 1962, 1963, 1965, 1967; national titles include Open Team 1953, 1956, 1959, 1961, Knockout Team 1955, 1956, 1960, 1962, 1963.

OSBORN, Florence (Mrs. Harold), of New Haven, Conn., bridge columnist and lecturer in the humanities; Bridge Editor of the New York *Herald Tribune* from 1936 until newspaper was discontinued in 1966, and previously of New York *American*. Writings include *How's Your Bridge Game?* and many magazine articles. Formerly conducted a bridge interview radio program, and has made many television appearances. Contributing Editor *Bridge Encyclopedia*. See BIBLIOGRAPHY, J.

OSELLA, Sergio, of Milan, Italy; npc Italian champions World Team Olympiad 1964, World Championships 1965, European Championships 1963, 1966.

OSHLAG, Richard J., of Memphis, Tenn., business and advertising manager ACBL Contract Bridge *Bulletin*, born 1945. Winner of several regional events including New York Winter Life Masters Pairs 1971, Mid-Atlantic Knockout Teams 1973, Mid-South Men's Pairs 1975.

ÖSTÖR, Dr. Ladislaus, of Munich, Germany, merchant, born 1904; represented Germany in European Championships 1954, 1957, 1959; national titles include Open Team six times, Open Pairs, and Individual.

OSTRICH, Dr. Nathan, of Lafayette, La., optometrist, born 1928; winner of several regional events including Mexican Nat'l Open Teams 1970, Men's Pairs 1969, Mixed Pairs 1971. Producer of TV series "Play Bridge with the Experts."

OSTROW, Albert A. (1910–1961), of Malverne, N.Y., was an authority on card games, and the author of numerous books, among them, *The Complete Card Player* and *The Bridge Player's Bedside Companion*. He was consultant on card games to the Association of American Playing Card Manufacturers 1960–61. See BIBLIOGRAPHY, B, K.

O'SULLIVAN, James de Courcy, of Brisbane, Australia, born 1924. Chairman WBF Zone 7 since 1973; President Australian BF since 1971.

OTSTOTT, Mrs. Herminia, of Rizal, Philippines, born 1926; represented Philippines Far East Women's Championship 1966, Hong Kong–Manila Interport tournament 1963; national titles include Women's Pairs 1957, 1958, Open Teams 1961, Mixed Teams 1967.

OTTLIK, Géza, of Budapest, Hungary, author, journalist, born 1912; one of the leading Hungarian novelists; editor of the Hungarian *Bridge Review;* winner of the International Bridge Academy's first "Article of the Year" award 1968; contributor to *Bridge World*.

OTTOLENGHI, Carlos (1907–1970), of Buenos Aires, Argentina, engineer; South American Champion 1948, 1958; won Argentine Open Team 1942, 1952, 1956, Open Pairs 1955. Won Gabarret Cup 1956.

OUDSHOORN, C. Leo, of The Hague, Doctor of Chemistry, born 1916; represented the Netherlands World Olympiad 1964, European Championships 1955, 1961, 1965. National successes include Open Teams 1962, 1964.

OUDSHOORN, Nicolaus Dirk (Nico), of Ryswijk, Holland, importer, born 1906; chief of Dutch Bridge-Rama, member of national technical staff for European Championships, tournament manager of European Championships 1963, 1965, 1966 and World Team Olympiad 1968, World Pair Olympiad 1974.

OUDSHOORN, Dr. Willem Adrajaan, of Rotterdam, Holland, physician, born 1909; represented Netherlands World Olympiad 1960, European Championships 1955, 1963; national wins include Open Team 1963, runner-up 1955, 1958, 1961.

OVALLE, Jorge, of Santiago, Chile, civil engineer; South American Champion 1951, second 1961; National Open Team Champion 1955, 1956, 1957, 1958, 1961, 1963.

OZORIO, L. A., of Hong Kong, businessman, born 1911; Far East Champion 1959, 1960; represented

Hong Kong Far East Championships on two other occasions; national titles include Open Teams, Master Teams, Open Pairs, Masters Pairs, Mixed Pairs.

P

PABIS TICCI, Camillo, of Florence, Italy, engineer, born 1920; one of the world's great players; World Champion 1963, 1964, 1965, 1966, 1967, 1968, 1969, 1972; runner-up European Championship 1963; national wins include Italian Cup 1961, Open Teams 1964. Former President Florence Bridge Association. Editor of revised *Bridge in Italy*.

PADGET, John E., of Seattle, Wash., bridge teacher, born 1945; winner of numerous regional titles including All-Western Knockout Teams 1972, Open Teams 1970, Bridge Week Masters Pairs 1971, Rogue River Knockout Teams 1973.

PADUA, Mrs. Leticia, de, of Rizal, Philippines, born 1930; represented Philippines Women's Pairs Olympaid 1962, Far East Championships 1963; won Far East Zone World Par contest 1963. Director Philippine Contract Bridge League.

PAES DE BARROS, Paulo Plinio, of São Paulo, Brazil, assessor, born 1941; South American Champion 1966, 1969, 1974; represented Brazil World Team Olympiad 1968, 1972, World Pair Olympiad 1970.

PAI, Tom Seek, of Honolulu, Hawaii, attorney, born 1921; won Hawaiian Men's Pairs 1956, Masters Pairs 1968.

PALOCZ, Eugenio, of Santiago, Chile, businessman; born in Hungary, now a Chilean citizen; represented Chile World Olympiad 1964, South American Championships 1956; won Chile International Trials 1959. Represented Hungary as national boxing champion 1922–23.

PALOCZ, Matilda Stark (Mrs. Eugenio), of Santiago, Chile, born in Hungary, became Chilean citizen. Represented Chile in World Women's Team Olympiad 1964. National winner of many swimming and tennis championships.

PAPASTAVROU, Dimitri J., of Greece, lawyer, bridge official and writer; represented Greece European Championships 1971; national successes include Team Trials 1971, Open Pairs 1973. Secretary General to Hellenic BF since 1974. Bridge columnist of Athens daily *Kathimerini*.

PARENT, Henri, of Montreal, Que., carpet retailer, born 1925; won Canadian Nat'l Open Teams 1960, Canadian-American Men's Pairs, Open Teams 1967; past President Montreal BL, Vice-President of District 1; Co-Chairman 1957 Summer Nat'l Planning Committee, ACBL Director since 1967.

PARIENTE, Dr. Jacques, of Paris, physician, born 1929; represented France World Pairs Olympiad 1962; European Championships runner-up 1959, represented France 1958, 1966, 1967; won French Open Team 1956.

PARKER, George W., of Millbrae, Calif., attorney and accountant, born 1933; winner of several regional events including Golden State Knockout Teams 1970, 1972, Polar Regional Knockout Teams, Men's Pairs 1974.

PARKER, Judy, of New York, N.Y.; won Summer Nat'l secondary Women's Pairs 1970, New York Winter Mixed Teams 1971, tied Tri-State Winter Open Teams 1974.

PARKER, Steven J., of Alexandria, Va., personnel counselor, born 1945; one of the leading East Coast players; won World Olympiad Mixed Teams 1974, Reisinger 1972, Fall Nat'l Mixed Pairs 1969, Spring Nat'l secondary Masters Pairs 1973, second Summer Nat'l Mixed Teams 1973; winner of many regional titles including Mid-Atlantic Knockout Teams 1974, Masters Pairs 1970, 1971, Open Pairs 1973.

PARR, Siddy, see FOX, MRS. SIDDY S.

PARTOS, George, of Miami Beach, Fla., retired bookkeeper, born 1907; formerly the owner of one of the largest private collections of bridge books and periodicals. Contributing Editor of *Bridge Encyclopedia*.

PASSELL, Marietta (Mrs. William), of Yonkers, N.Y., born 1935; one of the leading American women players; won VENICE CUP 1974, Spring Nat'l Women's Teams 1971, Summer Nat'l Mixed Teams 1972, Fall Nat'l Life Master Women's Pairs 1970, secondary Women's Teams 1968, 1969, Spring Nat'l secondary Women's Teams 1973, second Spring Nat'l Women's Teams 1973, World Bidding Contest 1969; winner of several regional championships including Southeastern Mixed Pairs 1966, 1967, Women's Teams 1974.

PASSELL, Michael J., of Mission Viejo, Calif., bridge professional, born 1947; one of the leading

West Coast players; won Spring Nat'l secondary Swiss Teams 1972, secondary Open Pairs 1974; winner of scores of regional titles including Mid-South Open Pairs 1970, Masters Pairs 1970, Mixed Pairs 1971, Pacific Southwest Knockout Teams 1973, Men's Pairs 1974.

PASSELL, William Lee, of Yonkers, N.Y., vice-president executive placement firm, bridge teacher, born 1930; one of the leading East Coast Players; won Summer Nat'l Mixed Teams 1972, Fall Nat'l Mixed Pairs 1960, secondary Men's Teams 1968, second World Bidding Contest 1969, Spring Nat'l Men's Pairs 1968, Summer Nat'l Comm. & Ind. Teams 1962; many regional successes include Eastern States Knockout Teams 1969, New England Fall Knockout Teams 1960, Mixed Teams 1958, Southeastern Mixed Pairs 1966, 1967, Keystone Knockout Teams 1974.

PATERNINA, Conchita Doriga de, of Madrid, Spain; represented Spain in many international tournaments including World Women's Team Olympiad 1972 (npc), European Championships 1974; national successes include two Ladies' Championships.

PATTERSON, J. Robert, of Milwaukie, Ore., attorney, born 1917; won Northwest Open Pairs 1961, 1962, Men's Pairs 1960.

PATTERSON, Lucille E. (Mrs. Gerald), of Sacramento, Calif.; won Spring Nat'l Women's Pairs 1964; many regional successes include Northwest Mixed Pairs 1955, Women's Pairs 1958, Desert Empire Open Teams 1956, Northern Rocky Mountain Open Teams 1958, Golden State Women's Pairs 1967, All-Western Women's Pairs 1968, Bridge Week Women's Pairs 1972. Member ACBL Goodwill Committee.

PATTON, Major Charles Lee (1851–1941), born in Mississippi, resident of New York City after 1888; pioneer of bridge organization from 1906. Originator of Patton movement (see TEAM-OF-FOUR MOVEMENT); one of those who claimed invention of the TAKE-OUT DOUBLE.

PAUL, Mary (Mrs. Maurice), of Toronto, Ont.; represented Canada World Women's Team Olympiad 1968, 1972; won Canadian-American Mixed Pairs 1971.

PAUL, Maurice, of Toronto, Ont., sales representative, bridge teacher, born 1923; won Marcus 1958; Canadian-American Open Teams 1957, Mixed Pairs 1971.

PAULS, Brian, of Winnipeg, Man., barrister, solicitor, bridge writer, and tournament director,

born 1940; won Leventritt Pairs 1966, 1968, Summer Nat'l President's Cup Pairs 1962; winner of several regional events including Mid-American–Canadian Masters Pairs 1963, Gopher Men's Pairs 1966, Open Pairs 1970. Director of Manitoba Unit.

PAULSEN, Erik, of Culver City, Calif., design engineer, born 1926; one of the leading American players; represented US World Pair Olympiad 1970; won Team Trials 1975, Chicago 1962, Blue Ribbon Pairs 1969, Reisinger 1968, 1974, 1975; second Vanderbilt 1963, Spring Nat'l Men's Pairs 1959, 1961, Reisinger 1966; many regional wins include Bridge Week Open Pairs 1961, 1962, Mixed Pairs 1961, Knockout Teams 1961, 1968, 1973.

PAVLICEK, Richard F., of Ft. Lauderdale, Fla., bridge teacher, born 1945; one of the leading players of the South; won Grand Nat'l Championship 1973; several regional victories including Southeastern Men's Teams 1970, Life Masters Pairs 1971.

PAVLIDES, Jordanis T., of London, England, company director, born 1903; World Champion 1955, European Champion 1954; also represented Great Britain European Championship 1955; Gold Cup 1949, Master Pairs 1948, and other national championships. Author of *One Page Guide to Bidding.*

PAYNE, Charles M., of South Laguna Beach, Calif., publisher's representative, born 1909; won Northwest Senior Masters Individual 1956, Desert Empire Open Teams 1965. Former President of Tucson BA, Director Western Conference.

PAYNE, Mrs. Houston, of Memphis, Tenn.; second Fall Nat'l Women's Team 1954; won Southern Conference Open Pairs 1962, Puerto Rico Open Teams 1973. Former Director Memphis Unit.

PEARSON, Don, of Sausalito, Calif.; won Spring Nat'l Men's Teams 1970, second Fall Nat'l Life Master Men's Pairs 1968; won ALACBU Open Teams 1969.

PEDERSON, Darryl, of Mercer Island, Wash., cost accountant, born 1936; winner of several regional championships including Puget Sound Knockout Teams 1970, 1971, 1972.

PELL, Margaret (Mrs. Murray), of Norfolk, Va., born 1922; won Fall Nat'l Senior Masters Individual 1960, Mid-Atlantic Fall Women's Pairs 1959.

PELUCCHI, Giovanni, of Milan, Italy, industrialist, born 1907; npc Italian Team European Championship 1962, 1966, 1967. President Milan Bridge Association. Organizer of 1958 World Championship. Author of several articles in *Bridge in Italy.*

PENDER, Peter A., of San Francisco, Calif., executive director of Bridge Professionals International, born 1936; one of the leading American players; won Mc Kenney 1966, Marcus 1958, Reisinger 1968, 1970, Fall Nat'l Life Masters Men's Pairs 1967; second Rockwell 1964, Leventritt Pairs 1964, Fall Nat'l Men's Teams 1967, Pan American Invitational 1974, 1975, numerous regional wins include New England Fall Masters Pairs 1958, Masters Teams 1959, 1960, All-American Open Teams 1966, Golden Gate Knockout Teams 1970, 1974, Open Teams 1971.

PEREIRA de SOUSA, Caio Luis, of São Paulo, Brazil, civil engineer, born 1905; South American Champion 1956, 1962; won Brazilian Open Team 1958, 1959, 1961.

PERES, Charles, of Chicago, Ill., bridge club owner, born 1930; won Morehead 1967, Summer Nat'l Masters Mixed Teams, Men's Pairs 1969; second Reisinger 1967, Spring Nat'l Open Pairs 1973; regional successes include District 11 Men's Pairs 1962, Central States Life and Senior Masters Teams 1962, Knockout Teams 1966, 1969, 1970.

PERKINS, Frank K., of Newton, Mass., engineer and bridge writer, born 1891, now deceased; won New England Knockout Teams 1930, 1934, 1937, 1939, 1941 (twice), and 1942, Men's Pairs 1943; second Reisinger 1931. Founder of New England BL 1937, and acted as its secretary, treasurer, and tournament director until 1946. His column in the Boston *Herald* was published from 1931 through the 1950s. Other writings include *Vital Tricks at Contract Bridge* (see BIBLIOGRAPHY, D), *Modern Contract Standards,* 1938, and articles for *The Bridge World.*

PERLMAN, Howard M., of Southfield, Mich., bridge and backgammon club owner, born 1943; second Grand National Championship 1974, Vanderbilt 1972; won Leventritt Pairs 1971, Fall Nat'l secondary Open Pairs 1974; winner of many regional championships including Central States Knockout Teams 1971, Open Pairs 1972, 1973, All-American Knockout Teams 1974.

PERLMAN, Mrs. Howard (formerly Linda Deaton), of Southfield, Mich., born 1945; winner of several regional events including Southeastern Women's Teams 1972.

PERROUX, Carl Alberto, of Modena, Italy, trial lawyer, born 1905; one of the leading personalities of the world of bridge; npc of winning Italian team World Championship 1957, 1958, 1959, 1961, 1962, 1963, 1965, 1966; European Championship 1951, 1956, 1957, 1958, 1959; former President Italian Bridge Federation; technical adviser Italian National Team. Author of the book *The Blue Team—Our Story of Bridge.*

PERUTZ, Sidney (Mrs. George), of Dallas, Tex., born 1933; won several regional events including Mid-South Summer Women's Pairs 1966, Texas Fall Mixed Pairs 1968.

PESTANER, James, of Pittsburg, Calif., radiation chemist, born 1924; won Spring Nat'l Men's Pairs 1959, Bridge Week Open Pairs 1960, Northern Rocky Mountain Men's Pairs 1965.

PETERS, Herbert, of Bristol, Va., attorney, born 1930; winner of several regional events including Mid-Atlantic Open Teams 1968, 1971, 1972.

PETERS, Thomas J., of Houston, Tex., born 1943; won Fall Nat'l secondary Special Pairs 1974; regional successes include Midwest Men's Pairs 1968, 1970, South Texas Swiss Teams 1974.

PETERSEN, Vibeke, of Copenhagen, Denmark, bridge teacher, born 1924; represented Denmark World Women's Team Olympiad 1964, European Women's Team Champion 1955, 1957. National titles include Women's Teams 1950, 1955, Open Teams 1958, 1959, Open Pairs 1962, Mixed Pairs 1958, 1960, 1961.

PETERSON, Harrison V., of Los Angeles, Calif., treasurer, born 1914; won Pacific Southwest Men's Pairs 1960, Open Teams 1966. Former President Los Angeles Unit.

PETERSON, Olive (1894–1965), of St. Davids, Pa., bridge teacher and author. An outstanding woman player associated closely with Milton C. Work, with whom she won many auction and contract championships; she conducted with him in 1933 one of the earliest Bridge Cruises on the SS *Carinthia* to the North Cape and Russia, lasting 36 days; subsequently she was associated with Charles Goren, especially at teachers' conventions; won Auction Bridge Nat'l Women's Pairs 1931; Women's Teams 1932; Fall Nat'l Women's Teams 1938, 1943, Nat'l Women's Pairs 1930, 1932, 1945, Nat'l Mixed Teams 1940, 1942, 1943, 1944, Fall Nat'l Mixed Pairs 1943; second Nat'l Women's Pairs 1935, Nat'l Women's Teams 1953. Vice-President Women's Auxiliary of ABL 1936; President Women's Nat'l Committee 1939; ACBL Secretary 1951. Writings include *Work-Peterson Accurate Valuation System, 101 Celebrated Hands, Simplified Digest of Culbertson System,* and *Common-Sense Contract.* See BIBLIOGRAPHY, H.

PETTERSON, Kelsey, of Long Beach, Calif., attorney, born 1911; represented North America World Championships 1965; won Spring Nat'l Men's Team 1962; second Vanderbilt 1964; many regional successes including Bridge Week Mixed Teams 1967, Open Pairs 1961, 1962, Masters Pairs 1973, All-Western Open Teams 1959, District 5 Open Teams

1965, Pacific Southwest Open Teams, Open Pairs 1966, Men's Pairs 1973. ACBL Director 1967–70; former president and attorney of Western Conference. Non-playing captain of Los Angeles team in *Sports Illustrated* Trophy matches.

PETTIJOHN, Mrs. Kenneth, of Indianapolis, Ind.; second Fall Nat'l Women's Teams 1966; won Midwest Open Teams, Women's Pairs 1960.

PETTIS, William C., of Washington, D.C., student, born 1948; winner of several regional events including Mid-Atlantic Knockout Teams 1973, 1974, Open Teams 1973, 1974.

PEYSER, Kenneth, of Chicago, Ill., business executive, born 1937; winner of several regional events including District 15 Knockout Teams 1974, 1975.

PHILIPPAS, Michael, of Montreal, Que.; winner of several regional championships including Oregon Trail Knockout Teams 1971, Men's Pairs 1970.

PHILIPPY, Julien P., of Camarillo, Calif., chemical engineer, born 1927; second US World Par tournament 1963; won Intercity title for Twin Cities 1962; won Gopher Open Team 1959.

PHILLEY, Mary. See WILLIAMS, MARY.

PHILLIPS, Duncan, of Toronto, Ont., lawyer; represented Canada World Pair Olympiad 1962, 1966, World Team Olympiad 1972, won Leventritt Pairs 1970; several regional wins include Canadian Nat'l Knockout Teams 1972, Open Teams 1958.

PHILLIPS, Hubert (1891–1964), of London, England, journalist and bridge writer. Editor of *British Bridge World* 1936–39, and one of the pioneers of bridge organization in England. For many years was internationally the most eminent author of intellectual and mathematical puzzles under the names "Caliban" and "Dogberry," and of cryptic crosswords; author of many general knowledge quiz books; essayist and leader-writer for the London *News Chronicle;* resident expert on Britain's most famous radio quiz program. Many bridge writings included *Brush Up Your Bridge, The Elements of Contract, Bridge at Ruff's Club* and *Bridge with Goren.* See BIBLIOGRAPHY, H, L.

PHILLIPS, Joyce (Mrs. Duncan), of Toronto, Ont.; represented Canada World Women's Team Olympiad 1964, World Pairs Olympiad 1966; regional successes include Canadian Nat'l Mixed Pairs 1971.

PHILLIPS, L. James, of Chicago, Ill., buyer, born 1935; won Fall Nat'l secondary Open Pairs 1966,

Spring Nat'l secondary Swiss Teams 1972; winner of several regional titles including Motor City Open Teams 1971, Central States Masters Pairs 1973, Tri-Unit Men's Pairs 1974.

PHILLIPS, Martin, of Chattanooga, Tenn., manufacturer, born 1916; won Southern Conference Open Pairs 1959, North American Rubber Bridge Championship 1963.

PIASKI, Edmund J., of Raleigh, N.C., accountant; winner of several regional events including Mid-Atlantic Knockout Teams 1973 (twice).

PIELSTICKER, Frances (Mrs. Peter), of Toronto, Ont., secretary; represented Canada Women's World Team Olympiad 1964.

PIETRI, Luis, of Philadelphia, Pa., insurance salesman, born 1931. One of the top-ranking players in the American Bridge Association; winner of more than a score of ABA national championships including every major title at least once, and Knockout Teams, Open Teams, and Open Pairs several times each. ACBL regional wins include Keystone Men's Swiss Teams 1971 (twice), 1972 (twice), and Puerto Rico Open Teams, Open Pairs, and Men's Pairs 1971.

PIGOT, David R. (1900–1965), of Dublin, Ireland, solicitor; between 1936 and 1949 was CBAI Champion and represented CBAI in international events both as player and npc. President CBAI, 1946; Vice-President CBAI 1955–65; member WBF Executive Committee, and contributed to the revision of the IMP scale and to the preparation of 1964 Olympiad regulations; member of EBL Executive Committee 1952–65 and chairman of EBL Tournament Committee 1957–65. Member of Editorial Advisory Board, *Bridge Encyclopedia.*

PIGOT, Peter, of Dublin, Ireland, economist, born 1932; represented Ireland World Pair Olympiad 1962, 1966, European Championships 1965, 1967, 1969, 1970, 1971, 1973, 1974, 1975; national wins include all major championships. Author of daily bridge column in *Irish Independent.*

PIKE, Robert C. (1932–1970), of Mexico City, Mexico, market research analyst; represented Mexico World Team Olympiad 1964, Pairs Olympiad 1962, 1966; won Mexican Olympiad Trials 1961, 1963, 1967, Mexican National Men's Pairs 1968.

PINTO, Rui, of Oporto, Portugal, engineer, born 1941; represented Portugal European Championships 1969, 1970, 1971; national wins include Open Teams once.

PIRO, Evelyn (Mrs. Ernest), of Port Orchard, Wash., apartment house owner and manager. One of the pioneers of bridge organization in the Northwest; responsible for the foundation of several tournaments including NORTHWEST REGIONAL and various units and clubs. Chairman Seattle Unit 1949, 1950, Portland Unit 1950, 1951; co-chairman Nat'l Goodwill Committee 1962; ACBL Director 1958–61 and 1964.

PISK, Dr. George M., of Austin, Tex., English professor, writer, born 1932; won Fall Nat'l secondary Masters Pairs 1974; winner of several regional titles including Texas Knockout Teams 1970, Capital City Knockout Teams 1972.

PITTALA, Vito, of Turin, Italy, professor of mechanical engineering, born 1927; World Champion 1973, 1975, third World Olympiad Mixed Pairs 1966; national successes include Open Teams 1971, 1972, 1974.

PLATE, August, of Houston, Tex.; regional successes include Mid-Winter Knockout Teams 1973.

POE, Edgar Allan (1809–49), American poet and critic, wrote a number of stories of mystery and occultism. He was interested in detection, cryptology, and whist. In his famous detective story, "The Purloined Letter," he embodied a fine analysis of the mental aspects of whist in the plot. He also discussed whist at some length in "The Murders in the Rue Morgue."

POLAK, Ebi J., of Antwerp, Belgium, diamond dealer and bridge columnist, born 1912; represented Belgium World Team Olympiad 1964, 1968, 1972, and in many European Championships; national titles include Open Team eight times, Mixed Teams twice, Open Pairs three times and five Master Individual events. First Life Master and top master-point holder in Belgium. Editor of Belgian magazine *Bridge.*

POLAK, Gunther, of Chicago, Ill., insurance investigator, born 1933; won Summer Nat'l Golder Pairs 1961; second Marcus 1959, Blue Ribbon Pairs 1964; numerous regional wins include Central States Life and Senior Masters Teams 1961, Mixed Pairs 1965, 1969, Masters Pairs 1973, 1974, Men's Pairs 1969, 1971, Knockout Teams, Open Pairs 1967.

POLÁK, Milos, of Prague, Czechoslovakia, research engineer. Represented Czechoslovakia in several international contests. National titles include Open Teams 1959, 1964, Open Pairs 1959, 1964.

POLISNER, Jeffrey D., of Orinda, Calif., attorney, born 1939; won Midwest Fall Open Teams 1963,

District 5 Mixed Pairs 1964, Golden Gate Masters Pairs 1973.

POLUNSKY, Harry, of San Angelo, Tex., food merchant, born 1895; owner of one of the largest private collections of books on playing cards and games played with them; contributor to various magazines, and Contributing Editor, *Bridge Encyclopedia.*

PONTIOUS, "Bitsy" (Mrs. Glenn), of Beaumont, Tex., tobacco wholesaler; won Fall Nat'l Mixed Pairs 1962; second Summer Nat'l Golder Pairs 1958; won Texas Masters Pairs 1957, Open Pairs 1961. Former President of Beaumont Unit.

POOL, W. Gerald, of Honolulu, Hawaii, bank comptroller, born 1908; won Hawaiian Masters Pairs and Hawaiian Mixed Pairs 1961. Former Chairman of Honolulu and Spokane units.

POPPER, Leslie, of Peabody, Mass., engineer, born 1937 in Hungary; winner of several regional events including New England Knockout Teams 1965, 1969, Masters Pairs 1974.

PORTEN, Ron von der. See VON DER PORTEN, RON.

PORTER, C. Finley, of Springfield, Mo., retired railroad purchasing agent, travel manager, born 1893; one of the pioneers of Midwest bridge; helped to organize the Midwest Bridge Conference and edit its monthly publication; former National Tournament Director, former President and member Board of Directors Chicago Contract Bridge Association.

PORTUGAL, Helen (Mrs. Morris), of Los Angeles, Calif., assistant sales manager; one of the leading American woman players; second World Women's Teams Olympiad 1964; represented US World Women's Team Olympiad 1960, World Women's Pair Olympiad 1962; won Life Masters Pairs 1960, Fall Nat'l Life Masters Women's Pairs 1961, Mixed Pairs 1951, 1953, Summer Nat'l Mixed Teams 1962, Spring Nat'l Women's Teams 1969; second Vanderbilt 1964, Fall Nat'l Women's Teams 1959, 1967, Spring Nat'l Women's Pairs 1961, Women's Teams 1963; regional successes include All-Western Open Teams 1956, 1958, Bridge Week Knockout Teams 1961, 1967, Open Teams 1951, 1960, 1961, Mixed Pairs 1948, Women's Pairs 1950, Holiday Knockout Teams 1972, Golden Gate Knockout Teams 1974.

PORTUGAL, Morris, of Los Angeles, Calif., bridge teacher, born 1916; one of the leading West Coast players; won Life Masters Pairs 1960, Fall Nat'l Mixed Pairs 1953, second 1965, Vanderbilt 1964; numerous regional successes include All-Western

Open Team 1958, Bridge Week Knockout Team 1956, 1961, Masters Team 1951, Open Team 1947, 1960, 1961, Masters Pairs 1957, Open Pairs 1946, Mixed Pairs 1951, 1953, Oregon Trail Mixed Pairs 1966, Open Teams 1973, Golden Gate Knockout Teams 1971.

POSTELL, J. A. (1890–1968), of Charlotte, N.C.; one of the leading bridge figures in North Carolina as a player of bridge whist, auction, and contract, manager, and organizer of Sectionals, Regionals, and charity games. Past President, Vice-President, Secretary, honorary board member Charlotte Bridge Association; former Editor of *Trump-It;* collaborated with Robert Brannon on a bridge column for the Charlotte *News* in the 1930s.

POTTER, Maj. John R., of Kirtland A.F.B., N. Mex., air force officer, born 1936; won Spring Nat'l secondary Swiss Teams 1972, tied 1971; regional wins include Music City Open Teams 1973.

POTTS, Edward E., of Bellevue, Wash., planning manager, born 1927; ACBL Regional Tournament Director; won several regionals including Northwest Mixed Pairs 1965. Former President Bellevue Unit.

POTTS, Mrs. William H., of Midland, Tex.; won North Texas Open Teams 1959, Women's Pairs 1961, District 15 Women's Pairs 1969.

POTVIN, Conrad J., of Inglewood, Calif., bridge teacher, born 1913; won Desert Empire Masters Pairs 1958, Open Pairs 1956, Bridge Week Knockout Team 1956, Mixed Pairs 1942, All-Western Open Pairs 1966.

POULDJIAN, Mrs. Esmerian, of Paris, France, born 1901; European Women's Team Champion 1939, 1956; second World Women's Team Olympiad 1960; represented France European Women's Team Championship 1965, npc 1967; played for France against Culbertsons in 1937; fourth Individual at Monte Carlo, with many international and national successes.

POULSEN, Elaine (Mrs. Allan), of Brisbane, Australia, physiotherapist, born 1929; Far East Women's Champion 1974; national wins include Women's Interstate Teams 1973, Women's Pairs 1973.

POWLEY, F. Bert, of Toronto, Ont., bridge club manager and tournament director, born 1906; won Marcus 1956, Canadian–American Men's Pairs 1959. Secretary-treasurer of former Ontario BL.

PRALL, Jack W., Toledo, Ohio, postal clerk, born 1914; President Northern Ohio BA 1956–58, Michi-gan Northern Ohio Conference 1961, 1962. ACBL Director 1964.

PRAY, Walter J., of Indianapolis, Ind., born 1886, now deceased; won American Whist League Open Pairs 1932, USBA Indiana Open Teams 1933, Ohio Open Teams 1933, Indianapolis Mixed Pairs 1933, Midwest Spring Open Teams 1945, Men's Pairs 1944, Western States Mixed Pairs 1936.

PRESSBERG, Leo, of Lawndale, Calif., cabinet-maker, born 1910, now deceased; won Nat'l Masters Individual 1959; several regional wins included Bridge Week Knockout Teams 1953, Masters Teams 1952, Mixed Teams 1960, 1965, Men's Pairs 1947, Pacific Southwest Masters Pairs 1970.

PRESSBURGER, John, of Munich; British national born in Czechoslovakia in 1913; represented Prague in matches against London and Leeds 1946, 1947, represented Germany World Team Olympiad 1968, World Pair Olympiad 1966, 1970, European Championships 1971, 1974; national successes include Czech Open Teams 1938, 15 German titles. Contributor to *Deutsches Bridge Verbands-Blatt;* bridge columnist of *Suddeutscher Zeitung.* Instrumental in development of WEISSBERGER CONVENTION.

PRESTON, Richard, of London, England, certified accountant, born 1907; represented England on many occasions in Camrose matches and in the 1962 World Pairs Olympiad; four times winner and four times runner-up in the Life Masters Pairs; won Gold Cup 1955, Crockford's Cup twice.

PRIDAY, Jane (Mrs. Richard A., formerly Mrs. Pedro Juan), of London, England, bridge teacher, born 1936; one of the leading women players in the world; won World Olympiad Women's Pairs 1966, Women's Teams 1964, European Women's Championships 1961, 1963, 1966; represented Great Britain European Women's Championships 1962, 1964, 1965, 1969, World Olympiad Women's Pairs 1970; won English Bridge Union Women's Teams 1966; in partnership with Mrs. J. Durran, second Life Masters Pairs 1966, the highest position ever gained by a women's pair.

PRIDAY, Richard Anthony, of London, England, timber merchant and bridge writer, born 1922; one of the leading British players; won European Championship 1961, represented Great Britain World Championships 1962, European Championships 1966; won Gold Cup 1964; English Mixed Teams Championship 1962; npc British Ladies' Team in World Teams Olympiad 1960; Council Member and selector of British Bridge League and English Bridge Union; bridge columnist for London *Sunday Telegraph.* Contributing Editor *Bridge Encyclopedia.* See also BUENOS AIRES AFFAIR.

PRIEST, David A., of North Hollywood, Calif., bridge professional, born 1940; winner of several regional events including Las Vegas Knockout Teams 1971, Golden State Knockout Teams 1973.

PRISYON, Jerome B. (Jerry), of North Woodmere, N.Y., sales manager, born 1927; a leading bridge figure in the New York area as a lecturer, administrator, Director, and former President of the Greater New York Bridge Association. Originated a novice program for the GNYBA, which included printed hand analyses. It was later adopted and expanded by the ACBL.

PROMBOIN, Ronald L., of Palo Alto, Calif., economist, born 1945; won District 21 Grand National 1974, several regional events including All-Western Men's Swiss Teams 1973.

PRONIEWICZ, Dr. Ferenc, of Budapest, Hungary, lawyer, born 1919; won Hungarian Open Teams 1955, 1957; member winning Hungarian team against Czechoslovakia 1963, Germany 1964, Belgium 1964, and Austria 1965.

PROSNITZ, Eugene, of New York, N.Y.; won Fall Nat'l secondary Men's Teams 1969; regional successes include Long Island Open Teams 1972.

PROTHRO, James T. ("Tommy"), of San Diego, Calif., football coach, born 1920; winner of several regional events including Rocky Mountain Knockout Teams 1969.

PUTTAERT, Louis, of Brussels, Belgium, bridge teacher, born 1914; represented Belgium World Team Olympiad 1964, 1972, World Pair Olympiad 1962, European Championships 1962, 1963, 1965, 1967, 1973, 1974; many national championships.

R

RABIN, Henry L., of Chicago, Ill., real estate developer, born 1935; winner of several regional events including Champagne Open Teams 1968, Open Pairs 1972, Central States Men's Pairs 1973.

RACHWALSKI, Kurt, of Frankfurt, Germany, businessman, born 1917; represented Germany World Team Olympiad 1960; and in European Championships 1956, 1957, 1958, 1959, 1961, 1963, 1965, 1966, 1967; national titles include Open Team, Open Pairs, and Individual, and won Austrian Pair contest.

RACIER, Robert, of Philadelphia, Pa., real estate broker, born 1895; won New York-New Jersey Open

Pairs 1959, Southeastern Open Team 1953, Men's Team 1953.

RAFFEL, Harry B. (1881–1953), of New York, N.Y., attorney; a leading New York player in the thirties; won Vanderbilt 1929, 1939, Eastern States Open Pairs 1935. assisted in preparation of Laws as representative of the New York Bridge Whist Club.

RAMSEY, Guy, of London, died 1959, journalist and author; writings include *Aces All* and many magazine articles. Bridge editor London *Daily Telegraph*. First President European (now International) Bridge Press Association (1958–59). See BIBLIOGRAPHY, K.

RAND, Dr. Nissan, of Tel Aviv, Israel, biochemist, born in Czechoslovakia 1930; represented Israel European Championships 1965, 1966, 1967, captain 1966, 1967; won Israel Open Pairs 1965, Tel Aviv Open Pairs 1964, 1965, Tel Aviv Open Teams 1964, 1967. Bridge columnist for leading Israeli newspaper.

RANDALL, Winslow H., of Redlands, Calif., publisher's representative and citrus farm manager, born 1897; ACBL Director and member of several of its committees, including Charity, Systems, Conventions and Tournament Regulations, and International Events. ACBL President 1959. President Western Conference 1955.

RANK, Peter C., of Los Angeles, Calif., lawyer, born 1938; one of the leading West Coast players; won McKenney 1965, Spring Nat'l Men's Pairs 1966, Fall Nat'l Mixed Pairs 1968; second Summer Nat'l Masters Mixed Teams 1969; winner of numerous regional titles, including Bridge Week Open Teams 1965, Master Men's Pairs 1971, Open Pairs 1974, Golden Gate Mixed Pairs 1966, 1968, Open Pairs 1968, 1969, Knockout Teams 1969, 1970, Open Teams 1971.

RAPÉE, George, of New York, N.Y., attorney and real estate investor, born 1915; one of the great bridge players of the world; World Champion 1950, 1951, 1953; represented North America World Championships 1958, 1969, and US World Team Olympiad 1960; won International Team Trials 1968. Has the best record of success in the three major national team championships, winning 21 and finishing second in 16; won Spingold 1944, 1948, 1950, 1952, 1957, 1968, Chicago 1945, 1947, 1953, 1954, 1956, Reisinger 1970, 1971, Vanderbilt 1946, 1950, 1951, 1955, 1956, 1957, 1959, 1970, Spring Nat'l Men's Teams 1975, Summer Nat'l Mixed Team 1960, Fall Nat'l Men's Pairs 1950, Summer Nat'l Non-Masters Pairs 1936, Masters Individual 1944, 1949, second Spingold 1943, 1947, 1955, 1960, 1961, 1966, Chicago 1948, 1950, Vanderbilt 1942, 1944, 1952, 1965, 1967, Reisinger 1968, 1969, 1972, Fall

Nat'l Men's Teams 1946, 1948, Spring Nat'l Men's Teams 1972, Summer Nat'l Mixed Teams 1952, 1968, Mixed Pairs 1955; regional successes include Reisinger 1951, Bridge Week Open Pairs 1950, Mid-South Spring Open Team 1960, Southeastern Open Team 1945. Co-author of the STAYMAN convention.

RAPHAEL, Selma (Mrs. Sheldon), of Chestnut Hill, Mass., bridge teacher; won New England Open Teams 1971, Women's Pairs 1954, Open Pairs 1959. Director New England BA and Eastern Mass. BA.

RAPPAPORT, Barbara, of Springfield, N.J., English teacher, born 1936; one of the leading women players; won Fishbein Trophy 1971; won Life Masters Pairs 1971, 1972, Spring Nat'l secondary Open Pairs 1971, Summer Nat'l secondary Women's Pairs 1971, Fall Nat'l secondary Mixed Pairs 1972, second Spring Nat'l Women's Teams 1969, 1971, Summer Nat'l Mixed Teams 1966, 1974, Fall Nat'l Life Master Women's Pairs 1973; winner of many regional championships including Eastern States Knockout Teams 1966, 1968, Women's Pairs 1964, Mixed Teams 1974. After sweeping the pairs events in a sectional tournament, she was named honorary Men's Pairs champion, so that her record would not be flawed.

RAPPLEYEA, Fred A., of Park Ridge, Ill., research director, born 1918; won All-American Open Teams 1954, 1957, Central States Open Teams 1956, Great Lakes Open Pairs 1959, Rocky Mountain Open Pairs 1965.

RAU, John, of New York, N.Y., sales executive, born 1908; with W. BARRETT credited with first using psychic bids in national tournaments; one of the youngest winners of major championships in the thirties; won Chicago 1930, Fall Nat'l Open Pairs 1934; second Vanderbilt 1935, 1936, Spingold 1936; regional wins include Eastern States Knockout Teams 1938; chief assistant to P. H. SIMS 1931–35, consultant on SIMS SYSTEM and books.

RAYMOND, Boris M. (1917–1967), of New York, N.Y., engineer; won Eastern States Open Pairs 1949, 1951, 1954, 1967, Masters Pairs 1961, Knockout Teams 1966, New York-New Jersey Open Pairs 1963.

RAYNE, Edward, of London, England, shoe manufacturer, born 1922; European Champion 1948; won Gold Cup 1949. Member of Portland Club Laws Committee which contributed to the preparation of the 1963 International Code.

READ, Gerard F., of Dublin, Ireland, insurance official, born 1916; represented Ireland World Team Olympiad 1964, European Championship 1953, 1954, 1955, 1957, 1958, 1959, 1963, 1966, 1967

(playing captain 1953, 1958, npc 1965); national wins include Irish Open Team three times, Men's Teams twice, CBA of Ireland Men's Pairs and Mixed Pairs twice.

REBNER, Mrs. Stella, of Los Angeles, Calif., born 1910 in Vienna; one of the leading American women players; second Women's Team World Olympiad 1964; won International Women's Team Trials 1963; won Nat'l Mixed Team 1952, 1953, Fall Nat'l Women's Team 1957, second Mixed Pairs; regional wins include All-Western Open Pairs 1958, 1959, Mixed Pairs 1958, Bridge Week Knockout Team 1953, Open Pairs 1959, Women's Pairs 1948, Women's Masters Pairs 1967, Mixed Teams 1966.

REED, Richard P., of Boulder, Colo., supervisory scientist, born 1934; won Spring Nat'l secondary Men's Pairs 1973, several regional championships including Missouri Valley Open Teams 1974, Open Pairs 1973.

REESE, Terence, of London, England, bridge author and journalist, born 1913. Learned bridge at the age of six, and played in tournaments at the age of fourteen. His numerous successes and infrequent failures in championships of every kind led him to be considered by many authorities the top-ranking player in the world. World Champion 1955; second World Team Olympiad 1960, World Pair Olympiad 1962; World Par Champion 1961; European Champion 1948, 1949, 1954, 1963; represented Great Britain World Team Olympiad 1964, World Championships 1965, and European Championships on five other occasions. In the 1965 World event, Reese and his partner Boris Schapiro were accused of conveying information about the heart suit through finger signals. Both were convicted by the World Bridge Federation, but were acquitted after a more exhaustive investigation by a special inquiry set up by the British Bridge League. (See BUENOS AIRES AFFAIR.) In his defense, Reese wrote *Story of an Accusation.* He has also won many British Championships, including the Gold Cup eight times and the Masters Pairs seven times. Reese was one of the originators of the ACOL system in the thirties, and of the LITTLE MAJOR. His many important contributions to the game include: the conduct of regular bridge radio programs; acting as Bridge-O-Rama commentator; bridge correspondent of the London *Observer* and *Evening News,* as well as other periodicals; editor of the British Bridge World 1955–62. Author of many books, including *Reese on Play, The Expert Game, The Bridge Player's Dictionary, The ACOL System Today, Play Bridge with Reese, Develop Your Bidding Judgment, Bridge for Tournament Players, Precision Bidding and Precision Play;* co-author *The Complete Book of Bridge, Backgammon — The Modern Game.* Since 1955 probably the most prolific author of bridge books. See BIBLIOGRAPHY, C, D, E, G.

REICH, Louis I., of Waltham, Mass., computer programmer, born 1949; winner of several regional titles including New England Open Teams 1973 (twice), Canadian–American Knockout Teams 1974.

REICHENBACH, Claude, of Paris, bridge club owner; represented Switzerland World Pair Olympiad 1960, European Championships 1951, 1958, 1959; national successes include Open Team 1956, 1957, 1958.

REICHMUTH, Mrs. B. C., of Billings, Mont., bridge teacher and tournament director; won Rocky Mountain Women's Pairs 1949, Northern Rocky Mountain Mixed Pairs 1959. A pioneer of duplicate bridge in Montana.

REIF, Rose, of Los Angeles, Calif., born 1895; second Fall Nat'l Women's Teams 1959; won Pacific Southwest Open Teams 1946, 1950, 1951, Masters Pairs 1948, Open Pars 1949, Women's Pairs 1958, 1965, Mixed Pairs 1952, with European successes prior to these.

REILLY, M. S. (Red), of Crete, Ill., bridge club owner, born 1896; won ABL Challenge Trophy 1936, Western States Open Pairs 1936, Central States Open Pairs 1938, Life and Senior Masters Teams 1962, Pairs 1965.

REINHOLD, Arthur E. ("Bud"), of Miami, Fla., furniture manufacturer, investor, born 1913; won Spingold 1973, Reisinger 1973, second Vanderbilt 1973; winner of many regional championships since 1970 including Mexican Nat'l Open Teams 1973, Masters Pairs 1974, Champagne Knockout Teams 1974, Open Teams 1974.

REISINGER, Curt H. (1891–1964), of New York, N.Y., financier and philanthropist, one of the principal patrons of contract bridge in its early years. By donations and loans made possible several early contract bridge tournaments, clubs, and books; donor of REISINGER TROPHY for Eastern States Knockout Teams. Third Fall Nat'l Open Pairs 1948. Positions have included Director USBA, President Greater New York BA, Chairman of ACBL. Honorary Member ACBL 1953.

REITH, George (1876–1939), of Yonkers, N.Y., stockbroker; one of the leading American bridge personalities; member of the most successful (Knickerbocker Whist Club) auction bridge team with P. H. Sims, S. Lenz, and others; devised Reith Count (6–4–3–2–1 point-count); wrote first book on one-over-one (see REITH'S ONE-OVER-ONE); won first Nat'l Contract Bridge Pair Championship 1929, Nat'l Mixed Pairs 1931, Nat'l Mixed Teams 1931, Chicago, 1932; second Vanderbilt 1930, Asbury Challenge Teams 1932; won Eastern States Knockout Teams 1930, Open Pairs 1929. Director Ameri-

can BL, Vice-President and Chief Executive Officer USBA. Author of the first "modern" book on auction bidding, *The Art of Successful Bidding,* and also of *Contract, Accurate Contract,* and *Reith's One-Over-One.* The Reith Trophy, in his memory, was donated to ACBL in 1940 for Eastern States Mixed Pairs. See BIBLIOGRAPHY, C, E.

REITHOFER, Dr. Max (1910–1969), of Vienna, Austria, corporation lawyer; second European Championships 1951, 1957; also represented Austria 1952, 1954, 1958, npc 1965. President Austrian Bridge Federation 1957–69.

REITMAN, Dr. Nelson R., of New Milford, N.J., dentist, born 1911; won Eastern States Mixed Pairs 1958, Mixed Team 1960, Men's Pairs 1961. Director New Jersey BA and chairman of its Conduct and Ethics Committee.

REMEY, Joan F., of Southfield, Mich., teacher; won Marcus Cup 1970, Spring Nat'l Open Pairs 1971, second summer Nat'l Mixed Teams 1971, Fall Nat'l Women's Teams 1960, Spring Nat'l Women's Teams 1965; many regional wins include All-American Women's Pairs 1959, 1974, Open Teams 1959, 1973.

REMEY, Vincent O., of Southfield, Mich; won Marcus Cup 1970, Spring Nat'l Open Pairs 1971, second Summer Nat'l Mixed Teams 1971, Life Masters Pairs 1948; many regional wins include All-American Open Teams 1959, 1973, Mixed Teams 1959, Men's Pairs 1965, Mixed Pairs 1959. ACBL Director since 1974. Contributor to *The Bridge World.*

RENNELS, Audrey, of Pleasant, Calif., won Summer Nat'l Commercial Teams 1972; regional successes include All-Western Women's Pairs 1970.

REQUARD, Daniel C., of Schaumburg, Ill., sales representative, born 1945; won Spring Nat'l secondary Swiss Teams 1972; several regional wins include Midwest Open Teams 1972, Open Pairs 1970.

RETHERS, Mrs. Robert, of Redwood City, Calif., bridge teacher, columnist and tournament director, born 1894; won Nat'l Mixed Team 1954; regional wins include Rocky Mountain Open Pairs 1950, Northwest Spring Mixed Pairs 1951.

REVELL, A. Richard, of Chicago, Ill., accountant, born 1916; won Fall Nat'l Men's Pairs 1950, Fall Nat'l Men's Team 1950, Summer Nat'l Golder Pairs 1949, 1955. All-American Open Team 1948, Central States Open Team 1949, Midwest Spring Open Team 1959.

REYES, José J., of Pasay City, Philippines, attorney, real estate broker, planter, and bridge columnist, born 1910; captain Philippine Team World Team Olympiad 1960; Far East Champion 1958; national titles include Open Team 1959, 1960, 1961, 1962, Open Pairs 1955, Individual 1957. Far East delegate to the World Bridge Federation, Chairman Far East Federation 1957–63; President Philippine CBL 1956–63.

REYES, Vicente, of Pasay City, Philippines, mechanical engineer and bridge columnist, born 1937; represented Philippines World Team Olympiad 1960, 1964; won National Open Team 1959, 1960, 1961, 1962, Knockout Team 1962, Open Pairs 1961, Men's Pairs 1957, Individual 1958.

REYNOLDS, Robert, of Miami, Fla., bridge teacher, born 1925; represented US World Pair Olympiad 1962; won Fall Nat'l Life Masters Individual 1960; second Vanderbilt 1960, Life Masters Pairs 1961; many regional wins including Florida Knockout Teams 1969, Men's Teams 1961, Men's Pairs 1959, Open Pairs 1964, Southeastern Men's Teams 1951, 1963, 1965, 1972, Knockout Teams 1968, Men's Pairs 1961, Open Teams 1951, 1959, Open Pairs 1960.

REYSA, Mrs. Gloria (formerly Gloria Turner), of Dallas, Tex., one of the leading Midwest women players; won Fall Nat'l Mixed Team 1957, 1961; second Vanderbilt 1951, Fall Nat'l Mixed Team 1953; several regional wins include Central States Open Team 1954, Open Pairs 1960, 1961, Big D Women's Teams 1974.

RHATIGAN, Jack, of Cottage Grove, Minn.; won Spring Nat'l Open Pairs 1973, tied Buffalo Centennial Open Teams 1974.

RHODES, Lady (Doris), of London, England, born 1898; represented England, Schwab Cup 1933; represented Great Britain, European Women's Championship four times, including wins 1951, 1952; and in World Women's Team Olympiad 1960. Also toured US as member of British women's team 1953.

RHODES, Kay (Mrs. Lester), of Novato, Calif., born 1910; an outstanding woman player with two unusual records—four consecutive wins Nat'l Women's Pairs with Margaret Wagar 1955, 1956, 1957, 1958, and seven consecutive seconds Fall Nat'l Women's Team 1952–58; won Chicago 1947, Nat'l Women's Pairs 1949; second Nat'l Mixed Team 1942, Women's Pairs 1944; regional wins include Mid-Atlantic Fall Women's Pairs 1952, Midwest Spring Open Pairs 1955, Eastern States Mixed Team 1949, and others.

RICE, Robert M., of Copenhagen, Denmark, managing director, born 1925; represented Norway in Scandinavian Team Championship 1962; won Norwegian National Team Championships 1962, East Danish Open Team 1959, Marcus 1954, second 1956.

RICHARDS, Ralph R. (1876–1943), of Detroit, Mich., bridge teacher, writer, and lecturer; joined the Whist Club of Chicago in 1897, developed into one of the great tournament players of the country. Contested at National tournaments from 1900; won the great whist trophies, some several times. In 1927 organized the American Auction Bridge League (subsequently the American BL), and became its first President. Donor of trophy for Auction Pairs; won American Whist League Auction Open Team 1926, Men's Team 1927, Men's Pairs 1930, Contract Chicago 1928, Fall Nat'l Open Pairs 1929. Author of *Championship Bridge,* co-author of *Common Sense Contract.*

RICHARDSON, Larry, of Kansas City, Mo., systems engineer, born 1941; won Fall Nat'l secondary Men's Pairs 1973; winner of several regional titles including Missouri Valley Knockout Teams 1971, 1974.

RICHARDSON, Nancy, of New York, N.Y.; won Summer Nat'l secondary Mixed Pairs 1971; regional wins include Florida Mixed Pairs 1973.

RICHMOND, David G., of Winnipeg, Man.; represented Canada World Pair Olympiad 1962.

RIELY, Terry, of Houston, Tex., sales representative; Mid-Winter Knockout Teams and Master Pairs 1973, Big D Bridge Week Open Pairs 1974.

RIESTER, William, of Columbus, Ohio; tied 2/3 Spring Nationals Men's Teams 1969; won Midwest Spring Life Masters Pairs 1972.

RIGMAIDEN, Roscoe N., of Philadelphia, Pa., general foreman US Post Office, born 1918. First in the American Bridge Association master-point rankings, and first winner of the William A. Friend award for most master points won in a year. Top-ranked player 1969–70. Won the leading player award in the ABA Summer Nationals 1966 and 1968, and the Spring Nationals 1969. Winner of all major ABA titles including Open Pairs twice and Open Teams twice. Member ABA Executive Board. Contributor to ABA *Bulletin.*

RIGGS, Polly (Mrs. J. E.), of West Newton, Mass.; won Fall Nat'l secondary Women's Pairs 1972;

regional wins include New England Mixed Pairs 1970.

RIORDAN, Beverly, of Ann Arbor, Mich., teacher, born 1928; winner of several regional events including Motor City Mixed Pairs 1971, 1973. First woman President Michigan BA.

RIPSTRA, J. G., of Wichita, Kan., mechanical contractor, born 1900; npc US Team World Championship 1958; second Chicago 1955, Fall Nat'l Men's Pairs 1949, many regional wins include Central States Open Teams 1953, Missouri Valley Open Teams 1953, 1959, Open Pairs 1953, Mid-South Spring Open Teams 1957, 1974, Open Pairs 1969, Knockout Teams 1965, Men's Pairs 1962. President ACBL 1957. Inventor of RIPSTRA convention.

RIVAS, Alvaro, of Bogotá. Colombia, lawyer, born 1921; represented Colombia South American Championships 1963, 1966, 1968, Caribbean Championships 1965; national titles include Open Teams 1963, Open Pairs 1965, 1966.

RIVAS Bernardo, of Bogotá, Colombia, economist, born 1923; represented Colombia South American Championships 1963, 1966, 1968; won National Open Teams 1961, 1963, Masters Pairs 1965; second Open Teams 1965, 1967.

RIVAS, Mrs. María Cristina de, of Bogotá, Colombia, born 1927; represented Colombia South American Championships 1963, South American Women's Championship 1964, 1965, 1966, 1967; South American Women's Champion 1968; national successes include first Open Teams 1961, 1963, Masters Pairs 1965; second Open Teams 1965, 1967, Masters Pairs 1968.

ROARK, Sandra. See TRENT, SANDRA.

ROBBINS, Ross F., of Boulder, Colo., scientist, born 1934; second Fall Nat'l Men's Teams 1964; won Rocky Mountain Master Pairs 1959.

ROBERTS, Dr. J. F., of Harwich Port, Mass., dentist, born 1889, deceased; won New England Spring Open Team 1953, Fall Mixed Team 1954. ACBL Director, President New England Conference.

ROBERTSON, L. R., of Dallas, Tex., real estate broker, born 1894; third Summer Nat'l Men's Pairs 1949; won North Texas Open Teams and Men's Pairs 1962, Texas Open Teams 1952, Mid-South Spring Men's Teams 1953. President Dallas Unit and Texas Regional.

ROBERTSON, Regis, of Prairie Village, Kans; winner of several regional events including District 15 Knockout Teams 1970, Open Teams 1969, Open Pairs 1969, Missouri Valley Knockout Teams 1972.

ROBINSON, Arthur Guy, of Villanova, Pa., bridge teacher, born 1936; one of the outstanding American bridge players; second World Team Olympiad 1964, 1968; represented US World Pair Olympiad 1962, 1966; North American World Championship 1963; won International Team Trials 1967, second 1962, third 1963; won Vanderbilt 1961, 1968, Reisinger 1966, 1967, Spring Nat'l Open Pairs 1962; second Vanderbilt 1965, Chicago 1961, Fall Nat'l Life Masters Individual 1960; third Fall Nat'l Men's Team 1962; won New England Fall Masters Team 1960, District 4 Open Pairs 1963, 1965, Open Teams 1964, 1965, District 5 Open Teams 1961, 1962, Keystone Open Teams 1960.

ROBINSON, Dr. Charles, of Fort Worth, Texas, gastroenterologist, born 1922; several regional wins include Missouri Valley Open Teams 1954, 1971, Republic of Texas Knockout Teams 1973. President Fort Worth Unit. Contributor to *Texas Bridge*.

ROBINSON, Frances (Mrs. Louis C.), of Philadelphia, Pa., won Fall Nat'l Women's Team 1947, 1949, Spring Nat'l Individual 1958; won Keystone Women's Pairs 1961, District 4 Women's Pairs 1960.

ROBINSON, Maurice, of New York, N.Y., attorney and social worker, born 1918; President of AMERICAN BRIDGE ASSOCIATION 1964–69 and one of its National Tournament Directors.

ROBINSON, Stephen W., of Alexandria, Va., computer specialist, born 1941; one of the leading American players; won World Olympiad Mixed Teams 1974, represented US World Olympiad Open Pairs 1974; won Herman Trophy 1972, Reisinger 1972, Blue Ribbon Pairs 1973, 1975, Spring Nat'l Men's Pairs 1972; second Fall Nat'l Life Masters Men's Pairs 1971, 1972, Spring Nat'l Men's Teams 1973, 1974, Men's Pairs 1973, 1974, Summer Nat'l Mixed Teams 1973; winner of many regional titles including Mid-Atlantic Knockout Teams 1971, 1974, Open Teams 1971, 1973, Open Pairs 1974, Men's Pairs 1969, 1971.

ROCCHI, Egisto, of Buenos Aires, Argentina, wholesale furrier, born 1922; represented Argentina World Championships 1959, 1961, 1962, 1963, 1965. World Team Olympiad 1964, 1968; South American Champion 1959, 1961, 1964; won Argentine Open Teams 1950, 1953, 1958, 1960. 1961. 1964, 1969, Open Pairs 1951, 1961, 1963, 1967. Director Argentine BA.

ROCKAWAY, Dr. Harold, of Sugar Land, Tex., psychiatrist, born 1926; won Herman Trophy 1964, Fall Nat'l Open Pairs 1953, Men's Teams 1953, Chicago 1964; second Spring 1954, Fall Nat'l Men's Teams 1956, Life Masters Men's Pairs 1964; regional successes include Texas Open Teams 1954, Open Pairs 1954.

ROCKAWAY, Tina (Mrs. Harold), of Houston, Tex.; won Spring Nat'l Women's Pairs 1970, Lone Star Swiss Teams 1975 as Mrs. Marc Freedman.

RODRIGUE, Claude, of London, England, stockbroker, born 1930; one of the leading British players; World Par Champion 1961; European Champion 1961; represented Great Britain in World Championship 1962, World Olympiad Open Pairs 1970, 1974, European Championships 1966, 1967, 1969, 1971, 1973, 1974, and Egypt in European Championship 1956; won Gold Cup in 1957, 1964, 1974, and many other national championships including Masters Individual and Mixed Pairs. Writings include contributions to *Bridge Magazine, British Bridge World,* and other periodicals.

RODRIGUE, Maria Elena C. de, of Buenos Aires, Argentina; South American Women's Champion 1957, 1961, 1962; represented Argentina World Olympiad Women's Teams 1972; national wins include Open Pairs 1970.

ROET, Leo, of Hallandale, Fla., born 1903; won Life Masters Pairs 1949, Fall Nat'l Men's Team 1949, Summer Nat'l Mixed Team 1951; second Fall Nat'l Open Pairs 1945, 1950, 1952.

ROGASNER, Mrs. Richard B., of Baltimore, Md., born 1919; won Mid-Atlantic Summer Women's Pairs 1962, District 4 Masters Pairs 1966. Secretary of Maryland BL.

ROGERS, Marty (Mrs. John), of Rancho Cordova, Calif.; several regional wins include All-Western Women's Pairs 1969, Rogue River Open Pairs 1973.

ROMANET, Dr. Bertrand, of Paris, physician and bridge writer, born 1921; World Champion 1956; World Par Champion 1963; European Champion 1955; won French Open Team 1950, 1951, 1954, 1962; many international and national successes; President Bridge Club of Physicians, Director of French Federation of Bridge. Inventor of Alpha System. Author of *Le Squeeze au Bridge,* 1954, and *Les Bases du Bridge Moderne,* 1957. Contributor to *Bridge Encyclopedia,* and many bridge periodicals. See BIBLIOGRAPHY, D, E.

RONCARELLI, Mrs. Mimi, of Montreal, Que.; bridge club proprietor; represented Canada Women's World Team Olympiad 1964; won Fall Nat'l Women's Team 1947; Canadian-American Open Teams 1960, Canadian Nat'l Open Teams 1963, New England Women's Pairs 1966, second Mixed Teams 1962.

ROOSEN, Russell, of Southfield, Mich., manager bridge studio, born 1908; one of Detroit's most prominent bridge figures in the early days of contract as a teacher, lecturer, instructor via radio, and problem composer. He has been Director of the Knickerbocker Bridge Club (Detroit) and columnist for the *Detroit Free Press.* His tournament achievements, beginning with a third-place finish in the ABL National Open Team 1931, include first All-American Open Teams 1955, Motor City Knockout Teams 1974. At exhibitions he demonstrated a remarkable memory by playing ten separate hands simultaneously while blindfolded.

ROOT, Peter C., of North Tonawanda, N.Y., attorney; second Fall Nat'l Open Individual 1954; won Canadian-American Men's Pairs 1955. President Upper New York Conference.

ROOT, William S., of Boca Raton, Fla., bridge teacher, lecturer, and writer, one of the world's outstanding players and teachers; born 1923; second World Team Olympiad 1968; represented North America World Championship 1967; won Chicago 1957, Spingold 1961, 1966, 1967, Vanderbilt 1968, Reisinger 1967, Summer Nat'l Men's Pairs 1953, Marcus 1957, 1960; second Team Trials 1967, third 1966; second Reisinger 1966, Spingold 1963, 1974, Spring Nat'l Men's Teams 1963; regional successes include Eastern States Knockout Teams 1960, 1961, 1966, 1968, Southeastern Open Teams 1954. National Tournament Director for the Intercollegiate Par-Hand Bridge Tournament and the National Industrial Recreation Association Par-Hand Bridge Tournament. Bridge columnist *American Legion Magazine.* Author *Introduction to Bidding, Contract Bridge Outlines* (see BIBLIOGRAPHY, C). Contributing Editor, *Bridge Encyclopedia.*

ROSA, Federico (1910–1972), of Milan, Italy, bridge writer and tournament director; co-founder of the Italian Bridge Federation in 1936; organizer and director of national and international bridge events. Secretary-General of the Italian Bridge Federation. Director of the *Bridge d'Italia,* and editor of a bridge column. Author of *L'A B C del Bridge.* Contributing Editor *Bridge Encyclopedia.*

ROSE, Albert (1908–1970), of London, England, textile converter; a leading European player; second World Team Olympiad 1960; represented Great Britain World Championship 1962 and World Pair Olympiad 1962; won European Championship 1961, second 1953; also represented Great Britain in European Championship 1957; won Gold Cup 1951, 1954, 1958, 1963, and other national championships.

ROSE, Irving N., of London, England, bridge club manager, born 1938; one of the leading British players; represented Great Britain World Pair Olympiad 1974, European Championships 1967, 1973, 1974, several Camrose Cups; national successes include Crockford's twice, Spring Foursomes three times.

ROSE, William, of London, England, textile merchant (1892–1941); one of the great British players of the thirties; won Gold Cup 1933 and 1934, and represented Britain in 1934 SCHWAB CUP match.

ROSEN, Edward L., of Chicago, Ill., bridge teacher, born 1929; one of the leading players of the Midwest; won Summer Nat'l Life Masters Pairs 1959, Spring Nat'l Mixed Pairs 1960, 1962; numerous regional wins include Central States Men's Pairs 1956, Open Teams 1958, Open Pairs, Knockout Teams 1965, Life and Senior Masters Teams 1960, Pairs 1954, Great Lakes Open Teams 1967, 1974. Director Chicago CBA.

ROSEN, Eunice (Mrs. William), of Highland Park, Ill., born 1930; won Summer Nat'l Mixed Team 1958, 1966; several regional wins include Central States Open Teams 1959, Women's Pairs 1963, Midwest Open Teams 1959, 1967, Open Pairs 1959.

ROSEN, William, of Highland Park, Ill., insurance salesman, born 1928; one of the outstanding American players of the postwar period; World Champion 1954; at twenty-five, the youngest player ever to win that title; represented North America World Championship 1955; won McKenney 1953, Spingold 1953, 1954, Life Masters Pairs 1953, Fall Nat'l Men's Pairs 1952, Summer Nat'l Masters Mixed Teams 1958, 1966, second 1965; many regional successes include Central States Open Teams 1962, Life and Senior Masters Pairs 1957, 1962, Masters Pairs 1969, Open Pairs 1963, Great Lakes Open Teams 1967, 1974. Director Chicago BL.

ROSENBERG, Beverly (Mrs. Howard), of Sherman Oaks, Calif.; second Spring Nat'l Women's Teams 1973, won Summer Nat'l secondary Master Women's Pairs 1972.

ROSENBERG, Irving, of Brooklyn, N.Y., service representative, born 1910; second Nat'l Senior Masters Individual 1955; won Eastern States Mixed Teams 1959.

ROSENBERG, Isadore, of Kansas City, Mo., office manager, born 1905; won Central States Open Teams 1953, Mississippi Valley Open Teams 1952, Open Pairs 1951, Missouri Valley Open Teams 1954, 1955, Men's Pairs 1954.

ROSENBERG, Milton, of Lombard, Ill., actuary, born 1944; one of the leading players of the Middle West; winner of many regional titles including District 15 Open Teams 1967, Open Pairs 1967, Central States Knockout Teams 1969, 1972, 1973, Open Pairs 1973. Director Chicago CBA.

ROSENBERG, Ronald, of Bronx, N.Y., accountant and purchasing agent, born 1921; won Spingold 1956; second Fall Nat'l Men's Teams 1951; regional wins include Eastern States Open Pairs 1965, Keystone Conference Open Pairs 1954, 1962, Men's Pairs 1952, 1953, 1954.

ROSENBLATT, Marvin, of Bristol, Conn., realtor, born 1929; winner of many regional titles including New England Fall Masters Teams 1952, 1958, 1962, 1967, 1969, Open Pairs 1967, Spring Teams 1963, 1970, Keystone Fall Swiss Teams 1973.

ROSENBLOOM, Edith (Mrs. George), of Miami Beach, Fla., won Spring Nat'l Mixed Pairs 1951; New York–New Jersey Women's Pairs 1961, Keystone Women's Pairs 1957.

ROSENBLOOM, James, of Scarsdale, N.Y., student, born 1954; winner of several regional events including Upper New York State Knockout Teams 1974, Open Teams 1973, Men's Teams 1973.

ROSENBLUM, Julius, of New Orleans, La.; one of the leading American bridge personalities; npc US Team World Championship 1951, 1966, 1967, 1968, alternate npc 1963; won Spring Nat'l Men's Pairs 1960; second Spingold 1954; numerous regional wins include Mexican Nat'l Open Pairs 1960, Men's Pairs 1962, Mid-South Open Teams 1944, 1949, Masters Pairs 1965, Open Teams 1965, Men's Pairs 1968, 1972. ACBL President 1951. Member of many ACBL committees including Executive Committee 1950–56, ACBL Director 1962–65. President World Bridge Federation 1970–76; Secretary 1966–70. IBPA Bridge Man of the Year 1975.

ROSENBLUM, Natalie (Mrs. Julius), of New Orleans, La.; as wife of and official hostess for the much-traveled former president and secretary of the World Bridge Federation, has been a familiar figure at numerous world and international events. A Life Master since 1957, her excellent record as a player includes wins in Southeastern Mixed Pairs 1953, Women's Teams 1958, Mexican Nat'l Women's Pairs 1962, Bermuda Mixed Pairs 1962.

ROSENBLUM, Robert D., of San Diego, Calif., bridge columnist, travel agent; won Pacific Southwest Masters Pairs 1967; District 22 Grand National 1975. Bridge columnist *San Diego Union* since 1968.

ROSENDORFF, Hans-Gunther, of Perth, Western Australia, librarian and bridge journalist, born Germany 1910; npc Australian Far East Women's

Championship team 1973, 1974; national successes include Individual 1965, 1966. Councillor Australian BF; author weekly column in *The West Australian* since 1956.

ROSENFELD, Louis M., of Baltimore, Md., bridge teacher, writer, tournament director, born 1907; won the Keystone Open Teams 1955. Former President Mid-Atlantic Bridge Conference, and Maryland BA. Author of two books on opening bids and opening leads.

ROSENKRANZ, Edith (Mrs. George), of Mexico, D.F.; represented Mexico World Pair Olympiad 1966, 1974, World Women's Pairs Olympiad 1962, 1970, World Women's Team Olympiad 1964; won Nat'l Mixed Pairs 1948, second Summer Nat'l Mixed Teams 1967; won Mexican Nat'l Open Teams 1974, Masters Pairs 1960, Mixed Pairs 1955, Bridge Week Open Pairs 1957, Pacific Southwest Mixed Pairs 1949.

ROSENKRANZ, Dr. George, of Mexico, D.F., chemist, born 1917; the leading Mexican player and theorist; represented Mexico in World Pair Olympiad 1962, 1966, 1970, 1974, and npc both Mexican teams World Team Olympiad 1964; won Vanderbilt 1975, Summer Nat'l Golder Pairs 1958, Fall Nat'l Men's Teams 1968, second Spingold 1967, Blue Ribbon Pairs 1974; many regional wins include Mexican Nat'l Mixed Pairs 1955, Open Teams 1955, 1956, 1958, 1969, 1971, 1974. Became first Life Master in Mexico; inventor of DYNAMIC NO TRUMP and MEXICAN TWO-DIAMONDS. Author of *The Romex System of Bidding*. Member, Editorial Board *Bridge Encyclopedia*. See BIBLIOGRAPHY, C.

ROSENTHAL, Louis L. (1904–1965), of Mount Prospect, Ill., lawyer; won All-American Open Teams 1957; Central States Open Pairs 1956, Men's Pairs 1957, Great Lakes Men's Pairs 1960, Midwest Spring Open Teams 1958.

ROSLER, Lawrence, of Murray Hills, N.J., physicist, born 1934; second World Par Championship 1961; won North American Zone World Par Championship 1963, Spring Nat'l Men's Pairs 1965, Eastern States Knockout Teams 1967, Open Pairs 1960. Co-inventor of ASTRO and ASTRO CUE-BID. Co-author of many *Bridge World* articles including "Bridge in the Sixties." Contributing Editor *Bridge Encyclopedia*. Former Chairman Advisory Committee National Intercollegiate Tournament and National Industrial Recreation Association Tournament Director. President New Jersey BL 1969–70.

ROSS, Harry, of Des Moines, Iowa, salesman, born 1928; winner of several regional events including Nebraska Knockout Teams 1973.

ROSS, Hugh, of Oakland, Calif.; won International Team Trial 1975; won Reisinger 1968, 1974, 1975; regional wins include Golden Gate Knockout Teams 1970.

ROSSANT, Simon (1903–1968), of New York, N.Y., haberdashery manufacturer; won Chicago 1941, 1947, Fall Nat'l Men's Pairs 1941; second Life Masters Pairs 1945, Chicago 1943, Vanderbilt 1946, 1954; won Eastern States Knockout Teams 1951; second Southeastern Men's Teams 1958. Co-author of RUSINOW LEADS.

ROSSIGNOL, Roger, of Caracas, Venezuela, businessman, born 1928; represented Venezuela World Team Olympiad 1960, 1964, 1968, World Pairs Olympiad 1966, World Championships 1966, 1967, South American Championships eleven times; South American Champion 1963, 1965, 1966; national wins include Open Teams nine times, Open Pairs, Mixed Teams.

ROTH, Alvin, of New York, N.Y., club proprietor, bridge teacher, and writer; one of the great players of all time, generally considered the most original bidding theorist of his bridge generation; second World Team Olympiad 1968; represented North America World Championships 1955, 1958, 1967; won Fishbein 1963, 1965, Spingold 1940, 1956, 1957, 1963. 1967, Chicago 1946, 1952, Vanderbilt 1943, 1963, 1968, Reisinger 1967, Fall Nat'l Men's Teams 1955, 1961, Summer Nat'l Mixed Teams 1952, 1953, 1955, 1965, Life Masters Pairs 1956, 1971, 1972, Fall Nat'l Open Pairs 1942, Spring Nat'l Open Pairs 1960, Fall Nat'l Mixed Pairs 1952, Spring Nat'l Men's Teams 1971, Mixed Pairs 1959, Masters Individual 1943, Men's Teams 1969; second International Team Trials 1967, third Spingold 1966; second Spingold 1943, 1945, 1953, 1961, Reisinger 1966, Chicago 1937, 1954, Fall Nat'l Open Pairs 1958, Men's Teams 1957, Mixed Teams 1945, Summer Nat'l Mixed Teams 1963, Nat'l Life Masters Pairs 1965; numerous regional successes include Eastern States Knockout Teams 1946, 1953, 1960, 1961, 1966, 1968, Open Pairs 1961, Men's Pairs 1960, New York-New Jersey Mixed Pairs 1965, Men's Pairs 1974. Writings include *Al Roth on Bridge, The Roth-Stone System, Bridge Is a Partnership Game, Modern Bridge Bidding Complete, Bridge for Beginners*. Co-inventor of the ROTH-STONE SYSTEM; his many contributions to bidding theory include the UNUSUAL NO TRUMP and the NEGATIVE DOUBLE. See BIBLIOGRAPHY, C, E.

ROTHFIELD, Jessel M., of Melbourne, Australia, company director, born 1917; won Far East Championships 1968, 1970, represented Australia Far East Championships 1967, 1969; npc Australian Bermuda Bowl Team 1971; won National Pairs 1970, ACBL Fall Nat'l Men's Teams 1969. President Australian Bridge Federation 1967–71; member World Bridge Federation Executive Council since 1970.

ROTHLEIN, Robert, of Orlando, Fla., general contractor; won Spingold 1958, second 1954; regional wins include Southeastern Open Team 1959, Men's Team 1954, 1956, 1966, 1968, Open Pairs 1956, 1957, Men's Pairs 1953, 1959, Mixed Pairs 1958, Governor Florida Unit.

ROTMAN, Daniel, of Skokie, Ill., bridge teacher and club owner, born 1932. One of the leading players of the Midwest. Won Life Masters Pairs 1959, Morehead 1967, Summer Nat'l Masters Mixed Teams 2969; second Spring Nat'l Open Pairs 1963, 1973, Men's Teams 1965, Reisinger 1967, Marcus 1959; many regional wins include Central States Knockout Teams 1966, 1969, Open Pairs 1960, 1969, Midwest Open Teams 1959, 1965, Mixed Pairs 1965.

ROTMAN, Florence (Mrs. Daniel), backgammon teacher; won Summer Nat'l Mixed Teams 1969; regional wins include Motor City Open Teams 1972.

ROTTECK, Dr. Heinz von, of Karlsruhe, Germany, brewery manager, born 1905; represented Germany European Championships 1961, npc 1965, 1966; three wins in German Open Teams. Chairman of the German Bridge Federation.

ROTZELL, Peggy (1929–1969), of Philadelphia, Pa., bridge teacher and writer; won Fall Nat'l Women's Teams 1956, 1958; second Summer Nat'l Mixed Teams 1959; regional successes include District 4 Open Teams 1962, Mixed Pairs 1964, Keystone Open Teams 1960, 1961, Mixed Pairs 1965, Open Pairs 1957, Women's Pairs 1963, Mid-Atlantic Fall Open Pairs 1960, New York–New Jersey Open Teams 1960, Women's Pairs 1960. Regular contributor to ACBL *Bulletin,* and author of two bridge books.

ROUDINESCO, Jean-Marc, of Paris, France, born 1932; European Champion 1966, 1970; represented France World Championships 1967, European Championships 1967. National titles include Open Teams 1963, 1965.

ROUSSOS, George P., of Greece, consulting engineer, born 1931; represented Greece European Championships 1967; national successes include Open Teams 1967. Executive Council Hellenic BF.

ROVERE, Ernest, of San Francisco, Calif., journalist, author, and travel agent; one of the leading bridge personalities; won Nat'l Mixed Teams 1955; regional wins include All-Western Open Pairs 1945, 1951, Men's Pairs 1948, 1957, 1958, Mixed Pairs 1955, Bridge Week Knockout Teams 1958, Mixed Teams 1942, Masters Pairs 1938, 1940, 1947, Men's Pairs 1948, Mixed Pairs 1939, Individual 1946, Rocky Mountain Open Pairs 1955. Bridge editor, San Francisco *Chronicle,* and commentator on radio and TV bridge programs in that city. Author of *Leads, Signals and Discards, Modern Point-Count*

Contract Bridge. Director ACBL 1957–60. Contributing Editor *Bridge Encyclopedia.* See BIBLIOGRAPHY, D, E.

ROWE, Nelson G., of Smyrna, Ga., professional tournament director, born 1913; President (four terms) Georgia unit, Associate National ACBL Tournament Director. ACBL Director 1956–57.

ROYAL, Herbert C., of Garden Grove, Calif., insurance investigator, born 1933; won Fall Nat'l Sub-National Masters Teams 1959, Bridge Week Individual 1967.

ROZEANU, Louis, of Haifa, Israel, professor of thermodynamics, born 1912; represented Israel World Team Olympiad 1964; national successes include Open Pairs 1962.

ROZECKI, Aleksander, of Warsaw, Poland, bridge writer and editor, born 1912; represented Poland World Team Olympiad 1964, European Championship 1957, and Mitropa Cup 1957; national titles include Open Team 1957, 1958, Individual 1961, second Open Pairs 1966. Executive editor *Brydz.* Co-author of two books for the less experienced player.

RUBBRA, Fredrick C., of Nassau, Bahamas, retired stockbroker; represented Bahamas World Team Olympiad 1972, World Pair Olympiad 1970; won Spring Nat'l secondary Swiss Teams 1974; winner of several regional titles including Puget Sound Knockout Teams 1973, Canadian Nat'l Open Teams 1974.

RUBENFELD, Moe, of Hollywood, Fla.; regional wins include Land of Coronado Knockout Teams 1974.

RUBENS, Gayle, of Miami Beach, Fla., born 1939; winner of several regional events including Keystone Women's Swiss Teams 1971, 1972, 1973.

RUBENS, Jeff, of Scarsdale, N.Y., Co-editor of *The Bridge World* since 1966, mathematician and bridge writer, born 1941; represented North America World Championship 1973; won International Team Trials 1972; won Spingold 1972, Spring Nat'l Men's Teams, Men's Pairs 1965; regional wins include Eastern States Knockout Teams 1970, New England Open Pairs 1964, Masters Pairs 1962, Masters Teams 1962; won Intercollegiate 1958; former Editor of *Bridge Journal;* co-chairman Advisory Committee for Intercollegiate Par Hand Tournament. Author of *Secrets of Winning Bridge;* co-author *Modern Bridge Bidding Complete, Bridge for Beginners.* Contributing Editor *Bridge Encyclopedia.* See BIBLIOGRAPHY, C, E.

RUBIN, Carl B., of Cincinnati, Ohio, lawyer and, since 1971, Judge US District Court for Southern

Ohio; President ACBL 1971; ACBL Director 1965–73; Director Cincinnati BA 1959–64, Midwest Conference 1963–65.

RUBIN, Ira S., of Paramus, N.J., mathematical computer engineer, born 1930; one of the world's great players; holds record number of three wins in Nat'l Men's Pairs; represented US World Team Olympiad 1960, World Championships 1966; won International Team Trials 1965, 1975, third 1967; won Reisinger 1969, 1974, 1975, Fishbein 1959, 1962, Vanderbilt 1965, 1966, Spingold 1956, 1959, 1966, Life Masters Pairs 1962, Blue Ribbon Pairs 1970, Spring Nat'l Men's Pairs 1958, 1961, 1962, Open Pairs 1961; second Spingold 1957, 1969, Vanderbilt 1968, 1969, 1971, Life Masters Pairs 1954, 1955, 1963, Summer Nat'l Mixed Teams 1957, Fall Nat'l Men's Pairs 1955, Open Teams 1965, co-winner Herman Trophy 1970; regional wins include Bridge Week Knockout Teams 1959, Eastern States Knockout Teams 1973, 1974. Inventor of RUBIN TRANSFERS, TWO-WAY TWO-BIDS.

RUBIN, Ronald D., of New York, N.Y., investment analyst, born 1948; won Spring Nat'l Men's Teams 1975, Fall Nat'l secondary Swiss Teams 1974; several regional wins include Fun City Open Teams 1973, Puerto Rico Open Teams 1971. Former ACBL regional tournament director.

RUBIN, Sam, of Antwerp, Belgium, diamond dealer, born 1926; represented Belgium several times in World Olympiads and European Championships; many national tournament successes.

RUBINOW, Morton L. (1927–1962), of New York, N.Y., bridge teacher; one of the leading American players; represented US World Team Olympiad 1960; won Herman Trophy 1959, Spingold 1959, Vanderbilt 1962, Fall Nat'l Open Pairs 1959, Spring Nat'l Men's Pairs 1961, Fall Nat'l Open Individual 1955; third Spingold 1962; won Reisinger 1962, New England Spring Open Pairs 1953, Eastern States Men's Pairs 1955, New England Fall Masters Pairs 1957. In 1959 pioneered bridge teaching through long-playing records, "Play Bridge with Morton Rubinow" and "Advanced Bridge Conventions."

RUBINOW, Sol I., of Scarsdale, N.Y., professor of biomathematics, born 1923; second Life Masters Pairs 1954, Spring Nat'l Men's Teams 1963, won Reisinger 1962, 1963, New England Spring Open Pairs 1953, Fall Masters Pairs 1957, 1960. Intercollegiate Chess Champion 1943. Brother of Morton Rubinow.

RUIA, Ramniwas R., of Bombay, president of manufacturing companies, born 1900; captain Indian Team World Team Olympiad 1960; national successes include Open Team 1959, Master Pairs 1960,

1961, second 1959, 1962. President All-India Bridge Federation, President Bombay CBA. Member executive committee WBF. Donor Ruia Gold Trophy 1960.

RUNEBERG, Lorenzo, of Helsinki, doctor of forestry, born 1916; represented Finland European Championships 1938, 1940, 1950, 1951, 1953, 1955, 1957, 1962; won Finnish Open Team 1948, 1950, 1951, 1952, Open Pairs 1938, 1946, 1947, 1955, 1957, Mixed Pairs 1960, 1961. Vice-President Finnish Bridge League.

RUNEBERG, Ulla (Mrs. Lorenzo), of Helsinki, Finland, born 1916; represented Finland Open Team European Championship 1962, Women's Team 1950, 1951, 1953, 1955, 1956, 1961; national successes include Open Team 1948, 1950, 1951, 1952, Open Pairs 1946, 1947, Mixed Pairs 1960, 1961.

RUNTZ, George de, of St. Louis, Mo., supervisor, born 1907; won Vanderbilt 1962, Mississippi Valley Open Teams 1959.

RUPP, Mrs. V. R., of Indianapolis, Ind., born 1906; second Fall Nat'l Women's Teams 1966; won Western States Mixed Pairs 1941, Open Teams 1942. Secretary of Central Indiana BA.

RUSH, Courtland, of St. Joseph, Mo., district sales manager, born 1917; many regional successes include Northwest Masters Pairs 1960, 1961, Open Team 1963, Oregon Trail Open Team 1966. Inventor of RUSH ASKING BID and BULLDOG SYSTEM.

RUSH, Doris (Mrs. G. Rufus), of Lubbock, Tex., born 1927; several regional wins include Texas Spring Open Teams 1962, Women's Pairs 1970.

RUSH, G. Rufus, of Lubbock, Tex., real estate developer and farmer, born 1923; won North Texas Open Team 1962, Northwest Masters Pairs 1965, District 15 Knockout Teams 1968.

RUSINOW, Sydney (1907–1953), of Newark, N.J., silver mine owner, businessman; won Vanderbilt 1933; second Life Masters Pairs 1934; won Eastern States Knockout Teams 1935, New England Knockout Teams 1935, New England Knockout Teams 1936, Open Pairs 1935. Designed a system of opening leads that bears his name. The original Rusinow principle was the lead of the lower of two honors. This was later refined to the lead of the lower of two touching honors.

RUSSELL, Clifford, of Miami, Fla., general contractor, born 1919; one of the leading American players; won Spingold 1963, Vanderbilt 1963; second Spingold 1954, 1972, Vanderbilt 1975,

Marcus 1955, Mixed Team 1964, Blue Ribbon Pairs 1963, 1970, Fall Nat'l Open Teams 1964; numerous regional wins include Southeastern Open Teams 1957, 1958, 1960. 1962, 1963, 1964, Men's Teams 1957, 1958, Men's Pairs 1955, 1960, 1963, 1964, Open Pairs 1963, 1964, Mixed Pairs 1968, Life Master Pairs 1968.

RUTHERFORD, Mrs. Allan, of Baltimore, Md.; Baltimore Team Champion 1933, 1934. Honorary member ACBL 1948.

RUTLEDGE, W. T., Jr., of Charleston, S.C., attorney, born 1939; won Fall Nat'l secondary Swiss Teams 1972; regional wins include Mid-Atlantic Spring Open Teams 1965.

RUTSTEIN, Donald, of Chicago, Ill., salesman, born 1927; winner of several regional events including Central States Open Team 1954, 1972, Knockout Team 1962.

RYAN, Mrs. George, of Indianapolis, Ind.; second Summer Nat'l Women's Pairs 1950, Fall Nat'l Women's Teams 1966; won All-American Open Pairs 1944, Central States Open Pairs 1949.

RYDER, Robert W., of Caldwell, N.J., consulting actuary, born 1935; won Fall Nat'l secondary Open Pairs 1969; several regional wins include Tri-State Open Teams 1967, Keystone Open Teams 1968, Men's Pairs 1974. Member New York Intercity Team 1968. Treasurer New Jersey Bridge League.

S

SAALE, Donald, of Chillicothe, Mo., born 1923; won Mid-American–Canadian Open Pairs 1959, Missouri Valley Open Teams 1960 and 1963, Open Pairs 1960.

SACHS, David S., of Baltimore, Md., actuary, born 1942; represented US World Olympiad Pairs 1970; second Spring Nat'l Open Pairs 1969, Summer Nat'l Mixed Teams 1970, 1974; several regional wins including Keystone Open Teams 1971, 1972, 1973, 1974.

SACHS, Edith, of New York, N.Y., real estate broker; won Summer Nat'l Mixed Teams 1973; regional wins include Eastern States Women's Pairs 1969.

SACHS, Herbert, of Pittsburgh, Pa.; winner of several regional championships including Motor City Open Teams 1970, Mid-Atlantic Open Teams 1970, Keystone Fall Open Teams 1973.

SACHS, Suzanne (Mrs. David S.), of Baltimore, Md., born 1933; one of the leading American women players; second Women's Pairs Olympiad 1966, third Women's Teams Olympiad 1968; represented US World Pairs Olympiad 1970; won Mott-Smith Trophy 1969, Spring Nat'l Women's Pairs 1965, Women's Teams 1966, second 1969, Open Pairs 1969; won Fall Nat'l Life Masters Women's Pairs 1967; second Summer Nat'l Mixed Teams 1970, 1974; regional successes include Keystone Women's Pairs 1966, Open Teams 1971, 1972, 1973, 1974.

SAID, Chuck, of Nashville, Tenn., bridge instructor and writer, born 1939; won Spring Nat'l secondary Open Pairs 1969, secondary Mixed Pairs 1972; several regional titles include Cambrian Shield Knockout Teams 1972, Open Teams 1972, Mid-Atlantic Master Pairs 1974.

ST. LUCE, Ralph, of Jamaica, physician, born 1934; represented Jamaica World Team Olympiad 1968, Central American and Caribbean Championships 1971, 1972, 1973, 1974, winning three times, second once; national wins include every major Jamaican title.

SAITO, Morse, of Kobe, Japan, English teacher and newspaper columnist. Author of bridge column in *Mainichi Daily News,* published in Tokyo and Osaka, since 1960.

SALTSMAN, Barbara (Mrs. David), of Montreal; represented Canada World Women's Teams Olympiad 1972; second Summer Nat'l Mixed Teams 1974; won Canadian-American Women's Pairs 1970.

SALTZ, Jack B., of New York, N.Y., account executive; second Summer Nat'l Mixed Teams 1974; regional wins include Fun City Knockout Teams 1973.

SAN, Tan Hok, of Surabaya, Indonesia, merchant, born 1923; Far East Champion 1962, second 1961; national titles include Open Team 1960, 1962, 1964, Open Pairs 1961.

SANDERS, Carol (Mrs. Thomas K.), of Nashville, Tenn., born 1932; one of the leading American women players; won Venice Cup 1975, represented US World Women's Pairs Olympiad 1962, 1974; won Spring Nat'l Mixed Pairs 1961, Women's Pairs 1962, Fall Nat'l Open Pairs 1964; second Chicago 1961,

Fall Nat'l Life Master Women's Pairs 1971, Spring Nat'l Open Pairs 1960; numerous regional successes include Mid-South Knockout Teams 1972, 1974 (twice), Masters Pairs 1970, 1972, 1973, Open Pairs 1971, Women's Pairs 1970, 1974, Mississippi Valley Open Teams 1958, Women's Pairs 1961, 1965.

SANDERS, Thomas K., of Nashville, Tenn., warehouse developer, born 1932; one of the leading players of the South; won Spring Nat'l Mixed Pairs 1961, Men's Pairs 1962, Fall Nat'l secondary Men's Teams 1974; second Spingold 1963, Chicago 1961, Reisinger 1973, Spring Nat'l Open Pairs 1960, Men's Pairs 1963; numerous regional successes include Mid-Atlantic Men's Team 1957, Open Teams 1970, Masters Pairs 1972, Southern Conference Masters Pairs 1959, Men's Pairs 1958, 1963, 1966, Mid-South Knockout Teams 1974, Men's Pairs 1974.

SANDGREN, Tore, of Stockholm, Sweden, army officer and bridge writer, born 1909; won World Bridge Olympic 1938; European Champion 1939, represented Sweden European Championship 1936, 1937, 1938, 1958; national titles include Open Team 1948, 1956. Bridge editor of the *Stockholm Expressen*.

SANTA COLOMA, Luis de, of Buenos Aires, Argentina, lawyer and landholder, born 1908; npc Argentine World Championship 1959, npc Argentine South American Championships 1967, 1971. President Argentine BA since 1967.

SANTAMARINA, Agustín, of Buenos Aires, Argentina, landholder, born 1934; represented Argentina World Team Olympiad 1964, 1968, 1972, World Championship 1965; South American Champion 1962, 1964; won Argentine Open Team 1956, 1965, 1967, 1970, 1973, 1974, Open Pairs 1959, 1960.

SANTAMARINA, Marcos, of Buenos Aires, Argentina, landholder, born 1931; represented Argentina World Championship 1963; South American Champion 1962; won Argentine Open Team 1956, 1968.

SANTOS, Jorge Monteiro Dos, of Lisbon, Portugal, lawyer, born 1941; represented Portugal European Championships 1969, 1970; national wins include Open Teams four times, and Open Pairs once.

SANTOS, Rui Silva, of Lisbon, Portugal, electrical engineer, born 1944; represented Portugal European Championships 1969, 1971; national wins include Open Teams twice.

SAPIRE, Leon, of Johannesburg, South Africa, attorney and bridge writer, born 1910; npc South African Open Teams and Women's Team World Olympiad 1960; national titles include Open Pairs 1955, second Open Teams 1958, Open Pairs 1956.

Founder and editor *Bridge Bulletin* since 1950. Former IBPA Vice-President; former executive member World Bridge Federation, founder and honorary Life Vice-President of Contract Bridge Council of South Africa.

SAPIRE, Max, of East London, South Africa, business executive and bridge writer, born 1918; represented South Africa World Team Olympiad 1960; won South African Pairs Par Contest 1954, second 1962; national titles include Open Teams 1957, Open Pairs 1955, second 1956, 1961, second Open Teams 1958, Par Contest 1954, 1962. Writings include magazine articles in *South African Bulletin* and *British Bridge World*. Author of book on Culbertson asking bids. Inventor of several bidding ideas including SOUTH AFRICAN TEXAS.

SARAVIA, Alfredo, of Buenos Aires, Argentina, real estate official, born 1908; represented Argentina World Championship 1963; South American Champion 1964; won Argentine Open Team 1940, 1941, 1947, 1954; Open Pairs 1944, 1959. Former President Argentine BA.

SARON, Robert, of St. Petersburg, Fla., pharmaceutical company president and bridge writer, born 1923; won Nat'l Comm. & Ind. Pairs 1961; Southeastern Open Teams 1962.

SARON, Sally (Mrs. Robert), of St. Petersburg, Fla., vice-president pharmaceutical company and registered nurse, born 1931; won Nat'l Comm. & Ind. Pairs 1961; Florida Women's Teams 1961, Mixed Pairs 1963, Southeastern Mixed Pairs 1963.

SAVDIE, Raymond, of Bogotá, Colombia, chemical engineer, born 1936 in Cairo, Egypt; represented Colombia South American Championships 1964, 1967, Caribbean Championships 1965; Caribbean Champion 1968; national titles include Open Teams 1967, Masters Pairs 1966, 1968; second Masters Pairs 1967.

SAVOSTIN, Nicolas, of Brussels, Belgium, sales manager and bridge writer, born 1906; represented Belgium World Team Olympiad 1960, 1964; third Mixed Team event Cannes 1962; third De La Rue International Pairs Championship 1957; represented Belgium in many European Championships; national titles include Open Teams, Mixed Teams, Open Pairs and Mixed Pairs. Contributor to magazines in Italy and Belgium.

SAYED, Floyd E., of Detroit, Mich., insurance salesman, born 1925; regional successes include Motor City Knockout Teams 1974, Open Teams, Open Pairs 1968. Former President of Michigan BA and a member of its Board of Directors.

SCAFFIDI, Sam, of Wintersville, Ohio, social worker, born 1935; won Midwest Fall Open Team 1960, Great Lakes Open Team 1962, District 5– Swiss Teams 1970. See STRIPED-TAIL APE DOUBLE.

SCALA, Wolfgang von, Graz, Austria, banker, born 1903; represented Austria European Championships 1939, 1955, 1966; national successes include Open Teams 1949, and German Open Teams 1939.

SCANAVINO, Eduardo, of Buenos Aires, Argentina, bridge teacher, born 1941; national wins include Open Teams 1966, 1973, 1974.

SCHALTZ, Peter, of Graasten Denmark, wholesaler, born 1950; won European Jr. Open Teams 1970; Nordic Jr. Open Teams 1971, 1973. Represented Denmark in European Open Teams 1975. Won all three major Danish national titles—Open Teams, Open Pairs, and Cup—1975.

SCHAPIRO, Boris, of London, England, croupier, born 1911; one of the leading players of the world; his partnership with Terence REESE has ranked as one of the world's best since 1948. World Champion 1955; second World Team Olympiad 1960, represented Great Britain in 1964 Team Olympiad, World Championships 1965; second in World Pairs Olympiad 1962 and won Mixed Team event; represented Great Britain in ten European Championships, winning in 1948, 1949, 1954, 1963; won CROWNIN-SHIELD TROPHY 1948; won Gold Cup 1946, 1947, 1948, 1950, 1952, 1953, 1956, 1960, 1964; won Master Pairs 1947, 1954, 1956, 1959, 1962, and many other national championships. Bridge editor London *Sunday Times.* In the 1965 World Championships Schapiro and his partner Terence Reese were accused of conveying information about the heart suit through finger signals. Both were convicted by the World Bridge Federation, but were acquitted after a more exhaustive investigation by a special inquiry set up by the British Bridge League. See BUENOS AIRES AFFAIR.

SCHAUFELBERGER, W. K. A., of Sydney, Australia, chief director of the New South Wales BA, born 1902; captain Australian Team World Team Olympiad 1960; captain Australian Open Team Champion 1947, 1948, 1949, 1950, 1952, 1954, 1955, 1957, 1961, won Open pairs 1954, 1959. Treasurer Australian Bridge Federation, Vice-President New South Wales BA.

SCHEINBERG, Martin R., of New York, N.Y., systems engineer, born 1930; won Fall Nat'l Men's Team 1960, Nat'l Non-Masters Pairs 1956; New England Fall Mixed Team 1960. Pioneer in scoring tournament results and predealing hands by electronic data-processing equipment. See COMPUTERS.

SCHEMEIL, Pierre, Paris, finance counsel, born 1921; represented Switzerland World Pairs Olympiad 1962; represented Lebanon European Championships 1952; represented Egypt European Championships 1953, 1954, 1958, 1959, 1961; national successes include French Open Team three times, Open Pairs 1963; Lebanese Open Team and Pairs; Egyptian Open Team, Open Pairs, Mixed Pairs; runner-up Swiss Pairs 1962.

SCHENKEN, Bee (Mrs. Howard), formerly Bee Gale, of New York, N.Y., born 1916; one of the world's most successful women rubber bridge players; won Fall Nat'l Mixed Pairs 1957, Women's Teams 1958, 1960, 1961, 1969, Spring Nat'l Women's Teams 1964, 1968, second 1963, 1967, Reisinger 1966, Summer Nat'l Mixed Teams 1958, Spring Nat'l Women's Pairs 1969; many regional wins include Eastern States Women's Pairs 1962, 1968, Southeastern Open Teams, Women's Teams 1958, Open Pairs 1974.

SCHENKEN, Howard, of New York, N.Y., real estate investor, bridge author and columnist, born in New York, N.Y., Sept. 28, 1903; one of the great players of the world, by the majority of US experts (as indicated by several polls) considered the best player of all time. Credited with introduction of several aspects of playing technique and deceptive play now standard, plus the WEAK TWO-BID, the forcing TWO-OVER-ONE, the prepared opening bid ("anticipation"), and other bidding devices. Schenken's Raymond Club team, 1927–29, first successfully broke the reign of the established men's clubs in tournament competition. After occasional appearances with the FOUR HORSEMEN and BID-RITE teams, Schenken was a founder of the FOUR ACES and participated in their long series of victories including victory over the French European champions in 1935 in the first official World Championship (see WORLD CHAMPIONSHIPS) and a winning tour of Europe in pair matches with M. T. Gottlieb, the next year. World Champion 1950, 1951, 1953; represented US World Olympiad 1960, and North American World Championships 1961, 1963, 1965. His five wins in the Life Masters Pairs 1931, 1933, 1934, 1941, 1943, and his ten wins in the Spingold 1934, 1936, 1938, 1939, 1943, 1945, 1948, 1950, 1952, 1960, the Vanderbilt won ten times, 1934, 1935, 1937, 1938, 1946, 1950, 1955, 1956, 1957, 1964, each constitutes a record. Other national wins include Reisinger 1968, Chicago 1957, 1963, Fall Nat'l Men's Team 1949, Mixed Team 1935, Mixed Pairs 1957, Master Individual 1932; second Spingold 1941, 1947, 1955, Chicago 1950, Vanderbilt 1930, 1931, 1932, 1941, 1945, 1952, 1959, 1962, 1967, Reisinger 1966, Mixed Teams 1931, 1936, 1958, Life Masters Pairs 1932. (See also USBA Championship.) ACBL Board of Directors 1937–38; honorary member IBPA 1973. Co-author of *Four Aces System of Contract Bridge,* 1935; author of *Better Bidding in Fifteen Minutes* and *Howard Schenken's Big Club* (see SCHENKEN SYSTEM), and *Education of a Bridge Player.* Took over Four Aces syndicated bridge column in 1943 and in 1957 merged it with R. L. Frey's to become co-author of longest continuously published nationally syndicated bridge feature. In 1970, he became the sole author of the column. Contributing Editor *Bridge Encyclopedia.* See BIBLIOGRAPHY, C, K.

SCHENONE, Dr. Luis (1910–1971), of Buenos Aires, Argentina, physician; represented Argentina World Championships 1963; South American Champion 1948, 1953; won Argentine Open Teams 1957, Open Pairs 1939, 1952, 1959.

SCHENONE, Mrs. Mercedes G. de, of Buenos Aires, Argentina; South American Women's Champion on seven occasions; represented Argentina World Women's Team Olympiad 1972; won Argentine Open Team 1951, 1965, 1971, Open Pairs 1957.

SCHERMER, John, of Seattle, Wash.; won Summer Nat'l secondary Open Pairs 1974; several regional wins include Bridge Week Knockout Teams 1974, Mount Shasta Knockout Teams 1974.

SCHEUER, Jerome, of Brookline, Mass., insurance broker, born 1889; won New England Knockout Teams twelve times, 1938, 1939, 1941 (twice), 1943, 1945, 1946 (twice), 1947, 1950, 1951, 1954, Open Teams 1950. Contributor to *Bridge Magazine* and *The Bridge World.* Contributing Editor *Bridge Encyclopedia.* Prominent as a lawn tennis official at the national and international levels.

SCHILTZ, Robert, of Nantes, France, commercial director and bridge writer, born 1909; European Champion 1953; won French Open Team 1948, 1953. Director French Bridge Federation. Writings include articles on American and European bridge systems for magazines.

SCHLEIFER, Meyer, of Los Angeles, Calif., bridge teacher, born 1908; one of the leading American players; represented US World Team Olympiad 1960; Inter-City Champion 1963, Summer Nat'l Life Master Pairs 1966, second Men's Pairs 1967; winner of a great many regional titles including All-Western Knockout Teams 1974, Masters Teams 1972, 1974, Masters Pairs 1943, Open Pairs 1942, 1943, 1947, Mixed Pairs 1965, Bridge Week Knockout Teams 1951, 1954, 1957, 1960, 1965, 1970, 1971, Masters Teams 1947, 1956, Mixed Teams 1956, 1961, 1967, Open Teams 1939, 1940, 1941, 1945, 1946, 1949, 1958, 1959, Masters Pairs 1943, 1963, Open Pairs 1942, 1943, 1947, 1948, Men's Pairs 1956, 1963.

SCHNEE, Lt. Col. Murray L., of Little Neck, N.Y., bridge teacher, born 1913; won New England Fall Masters Pairs 1956, Eastern States Knockout Teams 1966, second Men's Pairs 1956; won New York–New Jersey Open Teams 1965, Tri-State Teams and Team of Four 1970.

SCHNEIDEMAN, Leslie M., of Wellington, New Zealand, company director, born 1910; npc New Zealand Team in WBF Zone 7 competition 1968, 1969, World Team Olympiad 1972, npc New Zealand Women's Team Far East Championships 1971. New Zealand CBA President 1959–63, 1964–69, and since 1970; Zone 7 Delegate to WBF since 1970; WBF Executive Council since 1972.

SCHNEIDER, Karl, of Vienna, engineer, born 1904; one of the great players of the world; World Champion 1937, European Champion 1936; represented Europe in World Championship 1954; represented Austria five times, European Championship, second 1951, 1957; captain of Austrian national team for five years. Retired from international play since 1957.

SCHOENFELD, Brian L., of Alexandria, Va., accountant, born 1946; several regional wins include Mid-Atlantic Knockout Teams 1972, 1973, Swiss Teams 1974.

SCHOLIN, Rainer, of Helsinki, Finland, economist, born 1930; represented Finland European Championship 1956, 1959; Scandinavian Championship 1955, 1962; won Finnish Open Team 1958, 1960, 1962, 1963.

SCHOUCAIR, Henri A., of Beirut, Lebanon, engineer, born 1920; npc World Olympiad 1960; represented Lebanon European Championships 1954, 1956, 1957, 1959, 1962; national successes include Open Team and Open Pairs several times each. Former Chairman of Lebanese Bridge Federation.

SCHREIBER, Michael J., of Los Angeles, Calif., born 1952; winner of several regional titles including Desert Empire Open Teams 1972, Open Pairs 1970. Intercollegiate Champion 1973.

SCHREIBER, William, of Los Angeles, Calif.; winner of several regional titles including Desert Empire Open Teams 1972, Open Pairs 1970. Intercollegiate Champion 1973.

SCHULD, Diana, of Glen Head, N.Y.; second Life Masters Pairs 1967, won Summer Nat'l secondary Open Pairs 1973; regional wins include New England Open Teams 1971.

SCHULD, Frank, of Glen Head, N.Y.; second Life Masters Pairs 1967; won Summer Nat'l secondary Open Pairs 1973; regional wins include New England Open Teams 1971. Author, *The Simple Squeeze* (see BIBLIOGRAPHY, D).

SCHULLE, Kay, of La Jolla, Calif., winner of several regional events including Mount Shasta Knockout Teams 1974, Intermountain Open Teams 1974.

SCHWAB, Charles M. (1862–1939), noted US financier and steel magnate, patron of bridge. He was president of the Whist Club of New York, played on its teams, and was *ex officio* member of the committee that participated in the first International Code of Contract Bridge Laws, 1932. Donor of SCHWAB TROPHY for Anglo-American competition, 1933. He played regularly in the highest-stake bridge games on record, $1 per point in the US, approximately $2 per point in London (Portland Club).

SCHWAB, Clara (Mrs. Irving W., formerly Mrs. Dunlap Dwyer), of Springfield, Mo., born 1908; won Missouri Valley Women's Pairs 1954, Mixed Pairs 1961, Mississippi Valley Mixed Pairs 1955. Former ACBL Vice-President and Secretary, member National Goodwill Committee, President Southwest Missouri Unit.

SCHWAB, Irving W., of Springfield, Mo., attorney, born 1900; won Mississippi Valley Mixed Pairs 1955, Men's Pairs 1956, Missouri Valley Mixed Pairs 1961. Former President Missouri Valley Regional.

SCHWARTZ, Elmer I., Shaker Heights, Ohio, attorney, born 1903; won Chicago 1949, Fall Nat'l Men's Team 1958; second Spingold 1946, Chicago 1952; regional wins include Keystone Mixed Pairs 1953, All-American Men's Pairs, Mixed Pairs 1965.

SCHWARTZ, Mrs. Elmer I., of Shaker Heights, Ohio, born 1907; represented US World Women's Team Olympiad 1960; second Spring Nat'l Women's Teams 1938, Nat'l Pairs 1959; regional wins include Keystone Mixed Pairs 1953, All-American Open Pairs, Mixed Pairs 1965.

SCHWARTZ, Eugene, of Mercer Island, Wash., airline captain, born 1916; won Northwest Open Teams 1959, Masters Pairs 1960, 1961.

SCHWARTZ, Mrs. Joseph, of Anaconda, Mont., department store executive; won Northern Rocky Mountain Women's Pairs 1958, 1960, Open Teams 1958.

SCHWARTZ, Norman A., of Phoenix, Ariz.; winner of several regional events including Mid-Atlantic Open Teams 1971 (twice), Men's Pairs 1971.

SCHWARTZ. Peter L., of Quebec, Que., railway marketing manager, born 1934; won Canadian-American Open Pairs 1957, Open Team 1956, 1957.

SCHWARTZ, Richard C., of Brooklyn, N.Y., program analyst, born 1943; won Nat'l Comm. & Ind. Teams 1967, several regional wins including Tri-State Open Teams 1968, won Great Lakes Men's Pairs 1965.

SCHWARZ, Adrian, of Israel, engineer, born 1944; represented Israel World Team Olympiad 1968, 1972, European Championships 1970, 1971, 1973, 1974; national successes include Open Pairs 1968, 1969, 1971.

SCHWENCKE, John A., of North Palm Beach, Fla., real estate investor; won Spring Nat'l secondary Mixed Pairs 1971; several regional wins include Southeastern Open Teams 1967, Knockout Teams 1973, Men's Teams 1971, Open Pairs 1972.

SCOPE, Ivan H., of San Francisco, Calif., operations consultant; won secondary Blue Ribbon Pairs 1971; several regional wins include All-Western Masters Pairs 1970, Mixed Pairs 1970, California Capitol Knockout Teams 1972.

SCOTT, Ronald J., of Hamilton, New Zealand, dairy farmer, born 1930; represented New Zealand Far East Championships 1971; national successes include Open Teams 1973, 1974.

SCRIBBINS, Daniel, of Xenia, Ohio, equipment specialist, born 1912, deceased. Fourth-ranked player in American Bridge Association. Winner of many national titles, including Men's Pairs and Open Teams three times each and Mixed Pairs twice.

SEAMON, Rita (Mrs. William), of Miami Beach, Fla., won Summer Nat'l Mixed Teams 1974, second Nat'l Women's Pairs 1961; won Southeastern Mixed Pairs 1959, 1968.

SEAMON, William, of Miami Beach, Fla., banking executive and syndicated bridge columnist, born 1917; one of the leading American players; represented North America World Championships 1957; won Spingold 1956, 1963, Vanderbilt 1963, Grand National Championship 1973, Summer Nat'l Mixed Teams 1974, Mixed Pairs 1968; second Chicago 1954, Vanderbilt 1960, Spring Nat'l Men's Teams 1973, Fall Nat'l Men's Teams 1952; many regional successes include Southeastern Open Teams 1944, 1945, 1959, Men's Teams 1951, 1954, 1957, 1958, 1965, 1972, Masters Pairs 1962, 1963, Open Pairs 1947, 1949, 1954, 1963, Men's Pairs 1960, 1962, 1968, Mixed Pairs 1945. Brother of Mrs. Edith Kemp and Mrs. Anne Burnstein. Contributing Editor *Bridge Encyclopedia. See* FAMILY.

SEARS, Richard C., of Englewood Cliffs, N.J., actuary, born 1936; won New England Spring Open Team 1959, Knockout Team 1961, New England Fall Mixed Team 1957.

SEEWALD, Leo J., of South St. Paul, Minn., retired teacher, born 1908; second Goddard Pairs 1948. ACBL President 1964, Chairman Nat'l Master Point

Plan Committee, President Minnesota Unit, ACBL Director, Director Mid-American–Canadian Conference.

SEEWALD, Reine (Mrs. Leo J.), of South St. Paul, Minn., born 1899; second Goddard Pairs 1948; won Mid-American–Canadian Women's Pairs 1957. ACBL Secretary 1963.

SEGANDER, Mrs. Rut, of Karlsborg, Sweden, born 1917; won World Women's Team Olympiad 1968, European Women's Championships 1962, 1967, Scandinavian Women's Championships. National titles include Women's Pairs.

SEIDMAN, Solomon, of Brooklyn, N.Y., retired teacher and bridge lecturer; won Nat'l Open Individual 1949; several regional wins include Keystone Open Teams 1962, Fun City Knockout Teams 1970, Eastern States Knockout Teams 1972. Greater New York BA hospitality coordinator World Team Olympiad 1964; Chairman, GNYBA Board of Directors; former President GNYBA. Director ACBL since 1974.

SELIGMAN, Mrs. Barbara, of Dublin, Ireland, company director; represented Ireland World Pair Olympiad 1970, 1974, European Championships 1962, 1963, 1965, 1967, 1969, 1971, 1973, 1974, 1975; national wins include all major Irish titles.

SELIGMAN, Edith, née Seamon. See KEMP, EDITH.

SELYMES, Emery, of Seattle, Wash.; winner of several regional events including Puget Sound Knockout Teams 1970, 1971, 1972.

SERENY, Dr. George, of Toronto, formerly of Hungary, physician; represented Canada World Pairs Olympiad 1962; won Canadian-American Open Team 1959.

SERES, Thomas Peter ("Tim"), of Bronte, NSW, Australia, sales representative, born 1925 in Hungary; one of the world's great players; Far East Champion 1968, 1970; represented Australia World Championship 1971, World Team Olympiad 1960, 1964, 1968, captained the 1964 team; won National Open Teams 1948, 1949, 1950, 1952, 1954, 1955, 1957, 1959, 1961, 1962, 1963, 1964, 1965, 1967, 1974, Open Pairs 1954, 1961, 1962, 1964, 1965, Par Point 1952, 1962, 1963; WBF Zone 7 Champion 1970, 1971, 1974; won McCutcheon Trophy for most master points scored in 1974. Consulting editor *Australian Bridge;* contributing columnist *The Sun Herald;* IBPA Member. Discovered the SERES SQUEEZE.

SETHI, S. R., of Bombay, business executive, born 1918; represented India World Team Olympiad

1960; national successes include Open Team 1960, 1961; second Masters Pairs 1960, 1961.

SEXTON, F. Holton, of Greens Fork, Ind., real estate broker and dairy farm manager, born 1926; won Summer Nat'l secondary Mixed Pairs 1971; regional successes include Southern Conference Open Pairs 1954, Midwest Open Pairs 1960, Open Teams 1971, Florida Mixed Pairs 1973.

SHALLON, Marty, of Los Angeles, Calif., accountant, born 1952; second Spingold 1975, Spring Nat'l Men's Teams 1974; won Los Angeles Winter Knockout Teams 1974, 1975.

SHALOM, Felix, of Kingston, Jamaica, textile executive, born 1917; many national championship wins include Open Team fifteen times. Past president Jamaica Bridge Association.

SHANAHAN, Dorothy, of London, England, statistician; won World Women's Team Olympiad 1964; represented Great Britain European Women's Championship many times including wins in 1961 and 1963; won English Women's Team and Mixed Team twice each, and National Pairs once.

SHANBROM, Helen (Mrs. Al), of Ft. Lauderdale, Fla., retired teacher, born 1919; second Fall Nat'l Women's Teams 1960; won All-American Open Teams 1962, 1965, Great Lakes Open Team 1963, Midwest Spring Mixed Pairs 1959.

SHARIF, Omar, of Paris, France, formerly of Egypt, motion picture star, born 1932; represented UAR World Olympiad 1964, playing captain Egypt World Olympiad 1968. National wins include Inter-clubs 1960, 1962, 1963, 1964. Winner of the 1963 Golden Globe award, nominated for Academy Award 1963 for best supporting actor in *Lawrence of Arabia.* One of the most active promoters of bridge, making many public appearances on syndicated TV shows as a proponent of the game. Organized the Sharif Bridge Circus; participated in one of the highest stake set games in history. Winner IBPA-Simon award for Sportsman of the Year, 1974. Became co-author of Goren-Bridge newspaper column 1975. Member, with many former members of the BLUE TEAM, of the LANCIA BRIDGE TEAM, playing exhibition challenge matches in New York, Chicago, Los Angeles, and Miami in 1975. See also SET GAMES; SHARIF BRIDGE CIRCUS.

SHARP, Josephine ("Jo," formerly Mrs. R. G. Sharp & Mrs. Max Gutman), of Covington, Ky.; deceased, represented US Women's World Team Olympiad 1960; won Fall Nat'l Women's Team 1948, 1959, Women's Pairs 1947, 1948; second Mixed Team 1944; regional successes include All-American Mixed Pairs 1956, Midwest Spring Open Pairs 1958, Women's Pairs 1959, Southeastern Women's Teams

1955, Mid-South Spring Women's Pairs 1968, Southern Fall Open Teams 1964.

SHARP, Mrs. Judith, of Seattle, Wash., born 1902; second Fall Nat'l Women's teams 1965; won Pacific Southwest Women's Pairs 1957, 1961, and other regional events.

SHARP, Robert G., of Miami Beach, Fla., real estate broker, born 1910; one of the leading players of the South; won Grand National Championship 1973, Fall Nat'l Men's Teams 1959, Mixed Pairs 1966; second Open Individual 1957, Blue Ribbon 1964; numerous regional successes include Mississippi Valley Masters Pairs 1959, Open Pairs 1960, 1962, 1965, Open Teams 1965, Southeastern Knockout Teams 1967, Open Teams 1972, Men's Teams 1968. Former President Midwest Conference, Cincinnati BA.

SHARPLES, James, of Caterham, Surrey, England, bank clerk, twin brother of Robert, born 1908; runner-up European Championship 1958; also represented Great Britain 1956; won Gold Cup 1962, Masters Pairs 1950.

SHARPLES, Robert, of Caterham, Surrey, England, bank clerk, born 1908; runner-up European Championship 1958; also represented Great Britain 1956; won Gold Cup 1962; Masters Pairs 1950.

SHAUFEL, Elyakim, of Tel Aviv, Israel, engineer, born in Poland 1945; European Champion 1975; represented Israel World Olympiad 1972, World Pairs Olympiad 1972, European Championships 1966, 1967, 1969, 1971, 1973, 1974; national wins include Open Pairs 1966, 1967, 1972, 1973, 1974.

SHAW, Marshall T., of Grandview, Wash., farm corporation manager, born 1899; won Northwest Open Team 1950. Pioneered bridge in Washington State; Director Oregon BL.

SHEARDOWN, Percival E. ("Shorty"), of Toronto, Ont., bridge club manager, one of Canada's leading players, born 1911, started tournament bridge 1933; represented Canada World Team Olympiad 1960, 1968; won Spingold 1964, 1965, Fishbein 1964; second Life Masters Pairs 1964; regional wins include Canadian Nat'l Open Teams 1951, 1953, 1961, 1965, 1967, Masters Pairs 1971, Open Pairs 1969. One of the most consistent tournament winners before the inauguration of tournament and master-point ratings.

SHEEHAN, Robert, of London, physiologist and management consultant, born 1939; one of the leading British players; represented Great Britain World Team Olympiad 1972, World Pairs Olympiad 1974, European Championships 1971 (runner-up), 1973, 1974; national wins include Gold Cup 1972,

National Pairs, Spring Foursomes, several Camrose Cups. Contributor to *Bridge Magazine* and *Popular Bridge*.

SHEINWOLD, Alfred, of Beverly Hills, Calif., long of New York, N.Y., and born in London, England, 1912, bridge author and columnist, one of the most successful player-writer personalities. During World War II chief code and cipher expert, Office of Strategic Services, USA. An editor of *The Bridge World* 1934–63 successively as technical editor, managing editor, and senior editor; editor-in-chief *Autobridge* since 1938; bridge editor *Los Angeles Times* and syndicated columnist for L.A. Times Syndicate; contributing editor *Popular Bridge;* games editor *Argosy;* co-inventor KAPLAN-SHEINWOLD SYSTEM; editor *Bulletin* of ACBL 1952–58; pioneered bridge lessons on Pay TV 1963–64; npc North American Team World Championship 1975; see CAPTAIN; won Chicago 1958, Spring Nat'l Mixed Pairs 1963, Men's Team 1964; second Chicago 1959, Vanderbilt 1958; numerous regional successes include Eastern States Knockout Teams 1956, 1957, 1958, 1959, 1970, Mixed Teams 1957, Open Pairs 1955, Upper New York State Open Pairs 1957, 1959, All-Western Open Teams 1966. Author of many bridge books, notably *Five Weeks to Winning Bridge,* which sold more than 1,000,000 copies, and a series of *Pocket Books of Bridge Quizzes.* Prolific contributor to bridge magazines. Chairman ACBL National Laws Commission 1964–75; Chairman Appeals Committee 1966–70; Chairman ACBL Board of Governors 1970–73. Member Editorial Advisory Board *Bridge Encyclopedia.* See BIBLIOGRAPHY, C, D, E, F.

SHEINWOLD, Betty. See KAPLAN, BETTY.

SHEINWOLD, Patricia (formerly Mrs. Alfred, Beverly Hills, Calif., previously Mrs. Julian Adler, Baltimore, Md.), New York City writer and teacher, born 1924. Tournament successes include Spring Nat'l Women's Teams 1963; Keystone Conf. Open Teams 1955.

SHELNUTT, John L., of Atlanta, Ga.; regional wins include Motor City Mixed Pairs 1970.

SHEN, C. S., of Lafayette, Ind., professor of astrophysics, born 1933 in Nanking, China; one of the leading Far East players; second World Championships 1969 as member of the Chinese Team; represented China World Olympiad 1964, Far Eastern Championships 1962, 1963, 1966. National wins include Open Team 1955, 1956, Open Pairs 1955. One of the two best "Go" players in the US.

SHEN, K. W., of Bangkok, Thailand, merchant, born 1911; second World Championships 1969 as member of Chinese Team; Far East Champion 1961, 1966 as member of Thai team; represented Thailand World Championship 1967, World Olympiad 1964, Far East Championships 1960.

SHEPHERD, Richard, of Atlanta, Ga.; won Fishbein 1974, Spingold 1974, Summer Nat'l secondary Swiss Teams 1973; several regional wins including Mid-South Knockout Teams 1974, Open Teams 1970.

SHERBURN, Robert L., of Ada, Mich., steel purchasing agent, born 1943; regional wins include Motor City Masters Pairs 1973, Open Pairs 1970.

SHERIDAN, John K., of Indianapolis, Ind., insurance executive, born 1948; winner of many regional events including Indy 500 Knockout Teams 1973, All-American Open Pairs 1973, Men's Pairs 1974.

SHERMAN, Ruth (1903–1965), of New York, N.Y., one of the leading women players of the East Coast; won Chicago 1944, Vanderbilt 1953, Fall Nat'l Women's Team 1942, Mixed Team 1935, 1945, Spring Nat'l Mixed Team 1951, Fall Nat'l Women's Pairs 1944, 1949, Mixed Pairs 1948, 1950; second Chicago 1953, Fall Nat'l Women's Teams 1952, 1953, 1954, 1955, Life Masters Pairs 1946, Fall Nat'l Open Pairs 1947, Women's Pairs 1934, 1945, 1947; won Eastern States Knockout Teams 1954, Women's Pairs 1943, 1944, 1945, Keystone Open Teams 1954.

SHIVDASANI, B., of Bombay, business executive, born 1925; won national Masters Pairs 1959, second 1960, 1961.

SHMUKLER, Pauline (Mrs. Albert), of Miami Beach, Fla., bridge teacher, born 1913; second Fall Nat'l Women's Team 1946, 1954; won Mid-Atlantic Fall Mixed Pairs 1952, Keystone Conference Open Team 1952, 1955, Open Pairs 1959.

SHNEIDER, Alma, of Durban, S. Africa, bridge teacher; second World Women's Team Olympiad 1968, 1972; represented South Africa Women's Pairs Olympiad 1972; national successes include Open Teams 1965, 1967, Open Pairs 1971.

SHOFNER, Mrs. James C., of Burlington, N.C., bridge teacher, born 1920; won Mid-Atlantic Spring Women's Pairs 1958, second Summer Women's Pairs 1960, Spring Women's Pairs 1961.

SHOOP, Homer, of North Webster, Ind., bank president, born 1912; won Desert Empire Men's Pairs 1959, Midwest Fall Men's Pairs 1960, Upper New York State Men's Pairs 1959, Pacific Southwest Men's Pairs 1964, Polar Masters Pairs 1965.

SHORT, Karol F., of Miami, Fla.; regional wins include Southeastern Women's Pairs 1969 and Mixed Pairs 1972.

SHOUP, Russell O., of Dayton, Ohio, born 1947; regional wins include Motor City Masters Pairs 1974, Men's Pairs 1971.

SHRAGE, Dr. Marcus, of Dublin, Ireland, physician, born 1919; represented Ireland European Championship 1951, 1954, 1955, 1957, 1963, 1966, 1967; national successes include Irish Bridge Union Open Team and Mixed Pairs, CBA of Ireland Open Teams and Men's Teams.

SHUMAN, Kerri (Mrs. Michael), of Los Angeles, Calif., bridge professional; one of the leading American women players; won McKenney 1974, Fall Nat'l Mixed Pairs 1975, Spring Nat'l Women's Pairs 1972, secondary Swiss Teams 1974, second Women's Teams 1974, Fall Nat'l Mixed Pairs 1971, 1974; winner of a great many regional titles including Rocky Mountain Knockout Teams 1974, Masters Pairs 1974, All-Western Women's Teams 1973, Masters Pairs 1971.

SHUMAN, W. Michael, of San Mateo, Calif., bridge professional, born 1931; one of the leading West Coast players; won Spring Nat'l Men's Teams 1962, second 1974, Chicago 1961, Fall Nat'l Men's Pairs 1959, Spring Nat'l Open Pairs 1962; numerous regional wins include Bridge Week Knockout Teams 1961, 1968, Open Teams 1965, All-Western Open Teams 1959, Men's Pairs 1964, Life Masters Pairs 1973, Mid-Winter Knockout Teams 1974. Writings include contributions to *The Bridge World* and *American Bridge Digest.* Managing editor *Forum.*

SIDELL, Steven, of Seattle, Wash., investor, born 1947; won Zone 7 Grand National 1973; several regional wins include Oregon Trail Knockout Teams 1970, Open Pairs 1972; Klondike Swiss Teams 1974.

SIDES, William, of Van Nuys, Calif., banker; second Spingold 1975, Spring Nat'l Men's Teams 1974; regional wins include Bridge Week Knockout Teams 1973. One of the top ranking players of the American Bridge Association; set a record at 1969 ABA Summer Nationals by winning five major events and finishing second in another.

SIEBERT, Allan, of Little Rock, Ark., born 1942; won Fall Nat'l Men's Teams 1967, secondary Open Pairs 1973; regional successes include Southern Fall Masters Pairs 1962, Missouri Valley Open Teams 1971.

SIEBERT, David, of Little Rock, Ark., businessman, born 1940; won Fall Nat'l secondary Open Pairs 1973; several regionals wins, including Mid-South Masters Pairs 1972, Open Pairs 1970, second Men's Teams Fall Nationals 1967.

SIEMER, Marshall C. (1913–1966), of Bismarck, N.D., monument company owner; won Northern Rocky Mountain Men's Pairs 1959, Mixed Pairs 1958, Open Pairs 1965.

SIGURDSSON, Thorgeir, of Reykjavik, Iceland, accountant, born 1934; won Icelandic Open Teams 1958, 1960, and 1963, Open Pairs 1959, 1960. Represented Iceland European Championships 1967.

SIGURDSSON, Torin, of Reykjavik, Iceland, meteorologist, born 1931; won Icelandic Open Teams 1963, Open Pairs 1962, Reykjavik Open Teams 1963. Represented Iceland European Championships 1967.

SIGURHJARTARSON, Karl, of Reykjavik, Iceland, manager, born 1941; represented Iceland World Pair Olympiad 1974, European Championships 1970, 1973, 1974; national wins include Open Teams 1970, 1971.

SILBER, Albert J., of Southfield, Mich., lawyer, won All-American Open Teams 1959, Men's Pairs 1965, Great Lakes Open Pairs 1966, Open Teams 1968. Member Board of Governors, Goodwill Committee; former President Michigan BA.

SILBERWASSER, Roger, of Brussels, Belgium, bridge club manager, born 1923 in Austria; represented Belgium World Team Olympiad 1960, World Pair Olympiad 1962, European Championships 1961, 1966, 1967; national wins include Open Teams 1960, 1961, 1962, Open Pairs 1961, Masters Pairs 1961, 1963.

SILBORN, Mrs. Gunborg, of Norrköping, Sweden, born 1924; won World Women's Team Olympiad 1968, European Women's Championships 1967, Scandinavian Women's Championships 1964, 1966, and five National Women's titles.

SILBY, Mrs. Frances (formerly Mrs. Lawrence Singer), of Overland Park, Kan., retired psychiatric social worker; tied Summer Nat'l secondary Swiss Teams 1973; regional wins include Bermuda Women's Pairs 1974.

SILODOR, Sidney, of Havertown, Pa. (1906–1963), lawyer, bridge lecturer, writer, instructor, and one of the world's top players. He was on the North American team that won the World Championship in the first Bermuda Bowl matches in 1950 and also represented North America in that event in 1958 and 1961, as well as playing for the US in the World Olympiad of 1960. he won the MC KENNEY TROPHY in 1946, and set a record when he won the National Mixed Pairs five times, 1940, 1944, 1951, 1955, 1956. At his death he was a member of the National Board

of Directors of the ACBL and holder of the Open Pairs Championships, a title which he had first won in 1941 and again in 1945. He was also the third highest on the list of all-time master-point winners, with a total of 6,450—a figure great enough to hold that place until a year after his death when his total was surpassed by Norman KAY, who had been his regular partner. He was a director of ACBL and a former president of the Philadelphia Whist Association. His books included *Silodor Says, Contract Bridge According to Silodor and Tierney,* and *The Complete Book of Duplicate Bridge.* He was also author of many articles in *The Bridge World* magazine and a newspaper column. Other highlights of his tournament record include Vanderbilt 1944, 1945, 1950, 1955, 1956, 1957, 1959, 1960, Spingold 1943, 1951, 1957, Chicago 1942, 1943, Life Masters Pairs 1946, Nat'l Mixed Team 1941, 1943, 1944, 1950, 1954, 1956, 1961, Spring Nat'l Men's Pairs 1958, Masters Individual 1951; second Asbury Challenge Team 1936, Vanderbilt 1953, Spingold 1947, 1950, 1953, 1960, 1961, Chicago 1944, Life Masters Pairs 1943, 1956, Mixed Teams 1948, 1951, Men's Pairs 1962, and many regional successes. See BIBLIOGRAPHY, C, E, F.

SILVA, Lionel D. da, of Manila, Philippines, insurance underwriter, born 1911; represented Philippines World Team Olympiad 1960, 1964; Far East Champion 1957, 1958; represented Philippines Far East Championship 1959 through 1963; national titles include Open Teams 1956, Masters Pairs 1958, Open Pairs 1961, Individual 1956.

SILVER, Joseph, of Montreal, Que., public defender born 1941; one of the leading Canadian players; represented Canada World Pair Olympiad 1974; won Vanderbilt 1974, second Spring Nat'l Men's Team 1973, Summer Nat'l Mixed Teams 1974; winner of many regional events including New England Knockout Teams 1971, 1972, Open Teams 1969, Canadian-American Open Teams 1969, Open Pairs 1970.

SILVERMAN, H. M., of Norfolk, Va., real estate agent, born 1909; won Mid-Atlantic Fall Open Teams 1959, Spring Men's Pairs and Open Teams 1960.

SILVERMAN, Mrs. H. M., of Norfolk, Va., born 1921; won Mid-Atlantic Fall Women's Pairs and Open Teams 1959, Spring Open Teams 1960.

SILVERMAN, Jerome, of Mill Valley, Calif., account executive; won New York–New Jersey Men's Pairs 1959. ACBL President 1973; ACBL Treasurer 1970–72; Chairman ACBL Goodwill Committee 1975; ACBL Representative to WBF 1973–76; Trustee ACBL Charity Foundation 1974. Former President New Jersey BL and New York–New Jersey Bridge Conference; ACBL Director 1966–1975.

SILVERMAN, Neil, of New York, N.Y., estate researcher, born 1949; won Fall Nat'l secondary Swiss Teams 1974, secondary Men's Pairs 1974; regional wins include Puerto Rico Open Teams 1971, 1974.

SILVERMAN, Shirley (Mrs. Harry J.), of White Plains, N.Y., teacher, writer and executive of bridge supplies business, born 1928. Chairman ACBL Board of Governors since 1975; former President Westchester Unit. Member IBPA, ABTA.

SILVERSTEIN, Nate, of Memphis, Tenn., bridge teacher and bridge club manager, born 1909; numerous regional successes include Mid-South Spring Open Teams 1956, Open Pairs 1959, Summer Open Pairs 1962, Open Teams 1965, Fall Masters Pairs 1967, 1971, 1973, Mississippi Valley Open Teams 1965, ACBL Director 1968–71.

SILVERSTONE, Victor, of Glasgow, Scotland, chartered accountant, born 1940; represented Scotland in ten international matches; member of the victorious Camrose Trophy team once. National titles include Open Teams twice. One of four Scottish players to compete in the Sunday Times International Pairs Championships and the British Trials.

SIMITZ, Robert J., of Chicago, Ill., insurance supervisor, born 1924; second Summer Nat'l Golder Pairs 1955; won Central States Open Pairs 1955, Life and Senior Master Pairs 1954.

SIMMONS, Joyce H., of Charleston, S.C., manager, medical center; regional successes include Florida Open Pairs 1960, Mid-Atlantic Open Pairs 1972. Member, National Goodwill Committee.

SIMON, Adaline (Mrs. John E.), of St. Louis, Mo.; won Fall Nat'l Women's Team 1959, Midwest Spring Mixed Pairs 1956, Midwest Fall Open Team 1960, Mixed Pairs 1960, Mid-South Open Pairs 1957, Women's Pairs 1958, Mississippi Valley Master Pairs 1959, 1963, Missouri Valley Mixed Pairs 1957, Rocky Mountain Summer Open Teams 1956, Open Teams 1969.

SIMON, Andrzej, of Krakow, Poland, chemical engineer, bridge journalist, born 1934; represented Poland World Pairs Olympiad 1966; overall winner Beirut Festival 1968; won Beirut Festival Open Teams 1968, Juan-les-Pins Festival Open Teams 1965, second 1966. Secretary European Bridge League Junior Division; Assistant Secretary International Bridge Press Association. Editor IBPA *Bulletin* 1966, 1967.

SIMON, Edith, of Memphis, Tenn., ACBL Librarian. Administrative Secretary, Chicago CBA 1964–72. Contributing Editor, third edition, *Official*

Encyclopedia of Bridge. ACBL Goodwill and Charity Committee.

SIMON, Harold, of Los Angeles, Calif., pharmacist, born 1931; won several regionals including Desert Empire Open Teams 1960, Bridge Week Open Teams 1961, 1962.

SIMON, John E., of St. Louis, Mo., member of New York Stock Exchange, born 1897; one of the leading bridge personalities of the Midwest; represented US World Pair Olympiad 1962; won Fall Nat'l Men's Teams 1965, Spring Nat'l Men's Teams 1972, 1973, Fall Nat'l secondary Open Teams 1969; second Spring Nat'l Mixed Pairs 1960, Open Pairs 1961; many regional wins including Midwest Open Teams 1954, 1956, 1958, Mississippi Valley Open Team 1953, 1958, Missouri Valley Open Team 1955, 1961. ACBL Honorary Member 1962. Chairman of National Goodwill and Membership Committee from 1954; other executive positions include President Midwest Conference; President St. Louis Unit; Chairman Nat'l Championships in St. Louis 1953, 1963; Trustee ACBL Charity Foundation.

SIMON, S. J. (Simon Skidelsky, or "Skid") (1904–1948), novelist and bridge writer; one of the best-loved English bridge personalities; European Champion 1948 and represented Great Britain European Championships 1939. Many national wins include Gold Cup 1937, 1947. His many successful humorous novels in collaboration with ballet expert Carol Brahms include *Bullet in the Ballet, No Bed for Bacon,* and *Trottie True.* Bridge writings include the classic *Why You Lose at Bridge, Design for Bidding,* and *Cut for Partners.* One of the originators of the ACOL SYSTEM. See BIBLIOGRAPHY, C, E, H.

SIMONARSSON, Hallur, of Reykjavik, Iceland, journalist; represented Iceland European Championships 1967, 1969; national wins include Open Teams 1964, 1966, 1967, 1969, 1974.

SIMONARSSON, Simon, of Reykjavik, Iceland, contractor, born 1934; represented Iceland European Championships 1967, 1968, 1969, 1970; national wins include Open Teams 1964, 1966, 1967, 1969, 1974, Open Pairs 1969.

SIMONS, Edgar, of San Jose, Calif., professor of mathematics, born 1928; won Fall Nat'l Open Pairs 1960; regional wins include All-American Men's Pairs 1960, District 5 Open Teams 1963.

SIMPSON, Isabel (Mrs. Wallace), of Indianapolis, Ind., stenographer; won Fall Nat'l Non-Masters Pairs 1950; second Summer Nat'l Non-Masters Pairs 1950; won Midwest Women's Pairs 1958.

SIMPSON, Mrs. William C., of Plant City, Fla., office manager and bridge teacher, born 1919; won

Mid-Atlantic Fall Open Teams 1961, and several other regional successes. pioneered birdge in Columbia.

SIMS, Dorothy Rice (Mrs. P. Hal), (1889–1960), bridge author and player. Mrs. Sims was born June 24, 1889, at Asbury Park, N.J., daughter of Isaac L. Rice, first manufacturer of the submarine, and patron of chess and other recreational activities. From her teens she was active in competition, holding the US motorcycle speed championship for women (1911) and becoming one of the first US aviatrixes, in which capacity she met and married P. H. Sims (q.v.). She was noted as a sculptress and as an author in fields other than bridge, though she wrote several bridge books.

Acquiring an interest in bridge through her husband, Mrs. Sims became a successful player, and won several sectional and national championships in the early years of contract bridge. She is widely credited with "inventing" the psychic bid, but probably initiated only the popular name for it; however, she wrote the first book on the subject, *Psychic Bidding,* 1932. In 1935 she was her husband's principal partner in a 150-rubber match against E. and J. Culbertson, which the Simses lost (see CULBERTSON-SIMS MATCH). After Sims's death, she toured the world several times as a political correspondent for various newspapers. Won ABL Auction Women's Pairs 1929; American Whist League Open Team 1929, Open Pairs 1930; Contract Nat'l Mixed Team 1930, second Nat'l Mixed Team 1933, Chicago 1930; second Reisinger 1930. See BIBLIOGRAPHY, C.

SIMS, P(hilip) Hal (1884–1949), bridge author and system-maker, champion player. During the period 1932–34 he was considered by many the best American player, and his system had the largest expert following. Sims was born in Selma, Ala., Dec. 24, 1884. From 1906–16 he represented US banks in foreign countries. As a member of the US Army Air Corps in 1917 he met Dorothy Rice, a US aviatrix in transport service, whom he married. After World War I Sims devoted himself chiefly to competitive sports, in which he excelled, and to bridge. He held a national trapshooting record, and won the Artists' and Writers' Golf Tournament in 1937. In auction bridge he was a member of the highest-ranked team, the Knickerbocker Whist Club team, including S. Lenz, W. Liggett, G. Reith, and R. Leibenderfer. He was captain of the contract bridge team called the FOUR HORSEMEN, whose other members were W. Karn, O. Jacoby, and D. Burnstine. This team and its members won most of the principal American tournaments 1931–33.

The SIMS SYSTEM, a subjective approach based on Sims's desire to dominate every pair and team of which he was a member, left little impression on contract bridge methods used by experts from 1935 on; first- and second-hand opening one-bids were stronger than third- and fourth-hand bids; no trump bids were always strong but had wide limits; psychic bids were used freely; high pre-emptive bids were eschewed. In 1935, Mr. and Mrs. Sims tested this system in a 150-rubber match against Mr. and Mrs.

E. Culbertson, and were defeated (see CULBERTSON-SIMS MATCH). Nevertheless, the Sims books on his system are significant in bridge literature; they include *Money Contract,* 1932; *Master Contract* (his definitive work, largely by Sir D. Wernher), 1934; and several lesser books.

Sims was one of the most colorful characters in bridge history. His commanding presence (6'4" in height, more than 300 lbs. in weight, big-boned and muscular) augmented his claim to authority. For more than five years his mansion in Deal, N.J., was summer headquarters for the principal experts. He controlled the ABL for several years without holding formal office. He founded the Deal Club, a bridge club at which the principal US and international experts played from 1930 to 1935. His skill as a raconteur and his personal charm were proverbial. He died of a heart attack while bidding a hand in a game at the Havana Country Club, where he and Mrs. Sims spent their winters after 1946. See BIBLIOGRAPHY, E.

SINGER, Dr. Lav, of Zagreb, Yugoslavia, retired public attorney, born 1901; represented Yugoslavia in several European Championships in the 1930s; member of the team that finished second in 1935 and 1939; captain Yugoslav international teams from 1937 to World War II. President Yugoslav BF since 1967.

SINGLETON, Melvin E., of Butte, Mont., FBI investigator, born 1913; won Northern Rocky Mountain Open Teams 1959, Mixed Pairs 1963.

SINISCALCO, Guglielmo, of Naples, Italy, professor of civil engineering, born 1921; one of the world's great players; World Champion 1957, 1958, 1959, European Champion 1951, 1956, 1957, 1958, second 1952; won Italian Open Teams 1949, 1951, 1956, 1957, 1959.

SION, Steve, of Jamaica ·Plain, Mass., second Reiginger 1974; several regional wins including Metropolitan Knockout Teams 1974, Upper New York State Knockout Teams 1974.

SIU, M. C., of Hong Kong, businessman; represented Hong Kong Far East Championships three times; national victories include Open Teams, Masters Teams, Open Pairs, Masters Pairs, Mixed Pairs, Individual.

SKINNER, Eve (Mrs. Richmond H.), of Wilmington, Del., born 1899; second Fall Nat'l Mixed Pairs 1937; won New England Fall Mixed Team 1946, 1952, Women's Pairs 1948.

SKINNER, Col. Richmond H., of Wilmington, Del., US Army officer and bridge writer, born 1898; longtime member of New Hampshire Legislature; national lawn tennis official; one of the leading American bridge personalities; third Vanderbilt

1938; many regional wins include Eastern States Knockout Teams 1940, New England Fall Mixed Teams 1947, 1952, Knockout Teams, Masters Teams 1948, Men's Pairs 1946, Mixed Pairs 1947, 1948. Inventor of SKINNER PSYCHIC CONTROLS, SKINNER RESPONSES TO A ONE NO TRUMP OPENING, and SKINNER TWO-BIDS. Originated a point-count method in 1932 in which an ace was assigned 5 points, king 3 points, queen 2 points, and jack 1 point. ACBL President 1944; Past President Mid-Atlantic, Keystone, New England Conference. Member Executive Committee ACBL from formation through 1944.

SKOROUPO, Roman, of Helsingfors, Finland, businessman and bridge writer, born 1900; member Executive Committee of European Bridge League and Vice-Chairman of its Appeal Committee. Member World Bridge Federation tournament committee. Secretary-General Finnish Bridge League. Contributing Editor *Bridge Encyclopedia.*

SKOTTE, Mrs. Gulle, of Copenhagen, Denmark, born 1917; third World Women's Team Olympiad 1960; European Women's Champion 1948, 1955, 1957, second 1951, third 1963; Scandinavian Women's Team Champion 1947, 1951, 1955, 1961, 1962; national wins include Open Teams 1951, 1953, Open Pairs 1953, and the Women's Teams six times between 1945 and 1952.

SLAVENBURG, Cornelis, of Rotterdam, Holland, merchant, born 1917; won World Olympiad Open Pairs 1966; represented Netherlands World Championships 1966, World Olympiad Open Pairs 1970, European Championships 1951, 1959, 1965, 1966, 1967. National titles include Open Teams four times and Open Pairs three times.

SLEMMONS, George, of Bellevue, Wash.; won Spring Nat'l Men's Pairs 1974; winner of several regional titles including Puget Sound Knockout Teams 1970, 1971, 1972.

SLOAN, Jesse, of Van Nuys, Calif., real estate broker, born 1913; won Vanderbilt 1952; second Fall Nat'l Mixed Pairs 1937; regional wins include Southeastern Open Team 1940, Bridge Week Open Team 1962.

SMILDE, Roelof A., of Sydney, Australia, bridge teacher, born 1930; one of the leading Australian players; Far Eastern Champion 1968, 1970; represented Australia World Team Olympiad 1964, 1968, 1972; national successes include Open Teams 1958, 1961, 1962, 1963, 1965, 1974, Open Pairs 1974.

SMITH, Mrs. Carl H., of Goleta, Calif., born 1911; won Bridge Week Women's Pairs 1953, All-Western Women's Pairs 1956. Director Santa Barbara Unit, charter member of National Goodwill and Membership Committee.

SMITH, Curtis, of Pacific Palisades, Calif., engineer, born 1925; one of the leading players of the Southwest, won Spingold 1966, Fall Nat'l Open Pairs 1960; second Spingold 1972, Chicago 1960, 1964, Fall Nat'l Open Pairs 1953, Life Master Men's Pairs 1970, Life Masters Pairs 1963; winner of a great many regional titles including Texas Fall Open Pairs 1955, 1956, 1960, 1965, Open Teams 1956, Men's Pairs 1961, 1967, Mid-South Open Pairs 1968, Open Teams 1968, 1969, Knockout Teams 1971, Men's Pairs 1969. Author of *Bidding Through Logic* and inventor of the SMITH CONVENTION. See DEFENSE TO OPENING THREE-BID; BIBLIOGRAPHY, D.

SMITH, David W., of Greeneville, Tenn., behavior modification specialist, born 1944; represented Korea Far Eastern Championships 1969; second Grand National Championships 1973; won Beynon Pairs 1968; several regional wins include Champagne Masters Pairs 1972, Men's Pairs 1973.

SMITH, Edwin J., Jr. (1914–1970), of Grosse Pointe, Mich., steel salesman; one of the leading players of the Middle West; won Winter Nat'l Men's Teams 1951, Mixed Pairs 1958; second Summer Nat'l Open Teams 1952; third Spring Nat'l Open Pairs 1962; won Great Lakes Men's Pairs 1961, 1962, 1967, 1968, Mid-South Open Pairs 1962, All-American Open Teams 1966.

SMITH, Hazel (Mrs. Fred), of St. Petersburg, Fla., retired teacher; regional wins include Regina Women's Pairs 1965, Navajo Open Teams 1966, Canadian-Atlantic Mixed Teams 1968.

SMITH, Helen, of Philadelphia, Pa., insurance broker; won Golder Pairs 1973, Spring Nat'l secondary Masters Pairs 1972, second Fall Nat'l Mixed Pairs 1973; many regional wins include Keystone Knockout Teams 1973, Women's Teams 1972.

SMITH, Helen (Mrs. D. M. A.), of Toronto, Ont.; represented Canada World Women's Team Olympiad 1964; won Canadian Prairie Women's Pairs 1965.

SMITH, Helen Martin (Mrs. Stanley, formerly Mrs. A. M. Sobel & Mrs. Jack White) (1910–1969), universally ranked as probably the greatest woman bridge player of all time; born in Philadelphia. She enjoyed a brief stage career, including an appearance with the Marx Brothers in *Animal Crackers.* She was living in New York City when she won her first major national championship, the 1934 Women's Pair event. Shortly after her second marriage, to A. M. SOBEL (1937 to 1945, ending in divorce), she was invited by Ely Culbertson to represent the US, playing with Mrs. Culbertson and Charles Vogelhofer in a World Championship conducted by the International Bridge League in 1937 in Vienna, won by Austria. This was tacit recognition that Culbertson, like many other experts, considered her the equal of any male player, a view which became that of Charles Goren in 1940 when they won the National Open Pair title, their first of many championships, playing in what was to become one of the most enduring and successful partnerships in bridge history. Together they won the De La Rue International Invitation Pair Tournament in London in 1957, represented North America in the World Team Championship of 1957, and the US in the World Team Olympiad of 1960, and won many of the thirty-two national championships listed below, including the Life Masters Pair Championship twice. In 1963, after long residence in N.Y.C., Mrs. Sobel moved to Miami Beach, Fla.

In addition to her many championships, Mrs. Sobel won the McKenney Trophy for the best tournament record in 1944, and the Fishbein Trophy for the top performance in the Summer Nationals, 1958. By 1948 she had amassed the greatest number of master points of any woman, taking over the top spot from Mrs. Sally Young, and holding it uninterruptedly from 1964. She was the author, with Sam Fry, Jr., of *All the Tricks,* and of several magazine articles. Her tournament record includes wins in the Spingold 1944, 1947, 1951, 1956, 1960, Chicago 1941, 1943, 1950, 1957, Vanderbilt 1944, 1945, Fall Nat'l Women's Team 1939, 1943, 1944, 1945, 1946, Mixed Team 1941, 1943, 1944, 1948, 1954, Life Masters Pairs 1942, 1958, Open Pairs 1934, 1938, 1939, Mixed Pairs 1944, 1955, 1956, Summer Nat'l Mixed Teams 1968; second Spingold 1943, Chicago 1944, 1951, Vanderbilt 1942, 1949, 1950, 1953, 1955, 1962, Fall Nat'l Women's Team 1941, 1942, 1952, 1954, 1955, 1956, 1957, 1958, Mixed Team 1949, 1950, 1951, Life Masters Pairs 1953, Open Pairs 1938, Spring Nat'l Women's Pairs 1965, Summer Nat'l Women's Pairs 1947, Mixed Pairs 1933, 1940. Regional successes include Eastern States Knockout Teams 1943, Open Pairs 1941, Mixed Teams 1935, Women's Pairs 1943, 1944, 1945, Mixed Pairs 1942, 1943, Southeastern Open Team 1941, 1942, Women's Team 1952, Women's Pairs 1940, 1941, 1942, 1947, Mixed Pairs 1939, and many others. See BIBLIOGRAPHY, E.

SMITH, Herbert, of Burlingame, Calif., accountant, born 1932; regional wins include All-Western Knockout Teams 1970, Masters Pairs 1970, Men's Pairs 1974. Former President District 21 Organization.

SMITH, Leon E., of Jacksonville, Fla., computer programmer, born 1944; regional wins include Florida Open Teams 1974, Mixed Pairs 1970.

SMITH, Lois (Mrs. C. Arnholt), of San Diego, Calif.; regional wins include Desert Empire Mixed Pairs 1959. Member National Goodwill and Charity Committees.

SMITH, Paul C., of Pacific Palisades, Calif., retired business executive, born 1914; regional wins include Bridge Week Masters Pairs 1955, Central States Open Pairs and Open Teams 1940.

SMITH, Ronald, of St. Louis, Mo.; second Grand National Championships 1973; regional wins include Mid-South Open Teams 1972, 1974.

SMITH, Ronald L., of Opelika, Ala., mathematician, born 1947; second Grand National 1975; regional wins include Golden Gate Open Teams 1974, Palm Springs Open Pairs 1973.

SMITH, Terry, of Columbus, Ohio, bridge teacher, tournament director, born 1936; ACBL Tournament Coordinator 1968–70, Executive Assistant 1970–74. Member, Drafting Committee 1975 Laws of Duplicate. Contributing Editor *Bridge Encyclopedia.*

SMITH, Thomas M., of Greenwich, Conn., bridge editor and writer, born 1938; one of the leading American players; an original member of the PRECISION TEAM which won Spingold 1970, 1971, Vanderbilt 1972; winner of several regional titles including New England Knockout Teams 1968, Long Island Knockout Teams 1971, 1972. Intercollegiate Champion 1965. Contributor to *The Contract Bridge Bulletin* and *Bridge Journal.* Editorial manager second edition of *Official Encyclopedia of Bridge,* World Championship Handbooks 1966–72. Business manager ACBL *Bulletin* 1970–72. Editor Greater New York BA *Post-Mortem.*

SMITH, William (Bill), of Fort Myers Beach, Fla., formerly of Tarrytown, N.Y., retired teacher, born 1909; associate editor of ACBL *Bulletin* 1958–64. ACBL Regional Tournament Director.

SMOLEN, Michael, of Los Angeles, Calif., attorney, born 1940; won Fall Nat'l secondary Men's Teams 1971, second Spring Nat'l Men's Teams 1974; regional wins include Bridge Week Men's Pairs 1968, Knockout Teams 1973, Open Teams 1972, Orange County Knockout Teams 1974.

SMOLEN, Steve E., of Los Angeles, Calif., marketing executive, born 1946; won Summer Nat'l secondary Swiss Teams 1974; several regional wins include Oregon Trail Open Teams 1973, All-Western Masters Teams 1973.

SMOLENSKY, Mrs. Pat, of Calgary, Alta., bridge teacher, born 1924; represented Canada World Women's Pair Olympiad 1966; regional wins include Northern Rocky Mountain Women's Pairs 1959, Canadian Prairie Women's Pairs 1965.

SMYTH, Mrs. Dale, of Huntington Beach, Calif.; regional wins include Southern Conference Open Pairs 1954, Midwest Spring Open Pairs 1959, Southern Regional Women's Pairs 1968.

SNIDER, Wayne B., of Schaumberg, Ill., assistant traffic manager, born 1947; tied Summer Nat'l secondary Swiss Teams 1971; several regional wins including Indy 500 Open Teams 1973, Mississippi Valley Open Teams 1974.

SNITE, Fred Jr., of Miami Beach, Fla., died in 1955, having lived for the last nineteen years of his life in an iron lung. A regular competitor in ACBL tournaments, and Honorary Member ACBL in 1954.

SOBEL, Alexander M. (Al), of New York City, 1901–72, was the third person to be the National Tournament Manger for the ACBL, following Alfred M. Gruenther and Russell Baldwin, holding that position from 1942 until his retirement in 1969. Sobel directed tournaments from September 1934 in the US, Canada, Mexico, Argentina, France, Italy, England, and Brazil with guest appearances in Hong Kong, Tokyo, Philippines. His debut as manager of a major tournament was in 1935, when he substituted for Gruenther at the Eastern Championships, then a national tournament. He became the unofficial quiz master of the bridge players when the craze for quizzes about the time of "Ask Me Another" resulted in the bridge experts playing a similar game late at night after almost every tournament session. For three years, 1948–51, he wrote the questions for the Bob Hawk Lemac radio quiz. His commanding voice created a tournament directorial style; until the great crowds of the fifties, Sobel seldom needed a mircrophone. Married Helen Martin White 1937, divorced 1945. He became a member of the National Laws Commission 1943; former associate editor of the ACBL *Bulletin,* and author of "30 Days," a popular monthly diary column for that publication from 1944 until his retirement in 1969, when it became a bi-monthly column entitled "60 days." Former associate editor of *The Bridge World* magazine, former editor of *Bridge Forum,* Contributing Editor of *Bridge Encyclopedia.* First Honorary Member Japan Contract Bridge League, Honorary Member ACBL 1949.

SOBEL, Helen Martin. See SMITH, HELEN MARTIN.

SOKOLOWER, Lester, of Nutley, N.J., merchandiser, born 1931; won Keystone Mixed Pairs 1961, Bermuda Open Pairs 1968, New England Knockout Teams 1966, New York–New Jersey Open Teams 1966.

SOLAR, Rosa Maria Pascual Lacrest de, of Barcelona, Spain; represented Spain World Women's Pairs Olympiad 1974, European Women's Championships 1974; many national successes.

SOLODAR, John, of New York, N.Y., management consultant, bridge teacher, born 1940; won Fall Nat'l

Life Master Men's Pairs 1968; winner of many regional events including Southeastern Knockout Teams 1969, 1970, Eastern States Knockout Teams 1968. New York manager for Sharif's Bridge Circus 1968.

SOLODAR, Judi (Mrs. John) (Formerly Friedenberg), of New York, N.Y., retired stockbroker, born 1950; won Spring Nat'l Women's Teams 1971, second Reisinger 1974, Spring Nat'l Women's Pairs 1972; winner of many regional events including Motor City Open Teams 1968, Women's Pairs 1969, New York–New Jersey Mixed Pairs 1973.

SOLOMON, Charles J. (1906–1975), of Philadelphia, Pa., attorney, bridge teacher, and author; one of the leading players and personalities of bridge; represented US World Championships 1956, npc US Women's Teams 1960. Won Chicago 1937, 1938, 1939, 1944, Spring Nat'l Men's Teams 1965, Spingold 1955, Summer Nat'l Mixed Teams 1950, 1959, Life Masters Pairs 1946, Men's Pairs 1943, Masters Individual 1947; second Spingold 1939, 1944, Chicago 1953, 1959, Vanderbilt 1954, 1958, Fall Nat'l Men's Team 1955, 1960, Mixed Team 1939, 1940, Summer Nat'l Masters Pairs 1938, Spring Nat'l Open Pairs 1959, 1968, Fall Nat'l Mixed Pairs 1943, 1961, Masters Individual 1943, with many regional successes. President ACBL 1958. President World Bridge Federation 1964–68; Chairman of the Board since 1968; Vice-President 1958–64. Chairman of Board ACBL 1944, 1955, 1957; National Laws Commission 1940 to 1960. Author of *Slam Bidding and Point-Count* and *No Trump Bidding.* Bridge editor Philadelphia *Inquirer* from 1945. See BUENOS AIRES AFFAIR. See BIBLIOGRAPHY, C.

SOLOMON, Peggy (Mrs. Charles J., formerly Mrs. Benjamin Golder) of Philadelphia, Pa., born 1910; one of the leading American women players; third World Women's Pairs Olympiad 1966; won Chicago 1944, Summer Nat'l Mixed Teams 1949, 1950, 1959, Fall Nat'l Women's Teams 1957, 1963, 1964, 1965, Spring Nat'l Women's Teams 1964, 1968, Summer Nat'l Women's Pairs 1960; second Spingold 1944, Vanderbilt 1954, Chicago 1953, Nat'l Mixed Teams 1939, 1940, Spring Nat'l Women's Teams 1967, Fall Nat'l Women's Teams 1948, 1953, 1954, Mixed Pairs 1943, 1961, Life Masters Women's Pairs 1965, 1966, 1967. Regional successes include District 5 Mixed Pairs 1962, Eastern States Mixed Pairs 1944, Southeastern Open Teams 1955, 1956, Open Pairs 1940, Mixed Pairs 1940, 1947, and many more.

SOLOMONS, Patricia B., of Honolulu, HI, real estate broker; won Summer Nat'l secondary Commercial Teams 1970; several regional wins include Hawaii Open Teams 1973, Women's Pairs 1974.

SOLOWAY, Paul, of Los Angeles, Calif., bridge instructor, club owner, born 1941; one of the most successful American players; represented US World Team Olympiad 1972, North America World Championship 1973, 1975; won International Team Trials 1975, McKenney 1968, 1969, Nat'l Life Masters Men's Pairs 1965, Summer Nat'l Masters Mixed Teams 1966, Vanderbilt 1969, Grand National Championship 1974; second Vanderbilt 1971, Spingold 1973, Spring Nat'l Teams 1970, Men's Pairs 1969; a great many regional successes, including Bridge Week Knockout Teams 1969, 1970, Open Teams 1973, Open Pairs 1969, Men's Pairs 1966, 1967, Mixed Pairs 1966, 1971. Achieved a remarkable record in the 1967 Palm Springs Regional by winning four events, Open Teams, Masters Pairs, Men's Pairs, Mixed Pairs, and placing second in the Knockout Teams and third in the Open Pairs.

SONTAG, Alan, of New York, N.Y., tax accountant, and bridge professional, born 1946; one of the leading American players; represented US World Pair Olympiad 1974; won Vanderbilt 1972, Reisinger 1973, Spring Nat'l Men's Teams 1971, Fall Nat'l Life Master Men's Pairs 1971, *London Sunday Times* 1973, 1975; second Vanderbilt 1975, Life Masters Pairs 1972; many regional wins including Southeastern Knockout Teams 1970, Life Masters Pairs 1970, 1973, Open Pairs 1968. See PRECISION TEAM.

SORALAMPA, Col. Bhakdi, of Bangkok, Thailand, army dental surgeon, born 1910; npc Thai Team Far East Bridge Championships 1962, second Far East Bridge Championship 1960. National successes include Open Team 1962, Masters Individual 1954. Vice-President Far East Bridge Federation 1962–63. Secretary Contract Bridge League of Thailand 1962, Vice-President 1963.

SORRI, Kalevi, of Helsinki, Finland, born 1924; represented Finland European Championships 1953, 1954, 1957, 1965; national wins include Open Teams (eight times) and Open Pairs 1951.

SORRI, Keijo, of Helsinki, Finland, born 1926; represented Finland European Championships 1953, 1954, 1957, 1962, 1965; national wins include Open Teams (eight times) and Open Pairs 1951.

SOTO, Mrs. Ana de, of Bogotá, Colombia, born in Reus, Spain; represented Colombia South American Championships 1963, South American Women's Championships 1964, 1965, 1966, 1967; South American Women's Champion 1968; national successes include first Open Teams 1961, 1963; second Open Teams 1967, Masters Pairs 1968.

SPAIN, Elizabeth Patricia ("Pat"), of Los Angeles, Calif.; won Sub-Senior Masters Teams 1963, President's Pairs 1963, Fall Nat'l Flight B Women's Pairs 1965. Western Vice-President American Bridge Association; winner of many ABA national events.

SPERO, Richard L. (1932–1969), of Forest Hills, N.Y., attorney; won Spring Nat'l Open Pairs 1968, Eastern States Men's Teams 1967. Director Greater New York BA 1965–69; ACBL District Charity representative 1967.

SPICKETT, Dr. John Stuart, of Newport, Wales, born 1898; represented Wales in several international competitions; won National Open Teams 1957. Former President of the Welsh Bridge Union 1954–55, 1958–61; recognized for his outstanding service by being made Patron of the WBU.

SPICKETT, Mrs. Peggy, of Newport, Wales; represented Great Britain World Women's Pairs Olympiad 1962, and Wales in numerous Camrose Trophy and Lady Milne matches; won National Open Teams 1957, Women's Teams 1953, 1955, 1960, 1964, 1965.

SPIEGEL, Bernard ("Buddy"), of Memphis, Tenn., ACBL Tournament Division Manager, born 1947. Author of monthly column ACBL *Bulletin,* "Ruling the Game." Secretary National Laws Commission 1975, former ACBL Regional Tournament Director.

SPIEWAK, Walter, of Sudbury, Mass.; won Canadian-Atlantic Knockout Teams 1969, 1973, Open Teams 1969, Open Pairs 1974.

SPILIOPOULOS, Nicolas B., of Greece, lawyer, born 1913; co-founder Hellenic BF 1965; Vice-President Hellenic BF 1965–71 and since 1974; npc Greek Team European Championships 1969; national wins include Open Pairs 1966. Editor Hellenic BF *Bulletin.*

SPINGOLD, Nathan (Nate) (1886–1958), publicist, vice-president Columbia Motion Pictures, the most influential man in bridge administration 1937–43. Donor of the Spingold Trophy for the Masters Open Team in 1934, he was named Honorary Member ACBL 1936, and ACBL President 1938, and Chairman 1938–42. He was also president of the New York Cavendish Club.

SPITZ, Marshall R., of Marblehead, Mass., real estate, born 1943; won Golder Pairs 1973; regional wins include New England Masters Teams 1966, Knockout Teams 1967.

SPIVACK, Leo J., of Chicago, Ill., lawyer, born 1926; regional wins include Central States Knockout Teams 1971, District 11 Open Teams 1967. ACBL Director since 1970.

SPORING, Ann-Marie, of New York, N.Y., systems specialist, born 1930; regional wins include Eastern States Women's Teams 1967, Southeastern Women's Teams 1974.

SPOTTS, Robert L., of El Sobrante, Calif., program evaluator, born 1937; second Spring Nat'l Men's Teams 1967; won Bridge Week Knockout Teams, Mixed Teams 1968, Golden Gate Masters Pairs 1966, Knockout Teams 1972, Masters Teams 1973, Men's Pairs 1969.

SPURWAY, Paul, of Cardiff, Wales, accountant, born 1926; represented Great Britain World Pairs Olympiad 1962; English Open Teams 1959, Welsh Cup 1958, 1962, National Pairs 1959, 1962, 1964, Masters Pairs 1959, 1960, 1961.

SQUIRE, Norman, of London, England, club secretary and bridge writer, born 1907; won De La Rue International Par Tournament 1957; Gold Cup 1946, 1954, 1958; and other national championships. Competition editor of *Bridge Magazine* since 1948. Author of *The Theory of Bidding, Guide to Bridge Conventions, Bidding at Bridge,* and co-author of *Winning Points at Match-Point Bridge.* Many contributions to bidding theory include OUT-OF-THE-BLUE CUE-BID and development of the principle of FOURTH SUIT FORCING. Contributing Editor *Bridge Encyclopedia.* See BIBLIOGRAPHY, C, F.

STACHOWICZ, Dr. Jerzy, of Katowice, Poland, physician, born 1926; represented Poland European Championships 1962, 1966; won Hungarian Open Pairs 1959, Polish Open Teams 1959, Open Pairs 1960; second Open Pairs 1967.

STAFFORD, Jeff, of Pearisburg, Va.; won Mid-Atlantic Knockout Teams 1973 (twice), Open Teams 1973, 1974.

STAKGOLD, Alice (Mrs. Ivar), of Newark, Del.; won Summer Nat'l Mixed Teams 1969.

STAKGOLD, Ivar, of Newark, Del., mathematics professor, born 1925; one of the most successful American bridge players; represented US World Championships 1959 and World Team Olympiad 1960; won Mott-Smith 1958; won Spingold 1962, Chicago 1958, Vanderbilt 1958, Spring Nat'l Open Pairs 1958, Leventritt Pairs 1964, Summer Nat'l Masters Mixed Teams 1969; second Spingold 1958, Fall Nat'l Men's Teams 1957, Spring Nat'l Open Pairs 1963; many regional successes include Central States Life and Senior Masters Teams 1961, Knockout Teams 1966, 1970, New England Open Teams 1956, Knockout Teams 1954.

STAMPF, Abraham, of Israel, merchant, born 1937; represented Israel World Olympiad 1968, 1972, European Championships 1970, 1971, 1973, 1974; national successes include Open Pairs 1968, 1969, 1971.

STANLEY, Mrs. Emory D., Jr., of Seattle, Wash., winner of several regional events including Inter-

mountain Knockout Teams 1970, Desert Empire 1972, Yakima Valley Master Pairs 1974.

STANSBY, Jan (Mrs. Lew), of Oakland, Calif., law school professor, born 1943; won Spring Nat'l Women's Pairs 1974, Golden Gate Masters Pairs 1971.

STANSBY, Lew, of Oakland, Calif.; one of the leading American players; won Reisinger 1965, Vanderbilt 1967, Spingold 1975; regional wins include Golden Gate Masters Pairs 1971, 1974.

STAPPENBECK, Harry, of Uniondale, N.Y., bridge teacher; one of the leading East Coast players; second Spingold 1974; regional wins include New York–New Jersey Open Pairs 1970.

STARK, Eric, of Vancouver, B.C., retired, real estate, several regional wins include Northwest Open Teams 1956, Men's Pairs and Open Teams 1957.

STARK, Dr. Gary, of Portland, Ore., dentist, born 1931; won Spring Nat'l Men's Teams 1967; regional wins include Oregon Trail Knockout Teams 1974, Masters Pairs 1967.

STARR, Jeffrey C., of Huntington Woods, Mich., student and bridge professional, born 1949; second Grand National Championship 1974; many regional wins include All-American Knockout Teams, Open Teams, Masters Pairs, and Open Pairs 1974.

STARR, Robert E., of South Yarmouth, Mass., merchandise manager, born 1919; won Summer Nat'l Non-Masters Pairs 1947; winner of many regional events including New England Knockout Teams 1956, 1959, 1962, 1963, Open Teams 1952, 1954, 1958, 1962.

STAYMAN, Josephine "Tubby"(Mrs. Samuel), of New York, N.Y., gift-shop owner, born 1924; second World Olympiad Mixed Teams 1974, won Southeastern Open Teams 1972.

STAYMAN, Samuel M., of New York, N.Y., portfolio manager, investment company and bridge author, born 1909; one of America's leading players; World Champion 1950, 1951, 1953; second World Olympiad 1964; represented North America World Championship 1956 and US World Team Olympiad 1960; won Spingold 1942, 1944, 1948, 1950, 1952, 1955, 1959, Chicago 1945, 1947, Vanderbilt 1942, 1946, 1950, 1951, Summer Nat'l Life Masters Pairs 1965, Fall Nat'l Men's Teams 1952, 1962, Open Pairs 1959; second Spingold 1947, 1969, Chicago 1950, Vanderbilt 1944, 1945, 1952, 1969, Fall Nat'l Men's Teams 1948, 1955, Men's Pairs 1945, Life Masters Pairs 1950, Spring Nat'l Men's Teams 1965; regional successes include Eastern States Knockout Teams 1939, 1940, 1951, 1963, New York–New Jersey Open

Teams 1961, and others. Developed the STAYMAN convention, which shares with BLACKWOOD the distinction of being the most widely played convention throughout the world. ACBL Treasurer 1966–69, Trustee ACBL Charity Foundation. Author of *Expert Bidding, The Complete Stayman System of Contract Bidding;* and *Do You Play Stayman?* Contributing Editor *Bridge Encyclopedia.* See BIBLIOGRAPHY, C.

STEARNS, Sherman (1900–1965), of New York, N.Y., real estate broker; one of the leading American players of the thirties, and a member of the FOUR ACES TEAM during its later years; USBA National Open Team 1935, Open Pairs 1935, Vanderbilt 1938, 1941, Life Masters Pairs 1938; second Asbury Challenge Teams 1934, Chicago 1941, Vanderbilt 1931, Spingold 1934, Mixed Teams 1941; regional successes include Eastern States Open Teams 1934, Knockout Teams 1941, Mixed Teams 1941.

STEDEM, Joseph J., Wilmette, Ill., retired vice-president car rental company, born 1899; second National Senior Masters Individual 1952; won Mid-West Spring Open Pairs 1949, Central States Mixed Pairs 1950. President ACBL 1968; Honorary Member 1971. ACBL Director 1949–50 and from 1964–69; former President Midwest Bridge Conference; President Chicago CCBA 1948–49; President ACBL Charity Foundation 1973–74, Trustee 1972–75. Helped initiate the ACBL policy of holding national tournaments in many centers, begun in 1949.

STEEN, Douglas, of Seattle, Wash., physicist and economist, born 1927; one of the leading West Coast players until his retirement in 1956; World Champion 1954; won Spingold 1953, Nat'l Mixed Team 1952; second Fall Nat'l Men's Team 1953, Men's Pairs 1954; regional wins include Pacific Southwest Open Teams 1953, 1954, Masters Pairs 1949, Open Pairs 1952, 1953, Mixed Pairs 1954. Co-inventor of the BULLDOG SYSTEM, co-author of *Precision Power Bidding.* See BIBLIOGRAPHY, C.

STEEN, Harry S., of Beverly Hills, Calif., stockbroker, born 1922; regional wins include Pacific Southwest Open Teams 1957, 1958, Bridge Week Men's Pairs 1969.

STEGEMAN, Dr. Charles ("Chuck"), of Garden Grove, Calif., physician, born 1945; won Summer Nat'l secondary Swiss Teams 1971; regional wins include Iowa Open Teams 1971, Open Pairs 1971.

STEHLY, Paul E., of Minneapolis, Minn., salesman, born 1925; ACBL Associate National Tournament Director since 1968.

STEIL, Leo F., of Pt. Coquitlan, B.C., seaman, born 1925; won Northwest Open Teams 1962, Men's Pairs 1966, Masters Pairs 1967.

STEIN, James D., of Los Angeles, Calif., mathematician, born 1941; won Marcus Cup 1972, Spingold Consolation 1972; several regional wins include Bridge Week Masters Pairs 1969, 1974, Life Masters Pairs 1970.

STEIN, Joan S. (Mrs. Jack), of Milwaukee, Wis., born 1934; won Fall Nat'l Life Master Women's Pairs 1974, Tri-Unit Women's Pairs 1971.

STEIN, Sylvia, of Southfield, Mich., born 1921; one of the leading Midwest women players; represented US World Women's Pair Olympiad 1962, 1970, won Herman Trophy 1969, Nat'l Life Masters Individual 1958, Spring Nat'l Women's Pairs 1962, Women's Teams 1965, 1968, Life Master Women's Pairs 1969; second Summer Nat'l Mixed Teams 1965, 1967, Fall Nat'l Mixed Pairs 1958, Women's Teams 1960, Mixed Teams 1960, 1962, Life Masters Women's Pairs 1964, Spring Nat'l Women's Teams 1965, 1971; won All-American Women's Pairs 1959, 1960, Great Lakes Women's Pairs 1968, Motor City Open Teams, Open Pairs 1968.

STEINBERG, Philip, of St. Louis, Mo., shoe merchant, born 1904; won Central States Men's Pairs 1953, Mississippi Valley Mixed Pairs 1961, Missouri Valley Men's Pairs 1963.

STEINBERG, Ruth (Mrs. Philip), of St. Louis, Mo.; won many regional championships including Central States Open Pairs 1953, Women's Pairs 1951, Mixed Pairs 1954, Mississippi Valley Open Teams 1953, Women's Pairs 1963, 1969, 1972, Mixed Pairs 1965.

STEINER, Albert, of Cincinnati, Ohio, president of toy manufacturing company, born 1895; won Chicago 1933; Western States Mixed Pairs 1935. Co-donor of the STEINER TROPHY for the National Individual Masters Championship.

STEINER, George M., of Bellevue, Wash., student, born 1945; won Spring Nat'l Men's Pairs 1974; many regional wins, including Puget Sound Knockout Teams 1970, 1971, 1972, Mixed Pairs 1972. President Seattle Unit 1972.

STEINER, Philip, of Cincinnati, Ohio, retired vice-president of toy mfg. company, born 1901; won Chicago 1933, Western States Mixed Pairs 1935; second Open Teams 1941. ABL Vice-President 1936, Director 1930–38 and Committee Chairman 1934; ACBL Honorary Member 1937. Co-donor of the STEINER TROPHY for the National Individual Masters Championship.

STEINFELDT, Sherman Irving ("Irv"), of Minneapolis, Minn., company president, born 1918; winner of several regional titles including Pheasant Knockout Teams 1972, Gopher Open Teams 1972, Tri-Unit Men's Pairs 1973.

STEPHENS, Daisy (Mrs. W. A., Jr.), of Shreveport, La., born 1907; regional wins include Bermuda Women's Pairs 1972, Mexican Nat'l Women's Pairs 1967.

STEPHENSON, Barrett W., of St. Petersburg, Fla., racetrack calculator, born 1901; won Bridge Week Men's Pairs 1954, Mississippi Valley Men's Pairs 1954, Southeastern Mixed Pairs 1953.

STERN, Gerda, of Sydney, Australia, government interpreter, born 1925 in Poland; Far East Women's Champion 1973, 1974; represented Australia World Women's Team Olympiad 1968; national wins include Interstate Women's Teams 1964, 1967, 1972, 1974, Women's Trials 1971, 1973, 1974, Women's Individual 1973.

STERN, Dr. Paul (1892–1948), of Vienna, Austria, lawyer, bridge writer, and teacher, escaped to London, and became a naturalized British subject. A founder of the Austrian Bridge Federation 1928, he was its first president 1929. World Par Champion 1936, European Champion 1932, 1933, npc Austrian World Champion Team 1937, npc Austrian European Women's Champions 1935, 1936; inventor of VIENNA (AUSTRIAN) SYSTEM, author of *Stern Austrian System,* co-author *Two-club System of Bidding, Right Through the Pack,* and others. Number eleven on the Nazi list for extermination, he returned his World War I Iron Cross to the Nazi High Command with an insulting letter.

STERN, Richard I., Jr., of West Hollywood, Calif., data processing manager, born 1945; won Spring Nat'l secondary Open Pairs 1973; regional wins include Central States Open Teams 1974.

STERN, Roger D., of New York, N.Y., attorney, born 1934; npc North American Team World Championship 1973; second World Par Contest 1961; winner US Zone World Par Contest 1963; won Spring Nat'l Men's Teams 1965, Summer Nat'l Mixed Pairs 1969, Eastern States Open Pairs 1960, District 5 Open Pairs 1964, Rocky Mountain Men's Pairs 1967. Co-inventor of ASTRO and ASTRO CUE-BID; co-author of several *Bridge World* articles, including a series outlining a modern style of defensive bidding. First President District 24 Organization; Vice-Chairman National Appeals Committee.

STERNBERG, Elaine, of Park Forest, Ill.; second Spring Nat'l Women's Teams 1973; won Summer Nat'l secondary Women's Pairs 1972.

STETTEN, Jacques, of Paris, builder, born 1926; European Champion 1962, second 1961; represented France World Championship 1963, 1967, 1969, European Championships 1966; national titles include Open Teams 1961 and 1963.

STEVENSON, Juanita (Mrs. J. R., formerly Mrs. A. J. Strich) (1917–74), of Los Angeles, Calif., won Fall Nat'l Women's Teams 1955; won Pacific Southwest Masters Pairs 1957, Texas Mixed Pairs 1954.

STEWART, Lilly (Mrs. Edgar E.), of Laguna Hills, Calif., born 1910; won Northwest Open Teams 1954, 1958, Masters Pairs 1960, Women's Pairs 1960, 1962, Northern Rocky Mountain Open Team 1957.

STICKNEY, William L., of Evanston, Ill., born 1913; won All-American Open Pairs 1942 when playing duplicate for the first time, Central States Life and Senior Master Teams 1962; Florida Knock-out Teams 1967. Director, former President Chicago CBA.

STODDARD, Peggy (Mrs. Tom), of Laguna Hills, Calif., real estate broker; won Pacific Southwest Mixed Pairs 1953, All-Western Women's Pairs 1966. Member, National Goodwill Committee. Assisted her husband in many Western Division activities.

STODDARD, Tom, of Laguna Hills, Calif., born 1896; one of the outstanding personalities of American bridge, pioneer in bridge teaching and bridge-club management, founder of the PACIFIC BRIDGE LEAGUE, former ACBL executive. As a dealer in real estate and proprietor of a Los Angeles hotel in 1931, when most hotels were failing, Stoddard conceived the idea of making his hotel a center for bridge lessons and duplicate games. The project was a sensational success, at its peak employing eleven teachers and conducting duplicate games daily from nine thirty A.M. to midnight. In 1946 Stoddard turned over his bridge business to his associates, and in 1948 he agreed to amalgamation of the Pacific and national organizations, an arrangement consummated 1956. At this time Stoddard was elected President Emeritus of ACBL, Western Division, and an ACBL Director; he became ACBL Honorary Member 1960. He was founder and editor of the *Forum* of the Western Division, and was contributing editor to the *Bulletin* of the ACBL and to the *Bridge Encyclopedia.*

STOLKIN, Carol. See CRAWFORD, CAROL.

STONE, Abby, of Cardiff, Wales, commission agent, born 1901; represented Wales in international bridge from 1933 until he retired in 1960; numerous tournament and national successes.

STONE, Ben, of Detroit, Mich., industrial engineer and bridge writer, born 1908; won Canadian Nat'l Open Pairs 1960, Canadian–American Mixed Pairs 1966. Bridge contributor to Detroit newspapers.

STONE, Mrs. Godfrey B., of Southfield, Mich., born 1912; second Fall Nat'l Women's Teams 1960; won Rocky Mountain Open Teams 1948, 1950.

STONE, Janice Gilbert (Mrs. Tobias), of New York, N.Y., radio and television actress, mining executive; second World Women's Team Olympiad 1964; won International Women's Team Trials 1963, Spring Nat'l Women's Teams 1969, Fall Nat'l Women's Teams 1956, 1968, Life Masters Women's Pairs 1965, Summer Nat'l Mixed Teams 1965; second Spingold 1959, Nat'l Mixed Teams 1956, Fall Nat'l Women's Teams 1961, 1962, 1966; won Eastern States Open Pairs 1957, Mixed Teams 1958, Canadian–American Open Pairs 1956, All-American Open Teams 1956, Mid-Atlantic Open Teams 1957.

STONE, Kenneth, of Ft. Worth, Tex., accountant, born 1910; ACBL Associate National Tournament Director.

STONE, Marian (Mrs. Marvin), of Denver, Colo., born 1925; regional wins include Hawaiian Mixed Pairs 1969.

STONE, Robert F., of Cambridge Mass., economist, born 1946; won Golder Pairs, Summer Nat'l secondary Swiss Teams 1971; regional wins include New England Masters Pairs 1973.

STONE, Tobias, of New York, N.Y., bridge author, born 1921; one of the leading bridge players and personalities of the world, represented North America World Championships 1958 and US World Team Olympiad 1960. Held record for the most master points in any one national championships (Summer 1956); won McKenney 1956, Spingold 1956, 1957, Marcus 1960, Chicago 1952, 1961, Vanderbilt 1949, 1959, 1960, Life Masters Pairs 1956, Spring Nat'l Men's Teams 1963, Fall Nat'l Men's Teams 1961, Summer Nat'l Mixed Teams 1965, Open Pairs 1942, Men's Pairs 1947, Life Masters Individual 1953; second Spingold 1953, 1961, 1963, Vanderbilt 1969, Fall Nat'l Men's Teams 1959, Mixed Teams 1956, Life Masters Pairs 1942, 1958, Spring Nat'l Open Pairs 1958, Summer Nat'l Life Masters Pairs 1965, Fall Nat'l Men's Pairs 1952; regional successes include Eastern States Knockout Teams 1942, 1944, 1961, 1963, 1967, 1973, 1974, Mixed Teams 1958, Open Pairs 1957, 1961, and many more. Co-author of *Bridge Is a Partnership Game* and *The Bridge World* department "What Do You Play and Why?" Co-inventor of the ROTH-STONE SYSTEM; has made many contributions to bidding theory. See BIBLIOGRAPHY, C.

STOUT, Alan, of Tipton, Iowa, auditor, born 1949; won Spring Nat'l secondary Swiss Teams 1972; regional wins include Pheasant Knockout Teams 1973, Tri-Unit Masters Pairs 1974.

STRASBERG, David, of Miami, Fla., personnel and data processing consultant, born 1928; won Spingold 1970, Fishbein Trophy 1970; second Chicago 1958, Spring Nat'l Men's Pairs 1968, Summer Nat'l Mixed

Teams 1970; many regional wins include Eastern States Knockout Teams 1969, Masters Pairs 1956, Men's Pairs 1970. See PRECISION TEAM.

STRAUS, Dr. Ben, of Oakland, Calif., optometrist, born 1896; won All-Western Open Team 1937, 1938. One of the founders ACBL Western Division; first President Oakland Unit.

STREET, Robert P., of Seattle, Wash., tax accountant, born 1913; won Nat'l Mixed Pairs 1950, won Southeastern Men's Teams 1962, Northwest Open Pairs 1956, 1960, Men's Pairs 1950, 1956.

STREET, Venita (Mrs. Robert P.), of Honolulu, HI, born 1917; won Nat'l Mixed Pairs 1950, Northwest Masters Pairs 1952, 1954, 1955, Open Pairs 1950.

STRICKLAND, Fred E. III, of Atlanta, Ga., attorney, born 1945; won Fall Nat'l secondary Swiss Teams 1972, secondary Open Pairs 1974, Mid-Atlantic Men's Pairs 1970.

STROM, Louis André, of Stavanger, Norway, meteorologist, born 1927; represented Norway World Championship 1970, European Championships 1960, 1961, 1965, second 1969, Scandinavian Championships 1964, and on several other occasions; numerous national successes. Bridge columnist for local newspaper.

STROUSE, Clarence A., Jr. (1902–74), of Houston, Tex.; won Nat'l Mixed Team 1954, Fall Nat'l secondary Swiss Team 1973, second Men's Team 1956. Long a familiar tournament figure, he won many regional titles from 1939 to 1972, including Bridge Week Open Pairs 1954, Open Teams 1947.

STUART, Joel H., of Rego Park, N.Y., bridge club owner, born 1939; one of the leading American players; an original member of the PRECISION TEAM that won Spingold 1970, 1971, Vanderbilt 1972; Grand National Zonal Champion 1974, second Spring Nat'l Men's Teams 1968; winner of several regional titles including Long Island Knockout Teams 1971, 1972.

STUCKER, Robert, of Athens, Greece (formerly of Houston, Tex.), born 1930; represented US World Pairs Olympiad 1962; represented Greece European Championships (playing captain) 1970; second Fall Nat'l Open Pairs 1961, Spring Nat'l Men's Teams 1964 (see FORTUNE). Greek national wins include Open Teams 1967, 1968, 1974. Co-inventor of the BIG DIAMOND SYSTEM.

STYLE, Mrs. Agnes McQuistin Alexander, of Salisbury, Rhodesia, teacher, born 1906; one of the leading women players in Central Africa; won Central African Open Teams 1961, 1963, Open Pairs

1961, Salisbury Open Teams 1959, 1960, 1963, Open Pairs 1959, 1963; second Central African Open Teams 1962, Open Pairs 1963. Chairwoman, Salisbury Bridge Club.

SUCHARTKUL, Kovit, of Bangkok, Thailand, tin miner; Far East Champion 1961, 1963; second 1969 World Championships; represented Thailand in several Far East Championships.

SUDASNA, Col. Thakerngdef, of Bangkok, Thailand, army officer, born 1911; Far East Champion 1961, second 1960; Far East Zone World Par Champion 1961.

SUGAR, Paul, of Deerfield, Ill., lawyer and accountant, born 1928; winner of several regional events including Central States Knockout Teams 1964, Open Teams 1971, Tri-Unit Open Pairs and Swiss Teams 1973. Director Chicago CBA.

SUGENHEIMER, Ruth, of New Haven, Conn., school principal, born 1901; won New England Fall Open Teams 1961, Mixed Teams 1962, Mixed Teams 1960. Vice-President Connecticut BA.

SUGG, Richard, of Atlanta, Ga.; regional successes include Southeastern Men's Pairs 1970, 1973.

SULLIVAN, Michael J. (1894–1974), of Brisbane, Australia, accountant; World Par Zonal winner 1939, 1940, 1941; national titles include Par wins 1937, 1939, 1943, 1950, 1957. Co-founder World Bridge Federation in 1958, chairman of its Constitution Committee, and member of WBF Executive Board. Organizer 1951 Jubilee Year World Olympic, 1954 Bidding Championship; 1961 and 1963 World Bridge Federation Global Par Championships. Joint formulator of Laws of Par Point Contract Bridge 1963 (International Code).

SUNDSTROM, Patricia (Mrs. Raymond), of Indianapolis, Ind; regional wins include Midwest Women's Pairs 1970, 1971, Indianapolis 500 Women's Pairs 1973.

SUNG, Leslie L., of Hong Kong, former newspaper editor; represented Hong Kong in Far East Championships four times; national wins include Open Teams, Master Teams, Open Pairs, Mixed Pairs, Individual. Chairman Hong Kong Bridge Association.

SUSSEL, Mrs. Andrée, of Paris, antique dealer, born 1914; European Women's Team Champion 1956, represented France European Women's Championships 1958, 1959, 1962, 1965, 1966; won French Mixed Team 1962.

SUSSKIND, Alan, of Chicago, Ill., bridge club manager, born 1952; won Spring Nat'l secondary Swiss Teams 1973; regional wins include Mississippi Valley Open Teams 1974.

SUTHERLIN, John C., of San Francisco, Calif., portfolio manager, born 1936; second Fall Nat'l Mixed Pairs 1962, Spring Nat'l Men's Teams 1967; regional wins include Golden Gate Masters Pairs 1966, All-Western Life Masters Teams 1971, Hawaii Master Pairs 1973.

SUTHERLIN, Peggy Berry (Mrs. John), of San Francisco, Calif., born 1937; won Fall Nat'l Mixed Pairs 1972, second 1962; regional wins include Golden State Open Teams 1963, All-Western Women's Pairs 1965.

SUTTON, Iona, of Dallas, Tex., bridge teacher, born 1911; won Texas Women's Pairs 1959, Spring Open Teams 1968.

SUYCK, J. R. C. van Bemmel. See BEMMEL SUYCK, VAN.

SVARC, Henri, of Paris, factory manager, born 1928; one of the leading French players; European Champion 1966, 1970 second 1967; represented France World Team Olympiad 1964, World Championships 1967, 1969, World Pairs Olympiad 1962, European Championships 1954, 1956, 1958, 1959, 1965. National successes include Open Teams (three times) and Open Pairs.

SWAN, Mrs. Lester B., of Houston, Tex., publisher; won Fall Nat'l Mixed Pairs 1964, North Texas Masters Pairs 1961.

SWANSON, John, of Los Angeles, Calif., stamp dealer; represented North America World Championship 1971; won International Play-off 1970, Spring Nat'l Men's Teams 1970, Men's Pairs 1959, Vanderbilt 1969, Grand National Championship 1974; second Life Masters Men's Pairs 1968; winner of many regional titles including Pacific Southwest Open Teams, Masters Pairs 1964, Bridge Week Masters Pairs 1965, 1966, Open Teams 1973. Co-author, *Recap Bridge.*

SWANSON, Paul, of Morgantown, W. Va., entrepreneur, born 1932; one of the leading American players; represented US World Pair Olympiad 1974; co-winner of Mott-Smith Trophy 1972; won Life Masters Pairs 1973, Spring Nat'l Men's Teams 1972, Summer Nat'l secondary Swiss Teams 1973, second Chicago 1963, Reisinger 1973, Vanderbilt 1972; winner of numerous regional titles including Mid-Atlantic Open Teams 1970 (twice), Masters Pairs 1972, District 11 Knockout Teams 1971, Masters Pairs 1971.

SWARINGEN, Anita (Mrs. C. C.), of Greensboro, N.C., born 1907; regional wins include Mid-Atlantic Open Pairs 1958, Open Teams 1971.

SWARINGEN, C. C., of Greensboro, N.C., merchant, born 1904; regional wins include Mid-Atlantic Men's Pairs 1957, Open Teams 1971.

SWEARINGEN, Mrs. Harold P., of St. Louis, Mo., secretary; won Summer Nat'l Women's Pairs 1953; second Mississippi Valley Women's Pairs 1957.

SWEARINGEN, Stephen R., of Alexandria, Va., computer programmer, born 1943; highly successful in Mid-Atlantic competition since 1968; many regional wins include Mid-Atlantic Knockout Teams 1974, Open Teams 1968, 1971, 1972.

SWIMER, Ralph, of London, England, company director, born 1914; second World Team Olympiad 1960; represented Great Britain European Championship 1962, 1967, and World Pairs Olympiad 1962; national successes include Gold Cup 1955, Life Masters Pairs 1949, 1951, 1958, 1961, and many others; npc Great Britain World Championship 1965. See also BUENOS AIRES AFFAIR.

SWINNERTON-DYER, H. Peter F., of Cambridge, England, lecturer in mathematics, born 1927; second European Championship 1953; also represented Great Britain 1962; npc of winning Women's Team in European Championship 1961; won Gold Cup and English Open Teams 1963; second *Sunday Times'* International Pairs 1963.

SZURIG, Zbigniew, of Warsaw, Poland, born 1938; represented Poland World Team Olympiad 1964, European Championships 1963, 1965, npc Women's Teams 1966; second World Par contest 1963; won Hungarian Open Pairs 1959, Balaton Bowl 1963, Baltic Bowl 1964; national successes include first Open Teams 1962, 1963, 1964, 1966, 1968, Individual 1959; second Open Teams 1961, 1965. One of the leading Polish bridge theorists. Co-author of *Modern Bridge.*

T

TABAK, Mrs. Gabi, of Melbourne, Australia, born in Germany 1915; Far East Women's Champion 1973.

TAI, M. F., of Chang Hua, Taiwan, importer, born 1938; one of the leading Far East players; second World Championships 1969, 1970; represented China World Team Olympiad 1964, and several Far East Championships; national successes include Open Pairs 1963.

TALMADGE, Dorothy R. (Mrs. Rogers), of Denver, Colo.; won Fall Nat'l Life Master Women's Pairs 1968. One of the few licensed female helicopter pilots in the US.

TARLO, Joel, of London, lawyer, born 1905; European Champion 1963; represented Great Britain World Championship 1950, World Team Olympiad 1964, European Championships 1955, 1956, 1962, 1965, npc 1959. National wins include Gold Cup 1939, 1961.

TARLO, Louis, of London, England, lawyer, born 1911; represented Great Britain World Championship 1950; npc Great Britain World Team Olympiad 1972; European Champion 1950, represented Great Britain 1951, 1952, 1956, 1965, 1967, 1969; won Gold Cup 1939, 1951, 1954, 1957, 1960, 1974; won Masters Pairs 1952, 1965, 1970; npc Great Britain World Team Championship 1962, World Team Olympiad 1960, 1972, and European Championship 1961, 1963, 1970, 1971, 1973, 1974. Many executive positions include Vice-President and Chairman of English Bridge Union.

TARP, Kai, of Aarhus, Denmark, dentist. Represented Denmark in European Open Teams several times. National titles include Open Teams and Open Pairs. Author and co-author: *Modern Acol, Colonel Knuhrr & Co., Precision* (only Danish book on that system).

TATLOW, Major William B., of Tunbridge Wells, England, bridge supplies distributor and retired chartered accountant, born 1897; represented Wales Camrose Trophy matches three times; won Welsh National Pairs 1961. Former President Welsh Bridge Union; chief Recorder 1950 European Championships; tournament director 1961 European Championships.

TATOR, Dr. Robert B., of New York, N.Y., physician, born 1924; won Fall Nat'l secondary Masters Pairs 1973; many regional wins include New England Open Pairs 1966, Knockout Teams 1969, 1973, Open Team 1971.

TAUBE, Richard, of Washington, D.C., attorney, born 1933; winner of several regional events including Mid-Atlantic Open Teams 1972, 1974, Open Pairs 1972, 1973.

TAYLOR, Edward O., of Glendale, Calif., sales manager, born 1912; formerly one of the leading West Coast players; alternate for US Team World Team Olympiad 1964; fourth International Team Trials 1963; won Fall Nat'l Men's Team 1959, 1962, Open Pairs 1957, Life Masters Pairs 1963, Spring Nat'l Open Pairs 1959, Open Teams 1959, 1962; second Vanderbilt 1963, and fifteen regional wins.

TAYLOR, Eileen (Mrs. H. O.), of Auckland, N.Z., born 1908; represented New Zealand Far East Championships 1971, 1972, 1973; won New Zealand Open Teams 1957, 1959, 1960, 1961, 1962, 1963. As of 1964, second highest New Zealand master-point holder.

TAYLOR, Jeffrey F., of Kwajalein, Marshall Is., teacher, born 1941; Grand National Zonal Champion 1974; several regional wins include Oregon Trail Open Teams 1969, Masters Pairs 1971, Men's Pairs 1970. Intercollegiate Champion 1964.

TAYLOR, Pauline, of Detroit, Mich., decorative arts specialist, born 1911. President of the American Bridge Association 1969–73. Vice-President 1964–69. President of Detroit Unit 1956–61, and founder of first Women's Duplicate club there.

TEAGUE, Harriet (Mrs. Terry), of Birmingham, Ala.; regional wins include Southern Conference Open Teams 1963, Florida Open Pairs 1973, Bermuda Master Pairs 1974.

TEAGUE, Terry, of Birmingham, Ala., insurance agent; regional wins include Southern Conference Open Teams 1963, Mid-South Open Teams 1974, ACBL Director 1957–60.

TEEHANKEE, Eligio S., of Rizal, Philippines, business executive, born 1916; represented Philippines Far East Championships 1964; member Interport Team to Taipei 1962. National successes include Open Teams 1957, 1958, Men's Pairs 1958, 1961, Masters Pairs 1961, Knockout Teams 1963.

TEIXEIRA, Carlos Spinola, of Lisbon, Portugal, company director, born 1939; represented Portugal European Championships 1966, 1967, 1970, 1974; national wins include Open Teams four times, Open Pairs twice.

TELFER, Roy L., of Plymouth, England, army officer, born 1898. Many contributions to field of bridge mathematics include *Practical Odds at Bridge* and *Probabilities in Contract Bridge;* many articles in bridge magazines; tournament director 1961 European Championships. Contributing Editor *Bridge Encyclopedia.* See BIBLIOGRAPHY, M.

TEMMERMANN, Mrs. Simone de, of Paris, musician, born 1917; European Women's Teams Champion 1956, represented France European Championship 1955, 1959, 1961, 1965; winner French Mixed Teams 1960, Women's Teams 1955, 1960; Paris Mixed Teams 1960, Women's Pairs 1952, 1954, 1955, 1956, 1960, 1961.

TENCH, Stanley, of Ottawa, Ont., Director of Government Computer Centre, born 1929; won

Canadian-Atlantic Knockout Teams 1968, 1969, 1970; developed Tench movement. ACBL Associate National Tournament Director.

TEPPER, Mrs. Barbara, of Montclair, N.J., medical group administrator; won Summer Nat'l Women's Pairs 1967, Fall Nat'l Women's Teams 1967, second 1966, Spring Nat'l Women's Teams 1969, Marcus 1961; regional wins include Keystone Open Teams 1968.

TESSMER, Mrs. Carl F., of Belton, Tex., Far East Pair Champion 1961, representing Japan.

TEXTOR, Karel, of Prague, Czechoslovakia, technician, born 1926; represented Czechoslovakia European Championships 1966, 1967, against Poland 1961, 1962, and Hungary 1963; won Open Teams events 1962, 1963, 1964.

THÉRON, Dr. Georges (1922–1970), of Paris, physician and bridge writer; European Champion 1962, second 1967; represented France World Pairs Olympiad 1962, World Championships 1963, 1969, World Team Olympiad 1964, European Championships 1965; won French Open Teams 1952, Pairs 1962, with many more national successes. Writings include contributions to Pierre Albarran's *Encyclopédie,* articles for French and foreign magazines. Translated into French Olsen's *Mad World of Bridge.*

THEUS, Edgar, of Oklahoma City, Okla., attorney; second Fall Nat'l Life Master Men's Pairs 1966, Leventritt Pairs 1968; won Mid-South Spring Open Teams 1955, Open Pairs 1957, Texas Spring Masters Pairs 1965, Missouri Valley Open Teams 1961, Men's Pairs 1968. President ACBL 1969. ACBL Director and Chairman of its Membership and Promotion Committee. Past President Sooner Unit. Member WBF Executive Council 1971–73 and since 1975.

THOMAS, D. Michael, of Pittsburgh, Pa., sales executive, born 1938; won All-American Men's Pairs 1962, Mississippi Valley Open Teams 1968, Mid-American–Canadian Open Pairs 1967.

THOMAS, Frank, of Los Angeles, Calif., former leading boy actor of stage and screen; playwright, scriptwriter, and actor for radio and TV. In 1962 he retired from the theatrical side of the entertainment field to begin bridge teaching in association with George GOODEN, reaching as many as 18,000 students a year in department stores. Editor and publisher of *ABTA Quarterly* from 1969. Author of three bridge books, including *Sherlock Holmes, Bridge Detective* (in collaboration with Gooden) and *Sherlock Holmes, Bridge Detective, Returns.* Member IBPA.

THOMPSON, Mrs. M. L. (died 1975), of Indianapolis, Ind.; won Summer Nat'l Women's Pairs 1950, Fall Nat'l Women's Teams 1966, won Central States Women's Pairs 1943, 1945, Midwest Women's Pairs 1949, 1954, Open Teams 1971. ACBL Director; formerly President and Secretary Central Indiana BA and President Midwest Conference.

THOMSON, Doug, of Winnipeg, Man.; several regional wins include British Columbia Knockout Teams 1970, Men's Pairs 1972; Calgary Knockout Teams 1973.

THOMSON, J. Douglas, of Christchurch, New Zealand, physician; represented New Zealand in matches against Australia 1968, 1969, 1970, 1971; national wins include Pairs 1968, 1969, 1972, Interprovincial Teams 1967, 1969, 1971.

THORFINNSSON, Einar, of Reykjavik, Iceland, banker, born 1906; represented Iceland World Team Olympiad 1960; represented Europe World Championship 1950; represented Iceland European Championships 1950, 1951, 1958, 1971; national titles include Open Teams 1953, 1954, 1957, 1962, 1965, 1970, 1971, 1972, Open Pairs 1956.

THUMIM, Eugene, of Cleveland, Ohio, manufacturer's representative, born 1912; several regional wins include Eastern States Open Pairs 1956, All-American Open Teams 1958, Men's Pairs 1972.

THUMIM, Rose (Mrs. Eugene), of Cleveland, Ohio, bridge teacher; won Canadian-American Open Teams 1966, District 5 Open Teams 1967, Summer Nat'l Mixed Teams 1967.

THURRELL, Robert Freeman, Jr., of Wellesley Hills, Mass., life insurance executive, born 1920; won several regionals including Rocky Mountain Men's Pairs 1948, New England Open Teams 1967, and New England Open Pairs and Knockout Teams 1970.

TIERNAN, Agatha D., of Brandon, Vt., bridge teacher, writer and lecturer; second Spring Nat'l Women's Teams 1951; Honorary Secretary of the ACBL 1960. As a director at the Cavendish Club, she was granted the first club sanction for a monthly master-point game.

TIERNAN, Claire E., of Brandon, Vt., dress shop owner; second Fall Nat'l Women's Team 1951; won District 5 Open Teams 1958; Mixed Pairs 1958, Keystone Women's Pairs 1954.

TIERNAN, Mary Elizabeth, of Brandon, Vt., dress shop owner; won Nat'l Women's Teams 1956, second Women's Teams 1951; won Keystone Open Teams 1958, Women's Pairs 1954.

TIERNEY, Dr. John A., of Annapolis, Md., mathematical science administrator US Army, professor of mathematics USNA, born 1917; former Vice-President Maryland BA. Contributor to *The Bridge World* and co-author of *Contract Bridge: According to Silodor and Tierney.* See BIBLIOGRAPHY, E.

TIERNEY, William A., of Hacienda, Calif., manager insurance agency, born 1931; won All-Western Open Teams 1961, 1962, Bridge Week Masters Pairs 1961, 1966.

TIGHE, B. L., of Jackson, Miss., attorney, born 1905; won Mid-South Open Pairs 1966, Open Teams 1962, Southern Conference Open Teams 1960.

TILLES, Jules (1907–76), of Bronx, N.Y., bridge teacher, tournament director, and club owner, second Nat'l Mixed Pairs 1952; third Spingold 1951; won Eastern States Open Pairs 1943, 1950, 1954. Business manager of Greater New York BA 1957–72.

TINTNER, Léon, of Paris, publisher, born 1910 in Austria, French citizen since 1947; European Champion 1962; represented France in World Championships 1963, 1967, 1969, European Championships 1966; many national championships include Open Teams twice, and Inter-club twice.

TISH, Morris, of Skokie, Ill., professor of English, born 1918; second Marcus 1959, Summer Nat'l Golder Pairs 1953; won Central States Knockout Teams 1963, Men's Pairs 1952, Masters Teams 1958. Director Chicago CBL.

TOBIN, E. J. (1868–1953), born in Nova Scotia. Contributor to the Chicago *Record-Herald* and the *Daily Journal.* Won American Whist League Whist Open Team Championship 1911, 1913, Pairs Championship 1929, Chicago Whist Association Auction Pairs 1929, and American Whist League Contract Whist Championship 1934. One of the founders of American BL in 1927; retired to Florida and directed Greater Miami BL 1946–48. Author of *Sound Principles of Auction Bridge.*

TOLEDANO, John, of New Orleans, La., bridge teacher, born 1907; second Fall Nat'l Men's Teams 1956; won Mid-South Open Teams 1944, 1961, 1962, Men's Pairs 1944, Southern Conference Open Team 1960.

TOM, Merle, of Cedar Grove, N.J., attorney, born 1935; represented US World Pair Olympiad 1974, won Spring Nat'l Open Pairs 1972, Men's Teams 1974, Summer Nat'l Spingold Consolation 1970, second Vanderbilt 1974; winner of many regional events including Canadian-Atlantic Knockout

Teams 1973, Open Pairs 1972, New England Knockout Teams 1974.

TOMCHIN, Stanley, of New York, N.Y.; won Summer Nat'l Mixed Teams 1973.

TOSBATH, Aram, of Lebanon, Chief Meteorological Officer, Lebanese Weather Bureau, born 1903; represented Lebanon World Olympiad 1960, 1964, European Championships from 1952; national successes include Open Teams, Open Pairs, and Individual titles.

TOWNSEND, Mary Beth (Mrs. John J.), of Baton Rouge, La., dental assistant; second Spring Nat'l Women's Teams 1968; regional wins include Missouri Valley Women's Pairs 1958, South Texas Knockout Teams 1971.

TRAANE, Nils, of Brooklyn, N.Y., engineer, born 1925; composer of many double-dummy problems published in *The Bridge World* and the English *Bridge Magazine*.

TRAD, Antoine (Tony), of Geneva, Switzerland (formerly of Cairo, Egypt), former carton factory owner, born 1928; one of the leading Swiss players; represented Egypt European Championships 1954, 1956, 1961, 1962, Switzerland European Championships 1967; Egyptian national successes include Open Teams 1953, 1954, 1955, 1956, 1957, 1958, 1960, 1961, 1962, 1963, Open Pairs 1953, 1961, and many other titles in Egypt and Switzerland. Former technical advisor Egyptian Bridge Federation.

TRAUB, Alexander A., of Cape Town, South Africa, wool merchant and bridge writer, born 1911; national titles include Par event 1953, Open Teams 1955, 1962, second 1956, 1957. Author *Point-Count Expectancy Tables;* co-author of *Probabilities Contract Bridge;* editor *Practical Odds at Bridge;* translator of *Mathematical Theory of Bridge;* contributor to *Le Bridgeur.* Contributing Editor *Bridge Encyclopedia.*

TREADWELL, David R., of Wilmington, Del., planning associate, born 1912; Fall Nat'l Mixed Pairs 1969, secondary Swiss Teams 1974; winner of several regional titles including Keystone Knockout Teams 1973, Men's Teams 1970, Open Pairs 1960. Former President Delaware BA, President District 4, 1967–68 and 1973–74.

TREADWELL, George, of Lake Placid, N.Y.; regional wins include Golden State Men's Pairs 1969.

TRELDE, John, of Copenhagen, dentist, born 1921; represented Denmark European Championship Open Teams 1958, 1959, 1969, 1970, 1971. Won Danish Open Teams 1970, 1971. Invented many systems and conventions, including Copenhagen Convention, Trelde-lead and Trelde-asking bids.

TRENT, Paul, of New York, N.Y., attorney, born 1936; won Spring Nat'l Men's Teams 1969, 1971; winner of several regional events including Eastern States Open Pairs 1973, New England Masters Teams 1961, Masters Pairs 1970, Intercollegiate Par Championship 1957.

TRENT, Sandra (Mrs. Paul, formerly Mrs. Roark), of New York, N.Y.; won Summer Nat'l secondary Mixed Teams 1970, secondary Mixed Pairs 1969; regional wins include New England Masters Pairs 1968, Keystone Women's Pairs 1972.

TRÉZEL, Roger, of Paris, journalist, born 1918; one of the great players of the world. His partnership with Pierre Jaïs has been outstanding in international events. World Champion 1956, won World Team Olympiad 1960 and World Pairs Olympiad 1962, and represented France World Championship 1961. European Champion 1955, 1970; second 1956, 1959. Many national wins include Open Teams and Open Pairs. Writings include *La Clé du bridge, Cartes sur table,* and a series of booklets (Cahiers du bridge I–VIII). See BIBLIOGRAPHY, D.

TRITTER, Lorand, of Missouri City, Tex., account manager, born 1929; winner of many regional championships including Texas Knockout Teams 1970, 1971, Mid-American–Canadian Open Teams 1956, 1958, Masters Pairs 1965, South Texas Open Pairs 1974.

TROXEL, Richard B., of Wayzata, Minn., accountant, born 1932. One of the pioneers in the use of transfer bids over no trump openings.

TRUE, Robert H., Jr., of Newburgh, N.Y., born 1944, mathematician, historian of mathematics, bibliographer, a contributing editor of this *Encyclopedia* and American secretary of International Bridge Academy. Life Master since 1969, his research (1974–75) contributed greatly to clarifying the early history of BRIDGE, the probable origin of the name of the game, and the acquisition from Cambridge University Library of a copy of the 1886 pamphlet on BIRITCH, first recorded publication of rules of the game.

TRUSCOTT, Alan F., of New York, N.Y., a leading international player-writer, born 1925 in England; resident US since 1962; npc Bermuda Team World Olympiad 1964; represented Great Britain World Championship 1962; European Champion 1961, represented Great Britain European Championship 1951, 1958; national successes include Masters Individual 1953, 1958; won Fall Nat'l Men's Teams 1968, secondary Swiss Teams 1970, Summer Nat'l secondary Mixed Teams 1971; regional successes include Tri-State Open Teams 1968, Tri-State Men's

Pairs and Open Pairs 1972. Secretary British Bridge League 1957–62; Associate Editor ACBL *Bulletin* 1963–64. Bridge editor New York *Times* from 1964. Frequent contributor to *British Bridge World, The Bridge World,* and other magazines. Writings include *Contract Bridge* and *Bridge, The Great Bridge Scandal, Practical Bridge,* and *Master Bridge by Question and Answer;* co-translator of *Championship Bridge* (Le Dentu, *Bridge à la une*). Contributions to theory include RESTRICTED CHOICE. Executive Editor *Bridge Encyclopedia. See also* BUENOS AIRES AFFAIR. See BIBLIOGRAPHY, E.

TRUSCOTT, Dorothy Hayden (Mrs. Alan), of New York, N.Y., bridge teacher, mathematician; one of the great women players of the world. The only person to have competed in all four forms of major World Championships competition: Bermuda Bowl, World Olympiad Women's Teams, Open Pairs, Women's Pairs. Represented US World Women's Team Olympiad 1960, North America World Championships 1965; third World Open Pairs Olympiad 1966, Women's Pairs Olympiad 1962, 1974, Women's Team Olympiad 1968, 1972. Won Venice Cup 1974. In partnership with B. Jay BECKER, won three out of four restricted National Pairs Championships in a two-year period: Fall Nat'l Open Pairs 1962, Blue Ribbon Pairs 1963, Life Master Pairs 1964. Also won Fall Nat'l Women's Pairs 1961, Mixed Pairs 1959, Life Master Women's Pairs 1966, Spring Nat'l Women's Teams 1967, 1970, 1972, 1974, 1975, Summer Nat'l Women's Pairs 1959, secondary Mixed Teams 1971, Comm. & Ind. Teams 1958; second Vanderbilt 1964, Spingold 1965, 1968, Marcus 1959, Spring Nat'l Women's Pairs 1961, 1968, Women's Teams 1963, Summer Nat'l Mixed Teams 1957, 1960, 1967, 1972. Regional successes include New England Fall Mixed Teams 1958, Open Teams 1968, Tri-State Open Teams 1968, Southeastern Open Teams 1969, 1970, Bermuda Open Teams 1974. Author of *Bid Better, Play Better, Winning Declarer Play;* and several magazine articles. Contributing Editor *Bridge Encyclopedia.* See BIBLIOGRAPHY, C, D; BUENOS AIRES AFFAIR.

TSCHEKALOFF, Alex, of West Germany, formerly of Calif., computer programmer, born 1927; represented US World Pairs Olympiad 1970; won Fall Nat'l Life Masters Men's Pairs 1965, Blue Ribbons 1969; second Spring Nat'l Men's Pairs 1961, Sub-Senior Masters Teams 1951; numerous regional successes include Bridge Week Mixed Teams 1963, 1968, Open Teams 1967, Desert Empire Open Teams, Open Pairs 1960, Northwest Open Pairs 1962, Masters Pairs 1965, Open Teams 1961, 1966.

TSIANG, George, of Hong Kong, accountant; represented Hong Kong Far East Championships five times; won National Open Teams, Master Teams, Open Pairs, Mixed Pairs.

TSIANG, George Y. C., of Hong Kong, business executive, born 1919; Far East Champion 1959,

second 1963; national successes include many team and pair events. Vice-Chairman Hong Kong CBA for two years. Active in promotion of Far East Bridge Federation.

TSOU, Leslie, of Eugene, Ore., restaurateur, born 1919; Grand National Zonal Champion 1974; winner of numerous regional titles including Oregon Trail Knockout Teams 1970, Open Pairs 1969, All-Western Knockout Teams 1971, Peach Festival Knockout Teams 1974.

TUASON, Severo S. (1909–73), of Manila, Philippines, civil engineer; npc Philippine Team World Olympiad 1964; represented Philippines World Olympiad 1960; won Far East Championship 1959. Member WBF Executive Board.

TUBBS, Lewis G., of Arlington, Va., bridge instructor and club director, born 1902, deceased; second Summer Nat'l Master Mixed Teams 1954; ACBL Director 1965–68; former President Washington Bridge Association; author of *How We Teach and Play Contract Bridge.*

TUCKER, Dr. James L., of Abilene, Tex.; regional wins include Big D Knockout Teams 1972, Republic of Texas Knockout Teams 1973.

TUCKER, William F. E., of Downsview, Ont., accountant, born 1932; represented Bermuda World Olympiad 1964.

TUELL, David R., Jr., of Tacoma, Wash., attorney, born 1936; regional wins include Puget Sound Men's Pairs 1969, District 17 Men's Pairs 1973.

TURECKI, Dr. Stanley K., of New York, N.Y., child psychiatrist, born 1938 in Vilna, Poland, former resident of Sweden and South Africa; won Eastern States Men's Pairs 1970, Long Island Life Masters Pairs 1970, South African Open Teams 1965, 1967, 1968.

TURNER, Gloria. See REYSA, MRS. GLORIA.

TYLER, Frances, of Cincinnati, Ohio, bridge writer, born 1898; won Southern Ohio Mixed Pairs Championship 1935. Bridge columnist of the Cincinnati *Enquirer* since 1933, and one of the senior bridge columnists in the world.

U

UNAKUL, Dr. Sanong, of Bangkok, Thailand, professor of physiology, born 1920; Far East Champion

1961; national titles include Open Team 1959, Masters Pairs 1957, Individual 1948, 1953.

UNGER, George (1903–1968), of New York, N.Y., assistant manager CAVENDISH CLUB from 1947 until his death; won Chicago 1931; second Life Masters Individual 1937; auction wins include American BL Open Team 1931; regional wins Canadian–American Open Team 1933, South Jersey Open Team 1932, 1933, Individual 1933; second New Jersey Open Pairs 1931.

URBANIAK, Susan, of Mercer Island, Wash.; regional wins include Oregon Trail Knockout Teams 1972, Open Pairs 1974.

UTEGAARD, Helen (Mrs. John H.), of Bethesda, Md., one of the leading American women players; won Summer Nat'l Mixed Teams 1975, Women's Pairs 1965, Spring Nat'l Women's Teams 1971, 1973; winner of numerous regional titles including Eastern States Mixed Pairs, Women's Teams 1968, Mid-Atlantic Knockout Teams 1973, Open Pairs 1972, Women's Pairs 1970.

V

VAHALA, Vera, of Perth, Western Australia, born 1917 in Czechoslovakia; represented Australia World Women's Team Olympiad 1972, Far East Women's Championships 1971, vs. Australia 1969.

VAIL, Betty (Mrs. Thomas G.), of West Hartford, Conn., public relations director and bridge teacher, born 1905; won New England Mixed Team 1953, 1958, 1962, Swiss Teams 1969, Fall Open Teams 1961, Mixed Pairs 1953, 1957, Masters Women's Pairs 1969. Secretary New England Bridge Conference since 1955.

VALENTI, Anna (Mrs. Paolo), of Leghorn, Italy, born 1917; one of the world's greatest women players, sister-in-law and customary partner of Marisa BIANCHI; won World Women's Team Olympiad 1972, European Women's Champion 1970, 1971, 1973, 1974; represented Italy in many other European Women's Championships; other wins include European Common Market Women's Teams 1971, 1973, British Women's Teams 1973, Italian Cup twice, Italian Mixed Teams four times. See FAMILY.

VAN BEMMEL SUYCK. See BEMMEL SUYCK, J. R. C. VAN.

VAN BROOKS, J., of Oak Park, Mich., retired; won Nat'l Men's Teams 1951.

VAN DEN BORRE, Joseph (Jo), of Ghent, Belgium, public relations executive, tournament director, and columnist, born 1917; npc Belgian Women's Team World Olympiad 1964, and European Championship 1963; chief tournament director of Belgium; International Tournament Director of the World Bridge Federation since 1970. Author of bridge columns in many newspapers and contributor to many periodicals.

VAN HOOSE, Alf, of Birmingham, Ala.; regional wins include Mid-South Open Teams 1973, Open Pairs 1971.

VAN OSSEL, Lucienne, of Antwerp, Belgium; represented Belgium World Open Team Olympiad 1972, World Women's Team Olympiad 1960, 1964, 1968, World Women's Pairs Olympiad 1966, 1970, European Women's Championships 1961, 1963, 1965, 1966, 1970, 1974; national wins include Women's Pairs five times, Mixed Pairs twice. Top Belgian woman master-point holder.

VAN VLECK, Charles Edward (1886–1950), of New York, N.Y.; second Vanderbilt 1943; a pioneer of new bidding methods in the thirties. He originated the WEAK JUMP RESPONSES subsequently adopted by the ROTH-STONE SYSTEM, and advocated ultra weak WEAK TWO-BIDS. His system, which was based on the Vanderbilt Club, was probably the first to use the THREE-QUARTER NO TRUMP.

VAN ZANDT, Esta, of Houston, Tex., born 1929 in Calcutta, India; second Far East Women's Championships (represented Okinawa); second Spring Nat'l Women's Teams 1973; winner of many regional titles including Mid-South Open Teams 1971, Masters Pairs 1972, Mixed Pairs 1971, Missouri Valley Open Teams 1972, Women's Pairs 1970, 1972.

VANDERBILT, Harold S(tirling) (1884–1970), bridge authority whose revisions of auction bridge scoring principles created modern contract bridge, system-maker, and champion player. He was born at Oakdale, N.Y., into the richest and most famous American family of those times. He graduated from law school, then entered his family's railroad business, and for many years he was a successful business executive. His greatest fame in competitive fields is as a yachtsman—he successfully defended the America's Cup three times, and never lost an important race—and his revision of right-of-way rules, followed for all sailing vessels, are still known as the Vanderbilt Rules. Nevertheless his lasting fame is more likely to come from his contributions to bridge.

Vanderbilt took up bridge seriously in 1906, and his partnership with J. B. Elwell was considered the strongest in the US from 1910 to 1920. During that period the contract bridge principle—counting only bid tricks toward game—was often proposed and as often rejected, except for the limited success of plafond (see HISTORY OF BRIDGE). Experimenting with the proposed new game while on a cruise late in 1925, Vanderbilt originated the factors of vulnerability and inflated slam bonuses; and, a more decisive contribution, he produced a scoring table so balanced as to make nearly every aggressive or sacrifice bid an approximately even bet, allowing just enough differential to permit the exercise of nice judgment. Without such balance no game can be successful, and the original scoring table, which has not been materially altered, constitutes Vanderbilt's essential contribution to contract bridge.

The rapid spread of contract bridge from 1926 to 1929 is largely attributable to Vanderbilt's espousal of it; his social standing made the game fashionable. Vanderbilt's technical contribution was even greater. He devised the first unified system of bidding, being solely responsible for the artificial one club bid to show a strong hand, the negative one diamond response, the "strong" (16- to 18-point) no trump on balanced hands only, and the weak opening two-bid. These and his other principles were presented in his books, *Contract Bridge Bidding and the Club Convention,* 1929; *The New Contract Bridge,* 1930; *Contract by Hand Analysis,* 1933; and *The Club Convention Modernized.* 1964.

Vanderbilt was a member of the Laws Committee of the Whist Club of New York that made the American laws of contract bridge (1927, 1931) and the first international code (1932); then he became Chairman of that committee, and largely drafted the international code of 1935, the American code of 1943, and the international codes of 1948 and 1949. He remained Co-chairman of the National Laws Commission of the ACBL for the 1963 laws.

In 1928 Vanderbilt presented the Harold S. Vanderbilt Cup for a national team-of-four championship. This became and remained for many years the most coveted American team trophy, not least because of the replicas donated personally by Vanderbilt to the winners. In 1960 Vanderbilt supplied the permanent trophy for the World Bridge Federation's Olympiad team tournaments, and again adopted the policy of giving replicas to the winners.

As a player, Vanderbilt always ranked high. In 1932 and 1940 he won his own Vanderbilt Cup. He played by choice only in the strongest money games, and was a consistent winner. His regular partnership with W. von Zedtwitz was among the strongest and most successful in the US. In 1941 he retired from tournament bridge, but he continued to play in the most expert rubber bridge games, in clubs and at home.

In 1968, Vanderbilt spent more than $50,000 to re-create the lost molds for the replicas of the American trophy and to provide a quantity of replicas of both trophies sufficient to last from twenty to forty years. To perpetuate this practice of awarding individual replicas, Vanderbilt further bequeathed to the ACBL a trust fund of $100,000—a gift that wisely foresaw the possibility of inflation, but provided that excess funds, if any, can be donated in Vanderbilt's name to a charity of ACBL's choice. When last pur-

chased, replicas of the American trophy cost $600; of the Olympiad trophy, $500.

Many honors and distinctions have been awarded Vanderbilt: Commander of the Order of the British Empire for services as Director of British War Relief; Citizen of Athens for serving as President of Greek War Relief Association; honorary citizen of Nashville, Tennessee, for distinguished services as chairman of Trustees of Vanderbilt University; and others. In 1969, the World Bridge Federation made him its first honorary member. When a bridge Hall of Fame was inaugurated in 1964, Vanderbilt was one of the first three persons elected. See BIBLIOGRAPHY, C, E. Member Advisory Board *Bridge Encyclopedia*.

VANDERPORTEN, William S., of New Rochelle, N.Y., personnel relations; won Summer Nat'l Non-Masters Pairs 1940, Eastern States Men's Pairs 1958. 1958.

VEERABURUS, Manoo, of Bangkok, Thailand, professor, born 1928; represented Thailand World Olympiad 1964; Far East Champion 1963; national successes include Master Team 1963, Open Pairs 1963, Open Team 1964.

VEG, Dr. Lajos, of Budapest, Hungary, lawyer, born 1926; won Hungarian Open Teams 1966; member of the victorious Hungarian team in matches with Poland 1963, Germany 1964, and Brussels 1964.

VELASCO ORDONEZ, Eduardo M., of Buenos Aires, Argentina, bridge teacher, born 1923; national wins include Open Teams 1955, 1957, 1966, 1969.

VERDE, George A. (1904–1960), of Boston, Mass., lawyer, won New England Knockout Teams 1937, 1938, 1940 (twice), Open Pairs 1937, 1940, 1941.

VERGARA, Mrs. Etelvina S. de, of Buenos Aires, Argentina; won South American Women's Championship eight times; represented Argentine World Women's Team Olympiad 1964, 1972; won Argentine Open Teams 1937, Open Pairs 1937.

VERNAY, Colby K., of Lacon, Ill., born 1942; won Fall Nat'l secondary Men's Pairs 1971, Summer Nat'l secondary Open Pairs 1972; regional wins include Texas Fall Open Teams 1966.

VERNOFF, Lee (Mrs. Milton), of Los Angeles, Calif.; won Southeastern Women's Team four consecutive years, 1948–51, Women's Pairs 1944, 1945, Florida Individual 1949.

VERNOFF, Milton, of Los Angeles, Calif., insurance underwriter, born 1905; won Summer Nat'l Mixed Team 1938; many regional wins including Bridge Week Knockout Teams 1971, Masters Pairs 1953, Pacific Southwest Men's Pairs 1953, 1955,

1957, 1958, 1966, Rocky Mountain Men's Pairs 1955, Open Teams 1971, 1972. Former ACBL Director. Served as President Florida Unit 1947, California Unit 1960. Pioneered bridge on television in Florida.

VERNON, Francis, of Caracas, Venezuela, engineer, born 1934; represented Venezuela World Team Olympiad 1968, World Championships 1966, 1967; South American Champion 1965, 1966, and represented Venezuela in the 1968 South American Championships; won National Open Teams 1965, 1967, 1968.

VICKERY, Mrs. Robert (1870–1944), of Cambridge, Mass. Socially prominent bridge teacher in the Boston area from the 1910s to the 1930s. Her influence did much to advance and popularize the game in New England.

VINE, Frank, of Hamilton, Ont., attorney, born 1927; won Spring Nat'l Men's Pairs 1969; several regional wins include Canadian Nat'l Knockout Teams 1968, Men's Pairs 1968. Contributor to ACBL *Bulletin* and other bridge publications.

VIOLIN, Roxy, of Culver City, Calif., engineer, born 1929; Spring Nat'l Mixed Pairs 1970, second Fall Nat'l Life Master Men's Pairs 1973; won All-Western Masters Pairs 1964, Navajo Trail Mixed Pairs 1970.

VOGEL, Claude, of Chicago, Ill., college professor, born 1942; regional wins include Tri-Unit Knockout Teams 1971, Open Teams 1970.

VOGELHOFER, Charles C., of New York, N.Y., salesman; member of the Culbertson Team which finished second in the 1937 World Championships; won Eastern States Knockout Teams 1936. Former host at the Mayfair Club (New York).

VOIGT, Axel, of Risskov, Denmark, chemistry professor and bridge columnist, born 1908; represented Denmark World Team Olympiad 1960, and European Championship 1952, 1953, 1956, 1957, 1965, 1967. National successes include Open Teams 1941, 1952, 1956, 1957, 1960, 1961, 1963, 1964, 1965, 1966, 1973, 1974.

VON DER PORTEN, Ron, of San Francisco, Calif., bridge teacher, born 1936; one of the leading American players; represented North America World Championship 1962; third International Team Trials 1961; won Chicago 1962, Vanderbilt 1967, Spingold 1975; second Vanderbilt 1961, 1963, 1971; Blue Ribbon Pairs 1965, Spring Nat'l Men's Teams 1970; regional wins include All-Western Life Masters Teams 1972, Open Teams 1969, Masters Pairs 1962, Men's Pairs 1959, Open Pairs 1958, 1959, Bridge Week Knockout Teams 1966, 1971, Mixed Teams

1965. Author of *Introduction to Defensive Bidding* (see BIBLIOGRAPHY, C).

VON ELSNER, Don, of Hilo, Hawaii, real estate appraiser, bridge lecturer, and writer, born 1909; won Hawaiian Open Team 1952, Men's Pairs 1962, 1968. Author of many mystery novels in which bridge is featured, notably *How to Succeed at Murder Without Really Trying* in which the setting is a Hawaiian Regional, and several leading real-life experts play a part—the first book of the series featuring bridge pro Jake Winkman as the hero.

VON ZEDTWITZ, Waldemar K., linguist and lexicographer, one of the great players of all time, president emeritus of ACBL. He was born 1896 in Berlin, son of a German (Saxon) baron, to whose title he succeeded when his father died a few months after his birth, and of an American mother. Thereby he acquired dual citizenship, and after World War I he adopted US citizenship, relinquishing his title. A childhood spent in France, plus his American and German background, made him a trilingual native speaker; and his facility for and conversancy with many other languages, including the classical, as well as his scholarship in etymology, contribute to his international reputation as a linguist. In bridge, von Zedtwitz has been noted for versatility in playing with exponents of different systems. He was an early contributor to the CULBERTSON SYSTEM, a contributor and consultant in connection with the FOUR ACES SYSTEM, a member of the BRIDGE WORLD TEAM that won the first international matches (1930) in England and France, a member of one of the most successful all-time partnerships with H. S. VANDERBILT playing the club convention, and a regular partner of P. H. SIMS, S. G. CHURCHILL, the FOUR ACES, C. E. VAN VLECK, and many others. Later his regular partners included H. HARKAVY, Mrs. E. KEMP, and Mrs. B. BRIER. Beginning his tournament bridge career in 1923, von Zedtwitz won many national auction bridge championships and has won nearly all contract bridge championships. In 1930 he gave the GOLD CUP for Masters Pairs (now Life Masters Pairs) and won it the first year. He was honorary member ABL 1931, president ABL 1932, awarded the Wetzlar trophy 1936. When dissension threatened to break up the ACBL in 1948, the contesting factions agreed on von Zedtwitz as president and chairman with carte blanche; and in these positions he is credited with saving the League. Immediately upon rehabilitation of the League, at the end of 1949, he returned this power to the ACBL directors. He was a charter member of the NATIONAL LAWS COMMISSION, and as Co-chairman, played the most active role in preparation of the international code of 1963. A Director of the GNYBA, he was elected to the ACBL Board of Directors in 1962. As such he organized the ACBL Charity Foundation. (See CHARITY PROGRAM OF THE ACBL.) Upon his retirement in 1968 the ACBL Board of Directors presented him with a scroll in recognition of his outstanding contributions to bridge. He was a director of the WBF and chairman of its committee on INTERNATIONAL MATCH POINTS, being largely responsible for the schedule adopted in 1961, also Chairman of its Rules Committee for the 1964 Olympiad. Among his tournament successes are: won World Olympiad Mixed Pairs 1970, USBA Grand Nat'l Open Teams 1936, Mixed Pairs 1936; second Mixed Team 1935; won Spingold 1937, 1941, 1947, Chicago 1932, 1945, Vanderbilt 1930, 1932, 1940, Mixed Team 1940, 1942, 1945, 1965, Life Masters Pairs 1930, Open Pairs 1928, 1937, Men's Pairs 1946, Life Masters Individual 1936; second Spingold 1936, 1940, 1949, 1953, 1963, Chicago 1930, 1933, 1936, 1941, 1942, Vanderbilt 1937, 1938, 1943, 1945, 1960, Mixed Team 1933, 1935, 1956, Fall Nat'l Open Teams 1964, Life Masters Pairs 1933, 1939, Open Pairs 1935, Men's Pairs 1938, 1953; regional wins include All-Western Men's Pairs 1948, Bridge Week Mixed Teams 1948, Eastern States Knockout Teams 1935, 1944, 1973, 1974, Mixed Team 1934, Southeastern Open Team 1951, Men's Team 1951, Open Pairs 1947.

VORAJEE, Cassim Mahomed, of Johannesburg, South Africa, company director; chairman Southern Africa Bridge Federation 1964–1968; founding member and chairman of the Transvaal Contract Bridge Board of Control.

W

WACHTER, John E., of Wauwatosa, Wis.; won Fall Nat'l secondary Life Master Men's Pairs 1969; winner of several regional events including Gopher Knockout Teams 1971, Men's Teams 1969, 1970.

WAGAR, Margaret (Mrs. Wilkinson), of Atlanta, Ga.; bridge teacher and writer, one of the great American woman players of all time; npc US World Olympiad Women's Team 1968; shares with Kay Rhodes record number of wins in Women's Pairs 1944, 1955, 1956, 1957, 1958; won Life Masters Women's Pairs 1962, Spingold 1946, Marcus 1958, Chicago 1941, Fall Nat'l Women's Team 1940, 1943, 1944, 1945, 1946, 1964, 1965, Mixed Teams 1942, 1945, 1948, 1954, 1964, Open Pairs 1947, 1948, Mixed Pairs 1933, 1945, 1948, 1949; second Fall Nat'l Women's Team 1952, 1953, 1954, 1955, 1956, 1957, 1958, Summer Nat'l Life Masters Pairs 1943, Mixed Teams 1933, 1949, 1950, 1962, 1967, Spring Nat'l Women's Teams 1964. Numerous regional successes include Eastern States Women's Pairs 1937, 1965, Mid-Atlantic Mixed Pairs 1961, Open Teams 1960, 1966, 1967, 1968, Open Pairs 1966 (twice), 1971, Women's Pairs 1961, Masters Pairs 1968, Southeastern Women's Pairs 1939, 1940, 1941, 1942, 1947. Former Director ACBL.

WAGRODZKI, Krzysztof, of Warsaw, Poland, lawyer, born 1941; represented Poland European Championship 1967, Junior Championships 1968; won Polish Open Teams 1967; second Individual 1966, Mixed Pairs 1967.

WAINWRIGHT, Louise (Mrs. Stuyvesant), of New York, N.Y.; second Nat'l Mixed Pairs 1939, Mixed Team 1941; won Eastern States Mixed Team 1944. Donor of the Mrs. Stuyvesant Wainwright Trophy, Eastern States Women's Pairs, in play 1935.

WAINWRIGHT, Stuyvesant, of New York, N.Y., stockbroker, born 1895; second Summer Nat'l Mixed Team 1943. Vice-President of the Regency Club, New York. Member of Whist Club Committee on laws for international codes of 1932 and 1935; member of VANDERBILT CUP Committee 1928–57. Author of *Towie Tactics.*

WAKEMAN, Robert P., of Upper Montclair, N.J., systems engineer, born 1913; bridge Editor Newark *Evening News;* won Fall Nat'l Men's Teams 1960; regional wins include New England Fall Mixed Team 1960. Director New Jersey BL and its former bridge editor; contributing editor *Bridge Encyclopedia.*

WALDMANN, Arthur J., of New Preston, Conn., sales manager, born 1933; won Spring Nat'l Men's Pairs 1975, secondary Open Pairs 1970, second Spingold 1974; many regional wins include New England Open Pairs 1967, Masters Men's Pairs 1967, Masters Teams 1969, Swiss Teams 1970, Men's Pairs 1971.

WALLACE, Charlton, of Cincinnati, Ohio, bridge columnist, born 1904; won All-American Masters Individual 1946, Mid-Atlantic Open Pairs 1961, Midwest Spring Open Teams 1949, Open Pairs 1957. Bridge editor Cincinnati *Post-Times-Star* since 1933. Director AWL. President Midwest Association USBA 1936, Cincinnati BL 1938, contributing editor *Bridge Encyclopedia.* See BIBLIOGRAPHY, C.

WALLACE, Mrs. Charlton, of Cincinnati, Ohio; won Fall Nat'l Women's Teams 1947; All-American Open Pairs 1946, Midwest Spring Open Teams 1949.

WALLACE, Wilfred N. W., of Summer Hill, NSW, Australia, chemist, born 1908; World Par Champion 1937 with 100% score; national titles include Interstate Open Teams 1948, 1964, 1965, 1967, Open Pairs 1940, 1944, 1948, 1953, 1958, 1966. Vice-President New South Wales Bridge Association. Secretary Australian Bridge Federation.

WALSH, Alan D., of Sydney, Australia, systems analyst, born 1945; Far East Pairs Champion 1972; represented Australia Far East Championship 1972, 1973, 1974; national wins include Interstate Teams 1973.

WALSH, Miss Rhoda, of Hollywood, Calif., bridge professional and attorney; one of the leading American women players; third World Olympiad Women's Teams 1968; won Spring Nat'l Women's

Teams 1968, Women's Pairs 1968, 1972, Pairs 1968, Fall Nat'l Life Master Women's Pairs 1968, Spring Nat'l secondary Swiss Teams 1970; numerous regional wins include Bridge Week Mixed Teams 1965, 1969, 1970, Mixed Pairs 1966, 1974, Women's Pairs 1967, Open Teams 1972, 1973. Co-author of *Recap Bridge*.

WALSH, Richard R., of Van Nuys, Calif., stockbroker, born 1936; one of the leading American players; represented North America World Championship 1971; won International Play-off 1970, Vanderbilt 1969, Spring Nat'l Men's Teams 1970, Men's Pairs 1970; second Spingold 1959; numerous regional successes include Desert Empire Open Teams 1961, Open Pairs 1963, Men's Pairs 1962, Masters Pairs, Mixed Pairs 1967, Bridge Week Mixed Teams 1962, 1969, Mixed Pairs 1966, Masters Pairs 1965, 1966, Open Pairs 1965, Men's Masters Pairs 1967, Men's Pairs 1966, 1967.

WALSHE, Col. George Gordon J. (1873–1959), of London; represented England in ANGLO-AMERICAN MATCH 1934. One of the referees in the CULBERTSON-LENZ MATCH in 1932. Co-inventor of the CAB SYSTEM. Wrote under the pseudonym of "Yarborough" for the *Sunday Times*. Author of *Count to Win at Bridge, Let's Play CAB, Slams Made Simple;* co-author with F. Dudley Courtenay of *The Losing Trick Count, Standard Manual of Play, Standardized Code of Contract Bridge*. See BIBLIOGRAPHY, C.

WALVICK, Walter J., of McLean, Va., attorney, born 1942; won Fall Nat'l Life Master Men's Pairs 1975, second Summer Nat'l Life Masters Pairs 1974; winner of many regional events including Mid-Atlantic Knockout Teams 1971, 1972, Open Teams 1969 (twice).

WARNER, David, of Jenkintown, Pa., stockbroker, born 1911; second Nat'l Mixed Team 1947, Nat'l Mixed Pairs 1957; won District 4 Men's Pairs 1962, Eastern States Mixed Team 1958, Keystone Open Teams 1960, Men's Pairs 1965. Former ACBL Vice-President.

WARNER, Mrs. Greeley, of Pampa, Tex., secretary, born 1907; won Summer Nat'l Women's Pairs 1962, Desert Empire Open Pairs 1961.

WARREN, Mrs. Prescott, of Newton, Mass., born 1876. Prominent New England bridge teacher and radio lecturer in the twenties and thirties; won New England Women's Pairs 1931, 1933. Columnist for *Boston Transcript;* author of several books on auction and contract.

WARSHAUER, Bernard J., of Sumter, S.C., attorney, born 1920; won Spring Nat'l secondary Open

Pairs 1971; regional wins include Mid-Atlantic Knockout Teams 1972, 1973.

WARZEK, Frank G., of San Jose, Calif.; won Summer Nat'l Comm. & Ind. Teams 1969; regional wins include Golden Gate Men's Pairs 1973.

WATANABE, Clara, of Honolulu, Haw., bridge teacher; winner of many Hawaiian regional events, including Open Teams 1960, Open Pairs 1958, Women's Pairs 1959, 1969, 1972, 1974, Mixed Pairs 1960, 1970, 1972.

WATSON, Louis H. (1907–1936), of New York, N.Y.; a leading player of the thirties; until his sudden and untimely death, this most popular personality was considered by Culbertson to be his most likely successor. Won AWL Open Teams 1933, 1934, Open Pairs 1933, 1934, Asbury Challenge Teams 1932; second Asbury Challenge Teams 1933, Vanderbilt 1933, Fall Nat'l Open Pairs 1931, 1932. He was a widely followed analyst, acting as daily columnist for the New York *Post*, and as Technical Editor for *The Bridge World*. His writings included the classic *Watson on the Play of the Hand*, and *Contract Bridge*. See BIBLIOGRAPHY, D, E.

WEATHERBEE, Perley E., of South Portland, Me., electrical engineer, born 1896; won New England Open Teams 1951, Masters Pairs 1953, Individual 1953. One of original organizers of Maine Unit; former President New England Conference.

WEBSTER, H. T. (1885–1952), noted syndicated cartoonist, was best known for the character "The Timid Soul," which he created. He used bridge as the topic of many of his humorous pictures. He was born in West Virginia, and lived most of his adult life in New York. Co-author of cartoon books on bridge with Culbertson (1933) and Caswell Adams (1948). See BIBLIOGRAPHY, L.

WEED, Charles E., of Dallas, Tex., corporate vice-president, born 1931; won Grand Nationals 1975, Fall Nat'l secondary Swiss Teams 1973; winner of many regional titles including Mid-South Knockout Teams 1972, Open Teams 1973.

WEEKS, Thomas, of Dearborn, Mich., teacher and pilot, 1909–71. ACBL Associate National Tournament Director.

WEI, Charles C., of New York, N.Y., ship owner, born in Shanghai, China, 1914; npc of Chinese Team in World Olympiad 1964, World Championships 1969. Devised the PRECISION bidding system which was used successfully by the Chinese Team in 1969 and 1970 World Championships by the PRECISION TEAM in winning the 1970 and 1971 Spingolds and 1972 Vanderbilt, and by the Italian Team in winning the 1972 Olympiad and 1973 and 1974 World Championships. See SPONSORS. Regional successes include Puerto Rico Open Pairs 1970, New York Open Pairs 1974, holder of record score of 260 on 156 average in a one-session event. See HIGHEST SCORE. Author of many books and articles on Precision and Super Precision (see BIBLIOGRAPHY, C).

WEI, Katherine (Mrs. Charles), of New York, N.Y., writer and lecturer on the Precision System, born in Peking, China 1930; won Spring Nat'l Women's Teams 1971, secondary Women's Teams 1973, Fall Nat'l secondary Swiss Teams 1973, second Vanderbilt 1974, Spring Nat'l Women's Teams 1973; several regional wins include New England Knockout Teams 1974, Southeastern Women's Teams 1973.

WEICHSEL, Nancy (Mrs. Peter), of Flushing, N.Y.; winner of several regional events including Southeastern Life Masters Pairs 1973, Tri-State Open Pairs 1971.

WEICHSEL, Peter, of Flushing, N.Y., bridge professional, born 1943; one of the leading American players; won Spingold 1970, 1971, Vanderbilt 1972, Reisinger 1973, Fall Nat'l Life Master Men's Pairs 1971, second Life Masters Pairs 1972, Spring Nat'l Men's Teams 1968; won London Sunday Times 1975; many regional wins include Long Island Knockout Teams 1971, 1972, New England Knockout Teams 1968, Open Pairs 1968. Member New York Intercity Team 1968. See PRECISION TEAM.

WEILAND, Alexander, of Chicago, Ill., accountant, regional wins include Central States Open Teams 1972, Tri-Unit Open Teams 1972.

WEINBERG, Manuel M., of Frederick, Md., lawyer and company director, born 1907; won Mid-Atlantic Spring Open Pairs 1961, Summer Masters Pairs 1962, Fall Open Teams 1966.

WEINER, Mrs. George S., of Joplin, Mo., born 1905; won Missouri Valley Women's Pairs 1958, 1965, Keystone Mixed Pairs 1958.

WEINER, Leo B., of Chicago, Ill., bridge teacher and tournament director, born 1906; winner of Summer Nat'l Golder Pairs 1966; numerous regional championships including Central States Life and Senior Masters Teams 1957, Open Pairs 1943, 1953, Mississippi Valley Open Teams 1962, Men's Pairs 1951, 1953, 1956, Mixed Pairs 1957.

WEINSTEIN, Howard M., of Golden Valley, Minn., student, born 1953; won Spring Nat'l Non-Masters Pairs 1972; regional wins include Iowa Open Teams 1974, Men's Pairs 1974.

WEISBACH, Dean (Mrs. Frank), of Memphis, Tenn., ACBL executive, born 1911; ACBL Operations Division Manager since 1970, ACBL National Director 1956–70, the only woman to achieve this rank.

WEISBACH, Frank, of Memphis, Tenn., won Life Masters Pairs 1947; second Spingold 1951, Summer Nat'l Men's Pairs 1946; many regional wins include Midwest Spring Men's Pairs 1962, Mississippi Valley Men's Pairs 1968, Iowa Men's Pairs 1968, Tri-Unit Men's Pairs 1968.

WEISS, Albert ("Dingy"), of Miami Beach, Fla., retired, born 1900; one of the leading American players; won Vanderbilt 1963, 1965, Fall Nat'l Open Pairs 1939, 1951, Men's Teams 1946; second Spingold 1953, 1972, Life Master Pairs 1949, 1962, Life Master Individual 1945, Men's Teams 1952; many regional wins include All-American Open Teams 1938, 1939, Open Pairs 1938, Masters Individual, 1938, 1939, Southeastern Men's Teams, Open Pairs 1960, Open Teams, Knockout Teams 1968.

WEISS, Alexander, of New York, N.Y., president lithographing company, born 1897; won Vanderbilt 1948; Fall Nat'l Senior Masters Individual 1947; Eastern States Mixed Teams 1944. Former Chairman Charity Committee GNYBA, four times won second place in national drive.

WEISS, David J., of San Marino, Calif., psychology professor, born 1944; several regional wins include Pacific Southwest Masters Pairs 1969, Men's Pairs 1969, Bridge Week Open Pairs 1972.

WEISS, Larry, of Los Angeles, Calif., insurance broker and photographer; second Fall Nat'l Mixed Pairs 1970; winner of many regional titles including Bridge Week Knockout Teams 1963, 1965, Pacific Southwest Masters Pairs 1966, 1968, Navajo Trail Open Teams 1973. Author of several *Bridge World* articles on limit bidding and originator of the SIMPLIFIED CLUB system.

WEISS, Lawrence, of Brookline, Mass., attorney, born 1905; won Southeastern Open Teams 1944, New England Open Teams 1957, 1960, 1961, 1963, Mixed Pairs 1941, 1945, Knockout Teams 1938, 1939, 1941 (twice), 1942, 1945, 1957, 1961, 1964, Masters Teams 1950, Men's Pairs 1941, 1947. Chairman of committee to revise ACBL bylaws 1949; credited with devising administrative method used by ACBL since then. Former ACBL Vice-President and President of New England Bridge Conference. Author of *Contract Bridge: The Bidding Structure*. See BIBLIOGRAPHY, C.

WEITZNER, Jerome B., of Walnut Creek, Calif., salesman, born 1941; won Summer Nat'l Commercial Teams 1972; several regional wins include All-Western Men's Teams 1973, Hawaii Open Teams 1973.

WELCH, Lawrence J., of Indianapolis, Ind., realtor, born 1895; one of the most successful midwest players; won Chicago 1935, Central States Open Team 1939, 1943, All-American Open Team 1941, 1942, 1945, Masters Individual 1946.

WELLS, Nell (Mrs. George, formerly Nell Childs), of San Francisco, Calif., bridge teacher; one of the leading bridge personalities of the West Coast; first woman Life Master on the Pacific Coast; won Nat'l Mixed Teams 1946, 1951, 1955, All-Western Open Teams 1957, Bridge Week Open Teams 1948, 1957, Masters Pairs 1954, Open Pairs 1951, Women's Pairs 1942, 1961, and many others. Director of San Francisco Unit.

WENDT, Jay, of New York, N.Y., actuary, born 1928; won Spring Nat'l Comm. & Ind. Team 1958, Summer Nat'l Golder Pairs 1961; second Chicago 1961; won Eastern States Masters Pairs 1959, New England Mixed Teams 1958, New York–New Jersey Open Pairs 1965.

WENNBERG, Tom, of Gothenburg, Sweden, bridge teacher and columnist, born 1908; second European Championships 1948, and represented Sweden 1934, 1935; Scandinavian Champion 1948; national titles include Open Pairs 1961.

WERDELIN, Dr. Ole, of Copenhagen, Denmark, physician, born 1933; represented Denmark in European Championship 1961, 1965, 1973, 1974; won Danish Open Teams 1963, 1974.

WERDELIN, Stig, of Copenhagen, Denmark, lawyer, born 1937; represented Denmark in Team Olympiad 1972; European Championship 1961, 1970, 1971, 1973, 1974, 1975. Won Danish Open Teams six times 1963–75; Open Pairs 1972, 1973, 1974.

WERNER, Britta (Mrs. Einar), of Stockholm, Sweden, born 1912; won World Women's Team Olympiad 1968, European Women's Championships 1962, 1967; Scandinavian Women's Championships. National titles include Open Teams, Women's Pairs, and Mixed Pairs.

WERNER, Einar, of Stockholm, Sweden, doctor of mathematics, born 1901; one of the leading personalities in international bridge; represented Sweden World Championship 1950, 1953; European Champion 1939, 1952, second 1948, 1949, 1950; national titles include Open Teams 1942, 1944, 1948, 1951, 1952, Open Pairs 1941, 1942, 1943, 1945, 1946, 1949. Secretary Swedish Bridge League 1939–64. Chair-

man WBF Committee on International Match Points 1959–60, and assisted in their subsequent 1961 revision.

WERNHER, Sir Derrick J., Bt. (1889–1947), of London, England, and Deal, N.J.; succeeded to title in 1912 and lived in US between the two World Wars; served as British representative with International Red Cross in Geneva during World War II, and subsequently returned to London, where he died. A leading personality in American bridge in the thirties, he was one of the originators of the master-point system which became the basis of the later prosperity of the ACBL. ABL President 1933, and Chairman of its Master Plan Committee; AWL Director. Donor of the Wernher Trophy for Spring Nat'l Men's Pairs. Second Asbury Challenge Teams 1936; won Reisinger 1930.

WEST, Leslie H., of San Francisco, Calif., born 1944; winner of many regional events including Golden Gate Knockout Teams 1969, 1970, 1974, Golden State Knockout Teams 1970, Open Teams 1968.

WESTCOTT, Frank T. (1901–1974), of North Attleboro, Mass., engineer and contractor, one of the outstanding American bridge personalties; npc North American Team World Championship 1961 and US World Team Olympiad 1964; second Spring Nat'l Men's Team 1964; won New England Knockout Teams 1949, 1956, 1959, 1962, 1963, Mixed Teams 1946, 1948, 1949, 1950, 1956, Men's Pairs 1951, 1963, Mixed Pairs 1948, 1951, 1959, Spring Open Teams 1952, 1954, 1958, 1962, Open Pairs 1970, and a host of other important regional events. ACBL President 1960. Honorary Member 1968; former ACBL Director, President New England Bridge Conference, Eastern Massachusetts BA. Westcott Trophy awarded to winner of Summer Nationals Olympiad Fund Pairs.

WESTERFIELD, K. D. (Dan), of San Francisco, Calif., insurance adjuster, born 1912; won many regional events including All-Western Masters Pairs 1947, Bridge Week Knockout Teams 1952, Desert Empire Open Teams 1957, 1958, 1966.

WESTHEIMER, Gerald J. (Jeff), of New York, N.Y., commodity specialist, born 1934; fourth World Olympiad Open Pairs 1970; won Reisinger 1969, Marcus 1961; second Vanderbilt 1968, 1969, Spingold 1969.

WETZLAR, Edwin A., of New York, N.Y., died 1934; a leading personality in the early years of contract; won Vanderbilt 1928, Nat'l Mixed Teams 1933; second Vanderbilt 1929, AWL Open Pairs 1931, 1933; AWL Director. See WETZLAR TROPHY.

WHALEN, Vivian (Formerly Lavery), of Albertson, N.Y., bridge club owner; won Summer Nat'l secondary Mixed Pairs 1974, Fall Nat'l secondary Open

Teams 1974; winner of several regional titles including Eastern States Mixed Teams 1961, Mixed Pairs 1966, New York Winter Open Teams 1974.

WHITAKER, Mrs. Marjorie, of Johannesburg, South Africa (formerly of London, England), born 1916; won European Championship, Ladies' Series, 1959, also represented Great Britain in 1953, 1962, 1967; represented Great Britain in World Team Olympiad, Ladies' Series, 1960; won English Women's Teams 1960–63.

WHITE, Barry, of Portland, Ore., investor, born 1945; winner of several regional titles including Oregon Trail Open Teams 1972, Men's Pairs 1970, Peach Festival Knockout Teams 1974.

WHITE, Dorothy Collins, of Racine, Wisc., tournament director and bridge teacher, born 1904. ACBL Director 1964. Executive Secretary Wisconsin-Upper Michigan BA for more than fifteen years, she was known as "Mrs. Bridge" in Racine, Wisc.

WHITE, Matie (Mrs. Harold J.), of Cleveland, Ohio; second Winter Nat'l Mixed Pairs and Women's Teams 1933; regional wins include All-American Open Teams 1948, Women's Pairs 1952, Hawaiian Women's Pairs and Mixed Pairs 1956.

WHITE, Sam, of New York, N.Y., clerk, born 1917. A top ranking player in the American Bridge Association and winner of many national titles.

WHITEBROOK, Charles, of Ft. Lauderdale, Fla., advertising consultant; won Fall Nat'l Open Pairs 1949, Eastern States Open Pairs 1947, Florida Masters Pairs 1960, Southeastern Open Teams 1955, 1956, 1972. President Florida Unit, ACBL Director. Editor and publisher of *Florida Bridge News.* Co-chairman of Florida Nationals.

WHITEHEAD, Carolyn (Mrs. Allyn G.), of Washington, D.C., bridge teacher and tournament director, born 1896; regional wins include Bridge Week Knockout Teams 1952, Women's Pairs 1949, Rocky Mountain Women's Pairs 1954, Southeastern Women's Teams 1967.

WHITEHEAD, Wilbur C. (1866–1931), of New York, N.Y., one of the world's greatest bridge authorities. Member of team winning Vanderbilt Cup 1928, first time in play, second in 1929. His greatest contribution to bridge was necessarily in the days of auction, when he published *Auction Bridge Standards,* which explained the Whitehead system. He constructed the first table of quick tricks, and established a connection between playing tricks and quick tricks. See BIBLIOGRAPHY, A, E, H.

WHITESELL, William F., Sr., of Lake Oswego, Ore., realtor and bridge professional, born 1940;

winner of numerous regional events since 1970 including Oregon Trail Knockout Teams 1971, 1973, British Columbia Knockout Teams 1971, Open Pairs 1970, Men's Pairs 1973. Donated in 1930 the Wilbur C. Whitehead Trophy for winner of Summer Nationals Women's Pairs.

WIDDER, Dr. Lajos, of Budapest, lawyer and author, born 1893; European Champion 1938, Hungarian winner World Par Contest 1937; Hungarian Champion 1937–39, 1955, 1957. Writings include *Tournament Bridge* and *The Technique and Tactics of Bridge Playing.*

WIGNALL, John R., of Christchurch, New Zealand, stockbroker, born 1932; represented New Zealand World Championship 1974, World Team Olympiad 1972, Far East Championships 1964, 1971, 1973; national wins include Pairs 1964, 1965, 1970, 1971, 1973, 1974, Teams 1972.

WILDY, Marion E., of Aiea, Oahu, Hawaii, naval supplies supervisor; won Hawaiian Open Team 1956, Mixed Pairs 1957. President Honolulu Unit 1964.

WILEY, Kent, of Oak Park, Ill., government administrator, born 1937; won Fall Nat'l secondary Mixed Pairs 1969, Spring Nat'l secondary Swiss Teams 1972; winner of many regional events including Tri-Unit Open Pairs 1971, Men's Pairs 1972, 1974, Mixed Pairs 1969.

WILEY, Lois (Mrs. Kent), of Oak Park, Ill., chiropractic physician; the most successful blind player, a familiar sight at tournaments with her seeing-eye dog; won Fall Nat'l secondary Mixed Pairs 1969, Spring Nat'l secondary Swiss Teams 1972, 1973; many regional wins include Central States Open Teams 1969, 1974, Tri-Unit Open Pairs 1971, Mixed Pairs 1969.

WILKINS, Robert, of Memphis, Tenn., librarian, bridge teacher, and writer, ACBL executive, born 1911. National Tournament Director 1961–65, Tournament Coordinator 1965–68; Director of ACBL Elections and Director of Communications for the ACBL Board of Directors since 1968, Executive Secretary ACBL Charity Foundation 1969–73.

WILKINSON, Lee (Mrs. Harold), of Dallas, Tex., public relations and advertising agent; editor daily bulletins for Texas, Mid-South and Missouri Valley regionals and sectionals; former member publicity staff at national tournaments.

WILKOSZ, Andrezej, of Krakow, Poland, engineer, born 1935; represented Poland World Team Olympiad 1964, European Championships 1963, 1965; won Belgian Open Teams 1964, Beirut Festival Open Teams 1968, Polish Mixed Teams 1968, Open Pairs 1962; second Polish Open Teams 1967, 1968.

WILKS, Mrs. A. H., Jr., of Pittsburg, Kan.; won Mississippi Valley Women's Pairs 1956, Missouri Valley Mixed Pairs 1955, Women's Pairs 1957.

WILLIAMS, Don, of Kansas City, Mo., economist, born 1931; second Spring Nat'l Men's Teams 1962; regional wins include District 15 Open Teams 1967, 1969, Knockout Teams 1969, 1970.

WILLIAMS, Mary (Mrs. Tinker, formerly Philley), of Houston, Tex., attorney; winner of several regional championships including Texas Knockout Teams 1970, Mexican Nat'l Women's Pairs 1973. Former Secretary and Vice-President District 16.

WILLIAMS, Mrs. Phyllis L., of London, England, born 1907; European Women's Champion 1950, 1951, 1952; also represented Great Britain 1949, 1953, 1955, 1956, 1965, 1967; toured US 1953 as member of British Women's Team; national wins include Women's Teams 1952, 1956, 1964.

WILLIAMS, Robert Edward (1917–1974), of Sydney, Australia, born New Zealand; represented Australia World Team Olympiad 1960; national successes include Open Team 1947, 1948, 1949, 1950, 1952, 1959. Handsetter and organizer for Par Point Global Championships 1961, 1963, joint formulator Laws of Par Point Contract Bridge 1963, Vice-President Australian Bridge Council.

WILLIAMS, Dr. Sam, of Spring Valley, Calif.; regional wins include Pacific Southwest Open Pairs 1971, Men's Pairs 1969, District 17 Masters 1973.

WILLIAMS, W. W., Jr., of Raleigh, N.C., insurance salesman, born 1920; won Nat'l Senior Masters Individual 1955; regional wins include Mid-Atlantic Open Team 1961, 1962, 1971, 1972. Former President North Carolina Unit.

WILLIAMSON, Mrs. Vivian, of Roswell, N. Mex.; won Spring Nat'l Women's Pairs 1973.

WILLIS, Col. J. Tim, of Houston, Tex., bridge studio proprietor, born 1913; won Japanese Open Team 1952, Texas Conference Open Team 1962.

WILLNER, Olle, of Stockholm, Sweden, economic analyst, born 1923; originator of TRANSFER BIDS in 1953–54, which he described in a series of articles in the Swedish bridge magazine, *Bridge Tidningen*.

WILSON, Baden, of Dunedin, New Zealand, solicitor, born 1900; won Open Teams 1966. Former President New Zealand CBA.

WILSON, Bert, of Ventnor, N.J., bridge columnist, born 1915; won Mid-Atlantic Mixed Pairs 1963.

Publicity Director Philadelphia CBA. Co-author with C. SOLOMON of *Hold Our Bridge Hands*.

WILSON, Mrs. Jerome W., of Greenville, Miss., owner specialty shop, born 1914; won Mexican Nat'l Women's Pairs 1960, Mississippi Valley Open Team 1960, Women's Pairs 1957, Southern Conference Women's Pairs 1957, Golden Gate Individual 1968. Director Mississippi BA.

WILSON, Mike, of Vancouver, B.C., stockbroker, born 1950; born with no arms and only one leg, plays tournament bridge with a card rack as his only mechanical aid, using his toes to pick up his cards, sort them and keep score. Became a Life Master in 1974.

WILSON, Robert W. (1909–1965), of Lower Burrell, Pa., aluminum company employee. Organized Pittsburgh Industrial League for nineteen years. An authority on double-dummy problems, in which capacity he has contributed to the *Bulletin, The Bridge World* and many other magazines. Contributing Editor *Bridge Encyclopedia*.

WILSON, Walter, of Metairie, La. bridge teacher and writer, born 1910; ACBL associate National Tournament Director.

WILTON, Herbert C., real estate salesman, of Cincinnati, Ohio; second Summer Nat'l Mixed Teams 1958; won Great Lakes Open Teams 1962, Midwest Open Pairs 1968. Formerly President and Secretary of Cincinnati BA.

WINDLEY, Betty. See HADDAD, BETTY.

WINGES, Bert, of Ottawa, Ont.; regional wins include Canadian–American Open Pairs 1969, Men's Pairs 1970.

WINSLOW, T(homas) N(ewby) (1865–1942), bridge author and system-maker, born in North Carolina and later a resident of New Jersey. His system, introduced in a series of booklets beginning in 1930 and in the book *Win with Winslow* (1933), anticipated the FOUR ACES SYSTEM in its 1½–1–½ point-count and CANAPÉ in showing the lowest four-card suit first, regardless of the strength of that suit (◊ 9 7 6 3 would be shown before ♠ A K Q J x x). The object of the system was to exchange both distributional and high-card information early, often by artificial or semi-artificial bids. Several noted players including C. LOCHRIDGE used the Winslow System at its peak, 1932–33. The system failed because the defenders were given too much information and could play double-dummy defense, and often could use such information in their bidding.

WIRT, Sidney H. (1897–1954), of Brookline, Mass., stockbroker; one of the most successful New England players in the forties; won New England Knockout Teams 1935, 1940, 1945, 1946 (twice), 1947, 1950, 1951, Mixed Teams 1940, 1941, Open Pairs 1941, 1950, Men's Pairs 1936, 1946.

WISEMILLER, James P., of Columbus, Ohio, born 1943; won Spring Nat'l Open Pairs 1965; regional wins include Midwest Open Teams 1963, All-American Men's Pairs 1970.

WISER, John, of Beaconsfield, Que., former bridge club owner, born 1926; won Canadian–American Men's Pairs 1954, director TV program 1961–63, lecturing on bridge. ACBL National Tournament Director.

WIŚNIEWSKI, Jerzy, of Warsaw, Poland, jeweler, born 1928; represented Poland World Team Olympiad 1964; won Polish Open Pairs 1959, second 1958, 1966.

WITTES, Jon, of Los Alamitos, Calif., school psychologist, born 1942; won Golder Pairs 1969, Fall Nat'l secondary Open Teams 1968; many regional wins include Bridge Week Knockout Teams 1973, Men's Pairs 1971, All-Western Knockout Teams 1972, Little Bridge Week Knockout Teams 1974.

WOHLIN, Jan, of Stockholm, Sweden, bridge teacher, born 1924; one of the great players of Europe; represented Sweden-Iceland World Championship 1950, Sweden 1953; European Champion 1952, second 1948, 1949, 1950. Winner of many Scandinavian Championships and fifteen national titles. Co-inventor EFOS SYSTEM.

WOLDENBERG, Charles L., of New Orleans, La., secretary of liquor company, died 1968; won Rocky Mountain Open Pairs 1957, Texas Men's Pairs 1954, Mid-South Open Teams 1948, 1952, Open Pairs 1950.

WOLF, Jack, of Missouri City, Tex., sales manager, born 1934; regional wins include Missouri Valley Open Teams 1961, Open Pairs and Open Teams 1962, Mixed Pairs 1971, South Texas Unmixed Pairs 1974.

WOLFE, Edward C., of Cleveland, Ohio, born 1883, deceased, bridge expert, writer, whose success at whist and auction bridge helped make him one of the earliest of the recognized authorities on contract bridge. His ready wit and power of spontaneous analysis made him one of the most successful radio commentators, called by many the "McNamee of Bridge" (for Graham McNamee, a top raido commentator). A member of the Advisory Council of Bridge Headquarters, he helped draft the Official

System. After Culbertson's defeat of Lenz, he joined the Culbertson staff, organizing teachers' conventions and lecturing. Former contributing editor of *The Bridge World* and *British Bridge Magazine;* author of *The Play of the Cards at Contract Bridge.*

WOLFF, Elizabeth ("Betsey"), of Dallas, Tex., teacher, born 1937; won World Olympiad Mixed Teams 1972; second Spring Nat'l Women's Pairs 1971, Women's Teams 1973; several regional wins include South Texas Masters Pairs 1968, Knockout Teams 1971.

WOLFF, Robert, of Dallas, Tex., staff analyst corporate development, born 1932; one of the world's leading players; the only player to be World Champion in three different categories: Open Team World Champion 1970, 1971, World Olympiad Open Pair Champion 1974, World Olympiad Mixed Team Champion 1972; represented US World Team Olympiad 1972, North America World Championships 1973, 1974, 1975; won Spingold 1969, Vanderbilt 1971, 1973, Reisinger 1970, Grand Nationals 1975, Spring Nat'l Men's Teams 1969, 1972, 1973, Fall Nat'l secondary Swiss Teams 1974, Mott-Smith Trophy 1973, Pan-American Invitational Pairs 1974; second Spingold 1967, 1970, Vanderbilt 1970, Spring Nat'l Men's Teams 1969, Life Masters Pairs 1960, 1968, Fall Nat'l Open Teams 1964; winner of a great many regional titles including Bridge Week Knockout Teams 1955, Open Pairs 1968, Texas Spring Open Teams 1955, 1961, Knockout Teams 1968, Summer Open Pairs 1967, Fall Knockout Teams 1961, 1968, Open Teams 1963, 1967, 1968, 1973. Contributor to ACBL *Bulletin* (See ACES TEAM.)

WOLFF, Walter, Jr., of San Antonio, Tex., attorney, born 1927; won Marcus Cup 1955, Texas Open Teams 1955, 1961.

WONG, John, of San Diego, Calif., formerly of Tokyo, Japan, and Taiwan, Republic of China, computer specialist, born 1928; first Life Master in Japan; represented China World Olympiad 1964; represented Japan Far East Championships since 1958, captain 1959; runner-up Far East Open Team 1958, 1964; Far East Open Pairs Champion 1961; national successes include Takamatsu Open Team 1955, 1956, 1962, *Japan Times* Cup 1959, 1960, 1961, 1963, Mixed Pairs 1960, Masters Individual 1961, Trial Pairs 1962, Pacific Southwest Open Pairs 1966. Formerly editor of Japanese CBL Bulletin, Director of JCBL and Secretary.

WONG, Kok Leong, of Malaysia, oil executive, born 1925; represented Malaysia Far East Championships 1965, 1966, 1968, 1970, 1973, 1974.

WONG, Larry, of Portland, Jamaica, company director, born 1929; won Central American & Caribbean Championships 1971, 1972, 1974. Member Executive Committee of Jamaica BA 1972–73.

WOOD, Edson T. (1903–1963), of Indianapolis, Ind., real estate broker; one of the leading Midwest players; won Chicago 1935, second Fall Nat'l Open Pairs 1948, 1950; won All-American Open Teams 1941, 1942, 1945, Open Pairs 1948, Central States Open Teams 1939, 1943, Open Pairs 1944, 1951, Midwest Open Teams 1945. ACBL Director 1955. President Indiana Unit.

WOOD, Philip Arthur, of Vancouver, B.C., bridge club owner and bridge teacher, born 1921; won Northern Rocky Mountain Mixed Pairs 1966; ACBL National Tournament Director since 1968.

WOODARD, William F., of Albany, N.Y., computer science instructor, born 1947; winner of several regional titles including Upper New York State Open Teams 1974, Open Pairs 1970.

WOODRUFF, Fred M., of Kenner, La.; regional wins include Mid-South Open Teams 1972, Open Pairs 1972, Men's Pairs 1973.

WOODS, Mrs. H. A., of El Paso, Tex., bridge teacher; won Spring Nat'l Women's Pairs 1961, Texas Mixed Pairs 1953, Mexican Open Pairs 1957, Rocky Mountain Women's Pairs 1959.

WOODS, H. E., of Muncie, Ind., bank president, born 1909; won Missouri Valley Men's Pairs 1953; second Rocky Mountain Masters Pairs 1955, Mixed Pairs 1957, Open Pairs 1957.

WOODS, Mrs. Jo, of Little Rock, Ark., bridge teacher and writer; author of many books and booklets for bridge teachers and students including *Little Green Book* and *At the Bridge Table;* the former has had a bigger sale than almost any other comparable publication.

WOODSON, William B., of Matthews, N.C., electronic systems analyst, born 1921; regional wins include Southeastern Individual 1950, Mid-Atlantic Open Pairs 1954, 1964, Open Teams 1965, Summer Pairs 1961, Men's Pairs 1966. ACBL Director since 1973. Inventor of WOODSON TWO-WAY NO TRUMP. Author of *Woodson Two-Way No Trump; Woodson Electronic Bidding System.* See BIBLIOGRAPHY, C.

WOODWORTH, Robert M., of St. Petersburg, Fla., attorney, born 1911; regional wins include Florida Mixed Pairs 1960, 1963, Knockout Teams 1967, Life Masters Pairs 1974. Officer St. Louis, Mo., Unit, and Governor Florida Unit.

WOOLSEY, Christopher R. ("Kit"), of Arlington, Va., systems analyst, born 1943; one of the leading American players; represented US World Pair Olympiad 1974; won Blue Ribbons 1973, 1975,

Spring Nat'l Men's Pairs 1972, second Fall Nat'l Life Master Men's Pairs 1971, 1972, Spring Nat'l Men's Pairs 1973, 1974; regional wins include Mid-Atlantic Knockout Teams 1974, Open Teams 1969,1971, 1972, 1973.

WOOLWORTH, W. Howard, of Hialeah, Fla., formerly of Niagara Falls, N.Y., bridge columnist, born 1889. His bridge section in the Buffalo *Courier-Express,* which he conducted for more than thirty years, occupied more space than any other US bridge column, often a full newspaper page. He served as contributor and editor of *Florida Bridge News.*

WORK, Milton C. (1864–1934), the outstanding American authority on auction bridge, also a noted player and authority in whist and in contract bridge. He was born in Philadelphia and took three degrees at the University of Pennsylvania: A.B. (1884), and in finance (1885), and law (1887). He was an outstanding college athlete in baseball, then the principal college sport; in cricket, a favored game in Philadelphia; and in tennis, in which he twice won the national intercollegiate doubles championship. He was highly ranked also in golf, and was manager of the U. of P. football team. In 1893 he was coach and manager of the first US college cricket team to tour England.

From 1887 to 1917 Work practiced law in Philadelphia, eventually becoming senior partner in the firm of McCarthy, Work & DeHaven. In 1917 he took a leave of absence to tour the US with Wilbur C. WHITEHEAD, organizing bridge competitions and lecturing on bridge, to promote the sale of Liberty bonds. The success of the tour, coupled with the fact that his bridge books were already selling in large quantities, induced him to quit the practice of law, and adopt bridge as a career.

Work's whist career began as president of the U. of P.'s whist club where he organized and played in the first duplicate whist team-of-four match ever held between clubs (1881). He helped found the American Whist League (1893), and was captain of the Hamilton Club team of Philadelphia, which won several whist tournaments. Work's first book, *Whist of Today* (1895) was published at his own expense for a gift to friends, but it demonstrated the clarity of style for which his later books were so admired. He turned to bridge and then to auction bridge as those games became pre-eminent. His first book on auction bridge (1913) began a series that outsold all other bridge books by a wide margin until the appearance of E. Culbertson's *Blue Book* in 1930. From 1917 through 1931 Work was acknowledged the greatest bridge authority, with stature equivalent to that of Cavendish in whist before him and Culbertson and C. Goren in contract bridge after him. In 1965, he was elected to the Bridge Hall of Fame.

Work became a member of the laws committee of the Whist Club (New York) in 1909. He largely wrote and controlled the 1915 auction bridge laws, which revolutionized the scoring, and the 1917 laws, for which the contract bridge principle was first considered and rejected. He was an Honorary

Member of the American Bridge League and Honorary Chairman of its Laws Committee. As president of the United States Bridge Association (1933–34) he introduced into its Grand National tournaments the principle that every member of a team of four must play at least one session with each other member.

After having been a contributing editor, not very active, to all previous whist and bridge periodicals in the US, Work became a founder and chief editor of the earliest auction bridge magazines, the *Work-Whitehead Auction Bridge Bulletin* (1924–26) and its successor, the *Auction Bridge Magazine* (1927–29). Assisted by Whitehead, he served as chief authority on the first series of bridge games broadcast on radio (1926–29). In 1928 his fame was so great that he was paid $7,000 per week to give brief lectures on bridge in the course of vaudeville presentations.

Work's considerable fortune was substantially lost in the stock-market crashes of 1929–30, and he resumed some bridge activities from which he had retired. In 1931 he participated in the founding of BRIDGE HEADQUARTERS and the promulgation of the OFFICIAL SYSTEM, being chief architect of the system and principal author of its official books. Work had never been a contestant in important tournaments after the early years of whist competition, and as a player he was not highly rated by his peers, but in 1933–34 he resumed tournament play in contract bridge and won five consecutive sectional tournaments as member of a team that included Goren, Mrs. Olive Peterson, and Fred French. Work's prestige never suffered diminution, and his personal popularity was immense; in his later years he was called "the Grand Old Man of Bridge." See BIBLIOGRAPHY, A, C, E, H, J.

WUWUNGAN, P. Willy, of Jakarta, Indonesia, company president, born 1911; npc Indonesian Team World Championship 1974. Member WBF Executive Committee.

Y

YALIRAKIS, Dimitri, of Greece, civil engineer, born 1931; outstanding Greek player; represented Greece European Championships 1967, 1969, 1970, 1971; national wins include Open Teams 1966, 1968, 1969, 1970, 1971, 1972, 1973, 1974, Open Pairs 1965, 1968, 1970. Director Hellenic BF 1968–71.

YANKO, Richard, of Southfield, Mich., attorney, born 1939; winner of several regional titles including Motor City Knockout Teams 1973, Open Pairs 1969, Men's Pairs 1970.

YAP, Robert, of Manila, Philippines, insurance agent, born 1919; represented Philippines World Team Olympiad 1964; Far East Champion 1957, second 1962; national titles include Open Team 1960, Knockout Teams 1957, 1958, 1960, 1961, 1963,

Mixed Team 1957, 1958, Master Pairs 1957, Open Pairs 1955, Mixed Pairs 1956, 1957, 1958, 1959.

YAVITZ, Jerome A., of Miami Beach, Fla., real estate developer; won Summer Nat'l Mixed Teams 1974 and several regional events.

YELTON, Carey M., Jr., of Kenilworth, Ill., financial consultant and restaurateur, born 1934; regional wins include Central States Open Teams 1972, Southern Conference Open Teams 1961; won Intercollegiate Par 1953, 1954.

YOST, E. Lowell, of Wichita, Kan., company president, born 1922; second Fall Nat'l Life Master Men's Pairs 1970; regional wins include Republic of Texas Open Teams 1970.

YOU, Addie Lee (Mrs. E. W.), of Honolulu, Hawaii, portraitist in oils, born 1913; won Hawaiian Open Pairs 1959, 1963, Mixed Pairs 1959, Northern Rocky Mountain Mixed Pairs 1960.

YOU, Dr. E. W., of Honolulu, Hawaii, physician, born 1908; won Northern Rocky Mountain Men's Pairs 1960, Hawaiian Open Team, Masters Pairs and Mixed Pairs 1963.

YOUNG, Sally (Mrs. R. C.) (1906–1970), of Cynwyd, Pa.; seventeenth Life Master; one of the great American women players of all time; record number of seven wins in Nat'l Women's Team 1937, 1939, 1943, 1944, 1945, 1946, 1951, and three seconds in the same event, 1941, 1956, 1958; other wins include Chicago 1937, 1938, 1939, 1947, Fall Nat'l Open Pairs 1941, Women's Pairs 1936, 1938, 1939, 1946, Mixed Pairs 1940, Summer Nat'l Mixed Teams 1938, 1941, 1949, 1950, 1959; second Spingold 1939, Fall Nat'l Mixed Pairs 1934, Summer Nat'l Mixed Teams 1936, 1947; regional successes scored in Eastern States Mixed Teams 1942, 1946, 1958, and others.

YU KHE SIONG, Mrs. Margaret, of Manila, Philippines, born 1908; Far East Women's Champion 1967; represented Philippines Far East Championships on one other occasion, Taipei-Manila Interport tournament.

Z

ZABEL, Gunar, of Copenhagen, Denmark, civil engineer. President of Danish Bridge League 1969–75. Initiated master points, adult education in bridge, bridge material and book publishing and sale of bridge material by the League; increased its membership by 50%. Member Executive Committee of European Bridge League from 1973.

ZAKIN, Sandy, of Chicago, Ill., media advertising specialist, born 1940; regional wins include Gopher Open Teams 1973, Central States Women's Pairs 1974.

ZAMORA, Antonio, of Rizal, Philippines, interior designer, born 1919; Far East Champion 1957, won Far East Open Pairs 1962, Mixed Team 1963; national titles include Open Team 1958, Knockout Teams 1962, Master Teams 1959, Mixed Teams 1959, Open Pairs 1957, Mixed Pairs 1958.

ZANALDA, David, of Buenos Aires, Argentina, court official, born 1932; represented Argentina World Team Olympiad 1968, 1972; national wins include Open Teams 1970, Open Pairs 1968.

ZANANIRI, Marcel, of Cairo, Egypt, chemist, born 1915; represented Egypt World Team Olympiad 1964; International Tournament 1952, 1955; Open Team 1951, 1961, 1962, 1963, Open Pairs 1942, 1943. Technical Adviser Egyptian Bridge Federation.

ZAWISZA, Jerzy, of Wilmington, Del., bridge club manager, born 1908; second Fall Nat'l Men's Team 1960, New York-New Jersey Open Team 1959, Keystone Conference Men's Pairs 1961.

ZECKHAUSER, Richard J., of Cambridge, Mass., professor of political economy, born 1940; Team Trialist 1967; won Blue Ribbon Pairs 1966, Marcus 1963; second Spring Nat'l Men's Teams 1968; regional successes include New England Knockout Teams 1964, New York–New Jersey Men's Pairs 1962, Upper New York State Open Teams 1966. Intercollegiate Champion 1961.

ZEDTWITZ, Waldemar K. von. See VON ZEDTWITZ.

ZEVE, Vic D., of Fort Lauderdale, Fla., mortgage broker, born 1899; won Summer Nat'l Open Pairs 1952, Fall Nat'l Men's Team 1958. Author of *Method Bidding.*

ZILIC, John P., of Houston, Tex., accountant, born 1939; won Fall Nat'l Open Pairs 1966, regional wins include Gopher Men's Pairs, Open Teams 1962, Mid-Winter Knockout Teams 1973, Open Teams 1971.

ZILIC, Virginia (Mrs. John), of Houston, Tex.; several regional wins, including South Texas Open Teams 1974, Women's Pairs 1971.

ZIMMERMAN, James E., of Shaker Heights, Ohio, attorney, born 1942; winner of many regional events including Upper New York State Open Teams 1973, Masters Pairs 1973, Motor City Knockout Teams 1974. ACBL Director since 1973.

ZIRINSKY, Victor, of Hong Kong, businessman; represented Hong Kong Far East Championship six times; won National Open Teams, Masters Teams, Mixed Pairs. Vice-Chairman Hong Kong Bridge Association.

ZOLLER, Ray, of Jackson, Miss., salesman, born 1934; won Fall Nat'l Life Master Men's Pairs 1966; winner of many regional titles including District 5 Open Teams 1971, Masters Pairs 1964, Mixed Pairs 1971, Great Lakes Open Teams 1968, 1972.

ZOLLER, Nancy (Mrs. Ray, formerly Alpaugh), of Metairie, La., bridge teacher; won World Olympiad Mixed Teams 1972, second Spring Nat'l Women's Teams 1973; several regional wins including Mid-South Masters Pairs 1969, 1970, Women's Pairs 1973.

ZUCCHELLI, Sergio, of Bologna, pharmaceutical representative, born 1934; represented Italy Bermuda Bowl 1975; won London *Sunday Times* Pairs 1974, Common Market Junior Teams 1967; national wins include Italy Cup 1967, 1970, 1974, Open Teams 1967, 1970, 1971. Accused during the 1975 Bermuda Bowl of illicit communications through foot signals. See BERMUDA INCIDENT.

ZUMARAÁN, Ricardo, of Montevideo, Uruguay, farmer, born 1930; represented Uruguay in all South American Championships since 1959, and tied for first place in 1962; National successes include international team trials 1957, 1959, 1960, 1961, 1962, Open Teams 1958, 1960, 1961, 1963, Open Pairs 1957, 1958, Individual 1956; twice winner of the most points for the year.

ZWEIFEL, Dr. Paul, of Blacksburg, Va., professor of nuclear engineering, born 1929; won Canadian-American Open Teams 1955 and Upper New York State Open Teams 1956.

North American Championships

AMERICAN BRIDGE ASSOCIATION NATIONAL CHAMPIONSHIPS

OPEN TEAMS

1934	Dr. L. P. Rolerfort, D. E. Smith
	J. C. Graham, E. Clarke
1935	Dr. B. Withers, Dr. E. Brandon
	G. Gilmer, B. Gray, L. Grant
1936	P. E. Thomas, W. A. Friend, C. L. Long
	A. L. Parkinson, G. F. Benoit
1937 }	O. A. Moore, J. P. Holt
1938 }	O. Landry, L. Buser
1939	G. F. Benoit, W. A. Friend
	J. Niles, A. E. H. Hawkins
1940	O. A. Moore, L. Buser
	O. Landry, J. P. Holt
1941	C. E. Barron, K. D. Ross
	R. Alexander, L. A. Jones
1942	K. D. Ross, C. E. Barron
	A. L. Woolridge, D. M. Carr
1943	R. Banks, Dr. W. Richie
	A. Wilkes, G. Stewart
1944	O. A. Moore, Z. H. Brooks
	L. Scales, K. C. Brown, L. Clay
1946	C. Hanson, K. Cox
	S. White, R. Cunningham
1947	K. C. Brown, O. A. Moore
	L. Scales, Z. H. Brooks, L. Clay
1948	Mr. and Mrs. A. Woolridge
	V. Daly, K. D. Ross, D. M. Carr
1949 }	Mr. and Mrs. R. Alexander, L. Jones
1950 }	M. Garrett, C. E. Barron
1952	K. Cox, S. White
	A. Bishop, J. H. Smith
1953	A. Woolridge, C. Woolridge
	L. Goggins, G. Hall, G. Chapman
1954	K. Larson, R. Million
	M. Gertler, H. Bodman
1955 }	Dr. J. Henry, W. A. Friend
1956 }	
1957 }	R. Friend, L. Jones, R. Alexander
1958	A. Bishop, K. Cox
	J. Garcia, S. White
1959	C. Barron, F. O. Petite, O. Cassell
	O. C. Woolridge, D. Woolridge
1960	W. Mann, F. O. Petite
	C. Barron, O. Cassell
1961	R. Hamman, J. Becheley
	S. Rebner, W. Hanna
1962	R. Bratcher, M. Cocherell
	R. Landry, Dr. G. Ginn *tied with*
	Dr. J. Henry, Mrs. D. Brooks
	S. Jarett, R. Searcy
1963	J. Wilkins, A. Mells
	Mrs. J. Haley, C. Pyant
1964	L. Jones, Mrs. C. Woolridge
	Dr. J. Henry, R. Alexander
1965 }	Z. Allen, S. White, A. Mells
1966 }	B. Hudson, D. Scrivens
1967	G. Fowlkes, Dr. A. R. Flowers, G. Hall
	A. Wills, C. Pyant, J. H. Kerr
1968	L. Pietri, R. Rigmaiden, R. Smith
	J. Garcia, H. Steed, Dr. G. A. Ginn
1969	L. Jefferson, M. Schnee, D. Brooks
	S. Seidman, Dr. W. Lipton, J. Prisyon
1970	L. Pietri, R. Rigmaiden
	W. Sides, D. Fullwood
	A. Mells, A. Flowers
1971	M. Blumenthal, W. Landow, A. Sontag
	O. Cohen, H. Lewis, R. Becker
1972	A. Flowers, L. Pietri, D. Fullwood
	A. Kearse, A. Mells, W. Sides
1973	R. Rigmaiden, J. Williams, R. Price
	R. Halperin, H. Miller, Z. Allen
1974	R. Landry, C. Fredd
	S. and B. Lucas, Z. Allen

OPEN PAIRS

1934	Mr. and Mrs. L. Collins
1935	Dr. A. Curtis, Dr. W. Wethers
1936	Mrs. L. Goggins, H. Miller
1937	J. Holt, O. Moore
1938	G. Benoit, W. Friend
1939	L. Jones, J. McDougald
1940	H. Facey, L. Fields
1941	Dr. A. Curtis, A. Parkinson
1942	Mrs. L. Goggins, W. Friend
1943	L. White, C. Booker
1944	Mrs. E. Landry, E. Marsh
1946	L. Jones, R. Alexander
1947	K. Brown, L. Clay
1948	R. Watkins, E. Marsh
1949	Dr. F. Slaughter, W. Friend
1950	Mrs. Z. Rucker, R. Cunningham
1951	Mr. and Mrs. A. Herndon
1952	W. Friend, Dr. F. Slaughter
1953	L. Clay, Mrs. Z. Rucker
1954	H. Steed, W. Friend
1955	W. Friend, Maj. R. Friend
1956	J. Garcia, E. Marsh
1957	Mrs. M. Griffin, S. Gholston
1958	Dr. J. Henry, A. Bishop
1959	Mrs. Z. Hall, R. Alexander
1960	C. Pratt, J. Lee
1961	K. Cox, S. White
1962	W. Hampton, F. Tucker
1963	L. Pietri, R. Rigmaiden
1964	Dr. J. Henry, A. Bishop
1966	L. Pietri, R. Rigmaiden
1967	W. Sides, R. Price
1968	L. Pietri, R. Rigmaiden
1969	A. Wills, L. Berkley (Spring)
	A. Reid, Dr. M. Haley (Summer)
1970	R. Canty, S. Lee *tied with*
	D. Siegel, T. Griffith
1971	F. Davis, J. Dozier (Spring)
	J. Williams, R. Price (Summer)
1972	L. Pietri, A. Kearse (Spring)
	T. Griffith, G. Ginn (Summer)
1973	L. Pietri, A. Kearse (Spring)
	S. and F. Dunn (Summer)
1974	A. Mells, A. Flowers (Spring)
	F. Taylor, V. Banks (Summer)

ACBL CHAMPIONSHIPS
FALL NATIONAL CHAMPIONSHIPS

Open Teams. For the REISINGER TROPHY (originally for the CHICAGO TROPHY until 1965). A six-session event for Open Teams of Four, scored by Board-a-Match until 1975, when scoring was changed to international match points, with Swiss pairing through the first four sessions, and knockout matches thereafter. Contested as a four-session championship until 1966.

	WINNERS	RUNNERS-UP
1928	W. C. Whitehead, R. R. Richards E. A. Wetzlar, G. M. Scott	(In 1928, the Board-a-Match competition was for the Harold S. Vanderbilt cup.)
1929	R. W. Halpin, M. Cohen N. M. Wester, L. J. Haddad	C. R. Rilling, P. D. Parcells L. J. Kelly, C. R. Drake
1930	E. Culbertson, J. Carpenter W. J. Barrett, J. Rau	Mrs. and Mrs. P. H. Sims Mrs. E. Clement, W. von Zedtwitz
1931	W. Liggett, Mrs. N. N. Newman G. Unger, Mrs. E. Banfield	W. D. Karn, P. H. Sims O. Jacoby, D. Burnstine
1932	G. Reith, B. J. Becker W. von Zedtwitz, S. G. Churchill	E. Culbertson, O. Jacoby T. A. Lightner, M. T. Gottlieb
1933	C. A. Hall, R. M. Wildberg P. Steiner, A. Steiner	P. H. Sims, B. J. Becker S. G. Churchill, W. von Zedtwitz
1934	B. Rabinowitz, H. Dinkelspiel, Jr. M. Seiler, L. Jaeger	T. A. Lightner, M. D. Maier J. Mattheys, S. Stearns
1935	L. J. Welch, F. R. Buck J. E. Cain, E. T. Wood	Mr. and Mrs. E. Culbertson R. Frey, A. Morehead
1936	Mrs. J. A. Faulkner, P. E. Sheardown Mrs. W. M. Anderson, D. G. Farquharson	Mrs. L. Heiner, A. Glatt J. R. Smith, A. Weiss
1937	C. Goren, C. Solomon J. Crawford, Mrs. R. C. Young	W. Perry, S. Vorzimer A. Roth, O. Brotman
1938	C. Goren, C. Solomon J. Crawford, Mrs. R. C. Young	A. M. Barnes, B. Jarmel Mrs. E. Clement, W. von Zedtwitz
1939	C. Goren, C. Solomon J. Crawford, Mrs. R. C. Young B. J. Becker	A. Leibowitz, S. Kaplan E. N. Marcus, J. Cushing
1940	M. Glick, J. Glick H. Feinberg, L. Newman	E. R. Thomas, J. Sheern A. R. Dick, W. Potts
1941	Mrs. H. Sobel, S. Rossant Mrs. M. Wagar, P. Leventritt	L. Hazen, W. von Zedtwitz A. M. Barnes, C. Lochridge S. G. Churchill
1942	B. J. Becker, S. Silodor J. Crawford, C. Goren	W. von Zedtwitz, H. Fishbein S. G. Churchill, L. Hazen
1943	Mrs. H. Sobel, S. Silodor B. J. Becker, C. Goren	S. Rossant, S. Katz P. Leventritt, B. Lebhar
1944	R. Sherman, S. Becker Mrs. B. Golder, C. Solomon	B. J. Becker, S. Silodor Mrs. H. Sobel, C. Goren
1945	S. Stayman, G. Rapee W. von Zedtwitz, L. Hazen	J. Shore, A. Casner H. Ogust, H. J. Harkavy R. Hirschberg
1946	Mrs. E. J. Seligman, A. Roth J. Crawford, A. M. Barnes	S. O. Fenkel, F. Karpin S. Becker, L. Newman
1947	Mrs. R. C. Young, Mrs. L. M. Jaeger Mrs. P. Bacher, Mrs. L. Rhodes, *tied with* J. Crawford, T. A. Lightner G. Rapee, S. Stayman, *and* R. Appleyard, S. Rossant M. Berliant, M. A. Lightman	
1948	Mrs. R. Gordon, C. Sidway B. Elliot, G. Boeckh	S. Silodor, S. Stayman J. Crawford, G. Rapee
1949	R. Kahn, L. Hazen L. Hirsch, P. Leventritt J. Shore, *tied with* B. O. Johnson, Mrs. J. E. Folline L. B. Kabakjian, S. Aronson E. N. Marcus, *and* E. I. Schwartz, A. S. Goldsmith J. Glick, S. Mogal A. Landy	
1950	C. Goren, H. Sobel S. Silodor, B. J. Becker M. Field	E. Marcus, G. Rapee J. Crawford, H. Schenken S. Stayman
1951	C. Boland, C. B. Elliott M. M. Miller, P. E. Sheardown	C. Goren, S. Silodor B. J. Becker, M. Field H. Sobel

WINNERS	RUNNERS-UP
1952 Mrs. E. Kemp, A. Roth H. Harkavy, T. Stone	E. I. Schwartz, A. Goldsmith J. Glick, E. Cohen A. J. Frank
1953 J. Crawford, B. J. Becker G. Rapee, S. Stayman	Mr. and Mrs. C. Solomon R. Sherman, P. Leventritt H. Fishbein
1954 S. Silodor, B. J. Becker J. Crawford, G. Rapee	A. Roth, P. Kibler W. Seamon, I. Cohen
1955 B. Fain, P. Hodge O. Jacoby, J. Jacoby G. Heath	Dr. W. Lipton, V. Mitchell M. Nelson, J. G. Ripstra
1956 B. J. Becker, G. Rapee J. R. Crawford, S. Silodor	O. Jacoby, B. Fain D. Sutton, P. Hodge
1957 C. Goren, H. Sobel W. Root, H. Ogust H. Schenken	B. Fain, J. Gerber R. Barrett, P. Hodge H. Fishbein
1958 L. Harmon, A. Sheinwold I. Stakgold, R. Hirschberg E. Kaplan	A. Miller, J. Moran J. Wendt, D. Straberg
1959 L. Mathe, E. Taylor M. Schleifer, D. Oakie	J. Gerber, H. Fishbein C. Solomon, P. Hodge
1960 L. Mathe, O. Adams S. Lazard, W. Hanna	C. Smith, O. Jacoby G. R. Nail, M. Key
1961 T. Stone, A. Roth J. Crawford, S. Silodor N. Kay	R. Jordan, A. Robinson E. Murray, C. Coon, *tied with* H. Guiver, M. Shuman Mr. and Mrs. T. K. Sanders
1962 L. Mathe, E. O. Taylor H. Guiver, P. Allinger R. von der Porten, E. Paulsen, *tied with* E. Kantar, M. Miles D. Krauss, R. D. Hamman	
1963 C. Goren, H. Schenken P. Leventritt, H. Ogust B. Koytchou	D. Faskow, H. Sacks W. L. Flannery, P. Swanson
1964 J. Gerber, M. Key H. Rockaway, P. Hodge	E. Kemp, H. Harkavy, R. Wolff W. von Zedtwitz, C. Smith, C. Russell
1965 E. Kantar, M. Miles M. Lawrence, L. Stansby	P. Feldesman, M. Engel I. Rubin, R. Freeman
1966 E. Kaplan, N. Kay R. Jordan, A. Robinson	H. Ross, M. McMahan, L. Mathe G. Bare, H. Guiver E. Paulsen, *tied with* Mr. and Mrs. H. Schenken, A. Roth, W. Root
1967 A. Robinson, R. Jordan A. Roth, W. Root, E. Kaplan N. Kay	C. Peres, D. Rotman S. Altman, M. Becker
1968 H. Schenken, K. Larsen P. Pender, H. Ross E. Paulsen	R. Goldman, W. Eisenberg, E. Kantar R. Hamman, S. Lazard, G. Rapee
1969 I. Rubin, J. Westheimer W. Grieve, P. Feldesman	G. Rapee, S. Lazard, S. Kehela E. Murray, N. Kay, E. Kaplan
1970 J. Jacoby, R. Wolff R. Hamman, W. Eisenberg R. Goldman, M. Lawrence, *tied with* P. Pender, G. Baze A. Dionisi, W. Grieve G. Rapee	
1971 L. Mathe, D. Krauss E. Kaplan, W. Grieve, G. Rapee, N. Kay	P. Pender, G. Baze, H. Lewis, A. Dionisi
1972 S. Goldberg, S. Parker S. Robinson, L. Bluhm	G. Rapee, W. Grieve, S. Kehela, E. Murray
1973 A. Reinhold, P. Weichsel A. Sontag, R. Katz L. Cohen	P. Swanson, J. Blair, B. Greenberg, T. Sanders
1974 I. Rubin, F. Hamilton E. Paulsen, H. Ross	M. Jacobus, S. Sion, J. Merrill, J. Solodar S. Goldstein

Blue Ribbon Pairs. For the CAVENDISH TROPHY. A six-session Pairs event with two qualifying sessions, two semi-final sessions, and two final sessions. Entry is restricted to winners and runners-up in Regional Championships and high finishers in National Championships during the previous three years, members of current Grand National District Championship teams, members of current official teams representing the ACBL or member countries of the ACBL, together with the top 100 master-point holders.

	WINNERS	RUNNERS-UP
1963	D. Hayden, B. J. Becker	H. Harkavy, C. Russell
1964	L. Mathe, R. Hamman	R. G. Sharp, G. Polak
1965	C. Henke, J. Moran	M. Lawrence, R. Von der Porten
1966	C. Coon, R. Zeckhauser	Mrs. G. Goldstein, L. Ferer
1967	S. Kehela, W. Lebovic	L. Mathe, P. Feldesman
1968	Dr. R. Katz, L. Cohen	M. Lawrence, R. Goldman
1969	E. Paulsen, A. Tschekaloff	E. Murray, S. Kehela, *tied with*
		R. F. Morris, T. Hodapp,
		tied with R. H. Katz, L. Cohen
1970	I. Rubin, C. Burger	C. Russell, R. Freeman
1971	R. Bates, J. Grantham	M. Lawrence, H. Baron
1972	W. Kornfeld, R. Khautin	G. Hayden, M. Lair
1973	K. Woolsey, S. Robinson	M. Cappelletti, K. Cappelletti
1974	N. Kay, E. Kaplan	Dr. G. Rosenkranz, R. Bates

Open Pairs. A four-session event with two qualifying sessions and two final sessions. Played for the CAVENDISH TROPHY until 1963, when the Open Pairs became a secondary event with the introduction of the BLUE RIBBON PAIRS.

	WINNERS	RUNNERS-UP
1928	T. A. Lightner, W. von Zedtwitz	Mr. and Mrs. E. Culbertson
1929	W. E. McKenney, R. R. Richards, *tied with*	
	Mrs. S. Lovell, Mrs. E. Evans	
1930	P. S. Germain, Mrs. F. E. W. Bright	B. Foster, Mrs. E. M. Loftus
1931	P. H. Sims W. S. Karn	L. H. Watson, Mrs. O. Hilliard
1932	P. H. Sims, W. S. Karn	O. Jacoby, L. H. Watson
1933	C. A. Hall, R. M. Wildberg	S. Fry, Jr., W. von Zedtwitz
1934	C. Lochridge, J. Rau	H. J. Fishbein, H. Goldberg
1935	O. Jacoby, E. Hymes, Jr.	P. Parcells, C. W. Rilling
1936	W. Jacobs, R. Kempner	A. Paris, J. R. Smith
1937	W. von Zedtwitz, A. M. Barnes	H. Fishbein, P. Abramsohn
1938	Mrs. H. E. Funk, F. E. Bubna	Mrs. H. Sobel, A. Moyse, Jr.
1939	W. Jacobs, A. Weiss	M. Elis, P. Abramsohn
1940	Mrs. H. Sobel, C. H. Goren	H. Fishbein, H. Chanin
1941	Mrs. R. C. Young, S. Silodor	H. Fishbein, P. Abramsohn
1942	T. Stone, A. Roth	W. von Zedtwitz, H. Fishbein
1943	Mrs. R. C. Goldberg, Mrs. E. J. Seligman	M. Moss, N. Drucker
1944	A. Casner, R. Hirschberg	A. J. Frank, A. Goldsmith
1945	Mr. and Mrs. L. M. Jaeger	L. Roet, W. D. Levin
1946	B. J. Becker, S. Silodor	Mr. and Mrs. D. C. Carter
1947	Mrs. H. Sobel, Mrs. M. Wagar	S. Fry, R. Sherman
1948	Mrs. H. Sobel, Mrs. M. Wagar	P. Leventritt, E. T. Wood
1949	C. Whitebrook, G. E. Goldsmith	B. J. Becker, S. Becker
1950	J. Kushner, M. Kelliher	L. Roet, E. Wood
1951	A. Glatt, A. Weiss	R. Kahn, P. Leventritt
1952	I. Cohen, V. Zeve	P. Bacher, L. Roet
1953	B. Greenberg, H. Rockaway	C. K. Smith, D. Carter
1954	G. Heath, P. Hodge	F. A. Bombeck, D. C. Carter
1955	E. Hochfeld, M. Q. Ellenby	Mrs. J. Brier, W. von Zedtwitz
1956	B. Fain, P. Hodge	C. J. Solomon, N. Kay
1957	L. Mathe, E. O. Taylor	S. Lazard, P. Allinger
1958	Mrs. D. B. Hawes, Dr. J. Fisher	A. Roth, T. Stone
1959	S. Stayman, M. Rubinow	E. Hochfeld, W. Grieve
1960	O. Jacoby, C. Smith	Dr. E. Davidson, S. Becker
1961	P. Feldesman, I. Rubin	J. Blair, R. Stucker
1962	D. Hayden, B. J. Becker	E. Kantar, M. Miles
1963	A. Barfus, R. Schonan	D. S. Park, D. Rothlein
1964	S. Kehela, Mrs. C. Sanders	J. Blair, G. Cronin
1965	Mr. and Mrs. H. Feldstein	J. Jabon, D. Pedersen
1966	J. Zilic, D. Joyce	J. Klein, D. Garbett
1967	J. Wachter, Dr. R. Katz	P. Leon, D. Hocevar
1968	Mrs. A. Kluewer, R. N. Dallas	Dr. and Mrs. G. W. Stark
1969	R. Ryder, B. Birnholz	D. Darling, T. Lyons
1970	W. Johnson, P. Burka	R. LaCour, A. Childs
1971	J. Titone, I. Kostal	K. Taira, J. McKee

Life Masters Men's Pairs (MOUSER TROPHY). A four-session event with two qualifying sessions and two final sessions, restricted to Life Masters. Before 1963 restricted to National Masters and players of higher rank.

	WINNERS	RUNNERS-UP
1961	M. Manchester, L. Hays	M. Cohn, H. Hume
1962	S. Fuoto, V. Mitchell	K. Petterson, H. Kandler

WINNERS	RUNNERS-UP
1963 E. Murray, S. Kehela	C. J. Solomon, H. Fishbein
1964 C. Coon, R. Goldman	H. Rockaway, M. Key, *tied with* J. Blair
	Lt. Col. W. Christian
1965 A. Tschekaloff, P. Soloway	E. Kaplan, V. Mitchell
1966 C. Hudecek, R. Zoller	E. Theus, G. Kasle
1967 H. Lewis, P. Pender	W. Flannery, D. Faskow
1968 J. Solodar, H. Bethe	J. Swanson, D. Pearson
1969 C. Burger, J. Cayne	C. G. Jeans, N. Fischer
1970 H. MacLean, R. Andersen	C. Smith, E. Yost
1971 P. Weichsel, A. Sontag	K. Woolsey, S. Robinson
1972 M. Jacobus, L. Bart	K. Woolsey, S. Robinson
1973 E. Kaplan, N. Kay	E. Weiner, R. Violin
1974 G. Michaud, G. R. Nail	J. Gerber, D. Kaim

Life Masters Women's Pairs (Helen Sobel SMITH TROPHY). A four-session event with two qualifying sessions and two final sessions, restricted to Life Masters. Prior to 1963 restricted to National Masters and players of higher rank.

WINNERS	RUNNERS-UP
1961 H. Portugal, D. Hayden	J. Mueller, G. Goldstein
1962 M. Wagar, B. Kachmar	E. Kemp, A. Burnstein
1963 A. Burnstein, H. Baron	L. H. Gray, C. Arnold
1964 B. Kaplan, M. Alcorn	S. Stein, A. Gordon
1965 J. Stone, A. Sheaber	Mrs. J. Farrell, Mrs. C. Solomon
1966 D. Hayden, Mrs. D. B. Hawes	M. J. Farell, P. Solomon
1967 Mrs. J. Gruver, Mrs. D. Sachs	M. J. Farell, P. Solomon
1968 Mrs. R. Walsh, Mrs. D. Talmage	M. J. Farell, K. Blanchard
1969 S. Stein, G. Goldstein	K. Allison, G. Collier
1970 M. Passell, B. Cohn	L. Krauss, B. Mangan
1971 R. Bloomfield, D. Levinson	B. Kennedy, Mrs. T. Sanders
1972 R. Walsh, A. Kearse	D. Truscott, E. Hawes
1973 J. Deutsch, F. Arst	E. Kemp, B. Rappaport
1974 B. Larson, J. Stein	B. Rappaport, E. Kemp

Rockwell Trophy. A four-session Mixed Pair event with two qualifying sessions and two final sessions.

WINNERS	RUNNERS-UP
1946 A. Roth, Mrs. A. Burnstein	Mr. and Mrs. D. Carter
1947 C. H. Goren, Mrs. H. G. Ansin	J. Crawford, Mrs. M. Wagar
1948 J. Crawford, Mrs. M. Wagar	C. C. Johnson, Mrs. F. Myer
1949 J. Crawford, Mrs. M. Wagar	P. Leventritt, Mrs. P. Bacher
1950 P. Leventritt, Mrs. R. Sherman	Mr. and Mrs. W. Thiemann
1951 S. Silodor, Mrs. G. Rosenbloom	E. Burns, Mrs. S. Fairchild
1952 A. Roth, Mrs. A. Burnstein	Mr. and Mrs. J. Tilles
1953 Mr. and Mrs. P. Hodge	J. Gerber, Mrs. W. D. Mounce
1954 S. Haddad, Mrs. B. Windley	J. Moran, Mrs. C. Allen
1955 S. Silodor, Mrs. H. Sobel	G. Rapee, Mrs. A. Kempner
1956 S. Silodor, Mrs. H. Sobel	D. G. Farquaharson, Mrs. A. Gordon
1957 H. Schenken, Mrs. B. Gale	D. Warner, Mrs. D. Carter
1958 E. J. Smith, Jr., Mrs. C. Ross	L. Cohen, Mrs. S. Stein
1959 J. Crawford, Mrs. D. Hayden	S. Lazard, Mrs. S. Rebner
1960 W. Passell, Mrs. E. Abrams	P. Johnson, Mrs. S. Kransberg
1961 A. Comstock, Mrs. J. Muirhead	Mr. and Mrs. C. J. Solomon
1962 P. Levitt, Mrs. C. Holt	J. Sutherlin, P. J. Berry
1963 E. R. Murray, Mrs. A. Gordon	Mr. and Mrs. J. Brier
1964 Mrs. L. B. Swan, D. Morse	M. Alcorn, P. Pender
1965 Mr. and Mrs. E. Kaplan	Mrs. M. Klausner, M. Portugal
1966 Mr. and Mrs. R. Sharp	S. Lowery, Mrs. A. Blasband
1967 Mrs. J. Machlin, K. Woolsey	Mr. and Mrs. M. Cappelletti
1968 P. Rank, M. Johnson	J. Gerber, C. Klar
1969 Mr. and Mrs. S. Parker	E. Levitt, D. Treadwell
1970 G. Dawkins, C. Flournoy	M. Chilcote, L. Weiss
1971 L. Mathe, E. Mathe	B. Crane, K. Davis
1972 J. Mohan, P. Sutherlin	L. Ferer, G. Goldstein
1973 B. Chazen, M. Johnson	H. Smith, K. Cohen
1974 H. Utegaard, G. Caravelli	B. Crane, K. Shuman

SECONDARY CHAMPIONSHIPS

Non-Life Masters Men's Pairs. An event restricted to non-Life Masters. Contested as a three-session event with two qualifying rounds and one final round in 1963; a four-session event with two qualifying sessions and two final sessions from 1964 through 1969; and a two-session play-through event thereafter.

WINNERS	RUNNERS-UP
1963 J. Snelling, M. Cappelletti	H. Robinson, R. Asherman
1964 B. Grace, M. Harlow	A. W. Bishop, W. L. Zesiger
1965 K. Larsen, R. Eichler	S. Gross, S. Levy
1966 J. Locks, S. Schultz	W. Mullen, Dr. B. Sharp
1967 G. Kuchler, Jr., J. McMullin	J. Pasternack, D. Juran
1968 A. Granville, P. Greenberg	L. B. Stafford, G. Arthurs
1969 B. Yomtov, J. Foster	H. Jackson, J. A. Cross, Jr.
1970 R. Dombos, J. Longman	M. Mabry, R. Parramore
1971 E. Neff, M. Bischoff	G. Soules, V. Pang
1972 R. Fischer, K. Wong	M. Herbacsek, I. Fooshee
1973 J. Bayonne, S. Strachan	J. Saine, J. Saine, Jr.

Non-Life Masters Women's Pairs. An event restricted to non-Life Masters. Contested as a three-session event with two qualifying rounds and one final round in 1963; a four-session event with two qualifying sessions and two final sessions from 1964 through 1969; and a two-session play-through event thereafter.

WINNERS	RUNNERS-UP
1963 Mrs. M. Roehr, Mrs. R. Lewis	Mrs. R. L. Kunz, Mrs. G. Reintjes
1964 Mrs. H. Strasheim, Mrs. J. Truelson	Mrs. J. Miller, Mrs. J. D. Clyde
1965 E. Ferber, E. Spain	J. Colbert, E. Weinstein
1966 G. Cooper, F. Orner	Mrs. J. W. Baker, Dr. E. Auch
1967 D. Harmon, L. Jimerson	Mrs. A. Pope, Mrs. C. Smith
1968 P. Bergin, C. A. Shepard	Mrs. K. Godfrey, Mrs. M. Worger-Slade
1969 Mrs. J. C. McCleskey, Mrs. J. Caldwell	Mrs. R. G. Simon, Mrs. L. Peiser
1970 O. Davidson, Mrs. I. Rosenberg	R. Furbee, Mrs. J. Alspaugh
1971 J. Berken, B. Brasted	Mrs. E. Preston, V. Fuller
1972 E. Jacobson, H. Cheng	R. Woodman, J. Dockham
1973 D. Hill, R. Mercer	H. Gilbert, E. Lee

Men's Teams. A two-session event held in the Spring Nationals in 1962 and subsequently in the Fall Nationals, scored by Board-a-Match prior to 1971, when scoring was changed to international match points with Swiss pairing.

WINNERS	RUNNERS-UP
1962 K. Pettersen, H. Guiver	D. Williams, J. W. Hubbell
M. Shuman, T. K. Sanders	F. A. Bombeck, G. Michaud
A. Moyse, Jr.	
1963 P. Carson, A. R. Cohen	C. Coon, R. Stern
K. Forsythe, J. Alexander	F. Goldring, P. Bresner
1964 C. Miller, G. Pisk	R. Reed, R. F. Robbins
C. McFarland, W. Granberry	B. D. Troyer, S. Horn
1965 C. Goren, P. Hodge, J. Gerber	E. Barlow, W. E. Langlois
G. R. Nail, J. E. Simon	A. Chang, D. R. Davis
1966 N. Kay, V. Mitchell, P. Leventritt	R. Goldman, A. Coren
E. Kaplan, P. Feldesman	G. Hershman, E. Lazarus
1967 D. Siebert, A. Siebert	P. Pender, R. Goldman
J. Walton, W. Cook, Jr.	H. Lewis, T. Dionisi
1968 Dr. G. Rosenkranz, P. Hodge	J. Jacoby, Dr. J. Fisher
J. Gerber, W. Passell, A. Truscott	B. Crane, P. Rank
1969 G. Kasle, M. King, M. Lawrence	
R. Goldman, *tied with* G. Prosnitz	
K. Lebensold, J. Rothfield, W. Scott	
1971 P. Ivaska, M. Smolen, E. Davis	
T. Lesser, *tied with* N. Levin,	
Dr. S. Willner, W. Nakamura	
B. Evans	
1972 H. Guiver, A. Bricklin	A. Silber, V. Remey
S. Coolik, T. Sanders	J. Zimmerman, B. Hardies
	tied with G. Belski
	H. Sanders, D. Meyer
	M. Skinner
1974 J. Pietscher, R. Degen	J. Jacoby, C. Jackson
M. Griffith, A. Thomas	B. Keiden, J. Simon
	M. Lawrence, *tied with*
	J. Evans, S. Carver
	R. Boner, R. Labry

Women's Teams. A two-session event held in the Spring Nationals in 1962 and subsequently in the Fall Nationals, scored by Board-a-Match prior to 1971, when scoring was changed to international match points with Swiss pairing.

WINNERS	RUNNERS-UP
1962 Mrs. I. Bright, Mrs. M. Livingston Mrs. G. Crounse, Mrs. M. Cornillaud Mrs. E. M. Novak	E. Maupin, Mrs. E. C. Syrovatka A. Monheim, L. Solomon
1963 P. Rotzell, P. Solomon A. Blasband, O. Peterson	B. Schenken, M. Wagar A. Gordon, C. Sanders, *tied with* E. Abrams L. H. Gray, B. Campion, C. Arnold
1964 Mrs. C. Solomon, A. Gordon M. Wagar, M. J. Farell	C. Holt, Mrs. P. Love Mrs. S. Rubinson, M. B. Townsend
1965 M. Wagar, A. Gordon S. Stein, P. Solomon	W. Nepple, J. Sharp E. Breckman, Mrs. J. Peilen
1966 F. Thompson, Mrs. E. Lee A. Conroy, M. Erickson	B. Tepper, S. Johnson, J. Stone B. Rappaport, *tied with* Mrs. K. Pettijohn, Mrs. G. Ryan Mrs. R. Sundstrom, Mrs. V. R. Rupp, *tied with* Mrs. B. Halpern Mrs. E. Kramer, Mrs. A. Apter Mrs. G. Brown, C. Moscotti, *tied with* Mrs. P. Kantar, Mrs. J. West J. Dewitt, G. Cooper
1967 C. Krupp, B. Cohn M. Rosenthal, B. Tepper	A. Davis, G. Moss, H. Portugal Mrs. D. B. Hawes, M. Passell *tied with* Mrs. M. F. Meyer Mrs. A. Basset, Mrs. M. Katz B. Seago, Mrs. W. J. Nelson
1968 I. Alcone, J. Stone, K. Allison E. Levitt, *tied with* A. Davis C. Klar, S. Stein, B. Berkitz, *tied with* B. Schenken, G. Moss S. Johnson, M. Passell	
1969 B. Schenken, G. Moss M. Passell, S. Johnson	T. Michaels, G. Clarke J. Morse, Mrs. C. Stenger
1971 V. Burke, C. Jones M. Merryweather, J. Casalena	V. Meloan, K. Barnhill K. Good, M. Windhorst
1972 B. Brier, J. Stone, C. Klar T. Michaels, A. Davis	E. Alboum, A. Bean D. Silverman, S. Schaeffer, *tied with* M. Marr Mrs. R. Robb, J. Tina J. Einzigg, *tied with* T. Cohn, G. Clark, E. Marrs L. Karam, *tied with* R. Tabor, A. Gordon Mrs. R. Macy, Mrs. M. Henry
1974 L. Rivers, A. Westrom J. Rich, S. Chavers	C. Weidman, J. Guest V. Miller, E. Woods

Open Pairs.

Open Pairs. A two-session Pair event for non-participants in the BLUE RIBBON PAIRS.

WINNERS	RUNNERS-UP
1966 L. J. Phillips, A. Kearse	M. Ridley, S. Aldenderfer
1967 Mrs. R. Miller, Mrs. J. Packer	Mrs. J. Anderson, Mrs. M. Parsons
1968 J. Elliott, K. Rumph	Mr. and Mrs. R. Andersen
1969 H. J. Peck, D. B. Grove	J. Linhart, M. Spitz
1970 M. Schleifer, C. Baron	Mrs. E. Novak, Mrs. G. Crounse
1971 J. La Noue, C. Pitard	V. Pang, E. Fukushima
1972 D. Bhargava, D. Gerstman	P. Greenfeld, B. Bramley
1973 D. Siebert, A. Siebert	R. Andersen, W. Hascall
1974 Flight A: G. Hayden, R. Bates	L. Rautenberg, H. Chandross
Flight B: P. New, B. Hagedorn	D. Fizer, A. Fizer
Flight C: K. Benson, A. Bell	V. Weich, W. Ponder

Sub-National Masters Teams.

Sub-National Masters Teams. A two-session Board-a-Match event, restricted to players below the rank of National Master.

WINNERS	RUNNERS-UP
1958 A. W. James, W. R. Shaw G. E. Clark, D. N. MacKellar	Dr. F. Slaughter, S. Guy N. Miller, L. Willis
1959 Mrs. O. Bert, Mrs. J. W. Fleming S. Kessler, L. Katz	Mr. and Mrs. R. Sterett Mr. and Mrs. C. J. Veith
1960 G. Klorman, W. Colbert S. Ehrlich, E. Schulman	R. J. Rosenthal, L. L. Lehrburger D. Schoolman, L. Rosenthal, *tied with* J. Stein, W. Snavely, R. Weil P. Spiegelman, L. Snavely

WINNERS	RUNNERS-UP
1961 A. Hardwicke, Mrs. C. P. Hardwicke W. R. Long, D. Moody	Mr. and Mrs. W. L. Crothers O. Pierson, K. Pierson
1962 Mr. and Mrs. D. A. Drake Mr. and Mrs. F. Johnson, Jr., *tied with* E. B. Maxwell, D. K. McElfresh Mrs. W. V. Nold, Mrs. E. C. Maxwell	
1963 J. Titzel, R. P. Hodges M. N. Greenberg, H. D. Katz	J. Douglass, C. L. Clements H. Gottesman, J. L. Berry
1964 H. R. Janssen, R. E. Mangney Mrs. S. Edmonds, H. Edmonds	Mr. and Mrs. R. W. Hooks F. Spies, J. G. Tunnell, H. Lee
1965 Mr. and Mrs. W. R. Taft T. J. Smith, J. S. Farish	F. Laccabue, D. C. Handley L. Sleizer, D. M. Kurn, *tied with* W. D. McElwain, H. Betz M. D. Yeaman, E. A. Williams
1966 C. L. Shelton, M. Tiemeier E. Banks, W. Heard	B. Fleming, J. Fleming Mr. and Mrs. A. Creech
1967 Mr. and Mrs. W. M. Perry Mr. and Mrs. W. Barton	Mrs. R. Guercio, Mrs. L. Wagner Mrs. R. Nelson, Mrs. J. P. Aitken
1968 R. Jacobs, D. Blagdon J. Kasdan, A. Kandell	S. Maddocks, Mrs. P. Tasker-Brown C. A. Swentek, Mrs. P. M. Nugent

Commercial and Industrial Pairs. A two-session Pair event.

WINNERS	RUNNERS-UP
1958 Wyandotte Chemicals W. F. Pesold, E. Weipert	Welfare Department of Detroit A. Mells, E. Klein
1959 Douglas Aircraft R. Clark, R. Hamman	System Development Corporation P. Greenberg, H. Harman
1960 Halle & Stieglitz R. Levy, M. Sirot	New York Life H. Woodman, W. Miller
1961 Saron Pharmacal Company Mr. and Mrs. R. Saron	Humble Oil and Refining O. Pierson, W. Swan
1962 M. Cochrell, R. Bratcher	Mrs. C. Rockhill, Mrs. V. Miller
1963 Campus Hideaway B. Grace, L. Gerig	General Motors D. W. Brooks, J. White
1964 Saron Chemical Company Mr. and Mrs. R. Saron	Braniff Airways F. Jensen, J. J. Kee
1965 Bank of America G. Strohl, D. Geary	Fresno City Schools D. Flippin, M. Connolly
1966 Ford Motor Company R. Richman, B. Weinstock	Battelle Company W. Riester, N. Fischer
1967 McDonnell Douglas B. Sharp, D. Geers	El Paso Public Schools M. B. Long, Mrs. E. Hansen
1968 General Dynamics Convair W. B. Evans, T. G. Ludwig	Occidental Life Insurance S. Steen, K. Freyermuth
1969 Oldsmobile R. W. Bacon, R. J. Mosher	Stokell Corp. F. S. Degen, R. D. Stokell
1970 First Business Computing L. Green, L. Tritter	Tenneco, Inc. W. Such, B. Townsend

Senior Masters Individual (BEYNON TROPHY)

	WINNERS	RUNNERS-UP	THIRD
1947	A. Weiss	P. Ellett	B. O. Johnson
1948	N. Agran	S. Aronson	Dr. W. Hutchins
1949	C. Bowie	F. Karpin	B. Kaufman
1950	A. Goldstein	F. Karpin	J. H. Block
1951	J. Epstein	H. Bork	C. L. Berman
1952	H. Cohen	J. Stedem	A. Nusinoff
1953	W. E. Adams	N. B. Walts	G. S. Holtz
1954	D. Rutstein	R. Ludwig	S. Brown
1955	W. W. Williams, Jr.	I. Rosenberg	M. Rubinow
1956	Mrs. S. H. Salisbury	A. K. Darby	Mrs. E. S. Godfrey
1957	P. Feldesman	H. B. Deri	J. P. Hoover
1958	R. N. Miller	H. Tann	C. P. Weil
1959	T. Commander	A. Filipcic	Mrs. N. Riney
1960	Mrs. M. Pell	A. Lillico	G. Acker

Masters Individual (Karn Trophy 1931–33, STEINER TROPHY from 1934)

	WINNERS	RUNNERS-UP	THIRD
1931	W. S. Karn	R. L. Frey	O. Jacoby
1932	H. Schenken	D. Burnstine	R. L. Frey
1933	D. Burnstine	E. Murdoch	W. von Zedtwitz
1934	E. Murdoch	B. J. Becker	M. D. Maier
1935	O. Jacoby	D. Burnstine	C. Goren
1936	W. von Zedtwitz	M. D. Maier	B. J. Becker
1937	B. J. Becker	G. Unger	R. Appleyard
1938	Dr. R. Ecker, Jr.	H. Fishbein	E. Burns
1939	M. D. Maier	A. Landy	M. Field
1940	M. Elis	L. Hazen	C. Head
1941	L. Hazen	B. J. Becker	H. Fishbein
1942	H. Fishbein	Mrs. O. Peterson	Dr. A. Salasky
1943	A. Roth	C. Solomon	J. Glick
1944	G. Rapee	R. Chatkin	B. J. Becker
1945	C. Goren	A. Weiss	Mrs. W. L. Terry
1946	R. McPherran	M. Elis	A. Casner
1947	C. Solomon	J. Cushing	Dr. A. Steinberg
1948	B. J. Becker	M. Field	G. Rapee
1949	G. Rapee	B. J. Becker	J. R. Crawford
1950	M. Elis	R. Appleyard	Dr. W. Lipton
1951	S. Silodor	J. R. Crawford	H. J. Fishbein
1952	H. Fishbein	P. Leventritt	C. Head
1953	T. Stone	L. Hirsch	N. Kay
1954	E. Burns	F. A. Bombeck	Mrs. R. A. Briggs
1955	N. Kay	A. Roth, *tied with* B. J. Becker	
1956	J. R. Crawford	R. Appleyard	Mrs. I. Brall
1957	E. Kaplan	Dr. E. E. Karshmer	Dr. R. H. Israel
1958	S. Stein	J. Crawford	E. Murray
1959	L. Pressburg	F. L. Jackson	E. L. Rosen
1960	R. Reynolds	A. Robinson	Mrs. H. Bridegroom

Individual. Revived in 1966, a two-session Open event that replaced the two Individual championships that were discontinued in 1960.

	WINNERS	RUNNERS-UP
1966	Dr. I. J. Littman	C. Bavis
1967	B. L. Tighe	A. Hurd
1968	P. Mahoney	R. Bates
1969	Dr. E. F. Gudgel	P. Woodworth
1970	Mrs. E. Nix	L. DeWald, *tied with* T. Dix
1971	Mrs. C. Thomas	M. Erickson
1972	E. Hochberg	J. Wood
1973	R. Bishop	C. Williams
1974	I. Rasmussen	J. Rigopoulos

Charity Pairs. A one-session Charity Pair event for the Sadie MACHLIN TROPHY.

	WINNERS	RUNNERS-UP
1964	Mr. and Mrs. W. Passell	M. Galter, R. Anderson
1965	B. Crane, P. Rank	P. Read, M. Soules
1966	R. Zwack, R. Cutforth	M. B. Townsend, W. A. Baldwin
1967	M. Kahn, C. Kahn	G. Aime, A. Bagert
1968	J. Livezey, Mrs. W. W. Vosburgh	F. T. Adler, Mrs. M. Pasternak
1969	J. Carmena, P. Hawkins	A. Murman, Jr., M. Abel
1970	H. Pennington, C. Smith	D. Childs, Mrs. R. Rush
1971	C. Falk, F. Strickland	C. Pitard, R. Smith
1972	Mrs. W. Murphy, D. Rossell	C. Lenpiner, L. Lenpiner
1973	L. Deane, A. Callam	P. Davis, Dr. N. Ostrich
		tied with G. Baer, M. Taylor
1974	J. Howland, G. Tilly	K. Benson, D. Smith

Swiss Teams. A four-session team event scored by international match points, with two qualifying sessions and two final sessions.

	WINNERS	RUNNERS-UP
1970	L. Weiss, A. Truscott	A. Bricklin, A. Gerard
	C. Cronemiller, J. Carney	G. Ricci, J. Thomas
	R. Lord, M. Chilcote	J. Vandevoort, *tied with*
		P. Leon, S. Smolen
		R. Levick, F. Will, *tied with*
		B. Garozzo, C. Wei
		K. Wei, J. Becker
		V. Shen, E. Lazarus, *tied with*
		M. Lair, C. Vernay
		L. Dewey, J. Zilic, *tied with*
		M. Finch, B. Gentry
		G. Dawkins, J. Deegan
		W. Johnson

	WINNERS	RUNNERS-UP
1971	J. Darling, P. Darling Mr. and Mrs. R. Haller	J. Commons, B. McWilliams R. Harbin, L. Pressburg
1972	J. Rowley, L. Rowley B. Hutcheon, H. Buechler *tied with* T. Rutledge F. Merblum, C. Falk F. Strickland	
1973	E. Neff, M. Bischoff V. Potysman, C. Potysman	E. Neiger, M. Gurwitz H. Lilie, N. Weichsel J. King
1974	L. Rautenberg, V. Whalen, F. Whalen, H. Chandross	L. Eisenstein, R. Walsh B. Keiden, J. Apfelbaum

Swiss Teams Second Flight. A two-session team event scored by international match points, restricted to non-qualifiers from the four-session secondary Swiss Team event.

	WINNERS	RUNNERS-UP
1970	Mrs. E. Brandt, Mrs. E. Lee Mrs. B. Wilson, Mrs. E. Neville, *tied with* J. Martin, A. Meyer Mrs. F. Alderman, Mrs. W. Eubank, *tied with* Mrs. R. Cooper, Mrs. R. Swartz Mrs. B. Wilke, C. Allen	
1971	N. Posner, M. Hearst B. Voshall, G. Leeper	N. Levin, Dr. S. Willner W. Nakamura, D. Cox
1972	W. Adams, G. Effros R. Bassell, N. Felsinger	W. Wlavick, T. Weik M. Cappelletti, K. Cappelletti, *tied with* Mrs. F. Ganz R. von der Porten, G. Baze M. J. Farell, J. Fejervary
1973	C. Strouse, C. Weed B. Wolff, J. Jacoby J. Hooker	A. Bell, R. O'Leary R. Howard, D. Pelka
1974	R. Rubin, W. Root N. Silverman, M. Rosenblatt	H. Baer, M. Weed J. Hooker, J. DeWitt E. Van Zandt

Men's Pairs. A two-session event.

	WINNERS	RUNNERS-UP
1971	J. Gaer, C. Vernay	S. Robinson, M. Levy
1972	W. Rosner, P. Sidikman	G. Bloomer, W. Beckett
1973	L. Richardson, D. Kerr	J. Bookstaver, M. Gurwitz
1974	N. Silverman, P. Brennan	G. May, K. Benson

Women's Pairs. A two-session event.

	WINNERS	RUNNERS-UP
1971	M. Bergman, M. Gwozdzinsky	G. Erickson, Mrs. M. Close
1972	B. Bellino, B. Bentley, *tied with* P. Riggs, E. Katz	
1973	F. Arst, J. Christopher	B. Lavery, F. Kenigson
1974	D. Romm, S. Burns	C. Cole, M. Evans

Mixed Pairs. A two-session event.

	WINNERS	RUNNERS-UP
1970	A. Trenholm, S. Greenberg	S. Picus, R. Andersen
1971	M. McMahan, S. McMahan	K. Gorfkle, P. Sutherlin
1972	A. Roth, B. Rappaport	Mr. and Mrs. B. Wiener
1973	B. Doughty, P. LaCour	L. Jefferson, J. Pinto
1974	B. Chazen, C. Greenhut	K. Cohen, H. Smith

International Fund Pairs. A one-session event the proceeds of which are used to send ACBL teams to World Championship events.

	WINNERS	RUNNERS-UP
1970	B. Friedberg, M. Weil	A. Rodriguez, J. Anderson
1971	C. Wei, J. Becker	R. McKaig, J. Cullinan
1972	M. Yudin, K. Candela	C. Smith, Dr. L. Wiegman
1973	J. Bernard, R. Glenn	J. Lyons, R. Smith, *tied with* R. Emke, A. Olesak
1974	A. Bell, A. Siebert	E. David, K. Godfrey

OTHER SECONDARY EVENTS

(All two-session events)

1970

Open Teams Second Flight:	E. Kokish, D. Piafsky
	M. Cappelletti, K. Cappelletti
	B. Creed, A. Plate, L. Plate
	N. Lewis
Blue Ribbon Pairs Second Flight:	S. Cohn, L. Hetzer
	D. Darling, E. Banks
Life Master Men's Pairs Second Flight:	B. Economidy, W. Acker
	M. Wallington, V. Ellzey
Life Master Women's Pairs Second Flight:	Mrs. P. Terk, Mrs. B. Wilson
	J. Parker, S. Harris, *tied with*
	A. Gerard, L. Sharp, *tied with*
	C. Tornay, J. Stone
Open Pairs Second Flight:	D. Laird, C. Tupper
	M. Murphey, D. Cook
Mixed Pairs Second Flight:	P. Gowdey, M. Shira
	H. Smith, M. Blumenthal
Special Morning Pairs:	G. Fischer, Dr. B. Cearley
	D. Sakoski, K. Schutze

1971

Open Teams Second Flight:	V. Pang, K. Allison, E. Fukushima
	G. Soules, S. Lent
	S. Goldberg, K. Blackerby
	C. Dorn, W. Crossley
Blue Ribbon Pairs Second Flight:	I. Scope, B. Scope
	F. Rubbra, J. Linhart
Open Pairs Second Flight:	K. Taira, J. McKee
	G. Castro, J. Castro
Special Pairs:	J. Cole, R. Kerbel
	P. Benjamin, S. Lawrence

1972

Swiss Teams:	A. Cohn, T. Cohn, J. Gobert,
	D. Richardmeyer
	N. Ostrich, A. Davis
	K. Taira, D. Bhargava
Masters Pairs:	F. Hamilton, J. Murphy
	A. Cantor, S. Mayer
Non-Masters Pairs:	J. Haimes, E. Obrant
	D. Newman, D. Cantor
Special Pairs:	Dr. R. Lindquist, Dr. D. Williams
	W. Hunter, J. Loewenton
Special Pairs:	R. Clark, F. Brown
	M. Levine, H. Montague

1973

Swiss Teams:	K. Wei, J. Mitchell
	M. J. Farell, M. Johnson
	M. Tom, R. Andersen
	A. Truscott, D. Truscott,
	tied with P. Leon, S. Steinfeldt
	R. Levick, L. Pennario, *tied with*
	C. Davis, Z. Garabedian
	R. Hughes, R. Fiske, *tied with*
	D. Sacks, J. Van Ness
	I. Kostal, S. Wilson, *tied with*
	P. Marks, L. Engle, L. Marks
	G. Crain, V. Burke, *tied with*
	D. Crossley, B. Matthess
	V. Pang, B. Crossley
Masters Pairs:	C. Davis, R. Tator
	B. Crane, Dr. J. Fisher
Non-Masters Pairs:	D. Place, D. Lorhammer
	E. Omori, T. Schmitz
Open Pairs:	G. Crain, V. Burke
	E. Lewis, P. Benjamin
Mt. Charleston Pairs:	L. Harris, D. Cohen
	Mrs. D. Graham, Dr. P. Kronfeld
Eureka Pairs:	D. Lentz, M. Merrill
	K. Jolley, S. Larson
Tournament of Champions:	K. Petterson, P. Hawkins
	M. Meador, H. Mason

WINNERS	RUNNERS-UP
1974	
Swiss Teams:	C. Goppert, G. Hayden
	M. Lair, J. Gratham
	K. Wei, H. MacLean
	M. Feldman, R. Andersen
Masters Pairs:	Dr. G. Pisk, P. Hood
	I. Sternberg, C. Hultman
Open Pairs:	G. Lipsig, R. McGaffey
	J. Jacoby, J. Simon
Special Pairs:	C. Falk, F. Strickland
	T. Clarke, E. Susman
Special Pairs:	T. Peters, N. Coombs
	J. Brown, P. Ford

For the award to the player gaining the greatest number of master points, see HERMAN TROPHY.

SPRING NATIONAL CHAMPIONSHIPS

Vanderbilt Trophy. Originally a DOUBLE ELIMINATION Open Team event scored by international match points; usually nine or ten sessions. In 1966 the double elimination method was replaced by three qualifying sessions (subsequently reduced to two), followed by single elimination knockout matches. The preliminary qualifying sessions were dropped in 1970.

WINNERS	RUNNERS-UP
1928 R. R. Richards, G. N. Scott	
E. A. Wetzlar, W. C. Whitehead, *tied with*	
Mrs. S. Lovell, Mrs. R. L. Taylor	
A. Brown, N. Wester	
1929 H. B. Raffel, J. P. Mattheys	W. C. Whitehead, E. A. Wetzlar
L. Langdon, M. T. Gottlieb	R. J. Leibenderfer, G. M. Scott
1930 Mr. and Mrs. E. Culbertson	G. Reith, H. Schenken
W. von Zedtwitz, T. A. Lightner	W. Liggett, W. Malowan, *tied with*
	P. H. Sims, W. S. Karn
	O. Jacoby, H. Boscowitz
1931 P. H. Sims, W. S. Karn	W. Malowan, S. Stearns
O. Jacoby, D. Burnstine	H. Schenken, J. P. Mattheys
1932 P. H. Sims, W. S. Karn	R. Frey, C. Lochridge
W. von Zedtwitz, H. S. Vanderbilt	D. Burnstine, H. Schenken
1933 F. Rendon, P. Abramsohn	R. L. Frey, S. Fry, Jr.
S. Rusinow, B. Feuer	L. H. Watson, A. M. Barnes
1934 D. Burnstine, O. Jacoby	H. Boscowitz, C. Goren
H. Schenken, M. Gottlieb	C. Lochridge, J. Rau
R. L. Frey	
1935 O. Jacoby, H. Schenken	L. H. Watson, E. Hymes, Jr.
D. Burnstine, M. T. Gottlieb	M. D. Maier, S. Fry, Jr.
S. Stearns	
1936 F. D. Kaplan, P. Abramsohn	L. Langdon, W. Beinicke
H. Fishbein, I. Epstein	J. P. Mattheys, C. Goren
1937 H. Schenken, M. D. Maier	W. von Zedtwitz, C. Lochridge
D. Burnstine, O. Jacoby	H. S. Vanderbilt, B. J. Becker
S. Stearns	T. A. Lightner
1938 O. Jacoby, D. Burnstine	W. von Zedtwitz, B. J. Becker
M. D. Maier, H. Schenken	C. Lochridge, T. A. Lightner
S. Stearns	E. Hymes, Jr.
1939 H. Raffel, S. Dornbusch	T. A. Lightner, W. Bixby
M. Alexander, L. Hazen	Mrs. S. W. Peck, R. McPherran
S. Gintell	
1940 H. S. Vanderbilt, E. Hymes, Jr.	A. Brodsky, A. Schultz
C. Lochridge, W. von Zedtwitz	H. Rosenzweig, L. Lipschitz
R. McPherran	
1941 S. Stearns, M. Fuchs	O. Jacoby, H. Schenken
J. Crawford, R. McPherran	T. Lightner, B. J. Becker
	M. D. Maier
1942 L. Hazen, R. L. Frey	G. Rapee, H. Sobel
L. Bachner, S. M. Stayman	B. Jarmel, S. Fry, Jr.
S. Dornbusch	

WINNERS	RUNNERS-UP
1943 H. Fishbein, A. Roth T. Stone, F. Kaplan H. Fagin	W. von Zedtwitz, C. E. von Vleck M. Elis, P. Abramsohn E. O. Keller
1944 B. J. Becker, H. Sobel C. Goren, S. Silodor	R. L. Frey, L. Hazen G. Rapee, S. Stayman C. Lochridge
1945 H. Sobel, B. J. Becker C. Goren, S. Silodor	E. Hymes, Jr., T. Lightner W. von Zedtwitz, S. Stayman H. Schenken
1946 H. Schenken, J. Crawford G. Rapee, O. Jacoby S. Stayman	B. Lebhar, Jr., P. Leventritt S. Rossant, S. Katz W. von Zedtwitz
1947 J. Low, H. Fishbein L. Hirsch, H. Feinberg D. Clarren	B. Lebhar, Jr., L. Hazen S. Katz, P. Leventritt
1948 R. Appleyard, W. M. Lichtenstein J. Feigus, H. Sonnenblick A. Weiss	H. H. Goldberg, F. Hirsch A. Casner, J. Strasser A. Wolfe
1949 H. Fishbein, L. Hirsch M. Elis, C. Lochridge L. Hazen	H. Sobel, C. Goren B. J. Becker, M. Field O. Jacoby
1950 H. Schenken, S. Silodor J. Crawford, S. Stayman G. Rapee	H. Sobel, C. Goren B. J. Becker, M. Field
1951 B. J. Becker, J. Crawford G. Rapee, S. Stayman	B. Cohen, E. Hochfeld G. Turn, J. Hancock
1952 N. Drucker, J. Sloan I. Kass, M. Moss S. Mandell	G. Rapee, J. Crawford H. Schenken, S. Stayman B. J. Becker
1953 Dr. W. Lipton, P. Leventritt R. Sherman, R. Kahn E. Kaplan	C. Goren, H. Sobel M. Fields, S. Silodor A. Roth
1954 M. Moss, S. Mandell K. Apfel, N. Drucker F. Begley	S. Fenkel, S. Rossant M. Elis, S. Solomon Mrs. C. Solomon
1955 B. J. Becker, J. Crawford H. Schenken, S. Silodor G. Rapee	C. Goren, H. Sobel H. Ogust, B. Koytchou P. Leventritt
1956 B. J. Becker, G. Rapee H. Schenken, S. Silodor J. Crawford	Mr. and Mrs. L. Jaeger J. E. Low, W. M. Lichtenstein L. Hess
1957 B. J. Becker, G. Rapee H. Schenken, S. Silodor J. Crawford	O. J. Ray, M. Rubenfeld R. Bortstiber, R. Lichtenstein
1958 H. Fishbein, L. Hazen S. Fry, Jr., L. Harmon I. Stakgold	E. Kaplan, A. Sheinwold C. Solomon, N. Kay R. Hirschberg, R. Kahn
1959 S. Silodor, N. Kay B. J. Becker, G. Rapee J. Crawford, T. Stone	C. Goren, H. Sobel H. Schenken, H. Ogust P. Hodge, P. Leventritt
1960 S. Silodor, N. Kay T. Stone, J. Crawford	W. von Zedtwitz, E. Kemp W. Seamon, R. Arnold A. Weill, R. Reynolds
1961 R. Jordan, A. Robinson E. Murray, C. Coon	O. Adams, H. Guiver E. Kantar, R. von der Porten M. Miles
1962 Mr. and Mrs. J. Levitt G. Nash, G. deRuntz L. Kolker	C. Goren, H. Sobel H. Ogust, B. Koytchou P. Leventritt, H. Schenken
1963 H. Harkavy, E. Kemp A. Roth, C. Russell A. Weiss, W. Seamon	E. Taylor, E. Paulsen R. von der Porten, H. Guiver L. Mathe
1964 H. Schenken, P. Leventritt L. Mathe, E. Kantar R. Hamman, D. Krauss	B. J. Becker, D. Hayden I. Erdos, K. Petterson Mr. and Mrs. M. Portugal
1965 O. Jacoby, P. Feldesman Dr. J. Fisher, A. Weiss J. Jacoby, I. Rubin	R. Jordan, A. Robinson G. Rapee, B. Koytchou N. Kay, E. Kaplan
1966 P. Feldesman, I. Rubin L. Mathe, R. Hamman, S. Kehela	T. Stone, I. Erdos, R. Goldman W. Eisenberg, L. Harmon

1967	L. Mathe, M. Lawrence R. von der Porten, L. Stansby G. R. Nail, J. Jacoby	G. Rapee, S. Lazard P. Leventritt, P. Levitt H. Schenken
1968	E. Kaplan, N. Kay A. Robinson, R. Jordan W. Root, A. Roth	I. Rubin, J. Westheimer E. Kantar, R. Hamman
1969	R. Walsh, J. Swanson P. Soloway, G. Hallee	S. Stayman, V. Mitchell T. Stone, P. Feldesman I. Rubin, J. Westheimer
1970	E. Kaplan, N. Kay G. Rapee, S. Lazard E. Murray, S. Kehela	W. Eisenberg, R. Goldman R. Hamman, M. Lawrence R. Wolff, J. Jacoby
1971	W. Eisenberg, R. Goldman R. Hamman, J. Jacoby M. Lawrence, R. Wolff	R. von der Porten, K. Larsen P. Soloway, E. Kantar C. Burger, I. Rubin
1972	S. Altman, E. Neiger A. Sontag, J. Stuart P. Weichsel, T. Smith	P. Swanson, J. Blair F. Hamilton, H. Perlman
1973	R. Wolff, R. Goldman M. Lawrence, R. Hamman M. Blumenthal	A. Reinhold, E. Kantar W. Eisenberg, Dr. R. Katz L. Cohen
1974	J. Silver, E. Kokish R. Crossley, D. Crossley	K. Wei, S. Goldstein R. Andersen, M. Tom M. Feldman

Men's Teams. For the GOREN TROPHY. A four-session Board-a-Match event with two qualifying rounds and two final rounds. Contested as a three-session championship until 1972 and in 1975, held in the Fall Nationals until 1963.

	WINNERS	RUNNERS-UP
1946	A. Glatt, J. Bank A. Weiss, W. McGhee M. Adams	S. Silodor, G. Rapee A. M. Barnes C. Goren J. Crawford
1947	A. Landy, J. Glick S. Mogal, A. Goldsmith J. Kravatz	Dr. L. Mark G. Unger, J. Cohan R. Storr
1948	S. Mogal, A. Landy J. Glick, J. Ankus J. Law	E. N. Marcus S. Stayman G. Rapee J. Crawford
1949	H. Schenken, M. Levin L. Roet, A. Moyse, Jr.	W. Joseph Dr. R. Storr H. J. Gerst, J. Cohan
1950	E. Burns, D. Carter J. F. Carlin, A. R. Revell	R. Hirsch, M. Moss N. Drucker M. Vernoff R. Appleyard
1951	J. Van Brooks, J. Denny E. Dautell, A. Gutowsky E. J. Smith	R. Rosenberg F. Bickel J. Foreacre R. Lattomus
1952	O. Jacoby, S. Stayman C. Goren, S. Silodor C. Solomon	C. Kuhn, S. Katz W. Seamon A. Weiss
1953	G. Heath, B. Fain J. Gerber, H. Rockaway P. H. Hodge	A. Kauder H. Fishbein J. Moran, D. Steen C. Bishop
1954	A. Landy, J. Glick A. S. Goldsmith A. J. Frank, S. Mogal	O. Jacoby, J. Jacoby H. Chanin Dr. J. Fisher S. Lazard
1955	R. Hirshberg, N. Kay E. Kaplan, A. Roth R. Freeman	C. Solomon S. Stayman C. Goren P. Leventritt

	WINNERS	RUNNERS-UP
1956	J. Crawford, S. Silodor B. Fain, P. Hodge	O. Jacoby Dr. J. Fisher S. Lazard E. Hochfeld P. Allinger, *tied with* H. Rockaway J. J. Toledano C. A. Strouse B. Crane
1957	L. Mathe, E. Taylor M. Schleifer, D. Oakie	A. Roth, I. Cohen I. Stakgold D. Freeman J. C. Kunkel
1958	A. S. Goldsmith E. Schwartz, A. Landy V. Zeve, J. Glick	N. Kay, E. Kaplan R. Hirschberg R. Freeman
1959	I. Erdos, O. Adams O. Jacoby, R. Sharp	S. Silodor B. J. Becker J. Crawford T. Stone
1960	M. Schoenberg R. Wakeman, A. Messer C. Denby B. I. Humphreys	C. Solomon H. Fishbein P. Hodge, J. Gerber *tied with* J. Siverts J. Zawiscam W. Dumas D. McGee, *tied with* M. Paulshock D. Treadwell E. Reich J. R. Hughes
1961	T. Stone, A. Roth J. Crawford, N. Kay S. Silodor	G. R. Nail, M. Key S. Lazard E. Kaplan
1962	S. Stayman, V. Mitchell P. Feldesman, E. Murray R. Freeman, *tied with* L. Mathe, E. Taylor H. Guiver, P. Allinger	
1963	V. Mitchell, T. Stone S. Stayman P. Feldesman	S. Rubinow B. J. Becker W. Root, S. Silodor N. Kay

Year	Winners	Runners-Up
1964	A. Sheinwold, H. Guiver / I. Erdos, M. Lawrence	F. Westcott / C. Coon / G. R. Nail / R. Stucker
1965	H. Fishbein, C. Solomon / J. Rubens, R. Stern	P. Feldesman / V. Mitchell / S. Stayman / D. Rotman / S. Lazard
1966	E. Kaplan, N. Kay / P. Feldesman / R. Freeman	J. Flint, P. Pender / A. Dionisi, H. Lewis
1967	L. Jolma, Dr. G. Stark / T. Bussey, J. R. Dunlap / Dr. R. Patterson	J. Sutherlin, P. Read / R. Spotts, E. Barlow
1968	W. Eisenberg / M. Lawrence, R. Wolff / R. Goldman, J. Jacoby / I. Corn	M. Becker, J. Stuart / C. Coon, P. Weichsel / R. Zeckhauser
1969	A. Roth, P. Trent / J. Cayne, C. Burger	W. Eisenberg / R. Goldman / J. Jacoby / R. Hamman / R. Wolff / M. Lawrence, *tied with* M. J. Cohn / W. Reister / N. Fischer / C. MacCracken / P. Soloway / E. Kantar / R. Von der Porten / K. Larson
1970	L. Mathe, D. Krauss / R. Walsh, D. Bearson / J. Swanson, R. Bergovoy	B. Crane, Dr. J. Fisher / L. Cohen, G. Caravelli
1971	A. Roth, A. Sontag / B. Chazen, P. Trent	L. Mathe, D. Krauss / W. Grieve, G. Rapee / P. Pender, G. Baze
1972	J. Simon, J. Jacoby / R. Wolff, P. Swanson / J. Blair	S. Goldberg, S. Robinson / L. Gould, L. Bluhm, *tied with* C. Russell, W. Seamon / N. Kurlander, A. Roth / J. Crawford
1973	J. Simon, J. Jacoby / R. Wolff, G. Kasle / G. Hayden	J. Silver, E. Kokish / S. Robinson, M. Shuman / *tied with* M. Shallon / M. Smolen, H. Guiver / W. Sides
1974	R. Andersen / S. Goldstein, M. Tom / H. MacLean / M. Feldman	

Women's Teams. For the COFFIN TROPHY. A four-session event, scored by Board-a-Match until 1976; contested as a three-session championship until 1972 and in 1975, held in the Fall Nationals until 1963. In 1976 the event became a National Championship Women's Knockout event with Swiss qualifying.

Year	WINNERS	RUNNERS-UP
1933	G. Fenley, R. Field / J. Friedlander / C. Wallace	W. E. McKenney / H. Funk / H. J. White / G. A. H. Gardner
1934	W. E. McKenney / A. Rosenfeld / A. Rockwell / G. Hamilton	E. Banfield, E. Gross / D. Roberts / P. Gardner
1935	R. B. Fuller, H. White / F. Stratford / L. G. Quigley	W. E. McKenney / A. Rockwell / G. Hamilton / A. Rosenfeld
1936	R. B. Fuller, H. White / F. Stratford / L. G. Quigley	J. Faulkner / W. M. Anderson / G. Keedick / H. Haldeman
1937	J. H. Lemon / A. P. Stockvis / M. West, R. C. Young	R. B. Fuller, H. Sobel / L. G. Quigley / F. Stratford
1938	D. Tansill, S. A. Peck / G. Morris, O. Peterson	H. Fullerton / A. Rosenfeld / H. E. Funk / I. E. Schwarz / F. Stratford
1939	M. Ervin, H. Sobel / R. B. Fuller / J. J. Mitchell / R. C. Young	B. N. Katzen / S. DeYoung / M. Samberg
1940	A. Neuwirth, L. Zetosch / H. Levy, M. Wagar	W. E. McKenney / R. Horn / Ol. Hilliard / G. Planco
1941	W. P. Dickens, R. Scott / L. Buchannan / W. L. Terry	J. Rothschild / H. Sobel / R. B. Fuller / R. C. Young
1942	O. Peterson, R. Sherman / O. Hilliard, B. Golder	H. Sobel, J. E. Folline / D. Fuller / G. A. H. Gardner
1943	R. C. Young, J. E. Foline / H. Sobel, M. Wagar	B. Lebhar / F. Stratford / W. E. McKenney / G. Hirsch
1944	M. Wagar, H. Sobel / J. E. Folline, R. C. Young	M. Godfrey / J. J. Sullivan / C. W. Neeld / A. H. Todd
1945	R. C. Young, J. E. Folline / H. Sobel, M. Wagar	L. Goldstein / G. Schildmiller / A. Perlmutter / M. Butman
1946	R. C. Young, J. E. Folline / H. Sobel, M. Wagar	P. Bacher / A. Shmukler / L. Jaeger, M. Basher
1947	C. Wallace, M. Roncarelli / T. Lyons / W. M. Anderson, *tied with* R. Sondheim / L. C. Robinson / G. Illig, C. Stewart	
1948	C. Sidway, R. Gordon / J. Gutman, L. Goldstein	O. Peterson / C. Solomon / E. J. Seligman / R. C. Gilbert
1949	L. C. Robinson, H. Sabatt / R. H. Sondheim / C. T. Evans, *tied with* F. Eberson, E. P. Cotter / E. Boschan, K. McNutt	
1950	R. Gordon / A. W. Bowden / W. M. Anderson / G. E. Neil	M. F. Meyer / E. Feldman / R. Groves / J. Mathews / S. Fairchild
1951	R. C. Young / A. Burnstein / P. Bacher, J. Rosenfeld / E. Kemp	J. Steiner, C. Tiernan / A. D. Tiernan / H. E. Hathhorn / M. E. Tiernan
1952	S. Lipton, J. Moore / J. Begin, N. Matz	M. E. Harris / P. Adams / W. Keohane / H. D. Baker, *tied with* H. Sobel, K. Rhodes / R. Sherman / M. Wagar
1953	H. Feldstein, L. Goldstein / J. Glick, I. E. Schwarz	K. Rhodes / A. Kauder / R. Sherman / M. Wagar, *tied with* V. Sheronal, S. Lee / O. Peterson / C. Solomon

	WINNERS	RUNNERS-UP
1954	M. Harris, R. Fuller R. Ecker, M. Matz	R. A. Jervis T. B. Bouldin E. Hassler, H. Payne, *tied with* C. Solomon A. Shmukler M. Cohn, O. Peterson, *tied with* H. Sobel, K. Rhodes R. Sherman M. Wagar, *tied with* E. Folline, G. Reith L. Eisenman M. Alcorn
1955	P. Adams, C. Brall J. Strich, S. Johnson L. Eisenman	R. Sherman K. Rhodes, H. Sobel M. Wagar, *tied with* E. Kemp, M. Levin S. Young R. Steinberg A. Burnstein, *tied with* E. Neil, J. Gutman R. Gordon, B. Katzen E. Engleman
1956	J. Stone, P. Rotzell C. Sidway M. E. Tiernan	K. Rhodes, H. Sobel S. Young, M. Wagar
1957	S. Rebner, M. J. Kauder C. Solomon, M. Cohn	H. Sobel, K. Rhodes A. Gordon, M. Wagar
1958	R. Rotzell, C. Brall B. Gale, S. Johnson	K. Rhodes, H. Sobel S. Young, M. Wagar
1959	J. Simon, S. Kasle R. Sharp, M. Alcorn	H. Portugal M. Klausner J. Herb, R. Reif K. Dunn
1960	H. Schenken, R. Erde S. Johnson, B. Kachmar	H. Shanbrom M. Stone, J. Remey S. Stein
1961	H. Schenken, R. Erde S. Johnson, B. Kachmar	M. J. Farell T. Michaels P. Solomon, J. Stone
1962	E. Kemp, A. Burnstein S. Rebner, A. Kempner T. Warner	J. Stone G. McDaniel M. Kaplan T. Michaels
1963	T. Michaels, G. McDaniel C. Sanders, S. Stein P. Adler	H. Portugal M. Wagar B. Kachmar D. Layden A. Gordon
1964	B. Schenken, P. Solomon H. Baron, M. J. Farell	M. Wagar, A. Gordon D. Hayden H. Portugal
1965	J. Mitchell, B. Kaplan V. Heckel, E. Kemp	S. Stein, J. Remey C. Ruther, D. Polak
1966	F. Arst, C. Stolkin J. Deutsch, S. Stein, *tied with* T. Michaels, G. McDaniel N. Gruver, S. Sachs	
1967	A. Gordon, D. Hayden M. Wagar, E. J. Hawes	B. Schenken H. Baron M. J. Farell P. Solomon, *tied with* D. Bick, J. Ballard R. Needham V. Kirkwood
1968	B. Schenken, S. Johnson P. Solomon, M. J. Farell H. Baron, R. Walsh	M. O'Brien M. B. Townsend J. Frankel E. Van Zandt
1969	E. Kemp, V. Heckel J. Stone, K. Allison A. Kempner, H. Portugal	B. Tepper B. Rappaport N. Gruver, S. Sachs
1970	M J. Farell, D. Hayden J. Mitchell, M. Johnson E. J. Hawes, P. Solomon	R. L. Hawes F. Van Winkle F. Van Cleve D. Cowger
1971	K. Wei, J. Friedenberg G. Moss, M. Passell H. Utegaard	S. Stein, G. Goldstein E. Kemp, B. Rappaport R. Epstein

	WINNERS	RUNNERS-UP
1972	M. J. Farell, S. Picus D. Hayden, E. Hawes	F. Arst, J. Deutsch E. Rosen, C. Stolkin
1973	H. Utegaard, T. Michaels J. Morse, N. Gruver	Mrs. A. Noland, B. Wolff F. Beard, E. Van Zandt N. Alpaugh, *tied with* K. Wei, G. Moss J. Mitchell, M. Passell M. J. Farell, M. Johnson, *tied with* J. Christopher E. Sternberg, M. Peterson B. Rosenberg
1974	M. Johnson, D. Truscott J. Mitchell, G. Moss M. J. Farell, E. Hawes	H. Baron, K. Shuman C. Greenhut, T. Nugit

Open Pairs. For the SILODOR TROPHY. A four-session event consisting of two qualifying sessions and two final sessions.

	WINNERS	RUNNERS-UP
1958	L. B. Harmon I. Stakgold	A. Roth, T. Stone
1959	L. Mathe, E. O. Taylor	H. Fishbein C. Solomon
1960	R. Jordon, A. Roth	Mr. and Mrs. T. Sanders
1961	M. Hodges, H. Hume	J. E. Simon J. Denny
1962	A. Robinson, R. Jordan	M. Michaels M. Shuman
1963	S. Silodor, N. Kay	I. Stakgold D. Rotman
1964	O. Jacoby, B. Crane	L. Mathe, I. Erdos
1965	J. Biddle, J. Wisemiller	T. Stone, I. Erdos
1966	E. Kaplan, N. Kay	A. Roth, W. Root
1967	M. Genud, H. Cohen	P. Feldesman L. Mathe
1968	R. Spero, R. Blau	H. Fishbein C. Solomon
1969	R. Freedman, J. Mathis	Mr. and Mrs. D. Sachs
1970	B. Crane, Dr. J. Fisher	G. R. Nail G. L. Michaud
1971	B. Crane, Dr. J. Fisher, *tied with* V. Remey J. Remey	
1972	B. Crane, Dr. J. Fisher, *tied with* M. Granovetter, M. Tom	
1973	M. Hoffman, J. Rhatigan	D. Rotman, C. Peres
1974	B. Crane, Dr. J. Fisher	R. Andersen, H. MacLean

Men's Pairs. For the WERNHER TROPHY. A four-session event consisting of two qualifying rounds and two final rounds. Contested as a three-session championship from 1969 through 1971.

	WINNERS	RUNNERS-UP
1934	D. Burnstine, O. Jacoby	M. Elis, G. Kennedy
1935	F. French E. M. Cook, Jr.	C. Goren, L. Watson
1936	F. Kaplan Dr. R. H. Ecker, Jr.	B. Lebhar, Jr. S. Katz
1937	E. M. Cook, Jr. J. C. Kunkle	P. Abramsohn M. Elis
1938	C. Goren, B. J. Becker	M. Elis W. von Zedtwitz
1939	O. Jacoby, J. Crawford	M. Elis, H. Chanin
1940	M. D. Maier R. A. McPherran	H. Fishbein, M. Elis
1941	S. Rossant, J. E. Low	J. Davis, S. Silodor
1942	R. von Engel A. Goodman	M. Gross Dr. W. Lipton
1943	C. Solomon, C. Goren	Dr. R. H. Ecker, Jr. F. Kaplan

WINNERS	RUNNERS-UP
1944 S. Dornbusch	A. Casner
H. Goldberg	R. Hirschberg
1945 L. Hazen, S. Gintell	S. Stayman, G. Rapee
1946 W. von Zedtwitz	F. Weisbach
A. M. Barnes	L. Bernard, Jr.
1947 S. Mogal, T. Stone	M. Elis, M. Portugal
1948 F. Hirsch, S. Katz	L. Bernard
	H. Feldstein
1949 C. Goren, O. Jacoby	R. Nail, J. P. Ripstra
1950 P. A. Briggs.	G. Rapee, S. Silodor
A. R. Revell	
1951 E. Hochfield	C. Bishop
M. Q. Ellenby	A. Nusinoff
1952 W. Rosen, A. Grau	T. Stone
	H. Harkavy
1953 H. Harkavy, B. Root	J. R. Crawford
	W. von Zedtwitz
1954 E. R. Murray, D. Drury	M. Ellenby, D. Steen
1955 D. Drury, E. R. Murray	I. Rubin, V. Mitchell
1956 J. O. Jacoby, P. Allinger	R. Jordon, R. Sitnek
1957 J. W. Hubbell, D. Carter	J. Gerber, P. Hodge
1958 I. Rubin, W. Grieve	S. Silodor, N. Kay
1959 H. Fishbein, J. Gerber	E. Paulsen
	M. Shuman
1960 Maj. W. Christian	P. Hodge, D. Carter
J. Blair	
1961 P. Feldesman, I. Rubin	L. Mathe, P. Allinger
1962 P. Feldesman, I. Rubin	M. Miles, E. Kantar
1963 S. Kehela, B. W. Lebovic	A. Moyse, Jr.
	T. Sanders
1964 E. D. Weiner, G. Hays	D. Pederson
	D. Nemiro
1965 J. Rubens, L. Rosler	E. Murray, N. Kay
1966 B. Crane, P. Rank	M. Blumenthal
	M. Moss
1967 A. Price, R. Lawrence	E. Kantar
	S. Lazard
1968 K. Larsen, E. Lazarus	W. Passell
	D. Strasberg
1969 F. Vine, M. J. Martino	P. Soloway
	G. Halle
1970 D. Kaye, R. Walsh	E. Kaplan, N. Kay
1971 G. Belladonna	J. McKee, B. Kerr
B. Garozzo	
1972 K. Wolsey, S. Robinson	P. Heitner, M. Miles
1973 J. Kennedy, D. Hadden	S. Robinson, K. Woolsey
1974 G. Steiner, G. Slemmons	S. Robinson, K. Woolsey

This event was held in the Summer Nationals until 1963. A similar event was held at the Spring Nationals 1958–62 with the following results:

WINNERS	RUNNERS-UP
1958 S. Silodor, N. Kay	D. Harrison
	J. Denny
1959 J. Swanson, J. Pestaner	D. Oakie
	M. Schleifer
1960 J. Rosenblum, F. Hoadley	B. Creed
	S. Gould, Jr.
1961 M. Rubinow, T. Stone	A. Tschekaloff
	E. Paulsen
1962 P. Feldesman, I. Erdos	N. Kay, S. Silodor

Women's Pairs. For the WHITEHEAD TROPHY. A four-session event consisting of two qualifying rounds and two final rounds. Contested as a three-session championship from 1969 through 1971.

1930 O. Peterson, M. S. Zontlein	
J. Culbertson, E. Murdoch	
1931 V. Hansen, E. Murdoch	
E. Clement, O. Hilliard	
1932 J. S. Jones, O. Peterson	
M. S. Zontlein, F. Fitch	

1933 R. B. Fuller, C. Smith	
E. Clement, M. Black	
1934 H. Bonwit, H. White	
R. Sherman, T. Stern	
1935 M. Ulbrich, B. Teichman	
O. Peterson, R. B. Fuller	
1936 J. Jones, R. C. Young	
R. B. Fuller, M. Ervin	
1937 R. B. Fuller, M. Ervin	
J. H. Lemon, M. R. West	
1938 H. Sobel, R. C. Young	
D. Roberts, J. Gardner	
1939 H. Sobel, R. C. Young	
R. B. Fuller, D. B. Tansill	
1940 J. Waidlich, E. Atkinson	
G. Planco, H. Drescher	
1941 E. Seligman, M. P. Rosen	
R. Horn, G. Planco	
1942 E. Seligman, M. P. Rosen	
H. Bonwit, D. P. Hanson	
1943 E. Seligman, M. P. Rosen	
O. Hilliard, B. Lebhar	
1944 W. Wagar, R. Sherman	
P. Bacher, L. Rhodes	
1945 O. Peterson, B. M. Golder	
R. Sherman, M. Wagar	
1946 R. C. Young, E. J. Seligman	
A. Bernstein, G. Rosenbaum	
1947 M. Gutman, L. Goldstein	
H. Sobel, R. Sherman	
1948 M. Gutman, L. Goldstein	
M. Cunningham, H. M. Smith	
1949 R. Sherman, L. Rhodes	
C. P. Cunningham, H. M. Smith	
1950 M. Thompson, J. Kelly	
R. Buck, G. P. Ryan	
1951 E. Minear, R. A. Dunphy	
H. C. Wolfe, F. Fooshe	
1952 S. Fairchild, S. Lee	
M. Betzler, M. Hoffman	
1953 H. Swearingen, B. Weiner	
H. Feldstein, L. Goldstein	
1954 M. Alcorn, S. Neely	
M. Ritter, M. Levin	
1955 L. Rhodes, M. Wagar	
M. Nevins, C. Conklin	
1956 M. Wagar, L. Rhodes	
P. Halbestadt, R. Ecker	
1957 M. Wagar, K. Rhodes	
E. Kemp, T. Michaels	
1958 M. Wagar, K. Rhodes	
A. Smith, N. L. Cassibry	
1959 B. Adler, D. Hayden	
E. Schwartz, A. Gordon	
1960 M. J. Farell, C. Solomon	
E. A. Mahoney, J. F. Welch	
1961 R. Gordon, S. Haddad	
W. Seamon, S. Keith	
1962 C. Holt, G. Warner	
G. M. Sharum, K. Carter	
1963 K. L. Sargent, R. Tobin	
T. Michaels, G. MacDaniel	
1964 M. Alcorn, L. Patterson	
R. Ballantyne, L. Scott	
1965 J. Gruver, D. Sachs	
H. Sobel, A. Kempner	
1966 E. Kemp, V. Heckel	
T. Michaels, G. McDaniel	
1967 T. Michaels, G. McDaniel	
H. Baron, M. Johnson	
1968 R. Walsh, H. Baron	
D. Hayden, E. J. Hawes, *tied with*	
B. Kaufman, G. Cohen	
1969 G. Clarke, G. Noszka	
B. Schenken, S. B. Johnson	
1970 T. Rockaway, R. Klar	
J. Mitchell, G. Moss	
1971 J. Mitchell, A. Kearse	
B. Brier, B. Wolff	
1972 R. Walsh, K. Davis	
J. Solodar, G. Moss	
1973 A. Economidy, V. Williamson	
P. Eckard, M. Anderson	
1974 J. Stansby, P. Leary	
G. Moss, J. Mitchell	

This event was held at the Summer Nationals until 1962. A similar event was held at the Spring Nationals 1958–62 with the following results:

1958 M. J. Novak, B. Nail
      M. J. Root, W. J. Albersheim
1959 B. Epstein, B. Grossblatt
      B. Coombs, M. Klausner
1960 H. Feldstein, A. H. Mueller
      M. Jones, F. Eberson
1961 H. A. Woods, M. B. Long
      H. Portugal, D. Hayden
1962 S. Stein, C. Sanders
      J. Mitchell, B. Kaplan

SECONDARY CHAMPIONSHIPS

Mixed Pairs. A two-session event for the HILLIARD TROPHY.

WINNERS	RUNNERS-UP
1931 L. R. Ayres	O. Jacoby
Mrs. J. S. Jones, Jr.	E. Murdoch
1932 C. S. Lochridge	B. J. Becker
Mrs. N. N. Newman	Mrs. E. C. Kaiser
1933 F. Levy, M. Wagar	Dr. J. C. McClelland
	Mrs. R. J. White
1934 R. F. Kahn	C. Goren
Mrs. T. Greenbaum	Mrs. R. C. Young
1935 L. J. Haddad	M. J. Glick
Mrs. E. Evans	Mrs. P. Stratford
1936 W. Bixby	A. Glatt
Mrs. D. M. Healy	Mrs. L. Heiner
1937 H. J. Fishbein	J. Slutt
Mrs. S. Rush	Mrs. H. E. Latter
1938 F. D. Kaplan	R. Appleyard
Mrs. S. Rush	Mrs. H. Zetosch
1939 L. H. Fremont	O. Jacoby
Mrs. P. Stratford	Mrs. S. Wainwright
1940 S. Silodor	R. McPherran
Mrs. R. C. Young	Mrs. H. Sobel
1941 Mr. and Mrs. A. J. Glick	H. Feinberg
	Mrs. A. Bryant
1942 H. Fishbein	J. Crawford
Mrs. R. Sherman	Mrs. O. Peterson
1943 C. Goren	C. Solomon
Mrs. O. Peterson	Mrs. B. Golder
1944 S. Silodor, Mrs. H. Sobel	P. Leventritt
	Mrs. M. Gutman
1945 J. Crawford	I. Deuter
Mrs. M. Wagar	Mrs. A. Perlmutter
1946 H. Fishbein	Mr. and Mrs.
Mrs. P. Bacher	N. Perlstein
1947 M. Schleifer, B. Bysshe	H. Cale
	J. Ehrlenbach
1948 E. Miller, V. Leonard	H. Rethers
	D. Westerfield
1949 Mr. and Mrs. A. Kauder	Mr. and Mrs.
	H. J. Murphy
1950 R. Street, Mrs. V. Street	Mr. and Mrs.
	A. Kauder
1951 Mr. and Mrs. M. Portugal	Mrs. A. G. Whitehead
	D. Westerfield
1952 Mr. and Mrs. J. Dunn	Dr. E. Frischauer
	Mrs. M. Klausner
1952 Mr. and Mrs. M. Portugal	Mr. and Mrs.
	H. Bierman
1954 Mr. and Mrs. J. Dunn	Mrs. M. Lorber
	E. Hatcher
1955 Mr. and Mrs. J. Dunn	Mrs. E. Evans
	B. Crane
1956 J. Hancock, R. Million	Mr. and Mrs.
	T. Stone
1957 R. T. Adams	Mr. and Mrs.
M. K. Johnson	A. Kauder
1958 J. Gerber	Dr. and Mrs.
Mrs. M. J. Novak	W. A. Clunie

WINNERS	RUNNERS-UP
1959 A. Roth	Mrs. and Mrs.
Mrs. M. J. Farell	L. L. Mathe, *tied with*
	I. Erdos
	Mrs. S. Wantanabe
1960 E. Rosen, Mrs. S. Harris	Edgar Simon
	Mrs. B. Brandon
1961 Mr. and Mrs.	R. Jordan
T. K. Sanders	Mrs. H. Baron
1962 G. Marsee	E. Rosen
Mrs. J. Cook, *tied with*	Mrs. S. Harris
1963 I. G. Corn	A. Sheinwold
Mrs. C. Moore	Mrs. J. Mitchell
1964 O. Leesment	W. Rossman
Mrs. V. Whitney	W. Nepple, *tied with*
	Mr. and Mrs.
	J. Pestaner
1965 Mr. and Mrs. H. Beyer	K. Carter, G. Marsee
1966 F. Whiteley, J. Stinnett	J. Gerber, C. Klar
1967 H. Fishbein, C. Klar	G. Scalamandre
	J. Mitchell, *tied with*
	B. Jurovich
	A. McAlear
1968 M. Plaskow	V. Heckel, H. Ross.
Dr. J. J. Louis	
1969 C. Dobin, A. Danilenko	M. Johnson
	B. Crane
1970 G. Noszka, A. Danilenko	A. Davis, R. R. Violin
1971 S. Kasle, J. Schwencke	Mrs. E. Goodman
	C. Green
1972 C. Said, H. Armstrong	M. Cappelletti
	K. Cappelletti
1973 M. Chilcote, W. Lee	J. Gardner, E. Olson
1974 M. Becker, A. Kearse	A. Roth, B. Rappaport

Masters Pairs. A two-session pair event limited to players with 50 or more master points. Contested as a three-session event in 1970 and 1971.

WINNERS	RUNNERS-UP
1970 Dr. C. Pollock, B. Davis	A. Hoffman, S. Johnson
1971 M. Lair, M. Taylor	W. Cason, E. Cason
1972 K. Cohen, H. Smith	S. Smolen, P. Leon
1973 S. Robinson, S. Parker	T. Buckley, G. Nash
1974 F. Hamilton, I. Rubin	C. Greenhut, S. Robinson

Non-Masters Pairs. For the KEM CARD TROPHY. A two-session pair event limited to players with 0 to 49 master points, held in the Fall Nationals until 1966.

1937 R. A. Cook, C. W. Humphreys
      J. R. Chappell, Jr., P. Ellett
1938 Mr. and Mrs. E. W. Perry
      R. Michelson, H. Williams
1939 Mrs. E. Q. Crane, Mrs. R. H. Rishell
      R. Lloyd, A. A. Pope
1940 S. Gross, Mrs. P. Campbell
      M. Coleman, M. Feldman
1941 H. L. Oliver, R. Farber
      L. Kelner, M.Dupraw
1942 K. Cadwallader, A. Waterbury
      Mrs. F. R. Fitzgerald, Mrs. E. J. Speickhof
1943 H. Stein, Dr. M. Mitchell
      M. W. Goodman, R. Billig
1944 Mr. and Mrs. J. A. Gaynor
      Miss H. Costello, I. Reilly
1945 C. J. Bonney, B. Lampert
      C. L. Wood, Jr., R. Woolley
1946 F. Henderson, W. B. Bonds
      Mrs. G. Priestman, Mrs. W. C. DeMaris
1947 Mrs. M. D. Abuhove, Mrs. R. Miller
      Mrs. M. Hochheimer, J. Henig
1948 H. E. Loomis, J. G. McKay
      Mr. and Mrs. A. Jonap
1949 D. Kenner, S. Anderson
      S. Rubinow, A. Cohn

1950 Mrs. J. E. Morris, Mrs. W. Simpson
     S. Brown, Mrs. L. Wright
1951 Mrs. W. D. Selikoff, H. J. Blumenschine
     Mr. and Mrs. H. Hendee
1952 J. S. Moore, L. C. Hawkins
     L. Appleman, A. P. Weinberg
1953 R. J. Sarfaty, S. Greenberg
     Mrs. F. L. Ezell, Mrs. T. C. Sellers,
     tied with
     Mr. and Mrs. L. T. Sweet
1954 Dr. S. Gernazian, E. J. Early
     Dr. L. H. Spector, Mrs. B. W. Spector
1955 Sgt. E. L. Esh, Mrs. A. E. Esh
     F. Whitehead, D. A. Jones
1956 Mrs. M. Sharfstein, Mrs. M. Cohen
     Mrs. E. R. Nordine, W. A. McWaters
1957 Capt. W. Ginn, R. L. Mayer
     R. McKnight, S. Grandon
1958 Dr. R. Menczer, Dr. N. Bolton
     M. Kanter, W. Wintrub
1959 H. Royal, D. Harris
     H. Shaffer, L. Lerner
1960 Mr. and Mrs. B. Stephens
     Mr. and Mrs. J. Cordrey
1961 Mr. and Mrs. J. Russell
     Dr. J. Ravel, G. Ravel, *tied with*
     Mr. and Mrs. L. Roddie
1962 C. Berggren, R. Putnam, Jr.
     R. Barkley, S. Parker
1963 J. Titzel, R. P. Hodges
     Mrs. C. Meiner, Mrs. N. Jetson
1964 J. Shagman, E. Shagman
     D. Allen, Mrs. D. Allen
1965 G. Robinson, J. Reynolds
     G. Whyte, C. Robertson
1966 A. J. Iwaszko, E. Rodger
     J. F. Moses, H. Noble
1967 S. Lull, J. Sherman
     T. Bryant, W. Lee
1968 S. Rushing, R. Stampf
     A. Kallenberg, J. Roberts, *tied with*
     M. Moragne, L. Sayles
1969 R. D. Cooper, K. Ritchie
     J. A. Miller, W. J. Hale
1970 S. Minkoff, P. Minkoff
     P. Hann, S. Brown
1971 J. Jiles, J. Collins
     R. Snelsire, Mrs. H. Bungay
1972 H. Weinstein, R. Evarts
     T. Prince, D. Hennessey
1973 V. Morgan, R. Morgan
     S. Deets, M. Zlatic
1974 G. Remlinger, B. Sande
     B. Gorkin, F. Spears

1957 W. Wallace
     R. G. Sharp
1958 Mrs. F. Robinson
     J. Chodak
1959 J. Jabon
     L. Patrick
1960 D. Wolfson
     Mrs. L. L. Mason
1961 C. Woolsey
     L. A. Luther
1962 Mrs. I. Alcone
     E. Collins
1963 D. Geers
     Mrs. C. Richter, *tied with*
     Mrs. M. Haldeman
1964 Mrs. V. Kushner
     R. Chapman
1965 W. Lebovic
     Dr. F. Patterson
1966 J. L. Miller
     Mrs. R. Goldberg
1967 Cmdr. C. F. Cronemiller, Jr.
     H. Schaffer
1968 S. Parkas
     D. Hallman
1969 R. L. Fortune
     A. Kisin
1970 A. M. Wick
     F. T. Dong
1971 P. Clark
     L. Batra
1972 L. Grubner
     Mrs. B. Steger
1973 E. Dalton
     L. Grubner
1974 N. Brookes
     J. Rhoades

Open Pairs. A two-session Open Pair event.

1969 B. Crane, M. Johnson
     H. Latin, M. Bergen
1970 A. Waldmann, D. Faskow
     B. Crane, M. Johnson
1971 A. Roth, B. Rappaport
     T. Smith, M. Rosenblatt
1972 Mr. and Mrs. H. Eikleberry
     R. Grabel, B. Kelly
1973 M. Bernstein, G. DeFotis
     F. Hamilton, J. Starr
1974 B. Crane, M. Passell
     G. Tomczyk, P. Tinney

Individual. A two-session Open event for the BAIRD TROPHY.

1945 T. Samuels
     J. J. Foracre
1946 Mrs. A. S. Smith
     L. Held
1947 L. J. Kabakjian
     H. R. Storr, *tied with*
     Mrs. J. B. Folline
1948 O. Matthes
     S. A. Perrine
1949 S. Seidman
     A. E. Cohn
1950 E. Folline
     J. A. Jabon
1951 T. Denninger
     Mrs. G. H. Berry
1952 F. L. Blackmon, *tied
     with* N. W. White
1953 Mrs. M. R. McCrackin
     R. Ritter
1954 Dr. K. Chadwick
     F. C. Root
1855 M. Rubinow
     H. Harter
1956 S. Haddad
     I. Cohen

Charity Pairs. A one-session Charity event for the M. A. LIGHTMAN TROPHY.

	WINNERS	RUNNERS-UP
1959	B. Frost, D. Weld	Mrs. O. Schaefer
		M. Boucher
1960	Mrs. M. Sharfstein	Mrs. A. M. Byrd
	Dr. E. D. Dillon	F. Hughes
1961	Mrs. D. W. Gaignat	Mr. and Mrs.
	Mrs. A. C. Verner	E. M. Clark
1962	Dr. and Mrs. P. Castelle	A. Landy
		M. Manchester
1963	J. Walton, A. Siebert	B. Cook, D. Siebert
1964	E. Theus, H. Fishbein	C. Coon
		M. Lawrence
		tied with
		Mr. and Mrs.
		R. Hale
1965	Mr. and Mrs. M. Baff	Mrs. T. B. Ashcraft
		Mrs. L. Blackwood
1966	L. Oakley, H. Platt	W. Solomon
		Dr. R. Forbes
1967	Mr. and Mrs. R. Walsh	Mrs. L. P. Carmichael
		Mrs. F. D. Lippman

	WINNERS	RUNNERS-UP		WINNERS	RUNNERS-UP
1968	J. E. Bennett	D. Theodore	1974	D. Grant, B. Teshima	N. Sutherland, V. Norquay
	Mrs. I. C. Bennett	S. Weinberg		P. Prince, B. Crosby	S. Viswanathan
1969	S. Tiktin, A. Di Puccio	L. F. Iacueo			W. Fedynak, *tied with*
		J. Stroud			N. Ferguson, D. Messinger
1970	J. Solodar, J. Friedenberg	B. Crane			B. Stewart
		Dr. J. Fisher			H. McSheffrey, *tied with*
1971	J. Levinson, W. Rosen	M. J. Farrell, Mrs. F. Ganz			B. Livingston, B. Whamond
1972	O. Cromwell, E. Cromwell	S. Stein, Mrs. A. Mueller			H. Kleingeld
1973	Mr. and Mrs. E. Stuber	P. Westburg, S. Ellsworth			D. McCormick
1974	H. Utegaard, J. Morse	D. Rumsby, P. Smith			

International Fund Pairs. A one-session event, the proceeds of which are used to send ACBL teams to World Championship events.

	WINNERS	RUNNERS-UP
1970	J. Ehrlenbach	H. Craig, M. Dye
	Mrs. P. Lowden	
1971	Dr. R. Katz, J. Levinson	L. Michelman, J. Miller
1972	D. Margulis, R. Morrow	M. Passell, B. Cohn
1973	L. Kozlove, S. Tulin	H. Tannen, J. Goldstein
1974	L. McCauley, M. Doremus	D. Nudelman, D. Berry

Swiss Teams. A four-session team event, scored by international match points, with two qualifying sessions and two final sessions.

	WINNERS	RUNNERS-UP
1971	W. Cason, E. Cason	C. Sanders, B. Kennedy
	M. Sheets, W. Sheets	S. Lazarus, M. Passell
		E. Van Zandt
1972	Mr. and Mrs. H. Rasmussen	
	L. Hays, Mrs. J. Allen,	
	tied with L. Wiley	
	K. Wiley, L. Phillips	
	T. Brashler	
1973	B. Webber, F. Yang	
	B. Burger, J. Isackson,	
	tied with G. DeFotis	
	R. Anderson, A. Suskind	
	M. Bernstein, *tied with*	
	F. Singer, C. Jacob	
	B. Brick, S. Lapin	
	J. Joseph	
1974	F. Rubbra, K. Shuman	S. Scott, S. Kehoe
	B. Crane, B. Kehoe	P. Sutherlin, B. Hamman

Swiss Teams Second Flight. A two-session team event scored by international match points, non-qualifiers from the four-session secondary Swiss Team event.

	WINNERS	RUNNERS-UP
1971	J. Mackintosh, R. Allen	
	B. Wiglesworth	
	Mrs. R. Clift, *tied with*	
	J. Hayden, D. Gesell	
	Mrs. A. Singleton	
	L. Bailey, *tied with*	
	J. Potter, G. Kramer	
	L. Karp, D. Caton	
	H. Shoop	
1972	M. Passell, J. LaNoue	S. Scaffidi, W. Gardner
	J. Potter, R. Doughty	J. Isralsky, S. Cohn,
		tied with S. Steinfeldt
		S. Waletzky, B. Russ
		B. Price, *tied with*
		E. Blackwood, S. McComas
		W. MacDonald, J. Angel
1973	R. McCray, N. McCray	D. Hadden, D. Gerstman
	Dr. B. Hatch	J. Merrill, J. Wolstoncroft
	Dr. C. Hendricks	

OTHER SECONDARY EVENTS
(All two-session events)

1971

Open Pairs Second Flight:	Mrs. W. Carlen, Mrs. D. Foutch
	H. Baron, Mrs. H. Swisher
Men's Pairs Second Flight:	D. Morse, H. Fein
	H. Sexton, N. Fischer
Women's Pairs Second Flight:	P. Terk, B. Wilson
	Mrs. J. Watson
	Mrs. G. Roberts
Special Pairs:	W. Garrett, S. Das
	C. Watson, M. Camp
Special Pairs:	B. Warshauer, Mrs. W. Means
	Mrs. E. Short
	Mrs. R. Roberts

1972

Board-a-Match Swiss Teams:	J. Miller, J. Volpe
	R. McCoy
	Mrs. E. McGuide, *tied with*
	D. Requard, J. Diskin
	G. Alapas, A. Stout
Men's Swiss Teams:	H. Fein, D. Morse
	E. Kantar, R. Hamman
	B. Eisman, K. Wiley
	W. O'Loughlin
	V. Ragazzo, S. Scaffidi,
	tied with B. Gordon
	R. Baldwin, J. Conklin
	K. Blutreich
Women's Swiss Teams:	F. Arst, J. Deutsch
	C. Stolkin, S. Stein
	M. West, J. Stenger
	Mrs. G. Crounse
	R. Novak
Men's Pairs:	C. Braman, D. McGarry
	D. Requard, D. Smith
Women's Pairs:	Mrs. D. Buckshorn
	Mrs. F. Wright
	M. Erickson, A. Conroy
Non-Mixed Pairs:	R. Grabel, S. Landen
	S. Parker, S. Robinson
Special Pairs:	S. Graves, T. Hodapp
	D. Requard, D. Smith
Special Pairs:	Dr. J. Moberg
	Mrs. D. Greene
	H. Banks, Dr. R. Kiepfer

1973

Swiss Teams:	C. Bjerkan, L. Wiley
	L. McCaffery, B. Gardner
	J. Simon, J. Epstein
	J. Jacoby, M. Heller
	S. Greenberg
Men's Swiss Teams:	N. Humer, B. Bramley
	D. Dawson, B. Miller
	J. Startzel, C. Shannon
	T. Zelnic, D. Botch
Women's Swiss Teams:	K. Wei, G. Moss
	R. Epstein, A. Kearse
	M. Passell, S. Andersen,
	tied with F. Arst, J. Deutsch
	S. Stein, C. Crawford
Open Pairs:	C. Mahaffey, R. Stern, Jr.
	J. Isackson, B. Burger
Men's Pairs:	D. Reed, S. Horn
	F. Hamilton, J. Starr
Women's Pairs:	D. Henderson
	V. Meriwether
	S. Maxwell, J. Knapp

Special Pairs:	T. Hodapp, S. Graves
	R. Levin, R. Fischer
Special Pairs:	E. Reider, L. Moeller
	W. Schwarz, R. Simmons
1974	
Swiss Teams:	J. Simon, Dr. R. Katz
	R. Bates, L. Cohen
	G. Kasle, G. Caravelli
	C. Weed, M. Brachman
	J. Jacoby, D. Kaim
	R. Nail, *tied with*
	V. Mastron, S. Scott
	P. O'Brien, M. Portugal,
	tied with G. Nelson
	D. Fishman, V. Norquay
	P. Stochinsky, *tied with*
	S. Cimino, J. Cimino
	M. Wiggum, C. Wiggum,
	tied with P. Prince
	B. Teshima, R. Bolton
	J. Bolton
Mixed Swiss Teams:	D. Maurer, C. Jaskela
	E. Lee, C. Swanson
	D. Oakie, B. Creed
	V. Davis, M. Stanley,
	tied with E. Theus
	D. Winslow, P. Rhodes
	M. Anderson, *tied with*
	C. Cimino, J. Cimino
	M. Wiggum, C. Wiggum,
	tied with
	D. Breadwell, E. Levitt
	K. Cohen, H. Smith
	D. Treadwell, E. Levitt
	K. Cohen, H. Smith
Open Pairs: Flight A:	J. Beasy, J. Stewart
	R. Gish, M. Brice
Flight B:	J. Corwin, Mrs. L. Hoyer
	S. Cohen, J. Robison
Flight C:	J. McAvoy, D. Smith
	J. Bishop, I. Donnelly
Men's Pairs:	M. Kreutzer, N. Featherston
	G. Greighton, J. Beeson
Women's Pairs:	B. Ginsberg, I. Pingree
	K. Thorpe, J. Carlisle
Special Pairs:	H. McLennan, L. Black
	R. Ilfeld, R. Ilfeld
Early Risers Pairs:	D. Brown, P. Rowe
	D. O'Connor, E. Miskey

For the award to the player gaining the greatest number of Master Points see MOTT-SMITH TROPHY.

SUMMER NATIONAL CHAMPIONSHIPS

Challenge Teams of Four. For the ASBURY PARK TROPHY. The runner-up team in the regularly-scheduled portion of the event had the right to challenge the winners to a play-off. This right was never utilized. In the 1938 Summer Nationals this event was replaced by the Spingold Master Teams of Four.

	WINNERS	RUNNERS-UP
1930	E. Culbertson	P. H. Sims, W. S. Karn
	T. A. Lightner	M. Gottlieb, L. Langdon
	J. Culbertson	
	W. von Zedtwitz	
1931	W. S. Karn, P. H. Sims	
	D. Burnstine, O. Jacoby	Mrs. L. Roberts, T. LeGros
1932	O. Jacoby, L. H. Watson	S. G. Churchill, P. Stockvis
	M. T. Gottlieb	G. Reith, B. J. Becker
	T. A. Lightner	H. D. Lent
1933	O. Jacoby, D. Burnstine	Mrs. A. Rosenfeld
	H. Schenken, R. L. Frey	W. von Zedtwitz, S. Fry
		L. Watson, E. Hymes

	WINNERS	RUNNERS-UP
1934	J. Glick, W. F. Hopkins	S. Stearns, A. Moyse, Jr.
	A. Frank, C. H. Porter	Mrs. J. Culbertson, T. Lightner
1935	L. H. Watson, S. Fry, Jr.	H. H. Boscowitz, J. Rau
	E. Hymes, Jr., M. D. Maier	A. M. Barnes
	T. A. Lightner	C. Lochridge
1936	L. J. Haddad, M. S. Reilly	Sir. D. Wernher, S. Silodor
	A. Landy, P. Steiner	E. M. Goddard
	L. A. Bernard	H. J. Vogel
1937	D. Burnstine, O. Jacoby	F. Kaplin, A. M. Barnes
	M. D. Maier, H. Schenken	M. Ellis, P. Abramsohn
	C. H. Goren	H. H. Chanin

Master Teams of Four. For the SPINGOLD TROPHY. From 1934 through 1937, the Spingold was not part of a national tournament. In 1938, it replaced the CITY OF ASBURY PARK TROPHY Challenge Teams as an event at the Summer Nationals. At one time the Spingold was a DOUBLE ELIMINATION event scored by international match points, usually lasting nine or ten sessions, restricted to players of Senior Master rank and higher. In 1965, the Double Elimination Method was replaced by three qualifying sessions (subsequently reduced to two), followed by Single Elimination knockout matches. The preliminary qualifying sessions were dropped in 1970.

	WINNERS	RUNNERS-UP
1934	O. Jacoby, D. Burnstine	J. Glick, A. Frank
	H. Schenken, R. L. Frey	L. J. Haddad, C. Hall
	M. T. Gottlieb	
1936	O. Jacoby, D. Burnstine	W. von Zedtwitz
	B. J. Becker, H. Schenken	S. Fry, Jr.
		E. Hymes, Jr.
		M. D. Maier
1937	W. von Zedtwitz	P. Abramsohn
	S. Fry, Jr., T. A. Lightner	M. Elis, H. Fishbein
	E. Hymes, Jr.	L. Bernard, H. Goldberg
1938	B. J. Becker, M. D. Maier	F. Kaplan
	H. Schenken, O. Jacoby	A. M. Barnes, M. Elis
	D. Burnstine	C. S. Lochridge
1939	O. Jacoby, T. A. Lightner	C. Solomon
	M. D. Maier, H. Schenken	J. Crawford
	R. A. McPherran	Mrs. R. C. Young
		M. Fuchs, C. H. Goren
1940	B. Lebhar, S. Katz	W. von Zedtwitz
	O. Brotman, A. Roth	E. Hymes, Jr.
		S. Fry, Jr.
		C. Lochridge
		M. Fuchs
1941	W. von Zedtwitz	H. Schenken
	S. Fry, Jr., E. Hymes, Jr.	M. D. Maier
	A. M. Barnes	O. Jacoby
		B. J. Becker
		T. A. Lightner
1942	R. L. Frey, S. Stayman	C. Harvey, E. Marcus
	L. Hazen, S. Dornbusch	J. T. Feigus, S. Katz
	M. Seiler	
1943	H. Schenken, S. Silodor	H. Sobel
	C. H. Goren, J. Crawford	A. Roth, H. Fishbein
	E. Hymes, Jr.	G. Rapee, B. J. Becker
1944	H. Sobel, G. Rapee	C. Solomon
	B. J. Becker, S. Stayman	Mrs. B. Golder
		S. Becker, S. Fenkel
		E. G. Ellenbogen
1945	O. Jacoby, T. A. Lightner	W. von Zedtwitz
	S. Fry, Jr., H. Schenken	L. Hazen
	E. Hymes, Jr.	A. Roth, H. Fishbein
1946	W. Christian	A. Landy, E. Schwartz
	Capt. M. Hodges	A. S. Goldsmith
	M. Wagar, S. Mogal	J. Glick
1947	B. J. Becker, C. H. Goren	H. Schenken, G. Rapee
	H. Sobel, L. Hazen	S. Silodor, S. Stayman
	W. von Zedtwitz	J. Crawford
1948	G. Rapee, S. Stayman	A. Glatt, R. Halpin
	J. Crawford, M. Wagar	R. Kempner
	H. Schenken	O. Jacoby, J. Bank

MASTER TEAMS OF FOUR

	WINNERS	RUNNERS-UP
1949	A. S. Goldsmith	W. von Zedtwitz
	A. Landy, J. Glick	O. Jacoby, D. Clarren
	S. Mogal, B. Gowdy	J. Kraus, H. Chanin
1950	O. Jacoby, J. Crawford	C. Goren, S. Silodor
	H. Schenken, S. Stayman	H. Sobel, B. J. Becker
	G. Rapee	W. von Zedtwitz
1951	C. Goren, S. Silodor	A. Casner, C. A. Hall
	M. Field, H. Sobel	F. Weisbach
		A. Harvey
1952	H. Schenken, G. Rapee	A. Landy, S. Mogal
	B. J. Becker, J. Crawford	E. J. Smith, J. Glick
	S. Stayman	A. S. Goldsmith
1953	W. Rosen, M. Q. Ellenby	B. Lebhar, S. Katz
	C. Bishop, D. Oakie	D. Clarren, E. Burns
	D. Steen	A. Weiss, *tied with*
		D. Carter, A. Kincaid
		G. R. Nail
		F. A. Bombeck
		J. Hubbell, *tied with*
		W. von Zedtwitz
		Mrs. H. Kemp
		A. Roth, H. Harkavy
		T. Stone, *tied with*
		L. Mathe, M. Schleifer
		I. Erdos
		Dr. E. Fischauer
1954	W. Rosen, M. Ellenby	D. Carter, J. Hubbell
	C. Bishop, L. Mathe	J. Gerber
	J. Moran	F. A. Bombeck
		H. Rockaway, *tied*
		with A. Casner
		A. Harvey
		E. Burns, C. Russell
		tied with J. Rosenblum
		L. Rosen, S. Lazard
		B. Rothlein
		C. Neuman
1955	M. Field, R. Kahn	B. J. Becker
	L. Hazen, C. Solomon	H. Schenken
	S. Stayman	J. Crawford
		S. Silodor, G. Rapee
1956	H. Sobel, H. Ogust	
	B. Koytchou, P. Leventritt	
	W. Seamon, C. Goren, *tied*	
	with T. Stone, V. Mitchell	
	H. Harkavy, A. Roth	
	I Rubin, *tied with*	
	Dr. K. Apfel, L. Kelner	
	F. P. Begley, R. Abeles	
	R. Rosenberg	
1957	J. R. Crawford,	O. Jacoby, J. Jacoby
	B. J. Becker	M. Ellenby
	G. Rapee, T. Stone	E. Hochfeld
	S. Silodor, A. Roth	I. Rubin, I. Erdos
1958	R. Rothlein, C. Neuman	H. Fishbein, L. Hazen
	S. Lazard, W. Hanna	S. Fry, Jr.
	P. Allinger	L. B. Harmon
		I. Stakgold
1959	O. Jacoby, V. Mitchell	R. Freeman
	S. Stayman, M. Rubinow	M. Michaels
	I. Rubin, W. Grieve	A. Gabrilovitch
		R. Walsh
		J. Stone, F. Hoadley
1960	H. Schenken, P. Leventritt	G. Rapee, B. J. Becker
	C. Goren, H. Sobel	W. Grieve
	B. Koytchou, H. Ogust	R. Hirschberg
		S. Silodor, N. Kay
1961	E. Kantar, M. Miles	J. Crawford, G. Rapee
	W. Root, A. Gabrilovitch	S. Silodor, N. Kay
		T. Stone, A. Roth
1962	E. Kantar, M. Miles	G. R. Nail
	L. B. Harmon, I. Stakgold	G. Michaud
		J. Hubbell, J. Jacoby
		D. Carter
1963	C. Russell, H. Harkavy	T. Stone, W. Root
	Mrs. E. Kemp, R. Arnold	W. von Zedtwitz
	A. Roth, W. Seamon	R. Kahn
		T. Sanders, S. Kehela
1964	E. Murray, S. Kehela	B. Gowdy, F. Hoffer
	B. Elliott, P. Sheardown	R. Jotcham
		M. Altman
1965	E. Murray, S. Kehela	E. Kaplan, N. Kay
	B. Elliott, P. Sheardown	B. J. Becker
		D. Hayden
1966	I. Rubin, C. Smith	H. Ogust, W. Grieve
	W. Root, A. Roth	P. Levitt, G. Rapee
		S. Lazard
1967	E. Kaplan, N. Kay	R. Wolff, J. Gerber
	W. Root, A. Roth	G. Rosenkranz
		P. Hodge, D. Morse
1968	G. Rapee, E. Kaplan	B. J. Becker
	E. Murray, S. Kehela	D. Hayden
	S. Lazard, N. Kay	M. Becker
		S. Altman
1969	R. Goldman, R. Hamman	I. Rubin, S. Stayman
	W. Eisenberg, R. Wolff	V. Mitchell
	J. Jacoby, M. Lawrence	P. Feldesman
		W. Grieve
		J. Westheimer
1970	S. Altman, T. Smith	W. Eisenberg
	P. Weichsel, D. Strasberg	M. Lawrence
	J. Stuart	R. Goldman
		R. Wolff
		R. Hamman
		J. Jacoby
1971	J. Stuart, S. Altman	L. Mathe, D. Kraus
	E. Neiger, P. Weichsel	E. Kaplan, N. Kay
	T. Smith	
1972	B. J. Becker, M. Becker	C. Smith, B. Greenberg
	A. Bernstein, J. Rubens	C. Russell, E. Kemp
		A. Weiss, P. Brennan
1973	A. Reinhold, E. Kantar	M. Brachman, J. Jacoby
	Dr. R. Katz, L. Cohen	P. Soloway, J. Swanson
	W. Eisenberg	S. Lazard
1974	S. Goldberg, L. Bluhm	L. Mathe, A. Waldman
	R. Shepherd, L. Gould	P. Pender, H. Lewis
		H. Stappenbeck, W. Root

Life Masters Pairs. For the VON ZEDTWITZ GOLD CUP. A six-session event with two qualifying, two semifinal, and two final rounds, restricted to Life Masters.

	WINNERS	RUNNERS-UP
1930	P. H. Sims	Mr. and Mrs.
	W. von Zedtwitz	E. Culbertson
1931	D. Burnstine, H. Schenken	M. T. Gottlieb
		T. A. Lightner
1932	T. A. Lightner	D. Burnstine
	M. T. Gottlieb	H. Schenken
1933	H. Schenken, D. Burnstine	P. H. Sims
		W. von Zedtwitz
1934	R. Frey, H. Schenken	W. Malowan
		S. Rusinow
1935	T. A. Lightner, B. J. Becker	L. J. Haddad, C. Hall
1936	O. Jacoby, D. Burnstine	I. Epstein
		R. Appleyard
1937	S. G. Churchill	Mrs. R. B. Fuller
	C. Lochridge	Dr. H. J. Vogel
1938	S. Stearns, M. Elis	C. J. Solomon
		J. Crawford
1939	H. Fishbein, R. Appleyard	O. Jacoby
		W. von Zedtwitz
1940	H. Fishbein, M. Elis	S. Fry, Jr., M. Fuchs
1941	H. Schenken, M. D. Maier	O. Jacoby
		J. Crawford
1942	Mrs. H. Sobel, C. H. Goren	T. Stone
		P. Abramsohn
1943	H. Schenken, J. Crawford	Mrs. M. Wagar
		S. Silodor
1944	P. Leventritt, S. Katz	A. Casner
		R. Hirschberg
1945	M. A. Lightman	B. Lebhar, Jr.
	R. Appleyard	S. Rossant
1946	S. Silodor, C. Solomon	R. Sherman, L. Hazen
1947	A. Harvey, F. Weisbach	J. Crawford
		T. A. Lightner
1948	G. Churchill, C. Head	V. Remey, E. Coon
1949	Mrs. R. C. Gilbert, L. Roet	A. Glatt, A. Weiss
1950	Dr. C. W. Yorke	S. Stayman
	M. Sherwin	E. N. Marcus
1951	R. Kahn, P. Leventritt	N. Drucker, E. Kaplan
1952	W. Joseph, W. W. Jackson	A. Weiss, A. Glatt,
		tied with J. Crawford
		H. Schenken

WINNERS	RUNNERS-UP
1953 W. Rosen, M. Q. Ellenby	C. Goren, H. Sobel
1954 D. C. Carter, J. Hubbell	I. Rubin, V. Mitchell
1955 B. Fain, P. Hodge	I. Rubin, V. Mitchell
1956 A. Roth, T. Stone	J. R. Crawford
	S. Silodor
1957 H. S. Brown, M. Cohn	L. Kelner, F. Begley
1958 C. Goren, H. Sobel, *tied*	
with W. Landley, L. Levy	
1959 E. Rosen, D. Rotman	L. Weiss, S. Aronson
1960 Mr. and Mrs. M. Portugal	C. Smith, R. Wolff
1961 P. Feldesman, M. Miles	P. Kibler, R. Reynolds
1962 P. Feldesman, I. Rubin	E. Kemp, A. Weiss
1963 L. Mathe, E. Taylor	I. Rubin, C. Smith
1964 B. J. Becker, D. Hayden	B. Elliott
	P. Sheardown
1965 V. Mitchell, S. Stayman	A. Roth, T. Stone
1966 H. Baron, M. Schleifer	M. Freier, R. Reynolds
1967 L. Mathe, P. Feldesman	Mr. and Mrs. F. Schuld
1968 W. Eisenberg, R. Goldman	J. Jacoby, R. Wolff
1969 S. Kehela, E. Murray	C. Burger, J. Cayne
1970 P. Heitner, M. Moss	R. Freedman
	J. Mathis
1971 A. Roth, B. Rappaport	J. Jacoby, M. Brachman
1972 A. Roth, B. Rappaport	A. Sontag, P. Weichsel
1973 P. Swanson, J. Blair	J. Cayne, C. Burger
1974 G. R. Nail, G. Michaud	W. Walvick, T. Weik

Senior and Advanced Senior Masters Pairs. For the R. L. MILES TROPHY. A four-session event with two qualifying sessions and two final sessions.

WINNERS	RUNNERS-UP
1950 Mr. and Mrs. J. Winsten	D. Berning, S. Gaynor
1951 R. Fain, J. Rosenblum	Mrs. H. Glick
	A. Ritter
1952 Mrs. S. Lee, H. Feinburg	Mrs. A. van Ness
	Mrs. V. Harding
1953 Dr. R. Lloyd, E. H. Martin	
tied with	
M. Fisher, K. Rockwell	
1954 A. Fahrer, R. B. Troxel	R. G. Lesko
	P. A. Schwarz
1955 S. Rappaport, H. Wolpert	Mrs. B. Windley
	B. Sitnek
1956 Mrs. M. Nevins	B. Herb, G. Ateljenich
N. Gerstman	
1957 H. Solof, A. Levine	
tied with	
W. T. Dean, D. Conroy	
1958 Mr. and Mrs. F. Hopf	A. R. Cohen
	H. Wilton
1959 V. Lohmann, R. L. Muyres	I. Ewen, T. Griffin
1960 L. Hilbert, F. Lowe	Mr. and Mrs. S. Roe
1961 A. Brown, M. Mohr	Dr. R. Forbes
	J. Howell
1962 L. Shore, G. Tornay	H. MacLean
	R. DuFour
1963 G. Hallee, P. Soloway	F. Adams
	M. Neiman
1964 Mrs. L. Wilcox	A. Levine
Mrs. R. Gult, Jr.	G. A. Caravelli
1965 M. Levin, D. Levinson	D. Guerin, C. Sturm
1966 H. E. Pries, C. Gross	S. Goldstein, R. Rubin
1967 H. Thaw, A. Levy	K. Kadis, M. Drury
1968 J. Landon, H. Greenberg	J. Crumpacker
	H. Abrams
1969 Col. W. B. Foster	J. Carmena
B. C. Foster	P. Hawkins
1970 J. Lewis, M. Krevor	D. McGarry, L. Reich
1971 W. Geleerd, Jr.	D. Turner
M. Passman	B. Newman
1972 C. Patrias, W. Yue	J. Hall, R. Bell
1973 J. Friedberg, H. Looks	W. Post, A. Swonger
1974 D. Beers, D. Silberstein	E. Stein, K. Swenson

Master Mixed Teams. For the LEBHAR TROPHY (originally for the BARCLAY TROPHY until 1945). A four-session Board-a-Match event, restricted to Senior Masters and players of higher rank, with two qualifying rounds and two final rounds. In 1969 this event was played in three sessions.

BARCLAY TROPHY

WINNERS	RUNNERS-UP
1929 Mrs. M. K. Alexander	
M. M. Cohen	
R. Frankenstein	
Mrs. R. Fleischer	
1930 Mr. and Mrs. P. H. Sims	G. Reith
W. Liggett, Jr.	Mrs. R. B. Fuller
D. J. Wernher	W. C. Cogswell
	J. Farrar
1931 G. Reith, Mrs. R. B. Fuller	Mrs. H. D. Stahl
C. S. Lochridge	W. E. McKenney
Mrs. G. A. Bennett,	M. Beech, E. M. Baker
tied with	
D. Burnstine	
Mrs. V. Hansen	
H. Schenken	
Mrs. H. Scranton	
1932 H. H. Boscowitz	A. Gotthelf
Mrs. M. Black	Mrs. L. Bloomberg
S. Fry, Jr.	B. Cone, Mrs. S. Stern
Mrs. O. Hilliard	
1933 D. Burnstine	Mr. and Mrs.
Mrs. I. Stengel	P. H. Sims
E. Murdoch	Mrs. M. Wagar
E. A. Wetzlar	W. von Zedtwitz
1934 Mr. and Mrs. L. Bachner	Mrs. R. B. Fuller
Mr. and Mrs. J. Lemon	Dr. H. Vogel
	B. Collyer
	A. M. Barnes
1935 R. Sherman, H. Schenken	Mr. and Mrs. O. Jacoby
H. Bonwit, L. H. Watson	Mrs. E. Clement
	W. von Zedtwitz
1936 L. J. Haddad	H. Schenken
Mrs. E. Evans	H. Bonwit
R. McPherran, E. Whitney	B. J. Becker
	Mrs. R. C. Young
1937 P. Abramsohn, A. Naiman	Mrs. D. Roberts
M. Elis, E. Drescher	T. Legros
	Mrs. J. C. Gardner
	S. G. Churchill
1938 Mrs. R. B. Fuller	Mrs. A. Rockwell
Dr. H. J. Vogel	J. C. Kunkel
C. Goren	Mrs. G. B. Hirsch
Mrs. R. C. Young	M. Vernoff
1939 F. Stratford, A. Landy	Mrs. J. J. Mitchell
Mrs. V. Klein, R. Chatkin	E. G. Ellenbogen
	Mrs. B. Golder
	C. Solomon
1940 Mrs. O. Peterson	Mrs. B. Golder
H. Chanin	C. Solomon
Mrs. M. Black	Mrs. J. J. Mitchell
W. von Zedtwitz	E. G. Ellenbogen
1941 Mrs. H. Sobel, C. Goren	Mrs. S. Wainwright
Mrs. R. C. Young	O. Jacoby
S. Silodor	Mrs. W. A. Tucker
	S. Stearns
1942 W. von Zedtwitz	Mrs. E. Seligman
J. Crawford	P. Abramsohn
Mrs. O. Peterson	T. Stone
Mrs. M. Wagar	Mrs. L. Rhodes
1943 Mrs. H. Sobel	S. Wainwright
Mrs. O. Peterson	Mrs. P. Lightner
C. Goren, S. Silodor	W. Malowan
	Mrs. E. Hammond
1944 Mrs. H. Sobel	Mrs. M. Wagar
Mrs. O. Peterson	Mrs. Basher
C. Goren, S. Silodor	E. Cohn, J. Crawford
1945 R. Sherman	A. Roth
Mrs. M. Wagar	Mrs. E. J. Seligman
W. von Zedtwitz	Mrs. M. Elis
J. Crawford	H. Fishbein

(Contested 1946–1955 as a separate National event held on the West Coast.)

WINNERS	RUNNERS-UP
1946 Mr. and Mrs. G. Wells	R. Clarke
Mr. and Mrs. J. Dunn	E. M. Marcus
	M. Kaiser, C. Harvey
1947 Mrs. R. Eidem	
M. Schleifer	
B. Bysshe, D. Walther	
1948 Mrs. J. Rosenkranz	
W. von Zedtwitz	
Mr. and Mrs. M. Seiler	
1949 Mr. and Mrs. A. Kauder	
H. Cale, J. Ehrlenbach	
1950 Mr. and Mrs. A. Kauder	
H. Cale, J. Ehrlenbach	
1951 R. Smith, C. E. Million	
Mrs. G. Wells, J. Hancock	
1952 D. Oakie, Mrs. J. Moffat	
S. Rebner, D. Steen	
1953 B. Cohan, S. Rebner	
M. Klausner	
Dr. E. Frischauer	
1954 S. Rethers, C. A. Strouse	
A. Kempner, B. Crane	
1955 Mr. and Mrs. A. Kauder	
N. Wells, E. Rovere	

LEBHAR TROPHY

WINNERS	RUNNERS-UP
1946 S. Katz, Mrs. R. Kempner	H. Sobel
Mr. and Mrs. B. Lebhar, Jr.	C. Goren
	Mrs. J. E. Folline
	S. Silodor
1947 H. Fishbein	Mrs. J. E. Folline
Mrs. E. Seligman	D. Warner
Mrs. R. Goldberg	Mrs. R. C. Young
L. Kabakjian	P. Leventritt, *tied with*
	Mr. and Mrs.
	L. M. Jaeger
	Mrs. G. Strasser
	H. Harkavy
1948 J. Crawford, M. Wagar	Mrs. R. C. Goldberg
H. Sobel, C. Goren	L. Kabakjian
	H. Fishbein
	E. Seligman
1949 Mr. and Mrs. C. Solomon	H. Sobel, C. Goren
Mrs. R. C. Young	J. Crawford
P. Leventritt	M. Wagar
1950 Mr. and Mrs. C. Solomon	H. Sobel, C. Goren
Mrs. R. C. Young	J. Crawford
P. Leventritt	M. Wagar
1951 Mrs. L. N. Jaeger, L. Roet	C. Goren, H. Sobel
R. Sherman, R. Kahn	M. Field
	Mrs. R. W. Gordon
1952 Mrs. A. Burnstein	Mrs. D. B. Hawes
Mrs. E. Seligman	S. Silodor
A. Roth, H. Harkavy	G. Rapee, O. Peterson
	J. Crawford
1953 Mrs. A. Burnstein	M. J. Kauder
Mrs. E. Kemp	L. L. Mathe
H. Harkavy, A. Roth	G. Turner, E. Hochfeld
1954 H. Sobel, C. Goren	Mrs. F. Eberson
M. Wagar, S. Silodor	D. Murray
	Mrs. M. Boschan
	L. Tubbs
1955 Mrs. M. Michaels, A. Roth	Mrs. A. W. Bosden
Mrs. L. J. Goldstein	Mrs. R. W. Gordon
H. Harkavy	R. Freedman, D. Drury
	E. R. Murray
1956 Mrs. R. W. Gordon	Mr. and Mrs. T. Stone
E. R. Murray	B. Brier
Mrs. A. W. Bowden	W. von Zedtwitz
D. Drury	
R. Freeman	
1957 G. Turner, M. Ellenby	S. Johnson, D. Hayden
E. Kemp, H. Harkavy	S. Fry, Jr., I. Rubin
J. Crawford	O. Jacoby
1958 Mr. and Mrs. W. Rosen	B. J. Becker
Mrs. L. Goldstein, L. Ferer	Mrs. B. Adler
	Mr. and Mrs.
	H. Schenken

WINNERS	RUNNERS-UP
1959 Mr. and Mrs. C. Solomon	Mr. and Mrs.
P. Leventritt, S. Young	A. Sheinwold
R. Jordan	E. Kaplan
	L. B. Harmon
	P. Rotzell
1960 G. Rapee, A. Kempner	B. J. Becker, S. Silodor
B. A. Welch, W. Grieve	N. Kay, S. Stein
	D. Hayden
1961 R. Freeman	S. Lazard
Mrs. L. Robinson	Mrs. B. Kendrick
G. Turner, E. Hochfeld	L. Gurvich, J. Frankel
	Dr. J. Fisher
1962 E. Murray, A. Gordon	S. Silodor, S. Stein
C. Coon, H. Portugal	N. Kay, M. Wagar
1963 Mr. and Mrs. E. Kaplan	A. Roth
Mrs. S. Rebner, S. Lazard	Mrs. P. McDaniel
	I. Cohen
	Mrs. T. Michaels
1964 M. Wagar, J. Gerber	H. Hume, B. Jenkins
Mrs. D. B. Hawes	M. Cohen, M. Philley,
Dr. J. Fisher	*tied with*
	E. Kemp, H. Harkavy
	C. Russel, J. Yavitz
	V. Heckel
1965 T. Stone, J. Stone	S. Stein, W. Rosen
W. von Zedtwitz, A. Roth	C. Norton, B. Norton
B. Brier	C. Stolkin, A. Press
1966 Mr. and Mrs. W. Rosen	Mr. and Mrs.
J. Cayne, P. Soloway	H. Schenken
J. Dryer	A. Roth
	B. Rappaport
1967 Mr. and Mrs. M.	Dr. and Mrs.
Cappelletti	G. Rosenkranz
G. Shane, M. Moss	M. Wagar, N. Kay
	Mrs. H. Klar
	J. Gerber, *tied with*
	B. J. Becker
	D. Hayden
	Dr. J. Fisher
	Mrs. D. B. Hawes,
	tied with
	L. J. Goldstein
	L. Ferer
	F. Hamilton
	S. Stein
1968 H. S. Smith, O. Jacoby	Mr. and Mrs.
J. Jacoby, M. Brachman	E. Kaplan
	C. Stolkin, G. Rapee
1969 Mr. and Mrs. I. Stakgold	Mr. and Mrs. J. Farell
J. Cohn, C. Peres	P. Rank, M. Johnson
F. Orner, D. Rotman	B. Crane
1970 L. Mathe, E. Mathe	D. Strasberg
G. Bare, D. Bare	H. Strasberg
	K. Barbour
	M. Rosenthal
	W. Daly, *tied with*
	J. Adler, B. Adler
	D. Sachs, S. Sachs
1971 R. Andersen, S. Picus	V. Remey, J. Remey
J. Anderson, M. McCrary	D. Brooks, Z. Brooks
1972 W. Passell, M. Passell	Dr. J. Fisher
M. Moss, G. Moss	Mrs. D. B. Hawes
	D. Truscott, A. Truscott
	B. J. Becker
1973 P. Feldesman, S. Tomchin	J. Morse, S. Parker
E. Sacks, E. Alfandre	S. Robinson, B. Lipsitz
	P. Parker
1974 E. Kemp, J. Yavitz	D. Sachs, S. Sachs
W. Seamon, R. Seamon	J. Adler, B. Adler,
	tied with
	D. Fraser, S. Fraser
	B. Saltsman, J. Silver,
	tied with A. Kaminsky
	J. Saltz, S. Johnson
	M. Berger, M. Stocknoff,
	tied with A. Roth
	J. Crawford, C. Crawford
	B. Rappaport

Grand National Teams. For the Albert MOREHEAD TROPHY. A Team Event whose initial stages are con-

tested over the course of several months in districts throughout the ACBL. By the final stages, held at the Summer Nationals, the field has been reduced to the eight Zonal Championship Teams.

WINNERS	RUNNERS-UP
1973 W. Seamon, R. Arnold	J. Levitt, N. Kremer
R. Sharp, R. Pavlicek	R. Lord, R. Smith
J. Beery, J. Jaeger	B. Economidy, D. Smith
1974 P. Soloway, J. Swanson	S. Smith, D. Yanko
Dr. R. Katz, L. Cohen	F. Hamilton, C. Burger
W. Eisenberg, E. Kantar	H. Perlman, J. Starr

SECONDARY EVENTS

Sub-Senior Masters Teams. For the ROTHSCHILD TROPHY, a two-session Board-a-Match event restricted to players below the rank of Senior Masters.

WINNERS	RUNNERS-UP
1938 Mrs. A. Rosenfeld	Judge A. Del Mar
Mrs. E. M. Goddard	V. Miller
Mrs. B. D. Lavine	A. Dickman
Mrs. H. A. Steiner	L. C. Levy
1939 Mrs. F. Horn, Mrs. V. Klein	B. Foer, J. Presser
Mrs. G. Planco	C. Friedman, E. Sirota
Mrs. M. Ervin	
1940 A. R. Dick, E. R. Thomas	Mrs. E. Russell
J. T. Sheer, C. W. Potts	Mrs. A. Leary
	Mrs. S. Fry
	Mrs. M. D. Maier,
	tied with
	B. Hirschberg
	E. and H. Apfelbaum
	J. Van Moppes
1941 Mr. and Mrs. W. Cheeks	Mrs. B. Levine
	M. Levine
Mr. and Mrs. J. J. Wallendorf	Mrs. E. M. Goddard
	Mrs. H. A. Steiner
1942 Mrs. C. Van Slochem	Mrs. F. Lasarow
A. Jarmel	W. V. Kirk
Mrs. J. Daub, M. Strauss	J. Berson
	M. Rubenfeld
1943 Mrs. A. P. Hess	E. Theimer, G. R. Wolff
H. Frankenheimer	D. F. Geortner
Mrs. R. Rice, F. Slater	E. G. Scheck
1944 S. Freisinger, E. L. Saqui	G. Moore
Mr. and Mrs. R. Adams	Mrs. M. Aricson
	E. H. Brown
	J. A. Scarlett
1945 E. Theimer, L. A. Doyle	E. O. Dunaway
L. Sager, D. Goertner	J. F. Eck
	C. B. Groden
	Dr. W. Lipton
1946 O. Yablon, L. Blum	H. Mallinson
C. Lembeck, Dr. K. Apfel	N. Zampino
	W. Yablon, M. Roth
1947 A. Cantor, A. Gabrilovitch	E. W. Hertz
V. Mitchell, H. Mullaney	E. E. Bohm
	A. J. Arkin, E. Kaplan
1948 P. Sugar, M. Dagovitz	
R. Jonesi, N. Kaufman	
J. Weiner, *tied with*	
Mr. and Mrs. H. N. Daybach	
D. G. Horwitz	
Dr. A. G. Engel	
1949 Mrs. M. Gumblin	J. Millerd, J. Millerd
J. Gumblin	R. Casement
B. Randall, M. H. Daskais	E. L. Bel Beccaico
1950 L. McLean, H. Goldman	J. C. McGervey
L. Craig, L. A. Craig	P. A. Schwarz
I. E. Davis	F. Sorenson,
	C. E. Young, *tied with*
	S. Schwartz, Jr., J. Jay
	R. G. Westreich
	M. R. Louis, *tied with*
	Mrs. K. Moeching
	G. T. Humphreys
	J. R. Hughes
	C. B. Miller

WINNERS	RUNNERS-UP
1951 Dr. and Mrs.	W. B. Joachim
S. M. Transue	A. Tschekaloff
Mr. and Mrs.	G. W. Thompson
C. Lovenberg	C. W. Allen
1952 P. E. Gable, Sr.	T. Boggan, A. Sapowit
F. Westreich	T. Van Greyans
S. Schwartz, Jr.	C. Kish
Dr. M. Levitan	
1953 J. Embser, W. B. Gidcumb	R. T. Sarfaty
M. McCord, L. McCord	S. Greenberg
K. Gidcumb	J. E. Kraft
1954 Mrs. D. Currie, K. Boyle	J. L. Hallman
T. Burris, L. Sopkin, *tied*	
with E. C. Worden II	
R. C. Schreyer	
1955 B. McAdam, S. Lefler	L. Abrams, B. Harlow
R. M. Sherrill, M. Edelson	V. Wirpes
	J. Hudecek
1956 R. Lipton, Mrs. W. Slutsky	H. F. Bunn
B. Jereski	B. N. Everett, Jr.
Mrs. B. Braumstein	E. E. Bunn, P. Geary
1957 R. Walaitis, L. Kaplan	D. Murray
J. Levy, A. Levy	E. Weisenbacher
	Mr. and Mrs. J. D. Meehan
1958 Dr. E. Galler, L. Klein	Mr. and Mrs.
A. Weisbord, J. Taylor	M. Livingston
	P. Trinchieri
	Dr. D. Hendel
	T. Somma
1959 Mr. and Mrs. R. Swanson	Mr. and Mrs. P. Libby
C. Kouskolekas	F. Moyer, K. Narrod,
R. Whitcomb	*tied with*
	H. Hoyt, S. Grossman
	W. Stearns, D. Bier
1960 J. Esterkin, E. Grossblatt	Mr. and Mrs. S. Shane
B. Feldman, J. Micklin	M. Gerson
	J. Honigman
1961 S. Lipnick, R. Lambert	Dr. J. Henry, L. Jones
J. Jacobson, J. Hudgins	R. Alexander
M. Panella	Maj. R. Friend
1962 J. Schneider, Dr. P. Leck	W. Chaplin
Mrs. J. McGuiness	L. Pinsonneault
Mrs. G. Anderson	L. Settle, R. Kruse
	R. Fishman, *tied with*
	W. Thompson
	W. Mamecke
	P. Langetsmo
	R. Zeiffert
1963 Dr. K. Mannings, C. Clarke	W. Strum, J. Serling
E. Spain, G. Dobbs	W. Bockwoldt
	L. Vaugh, Jr.
1964 G. Shorting, G. Turner	J. Dixon, C. North
J. Pollock, M. Coutts	R. Jaffe, R. Bartlett
	G. Cohen, *tied with*
	Mr. and Mrs. A. Kraus
	H. Houston, J. Stock
1965 B. Ascheim, R. Holber	R. Keating, S. Dowd
E. Strossberger, J. Black	L. Lutz, R. Cashner,
	tied with
	D. Searcy, C. Searcy
	A. Hamilton
	R. Ciaffone
1966 R. Maik, J. Farrell	D. J. Young, I. Laasi
J. Wallen, H. McConnell	C. Barrere, R. Anziani
1967 K. Comins, R. Elder	J. M. Cote
M. Bergen, R. Betz	J. P. Dagenais
	P. Herbert, P. Lucien,
	tied with
	R. Springett
	T. Springett
	M. Anderson
	J. Anderson,
	tied with
	D. Andrews
	D. Deaves, K. Murray
	R. Wigdor
	A. Brownbill
1968 R. A. Engen	Mr. and Mrs.
J. McAllister, G. R. Brings	J. Orleck, Mr. and
P. D. Schwarz	Mrs. J. Lester
1969 D. Blagdon, H. Einberg	D. Wilczynski
L. Finkelman, S. Kurman	D. M. Weiner
	R. Jacobs, D. Nash

WINNERS	RUNNERS-UP
1970 D. Olson	F. Veres, E. Sachs
M. Throckmorton	F. Chen, W. Linskey
S. Blickman, T. Lundeen	
1971 S. Yellen, B. Reddy	S. Volk, Mrs. C. Huston
J. Carlson, B. Adelman	K. Bley, R. Giniss

Goddard Pairs. Two-session, separate flight events for Men's and Women's Pairs, restricted to Senior Masters and players of higher rank. Contested as a second flight for non-qualifiers of the National Men's and Women's Pairs until those events were moved to the Spring National in 1963.

WINNERS	RUNNERS-UP
1941 S. Kaufer, M. N. Schwartz	Mr. and Mrs. William Cheeks
1942 W. V. Kirk	J. Glick
Mrs. F. Lasarow	M. A. Lightner
1943 E. Lembek, A. Jarmel	H. Ogust, A. Casner
1944 Mrs. R. W. Gordon	
F. Stratford	
1945 N. Hyman, L. C. Levy	Mrs. R. S. Weeks
	J. Friedlander
1946 Mrs. J. Glick, V. Vaughan	T. G. Scharf, F. Hirsch
1947 L. Weiss, S. Aronson	L. Coons
	Mrs. B. Lebhar
1948 Mrs. W. J. Donaldson	Mr. and Mrs.
I. Half	L. J. Seewald
1949 J. Geilfuss, M. Lederer	S. Heinrick
	L. Lazarus
1950 E. J. Smith, J. Denny	Mrs. R. Moore
	Mrs. J. Miller
1951 J. L. Holton, H. Lees	Mrs. O. T. Turner
	Mrs. W. R. Williams
1952 F. Wescott	M. R. May, R. Lesser
Mrs. W. Keohane	
1953 M. Ellenby, P. Sugar	A. Bell, James Miller
1954 H. Harkavy	J. C. Barefoot, Jr.
F. A. Bombeck	W. H. Holderness
1955 G. Droder, W. A. Rohr	S. De Lott, H. Mendel
1956 J. Leonard, A. Tschekaloff	W. E. McCorquodale
	J. Grindsfelder
1957 Mrs. W. Keller	G. Brown, G. Kent
Mrs. V. Schick	
1958 A. Robinson, R. Sitnek	G. Davidson
	J. Schoenfield
1959 I. Berkson, L. Lehman	D. King, J. Parish
1960 M. Vernoff, J. Farell	R. Miller
	G. Gallagher
1961 MEN'S I. Guttman	R. Miller, R. Hunt
R. Sharp	
WOMEN'S L. Albright	Mrs. L. Amster
Mrs. C. F. Posluszny	Mrs. H. Breakey
1962 MEN'S R. N. Miller	M. Michaels
G. Anderson	R. Arnold
WOMEN'S L. Jacobs	Mrs. W. Veurink
Mrs. C. E. Hartwell	Mrs. L. Cudahy
1963 MEN'S G. Hershman	G. Hallee, P. Soloway
E. Lazarus	
WOMEN'S A. Bowden	B. McGlaughin
N. Rippon	B. R. Whitney
1964 MEN'S R. Sharp	J. Sutcliffe
C. Hudecek	P. Rosenburg
WOMEN'S P. Solomon	T. Michaels
A. Blasband	G. McDaniel
1965 MEN'S D. Cox	H. Stern, B. Saxe
J. Mathis	
WOMEN'S H. Utegaard	S. Lazarus, J. Frankel
L. Mark	
1966 MEN'S L. Weiss	R. Halperin
K. Larsen	G. Caravelli
WOMEN'S J. Dryer	Mrs. R. McMillan
R. Walsh	B. Messer
1967 MEN'S R. Perry	M. Schleifer, G. Kasle
O. Sweet	
WOMEN'S B. Tepper	L. Durham
Mrs. B. Birnholz	Y. Conklir

WINNERS	RUNNERS-UP
1968 MEN'S T. J. Parris	J. C. Anderson
J. Nash	A. M. Seltzer
WOMEN'S S. A. Swander	Mrs. G. Harnack
D. Orlett	Mrs. H. M. Macken
1969 MEN'S M. Ingberman	P. Ivaska, E. Davis
C. Peres	
WOMEN'S B. Epstein	C. Jones
M. Donnerstag	C. Fullbright
1970 MEN'S R. Zeckhauser	R. Freedman
M. Klein	C. Lamprey, *tied with*
	H. Stappenbeck
	R. Budd
WOMEN'S J. Parker	H. Cale, F. Smith
S. Harris	
1971 MEN'S C. Lamprey	L. Kozlove, J. Sheridan
A. Waldmann	
WOMEN'S B. Rappaport	L. Wiley, C. Protko
R. Epstein	
1972 MEN'S D. Paulsen	R. Smith, M. Passell
L. Elliott	
WOMEN'S B. Rosenberg	K. Wei, M. Passell
E. Steinberg	

Mixed Pairs. A two-session Mixed Pairs event, restricted to players of Senior Master rank and higher.

WINNERS	RUNNERS-UP
1963 Mrs. J. Stone, J. Sloan	D. Bagby, L. Andrews
1964 Mrs. G. Crounse	Mrs. D. B. Hawes
R. Lawrence	Dr. J. Fisher
1965 Mrs. D. Brechner	G. Cronin, J. Epstein
M. Moss	
1966 Mr. and Mrs. M. Cohn	B. Bloch, H. Mobley
1967 E. Kaplan, J. Kay	Mr. and Mrs. M. Cappelletti
1968 E. Kemp, W. Seamon	W. Flannery
	G. Clarke
1969 R. Stern, S. Roark	N. Smolen
	M. Abrams
1970 N. Lewis, G. Kasle	J. Furman, H. Lilie
1971 N. Richardson, H. Sexton	G. Kugar, L. Kugar
1972 H. Baron, M. Lawrence	B. Troyer, J. Troyer
1973 R. Doughty, P. LaCour	J. Grantham
	Mrs. O. Veselka
1974 Flight A: N. Rosen	E. Sacks, D. Khautin
B. Goldstein	
Flight B: V. Whalen	S. Weng, R. Weng
B. Ryder	
Flight C: B. Sartorius	H. Holtzclaw, G. Clarke
L. Keaveny	

Masters Teams. For the MARCUS CUP. A two-session Team event restricted to players of Senior Master rank and higher, scored by Board-a-Match until 1972, when scoring was changed to international match points with Swiss pairing.

WINNERS	RUNNERS-UP
1946 E. Murdoch. C. Croden	Mrs. L. Goldstein
J. Shore, H. Harkavy	G. Schildmiller
	M. Basher
	L. A. Bernard
1947 Mr. and Mrs. H. Zacks	Mrs. E. Folline
C. Sanders, J. Cushing	Mrs. S. Landauer
	C. Shapiro, H. Gerst
	Dr. A. Salasky
1948 R. Nail, F. A. Bombeck	M. Levin, P. Bacher
M. Adams, E. Wood	Mr. and Mrs. L. Jaeger
	P. Leventritt
1949 H. S. Brown, I. Deuter	R. Sherman
S. Delott, J. F. Carlin	H. Sonnenblick
	Dr. W. Lipton
	W. M. Lichtenstein
	E. Kaplan
1950 Mr. and Mrs. H. Lackman	P. Godin, M. Blain
Mr. and Mrs. H. Feldstein	E. Beausoleil
Mrs. L. Goldstein	J. J. Perrault

WINNERS	RUNNERS-UP	WINNERS	RUNNERS-UP
1943 R. Tyson, A. J. Mills	H. Goldsmith	1962 J. Philippy, D. Horwitz	R. Roosen, J. Remey
	J. Weisman	1963 D. Krauss, R. Hamman	O. Jacoby, R. Wolff
1944 F. W. Hawke, L. Hamilton	Mrs. D. Schwartz	1964 I. Stakgold, L. Harmon	P. Pender
	J. D. Boyd		Mrs. J. Begin
1945 Mrs. P. Adams	Mrs. J. A. Donaldson	1965 R. Balanow, S. Honet	Dr. L. Fogelson
S. Freisinger	A. Fineman		R. Wolf
1946 L. C. Levy, N. Hyman	L. Blum, C. Lembeck	1966 B. Pauls, L. Oakey	S. Rebner, H. Flint
1947 R. Starr, R. S. Fox	M. Roth, O. Yablon	1967 J. Jacoby, Mrs. J. Simon	O. Jacoby, W. Rosen
1948 T. Fenwick, P. G. Hopkins	Dr. K. Uba, T. Tanabe	1968 H. Wolch, B. Pauls	Dr. J. Kraft, E. Theus
1949 E. R. Murray	J. Burns, P. Olsen	1969 J. Miller, N. Erickson	P. Leon, G. Hann
J. J. Scanlon		1970 D. Brooks, D. Phillips	S. Perutz, R. Wolff
1950 S. Babich, L. Hardy	Mrs. W. Simpson	1971 H. Perlman, F. Hamilton	N. Schwartz, K. Woolsey
	Mrs. S. R. Richardson		
1951 Mr. and Mrs. C. Neuman	Mr. and Mrs.		
	J. Adler, Jr.		
1952 J. J. Klink	L. A. Richman		
R. Schreitmueller	S. Polasky		
1953 J. Chasson, L. Weil	C. Weathered		
	Mrs. G. Weathered		
1954 T. D. O'Keefe	G. Caragian		
R. W. Trares	O. E. Whiteside		
1955 D. J. McDonald, I. Rooks	R. B. McAdam		
	R. M. Sherrill		
1956 R. Hecht, M. Scheinberg			
tied with			
N. Appel, S. Cohen			
1957 S. Berg, S. Polsky	D. Langreth, E. Berg		
1958 Mr. and Mrs. C. Walker	A. Weisbord, L. Klein		
1959 Mrs. G. Bass, T. Leverenz	Mr. and Mrs. A.		
	Hertzberg		
1960 Lt. F. Murphy, E. Hayes	S. Aaronson		
	W. G. Conrad		
1961 Lt. Col. and	M. Veeraburus		
Mrs. A. Hurow	J. Gray		
1962 B. Pauls, D. Thompson	R. Kitchel, L. Heifetz		
1963 G. H. Dobbs, E. Spain	M. Smolen		
	J. Thompson, *tied with*		
	G. Bassman, A. Fonyo		
1964 Mr. and Mrs. G. Robertson	G. R. Darrow		
	C. M. Burnett		
1965 G. Chait, F. Slate	P. Gama-lobo, B. Pike		
1966 G. Afendoulis	B. Ashley, C. Adler		
J. Theodore			
1967 K. Beckett, H. A. Sutton	T. Pivko, E. Kallos		
1968 W. S. Grey, L. Cadwell	R. Joseph, P. Levee		
1969 M. Schwartz, R. J. Wiley	D. Wilczynski		
	M. Nash		
1970 L. Chui, P. Chye	S. Zucker, R. Stone		
1971 D. White, R. Hupf	L. Rabideau, D. Taylor		
1972 P. Michael, S. Michael	R. Berger, A. Peterson		
1973 J. Farmer, S. Bloom	R. Hume, B. Brown		
1974 B. Hoffman, B. Logan	J. Petree, R. Fidler		

Beynon Pairs. A two-session pair event for the George W. BEYNON TROPHY, restricted to non-qualifiers of the Senior and Advanced Senior Masters Pair championship. The BEYNON TROPHY was first awarded in 1966, although the non-Life Master eliminees had competed as a separate flight since 1964.

WINNERS	RUNNERS-UP
1964 Mr. and Mrs. H. Bloom	W. Robinson, K. Oddy
1965 Mr. and Mrs. A. Fonyo	M. Cammarath
	R. Fitzwater
1966 Mrs. L. Volker, A. Efnor	R. H. Lea, G. E. Kirk
1967 Dr. and Mrs. A. Rosen	Mr. and Mrs. S. Salvin
1968 Dr. J. Wotiz, D. Smith	D. M. Burke
	J. D. Barber
1969 Mr. and Mrs. N. H. Wills	J. Shanberg
	P. S. Levin
1970 L. Lau, J. Klayman	C. Allen
	R. Houtrow
1971 A. Guschwan, O. Mullenbach	R. Brody, G. Brody

Leventritt Pairs. A two-session pair event for the Peter LEVENTRITT TROPHY, restricted to non-qualifiers of the Life Masters Pair championship.

WINNERS	RUNNERS-UP
1950 Mrs. J. H. McCarthy	M. Catlin, J. Fourness
Mrs. W. H. Lehman	
1951 S. Landauer, E. Folline	W. H. Holderness
	W. B. Woodson
1952 S. Fink, H. Feinberg	M. Cytron
	N. Silverstein
1953 Mr. and Mrs. J. Skinner	Mrs. S. Lee, M. Moss
1954 F. Berger, S. Lazard	Mrs. L. C. Robinson
	B. Kaufman
1955 J. Millerd, J. Millerd	Mrs. M. Thompson
	J. Ditto
1956 Mrs. S. Neuwirth	S. Fairchild, J. Low
M. Gross	
1957 O. Jacoby, J. Jacoby	F. Bellinger
	R. Freedman
1958 W. Rosen, P. Szecsi	Mr. and Mrs.
	T. Teague
1959 J. Rosenblum, J. Glick	Mrs. D. Howard
	Mrs. R. Charles
1960 Mrs. D. B. Hawes	Dr. W. Lipton
M. Wagar	J. Friedlander
1961 Mrs. J. Robinson, D. Cox	C. Burger, M. Lipin

Charity Pairs. For the MID-ATLANTIC CUP. A one-session Charity Pair event.

WINNERS	RUNNERS-UP
1951 Mrs. W. H. McKaig	M. Roberts
Mrs. C. W. Kenney	C. C. Lovenberg
1952 R. T. Haas, R. Reynolds	E. Rosen, R. Simitz
1953 M. Michaels, V. Zeve	C. Neuman
	S. Heinrick
1954 G. Willett, G. B. Stone	Mr. and Mrs. G. May
1955 D. Drury, Dr. E. E. Jones	Mrs. W. Albersheim
	J. Foreacre
1956 G. R. Nail, F. A. Bombeck	Mr. and Mrs. C. J. Solomon
1957 Mrs. J. Ellis, C. A. Salzman	S. Lazard, W. Hanna
1958 S. Lazard, W. Hanna	I. J. Horwitz
	B. Siegel
1960 M. Cocherell, R. Bratcher	W. Hughes, M. Patton,
	tied with R. Shepherd
	H. R. Hall
1961 L. Kelner, R. Freedman	Gen. A. M. Gruenther
	C. Solomon
1962 L. Gurvich, J. Frankel	R. von der Porten
	M. Miles
1963 Mrs. F. Aydelotte	D. Crossley
Mrs. H. W. Devine	W. Crossley
1964 P. L. Ross, R. E. Lewis	K. R. Barbour
	Mrs. M. Rosenthal
1965 D. Hocevar, P. Leon	O. Jacoby, R. Wolff
1966 R. Sharp, A. Steinberg	J. Jacoby
	Mrs. S. Perutz
1967 J. Landeryou, D. Brander	H. Sachs, P. Swanson
1968 R. Rubin, C. Coon,	
tied with	
J. P. Ivaska, Jr.	
K. Woolsey	
1969 J. Cahill, M. J. Cooling,	
tied with	
P. Hunt, P. Patenade	

	WINNERS	RUNNERS-UP
1970	F. Egger	S. Goldstein
	Dr. N. Williams	J. Fajgelzon, *tied with*
		R. Wigdor, F. Forbes
1971	B. Rappaport, G. Moss	Mrs. G. Breick
		Mrs. L. Singer
1972	M. Walker, W. Walker	D. Drebes, E. Hagerman,
		tied with M. Brumley,
		Z. Tolentino
1973	G. Sydnor, J. Armstrong	Mrs. R. Eisenman
		M. Meridith
1974	J. Apfelbaum, L. Galvin	R. Rhoads, A. Katz

Swiss Teams. For the Col. Russell J. BALDWIN TROPHY. A four-session team event, scored by international match points, with two qualifying sessions and two final sessions.

	WINNERS	RUNNERS-UP
1971	J. Weinstein, D. Cohler	
	J. Premo, W. Snyder,	
	tied with C. Stegeman	
	D. Nicklasson, J. Leary	
	K. Hanson, *tied with*	
	J. Albright, P. Becker, B. Moyers,	
	W. Hale, *tied with*	
	L. Finkel, J. Morse	
	R. Becker, M. Thompson	
1972	D. Mraz, J. Mohan	S. Evans, B. Tucker
	J. Grantham, M. Shuman	B. Bell, J. Hall
	N. Anderson	M. McCoy, R. Gold
1973	J. Landau, P. Clark	B. Newman, K. Newman
	J. Ruben, J. Walters	S. Burger, P. Doran
	A. Reiver, J. Loiselle	B. Ciaffone
1974	Flight A: J. Adlersberg	J. Machotka, F. Arst
	E. Nevins	D. Temkin, R. Rich,
	F. Singer	*tied with* P. Tobias
	B. Parker	A. Stauberg, M. Bluestein
		R. Katraganda, S. Bandes
	Flight B: P. Leon	S. Garbose, D. Nelson
	S. Smolen	R. Goddard, F. Baril,
	E. Levitt	*tied with* J. Mitchell
	D. Treadwell	G. Moss, M. J. Farell
		D. Truscott

Swiss Teams Second Flight. A two-session team event scored by international match points, restricted to non-qualifiers from the four-session secondary Swiss Team event.

	WINNERS	RUNNERS-UP
1971	R. Stone, A. Cokin	J. Anderson, L. Tsou
	C. Yost, W. Dechert	R. DuFour, K. Gorfkle
1972	S. Hudgens, J. Toy	W. Ragland, H. Oliver
	D. Gerstman, P. Mollemet	R. Gerould, B. Cobb,
		tied with J. Raushenbush
		R. Humphreys
		Mrs. J. Milowski
		Mrs. E. Frey, *tied with*
		V. Brink, Mrs. A. Cain
		V. Gilbert, E. Brockman
1973	A. Hussein, J. Stone	P. Ossip, R. Gold
	B. Brier, S. Cox	J. Horowitz, L. Bausher,
		tied with W. Vinson
		Mrs. R. Macy
		Mrs. R. Henry, C. Heine
		tied with R. Pearson
		A. Jackson, J. Taylor
		M. Hutchinson

Open Pairs. A two-session Pair event.

	WINNERS	RUNNERS-UP
1971	Mr. and Mrs. B. Nelson	A. Graves, K. Gorfkle
1972	C. Vernay, P. Womack	G. Sullivan, T. Hause
1973	F. Schuld, D. Schuld	D. Berkowitz, B. Sartorius
1974	J. Schermer, B. Bramley	K. Evans, L. Bart

Non-Masters Pairs. A two-session event restricted to players below the rank of Senior Master.

	WINNERS	RUNNERS-UP
1971	W. Leonard, B. Leonard	P. Tavins, H. Holtzman
1972	B. Boje, R. Burton	B. Enestein, J. Gonsiewski,
		tied with J. Brackle
		P. Patrick
1973	Dr. A. Steinberg	
	P. Bloch, *tied with*	
	D. Leibowicz	
	C. Clayton	
1974	M. Markovitz, B. Bloom	F. Weisser, P. Purdy

Olympiad Pairs. A one-session Pair event, the proceeds of which are used to send ACBL teams to World Olympiads.

	WINNERS	RUNNERS-UP
1971	A. Van Hoose, B. Yomtov	I. Bremler, E. Bloom
1972	C. Greenhut, B. Staats	L. Harris, R. Howard
1973	R. Gladfelter, R. Sheline	Mrs. V. Block, J. Robertson
1974	P. Rander, W. Cook	G. Schanzer, A. Dworetzky

Individual. A two-session Open event, awarded the William H. KEOHANE TROPHY since 1973.

	WINNERS	RUNNERS-UP
1971	P. Hawkins	G. Dye
1972	G. Oehm	T. Turk, *tied with*
		Mrs. W. Miller
1973	R. Hume	J. Harrison
1974	R. Orne	P. Hollander

OTHER SECONDARY EVENTS

(All two-session events unless indicated otherwise)

1971		
Master Mixed Teams Second Flight:		B. J. Becker, D. Hayden
		A. Truscott, E. Hawes
		Dr. J. Fisher
		Dr. L. Melander
		A. Melander
		D. Marcus
		E. Marcus
President's Pairs Second Flight (one-session):		S. Katz, N. Paulos
		P. Flatowicz, J. Traudt,
		tied with P. Cipriani
		E. Tierney
Special Pairs:		R. Shair, J. Shair
		R. McNeil, H. Wing
1972		
Spingold Consolation Teams:		K. Lebensold, B. Miller
		S. Goldstein, N. Humer
		D. Joyce, J. Stein
		D. Mordecai
		J. Bitman
		R. Lesko
		Col. W. Christian

Non-Master Swiss Teams:	S. Allen, S. Strauss	Men's Pairs:	B. O'Neill, T. Hollcroft
	A. Petronella, K. Boudreau		R. Potter, J. Potter
	R. Burton	Women's Pairs:	M. Dyer, N. Holland
	R. Anderson		C. Sanders
	S. Anderson		B. Kennedy
	B. Boje, *tied with*	Novice Pairs:	D. Long, D. Becker
	M. Metz, M. Metz		G. Livingston
	J. Dodson, B. Bosley,		D. Livingston
	tied with D. Wright	Special Pairs:	W. Hollingsworth
	M. Holtz, F. Collins		J. Gargrave
	M. Happer, *tied with*		W. Gorden
	Mrs. J. Trefzger		R. Woodman
	G. Trefzger	Special Pairs:	R. Andersen
	S. Michael		S. Andersen
	P. Michael		R. Zeckhauser
Men's Pairs:	J. Mohan, S. Beard		M. Klein
	C. Weed, J. Titus		
Women's Pairs:	B. Kennedy	1974	
	Mrs. T. Sanders	Open Pairs:	J. Hilton, J. Scibelli
	A. Goldman		M. Smolen, E. Kokish
	E. Abrams, *tied with*	Men's Pairs:	B. Pollack, J. Linhart
	C. Greenhut		B. Bramley, L. Reich
	H. Baron	Women's Pairs:	F. Beard, M. Weed
Non-Master Men's Pairs:	B. Creech, G. Bennett		R. Haggerty
	K. Bach, D. Los		B. Sturm
Non-Master Women's Pairs:	Mrs. J. Reinhardt	Executive Pairs:	Dr. A. Sternberg
	Mrs. E. Colson		S. Aldenderfer, *tied with*
	Mrs. N. Sheneman		D. Gross, S. Root
	I. Dennis	VIP Pairs:	E. Gross
Special Pairs:	J. Brissman, J. Rieser		H. Schoenfrank
	T. Clarke, K. Schutze		A. Radin
Special Pairs:	L. Bausher		W. Herrmann
	Mrs. H. Adair	Special Pairs:	J. Isackson
	D. Bond, C. Bond		M. Hubbard
			D. Cummings, L. Cara
1973		Special Pairs:	J. Gardner, S. Haver
Open Pairs:	Dr. A. Feingold		Mrs. C. Seward
	M. Siegrist		J. Rudy
	M. Lair, H. Utegaard		

ACBL CONTINENTWIDE GAMES

	WINNERS	RUNNERS-UP
1962 (Summer)	Mr. and Mrs. J. Wallendorf	M. Phillips, W. Landis
1963 (Spring)	Mrs. E. Obie, Mrs. L. Mellett	M. Zealfar, S. Wynberg, *tied with*
		F. Pignato, Mrs. R. Ward
(Summer)	Mrs. E. Klein, Mrs. C. Ford	Dr. and Mrs. J. Tierney, *tied with*
		F. Jensen, Mrs. N. Taylor
(Fall)	W. Stauffer, W. Kpoacz	R. Nelson, R. Bretlow
1964 (Spring)	Mrs. F. Hull, Maj. L. Hine	R. Alonzo, B. Dozier
(Summer)	Mrs. A. Inklebarger, J. Boudreaux	H. Kaufmann, R. Rockhold
(Fall)	M. Rosenthal, K. Barbour	Mr. and Mrs. W. Passell
1965 (Spring)	R. Wall, B. Bratcher	G. Rathwick, J. Jester
(Summer)	C. Orr, Mrs. C. Scholer	W. Vanderporten, B. Strauss
(Fall)	Mrs. M. Cunningham, Mrs. K. Cowing	Mrs. M. Kintz, Mrs. W. French
1966 (Spring)	C. Duchene, P. Marson	Mrs. C. Kantrow, Mrs. A. Villavaso
(Summer)	Mr. and Mrs. T. Sanders	Mrs. A. Cates, M. Cohen
(Fall)	Mr. and Mrs. J. Meyer	C. Gilmore, D. Scrivens
1967 (Winter)	Mr. and Mrs. S. Cohen	G. Soucy, J. Currie
(Spring)	Dr. L. Grant, Mrs. L. McConnell	Dr. N. Ostrich, J. Elsbury
(Summer)	Mr. and Mrs. S. Fishburne	E. Paulsen, M. Edwards
(Fall)	A. Romm, D. Caro	Mrs. J. Peyton, W. Metzler
1968 (Winter)	Dr. J. Sheridan, Mrs. E. Dwyer	Dr. R. Weissman, Mrs. G. Kennedy
(Spring)	J. Kozlove, C. Bensinger	D. Myers, Mrs. S. Ondeck, *tied with*
		B. Anderson, D. McGee
(Summer)	P. Buechler, L. Lang	D. Swig, T. Smith
(Fall)	W. Odierna, J. Locks	B. and K. Bambrick
1969 (Winter)	J. Panepinto, J. Singmaster	D. and S. Sachs
(Spring)	M. Londry, S. Loyst	T. Reece, E. Sparks
(Summer)	L. St. Jean, T. Riely	C. and J. Banzhaf
(Fall)	D. and B. Lowe	M. Smith, J. Marshall
1970 (Winter)	Mrs. M. St. John, Mrs. A. Graham	Mr. and Mrs. L. Keefe
(Spring)	G. Polonsky, L. Hansen	B. and A. Economidy
(Summer)	H. Rosenkranz, G. Wiswell	Dr. M. Alexander, S. Russak
(Fall)	L. Kessler, R. Mayfield	Mr. and Mrs. H. Feldstein

WINNERS		RUNNERS-UP
1971	(Winter) Ś. Zabaglo, J. Imholte	Mr. and Mrs. S. Sutton
	(Spring) Mr. and Mrs. N. Moore	J. Angel, H. Harrison
	(Summer) G. Afendoulis, J. Theodore	B. Fraser, S. Timmerman
	(Fall) H. Kandler, B. Stutzer	B. Lomholt, M. Engel
1972	(Winter) E. Murray, S. Kehela	R. Lee, L. Waldman
	(Spring) E. Butler, G. Scott	D. Scheinman, M. Wheatley
	(Summer) J. DeCostas, D. Caballero	H. Smith, E. McCarkle
	(Fall) D. MacNeil, T. Boutilier	C. Hudecek, R. Sheline
1973	(Winter) J. Wood, M. Roberts	S. Touchtidis, R. Howard
	(Spring) H. Jagasia, S. Gupta	Mrs. J. Blaney, R. Powell, *tied with* P. Lange, W. Frost
	(Summer) C. Nelson, D. Sakoski	G. Espy, L. Weaver, *tied with* Mr. and Mrs. W. Dillingham
	(Fall) J. Kivel, R. Taube	M. Slaven, A. Karim
1974	(Winter) R. Wagner, M. Gore	K. Bley, S. Volk
	(Spring) M. Shipton, C. Burge	E. Mersky, S. Nobles
	(Summer) C. and W. Sturm	J. Reach, E. Smith
	(Fall) M. Conn, A. Wolf	R. and I. Benedicto
1975	(Winter) K. Benson, A. O'Grady	R. Agosti, D. Paddleford

INTERCOLLEGIATE CHAMPIONSHIPS

1940   Radcliffe
1941   Harvard
1942   Princeton
1946   Cornell
1947   University of California (first time on a national basis)
      Charles W. Drake, Philip J. Smith
1948   Capital University, Columbus, Ohio
      Charles Krueger, Luther Schleisser, Jr.
1949   Wayne University, Detroit
      Dorsey Brooks, Clifford Bishop
1950   Massachusetts Institute of Technology
      Martin Cornish, Jr., Richard Lesser
1951   Washburn University, Topeka, Kansas
      Gerald Michaud, Bradley Post
1952   Rice Institute, Houston, Texas
      John Harris, Richard Sutton
1953   Purdue University (N-S)
      Frank McClure, Carey Yelton, Jr.
      Princeton University (E-W)
      David Bradley, Harlow Lewis
1954   Purdue University (N-S)
      Carey Yelton, Jr., Herman Rose
      Dartmouth (E-W)
      Robert Sokolsky, Harry Connaro
1955   Whitman College (N-S)
      William Click, Robert Luther
      University of Texas (E-W)
      Charles Callery, Charles Miller
1956   Harvard (N-S)
      Boyd Everett, Jr., Franklin Bunn
      Dartmouth (E-W)
      Frank Barteaux, Jr., John Strong, Jr.
1957   Cornell (N-S)
      Paul Trent, Frank Goldring
      Oberlin (E-W)
      Danny Kleinman, Dick Recht
1958   University of Iowa (N-S)
      Terry Campbell, Peter Kemble
      Cornell (E-W)
      Robert Ewen, Jeffrey Rubens
1959   Columbia University (N-S)
      Sanford Reder, James Becker
      Princeton (E-W)
      John O'Neil, Willard Speakman
1960   Columbia University (N-S)
      Sanford Reder, James Becker
      North Carolina State College (E-W)
      Robert Smith, Richard Stanton
1961   Harvard (N-S)
      Richard Zeckhauser, Roman Weil
      Stanford (E-W)
      Roger Tippy, Mort Goerman
1962   University of Iowa (N-S)
      Robert Pugh, Larry Friedman
      Lake Forest (E-W)
      Richard Berger, James Bert

1963   Lake Forest (N-S)
      Richard Berger, James Bert
      University of Illinois (E-W)
      Robert Ewen, Darrell Penrod, *tied with* University of California at Berkeley
      Willard Nutting, Hugh Ross
1964   University of Texas (N-S)
      Dan Leightman, George Kirkwood
      University of Oregon (E-W)
      Dale Foster, Jeff Taylor
1965   *1st* Cornell University
      Thomas Smith, Emil Tobenfeld
      2nd University of Wisconsin
      Larry Cohen, Richard Katz
1966   *1st* University of Wisconsin
      Larry Cohen, Richard Katz
      2nd University of Minnesota
      Richard Dufour, Morrie Freier
1967   *1st* Rensselaer Polytechnic Institute
      Gerald Cohen, Tony Rosenstein
      2nd University of Colorado
      Michael Copeland, Robert Wherry
1968   *1st* University of Maryland
      Jeff Hand, John Richards II
      2nd University of Michigan
      Daniel Suty, Ronald Gerard, *tied with* Rensselaer Polytechnic Institute
      Frank Hacker, Gary Weldin
1969   *1st* Rice University
      Michael Finch, Delmas Parker
      2nd University of Utah
      Ron Rosenthal, Reed Coray
1970   *1st* University of Virginia
      Bruce Platt, E. Craig Kennedy, Jr.
      2nd University of Florida
      Patricia Sprague, Markland Jones
1971   *1st* Louisiana State University
      Dennis Conlon, Charles Crosby
      2nd University of North Carolina
      William Wisdom, Douglas Stewart
1972   *1st* SUNY at Stony Brook
      Sheo Khetan, Raghunath Khetan
      2nd University of Washington
      John Schermer, Neil Chambers
1973   *1st* Loyola University of Los Angeles
      Bill Schreiber, Mike Schreiber
      2nd University of Alabama
      Ann Hubmaier, Bob Dennard
1974   *1st* University of California at San Diego
      Douglas DePoister, Barry Rothstein
      2nd University of Pennsylvania
      Max Bazerman, Marc Nathan
1975   *1st* University of Missouri
      Thomas Allan, Lee Goodman
      2nd Yale University
      Jeff Juster, Andrew Markowitz

APPENDIX II

ACBL REGIONAL CHAMPIONSHIPS

Regional Tournaments are listed alphabetically in the Index below, showing the District in which the results of each tournament are reported.

INDEX TO REGIONALS

NAME OF TOURNAMENT	DISTRICT	PAST TOURNAMENT SITES
ALACBU	23	Los Angeles, Cal.
All-American	5	Cleveland, Akron, Toledo, O.; Detroit, Mich.
All-Western	21	San Francisco, Cal.
Beef State: *see* District 14	14	
Bermuda	7	Hamilton; Southampton
Big D: *see* Texas Spring, Texas Midwinter	16	Dallas, Tex.
Big D Bridge Week: *see* Texas Midwinter	16	
Big Sky: *see* District 18	18	
Bridge Week	23	Los Angeles, Cal.
Bridge Week	6	Washington, D.C.
British Columbia: *see* Pacific Northwest	19	
Buffalo: *see* Canadian Prairie	2	Winnipeg, Man.
Buffalo Centennial: *see* Canadian Prairie	2	Winnipeg, Man.
Calgary: *see* District 18	18	
California Capital: *see* Central California	21	Sacramento, Cal.
Cambrian Shield	2	Sault Ste. Marie, Sudbury, Ont.
Canadian	18	Edmonton, Calgary, Alta.; Regina, Sask.
Canadian-American (Can-Am)	1	Montreal, Quebec; Ottawa, Kingston, Ont.
Canadian-Atlantic (Can-At)	1	Fredericton, Moncton, N.B.; Halifax, N.S.
Canadian-National	2	Toronto, Ont.
Canadian Prairie	2	Winnipeg, Man.; Thunder Bay, Ont.
Canadian Prairie	14	Fargo, N.D.
Canadian Thanksgiving: *see* District 18	18	
Capital City	16	Austin, Tex.
Central California	21	Stockton, Sacramento
Central States	13	Chicago, Ill.
Champagne	8	Belleville, Springfield, DeKalb, Ill.; South Bend, Ind.
Charlotte: *see* Mid-Atlantic Fall	7	
Cheyenne Frontier: *see* District 17	17	
Crater Lake: *see* District 20	20	
Desert Empire	17	Phoenix, Tucson, Ariz.; Las Vegas, Nev.
Disneyland: *see* Southern California	22	
District 2: *see* Canadian Prairie	2	
District 4: *see* Keystone Fall	4	
District 5	5	Pittsburgh, Pa.
District 11	11	Cincinnati, Dayton, O.; Lexington, Ky.; Indianapolis, Clarksville, Ind.
District 14	14	Nebraska; South Dakota
District 15	15	Amarillo, Tex.; Wichita, Kans.
District 17	17	Las Vegas, Nev.; Cheyenne, Wyo.
District 18	18	Saskatoon, Regina, Sask.; Calgary, Alta.; Billings, Mont.; Boise, Ida.
District 20	20	Medford, Ore.; Redding, Cal.
District 22	22	Bakersfield, San Bernardino, Cal.
Eastern States	24	New York City
Fall Midwest: *see* Midwest Fall	11	
Fleur-De-Lys	1	Montreal, Quebec City, Que.
Florida	9	Clearwater, Jacksonville, Sarasota, Daytona Beach, St. Petersburg
Fun City	24	New York City

Gem State: *see* District 18	18	
Golden Gate	21	San Jose, Oakland, Sacramento, Santa Rosa, Cal.
Golden State	22	Fresno, Bakersfield, Monterey, Palm Springs, Cal.
Gopher	14	Minneapolis, St. Paul, Minn.
Great Lakes	12	Toledo, O.; Grand Rapids, Lansing, Port Huron, Mich.
Gulf Coast Mid South	10	Mobile, Ala.
Hawaii	20	Honolulu
Holiday	20	Reno, Stateline, Nev.; Portland, Ore.
Indy 500: *see* District 11	11	
Inland Empire	19	Yakima, Spokane, Wash.
Inland Empire: *see* District 22	22	San Bernardino, Cal.
Intermountain	18	Boise, Ida.; Salt Lake City, Utah; Billings, Mont.
International City: *see* Texas Summer	16	El Paso, Tex.
Iowa	14	Davenport, Des Moines, Sioux City, Cedar Rapids
Keystone	4	Atlantic City, N.J.
Keystone Fall	4	Lancaster, Philadelphia, Pa.; Wilmington, Del.
King Cotton: *see* Texas Spring	16	
Klondike: *see* Canadian	18	
Land of Coronado	15	Amarillo, Tex.
Las Vegas: *see* Desert Empire; District 17	17	
Little Bridge Week: *see* Los Angeles Winter	23	
Long Island	24	Westbury, Hempstead, N.Y.
Los Angeles Winter	23	Los Angeles, Cal.
Metropolitan: *see* Fun City	24	
Mexican Nationals	16	Mexico City
Mid-American-Canadian	14	Canada; Dakotas; Iowa; Nebraska
Mid-Atlantic Fall	6	Baltimore, Md.; North Carolina, Richmond, Va.; Washington, D.C.
Mid-Atlantic Fall	7	Charlotte, Winston-Salem, N.C.
Mid-Atlantic Independence Day	6	Baltimore, Md.; Virginia
Mid-Atlantic Spring	6	Norfolk, Virginia
Mid-Atlantic Spring	7	Gatlinburg, Tenn.; Durham, N.C.
Mid-Atlantic Summer	6	Baltimore, Md.; Norfolk, Roanoke, Richmond, Va.
Mid-Atlantic Winter	7	Charleston, Myrtle Beach, Greenville, S.C.
Mid-South Fall	10	Arkansas; Louisiana; Mississippi; Alabama; Western Tennessee
Mid-South Spring	10	Arkansas; Louisiana; Mississippi; Alabama; Western Tennessee
Mid-South Summer	10	Arkansas; Louisiana; Mississippi; Alabama; Western Tennessee
Midwest Fall	11	Columbus, O.; Louisville, Lexington, Ky.
Midwest Spring	11	Indianapolis, Ind.; Louisville, Ky.; Columbus, Cincinnati, O.
Mid-Winter	16	Houston, Tex.
Midwinter: *see* Holiday	20	
Midwinter Holiday: *see* Holiday	20	
Mississippi Valley	8	St. Louis, Mo.
Missouri Valley	15	Kansas City, Mo.; Tulsa, Oklahoma City, Okla.; Wichita, Kan.
Motor City	12	Detroit, Mich.
Mount Shasta: *see* District 20	20	
Music City 1973: *see* Mid-South Fall	10	Nashville, Tenn.
Navajo Trail	17	Las Vegas, Nev.; Albuquerque, N.M.
Nebraska 1973: *see* District 14	14	
New England	25	Hartford, Norwich, Conn.; Boston, Hyannis, Chicopee, Mass.; Bretton Woods, N.H.
New England Fall	25	Boston, Hyannis, Mass.; Portland, Me.
New England Individual	25	Boston, Mass.
New England Knockout	25	Hartford, Norwich, Conn.; Boston, Hyannis, Chicopee, Mass.; Bretton Woods, N.H.

New England Masters	25	Hartford, Norwich, Conn.; Boston, Hyannis, Chicopee, Mass.; Bretton Woods, N.H.
New York-New Jersey	3	McAfee, Asbury Park, N.J.; Grossinger, Swan Lake, South Fallsburg, N.Y.
New York Winter	24	New York City
Northwest: *see* Pacific Northwest	19	
Northwest Rocky Mountain: *see* Intermountain	18	
Orange County: *see* Southern Calif.	22	
Oregon Trail	20	Eugene, Portland, Ore.
Pacific Northwest	19	British Columbia; Washington
Pacific Southwest	22	San Diego, Coronado, Cal.
Palm Springs: *see* Southern California	22	
Peach Festival: *see* Pacific Northwest	19	
Pheasant 1970: *see* District 14	14	
Pikes Peak: *see* Rocky Mountain	17	
Polar	19	Anchorage, Alaska
Puerto Rico	9	San Juan
Puget Sound	19	Seattle, Wash.
Republic of Texas	16	Fort Worth
Rocky Mountain	17	Denver, Colorado Springs, Colo.
Rogue River Valley: *see* District 20	20	Medford, Ore.
Silver Anniversary 1974: *see* District 14	14	
Southeastern	9	Miami Beach, Fla.
Southern California	22	Anaheim, Palm Springs
Southern Conference	10	Tennessee; Alabama; Georgia
South Saskatchewan: *see* District 18	18	
South Texas: *see* Texas Fall	16	
Texas Fall	16	San Antonio, Corpus Christi
Texas Mid-Winter	16	Houston, Dallas
Texas Spring	16	Lubbock, Dallas
Texas Summer	16	El Paso, Austin, Fort Worth
Thanksgiving	7	Atlanta, Ga.
Tri-State	3	Grossinger, N.Y.
Tri-Unit	13	Chicago, Ill.; Milwaukee, Madison, Green Bay, Wisc.
Upper New York State	3	Albany
Upper New York State	4	Syracuse, Rochester
Upper New York State	5	Buffalo
Western States	11	Columbus, Cleveland, Cincinnati, O.; Pittsburgh, Pa.; St. Louis, Mo.; Detroit, Mich.; Indianapolis, Ind.
Winter; *see* New York Winter	24	
Yakima Valley: *see* Inland Empire	19	

DISTRICT 1 (Quebec, eastern Ontario, Nova Scotia, New Brunswick, Newfoundland, Prince Edward Island)

CANADIAN-AMERICAN

KNOCKOUT TEAMS

1972   R. Fleischman, K. Allison, S. Forbes, J. Laskin, R. Wigdor

1973   D. Clark, N. Sugarman, J. Springer, J. Shinehoft, D. Bryce

1974   M. Bright, M. Cummings, R. Cohen, R. Kehoe, N. Humer, L. Reich

OPEN TEAMS

1951   Mrs. D. Prevost, C. Mignault, Mr. A. LeClaire, Mrs. R. Carrière

1952   C. A. Geffrion, A. Goodman, E. J. Marsh, S. Gold, R. Cohen

1953   J. Friedlander, M. DeLeeuw, E. Katz, Mrs. R. W. Gordon

1954   H. Foering, Jr., A. Goodman, R. Cohen, S. Gold, *tied with* Mrs. E. R. Complin, G. B. Hebert, D. Andress, Mrs. E. G. Maloney

1955	M. F. Braunstein, R. Ludwig
	P. Zweifel, R. E. Brown
1956	Mrs. J. Begin, P. Schwartz
	B. Marsh, D. Fisfsky
1957	Mrs. J. Begin, M. Paul
	R. Cohen, P. Schwartz
1958	C. S. Hirschey, W. Truesdale Clarke
	J. R. Barrington, M. Raikes
1959	D. DaCosta, Dr. G. Sereny
	M. Miller, C. Boland
1960	M. Roncarelli, W. Solomon
	J. Ross, H. Ross
1961	Dr. E. Jones, D. Cowan
	D. Saltsman, F. Hoffer
1962	N. Gerstman, A. Lando
	B. Crissey, I. Goodman
1963	Mrs. A. Gordon, E. Murray
	B. Elliott, P. Sheardown
	S. Kehela
1964	C. Coon, M. Altman
	F. Hoffer, R. Jotcham
1965	Mrs. J. Begin, D. J. Silver
	B. Droyon, H. Maldaver
1966	S. Gold, A. Goodman
	P. Nagy, Mr. and Mrs. E. Thumin
1967	A. Doane, B. Croswell
	S. Blum, R. Jotcham, *tied with*
	H. Parent, J. Findley
	S. Gold, A. Goodman
1968	J. Laskin, T. R. Gree
	C. A. Lindsay, J. B. Johnston
	A. N. Stevens
1969	F. Hoffer, J. Silver
	M. Altman, S. Aarons
	R. Jotcham
1970	J. Solodar, M. Blumenthal
	R. Lipsitz, A. Waldman
1971	D. Bryce, Dr. D. Snikeris
	S. Chernin, Mrs. R. Stephens
1972	J. Norton, C. Lindsay
	J. Lloyd, J. Stevens
1973	H. Cukoff, E. Kokish
	J. Silver, G. Mittleman
1974	G. Ardern, D. Clark
	S. Lezwoff, B. Baran

MASTERS PAIRS

1968	Mrs. H. Kugler, L. Berman
1969	S. Gold, P. Nagy
1970	M. Blumenthal, J. Solodar
1971	E. Levitt, D. Treadwell
1972	F. Lerner, D. Lindop
1973	I. McKinnon, H. Currie
1974	R. Jotcham, G. Jotcham

OPEN PAIRS

1951	E. Beausoleil, G. L'Espérance
1952	Mrs. J. Begin, B. Cohen
1953	Mrs. W. Merriman, H. Foering, Jr.
1954	E. Hamel, P. Charette
1955	J. Fetsko, J. Asber
1956	Mr. and Mrs. T. Stone
1957	Mrs. J. Begin, P. Schwartz
1858	D. Thurber, F. Palen
1959	Mrs. R. Carrière, Mrs. D. Prevost
1960	F. Thurner, A. Derby
1961	F. Goldring, C. Coon
1962	E. R. Murray, A. Lando
1963	Mrs. J. Begin, D. Tait
1964	E. Viires, J. Raynault
1965	B. Elliott, P. Sheardown
1966	J. E. Cullinan, Jr., Mrs. R. H. McKaig
1967	C. Hirschey, B. Sanders
1968	M. Altman, F. Hoffer
1969	B. Provencher, B. Winges
1970	J. Silver, E. Kokish
1971	M. Feldman, M. Blumenthal
1972	Dr. G. Rao, J. Edwards
1973	L. Ruderman, J. Burtin
1974	D. DiFelice, S. Gangwal

MEN'S PAIRS

1951	C. A. Geoffrion, J. Raynault
1952	G. Klein, B. Marsh
1953	C. Hirschey, T. Clarke
1954	J. Wiser, G. L'Espérance
1955	F. G. Root, F. F. Janik
1956	S. Gold, A. Goodman
1957	R. Cohen, S. Gold
1958	N. Duchesne, R. Olivier
1959	L. Woodcock, B. Powley
1960	E. Murray, S. Kehela
1961	R. Olivier, H. Laliberte
1962	C. Olson, Dr. R. Forbes
1963	Dr. W. S. Hutchins, E. Stanton, Jr.
1964	C. Hirschey, B. Sanders
1965	J. Benoit, M. Cappelletti, *tied with*
	Dr. W. Hutchins, M. Melton
1966	M. Kuttis, E. Viires
1967	H. Parent, R. Binsky
1968	S. Baker, G. Dahan
1969	L. Rosenbaum, C. Saragea
1970	D. Clark, B. Winges, *tied with*
	M. Rosenbloom, F. Gauthier
1971	M. Blond, G. Benesh

WOMEN'S PAIRS

1951	O. V. Giddings, W. O. Lewis
1952	S. A. Maloney, J. Hazel
1953	W. H. McKaig, C. W. Kenney
1954	W. M. Anderson, J. G. Boeckh
1955	C. Mercer, H. Dutcher, *tied with*
	C. W. Kenney, W. H. McKaig
1956	A. Maheu, J. Hazel
1957	R. Fitts, F. Drummond
1958	E. Ackerman, F. Harding
1959	E. E. Taylor, R. Gordon
1960	V. E. Maurer, W. H. McKaig
1961	A. Gordon, E. R. Complin
1962	D. W. Spurlock, C. W. Fite
1963	A. Gordon, V. Maurer
1964	A. Gordon, V. Maurer
1965	Mrs. J. Begin, Mrs. I. Reingold
1966	Mrs. J. Begin, Mrs. I. Reingold
1967	K. Blakeney, C. MacDonald
1968	I. Reingold, Mrs. P. Bandler
1969	B. Siblin, E. Nagy
1970	Mrs. B. Saltsman, Mrs. E. Nagy
1971	Mrs. L. Arseneault, Mrs. L. DuFour

MIXED PAIRS

1951	Mrs. J. Begin, E. Marsh
1952	Mrs. R. Perrault, C. A. Geoffrion
1953	Mrs. N. J. Speickhoff, W. Joseph
1954	Mrs. E. R. Complin, Rev. L. A. Tobin
1955	Mrs. J. H. Smith, V. Dirvin
1956	Mrs. F. LeClaire, A. Derby
1957	Mrs. P. Brochu, P. E. Laguex
1958	Miss H. Harrow, N. M. Burns
1959	Mrs. R. Gordon, E. Murray
1960	Mr. and Mrs. R. Edney
1961	Mrs. A. Gordon, E. Murray
1962	Mrs. I. Reingold, D. DaCosta
1963	Mrs. J. R. Barrington, S. Gold
1964	Mrs. M. Roncarelli, W. Solomon
1965	P. Pender, Mrs. A. Gordon
1966	Mr. and Mrs. B. Stone
1967	R. Milgram, I. Burke
1968	J. Cohen, Mrs. A. Cohen
1969	Mrs. R. Foland, J. Robinson
1970	Mrs. J. Hall, F. Sontag
1971	Mr. and Mrs. M. Paul

CANADIAN-ATLANTIC

KNOCKOUT TEAMS

1968	F. Westcott, C. Coon
	R. Bambrick, D. Stothart
	H. Francis, S. Tench

1969 C. Hirschey, E. O'Reilly
       S. Tench, H. Francis
       W. Spiewak
1970 H. Francis, E. O'Reilly
       S. Tench, P. Heitner, A. Lifschitz
1971 A. Doane, D. Oulton
       G. Caldwell, G. Hatfield
1972 N. Ferguson, Mr. and Mrs. T. Clark
       Mr. and Mrs. D. Gamble
1973 P. Heitner, A. Heitner
       W. Spiewak, D. Beer, M. Tom
1974 K. Cox, T. Kasday
       E. Spear, J. Giard
       R. Bojar, B. Lewis

OPEN TEAMS

1968 R. Bambrick, C. Coon
       D. Stothart, F. Westcott, *tied with*
       Mrs. M. Fraser, Mrs. D. MacDonald
       R. Smith, D. Davis
1969 P. Heitner, K. Lebensold
       D. Beer, W. Spiewak
1970 Mr. and Mrs. E. O'Reilly
       P. Heitner, A. Lifschitz
1971 E. Murray, A. Hobart
       B. Black, R. McKenzie
1972 Mr. and Mrs. P. LaVallee,
       F. Suzman, J. Malley
1973 A. Hobart, R. Brown
       S. Lewis, A. Doane
1974 K. Cox, T. Kasday
       E. Spear, J. Giard

MASTERS PAIRS

1971 H. Keffer, T. Lagan
1972 G. Effros, L. Bauscher

OPEN PAIRS

1968 C. Coon, F. Westcott
1969 G. Caldwell, G. Hatfield
1970 E. Keohane, F. Westcott
1971 Mr. and Mrs. E. Mills
1972 M. Granovetter, M. Tom
1973 M. Feldman, M. Bright
1974 G. Caldwell, W. Spiewak

MIXED PAIRS

1968 Mr. and Mrs. F. Smith
1969 E. Kays, R. Hambly
1970 W. Jamison, Mrs. W. Jamison
1971 G. Julien, Mrs. M. Bilodeau
1972 Mr. and Mrs. F. Eichman
1973 R. Mingo, I. Spencer, *tied with*
       Mr. and Mrs. A. May
1974 M. Bright, N. Humer

FLEUR-DE-LYS

KNOCKOUT TEAMS

1972 A. Laliberte, J. Patry
       J. Bernier, G. Bilodeau
1973 J. Silver, G. Mittleman
       E. Kokish, S. Kokish
       D. Gordon, C. Lamprey
1974 B. Winges, A. McDonald
       B. Provencher, P. Schmaltz

OPEN TEAMS

1972 A. Altay, D. Lindop
       J. Sabino, H. Abel
1973 B. Winger, B. Bowman
       A. McDonald, M. Delaney
1974 Dr. A. Feingold, G. Holland
       J. Bowman, B. Bowman

MASTERS PAIRS

1972 H. Banks, J. Appleton, Jr.

1973 R. Wigdor, M. Rosenbloom
1974 H. Creed, T. Margollan

OPEN PAIRS

1972 P. Hollander, R. Lebi
1973 A. McDonald, J. Bowman
1974 B. Cohen, D. Stothart

DISTRICT 2 (Manitoba, central and western Ontario)

CAMBRIAN SHIELD

KNOCKOUT TEAMS

1972 G. Hann, C. Said
       P. Leon, F. Hamilton
1973 Dr. A. Feingold, M. Caley
       J. Bowman, T. Edwards-Davies
1974 P. Leon, D. Hocevar
       C. Bishop, R. Huggard
       F. Will, J. Buchheister

OPEN TEAMS

1972 E. Murray, S. Forbes
       F. Hamilton, C. Said
1973 S. Chevalier, F. Gautheir
       F. Asselin, J. Gosselin
1974 G. Polonsky, J. Arblaster
       B. Riordan, R. Huggard

MASTERS PAIRS

1972 R. Kruse, D. Nicklasson
1973 K. Allison, T. Greer
1974 J. Aceti, J. Ross

OPEN PAIRS

1972 J. D. King, M. Passell
1973 D. Lindop, A. Altay
1974 J. Peterson, J. Wier

CANADIAN NATIONAL

KNOCKOUT TEAMS

1968 F. Vine, H. Bork
       J. O'Dowd, M. J. Martino
1969 W. Eisenberg, R. Goldman
       M. Lawrence, R. Hamman
       J. Jacoby, R. Wolff
1971 D.Cowan, F. Bandoni, C. Bishop
       D. Hocevar, P. Leon, G. Hann
1972 E. Murray, S. Kehela, D. Phillips
       G. Charney, W. Crissey, B. Gowdy
1973 G. Mittleman, E. Kokish, S. Kokish
       D. Gordon, D. Lindop, A. Altay
1974 J. Starr, B. Newman, F. Hamilton
       S. Landen, F. Bell

MASTERS TEAMS

1968 L. Takefman, R. Milgram
       F. E. Dyson, S. Bramson
1969 J. R. Stevens, Mrs. F. A. Isaacs
       C. A. Lindsay, J. M. Norton, *tied with*
       R. Fleischman, R. Lipsitz
       D. Faskow, B. Chazen
       M. Blumenthal

MASTERS PAIRS

1967 F. T. Will, R. Levick
1969 L. Popper, N. D. Humer
1970 R. Wilton, R. Chapman
1971 E. Horning, P. Sheardown
1972 B. Weinstock, R. Rogalski
1973 J. Starr, F. Hamilton
1974 W. Lebovic, F. Bandoni

OPEN TEAMS

1951	C. B. Elliott, R. Funston
	B. Gowdy, P. Sheardown
1952	P. E. Sheardown, B. Gowdy
	C. B. Elliott, R. Funston
1953	P. Sheardown, C. B. Elliott
	R. Funston, B. Gowdy
1954	Mrs. M. E. Maloney, D. Andress
	Mrs. F. R. Complin, C. O. Hebert
1955	Mr. and Mrs. W. Anderson
	M. M. Miller, J. C. Boland
1956	P. E. Sheardown, C. B. Elliott
	D. Drury, E. R. Murray
1957	Mrs. R. Gordon, E. Katz
	R. Freedman, J. Friedlander
1958	D. E. Phillips, M. T. King
	D. Hart, J. O'Dowd, L. Woodcock
1959	E. Murray, C. B. Elliott
	G. Charney, S. Kehela
1960	O. Boyd, H. Parent
	F. Hoffer, M. Altman
1961	E. Murray, P. Sheardown
	S. Kehela, D. DaCosta
	C. B. Elliott
1962	D. Cowan, Dr. E. Jones
	B. Mathers, R. Gray
1963	Mrs. J. Begin, Mrs. M. Roncarelli
	M. Paul, B. Solomon
1964	J. Honigman, C. Burger
	D. Brooks, G. Marsee
1965	E. Murray, S. Kehela
	P. Sheardown, B. Elliott
1966	J. Howell, Dr. R. Forbes
	R. Gray, M. M. Miller
1967	E. Murray, S. Kehela
	P. Sheardown, B. Elliott
1970	J. Silver, E. Kokish
	J. Meerof, R. Binsky
	G. Mittleman
1971	Dr. A. Feingold, B. Lagowski
	G. Noszka, F. Bandoni
1972	Mr. and Mrs. W. Van Court
	V. Ragazzo, S. Haver, *tied with*
	C. Elliott, M. Cummings
	J. Laskin, S. Forbes
1973	B. Winges, R. Bartlett
	C. Clark, L. Takefman
	R. Chow, *tied with*
	Dr. A. Feingold, B. Lagowski
	D. Fraser, S. Schamroth, *tied with*
	J. Carruthers, J. Cunningham
	A. Lalonde, L. Vine
1974	F. Rubbra, R. Walsh
	L. Reich, B. Kehoe

OPEN PAIRS

1952	B. Cohen, E. Marsh
1953	J. Swenholt, T. Clarke
1954	Miss H. B. Harrow, Miss H. V. Roberts
1955	C. B. Elliott, P. Sheardown
1956	A. Ross, J. W. McDonald
1957	E. R. Murray, D. Drury
1958	E. R. Murray, C. B. Elliott
1959	M. Altman, F. Hoffer
1960	B. Stone, H. Maldaver
1961	P. Trent, H. Creed
1962	E. R. Murray, C. B. Elliott
1963	G. Cooke, H. Stephenson
1964	C. G. Jeans, E. C. Bissell
1965	H. Bethe, T. Smith
1966	H. Hoffer, M. Altman
1967	Mrs. L. P. Bott, Jr., C. H. Urban
1968	J. Cayne, C. Burger
1969	B. Elliott, P. Sheardown
1970	Mr. and Mrs. R. Edney
1971	N. Unger, R. Selikoff
1972	J. Guoba, A. Greenspan
1973	M. Tom, H. Cukoff
1974	J. Merrill, W. Woodard

MEN'S PAIRS

1959	J. B. Robinson, L. Woodcock
1960	C. B. Elliott, B. Gowdy
1961	R. J. Hart, A. W. James
1962	P. Sheardown, B. Dwyer
1963	A. Landy, E. R. Murray
1964	L. Cheney, W. Lande
1965	M. M. Wallace, W. A. Allison
1966	R. Lipsitz, R. K. Fleischman
1967	W. Pollack, H. Allen
1968	M. J. Martino, F. Vine
1969	H. Creed, A. Goodman
1970	E. Murray, D. Phillips
1971	B. Pollack, M. Martino
1972	S. McCallum, H. Jacobs
1973	R. Pugh, W. Conkie
1974	S. Aarons, A. Kisin

WOMEN'S PAIRS

1959	J. R. Barrington, K. Buckman
1960	H. Toffee, C. McGill
1961	S. Reynolds, J. G. Boeckh
1962	A. Gordon, J. Begin
1963	P. Simmons, I. Hall
1964	D. Schick, L. Davidson
1965	Mrs. A. N. MacTavish, Mrs. W. E. Weber
1966	A. Gordon, Mrs. R. K. Cunningham
1967	Mrs. C. Levin, Mrs. P. Bandles
1968	Mrs. R. Appleby, Mrs. M. Boyd-Bowman
1969	K. Alexander, S. Forbes
1970	B. Peterson, L. Brown
1971	I. Hodgson, L. Waldman
1972	Mrs. M. Wagner, Mrs. M. Morgan
1973	Mrs. F. Isaac, Mrs. R. Pearce
1974	S. Robinson, R. Frankel

MIXED PAIRS

1952	C. B. Elliott, M. Bell
1953	B. Gowdy, Mrs. R. X. Cunningham
1954	Mrs. J. A. Regan, N. M. Burns
1955	M. Raikes, Mrs. R. X. Cunningham
1956	B. Sheriff, Mrs. H. A. Russell
1957	A. Ross, Mrs. H. Johnston
1958	N. M. Burns, Miss H. B. Harrow
1959	S. Kehela, Mrs. C. Fisher
1960	H. Bork, R. Poder
1961	R. Freeman, Mrs. W. C. Robinson
1962	S. Kehela, Mrs. C. Fisher
1963	J. Ross, J. Begin
1964	B. Elliott, Mrs. A. Gordon
1965	Mrs. J. Begin, D. DaCosta
1966	Mrs. R. T. Broad, J. R. Stevens
1967	M. Bowden, H. Creed
1968	S. Forbes, F. E. Dyson
1970	Mrs. R. Brenan, C. Lindsay
1971	Mrs. J. Phillips, M. Martino
1972	Dr. and Mrs. S. Marinker
1973	D. DiFelice, M. Lerner

OPEN INDIVIDUAL

1955	R. Holliday
1957	M. Timanoff
1958	D. DaCosta

CANADIAN PRAIRIE

KNOCKOUT TEAMS

1972	D. Thomson, B. Pauls
	H. Wolch, R. Weikle
	L. Oakey
1973	G. Watkinson, H. Scollie
	B. Weiler, M. Weiler
1974	C. Goppert, G. Hayden
	G. Kasle, M. Passell
	M. Lair

OPEN TEAMS

1965	O. Leesment, K. van Renesse
	J. Murphy, Dr. F. Patterson
1967	J. Marsch, B. Pauls
	H. Wolch, D. Thomson
1968	C. M. Shefchik, J. Schoenecker
	R. De Harpporte, D. Egholm
1969	J. Hall, D. Horwitz
	J. Lee, E. Langer
1970	Mrs. L. Smithen, Mrs. E. Marquart
	G. Sekhar, B. Pippy, W. Dare
1971	A. DeGroot, N. Levi
	R. Seabrook, L. Carscadden
1973	A. DeGroot, W. McTavish
	L. Carscadden, D. Cannell
1974	Dr. D. Schmeiser, G. Sugarman
	T. Braun, A. d'Entremont, *tied with*
	J. Leary, J. Larsen
	J. Rhatigan, J. Hugstad

MASTERS PAIRS

1967	S. Kehela, W. Lebovic
1970	D. Kantor, H. McLean
1972	Mrs. H. Promislow, N. Promislow
1974	H. Siegelman, J. Brothers

OPEN PAIRS

1965	S. Brooks, G. Mitchell
1967	E. Dayboch, M. Freier
1968	E. Dayboch, M. Freier
1969	Mrs. M. Enstrom, Mrs. Y. Gauthier
1970	R. Andersen, A. Seltzer
1971	E. Mersky, L. Oakey
1972	R. Andersen, B. Coleman
1973	R. Weikle, R. Kruse
1974	J. Carruthers, A. Kisin

MEN'S PAIRS

1965	D. Thomson, L. Oakey
1967	R. Weikle, L. Oakey
1968	D. Thomson, J. Halper
1969	K. Sandiford, B. Wolk
1970	B. Pauls, L. Oakey
1971	G. Polonsky, L. Hansen
1972	R. Andersen, H. MacLean

WOMEN'S PAIRS

1965	Mrs. H. Smith, Mrs. P. Smolensky
1967	Mrs. W. Williams, M. Phillips
1968	E. Dayboch, J. Schoenecker
1969	Mrs. G. Gustafson, Mrs. C. Nicholson, *tied with*
	Mrs. M. Landa, Mrs. T. Sornsin
1970	E. Mersky, J. Shoenecker
1971	Mrs. W. Acheson, Mrs. M. Cullum
1972	M. Shaffer, I. Udow

MIXED PAIRS

1967	R. Smithen, J. Chasanoff

DISTRICT 3 (Northern and central New Jersey, eastern New York State)

NEW YORK-NEW JERSEY CONFERENCE

OPEN TEAMS

1958	J. Gallaher, V. Mitchell
	M. Rubinow, D. Strasberg
1959	N. Kay, T. Stone
	J. R. Crawford, S. Silodor
1960	T. Michaels, I. Cohen
	P. Rotzell, R. Sitnek
1961	S. Stayman, P. Feldesman
	Mr. and Mrs. V. Mitchell
	D. Strasberg

1962	Dr. and Mrs. S. Warner
	J. Solodar, R. Reisig
1963	Mrs. S. Johnson, Lt. Col. W. Christian
	R. Sitnek, P. Pender
1964	R. Sitnek, B. Raymond
	Lt. Col. W. Christian, S. Johnson
1965	Lt. Col. M. Schnee, Dr. K. Apfel
	V. Shen, A. Rich
1966	R. Budd, M. Ginsberg
	L. Sokolower, H. Stappenbeck
1967	H. Smith, M. Carson
	W. Landow, R. Alexander
1968	J. Solodar, P. Weichsel
	C. Coon, M. Rosenblatt
1969	Mr. and Mrs. M. Cappelletti
	S. Parker, D. Parker
1970	P. Heitner, H. Bethe
	T. Griffin, K. Allison
1971	P. Levin, L. Ribner
	M. Becker, M. Blumenthal
	S. Leibowitz
1972	Mrs. M. Mignocchi, M. Mignocchi
	J. Becker, E. Becker
1973	H. Lilie, B. Sartorius
	D. Berkowitz, M. Gurwitz
1974	B. Bramley, L. Reich
	S. Labins, C. Lamprey

OPEN PAIRS

1958	E. Lowenthal, D. Bird, *tied with*
	Mr. and Mrs. C. A. Schofield
1959	M. Lees, R. Racier
1960	J. Siegelman, M. Ginsberg
1961	P. Feldesman, D. Strasberg
1962	Dr. and Mrs. B. Bronstein
1963	B. Raymond, F. Dossenbach
1964	C. Coon, M. Rosenblatt
1965	F. Dossenbach, J. Wendt
1966	M. Carson, W. Landow
1967	D. Mason, T. Griffin
1968	L. Cohen, A. Jacoby
1969	D. Sachs, S. Sachs
1970	P. Heitner, H. Stappenbeck
1971	H. Lewis, T. Dionisi
1972	J. Stuart, G. Neiger
1973	R. Gerard, P. Cowan
1974	W. Gough, P. Brady

MEN'S PAIRS

1958	E. Kaplan, M. Rubinow
1959	C. Friedman, J. Silverman
1960	E. Bitz, W. Bitz
1961	J. Westheimer, M. Ginsberg
1962	D. Zeckhauser, P. Spiegelman
1963	A. Malasky, G. Prosnitz
1964	D. Mason, W. Passell
1965	Dr. N. Buch, Dr. M. Halper
1966	L. Fattel, Dr. A. Spiegel
1967	A. Norton, B. Nathanson
1968	L. Levy, D. Mason
1969	L. Popper, C. Davis
1970	A. Weinstein, F. Stewart
1971	M. Moss, H. Bethe
1972	R. Didowski, J. Wayne
1973	B. Chazen, H. Feldheim
1974	A. Roth, A. Hussein

WOMEN'S PAIRS

1958	O. Neustadt, P. Lee
1959	C. Brail, M. Harris
1960	P. Rotzell, M. Gordon
1961	E. Rosenbloom, D. Voorhees
1962	R. Cohen, K. Kolsby
1963	M. Bloch, H. Smith
1964	L. Brown, J. Klein
1965	A. Kotzen, B. Kauffman
1966	Mrs. D. Brechner, M. Kaplan
1967	A. Kotzen, B. Kauffman
1968	C. Cohen, E. Schwartz

1969 B. Tepper, B. Rappaport
1970 M. Kelly, J. Carroll
1971 G. Moss, J. Solodar
1972 Mrs. M. Sweet, Mrs. B. Alperin
1973 D. Hughes, M. Mannes
1974 M. Passell, D. Truscott

MIXED PAIRS

1958 Mrs. J. James, B. Hirschberg
1959 J. Stone, A. Gabrilovitch
1960 L. Allen, Dr. S. Warner
1961 Mrs. J. Silverman, C. Friedman
1962 A. Sheaber, D. Mason
1963 Mrs. M. Charles, E. Bernstein
1964 B. Rappaport, A. Roth
1965 B. Rappaport, A. Roth
1966 N. Cook, B. Longton
1967 W. Ecker, Dr. E. Theimer
1968 J. Solodar, E. Alfandre
1969 C. Coon, I. Alcone
1970 P. Nixon, B. Miller
1971 M. Epstein, R. Epstein
1972 H. Lilie, J. Furman
1973 H. Lilie, J. Solodar
1974 A. Romm, R. Nilsen

INDIVIDUAL

1958 J. Siegelman

TRI-STATE

OPEN TEAMS

1967 J. Barnicle, M. Mohr
      F. Burstein, R. Ryder
      R. Celler
1968 B. J. Becker, D. Hayden
      H. Fein, R. Schwartz
      A. Truscott
1969 R. Abelson, C. Winters
      S. Dow, Jr., M. Edwards
1970 M. Schnee, T. Hirsch
      S. Seidman, J. Becker
      J. Bennett
1971 A. Roth, A. Sontag
      B. Rappaport, B. Chazen
1972 S. Altman, E. Neiger
      A. Sontag, J. Stuart
      P. Weichsel, T. Smith
1973 S. Pashkin, T. Trifon
      F. Melman, R. Wahl
1974 C. Friedman, N. Nathanson
      K. Parker, J. Parker, *tied with*
      S. Altman, T. Smith
      S. Labins, C. Lamprey

MASTERS PAIRS

1972 A. Cantor, R. Bowers
1973 M. Granovetter, M. Blumenthal
1974 B. Cohen, B. Kehoe

OPEN PAIRS

1967 N. Gerstman, J. Slater
1968 W. Herrmann, H. Smith
1969 J. S. Goldberg, I. Boris
1970 W. Kornfield, R. Khautin
1971 N. Weichsel, P. Weichsel
1972 D. Hayden, A. Truscott
1973 N. Humer, B. Miller
1974 A. Roth, B. Rappaport

MEN'S PAIRS

1967 N. Gerstman, H. A. Gerstman
1968 M. A. Berger, E. Andreasian
1969 J. Becker, S. de Satnick
1970 J. D. King, M. Berger
1971 H. Fein, D. Strasberg
1972 B. J. Becker, A. Truscott

1973 H. Lilie, G. Hampar
1974 N. Humer, B. Miller

WOMEN'S PAIRS

1967 A. Davis, H. Strasberg
1968 Mrs. R. Goldberg, M. Fingerle
1969 S. Spero, S. Palmer
1970 Mrs. W. Wolfe, Mrs. P. J. Mahrer
1971 V. Habicht, S. Petty
1972 J. Schwartz, P. Rutkin
1973 R. Epstein, B. Rappaport
1974 E. Sudikoff, S. LeSavoy

MIXED PAIRS

1967 R. G. Hewitt, A. Bronstein
1968 Mr. and Mrs. G. Brown
1969 Mr. and Mrs. L. Strauss
1970 V. Penick, M. Cohen
1971 V. Habicht, R. Becker

UPPER NEW YORK STATE
(*See also* Districts 4 and 5)

KNOCKOUT TEAMS

1974 J. Merrill, P. Boyd
      C. Martel, S. Sion
      R. Grabel, J. Rosenbloom

OPEN TEAMS

1970 R. Freedman, J. Mathis
      B. Miller, M. Feldman
1974 R. Woodard, G. Cohen
      M. Bergen, R. Harvey

MEN'S TEAMS

1974 P. Clark, G. Lublin
      J. Conway, P. DePorte

WOMEN'S TEAMS

1974 J. Karlen, J. Noll
      M. Merriman, J. Flack

MASTERS PAIRS

1970 Mrs. W. Merriman, E. Hatch
1974 S. Paskin, M. Storfer

OPEN PAIRS

1970 W. Woodard, M. Bergen
1974 R. Miller, J. Saxe

MEN'S PAIRS

1970 R. Walford, G. Ainslie
1974 P. Boyd, J. Merrill

WOMEN'S PAIRS

1970 E. Scatassa, J. Portale
1974 R. MacLeod, P. Mann

MIXED PAIRS

1970 E. Garfield, C. Davis

DISTRICT 4

KEYSTONE CONFERENCE

KNOCKOUT TEAMS

1973 D. Treadwell, E. Levitt
      R. Raskin, C. Jeans
      H. Smith, K. Cohen

OPEN TEAMS

1952   E. Jaye, A. Shmukler
     N. Kay, E. Kaplan
1953   H. Knopf, F. Bellinger
     S. O'Hagen, R. Rovner
1954   R. Sherman, E. Kaplan
     J. Moran, R. Kahn
     R. Hirschberg, *tied with*
     D. Bayless, R. Wayne
     M. J. Root, M. Feldman
1955   Mr. and Mrs. J. Adler
     Mrs. E. Behrend, L. Rosenfeld, *tied with*
     Mrs. A. Shmukler, S. Becker
     J. McGervey, E. Jaye
1956   D. Wolfson, C. Braman
     W. C. Hall, Mrs. H. M. Steiger, *tied with*
     D. Murray, A. Roth
     Mr. and Mrs. S. Haddad
1957   N. Kay, E. Kaplan
     R. Hirschberg, A. Sheinwold
1958   R. Alexander, C. Coon
     D. Strasberg, E. Murray
     H. Creed
1959   T. Michaels, I. Cohen
     W. Christian, F. Hoadley
1960   P. Rotzell, R. Sitnek
     A. Robinson, P. Pender
     L. Harmon
1961   Mr. and Mrs. S. Haddad
     P. Rotzell, S. Aronson
1962   E. Kaplan, E. Sheinwold
     N. Kay, R. Jordan
     A. Gabrilovitch
1963   S. Johnson, O. Jacoby
     P. Trent, Lt. Col. W. Christian
1964   W. Flannery, H. Sachs
     D. Faskow, P. T. Swanson
1965   H. Lewis, M. Blumenthal
     H. Smith, J. Asber
     T. Dionisi
1966   Mr. and Mrs. M. Cappelletti
     L. Popper, J. Benoit
1967   A. Bernstein, S. Tomchin
     E. Manfield, B. Chazen
     T. Smith
1968   W. Landow, M. Carson
     J. Cayne, B. Tepper, *tied with*
     R. Ryder, F. Burstein
     R. Celler, M. Mohr
1969   A. Sontag, K. Garber
     J. Bookstaver, R. Abelson, *tied with*
     Mr. and Mrs. M. Cappelletti
     S. Parker, B. Parker
1970   B. Gough, R. Raskin
     J. Locks, L. Silberman
1971   Mr. and Mrs. J. Adler
     Mr. and Mrs. D. Sachs
1972   Mr. and Mrs. J. Adler
     Mr. and Mrs. D. Sachs
1973   Mr. and Mrs. J. Adler
     Mr. and Mrs. S. Sachs
1974   Mr. and Mrs. J. Adler
     Mr. and Mrs. D. Sachs

MEN'S TEAMS

1971   M. Blumenthal, L. Pietri
     J. Cohen, A. Coren
1972   M. Blumenthal, J. Cohen
     L. Pietri, E. Shapiro
1974   J. Killaly, R. McGiboney
     F. Corredine, A. Anderson

WOMEN'S TEAMS

1971   A. Kotzen, G. Rubens
     N. Gruver, B. Adler, *tied with*
     I. Slabey, E. Silver
     A. Gittleman, M. Gaynor
1972   J. Kay, H. Smith
     E. Levitt, R. Blumenthal, *tied with*
     B. Adler, G. Rubens, J. Solodar, G. Rabinowitz

1974   L. Perlstein, J. Tucker
     M. Kelly, J. Carrol, *tied with*
     L. Rothman, B. Weeks
     M. Knox, S. Wigner

MASTERS PAIRS

1968   E. O'Neill, L. Roth
1969   M. Blumenthal, S. Leibowitz
1970   H. Bethe, R. Fleischman
1971   J. Morse, S. Robinson
1972   M. Bergen, R. Oshlag
1973   C. Gray, M. Garner
1974   M. Blumenthal, S. Leibowitz

OPEN PAIRS

1952   J. R. Crawford, S. Silodor
1953   P. Lisse, J. Mylott
1954   R. Rosenberg, F. Bickel
1955   M. A. Tergis, C. Bowie
1956   C. Bishop, B. Williams
1957   P. Rotzell, R. Sitnek
1958   R. Jordan, A. Gabrilovitch
1959   Mrs. A. Shmukler, Mrs. J. Kaplan
1960   D. Treadwell, M. Paulshook
1961   Mr. and Mrs. J. Adler
1962   R. Rosenberg, F. Bickel
1963   Dr. W. H. Rogers, E. Gardner
1964   D. Darling, T. Ekel
1965   B. Kauffman, A. Kotzen
1966   S. Parker, J. Hand
1967   E. O'Neill, D. Kaufman
1968   Mr. and Mrs. R. Lattomus
1969   K. Rhodes, H. Itkin
1970   S. Parker, Mrs. S. Parker
1971   V. Chernoff, J. Bennett
1972   S. Parker, S. Robinson
1973   P. Boyd, B. Pettis
1974   J. Locks, F. Klat

MEN'S PAIRS

1952   R. Rosenberg, F. Bickel
1953   R. Rosenberg, F. Bickel
1954   R. Rosenberg, A. E. Goodman
1955   W. O. Warren, H. E. Potts
1956   A. Ritter, J. C. Donaldson
1957   R. Freeman, I. Cohen
1958   D. Warner, F. O'Keefe
1959   J. Grinsfelder, J. Fish
1960   E. Gerard, L. Lipstein
1961   H. Confer, B. L. Graham
1962   O. Jacoby, C. Coon
1963   J. Rintels, A. Fribourg
1964   W. Flannery, H. Sachs
1965   D. Warner, A. Cohen
1966   S. Becker, R. Becker
1967   W. Butcher, J. Bennett
1968   M. Blumenthal, S. Leibowitz
1969   C. Friedman, D. Kaufman
1970   M. Garner, L. Kesselman
1971   J. Lipman, F. Balas
1972   J. Becker, W. Esberg
1973   M. Bergen, B. Woodard
1974   J. Looby, B. Ryder

WOMEN'S PAIRS

1952   W. W. Sketchley, L. M. Baker
1953   H. R. Hathorn, B. Katzen
1954   M. E. Tiernan, C. Tiernan
1955   R. Goldberg, S. Scheiner
1956   J. R. Younkin, R. Metzler
1957   T. Sabott, E. Rosenbloom
1958   J. Q. Gaynor, E. Mitchell
1959   R. Feldman, R. Jandorf
1960   L. Brown, L. Amade
1961   L. C. Robinson, E. Berkovits
1962   R. Erde, I. Silbertstein
1963   O. Peterson, P. Rotzell
1964   J. Kolsby, M. Rosen
1965   F. Felman, H. Weiner
1966   Mrs. J. A. Gruver, Mrs. D. Sachs
1967   A. Kotzen, B. Kauffman

1968	A. Cantor, D. Brechner
1969	Mrs. J. Weinrott, Mrs. J. Segal
1970	Mrs. E. Wilson, Mrs. W. Lewis
1971	Mrs. M. Byrne, Mrs. J. Embury
1972	G. Moss, S. Roark
1973	T. Michaels, N. Gruver
1974	E. Lefkowitz, S. Hyman

MIXED PAIRS

1952	H. Nolan, J. C. Dougherty
1953	Mr. and Mrs. E. Schwartz
1954	Mr. and Mrs. A. Goodman
1955	R. Goldberg, J. Chodak
1956	Mr. and Mrs. C. Solomon
1957	Mrs. I. Brall, R. Hirschberg
1958	Mr. and Mrs. G. Weiner
1959	Mrs. A. Blasband, S. Lowery
1960	Mrs. M. J. Root, C. Dewey
1961	V. Lavery, L. Sokolower
1962	L. Levy, A. Sporing
1963	Mr. and Mrs. S. Haddad
1964	Mrs. M. Altman, D. Pavlista
1965	N. Kay, P. Rotzell
1966	Mrs. H. L. Cromer, J. L. Coppie
1967	P. Weichsel, G. Collier

KEYSTONE FALL

KNOCKOUT TEAMS

1974	S. Leibowitz, M. Blumenthal
	W. Passell, A. Gabrilovitch

OPEN TEAMS

1961	E. C. Worden, D. Pattison
	R. Schreyer, J. Siverts, *tied with*
	Mr. and Mrs. L. Feirman
	Dr. and Mrs. T. Ginsburg
1962	P. Rotzell, L. B. Harmon
	D. Mason, S. Seidman
1963	P. Flynn, J. Polchinski
	C. Bennett, J. E. Bennett
1964	N. Kay, E. Kaplan
	R. Jordan, A. Robinson
1965	N. Kay, E. Kaplan
	R. Jordan, A. Robinson
1966	P. Pender, J. Flint
	H. Lewis, A. Dionisi
1967	C. L. Antrobus, T. D. Vinson
	Mrs. G. C. Braham, W. R. Williams
1968	E. Lazarus, D. Sachs
	P. Feldesman, J. Solodar
1969	M. Blumenthal, W. Landow
	Mr. and Mrs. D. Sachs
1970	M. Silver, M. Rabinowitz
	S. Raffel, G. Cohen
1971	R. Lipsitz, P. Parker
	S. Parker, M. Rosenblatt
1973	N. Rosen, B. Goldstein
	E. Economidis, T. Robinson (Spring)
	F. Hamilton, M. Rosenblatt
	D. Faskow, H. Sachs (Fall)
1974	R. Blau, C. McGinley
	W. Gough, W. May

MEN'S TEAMS

1970	S. Becker, R. Becker, J. Resnick,
	E. Davidson, *tied with*
	D. Treadwell, S. Robinson
	E. Lazarus, B. Lewis, *tied with*
	M. Blumenthal, P. Swanson
	D. Faskow, A. Gabrilovitch
1971	S. Leibowitz, L. Pietri
	M. Blumenthal, A. Gabrilovitch

1973	S. Leibowitz, M. Blumenthal
	L. Pietri, A. Gabrilovitch

WOMEN'S TEAMS

1970	P. Miller, F. Egger
	Mrs. R. Wade, Mrs. A. Lytle
1971	Mrs. L. Van Antwerp, Mrs. H. West
	Mrs. B. Molovinsky, E. Auch
1973	P. Lapides, A. Kotzen, B. Adler, G. Rubens

MASTERS PAIRS

1966	Mrs. R. B. Rogasner, E. Pierson
1967	M. Garner, C. Gray
1968	D. Oken, R. J. Oken
1969	Mrs. J. Livezey, Jr., J. Livezey III
1970	J. Morse, S. Robinson
1971	S. Robinson, J. Morse
1973	R. Andersen, M. Epstein (Spring)
	F. King, J. Kivel (Fall)
1974	J. Levy, R. Gerard

OPEN PAIRS

1961	W. Eisenberg, M. Ginsberg
1962	S. Silodor, N. Kay
1963	R. Jordan, A. Robinson, *tied with*
	M. Carson, W. Landow
1964	N. Kay, E. Kaplan
1965	A. Robinson, R. Jordan
1966	Mrs. K. Fillingham, W. Gough
1967	J. Eatherly, M. Aronson
1968	M. West, J. P. Schiff
1969	Mrs. P. C. Miller, G. Robbins
1970	Dr. R. Saylor, Dr. S. Lebengood
1971	M. Granovetter, M. Tom
1973	R. Alexander, H. Cohen, *tied with*
	R. Andersen, S. Andersen (Spring)
	J. Kivel, F. King (Fall)
1974	C. Lamprey, A. Kearse

MEN'S PAIRS

1961	A. R. Milio, E. Van Cott
1962	D. Warner, A. Cohen
1963	O. Jacoby, C. Henke
1964	A. Grant, I. Nelson
1965	L. Klein, M. Nagel
1966	P. Pender, J. Flint
1967	W. Flannery, H. Sachs
1968	R. Wegman, R. Spritzer
1969	R. Peterson, D. Per-Lee
1970	P. Brady, F. Brown
1971	M. Blumenthal, A. Gabrilovitch
1973	A. Rich, G. Graham (Spring)
	E. Junkur, F. Gillespie (Fall)
1974	H. Chandross, B. Yellis

WOMEN'S PAIRS

1961	L. C. Robinson, E. Berkovitz
1962	E. Levitt, M. H. Welch
1963	R. Bronne, M. Chernoff
1964	D. Byrne, M. Forker
1965	Mrs. D. S. Sachs, Mrs. J. A. Gruver
1966	Mrs. W. W. Vosburgh, Mrs. C. Felton
1967	A. Kotzen, Mrs. G. H. Rubens
1968	Mrs. D. Solomon, Mrs. L. J. Muskin
1969	E. M. Dumas, Mrs. W. F. Sheldon
1970	R. Sachs, S. Parr
1971	M. Tamres, G. Moore
1973	A. Kotzen, G. Rubens (Spring)
	J. Tiderman, J. Vineyard (Fall)
1974	A. Lane, R. Tabor

MIXED PAIRS

1963	A. Alexander, B. Kauffman
1964	N. Kay, P. Rotzel
1965	Mrs. D. A. Mott, E. W. Douglas

UPPER NEW YORK STATE
(*See also* Districts 3 and 5)

OPEN TEAMS

1969   Mrs. R. McKaig, J. Cullinan, Jr.
      J. Landon, J. Edwards
1972   B. Bowman, B. Curry,
      A. McDonald, J. Bowman
1973   S. Sun, J. Rosenbloom
      D. Ross, S. Maitra, *tied with*
      J. Zimmerman, D. McGarry
      H. Akturk, P. Leon

MEN'S TEAMS

1972   H. Resnick, H. Penner.
      R. Stone, R. Ekeblad
1973   L. Bart, J. Merrill
      J. Rosenbloom, R. Bartlett

WOMEN'S TEAMS

1972   J. Morse, S. Neilson
      H. Utegaard, S. Linkovsky,
      tied with A. O'Brien, Mrs. W. Merriman
      Mrs. H. Penner, J. Noll
1973   Mrs. W. Harper, Mrs. R. Binning
      Mrs. D. Myer, Mrs. M. Ruta

MASTERS PAIRS

1969   D. Andrews, G. Chapman
1972   E. Kokish, M. Blumenthal
1973   J. Zimmerman, D. McGarry

OPEN PAIRS

1969   P. Heitner, B. Chazen
1972   R. Freedman, J. Mathis
1973   E. Hatch, F. Neuberger

MEN'S PAIRS

1969   F. Root, M. Morris
1972   H. Resnick, D. Gerstman
1973   T. Clarke, J. Cullinan

WOMEN'S PAIRS

1969   Mrs. F. Lisowski, Mrs. M. Instance
1972   J. Morse, H. Utegaard
1973   Mrs. A. Goldman, Mrs. B. Lawrence

MIXED PAIRS

1969   Mrs. B. Ku, Dr. D. Sun

DISTRICT 5   (Western Pennsylvania, northeastern Ohio, northern West Virginia, western Maryland, western New York)

ALL-AMERICAN

KNOCKOUT TEAMS

1974   S. Smith, W. Rosen, J. Starr
      H. Perlman, F. Hamilton

OPEN TEAMS

1938   A. Glatt, A. Weiss
      R. Kempner, W. Jacobs
1939   A. Glatt, A. Weiss
      R. Kempner, W. Jacobs

1940   Dr. H. Bernstein, J. Carlin
      S. Delott, A. Stracke
      N. Kent
1941   F. R. Buck, L. J. Welch
      J. E. Cain, E. T. Wood
1942   R. W. Lee, L. J. Welch
      J. E. Cain, E. T. Wood
1943   S. Heinrick, D. B. Clarren
      W. Zeigler, G. E. Neil
1944   A. Weiss, R. W. Halpin
      J. C. Bank, D. Clarren
      M. D. Adams
1945   F. R. Buck, L. J. Welch
      E. T. Wood, J. Van Brooks
1946   M. O'Brien, J. J. Kaplan
      L. Goren, R. M. Carter
1948   Mrs. B. Agruss, J. Krause
      C. Bishop, A. R. Revell
1952   Mrs. H. J. White, H. Creed
      Mrs. H. E. Hathorn, J. Mylett
1953   C. Goren, A. S. Goldsmith
      O. S. Emrich, S. Fink
1954   F. Rappleyea, E. Hyere
      R. Healy, L. Garner
1955   C. Bishop, J. Denny
      R. Roosen, E. Samuel
1956   Mrs. and Mrs. T. Stone
      V. Mitchell, R. E. Mnuchin
1957   L. Rosenthal, G. Turner
      E. Hochfeld, F. Rappleyea
1958   A. C. Bell, J. Biddle
      R. G. Sharp, E. Thumin
1959   J. and V. Remey
      W. Mouser, A. J. Silber
1960   P. H. Sheardown, D. Phillips
      R. E. Dwyer, D. Cowan
      Dr. E. Johns
1961   R. Paulson, Dr. R. Rovner
      F. Bollinger, A. Bell
1962   S. Stein, H. Shanbrom
      J. Young, J. Dillon
1963   I. Deuter, E. J. Smith, Jr.
      O. Jacoby, P. Levitt
1964   G. Marsee, W. Reister
      R. Zoller, F. H. Sexton
1965   Dr. B. Breakey, J. Gittleman
      H. Shanbrom, A. Shanbrom
1966   J. Flint, P. Pender
      Mrs. H. S. Smith, E. J. Smith, Jr.
1967   Mr. and Mrs. J. Denny
      R. Vichill, S. Stacey
1968   J. Alexander, Mr. and Mrs. M. Low
      R. Morris, T. Hodapp, *tied with*
      M. J. Cohn, L. J. Cohen
      D. Brooks, B. Werbe
      W. Panzer
1969   E. J. De Witt, H. D. Keirns
      R. M. Sacks, M. Trikilis
1970   M. Kane, Dr. G. Chappell
      H. Kohn, F. Root
1971   A. McGilvrey, N. Phelps
      M. Irwin, F. Egger
1972   H. Mouser, M. Neher, Mr. and Mrs. R. Koopman
1973   J. Zimmerman, B. Hardies
      J. Remey, V. Remey
1974   F. Hamilton, J. Starr
      F. Bell, S. Landen

MASTERS PAIRS

1974   F. Hamilton, J. Starr

OPEN PAIRS

1938   A. Glatt, A. Weiss
1939   W. Jacobs, R. Kempner
1940   A. Glatt, M. Kirshbaum
1941   Dr. and Mrs. E. J. Hunt
1942   L. C. Quigley, W. L. Stickney, Jr.
1944   Mr. and Mrs. G. P. Ryan
1945   Mr. and Mrs. D. C. Carter

1946	Mrs. H. Mason Smith, Mrs. C. Wallace
1947	Dr. R. Staff, E. O'Bryan
1948	H. Feinberg, E. Wood
1949	C. S. Hoblit, H. Beyer
1952	R. Ittenbach, S. Kasle
1953	Mrs. H. M. Foulke, Mrs. J. T. Tobin
1954	R. Arnold, M. H. Freier
1955	M. Jacobs, Dr. W. Greenburg
1956	D. C. Carter, J. G. Ripstra
1957	B. Creed, W. H. Howe
1958	B. Creed, W. H. Howe
1959	D. Rotman, E. Rosen
1960	C. Mitchell, H. R. Biddle
1961	B. Sharp, G. Polak
1962	Mr. and Mrs. H. Goetz
1963	M. Arndt, Dr. L. W. Melander
1964	E. I. Schwartz, A. Landy
1965	Mrs. F. White, Mrs. F. Morrison
1966	B. Ceifetz, H. Shevitz
1967	G. Noszka, Dr. N. S. Williams
1968	M. Arndt, B. Hardies
1969	S. M. Cohn, J. Hohenstein
1970	L. Louk, R. Weston
1971	A. Fahrer, M. Low
1972	L. Kozlove, J. Sheridan
1973	J. Sheridan, L. Kozlove
1974	J. Starr, F. Hamilton

MEN'S PAIRS

1946	C. S. Hoblit, J. Carlin
1947	I. Deuter, J. G. Ripstra
1948	H. Byer, C. S. Hoblit
1949	C. S. Hoblit, J. Carlin
1952	A. L. Greenspun, Dr. M. Isvitin
1953	J. Cohan, O. S. Emrich
1954	D. Carter, S. Lazard
1955	J. Bishop, E. J. Smith, Jr. *tied with*
	I. A. Klar, M. Jacobs
1956	T. Stoner, A. Cohn
1957	W. Jones, J. L. Johnson
1958	C. Braman, R. H. Partenfelder
1959	I. Deuter, C. P. Weil
1960	R. Jordan, E. Simons
1961	T. Bladen, Dr. L. W. Melander
1962	Cpl. D. M. Thomas, C. Klayer
1963	J. Hartford, G. Shaffer
1964	W. Reister, G. Marsee
1965	V. Remey, A. J. Silber
1966	E. Berman, D. Kelston
1967	M. Arndt, S. Friedlander
1968	G. Lamproplos, S. Friedlander
1969	P. T. Swanson, H. Sachs
1970	J. Wisemiller, G. Potts
1971	J. Adams, D. Barbaris
1972	E. Thumim, D. McGarry
1973	F. Hamilton, C. Said
1974	J. Sheridan, L. Kozlove

WOMEN'S PAIRS

1939	H. M. Smith, J. Lefler
1940	L. G. Quigley, F. Meyer
1941	L. Mackie, B. Fritz
1942	A. MacMillan, B. A. Meixner
1944	P. Steinberg, H. Lees
1945	P. Steinberg, H. Lees
1946	M. McKinley, A. Briggs
1948	C. G. Taylor, H. B. May
1952	E. Engelman, M. C. Monett
1953	E. J. Jungerford, M. Scalabrino
1954	E. A. Styne, G. Majek
1955	Mrs. S. Kaplan, S. Rollins
1956	V. R. Schick, R. C. Dabney
1957	J. Halloran, W. A. Shideler
1958	P. Cohn, J. Remey
1959	S. Stein, C. Ross
1960	S. Stein, M. Ver Linden
1961	H. Carney, J. Ruther
1962	J. Halloran, R. K. Jones
1963	E. Argersinger, A. Gordon

1964	Mrs. P. Miller, Mrs. N. Soldinger
1965	J. Collier, B. R. van Kainen
1966	H. Hendee, L. Porter
1967	Mrs. J. Denny, Mrs. J. Russell
1968	C. Chaney, Z. Allen
1969	Mrs. J. Rosenthal, Mrs. L. Schlessinger
1970	Mrs. J. Wade, Mrs. A. Lyle
1971	E. Welsby, Mrs. R. Kline
1972	Mrs. E. Marquard, Mrs. H. Peters, *tied with*
	A. Kelly, M. Taylor
1973	C. Schoenberger, M. Ballon
1974	J. Remey, B. Riordan

MIXED PAIRS

1938	O. Reilly, J. Kravatz
1939	J. J. Jacobs, K. R. Gallagher
1940	F. Meyer, G. Neeves
1941	F. Nelson, L. B. Weiner
1942	R. B. Johnstone, M. Rothman
1943	Mr. S. W. O. Bennett, Dr. S. Manheimer
1944	E. Johnstone, D. Clarren
1945	J. D. Cook, M. Fleig
1946	L. Albright, P. X. Marsh
1948	Mrs. H. J. White, W. M. Fulton
1952	A. Baum, E. Baum
1953	H. Creed, Mrs. H. E. Hathorn
1954	R. V. Kaimann, L. J. Berg
1955	L. Harvie, G. Marsee
1956	J. Gutman, R. G. Sharp
1957	J. Rodkin, C. Petersen
1958	B. Way, E. Rosen, *tied with*
	Mr. and Mrs. R. G. Sharp
1959	V. and J. Remey
1960	M. Hammerstein, F. Morganroth
1961	D. Cowan, Mrs. S. Reynolds
1962	C. Berger, J. Honigman
1963	D. M. Thomas, Mrs. W. C. Miller
1964	Mr. and Mrs. E. I. Schwartz
1965	C. Bishop, A. Gordon
1966	A. Argersinger, A. Price
1967	Mrs. M. D. Allison, W. C. Smith, *tied with*
	D. Schick, W. F. Fees, Jr.
1968	J. Friedenberg, P. Leon
1969	J. Denny, J. Denny
1970	Mrs. D. West, J. Shelnutt
1971	P. Miller, D. McGarry
1972	Mr. and Mrs. J. Richling
1973	Mrs. R. Brubaker, M. Melamed

MASTERS INDIVIDUAL

1938	A. Weiss
1939	A. Weiss
1940	G. Neeves
1941	P. Leventritt
1942	R. P. Cunningham
1944	B. Fain
1945	G. Carlton
1946	C. Wallace

DISTRICT 5

KNOCKOUT TEAMS

1974	F. Cymerman, M. Bazerman
	M. Nathan, R. Ostifield

OPEN TEAMS

1958	Mr. and Mrs. H. Glick
	M. E. Tiernan, C. Tiernan
	H. Fuss
1960	Mr. and Mrs. R. G. Lesko
	E. Klawier, G. Closson
	J. P. McGervey
1961	S. Silodor, N. Kay
	R. Jordan, A. Robinson

1962 S. Silodor, N. Kay
      R. Jordan, A. Robinson
      O. Jacoby
1963 O. Jacoby, J. Lowenthal
      Mr. and Mrs. C. Solomon, *tied with*
      E. Simons, Z. Jabbour
      C. Hudeck, M. J. Cohn, *tied with*
      C. Bishop, M. J. Talbot
      Dr. J. L. Henry, A. A. Bishop
      J. M. Hinton, *tied with*
      P. E. Sheardown, J. B. Howell
      R. Robinson, M. Abrams
1964 E. Simmons, C. Burger
      M. Lipin, Z. Jabbour
1965 D. Hayden, B. J. Becker
      K. Petterson, I. Erdos
1966 M. Carson, W. Walvick
      T. Lyon, M. Garner
1967 Mr. and Mrs. E. Thumin
      R. Vichill, Dr. T. W. Babb
1968 Mr. and Mrs. V. Remey
      P. Leon, D. Hocevar
1969 S. Margulis, H. M. Perlman
      J. Friedenberg, S. C. Ruskin
1970 G. Mitchell, H. Creed
      G. Robbins, S. Scaffidi
1971 R. Zoller, H. Perlman
      F. Hamilton, H. Bethe
1972 J. Zimmerman, B. Hardies
      J. Remey, V. Remey
1973 L. Bart, K. Peyser
      J. Merrill, J. Gardner
1974 L. Kozlove, J. Sheridan
      F. Hamilton, J. Starr

MASTERS PAIRS

1961 H. Fishbein, R. G. Sharp
1962 O. Jacoby, J. Lowenthal
1963 K. Bhavnani, J. P. Burg
1964 R. Zoller, M. Moss
1965 J. Hovandec, J. Hohenstein
1966 A. Knaus, E. Moorehead
1967 G. Robbins, Mrs. M. L. Reich
1968 F. Hamilton, C. Burger
1969 F. Hamilton, C. Burger
1970 M. Miller, R. Stevens
1971 M. Arndt, B. Hardies
1972 Mr. and Mrs. E. Reich
1973 G. Hershman, L. Lee
1974 J. Sheridan, L. Kozlove

OPEN PAIRS

1958 A. J. Feigus, Dr. P. Castelle
1960 K. Bhavnani, J. P. Burg
1961 S. Silodor, N. Kay
1962 S. Silodor, N. Kay
1963 E. L. Rosen, S. J. Wright
1964 J. Lowenthal, R. Stern
1965 B. J. Ceifetz, H. A. Shevitz
1966 F. Weisbach, C. P. Weil
1967 F. Mikitaw, R. LaFleur
1968 R. M. Sacks, B. Garson
1969 K. Rhodes, H. Itkin
1970 W. Scott, W. Lewis
1971 E. Reich, C. Midelburg
1972 A. MacAslan, D. MacAslan
1973 B. Visokey, R. Fox
1974 B. Visokey, R. Fox

MEN'S PAIRS

1958 H. Auslander, J. Gelman
1960 Dr. R. Israel, J. R. Israel
1961 F. P. Kilchenstein, M. J. Cohn
1962 N. Kay, A. Landy
1963 H. L. Feldman, B. Baldwin
1964 I Deuter, G. Marsee
1965 J. Watson, G. Brown
1966 H. Sachs, S. Ruskin

1967 C. J. Solomon, M. J. Cohn
1968 W. Flannery, H. Sachs
1969 C. Solomon, R. G. Sharp
1970 D. Faskow, P. Swanson
1971 S. Parker, M. Blumenthal
1972 R. Ayers, P. Hall
1973 J. Starr, B. Newman
1974 R. Fox, B. Ayers

WOMEN'S PAIRS

1958 M. Gladstein, G. Sander
1960 S. Harrold, H. B. Hall
1961 P. R. McGuigan, J. R. John
1962 B. Halpern, L. J. Bloch
1963 H. M. Siegel, G. Hertz
1964 Mrs. W. Moldovan, Mrs. J. Ratesie
1965 A. Melander, Mrs. J. Halloran
1966 Mrs. T. Michaels, Mrs. G. McDaniel
1967 N. Phelps, Mrs. R. Getty
1968 Mrs. H. Heller, G. Moore
1969 Mrs. J. Wise, Mrs. M. Tamres
1970 L. Semler, S. Parr
1971 Mrs. P. Corell, Mrs. J. Parks
1972 B. Letzer, S. Schubiner
1973 K. Cummings, P. Cummings
1974 Mrs. R. Pierce, Mrs. W. Steffee

MIXED PAIRS

1958 C. Tiernan, Dr. R. Israel
1960 Mr. and Mrs. J. Denny
1961 M. S. Silverman, J. Wise
1962 Mr. and Mrs. C. Solomon
1963 K. Carter, F. Hamilton
1964 Mrs. J. Halloran, J. Polisner
1965 Mrs. R. Wade, J. C. Lopeman
1966 Mrs. R. Fields, B. Sokol
1967 Mr. and Mrs. A. Cohn
1968 Mr. and Mrs. C. Solomon
1969 L. Slusser, C. G. Jeans
1970 J. Remey, V. Remey
1971 L. Deaton, R. Zoller
1972 J. Wyatt, R. Ayers
1973 R. Hoffman, H. LeBow
1974 W. Walter, A. Fiscus

UPPER NEW YORK STATE
(*See also* Districts 3 and 4)

OPEN TEAMS

1956 S. Lorvan, R. C. Lesser
      W. May, Dr. P. Zweifel
1957 A Sheinwold, E. Kaplan
      N. Kay, I. Stakgold
1958 R. Freeman, L. Harmon
      N. Kay, R. Walsh
      Mrs. E. P. Cotter
1959 E. Murray, B. Elliott
      R. Freeman, R. Walsh
      A. Sheinwold
1960 Mrs. R. Gordon, J. Friedlander
      R. P. Freedman, A. Landy
1961 M. Rosenblatt, C. Coon
      C. Davis, Jr., F. T. Westcott
1962 C. Coon, C.Davis
      F. T. Westcott, M. Rosenblatt
1963 W. Flannery, P. Swanson
      D. Faskow, R. Lesko
      H. Sachs
1964 A. Landy, E. Katz
      J. L. Mathis, R. P. Freedman
1965 B. Crane, G. Marsee
      E. Murray, S. R. Kehela
1966 C. P. Davis, Jr., C. Coon
      R. Zeckhauser, M. Rosenblatt
      F. T. Westcott

1967 F. Bellinger, R. Meyer
      Mr. and Mrs. G. Fried
1968 Dr. W. Werner, D. A. Collins
      S. Kantor, M. Melton
1969 Mrs. R. H. McKaig, J. E. Cullinan, Jr.
      J. Landon, J. M. Edwards
1971 R. Freedman, J. Mathis
      M. Martino, F. Vine, *tied with*
      J. Zimmerman, B. Hardies
      R. Alexander, E. Jones, *tied with*
      J. Silver, E. Kokish
      R. Lipsitz, M. Blumenthal

MASTERS PAIRS

1964 E. Lazarus, Dr. H. P. McDonald
1965 R. P. Freedman, J. L. Mathis
1966 N. M. Hall, F. Sontag, *tied with*
      J. E. Cullinan, Jr., J. Burgess
1967 A. Lando, W. J. Crissey
1968 H. Nuckols, M. Bergen
1969 D. Andrews, G. Chapman
1971 R. Cofer, R. Spitzner

OPEN PAIRS

1956 Mr. and Mrs. C. D. Mercer
1957 E. B. Katz, R. Freedman
1958 C. Coon, F. T. Westcott
1959 Dr. R. Israel, E. Majeroni
1960 A. Aroneck, E. Smith
1961 Mrs. M. E. W. Torok, F. Hess
1962 Mr. and Mrs. J. McElwain
1963 E. Murray, S. Kehela
1964 Mrs. M. M. Rheault, J. Goda
1965 B. Crane, G. Marsee
1966 Mrs. C. Bunnecke, M. Melton
1967 M. I. Arndt, B. H. Hardies
1968 S. Kantor, M. Melton
1969 P. Heitner, B. Chazen
1971 Mr. and Mrs. G. Fried

MEN'S PAIRS

1956 C. Hirschey, C. W. Spencer
1957 P. Feldesman, L. Kelner
1958 H. J. Behm, T. Clarke
1959 H. Shoop, M. Shuman
1960 Dr. R. Israel, E. Majeroni
1961 C. Jack Bonney, D. L. Stanton
1962 M. McMartin, J. Becker
1963 Lt. Col. C. S. Hartnoll, V. Dimarco
1964 S. Berg, M. W. Goodman
1965 W. Lebovic, S. Kehela
1966 S. Poskanzer, M. Melton
1967 S. Kehela, S. Aarons
1968 W. Merriman, E. Hatch
1969 F. C. Root, M. M. Morris
1971 J. Smith, L. Spalding

WOMEN'S PAIRS

1956 M. Nevins, R. Gordon
1957 C. Gillette, H. Penner
1958 Mrs. M. Nevins, Mrs. A. Gordon
1959 C. N. Frank, C. J. Dennis
1960 M. H. McKaig, V. E. Maurer
1961 A. Sheabor, R. Hewitt
1962 E. H. Hunt, J. D. Reardon
1963 Mrs. A. N. McTavish, Mrs. W. E. Weber
1964 A. Gordon, A. Wright
1965 Mrs. G. Fried, Mrs. M. McKenna
1966 Mrs. W. H. McKaig, Mrs. T. J. Peterson, Jr.
1967 Mrs. G. R. Johnson, Mrs. S. B. Rose
1968 Mrs. R. Appleby, Mrs. E. F. Gudgel
1969 Mrs. F. S. Lisowski, Mrs. M. C. Instance
1971 Mrs. G. Morgan, Mrs. R. Vander Laan

MIXED PAIRS

1956 Mrs. W. H. McKaig, G. Hirschey
1957 Mrs. R. Gordon, E. B. Katz
1958 Mrs. R. Gordon, E. B. Katz
1959 Mrs. N. Freedman, K. A. P. Stepanian
1960 Mrs. R. Gordon, E. B. Katz
1961 Mrs. A. Godfrey, Dr. M. M. Sandler
1962 Mrs. V. Lavery, Dr. J. Manos
1963 Mrs. M. G. McKenna, E. B. Katz
1964 Mrs. C. Letcher, F. L. Root
1965 Mrs. M. G. McKenna, E. B. Katz
1966 Mrs. W. J. Albersheim, C. Coon
1967 Mrs. J. Phillips, D. Cowan
1968 Mrs. H. Hobbs, Rev. L. A. Tobin
1969 Mrs. B. Ku, Dr. D. Sun
1971 Rev. T. Kemp, Mrs. J. Schlaerth

DISTRICT 6   (Virginia, Washington, D.C., most of Maryland)

BRIDGE WEEK

KNOCKOUT TEAMS

1974 T. Michaels, R. Henderson
      M. Philley, W. Christian
      J. Morse, H. Utegaard

OPEN TEAMS

1974 S. Swearingen, R. Joyce
      N. Nickell, B. Pettis

MASTERS PAIRS

1974 A. Frankel, P. McManus

OPEN PAIRS

1974 R. Joyce, S. Swearingen

MEN'S PAIRS

1974 D. Treadwell, K. Cohen

WOMEN'S PAIRS

1974 B. Adler, A. Lane

MID-ATLANTIC FALL

KNOCKOUT TEAMS

1971 W. Walvick, S. Robinson, T. Weik
      E. Manfield, S. Aronson
1972 B. Schoenfeld, J. Murphy
      S. Goldberg, L. Bluhm

OPEN TEAMS

1971 Mr. and Mrs. L. Allen
      S. Swearingen, R. Joyce
1972 K. Wei, C. Wei, V. Mitchell
      J. Mitchell, B. Passell, M. Passell

MASTERS PAIRS

1971 L. Bluhm, L. Ballentine
1972 L. Bluhm, S. Goldberg

OPEN PAIRS

1971 R. Beall, E. Simmons
1972 A. Kravetz, H. Ketchum

MEN'S PAIRS

1971 J. Kivel, D. Darling

WOMEN'S PAIRS

1971 Mrs. L. Allen, Mrs. L. Harlston

MID-ATLANTIC INDEPENDENCE DAY

KNOCKOUT TEAMS

1972 W. Walvick, S. Aronson, M. Cappelletti, K. Cappelletti
1973 R. Ewen, R. Oshlag, Dr. F. Mastrola, B. Bragin
      M. Bergen, W. Woodard
1974 J. Apfelbaum, A. Fisher, J. Lambert, L. Edwards

OPEN TEAMS

1966 G. R. Nail, J. Gerber
      J. G. Ripstra, Mrs. E. A. Mahony
1967 D. Hocevar, P. Leon, H. Sachs
      P. Swanson, *tied with*
      E. Manfield, R. Fleischman
      R. Schwartz, S. Goldstein
1968 Mr. and Mrs. J. Adler
      E. Lazarus, T. Weik
1969 M. Blumenthal, S. Lapides
      D. Faskow, K. Woolsey
1970 D. Faskow, H. Sachs
      P. Swanson, C. Jeans
1971 B. Lewis, N. Schwartz
      K. Woolsey, S. Robinson
1972 V. Davis, F. Hultman
      W. Williams, C. Fulton
1973 R. Lipsitz, P. Parker
      K. Woolsey, S. Parker, *tied with*
      R. Pies, S. Pies, J. Kivel, M. Kivel
1974 J. Banks, B. Lindsay, J. Robert, A. Duncker

MASTERS PAIRS

1966 D. Bier, M. J. Daniels
1967 Mrs. J. Vastine, J. O. Lipman
1968 Maj. E. R. Lewis, J. Kivel
1969 B. Greenberg, M. Glass
1970 Mr. and Mrs. M. Moss
1971 S. Parker, M. Garner
1972 J. Cohen, D. Darling, *tied with* G. Hann, J. Brinley
1973 A. Wilhide, M. Carroad
1974 J. Livezey, P. Brady

OPEN PAIRS

1966 M. Wagar, B. Crane
1967 Mr. and Mrs. D. Sachs
1968 D. Freese, E. Bowen
1969 D. Lazarus, K. Woolsey
1970 H. Bethe, B. Chazen
1971 J. Bookstaver, E. Neiger
1972 J. Morse, H. Utegaard
1973 R. Taub, K. Woolsey
1974 Mr. and Mrs. W. Snyder

MEN'S PAIRS

1966 W. B. Woodsen, J. W. Norwood, Jr.
1967 H. Sachs, P. Swanson

1968 T. Ekel, J. Deutschberger, *tied with*
      J. Stafford, L. Barnett
1969 N. Nickell, F. Garson II
1970 T. Lyon, H. Cappelletti, *tied with*
      R. Perry, H. Monyer
1971 D. Darling, J. Kivel
1972 H. Peters, W. Roberts
1973 W. Vinson, T. Patton

WOMEN'S PAIRS

1966 J. M. Clayton, Mrs. L. F. Buschbaum
1967 Mrs. J. Miller, Mrs. M. Wasserman
1968 Mrs. E. L. Henson, Mrs. M. N. Anderson
1969 S. Parr, S. R. Heinsohn
1970 Mrs. L. DuPont, Mrs. H. Hirsty
1971 J. Morse, J. Stenger
1972 J. Wilcox, Mrs. T. Sikora
1973 E. Berman, G. Berns

MIXED PAIRS

1967 Mr. and Mrs. T. Ekel
1968 Mrs. H. Utegaard, M. Blumenthal
1969 E. Wolf, K. Zendig
1971 S. Sachs, D. Sachs

MID-ATLANTIC SPRING

KNOCKOUT TEAMS

1973 B. Pope, B. Schoenfeld, P. Boyd
      D. Taube, B. Moran, P. Lesnik

OPEN TEAMS

1973 V. Chernoff, L. Bart, C. Bowie, J. Rengstorff

OPEN PAIRS

1973 L. Bluhm, S. Swearingen

MEN'S PAIRS

1973 L. Poe, M. Rind

WOMEN'S PAIRS

1973 B. Adler, P. Lapides

MID-ATLANTIC SUMMER

KNOCKOUT TEAMS

1962 Dr. J. Henry, J. Hudgins
      Dr. M. Lipsett, T. Ekel, D. Darling
1970 W. Eisenberg, R. Goldman, R. Wolff
      R. Hamman, M. Lawrence, J. Jacoby
1972 S. Catlett, R. Hamilton
      B. Wick, B. McCallon
1973 J. Stafford, J. Morse
      J. Piaski, H. Utegaard
1974 N. Nickell, S. Swearingen, W. Pettis
      W. Roberts, L. Ballentine

OPEN TEAMS

1960 Mrs. M. L. Fisher, E. L. Allen
      R. Shankie, C. Duffy

1961	Mrs. W. C. Simpson, Mrs. M. Yates
	R. F. McMahan, W. W. Williams, *tied with*
	Dr. A. C. Current, Jr., J. Warlick
	B. Beghardt, J. S. Mitchell
1962	Mr. and Mrs. J. M. Keating
	Mrs. E. Pratt, J. A. Armstrong
1963	Lt. Col. W. Christian, S. Aronson
	R. Sitnek, A. Gabrilovitch
1964	Mr. and Mrs. H. Schenken
	A. Gabrilovitch, I. Stakgold
1965	Mr. and Mrs. E. Harlow
	W. Jones, D. J. Harris, *tied with*
	Mr. and Mrs. J. Kivel
	E. Lazarus, D. Darling
1966	H. Hess, J. L. Coppie
	R. Clark, W. Weinberg, C. L. Crum
1967	M. Wagar, Mr. and Mrs. R. Freeman
	H. R. Hall, R. Shepherd
1968	Mr. and Mrs. M. Cappelletti
	M. Blumenthal, S. Lapides
1969	Mr. and Mrs. H. H. Swisher
	J. Brenner, A. Bricklin, A. Gerard
1970	Mr. and Mrs. M. Cappelletti
	E. Kokish, J. Silver
1972	M. Lipsett, J. Morse, T. Ekel
	D. Darling, *tied with* S. Lapides,
	R. Taube, K. Woolsey. J. Cohen
1974	E. Marrs, R. Taube, P. Brady
	J. Livezey, B. Schoenfeld

MASTERS PAIRS

1960	Mr. and Mrs. J. E. Clinkinbeard
1961	S. Lourie, A. L. Brewington
1962	J. Coppie, M. Weinberg
1963	D. M. Lipsett, Dr. R. Rovner
1964	Mrs. D. Evans, L. Tubbs
1966	P. Harrison, T. Ekel
1967	Mrs. R. C. Williams, Mrs. J. Addlestone
1969	Mrs. E. E. Shouse, J. Clayton
1970	Mr. and Mrs. S. Parker
1972	M. and K. Cappelletti
1973	N. Holthouse, W. Glover
1974	R. Leonard, R. Burton

OPEN PAIRS

1960	P. Rotzell, R. Sitnek
1961	P. Sowers, C. Wallace
1962	R. Baum, M. Borindky
1963	Mr. and Mrs. B. M. Rainier
1964	J. Norwood, W. B. Woodson
1965	O. Jacoby, J. Jacoby
1966	S. Swearingen, H. Peters
1967	Mr. and Mrs. L. C. Allen
1968	J. M. Edwards, J. Landen
1969	C. Fulton, H. A. Petrea
1970	Mr. and Mrs. S. Parker
1972	S. Lapides, R. Taube
1973	E. Solomon, M. Nelson
1974	S. Robinson, R. Henderson

MEN'S PAIRS

1960	A. Gabrilovitch, R. Jordan
1961	D. and D. Caton
1962	E. Fleischer, L. Friedberg
1963	D. Murray, J. R. Chappell, Jr.
1964	T. A. Troop, D. M. Peebles, Jr.
1965	C. Price, C. Crum
1966	B. J. Becker, E. W. Spickard
1967	R. Freeman, H. R. Hall
1968	M. Cappelletti, T. Hirsch
1969	H. L. Abrams, A. Van Hoose
1970	S. Swearingen, H. Peters

WOMEN'S PAIRS

1960	W. Lusby, R. Roberts

1961	K. S. Fortson, H. K. Smith
1962	R. Rogasner, W. O'Loughlin, *tied with*
	R. Roberts, H. Phillips
1963	E. Wilson, A. Buist
1964	Mrs. A. West, Mrs. G. Carroll
1965	Mrs. A. Kotzen, Mrs. M. Rubens
1966	Mrs. W. E. Dillon, Mrs. F. T. Wolford
1967	Mrs. J. H. Toledano, E. Foley
1968	Mrs. C. Blumenthal, B. Adler
1969	Mrs. B. Cohn, Mrs. J. Remey
1970	H. Utegaard, A. Burger

MIXED PAIRS

1960	Mrs. L. Eisenman, R. Harrison
1961	Mrs. W. Wagar, W. Davis
1962	B. Adler, A. Goldberg
1963	H. Nathan, Bert Wilson
1964	B. Adler, A. Goldberg
1965	Mrs. E. Wilson, Jr., R. Taube
1968	Mr. and Mrs. W. O'Loughlin
1970	J. Tierney, Mrs. M. Tierney

DISTRICT 7 (North Carolina, South Carolina, Georgia, Bermuda, eastern Tennessee)

BERMUDA

OPEN TEAMS

1962	F. Westcott, Dr. J. Manos
	R. Fox, C. Davis, Dr. R. Tator
1966	M. Siebert, S. Siebert
	B. Reid, D. Reid
1968	Dr. and Mrs. W. Melander
	Mr. and Mrs. V. Remey
1970	F. T. Westcott, Dr. R. Tator
	Dr. J. T. Manos, R. S. Fox
	R. W. McVay
1972	R. Fox, F. Westcott, C. Davis
	Dr. J. Manos, Dr. R. Tator, *tied with*
	R. Miller, A. Spielholz, H. Horowitz
	T. Gray, *tied with* Mr. and Mrs. H. Sachs
	Mrs. W. Albersheim, Mrs. M. Root,
	tied with Mr. and Mrs. E. Kaplan
	J. Rosenblum, N. Silverstein
1974	T. Saunders, F. Freda
	A. Truscott, D. Truscott

MASTERS PAIRS

1968	Mrs. D. Apple, Mrs. C. Samberg
1970	Mr. and Mrs. I. Gershkoff
1972	Mr. and Mrs. A. Derby
1974	Mr. and Mrs. T. Teague

OPEN PAIRS

1962	R. Frey, H. Schenken
1966	C. Krupp, P. Trent
1968	M. Ginsberg, L. Sokolower
1970	P. Beyer, Mrs. B. Pope
1972	J. Barna, A. Derby
1974	B. Kaplan, E. Kaplan

MEN'S PAIRS

1962	Dr. R. Tator, C. Davis
1966	C. Davis, Dr. R. Tator
1968	Maj. F. O'Neill, P. Willcocks
1970	A. Oszy, T. Clarke
1972	T. Denninger, H. Sachs
1974	D. Brooks, Dr. L. Melander

WOMEN'S PAIRS

1962   Mrs. C. Foster, Mrs. A. Wilmot
1966   Mrs. E. Leahy, M. Hartley
1968   Mrs. G. Galespie, Mrs. H. Wolf
1970   Mrs. H. Katzen, Mrs. W. L. Lewis
1972   Mrs. G. Nelson, Mrs. W. Stephens
1974   E. Abrams, Mrs. L. Singer

MIXED PAIRS

1962   Mr. and Mrs. J. Rosenblum
1966   Mr. and Mrs. E. Hoffman

MID-ATLANTIC FALL

KNOCKOUT TEAMS

1972   B. Moran, S. Gregory
       J. Murphy, E. Marrs
1973   B. Schoenfeld, J. Looby
       S. Gregory, M. Tierney
1974   S. Leibowitz, M. Blumenthal, S. Parker
       S. Robinson, K. Woolsey, L. Bluhm

OPEN TEAMS

1952   W. B. Joachim, A. Tschekaloff
       S. Judd, A. Danilenko
1953   C. J. Bonney, M. Bonney
       F. Yagi, G. R. Wolff
1954   D. J. Harris, Mrs. C. McGhee
       J. G. Stone, M. Fisher
1955   Mr. and Mrs. C. Solomon
       Mr. and Mrs. N. Agran
1956   Mrs. J. E. Folline, R. L. Miles, Jr.
       L. Eisenman, R. Freeman
1957   Mr. and Mrs. T. Stone
       J. R. Crawford, S. Silodor
1958   J. E. McCabe, R. Lovill, Jr.
       I. Deuter, C. P. Weil
       J. Remey
1959   Mr. and Mrs. B. M. Rainier
       Mr. and Mrs. H. Silverman
1960   R. Jordan, N. Kay
       Mr. and Mrs. T. Sanders
       M. Wagar
1961   Mr. and Mrs. J. W. Norwood, Jr.
       H. R. Hall, F. Blackman
1962   Mrs. L. Robinson, E. Murray
       R. Freeman, H. Hume
       B. Hughes
1963   G. Davidson, H. Hume
       B. Hughes, M. J. Cohn
       H. R. Hall
1964   Mrs. J. Folline, R. L. Miles, Jr.
       N. Berlin, Mr. and Mrs. R. Freeman
1965   R. MacNab, Mr. and Mrs. J. Norwood, Jr.
       M. Powell, W. B. Woodsen
1966   M. Wagar, B. Crane, R. H. Govan
       Mr. and Mrs. R. Shepherd
1967   E. J. Earley, Mrs. B. Jenkins
       Mr. and Mrs. H. R. Hall, J. Dodd
1968   H. G. Peters, J. K. Sheridan
       S. R. Swearingen, R. Joyce
       N. Nickell
1969   W. N. Eskridge, Mrs. J. Mackintosh
       J. J. Gottlet, J. Shelnutt
1970   A. Bernstein, M. Blumenthal
       D. Faskow, P. Swanson
1972   S. Leibowitz, M. Blumenthal
       N. Nickell, T. Callaham
       H. Peters
1973   J. Piaski, R. Joyce
       L. Barnett, B. Pettis
       J. Stafford
1974   J. Stafford, B. Pettis
       Dr. L. Barnett, R. Joyce
       J. Piaski

MASTERS PAIRS

1959   A. Vatz, G. Wolfe
1960   Mr. and Mrs. J. E. Clinkinbeard
1961   M. Cowell, W. B. Woodson
1962   J. W. Norwood, Jr. B. Warshauer
1964   R. C. Spikes, E. Chauncey
1965   Mr. and Mrs. R. Freeman
1966   M. Blumenthal, W. Walvick
1967   D. Faskow, W. Flannery
1968   C. Smith, Mrs. W. L. Corbin
1969   J. Hand, D. Bragin
1970   T. Callaham, P. McManus
1973   G. Hayden, M. Passell
1974   D. Darling, F. King, *tied with*
       R. Mourer, L. Horton

OPEN PAIRS

1952   S. Silodor, J. Crawford
1953   J. Parish, B. O. Johnson
1954   W. B. Woodson, R. J. Lovill, Jr.
1955   R. Jordan, R. Sitnek
1956   R. C. Olson, E. F. Gambill
1957   A. Roth, Mrs. B. Haddad
1958   Mr. and Mrs. C. C. Swaringen
1959   Mrs. V. Dye, G. Whitehead
1960   Mrs. J. E. Clinkinbeard, Mrs. A. H. Fay
1961   S. Aronson, M. Chaitt
1962   Mr. and Mrs. A. Strom
1963   W. L. Williams, P. H. Wuille
1964   R. F. Ling, H. Dillenbeck
1965   J. D. Cobb, B. Robbins
1966   M. Wagar, B. Crane
1967   H. R. Hall, E. J. Earley
1968   Mr. and Mrs. G. Carter
1969   J. Lay, Jr., F. Marshall
1970   G. Roberts, L. Gould
1972   S. Goldberg, S. Robinson
1973   S. Parker, L. Bluhm
1974   D. Hoffner, M. Shaw

MEN'S PAIRS

1952   R. L. Nelson, S. M. Epstein
1953   D. Murray, S. Katz
1954   H. Gerst, R. Farber
1955   A. Roth, S. Haddad
1956   W. M. Davis, H. P. Deal
1957   N. Berlin, H. Gerst
1958   P. M. King, Jr., W. M. Davis
1959   D. Murray, R. Banner
1960   S. B. Broadfoot, J. Norwood, Jr.
1961   J. Norwood, S. B. Broadfoot
1962   E. Fleischer, L. Friedberg
1963   W. Ridenour, J. C. Barefoot
1964   G. Smith, J. H. Slager
1965   C. C. Swaringen, L. Thomas
1966   P. Pender, R. Sitnek
1967   J. C. Masson, E. Mendell
1968   R. J. Lovill, Jr., K. S. Anderson, Jr.
1969   P. Lesnik, D. File
1970   G. Roberts, F. Strickland
1972   C. Thomas, H. Deal
1974   G. Kasle, G. Hayden

WOMEN'S PAIRS

1952   K. Rhodes, L. Eisenman
1953   S. W. Alcorn, W. Howard
1954   R. Bayliss, A. J. Rosenbloom
1955   L. Meyer, W. Howard
1956   F. C. Sydnor, J. Jackson, Jr.
1957   D. Epstein, H. Bernstein
1958   C. Mitchell, W. David
1959   H. Silverman, M. Pell
1960   Mrs. E. W. Cummings, Mrs. C. C. Swaringer
1961   H. E. Wagnon, J. Boone
1962   R. Rogasner, W. O'Loughlin, *tied with*
       R. Roberts, R. Phillips

1963   J. S. Carter, S. Schechter
1964   Mrs. M. B. Mowry, Mrs. E. W. Bailey
1965   Mrs. E. Davis, Mrs. B. Haynes
1966   Mrs. S. Mirsky, Mrs. B. Pories
1967   Mrs. J. E. Clinkinbeard, Mrs. I. B. Cohen
1968   Mrs. C. Lundin, Mrs. H. W. Holmes
1969   Mrs. L. W. McIlhany, P. Phetteplace
1970   Mrs. W. Hoffman, Mrs. R. Broughton
1972   Mrs. R. Lamp, L. Maybin
1974   N. Walker, R. Myers

MID-ATLANTIC SPRING

KNOCKOUT TEAMS

1973   M. King, D. Fisher
      B. Warshauer, R. McMahan
1974   C. Goppert, F. McBride
      G. Kasle, G. Hayden, M. Passell

OPEN TEAMS

1957   Mr. and Mrs. H. Coplon
      Mrs. A. Marks, C. Johnson
1959   B. C. Morrow, I. Wilson
      A. C. Current, Jr., J. Warlick
1960   Mrs. A. Nordlinger, H. Gerst
      Mr. and Mrs. H. Silverman
1961   A. Sheinwold, I. Stakgold
      R. Freeman, A. Gabrilovitch
      Mrs. W. C. Robinson
1962   Mrs. L. Robinson, S. Kehela
      R. Freeman, W. W. Williams
      Dr. R. Melton, *tied with*
      Mrs. H. Richardson, W. B. Woodson
      Dr. H. McDonald, M. J. Cowell
1963   Dr. and Mrs. C. Hall, Jr.
      R. T. Smith, Col. J. Day
      H. R. Hall
1964   D. Carter, Mrs. E. A. Mahony
      L. Starr, J. Griscom
1965   L. Silverfield, Mrs. J. Bernard, Jr.
      W. T. Rutledge, Jr., R. Fechter
1966   C. L. Fulton, W. W. Williams, Jr.
      R. Ashton, R. Glenn
1967   M. Blumenthal, W. Walvick
      L. Popper, Mr. and Mrs. M. Cappelletti
1968   B. J. Becker, D. Hayden
      M. Wagar, B. Crane
1969   E. Lazarus, M. Blumenthal
      D. Treadwell, W. Walvick
1970   Mr. and Mrs. T. Sanders
      Mr. and Mrs. M. Cohn
1971   Mr. and Mrs. L. Allen
      C. Fulton, W. Williams
1972   Mrs. L. Perdue, Mrs. E. Grady, Mrs. H. Long
      Mrs. T. Maurer, *tied with* G. Fraction
      W. Knight, M. Hogan, S. Cox,
      tied with J. Sheridan, L. Kozlove
      N. Fischer, T. Hodapp, *tied with*
      M. Granovetter, E. Rogers, R. Pavlicek
      F. Rubbra, *tied with* S. Swearingen
      L. Bluhm, T. Callaham, R. Joyce
1973   S. Goldberg, J. Murphy
      L. Bluhm, S. Robinson
1974   K. Reitz, Mrs. J. Ingram, C. Eckles
      Mrs. F. Fister, *tied with* L. Axtell
      L. Griffey, L. Smith, B. Dennard,
      tied with C. Wall
      Mrs. J. Chapman, M. Little, S. Locke

MEN'S TEAMS

1956   N. Berlin, Dr. E. S. Berlin
      E. Harlow, R. L. Miles
      W. Jones
1957   F. McBridge, C. C. Swaringen
      T. K. Sanders, H. Hume

WOMEN'S PAIRS

1956   R. O. Rogers, P. Cole
      J. A. Dearing, A. B. Fairley

MASTERS PAIRS

1956   Mrs. T. Michaels, C. C. Lovenberg
1961   A. Sheinwold, I. Stakgold
1962   Mrs. B. R. Hughes, Mrs. J. N. Parr
1963   R. A. Ashton, R. Hamilton
1964   Mr. and Mrs. R. Sharp
1965   W. W. Williams, Jr., R. A. Ashton
1966   Mr. and Mrs. L. C. Allen
1967   S. Robinson, J. Cohen
1968   M. Wagar, B. Crane
1969   E. Ryan, G. J. Smith
1970   Mrs. B. Jenkins, Mrs. H. Hume
1971   Mrs. W. Latzell, E. Norberg
1972   P. Swanson, G. Moss
1973   C. Thomas, T. Van Zant
1974   Mrs. H. Knight, C. Said

OPEN PAIRS

1957   W. Bell, W. E. McCaskill
1959   G. L. Cox, S. Robinson, Jr.
1960   Mrs. M. Fisher, E. Allen
1961   Mrs. A. Fischer, M. Weinberg
1962   Mr. and Mrs. E. L. Kulbersh
1963   J. Sauls, I. Barin
1964   J. I. McCabe, Sr., J. I. McCabe, Jr.
1965   L. Bluhm, N. Smith
1966   E. Reinstein, R. Rosenberger
1967   M. J. Welles, J. Deutschberger
1968   W. McCallon, W. Wick, Jr.
1969   Mrs. L. C. Allen, L. C. Allen
1970   Dr. R. Melton, L. Hetzer
1971   B. Pope, S. Gregory
1972   R. Steele, Mrs. M. Mashburn
1973   R. McMahan, J. Harris
1974   D. Landers, J. Fitzgerald

MEN'S PAIRS

1959   W. K. Brown, R. Glenn
1960   H. M. Silverman, N. Berlin
1961   D. Rosenbloom, H. M. Kritzik
1963   H. R. Fechter, R. F. McMahan, *tied with*
      J. E. Travis, T. M. Byer
1964   F. Weisbach, F. McBride
1965   M. Michaels, S. Aronson
1966   R. Glenn, A. L. Kenton
1967   M. Blumenthal, E. Lazarus, *tied with*
      Dr. A. C. Current, C. D. Thomas, Jr.
1968   W. E. Thomas, J. J. Hudson
1969   S. W. Robinson, T. Lyon
1970   R. Kaiser, Jr., S. Goldberg
1971   D. Hudgins, R. Glenn
1972   M. Moss, D. Faskow
1974   J. Andersen, J. Thames

WOMEN'S PAIRS

1957   N. H. Rodenberg, N. Phillips
1959   D. Sechrest, D. C. Wright
1960   F. Sims, J. W. Stott
1961   M. Wagar, J. E. Folline
1963   D. Brown, J. Rountree
1964   J. Reidelbach, F. Meyer
1965   Mrs. D. C. Wright, Mrs. D. R. Dunlop
1966   Mrs. F. F. Huffman, Mrs. W. DuBose
1967   Mrs. E. W. Cummings, Mrs. W. D. Fobert
1968   Mrs. F. P. Barry, Mrs. L. Allen
1969   Mrs. R. A. Small, Mrs. H. Berg
1970   Mrs. H. Peek, Mrs. W. Milner
1971   Mrs. J. Rhodes, Mrs. R. Critcher
1972   Mrs. L. Harleston, Mrs. L. Allen
1974   G. Long, J. King

MIXED PAIRS

1956 Mr. and Mrs. J. R. Chappell, Jr.
1957 Mrs. W. Howard, H. G. Gerst
1959 Mr. and Mrs. A. Stidham
1960 Mrs. B. Torrey, S. W. Bliley
1961 Mr. and Mrs. E. S. Harlow
1963 B. Bratcher, M. Cocherell

MID-ATLANTIC SUMMER

KNOCKOUT TEAMS

1971 S. Goldberg, R. Shepherd
      L. Bluhm, L. Gould
1973 J. Stafford, B. Pettis
      B. Moran, J. Piaski, N. Nickell
1974 B. Reinhold, L. Cohen, Dr. R. Katz, K. Shuman

OPEN TEAMS

1971 H. Clinkinbeard, J. Clinkinbeard
      Mr. and Mrs. H. Peters, W. Robert
1973 M. King, D. Fisher, R. Maybin
      L. Maybin, *tied with* J. Lay, B. McNeely
      A. Cox, R. Jones
1974 C. Goppert, G. Kasle, G. Hayden
      M. Passell, R. LaCour

MASTERS PAIRS

1971 T. Hodapp, N. Fischer
1973 J. Jacoby, H. Nolan
1974 B. Crane, Dr. J. Fisher

OPEN PAIRS

1971 G. Michaud, E. Yost
1973 L. Kozlove, J. Sheridan
1974 F. McBride, L. Bart

MEN'S PAIRS

1971 E. Earley, J. Dodd
1973 J. Felts, L. Spilman

WOMEN'S PAIRS

1971 C. Sanders, B. Cohn
1973 Mrs. J. Novak, Mrs. P. Ambery

MID-ATLANTIC WINTER

KNOCKOUT TEAMS

1972 Mrs. M. King, D. Fisher
      B. Warshauer, Mrs. W. Means
1973 A. Barrett, J. Murphy
      W. Murphy, R. Arnold
      G. Mahaffee, R. LaCour
1974 T. Collins, L. Bluhm
      R. Shepherd, B. Moran
      J. Looby

OPEN TEAMS

1965 R. L. Miles, N. Berlin, J. Hudgins
      Mr. and Mrs. R. Freeman
1966 J. Flint, P. Pender
      S. Aronson, M. Blumenthal

1967 S. Catlett, R. H. Hamilton
      W. Wick, Jr., W. McCullom
1968 R. Govan, D. Heller
      D. Pruitt, L. Bluhm
1969 W. Walvick, D. Treadwell
      M. Blumenthal, S. Lapides
1970 E. Pinckney, C. Brown
      H. Edwards, T. Devereau
1971 C. Swaringen, A. Swaringen,
      Mrs. W. Randall, A. Foreman, *tied with*
      Mrs. B. Miller, Mrs. C. Felton
      Mrs. L. Copses, M. Garber
1972 E. Gay, W. Howe, E. Mason
      D. Wittrup, *tied with* K. Anderson
      L. Ballentine, J. McCabe, L. Bluhm,
      tied with A. Raeuber, Mrs. L. Galloway
      Mrs. W. Bomar, F. Harb, J. Ferguson
1973 L. Kozlove, J. Sheridan
      M. Blumenthal, M. Lair
1974 L. Smith, L. Griffey, L. Axtell, B. Dennard

MASTERS PAIRS

1965 Dr. C. Duffy, W. W. Williams, Jr.
1966 Mr. and Mrs. H. Gould
1968 Mr. and Mrs. R. Freeman
1969 D. Thompson, K. Grunwald
1970 Mrs. F. A. James, Mrs. W. V. Turner
1971 N. Berlin, S. Catlett
1972 R. Loville, L. Ballentine
1973 B. Crane, T. Sanders
1974 N. Crawford, Mrs. V. Randall

OPEN PAIRS

1965 M. Blumenthal, S. Aronson
1966 R. L. Wilhide, C. M. Boteler
1967 Mr. and Mrs. J. Adler, Jr.
1968 W. Flannery, P. Swanson
1969 W. W. Williams, Jr., J. Greiner
1970 E. Mendell, J. Masson
1971 M. Wagar, R. Govan
1972 S. Swearingen, Mrs. P. Simmons
1973 L. Gould, L. Bluhm
1974 D. Fisher, B. Fechter

MEN'S PAIRS

1966 J. Flint, P. Pender
1967 R. V. Schreiber, G. Kaufman
1968 L. Bluhm, R. Govan
1969 R. Joyce, S. Swearingen
1970 S. Goldberg, M. Cohn
1971 F. Rubbra, J. Linhart, *tied with*
      N. Schwartz, S. Robinson
1973 B. Crane, Dr. J. Fisher

WOMEN'S PAIRS

1966 A. Kotzen, B. Kaufman
1967 Mrs. J. A. Gruver, Mrs. D. S. Sachs
1968 Mrs. E. C. McMahan, Mrs. B. M. Lanford
1969 Mrs. E. W. Cummings, Mrs. W. D. Fobert
1970 Mrs. G. Murray, Mrs. G. McKneely
1971 Mrs. F. Barry, Mrs. L. Allen, *tied with*
      Mrs. W. Thompson, Mrs. L. Ingram
1973 L. Maybin, M. King

MIXED PAIRS

1967 R. V. Schreiber, Mrs. C. Wilhide

THANKSGIVING

KNOCKOUT TEAMS

1972 M. Cohn, S. Coolik, S. Swearingen
      N. Nickell, W. Roberts

OPEN TEAMS

1972 J. Popkin, F. Garson,
       T. Rutledge, J. Simmons
       S. Swearingen, *tied with*
       L. Gould, S. Goldberg,
       L. Bluhm, R. Shepherd, S. Robinson

OPEN PAIRS

1972 C. Sanders, S. Coolik

MEN'S PAIRS

1972 Dr. J. Fisher, G. Polak

WOMEN'S PAIRS

1972 C. Sanders, B. Cohn

DISTRICT 8 (Illinois except Chicago area, eastern Missouri, western Kentucky, northern Indiana)

CHAMPAGNE

KNOCKOUT TEAMS

1974 B. Reinhold, Dr. R. Katz
       L. Cohen, B. Wolff

OPEN TEAMS

1967 R. Cruise, G. Caravelli
       M. Rosenberg, D. Rutstein
1968 S. Leavitt, P. Sugar
       A. Astrologes, H. Rabin
1969 Dr. R. Katz, L. Cohen
       A. Schmidt, J. Schmidt
1970 C. Tidball. M. Sorg
       Mrs. R. Moore, L. Wieser
1971 B. Crane, G. Caravelli
       L. Cohen, M. Rosenberg
1972 E. Singleton, Jr., D. Jordan
       P. Slatt, F. Binder, Jr.
1973 R. Grantham, J. Grantham
       C. Goppert, G. Hayden
1974 B. Reinhold, Dr. R. Katz, L. Cohen
       K. Shuman, B. Crane, B. Wolff

MASTERS PAIRS

1970 J. LaNoue, R. Pitard
1971 D. Nicklasson, L. Oakey
1972 N. Ehrlich, D. Smith
1973 M. Rosenberg, G. Caravelli
1974 G. Caravelli, Dr. J. Fisher

OPEN PAIRS

1967 E. Rosen, P. Sugar
1968 G. Caravelli, M. Rosenberg
1969 J. Wachter, G. Polak
1970 Mrs. G. Crounse, Mrs. E. Novak
1971 M. Mueller, A. Cieslak
1972 F. Walters, H. Rabin
1973 G. Caravelli, J. Mandell
1974 G. Morell, S. Collier

MEN'S PAIRS

1967 H. Bud. J. Chmielowiec

1968 R. Lawrence. R. M. Esch
1969 B. Coleman, L. Oakey
1970 H. MacLean, R. Andersen
1971 M. Spitz, K. Hanson
1972 J. Herrmann, S. Goldberg
1973 D. Smith, B. Jackson
1974 C. Dennen, J. Jacoby

WOMEN'S PAIRS

1967 F. Arst, J. Deutsch
1968 F. Arst, J. Deutsch
1969 V. Heckel, J. DeWitt
1970 Mrs. M. Soffer, Mrs. L. Epstein
1971 Mrs. E. Argersinger, M. Wagar
1972 M. Miller, P. Doran
1973 B. Merida, C. Heimer
1974 G. Grant, M. Stracke

MIXED PAIRS

1967 Mrs. W. Stein, D. Cook
1968 J. Zilic, D. Witte
1969 F. Arst, J. Wachter

MISSISSIPPI VALLEY

OPEN TEAMS

1951 G. Turner, M. Q. Ellenby
       E. Hochfeld, W. Grieve
1952 J. G. Ripstra, I. Rosenberg
       J. Hubbell, A. R. Kincaid
1953 C. Benjamin, Mrs. P. Steinberg
       A. Marian, C. K. Smith, *tied with*
       O. Jacoby, J. Jacoby
       J. Cohan, J. Simon
       A. Weiss
1954 P. Ochs, C. Wiley
       J. Epstein, R. Woodworth
1955 J. Epstein, D. Carter
       P. Ochs, C. Wiley, *tied with*
       Mr. and Mrs. G. Rosenschein
       Mr. and Mrs. J. E. Johnson
1956 S. Lazard, B. Hanna
       F. A. Bombeck, J. Jacoby
       O. Jacoby
1957 E. Melchior, L. Tiller
       R. O. Groves, C. Finch
1958 Mr. and Mrs. G. R. Nail
       Mr. and Mrs. T. K. Sanders
1959 P. Ochs, B. McClintock
       Mr. and Mrs. J. Levitt
       G. De Runtz
1960 Mr. and Mrs. R. M. Braznell
       A. Smith, Mrs. J. Wilson
1961 M. Hochfeld, I. Stakgold
       G. Turner, M. Ingberman
1962 L. Weiner, G. Nash
       L. Kolker, C. Willey
1963 D. Carter, G. Michaud
       Mr. and Mrs. O. Jacoby
       P. Levitt
1964 F. C. Rubbra, H. Shoop
       J. J. Leach, J. Moran
       C. Henke
1965 R. Sharp, N. Silverstein
       G. Treadwell, M. Bright
       M. Thomas
1966 G. Kasle, C. Smith
       Mr. and Mrs. C. Kittle
1967 B. Crane, G. Marsee
       W. Rosen, G. Polak
1968 D. M. Thomas, G. Polak
       J. Blair, D. Williams
1969 P. L. Sincoff, Ed Melchior
       M. J. Cohn, A. McNeiley
1970 M. Ledeen, H. Bethe
       D. Faskow, P. Swanson

1971 B. Crane, G. Caravelli
     M. Rosenberg, H. Perlman
1972 D. Rutstein, J. Mandell
     A. Weiland, C. Yelton
1973 J. Schneider, N. Schneider
     C. Wiley, E. Wiley
1974 A. Susskind, M. Bernstein
     W. Snider, S. Rose

MASTERS PAIRS

1959 Mrs. J. Simon, R. G. Sharp
1966 J. Jacoby, B. Trenholm
1967 L. Kolker, D. Carter
1968 B. Creed, Mrs. V. Davis
1969 Mr. and Mrs. R. L. Christensen
1970 D. Cammarata, R. McClintock
1971 C. Said, Dr. P. Volpe
1972 E. Schulte, Jr., J. Spear
1973 H. Miller, Jr., J. Weiner
1974 E. Lester, B. Larson

OPEN PAIRS

1951 A. Kincaid, I. Rosenberg
1952 M. Wagar, D. Carter
1953 D. Carter, J. Levitt
1954 M. Q. Ellenby, G. Turner
1955 A. P. Harvey, Jr., F. Weisbach
1956 J. W. Hubbell, W. J. Gilbert
1957 A. B. Mariam, C. Levitt
1958 C. Smith, J. Epstein
1959 G. Turner, E. Hochfeld
1960 R. Sharp, B. Crane
1961 G. Nash, J. Levitt
1962 R. Sharp, B. Crane
1963 E. Rosen, A. Simon
1964 B. Crane, J. Epstein
1965 R. Sharp, L. Clark
1966 R. Amann, K. Woolsey
1967 B. Crane, G. Marsee
1968 H. Rabin, S. Rabin
1969 P. Arnall, T. Kniest
1970 D. Faskow, P. Swanson
1971 B. Crane, G. Caravelli
1972 D. Rutstein, J. Mandell
1973 S. Graves, T. Hodapp
1974 B. Crane, G. Caravelli

MEN'S PAIRS

1951 G. Rosenschein, L. B. Weiner
1952 M. Ellenby, B. Kaufman
1953 D. Goldberg, L. B. Weiner
1954 M. W. Bierbaum, B. Stephenson
1955 A. P. Harvey, Jr., J. G. Ripstra
1956 I. Schwab, L. B. Weiner
1957 O. Jacoby, A. Bell
1958 P. Feldacker, D. C. Carter
1959 B. Crane, J. Epstein
1960 J. Epstein, T. Sanders
1961 M. Lopata, M. Heller
1962 L. Kolker, J. Levitt
1963 L. Kolker, J. Levitt
1964 C. Smith, N. Silverstein
1965 F.Ensminger, B. Matthews
1966 J. Epstein, G. Polak
1967 M. Heller, D. Carter
1968 J. H. Nieberding, F. Weisbach
1969 Dr. G. H. Berndsen, D. E. Williams
1970 M. Lopata, M. Heller
1971 C. Said, Dr. P. Volpe
1972 G. Hayden, R. Bates
1973 D. Carter, R. Lord
1974 J. Rosenschein, B. Muir

WOMEN'S PAIRS

1952 M. Cytron, M. Newbill
1953 M. Cytron, M. Newbill

1954 D. C. Carter, R. A. Jervis
1955 L. Amster, C. Brumfiel
1956 L. W. Rigney, Mrs. A. H. Wilks, Jr.
1957 V. G. Scoggin, J. Wilson
1958 C. G. Cody, G. V. Gerbig
1959 G. Wolfe, J. Gray
1960 J. Halloran, D. Carter
1961 C. Sanders. W. H. Adams
1962 H. L. Levin, E. N. Carlson
1963 P. Steinberg, J. Levitt
1964 R. Steinberg, J. Levitt
1965 Mrs. T. Sanders, Mrs. C. Wiley
1966 Mrs. M. Bloom, Mrs. A. Rosenberg
1967 Mrs. H. L. Levin, Mrs. E. E. Goodman
1968 Mrs. E. Gordon, Mrs. C. M. Buckner
1969 M. Bright, Mrs. P. Steinberg
1970 Mrs. L. McConnell, Mrs. E. Novak
1971 L. Stelzer, S. Roberts
1972 M. Bright, R. Steinberg
1973 Mrs. P. Sincoff, Mrs. M. Kramer
1974 Mrs. R. Loewenstein, Mrs. H. Collins

MIXED PAIRS

1951 Mrs. M. Schwabe, F. Hayden
1952 B. Crane, Mrs. G. Rosenschein
1953 Mrs. S. Fairchild, J. E. Simon
1954 Mr. and Mrs. M. W. Bierbaum
1955 Mrs. D. Dwyer, I. W. Schwab
1956 C. Levitt, A. C. Bell
1957 Mrs. D. C. Carter, P. Portnoy
1958 Mrs. B. Morris, L. T. Robinson
1959 B. Crane, Mrs. E. Evans
1960 K. O'Keefe, M. Heller
1961 Mrs. I. Bright, Sr., P. Steinberg
1962 Mr. and Mrs. G. R. Nail
1963 Mrs. F. L. Rhodes, D. Carter
1964 Mrs. M. Bloom, G. Polak
1965 A. Weiss, Mrs. P. Steinberg
1966 Mr. and Mrs. F. Eckert
1967 Mrs. P. Sincoff, E. Melchior
1968 J. Levitt, A. Rosenberg
1969 Mrs. S. Dorn, P. Feldacker
1970 E. Bransford, L. Hetzer
1971 Mrs. W. Wood, J. D. King
1972 G. Spitzer, P. Portnoy
1974 J. Levitt, A. Rosenberg

MASTERS INDIVIDUAL

1961 M C. Ballard
1962 J. J. Parish
1963 C. Garvey, Jr.

INDIVIDUAL

1953 W. Cantrall
1954 Mrs. M. W. Bierbaum
1955 J. Halliburton
1957 S. A. Miller

DISTRICT 9 (Florida, Puerto Rico)

FLORIDA

KNOCKOUT TEAMS

1967 R. Woodworth, W. Stickney
     A. Gerard, A. Bricklin
1968 H. Fishbein, P. Feldesman
     S. Katz, R. Sharp
     F. Hirsch, H. Fein
1969 C. Russell, R. Arnold
     C. Smith, B. Reynolds

1970 R. Halperin, S. Halperin
J. Denny, A. J. Astrologes
T. Mahaffey
1972 A. Gerard, J. Thomas
L. Wiley, K. Wiley
1973 Mrs. W. Loudermilk, Mrs. A. Lea
Mr. and Mrs. D. Hogan
1974 L. Smith, L. Griffey
A. Barfus, B. Dennard

MEN'S TEAMS

1959 S. Katz, J. C. Kunkel
R. Appleyard, F. Blackson
1960 J. C. Kunkel, S. Katz
F. Hirsch, F. Blackson
R. Appleyard
1961 H. Braverman, L. Ferer
B. Reynolds, W. Seamon
1962 H. Harkavy, C. Russell
D. Warner, C. Kuhn
R. Arnold

WOMEN'S TEAMS

1959 V. L. Carlson, H. B. Freeman
H. E. Spitz, M. McCord
1960 R. Slentz, S. Royal
J. Hillegass, M. Hudson
1961 V. Alderman, A. Gerard
A. D. White, B. Saron
1962 C. Arnold, T. H. Gray
B. Champion, E. Abrams

LIFE MASTERS PAIRS

1967 C. Russell, E. Kemp
1968 Mr. and Mrs. G. L. Awad
1969 J. Brenner, R. Schoenau
1970 H. Raymond, Mrs. J. McPeel Berg
1972 K. Cohen, H. Smith
1973 Mrs. A. O'Grady, B. Moore
1974 E. Schulte, R. Woodworth

MASTERS PAIRS

1959 J. C. Kunkel, W. Seamon
1960 C. H. Whitebrook, H. Rosene
1961 A. H. Barr, Mrs. S. Kirtland
1962 E. Kemp, C. Russell
1963 J. A. Schwenke, J. D. Bacon
1964 C. Lefkowitz, R. Schoenau
1965 Mrs. I. Rayburn, T. Dean
1966 Mrs. C. Flattery, Mrs. B. Englander
1967 O. Goddard, N. Lazarus
1968 G. B. Barrs, R. Pavlicek
1969 F. Babiarz, J. Saville
1970 F. Babiarz, Mrs. J. Shachtman
1972 Mr. and Mrs. W. Murphy
1973 Mr. and Mrs. P. Graegin
1974 Mrs. W. McDonald, Mrs. W. Robinson

OPEN PAIRS

1960 Mrs. H. P. Simmons, Mrs. E. Wilson
1961 L. Ferer, G. Goldstein
1962 M. Michaels, R. Arnold
1963 J. A. Schwenke, J. D. Bacon
1964 E. Kemp, R. Reynolds
1965 Mr. and Mrs. R. Rothlein
1966 R. W. Mitchell, P. Carson
1967 T. Horning, F. Horning
1968 A. Lefkowitz, A. Barfus
1969 M. Passell, J. Barrow
1970 A. Barfus, R. Schwartz
1972 G. Merrill, Mrs. A. Winter
1973 Mr. and Mrs. T. Teague
1974 G. Mitchell, H. Neuffer

MEN'S PAIRS

1959 R. Reynolds, J. C. Kunkel
1965 C. E. LePaige, W. Mussallem
1966 J. Fox, A. Bricklin
1967 P. Piedmont, D. King
1968 E. A. Jones, P. F. Oreffice
1969 H. Darden, W. Landly
1970 E. Jaye, C. P. Weil
1972 W. Seamon, S. Mandell
1973 A. Cokin, J. Mahaffey, *tied with*
R. Sugg, R. Norton
1974 R. Saron, R. Glenn

WOMEN'S PAIRS

1959 P. Miller, M. Ray
1965 J. Clark, Mrs. W. Stem
1966 Mrs. E. J. Lewis, Mrs. E. Andrews
1967 H. Colby, M. Loudermilk
1968 J. M. Young, J. T. Oxford
1969 E. Palmer, Mrs. N. M. Pate
1970 Mrs. A. McDonald, Mrs. J. T. Ecklund
1972 Mrs. J. Oxford, S. Young
1973 Mrs. J. McCorquodale, J. Young
1974 J. Kelley, E. Maupin

MIXED PAIRS

1963 Mrs. R. Saron, R. Woodworth
1964 Mrs. H. Ameisen, G. F. Davis
1965 J. Thomas, F. Carrieri
1966 Mr. and Mrs. M. Noble
1967 L. Ferer, G. Goldstein
1968 M. L. Holley, D. L. Hogan
1969 B. Koorey, H. Florea
1970 L. E. Smith, Mrs. D. J. Neville
1972 R. Woodworth, A. Barrett
1973 N. Richardson, F. Sexton
1974 L. Griffey, Mrs. M. Hudson

INDIVIDUAL

1960 Mrs. E. Maupin
1961 L. Manson, *tied with* A. Nielsen
1963 M. Waldron
1964 H. G. Aaron
1965 T. Gemzell
1966 Mrs. A. Johnson
1967 F. Zearfoss
1969 G. Powers
1969 H. Lent, Jr.
1970 Mrs. R. Wetherington
1974 F. Redman

PUERTO RICO

OPEN TEAMS

1969 R. Nachman, N. Nachman
H. Solomon, R. Solomon
1970 J. Glick, V. Glick
Mr. and Mrs. G. Rosenschein
S. Alpert
1971 L. Pietri, M. Garner
N. Silverman, R. Rubin
1972 D. Eboli, R. Cappali
K. Kristansen, F. Higginbotham
Mrs. C. Lee, *tied with* C. Wei
K. Wei, J. Mitchell
M. Granovetter, V. Mitchell
1973 Dr. R. Goodman, R. Hetzer
D. Payne, R. Carvel, *tied with*
B. Reinhold, P. Weichsel
N. Weichsel, K. Larsen
B. Eisenberg, Mrs. M. Dornfeld
1974 Z. Granovetter, M. Granovetter
J. Looby, N. Silverman

MASTERS PAIRS

1967   W. Seamon, C. Russell
1968   Mr. and Mrs. R. Sharp
1973   E. Nevins, F. Singer
1974   K. Wei, R. Andersen

OPEN PAIRS

1967   Mr. and Mrs. V. Remey
1968   F. Higginbotham, K. Kristiansen
1969   Mrs. R. J. Rosenthal, R. J. Rosenthal
1970   C. Wei, J. Becker
1971   L. Pietri, M. Garner
1972   K. Kristiansen, F. Higginbotham
1973   L. Edwards, J. Brinley
1974   C. Hinckley, B. Eboli

MEN'S PAIRS

1967   R. Reynolds, R. Sitnek
1968   J. Rosenblum, N. Silverstein
1969   J. Weintraub, W. Seamon
1970   T. Smith, F. Higginbotham
1971   L. Pietri, M. Garner
1972   M. Granovetter, Z. Granovetter
1973   M. Moss, J. Saltz
1974   D. Eboli, R. Cappalli

WOMEN'S PAIRS

1967   R. Zellinger, P. Halberstadt
1968   P. Levin, J. Mason
1969   Mrs. R. J. Rosenthal, G. Simon
1970   J. Mason, B. Birnholz
1971   Mrs. B. Eboli, J. Costas
1972   Mrs. J. Sykes, Mrs. F. Willis
1973   J. Mitchell, G. Moss
1974   M. Cooke, C. Grossman

MIXED PAIRS

1967   Dr. and Mrs. H. Nachman
1968   P. Levin, L. D. Ribner
1969   D. Sendral, M. Paris
1970   R. Russo, A. Russo
1971   Mr. and Mrs. H. Schenken
1972   Mrs. A. Gerard, A. Bricklin

SOUTHEASTERN

1967   N. Silverstein, J. Jacobs
      R. Rothlein, R. Sharp
      A. Barfus
1968   P. Oreffice, J. Jaeger
      P. Levin, J. Scanlan
      A. Weiss, R. Reynolds
1969   P. Feldesman, J. Solodar
      R. Zoller, C. Burger
      M. Ingberman
1970   A. Sontag, M. Moss
      J. Solodar, W. Passell
      K. Larsen, R. Zoller
1973   B. Hamman, J. Schwencke
      J. Jacoby, G. Hayden
      G. Kasle

OPEN TEAMS

1931   S. J. Rockwell, T. Barrett
      L. H. Watson, W. K. Barrett
1933   E. T. Barco, W. A. Clark
      E. C. Moore, B. T. Groene

1934,   W. Cary, J. E. Tyner
      J. Hardesty, J. A. Walton
1936   Mrs. A. S. Terry, H. Homa
      E. Cohen, M. Goldstein
1937   B. Parks, D. C. Carter
      E. Cohen, A. Terry
1938   L. Thurtell, W. M. McIntyre
      L. Morris, J. C. Kunkel
1939   A. S. Goldsmith, H. Feinberg
      S. L. Guggenheim, S. Fink
1940   P. Abramsohn, J. Slutt
      C. W. Hutzler, H. Chanin
      Mrs. M. Wagar
1941   Mrs. H. Sobel, C. Goren
      Mrs. B. Golder, C. Solomon
1942   Mrs. H. Sobel, C. Goren
      Mrs. B. Golder, C. Solomon
1943   Mr. and Mrs. J. J. Wallendorf
      Dr. W. V. Kirk, Mrs. F. Lasarow
1944   Mrs. A. Tarr, W. E. McKenney
      W. Seamon, L. Weiss
      I. Epstein
1945   W. Brown, W. Seamon
      G. Rapee, I. Epstein
      M. Vernoff
1946   Mrs. M. Basher, E. Cohn
      C. Goren, D. Farquharson
1947   Mr. and Mrs. R. Scott
      Mr. and Mrs. R. C. Burleigh
1951   M. Bender, J. Ankus
      A. Eber, R. Reynolds, *tied with*
      T. Stone, E. Kemp
      W. von Zedtwitz, H. Harkavy
1952   H. Kemp, A. Roth
      M. Michaels, R. Sitnek
1953   Mr. and Mrs. J. Glick
      B. Root, M. Turk
      E. Cohen, *tied with*
      J. Kunkel, R. Racier
      F. Bickel, R. Rosenberg
      A. Goodman
1954   Mr. and Mrs. J. Glick
      M. Turk, W. S. Root
      E. Cohen
1955   Mr. and Mrs. C. Solomon
      C. Whitebrook, J. Rosenblum
1956   Mr. and Mrs. C. Solomon
      C. Whitebrook, J. Rosenblum
1957   Mrs. A. Cavanaugh, Mrs. P. Remlinger
      Mrs. F. J. Niver, Mrs. T. McKenna
1958   Mrs. B. Brier, Mrs. B. Gale
      A. Eber, C. Russell, *tied with*
      Mrs. V. Alderman, Mr. and Mrs. R. Werdling
      E. Cohen, Mrs. W. Hoffman
1959   B. Reynolds, B. Seamon
      B. Rothlein, C. Neyman
1960   A. Eber, J. Kravatz
      H. Harkavy, C. Russell
1961   Mr. and Mrs. J. Barth
      Mr. and Mrs. S. Kirtland
1962   B. Sharp, I. Guttman
      M. Lipin, B. Saron
      A. Lefkowitz, *tied with*
      E. Kemp, C. Russell
      A. Eber, R. Sitnek
1963   E. Kemp, C. Russell
      A. Eber, O. Jacoby
1964   E. Kemp, A. Eber
      C. Russell, R. Reynolds
1965   B. Haddad, S. Haddad
      P. Pender, R. Sitnek
1966   M. Michaels, Mrs. L. J. Goldstein
      L. Ferer
      Mr. and Mrs. A. H. Mueller
1967   A. Steinberg, J. A. Schwencke
      K. Kristiansen, J. Swanson
1968   A. Weiss, A. Barrett
      J. Levinson, R. Arnold
      S. I. Steinfeldt
1969   B. J. Becker, D. Hayden
      D. Morse, H. Fein
1970   D. Hayden, D. Morse
      H. Fein, W. August

1971   Mr. and Mrs. H. Schenken, W. Seamon
      J. Weintraub, S. Katz, *tied with*
      H. Fein, D. Morse
      R. Crown, G. R. Nail, *tied with*
      A. Reinhold, E. Hochfeld
      K. Larsen, A. Weiss, *tied with*
      H. Fishbein, F. Hirsch
      Dr. R. Tator, R. Fox
      F. Dossenbach, *tied with*
      Mrs. P. Levin, J. Lowe
      L. Heinrich, L. Ribner, *tied with*
      Mr. and Mrs. K. Wiley
      Mr. and Mrs. B. Ohmann, *tied with*
      S. Jaeger, J. Kinard
      S. Perry, B. Shaw
1972   Mr. and Mrs. S. Stayman
      A. Rand, R. Rand
      V. Mitchell, P. Parella, *tied with*
      W. Passell, F. Rubbra
      M. and Z. Granovetter, *tied with*
      Mr. and Mrs. T. Lagan
      H. Keffer, Mrs. H. Keffer
      A. Doane, *tied with*
      R. Sharp, R. Sharp
      G. Fischer, A. Fischer
      A. O'Grady, *tied with*
      M. Moss, G. Moss, J. Mitchell
      M. Passell, *tied with*
      Mr. and Mrs. E. Lowenthal
      Mr. and Mrs. J. Low
      C. Whitebrook, I. Fisher, *tied with*
      E. Short, K. Short
      Mr. and Mrs. R. Sugg
1973   T. Reid, H. Rabin
      F. Walters, A. Samuels
1974   C. Bishop, Dr. L. Weisman
      R. Schwartz, C. Davis
      B. Butcher

MEN'S TEAMS

1951   W. von Zedtwitz, W. Seamon
      J. Ankus, A. Eber
      R. Reynolds
1952   L. Levy, J. Glick
      A. Landy, J. Rosenblum
      N. Silverstein
1953   F. Bickel, L. Jaeger
      R. Rosenberg, M. Seiler
1954   L. Ferer, W. Seamon
      R. Rothlein, F. Nickols
      A. Roth
1955   I. Cohen, J. Kunkel
      A. Roth, N. Kay
      M. Michaels
1956   C. Solomon, R. Sitnek
      C. Neuman, R. Rothlein, *tied with*
      M. Gross, Dr. A. Salasky
      R. Rosenberg, C. Woldenberg
1957   W. Seamon, C. Russell
      H. J. Harkavy, T. Stone
1958   W. Seamon, C. Russell
      H. Harkavy, R. Arnold
      A. Eber
1959   Dr. A. Salasky, M. Gross
      P. Feldesman, E. Lowenthal
1962   I. Buttman, Lt. Col. W. Christian
      B. Sharp, M. Lipin
      R. Sitnek
1963   W. Seamon, F. Hirsch
      P. Kibler, P. Pender
      R. Reynolds
1964   W. Seamon, R. Reynolds
      S. Katz, J. Weintraub
1965   W. Seamon, S. Katz
      J. Weintraub, R. Reynolds
1966   J. Brier, J. Jacobs
      R. Rothlein, I. Kass
1967   G. Kasle, R. Wolff
      I. Erdos, F. De Marigny
1968   I. Guttman, R. Rothlein
      A. Barfus, R. Sharp

1969   G. Treadwell, C. Kittle
      M. Lipin, P. Stern
      S. W. Weingarden
1970   G. Kasle, M. Carson
      R. Pavlicek, M. King
1971   J. Schwencke, G. Fischer
      G. Kasle, J. Brenner
1972   J. Weintraub, B. Reynolds
      S. Katz, B. Seamon
      H. Schenken
1973   L. Ribner, J. Shakofsky
      M. Moss, S. Altman
      V. Mitchell
1974   R. Huggard, C. Bishop
      J. Harwood, J. Denney, *tied with*
      F. McBride, B. Moss
      R. Coren, A. Coren, *tied with*
      F. Whiteley, D. Curtis
      J. Epstein, J. Ripstra, *tied with*
      T. Mahaffey, R. Pavlicek
      J. Berry, P. Richmond

WOMEN'S TEAMS

1951   M. Vernoff, J. Lyell
      M. Gross, F. J. Niver
1952   H. Sobel, P. Bacher
      E. Seligman, J. Rosenfield
1953   P. Bacher, A. Burnstein
      J. Jaeger, E. Neuman, H. Sobel
1954   E. F. Cohn, O. Peterson
      J. C. Kunkel, J. Kaplan
1955   R. Gilbert, E. Kemp
      M. Levin, E. Eber
      A. Burnstein
1956   E. Kemp, L. Eber
      P. Levin, A. Burnstein
1957   G. Wallendorf, L. C. Childress
      J. Leyell, B. Windt
      E. Kirtland
1958   M. Levin, J. Rosenblum
      B. Gale, J. Gardner
      L. Jaeger
1959   N. Agran, G. Goldman
      A. Myers, A. Gittelman
1962   C. Arnold, T. H. Gray
      B. Champion, E. Abrams
1963   E. Abrams, Mrs. I. Arnold
      Mrs. T. H. Gray, B. Champion
1964   E. Abrams, C. Arnold
      B. Champion, Mrs. T. H. Gray
1965   A. Kempner, H. Sobel
      P. Levin, B. Hermanson
      Mrs. W. Keohane
1966   E. Kennedy, L. Rudnick
      A. Weiss, S. Shapira
1967   M. Cunningham, C. Arnold
      Mrs. T. Gray, Mrs. A. G. Whitehead
1968   E. Evans, G. Roberts
      Mrs. S. Perlow, M. Beaver, *tied with*
      Mrs. J. Lyell, D. Grady
      Mrs. J. Barth, W. Childress
1969   L. Lyell, L. Barth
      W. Childress, D. Grady
1970   G. Goldstein, A. Schwartz
      Mrs. H. Feldstein, Mrs. A. Mueller
1971   N. Lewis, B. Brier
      Mrs. M. Clark, E. Abrams
1972   W. Sameroff, J. Solodar
      L. Deaton, E. VanZandt
1973   J. Theus, J. Bernard
      Mrs. J. Berg, E. Evans, C. Falk
      tied with K. Wei, G. Moss
      J. Mitchell, B. Kennedy
1974   B. Brier, A. Sporing
      P. Smith, N. Lewis
      M. Passell

LIFE MASTERS PAIRS

1967   S. Adamowski, S. I. Steinfeldt

1968   C. Russell, C. Smith
1969   Mr. and Mrs. H. Schenken
1970   A. Sontag, J. Solodar
1971   R. Pavlicek, M. Carson
1972   M. Carson, M. Blumenthal
1973   A. Sontag, N. Weichsel
1974   C. Davis, B. Butcher

MASTERS PAIRS

1961   Mr. and Mrs. S. Keith
1962   R. Arnold, W. Seamon
1963   Mrs. C. Munn, H. Harkavy
1964   F. Holtzman, A. Bricklin, *tied with*
       Mrs. L. Goldstein, L. Ferer
1965   S. Braverman, J. Kaiserman
1966   Mrs. W. Barrett, Mrs. D. Kelly
1967   Mrs. M. A. Winters, Mrs. J. E. Brooks
1968   A. Russo, B. Lazarus
1969   Mr. and Mrs. R. W. Byrns
1970   M. Farinas, Mrs. J. Rybovich
1971   F. Faulds, R. Stanger
1972   Mr. and Mrs. J. Abrams
1973   B. Elliott, H. Hopson
1974   B. Moss, R. Coren

OPEN PAIRS

1931   Mrs. E. Calhoun, S. Lenz
1933   C. Swisher, F. Pumpelley
1934   M. Adams, H. E. Hartman
1936   Mrs. A. S. Terry, E. Cohen
1937   Mrs. M. Wagar, F. Levy
1938   M. Elis, P. Abramsohn
1939   R. Weidling, W. Brown
1940   Mrs. B. Golder, C. Solomon
1942   Mrs. W. E. McKenney, P. Leventritt
1943   Mrs. E. Rishell, R. Bishop
1944   Mrs. J. Leyell, J. G. Staples
1945   W. E. McKenney, E. J. Tobin
1946   Mrs. M. Meyer, S. W. Kirtland
1947   W. von Zedtwitz, W. Seamon
1949   T. Stone, A. Roth
1950   T. Stone, A. Roth
1951   E. Seligman, T. Stone
1952   P. Abramsohn, M. Bender
1953   M. A. Lightman, N. Silverstein
1954   W. Seamon, S. Mogal
1955   P. Abramson, F. Kaplan
1956   C. Neuman, R. Rothlein
1957   C. Neuman, R. Rothlein
1958   M. Bender, W. Dunberg
1959   W. Thieman, J. Gelman
1960   A. Weiss, B. Reynolds
1961   Mr. and Mrs. M. Cooper
1962   R. Sitnek, S. Haddad
1963   W. Seamon, C. Russell
1964   E. Kemp, C. Russell
1965   A. Barfus, A. Lefkowitz
1966   Mrs. and Mrs. P. Brennan, Jr.
1967   M. Reubenfeld, Dr. H. Weinstock
1968   A. Sontag, G. Collier
1969   P. Feldesman, M. Ingberman
1970   I. Blocker, G. Powers
1971   R. Dennard, L. Griffey
1972   G. Kasle, J. Schwencke
1973   G. Bode, K. Rasmussen
1974   H. Schenken, B. Schenken

MEN'S PAIRS

1946   D. Carter, J. G. Ripstra
1947   P. Abramsohn, D. Farquharson
1951   Dr. R. Wilson, H. Houtz
1952   L. Levy, J. Glick
1953   R. Rothlein, B. Greenberg
1954   J. C. Kunkel, Dr. A. J. Steinberg
1955   A. Miller, C. Russell
1956   A. Casner, S. Katz
1957   T. Stone, S. Lazard

1958   H. J. Fishbein, Dr. H. R. Storr
1959   R. Sitnek, R. Rothlein
1960   J. Kunkel, W. Seamon
1961   R. Reynolds, C. Neuman
1962   Dr. C. Kuhn, W. Seamon
1963   O. Jacoby, C. Russell
1964   P. Levitt, C. Russell
1965   M. Moss, A. Sinoyan
1966   B. Crane, G. Marsee
1967   R. Fox, C. Davis
1968   Dr. I. B. Cippes, W. Seamon
1969   H. Fein, D. Morse
1970   R. Sugg, R. Mitchell
1971   J. Lyell, S. Kirtland
1972   I. Kass, M. Moss
1973   T. Hodapp, R. Henderson
1974   R. Huggard, C. Bishop

WOMEN'S PAIRS

1938   R. Bennett, F. J. Niver
1939   A. S. Terry, M. Wagar
1940   H. Sobel, M. Wagar
1941   H. Sobel, M. Wagar
1942   H. Sobel, M. Wagar
1943   *F. Lasarow, J. J. Walldendorf, N. Young
1944   M. Gross, M. Vernoff
1945   M. Gross, M. Vernoff
1946   A. Baldassare, J. Rubin
1947   H. Sobel, W. Wagar
1951   S. O. Grinberg, A. Burnstein
1952   J. Peyton, A. Cavanaugh
1953   P. Bacher, E. Neuman
1954   P. Levin, E. Neuman
1955   R. Gilbert, E. Kemp
1956   F. Johnson, L. C. Childress
1957   G. M. Smith, T. B. Bouldin
1958   E. Kemp, J. Kunkel
1959   W. L. Rice, W. E. Woods
1960   E. Kemp, S. Keith
1961   J. Leyell, B. Windt
1962   C. Arnold, T. Gray
1963   W. Seamon, S. Keith
1964   D. Machamer, J. Cromer
1965   Mrs. G. Goldman, Mrs. M. Root
1966   J. Jaeger, P. Levin
1967   E. Evans, L. Brooks
1968   Mrs. O. Ellis, Mrs. H. Wise
1969   A. Barrett, K. F. Short
1970   G. Goldstein, A. Schwartz
1971   Mrs. W. Derbyshire, Mrs. C. Hering
1972   Mrs. W. Keohane, Mrs. S. Perlow
1973   H. Utegaard, T. Michaels
1974   P. Cohen, B. Greenberg

MIXED PAIRS

1931   Miss M. Irvin, P. S. Langdon
1932   Mrs. H. N. Page, W. Cary
1933   Mr. and Mrs. L. Crane
1934   Mrs. L. Baker, J. Follette
1936   Miss B. Peiser, C. Daly
1937   Mrs. C. G. Chapman, L. D. Joel
1938   Mrs. A. S. Terry, B. Parks
1939   Mrs. H. Sobel, A. M. Barnes
1940   Mrs. B. Golder, C. Solomon
1941   Mrs. J. H. Meyering, E. J. Tobin
1942   Mr. and Mrs. B. Fain
1943   Mr. and Mrs. J. J. Wallendorf
1944   Mr. and Mrs. J. Glick
1945   Mrs. A. Tarr, W. Seamon
1946   Mrs. O. Hilliard, A. Jarmel
1947   Mrs. B. Golder, C. Solomon
1951   E. Kemp, T. Stone
1952   P. Bacher, C. Goren
1953   F. J. Niver, B. Stephenson
1954   Mrs. and Mrs. J. Rosenblum
1955   Mr. and Mrs. E. Cohen
1956   Mr. and Mrs. S. Lazard

---

*One of the original partners was forced to retire because of illness.

1957 E. Kemp, M. Lobell
1958 Mr. and Mrs. R. Rothlein
1959 Mrs. W. Seamon, J. Kunkel
1960 Mr. and Mrs. M. Cooper, *tied with*
      A. Mims, A. Eber
1961 Dr. F. C. Chandler, Mrs. S. Harrold
1962 P. Woods, R. W. Donaldson
1963 Mrs. C. Munn, H. Harkavy
1964 Mrs. L. Goldstein, L. Ferer
1965 A. Barfus, E. Zimmerman
1966 Mr. and Mrs. W. Passell
1967 Mr. and Mrs. W. Passell, *tied with*
      A. Bricklin, J. Bates
1968 R. Seamon, C. Russell
1969 Mr. and Mrs. D. Tuell, *tied with*
      J. K. Mancini, M. Meyer
1970 K. Short, E. Short
1971 Mrs. J. Thomas, L. Thomas
1972 B. Riordan, R. Huggard
1973 B. Crane, T. Michaels
1974 K. Wiley, L. Wiley

INDIVIDUAL

1934 E. H. Cohen
1946 Mrs. L. Rautenstrauch
1947 M. Vernoff
1952 G. Byrnes
1954 W. V. Kirk
1955 F. Stresau
1956 Mrs. G. Wilson
1957 G. Ellinicos
1958 Made into Non-Master
1959 S. J. Wikler

DISTRICT 10 (Arkansas, Louisiana, Mississippi, Alabama, western Tennessee)

GULF COAST MID-SOUTH

OPEN TEAMS

1972 G. Daniels, F. Connor
      C. Watson, H. Kaufmann, *tied with*
      B. Craig, B. Crockett
      H. McCabe, Mrs. C. Beveridge, *tied with*
      F. Hamilton, N. Schwartz
      M. Hunt, B. Greenberg, *tied with*
      W. Lewis, J. Arledge III
      C. Pierce, J. Floyd, *tied with*
      R. Logan, J. Bush
      G. Ginsburg, K. Fonte, *tied with*
      Mrs. A. Fell, Mrs. W. Barber
      Mrs. C. Warner, Mrs. R. Miller

MASTERS PAIRS

1972 N. Alpaugh, B. Greenberg

OPEN PAIRS

1972 F. Hamilton, M. Hunt

MEN'S PAIRS

1972 G. Randall, Dr. R. Green

WOMEN'S PAIRS

1972 Mrs. J. Scott, Mrs. J. Ramsey

MID-SOUTH FALL

KNOCKOUT TEAMS

1974 L. Bluhm, R. Shepherd, Mr. and Mrs. J. Gibbons
      C. Sanders, J. Rainey

OPEN TEAMS

1967 P. Deal, P. Munafo
      G. Kendall, N. Duvic, *tied with*
      J. A. Rockhold, H. Rockhold
      M. B. Townsend, M. Genud
      P. Soloway
1968 A. Plate, D. Horner
      B. J. Wilson, C. Downs
1969 W. A. Brown, Dr. J. Griscom
      J. Kirkpatrick, C. Smith
1970 L. Gould, S. Goldberg
      L. Bluhm, R. Shepherd
1971 D. Conlon, G. Cordes
      C. Carpenter, E. Gordon, Jr.
1973 W. Hollingsworth, R. Potter
      Capt. J. Potter, J. Gargrave
1974 T. Teague, E. Murdoch
      Dr. C. Burnham, J. Ripstra

MEN'S TEAMS

1973 T. Sanders, M. Lair
      M. Passell, B. Greenberg
      J. Jacoby, N. Silverstein

WOMEN'S TEAMS

1973 H. Utegaard, N. Gruver
      M. Townsend, T. Michaels
      tied with E. Lynch, J. Judy
      R. Francis, K. Shropshire

LIFE MASTERS PAIRS

1968 Mrs. N. C. Duvic, Mrs. W. A. Kuhn

MASTERS PAIRS

1967 J. L. Rosenblum, N. Silverstein
1969 R. Doughty, J. LaNoue
1970 N. Alpaugh, N. Silverstein
1971 J. Kennedy, L. Howard
1973 F. McBride, R. Shepherd
1974 J. Bernard, R. Glenn

OPEN PAIRS

1967 J. Jacoby, C. Kittle
1968 V. Ellzey, K. Robertson
1969 D. Requard, D. Fisher
1970 M. Passell, D. Caton
1971 B. Kennedy, C. Sanders
1973 B. Crane, G. Caravelli
1974 E. Murdoch, Dr. C. Burnham

MEN'S PAIRS

1967 O. Jacoby, F. Berger
1968 P. Connelly, J. Rosenblum
1969 C. Smith, Dr. J. Griscom
1970 J. Barrow, D. Daton
1971 F. Conner, H. Herbst
1973 M. Lair, M. Passell
1974 F. Stewart, T. Sanders

WOMEN'S PAIRS

1967 Mrs. A. C. Winters, Mrs. B. Floyd
1968 Mrs. B. D. Looney, Mrs. J. A. Brill
1969 Mrs. M. Hulan, Mrs. A. Dunhill
1970 G. Sangaree, Mrs. L. Hanahan
1971 A. McHann, S. Harrison
1973 B. Fleck, B. Austin
1974 B. Kennedy, C. Sanders

MIXED PAIRS

1967 F. Hoadley, Mrs. E. W. Alpaugh
1968 Mrs. H. G. Gardiner, Dr. C. Robinson
1971 M. Passell, C. Watson
1974 M. Cohn, B. Cohn

MID-SOUTH SPRING

KNOCKOUT TEAMS

1965   Mrs. M. Levin, A. Weiss
      G. Willett, J. G. Ripstra
1970   F. Hoadley, J. LaNoue
      Col. W. Christian, J. Linhart
1971   G. Kasle, P. Soloway
      C. Smith, R. and C. Kittle
1973   J. Jacoby, M. Chang, R. Dreyfus
      L. Gurvich, J. Frankel, B. Nail
1974   M. Brachman, J. Jacoby, S. Lazard
      P. Soloway, M. Passell

OPEN TEAMS

1941   C. P. Williams, J. Gerber
      B. Fain, P. Hodge
1942   B. Fain, J. Gerber
      Mrs. F. H. Gerson, P. Hodge
1943   Mrs. L. B. Buchanan, Mrs. R. Scott
      Mrs. E. C. McGarity, L. D. Boone
1944   L. Zilberman, J. Rosenblum
      Mr. and Mrs. J. Toledano
      Dr. R. Greene
1945   A. McKeen, L. Shurlds
      Mrs. W. L. Terry, Mrs. J. J. Ogden
1946   P. Harrison, Capt. M. Hodges
      Capt. W. Christian, E. Murdoch
1947   Mr. and Mrs. G. Green, Jr.
      Mr. and Mrs. J. W. McCormick
1948   J. L. Rosenblum, L. Rosen
      Dr. R. Greene, R. J. Pitard
      W. Herbert
1949   E. Murdoch, L. Herman
      O. Jacoby, J. Rosenblum
1950   Mrs. E. Feldman, Mrs. M. Parsons
      H. Teles, Mrs. R. Groves
1952   R. Y. Barrett, C. Woldenberg
      J. Gerber, R. Sharp
1953   Mrs. J. Potts, Mrs. B. D. Brandon
      Mrs. L. Tiller, Mr. and Mrs. C. Finch
1954   O. Jacoby, J. Jacoby
      H. Chanin, D. Westerfield
1955   S. Fairchild, B. Gentry
      E. Theus, J. W. Torbett
1956   C. Goren, D. Carter
      Mr. and Mrs. J. Glick
1957   J. G. Ripstra, Mrs. J. Krebs
      Mr. and Mrs. P. Merry
      Mrs. L. Durham
1958   A. McKeen, R. Michaelson
      J. H. Slager, H. K. Slager
1959   Mr. and Mrs. D. C. Carter
      B. Fain, Dr. G. Rosenkranz
      W. G. Cook, Jr.
1960   W. Grieve, G. Rapee
      C. Smith, J. A. Rockhold
1961   J. A. Rockhold, R. Rockhold
      E. Robertson, C. Smith
      L. Anderson
1962   F. Berger, L. Gurvich
      Mrs. J. Frankel, F. J. Pitard
1963   J. Skinner, Mrs. J. Skinner
      F. W. Hughes, Mrs. W. W. Corn
1964   Mr. and Mrs. O. Jacoby
      N. Silverstein, P. Levitt
      S. Lazarus
1965   S. Lazarus, J. Frankel
      P. Levitt, L. Gurvich
      R. Pitard
1966   Mr. and Mrs. D. Clay
      Mrs. K. S. Reinhardt, Mrs. R. A. Riley
1967   J. Frankel, L. Gurvich
      B. Crane, G. Marsee
1968   P. Levitt, S. Lazarus
      J. Tallant, C. Duncan
      Col. W. Christian
1969   R. Doughty, G. Tilly
      F. Whitely, D. Landers

1970   J. Tallman, Mrs. E. Simmons
      Mrs. F. Likins, Mrs. E. Thompson, *tied with*
      M. Nelson, F. Hoadley
      J. LaNoue, J. G. Ripstra
1971   H. Adams, D. Adams
      H. Katz, J. Hudgins
      B. Durbin
1972   F. Woodruff, R. Smith
      L. Hetzer, M. Shapiro
1973   Dr. J. Fisher, C. Weed
      J. Kennedy, B. Kennedy
      F. Berger, S. Coolik, *tied with*
      L. Gurvich, J. Frankel
      S. Lazarus, A. Davis
      G. McDaniel, Dr. N. Ostrich, *tied with*
      P. Munafo, Mrs. F. Stickney
      F. Hughes, M. Byrd
1974   T. Frick, J. Foote
      B. Foote, K. Bradley

MASTERS PAIRS

1957   L. Stan, R. Hunter
1958   Mrs. J. F. Welch, K. W. Robertson
1959   Mrs. B. Burns, Mrs. J. N. Morrell
1960   Mrs. A. W. Harrison, Mrs. J. T. Brown
1961   Mrs. M. Meyer, T. Hirsch
1962   P. Connelly, O. Jacoby
1963   D. Morse, G. Dawkins
1964   Mr. and Mrs. T. Sanders
1965   J. Rosenblum, J. Jacoby
1966   Mr. and Mrs. D. Clay
1967   B. Crane, G. Marsee
1968   J. Walton, L. Sharp
1969   F. Berger, B. L. Tighe
1970   M. Passell, J. Potter
1971   Dr. R. Greene, A. Gutowsky
1972   C. Sanders, E. Van Zandt, *tied with*
      B. Theobald, L. Wilson
1973   N. Silverstein, F. Hoadley
1974   W. Irby, K. Bains

OPEN PAIRS

1941   A. McNeile, R. Woodworth
1942   Mrs. J. J. Ogden, J. Floyd
1943   L. Shurlds, E. Murdoch
1944   Dr. and Mrs. R. D. Furlong
1945   Sgt. R. Appleyard, M. A. Lightman
1946   L. Krause, J. Rosenfield, Jr.
1947   Mrs. J. Rosenfield, Jr., E. Murdoch
1948   Mrs. G. Foley, Mrs. R. J. Pitard
1949   J. Gerber, P. Hodge
1950   N. Wallfisch, C. Woldenberg
1952   E. Murdoch, N. P. Howell
1953   Mrs. M. F. Meyer, L. Zilbermann
1954   M. Levin, P. Leventritt
1955   Mrs. J. T. Brown, C. Holt
1956   J. Glick, J. Lewis
1957   A. P. Simon, Jr., E. Theus
1958   L. S. Gurvich, S. H. Lazard
1959   Dr. J. Fisher, N. Silverstein
1960   J. Heymann, R. E. Craig
1961   J. L. Rosenblum, F. Hoadley
1962   J. Gerber, E. Smith, Jr.
1963   O. Jacoby, P. Levitt
1964   O. Jacoby, M. Thomas
1965   N. Kramer, J. Murphy
1966   Mrs. B. L. Tighe, N. Arnold
1967   Mrs. E. L. Goodman, P. Weiss
1968   C. Smith, C. Kittle
1969   A. Childs, L. Lockwood
1970   Mr. and Mrs. J. Kennedy
1971   H. Abrams, A. VanHoose
1972   F. Woodruff, R. Capps
1973   F. Hoadley, D. Caton
1974   D. Foote, D. Phillips

MEN'S PAIRS

1941   R. C. Burleigh, L. D. Boone
1942   B. Fain, P. Hodge

1943 J. R. Bailey, J. P. Risics
1944 B. Fain, Lt. C. Husted
1945 Lt. A. Harris, L. D. Boone
1946 C. N. Coleman, P. Harrison
1947 E. Jordan, W. M. Nelson
1948 B. Fain, P. Hodge
1949 C. N. Coleman, J. Farrar
1950 H. Early, M. Soniat
1952 A. McKeen, P. Connelly
1953 R. Sharpe, L. R. Robertson
1954 D. Westerfield, J. Jacoby
1956 J. Jacoby, O. Jacoby
1957 G. L. Michaud, D. Carter
1958 S. Greenberg, A. J. Blair, Jr.
1959 R. Greene, B. Greenberg
1960 M. Cohn, T. Sanders
1961 J. Jacoby, Dr. J. W. Fisher
1962 R. D. Sheffield, J. G. Ripstra
1963 R. H. Dreyfus, S. Lazard
1964 J. Jacoby, Dr. J. Fisher
1965 C. Coon, P. Pender
1966 J. Gerber, D. Morse
1967 D. Siebert, J. Walter
1968 J. Potter, R. Potter
1969 T. Golding, C. B. Roesch
1970 Dr. J. Fisher, F. Berger
1971 J. Barrow, D. Caton
1972 S. Coolik, E. Oxford
1973 J. Miller, F. Woodruff
1974 P. Soloway, M. Brachman

WOMEN'S PAIRS

1942 M. L. Murphy, M. Ratliff
1943 F. Bonck, T. Casey
1944 M. Meyer, J. Toledano
1945 R. Scott, R. C. Burleigh
1946 M. L. Oldham, M. Davis
1947 A. H. Hodgson, G. McGhee
1948 Mrs. L. Rosen, E. Murdoch
1949 J. Rosenblum, E. Murdoch
1950 Mrs. R. Tete, Mrs. L. Galatoire
1952 L. C. Barrow, C. Shepherd
1953 Mrs. R. J. Pitard, Mrs. E. Foley
1954 D. Rosenfeld, M. Parsons
1955 J. T. Brown, C. Holt
1956 J. Glick, P. Remlinger
1957 R. T. Lucas, C. Bonnell
1958 J. Simon, C. M. Newbill
1959 Mrs. R. J. Pitard, Mrs. J. T. Brown
1960 E. E. Rackle, H. C. Evans
1961 E. C. Thompson, N. Jost
1962 H. E. Wagnon, J. W. Boone
1963 J. Rosenblum, E. Murdoch
1964 R. Steinberg, G. Rosenschein
1965 Mrs. F. Miers, K. Thalheimer
1966 A. Villavaso, G. Aillet
1967 Mrs. P. V. Hitt, Mrs. J. T. Martin
1968 Mrs. C. R. Ault, Mrs. J. Sharp
1969 Mrs. B. Chancey, Mrs. J. Brazille
1970 Mrs. E. Bransford, Mrs. G. Sanders
1971 D. Kaiser, G. Goff
1972 P. Leonard, Mrs. G. Roberts
1973 M. Townsend, P. LaCour
1974 D. Adam, L. Goodman

MIXED PAIRS

1941 Mrs. M. Windsor, C. P. Williams
1942 Mrs. J. J. Ogden, J. Floyd
1943 Mrs. E. Campbell, J. McCormick
1944 Mrs. G. F. Foley, L. Kershenbaum
1945 L. Robbins, Lt. H. R. Regelin
1946 H. Rice, G. Coffin
1947 Mrs. M. Meyer, L. Levy
1948 F. Berger, Mrs. Marshall
1949 Mrs. D. B. Hawes, B. Fain
1950 H. Moore, J. Jabon
1952 Mr. and Mrs. T. C. Drake
1953 Mrs. L. Tiller, J. Simon
1954 Mrs. P. Levin, P. Leventritt
1955 Mrs. S. Fairchild, J. D. King

1956 Mr. and Mrs. L. Terry
1957 A. Davis, F. Berger
1958 Mrs. J. T. Brown, F. Berger
1959 Mrs. T. J. Hickman, J. Blair
1960 Mrs. F. Eberson, J. Lewis
1961 Mrs. J. F. Welch, J. Kennedy
1963 Mrs. T. Youngblood, H. Cage
1964 Mr. and Mrs. T. Sanders
1965 Mrs. D. B. Hawes, P. Rank
1966 Mrs. L. R. Smith, J. L. Hyland
1968 Mr. and Mrs. C. Brown
1969 Mrs. D. Hawes, J. Bromberg
1970 Col. and Mrs. J. Stephenson
1971 E. Van Zandt, A. Reinhold
1972 Mrs. D. Siebert, C. Clay
1973 G. Elzen, Mrs. A. Schexnayder

NON-MIXED PAIRS

1974 P. Soloway, M. Passell

MASTERS INDIVIDUAL

1942 Mrs. P. Mooney
1943 Mrs. C. Levy
1944 Mrs. W. L. Terry
1947 Mrs. J. Ogden
1948 M. Hodges
1950 Mrs. L. Galatoire
1953 W. Wilson, Jr.
1954 Mrs. C. L. Woldenberg
1955 J. C. Baird
1957 Mrs. D. W. Spurlock
1958 Mrs. N. Burgner

MID-SOUTH SUMMER

KNOCKOUT TEAMS

1968 J. Jacoby, R. Wolff
      M. Lawrence, W. Eisenberg
      R. Goldman
1972 J. Kennedy, B. Kennedy
      C. Sanders, J. Blair
      B. Greenberg, C. Weed
1974 C. Sanders, T. Sanders
      J. Blair, B. Greenberg
      S. Greenberg

LIFE MASTERS PAIRS

1968 J. Jacoby, R. Wolff

OPEN TEAMS

1960 F. Berger, Dr. R. Greene
      Mr. and Mrs. O. Jacoby
1961 Mr. and Mrs. J. Jacoby
      O. Jacoby, C. Finch
      S. Greenberg
1962 J. Toledano, F. Hughes
      A. Byrd, J. Floyd
      B. Tighe
1963 A. Gutowsky, S. Greenberg
      Mrs. N. Alpaugh, Dr. R. P. Greene
1964 D. Reid, I. Corn
      Mrs. D. Moore, M. Hodges
1965 J. Rosenblum, N. Silverstein
      G. Treadwell, M. Bright
      M. Thomas
1966 O. Jacoby, D. Morse
      P. Levitt, S. Lazarus
1967 C. Holt, M. B. Townsend
      M. Finch, G. Dawkins
1968 C. Smith, S. Lawrence
      E. Van Zandt, Mrs. A. W. Noland
1969 H. Baron, P. Soloway
      Mrs. J. Simon, G. Kasle
      N. Anderson

1970	O. Jacoby, L. Gurvich
	J. Frankel, J. Linhart
	J. Jacoby
1971	J. Zilic, V. Zilic
	E. Van Zandt, S. Lazarus
1972	K. Petterson, P. Hawkins
	K. Bradley, O. Moore
1973	J. Foster, A. Van Hoose
	J. Rainey, W. Jones
1974	M. Shapiro, L. Kolker
	R. Smith, D. Malec
	R. Oshlag

MASTERS PAIRS

1960	M. G. Wallington, V. Ellzey
1961	L. Green, J. Driscoll
1962	B. Lazard, S. Lazard, *tied with*
	J. Jacoby, G. R. Nail
1963	S. Lazard, Dr. R. P. Greene
1964	S. Lazard, Dr. R. P. Greene
1965	R. Stoll, J. Gerber
1966	J. LaNoue, P. Munafo
1967	B. Pontius, Dr. E. D. Dillion
1968	Mrs. E. Balding, Mrs. H. Bell
1969	Mrs. E. S. Alpaugh, P. Munafo
1970	Mrs. M. O'Brien, Mrs. C. Sanders
1971	N. Silverstein, J. Colglazier
1972	J. Blair, D. Siebert
1973	B. Kennedy, C. Sanders
1974	S. Greenberg, M. Lair

OPEN PAIRS

1960	Mrs. J. D. Stephenson, Lt. J. Payton
1961	O. Jacoby, J. Jacoby
1962	J. Glick, N. Silverstein
1963	F. Hoadley, R. Dreyfus
1964	G. Pisk, H. A. Cohen
1965	S. Lazarus, P. Levitt
1966	S. Lazarus, P. Levitt
1967	J. Duval, W. Riddle
1968	P. Hood, G. M. Pisk
1969	J. G. Ripstra, M. Nelson
1970	C. Holt, C. Robinson, *tied with*
	D. Siebert, A. Siebert
1971	R. Doughty, Dr. R. Greene
1972	D. Kaiser, R. Kaiser
1973	T. Radjef, D. Hill
1974	M. Blumenthal, S. Leibowitz

MEN'S PAIRS

1960	J. Jacoby, J. Spessard
1961	L. Brown, D. Clay
1962	F. Hoadley, L. Gurvich
1963	S. Lazard, R. Dreyfus
1964	F. H. Condon, J. D. Colglazier
1965	G. Dawkins, B. Gentry
1966	T. Wood, Jr., Dr. C. S. Merlin
1967	Dr. H. Oddie, D. Ball
1968	F. Hamilton, C. Bishop
1969	T. L. Radjef, J. Walton
1970	G. Michaud, L. Richardson
1971	S. Coolik, E. Oxford
1972	M. Passell, J. Rosenblum
1973	F. Hoadley, P. Munafo
1974	R. Teel, M. Davis

WOMEN'S PAIRS

1960	C. W. Coleman, T. Caspary
1961	T. Potts, W. A. Stephens
1962	G. Van Geffen, C. Van Geffen
1963	W. J. Nelson, S. Morais
1964	E. G. Chilleteau, A. B. Hurd
1965	Mrs. J. H. Toledano, Mrs. A. W. Harrison, *tied with*
	Mrs. R. Gaston, Mrs. C. Kantrow
1966	Mrs. S. Beard, Mrs. G. Perutz

1967	C. Hurd, R. O. Groves
1968	M. Brachman, S. Lazarus, *tied with*
	Mrs. J. Rosenblum, Mrs. M. Levin
1969	Mrs. J. F. Kennedy, Mrs. D. B. Dawes
1970	J. Littrell, M. Bennett
1971	T. Bassett, Mrs. R. Kaiser
1972	Mrs. C. McInnis, Mrs. H. Werner
1973	N. Alpaugh, E. Van Zandt
1974	G. Colley, R. Horwitz

MIXED PAIRS

1960	Mrs. C. Smith, D. Carter
1961	H. Sobel, R. Golden
1962	J. Frankel, L. Gurvich
1963	A. Gutowsky, Mrs. N. Alpaugh
1964	C. Strouse, Mrs. J. M. Mathews
1965	B. Wolff, C. Miller
1966	L. Gurvich, J. Frankel
1967	M. B. Townsend, G. R. Nail
1968	Mrs. E. S. Alpaugh, P. Munafo
1969	Dr. M. Anderson, Mrs. M. H. Hall
1970	L. Gurvich, J. Frankel
1971	Mrs. R. Schoenau, A. Dovell
1972	Mrs. H. Gardner, Dr. C. Robinson

SOUTHERN CONFERENCE FALL*

OPEN TEAMS

1952	M. A. Lightman, Mrs. Z. Glover
	Nate Silverstein, Louis Levy
1953	C. Goren, Mrs. M. Wagar, J. A. Walton
	N. Chanin, M. Hodges
1954	E. F. Roy, Mrs. P. Eberson
	T. Spiewack, J. H. Moore
1955	S. Smith, M. A. Anderson
	Mrs. S. Johnson, R. M. Carter
1956	J. Glick, M. Turk, N. Silverstein
	R. Michelson
1957	Mrs. A. D. White, J. K. West, A. Massie
	Mrs. W. LeSeuer, Mrs. R. Ronn
1958	F. Berger, L. Gurvich, S. Lazard
	N. Silverstein, Dr. J. Fisher
1959	Mr. and Mrs. R. G. Sharp
	Mr. and Mrs. S. Kasie
1961	J. George, D. Hart, J. Kay, Jr.
	L. Loeb, C. Yelton
1962	E. Blackwood, Dr. D. Trapp
	Mrs. S. Davis, S. Lanier, *tied with*
	Mr. and Mrs. T. K. Sanders
	Mrs. M. Wagar, H. Hume
	M. Cohn
1963	E. Murdoch, Dr. C. Burnham
	Mr. and Mrs. T. Teague
1964	Mr. and Mrs. R. Freeman
	Mr. and Mrs. R. Sharp
1965	P. Weiss, R. Sharp
	B. Creed, L. Clark

MASTERS PAIRS

1957	Mrs. M. Wagar, A. Miller
1958	W. H. Adams, T. K. Sanders
1959	Mr. and Mrs. T. K. Sanders
1961	W. B. Woodson, J. McDonald
1962	Mr. and Mrs. A. Siebert
1963	H. R. Hall, V. Davis
1964	J. H. Armstrong, Dr. C. Duffy
1965	J. Jacoby, N. Silverstein

OPEN PAIRS

1952	L. Campbell, F. H. Richmond
1953	Mr. and Mrs. J. Glick
1954	F. H. Sexton, Mrs. D. Smyth
1955	Mrs. P. Semonin, C. Klayer

* This tournament was discontinued in 1966.

1956   L. Zollinger, C. Inman, Jr.
1957   M. Turk, J. Glick
1958   N. Silverstein, M. A. Lightman
1959   J. McKenzie, M. Phillips
1961   M. Cohn, H. Hume
1962   E. Murdoch, Dr. C. Burnham, *tied with*
       Mrs. H. Payne, Mrs. R. C. Shuptrine
1963   Mrs. G. Spencer, Mrs. R. Mourer
1964   Capt. H. Hertzberg, Mrs. M. Yates
1965   C. Smith, C. Kittle

MEN'S PAIRS

1952   M. A. Lightman, S. J. Maxwell
1953   J. E. Beagin, P. Herndon, *tied with*
       W. Downs, J. Caller
1954   A. Kincaid, F. A. Bombeck
1955   B. Goldberg, W. A. Peale
1956   J. Glick, M. Turk
1957   D. Carter, J. D. Daniel
1958   W. H. Adams, T. K. Sander
1959   T. K. Sanders, H. Hume
1961   G. Harris, D. Krakowski
1962   Dr. C. Burnham, T. Teague
1963   S. A. Baker, Dr. D. P. Edmundson
1964   S. Neely, M. Bell
1965   L. Levinson, R. Read

WOMEN'S PAIRS

1952   L. Lusky, R. Hunter
1953   C. Campbell, G. Barrett
1954   J. Bailey, J. E. Clinkinbeard
1955   J. Rosenfield, S. Johnson
1956   M. Hudson, E. L. Crew
1957   V. C. Scoggin, J. Wilson
1958   S. Lazard, J. Frankel
1959   J. Pearson, C. W. Peterson
1961   R. E. Thompson, S. W. Seagull
1962   L. Haynes, J. M. Clayton
1963   R. Ruppel, R. Burton
1964   E. Murdoch, Mrs. T. H. Teague
1965   Mrs. M. Porter, Mrs. J. Spence

MIXED PAIRS

1952   Mrs. E. L. Crew, C. E. Wilson
1953   Mrs. E. L. Crew, C. E. Wilson, *tied with*
       Mrs. J. B. McConnel, J. A. Walton
1954   Mrs. E. J. Ittenback, I. Spiewack
1955   G. Smith, C. H. Hall
1956   Mrs. J. T. Brown, F. Berger
1957   M. Cytron, D. Carter
1958   Mrs. J. S. Roleson, M. Turk

SOUTHERN CONFERENCE SPRING*

OPEN TEAMS

1963   Mr. and Mrs. J. McKenzie, Sr.
       Mrs. J. Hemphill, Mrs. P. Attaway
1964   Mrs. L. Lerman, R. M. Carter
       Mr. and Mrs. R. G. Sharp, *tied with*
       J. H. Moran, C. Henke
       J. D. King, J. J. Leach
       F. C. Rubbra
1965   H. R. Hall, H. Hume
       G. Cronin, J. Blair
       B. Jenkins
1966   R. Morris, J. L. Bowman
       Capt. E. R. Lewis, Mrs. D. Lewis

MASTERS PAIRS

1963   Mr. and Mrs. R. Sharp
1965   H. R. Hall, M. Wagar
1966   P. Pender, J. Flint

---

* This tournament was discontinued in 1967.

OPEN PAIRS

1963   Mr. and Mrs. R. Sharp
1964   H. Baron, B. Crane
1965   J. I. Meyers, G. Elder
1966   C. Smith, Dr. R. Farris

MEN'S PAIRS

1963   T. Sanders, H. Behm
1964   R. M. Carter, L. Roberts
1965   C. Miller, D. Morse
1966   B. Crane, T. Sanders

WOMEN'S PAIRS

1963   W. E. Thompson, G. A. Davis
1964   J. Morris, C. Mahan
1965   C. Fox, F. Hultman
1966   Mrs. H. Peters, Mrs. J. E. Clinkinbeard

MIXED PAIRS

1964   Mrs. E. E. Shouse, A. Marler

DISTRICT 11   (Central and southern Indiana, central and southern Ohio, most of Kentucky, southern West Virginia)

DISTRICT 11

KNOCKOUT TEAMS

1969   Mr. and Mrs. M. Cohn, P. Leon
       R. K. Fleischman
1971   J. Blair, M. Blumenthal
       P. Swanson, D. Faskow
1973   F. Hamilton, K. Cohen, M. Blumenthal
       P. Leon, J. Sheridan, L. Kozlove
1974   C. Bauer, B. Neikirk, R. Baron
       D. MacAslan (Winter)
       Dr. H. Stocker, S. Murstein, P. Palm
       B. Staples (Spring)

OPEN TEAMS

1962   J. and J. Denny, S. Stein
       Mrs. J. Halloran, G. Marsee
1963   J. Beebe, W. Riester
       Mr. and Mrs. W. O'Hara
1964   J. Simon, J. Denny
       P. Matthews, W. Long
1965   A. Bombeck, M. Thomas
       J. Blair, P. Swanson
1966   K. Woolsey, J. Hrones, Jr.
       J. Levinson, J. Passel
1967   J. W. Levinson, D. Rotman
       Dr. D. Kitzes, L. J. Spivack, *tied with*
       K. Austin, J. Angel, H. Marsh, S. Zimmerman
1968   J. Groben, D. Kahane
       W. Morris, J. Winkler
1969   J. J. Feld, T. Todd
       S. D. Zimmerman, M. Ferguson
1970   Mr. and Mrs. E. Cain
       D. Morrow, J. R. Mathews
1971   Mrs. J. Clinkinbeard, J. Lay
       R. Stone, A. Cokin
1972   G. Potts, J. Wisemiller
       J. Biddle, C. Kopp
1973   W. Snider, R. Katz
       H. Rabin, G. Chait
1974   B. Coombs, R. Koopman
       S. Cohn, J. Gargrave (Winter)
       F. Hamilton, J. Sheridan
       J. Starr, C. Bishop
       L. Kozlove (Spring)

LIFE MASTERS PAIRS

1972 N. Fisher, T. Hodapp

MASTERS PAIRS

1964 H. Baron, B. Crane
1965 R. Sharp, L. M. Clark
1966 R. Zoller, P. Leon
1969 N. Coombs, Jr., G. Steuernagel
1970 Mr. and Mrs. J. A. Gordon
1971 P. Swanson, J. Blair
1972 M. Lipp, J. Dink, Jr.
1974 C. Said, S. Tallent (Winter)
     R. Walsh, K. Shuman (Spring)

OPEN PAIRS

1962 S. Harris, E. Rosen
1963 M. Cohn, P. Scezci
1964 C. Coon, M. Moss
1965 J. Blair, P. Swanson
1966 W. Flannery, P. Swanson
1967 M. Angell, W. K. Smith
1968 F. Hamilton, H. Perlman
1969 T. Clarke, J. D. King
1970 K. Rhodes, H. Itkin
1971 J. Biddle, J. Wisemiller
1972 S. Sherman, D. Boughman
1973 M. Blumenthal, S. Leibowitz
1974 J. Sheridan, L. Kozlove (Winter)
     J. Morrison, J. Wyatt (Spring)

MEN'S PAIRS

1962 J. Yavitz, C. Peres
1963 Lt. N. Coombs, R. Zoller
1964 C. Coon, M. Moss
1965 N. Silverstein, G. Treadwell
1966 E. R. McKinney, Jr., D. Guerin
1967 J. Beard, T. Johnson
1968 J. Finegan, M. Keisler
1969 T. Peters, R. Brown
1970 T. Hodapp, S. Cohn
1971 A. Kaseman, Dr. C. Bishop
1973 W. MacDonald, R. Calhoun
1974 M. Aliotta, R. Huggard

WOMEN'S PAIRS

1962 W. Eckhart, C. Maudlin
1963 A. Pacella, J. Baum
1964 D. Johnson, C. Wallace
1965 Mrs. I. Rosenbaum, Mrs. M. L. Thompson
1966 B. Hartley, Mrs. W. M. Baughn
1967 Mrs. M. Thompson, A. Gordon
1968 Mrs. E. Argersinger, Mrs. G. Rosenschein
1969 Mrs. E. Reich, G. E. Neil
1970 Mrs. G. Crounse, Mrs. F. Eberson
1971 Mrs. T. Sanders, L. Hanson
1973 Mrs. A. Falender, Mrs. R. Sundstrom
1974 Mrs. J. Pattison, L. Kleve

MIXED PAIRS

1963 G. E. Neil, T. Sines
1964 J. Sharp, F. Ensminger
1967 F. Weisbach, Mrs. J. Hamilton
1968 Mrs. L. W. McConnell, T. C. Ezzell

MIDWEST FALL

KNOCKOUT TEAMS

1973 M. Hunter, D. Carmeris
     S. Cox, C. Ferry

OPEN TEAMS

1959 Mr. and Mrs. W. Rosen
     B. Casement, A. Habel
1960 Mr. and Mrs. J. Simon
     Mr. and Mrs. J. Denny, *tied with*
     S. Harris, E. Rosen
     F. Pettijohn, S. McComas, *and*
     B. Creed, S. Scaffidi
     J. Biddle, C. Rudecek
1961 W. Rosen, A. Leavitt
     E. Rosen, B. Crane
1962 B. Crane, R. Sharp
     W. Rosen, E. Rosen
     A. Leavitt
1963 J. Biddle, J. Polsner
     B. Riestner, J. Wisemiller
1964 E. Rosen, A. Zeh
     B. Farber, W. Vaughan
     J. Wachter
1965 M. Altman, G. Turner
     D. Rotman, R. Mosher
1966 J. Flint, P. Pender
     H. Flint, J. Denny
1967 Mr. and Mrs. W. Rosen
     G. Polak, B. Crane
1972 W. Snider, L. Gould
     L. Bluhm, J. Piaski
1973 B. Crane, K. Shuman
     G. Caravelli, Dr. J. Fisher
1974 C. Hudecek, F. McClure
     L. Willinger, D. Bondy
     B. Hale

MASTERS PAIRS

1972 J. Zimmerman, B. Hardies
1974 R. Shoup, B. Coombs

OPEN PAIRS

1959 J. Wachter, J. Hanley
1960 P. H. Sexton, P. D. Mathews
1961 B. Crane, R. Sharp
1962 E. Hochfeld, W. Rosen
1963 G. Polack, C. Ruther
1964 H. Miller, J. Weiner
1965 Mr. and Mrs. W. Mann
1966 J. Flint, P. Pender
1967 W. Zurfluh, G. Durgin
1972 H. Gordon, D. Walker
1973 Z. Johantgen, Mrs. W. Crawford
1974 G. Hartleben, K. Hartleben

MEN'S PAIRS

1959 J. Felfuss, A. Lindberg
1960 H. Shoop, C. B. Knuff
1961 J. Wachter, R. Shepard
1962 M. Heller, M. Lopata
1963 O. Jacoby, P. Levitt
1964 H. Schenken, I. Stakgold
1965 F. W. Carlson, S. Koritala, *tied with*
     A. Bell, R. Amann
1966 W. Brown, S. C. Follmer
1967 J. Kamin, L. Mines
1973 C. Bauer, D. Boxley

WOMEN'S PAIRS

1959 E. Benjamin, D. Bramhall
1960 W. MacLeod, R. G. Watson
1961 S. Leavitt, C. Stolkin
1962 C. Piowaty, E. H. Charlton
1963 P. Paris, P. H. Miller
1964 F. Arst, H. Baron
1965 L. Herzberg, E. Hyre
1966 Mrs. R. Decker, Mrs. D. Fuller
1967 J. Cohn, J. Sage
1973 G. Funk, Mrs. K. Nielsen

MIXED PAIRS

1959 A. Klein, F. Ensminger
1960 Mrs. J. Simon, J. Denny
1961 Mr. and Mrs. M. Cooper
1962 Mrs. J. French, M. Cooper
1963 J. L. Bowman, K. O'Keeffe
1964 C. Ruther, S. Honet
1965 F. Orner, D. Rotman
1966 Mrs. R. Gordon, P. Pender
1967 B. Larson, H. Pickett

MIDWEST SPRING

KNOCKOUT TEAMS

1972 H. Mouser, Jr., N. Butcher
      L. Secrist, L. Vild

OPEN TEAMS

1944 J. Van Brooks, R. A. Malchie
      H. Feinberg, A. Levy
1945 E. Wood, C. Nafe
      W. M. Zeller, W. Pray
1946 M. Adams, J. Banks
      O. Jacoby, J. Kravatz
1947 A. S. Novak, A. E. Stein
      J. Epstein, P. Ochs
      R. M. Woodworth
1948 J. Halencamp, C. A. Hall
      Mr. and Mrs. H. Feldstein
1949 Mr. and Mrs. C. Wallace
      J. Halenkamp, C. Hall
      S. Sublette
1950 G. R. Nail, E. Wolter
      I. Rosenberg, F. A. Bombeck
1951 H. Doern, S. Delott
      J. Carlin, Dr. H. McDaniels
1952 A. A. Rosen, B. Kaufman
      M. Ellenby, E. Hochfeld
1953 J. Lennon, S. Hoblitt
      F. Ensminger, M. Van Pelt
      J. Van Brooks
1954 D. Carter, J. G. Ripstra
      J. E. Simon, A. Harvey
      R. M. Carter
1955 C. Bensinger, S. Katz
      J. Glick, M. Turk
1956 Mrs. P. Steinberg, J. E. Simon
      M. Cytron, J. J. Parish
1957 J. Jacobs, E. E. Stimming
      E. G. Dautell, C. J. Hudecek
1958 Mr. and Mrs. R. Sharp
      J. E. Simon, L. Weiner
      L. Rosenthal
1959 J. Rodkin, R. Revell
      D. Rotman, E. L. Rosen
1960 I. Stakgold, I. Berkson
      W. Rosen, A. Sheinwold
      A. Glatt
1961 A. C. Bell, G. Polak
      R. Cruise, J. Blair
      R. Vission
1962 Mr. and Mrs. R. Sharp
      Mrs. W. Miller, B. Creed
      T. Mahaffey, Jr.
1963 M. Cocherell, B. Bratcher
      R. Jerles, G. R. St. Pierre
1964 Mrs. S. Lerman, R. M. Carter
      Mr. and Mrs. R. Sharp, *tied with*
      J. H. Moran, C. Henke
      J. D. King, J. J. Leach
      F. C. Rubbra
1965 H. Hume, J. Blair
      P. Swanson, M. Low
      Mrs. T. K. Sanders
1966 A. J. Astrologes, J. Levinson
      R. Halperin, G. Caravelli

1967 B. Crane, G. Marsee
      G. Polak, R. G. Zoller
1968 Mr. and Mrs. W. H. Dillingham
      Mrs. H. Baird, Mrs. C. Hall
1969 D. Faskow, H. Sachs
      P. Swanson, M. Blumenthal
      D. Fleischman
1970 Mr. and Mrs. R. Bland
      Mrs. J. Davis, J. Gormong, *tied with*
      L. J. Phillips, J. Zilic
      G. Caravelli, M. Altman
1971 D. Thompson, B. Matthews
      D. Carter, B. Phillips (Swiss)
      D. Thompson, B. Matthews
      D. Carter, H. Lackman, *tied with*
      H. Sexton, N. Richardson
      C. Stemming, J. Epstein (Board-a-Match)
1972 F. Hamilton, H. Perlman
      L. Deaton, P. Swanson, *tied with*
      J. Sheridan, L. Kozlove
      D. Smith, D. Requard
1973 J. Gardner, A. Falk
      D. Swarthout, J. Fatka

MASTERS PAIRS

1968 J. Reel, N. Coombs
1969 W. A. Epperson, L. Roberts
1970 Mrs. J. Danner, L. Laughner
1971 J. Kozlove, L. Kozlove
1972 W. Riester, J. Biddle
1973 J. Davis, E. Hatch

OPEN PAIRS

1944 Mrs. R. Buck, T. Mahaffey
1945 Mrs. L. J. Goldstein, G. Schildmiller
1946 S. A. Fink, A. S. Goldsmith
1947 A. Harvey, F. Weisbach
1948 E. Babin, A. Goldsmith
1949 J. J. Stedem, G. Alderton
1950 M. Goldman, E. Burns
1951 J. Hancock, E. Hochfeld
1952 J. Wachter, H. Heberlein
1953 G. Turner, V. Bennahum
1954 A. Harvey, R. Carter
1955 A. Harvey, Mrs. L. Rhodes
1956 H. S. Brown, V. Remey
1957 C. A. Hall, C. Wallace
1958 Mr. and Mrs. R. Sharp
1959 Mrs. D. Smyth, E. Isralsky
1960 Mr. and Mrs. T. K. Sanders
1961 J. Cayne, G. Polak
1962 B. Crane, J. Epstein
1963 G. Mitchell, W. Riester
1964 H. Baron, B. Crane
1965 B. Crane, M. Wagar
1966 W. K. Smith, O. M. Angell
1967 B. L. Ascheim, L. Deaton
1968 Mr. and Mrs. H. C. Wilton
1969 H. Bethe, A. Waldmann
1970 L. Hetzer, D. Requard
1971 M. and L. Low
1972 H. Perlman, F. Hamilton
1973 J. Starr, F. Hamilton

MEN'S PAIRS

1944 E. Blackwood, W. Pray
1945 J. E. Cain, R. Kempner
1946 O. Jacoby, A. Gutowsky
1947 H. W. Clow, E. R. Page
1948 J. Kravatz, M. Adams
1949 W. von Zedtwitz, S. Hoblitt
1950 J. Winston, C. Berman
1951 J. Kozlove, L. Goren
1952 J. Millerd, A. C. Bell
1953 E. Berman, J. P. Utz
1954 E. J. Crooks, Dr. P. Bernstein

1955 H. H. Logan, Judge B. G. Mathews
1956 C. Bishop, L. J. Cohen
1957 B. F. Camin, R. Toffler
1958 J. L. Johnson, W. A. Jones
1959 J. Simon, J. Denny
1960 J. Schwartz, C. Bauer
1961 P. Mathews, F. Holton
1962 F. Weisbach, N. Marx
1963 R. Sharp, B. Crane
1964 R. M. Carter, L. Roberts
1965 H. Hume, J. Blair
1966 J. Levinson, E. Schless
1967 M. Low, A. Bell
1968 M. Hargrove, T. Peters
1970 N. Coombs, T. Peters
1971 B. Penton, J. Johnson
1972 R. Rudolph, N. Frank
1973 L. Robinson, B. Precker

WOMEN'S PAIRS

1944 E. J. Ittenbach, R. E. Duncan
1945 J. Gutman, H. M. Smith
1946 A. W. Bowden, W. H. Anderson
1947 Mrs. P. Steinberg, S. L. Cytron
1948 Mrs. L. Goldstein, Mrs. H. Feldstein
1949 J. Kelley, M. L. Thompson
1950 Mrs. A. E. Fey, Mrs. L. R. Anderson
1951 K. Wood, H. W. Lackman
1952 A. Mohl, A. J. Leonard
1953 J. Sanford, T. F. Barnes
1954 M. L. Thompson, S. A. Brower
1955 M. Cytron, Mrs. P. Steinberg
1956 M. Hardy, J. Y. Brown
1957 W. W. Gill, J. Halloran
1958 J. E. Morris, W. Simpson
1959 J. Sharp, G. Rosenschein
1960 S. Kasle, K. Pettijohn
1961 K. Baum, M. L. Berg
1962 H. H. Baum, J. Berg
1963 Mrs. G. Kerr, Mrs. R. Troxel
1964 J. Morris, C. Mahan
1965 G. E. Neil, E. E. Reich
1966 D. Levinson, N. Rohr
1967 Mrs. E. F. Romminger, Mrs. C. G. Priem
1968 Mrs. D. Smyth, Mrs. R. McNutt
1970 M. A. Falender, Mrs. R. Sundstrom
1971 Mrs. A. Fallender, Mrs. R. Sundstrom
1972 M. Barthel, M. Smith
1973 G. Hildebrand, M. Frees

MIXED PAIRS

1944 Mrs. M. Gutman, F. R. Buck
1945 Mrs. J. Kelly, O. K. Fraunstein
1946 F. Stratford, M. S. McComas
1947 Mrs. H. A. Bridges, L. Herman
1948 Mrs. E. D. Tyler, W. von Zedtwitz
1949 M. Flasher, J. Cohan
1950 Mrs. C. C. Caldwell, A. Grau
1951 Mrs. J. Y. Brown, N. W. Jordan
1952 Mr. and Mrs. H. F. Heberlein
1953 Mr. and Mrs. J. Gelman
1954 M. Malchie, Dr. E. A. Hochman
1955 M. Cytron, G. Nash
1956 Mrs. I. W. Campbell, R. F. Morris, *tied with*
        Mrs. J. Simon, R. Sharp
1957 C. A. Hall, J. Halenkamp
1958 Mr. and Mrs. T. K. Sanders
1959 H. Shambron, Dr. W. Barron
1960 Mrs. E. A. Mahoney, D. Carter
1961 Mrs. T. R. Sanford, O. Jacoby
1962 Mr. and Mrs. J. R. Hughes
1963 Mr. and Mrs. J. Berg
1964 Mrs. E. E. Shouser, A. Marler
1965 G. Kasle, E. Zeve
1966 G. Cooper, G. Polak
1967 Mr. and Mrs. R. Sharp

INDIVIDUAL

1956 L. Jaffe

WESTERN STATES

TEAM OF FOUR

1934 S. B. Fink, O. S. Emrich
        E. Babin, A. L. Siegel
1935 C. Hall, R. M. Wildberg
        C. Porter, W. Hopkins
1936 A. Landy, J. Glick
        M. Glick, J. H. Higgins
1937 C. N. Bensinger, W. S. Lapp
        T. Clarke, D. L. Street
1938 R. J. Henderson, H. Auslander
        H. Quinlivan, E. C. Donaghey
1939 J. E. Simon, A. E. Stein
        G. Scherck, C. C. Lockett
        T. Faulkner
1940 Mr. and Mrs. D. Carter
        A. R. Kincaid, F. A. Bombach
1941 F. DuRelle, J. F. Taylor
        D. L. Street, J. Cleve Iler, Jr.
1942 Mrs. A. Coffin, Mrs. E. J. Ettenbach
        Mr. and Mrs. V. R. Rapp
1943 M. Adams, Mrs. A. Whitehead
        H. C. Keubler, J. W. Denny
1944 J. E. Cain, L. Roet
        Mrs. L. Rhodes, H. Ogust

OPEN PAIRS

1934 S. B. Fink, O. S. Emrich
1935 C. H. Porter, W. F. Hopkins
1936 R. W. Halpin, M. S. Reilly
1937 A. S. Goldsmith, M. J. Nagusky
1938 A. Landy, J. Glick
1939 E. J. Babin, S. B. Fink
1940 Mr. and Mrs. C. Wallace
1941 Mr. and Mrs. D. Carter
1942 Mrs. E. Hill, M. Kaiser
1943 F. Nelson, A. Marks
1944 Mrs. E. A. Oberrecht, F. Schneider

WOMEN'S PAIRS

1937 Mrs. H. J. White, F. Klein
1938 Mrs. E. B. Culp, G. Lear
1939 Mrs. L. Tuholske, Mrs. H. Tenenbaum
1940 Mrs. W. L. Terry, Mrs. W. L. Dickens
1941 Mrs. W. L. Dickens, Mrs. L. B. Buchanan
1942 J. Dunlap, Mrs. G. T. Atkins
1943 Mrs. B. T. Lawrence, Mrs. A. W. McNeiley
1944 Mrs. C. J. Sweeney, Mrs. A. Bridges

MIXED PAIRS

1935 Mrs. J. Friedlander, P. Steiner
1936 Mrs. F. E. Ittenbach, W. J. Pray
1937 Mrs. H. J. White, W. M. Fulton
1938 Mr. and Mrs. C. M. Whitehead
1939 Mrs. M. A. Clark, T. Faulkner
1940 Mr. and Mrs. D. Miller
1941 Mr. and Mrs. V. R. Rupp
1942 Mrs. O. Frisch, M. Hennrich
1943 F. Ensminger, Mrs. M. Gutman
1944 Mrs. R. E. Duncan, T. C. Alexander

MASTERS INDIVIDUAL

1941 E. E. Stein
1942 L. C. Hagemeyer

DISTRICT 12 (Northwestern Ohio, most of Michigan)

GREAT LAKES

OPEN TEAMS

1959 P. G. Kraut, G. R. Targett
      J. Harrison, K. Austin
1960 S. Fink, N. Fribourg
      C. Braman, A. Szabo, *tied with*
      H. E. Hathorn, J. Nischwitz
      J. D. Meehan, W. R. Gubbins
1961 M. J. Cohn, G. Marsee
      J. Young, F. Sayed
1962 H. Wilton, H. Sexton
      J. Biddle, S. Scaffidi
      G. Mitchell
1963 F. Ensminger, C. Bishop
      J. Van Brooks, L. Cohen, *tied with*
      J. Young, D. Dillon
      S. Stein, H. Shanbrom, *tied with*
      D. Smith, A. Price
      Dr. H. McDonald, M. Arndt
1964 I. Farber, S. Lawrence
      Dr. D. D. Grove, W. Rife
1965 A. Gordon, N. Gerstman
      M. Altman, D. Rutstein
1966 W. Flannery, D. Faskow
      S. Ruskin, P. Swanson
1967 J. Levinson, W. Rosen
      E. Rosen, G. Polak
1968 M. Cohn, A. Silber
      R. Zoller, J. Rosentiel
1969 H. Pearlman, S. Margulis
      G. Hann, C. Said
1970 D. Cowan, M. Cummings
      D. Phillips, B. Elliot
1971 D. Yanko, M. Maddox
      H. Shevitz, G. Hann
1972 H. Perlman, F. Hamilton
      C. Burger, R. Zoller
1973 R. Shoup, R. Koopman
      D. Linton, J. Gargrave
1974 B. Stuart, P. Fodor
      A. Korde, R. Kuusik, *tied with*
      H. Perlman, J. Starr
      F. Hamilton, B. Rosen, *tied with*
      W. Buhl, J. DeSerio
      R. Pearl, N. Markakis, *tied with*
      D. Suty, G. Owens
      M. Maddox, M. Maddox, *tied with*
      E. Rosen, J. Rosen
      A. Susskind, S. Rose

MASTERS PAIRS

1974 R. LaCour, M. Passell

OPEN PAIRS

1959 F. Rappleyea, M. Pike
1960 W. Gardiner, I. Zucker
1961 S. Stein, G. Marsee
1962 M. Charfoos, B. Perkers
1963 A. Gordon, N. Gerstman, *tied with*
      C. Burger, M. Ingberman
1964 L. Price, G. Brownlee
1965 D. Brooks, J. White
1966 M. J. Cohn, A. J. Silber
1967 F. Hamilton, E. Banghart
1968 G. Caravelli, M. Rosenberg
1969 H. Pearlman, S. Margulis
1970 J. Gowdy, D. Vincze
1971 M. Low, G. Caravelli
1972 R. Halperin, H. Miller, Jr.
1973 D. Faskow, P. Swanson
1974 G. Hann, H. Akturk

MEN'S PAIRS

1959 F. Sayed, H. Philp
1960 L. L. Rosenthal, H. Behm
1961 B. Crane, E. J. Smith
1962 B. Crane, E. J. Smith
1963 B. Hughes, R. Halperin
1964 F. Weisbach, J. Weismiller
1965 R. Schwartz, R. Sherburn
1966 C. Bishop, J. M. Hinton
1967 G. Marsee, E. J. Smith, Jr.
1968 E. J. Smith, F. Hamilton
1969 B. J. Becker, C. Burger
1970 M. Maddox, V. Remey
1971 J. Alexander, J. Zimmerman
1972 L. Cohen, S. Kahn
1973 F. Bell, S. Landen
1974 R. LaCour, M. Passell

WOMEN'S PAIRS

1959 E. Argersinger, W. McLean
1960 R. French, S. Glass
1961 E. Epstein, R. Leland
1962 R. Barbaris, R. L. Deaton
1963 D. Johnson, M. Schneider
1964 R. K. Jones, A. Goldsmith
1965 F. Miller, M. Bellson
1966 B. Garson, Mrs. N. Bianco
1967 Mrs. R. W. Prange, Mrs. H. Sherwin
1968 S. Stein, J. Friedenberg
1969 S. Stein, J. Friedenberg
1970 A. Gust, L. Goldsmith
1971 R. Kaplan, Mrs. V. Melkovian
1972 J. Remey, R. Dillon
1973 S. Waterstone, R. Brownstein
1974 L. Menthen, A. Dickinson

MIXED PAIRS

1962 M. G. Abrams, W. L. Flannery
1963 Mr. and Mrs. G. Stewart
1964 Mr. and Mrs. M. Kane
1965 L. Goldsmith, S. Heinrich
1966 Mr. and Mrs. M. Kane
1967 Mr. and Mrs. M. Maddox
1968 Mr. and Mrs. M. Maddox
1969 V. Remey, J. Remey
1970 E. Brown, L. Jay
1971 A. Argersinger, P. Leon
1972 Mrs. J. Nangle, D. Pratt
1973 D. Doran, M. Smith

MOTOR CITY

KNOCKOUT TEAMS

1973 S. Smith, R. Yanko
      J. Starr, H. Perlman, F. Hamilton
1974 R. Roosen, V. Remey
      F. Sayed, D. McGarry, J. Zimmerman

OPEN TEAMS

1967 S. Fenkel, R. Peters
      H. Shevitz, R. Yanko
1968 S. Stein, J. Friedenberg
      F. Sayed, P. Leon
1969 H. Perlman, S. Margulis
      D. Katz, L. Cohen
1970 Z. Brooks, D. Brooks
      H. Sachs, D. Ruskin
1971 M. Low, G. Polak
      L. Phillips, G. Caravelli
1972 Mr. and Mrs. D. Rotman
      J. DeWitt, C. Peres
1973 M. Cummings, B. Elliott
      R. Freedman, S. Isaacs

1974   H. Mouser, J. Isralsky
      R. Koopman, J. Gargrave

MASTERS PAIRS

1973   P. Leon, R. Sherburn
1974   J. Gargrave, R. Shoup

OPEN PAIRS

1967   C. Burger, F. Hamilton
1968   S. Stein, F. Sayed
1969   D. Yanko, J. Starr
1970   B. Sherburn, A. Banghart
1971   L. Deaton, N. Fischer
1972   B. Ferguson, J. Carruthers
1973   E. Shepherd, G. Vella
1974   B. Webber, P. Stern

MEN'S PAIRS

1967   H. Kreitzburg, E. Moorehead
1968   S. Berg, R. Zoller
1969   D. Searcy, D. Swarthout
1970   C. Bishop, D. Yanko
1971   Dr. H. Stocker, Dr. R. Shoup
1972   Dr. J. Fisher, B. Crane
1974   C. Bishop, A. Bricklin

WOMEN'S PAIRS

1967   C. Gordon, J. Maddocks
1968   A. Argersinger, M. Wagar
1969   S. Stein, J. Friedenberg
1970   J. Halloran, P. Miller
1971   P. Miller, J. Halloran
1972   G. French, Mrs. R. Porter
1974   F. Schwartz, M. Feldman

MIXED PAIRS

1967   C. Denninger, J. Maddocks
1968   Mr. and Mrs. R. Andersen
1969   J. Remey, R. Roosen
1970   Mrs. D. West, J. Shelnut
1971   B. Riordan, R. Sherburn
1972   Dr. and Mrs. R. House
1973   B. Riordan, R. Huggard

DISTRICT 13 (Most of Wisconsin, Chicago area, Upper Michigan Peninsula)

CENTRAL STATES

KNOCKOUT TEAMS

1962   A. Leavitt, M. Ingberman
      W. Rosen, A. Glatt
      D. Rutstein, A. Press
1963   M. Ely, M. Tish
      J. Higaschiuchi, W. Hiura
      J. Ditto
1964   E. Rosen, S. Leavitt
      P. Sugar, C. Norton
      B. Norton
1965   E. Rosen, L. Cohen
      R. Katz, J. Wachter
      W. Vaughan
1966   C. Peres, M. Ingberman
      D. Rotman, I. Stakgold
      M. Ellenby
1967   Mr. and Mrs. W. Rosen, G. Polak
      B. Norton, L. Ferer

1968   O. Jacoby, Mr. and Mrs. M. Brachman
      P. Levitt, P. Soloway
      E. Hochfeld
1969   M. Rosenberg, G. Caravelli
      D. Rotman, C. Peres
      M. Ellenby, B. Norton
1970   E. Hochfeld, R. Amann
      C. Peres, I. Stakgold
1971   Dr. R. Katz, L. Spivack
      J. Levinson, F. Hamilton
      C. Burger, H. Perlman
1972   G. Caravelli, L. Cohen
      M. Rosenberg, R. Andersen
1973   G. Caravelli, L. Cohen
      Dr. R. Katz, M. Rosenberg
      R. Andersen
1974   M. Garner, J. Weiner
      C. Urban, H. Miller, Jr.

LIFE AND SENIOR MASTERS TEAMS

1957   L. B. Weiner, M. Q. Ellenby
      E. Hochfeld, Mrs. G. Turner
      T. Fenwick
1958   W. Blank, S. Kasle
      Mr. and Mrs. R. Sharp
1959   Mr. and Mrs. W. Rosen
      L. Ferer, G. Goldstein
1960   E. Rosen, W. Hiura
      K. Higaschiuchi, S. Harris
1961   E. Hochfeld, I. Stakgold
      G. Polak, Mrs. G. Turner
      R. Freeman, *tied with*
      G. Marsee, Mrs. D. J. Cook
      R. Casement, W. L. Stickey
1962   M. S. Reilly, V. Heckel
      J. Yavitz, C. Peres
1964   S. Leavitt, A. Leavitt
      M. Low, J. Blair

MASTERS PAIRS

1952   Mrs. F. Arst, M. Fleig
1953   H. Doern, S. Delott
1954   E. Rosen, R. Simitz
1955   T. Fenwick, J. McGervey
1956   E. Hochfeld, M. Q. Ellenby
1957   W. Rose, T. Fenwick
1958   F. Arst, L. Rosenthal
1959   R. Wolf, L. Weiner
1960   J. D. King, C. Ruther
1961   Mrs. E. A. Mahony, D. Carter
1962   W. Rosen, M. Ingberman
1963   S. Leavitt, J. Gayne
1964   S. Leavitt, P. Sugar
1965   M. S. Reilly, J. Heckel
1966   M. Lawhorn, B. Sides
1967   R. Hemmings, H. Rabin
1968   A. Kurti, J. Martin
1969   A. Leavitt, W. Rosen
1970   S. Halperin, A. Astrologes
1971   M. Madsen, J. White
1972   V. Levin, P. Schiffert
1973   G. Polak, L. Phillips
1974   R. Melson, T. Beckman (Winter)
      A. Leavitt, G. Polak (Spring)

OPEN TEAMS

1935   R. Kempner, C. W. Rilling
      M. H. Besser, A. Glatt
1936   E. Culbertson, L. J. Haddad
      R. W. Halpin, W. Jacobs
1937   Mrs. P. Parcells, J. K. Howe
      Mrs. E. Evans, W. Bixby
1938   W. Jacobs, A. Glatt
      R. Kempner, A. Weiss
1939   E. T. Wood, Dr. C. Nafe
      L. J. Welch, F. R. Buck
1940   A. O. Stracke, N. Kent
      J. F. Carlin, S. Delott
1941   Mr. and Mrs. R. B. Johnstone
      M. S. Reilly, P. Smith
      G. A. Carlton, J. Howe

1942 N. Kent, S. Delott
      M. Fleig, J. Carlin
1943 J. Cain, F. R. Buck
      E. T. Wood, L. J. Welch
1944 A. Bryant, H. Feinberg
      J. M. Mathews, D. B. Clarren
1949 Mrs. B. Agruss, J. Carlin
      A. Richard Revell, S. Delott
1951 H. Doern, H. McDaniel
      S. Delott, M. H. Daskais
1952 W. Blank, J. Jacobs
      M. Adams, J. Kravatz
      E. T. Wood
1953 M. Cytron, J. G. Ripstra
      D. Carter, I. Rosenberg
1954 G. Turner, E. Hochfeld
      P. Sugar, D. Rustein
      T. Thomas
1955 W. L. Bland, S. Kasle
      J. Jacobs, J. Epstein
1956 F. Arst, M. Fleig
      J. Bank, M. Adams, *tied with*
      I. N. Garn, R. J. Healy
      F. Rappleyea, R. Hemmings
1964 Mr. and Mrs. A. E. May
      Mr. and Mrs. J. Fourness
1968 Mr. and Mrs. A. E. May
      Mr. and Mrs. J. Fourness
1969 Mr. and Mrs. R. Solomon, I. Kipnis
      Mr. and Mrs. R. Hirsch, *tied with*
      G. Sourlis, Mr. and Mrs. K. Wiley
      M. Peterson, J. Christopher
1970 Mr. and Mrs. M. Nelson
      L. Mines, J. Kamin
1971 B. Hemmings, Mrs. R. Simitz
      R. Sundby, D. Uphoff (Winter)
      S. Leavitt, J. Wachter
      P. Sugar, C. Urban (Spring)
1972 D. Rutstein, J. Mandell
      C. Yelton, A. Weiland (Winter)
      W. Orton, C. Vernay
      D. Botch, Dr. B. Hoenk (Spring)
1973 T. Brashler, M. Snodell
      J. Sturgis, K. Dubrau (Winter)
      C. Weil, D. Florida
      R. Fiesner, J. Kulig, Jr. (Spring)
1974 R. Stern, J. Mandell
      S. Robinson, R. Henderson (Winter)
      D. Yanko, L. Coggan
      S. Landen, F. Bell (Spring)

OPEN PAIRS

1936 L. E. Hart, Jr., J. K. Howe
1937 M. H. Besser, A. Glatt
1938 M. S. Reilly, R. W. Halpin
1939 R. Kempner, W. Jacobs
1940 J. Bank, P. Smith
1941 Dr. A. W. Maier, C. H. Brecher
1942 A. Weiss, A. Gutowsky
1943 L. B. Weiner, A. R. Revell
1944 E. T. Wood, J. Van Brooks
1945 J. Kravatz, A. Bryant
1946 H. Feinberg, D. B. Clarren
1947 C. L. Woldenberg, S. N. Ruttenberg
1949 Mr. and Mrs. G. P. Ryan
1951 J. Jacobs, E. Wood
1952 Mrs. E. Evans, B. Cohen
1953 Mrs. P. Steinberg, L. Weiner
1954 Mrs. H. Klein, J. W. Martin
1955 R. Denner, R. Simitz
1956 M. Cunningham, L. L. Rosenthal
1957 M. Lawhorn, B. Chandler
1960 G. Turner, E. Hochfeld
1961 G. Turner, E. Hochfeld, *tied with*
      Mrs. E. A. Mahony, D. Carter
1962 M. Low, J. Blair
1963 E. Hochfeld, W. Rosen
1964 A. Kincaid, Dr. M. L. Mooney
1965 J. Wachter, E. Rosen
1966 R. Katz, L. Cohen
1967 B. Crane, G. Polak
1968 S. Leavitt, P. Sugar
1969 D. Rotman, E. Rosen

1970 R. Huggard, M. Aliotta
1971 Dr. and Mrs. F. Griffin
1972 H. Perlman, F. Hamilton (Winter)
      G. Caravelli, L. Cohen (Spring)
1973 L. Cohen, Dr. R. Katz (Winter)
      H. Perlman, M. Rosenberg (Spring)
1974 J. Welander, D. Sershon (Winter)
      K. Wiley, L. Wiley, *tied with*
      B. Crane, K. Shuman (Spring)

MEN'S PAIRS

1946 J. A. Eskin, J. W. Cannon, Jr.
1947 M. Fleig, F. Chemelick
1949 B. Cohen, R. Appleyard
1951 R. Halpin, J. Chestnut
1952 A. Glatt, D. Daskais
1953 E. Melchior, P. Steinberg
1954 S. Delott, R. H. Mendal
1955 M. Fleig, E. Hyers
1956 E. Rosen, J. P. Miller
1957 L. Rosenthal, R. Scollay
1960 E. Hochfeld, D. Rotman
1961 R. Schulman, J. Foster
1962 R. Gottlieb, W. Katz
1963 A. Sheinwold, M. Ingberman
1964 A. Bell, D. M. Thomas
1965 R. Kay, A. Astrologes
1966 J. Levinson, A. Astrologes
1967 G. Caravelli, R. Halperin
1968 M. Bernstein, M. Wolock
1969 P. Swanson, G. Polak
1970 E. Post, A. Franzese
1971 G. Polak, A. Leavitt
1972 J. Leary, K. Hanson
1973 W. Snider, H. Rabin
1974 J. Nieberding, G. Kugar

WOMEN'S PAIRS

1940 L. G. Quigley, A. G. Whitehead
1941 R. B. Johnstone, H. W. Sax
1942 H. L. Dick, R. P. Cunningham
1943 J. R. Kelley, M. Thompson
1944 P. Steinberg, H. Lees
1945 M. L. Thompson, J. R. Kelley
1946 M. G. Kearns, W. Burton
1947 P. Marks, R. Swindell
1949 H. Rohner, B. Travelletti
1951 L. Durham, P. Steinberg
1952 R. K. Akin, J. Mohl
1953 G. Sumner, P. Ford
1954 A. DeAlarco, R. W. Reagan
1955 G. LaBounty, J. C. Peebles
1956 H. O'Brien, M. Gould
1957 F. Arst, I. Garn
1960 F. Bloomfield, J. Bauer
1961 F. Arst, J. Rodkin
1952 F. Arst, J. Rodkin
1963 S. Leavitt, W. Rosen
1964 M. Bloom, N. Soffer
1965 F. Arst, J. Deutsch
1966 Mrs. G. Faris, A. Gordon
1967 F. Arst, J. Deutsch
1968 Mrs. N. Welch, Mrs. T. Ludwig, *tied with*
      F. Heifner, Mrs. H. Yedor
1969 E. Kemp, V. Heckel
1970 H. Hirsh, M. Metz
1971 F. Rotman, V. Heckel
1972 N. Rohr, A. Kurti
1973 S. Flaxman, B. King
1974 S. Halperin, S. Zakin

MIXED PAIRS

1939 Mrs. L. P. Cook, R. Kempner
1940 Mrs. R. Akin, E. C. Grage
1941 Mr. and Mrs. W. H. Tallmann
1942 Mrs. P. Spink, A. Gutowsky
1943 Mrs. F. Meyer, W. W. McGhee
1944 Mrs. M. Cunningham, L. B. Weiner
1945 Mrs. J. M. Ray, C. G. Chase
1946 Mrs. M. McKinley, L. B. Weiner
1947 Mrs. D. J. Cook, J. Kravatz
1949 Mrs. P. M. Spink, J. Kempner

1950	Mrs. B. Agruss, J. J. Stedem
1951	Mrs. P. N. Marks, L. Ferer
1952	Mrs. B. L. Travelletti, R. T. McKearnan
1953	Mrs. J. Fox, V. Bennehum
1954	Mrs. P. Steinberg, A. McNeily
1955	E. Count, K. A. Higaschiuchi
1956	M. Beasley, C. P. Rumpf
1957	T. Wilder, A. Conroy
1958	Mrs. R. Briggs, A. Bell
1959	R. Dowd, P. Szesci
1960	G. Harris, D. Rotman
1961	E. Hubbard, W. Kriebel
1962	S. and M. Nelson
1963	M. Bridegroom, R. Balanow
1964	D. Polak, W. Rosen
1965	G. Turner, G. Polak
1966	M. Erickson, I. Guttman
1967	M. Deutsch, J. Deutsch
1968	B. Charney, G. Hartsman
1969	T. Leavitt, G. Polak
1970	J. Deutsch, G. Chait
1971	B. Price, J. Williams
1972	Mrs. M. Tonn, R. Tonn
1973	Mr. and Mrs. W. Tatting

INDIVIDUAL

1944	W. E. McGhee, R. B. Johnstone
	J. C. Bank
1945	H. Lees
1946	M. Cunningham
1947	A. E. Briggs
1954	R. Chapman
1955	R. Terp
1960	J. Yavitz
1964	M. Ozaki
1965	B. Price
1966	J. Stade
1967	C. Blackwell
1968	R. Brody
1969	D. Corbin
1970	C. Said

TRI-UNIT

KNOCKOUT TEAMS

1969	E. Hochfeld, D. Rotman
	C. Peres, R. Amann
1971	M. Case, T. Brashler
	M. Marmer, C. Vogel
1974	R. Andersen, J. Starr
	F. Hamilton, H. MacLean
	G. Caravelli

OPEN TEAMS

1968	J. Wachter, Dr. R. Katz
	L. Cohen, H. Bethe
	Dr. W. Vaughan
1969	M. Polonsky, H. Deyne
	Mr. and Mrs. F. Golec
1970	C. Vogel, C. Stringer
	A. Ramer, M. Case
1971	J. Tani, R. Tani
	J. Gerken, M. Vonesh
1972	D. Smith, L. McCaffrey
	W. Snider, B. Gardner, *tied with*
	D. Rutstein, J. Mandell
	A. Weiland, C. Yelton
1973	R. Rich, R. Hoffman
	B. Mammoser, J. Stokes
1974	A. Leavitt, S. Leavitt
	P. Sugar, G. Polak

MASTERS PAIRS

1969	L. Spivack, C. Burger
1971	E. Merski, L. Oakey
1972	M. Granovetter, D. Massey
1974	C. Vernay, A. Stout

OPEN PAIRS

1968	W. Rosen, J. Levinson
1969	N. Knutsen, P. Warden

1970	Dr. R. Katz, L. Cohen
1971	L. Wiley, K. Wiley
1972	D. Smith, D. Requard
1973	S. Leavitt, P. Sugar
1974	F. Hamilton, J. Starr

MEN'S PAIRS

1968	S. Adamowski, F. Weisbach
1969	N. Fink, R. Jarrett
1970	J. Startzel, B. Gardner
1971	L. Oakey, D. Nicklasson
1972	J. Wachter, K. Wiley
1973	I. Steinfeldt, L. Tritter
1974	L. Phillips, K. Wiley

WOMEN'S PAIRS

1968	Mrs. H. Denison, Mrs. C. Pohland
1969	Mrs. E. N. Wier, Mrs. R. D. Risch
1970	J. Deutsch, F. Arst
1971	J. Wilkinson, J. Stein
1972	J. Deutsch, G. Harris
1973	D. Coakley, H. Schnarsky
1974	S. Simon, G. Weber

MIXED PAIRS

1968	S. Harris, J. Zilic
1969	L. Wiley, K. Wiley
1970	K. Feiler, D. Polcrack
1971	D. Kantor, H. MacLean
1973	B. Gardner, D. Witte

DISTRICT 14 (North Dakota, South Dakota, Minnesota, Iowa, Nebraska, one county of northwestern Wisconsin)

CANADIAN PRAIRIE

KNOCKOUT TEAMS

1972	H. MacLean, D. Kantor
	B. Coleman, A. Stout

OPEN TEAMS

1969	J. Hall, D. Horowitz
	J. Lee, E. Langer
1972	L. Oakey, K. Klimmek
	T. Wernz, S. Bender, *tied with*
	P. Lewis, G. Mogen
	M. Lightle, C. Lowless

OPEN PAIRS

1969	D. Rossen, E. Chernick
1972	Mr. and Mrs. L. Udow

MEN'S PAIRS

1969	K. Sandiford, B. Wolk
1972	T. Beckman, H. Weinstein

WOMEN'S PAIRS

1969	G. Gustafson, C. Nicholson, *tied with*
	Mrs. M. Landa, Mrs. T. Sornsin
1972	Mrs. C. Engebretson, Mrs. E. Nelson

DISTRICT 14

KNOCKOUT TEAMS

1970	R. Du Four, Jr., H. MacLean
	D. Kantor, F. Hamilton
1971	R. LaCour, H. Tepperman
	J. McKee, M. Passell
1972	G. Kotulski, D. Kantor
	S. Steinfeldt, L. Tritter
	H. MacLean, A. Stout

1973 J. Jacoby, J. Nash
P. Levitt, P. Galter
H. Ross
1974 C. Goppert, M. Passell
M. Lair, J. Grantham
H. Divis

OPEN TEAMS

1968 Mrs. A. L. Bauer, Mrs. R. A. Bauer
Miss V. Christensen, Mrs. J. P. Holland
1969 L. Hoberman, Mrs. F. E. Watters
S. Greenberg, R. Hoberman
1971 E. Mersky, M. Freier
E. Daybock, L. Oakey
1972 L. Phillips, G. Polak
Dr. J. Fisher, R. Andersen
J. Blair, G. Caravelli
1973 R. Wolff, J. Jacoby
J. King, G. Kasle
P. Hawkins
1974 T. Fox, R. Leonard
H. Siegelman, J. Brothers

MASTERS PAIRS

1968 C. E. Cramer, M. Moore
1969 P. Orlett, R. Robertson
1970 W. Pinsonneault, P. Winter
1971 D. Nicklasson, C. Stegeman
1972 Dr. J. Fisher, G. Polak
1973 J. Jacoby, G. Caravelli, *tied with*
R. LaCour, P. Hawkins
1974 R. Du Four, F. Hamilton

OPEN PAIRS

1968 D. Egholm, L. Oakey
1969 L. Tonkin, B. Crooks
1970 W. Erickson, P. Langsetmo
1971 B. Furnish, B. Muir
1972 J. Hall, S. Moss
1973 B. Crane, Dr. J. Fisher
1974 A. Bangs, M. Howland

MEN'S PAIRS

1968 H. Nicholas, D. Robinson
1970 D. Nicklasson, C. Stegeman

WOMEN'S PAIRS

1968 Mrs. T. Bunn, Mrs. A. Lampert
1970 Mrs. C. Hamilton, Mrs. E. Benton

GOPHER

KNOCKOUT TEAMS

1967 D. Clarren, N. Dockman
H. MacLean, R. Anderson
1968 D. Horwitz, M. Freier
E. Dayboch, J. Wachter
J. Hall
1969 M. Freier, E. Dayboch
D. Horwitz, J. Hall
1971 D. Clarren, D. Kantor
H. MacLean, J. Wachter
L. Cohen, G. Caravelli

OPEN TEAMS

1958 N. Dockman, N. Justice
D. Clarren, M. Freier
1959 J. Philippy, W. Scheuneman
F. Green, I. Levin
1960 N. Dockman, P. Levitt
Mrs. S. Shapiro, D. Horwitz
1961 F. Green, I. Levin
J. Philippy, H. Wolpert
1962 A. Bell, J. Zilic
G. Polak, J. Wachter
1963 D. Clarren, N. Dockman
E. Langer, J. Lee

1964 A. Zeh, E. Rosen
E. Vaughan, K. Christiansen
J. Wachter
1965 M. Freier, E. Dayboch
N. Justice, R. Troxel
D. Horwitz
1966 D. Horwitz, J. Hall
J. Lee, E. Langer
1967 D. Clarren, E. Dayboch
M. Freier, J. Wachter
G. Marsee
1969 J. Hall, J. Lee
E. Langer, D. Horwitz
1970 J. Hall, J. Lee
E. Langer, D. Horwitz
1972 J. Benedict, H. Moss
S. Steinfeldt. H. Ross
1973 J. Cohn, S. Zakin
R. Stern, G. Chait
1974 M. Freier, E. Dayboch
L. Tritter, F. Green

MASTERS TEAMS

1968 E. Mersky, L. Oakey
J. Schoenecker, R. DeHarpporte

MASTERS PAIRS

1958 M. Freier, E. Dayboch, *tied with*
L. Magee, Mrs. M. S. Levitt
1959 E. Langer, P. Pink
1960 D. Clarren, A. Bell, *tied with*
A. Simmons, R. LaDue
1961 Mrs. D. Kennedy, Mrs. L. Thornburg
1962 Mrs. H. Mott, H. Platt
1963 A. Weiner, Mrs. B. Torrey
1964 F. C. Rubbra, J. Moran
1965 Mrs. J. Peilan, W. Wheeler
1966 J. Lee, E. Langer
1967 D. Faskow, G. Marsee
1968 Mrs. I. Rosen, E. Mersky
1969 C. M. Shefchik, D. King
1970 E. Mersky, D. Thomson
1971 J. Mitchell, N. Justice
1972 R. McCray, K. Hanson
1973 D. Kantor, H. MacLean
1974 G. Chait, H. Miller, Jr.

OPEN PAIRS

1958 T. Wilder, L. O. Benson
1959 P. Levitt, N. Dockman
1960 H. Wolpert, F. Green
1961 M. Pike, F. Rappleyea
1962 H. Wolpert, F. Green
1963 W. H. Campbell, J. H. Tidball
1964 Mr. and Mrs. J. Cummings
1965 D. L. Williams, G. E. Schnurr
1966 J. Lee, E. Langer
1967 J. Philippy, F. Green
1968 J. Larsen, D. Nicklasson
1969 Mrs. H. M. Macken, J. Hugstad
1970 D. Thomson, B. Pauls
1971 Mr. and Mrs. I. Rosen
1972 G. Chait, G. Polak
1973 R. Stern, G. Chait
1974 Mrs. J. Christo, R. Countryman

MEN'S PAIRS

1958 H. Wolpert, I. Levin
1959 D. Clarren, E. Rosen
1960 D. Clarren, D. Horwitz, *tied with*
J. Lee, J. Gustafson
1961 R. Roddewig, R. Shulman
1962 A. Bell, J. Zilic
1963 D. G. Dalbey, R. E. Anderson
1964 J. Wachter, M. Freier
1965 J. Wachter, E. Kantar
1966 H. MacLean, D. Rockstad
1967 B. Pauls, M. Kaplan
1968 R. Gasway, A. Malmon
1969 J. Wachter, D. B. Clarren

1970   J. Wachter, D. B. Clarren
1971   G. Caravelli, H. MacLean
1972   W. Snider, B. Gardiner
1973   J. Hall, M. Schneider
1974   M. Freier, L. Tritter

WOMEN'S PAIRS

1958   J. Peilen, B. Litman
1959   M. S. Levitt, B. J. Galter
1960   M. Meyer, E. E. Green
1961   T. F. Hassett, N. Grue
1962   L. M. Cubbison, B. T. Anderson
1963   E. Marquart, S. Shapiro
1964   A. Strom, G. Fismen
1965   D. King, Mrs. E. P. Stuhlman
1966   Mrs E. Mersky, Mrs. N. Grue
1967   Mrs. A Whittle, Mrs. L. Udow
1968   Mrs. D. Oxman, Mrs. J. Norman
1969   Mrs. C. P. Doll, Mrs. I. M. Rasmussen
1970   Mrs. N. Grue, Mrs. M. Hill
1971   B. Morris, D. Kantor
1972   M. Annis, B. Larson
1973   Mrs. G. Schochet, S. Moss
1974   M. Cravaack, Mrs. L. Young

IOWA

KNOCKOUT TEAMS

1972   T. French, R. Andersen
       H. MacLean, D. Kantor

OPEN TEAMS

1970   Mrs. E. Mersky, Mrs. E. Dayboch
       M. Freier, L. Oakey
1971   C. Stegeman, D. Nicklasson
       J. Larsen, R. Du Four, Jr.
1972   B. Staton, C. Allen
       J. Casper, J. Thurtell
1973   C. Cummins, J. Oxley
       H. Ross, V. Anderson, *tied with*
       H. Everley, B. Byrne
       J. Matulef, J. Hall
1974   R. Weikle, J. Hall
       H. Weinstein, T. Beckman

MASTERS PAIRS

1968   G. Caravelli, M. Rosenberg
1969   Mrs. E. D. Shipley, D. Rockstad
1971   B. Crane, G. Caravelli
1972   R. Andersen, T. French
1973   S. Schiller, J. Lanteri
1974   E. Rosen, J. Rosen

OPEN PAIRS

1968   E. Mersky, L. Oakey
1969   J. Wexler, G. Caravelli
1970   Mr. and Mrs. L. Herbster
1971   C. Stegeman, D. Nicklasson
1972   Dr. J. Gustafson, I. Steinfeldt
1973   Dr. J. Fisher, G. Polak
1974   K. Wiley, L. Wiley

MEN'S PAIRS

1968   S. Adamowski, F. Weisbach
1969   J. Wexler, G. Caravelli
1970   G. Polak, C. Vogel
1971   B. Crane, R. Kaye
1973   H. MacLean, R. Du Four, Jr.
1974   J. Hall, H. Weinstein

WOMEN'S PAIRS

1968   Mrs. B. Morris, Mrs. J. Tew
1969   Mrs. M. Oliver, Mrs. B. R. Goodall
1970   Mrs. F. Arst, Mrs. J. Deutsch
1971   Mrs. L. Beers, Mrs. W. Cushing
1973   K. Kenna, M. Long
1974   J. DeWitt, E. Van Zandt, *tied with*
       E. Kaufman, M. Markley

MID-AMERICAN–CANADIAN

OPEN TEAMS

1955   R. Arnold, H. Harvey
       R. Bullock, L. Lazarus
       E. Langer, *tied with*
       J. J. Cohen, G. R. Wilson
       Mr. and Mrs. J. Millunchick
1956   Mrs. S. Shapiro, I. Berkson
       L. Tritter, C. Wetmore
1957   W. A. Schueneman, H. Harvey
       M. Reuben, E. Langer
1958   M. A. Goldberg, Mr. and Mrs. J. J. Bowers
       L. Tritter, E. Dayboch
1959   O. Jacoby, G. Michael
       W. Gilbert, J. Hubbell
1960   E. Dayboch, M. Freier
       B. Casement, A. Habel, Jr.
1961   D. Clarren, J. Lee
       E. Langer, N. Dockman
1962   D. Clarren, J. Lee
       E. Langer, N. Dockman, *tied with*
       R. Bullock, D. DuFour
       H. McLean, R. Weikle
1963   D. Clarren, J. Mitchell
       F. Green, I. Steinfeldt
       M. Fiterman
1964   D. Kantor, H. MacLean
       Mrs. E. Mersky, R. Anderson
1965   G. Krook, J. Larsen
       L. Oakey, D. Nicklasson, *tied with*
       H. MacLean, D. Kantor
       Mrs. B. Morris, C. M. Shefchik
1966   J. Wachter, G. Hartsman
       L. Cohen, M. Ledeen
1967   A. Mitchell, W. J. Schleusener
       J. Nelson, J. H. Smith

MASTERS PAIRS

1956   J. Terry, E. W. Hyers
1957   Mr. and Mrs. T. C. Krikac
1958   A. C. Bell, D. Clarren
1959   P. Galter, P. Levitt
1960   A. Bell, P. Levitt
1961   H. Meyers, B. King
1962   A. Myers, J. Klein
1963   D. Thomson, B. Pauls
1964   J. Nelson, Mrs. F. Mitchell
1965   C. Betcke, L. Tutter
1966   H. MacLean, D. Kantor
1967   N. Abrahamson, W. J. Schleusener

OPEN PAIRS

1955   J. Millerd, A. C. Bell
1956   I. A. Berkson, F. Schneller
1957   D. J. Cannell, H. C. MacFarlane
1958   V. Meriwether, Dr. D. M. Danes
1959   E. Wolter, D. Saale
1960   J. Corisis, G. Banck
1961   R. Balanow, B. Cruise
1962   I. Levin, J. C. Mitchell
1963   I. Steinfeldt, M. Galvin
1964   D. Carter, G. Michaud
1965   Mrs. H. Mott, Mrs. G. Specker
1966   J. Leary, S. Nisam
1967   D. M. Thomas, J. Blair

MEN'S PAIRS

1955   H. Harvey, R. Bullock
1956   H. E. Churchill, H. H. Klein
1957   Dr. W. W. Sands, E. L. Rosen
1958   A. C. Bell, D. Clarren
1959   Dr. W. W. Sands, E. L. Rosen
1960   D. Clarren, D. Horwitz
1961   Dr. C. T. Hsu, C. Colvin
1962   R. Weikle, R. DeHarpporte
1963   J. Fox, H. MacLean
1964   P. Sokolof, L. Tritter
1965   J. Hall, D. Horwitz
1966   R. Weikle, L. Oakey
1967   L. Magee, R. Lord

WOMEN'S PAIRS

1955   M. Mulford, C. Charlet
1956   G. Schachet, B. A. Marvy
1957   N. Grue, L. J. Seewald
1958   E. Dayboch, L. Jacobs
1959   G. Rosenberg, S. Browne
1960   F. E. Watters, W. J. Brennan
1961   N. Oram, L. Bishop
1962   M. Soloman, A. Meyers
1963   F. F. Hasselt, R. Brink
1964   Mrs. E. Taber, D. Wilson
1965   Mrs. O. F. Meredith, Mrs. G. Kuhns
1966   Mrs. R. Farha, Mrs. A. Reed
1967   Mrs. W. F. Adams, Mrs. R. L. Stewart

MIXED PAIRS

1965   D. Kantor, H. MacLean
1966   Mr. and Mrs. H. Schenken
1967   Mr. and Mrs. I. Steinfeldt

OPEN INDIVIDUAL

1955   C. Hoyt, *tied with*
       J. Bockwitz
1959   G. L. Judge
1960   V. Christensen

DISTRICT 15 (Kansas, western Missouri, Oklahoma, one county of northwestern Texas)

DISTRICT 15

KNOCKOUT TEAMS

1967   M. Lawrence, H. Ross
       J. Jacoby, R. Wolff
       W. Eisenberg, I. Corn, Jr.
1968   A. Kincaid, R. Ayres
       J. Hubbell, C. Rush
       G. Michaud, L. Richardson
1969   J. Hubbell, D. Williams
       G. Michaud, L. Richardson
1970   J. Russell, R. Robertson
       D. Williams, T. Lux
       P. Orlett
1974   G. Michaud, B. Nail
       A. Bell, K. Peyser
       L. Richardson, D. Kerr

OPEN TEAMS

1967   J. Wolf, D. Keleher
       L. Richardson, D. Williams, *tied with*
       B. Crane, T. French
       G. Polak, M. Rosenberg
       G. Caravelli
1968   A. Kincaid, R. Ayres
       A. Bombeck, Mr. and Mrs. L. Magee
1969   J. Hubbell, D. Williams
       B. Crooks, R. Robertson
       H. Cassidy
1970   E. Banks, J. Blair
       S. Greenberg, H. Bethe
1974   M. Brachman, J. Jacoby
       P. Soloway, M. Passell

MASTERS PAIRS

1967   Mrs. V. Meriwether, Dr. G. Ginns
1968   Mrs. A. Peterson, Mrs. M. Holloway
1969   J. D. Shaw, J. Knudsen
1970   J. Russell, P. Orlett
1974   J. Jeffrey, P. Hawkins

OPEN PAIRS

1967   G. Caravelli, M. Rosenberg
1968   A. Kincaid, R. Ayres
1969   J. C. Anderson, H. C. Halsted
1970   J. Hancock, W. Gibbs
1974   B. Crane, G. Caravelli

MEN'S PAIRS

1967   M. Lawrence, H. Ross
1968   D. Shapiro, P. Orlett
1969   G. Michaud, L. Richardson
1970   J. Gerber, D. Kaim

WOMEN'S PAIRS

1967   Mrs. E. Clark, R. Mills
1968   Mrs. V. Watkins, Mrs. F. Walters
1969   Mrs. D. Stewart, Mrs. W. H. Potts
1970   Mrs. R. Wilson, Mrs. W. Roye

MIXED PAIRS

1967   Mrs. S. Sweet, R. Robertson
1968   G. Anderson, Mrs. L. Bunn
1969   Mr. and Mrs. S. Beard

LAND OF CORONADO

KNOCKOUT TEAMS

1972   G. Kasle, G. Hayden
       R. Bates, R. Grantham
       J. King
1974   M. Rubenfeld, H. Divis
       J. King, J. Grantham
       M. Lair

OPEN TEAMS

1972   G. Kasle, R. Bates
       G. Hayden, R. Grantham
       J. King
1974   C. Goppert, G. Kasle
       G. Hayden, J. Grantham
       R. LaCour

MASTERS PAIRS

1972   J. Janitschke, C. Janitschke
1974   J. Griffin, B. Martin

OPEN PAIRS

1972   B. Martin, E. Rudes
1974   J. Janitschke, C. Janitschke

MEN'S PAIRS

1972   R. Bates, G. Hayden

WOMEN'S PAIRS

1972   Mrs. D. Park, Mrs. D. Walker

NON-MIXED PAIRS

1974   M. Kaplan, N. Haflich

MISSOURI VALLEY

KNOCKOUT TEAMS

1969   J. G. Ripstra. M. Nelson
       B. Christian, J. Linhart
1970   M. Brachman, P. Soloway
       R. Henderson, J. Mohan
       B. Shutts
1971   J. Blair, B. Greenberg,
       J. Jacoby, M. Brachman
       S. Greenberg, P. Swanson (Spring)
       G. R. Nail, J. Hubbell
       L. Richardson, G. Michaud (Fall)
1972   D. Williams, P. Orlett
       W. Crooks, R. Robertson

1973 P. Soloway, M. Brachman
M. Passell, M. Lair (Winter)
O. Swander, S. Swander
L. Magee, J. Hubbell
W. Crooks (Summer)
A. Reinhold, Dr. R. Katz
L. Cohen, K. Larsen (Fall)
1974 B. Greenberg, J. Jacoby
M. Brachman, B. Wolff
B. Goldman, S. Greenberg

OPEN TEAMS

1952 A. Kincaid, F. A. Bombeck
J. W. Hubbell, B. L. Greenberg
1953 D. Westerfield, Mrs. E. Miller
J. G. Ripstra, Mrs. V. Bailey
1954 C. Robinson, I. Rosenberg
G. Nash, D. Carter
F. Carter
1955 Mr. and Mrs. David Carter
J. Simon, I. Rosenberg
C. Rosenberg
1958 O. Jacoby, Mrs. W. B. Johnson
A. Bell, Mrs. G. Sheehan
1959 A. Kincaid, W. Gilbert
J. W. Hubbell, J. G. Ripstra
G. Willett
1961 E. Theus, J. Wolf
Mrs. S. Alcorn, J. Simon
1962 P. Levitt, F. A. Bombeck
R. Ayres, J. Wolf
1963 A. Gutowsky, M. Moore
Mrs. J. Cheever, Mrs. J. Inman
1964 J. G. Ripstra, J. W. Hubbell
R. Ayres, B. Grace
1965 M. Thomas, P. Swanson
J. Blair, B. Jenkins
H. Hume
1966 O. Jacoby, J. Jacoby
Mr. and Mrs. M. Brachman
M. Thomas
1967 R. Lord, J. Showalter
A. M. Seltzer, J. Fellows
1968 Mr. and Mrs. L. Magee
N. Kremer, R. Lord
1969 Mrs. E. Coffey, Mrs. N. Phillips
Mrs. J. Meyer, Mrs. B. Grisham
1970 Dr. J. Fisher, H. Baer
C. Weed, Mrs. D. Hawes
1971 Dr. C. Robinson, J. Swindle
J. Spessard, S. Turner, *tied with*
K. Bradley, M. Merry
Mr. and Mrs. L. Magee, *tied with*
B. Creed, V. Davis
Dr. T. Teel, J. Torbett III, *tied with*
Mr. and Mrs. J. Weddle
B. Layton, B. Weingrad (Spring)
J. Blair, Col. W. Christian
A. Siebert, D. Siebert (Fall)
1972 E. Van Zandt, C. Smith
J. Barrow, B. Greenberg
S. Greenberg
1973 P. Soloway, M. Brachman
H. Noland, Dr. J. Fisher
J. Jacoby, B. Crane (Winter)
M. Blumenthal, Dr. J. Fisher
G. Caravelli, M. Rosenberg (Summer)
B. Greenberg, P. Fields
O. Jacoby, G. Michaud (Fall)
1974 J. Janitschke, M. Kaplan
D. Reed, B. Harrison

MASTERS PAIRS

1957 M. Low. K. Bullock
1959 Mr. and Mrs. P. Brennan, Jr.
1961 Mrs. D. B. Hawes, O. Jacoby
1962 G. Cubbon, C. Simon
1963 Mrs. L. A. Jervis, Mrs. E. Coffey
1964 Mr. and Mrs. M. Beegle
1965 H. Hume, J. Jacoby

1966 J. C. Anderson, L. V. McKinley, Jr.
1967 Mrs. J. Rosen, Mrs. L. Knight
1968 G. R. Nail, W. Brown
1969 D. Orlett, W. Hill
1970 L. Richardson, G. Michaud
1971 B. Kennedy, Mrs. A. Hagert (Spring)
G. R. Nail, L. Richardson, *tied with*
C. Hipsh, M. Hipsh (Fall)
1972 J. Fitzgerrell, R. Bates
1973 G. Kasle, R. Bates, *tied with*
T. Gibson, L. McLaughlin (Winter)
K. Bradley, B. Grace (Summer)
Dr. R. Greene, Col. W. Christian (Fall)
1974 B. Crane, Dr. J. Fisher

OPEN PAIRS

1952 Mrs. J. C. Fairchild, W. L. Curtis
1953 Mrs. V. Bailey, J. G. Ripstra
1954 J. Gerber, O. Jacoby
1955 I. Erdos, L. Wolfers
1957 F. A. Bombeck, R. Ayres
1958 O. Jacoby, A. Bell
1959 L. McLaughlin, E. J. Rogers, Jr.
1961 A. Kincaid, R. Ayres
1962 S. Crooks, J. Wolf, *tied with*
A. Gutowsky, T. Brown
1963 E. Monroe, K. Stenger, *tied with*
Mr. and Mrs. R. Cundiff
1964 F. B. Lowe, Mrs. C. O. Hackley
1965 D. Carter, J. Hubbell
1966 J. Jacoby, Mrs. M. Brachman
1967 Mrs. J. Cheever, W. A. Springall
1968 J. K. Cronin, Mrs. S. Sweet
1969 R. Robertson, D. Williams
1970 R. Nail, D. Lair
1971 Mrs. D. Frandsen, Mrs. C. White (Spring)
B. Crane, G. Caravelli (Fall)
1972 R. Smith, R. Lord
1973 D. Mordecai, D. Reed (Winter)
G. McDaniel, T. Hodapp (Summer)
B. Crane, K. Shuman (Fall)
1974 B. Crane, Dr. J. Fisher

MEN'S PAIRS

1952 W. H. James, J. H. Cullinan
1953 H. E. Woods, W. H. Theiman
1954 C. Robinson, I. Rosenberg
1955 P. Barnes, J. P. Hoover
1957 F. A. Bombeck, R. Ayres
1958 G. Cubbon, W. C. Hainline
1959 D. Carter, L. Kolker
1961 G. R. Nail, A. Kincaid
1962 W. Bunyan, M. Beegle
1963 G. Rosenstein, P. Steinberg
1964 R. D. Hall, J. T. Chaney
1965 Dr. M. Mooney, A. Kincaid
1966 B. L. Gariepy, J. L. Foote
1967 T. C. French, D. Keheler
1968 E. G. Theus, Dr. J. E. Kraft
1969 W. L. Crooks, D. Williams
1970 P. O'Konski, J. Oxley
1971 J. Jacoby, S. Beard, *tied with*
M. Passell, J. Zilic (Spring)
L. McKinney, Jr., P. Hawkins (Fall)
1972 D. Holmes, W. Hedden
1973 M. Harlow, B. Shutts

WOMEN'S PAIRS

1952 J. C. Fairchild, S. Lee
1953 C. C. Neff, W. H. Theiman
1954 D. Dwyer, L. Durham
1955 M. Lagle, M. L. Mooney
1957 B. Harding, A. H. Wilks
1958 J. J. Townsend, L. Harrington
1959 G. Weiner, B. Weiner
1961 N. Cram, W. Bishop
1962 V. Bailey, C. F. Newland

1963	P. Steinberg, G. Rosenstein
1964	D. Broyles, M. Lagle
1965	Mrs. G. Weiner, B. Weiner
1966	Mrs. C. W. Broyles, Mrs. E. T. Martin
1967	Mrs. J. James, Mrs. G. Reintjes
1968	Mrs. D. Frandsen, Mrs. D. R. Davis
1969	Mrs. P. Jensen, F. Thompson
1970	S. Lazarus, E. Van Zandt
1971	S. Lazarus, E. Van Zandt (Spring)
	G. Cronin, M. Cheever (Fall)
1972	J. Steele, E. Van Zandt
1973	S. Swander, L. Magee

MIXED PAIRS

1952	B. Salmon, H. Greenberg
1953	Mrs. D. Bombeck, F. Hoadley
1954	Mrs. P. Steinberg, J. Simon
1955	E. H. Scurlock, Mrs. A. H. Wilks, Jr.
1957	Mrs. J. Simon, J. Jacoby
1958	O. Jacoby, Mrs. W. B. Johnson
1959	Mrs. M. Alcorn, M. Michaels
1962	J. Taylor, E. Friedman
1963	V. V. Anderson, Jr., Mrs. G. Weiner
1964	F. A. Bombeck, Mrs. S. Sweet
1965	Mr. and Mrs. T. K. Sanders
1966	L. McLaughlin, Mrs. P. K. French
1967	Dr. W. A. Grosjean, Mrs. P. Wilcox
1968	Mrs. G. Reardon, A. R. Phillips
1969	P. J. O'Connell, Mrs. A. Vogt
1970	W. Mann, Mrs. W. Mann
1971	J. and M. Wolf (Spring)
	J. Zilic, V. Zilic (Fall)
1972	M. Conway, G. Conway

INDIVIDUAL

1952	R. T. Brennan
1954	S. L. Haffamier
1955	Mrs. L. Cameron
1957	E. Eastman
1958	F. E. Adams
1959	Mrs. W. H. Bridges

DISTRICT 16 (Mexico, most of Texas)

MEXICAN NATIONAL

OPEN TEAMS

1955	R. Y. Barrett, J. Mothershed
	H. Lesky, P. R. Friedberg, *tied with*
	Dr. G. Rosenkranz, Dr. L. N. Leishman
	V. E. Laska, G. Mandoki
1960	J. Barth, C. Strouse
	Dr. J. W. Fisher, Mrs. J. L. Kendrick
1961	Mrs. L. F. Storr, F. Herring
	Mrs. C. Smith, J. C. Tucker
1962	Mrs. R. Goble, Dr. J. Fisher
	H. Lesky, R. Friedberg
1964	A. Kempner, J. Herb
	C. Strouse, M. Weil
	R. Fischer, *tied with*
	J. Rosenblum, P. Levitt
	N. Silverstein, Dr. J. Fisher
1965	J. Jacoby, R. Kittle
	C. Kittle, Mrs. S. Lee
	G. Treadwell
1966	G. R. Nail, G. Kasle
	Mr. and Mrs. R. Wolff
	A. de Marigny
1967	A. de Marigny, J. Jacoby
	R. Wolff, G. R. Nail
	M. Cohn
1968	R. Wolff, M. Lawrence
	J. Jacoby, W. Eisenberg
	R. Boldman

1969	Dr. G. Rosenkranz, D. Morse
	J. Gerber, M. Wagar
	D. Hayden
1970	Dr. N. Ostrich, Dr. A. D. Ostrich
	S. Greenberg, M. Stine
1971	Dr. G. Rosenkranz, M. Reygadas
	G. R. Nail, D. Morse
	J. Gerber
1972	T. Sanders, C. Sanders
	M. Cohn, B. Cohn
	H. Guiver, T. Prothro
1973	A. Reinhold, B. Eisenberg
	R. Walsh, T. Nugit
1974	Dr. G. Rosenkranz, E. Rosenkranz
	S. Dubson, R. Bates
	J. Grantham, *tied with*
	L. Andrews, J. Steehler
	L. Mills, J. Mitchell, *tied with*
	M. Brachman, P. Soloway
	M. Passell, J. Jacoby

MASTERS PAIRS

1960	Mrs. G. Rosenkranz, C. Strouse
1961	Mrs. M. F. Ruffner, W. Leipen
1964	J. Rosenblum, P. Levitt
1965	Dr. C. Burnham, Mrs. E. Murdoch
1966	C. Smith, Mrs. A. W. Noland
1967	Mrs. G. Litwinczak, Mrs. L. Mana
1968	A. Kluewer, R. N. Dallas
1969	D. Morse, Dr. G. Rosenkranz
1970	J. D. King, L. M. Sharp
1971	M. Fogarty, M. Covarrubias
1972	M. Passell, T. Sanders
1973	V. Davis, B. Creed
1974	B. Reinhold, B. Eisenberg

OPEN PAIRS

1955	B. Crane, Mrs. M. Weissman
1960	Dr. L. N. Leishman, J. Rosenblum
1961	D. E. Morse, G. Dawking
1962	C. Fua, W. Leipen
1964	J. Rosenblum, N. Silverstein
1965	J. Murphy, Mrs. C. Duncan
1966	Mr. and Mrs. R. Wolff
1967	Mr. and Mrs. H. P. Cohen
1968	C. Klar, C. Strouse
1969	A. Harrison, R. T. Williams
1970	A. Harrison, R. T. Williams
1971	G. Kasle, Dr. J. Tucker
1972	F. Atiyeh, G. Malhame
1973	H. Baron, M. Passell
1974	Dr. G. Rosenkranz, R. Bates

MEN'S PAIRS

1955	C. Fua, R. Resiere
1960	G. R. Nail, G. Howard
1961	J. Pike, M. Block
1962	C. Fua, J. Rosenblum
1964	J. Rosenblum, C. Fua
1965	D. Carter, N. Silverstein
1966	J. Jacoby, R. Wolff
1967	R. Wolff, A. de Marigny
1968	R. Pike, O. Duran
1969	Dr. N. Ostrich, Mrs. M. A. Stine
1970	D. Morse, M. Moss
1971	W. Leipen, M. Reygadas
1972	C. Smith, C. Phippin
1973	J. Grantham, M. Lair
1974	R. Fensterwald, J. Becker

WOMEN'S PAIRS

1955	E. Casoman, A. Smith
1960	T. Golding, J. Wilson
1961	A. Duran, J. Richmond
1962	J. Rosenblum, J. Frankel
1964	C. Buchman, C. McIntyre
1965	Mrs. C. Duncan, J. Murphy
1966	Mrs. A. Davis, H. Baron
1967	Mrs. W. A. Stephens, Mrs. E. Strother
1968	Mrs. C. T. Hester, Mrs. D. Hester
1969	Mrs. G. H. Kaercher, Mrs. J. L. Fleming

1970	Mrs. E. Abrams, H. M. Owens
1971	M. Fogarty, M. Cespedes
1972	C. Sanders, B. Cohn
1973	T. Michaels, M. Philley
1974	N. Gruver, H. Utegaard

MIXED PAIRS

1955	Dr. and Mrs. G. Rosenkranz
1960	Mrs. J. Timon, A Harrison, *tied with*
	Mrs. B. Weissman, C. Fua
1961	M. S. Fogarty, W. Leipen
1962	W. S. Clymore, J. Ferguson
1964	A. Davis, J. Hooker
1965	J. Jacoby, Mrs. S. Lee
1966	Mrs. J. Gerard, J. Menkes
1967	Mr. and Mrs. M. J. Cohn
1968	J. Vaughan, Mrs. M. B. Killian
1969	W. F. Muthard, E. J. English
1970	Mr. and Mrs. M. Moss
1971	A. Davis, N. Ostrich
1972	Mrs. W. Lewis, H. Guiver
1973	Mrs. F. Taylor, R. Taylor
1974	M. Mignocchi, J. Becker

OPEN INDIVIDUAL

1955	S. Goldring
1960	L. B. de Celis
1961	F. K. Thompson

TEXAS FALL

KNOCKOUT TEAMS

1968	I. Corn, J. Jacoby
	R. Wolff, W. Eisenberg
	R. Goldman, M. Lawrence
1969	Dr. G. Rosenkranz, J. Gerber
	P. Hodge, G. R. Nail
	D. Morse, Dr. H. Rockaway
1970	L. Tritter, M. Philley
	G. McDaniel, S. Honer
	G. Pisk
1971	G. Dawkins, B. Hagedorn
	C. Holt, M. Townsend
	C. Flournoy, B. Wolff

OPEN TEAMS

1952	Mrs. J. M. Mathews, R. Sharpe
	F. Stilwell, L. R. Robertson
1953	E. McKale, L. Longfeld
	E. Sandstrom, J. H. Moran
1954	B. Fain, G. Heath
	P. Hodge, H. Rockaway
	O. Jacoby
1955	W. Wolff, Jr., R. Wolff
	B. Fain, J. Musumeci
	P. Zeller
1956	E. A. Jacobson, W. O. Curry
	O. Rosenschein, D. W. Dye
1957	C. Flournoy, B. L. Kickman
	A. Gutowsky, C. K. Smith
1959	Mrs. D. B. Hawes, Dr. J. W. Fisher
	O. Jacoby, J. Jacoby
1960	Mrs. D. B. Hawes, Dr. J. W. Fisher
	Mr. and Mrs. O. Jacoby
	J. Jacoby
1961	E. J. Hawes, C. Gabriel
	R. Wolff, W. Wolff
	J. Musumeci
1962	B. Fain, V. Emanuel
	J. Levy, Col. T. Willis
	W. Herbert
1963	J. Gerber, P. Hodge
	E. J. Smith, Jr., A. Gutowsky
1964	B. Creed, M. Thomas
	M. Cohn, J. Taylor
1965	L. Tritter, S. Emery
	E. Dayboch, M. Frier
	M. Philley

1966	L. Krauss, J. D. Vaughan
	C. Vernay, B. Economidy
	Mrs. A. L. Graham
1967	G. R. Nail, J. Jacoby
	R. Wolff, A. de Marigny
1968	I. Corn, J. Jacoby
	R. Wolff, W. Eisenberg
	R. Goldman, M. Lawrence
1969	E. Van Zandt, C. Smith
	J. Jacoby, Mrs. A. W. Noland, *tied with*
	A. Childs, Dr. B. L. Clearly
	G. Tilly, M. Woodruff
1970	B. Creed, V. Davis
	E. Cohen, J. Cosentino
	J. King
1971	G. Dawkins, D. Horner
	A. Plate, L. Plate
	C. Flournoy
1973	B. Hamman, B. Wolff
	C. Weed, J. Hooker
1974	V. Zilic, J. Zilic
	T. Peters, B. Fiske
	R. Beall

MIXED TEAMS

1965	D. Carter, M. B. Townsend
	G. Cronin, J. Blair

MASTERS PAIRS

1954	A. Gutowsky, E. J. Smith, Jr.
1956	P. C. Fewell, A. Roth
1957	Mrs. G. Pontious, Mrs. A. Davis
1959	F. A. Pryor, Mrs. J. Kendrick
1960	Mrs. S. Basil, Mrs. R. H. Tompkins
1961	B. Acker, M. Gouger
1962	H. E. Barnard, J. Mark
1963	J. Gerber, P. Hodge
1964	C. Wright, J. Clinton
1965	P. Hodge, D. Morse
1966	M. Frier, B. Acker
1967	Col. E. G. Stutton, B. M. Brown
1968	B. Wolff, B. H. Hagedorn
1969	Mrs. A. W. Noland, J. Jacoby
1970	R. Norwood, B. Norwood
1971	J. Sullivan, M. Reid
1973	P. Burka, K. Schutze
1974	J. Hooker, K. Jones

OPEN PAIRS

1952	R. Dreyfus, Dr. J. W. Fisher
1953	E. McKale, J. H. Moran
1954	H. Rockaway, O. Jacoby
1955	D. Carter, C. Smith
1956	O. Jacoby, C. Smith, *tied with*
	G. Heath, P. Hodge
1957	S. Lazard, Dr. J. W. Fisher
1959	E. A. Jacobson, O. Jacoby
1960	E. K. Smith, Dr. R. G. Farris
1961	Mrs. G. Pontious, Mrs. A. Davis, *tied with*
	K. Parker, J. Parker
1962	Mrs. A. Blasband, S. Lowery
1963	Mr. and Mrs. L. Roddy
1964	J. Gerber, J. Yates
1965	B. Crane, C. Smith
1966	B. Crane, G. Polak
1967	P. Harrison, B. Adams
1968	M. Mangan, B. J. Wagner
1969	D. Keleher, K. Jones
1970	A. Palmer, W. Burbridge
1971	J. Adams, C. Coleman
1973	B. Hamman, Dr. C. Robinson
1974	Dr. G. Pisk, L. Tritter

MEN'S PAIRS

1952	J. Moran, J. B. Kennedy
1953	Dr. J. Fisher, R. Dreyfus
1954	C. Woldenberg, W. M. McGhee
1955	G. Heath, R. Y. Barrett
1956	A. Roth, R. Smith
1957	S. Lazard, Dr. J. Fisher

1959   O. Jacoby, M. Gouger
1960   R. W. Mitchell, E. A. Meyers
1961   C. Smith, G. Treadwell
1962   R. A. McAlpin, C. Coleman
1963   D. Morse, P. Harrison
1964   B. Gentry, M. Finch
1965   J. Jacoby, E. G. Burke
1966   B. Johnson, J. Bromberg
1967   C. Smith, G. R. Nail
1968   B. Creed, B. H. Hagedorn
1969   B. Kuenstler, D. Fizer
1970   G. Kasle, Dr. N. Ostrich
1971   L. Tritter, C. Weed
1973   L. Dreyfus, P. Burka

WOMEN'S PAIRS

1952   E. E. Ellis, W. A. Stephens
1953   J. C. Hedrick, R. L. Carruth
1954   R. T. Lucas, C. M. Newbill
1955   J. R. King, J. G. Davis
1956   R. Groves, L. Tiller
1957   S. Basil, R. M. Tompskins
1959   T. Barnard, H. Wagnon
1960   D. B. Hawes, J. A. Welch
1961   A. Harper, W. M. Remick
1962   F. Mathews, B. Gentry
1963   S. Beard, A. W. Patterson
1964   Mrs. F. Seikel, Mrs E. Jones, *tied with*
       Mrs. K. Peery, Mrs. I. Sutton
1965   Mrs. J. M. Curran, Jr., Mrs. R. W. McCullough
1966   Mrs. P. McDaniel, Mrs. D. Philley
1967   Mrs. H. Mason, Mrs. M. B. Killian
1968   Mrs. H. Reid, Mrs. O. Veselka
1969   C. Winfield, M. Hastings
1970   Mrs. R. White, Mrs. C. Westbrook
1971   S. Lillienstern, V. Zilic
1973   J. Titus, F. Beard

MIXED PAIRS

1952   Mrs. A. Crank, Lt. Col. C. C. Merrifield
1953   Mrs. H. A. Woods, S. Shuford
1954   Mrs. J. Strich, Dr. G. Rosenkranz
1955   S. Fairchild, C. Russell
1956   Mrs. J. Bashara, R. D. Cheatwood
1957   Mrs. D. L. Pieratt, A. Fishl
1959   Mrs. H. A. Woods, M. Calisch, Jr.
1960   Mrs. D. B. Hawes, Dr. J. W. Fisher
1961   J. C. Ferguson, V. G. LeLaurin
1962   Mrs. C. Weed, J. Cayne
1963   Mrs. S. Camp, D. Morse
1964   Mrs. B. Jenkins, D. C. Carter
1965   Mr. and Mrs. S. Lawrence
1966   A. Trenholm, H. Baer
1967   J. Gerber, C. Klar
1968   J. Jacoby, S. Perutz
1969   J. Vaughan, S. Gibson
1970   J. Mathis, S. Kasle
1971   B. Economidy, M. Hagedorn
1973   Mrs. N. Goodloe, R. LaCour
1974   G. R. Nail, B. Nail

OPEN INDIVIDUAL

1954   D. Hooper
1955   M. Freedman
1957   S. P. McCalla
1959   Mrs. W. H. Fair, Jr.

NON-MIXED PAIRS

1974   A. Gutowsky, J. Wolf

TEXAS MIDWINTER

KNOCKOUT TEAMS

1971   J. Crawford, O. Jacoby
       L. Tritter, C. Smith
1972   B. Hamman, C. McFarland
       G. Kasle, Dr. J. Tucker
       B. Hamman

1973   J. Zilic, V. Zilic
       T. Riely, A. Plate
       E. Wold
1974   M. Brachman, M. Brachman
       J. Jacoby, P. Soloway
       M. Passell

OPEN TEAMS

1971   F. Berger, Dr. J. Fisher
       B. Wolff, C. Weed
       A. de Marigny, *tied with*
       Mr. and Mrs. A. Plate, D. Horner
       E. Hawes, *tied with*
       J. Elwood, B. Frohman
       D. Furman, L. Laird, *tied with*
       P. Soloway, J. Jacoby
       Mr. and Mrs. C. Kittle, *tied with*
       J. Barrow, L. Hetzer
       J. Zilic, B. Crews
1972   G. Dawkins, B. Hagedorn
       C. Flournoy, G. Pisk
1973   J. Jacoby, B. Wolff
       Dr. J. Fisher, C. Weed
       C. Weed
1974   C. Gabriel, M. Chang
       B. Wolff, Dr. C. Crossley

MEN'S TEAMS

1974   K. Bains, T. Edwards
       W. Irby, S. Williams, *tied with*
       B. Trenholm, E. Groner
       C. Scallon, A. LeBendig

WOMEN'S TEAMS

1974   M. Brachman, B. Hamman
       C. Reysa, J. Titus, *tied with*
       B. Bowling, E. Piwetz
       E. McGee, Mrs. F. Fredrickson

MASTERS PAIRS

1971   P. Holdge, S. Honet
1972   M. Chang, J. Jacoby
1973   M. Passell, T. Riely
1974   D. Siebert, A. Siebert

OPEN PAIRS

1971   F. Smith, B. Martin
1972   Mrs. J. McLean, Mrs. M. Robinson
1973   B. Goldman, M. Blumenthal
1974   T. Riely, E. Wold

MEN'S PAIRS

1971   K. Perry, C. Claflin
1972   J. Vaughn, S. Toplansky
1973   R. Hargrove, J. Hargrove
1974   R. LaCour, M. Lair

WOMEN'S PAIRS

1971   F. Beard, B. Wolff
1972   R. Fox, M. Cheney
1973   D. Sanders, M. Duttenhofer
1974   M. Farell, E. Ganz

MIXED PAIRS

1971   J. Broussard, C. Borden
1972   A. Davis, L. Howard
1973   M. Passell, H. Baron

NON-MIXED PAIRS

1974   T. Gibson, H. Divis

TEXAS SPRING

KNOCKOUT TEAMS

1968   A. de Marigny, R. Wolff
       C. Smith, P. Levitt
       D. Morse

1969   P. Harrison, B. Adams
       A. Gutowsky, L. McLaughlin
1970   Mr. and Mrs. M. Brachman
       P. Soloway, G. Dawkins
       Mr. and Mrs. M. Moss
1972   J. Jacoby, G. Ricci
       Mrs. A. Noland, L. Tritter

OPEN TEAMS

1958   Mrs. E. Evans, B. Crane
       C. Strouse, Jr., B. Greenberg
       A. J. Blair, Jr.
1959   Mrs. W. R. Potts, Mrs. H. P. Hubbard
       Mrs. A. A. Moore, J. Torbett
1960   S. Lazard, J. Gerber
       A. Bombeck, P. Hodge
1961   Mrs. D. B. Hawes, S. Lazard
       C. Gabriel, Dr. J. W. Fisher
       R. Wolff
1962   Mr. and Mrs. R. Rush
       J. Lewis, L. R. Robertson
1963   Mrs. D. B. Hawes, S. Lazard
       Dr. J. W. Fisher, R. Wolff
1964   C. Smith, R. Lee
       J. Jacoby, Mrs. A. W. Noland
1965   Mrs. E. L. Powell, Mrs. T. Allen
       Mrs. C. E. Bast, Mrs. C. B. Bryant
1966   J. Gerber, G. R. Nail
       Mrs. E. A. Mahoney, P. Hodge
1967   G. Kasle, B. Economidy
       M. Reid, B. Baker
       Mrs. I. C. Mundy, *tied with*
       Mrs. E. S. Alpaugh, Dr. R. Greene
       M. B. Townsend, Mrs. J. E. Kennedy
1968   C. R. Davison, N. Chambers
       Mrs. L. N. Simmons, Mrs. I. Sutton
1969   C. Weed, S. Perutz
       Mr. and Mrs. R. Wolff
1970   Mrs. K. Hartman, Mrs. C. Hellums
       Mrs. B. A. Strickland, Mrs. N. B. Vaughan
1972   P. and K. Brennan, J. Tucker, G. Kasle
       R. Bates, G. Hayden

MIXED TEAMS

1966   Mr. and Mrs. O. Jacoby
       R. Smith, M. Cutler

LIFE MASTERS PAIRS

1966   Dr. R. Farris, C. K. Smith

MASTERS PAIRS

1960   J. Titus, D. Reid
1961   Mrs. L. B. Swan, Mrs. W. K. Wood
1962   Mrs. L. Horner, B. Matthews
1963   O. Jacoby, B. Crane
1964   Mrs. J. Duncan, Mrs. R. H. Weaver
1965   G. Kasle, E. Theus
1966   S. D. Turner, Mrs. C. Word
1967   Mrs. R. H. Patton, C. McFarland
1968   C. R. Davison, N. Chambers
1969   A. Gutowsky, P. Harrison
1970   N. Jensen, F. Jensen
1972   W. Copson, R. Holmes

OPEN PAIRS

1958   G. Heath, P. Hodge
1959   M. Key, G. R. Nail
1960   E. Jennings, B. Slay
1961   O. Jacoby, R. Wolff
1962   Mrs. L. T. Barber, Mrs. R. Jackson
1963   B. Crane, B. Greenberg
1964   G. Kasle, B. Adams
1965   Mrs. C. C. Bledsoe, Mrs. H. P. Bunch
1966   H. T. Siefen, J. W. Stuart
1967   Mrs. F. Matthews, Mrs. D. Garrett
1968   J. Jacoby, Mrs. M. Brachman
1969   Mrs. L. Harris, Mrs. F. B. Shank
1970   J. Patterson, J. Littrell
1972   J. Jacoby, M. Chang

MEN'S PAIRS

1958   C. Smith, J. G. Ripstra
1959   C. Miller, T. Higgins
1960   D. Carter, J. A. Rockhold
1961   S. Greenberg, J. Taylor
1962   J. Yates, A. D. Fryman
1963   J. Yates, A. D. Fryman
1964   O. Jacoby, M. Gouger
1965   B. Adams, P. Harrison
1966   B. Adams, G. Smith
1967   D. Morse, C. Miller
1968   P. Harrison, B. Adams
1969   M. Bruce, R. L. Rosenwald, Jr.
1970   R. Smith, J. D. King
1972   J. Roberts, L. Roberts

WOMEN'S PAIRS

1958   I. Barnard, M. Lichtenstein
1959   M. Sharfstein, M. Lipoff
1960   L. W. Killiam, W. H. Potts
1961   J. N. Allison, W. H. Potts
1962   W. L. Meadows, V. P. Weiss
1963   G. Pontious, J. W. Stuart
1964   M. Weller, Mrs. A. R. Klaus
1965   Mrs. J. Boren, Mrs. E. Shannon
1966   Mrs. F. Hare, Mrs. F. Welch
1967   Mrs. A. Cahn, Jr., Mrs. R. Schultz
1968   Mrs. S. Mark, Mrs. Z. Morphew
1969   Mrs. W. W. Carter, Mrs. D. A. Donaldson
1970   Mrs. G. R. Rush, M. Dusek
1972   Mrs. L. Mitchell, Mrs. S. Mead

MIXED PAIRS

1959   Mr. and Mrs. J. Levy
1960   Mrs. A. C. Vernor, P. Hodge
1961   Mrs. C. Yost, G. Michaud
1962   Mr. and Mrs. W. Wolfforth
1963   R. Smith, W. B. Hisel
1964   J. Gerber, Mrs. P. McDaniel
1965   P. Pandres, Dr. R. E. Day
1966   Mr. and Mrs. J. Boone
1967   T. Michaels, Dr. A. Salasky
1968   V. Miller, R. Layton
1969   P. Soloway, M. Brachman
1970   H. Baer, B. Wolff

TEXAS SUMMER

KNOCKOUT TEAMS

1967   O. Jacoby, Mr. and Mrs. M. Brachman
       S. Lazard, P. Levitt
1970   Dr. J. Fisher, C. Weed
       Mrs. D. Hawes, J. Blair
       G. Dawkins, B. Hagedorn
1971   B. Goldman, B. Hamman
       M. Lawrence, B. Wolff
1972   R. Wolff, Dr. G. Pisk
       P. Hood, L. Tritter
       C. Strouse
1973   Dr. J. Tucker, Dr. C. Robinson
       G. Hayden, G. Kasle
       B. Hamman
1974   B. Creed, V. Davis
       J. Brownlee, J. Griffin
       S. Lawrence, F. Lawrence

OPEN TEAMS

1967   Dr. J. Fisher, Mrs. D. B. Hawes
       B. Crane, G. Polak
1968   G. B. Gray, Mrs. B. J. Wilson
       W. L. Desmuke, Mrs. H. Witt
1969   P. Soloway, G. Dawkins
       Mr. and Mrs. M. Brachman
       B. Hagedorn

1970   C. Smith, D. Siebert
      J. Blair, J. Ritter
      E. Yost
1971   B. Goldman, B. Wolff
      Mr. and Mrs. E. Burke
1972   C. Smith, C. Weed
      J. Blair, B. Greenberg
      P. Swanson
1973   O. Jacoby, T. Ried
      B. Hamman, P. Levitt
1974   G. Pisk, P. Hood
      S. Horn, P. Horn
      M. Kaplan

MASTERS PAIRS

1967   W. McGrew, Mrs. H. L. Mott, *tied with*
      R. E. Rinkus, G. S. Morrow
1968   W. Fannin, J. Puscas
1969   Mr. and Mrs. R. Carmichael
1970   P. Levitt, S. Lazarus
1971   R. Schmieder, G. Hayden
1972   P. Swanson, J. Miller
1973   M. Brachman, P. Soloway
1974   J. Janitschke, C. Janitschke

OPEN PAIRS

1967   R. Wolff, Mrs. M. B. Killian
1968   J. D. King, Mrs. W. L. Corbin
1969   J. Jacoby, M. Brachman
1970   J. Gerber, C. Klar
1971   B. Wolff, B. Hagedorn
1972   R. Capps, F. Woodruff
1973   M. Brachman, J. Jacoby
1974   H. Baer, C. Jackson

MEN'S PAIRS

1967   P. Levitt, S. Lazard
1968   M. Carroll, A. Harrison
1969   S. Coolik, G. Treadwell
1970   Dr. C. Robinson, Dr. H. Gardiner, *tied with*
      A. Gutowsky, J. Jelsma
1971   G. Gault, G. Good
1972   R. Hamman, Dr. C. Robinson
1973   B. Acker, B. Hagedorn
1974   J. Puscas, B. Fannin

WOMEN'S PAIRS

1967   Mrs. W. N. Dale, P. MacLean
1968   A. Davis, Mrs. J. W. Rodes
1969   Mrs. L. French, Mrs. J. Hopper
1970   Mrs. T. Sanders, Mrs. J. Kennedy
1971   F. Beard, B.Wolff
1972   A. Davis, P. Drury
1973   P. Pandres, V. Davis
1974   E. Van Zandt, H. Noland

MIXED PAIRS

1967   Mr. and Mrs. C. Weed
1969   J. Jacoby, S. Perutz
1970   S. Lawrence, Mrs. N. Goodloe
1972   L. Oliver, R. Walker
1973   Dr. G. Pisk, P. Hood
1974   L. Childs, D. Childs

DISTRICT 17 (Arizona, New Mexico, Colorado, southern and eastern Wyoming, southern and eastern Nevada, one county of Utah)

DESERT EMPIRE

KNOCKOUT TEAMS

1967   D. Conlin, R. Cash
      H. Segal, N. Schwartz
      L. Marks, P. Marks
1969   P. Soloway, H. Baron
      G. Kasle, L. West
      B. O'Malia
1970   N. Anderson, J. Mohan
      P. Soloway, H. Baron
      R. Henderson, T. Lux
1971   Mrs. W. Chilcote, A. Evans
      D. Priest, L. Weiss
1972   S. Sadowsky, G. Kasle
      G. Hayden, D. Oakie
      Mrs. E. Stanley, W. Truman
1973   J. Schwenke, G. Kasle
      G. Hayden, J. Jacoby
1974   M. Hardy, P. Marks
      M. Gaer, J. Gaer
      B. Truman, M. Kaplan

OPEN TEAMS

1956   Mr. and Mrs. C. Bull
      Mr. and Mrs. G. Patterson
1957   M. Klausner, M. Schleifer
      D. Westerfield, B. Isaacs
1958   Mrs. S. Klausner, M. Schleifer
      D. Westerfield, B. Isaacs
1959   F. Flanagan, R. Cash
      G. Farley, D. Conlin
      L. Goren
1960   M. J. and J. Farell
      A. Tschekaloff, H. Simon
1961   D. Walsh, H. Guiver
      J. M. D. Oakie, E. Burns
1962   R. R. Hislop, R. A. Cash
      C. F. Crossley, Sr., Dr. C. F. Crossley, Jr.
1963   R. Cash, C. F. Crossley, Sr.
      A. Burnstein, Dr. C. F. Crossley, Jr.
1964   G. Bare, G. Hallee
      R. Henderson, P. Soloway
1965   R. L. Tripp, C. Payne
      J. Griffing, Mr. and Mrs. R. McCracken
1966   Mrs. J. Farell, Mrs. L. J. Newman
      K. D. Westerfield, R. Cash
      B. Crane
1968   M. Bartosik, H. Kurtzman
      J. Carney, A. Weiss
1971   H. Guiver, G. Bare
      M. McMahon, E. Paulsen
1972   J. Swanson, P. Soloway
      C. Phillips, A. Evans
      D. Priest, *tied with*
      C. Dunn, K. Downs
      S. Kasle, I. Sadowsky, *tied with*
      H. Baron, M. Shuman
      R. Henderson, J. Mohan, *tied with*
      B. Crane, Dr. J. Fisher
      B. Schreiber, M. Schreiber
1973   J. King, R. LaCour
      N. Erickson, Mrs. J. Howard
      E. Pace
1974   M. Brachman, P. Soloway
      L. Mandel, I. Cohen

MASTERS PAIRS

1956   L. Wolfers, Mrs. W. H. Thieman
1957   Mrs. W. M. Godfrey, B. Groetzinger
1958   T. Foster, C. Potvin
1959   I. Erdos, H. H. Law
1960   M. Klausner, M. Schleifer
1961   E. Burns, H. Guiver
1962   Mrs. F. L. Apt, G. W. Wilson
1963   Mrs. J. J. Azar, Mrs. D. B. Fisher

1964 Mr. and Mrs. D. Drury
1965 R. S. Wolff, M. Wilson
1966 Mrs. R. Kohler, I. Erdos
1967 Mr. and Mrs. R. Walsh
1968 Mr. and Mrs. G. R. Leenerts
1969 D. Heywood, B. Ziegler
1970 Mr. and Mrs. A. Herzberg
1971 T. Primmer, S. Turner
1972 J. Mohan, J. Grantham
1973 M. Blumenthal, N. Anderson, *tied with*
      H. Portugal, E. Herbert
1974 Mrs. T. Thompson, H. Arnstein

OPEN PAIRS

1956 C. Potvin, A. W. Olsen
1957 Mrs. M. M. Hopps, J. Ehrlenbach
1958 S. Rebner, B. Crane
1959 O. Jacoby, C. Russell
1960 E. Paulsen, A. Tschekaloff
1961 Mrs. F. Roach, Mrs. G. Warner
1962 O. Jacoby, M. Shuman
1963 R. Walsh, H. Handler
1964 B. Crane, P. Rank
1965 B. Crane, P. Rank
1966 B. Crane, P. Rank
1967 Mrs. A. W. Noland, Mrs. E. Van Zandt
1968 N. Schwartz, L. Marks
1969 H. Steen, G. A. Civetta
1970 B. Schreiber, M. Schreiber
1971 S. Smolen, B. Schreiber
1972 P. Soloway, M. Brachman
1973 P. Hawkins, K. Petterson
1974 J. Jeffrey, P. Hawkins, *tied with*
      F. Aspell, G. May

MEN'S PAIRS

1956 R. Cash, D. Oakie
1957 E. H. Scurlock, A. Scribner
1958 R. Cash. M. Schleifer
1959 M. Shuman, H. Shoop
1960 J. Kiamy, B. Isaacs
1961 F. S. Flanagan, D. Neal
1962 M. Portugal, R. Walsh
1963 M. Ribyat, T.Christianson
1964 B. Naness, J. T. McEntree
1965 L. Dewey, W. M. Anderson
1966 L. Marks, T. Adler
1967 P. Soloway, R. Walsh
1968 S. Lawrence, R. Spotts
1969 T. Mayr, M. Portugal
1970 H. Friedman, P. Robbins
1971 A. Reinhold, E. Kantar
1972 P. Benjamin, E. Fukushima
1973 M. Rubenfeld, J. King
1974 J. Grantham, J. Jacoby

WOMEN'S PAIRS

1956 J. M. Foote, K. Hobbs
1957 C. Baldwin, C. Briggs
1958 M. Anderson, M. McComber
1959 M. J. Farell, P. Heidelberger
1960 S. W. Attwood, C. R. Hesler
1961 D. Blakemore, R. Howard
1962 R. D. Brown, F. Greene
1963 L. S. Skinner, M. Clark
1964 P. Drury, H. Baron
1965 C. Morriss, F. Blackwell
1966 Mrs. J. C. Butler, Mrs. A. W. Sidles
1967 Mrs. A. W. Noland, Mrs. E. Van Zandt
1968 Mrs. J. Fahrendorf, L. Harmonson
1969 Mrs. M. R. McCrackin, P. Waggoner
1970 Mrs. B. Stuart, Mrs. L. Anderson
1971 Mrs. H. Knowles, H. Baron
1972 J. Carney, M. Chilcote
1973 D. Jonas, K. Shuman, *tied with*
      R. Grantham, S. Kasle

1974 B. Downey, F. Reiner, *tied with*
      K. Shuman, C. Greenhut

MIXED PAIRS

1956 W. C. Guenther, M. Hertel
1957 M. Klausner, M. Schleifer
1958 M. Klausner, M. Schleifer
1959 Mrs. C. A. Smith, Dr. C. H. Swartz
1960 M. Klausner, M. Schleifer
1961 R. Groves, B. Seelman
1962 C. Garrett, D. Holt
1963 Mrs. M. Barrett, E. J. Herbert
1964 C. Dibblee, O. A. Mowry
1965 L. Peterson, L. C. Dewey
1967 C. J. Brong, Mrs. M. Rustad, *tied with*
      Mr. and Mrs. R. Walsh
1970 H. Baron, J. Mohan
1971 J. Stein, H. Baron

DISTRICT 17

KNOCKOUT TEAMS

1972 H. Baron, M. Shuman
      K. Gorfkle, M. Passell

OPEN TEAMS

1972 B. Crane, Dr. J. Fisher
      J. Jacoby, C. Weed
1973 P. Soloway, B. Schreiber
      M. Schreiber, H. Baron
1974 D. Guerin, M. Ralph
      R. Lipton, L. Kassis

MASTERS PAIRS

1972 H. Baron, M. Shuman
1973 S. Williams, J. McKee
1974 J. Jacoby, C. Dennen

OPEN PAIRS

1972 J. Jacoby, C. Weed
1973 K. Gorfkle, B. Whitesel
1974 H. Perlman, J. Starr

MEN'S PAIRS

1972 R. Bates, G. Kasle
1973 D. Tuell, G. Steiner
1974 R. LaCour, K. Petterson

WOMEN'S PAIRS

1972 Mrs. M. Webster, Mrs. C. Gunter
1973 P. Eckard, L. Kasle
1974 K. Shuman, R. Walsh

NAVAJO TRAIL

KNOCKOUT TEAMS

1967 Mrs. P. Lowden, J. Ehrlenbach
      G. Kasle, L. Marks
      P. Marks
1968 M. Bartosik, R. L. Grime
      J. D. Duke, A. McAlear
1969 N. Greenberg, L. Bushnell
      P. Drury, R. Luebkeman

1970 A. Burnstein, P. Kaye
      J. Perry, M. Agay
      M. Vernoff, C. Kaye
1971 J. Mohan, J. Padget
      J. King, H. Baron
      R. Henderson
1973 K. Petterson, P. Hawkins
      F. Smith, J. Erickson
      R. LaCour

OPEN TEAMS

1966 Mrs. V. D. Rowley, H. F. Coray
      J. McEntree, Mrs. F. Smith
1967 Mrs. W. Achning, R. Wolff
      G. Polak, J. Jacoby
      B. Crane
1968 T. Cochran, Mrs. E. D. Giffen
      Mrs. P. M. McClanahan, S. O. Benzon
1969 Mr. and Mrs. H. A. Woods, Jr.
      B. Martin, E. Rudes
1971 Mrs. H. Woods, M. Long
      F. Downing, R. Osthues, *tied with*
      J. Kahan, D. Mordecai
      L. Kahan, S. Horn
      D. Reed, *tied with*
      F. Clark, K. Geffen
      M. Stone, W. Ragland, *tied with*
      Mr. and Mrs. P. Brennan, L. Dewey, M. Lair
1973 J. Jacoby, J. McIlroy
      V. McIlroy, L. Weiss
      M. Chilcote

MASTERS PAIRS

1966 G. R. Lee, Mrs. V. D. Rowley
1967 Mrs. R. L. Wood, Mrs. H. H. Conger
1968 M. Blustein, M. Blustein
1969 J. D. King, Mrs. M. McCrory
1970 Mrs. E. King, B. King
1971 E. Sussex, R. Sussex
1973 B. Crane, K. Shuman

OPEN PAIRS

1966 B. Crane, M. Anticouni
1967 H. St. John, T. Callaham
1968 Mrs. D. R. Huston, J. A. Cramer
1969 B. L. Harrison, R. Reed
1970 R. Matthess, R. Walsh, *tied with*
      B. Crane, Dr. J. Fisher
1971 B. Crane, M. Jones
1973 B. Schmieder, J. Grantham

MASTERS MEN'S PAIRS

1971 D. Reed, S. Horn

MEN'S PAIRS

1966 A. L. McAlear, F. J. Walker
1967 B. Crane, G. Polak
1968 R. Plowman, R. Summerhayes
1969 R. L. Tripp, J. F. Griffin
1970 D. Mordecai, D. Salkoff
1971 J. Mohan, R. Henderson
1972 W. Vail, R. Esch

MASTERS WOMEN'S PAIRS

1971 J. Brownlee, L. Hyder

WOMEN'S PAIRS

1966 H. Sykes, Mrs. E. M. Gabriel
1967 M. Frampton, Mrs. J. Vickers
1968 Mrs. A. Cook, Mrs. J. Wertz
1969 S. Berryhill, M. J. Jones
1970 H. Baron, A. Arndt
1971 Mrs. J. Marks, Mrs. J. Hobson
1972 B. Schmieder, H. Baron

MIXED PAIRS

1970 B. King, R. Violin

INDIVIDUAL

1969 Z. Colby

ROCKY MOUNTAIN

KNOCKOUT TEAMS

1967 K. Petterson, H. Moore
      J. Spadero, M. Portugal
      L. West, M. Schleifer
1968 J. Kahan, L. Kahan
      D. Mordecai, M. Senti
1969 J. J. Farrell, K. Blanchard
      M. Genud, T. Prothro
      J. P. Miller, H. Guiver
1970 H. Baron, P. Soloway
      R. Henderson, J. Anderson
1971 H. Baron, N. Anderson
      J. Mohan, D. Ashley
1972 H. Bethe, J. Farell
      M. J. Farell, D. Reed
      J. Bitman, D. Mordecai
1973 R. Kaye, G. Hayden
      Capt. J. LaForce, N. Greenberg
      A. Kaminsky
1974 A. Reinhold, K. Shuman
      L. Cohen, Dr. R. Katz
      E. Kantar

OPEN TEAMS

1948 E. Herz, Dr. J. A. Wolf
      Mrs. W. L. Zent, Mrs. T. Kahan *tied with*
      Mr. and Mrs. G. B. Stone
      Mrs. F. J. Terhune, P. Turner
1949 M. Parker, T. Bailey
      J. G. Ripstra, J. Hopkins
1950 Mr. and Mrs. G. B. Stone
      Mr. and Mrs. W. W. Sanders
1951 G. Thieman, J. Bitman
      J. Gelman, W. Thieman
1952 H. L. Thurtell, J. Kahan
      S. Fairchild, J. Simon
1953 G. R. Nail, J. G. Ripstra
      M. Thomas, G. Michaud
      J. Hopkins
1954 Mrs. A. Kauder, D. Steen
      I. Erdos, W. Hanna
1955 K. Patterson, E. Thygeson
      B. Coombs, A. O. Jones
1956 M. Newbill, R. Steinberg
      Mr. and Mrs. J. Simon
      L. Weiner
1957 L. Kahan, J. Kahan
      H. L. Thurtell, J. Bitman
1958 Mr. and Mrs. J. Kahan
      R. Thurtell, M. McClure
1959 R. Thurtell, J. Kahan
      L. Kahan, J. Bitman
1960 A. R. Mayer, B. Aisenberg
      K. Kaane, R. Baptist
1961 P. Brennan, Jr., D. Mordecai
      I. Stakgold, P. Pender
1962 L. Kahan, J. Bitman
      J. Kahan, H. L. Thurtell
      J. McClure
1963 D. Oakie, Mrs. A. Coleman
      M. Klausner, M. Schleifer
1964 Mr. and Mrs. J. Kahan
      R. Thurtell, J. Bitman
      J. McClure
1965 Dr. and Mrs. J. Cline
      Mrs. P. Clarke, Mrs. K. Yingling
1966 H. Baron, P. Pender
      Mr. and Mrs. J. Flint, *tied with*
      B. Bratcher, M. Cocherell
      P. Yates, J. Kelly
1967 Mr. and Mrs. R. Walsh
      Mr. and Mrs. J. Farell

1968   R. Rowley, G. Hays
      L. Voigt, C. Dibblee
1969   J. Carney, F. Aspell
      D. Mordecai, T. Callaham
      W. Baldwin, E. Theus
1970   S. Crain, J. Padget
      J. Herriot, D. Afdahl
1971   G. Kasle, Mrs. F. Proctor
      R. Cobb, N. Cobb
1972   D. Mordecai, E. Mordecai
      J. Bitman, J. McClure
      H. Bethe, E. Bronson, *tied with*
      D. Arlen, Mrs. H. Bleakley
      J. Cramer, Mrs. D. Scott, *tied with*
      V. McIlroy, J. McIlroy
      J. Jacoby, M. Chilcote
      L. Weiss, *tied with*
      Mrs. S. Sweeney, K. Leiker
      Mr. and Mrs. G. Mason
1973   G. Vince, E. Walker
      N. Walker, B. Puryear
1974   M. Thieman, Mrs. D. Dwight
      Mrs. D. Myers, Mrs. J. Mohler

MASTERS PAIRS

1950   W. L. Crooks, G. R. Nail
1951   S. Rebner, J. H. Moran
1952   F. D. Cheatwood, A. P. Simon
1953   S. Fairchild, J. Winston
1954   Mrs. A. Kauder, B. Thompson
1955   R. Cash, R. R. Hislop
1956   H. O. Reid, Mrs. J. McKenna
1957   Mrs. W. Thieman, R. Groetsinger
1958   F. Budlong, J. C. Ehrlenbach
1959   R. P. Reed, R. F. Robbins
1960   Mrs. A. T. Sweet, R. S. Allen
1961   K. Stenger, E. Monroe
1962   I. Erdos, M. Turk
1963   Mr. and Mrs. J. Farell
1964   G. Halle, P. Soloway
1965   M. Carwin, Mrs. C. Jeffrey-Smith, *tied with*
      H. Moore, M. Portugal
1966   D. Mordecai, J. A. Kahan
1967   L. West, R. Henderson
1968   Mr. and Mrs. J. Farell
1969   R. Baptist, J. P. Miller
1970   B. Crane, Dr. J. Fisher
1971   M. Lair, L. Dewey
1972   J. Janitschke, C. Janitschke
1973   C. Janitschke, M. Kaplan
1974   K. Shuman, J. Grantham

OPEN PAIRS

1948   Mr. and Mrs. R. P. Bean
1949   T. Bailey, J. G. Ripstra
1950   H. Rethers, E. Miller
1951   S. Rebner, J. H. Moran
1952   I. Epstein, C. Hart
1953   B. Berkitz, W. Hanna
1954   I. Levine, O. M. Rye
1955   E. Rovere, J. Bitman
1956   M. J. Kauder, J. Farell
1957   Mr. and Mrs. C. L. Weldenberg
1958   W. R. McWilliams, J. Wright
1959   M. Shuman, A. Bell
1960   M. Klausner, M. Schleifer
1961   B. L. Harrison, Mrs. W. E. LaVelle
1962   Mrs. E. A. Mahoney, D. Carter
1963   O. Jacoby, P. Harrison
1964   R. Walsh, G. Bare
1965   F. Rappleyea, J. Zilic
1966   J. Linhart, R. P. Baptist
1967   Mr. and Mrs. R. Walsh
1968   H. Moore, M. Portugal
1969   D. Forster, J. Taylor
1970   B. Crane, Dr. J. Fisher
1971   M. McCrory, G. Kasle, *tied with*
      C. Graham, D. Jordan
1972   M. Stone, Mrs. J. Lankton
1973   B. Crane, Dr. J. Fisher
1974   J. Bitman, D. Mordecai

MEN'S PAIRS

1948   R. Thurrell, L. Wolfe
1949   G. Ford, L. Goldstein
1950   M. Coff, L. Horwitz
1951   H. Coray, D. Buie
1952   M. Thomas, M. Nelson
1953   W. Hanna, D. Steen
1954   W. Hanna, D. Steen
1955   L. Mathe, M. Vernoff
1956   M. W. Bierbaum, P. H. Katt
1957   E. Herz, D. Mordecai
1958   R. Galena, G. Ford, Jr., *tied with*
      W. Thieman, J. Haley
1959   R. G. Sharp, S. Kasle
1960   R. D. Hutchinson, J. Ehrlenbach
1961   E. L. Bookins, M. Derby
1962   C. Hanks, J. Moran
1963   R. Baptist, Dr. C. F. Crossley, Jr.
1964   P. Brennan, D. Mordecai
1965   Capt. R. Kibler, J. A. Yates
1966   N. O. Haflich, M. D. Copeland
1967   R. Stern, J. Cramer
1968   M. Genud, L. West
1969   G. Graham, M. Genud
1970   S. Horn, D. Reed
1971   P. Soloway, D. Ashley
1972   J. McKee, D. Parker
1973   M. Lair, R. Henderson
1974   R. Kaye, M. Shuman

WOMEN'S PAIRS

1948   D. C. DeWitt, E. Zent
1949   B. C. Reichmuth, J. L. McClellan
1950   T. R. Burnett, C. Berry
1951   C. C. Neff, J. McKenna
1952   C. B. Lee, C. Neff
1953   A. Neal, T. C. Lee
1954   M. Klausner, C. Whitehead
1955   A. F. Moline, C. Morgan
1956   J. C. Allen, V. D. Roberts
1957   W. C. Godfrey, C. Morgan
1958   V. Leonard, N. Dukes
1959   A. F. Mottelson, H. A. Woods
1960   D. Walker, W. E. Swart
1961   B. English, S. Bishop
1962   W. J. Byrd, L. J. Ward
1963   J. McKenna, C. C. Neff
1964   O. V. Durbin, G. P. Ruppert
1965   F. Leventhal, F. Reed
1966   Mrs. E. B. Still, Mrs. J. M. Holbrook
1967   Mrs. R. H. Pyle, C. Pratt
1968   J. W. Anderson, Mrs. M. Mier
1969   M. Senti, B. L. Harrison
1970   Mrs. W. Godfrey, Mrs. S. Hollingsworth
1971   Mrs. F. Glenn, Mrs. A. Fearheiley
1972   Mrs. S. Occhipiniti, Mrs. D. Rees
1973   N. Austermann, S. Cohen
1974   J. Kelly, J. Sloop

MIXED PAIRS

1950   Mrs. S. Emerson, J. Miller
1951   Mrs. R. S. Parker, H. Love
1952   S. Hanna, W. Hanna
1953   S. Rebner, C. Strouse
1954   Mrs. J. Barth, J. Barth
1955   Mr. and Mrs. M. H. Howard
1956   Mrs. W. Klausner, J. Moran
1957   M. Klausner, M. Schleifer
1958   Mrs. C. C. Neff, J. Kahan
1959   S. Harris, E. Rosen
1960   Mrs. J. Farell, B. Crane
1961   S. Harris, E. Rosen
1962   Mrs. L. S. Skinner, R. S. Allen
1963   Mrs. J. B. Wilson, H. W. Christ
1964   Mrs. R. H. Alderson, H. W. Holtzclaw
1965   H. Baron, P. Rank
1966   Mrs. E. B. Still, W. P. Mullen
1967   R. Kaye, Mrs. V. L. Baptist
1968   S. Horn, P. Horn
1969   J. Farley, B. Schmidt
1970   H. Baron, D. Mordecai
1971   J. Trussell, R. Neumann

INDIVIDUAL

1948   Mrs. B. C. Reichmuth
1969   J. Irish

DISTRICT 18 (Alberta, Saskatchewan, Montana, northwestern Wyoming, most of Idaho, most of Utah)

CANADIAN

KNOCKOUT TEAMS

1970   P. Soloway, M. Schleifer
      Mrs. E. A. Mahoney, M. J. Farell
      Dr. V. Mastron
1971   J. Anderson, R. DuFour
      J. Martineau, A. Graves
      K. Gorfkle
1972   M. J. Farell, Mrs. E. Mahoney
      N. Anderson, R. Teshima, B. Pritchard
      P. Prince
1973   D. Thomson, J. Marsch
      A. Graves, L. Oakey
1974   C. Goppert, M. Passell
      H. Baron, G. Hayden
      R. LaCour

OPEN TEAMS

1968   H. Baron, M. Portugal
      L. West, N. Anderson
1969   A. G. Hampson, R. G. Phelps
      C. W. Wilkinson, W. Hepperle
1970   S. Anderson, K. Gorfkle
      N. Anderson, L. Weiss
1971   J. Anderson, R. DuFour
      K. Gorfkle, A. Graves, *tied with*
      Mrs. D. Mitchell, G. Mitchell
      B. Stewart, A. d'Entremont
      J. Phillips, *tied with*
      M. Balych, E. Dressler
      K. Chao, O. Soice
1972   C. Wilson, J. Whillis
      C. Ashman, C. Fergie, *tied with*
      M. Thomas, J. Kittlitz
      R. Kittlitz, F. Ratai, *tied with*
      G. Sagen, F. Waters
      Mr. and Mrs. P. Betz
1973   T. Gould, L. Racette
      P. Lopushinsky, S. Viswanathan
1974   B. Krapko, J. Donaldson
      S. Sidell, P. Hagen, B. Connop

MASTERS PAIRS

1968   Mrs. M. R. Mrazek, J. Landeryou
1969   J. C. Anderson, J. Taylor
1970   J. C. Anderson, J. Taylor
1971   R. DuFour, J. Anderson
1972   A. Graves, N. Chambers
1973   A. McAlear, D. McAlear
1974   L. Betts, J. Kerger

OPEN PAIRS

1968   H. Baron, M. Portugal
1969   B. L. Harrison, D. Reed
1970   D. Thomson, Mrs. H. Promislow
1971   R. DuFour, J. Anderson
1972   R. MacDuff, O. Mowry
1973   R. Johnson, D. Wilkeson
1974   H. Heard, M. Portugal

MEN'S PAIRS

1968   O. Nelson, R. D. Hutchinson
1969   R. Wobick, K. Waters
1970   K. Gorfkle, S. Sidell
1971   Dr. J. Averback, G. Sekhar

1973   J. Marsch, B. Smith
1974   G. Hayden, R. LaCour

WOMEN'S PAIRS

1968   M. J. Farell, Mrs. E. A. Mahoney
1969   M. J. Farell, Mrs. E. A. Mahoney
1970   Mrs. H. Larson, Mrs. E. Rutledge
1971   Mrs. J. Byorth, Mrs. J. Biggle
1973   L. Solinger, R. Price
1974   R. Bateman, M. Treadway

MIXED PAIRS

1968   G. E. Joneson, Mrs. M. Hall
1969   M. J. Farell, R. Spotts
1970   H. Baron, D. Forster
1972   B. and G. Haller
1973   L. Barton, L. Ellestad

DISTRICT 18

KNOCKOUT TEAMS

1970   V. Mastron, M. J. Farell
      Mrs. E. Mahoney, M. Portugal
      P. Soloway
1971   K. Gorfkle, R. DuFour
      A. McAlear, V. White
      M. Adkins, Dr. B. Bryson
1973   D. La Fleur, J. Grantham
      M. Shuman, H. Baron,
      R. Bates, J. Mohan
1974   M. Passell, H. Baron
      P. Soloway, M. Brahman
      M. Lair

OPEN TEAMS

1971   B. Jurovitch, S. Roan
      R. Castle, G. Williamson
      L. Poppler, S. Thomas, *tied with*
      J. Elliott, C. Crawford
      Mr. and Mrs. P. Betz, *tied with*
      A. McAlear, R. Rolfson
      Mrs. L. Torgrimson, R. DuFour
1972   D. Thomson, H. Smithen
      D. Levin, R. Kurse, *tied with*
      Dr. K. Paine, Dr. M. Tyrrell
      D. Schmeiser, J. Howard, *tied with*
      J. Padget, R. Bolton
      D. Schopflocher, D. Carson
      K. Schulle
1974   G. Steiner, J. Schermer
      M. Blumenthal, M. Gurwitz

MASTERS PAIRS

1970   Dr. A. Cook, J. Balfour
1971   B. Crane, R. Kaye
1972   M. Johnson, K. Johnson
1974   P. Soloway, M. Brachman

OPEN PAIRS

1970   V. Mastron, M. Portugal
1971   W. Whitesel, L. Tsou
1972   M. Shuman, H. Baron
1974   B. Crane, Dr. J. Fisher

MEN'S PAIRS

1970   G. Mitchell, A. d'Entremont
1971   K. Gorfkle, J. Padget
1972   D. Schopflocher, D. Carson
1974   P. Soloway, M. Passell

WOMEN'S PAIRS

1970   S. Harris, M. Sollod
1971   Mrs. S. Helmer, Mrs. C. Hestekin
1972   L. Thierman, P. Smolensky
1974   P. Angle, K. Schulle

INTER-MOUNTAIN

KNOCKOUT TEAMS

1968   H. Baron, P. Soloway
      M. Portugal, B. Levan
      L. West, C. MacCracken
1969   B. O'Malia, G. Kasle
      C. MacCracken, H. Baron
      P. Soloway
1970   D. Oakie, Mrs. E. Stanley
      Mrs. R. Williams, K. Allison
1971   D. Adams, D. Buie
      R. Carone, R. MacDuff
1972   M. J. Farell, Mrs. E. Mahoney
      C. Dorn, K. Blackerby
      L. Tsou, R. Henderson
1973   M. Portugal, H. Baron
      M. Passell, M. Rubenfeld
      J. King
1974   M. Passell, H. Baron
      R. LaCour, G. Kasle
      G. Hayden

OPEN TEAMS

1956   J. Jackson, Mrs. L. Thompson
      Dr. and Mrs. E. C. Goblirsch
      H. Edwards
1957   Mrs. E. Stewart, D. Hopkins
      Mrs. E. Nepple, E. Oke
1958   L. and G. Patterson
      I. Epstein, A. Hicks
1959   M. E. Singleton, B. Goodman
      A. C. Felt, J. H. Schwarts
1960   Dr. and Mrs. J. M. Hickes
      Mrs. G. Nilson, B. O'Mahoney, *tied with*
      E. Paulsen, M. Shuman
      M. J. Farell, I. Zorn
      A. Bell
1961   J. Moran, D. Oakie
      H. Haugsten, Mrs. J. Meier
1962   P. Pender, M. S. Lawrence
      H. Baron, P. C. Rank
1963   J. Budd, A. Hicks
      Mrs. M. S. Nemer, Mrs. L. S. Gordon
1964   R. Speicher, B. Dougherty
      Mr. and Mrs. H. Doughty
1965   H. Baron, P. Rank
      M. Lawrence, J. Moran
      C. Henke
1966   H. Baron, M. Schleifer
      P. Pender, J. Flint, *tied with*
      F. Cady, K. Gorfkle
      G. Steiner, N. Featherston
1967   C. Kramer, R. Hicks
      Mr. and Mrs. R. McLaughlin, *tied with*
      D. Schulte, H. Baron,
      J. Moran, P. Rank
      M. Johnson
1968   Mrs. A. S. Brown, Mrs. S. Barbo
      Mrs. R. Faus, Mrs. B. DeTour
1970   H. Baron, R. Henderson
      T. Lux, N. Anderson
      J. King
1971   N. and J. Berken, P. and P. Eagan, *tied with*
      A. McAlear, D. McAlear
      F. and M. Walker
1972   C. Wilson, D. Brown
      J. Erickson, M. Chomyn
1973   G. Kasle, R. Bates
      G. Hayden, J. Mohan
      J. King
1974   J. Hooker, Dr. J. Fisher
      K. Shuman, J. Grantham
      K. Schulle, J. Schermer

MASTERS PAIRS

1956   Mrs. R. Bartholomew, Mrs. J. J. Parker
1957   F. Carpenter, N. Ballard, *tied with*
      R. MacNab, M. Manchester
1958   G. McCann, J. Ehrlenbach
1959   M. Hutchinson, D. Oakie
1960   C. Rush, I. Epstein

1961   P. Rank, D. Krauss
1962   R. Bratcher, M. Cocherell
1963   Mrs. E. S. Mahoney, D. Carter, *tied with*
      Mrs. C. J. Stormwind, P. Carlin
1964   W. E. Ensminger, J. D. Shortridge
1965   Mrs. M. M. McGill, D. Oram
1966   D. Oakie, B. E. O'Malia
1967   M. Johnson, P. Rank
1968   H. Baron, P. Soloway
1969   Mrs. D. R. Houston, M. Bozeman
1970   N. Anderson, R. Henderson
1971   B. Crane, Dr. J. Fisher
1972   D. Mraz, J. Mohan
1973   M. Passell, H. Baron
1974   H. Heard, M. Portugal

OPEN PAIRS

1956   M. Harkleroad, A. E. Hill
1957   R. Hendershott, J. Donelly
1958   F. Carpenter, J. L. Donelly
1959   Mrs. O. Heidelberger, J. Ehrlenbach
1960   I. Epstein, A. Hicks
1961   H. Guiver, A. Tschekaloff
1962   Mr. and Mrs. T. E. Bussey
1963   O. Jacoby, P. Levitt
1964   H. Baron, H. Shoop
1965   L. A. Jordan, M. C. Siemer
1966   C. Henke, J. Moran
1967   J. Kamb, C. Hansen
1968   Mrs. S. Thomas, K. Hummel
1969   P. Soloway, H. Baron
1970   R. Henderson, H. Baron
1971   S. Smolen, C. MacCracken
1972   M. Shuman, H. Baron
1973   B. Crane, Dr. J. Fisher
1974   R. LaCour, H. Baron

MEN'S PAIRS

1956   D. Oakie, G. F. Shaw
1957   B. Ignatz, G. Welch
1958   G. McCann, J. Ehrlenbach
1959   M. C. Siemer, L. G. Shadoan
1960   I. Erdos, Dr. E. W. You
1961   D. Oakie, M. Hodges
1962   R. Borg, W. Weinstein
1963   P. Larson, W. C. Peterson
1964   M. E. Singleton, Dr. R. W. Thometz
1965   J. Pestaner, J. Linhart
1966   P. Pender, J. Flint
1967   O. Leesment, K. Van Renesse
1968   B. May, B. Crapko
1969   M. Portugal, V. Mastron
1970   O. Leesmont, M. Squier
1971   B. O'Malia, G. Kasle
1972   T. Quinlan, M. Adkins
1974   G. Kasle, J. Grantham

WOMEN'S PAIRS

1956   J. E. Harris, J. J. Parker
1957   W. Mozzone, T. Lantry
1958   A. C. Felt, J. H. Schwart
1959   H. Joffe, P. Smolensky
1960   A. C. Felt, J. H. Schwartz
1961   J. Ruhle, B. Goodman
1962   V. Galena, N. E. Vincent
1963   M. Bybee, A. F. Skinner
1964   A. Skinner, E. Erlandson
1965   Mrs. L. J. Egan, Mrs. J. E. Rodgers
1966   H. Baron, H. Flint
1967   M. McGill, J. Millward, *tied with*
      M. J. Farell, M. Mahoney
1968   M. J. Farell, Mrs. E. A. Mahoney
1969   Mrs. J. Hewitt, Mrs. E. E. LaFrance
1970   Mrs. L. Stratton, Mrs. R. Haller
1971   S. Jones, Mrs. C. Hyatt
1972   C. Smith, H. Gregory
1974   L. Gunther, J. Madrid

MIXED PAIRS

1956   R. Leber, J. Frederick
1957   Mrs. S. de Mers, L. Jordan

1958 O. Griffith, M. C. Siemer
1959 Mr. and Mrs. A. Scribner, *tied with*
      Mrs. B. C. Reichmuth, A. Lipsker
1960 A. L. You, I. Erdos
1961 Mrs. J. Farell, P. Rank
1962 Mr. and Mrs. H. W. McGlynn
1963 Mrs. K. Mulholland, M. E. Singleton
1964 E. Herbert, B. G. Wills
1965 Mrs. S. Ondeck, H. A. McLane
1966 P. Wood, B. Coerner
1967 Dr. W. I. Lukas, S. Hartley
1968 D. Morris, B. Patrick
1969 M. Bartosik, M. Triplitt
1974 C. Roberts, Mrs. J. Hickes

INDIVIDUAL

1968 V. White

DISTRICT 19 (British Columbia, Alaska, Washington, portion of western Idaho)

INLAND EMPIRE

KNOCKOUT TEAMS

1970 G. Steiner, J. Donaldson
      A. Graves, N. Chambers
1971 D. Oakie, Mrs. E. Stanley
      J. Jabon, Dr. E. Christopherson
1972 H. Baron, R. Henderson
      J. Padget, L. Tsou
      J. Mohan
1973 J. Mohan, D. LaFleur
      J. Grantham, R. Bates
      M. Passell, G. Hayden
1974 C. Goppert, R. LaCour
      P. Soloway, G. Hayden
      M. Passell

OPEN TEAMS

1971 N. and J. Ballard, C. Baird
      B. Luebkeman, *tied with*
      J. Person, B. Person
      M. Curtis, Mrs. L. Hopkins, *tied with*
      N. Sutherland, D. McKinney
      J. Erickson, M. Chomyn, *tied with*
      G. Slemmons, D. Sletterholm
      P. Goodin, D. Pederson
1972 J. Schermer, N. Chambers
      K. Gorfkle, A. Graves
1973 K. Scholes, S. Sidell
      H. Lortz, D. Brown
1974 G. Steiner, G. Slemmons
      C. Baird, J. Anderson

MASTERS PAIRS

1971 J. Anderson, J. Sullivan
1972 W. Whitesell, R. Henderson
1973 H. Lortz, S. Sidell
1974 D. Oakie, Mrs. E. Stanley

OPEN PAIRS

1970 P. Soloway, H. Baron
1971 B. Hitchens, Dr. R. Tracy
1972 T. Hammond, M. Bailey
1973 M. Passell, H. Baron
1974 S. Smolen, P. Rank

MEN'S PAIRS

1970 W. Whitesell, D. Jones
1971 J. Padget, N. Anderson
1974 L. Betts, G. Harper

WOMEN'S PAIRS

1970 Mrs. L. Austin, Mrs. R. Kershaw
1971 J. Ballard, C. Baird
1974 M. Blustein, S. Urbaniak

PACIFIC NORTHWEST

KNOCKOUT TEAMS

1969 F. Hagan, P. Novak
      B. Hendershott, G. Hays
      B. Crapko
1970 B. Crapko, P. Novak
      D. Thomson, J. Marsch
      D. Shapiro
1971 L. Tsou, J. Anderson
      W. Whitesell, M. Phillippas
1972 N. Chambers, D. Mehaffey
      B. Eisenberg, K. Hiatt
      J. Schermer
1973 J. Martineau, D. Afdahl
      R. Christie, A. Gammie
1974 B. White, C. Earl
      R. Fleischman, A. Bell
      L. Tsou

OPEN TEAMS

1949 Mr. and Mrs. S. Meyer
      S. Gordon, M. Perlman
1950 H. Holmes, S. Ungar
      C. Holbrook, M. Shaw
1951 W. Mozzone, Mrs. N. A. Currie
      F. Yagi, T. Yagi
1952 A. C. Duby, W. Russman
      D. Harkleroad, G. V. Voight
1953 Mr. and Mrs. D. Harkleroad
      E. McKale, J. H. Moran
1954 Mrs. T. O. Amos, Mrs. E. Stewart
      A. Wright, Jr., A. Doran
1955 N. Ballard, J. Donnelly
      B. Street, M. Manchester
1956 E. Stark, A. Hicks
      I. Epstein, A. Davidson
1957 M. McKenzie, D. Cahill
      W. Rossman, H. Dear
1958 B. Lapidus, N. Turnbull
      G. Yoxall, E. Adams
1959 Dr. E. Schwartz, C. F. Crossley, Jr.
      C. Lewis, R. Beste
1960 A. Zelikowsky, W. G. Schmidt
      J. Costello, R. Melosh
1961 M. Curtis, L. Fox
      R. Beste, C. Lewis
1962 D. Bick, A. Zelikowsky
      J. Donaldson, L. Steil
      R. Berg
1963 Mrs. L. Hills, B. Young
      A. Brown, P. Helland (Spring)
      P. Crowder, E. Selymes
      Dr. D. Federson, R. McDonald (Fall)
1964 D. D. Bick, M. Vernon
      M. Stacklies, B. Crapko (Spring)
      A. Wright, P. Novak
      D. Norton, J. Norton (Fall)
1965 R. J. Waite, D. A. Moore, Jr.
      Mrs. F. B. Sole, Mrs. M. D. Boyer (Spring)
      A. J. Wright, P. Novak
      D. Norton, J. Norton (Fall)
1966 B. Nilsson, L. Frandsen
      F. Baldwin, L. Belzberg (Spring)
      P. Pender, J. Flint
      A. Tschekaloff, R. B. Henderson (Fall)
1967 M. Lawrence, L. West
      H. Moore, P. O'Brien
      M. Portugal (Spring)
      Mr. and Mrs. R. Walsh, L. West
      M. Lawrence (Fall)

1968   J. Powell, Mrs. K. Moody
      Mrs. L. Mason, H. Fisher
1971   A. Hicks, M. Smith
      J. Dickie, M. Strebinger
1972   G. Rath, D. Birnie
      G. Mackenzie, B. Johnston
      E. Bishop
1973   J. Anthony, R. Ohmart
      H. McAllister, S. Metzger, *tied with*
      J. Garrison, P. Dunn
      H. Lortz, K. Scholes
1974   P. Nixon, J. Andrews
      G. Harper, L. Betts

MASTERS PAIRS

1952   Mr. and Mrs. R. Street
1953   B. Johnson, A. Landy
1954   B. Street, V. Street
1955   Mr. and Mrs. R. Street
1956   A. J. Wright, Jr., C. Koch
1957   A. Hicks, I. Epstein
1958   H. Haugsten, D. Oakie
1959   Mrs. J. Meier, D. Oakie
1960   L. Stewart, L. T. Oke
1961   L. Barde, J. Jabon
1962   M. L. Hutchinson, C. Henke
1963   M. Bruce, D. D. Crapke
1964   A. Hicks, J. R. Jacobs (Spring)
      C. Rush, R. Hendershott (Fall)
1965   P. D. Lit, H. Shoop (Spring)
      R. Henderson, A. Tschekaloff (Fall)
1966   K. van Renesse, B. Crapko (Spring)
      R. J. Donaldson, P. Hagan (Fall)
1967   L. Steil, P. Novak (Spring)
      J. Kamb, L. Steil (Fall)
1968   Mrs. T. Hansen, Mrs. L. E. Krause
1969   J. C. Anderson, D. Nemiro
1970   P. Soloway, H. Baron
1971   D. Brander, J. Donaldson
1972   B. White, C. Cleveland
1973   B. Palmer, J. Jabon

OPEN PAIRS

1949   W. Powell, A. Vosburg
1950   M. Manchester, V. Summers
1951   M. Orme, R. Street
1952   G. New, N. P. Monson
1953   J. H. Moran, J. Hennecke
1954   R. Street, L. Graham
1955   E. Bunnell, E. Stark
1956   B. Street, L. Graham
1957   Mr. and Mrs. C. G. Koch
1958   T. Myers, E. Kirkwood
1959   M. Klausner, M. Schleifer
1960   N. Ballard, R. Street
1961   M. Orme, J. W. Patterson
1962   E. Paulsen, A. Tschekaloff
1963   Mrs. L. Hills, O. Leesement (Spring)
      D. Lefebvre, L. W. Hawkins (Fall)
1964   E. Paulsen, R. R. Walsh (Spring)
      J. Taylor, D. E. Forster (Fall)
1965   L. Kramer, D. A. Oakie (Spring)
      J. Jabon, D. Pedersen (Fall)
1966   M. Sacklies, K. van Renesse (Spring)
      B. Crane, P. Rank (Fall)
1967   F. Schaefers, J. Taylor (Spring)
      W. Silver, A. Oaks (Fall)
1968   D. Moore, L. Patrick
1969   H. Baron, P. Soloway
1970   W. Whitesell, M. Miller
1971   R. and R. Wakeman
1972   N. Divinsky, A. Graves
1973   J. Anthony, J. Andrews
1974   K. Larsen, M. Lawrence

MEN'S PAIRS

1949   I. Epstein, H. P. Holmes
1950   E. Cahill, R. Street
1951   J. Ehrlenbach, H. Edwards

1952   C. Wyman, C. Holbrook
1953   W. Hanna, D. Steen
1954   E. Cahill, B. Street
1955   O. Leesment, M. Bruce
1956   E. Cahill, R. Street
1957   M. Stackles, E. Stark
1958   E. Adams, M. Stackles
1959   C. Wyman, H. Craig
1960   E. Patterson, S. Hicks
1961   J. Goldie, S. Marinker
1962   B. Haness, J. T. McEntee, *tied with*
      D. Pederson, R. Hendershott
1963   O. Leesment, J. Beeson (Spring)
      D. Lefebvre, E. Selymes (Fall)
1964   E. Stark, M. Stackles (Spring)
      P. Pender, D. Drury (Fall)
1965   Lt. Col. M. F. Murtha, R. W. Volkwine (Spring)
      P. Lit, H. Ross (Fall)
1966   B. Nilsson, L. Frandsen (Spring)
      L. Steil, G. Hays (Fall)
1967   E. Stark, J. Ribeyre (Spring)
      G. Hays, C. Berry (Fall)
1968   Dr. R. Tracy, R. Hitchens
1969   D. Grant, L. Barton
1970   J. Kamb, D. Smith
1972   A. Graves, D. Thomson
1973   W. Whitesell, A. Bell
1974   F. Hagen, B. Hendershott

WOMEN'S PAIRS

1949   R. W. Nelson, R. Kelley
1950   A. Rosenkrans, H. Brunn
1951   V. Duncan, G. Elmes
1952   L. Green, Mrs. K. Leaverton
1953   L. Wheeler, G. Wilson
1954   W. Mozzone, L. Creary
1955   W. Nepple, L. T. Oke
1956   L. Hills, H. Edwards
1957   D. Hopkins, C. M. Lewis
1958   W. Flaherty, T. Lantry
1959   E. Nepple, L. T. Oke
1960   L. Stewart, J. Kennedy
1961   E. Warren, E. Cleworth
1962   Mrs. E. G. Kauffman, Mrs. D. W. Creary
1963   B. J. Jurovich, D. K. Ribar (Spring)
      W. Price, E. Cleworth (Fall)
1964   D. D. Bick, R. G. Needham (Spring)
      Mrs. L. M. Arnold, D. Norton (Fall)
1965   M. L. Hutchinson, Mrs. M. E. Berg (Spring)
      Mrs. C. R. Gilman, T. Pinkerton (Fall)
1966   Mrs. M. Stone, Mrs. V. Roberts (Spring)
      D. Norton, Mrs. L. M. Arnold (Fall)
1967   P. Hagel, V. Acres (Spring)
      Mrs. M. Mansfield, Mrs. F. Westwood (Fall)
1968   Mrs. W. S. Parker, Mrs. M. Walker
1969   Mrs. T. Kersey, Mrs. H. Reid
1970   H. O'Rourke, M. Marlow
1972   D. Allen, M. Scott
1973   J. Redcliffe, Mrs. C. Van Viegen
1974   D. Campbell, I. Waters

MIXED PAIRS

1949   D. Breher, W. Leary, Sr.
1950   Mr. and Mrs. C. B. Manke
1951   H. Rethers, E. Styer
1952   Mrs. S. Wilson, H. Craig
1953   Dr. and Mrs. H. F. Basford
1954   M. Hall, T. Burns
1955   Mr. and Mrs. G. Patterson
1956   M. Agay, C. Fantone
1957   M. Orme, L. T. Oke
1958   J. L. Meier, J. Ehrlenbach
1959   M. Hutchinson, L. Baker
1960   L. Arnold, D. Lefebvre
1961   E. Gordon, P. Burke
1962   W. Nepple, R. Kirkwood
1963   A. Brown, R. C. Werner (Spring)
      M. Grinstein, K. Bruce (Fall)

1964	M. A. Adams, A. Marsh (Spring)
	Mr. and Mrs. D. R. Tuell (Fall)
1965	P. A. Prahl, E. E. Potts (Fall)
1966	E. Gordon, L. Steil (Spring)
	G. Hays, J. R. Daling (Fall)
1967	M. Powell, O. Jacoby (Spring)
	M. J. Farell, C. MacCracken (Fall)
1969	Mrs. M. McGill, D. Folinsbee

INDIVIDUAL

1969	Mrs. H. A. Anderson

POLAR

KNOCKOUT TEAMS

1971	Maj. and Mrs. R. Towne
	Maj. and Mrs. H. Enbysk
1974	D. Landauer, B. Landauer
	G. Parker, L. Parker

OPEN TEAMS

1971	Mrs. G. Middleton, Mrs. K. McCasky
	Mrs. D. Anderson, Mrs. N. Gregg
1974	P. Jones, T. Schleppegrell
	Capt. D. Day, M. Richens, *tied with*
	R. Wendte, A. Marek
	H. Enbysk, D. Enbysk

MASTERS PAIRS

1971	E. Young, D. Moore
1974	M. Oneck, D. Myers

OPEN PAIRS

1971	Mrs. J. Kendrick, Dr. J. Fisher, *tied with*
	J. Kendrick, P. Sparks
1974	D. Oakie, Mrs. E. Stanley

MEN'S PAIRS

1971	H. Fisher, J. Beeson
1974	D. Landauer, G. Parker

WOMEN'S PAIRS

1971	M. J. Farell, Mrs. J. McLucus
1974	L. Farrell, B. Aharrah

MIXED PAIRS

1971	Mrs. D. Anderson, D. Moore
1974	J. Kendrick, B. Kendrick

PUGET SOUND

KNOCKOUT TEAMS

1968	J. Kamb, C. Hansen
	M. Bailey, T. Hammond
1969	J. Kamb, C. Hansen
	M. Bailey, T. Hammond
1970	G. Steiner, E. Selymes
	G. Slemmons, D. Pederson
1971	G. Steiner, G. Slemmons
	D. Pederson, E. Selymes
1972	E. Selymes, G. Slemmons
	D. Pederson, G. Steiner

1973	F. Rubbra, R. Walsh
	M. Lawrence, N. Anderson
1974	K. Hiatt, K. Shuman
	M. Gurwitz, R. LaCour

OPEN TEAMS

1968	R. Hitchens, F. Cady
	R. Tracy, D. Setterholm
	D. Glad
1971	M. Farman, C. Farman
	Dr. J. Farman, G. Farman
1972	W. Whitesell, S. Sather
	O. Mowry, P. Novak
	B. Crapko
1973	B. Crane, Dr. J. Fisher
	R. Henderson, A. Graves
1974	C. Earl, Dr. E. Christopherson
	T. Kinakin, L. Pfefer

MASTERS PAIRS

1968	E. Murray, V. R. Smith
1969	J. Jabon, T. Taft
1970	W. Whitesell, D. Jones
1971	K. Gorfkle, J. Padget
1972	R. Norberg, D. Metcalf
1973	B. Crane, Dr. J. Fisher
1974	B. Crane, K. Shuman

OPEN PAIRS

1968	B. Crane, P. Rank
1969	A. McAlear, G. Hays
1970	J. Anderson, R. Henderson
1971	J. Padget, N. Anderson
1972	R. MacDuff, T. Suchanis
1973	C. Baird, J. Anderson
1974	D. Nudelman, M. Adkins

MEN'S PAIRS

1968	D. Bennett, S. Sidell
1969	D. Tuell, Jr., E. L. McNeal
1970	K. Gorfkle, R. Henderson
1971	J. Anderson, L. Tsou
1972	E. Chow, J. Thomas
1973	B. Hitchens, E. Giese
1974	R. Feist, R. Johansen

WOMEN'S PAIRS

1968	A. Bean, B. Akin
1969	Mrs. E. Tennyson, Mrs. F. Pigato
1970	Mrs. L. Dudley, E. Cole
1971	Mrs. F. Peters, Mrs. L. Seinfeld
1972	R. Bratcher, F. O'Malia
1973	S. Urbaniak, O. Andrews
1974	K. Cunneen, M. Otness

MIXED PAIRS

1968	W. Nepple, B. Naness
1969	D. Busch, B. Gilman
1970	Mrs. R. Douglas, J. Costello
1971	B. Bedayan, V. Seglins
1972	G. Steiner, M. Blumenthal, *tied with*
	M. Jackson, B. Hagen
1973	S. Bruno, L. Blumenthal
1974	R. Purves, E. Lee

INDIVIDUAL

1968	J. Banks
1974	K. Powers

DISTRICT 20 (Oregon, northern California, northern Nevada, Guam, Wake, Hawaii, portion of western Idaho)

DISTRICT 20

KNOCKOUT TEAMS

1972 R. Henderson, L. Tsou
J. Grantham, R. Bates
1973 B. Crossley, D. Crossley
R. Henderson, V. Pang
J. Padget, K. Gorfkle
1974 M. Gurwitz, B. Crossley
J. Schermer, K. Schulle
M. Lawrence

OPEN TEAMS

1970 D. Cook, L. Baumann
Mr. and Mrs. C. Million
1972 R. Bates, G. Hayden
P. Rank, J. Grantham
1973 M. J. Farell, E. Ganz
L. Tsou, K. Blakerby
1974 W. Whitesell, C. Earl
R. LaCour, P. O'Brien, *tied with*
S. Smolen, P. Rank
N. Moss, E. Fukushima

MASTERS PAIRS

1972 B. Crane, Dr. J. Fisher
1973 O. Mowry, R. Norberg, *tied with*
K. Blackerby, L. Tsou
1974 G. Gates, L. West

OPEN PAIRS

1970 H. Baron, R. Henderson
1972 M. J. Farell, Mrs. F. Ganz
1973 J. Rogers, M. Rogers
1974 P. O'Brien, S. Dow

MEN'S PAIRS

1970 S. Clarke, R. MacWilliamson

WOMEN'S PAIRS

1970 Mrs. E. Wilson, Mrs. D. Parker

HAWAII

KNOCKOUT TEAMS

1967 J. Hancock, P. Vakil
M. Lawrence, K. Larsen
M. Schuman, R. Spotts
1970 N. Ballard, F. Cady
F. Hagen, D. Glad

OPEN TEAMS

1952 M. Harvey, C. Garvey
Mr. and Mrs. D. von Elsner
1953 Mr. and Mrs. W. Edwards
M. Hoffman, M. Anderson
1955 D. Oakie, C. Davidson
Mr. and Mrs. R. D. Hutchinson

1956 V. Anastasopolus, H. Fishel
F. Donnell, M. Wildy
1957 Dr. E. Cheim, T. S. Pai
H. Fishel, F. Donnell
1958 B. Coombs, F. Donnell
T. S. Pai, H. Fishel
1959 E. Cheim, F. Donnell
H. Fishel, T. S. Pai
1960 D. Oakie, C. Watanabe
V. Anastasopolus, G. Pool
1961 M. Hodges, R. Groves
Mr. and Mrs. N. Agran
1962 F. Wong, W. Ishii
W. Kau, W. Motokane, *tied with*
B. H. Marliave, T. Hervey
B. Juett, A. Hurlimann
1963 I. Erdos, T. S. Pai
H. Settle, Dr. E. W. You
1964 M. Schleifer, Mr. and Mrs. J. Farell
B. Crane, Mrs. E. A. Mahoney
1965 H. Baer, O. Jacoby
J. Jacoby, A. Weiss
1966 Mr. and Mrs. J. Farell, P. Rank
D. Oakie, Mrs. E. A. Mahoney
1967 Mr. and Mrs. R. Walsh
P. Soloway, J. Swanson
1968 L. Hofacre, P. Drury
C. MacCracken, W. H. Escue
J. Weitzner
1969 P. Rank, Dr. J. Fisher
Mrs. E. A. Mahoney, M. J. Farell
C. MacCracken
1971 Col. J. Kiernan, S. Kiernan
M. O'Bradovitch, I. Berns
1972 B. Crane, Dr. J. Fisher
M. J. Farell, J. Farell
Mrs. E. Mahoney, N. Anderson
1973 P. Solomons, J. Weitzner
R. Promboin, L. Hofacre
1974 M. Carlos, G. Kasle
G. Hayden, R. Bates
N. Erickson

MASTERS PAIRS

1952 J. M. Mardick, C. Powell
1953 B. Johnson, J. C. Kunkel
1955 Mr. and Mrs. C. E. Million
1956 J. L. Meier, D. Oakie
1957 B. Howell, C. Johnson
1958 D. E. Davis, Dr. J. N. Konde
1959 S. Heinz, G. Gooden
1960 J. H. Chang, A. Sakuma
1961 J. H. Chang, G. Pool
1962 L. J. Graham, G. A. Ginn
1963 Dr. E. W. You, I. Erdos
1964 Mrs. E. A. Mahoney, M. Schleifer
1965 I. Erdos, Dr. W. S. You
1966 H. Baron, K. Petterson
1967 P. Soloway, R. Walsh
1968 T. S. Pai, H. A. Settle
1969 Dr. J. Fisher, P. Rank
1970 M. J. Farell, Mrs. E. A. Mahoney
1971 M. Johnson, M. Carlos
1972 Dr. and Mrs. E. Low
1973 J. Sutherlin, G. Chang
1974 G. Ebesu, D. Coleman

OPEN PAIRS

1952 F. Kirwin, Dr. E. Cheim
1953 V. Anastasopulos, H. Fishel
1955 B. Coombs, J. Bomash
1956 E. Nicholson, S. D. Ingraham, Jr.
1957 H. A. Graham, A. Stacy
1958 D. Oakie, C. Watanabe
1959 A. L. You, I. Erdos
1960 Mrs. E. F. Hobart, M. Murtha
1961 Mr. and Mrs. J. Farell
1962 R. Kimura, A. Iwahara

1963 H. Baron, B. Crane
1964 H. Moore, M. Portugal
1965 Mr. and Mrs. S. Schloss
1966 G. Kasle, Mrs. L. H. Lanning
1967 W. Nutting, L. Weiss
1968 P. Rank, J. Farell
1969 H. Baron, P. Soloway
1970 H. A. Settle, D. Von Elsner, *tied with*
     B. Crane, P. Rank
1971 B. Crane, P. Rank
1972 B. Crane, Dr. J. Fisher
1973 K. Shuman, Dr. J. Fisher
1974 B. Levan, N. Anderson

1966 H. Baron, P. Rank
1967 P. Soloway, Mrs. R. Walsh
1968 Mr. and Mrs. F. Cady
1969 Mr. and Mrs. M. Stone
1970 W. Ishii, C. Watanabe
1971 S. Zakin, L. Phillips
1972 C. Watanabe, G. Chang
1973 P. Smith, Z. Zimmerman
1974 B. Levan, J. Padget

HOLIDAY

KNOCKOUT TEAMS

1970 A. Hunte, E. Nagy
     J. Gaer, M. Gaer
1971 N. Chambers, K. Gorfkle
     A. Graves, D. Forster
1972 J. Janitschke, C. Janitschke
     J. Miller, M. Kaplan
1973 M. Passell, M. Portugal
     H. Portugal, H. Baron
     M. Lair, D. Priest
1974 K. Shuman, M. Shuman
     E. Paulsen, B. Crossley
     D. Crossley

MEN'S PAIRS

1952 W. H. Dumas, J. D. Clarke
1953 B. Johnson, J. C. Kunkel
1955 B. D. Hutchinson, D. Oakie
1956 T. S. Pai. H. L. Fishel
1957 G. Gooden, H. Fishel
1958 R. A. Beausoleil, G. Andreozzi
1959 W. S. Stein, L. H. Canfield
1960 G. Gooden, H. Fishel
1961 R. Donnell, H. Fishel
1962 H. A. Settle, D. von Elsner
1963 L. F. Cox, M. Kivel
1964 M. Schleifer, M. J. Hodder
1965 J. Farell, P. Rank
1966 K. Petterson, G. Bare
1967 M. Lawrence, P. Soloway
1968 F. Donnell, D. Von Elsner, *tied with*
     E. B. Anderson, M. E. Hole
1969 A. Levy, G. Chang
1970 P. Soloway, I. Berns
1971 R. Odlin, E. Wright
1972 N. Levi. H. Friesen
1973 N. Erickson, R. Promboin
1974 J. Grantham, N. Anderson

OPEN TEAMS

1970 V. Mastron, M. Portugal
     H. Portugal, N. Anderson
1971 J. Dunlap, H. Gagnon
     T. Weeg, J. Marsh
     D. Bussey
1972 A. Tschekaloff, J. Padget
     J. Mohan, R. Henderson
1973 H. Ross, M. Ross
     S. Nedham, J. Nedham
1974 B. O'Malia, M. Jacobus
     G. Kasle, P. Orlett

WOMEN'S PAIRS

1952 F. Kirwin, L. Wilcox
1953 J. Strich, V. Lewis
1955 A. Pratt, K. Abbott
1956 H. J. White, M. L. Cleaton
1957 B. Epstein, B. Coombs
1958 C. Morgan, A. R. Falb
1959 V. Anastasopulos C. Watanabe
1960 B. Ingham, J. White
1961 M. J. Farell, E. A. Mahoney
1962 M. Bonner, E. Oakley
1963 K. Mullins, M. E. Facer
1964 Mrs. E. M. Clark, L. Durham
1965 M. J. Farell, Mrs. E. A. Mahoney
1966 Mrs. J. Cahill, Mrs. M. J. Cooling
1967 G. Lowree, Mrs. S. F. Cyborowski
1968 Mrs. J. L. Fleming, M. Kroney
1969 C. Watanabe, V. Anastasopulos
1970 P. Wagner, P. Sutherlin
1971 J. Schroeder, Mrs. A. Greenberg
1972 C. Watanabe, B. Char
1973 Mrs. K. Mills, Mrs. R. Elliott
1974 P. Solomons, C. Watanabe

MEN'S TEAMS

1974 S. Skinner, R. LaCour
     M. Zwerling, R. Smith

WOMEN'S TEAMS

1974 G. Gates, L. Rogers
     A. Rennels, M. Bright

MASTERS PAIRS

1968 S. Haber, M. E. Miller
1969 G. Baze, K. Jensen
1970 H. Raymond, J. Chrysler
1971 J. Thomas, H. Ellis
1972 E. Paulsen, H. Ross
1973 M. Lair, M. Passell
1974 S. Miki, F. Warzek

MIXED PAIRS

1952 V. Anastasopulos, H. Fishel
1953 Mr. and Mrs. B. O. Johnson
1955 Adm. and Mrs. J. L. Herlihy
1956 H. J. White, H. Fishel
1957 V. Anastasopulos, M. Wildy
1958 M. Harvey, H. Yokoyama
1959 I. Erdos, A. L. You
1960 C. Goren, C. Watanabe
1961 Mrs. L. M. Amster, G. Pool
1962 B. Char, C. Goren
1963 A. L. You, I. Erdos
1964 I. Erdos, A. L. You
1965 J. UpdeGraff, L. Dashiell, *tied with*
     Mr. and Mrs. J. Farell

OPEN PAIRS

1968 D. Crossley, R. Crossley
1969 J. Wittes, J. P. Ivaska
1970 M. Brachman, P. Soloway
1972 W. Cederborg, J. Farell
1973 P. Rank, P. Pender
1974 M. Blumenthal, G. Hayden

MEN'S PAIRS

1968 J. Lebbert, S. Rubin
1969 P. Soloway, J. Wittes
1970 R. Booth, D. Sweet
1971 W. Whitesell, M. Philippas, *tied with*
     J. Martineau, P. Hagen

WOMEN'S PAIRS

1968   Mrs. J. B. York, Mrs. M. Reiter
1969   B. Selby, E. Siepler
1970   H. Baron, Mrs. H. Swisher
1971   Mrs. B. Cotton, Mrs. C. Lewis

OREGON TRAIL

KNOCKOUT TEAMS

1967   Mr. and Mrs. D. Drury, J. Moran
        H. Baron, M. Schleifer
1968   M. Manchester, D. Forster
        J. Farley, W. Silver
        D. Jones, G. Kasle
1969   R. Kaye, Mr. and Mrs. R. Walsh
        J. P. Ivaska, L. West
1970   L. Tsou, G. Parker
        S. Sidell, M. Miller
        K. Blackerby
1971   A. Graves, W. Whitesell
        H. Fuller, H. Antonson
        M. Philippas
1972   M. and M. Blustein, R. and S. Urbaniak
        J. Jabon
1973   J. Ashton, W. Whitesell
        D. Metcalf, W. Rossman
        A. Hicks, D. Jones
1974   L. Jolma, M. Jolma
        G. Stark, B. Whitesel
        B. Rossmann, M. Larson

OPEN TEAMS

1958   E. Stewart, R. Hopkins
        E. Oke, E. Nepple
1960   M. Klausner, M. Schleifer
        M. Agay, M. Orme
1961   D. Krauss, G. Bare
        H. Guiver, R. Walsh
1962   M. J. Farell, A. Cohn
        P. Rank, M. Orme
1963   D. Lefebvre, J. Jabon
        J. Ehrlenbach, C. Rush
1965   M. K. Johnson, P. Rank
        B. Crane, R. T. Adams
1966   J. Jabon, R. Hendershott
        C. Rush, G. Hays
1967   W. Silver, M. Lawrence
        D. L. Jones, A. W. Oaks
        C. MacCracken
1968   B. Crane, J. Jabon
        Mrs. P. Drury, C. MacCracken
        M. Johnson
1969   J. C. Anderson, D. Forster
        J. Taylor, J. Farley
1970   H. Antonson, H. Fuller
        W. Whitesell, N. Chambers
        D. Mehaffey
1971   G. Slemmons, G. Steiner
        D. Pederson, E. Selymes
1972   C. and J. Cleveland, K. Gisler
        B. White, C. Earl
1973   B. O'Malia, N. Moss
        S. Smolen, M. Portugal
        P. O'Brien
1974   J. Andrews, J. Andrews
        M. Hunt, D. Meador

MEN'S TEAMS

1971   E. Selymes, G. Steiner
        G. Slemmons, D. Pederson

WOMEN'S TEAMS

1971   W. Nepple, J. Sharp
        P. Prahl, E. Brockman

MASTERS PAIRS

1958   J. Kiamy, B. Isaacs
1960   E. Schwartz, C. Rush
1961   E. Schwartz, C. Rush
1962   J. Littrell, J. Jabon
1963   J. Ballard, N. Ballard
1965   Dr. C. C. Cruikshank, Dr. R. E. Tracy
1966   Mrs. R. E. Diehl, Mrs. R. W. Carrico
1967   Dr. G. Stark, J. Stark
1968   M. Adkins, G. Hays
1969   T. H. Craig, B. Rossman
1970   R. Haller, Mrs. R. Haller
1971   J. Taylor, R. DuFour
1972   P. Burns, R. Mudd
1973   D. Perkins, B. Naness
1974   R. LaCour, P. O'Brien

MASTER MEN'S PAIRS

1971   F. Squire, J. Squire

MASTER WOMEN'S PAIRS

1971   J. Ballard, C. Baird

OPEN PAIRS

1958   B. Lapidus, N. Turnbull
1960   B. Crane, P. Rank
1961   B. Crane, P. Rank
1962   M. Orme, J. Patterson
1963   F. Ganz, D. Oakie
1965   P. Rank, B. Crane
1966   P. D. Lit, M. Lawrence
1967   K. Christiansen, D. Setterholm
1968   A. J. Wright, C. G. Robson
1969   D. W. Willing, L. Tsou
1970   B. Crane, P. Rank
1971   P. Hitchens, Dr. R. Tracy
1972   S. Sidell, D. Lewis
1973   D. Gold, R. MacDuff
1974   J. Jabon, S. Urbaniak

MEN'S PAIRS

1958   A. Hicks, R. Hendershott
1960   A. Allison, J. Ehrlenbach
1961   M. Agay, M. Shuman
1962   L. M. Fox, F. Beirne
1963   I. Erdos, J. Brown
1965   D. Oram, D. Kemmard
1966   D. Brown, L. Hawkins, *tied with*
        J. Donnelly, G. Gruger
1967   G. Kasle, G. Morton
1968   B. Crane, G. Hays
1969   W. Schmitz, J. McVay
1970   M. Philippas, J. Taylor, *tied with*
        J. Cleveland, B. White
1971   A. McBeth, F. King
1972   C. Dorn, K. Blackerby
1973   J. Strauch, B. Crapko
1974   B. Berger, H. Allahverdian

WOMEN'S PAIRS

1958   L. Patterson, L. Wheeler
1960   H. Herron, C. Slick
1961   M. Jolma, R. M. Robson
1962   L. Stewart, M. L, Kahmann, *tied with*
        P. Hutchinson, F. Aydelotte
1963   J. E. Van Winkle, M. V. Young
1965   Mrs. J. M. Willis, Mrs. J. M. Weaver
1966   Mrs. F. R. Baker, Mrs. R. T. Jones
1967   Mrs. J. W. Eckersley, Mrs. M. V. Young
1968   R. Vaughn, Mrs. M. E. Berg
1969   M. Rash, Mrs. W. E. Ritchie
1970   F. Van Winkle, D. Cowger
1971   M. J. Farell, Mrs. F. Ganz

1972 M. Larson, D. Berry
1973 E. Brockman, P. Prahl
1974 M. Jolma, E. Birnbach

MIXED PAIRS

1958 M. Klausner, M. Schleifer
1960 M. Klausner, M. Schleifer
1961 M. Manchester, L. Strebinger
1962 L. Wheeler, M. Orme
1963 H. Haugsten, J. E. Ehrlenbach
1965 H. Haugsten, D. L. Jones
1966 H. Moore, M. Portugal
1967 R. Norberg, Mrs. F. VanCleve
1968 J. Pearcy, M. V. Laylor
1969 M. R. Blustein, D. Pedersen
1971 V. and J. McVay
1972 J. Anderson, C. Davis
1973 M. Passell, H. Baron
1974 M. Kinney, H. Kinney

INDIVIDUAL

1968 Mrs. W. R. Taft
1969 Mrs. J. W. Kruse

DISTRICT 21 (North central California)

ALL-WESTERN

KNOCKOUT TEAMS

1967 P. Rank, R. Adams
     P. Pender, M. Johnson
     J. Swanson, P. Soloway
1968 K. Larsen, G. Baze
     A. Hunte, C. Dorn
1969 M. Lawrence, B. Hamman
     B. Bergovoy, K. Larsen
     J. Swanson
1970 H. Baron, M. Dagovitz
     H. Smith, N. Anderson
1971 J. Fejervary, C. Dorn
     K. Blackerby, J. Swanson
     L. Tsou, M. Lawrence
1972 J. Padget, R. Henderson
     J. Wittes, N. Erickson
     A. Graves, K. Gorfkle
1973 B. Matthess, B. McWilliams
     J. Robison, J. Roth
1974 M. Schleifer, D. Krauss
     M. Vernoff, A. Spreckles
     R. von der Porten

MASTERS TEAMS

1971 R. Spotts, J. Sutherlin
     P. Vakil, E. Barlow
1972 M. Schleifer, R. von der Porten
     A. Hammel, K. Larsen
1973 K. Gorfkle, S. Smolen
     C. Greenhut, A. Graves
     D. Ashley
1974 M. Schleifer, D. Krauss,
     R. von der Porten, A. Spreckles, *tied with*
     B. Staats, M. Singer
     H. Brody, F. Lee

OPEN TEAMS

1956 L. Patterson, F. Carpenter
     Mr. and Mrs. B. Ignatz
1957 N. Wells, D. Cook
     M. Klausner, E. Frischauer

1958 Mr. and Mrs. J. Farell
     Mr. and Mrs. M. Portugal
1959 M. Shuman, E. Kantar
     H. Guiver, K. Petterson
     A. Tschekaloff
1960 M. Johnson, R. Adams
     F. Jackson, I. Scope
1961 P. Allinger, L. Mathe
     M. G. Kamens, B. Tierney
1962 L. Mathe, P. Allinger
     M. G. Kamens, B. Tierney
1963 V. Hull, D. Cook
     D. Ashley, D. Kleinman
1964 R. Walsh, H. Guiver
     M. McMahan, M. Gilbert, *tied with*
     M. Dagovitz, F. Lee
     B. Bergovoy, R. B. Henderson
1965 R. Lander, J. Linhart
     E. Hirsch, J. Stein, *tied with*
     M. Schleifer, D. Drury
     A. Coleman, D. Oakie
1966 E. Mathe, L. Mathe
     A. Sheinwold, L. Pressburg
1967 H. Baron, D. Romm
     L. West, J. Wittes
     J. P. Ivaska
1968 C. Dorn, W. Corbin
     W. J. Gilbert, I. Scope
     C. Buckley
1969 P. Soloway, M. Brachman
     R. von der Porten, J. Fejervary
1970 R. McConnell, M. Savage
     R. Henderson, J. Padget
     M. Edwards

MEN'S TEAMS

1973 W. Cederborg, T. Tracy
     J. Weitzner, A. Bell
     R. Promboin, E. Hirsch

WOMEN'S TEAMS

1973 E. Jaccard, M. Mazza
     S. Cole, V. Bigelow
     J. Omo, *tied with*
     R. Epstein, H. Baron
     K. Shuman, G. Gates
     C. Greenhut

MASTERS PAIRS

1939 J. Sherman, C. Strouse
1940 W. Herbert, E.Rovere
1941 M. Bailey, W. Hayhurst
1942 F. Fee, D. Davis
1943 M. Schleifer, N. Perlstein
1944 Mrs. S. Klausner, Dr. E. Frischauer
1945 C. Strouse, N. Perlstein
1946 Mr. and Mrs. A. Kauder
1947 D. Westerfield, E. Rovere
1956 F. Fee, G. J. Dunn
1957 H. Schmidt, B. Krems
1958 H. Kandler, E. Paulsen
1959 G. H. Buckley, F. M. Ganz
1960 Mr. and Mrs. J. Farell
1961 I. Scope, F. L. Jackson
1962 D. Krauss, R. von der Porten
1963 N. Walsh, H. L. Ross
1964 B. King, R. Violin
1965 J. Lyon, P. Allinger
1966 K. Dunn, D. Cook
1967 H. Kandler, E. Bailey
1968 H. Moore, M. Portugal
1969 A. Bell, C. Vogel
1970 I. Scope, H. Smith
1971 K. Davis, H. Guiver
1972 P. Pender, P. Rank
1973 S. Levey, B. Giragosian, *tied with*
     J. Grantham, M. Shuman
1974 G. Steiner, M. Blumenthal

OPEN PAIRS

1935 H. Pemberton, R. Puffer
1936 J. Meyer, H. Merkle
1937 J. Ehrlenbach, E. Taylor
1938 W. Savery, J. Muckey
1939 J. Ehrlenbach, E. Taylor
1940 M. Bailey, H. Pemberton
1941 D. Oakie, W. Turner
1942 M. Schleifer, L. Mathe
1943 M. Schleifer, M. L. Mendelsohn
1944 Mrs. S. Klausner, Dr. E. Frischauer
1945 E. Rovere, D. Westerfield
1946 H. Friedrich, M. Portugal
1947 L. Mathe, M. Schleifer
1956 J. Dunn, R. Blench
1957 J. Prager, F. Jackson
1958 S. Rebner, R. von der Porten, *tied with*
      R. Walker, J. Blattner
1959 S. Rebner, R. von der Porten
1960 B. Ignatz, G. Eveleth
1961 L. Newman, D. Cook
1962 M. Alcorn, P. Pender
1963 L. Weiss, M. McMahan, *tied with*
      R. Hamman, D. Krauss
1964 I. Erdos, M. Turk
1965 R. Lander, M. Lawrence
1966 M. Klausner, C. Potvin
1967 Mr. and Mrs. J. Farell
1968 T. Lesser, D. Romm
1969 R. B. Henderson, M. Edwards
1970 P. Rank, M. Johnson
1971 B. Nutting, L. Stansby
1972 H. Brody, K. Peyser
1973 B. Crane, Dr. J. Fisher
1974 L. Taggart, J. Lenze

MEN'S PAIRS

1945 C. Harvey, W. L. Jones
1946 E. Sandstrom, E. Taylor
1947 L. Pressburg, J. Ehrlenbach
1956 E. H. Noffsinger, A. G. Kridl
1957 M. Vernoff, E. W. Rovere
1958 C. E. Million, E. W. Rovere
1959 R. von der Porten, G. Eveleth
1960 Dr. H. Tsang, F. Savstrom
1961 B. Juett, B. Marliave
1962 R. Sitnek, P. Pender
1963 W. A. Lang, J. Ehrlenbach
1964 P. Pender, M. Shuman
1965 J. Gladfelter, R. Hendershott
1966 G. Morton, R. Walker
1967 P. Soloway, R. Walsh
1968 G. Mattos, G. L. Toone
1969 D. Roberts, J. Bjorklund
1970 P. Pender, G. Baze
1971 A. Haas, G. Solberg
1972 J. Grantham, J. Mohan
1973 M. Dagovitz, G. Strohl
1974 R. LaCour, H. Smith

WOMEN'S PAIRS

1936 C. C. Dickson, H. P. Watson
1937 V. O. Leonard, M. M. Mortimore
1938 B. Bates, J. de Costa
1939 S. Hutten, M. Gillingham
1940 H. Brunn, M. H. Jordon
1941 A. Wesson, M. Criswell
1942 I. Oeschger, N. Childs
1943 E. Gibbons, R. E. Kirkman
1944 I. Oeschger, N. C. Well
1945 H. Brunn, J. Dunn
1946 C. Smith, J. Dunn
1947 V. O. Leonard, M. M. Mortimore
1956 C. H. Smith, J. Garrigan
1957 B. Coombs, C. Fantone
1958 V. Bennayan, S. Clark
1959 J. Heimburger, J. Shaw
1960 S. Davis, R. Gaumer

1961 P. Long, K. Mausser
1962 G. Frioux, A. R. Chapman
1963 W. Herman, M. Puncochar
1964 M. McElfish, B. Coombs
1965 S. Harris, P. J. Berry
1966 Mrs. P. Stoddard, Mrs. L. J. Newman
1967 J. McDonald, B. Borquin
1968 L. Patterson, E. Weil
1969 S. Clark, M. Rogers
1970 M. Roberts, A. Rennels
1971 M. Gaer, L. Baumann
1972 A. Kearse, K. Singer
1973 D. Rushing, H. Miller
1974 J. Draga, M. Murnig

MIXED PAIRS

1956 V. Leonard, H. Feinberg
1957 V. Leonard, V. Gerther
1958 S. Rebner, W. Hanna
1959 J. Brinley, Mrs. A. H. Schreek
1960 P. Medford, E. Paulson
1961 Mr. and Mrs. G. Awad
1962 C. Potvin, K. Blanchard
1963 M. Alcorn, P. Pender
1964 N. Walsh, R. Walsh
1965 Mrs. E. A. Mahony, M. Schleifer
1966 Mr. and Mrs. H. L. Smith
1967 K. Taira, E. Shampanier
1968 W. Corbin, D. Corbin
1969 H. Moore, M. Portugal
1970 I. Scope, B. Scope
1971 E. Davis, G. Herrington
1972 H. Smith, L. Smith
1973 P. Vakil, M. Vakil
1974 G. Gates, L. West

INDIVIDUAL

1968 A. Grisham

CENTRAL CALIFORNIA

KNOCKOUT TEAMS

1971 M. and G. Gaer
      E. Nagy, M. Levison
1972 K. Blackerby, C. Dorn
      M. Miller, H. Smith
      I. Scope, L. Tsou
1973 K. Blackerby, C. Dorn
      J. Hayashi, H. Rhodes
      M. Miller
1974 E. Neiger, D. LaFleur
      J. Grantham, J. Mohan
      M. Lawrence

OPEN TEAMS

1971 J. Singer, M. Guagliardo
      G. Nicholas, T. Ansnes
1972 A. Hunte, L. Maes
      E. Nagy, H. Brody
1973 E. Nagy, A. Hunte
      B. Spotts, L. Stansby
1974 Mrs. C. Gilkeson, M. Shuman
      P. Soloway, J. Swanson
      F. Hamilton

MASTERS PAIRS

1971 D. Bhargava, J. Houde
1972 A. Hunte, E. Nagy
1973 L. Mandel, I. Cohen
1974 S. Levey, S. Levey

OPEN PAIRS

1971   R. Borden, L. Wasselle, *tied with*
       M. Gaer, N. Anderson
1972   J. and A. Kauder
1974   B. Crane, P. Rank

MEN'S PAIRS

1971   R. McConnell, R. Henderson
1972   R. McConnell, J. Sutherlin

WOMEN'S PAIRS

~~1971   Mrs. B. Zahlos, Mrs. C. Crawford~~
1972   L. Patterson, E. Weil

MIXED PAIRS

1974   P. Sutherlin, J. Sutherlin

GOLDEN GATE

KNOCKOUT TEAMS

1967   M. Moss, P. Soloway
      H. Baron, R. Walsh
1968   I. Corn, Jr., R. Wolff
      J. Jacoby, M. Lawrence
      R. Goldman, W. Eisenberg
1969   L. West, M. Johnson
      P. Pender, P. Rank
      C. MacCracken
1970   P. Pender, H. Ross
      G. Baze, L. West
      P. Rank
1971   J. McKee, P. Soloway
      M. Portugal, V. Mastron
      K. Gorfkle
1972   M. Shuman, H. Baron
      J. Padget, J. Mohan
      B. Spotts
1973   J. Farell, M. J. Farell
      D. Williams, W. Cederborg
1974   P. Pender, L. West
      D. Crossley, B. Crossley
      D. Smith, M. Lawrence

MASTERS TEAMS

1973   E. Hirsch, R. Spotts
      S. Nedham, J. Nedham

OPEN TEAMS

1964   F. Lee, M. Dagovitz
      B. Bergovoy, N. G. Turk
1966   R. Walsh, J. Swanson
      M. Lawrence, H. Guiver
1967   B. Crane, Mr. and Mrs. J. Farell
      Mrs. E. A. Mahony, H. Kandler
1968   P. Soloway, H. Ross
      B. Bergovoy, J. Hancock
1969   P. Pender, G. Baze
      C. MacCracken, K. Larsen
      C. Dorn
1971   P. Pender, P. Rank
      M. Johnson, G. Baze
      B. Sanner
1972   W. Miller, G. Sturges
      G. Griffith, J. Franks
1974   K. Blackerby, J. Hayashi
      R. Smith, J. Onstott

MASTERS PAIRS

1962   M. J. Farell, Mrs. E. A. Mahony
1964   S. Schloss, E. D. Weiner

1966   J. C. Sutherlin, R. Spotts
1967   K. Larsen, J. Hancock
1968   J. Hancock, G. Kasle
1969   I. Han, M. Miller
1970   B. Bratcher, M. Bartosik
1971   Mr. and Mrs. L. Stansby
1972   R. Walsh, P. Maier
1973   B. Bergovoy, J. Polisner
1974   B. Nutting, L. Stansby

OPEN PAIRS

1962   D. Drury, P. A. Pender
~~1964   M. Lawrence, P. J. Berry~~
1966   B. Bergovoy, H. Portugal
1967   K. Larsen, J. Hancock
1968   B. Crane, P. Rank
1969   P. Rank, M. Johnson
1970   W. Slife, A. Slife
1972   R. Henderson, J. Wittes
1973   J. Weisberg, S. Clark
1974   L. Rogers, L. Stansby

MEN'S PAIRS

1962   R. R. Walsh, E. Bailey
1964   D. Drury, D. B. Cook
1966   G. Kasle, M. Levison
1967   C. Barrere, M. Lawrence
1968   B. Ignatz, N. Anderson
1969   P. Read, R. Spotts
1970   R. Sanner, R. Booth
1972   T. Prothro, N. Erickson
1973   F. Warzek, J. Hayashi

WOMEN'S PAIRS

1962   E. A. West, R. H. Ryder
1964   F. A. Shields, H. M. Middleton
1966   M. M. Costello, Mrs. R. M. Schneider
1967   Mrs. C. B.Schmidt, Mrs. R. Gohn
1968   M. J. Farell, K. Blanchard
1969   Mrs. W. S. Johnson, Mrs. S. Rice
1970   B. Walker, L. Patterson
1972   J. Mitchell, S. Nedham
1973   M. Soules, N. Wells

MIXED PAIRS

1962   M. Klausner, M. Vernoff
1964   M. Portugal, B. Levan
1966   P. Rank, E. Schulte
1967   B. Crane, M. J. Farell
1968   P. Rank, R. Walsh
1969   P. Sutherlin, R. B. Henderson
1970   J. Anderson, M. Churchill
1971   P. Drury, R. LaCour

INDIVIDUAL

1968   J. Wilson
1969   R. J. Purcott
1970   V. Roberts

DISTRICT 22 (Central and southern California, excluding Los Angeles area)

DISTRICT 22

KNOCKOUT TEAMS

1973   B. O'Malia, G. Kasle
      G. Hayden, R. Bates

1974 E. Neiger, R. Bates
      D. LaFleur, J. Mohan
      J. Grantham

OPEN TEAMS

1973 D. McClintock, J. McClintock
      A. Daniels, D. Spahlinger
      G. Frankson
1974 I. Cohen, P. Ivaska
      L. Mandel, J. Wittes

MASTERS PAIRS

1973 G. May, D. Greenwald
1974 M. Ralph, D. Guerin

OPEN PAIRS

1973 H. Kandler, W. Moore
1974 R. LaCour, C. Greenhut

MEN'S PAIRS

1974 R. Smith, J. Onstott

WOMEN'S PAIRS

1974 J. Cohen, M. Abrams

GOLDEN STATE

KNOCKOUT TEAMS

1968 S. Blum, A. Wood
      J. Levey, S. Levey, Jr.
      C. Wood, M. L. Bert
1969 P. Soloway, M. Schleifer
      Mr. and Mrs. C. Baron, C. Phillips
1970 G. Parker, I. Scope
      L. West, K. Jensen
      W. Cederborg
1971 H. Baron, M. Shuman
      N. Anderson, J. Anderson
1972 B. O'Malia, G. Parker
      G. Kasle, G. Hayden
1973 M. Passell, H. Baron
      J. Robinson, D. Priest

OPEN TEAMS

1963 Mr. and Mrs. S. E. Schloss
      Mrs. N. D. Chasnoff, W. S. Ashton, *tied with*
      H. Utegaard, P. J. Berry
      P. Lynch, R. Spotts
      G. G. Hays
1965 Mr. and Mrs. K. Petterson
      M. Turk, I. Erdos
1966 L. Mathe, M. McMahan
      G. Bare, H. Ross
      E. Paulsen
1967 J. Ross, H. Ross
      K. Larsen, B. Bergovoy
1968 Mrs. R. Walsh, M. Smolen
      L. West, C. MacCracken
1969 P. Soloway, H. Baron
      M. Brachman, J. Wittes
1971 Mr. and Mrs. J. Kauder
      L. Weiss, C. Kalme
1972 H. Baron, M. Passell
      P. Pender, P. Rank, *tied with*
      A. LaFleur, D. LaFleur
      N. Anderson, M. Shuman
      K. Shuman, J. Mohan

1973 J. Mohan, D. LaFleur
      J. Grantham, M. Lawrence
      E. Neiger

MASTERS PAIRS

1963 M. Lawrence, R. Spotts
1965 D. C. James, Mrs. M. Askew
1966 Mrs. R. A. Pfahler, Mrs. R. Conway
1967 T. Richmond, J. Rogers
1968 E. D. Weiner, H. Baron
1969 H. Baron, R. Henderson
1970 T. Kasday, P. Ivaska
1971 A. Tschekaloff, E. Davis
1972 B. Crane, Dr. J. Fisher
1973 B. Kerr, D. Guerin

OPEN PAIRS

1963 E. J. Barlow, E. Bailey
1965 P. Kayfetz, W. Nutting
1966 M. Lawrence, M. Miles
1967 B. Crane, P. Rank
1968 J. Hallee, P. Soloway
1969 B. Waite, A. Arndt
1970 B. Crane, M. Jones
1971 J. Anderson, S. Goldberg
1972 R. LaCour, G. Hayden
1973 M. Levison, B. Hamman

MEN'S PAIRS

1963 K. Petterson, E. B. Andersen
1965 E. Kantar, J. Wack
1966 M. Lawrence, P. Soloway
1967 W. Tivol, R. Anziani
1968 A. Kasday, J. P. Ivaska, Jr.
1969 S. Coolik, G. Treadwell
1970 G. Kasle, D. Carter
1971 K. Gorfkle, W. Cederborg
1972 M. Passell, J. Mohan

WOMEN'S PAIRS

1963 L. J. Newman, N. Wells
1965 B. Epstein, M. Donnerstag
1966 Mrs. M. C. Mansella, Mrs. C. H. Van Pelt
1967 R. Hawks, L. Patterson
1968 A. Grisham, M. Rogers
1969 M. Heumann, A. Kempner
1970 M. Kovac, H. Baron
1971 D. Koren, B. Hays
1972 M. J. Farell, Mrs. F. Ganz

MIXED PAIRS

1963 M. Portugal, B. Levan
1965 M. Portugal, B. Levan
1966 B. Crane, M. Anticouni
1967 P. Soloway, Mrs. L. Newman
1968 C. Harding, Jr., M. J. Farell
1969 Mrs. B. W. Meyer, P. Soloway

INDIVIDUAL

1968 Mrs. M. H. Ragle

PACIFIC SOUTHWEST

KNOCKOUT TEAMS

1967 H. Kandler, H. Baron
      D. Ashley, L. West
1968 E. Paulsen, G. Bare
      M. McMahan, H. Guiver

1969	B. O'Malia, M. Bartosik
	R. Geller, R. McDonnell
1970	A. Bell, H. Kandler
	B. Amer, E. Davis
1971	H. Kandler, A. Bell
	N. Anderson, H. Baron
	P. Heitner
1972	H. Baron, R. Henderson
	P. Soloway, M. Shuman
	J. Mohan
1973	R. Henderson, M. Passell
	P. Ivaska, J. Wittes
1974	D. Pelka, T. Reynolds
	R. Howard, R. Radwin

OPEN TEAMS

1946	Mr. and Mrs. S. Klausner
	R. Reif, Dr. E. Frischauer
1949	J. Dunn, L. Mathe
	M. Portugal, W. Waterman
1950	M. Schleifer, H. Edwards
	H. Cale, J. Ehrlenbach, *tied with*
	M. Klausner, R. Reif
	Dr. E. Frischauer, W. Kivi
1951	M. Foote, R. Cash
	Mrs. A. G. Whitehead, D. Westerfield, *tied with*
	R. Reif, W. Hanna
	M. Klausner, Dr. E. Frischauer
1952	D. Walther, M. Schleifer
	Mr. and Mrs. J. Dunn
1953	I. Erdos, H. Murphy
	L. Mathe, D. Steen
1954	H. Feinberg, D. Steen
	N. Kaufman, W. Hanna
1955	J. Cantor, S. W. Smith
	A. Silverman, B. Dayton
1956	R. Evans, G. May
	Mr. and Mrs. R. J. Marks
1957	M. Klausner, H. Portugal
	Dr. E. Frischauer, J. Herd
	H. Steen
1958	M. Klausner, H. Portugal
	Dr. E. Frischauer, J. Herd
	H. Steen
1960	M. Klausner, M. Schleifer
	Mr. and Mrs. J. Dunn
1961	M. Klausner, M. Schleifer
	Mr. and Mrs. J. Dunn
1963	M. Shuman, K. Ashe
	J. W. Murphy, D. Ashley
1964	J. Swanson, N. Walsh
	H. Ross, R. Spotts
1965	L. Israel, I. Erdos
	F. Silver, M. Cappelletti
	L. DeBurger
1966	Mr. and Mrs. K. Petterson
	Mr. and Mrs. G. Bare
	H. V. Peterson
1967	H. Kandler
	Mr. and Mrs. J. Farell
	R. Henderson, B. Crane
1968	Mrs. B. W. Meyer, J. Dryer
	J. Dryer, H. Guiver
	H. Tippins
1969	J. Swanson, P. Bradford
	R. Adams, T. Tracy
1971	M. Schleifer, M. Vernoff
	R. von der Porten, Mrs. C. Hammel
1972	Mrs. C. Hammel, R. von der Porten
	M. Vernoff, M. Schleifer
	D. Mordecai
1973	M. J. Farell, J. Farell
	N. Anderson, Mrs. F. Ganz
1974	R. Doughman, L. Jelusich
	R. Zellmer, C. Evans

MASTERS PAIRS

1946	Mr. and Mrs. E. Ackerman
1947	R. Cash, H. Norman
1948	M. Klausner, R. Reif

1949	D. Steen, C. Rush
1950	L. Mathe, A. Kauder
1951	Mr. and Mrs. M. Portugal
1952	P. Wood, S. Lazard
1953	B. Cohen, C. Strouse
1954	V. Hammels, R. Hislop
1955	A. Baron, L. Mathe
1956	M. J. Kauder, J. Farell
1957	S. Rebner, J. Strich
1958	E. Kantor, Dr. J. Etkin
1960	Mrs. H. Hope, E. McDuffee
1961	G. Eveleth, D. Cutler
1963	M. McMahan, G. W. Bare
1964	R. Walsh, J. Swanson
1965	P. Soloway, R. Henderson
1966	J. Spadero, L. Weiss
1967	Dr. L. Laughlin, R. D. Rosenblum
1968	R. Clark, L. Weiss
1969	J. Hoersch, D. Weiss
1970	J. Millerd, L. Pressburg
1971	B. Crane, B. Messer
1972	P. Soloway, M. Brachman
1973	B. O'Malia, G. Kasle
1974	R. Radwin, C. Williams

OPEN PAIRS

1946	W. McKenney, C. Strouse
1947	K. D. Westerfield, J. Hancock
1948	M. Klausner, Dr. E. Frischauer
1949	R. Reif, M. Klausner
1950	M. Klausner, A. Kauder
1951	J. Wright, S. Rebner
1952	D. Oakie, D. Steen
1953	L. Mathe, D. Steen
1954	M. Klausner, M. Schleifer
1955	M. Klausner, M. Schleifer
1956	B. Dayton, R. Fischer
1957	Mr. and Mrs. A. Kauder
1958	W. R. McWilliams, J. Wright
1960	R. Cheng, A. Fletcher
1961	A. Blinder, J. Nedham
1963	H. Portugal, H. Steen
1964	T. Lesser, D. Romm
1965	Mr. and Mrs. J. Farell
1966	J. Wong, K. Petterson, *tied with*
	B. Crane, P. Rank
1967	K. Larsen, M. Lawrence
1968	H. Kandler, D. Ashley
1969	H. Kandler, D. Ashley
1970	A. Tschekaloff, D. Ashley
1971	Dr. S. Williams, R. Henderson
1972	G. Bare, H. Guiver
1973	D. LaFleur, J. Mohan
1974	M. McFaddin, J. George

MEN'S PAIRS

1947	K. D. Westerfield, J. Hancock
1948	H. Norman, R. Cash
1949	H. Smith, G. Troutt
1950	Dr. E. Frischauer, J. Hennicke
1951	C. P. Williams, J. Dunn
1952	M. Manchaster, R. Marks
1953	M. Vernoff, J. Cantor
1954	W. Hanna, C. E. Million
1955	M. Vernoff, J. Cantor
1956	W. Hanna, S. Lazard
1957	H. Guiver, M. Vernoff
1958	D. Cook, C. Lane
1960	G. Gallegher, H. V. Peterson
1961	J. Dunn, E. Paulsen
1963	R. Walsh, A. Sheinwold
1964	H. Shoop, E. Herbert
1965	M. Bartosik, P. Lit
1966	A. Pounds, M. Vernoff
1967	E. M. Cook, Adm. W. H. Ginn
1968	A. De Voss, E. Belasco
1969	D. Weiss, S. Williams
1970	M. Adkins, J. McKee
1971	R. O'Leary, D. Pelka, *tied with*
	G. Shephard, W. Moore

1972   J. Buchheister, E. Davis
1973   K. Petterson, P. Hawkins
1974   M. Passell, M. Lair

WOMEN'S PAIRS

1947   J. Rae, F. Newcomb
1948   B. B. Morris, M. J. Kauder
1949   A. Goldfine, E. Goldfine
1950   M. Klausner, M. J. Kauder
1951   M. Owens, J. Hovis
1952   H. Feldman, D. Moody
1953   H. Portugal, K. Mausser
1954   E. Caseman, B. Kelly
1955   B. Berkitz, M. Moran
1956   R. Bay, B. Allen
1957   J. Sharpe, J. M. Foote
1958   M. Klausner, R. Reif
1960   M. J. Farell, K. Blanchard
1961   J. Sharp, H. C. Best
1963   R. Heim, D. van Syke
1964   M. L. Morrison, J. A. Harnage
1965   R. Reif, B. Sakamoto
1966   J. Dryer, R. Walsh
1967   Mrs. M. Klausner, Mrs. C. Baron
1968   S. Shannon, G. Seacat
1969   G. Borthwick, G. De Jonge
1970   M. Soules, V. Brown
1971   M. Abrams, Mrs. D. Acre
1972   R. Grantham, T. Heath
1973   M. J. Farell, Mrs. F. Ganz
1974   K. Shuman, H. Baron

MIXED PAIRS

1946   Mrs. H. Gross, H. Mendelsohn
1947   H. Cale, J. Ehrlenbach
1948   Mr. and Mrs. M. Portugal
1949   Mrs. J. Rosenkranz, J. Moran
1950   M. Klausner, Dr. E. Frischauer
1951   Mr. and Mrs. M. Portugal
1952   I. Erdos, R. Reif
1953   P. Stoddard, D. Z. Davis
1954   Mrs. A. C. Whitehead, D. Steen
1955   Mr. and Mrs. F. Ullrich
1956   M. Klausner, M. Schleifer
1957   M. J. Kauder, J. Farell
1958   M. Klausner, M. Schleifer
1960   Mrs. E. A. Mahony, D. Carter
1961   B. Crane, H. Baron
1963   I. Erdos, Mrs. R. Kohler
1964   H. Baron, M. Schleifer
1965   G. Angel, A. Lapins
1966   Mrs. C. Munn, D. Krauss
1967   J. Gertmenian, A. Ramo
1968   M. McMahan, S. McMahan
1969   A. Arndt, A. Bell

INDIVIDUAL

1965   F. Dilley
1968   K. Daane

SOUTHERN CALIFORNIA

KNOCKOUT TEAMS

1971   M. J. Farell, J. Farell
    M. McCrory, J. Padget
    W. Cederborg, P. O'Brien
1972   A. Bell, D. Weiss
    D. Guerin, B. Amer
    J. Strauch, J. Hoersch
1973   B. Hamman, B. Hamman
    J. Fejervary, G. Baze
    W. Corbin

1974   M. Smolen, B. Sides
    J. Wittes, T. Lesser
    P. Ivaska, E. Davis

OPEN TEAMS

1970   H. Peterson, Dr. E. Fradkin
    T. Lesser, D. Bare
    P. Van Hook
1971   B. Crane, Dr. J. Fisher
    G. Bare, E. Paulsen
1972   I. Kostal, A. Paul
    R. Dallas, A. Kluewer
1973   D. Weiss, J. Rosenstiel
    B. Schreiber, S. Williams
1974   M. Minken, J. Minken
    K. Petterson, P. Hawkins
    M. Portugal, H. Portugal

MASTERS PAIRS

1970   T. Lolli, S. Dollar
1971   M. Smolen, A. Tschekaloff
1972   K. Davis, P. Rank
1973   K. Petterson, P. Hawkins
1974   J. Bechely, M. Miles

OPEN PAIRS

1970   P. Kantar, A. Gordon
1971   B. Crane, J. Farell
1972   B. Crane, Dr. J. Fisher
1973   R. Smith, R. Logan
1974   R. LaCour, C. Greenhut

MEN'S PAIRS

1970   J. King, N. Anderson
1971   L. West, W. Cederborg
1972   W. Corbin, G. Baze

WOMEN'S PAIRS

1970   S. Nolan, Mrs. M. Hurley
1971   A. Kempner, B. Schenken
1972   Mrs. J. Michel, P. Leary

DISTRICT 23 (Los Angeles area)

ALACBU WINTER. A special four session red-point tournament awarded for 1969 only.

SWISS TEAMS

1969   D. Pearson, N. Erickson
    J. Swanson, R. Walsh
    J. Weitzner

OPEN PAIRS

1969   H. Heard, N. Anderson

BRIDGE WEEK

KNOCKOUT TEAMS

1951   A. Kauder, L. Mathe
    M. Schleifer, E. Taylor
1952   M. Klausner, Dr. E. Frischauer
    Mrs. A. Whitehead, D. Westerfield

1953 S. Rebner, H. Feinberg
L. Pressburg, Dr. A. Strich
1954 A. Kauder, M. Schleifer
E. Taylor, L. Mathe
1955 E. Kantar, J. Becheley
R. Wolff, M. Miles
A. Okuneff
1956 A. J. Strich, J. Moran
R. Hislop, C. Potvin
1957 L. Mathe, E. Taylor
M. Schleifer, D. Oakie
1958 E. Kantar, M. Miles
I. Erdos, E. Rovere
1959 I. Erdos, I. Rubin
O. Adams, E. Kantar
E. Rovere, M. Miles
1960 P. Allinger, D. Oakie
M. Schleifer, L. Mathe
1961 E. Paulsen, H. Portugal
M. Portugal, M. Shuman
A. Baron, J. Werner
1962 L. Weiss, W. McWilliams
M. Moss, J. Sloan
R. Ryder, W. Blank
1963 J. Swanson, H. Ross
M. Lawrence, H. Guiver
1964 R. Hamman, D. Krauss
E. Kantar, M. Miles
H. Cohen
1965 Mrs. A. S. Coleman, D. A. Oakie
M. Schleifer, D. Drury
1966 R. Hamman, D. Krauss
L. Mathe, R. von der Porten
1967 H. Guiver, M. Lawrence
Mr. and Mrs. M. Portugal, B. Crane
1968 M. Shuman, R. Spotts
R. Henderson, H. Ross
A. Tschekaloff, E. Paulsen
1969 P. Soloway, H. Baron
J. Hallee, M. Brachman
M. Brachman, M. J. Farell
1970 Mr. and Mrs. M. Brachman
H. Baron, P. Soloway
M. Schleifer, G. Hallee
1971 Mrs. C. Hammel, K. Larsen
R. von der Porten, M. Schleifer
M. Vernoff
1972 B. Reinhold, B. Eisenberg
E. Kantar, J. Cansino
R. Sheehan, M. Miles
1973 M. Smolen, E. Paulsen
B. Sides, P. Ivaska
J. Wittes, G. Bare
1974 M. Miles, J. Bechely
J. Schermer, M. Gurwitz

MASTERS TEAMS

1947 R. Eiden, M. Schleifer
B. Bysshe, D. Walther
1952 M. Breslauer, L. Mathe
L. Pressburg, A. Strich
1953 Mr. and Mrs. A. Kauder
H. Murphy, I. Erdos
1954 S. Fairchild, Mrs. R. Kempner
L. Kramer, R. Kempner
1955 Mrs. B. B. Alston, D. Weld
B. Coombs, P. Allinger
1956 A. Baron, M. Schleifer
I. Erdos, L. Mathe

OPEN TEAMS

1936 C. Schwartz, W. Graff
J. S Meyer, T. Harry Merkle
1937 G. Gooden, Dr. B. L. Strauss
W. Turner, D. Oakie
1938 G. Gooden, Dr. B. L. Strauss
W. Turner, D. Oakie
1939 J. Ehrlenbach, E. Taylor
M. Schleifer, L. Mathe

1940 L. Mathe, M. Schleifer
J. Ehrlenbach, E. Sandstrom
1941 D. Burnstine, L. Mathe
R. A. Puffer, Jr., M. Schleifer
1942 M. Lipsett, F. Thompson
M. Merkle, E. Ackerman
1945 J. Ehrlenbach, E. Taylor
N. Perlstein, M. Schleifer
1946 L. Mathe, M. Schleifer
E. Taylor, J. Ehrlenbach
1947 D. Bruce, J. H. Moran
M. Portugal, H. Frederick
C. Strouse, Jr.
1949 M. Schleifer, R. Puffer, Jr.
E. Taylor, L. Mathe
1957 J. and J. Millerd
A. Bell, M. Miles
1958 L. Mathe, D. Oakie
M. Schleifer, E. Taylor
1959 E. Taylor, L. Mathe,
M. Schleifer, D. Oakie
1960 Mr. and Mrs. M. Portugal
H. Kandler, S. Levy
1961 Mr. and Mrs. M. Portugal
H. Kandler, S. Levy, *tied with*
M. Miles, H. Simon
E. Kantar, J. Hancock
1962 H. Simon, E. Kantar
J. Becheley, R. Hamman
1963 N. Walsh, J. Swanson
W. J. Linhart, W. R. McWilliams
1964 D. Deery, H. Cohen
M. Johnson, R. Adams
1965 H. Baron, M. Shuman
A. Kauder, M. Johnson
P. Rank
1966 H. Tippins, C. N. Tsu
J. Dryer, J. Dryer
1968 J. Roth, R. L. Balisok
E. Davis, I. Kostal
1969 J. Jacoby, R. Wolff
R. Goldman, W. Eisenberg
M. Lawrence
1970 H. Kandler, A. Bell
M. Savage, T. Lesser
B. Amer, E. Davis
1971 R. Bates, E. Herbert
H. Wick, H. Segal (Board-a-Match)
J. Fejervary, L. Genud
B. Eisenberg, V. Calamaro (Swiss)
1972 D. Ashley, M. Smolen
D. Henderson, R. Walsh
G. Baze
1973 Dr. P. Forbes, R. Adams
J. Swanson, P. Soloway (Board-a-Match)
M. Kovac, N. Anderson
R. Walsh, M. Lawrence (Swiss)
1974 D. Dautell, H. Stern
J. Rosenstiel, C. Mitchell

MEN'S TEAMS

1974 R. Jenson, C. Conan
D. Cooksey, F. Prior

WOMEN'S TEAMS

1974 E. Young, M. Hurd
S. Pond, C. Gnam, *tied with*
E. McDermott, V. Carrera
P. Hinkle, D. Barron, *tied with*
B. Pritchard, M. Emrich
L. Newman, E. Montwill

MIXED TEAMS

1937 H. Watson, R. Oakley
R. Baehr, C. Arnoldy
1938 R. O'Brien, B. Dethridge
H. Pemberton, J. Ehrlenbach, *tied with*
M. O'Brien, I. Oeschger
C. Schwartz, J. Meyer

1939 Mr. and Mrs. S. Kapp
      Mr. and Mrs. G. Troutt
1940 L. Senderman, H. Merkle
      Mrs. C. Johanson, E. Sandstrom
1941 M. Kaiser, L. Mathe
      C. Arden, J. Ehrlenbach
1942 L. Senderman, D. Westerfield
      B. Stilwell, E. Rovere
1943 Lt. Col. and Mrs. H. Vanderluis
      Mr. and Mrs. H. Bowman
1944 A. Goldfine, H. Burnstein
      E. Goldfine, F. Reif
1945 F. Cohn, C. Schwartz
      J. Cummings, G. Bergmans
1946 Mr. and Mrs. G. Wells
      Mr. and Mrs. J. Dunn
1947 R. Eidem, M. Schleifer
      B. Bysshe, D. Walther
1960 Mr. and Mrs. J. Farell
      J. Herb, B. Crane, *tied with*
      R. Eiden, J. Atchley
      L. Pressburg, Mrs. B. W. Meyers
1961 Mr. and Mrs. J. Dunn
      M. Klausner, M. Schleifer
1962 Mr. and Mrs. R. Walsh
      D. Cook, L. Newman
      H. Kandler
1963 Mr. and Mrs. L. Mathe
      F. Meyer, H. Guiver
      A. Tschekaloff
1964 H. Baron, H. Portugal
      B. Crane, E. Paulsen
1965 R. Lander, L. Weiss
      L. Pressburg, E. Landow, *tied with*
      Mrs. C. Munn, Mrs. A. S. Coleman
      D. Drury, R. von der Porten
1966 S. Rebner, F. Tsacnaris
      P. Soloway, W. R. McWilliams
1967 Mr. and Mrs. K. Petterson
      M. Klausner, M. Schleifer
1968 D. Lawrence, R. Spotts
      P. Sutherlin, H. Ross
1969 R. Walsh, R. Walsh
      H. Kandler, B. Crane
      M. J. Farell
1970 R. Walsh, W. Blank
      F. Tsacnaris, D. Ashley

MASTERS PAIRS

1938 D. Westerfield, E. Rovere
1939 J. Sherman, C. Strouse, Jr.
1940 E. Rovere, W. Herbert
1941 M. O'Brien, W. Hayhurst
1942 F. Fee, D. Davis
1943 M. Schleifer, N. Perlstein
1944 M. Klausner, Dr. E. Frischauer
1945 N. Perlstein, C. Strouse, Jr.
1946 Mr. and Mrs. A. Kauder
1947 D. Westerfield, E. Rovere
1949 L. Mathe, E. Taylor
1951 M. Klausner, A. Kauder
1952 J. Ehrlenbach, H. Edwards
1953 M. Vernoff, H. Bierman
1954 Mr. and Mrs. L. Newman
1955 P. C. Smith, F. Meyers
1956 J. C. Atchley, E. Sullivan
1957 M. Portugal, A. Baron
1958 W. R. McWilliams, J. Wright
1959 M. Klausner, J. Ehrlenbach
1960 C. Harvey, D. Conlin
1961 W. Tierney, M. G. Kamens
1962 Mrs. B. W. Meyer, H. Guiver
1963 A. Coleman, M. Schleifer
1964 H. Guiver, D. Deery
1965 R. Walsh, J. Swanson
1966 R. Walsh, J. Swanson
1967 T. Kasday, J. P. Ivaska, Jr.
1968 E. Barlow, E. Bailey
1969 A. Okuneff, J. Stein
1970 D. Joyce, J. Stein
1971 R. McConnell, J. Padget

1972 J. Druer, J. Sharron
1973 K. Petterson, P. Hawkins
1974 J. Stein, D. Joyce

OPEN PAIRS

1935 H. Pemberton, R. Puffer
1936 J. Meyer, H. Merkle
1937 J. Ehrlenbach, E. Taylor
1938 W. Savery, J. Muckley
1939 J. Ehrlenbach, E. Taylor
1940 M. O'Brien, H. Pemberton
1941 D. Oakie, W. Turner
1942 L. Mathe, M. Schleifer
1943 M. Schleifer, M. L. Mendelsohn
1944 M. Klausner, Dr. E. Frischauer
1946 H. Frederick, M. Portugal
1947 L. Mathe, M. Schleifer
1948 L. Mathe, M. Schleifer
1949 Mr. and Mrs. A. Kauder
1950 G. Rapee, R. Kempner
1951 E. Taylor, L. Mathe
1952 W. Jones, A. S. Montgomery
1953 Mrs. J. Moffat, M. Miles
1954 Mr. and Mrs. A. Kauder
1955 Mr. and Mrs. A. Kauder
1956 S. Lazard, P. Allinger
1957 E. Taylor, L. Mathe
1958 E. Kantar, M. Miles
1959 S. Rebner, B. Crane
1960 P. Allinger, J. Pestaner
1961 K. Petterson, E. Paulsen
1962 E. Paulsen, K. Petterson
1963 Mr. and Mrs. J. Farell
1964 B. Crane, H. Baron
1965 R. Walsh, M. McMahan
1966 J. Flint, P. Pender
1967 Mrs. S. Murphy, R. Kerr
1968 W. Eisenberg, R. Wolff
1969 P. Soloway, M. Brachman
1970 D. Mordecai, N. Schwartz
1971 E. Keeler, J. Lindsay
1972 D. Weiss, J. Hoersch
1973 B. Crane, Dr. J. Fisher
1974 B. Crane, P. Rank

MASTERS MEN'S PAIRS

1965 K. Larsen, H. Ross
1966 W. Tierney, D. C. Wurdeman
1967 R. Walsh, G. Hallee, *tied with*
      L. West, D. Pearson
1968 B. Crane, M. McMahan
1970 R. McKnight, S. Crandon
1971 B. Crane, P. Rank

MEN'S PAIRS

1945 C. Harvey, W. L. Jones
1946 E. Sandstrom, E. Taylor
1947 L. Pressburg, J. Ehrlenbach
1948 E. Rovere, W. von Zedtwitz
1950 Dr. E. Frischauer, L. L. Mathe
1951 R. Sharp, D. Ingham
1952 R. Kempner, A. Kramer
1953 E. Quade, E. Andersen
1954 B. Stephenson, M. Nelson
1955 I. Marker, M. Breslauer
1956 J. Dunn, M. Schleifer
1957 S. Lazard, P. Allinger
1958 M. Vernoff, E. M. Cook, Jr.
1959 D. Sullivan, W. Keller
1960 J. Dunn, P. Allinger
1961 T. Adler, L. Marks
1962 E. Taylor, H. Guiver
1963 M. Hodder, M. Schleifer
1964 R. Walsh, E. Bailey
1965 R. A. Hislop, R. Kempner
1966 P. Soloway, R. Walsh
1967 P. Soloway, R. Walsh
1968 M. Smolen, B. Amer

1969	H. Steen, G. Civetta
1970	L. Kaye, J. Rygh
1971	J. Wittes, P. Ivaska
1972	J. Kauder, H. Guiver
1973	L. Cohen, Dr. R. Katz
1974	H. Farnsworth, J. Robison

MASTERS WOMEN'S PAIRS

1965	M. Johnson, H. Baron
1966	M. Anticouni, B. Feldman
1967	S. Rebner, A. Kempner
1968	E. Schulte, M. Johnson
1970	M. Futterman, M. Graham
1971	J. Cohen, H. Cale

WOMEN'S PAIRS

1936	H. Watson, C. Dickson
1937	V. Leonard, M. Mortimore
1938	B. Bates, J. De Costa
1939	M. Gillingham, S. Hutton
1940	H. Brunn, M. H. Jordan
1941	A. Wesson, M. Criswell
1942	I. Oeschger, N. Childs
1943	E. Gibbons, R. E. Kirkman
1944	I. Oeschger, G. Wells
1945	H. Brunn, J. Dunn
1946	J. Dunn, C. Smith
1947	V. Leonard, M. Mortimore
1948	R. Clarke, S. Rebner
1950	J. Duprau, H. Portugal
1951	G. Wallach, B. Allen
1952	D. Rickards, K. Hobbs
1953	C. Smith, J. Garrigan
1954	H. Cale, B. Bysshe
1955	M. Cartwright, H. P. Cavanaugh
1956	D. Lorber, M. Klausner
1957	L. Morrison, H. Hope
1958	J. Wright, K. Dunn
1959	J. Dunn, J. Herb
1960	H. Baron, P. Medford
1961	H. Gross, N. Wells
1962	E. O'Hara, S. G. Kelsey
1963	S. Dollar, W. Kent
1964	E. Bishop, E. Hirschfeld
1965	R. M. Gale, Mrs. L. M. Ryel
1966	M. Kovac, Mrs. A. Scharfe
1967	H. Baron, R. Walsh
1968	A. Kempner, Mrs. P. Laverty
1969	M. J. Farell, K. Blanchard
1970	K. Van Hook, P. Wittes
1971	Mrs. B. Meyer, T. Nugit
1972	D. Ferris, B. Norbury
1973	F. Tsacnaris, P. Wittes
1974	S. Hinman, P. Callahan

MIXED PAIRS

1936	Mrs. H. Moscovitz, G. Wooten
1937	E. Cooney, W. Schroeder
1938	M. Kaiser, L. Mathe
1939	Mrs. A. Childs, E. Rovere
1940	M. Glazer, H. Gross
1941	C. Arden, J. Ehrlenbach
1942	C. Potvin, H. Remley
1943	Lt. Col. and Mrs. H. Vanderluis
1944	Mrs. J. Rae, W. Wolf
1945	H. Brunn, D. Westerfield
1946	P. Bacher, H. J. Fishbein
1947	B. Bysshe, M. Schleifer
1949	Mr. and Mrs. A. Kauder
1951	Mr. and Mrs. M. Portugal
1952	Mr. and Mrs. J. Dunn
1953	Mr. and Mrs. M. Portugal
1954	Mr. and Mrs. J. Dunn
1955	Mr. and Mrs. J. Dunn
1956	J. Hancock, R. Million

1957	M. Johnson, R. T. Adams
1958	R. Kempner, Mrs. B. W. Meyer
1959	Mr. and Mrs. L. Mathe
1960	Mr. and Mrs. A. Jones
1961	H. Portugal, E. Paulsen
1962	Mr. and Mrs. H. Bierman
1963	Mr. and Mrs. K. Petterson
1964	D. Wheelock, L. Weiss
1965	C. Tucker, J. Ehrlenbach
1966	Mr. and Mrs. R. Walsh
1967	Mrs. E. Hirschfeld, H. Kleigman
1968	B. Levan, P. Benjamin
1969	A. Pounds, L. Patterson
1970	G. Herrington, E. Davis
1971	P. Kantar, P. Soloway
1972	H. Baron, J. Mohan
1973	S. Kehoe, R. von der Porten
1974	R. Chapin, R. Walsh

NON-MIXED PAIRS

1972	B. Crane, Dr. J. Fisher
1973	L. Tsou, O. Mowry
1974	D. Kleinman, S. Wilson

INDIVIDUAL

1936	J. Sherman
1937	G. Sherman
1938	G. Sherman
1939	J. Moran
1940	C. L. Taylor
1941	J. Muckey
1947	S. Bonner
1948	Mrs. G. C. Reinkins
1949	A. W. Green
1950	E. Thygeson
1951	N. Karoly
1957	Mrs. F. M. Harris
1958	Mrs. C. George
1959	Dr. H. J. Wells
1960	J. C. Atchley
1967	H. C. Royal
1968	M. Ryan, *tied with*
	M. Prichard
1969	R. Edwards

LOS ANGELES WINTER

KNOCKOUT TEAMS

1972	M. Skinner, S. Skinner
	W. Whitesell, R. Bates
	J. Grantham
1974	R. Garber, S.Evans
	M. Shallon, H. Guiver
	J. Wittes

OPEN TEAMS

1974	L. Ryan, J. Ryan
	L. Mitchell, G. Hayden

MASTERS PAIRS

1972	Dr. J. Fisher, B. Crane
1974	M. Masterson, F. Meyer, *tied with*
	R. Felton, J. Little

OPEN PAIRS

1972	J. Anderson, N. Erickson

DISTRICT 24 (New York City and Long Island)

EASTERN STATES

KNOCKOUT TEAMS (REISINGER)

1930 G. Reith, Sir D. J. Wernher
     W. Liggett, Jr., P. H. Sims
1931 J. Barth, F. A. Rendon
     H. Schenken, D. Burnstine
1932 W. Karn, P. H. Sims
     O. Jacoby, D. Burnstine
1933 H. Schenken, D. Burnstine
     R. L. Frey, C. Lochridge
1934 O. Jacoby, D. Burnstine
     H. Schenken, M. T. Gottlieb
1935 A. M. Barnes, B. J. Becker
     S. Fry, Jr., S. Rusinow
1936 F. D. Kaplan, C. C. Vogelhofer
     M. Elis, I. Epstein
1937 C. Lochridge, W. von Zedtwitz
     A. M. Barnes, S. G. Churchill
1938 S. Fry, Jr., J. Rau
     T. Le Gros, S. G. Churchill
     C. Lochridge
1939 S. Fry, Jr., J. Rau
     T. Le Gros, S. G. Chruchill
     C. Lochridge
1940 M. Elis, S. Stayman
     R. Skinner, M. Fuchs
     M. Seiler
1941 Mrs. S. Wainwright, O. Jacoby
     J. Crawford, C. Lochridge
     S. Stearns
1942 B. J. Becker, S. Becker
     G. Rapee, H. J. Fishbein
     T. Stone
1943 Mrs. H. Sobel, C. Goren
     P. Leventritt, H. Schenken
1944 H. Fishbein, W. von Zedtwitz
     T. Stone, C. Lochridge, L. Hazen
1945 Mr. and Mrs. L. M. Jaeger
     J. Low, W. M. Lichtenstein
     H. Sonenblick
1946 H. J. Fishbein, A. Roth
     L. Hirsch, R. Hirschberg, O. Brotman
1947 Dr. W. Lipton, C. B. Groden
     J. T. Feigus, J. Friedlander
1948 C. Sanders, J. Cushing
     Mr. and Mrs. H. Zacks
1949 C. Groden, J. Shore
     A. N. Goldstein, J. T. Feigus
     Dr. W. Lipton
1950 L. Axmann, Mrs. L. Klehmet
     A. Rosen, L. Blum, I. Kass
1951 G. Rapee, J. R. Crawford
     S. Stayman, B. Lebhar, Jr., S. Rossant
1952 R. Hirschberg, A. Casner
     L. Hirsch, S. Mogal
1953 L. Glucksman, W. Yablon
     O. Yablon, M. Roth, N. Neiger
1954 E. Kaplan, R. Sherman
     E. Jaye, N. Kay
     B. Koytchou
1955 G. Boehm, Dr. W. Lipton
     E. Loewenthal, V. Mitchell
1956 E. Kaplan, R. Kahn
     R. Hirschberg, A. Sheinwold, N. Kay
1957 E. Kaplan, R. Kahn
     R. Hirschberg, A. Sheinwold, N. Kay
1958 E. Kaplan, A. Sheinwold
     R. Hirschberg, R. Kahn, N. Kay
1959 E. Kaplan, R. Hirschberg
     R. Kahn, A. Sheinwold
     L. B. Harmon, N. Kay
1960 A. Roth, W. Grieve
     W. Root, A. Gabrilovitch
     R. Jordan, R. Freeman

1961 A. Roth, T. Stone
     W. Root, R. Freeman
     A. Gabrilovitch, R. Jordan
1962 P. Feldesman, S. Rubinow
     Mr. and Mrs. V. Mitchell
     M. Rubinow, S. Stayman
1963 S. Rubinow, S. Stayman
     Mr. and Mrs. V. Mitchell
     T. Stone, P. Feldesman
1964 Mr. and Mrs. V. Mitchell
     S. Stayman, P. Feldesman, R. Mnuchin
1965 M. Moss, J. Bennett
     M. Blumenthal, H. Lewis
     A. H. Dionisi
1966 A. Roth, M. Schnee
     Dr. K. Apfel, W. Root
     B. Raymond, B. Rappaport
1967 T. Stone, J. Crawford
     O. Jacoby, A. Messer
     L. Rosler
1968 A. Roth, W. Root
     R. Chafetz, J. Solodar
     R.Dorfman, B. Rappaport
1969 H. Schenken, D. Strasberg
     P. Leventritt, R. Crown
     D. Kahn, W. Passell
1970 E. Kaplan, L. Harmon
     J. Rubens, A. Scheinwold
     N. Kay, M. Ingberman
1971 H. Fein, B. J. Becker
     M. Becker, R. Chafetz
     A. Bernstein
1972 D. and J. Mason, S. Seidman
     G. and M. Awad
1973 W. von Zedtwitz, P. Feldesman
     T. Stone, I. Rubin
     K. Larsen, B. Brier
1974 W. von Zedtwitz, T. Stone
     P. Feldesman, B. Brier
     I. Rubin, K. Larsen

MEN'S TEAMS

1967 H. Robinson, A. Ruttenberg
     M. Engel, J. Mechutan
     M. Friedman
1968 P. Heitner, L. Orange
     S. Altman, R. Spero
1969 M. Gurwitz, D. Bloch
     H. Lilie, G. L. Awad
     G. Prosnitz, *tied with*
     A. Neidle, J. Hester
     H. Woodman, R. DeMartino
     W. A. Johnson, *tied with*
     I. Sklarew, M. Goodman
     R. L. Billig, R. Back

WOMEN'S TEAMS

1967 B. Birnholtz, J. Carroll
     D. Silverman, S. Bederson
     A. Sporing
1968 H. Smith, A. Kotzen
     H. Utegaard, E. Levitt
1969 Mrs. C. Smith, Mrs. R. P. Kindler
     Mrs. D. Cohen, Mrs. A. Penick
     Mrs. A. West

MIXED TEAMS

1933 O. Jacoby, Mrs. F. Furlow
     T. A. Lightner, Mrs. L. Peck
1934 W. von Zedtwitz, Mrs. S. Furlow
     Mr. and Mrs. O. Jacoby
1935 Mrs. H. Sobel, H. Schenken
     H. Bonwit, L. M. Watson
1936 I. Epstein, Mrs. E. Drescher
     B. Collyer, A. Leibowitz

1937   H. Schenken, H. Chanin
      H. Bonwit, Mrs. M. Wagar
1938   H. Schenken, H. Bonwit
      M. Elis, Mrs. E. Drescher
1939   Mr. and Mrs. J. H. Lemon
      Dr. and Mrs. L. W. Lord
1940   Mr. and Mrs. G. W. Kennedy
      Mrs. S. Wainwright, W. Malowan
1941   Mrs. S. Wainwright, W. Malowan
      Mrs. W. A. Tucker, S. Stearns
1942   Mrs. R. C. Young, Mrs. B. Golder
      C. Goren, C. Solomon
1943   Mrs. L. W. Noel, F. D. Kaplan
      Mrs. P. Bacher, M. Levin
1944   Mrs. S. Wainwright, W. Malowan
      Mrs. W. A. Tucker, W. Bixby
1945   Mr. and Mrs. S. Kreps
      C. Little, L. Sager
1946   P. Leventritt, S. Katz
      Mrs. R. C. Young, Mrs. L. Jaeger
1947   Mrs. P. Bacher, Mrs. J. D. Gardner
      L. Jaeger, M. Levin
1949   Mrs. H. Sobel, Mrs. K. Rhodes
      R. Kahn, S. Fry, Jr.
1955   Mr. and Mrs. I. Brall, E. Jaye
      Mrs. D. Woodington, E. Kaplan
1956   C. Goren, Mrs. E. Kemp, S. Stayman
      Mrs. R. Sherman, R. Kahn, *tied with*
      Mr. and Mrs. L. Jaeger, Mrs. P. Gardner
      W. Slattery, *tied with*
      Mrs. C. Gilbert, Mrs. V. Klein
      Dr. K. Apfel, L. Kelner, A. Greene
1957   Mr. and Mrs. A. Sheinwold
      Mrs. B. Pearly, L. Harmon
1958   Mr. and Mrs. T. Stone, D. Warner
      Mrs. R. C. Young, R. Jordan
1959   Mrs. J. Gardner, H. Benjamin
      D. Tourance, I. Rosenberg
      A. Ritter
1960   Mrs. O. Eichmann, Mrs. G. Montgomery
      Dr. W. V. Lipton, Dr. N. Reitman
1961   Mrs. M. Harris, Mrs. V. Lavery
      Dr. R. Tator, Dr. J. Manos, *tied with*
      Mrs. W. Keohane, Mrs. T. Griffin
      F. T. Westcott, R. Brown
1962   Mrs. D. Robinson, Mrs. S. Baderson
      M. Kassay, G. Hochman
1963   F. Carroll, Mrs. E. Long
      Mr. and Mrs. G. Gibson
1964   Dr. and Mrs. S. Warner
      A. Messer, B. Tepper
1965   E. Schwartz, J. Bennett
      I. Bennett, M. Moss
1966   Mr. and Mrs. M. Feld
      E. Lazarus, D. Aiken
1967   C. Coon, J. Bennett, Jr.
      Mrs. W. Albersheim, Mrs. I. Bennett
1968   Mr. and Mrs. L. Harmon
      C. Brall, P. Pender
1969   J. Mason, D. Mason
      J. Becker, E. Alfandre

MASTERS PAIRS

1951   S. Fry, Jr. P. Leventritt
1952   Dr. W. Lipton, I. Rubin
1953   F. Atiyeh, G. Malhame
1954   I. Rubin, I. Martin
1955   L. Glucksman, M. Newman
1956   D. Strasberg, I. Rubin
1957   N. Kay, R. Hirschberg
1958   S. Fry, Jr., L. B. Harmon
1959   J. Wendt, H. Lavine
1960   R. Kahn, A. Meredith
1961   P. Feldesman, B. Raymond
1962   H. Brandon, F. Carroll
1963   Mrs. A. Cantor, L. Tritter
1964   R. Kahn, E. Loewenthal
1965   J. Benoit, M. Cappelletti
1966   Mr. and Mrs. V. Mitchell
1967   R. Rosenberg, R. Lattomus

1968   Dr. K. Apfel, N. Drucker
1969   M. Melton, S. Kantor
1970   C. Tornay, S. Goldstein

OPEN PAIRS (GOLDMAN)

1929   O. Jacoby, G. Reith
1930   G. Mott-Smith, R. L. Frey
1931   W. C. Cogswell, N. Bonney
1932   W. Liggett, Jr., S. S. Lenz
1933   Mrs. G. E. Perpall, F. E. Bailey
1934   O. Jacoby, D. Burnstine
1935   H. N. Raffel, M. Alexander
1936   J. G. Wetzlar, S. Cunningham
1937   H. Fishbein, L. Bernard
1938   R. Chatkin, M. Fuchs
1939   F. D. Kaplan, H. Ziman
1940   C. S. Lochridge, M. D. Maier
1941   Mrs. H. Sobel, C. Goren
1942   A. Moyse, R. L. Frey
1943   A. Goldstein, J. Tilles
1944   Mrs. K. Beghold, E. F. Smith
1945   J. Friedlander, N. Drucker
1946   H. Harkavy, A. Casner
1947   R. Kahn, C. H. Whitebrook
1948   Dr. K. Apfel, F. Begley
1949   A. Goldstein, B. M. Raymond
1950   J. Tilles, E. I. Phillips
1951   E. Kaplan, B. Raymond
1952   B. Lebhar, S. Rossant
1953   O. Jacoby, H. Fishbein
1954   J. Tilles, B. Raymond
1955   O. Jacoby, A. Sheinwold
1956   A. W. Leeds, E. Thumim
1957   Mr. and Mrs. T. Stone
1958   J. Gallaher, V. Mitchell
1959   H. Berger, Dr. G. Rothenberg
1960   L. Rosler, R. Stern
1961   T. Stone, A. Roth, *tied with*
      S. Seidman, N. Neiger
1962   V. Shen, B. Borak
1963   R. Jotcham, J. Guertin
1964   E. Jaye, S. Becker
1965   F. Bickel, R. Rosenberg
1966   J. Kauder, A. Nichols
1967   B. Raymond, S. Altman
1968   C. Burger, J. Cayne
1969   A. Bernstein, R. Chafetz
1970   V. Chernoff, C. Bowie
1971   J. Asber, T. Dionisi
1972   R. Freedman, D. Loomis
1973   C. Krupp, P. Trent
1974   P. Berger, S. Hanna

MEN'S PAIRS

1952   R. Michelson, G. Kennedy
1954   Dr. W. Lipton, E. Loewenthal
1955   Dr. K. Apfel, M. Rubinow
1956   F. T. Westcott, B. Koffman
1957   I. Cohen, R. Freeman
1958   B. Strauss, W. Vanderporten
1959   H. Fishbein, H. Goldberg
1960   A. Roth, S. Haddad
1961   Dr. N. Reitman, Dr. W. Lipton
1962   M. Zipser, R. Wegman
1963   V. Bennahum, D. Halper
1964   R. Eisenberg, S. Palmer
1965   Dr. W. Lipton, R. Bortstiber
1966   L. Kass, M. Cohn
1967   R. DeMartino, H. Woodman
1968   A. Osborn, R. Green, *tied with*
      R. DeMartino, H. Woodman
1969   E. Manfield, A. Sontag
1970   Dr. S. Turecki, D. Strasberg
1971   K. Cox, F. Westcott
1972   R. Khautin, W. Kornfeld
1973   B. Ryder, J. Looby
1974   J. Wendt, R. Lanke

WOMEN'S PAIRS

1935	M. Kalman, G. Planco
1936	M. Frey, G. Planco
1937	R. Sherman, M. Wagar
1938	S. Dykman, N. Noel
1939	M. D. Rothschild, R. B. Fuller
1940	W. E. McKenney, G. B. Hirsch
1941	B. Cook, E. Seligman
1942	B. Cook, E. Seligman
1943	H. Sobel, R. Sherman
1944	H. Sobel, R. Sherman
1945	H. Sobel, R. Sherman
1946	R. Adams, M. Hochheimer
1947	J. Jaeger, P. Bacher
1948	C. Van Slochem, A. Hess
1950	G. Gibson, D. Brooks
1951	P. Adams, M. Harris
1952	A. Albersheim, B. C. Martin
1953	C. Gibson, B. Brooks
1954	J. Mitchell, O. Reilly
1955	W. Ecker, I. Goldman
1956	C. Gilbert, E. Mallinson
1957	M. Harris, P. Adams
1958	M. Rosen, R. Ecker
1959	M. Bonney, H. Simon
1960	D. Rosenfield, D. Berning
1961	M. E. Silver, A. Gittelman
1962	B. Schenken, S. Johnson
1963	M. Rosen, W. Ecker
1964	B. Rappaport, E. Asherman
1965	M. Wagar, C. Sanders
1966	J. Jaeger, Mrs. A. Grinberg
1967	Mrs. V. Mitchell, U. Blanton
1968	B. Schenken, S. Johnson
1969	G. Ritter, E. Sacks
1970	M. Altman, D. Schuld
1971	F. Fear, H. Tax
1972	A. Heitner, S. Levenson
1973	B. Loop, P. Frenkel
1974	N. Goldfarb, A. Kurland

MIXED PAIRS

1941	Mrs. J. Gardner, H. D. Halstead
1942	Mrs. H. Sobel, E. Hymes, Jr.
1943	Mrs. H. Sobel, E. Hymes, Jr.
1944	Mrs. B. Golder, C. Solomon
1945	Mrs. B. Cook, A. Casner
1946	Mrs. H. Levy, M. Schwartz
1947	Mrs. F. W. Solomon, J. Shore
1948	Mrs. H. Levy, M. Schwartz
1949	Mr. and Mrs. L. M. Jaeger
1950	Mrs. P. Adams, A. L. Gotthelf
1951	Mr. and Mrs. M. Agran
1952	Mrs. S. Fox, K. Garlinger
1953	Mrs. A. P. Hess, E. Bauer
1954	Mrs. W. Albersheim, J. Foreacre
1955	Mrs. B. Pearly, B. Mitchell
1956	Mrs. C. Gilbert, Dr. K. Apfel
1957	Mr. and Mrs. H. Fishbein
1958	Mrs. G. Montgomery, Dr. N. Reitman
1959	Mr. and Mrs. H. Levitt
1960	Mr. and Mrs. H. Levitt
1961	Mrs. E. Kemp, E. Seligman
1962	Mr. and Mrs. E. Kaplan
1963	Mr. and Mrs. J. Greenwood
1964	Mrs. S. Kransberg, C. Davis
1965	Mr. and Mrs. M. Feld
1966	V. Lavery, A. Bernstein
1967	B. Cagan, T. Smith
1968	H. Utegaard, M. Blumenthal
1969	V. Mitchell, M. Ribner
1970	H. Smith, A. Dionisi

INDIVIDUAL

1952	L. Kelner
1954	J. Arbee

1955	J. McCormick
1956	E. Panossian
1957	E. J. Seligman
1959	Mrs. J. Epstein
1960	J. Aldridge
1967	J. Melrose
1968	J. Grassi
1969	J. Becker

FUN CITY

KNOCKOUT TEAMS

1970	D. Mason, J. Mason
	G. Awad, M. Awad
	S. Seidman, M. Mohr
1971	T. Griffin, E. Griffin
	T. Dionisi, C. Lamprey
	M. Blumenthal, H. Lewis
1972	K. Lebensold, S. Goldstein
	G. Tornay, L. Levy
	L. Popper, M. Feldman
1973	J. Saltz, A. Kaminsky
	M. Lawrence, A. Kearse
1974	J. Cayne, P. Weichsel
	N. Weichsel, S. Sion
	J. Rosenbloom, C. Lindenman

OPEN TEAMS

1973	R. Lipsitz, B. Ewen
	S. Stayman, M. Tom
	R. Rubin, M. Granovetter
1974	C. Russell, A. Sontag
	P. Weichsel, A. Roth
	B. Rappaport, J. Stuart

MASTERS PAIRS

1972	R. Ekeblad, G. Hahn

OPEN PAIRS

1970	P. Feldesman, B. Grieve
1971	J. Feigus, A. Greene
1972	A. Roth, B. Rappaport
1973	R. Stern, S. Stern
1974	C. Wei, M. Tom

MEN'S PAIRS

1970	P. Kramer, P. Cowan
1971	H. Bethe, S. Goldberg
1972	K. Garber, M. Epstein
1973	N. Phillips, D. Stewart

WOMEN'S PAIRS

1970	E. Sudikoff, R. Grossman
1971	C. Furman, S. Krellenstein
1972	B. Brier, C. Lomaskin
1973	D. Schuld, M. Altman

MIXED PAIRS

1970	E. Keohane, F. Westcott
1971	G. Collier, A. Sontag
1974	B. Braucher, A. Roy

INDIVIDUAL

1974	J. Saxe

LONG ISLAND

KNOCKOUT TEAMS

1968   Mr. and Mrs. T. Griffin, R. Brown
     A. Dionisi, R. Ewen, A. Messer
1969   Mr. and Mrs. S. Palmer
     Mr. and Mrs. G. Awad, D. Mason
1970   I. Ewen, L. Ewen
     R. Bowers, S. Bowers
1971   J. Stuart, E. Neiger
     P. Weichsel, S. Altman
     T. Smith
1972   T. Smith, P. Weichsel
     G. Neiger, S. Altman
     A. Sontag, J. Stuart

OPEN TEAMS

1967   J. Bennett, W. Butcher
     M. Rosenblatt, A. Waldmann
1972   J. and A. Tucker, P. Ross
     E. Prosnitz, M. Friedman
1973   Dr. E. Etkind, S. Earl
     J. Strauss, L. Bausher
1974   W. Natbony, M. Radin
     M. Jacobus, S. Sion

MASTERS PAIRS

1968   P. Atiyeh, C. McLaughlin
1969   W. August, D. Hayden
1970   A. Bernstein, Dr. S. Turecki

OPEN PAIRS

1967   G. Moss, M. Spitz
1968   R. Ryder, G. Hochman
1969   H. Itkin, K. Rhodes
1970   R. Feld, M. Feld
1971   M. Moss, G. Moss
1972   L. St. Jean, M. Rosenberg
1973   A. Kurland, T. Riely
1974   M. Tom, M. Granovetter

MEN'S PAIRS

1967   C. Brenner, C. MacCracken
1968   M. Steinfeld, W. Meltzer
1969   R. J. Becker, L. Finkel
1970   E. Andresian, M. Berger
1971   F. Mela, M. Granovetter
1972   Dr. S. Kantor, R. Becker
1973   B. Yadgaroff, M. Mirźoeff
1974   R. Taylor, G. Prosnitz

WOMEN'S PAIRS

1967   J. Orange, C. Tornay
1968   E. Sacks, Mrs. M. Ritter
1969   E. Sacks, G. Ritter
1970   N. Half, M. Suran
1971   I. Bennett, E. Keohane
1972   L. Perlstein, M. Gwozdzinsky
1973   B. Powsner, M. Silverman
1974   J. Mitchell, J. Roberts

MIXED PAIRS

1967   J. Oates, H. Sachs
1968   Mr. and Mrs. J. Goldberg
1969   Mr. and Mrs. M. Cappelletti
1970   G. Awad, M. Awad
1971   E. Miller, D. Berkowitz

NEW YORK WINTER

OPEN TEAMS

1972   B. J. Becker, J. Rubens
     M. Becker, R. Stern
     A. Bernstein, *tied with*
     A. Roth, B. Rappaport
     N. Silverman, R. Rubin
1973   A. Schoenfeld, F. Begley
     D. Halper, Dr. K. Apfel
     P. Goodman
1974   J. Rengstorff, E. Kayser
     N. Schwantes, B. Erickson

MIXED TEAMS

1971   P. Heitner, A. Heitner
     K. Parker, J. Parker

LIFE MASTERS PAIRS

1971   M. Bergen, R. Oshlag

OPEN PAIRS

1972   A. Kaminsky, C. Papazian
1973   G. Moss, M. Moss
1974   R. Grabel, M. Rosenberg

MEN'S PAIRS

1971   C. Lamprey, S. Labins
1974   Dr. G. Elkind, Dr. D. Reider

WOMEN'S PAIRS

1971   P. Jenshel, R. Rosenfeld
1974   M. Altman, V. Whalen

MIXED PAIRS

1972   J. Solodar, J. Solodar
1973   R. Marshall, D. Goldsmith˙

DISTRICT 25 (Connecticut, Maine, Massachusetts, New Hampshire, Rhode Island, Vermont)

NEW ENGLAND

KNOCKOUT TEAMS

(When two results are given, the first names represent the winners of the Boston Chess Club event, and the second the winners of the Cavendish Club event.)

1930   N. S. Kelly, J. A. Farrer
     P. R. Ammidon, F. K. Perkins
1931   P. H. Sims, W. S. Karn
     D. Burnstine, W. Malowan
1932   F. M. Howe, Mrs. F. Harding
     F. D. Pollard, Mrs. H. Mann
1933   Mrs. W. J. Lyons, Mrs. F. Merrill
     E. Brown III, C. Head
1934   N. S. Kelly, F. K. Perkins
     J. F. Barry, C. Head
1935   J. A. Farrer, R. Chase
     S. Wirt, R. Ells

1936 W. Malowan, S. Rusinow
      Mr. and Mrs. R. L. Frey
1937 Mr. and Mrs. C. Harvey
      F. K. Perkins, E. Marcus
1937 W. Towne, P. McNulty
      G. Verde, J. Silin
1938 N. Kelley, L. Weiss
      J. Scheuer, C. C. Harvey
1938 J. A. Farrer, R. Elzholz
      G. Verde, J. Silin
1939 C. Head, L. Weiss
      J. Scheuer, S. Weiss
1939 E. N. Marcus, S. Green
      Mrs. M. Levine, F. K. Perkins
1940 G. Verde, A. Bell
      J. A. Farrer, P. McNulty
1940 G. Verde, S. Wirt
      A. Bell, J. A. Farrer
1941 F. K. Perkins, C. Head
      J. Scheuer, E. Marcus, L. Weiss
1941 C. Head, J. Scheuer
      F. K. Perkins, L. Weiss
      E. N. Marcus
1942 L. Weiss, A. Howard
      E. Marcus, F. K. Perkins
1942 W. Campbell, B. Ruiter
      P. McNulty, W. Hopkins
      Dr. J. F. Roberts
1942 W. Campbell, R. Ruiter
      P. McNulty, W. Hopkins
      Dr. J. F. Roberts
1943 J. Scheuer, F. W. Solomon
      M. B. Casson, A. H. Jacobson
1943 P. Johnson, R. Fisher
      R. Martens, M. Marks
      Y. Barkan
1944 Mrs. H. Ansin, C. Goren
      E. Marcus, H. Fagan
1944 Mrs. H. Ansin, E. N. Marcus
      B. Levin, S. Green
      W. Silver
1945 Mrs. H. Ansin, L. Weiss
      E. Marcus, R. Elzholz
      B. Levin
1945 M. Casson, J. Scheuer
      C. Head, S. Wirt
1946 J. Scheuer, M. Casson
      C. Head, S. Wirt
1946 M. Casson, J. Scheuer
      C. Head, S. Wirt
1947 J. Scheuer, M. Casson
      C. Head, S. Wirt
1948 K. P. Hill, R. H. Skinner
      Mr. and Mrs. H. Zacks
1949 Mrs. W. Keohane, H. D. Baker
      R. Baker, F. Westcott
1950 M. B. Casson, J. J. Liston
      A. H. Morehead, J. Scheuer
      S. Wirt
1951 J. Scheuer, S. Wirt
      J. Liston, A. H. Morehead
      C. Head
1952 M. L. Meltzer, I. Stakgold
      R. C. Lesser, L. Katz
1953 Mr. and Mrs. H. D. Baker
      R. Cox, J. W. Ryan
1954 C. Head, E. Kaplan
      J. Scheuer, I. Stakgold
1955 B. Goldman, F. W. Solomon
      M. Casson, K. P. Hill
1956 F. Westcott, R. Baker
      R. Fox, R. Starr
1957 L. Weiss, W. P. Grieve
      C. Coon, G. Durgin
      A. Tschekaloff
1958 C. Kemball, P. Feldman
      C. Coon, P. Johnson
      R. Sears
1959 F. Westcott, R. Fox
      R. Starr, R. Baker .

1960 W. Butcher, Mrs. L. Garfield
      Dr. G. Dorfman, E. Abrams
      W. Passell
1961 W. Levin, D. Cliff
      C. Coon, R. Sears
      L. Weiss
1962 F. Westcott, R. Baker
      R. Fox, R. Starr
      H. Bernstrom, H. Calder
1963 F. Westcott, R. Baker
      R. Starr, R. Fox
      C. Davis
1964 F. Goldring, C. Coon
      R. Sears, R. Zeckhauser
      L. Weiss
1965 F. Silver, J. Benoit
      J. Goldberg, L. Popper
      M. Cappelletti
1966 R. Blau, L. Sokolower
      J. Lowenthal, P. Heitner
1967 S. Labins, C. Sonnenschein
      M. Spitz, M. Marcus
      K. Bhavnani, R. Schreitmueller
1968 A. Bernstein, H. Feldheim
      P. Weichsel, T. Smith
1969 C. Davis, Dr. R. Tator
      L. Weiss, L. Popper
      N. Humer, J. Goldberg
1970 B. Chazen, R. Budd
      C. Lamprey, S. Labins
1971 J. Silver, E. Kokish
      M. Blumenthal, R. Lipsitz
1972 J. Silver, E. Kokish
      M. Gurwitz, J. Bookstaver
1973 C. Davis, N. Humer
      B. Miller, Dr. R. Tator
1974 D. Dawson, J. Dawson
      J. Stiefel, J. Bennett
      M. Keszycki, B. Hughes (Winter)
      K. Wei, S. Goldstein
      K. Lebensold, M. Tom
      R. Andersen, M. Feldman (Spring)

MASTERS TEAMS

1948 R. H. Skinner, P. Herrmann
      P. Katzenstein, S. Gold
1949 Mr. and Mrs. H. Zacks
      K. P. Hill, Mrs. W. H. Keohane
1950 E. N. Marcus, L. Weiss
      Mrs. C. Hootstein, S. Aronson
1951 H. Ballou, H. D. Baker
      W. Offner, P. A. Kerwick
1952 E. N. Marcus, P. Johnson
      J. B. Kushner, M. H. Kelleher
1953 Mr. and Mrs. H. Zacks
      S. Fox, H. Mullaney
1954 R. Fels, J. Gildea
      P. Herrmann, H. Palmer
1955 E. Kaplan, A. Sheinwold
      I. Stakgold, S. Rubinow
1956 A. Tschekaloff, C. Coon
      G. Durgin, D. Cliff
1957 E. Kaplan, A. Sheinwold
      L. B. Harmon, I. Stakgold
1958 R. Lesser, W. May
      M. Rosenblatt, C. Coon, *tied with*
      H. B. Bernstrom, M. G. Calder
      Mr. and Mrs. D. Baker
1959 P. Pender, R. Sitnek
      J. Moran, R. Levine
1960 N. Kay, R. Jordan
      A. Robinson, P. Pender
1961 M. Engel, L. J. Phillips
      P. Trent, N. Altman
1962 R. Mosher, J. Rubens
      D. Kitzes, W. Bradley
1963 Mr. and Mrs. P. Heitner
      I. Ewen, E. Prosnitz

1964	Mr. and Mrs. M. Feld
	I. Boris, P. Brenner
1965	J. E. Bennett, Lt. Col. W. Christian
	G. Shane, M. Moss
1966	S. Labins, C. Lamprey
	M. Marcus, C. Sonnenschein
	M. Spitz
1967	R. Lipsitz, A. Waldmann
	M. Rosenblatt, W. Butcher
1968	F. Merblum, H. Merblum
	M. Magnus, D. Corbin
1969	J. Solodar, H. Bethe
	A. Waldmann, M. Rosenblatt
1970	Mr. and Mrs. M. Feld, J. Bennett
	M. Keszycki, *tied with*
	M. Blumenthal, R. Lipsitz
	S. Labins, C. Lamprey
1971	J. Appleton, J. McDermott
	B. Braucher, C. Morrell
1972	J. Appleton, J. McDermott
	W. Braucher, C. Morrell
1974	B. Goldsmith, R. Weiss
	S. Ligas, L. Gillespie

1971	C. Davis, Dr. R. Tator
	C. Zegar, H. Feldheim
1972	S. Raphael, H. Palmer
	S. Cohen, A. Thall
1973	E. Kokish, S. Kokish
	J. Silver, D. Gordon
	G. Mittleman (Spring)
	B. Bramley, C. Lamprey
	L. Reich, S. Labins (Summer)
	B. Bramley, C. Lamprey
	L. Reich, S. Labins (Fall)
1974	M. Kuka, R.Gilbertson
	C. Moxey, R. Hughes, *tied with*
	S. Hewitt, R. Hewitt
	G. Fernandes, W. Fernandez, *tied with*
	M. Agranoff, R. Briley
	S. Slitt, M. Lawrence, *tied with*
	J. Logan, A. Logan
	R. Graham, C. Graham (Winter)
	S. Ligas, L. Gillespie
	B. Goldsmith, R. Weiss (Spring)
	A. Albersheim, E. Keohane
	K. Kadis, U. Nayak (Summer)

OPEN TEAMS

1948	J.B. Kushner, S. Wilson
	R. Fels, D. Goldschmidt
1949	J. B. Kushner, S. Wilson
	R. Fels, D. Goldschmidt
1950	Mrs. F. W. Solomon, J. Scheuer
	J. J. O'Donnell, S. M. Gottlieb
1951	Mrs. W. Keohane, K. Hill
	E. F. Abbott, Jr., P. E. Weatherbee
1952	F. Westcott, R. Starr
	R. Fox, W. H. Johnson
1953	Mr. and Mrs. E. Ackerman
	Mrs. F. Harding, P. Johnson
1954	F. Westcott, R. P. Baker
	R. Fox, R. Starr
1955	P. Johnson, L. Katz
	M. F. Braunstein, R. Ludwig
1956	E. Kaplan, A. Sheinwold
	C. Coon, I. Stakgold
1957	W. Grieve, L. Weiss
	G. Durgin, W. Levin
	D. Cliff
1958	R. Baker, R. Starr
	R. Fox, F. Westcott
1959	C. Coon, R. Sears
	W. Levin, D. Cliff
1960	D. Cliff, W. Levin
	C. Coon, L. Weiss
1961	D. Cliff, C. Coon
	W. Levin, L. Weiss
1962	F. Westcott, R. Fox
	R. Baker, R. Starr
1963	C. Coon, L. Weiss
	S. Aronson, W. Levin
1964	J. Carney, P. Sorter
	M. Engel, F. Lindon
1965	A. Gordon, N. Gerstman
	M. Kassay, R. Brown
1967	Mrs. W. Keohane, R. Thurrell
	A. Oszy, Z. Garabedian
1968	T. Griffin, P. Heitner
	J. Lowenthal, R. Crown, *tied with*
	D. Hayden, B. J. Becker
	S. Becker, M. Becker, *tied with*
	R. Easterbrook, W. Adams
	E. Delahanty, J. Hunt, *tied with*
	K. Parker, J. Parker
	J. Segel, I. Zippert
	L. Schwartz (Winter)
	E. Keohane, R. Thurrell
	A. Oszy, Z. Garabedian (Spring)
1969	R. Cohen, B. Marsh
	E. Kokish, J. Silver
	N. Nagy
1970	A. Waldmann, M. Rosenblatt
	M. Moss, M. Blumenthal

MIXED TEAMS

1935	Mr. and Mrs. C. Harvey
	Mr. and Mrs. A. K. Howard
1936	R. Vahey, J. J. Liston
	Mrs. F. J. Robinson, A. N. Guimerais
1937	R. Vahey, J. J. Liston
	Mrs. F. J. Robinson, A. N. Guimerais
1938	Mr. and Mrs. C. Harvey
	Mrs. M. Levine, E. N. Marcus
1940	Mrs. W. B. Bacon, S. Wirt
	Mr. and Mrs. C. Barnet
1941	Mr. and Mrs. C. Barnet
	Mrs. W. B. Bacon, S. Wirt
1942	Mr. and Mrs. R. Olsen
	Mrs. W. Keohane, O. Hart
1943	Mrs. H. Ansin, E. N. Marcus
	Mrs. C. Hootstein, E. Clarke
1944	Mrs. W. Hermanson, W. M. Noble
	Mrs. D. Wilber, F. Carpenter
1945	Mr. and Mrs. M. Casson
	Mrs. F. Solomon, J. J. O'Donnell
1946	Mrs. W. Keohane, K. P. Hill
	Mrs. R. Skinner, F. Westcott
1947	Mr. and Mrs. E. B. Ackerman
	Mrs. M. Harris, R. H. Skinner
1948	Mrs. W. Keohane, K. P. Hill
	Mrs. A. G. Whitehead, F. T. Westcott
1949	Mrs. W. Keohane, K. P. Hill
	Mrs. S. I. Raphael, F. T. Westcott
1950	Mrs. W. Keohane, K. P. Hill
	Mrs. S. I. Raphael, F. T. Westcott
1951	Mrs. F. W. Solomon, J. J. O'Donnell
	Mrs. F. Harding, L. Weiss
1952	Mrs. C. N. Lovenberg, J. H. Creedon
	F. Johnson, M. Jones, *tied with*
	Mr. and Mrs. J. Kunkel
	Col. and Mrs. R. H. Skinner, *tied with*
	Mrs. C. Hootstein, C. Clancey, Jr.
	Dr. C. G. Barrett, Mrs. N. Hartigan
1953	Mrs. T. G. Vail, W. W. Mansfield
	H. Sweeney, R. Starr
1954	Mrs. W. Bailey, J. W. Lee
	Mrs. F. Rosen, Dr. J. F. Roberts
1955	Mr. and Mrs. H. D. Baker
	Mr. and Mrs. E. D. Noyes
1956	Mrs. W. Keohane, F. Westcott
	C. Kemball, G. Durgin
1957	P. Feldman, P. Johnson
	F. Harding, R. Sears
1958	W. Passell, E. Abrams
	E. G. Wendt, D. Hayden
	D. Strasberg
1959	Mr. and Mrs. N. Curry
	Mrs. N. Coutant, S. Kantor
1960	Mr. and Mrs. M. Scheinberg
	Mr. and Mrs. R. Wakeman

1961 R. Sugenheimer, W. Adams
     W. Mansfield, Mrs. T. G. Vail
     W. Mansfield, Mrs. T. G. Vail
1962 R. Sugenheimer, W. Adams
     W. Mansfield, Mrs. T. G. Vail
1963 Mr. and Mrs. J. McElwain
     Mrs. W. J. Albersheim, C. Coon, *tied with*
     Mr. and Mrs. H. Poock
     Mrs. S. Kransberg, W. Butcher
1964 V. Lavery, Dr. J. T. Manos
     M. Harris, Dr. R. Tabor
1965 Mr. and Mrs. M. Feld
     Mrs. W. J. Albersheim, C. Coon
1966 G. Kransberg, C. Davis
     M. Moss, G. Shane
1967 Mrs. M. Rosenthal, K. Barbour
     Mr. and Mrs. M. Cappelletti
1968 Mr. and Mrs. M. Schneider
     J. Livezey, Mrs. W. W. Vosburgh
1969 D. Faskow, M. Blumenthal
     G. Cohen, H. Smith, *tied with*
     N. Gerstman, Mrs. J. Elms
     D. Scheffer, M. Rheault, *tied with*
     W. Adams, Mrs. M. Clark
     W. Mansfield, B. Vail, *tied with*
     Mrs. P. Finkle, Dr. R. Farrelly
     B. Starr, Mrs. E. Slack
     Mrs. A. Stone
1970 A. Waldmann, E. Alfandre
     N. Drucker, C. Graham
1971 C. Davis, E. Garfield
     D. Schuld, F. Schuld
1972 S. Linkovsky, E. Kokish
     L. Labins, S. Labins

MASTERS PAIRS

1942 A. H. Jacobson, S. Aronson
1946 F. I. Carpenter, A. L. Markson
1947 E. F. Abbott, Jr., S. E. Thoits
1948 A. H. Jacobson, P. Johnson
1949 E. N. Marcus, S. M. Stayman
1950 W. H. Johnson, R. P. Baker
1951 W. Hopkins, H. K. Williams
1952 E. N. Marcus, P. Johnson
1953 P. Weatherbee, E. F. Abbott, Jr.
1954 R. Ludwig, L. Katz
1955 J. Mechutan, E. Van Cott
1956 Dr. W. V. Lipton, M. L. Schnee
1957 S. Rubinow, M. Rubinow
1958 P. Pender, R. Sitnek
1959 R. Lesser, W. May
1960 S. Rubinow, D. Strasberg
1961 H. B. Bernstrom, M. G. Calder
1962 J. Rubens, R. Mosher
1963 H. Bernstrom, M. G. Calder
1964 M. Cappelletti, J. Benoit
1965 B. Fourierzos, M. Magnus, Jr.
1966 P. Pender, J. Flint
1967 R. Fleischman, P. Leon
1968 G. Moss, S. Roark
1969 P. Heitner, B. Chazen (Winter)
     M. L. Cushner, G. Nash (Fall)
1970 C. Krupp, P. Trent
1971 R. Freedman, E. Krugman
1972 A. Albersheim, C. Coon
1973 R. Ekeblad, R. Stone
1974 B. Miller, L. Popper (Summer)
     R. Newberg, P. McDevitt (Fall)

OPEN PAIRS

1932 Mrs. F. Robinson, H. J. O'Meara
1933 M. Casson, W. Campbell
1934 E. N. Marcus, W. R. Silver
1935 W. Malowan, S. Rusinow
1936 R. Vahey, J. J. Liston
1937 G. Verde, J. Silin
1937 R. Ecker, J. Cushing
1938 G. Tolman, Jr., A. L. Moeldner
1938 A. Morehead, G. Mott-Smith
1939 N. Bonney, F. Edlin

1939 E. Clarke, P. Sweet
1940 W. Bixby, Mrs. S. W. Peck
1940 G. Verde, A. Bell
1941 B. Linderman, S. Wirt
1941 Mrs. R. H. Mason, Mrs. D. W. Wilber, *tied with*
     G. Verde, S. Aronson
1942 L. Goff, R. B. Hartley
1942 M. Casson, C. Kopelman
1943 L. Goff, R. B. Hartley
1943 L. Hazen, E. N. Marcus
1944 Lt. and Mrs. A. Kauder
1944 M. Channen, A. Markson
1945 J. Albert, M. Wayner
1945 B. Goldman, L. Plotkin
1946 Mrs. R. Hartley, H. Cohn
1946 K. P. Hill, A. Bell
1947 J. J. O'Donnell, A. Jacobson
1948 S. M. Stayman, E. N. Marcus
1949 S. B. Cotzin, M. L. Meltzer
1950 S. H. Wirt, M. B. Casson
1951 Mr. and Mrs. E. Ackerman
1952 R. Fox, W. H. Johnson
1953 S. Rubinow, M. Rubinow
1954 Mr. and Mrs. R. Hartley
1955 Mrs. M. Cabral, C. Coon
1956 A. Leeds, E. Thumim
1957 A. Leeds, E. Thumim
1958 H. Poock, H. G. Francis
1959 R. Talbot, S. Raphael
1960 D. Cliff, W. Levin
1961 D. Creedon, P. Kerwick
1962 F. Goldring, C. Coon
1963 W. Butcher, M. Rosenblatt
1964 R. Mosher, J. Rubens
1965 R. Cohen, P. Pender
1966 C. Davis, Dr. R. P. Tator
1967 A. Waldmann, M. Rosenblatt
1968 J. Solodar, P. Weichsel
1969 R. Cohen, B. Marsh
1970 F. Westcott, R. Starr (Spring)
     E. Keohane, R. Thurrell (Winter)
1971 R. De Martino, H. Woodman (Winter)
     S. Ekeblad, M. Feldman (Spring)
1972 C. Wallace, M. Schwalb (Winter)
     P. Hollander, H. Cukoff (Spring)
1973 J. Trevis, M. Bonney (Winter)
     J. Roche, A. Levesque (Spring)
     M. Backer, L. Backer (Summer)
1974 S. Sion, J. Rosenbloom (Spring)
     W. Woodard, J. Merrill (Summer)

MASTERS MEN'S PAIRS

1967 A. Waldmann, M. Feld
1968 W. Butcher, B. Chazen
1969 R. Sidman, E. Spiegel
1970 W. Henry, J. Wadas
1971 S. Labins, C. Lamprey
1972 R. Stokey, E. Sullivan

MEN'S PAIRS

1935 E. N. Marcus, S. Green
1936 S. Wirt, H. White
1937 H. Keller, L. Goff
1938 E. N. Marcus, S. Aronson
1939 F. Edlin, N. Bonney
1940 W. M. Noble, G. Hatch
1941 L. Weiss, E. Marcus
1942 W. M. Noble, B. Ruiter
1943 F. K. Perkins, E. N. Marcus
1944 N. S. Kelly, K. P. Hill
1945 J. J. O'Donnell, A. Bell
1946 S. Wirt, R. Skinner
1947 L. Weiss, S. Aronson
1948 D. Goldschmidt, G. H. Linde
1949 J. Albert, M. Wayner
1950 W. H. Johnson, R. P. Baker
1951 F. Westcott, R. E. Starr
1952 B. Goldman, M. Casson
1953 C. Clancy, G. E. Closson

1954 R. Arthur, D. Gaudette
1955 R. Ludwig, P. Johnson
1956 R. Ludwig, P. Johnson
1957 F. Hess, T. J. Heeney
1958 D. Gaudette, C. Ruggiero
1959 H. B. Bernstrom, D. Baker
1960 S. Kantor, C. R. Greenhow
1961 M. Harris, L. Berrouard
1962 S. Labins, R. Hoffman
1963 F. Westcott, R. Starr
1964 E. C. Phillips, C. M. O'Connor (Spring)
     D. Mason, W. Passell (Fall)
1965 Dr. E. Etkind, Dr. H. F. Bunn
1966 M. Feld, B. Levin
1967 R. Lipsitz, S. Labins
1968 F. Merblum, H. Merblum
1969 H. Cohen, R. Borod
1970 R. Kehoe, B. Miller
1971 M. Rosenblatt, A. Waldmann
1972 M. Feld, J. Bennett
1974 D. Bhargava, D. Probst

MASTERS WOMEN'S PAIRS

1967 Mrs. L. T. Le Savoy, Mrs. S. Epstein
1968 G. Kransberg, E. Garfield
1969 B. Vail, W. Clark
1970 P. Jones, Mrs. S. Fromm
1971 J. Solodar, G. Moss
1972 M. Campbell, A. Cortner, *tied with*
     E. Katz, P. Riggs

WOMEN'S PAIRS

1931 E. F. Bancroft, P. Warren
1932 R. M. Kimball, C. Smith
1933 E. Bancroft, P. Warren
1934 F. J. Robinson, R. Vahey
1935 P. H. Blanding, S. B. Levy
1936 T. L. Haugen, J. F. Kutz
1937 W. B. Bacon, E. F. Bancroft
1938 N. Levine, M. Casson
1939 W. Flanders, W. S. David
1940 F. J. Robinson, E. J. Ziegler
1941 W. J. Lyons, D. Golden
1942 W. Keohane, E. Olsen
1943 H. Ansin, C. Hootstein
1944 W. Davis, W. Flanders
1945 F. Harding, F. Solomon
1946 F. Harding, F. Solomon
1948 W. Keohane, R. Skinner
1949 S. Raphael, A. Ramer
1950 W. Keohane, M. Levine
1951 L. H. Rogers, H. Stieglandt
1952 F. Harding, F. Solomon
1953 M. McCarthy, R. Hartley
1954 S. Raphael, F. Hootstein
1955 S. Johnson, R. Krupa
1956 W. Hanlon, W. Albersheim
1957 E. Silverton, L. Hummel
1958 H. Steiglandt, F. L. Rosen
1959 J. McElwain, F. Harding
1960 D. Goldman, A. Welansky
1961 W. Slutsky, A. Godfrey
1962 K. Creedon, H. Walcott
1963 J. Goldman, A. Gottlieb
1964 T. Michael, S. Johnson (Spring)
     L. Sagalyn, M. Hartley (Fall)
1965 Mrs. T. J. Dye, Mrs. E. Joiner
1966 S. Thornton, A. Roncarelli
1967 P. Prager, R. Grossman
1968 Mrs. E. Dunham, Mrs. M. Prouty
1969 E. Wynn, Mrs. A. Stone
1970 E. Garfield, M. Bright
1971 J. Cunningham, C. Weiss
1972 D. Smith, S. Smith
1974 H. Reznikoff, M. O'Neal

MIXED PAIRS

1930 A. Holt, R. Vahey
1931 K. Tufts, J. A. Farrer
1932 Mrs. J. Rock, J. A. Farrer
1933 Mrs. W. J. Lyons, E. Brown III
1934 Mrs. C. Smith, J. F. Barry
1935 Mr. and Mrs. C. C. Harvey
1936 Mrs. V. A. Hicks, J. Holden
1937 Mr. and Mrs. R. M. Kimball
1937 Mrs. W. M. Hurd, S. Weiss
1938 Mrs. N. Levine, E. N. Marcus
1938 Mrs. H. Cohn, P. McNulty
1939 Mrs. F. Harding, Dr. F. Rouillard
1939 Mr. and Mrs. B. Levin, *tied with*
     Mrs. F. Harding, Dr. F. Rouillard
1940 Mrs. R. Harvey, R. Elzholz
1940 Mr. and Mrs. M. Casson
1941 Mrs. F. Solomon, E. Marcus
1941 Mrs. F. Harding, L. Weiss
1942 A. Bell, Mrs. W. J. Lyons
1942 Mrs. F. Harding, B. Ruiter
1943 Mrs. W. M. Hurd, W. Hopkins
1943 Mr. and Mrs. N. S. Kelly
1944 Mrs. D. Golden, B. Goldman
1944 Mrs. J. B. Rooney, O. Westbury
1945 Mrs. F. Harding, L. Weiss
1945 Mr. and Mrs. M. Casson
1946 E. N. Marcus, Mrs. H. Ansin
1946 Mrs. H. Ansin, C. Goren
1947 Mrs. H. Cohn, R. Wechsler
1948 Mrs. W. Keohane, F. Westcott
1949 Mrs. C. Hootstein, S. Aronson
1950 Mrs. L. H. Rogers, B. Breitstein
1951 Mrs. W. Keohane, F. Westcott
1952 Mrs. T. G. Vail, D. Goldschmidt
1953 Mrs. T. G. Vail, W. W. Mansfield
1954 Mrs. W. Bailey, J. W. Lee
1955 I. Finlay, C. P. Davis, Jr.
1956 P. Cabral, Mrs. L. Garfield
1957 C. Graham, R. Easterbrook
1958 Mrs. F. Harding, C. Coon
1959 Mrs. W. Keohane, F. Westcott
1960 R. Ryans, D. Wynne
1961 Mrs. R. Walcott, R. S. Fox
1962 Mrs. W. J. Albersheim, C. Coon
1963 F. Johnson, R. McVey
1964 A. Cantor, A. Rich
1965 Mrs. W. J. Albersheim, C. Coon
1966 M. Rosenthal, K. Barbour
1967 M. Rosenthal, K. Barbour
1968 Col. A. Abbott, Mrs. M. Hartley
1969 E. Schwartz, W. Butcher
1970 P. Riggs, R. Rosen
1971 G. Moss, M. Moss
1972 S. Linkovsky, E. Kokish
1973 L. Roth, E. Roth
1974 M. Lehner, G. Melikan

NEW ENGLAND INDIVIDUAL

1945 K. Hill
1946 M. Channen
1947 S. Thoits
1948 M. Casson
1949 R. Fells
1950 A. Markson
1951 E. F. Abbott, Jr.
1952 R. Fox
1953 P. Weatherbee
1954 J. W. Lee
1955 A. Shaghalian
1956 K. Edmunds
1957 F. Rosen
1958 C. Farell
1959 Dr. A. Ramer
1960 E. D. Noyes
1961 J. Hunt
1962 J. Bauer
1963 H. Johnson, Jr.
1964 Dr. S. Sheiman
1965 J. Hunt
1966 M. Feld
1967 K. B. Edmunds
1968 E. Mentuck
1969 L. Weiner
1970 J. Tang
1971 D. Lenk
1972 V. Habicht
1973 D. Silberstein
1974 D. Scott

International Championships

EUROPEAN CHAMPIONSHIPS

OPEN CHAMPIONSHIPS
WINNERS   RUNNERS-UP

1932 Scheveningen, Holland

Austria	Holland
Dr. P. Stern	Dr. E. C. Goudsmit
E. Pollak	Dr. F. W. Goudsmit
L. Urvater	B. Einhorn
S. Fleischmann	G. Borel
	Dr. J. R. C. van Bemmel Suyck

1933 London, England

Austria	Holland
S. Fleischmann	Dr. E. C. Goudsmit
W. Herbert	Dr. F. W. Goudsmit
P. von Kaltenegger	B. Einhorn
E. R. H. Pollak	J. de Kuyper
Dr. P. Stern	Dr. J. R. C. van Bemmel Suyck

1934 Vienna, Austria

Hungary	Holland
E. Alpar	Dr. E. C. Goudsmit
R. Cohen	Dr. F. W. Goudsmit
L. Decsi	B. Einhorn
F. von Leitner	Dr. J. R. C. van Bemmel Suyck
A. Keleti	S. van Houton
L. Klor	L. B. Zeldenrust

1935 Brussels, Belgium

France	Hungary
Baron R. de Nexon	E. Alpar
P. Albarran	R. Cohen
A. Aron	L. Decsi
J. Broutin	G. Ferenczy
G. Rousset	L.Klor
S. Venizelos	A. Keleti

1936 Stockholm, Sweden

Austria	Hungary
H. Jellinek	E. Alpar
Dr. P. von Kaltenegger	R. Cohen
E. R. H. Pollak	L. Decsi
K. Schneider	A. Keleti
	L. Klor

1938 Oslo, Norway

Hungary	Norway
G. E. Zichy	R. Abrahamsen
E. Bokor	L. Christiansen
G. Ferenczi	R. Halle
L. Klor	R. Larssen
A. Por	J. Magnussen
Dr. L. Widder	T. Sommervelt

1939 The Hague, Holland

Sweden	Yugoslavia
R. Kock	Dr. L. Singer
J. Neumann	Dr. J. Fischer
T. Sandgren	G. Klein
E. Werner	J. Klein
	I. D. Marjanovic
	G. Stern

1948 Copenhagen, Denmark

Great Britain	Sweden
L. W. Dodds	E. Werner
K. W. Konstam	R. Kock
E. Rayne	N. Lilliehöök
B. Schapiro	J. Wohlin
T. Reese	K. Sundin
S. J. Simon	R. Wennberg
M. Harrison-Gray (capt.)	

1949 Paris, France

Great Britain	Sweden
K. W. Konstam	R. Kock
A. Meredith	E. Werner
B. Schapiro	J. Wohlin
T. Reese	N. Lilliehöök
S. J. Simon	P. Brome
M. Harrison-Gray (capt.)	J. Kjelldahl

1950 Brighton, England

Great Britain	Sweden
J. C. H. Marx	R. Kock
K. W. Konstam	E. Werner
L. W. Dodds	J. Wohlin
N. Gardener	P. Brome
L. Tarlo	J. Kjelldahl
M. Harrison-Gray (capt.)	

1951 Venice, Italy

Italy	Austria
P. Baroni	H. Eisler
E. Chiaradia	L. Gulyas
P. Forquet	H. Gruber
A. Ricci	K. Klimt
M. Franco	M. Reithoffer
G. Siniscalco	K. Schneider
C. A. Perroux (npc)	W. Marschner (npc)

1952 Dun Laoghaire, Ireland

Sweden	Italy
G. Anulf	E. Chiaradia
R. Kock	M. Franco
R. Larsen	M. Giovine
E. Werner	G. Siniscalco
N. Lilliehöök	P. Baroni
J. Wohlin	C. Zeuli
T. Ljungberg (npc)	C. Perroux (npc)

1953 Helsinki, Finland

France	Great Britain
J. Amouraben	L. Dodds
M. Kornblum	K. Konstam
Dr. F. Hervouët	N. Gardener
P. Ghestem	A. Rose
R. Schiltz	H. P. F. Swinnerton-Dyer
R. Bacherich	Mrs. A. L. Fleming
R. de Nexon (npc)	R. F. Corwen (npc)

1954 Montreux, Switzerland

Great Britain	France
L. W. Dodds	P. Jaïs
K. W. Konstam	F. Bodier
G. Schapiro	P. Figeac
T. Reese	P. J. Guerin
A. Meredith	H. Svarc
J. Pavlides	R. Trézel
R. F. Corwen (npc)	R. de Nexon (npc)

1955 Amsterdam, Holland

France	Italy
P. Jaïs	E. Chiaradia
R. Trézel	N. Sabetti
P. Ghestem	M. d'Alelio
R. Lattes	M. Franco
R. Bacherich	M. Giovine
G. Romanet	A. Ricci
R. de Nexon (npc)	Dr. P. V. Valenti (npc)

1956 Stockholm, Sweden

Italy	France
W. Avarelli	P. Ghestem
G. Belladonna	R. Bacherich
E. Chiaradia	H. Svarc
M. d'Alelio	G. Bourchtoff
P. Forquet	P. Jaïs
G. Siniscalco	R. Trézel
C. A. Perroux (npc)	R. de Nexon (npc)

1957 Vienna, Austria

Italy	Austria
W. Avarelli	Dr. M. Reithoffer
G. Belladonna	H. Eisler
E. Chiaradia	K. Klimt
M. d'Alelio	H. Hartwich
P. Forquet	Dr. Gluttig
G. Siniscalco	K. Schneider (capt.)
C. A. Perroux (npc)	

1958 Oslo, Norway

Italy	Great Britain
W. Avarelli	T. Reese
G. Belladonna	B. Schapiro
E. Chiaradia	J. Sharples
M. d'Alelio	R. Sharples
P. Forquet	M. Harrison-Gray
G. Siniscalco	A. Truscott
C. A. Perroux (npc)	R. F. Corwen (npc)

1959 Palermo, Italy

Italy	France
W. Avarelli	P. Jaïs
G. Belladonna	R. Trézel
B. Bianchi	G. Bourchtoff
R. Manca	C. Delmouly
P. Forquet	Dr. J. Pariente
E. Chiaradia	H. Svarc
C. A. Perroux (npc)	R. de Nexon (npc)

1961 Torquay, England

Great Britain	France
N. Gardener	P. Ghestem
A. Rose	R. Bacherich
C. Rodrigue	L. Malabat
K. W. Konstam	C. Deruy
R. A. Priday	J. Herschmann
A. Truscott	J. Stetten
L. Tarlo (npc)	R. de Nexon (npc)

1962 Beirut, Lebanon

France	Italy
R. Bacherich	G. Belladonna
P. Ghestem	M. d'Alelio
G. Desrousseaux	B. Bianchi
G. Theron	M. Brogi
J. Stetten	G. Messina
L. Tintner	C. Pabis Ticci
R. de Nexon (npc)	G. Pelucchi (npc)

1963 Baden-Baden, Germany

Great Britain	Italy
J. Flint	B. Bianchi
M. Harrison-Gray	G. Brogi
K. Konstam	E. Chiaradia
T. Reese	M. d'Alelio
B. Schapiro	G. Messina
J. Tarlo	C. Pabis Ticci
L. Tarlo (npc)	S. Osella (npc)

1965 Ostend, Belgium

Italy	Netherlands
P. Astolfi	M. Blitzblum
G. Belladonna	P. Boender
B. Bianchi	J. T. M. Kreyns
V. Gandolfi	C. L. Oudshoorn
G. Messina	A. Rijke
R. Mondolfo	C. Slavenburg
A. Tracanella (npc)	G. Kramer (npc)

1966 Warsaw, Poland

France	Netherlands
J. M. Boulenger	M. Cats
H. Svarc	C. Kaiser
J. M. Roudinesco	J. C. Kokkes
J. Parlente	G. Kramer
L. Tintner	J. T. M. Kreyns
J. Stetten	C. Slavenburg
R. Huni (npc)	J. Nellis (npc)

1967 Dublin, Ireland

Italy	France
G. Belladonna	H. Svarc
R. Mondolfo	J. M. Boulenger
B. Bianchi	J. Parlente
G. Messina	J. M. Roudinesco
C. Bresciani	Dr. G. Theron
O. Bellentani	G. Desrousseaux
A. Tracanella (npc)	R. Huni (npc)

1969 Oslo, Norway

Italy	Norway
G. Belladonna	E. Höie
B. Bianchi	T. Jensen
P. Frendo	K. Koppang
B. Garozzo	B. Larsen
G. Messina	A. Ström
R. Mondolfo	W. Varnäs
Barsotti (npc)	B. Baardsen (npc)

1970 Estoril, Portugal

France	Poland
J. M. Boulenger	Klapper
P. Jaïs	L. Lebioda
J. M. Roudinesco	J. Nowak
J. L. Stoppa	J. Pietruk
H. Svarc	A. Wilkosz
R. Trézel	Zimnielski
R. Huni (npc)	

1971 Athens, Greece

Italy	Great Britain
G. Belladonna	J. Cansino
B. Bianchi	C. Dixon
B. Garozzo	J. Flint
G. Messina	A. Priday
F. Meyer	C. Rodrigue
R. Mondolfo	R. Sheehan
U. Barsotti (npc)	L. Tarlo (npc)

1973 Ostend, Belgium

Italy	France
G. Belladonna	J. M. Boulenger
D. de Falco	C. Guiton
A. Franco	P. Jaïs
B. Garozzo	M. Lebel
R. Pedrini	C. Mari
A. Vivaldi	H. Svarc
S. Salvetti (npc)	C. DeRuy (npc)

1974 Herzliya, Israel

France	Italy
J. M. Boulenger	O. Bellentani
M. Lebel	B. Bianchi
F. Leenhardt	C. Bresciani
C. Mari	G. Matteucci
H. Svarc	C. Mosca
E. Vial	S. Sbarigia
R. Bacherich (npc)	U. Barsotti (npc)

1975 Brighton, England

Italy	Israel
S. Di Stefano	J. Frydrich
A. Franco	M. Hochzeit
B. Garozzo	S. Lev
O. Milani	Y. Levit
C. Mosca	P. Romik
S. Sbarigia	E. Shaufel

Women's Championships

1935 Brussels, Belgium

Austria
Mrs. G. Brunner
Mrs. M. Boschan
Mrs. E. Ernst
Mrs. G. Joseffy
Mrs. Mandl
Mrs. R. Markus

1936 Stockholm, Sweden

Austria
Mrs. G. Brunner
Mrs. M. Boschan
Mrs. E. Ernst
Mrs. G. Joseffy
Mrs. Mandl
Mrs. R. Markus

1938 Oslo, Norway

Denmark
Mrs. K. Kolle
Mrs. E. Lundsteen
Mrs. A. Hillerup
Mrs. D. Wilming

1939 The Hague, Holland

France
Mrs. Behr
Mrs. de Montaigu
Mrs. Martin
Mrs. Pouldjian

1948 Copenhagen, Denmark

Denmark
Mrs. E. Dam
Mrs. G. Kieldsen
Mrs. R. Fraenckel
Mrs. D. Wilming
Mrs. V. Thostrup

1949 Paris, France

Denmark
Mrs. D. Wilming
Mrs. R. Fraenckel
Mrs. L. Damm
Mrs. E. Dam

1950 Brighton, England

Great Britain
Mrs. N. Renshaw
Mrs. P. M. Williams
Mrs. R. Evans
Mrs. F. Gordon
Mrs. A. Crisford
Mrs. P. Carr
Col. G. J. G. Walshe (npc)

1951 Venice, Italy

Great Britain
Mrs. R. Evans
Mrs. F. Gordon
Mrs. A. L. Fleming
Mrs. R. Markus
Lady D. Rhodes
Mrs. P. M. Williams
Dr. S. Lee (npc)

1952 Dun Laoghaire, Ireland

Great Britain
Mrs. R. Evans
Mrs. F. Gordon
Mrs. A. L. Fleming
Lady D. Rhodes
Mrs. R. Markus
Mrs. P. M. Williams
E. Kempson (npc)

1953 Helsinki, Finland

France
Mrs. S. Baldon
Mrs. Devries
Mrs. G. Bourchtoff
Mrs. Morand
Mrs. M. C. de Montaigu (capt.)

1954 Montreux, Switzerland

France
Mrs. S. Baldon
Mrs. G. Bourchtoff
Mrs. Devries
Mrs. Martin
Mrs. M. C. de Montaigu
Mrs. Morand
A. Larrivoire (npc)

1955 Amsterdam, Holland

Denmark
Mrs. O. Damm
Mrs. L. Schaltz
Mrs. V. Petersen
Mrs. R. Fraenckel
Mrs. G. Skotte

1956 Stockholm, Sweden

France
Mrs. C. Bedin
Mrs. C. Martin
Mrs. Devries
Mrs. S. de Temmermann
Mrs. E. Pouldjian
Mrs. A. Sussel
A. Larrivoire (npc)

1957 Vienna, Austria

Denmark
Mrs. O. Damm
Mrs. Detlevsen
Mrs. R. Fraenckel
Mrs. V. Petersen
Mrs. G. Skotte
E. Varn (npc)

1958 Oslo, Norway

Denmark
Mrs. A. Faber
Mrs. R. Fraenckel
Mrs. G. Ljungberg
Mrs. O. Damm
Miss M. Nyholm
N. Funding (npc)

1959 Palermo, Italy

Great Britain
Mrs. F. Gordon
Mrs. A. L. Fleming
Mrs. R. Markus
Mrs. M. Whitaker
Mrs. M. Edwards
Mrs. G. E. Higginson
E. Leader-Williams (npc)

1961 Torquay, England

Great Britain
Mrs. F. Gordon
Mrs. R. Markus
Mrs. J. Juan
Miss D. Shanahan
Mrs. J. Durran
Mrs. M. Hiron
H. P. F. Swinnerton-Dyer (npc)

1962 Beirut, Lebanon

Sweden
Mrs. I. L. Larsson
Mrs. M. Rex
Mrs. R. Segander
Mrs. B. Werner
Mrs. E. Friberg
Mrs. L. Saabye-Christiansen (npc)

1963 Baden-Baden, Germany

Great Britain
Mrs. A. L. Fleming
Mrs. F. Gordon
Mrs. J. Juan
Mrs. R. Markus
Mrs. M. Moss
Miss D. Shanahan
H. Franklin (npc)

1965 Ostend, Belgium

France
Mrs. de Gailhard
Mrs. C. Martin
Mrs. A. Pouldjian
Mrs. A. Sussel
Miss S. de Temmermann
Mrs. J. Velut
M. Gadelle (npc)

1966 Warsaw, Poland

Great Britain
Mrs. J. Durran
Mrs. F. Gordon
Mrs. B. Harris
Mrs. J. Juan
Mrs. R. Markus
Miss D. Shanahan
H. Franklin (npc)

1967 Dublin, Ireland

Sweden
Mrs. G. Blom
Mrs. G. Jarpner
Miss M. Moore
Mrs. R. Segander
Mrs. G. Silborn
Mrs. B. Werner
Mrs. L. Saabye (npc)

1969 Oslo, Norway

France
Mrs. C. Brochot
Mrs. M. Devries
Mrs. M. Kitabji
Mrs. M. Serf
Mrs. A. Sussell
Miss S. de Temmermann
C. Delmouly (npc)

1970 Estoril, Portugal

Italy
Mrs. M. Bianchi
Mrs. R. Jabes
Mrs. A. Robaudo
Mrs. L. Romanelli
Mrs. A. Valenti
Mrs. M. Venturini
G. Pelucchi (npc)

1971 Athens, Greece

Italy
Mrs. M. Bianchi
Mrs. R. Jabes
Mrs. A. Robaudo
Mrs. L. Romanelli
Mrs. A. Valenti
Mrs. M. Venturini
G. Pelucchi (npc)

1973 Ostend, Belgium

Italy
Mrs. M. Bianchi
Mrs. L. Canessa
Mrs. R. Jabes
Mrs. A. Robaudo
Mrs. A. Valenti
Mrs. M. Venturini
G. Pelucchi (npc)

1974 Herzliya, Israel

Italy
Mrs. M. Bianchi
Mrs. L. Capodanno
Mrs. M. Dandrea
Mrs. R. Jabes
Mrs. A. Robaudo
Mrs. A. Valenti
G. Pelucchi (npc)

1975 Brighton, England

Great Britain
Mrs. C. Esterson
Miss N. Gardener
Mrs. F. Gordon
Mrs. S. Landy
Mrs. R. Markus
Mrs. R. Oldroyd
G. Cook (npc)

FAR EAST CHAMPIONSHIPS
OPEN WINNERS

1957 Manila, Philippines

Philippines
S. Chua
A. Zamora
L. da Silva
R. Yap
C. Ballesteros
F. Leung

1958 Tokyo, Japan

Philippines
J. J. Reyes
S. Chua
L. da Silva
R. Hernandez
A. Teehankee
V. Reyes
S. A. Tuason (npc)

1959 Taipei, Formosa

Hong Kong
Y. T. Fong
L. A. Ozorio
H. Kuai
V. Zirinsky
G. Tsiang
Y. M. Chu
D. Miao (npc)

1960 Hong Kong

Hong Kong
Y. T. Fong
L. A. Ozorio
W. Wong
D. Chen
H. Kuai
A. Ouan
D. Miao (npc)

1961 Bangkok, Thailand

Thailand
K. Suchartkul
S. Nandhabiwat
T. Sudasna
E. R. Gaan
S. Unakul
K. W. Shen
T. Raenkham (npc)

1962 Manila, Philippines

Indonesia
O. K. Hian
T. H. San
M. W. Haznam
Djanwar
T. O. Gie
T. K. Say
S. B. Hwei (npc)

1963 Taipei, Formosa

Thailand
K. Suchartkul
B. Nantaterm
U. Isrankul
S. Nandhabiwat
M. Veeraburns
B. Gimkiewicz
S. Sirisuay (npc)

OPEN WINNERS   WOMEN'S WINNERS

1964 Tokyo, Japan

Indonesia
L. H. Po
B. Hutagalung
P. Sanbudhi
K. Sudianto
J. A. Fransz
O. T. Goan
F. J. Inkiriwang (npc)

Thailand
Mrs. S. Chang
Mrs. G. Huang
Mrs. P. Pibulsonggram
Mrs. C. Sooksawasdi

1965 Hong Kong

Thailand
K. Suchartkul
A. Boonsupa
M. Veeraburus
V. Rasmidatta
P. Narabhallobh
U. Israngkul

Malaysia
Mrs. G. Loh
Mrs. L. Lim
Mrs. R. G. Fraser
Mrs. G. W. Arnott
Mrs. S. Bradley
Mrs. D. Peddie

1966 Bangkok, Thailand

Thailand
K. W. Shen
B. Gimkiewicz
E. R. Gaan
S. Nandhabiwat
S. Pothisuwan
P. Vanigbandhu
Dr. M. Suebsaeng (npc)

Thailand
Mrs. S. Chang
Mrs. G. Huang
Mrs. M. Dibavadi
Mrs. I. Chandarasomboon
Mrs. C. Sooksawasdi
Mrs. P. Pibulsonggram
Lt. A. Boonsupa (npc)

1967 Manila, Philippines

Republic of China
Y. J. Hsi
M. F. Tai
K. H. Huang
H. T. Lin
C. W. Liaw
C. C. Wei (npc)

Philippines
Mrs. M. Cacho
Mrs. H. Small
Miss R. Cacho
Miss I. Tubangui
Miss H. Tubangui
Mrs. M. Yu
W. Wong (npc)

1968 Kuala Lumpur, Malaysia

Australia
J. Rothfield
N. Rothfield
T. Seres
R. Smilde
W. Scott
J. Borin

Philippines
Mrs. C. LaGuardia
Mrs. L. Galpert
Mrs. C. Palmer
Mrs. P. Tuason
Mrs. I. Tubangui
S. Tuason (npc)

1969 Taipei, Taiwan

Republic of China
K. Cheng
V. Chow
C. Hsoia
P. Huang
C. Lee
M. Tai

1970 _____

Australia
R. Klinger
M. McMahon
J. Rothfield
T. Seres
R. Smilde

1971 Melbourne, Australia

Republic of China
C. Chen
C. Cheng
C. Huang
H. Lin
C. Lu
M. Tai

1972 Singapore

Indonesia
M. Aguw
J. Fransz
H. Lasut
F. Manoppo
M. Manoppo
E. Najoan
D. Sacul
F. Walujan
D. Masengri (npc)

1973 Hong Kong

Indonesia

Australia
F. Beale
R. Eaton
G. Stern
W. Lipscomb
M. McMahon
G. Tabak
H. Rosendorff (npc)

1974 Manila, Philippines

Indonesia

Australia
P. Brown
R. Eaton
G. Stern
W. Lipscomb
M. McMahon
E. Poulsen
H. Rosendorff (npc)

SOUTH AMERICAN CHAMPIONSHIPS

OPEN WINNERS   WOMEN'S WINNERS

1948 Buenos Aires, Argentina

Argentina
R. Argerich
A. J. Blousson
C. Cabanne
A. Castro
C. Ottolenghi
L. Schenone

Argentina
C. M. de Basavilbaso
J. M. de Crámer
C. de Luro
S. R. de Piacentini
E. S. de Vergara
M. Guerrico

1949 São Paulo and Rio de Janeiro, Brazil

Brazil	Argentina
M. Alvarenga	E. S. de Vergara
M. de Couver	M. Guerrico
R. Cusano	
A. Figueredo	
A. Frugoli	
S. Leite Ribeiro	
R. Reis	
N. Schloman	
A. Taubkin	
A. Trompowsky	
U. Viana	

1950 Montevideo, Uruguay

Argentina	Argentina
C. Cabanne	I. M. G. de Casado
F. de Corral	M. Guerrico
A. Olmedo	E. Pérez Mendoza
J. Quesada	M. E. Quesada
M. Ugarte	

1951 Santiago, Chile

Chile	Argentina
A. Aguero	I. M. G. de Casado
A. Carrasco	M. L. V. de Mihura
C. Doren	E. S. de Vergara
J. Guzmán	E. C. de Vidal
A. Herrera	
J. Ovalle	
J. Suárez	
J. Subercasseaux	

1953 Punta del Este, Uruguay

Argentina	Argentina
R. Argerich	I. M. G. de Casado
C. Cabanne	M. L. V. de Mihura
A. Castro	E. S. de Vergara
A. Olmedo	M. Guerrico
L. Schenone	E. Pérez Mendoza
	L. Vivot

1954 São Paulo, Brazil

Argentina	Brazil
M. A. Benedit	F. Estella
C. Cabanne	D. Machado
A. Castro	S. Salles Godoy
H. Crámer	L. Stefani
C. F. Dibar	L. Vasconcellos
A. Gabarret	M. Villalobos

1955 Buenos Aires, Argentina

Brazil	Brazil
E. Amaral	M. Farias
M. Alvarenga	E. L. Dos Santos
L. Decsi	D. Machado
N. Mandler	R. F. de Mello
J. Murtinho	L. Stefani
C. Souto	L. Vasconcellos

1956 Lima, Peru

Brazil	Brazil
M. Alvarenga	M. Farias
M. Giorgetti	E. L. Dos Santos
C. L. Pereira de Sousa	D. Machado
N. Mandler	L. Stefani
N. Martins Ferreira	L. Vasconcellos
J. Murtinho	

1957 Santiago, Chile

Argentina	Argentina
A. J. Blousson	I. M. G. de Casado
C. Cabanne	M. E. C. de Rodrigué
A. Castro	E. S. de Vergara
H. Crámer	E. Pérez Mendoza
M. Lerner	M. E. Quesada
A. Olmedo	L. Vivot

1958 Punta del Este, Uruguay

Argentina	Brazil
A. Berisso	S. Godoy
A. J. Blousson	E. L. Dos Santos
A. Castro	E. Rodrigues
C. F. Dibar	R. Schmieder
A. Jaques	L. Siqueira
C. Ottolenghi	L. Stefani

1959 Santos, Brazil

Argentina	Brazil
A. Berisso	S. Almeida
D. Blum	M. Faria
C. Cabanne	R. Figueira de Mello
R. Calvente	D. Machado
A. Jaques	R. Petzold
E. Rocchi	L. Vasconcellos

1961 Lima, Peru

Argentina	Argentina
L. Attaguile	I. M. G. de Casado
A. Berisso	M .E. C. de Rodrigué
C. Cabanne	M. G. de Schenone
R. Calvente	E. S. de Vergara
A. Jaques	E. Pérez Mendoza
E. Rocchi	M. E. Quesada

1962 Buenos Aires, Argentina

Argentina	Argentina
L. Attaguile	I. M. G. de Casado
A. Berisso	M .E. C. de Rodrigué
D. Blum	M. G. de Schenone
C. Cabanne	E. S. de Vergara
A. Santamarina	M. T. P. de Espinosa Paz
M. Santamarina	M. E. Quesada

1963 Caracas, Venezuela

Venezuela	Peru
E. Lloynaz	P. de Alaez
M. Gonzalez-Vale	E. de Bozzo
M. Onorati	M. de Foccaci
M. Straziota	E. de Carbone
R. Rossignol	Z. de Fleischman
D. A. Berah	A. de Isnardi
R. Benaim (npc)	

1964 Montevideo and Punta del Este, Uruguay

Argentina	Argentina
L. Attaguile	E. C. de Aguirre
D. Blum	I. M. G. de Casado
C. Cabanne	A. N. de Engel
E. Rocchi	H. S. de Lippstadt
A. Santamarina	E. S. de Vergara
A. Saravia	M. E. Quesada

1965 Santiago, Chile

Venezuela	Brazil
R. Benaim	S. Jung
D. Berah	N. Miranda Jordao
M. Onorati	Y. Paez de Barros
R. Rossignol	V. Sampaio
R. Straziota	L. Sequeira
F. Vernon	L. Vasconcellos

1966 São Paulo, Brazil

Venezuela	Brazil
R. Benaim	T. Chammas
D. Berah	M. Faría
E. Loynaz	M. E. Miranda Jordao
R. Romanelli	R. Figueira de Mello
R. Rossignol	S. Salles Godoy
F. Vernon	D. Vasconcellos

tied with
Uruguay
M. Brito del Pino
L. P. de Castillo
E. M. de Ham
R. D. de Methol
B. Philipstal
E. M. G. de Zumarán

1967 Lima, Peru

Brazil	Uruguay
P. P. Assumpção	M. Brito del Pino
M. Giorgetti	L. P. de Castillo
G. Golefarb	E. M. de Ham
E. Nahmias	R. D. de Methol
G. Pinheiro Chagas Filho	B. Philipstal
A. Porto D'Ave Filho	E. M. G. de Zumarán

1968 Bogota, Colombia

Brazil	Colombia
M. Castelo Branco	A. Echeverri González
R.Figueira de Mello	M. Marulanda de Ferrer
D. Martims Coutinho	M. O. Vélez de Hortet
P. P. Assumpção	M. C. Rivas de Rivas
G. Pinheiro Chagas Filho	A. Pinzón de Soto
A. Porto D'Ave Filho	E. Osorio de Vélez
P. S. Brun (npc)	R. Escovar (npc)

1969 Buenos Aires, Argentina

Brazil	Peru
P. P. Assumpção	M. D. de Denegri
P. P. de Barros	Z. de Fleischman
E. Bastos	B. de Magnani
P. P. Branco	E. de Piana
G. Chagas	A. de Plucker
S. Ferreira	P. de Velarde

1970 Caracas, Venezuela

Brazil	Colombia
E. Amaral	T. de Mandowsky
P. P. Assumpção	R. de Nunez
G. Chagas	M. de Prieto
G. Cintra	M. C. R. de Rivas
C. Fonseca	A. P. de Soto
T. Kenedi	O. de Zuloaga

1971 Montevideo, Uruguay

Brazil	Uruguay
P. P. Assumpção	E. M. de Ham
A. D'Ave	R. D. de Methol
S. Barbosa	M. C. A. de Meyer
M. Branco	M. B. del Pino
O. de Faria	B. Philipsthal
C. Fonseca	L. de Pineyruá

1972 Santiago, Chile

Brazil	Brazil
P. P. Assumpção	L. Cintra
M. Branco	G. Leal
P. P. Branco	D. Machado
G. Chagas	M. E. Murtinho
G. Cintra	M. H. de Oliveira
C. Fonseca	D. Vasconcellos
A. D'Ave (npc)	

1973 Rio de Janeiro, Brazil

Brazil	Brazil
P. P. Assumpção	L. Cintra
M. Branco	S. Fujihura
P. P. Branco	G. Garmegna
G. Chagas	L. M. Gil
G. Cintra	M. E. Murtinho
C. Fonseca	H. Nogueira

1974 Lima, Peru

Brazil	Uruguay
M. Amaral	V. B. de Beer
P. P. Assumpção	R. D. de Methol
P. P. de Barros	M. C. A. de Meyer
G. Chagas	M. B. del Pino
N. Ferreira	B. Philipsthal
S. Ferreira	L. de Pineyruá

KEY: Many thousands of books have been written on bridge; this bibliography attempts to list those which have permanent value, under fifteen subdivisions; in this category the books are listed alphabetically, by author. All publishers, unless otherwise indicated, are American. Where there has been more than one edition, the earliest and latest dates are given.

A HISTORY Whist, Bridge, and Auction Bridge	G MATCH AND TOURNAMENT RECORDS
B ANTHOLOGIES	H HAND COLLECTIONS
C BIDDING (including Systems)	J PROBLEMS, QUIZZES, and PUZZLES
D PLAY	K BIOGRAPHY
E BIDDING AND PLAY (in combination)	L HUMOR AND POETRY
F DUPLICATE BRIDGE (Bidding, Play, and Tournament Directing)	M MATHEMATICS
	N LAWS

Books of historic significance and books of importance for the purposes of a modern technical bridge library have been separately indentified as follows:

* Books marked thus made a major contribution to the technical development of the game.

† Books marked thus are optional requirements for a modern technical bridge library.

‡ Books marked thus are mandatory requirements for a modern technical bridge library.

AUTHOR	TITLE	PUBLISHER	PAGES	DATES

A HISTORY Whist, Bridge, and Auction Bridge

AUTHOR	TITLE	PUBLISHER	PAGES	DATES
Benham	Playing Cards: History of the Pack	Ward, Lock (London & Melbourne)	196	1931
		Spring Books		1957
Bullet	Recherches Historiques sur les Cartes à Jouer	J. Deville (Lyons)	166	1757
Burney	*Treatise on the Game of Whist	Thos. & Wm. Boone	87	1823
Cavendish (Henry Jones)	Card Essays and Card Table Talk	Thos. De La Rue (London)	260	1879
Cavendish (Henry Jones)	*Cavendish on Whist	De La Rue	320	1863
Chatto	Facts and Speculations on the Origin and History of Playing Cards	John Russell Smith (London)	343	1848
Cotton	Compleat Gamester			1674
Dalton, W.	Auction Bridge up to Date	Saturday Bridge	210	1906–08
Deschapelles	Traité du Whiste	Perrotin (Paris)		1840
Elwell	*Advanced Bridge	Scribner's	207	1904
Elwell	Elwell on Bridge	Scribner's	136	1902–11
Elwell	*Auction Bridge	Scribner's		1912
Ferguson, W.	Auction Bridge	Davison	64	1915–29
Foster	Foster on Auction	Dutton	300	1920–26
Foster	Foster's Bridge Manual	Brentano's	200	1903
Foster	Foster's Whist Manual	Brentano's	168	1890–1904
Hargrave	A History of Playing Cards	Houghton Mifflin	468	1930
		Dover (Paperback)	462	1966
Hoyle	*A Short Treatise on the Game of Whist	T. Osborne (London)	86	1743–50
Kaiser	British Playing Card Stamp Duties, etc.	American Philatelic Society	64	1960
Kolb	Old Playing Cards, 15th to 19th Century	Hungaria (Budapest)	84	1940
Lenz	*Lenz on Bridge	Simon & Schuster	379	1926
Lenz, Rendel	How's Your Bridge?	Simon & Schuster		1929
Mathews	*Advice to the Young Whist Player	Meyler & Son (England)	64	1819
Payne	*Maxims for Playing the Game of Whist with All Necessary Calculations	Payne & Son (England)	67	1777
Pole	Evolution of Whist	Longmans (London & NYC)	269	1895
Pole	*Philosophy of Whist	Longmans	144	1883
Portland and Arlington Clubs	The Laws and Principles of Whist	Portland and Arlington Clubs	139	1873–98
Portland (James Hogg)	The Whist Table	John Hogg (London)	472	1894
Reith	*The Art of Successful Bidding	Doubleday	227	1928

AUTHOR	TITLE	PUBLISHER	PAGES	DATES
Rendel (see Lenz)	*How's Your Bridge?*			
Seymour	*The Court Gamester*	Curll & Wilford (London)	94	1734
Shepard	*Expert Auction*	Harper & Bros.	245	1913–16
Shepard	*Scientific Auction Bridge*	Harper & Bros.	241	1913–14
Singer	*Researches into the History of Playing Cards*	Robert Triphook (London)	378	1816
Tiley	*A History of Playing Cards*	Crown	192	—
Whitehead	**Auction Bridge Standards*	Stokes	314	1918
Whitehead	*Whitehead's Conventions of Auction Bridge*	Stokes	243	1914
Work	**Auction Bridge Complete*	J. C. Winston	500	1913–28

B ANTHOLOGIES

AUTHOR	TITLE	PUBLISHER	PAGES	DATES
Cole, Edwards	*Grand Slam*	Putnam	224	1975
Edwards (see Cole)	*Grand Slam*			
Frey	*Bridge for Women*	Doubleday	221	1967
		Funk & Wagnalls	224	1970
Goren	*Bridge Is My Game: Lessons of a Lifetime*	Doubleday	190	1965
Goren	*The Sports Illustrated Book of Bridge*	Time, Inc.	520	1961
Hart	*The Bridge Players' Bedside Book*	Eyre & Spottiswoode (London)	160	1939
Hervey	*The Bridge Players' Bedside Book*	Faber & Faber (London)	116	1964
Jacoby, Morehead	*Fireside Book of Cards*	Simon & Schuster	365	1957
Jaïs, Le Dentu, Truscott	*L'Aristocratie du Bridge*	Balland (Paris)	317	1973
Le Dentu (see Jaïs)	*L'Aristocratie du Bridge*			
Le Dentu	*Bridge à La Une*	Fayard (Paris)	428	1965
Le Dentu	*‡Championship Bridge* (trans. by A. Truscott and A. Kearse)	Harper & Row	308	1974
Mackey	*The Walk of the Oysters*	W. H. Allen (London)	197	1964
Mollo	*Bridge Immortals*	Faber & Faber (London)	191	1967
		Hart	191	1968
Morehead (see Jacoby)	*Fireside Book of Cards*			
Olsen	*Mad World of Bridge*	Holt, Rinehart & Winston	239	1960
Ostrow	*Bridge Player's Bedside Companion*	Prentice-Hall	391	1956
Truscott (see Jaïs)	*L'Aristocratie du Bridge*			

C BIDDING (including Systems)

AUTHOR	TITLE	PUBLISHER	PAGES	DATES
Anderson (see Wolf)	*The Subtle Club*			
Avarelli (see Belladonna)	*Roman Club System of Distributional Bidding*			
Baron, Meredith	**Baron System of Contract Bridge*	Contract Bridge Equipment Co. (Leeds)	160	1948
Barrow (see Cohen, B.)	*Acol Without Tears*			
Barton	*Barton System*	Little & Ives	80	1934
Beasley	*Beasley Contract Bridge System*	Assoc. Newspapers (London) Morrison & Gibbs (London)	128	1935
Belladonna, Avarelli	**Roman Club System of Distributional Bidding*	Simon & Schuster	162	1959
Belladonna, Garozzo	*‡Precision and Super Precision*	Putnam	237	1975
Belladonna (see Wei)	*Summary of Super Precision*			
Bissell	*Bissell System: Distributional Method of Bidding*	Columbia U. Press	316	1936
Blackwood	*Blackwood on Bidding*	Bobbs-Merrill	215	1956
Blackwood	*Blackwood on Slams*	Prentice-Hall	160	1970
Blackwood, Wallace	**Blackwood Slam Bidding*	Bruelheide	64	1941
Boland, Law	*Accurate Contract Bidding*	Barrie Books (London)	84	1931
Bose Mullick	*The Relay Club*	Allied (Bombay)	344	1975
Brannon	*The Incomparable Club Convention*	New Press (Charlotte, N.C.)	88	1935
Brown	*Bidding Craft*	Duckworth (London)	133	1962
Budin, Kornfeld	*Bridge Players Digest of Conventions*	Budin Press	32	1962
Burnstine (see Four Aces)	*Four Aces System of Contract Bridge*			
Burnstine	*The Four Horsemen's One-over-One Method of Contract Bidding*	Walter J. Black, Inc.	118	1932
Butler, Stern	*Two Clubs System of Bidding*	Faber & Faber (London)	300	1946
Churchill, Ferguson	**Contract Bidding Tactics at Match Point Play*	Ad Press	323	1936
Coffin	*Acol and the New Point Count*	Duckworth (London)	56	1953
Coffin	*Natural Big Club*	Coffin	192	1969
Coffin	*The Weak No Trump*	Eaton Press (Mass.)	32	1956
Coffin	*Winning Duplicate*	B. Humphries	146	1933
Cohen, B., Barrow	*Acol Without Tears*	Allen & Unwin (London)	287	1961
Cohen, B., Reese	**Acol System of Contract Bridge*	Contract Bridge Equipment Co. (Leeds)	127	1938–56
Cohen, L., Katz, Sundby	*†Breakthrough in Bridge*	Breakthrough Enterprises	175	1974
Courtenay	*Standardized Code of Contract Bridge Bidding*	Bridge Headquarters	107	1937
Courtenay	**The System the Experts Play*	Bridge Headquarters	176	1935
Crane	*Crane System of Modern Contract Bidding*	East Anglian Daily Times (London)	107	1948
Criticus	*Contract Simplicitas*	Jenkins, Ltd. (London)	332	1933
Crowhurst	*Precision Bidding in Acol*	Pelham (London)	240	1974
Culbertson, E.	**Contract Bridge Blue Book*	Bridge World	599	1930
Culbertson, E.	*Culbertson's Summary*	Bridge World	64	1931
Culbertson, E.	*Point Count Bidding*	J. C. Winston	171	1952
Disbrow (see Solomon)	*Slam Bidding and Point Count*			

AUTHOR	TITLE	PUBLISHER	PAGES	DATES
Dormer (see Reese)	The Acol System Today			
	Blueprint for Bidding (American title)			
Dormer	†Powerhouse Hands	Prentice-Hall	223	1975
Drury	The Drury Two Club Convention		46	1969
Duncan	New Dimension Bidding in Contract Bridge	Robert B. Luce Inc.	308	1963
Eastgate, McKillop	Modern Gladiator System	Whitcombe & Tomes		
		(New Zealand)	67	
Ewen	‡Doubles for Takeout, Penalties and Profit	Prentice-Hall	278	1973
Ewen	‡Preemptive Bidding	Prentice-Hall	162	1975
Feldheim	†Weak Two-Bid in Bridge	Barclay Bridge Supplies	105	1971–73
Ferguson (see Churchill)	Contract Bidding Tactics at Match Point Play			
Fishbein	Fishbein Convention	Crown	83	1960
Forquet (see Garozzo)	The Italian Blue Team Bridge Book			
Foss	*Simplified Contract Bidding	Gane & Son	67	1935
Four Aces	*Four Aces System of Contract Bridge	Random House	302	1935
Fox	Sound Bidding at Contract	E. Arnold (London)	254	1954
Frey (see Four Aces)	Four Aces System of Contract Bridge			
Garozzo (see Belladonna)	Precision and Super Precision			
Garozzo, Forquet	‡The Italian Blue Team	Grosset & Dunlap	292	1970
Garozzo (see Wei)	Summary of Super Precision			
Garozzo, Yallouze	†The Blue Club	Faber & Faber (London)	170	1970
Gerber	*The Four Club Bid: a Slam Convention	Texas Bridge	28	1942
Goldman	†Aces Scientific	Goldman	250	1973
Goren	Advanced Bidding: A Tutor Text	Doubleday	342	1963
Goren	Goren Settles the Bridge Arguments	Hart	429	1974
Goren	The Italian Bridge System	Doubleday	216	1958
Goren	*†Point Count Bidding	Simon & Schuster	154	1951
Goren	†The Precision System	Doubleday	228	1971
Goren	Standard Book of Bidding	Doubleday	308	1944
Gottlieb (see Four Aces)	Four Aces System of Contract Bridge			
Hanna, Steen	Precision Power Bidding: the Bulldog System	Coffin	104	1956
Hardy	†Five Card Majors, Western Style	Hardy	94	1974
Hart (see Kempson)	Quintessence of CAB			
Hart (see Stern)	Vienna System of Contract Bridge			
Hayden	†Bid Better, Play Better	Harper & Row	196	1966
		Award Books		1967
Heath	*Seven-Eleven: A Manual of the Heath System	McDonald & Co.	55	1933
Ingram	Ingram One Club	Eyre & Spottiswoode (London)	96	1935
Jacoby (see Four Aces)	Four Aces System of Contract Bridge			
Jacoby	Point Count Bidding Made Easy	Arco	31	
Jacoby	What's New in Bridge	Hanover House	158	1954
Jannersten	†Precision Bridge	Allen-Unwin (London)	224	1972
Kantar	†Bridge Bidding Made Easy	Wilshire Books	256	1972
Kantar	‡Bridge Conventions	Wilshire Books	124	1972
Kaplan	†Competitive Bidding in Modern Bridge	Fleet	192	1965
Kaplan	*†Complete Italian System of Winning Bridge	Washburn	159	1959
Kaplan	Kaplan Sheinwold Updated	Bridge World	42	1973
Kaplan, Sheinwold	*‡How to Play Winning Bridge: Kaplan-	Fleet	256	1958–63
	Sheinwold System	Collier	224	1962
Karpin	*Karpin Point Count System	Kaufman (Washington, D.C.)	89	1949
Katz (see Cohen, L.)	Breakthrough in Bridge			
Kelsey	Slam Bidding	Faber & Faber (London)	200	1973
Kempson, Hart	Quintessence of CAB	Nicholas Kaye (London)	160	1959
Kennedy	The Kennedy System of Bridge	Arco	281	1965
Kushner	T.N.T. System of Bidding			
Law (see Boland)	Accurate Contract Bidding			
Lea	Bridge Is Easy with the Lea System	R. H. Lea	194	1965
Lederer	*Lederer Bids Two Clubs	Williams & Moregate (London)	220	1934
Lenz	My System of Contract Bridge	Simon & Schuster	93	1930
McKillop (see Eastgate)	Modern Gladiator System			
Meredith (see Baron)	Baron System of Contract Bridge			
Miller	Point Count Bidding	R. A. Miller	32	1947
Mollo	Bridge: Modern Bidding	Faber & Faber (London)	124	1961
Mollo	*†Streamlined Bridge: or Bidding	Christopher Johnson		
	Without Tears	(London)	256	1947
Monk	Le Bridge: Système Complet des	Albin Michel (Paris)	276	1970
	Enchères Modernes			
Morehead	*‡Morehead on Bidding	Macmillan	374	1964
Morehead	‡Morehead on Bidding (Frey ed.)	Simon & Schuster	447	1974
Mott-Smith	Contract Bridge and Advanced Auction Bidding	Minton, Balch	281	1927
Mundy	The Direct British System of Contract Bidding	Rich & Cowan	176	1932
Nail, Stucker	Revolution in Bridge	Naylor	325	1965
Noall	Contract Bridge: Australian One Club	Angus & Robertson (Sydney)	109	1959
	System			
Perkins	Simplified Contract Standards	Coffin	80	1939
Reese	‡Develop Your Bidding Judgement	Sterling	254	1962
		Cornerstone	192	1964
Reese	Modern Bidding and the Acol System	Nicolson & Watson (London)	128	1952–60
Reese (see Cohen)	Acol System of Contract Bridge			
Reese, Dormer	*‡The Acol System Today	E. Arnold (London)	163	1961
	*‡Blueprint for Bidding (American title)	Sterling		1962

AUTHOR	TITLE	PUBLISHER	PAGES	DATES
Reith	*Contract*	John Day	250	1929
Reith	*Contract Bidding*	John Day	37	1930
Reith	*One over One System of Contract Bidding*	Knickerbocker	50	1932
Root	*Introduction to Bidding*	Prentice-Hall	151	1967
Rosenkranz	*The Romex System of Bidding*	World Publishing	325	1970
Rosenkranz	†*Win with Romex*	Crown	420	1975
Roth	*Roth-Stone System*	Melville	176	1953
Roth, Rubens	†*Modern Bridge Bidding Complete*	Funk & Wagnalls	512	1968
Roth, Stone	*‡Bridge Is a Partnership Game: the Roth-Stone System*	Dutton	237	1958
Rubens (see Roth)	*Modern Bidding Complete*			
Sapire	*Accurate Slam Bidding at Contract (Asking Bids)*	Bridge World	63	
Schenken	*‡Better Bidding in Fifteen Minutes*	Simon & Schuster	192	1963
Schenken (see Four Aces)	*Four Aces System of Contract Bridge*			
Schenken	*‡Howard Schenken's Big Club*	Simon & Schuster	224	1968
Sharif	*How to Play the Blue Team Club*	Stancraft Products	48	1970
Sheinwold (see Kaplan)	*Kaplan-Sheinwold System of Winning Bridge*			
Silodor	*Silodor Says*	Pageant Press	240	1952
Simon	*Design for Bidding*	Nicolson & Watson (London)	268	1949
Sims, D.	*Psychic Bidding*	Vanguard Press	87	1932
Sims, P. H.	*Master Contract*	Simon & Schuster	348	1934
Sims, P. H.	*Money Contract*	Simon & Schuster	246	1932
Smith, C.	*Bidding Through Logic*	Houston (Tex.)	185	1962
Smith (see Stern)	*Vienna System of Contract Bridge*			
Solomon	*No Trump Bidding*	7 Stars (N.J.)	49	1946
Solomon, Disbrow	*Slam Bidding and Point Count*	Macrae Smith	281	1951
Squire	*Bidding at Bridge*	Penguin (London)	191	1965
Squire	*Guide to Bridge Conventions*	Duckworth (London)	138	1958
Squire	*†Theory of Bidding*	Duckworth (London)	280	1957
Stayman	*Complete Staymen System of Contract Bidding*	Rinehart	233	1956
Stayman	*‡Do You Play Stayman?*	Odyssey	207	1965
Stayman	*Expert Bidding at Contract Bridge*	Wellington	144	1951
Stayman	*Highroad to Winning Bridge*	Cornerstone Library	192	1970
Steen (see Hanna)	*Precision Power Bidding: the Bulldog System*			
Stern	*Stern Austrian System*	Harrap (London)	192	1938
Stern (see Butler)	*Two Club System of Bidding*			
Stern, Hart, Smith	*Vienna System of Contract Bridge*	Jenkinson	249	1948
Stone (see Roth)	*Bridge Is a Partnership Game*			
Stucker (see Nail)	*Revolution in Bridge*			
Sundby (see Cohen, L.)	*Breakthrough in Bridge*			
Vanderbilt	†*The Club Convention*	Scribner's	186	1964
Vanderbilt	*Contract Bridge: Bidding and the Club Convention*	Scribner's	251	1929
Von der Porten	*Introduction to Defensive Bidding*	Prentice-Hall	151	1967
Wallace (see Blackwood)	*Blackwood Slam Bidding*			
Walshe	*Count to Win at Bridge*	E. Benn (London)	147	1948
Walshe	*Let's Play Cab*	Methuen (London)	71	1945
Wei	*Bidding Precisely*	Precision Headquarters	210	1974
Wei	†*Precision Bidding in Bridge*	Barclay Bridge Supplies	112	1969
Wei	*Simplified Precision Bridge*	Precision Headquarters	64	1972
Wei, Belladonna, Garozzo	*Summary of Super Precision*	Precision Headquarters	28	1974
Weiss	*Contract Bridge: The Bidding Structure*	Garden Press	376	1942
Wolf, Anderson	*The Subtle Club*	Wand Books	187	1974
Woodson	*Woodson Electronic Bidding System*	Greensboro Printing (N.C.)	63	1958
Woodson	*Woodson Two-Way No Trump*	Greensboro Printing (N.C.)	31	1953
Work	*The Official System of Contract Bridge*	J. C. Winston	235	1931
Yallouze (see Garozzo)	*The Blue Club*			

D PLAY

AUTHOR	TITLE	PUBLISHER	PAGES	DATES
Andersson, Coffin	†*Sure Tricks*	David McKay	255	1950
Barrow (see Cohen)	*Opening Leads to Better Bridge*			
	Your Lead, Partner			
Bellanger, Roussière	*Les Impasses du Bridge: Étude Scientifique et Solutions Pratiques d'après une Théorie Nouvelle*	Librairie Plon (Paris)	424	1936
Brown	*‡Winning Defense*	Duckworth (London)	343	1952–60
Brown	*Winning Tricks*	Duckworth (London)	300	1947
Cioffi	*Bridge Endings*	Coffin	127	1953
Coffin	†*Bridge Play Four Classics*	Coffin	960	1975
Coffin	*Bridge Play from A to Z*	Faber & Faber (London)	352	1954
Coffin	*Double Dummy Bridge*	Coffin	192	1967
Coffin	*End Plays*	Duckworth (London)	212	1950
Coffin (see Andersson)	*Sure Tricks*			
Cohen, Barrow	*Opening Leads to Better Bridge*	A. S. Barnes & Co	96	1964
	Your Lead, Partner	Allen & Unwin (London)	96	1963
Cohen, R.	*Elements of Play*	Barclay	63	1958
Courtenay	*Standard Manual on Play*	Methuen (London)	95	1938
Culbertson	*Contract Bridge Red Book on Play*	J. C. Winston	616	1934

AUTHOR	TITLE	PUBLISHER	PAGES	DATES
Culbertson	*How to Lead and Play: Self Instructor*	Bridge World	64	1934
Eng	‡*Bridge Squeezes Illustrated*	Eng	185	1973
England, Reford	*The Play of the Cards*	De La Rue (London)	223	1934
Ewen	*‡*Opening Leads*	Prentice-Hall	236	1970
Flint, North	*Match Your Skill against the Masters*	Stein & Day	208	1972
Freehill	*The Squeeze at Bridge*	Faber & Faber (London)	126	1946
Gardener (see Mollo)	*Card Play Technique*			
Goren	*Better Bridge for Better Players*	Doubleday	538	1942
Goren	‡*Play and Defense*	Doubleday	489	1974
Hathorn (see Nail)	*How to Play the Hand*			
Hayden	*Winning Declarer Play*	Harper & Row	280	1969
Jannersten	†*Cards on the Table*	Allen-Unwin (London)	207	1972
	Card Reading (American title)	Hart	207	1972
Kantar	‡*Complete Defensive Bridge Play*	Wilshire Books	528	1974
Kantar, Stanley	*Gamesman Bridge*	Liveright	177	1972
Kantar	*Introduction to Declarer's Play*	Prentice-Hall	160	1967
Kantar	*Introduction to Defender's Play*	Prentice-Hall	160	1968
Kantar	*Test Your Bridge Play*	Wilshire Books	201	1974
Karpin	†*The Art of Card Reading*	Harper & Row	232	1973
Karpin	‡*The Finesse*	Prentice-Hall	273	1972
Karpin	*How to Play and Misplay Slam Contracts*	Harper & Bros.	171	1962
Karpin	*How to Play Slam Contracts*	Collier	191	1964
Karpin	‡*The Play of the Cards*	Bridge Quarterly	506	1958
Karpin	†*Winning Play in Contract Bridge; Strategy at Trick One*	Coffin Dell (paperback)	288	1964
Kelsey	*‡*Advanced Play at Bridge*	Hart	192	1968
Kelsey	*‡*Killing Defense at Bridge*	Hart	192	1967
Kelsey	†*More Killing Defense*	Hart	192	1972
King	*Squeeze in Valhalla*	Carlton Press	300	1964
Lavinthal	*†*Defense Tricks*	Coffin	192	1963
Lawrence	‡*How to Read Your Opponent's Cards*	Prentice-Hall	175	1973
Love	†*Bridge Squeezes Complete*	Barclay Dover	260	1959 1968
Love	*Squeeze Play in Bridge*	R. R. Smith	183	1951
Mallon	*Opening Leads and Signals in Contract Bridge*	Collier	158	1969
Miles	*‡*All 52 Cards*	Exposition Press	142	1963
Mollo	*Test Your Defense*	Prentice-Hall	311	1972
Mollo, Gardener	‡*Card Play Technique*	Geo. Newnes, Ltd. (London)	381	1955
Nail, Hawthorn	*How to Play the Hand*	Texas Bridge	73	1961
North (see Flint)	*Match Your Skill against the Masters*			
Parson	*Fall of the Cards*	Little, Brown	280	1959
Perkins	*Vital Tricks at Contract Bridge*	Joiner & Steele (London) (original American ed., 1936)	96	1953
Reese	*‡*The Expert Game*	E. Arnold (London)	140	1958
	Master Play (American title)	Coffin		1960
Reese	*‡*Play Bridge with Reese*	Sterling	251	1960
Reese	*†*Reese on Play*	E. Arnold (London)	232	1948
Reford, (see England)	*The Play of the Cards*			
Romanet	*Le Squeeze au Bridge*	Grasset (Paris)	414	1954
Rosencrans	*Squeezes, Coups, and End Plays*	Rosencrans Publishing Co.	68	1965
Roussière (see Bellanger)	*Les Impasses au Bridge: Étude, etc.*			
Rovere	*Leads, Signals and Discards*	(pamphlet)		1941
Schuld	*The Simple Squeeze*	Drake	223	1974
Sheinwold	*First Book of Bridge: How to Improve Your Play*	Sterling Barnes & Noble		1953
Sheinwold	*Second Book of Bridge: Play of the Hand*	Sterling Barnes & Noble	153	1954
Sheinwold	*A Short Cut to Winning Bridge*	Fleet	160	1961
Stanley (see Kantar)	*Gamesman Bridge*			
Trézel	*Cahiers de Bridge*	Trézel (France)		1956–64
Watson	*Play of the Hand at Bridge*	Copeland	475	1934–58
Wolfe	*The Play of the Cards*	J. C. Winston	251	1932

E BIDDING AND PLAY (in combination)

Abrahams	*Brains in Bridge*	Horizon Press	262	1964
Albarran	*Encyclopédie du Bridge Moderne*	Librairie Arthème Fayard (Paris)	800	1957
Albarran, Jaïs	*How to Win at Rubber Bridge*	Barrie Books (London)	191	1959
Bailey, Oeschger	*Bridge for the Joneses*	Morrow	331	1947
Barclay	*Learn Bridge Fast*	David McKay	125	1944
Barrow (see Cohen)	*ABC of Contract Bridge*			
Blackwood	*Bridge Humanics*	Drake House (Indianapolis)	255	1949
Brannon	*Fool Proof Contract*	R. M. Brannon	169	1933
Buller	*How to Play Contract Bridge*	The Star (London)	144	
Coffin	*Learn Bridge the Easy Way*	C. Branford	128	1950
Cohen, B.	*ABC of Contract Bridge*	Anthony Blond (London)	288	1964
Cook	*Learn to Play Winning Bridge*	D. J. Cook	92	1967
Courtenay	*Standardized Contract Bridge Complete*	Bartholomew	160	1941
Crawford	*Crawford's Contract Bridge*	Grosset & Dunlap	367	1953
Culbertson, E.	**Contract Bridge Complete: Gold Book of Bidding and Play*	J. C. Winston	603	1936–54

AUTHOR	TITLE	PUBLISHER	PAGES	DATES
Culbertson, E.	Contract Bridge for Everyone	J. C. Winston	118	1948
Culbertson, E.	The Official Culbertson System of Contract Bridge	J. C. Winston	399	1944
Culbertson, J.	Contract Bridge for Beginners	J. C. Winston	221	1939–41
Dormer (see Reese)	Complete Book of Bridge			
Dormer (see Reese)	How to Play a Better Game of Bridge			
Ewen	Contract Bridge: How to Improve Your Technique	Franklin Watts	64	1975
Flint, North	Tiger Bridge	Simon & Schuster	192	1970
Foster	Foster's Contract Bridge	Greenberg	121	1927
Fox	Begin Bridge	Elliot Right Way	125	1973
Frey	How to Win at Contract in Ten Easy Lessons	Fawcett Pub.	288	1961
Fry	Better Bridge	Leisure League (booklet)	109	1935
Fry	How to Win at Bridge with Any Partner	Golden Press	144	1960
Gardener (see Mollo)	Bridge for Beginners			
Goldstein, A.	Common-Sense Bridge for the Intermediate Player	Arco	80	1959
Gooden	Contract Bridge, Bidding and Play	G. S. Gooden	150	1969
Goren	*Contract Bridge Complete	Doubleday	498	1951–57
Goren	Contract Bridge in a Nutshell	Doubleday	128	1947
Goren	Contract Bridge Made Easy	Doubleday	96	1948
Goren	The Elements of Bridge	Doubleday	420	1960
Goren	‡Goren's Bridge Complete	Chancellor Hall	562	1963
Goren	Goren's Easy Steps to Winning Bridge	Franklin Watts, Inc.	287	1964
Goren	Winning Partnership Bridge	Random House	183	1961
Harkness	Invitation to Bridge	Simon & Schuster	306	1950
Hathorn	Secrets of Tactical Bridge	Texas Bridge	85	1961
Ingram	How to Win at Bridge	Eyre & Spottiswoode (London)	126	1950
Jacoby, O. & J.	Win at Bridge with Jacoby and Son	G. P. Putnam's Sons	222	1966
Jacoby, O. & J.	Win at Bridge with Jacoby Modern	Enterprise Publications	128	1970
Jaïs	Apprendez à Mieux Jouer au Bridge	Julliard (Paris)	582	1957
Jaïs (see Albarran)	How to Win at Rubber Bridge			
Kantar	A Comprehensive Bridge Manual for Beginners	Kantar	122	1965
Kaplan	*‡Winning Contract Bridge Complete	Fleet	434	1964
Karn	Karn's Bridge Service	Long & Smith	361	1933
Kearse	‡Bridge Conventions Complete	Hart	624	1975
Kelsey	Improve Your Bridge	Hart	191	1971
Kelsey	Match-Point Bridge	Faber & Faber (London)	239	1970
Karpin	Psychological Strategy in Contract Bridge	Harper	325	1960
Kempson	Contract Bridge, How to Play It	Emerson Books	164	1957
Kerwin	Partnership Contract	Wm. Morrow	180	1934
Le Dentu	Bridge Facile	Fayard (Paris)	446	1970
Lenz	Lenz on Contract Bridge	Simon & Schuster	131	1929
Liggett	Contract Bridge Summary			1931
MacLeod	Bridge Is an Easy Game	Falcon Press (London)	244	1952
Markus	Common Sense Bridge	Random House	171	1973
Mayer	Money Bridge	Van Nostrand	258	1954
Michaels, Cohen	Ideal Student Textbook	Barclay	48	1957
Miles	†Marshall Miles Teaches Logical Bridge	Exposition Press	319	1967
Mollo	Bridge with a Master	Barnes & Co.	102	1960
Mollo	Bridge Psychology	Duckworth (London)	127	1958
Mollo	Success at Bridge	Newnes (London)		1964
Mollo, Gardener	Bridge for Beginners	Barnes & Co.	160	1960
Morehead	Bridge the Expert Way	Bridge World Accessories	62	1953
Morehead	‡Contract Bridge Summary	Macmillan	126	1963
North (see Flint)	Tiger Bridge			
Oeschger (see Bailey)	Bridge for the Joneses			
Phillips, Reese	The Elements of Contract	British Bridge World	271	1937
Reese	‡Advanced Bridge	Sterling (London)	464	1973
Reese	†Bridge for Bright Beginners	Sterling	151	1965
Reese	Your Bridge Questions Answered	Jordan & Sons (London)	136	1951
Reese	†Precision Bidding and Precision Play	Sterling (London)	153	1973
Reese (see Phillips)	The Elements of Contract			
Reese, Dormer	‡Complete Book of Bridge·	Dutton	486	1974
Reese, Dormer	†How to Play a Better Game of Bridge	Stein & Day	181	1969
Rendel (see Lenz)	Lenz on Contract Bridge			
Romanet	*Les Bases du Bridge Moderne	Albin Michell (Paris)	368	1958
Roth, Rubens	Bridge for Beginners	Funk & Wagnalls	216	1970
Rovere	†Contract Bridge Complete	Simon & Schuster	844	1973
Rovere	Point Count Contract Bridge Complete	Random House	710	1954–64
Rovere	Contract Bridge Complete	Simon & Schuster	834	1965
Rubens	The Secrets of Winning Bridge	Grosset & Dunlap	241	1969
Rubens (see Roth)	Bridge for Beginners			
Sheinwold	Complete Bridge Course First Book of Bridge Second Book of Bridge—Play of the Hand Third Book of Bridge—How to Bid and Play in Duplicate Tournaments Fourth Book of Bridge—How to Improve Your Game	Sterling Pub. Permabooks	640	1959
Sheinwold	*‡Five Weeks to Winning Bridge	Permabooks	498	1960
		Trident	548	1964

AUTHOR	TITLE	PUBLISHER	PAGES	DATES
Shepard	*Correct Contract Bridge*	Doubleday	265	1929
Silodor, Tierney	*Contract Bridge According to Silodor and Tierney*	Stanley Allen	442	1961
Simon	*†Why You Lose at Bridge*	Simon & Schuster	159	1946
Sobel	*All the Tricks*	Greenberg	245	1949
Solomon, Disbrow	*How to Bid and What to Lead*	Macrae Smith	128	1953
Tait	*Bridge Challenge*	Wolf (London)	141	1974
Tierney (see Silodor)	*Contract Bridge According to Silodor and Tierney*			
Truscott	*Bridge: Successful Play from First Principles*	Oldbourne (London)	159	1961
Vanderbilt	*Contract by Hand Analysis*	The Bridge World	165	1933
Watson	*Outline of Contract Bridge*	Grosset & Dunlap	333	1934
Whitehead	*What to Do and Why*	Frederick A. Stokes	183	1931
Woods	*Little Green Book, Artificial Bids, Leads, Signals*	Little Rock (booklet)	32	1958
Work	*Contract Bridge for All*	J. C. Winston	243	1929–31
Young	*Bridge for People Who Don't Know One Card from Another*	Follet	127	1965

F DUPLICATE BRIDGE (Bidding, Play, and Tournament Directing)

AUTHOR	TITLE	PUBLISHER	PAGES	DATES
Andersen (see Wei)	*†Match Point Precision*			
Benjamin, Kempson	*Tournament Bridge for Everyone*	Faber & Faber (London)	200	1963
Beynon	**Tournament and Duplicate Bridge*	Stuyvesant	270	1944–62
Beynon	*‡Bridge Director's Manual* (6th ed., rev.)	Coffin	192	1962
Bruelheide	*Duplicate Bridge Guide*	Bruelheide	64	1938
Coffin	*Perfect Plays and Match Point Ways*	Coffin	160	1973
Culbertson, E.	** Bidding and Play in Duplicate Contract Bridge*	J. C. Winston	271	1946
Dormer (see Reese)	*Bridge for Tournament Players*			
Farrington	**Duplicate Bridge Movements*	Farrington	98	1960
Fox	*Duplicate Bridge*	St. Martin's	160	1974
Fox	*Duplicate Bridge, Its Procedures and Tactics*	E. Arnold (London)	143	1955
Groner	*‡Duplicate Bridge Direction*	Barclay Bridge Supplies	224	1967
Groner	*‡Duplicate Bridge Direction: A Complete Handbook*	Barclay Bridge Supplies	224	1972
Gruenther	**Duplicate Contract Complete*	Bridge World	328	1933
Harrison-Gray (see Squire)	*Winning Points at Match-Point Bridge*			
Hathorn, Nail	*How to Play Championship Duplicate Bridge*	Texas Bridge	69	1963
Jourdan	*ABC of Duplicate Bridge Direction*	Coffin	96	1967
Kaplan	*†Duplicate Bridge, How to Play, How to Win*	Bantam Books	149	1966
		Hearthside Press	152	1968
Karpin (see Kay)	*The Complete Book of Duplicate Bridge*			
Karpin	*Winning Play in Tournament and Duplicate Bridge: How the Experts Triumph*	New American Library	241	1968
Kay, Silodor, Karpin	*‡The Complete Book of Duplicate Bridge*	G. P. Putnam Sons	496	1965
		Barnes & Noble	496	1969
Kelsey	*†Match Point Bridge*	Faber & Faber (London)	239	1970
Kempson (see Benjamin)	*Tournament Bridge for Everyone*			
Miles	**‡How to Win at Duplicate Bridge*	Exposition Press	463	1957
Nail (see Hathorn)	*How to Play Championship Duplicate Bridge*	Exposition Press	463	1957
Parker	*Let's Play Duplicate—Actual Duplicate in the Home*	Miller Quarles, vol. 1		1961
		vol. 2		1963
Reese, Dormer	*†Bridge for Tournament Players*	Robert Hale	173	1968
Sheinwold	*Third Book of Bridge—How to Bid and Play in Duplicate Tournaments*	Sterling	157	1954
Silodor (see Kay)	*The Complete Book of Duplicate Bridge*			
Squire, Harrison-Gray	**†Winning Points at Match-Point Bridge*	Faber & Faber (London)	151	1959
Wei, Andersen	*†Match Point Precision*	Monna Lisa	195	1975

G MATCH AND TOURNAMENT RECORDS

EDITOR

EDITOR	TITLE	PUBLISHER	PAGES	DATES
Albarran (see Bellanger)	*Les 102 Donnes d'un Grand Match*			
Aron (see Bellanger)	*Les 102 Donnes d'un Grand Match Australian World Par Hands*			1951
Bellanger, Albarran, Aron, Venizelos	*Les 102 Donnes d'un Grand Match*	Grasset Pub. (Paris)	189	1933
Culbertson, E.	**Famous Hands of the Culbertson-Lenz Match*	Bridge World	437	1931
Culbertson, E.	*300 Contract Bridge Hands—First World Bridge Championship* (England vs. US)	Bridge World	380	1933
Culbertson, E.	*World Bridge Olympic Hands*	Bridge World		1932
Filarski, Hirsch	*Tournament Book of the 2nd World Olympiad Pairs*	Elseviers Weekblad (Amsterdam)	206	1966
Francis	*World Bridge Championship* (Italy, US Aces, Brazil, North America, Indonesia)	ACBL	216	1973
Francis	*World Bridge Championship* (Italy, North America, Brazil, France, Indonesia, New Zealand)	ACBL	192	1974
Franklin (see Reese)	*World Bridge Championship 1955*			

AUTHOR	TITLE	PUBLISHER	PAGES	DATES
Frey	*International Team Playoff*	ACBL	96	1969
Frey	*Team Trials*	ACBL		1964
Frey	*Team Trials*	ACBL		1965
Frey	*Team Trials*	ACBL	144	1966
Frey	*World Championship* (United States, Italy, and Argentina)	ACBL	158	1958
Frey	*World Championship* (United States, Italy, and Argentina)	ACBL	160	1959
Frey	*World Bridge Olympiad* (France, Great Britain, Italy, and United States)	ACBL	136	1960
Frey	*World Championship* (Italy, North America, France, and Argentina)	ACBL	132	1961
Frey	*World Championship* (Italy, North America, Great Britain, and Argentina)	ACBL	118	1962
Frey	*World Championship* (Italy, North America, France, and Argentina)	ACBL	120	1963
Frey	*World Bridge Olympiad* (Italy, U.S.A., Canada, Great Britain, and 25 others)	ACBL	192	1964
Frey	*World Bridge Championship* (Italy, North America, Great Britain, Argentina)	ACBL	192	1965
Frey	*World Bridge Championship* (Italy, North America, Thailand, Venezuela, Netherlands)	ACBL	224	1966
Frey	*World Bridge Championship* (Italy, France, North America, Thailand, Venezuela)	ACBL	224	1967
Frey	*World Bridge Olympiad* (Italy, U.S.A., Canada, Netherlands, and 29 others)	ACBL	192	1968
Frey	*World Bridge Championship* (Italy, North America, France, Nationalist China, Brazil)	ACBL	224	1969
Herts (see Kerwin)	*Expert Misbidding*			
Hirsch	*World Bridge Championship* (Italy, North America, Norway, Nationalist China, Brazil)	ACBL	224	1970
Hirsch	*World Bridge Championship* (US Aces, France Australia, China, Brazil, North America)	ACBL	224	1971
Hirsch (see Filarski)	*Tournament Book of the 2nd World Olympiad Pairs*			
Kempson	*Championship Hands*	Joiner & Steele (London)	59	1950
Kempson	*Bridge Match in Dublin*	Waddington (Leeds, England)		1958
Kerwin, Herts	*Expert Misbidding* (Culbertson-Lenz 1931)	Covice-Friede	140	1932
McKenney	*Par Bridge—Hands for Replay*	Circa		1938
	National Intercollegiate Bridge Tournaments	Barclay & Assoc. of American Card Man.		1956–64
Moyse, Sheinwold	*World Championship, U.S.A., Sweden*	ACBL	136	1953
	World Championship, U.S.A., France	ACBL	80	1954
Moyse, Sheinwold	*World Championship, U.S.A., Great Britain*	ACBL	120	1955
	World Championship, U.S.A., France	ACBL	84	1956
Moyse, Sheinwold	*World Championship* (United States, Italy)	ACBL	126	1957
Reese, Franklin	*World Bridge Championship* (Great Britain v. US)	De La Rue (London)		1955
Smith	*World Bridge Olympiad* (Italy, US, Canada, France, and 35 others)	ACBL	224	1972
Sullivan, Williams	*World Par Hands*	World Bridge Federation	40	1961–63
Venizelos (see Bellanger)	*Les 102 Donnes d'un Grand Match*			

H HAND COLLECTIONS

AUTHOR	TITLE	PUBLISHER	PAGES	DATES
Becker	*Becker on Bridge*	Grosset & Dunlap	128	1971
Corn	*Play Bridge with the Aces*	Fawcett	224	1972
Darvas, Hart	**Right Through the Pack*	Stuyvesant House	328	1947
Darvas, Lukacs	*†Spotlight on Card Play*	Barclay	160	1960
Gooden, Thomas	*Sherlock Holmes, Bridge Detective*	Thomas	122	1973
Goren	*Bridge Mystery Deals*	Heines	64	1964
Goren	*Championship Bridge with Charles Goren*	Doubleday	255	1964
Goren	*The Best of Championship Bridge*			
Harrison-Gray	*Country Life Book of Bridge*	Hamlyn Group (London)	160	1973
Hart (see Darvas)	*Right Through the Pack*			
Jannersten (see Mollo)	*The Best of Bridge*			
Jannersten	*Bridge Writer's Choice 1964*	International Bridge Press Association (Sweden)		1965
Jannersten	*Bridge Writer's Choice 1968*	International Bridge Press Association (Sweden)		1968
Jelks, Schmitt	*Trick Taking Potential*	Jett	80	1974
Kauder	*The Bridge Philosopher*	Kauder	144	1972
Kempson	*Contract Bridge Hands*	Faber & Faber (London)	96	1950
Le Dentu	*120 Donnes et Problèmes du Bridge*	Presses Pocket (Paris)	189	1975
Lukacs (see Darvas)	*Spotlight on Card Play*			
Lukacs (see Milnes)	*Bridge Hands for the Connoisseur*			
Markus	*Aces and Places*	Bodley Head (London)		1972
		Drake	140	1973
Markus	*†Bid Boldly, Play Safe*	Blond (London)	212	1966
		Hawthorn	212	1968
McKenney	*Contract Bridge (Bidding and Playing Hands from Championship Tournaments)*	(booklet)	(unpaged)	1935

AUTHOR	TITLE	PUBLISHER	PAGES	DATES
Miller	*Bridge Brilliance and Blunders*	Dow Jones	222	1974
Milnes, Lukacs	†*Bridge Hands for the Connoisseur*	Barclay	127	1974
Mollo, Jannersten	†*The Best of Bridge*	Faber & Faber (London)	223	1973
Peterson (see Work)	*101 Celebrated Hands*			
Phillips	*Bridge with Goren*	Citadel Press	128	1960
Phillips	*Bridge at Ruff's Club*	Batchworth Press (London)	248	1951
Phillips	*Bridge with Mr. Playbetter*	Batchworth Press (London)	219	1952
Schmitt (see Jelks)	*Trick Taking Potential*			
Simon, S. J.	*Cut for Partners*	Nicholson & Watson (London)	128	1950
Smith, A. J.	*Contract Chronicles*	Grayson & Grayson (London)	52	1936
Solomon, Wilson	*Hold Our Bridge Hands*	Lefax, Inc.	139	1969
Stern, Smith, A. J.	*Sorry Partner*	Faber & Faber (London)	141	1945
Thomas (see Gooden)	*Sherlock Holmes, Bridge Detective*	Thomas	200	1975
Thomas	*Sherlock Holmes, Bridge Detective Returns*			
Truscott	†*Master Bridge through Question and Answer*	Quadrangle Books	252	1971
Tuite	*Contract Bridge for Iris*	Geoffrey Bles (London)	125	1930
Tuite	*Mrs. Pottleton's Bridge Parties*	Simon & Schuster	154	1928
Whitehead	*Championship Bridge Hands*	Stokes		1929
Wilson (see Solomon)	*Hold Our Bridge Hands*			
Work, Peterson	*101 Celebrated Hands*	J. C. Winston	215	1933

J   PROBLEMS, QUIZZES, AND PUZZLES

Cohen, B.	*Playing Better Bridge*	A. S. Barnes		1964
Cohen, B.	*Test Your Bridge*	Arco (London)	227	1962
Darwen	†*Bridge Magic*	Faber & Faber (London)	213	1973
Foster	*Vanity Fair's Bridge Problems*	Horace Liveright	198	1932
Goren	*Bridge Quiz Book*	Permabooks	184	1949
Kempson, Ritch	*Bridge Quiz*	Contract Bridge Equipment Co. (Leeds)	215	1949
Kempson	*First Pocket Book of Bridge Problems*	Barclay	79	1961
Kempson	*More Bridge Quizzes*	Wm. Jackson (London)	109	1952
Kempson, Lukacs	*Second Book of Bridge Problems*	Barclay	80	1962
Lukacs (see Milnes)	*Improve your Dummy Play*			
Martin	*Bridge Word Puzzles*	White Arts	140	1973
Milnes, Lukacs	*Improve your Dummy Play*	Barclay Bridge Supplies	80	1969
Osborn	{ *How's Your Bridge?*	Faber & Faber (London)	212	1949
	How's Your Bridge Game? (American title)	McGraw-Hill	201	1948
Ritch (see Kempson)	*Bridge Quiz*			
Sheinwold	*The Pocket Book of Puzzles* (Nos. 1-6)	Pocket Books	(6 vols.) 191	1970-71

K   BIOGRAPHY

Culbertson	*Strange Lives of One Man*	J. C. Winston	693	1940
Dunne, Ostrow	*Championship Bridge as Played by Experts;* later ed., *Contract Bridge as Played by the Experts*	McGraw-Hill	251	1949
		Coffin		1952
Ramsey	*Aces All*	Museum Press (London)	204	1955
Schenken	*Education of a Bridge Player*	Simon & Schuster	286	1973

L   HUMOR AND POETRY

Calhoun (see Webster)	*Who Dealt This Mess?*			
Goren	*Bridge Players Write the Funniest Letters*	Doubleday	148	1968
James	*What the Hell Is Trumps*	A. S. Barnes	91	1969
Lakefield (see Stein)	*Bridge and Gin Gambitry*			
Lind	*Psychotics, Neurotics and Bridge Players*	Simons Pub. (Santa Fe, N.M.)	58	1961
Mollo	*Bridge in the Fourth Dimension*	Faber & Faber (London)	160	1974
Mollo	*Bridge in the Menagerie*	Hawthorn	224	1967
Phillips	*You Can Play and Laugh*	Faber & Faber (London)	269	1934
Stein, Lakefield	*Bridge and Gin Gambitry*	Home Library Press	158	1963
Webster, Calhoun	*Who Dealt This Mess?*	Doubleday	174	1948

M   MATHEMATICS

Borel, Cheron	‡*Mathematical Theory of Bridge* (trans. by A. Traub)	Monna Lisa Precision	434	1975
Borel, Cheron	*Théorie Mathématique du Bridge*	Gauthier-Villars (Paris)	424	1940-55
Frost	†*Bridge Odds Complete*	Coffin	96	1971
Goren	*Go with the Odds*	MacMillan	308	1969
Jacoby	*How to Figure the Odds*	Doubleday	215	1947
Kibler, Telfer, Traub	*Probabilities in Contract Bridge*	Frost	103	1963
Levinson	*Science of Chance*	Faber & Faber (London)		1952
Northrop, Stein	*Mathematical Odds in Contract*	Williams & Morgan, Ltd. (London)		1933
Telfer	*Practical Odds at Bridge*	Traub (Capetown)	114	1961
Telfer (see Kibler)	*Probabilities in Contract Bridge*			
Traub (see Kibler)	*Probabilities in Contract Bridge*			

AUTHOR	TITLE	PUBLISHER	PAGES	DATES
N LAWS				
Whist Club, N.Y.	*The Laws of Contract Bridge*	J. C. Winston	54	1932
Nat'l Laws Commission	*The Laws of Duplicate Contract Bridge*	ABL, USBA	64	1933
Whist Club, N.Y.	*The Laws of Contract Bridge*	J. C. Winston	51	1935
Nat'l Laws Commission	*The Laws of Duplicate Contract Bridge*	J. C. Winston	91	1935
Nat'l Laws Commission	*The Laws of Contract Bridge*	J. C. Winston	62	1943
Nat'l Laws Commission	*The Laws of Contract Bridge*	J. C. Winston	47	1948
Nat'l Laws Commission	*The Laws of Duplicate Contract Bridge*	J. C. Winston	67	1948
Nat'l Laws Commission	*The Laws of Contract Bridge*	Crown	62	1963
Nat'l Laws Commission	*The Laws of Duplicate Contract Bridge*	Crown	78	1963
Nat'l Laws Commission	*‡Laws of Duplicate Contract Bridge*	ACBL	102	1975